New

AMERICAN NATIONAL BIOGRAPHY

AMERICAN
NATIONAL BIOGRAPHY

Published under the auspices of the
AMERICAN COUNCIL OF LEARNED SOCIETIES

General Editors

John A. Garraty
Mark C. Carnes

VOLUME 8

OXFORD UNIVERSITY PRESS
New York   1999   Oxford

OXFORD UNIVERSITY PRESS

Oxford   New York
Athens   Auckland   Bangkok   Bogotá
Buenos Aires   Calcutta   Cape Town   Chennai
Dar es Salaam   Delhi   Florence   Hong Kong   Istanbul
Karachi   Kuala Lumpur   Madrid   Melbourne   Mexico City
Mumbai   Nairobi   Paris   São Paulo   Singapore
Taipei   Tokyo   Toronto   Warsaw
and associated companies in
Berlin   Ibadan

Published by Oxford University Press, Inc.,
198 Madison Avenue, New York, New York 10016
http://www.oup-usa.org

Funding for this publication was provided in part by
the Andrew W. Mellon Foundation, the Rockefeller Foundation,
and the National Endowment for the Humanities,
a federal agency.

Library of Congress Cataloging-in-Publication Data

American national biography / general editors, John A. Garraty, Mark C. Carnes
p.   cm.
"Published under the auspices of the American Council of Learned Societies."
Includes bibliographical references and index.
1. United States—Biography—Dictionaries.   I. Garraty, John Arthur,
1920–   .   II. Carnes, Mark C. (Mark Christopher), 1950–   .
III. American Council of Learned Societies.
CT213.A68   1998   98-20826   920.073—dc21   CIP
ISBN 0-19-520635-5 (set)
ISBN 0-19-512787-0 (vol. 8)

Printing (last digit): 9 8 7 6 5 4 3 2 1

Printed in the United States of America
on acid-free paper

F

CONTINUED

FISHBERG, Maurice (16 Aug. 1872–30 Aug. 1934), physician, anthropologist, and Jewish community worker, was born in Kamenets-Podolski, Russia, the son of Philip Fishberg and Kate Moverman. Raised in a traditional Jewish household, Fishberg was introduced to modern scientific study in a Russian government school before immigrating to the United States in 1890. He attended the Medical College of New York University, where he received his M.D. in 1897. That same year he married Bertha Cantor; they had two children. Fishberg was initially engaged in private practice on New York's Lower East Side, later securing a post as chief medical examiner for the city's United Hebrew Charities. There Fishberg treated immigrant patients who relied on the support of the Jewish community and made recommendations to community leaders on how social conditions and medical care for the Jewish poor could be improved. While at the United Hebrew Charities, Fishberg became concerned with the attempts of immigration restrictionists to paint Jewish immigrants as carriers of disease. His early medical scholarship, therefore, mustered scientific data in an attempt to dispel myths concerning "Jewish pathology," particularly the common accusation that immigrants were responsible for the spread of tuberculosis. Fishberg demonstrated, in fact, that Jews were more immune to tuberculosis than other immigrants, a fact he attributed to their religious customs and previous exposure to urban life in European towns and cities.

In the course of his early medical research on Jews, Fishberg began to see that claims of a Jewish predisposition to disease were part of a larger nativist discourse that cast Jews and other Southern and Eastern European immigrants as racial aliens. As a result, beginning in 1902 he conducted several anthropological investigations, hoping to determine the significance of race to the adaptation of Jewish immigrants to the United States. Fishberg's first anthropological studies, though skeptical of biological determinism, conceived of the Jews as a distinct racial group. Increasingly after 1903, however, he began to reject this position, arguing that the Jews were not a pure race but a racial composite, having mixed thoroughly during their long history with surrounding populations. After extensive fieldwork conducted in European countries and in North Africa during the following years, Fishberg concluded that there were no enduring racial differences between Jews and the non-Jews among whom they lived.

In 1911, when the movement for immigration restriction was intensifying, Fishberg published *The Jews: A Study of Race and Environment*, in which he argued that environment, not race, was responsible for the cultivation of so-called Jewish characteristics. The book represented the largest collection of anthropological data on the Jews ever published, including material on physical characteristics, vital statistics, criminality, intermarriage, and conversion. Fishberg argued that the distinctiveness of Jews was a product of their isolation in European ghettoes and that when immigrants entered a non-Jewish social environment, their so-called racial characteristics began to disappear. Based on his findings, Fishberg predicted the speedy assimilation of Jews in the United States and other English-speaking countries.

Fishberg intended his book not only to refute the claims of nativists, but to counteract the efforts of those Jews interested in cultivating Jewish national and cultural distinctiveness, which he saw as an obstacle to their successful political and social integration. Zionism and other movements stressing Jewish particularism, wrote Fishberg, were dangerous because they often expressed Jewish identity in terms of race. According to Fishberg, religion was the only viable form of Jewish identification, and even that distinction was being obliterated by the assimilatory power of the United States. The book had a mixed reception among Jewish community leaders, who praised Fishberg's scientific method but were uncomfortable with his conclusions. Zionists attacked his book for its prediction of Jewish "self-effacement," and even the Reform rabbinate, which favored a deracinated view of Jewish identity, objected to its bleak predictions concerning the future of American Judaism.

After the appearance of *The Jews*, Fishberg put aside the field of anthropology and devoted his activity to the study and treatment of pulmonary diseases. About this time he joined the staff of Montefiore Hospital, a Jewish-sponsored institution concerned with the spread of tuberculosis among Jews, serving as director of the tuberculosis service and the hospital's Bedford Sanitarium. Fishberg made important discoveries concerning the incidence of tubercular infection in school-age children and helped to introduce the pneumothorax treatment of the disease. In 1916 he published his *Treatise on Pulmonary Tuberculosis*, which became a standard text on the topic and was reissued in four editions before 1932. Fishberg served as clinical professor of medicine at the Bellevue Hospital Medical College (now part of New York City University) from 1915 to 1928. He died in New York City.

Fishberg was the most important American scholar to undertake a study of the anthropology of the Jews. He also made important contributions in the diagnosis and treatment of tuberculosis and other pulmonary diseases. At a time when Jews were commonly stigmatized by racial theories and accusations that they spread disease, Fishberg's scientific work made him an important agent of Jewish adjustment to the United States. As an anthropologist and physician of wide repute, he was able to contest the conclusions of medical and racial science with an authority few others in the Jewish community could wield. His disagreements with the Jewish community over Jewish cultural and national distinctiveness, however, reveal the difficulties American anthropology posed for ethnic expression as long as it did not neatly distinguish between race and culture.

• Fishberg's papers are not known to have survived. His published writings, however, offer a rich field for research. Aside from those mentioned above, the most important are his "Materials for the Physical Anthropology of the Eastern European Jews," *Memoirs of the American Anthropological and Ethnological Societies* 1 (1905–1907): 1–146, and his Yiddish polemic against Zionism, *Di gefahr fun die idishe natsyonalistishe bavegung* (1906). For a survey and analysis of his early medical writings on Jews, see Alan M. Kraut, *Silent Travelers: Germs, Genes, and the "Immigrant Menace"* (1994). A lengthy biographical sketch of Fishberg was published by Yoel Slonim in the New York Yiddish daily *Der Tog*, 30 Apr. 1925. An obituary is in the *New York Times*, 31 Aug. 1934.

ERIC L. GOLDSTEIN

FISHER, Ada Lois Sipuel (8 Feb. 1924–18 Oct. 1995), civil rights pioneer, lawyer, and educator, was born in Chickasha, Oklahoma, the daughter of Travis B. Sipuel, a minister and later bishop of the Church of Christ in God, one of the largest black Pentecostal churches in the United States, and Martha Bell Smith, the child of a former slave. Her parents moved to Chickasaw, Oklahoma, shortly after the Tulsa race riot of 1921.

Her brother Lemuel had initially planned to challenge the segregationist policies of the University of Oklahoma. After returning from service in World War II, he went to Howard University Law School instead because he did not want to delay his career with protracted litigation. Ada, who was younger and had been in college during the war, was willing to delay her legal career for the opportunity to challenge segregation. She entered Arkansas A & M College on a scholarship in 1941 but transferred to Oklahoma State College for Negroes (now Langston University) in 1942 and graduated in 1945. In 1944 she married Warren W. Fisher, a longtime family friend and son of a Baptist minister. They had two children.

In 1946 she applied for admission to the University of Oklahoma School of Law, at the time the state's only law school. Following its segregationist policies, the university rejected her application solely on the basis of her race. In an extraordinary meeting, Dr. George L. Cross, the university's president, asserted that but for her race Sipuel would be admitted to the law school. He then willingly put this statement in writing, setting the stage for her lawsuit. Although already married at the time, she sued under her maiden name, and thus the case was known as *Sipuel v. Board of Regents of the University of Oklahoma*.

Two Oklahoma state courts upheld the university. Thurgood Marshall, a litigator with the National Association for the Advancement of Colored People (NAACP) Legal Defense and Education Fund, took her case to the U.S. Supreme Court. The Court issued a "per curium" decision, summarily reversing the Oklahoma courts. The Supreme Court relied on the precedent in *Missouri ex rel. Gaines v. Canada* (1938), which had required Missouri to open its only state law school to African Americans and ordered the University of Oklahoma to admit Sipuel to law school. Initially the state tried to avoid the decision by creating a separate and thoroughly bogus law school for blacks. In the summer of 1949 university officials finally allowed Sipuel to register for classes. She thus became the first African-American woman to attend a previously all-white law school in the South.

By the time the law school allowed her to register, the semester had already begun. The law school gave Fisher (by this time she was married and pregnant) a special chair marked "colored" and roped off from the rest of the class. Despite this her classmates and teachers welcomed her and shared notes with her. Students studied with her and helped her catch up on the material she had missed. She was forced to eat in a chained off and guarded area of the law school cafeteria, but she recalled many years later that "white students would crawl under the chain and eat with me" when the guards were not around. Adding to these circumstances and the usual difficulties of law school were the pressure of the lawsuit and the need to succeed for all those who had supported her suit. "I knew the eyes of Oklahoma and the nation were on me," she would later say. Moreover, her lawsuit and tuition were supported by hundreds of small donations. "I owed it to those people to make it," she recalled.

She graduated from the law school in 1951 and in 1952 began practicing law in her hometown of Chickasha. In 1954 she represented a client before the Oklahoma Supreme Court. In 1957 she joined the faculty at Langston University, where she served as chair of the social sciences department and later assistant vice president for academic affairs. She later returned to the University of Oklahoma, where in 1968 she earned a masters degree in history. In 1987–1988 she served as assistant vice president for academic affairs and later as director of the Urban Center at Langston University before retiring to become counsel to Automations Research Systems in Virginia. In 1988 the Oklahoma Legislative Black Caucus honored her achievement in pursuing justice in *Sipuel v. Board of Regents of the University of Oklahoma*. On the fortieth anniversary of the U.S. Supreme Court's decision (1974–1975), she served on the Advisory Committee on Civil Rights for the Oklahoma Regents for Higher Education. Throughout her career she remained active in civil rights organizations, working with the Urban League, the NAACP, and the American Civil Liberties Union. In 1991 the University of Oklahoma gave her the honorary doctorate of humane letters, and in 1992 Oklahoma governor David Walters appointed her to the

Board of Regents of the University of Oklahoma. Fisher noted, "This appointment completes a 45-year cycle." She planned to bring "a new dimension to university policies. Having suffered severely from the bigotry and racial discrimination as a student, I am sensitive to that kind of thing." She died in Oklahoma City.

• The best source of details of Fisher's life is her posthumously published autobiography, *A Matter of Black and White: The Autobiography of Ada Lois Sipuel Fisher* (1996), written with Danny Globe. Brief biographical information is available in *Who's Who among Black Americans, 1992–93*. For the background regarding her case, see Richard Kluger, *Simple Justice* (1976). Newspaper stories about her can be found in *Tulsa World*, 28 Apr. 1992; Gannett News Service, 29 Apr. 1992; United Press International, 2 May 1988; the *New York Times*, 5 June 1992; *Tulsa World*, 17 Sep. 1994; the *Dallas Morning News*, 20 Oct. 1995; and the *Washington Post*, 21 Oct. 1995. Obituaries are in the *Washington Post*, 21 Oct. 1995, and in most other national newspapers between 19 Oct. and 22 Oct. 1995.

PAUL FINKELMAN

FISHER, Alfred Joseph. *See* Fisher, Frederic John.

FISHER, Alvan (9 Aug. 1792–13 Feb. 1863), portrait, genre, and landscape painter, was born Alvin Fisher in Needham, Norfolk County, Massachusetts, the son of Aaron Fisher, a disabled revolutionary war veteran on government pension, and Lucy Stedman. In 1811, at the age of nineteen, with no artistic tradition in his family, Fisher began a three-year apprenticeship under John Ritto Penniman, who maintained a studio in the Roxbury section of Boston. Fisher was introduced not only to the rudiments of painting but also to a community of craftsmen and artists in the greater Boston area. After he left Penniman's studio in 1814, Fisher embarked on a prolific career that lasted for nearly fifty years.

Fisher almost immediately painted several innovative winter pieces that combined elements of both genre and landscape, such as *A Roadside Meeting: Winter* (1815, Virginia Museum, Richmond) and *Winter in Milton* (1815, Montclair Art Museum, N.J.). These were picturesque images of New England life, evoking the character of seventeenth-century Dutch art. The general effect of the scene was more important to Fisher than a specific depiction of the site.

His continued reverence for American scenery was reinforced by an intensive commitment to landscape subjects. He was one of America's earliest landscape painters, a seminal figure of the Hudson River school. In search of nature's beauty, he traveled extensively, visiting the Connecticut River valley (1817) and Niagara Falls (1820). Many landscape images resulted from these early sketching trips, including a pair of paintings that depict companion views of Niagara Falls (1820; National Museum of American Art, Smithsonian Institution). To ensure a comfortable standard of living for himself, he also accepted portrait commissions, painting middle-class New Englanders as well

as animals such as American Eclipse, the celebrated racehorse (c. 1822–1823, Munson-Williams-Proctor Institute, Utica, N.Y.). Around 1820 Fisher began to use the spelling "Alvan" rather than "Alvin" in his personal papers. No reason for the change is known, but it does suggest an attempt to establish a sense of refined gentility. He retained the second spelling for the remaining years of his career.

In 1825 Fisher traveled to Europe, his only trip abroad and the first by an American landscape painter. Accompanied by his younger brother John Dix, who was studying medicine, he visited England, France, Switzerland, and Italy. For the artist, it provided a marvelous opportunity to see examples of the Old Masters as well as contemporary English and French paintings. On his return in late 1826, he sought professional recognition and quickly became a major figure in the Boston art scene. He established his studio on Washington Street and regularly contributed to the gallery exhibits at the Boston Athenaeum. In 1827 Fisher married Lydia Ellis of Dedham. They had one child.

In the 1830s Fisher frequented the White Mountains and the upper coast of Maine, spots that were not yet common destinations for other landscape artists. Fisher's paintings, based on his diligent exploration of New England sites, helped to popularize many unrecognized places of unspoiled beauty. He created images in the Claudian mode, based on the recurring compositional elements used by seventeenth-century painter Claude Lorrain, including tall, graceful trees that frame the scene, scooped-out centers with a body of water, distant mountain ranges, and a small figure or anecdotal group positioned in the foreground for scale. Fisher's landscapes were well received. With exhibitions in New York, Philadelphia, Baltimore, Washington, and Natchez, the artist cultivated an audience far beyond Boston.

Fisher was a successful businessman and artist, organizing four solo large-scale sales in 1843, 1847, 1852, and 1857. With investments in real estate and railroad stocks, he enjoyed a comfortable life in Dedham, where he had moved from Boston in 1846. Fisher was fortunate to see landscape painting gain acceptance in the United States. As one of the earliest artists to travel around New England depicting picturesque sites based on direct observation, Fisher inspired other artists to visit these same places of charming beauty. He also helped to elevate the public taste for American landscape subjects. By the final years of his career, Americans were drawn to more sublimely spectacular scenes than the pastoral eastern subjects that Fisher had been painting. After his death in Dedham, Fisher's contribution to the development of American art was quickly forgotten.

• Numerous sketchbooks as well as Fisher's first account book are in the M. and M. Karolik Collection at the Museum of Fine Arts, Boston. A chronological study of Fisher's career as a landscape painter and an extensive bibliography, both primary and secondary, can be found in Fred B. Adelson,

"Alvan Fisher (1792–1863): Pioneer in American Landscape Painting" (Ph.D. diss., Columbia Univ., 1982). See also three articles by Adelson: "An American Snowfall: Early Winter Scenes by Alvan Fisher," *Arts in Virginia* 24, no. 3 (1983–1984): 2–9; "Alvan Fisher in Maine: His Early Coastal Scenes," *American Art Journal* 18, no. 3 (1986): 63–73; and "Home on La Grange: Alvan Fisher's Lithographs of Lafayette's Residence in France," *Antiques* 134 (1988): 152–57. For earlier research on Fisher, see Charlotte B. Johnson, "The European Tradition and Alvan Fisher," *Art in America* 41, no. 2 (Spring 1953): 79–87; Mabel M. Swan, "The Unpublished Notebooks of Alvan Fisher," *Antiques* 68 (1955): 126–29; and Robert C. Vose, Jr., "Alvan Fisher, 1792–1863: American Pioneer in Landscape and Genre," *Connecticut Historical Society Bulletin* 27 (1962): 97–117.

FRED B. ADELSON

FISHER, Charles Thomas. *See* Fisher, Frederic John.

FISHER, Dorothy F. Canfield (17 Feb. 1879–9 Nov. 1958), author and educational leader, was born Dorothea Frances Canfield in Lawrence, Kansas, the daughter of James Hulme Canfield, a professor of economics and sociology at the University of Kansas, and Flavia A. Camp, an artist. As a child Dorothy summered with relatives in Arlington, Vermont. In 1890 she went to Paris with her mother, visited her mother's studio in the Latin Quarter, and attended a convent school.

In 1891 Fisher's father became chancellor of the University of Nebraska, and the family moved to Lincoln. In 1895 they moved to Columbus, Ohio, where he was the president of Ohio State University. After graduating from high school in Lincoln, Fisher enrolled at Ohio State. In 1899 she received her Ph.B. In March 1902 she published "Holy Week in Spain" in the *New York Times*; that fall she traveled in Europe with novelist Willa Cather, whom she had met in Nebraska in 1891. In 1904 Fisher earned a Ph.D. in Romance languages from Columbia University, where her father had become the first to hold the post of librarian. Her dissertation was published under the title *Corneille and Racine in England* (1904).

Fisher then declined an offer to teach French and German at Western Reserve University in Cleveland and remained instead with her aging parents in New York City. She became a secretary at the experimental Horace Mann School, began to publish short stories and poetry (1905), and coauthored *Elementary Composition* (1906). In 1907 she married John Redwood Fisher, a Columbia football star; they had two children. In 1907 she also inherited her great-grandfather's farm in Arlington, to which she and her husband moved permanently. In 1911 she met Maria Montessori in Rome and was impressed by her method of educating children.

In 1912 Fisher engaged Paul Reynolds, the distinguished literary agent, who helped promote her novels *The Squirrel-Cage* (1912) and *The Bent Twig* (1915) and her collection of stories *Hillsboro People* (1915). After her husband went to France in April 1916 to be an ambulance driver and driver trainer, Fisher and their two children joined him in August. For two years she operated a camp commissary, helped rehabilitate war-blinded French soldiers, and set up convalescent homes for children in France and in the Basque country. Her next novels, about one couple, were *The Brimming Cup* (1921) and *Rough-Hewn* (1922). Her controversial novel, *The Home-Maker*, appeared in 1924. In 1926 the Book-of-the-Month Club was founded, with Henry Seidel Canby as chairman and Fisher, Heywood Broun, Christopher Darlington Morley, and William Allen White as members of the book-selecting committee. Fisher published *Her Son's Wife* (1926), after which came *The Deepening Stream* (1930), perhaps her best novel. In 1931 she was elected to membership in the National Institute of Arts and Letters. Her novel *Bonfire* (1933) upset reviewers but delighted readers.

Fisher's last decades were marked by unremitting publication, most notably her novel *Seasoned Timber* (1939). She also helped organize the Children's Crusade to bring Jewish refugees from Hitler's Germany to America in 1939. Fisher retired from the Book-of-the-Month Club in 1951, having evaluated fifteen books a month for a quarter of a century. She died in Arlington, Vermont.

Fisher is noteworthy for her novels about marital and family struggles and triumphs. *The Squirrel-Cage* tells of a sweet girl's difficulties in her marriage to a hard-driving Ohio executive. *The Bent Twig* dramatizes a spirited and fortunately practical heroine's choices—comfort versus conscience—separately offered by contrasting suitors. Middle-western campus life is in the background, and racial prejudice and alcoholism are portrayed. *The Brimming Cup* presents the struggle of Marise Crittenden when the intensity of love for her husband Neale diminishes and she meets the more suave Vincent Marsh. Neale sagely realizes that Marise alone should make a choice with which she can live happily. In this novel too, Fisher bravely criticizes racial prejudice. *Rough-Hewn*, though published after *The Brimming Cup*, presents Neale and Marise from childhood to love and marriage. Marise's early years in Europe reflect Fisher's knowledge of the French and the Basques, while Neale's early life is based on that of Fisher's husband.

In Fisher's *The Home-Maker*, a businessman hates his work, and his extremely efficient wife dislikes housework and child rearing. When he is homebound by a crippling accident, she embarks on a successful career while he nurtures the children—all in the face of what Fisher rebukingly labels "Tradition." *Her Son's Wife* dramatizes the perils of being a take-charge, perfectionist mother-in-law. She is the widowed Mary Bascomb, perhaps Fisher's most complex heroine. In *The Deepening Stream*, a professor and his wife compete for control, which hurts their daughter until she senses their spiritual rapport. She matures in a happy marriage, accompanies her husband to France with their two children in 1915 when he joins the ambulance corps, and is disillusioned—as Fisher was—by postwar materialistic politics. *Bonfire* shows the uproar a Vermont physician causes when he brings Lixlee, his backwoods siren of a bride, into his sedate village. *Seasoned Timber* (1939) features Timothy Coulton Hulme, the freedom-loving, middle-aged principal of a rural Vermont academy who refuses a trustee's huge bequest because it has profascist, anti-Semitic strings attached. Hulme was the middle name of Fisher's beloved father, also a moral academician.

Fisher's *A Montessori Mother* (1912), *A Montessori Manual* (1913), and *Mothers and Children* (1914) helped introduce the Montessori method in the United States. In *A Harvest of Stories* (1951) Fisher collected twenty-seven of her best short stories, including two masterpieces—"The Bedquilt" (1906), about a farm woman whose one talent is making quilts, and "Sex Education" (1945), presenting three versions of one encounter in a cornfield. *Home Fires in France* (1918) and *The Day of Glory* (1919) are collections of short stories about French bravery and the futility of war. Fisher translated two Italian books: Giovanni Papini's *Life of Christ* in 1923 and Adriano Tilgher's *Work: What It Has Meant to Men through the Ages* in 1932. *Basque People* (1931) contains eight stories about a race of people Fisher observed and respected.

Fisher wrote much fiction for juvenile readers, the best being the classic *Understood Betsy* (1917). She also wrote nonfiction for such audiences, including *Our Young Folks* (1943), a manual on how to instill responsibility in children, and *Fair World for All . . .* (1952), a book about human rights that featured a foreword by Eleanor Roosevelt, who in 1958 called Fisher one of the ten most influential women in America.

Fisher's varied works lost favor after her death, perhaps because of their generally conservative didacticism. Modernist critics prefer fiction by her more experimental contemporaries. All the same, she effectively wrote and acted against political tyranny of all sorts, racism, and the degradation of women, and she encouraged the development of the best in everyone, often within the institution of marriage.

• Fisher's papers, approximately 3,000 in number, are in at least fifty-eight repositories. The bulk are in libraries at Columbia University, Princeton University, and the University of Vermont. Many other papers are at the American Academy of Arts and Letters in New York City; the Houghton Library at Harvard University; and the Social Welfare History Archives at the University of Minnesota. In *Vermont Tradition* (1953) and *Memories of Arlington, Vermont* (1957), Fisher extols her adopted state and its rugged people. Biographies include Elizabeth Yates, *Pebbles in a Pool: The Widening Circles of Dorothy Canfield Fisher's Life* (1958); Ida H. Washington, *Dorothy Canfield Fisher: A Biography* (1982); and Mark J. Madigan, ed., *Keeping Fires Night and Day: Selected Letters of Dorothy Canfield Fisher* (1993). Bradford Smith, "Dorothy Canfield Fisher," *Atlantic Monthly*, Aug. 1959, pp. 73–77, is an engaging personality analysis. Alice Payne Hackett, *60 Years of Best Sellers, 1895–1955* (1956), lists *The Brimming Cup* and *The Home-Maker* as the most popular of Fisher's several bestselling novels. Joseph J. Firebaugh, "Dorothy Canfield and the Moral Bent," *Educational Forum* 15 (Mar. 1951): 283–94, discusses her treatment in *The Deepening Stream* of marriage and family life, success, the environment, religion, war, and especially education. Frederick A. Pottle, "Catharsis," *Yale Review* 40 (June 1951): 621–41, discusses the genesis of Fisher's "The Bedquilt." Arthur Hobson Quinn, *American Fiction: An Historical and Critical Survey* (1936), and Edward Wagenknecht, *Cavalcade of the American Novel: From the Birth of the Nation to the Middle of the Twentieth Century* (1952), treat Fisher with admiration. Charles Lee, *The Hidden Public: The Story of the Book-of-the-Month Club* (1958), discusses Fisher's work for the club. An obituary is in the *New York Times*, 10 Nov. 1958.

ROBERT L. GALE

FISHER, Edward Francis. *See* Fisher, Frederic John.

FISHER, Fred (30 Sept. 1875–14 Jan. 1942), composer and lyricist of popular songs, was born Alfred Breitenbach in Cologne, Germany, the son of Max Breitenbach and Theodora (maiden name unknown). He spent his earliest years in Germany before his family immigrated to the United States, where his parents became citizens. When he reached his teen years, young Alfred's life was filled with remarkable adventures that were typical of the dime novels of the day. At the age of thirteen he ran away from home to enlist in the German navy. A few years later he joined the French Foreign Legion before immigrating back to America on a cattle boat in 1900. Settling in Chicago and changing his name to Fred Fisher, he learned to play the piano from a black barroom pianist in hopes of becoming a popular songwriter.

Fisher began his prolific songwriting career in earnest in 1904 and was prosperous enough within a year to open his own publishing house (in brief partnership with songwriter Joseph McCarthy), which was enormously successful. His first hit song, "If the Man in the Moon Were a Coon," for which he wrote both music and lyrics, sold in excess of three million copies in 1906. Fisher's songs, like many others of his day, featured ethnic and racial stereotypes that seem ludicrous today. However, they were extremely popular with early twentieth-century audiences. Fisher also excelled at songs featuring geographical images, such as "Norway" (1915), "Siam" (1915), and one of his greatest and most lasting successes, "Chicago" (1922). Although he composed numerous ballads, his most effective works were comic songs, for which he was adept at inventing odd rhythms to suit the comic lyrics.

From 1906 to the early 1920s Fisher wrote a long string of commercial song successes, many of which evoke the spirit of the first two decades of the twentieth century. The most popular of these were "Any Little Girl That's a Nice Little Girl" (1910, with lyrics by Thomas J. Gray), "Come, Josephine, in My Flying Machine" (1910, with lyrics by Alfred Bryan), and "When I Get You Alone Tonight" (1912, with lyrics by Bryan). In 1913 Fisher's "Peg o' My Heart," also with lyrics by Bryan, was suggested by the title of a popular Broadway play featuring the incandescent actress Laurette Taylor. The song scored a hit in the

Ziegfeld *Follies of 1913* when it was introduced by José Collins. In 1914 singer/comedian Al Jolson was instrumental in popularizing a typical Fisher novelty song, "Who Paid the Rent for Mrs. Rip Van Winkle?" (with lyrics by Bryan). Among other hits from Fisher's pen were "There's a Little Spark of Love Still Burning" (1914, with lyrics by Joe McCarthy), "Ireland Must Be Heaven for My Mother Came from There" (1916, with lyrics by McCarthy and Howard Johnson), "There's a Broken Heart for Every Light on Broadway" (1915, with lyrics by McCarthy), "They Go Wild, Simply Wild, Over Me" (1917, with lyrics by McCarthy), "Oui, Oui, Marie" (1918, with lyrics by Bryan and McCarthy), and "Lorraine, My Beautiful Alsace Lorraine" (1917, with lyrics by Bryan). The last was particularly popular during the years of World War I, as was Fisher's greatest popular success, "Dardanella" (1919, with lyrics by Fisher set to a tune originated by Felix Bernard as "Turkish Tom Tom"). It sold over six million records and two million copies of sheet music. (In 1943 dramatist Tennessee Williams chose this song to evoke the World War I era in his great drama *The Glass Menagerie*). Typically for Fisher, who was thought of as "difficult" and eccentric by many of his contemporaries, this remarkably successful song was entangled for many years in various lawsuits over ownership that dragged on until the 1960s. Similarly, when composer Jerome Kern used Fisher's technique of a recurring bass rhythm (later used frequently in the boogie-woogie music of the late 1930s) for his song "Ka-luia," Fisher sued and was awarded $250 damages.

Following World War I, Fisher's outstanding song successes were "Daddy, You've Been a Mother to Me" (1920), "When the Honeymoon Was Over" (1921), and the aforementioned "Chicago," all with both music and lyrics by Fisher, and "Fifty Million Frenchmen Can't Be Wrong" (1927, with lyrics by Billy Rose and Willie Raskin), "When the Morning Glories Wake Up in the Morning" (1927, with lyrics by Rose), and "Happy Days and Lonely Nights" (1929, with lyrics by Rose). In the early 1920s Fisher moved to Hollywood, where he composed the scores for several silent films. When the transition was made to sound film in 1927, some of his songs were included in two early talkies, *Hollywood Revue of 1929* and *Their Own Desire* (1930), and he wrote "I'd Rather Be Blue" (with lyrics by Rose) for Fanny Brice's first film, *My Man* (1928). Other movie songs by Fisher that were popular include "I Don't Want Your Kisses" (with lyrics by Fisher) for *So This Is College* (1929), "Ich Liebe Dich" (with lyrics by Martin Broones) for *Wonder of Women* (1929), and "Girl Trouble" (lyrics by Fisher) and "Dust" (music by Andy Rice) for *Children of Pleasure* (1930). After this extraordinary period of feverish activity, Fisher wrote few songs after 1930, although his "Your Feet's Too Big" (lyrics by Ada Benson) was popularized by Fats Waller in 1936.

Fisher's work included songs of every kind, but aside from a few ballads and love songs, it was his comic songs that were generally recognized as his out-standing efforts. Fisher's songs remained popular even toward the end of his life. In 1941 his song "Whispering Grass" (with lyrics by his daughter Doris), was the top song on the BBC Hit Parade. Doris Fisher also wrote songs for several movies, often in collaboration with Allan Roberts. Some of her co-compositions include "You Always Hurt the One You Love" (1944) and "Put the Blame on Mame" (1946). Fisher's sons, Marvin and Dan, were also songwriters.

Seriously ill during the last years of his life, Fisher despaired and committed suicide by hanging himself in New York City. In 1949 a highly fictionalized film version of his life, *Oh, You Beautiful Doll*, featured S. Z. "Cuddles" Sakall as Fisher and was released by 20th Century–Fox. Adapted from an original story by Albert and Arthur Lewis and a screenplay credited to George Jessel, Fisher's movie biography also featured June Havoc and Mark Stevens in the cast. Curiously enough, the title song was not by Fisher, but the score of the film is otherwise laced with his most enduring songs.

• For information on Fisher, see W. Craig, *Sweet and Lowdown: America's Popular Song Writers* (1978), and "The Honor Roll of Popular Songwriters. No. 13: Fred Fisher," *Billboard*, 19 Mar. 1949, p. 46. Obituaries are in *Metronome*, Feb. 1942; the *New York Herald Tribune*, 15 Jan. 1942; and *Newsweek*, 26 Jan. 1942.

JAMES FISHER

FISHER, Frederic John (2 Jan. 1878–11 July 1941), **Charles Thomas Fisher** (16 Feb. 1880–8 Aug. 1963), **William Andrew Fisher** (21 Sept. 1886–20 Dec. 1969), **Lawrence P. Fisher** (19 Oct. 1888–3 Sept. 1961), **Edward Francis Fisher** (23 Feb. 1891–17 Jan. 1972), and **Alfred Joseph Fisher** (7 Dec. 1892–9 Oct. 1963), automobile industry pioneers, were the sons of Lawrence B. Fisher, a blacksmith, and Margaret Theisen. The family also included a youngest son, Howard Albert, and four sisters. Fred and Charles were born in Sandusky, Ohio; the other brothers were born in Norwalk, Ohio, where they all grew up and worked for their father in his blacksmith and carriage shop. Fred attended a Catholic parochial school and left after finishing eighth grade so that he could work full time for his father. He later studied two years at a business college in Sandusky.

In the 1890s Charles and Fred Fisher traveled as artisans and plied their carriage-making skills. From 1901 to 1902 Charles worked in Detroit with the C. R. and J. C. Wilson Carriage Company, which as the world's largest manufacturer of horse-drawn carriage bodies was beginning to manufacture automobile bodies. The brothers later worked with the Chancey Thomas Company of Boston, one of the most prestigious American buggy shops. Boston was then considered one of the premier coach-building cities in the country, but Charles and Fred also worked in various other cities, including New York, Chicago, Philadelphia, and Pittsburgh. In 1902 Fred was hired by the C. R. and J. C. Wilson Carriage Company and later that year was promoted to the position of superintendent; two years later he induced Charles to return as his assistant.

In 1908 Charles, who was married and starting a family, asked for a $5-a-week raise but was refused. As a result, both Charles and Fred quit their positions at the Wilson company and pooled resources with their only relative in Detroit, an uncle named Albert A. Fisher, to form the Fisher Body Company in July 1908. Albert, whose successful Standard Wagon Works was already making automobile carriages for Henry Ford, supplied 60 percent of the $50,000 in capital needed to start the company. The Fisher brothers planned to make closed "all-weather" bodies, foreseeing a time when Americans would drive in all seasons of the year, but they faced skeptical automobile manufacturers who believed that Americans would not like being confined behind glass and would enjoy driving only in the open air. As a result, until the 1920s most of the bodies that the Fisher Body Company made were open; in fact, as late as 1919 most automobiles manufactured in America had open bodies. Closed bodies remained unpopular not because motorists resisted confinement but rather because cars with closed bodies were unreasonably expensive. During the 1920s automobile manufacturers finally began to price their closed-body cars more competitively with open-body cars. By 1927, 85 percent of automobiles made in America had closed bodies. This switch to closed bodies, which the Fisher brothers helped to effect, represented a major transformation of the American automobile industry.

Albert Fisher was one of those who subscribed to the idea that the public would not take to riding in an enclosed body. He resisted the Fisher brothers' predilection for closed bodies and soon wanted to pull out of their business. Albert's departure could have spelled financial trouble for the Fishers, but Louis Mendelssohn, an architect and engineer who served as a director of the Herreshoff Motor Company, a builder of luxury cars, stepped in and bought out Albert's share in the company. Mendelssohn became chairman of the firm and installed his brother Aaron as head bookkeeper and secretary. The Mendelssohns stayed with the company until 1926, and their infusion of new money and confidence allowed it to prosper and expand production. The new Fisher Body enterprise also benefited from new orders, such as a 1910 Cadillac Motor Car Company request for 150 closed bodies, which it wanted delivered within several months. The brothers astounded skeptics by successfully completing the order on time. Later that year they renamed their operation the Fisher Closed Body Company. Another opportunity came when the Herreshoff Motor Company ordered 500 bodies.

In 1912 the Fisher brothers organized the Fisher Body Company of Canada, Ltd., based in Walkerville, Ontario. In that year Lawrence came to Detroit and joined his brothers' operation as superintendent of paint and trim. The following year Edward and Alfred graduated from the Andrew F. Johnson Carriage and Automobile Drafting School in New York, and both

began to work for Fisher Body Company, with Alfred becoming a vice president and chief engineer. In 1915 William, who was in Norwalk operating the Fisher Auto Top Company, a supplier of canvas car roofs, also joined his brothers in Detroit to work for their burgeoning business. In 1916 the Fisher Body Corporation was formed from a merger of the brothers' U.S. and Canadian operations. The new enterprise had an annual productive capacity of 370,000 units.

One explanation for the immediate success of the Fisher brothers' enterprise lay in the quality and craftsmanship of their product. Fisher bodies, designed specifically for automobiles, were attractive and stylish but also able to withstand the stress of high-speed, power-driven vehicles, which in the early days of the industry vibrated violently and had to travel on crude dirt roads. By contrast, many of their competitors simply modified designs for horse-driven carriages, and as a result, their products lacked the strength and durability of the Fisher bodies. As the quality of its product received recognition, the company became the world's largest manufacturer of automobile bodies, its customers including such renowned automakers as General Motors, Ford, Chrysler, Dodge, Packard, Hudson, Studebaker, Buick, and Wills Sainte Claire. In 1914 the business manufactured 105,000 bodies, a remarkable number for the time, and by 1920 its annual production had increased to 328,978. Profits jumped from $369,321 in 1913–1914 to $1.4 million in 1915–1916. During World War I, under government contract, the Fisher Body Company built a manufacturing plant and made military aircraft bodies; from 1917 to 1918 the company built 2,005 aircraft. During the 1920s it built or bought at least twenty plants at various sites in the United States and made several important acquisitions, including the Fleetwood Body Corporation, the Ternstedt Manufacturing Company, and the International Metal Stamping Company.

In making automobile bodies, the Fisher brothers helped to pioneer a number of new manufacturing techniques, including sheetmetal stamping and precision woodworking in mass production; the latter featured interchangeable wooden components and thereby dispensed with the need for individual hand-fitting. The interchangeability of parts allowed the brothers' operation to increase output while lowering unit costs, thereby increasing profits. The brothers also were the first manufacturers to use lacquer rather than paint on automobile bodies, and they introduced side window vents as well as the rubber weather strip for windshields. The Fishers continued to use wood framing in their car bodies until 1937, long after other car manufacturers had adopted all-metal bodies. But the Fishers put themselves at the vanguard of the industry in the mid-1930s when they unveiled the Turret Top, an all-steel, seamless roof that the entire automobile industry soon adopted.

During their early years of automobile body production the Fisher brothers considered starting up their own automobile manufacturing company. The obvious advantages would be that they already had expertise in making a major car component, the body, and producing complete cars would ensure their body-making division a constant and reliable customer, namely, their own prospective car-manufacturing operation. Moreover, the brothers would be able to control the cost of their closed-body vehicles and thus make them more competitive with open-body cars. However, although they seriously entertained the idea of manufacturing their own automobiles, the brothers never made a final commitment to it; talk of Fisher cars ended after World War I, when it became clear that some of the country's premier automakers, including Ford, General Motors, and Studebaker, were interested in buying out the Fisher Body Company.

General Motors eventually acquired the Fisher Body Company in a two-stage process. The first step took place in 1919, when the Fisher brothers sold a 60 percent interest in their company to GM. At that time, GM was undergoing an ambitious expansion program under the direction of president William C. Durant, and the Fisher brothers' business was one of the more profitable companies he acquired. The new arrangement, which included an agreement to furnish bodies for all GM cars, gave the Fisher brothers an assured market that was large enough to accommodate their considerable production capacity. After striking this deal with GM, they refrained from contracting with outside automakers with the notable exception of Walter P. Chrysler, whose firm received open bodies from the Fishers during the mid-1920s. After finishing out their contract with Chrysler, the Fisher brothers made bodies exclusively for GM. BODY BY FISHER, with its emblem of a Napoleonic coach in profile, became an important slogan and selling point for GM cars.

Under the new arrangement with GM, the Fisher brothers continued to manage their division, and some of them also assumed important roles in the GM corporate structure. In 1922 Fred became a director at GM as well as a member of the corporation's executive committee. Two years later Fred, Charles, and Lawrence left the Fisher Body Corporation to join GM management. Fred was made a vice president and a member of GM's finance committee, whereas Charles became a vice president and director. Lawrence also became a GM director in 1924 and the following year was named a vice president, a member of GM's executive committee, and president and general manager of Cadillac operations. As president of Cadillac until 1934, Lawrence, the most flamboyant of the Fisher brothers, oversaw a $5 million expansion program that boosted the division's annual production capacity to 60,000 cars. In 1930 he introduced America's first sixteen-cylinder automobile, the Cadillac V-12. Lawrence was responsible also for bringing Harley Earl to Detroit to work for GM; Earl, a pioneer in automobile styling, influenced the shape of American automobiles for decades. In 1941 Lawrence became a vice president in charge of the Fisher Body Division.

The second stage of the GM buyout came in 1926, when GM bought the remaining stock of the Fisher

Body Corporation for a reported $208 million. It was a staggering sum for its day, and the story of how the Fisher brothers parlayed an original investment of $50,000 into such a lucrative sale is legendary in the annals of automobile history. The company became the Fisher Body Division of GM, and under the direction and control of the parent company it continued to produce all bodies for GM cars. The six Fisher brothers each received a position in the GM corporation or one of its divisions. William became the first president of the Fisher Division, Alfred worked as a vice president, and Edward served as chief engineer, a title he held until 1934, when he became general manager of the Fisher Body Division. By the time GM absorbed it, the division was producing more than half a million car bodies per year and employing 40,000 workers in forty-four plants. When the stock market crashed in October 1929, the Fisher family was one of the richest in America, their fortune estimated at over $3 billion.

In 1920 the Fisher brothers became the first tenants of the new GM Building in downtown Detroit, where they based their operations for the next eight years. In 1927 they began construction of the $9 million, 29-story Fisher Building, which was designed by architect Alfred Kahn and completed in 1928. Located in downtown Detroit, the Fisher Building served as the headquarters for the Fisher brothers' various operations and was connected to the GM Building by an underground tunnel. The brothers held the twenty-fifth through twenty-seventh floors of the building. Fisher & Company, a family-owned investment firm founded in 1924, occupied the twenty-fifth floor; their offices were located on the twenty-sixth floor, where the brothers' affinity for fine wood craftsmanship was apparent in the exquisite wooden paneling and hand-carved wooden furniture; and the twenty-seventh floor featured a luxurious dining room where the brothers met daily for lunch. The Fisher brothers sold the building in 1963, and it later was a designated Michigan historical landmark.

Both Fred and Charles Fisher continued as GM vice presidents until 1934. Charles resigned to become president of Fisher & Company; Fred served as its chairman. Its interests included vast amounts of lumber and land. Charles also became president of a personal investment firm, Prime Securities Company. During the 1920s the Fishers had engaged in considerable stock market speculation, but heavy losses resulting from the 1929 crash forced them to withdraw from large-scale trading.

In 1940 Edward became a vice president of GM while also continuing as general manager of its Fisher Body Division. During World War II the division made various armaments, including tanks, for the U.S. armed services. Alfred, who was active in the management of Fisher & Company, continued as chief engineer and vice president of Fisher Body Division until 1944. That same year the Fisher brothers surprised the automobile industry by leaving their executive posts at GM. The brothers explained at the press conference announcing their retirement that there was no acrimony with GM; rather, their departure stemmed from their desire to leave the business together, since they had started their enterprise together and had worked as a team throughout their careers. Lawrence and Edward continued as directors of GM, Lawrence until his death in 1961 and Edward until his retirement in 1969, the latter event marking the end of forty-eight years of GM board membership for the Fisher brothers.

One of the most closely knit business families in American history, the Fisher brothers were intensely private; they so avoided publicity that many aspects of their private lives remain inscrutable. After the death of their father in 1921, Fred served as the acknowledged leader of the clan until his death in 1941, whereupon leadership responsibilities devolved to Charles. From 1914 to 1963 the brothers met daily for lunch to exchange ideas and discuss problems and policies. Deeply respectful of age, they positioned the eldest at the head of the table and arranged themselves in descending order of age, with the youngest at the foot of the table. These lunches were private and exclusively for the brothers. Although they occasionally disagreed in private, the brothers almost always stood together on major decisions, which led outsiders to comment that they were essentially one person. All of the brothers had an equal say in deciding business policies, and they all shared equally in business profits.

After leaving GM, the Fisher brothers remained active in the business world, serving as directors of numerous corporations and taking prominent roles in the community affairs of Detroit. Their active role in that city led them to be called "Detroit's first family." They gave extensively but unpretentiously to charity, donating money to schools, churches, and cultural institutions and founding orphanages and nursing homes. Among the institutions in and around Detroit that they helped to establish were the Fisher Home for the Aged, the Sarah Fisher Home for Orphaned Children (named after Charles's wife), the Fisher branch of the Detroit YMCA, the Fisher Administration Center at the University of Detroit, and a nurses' home at Providence Hospital. They also donated $1 million for the Fisher-Titus Hospital in the younger brothers' hometown of Norwalk.

Fred married Burtha Meyers in 1908. Charles and his wife, Sarah W. Kramer, whom he married in 1901, had four sons and two daughters. William married Lura Mary Titus in 1908; they had one son. Lawrence married Dolly Roach in 1951. Alfred married Alma Cripps in 1918; they had five children. Edward married Adeline Wink in 1916; she died in 1954. The couple had three daughters. The seventh and youngest Fisher brother, Howard Albert, was not active in auto bodymaking but managed the Fisher Building. All of the Fisher brothers died in Detroit.

• Literature on the Fisher brothers is sparse. The National Automotive History Collection of the Detroit Public Library maintains files on the Fisher brothers. The Historical Collection of the GMI Engineering and Management Institute in Flint, Mich., contains several articles and publicity releases on the Fishers. Among the articles are Malcolm Bingay, "The Story of Frederic J. Fisher, an Epic of Great Family Fidelity," *Detroit Free-Press*, 15 July 1941, and Jack Crellin, "Fisher Brothers—7 Brilliant Lives Cloaked in Privacy," *Detroit News*, 31 Jan. 1965. Obituaries are in the *Detroit News* and the *Detroit Free-Press*, 4 Sept. 1961, 10 Aug. 1963, 10 Oct. 1963, 22 Dec. 1969, and 17 Jan. 1972, and in the *New York Times*, 12 July 1941, 4 Sept. 1961, 9 Aug. 1963, 10 Oct. 1963, 22 Dec. 1969, and 18 Jan. 1972.

YANEK MIECZKOWSKI

FISHER, Frederick Bohn (14 Feb. 1882–15 Apr. 1938), Methodist minister, bishop, and missionary, was born in Greencastle, Pennsylvania, the son of James Edward Fisher and Josephine Bohn-Shirley. In the early 1890s his father moved his family to Muncie, Indiana, to take advantage of the economic opportunity in a growing industrial center. In 1899 Fisher graduated from high school in Muncie. He received a B.A. from Asbury College in 1902, and from 1907 to 1909 he did graduate work at Boston University and Harvard. He received an S.T.B. from Boston University School of Theology in 1909 and an S.T.D. from Boston University in 1930. He married Edith Jackson in 1903. After her death, he married Welthy Honsinger in 1924. There is no record of children from either marriage.

Fisher was licensed as a Methodist exhorter in 1900 and as a local preacher by the North Indiana Conference in 1902. He was ordained a deacon in 1904, and he was ordained an elder by Bishop F. W. Warne, Meerut, India, in 1905. From 1902 to 1904 he served Beamer Chapel and Hopewell, Kokomo, Indiana, but between 1904 and 1906 he was a missionary in Agra, India. He returned to the United States and ministered to North Cohasset Methodist Church in Massachusetts in 1906–1907 and to First Methodist Church, Boston, from 1907 to 1910. Between 1910 and 1912 he was field secretary of the Board of Foreign Missions, and from 1912 to 1916 he was secretary of the Laymen's Missionary Movement of the Methodist church. Internationally, he attended the World Missionary Conference in Edinburgh, Scotland, in 1910; he served as associate general secretary of the Laymen's Missionary Movement (United States and Canada) in 1916–1917; he toured Oriental mission fields in 1917–1918; he served on the Centenary Committee for the denomination and New York area from 1918 to 1920; and he was director of the Industrial Relations Department Interchurch Movement in 1919–1920.

At the General Conference in 1920 Fisher, back in the North Indiana Conference, was elected a bishop of the Methodist Episcopal church at age thirty-eight and assigned to Calcutta, India. From 1920 to 1930 he served as bishop and immersed himself in Indian culture in an effort to relate Methodism to the local situation. He came to know Mohandas Karamchand Gandhi, and upon Fisher's return to the United States he lectured on Gandhi to American audiences. It was Fisher who is credited with inspiring E. Stanley Jones to become a missionary to India. As an advocate of the Indianization of the Methodist enterprise in India,

Fisher also promoted the development of an international church polity whereby all Christians could be in fellowship and communion. Because of the administrative demands on him as a bishop (such as travel, judicial trials, and financial and temporal management), Fisher resigned the episcopal office in 1930. He thus became the first Methodist bishop to seek release, except for reasons of health, from episcopal duties in 150 years. Back in the United States he pastored at First Methodist Church in Ann Arbor, Michigan, from 1930 to 1934 and at Central Methodist Church in Detroit from 1934 to 1938.

A dynamic preacher, lecturer, and leader, Fisher was in demand. He was Fondren lecturer at Southern Methodist University in 1931; Earl lecturer at Pacific School of Religion in 1932; Beemer lecturer at De-Pauw University in 1932; special lecturer at Boston University in 1924, 1928, and 1930; lecturer at Syracuse University in 1933; lecturer at Morningside College in 1934; Adams lecturer at Indiana University in 1936; and Cole lecturer at Vanderbilt University in 1937. His published writings include *The Way to Win* (1915); *Gifts from the Desert* (1916); *India's Silent Revolution*, with Gertrude Marvin Williams (1919); *Garments of Power* (1920); *Which Road Shall We Take?* (1923); *Indians in South Africa* (1924); *Building the Indian Church*, with Walter Brooks Foley (1929); *Personology* (1930); *The Living Christ in the Modern World* (1931); *That Strange Little Brown Man Gandhi* (1932); *Can I Know God?* (1934); *The Man That Changed the World* (1937); and *How to Get Married and Stay That Way* (1938). He held membership in the International Society of Theta Phi, was a fellow of the American Geographical Society and the Royal Geographical Society, and was a Freemason.

Fisher was a large man physically and intellectually and had a commanding presence. A wide reader, serious thinker, and generous contributor of his means to good causes, he emphasized the evangelical and prophetic traditions of the Christian ministry rather than the ecclesiastical and technical aspects of administration. By championing the Indianization of the Methodist church in India, he hastened the day when the denomination promoted native leadership in its foreign missions. He also sought to move his denomination toward more democratic reforms, which would make unity with other free Christian bodies a natural step. He died on Good Friday in Detroit, Michigan.

• Sources on Fisher include "Frederick Bonn Fisher," *Encyclopedia of World Methodism*, vol. 1 (1974); Welthy Honsinger Fisher, *Frederick Bohn Fisher: World Citizen* (1944); *Christian Century*, 2 July 1930; and Francis V. McConnell, *By the Way: An Autobiography* (1952). An obituary is in the *New York Times*, 16 Apr. 1938.

FREDERICK V. MILLS

FISHER, George Park (10 Aug. 1827–20 Dec. 1909), historian of Christianity, was born in Wrentham, Massachusetts, the son of Lewis Whiting Fisher and Nancy Fisher. After graduating from Brown University in 1847, Fisher enrolled briefly at Yale Divinity School and Auburn Theological Seminary before completing his professional education at Andover Seminary in 1851, where he was influenced by Edwards Amasa Park, an advocate of the New England theology based on the thought of Jonathan Edwards. From 1852 to 1854, Fisher studied in Germany, imbibing the historical method, with its attention to detail and the literary and critical analysis of historical texts, that was sweeping German intellectual circles, especially in Tübingen. Consequently, Fisher believed that Christianity, both as a religion and as an institution, should be subjected to the same scholarly scrutiny that applied to all social institutions. In keeping with the German academic approach to historical scholarship, he saw his task as laying bare the facts and drawing presumably objective conclusions from them. His insistence on this understanding of historical method remains one of his most important contributions to American intellectual life.

Returning to the United States in 1854, Fisher accepted the Livingston Professorship of Divinity at Yale. Since the post included serving as pastor in the college church, he was also ordained to the Congregationalist ministry. This appointment began a lifelong career at Yale. In 1860 he married Adeline Louisa Forbes, with whom he had two sons and one daughter. The following year, Fisher became professor of ecclesiastical history at Yale Divinity School, serving until his retirement in 1901. He was also dean of the divinity school from 1895 to 1901. As a teacher, Fisher was noted for his witty and anecdotal style.

Fisher's work combined historical analysis with a commitment to establishing a solid intellectual grounding for Christian belief. This dual focus led him to explore early church history in *The Beginnings of Christianity* (1877) and the development of Christian thought in *History of Christian Doctrine* (1896). His concern for demonstrating that Christian belief was reasonable provided the basis for *Faith and Rationalism* (1879). In this work, which went through several editions, Fisher argued that faith was grounded both in the intellect and in the feelings, especially one's experience of conscience and dependence on supernatural power. This awareness made the moral teachings of Christianity reasonable, for experience revealed the reality of sin and the pervasiveness of mystery in human life. Stark rationalism, Fisher claimed, ignored both sin and mystery. Similar themes undergirded other apologetic works, such as *The Christian Religion* (1882), *The Grounds of Theistic and Christian Belief* (1883), *Manual of Christian Evidences* (1890), *The Nature and Method of Revelation* (1890), and *Manual of Natural Theology* (1893). Fisher's *History of the Reformation*, first published in 1873 and revised in 1906, became the standard textbook for a generation of students. He also wrote a widely used *History of the Christian Church* (1887).

German scholarship encouraged Fisher to place religious developments in their larger cultural context, for he was convinced that the history of Christianity could be understood only through the interaction of religious and secular forces. This broader interest resulted in his *Outlines of Universal History* (1885) and *Brief History of the Nations* (1896). He also explored his New England roots in a study of early American history, *The Colonial Era*, published in 1892.

Fisher was active in promoting the more general academic study of history. He served as president of both the American Historical Association and the American Society of Church History. In addition, through his editorship of *New Englander* and its successor, *New Englander and Yale Review*, he was able to reach a larger, nonacademic audience.

Although historical scholarship in the later twentieth century has moved well beyond his understanding of fact and objectivity, Fisher made a signal contribution in his attention to historical method and detail, his application of critical tools to Christian sources, and his construction of an apologetic for Christian belief based on the resonance between doctrine and the actual human experience that made such belief plausible.

Fisher died in New Haven eight years after his retirement from Yale.

• The Yale Divinity School library is the repository for the George Park Fisher Papers. Letters from Fisher may also be found in the Franklin E. Smith Papers, Duke University, and the Samuel W. Marvin Correspondence, University of Virginia. In addition to numerous scholarly articles, Fisher wrote *History of the Church in Yale College* (1858), *The Supernatural Origins of Christianity* (1865), *Life of Benjamin Silliman* (1866), and *Discussions in History and Theology* (1880). He also edited and wrote the introduction to one work by Jonathan Edwards, *An Unpublished Essay of Edwards on the Trinity* (1903). There is no critical biography and only brief references to him in scholarly works on the history of New England religious thought. An obituary by his successor at Yale, Williston Walker, appears in the January 1910 issue of *Yale Divinity Quarterly*.

CHARLES H. LIPPY

FISHER, Ham (1901–27 Dec. 1955), cartoonist, was born Hammond Edward Fisher in Wilkes-Barre, Pennsylvania, the son of Edward John Fisher, a businessman, and Sadie Breakstone. With little taste for studies—"Mathematics and kindred subjects bored me," he recalled in 1948, "and I barely lurched through high school"—he dreamed of being a cartoonist from the age of six, and he remembered being "thrown out of every class for drawing pictures." He managed to finish high school in 1918, however, and drove a truck for his father until the family business failed that year. Then he worked for a time as a salesman before landing a job as editorial and sports cartoonist and part-time advertising salesman with the *Wilkes-Barre Herald* in 1919. The next year he moved to the larger *Times-Leader*, where he had the chance to report the local news and write a column as well as draw cartoons. In 1925 he and a friend started their own paper in Wilkes-Barre, but the enterprise lasted less than a year.

Sometime around 1920 Fisher met a simple, good-natured boxer and found the idea for his comic strip

Joe Palooka. He rushed back to his office, wrote a plot outline, and made some sketches for a strip featuring a powerful but warm-hearted pugilist. Fisher made repeated forays to New York to interest the syndicates in distributing the strip, but with no success. Finally in 1927 he moved to New York to improve his chances. He kept a job selling advertising at the *Daily News* for two years while he tried to sell *Joe Palooka*. At last his break came in 1929 when he became a salesman for the McNaught Syndicate. The president, Charles V. McAdam, agreed to give *Palooka* a chance the next year but first wanted Fisher to try to sell a new strip, *Dixie Dugan*. The strip, recounting the adventures of a show girl, had been sold to only two papers, but in forty days Fisher persuaded thirty papers to take it, a syndicate sales record. McAdam was so impressed he urged him to stay on the sales staff, but Fisher refused to give up on his brainchild. When his boss went on vacation, Fisher set out on his own and sold the strip to twenty papers in three weeks. *Joe Palooka* was launched successfully on 19 April 1930 and quickly established itself as one of the most popular strips in the country.

At the peak of *Joe Palooka*'s popularity, during the 1950s, its syndicate claimed sales to some 1,000 newspapers worldwide and a readership of more than 100 million. The strip was translated into fourteen languages and appeared in virtually every medium. In 1932 there was a network radio show about the boxer; in 1934 a feature film was made with Stu Irwin as Joe and Jimmy Durante as his manager; in 1936 and 1937 Joe was featured in six comedy shorts; during the 1940s and 1950s Hollywood produced nineteen full-length *Joe Palooka* films and the reprint comic book *Joe Palooka Comics* was selling more than a million copies a month; and in 1954 a syndicated television series was based on the strip. It had a large readership among boxing fans, but its audience extended far beyond the sports audience. Historian Jerry Robinson wrote in 1974 that the strip "was also a classic confrontation of good versus evil, the virtuous and innocent versus the corrupt and corrupters. Joe Palooka was a young heavyweight champion, simple, big-hearted, incorruptible, with a perfect physique and a dynamic left cross" (Robinson, p. 123). Other regular characters in the strip, including Joe's flashy manager Knobby Walsh, his youthful sidekick Jerry Leemy, his attractive, upper-class sweetheart (and, from 1949, wife) Ann Howe, his devoted trainer Smokey (or Smoky), and his loving mother Ma Palooka, were all stock types used to further the plots, but "the gentle knight" remained the focus of all action.

Fisher relied on assistants to help him with his somewhat inept drawing, employing the services of Wilkes-Barre friend Phil Boyle from 1930, Al Capp in 1933, and Mo Leff from 1934 onward, but the scripting remained essentially his own. The strip was never sophisticated graphically but owed its popularity to its clearly defined characters and its blend of adventure, suspense, humor, and sentiment. The tightly plotted stories were believable, by comic-strip standards, and were made more so by being set in recognizable places and including such real-life notables as Jack Dempsey, Claudette Colbert, and Franklin D. Roosevelt. The strip also kept up with the times. Its patriotic hero was the first adventure-strip character to enter military service, enlisting on 29 November 1940, more than a year before the United States entered the war. Though he was "the heavyweight cham-peen of the world," he never took advantage of his celebrity, declining a commission, with characteristic modesty, because he recognized that he did not know enough to be an officer. This combination of heroism and humility made Joe Palooka one of the most engaging personifications of American virtue during the war, and Fisher often contributed the champ's services to support military recruitment, education, and morale.

Fisher was a shrewd businessman who negotiated his own contracts very successfully, and by the middle 1940s he was earning more than $250,000 a year from his work. He was less successful in his personal life. His marriage to Carolyn Graham, contracted in 1936, dissolved in a messy divorce in 1943. The couple had one child. He married a woman many years his junior named Marilyn in 1954, but the two spent little time together, and he grew increasingly isolated. A difficult man to work with, he maintained a bitter feud with his onetime assistant Al Capp, begun in 1933 when Capp took a hillbilly character Fisher claimed as his own creation as a model for the hero of his own strip, *Li'l Abner*. Fisher attacked Capp frequently on public platforms and in print, and Capp lampooned Fisher mercilessly in his strip and wrote a piece in the *Atlantic Monthly* describing his former employer (without naming him) as "a veritable gold mine of human swinishness." Fisher retaliated by accusing Capp of including hidden pornographic imagery in *Li'l Abner* and sent photostats of the allegedly obscene material to the news media. Capp's lawyers had no trouble proving that Fisher had doctored the art. In February 1955 the National Cartoonists Society charged Fisher with using artwork that was "altered, tampered with and . . . not a true reproduction" and expelled him.

Shortly after Christmas that year, Fisher took an overdose of sleeping pills and died in his New York studio, leaving two notes complaining of his health. The *New York Daily Mirror*'s sports editor Dan Parker wrote of him on 30 December, "Ham Fisher, who piggy-backed to fame and fortune on the broad shoulders of a lovable pugilist named Joe Palooka . . . had everything one could ask of life when he reached the top except health, happiness and the desire to live." The strip lived on, however, continued by his assistant Mo Leff, who wrote and drew it until October 1959, when it was taken over by Tony di Preta. Described by Denis Gifford as "the most successful sporting strip of all time," Fisher's creation lasted until 4 November 1984.

• Material on Fisher is in "Comics—and Their Creators," *Literary Digest*, 17 Nov. 1934, p. 11; "Fourth Estate," *Newsweek*, 18 Dec. 1939, p. 42; and "Number 2 in a Series Devoted to America's Top Comic Strips," *Collier's*, 16 Oct. 1948, p. 28. For contemporary comments on *Joe Palooka*, see "Re-converting Palooka," *Newsweek*, 3 Sept. 1945, p. 68; "Palooka and Ann?—Yes," *Newsweek*, 7 June 1948, p. 56; Joe Brumby, "Joe Palooka, Perennial Champ," *Look*, 14 Oct. 1947, pp. 92–99; and "Mr. and Mrs. Palooka," *Time*, 27 June 1949, p. 4. The feud between Fisher and cartoonist Al Capp was reported in Al Capp's denunciation of Fisher, "I Remember Monster," *Atlantic Monthly*, Apr. 1950, pp. 54–57, and in "Capp vs. Fisher," *Time*, 14 Feb. 1955, p. 76, and 28 Feb. 1955, p. 49.

Entries on Fisher are in Maurice Horn, ed., *World Encyclopedia of Comics* (1976), and Ron Goulart, ed., *The Encyclopedia of American Comics* (1990), and his life and work are discussed in such histories of the medium as Coulton Waugh, *The Comics* (1947); Stephen Becker, *Comic Art in America* (1959); Jerry Robinson, *The Comics* (1974); Denis Gifford, *The International Book of Comics* (1984); Robert C. Harvey, *The Art of the Funnies* (1994); and Ron Goulart, *The Funnies* (1995). An obituary is in the *New York Times*, 5 Jan. 1956.

DENNIS WEPMAN

FISHER, Irving (27 Feb. 1867–29 Apr. 1947), economist, was born in Saugerties, New York, the son of George Whitefield Fisher, a minister, and Ella Westcott. One of four children, he was the oldest who survived childhood. The family lived for twelve years in Peace Dale, Rhode Island, where his father occupied the Congregational pulpit, then moved to Missouri. His father, who had studied divinity at Yale, died of tuberculosis just a few months before Fisher himself began as an undergraduate there in 1884. Fisher helped to support the family with prize scholarships and income from tutoring. At his graduation in 1888, he was awarded $500 per year for postgraduate study. He also earned money in other ways, such as a summer (1890) spent near St. Paul tutoring the sons of J. J. Hill, the railroad baron. He wrote at the time that Hill's enormous wealth was thoroughly justified, since he trebled the value of his railroad and provided an immense benefit to farmers "through his special sagacity." Later he repented of his enthusiasm, calling Hill "a shrewd man but unreliable to the last degree."

Graduate study at Yale in the late nineteenth century was not strictly departmentalized. Fisher studied mathematics under Josiah Willard Gibbs and political economy with William Graham Sumner. When the time came for a doctoral dissertation, Sumner suggested he combine the two fields, and this was how Fisher came to write one of the earliest works of mathematical economics by an American. The dissertation was published in 1892 in the *Transactions* of the Connecticut Academy of Arts and Sciences and rapidly won him an international reputation. In those years Yale recruited its faculty almost exclusively from among its own students, and Fisher was hired to teach mathematics. He never left, though in 1895 he was reassigned to the faculty of social and political science.

In 1893, after a two-year courtship, Fisher married Margaret Hazard, whom he had known casually in childhood. Her father was woolen goods manufacturer Rowland Hazard, and the marriage greatly improved Fisher's finances. Hazard built his daughter a palatial house in New Haven as a wedding present. The couple occupied that house until Margaret's death in 1940, raising in it three children. The first year of their marriage was spent touring Europe and meeting economists in Britain, France, Switzerland, Austria, and Italy.

In 1898 Fisher was promoted to full professor. He also began suffering from tuberculosis. Yale granted him an extended leave of absence, from which he returned in 1901. He began treatment under the fresh-air regime of a Dr. Trudeau in Saranac, New York, then went west to take advantage of the dry air in Colorado and California. This bout with serious illness probably was responsible for his considerable interest in matters of health. His bestselling book, by far, was a health manual called *How to Live*. The advice it contained reflected his view that "man has upset his pristine animal mode of living and needs to find scientific ways to restore the equilibrium. Most of the present-day problems of hygiene arise from introducing, uncompensated, the effects of certain devices of civilization." These were to be combated by avoiding alcohol and tobacco, masticating food fully, and filling houses with fresh air. Such advice, delivered tirelessly, caused him to be regarded, around New Haven at least, as a health faddist. This reputation was not greatly alleviated by his regular pilgrimages to Battle Creek, Michigan, to practice "biologic living" with John Harvey Kellogg, or by his writings in favor of prohibition, or by his exotic exercise habits, or even by his late conversion to a diet of fruit and vegetable juices. Ostensibly writing about astronomer Simon Newcomb in the *Economic Journal*, but really lamenting the refusal of colleagues to take his medical advice seriously, Fisher complained that "once a man's name becomes associated with a particular department of knowledge like astronomy, any attempts to contribute to other departments encounter a prejudice which it is difficult to overcome" (19 [1909]: 641).

Fisher's economic research was marked above all by an ideal of quantification. Political economy, as the discipline had traditionally been known, underwent an important theoretical change in the 1870s and 1880s. The new neoclassical theory identified value with utility, or more precisely with the utility of the last increment of a product consumed. Because utility was defined "at the margin," this increment could be regarded mathematically as a derivative. That is, the new marginal utility theory permitted the calculus to enter economics as the fundamental basis of theory. This was why Sumner could recommend that Fisher join his study of political economy to that of mathematics. He relied for his dissertation mainly on books by the British economist William Stanley Jevons and by two Germans, Rudolf Auspitz and Richard Lieben.

While Fisher always esteemed mathematical economics highly, he wrote rather little of it himself after 1892. Even his dissertation revealed a strong preference for measurement over logical deduction. Joseph Schumpeter remarked in an eloge prepared for the Econometric Society—of which Fisher himself was a founder—that Fisher's economics cannot be separated

from his statistics: "Throughout and from the start, Fisher aimed at a theory that would be statistically operative, in other words, at not merely quantitative but also numerical results." Fisher's dissertation began with an argument that economists should not trouble themselves with utilitarian psychology but need only attend to desires as reflected in economic behavior. He proposed that utility, in this sense, could be scaled and indeed measured in "utils." Fisher's first major work was also distinguished by its use of hydraulic constructions to model economic processes. Since utility was represented in these models as height, the equality of utilities of different goods at the margin was equivalent to the tendency of water to reach equilibrium at a single level.

In later work Fisher occasionally returned to the theory of marginal utility. In a 1927 festschrift for John Bates Clark, for example, he tried to show how interpersonal comparisons of utility could be made, so that one could reckon the advantages of shifting income from the rich to the poor. But after 1892 his economic interests shifted decisively in the direction of economic accounting and monetary theory. Both reflected unambiguously his lifelong commitment to economic measurement. He argued for the centrality of accounting to economics in the *American Economic Review*: "Any quantitative economic concept, to be of any use, should be capable of actual measurement. Accounts represent primarily those measures of business which are practical. They apply to business the acid test of practical workability—a test which might have saved much useless labor and disputation in economic literature" (20, no. 4 [1930]: 603).

In 1906 Fisher published *The Nature of Capital and Income* in which he tried to make these concepts clear. At its center was a distinction based on another hydraulic analogy: capital, like a lake, has no temporal dimension; income is a flow, like a river. He considered the latter the more fundamental concept. The value of capital is nothing other than a measure of an expectation of future income discounted by an interest rate, and, as the stock market clearly shows, the worth of a firm is by no means equivalent to the resale value of its property and equipment. He argued that income for tax purposes should mean present consumption, and should not include invested earnings. To label as "income" both the initial investment and its yield was absurd, and to tax them as such was unjust. Accordingly, he favored a consumption tax rather than a conventional income tax.

His first important work on money, significantly, was published in 1896, the year that William Jennings Bryan ran for the presidency on a ticket that backed the populist campaign for bimetalism in order to increase the money supply. Fisher was not unsympathetic. He presented extensive evidence of deflation over the previous two decades. He conceded that this had made the repayment of debts a great hardship for many. Farmers, he allowed, had a point in complaining about what Bryan, famously, called a cross of gold. Fisher added, though, that this increase in the value of gold was partially reflected in interest rates. To monetize silver would not rectify old injustices but might simply create new ones. In later writings he regretted that he had dealt too harshly with the bimetalists. Already in 1896 he expressed a hope that the monetary unit might somehow be made less variable.

His *The Rate of Interest* (1907) became famous for its defense of an "impatience" theory of interest. Interest derives most fundamentally from a preference for present earnings over future earnings, which is itself due in part to the possibility of investing that revenue productively. Monetary theory entered here, too, since "nominal" interest rates can be translated into real ones only by taking account of the changing value of money. In *The Purchasing Power of Money* (1911), he argued that the value of money is determined by its quantity. The relevant quantity for understanding prices is not a volume but a flow, the product of monetary volume (currency plus checking deposits) and velocity. Volume and velocity, he explained, are both "extremely definite," and the study of money can be "an exact science, capable of precise formulation, demonstration, and statistical verification." He presented in this book his fundamental monetary equation: the product of the volume of money and its rate of circulation is equal to the summed prices of all goods purchased.

This equation defined for Fisher a statistical problem. He undertook to measure all the relevant quantities and began in 1911 to publish them each year in an "equation of exchange." Soon after he began a major project to measure the purchasing power of money by keeping track of changes in the prices of a wide range of commodities. In the 1920s his enlarged home became the site of an "Index Number Institute," staffed by a dozen assistants and then, in addition, by a professional economic statistician, Max Sasuly. The institute published a weekly report, which was sent out to newspapers throughout the world. It also provided the calculations for much of his own work, especially the monumental study of 1922, *The Making of Index Numbers*.

By this time Fisher's monetary interests had coalesced into a reform campaign to stabilize the currency. Already in 1911 he explained the expansions and contractions of money that others were calling "business cycles" as monetary in origin. When prices rise, interest rates lag behind, so that real interest rates fall, perhaps even becoming negative. This leads businesses to borrow excessively and to overinvest. When interest rates catch up, some firms will be unable to make payments. Banks try to build up their shrinking reserves by calling in their loans; this contracts the money supply, causes prices to fall, and leaves businesses in a still more precarious situation, since they have to pay back their loans with appreciated money. Eventually interest rates fall too far and the expansionist phase begins over again.

Fisher proposed that this and other problems could be avoided by introducing a "compensated dollar." Using one of his index numbers to measure the changing value of money, Fisher theorized that the value of money could be steadied by increasing or decreasing appropriately the quantity of gold for which a dollar could be exchanged. This came to seem all the more urgent during the depression of the 1930s, which Fisher explained as mainly a consequence of an ill-timed monetary contraction. A tireless reformer and campaigner, he devoted a particularly great effort to this cause, writing several books and hundreds of technical reports and newspaper columns in favor of a dollar that would be as well standardized as the foot and the pound. Stable money, he wrote, can reduce "social injustice, social discontent and social inefficiency." He took advantage of his increasing access to political power to push his monetary scheme. In 1927, most memorably, he obtained an audience with Mussolini in Rome for this purpose. In that case and others, he mistook the courtesy of his reception for an intention to act.

In 1925 he identified four great causes to which his life was devoted: "the abolition of war, disease, degeneracy, and instability in money." The first of these inspired him to write a book and a flood of popular articles on behalf of American membership in the League of Nations. He even became active in the 1920 presidential campaign of James Cox. Disease was to be combated mainly through improved diet, exercise, and fresh air. He also favored public action to improve the national health, for which he furnished quantitative arguments. In a 1909 report for the National Conservation Commission under Theodore Roosevelt, he reckoned that an infant was worth $25 and an average person $2,900, making the total (net) value of the population some $250 billion. This, he explained, greatly surpassed all other wealth and justified strenuous public-health efforts. He later held that prohibition could increase national production by $6 billion annually.

The centerpiece of his campaign against degeneracy was eugenics. He urged the importance of eugenic measures in his bestselling *How to Live* and also in speeches and newspaper columns. He participated in conferences on "race betterment" and organized the American Eugenic Society in the early 1920s. He argued that the worst effect of the war was its "waste of germ plasm" and proposed that the "small stature characteristic of Frenchmen" was a result of the death of its finest in Napoleon's campaigns. "It is the quality rather than the quantity of life that should be held precious," he wrote. War might even be praiseworthy if it "would weed out only the criminal, the vicious, the feebleminded, the insane, the habitual paupers, and others of the defective classes" (*New York Times*, 25 July 1915).

Fisher poured great quantities of his own money into these campaigns. During the 1920s he became extremely wealthy, mainly in consequence of a card-index system he invented and marketed. His Index Visible Company was merged in 1926 with its chief competitor into Remington Rand and later enlarged to form Sperry Rand. Fisher, already a major stockholder, purchased massively on margin in the late 1920s, then lost everything in the depression, which he conspicuously failed to anticipate. He had to be rescued from bankruptcy by his sister-in-law. Yale helped by buying his house and renting it back to him. Late in life, according to his son, he was always looking to recover his fortune by investing in new companies with explosive growth potential and thereby became a soft touch for investment scams. He remained active as an economist and reformer until the end of his life, with his last years devoted above all to reducing monetary instability by requiring banks to hold 100 percent of checking deposits in reserve. At the time of his death in New York City he still resided in New Haven.

Fisher always wanted economics to matter for policy decisions. As president of the American Economic Association, in 1918 he proposed: "If we jealously guard our independence and impartiality we shall gain for our profession the enviable position of being the logical arbiters of the class struggle now beginning—arbiters which both sides can trust" (*American Economic Review* 9, supp. [1919]: 11). It may be doubted that Fisher heeded his own advice. In any case, none of his great reform campaigns succeeded. While his was a prominent voice in American public discourse for some three decades, his influence has been most enduring in government uses of economic quantification and within the discipline of economics itself. Schumpeter predicted in 1948 that "his name will stand in history principally as this country's greatest scientific economist." This sentiment was echoed in 1967 by Paul Samuelson and in 1987 by James Tobin. His work has inspired a huge professional literature, both in the more abstract and in applied areas of economic research.

• Fisher's papers, including nearly all his 2,425 publications, are held by the Sterling Library of Yale University. The publications are listed in a compilation by Fisher's son, Irving Norton Fisher, *A Bibliography of the Writings of Irving Fisher* (1961). The best source on Fisher's life is also by Irving Norton Fisher, *My Father Irving Fisher* (1956). This is a remarkably fair-minded account and includes extensive excerpts from some letters and from his major published works. It is the source of unattributed quotations in the article above. There is very little serious historical scholarship on Fisher. Some useful assessments of his work by economists include obituaries by Max Sasuly, "Irving Fisher and Social Science," *Econometrica* 15 (1947): 255–78, and Joseph Schumpeter, *Ten Great Economists* (1951), pp. 222–38, and the biographical sketch by James Tobin in *The New Palgrave: A Dictionary of Economics*, vol. 2 (1987), pp. 369–76. See also Robert L. Allen, *Irving Fisher: A Biography* (1993). On Fisher in an intellectual and academic context, see William J. Barber, "The Fortunes of Political Economy in an Environment of Academic Conservatism: Yale University," in *Breaking the Academic Mould*, ed. Barber (1988), and Dorothy Ross, *The Origins of American Social Science* (1991).

THEODORE M. PORTER

FISHER, Lawrence P. *See* Fisher, Frederic John.

FISHER, Mary (1623–1698), pioneer Quaker preacher and missionary, was born in Pontefract, Yorkshire, England. Nothing is known of her parents and educa-

tion. She was a servant girl in a home in Selby when she was converted to Quakerism by George Fox in 1651. She wrote an excellent if crabbed handwriting and expressed herself clearly.

In 1652 she was one of six Quakers imprisoned for sixteen months in York Castle for rebuking the "priest" at Selby. Together the Quakers published a tract, *False Prophets and False Teachers Described*. Released in 1653, she went with an older Quaker woman, Elizabeth Williams, on a preaching trip through the Fen country. In December they spoke to the undergraduates of Sidney Sussex College in Cambridge, telling them that "they were Antichrists, and that their College was a Cage of unclean Birds, and the Synagogue of Satan." Summoned by the students, the constable conducted the women to the mayor, who ordered them whipped at the market cross "until the blood ran down their bodies." The order was carried out, Fisher and Williams becoming the first Quakers to be publicly flogged.

The punishment only increased Fisher's zeal. Twice more she was imprisoned, again in York and in Buckinghamshire for rebuking "priests." Then in late 1655 she set off for the New World in the company of an older woman, Anne Austin. The two landed first in Barbadoes, then, in July 1656, in Puritan Boston, the first Quakers to reach the American colonies.

The Puritans feared the Quakers, whom they viewed as heretics, and the travelers were immediately seized, thrown into prison, stripped naked, and searched intrusively for signs of witchcraft. Their books and pamphlets were burned, and their jail window was boarded up; they might have starved had an elderly Puritan not bribed the jailer to allow him to provide them food. After five weeks they finally were shipped back to Barbados, and from there they returned to England.

Fisher's next, and most famous, missionary effort occurred the following year when she joined a group of six Quakers, three men and three women, traveling to the Mediterranean. After many adventures they reached Smyrna in Turkey, where the English consul sent them back to Venice. A storm at sea forced them to land on the island of Zante. At that point Fisher left her companions and somehow made her way over 600 miles across Greece and Thrace to Adrianople in Turkey. She believed herself to be on a divine mission to address the young Sultan Mahomet IV, to tell him that she had a message for him from "the Most High God." She persuaded the grand vizier to arrange an interview; the sultan listened to her gravely and said that he had understood every word and that he believed what she had said was true. He offered her an escort to see her safely back to Constantinople, but she declined and managed the trip alone.

Back in England Fisher continued to preach. In 1662, at the age of thirty-nine, she married William Bayly, a noted Quaker minister and writer who was also a sea captain. According to Gerard Croese, a seventeenth-century historian, Bayly chose Fisher because of her "great endowments not only of mind and wit but dexterity and experience." Later that year Bayly was arrested in London for refusing to remove his hat and was beaten by a soldier. When Mary Fisher Bayly reproved the officer, he struck her on the mouth and threw her to the ground, although she was pregnant. The child (her first) was born normally, and the couple had two additional children before Bayly drowned at sea in 1675. Three years later she was married a second time, to John Cross, of Southwark, and with him and her three children she emigrated to Charleston, South Carolina, in 1682, becoming part of a small pioneer Quaker settlement in that city. Cross died in 1687. Ten years later, a Quaker traveler, Robert Barrow, wrote to his wife that after being shipwrecked off Florida he had as his nurse Mary Fisher, "she that spake to the Great Turk."

In 1698 Fisher died in Charleston, leaving substantial properties in the city to her three children. Her pioneering work was kept alive by one granddaughter, Sophia Hume, who became an important Quaker writer and traveling minister.

• Letters from Mary Fisher to George Fox, Thomas Aldam, and others are at Friends House, London. A contemporary account of her whipping in Cambridge appears in *The First New Persecution; or, A True Narrative of the Cruel Usage of Two Christians by the Present Mayor of London* (1654); of her treatment in Boston, in George Bishop, *New England Judged* (1661); of her visit to the sultan and subsequent marriage, in Gerard Croese, *The General History of the Quakers* (1696); and of her beating on the streets of London, in Joseph Besse, *A Collection of the Sufferings of the People Called Quakers* (1753). There are chapters on her life in Mabel R. Brailsford, *Quaker Women* (1915), and in *Quaker Biographies*, vol. 2 (1912). Good treatments are in Rufus Jones, *The Quakers in the American Colonies* (1911; repr. 1962); William Braithwaite, *The Beginnings of Quakerism* (1912); and Nancy Hardesty, "Early Quaker Women Defy Persecution," *Evangelical Friend* 9, no. 3 (1975): 9–10. Material on her life in Charleston can be found in George Vaux, "Friends in Charleston, S.C.," *The Friend* 60, no. 12 (1909): 403–4, 411–13.

MARGARET HOPE BACON

FISHER, M. F. K. (3 July 1908–22 June 1992), writer, was born Mary Frances Kennedy in Albion, Michigan, the daughter of Rex Brenton Kennedy, a newspaper editor, and Edith Oliver Holbrook, a real estate broker. When Fisher was three years old, the family moved to the Quaker community of Whittier, California, where her father took over the editorship of the local newspaper. The Kennedys were Episcopal and somewhat "outside the faith" in their new home. Rex Kennedy continued as editor of the *Whittier News* for forty years. His and his wife's appreciation of writing and proper manners, the literary, artistic, and odd cohorts of the household all contributed to Fisher's intellectual, social, and imaginative growth.

Fisher's parents encouraged her learning, and she read early and much. Looking at herself retrospectively and with dry wit, she discerned precocious powers of observation and philosophy as well as the seeds of her life's passion in the girl she was: "When I was

about five, I began to suspect that eating something good with good people is highly important. By the time I was ten I not only knew, for myself, that this theory was right but I had added to it the companion idea that if children are given a chance to practice it, they will stand an even better chance of being keen adults" (*To Begin Again*, p. 50).

Epiphany apparently came at the age of six. Though she of course did not know it then, Fisher was beginning to collect the experiences that would define her career and her life: "My mother took us twenty-five miles each way on the trolley to see [*H. M. S. Pinafore*] and have our first meal in public, which she and my father decided—with no dispute—should be as fine as possible . . . the small room lighted with candles behind pink silk lampshades, with incredible expanses of snow-white linen, and a forest of glasses sparkling everywhere at our eye level, and with a fine, thin-nosed man dressed in black to take care of us— only us" ("The First Cafe" in *As They Were*, p. 85).

"Home" schooling included cooking, and Fisher greatly enjoyed preparing meals for her family. After public school in Whittier, Fisher attended the Bishop's School, a boarding school, which was where she ate her first raw oyster—an act that sealed her fate.

In 1927 Fisher enrolled in Illinois College, but moved back to California and Whittier College and then briefly attended Occidental College and the University of California at Los Angeles, where she met the poet Alfred Young Fisher. She did not finish her course of study at UCLA, but she and Alfred were married on 5 September 1929. Two weeks later they were off to Dijon, France, where Alfred entered the university's doctoral program.

As Fisher later remarked, Dijon "made" her. She learned the French language, literature, culture, food, wine, and idiosyncrasies; she learned cooking, she learned life, and she learned to be herself. She studied at the University of Dijon and the École des Beaux Arts but did not take a degree; she later bemoaned her lack of seriousness in getting a formal education. At this time she began writing seriously, keeping journals, composing stories and essays. She and her husband returned to California in 1932, unprepared for the America of the Great Depression. The Fishers lived at the Kennedy home in Whittier and at the Laguna Beach cottage built by Rex Kennedy around 1914. It was two years before Alfred was offered a job as an English instructor at Occidental College. To supplement that income Fisher worked at a frame shop that also sold pornographic postcards.

During those two years Fisher met many of her lifelong friends, including Lawrence Powell, his wife Fay, and Gloria Stuart Sheekman, the actress and artist. She and Alfred also met Dillwyn Parrish, a painter and relative of the artist Maxfield Parrish. Dillwyn, known as Timmy and Tim, was the senior member of the group of friends, being fourteen years older than Fisher. Alfred and Tim both encouraged Fisher's authorial inclinations; she had already published an article, "Pacific Village," in *Westways* (1934) and had been scribbling essays drawn from her readings of old cookbooks. Parrish suggested that she mix personal essays in with the historical ones and, more as literary amusement for her husband and her friend, Fisher submitted *Serve It Forth* to Harper. They published it in 1937.

Serve It Forth was a success in the rarefied world of culinary writing, where Fisher's unusual approach to considering food had many readers thinking she was a man, especially since she used masculine-sounding initials rather than her first name. She was set on the path she would never leave for the rest of her life. Parrish and his wife had divorced in 1934, and in 1937 he and the Fishers tried to make a go of communal life at the crumbling farmhouse and vineyard Parrish had bought in Vevey, near Bern, Switzerland. The idea was a pipedream; Alfred decamped to Smith College in Northampton, Massachusetts, and Fisher returned to California with the announcement she was divorcing Alfred and marrying Tim.

Fisher and Parrish began a life together in Vevey, where they tried to make the best of the perpetual pain that Parrish suffered after an embolism forced the amputation of one of his legs. They even managed joint authorship of a light-hearted novel, *Touch and Go* (1939), using the nom de plume Victoria Bern. In 1940 they returned to California, married, and set up their home, Bareacres, near Hemet, where Fisher resumed writing and Parrish painted, through the pain, every day. Parrish contracted Breuger's disease, which was progressive and incurable, and in the summer of 1941 he shot himself, finally ending his pain but leaving Fisher alone with a continuing sorrow.

Fisher briefly retreated to Mexico, where her brother David and her sister Norah and Norah's husband were living. But David too committed suicide shortly thereafter and Fisher returned to the sad but familiar solace of the little ranch near Hemet. Bareacres remained Fisher's haven for sixteen years, though by 1942 she was also living in Hollywood where she was a model for the avant-garde photographer Man Ray and a sometime screenwriter for Paramount Studios. She kept up her prolific freelance writing—magazine articles, essays, and books—because she was a writer to her bones, and she had to support herself. *Consider the Oyster* (1941) was followed by *How to Cook a Wolf* (1942), a shocking title that actually gave entertaining and practical advice on how to handle wartime rationings and deprivations. *The Gastronomical Me*, in which Tim Parrish is reincarnated as Chexbres, came in 1943. Literary critics as well as food critics were beginning to notice her work and, in it, a new and unusual literary voice.

The 1940s were highly productive and hectic years for Fisher: two daughters (Anna, born in 1943, and Mary, called "Kennedy," in 1946); marriage to literary agent Donald Friede in 1945; the collection *Here Let Us Feast: A Book of Banquets* (1946); a novel *Not Now But Now* (1947); and the seminal translation of Brillat-Savarin's *The Physiology of Taste* (1949). Fisher credited Friede with getting her to do—"under duress"—the

Brillat-Savarin translation. It was immediately acclaimed, whereas her novel had not been. Yet Friede still felt that she should focus on novels. Artistic differences, financial problems, parenting, and ill health all took their toll. Fisher and the girls had moved back to her family's home in Whittier by 1949 and the marriage ended in divorce in 1951.

Friede and Fisher remained friends, however, and it was his suggestion that resulted in the compilation of her first five books into *The Art of Eating* (1954), which remained in print for decades and which provided much-needed income for the hard-pressed single mother of two. Fisher had been working for her father at his newspaper. He died in 1953 and, a few years later, using their savings and a small inheritance, Fisher and her daughters moved to Europe for four years. The money would last longer there, and Fisher wanted her children to learn about other languages and cultures.

Financial necessity also spurred the production of *A Cordiall Water: A Garland of Odd and Old Recipes to Assuage the Ills of Man and Beast* (1961), Fisher's historical meditation on and collection of folk medicine that she always considered her best book. In 1962 she moved back to California after her daughters were ready to go out on their own. *The Story of Wine in California* was published that year. As much as Fisher loved France, as much as her work is about France, her work is also a paean to her love of the Golden State: Though not "born" a Californian, she wrote, "I truly think I am one."

Early in 1964 Fisher traveled to the one place she would never write about, the Piney Woods School in Mississippi. She went there as a volunteer to teach English, a white teacher in a school for black students. She and her students did well together, but she was not invited back because she was a "troublemaker"— what kind of trouble Fisher never specified. So, late in 1964 she returned to California and to her writing. More books followed, along with a journey to Paris, where she began her friendship with writer Janet Flanner and a brief run as a columnist ("Gastronomy Recalled") for the *New Yorker*. In 1971 she published her memoir of her childhood in Quaker Whittier, *Among Friends*, sold her St. Helena home and bought a small ranch in Glenn Ellen, California, and then went off to travel around France for six years with her sister Norah. Upon her return, her work became more overtly memoirs of places and people and meals.

Fisher's work was widely acclaimed. W. H. Auden said that nobody in America wrote better prose, and John Updike called her "a poet of the appetites." She garnered numerous honors and awards, both literary and culinary. By 1991, when she was elected to the American Academy of Arts and Letters, she had endured arthritis, failing eyesight, and the ravages of Parkinson's disease. She "wrote" by whispering into a tape recorder words that her secretary would transcribe. In such works as *Sister Age* (1983) and the posthumously published *To Begin Again: Stories and Memoirs, 1908–1929* (1992), she examined with wit and compassion the fears, vagaries, and indignities of old age as well as its consolations and rewards. In *To Begin Again*, she also explained that, when she was a child, her family teasingly warned "gullible listeners" that she never spoiled a story by sticking to the truth. This is a plain lie, because I do not lie. But I have never seen any reason to be dull" (pp. 3–4). Fisher died at home, on her Glen Ellen ranch in the wine country of northern California.

Fisher's writing is cool passion and vintage quality, a simultaneity of objective and subjective perspectives. Alchemy is what she performed. Practical, personal, and profound, her books are about food, its preparation and reception. She never set a table without setting a scene; to offer something bare of context would never have occurred to her. Innumerable critics, writers, and readers have recognized the brilliant prose and literary pearls slyly content to be clothed in the seeming ordinariness of cookery, just as the oyster shell covers the dual and different delicacies of flesh and gem. A sometimes demanding and difficult personality, Fisher in person could recall the stereotypical image of a chef—impossible, irritable, quirky, and a genius. And as a chef M. F. K. Fisher took the ingredients of life and created unique writings of universal appeal, much the way the oyster creates the pearl.

• Fisher's papers are archived in the Schlesinger Library at Radcliffe College. Her work comprises an informal (though calculated) autobiography. Her works not mentioned above include *An Alphabet for Gourmets* (1949); *Maps of Another Town: A Memoir of Provence* (1964); *The Cooking of Provincial France* (1968); *With Bold Knife and Fork* (1969); *Among Friends* (1970); *A Considerable Town* (1978); *As They Were* (1982); *Spirits of the Valley* (1985); *The Standing and the Waiting* (1985); *Dubious Honors* (1988); *Answer in the Affirmative and the Oldest Living Man* (1989); *Long Ago in France: The Years in Dijon* (1991); *Stay Me, Oh Comfort Me: Journals and Stories, 1933–1941* (1993); *Last House: Reflections, Dreams, and Observations, 1943–1991* (1995); and *The Boss Dog* (1991), a novel. Jeannette Ferrary's *Between Friends: M. F. K. Fisher and Me* (1991) is a form of biographical valuation, extended interview, and personal reminiscence. See also David Lazar, ed., *Conversations with M. F. K. Fisher* (1992). For other assessments, see Christopher Benfey, "In the Company of M. F. K. Fisher," *Boston Review* 9 (Oct. 1984): 9–11; Mary Hawthorne, "A Hunger Artist," *New Yorker*, 11 Jan. 1993; David Lazar, "The Useable Past of M. F. K. Fisher: An Essay on Projects," *Southwest Review* (1992): 515–31; Jan Morris, "Marseille Ramble," *New York Times Book Review*, 4 June 1978; Ruth Reichl, "M. F. K. Fisher," *Los Angeles Times Book Review*, 6 June 1991; Raymond Sokolov, "On Food and Life and Herself," *New York Times Book Review*, 6 June 1982; and Brenda Wineapple, "Feasting on Life," *Women's Review of Books*, March 1993. Obituaries are in the *New York Times*, the *Los Angeles Times*, and the *Washington Post*, all 24 June 1992; and the *Times* (London), 29 July 1992.

E. D. LLOYD-KIMBREL

FISHER, Rudolph (9 May 1897–26 Dec. 1934), Harlem Renaissance author and physician, was born in Washington, D.C., the son of John Wesley Fisher, a clergyman, and Glendora Williamson. Fisher was raised in Providence, Rhode Island, and in 1919 received his B.A. from Brown University, where he studied both English and biology. Fisher's dual interests, literature and science, were reflected in his achievements at Brown, where he won numerous oratorical contests and was granted departmental honors in biology; the following year he received an M.A. in biology. In 1920 Fisher returned to Washington to attend Howard University Medical School. He graduated with highest honors in June 1924 and interned at Washington's Freedman's Hospital. Later that year Fisher married Jane Ryder, a local teacher, with whom he had one son.

When Fisher moved to New York in 1925, he made rapid advances in both of his careers as a doctor and a writer. As a bright young physician, Fisher became a fellow of the national Research Council at Columbia University's College of Physicians and Surgeons. There he studied bacteriology, pathology, and roentgenology (the use of X-rays) for two years before opening up his own practice and publishing the results of his independent scientific research. Fisher was also an instant success as a fiction writer, publishing four short stories during his first year at Columbia. His story, "The City of Refuge," is an ironic tale that juxtaposed Harlem's promise with its inevitable shortcomings. The story appeared in the prestigious *Atlantic Monthly* (Feb. 1925), a first for a Harlem Renaissance writer, and was included in Edward J. O'Brien's *Best Short Stories of 1925* later that same year. From this point onward, Fisher's career as a writer would be characterized by his ability to place his stories in traditionally white, mainstream publications such as the *Atlantic Monthly* and *McClure's*, as well as in the black publications such as *Crisis* and *Opportunity*. His stories deal with the conflict between the values of southern black folk and the demands of northern urban life as well as the effects of interracial and intraracial prejudice on Harlem's inhabitants.

Fisher's first novel, *The Walls of Jericho* (1928), explores how America's equating white skin with economic opportunity increased class antagonism in Harlem. Warmly received by black critics because the novel lacked the exotic and erotic sensationalism of many insider exposés of Harlem, *The Walls of Jericho* examines the antagonisms between the black proletarians, or "rats," and the black middle and upper classes, or "dickties." Although his often comic and ironic dissection of Harlem society skewered upper-class pretensions as well as lower-class ignorance, Fisher nevertheless concluded his novel with a utopian resolution: a truck-driving furniture mover, Joshua "Shine" Jones, overcomes his enmity for a wealthy lawyer, Fred Merrit, who in turn provides him with the opportunity to start his own business.

Following the publication of his novel, Fisher pursued various positions that confirmed not only his continued commitment to a dual career in medicine and writing, but also his willingness to act as public educator within his community. In 1929 he was appointed superintendent of the International Hospital on Seventh Avenue, a position he held through 1932. In addition, he worked as a roentgenologist for the New York Health Department from 1930 to 1934, served on the literature committee of the 135th Street Young Men's Christian Association, and lectured at the 135th Street Branch of the New York Public Library.

Fisher's next novel, *The Conjure-Man Dies: A Mystery Tale of Dark Harlem* (1932), generally recognized as the first black detective novel, is an elaborately plotted work that utilizes flashbacks in order to reconstruct the mystery behind the puzzling murder of a conjurer who later appears alive after the disappearance of the corpse. *The Conjure-Man Dies* allowed Fisher to continue his exploration of Harlem's social climate, while also indulging his interest in science and medicine through his fictional creation, Dr. John Archer. Summoned to examine the murdered corpse, Archer becomes the cerebral assistant to a local police detective, Perry Dart, in the ensuing investigation. Using medical discussions about the properties of blood and scientific debates about determinism, Fisher weaves an eerie tale.

Although he intended *The Conjure-Man Dies* to be the first in a series of Harlem-based detective novels featuring Archer and Dart, Fisher completed only one sequel, *John Archer's Nose*, a novelette published posthumously in January 1935 in *Metropolitan* magazine. Fisher did, however, complete a dramatic treatment of his earlier detective novel, titled *Conjur' Man Dies*, that was staged in 1936 at the Lafayette Theatre in Harlem to mixed reviews.

Rudolph Fisher was killed, ironically, by the intellectual curiosity that fueled his substantial achievements. Exposed to lethal radiation during his work with newly developed X-ray equipment, the multitalented writer known for his acerbic wit was stricken with intestinal cancer and died a tragically early death in New York City. Despite his substantial artistic contributions to the Harlem Renaissance, Rudolph Fisher remained underappreciated by literary scholarship through the end of the twentieth century.

• Letters from Fisher written to Carl Van Vechten are in Yale University's Beinecke Rare Book and Manuscript Library, New Haven, Conn. Other materials pertaining to Fisher's life and work are in the Schomburg Center for Research in Black Culture, New York Public Library. Some of Fisher's other major stories are "The South Lingers On" (1925), "Ringtail" (1925), "High Yaller" (1925), "The Promised Land" (1927), "Blades of Steel" (1927), "Guardian of the Law" (1933), and "Miss Cynthie" (1933). His most famous nonfiction essay is "The Caucasian Storms Harlem" (1927). Four unpublished stories are in the Brown University Archives, Providence, R.I. The best discussions of Fisher's work, particularly his novels, remain in larger works of literary and cultural history such as Nathan Irvin Huggins, *Harlem Renaissance* (1971); David Levering Lewis, *When Harlem Was in Vogue* (1981); and Bernard W. Bell, *The Afro-American Novel and Its Tradition* (1987). Obituaries are in the *New York Times*, 27 Dec. 1934, and the *New York Age*, 5 Jan. 1935.

MICHAEL MAIWALD

FISHER, Sydney George (11 Sept. 1856–22 Feb. 1927), lawyer and historian, was born in Philadelphia, Pennsylvania, the son of Sidney George Fisher and Elizabeth Ingersoll. His father, a prominent Philadelphia attorney, was active in public affairs and contributed numerous essays to the popular press on political and constitutional issues.

Sydney's childhood was spent on his father's farm and country estate, where he acquired a lifelong devotion to nature and outdoor activities, particularly yachting, fishing, and swimming. Orphaned at age sixteen, he undertook preparatory studies at St. Paul's School in Concord, New Hampshire. In 1879 he received a B.A. from Trinity College at Hartford, Connecticut, where he honed his literary skills as editor of the school magazine. Subsequently, he pursued legal studies at Harvard College for two years and was admitted to the Pennsylvania bar in 1883.

While studying law, Sydney followed in his father's footsteps as a political essayist. In 1880 he initiated a national discussion of civil service reform with an article in the *New York Nation* that attacked the spoils system. A subsequent series of articles led directly to the formation of civil service reform societies throughout the country and thereby indirectly to passage of the federal Civil Service Act of 1883. In 1895–1896 Fisher published three articles against unrestricted immigration, which argued that it had a negative effect on national character, culture, and wage levels. His essays captured the attention of both conservative intellectuals and liberal labor leaders, helping to spur the formation of the Immigration Restriction League.

Fisher turned his attention to historical writing with the publication of three books on the colonial period: *The Making of Pennsylvania* (1896), *Pennsylvania: Colony and Commonwealth* (1897), and *The Evolution of the Constitution* (1898). Although academic historians dismissed his work on Pennsylvania history as impressionistic and careless, his book on the Constitution documents with meticulous effort that the Constitution "is a development of Progressive history and not an isolated document struck off at a given time" as a result of divine inspiration or individual genius. Fisher challenged the established interpretations of George Bancroft, C. Ellis Stevens, and Douglas Campbell. To support this challenge, in *The Evolution of the Constitution* Fisher was the first to collate all the provisions of the colonial charters and early state constitutions that related to the same subjects. As a result, students of the Constitution were now able to determine the origin of clauses in the federal Constitution by identifying those clauses in previous documents. The book went through three editions because of widespread demand. Fisher's two-volume social history, *Men, Women, and Manners in Colonial Times* (1898), enjoyed similar success, also appearing in three editions.

However, it was publication of *The True Benjamin Franklin* (1899) that established Fisher as a notable figure among the new critical realists who began challenging conservative historians in the late 1890s and who, subsequently, provided an intellectual foundation for the Progressive movement with their muck-raking histories. Fisher made other contributions to this genre, including *The True William Penn* (1900), published in four editions; *The True Daniel Webster* (1911); and *The American Revolution and the Boer War: An Open Letter to S. F. Adams* (1902), an anti-imperialist tract directed against the historian Charles Francis Adams.

Yet, Fisher's most significant contribution to the new critical realism was *The True Story of the American Revolution* (1902), published in five editions. This book, perhaps his single most influential work, charged that widely accepted histories of the American Revolution were full of purposeful omissions designed consciously "to build up nationality, and to check sectionalism and rebellion" among ordinary citizens of the United States. Despite its attack on the historical profession, it was received favorably by a new generation of progressive historians. The book was subsequently revised and republished in 1908 as the expanded, two-volume version, *The Struggle for American Independence*.

Although not widely read, Fisher's one methodological essay, "The Legendary and Myth-Making Process in Histories of the American Revolution," made an insightful contribution to historiographic theory. This essay was read before the American Philosophical Society and published in its *Proceedings* (50, no. 204 [Apr.–June 1912]). In 1919 Fisher published *The Quaker Colonies: A Chronicle of the Proprietors of Delaware*, part of the Chronicle of America series, as his final contribution to critical realism.

In addition to his legal practice and historical writing, Fisher was deeply interested in education. Indeed, his initial foray into historical writing was *Church Colleges: Their History, Position and Importance with Some Account of the Church Schools* (1895), a book that surveys the development of Episcopalian higher education institutions in the United States. Fisher served many years on the board of trustees of Trinity College and was president of the board at the end of his life. He also served as a trustee of the Institution for the Education of the Blind and the Library Company of Philadelphia. Indeed, Fisher's last book, *American Education* (1917), grew out of his service as a trustee and dealt with the expanding role of education in American democracy.

Fisher often spent his winters in Florida on a houseboat on the Kissimmee River, where he pursued his enduring love of water sports. He remained an avid yachtsman and eventually took up permanent residence at the Corinthian Yacht Club in Essington, Pennsylvania, where he died. He was never married.

A prolific author, Fisher developed a reputation that rests primarily on his contributions to the development of a new critical realism in reinterpreting the political history of the American Revolution and the development of the U.S. Constitution.

• Some miscellaneous papers of Sydney George Fisher are kept in Philadelphia at the Historical Society of Pennsylvania. Papers dating from 1875 to 1895 are found in the collection of his father, Sidney George Fisher, 1832–1895. The Sydney L. Wright Collection, 1852–1927, also includes some correspondence, business, and financial papers of Sydney George Fisher from 1911, owing to the fact that the Wright family is connected to the Fisher family through descent and marriage. Sydney George Fisher's genealogical background can be traced on his mother's side in L. D. Avery, *A Genealogy of the Ingersoll Family in America, 1629–1925* (1926). Sydney George Fisher did not write an autobiography. Brief biographical accounts of his life and work are in various biographical directories. Obituaries are in the *Philadelphia Inquirer*, 22 Feb. 1927, and the *New York Times*, 23 Feb. 1927.

CLYDE W. BARROW

FISHER, Vardis Alvero (31 Mar. 1895–9 July 1968), novelist, was born in Annis, Idaho, the son of Joseph Oliver Fisher and Temperance Thornton, Mormon pioneers. At age six he moved with his family to the isolated Antelope Hills along the main fork of the Snake River. This majestic and violent wilderness territory became the setting for many of his novels. His dominating and overzealous mother wanted her sons to leave the backcountry and succeed in the outside world, while his silent frontiersman father treated him harshly. Having an introverted spirit, "overdeveloped idealism," and deep distrust of human motives, Fisher felt that his childhood "tortured" him and drove him "almost to lunacy." He and his brother moved by themselves to a hut near Rigby, Idaho, to attend high school. During this time he rejected the Mormon faith of his parents.

Fisher started college at the University of Utah in 1915. In 1917 he married Leona McMurtrey, his childhood sweetheart. He went into the air force during World War I but resigned in opposition to its authoritarian hierarchy. He then trained briefly as an army corporal. After the war he returned to the University of Utah, where he was granted a B.A. in 1920. Between 1920 and 1925 he studied at the University of Chicago, where he received an M.A. and Ph.D. in English.

Fisher and his wife had two sons before she committed suicide in 1924, despondent over the differences in their intellectual natures and desires. Fisher blamed her death on conflicts in his own personality and began to scrutinize himself through his writing. In doing so he also carefully examined human nature, especially what he saw as evasions and self-deception.

Fisher returned to the University of Utah in 1925 as an assistant professor of English but found teaching unrewarding and the political influence of the Mormon church stultifying. He published his first book, a sequence of seventy-three sonnets entitled *Sonnets to an Imaginary Madonna*, in 1927. In 1928 he married Margaret Trusler, a fellow student at Chicago. His first novel, *Toilers of the Hills*, a realistic account of farming struggles in Fisher's own Antelope Hills country, was published that same year, and with this credential he secured a teaching position at Washington Square College of New York University. Here he became friends with Thomas Wolfe, with whom he is often compared.

Fisher spent the summer of 1930 touring Europe on bicycle with his wife. He then returned with her to his childhood home in Idaho, where his sons had been living with his parents since their mother's suicide, and he dedicated himself to writing. While improving the farm for his parents, whom he had begun to appreciate, Fisher wrote another regional novel, *Dark Bridwell* (1931). Both this novel and the first were praised, although they were not commercially successful. He nevertheless began work on his autobiographical tetralogy. Earning little money from his literary efforts, he supplemented his income by teaching two summers at the University of Montana (1932 and 1933) and then working as Idaho director of the WPA Writers' Project (1935–1939).

The first novel of Fisher's tetralogy, *In Tragic Life* (1932), based on the struggles of his own life, was praised by critics for its honesty and sensitivity. It also brought him to national attention: in 1933 a new edition was published jointly by the original printer, Caxton, and by Doubleday, Doran. Its dust jacket was done by Grant Wood. Caxton and Doubleday, Doran continued joint publication of the next three novels of the tetralogy, whose hard-hitting realism appealed to depression-era readers.

Fisher's third son was born in 1937, but he and Margaret divorced in 1939. That year he received the Harper Prize for fiction for *Children of God*, a fictionalized account of the beginnings of Mormonism, which became Fisher's most widely known and critically and popularly successful novel.

In 1940 Fisher married Opal Laurel Holmes, and they settled on undeveloped land among the Thousand Springs on the Snake River near Hagerman, Idaho. Here he began writing the *Testament of Man* (1943–1960), a series of twelve novels.

In his fiction Fisher tried to show the development of human morals and conscience. He criticized Marxists and Freudians for their ignorance of human nature and of social and group interactions. He asserted that human beings have within them both an egoistic drive, based on racial individualism, and a communal drive. Fisher's work, however, began to be criticized as being too autobiographical, didactic, and voluminous, and his literary reputation began to decline. His works were at times undisciplined and preachy, and personally he was temperamental and obstinate. After the fifth novel of the *Testament* series, Fisher's publisher dropped him. Abelard Press published the two middle novels of the series, *The Valley of Vision* (1951) and *The Island of the Innocent* (1952), which cover the times of the biblical Solomon and the Maccabean wars, but after these Abelard also dropped Fisher's works. Not only were the novels potentially offensive in their fictionalized accounts of Bible stories, but Fisher's writing had become strident. Fisher continued to write but had trouble finding a publisher. Finally, Alan Swallow's Denver publishing firm created a subscription list to support the rest of the *Testament* project and printed and promoted the rest of the series.

Before his death, Fisher taught writing as artist-in-residence at the College of Idaho. His work experienced a modest revival in the later 1950s and early 1960s, and his final novel, *Mountain Man: A Novel of Male and Female in the Early American West* (1965), was well received and made into the movie *Jeremiah Johnson*, starring Robert Redford.

Fisher's place in American letters is now firm as the first significant Rocky Mountain regionalist and as a novelist of ideas (in *Mountain Man*, for example, he presented the problems of dying frontiers, overpopulation, and the need for conservation). When he died in Twin Falls, Idaho, he and his wife were finishing a joint project, *Gold Rushes and Mining Camps of the Early American West* (1968).

• Vardis Fisher's papers can be found in the Yale Collection of American Literature. Major published works not cited in the text include *Passions Spin the Plot* (1934), *We Are Betrayed* (1935), *The Neurotic Nightingale* (1935), *No Villain Need Be* (1936), *April: A Fable of Love* (1937), *Odyssey of a Hero* (1937), *Forgive Us Our Virtues: A Comedy of Evasions* (1938), *The Idaho Encyclopedia* (editor) (1938), *Idaho Lore* (editor) (1939), *City of Illusion* (1941), *Darkness and the Deep* (1943), *The Mothers* (1943), *The Golden Rooms* (1944), *The Caxton Printers in Idaho: A Short History* (1944), *Intimations of Eve* (1946), *Adam and the Serpent* (1947), *The Divine Passion* (1948), *God or Caesar: The Writing of Fiction for Beginners* (1953), *Pemmican* (1956), *Jesus Came Again* (1956), *A Goat for Azazal* (1956), *Peace Like a River* (1957), *A Tale of Valor: A Novel of the Lewis and Clark Expedition* (1958), *My Holy Satan* (1958), *Love and Death: The Complete Stories of Vardis Fisher* (1959), *Orphans and Gethsemane* (1960), *Suicide or Murder? The Strange Death of Governor Meriwether Lewis* (1962), and *Thomas Wolfe as I Knew Him, and Other Essays* (1963).

A bibliography of Fisher's works has been compiled by George Kellogg, "Vardis Fisher: A Bibliography," *Western American Literature* 5 (Spring 1970): 45–64. A major examination of his life and works is by Joseph M. Flora, *Vardis Fisher* (1965), and an update by Flora appears in *American Novelists, 1910–1945*, vol. 9 of *Dictionary of Literary Biography*. A brief work that covers Fisher's work through his death is Wayne Chatterton, *Vardis Fisher: The Frontier and Regional Works* (1972). Tim Woodward, *Tiger on the Road* (1989), is a nonacademic biography that provides important information gained from personal interviews with Fisher's family and friends. See also George Day, *The Uses of History in the Novels of Vardis Fisher* (1968), and David Rein, *Vardis Fisher: Challenge to Evasion* (1938).

ANN W. ENGAR

FISHER, Walter Lowrie (4 July 1862–9 Nov. 1935), urban reformer and secretary of the interior, was born in Wheeling, Virginia (now W.Va.), the son of Daniel Webster Fisher, a Presbyterian clergyman and college president, and Amanda D. Kouns. For one year he attended Marietta College in Ohio before transferring to Hanover College, Indiana, in 1880. After graduation in 1883, he worked as a law clerk with the firm of Dexter, Herrick, and Allen in Chicago until he passed the Illinois bar examination in 1888. He formed a partnership with Rudolph Matz, whose family connections helped secure Fisher an appointment as special assessment attorney for Chicago, representing the department of public works. Although he performed well, Dewitt C. Cregier, the newly elected mayor, replaced him with Clarence Darrow in 1889.

Fisher resumed private practice in his law firm, which added several other partners over the years. In 1891 he married Mabel Taylor of Boston. They had seven children.

During the late nineteenth century, Chicago was beset with political corruption and boss politics, being described by Lincoln Steffens as "first in violence, deepest in dirt; loud, lawless, unlovely, ill-smelling, irreverent, new; an overgrown gawk of a village, the 'tough' among cities, a spectacle for the nations" (Steffens, p. 563). This milieu prompted the founding of the Municipal Voters League, which Fisher joined in 1896. He became its secretary in 1899 and its president in 1906.

Fisher's most immediate concern as a reformer was the Chicago public transportation system. As a self-taught reform expert in the field, he fought Charles Tyson Yerkes, a private owner of streetcar facilities, who controlled the city's streetcars. Following a protracted struggle, in 1903 the Illinois legislature passed a bill Fisher had written, which retained local community control of street railways under charters issued by cities for a limited duration. It also allowed city councils to revoke franchises and operate traction lines on their own.

This legislation caused an outcry for public ownership, something Fisher did not support. After Mayor Edward F. Dunne fumbled in his effort to establish a city-owned transit system, in 1906 he appointed Fisher as special traction attorney. While in office Fisher negotiated a compromise with the privately owned company that protected Chicago's citizenry and was fair to street railway investors. Differences with Dunne soon caused him to resign, but the city council convinced him to stay on as its employee. Ida M. Tarbell credited Fisher's success in the matter as the result of generosity, knowledge, and ability as well as "amazing patience with those who differed from him" (Tarbell, p. 138).

By 1906 his fame as a traction reformer had spread, and leaders of other cities regularly asked his assistance in these matters. His reform beliefs were typical of urban progressives. He supported efficient and expert government, feeling that the public should be led to proper decisions. He favored the city-manager form of government, with educated professionals and businessmen as policy makers. Although he spoke of "vigorous, independent, and intelligent American working-men" being members of city councils (Gould, p. 171), his record in trying to elect such men was scanty if not nonexistent.

A Republican, Fisher believed city government should be nonpartisan and avoid state and national party issues. He was responsible for improvements in handling city funds and in the city police force. He

played a role in discrediting and removing William Lorimer, the former Republican boss of Chicago, from the U.S. Senate in 1912. Fisher held memberships and offices in a variety of reform groups, some of which he helped found. They included Chicago's University Club, City Club, and Commercial Club, as well as the National Civil Service Reform League, the Conservation League of America, and the National Conservation Association.

Through the latter organizations he became a friend and confidant of Gifford Pinchot, a conservationist and the chief forester of the United States, and James R. Garfield, Theodore Roosevelt's secretary of the interior. William Howard Taft appointed Fisher to the Federal Railroad Securities Commission in 1910, and although Major Archie Butt, military aide to President Taft, found the Chicagoan "the reformer type and therefore to be suspected" (*Taft and Roosevelt*, vol. 2, p. 670), the president named him secretary of the interior following Richard A. Ballinger's resignation in 1911. Ballinger had run afoul of conservationists as a result of the so-called Ballinger-Pinchot Affair, which concerned the leasing of coal lands in Alaska. Taft, who had removed Pinchot from office, was beset by advisers who wanted him to end Ballinger's tenure, which he did by accepting the secretary's resignation. Fisher's appointment was political window dressing. Nevertheless, he spent a great deal of his term, which lasted until March 1913, on affairs concerning Alaska. He recommended its government be reorganized and it be granted territorial status. He also promoted railroad building and greater leasing of coal lands in the area. In addition to being a champion of "rational use" of public lands, for example, favoring reforesting projects, he was an advocate of national parks.

Fisher returned to Chicago and the practice of law in 1913 and remained active in civic affairs, especially giving advice concerning public transportation and conservation. In addition to the book *Alaskan Coal Problems* (1911), he published several journal and magazine articles on reform topics. He died at home in Winnetka, Illinois.

Fisher was an energetic and devoted advocate of responsible government who believed that good government was possible only with good people leading the way. Some of his methods to achieve this end caused him to be labeled by a few as a "reform boss." Generally, he was an excellent example of the urban progressives.

• Fisher's papers are in the Library of Congress. The best assessments of him as a Chicago reformer are Alan Brant Gould, "Secretary of the Interior Walter L. Fisher and the Return to Constructive Conservation: Problems and Policies of the Conservation Movement, 1909–1913" (Ph.D. diss., West Virginia Univ., 1969) and "Walter L. Fisher: Profile of an Urban Reformer, 1880–1910," *Mid-America* 57 (July 1975): 157–72; and Joel Arthur Tarr, *A Study in Boss Politics: William Lorimer of Chicago* (1971). Opinions of two contemporaries and well-known muckrakers are to be found in Lincoln Steffens, "Chicago: Half Free and Fighting On," *McClure's Magazine*, Oct. 1906, pp. 563–77, and Ida M. Tarbell,

"How Chicago Is Finding Herself," *American Magazine*, Dec. 1908, part 2, pp. 124–38. For Fisher's years as a member of Taft's cabinet see *Taft and Roosevelt: The Intimate Letters of Archie Butt, Military Aide* (2 vols., 1930); *The Letters of Theodore Roosevelt*, ed. Elting E. Morison (8 vols., 1951–1954); Elmo R. Richardson, *The Politics of Conservation: Crusades and Controversies, 1897–1913* (1962); James L. Penick, Jr., *Progressive Politics and Conservation: The Ballinger-Pinchot Affair* (1968); and Henry F. Pringle, *The Life and Times of William Howard Taft: A Biography* (2 vols., 1939). An obituary is in the *New York Times*, 10 Nov. 1935.

ROBERT S. LA FORTE

FISHER, William Andrew. *See* Fisher, Frederic John.

FISHER, William Arms (27 Apr. 1861–18 Dec. 1948), composer and music editor and publisher, was born in San Francisco, California, the son of Luther Paine Fisher and Katharine Bruyn Arms, both from families whose ancestry dated back to colonial Massachusetts. For more than fifty years, Luther Fisher was the owner of an advertising agency. William attended school in nearby Oakland and studied music with John P. Morgan. In 1890 Fisher moved to New York City and began studies in harmony with composer Horatio Parker; he also took singing lessons in London. During this time, Fisher taught briefly at the newly established National Conservatory of Music in New York. While there, he was also a student of the famous Bohemian composer Antonín Dvořák, who was director of the conservatory from 1892 to 1895.

Fisher was invited to attend the premiere of Dvořák's Symphony in E Minor (*From the New World*), op. 95, performed by the Philharmonic Society under the direction of Anton Seidl at Carnegie Hall on 15 December 1893. Dvořák had composed the work in New York and orchestrated most of it earlier that year while on a summer vacation in Spillville, Iowa, the center of a large Czech community. Fisher was so moved by the symphony's slow movement, marked *Largo*, that many years later he wrote his own song based on its theme. Called "Goin' Home," the song was published in 1922 and quickly became his most popular work. In his preface, Fisher described the emotions he felt while at the symphony premiere in 1893, writing that "at the close of the *Largo*, so moving was the performance, so touched to the heart was the great audience, that . . . all about the hall, people sat with the tears rolling down their cheeks."

"Goin' Home" was not actually a Negro spiritual (though it has been incorrectly identified as such), but Fisher did arrange some spirituals for voice and piano, attempting to give rich expression to this indigenous musical form. His collection *70 Negro Spirituals* includes well-known titles such as "Deep River," "Ev'ry Time I Feel the Spirit," "Steal Away," and "Swing Low, Sweet Chariot." He also was a composer of mostly vocal music, including many anthems and sacred choruses and more than seventy-five songs. His important song collections include *Echoes of Naples, A Child's Garden of Verses, Three Shelly Songs, Foster's Choral Book, Bible Songs*, and the op. 2, 15, and 18 collections. The style of his music is simple and straightforward, somewhat like that of his American contemporaries Dudley Buck and George Whitefield Chadwick.

Fisher is best known, however, as a music editor and publisher. Beginning in 1897 he worked for the Oliver Ditson Company in Boston, the largest music publisher of its day (and the publisher of "Goin' Home"). Hired initially as director of publications with the task of improving sales, Fisher set about producing a series of popular educational works. Among his most successful titles were The Music Student's Library (begun in 1897 and numbering more than forty volumes), The Musician's Library (initiated in 1903 and comprising almost one hundred volumes), and The Music Student's Piano Course (begun in 1918 and numbering twenty volumes). He also edited the collection *Sixty Irish Songs* (1915). Fisher became vice president of Oliver Ditson in 1926 and served in that post until his retirement in 1937.

Fisher was one of the first editors to recognize the importance of early American music. During the 1930s he compiled the following collections of American music from earlier centuries: *Ye Olde New England Psalm-Tunes 1620–1820* (1930), *The Music That Washington Knew* (1931), and *Father Kemp's Old Folks Concert Tunes* (1934); the last collection was originally produced by Robert Kemp and published in three editions (1860, 1874, 1889). Some of the music in these three volumes was extensively altered from the original work, but they are still useful for performance, and the historical notes are informative and incisive. Fisher arranged some of the songs for voice and keyboard to make them attractive to a wider audience.

In addition to these collections, Fisher published several books on the subject of early American music. The first, *Notes on Music in Old Boston* (1918), is an appealing history containing many facsimiles of eighteenth- and nineteenth-century music and fine old photographs. Another, *One Hundred and Fifty Years of Music Publishing in the United States* (1934), deals with the years from 1783 to 1933. A third, *Music Festivals in the United States* (1934), describes those festivals in existence at that time. Fisher joined ASCAP in 1926 and also served as president of the Music Publishers Association and of the Music Teachers National Association.

In 1922 Fisher married Emma Roderick Hinckle, the daughter of a Methodist minister. (Fisher himself was a Unitarian.) The couple had no children. For many years they lived in the Boston suburb of Brookline, where Fisher died.

The tone of most of Fisher's writings was objective and reserved. Only when writing about the Oliver Ditson Company, where he worked for forty years, did he let his personal pride come through. In the preface to *Notes on Music in Old Boston*, for example, he describes the new location of the Ditson building, at 178–79 Tremont Street, across from Boston Common, as "altogether fitting, for in its vicinity were issued the first book printed in America [1640], the first treatise on singing [1647], the first printed music [1698], the first music instruction book [1721], and the first book wholly of American composition [1770]." He ends the book with a brief history of the company, the last chapter focusing entirely on the new ten-story building, which contained all of the music in the Ditson catalog, "more than 13,000 numbers." He gives a detailed description of each floor, saving his highest praise for the top floor, which he calls "the crowning feature of the entire building" because of the room set apart for the president and directors' meetings. On the mantel in that room was a motto attributed to Socrates, which he translates from the Greek as Make Music and Work Making It. This motto could just as well represent Fisher's dedication to early American music and to American music publishing in general.

• Fisher's extensive notes on American newspapers, which include music quotes, are in the Special Collection of the Mugar Library at Boston University. Information on Fisher's work can be found in American Society of Composers, Authors and Publishers (ASCAP), *Biographical Dictionary*, 3d ed. (1966), as well as the standard biographical source books. Obituaries are in *Etude*, Mar. 1949; *Musical America*, 1 Jan. 1949; the *New York Times* and the *Boston Globe*, both 20 Dec. 1948.

ROGER L. HALL

FISK, James (1 Apr. 1834–7 Jan. 1872), financial speculator, was born in Pownal, Vermont, the son of James Fisk, a country peddler; his mother's name is unknown. He was four years old when his mother died and his father moved to Brattleboro and married Love B. Ryan. He left school at age twelve to accompany his father on peddling trips, became a waiter two years later when his father built a temperance hotel, and joined the Van Amberg Circus as a roustabout and ticketseller when he was fifteen. Returning home at age eighteen, he reorganized his father's peddling business and married Lucy Moore in 1854. They had no children.

By 1852 he had bought his father out and had five wagons on the road, all gaily painted like circus wagons. His jobbing for Jordan Marsh Company in Boston led to his leaving peddling in 1860 to become a wholesale salesman for Jordan's. He prospered in this role with the coming of the Civil War, setting up a hospitality suite for the firm at Willard's Hotel in Washington, where he began securing government textile orders. His energy and audacity, which embraced both buying a Vermont mill so Jordan's could corner a type of textile and smuggling cotton out of the Confederate States for Jordan's mills, led to a partnership, but his fast and loose methods of doing business resulted in his being bought out in 1864 for $60,000. With the proceeds, Fisk briefly ran his own textile jobbing house in Boston, then lost heavily in a brokerage operation in New York; he made a profit selling Confederate bonds in the London market through an agent but lost everything on Wall Street.

Back in Boston, he borrowed money to buy a patent for a textile weaving machine from which he made a fortune. He served as a go-between for the financier Daniel Drew in selling the Stonington Steamship Line and made enough to open a new brokerage office, Fisk and Belden. When Drew, director and treasurer of the Erie Railway, made another fortune in 1868 selling Erie stock short and buying it back low, Fisk made his own fortune in brokerage fees and insider trading. He soon became a director of the Erie and teamed up with Drew and Jay Gould to sell watered stock to Commodore Vanderbilt. In the aftermath, they had to flee to New Jersey in 1868 to avoid writs of arrest, and they spent half a million dollars to bribe the New York state legislature to pass legislation legalizing their overissue of stock.

Fisk and Gould then squeezed Drew out of the railway, Gould becoming president and treasurer, Fisk comptroller and managing director. At once they realized a $3 million profit by raiding the United States Express Company. They then issued 235,000 shares of new stock, an increase in the capital stock of $23.5 million, sold short, and made millions. Falling out with Drew, who had come into the scam with them, they lost all their profits in 1868 pushing the stock value up in an attempt to destroy him. At year's end, they topped off the performance by buying Pike's Opera House at Twenty-third Street and Eighth Avenue for Erie's offices.

In the following year, they failed in a bid to take over the Albany and Susquehanna Railroad in a complex battle of writs, property seizures, and the Battle of the Tunnel, a clash of dueling locomotives and hand-to-hand combat of hundreds of laborers fifteen miles west of Binghamton. At the same time Fisk was refurbishing the Narragansett Steamship Company, in which he had bought a controlling interest, and commissioning two 176-foot ferryboats, the James Fisk Junior and the Jay Gould, for the Erie ferry across the Hudson. He was also joining with Gould in another high-stakes game, trying to manipulate President Ulysses S. Grant in an attempt to corner the gold market. When it all went wrong on the infamous Black Friday (24 Sept. 1869), Gould had made $11 million, half of Wall Street was bankrupt, and Fisk was hiding in the Opera House and repudiating his debts by assigning them to his bankrupt partner, William Belden.

To the investing public, Fisk was the villain of the piece and his insouciant testimony before Representative James Garfield's Banking and Finance Committee evidenced his depravity. Yet the larger public forgave him his trespasses because of his good humor and his colorfulness. When he established the "Grand Spectacular Opera Bouffe Company" to perform comic operas in the theater that was Erie Company headquarters, it was no more than art mirroring life. When he dressed as an admiral to ride his ferryboats, people laughed and applauded, and they enjoyed it no less when he bought himself a colonelcy in the Ninth New York State National Guard.

But on January 1871 his long-term liaison with and lavish support of a mistress, Helen Josephine ("Josie")

Mansfield, became public and tarnished his image. In June when Fisk was marching down Eighth Avenue at the head of his troops on Orange Day, a Protestant commemoration, the parade was attacked by irate Irish Catholics, a riot erupted in which forty-five people were killed, and Fisk had to flee for his life down alleys and through backyards. Amid continuing troubles over Erie affairs, Josie Mansfield and her new lover, Edward Stokes, separately sued Fisk for a total of $250,000, threatening to make public his love letters. Dogged by their suit and others aimed at his role in Erie, forced out of the vice presidency of the railroad, and obliged to see his position as comptroller and director jeopardized, Fisk's courage never failed him. After the second hearing of the case on 6 January 1872, Stokes shot Fisk at the Grand Central Hotel. Fisk died the following morning.

A corpulent man, blond with an impressive mustache, bejeweled, and floridly dressed, Fisk bubbled with bonhomie and good humor. No country bumpkin, though he often affected the role, he was astute both about financial dealings and about people and had more than his share of courage. For all that, he was amoral in business and morally casual in personal matters, his attitude summed up in his tongue-in-cheek comment about a failed venture: "Nothing is lost save honor." He was more flamboyant but no worse than other financial speculators of the post–Civil War period, a group who pursued personal enrichment at the expense of public safety and the interest of their investors as well as of the economy and society in general.

• The most careful and complete biography of Fisk is W. A. Swanberg, *Jim Fisk: The Career of an Improbable Rascal* (1959). Matthew Josephson in his *The Robber Barons* (1934) sketches Fisk unforgettably in the context of his peers. Also useful is Robert H. Fuller [Robert Higginson], *Jubilee Jim: The Life of Colonel James Fisk, Jr.* (1928). A great many sensationalistic biographies were rushed into print on Fisk's death, the best of which are George L. Barclay, *Life, Adventures, Strange Career and Assassination of Col. James Fisk, Jr.* (1872); Willoughby Jones, *James Fisk, Jr.: The Life of a Green Mountain Boy* (1872); and R. W. McAlpine, *Col. James Fisk, Jr.* (1872). Genealogical and biographical material are available in F. C. Pierce, *Fiske and Fisk Family* (1896). A withering contemporary analysis of the railroad wars by a famous diplomat and his historian son is Charles Francis Adams and Henry Adams, *Chapters of Erie* (1871). E. H. Mott, *Between the Ocean and the Lakes: The Story of Erie* (1899), provides interesting detail on the rail line. For the attempt to corner the gold market, Kenneth D. Ackerman, *The Gold Ring: Jim Fisk, Jay Gould, and Black Friday, 1869* (1988), is indispensable. See also the obituary in the *New York Daily Tribune*, 8 Jan. 1872.

JOSEPH M. McCARTHY

FISK, James Brown (30 Aug. 1910–10 Aug. 1981), physicist and science administrator, was born in West Warwick, Rhode Island, the son of Henry James Fisk, a businessman, and Bertha Brown. Fisk's childhood was spent at various places. When he was several years old, the family moved to Tacoma, Washington, and later to Long Beach, California. The early death of his mother sent Fisk and his siblings to their maternal grandparents in Providence, Rhode Island. Fisk went to the Providence Technical High School before enrolling in the Massachusetts Institute of Technology (MIT) in 1927.

Fisk received a broad education in science and engineering at MIT, majoring in aeronautical engineering, a field made popular by Charles Lindbergh's recent solo flight across the Atlantic. After graduation in 1931, he remained at MIT as a research assistant for Charles Stark Draper, the rising aeronautic engineer. Then, in 1932, encouraged by Draper and supported by a Proctor Travelling Fellowship, Fisk sailed for England to study nuclear physics at Cambridge University, with residence at Trinity College. While there, he worked in the famed Cavendish Laboratory and published two papers (one with a coauthor) on gamma rays. In 1934 he returned to MIT to complete his dissertation, "The Scattering of Electrons from Molecules," which extended the quantum theory of electron-scattering from that involving monatomic to diatomic molecules. He received his Ph.D. in theoretical physics in 1935.

During 1935–1936 Fisk taught physics at MIT. Then he moved to Harvard University as a junior fellow in its Society of Fellows. There he investigated the disintegration of nuclei by high-energy radiation and built, with a colleague, a Van de Graaff electrostatic accelerator for nuclear research. An associate professorship in physics brought Fisk to the University of North Carolina, Chapel Hill, in 1938, the same year he married Cynthia Hoar of Concord, Massachusetts; they would have three children. They did not stay long in North Carolina because in 1939 Mervin J. Kelly, then director of research at the AT&T Bell Telephone Laboratories in New Jersey, recruited Fisk for its electronics research department. William Shockley, Fisk's former colleague at MIT and now at Bell Labs, had recommended Fisk to Kelly.

World War II transformed Fisk from a promising young physicist into a distinguished scientist and scientific organizer. During the war he headed a group at Bell Labs to reproduce and improve a powerful microwave generator called the magnetron. Invented in Britain, the device later became the heart of radar, which contributed so much to the Allied victory. To perfect radar, Fisk's group cooperated closely with the radiation laboratories at both MIT and Columbia University. Fisk's knowledge of nuclear physics also found use when a comprehensive report on nuclear fission that he coauthored with Shockley, in August 1940, alerted the British to the plutonium route to an atomic bomb. At the end of the war, Fisk was appointed assistant director of physical research in charge of electronics and solid-state research at Bell Labs. He organized the superb team of scientists who two years later invented the transistor.

Fisk's career took unexpected turns in the postwar period. In late 1946 he was offered a professorship at Harvard. Before he could accept it, however, Carroll

L. Wilson, a former classmate at MIT and now general manager of the newly established Atomic Energy Commission (AEC), "drafted" him to become the AEC's first director of research in January 1947. In this position, Fisk helped revitalize the national laboratories the AEC inherited from the wartime Manhattan Project and further their research and development of nuclear weapons. Concerned about the shortage of scientific manpower in the field of nuclear weapons research, Fisk at first resisted calls by scientists to expand the AEC's support of basic research at universities. But later he did bring the AEC into a joint program with the navy to sponsor high-energy physics and expand AEC support of science at universities.

In August 1948 Fisk left the AEC for the Gordon McKay Professorship in Applied Physics at Harvard. This second academic job did not last long either. Kelly won Fisk back with an offer of director of physical research at Bell Labs in June 1949. Because of his broad understanding in science and engineering and his quietly effective leadership, Fisk advanced rapidly within Bell Labs to become vice president for research in 1954, executive vice president in 1955, and finally president in 1959. In these positions, Fisk gave scientists and engineers the freedom to do research and publish their findings. During his tenure, Bell Labs, the premier industrial laboratory in the world, continued to play a leading role in communication technology, which was revolutionized by the use of satellites, and in military research and development, such as on the controversial antiballistic missile system (ABM).

Fisk himself remained a major adviser to the U.S. government, with membership on the AEC's General Advisory Committee, the Science Advisory Committee of the Office of Defense Mobilization (ODM-SAC), and its successor, the President's Science Advisory Committee. In 1954–1955 Fisk was associate director of the ODM-SAC's Technological Capability Panel, which, under the direction of James R. Killian, president of MIT, produced a report to the National Security Council that decisively accelerated the U.S. missile and other defense programs.

Fisk rose to national prominence in 1958 when President Dwight D. Eisenhower appointed him head of the U.S. (and western) delegation to the Geneva conference of experts on a nuclear test ban. From 1 July to 21 August, western and eastern experts sought to devise ways to detect clandestine nuclear tests in preparation for a possible test-ban treaty to control the arms race and to allay fears of radioactive fallout from nuclear tests. The resulting agreement, which included proposals for control stations on both U.S. and Soviet territories, was hailed as a major breakthrough in the Cold War. Although subsequent technical developments proved the Geneva system to be inadequate, it nevertheless began the process that eventually led to the Limited Test Ban Treaty in 1963.

Fisk retired from the presidency of Bell Labs in 1973 and remained chairman of its board for another year. He died in Elizabethtown, New York.

A major player in the American military-industrial complex, Fisk had a life and a career that reflected the increasing interdependence of science, technology, and society in the twentieth century. His scientific, engineering, and organizational talents enabled him to cross between basic and applied research and move easily among academe, industry, and government. In each, he was recognized as a versatile physicist and outstanding scientific organizer.

• There is no known collection of Fisk's papers nor a full-length biography of him. Richard G. Hewlett and Francis Duncan, *Atomic Shield: A History of the United States Atomic Energy Commission*, vol. 2: *1947–1952* (1969), provides information on Fisk's service in the AEC. James R. Killian, Jr., *Sputnik, Scientists, and Eisenhower: A Memoir of the First Special Assistant to the President for Science and Technology* (1977), describes Fisk's role as a science adviser to the U.S. government. On the Geneva conference of experts on a test ban in 1958 and Fisk's performance as chairman of the western delegation, see Harold Karan Jacobson and Eric Stein, *Diplomats, Scientists, and Politicians: The United States and the Nuclear Test Ban Negotiations* (1966). The best obituary is by his Bell Labs colleague William H. Doherty, "James Brown Fisk," National Academy of Sciences, *Biographical Memoirs* 56 (1987): 91–116, which includes a selected bibliography of Fisk's publications.

ZUOYUE WANG

FISK, Wilbur (31 Aug. 1792–22 Feb. 1839), Methodist minister and educator, was born in Brattleboro, Vermont, the son of Isaiah Fisk, a farmer and public official, and Hannah Bacon. He studied both independently and at the common school in Pecham, Vermont. In 1812 he entered the sophomore class of the University of Vermont but graduated from Brown University in 1815. At first he studied law with Isaac Fletcher in Lyndon, Vermont, but partly due to frail health he turned to teaching. Having been raised in a devout Methodist home, he was licensed to preach on 14 March 1818. That June he joined the New England Conference of the Methodist Episcopal church and entered into full connection in 1820. He was ordained elder in 1822. His first appointment was the Craftsbury circuit in Vermont, then the Charlestown charge in Massachusetts, and next the Vermont district as presiding elder (district superintendent). In 1825 he was elected principal of the newly organized Wesleyan Academy in Wilbraham, Massachusetts. He married Ruth Peck of Providence, Rhode Island, in June 1823.

Fisk was the first Methodist minister within the eastern states to hold an earned college degree. This preparation recommended him for election as chaplain to the Vermont legislature before whom he delivered the election sermon in 1826. He was chosen by the New England Conference as a delegate to the General Conferences of 1824, 1828, and 1832. The Methodist church in Canada (1828) and the Methodist Episcopal church in America (1836) elected him bishop, but in both instances he declined giving priority to his work in education. Within the denomination he was active in promoting the formation of educational societies, temperance reform, a Sunday school and Tract society, and missions. His efforts along with those of Nathan Bangs were responsible for the creation of the Methodist Sunday School Union in 1827. In 1831 when Wesleyan University in Middletown, Connecticut, was chartered, he was chosen its first president. The General Conference Temperance Committee was a direct result of Fisk's "Address to the Members of the Methodist Episcopal Church, on the Subject of Temperance" (1832). He was instrumental in recruiting Jason Lee in 1833 to be the first Methodist missionary to the Flathead and Nez Perce Indians of Oregon. In 1836, when Wesleyan granted Fisk a leave to travel to Europe, in the hope it would improve his health, the General Conference requested him to represent them to the British Wesleyan Conference as did the American Bible Society.

On the subjects of theology and slavery Fisk engaged in public controversy. Due to his training, he was the first among American Methodists to effectively represent the Arminian theological position that Salvation was a possibility for all, as opposed to Calvinism's predestination and Unitarianism's belief that the deity existed only in one person. But it was his support of the American Colonization Society that led to a decline in his influence within New England Methodism. As a "moderate," he abhorred slavery and opposed abolitionism because he feared the latter would divide the church and nation. In 1835 Orange Scott, LaRoy Sunderland, and Shipley Willson, all passionate abolitionists, publicly challenged Fisk's views and moved the New England Conference to aid abolitionism.

It was in the field of education that Fisk demonstrated remarkable ability, first at Willbraham Academy (1826–1831) and then at Wesleyan University (1831–1839). He stressed educational opportunity for both sexes and in his five years at Willbraham over 350 students attended. As a successful fundraiser he was able to recruit a faculty and develop a strong academic program. He is credited with introducing a "modified diploma," which eventually became a bachelor of science degree, and awarding advanced standing to students based on entrance examinations. A work program and financial aid were designed to assist students with limited resources. At Wesleyan he continued these practices and insisted, in a day of denominational rivalry, that no religious or creedal test be required for admission. His promotion of education in the General Conference prompted that body to provide funds for training home and foreign missionaries at Wesleyan. Known as the "Father of American Methodist education," he died in Middletown, Connecticut.

• The Wilbur Fisk Papers are in Wesleyan University Library, Special Collections. There are thirteen boxes of personal papers plus additional volumes of his published writings and individual pamphlets. Biographies by Joseph Holdrich, *The Life Of Wilbur Fisk, D.D.* (1842), and George Prentice, *Wilbur Fisk* (1890), are useful. Dissertations by David Markle "Wilbur Fisk: Pioneer Methodist Educator" (Ph.D. diss., Yale Univ., 1935) and Douglas J. Williamson, "The Ecclesiastical Career of Wilbur Fisk: Methodist Educa-

tor, Theologian, Reformer, Controversialist" (Ph.D. diss., Boston Univ., 1988), are excellent sources. See also *Encyclopedia of World Methodism* (2 vols., 1974).

FREDERICK V. MILLS, SR.

FISKE, Bradley Allen (13 June 1854–6 Apr. 1942), naval officer and inventor, was born in Lyons, New York, the son of William Allen Fiske, an Episcopalian minister, and Susan Matthews Bradley. After obtaining his primary education in a public school and then a private military school in Cincinnati, Ohio, where the family had moved, Fiske was nominated as a candidate to the U.S. Naval Academy in 1870. He served as secretary and treasurer of his class and graduated second in the class of 1874. He then began serving in a navy that had reached its post–Civil War nadir.

What most set Fiske apart was his experimenting in such fields as optics and electricity. Among his earliest inventions were an electric log (to measure the distance a ship covered), a sounding machine (fathometer), and a flashing light communications apparatus. His sale of a mechanical pencil patent enabled him to be financially solvent when, in 1882, he married Josephine Harper, the daughter of a director of the publishing firm of Harper and Brothers; she died in 1919. The couple had one child.

Granted a year's leave to study electricity, Fiske wrote a textbook on the subject. He then supervised the installation of electric power in navy ships, beginning with the four steel steamers authorized in 1883. A central electrical station was built below the waterline to provide power for searchlights, training and firing guns, telephones, hoisting ammunition, and the like, thereby revolutionizing naval gunnery and internal and external communications. By 1890 Fiske had electrified almost all controls in the pilot house, and in addition he had improved torpedo control. In 1894 came his stadimeter, a hand-held optical device that measures distance to an object.

Fiske served on a gunboat in Manila Bay during the Spanish-American War and Filipino insurrection. He also advocated improving naval administration by adopting a naval general staff. Instead, in 1900 the General Board of the Navy was created. While he climbed the ladder to flag rank in 1912 and second in command of the fleet, Fiske also patented a torpedo plane and worked unceasingly for a general staff. Between 1913 and 1915, while aide for operations to Secretary of the Navy Josephus Daniels, Fiske attempted unsuccessfully to persuade Daniels to adopt a general staff, but in 1915 Congress passed legislation creating the Office of Chief of Naval Operations. Fiske further irked Daniels by demanding that the United States, even though still neutral in the Great War, prepare for a war he felt was imminent. Daniels sent him to the Naval War College until he was retired for age in 1916. Fiske's glee when the Republicans won the elections of 1920 is evident in his writing to Admiral William S. Sims, "Gee Whiz. Holy Smoke, Great Scott. Sulking Moses, Caesar's ghost. Uh-hell. What an a—

kicking" (W. S. Sims Papers, Manuscript Division, Library of Congress, 6 Nov. 1920).

Fiske set a new record by serving as president of the U.S. Naval Institute from 1911 to 1923. He also published six books and sixty-two articles. Among his most important books are *The Navy as a Fighting Machine* (1916; repr. 1988) and his memoirs, *From Midshipman to Rear-Admiral* (1919). He died in New York City.

• Only two parts of the many diaries Fiske kept still exist. Among his most important articles are "The Naval Profession," U.S. Naval Institute *Proceedings (USNIP)* 33 (June 1907): 475–78; "Naval Power," *USNIP* 37 (June 1911): 683–736; "Naval Policy," *North American Review* 203 (Jan. 1916): 63–73; and the posthumously published "Air Power," *USNIP* 68 (May 1942): 686–94. A full biography is Paolo E. Coletta, *Admiral Bradley A. Fiske and the American Navy* (1979). Discussions of Fiske's role as an inventor and military reformer can be found in three volumes by Elting E. Morison, *Admiral Sims and the Modern American Navy* (1942), *Men, Machines, and Modern Times* (1966), and *War of Ideas: The United States Navy 1870–1890* (1969), and in Eric Sterner, "Bradley Fiske, Reformer," *Naval History* 7 (Spring 1993): 21–24. A good and succinct appraisal of Fiske is Benjamin Franklin Cooling, "Bradley Allen Fiske: Inventor and Reformer in Uniform," in *Admirals of the New Steel Navy: Makers of the American Naval Tradition, 1880–1930*, ed. James C. Bradford, (1990). An obituary is in the *New York Times*, 7 Apr. 1942.

PAOLO E. COLETTA

FISKE, Daniel Willard (11 Nov. 1831–17 Sept. 1904), librarian and book collector, was born in Ellisburg, New York, the son of Daniel Haven Fiske and Caroline Willard. Called "Willard" from childhood, he learned to read at age three, and during the 1840 presidential campaign the youngster read political news to village residents. Fiske attended Cazenovia Seminary and Hamilton College in New York State but in 1850 left to study Scandinavian languages at the University of Uppsala. During that time he served as a European correspondent for several American periodicals. In 1852 he returned to New York City to become first assistant librarian at the Astor Library. There he honed strongly held beliefs that libraries ought to develop circulating collections for the public and large reference collections for scholarly research; except for works of "bare-faced immorality," he argued, no books should ever be rejected from reference collections.

Between 1857 and 1868 Fiske engaged in a variety of activities. He coedited the *American Chess Monthly* from 1857 to 1860 and compiled the *Book of the First American Chess Congress* in 1859. Between 1859 and 1863 he was contributor on Scandinavian countries and languages for Appleton's *New American Cyclopedia*, and from 1859 to 1860 he served as general secretary of the American Geographical Society. Fiske returned to Europe in 1861 as an attaché to the U.S. Legation in Vienna and in 1863 became correspondent for the *Syracuse Daily Journal*. In 1865 he started a bookselling business in Syracuse and in 1867 became correspondent for the *Hartford Courant*. A year later

he accepted a position as professor of North-European languages and librarian at Cornell University, which had recently opened its doors.

As librarian, Fiske expanded the collection from its 15,000 volumes by acquiring the personal libraries of Goldwin Smith, Franz Bopp, and Jared Sparks, and he immediately extended library hours from one or two on certain weekdays to nine daily. In 1872 he presided over the move to and opening of a new library building donated by John H. McGraw. As professor, Fiske taught German, Swedish, Danish, and especially Icelandic, for which as early as 1852 he had developed a deep affinity and a sizeable book and pamphlet collection. "I am deeply and truly interested in Iceland," he wrote at age twenty to an Icelandic scholar in a letter preserved in the National Library. "I see in the small but noble people which inhabit it the same flesh, blood, and spirit as my own nation is made of, and the same elements which compose the English and American character." Fiske visited Iceland for the first time in 1879.

In July 1880 Fiske married Jennie McGraw, a tubercular invalid who was heir to the considerable estate of her father, John McGraw. Given her condition, Fiske renounced any claim on his wife's property before their marriage, but by that time he had already developed a reputation as an opportunist who lived on other people's money. (One of his students had paid for his 1879 trip to Iceland.) Jennie died a year after they were married. When the will was initially probated, no one objected. Fiske got $300,000 and McGraw family members $550,000. Cornell received $200,000 for a new library plus unrestricted use of Jennie's residual estate, which pushed the total value of the bequest to Cornell to over $1 million.

At that time, however, and unbeknownst to Fiske, Cornell was operating under a New York charter that debarred it from holding more than $3 million worth of property. After he learned that the state legislature had quietly revised Cornell's charter on 12 May 1882 so that it could legally accept the gift, he brought suit to break his wife's will. He also resigned from the university and left for Europe, where in 1883 he took up residence in a spacious Florentine villa. For years the "Great Will Case" dragged through the courts. An Ithaca surrogate court ruled in Cornell's favor in 1886, but the New York Supreme Court reversed the judgment in 1887. Finally, in 1890 the U.S. Supreme Court sustained the reversal. After payment of legal fees totaling $280,000, Fiske received $500,000, the McGraw family $1 million.

From his base in Florence, Fiske devoted the rest of his life to bibliophilistic interests, entertaining friends and visitors, and advocating for Egypt to adopt a romanized alphabet for the Arabic language. Over the years he amassed significant Dante, Petrarch, and Rhaeto-Roman language collections, and he added substantially to his already impressive Icelandic history and literature collections. These books were eventually willed to Cornell after his death in Frankfurt,

Germany, as was a $500,000 endowment to maintain them.

Daniel Willard Fiske did not always abide by the conventions of the social circles in which he traveled. To many of his contemporaries, he looked like a self-indulgent opportunist all too willing to exploit other people's good fortune. This impression was reinforced by his actions in the "Great Will Case." To others, however, he was appreciated as an excellent librarian, a superb book collector, a generous host, and a significant benefactor.

• Fiske's papers are in the Rare Books and Manuscript Collections at Cornell University. See also the Jennie McGraw Fiske Estate Papers (1877–1891) in the Douglas Boardman Collection and the Andrew Dickson White Papers in the Rare Books and Manuscripts Collection, both at Cornell. The "Great Will Case" is wittily discussed in Morris Bishop, *A History of Cornell* (1962). See also Horatio S. White, ed., *Memorials of Willard Fiske* (3 vols., 1920–1922), and White, *Willard Fiske, Life and Correspondence* (1925). An obituary is in *Library Journal* 29 (Oct. 1904): 534–35.

WAYNE A. WIEGAND

FISKE, Fidelia (1 May 1816–26 July 1864), missionary and educator, was born in Shelburne, Massachusetts, the daughter of Rufus Fisk, a farmer and cooper, and Hannah Woodward. (Descended from William Fiske, who had settled in Salem in 1637, she preferred that spelling of her surname.) Her father instructed her in the Bible and encouraged her avid reading, including such works as Cotton Mather's *Magnalia Christi Americana* and Timothy Dwight's *Theology Explained and Defended*, both of which she read as a youngster. Companion as well as mentor, her father was always a presence in Fiske's life, even after his death during her college years; at one difficult juncture in her missionary career his appearance in a dream resolved her fears. After early religious struggles in which God appeared "cruel and unjust," she accepted "the Creator's terms of mercy" and at age fifteen professed faith and joined the Congregational church.

Two years later Fiske began six years of teaching in district schools, then in 1839 she enrolled in Mary Lyon's new Mount Holyoke Seminary. After missing a year of study due to typhoid fever, she was graduated in 1842, declined a minister's offer of marriage, and became a teacher at the seminary. In January 1843 Justin Perkins, pioneer of a mission to Persia, came to the campus to find teachers for a new girls' school. Lyon, an enthusiast for missions, had dedicated her seminary to that cause. No doubt influenced by the example of an uncle, Pliny Fisk [*sic*], a pioneer missionary in the Near East, Fiske responded to Perkins's appeal. When her mother objected Lyon bundled the young teacher into an open sleigh, drove thirty miles with her through formidable snowdrifts, and spent much of the night talking and praying with Fiske's family. Hannah Fiske's objections were overcome, and on 1 March 1843 Fidelia Fiske sailed from Boston under the auspices of the American Board of Commissioners for Foreign Missions. On the final leg of her voyage Fiske had as a fellow passenger a Persian who had acquired a beautiful girl from the Republic of Georgia, of about fourteen years, in the Constantinople slave market for $1,000 and an African woman for $400—a vivid introduction to women's life in the region she was entering.

Arriving at Oroomiah (Rezaiyeh, Iran), Fiske joined the American board's Nestorian Mission, whose efforts were directed to the Syriac-speaking people belonging to the ancient Eastern church named for the fifth-century theologian Nestorius, who was condemned at the Council of Ephesus in 431 for over-emphasizing the duality of the divine and human natures of Christ. The mission aimed at reforming the ancient church and improving the lives of the people, largely through education and Protestant religious teaching. While learning the language (she wrote of "poring with delight over my Syriac") and the life and customs of the people, Fiske set about establishing a boarding school whose pupils would be under her constant care and influence as teacher, housekeeper, chaplain, and surrogate mother. Fiske thought educating village girls would greatly improve their hygiene, health, manners, morals, intelligence, and prospects in life; they appeared to her, with reason, as unkempt, ignorant, undisciplined, and prone to lie, with no prospects of breaking the immemorial patterns of village life. She envisaged for them a spiritual awakening, improved style of living, and the possibility of being teachers of their people or wives of pastors being trained at the mission school for boys. In spite of strong objections—especially from Persian women—to the education of girls, she persuaded a few families with promising daughters to entrust them to her care. From a first class of six, the Fiske Female Seminary gradually grew through fifteen years to a student body of forty. Centered in the Bible, the curriculum came to include arithmetic, geography, physiology, natural philosophy, and history. The school was organized like a household in which pupils shared all the daily chores—a system similar to the regimen at Mount Holyoke.

Early on Fiske enlisted the help of her best pupils in teaching others, and in 1847 she was joined by Mary Susan Rice from Mount Holyoke. Through her firm and loving guidance the local girls, who often came to her ragged, unkempt, and unruly, became models of cleanliness, order, and piety, and most of them became effective teachers. Many were deployed during vacation months as leaders of village Sunday schools and later as teachers in charge of regular schools. Some married graduates of the boys' school and undertook with them the work of education and evangelism in villages throughout the region. Fiske sought to bring each pupil to a personal faith and the earnest practice of prayer, believing that merely secular education, no matter how excellent, was not the business of missions.

In addition to work in her school, Fiske visited in village homes, sometimes making strenuous horseback tours in the mountains. She would provide instruction in literacy and child care as well as religion, sometimes sitting with weavers at the loom or talking with women working in cotton fields. A colleague described her chief characteristic as "*lovingness* . . . guided by an unusually quick intelligence"; another noted that "it was not love alone that gave her magnetic power; but with it, strong sense, tact, discretion to say just the right word . . . and at the right time" (Fiske, pp. 414, 406). She delighted in offering hospitality to the many travelers who came by and often was involved in visiting and nursing the sick.

Fiske suffered increasingly from ophthalmia and by 1858 was forced to return home, where she became active again at Mount Holyoke, conducting devotionals, counseling students about their faith, fostering the recurrent religious revivals, and visiting the seminary's affiliated institutions at Oxford and Painesville, Ohio (later Western College and Lake Erie College.) Fiske was an effective speaker, and her "parlor meetings" attracted many to the missionary cause, but for reasons of decorum she declined to speak to mixed audiences of men and women. Hoping to return to Persia, she turned down an invitation to become principal of Mount Holyoke, but her health did not permit her to leave Massachusetts. Instead, in her last years she compiled *Memorial: Twenty-fifth Anniversary of the Mt. Holyoke Seminary* (1862) and worked on *Recollections of Mary Lyon* (1866), the latter published posthumously. During the spring of 1864 she devoted herself to encouraging a religious revival at the seminary, and she died a few months later at her home in Shelburne of "acute inflammation of the lymphatic vessels."

Among the many tributes from both Persians and Americans was that of Rufus Anderson, the most important American missionary leader of the nineteenth century; she possessed, he wrote, "a combination of qualities, intellectual and emotional, surpassing anything I had ever seen in any other person. . . . She seemed to me the nearest approach I ever saw, in man or woman, in the structure and working of her whole nature, to my ideal of our blessed Savior, as he appeared in his walks on Earth" (vol. 2, pp. 281–83). Fiske was one of the earliest of the nineteenth-century women missionaries who achieved and modeled a career of service in the public sphere with significant freedom and responsibility.

• The Mount Holyoke College Library/Archives has an extensive collection of Fidelia Fiske material, including her correspondence (1843–1864) and writings as well as biographical materials and memorabilia and photographs (1842–1864, 1912) of Fiske and Fiske Female Seminary. The best biography is Daniel T. Fiske (probably a cousin), *The Cross and the Crown; or, Faith Working by Love, as Exemplified in the Life of Fidelia Fiske* (1868), which contains large extracts from her letters. A second biography is by Thomas Laurie: *Woman and Her Savior in Persia* (1863), which was written largely from materials provided by Fiske herself. The *Missionary Herald* of the American Board has an obituary, vol. 60 (1864): 257–60; other issues contain reports on her work and school, such as those in vol. 48 (1852): 65–70, 206, 240–41, and 338–39; see also vol. 50 (1854): 67, and vol. 55 (1859):

57. A number of references in Elizabeth Alden Green, *Mary Lyon and Mount Holyoke, Opening the Gates* (1979), situate Fiske in the life of the college. Rufus Anderson, *History of the Missions of the American Board of Commissioners for Foreign Missions to the Oriental Churches*, (2 vols., 1872), refer to Fiske's life and work.

DAVID M. STOWE

FISKE, Harrison Grey (30 July 1861–2 Sept. 1942), theatrical editor and manager-producer, was born in Harrison, New York, the son of Lyman Fiske, a hotel owner, and Jennie Durfee. Fiske's well-to-do family moved to New York City when he was a child, and there he developed a lifelong passion for the theater. He was educated by tutors and at private schools and traveled in Europe. Thanks to family influence with the owners of the papers, while still an adolescent Fiske began reviewing plays for two newspapers, the *Jersey City Argus* and the *New York Star*. During his one year at New York University, he began contributing to a theatrical weekly, the *New York Dramatic Mirror*. He decided that year to make theatrical journalism his profession. His father bought an interest in the *Dramatic Mirror*, and Fiske, barely eighteen, became its editor in 1879.

Under the young man's devoted editorship, the weekly publication became more than a journal of stage information; it became the guardian of the theater's managerial and artistic standards. Fiske was determined to bring about better conditions for the artists of the theater and to protect them against managerial exploitation. He succeeded in establishing the Actors' Fund in 1882 to aid destitute actors. He also worked to bring about the passage of laws to protect playwrights against piracy of their works. In 1883 Fiske bought a third share of the *Dramatic Mirror* and in 1888 became its sole owner.

Fiske, though large in height and girth, was a personable young man skilled in the arts of gracious living. One interviewer described his appearance as that of "the ideal New York man of position, handsome, well bred, and well dressed" (*Washington Post*, 4 Mar. 1906). In 1886 bachelor Fiske turned his attention to courting a rising young actress, Mary Augusta Davey (known as Minnie Maddern), as passionate as he in her devotion to the theater. They married in 1890, more from their shared love of the theater than from ardent personal attraction. She, a stage professional from childhood, was only sketchily educated and retired from acting after marriage, the better to absorb her husband's broader knowledge of life and the drama. She never gave up thoughts of the stage, however, having no desire for children or domesticity. In 1893 she returned to the stage in a tragedy, *Hester Crewe*, written by Fiske. It did not succeed; Fiske wrote several plays, and none succeeded.

In 1894 her triumphant success in a performance of the demanding role of Nora in *A Doll's House* changed Fiske's life as well as her own. Reports of theatergoers' acclaim for Mrs. Fiske's performance went nationwide. A national tour in the play was immediately called for. Her biographer Archie Binns wrote: "[The public] had seen Minnie Maddern, the winsome and the capricious, suddenly loom up as a great actress. . . . Now [Fiske] saw that her career was more important than his, and his life would have to be changed to fit hers." Ever the theater lover, he was wholehearted in support of "the clear light of genius."

While continuing as editor of the *Dramatic Mirror*, Fiske over the next years became more and more involved in managing the career of the great star that Minnie Maddern Fiske became. At first he was simply a silent partner in management, letting others handle actual production. In 1897, however, the producer of Mrs. Fiske's *Tess of the D'Urbervilles* withdrew before the play opened, pleading lack of funds. Fiske, believing in the play's dramatic value, stepped in. Once in, having experienced the excitement of the play's great success, he remained active as his wife's producer.

Both husband and wife, beginning in 1897, were swept up in a shared twelve-year campaign against a business group's attempt to dominate the commercial theater. Six managers and theater owners, led by Marc Klaw and A. L. Erlanger, had gained control of bookings for nearly all the major playhouses across the nation and proposed to offer them only to stars and producers who booked exclusively through their organization, known as the Theatrical Syndicate. The Syndicate people wanted Fiske, who was both editor of the *Dramatic Mirror* and producer-husband of a star, on their side. He was approached early and offered very favorable terms to send his wife's touring productions to their theaters.

Fiske refused to go along. As he put it years later, he "realized that the establishing of such a syndicate meant the degeneracy of the stage . . . " (*Washington Post*, 4 Mar. 1906). The more he learned of the Syndicate's operations, the more Fiske recognized it as a trust, or monopoly, that would begin by dictating financial terms to theater professionals and end by strangling artistic innovation in the theater in the name of commercial caution. After he turned the group's representative out of his office, the Syndicate made continued attempts to silence him, but "Fiske publicized every attempt . . . to win him over and every threat they made to quiet him," according to theater historian Monroe Lippmann.

Fiske succeeded in alerting the theatrical world. In years to follow, many stars and producers proclaimed they would never bow to the Syndicate, only to defect under financial pressures brought by that organization. The Fiskes alone persevered as a matter of principle. For years, the Syndicate barred all New York theaters to Mrs. Fiske, until Fiske was able by subterfuges to lease—and renovate at great expense—one antiquated playhouse that became available. The Manhattan Theatre became Mrs. Fiske's New York showcase from 1901 to 1906. She was still barred from the majority of the nation's suitable playhouses in other cities.

While Mrs. Fiske toured the country in whatever decrepit non-Syndicate theaters could be found or act-

ed in skating rinks, assembly halls, or tents, Fiske used the *Dramatic Mirror* to inveigh against the machinations of the Syndicate. He published a number of supplements detailing its workings and willingly fought a libel suit brought against him by the Syndicate, because it allowed him to make public the private agreements made among the members of the Syndicate. The suit was finally dismissed.

It was a long, expensive fight: tours carried out under adverse conditions lost the Fiskes much of the money Mrs. Fiske's potential successes in these years might have earned. It was also a brutal fight, fiercely personal, that once led to fisticuffs between Erlanger and Fiske. In 1909, however, the Fiskes' battle against theatrical monopoly ended with the rise of a rival syndicate headed by the Shubert brothers, who controlled enough theaters to return competition and independence to bookings. By 1910 Fiske could once again choose any New York theater for his wife's plays.

The couple's achievements, even under adversity, were considerable. Mrs. Fiske, in a series of productions, had become a leading interpreter of Ibsen's plays. The pair had also encouraged the work of young American playwrights, bringing plays by Langdon Mitchell, Edward Sheldon, and Harry James Smith to success. Fiske had some achievements of his own, also. He had introduced Bertha Kalich, the great star of the Yiddish theater, to the English-speaking theater. He had given actor George Arliss his first starring role.

Fiske's record as a producer was not unblemished, however, especially in financial matters. He had inherited no wealth from his high-living father, but carried on his father's free-spending style. In his theatrical productions he sought artistic quality above all, and that brought higher costs and lower profits. The closing of the Manhattan Theatre in 1906 was due to losses Fiske had incurred there.

In 1911 Fiske took his deepest plunge into the risks of theatrical production. That year, with Mrs. Fiske having one of her great successes in the farce-comedy *Mrs. Bumpstead-Leigh*, he sold the *Dramatic Mirror*—the couple's only steady source of income. He entered into production of an elaborate Arabian Nights fantasy, *Kismet*, starring Otis Skinner. The play demanded a cast of dozens and elaborate scenic effects. Artistically, Fiske's career as a producer reached its crest with *Kismet*. The play made a huge success with the public and ran from 1911 through 1914 in New York and on the road, but profits were minimal because of high production costs. Then Fiske's attempt to make dancer Lydia Lopokova an actress in a 1914 production, *Just Herself*, failed utterly and disastrously. By the end of 1914, Fiske was in bankruptcy court.

Fiske and his wife remained loyal professional partners, though their marriage had deteriorated to the point that they lived in separate residences. They continued to work together on productions for her. By 1914 Mrs. Fiske was in her fifties, the New York theatergoing public's tastes were changing, and the popularity of moving pictures was eating away at the "road," where Mrs. Fiske had her most loyal following. Never again did the pair know the success of earlier days. Neither did Fiske's prudence as a manager improve. In Allen Churchill's words, he followed "an unsteady course between the brilliant and the disastrous. In the end, disaster won . . . " A failed revival of *Much Ado about Nothing* brought Fiske back to bankruptcy in 1927. His wife's death in 1932 effectively ended Fiske's career in the theater, and he spent the last years of his life living quietly and working on a never-published autobiography. He died in New York City. His place in American theatrical history had been assured years before, by his long, courageous, principled battle against the monopolistic power of the Theatrical Syndicate.

• The papers of Fiske are in the Library of Congress, Washington, D.C. Materials on his life and career are in the Billy Rose Theatre Collection at the New York Public Library for the Performing Arts, Lincoln Center. His work as a theatrical journalist is analyzed in Paul Roten, "The Contributions of Harrison Grey Fiske to the American Theatre as Editor of the *New York Dramatic Mirror*" (Ph.D. diss., Univ. of Michigan, 1962). His part in the fight against the Syndicate is considered, based on a 1936 interview with Fiske, in Monroe Lippman, "The History of the Theatrical Syndicate: Its Effect upon the Theatre in America" (Ph.D. diss., Univ. of Michigan, 1937). Much material about Fiske's life with his wife, based on his manuscript autobiography, is found in Archie Binns, *Mrs. Fiske and the American Theatre* (1955). Other views of the way his life intertwined with his wife's are in Allen Churchill, *The Great White Way* (1962). A view of Fiske in midcareer is in Marie B. Schrader, "Harrison Grey Fiske: A Chat with the Noted New York Editor, Manager, and Dramatist," *Washington Post*, 4 Mar. 1906. Obituaries are in the *New York Times* and the *New York Herald-Tribune*, both 4 Sept. 1942.

WILLIAM STEPHENSON

FISKE, John (11 Apr. 1744–28 Sept. 1797), naval officer and merchant seaman, was born in Salem, Massachusetts, the son of the Reverend Samuel Fiske, a Christian minister, and Anna Gerrish. Besides the educational instruction he received from his father, Fiske attended local schools. At an early age, he determined to make his living as a sailor, and by the time he was twenty-one he commanded a brigantine in trade with Spanish ports. In 1766 he married Lydia Phippen, with whom he had a large family. An outgoing, garrulous man, he was appreciated by those who were employed by him because of his handsome largesse and his congenial spirit as a master.

In 1775 Fiske was pressed by his friends and neighbors to assume a leading part in organized protests against Britain's policies toward its American colonies. At that time he became a member of the Salem committee of safety and correspondence, and the following year he moved on to the larger stage of Massachusetts colonial resistance. In 1776 the Massachusetts General Court established a small provincial (later state) navy to resist English encroachments upon the colony's liberties and on 20 April gave Fiske the second naval officer's commission awarded by that body (the first was

given to Captain Jeremiah O'Brien), to be captain of the brigantine *Tyrannicide*. Quickly Fiske recruited officers and crew for his ship, and in July he sailed from Salem on his first cruise against enemy merchant vessels in the Atlantic shipping lanes. Over the next two months, he captured four prizes, sometimes having to fight for them, and for the remainder of the year was in and out of port on numerous expeditions. In February 1777 he took command of the brigantine *Massachusetts* and in company with two other warships, the *Tyrannicide* under Captain Jonathan Haraden and the *Freedom* under Captain John Clouston, plus a number of privateers, sailed into European waters to harass British shipping. Taking twenty-five prizes, again sometimes having to use force, he and his comrades were generally successful above the norm and in July returned home to the praise of their fellow citizens. Wasting little time in port, Fiske went back to sea in September, cruising off the West Indies and seizing more prizes. When he sailed once more into Salem in October, he discovered that charges had been made against his honor as a naval officer and demanded a public hearing. Although vindicated, he refused any further service in his state's navy. When asked in 1778 to take command of the *Hazard* and resume his naval career, he declined.

Instead, Fiske used the wealth he had accumulated in the past two years from his prizes to establish himself as a merchant in his native Salem, and for the remainder of his life he lived there comfortably with his family. Following the death of his first wife in 1782, he married Martha Lee Hibbert in 1783. She died in 1785, and the following year he wed Sarah Wendell Gerry, who along with three of his children by his first marriage outlived him. Over the years, as he accumulated considerable wealth and standing in Salem, he became famous for his generous hospitality to friends and strangers.

From time to time, Fiske purchased merchant vessels that he sent on trading voyages to the East and West Indies, Europe, and Africa. Continuing to stand high in the esteem of his neighbors, he was rewarded with various offices. In 1791 he was chosen master of the Salem Marine Society, an office that he used to lobby Congress to install navigational aids along the coast of Massachusetts. A year later, he was appointed major general of the state militia and employed his rank and reputation to improve the lot of common soldiers by giving attention to their food, clothing, and shelter and by not aggrandizing money to himself that was supposed to be spent on the militia. Despite his accomplishments as a militia officer, he was most remembered by his friends and posterity for his naval exploits, particularly his sanguinary sea combats, during the revolutionary war.

• Details of Fiske's life are in a eulogy by William Bentley, *A Funeral Discourse* (1797). Other bits are gleaned from *Laws of the Salem Marine Society* (1914), Frederick Clifton Pierce, *Fiske and Fisk Family* (1896), and Joseph Barlow Felt, *Annals of Salem* (1827). Fiske's naval career is discussed in Gardner

Weld Allen, *A Naval History of the American Revolution* (1913), and Charles Oscar Paullin, *The Navy of the American Revolution* (1906). Henry F. Howe, *Massachusetts: There She Is—Behold Her* (1960), has useful information on the European cruise of 1777. William M. Fowler, *Rebels under Sail: The American Navy during the Revolution* (1976), provides background on the Massachusetts navy in overall rebel navy strategy.

PAUL DAVID NELSON

FISKE, John (30 Mar. 1842–4 July 1901), historian and popularizer of evolutionary science, was born Edmund Fisk Green in Hartford, Connecticut, the son of Edmund Brewster Green, a lawyer and Whig journalist, and Mary Fisk Bound. When his father's political journalism proved financially unsuccessful, his parents sent the one-year-old child to live with his grandmother Polly Fisk Bound and great-grandfather John Fisk in Middletown, Connecticut. In 1855, after the death of his father and his mother's remarriage to Edwin Wallace Stoughton, a successful lawyer and later U.S. minister to Russia, he agreed to his grandmother's request that he legally adopt her father's name since he was the only male descendant of his great-grandfather (he added the "e" to his name in 1860).

Fiske grew up in an orthodox Christian family, formally joining the North Congregational Church in Middletown at the age of fourteen. A shy boy, he spent much of his time reading, exploring current literature, and discovering new attitudes to the world that shook his religious faith. At eighteen he declared himself an "infidel" and a convert to the positive philosophy of Auguste Comte, whose rational, scientific system of thought provided Fiske with a comprehensive explanation of the universe. His open rejection of his upbringing precipitated a family crisis that was resolved by his removal to Cambridge, Massachusetts, where he prepared for admission to Harvard College, entering as a sophomore in 1860. He found the required studies uninspiring and spent most of his time on a self-directed, wide-ranging reading and study program in history and philosophy, also teaching himself the elements of a dozen languages, which he hoped to use to prepare for a career as a philologist.

While exploring Boston bookshops, Fiske stumbled on the work of Herbert Spencer. He reacted with enthusiasm, telling his mother that Spencer "has discovered a great law of evolution in nature, which underlies all phenomena, & which is as important & more comprehensive than Newton's law of gravitation" (Berman, pp. 36–37). Fiske's enthusiasm for Spencer's philosophy of evolution never waned; much of his career would be devoted to applying his understanding of Spencer to linguistics, philosophy, religion, and history.

In 1863, the year he graduated from Harvard, Fiske published "The Evolution of Language" in the October *North American Review*, in which he argued that the classification systems created by the great nineteenth-century philologists were not simply descriptive, but also revealed a developmental progression from the simplest language, Chinese, to the most advanced and civilized languages, the Indo-European. He continued to write reviews and articles while studying at Harvard Law School (LL.B., 1865) and during a brief unproductive career as a lawyer. In 1864, with support from his mother and stepfather, he married Abby Morgan Brooks of Petersham, Massachusetts; they had six children.

New opportunities opened up for Fiske when Charles William Eliot became president of Harvard and began to develop postgraduate education in the arts and sciences. He invited Fiske to give a series of lectures on positive philosophy in 1869–1870. Manton Marble, an admirer of Spencer, published all eighteen lectures—as well as nineteen new ones Fiske wrote for the next academic year—in his *New York World*, printing the first four on the front page.

Fiske failed to obtain a position teaching history at Harvard due to opposition within the governing boards to placing a positivist, whose religious ideas seemed almost atheistic, on the faculty. Instead, Eliot appointed him assistant librarian in 1872. His library duties took little time, permitting him to continue to write articles, lecture, and revise his Harvard lectures, eliminating praise of Comte and moving closer to Spencer's positions. In 1873 he traveled to England for a year's stay, financed by his Boston admirers, to prepare his manuscript for publication. He thoroughly enjoyed his social and intellectual success in England; Spencer, Thomas Henry Huxley, Charles Darwin, George Eliot, and Sir Charles Lyell welcomed him to their homes and clubs and advised him on his revision.

In *Outlines of Cosmic Philosophy* (2 vols., 1874), a title Fiske kept despite Spencer's objections to the word "cosmic," Fiske demonstrated his mastery of Spencer's philosophy of evolution. Not only did he explain, in much clearer language than the original, material that Spencer's published work had covered, but he went on to apply these ideas to matters of social evolution that Spencer had not yet explored. He also showed much more interest in the religious implications of evolution, arguing that there was no conflict between science and religion because Spencer's concept of the "Unknowable" was the basis of all religion.

The *Cosmic Philosophy* earned Fiske a reputation as a philosopher but did little to advance his position at Harvard. He welcomed an 1878 offer to give six lectures on American history for the Old South Association; in 1879 he resigned his Harvard library position and thereafter earned his living as a freelance lecturer and writer. Success came slowly; not until the Houghton Mifflin Company, in 1888, put him on an annual retainer did the financial stringency of the 1880s begin to ease. During that decade Fiske developed the process by which he wrote and marketed his historical works. Initially written as a series of lectures during lengthy tours that took him to northern cities from Maine to Oregon and as far south as Richmond, Virginia, they were later published as magazine articles and finally as books.

Fiske stated the philosophic basis of his histories in three lectures first given in 1879 and 1880 and published as *American Political Ideas Viewed from the Standpoint of Universal History* (1885). Drawing on the work of British historians who viewed Parliament as the acme of European ideas of freedom and self-government, he argued that the United States had evolved even further. The New England town meeting was the purest form of local government and the American Federal Union the highest form of representative government. English settlers carried these ideas to a new land where a new nation could evolve, "equipped as no other nation had ever been, for the task of combining sovereignty with liberty, indestructible union of the whole with indestructible life in the parts" (Fiske, *Beginnings of New England*, p. 56). The final lecture, "Manifest Destiny," the most popular of his lectures, predicted the peaceful spread of English and American political ideas across the globe, ushering in a millennium of freedom and peace.

The first of Fiske's historical series to be published, *The Critical Period of American History, 1783–1789* (1888), argued that the years 1783–1789 were critical not just because of economic and political turmoil, as some have read the book, but because the adoption of the Constitution was the decisive step by which the United States advanced English political ideas of representative government to a new and higher level. *The Beginnings of New England* (1889) and *The American Revolution* (2 vols., 1891) were smoothly written anecdotal accounts based on secondary sources that could be read (and heard) as fascinating detail or as illustrations of his basic thesis. Only in *The Discovery of America* (2 vols., 1892) did he use primary sources, footnoting printed sources in a dozen languages on points in controversy. *Old Virginia and Her Neighbours* (2 vols., 1897), *The Dutch and Quaker Colonies in America* (2 vols., 1899), and *New France and New England* (1902) filled chronological gaps in his history with well-written if unoriginal narratives.

During the 1880s, as financial and family problems worsened, Fiske began to lecture on religion, replacing the abstract reconciliation of science and belief in his *Cosmic Philosophy* with discussions of the emotional consolation he found in the idea of an immanent deity guiding evolution to produce humanity as the crown of creation. He wrote:

He who has mastered the Darwinian theory, he who recognizes the slow and subtle process of evolution as the way in which God makes things come to pass, . . . sees that in the deadly struggle for existence that has raged throughout countless aeons of time, the whole creation has been groaning and travailing together in order to bring forth that last consummate specimen of God's handiwork, the Human Soul. (Fiske, *Studies in Religion*, pp. 19–20)

Collected in 1902 as *Studies in Religion*, the lectures "The Destiny of Man in the Light of His Origins," "The Idea of God as Affected by Modern Knowledge," and "Through Nature to God" were given in many cities, sometimes as Sunday guest sermons, as Fiske toured with his history lectures.

In the 1890s Fiske's optimistic faith in the peaceful evolution and expansion of American democracy weakened. The rise of urban political machines based on the votes of immigrant citizens troubled him. When a group of young Harvard graduates formed the Immigration Restriction League in 1894 and offered him the presidency, he accepted, although he apparently did not attend any meetings. William Jennings Bryan's 1896 free silver campaign led Fiske to abandon his lifelong allegiance to the Democratic party. The Spanish-American War caused even more intellectual discomfort. Fiske's Manifest Destiny expected peaceful expansion through consent; at first he opposed annexation of the Philippines, then reluctantly supported the move.

Fiske's health deteriorated in his last years; he complained of shortness of breath. A period of hot, muggy weather in June 1901 sent him from Cambridge to Gloucester, Massachusetts, for the sea air, where he died as the nation celebrated its 125th birthday.

Fiske's work drew audiences partly because of his literary skills but even more because his ideas spoke so eloquently to the needs of his time. He became the most popular historian of his generation, though not a bestselling author in the modern sense; few of his books sold as many as 15,000 copies in their year of issue. Academics might fault his scholarship, but to educated audiences across the United States who came to his lectures and bought his books, he presented a view of their past that appealed to their national pride and a reconciliation of science and religion that eased accommodation to the challenge of evolutionary thought.

• The family collection of Fiske letters, lectures, and book manuscripts is in the Huntington Library, San Marino, Calif. The Manton Marble Papers in the Library of Congress and various collections in the Harvard University Archives and the Houghton Library of Harvard University hold significant manuscripts. John Spencer Clark, *The Life and Letters of John Fiske* (2 vols., 1917), is an uncritical biography but is the most useful edition of his letters. *The Letters of John Fiske*, edited by his daughter, Ethel F[iske] Fisk (1940), is heavily edited and unreliable. His work was collected as *The Historical Writings of John Fiske* (12 vols., 1902) and *The Miscellaneous Writings of John Fiske* (12 vols., 1902). Milton Berman, *John Fiske: The Evolution of a Popularizer* (1961), includes an annotated bibliography. See also Jennings B. Saunders, "John Fiske," in *The Marcus W. Jernegan Essays in American Historiography*, ed. William T. Hutchinson (1937), pp. 144–70; H. Burnell Pannill, *The Religious Faith of John Fiske* (1957); Bruce Kuklick, *The Rise of American Philosophy* (1977); Lewis O. Saum, "John Fiske and the West," *Huntington Library Quarterly* 48 (1985): 47–58; and Jon H. Roberts, *Darwinism and the Divine in America* (1988). Significant obituaries are in the *Nation*, 11 July 1901; *Harper's Weekly*, 20 July 1901; *Critic*, Aug. 1901; and *International Monthly*, Oct. 1901.

MILTON BERMAN

FISKE, Minnie Maddern (19 Dec. 1864?–15 Feb. 1932), actress, playwright, and director, was born Marie Augusta Davey in New Orleans, Louisiana, the daughter of Thomas Davey, an actor-manager, and Minnie Maddern, a musician and actress. As an infant she performed during the entr'actes in her parents' company. Her dramatic debut occurred at the age of three, as the duke of York in *Richard III*. A succession of child parts followed, and she became a prodigy patterned after Lotta Crabtree and Clara Fisher, appearing opposite major performers of the 1860s and 1870s, including Laura Keene, Junius Brutus Booth, Barry Sullivan, Carlotta Leclercq, Edward Loomis Davenport, Sarah Scott-Siddons, Emma Waller, and Joseph Jefferson. Her parents separated when she was very young, and she was in her mother's custody during this period of intense touring and New York apprenticeship. Many accounts acknowledge that she was educated in convents in Cincinnati, St. Louis, and possibly Montreal, but the chronology is uncertain and formal schooling was minimal. Following her mother's death in 1879, she was raised by her maternal aunt Emma Stevens, whose daughter Emily also had a stage career.

Fiske's apprenticeship exposed her to a wide range of parts requiring skill in tragedy, melodrama, comic opera, travesty roles, and even the old woman line of business (the Widow Melnotte in Edward Bulwer-Lytton's *The Lady of Lyons*). She became a full-fledged star in 1882–1883 with the success of *Fogg's Ferry*, by Charles E. Callahan, and *Caprice*, by Howard Taylor (1884), "protean pieces" patterned after her unique talent. During the tour of *Fogg's Ferry* she wed one of the orchestral musicians, LeGrand White. This marriage was brief. Until her second marriage to Harrison Grey Fiske (a playwright and the editor and publisher of the *New York Dramatic Mirror*, the leading trade paper) in 1890 she was always known professionally as Minnie Maddern.

The actor and dramatist Dion Boucicault described Fiske as "no radiant *Juliet*, no stately *Pauline*, no majestic *Parthenia*. Here is only an odd morsel of humanity, half child, half woman; a creature with thin, wiry body, a pale face, nervous lips and wonderful eyes" (quoted in John Bouvé Clapp and Edwin Francis Edgett, *Players of the Present* [1899–1901], pp. 109–10). This explains her attraction as a child and ingenue performer. During the first three years of her marriage to Fiske she did not appear on stage but composed several plays (including *The Rose*, *The Eyes of the Heart*, *Fontenelle*, *A Light for St. Agnes*, and *Countess Roudine*), most of which were produced. During this sabbatical she came under the influence of European modernists, observing Elenora Duse on her first American tour and following the controversies surrounding Henrik Ibsen's plays, especially during the 1889–1894 seasons. She resumed acting in late 1893 in her husband's play *Hester Crewe*; shortly after she was acclaimed as Nora in Ibsen's *A Doll's House* in a single benefit performance.

During the rest of the 1890s Fiske's repertoire alternated between the "advanced drama"—most notably adaptations of Thomas Hardy's *Tess of the D'Urbervilles* (1897) and William Makepeace Thackeray's *Vanity Fair* (*Becky Sharp*, 1899)—and the most frivolous plays of the established repertoire, such as *Frou-Frou* (1894) and *Divorçons* (1897). This is typical of Ibsen's champions; the same pattern is evident in Janet Achurch and Elizabeth Robins, actresses who did much to promote opportunities for psychologically realistic acting and for new playwrights in England, while making their living in trivial comedies and outdated melodramas. Equal strength in comedy and tragedy, therefore, helped to forge the new hybrid style. Fiske's contribution to the history of acting in the United States was to foreground the internal processes of characters, giving subtext precedence over overt signals such as asides or monologues. She specialized in playing women who would not or could not speak about what they knew, and so she had to develop methods (such as pauses and nonlinguistic sounds) to indicate their state of mind.

In 1901 the Fiskes embarked on the management of the Manhattan Theatre, establishing a company that aimed to bring the ideals of ensemble acting and minute attention to every detail of production to the United States. The repertoire was not exclusively modernist, but productions of *Hedda Gabler*, *A Doll's House*, *Rosmersholm*, Paul Heyse's *Mary of Magdalene*, and Langdon Mitchell's *The New York Idea* paralleled the objectives of the European free theater movement until the experiment collapsed as a resident company in 1906–1907 (tours continued until 1914). In 1908 she produced *Salvation Nell*, a play by Edward Shelton, the first product of George Pierce Baker's Harvard course to reach Broadway. Her performance was infamous for the sequence in which she held her drunken lover's head in her lap, motionless and silent, for ten minutes.

Unlike most players of the period, Fiske was not in the employ of the Theatrical Syndicate, which, from 1896, controlled a large number of theaters and forced companies to accept its dates, routes, and terms. This had two chief implications: first, she tried to surround herself with an entire complement of skilled performers, eschewing the single "star" system, and second, she had no access to booking the vast majority of bona fide theaters in New York and throughout the nation. The Fiskes' opposition to the Syndicate's star vehicles and stranglehold on real estate forced them to hire venues completely out of keeping with Minnie's fame. When an entente was reached in 1909 and the Syndicate allowed *Salvation Nell* to be booked into their theaters on independent terms, a series of critical but not financial successes ensued. They were forced to sell the *New York Dramatic Mirror* in 1911, and Harrison declared bankruptcy in 1914. By this time the couple were estranged and had parted on amicable terms; years of touring kept her on the road while he remained in New York.

Fiske appeared in at least two film versions of her stage roles, as Tess in *Tess of the D'Urbervilles* (1913) and as Becky Sharp in *Vanity Fair* (1915), but after 1915 she stuck to live performance. Revivals and pot-boilers paid the bills, but productions by Elmer Rice, Richard Brinsley Sheridan, and Shakespeare are also notable. Her last performance occurred in Chicago late in 1931. She collapsed and three months later died at her home in Long Island, ending a sixty-five year career.

Fiske's acting has been described in diametrically opposed ways: stagey and nervous as well as consummately true to life. Her voice was sometimes criticized for overemployment of staccato passages and other times for slurring, though whether the power and control she acquired working in huge mid-nineteenth-century theaters had simply gone out of vogue or whether she was indulging in idiosyncrasy for growing naturalist tastes is impossible to definitively determine. She was conscious of the rules of acting and so could deliberately break them—such as speaking while facing upstage—paradoxically garnering the audience's full attention when a more orthodox actor might simply have been judged inept. Toward the end of her career, her technique of subtextually evoking characters' emotional lives had been absorbed into the general acting vocabulary; when she ceased to innovate, these "signatures" that she had taught audiences to recognize and appreciate seemed like clichéd claptraps from a bygone era. Her directing skills, particularly in the first decade of the twentieth century, brought her theater in line with the practices of the Moscow Art Theatre under Stanislavsky, though this was a coincidence. Her playwriting represents some of the first attempts to create an Americanized idiom in the realist school, capitalizing on Ibsen's and Duse's lead in creating complex characterizations for actresses.

Fiske had no biological children but in 1922 adopted an abandoned infant whom she named Danville Maddern Davey. She was an activist on behalf of animal rights, opposing trapping, bullfighting, and abuse of cart horses, serving as the first vice president of the International Humane Association. She was honored by Smith College in 1926 for being "the foremost living actress" and received the Good Housekeeping Award in 1931 in recognition of being among the twelve greatest living women.

• Manuscript materials relating to Fiske are deposited at Harvard College Library (Harvard Theatre Collection), the New York Public Library, the University of Texas at Austin (Hoblitzelle Theatre Arts Library), and the Library of Congress. The Library of Congress also holds materials in the Prints and Photographs Division and the only known copy of the 1915 Kleine-Edison film of *Vanity Fair* (American Film Institute). Of her plays, only *A Light from St. Agnes* (1905?) has been published. *Mrs. Fiske: Her Views on Actors, Acting, and the Problems of Production*, as recorded by Alexander Woollcott, is an important source (1917), along with Archie Binns's biography, *Mrs. Fiske and the American Theatre* (1955). Recent dissertations include Elizabeth Lindsay Neill, "The Art of Minnie Maddern Fiske: A Study of Her Realistic Acting" (Ph.D. diss., Tufts Univ., 1970); Mary Ann Angela Messano-Ciesla, "Minnie Maddern Fiske: Her Battle with the Theatrical Syndicate" (Ph.D. diss., New York Univ., 1982); and Ellen Donkin, "Mrs. Fiske's 1897 *Tess of the D'Urbervilles*: A Structural Analysis of the 1897–98 Production" (Ph.D. diss., Univ. of Washington, 1982). An obituary is in the *New York Times*, 17 Feb. 1932.

TRACY C. DAVIS

FITCH, Asa (24 Feb. 1809–8 Apr. 1879), entomologist, agriculturist, and historian, was born in Salem (Washington County), New York, the son of Asa Fitch, a physician and judge, and Abigail Martin. Fitch spent his childhood on the family farm, where he developed a fascination with natural history and a deep sense of religious conviction. He received a liberal education at academies in Salem, New York, and Bennington, Vermont, from 1822 to 1824, and in 1826 he entered the Rensselaer School (now Rensselaer Polytechnic Institute), a new school for scientific education in Troy, New York. There he learned the importance of experimenting and learning by doing, and he became convinced that economic and social enrichment would result from the application of science to the common purposes of life. In 1826 he accompanied students and faculty on a scientific tour of the recently opened Erie Canal. Under the instruction of Amos Eaton, he became acquainted with all branches of natural history and began a lifelong interest in insects. Graduating in 1827, he then attended the Vermont Academy of Medicine, Castleton, and Rutgers Medical College, New York City, and received an M.D. from the former institution in 1829. He spent the winter of 1830–1831 on the western frontier in Illinois.

Fitch married Elizabeth McNeil in 1832; they had six children. Shortly after they married, the couple moved to Stillwater, New York, where Fitch practiced medicine and took an active interest in the moral and intellectual advancement of the community. In the spring of 1838, they moved to Salem, New York, where he managed the family farm, took leading roles in local educational pursuits, and became involved in management of the Washington County Agricultural Society. He soon abandoned medicine, regarding himself as too honest to compete with the quacks. He pursued natural history interests with a sense of religious purpose and eventually established a well-defined plan to devote his life to the study of insects.

By 1840, insect damage and soil depletion were making the need for agricultural research evident. In 1845 and 1846 Fitch published articles on the wheat fly, Hessian fly, and related species in Ebenezer Emmons's *American Quarterly Journal of Agriculture and Science*. These and other early articles received wide acclaim from American and European agriculturists and scientists. In 1846 Fitch was recruited to assist with preparation of Emmons's *Insects of New York* (1855) for the voluminous Natural History of New York series. In 1847 the State Agricultural Society engaged him to conduct a model survey in Washington

County. He prepared for the historical portion of that survey by interviewing elderly residents. His report, "Historical, Topographical and Agricultural Survey of the County of Washington," which appeared in the 1848 and 1849 volumes of the *Transactions of the New York State Agricultural Society*, led to his election to membership in the New York and New Jersey Historical Societies. In 1851 Fitch published a descriptive catalog of about 300 insect specimens, including six new genera, eighty-five new species, and five new subspecies, that had been collected for the New York State Cabinet of Natural History (now the New York State Museum).

Aware of a lack of practical information in the state's natural history series and the need for thorough study of agricultural pests, the New York state legislature appropriated $1,000 in 1854 to the New York State Agricultural Society for an entomological survey. On 4 May the society appointed Fitch the first salaried, professional entomologist in the United States. Legislative appropriations continued through 1872.

During his career, Fitch described thirteen new genera and 451 new species and subspecies in fifteen arthropod orders and 107 families. He named many of the most destructive North American orchard and crop pests and studied their life histories in search of practical and effective strategies for destroying the pests or shielding vegetation from attack. His emphasis on natural history led to many useful and novel pest control strategies that involved sanitation, adjustment of planting times, fertilization, selection of resistant varieties, manipulation of predators and parasites, and baiting. In one of his most innovative proposals, in 1855 Fitch suggested importing live specimens of European parasites to help control introduced insects that were destroying American wheat crops, a practice that is now considered conventional biological control. Fitch encouraged experimentation with various materials to shield vegetation from insect attack, and by 1860 he employed an early spraying device for drenching vegetation with various toxic and repellant mixtures. By the time that he retired from service as the state's entomologist in 1873, Paris green, the first important stomach poison, was in common use against the Colorado potato beetle, and the insecticide era was underway.

Through his more than 140 publications, Fitch taught practical entomology and refuted charlatans who promoted ineffective insect control methods. His fourteen official reports on the injurious and beneficial insects of New York State were published in the *Transactions of the New York Agricultural Society* between 1855 and 1872. Based on original observations and written in simple language for both scientists and farmers, these reports were a stimulus and model for later professional entomologists and remained in demand for decades. Through them Fitch aroused the attention of citizens and government to the importance of entomology and inspired similar investigations in other states. Throughout his career he wrote articles for various farm papers, especially the *Country Gentleman* and the *Cultivator*.

Characterized as humble and gentle in demeanor, Fitch rarely gave formal lectures on entomology, and he never published in prestigious scientific journals. Quietly working in scientific isolation at his rural home in Salem, New York, Fitch became preeminent among the world's pioneer entomologists. In 1858 the Société Imperiale et Centrale d'Agriculture in Paris reviewed Fitch's early reports and awarded him a gold medal. He was also elected to membership in entomological societies in Philadelphia and in France, Germany, and Russia.

After his retirement, Fitch worked on his vast insect collection, his Washington County history notes, Fitch family genealogy notes, and civic and church matters. He died at home in Salem, New York.

• Fitch's diary is in Sterling Memorial Library, Yale University. His notes on the history of Washington County and on the genealogy of the Fitch family in America are in the collection of the New York Genealogical and Biographical Society, New York City. Most of his lengthy manuscript catalog of insects is at the New York State Museum. A modern assessment of his life as an entomologist is Jeffrey K. Barnes, "Asa Fitch and the Emergence of American Entomology, With an Entomological Bibliography and a Catalog of Taxonomic Names and Type Specimens," *New York State Museum Bulletin* 461 (1988): 1–120. Samuel Reznick used Fitch's diary extensively in "A Traveling School of Science on the Erie Canal in 1826," *New York History* 40 (1959): 255–69; *Education for a Technological Society: A Sesquicentennial History of Rensselaer Polytechnic Institute* (1968); "A Course of Medical Education in New York City in 1828–29: The Journal of Asa Fitch," *Bulletin of the History of Medicine* 42 (1968): 555–65; "The Study of Medicine at the Vermont Academy of Medicine (1827–29) as Revealed in the *Journal of Asa Fitch*," *Journal of the History of Medicine and Allied Sciences* 24 (1969): 416–29; ("Diary of a New York Doctor in Illinois—1830–1831," *Journal of the Illinois State Historical Society* 54 (1961): 25–50); and "The Religious Life and Struggle of a New York Scientist, 1809–1879," *New York History* 53 (1972): 411–36.

JEFFREY K. BARNES

FITCH, Clyde (2 May 1865–4 Sept. 1909), playwright, was born William Clyde Fitch in Elmira, New York, the son of William Goodwin Fitch, a captain in the Union army, and Alice Maud Clark. He survived a sibling who died in infancy; as a result, his childhood was carefully watched over by his protective mother. Though a frail child who was often sent to relatives in the country to recuperate, Fitch possessed a lively imagination, which he freely expressed in impromptu theatricals with neighborhood children. Even at a young age, however, schoolmates mocked his eccentricity, his effeminate mannerisms, and his love for ornate dress. Upon the completion of his studies at Holderness, a boarding school for boys in New Hampshire, he entered Amherst in 1882, where his colorful appearance earned him both popularity and still more ridicule. But despite his classmates' derision, "Billy"

Fitch remained true to his own aesthetic vision and became active in designing, staging, and acting in theatricals throughout his tenure at Amherst.

Although his father wanted him to become an architect, Fitch had literary aspirations and in the fall after his graduation made his way to New York. After unsuccessful attempts to sell several plays, Fitch moved through a variety of jobs, giving public readings, tutoring, and writing short pieces for periodicals. Ultimately, he made his first trip to Europe in 1888, visiting Paris and London and acquainting himself with Walter Pater and the Aesthetic Movement. Upon his return to New York, his friendship with the dramatic critic for the *New York Times*, Edward A. Dithmar, resulted in an opportunity that was to change the course of his life. Dithmar recommended Fitch to the actor Richard Mansfield, who was looking for someone to write a play about Beau Brummel. Though the construction of *Beau Brummel* was fraught with difficulty owing to the star's excitable temperament and reluctance to share credit, the play opened on 17 May 1890 in the Madison Square Theater to great popular success, if mixed critical reviews.

Fitch's subsequent career included thirty-three original plays as well as twenty-three adaptations. After 1890, New York dramatic seasons were usually marked by the presence of not just one, but two or three of Fitch's works. Indeed, the 1901 New York opening of *Lover's Lane* faced competition from three other Fitch plays. The early works that followed *Beau Brummel*, such as *Nathan Hale* (1898) and *Barbara Frietchie* (1899), were historical, exemplifying Fitch's continual emphasis on American themes. They placed romantic scenarios in historical settings, and good always emerged triumphant by the end of these moralistic plays. Midway through his career, Fitch moved away from melodrama and closer to a theatrical realism that took as its subject the upper reaches of New York society. It is important to point out, however, that Fitch's realism was still infused with much emotion, which to him enhanced the believability of a play. Although with his 1907 play *The Truth*, Fitch yet again entered on a new phase of his career, moving even farther away from melodramatic twists, his writing was continually derided as too overwrought by critics. Fitch, however, still saw melodrama and "real" emotion as two different entities, continually insisting on the necessity of the latter.

Despite this evolution as an artist, his reception remained as mixed as his methods for the duration of his playwriting efforts over the next twenty years. While his plays continued to be wildly popular with audiences, garnering Fitch as much as $250,000 a year in the later years of his career, he never won complete critical admiration. It became customary to damn Fitch with faint praise; even critics who liked his plays asserted that they could be made better with more attention to their crafting. Often he was given credit for being little more than a "theatrical dressmaker," hastily fashioning a new piece for some leading lady. Though his critics certainly were right that many of

Fitch's plays were vehicles for leading actors of the day (they included many strong roles for women) and that Fitch's work pace was frenetic, his reputation as a reckless author was based on misconceptions about his artistic process. For Fitch, writing was the final step in what was a long, careful period of reflection on each play and the individual natures and foibles of its characters, turning them over and over in his mind.

Fitch's rapid pace did take its toll on his health, however; he progressively wore himself down during the later years of his career. Though he built himself a country retreat, "Quiet Corner," in Greenwich, Connecticut, his health worsened, and his output radically decreased. On a tour of Europe to recuperate his health, he suffered an attack of appendicitis and died in 1909 at Chalons-sur-Marne, France.

Fitch always remained something of an aberration in the competitive theatrical world—and not just because of his colorful appearance. He was a genial man who consistently encouraged other artists, actors, and aspiring playwrights alike, insisting that there was room for all in the theatrical establishment. He was at ease conversing on any manner of subjects, and as his career progressed, he would diversify his own artistic role, taking a larger and larger part in the production and staging of his plays. Fitch's marginalized status in the dramatic canon was, and still is, due in large part to his role as a transitional figure in the history of American theater as it moved from melodrama to realism. He at once embraced color and spectacle while still striving to produce real instances from American life on his stage—and he was among the first playwrights to do so. For Fitch, creating an intricate photograph of an event became a means for telling a story more effectively, rather than an end in itself or an obsession with frivolous detail or captivating spectacle. As he himself emphasized in an article for *Harper's Weekly*, "I am trying especially to reflect our own life of the present, and to get into the heart of the picture made by the past. To do this I do not consider any detail too small, as long as it is not boring." Though this may date his plays or seem to limit their artistry, it makes them no less important as evidence of the developing maturity of the American theater, which was steadily approaching the important realism that had already made its inroads in fiction and European drama.

• Amherst College contains the largest collection of Fitch's papers, while the New York Public Library also contains an assortment of play manuscripts and promptbooks. Fitch's works not mentioned above include, among others, *Frederic Lemaitre* (1890), *The Masked Ball* (1892), *An American Duchess* (1893), *Mistress Betty* (1895), *The Head of the Family* (1898), *The Way of the World* (1901), and *Major Andre* (1903). Three book-length studies of Fitch are Archie Bell's *The Clyde Fitch I Knew* (1909); *Clyde Fitch and His Letters*, ed. Montrose J. Moses and Virginia Gerson (1924); and James J. Murray's "The Contribution of Clyde Fitch to the American Theater" (Ph.D. diss., Boston Univ., 1950). Brief biographies of Fitch can be found in several histories and anthologies of American drama, including Margaret G. Mayorga's *A Short History of the American Drama* (1932); Montrose J. Moses's *Representative Plays by American Dramatists*, vol. 3 (1964); Walter J. Meserve's *An Outline of American Drama* (1965); John Geoffrey Hartman's *The Development of American Social Comedy from 1787 to 1936* (1971); and Arthur Hobson Quinn's *A History of the American Drama from the Civil War to the Present Day*, vol. 1 (1972). William Dean Howells gives interesting commentary on Fitch in his article "Some New American Plays," reprinted in Alan S. Dowen, ed., *American Drama and Its Critics* (1965).

ANN M. FOX

FITCH, James (2 Aug. 1649–10 Nov. 1727), Connecticut land speculator and magistrate, was born in Saybrook, Connecticut, the son of the Reverend James Fitch and Abigail Whitfield. In 1659 his father led a group of people to settle the town of Norwich, situated where the Quinebaug and Shetucket rivers combine to form the Thames. Fitch was raised largely on the frontier in close proximity to the Indians, with whom his father had numerous contacts. He gained knowledge of the unsettled lands in eastern Connecticut and learned to manipulate the Native Americans who controlled them. Fitch served in King Philip's War, was chosen commissioner or justice of the peace for Norwich (1678–1680), was selectman (1679–1680), was appointed treasurer of New London County in 1679, and made captain of the Norwich trained band in May 1680. In 1677 he married Elizabeth Mason, daughter of Deputy Governor John Mason, leader of Connecticut forces in the Pequot War. She was the younger sister of his stepmother, the second wife of the Reverend James Fitch. They had four children who survived infancy. After her death in October 1684, Fitch married Alice Bradford Adams, widow of the Reverend William Adams of Dedham, Massachusetts, in May 1687; he fathered eight more children.

In the wake of King Philip's War, Fitch secured deeds in 1680 and 1684 from Owaneco, chief of the Mohegans, to two huge tracts in northeastern Connecticut, the Quinebaug and Wabbaquasset lands, encompassing more than one thousand square miles, thus making him the largest landowner in the colony. Fitch's purchase of the two tracts of land set the stage for most of his future political career, as he became the leader of the colony's "native right" men, people who believed that although royal charters gave Englishmen the right to govern, the charters did not grant them ownership over land, which only the Native Americans had the right to convey. In addition, his acquisition of these Indian lands drew him into conflict with Wait-Still and Fitz-John Winthrop, powerful sons of Governor John Winthrop, Jr., who claimed some of the same territory.

Fitch was first elected deputy to the General Court from Norwich in April 1678, a position to which he was reelected the next five legislative sessions between October 1678 and October 1680. He was first nominated for a seat on Connecticut's twelve-man upper house in October 1679 and was elected to that body in May 1681. Fitch strongly opposed Connecticut's incorporation into the Dominion of New England, although he accepted a justice of the peace's commission

from Governor Edmund Andros. A lifelong supporter of charter government, he led the fight to restore the old government in 1689. When news of the Glorious Revolution reached Connecticut, the former leaders, led by former Governor Robert Treat, Secretary John Allyn, and the Winthrops, procrastinated. Fitch, however, called for new elections to be held in Hartford on 9 May 1689, the reestablishment of charter government, and the dismissal from their former offices of those who had surrendered too easily to Andros. He achieved his first two goals, but the freemen voted to restore all the old magistrates to office. Fitch and his allies hoped to turn out the old rulers in the election of 1690, but delay gave the friends of Treat and the Winthrops the opportunity to retain power. Election laws were modified both to loosen the requirements for becoming a freeman and to make it more difficult to defeat incumbents. The new freemen responded by continuing the old rulers in office. Fitch articulated his views on the efficacy of charter government and the wrongheadedness of Connecticut's leaders in two hotly worded but not extant manuscript pamphlets, "A Plain Short Discourse" (1691) and "A Little of Much" (1692), regarded as "two scurrillous libels" by some of his opponents.

Immediately after the restoration of charter government in Connecticut, Fitch and Nathan Gold of Fairfield were appointed by the General Court to travel to New York City to meet Captain Jacob Leisler and the other captains "to giue there best aduice . . . in any thing wherein they may be helpfull" (Trumbull and Hoadly, vol. 3, p. 468) in instituting a government favorable to the new monarchs William and Mary. Fitch was selected to a commission to settle the boundary with Massachusetts in May 1695, appointed to the committee to revise Connecticut's laws in October 1696, chosen major of the New London County militia that same session, placed in charge of the fort in New London in August 1697, and served on a 1698 committee to settle the boundary between Connecticut and Rhode Island.

During the 1690s Fitch continued to oppose the colony's traditional rulers through his leadership of the "native right" men, his attempts to arouse popular passions against the colony's traditional leaders, and most importantly through his efforts to settle families in new towns on the land he had purchased from the natives of eastern Connecticut. From his base of power in New London County and his alliance with other important figures in the county, Fitch began to move tenants into the Quinebaug country in the early 1690s. He settled his family in what became the town of Canterbury in 1697. The Winthrops responded by sending their own tenants into the region, with the result that the area became enmeshed in conflict. Fitch's control of the New London County Court gave him the initial advantage.

Fitch might well have gained total political control over Connecticut but for the success of Fitz-John Winthrop's mission to London to gain formal confirmation of the colony's 1662 charter. When news reached Connecticut in December 1697 of Winthrop's triumph, the old order quickly struck to secure their advantage and defeat their most implacable opponent. Previously, county courts were presided over by local councillors like Fitch, but new legislation in May 1698 vested control of the county courts in the general assembly. Worse yet, Winthrop was elected governor of Connecticut in the 1698 elections. Fitch was replaced as presiding officer over the New London County Court and lost his council seat in 1698, although he regained it in 1700. His allies in the upper house dwindled as some died and others were defeated for reelection. Fitch struggled to discredit Governor Winthrop, and although this effort proved to be unsuccessful, he continued to wield considerable power for much of the next decade. In 1706 and 1707, however, the legislature investigated all Indian claims in eastern Connecticut and deprived Fitch of control of all remaining lands he claimed through deeds from Owaneco. Two years later, in 1709, he was defeated for reelection. In poor health, Fitch made a final effort to sell lands in eastern Connecticut by issuing a proclamation on 22 March 1717 "to give further encouragement for the settling of a new town" (Larned, vol. 1, p. 151), in direct opposition to an order from Governor Gurdon Saltonstall prohibiting such an action. He was ordered to desist by the sheriff of New London County, refused to obey, was condemned by the general assembly in May 1717, and was forced to apologize for his behavior. In March 1723 the elderly Fitch had a poem published in the *New England Courant* on the Anglican heresies at Yale College, an institution he had supported with a large gift of land in 1701. Fitch died in Canterbury four years later.

James Fitch for a period of some twenty years was an extremely powerful political figure in Connecticut. His aristocratic enemies who represented the traditional rulers of the colony characterized him as "Black-James" or the "great Land pirat," and Fitch and his allies were considered "the principall bane and Ruin of our Ancient Order and Peace" (Bushman, p. 102). In his leadership of a faction devoted to charter government and "native right," and his reputation as "the cheife patron of theire charter privelages" (*Massachusetts Historical Society Collections*, 6th ser., vol. 5, p. 112), Fitch exerted a major, albeit disturbing, influence over the affairs of the colony and played a critical role in the evolution of Connecticut society, from one stressing traditional Puritan values to one emphasizing more acquisitive and assertive Yankee ones.

• No major collection of Fitch papers exists, although significant material about him can be found in a number of sources. Letters and documents by and about Fitch have been published in several works, most notably "The Winthrop Papers," *Massachusetts Historical Society Collections*, 5th and 6th ser.; Ellen D. Larned, *History of Windham County, Connecticut*, vol. 1 (2 vols., 1874, 1880); "The Wyllys Papers," *Connecticut Historical Society Collections* 21 (1924); and "Early Letters and Documents Relating to Connecticut," *Connecticut Historical Society Collections* 24 (1932). Additional material is in the Winthrop Manuscripts, Massachusetts Historical Society; and in the Connecticut Archives, Connecticut State Library, especially in Civil Officers 1st ser.; Colonial and State Boundaries, 1st ser.; Crimes and Misdemeanors, 1st ser.; Indians; Miscellaneous, 1st ser.; Private Controversies; and Towns and Lands, 1st ser. J. Hammond Trumbull and Charles J. Hoadly, eds., *The Public Records of the Colony of Connecticut*, vols. 3–6 (15 vols., 1850–1890), is invaluable.

Most information known about Fitch comes from his enemies, like the correspondents in *The Winthrop Papers* and royalist Gershom Bulkeley in "Will and Doom, or the Miseries of Connecticut by and under an Usurped Power," *Connecticut Historical Society Collections* 3 (1895): 79–269. An important article is James M. Poteet, "More Yankee Than Puritan: James Fitch of Connecticut," *New England Historical & Genealogical Register* 133 (Apr. 1979): 102–17. Further information can be found in Frances Manwaring Caulkins, *History of Norwich, Connecticut from Its Possession by the Indians, to the Year 1866* (1866); Roscoe Conkling Fitch, *History of the Fitch Family* (2 vols., 1930); and Thomas M. Jodziewicz, "Charters and Corporation, Independence and Loyalty," *Connecticut History* 29 (Nov. 1988): 27–46. Richard L. Bushman, *From Puritan to Yankee: Character and Social Order in Connecticut, 1690–1765* (1967), and Richard S. Dunn, *Puritans and Yankees: The Winthrop Dynasty of New England 1630–1717* (1962), were responsible for rediscovering Fitch and emphasizing his importance in what they and Poteet characterize as the colony's transformation from Puritan to Yankee in the late seventeenth and early eighteenth centuries.

BRUCE P. STARK

FITCH, John (21 Jan. 1743–June or July 1798), inventor and craftsman, was born in Windsor, Connecticut, the son of Joseph Fitch and Sarah Shaler, farmers. His father came from neighboring Hartford and his mother from Bolton. His mother died before he was five; his father married Abigail Church of Hartford two years later. Most of what is known about Fitch comes from an autobiographical sketch written between 1790 and 1792, when he was alone and embittered, convinced that he had been cheated by life. Although he had by then put aside the Calvinistic Presbyterianism of his upbringing and replaced it with a rationalistic deism, he still tended to pass judgment on those he felt had failed him. His memories of childhood were few and unhappy. He described his father as uncaring, even tyrannical. Unjust treatment by an older brother "forbode" his "future rewards," he reminisced—with the irony intended (*Autobiography*, p. 23).

Fitch showed an independent streak, a desire to pursue a career of his own choosing, early on. He had just four or five years of public school before he was kept at home to help run the farm. He read voraciously in his spare time, particularly geography and arithmetic texts, and he taught himself surveying in his early teens. He thought about a life at sea but quickly gave up the idea after a few weeks on a vessel engaged in the coastal trade. He then apprenticed himself to two clockmakers in succession, neither of whom taught him enough to become a journeyman. He spent most of those years performing mundane tasks and learning a little brass work. By 1765 relatives had bought out his indenture and he did enough business at a small brass foundry to repay his debts. When he married

Lucy Roberts of Simsbury in December 1767, he apparently did so with no great passion. He abandoned Lucy and an infant son just over a year later "and have never since found my way back" (*Autobiography*, p. 45). His wife, he learned after leaving, had been pregnant with a daughter. When he finally returned to Windsor in 1794 and visited with his grown children it was too late to mend familial fences. The closest that Fitch came to a family life was an odd relationship during his Pennsylvania years with a widow, Mary Krafft, who was in turn involved with his married business partner, Henry Voight.

Earlier in the year of his marriage, Fitch had tried to start a potash manufacturing business with a couple of other young men. The enterprise failed and Fitch, again in debt and trapped in a loveless marriage, left Connecticut and wandered to New Jersey in 1769. For a time Fitch improved his fortunes. He lived in Trenton from 1769 to 1775 and went from making brass buttons and repairing an occasional clock to a modestly successful silversmithing business. As before, Fitch basically taught himself, and surviving pieces attest to his craft skills. A militia lieutenant and gunsmith with the outbreak of war, his trade was disrupted, and personality conflicts—a recurrent problem—brought an embarrassing end to his military service. He traveled down the Ohio River to Kentucky in 1780 in an attempt to survey various tracts and recoup his financial losses through land speculation. On a second trip down the Ohio in 1782 for the same purpose, he and his companions were captured by Indians, taken to Detroit, and handed over to the British. From there Fitch went to a prisoner-of-war camp below Montreal, where he remained until he was released on parole and given passage to New York City. He came ashore on Christmas Day 1782, after nearly nine months in captivity.

Fitch took up residence in Bucks County, Pennsylvania. Undeterred by his frontier experience to that point, he resumed his land jobbing and joined with associates in a newly formed company, this time to survey more than 250,000 acres along the Muskingum and Hockhocking rivers in the Ohio country. After yet another trip down the Ohio River, he returned to Bucks County and in 1785 produced a map that showed his abilities as both cartographer and engraver—once more, self-taught skills. But Congress's organization of western lands invalidated private claims, and Fitch's efforts came to naught.

Fitch was about to prove his genius in an entirely new field: steam navigation. Thinking "that there might be a force governed by steam," he "gave over the Idea of Carriages but thought it might answer for a Boat and better for a first rate man of war" (*Autobiography*, p. 113). How Fitch got turned in this direction is not clear. He professed to have never read about steam engines and denied having heard of anyone using steam to propel boats before it occurred to him in April 1785. He did subsequently read treatises on steam, and he talked with William Henry of Lancaster, who years before had contemplated building a

steamboat, but much of what Fitch did from 1785 on came from his own trial-and-error approach to experimentation. Because he became obsessed with establishing his claim to "originality" and was embroiled in a contest to prove his claim, it was in Fitch's interest to plead ignorance of what others had done. Therefore establishing a precise chronology is all but impossible.

In any event, before the end of 1785 Fitch had designed an engine and boiler that utilized the same principles as a Newcomen atmospheric engine, and he built a model of a proposed steam-driven boat that used side-mounted paddles connected by an endless chain. He submitted his model to the American Philosophical Society, though he probably never made a full-scale version. Collaborating with watchmaker Henry Voight, Fitch constructed a boat that he was able to demonstrate on the Delaware River on 22 August 1787. Spectators included men attending the Constitutional Convention. This boat was powered by a Watt-type engine with a separate condenser, and the engine transmitted power to oars mounted to stroke in paddle fashion, six oars to each side of the boat. In 1789 Fitch and Voight switched to a newer, double-acting engine and shifted the driving paddles to the rear of the boat. Fitch even had the satisfaction of seeing his third boat run a successful Burlington-Philadelphia-Trenton packet service in 1790. Despite a summer of service and perhaps a total of 2,000 miles on the Delaware at a notable eight miles per hour—twice the speed of the 1787 model—Fitch's boat was a commercial failure. His backers lost interest and his 1791 model, the *Perseverance*, was doomed—ironically, for lack of perseverance.

Inadequate financing and technical problems proved inescapable. Nor did there seem to be a great public demand for steamboat travel. Equally vexing to Fitch was his competition with James Rumsey of Maryland. Rumsey designed a steamboat that ran by direct force—jet propulsion. Although he did not publicly demonstrate a working model until December 1787, he claimed to have thought of using steam power as early as 1784 and competed with Fitch as the originator of the idea in a practical form. Fitch and Rumsey battled for some six years, from 1785 to 1791, taking their arguments to the Continental Congress, state legislatures, and the American Philosophical Society. They even formed companies to attract investors. Virtually every leading politician and scientist in the middle states became caught up in the controversy at one point or another. Fitch won some rounds, securing state patents that gave him a monopoly on steam navigation in New York, New Jersey, Pennsylvania, Delaware, and Virginia. But Rumsey, even if he ended up with fewer state patents, had the backing of more prominent men: George Washington, Thomas Jefferson, and Benjamin Franklin.

By 1790 neither Fitch nor Rumsey would compromise; both wanted full credit for discovery and an exclusive right to all forms of steam navigation. Their dispute pressed home the need for federal patents to replace the chaos of the existing state system, and the

Patent Act of 1790 can in part be attributed to them. Even though both men received federal patents on the same day—26 August 1791—neither was satisfied. Rumsey had already sailed for England in 1788, only to die there in 1792 after coming tantalizingly close to success. Fitch left for Europe the next year, hoping to stimulate interest in his steam boat designs. He went first to France, then to England, and returned to the United States in 1794, with almost nothing to show for his efforts.

Fitch eventually drifted to Bardstown, Kentucky, thinking that he might be able to make good on claims to land that he had surveyed near there more than a decade before. Unsuccessful at that, he became a pathetic figure. Some people pitied him; others offered only ridicule. By 1798 he was ready to give up. "This is a damn wicked world," he had once lamented (*Autobiography*, p. 128). He apparently committed suicide in Bardstown by taking an overdose of opium pills that had been prescribed for insomnia. He was buried in an unmarked grave, which remained that way until 1910, when the local chapter of the Daughters of the American Revolution provided a simple plaque, like that for other veterans. It said nothing of his being an inventor.

In 1790, when one of his boats began steaming on the Delaware, Fitch took grim satisfaction that although neither "the World nor his country" thanked him for it, no one could take from him credit "for one of the Greatest and most useful arts that was ever introduced" (*Autobiography*, p. 193). If Fitch hoped that posterity would be kinder to him than his contemporaries, he would have been disappointed. In the popular mind Robert Fulton is the inventor of steamboats, even though Fulton's first success came seventeen years after Fitch's. The fate of John Fitch is proof that in some sense Fulton deserves that title: before Fulton there had been many experiments but no long-term successes. Fitch ended his days in poverty and obscurity, and yet as a steamboat pioneer he helped open the way for Fulton. There were actually many inventors of the steamboat; John Fitch should be remembered as one of them.

• Frank Prager edited Fitch's *Autobiography* (1976) from the manuscript owned by the Library Company of Philadelphia. Fitch divided his autobiography into two parts: a sketch of his life from 1743 to 1785 and a history of his steamboat work from 1785 to 1790. Fitch compiled the latter from a larger set of papers now housed at the Library of Congress. Rumsey criticized Fitch in *A Short Treatise on the Application of Steam* (1788), and Fitch responded with *The Original Steamboat Supported or a Reply to James Rumsey's Pamphlet* (1788), which drew a retort from Joseph Barnes, *Remarks on Mr. John Fitch's Reply to Mr. James Rumsey* (1788). Thompson Westcott, *The Life of John Fitch: The Inventor of the Steamboat* (1857), was not the first Fitch biography, but it is the best one done to that point and has details found nowhere else. Readers should keep in mind that Westcott set out to right a historiographic wrong, so he was passionate in his defense of Fitch. James Thomas Flexner, *Steamboats Come True* (1944; repr. 1992), stands as the best study overall. True to

his desire to connect "the behavior of people with the growth of ideas," Flexner put Fitch, Rumsey, and Robert Fulton into context as steamboat pioneers. Frank Prager's "The Steamboat Pioneers before the Founding Fathers" and "The Steam Boat Interference, 1787–1793" appeared in the *Journal of the Patent Office Society* 37 (1955): 486–522, and 40 (1958): 611–43. Brooke Hindle, *Emulation and Invention* (1981), includes an insightful chapter on Fitch and Rumsey. Neil L. York's *Mechanical Metamorphosis* (1985) reviews the Fitch-Rumsey battle in connection with the emergence of federal patent law.

NEIL L. YORK

FITCH, Thomas (c. 1700–18 July 1774), lawyer and colonial governor, was born in Norwalk, Connecticut, the son of the well-to-do Thomas Fitch and Sarah (maiden name unknown). His great-grandfather, also named Thomas Fitch, was one of the founders of the town. Three years after he graduated from Yale College (1721), Fitch married Hannah Hall of New Haven; they had ten children. By 1726, Fitch was serving occasionally as the substitute minister for the Norwalk Congregational church, although there is no record of his ever being formally ordained.

Elected to the lower house of the General Assembly in 1726 as a deputy from Norwalk, and reelected in 1727, 1729, and 1730, Fitch was elevated to the governor's council or upper house in 1734 and 1735. From 1740 to 1751 he was annually reelected to the council before he was chosen deputy governor, 1751–1754. In 1754 Fitch was elected governor over Roger Wolcott, who was implicated in the plundering of a Spanish merchant vessel in New London, a situation that had moved British authority to demand colony restitution. This was the first time an incumbent governor was defeated for reelection in the colony's history. Before Fitch became the second incumbent Connecticut governor denied reelection (1766), he served ably as a wartime colonial leader during the last imperial war, the French and Indian War (1754–1763). At the same time, he also experienced first the developing internal threat to the colony's political and religious status quo and then the simultaneous, revived British efforts to create a revenue from and to tighten control over its American colonies after 1763, an initiative widely perceived in Connecticut as an external assault on the standing order.

For a generation before Fitch's election as governor, Connecticut's New Lights had railed against a religious establishment, embodied in the Saybrook Platform, which created county associations or consociations of ministers and lay messengers with ecclesiastical authority over the county's congregations. The platform also allowed the use of the half-way covenant, a compromise that granted partial church membership to those who could not testify to a saving or conversion experience. Calling for a return to this earlier test for the creation of a church membership of visible saints, the adherents of the Great Awakening, or New Lights, attacked the standing religious order in a variety of enthusiastic ways, from creating separate congregations to endorsing sympathetic political candidates. Strongest in the rapidly developing eastern counties of New London and Windham, the New Light insurgency was amplified after the 1750s by extensive popular support in those same counties for the efforts of the Susquehannah Company, a response to particular economic and expansionist currents in the colony. Organized in the mid-1750s in Windham, the company sought to take advantage of the sea-to-sea Connecticut boundaries mentioned in the colony's 1662 royal charter by settling the northern third of Pennsylvania. Intended to create opportunities for land-poor Connecticut inhabitants and land speculators alike, the scheme offended not only Pennsylvania, but royal authorities as well. Sensitive to any issues that might bring royal scrutiny on his largely self-governing colony, and endanger the colony charter, Fitch opposed the company's initiative in the early 1760s. While he also opposed the New Light offensive against Connecticut's religious establishment, and came to personify the western Connecticut, conservative standing political and religious order that eastern elements were seeking to overturn in the mid-eighteenth century, Fitch was not completely unsympathetic to the dissidents. In 1765 he published anonymously *An Explanation of Say-Brook Platform; The principles of the consociated churches in the Colony of Connecticut: collected from their Plan of Union. By one that heartily desires the Order, Peace and Purity of these Churches*, a pamphlet that argued against what he claimed was a nonexistent judicial authority in the county consociations even as he accepted the presbyterian church system established by the Saybrook Platform (1708). Ironically, though, it was the external, British imperial assault that created the context within which Fitch and his conservative allies were defeated.

When news of a proposed stamp act reached Connecticut in May 1764, the assembly directed a committee to prepare an appropriate negative response. Drafted chiefly by Fitch, *Reasons why the British Colonies in America, Should not be Charged with Internal Taxes, by Authority of Parliament; Humbly offered for Consideration in Behalf of the Colony of Connecticut* was one of the first official colonial responses to the proposal. The pamphlet argued that in effect, according to the English constitution, no taxes could be voted by Parliament concerning Connecticut unless the colony was represented in Parliament, which it was not. Yet Parliament did have the right to raise revenues in the colonies, but by means of duties on commerce. In other words, Parliament could regulate the external sphere, but not the internal sphere, levying commercial duties but not direct taxes. The latter sphere was within the competence of Connecticut's own chartered government. The response satisfied the colony's assembly, but not the British government, which passed the Stamp Act in early 1765.

While still opposed to the act itself, Fitch and four council members took the required oath to see to its observance in their colony, an extremely unpopular position to take in Connecticut, where a loud and turbulent majority was against the act. Fitch offered an explanation of his actions in early 1766 in a pamphlet entitled *Some Reasons that influenced The Governor to take, and The Councillors to administer The Oath, Required by the Act of Parliament; commonly called the Stamp Act. Humbly submitted to the Consideration of the Publick*, in which he contended that his actions followed from his oath taken as governor to obey king and parliament. Not only would he have personally run the risk of a large fine if he had not taken the stamp act oath, but the colony itself might have lost its charter in the face of such insubordination. The eastern, radical interests completed their control over Connecticut's government in the May 1766 election, however, when Fitch and the four councillors were defeated. During the last eight years of his life, Fitch was regularly a candidate for the governor's council, but he was never successful. Norwalk, though, did elect him a town deputy in 1772.

Fitch was a prominent attorney and served his colony on a variety of committees that dealt with legal questions. He was the principal member of a committee that completed a revision of Connecticut's laws in 1750. He also served as a justice of the peace and as the chief judge of the Superior Court while he was deputy governor.

Just a few days before Fitch's death in Norwalk, Connecticut's delegates to the First Continental Congress were chosen. The juxtaposition of events was of symbolic significance as the Connecticut government, moving rapidly toward revolution, took no official notice of the ex-governor's death. Radicals, or Whigs, were not overly sensitive to the passing of conservatives in the American colonies in the mid-1770s. Fitch, though, had served his colony well, with integrity and a firm attachment to principle. The more traditional standing order he celebrated, however, had been replaced by the time of his death by a new order, an establishment that, at least for a time, would have little use for a society marked by conservative hues and bounded by imperial tones.

• Volumes 17 and 18 of the Connecticut Historical Society's *Collections* (1918, 1920) contain *The Fitch Papers: Correspondence and Documents during Thomas Fitch's Governorship of the Colony of Connecticut, 1754–1766*. Charles J. Hoadly, ed., *Public Records of the Colony of Connecticut, 1636–1776*, vols. 10–12 (1850–1890), cover Fitch's years as governor, as do appropriate volumes in the Connecticut Archives, Connecticut State Library. Fitch's *Reasons Why* is included in Bernard Bailyn, ed., *Pamphlets of the American Revolution, 1750–1776* (1965). There is an entry for Fitch in Franklin B. Dexter, *Biographical Sketches of the Graduates of Yale College*, vol. 1 (1885). Especially useful in understanding the historical context is Richard L. Bushman, *From Puritan to Yankee: Character and the Social Order in Connecticut, 1690–1765* (1967); Oscar Zeichner, *Connecticut's Years of Controversy, 1750–1776* (1949); Christopher Collier, *Roger Sherman's Connecticut:*

Yankee Politics and the American Revolution (1971); and Edmund S. and Helen M. Morgan, *The Stamp Act Crisis: Prologue to Revolution* (1953).

THOMAS W. JODZIEWICZ

FITE, Warner (5 Mar. 1867–23 June 1955), educator and philosopher, was born in Philadelphia, Pennsylvania, the son of George Fite, a fire insurance salesman, and Sallie Gibbs Liddle. Fite attended Haverford College and received his A.B. in 1889. After a year at the Philadelphia Divinity School (Episcopal), he entered the Ph.D. program in philosophy at the University of Pennsylvania. As part of his studies, he studied abroad at the University of Berlin from 1891 to 1892 and at the University of Munich from 1892 to 1893. After his return to the United States, he received his Ph.D. in 1894. That fall he began his teaching career as an instructor in philosophy at Williams College in Massachusetts. While there, Fite also served as dean of faculty from 1895 to 1897. He then moved to Chicago, where he taught in the psychology department at the University of Chicago from 1897 to 1903. During his tenure there, he wrote *An Introductory Study of Ethics* (1903), a college text book in ethics. Reviewers of this text admired Fite's clarity and avoidance of philosophical jargon, but they found his argument to be weak and felt that his attempt to prove the fundamental philosophical unity of hedonism and idealism was unnecessary and detracted from the excellence of the first part of the study.

From 1903 to 1906 Fite served at the University of Texas as an instructor in philosophy. He then accepted a position at Indiana University in Bloomington, where he taught from 1906 to 1915. While at Indiana, he published *Individualism* (1911), a collection of four lectures he had presented at the University of Chicago in 1909. He also wrote several articles criticizing university education departments (*Nation*, 11 Sept. 1911) and the new realism of Bertrand Russell (*Nation*, 9 Feb. 1914). In another article, he argued against women's suffrage, claiming that the female mind was equivalent to the male mind just before it reached maturity. Since only mature men and not all men were given the vote, Fite believed that women were unable to fulfill this responsibility (*Nation*, 2 Feb. 1913).

In 1915 Fite became professor of philosophy at Princeton University, where he was appointed Stuart Professor of Ethics in 1917 and taught until his retirement in 1935. While at Princeton he published a number of works, including a two-part essay on the principles of advertising (*Unpopular Review*, July and October, 1915), and a critique of Sigmund Freud's "weird, grotesque, uncanny and bestial" psychology (*Nation*, 10 Aug. 1916). In another essay, he attacked the scientific argument against birth control, arguing that human evolution and intelligence allowed a married couple to make decisions regarding the number of children they would have (*International Journal of Ethics*, Oct. 1916). He also published essays on discipline (*Unpopular Review*, Oct. 1918) and a study of the scientific method used to study the mind (*Atlantic Month-*

ly, Dec. 1918). Throughout these articles, Fite maintained his criticism of views that studied the brain at the expense of the mind and argued for the importance of individuals over the interests of society. In 1924 Fite, who believed that crossword puzzles improved logic skills, offered a prize to the student who could construct a puzzle with two different complete solutions.

In 1925 Fite published *Moral Philosophy*. He translated *Mist*, a work by his close friend Miguel de Unamuno, the Spanish philosopher, in 1928, followed by *The Living Mind* (1930) and the controversial *The Platonic Legend* (1934). In the latter, Fite admitted that he found Plato "rather repellent" and argued against the idealization of Plato to a nonphilosophical audience. In his review, Irwin Edman argued that Fite's account of Plato made it "impossible to account for the hold Plato has over the imagination of Professor Fite," unless Plato was a greater poet and artist than Fite was willing to admit (*New York Times*, 9 Dec. 1934).

The same year, Fite was elected president of the Eastern Section of the American Philosophical Association. In his presidential address, "The Philosopher and His Words," he questioned the definition of philosophy as universal thought. His last publication, *Jesus the Man: A Critical Essay* (1946), was nearly as controversial as *The Platonic Legend* had been. In this work, he argued that Jesus was not God, but was a "God-intoxicated man."

Fite married Esther Wallace Sturges in 1901; they had four children. Esther died in 1916, and he married Florence Odell in 1930; they had no children. He died in Philadelphia, Pennsylvania.

Although a relatively unknown figure in the history of Western philosophy, Fite represents the quintessential American philosopher. Not adhering to any one school of thought, he addressed contemporary social issues and tackled philosophical views that had frequently been taken for granted. Moreover, his criticisms have a timelessness that makes them as provocative now as they were in his life time. Well known in Europe, he maintained correspondences with Miguel de Unamuno and the Italian philosopher Benedetto Croce.

• Fite's papers are in the Seeley G. Mudd Manuscript Library, Princeton University. An obituary is in the *New York Times*, 24 June 1955.

COLLEEN K. FLEWELLING

FITHIAN, Philip Vickers (29 Dec. 1747–8 Oct. 1776), tutor and chaplain, was born in Greenwich, New Jersey, the son of Joseph Fithian and Hannah Vickers, farmers. He was educated at Enoch Green's school in Deerfield, New Jersey, and received an A.B. in 1772 and an A.M. in 1775 from the College of New Jersey (Princeton), where he studied theology and Greek with the Reverend Andrew Hunter.

Fithian worked as a tutor in the home of Robert Carter of Nomini Hall in Westmoreland County, Virginia, from 1 November 1773 until 20 October 1774.

While working in Virginia Fithian kept a journal and wrote letters (published in 1900 and reissued in 1943) that present a classic analysis of the Virginia aristocracy on the eve of the American Revolution. "I believe the Virginians have, of late, altered their manner very much," he wrote to his former teacher, Enoch Green, on 1 December 1773, "for they begin to find that their estates, even by small extravagance, decline, grow involved with debt; this seems to be the spring which induces the people of fortune, who are the pattern of all behaviour here, to be frugal and moderate" (Farish, p. 35). That prescient observation anticipated modern scholarship by linking the planters' straited circumstances in the tobacco trade with three other elements: the powerful cultural model that planters set for the rest of the white population, the deep aversion to economic dependency on British creditors that began to curb the material appetites of the aristocracy, and the web of political goals and personal inhibitions that in the eighteenth century was called "moderation."

The model set by such men as Fithian's employer and friend Robert Carter was a complex one. Carter's 650-volume library, which Fithian cataloged, ranged widely and included classics and works on the Enlightenment, religion, and the British libertarian tradition. "Mr. Carter is sensible, judicious, much given to retirement and study; his company and conversation are always profitable. His main studies are law and music, . . . the latter of which seems to . . . nourish as well as entertain his mind!" (Farish, p. 64) But for those members of the gentry who lacked Carter's discipline and secure wealth, more visible badges of success earned Fithian attention and deference: the "amazing property" of slavery "blows up the owners to an imagination which is visible to all" so "that they are exalted . . . much above other men in worth and precedency." Only "honour" and "mental acquirements," Fithian believed, conferred more social status that did land and slaves (Farish, p. 211). A Princeton degree, he explained to John Peck, his successor at Nomini Hall, was the social equivalent of £10,000, but Fithian admonished Peck to presume to only half that much social distinction in order to avoid gambling, fencing, and horse racing, in which he would be ill equipped to compete.

Fithian's description of the architecture of Nomini Hall emphasized not just its grandeur but also the way house design reinforced the master's authority. The dining room and central hallway allowed for formality when strangers and guests were present and furnished space for familial and household hubbub at other times. Meals had their own ceremony of social obligations acknowledged and performed, and the seating arrangement at dinner underscored the status of honored guests and humbler supplicants. Fithian concluded that this attention to spatial detail and social convention was intended to conserve virtue through efficiently maintaining the social hierarchies of society. To exert his authority over his slaves, Carter—despite his culture and education—resorted to cruelty. If the slaves were suspected of "sullenness, obstinacy, or idleness," they were strapped upright on a thick board with their feet just touching a sharp peg onto which they would be lowered if their answers to questions were unsatisfactory. "There is a righteous God who will take vengeance on such inventions!" (Farish, p. 51) Fithian maintained.

Fithian realized that in highly oral and visible cultures such as his own, social success and moral reputation depend primarily on circumspection and self-control. He advised his successor at Nomini Hall to "extend the limits of your acquaintance" because well-placed friends were a "considerable advantage." "Yet attempt [such familiarization] slowly and with the most jealous circumspection," he warned. One rash or presumptuous social move could threaten an outsider with "total, if not immediate ruin. . . . In all promiscuous company, be as silent and attentive as decency will allow you" (Farish, pp. 212–13). Fithian modeled the behavior he advocated on Horace's admonition to "love close retirement and a life by stealth."

After returning to New Jersey, Fithian was licensed by the Presbytery of Philadelphia on 6 December 1774. Later that month he was part of a Whig mob that seized and destroyed a shipment of tea in Greenwich, New Jersey. During the next year he made several missionary tours for the Donegal Presbytery into western Pennsylvania, Maryland, and Virginia. Also in 1775 Fithian married Elizabeth Beatty, following a five-year courtship. The marriage was childless.

The Revolution overtook Fithian's new career and marriage. At the College of New Jersey, his graduation oration defended the typically republican proposition that "political jealousy is a laudable passion," a doctrine reinforced by the college's president John Witherspoon. On 26 June 1776 he was appointed chaplain in the New Jersey militia and spent most of that summer visiting field hospitals, before dying of dysentery in New York.

• Biographical information on Fithian is in Richard A. Harrison, ed., *The Princetonians, 1769–1775* (1980). Hunter Dickinson Farish, ed., *Journal & Letters of Philip Vickers Fithian, 1773–1774* (1943), records his experience in Virginia. Rhys Isaac, *The Transformation of Virginia, 1740–1790* (1982), discusses Fithian's value as a source on architectural history.

ROBERT M. CALHOON

FITLER, Edwin Henry (2 Dec. 1825–31 May 1896), cordage manufacturer, was born in Philadelphia, Pennsylvania, the son of William Fitler, a successful tanner and leather merchant, and Elizabeth Wonderly. His father provided very well for his family, including giving his son a fine academic education. Fitler planned to make law his profession and thus arranged to enter the office of Charles E. Lex. He studied with Lex four years but found he had no sustaining interest in the law; he was deeply interested in mechanics and engineering. However, he evidently learned enough about law that in his distinguished business career of more than forty-five years he was never involved in litigation. To pursue his true passion, in 1846, at age twenty-one, Fitler went to work for his brother-in-law,

George J. Weaver, who managed a well-established cordage firm (Weaver's father had founded the firm in 1816). The firm already had two factories, one for manila and tarred ropes, the other for fine yarns and jute, with a combined annual capacity of 4.5 million pounds. This offered Fitler ample opportunity to engage his interests.

Within two years Fitler supposedly knew every aspect of cordage manufacture as well as any workman. Probably in part because of that intense involvement, he was made a partner in 1848. With his position secure, he soon married Josephine R. Baker, with whom he had four children. Fitler proceeded to take responsibility for developing and introducing a range of important labor-saving machinery. As a result, Weaver, Fitler & Co. was the first firm in the United States to spin manila yarns and rope by machine. In 1859 Fitler bought out his partners and renamed the company Edwin H. Fitler & Company; except for a brief foray into politics in the late 1880s, it was the focus of his energies and talent for his whole life. Fitler apparently had excellent labor relations; no strike was ever reported at his works. He was also intensely patriotic, and during the Civil War he raised and personally equipped a regiment from among his own employees.

In 1880 Fitler made his most significant impact on American business and economic history. Manufacturers of grain harvesters were in a hot competitive battle to develop better binding technology. The industry leader, McCormick Harvesting Machine Company of Chicago, produced a reliable wire binder, but the use of wire had come under widespread criticism because occasional bits of wire damaged milling machinery or injured cattle. The Deering Company had developed what appeared to be an excellent binder that used twine but was constantly defeated by the twine. Traditional twines, unable to withstand the heavy tension exerted by the knotter, frequently broke. Made from soft fibers like jute, they quickly succumbed to heat caused by friction and burned or damaged the equipment. William Deering believed that manila could be used to make a successful binder twine but could find no manufacturer willing to try, until he came to Fitler. Fitler was initially reluctant to pursue the idea, because he recognized that to make the product Deering wanted would require a new line of machinery, a major investment for what was essentially a nonexistent market. But Deering promised to buy ten carloads if Fitler made a suitable product. Fitler modified a Todd & Rafferty jenny and then developed a twine made of a single ply of pure manila with a very hard twist—more turns per inch than anyone had ever before attempted with any fiber—and produced nearly 700 feet of twine from each pound of manila. Deering sent it for testing in the early wheat harvest in Texas; a telegram reported the results: "Manila splendid." Within four years the wire binder was dead, displaced by tens of thousands of twine binders, creating an unprecedented market for cordage. In 1892, with annual capacity of 10,000 tons, the Fitler

Company was one of the three major cordage producers in the country.

Fitler was active in creating and sustaining the American Cordage Manufacturers Association, for which he served many terms as president. But he was also fiercely independent and was the only significant cordage manufacturer to hold out against the predations of the National Cordage Trust when it sought to monopolize the industry between 1888 and 1893, the year it collapsed, dragging Wall Street and the nation into one of its severest recessions.

For most of his life, Fitler took little part in civic affairs. But he was active in organizing and promoting Philadelphia's great Centennial Exposition of 1876 and served on its board of finance. He also was a founder of the Philadelphia Art Club and supported the Union League of Philadelphia, for which he served several years as vice president and then from 1890 to 1893 as president. He also was elected in 1892 president of the board of trustees of Jefferson Medical College and sat on the boards of a local bank and a regional railroad. Fitler largely avoided politics, but after a change in the city charter created a mayoralty with sweeping managerial responsibility—possibly the widest powers of any city executive at the time—he agreed to run for mayor. In one of the most lopsided elections in Philadelphia history, he won by more than 30,000 votes in February 1887. He was by all accounts both very successful in handling the office with its new breadth of responsibility and hugely popular; at the Republican convention in Chicago in 1888, the Philadelphia delegation nominated him for president. Fitler retired from the mayoralty in 1891. He died at his country estate near Philadelphia.

• There are a few original documents touching on Fitler's life in the Deering papers incorporated in the McCormick collections housed at the State Historical Society of Wisconsin. Twenty-five Fitler letters from 1879 to 1881 are in folder 573 of the Edwin Forrest Collection at the University of Pennsylvania. See also Edwin T. Freedley, *Philadelphia and Its Manufactures: A Handbook* (1859); John J. MacFarlane, *Manufacturing in Philadelphia, 1683–1912* (1912); and John F. Steward, *The Reaper* (1931). Obituaries are in the *Philadelphia Press*, the *Philadelphia North American*, and the *Philadelphia Public Ledger*, all 1 June 1896.

FRED CARSTENSEN

FITTON, James (10 Apr. 1805–15 Sept. 1881), missionary, educator, and author, was born in Boston, Massachusetts, the son of Abraham Fitton, a wheelwright and immigrant from the traditionally Catholic outpost of Preston, Lancashire, England, and Sarah Williams, a native of Wales. Raised in Boston and Roxbury, he attended public schools and a small parochial school in Boston. Inspired by his parents, members of the first Catholic congregation in Boston, he attached himself at an early age to the church and served as an acolyte in Holy Cross Cathedral in Boston.

Bishop John de Cheverus subsequently encouraged him to seek the priesthood, and in 1822 sent him to Quebec to study Latin and Greek with a tutor. In

1824–1825 he attended a Catholic academy in Claremont, New Hampshire, and in December 1825 he and William Wiley became the first novitiates in the Diocese of Boston. Fitton received his theological training from Benedict Joseph Fenwick, second bishop of Boston, who ordained him on 23 December 1827.

In 1828, partly to stem missionary efforts of the Congregationalists, Fenwick dispatched Fitton to work as a resident priest and teacher among the Passamaquoddy in Eastport and Old Town, Maine. The privations of this experience inured him to the rigors of an itinerant missionary and left him with a lifelong affection for the Passamaquoddy, whom he described as "devoted Christians of the forest."

In 1830, following itinerant missionary work in Burlington, Vermont, Fitton moved to Hartford, Connecticut, where he founded Trinity Church (1831) and served as pastor. He was also a circuit rider, touring mill towns throughout Connecticut to say predawn masses for Irish immigrants in barns, cottages, and fields. During this era of anti-Catholic bigotry, he often encountered antagonists who believed priests to be—in his words—"unearthly [and] wholly different from any other mortal." In his *Sketches of the Establishment of the Church in New England* (1872), he also wrote about "urchins" who "hooted" and hurled stones during mass, and tavern keepers in Connecticut who refused him lodging.

In the early 1830s Fitton's itinerancy ranged beyond Connecticut to include central and western Massachusetts and portions of New Hampshire. He also participated in a vigorous campaign to refute an outpouring of anti-Catholic literature from nativist sources. He edited the Hartford newspaper *Catholic Press*, wrote pamphlets, lectured, and translated devotional books and tracts. He also advocated the protemperance position favored by Fenwick and his successor, John Bernard Fitzpatrick, and organized several Catholic temperance societies.

Beginning in 1836 Fitton concentrated much of his missionary work in and around Worcester, Massachusetts. He opened five mission stations to proselytize among Irish immigrants employed on the railroads and canals and in the orchards, tanneries, and textile mills of the Blackstone Valley. He also cultivated friendships with benevolent, liberal-minded Protestants, such as William Lincoln in Worcester, and artfully relied upon them to arrange the sale of land that otherwise would have been unavailable for a Catholic church or school. His most notable achievement during his years in Worcester was opening Mount St. James Academy, a school for boys similar to the short-lived academy he had attended in New Hampshire. In 1843, after Fitton transferred the school to Fenwick, it was reorganized as a Jesuit institution, the College of the Holy Cross.

Transferred in 1844 to Rhode Island, Fitton gradually relinquished his duties as a missionary. As a parish priest in Newport, he promoted the liturgical practices of the European-inspired Catholic Revival and the movement within the Church to impart Gothic Revival imagery to houses of worship. With support from parishioners and influential Catholic benefactors (including Catherine Carroll Harper), he successfully raised funds for construction of St. Mary's Church (1849), an ornate Gothic Revival church and one of the first major works of church architect Patrick Charles Keely.

In 1855 Fitton returned to his native city. Succeeding his colleague Wiley in the pastorate of East Boston, he supervised the ambitious project of constructing the Church of the Most Holy Redeemer Church (1857, P. C. Keely, architect). He also resumed a familiar role of ministering to impoverished Irish immigrants, who lived and worked along the waterfront.

In the 1850s Fitton participated in a major triumph over anti-Catholic discrimination in Boston, when he became one of the first Catholic curates permitted to counsel hospital patients and prisoners on Deer Island. With profound satisfaction, he also wrote during this era about the growth of the church in his lifetime. He noted, in particular, the "glorious sight" of religious processions in public streets and marveled how "every foot" of his parish was occupied on Sundays.

During his 26-year residence in East Boston, Fitton enjoyed a wide circle of friends, including the Unitarian clergyman Warren H. Cudworth. He founded three parishes, three literary societies, and three parochial schools, and he was a leading proponent of Catholic parochial education.

Described as "rugged" and "taciturn," Fitton was instrumental in carrying Catholicism to remote areas of New England at a time when the church had few resources to commit to the prodigious task of preserving the traditional faith of Irish-Catholic immigrants. When he died in Boston, he was remembered as "the great Missionary of New England," a heroic figure among Catholics in six states. His achievements among the pioneering Catholic missionaries in the nineteenth century parallel those of the two émigré priests, Pierre de Smet and Charles Nerinckx.

• Only a small collection of manuscripts relating to Fitton are in the archives of the College of Holy Cross and the Archdiocese of Boston. His *Sketches* has only traces of autobiographical material obscured in third-person references ("the Missionary"). The leading sources are a monograph by L. P. McCarthy, *Sketch of the Life and Missionary Labors of Rev. James Fitton* (1908), and Robert H. Lord, et al, *History of the Archdiocese of Boston* (3 vols., 1944). See also a brief but informative account by one of his benefactors, William Lincoln, *History of Worcester* (1862), and a scholarly assessment of his role in the rise of Catholicism in New England, Vincent A. Lapomarda, *The Jesuit Heritage in New England* (1977). A lengthy obituary is in the Boston diocesan newspaper, the *Pilot*, 24 Sept. 1881.

JEFFREY CRONIN

FITTS, Dudley (28 Apr. 1903–10 July 1968), translator and poet, was born in Haverhill, Massachusetts, the son of Dudley Thomas Fitts, a bookkeeper, and Edith Kimball Eaton. He attended Harvard University, where he edited the *Harvard Advocate*; he graduated in 1925. His first serious poems appeared in 1930 in *Poetry* and *transition*. He also published in the *Atlantic Monthly*, *Criterion*, and other magazines.

Beginning in 1927 Fitts taught English at the Choate School in Wallingford, Connecticut. In 1939 he married Cornelia Butler Hewitt, with whom he had two children. In 1941 he left Wallingford to teach at Phillips Academy in Andover, Massachusetts, where he lived with his family until his death.

Fitts's first book, *Two Poems*, appeared in 1932, followed by his only collection, *Poems (1929–1936)*, in 1937. Influenced by Ezra Pound and T. S. Eliot as well as by modern Spanish poetry, Fitts's poems often seem poised between disillusionment and jaded aestheticism, mixing, as his modernist masters did, classical allusion and jazz-age slang. It was a style that, for some readers in the more socially conscious 1930s, had played itself out in the previous decade. William Rose Benet, reviewing *Poems*, commented that Fitts was "highly intellectual, wayward, and quite difficult" but also gifted with "a subtle mind, sensitivity to beauty, [and] an esoteric sense of humor."

Although his own poetry attracted only brief attention and was rarely anthologized, Fitts's adaptations from the Latin and Greek were widely known and celebrated: the *Alcestis* of Euripedes, with Robert Fitzgerald (1936); *One Hundred Poems from the Palatine Anthology* (1938); *More Poems from the Palatine Anthology in English Paraphrase* (1941); Sophocles's *Oedipus Rex*, with Robert Fitzgerald (1949); Aristophanes's *Lysistrata* (1954) and *The Frogs* (1955); *Poems from the Greek Anthology in English Paraphrase* (1956); Aristophanes's *The Birds* (1957); *The Oedipus Cycle*, with Robert Fitzgerald (1958); a translation of Aristophanes's *Thesmophoriazusae* titled *Ladies' Day* (1959); *Four Comedies* (1962); and *Sixty Poems of Martial* (1967). Fitts also edited three collections of Greek plays in English and wrote forewords to other translations and collections.

Unlike many translators, Fitts took considerable liberties with the texts he translated, in an effort to replicate, in modern, colloquial English, the freshness as well as the semantic complexity of his originals. Thus, in *The Birds*, the battle of Orneai—a pun in the Greek—is translated "Gettysbird." Most critics agreed that Fitts's invention and the exuberant colloquial style were in keeping with the spirit of the original plays and poems. Thus Brooks Atkinson wrote of Fitt's translation of *Lysistrata* that "the modern theater-goer can only welcome the success with which Mr. Fitts has recreated the furious, scornful vitality of a satirical dramatist who had principles as well as skill" (*New York Times*, 11 July 1968). Some of his adaptations of ancient lyrics suggest the Poundian injunction to "make it new," at the same time capturing classical humor and economy. One example, from Lucilius (in *One Hundred Poems from the Palatine Anthology*), is retitled "A Valentine for a Lady":

Darling, at the Beautician's you buy
Your [a] hair
    [b] complexion
    [c] lips
    [d] dimples, &
    [e] teeth.
For a like amount you could just as well buy a face.

In addition to his classical adaptations, Fitts translated a number of poems from the Spanish and Portuguese and edited the *Anthology of Contemporary Latin-American Poetry*. He was also recognized as a literary critic and contributed numerous articles and reviews to the *Saturday Review of Literature* and the *New York Times Book Review*.

Active in the world of poetry, Fitts received numerous honors and distinctions. He served on the poetry jury for the National Book Awards in 1954 and 1960; was named Phi Beta Kappa Poet at Harvard University in 1961; served as editor of the Yale Series of Younger Poets from 1960 until his death; was made a member of the National Institute of Arts and Letters in 1963; was a Jonathan Edwards College Fellow at Yale University from 1964 to 1968; was appointed chancellor of the Academy of American Poets in 1967; and was awarded a doctorate of letters from Columbia University in 1968, one month before his death in a hospital in Lawrence, Massachusetts.

• Fitts's personal papers are housed at the Phillips Academy, Andover, Mass. For a general discussion of his work, see "The 1920's," in *A History of American Poetry 1900–1940*, ed. Horace Gregory and Marya Zaturenska (1946). For reviews of Fitts's *Poems 1929–1936*, see William Rose Benet's column "The Phoenix Nest: Contemporary Poetry," *Saturday Review*, 3 July 1937, p. 18, as well as T. C. Wilson, "Sentiment and Form," *Poetry* 51 (1937): 107. Other reviews of that volume appeared in *Books*, 25 July 1937, p. 16, and the *Boston Transcript*, 28 Aug. 1937, p. 3. For a review of the translation of *Lysistrata*, see John Ciardi, "Strictness and Faithfulness," *Nation*, 19 June 1954, p. 525. Obituaries are in the *New York Times*, 11 July 1968; the *Washington Post*, 12 July 1968; and *Publishers Weekly*, 5 Aug. 1968.

MELISSA FABROS

FITZ, Reginald Heber (5 May 1843–30 Sept. 1913), physician, was born in Chelsea, Massachusetts, the son of Albert Fitz, a diplomat, and Eliza Roberts Nye. Fitz attended Chauncy Hall preparatory school in Boston and enrolled at Harvard College in 1858. An undistinguished and unenthusiastic student, he left Harvard in the middle of his junior year to seek his fortune in the booming copper fields of Michigan's Upper Peninsula. After a little more than a year of this adventure, he decided that his initial career path was not so bad after all. "I find that it will be much pleasanter to become a professional man," Fitz wrote to his family, "and live moderately and free from care than to become rich and have my mind continually harassed with care and anxiety" (quoted in Leach, p. 109). He returned to Harvard in the fall of 1862 and graduated with an A.B. in the spring of 1864.

After graduating Fitz began the study of medicine as an apprentice under a prominent Cambridge physician and Harvard medical professor, Jeffries Wyman. In the fall of 1865 he enrolled at Harvard Medical School. Before finishing his studies there, he won an appointment in April 1867 as house physician at the Boston City Hospital. Fitz maintained his hospital responsibilities during his final year of medical school and graduated with an M.D. in June 1868. He then traveled to Europe for two years of advanced study. He first went to Vienna, where he worked for almost a year under the renowned pathologists Karl Freiherr von Rokitansky and Joseph Skoda, who instilled in him a strong belief in the constant need to test and improve medical understanding through rigorous comparison of clinical diagnoses with autopsy findings. Fitz spent the second half of his European tour in the Berlin laboratory of another famous pathologist, Rudolf Virchow, who advocated that all disease occurred at a cellular level. In Virchow's laboratory Fitz achieved great facility in the microscopic examination of diseased tissue; the results of his research on histological aberrations found in bronchiectasis were published in Virchow's prestigious journal, *Archiv für pathologische Anatomie und Physiologie* (51 [1870]: 123–26).

Fitz returned to Boston in 1870 invigorated by his experiences in Europe and with his professional credentials considerably enhanced. He set up a private medical practice and quickly secured teaching and hospital positions: in 1871 he was named an instructor in pathological anatomy at Harvard Medical School and was appointed as a pathologist at Massachusetts General Hospital. He rose rapidly to positions of influence at these two institutions, with which he would remain associated until his retirement almost four decades later. He married Elizabeth Loring in 1879; they had four children.

At Harvard Medical School, Fitz was an early and influential proponent of Virchow's cellular pathology. Eager medical students packed into halls to hear him deliver lectures in a style vividly recalled by a former student: "He had a habit of tilting his head backward, closing his eyes, talking with extreme rapidity and fluency, never missing a word, for 61 minutes in the hour. . . . It was as if he read a carefully prepared lecture from the inside of his eyeballs" (quoted in Leach, p. 110). As a member and long-time chair of a Harvard curriculum committee, Fitz also played a significant role in bringing more rigor and in particular more emphasis on laboratory and clinical instruction to medical education at Harvard. These reforms resonated well beyond Harvard, becoming a model for widespread reforms in American medical education during the late nineteenth and early twentieth centuries.

Fitz is best remembered, however, for his identification of acute appendicitis as a frequent cause of death from peritonitis. In a paper delivered on 17 June 1886 at a meeting of the Association of American Physicians in Washington, D.C. (published later that year in the *Transactions of the Association of American Physicians* 1: 107–35), Fitz coined the term "appendicitis," offered techniques for clear diagnosis of the disorder, and advocated prompt surgical removal of the vermiform appendix if symptoms persisted. He had drawn his conclusions from many autopsies he had performed at Massachusetts General Hospital and from a wide, systematic review of medical literature. In making sense of the abundant data he had gathered on frequently fatal peritonitis, usually associated with the ileum, he had employed great powers of synthesis. As one of his contemporaries put it, Fitz was "not an investigator in the sense that he carried out or led original, experimental research," instead Fitz possessed "penetrating clearness of vision [that] enabled him to extract, as could no one else, from a mass of apparently unrelated observations, the concise, clear clinical picture" (quoted in Brooks and Brooks, p. 36). Fitz's call for aggressive surgery in cases of appendicitis found prompt reception in most of the medical community, at least partially because he was *not* himself a surgeon. Surgeons were often perceived by more medically oriented colleagues as aggressive and simplistic in their desire to slice out troublesome organs; Fitz, the pathologist, could not be dismissed as an over-eager surgeon with a sharp scalpel.

Three years after his paper on appendicitis, Fitz offered a major synthetic analysis of another, though less common, abdominal affliction, acute pancreatitis. In a lecture delivered before the New York Pathological Society on 16 February 1889 (published a few days later in the *Boston Medical and Surgical Journal* 120: 181–87, 205–7, 229–35), Fitz adroitly distinguished between pancreatitis and other forms of abdominal distress, and he drew neat distinctions among the hemorrhagic, suppurative, and gangrenous forms of pancreatitis.

Fitz died in Brookline, Massachusetts, five years after his retirement at the mandatory age of sixty-five from Harvard and Massachusetts General Hospital. Several weeks after his death, colleagues gathered for a memorial meeting at Harvard Medical School. The dean of the school offered a fitting summation of Fitz's legacy: "Many have sought truth, but it is rare to have found and taught it so clearly that the lives of thousands and thousands were saved thereby" (quoted in Morrison [1946], p. 269).

• Fitz's papers are in the Harvard Medical School Archives, Francis A. Countway Library of Medicine, Harvard University. The author of many articles, Fitz cowrote, with Horatio C. Wood, *The Practice of Medicine* (1897). Hyman Morrison contributed three useful articles on Fitz to the *Bulletin of the History of Medicine*: "The Chapter on Appendicitis in a Biography of Reginald Heber Fitz," vol. 20 (1946): 259–69; "Reginald Heber Fitz's Contribution to the Understanding of Acute Pancreatitis," vol. 22 (1948): 263–72; and "The Borderland of Medicine and Surgery as Conceived by Reginald Heber Fitz," vol. 22 (1948): 680–84. Pieces containing biographical information on Fitz appeared to mark the centenaries of his two most famous medical contributions: Stewart

M. Brooks and Natalie A. Brooks, "Appendicitis at 100," *American Heritage* 37 (Apr.–May 1986): 34–37; and Steven D. Leach et al., "Acute Pancreatitis at Its Centenary: The Contribution of Reginald Fitz," *Annals of Surgery* 212 (1990): 109–13.

JON M. HARKNESS

FITZGERALD, Alice (13 Mar. 1875–10 Nov. 1962), nurse and public-health administrator, was born Alice Louise Florence Fitzgerald in Florence, Italy, the daughter of Charles H. Fitzgerald and Alice Riggs Lawrdson. Her parents, both from Baltimore, Maryland, were independently wealthy and chose to live in Florence. Alice was taught by governesses, became proficient in English, French, German, and Italian, attended the Convent of the Sacred Heart in Florence, and then went to a finishing school in Switzerland.

Fond childhood memories of a nurse who had cared for Fitzgerald were reinforced in 1892 by a visit to Kaiserwerth, a well-run Protestant hospital near Stuttgart, Germany. Two years later, while visiting an aunt in Baltimore, she learned that Johns Hopkins University had a training school for nurses, and she determined to attend it. When she reached the school's minimum required age of twenty-five, she was delayed by family commitments until 1902, when, despite her parents' strong opinions that nursing was not a suitable pursuit, she entered the Nurses Training School of Johns Hopkins. She was included in the graduating class of 1906 although, because of absence to tend her mother in an illness, she did not complete the course until 1907.

Fitzgerald became a head nurse at Johns Hopkins Hospital in 1906. On vacation in Italy in December 1908 she volunteered to help the Italian Red Cross after an earthquake devastated Messina, and she was assigned to a hospital in Naples to which the injured were transported. Her receipt of the Italian Red Cross Disaster Relief Medal in 1909 changed her parents' views against nursing.

Fitzgerald returned to Johns Hopkins, but in 1911 she went to Bellevue Hospital in New York City to reorganize the nursing facilities in the operating rooms that were used by surgeons from four local medical schools. In 1912 she became superintendent of nurses at General Hospital in Wilkes-Barre, Pennsylvania. There some patients were victims of mine explosions, and many patients were Polish, so she learned that language to interpret for them. In 1914 she became superintendent of nurses at the Robert W. Long Hospital in Indianapolis, Indiana, and began a program to train public-health nurses in that state. The next year she became head nurse at Dana Hall, a girls' school in Wellesley, Massachusetts.

Before the United States entered World War I English nurse Edith Cavell was shot in Belgium by Germans for helping British soldiers escape, and a group in Boston decided to pay the costs of an American nurse to serve with the British army. Fitzgerald accepted the position of Edith Cavell Memorial Nurse early in 1916, reported to the British War Office in London, and was sent to Boulogne, France. While working in a hospital that treated wounded soldiers, she continually asked to be sent closer to the war front, a request that was granted late in 1916 when she was sent to a muddy frontline field hospital jammed with wounded and shell-shocked patients. Her previous experience with injured patients helped her handle nursing duties heroically. After leave in England, she returned to Boulogne from January to December 1917, when she was released to join the American Red Cross in France because the United States had entered the war. She was assigned to Rimini, Italy, to help with refugees fleeing from the German military advance. In early 1918, with headquarters in Paris, she became the liaison among the American Red Cross, the American Army Medical Service, and the French military medical service to provide bilingual nurses in French hospitals for wounded American service personnel. This successful program entailed a great deal of traveling in war torn areas. When the war ended in 1918, Fitzgerald spent some time in Germany arranging for the nursing of sick American prisoners. Through the years her ability in languages was invaluable.

In 1919, under the Commission of the American Red Cross to Europe, Fitzgerald became chief nurse for the war-devastated countries of Europe and the Middle East. Her goal was to establish training programs for nurses to help in rural areas. She began in Belgium, which soon set up nursing schools and adopted without change her wording in recommending public-health measures and for providing nurses in rural districts. Within a year, under her jurisdiction, successful nursing training programs were also set up in the Netherlands, Czechoslovakia, and Germany. When an international program was established in late 1919 as the League of Red Cross Societies, Fitzgerald was elected its first director of nursing. She established an international training school for nurses in London at the King's College for Women, a medical school. It opened in 1920 with women students from seven nations, and enrollment increased for some years.

In 1922 Fitzgerald considered her international work well established, so she resigned and returned to the United States. For two months she was on a speaking tour for the American Red Cross. Later that year she went to the Philippines to advise on public-health nursing for the Rockefeller Foundation and in cooperation with Governor-General Leonard Wood. After considerable traveling in rural areas, she established a nursing school at Baguio, which was an immediate success, and she arranged for other training programs in outlying areas until 1923. From 1925 to 1928 she was in Siam (Thailand) to improve nursing programs at the request of the Rockefeller Foundation and the Siamese royal family.

Fitzgerald never married. She returned to the United States in 1929, advised the state of Maryland on nursing and public-health programs, became director of nurses at the Polyclinic Hospital in New York City from 1931 to 1937, then ran a residence hall for nurses at Sheppard-Pratt Hospital in New York City until 1948. She moved into a retirement home in New York City, where she died. Fitzgerald's accomplishments in nursing and training programs advanced the profession considerably and were highly regarded in many countries. She respected differences in cultures and thus was able to persuade government officials, royalty, and local people of the importance of nursing and public-health programs.

• Some personal letters and other Fitzgerald records are in the archives of the School of Nursing and Nursing Service at Johns Hopkins Hospital. A biography for juveniles is Iris Noble, *Nurse around the World: Alice Fitzgerald* (1964).

ELIZABETH NOBLE SHOR

FITZGERALD, Edward (16 Oct. 1833?–21 Feb. 1907), Roman Catholic bishop, was born in Limerick, Ireland, the son of James Fitzgerald and Joanna Pratt. He immigrated with his family to Cincinnati, Ohio, in 1849 and entered the Lazarist Seminary in Barrens, Missouri, the following year. In 1852 he transferred to Mount St. Mary of the West in Cincinnati and then, in 1855, to Mount St. Mary's Seminary in Emmitsburg, Maryland, from which he graduated in June 1857.

Fitzgerald was ordained by Archbishop John Purcell in August 1857 and was sent to St. Patrick's Church in Columbus, Ohio, to begin his first pastorship. There he replaced James Meagher, whose recent transfer by Purcell had created a revolt among members of the parish's lay trustees—a board of individuals who helped the pastor run the parish, particularly in regard to fiscal matters. The trustee system, which was modeled after Protestant congregations and was necessary under contemporary U.S. laws pertaining to the incorporation and legal protection of churches, was often troublesome within Catholic ecclesiology. Some trustees came to believe that they and not the bishop had the right to control the administration of the parish, including the hiring and ousting of pastors.

The trustees of St. Patrick's, led by the church organist William Kehoe, had taken control of the church building and barred entrance to both priests and laymen. Purcell responded by excommunicating the trustees and placing under interdict all parishioners who would not sign a statement condemning their actions. Fitzgerald stayed at a nearby parish after his arrival; within two months he had unified St. Patrick's and inspired forgiveness and contrition among its parishioners. His nine-year tenure at the parish saw its growth in every phase, including St. Patrick's School, the administration of which Fitzgerald turned over to the Brothers of the Holy Cross from Notre Dame, Indiana.

In February 1867 Fitzgerald was consecrated by Purcell as the bishop of Little Rock, Arkansas. The impoverished diocese, which covered all of Arkansas and parts of Indian Territory, had been without a bishop since 1862 and was badly fragmented by the Civil War. Only five priests ministered to the diocese's 1,600 communicants, who were scattered throughout the region and often lacked the disciplines of the faith.

The struggle of his people to survive as practicing Catholics in this harsh and markedly Protestant frontier became Fitzgerald's lifelong concern. After arriving in March, he immediately began visiting his congregations, often traveling on horseback or by stagecoach. Under his pastoral care, the diocese began to spring to life. During his years as bishop, twenty-nine schools and eight academies were established. St. Andrew's Cathedral in Little Rock, dedicated in November 1881, was both conceived and implemented by him. In response to the dearth of secular priests in the diocese, Fitzgerald invited several religious groups to Arkansas to administer to schools and charitable institutions. Among these were Subiaco College (1887), founded by Benedictines from St. Meinrad, Indiana; a hospital in Eureka Springs, founded by Sisters of Mercy from St. Louis (1901); and an abbey near Morrilton, founded by the Fathers of the Holy Ghost (1879).

In 1870 Fitzgerald left the obscurity of Little Rock to attend the Vatican Council in Rome. Among the many doctrinal issues set for clarification at the council was the doctrine of papal infallibility, which maintains that the papacy is immune from error when officially defining matters of faith and morals for Roman Catholics. Although well accepted by the Catholic world in 1870, the doctrine had never been defined as dogma. A minority of bishops, including Fitzgerald and his mentor Purcell, were skeptical of the need to define the doctrine and voiced their dissent in Rome. Fitzgerald, knowing that his opinion was not gaining him friends at the Vatican, wrote to the mother superior of a convent in Arkansas on 25 April 1870: "There is no chance the Holy Father will take me from Arkansas, except to put me in the prisons of the Inquisition, perhaps. I have not been in his good book since coming to Rome."

The trial ballot on infallibility took place on 13 July 1870, with Fitzgerald and 87 other bishops voting against (*non placet*) out of 601. Although many of those who questioned the doctrine left Rome to avoid having to officially cast negative votes, Fitzgerald remained. The final vote was taken on 18 July: out of 535 voting bishops, 533 voted for the acceptance of the doctrine, including 24 Americans, and 2 voted *non placet*. The two were Luigi Riccio, the bishop of Cajazzo, Italy, and Fitzgerald. Immediately after the vote, however, Fitzgerald made clear his devotion to the pope and his acceptance of the doctrine.

While it is remarkable that Fitzgerald stayed to vote against what he knew was a doctrinal cornerstone of the church to which he had devoted his life, it is unlikely that he did so for theological reasons. A decade later, in an address titled "After Ten Years, the Vatican Council," Fitzgerald stated that he had "held and taught before going to Rome" the validity of papal infallibility. Nevertheless, he had felt compelled to vote against its adoption as dogma because "it is one thing to hold a given doctrine as the most probable, or even as certain in the face of other conflicting views; quite a different thing to aid by my vote to impose a new obligation on Catholics, and, as it appeared to me then, to place a new obstacle in the path of others seeking a union with the Catholic Church."

This practical ecumenism became the source of further dissent by Fitzgerald at the Third Plenary Council of Baltimore in 1884, at which the American bishops studied the role of Catholic schools in American Catholic life. American public schools were seen by the bishops as essentially indifferent to religious and moral matters and thus unacceptable for Catholic children. A decree was entertained that would require Catholic parents to send their children to parochial schools. Fitzgerald argued that, while Catholics had a dire obligation to instruct children in religion (particularly the catechism), the teaching of secular subjects was not the responsibility of the church.

Fitzgerald's career as an American Catholic bishop clearly reflected his role as the leader of a minority religious body in a rugged, often hostile theological landscape. He believed that theology, though vital, must sometimes be set aside for reasons of economic and cultural survival. He desired the well-being of all those under his spiritual care, and his devotion to the people of Arkansas made him a beloved figure among the state's Catholics and non-Catholics alike. He retired in 1906 to St. Joseph's Infirmary in Hot Springs, Arkansas, where he died.

• Fitzgerald's papers, including sermons, manuscripts, and correspondence, are at the Archives of the Diocese of Little Rock and the Archives of the Archdiocese of Cincinnati. An extensive account of Fitzgerald's career is in Clay M. O'Dell, "An American Catholic: Edward Fitzgerald, Second Bishop of Little Rock" (master's thesis, Graduate Theological Union, Berkeley, Calif., 1994). His involvement with the trustee controversy at St. Patrick's is discussed in Donald M. Schlegal, "The Rocks on Which We Split," *Bulletin of the Catholic Record Society of the Diocese of Columbus* 8, no. 3 (Mar. 1988): 17–26. Information concerning his role at the Vatican Council is in John Tracy Ellis, ed., *Documents of American Catholic History* (1967) and *Perspectives in American Catholicism* (1963). Francis P. Cassidy, "Catholic Education in the Third Plenary Council of Baltimore," *Catholic Historical Review* 34, no. 3 (Oct. 1948): 257–305, discusses his views on Catholic schools. An obituary is in the *Arkansas Gazette*, 22 Feb. 1907.

JAY MAZZOCCHI

FITZGERALD, F. Scott (24 Sept. 1896–21 Dec. 1940), writer, was born Francis Scott Key Fitzgerald in St. Paul, Minnesota, the son of Edward Fitzgerald, a businessman, and Mary "Mollie" McQuilan. Fitzgerald was always haunted by his father's taking a job as a salesman for Procter & Gamble in 1898 following the business collapse of his St. Paul furniture factory, the American Rattan and Willow Works. Between 1898 and 1908, the years of his father's employment by Procter & Gamble, the family lived in Buffalo and Syracuse, New York. By the time they moved back to St. Paul in July 1908, Fitzgerald knew that his mother was the financial support of the family and that his father's confidence had ebbed. His father was fifty-five when he lost his job as a salesman. Fitzgerald said twenty-eight years later, "That morning he had gone out a comparatively young man, a man full of strength, full of confidence. He came home that evening, an old man, a completely broken man. He had lost his essential drive. . . . He was a failure the rest of his days" (Bruccoli, *Grandeur*, p. 22). Fitzgerald got his name from his father's forebears, the Scotts and the Keys of Maryland, and his lineage did in fact link him to Francis Scott Key, author of the words to "The Star-Spangled Banner." Fitzgerald's mother inherited a portion of her father's wealth, $266,289, which in 1890 was a substantial sum. Thus when her husband proved unsuccessful in business, her money sustained the family. By the time Fitzgerald's parents had married in 1890, Mollie was independently wealthy—or was about to be after her mother's death. Fitzgerald was spoiled by his mother, whom he later described as "half insane with pathological nervous worry" (Bruccoli, *Grandeur*, p. 15). After his marriage to Zelda Sayre in 1920, Fitzgerald rarely saw his mother.

In September 1913 Fitzgerald entered Princeton University as a member of the class of 1917 and met John Peale Bishop and Edmund Wilson, who became lifelong friends. Fitzgerald was active in the Triangle Club, which produced musicals, and in writing for college publications, such as the *Nassau Literary Magazine*. In early January 1915, during his Christmas vacation, Fitzgerald met Ginevra King in St. Paul. She was his first serious romance, which ended suddenly when he overheard her father supposedly say, "Poor boys shouldn't think of marrying rich girls." Never a keen student, Fitzgerald spent too much of his time writing and acting in Triangle shows, working on the *Princeton Tiger*, and participating in other extracurricular activities. In December 1915 Fitzgerald dropped out of Princeton because of poor grades and for health reasons; when he returned he became a member of the class of 1918.

As American involvement in World War I deepened, Fitzgerald (on the verge of flunking out once again) received a commission as a second lieutenant in the infantry in October 1917. In November 1917 he reported to a unit under the command of Captain Dwight D. Eisenhower at Fort Leavenworth, Kansas. There, on weekends at the Officers' Club, Fitzgerald began writing the first draft of a novel, "The Romantic Egotist." In February 1918 he was assigned to Camp Taylor in Louisville, Kentucky. By then he had finished the first draft of "The Romantic Egotist" and while on leave at Princeton sent the novel to Scribners. Fitzgerald, who was no better as an officer than he had been as a student, was transferred to Camp Sheridan near Montgomery, Alabama, in June 1918. At a weekend dance at the Montgomery Country Club that July, he met the woman who would change his life, Zelda Sayre.

In August Scribners declined his novel and in October rejected a revision. Maxwell Perkins, an editor at Scribners, nevertheless held out future hope for the novel's publication, given another revision. In November Fitzgerald, along with his unit, was sent to Camp Mills, Long Island, preparatory to embarkation, but the war ended before he could be sent overseas. In February 1919 Fitzgerald was discharged from the army. He went to New York City to work at the Barron Collier advertising agency while revising his novel and trying to publish short stories. Deeply in love with Zelda, he returned to Montgomery in April, May, and June to try to convince her to marry him. But in June, still reluctant, she broke their engagement. During that spring Fitzgerald succeeded, however, in making his first sale to a commercial magazine, the *Smart Set*, which accepted his story "Babes in the Woods." In July Fitzgerald quit his advertising job and went home to St. Paul to rewrite his novel in his parents' attic. Meanwhile, Zelda insisted that she could not marry him until he had some financial security. To Fitzgerald, this meant he had to become established as an author.

In September 1919 Perkins notified Fitzgerald that his revised manuscript—now called "This Side of Paradise"—had been accepted for publication. Ecstatic, Fitzgerald wrote back, "Of course I was delighted to get your letter and I've been in a sort of trance all day." He asked whether an earlier publication date was possible because "I have so many things dependent on its success—including of course a girl—not that I expect it to make me a fortune but it will have a psychological effect on me and all my surroundings and besides open up new fields" (Turnbull, *Letters*, p. 139). In 1936, recalling his anguish over Zelda's hesitation to marry, Fitzgerald said that "during a long summer of despair I wrote a novel instead of letters, so it came out all right, but it came out all right for a different person. The man with the jingle of money in his pocket who married the girl a year later would always cherish an abiding distrust, an animosity, toward the leisure class—not the conviction of a revolutionist but the smouldering hatred of a peasant" ("Pasting It Together," repr. in *The Crack-Up*). The publication of *This Side of Paradise* on 26 March 1920 brought Fitzgerald money, success, and Zelda. They were married on 3 April 1920 in New York at St. Patrick's rectory, and they honeymooned in the city at the Biltmore Hotel. Seventeen years later Fitzgerald wrote in "Early Success," a rueful reminiscence, "Counting the bag, I found that in 1919 I had made $800 by writing, that in 1920 I had made $18,000, stories, picture rights and book."

Although *This Side of Paradise* seems dated today, at the time it was a daring, revealing book about the generational gap in manners and morals. Few Victorian parents knew what their sons and daughters were doing in private, in cars and at dances. In its portrayal of cultural changes that resulted from World War I, the novel shocked those whose standards of conduct had been formed earlier. Nevertheless, Fitzgerald was now seen as the chronicler of the Jazz Age, of flaming youth, of the flapper—a reputation that would constantly plague him even in his obituaries. From then on the Fitzgeralds traveled between the United States and Europe, indulging themselves in parties and liquor. While his income during the 1920s rose steadily, Fitzgerald and his wife always spent more than he earned.

When Edmund Wilson reviewed *This Side of Paradise*, he observed that the book's "chief weakness is that it is really not *about* anything: its intellectual and moral content amounts to little more than a gesture—a gesture of indefinite revolt" (Wilson, p. 28). But an attitude of revolt among the young was in the air at the time, and Fitzgerald's rendering of it was so potent that much of his subsequent work was shadowed by his first novel. When Fitzgerald published *The Beautiful and Damned* in March 1922, reviewers were disappointed that it did not strike the sort of spark found in *This Side of Paradise*. The novel concerns the disintegration of Anthony and Gloria Patch while they await an inheritance. Unwilling or unable to moderate their careless spending and weakness for drink, they are in the end too worn out to participate in life. Many critics think of the novel as a portrait of the Fitzgeralds' marriage, uncannily accurate in its portent. Owing to Scott Fitzgerald's high income from the publication of short stories in popular magazines, and subsequently in collections such as *Flappers and Philosophers* (1920) and *Tales of the Jazz Age* (1922), the couple could for a while continue their extravagant style of living in Europe. But they returned to St. Paul in August 1921 because of the impending birth of their daughter, Scottie (Frances Scott Fitzgerald), their only child.

In May 1924 the Fitzgeralds were again in Europe, this time in Paris and on the Riviera; a year later, Scribners published *The Great Gatsby*, the novel that secured Fitzgerald's enduring fame. He had reached his full maturity as a writer. The work is often described in terms of a meditation or vision of America because of its judicious use of myth, metaphor, and history. When Fitzgerald was first thinking about his third novel in July 1922, he wrote Perkins that he wanted "to write something *new*—something extraordinary and beautiful and simple [and] intricately patterned" (qtd. in Bruccoli, *Grandeur*, p. 170). He knew that he was working near his peak—his artistic conscience was pure during the ten months of writing *Gatsby*. In April 1924 he wrote to Perkins from Great Neck, Long Island, "I feel I have an enormous power in me now, more than I've ever had in a way. . . . This book will be a consciously artistic achievement and must depend on that as the first books did not" (Turnbull, *Letters*, p. 163).

If *The Great Gatsby* has any claim to being the great American novel, it is because of what it stands for, not for the specifics of the story. The somewhat nebulous Jay Gatsby represents the quest inherent in the American dream; Daisy Buchanan, its fulfilment. At a more basic level, the novel poignantly portrays the age-old theme of poor boy meets rich girl, with the poor boy ending up a sacrificial lamb. To a considerable extent the story turns on differences in social class: the presumptuousness of the very rich (Tom and Daisy Buchanan) versus new money (Gatsby) that strives for position and command of society. In moving his story from the American West to the East, Fitzgerald set up a metaphorical equivalent for America itself. Nick Carraway, the observer-narrator, summarizes the Buchanans' life at the end of the novel succinctly: "They were careless people, Tom and Daisy—they smashed up things and creatures and then retreated back into their money or their vast carelessness, or whatever it was that kept them together, and let other people clean up the mess they had made."

When T. S. Eliot read the novel, he wrote Fitzgerald that it was a "remarkable book" and that "it seems to me to be the first step that American fiction has taken since Henry James" (letter of 31 Dec. 1925, repr. in *The Crack-Up*). Following the reappraisal of Fitzgerald that occurred when Arthur Mizener wrote *The Far Side of Paradise* (1951), *The Great Gatsby* and its author have steadily held the interest of scholars. Even if one reads the novel only for the quality of its prose, the rewards are high. Some lines near the end say more about the American dream than many entire books:

I became aware of the old island here that flowered once for Dutch sailors' eyes—a fresh green breast of the new world. Its vanished trees, the trees that had made way for Gatsby's house, had once pandered in whispers to the last and greatest of all human dreams; for a transitory enchanted moment man must have held his breath in the presence of this continent, compelled into an aesthetic contemplation he neither understood nor desired, face to face for the last time in history with something commensurate to his capacity for wonder.

There is great significance in the emphasis on "last time," for if it was the last time, then part of Gatsby's tragedy is that he brings an enormous capacity for wonder to a woman and to an entire way of life that fail to measure up to his longings. There is no way, in other words, that Gatsby could have found the means for the fulfillment of his dream. Fitzgerald's indictment is not merely of the "careless" Buchanans but of the cynicism and corruption that have killed the American dream.

Fitzgerald's contemplation of America and its society was marred somewhat while he was working on *Gatsby* because Zelda began an affair with French aviator Edouard Jozan in June 1924. Scott locked Zelda in her room, and the French military transferred Jozan to another post. Whether the affair amounted to only a flirtation or—much more likely—something more intimate, it deeply upset Scott. After all, Zelda had been his "golden girl," his princess in an ivory tower, and he was trying to finish the book he knew represented his best work.

In late April 1925, following the publication of *The Great Gatsby*, Fitzgerald met Ernest Hemingway at the Dingo Bar in Paris near Montparnasse and the boulevard Raspail. Hemingway's condescending account of their first meeting, in *A Moveable Feast* (1964), should not be taken too literally; it was written nearly forty years later, and Hemingway made himself out to be a wiser, more knowing person than is plausible. There is more than a grain of truth, however, in Hemingway's account of Fitzgerald's inability to hold his liquor and tendency to become impossibly tedious when drunk. Also grounded in fact were Hemingway's snide remarks on Fitzgerald's sexual worries.

For nearly a decade thereafter, while calamity surrounded him, Fitzgerald worked on the manuscript that became *Tender Is the Night* (1934). In April 1930 Zelda suffered her first nervous breakdown, and most of the rest of her life she was under institutional care. Faced with the costs of Zelda's hospitalization and of their daughter's schooling, along with the deepening economic depression in the United States and Europe, Scott soon realized that his finances were in a perilous condition. *Tender Is the Night* did not sell well, a disappointment for which a variety of reasons have been advanced. Living in Baltimore, Fitzgerald became depressed and morose. His income had dropped from an all-time high in 1931 of $37,599 to an alarming $10,180.97 in 1936.

Tender Is the Night is the story of a talented young psychiatrist, Dick Diver, who marries one of his wealthy patients, Nicole Warren. The story incorporates some of Zelda's mental troubles and their more technical aspects based on medical reports that Scott had received. It also deals in part with the life of Gerald and Sara Murphy, wealthy American expatriates whose house at Cap d'Antibes was similar to the Divers'. By fusing several people and several stories into a composite, Fitzgerald may have lost the central thread of the story; only decades later was the novel regarded more highly than it was at the time of its publication. At the end Dick Diver is exhausted by the need to care for Nicole and by other responsibilities; when she is cured, he is dismissed. As Nicole's sister, Baby Warren, says, "That's what he was educated for." It is again the classic Fitzgerald formula of poor boy meets rich girl and is destroyed by her. In his short story "The Rich Boy," published in 1926, Fitzgerald announced his predominant theme for the years to come:

Let me tell you about the very rich. They are different from you and me. They possess and enjoy early, and it does something to them, makes them soft where we are hard, and cynical where we are trustful, in a way that, unless you were born rich, it is very difficult to understand. They think, deep in their hearts, that they are better than we are because we had to discover the compensations and refuges of life for ourselves. Even when they enter deep into our world or sink below us, they still think that they are better than we are. They are different.

Tender Is the Night reflects Fitzgerald's own ambivalence about the very rich, his marriage, and his future. Once Dick Diver is back in America, he just fades away in the Finger Lakes region of New York State. Nicole has a new admirer, Tommy Barban, a soldier of fortune and a mercenary, and Baby, single and alone, has her money and social standing. Dick Diver, though, is left with nothing other than the practice of medicine.

In July 1937 Fitzgerald, deeply in debt, accepted an offer to work on scripts in Hollywood for $1,000 per week; two previous stints there, in 1927 and 1931, had not had happy results. This time, soon after his arrival, he met Sheilah Graham, a gossip columnist, who became his companion and remained with him until his death. Fitzgerald received only one screen credit—for the script of *Three Comrades* (1938)—as a result of his efforts that summer and fall, but in December his contract with Metro-Goldwyn-Mayer was renewed for $1,250 per week. Between bouts of recurrent tuberculosis, Fitzgerald worked at home on scripts, and he was beginning to pay off his debts to Scribners, to his agent, Harold Ober, and to the hospital back east where his wife was staying.

Zelda had entered Highland Hospital in Asheville, North Carolina, in 1936. Not long before Scottie entered Vassar College, in July 1938, Scott wrote to his daughter about his relationship with her mother:

When I was your age I lived with a great dream. The dream grew and I learned how to speak of it and make people listen. Then the dream divided one day when I decided to marry your mother after all, even though I knew she was spoiled and meant no good to me. I was sorry immediately I had married her but, being patient in those days, made the best of it and got to love her in another way. . . . She realized too late that work was dignity . . . but it was too late and she broke and is broken forever. (Turnbull, *Letters*, p. 32)

Although Fitzgerald saw Scottie only infrequently during his years in Hollywood, he continued to write to her often and in detail, and the letters, edited by Andrew Turnbull and published in 1965, constitute a remarkable personal and literary legacy. Scott also visited Zelda on occasion, having maintained a residence in Asheville, and even went with her on trips to South Carolina (Sept. 1937), Virginia (Mar. 1938), and Florida (Feb. 1939). After he died, however, she lived most of the time at Highland Hospital until her death, in a fire, in 1948.

In October 1939 Fitzgerald began working on *The Last Tycoon*, based on his observations and understanding of the inside of the studios and the external political atmosphere. He finished nearly one-half of it and outlined chapters for the rest in detail. He was only forty-four when he succumbed to a heart attack at Sheilah Graham's apartment at 1443 North Hayworth Avenue, Hollywood.

The Last Tycoon gives every evidence that Fitzgerald had returned to the sharpness and vision of *The Great Gatsby*; with only an incomplete text to go by, one can only speculate what he might have done with the novel. Edmund Wilson shaped an edition of the unfinished book for Scribners, which published it in 1941. More than half a century later, however, scholar Matthew J. Bruccoli reedited the novel, incorporating much that Wilson had left out or could only guess at; the enlarged version appeared in 1993.

Fitzgerald had an acute sense of history, a natural talent for writing, and a large view of America and Americans. Stephen Vincent Benét perhaps summed up Fitzgerald's posthumous stature best in his review of *The Last Tycoon* for the *Saturday Review of Literature* (6 Dec. 1941): "You can take off your hats now, gentlemen, and I think perhaps you had better. This is not a legend, this is a reputation—and, seen in perspective, it may well be one of the most secure reputations of our time" (Bryer, *Critical Reception*, pp. 375–76). That reputation was sustained by the approximately 160 short stories Fitzgerald published during his lifetime. As the author of *The Great Gatsby*, however, he became a bright star in the firmament of American literature and acquired the aura of a near-legendary figure. Perhaps that aura has faded some with the increasing interest in and sympathy for Zelda Fitzgerald, but Scott Fitzgerald will always remain central to a culture haunted by the elusive "American dream."

• Fitzgerald's papers and remaining books are in the Firestone Library, Princeton University. Among collections of letters, *The Letters of F. Scott Fitzgerald*, ed. Andrew Turnbull (1963), is the first and most valuable. See also *The Correspondence of F. Scott Fitzgerald*, ed. Matthew Bruccoli and Margaret Duggan (1980); *F. Scott Fitzgerald: A Life in Letters*, ed. Bruccoli (1994); *As Ever, Scott Fitz: Letters between F. Scott Fitzgerald and His Literary Agent Harold Ober, 1919–1940*, ed. Bruccoli (1973); *Dear Scott, Dear Max: The Fitzgerald-Perkins Correspondence*, ed. John Kuehl and Jackson Bryer; and *Scott Fitzgerald: Letters to His Daughter*, ed. Turnbull (1965). The novels and short stories that Fitzgerald published in book form in his lifetime appeared then and long after his death under the imprint of Charles Scribner's Sons; several reissues were brought out by an associated imprint, Collier Books (Macmillan). The definitive version of *The Great Gatsby*, edited by Bruccoli with informative notes, was published by Collier in 1992. Bruccoli's reworking of "The Last Tycoon" manuscript was published in the Cambridge Edition of the Works of F. Scott Fitzgerald as *The Love of the Last Tycoon: A Western* (1993). Textual studies of note include James L. W. West, *The Making of "This Side of Paradise"* (1983); Bruccoli, *The Composition of "Tender Is the Night"* (1963) and *Reader's Companion to F. Scott Fitzgerald's "Tender Is the Night"* (1996); and Bruccoli, *"The Last of the Novelists": F. Scott Fitzgerald and "The Last Tycoon"* (1977). *The Crack-Up*, ed. Edmund Wilson (1945), includes published and unpublished essays, notebook entries, and correspondence by Fitzgerald, plus letters to him by Gertrude Stein, Edith Wharton, T. S. Eliot, Thomas Wolfe, and John Dos Passos. All available reviews of Fitzgerald's books and his obituaries appear in Bryer, ed., *F. Scott Fitzgerald: The Critical Reception* (1978). Bryer, *The Critical Reputation of F. Scott Fitzgerald* (2 vols., 1967–1984), is a complete bibliographical study covering 1920–1981 for books, articles, and sections of books by and about Fitzgerald. Bruccoli, *F. Scott Fitzgerald: A Descriptive Bibliography* (1972; rev. ed., 1987), lists articles and books by Scott and a few by Zelda. Among numerous biographies are Arthur Mizener, *The Far Side of Paradise* (1951; rev. ed., 1965); Turnbull, *Scott Fitzgerald: A Biography* (1962); Bruccoli, *Some Sort of Epic Grandeur* (1981); Scott Donaldson, *Fool for Love: F. Scott Fitzgerald* (1983); James R. Mellow, *Invented Lives: F. Scott and Zelda Fitzgerald* (1984); and Jeffrey Meyers, *Scott Fitzgerald* (1994). Wilson, *The Shores of Light* (1952), views Fitzgerald from the vantage point of a fellow Princetonian, friend, and critic. Milton R. Stern, *The Golden Moment* (1971), focuses entirely on Fitzgerald's work, with fruitful results and insights.

ROBERT A. MARTIN

FITZGERALD, John Francis (11 Feb. 1863–2 Oct. 1950), mayor of Boston and maternal grandfather of U.S. president John F. Kennedy and U.S. senators Robert F. Kennedy and Edward M. Kennedy, was born in Boston, Massachusetts, the son of Irish immigrants Thomas Fitzgerald and Rosanna "Rose" Cox. Although Thomas Fitzgerald was part of the "Famine Irish" migrations of the 1840s and 1850s, he was able to join his brother in the grocery and liquor business in Boston's North End. John Fitzgerald graduated from Boston Latin School and entered Harvard Medical School. However, the death of his father in 1885 forced him to find a job. Turning to ward leader Matthew Keany for help, Fitzgerald obtained a post in the Boston Customs House. He soon started his own insurance business and became immersed in the turbulent, congenial world of Democratic ward politics.

Fitzgerald (known as "Johnny Fitz," "Fitzy," or "Honey Fitz"), a small, garrulous, gregarious man, was a natural leader, most significantly in Matt Keany's Ward 6 political organization. With Keany's backing he was elected to the Boston Common Council in 1891. When Keany died in 1892, Fitzgerald assumed ward leadership and was elected to the Massachusetts senate. In 1894 he successfully challenged the local Democratic incumbent in the U.S. House of Representatives, where he served three terms. During his whirlwind political rise, Fitzgerald supported such issues as unrestricted immigration, labor legislation, and local betterments. In 1889, at the beginning of this decade of political growth, Fitzgerald married Mary Josephine "Josie" Hannon; the couple had six children.

In 1900, when Fitzgerald returned his undivided attention to Boston politics, the city was at a critical juncture. In the era of "the shame of the cities," Boston had been noted for its good government and as a city where municipal services were responsive, and politics were reasonably honest. There was no city political machine in nineteenth-century Boston; rather, an alliance of well-born Yankee Democrats and Irish political leaders maintained a standard of responsible governance. The city's principal social problem was not corruption, but a deep-seated anti-Catholicism. However, by 1900 in a historic transition, the Irish were poised to dominate the city's politics; at the same time, this traditional standard of governance was increasingly challenged by a vigorous and often raucous generation of younger Irish ward leaders.

Recognizing the futility of challenging the incumbent mayor, the revered Patrick Collins, Fitzgerald bought a weekly newspaper, the *Republic*, continued his local political activities, and waited. Upon Collins's unexpected death in 1905, the "Napoleon of Ward 6" announced his candidacy for mayor. This declaration alarmed other ward bosses, who feared his growing power, and the reformers in the Good Government Association (the GooGoos), who feared that he would create a corrupt political machine. Following a bitterly fought election, Fitzgerald was narrowly elected in December 1905.

Fitzgerald's early actions as mayor confirmed the reformers' worst fears: he appointed cronies to critical city posts and awarded municipal contracts on a patronage basis. Reformers sought a state investigation, but Fitzgerald headed them off by proposing an independent finance commission (the Fin Com), to be headed by former Yankee mayor Nathan Matthews, to conduct the investigation. Matthews had been a Fitzgerald supporter in 1905, but unknown to Fitzgerald, he had become bitterly disillusioned with his former ally. Under Matthews's leadership the Fin Com held dramatic public hearings during the fall of 1907 that produced evidence of contract fraud and political chicanery. Although the investigators could not link Fitzgerald directly with the fraud, the scandals were enough to defeat him when he ran for reelection in December 1907.

These revelations were minor compared with those raked up in New York and other contemporary cities, but for Boston they were shocking. Boston reformers did what reformers did elsewhere: they sought a new city charter to cripple ward-based political power and put additional strength in the hands of the mayor. The new charter was approved by the voters in 1909, and the critical election to choose the first reform mayor took place in January 1910.

Carrying the reform banner in this contest was the city's principal investment banker and progressive reformer, James Jackson Storrow. Storrow had a strong record as civic leader, school reformer, and friend to Irish Catholics, but he was rich and a Protestant. His opponent was John F. Fitzgerald. Heartened by the failure of the Fin Com to link him directly to corruption, Fitzgerald sought reelection by crying for vindication and charging that Storrow was trying to buy the election at the expense of poor Irish Catholics. Sinking to his opponent's level, Storrow became a shrill reformer crying out against "Fitzgeraldism." The campaign divided the city along ethnic lines, with Fitzgerald winning by 1,400 of the 95,000 votes cast.

Watched by the state-run Finance Commission and Civil Service Commission, Fitzgerald was careful to live within the law during his second term. The city payroll swelled as he continued the Boston commitment to more streets, playgrounds, schools, and bathhouses. He went out of his way to seek accommodation with the business interests of the city, calling for a "Bigger, Busier, Better Boston." Constantly on the move, he attended all manner of civic functions. His political position appeared impregnable.

Abruptly Fitzgerald fell from political power. He had declared that he would not seek reelection in 1914, then changed his mind and announced his candidacy. This about-face challenged the plans of another ambitious Democrat, U.S. congressman James M. Curley. Furious, Curley threatened to expose Fitzgerald's dalliance with "Toodles," a local chorus girl, unless he got out of the race. Under intense pressure from his family, Fitzgerald reluctantly capitulated to Curley's threat and withdrew in December 1913.

Although Fitzgerald remained on the city and state political scene for three more decades and often ran for office—for U.S. senator in 1916 and 1942, for U.S. representative in 1918, for governor in 1922 and 1930—he was never elected. He was pushed aside by two men who dominated Democratic politics for the first half of the twentieth century. In city politics, Mayor Curley was an audacious brawler, Yankee-baiter, exploiter of the political system, and champion of the poor. On the state level, Irish Democratic politics belonged to governor and then U.S. senator David I. Walsh, whose dignified, conservative, accommodationist stance accorded him bipartisan support. Caught between these two men, Fitzgerald could not find a leadership role, and his career petered out in decades of irrelevance. As "Honey Fitz" he continued on the public stage by holding honorary positions and singing his trademark tune, "Sweet Adeline." He died in Boston.

Although a critical figure in Boston politics in the early part of the twentieth century, both as a figure in the transition from Yankee to Irish political dominance and as a catalyst for political reform, Fitzgerald is remembered less for his own political role than for his kinship to his Kennedy grandsons.

• There are no Fitzgerald papers, but the Rose Fitzgerald Kennedy Papers at the John F. Kennedy Library, Boston, Mass., contain some Fitzgerald material. Boston *City Documents* (1905–1907, 1910–1914) contain speeches and other public writings. Volumes 1–4 of the Boston Finance Commission, *Report of the Finance Commission* (1909) contain much of the record of his first administration; volumes 5–9 continue into his second administration. The Kennedy Library contains oral histories by several of Fitzgerald's contemporaries.

There is no definitive biography of Fitzgerald. Doris Kearns Goodwin, *The Fitzgeralds and the Kennedys* (1987), contains valuable material on his personal life and mayoral years. John Henry Cutler, *"Honey Fitz": Three Steps to the White House; the Life and Times of John F. "Honey Fitz" Fitzgerald* (1962), is an informal study. Reminiscences appear in the autobiography of his daughter Rose Fitzgerald Kennedy, *Times to Remember* (1974), and in her biography by Gail Cameron, *Rose: A Biography of Rose Fitzgerald Kennedy* (1971).

Fitzgerald's career in Boston and Massachusetts politics spanned a half-century, and it must be patched together from a variety of sources. Richard Abrams, *Conservatism in a Progressive Era: Massachusetts Politics, 1900–1914* (1964), includes information on his mayoralty, and J. Joseph Huthmacher, *Massachusetts People and Politics, 1919–1933* (1969), describes his subsequent state activities. For contemporary Boston politics, see sources for Fitzgerald's more noted contemporary, James M. Curley, Ronald Formisano and Constance Burns, *Boston 1700–1980: Evolution of Urban Politics* (1984), contains useful articles.

Obituaries are in the *New York Times* and the *Boston Globe*, 3 Oct. 1950.

CONSTANCE K. BURNS

FITZGERALD, Zelda (24 July 1900–10 Mar. 1948), wife of F. Scott Fitzgerald, writer, and artist, was born in Montgomery, Alabama, the daughter of Anthony D. Sayre, an associate justice of the Supreme Court of Alabama, and Minnie Buckner Machen. Zelda grew up in a privileged and secure home. As the baby of the family, she was indulged and spoiled as a child, and at a young age she began to develop eccentric, self-centered behavior. In 1909 she began studying ballet, which became a lifetime interest. Zelda was known as an excellent athlete, particularly in her habit of diving from high places on a dare. When she was seven, the family moved to 6 Pleasant Avenue in Montgomery, Zelda's permanent home until her marriage.

In 1914 Zelda entered Sidney Lanier High School, where she was an indifferent student but still managed to maintain a "B" average during her first year. Increasingly attracted to boys, she became a restless and undisciplined personality, addicted to pranks and with a disregard for the more traditional values of behavior and dress that characterized Montgomery. By the time she was fifteen, she had become strikingly beautiful. Involved with the country club set in Saturday night dances, she often would sneak out during intermissions to smoke, drink liquor, and neck in the cars. She soon had dates every night of the week. Her friendships were mostly with men. Her father forbade her to go out at night, but she often climbed out her bedroom window. She seemed to be immune to social criticism because of her father's position as a judge, and by the time she graduated from high school in 1918, she was known as the belle of Alabama. She was voted "prettiest and most attractive girl in her class" when she graduated. By this time Zelda was completely unconventional in manner and dress and was encouraged in her escapades by her mother while opposed by her father, who had become increasingly distant.

With the advent of World War I, in 1918 Montgomery felt the influence of troops sent to Camp Sheridan, a training camp just outside Montgomery for officers. Among those sent to Camp Sheridan was F. Scott Fitzgerald. In July 1918 Scott and Zelda met at a country club dance in Montgomery and immediately were attracted to each other. Scott at the time was writing a novel, *The Romantic Egotist*, which was initially rejected by Scribners. After a revision, in which Zelda appears as Rosalind, and a new title, *This Side of Paradise*, the novel was accepted. Zelda had some doubts about marrying Scott (who by this time had been discharged from the army) but was persuaded by Scott's frequent visits to Montgomery in 1919 and by the novel's tremendous popularity upon publication in March 1920. Her family was opposed to the match, and her parents did not attend the wedding in New York on 3 April 1920.

Scott emerged as one of the most popular and wealthy writers of the 1920s, and he and Zelda embarked on a restless life divided between America and Europe, where they were key figures in the expatriate American community in France. On 26 October 1921 their daughter was born. Thrust into the limelight as spokespersons for the Jazz Age, neither Scott nor Zelda could see the end of the decade as bringing about a change in their hectic life of parties, liquor, and spending beyond their income. Zelda contributed some short pieces to magazines and served as the model for many of Scott's attractive women characters.

While in Europe in 1930, Zelda had her first breakdown. Her story after that is largely one of confinement. After brief stays in two clinics in Europe, Malmaison outside Paris and Valmont in Switzerland, on 5 June 1930 she entered Prangins clinic at Nyon, Switzerland. In September 1931 she was released from Prangins (supposedly better), and the Fitzgeralds returned to America. Following the death of her father in November 1931, Zelda suffered a second breakdown and in February 1932 entered Phipps Psychiatric Clinic in Baltimore, where she wrote her version of the marriage, *Save Me the Waltz* (1932), in six weeks. Scott, who was working on *Tender Is the Night* (1934) with difficulty, objected to her use of the same material. A rather difficult confrontation and examination ensued with the Fitzgeralds airing their complaints against each other in sessions with Zelda's psychiatrist. In June 1932 Zelda was discharged from Phipps.

From 29 March to 30 April 1934 Zelda's artwork was exhibited in New York to minor acclaim. She had not been so lucky with an earlier play, *Scandalabra*, produced by the Vagabond Junior Players in Baltimore in 1933. The play failed to attract attention.

In April 1936 Zelda entered Highland Hospital in Asheville, North Carolina. She was self-confined and periodically went back to Montgomery to live with her mother. On 10 March 1948 a fire broke out on the top floor where Zelda was living, and she burned to death.

One of the most attractive personalities of the Jazz Age, Zelda collaborated with Scott on articles and short stories, wrote a play and a novel, painted numerous pictures, and tried very hard to establish herself as a ballet dancer. If she started out thinking the good life would go on forever, she was not alone in her thinking. Scott once wrote to Zelda that "we ruined each other" (Mellow, p. 135).

• The principal location of the Fitzgeralds' letters is Princeton University, Rare Books and Special Collections department. Zelda's writings are collected in *Zelda Fitzgerald: The Collected Writings*, ed. Matthew J. Bruccoli (1991), which includes *Save Me the Waltz*, *Scandalabra*, her short stories, and her articles, along with her letters to Scott. A standard biography is Bruccoli, *Some Sort of Epic Grandeur* (1981). Books are usually written on the Fitzgeralds together, but a few focus on Zelda. Koula Hartnett, *Zelda Fitzgerald and the Failure of the American Dream for Women* (1991), and Nancy Milford, *Zelda* (1970), focus on Zelda exclusively. Eleanor Lanahan, ed., *Zelda: An Illustrated Life* (1996), is a collection of eighty of Zelda's paintings assembled by her granddaughter. James R. Mellow, *Invented Lives: F. Scott and Zelda Fitzgerald* (1984), is a joint biography, as is Sara Mayfield, *Exiles from Paradise: Zelda and Scott Fitzgerald* (1971). Biographies that focus on Scott but nevertheless contain much of interest on Zelda are Scott Donaldson, *Fool for Love* (1983); Jeffrey

Meyers, *Scott Fitzgerald* (1994); Henry Dan Piper, *F. Scott Fitzgerald: A Critical Portrait* (1965); and Andrew Turnbull, *Scott Fitzgerald* (1962).

ROBERT A. MARTIN

FITZHUGH, George (4 Nov. 1806–30 July 1881), lawyer and author, was born in Prince William County, Virginia, the son of George Fitzhugh, a physician and small-scale planter, and Lucy Stuart. When Fitzhugh was six years old, the family moved to a plantation near Alexandria, Virginia. Obtaining a poor education in a field school, he partly educated himself. After reading for the law, he married Mary Metcalf Brockenbrough in 1829, possessed through marriage a small plantation near Port Royal, Virginia, and moved there with his wife, with whom he had nine children, six of whom survived infancy. He practiced law in Port Royal but disliked the profession, once admitting that his long-winded clients bored him, and often defended criminals. Favoring slavery, he was distressed by two socioeconomic problems: agitation in Virginia caused by increasing numbers of free blacks, and resistance to the extension of slavery into territories gained after the Mexican War (1846–1848).

In 1849 Fitzhugh published a pamphlet titled *Slavery Justified*. In embryonic form it contains many of his later arguments, which he eventually expressed in scores of articles and editorials. His *Sociology for the South; or, The Failure of Free Society* (1854), the first American book with the word *sociology* in its title, reprints *Slavery Justified* as an appendix and proved popular with many southern readers.

In 1855 Fitzhugh visited Boston, Massachusetts, and New Haven, Connecticut, where he lectured, discussed the subject of slavery with abolitionists such as Stephen Pearl Andrews and Harriet Beecher Stowe, and grew more firmly convinced of the rightness and necessity of keeping southern blacks enslaved. At this time he temporarily opposed reopening the slave trade, wrote a friend that he privately saw some evils in slavery but could not say so in print, and yet argued that employment of plantation slaves in the South made more economic sense than employment of "wage slaves" did in the North. As proof he cited the deplorable conditions of oppressed factory workers in England, about which he had read in British journals and in the works of Thomas Carlyle, one of his favorite authors.

Fitzhugh's *Cannibals All! or, Slaves without Masters* (1857) expands on articles he had published in the *Richmond Enquirer* and in *De Bow's Review* beginning in 1855. James Dunwoody Brownson De Bow, founder of this review in 1846, was an advocate of slave labor who met and liked Fitzhugh in Washington, D.C., probably in 1857. In 1857 and 1858, during the administration of President James Buchanan, Fitzhugh was a law clerk in Washington, D.C., in the land claim department of the office of Attorney General Jeremiah Sullivan Black. In 1859 Fitzhugh's advocacy of the resumption of the slave trade caused pro-Union southern friends to desert him. When North-South conflict seemed inevitable, Fitzhugh went so far as to praise war as a noble adventure sanctioned by God.

Fitzhugh also wrote essays on literary topics, mainly to tout the work of southern authors. He once opined that it was more important for southerners to write their own books than to manufacture their own shoes. His reputation, however, is based only on his *Sociology for the South* and *Cannibals All!* In these two ill-organized but absorbing works he tries to demonstrate that slavery is natural and benefits not only white masters but also their black servants, who, without white overseers, would perish. He argues that the capitalistic system in the North ruins rich masters, idle landlords, and wage-dependent workers, who are all dangerously removed from the nurturing land. He theorizes that any society following Scottish economist Adam Smith's laissez-faire proposals will find its "freedom" collapsing into chaos. Fitzhugh hoped to avert a military clash between the North and the South by convincing both sides of the validity of his socioeconomic thesis that security is better than freedom. He argues that a master race evolved in America in the form of patriarchal southern aristocrats out of British cavaliers and that this chivalric group is superior to northern capitalists, who evolved from Anglo-Saxon serfs. Inconsistently, in his written work he was also simultaneously calling for an increase in industrial productivity in the South, in imitation of northern manufacturing successes. And, although in *Cannibals All!* he defined blacks as belonging to the human race, in 1861 he adopted De Bow's fulmination that blacks were forever members of an inferior breed.

In 1862, a year after the Civil War began, Fitzhugh moved to Richmond and clerked in the Treasury Department of the Confederacy. After the war he became a judge in the Freedmen's Court, which was part of the Freedmen's Bureau. He continued to contribute to *De Bow's Review* until 1867 and published in *Lippincott's Magazine* in 1869 and 1870. A year after his wife's death in 1877, he began to live in Frankfort, Kentucky, with his son. In 1880 he moved again, to be with his daughter in Huntsville, Texas, where, suffering from both insomnia and near-blindness, he died.

• Most of Fitzhugh's papers are no longer extant. Some correspondence is in the James Dunwoody Brownson De Bow Papers and in the George Frederick Holmes Collection, both in the William R. Perkins Library of Duke University; and in the Department of War Records, the Files of the Attorney General, and the Freedmen's Bureau Collection, all in the National Archives, Washington, D.C. Selections from Fitzhugh's works are in *Ante-Bellum Writings of George Fitzhugh and Hinton Rowan Helper on Slavery*, ed. George Wish (1960). Harvey Wish, *George Fitzhugh: Propagandist of the Old South* (1943), is a detailed critical biography. A balanced brief treatment of Fitzhugh is in Jay B. Hubbell, *The South in American Literature, 1607–1900* (1954). Edmund Wilson, *Patriotic Gore: Studies in the Literature of the American Civil War* (1962), compares Fitzhugh, William John Grayson, and Helper as fellow apologists for slavery. Fitzhugh's defense of slavery is variously treated in Eugene D. Genovese, *The World the Slaveholders Made: Two Essays in Interpretation* (1969); Fred Hobson, *Tell about the South: The Southern Rage to Explain* (1983); Lewis P. Simpson, "The Mind of the Antebellum South," in *The History of Southern Literature*, ed. Louis D. Rubin, Jr., et al. (1985), pp. 164–74; and Louis D. Rubin, Jr., *The Edge of the Swamp: A Study in the Literature and Society of the Old South* (1989). An obituary is in the *Fredericksburg (Va.) News*, 15 Aug. 1881.

ROBERT L. GALE

FITZHUGH, William (1651–21 Oct. 1701), lawyer and planter, was born in Bedford, England, and was baptized there on 10 January 1651, the son of Henry Fitzhugh, a woolen draper, and Mary King, the daughter of the vicar of Tempsford in Bedfordshire. The Fitzhughs had been a prominent middle-class family in Bedford for many generations. William received a classical grammar school education in England and read law in the office of an English lawyer before emigrating to the Northern Neck of Virginia. The exact date of his settling in Virginia is unknown, but it was sometime before February 1674. Later that year he married Sarah Tucker of Westmoreland County, Virginia. She was eleven years of age and a member of a prosperous and well-connected family. They would have six children.

William and Sarah Fitzhugh set up housekeeping in Stafford County on the Potomac River on a tract of land that would be increased over the years into an extensive holding. Fitzhugh had an active law practice in the Northern Neck, his clients being wealthy planters such as Richard Lee, Robert Beverley, and Ralph Wormeley, as well as the more humble persons of his county. Fitzhugh also engaged in land speculation, plantation management, and what later became known as the import-export business. Beginning with a small amount of capital from his wife's inheritance and perhaps a small amount of money from his father, Fitzhugh built up a large fortune through an active lifetime of constant and diligent work.

In 1677 Fitzhugh was elected to the General Assembly to represent Stafford County in the House of Burgesses. He remained in the legislature until 1685 and sat again in 1693. Soon after his first election, he rose to become one of the leaders of that assemblage. This was a period of tense partisan politics in Virginia as well as in England. Fitzhugh was allied with the royal governor and the conservatives. In 1685 he was a supporter of James II while his county was being represented in the General Assembly by Whigs. In that same year, a bill of impeachment, the first in America, was passed against him. He was accused of making false claims for moneys due to him from Stafford County. The accusation appears to have been politically motivated and untrue, and his own political friends prevented his being brought to trial.

Fitzhugh's legal and political prominence also resulted in another important position, this one being of significant financial importance. From 1693 to the end of his life, he and his law partner, George Brent, were the resident land agents for the Fairfax Proprietary of the Northern Neck. During this time, Fitzhugh purchased large tracts of the proprietary.

Fitzhugh sat as a justice of the peace on the Stafford County Court from 1684 to 1691. Also in 1684 he was appointed lieutenant colonel of the Stafford County militia. He was one of the original trustees of the College of William and Mary. These appointments reflected his political importance, social rank, and financial success. Fitzhugh died at "Ravensworth," his home in Stafford County, Virginia.

• Fitzhugh's surviving correspondence, which is at Harvard University, gives a useful insight into his life and an unusual glimpse of his times. There is a detailed sketch of the life of Fitzhugh preceding an edition of his letters by Richard Beale Davis, *William Fitzhugh and His Chesapeake World 1676–1701* (1963).

W. HAMILTON BRYSON

FITZPATRICK, Benjamin (30 June 1802–21 Nov. 1869), governor of Alabama and U.S. senator, was born in Greene County, Georgia, the son of William Fitzpatrick, a Georgia state legislator, and Anne Phillips. Benjamin, orphaned at seven, received only the most rudimentary education. When he was fourteen, he came to the area that would later be Alabama to manage lands that had been acquired by his older brother. He read law under Montgomery mayor Nimrod E. Benson and was admitted to the bar in 1823. In the same year the state legislature elected him a circuit solicitor and reelected him in 1825. After 1827 he devoted himself to cotton planting. His slaveholding grew from 24 persons in 1830, to 50 in 1840, and to 106 in 1850. By 1860 Fitzpatrick's real estate was valued at $60,000, his personal property at $125,000.

In 1827 Fitzpatrick married Sarah Terry Elmore, thereby allying himself with one of the most prominent families in the state. Before her death in 1837, she and Fitzpatrick had six sons. In 1846 he married Aurelia Rachel Blassingame and by her had a seventh son.

Fitzpatrick served as a Democratic candidate for presidential elector in 1840 and successfully canvassed the state for Martin Van Buren. The following year the Democrats nominated him for governor, and he received 57 percent of the vote against Whig James W. McClung.

Fitzpatrick's years as governor were dominated by questions surrounding the state-owned Bank of Alabama, which had been badly damaged by the Panic of 1837. Fitzpatrick's cautious nature made him wish to save the institution. He recommended that the mismanaged branch at Mobile be liquidated but sought merely the reform of the main bank and the other three branches. The legislators wished to go further, however, and in 1843 Fitzpatrick signed legislation to liquidate all four of the branches and to preserve only the main bank of Tuscaloosa. This proved very popular because it seemed to represent a blow at the wealthy speculators whom the Jacksonians blamed for the depression, and in August Fitzpatrick was reelected to a second term without opposition. Thereupon he moved to a harder line. In 1845 he signed the bill abolishing the state banking system altogether.

In November 1848 Fitzpatrick was appointed to the U.S. Senate to succeed his former brother-in-law Dixon H. Lewis, who had died. But when the state legislature met in 1849, Fitzpatrick was defeated for the seat by Jeremiah Clemens, the candidate of dissident north Alabama Democrats who formed a coalition with the Whigs.

In January 1853 Fitzpatrick was appointed to the Senate again, to succeed William R. King, who had resigned. Fitzpatrick was overwhelmingly elected to the seat by the legislature in November, and in 1855 he was chosen for a full term over the Know Nothing nominee, Luke Pryor.

In the Senate Fitzpatrick devoted much attention to the question of the public lands. He strongly supported the Graduation Act of 1854 that reduced the minimum price of land in proportion to its quality and the number of years that it had remained unpurchased, and he fought to gain preemption rights for squatters on lands granted to railroads. He favored the Homestead Bill of 1860 but later refused to vote to override President James Buchanan's veto of it. He served as president pro tempore of the Senate from December 1857 to his resignation in January 1861. In June 1860 the Baltimore Democratic convention nominated him for vice president on the ticket with Stephen A. Douglas, but at the urging of his political allies in Alabama he declined the position.

Fitzpatrick's enthusiasm for the doctrine of popular sovereignty earned him increasing opposition from William Lowndes Yancey and his group of young southern-rights Democrats. When Fitzpatrick sought reelection to the Senate in 1859, the Yanceyites blocked the resolution to bring on the election. In the secession-convention election of December 1860, Fitzpatrick sought to defeat the Yanceyite faction, which was advocating separate-state secession, by endorsing instead the cooperative secession of the southern states. But this proposal gained significant support only in northern Alabama.

In November 1863 the legislature deadlocked in choosing a member of the Confederate Senate. Fitzpatrick's name was then placed in nomination, but he was defeated after twenty ballots. In the summer of 1865 Fitzpatrick was elected to represent Autauga County in the constitutional convention called under the terms of Presidential Reconstruction and was unanimously chosen its president. But this constitution was voided, and he was disfranchised by the Military Reconstruction Acts of 1867. Fitzpatrick died at his Autauga County plantation and was buried in Montgomery.

• A small collection of Fitzpatrick's papers is held by the Southern Historical Collection of the University of North Carolina, Chapel Hill. His gubernatorial correspondence is at the Alabama Department of Archives and History, Montgomery, which also holds a few of his personal papers. His career has not been well studied, but see William W. Duncan, "The Life of Benjamin Fitzpatrick" (M.A. thesis, Univ. of Alabama, 1930), and J. Mills Thornton III, *Politics and Power in a Slave Society: Alabama, 1800–1860* (1978).

J. MILLS THORNTON III

FITZPATRICK, John (21 Apr. 1870–27 Sept. 1946), labor leader, was born in Athlone, Ireland, the son of John Fitzpatrick, a farmer and horseshoer, and Adelaide Clarke. His mother died when he was one year old and his father died when he was ten, so in 1882 he moved to Chicago to live with his uncle. His only formal education in the local grammar school ended with his father's death. He worked for three years in meat packing and then learned the trade of farrier. In 1886 he joined the International Union of Journeymen Horseshoers, a membership he was to retain throughout his life. Over the next ten years he held the offices of vice president, treasurer, president, and business agent of Local No. 4 of the Horseshoers.

In 1896 Fitzpatrick helped launch the Chicago Federation of Labor (CFL), an organization established by reform-minded unionists frustrated with the corrupt William C. Pomeroy's domination of the Trades and Labor Assembly. Fitzpatrick soon emerged as a leader in the CFL, serving as its president from 1899 to 1901. In the early years of the century he struggled with corrupt building-trades influence within the new federation, forging alliances with many of Chicago's leading reformers, such as Jane Addams and Raymond Robins. Fitzpatrick regained the CFL presidency in 1905 and held it until his death. Under his influence, the CFL became an important center of progressive unionism in America, experimenting with industrial forms of union organization and independent political action—activities that were not sanctioned by the more conservative American Federation of Labor (AFL).

In 1917 Fitzpatrick and William Z. Foster set out to organize the Chicago meat-packing industry. They formed the Stock Yards Labor Council, which represented all of the craft unions with jurisdiction in the stockyards and functioned as a protoindustrial union. The council enjoyed a fair amount of success until, weakened by jurisdictional disputes and racial antagonism, it was destroyed in 1921–1922. Fitzpatrick also collaborated with Foster on the national steel campaign, organized along similar semi-industrial lines, which culminated in the massive but unsuccessful 1919 steel strike.

In late 1918 Fitzpatrick and the CFL began to organize an Independent Labor party. On 17 November, six days after the end of the First World War, the CFL issued a social-democratic platform, "Labor's 14 Points," which called for the right to organize, the eight-hour workday, a minimum wage, full employment, government ownership of public utilities including the stockyards, and labor representation in government and the postwar peace settlements. Fitzpatrick ran for mayor of Chicago in the spring of 1919 on the Labor party ticket, coming in fourth. The La-

bor party expanded quickly but was similarly unsuccessful in the 1920 national elections, and its national organization collapsed shortly thereafter. Fitzpatrick kept the Illinois party, which had become the Farmer-Labor party, alive until 1923, when a merger with the Communist-led Workers' party resulted in the Communist domination of the new Federated Farmer-Labor party (FF-LP). Fitzpatrick became thoroughly disheartened by the whole affair, and the new FF-LP soon disintegrated. Although he retained the post of president of the CFL for another two decades, Fitzpatrick was never again the dynamic force within the labor movement that he had been. In the 1930s he, like most AFL leaders, was hostile to the radicalism of the emerging Congress of Industrial Organizations. He died in Chicago.

The most remarkable aspect of Fitzpatrick's career was his ability to remain independent from the AFL, an organization that provided both his legitimacy (the CFL was composed of AFL unions) and his salary (for most of his life he was employed as an AFL organizer). His initiative in organizing mass-production workers directly contradicted the AFL's official commitment to craft unionism and displayed a willingness to organize Slavic and African-American workers, a position that was not common in the AFL at the time. His experiments with independent labor politics conflicted with the AFL's policy of working with the established political parties. Although he never embraced socialism as a creed, his Labor party's political platform was social-democratic in orientation, and he was tolerant of and willing to work with radicals such as Foster.

• Fitzpatrick's papers are at the Chicago Historical Society. Information on the CFL and Fitzpatrick's role in its history can be found in the *New Majority*, the publication of the CFL. John Keiser, "John Fitzpatrick and Progressive Unionism, 1915–1925" (Ph.D. diss., Northwestern Univ., 1965), addresses his contributions. A contemporary account of the period's events is found in William Z. Foster, *The Great Steel Strike and Its Lessons* (1920). Other sources that address unionization include David Brody, *The Butcher Workmen: A Study of Unionization* (1964) and *Steelworkers in America: The Nonunion Era* (1960). The movement's socialist and communist characteristics are discussed in Edward P. Johanningsmeier *Forging American Communism* (1994), and James Weinstein, *The Decline of Socialism in America: 1912–1925* (1967). Obituaries are in the *Chicago Tribune*, 28 Sept. 1946, and the *New York Times*, 29 Sept. 1946.

JONATHAN KISSAM

FITZPATRICK, John Bernard (15 Nov. 1812–13 Feb. 1866), Roman Catholic bishop, was born in Boston, Massachusetts, the son of Bernard Fitzpatrick, a tailor, and Eleanor Flinn, a former schoolteacher. His parents were natives of Tullamore, Ireland, and had moved to Boston, via Baltimore, in 1805. His mother tutored Fitzpatrick at home, after which he studied at the Adams School, the Boylston School, and, from 1826 to 1829, the Boston Latin School, where he studied the classics. In 1829, to begin preparation for the priesthood, he entered the Collège de Montréal, studying under Société de Saint-Sulpice priests. Four years later he publicly defended his thesis in English, French, Greek, and Latin with such skill that he was appointed to a faculty position while he continued his studies. After graduating in 1837 he went to Paris for three years. During this time, he studied at the Grand Séminaire de Saint-Sulpice and taught the catechism in French to sons of aristocrats living in the fashionable Faubourg St. Germain. He presided as a master at theological conferences and was appointed a subdeacon and then a deacon in 1839. He was ordained as a priest in 1840.

Fitzpatrick returned to Boston in 1840 to accept an appointment at the cathedral there. Because of his brilliance and tact, he rose rapidly to his final position of eminence. He was consecrated bishop of Callipolis and coadjutor of Boston at a ceremony in Georgetown, District of Columbia, in 1844. When Benedict Joseph Fenwick, bishop of Boston, died in 1846, Fitzpatrick succeeded to the See of Boston.

Fitzpatrick served resolutely and with diplomacy. The problems he handled over a period of two decades were of three general sorts. The Brahmin establishment in Boston had to be persuaded to be tolerant of the dispossessed Irish immigrants whom they mainly disliked and whose Catholic religion most of them reviled—partly through ignorance. The Irish populace had to be cajoled into permitting themselves to be controlled by domineering city leaders and into conforming to their standards—for a time at least. And, when the Civil War began, the Irish had to be persuaded to be loyal to the federal government and talked out of using the national crisis as an excuse for violent reprisals against prejudiced Protestant authorities.

Fitzpatrick was largely successful. He organized the diocese to meet the needs of thousands of Irish who, because of the Potato Famine of 1845–1849, left their homeland to settle in Boston. His diocese also sent substantial relief funds and tons of supplies to Ireland, to aid families remaining behind. (Non-Catholic Bostonians were also generous, as were Americans in general.) Protestant Bostonians objected to the unchecked influx of impoverished, unskilled Irish Catholics whom they saw as causing taxes to rise, wages to fall, disease, drunken brawling, and crime. In response to many provocations, Fitzpatrick preached patience, self-control, tolerance, and pro-Americanism. He advised his parishioners to moderate their intake of alcohol but not to favor prohibition, to avoid establishing secret societies of "Hibernians," and to vote for conservative Whig candidates rather than for liberal Democratic ones. He developed amicable relationships with several national and regional political, commercial, professional, and cultural leaders over the years.

Fitzpatrick oversaw the construction of seventy-one new churches in his diocese but steadfastly refused to spend limited funds on parochial schools. He fought to build Catholic orphanages and hospitals, to enable priests to visit Catholic patients in city hospitals, and to expand Catholic cemetery facilities. He saw to the rebuilding of Holy Cross College in Worcester after a disastrous fire in 1852. He urged passive resistance to harassment of Catholic pupils in public schools—until dramatic trouble erupted. In 1859 a Catholic boy was beaten by a teacher for refusing to recite Protestant prayers. Fitzpatrick wrote the Boston School Committee complaining that it had habitually violated Catholic citizens' constitutionally guaranteed religious liberties. He also supported the injured pupil's parents in a lawsuit against the teacher. The suit failed in a court dominated by Know Nothing nativist politicians. But Fitzpatrick was gratified when school procedures were liberalized and when a Catholic priest was welcomed as a member of the Boston School Committee. The year 1861 saw the start of construction of Boston College for Catholic lay students. The college was the result of the Jesuit priest John McElroy's years of effort and Fitzpatrick's diplomatic maneuvering.

During the years just before the Civil War, Fitzpatrick declined to state any official position regarding slavery, abolition, or efforts at compromise. But when the conflict began, he supported the Union cause, as did a vast majority of his parishioners. He fought for the religious rights of Catholic soldiers, including access to Catholic chaplains. Though in poor health, he conferred with Catholic priests and pro-Catholic secular leaders in Europe in 1862–1864, visiting Italy and France but making Brussels his headquarters—quite possibly to counteract Confederate diplomatic strategies in Catholic countries there. Once back in Boston, Fitzpatrick resumed some of his duties as bishop, but he never fully regained his strength. He had suffered minor paralytic strokes since the mid-1850s and succumbed to a final one in Boston. Fitzpatrick is notable as a skilled advocate of sociopolitical accommodation during potentially catastrophic times. He loved Boston, his birthplace; he also loved the Irish, his people. His dignity and wisdom made a permanent impression on virtually every leading Bostonian. With remarkable success, he steadily advocated gradual, evolutionary progress, always within the law.

• Fitzpatrick's papers, including his daily journal, are in the Archives of the Archdiocese of Boston. Thomas H. O'Connor, *Fitzpatrick's Boston, 1846–1866: John Bernard Fitzpatrick, Third Bishop of Boston* (1984), contains the definitive treatment of Bishop Fitzpatrick. Cecil Woodham-Smith, *The Great Hunger: Ireland, 1848–1849* (1962), details the Potato Famine and its widespread consequences. Obituaries are in the *Boston Advertiser*, 14 Feb. 1866, and the *Boston Journal* and the *Boston Post*, both 16 Feb. 1866.

ROBERT L. GALE

FITZPATRICK, John Clement (10 Aug. 1876–10 Feb. 1940), archivist, was born in Washington, D.C., the son of James Nicholas Fitzpatrick, a financial clerk of the U.S. Senate, and Elizabeth Ann Combs. He graduated from Washington High School in 1894 and for three years worked as a journalist for the *U.S. Government Advertiser*. In 1897, the year the Library of Congress established its Manuscripts Division, Fitzpatrick was appointed by Librarian of Congress John Russell Young as an entry technician in the division. Upon his arrival, Fitzpatrick was assigned the task of calendaring (a laborious process of item indexing manuscripts) the George Washington papers, a project he finally completed in 1909. As he worked on this project, he assumed greater responsibility for the Manuscripts Division. In 1908 he was appointed chief clerk, which meant he had charge of its administrative duties, and he held this position until his acrimonious departure in 1928. During his tenure at the library he produced the *Handbook of Manuscripts in the Library of Congress* (1918) and edited *The Autobiography of Martin Van Buren* (1920), as well as producing documentary editions of the Continental Congress journals and George Washington's diaries. He left the library when he was passed over to become chief of the Manuscripts Division in favor of historian John Franklin Jameson.

After he left the library, Fitzpatrick became the editor for the George Washington Bicentennial Commission, returning to his preferred work on the Washington manuscripts. From 1931 to 1944 Fitzpatrick, with the assistance of a small staff, produced thirty-nine volumes of Washington papers. His earlier work at the library and this project moved Fitzpatrick into the circle of preeminent scholars and other researchers and archivists who were laboring in the early twentieth century to preserve America's documentary heritage. He also served as president of the American Catholic Historical Association in 1928–1929. Fitzpatrick was disappointed, however, in not being named first archivist of the United States in 1934, probably because he lacked any advanced degrees.

While Fitzpatrick has been closely associated with his work on the Washington manuscripts, his main contribution was his authoring of the *Notes on the Care, Cataloguing, Calendaring and Arranging of Manuscripts* published in 1913 by the Government Printing Office. Written because of the constant requests for assistance by other archival and historical manuscripts repositories as to how the Library of Congress was handling its voluminous manuscript collections, *Notes* became an instant bestseller in the young American archival community. It remained until the 1930s the basic American text in the archival field, going through three editions and a final reprinting in 1934.

Notes described eighty-four different topics related to the administration of historical manuscripts, ranging from basic arrangement and description (cataloging) to preservation issues. The centerpiece of Fitzpatrick's work was his description of a "chronologic-geographic" system of arranging manuscripts, a process that was later criticized by archivists because it threatened other basic archival principles such as provenance and original order. Fitzpatrick's use of this system revealed his predilection that the historical researcher is the main user of such documents and that they should be arranged in a manner that facilitates such use. Nearly a quarter of *Notes* was devoted to the calendaring system, not a surprising characteristic given that Fitzpatrick's first decade had been involved in such work. Fitzpatrick was also active with the American Historical Association's Public Records Commis-

sion and was a consistent advocate for that commission's efforts to develop a basic primer for the management of public records (this work was never completed).

Fitzpatrick died in Washington, D.C. He had been married twice, first to Louise Tracy Hull in 1908 (she died in 1911) and then to Elizabeth Veronica Kelly in 1922 (she died in 1933). Fitzpatrick had one child. Among his accomplishments, Fitzpatrick also designed posters for government agencies, and in 1932 he helped to revive the Purple Heart, a military decoration originally developed by George Washington.

Despite a start as a minor federal bureaucrat, Fitzpatrick had a major influence on the way American archivists managed historical documents and archival records. Fitzpatrick wrote the first major American archival manual, one that influenced two generations of archivists and manuscripts curators. He also produced a major edition of George Washington's papers that remained a vital source for historians of early America for generations.

• Fitzpatrick's papers are at the Library of Congress. Today Fitzpatrick is largely unknown to archivists, documentary editors, and historians. The most thorough treatment of his career is in Robert D. Reynolds, Jr., "The Incunabula of Archival Theory and Practice in the United States: J. C. Fitzpatrick's *Notes on the Care, Cataloguing, Calendaring and Arranging of Manuscripts* and the Public Archives Commission's 'Primer of Archival Economy,'" *American Archivist* 54 (1991): 466–82.

RICHARD J. COX

FITZSIMMONS, Frederick Landis (28 July 1901–18 Nov. 1979), baseball pitcher, manager, and coach, was born in Mishawaka, Indiana. (His parents' names are unknown.) Fitzsimmons grew up on a farm near his birthplace and played several sports in high school. After graduation in 1919, he entered professional baseball, pitching three seasons for Muskegon, Michigan, of the Central League (Class B). The right-hander spent the 1923 and 1924 seasons with Indianapolis of the American Association. He was married there in 1924 to Helen Louise Burger, with whom he had one child. The following season he again played with Indianapolis before beginning a nineteen-year National League career with the New York Giants in August 1925. Over the next nine seasons he averaged better than 15 wins each year. Although he had only one 20-game victory year, in 1928, his 19–7 season in 1930 led all National League pitchers in winning percentage (.731). He had a 16–11 record in 1933, joining Hall of Fame left-hander Carl Hubbell and right-handers Hal Schumacher and Roy Parmelee in pitching the Giants to a surprise pennant and World Series win.

"Fat Freddie," as the chunky 5'11", 200-pounder was called, began experiencing arm problems in 1935, and in midseason 1937 he was traded to the Brooklyn Dodgers in a deal that backfired on the Giants as Fitzsimmons pitched effectively for another four years. He had a remarkable 16–2 campaign for the Dodgers in 1940 to again lead all National League pitchers in winning percentage with a major league record at the time of .889. His last noteworthy season came in 1941 when the forty-year-old pitcher, used on a spot basis, had a 6–1 record. He was a hard-luck pitcher in three World Series, compiling an 0–3 record and a 3.86 earned run average. During his career in the majors, he posted an impressive 217–146 won-lost record (.598) with a 3.51 ERA.

Fitzsimmons, a knuckleball specialist, had a unique pitching style that added to his effectiveness. He pitched as though pivoting on a turntable, looking in at the hitter as he began his windup, then rotating his body toward second base before swinging around to face the plate just before releasing the ball. Sportswriter Red Smith wrote: "No matter where you sit in the ballpark, there is an instant in his windup when he is looking you in the eye." In addition, Fitzsimmons was one of the best fielding pitchers of his time and one of the better hitting pitchers, with 231 lifetime hits, which included 14 home runs.

Fitzsimmons is remembered as a fierce competitor who fought a continuing battle against injuries as well as opposing hitters. A quintessential appearance occurred on 5 September 1931. He pitched seven strong innings in a win against the Brooklyn Dodgers, yielding only three hits and hitting a home run to put the Giants in the lead. In the top of the seventh inning, a Brooklyn batter slashed a drive back to the box that struck Fat Freddie in the pit of the stomach, knocking him flat. Then, barely recovered in the bottom of the inning, he was hit in the head by a pitch while batting and again collapsed in a heap. After a few minutes, he got to his feet and walked slowly off the field only to collapse again in the Giants' clubhouse. Yet, despite a ruptured blood vessel in his head, the rotund knuckleballer characteristically missed only one turn on the mound. He was not as fortunate, however, in the 1941 World Series when a Yankees' batter lined a wicked drive that severely bruised his left kneecap, forcing him out of the game and costing him the chance at a well-pitched victory.

A sportswriter wrote of Fitzsimmons: "Freddie was from the old school. He knocked down line drives with his legs, and he was forever challenging batters and umpires." Leo Durocher wrote: "Off the field, Freddie was as nice a man as you would want to meet. [But] once he gets out on the mound, you just couldn't talk to him. He'd snap his head at you and stomp around and snarl out his words like a lion chasing a piece of meat."

Fitzsimmons was a pitcher-coach for the Dodgers in 1943, in his last active season before taking over as manager of the Philadelphia Phillies in midseason of that year. He managed the club to a poor 105–181 (.367) record before his dismissal in the middle of the 1945 season. Subsequently, he coached for the Boston Braves, New York Giants, Chicago Cubs, Kansas City Athletics, and in the minor leagues. Fitzsimmons's hiring as pitching coach by the Giants in 1949 caused an uproar as his previous employer, the Braves, claimed the Giants had been guilty of "tampering"

—that is, the Giants had discussed hiring Fitzsimmons while he was still under contract to the Braves. As a result, baseball commissioner Happy Chandler fined Fitzsimmons and Giants manager Durocher and suspended Fitzsimmons for a month.

In addition to his extensive involvement in major league baseball, Fitzsimmons had a short career as a professional football executive. Philadelphia Phillies owner William D. Cox purchased the Brooklyn Dodgers franchise in the short-lived All-America Football Conference in October 1945 and hired Fitzsimmons, deposed as Phillies manager just three months earlier, as his football team's general manager. Fitzsimmons remained in the position until February 1948. Fitzsimmons died in Yucca Valley, California.

• Biographical accounts of Fitzsimmons's career can be found in Jack P. Lipton, *Biographical Dictionary of American Sports—Baseball* (1987); Mrs. Freddie Fitzsimmons, "I Married Baseball," *Coronet*, Sept. 1955; and Fred Stein and Nick Peters, *Giants Diary—A Century of Giants Baseball in New York and San Francisco* (1987). The most up-to-date compilations of his playing records are in John Thorn and Pete Palmer, eds., *Total Baseball*, 3d ed. (1993), which was used in this article, and Macmillan's *Baseball Encyclopedia*, 9th ed. (1993). There is no full biography of Fitzsimmons, but an extensive file of clippings is in the National Baseball Library in Cooperstown, N.Y. An obituary is in the *New York Times*, 8 Dec. 1979.

FRED STEIN

FITZSIMMONS, James Edward. *See* Fitzsimmons, Sunny Jim.

FITZSIMMONS, Robert (26 May 1863–22 Oct. 1917), boxer, was born at Helston, Cornwall, England, the son of James Fitzsimmons, a police constable and, later, a blacksmith, and Jane Strongman. According to Gilbert Odd, Fitzsimmons may have had the middle name James, even though his birth certificate lists only his first name and surname (The Fighting Blacksmith, pp. 254–55). His family emigrated to Lyttelton, New Zealand, when he was eight years old. He left school at the age of twelve and worked for a while at odd jobs and house painting. Then he joined his older brother at Timaru, New Zealand, and worked as a blacksmith.

While living at Timaru, Fitzsimmons became an amateur boxer and was New Zealand lightweight champion from 1880 to 1882. He then turned professional and won two fights conducted under the rules of the London Prize Ring. In 1883 he went to Sydney, Australia, where he remained until 1890, working as a blacksmith and pursuing a professional boxing career. He boxed more than forty times, mostly four-rounders in which no official decision was given. He gradually acquired a reputation and fought for the Australian middleweight title in February 1890 but, as he later claimed, accepted a bribe and faked a knockout loss to the champion, Jim Hall.

In April 1890 Fitzsimmons was recruited by a California boxing promoter to come to the United States, becoming an immediate success and scoring knockouts in his first three fights. At 5′11½″ and weighing only about 150 pounds at this time, Fitzsimmons then fought for the recently invented world middleweight title, which he won by knocking out the reigning champion, Jack Dempsey, the "Nonpareil," at New Orleans in January 1891. Fitzsimmons won all but one of his battles over the next several years, including a knockout of Hall in 1893, soon after which he became a naturalized citizen of the United States. He was prevented from winning a fight in Boston with Joe Choynski, whom he had beaten badly, when the referee declared a draw after the police stopped the fight to save Choynski. In September 1894 he defended the middleweight title with a two-round knockout of Dan Creedon.

In November Fitzsimmons engaged Con Riordan in an exhibition at Syracuse, New York. Riordan, drunk when he entered the ring, was quickly knocked out and died shortly thereafter. Fitzsimmons was brought to trial for manslaughter but was found innocent on 3 July 1895. He was matched to fight James J. Corbett for the world heavyweight title in October 1895 at Corpus Christi, Texas, but the fight was prevented when the Texas Senate hurriedly passed a law that made prizefighting a criminal offense.

Fitzsimmons had two important fights in 1896. He won a one-round knockout over Peter Maher in a bout held on a sand island in the Rio Grande near Langtry, Texas, to escape the attempts of authorities to prevent it. His second fight with Tom Sharkey in San Francisco was refereed by gunfighter Wyatt Earp. Fitzsimmons soundly beat Sharkey, knocking him out in the eighth round. However, Earp disqualified him for an alleged low blow seen by no one else.

Fitzsimmons then challenged Corbett for the heavyweight championship on 17 March 1897 at Carson City, Nevada. For thirteen rounds, Corbett outboxed his foe, although Fitzsimmons sought to land a knockout punch. In the fourteenth round Fitzsimmons finally delivered a short, powerful left, the famous "solar plexus" punch, just below the ribs, followed by a right to the jaw, and Corbett collapsed. Fitzsimmons won the title although officially weighing only 167 pounds, ten more than he actually weighed, according to his friend Jim Coffroth.

Fitzsimmons fought flat-footed, shuffling aggressively after his opponent at all times. He punched accurately and powerfully with both hands and was one of the most effective body-punchers in ring history. He had a large torso but spindly knock-kneed legs. His body was covered with large freckles, and his sparse hair was auburn, almost red, giving rise to the nicknames "Freckled Bob" and "Ruby Robert." He was a good-natured man and liked to play practical jokes. He spoke with a cockney-like Australian accent, liked to sing hymns in a tenor voice, and sometimes gave way to emotions, as when he sought a duel with a young man for paying undue attention to his wife.

Outside the ring Fitzsimmons was certainly one of the most colorful fighters who ever lived. He was generous, a spendthrift, and claimed that managers and boxing promotors swindled him out of most of his ring earnings. For years the sporting pages detailed his pranks and misadventures. He was immensely fond of animals and, while training for a fight, he often wrestled publicly with his lion cub or his great dane. His pets were the cause of considerable grief and injury to him; he was badly bitten by a monkey and a mongoose and once nearly electrocuted when his lion lunged playfully at him and instead struck a high-voltage line.

In 1899, in his first heavyweight defense, Fitzsimmons was defeated by James J. Jeffries, who knocked him out in the eleventh round. In 1900 he made a comeback, knocking out Sharkey and two other opponents. In 1902 he fought Jeffries again, at San Francisco, in a match that ended in controversy. He whipped Jeffries for seven rounds, but in the eighth Fitzsimmons received a body punch, dropped his arms, said something to Jeffries, took a punch to the jaw, and fell to the floor to be counted out. Rumors of a faked fight circulated, but no evidence was produced, and Fitzsimmons always maintained that he was disabled by the body punch that landed just before the knockout blow.

In 1903 Fitzsimmons won his third championship, outpointing George Gardner to win the light heavyweight title. He held the title until 1906, when he was badly defeated by "Philadelphia" Jack O'Brien. He continued to fight occasionally and had two minor fights as late as 1914, at the age of fifty.

Fitzsimmons was married four times, first (date unknown) in Australia to Alice Jones, with whom he had one child and whom he divorced in 1893, just before marrying Rose Julian, an acrobat, in 1894. They had three children, and Rose's brother, Martin Julian, became his manager. After she died in 1903 Fitzsimmons the same year married Julia May Gifford, a singer in a touring company to which he also belonged, but they soon parted. Finally he married Temo Ziller Slomonin in 1915. He had no children with his last two wives. He spent most of his later years in vaudeville, living in Brooklyn, New York, and Dunellen, New Jersey. He died of pneumonia in Chicago while on a vaudeville tour. He was an inaugural inductee into the International Boxing Hall of Fame in 1990.

• Fitzsimmons is the author of *Physical Culture and Self Defense* (1901). The *Philadelphia Item* is a gold mine of information on the fights and other activities of Robert Fitzsimmons from 1890 to 1912. Three books have been written about him: Richard K. Fox, *Bob Fitzsimmons: His Life and Battles* (1895); Robert H. Davis, *"Ruby Robert" Alias Bob Fitzsimmons* (1926); and Gilbert Odd, *The Fighting Blacksmith: A Biography of Bob Fitzsimmons* (1976). Odd's book is by far the most authoritative and factual of the three. John Hogg of Brisbane, Australia, provided a record of Fitzsimmons's fights there. Herbert G. Goldman, ed., *The 1986–87 Ring Record Book*, contains an accurate record of Fitzsimmons's fights after he left Australia. The *Ring* magazine published many articles on Fitzsimmons; see especially James W. Coffroth, "Coffroth Picks Bob Fitzsimmons in Three Places on His All-Time Boxing Team" (Dec. 1926); Charley Harvey, "When Wyatt Earp's Gun Silenced Enraged Fight Fans" (Mar. 1929); Jim Nasium, "When Fitz and Maher Put Langtry on Map" (June 1930); Will Lawless, "Bob Fitzsimmons—The True Story of the Early Career of the Great Triple Champion" (Sept. 1930); and Daniel M. Daniel, "Golden Anniversary of Fitz-Corbett" (May 1947). An obituary is in the *New York Times*, 22 Oct. 1917.

LUCKETT V. DAVIS

FITZSIMMONS, Sunny Jim (23 July 1874–11 Mar. 1966), thoroughbred horse trainer, was born James Edward Fitzsimmons in Brooklyn, New York, the son of George Fitzsimmons, a farmer and vegetable huckster, and Catherine Murphy. In 1879, the exact site of Fitzsimmons's birth in the Sheepshead Bay section of Brooklyn became the new Sheepshead Bay Racetrack. Significantly, Fitzsimmons's earliest childhood experiences were filled with the sights, sounds, and smells of horses and racetracks, an environment in which he lived and worked for the rest of his life.

Because of the extreme poverty of his Irish immigrant parents, Fitzsimmons had little opportunity for formal education. By the age of five, in order to help his family survive, Fitzsimmons was asked to drive his father's horse-drawn vegetable wagon. Within a year he began the routine of rising at 3:45 A.M. and working eleven-hour days. Before his eleventh birthday he labored as a blacksmith's assistant, a lunch-wagon driver, and a cook and stablehand for the Brennan Stables in Sheepshead Bay, and in 1885 he was hired as an exercise boy and apprentice rider for the Dwyer Stables in Sheepshead, in exchange for two meals per day, a cot in a barn and $10 per month. At about this time, Fitzsimmons met George "Fish" Tappen, another boy who was fascinated with horses. They became fast friends, and Tappen worked as Fitzsimmons's valet and assistant trainer for the next seventy years.

In August 1889 the 84-pound Fitzsimmons rode his first professional race on a horse named Newburgh. He finished out of the money and was not allowed to ride for the Dwyer Stables again. Disillusioned, Fitzsimmons tested his skills at many of the small racetracks in New Jersey, Kentucky, Maryland, Virginia, and southern Ohio and managed to scratch out a subsistence living. In September 1890 he rode his first winner, a four-year-old named Crispin. During this same period he worked briefly for a horse owner with a famous name: Frank James, the brother of the notorious outlaw, Jesse James. By mid-1891 Fitzsimmons was earning enough money to start a family. That year he married Jeannie Harvey; they had six children.

For the next decade the Fitzsimmons family struggled to survive on the outlaw circuit. The worst problem was Fitzsimmons's increasing difficulty making the weight requirement as a jockey. In order to keep working, he exercised vigorously, sweated in steam baths, took laxatives and literally starved himself. In doing so, he reduced his natural weight of 140 pounds to a cadaverous 105 pounds. He managed to keep his family together by using these draconian measures, but he also risked his health to the point that he induced a case of the disfiguring spinal arthritis, which

by the time he reached middle age caused him to stoop over almost double.

In 1907, with his back pain increasing, Fitzsimmons gave up riding altogether and devoted himself fulltime to training racehorses in Sheepshead Bay. Still living on the edge of poverty at age thirty-six, his dedication and hard work finally began to pay off when he was hired by New York financier J. E. Davis to train a select few first-rate thoroughbreds. Fitzsimmons's success with Davis's horses caught the eye of James F. Johnson, who owned the prestigious Quincy Stables. His association with Johnson put Fitzsimmons for the first time in close contact with the moneyed class. His demonstrable ability to make bad horses good and good horses better was now being noticed by many rich owners, and Fitzsimmons received ten percent of every purse. Fellow trainer Johnny Nerud characterized Fitzsimmons's talent this way: "He's got the touch to make a billy goat run." One of his few disappointments during these early years of success came when, in an effort to save money for Johnson, Fitzsimmons was the last man to drop out of the bidding for the famous stallion, Man 'o War. Nevertheless, Fitzsimmons's reputation for honesty, integrity, and the knack for training consistent winners impressed many who loved horse racing, including journalists. With Fitzsimmons's popularity growing in proportion to the number of winners he produced, George Daley, a sportswriter for the New York *World*, began a column in 1914 by saying, "Jimmy Fitzsimmons—Sunny Jim they ought to call him because of a disposition that ever makes for a happy smile—had three good ones at Jamaica yesterday." The names of the winning horses were soon forgotten, but the nickname stuck, as did "Mr. Fitz," the name favored by his closest friends and associates.

In 1924 Fitzsimmons entered the world of big-time racing when he was hired by New York banker William Woodward as head trainer for the Belair Stud Farm, one of the great racing establishments in America. In 1925 he was also hired by Mrs. Henry Carnegie Phipps and Ogden L. Mills (who would later become secretary of the treasury under President Herbert Hoover) to train for the Wheatley Stables. With these top positions, Fitzsimmons gained control of many of the finest thoroughbred horses in the United States, often training as many as fifty per year. He always had a realistic assessment of the nature of his job: "You can't add anything to a horse that's not in him. If you can bring out the best in any horse you've done your job well."

Fitzsimmons produced his first great champion in 1930 when three-year-old Gallant Fox, with veteran jockey Earl Sande aboard, won the Wood Memorial and then the Triple Crown, finishing first in the Kentucky Derby, the Preakness, and the Belmont Stakes. Gallant Fox earned $308,165 and was named horse of the year. After developing Faireno and Dark Secret into big earners, Fitzsimmons produced his second Triple Crown winner, Omaha, in 1935. Later that year he trained the legendary Seabiscuit before Belair

Farms sold him. Other great stallions Fitzsimmons handled during the late 1930s were Granville, who won Horse of the Year honors in 1936; and his best speed horse, Johnstown, who won the Withers Stakes, the Dwyer, and two legs of the Triple Crown in 1939. The most successful fillies he trained were Vagrancy, Busanda, High Voltage, and Misty Morn.

From the years following World War II until his retirement in 1963, Fitzsimmons was considered a master horse trainer by those who knew racing best. One of the most famous horses from Fitzsimmons's glory years was the huge bay colt Nashua, who easily won the Preakness and Belmont Stakes in 1955 but was upset by Swaps in the Kentucky Derby. As a reaction to this defeat, perhaps Fitzsimmons's greatest single victory came in August 1955 when Nashua beat Swaps by six and one-half lengths in a highly publicized $100,000 match race in Chicago, and was named horse of the year. In his three years of racing Nashua won a total of $1,288,565, a record at the time. Fitzsimmons's last great stallion was Bold Ruler, another horse of the year and winner of twenty-three races, including the 1957 Preakness, the Wood Memorial, and the Flamingo. He was also the sire of Secretariat, perhaps the greatest thoroughbred in the twentieth century.

In addition to his training of high-profile racehorses, Fitzsimmons kept his own modest stable with the help of his sons, James and John. He also owned a business that manufactured Bigeloil, a cure-all liniment that he recommended for horses and humans alike. In his later years Fitzsimmons became moderately wealthy and was able to build an estate called "Fitzsimmonsville" on the banks of northern New York's Lake Desolation near Saratoga Spa, the site of his favorite racetrack. His horses won ten Saratoga Cups.

Racing experts agree that Fitzsimmons's greatest strength as a trainer was the conditioning of his horses for distance races. In his last race, Nashua set a record in winning the two-mile Jockey Club Gold Cup in 1956 with a time of 3:20⅖. All-time great jockey Eddie Arcaro, who rode both Nashua and Bold Ruler to victory, paid Fitzsimmons this high tribute: "Getting a horse ready for a distance race Mr. Fitz is the greatest trainer who ever lived." Remarkably, Fitzsimmons stayed near the top of his profession until his retirement at age eighty-nine, when he led the list of stakes winners at Saratoga. His biographer, Jimmy Breslin, made this observation in *Sunny Jim: The Life of America's Most Beloved Horseman* (1962): "In what other business could an eighty-year-old man win something called the Futurity."

In his long career Fitzsimmons trained winners of 2,275 races and marked some 250 stakes victories, including the Kentucky Derby three times, the Preakness four times, the Belmont Stakes and the Dwyer six times each, the Jockey Club Gold Cup seven times, and the Realization and the Wood Memorial eight times. His horses won purses of over $13 million. In 1956, when asked the secret of his success as a trainer,

Fitzsimmons gave this answer: "Thing is, that's the horses's business, running. . . . He feels like he just plain *got* to run, that's all. Well, part of my job is to train him so he'll feel exactly that way, crazy to run, at exactly the right time, at exactly the time they go to the post. Sometimes I do it, sometimes I don't." Fitzsimmons did it exactly right most of the time. He died in Miami, Florida.

• An excellent summary of his life and career in racing is included in Robert Riger, *The Athlete: An Original Collection of Twenty-five Years of Work* (1980). Fitzsimmons is also featured in Frank Litsky, *Superstars* (1975). Riger explores Fitzsimmons's displeasure with the decline in sportsmanship in American racing in "Sunny Jim's Lament," *Esquire*, Aug. 1963, pp. 83–86. John McNulty presents an affectionate look at Fitzsimmons with one of his favorite horses in "A Visit with Mr. Fitz and Nashua," *Colliers*, 30 Mar. 1956, pp. 21–23. See also Arturo Gonzalez and Janeann Gonzalez, "Life Begins at 40 (x2)," *New York Times Magazine*, 19 June 1958, p. 11. Two colorful articles marking Fitzsimmons's retirement are "Sunny Jim Bows and Turns Himself Out to Pasture," *Life*, 28 June, 1963, p. 44; and George Ryall, "Sunny Jim," *Blood-Horse*, 13 and 20 July 1963. Sportswriter Red Smith included a posthumous tribute to Fitzsimmons in *To Absent Friends* (1982). Obituaries are in the *New York Times*, 12 Mar. 1966, and *Blood-Horse*, 19 Mar. 1966.

BRUCE L. JANOFF

FITZSIMONS, Thomas (1741–26 Aug. 1811), congressman and merchant, was born in Ireland. No information about his parents or his early life is available. He emigrated to Philadelphia, Pennsylvania, in 1760 and found work as a clerk in a countinghouse. In 1763 he married Catharine Meade, daughter of wealthy merchant Robert Meade; he became a partner with his brother-in-law in George Meade & Company, which conducted a considerable business in the West Indies.

With the onset of the revolutionary crisis with Great Britain, Fitzsimons played an active role as a member of Philadelphia's Committee of Correspondence and other revolutionary committees. When the revolutionary war broke out, he commanded a volunteer company of home guards and fought during the Trenton campaign of 1776. Thereafter he held a variety of state offices during the war including membership on Pennsylvania's Council of Safety and the state's Navy Board. In 1779 he was appointed to Philadelphia's Committee of Inspection, which was charged with regulating prices. In 1780 Fitzsimons's firm subscribed £5,000 to support the Continental soldiers encamped during the harsh winter at Morristown, New Jersey. A year later, in an effort to strengthen the finances of the United States, he helped found the Bank of North America, the first bank in the United States. He served on the bank's board of directors until 1803.

In 1779 Fitzsimons became a member of Pennsylvania's elitist Republican Society, a proto-Federalist group that favored amending Pennsylvania's radical constitution of 1776. Elected to the Continental Congress in 1782 and 1783, he advocated increasing the powers of Congress through an impost on trade. He also supported efforts to pay Continental soldiers their back wages before they demobilized. The following year, he was appointed to Pennsylvania's Board of Censors. From 1785 to 1789 he represented Philadelphia in the state assembly, during which time the Pennsylvania legislature appointed him a delegate to the federal Constitutional Convention. At the convention he repeatedly voted to strengthen the powers of the central government. He favored giving Congress authority to tax exports as well as imports, opposed universal suffrage, and approved the motion to give the House of Representatives equal authority with the Senate to ratify treaties.

Beginning in 1789, Fitzsimons served three successive terms in the new U.S. House of Representatives, where he functioned as Secretary of the Treasury Alexander Hamilton's chief representative. Throughout his congressional career, he supported vigorously the Federalist party's economic program, voting for Hamilton's proposals for funding and assumption of the national debt by the United States and a protective tariff for American industry.

Fitzsimons was defeated in 1794 by Democrat John Swanwick and never again stood for public office. He did, however, serve the United States as a Jay Treaty commissioner, assigned to resolve the prerevolutionary debts that Americans owed British merchants, and he continued to take a lively interest in public affairs. He disapproved of the French Revolution, accused the Democratic-Republican Societies of fomenting the Whiskey Rebellion, and in 1803, in concert with other prominent Philadelphia merchants, petitioned Congress for $2 million in reimbursements for French depredations of American commerce between 1792 and 1795. He denounced President Thomas Jefferson's Embargo Act as oppressive to commerce and ineffective as a means of coercion. In 1810, as a member of a committee of Philadelphia merchants, he urged Congress to recharter the Bank of the United States.

Along with an illustrious political career, Fitzsimons achieved prominence in business activities and civic affairs. A founder and trustee of the Insurance Company of North America, he was also, in 1801, elected president of the Philadelphia Chamber of Commerce. He served as a trustee of the University of Pennsylvania from 1791 until 1811 and throughout his life promoted public education. In 1805 Fitzsimons went bankrupt, a result of debts he had assumed to support the speculative land schemes of Robert Morris and others. Fitzsimons regained some of his wealth, but his prestige was diminished from that time onward. He contributed generously to Catholic philanthropies, becoming the largest contributor to the construction of Philadelphia's St. Augustine's Church. Fitzsimons died in Philadelphia.

• A handful of Fitzsimons's letters and his journal (1781–1785) are in the Historical Society of Pennsylvania. Biographical sketches of Fitzsimons's life include Henry Flanders, "Thomas Fitzsimons," *Pennsylvania Magazine of History and Biography* 2 (1878); J. T. Scharf and T. Westcott, *History of Philadelphia*, vol. 1 (1884); Martin I. J. Griffin, "Thomas Fitzsimons: Pennsylvania's Catholic Signer of the Constitution," *Records of the American Catholic Historical Society of Philadelphia*, vol. 2 (1889); James A. Farrell, "Thomas Fitzsimons: Catholic Signer of the American Constitution," *Records of the American Catholic Historical Society of Philadelphia*, vol. 39 (1928); and *Biographical Directory of the United States Congress, 1774–1989*. See also Lawrence Lewis, Jr., *A History of the Bank of North America* (1882).

E. WAYNE CARP

FIXX, James Fuller (23 Apr. 1932–20 July 1984), writer, was born in New York City, the son of Calvin Henry Fixx, a journalist, and Marlys Fuller. After completing his primary education, he attended the Garden Country Day School in Jackson Heights, New York, from 1947 to 1948, and he graduated from the Trinity School in New York City in 1951. Fixx attended Indiana University from 1951 to 1952 and then served as a clerk in the U.S. Army from 1952 to 1954 in Pusan, South Korea. In 1955 he entered Oberlin College and majored in English literature, with the goal of becoming either a journalist or a teacher. While studying at Oberlin, Fixx worked as a reporter and feature writer for the Oberlin *News Tribune*. He graduated from Oberlin in 1957 and married Mary Jeannette Durling, also an Oberlin graduate, in June of that year; the couple had four children before they divorced in 1973.

Fixx began a career in journalism as a reporter, feature writer, and drama critic for the *Sarasota (Fla.) Journal* in 1957. Returning to New York in 1958, he worked as a stringer and researcher for *Time* magazine before becoming a textbook editor for Henry Holt and Company, Inc., in 1959. That year Fixx won the Danforth Scholarship for graduate study in education, but he turned it down and became instead the feature editor for the *Saturday Review*. Six years later he joined *McCall's* as a senior editor and within a month became the executive editor of the popular women's magazine. In 1969 Fixx left *McCall's* to join the editorial staff of *Life* magazine, becoming a senior editor. Throughout 1970 he worked as a freelance writer and contributing editor to the *Christian Herald*, the *New York Times*, and *Time*. In 1971 Fixx left *Life* and joined *Audience Magazine* as an articles editor. After *Audience* folded in 1973, he worked as the managing editor of *Horizon*, but devoted more time to freelance writing. In 1974 Fixx married Alice Kasman; the marriage produced no children and ended in divorce.

Fixx's first book was *Games for the Superintelligent* (1972), a collection of math, logic, and word puzzles designed to stump the members of Mensa, an organization to which Fixx belonged, consisting of people with IQs over 140. Four years later he authored a companion volume of brain teasers, *More Games for the Superintelligent*. The publication of *The Complete Book of Running* in 1977 catapulted Fixx into the limelight of the physical fitness craze that had captured the United States since the late 1960s, making him an authority on running, a millionaire, and an international celebrity. Before starting the book, Fixx had been running for nearly eight years to lose weight. While Fixx was a newspaper reporter and magazine editor, his weight had ballooned over 200 pounds and he smoked over a pack of cigarettes a day. Like millions of other Americans during the 1970s, Fixx began participating in the grueling 26.2-mile marathon foot race. *The Complete Book of Running*, which described in detail every possible aspect of the sport, remained on the *New York Times* bestseller list for nearly two years and netted Fixx $600,000 in 1978 and over $900,000 in 1979. In 1978 Fixx wrote a third book of puzzles, *Solve It!*, and, in revising *The Complete Book of Running*, produced an entirely new book, *Jim Fixx's Second Book of Running* (1980). In 1982 he wrote *Jackpot!*, an autobiographical account of his rise to celebrity, including his two divorces. Fixx died from a heart attack while running on a rural highway near Harwick, Vermont. Although his death precluded his completion of *Maximum Sports Performance*, Random House in conjunction with Nike, Inc., completed and published the volume posthumously in 1985.

Fixx's death came as a shock to the millions of running enthusiasts around the world, many of whom took up the sport after reading his popular books. Although he had been running nearly ten miles a day for nearly fifteen years, he was a candidate for a heart attack, especially since his father had suffered a heart attack at age thirty-five and had died of another attack at age forty-three. In fact, Fixx's awareness of his disposition to heart attacks probably had contributed to his decision to begin jogging in the late 1960s. Fixx's autopsy revealed not only extensive coronary heart disease—the three main arteries to his heart were narrowed 80 to 99 percent—but also scar tissue from three mild heart attacks, one of which had occurred within two weeks of his death. In his books about running, Fixx wrote optimistically about the extent to which running could prevent heart disease, make the body immune to heart attack, and postpone old age. In effect, Fixx became a martyr through his quest for everlasting health and longevity, a goal that had captured health reformers for centuries. While some credit Fixx with launching the running boom of the 1970s, his contribution was actually one of several factors, including the publication of Kenneth H. Cooper's *Aerobics* (1968) and the gold medal–winning performance of Frank Shorter in the 1972 Olympic marathon.

• An extensive biographical file on Fixx is in the Oberlin College archives. For the historical context of the fitness boom of the late twentieth century, consult Jack W. Berryman and Roberta J. Park, eds., *Sport and Exercise Science: Essays in the History of Sports Medicine* (1992); Harvey Green, *Fit for America: Health, Fitness, Sport and American Society* (1986); James C. Whorton, *Crusaders for Fitness: The History of American Health Reformers* (1983); Patricia A. Eisenman and Robert Barnett, "Physical Fitness in the 1950s and 1970s: Why Did One Fail and the Other Boom?" *Quest* 31 (1979): 114–22; and Benjamin G. Rader, "The Quest for Self-Sufficiency and the New Strenuous Life: Reflections on the Strenuous Life of the 1970s and 1980s," *Journal of Sport History* 18

(1991): 255–66. Obituaries are in the *New York Times* and the *Los Angeles Times*, both 22 July 1984; the *Chicago Tribune*, 23 July 1984; and *Newsweek* and *Time*, both 30 July 1984.

ADAM R. HORNBUCKLE

FLAGET, Benedict Joseph (7 Nov. 1763–11 Feb. 1850), Roman Catholic bishop, was born in Contournat, Auvergne, France, the son of Antoine Flaget and Anne Chomette, peasants. His father died before his birth, and his mother died when he was three; he was raised by his maternal aunt. After attending the College of Billom and the Sulpician seminaries at Clermont and Issy, he was ordained a priest in 1788. He joined the Society of St. Sulpice, commonly called Sulpicians, a community of diocesan priests engaged in conducting seminaries. He then taught theology at the seminary of Nantes. When the French Revolution closed the country's seminaries, Flaget immigrated in 1792 to the United States, where Sulpicians had opened the country's first Catholic seminary at Baltimore, Maryland, the previous year. With the seminary faculty already filled, Flaget ministered to French-speaking Catholics at Vincennes, Northwest Territory (now Ind.), and environs until 1795. He was then instructor and vice rector of Georgetown College, Washington, D.C., until 1798, when he joined Sulpicians starting a seminary in Havana, Cuba. In 1801 he joined the faculty of St. Mary's Seminary in Baltimore.

In 1808 Flaget was appointed bishop of the newly created diocese of Bardstown, Kentucky, a jurisdiction encompassing Kentucky, Tennessee, and areas of the Northwest Territory. Reluctantly he accepted and was consecrated a bishop by Archbishop John Carroll in Baltimore in 1810, arriving in Bardstown in June 1811. As bishop he began to establish diocesan institutions with the assistance of personnel and funding from abroad. He founded St. Thomas Seminary in 1811 near Bardstown and completed St. Joseph's Cathedral in 1819. He invited the Sisters of Loretto, the Sisters of Charity of Nazareth, and Dominican sisters to staff Catholic schools and welcomed the Society of Jesus (Jesuits) to the diocese in 1831 to staff a college. He also made strenuous travels for pastoral visits throughout his vast diocese.

Despite an outward calm and personal graciousness, Flaget was sensitive to conflict and suffered melancholia. Believing that his health was failing, he resigned his see in 1832 and was succeeded by John Baptist David, his coadjutor bishop since 1819. This change of bishops produced a major crisis in early Kentucky Catholic history as David's personality had not appealed to local clergy and laity who were stirred to organized opposition. David thereupon resigned, and the pope reappointed Flaget in 1833 along with a new coadjutor bishop, Guy Ignatius Chabrat.

In church affairs outside his diocese, Flaget attended the American bishops' provincial councils of 1829 and 1840. In 1835 he visited Rome to report on his diocese. On that occasion, he agreed to the pope's request to promote membership in the French-based Society for the Propagation of the Faith, which funded missionary dioceses, by visiting every French diocese. He returned to Kentucky in 1839.

Because of the creation of several new dioceses in the region, Flaget's jurisdiction was limited to Kentucky by 1837. In his declining years his coadjutor bishop, Martin J. Spalding, assisted in administering the diocese. Known as the "Patriarch of the West" in Catholic circles because of his forty years as bishop, Flaget died in Louisville, which had become the seat of his diocese in 1841.

• Flaget's personal papers were not preserved, though a considerable number of his letters to contemporaries can be found in various collections at the University of Notre Dame Archives, the Archives of the Archdiocese of St. Louis, the Archives of the Archdiocese of Baltimore, the Sulpician Archives at St. Mary's in Baltimore and at St. Sulpice in Paris, France, and the archives of Kentucky-based religious orders such as the Sisters of Charity of Nazareth and the Sisters of Loretto. Charles Lemarié located Flaget's extant letters for the massive *A Biography of Msgr. Benedict Joseph Flaget, 1763–1850*, trans. Mary Wedding (3 vols., 1992); the French original is *Le Patriarche de L'Quest: Flaget* (3 vols., 1982–1983). Scholarly but dated biographies are Herman J. Schauinger, *Cathedrals in the Wilderness* (1956), and Martin J. Spalding, *The Life, Times and Character of Bishop Flaget* (1852; repr. 1969). His life is carefully interpreted in Clyde F. Crews, *An American Holy Land: A History of the Archdiocese of Louisville* (1987).

JOSEPH M. WHITE

FLAGG, Azariah Cutting (28 Nov. 1790–24 Nov. 1873), newspaper editor and politician, was born in Orwell, Vermont, the son of Ebenezer Flagg and Elizabeth Cutting. In 1801 his parents apprenticed him to a cousin, a Burlington, Vermont, printer who over a period of five years taught him the trade. For the next five years, he was engaged in printing and publishing, and in 1811 he moved to Plattsburgh, New York. Two years later he founded the Plattsburgh *Republican*, a weekly newspaper he conducted until 1825. In 1814 he married Phoebe Maria Cole, with whom he had several children. Small of stature, unconventional and untidy in dress, Flagg was a prodigious worker and a hard-hitting journalist in the best tradition of political journalism during the 1820s. A veteran of the War of 1812, during which he served in the defense of Plattsburgh, New York, Flagg's patriotic views were popular with the citizens of his adopted hometown, and they elected him to the legislature three times from 1823 to 1826. In the legislature, he made such a mark in matters of state finance that he was brought to the attention of DeWitt Clinton. Under Clinton's patronage, Flagg was appointed secretary of state. He moved to Albany, New York, in 1826.

Flagg soon broke with Clinton to join Martin Van Buren's Bucktail faction of the Jeffersonian Republican party. He formed a close personal and political friendship with Van Buren, Silas Wright, and William L. Marcy, who were creating what would become the Democratic party in the state. A leading member of a small group of politicians that came to be known as the "Albany Regency," Flagg served as comptroller of the state from 1834 to 1839 and from 1842 to 1846 and as the Regency's principal manager of state politics during the absences of Van Buren, Wright, and Marcy, who were frequently occupied in Washington.

A caustic critic of Nicholas Biddle (1786–1844) and of the second Bank of the United States, Flagg's editorials in the *Albany Argus* on that subject gained him a wide readership among Jacksonian Democrats during the early 1830s. Although closely identified with New York politics, his reputation as a financial expert, skillful editorial writer, and gifted public servant was promoted by Van Buren, Wright, and other prominent New Yorkers in Washington. Flagg soon became an important and respected figure among the national leaders of the Democratic party.

A Jacksonian in politics and a dedicated agrarian by conviction, Flagg believed the free, independent farmer formed the basis of all human society. Consequently, he supported free trade, hard money, and above all states' rights, though he vehemently opposed John C. Calhoun's doctrine of state sovereignty and nullification.

In 1842 Flagg was instrumental in pushing the so-called "stop and tax policy" that reversed the expansive economic program of William H. Seward's Whig administration in New York. These conservative fiscal measures provided appropriate funding for the debt and preserved the state from threatened insolvency. From 1837 through 1842 the issues of state banking and state funded internal development split the Democratic party in New York into two factions. Flagg became a prominent spokesperson for conservative economic policies locally and for opposition to southern domination of the party nationally. Denominated the "Barnburners," Flagg's group opposed the "Hunkers," who championed state support for banking and transportation and who acquiesced in southern control of the national party organization.

After the election of James K. Polk to the presidency in 1844, Van Buren and Wright, leaders of the Barnburners, proposed Flagg for secretary of the Treasury. Polk rejected their advice and in fact appointed a disproportionate number of Hunkers to important federal posts, thus contributing to the eventual breakup of the national party organization into northern and southern wings.

Always opposed to slavery in principle, Flagg supported the Wilmot Proviso, which would prohibit the introduction of slavery into the territories, and endorsed the Free Soil party in 1848 with others of the Barnburner faction. After the presidential election, he returned to the Democratic party. Flagg moved to New York City in 1846, where he became city controller in 1852, a position he held for seven years. His tenure was characterized by his customary careful accounting policies and budgetary restraints.

Flagg remained interested in politics and economic issues for the remainder of his life. He became a member of the Republican party after 1854 and supported its policies during the Civil War. Although blind by

1859, he nevertheless continued to be active in public affairs, assisted by his daughters, who kept him abreast of the political, social, and economic issues of the day. He died at his home on London Terrace and Twenty-third Street in New York City, the last surviving member of the 1823 New York State legislative session.

• Flagg's correspondence with Van Buren, Wright, and other notables of his era is in the New York Public Library, but some additional letters are in the Van Buren and Marcy papers at the Library of Congress, the John A. Dix Papers at Columbia University, and the Samuel J. Tilden Collection at the New York Public Library. Flagg himself set forth his hard money views in his *Banks and Banking in the State of New York* (1868). No biography or memoirs trace his important political career. Two excellent though biased political histories of New York are good sources for Flagg's activities: Jabez D. Hammond, *History of Political Parties in the State of New York* (2 vols., 1846), and De Alva Stanwood, *A Political History of the State of New York* (3 vols., 1909). Ransome H. Gillet, *Life and Times of Silas Wright* (2 vols., 1874), is a useful compendium. John A. Garraty's modern biography, *Silas Wright* (1949), must be consulted for comments on Flagg, Wright's closest friend. John Niven, *Martin Van Buren, the Romantic Age of American Politics*, and Arthur Schlesinger, Jr., *The Age of Jackson*, deal with Flagg's role in the party battles and the economic and financial contests of the Jacksonian Era. Robert V. Remini, *Martin Van Buren and the Making of the Democratic Party* (1954), is also a valuable source for Flagg's relationship with the Albany Regency. Flagg's obituaries in the New York *Tribune* and the *New York Times* are brief and of little value.

JOHN NIVEN

FLAGG, Edmund (24 Nov. 1815–1 Nov. 1890), author and civil servant, was born in Wiscasset, Maine, the son of Edmund Flagg and Harriet Payson. He graduated with distinction from Bowdoin College in 1835. Later that year he moved with his widowed mother and sister to Louisville, Kentucky, where he briefly taught the classics in a boys' school. The following summer, he explored the Illinois and Missouri prairies and published in the *Louisville Daily Journal* a few essays based on his observations called "Tales of a Traveller." Their popularity helped Flagg establish a connection with the *Journal* lasting until 1861. He studied law in St. Louis in 1837–1838, passed the bar, and published some articles in the *St. Louis Daily Commercial Bulletin*, of which he was associate editor briefly. He reissued his travel sketches as *The Far West* (2 vols., 1838). Returning to Kentucky in 1839, he became comanager of the *Louisville News Letter*.

Poor health forced Flagg to move to Vicksburg, Mississippi, where he became a partner in a law firm. By this time, he had begun to publish poems and romantic fiction and to distribute some of his plays. He also edited the *Vicksburg Daily Whig*. The rival newspaper was the *Sentinel*, whose fiery editor held opposing opinions. The two men quarreled over politics and fought a duel in which Flagg was wounded. In 1842 Flagg moved to Marietta, Ohio, where he edited the *Weekly Gazette* for two years, after which he returned

to St. Louis, edited the *Evening Gazette*, became a court reporter, published a book on *Mutual Insurance* (1846), and polished some of his plays.

In 1849 Flagg entered the field of international diplomacy. He served as secretary to the American minister in Berlin and traveled widely in Europe. In 1849 he also published *Edmond Dantes*, which was advertised as a continuation of the plot and in the style of Alexandre Dumas's famous novel *The Count of Monte Cristo*. Largely by means of stilted dialogue, Flagg's novel presents Dantes as the deputy of Marseilles whose formidable intelligence, wealth, and eloquence make him the secret power behind the French revolution of February 1848. Flagg returned to St. Louis to resume his law practice but was quickly appointed consul to the port of Venice, in 1850. While there, he was also foreign correspondent for several American newspapers. He returned to St. Louis in 1852, edited its *Democratic Times*, and wrote *Venice: The City of the Sea* (1853). He also contributed several essays to the *United States Illustrated* in 1853–1854, in which he described urban and rural locales in the West.

Flagg moved to Washington, D.C., in 1854. While there, he was a statistician in the Department of State (1854–1857), a journalist (1858–1860), and the Department of the Interior official in charge of issuing copyrights (1861–1870). The most significant of several he wrote was the massive *Report of the Commercial Relations of the United States with All Foreign Nations* (4 vols., 1856–1857); 20,000 copies were printed, and the work was commended for its copious details. Married in 1862 to Kate Adeline Gallaher of West Virginia, Flagg moved with his wife in 1871 to "Highland View," a farm near Falls Church, Virginia. The couple had four children, one of whom who died in early infancy. The continuing popularity of *Edmond Dantes* encouraged him, though tardily, to follow it with *Monte Cristo's Daughter* (date unavailable, not later than 1880, often reprinted). He also wrote *De Molai: The Last of the Military Grand Masters of the Order of Templar Knights* (1888). Detailing the efforts of King Philip IV of France to centralize his power by suppressing the Order of Templars, *De Molai* combines erudite criticism of both King Philip and his Avignonese pope, Clement V, with praise of brave old Jacques de Molay, burned at the stake in 1314 during the French Inquisition. The novel features a melodramatic subplot involving two women vying for a handsome young Templar.

Flagg wrote several historical dramas, the best being *Mary Tudor* (1844) and *Catherine Howard* (1847). He also wrote several historical romances based on Victor Hugo's dramas, the best being *Ruy Blas*, published in 1845 in the *New World*, edited by Park Benjamin (1809–1864), who had also published as *New World* "extra numbers" in 1843 Flagg's short stories "Francis of Valois; or, The Curse of St. Valliar: A Tale of the Middle Ages" and "Carrero; or, The Prime Minister." The most noteworthy of Flagg's many poems scattered in various newspapers were featured in *The Native Poets of Maine* (1854). Two were anthologized in *The Poets and Poetry of the West* (1864). The subtitle of Flagg's detailed, informative, but stilted *Far West* indicates its scope: *A Tour beyond the Mountains, Embracing Outlines of Western Life and Scenery; Sketches of the Prairies, Rivers, Ancient Mounds, Early Settlements of the French, Etc., Etc.* His painstakingly thorough *Venice: The City of the Sea* displays great descriptive power but is less pictorial than historical, as is indicated by its subtitle, *From the Invasion by Napoleon in 1797 to the Capitulation to Radetzky in 1849; with a Contemporaneous View of the Peninsula.* Perhaps the most readable today of anything from Flagg's tireless pen is his solid *De Molai.*

Flagg died at his Virginia farm home. In his day, he was popular and respected as a versatile literary romancer and also as an expert on foreign affairs. Now, however, he is an all-but-forgotten figure. His energy, ambition, and diverse interests impelled him to seek success in too many fields.

• The following contain biographical information: William T. Cogeshall, ed., *The Poets and Poetry of the West: With Biographical and Critical Notices* (1864), p. 201; "The Late Edmund Flagg," *Washington Evening Star*, 17 Jan. 1891; and "Class of 1835," *Library Bulletin of Bowdoin College*, no. 1–4 (June 1891–June 1895), pp. 45–46. The following provide bibliographical data: "List of the Published Writings of Edmund Flagg," *Library Bulletin of Bowdoin College*, no. 1–4 (June 1891–June 1895), pp. 36–38, and Richard Fyfe Boyce and Katherine Randall Boyce, *American Foreign Service Authors: A Bibliography* (1973), pp. 111–12.

ROBERT L. GALE

FLAGG, Ernest (6 Feb. 1857–10 Apr. 1947), architect and urban reformer, was born in Brooklyn, New York, the son of Jared Bradley Flagg, a clergyman and artist, and Louisa Hart. After his mother's death in 1872, Flagg abandoned his formal education and found employment in a series of marginal businesses in New York City. Later he worked as a developer in partnership with his father and brother, an experience that stimulated his interest in architecture and urban reform. Flagg's cousin Cornelius Vanderbilt II provided financial support for his study at the École des Beaux-Arts in Paris (1889–1890). There Flagg joined the atelier of Paul Blondel and was joined by Walter B. Chambers, with whom he later formed a flexible partnership.

As a result of his study in Paris, Flagg gained an exceptionally accurate understanding of beaux-arts methods and theory. Through learning from Blondel and studying the writings of the mid-century theorist Charles Blanc, Flagg learned the concept of *parti*, or "the logical solution of the problem from his [the architect's] dual standpoint as constructor and artist" from Paul Blondel and the writings of midcentury theorist Charles Blanc. In the 1890s this concept reconciled the diverse objectives that had characterized late beaux-arts theory and design: art and science, aesthetics and technology, intuition and reason.

Flagg returned to the United States in 1891. Armed with the business acumen he had acquired during his early career and well trained in beaux-arts theory and design, Flagg began a forty-year practice producing innovative designs for institutions, skyscrapers, and urban housing for the privileged as well as for the working classes. Among the American architects of his generation, Flagg promoted the broadest spectrum of beaux-arts theory and design. Based on his notion of *parti*, a theory of choice, Flagg stressed academic classicism, idealism, and ceremonial planning. He also regarded as optional design solutions the legacies of structural rationalism and the néo-grec movement (a French development in which architects of rationalist persuasion, most notably Henri Labrouste, sought to adopt the reasoned principles of Greek and Byzantine architecture). Flagg's methods considered the special needs of each building type or program. Private institutions such as the Corcoran Gallery of Art, Washington, D.C. (1892–1897), and St. Luke's Hospital in New York City (1892–1897), as well as public institutions such as the U.S. Naval Academy complex at Annapolis, Maryland (1896–1908), combined academic classicism and idealism with formal beaux-arts planning and an emphasis on public space, all of which were characteristic of what he called "the French school."

Some of Flagg's most inventive designs were for commercial and utilitarian buildings. An early proponent of skeletal steel framing, Flagg employed it for the Singer Tower at 149 Broadway in New York City (1896–1898; 1906–1908; demolished 1967–1968). The 47-story tower was the first of the skyscrapers of needle-like proportions that later characterized the spectacular New York skyline of the 1920s and 1930s. On its completion in 1908, the 612-foot Singer Tower became the tallest building in the world. Its metal cross-bracing, modeled after the trussed structure of the 1889 Eiffel Tower in Paris, countered torsion twisting. The Singer skyscraper also demonstrated Flagg's solution to zoning reform—a tower, set back and restricted to one-quarter of its site, thus permitting it to rise indefinitely—that was later incorporated into the New York Zoning Resolution of 1916. Other commercial and utilitarian buildings united French aestheticism with structural rationalism, inspired by Eugene Emmanuel Viollet-Le-Duc and his followers. In his design for the Singer Loft Building in New York City (1902–1904), Flagg conveyed a reasoned approach to architecture as decorated structure. The Singer Loft illustrates Flagg's attempt to introduce a rational architecture to America by uniting the American system of skeletal framing with a French approach to decorated construction. From a structural point of view, the Singer Loft Building is inventive. However, it raises a conflict between rationalism and functionalism—between rendering the structure explicit and, at the same time, attempting to fireproof it. In the Scribner Building at 597 Fifth Avenue, New York City (1912–1913), Flagg's design was especially French, reflecting some of the best Parisian commercial architecture of the early Third Republic (1871–1900). At Scribner's Flagg employed a steel frame (covered with a thin veneer of limestone) to support the structure and thereby permit a daringly open storefront of ornamental iron and transparent glass. Nowhere in Manhattan was the rational correspondence between exterior and interior more explicitly and eloquently affirmed.

In domestic architecture Flagg was considerably less committed to the orthodoxy of "the French school." In his domestic designs he often employed a hybrid of colonial revival and "modern French Renaissance" styles in the belief that such building would advance the search for a national style of architecture in America as a logical evolution from historical precedents. Flagg synthesized these styles in his townhouse at 109 East Fortieth Street, New York City (1905–1907; demolished), and his country house, "Stone Court," on Staten Island (1898–1899; 1907–1909), as well as in the Alfred Corning Clark House, Riverside Drive, New York City (1898–1900; demolished).

Flagg is regarded as a committed urban reformer and, according to the New York architect I. N. Phelps Stokes, the "father of the modern model tenement in this country." His light-court plan (configured on a 100′ × 100′ lot) replaced the notorious 'dumb-bell' plan (employing a standard 25′ × 100′ city lot) and was first realized in his Alfred Corning Clark buildings, New York City (1896–98; demolished), built by the City and Suburban Homes Company. Flagg later formed his own company to build fireproof tenement housing in New York City and Flagg Court, an apartment complex in Brooklyn, New York (1933–1937).

Flagg was also an ingenious inventor and a student of classical systems of proportion. He registered more than thirty U.S. patents, most of which improved on house construction techniques. After World War I he adapted Greek principles of proportion to small home design and construction, also inventing an economical method of concrete and stone construction that later influenced Frank Lloyd Wright. Flagg published many of his designs, including the Staten Island cottage "Bow-Cot" (1917), in *Small Houses: Their Economic Design and Construction* (1922).

Flagg was one of the most inventive beaux-arts architects in America. He did not achieve professional recognition until 1911, when he was elected to the American Institute of Architects. Flagg advanced the cause of French classicism in America, challenged a generation of architects to reject revivalism based on "archaeology" in favor of a reasoned approach to design based on Beaux-Arts principles, promoted height and density reform for skyscrapers, and improved housing for the urban poor.

In 1899 Flagg married Margaret Elizabeth Bonnell of Staten Island; they had one child. Flagg died in New York City.

• The most extensive collection of Flagg's papers, both personal and professional, is at the Avery Architectural and Fine Arts Library, Columbia University. Flagg's architectural writings include "The École des Beaux-Arts," *Architectural Record* 3 (Jan.–Mar. 1894): 302–13, (Apr.–June 1894): 419–28, and 4 (July–Sept.): 38–43; "The New York Tenement-House Evil and Its Cure," *Scribner's Magazine*, July 1894, pp. 108–17; "Influence of the French School on Architecture in the United States," *Architectural Record* 4 (Oct.–Dec. 1894): 210–28; and "The Limitation of Height and Area of Buildings in New York," *American Architect and Building News*, 15 Apr. 1908, pp. 125–27. He is also the author of *Genealogical Notes on the Founding of New England: My Ancestors Part in That Undertaking* (1926) and *The Parthenon Naos* (1928). The most comprehensive analysis of Flagg's architectural career is Mardges Bacon, *Ernest Flagg: Beaux-Arts Architect and Urban Reformer* (1986). Other publications include two articles by Harry W. Desmond, "The Works of Ernest Flagg," *Architectural Record* 11 (1902): 1–104, and "A Rational Skyscraper," *Architectural Record* 15 (1904): 274–84. An obituary is in the *New York Times*, 11 Apr. 1947.

MARDGES BACON

FLAGG, James Montgomery (18 June 1877–27 May 1960), artist and author, was born in Pelham Manor, New York, the son of Elisha Flagg, a businessman, and Anna Elida Coburn, a socialite. Flagg attended public schools in Brooklyn and New York City, then a private institution called Dr. Chapin's School (1889–1891), and finally the Horace Mann School in New York (1891–1893). When he was twelve, he sold a drawing to the children's magazine *St. Nicholas* for $10. At fourteen he sold another, to *Life*, for $8. At sixteen he was on the staff of both *Life* and *Judge* and was sent by the editor at *St. Nicholas* to report on the World's Columbian Exposition (Chicago, 1893). He took what he later called useless lessons at the Art Students League in New York (1894–1898) and in Bushey, England (1898–1899).

Back home in 1899, Flagg married St. Louis socialite Nellie McCormick, eleven years his senior; they had no children. At this time his parents were living in London, where his father was manager of the American Express office. Overseas again, Flagg drew sketches for his *Yankee Girls Abroad* (1900) and also studied painting in Paris (1899–1900) under Victor Marec, whose vivid portrait he painted and exhibited in the Paris Salon of 1900. During the next four years Flagg and his wife traveled to California—including Hollywood—Florida, and Virginia and summered in Europe.

Beginning in 1904 Flagg maintained a New York residence. He had a studio on West Sixty-seventh Street until 1921 and thereafter on West Fifty-seventh Street. He enjoyed a phenomenal career as an illustrator in pen and ink and in brush and scratch; as a portraitist in oil, watercolor, charcoal, and tempera; and as a saucy author. As covers and inside, his pictures appeared in the humorous magazines *Life* and *Judge* and in *Cosmopolitan, Everybody's, Good Housekeeping, Harper's, Harper's Weekly, Liberty, Redbook, Scribner's,* and *Woman's Home Companion*. Often a picture by Flagg was published somewhere every week. He drew cartoons to ridicule advertisers' slogans—for example, a hungry lion captioned "I'd Walk a Mile for a Camel!" He published the following books of illustrations, texts, and humorous short poems: *Tomfoolery* (1904), "*If*": *A Guide to Bad Manners* (1905), *Why They Mar-*

ried (1906), and *All in the Same Boat* (1908). He published satirical illustrations in his *City People* (1909) and *The Well-Knowns as Seen by James Montgomery Flagg* (1914), wrote and illustrated *The Adventures of Kitty Cobb* (1912) about a country girl seeking love and adventure in the city, and published two collections of satirical short stories: *I Should Say So* (1914) and *The Mystery of the Hated Man* (1916). His targets include marriage and motherhood, children, pets, dinner parties and picnics, politics and Prohibition. He joined many clubs and even cofounded one, the Dutch Treat Club (1911). With his rapierlike wit, natty attire, and handsome features, highlighted by satanic eyebrows, he was extremely popular with advertising agents, actors, singers, celebrities of various sorts, and society leaders.

In 1917, when the United States entered World War I, Governor Charles S. Whitman of New York appointed Flagg military artist of the state. Flagg also joined a group of fellow artists to form the Division of Pictorial Publicity to create posters on order from various federal agencies in Washington, D.C. He drew and designed forty-six posters that were used nationally. Best known was his 1917 picture of Uncle Sam, with white hat, blue hatband and jacket, white shirt, red neckpiece, white hair and goatee, staring eyes, aquiline nose, jutting lower lip, and his right index finger pointed at the viewer over a caption reading, "I Want You for U.S. Army/Nearest Recruiting Station." Four million copies were lithographed for wide distribution, and it became the most famous poster in the history of popular art. Flagg used his own face as a model for Uncle Sam's. Flagg's "Tell That to the Marines," also popular, shows a tough American in civilian clothes pulling off his coat to fight, on learning by newspaper headline of German wartime atrocities. For this poster, Flagg, a skillful sculptor, made a clay model. Flagg sketched a free portrait of any person who purchased a $1,000 Liberty Bond, and he was active in writing and supervising the production of American Red Cross and U.S. Marine movies.

In 1917 and 1918 Flagg wrote scripts for and helped produce twenty-four short silent films and even acted in a few. The first twelve comprised a series called *Girls You Know*. In the 1920s and 1930s, by which time he was earning up to $75,000 annually, he drew and painted pictures of Hollywood's most celebrated stars, from William S. Hart and W. C. Fields to Greta Garbo and John Barrymore, and dozens in between. More detailed, finished, and expressive are his oil portraits, especially those of Ethel Barrymore, John Barrymore, Irwin Shrewsbury Cobb, Booth Tarkington, and Mark Twain.

In 1923 Nellie Flagg died. A year later Flagg married Dorothy Virginia Wadman, formerly one of his models; the couple had one child. They took a riotous honeymoon by driving from New York to California and back again. The literary result was Flagg's *Boulevards All the Way—Maybe* (1925), which he also illustrated. Reviewers found the breezy report of "super driver" and "motor queen" concerning roads, weath-

er, and Americans encountered either carefree, amiable, and humorous, or cheap and jaunty.

Never a faithful husband, Flagg associated from 1929 to 1937 with Ilse Hoffmann, his young, petulant, German-born model who was half his age. He later called her the one love of his life. The unbalanced woman boasted of other lovers, married unhappily elsewhere, returned briefly to Flagg, and committed suicide in her apartment in 1937. Meanwhile, his second wife suffered a hushed-up, permanent psychiatric breakdown, and he institutionalized her privately at his expense. In 1936 and 1937 Flagg and his father relished summer transatlantic voyages and fun in Europe. In 1937 Flagg met President Franklin Delano Roosevelt, in connection with posters about forest fires for the U.S. Department of Forestry.

Flagg relished his popularity—even notoriety—and capitalized on it by frequently speaking in public and on the radio. When World War II began, he designed recruitment and Red Cross posters. He also created a campaign poster for Roosevelt's reelection. Some 400,000 copies of his famous 1917 Uncle Sam poster were also reprinted and widely displayed. By the early 1940s Flagg's health began to fail, and his eyesight grew weaker. Even so, he published *Roses and Buckshot* (1946), his cocky, unrestrained autobiography. Though valuable for its revelations about Flagg and his notable friends (and enemies), it is not altogether reliable as to dates and facts—which some reviewers were quick to point out. Among his several other publications is *Celebrities* (1951), a collection of his Hollywood drawings, with glib running commentary. Flagg was miserably unhappy during his final years. He hated both the absence of his old peers and his increasing physical debility. He died in New York City.

Flagg was popular for his clean-lined art more than he was of value for his professional opinions. In his practice and his criticism, he remained static. For example, he regarded women as mainly of interest for their physical charms, and he delighted in ridiculing artists more experimental than he was, especially the French impressionists and Pablo Picasso. He said that Auguste Renoir's works would seem to have been painted with lipstick and pillow feathers, while Picasso's resembled graffiti in chalk by nasty boys. All the same, his Uncle Sam, with its burning intensity, remains a permanent icon.

• Susan E. Meyer, *James Montgomery Flagg* (1974), contains an informative biographical and critical text and is lavishly illustrated. An obituary is in the *New York Times*, 28 May 1960.

ROBERT L. GALE

FLAGG, Josiah (28 May 1737–30 Dec. 1794), musician and soldier, was born in Woburn, Massachusetts, the son of Gershom Flagg, and Martha Johnson. Sometime before 1747 Josiah moved with his family to Boston, where one of his boyhood friends was Paul Revere. In about 1750 Flagg, Revere, and five other boys formed themselves into a society of bell ringers and petitioned Christ (Episcopal) Church for permission to play on the church's bells. The exact manner of Flagg's musical education is not known. It is likely that he attended one or more singing schools in the Boston area and perhaps took lessons from the organist at Christ Church. His subsequent activities reveal him to have been a well-rounded musician who was aware of recent fashions in European music. In 1760 he married Elizabeth Hawkes; they had eight children.

In 1764 Flagg compiled and published *A Collection of the Best Psalm Tunes*, for which Revere did the engraving. This volume contained 119 pieces of sacred music, making it the largest music collection printed in America to that time. It was also the first New England tunebook to contain pieces in more than three parts. Two other important features of the book—a heavy reliance on European tunes and the use of American-made paper—were pointed out in the compiler's preface: "however we are oblig'd to the other side the Atlantick *chiefly*, for our Tunes, the Paper on which they are printed is the Manufacture of our own Country." A handful of the tunes have not been traced to European origins and may have been written by Americans. At least sixty pieces received their first American printings in this book, one of which, a "March of Richard 3d," the earliest publication of music by George F. Handel in the New World; the piece was an arrangement from Handel's opera *Riccardo Primo*.

Two years later Flagg published another tunebook, *Sixteen Anthems . . . to Which Is Added, a Few Psalm Tunes* (1766), for which he did the engraving himself. As with *A Collection of the Best Psalm Tunes*, *Sixteen Anthems* focused on British music. Unlike the earlier volume, however, *Sixteen Anthems* emphasized lengthier pieces; this was the largest collection of anthems—extended musical settings of prose texts—that had yet appeared in America. Flagg advertised himself as a teacher of singing schools during this period, and both *A Collection of the Best Psalm Tunes* and *Sixteen Anthems* were designed primarily for this use. Flagg might also have been involved in the production of William Billings's *New-England Psalm-Singer* (Boston, 1770), the earliest tunebook to contain only music by an American composer. Flagg was listed on the title page as one of the salesmen of Billings's tunebook. Furthermore, the *New-England Psalm-Singer* was engraved with the same tools as *Sixteen Anthems*, suggesting that Flagg might have done this work or at least lent his equipment to Billings.

A different side of Flagg's musical ability was revealed between 1769 and 1773, when he organized and performed in a series of at least six public concerts held in Boston and one in Providence, Rhode Island (1771). Several of the Boston concerts were accompanied by a Band of the 64th Regiment that Flagg claimed to have organized and trained. He also appeared in the Boston programs as vocal soloist, and perhaps as conductor and organist. Music by Handel and other European composers played a prominent

part in the concerts, but a few compositions by recent American immigrants such as W. S. Morgan were included as well.

In addition to these musical activities, Flagg earned at least part of his living in Boston as a jeweler. He was involved in the Sons of Liberty, a proindependence group in which his friend Revere was also active.

Flagg apparently moved from Boston shortly after his 1773 concert there, for the outbreak of the American Revolution found him in Rhode Island, where he served as a major in the state's armed forces. In 1779 he was promoted to lieutenant colonel, a rank he still held at the war's end. Sometime between 1784 and 1790 he returned to Boston, where he set up shop as an engraver. He remained in Boston until his death from unknown causes.

Flagg is not known to have participated in any musical activities after 1773. However, he was not forgotten by the Boston musical world, for a month after his death a benefit concert was arranged for his widow, which netted the sum of $102.

Flagg was one of early America's most versatile musicians. Many eighteenth-century American musicians participated either in teaching singing schools and compiling tunebooks or in concertizing; Flagg did both. His known musical activities included work as an impresario, bell-ringing, singing, playing the organ, teaching, editing and publishing music, and possibly conducting as well; the only significant omission from this list is composition. He was an early advocate of the music of Handel and other European classical composers and helped direct the attention of Americans to recent trends in transcontinental music. At the same time, his activities helped to promote American musicians and compositions, not to mention American independence.

• The fullest account of Flagg's life and work is David W. Music, "Josiah Flagg," *American Music* 7 (1989): 140–58. Information on his tunebooks can be found in Ralph T. Daniel, *The Anthem in New England before 1800* (1966), and especially Allen Perdue Britton et al., *American Sacred Music Imprints, 1698–1810: A Bibliography* (1990). Flagg's Boston concerts are discussed in O. G. Sonneck, *Early Concert-Life in America (1731–1800)* (1907). Reprints of eighteenth-century Boston newspaper advertisements and some other contemporary documents related to Flagg are found in *Music in Colonial Massachusetts, 1630–1820*, vol. 2: *Music in Homes and in Churches* (1985).

DAVID W. MUSIC

FLAGG, Josiah Foster (11 Jan. 1789–20 Dec. 1853), dentist and artist, was born in Boston, Massachusetts, the son of Josiah Flagg, Jr., the first dentist born in the United States; his mother's maiden name was probably Foster. He is often confused with John Foster Brewster Flagg, his brother, and Joseph Foster Flagg, his nephew, both of whom also became prominent dentists. As a boy he displayed little interest in book learning and instead preferred farm chores and working with wood. At age sixteen he became an apprentice cabinetmaker and shortly thereafter developed an intense desire to obtain a scholastic education. After completing the course of study at an academy in Plainfield, Connecticut, in 1811 he began studying medicine with J. C. Warren, a Boston physician. During the next two years he designed the bone-forceps for cutting bone and removing the resultant fragments. He also carved the woodcut engravings of the pictures and diagrams that illustrate Warren's *Anatomical Description of the Arteries of the Human Body* (1813), a translation of a work by the Swiss anatomist Albrecht von Haller. Shortly thereafter Flagg enrolled in Boston Medical College, from which he received an M.D. in 1815.

That same year Flagg opened a medical and surgical practice in Dover, New Hampshire, which he later relocated to Uxbridge, Massachusetts. In 1818 he married Mary Wait; they had no children. That same year he relocated his practice to Boston at Warren's insistence. Within a year he was devoting the greatest part of his attention to dentistry and for a number of years was the only dental surgeon in Boston. He authored *The Family Dentist* (1822), a treatise on the structure and formation of human teeth and the diseases that afflict them, in which he attacked the deleterious and widespread practice of removing cavities by filing or sawing through healthy portions of dental enamel and advocated instead the removal of caries by means of small knives or similar cutting instruments. In 1828 he designed a set of adjustable forceps that could be adapted to fit the neck of any tooth regardless of its size or shape.

Shortly thereafter Flagg turned his attention to the manufacture of artificial teeth. At the time most false teeth were either carved from ivory or fashioned from the teeth of hippopotamuses, cows, or humans; none of these materials offered the requisite durability. Some artificial teeth were made from French porcelain, but although they did not deteriorate, they looked too unnatural to be satisfactory. The first teeth Flagg produced, which were shaped from clay and then baked in a kiln, looked genuine enough but lasted no longer than any of the others. Two years later he began collaborating with N. C. Keep, a fellow dentist; after examining and rejecting a variety of materials such as mineral paste and metal they worked closely for about six months with a minerologist, who provided them with a substantial amount of high-grade feldspar, and a chemist, who developed a coating that was comparable in durability and color to tooth enamel. In 1833 Flagg and Keep developed a method for molding porcelain teeth that were incorruptible and appeared to be real. This method was used to manufacture artificial teeth for a number of decades and proved to be so lucrative that some dentists refused to teach it to their apprentices.

In 1844 Flagg began experimenting with an improved method for preparing a decayed tooth for a filling. At the time, cavities were removed by rotating a metal burr between finger and thumb; the exposed nerve that often resulted normally was not removed before the gold-leaf filling was inserted, frequently

causing the patient much unnecessary pain at a later date. Three years later Flagg developed a drill adapted partly from a finger-ring / drill-socket device invented by Amos Westcott, a dentist and inventor in Syracuse, New York, and partly from the bow drill used by watchmakers. He then used this device to drill into the tooth's pulp chamber and remove the nerve ending as well as the cavity before filling the tooth.

Despite attaining a large and profitable dental practice, Flagg remained interested in general medicine and surgery all his life. In 1821 he adapted Desault's apparatus, essentially a bandage used to set broken collarbones, so that it could be used on fractured thigh bones as well, and in 1828 he developed the box or trough splint for setting the longer bones.

In 1839 Flagg became one of the first physicians in the United States to promote publicly the practice of homeopathy, a school of medicine that holds that a patient's condition can best be cured by administering minute doses of drugs or treatments that induce in healthy individuals the same symptoms from which the patient suffers. Despite the fierce opposition of many of his medical colleagues, he conducted a series of scientific experiments concerning the principles of homeopathy and subscribed to these principles until his death.

In 1846 Flagg became involved in the so-called ether controversy. That same year William T. G. Morton, a Boston dental surgeon, had successfully employed during a tooth extraction an anesthetic he called "letheon." When Morton attempted to obtain a patent, Flagg's brother showed that letheon was nothing more than washed sulfuric ether, whereupon Flagg became a vociferous opponent of granting the rights to its use to any one individual. After much heated debate, Morton's application was withdrawn, and ether was made available to the medical community at large.

In 1840 Flagg became a charter member and first vice president of the American Society of Dental Surgeons. He also played an instrumental role in the establishment of the Boston School of Design for Women. He died in Boston.

Flagg was one of the foremost dental surgeons of his day. His primary contribution to dentistry consists of his development of a process for making natural-looking, long-lasting artificial teeth.

• Flagg's papers have not been located. A biography is in Burton Lee Thorpe, *Biographies of Pioneer American Dentists and Their Successors*, vol. 3 of *History of Dental Surgery*, ed. Charles R. E. Koch (1910), pp. 123–28. An obituary is in the *Boston Medical and Surgical Journal*, 11 Jan. 1854.

CHARLES W. CAREY, JR.

FLAGG, Wilson (5 Nov. 1805–6 May 1884), naturalist and writer, was born Thomas Wilson Flagg in Beverly, Massachusetts, the son of Isaac Flagg and Elizabeth Frances Wilson. An 1821 graduate of Phillips Andover Academy, he also studied medicine (at Harvard and elsewhere) but never became a practicing physician. He married Caroline Eveleth in 1840 and lived in Massachusetts throughout his life. He was a writer for a number of magazines, including the *Atlantic Monthly*. As Wilson Flagg (he dropped "Thomas") he was the author of several influential books. Beginning in 1857, with the publication of *Studies in the Field and Forest*, the world of nature became his overriding concern and a theme which continued through his subsequent writings. Flagg was also a devoted family man who was disdainful of "personal adventure." In a dedication to *Woods and By-Ways of New England* (1872), Flagg spoke of the satisfactions of his family life—with his wife and two sons—as being the source of his happiness.

Flagg's numerous writings vary widely in quality. An early volume, *Analysis of Female Beauty* (1834), in verse and prose, is a work of scant merit, and perhaps served as little more than a kind of apprenticeship for later, more substantial writings. *The Tailor's Shop* (1844) is also a badly flawed work, an imitative and mostly unsuccessful attempt at satire. Flagg's writings about nature, however, reveal him as a thoughtful and systematic observer who had sympathy with and concern for the natural environment. Although he limited himself to studies which were close to home and relatively easy to perform, Flagg wrote about his topic directly and convincingly. One of Flagg's articles in the *Atlantic*, "The Birds of the Pasture and Forest" (Dec. 1858), captured the interest of the naturalist John Burroughs.

In 1857 Henry David Thoreau wrote a letter to his friend Daniel Ricketson in which he evaluated Flagg's writings on nature. Flagg, said Thoreau, seemed a serious writer, but "he is not alert enough. He wants stirring up with a pole." Thoreau went on to characterize Flagg's "style" as "singularly vague" and lacking in the excitement generated by new ideas. Flagg took note of the comments made by Thoreau but seemed unconcerned—he was, he asserted, a person who had enjoyed living a "retired" life which was lacking in "enthusiasm." Although Thoreau expressed the hope that a person who wrote about nature would develop an enthusiasm for it, Flagg's appreciation of the natural world remained rather detached and quiet.

Flagg's love of nature may have been a weakness, as well as his greatest strength, in writing. One critic objected that his *Woods and By-Ways* was written in the "manner of a catalogue." Although Flagg condemned the "popular writers on nature's aspects," his own style could be characterized as more "popular" than serious. Recommending "old roads" to his readers, he comments: "The old road is bordered with wild shrubbery, groups of trees of bold and irregular growth—there is no sameness." In the sentence, a rather typical one, a lack of serious artistic purpose is apparent—there is none of the detail which one finds, for example, in the writings of Thoreau or of Burroughs. Flagg argued that his stylistic purpose was 'clearness and simplicity' and added that he avoided using metaphors because they 'tend to obscurity.' Flagg's artistic ability was unmistakably minor; nevertheless, he must be considered a writer of some historical importance. His contribution to an emerging American literature was as a member of a group of writers (which included Thoreau, Lowell, Burroughs, T. W. Higginson, and others) that established the "nature essay" as a distinct and legitimate genre. Flagg died in Cambridge, Massachusetts.

• Works of Flagg not previously mentioned are *Mount Auburn: Its Scenes, Its Beauties, and Its Lessons* (1861); *A Prize Essay on Agricultural Education* (1858); and *The Birds and Seasons of New England* (1875), which, along with *The Woods and By-Ways of New England*, was divided into three volumes in 1881: *Halcyon Days, A Year with the Birds*, and *A Year among the Trees*. N. G. and L. C. S. Flagg, *Family Records of the Descendents of Gersham Flagg* (1907), is a source of biographical information. See also W. G. Barton, "Thoreau, Flagg, and Burroughs," *Essex Institute Historical Collections* (Jan.–Mar. 1885). An obituary appears in the *Boston Transcript*, 7 May 1884.

RICHARD E. MEZO

FLAGLER, Henry Morrison (2 Jan. 1830–20 May 1913), businessman and railroad promoter, was born in Hopewell, just outside of Canadaigua, New York, the son of the Reverend Isaac Flagler, a Presbyterian minister, and Elizabeth Morrison. As a pioneer missionary preacher, Isaac Flagler earned no more than $300 to $400 a year. Henry attended the local district school until he was fourteen, when he decided to strike out on his own. He walked to the Erie Canal and worked his way west on a canal boat until he reached Buffalo, New York, where he took a lake boat to Sandusky, Ohio. South of Sandusky in the small town of Republic, Flagler joined a half brother, Daniel M. Harkness, who helped him get a clerkship in a country store at five dollars a month plus board. He saved his money both at Republic and at another store in Fostoria, Ohio. Having gained both experience and capital, Flagler in about 1850 moved to Bellevue, south of Sandusky, where he became a grain commission merchant. Some of the other Harknesses, relatives of his mother, lived in Bellevue. In 1853 Flagler married Mary Harkness, niece of Stephen V. Harkness, a leading citizen of Bellevue. The couple had three children. Flagler shipped grain to John D. Rockefeller, who was then engaged in the grain business in Cleveland, Ohio. Flagler also had an interest in a distillery in Bellevue but gave it up because he had conscientious scruples about the liquor traffic. During his decade in Bellevue, Flagler prospered, and by 1860 he had accumulated some $50,000 in the produce and grain business. Early in the 1860s Flagler moved to Saginaw, Michigan, a lumber and grain center. He sank several wells for the manufacture of salt and made some money from the heavy demand for salt during the Civil War. Massive overproduction followed the war's end, and the stiff competition soon put Flagler heavily in debt. The Flagler family moved to Cleveland late in 1865, and Stephen Harkness lent Flagler the money to establish a general merchandise firm. Within a rather short period Flagler fought his way back to prosperity. In the meantime brothers John D. and William Rockefeller had established an oil refinery in Cleveland.

When Flagler joined Rockefeller in 1866, he was nine years older than the senior partner. At age thirty-six Flagler was a dynamic and distinguished looking man with keen eyes, clean-cut features, and heavy dark hair and mustache. Polished and confident in speech, he had an alert and incisive mind. The two men were similar in several ways. Both had been born in western New York, had made early strides in business, had strong inclinations toward entrepreneurship, and had deep beliefs in religion. The two men quickly became good friends and daily discussed business affairs as they walked from the office to their Euclid Avenue homes. But Flagler and Rockefeller had different strengths that complemented each other. Flagler was energetic, bold, and aggressive, while Rockefeller was more deliberate, thoughtful, and judicious. Flagler could easily grasp the essentials of a problem and would prepare and draw up contracts that Rockefeller found very useful. Flagler invested his own modest capital in the growing oil firm and convinced his wife's uncle, Stephen Harkness, to invest even larger amounts as a silent partner. In 1867 the name of the Cleveland-based oil firm was changed from Rockefeller & Andrews to Rockefeller, Andrews & Flagler. Before long it was generally believed that next to Rockefeller himself, Flagler was the strongest partner in the firm. The third partner, Samuel Andrews, played only a minor role in the top management of the firm, dealing mainly with the technical work of refining. Flagler was the partner who arranged for large railroad rebates for the shipment of oil. Having earlier been a shipper of heavy grain traffic, Flagler knew many railroad officials. Earlier, during the summer, the firm had shipped much oil by lake and canal. Flagler now offered to stop these water shipments, move all the firm's oil by rail, and ship sixty carloads of oil every day of the year. In return he asked for a large rebate on all oil shipments, and the railroads agreed.

In 1870 the partnership of Rockefeller, Andrews & Flagler was replaced by the new Standard Oil Company of Ohio, with $1 million of stock. John D. Rockefeller was president, and Flagler was secretary and treasurer. The new firm prospered as it built and acquired additional oil refineries. Its earnings in 1873 reached $538,000, permitting a dividend of 15 percent. Flagler also played an important role in a merger of several major pipelines. In the late 1870s when severe legal problems began to threaten the Standard Oil Company of Ohio, Flagler helped create a giant trust arrangement to hold the numerous properties owned by the Rockefeller partners. In 1877 the Flaglers moved from Cleveland to New York City. Later, in 1882 Flagler was elected president of the newly formed Standard Oil Company of New Jersey. In 1883 the Rockefeller partners had total assets of nearly $73 million with net earnings for the year of more than $11 million. When Flagler gave up his active management

as a Rockefeller partner in the early 1880s, a fair estimate of his wealth would be between $10 and $20 million. He continued as a vice president until 1908 and as a director until 1911.

In 1882 Flagler had invested some money in Henry B. Plant's Investment Company, which planned to acquire railroads and hotels in Florida and other southern states. Flagler's wife, Mary Harkness Flagler, died in 1881. Two years later Flagler married Mary's nurse, Ida Alice Shourds. Their delayed honeymoon was in December of that year, and Flagler decided to visit Jacksonville and St. Augustine on Florida's northeast coast. Flagler was charmed with the climate and beauty of St. Augustine, one of the oldest towns in the United States. Flagler knew that a number of rich Americans each year spent part of their winter on the sunny shores of the French and Italian Riviera. He came to believe that many wealthy Americans could be induced to take winter vacations in Florida if the hotel and travel accommodations were properly upgraded and improved. Flagler decided to create an "American Riviera" in Florida. In the early 1880s Florida was a rural and undeveloped state. Its population in 1880 of 270,000 was only a sixth that of Georgia and a fifth that of Alabama. The bulk of Florida's population was in the northern half of the state, and the density of population in the southern half was less than two persons per square mile. In 1880 Florida had only 518 miles of railroad, far less than any other southern state. The railroads were all located in northern Florida, and many of them were narrow gauge.

In 1885 Flagler began to build at St. Augustine the Ponce de Leon, a large, magnificent hotel constructed of poured concrete and costing well over $1 million by the time it opened in January 1888. Also in the late 1880s he built a second hotel nearby, the Alcazar. Finding it difficult to get building materials delivered to St. Augustine, he purchased the rickety, narrow-gauge Jacksonville, St. Augustine & Halifax Railway. Flagler soon upgraded the 36-mile road and changed it to standard gauge. In 1889 he built a steel railway bridge over the St. Johns River to replace the ferry at Jacksonville. In 1892 the Flaglers built a fifteen-room winter home at St. Augustine named "Kirkside." Flagler acquired or built other railroads south of St. Augustine, and soon he owned resort hotels both at Ormond and Daytona Beach. Flagler's hotels were quickly crowded with visitors, but his railroads needed more business, especially additional freight traffic. Florida was a promising agricultural region, and soon fruit and pineapple crops were moving north over Flagler's railroad. In 1892 his railroad was renamed the Jacksonville, St. Augustine & Indian River Railway. By early 1893 Flagler's freight trains were hauling fruit out of Cocoa, 63 miles south of Daytona Beach and 175 miles south of Jacksonville. By 1894 Flagler's railroad was extended more than a hundred miles further south to Lake Worth and Palm Beach. He at once built two more large resort hotels, the Royal Poinciana and the Breakers. Both hotels were soon as popular as the earlier resorts in northern Florida. In the winter of 1894–1895 Florida experienced the coldest weather in a century. Severe cold both in December and February ruined the citrus crop and killed vegetables and coconut palms as far south as Palm Beach. Flagler moved quickly to aid the impoverished farmers. He gave free seed to the growers; fertilizer was hauled free of charge on his railroad. Flagler also made personal loans to some destitute farmers. In 1895 Flagler's railroad was renamed the Florida East Coast Railway.

Sixty-five miles south of Palm Beach and east of the Everglades, the Miami River flowed into Biscayne Bay. The few settlers living in the area had been untouched by the bad freeze of 1894–1895. Some of the residents along the Miami River urged Flagler to extend his railroad south to the Biscayne Bay. When Julia Tuttle, who owned 640 acres on Biscayne Bay, offered a major portion of her property as an inducement, Flagler agreed to extend the railroad down to the Miami River. The Florida East Coast Railway was completed to Miami, 365 miles south of Jacksonville, in April 1896. Flagler at once started to build the five-story Royal Palm Hotel. He also financed a sewage system, an electric power plant, and a waterworks for the infant city of Miami. As he had earlier done in St. Augustine, Flagler also helped in the building of churches in Miami. By this time Flagler had an interest in several land companies along the Florida East Coast Railway. He also controlled the Florida East Coast Steamship Company, which offered passage from Miami to Key West and Nassau.

During the mid-1890s the mental condition of Flagler's second wife began to deteriorate, and in August 1899 she was ruled legally insane. In April 1901 the Florida legislature passed an act making incurable insanity a cause for divorce. Flagler divorced his wife and a few months later married Mary Lily Kenan, a lady several years his junior. His new wife wanted to live in Palm Beach, and Flagler built her a large mansion there, which she named "Whitehall." The residents of Florida had mixed views of Flagler. Many were critical of the divorce and his third marriage and also called him a rich carpetbagger. Others viewed him as a generous empire builder and the father of Miami. Flagler was a lifelong Republican but took no active role in politics.

In 1903–1904 the railroad was extended twenty-eight miles south of Miami to Homestead. In July 1905 Flagler announced he would build the Florida East Coast line across the Florida Keys to Key West, 156 miles southwest of Miami. Many people called the project "Flagler's Folly," but a force of nearly 3,000 workers laid the rails across dozens of small islands and many long bridges to reach Key West early in 1912. The expense of bridging the Florida Keys pushed Flagler's total investment in Florida in thirty years to about $50 million. In a sense the Flagler years with Rockefeller had been a time of making money, while the time in Florida had been years of spending money. Many of his civic gifts in Florida were anonymous. Flagler enjoyed his role of builder of a state and

felt a sense of responsibility both to the settlers in Florida and the workers on his railroad. After his death in Palm Beach he left an estate valued at nearly $100 million.

• Some of Flagler's correspondence is in the Flagler collection, Flagler Museum, Palm Beach, Florida. The best biography of Flagler is Sidney W. Martin, *Florida's Flagler* (1949). Excellent material on Flagler's partnership with John D. Rockefeller can be found in Allan Nevins, *Study in Power* (1953). A brief history of the Florida East Coast Railway is Seth Bramson, *Speedway to Sunshine* (1984). His railroad career is reviewed in his obituary in *Railroad Gazette*, 23 May 1913.

JOHN F. STOVER

FLAHERTY, Robert Joseph (16 Feb. 1884–23 July 1951), filmmaker, was born in Iron Mountain, Michigan, the son of mining authority Robert Henry Flaherty and Susan Klöckner. After sporadic early education in Minnesota, Michigan, and Ontario, followed by an unsuccessful period at Upper Canada College in Toronto, Canada, in 1898, Flaherty attended the Michigan College of Mines in 1902. There he met the daughter of mineralogist and geologist Lucius L. Hubbard, Frances Hubbard, whom he married in 1914. The couple had three children.

Leaving before graduation, Flaherty became a surveyor for the Grand Trunk Pacific Railroad and worked in this capacity from 1906 to 1908. Through his father, in 1910 Flaherty was hired by Sir William Mackenzie, a mining and railroad magnate, to search for iron ore in the Nastapoka Islands and, the next year, in the Belcher Islands. For these expeditions, Mackenzie provided still photographic equipment so that Flaherty could record cultural and geological features. In 1912 Mackenzie sent Flaherty to Rochester, New York, for instruction in motion picture photography and processing. Flaherty then traveled to Baffin Island and the Belcher Islands (1913–1914) and shot 14,000 feet of film that was edited and shown in Toronto in 1915.

In 1915 Flaherty convinced Mackenzie to fund another expedition to the Belchers, resulting in an expanded version of his first movie. But the collapse of Mackenzie's Canadian Northern Railway led to the loss of sponsorship for Flaherty. The filmmaker spent the next few years lecturing, working on a book about his northern experiences, and searching for sponsorship of another film venture.

In 1920 Flaherty persuaded Captain Thierry Mallet of the fur-trading concern Revillon Frères to produce a feature film to celebrate the company's 200th anniversary. Relocating to the Revillon outpost at Port Harrison (now Inoucdjouac), Quebec, in 1920, Flaherty began work on depicting the life of Allakariallak (Nanook) and his family.

Flaherty involved the local community in the production. The film's subjects suggested sequences and assisted with behind-the-camera production work. Flaherty structured his project around the heroic struggle for existence in a harsh climate, with emphasis on the dangers of walrus hunting and unexpected storms. *Nanook of the North* (1922) was a landmark in documentary film in that its narrative appeared to derive from the culture being observed rather than from the culture of the observer. This technique that Flaherty called "natural drama" drew upon both the observations of the filmmaker and the creative participation of the documentary's subjects. This pioneering attempt at salvage ethnography, led to criticism by authorities such as Vilhjalmur Stefansson who characterized *Nanook* as "a most inexact picture of the Eskimo's life" (quoted in Iris Barry, *Let's Go to the Pictures* [1926]).

Flaherty filmed his next project in Polynesia. He relocated to the island of Savaii in Samoa, where he planned to document the lives of natives untouched by European civilization. He decided to use panchromatic film, giving superior rendition of the natural settings and making this project among the first to use the new technology. Despite the beauty of Savaii, Flaherty was unable to discover a tropical equivalent to the Inuit's noble struggle for existence. Flaherty eventually found his theme through the revival of a painful tattooing ritual that long had been discouraged by missionaries.

The finished *Moana* (1926) was a disappointment at the box office, although much admired by critics, inspiring John Grierson to coin the word "documentary" while reviewing *Moana* in the *New York Sun*. Flaherty then directed two short sponsored films, *The Pottery Maker* (1925) and *The Twenty-Four Dollar Island* (1927), before receiving an offer from Metro-Goldwyn-Mayer (MGM) to film Frederick O'Brien's *White Shadows in the South Seas*. During production in Tahiti, Flaherty's relations with the cast and crew soon deteriorated. Three weeks before filming was completed, Flaherty left MGM.

Moving to Santa Fe, New Mexico, Flaherty developed a project first initiated by his wife and brother on the natives of the Acoma Pueblo. In 1928 he interested Fox Film in a "Nanook of the Desert" story depicting the struggle of the Acoma Indians against the arid terrain and their Navajo enemies. The production of *Acoma* was plagued by poor weather and disease. When a fire at the base camp destroyed some of the footage and the introduction of sound rendered this silent film obsolete, Fox Film put an end to the production.

In partnership with German director Friedrich Wilhelm Murnau, Flaherty established the independent Flaherty-Murnau Productions in 1929. That same year, on the promise of backing from the Colorart Studio, the two directors left for Tahiti to make a sound and color film. Disagreements with Colorart and the lack of promised funding left the filmmakers stranded in Papeete. Hence, using Murnau's money, Flaherty and Murnau codirected *Tabu* (1931). But Flaherty's passion for natural drama clashed with Murnau's expressionist style. Since Murnau held the purse strings, Flaherty lost control of production and his contribution to the final shape of the film was limited. Disillusioned by his recent experiences, Flaherty character-

ized the American film industry by saying, "Hollywood is like sailing over a sewer in a glass-bottomed boat" (Rotha, p. 5).

In 1931 Flaherty was hired by the Empire Marketing Board in London to film *Industrial Britain* (1931), which applied the style of Flaherty's ennobling portraiture to depictions of English working people. Reading J. M. Synge's *Riders to the Sea* and *The Aran Islanders* led Flaherty to his next project, *Man of Aran* (1934), which depicted the traditional lives of the inhabitants of Ireland's Aran Islands and their struggle to wrest a living from Aran's rocky soil and the sea. Practicing the same kind of salvage ethnography as in his earlier films, Flaherty revived the vanished practice of hunting basking sharks from fragile curraghs. Although criticized for risking the lives of his cast and crew and for romanticizing the lives of Araners, this film was awarded the Grand Prix at the Venice Film Festival in 1934 and was successful at the box office.

Flaherty then joined forces with producer Alexander Korda to adapt Rudyard Kipling's *Toomai of the Elephants* to the screen. When filming fell behind schedule, Korda sent his brother Zoltan Korda and veteran Hollywood director Monta Bell to speed up production. Control of production eventually shifted to Zoltan Korda. *Elephant Boy* (1937), was a costly failure and Flaherty's prospects were grim.

Rescue came in the form of a telegram in 1939 from Pare Lorentz, head of the new U.S. Film Service. Lorentz, a prominent film critic turned documentary director, asked Flaherty to make a short film on the activities of the Agricultural Adjustment Administration. *The Land* (1942) recorded the human cost and devastated landscape of the depression-era dustbowl and proposed crop limitation and new agricultural techniques as a solution. *The Land* effectively conveyed Flaherty's social engagement and rage at the agricultural disaster of the 1930s. By the time of the film's limited release in 1942, wartime economic conditions and an end to the drought made it obsolete.

In 1941–1942 John Grierson, head of the National Film Board of Canada, contacted Flaherty to direct a film about the Canadian naturalist Jack Miner. Although Flaherty shot a test reel in Canada, the project was abandoned when Flaherty was hired in May 1942 by Frank Capra, who then headed the War Department Film Division in Washington, D.C. Flaherty was put in charge of a weekly newsreel called *The State of the Nation*. When nine months of work failed to produce a single episode of the newsreel, Flaherty's unit was closed down.

In 1944 Roy Stryker approached Flaherty on behalf of Standard Oil of New Jersey, which wanted to sponsor a film dealing with the company's oil exploration in Louisiana. The film's theme of the introduction of modern technology to a traditional culture was complimented by Flaherty's concern for the relationship of his characters to nature.

Louisiana Story met with critical success. The film's release was preceded by a 1947 reissue of *Nanook of the North*. The postwar fashion for cinematic realism (popularized by the success of Italian neo-realist films) revitalized acceptance of Flaherty's style. The U.S. State Department sent Flaherty and his films on a tour of Germany, and the filmmaker was honored with a doctorate from the University of Michigan and with a retrospective of his work at the Museum of Modern Art. At the time of his death at the family farm outside Brattleboro, Vermont, Flaherty had begun the direction of his biggest budget film—*This Is Cinerama*—for producers Michael Todd and Lowell Thomas.

The trajectory of Flaherty's career, as notable for its failures as its successes, has made his place in film history controversial. He is hailed as the father of documentary and ethnographic film and denounced as an agent of imperialism. His films are praised as masterpieces of natural drama or nonpreconception and criticized for their nineteenth-century romantic narratives and misrepresentations of native cultures. Although much of Flaherty's work was done within the commercial motion picture industries in the United States and the United Kingdom, he has become canonized as the patron saint of oppositional film practices. The location of Flaherty's work at the interstitial sites of opposing views of film history ensures that interpretations of his career will differ.

• The Robert J. Flaherty Papers are held at Columbia University. His photographic materials are held at the Robert and Frances Flaherty Study Center, Claremont College, Claremont, Calif.; and at the National Archives of Canada, Ottawa. Flaherty wrote the following books: *My Eskimo Friends* (1924); *The Captain's Chair: A Study of the North* (1938); and *White Master* (1939). Considerations of Flaherty's career can be found in Richard Barsam, *The Vision of Robert Flaherty* (1988); Jo-Anne Birnie-Danzker, ed., *Robert Flaherty: Photographer/Filmmaker* (1979); Arthur Calder-Marshall, *The Innocent Eye: The Life of Robert J. Flaherty* (1963); Richard Griffith, *The World of Robert Flaherty* (1953); Paul Rotha, *Robert J. Flaherty: A Biography*, ed. Jay Ruby (1983); and Pat Mullen, *Man of Aran* (1935; repr. 1970). Also, selected reviews of Flaherty's most noted films can be found in the critical anthology Lewis Jacobs, ed., *The Documentary Tradition From Nanook to Woodstock* (1971). See also Robert Flaherty, "How I Filmed *Nanook of the North*," *Film Makers on Filmmaking*, ed. Harry M. Geduld (1967). An obituary is in *Variety*, 25 July 1951, p. 55.

MARK LANGER

FLANAGAN, Edward Joseph (13 July 1886–15 May 1948), Roman Catholic priest and founder of Boys Town, was born in Leaberg, County Roscommon, Ireland, the son of John Flanagan, a farm manager, and Honora Larkin. His first formal education was at Summer Hill College, a boarding school in Sligo, Ireland. Flanagan was inspired as a teenager by his older brother Patrick, who had graduated from a Dublin seminary and been ordained a priest. He planned to attend the same Dublin seminary but instead ventured to the United States in 1904 at the age of eighteen. Prompting his decision to immigrate was his sister Nellie, who had returned to visit him in Ireland after spending several years in America. She enthralled him

with stories of life there and convinced him of the many advantages America held for his vocational training.

With an uncle's support, Flanagan attended Mount St. Mary's College in Emmitsburg, Maryland, earning a B.A. in 1906 and an M.A. in 1908. He also studied at St. Joseph's Seminary in Dunwoodie, New York, in 1906 and early 1907. It was while in New York that Flanagan began visiting the terminally ill. The long hours spent in study and in traveling to hospital wards nearly drove him to exhaustion, which led to a lung infection requiring months of bed rest. He was forced to withdraw from St. Joseph's. While still in the last stages of recovery, he became determined to finish his education. In the fall of 1907, he enrolled at the Gregorian University in Rome, Italy. Within six months his illness returned, compelling him to withdraw once again from academic life. By the summer of 1908, Flanagan was able to enroll at the University of Innsbruck, Austria, where the alpine air would not inflame his weakened lungs. He spent three years studying theology and in 1912 was ordained a priest at St. Ignatius Church in Innsbruck.

Following graduation, Flanagan returned to the United States, to become assistant pastor of St. Patrick's Church in O'Neill, Nebraska, where he served from 1912 to 1913. Between 1913 and 1916, he was assigned as assistant pastor of St. Patrick's Church in Omaha, Nebraska. During his tenure there he began dedicating his life to the troubled and underprivileged. In 1914 he founded the Workingmen's Hotel, which provided lodging to homeless men and itinerant workers. To protect the younger men, Flanagan segregated them to the upper floors of the hotel. He quickly became convinced that the youngest men, boys really, responded best to rehabilitation. Encouraged, he began concentrating all of his efforts toward the destitute and delinquent youth he saw on the streets or read about in the paper. In 1917 he founded (with borrowed money) the Home for Homeless Boys, which started with five boys, three of whom were referred by Juvenile Court. The home soon became crowded, and Flanagan began making plans to move. A year later he moved to Douglas County, eleven miles west of Omaha, and established Boys Town. In 1919, he became a naturalized American citizen.

Boys Town had a difficult start financially. Few in Omaha or the local church supported Flanagan. In fact, as Flanagan's debts mounted, the bishop of Omaha threatened to close his home. Flanagan, however, cleverly publicized Boys Town's plight in several ways. He would greet celebrities passing through the area with the Boys Town band. This tactic resulted in newspaper coverage of both the celebrity and Boys Town. He also conducted a massive writing campaign asking for donations and support. He was able to raise thousands of dollars when notables such as Babe Ruth and Jack Dempsey visited Boys Town. The church, finally convinced of the value of Flanagan's work, began to increase its contributions as well.

Boys Town became famous for its innovative approach to reforming youngsters' lives. Paternal in his treatment of the residents, Flanagan ignored the standard practices of his time. Most remarkably, he abandoned corporal punishment, believing that extrinsic factors contributed more to delinquency than anything else. He established academic, vocational, and recreational programs designed to serve as correctives for parental neglect and abuse. Life at Boys Town was highly structured with the thought that boys kept busy would keep out of trouble. To change a child's behavior, Flanagan believed in heaping praise when rules were followed and constructive criticism when they were not. When a boy followed accepted behavior on a consistent basis, he received not only constant praise but added privileges. By following this simple formula, Flanagan felt he could motivate children to act appropriately.

From its beginning Boys Town was nonsectarian and open to all races. Flanagan created a self-governing city entirely run by boys. He included a mayor's office, town council, fire chief, park commissioner, and sanitation department. The "municipal" positions were all held by boys in an attempt to nurture their sense of responsibility and self-esteem. As director and secretary-treasury of Boys Town, Flanagan also oversaw its incorporation as a village in 1936. Upon incorporation, Boys Town gained legal status for its boys-run government as a municipality.

Flanagan soon met with great success as graduates of Boys Town, once labeled hopeless, became productive members of society. Thoughts on juvenile rehabilitation and care were forever changed as Boys Town presented a viable alternative to programs based only upon harsh disipline. The importance of environment to a child's development could no longer be denied. Other juvenile institutions began experimenting with and adopting many of Flanagan's theories on rehabilitation. Priests went to Boys Town to study the curriculum and learn firsthand Flanagan's theories on juvenile development, and many went on to open similar facilities across America. Flanagan's adage, "There's no such thing as a bad boy—only bad environment, bad thinking, and bad training," was not only a slogan but a rallying cry for those seeking to overhaul juvenile treatment programs.

Thanks to the success of Boys Town, Flanagan was considered an expert on juvenile delinquency and treatment. He served ten years as the president of the Omaha Welfare Board. He was also a member of the children's committee of the National Conference of Catholic Charities. In 1937 he was named a domestic prelate by Pope Pius XI. He gained worldwide fame in 1938 when Metro-Goldwyn-Mayer made the first of two successful films about his life. The first film, *Boys Town*, starred Spencer Tracy as Father Flanagan and Mickey Rooney as a troubled youth. A sequel, *Men of Boys Town*, was made in 1941. Flanagan was appointed a member of Attorney General Tom Clark's advisory panel to study juvenile delinquency, and in 1947, at the request of the U.S. War Department, he was asked to visit child-care facilities in Japan and Korea. The next year he extended his tour to include the war-torn countries of Europe. He died while in Berlin.

Flanagan founded Boys Town to rehabilitate and offer hope to abused, neglected, and delinquent boys. His reputation for tolerance and his renowned public relations skills gained him widespread popularity, which he cleverly parlayed into contributions for his beloved Boys Town. He is remembered for revolutionizing juvenile institutions and for innovative approaches to child care and development.

• Flanagan's papers are in Boys Town, Omaha, Nebr. Many of his writings are also contained in *Father Flanagan's Home Journal* and its successor, the *Boys Town Times*. A dated but useful account of Flanagan's philosophy is contained in *Understanding Your Boy* (1950) published under his name. See also Gladys Shultz, "Boy Handling Tips from Boys Town," *Better Homes and Gardens*, Mar. 1940, pp. 42–43, and Flanagan's statement to the U.S. Congress, Senate, *Wartime Health and Education*, Hearings before a Subcommittee of the Committee on Education and Labor, 78th Cong., 1st sess., 30 Nov. 1943, pp. 66–71. Biographical Studies include Fulton and Will Oursler, *Father Flanagan of Boys Town* (1949); Charles Graves, *Father Flanagan* (1972); and Clifford Stevens, "Father Flanagan of Boys Town," *America*, Nov. 1986, pp. 286–89. For a discussion concerning the development of Boys Town after Flanagan's death see Brian Jendryka, "Flanagan's Island," *Policy Review* (Summer 1994): 44–51. An obituary is in the *New York Times*, 15 May 1948.

TIMOTHY F. WELLS

FLANAGAN, Hallie Mae Ferguson (27 Aug. 1890–23 July 1969), theater educator, administrator, and director, was born in Redfield, South Dakota, the daughter of Frederic Miller Ferguson, a businessman, and Louisa Fischer. Throughout her childhood, Hallie's father encouraged her to believe in her uniqueness and individual potential, while her mother instilled in her a selflessness of putting others before herself. These conflicting ideas would haunt Hallie throughout her life as she tried to balance a career and a family. She sometimes believed she had failed as a wife and mother because she had devoted too much of herself to her career.

In 1911 Hallie graduated from Grinnell College in Grinnell, Iowa, and began teaching at Sigourney High School. The following year she married her college sweetheart, Murray Flanagan, an insurance salesman; they had two children before his death in 1919. Hallie Flanagan then began teaching again, first in the local high school and then assisting at Grinnell College. In 1922, however, her older son died of spinal meningitis. To ease the pain of her loss, Flanagan threw herself into her work—directing at the Colonial Theatre in Grinnell and teaching theater at Grinnell College.

Writing had always interested Flanagan, and at Grinnell she turned her attention to playwriting. Although encouraged by friends to try acting, Flanagan thought playwriting would allow her to spend more time at home. One of her plays, *The Curtain*, won a playwriting contest and was produced by the Des Moines Little Theatre. Accepted into Harvard professor George Pierce Baker's 47 Workshop for playwriting, she became his assistant. She believed Baker taught her everything she learned about the theater. In 1924, after completing her A.M. at Radcliffe College, Flanagan returned to Grinnell College but soon moved on to teach at Vassar College in Poughkeepsie, New York. She wanted to build a strong, innovative theater program at Vassar, but receiving a Guggenheim Fellowship to study abroad interrupted her plans for a year.

Baker had suggested that Flanagan travel to see the innovative European theater, and the fellowship enabled her to do so. During her year abroad she saw not only new plays but also new methods of staging. Flanagan was particularly impressed by the Soviet Union's employment of drama as an instrument of social and political change. She talked with many theater practitioners, being particularly affected by Meyerhold, a leader in the Russian experimental theater revolt, and developing a special relationship with Edward Gordon Craig, also known for his innovative theatrical ideas. When she completed her trip Flanagan returned to Vassar, where she began to put all she had learned into practice—the result was the Vassar Experimental Theatre. Her work at Vassar was progressive; while there she directed a production of Euripides' *Hippolytus* in Greek and a number of agit-prop plays that presaged the later Living Newspaper productions of the Federal Theatre.

In 1934 Flanagan married Philip Davis, a professor of Greek at Vassar, but continued to use Flanagan as her professional name. The couple had no children. In 1935 Harry Hopkins, a friend from her days at Grinnell, offered Flanagan an opportunity she could not refuse—but one that would make her choose once again between family and career. Hopkins, head of the Works Progress Administration, wanted Flanagan to run the Federal Theatre Project (FTP). Although the job would keep her away from home for long periods, her husband encouraged her to take it because "all the forces of your life have led to it."

Flanagan saw the Federal Theatre Project as more than a work relief program. She wanted to develop a national theater that would be able to continue even after federal subsidy ended. She believed in "creating a national theatre and building a national culture." The key, she thought, was to make theater a vital part of communities. She was not alone in this idea. Many of the artists who joined the project, including playwright Elmer Rice, believed that commercialism was killing the theater. She also thought that the theater needed to reflect society more closely to reach more people. The project was divided into four sections: a popular-price theater, the Living Newspaper, the Negro theater, and the experimental theater, with offices nationwide.

The achievements of the FTP are numerous and diverse. Most important, the FTP provided employment for out-of-work theater personnel. More than 12,000 people in 158 theaters in twenty-eight states were employed by the FTP. The Negro unit employed 851 blacks and produced seventy plays. The FTP had a Yiddish unit, a children's theater unit, a dance unit, and a puppet unit. These groups performed in parks, halls, hospitals—all evidence of Flanagan's commitment to bringing the theater to the people. Because admission was free or for a nominal fee the productions of the FTP reached a broad audience. Its houses averaged 500,000 weekly, and its productions were seen by more than thirty million people. Sixty-five percent of its audience had never before been to the theater.

Flanagan's objective was "to make theatre out of everyday factual materials . . . to dramatize [the] struggle to turn the great natural and economic and social forces of our time toward a better life for more people." Accordingly, the most innovative and controversial dramas of the FTP were the Living Newspaper productions. They employed large numbers of actors and attempted to document current social and political issues. The more effective of the Living Newspaper productions were *Ethiopia* (1934), concerned with U.S. foreign relations; *Triple-A Plowed Under* (1935), taken from the Supreme Court finding that the Agriculture Adjustment Act was unconstitutional and concentrating on the plight of the farmer caught between the depression and drought; and *One Third of a Nation* (1938), concerned with the reality of slum life in America and an attack on the watering-down of the Wagner-Steagall Act—all three topical, controversial, and political.

The political nature of these productions and their close association with New Deal government contributed to the demise of the FTP. Brought before the House Un-American Activities Committee, Flanagan ardently defended the FTP, but nevertheless Congress voted to end its funding on 30 June 1939. What the project achieved and that it lasted as long as it did was due largely to the vision and tenacity—what producer-director John Houseman would call the "ferocity of a roused lion"—of Flanagan.

After the FTP ended, Flanagan returned to Vassar College and with a small staff wrote *Arena* (1940), the story of the FTP. She divided her time among the book, her family, and the Experimental Theatre. In February 1940 Davis died, and once again she relied on work to relieve the pain of loss.

In 1942 Flanagan became dean at Smith College. She held that position until 1946, when she became a full-time professor in the theater department, remaining there until her retirement in 1955. In 1957 she received the Creative Arts Award from Brandeis University, and in 1968 she received a citation from the National Theatre Conference. After Flanagan died in Old Tappan, New Jersey, a memorial attended by more than 300 people was held at the Vivien Beaumont Theatre at Lincoln Center.

Flanagan committed her life to the development of theater arts within the liberal arts curriculum and to the development of the theater within the wider community. She believed theater should "be a part not apart from everyday existence." It was her conviction that a living, changing theater could do this. Her innovative work in educational theater and the FTP are concrete examples of her belief that theater must continually try to push the boundaries if it is to remain a living art. Her vision of an American theater, which began with the FTP, is summed up in the final pages of *Arena*: "the ten thousand anonymous men and women—the et ceteras and the and-so-forths who did the work, the nobodies who were everybody, the somebodies who believed it—their dreams and deeds were not the end. They were the beginning of a people's theatre in a country whose greatest plays are still to come." While Flanagan's vision for American theater was not wholly realized, theater historian Francis Fergusson asserts that "in a crucial experiment [Flanagan] demonstrated the potential theatre life of this country." Houseman, who worked with her on the FTP, eulogized that Flanagan "turned a pathetic relief project into what remains the most creative and dynamic approach that has yet been made to an American National Theatre."

So clearly associated with the New Deal Administration, it was inevitable that the FTP would become the focus of political debate and suffer the same fate as its sponsor. While Flanagan tried to keep the FTP from becoming a political toy, the need to address the social issues that led to its creation was stronger than the threat of Senator Joseph McCarthy. Flanked by conservatives who saw the FTP as a Communist infiltration into the U.S. government and the radicals who felt the FTP was not political enough, Flanagan managed to produce a diverse repertoire of styles and themes for an equally diverse audience.

• The largest collection of Flanagan's personal and professional papers is in the Billy Rose Theatre Collection at the New York Public Library for the Performing Arts at Lincoln Center. In addition, the archives at Grinnell College, Vassar College, and Smith College have various materials relating to her tenure at these institutions. A large collection of materials, including her unpublished autobiography, "Notes on My Life," is in the private collection of her family. Her stepdaughter, Joann Davis Bentley, wrote her biography, *Hallie Flanagan: A Life in the American Theatre* (1988). Flanagan's other published works include *Shifting Scenes of the Modern European Theatre* (1928), a memoir of her Guggenheim trip, and *Dynamo: The Story of a College Theatre* (1943), an account of her work with the Vassar Experimental Theatre. Flanagan also wrote a large number of articles for journals such as *Theatre Arts Monthly* throughout her career. One dissertation that looks specifically at Flanagan's achievements as an educator is Barbara Mendoza, "Hallie Flanagan: Her Role in the American Theatre, 1924–1936" (NYU, 1976). Others include Patricia Ridge, "The Contributions of Hallie Flanagan to the American Theatre" (Univ. of Colorado, 1971), and Cheryl Diane Swiss, "Hallie Flanagan and the Federal Theatre Project: An Experiment in Form" (Univ. of Wisconsin, 1982). Articles concerning her career are Helen Krich Chinoy and Linda Walsh Jenkins, eds., *Women in American Theatre* (1987), and Karen Malpede, ed., *Women in Theatre* (1991). An obituary is in the *New York Times*, 24 July 1969; the memorial by Houseman was published in the newspaper on 3 Aug. 1969.

MELISSA VICKERY-BAREFORD

FLANAGAN, John J. (9 Jan. 1873–4 June 1938), track and field athlete and coach, was born of poor farming parents in Kilmallack, Limerick County, Ireland (his parents' names are unknown). As a boy, Flanagan could run, jump, and throw heavy weights with success against anyone in the county, and this in a nation that had been a world leader for a century in such sporting activities.

On 9 September 1895, the young Flanagan, standing 6' tall and weighing 201 pounds, stepped into the nine-foot-diameter dirt circle and threw the 16-pound iron ball, or "hammer," suspended from a 48-inch piano wire, a distance of 145 feet—a world record. On that same day in 1895 he won the Irish "all around" title (running, jumping, throwing), and he soon immigrated to the United States, where he remained until 1911. In New York City he joined thousands of new Irish immigrants, many of them employed by the police and fire departments. Police officer Flanagan joined the Irish-American Athletic Club and soon gained athletic notoriety for his skill in throwing the hammer, the discus, the shot, and the 35- and 56-pound weights. His companions were Patrick J. Ryan, Ralph Rose, James S. Mitchell, Martin Sheridan, Matthew McGrath, and Patrick McDonald—all future national, Olympic, and world champions in weight-throwing, all huge men, and all of them called "The Irish-American Whales." Flanagan was their leader, described by contemporary track-and-field expert Arthur Ruhl as "a big man—a black, shaggy, hirsute animal, the perfect picture of a hurler of weights."

The American hammer circle was seven feet in diameter. Accelerated speed and greater centrifugal force generated by two rotational turns with the hammer (rather than the traditional one turn) were deemed nearly impossible by experts. When Flanagan first attempted the double turn, he fell flat on his back. But as his colleague Mitchell wrote: "Flanagan stuck at it, for weeks and weeks, he tried again and again, went turning, twisting and wriggling all over a ten-acre field until he mastered the intricacy of the double revolution." An *Outing* magazine correspondent was in Paris for the second Olympic Games in 1900 and wrote about how Flanagan's two turns won him the gold medal "with a throw of 167'4"." He won again in St. Louis in 1904 with 168'1" and in London (1908) with 170'4¼"—the first to reach that plateau. He also became the first to exceed 180 feet when on 24 July 1909, in Hartford, Connecticut, he spun three times inside the circle and set a world record of 184'4". Track expert Frederick A. M. Webster wrote that Flanagan deserved the record, for, "after striving untiringly for three long years, he at last mastered that third turn."

Flanagan was a robust thirty-six years of age, world champion, three-time Olympic champion and six-time national winner in the 56-pound weight throw, always against Irish-American teammates who frequently outweighed him by seventy pounds. President Theodore Roosevelt shook his hand on Flanagan's return from London, exclaiming: "This is a big man, all right. . . . Your throw over in the Olympic Games was fine. I congratulate you." Flanagan and his cadre of "Whales" dominated American and Olympic circles in the pre–World War I era. In the *New York Times* obituary, Flanagan's name "was recalled forcibly at Amsterdam in 1928" when a U.S. competitor, for the first time, failed to win the hammer throw. The victor was a young medical doctor, Patrick O'Callagham, of the Irish Free State, who had been taught the art and science of hammer throwing by Flanagan. There were bigger and stronger men than Flanagan, wrote James Brendon Connolly, the 1896 Olympic triple jump champion, "but none possesses his skill, nervous energy, and rhythm in action." The former secretary of the Amateur Athletic Union, Daniel J. Ferris, remembered Flanagan and his Irish-American friends. "They trained very hard, ate seriously, and won."

Flanagan resigned from the police department on 13 August 1910; all three major New York City newspapers took note of the fact. He returned to his native Ireland to become head of the Flanagan clan at Kilmallack, succeeding his father, and coached young Irish weight-throwers of the next generation. He never married, but he left a legacy, or "family," of athletes on both sides of the Atlantic. He died in the village of his birth.

• The clearest verbal pictures of Flanagan come from eyewitnesses. See *Outing*, Sept. 1900, p. 705; and July 1908, p. 387–402; James Mitchell, *How to Become a Weight Thrower* (1910), p. 13; *Collier's*, 5 Sept. 1908, pp. 12–13; *World Today*, 10 Mar. 1906, pp. 281–85; F. A. M. Webster, *Athletes of Today* (1929), p. 301; Webster, *Great Moments in Athletics* (1947), p. 183; *1908 British Report Fourth Olympiad* (1909), p. 89; Charles J. P. Lucas, *The Olympic Games, 1904* (1905), p. 88; and Webster, *Olympic Cavalcade* (1948), p. 154. See also *Irish Historical Studies* 15 (Sept. 1967): 438–45, and Bill Mallon and Ian Buchanan, *Quest for Gold: The Encyclopedia of American Olympians* (1984), p. 297. For several of Flanagan's greatest throws, see *New York Daily Tribune*, 13 Sept. 1908, p. 8, and 25 July 1909, p. 9; and *New York Times*, 13 June 1909, p. 4, and 25 July 1909, p. 52. Obituaries appear in the *New York Times* and *New York Herald Tribune*, both 5 June 1938.

JOHN A. LUCAS

FLANAGAN, William (14 Aug. 1923–1 Sept. 1969), composer and journalist, was born in Detroit, Michigan, the son of William Flanagan and Elona (maiden name unknown), both of whom worked for the American Telephone and Telegraph Company. As his was a nonmusical family, Flanagan received very little training as a child besides exposure to the scores of Max Steiner in the movie theaters of the thirties. By the age of fifteen, however, Flanagan's innate talent enabled him to reproduce Steiner's lush, romantic style during services at the University of Detroit High School, where he was chapel organist.

During his college education at the University of Detroit and the University of Michigan, Flanagan had in mind a career in journalism, but in 1945 he succumbed to the increasing strength of his desire to pursue a musical career. For the next three years he studied composition at the Eastman School with Bernard

Rogers and Burrill Phillips, and in the summers of 1947 and 1948 he worked at Tanglewood with Samuel Barber, Arthur Honegger, and Aaron Copland. Copland was one of his two most important musical influences; the other was David Diamond, with whom he studied in New York between 1948 and 1950. At this time, he also began living in Greenwich Village with the playwright Edward Albee, who was then trying to find his place in the literary world.

With the exception of a brief stint as an instructor at the short-lived School of American Music, Flanagan earned his living for the next twenty years primarily as a journalist. He wrote essays on music for many periodicals, composed "sleeve" commentaries for almost a dozen record companies, and was an important critic and reviewer for *Musical America*, the *New York Herald Tribune*, and *Stereo Review*. While writing for the *Herald Tribune*, Flanagan came to know John Gruen and Lester Trimble, two other young composers reviewing for the paper, both of whom later spoke highly of Flanagan's intellect and personal qualities. Another of his close associates was Ned Rorem, with whom Flanagan organized a concert series called Music for the Voice by Americans. This series, which ran from 1959 to 1962, presented and often premiered songs by Virgil Thomson, Diamond, Daniel Pinkham, and Gruen, as well as by Rorem and Flanagan themselves.

The song was always Flanagan's favorite medium. He explained that he was initially drawn to the genre because he believed himself lacking in the technique required for the composition of longer forms, but in time he applied his vocal orientation to the composition of a handful of orchestral, piano, and chamber works. His growing body of songs demonstrated his personal convictions regarding the art of word setting, which he expressed verbally in these terms: "The vocal line," wrote Flanagan, "is a song's most elusive property. Its curve, its metrical pulse, should be one with the rhythmic flow of the language" (quoted in Ned Rorem, *Bulletin of the American Composers' Alliance* 9, no. 4 [1961], p. 15). The unique style of his songs demonstrates effective vocal contours and elegant prosody, and they are coupled with a harmonic vocabulary that derives from Copland, Stravinsky, and the mid-century language of Broadway, yet is unmistakably his own. The high quality of Flanagan's settings was attested to by Virgil Thomson, generally a harsh critic of songs by American composers, who declared in 1970 that "the songs of William Flanagan have a soaring intensity all unusual to the English language."

Flanagan's choice of texts ranged from works by the English writers John Donne, Siegfried Sassoon, and A. E. Housman, to those of such Americans as Walt Whitman, Herman Melville, and Howard Moss, the longtime poetry editor for the *New Yorker* magazine. The Moss settings were among Flanagan's most successful, as were several songs to words by Albee. Although Flanagan and Albee had moved to separate quarters in the late 1950s, they nevertheless remained friends and collaborated on a number of projects. Flanagan wrote incidental music for Albee's plays *The Sandbox* (1961), *The Ballad of the Sad Cafe* (1963), and *Malcolm* (1966), and Albee supplied libretti for two Flanagan operas: *Bartleby* (1961) and *The Ice Age*, which was never completed.

The 1960s brought long-awaited, if short-lived, recognition to Flanagan as a composer. He received the National Institute of Arts and Letters Award in 1967 and a Pulitzer nomination (1968) for his *Another August* for soprano and orchestra, as well as several major recordings, commissions, and performances of his compositions by the Detroit and Philadelphia orchestras.

Tragically, on 1 September 1969, Flanagan was found dead in his New York apartment from an overdose of barbiturates. His saddened musical colleagues surmised that he had succumbed to the difficulties of being, in Rorem's words, "an unappreciated conservative in a time of artistic upheaval" (1980, p. 630).

Flanagan's most important musical legacy is his songs. These demonstrate a dramatic flair for word setting, an affective lyricism, and a style that combines diatonic chromaticism with the rhythmic and harmonic overtones of Broadway. Flanagan the writer is largely unknown to the late twentieth-century musical public. Two volumes on American music and American theater were left uncompleted at the time of his death, and many of his fine critical reviews and articles still await collection and publication in book form.

• Flanagan's principal publishers are Peer Southern and C. F. Peters. His manuscripts are held by the New York Public Library and Broadcast Music, Inc. Two articles of special interest among the many that Flanagan published are "How to Succeed in Composing Without Really Succeeding," *Bulletin of the American Composers' Alliance* 11 (1963): 8, and "The Critics Confess: My Ten Favorite Composers," *Hi Fi/Stereo Review* 19 (Sept. 1967): 68. A complete listing of his works appears in the entry by Ned Rorem in the *New Grove Dictionary of Music and Musicians*, ed. Stanley Sadie, 6th ed. (1980). For essays on Flanagan's life and work, see Rorem's collections *Music and People* (1967), *Critical Affairs* (1970), and *Settling the Score* (1988). See also Peter Reilly, "William Flanagan," *Stereo Review* 21 (Nov. 1968): 134; Lester Trimble, "William Flanagan (1923–1969)," *Stereo Review* 23 (Nov. 1969): 118; and John Gruen, *The Party's Over Now: Reminiscences of the Fifties—New York Artists, Writers, Musicians, and Their Friends* (1972). A substantial treatment of Flanagan as a songwriter can be found in Ruth C. Friedberg, *American Art Song and American Poetry*, vol. 3 (1987). An obituary is in the *New York Times*, 2 Sept. 1969.

RUTH C. FRIEDBERG

FLANAGIN, Harris (3 Nov. 1817–23 Oct. 1874), governor of Arkansas, was born in Roadstown, Cumberland County, New Jersey, the son of James Flanagin, who was a farmer and in the furniture and undertaking businesses, and Mary Harris. He attended a local common school, where he was an excellent student. His family allowed him to continue his education at a Quaker school even though they were Baptists. In 1835 he moved to Frankfort, Pennsylvania, where he taught mathematics and English at Clermont Seminary. A year later he opened his own school at Paoli, Illinois. In Illinois he also studied law and passed the bar.

In 1838 Flanagin moved to Arkansas, settling first at Pine Bluff, then Little Rock, then Greenville in Clark County in 1839 and Arkadelphia in 1842. He established a successful law practice, purchased a farm and slaves, and speculated extensively in land with Benjamin Duncan, a friend from Clermont Seminary. His social activities during the 1840s reflected the career of an individual rising to local prominence. He joined the Masonic lodge and was a member of the local militia, which elected him captain in 1847. He married Martha Elizabeth Nash, daughter of a landowner, in 1851 and was thereafter active in the local Presbyterian church. The couple had three children.

Flanagin showed an early interest in politics. In 1841 Clark County sheriff Willis S. Smith appointed him deputy sheriff, reflecting Flanagin's association with this prominent early settler, landowner, and Whig politician. In 1842 Flanagin ran for the state legislature as a Whig and was elected, but he did not seek reelection. In 1848 he was chosen for the state senate, where he achieved some notoriety when he introduced a resolution to change the names of all males named Martin or Martin Van Buren, the former Democratic president, to Lewis or Lewis Cass, the Whig nominee. His Whig affiliation, however, limited his opportunities for a state office in a state dominated by the Democratic party, so during the 1850s his political career remained inactive.

Flanagin ran for the state secession convention of 1861, supporting immediate withdrawal from the Union. Once elected, he played an important role by writing the state's Confederate constitution, and he earned a reputation as a cautious and conservative leader. Following Arkansas's secession in May 1861, Flanagin joined the army. He organized a company that became Company E, Second Arkansas Mounted Rifles, and was elected its captain. He saw service at Wilson's Creek and Pea Ridge, where after the death of Colonel James McIntosh, Flanagin was appointed commander of the regiment. In 1862 a combination of prominent Democrats and prewar Whigs nominated him, while he was with his regiment in Tennessee, for the governorship in opposition to the incumbent, Henry M. Rector. He defeated Rector decisively and returned to Little Rock, taking office on 15 November 1862.

Flanagin assumed the governor's office at a time when Arkansas was on the verge of collapse. The Confederate army and state authorities had been driven from most of the counties in the north and along the Mississippi River. Many of the regiments raised within the state had been diverted east of the Mississippi River, and neither the Confederacy nor the state had a force sufficient to resist a major invasion. Both soldiers and civilians suffered from shortages of food and supplies. When, in September 1863, a Federal column marched on Little Rock, it faced minimum resistance and easily captured the capital and established control over most of the state north of the Arkansas River. Flanagin's government fled to Washington, in the southwestern part of the state.

As governor, Flanagin was an active and brave military leader, personally commanding the state militia and participating in the battle of Helena on 4 July 1863 as a volunteer aide-de-camp to General Theophilus Holmes. His constitutional views, however, limited his action as the state's civil leader. While other governors of the Trans-Mississippi Department assumed an active role in procuring supplies and developing essential industries, Flanagin refrained from such efforts, because he believed that he lacked constitutional or legislative authority. He also resisted what he considered to be unconstitutional interference in civilian affairs by military officials. His inaction drew the criticism of many, including the department commander, General Edmund Kirby Smith, who believed that the executive needed to take more decisive action in the war crisis.

As the war ended, Flanagin tried to bring about a reconstruction of the state government in a way that would minimize political upheaval. He sent a delegation to Little Rock to consult with the Unionist government of Isaac Murphy. They proposed that Confederate state officials resign in favor of the Murphy state government in return for that government's recognition of the legality of the county governments still in Confederate hands. General Joseph J. Reynolds, Federal commander in Arkansas, blocked this plan. With the ultimate Confederate surrender in the western theater, Flanagin himself surrendered, signed his parole, and returned to his home in Arkadelphia.

At home Flanagin resumed his law practice and farming. He also renewed his active support for the development of his local community. In 1867 he was named treasurer of the Presbyterian Synodical College. That same year he also became president of the board of trustees of the Arkansas Institute for the Blind.

At the same time, while he held no elective office, Flanagin emerged as an important leader and strategist for the state Democratic party. He was active in party conventions and attended the Democratic National Convention in 1872 but primarily engaged in an extensive dialogue with other Democrats about the best means of overthrowing Republican rule. Flanagin was a strong proponent of fusionist policies, urging other leaders to back bolting Republicans who could be used to bring about an end to Reconstruction. In 1872 he supported Joseph Brooks, part of the "brindletail" Republican faction and the more radical candidate on racial issues, over Elisha Baxter, the regular or "minstrel" candidate. Ultimately, fusion strategy brought about an end to Reconstruction in Arkansas, but only after Flanagin and other Democrats threw their support in 1874 to Baxter, who supported changes in state franchise laws that allowed a return of the Democrats to power.

Following the overthrow of the Republican regime, Flanagin was elected to the constitutional convention of 1874, where he played a prominent role in the Judiciary Committee and the Committee on Revision. At least one contemporary considered him to be the father of that constitution. Overworked and suffering from dysentery, in the last days of the convention he returned to Arkadelphia, where he died.

• A few of Flanagin's personal and gubernatorial papers are in the Harris Flanagin Papers and the Kie Oldham Collection in the Arkansas History Commission, Little Rock. Short scholarly treatments of Flanagin's life are provided in Farrar Newberry, "Harris Flanagin," *Arkansas Historical Quarterly* 17 (Spring 1958): 3–20; and Michael Dougan, "Harris Flanagin," in *The Governors of Arkansas*, ed. Timothy P. Donovan and Willard B. Gatewood, Jr. (1981). An obituary is in the *Arkansas Gazette*, 24 Oct. 1874.

CARL H. MONEYHON

FLANDERS, Ralph Edward (28 Sept. 1880–19 Feb. 1970), industrialist and U.S. senator, was born in Barnet, Vermont, the son of Albert Wellington Flanders, a farmer and woodworker, and Mary Lizzie Gilfillan, a schoolteacher. At the age of six his family moved to Pawtucket, Rhode Island, and two years later to a farm near Lincoln, Rhode Island. Graduating from a country school at fifteen, the eldest of nine children in a poor family that needed his wages, he became an apprentice machinist.

Flanders absorbed the elements of mechanical engineering and drafting in his employer's shop. An ambitious worker, he studied mechanical drawing at night school and engineering from a correspondence school. Early in his career he displayed striking qualities—at nineteen he presented management with a petition calling for workers to be given Saturday afternoons off in summer; he made inventions and wrote articles on machine designing. Flanders's articles led to his appointment in 1905 as associate editor of *Machinery*, which took him to New York for five years and inspired articles that he later converted into two books about gears. Disliking New York, he welcomed the opportunity to return to Vermont, where he said "he found himself" working as a sales engineer and making mechanical improvements in gear cutting for Jones and Lamson Machine Company in Springfield. In 1911 he married Helen E. Hartness, who framed a career as an author, lecturer, and ballad collector. She also was the daughter of the company's president, an office to which Flanders succeeded in 1933. They had three children. His reputation as an industrialist spread in the 1920s and 1930s and along with it came a reputation for concern about economics and social problems. Through speeches and books he publicized his ideas about a responsible capitalism that avoided wide swings in production and employment and raised the standard of living for workers.

Flanders entered public life as a Republican during the New Deal and World War II years, holding a series of government appointments, including service on the War Production Board. Failing to win nomination as U.S. senator in 1940, he was appointed in 1946 to fill an unexpired Senate term and later in the year won election with labor support. During his dozen years in the Senate Flanders served on the committees for banking and currency, civil service, post office, housing, finance, armed services, and Truman's Economic Report. He joined early the "Young Turks," demanding a larger Senate role for junior members. Offering his own view of Vermont Republicanism, he observed to conservative leader Robert Taft, "I wish the whole party leadership were more positively interested in people." At different times he described himself as a "liberal" and a "Tory."

In domestic affairs Flanders voted for the Taft-Hartley labor law, which did not please his labor constituency; the Taft-Ellender-Wagner housing law, championing its slum clearance provisions; and the Civil Rights Act of 1957. He did not vote on the conservative McCarran Internal Security Act. In foreign affairs he supported the Truman Doctrine, the Selective Service Act of 1948, the Marshall Plan, the Eisenhower Doctrine, and the Atoms for Peace Treaty. He opposed the North Atlantic Treaty Organization (NATO) Treaty, urged revision of the veto clause being abused by the Soviet Union in the United Nations Security Council, and approved of the Bricker amendment, which aimed to restrict presidential power to negotiate treaties and executive agreements.

A self-made Yankee, Flanders stood for a large measure of self-reliance and self-discipline, faith in moral law, and an expanding economy that provided more goods and wealth for all. He envisioned a cooperative world order in which nations found a mutuality of interest. He considered his activity for economic development his most important work. Though a friend of Senator Taft, Flanders early supported Dwight Eisenhower for the presidency in 1952; he wrote to Eisenhower that he was uncomfortable with "lifelong Republicans." Attentive to his Vermont constituency, giving weekly radio chats, he handily won reelection in 1952.

As he entered his second term, Flanders was distressed by the irresponsible conduct of his fellow Republican senator Joseph R. McCarthy. Exploiting a national fear of communism since 1950, McCarthy had leveled without verification charges of communist influence against employees in the State Department and the army. Few members of either party dared to challenge his demagoguery. Early in March 1954, in a Senate speech, Flanders warned that McCarthy's activities were "to an extent dangerous to our future as a nation." Several weeks later he sharpened his criticism, comparing McCarthy's methods with Hitler's.

Televised hearings of McCarthy's charges against the army in the spring of 1954 had heightened excitement over McCarthyism and served to discredit McCarthy. Flanders announced at the hearings that he intended to propose that McCarthy be removed from his committee posts; on 11 June Flanders introduced a resolution to remove McCarthy. Within his party were many who opposed his move, including the majority leader, William E. Knowland—who called a press conference to denounce the resolution—while the White House remained passive.

An anti-McCarthy group called the Clearing House, child of the National Committee for an Effective Congress, took charge of the campaign to force a reluctant Senate to act. "I will not let this session of Congress end without providing the Senate with an opportunity to go clearly on record on this issue," Flanders declared at a press conference arranged by the group. When the Senate Republican Policy Committee announced its unanimous opposition to his resolution, Flanders altered his resolution to call for censure of McCarthy.

On the night of 30 July, in a Senate chamber filled with gallery spectators, Flanders told a hushed, tense audience that McCarthy's conduct was unbecoming a senator, contrary to senatorial traditions, and tended toward bringing the Senate into disrepute. Senator Everett Dirksen rose to denounce the resolution as the work of communists and left-wingers. The usually astute *New York Times* journalist James Reston privately expressed doubt that Flanders could muster the votes to pass his resolution.

The Senate's sense of its tradition—only five times in 165 years had it censured a member—and the imminence of the congressional elections in November, with many voters supporting McCarthy, led to a decision to appoint a bipartisan committee to conduct "judicial" hearings. Vainly resisting that move, Flanders nonetheless supplied the committee with thirty-three charges. He had forced the Senate to act, and on 27 September 1954 the committee unanimously recommended censure. The November elections gave the Democrats control of both houses, and in December after bitter debate, the Senate voted for censure, 67 to 22. The Vermont Yankee had prevailed against one of the nation's most dangerous demagogues as well as against his party's leadership.

Flanders the pariah became a hero. He had led the charge to smash McCarthyism and dissipate the hysteria that no other senator had found the courage and persistence to challenge. He retired from the Senate in 1958 and wrote his autobiography, *Senator from Vermont.* He died in Springfield, Vermont.

• Syracuse University holds the Flanders papers and has published a register. Flanders's autobiography, *Senator from Vermont* (1961), is indispensable. He also wrote *Platform for America* (1936), *Toward Full Employment* (1938), *The American Century* (1950), and *Letter to a Generation* (1956). Robert Griffith, *The Politics of Fear: Joseph R. McCarthy and the Senate* (1970), is helpful on the McCarthy episode.

JAMES A. RAWLEY

FLANNAGAN, John Bernard (7 Apr. 1895–6 Jan. 1942), sculptor, was born in Fargo, North Dakota, the son of Martin H. Flannigan, a policeman, and Marguerite McDonnell, a former teacher. (According to the biographer Robert J. Forsyth, genealogical records indicate discrepancies in the spelling of the family surname.) Raised in modest circumstances in Fargo,

Flannagan enjoyed childhood visits to his paternal uncle's Minnesota farm. He developed a love for animals that later found expression in his carved sculpture.

In 1901, when Flannagan's father died, the family suffered economic hardship and separation. By 1905, Flannagan's mother was forced to place her three sons in St. Otto's Orphanage in Little Falls, Minnesota, while she worked at St. Francis Hospital in Breckenridge. In 1910, after completing training as a practical nurse, she and her sons were reunited, but the five-year separation had left psychological marks on Flannagan. After attending St. John's University, a preparatory school, from 1910 to 1913, he sought full-time employment in Minneapolis to help support his family. At age eighteen, having decided to become an artist, he enrolled in night classes at the Minneapolis School of Arts. In 1916 Flannagan's youngest brother died of tuberculosis. Torn between family duty and his desire to pursue an artistic career, Flannagan considered his brother's death emblematic of the futility of his filial devotion. This loss triggered his decision to study art full time and fueled his ambition to move to New York City. After the United States had entered World War I in 1918, Flannagan enlisted in the U.S. Merchant Marine and severed all contact with his mother and surviving brother.

When he was released from service in 1919, Flannagan settled in Greenwich Village in New York. Before leaving for active duty, he had submitted two paintings to the third annual exhibition of the Society of Independent Artists. Intent on pursuing an artistic career, Flannagan sought out former Minneapolis art students who had also migrated to New York. His artist friends helped him find part-time night work as a security guard for Holmes Electrical Protective Service. When he was no longer able to support himself with part-time work, Flannagan reenlisted as a seaman. He left the Merchant Marine in 1922 and was subsequently hired as a farmhand at the home of the American artist Arthur B. Davies in Congers, New York. A well-respected member of the New York art world, Davies encouraged Flannagan and included his work in a group exhibition in January 1923 at the Montross Gallery in New York City.

The rocky countryside and rural life in Congers, and Flannagan's own experiments in relief painting, contributed to his decision to abandon painting and devote himself instead to sculpture. Encouraged by Davies's support, Flannagan established a studio on Patchin Place in Greenwich Village. His carved wood sculptures were accepted for exhibitions at the Whitney Studio Club, and collectors began acquiring his work. During the 1920s, Flannagan received spiritual and financial support from his neighbor and mistress, Florence Rollins, the personnel director of an insurance agency. In 1925 Rollins purchased property and began building a home in New City, on the west bank of the Hudson River in Rockland County. There Flannagan began using local stone to carve his sculptures and began developing his credo of direct carving.

Flannagan, like many progressive artists in the United States and Europe, believed that hand craftsmanship and the use of natural materials would revitalize the art of sculpture. Renouncing modeling and bronze casting, Flannagan chose to carve images from wood or stone without the use of assistants, preliminary maquettes, or techniques for mechanical enlargement. Instead, he carved directly in order to discover what he would later term "the Image in the Rock." In a 1941 essay of that title, Flannagan explained, "Often there is an occult attraction in the very shape of a rock as sheer abstract form. . . . It [carving] partakes of the deep pantheistic urge of kinship with all living things and the fundamental unity of all life. . . . To that instrument of the subconscious, the hand of the sculptor, there exists an image within every rock. The creative act of realization merely frees it" (published posthumously, *Magazine of Art*, Mar. 1942). In *Triumph of the Egg I* (1937, Museum of Modern Art, New York), one of Flannagan's mature stone carvings, the boldly simplified form of a newly hatched bird emerges from the rough-hewn broken egg to create a memorable image of birth and renewal. Flannagan, together with Robert Laurent and William Zorach, became the principal exponent of direct carving in the United States.

In 1926 Flannagan met Carl Zigrosser, the director of the Weyhe Art Gallery. Zigrosser not only organized Flannagan's first solo exhibition, but he also arranged to pay Flannagan a stipend in return for his granting the gallery the rights to exclusive representation of his work. The arrangement ensured Flannagan a measure of financial security and independence. He ended his affair with Rollins in 1928 and married Grace McCoy the following year. The couple had one daughter. In 1930 the Weyhe gallery financed the couple's year-long sojourn in Ireland. Long fascinated by the country of his ancestors, Flannagan believed that life in rural Ireland would prove compatible with his artistic credo of direct carving. With the support of a Guggenheim Fellowship, Flannagan and his family returned to Ireland in 1932; he derived artistic inspiration from his experiences abroad.

Flannagan suffered from periodic bouts of alcoholism, which intensified when he returned to New York in 1933. In September 1934, after an attempted suicide, he was committed first to Bellevue Hospital in New York City and then to Bloomingdale Hospital in White Plains. He was subsequently released after seven months of treatment. Flannagan's wife then separated from him, taking their daughter with her, and Flannagan was forced to find a new studio and build a new life. He established a relationship with Margherita La Centra, a young woman from Boston, who became his second wife in 1935; they had no children.

Flannagan won a commission in 1937 for the figure of a goldminer from the Fairmount Park Association in Philadelphia. The large scale of this prestigious commission necessitated a departure from direct carving and required the use of assistants. His work on the commission was delayed several months when he suffered a broken leg in an automobile accident. The monument was completed in May 1938. In the summer of 1939 Flannagan, inebriated at the time, was struck by an automobile, suffered a concussion, and underwent a series of brain operations. He never fully recovered from his injuries. Deeply in debt, Flannagan authorized the Weyhe gallery and his new dealer, Curt Valentin, to produce bronze and cast stone editions of his earlier carvings. In 1940 Flannagan's *Figure of Dignity* won the Schilling Award and was purchased by the Metropolitan Museum of Art. Valentin meanwhile promised to organize a retrospective of Flannagan's work. Plagued by complications from his accident and too weak to continue the strenuous work of carving directly, Flannagan committed suicide in January 1942.

Flannagan left behind carved sculptures that exemplify the vitality and modern innovations of the direct carving movement. While his few monumental sculptures, such as the *Goldminer*, were less than fully successful, Flannagan's intimately scaled carvings of animals and human figures eloquently embody themes of birth, death, and mystical renewal. A troubled but gifted sculptor, Flannagan contributed to the growth of modern art in the United States during the interwar period.

• Flannagan's papers, including correspondence, a journal, and manuscripts, are in the Archives of American Art, Smithsonian Institution. Additional material on Flannagan in the Archives of American Art includes the Carl Zigrosser Papers and research papers donated by Robert J. Forsyth. Flannagan's correspondence is published in Margherita Flannagan, ed., *Letters of John B. Flannagan* (1942), with an introduction by W. R. Valentiner. Flannagan's credo, "The Image in the Rock," was republished in Dorothy C. Miller, ed., *The Sculpture of John B. Flannagan* (1942), with an introduction by Carl Zigrosser. The most complete account of Flannagan's life is Forsyth, "John B. Flannagan: His Life and Work" (Ph.D. diss., Univ. of Minnesota, 1965). Useful essays include Joseph S. Bolt, "A Note on John B. Flannagan's *Bear*," *North Carolina Museum of Art Bulletin* 9, nos. 3 and 4 (Mar. 1970): 14–19; and Forsyth, "A Head by John B. Flannagan," *Register of the Spencer Museum of Art* (Lawrence, Kans.) 5, no. 6 (Fall 1978): 19–27. For Flannagan's role in the direct carving movement, see Judith Zilczer, "The Theory of Direct Carving in Modern Sculpture," *Oxford Art Journal* 4, no. 2 (Nov. 1981): 44–49.

JUDITH ZILCZER

FLANNER, Janet (13 Mar. 1892–7 Nov. 1978), journalist, was born in Indianapolis, Indiana, the daughter of Frank W. Flanner, a funeral director and philanthropist (founder of Flanner House, a settlement house), and Mary Ellen Hockett, a retired teacher and amateur actress. She attended the University of Chicago for two years (1912–1914) without graduating and then married William Lane Rehm in 1918 after a short period working on the *Indianapolis Star* (1917–1918) as assistant drama editor and then as a film columnist. (Flanner liked to say that she wrote the first film criticism in the United States.)

In New York City with her husband Flanner worked mainly as a freelance writer and became acquainted with members of what would later be known as the Algonquin Round Table, a group of literary and theatrical people who lunched together daily at the Algonquin Hotel on West Forty-fourth Street during most of the 1920s. Known for their caustic wit and barbed repartee, they included *New York Times* drama critic Alexander Woollcott, columnist Franklin Pierce Adams, journalists Heywood Broun and Ruth Hale, writers Dorothy Parker and Robert Sherwood, humorist Robert Benchley, and illustrator Neysa McMein. Flanner also met *New York Tribune* drama writer Solita Solano, whom she accompanied to Greece and Turkey in 1921 when Solano was on assignment for *National Geographic* magazine. Flanner, who had kept her maiden name when she married, was divorced in 1926, but by the fall of 1922 she and Solano had settled on the Left Bank of Paris near other American expatriates and lesbians.

In 1925, just before the publication of her first and only novel, *The Cubical City*, Flanner was hired by the fledgling *New Yorker* magazine, founded by her New York friends Harold Ross and Jane Grant. Her assignment was to provide "anecdotal and incidental stuff of places familiar to Americans and on people of note," according to Grant. Under the pseudonym "Genêt," which Ross suggested for Flanner since in the early days of the magazine all contributors had to write under pseudonyms, Flanner contributed a fortnightly column in which she covered the entire Paris scene, from fashion to books to general trends, from the dance of Isadora Duncan ("like a glorious bounding Minerva in the midst of a cautious corseted decade") to the landing of aviator Charles Lindbergh, from the races at Longchamps to the death of French premier Georges Clemenceau (he "asked to be buried standing upright. The position suited him"). In a mordant, witty style consistent with the detached sophistication of the magazine itself, especially during the 1920s, Flanner presented the point of view of the French, not of herself, or so she later maintained. She did not analyze; instead, she provided her readers with brisk, informed, and perceptive accounts of French cultural and social life.

During the 1930s Flanner's province enlarged to include current European events, and in addition to her "Letter from Paris" column she also contributed occasional letters from cities such as London, Berlin, Vienna, and Budapest. In 1936 she covered the Olympic Games in Berlin; that same year she published a three-part profile of Adolf Hitler that earned both admiration and contempt, for it seemed to some to evade the realities of nazism. During the late 1930s Flanner increasingly covered political events and crises. She closely monitored the Popular Front and the last days of the Third Republic in a style that was still witty, incisive, and elegant but that refrained, as much as possible, from personal judgment.

Just after war was declared in September 1939, Flanner left France for the United States, where she remained until 1944, covering Europe from afar and writing profiles of public figures like Thomas Mann, Wendell Willkie, Bette Davis, and Marshal Philippe Pétain (the latter published in book form as *Pétain: The Old Man of France*, 1944). After returning to France to report for the *New Yorker* on the end of the war and its devastating aftermath, Flanner's trenchant, stirring prose earned her France's highest honor, induction into the Legion of Honor. These pieces, collected in the volume *Paris Journal, 1944–1965*, won the National Book Award in 1966 as the "narrative of the culture of a nation in transition" and demonstrate the way war's aftermath altered her prose style. Though still elegant, it also expressed her own dramatic estimation of the condition of postwar Europe: "Europe has been the victim of cannibalism, with one country trying to eat the other countries, trying to eat the grain, the meat, the oil, the steel, the liberties, the governments, and the men of all the others," she wrote in December 1944.

The half-consumed corpses of ideologies and of the civilians who believed in them have rotted the soil of Europe, and in this day of the most luxurious war machinery the world has ever seen, the inhabitants of the Continent's capital cities have been reduced to the primitive problems of survival, of finding something to eat, of hatred, of revenge, of fawning, of being for or against themselves or someone else, and of hiding, like savages with ration cards.

Several other essays, particularly her profiles, were also collected and published in book form. *Men and Monuments* (1957) consists of her profiles of writer André Malraux and artists Henri Matisse, Pablo Picasso, and Georges Braque, as well as a long essay on the American armed service division devoted to recovering art objects pillaged during the war. *Paris Was Yesterday, 1925–1939* (1971) includes some of Flanner's best early writing and profiles, and *Paris Journal, 1965–1971* (1971) compiles Flanner's later contributions to the *New Yorker*.

Dividing her time between New York and France, Flanner continued to write for the *New Yorker*, covering the rise and fall of Charles de Gaulle, the Algerian crisis, the student demonstrations of May 1968, existentialism, art, film, and music, until 1975, when she retired from her fifty-year tenure as the magazine's unfailingly curious, sharp-tongued, and beloved Paris correspondent. She died in New York City.

• The major collection of Flanner's papers is the Flanner/Solano archive at the Library of Congress. The *New Yorker* magazine files are in the New York Public Library. Anthologies of her writings besides those mentioned in the text include *An American in Paris* (1940); *London Was Yesterday, 1934–1939* (1975); and *Janet Flanner's World: Uncollected Writings, 1932–1975* (1979). A complete bibliography is available in Brenda Wineapple, *Genêt: A Biography of Janet Flanner* (1989), and a selection of letters is available in *Darlinghissima: Letters to a Friend*, ed. Natalia Danesi Murray (1985). See also Margaret Anderson, *The Fiery Fountains* (1951); John C. Broderick, "Paris between the Wars: An Unpublished Memoir by Solita Solano," *Quarterly Journal of the Library of Congress* (October 1977): 306–14; and Glenway Wescott, "The Tri-Colored Rainbow," *New York Herald Tribune*, 19 Dec. 1966. An obituary is in the *New Yorker*, 20 Nov. 1978.

BRENDA WINEAPPLE

FLATT, Lester (28 June 1914–11 May 1979), bluegrass singer, musician, and songwriter, was born Lester Raymond Flatt in Overton County, Tennessee, the son of Isaac Flatt and Nancy Haney, sharecroppers and amateur musicians. After rudimentary schooling, Flatt became a mill worker at the age of seventeen. That same year (1931) he married Gladys Lee Stacey, with whom he later would have one daughter. Flatt moonlighted from his job at the textile mill as a guitar player and singer in several local bands, including the Harmonizers and the Happy-Go-Lucky Boys, until 1939. Then, at the age of twenty-five, Flatt left home to join Charlie Monroe's band and subsequently became a professional traveling mandolinist, playing traditional, though commercial, music.

Flatt's experience with Monroe brought his clear tenor voice to the attention of the bandleader's brother, the legendary Bill Monroe, and in 1944 Flatt became one of Bill Monroe's traveling Bluegrass Boys. Flatt's ability to "bend" notes into "blue notes" enabled Monroe to meld the traditional mountain music he had heard and played as a boy with the blues music with which he was becoming more familiar. Against Flatt's strong but unassuming voice Monroe placed his indescribably soulful high tenor; their harmonies produced the "high lonesome" sound that is inevitably present in any description of this band's oeuvre. The result was a truly original American musical form. Almost immediately after the addition of Flatt, who also played guitar and wrote songs, and a young banjo picker from North Carolina named Earl Scruggs, Bill Monroe and His Bluegrass Boys became one of the most popular musical groups of the post–World War II era. Their records, most notably two singles, "Kentucky Waltz" (Columbia 20013, 1946) and "Blue Moon of Kentucky" (Columbia 20370, 1947), sold hundreds of thousands of copies and reached hundreds of thousands of listeners over the powerful radio station WSM, which broadcast the seminal Grand Ole Opry from Nashville, Tennessee, every Saturday evening. The group was so popular and so influential that its name became eponymous with the vibrant new style of American folk music that continues to flourish.

Flatt spent four years with the Bluegrass Boys, during which time he further honed his voice and grew into a remarkably original and economical songwriter and guitar player. By 1948 he had already gone a long way toward defining what it meant to sing, write, and play bluegrass, and the ascending flourish of a guitar lick at the end of each chorus and verse of a song that characterizes this musical style is still known as "the Flatt run."

Flatt and Scruggs left the Bluegrass Boys in 1948, at the height of the band's popularity. For a brief period they had a short spot on Mac Wiseman's "Farm and Fun Time" show broadcast on radio station WCYB in Bristol, Virginia, and their popularity grew rapidly from that point on. Flatt and Scruggs made American music history by forming a band that continued in Monroe's general style but took bluegrass, as the form was coming to be known, in exciting new directions. At the same time, another band, the Stanley Brothers, also emerged in the style of Bill Monroe, so in 1948 bluegrass became a genre, whereas before it had been one band's original sound. Flatt and Scruggs, already recognized as the finest bluegrass musicians of their generation, formed the Foggy Mountain Boys, with Flatt as singer, guitarist, and master of ceremonies. The group became the most popular bluegrass band in history, quickly eclipsing Monroe's success. Flatt and Scruggs made more live appearances in the 1950s and 1960s than any other bluegrass or country-western musician. The Foggy Mountain Boys and the incarnation of the Bluegrass Boys that included Flatt and Scruggs are the bands against which all other bluegrass groups will forever be measured.

The folk revival of the early 1960s introduced American crowds made up primarily of college students to the practitioners of indigenous forms of American music, such as bluegrass and the blues. In 1962, at the height of this revival, Flatt and Scruggs played to a raucous, sold-out crowd at Carnegie Hall in New York City, an indisputable sign that the band had arrived on the American popular music scene. In 1962 Flatt's tune "The Ballad of Jed Clampett," the theme song to the forgettable but momentarily popular "Beverly Hillbillies" television program, became the first bluegrass song to hit number one on *Billboard* magazine's country chart. Flatt and Scruggs's "Foggy Mountain Breakdown" (recorded in 1942), the theme song to the acclaimed motion picture *Bonnie and Clyde* (1968), exposed their music to an even wider audience.

After Flatt and Scruggs went their separate ways in 1969, Flatt continued to explore new avenues in traditional bluegrass as the leader of the Nashville Grass, one of the most popular bluegrass bands of the 1970s. Flatt's new band reportedly logged more than ten thousand miles per month as it toured North America. He also had a regular spot on the Grand Ole Opry and continued to write, record, and tour almost until the moment of his death in a hospital in Nashville, the city that he as much as anyone had helped to transform into the worldwide center of country music.

Lester Flatt's songwriting, singing, and guitar picking continue to influence bluegrass and country-western musicians. Even the most knowledgeable of bluegrass experts—to say nothing of the millions of avid listeners—are likely to think of Flatt's style in trying to define bluegrass music. Certainly it was his decision to break away from his mentor Bill Monroe's greatest band that ensured the development of bluegrass music beyond the confines of the Bluegrass Boys. Thanks in large part to Flatt's prodigious creative output, bluegrass music continues to thrive.

• A biography is Jake Lambert and Curly Sechler, *The Good Things Outweigh the Bad: A Biography of Lester Flatt* (1982). For more on Flatt's role in the development of bluegrass see Robert Cantwell, *Bluegrass Breakdown: The Making of the Old Southern Sound* (1984), and Neil V. Rosenberg, *Bluegrass: A History* (1985). For a sample of his music, try *The Original Bluegrass Band*, with the Bluegrass Boys (Rounder Records 06); *Changin' Times*, with the Foggy Mountain Boys (Columbia Records CS 09596); *The Original Sound*, with the Foggy Mountain Boys (Mercury Records MC 20773); *Lester Raymond Flatt* (Flying Fish Records 015); and *Best of Lester Flatt* (Victor Records ALLI-0578). An obituary is in the *New York Times*, 12 May 1979.

J. TODD MOYE

FLAVIN, Martin Archer (2 Nov. 1883–27 Dec. 1967), writer and businessman, was born in San Francisco, California, the son of Martin J. Flavin, a merchant, and Louise Archer. At the age of four he saw a production of *Romeo and Juliet*, which "made an indelible impression" (*Wilson Bulletin* 5 [Jan. 1931]: 292) on him. His father died while Martin was still a child; his mother remarried soon after, and the family moved to Chicago. Martin attended public schools there and began writing plays at age twelve, producing them with friends in the basement of his home. He attended the University of Chicago (1903–1905), where he was active in all phases of dramatic production, preferring at that time the comic opera. After two years he withdrew and turned to writing short stories, supporting himself with a night job on the *Chicago Tribune*. In 1906 he began working for a wallpaper manufacturing firm in Joliet, Illinois, with the plan of returning to writing when he was more mature. In 1914 he married Daphne Virginia Springer. They had one daughter and were divorced in 1917. He was in officer candidate school in the field artillery during the latter part of World War I. At the end of the war, combining his jobs of president of one company and vice president of another, he returned to writing, concentrating on his first love, the theater. What followed was a series of one-act plays, which suggested a real talent for playwriting. The best of these were collected in the book *Brains and Other Plays*, published by Samuel French in 1926. In 1919 he married Sarah Keese Arnold and settled near Carmel, California; they had two sons.

His first success in full-length drama was *Children of the Moon*, which ran on Broadway for more than 100 performances in 1923. Concerned with an overprotective, selfish mother and family madness, the drama elicited comparisons of the playwright with Henrik Ibsen. He retired from his businesses in 1926, but it was not until 1929 that he again achieved success on Broadway, this time with three dramas in the same season. The most notable of the three, *The Criminal Code*, won the New York Theatre Club Medal for the best play of the season. Inspired by a visit to San Quentin and critical of the justice system, the play held the stage for 174 performances. A second play,

Broken Dishes, a comedy, received good reviews and ran 178 performances. For a time in the early 1930s he worked in Hollywood as a screenwriter but continued writing plays. In 1935 he again had three plays in production: two on Broadway and one in noncommercial theater. None of these were successful, though one, *Achilles Had a Heel*, panned by some as confusing, received an excellent review by critic Grenville Vernon. The next season the failure of his thirteenth full-length production, *Around the Corner*, was, Flavin said, "the straw that broke the camel's back" (*Current Biography*, 1943); at this point he stopped writing for the stage, though he did for a short time teach playwriting at Stanford.

Following the death from a fall of his second wife in 1937, Flavin turned to writing long fiction. His first novel, *Mr. Littlejohn*, appeared in 1940, the same year he married Cornelia Clampett Bell. A modern picaresque story of a businessman tired of it all, the book met with some success, one critic comparing it favorably with *Tristram Shandy*. His second novel, *Corporal Cat*, appeared in 1941. Its story of the brief career of a German paratrooper who parachutes behind his own lines and is unwittingly killed by his own people was even more unconventional than his first. His next novel scored his greatest success: *Journey in the Dark* won the Harper Prize in 1943 and the Pulitzer Prize for fiction in 1944. A rags-to-riches story (with strong doses of autobiography), it is generally engaging, especially in its account of Sam Braden's growing up in Wyattville, a small Iowa town along the Mississippi River. Clifton Fadiman, one of the Pulitzer judges, characterized the book as "intelligent and conscientious," and the reviews were generally positive. Flavin's fourth novel, *The Enchanted*, appeared in 1947. The story of seven orphans stranded on a desert island, it was almost universally panned by reviewers. Ten years later came his last novel, *Cameron Hill*, a riches-to-rags story; his hero, Cameron Bradley, loses everything of importance—wealth, love, opportunity—and ends up strangling a prostitute.

After a move to Pebble Beach in 1946, Flavin spent the last twenty years of his life as a journalist, traveling extensively and writing of his observations and experiences. From a trip to South Africa in 1948 came the book *Black and White*, published in 1950, excerpts of which appeared first in *Harper's* magazine. In the fall of that year he and his wife set out from San Francisco for a trip around the world. From this journey came articles in *Harper's* on refugees in Korea, problems in India, and conditions in Berlin. In 1962 he published *Red Poppies and White Marble*, a travel book tracing the antiquities of the Riviera. He and his third wife were divorced in 1963. Flavin died in Carmel, California.

Flavin never fulfilled his promise in either drama or fiction; perhaps twenty years spent in each genre was not enough. John Gassner called him one of "our lost playwrights" (*Theatre Arts*, Aug. 1954). And critic W. J. Stuckey rated *Journey in the Dark* one of the worst choices for the Pulitzer Prize, calling it "a series of badly written, disconnected incidents which the author attempts to force into significance."

• The Emma Mills Memorial Library Collection contains typescripts of works and letters of Flavin. A brief discussion of *Journey in the Dark* is in W. J. Stuckey, *The Pulitzer Prize Novels: A Critical Backward Look* (1966). Obituaries are in the *New York Times*, 28 Dec. 1967; *Publishers Weekly*, 8 Jan. 1968; *Current Biography* (Feb. 1968); *Books Abroad* (Spring 1968); and *Britannica Book of the Year* (1968).

RICHARD BOUDREAU

FLEESON, Doris (20 May 1901–1 Aug. 1970), journalist, was born in Sterling, Kansas, the daughter of William Fleeson, a clothier, and Helen Hermione Tebbe. Fleeson was educated in public schools and at the University of Kansas, graduating with a degree in English in 1923.

Influenced by reading the work of fellow Kansans William Allen White of the *Emporia Gazette* and Edgar Watson Howe at the *Atchison Globe*, Fleeson chose a career in journalism. Her first reporting job was with the *Pittsburg (Kans.) Sun*, and she later served as society editor for the *Evanston (Ill.) News-Index* in 1926. She wanted to work for a major newspaper in Chicago or New York City. Fleeson briefly served as city editor for the *Great Neck News* on Long Island starting in December 1926, but after learning of a *New York Daily News* reporting vacancy in 1927 Fleeson obtained an interview with the editor and got the job covering crime and legal affairs immediately. Her articles analyzing state and local government scandals brought her important attention. She married another *Daily News* reporter, John O'Donnell, in 1930; they had one child. The couple wrote a column about politics and politicians entitled "Capitol Stuff" for the Washington bureau of the *Daily News* beginning in 1933.

The Great Depression took its toll on newspaper reporters as well as other professionals. *New York World-Telegram* columnist Heywood Broun invited Fleeson to join him in promoting "A Union of Reporters." He recruited Fleeson because he believed the *Daily News* was more sympathetic to editorial workers and reporters than most other newspapers. In 1933 Fleeson met with other New York editorial writers at Broun's house to organize the Guild of New York Newspaper Men and Women. Soon the organization expanded, changing its name to the American Newspaper Guild, and Fleeson was a member of the Guild's original executive committee. She also joined a Guild lobbying group that traveled to Washington to meet with the National Recovery Administration to appeal for a minimum wage of $35 per week for reporters.

Among other honors, Fleeson was the first female reporter allowed to travel with President Franklin Roosevelt in 1933 and was elected president of the Women's National Press Club in 1937. She won the first reporting award given by the New York Newspaper Women's Club in 1937 for covering the 1936 Republican Convention and a second Club award in 1943 for an article about Wendell Willkie's fight for the 1944 Republican nomination. Following her divorce from O'Donnell in 1942 and a brief trip to Europe, the *Daily News* assigned Fleeson to write radio news. Unhappy with what she considered a menial task, Fleeson resigned in 1943 and became a war correspondent for *Woman's Home Companion* magazine. Over the next two years she wrote ten articles about various aspects of World War II, including the Allied landings in Italy (1943) and France (1944).

Upon returning to the United States in 1945, Fleeson began writing a political column from Washington, D.C. The column was published by the *Washington Star* and the *Boston Globe*, and before the end of 1945 Fleeson had arranged to market her column with the Bell Syndicate, thus following Dorothy Thompson as the second woman to write a syndicated political column. In 1954 Fleeson switched her column to the United Features Syndicate. In the late 1950s, at its peak, Fleeson's column appeared in more than 100 newspapers.

Fleeson made a point of finding her own sources, often at social events, rather than relying on press briefings by government officials. She revealed a private feud between Supreme Court justices Robert H. Jackson and Hugo Black, quoted President Harry Truman's off-the-record critical remarks that military deserters in the Korean War resided in parts of the nation supporting General Douglas MacArthur, and predicted accurately Dwight D. Eisenhower's resignation as NATO commander in 1952 in preparation for seeking the Republican nomination for president.

Fleeson's pointed and passionate writing style continued to earn her awards during the 1950s. She won the Headliner Award for 1950, sponsored by the women's professional journalism society Theta Sigma Phi. In 1954 she was the first woman to win the Raymond Clapper Award presented by the American Society of Newspaper Editors for meritorious service. Describing herself as a "nonpartisan liberal," Fleeson did not hesitate to criticize Democratic presidents such as Truman. She was most complimentary of Democratic party presidential nominee Adlai Stevenson during the 1952 and 1956 campaigns and offered criticism of John Kennedy's policies early in his administration. Fleeson married Dan A. Kimball, former secretary of the navy and president of Aerojet Corporation, in 1958. She covered her last presidential campaign in 1964. She became ill that year but continued to write her column until 1969. She died in Washington.

Doris Fleeson made an indelible impression on American journalism by her insider reporting and political columns, which were marked by an irreverence for virtually all politicians. By enduring and overcoming societal prejudices, she demonstrated that women could compete with men in the profession. Fleeson assisted young female journalists, such as Mary McGrory, and inspired later generations by her example.

• Fleeson's papers are housed in the Spencer Research Library at the University of Kansas, Lawrence. The best biographical source is Terry Hynes, "Doris Fleeson," in *Dictionary of Literary Biography: American Newspaper Journalists,* *1926–1950,* ed. Perry J. Ashley (1984). Another biographical source is Barbara Belford, *Brilliant Bylines: A Biographical Anthology of Notable Newspaperwomen in America* (1986). Fleeson's role in founding the American Newspaper Guild is covered in Daniel J. Leab, *A Union of Individuals: The Formation of the American Newspaper Guild, 1933–1936* (1970). Her obituary is in the *New York Times,* 2 Aug. 1970.

DANIEL WEBSTER HOLLIS III

FLEET, Thomas (8 Sept. 1685–21 July 1758), printer and publisher, was born in Shropshire, England (parents unknown). He apprenticed and served as a journeyman printer in England, but, according to Isaiah Thomas, a youthful show of disdain toward the Anglican church forced him to emigrate to America. Fleet arrived in Boston around 1712 and soon established a printing house in Pudding Lane. Perhaps his earliest imprint was the fourth edition of John Hill's *Young Secretary's Guide* (1713). Fleet would reprint the work many times during his printing career. Also in 1713 Fleet printed several items by Cotton Mather, whose works would become another staple of Fleet's business during the next decade and a half. In 1715 Fleet entered an informal partnership with Thomas Crump. Their joint imprints include many items, largely religious: sermons by Cotton Mather and Benjamin Colman and popular devotional manuals including the first American printing of Jabez Earle's *Sacramental Exercises* (1715); James Janeway's *Three Practical Discourses* (1715); and Matthew Henry's *Communicant's Companion* (1716). Back on his own in 1717, Fleet decreased his output somewhat, but he continued publishing religious items. He helped contribute to the popularity of the Indian captivity narrative by reprinting editions of both Mary Rowlandson's *Soveraignty and Goodness of God* (1720) and John Williams's (1664–1729) *Redeemed Captive, Returning to Zion* (1720).

The first religious controversy Fleet took part in concerned John Checkley and the authority of the Anglican church. In 1719 Fleet published Checkley's edition of a work by English pamphleteer Charles Leslie, *Religion of Jesus Christ the Only True Religion; or, A Short and Easie Method with the Deists,* and the following year he printed Checkley's *Choice Dialogues between a Godly Minister and an Honest Countryman Concerning Election and Predestination* (1720). Onto both tracts, Checkley appended documents from Ignatius that affirmed the primitive authority of bishops. In 1723 Checkley had Fleet print his *Modest Proof of the Order and Government Settled by Christ and His Apostles* in which he argued the apostolic origins of the episcopacy. Prominent Boston clergymen Edward Wigglesworth (1693–1765) and Jonathan Dickinson published responses, and Checkley again enlisted Fleet's services to print *A Defense of . . . A Modest Reproof* (1724) and *A Letter to Jonathan Dickinson* (1725). The pamphlets were avidly read among high and low church members. Fleet quickly recognized the profitability of becoming involved in Checkley's pamphlet war, but he had become a careful enough businessman to avoid direct involvement with the controversy. Fleet's support of Checkley never alienated him from the Puritan community. Throughout the early 1720s he continued to print many of Cotton Mather's works, including *A Father Departing* (1723), Mather's notable funeral sermon for Increase Mather. In one instance, however, Fleet openly defied the Puritan hegemony. As Clyde Duniway points out, although Fleet's contributions to James Franklin's antiauthoritarian *New England Courant* were probably unknown to the Boston officials, he publicly supported Franklin by posting £50 bail in his 1733 libel trial.

In the late 1720s Fleet diversified his printing output. From 1729 through 1731 he was printer to the Massachusetts House of Representatives. In early 1731 he moved his operation to Cornhill, where he sold books and held auctions. After John Draper began printing Jeremiah Gridley's Boston *Weekly Rehearsal* in September 1731, Fleet took over printing the paper starting 21 August 1732. Fleet assumed editorial responsibilities with the 2 April 1733 issue, in which he wrote, "The publisher of this paper declares himself of no Party, and invites all Gentlemen of Leisure and Capacity, inclined on either Side, to write any thing of a political Nature, that tends to enlighten and serve the Publick, to communicate their Productions, provided they are not overlong, and confined within Modesty and Good Manners; for all possible Care will be taken that nothing contrary to these shall ever be here published" (quoted in Thomas, p. 247). While Fleet's paper often contained worthy belletristic essays, he was reluctant to include poetry. A headnote introducing the first poem he printed in the *Weekly Rehearsal* (27 Jan. 1735) stated, "I confess that Poetry does not look over graceful in a *News-Paper*." The most notable poem Fleet printed was Mather Byles's "The Comet: A Poem" (*Boston Evening Post*, 20 Feb. 1744). In August 1735 Fleet changed the *Weekly Rehearsal* into the *Boston Evening Post*, which he published until his death. Calling the *Evening Post* "the best newspaper then published in Boston," Isaiah Thomas wrote: "The selection of entertaining and amusing pieces from London publications, and some of Fleet's own humorous paragraphs gave it animation, and its news were well selected and seasonably published. It interfered very little with political controversy, and not greatly with religious disputes."

In the late 1730s Fleet recognized the commercial possibilities of the Great Awakening, and many of his subsequent imprints concern the popular religious revival. Though he had avoided becoming personally involved with controversy, he could not disguise his contempt for George Whitefield. Describing the humbling effects of the same comet that had inspired Mather Byles, Fleet wrote, "there will be reason to think that the Comet is the most profitable Itinerant Preacher, and friendly NEW LIGHT, that has yet appeared among us." Fleet's *Evening Post* contained articles both defending and vilifying Whitefield, and he separately printed many indictments of Whitefield by prominent Boston divines, including Nathaniel

Henchman, Samuel Niles, and Edward Wigglesworth (1693–1765). When Whitefield's appearance coincided with a spell of inclement weather in 1754, Fleet included a poem in the *Evening Post* that begins, "When Whitefield comes, 'Tis fair: A Fog ensues . . . " (21 Oct. 1754).

Fleet's remarks about Whitefield reveal both humor and commercial prudence. His wit often evidenced itself in the pages of the *Evening Post*. Isaiah Thomas devoted much of his lengthy essay on Fleet to his favorite excerpts from the *Evening Post*, summing up, "Fleet was industrious and economical; free from superstition; and possessed a fund of wit and humor, which were often displayed in his paragraphs and advertisements." Fleet's career shows his maturity as a printer. His early experience in England taught him to tread lightly toward the established church, and his subsequent activities in New England show that he learned his lesson. Avoiding direct conflict with the Puritan hegemony, Fleet ably served Boston's reading community through the first half of the eighteenth century.

• For Fleet's imprints, see Charles Evans, *American Bibliography* (1903–1934). Information concerning Fleet within Evans is easily accessible using Roger Pattrell Bristol, *Index of Printers, Publishers, and Booksellers Indicated by Charles Evans in His American Bibliography* (1961). See also Bristol's *Supplement to Charles Evans' American Bibliography* (1970). Fleet's newspapers are discussed in Clarence S. Brigham, *History and Bibliography of American Newspapers 1690–1820* (1947). Other sources include Isaiah Thomas, *The History of Printing in America*, ed. Marcus A. McCorison (1970); J. A. Leo Lemay, *A Calendar of American Poetry in the Colonial Newspapers and Magazines* (1972); Benjamin Franklin V, ed., *Boston Printers, Publishers, and Booksellers: 1640–1800* (1980); and Clyde Duniway, *The Development of Freedom of the Press in Massachusetts* (1906).

KEVIN J. HAYES

FLEETE, Henry (c. 1602–c. 1661), English colonial merchant and Indian interpreter, was born in County Kent, England, the son of William Fleete, a lawyer and country squire, and Deborah Scott. Residing in America after 1621, Fleete is best known for pioneering the Potomac River beaver trade between the late 1620s and early 1630s and for guiding Lord Baltimore's colonists to their first Maryland settlement in March 1634.

Fleete was well connected to other leading gentry families in Kent, including the Wyatts of Boxley Abbey and the Scotts of Scot's Hall, but his dim prospects for landed inheritance or a university education as a sixth son prompted him to seek his fortune in the new colony of Virginia. His father, an investor in the Virginia Company of London since 1612, joined other influential Kentish gentlemen in sending their funds and their sons to Chesapeake Bay. Fleete arrived in Virginia in November 1621 with his second cousins—the colony's new governor, Sir Francis Wyatt, and the Reverend Hawte Wyatt—and others from Kent, including George Sandys, a notable poet and new treasurer of the colony, and Virginia's first surveyor, William Claiborne, a recent Cambridge graduate.

Fleete's youth and inexperience might have consigned him to historical oblivion had it not been for the massive Indian attack that devastated dozens of English settlements only five months after his arrival. The Powhatan Uprising of 22 March 1622 killed at least 330 colonists in a single day—about one-fourth of the total in Virginia—and wiped out a decade of English progress. Colonists of every social class died in that terrifying attack, creating unprecedented opportunities for survivors, like Fleete, with the luck and pluck to grasp them.

Fleete's new career began in March 1623 when he was captured during an Indian ambush of Captain Henry Spelman's expedition along the Potomac River. Spelman and most of his men were slain, but Fleete survived to spend the next four years as a prisoner of the Nacotchtank (Anacostan, Nacostine) Indians near present-day Washington, D.C. He later commented that this experience enabled him to be "better proficient in the Indian language than mine own" and thus "more able that way" to pursue his future course as an Indian interpreter and fur trader. Fleete's extensive knowledge of southern Algonquian dialects and Indian trading customs would propel him into a prominent position of lifelong influence matched by only a few colonists.

By some unknown means, Fleete turned up in London in 1627 actively soliciting investors to help him procure the luxurious "black fox" and other fine pelts from the Potomac River area. In September of that year, he returned to the Chesapeake as a factor (local trading agent) in a hundred-ton ship, *Paramour*, owned by wealthy London merchant William Cloberry. Huge profits eluded him, but by 1631 Fleete and his three younger brothers (Edward, Reginald, and John) were factors for George Griffith and Company, engaged in transporting many kinds of regional products from port to port along the Atlantic Coast. They would convey provisions from London to New England, take Indian trade items from there to the Chesapeake, ship Virginia maize back to New England, and finally sail back to Britain with a rich store of Potomac beaver pelts aboard Griffith's eighty-ton bark, *Warwick*.

According to Fleete's intriguing but little-known "Breife Journall," which detailed his trading activities between July 1631 and September 1632, he had to teach the Algonquians along the lower Potomac River how to preserve their beaver pelts for market, because they had traditionally burned them as trash. But he also described his encounters with distant Iroquoian tribes who possessed thousands of prime, well-processed beaver pelts and were very sophisticated about European products. On 10 July 1631 Fleete met with a delegation of "Usserahak" Indians from a huge village located many days beyond the falls of the Potomac, but he was embarrassed by his paltry trade goods: "I had but little, not worth above 100 pound starlinge, and such as was not fitt for these Indians to trade with,

who delight in hatchets, and knives of large size, broadcloth and coats, shirts, and Scottish stockins." The next day other Indians arrived from a distant, rival tribe, dressed in beaver coats trimmed with red fringe and carrying English metal axes from a Thames River merchant he knew. "Their language was haughty and they . . . demanded to see my truck, which, upon view, they scorned."

Hard-to-satisfy native customers were the least of Fleete's concerns, however, since his uncanny success in locating vast stores of rich furs produced jealousy among Indians and Englishmen alike. The Nacotchtanks blocked trade goods and furs from crossing the Potomac River falls in either direction, while Virginians claimed the beaver pelts that Fleete's Algonquian friends had been saving for him. In July 1632 representatives of Virginia's Council of State intercepted his ship and escorted him to Jamestown as an interloper. Governor John Harvey wanted to share in Fleete's profits and even authorized him to ignore his debts to Griffith and Company, while rival fur traders on the council, especially William Claiborne, tried to prohibit Fleete's access to Indian trappers along the Potomac.

Resisting a loss of independent business control in either case, Fleete joined forces with Lord Baltimore's first Maryland colonists when they sailed into the northern Chesapeake in March 1634. Cecil Calvert, lord proprietor of Maryland, had a royal charter that gave him control of all the prime beaver territories in the bay. He formed a business alliance with Fleete, the bilingual entrepreneur, and the Piscataway Indian trappers of the lower Potomac River. Dependent on the natural resources and native peoples of the Potomac, this intercultural interest group sought mutual military security and trading profits in the face of violent hostility from Claiborne and his colonists on nearby Kent Island, who now had to enter Maryland territory illegally to retrieve the annual fur harvest from the powerful Susquehannocks at the head of the bay.

Little is known of Fleete's family life. His brothers disappear from the records very early, and he married a widow, Sarah Burden, rather late in life. They had one child, Henry Fleet (all subsequent generations dropped the final e).

In 1653 the Virginia General Assembly recognized Fleete's pathbreaking contributions as an explorer and entrepreneur by granting him a special license to seek out and enjoy the "benefits, profit and trade in places where no English have ever been." Fleete's greatest legacy, however, was the intercultural cooperation he promoted between natives and newcomers as an invaluable interpreter and negotiator. He successfully tutored Governor Leonard Calvert of Maryland in the Indian "Customes of [the] Country" so as to make the local Algonquians "glad of our company" and thus avoid the bloody blunders that had disrupted Jamestown's early decades. Fleete's special talents were recognized and sought out by Marylanders and Virginians alike; between June 1644 and April 1646 *both* Chesapeake colonies, though locked in a virtual civil war, picked Fleete to arrange truces with Indians as different as the Iroquoian Susquehannocks far to the north and the Algonquian Pamunkeys/Powhatans far to the south.

Fleete died between April 1660 and May 1661 in Northumberland County, Virginia.

• An indispensable primary source is Fleete's own "Breife Journal of a Voyage Made in the Barque Warwick to Virginia & Other Parts of the Continent of America [4 July 1631–14 September 1632]," a twelve-page manuscript dated 22 Feb. 1633 in the Lambeth Palace Library, London. It has never been published in its entirety, and the versions by Edward D. Neill—*The English Colonization of America during the Seventeenth Century* (1871) and *The Founders of Maryland* (1876)—are seriously flawed, with many omissions.

The skimpy genealogical details on Fleete are compiled in Betsy Fleet, *Henry Fleet: Pioneer, Explorer, Trader, Planter, Legislator, Justice, & Peacemaker* (1989), and Virginia M. Meyer and John Frederick Dorman, eds., *Adventurers of Purse and Person: Virginia, 1607–1624/5*, 3d ed. (1987). Inexplicably, none of the four Fleete brothers appears in Edward A. Papenfuse et al., eds., *A Biographical Dictionary of the Maryland Legislature, 1635–1789* (2 vols., 1979, 1985). Informative secondary sources include Raphael Semmes, *Captains and Mariners of Early Maryland* (1937); J. Frederick Fausz, "Present at the 'Creation': The Chesapeake World That Greeted the Maryland Colonists," *Maryland Historical Magazine* 79, no. 1 (Spring 1984): 7–20; Fausz, "'To Draw Thither the Trade of Beavers': The Strategic Significance of the English Fur Trade in the Chesapeake, 1620–1660," in *Le Castor Fait Tout: Selected Papers of the Fifth North American Fur Trade Conference, 1985*, ed. Bruce G. Trigger et al. (1987); and Fausz, "Merging and Emerging Worlds: Anglo-Indian Interest Groups and the Development of the Seventeenth Century Chesapeake," in *Colonial Chesapeake Society*, ed. Lois Green Carr et al. (1988).

J. FREDERICK FAUSZ

FLEISCHER, Max (19 July 1883–11 Sept. 1972), and **Dave Fleischer** (14 July 1894–23 June 1979), animators and the joint heads of Fleischer Studios, were the sons of William Fleischer, a tailor and part-time inventor, and Amalia (maiden name unknown). Max was born in Vienna, Austria, and Dave was born in New York City, where their parents moved when Max was four. Two of their brothers, Joe and Lou, also made significant contributions to Fleischer Studios. The Fleischers were relatively well off during their early years in America, but with the introduction of mass-produced clothing, they slid into poverty. The family moved to Brooklyn and relocated frequently. The children attended public schools, and both Max and Dave showed an early flair for drawing. Max attended high school in the evening and received additional training at the Art Students League and Cooper Union.

Dave left school at a relatively young age and worked at various odd jobs. He had stints as an usher at New York's Palace Theater, as an artist at the Walker Engraving Company, and as a film cutter at Pathé Frères.

In 1900 Max began to work as an errand boy at the *Brooklyn Daily Eagle*. By 1904 he was a staff artist. In 1905 he married his childhood sweetheart, Essie Gold;

they had two children. After he left the *Eagle*, Max briefly did artwork for two companies and then became art editor of *Popular Science Monthly* in 1914. There his childhood interest in mechanical matters was reignited.

In fact, it was a mechanical problem that pulled Max Fleischer into the field of animation. Early animation was frequently very choppy. Max theorized that if live-action footage were traced, frame by frame, fluid motion could be achieved. He enlisted the help of his brothers Dave and Joe, and the three developed the Rotoscope, a camera mounted under a piece of frosted glass with a crank to advance the film, so each frame could be traced.

It took the brothers a week to build the Rotoscope, but it was a full year before they finished their first cartoon. Dave donned a clown suit, and Max and Joe filmed him. Then they traced the clown on the Rotoscope. Work on the cartoon was completed in 1916, and a patent for the Rotoscope came through a year later.

Max interested a former colleague from the *Eagle*, pioneering animator John Randolph Bray, in their cartoon, and Bray hired Max and Dave to produce a cartoon a month for his Bray Pictograph series.

After the United States entered World War I, Max was one of the Bray Studios employees who was assigned to make army training films from 1917 to 1918. Dave joined the army in 1917 and was assigned to edit and cut film. Three days before joining the army, he married Ida Sharnow; they had two children.

After the war, Max and Dave returned to Bray Studios. Their Out of the Inkwell series was created in 1919, and in 1921 they left Bray to form their own company, Out of the Inkwell Films, Inc.

Within a year, Max was concentrating on the business side, while Dave came up with scenarios for the cartoons and added gags and special bits. The actual drawing was done by staff animators. On the finished cartoons, Max was credited as the producer and Dave as the director, although in reality, Max acted as the executive producer, while Dave acted as the producer and dialogue director of all their cartoons.

The Fleischer cartoons were marked by zany inventiveness. Live action was mixed with animation. Max Fleischer, playing himself, opened each cartoon. He would dip his pen into an inkwell, and in a few strokes Koko the Clown (the Fleischers' signature character from the moment Dave donned the clown suit) would emerge and begin to move.

Another Fleischer innovation was a white ball that bounced over the words of a song, hitting each syllable when it was supposed to be sung. Their Song Car-Tunes, introduced in 1924, were an immediate hit. The Fleischers were also the first animators to experiment with sound, and they produced several Sound Car-Tunes in 1926 and 1927.

In 1924 Max and Dave established an independent studio, Red Seal Pictures, to distribute their cartoons and produce live-action movies. It failed. The Fleischers may have lost as much as $1 million and found themselves unable to pay even their lab bills. They were bailed out in 1927 by an investor whose ethics proved to be unreliable. In January 1929 Max filed a bankruptcy petition. Paramount, which had begun distributing the Fleischers' cartoons in 1927, joined Max and Dave in setting up a new corporation, Fleischer Studios, Inc., with Max as president and Dave as vice president. But Paramount retained 51 percent of the stock and held the copyrights to the cartoons.

Meanwhile, the success of Walt Disney's "Steamboat Willie" in 1928 changed the cartoon landscape. Sound became the norm, Disney became the industry's leader, and Disney lured many of the Fleischers' top animators to California. Ironically, at the same time that the studio lost many of its top animators, it also entered its period of greatest creativity. Meticulous care was the hallmark of Disney cartoons; the Fleischers' efforts were marked by freewheeling verve. Animators were given loose story lines and were encouraged to embellish as they went along. A maximum number of gags were stuffed into each Fleischer cartoon, and coming up with extra gags was Dave's particular specialty. During the 1920s Max Fleischer was arguably the best-known animator in America, by virtue of his appearances with Koko the Clown. Even after the ascendancy of Disney, Fleischer Studios held its own, running a close second throughout the 1930s.

With the advent of sound, Koko was temporarily retired. In the Fleischers' sixth Talkatoon, "Dizzy Dishes" (1930), a new star emerged. Betty Boop, the creation of animator Grim Natwick, started out as a female dog with some human characteristics. In 1932, she emerged as a full-fledged human and became the first female cartoon character to be a lead in her own right. Her trademarks were a squeaky voice, the catch phrase "boop oop a doop," and a garter that her dangerously short skirt never quite concealed. She frequently was beset by lascivious villains, and the tone of her cartoons was decidedly risqué. The movie industry's adoption of the Hayes Code in 1934 forced the Fleischers to tone down their endearing vamp. She continued to headline cartoons through 1939, but she was never quite the same. Luckily, the Fleischers had developed another cartoon superstar. Popeye, already a popular King Features comic strip character, made his cartoon debut in "Popeye the Sailor" (1933) and was an immediate hit.

In December 1937 Walt Disney upped the ante among animators with the release of *Snow White*, the first full-length animated movie. In February 1938 the Fleischers announced that they would build a $300,000 animation studio in Miami to produce full-length feature cartoons.

The attraction of Florida was threefold: land was cheap, the state of Florida was not supportive of union activity (in 1937, there had been a bitter six-month strike at Fleischer Studios), and Miami offered tax advantages. But it was Paramount that encouraged the move and bankrolled construction of the new studio with a ten-year loan.

Gulliver's Travels, a favorite book of Max's, was chosen as Fleischer Studios' first full-length vehicle. But the Fleischers were operating under serious handicaps. The staff of 200 in New York was expanded to 500 in Miami, and many of the new employees had little experience. *Snow White* was four years in the making; *Gulliver's Travels*, which premiered in December 1939, was rushed through production in twenty months. It was a success at the box office, but it didn't stand up to comparisons with *Snow White*.

Work on a second cartoon feature began almost as soon as *Gulliver's Travels* was completed, and the Fleischers also continued to produce cartoon shorts, including an adaptation of the comic book "Superman" that was both an artistic and a popular success.

The Fleischers' second full-length feature, *Mr. Bug Goes to Town* (1941), flopped. It received only lukewarm praise from critics, and Paramount gave it little promotional support. Meanwhile, Max and Dave, who had always had an uneasy partnership, were feuding.

In 1942, in a move that is difficult to fathom, Paramount demanded immediate repayment of approximately $100,000, which was still outstanding on the ten-year Miami studio loan. The Fleischers were in a vulnerable spot. Max Fleischer carefully had patented dozens of inventions, but Paramount held the copyrights to Fleischer Studios' most valuable asset, its cartoon library. And since the Fleischers tended to emphasize their technological innovations, rather than their integral role in the creation of Fleischer Studios' remarkable cartoons, Paramount apparently underestimated their contributions and assumed that it could run the Fleischers' studio better than they could.

Paramount's move probably was illegal, since the balance of the loan was not due, but animosity between Max and Dave had become so intense that neither had any interest in cooperating with the other to mount a legal challenge. It was not until seven years later that Max sued, and by then too much time had passed for the Fleischers to get legal redress. Paramount retained most of the studio's employees and renamed it Famous Studios. Quality began to fall almost immediately.

Neither Max nor Dave was as successful on his own as they had been together. Max joined the Jam-Handy Company in Detroit, where he worked on commercial films. He remained active in various projects up until his death in Woodland Hills, California.

Dave moved to Hollywood in 1942 to head Columbia Pictures' cartoon unit. The freewheeling Fleischer style didn't transplant well, and the job lasted only two years. After a divorce from his first wife, he married Mae Schwartz; he had no children with his second wife. In 1944 he was hired at Universal Pictures, where he contributed gags, special effects, and extra bits to the studio's live-action movies. He worked there until his retirement in 1967. He also died in Woodland Hills.

After the demise of Fleischer Studios, Max and Dave never spoke to each other again.

• Leslie Cabarga, *The Fleischer Story*, rev. ed. (1988), is the most complete bibliography available on the Fleischer brothers. Leonard Maltin, *Of Mice and Magic: A History of American Animated Cartoons*, rev. ed. (1987), contains a history of Fleischer Studios and a valuable survey of its work. Insights into the personalities of Max and Dave can be gleaned from sections of Shamus Culhane, *Talking Animals and Other People* (1986), and Richard Fleischer, *Just Tell Me When to Cry: A Memoir* (1993). See also Giannalberto Bendazzi, *Cartoons: One Hundred Years of Cinema Animation* (1994); Grace Jeromski, ed., *International Dictionary of Films and Filmmakers* (1988); Mark Langer, "Institutional Power and the Fleischer Studios," *Cinema Journal* (Winter 1991): 3–22; and Film Dope (Feb. 1979): 27–35. Max's obituary is in *Variety*, 13 Sept. 1972; Dave's obituary is in *Variety*, 4 July 1979.

LYNN HOOGENBOOM

FLEISCHER, Nat (3 Nov. 1887–25 June 1972), boxing journalist and editor, grew up on New York's Lower East Side, a child of immigrants Haskell Fleischer, a tailor, and Anna Singer. Fleischer's interest in boxing was kindled in 1899 by the first fight he attended, one in which Terrible Terry McGovern knocked out Pedlar Palmer. At age twelve Fleischer briefly became an amateur featherweight. He graduated from the City College of New York (B.S., 1908), where he sprinted for the track team, managed the basketball team, and was a college correspondent for several newspapers. By his junior year he was a part-time cub reporter for the New York *Press*. He became a full-time member of the *Press*'s sports staff after college and was also a postgraduate chemistry student at New York University. An explosive experiment ended his academic career, and he became an elementary school teacher while still working full time as a sportswriter. He spent two summers as a playground teacher, organizing the Public School Athletic League's first Fourth of July schoolboy track and field meet. Despite his slight, 5′3″ stature, he served during World War I as an army fitness instructor.

Fleischer was part of an outstanding sports staff on the *Press*, but his first important news assignment occurred 14 April 1912 when he received the flash that the *Titanic* was sinking. His best reporting work came when he discovered that defendants in the notorious Rosenthal murder case of 1912 had secured $50,000 for their legal fees by employing East Side boxers and promoters to extort $100–$150 apiece from neighborhood merchants.

Fleischer worked as a sports editor from 1916 through 1929, first for the *New York Sun-Press* and later for the *Morning Herald*, the *Mail-Telegram*, and the *Evening Telegram*. He lost his last position in 1929 when Scripps-Howard bought Frank Munsey's *New York Telegram* and merged it with the *World*. He married Gertrude Phillips in 1917; they had one child.

In 1920 Fleischer supported passage of the Walker Act that legalized boxing in New York state. Beginning in 1923, he occasionally represented promoter Tex Rickard overseas and was Rickard's confidant in several boxing deals. Fleischer also played an important role in the construction of the third Madison Square Garden. In 1923, when Rickard's lease on the old Garden was about to lapse, the *Telegram*, for which Fleischer was sports editor, published his front-page story on the need for a new arena along with architectural plans for one produced by sports promoter Dinty Scanlon. Fleischer investigated potential sites and recommended a car barn belonging to the bankrupt Manhattan Railway Company. Rickard met with Fleischer and Scanlon, and three months later his syndicate purchased the barn at 50th Street and Eighth Avenue. Rickard dismissed Fleischer's contribution but eventually paid Fleischer $2,500 and some stock for his work. In 1926 Fleischer "discovered" in Germany future heavyweight champion Max Schmeling, then a light heavyweight in only his second year of professional boxing. Fleischer was offered a comanagership, which he refused out of friendship and on principle, since it would have been a conflict of interest with his journalism career. He did agree to help represent the German boxer in the United States for 10 percent of his earnings, which he never collected, for the same reasons. Fleischer also advised and was overseas representative for Mike Jacobs, who succeeded Rickard as boxing's leading impresario.

Fleischer's greatest contribution to the sport was as editor and publisher of the monthly magazine *Ring*, "the Bible of Boxing," which first appeared on 10 February 1922 with a 2,700 print run. State legislators were considering proposals to ban boxing, and Fleischer suggested to Rickard that a boxing periodical could promote the sport. When Rickard offered no support, Fleischer started *Ring* largely on his own with some help from Ike Dorgan, Rickard's public relations chief, Madison Square Garden treasurer Frank Coultry, and I. C. Brenner of *Golfer's Magazine*. In only one year, *Ring* expanded its page count by more than half and reached a circulation of 13,000. By 1940 distribution had surpassed 200,000 copies. The magazine reviewed recent fights, reported on upcoming bouts, offered features on prominent fighters, and answered queries from readers. Fleischer used *Ring* to campaign for fair play in sports. In 1922 *Ring* led an unsuccessful crusade to break the color barrier in the heavyweight division and get number-one contender Harry Wills a championship match against Jack Dempsey. Monthly rankings of boxers were initiated in February 1925. Rickard was the first selector, but he had limited familiarity with fighters in lighter weight divisions. After Rickard's death in 1929, former heavyweight champion Jack Dempsey did the rating for one year, followed by Madison Square Garden matchmaker Tom McArdle, whose involvement was a conflict of interest. Starting in 1933, Fleischer issued the ratings, considered definitive in the boxing community, relying on the evaluations of worldwide correspondents. So important were *Ring*'s rankings that by the early 1950s underworld boxing figure Frankie Carbo threatened to make the magazine disappear from New York City newsstands unless a particular fighter gained "top ten" standing. Fleischer purchased the *Police Gazette* in 1932, and beginning in

1942 he edited the *Ring Record Book and Boxing Encyclopedia*. During World War II the magazine sponsored lectures and movies in military camps and hospitals and distributed sports equipment through the Serviceman's Athletic Fund.

Fleischer used *Ring* to promote boxing and seldom published stories detrimental to the sport. In 1967 when the World Boxing Association withdrew recognition of Muhammad Ali for claiming exemption from the draft on religious grounds, *Ring* continued to recognize him as champion through 1971 when the Supreme Court ruled in Ali's favor.

The preeminent historian of boxing, Fleischer wrote more than fifty books, mainly biographies and histories, beginning in 1929 with *Training for Boxers*, which sold nearly a million copies. He preferred the fighters of his youth, rating Jack Johnson the best heavyweight, Kid McCoy the best light heavyweight, and Stanley Ketchel, the best middleweight of all time. "Mr. Boxing" maintained the Boxing Hall of Fame and an outstanding collection of memorabilia at his Madison Square Garden office.

Fleischer died in Atlantic Beach, New York, shortly after his retirement from *Ring*. As the preeminent boxing journalist, he attended virtually all important bouts in the twentieth century and officiated in more than a thousand fights, among them probably more foreign matches than any other American. Fleischer was the leading popular historian of the ring and tried to stress the sport's positive features over its negative qualities. His judgments on boxers' abilities and performance were considered gospel. *Ring* remained the magazine of record for prize fighting after his death but was less authoritative than during his tenure.

• Fleischer's autobiography, *50 Years at Ringside* (1960), provides considerable information about his youth, his career in journalism, his work with Rickard and Jacobs, and his reminiscences of outstanding fights. On his career in the 1920s see also Randy Roberts, *Jack Dempsey: The Manassa Mauler* (1979). For an obituary, see *New York Times*, 26 June 1972.

STEVEN A. RIESS

FLEISCHMAN, Doris E. (18 July 1891–10 July 1980), public relations counsel, was born in New York City, the daughter of Samuel E. Fleischman, a lawyer, and Harriet Rosenthal. She received a bachelor's degree from Barnard College in 1913 and the next year was hired as a women's page writer by the *New York Tribune*, where in 1915 she was the first woman to cover a prize fight for a major newspaper. She advanced to assistant women's page editor before leaving in 1916; she then did freelance newspaper writing and fundraising work.

In 1919 she was the first employee hired by Edward L. Bernays, who had just opened an office providing what he called "publicity direction." As a prolific staff writer, Fleischman spent most of her time writing and placing news releases. But her work expanded in 1920 when the organization took on a new client, the National Association for the Advancement of Colored People (NAACP), which was holding its first national convention in the South and was concerned about negative, and possibly violent, local reaction. Working by herself, out of Atlanta, Georgia, Fleischman met with government officials and local editors during the week before the convention, helping calm a tense situation. Bernays joined her during the convention, and together they followed up on her media contacts, produced constant news releases, and helped obtain extensive positive coverage for the meeting. Decades later she said this work had affected her more deeply than anything else she did during her career.

When Fleischman and Bernays married in September 1922, she became an equal partner with him in their firm, known as Edward L. Bernays, Counsel on Public Relations. Together they were among a handful of people who founded the field of public relations, going on to help establish many of its principles, methods, and ethics. Inventing the term "public relations counsel," they were leaders in widening the profession beyond press agentry to actions that had a much broader influence on public opinion and behavior. Their New York firm was one of the country's premier public relations operations from the 1920s through the 1950s, with clients that included five U.S. presidents and an impressive list of well-known companies, government bodies, and educational and cultural institutions.

Their success was due in large part to their complementary personalities and professional strengths; in synergy, they were able to develop the kinds of innovative and effective campaigns that neither could have created individually. Both of them called their relationship a "24-hour-a-day partnership," and they benefited from their close, constant contact with each other, which gave them limitless opportunities to discuss their work and test out ideas—an important advantage since theirs was a new, rapidly developing field with few rules or precedents.

Fleischman was a strong, fast writer and editor, possessed a quick, original mind, and was highly imaginative. She also had excellent interpersonal skills and was an exceptional judge of people. She was more practical and organized than her husband, who was good at envisioning the large picture—whether it was a single campaign or the development of public relations overall—and was more of a theoretician and philosopher. He saw himself as a scientist and was heavily influenced by the ideas of his uncle, Sigmund Freud, and by other research in the social and behavioral sciences.

Their most striking difference, though, was in their visibility. Outgoing, supremely self-confident, and a brilliant self-promoter, Bernays constantly called attention to himself, wrote and spoke extensively, and received frequent media coverage. In contrast, Fleischman was modest and private, seldom sought the spotlight, and did not seem to need public validation of her accomplishments. Thus Bernays was able to take virtually all of the credit for the firm's work, despite later admitting that Fleischman was equally responsible for it.

Much of Fleischman's lack of visibility can be explained by a key disparity in her and her husband's professional responsibilities: after her marriage, she had no client contact. Bernays met with their clients, then reported on those meetings to Fleischman. He claimed most clients would not have taken advice from a woman while many would not have hired the firm if they had known he had a woman partner. And she apparently did not complain.

But Fleischman was thrust into the public eye by actions unrelated to her public relations work. A member of the Lucy Stone League, she kept her birth name when she married Bernays in 1922. When the couple arrived at the Waldorf-Astoria for their honeymoon weekend and she signed the register as "Miss Doris E. Fleischman," more than 200 newspapers nationwide carried reports that, for the first time, a married woman had been permitted to register at this hotel using her birth name. She received similar newspaper attention three years later when, after fighting the State Department, she became the first married woman to receive a U.S. passport in her birth name.

She was known personally and professionally by that name for three decades, using it on the book about careers for women that she edited in 1928 and on seven book chapters and magazine articles that she wrote in the 1930s and 1940s. But the cover page of her semiautobiographical book, *A Wife Is Many Women* (1955) identified her as Doris Fleischman Bernays, and she essentially gave up her birth name after that date.

Fleischman and Bernays had two daughters. In 1961 they moved to Cambridge, Massachusetts, saying they were retiring. But instead they quickly started a new, much smaller public relations business that they ran out of their home and were still operating when Fleischman died in Cambridge.

Certainly Fleischman is the most important woman in public relations history. She helped found and form the field and had a remarkable career as an equal partner with her husband in what was for three decades one of the country's most influential and successful public relations firms. But her pioneering work was scarcely noticed at the time, in large part because her extraordinarily visible husband took so much credit for their joint efforts. Thus, although Bernays has frequently been called (and liked to call himself) "the father of public relations," Fleischman's work has only begun to be acknowledged and understood.

• Fleischman's papers—known as the Doris Fleischman Bernays Papers—are in the Schlesinger Library on the History of Women in America at Radcliffe College. Additional manuscript materials on her are in the Edward L. Bernays Papers at the Library of Congress. She edited *An Outline of Careers for Women: A Practical Guide to Achievement* (1928), which contains a chapter by her on women in public relations, and she wrote a similar chapter for Edward L. Bernays, ed., *An Outline of Careers: A Practical Guide to Achievement by Thirty-Eight Eminent Americans* (1927). Her best-known article, in which she announced that she was taking her husband's last name, is "Notes of a Retiring Feminist," *American Mercury* (Feb. 1949): 161–68.

Her husband's autobiography, *Biography of an Idea: Memoirs of Public Relations Counsel Edward L. Bernays* (1965), contains many scattered and anecdotal references to Fleischman. Using the pseudonym Henry Raymond, Bernays wrote a long profile of Fleischman titled "Miss Versatility: A Rather Unusual Sketch of the Rather Unusual Career of Doris E. Fleischman" in *The American Hebrew* (Feb. 1927): 438.

Two articles on Fleischman by Susan Henry are "Anonymous in Her Own Name: Public Relations Pioneer Doris E. Fleischman," *Journalism History* 23, no. 2 (Summer 1997): 50–62, and "Dissonant Notes of a Retiring Feminist: Doris E. Fleischman's Later Years," *Journal of Public Relations Research* 10, no. 1 (Winter 1998): 1–33. A listing of books and articles that contain references to her can be found in Keith A. Larson, *Public Relations, the Edward L. Bernayses and the American Scene: A Bibliography* (1978). Obituaries are in the *New York Times*, and the *Boston Globe*, both 12 July 1980.

SUSAN HENRY

FLEISCHMANN, Charles Louis (3 Nov. 1834–10 Dec. 1897), yeast manufacturer and inventor, was born near Budapest, Hungary, the son of Alois (or Abraham) Fleischmann, a distiller and yeast maker, and Babette (maiden name unknown). Following his education in Vienna and Prague, Fleischmann began his business career at age nineteen as a general store clerk in Tàsgendorf, Austria. He emigrated to the United States as did his six siblings. While eating at his sister's wedding in New York in 1866, he concluded that the inferior liquid yeast used in baking resulted in a poor quality American bread and determined to create a reliable, solid yeast. After the wedding Fleischmann returned to Austria to retrieve a superior strain of yeast that his father had developed. Returning to the United States permanently, he worked in a New York City distilling business for two years before moving in 1868 to Cincinnati, Ohio.

In partnership with his brother Maximilian Fleischmann and James W. Gaff in a Cincinnati distillery, Charles Fleischmann persuaded his partners to include baker's yeast as a product line. Working from the process patented on 26 April 1870 by his brother Henry, Fleischmann manufactured "a compressed yeast, suitable for baking and other purposes, prepared from the froth or scum formed during the fermentation of 'mash' used for the manufacture of malt or spirituous liquors" (Patent no. 102,387). Consumers did not readily accept the new yeast. Gaff, Fleischmann and Company nearly failed until it created an exhibit at the 1876 Philadelphia Centennial Exposition that demonstrated the yeast-making process, set the dough, baked the bread; the partners then served their bread at an attached restaurant. The combination of their popular Model Vienna Bakery exhibit, profitable restaurant, and high-visibility advertising ensured the success of Fleischmann's yeast. Fleischmann wisely offered one of the first industrial services to accompany his yeast via a circular that promised that "a practical baker will be sent to give instructions in its use when necessary." Because yeast must be used fresh, the company devised a daily delivery-wagon system to grocers, becoming famous for its regularity and ability to outmaneuver natural disasters to deliver. They spun off malt, syrup, vinegar, and feed by-products into separate brands. The company's home plant was located in Riverside, outside Cincinnati, with additional factories in Blissville and Greenpoint, New York, and East Millstone, New Jersey.

When Gaff died in 1879, the Fleischmann brothers continued the partnership; Maximilian bought Gaff's interest in 1883, and they changed the company name to Fleischmann and Company. After Maximilian's death in 1890, Charles Fleischmann ran the company as sole proprietor from the New York City offices until his own death. By 1900 the company operated the world's largest yeast plant at Charles Point in Peekskill, New York, with branch offices in major cities across the country.

Fleischmann patented thirteen inventions between 1866 and 1888 for his own business and for other business interests, including distilling apparatus (which financed his initial business and became the foundation of his fortune), two improved cotton gins, a cottonseed oil extraction process, sewing machine improvements, an improved plow, a process for aging liquors and spirits and for producing aromatic ethers, two apparatuses for rectifying alcoholic liquors, a revivifying charcoal used in rectifying spirits, a device for overcoming the dead points of cranks, a duplex pedal motor, and a treatment of prairie soil to obtain useful products from it. His other numerous business interests included partnerships in the Buffalo Distilling Company and the Baltimore Manufacturing Company, presidency of the Cincinnati Commercial Tribune Company, directorship of the Cincinnati Cooperage Company, and organizer in 1887 of the Market National Bank of Cincinnati, of which he was president from 1889 until his death.

Fleischmann became active in civic and Republican political affairs. He counted among his friends the governor and later president William McKinley, who appointed him as an aide on his staff from 1892 to 1893. He served as the appointed fire commissioner of Cincinnati from 1886 to 1890, a trustee of Longview Hospital, a delegate to the Republican National Conventions of 1880 and 1884, and as an Ohio state senator from the First District from 1880 to 1881 and again from 1896 to 1897. Two of the bills he introduced proposed installing electric lighting in the state house, initially ridiculed but later implemented, and building a governor's mansion, which was defeated by the house.

Charles Fleischmann had married Henrietta Robertson in her native New York City sometime between 1866 and 1869. Of their three children, a son, Julius, operated a harness-racing stable with his father in Millstone, New Jersey, after Charles's doctor suggested in 1890 that horseback riding outdoors would improve his health. As with the yeast business, Fleischmann threw himself and his money wholeheartedly into the risky racing business. He added thoroughbred racing, campaigning them in New York, Ohio, and Kentucky while his harness horses competed in Vienna, Austria. Fleischmann & Son operated an extensive racing stable in Cincinnati and three large stock farms in New Jersey. They purchased the 1895 Kentucky Derby winner, Halma, for $25,000 and raced him to stakes victories along with Vespers, St. Maxim, and other sons of Himyar.

Fleischmann's other interests included a French art collection, piano playing by ear, and donating to local charities and educational institutions. Fleischmann owned the "Schloss," an estate in the Catskill Mountains of New York, around which the town of Fleischmann, named in his honor, grew. He belonged to the New York, Atlantic, and Larchmont yacht clubs as the owner of the steam yacht *Hiawatha*. Fleischmann died at his home in Avondale, a suburb of Cincinnati, leaving an estate of approximately $2 million to his family after modest bequests to the Associated Charities, Hebrew Relief Union, the Jewish Home, Catholic Orphan Asylum, Protestant Orphan Asylum, Colored Orphan Asylum, and Jewish Hospital.

Charles Louis Fleischmann changed the way commercial bakers and homemakers made their bread through marketing a baker's yeast that produced consistent results. In addition to the products he developed, Fleischmann's inventiveness with processes and equipment benefited several industries, particularly distilling. In his later years, Fleischmann split his time actively among three pursuits—his business, horse racing, and the state legislature—positively influencing three distinct segments of American life in the nineteenth century.

• Henry Weigl in *Nation's Business*, Jan. 1971, pp. 90–91, notes Fleischmann's contributions to the baking industry and provides biographical information. An assessment of his political career appears in James K. Mercer and C. N. Vallandigham, *Representative Men of Ohio, 1896–1897* (1896). An obituary is in the *New York Times*, 11 Dec. 1897.

SUSAN HAMBURGER

FLEMING, John Adam (28 Jan. 1877–29 July 1956), geophysicist and scientific administrator, was born in Cincinnati, Ohio, the son of Americus Vespucius Fleming, an engineer, and Katherine Barbara Ritzmann. Several other ancestors had been engineers, a fact that Fleming said influenced his choice of study. Fleming studied at the University of Cincinnati from 1895 to 1899, earning a B.S. in engineering. After graduation he became assistant engineer in redesigning the Convention Building of the Sängerbund Society in Cincinnati. That year he passed his federal civil service examination and joined the U.S. Coast and Geodetic Survey (USCGS) as an aide in the newly established Division of Terrestrial Magnetism. The chief of this division, Louis Agricola Bauer, a trained engineer, had taught physics and geophysics at the University of Cincinnati during Fleming's student years. This began a long association.

Fleming continued with the USCGS until 1903. His main assignment was to design and construct special geomagnetic observatories, a task that capitalized on his engineering education. These buildings required nonmagnetic materials and the maintenance of a nearly constant temperature. He supervised the building of observatories in Alaska and Hawaii and of the main USCGS observatory at Cheltenham, Maryland.

In 1903 Fleming married Henrietta Catherine Barbara Ratjen, with whom he had one child. In 1903–1904 he resigned from the survey to become a partner in Vulcan Copper Works in Cincinnati, where he developed methods for chemical manufactures. He also joined his brother in a construction business. In 1904 he returned to part-time employment with USCGS as magnetic observer and also began a career transition. In 1904 his colleague Louis Bauer founded the Department of Terrestrial Magnetism (DTM) at the new Carnegie Institution of Washington, D.C. Fleming worked simultaneously there and at USCGS. Fleming's activities at DTM resembled those at USCGS. He designed DTM's Standardizing Magnetic Observatory, used for calibrating magnetometers. He set up the instrument-making shop and had charge of designing new types of magnetic instruments; these became models of accuracy and portability for geomagnetic surveying worldwide. Fleming participated in DTM magnetic surveys in Central America, reflecting the broader geographic scope of a nongovernmental research laboratory. By 1910 his work at DTM required his full attention and he resigned from USCGS.

The DTM's primary initial goal was a global survey of the earth's magnetism, except where nations were themselves surveying. The causes of geomagnetism could not be understood, it was thought, until the magnetic field was adequately described. The DTM's was the first global magnetic survey. Fleming contributed essentially to this effort. He was appointed chief magnetician (1904), chief of the Observatory Division (1916), chief of the Magnetic Survey Division (1919), assistant director of DTM (1922), and acting director (1929). He was director from 1935 until his retirement in 1946. He selected DTM scientific staff, helped plan magnetic surveys, and was in charge of establishing DTM's two important geophysical observatories in Australia and Peru. In 1913, his wife having died, he married her sister, Carolyn Ratjen.

As Bauer's leadership at DTM faded due to illness during the 1920s, Fleming's role increased. He completed the global survey in the 1930s, though he continued limited surveying into the 1940s to study geomagnetic secular variation. Analysis of the survey results also continued. The last volume of results (1947), with earlier volumes, is still accepted as an essential source of geomagnetic data. He guided DTM into new experimental studies of magnetization by rotation, of the structure of the ionosphere, and of atomic physics. These projects diverged significantly from Bauer's program, partly because the global survey was completed and partly because Fleming directed research toward geophysical studies beyond geomagnetism.

Fleming participated in war-related work in both world wars. In World War I he helped develop a magnetically triggered underwater mine and instruments for detecting submarines. During World War II he supervised numerous contracts with the armed forces, including the development of the proximity fuse (for which Merle A. Tuve had more immediate responsibility), studies of radio transmission and the ionosphere, and the completion of the analysis of world magnetic data.

According to Tuve, who succeeded Fleming as DTM director, Fleming was an administrator with "unusual gifts." Tuve stated that Fleming praised even small accomplishments, warned against undue pride, insisted on clear expression in publications, and won all battles as editor. Fleming edited all DTM publications personally, indicating how strictly he administered the department. Moreover, because he edited *Terrestrial Magnetism and Atmospheric Electricity* (now *Journal of Geophysical Research*) from 1928 to 1948, his leadership extended to the larger geophysical community. Fleming exercised influence, too, in his support of the American Geophysical Union. He was secretary of the AGU Section on Terrestrial Magnetism and Electricity (1920–1929), AGU general secretary (1925–1947), and honorary president for life (from 1947). He edited the AGU's *Transactions*, organized its annual meetings, and was its insistent dues collector. He shaped and nurtured an entire discipline through these activities, encouraging research areas as diverse as isostatic crustal studies and solar-terrestrial relations, while working to strengthen the discipline's institutional base.

Fleming's publications include five volumes in the Carnegie Institution series Researches of the Department of Terrestrial Magnetism. He edited volume 8 in the National Academy of Sciences' series Physics of the Earth, *Terrestrial Magnetism and Electricity* (1939). He provided Sydney Chapman and Julius Bartels several "sabbaticals" at the DTM to write their classic *Geomagnetism* (1940). He published more than 100 articles, including "Geomagnetic Secular Variations and Surveys," given in 1945 as the third Charles Chree Lecture, which summarized the conclusions of his career.

Although Fleming made no single important discovery and contributed no great theoretical development, he was widely respected by those who did. He was an important instrument designer and an insightful and indefatigable scientific administrator. He was one of the most important individuals in the institutionalization of geophysics in twentieth-century America. These accomplishments were recognized through election to the National Academy of Sciences (1938), receipt of the AGU's William Bowie Medal (1941) and the Chree Medal of the Physical Society (London) (1945), and the posthumous creation of an award in his name by the AGU. He died in San Mateo, California, where he had retired.

• Some of Fleming's papers are in the National Archives in the records of the U.S. Coast and Geodetic Survey and at the Carnegie Institution. The location of other personal papers is not known. Fleming's Chree lecture was published in the *Proceedings of the Physical Society (London)* 58 (1946): 213–47.

His career is discussed in Merle A. Tuve, "John Adam Fleming, January 28, 1877–July 29, 1956," National Academy of Sciences, *Biographical Memoirs* 39 (1967): 104–40. Tuve's article includes an extensive bibliography. An obituary is in the *Washington Evening Star*, 31 July 1956.

GREGORY A. GOOD

FLEMING, Walter Lynwood (8 Apr. 1874–3 Aug. 1932), historian, was born near Brundidge, Alabama, the son of William LeRoy Fleming, a prosperous farmer before the Civil War and a veteran of the war, and Mary Love Edwards. He received his B.S. from Alabama Polytechnic Institute (later Auburn University) in 1896 and earned his M.S. there a year later. He was teaching there when he volunteered in the Spanish-American War. After enlisting in May 1898 as a private, he obtained a commission as second lieutenant of the Third Alabama Infantry Regiment (Colored) in July 1898 and served in Alabama and Florida as a white officer of a black unit until March 1899. He considered a career in the military but instead returned to Alabama Polytechnic and in 1900 enrolled at Columbia University to do graduate work in history. There he studied with men in a wide range of social science disciplines, especially historian William Archibald Dunning, and earned an M.A. in 1901 and the Ph.D. in 1904. He married Mary Wright Boyd in 1902; they had four children.

At about the time he enrolled at Columbia, Fleming published an essay, "The Buford Expedition to Kansas," in the *American Historical Review* 6 (Oct. 1900). Exemplifying his interest in his home state and the sectional crisis of the Middle Period, the article focused on an Alabamian, Jefferson Buford, who had sought to foster proslavery settlement in Kansas in the 1850s. Displaying Fleming's commitment to work in primary sources, it relied in part on letters he had found in the possession of Buford family members.

Recognizing the need for scholarship on the Reconstruction era, Fleming set out to study the period in Alabama. As he explained at the time: "The Southern people have not rushed into books with their knowledge of things. Consequently, the younger generation knows little of the post bellum troubles except thro' tradition, which is not very lasting, and thro' prejudiced accounts written in Mass. [*sic*] or Ohio" (as quoted in Stephenson, p. 95). The son of an Alabama planter dispossessed by emancipation, Fleming set out to bring another perspective, correct such biases, as he saw them, and provide an enduring history. His dissertation, published as *Civil War and Reconstruction in Alabama* in 1905, displayed his prodigious research, felicitous writing style, and interpretive powers. For it he collected and examined a wide range of documentary materials and spoke or corresponded with elderly Alabamians of both races.

James Ford Rhodes and Fleming's mentor William A. Dunning soon relied on his findings when they wrote more general histories of Reconstruction. Dunning, the early twentieth century's preeminent historian of Reconstruction, also directed dissertations on

other states, among them Mississippi and Georgia, that, with Fleming's, constitute what are known as the Dunning studies of Reconstruction for their careful historical work but their antipathy for the Republican policies of the time.

Fleming followed his first book with the two-volume *Documentary History of Reconstruction: Political, Military, Social, Religious, Educational and Industrial, 1865 to the Present Time* (1906–1907), which incorporated a broad conception of history, far beyond the confines of politics and diplomacy that tended to circumscribe the study of history in his time. As late as 1966 David Donald characterized it as "the broadest and best balanced collection of original sources on the Reconstruction era."

Fleming taught at West Virginia University from 1904 to 1907 and then at Louisiana State University from 1907 to 1917, when he went to Vanderbilt University. In 1919 he published *The Sequel of Appomattox: A Chronicle of the Reunion of the States* (1919), an interpretive work that broadened to the entire South the scope of his Alabama book. He became dean of Vanderbilt's College of Arts and Sciences in 1923 and later directed the graduate school there. He returned to full-time teaching in 1926 and published *The Freedmen's Savings Bank: A Chapter in the Economic History of the Negro Race* in 1927. Ill health forced his retirement in 1928, and he died in Nashville four years later of pneumonia after a stroke. A posthumous publication, *Louisiana State University, 1860–1896*, appeared in 1936.

Fleming's greatest scholarly output came between about 1902 and 1912. A central reason for the decline thereafter was how much time he spent at both Louisiana and Vanderbilt in administration and working to build up a center of graduate study in the South. He also served on the editorial board of the *Mississippi Valley Historical Review* (later the *Journal of American History*) for its first eight years of publication (1914–1922). Professional colleagues appreciated his manifold contributions as scholar and administrator, and some of his colleagues at Vanderbilt displayed their esteem by dedicating *I'll Take My Stand: The South and the Agrarian Tradition* to him when they published it in 1930: "This book is dedicated in love and admiration to Walter L. Fleming . . . [,] to whom some of the contributors owe doctrine and example, and all would offer this expression of perfect esteem."

Fleming became known as perhaps the premier historian of his generation—the generation after William A. Dunning—of the South during the Civil War and Reconstruction eras. His accomplishments went beyond his breadth of research, work in primary sources, and integration of various facets of social and cultural history. He did something in *Civil War and Reconstruction in Alabama* rarely emulated through the next seventy years when he followed through on his insight that, to comprehend the post–Civil War years, one must understand the developments of the prewar and wartime periods. He also insisted: "The negro is the central figure in the reconstruction of the south.

Without the negro there would have been no Civil War. Granting a war fought for any other cause, the task of reconstruction would, without him, have been comparatively simple" (*Sequel of Appomattox*, p. 34). Yet Fleming's limitations related to the same insights, when he observed, from the vantage point of the early twentieth century, that the black codes of the immediate postwar years, "with few exceptions, were timely and sensible, and in substance had long been and still are on the statute books of most of the states of the Union" (as quoted in Green, p. 508).

Recent historians have found Fleming's research more compelling and enduring than his perspective. As early as the 1930s one critic, pioneer black historian Horace Mann Bond, chided Fleming for exaggerating the racial texture of Reconstruction politics. Seeing instead a clash of railroad corporations—the Alabama and Chattanooga versus the Louisville and Nashville—Bond spoke of Fleming's "delightful naivete" and rejected his "strictly racial and sectional interpretation of the period." Viewing the Republican and Democratic parties as "only the obverse aspects" of these two great railway enterprises, Bond suggested that "the basic economic issue of the campaign of 1874 in Alabama was to determine which of the financial interests involved would be able to make the best possible settlement with a state government bankrupted by the earnest efforts of both."

Beginning in the 1960s a new generation of students offered major revisions of the "Dunning studies" for every state of the former Confederacy. Central to their approach was a greater attention to and more favorable view of black southerners in the years before as well as after emancipation. Fleming had supplied perhaps the strongest of the Dunning studies, but other voices insisted on being heard a century after the events his research helped bring to light.

• Fleming's papers are at the New York Public Library, Louisiana State University, and the Alabama Department of Archives and History. Assessments of his life and work appear in Fletcher M. Green, "Walter Lynwood Fleming: Historian of Reconstruction," *Journal of Southern History* 2 (Nov. 1936): 497–521; William C. Binkley, "The Contribution of Walter Lynwood Fleming to Southern Scholarship," *Journal of Southern History* 5 (May 1939): 143–54; Horace Mann Bond, *Negro Education in Alabama: A Study in Cotton and Steel* (1939); Wendell Holmes Stephenson, *The South Lives in History: Southern Historians and Their Legacy* (1955); David Donald's introduction to a reprint edition of the *Documentary History of Reconstruction* (1966); and Beth Taylor Muskat, "The Ironic Military Career of Walter Lynwood Fleming," *Alabama Review* 44 (Oct. 1991): 269–84. Obituaries are in the *Nashville Banner*, 3 and 4 Aug. 1932, and the *American Historical Review* 38 (Oct. 1932): 182.

PETER WALLENSTEIN

FLEMING, Williamina Paton Stevens (15 May 1857–21 May 1911), astronomer, was born in Dundee, Scotland, the daughter of Robert Stevens, the proprietor of a carving and gilding business and also a photographer, and Mary Walker. Williamina was educated in the Dundee public schools, where from age fourteen she was a pupil-teacher. She continued teaching until her marriage to James Orr Fleming, also of Dundee, in 1877. In December 1878 the couple emigrated to Boston, Massachusetts, but the marriage soon failed, and they separated in 1879. Needing to support herself, the pregnant Williamina Fleming found employment as a domestic in the household of E. C. Pickering, director of the Harvard College Observatory. When he realized Fleming's educational background and intelligence, Pickering in 1881 hired her to do clerical and computing work at the observatory. Except for a short trip back to Scotland to give birth to her child (in October 1879), Fleming remained at Harvard the rest of her life. She lived in an era of rapidly developing celestial photography, when new discoveries abounded.

In 1885 Fleming began the first determinations of the photographic magnitudes of more than 2,600 stars, mostly brighter than fifteenth magnitude (Pickering, 1889). Later she published magnitudes to about 10.0 and spectral classes for stars in forty-five Standard Regions (Fleming, 1911).

The Henry Draper Memorial was established in 1886, providing funds to permit a large-scale program of celestial photography at the observatory. Fleming was put in charge of classifying spectra for the first *Draper Catalogue*. The Pickering-Fleming system of classification arranged the majority of the spectra alphabetically from A to M in order of increasing complexity in the appearance of the patterns of dark lines, and added other letters for less common spectra or "peculiar stars." Published in 1890, the catalogue contained 10,351 stars, mostly brighter than seventh magnitude, and it was the first comprehensive catalogue of photographic stellar spectra.

Harvard's Boyden Station was established in Arequipa, Peru, in 1891. Fleming carefully examined the plates from both the northern and southern telescopes, and assigned a "quality" to each plate. Scrutinizing around 200,000 plates, she discovered many unusual objects. In addition to stars with peculiar spectra, she recorded ninety-one meteor trails and found spectra of two meteors.

Among the stars with peculiar spectra, Fleming noted that some proved to be variable, particularly novae and long period variables. Hence she inferred that such stars could be assumed to be variable upon the discovery of just one spectrum showing the same peculiarity. She was the first person to discover a nova by photography—Nova Persei 1887. Of the twenty-four novae detected worldwide between 1881 and 1911, she discovered ten. Her first discovery of a long period variable by means of its spectrum was R Caelum in 1890. In all, she discovered over 300 variable stars, most of them on the basis of their spectral peculiarities.

Besides her extensive research, Fleming edited all the observatory publications, supervised a dozen female "computers," and participated in the selection of new employees. Thus she played a role in the appointments of three women astronomers who became famous—Antonia Maury, Annie J. Cannon, and Henrietta Leavitt; all three, and Fleming herself, had craters on the far side of the Moon named for them.

In 1899 Fleming received a Harvard Corporation appointment with the title curator of astronomical photographs. This was the only such appointment awarded a woman at Harvard until 1938, when Cecilia Payne-Gaposchkin and Annie J. Cannon received appointments as Astronomers. Fleming received numerous honors; she was an honorary fellow in astronomy at Wellesley College (1906) and honorary member of the Royal Astronomical Society (1906), and she was awarded the gold medal of the Mexican Academy of Sciences (1910). At the World's Fair in Chicago in 1893 Fleming gave a talk, "A Field for Woman's Work in Astronomy," concluding "While we cannot maintain that in everything woman is man's equal, yet in many things her patience, perseverance and method make her his superior" (1893, p. 688).

Her achievements notwithstanding, Fleming was not happy with her situation. As editor of the many observatory publications, she was distressed that she had too little time for research. She considered her salary degrading in comparison with what men with similar qualifications received. As curator of the astronomical plate collection, she was annoyed that the photographers at Arequipa were examining the plates before shipping them to America, discovering objects with unusual spectra—a domain she considered exclusively hers.

As a supervisor Fleming had a reputation as a firm disciplinarian, but all praised her warm friendliness. At the height of her career, she died in Boston of pneumonia. Pickering in his eulogy noted that Fleming's record as a discoverer of objects with peculiar spectra was unequaled; he added, "Her gifts as an administrative officer, especially in the preparation of the *Annals*, although seriously interfering with her scientific work, were of the greatest value to the Observatory" (*Annual Report for 1911*, p. 4).

The British astronomer H. H. Turner commented:

As an astronomer Mrs. Fleming was somewhat exceptional in being a woman; and in putting her work alongside that of others, it would be unjust not to remember that she left her heavy daily labours at the observatory to undertake on her return home those household cares of which a man usually expects to be relieved. She was fully equal to the double task. . . . and it is perhaps worthy of record, as indicating how lightly the double burden sat on her, that she yielded to none in her enjoyment of a football match, especially a match between Harvard and Yale. (1912, p. 263)

Fleming published twenty-eight articles in her own name, but much of her work was published by Pickering in about fifty titles. He gave her credit, however, for having supplied the bulk of the observational data and analyses. Fleming was an important leader in spectral classification, but perhaps her greatest achievement was her influence as a role model. Her research provided stepping-stones for younger women, extending the investigations she began.

• Fleming's personal records are at the Harvard University Archives. These were investigated by Pamela Mack, "Straying from Their Orbits: Women in Astronomy," in *Women of Science: Righting the Record*, ed. by G. Kass Simon and P. A. Farnes (1990). Fleming, "A Field for Women's Work," *Astronomy and Astro-Physics* 12 (1893): 638–89, is an excellent account of her own and contemporary women's work at Harvard. On her life and career see also Solon I. Bailey, *The History and Work of Harvard Observatory* (1931); B. Z. Jones and L. G. Boyd, *The Harvard College Observatory* (1971); and Margaret W. Rossiter, *Women Scientists in America* (1982).

Fleming's most important research results were published in the *Annals of Harvard College Observatory*. Those before 1900, authored by Pickering, include "A Photographic Determination of the Brightness of Stars," 18 (1889): 119–14; "The Draper Catalogue of Stellar Spectra," 27 (1890); "Spectra of Stars in Clusters," 26 (1897): 260–86; "A Photographic Study of Variable Stars," 47 (1907); "Spectra and Photographic Magnitudes of Stars in Standard Regions," 71 (1911): 27–45; and "Stars Having Peculiar Spectra," 56 (1912): 165–49. Obituaries evaluating her achievements and character include E. C. Pickering, *Harvard Observatory Annual Report for the Year Ending September 30, 1911*, p. 4; *Harvard Graduates Magazine* 20 (1911): 49–51; Annie J. Cannon, *Astrophysical Journal* 6 (1911): 314–17; and H. H. Turner, *Monthly Notices of the Royal Astronomical Society* 72 (1912): 261.

DORRIT HOFFLEIT

FLESCH, Rudolf Franz (8 May 1911–5 Oct. 1986), readability researcher and educational critic, was born in Vienna, Austria, the son of Hugo Flesch and Helene Basch. He earned a doctorate in law from the University of Vienna in 1933. After immigrating to the United States in 1938, he married Elizabeth Terpenning in 1941. They had six children. He earned a Ph.D. in library science from Columbia University in 1943 and became a citizen in 1944.

Working out of the Readability Laboratory of the American Association of Adult Education at Columbia Teachers College, Flesch began his educational research by calling attention to the limitations of a very influential study in the newly developed field of adult reading comprehension tests, William Gray and Bernice Leary's *What Makes a Book Readable* (1935). In his early monograph, *Marks of Readable Style: A Study in Adult Education* (1943) and later in his bestselling *The Art of Plain Talk* (1946), Flesch offered what he thought to be a scientific method for achieving a plain, understandable prose. He advocated an unadorned style, with shorter paragraphs, shorter sentences, fewer prefixes and suffixes, and greater use of colloquial American English. He equated such plain talk with progressive politics, especially with the New Deal policies of Franklin Delano Roosevelt. "Democracy could be defined," Flesch said, "as government by plain talk" (*New York Times*, 6 Oct. 1986).

Flesch developed two formulas for measuring the relative readability of any given passage: one measures reading ease, the other measures "human interest." He was particularly interested in making more readable books available for the layperson for "self-education" (*Marks*, p. 39). Initially aimed at the teacher, librarian, or book publisher who was interested in making more materials available to an adult population perceived to have insufficient reading skills, this early work was most influential among journalists, advertising copywriters, and businesspeople interested in communicating with a mass audience. Flesch's work, however, was not without its critics. The writer E. B. White, for example, commented that "communication by the written word is a subtler (and more beautiful) thing than Dr. Flesch and General Motors imagine" (*The Second Tree from the Corner*, 1954, pp. 165–67). GM was one of Flesch's industry clients; he acted as a readability consultant, giving advice about how to streamline their business publications and advertising.

Settling at the close of World War II in Dobbs Ferry, New York, Flesch became a freelance writer, lecturer, and editorial consultant. While a consultant for the Associated Press, he produced the influential *AP Writing Handbook* (1951). He also wrote a series of how-to guides, including *How to Write Better* (1951) and *The Art of Clear Thinking* (1951). But perhaps none of his work had as much impact as the bestselling *Why Johnny Can't Read: And What You Can Do about It*. With this 1955 polemic, Flesch turned his attention from readability research to the nation's schools. This book "took the nation by storm," according to Jeanne Chall. "Flesch challenged—strongly, clearly, and polemically—the prevailing views on beginning reading instruction, which emphasized teaching children by a sight method" (*Learning to Read* [1967], p. 3). Flesch blamed the sight method, or the look-say approach to reading instruction, for the nation's increasing number of illiterates. He urged that the nation institute a phonics approach—teaching the correspondence of letters and sounds. The educational press attempted to refute Flesch's blanket claim that American children were taught only through the look-say method, but according to reading researcher Carole Riedler, one-half of the book reviews in mass magazines agreed with Flesch's criticism, confirming that he was in line with popular impressions, and the other half were noncommittal (Chall [1967], p. 183). Flesch's book was instrumental in raising public awareness of reading methods and the importance of parents' reading to their children. Instruction in phonics increased across the nation, though never in quite the wholesale fashion Flesch wanted, and never without strong opposition from reading theorists, especially those who advocated a holistic, or whole-language, approach to integrated language learning. Unlike the building-block system Flesch advocated (working from letter/sound correspondences to parts of words to whole words and eventually to meaning units), holistic approaches were based on how children learn to make sense of a variety of sign systems, not piece by piece in isolation, but as wholes in real-life contexts (reading cereal boxes is an everyday instance of how children make sense of signs in real-life contexts). *Why Johnny Can't Read* is often cited as having raised public awareness not only of

reading instruction but of what was perceived as a national literacy crisis, a perception reinforced by growing national concern over the nation's ability to compete against the Soviet Union in space exploration and also, more broadly, the ability of Americans to compete in the world economic arena. But it is generally conceded that Flesch had less influence in professional educational circles (*Becoming a Nation of Readers: The Report of the Commission on Reading* [1985], p. 36).

After the popular success of *Why Johnny Can't Read*, Flesch spoke to such national educational and professional organizations as the College Composition and Communication Conference, and he continued to write the sorts of "layman's books" he had advocated early in his career; he contributed to various journals; he continued to write letters to the editor warning the public of the weaknesses in public school reading instruction; and he produced a number of handbooks for people in business and law. One of the last books he wrote, however, was a return to the theme of his 1955 bestseller. In *Why Johnny Still Can't Read: A New Look at the Scandal of Our Schools*, published in 1981, Flesch examined once again the limitations of reading instruction and the importance of adopting a phonics approach.

Throughout his career, Flesch opposed obfuscation in business and government documents. He targeted especially "federalese," or bureaucratic jargon, and "gobbledygook" or any confusing, meaningless language. He was a tireless advocate of a more efficient, more democratic prose style, and more efficient, more democratic reading instruction. As such, his work can be seen as part of an older "plain style" tradition dating back to early language and educational reform movements in sixteenth- and seventeenth-century England. Plain-style advocates often contended that plainer language made truth more visible and was therefore more appropriately the language of mass instruction. Critics have long argued that plain style might itself "obscure" because it might oversimplify. That criticism, in fact, has been leveled against Flesch's work. But part of Flesch's popular appeal seems to have been precisely his ability to simplify the complex and capture the public's attention with his own snappy, forceful style. As an educational Jeremiah, Flesch was a force to be reckoned with. A measure of his success can be found in the number of authors of books and articles on literacy who have had to distinguish their own approaches to language reform and reading instruction from that of Rudolf Flesch. In E. D. Hirsch's *The Philosophy of Composition* (1977), in the U.S. Department of Education's *Becoming a Nation of Readers*, in debates over legal language reform, and among journalists, Flesch's position on language and learning have had to be acknowledged even if his positions are subsequently dismissed as too simple. Flesch's solutions to complex problems may be judged inadequate by educational experts, but his ability to focus much-needed public attention on schools was extraordinary. He died at Dobbs Ferry, New York.

• Flesch's "Estimating the Comprehension Difficulty of Magazine Articles," *Journal of General Psychology* 28 (1943): 63–80, *A New Readability Yardstick* (1948), and *How to Test Readability* (1951) lay out the readability formula. *What Can You Do about Readability* (1941), *The Way to Write*, written with A. H. Lass (1947), *Some Writing Hints* (1948), *The Art of Readable Writing* (1949), "Let's Face the Facts about Writing: A Look at Our Common Problems" in *College English* (1950), and the *Instructor's Guide to How to Write Better* (1951) all make use of the basic premises behind readability formulas to argue for "plain talk." Flesch was a frequent writer of letters to the *Times* editor. The last contribution on the literacy crisis was published the day after he died, suggesting something of his persistence. Some biographical information can be culled from introductions to Flesch's numerous books. See especially Lymon Bryson's foreword to *The Art of Plain Talk* (1946). For some biographical information as well as an indication of the critical reception of his ideas, see, for example, the *New York Times*, 5 May 1946. The readability literature is vast. George Klare's *The Measurement of Readability* is still a useful overview (1963). Jeanne Chall's *Readability: An Appraisal of Research and Application* (1958) and the 1983 revision of her 1967 work, *Learning to Read: The Great Debate*, offer a sympathetic appraisal of readability research—including Flesch's part in the larger field—and its implications for curricula. For a more critical look, see Patrick Shannon et al., *Broken Promises: Reading Instruction in Twentieth-Century America* (1989). Marion Blake's bibliography on *Plain Language and the Law* (1986) and the audiotape of a symposium on legal language reform held at Indiana University School of Law in 1980, *A Gathering on Plain English in a Complex Society*, suggests the extent to which Flesch has influenced legislation mandating change in legal language practice. An influential expansion of Flesch's ideas and application of readability formulas to the business world can be found in Robert Gunning's *The Technique of Clear Writing* (1952). For an early critique of such applications, see "The Language of Business," a *Fortune* magazine article reprinted in *Toward Liberal Education* (1957). For an accessible overview of the history of plain style, see Michael Halloran and Merrill Whitburn's "Ciceronian Rhetoric and the Rise of Science: The Plain Style Reconsidered" in *The Rhetorical Tradition and Modern Writing* (1982). The *New York Times* obituary, 7 Oct. 1986, is the most complete overview of Flesch's life to date.

KATHRYN T. FLANNERY

FLETCHER, Alice Cunningham (15 Mar. 1838–6 Apr. 1923), anthropologist and reformer of U.S. Indian policy, was born in Havana, Cuba, the daughter of Thomas Gilman Fletcher, a lawyer in New York City, and Lucia Adeline Jenks. Her parents were in Cuba to see if the climate there would help her father's tuberculosis; it did not. The family returned to New York, where her father died when she was twenty months old; her mother was eventually married again, to Oliver C. Gardiner, giving her a stepfather from whose unwanted attentions she fled in her midteens. She was taken in by a wealthy hardware merchant, Claudius Conant, whose daughters were her schoolmates at the Packer Collegiate Institute in Brooklyn, New York. Fletcher served for a time as governess to the younger children in the Conant family and then was set up by Claudius Conant to be financially independent. Fletcher's difficult teenage years led her to revere her father, whom she had scarcely known. She cherished family stories about him, was proud of being musical, as he was, and liked to identify with his name, thinking of herself as an "archer" (a cognate of "Fletcher"), inclined to "aim her arrows at the sun."

Around 1870 Alice Fletcher moved to New York City, intending to pursue her interest in the arts. She soon joined Sorosis, one of the first women's clubs in the country, and in 1873 helped to organize the Association for the Advancement of Women (AAW), a nationwide group modeled on the American Association for the Advancement of Science (AAAS). The AAW was a moderate reform group led by Julia Ward Howe, Mary Livermore, and Maria Mitchell that sought to promote education and professional careers for women. Inspired by their example and needing, as a result of financial reverses, to earn her own living, Fletcher looked around for a professional career.

Her first choice was public lecturing. Seeking information for a series of lectures on "Ancient America," she went to the Peabody Museum of American Archaeology and Ethnology at Harvard, where she met the nation's leading archaeologist, F. W. Putnam, and in 1879 became one of his first converts to the new science of anthropology. Fletcher spent some months in the museum examining artifacts until she met a party of Omaha Indians who were on a tour of the East, and her interest turned from the field of archaeology to that of contemporary Indian life.

In 1881 Fletcher went west to camp among the Sioux and to visit the Omahas on their reservation in Nebraska. The six-week camping trip on the Sioux Reservation in Dakota Territory was her "rite of passage" into anthropology. Often disoriented, lonely, and depressed, she was nevertheless a serious observer and conscientious about taking notes. On her return she published "Five Indian Ceremonies" (*16th Annual Report*, Peabody Museum of American Archaeology and Ethnology [1884], pp. 260–333), her first major scientific work. Fletcher's journey, undertaken solely for scientific purposes, marks her as one of the small group of ethnographers who in the early 1880s initiated the fieldwork tradition in that branch of anthropology.

Fletcher intended to make more scientific studies of Indian life, especially the life of Indian women, but became caught up instead in the Omahas' struggles to avoid being moved to Indian Territory (present-day Oklahoma). In 1881 she helped the Omahas write a petition asking Congress to grant them individual titles to their land in Nebraska. When no response came, Fletcher went to Washington herself to lobby on its behalf. When the special act for the Omahas was passed in 1882, she was appointed a special agent for the Bureau of Indian Affairs and charged with carrying out the provisions of the act.

Fletcher spent a year on the Omaha reservation, dividing the land into individual parcels of land: 160 acres for each head of family, 80 acres for each single adult, 40 acres for each child. The allotment work gave her an unusual opportunity to observe Indian life, and it cemented her ties with the family of Omaha chief Joseph La Flesche, whose son Francis worked as her field assistant. It was the start of a forty-year collaboration between the two. La Flesche, who cared for Fletcher when she fell seriously ill on the reservation with rheumatoid arthritis, became her informant, then her colleague and co-worker, and finally an ethnologist in his own right. In 1890 Fletcher, who never married, adopted La Flesche informally as her son, and thereafter they shared a home in Washington, D.C.

Fletcher's year on the Omaha reservation, her public speaking on behalf of the Indians, and a government report she wrote on *Indian Education and Civilization* (1888) led her to be widely recognized as an expert on Indian affairs. An opponent of the agency system in which Native Americans were considered wards of the U.S. government and confined to reservations under the control of a federal agent, she helped to write and lobbied for the Dawes Act of 1887, the goal of which was to break up reservations and improve the lot of Indians by giving them education, citizenship, and private ownership of homesteads while at the same time opening some of the reservation lands to white settlers. When the Dawes Act was passed, she was hired to carry out its provisions among the Winnebagos and the Nez Perces. The failure of the allotment program—much of the land ended up in white hands—has cast a shadow on Fletcher's reputation. By 1898 Fletcher realized that the allotment program probably had been a mistake, but she never admitted this publicly. Instead she quietly withdrew from government work and politics and devoted the rest of her life to scientific study.

In 1890 Fletcher was awarded a lifetime fellowship founded for her at the Peabody Museum by Mary C. Thaw. By virtue of the Thaw fellowship, Fletcher became the first woman to hold an academic position at Harvard, albeit one with no teaching or other formal responsibilities. With La Flesche she wrote "A Study of Omaha Indian Music" (*Archaeological and Ethnological Papers*, Peabody Museum of American Archaeology and Ethnology, vol. 1 [1893]), the first monograph of the music of a single tribe, and the classic ethnography, *The Omaha Tribe* (1911), the culmination of their scholarly collaboration. For several years in the early 1900s she did research on the Pawnees with James R. Murie, publishing with him *The Hako: A Pawnee Ceremony* (1904). She also wrote more than thirty entries for the *Handbook of the American Indians North of Mexico* (1907, 1910).

Fletcher, whose appearance and demeanor often reminded her friends of Queen Victoria, held many professional offices. She was an early proponent of the preservation of archaeological monuments in the United States and was a major force behind the founding in 1909 of the School of American Archaeology (later School of American Research) in Santa Fe, New Mexico. An honorary bronze plaque hanging in the patio of the art museum in Santa Fe bears the following words from her last book, a collection of *Indian Games and Dances* (1915): "Living with my Indian friends I found

I was a stranger in my native land. As time went on, the outward aspect of nature remained the same, but a change was wrought in me. I learned to hear the echoes of a time when every living thing even the sky had a voice. That voice devoutly heard by the ancient people of America I desired to make audible to others."

Fletcher died in Washington, D.C. She was a pioneering field worker, the first significant woman anthropologist in the United States, and one of the leading anthropologists of her generation. Her legacy as a reformer of U.S. Indian policy is more ambiguous because the Dawes Act, which she so strongly supported, is generally regarded as a failure. Yet she had tried to help a people who turned to her in their distress. Above all, she sought to help Indians and whites understand one another, for she believed that it was only a mistrust growing out of ignorance that kept them apart.

• The professional papers of Alice Fletcher and Francis La Flesche are in the National Anthropological Archives at the Smithsonian Institution. Other significant collections are in the Putnam papers at the Harvard University Archives, the Barrows papers at Houghton Library, Harvard, the La Flesche family papers at the Nebraska State Historical Society, the Dawes papers at the Library of Congress, and the Records of the Bureau of Indian Affairs. A major biographical study is Joan Mark, *A Stranger in Her Native Land: Alice Fletcher and the American Indians* (1989). See also E. Jane Gay, *With the Nez Perces: Alice Fletcher in the Field, 1889–92*, ed. Frederick E. Hoxie and Joan Mark (1981); Nancy O. Lurie, "Women in Early American Anthropology," in *Pioneers of American Anthropology*, ed. June Helm (1966), pp. 29–83; Mark, "The American Indian as Anthropologist: Francis La Flesche," *Isis* 73 (1982): 497–510; and the memorial by Walter Hough, "Alice Cunningham Fletcher," *American Anthropologist* 25 (1923), 254–57.

JOAN MARK

FLETCHER, Benjamin (14 May 1640–28 May 1703), imperial commander in Ireland, New York, New Jersey, and Pennsylvania, was born in London, England, the son of William Fletcher, a royal army officer, and Abigail Vincent. William Fletcher was killed at the siege of Gloucester in 1643. Twenty years later, Benjamin Fletcher emerged in Ireland as a cavalry officer in the royal army of occupation, cornet to John, Lord Berkeley, brother of Sir William Berkeley and president of the province of Connacht. Fletcher had made his way in the Dublin demimonde, so his Anglo-Irish enemies afterward recalled, as an actor, barber, and valet, perhaps to Lord Athlone. Certainly Lord Athlone; James Butler, the great duke of Ormonde; and Sir Robert Southwell, the pioneering imperial bureaucrat, became Fletcher's patrons and supported Fletcher in Connacht after his troop was disbanded in 1672. There he became captain of an independent company of infantry by 1677. In 1685 Fletcher was purged as a Protestant when King James Catholicized the army in Ireland.

With many other Protestant officers (including his nemesis, Richard Coote, earl of Bellomont), who afterward displaced him in New York and attacked his administration there, Fletcher retreated to England. There, King James's Catholicism provoked William of Orange's invasion and the desertion to him of the Protestant professional military. Fletcher had been commissioned captain of the key regiment, Princess Anne's, the Portsmouth mutineers, in September 1688, and he became major during the Glorious Revolution. In August 1689 Fletcher's regiment was committed by the new king, William III, to the reconquest of Ireland. Fletcher was one of the few English officers to emerge with credit from the invading army's debacle at Dundalk Camp. There Fletcher was assiduous in tending to his men. He served at the battle of the Boyne on 1 July 1690 and fought in the savage Irish guerrilla war.

In 1691 Southwell put Major Fletcher's name before William Blathwayt, secretary at war and of plantations and state, for the command of New York. As Blathwayt recalled, "His Majesty Having of his own choice in considering of his Services during the whole war of Ireland" selected Fletcher for "New York as a person very fitt to manage the Warr in those Parts." Fletcher was brevetted colonel by the king on 9 March 1692. He crossed the Atlantic in company with Sir Edmund Andros, who was outbound to command Virginia, and landed from HMS *Wolfe* in New York with his wife, daughter, nineteen servants, munitions, and a corps of Anglo-Irish officer cadets on 30 August 1692. (His wife's name, the date of their marriage, and the total number of their children are unknown.)

Like the rest of England's empire in America, New York was still reverberating from the revolution. Its New York leaders, the Protestant dissenter Jacob Leisler and the English libertarian Jacob Milburne, had been judicially murdered by the provincial ancien régime in May 1691. Rehabilitation of the New York martyrs became the cause of the English Whigs, defenders of the revolution. The preservation of New York's old order was advocated by the English Tories, champions of Anglican religious obedience. Fletcher brought with him Queen Mary's Whig-inspired offer of conditional pardon for the surviving Leislerians, but he was himself a Tory appointee, as he made clear by his successful campaign to establish the Church of England in New York and to endow its mother parish, Trinity Church, with "the King's Farm" in Manhattan, the basis of Trinity's fabulous wealth.

The remainder of Fletcher's program was essentially that of his predecessor, Andros: to recruit men and money from all the English colonies to defend the Albany frontier and to support the Anglo-Iroquoian alliance (which Andros had negotiated with Daniel Garacontié, the eminent Onondaga). The results were disappointing. The distances of New York's frontiers from its metropolis and the province's deficits of money and men (deepened by Fletcher's systematic fraud) exposed the Iroquois to French raids on their towns. Fletcher's attempts to enforce the royal quota system of intercolonial defense excoriated the isolationist sensibilities of both the New England and the Chesapeake colonies.

Only in the middle colonies, where he took command personally, did Fletcher get results. New Jersey contributed nearly full quotas of men to the Albany frontier. In Pennsylvania (1693–1695), Fletcher stimulated a political upheaval, out of which the assembly emerged to prevail over the proprietor, William Penn, at the price of modest cash contributions to the New York war effort in violation of the Friends' pacifism.

Raised in the rough school of Irish garrison government, Fletcher used his garrison companies and naval crews to control city elections in New York. He gave huge land grants to his political followers. He kept up the provincial army by drafts from the militia, officered it with Anglo-Irish cadets, supplied it poorly by corrupt commissaries, and paid for all with funds authorized by councillors and assemblymen, whom he rewarded with permission to connive at piracy and engage in illegal trade.

So long as the war went on and the Tories stayed in office, Fletcher's excesses were overlooked. When the war ended, the Whigs and their new Board of Trade gained oversight of the plantations and replaced Fletcher with Bellomont. The Irish earl arrived in New York in April 1698. He quickly exhibited a Whiggism that verged on hysteria, issuing proclamations against profanity, alcohol, sex, and violations of the Sabbath. Before Bellomont's charges of connivance with pirates and misappropriation of funds against Fletcher could be resolved by the Board of Trade, however, Anglo-American politics again took on a Tory tint. The board's report of March 1699 merely admonished Fletcher for carelessness in dealing with pirates and criticized his excessive land grants. As King William himself was guilty on both fronts, for example, he patronized the New York pirate William Kidd and made huge land grants to Irish favorites such as Bellomont, he ordered Fletcher's bond discharged. The colonel retired to Dublin, where he died, much damaged in reputation but fully representative of the English Restoration and revolutionary empire's militant administration.

• Aside from the papers of William Blathwayt in the British Library and miscellaneous papers in the New-York Historical Society, the primary sources for Fletcher's administrations are in E. B. O'Callaghan, ed., *The Documentary History of the State of New York* (1850) and *Documents Relative to the Colonial History of the State of New York . . .* (1853–1855); and J. W. Fortescue et al., eds., *Calendar of State Papers, Colonial Series, America and West Indies*, vols. 13–21 (1901–1913). The chief secondary source is James S. Leamon, "War, Finance, and Faction in Colonial New York: The Administration of Governor Benjamin Fletcher, 1692–1698" (Ph.D. diss., Brown Univ., 1961). See also Leamon, "Governor Fletcher's Recall," *William and Mary Quarterly*, 3d ser., 20 (1963): 527–42; on the same subject, Stephen Saunders Webb, "William Blathwayt, Imperial Fixer: Muddling through to Empire, 1689–1717," *William and Mary Quarterly*, 3d ser., 26 (1969): 373–415; and Gertrude Ann Jacobsen, *William Blathwayt* (1932). On commissaries and corruption, see Lawrence H. Leder, *Robert Livingston* (1961); on piracy and politics, see Robert C. Ritchie, *Captain Kidd* (1986); and on Restoration Ireland and American empire, see Webb, *The Governors General* (1979; repr. 1987) and *Lord Churchill's Coup* (1995). On the Pennsylvania episode, see Charles M. Andrews, *The Colonial Period of American History*, vol. 3 (1937), and Gary B. Nash, *Quakers and Politics 1681–1726* (1968).

STEPHEN SAUNDERS WEBB

FLETCHER, Benjamin Harrison (13 Apr. 1890–10 July 1949), African-American union activist, was born in Philadelphia, Pennsylvania. The record covering Fletcher's early years is sparse, containing no mention of his parents, childhood, or education. As a teenager he evidently secured work at various odd jobs in and around his home town. He soon drifted into casual work on the waterfront, where he came in contact with a steady stream of radical agitators connected with the Industrial Workers of the World (IWW), or Wobblies. Much of what the Wobblies had to say to the port's unorganized longshoremen appealed to the young Fletcher, particularly their vision of interracial solidarity and worker militancy. So in 1911 he offered his services as a corresponding secretary for a citywide local of the IWW. It was an association that would last a lifetime. Fletcher married and had at least one child, but no details are available.

Fletcher's life was deeply intertwined with the organizational history of the port's dockworkers, members of Local 8, affiliated with the IWW's Marine Transport Workers Industrial Union. Formed in 1913 following a strike on the city's docks, Local 8 successfully combined revolutionary IWW leadership—of which Fletcher was an important part—with sound organizational principles modeled after the more established American Federation of Labor (AFL) craft unions. This hybrid species of unionism, virtually unknown in the United States, has confounded labor theorists ever since. For some, Local 8 "differed not one whit from a conservative union of the A.F. of L" (Spero and Harris, p. 335), whereas others saw Philadelphia's longshoremen as "the vanguard of American labor" (*Messenger*, Oct. 1921, p. 263). In fact, the Wobbly union was both. While Local 8 followed many of the AFL's proven organizational methods, including the imposition of high initiation fees and limited membership, it departed from the usual "business union" in several ways, most notably in its racial policies. In addition to enforcing complete and full integration of the workforce, Local 8 mandated rotation in office between white and black union leaders: one month, an African American served as local president with a white vice president; the next month this pattern was reversed. In an industry otherwise known for its practice of racial separatism, Local 8's egalitarianism was a most remarkable achievement.

Local 8's progressive racial policies were largely attributable to its indigenous black leadership, particularly Fletcher, whose reputation among his fellow workers was second to none. Jack Lever, a longshoreman who worked alongside Fletcher in the early days, remembered him as simply "one of the best organizers I knew" (Black Workers in America Collection, p. 28). Articulate and charismatic, Fletcher blossomed into a leading national spokesman for the African-American working class. Recognizing his considerable talents, the IWW in 1915 temporarily reassigned Fletcher to Boston, Baltimore, and other North Atlantic cities to organize dockworkers. But his crowning achievement was organizing the port of Philadelphia, where Local 8 almost doubled in size to nearly six thousand members by 1917.

Partly as a consequence of Fletcher's growing following on the docks, he was indicted by the Department of Justice in 1917. Charged with various acts of subversion and disloyalty during wartime, Fletcher was tried along with 165 other IWW leaders in Chicago's federal court amid a growing national hysteria focused on the dangers of "bolshevism" and radicalism. Fletcher, the lone black defendant, did not testify on his own behalf, and no questions were asked of him by the prosecution. The case against him rested on several letters that were read at his trial.

Fletcher's real crime, as revealed in a confidential report from the justice department, was being "a Negro who had great influence with the colored stevedores . . . in building up the Marine Transport Workers Union which at time of indictment had become so strong that it practically controlled all shipping on the Atlantic Coast" (Foner, p. 59). In 1918 Fletcher was summarily convicted on four counts, sentenced to ten years in jail, and fined $30,000. Even at his sentencing Fletcher retained his dry sense of humor, reprimanding the judge for "using poor English today. His sentences are too long" (Seraile, p. 221). On 30 October 1922 he was released from prison under a conditional pardon that he "stay out of trouble," signed by President Warren G. Harding. The next day Fletcher was back on the Philadelphia docks, offering his assistance to the longshoremen who were in the midst of a strike.

The strike that year was crushed. Growing dissension in the ranks of longshoremen led many to affiliate with the rival International Longshoremen's Association (ILA), affiliated with the AFL. When the national office of the IWW refused to assist Local 8 in its life-and-death struggle with the ILA, Fletcher marshaled his supporters and together they struck out on their own, forming the Independent Longshoremen's Union in the spring of 1923. It was a painful parting of the ways for Fletcher, and, after a year's absence, he led his integrated membership back into Local 8. Increasing employer and government favoritism for the more conservative ILA placed the Wobblies at a serious disadvantage in the intensifying contest for union loyalty. Following a string of minor skirmishes throughout the port, many of Local 8's key leaders switched allegiance to the ILA in 1925, bringing to a close the IWW's brief but illustrious history on the docks.

Fletcher, a man of principle, refused to follow his former comrades into the ILA. His decision was not without its costs, both personally and professionally, for it meant that Fletcher's career in the labor movement was effectively over. Indeed, he was not heard from for several years, surfacing briefly in 1931 on the streets of New York City, where he held his listeners "spellbound" for over an hour. "I have heard all the big shots of the labor movement over a period of 25 years from coast to coast," wrote an AFL official who was in the audience, "and it is no exaggeration when I state that this colored man . . . is the only one I ever heard who cut right through to the bone of capitalist pretensions . . . with a concrete constructive working class union argument" (*Industrial Solidarity*, 11 Aug. 1931, p. 4). It was to be Fletcher's last known public address. A victim of failing health, he suffered a stroke two years later that all but silenced this gifted orator. Further restricted by a heart attack in 1945, he eventually died at his home in Brooklyn—with his membership in the IWW current and paid up.

• Fletcher's papers are in the Abram Harris Collection, deposited in the Moorland-Spingarn Research Center at Howard University. The only published biographical materials devoted to Fletcher are a brief overview by Irwin Marcus, "Benjamin Fletcher: Black Labor Leader," *Negro History Bulletin* 35 (Oct. 1972): 138–40, and a more extensive scholarly discussion by William Seraile, "Ben Fletcher, I.W.W. Organizer," *Pennsylvania History* 46 (July 1979): 213–32. For a more personal look at Fletcher, see the brief references to him in oral histories conducted with Jack Lever in the Black Workers in America Collection at Wayne State University, and with James Fair in *Solidarity Forever: An Oral History of the IWW* (1985). Insight into both Fletcher and the union he led can be gained from reading selected issues of the *Messenger*, a radical black monthly, from 1918 to 1923, including articles by Fletcher himself appearing in the June and July 1923 issues. Brief discussions of Local 8 can be found in Sterling D. Spero and Abram L. Harris, *The Black Worker: The Negro and the Labor Movement* (1931), and Philip S. Foner, "The IWW and the Black Worker," *Journal of Negro History* 55 (Jan. 1970): 45–64.

HOWARD KIMELDORF

FLETCHER, Bridget Richardson (23 Apr. 1726–8 June 1770), hymnist and religious poet, was born in Chelmsford, Massachusetts, the daughter of Zachary and Sarah Richardson. Although little is known about Fletcher's childhood, her parents were probably farmers, as Middlesex County was largely an agricultural region and Fletcher herself writes in Hymn 2 that she did not spring from a prophet's line, but "only of an herdsman." Whether or not Fletcher had any formal education is uncertain. Her ability to read and write should be noted, however, since only 40 percent of women were literate during this period, and schools frequently did not admit female students. On 15 February 1745, she married Timothy Fletcher, Jr., of Westford, Massachusetts, a small community adjoining Chelmsford. She probably lived the rest of her life in this town, as the title page of her volume of hymns indicates that she is "late of Wesford [*sic*]." Between 1747 and 1762 the Fletchers had three sons and three daughters; one daughter died in infancy.

Fletcher's life probably continued to revolve around farming. She writes in Hymn 2 that she is "a fruit gath-

erer, / If not of the sycamore, / It is from these the apple trees, / Which here we have in store." She did not begin writing verse until fairly late in her life. Evidence suggests that she composed the hymns in chronological order, and in Hymn 7, one of her earliest hymns, Fletcher remarks that she is forty-two. That dates this early hymn at 1768, just two years before her death. In these few years, however, Fletcher wrote prolifically. Although the only extant text of her work is incomplete, it contains eighty-two hymns.

Many of Fletcher's poems address her struggle to maintain her religious faith as she experiences dark times and as she deals with her fear of death. In Hymn 3, for example, she speaks of the "dark road" of death and describes this world as a "wilderness" of care and suffering. Frequently, however, Fletcher transfers her fear to a reliance on God's grace. In her study of early American women poets, Pattie Cowell observes that Fletcher's hymns map a path of spiritual growth with the later hymns expressing more spiritual confidence than the early hymns.

Stylistically, most of Fletcher's hymns conform to standard eighteenth-century ballad stanza and meter. Her poetic imagery derives largely from biblical and popular poetic convention. She frequently describes the Christian life as a warfare, or a journey, and uses images of prison, nighttime, and darkness to describe her spiritual desolation, while images of light, day, and feasting describe spiritual joy.

Whether or not Fletcher intended her poems for publication is uncertain. Many of her hymns seem written primarily for particular spiritual occasions in her personal life. At times, however, as the preface to her book notes, Fletcher shared her poems with family and friends to comfort or strengthen them in their own struggles.

Fletcher also seems aware of an audience beyond herself and her immediate friends and family. Unsure about her own poetic ability and fearful of receiving publicity, Fletcher writes in Hymn 2, "A tear I'd drop now if I thought / That I should surely rob, / Oh! the most high, of his glory, / From whence comes all my good."

Fletcher did not live to see her poetry published. She died at the age of forty-four, as her preface laments, "at the meridian of life." Briefly describing her last weeks, the preface notes that her death was unexpected. She had been sick for three weeks, but as she had passed through many difficulties in her life, she expected that God would carry her through this sickness as well. Just before her death, however, Fletcher was resigned to her fate.

After her death, friends and family collected Fletcher's verse and prepared it for publication by adding titles and doing minor editing. The preface begs the readers to allow for "the many inaccuracies of the female pen," considering that the advantages for "polite learning" are few for women "in this society." Similarly, the preface reminds the reader that Fletcher's sudden death made her unable to edit or prepare these poems for publication; thus, she should not be held responsible for the roughness of the verse.

Published in 1773 by Isaac Thomas, Fletcher's *Hymns and Spiritual Songs* appeared largely as a memorial to its author. While it is unlikely that Fletcher will ever be considered a major American poet, her verse provides important insights into the spiritual life of one eighteenth-century woman, and the religious and poetic conventions of her culture. Moreover, it establishes Fletcher as one of the earliest known women poets published in colonial America.

• The only manuscript of Fletcher's volume of hymns is in the American Antiquarian Society Library, Worcester, Mass. The only critical assessment of Fletcher's poetry to date is in Pattie Cowell's *Women Poets in Pre-Revolutionary America* (1981).

SUZANNE M. ZWEIZIG

FLETCHER, Frank Friday (23 Nov. 1855–28 Nov. 1928), naval officer, was born in Oskaloosa, Iowa, the son of James Duncan Fletcher, a saddle and harness maker, and Nancy Power Jack. After being educated in Iowa's public school system and working on a farm as a boy, Fletcher received an appointment to the U.S. Naval Academy in Annapolis, Maryland, from Congressman William Loughbridge, representing Iowa's Fourth District, in September 1870. Graduating from the academy in June 1875, Fletcher served initially in the screw sloop *Tuscarora*. Appointed ensign in July 1876, he served successive tours of sea duty in the screw sloop *Lackawanna* and the sloop of war *Constellation*.

Fletcher next served in the screw sloop *Ticonderoga* as it carried Commodore Robert W. Shufeldt on a globe-girdling cruise, a portion of which was dedicated to the negotiation of a commercial treaty with Korea. Appointed master in April 1882, Fletcher worked in the Hydrographic Office in Washington, D.C., before he journeyed to the west coast of South America for special duty with Lieutenant Commander Charles H. Davis (1845–1921) on an expedition "for [the] telegraphic determination of longitudes in Central and South America." Promoted to lieutenant, junior grade, in March 1883, Fletcher served next in the screw steamer *Quinnebaug* on the European Station (1884–1887). During his time in the *Quinnebaug*, he developed a proposal that ships at sea display range lights to reduce the number of collisions—a safety feature eventually adopted in 1890.

Fletcher reported to the Washington Navy Yard in 1887 for duty in the Bureau of Ordnance. Appointed lieutenant in February 1889 while at the bureau, he perfected a breech-closing mechanism for firearms that would bear his name. He also helped to otherwise increase the efficiency of quick-firing weapons and to develop better telescopic sights and breech plugs. In December 1892 Fletcher received his first sea command, the torpedo boat *Cushing*—then attached to the Naval Torpedo Station, Newport, Rhode Island—for which he developed a trainable torpedo tube mount.

After a year in the new coast defense battleship *Maine* (Sept. 1895–Sept. 1896), he returned to the Naval Torpedo Station to work on a number of armor factory and gun factory boards. In 1895 he married Susan Hunt; they had two children. Returning to the Bureau of Ordnance in April 1898, he eventually rose to be assistant bureau chief. In the summer of 1898, shortly before the end of hostilities with Spain, he was given command of the converted gunboat *Kanawha*.

Following the Spanish evacuation of Cuba in 1898, Fletcher took charge of the town of Gibara. He was reassigned later the same year to command the surveying ship *Eagle* as it gathered hydrographic data off the coast of Cuba. He was promoted to lieutenant commander in 1899. Detached in 1901, he served a brief tour of duty at the Washington Navy Yard before he became inspector of ordnance in charge of the Naval Torpedo Station at Newport in June 1902. During his time at the helm, the station proved active in the development of the submarine and its application to modern warfare. Promoted to commander while at Newport, he was detached in November 1904 to journey to the Asiatic Station.

After a brief tour as chief of staff to Rear Admiral Charles J. Train, commander in chief, Asiatic Fleet, Fletcher commanded the cruiser *Raleigh* in 1905 before he traveled to the Naval War College for instruction in 1907. He next served as a member of the Special Board on Naval Ordnance with additional duty on the General Board, the navy's highest ranking policy advisory body. Promoted to captain in 1908, Fletcher was given command of the battleship *Vermont* later the same year.

Returning to Washington in 1910, he became the Navy Department's aide for matériel, a position that had emerged from recommendations of the board chaired by Rear Admiral William Swift, which had dealt with Navy Department reorganization. As aide for matériel, Fletcher scrutinized requests for repairs to naval vessels to determine whether or not the "final military value" of the ship in question justified the expenditure of funds. Promoted to flag rank in 1911, Fletcher then commanded a succession of divisions of the Atlantic Fleet: the Fourth (1912), Second (1913), and Third (1913). In February 1913 he was put in charge of American naval forces operating off the east coast of Mexico.

In April 1914 Fletcher directed the operations of the expeditionary force that seized and occupied the city of Veracruz, Mexico, preventing the landing of munitions to General Victoriano Huerta's regime. In recognition of his "distinguished conduct in battle" at Veracruz, directing the landings and occasionally being under fire, the admiral received the Medal of Honor. President Woodrow Wilson, who had hoped the affair would oust Huerta from power, consequently praised Fletcher as a man "with a touch of statesmanship about him."

In March 1915 Fletcher assumed the post of commander in chief, Atlantic Fleet, a position in which he remained until June 1916. Reverting to the permanent rank of rear admiral, he then spent the remainder of his time on the active list on the General Board and as the navy's representative on the War Industries Board. After the armistice, he advised the American Disarmament Commission at Geneva. Fletcher retired from active duty on 23 November 1919, having reached the statutory retirement age of sixty-four years, and received the Distinguished Service Medal in 1923 for his "exceptionally meritorious service." He served on the Morrow Board in 1925 as it weighed the "best means of developing and applying aircraft to national defense." Fletcher died in New York City and was eulogized by former secretary of the navy Josephus Daniels as a man "of wisdom and ability . . . upon whom I learned to rely."

• Fletcher's papers are at the Manuscripts Department, University of Virginia Library, Charlottesville. The biographical (ZB) files of the Operational Archives Branch, Naval Historical Center, contain biographical material, as does the Ship Name and Sponsor File for the destroyer *Fletcher* (DD-445), which was named in his honor in 1942, in the Ships' Histories Branch of the Naval Historical Center. Recollections of Fletcher's service are in E. David Cronon, ed., *The Cabinet Diaries of Josephus Daniels, 1913–1921* (1963), and an evaluation of his role in the Veracruz intervention of 1914 is in Richard D. Challener, *Admirals, Generals, and American Foreign Policy, 1898–1914* (1973). Published documents concerning Fletcher's role at Veracruz are in *Papers Relating to the Foreign Relations of the United States: With the Address of the President to Congress [of] December 8, 1914* (1922). His testimony in the post–World War I controversy over the navy's preparedness in the conflict can be found in U.S. Congress, Senate, *Hearings before the Subcommittee of the Committee on Naval Affairs, United States Senate*, vol. 1, pt. 2, 66th Cong., 2d sess., 1921. An obituary is in the *Army and Navy Journal*, 1 Dec. 1928.

ROBERT JAMES CRESSMAN

FLETCHER, Frank Jack (29 Apr. 1885–25 Apr. 1973), naval officer, was born in Marshalltown, Iowa, the son of Thomas Jack Fletcher and Alice Glick. Fletcher graduated from the U.S. Naval Academy in 1906, was commissioned an ensign in 1908, and received his first command, of the destroyer *Dale* in the Asiatic Torpedo Flotilla, in 1910. As an aide to his uncle, Rear Admiral Frank Friday Fletcher, Frank Jack Fletcher saw action in 1914 at Veracruz, Mexico. In command of the transport *Esperanza*, Fletcher's demonstrated bravery in moving 350 refugees to safety earned him the Congressional Medal of Honor. He then went to the Atlantic Fleet as flag lieutenant. In 1917 he married Martha Richards.

During World War I, Fletcher was promoted to lieutenant commander and commanded the destroyer *Benham* on convoy escort and patrol duty. He won the Navy Cross for service in submarine-infested waters in 1918.

Fletcher's postwar assignments included destroyers, a submarine tender, and command of a submarine base in the Philippines, where he served in suppressing a 1924 insurrection. After graduating from the U.S. Naval War College in 1930 and the U.S. Army War College in 1931, Fletcher became chief of staff of the Asiatic Fleet. He served as aide to Secretary of the Navy Claude A. Swanson from 1933 to 1936 before returning to sea duty as captain of the battleship *New Mexico*. Fletcher had high-profile staff assignments with the Bureau of Personnel from 1938 to 1939, was promoted to rear admiral, and then commanded cruiser divisions in the Pacific.

Fletcher's first assignment in World War II was command of Task Force Fourteen on a mission to reinforce Wake Island. Despite having to rely on a slow oiler with a maximum speed of only 12.75 knots, he was proceeding on schedule when ordered to abort the mission because of the Japanese capture of Wake Island. Fletcher, who flew his flag from the heavy cruiser *Astoria* instead of from the task force's carrier *Saratoga*, was still learning about naval aviation and the central role that carriers were to play in the war against Japan.

After a brief reassignment to cruisers, Fletcher formed Task Force Seventeen around the carrier *Yorktown* in early 1942 and escorted a convoy bound for Samoa. He participated in the February raid on the Marshall and Gilbert Islands, led Task Force Seventeen into the South Pacific, joined Task Force Eleven in attacking Japanese ships in New Guinea in March, and then remained on patrol in the Coral Sea to guard the line of communications between Hawaii and Australia.

In May, at the battle of the Coral Sea, Fletcher and Rear Admiral Aubrey W. Fitch engaged larger Japanese forces in history's first carrier versus carrier naval battle. The Americans lost the fleet carrier *Lexington*, a fleet oiler, and a destroyer in exchange for sinking the light carrier *Shoho*. This tactical defeat was a strategic victory, however, because the threatened Japanese invasion of Port Moresby was averted, communications with Australia remained open, and the damaged Japanese carriers *Shokaku* and *Zuikaku* were unavailable for the upcoming battle of Midway.

After taking the battered *Yorktown* back to Pearl Harbor for hasty repairs, Fletcher raced to join Rear Admiral Raymond A. Spruance in June near Midway Island, where American aircraft sank four Japanese fleet carriers for the loss of the *Yorktown*. The battle of Midway was the turning point in the Pacific war. Fletcher was promoted to vice admiral and awarded the Distinguished Service Medal; nevertheless, some critics minimized his contributions at Midway and gave most of the credit to Spruance.

Fletcher has been criticized also for his handling of the three-carrier task force supporting the First Marine Division's assaults on Tulagi and Guadalcanal. Although the Marine transports were overly slow in unloading, Fletcher decided to withdraw the carriers on schedule; because the carriers represented the navy's main offensive force in the Pacific, keeping them exposed to the threat of strikes from land-based and possibly carrier-based aircraft was too dangerous. He committed his force to repulse the Japanese counterattack toward Guadalcanal, and in the resulting battle of the Eastern Solomons the Japanese badly damaged the carrier *Enterprise* but lost the carrier *Ryujo* and at least ninety aircraft. Fletcher, wounded on 31 August when his flagship *Saratoga* was torpedoed, returned to the United States for recovery.

In November Fletcher became commandant of the Thirteenth Naval District and Northwestern Sea Frontier. He was unable to return to sea duty despite the recommendation of his commander, Admiral Chester W. Nimitz, because Admiral Ernest J. King, commander in chief, U.S. Fleet, criticized Fletcher's lack of aviation experience and distrusted the prewar connections he had made during high-level staff assignments in Washington. From 1943 to 1945 Fletcher commanded the naval forces of the North Pacific area. Using warship raids and air strikes, his forces tied down Japanese troops around the Kuril Islands and northern Japan. After the Japanese surrender, Fletcher oversaw the occupation of northern Honshū and Hokkaidō.

In December 1945 Fletcher joined the navy's General Board, which advised the secretary of the navy, and served as chairman from May 1946 until May 1947, when he was promoted to full admiral and retired. He died at the Naval Hospital in Bethesda, Maryland.

Fletcher's commands in World War II culminated his successful naval career. Despite his lack of experience with naval aviation, Fletcher commanded carrier task forces in three of the six carrier versus carrier duels in the war against Japan. His strategic victories at Coral Sea and Midway came when Japanese strength was at its greatest relative to Allied forces and when the Japanese navy held its most significant advantages in pilot experience and familiarity with multicarrier operations. Despite his critics' charges that he was unaggressive, timid, overly concerned about refueling instead of acting decisively, and willing to leave the marines in the lurch at Wake Island and Guadalcanal, an objective assessment of the available evidence shows that Fletcher was a competent and capable commander in both sea and administrative assignments.

• John B. Lundstrom offers a favorable view of Fletcher's World War II career in a two-part article, "Frank Jack Fletcher Got a Bum Rap," *Naval History* 6, no. 2 (Summer 1992): 22–27, and *Naval History* 6, no. 3 (Fall 1992): 22–28. Lundstrom provides more general background for Fletcher's early campaigns in *The First South Pacific Campaign: Pacific Fleet Strategy, December 1941–June 1942* (1976). A less sympathetic view appears in Samuel Eliot Morrison, *History of the United States Naval Operations in World War II*, vols. 3–5 (15 vols., 1947–1962). Other works that deal with Fletcher's World War II commands include George C. Dyer, *The Amphibians Came to Conquer: The Story of Admiral Richmond Kelly Turner* (1972); E. B. Potter, *Nimitz* (1976); and H. P. Willmott, *The Barrier and the Javelin: Japanese and Allied Pacific Strategies February to June 1942* (1983). The role Fletcher played in the Veracruz expedition is treated in Jack Sweetman, *The Landing at Vera Cruz: 1914* (1968). Fletcher's obituary is in the *New York Times*, 26 Apr. 1973.

FRANCIS C. STECKEL

FLETCHER, Henry Prather (10 Apr. 1873–10 July 1959), diplomat and Republican party leader, was born in Greencastle, Pennsylvania, the son of Lewis Henry Clay Fletcher, a bank cashier, and Martha Ellen Rowe. Fletcher's mother died prematurely in 1882, leaving his father to raise eight children alone. Two years later his father accepted an auditor's position with the Cumberland Railroad, and the family moved to Chambersburg, Pennsylvania. After graduating from a nearby private academy, Fletcher served as district court reporter and read law with his uncle, D. Watson Rowe. He passed the bar examination in 1894 and subsequently formed a law partnership with his uncle and became active in the local Republican party. Later, Fletcher would perceive his lack of a college education as a personal shortcoming, despite receiving honorary law degrees from several institutions.

Caught up in the excitement and patriotic fervor surrounding the Spanish-American War, Fletcher asked Senator Matthew Quay in 1898 to assist him in gaining a commission with the First Volunteer Cavalry Regiment, more popularly known as the "Rough Riders." He joined K Troop and went to Cuba but never fought under fire. At the end of the war Fletcher decided to remain in the army and with the help of Senator Quay received a temporary commission as first lieutenant. Later, he served in various capacities as a junior officer in the Philippines until 1901. Participation in the occupation of the Asian country reinforced Fletcher's paternalistic views toward less-developed peoples and convinced him of the benevolent effect of America's economic expansion abroad.

His experiences in Spain's former colonies also gave Fletcher a lifelong interest in Hispanic culture and a taste for foreign service. At the end of his tour of duty, Fletcher used his Rough Rider connections to secure from President Theodore Roosevelt an appointment as second secretary to the legation in Cuba (1902–1903). Moving on to China (1903–1905) and, later, Portugal (1905–1907), he returned, a seasoned diplomat, to China as first secretary in 1907. A strong advocate of Dollar Diplomacy—the effort by President William Howard Taft and Secretary of State Philander C. Knox to increase American security and influence by persuading American bankers to displace European creditors in China and the Caribbean—Fletcher discovered a sympathetic friend while in China in Consul Willard Straight. Through Straight, Fletcher met several Wall Street figures such as Thomas Lamont and J. P. Morgan. It was within this rarefied atmosphere of wealth and position that Fletcher also met the socialite Beatrice Bend. Insecure about his own financial status, he courted her for eight years before their marriage in 1917; they had no children.

Meanwhile, Fletcher amassed an enviable foreign service record that was duly rewarded by his designation in 1909 as minister to Chile. After Woodrow Wilson's election in 1912, Fletcher's reputation for professionalism protected him from Secretary of State William J. Bryan's purge of Republicans in the foreign service in order to make room for "deserving Democrats." In fact, when the Santiago legation achieved embassy status in 1914, Fletcher became the first American ambassador to Chile.

Success at his post in Chile led to Fletcher's next and most challenging post, Mexico. Because of his understanding of Latin America and President Wilson's hope that Fletcher's Republican ties might disarm administration critics, he was named ambassador to Mexico in the fall of 1915. During his tenure Fletcher faced several major crises, including Francisco Villa's raid into the United States, General John Pershing's punitive expedition into Mexico, and German Foreign Secretary Arthur Zimmermann's infamous note, inviting Mexico in the event of war to attack the United States. Fletcher's most difficult problem, however, was Mexico's claim to subsoil rights, a position that jeopardized the Mexican holdings of U.S. oil companies. Uncharacteristically, Fletcher lost his patience during the dispute and recommended aggressive retaliation to an unreceptive Wilson. After negotiating a face-saving truce between the Venustiano Carranza regime and U.S. oil producers, Fletcher resigned his post in January 1920.

This low point in Fletcher's career was followed by years of diplomatic eminence. During the Republican decade of the 1920s Fletcher served as undersecretary of state (1921–1922) and headed embassies in Belgium (1922–1924) and Italy (1924–1929). He also led the U.S. delegation to the Fifth (1923) and Sixth (1928) Pan-American Conferences, as well as to the International Conference for the Protection of Literary and Artistic Property (1928). Later, he worked on the Forbes Commission to Haiti (1930) and chaired the U.S. Tariff Commission (1930–1931). In addition, Fletcher continued his active role in party politics; he chaired the Republican National Committee from 1934 to 1936 and served as a counselor to its executive body until 1944. In that year Secretary of State Cordell Hull asked Fletcher to be his special advisor at the Dumbarton Oaks Conference. Afterward, Fletcher retired from public life to his home in Newport, Rhode Island, where he died fifteen years later. A conservative and graceful representative of his era, Fletcher proved to be an intelligent and effective individual whose hard work and good fortune enabled him to enjoy a distinguished diplomatic career.

• The Henry P. Fletcher Papers are located in the Library of Congress and contain over 6,500 items including correspondence, speeches, clippings, and memorabilia. In addition, his diplomatic career is well documented. Published items are included in the appropriate volumes of *Papers Relating to the Foreign Relations of the United States*; unpublished items are located in the National Archives, Record Group 43 (Records of International Conferences, Commissions and Expositions) and 59 (General Records of the Department of State). The most complete biography available is by Olivia Frederick, "Henry P. Fletcher and United States Latin-American Relations, 1910-1930" (Ph.D. diss., Univ. of Kentucky, 1977).

Fletcher makes an appearance in dozens of books devoted to U.S. diplomacy in the first third of the twentieth century. Of all the areas where Fletcher served, from China to Italy, his diplomatic persona is best revealed by his assignment to Mexico. For further information and analysis of this important episode see Mark T. Gilderhus, *Diplomacy and Revolution: U.S.-Mexican Relations under Wilson and Carranza* (1977); P. Edward Haley, *Revolution and Intervention: The Diplomacy of Taft and Wilson with Mexico, 1910-1917* (1970); and Robert Freeman Smith, *The United States and Revolutionary Nationalism in Mexico, 1916-1932* (1972).

JAMES K. LIBBEY

FLETCHER, Horace Page (10 Aug. 1849–12 Jan. 1919), dietetic reformer, was born in Lawrence, Massachusetts, the son of Isaac Fletcher, a stone contractor, and Mary Ann Blake. Throughout his life, Fletcher was driven by an insatiable wanderlust. He once referred to himself as "Bohemian Van Fletch, of every-where-and-anywhere-so-long-as-there-was-fun-there" (*San Francisco Argonaut*, 18 Aug. 1902). A "dangerous restlessness," as he later told a friend, caused his parents to place him at the age of five with relatives on a farm in Howard, New York. He returned to Lawrence in 1859, and at the age of fifteen, he joined the merchant firm of Russell and Company. That same year, he departed for the Far East, where he spent much of the next ten years as a clerk and sailor. He received only a year of higher education, spending 1867–1868 at the Chandler Scientific Department of Dartmouth College.

By the late 1870s Fletcher had become a prosperous businessman in San Francisco. Until 1883 he was a partner in Shattuck and Fletcher, manufacturers of printing inks, and in the 1880s owned an oriental import firm, Ichi Ban, a business that took him frequently to Japan. During the anti-Chinese Sandlot Riots of 1877–1878, Fletcher became a lieutenant colonel in the National Guard.

Fletcher was an accomplished gymnast and crack rifle shot in this period and from 1878 to 1883 was president of the Olympic Club of San Francisco. In 1878 he patented a ball target for trap shooting and toured the United States in a show with Doc Carver, "the rifle king." His first book, *A.B.C. of Snap Shooting* (1880), described his techniques. These were adopted by the army, which in 1881 issued a troop manual that he co-authored with Charles A. Totten. In 1881 Fletcher married Grace Adelaide Marsh, who already had one child. He had no children of his own.

In 1889 Fletcher moved to New Orleans, where his wealth and gregarious nature made him a popular figure in society. Although officially the manager of the New Orleans branch of the I. D. Fletcher Company (a family firm that manufactured creosote, roofing, and other building materials) until 1897, he allowed travel and personal interests to take increasing precedence over business. From 1892 to 1894 he was president of the Opera Guarantee Association, which produced performances at the French Opera House in New Orleans. By 1895 he had devoted himself fully to writing.

After producing books on child welfare and on the importance of cheerful attitudes, Fletcher published *What Sense?, or Economic Nutrition* (1898), which explained the dietetic system later called Fletcherism, or, by detractors, "the chew chew cult." Fletcherism entailed chewing food until it became liquid, when "nature's food filter" (which Fletcher claimed existed in the throat) would open so that fluid could be swallowed and any solid residue spat out. The body thus digested a greater proportion of the food, Fletcher thought, and received perfect nutrition from a smaller amount of food. Let the appetite be one's guide, he taught: eat only when hungry and never when in a bad mood. Fletcher considered his system a philosophy of life and in later writings promised more than physical benefits and monetary savings. "Husbands who fletcherize faithfully," he claimed in an article in *Harper's Bazar*, "lose taste for alcoholic drinks" (Aug. 1908). He and his supporters believed that Fletcherism would eliminate poverty and vice. "For a multitude temperance, purity, and prosperity would take the place of intemperance, impurity, and failure," wrote the Reverend Francis E. Clark, editor of the *Christian Endeavor World* (11 Mar. 1909).

In 1900 Fletcher moved to Venice, Italy, where he leased a mansion (renamed the Palazzo Saibante—the Palace of Health) on the Grand Canal. Subsequently, he toured extensively in Europe and between 1901 and 1904 produced many articles on travel and topical events for the *San Francisco Argonaut*. In 1901 Fletcher met Ernest Herbert van Someren, an English physician (and later his son-in-law), who brought Fletcherism to the attention of the scientific world. By 1904 Fletcher had gained such influential converts as Russell H. Chittenden, a professor of physiology at Yale. Between 1906 and 1910 Fletcherism was a popular fad, and "munching clubs" became all the rage among the social elite of the United States and Europe. Nicknamed "The Great Masticator," Fletcher wrote prolifically and lectured on food reform and social issues in these years; he himself was the subject of dozens of articles in the popular and scientific press. Recognition of his stature in American popular culture came in 1909 when Dartmouth College awarded Fletcher an honorary M.A.

Among the societies to which Fletcher belonged in this period were the American Association for the Advancement of Science, the Health and Efficiency League of America (which he helped form in 1909), the Committee of One Hundred on National Health, the National Committee for Mental Hygiene, and the National Food Reform Association, which was active in Europe.

As Fletcherism gained in popularity, Fletcher gradually increased the frequency and length of his visits to the United States; by 1908 he was seeing little of his family, who remained in Venice. From 1909 to 1910 he rented an apartment in New York City, where he conducted "kindergarten muncheons" for slum children. All fads have a limited lifespan; by 1910 Ameri-

cans were tiring of Fletcherism. At the end of that year Fletcher moved to Copenhagen, where he enjoyed the support of Danish physiologist Mikkel Hindhede. By now estranged from his wife, Fletcher was accompanied by Helen, the marquise de Chamberay, whom he had met in New York. For several years the two traveled around central Europe collecting material for a book on "child conservation," Fletcher's term for welfare programs protecting orphans and other needy children; the work was never published. In 1913 Fletcher and de Chamberay moved to Brussels. When World War I broke out, Fletcher joined the Commission for Relief in Belgium as general assistant and publicist. He served in Belgium through 1915 and in the United States through 1916. He then returned to Copenhagen, where he died of bronchitis during the postwar influenza epidemic.

Although his theories were mistaken, Fletcher contributed to the advancement of nutritional science by inspiring professional researchers to investigate metabolism and food needs. One outcome, resulting from Chittenden's interest in Fletcher, was a reduction in the recommended level of protein in the diet. Fletcher also helped spread awareness of the value of healthy eating habits among the general public. For years after his death, the term "Fletcherism" continued to be used as a synonym for thorough chewing and was still appearing into the 1990s in *Webster's New World Dictionary*.

• Fletcher's papers are in the Houghton Library, Harvard University. His books on cheerfulness include *Menticulture, or the ABC of True Living* (1895), *Happiness As Found in Forethought Minus Fearthought* (1897), and *Optimism, A Real Remedy* (1908). *That Last Waif; or, Social Quarantine* (1898), outlines his first ideas on "child conservation." *Nature's Food Filter* (1899), *The AB-Z of Our Own Nutrition* (1903), and *Fletcherism: What It Is; or How I Became Young at Sixty* (1913), explain his dietetic theories. For some contemporary articles by supporters see Isaac Marcosson, "Perfect Feeding of the Human Body," *World's Work*, Feb. 1904 pp. 4457–60; Michael Williams, "Fletcherizing with Fletcher," *Good Housekeeping*, May 1908, pp. 502–5; and Elbert Hubbard, "The Gentle Art of Fletcherizing," *Cosmopolitan*, Dec. 1908, pp. 48–53. Russell H. Chittenden describes his tests of Fletcher's claims in "The Influence of Diet on Endurance and General Efficiency," *Popular Science Monthly*, Dec. 1907, pp. 536–41. William Dana Orcutt, a personal friend, included a sketch of Fletcher in *Celebrities Off Parade* (1935). Fletcher is also portrayed as a character in Orcutt's novel *The Spell* (1909) in the role of the genial amateur philosopher and world traveler, "Henry Peabody Cartwright." For Fletcher's nutritional theories and historical importance see Ronald Deutsch, *The New Nuts among the Berries* (1977), Harvey Green, *Fit for America: Health, Fitness, Sport and American Society* (1986), Harvey Levenstein, *Revolution at the Table* (1988), and James Whorton, *Crusaders for Fitness* (1982). See also L. Margaret Barnett, "The Impact of 'Fletcherism' on the Food Policies of Herbert Hoover during World War I," *Bulletin of the History of Medicine* 66 (June 1992): 234–59. An obituary is in the *New York Times*, 14 Jan. 1919.

L. MARGARET BARNETT

FLETCHER, Inglis (20 Oct. 1879–30 May 1969), novelist, was born Minna Towner Inglis Clark in Alton, Illinois, the daughter of Maurice William Clark, a railroader and employee of the Canadian Pacific Railroad, and Flora Deane Chapman, an amateur actress and writer. A tomboy and a reader whose early love for Sir Walter Scott's romances never diminished, Inglis, known as "Peggy," enjoyed listening to family tales "of olden days," especially of battles, and she incorporated them into her own youthful stories. Later her interest in the fine arts led her to study sculpture at Washington University in St. Louis, which she left to marry John "Jack" George Fletcher, a mining engineer, in April 1902. His job took them to rough mining camps in California, Oregon, and Alaska.

The title of Fletcher's autobiography, *Pay, Pack, and Follow* (1959), indicates the role of the wife of a mining engineer: when he finished a job and moved on, she was to pay the bills, pack up their household, and follow him to the next camp—a process she repeated some twenty times during their first ten years. These mining camp experiences gave her the material for her first sale. An independent film company paid her $100 for a story synopsis based on the tale of Dan Haskell's death in defense of the miners' payroll. The sale of that script, *Express Messenger*, in February 1920, followed by the sale of another, *The Western Gate*, later that year convinced her for the first time that she could earn money by writing.

After their first baby died, Jack left mining to accept various positions, eventually beginning a 25-year career at Standard Oil. The family moved first to Oakland, where in July 1911 their son John Stuart was born, then to Port Townsend, Washington, and finally to Spokane, where during World War I Fletcher took an active leadership role in the Red Cross. Although she continued writing, it was not until she met the explorer Vilhjalmur Stefansson in 1921 and received encouragement from him that she wrote her first novel, using her Alaskan experiences. When the publisher returned it for revision, she thought it had been rejected and burned the manuscript. However, her collection of tributes to Stefansson, to which she also contributed a biographical sketch, saw publication in 1925; that same year the Fletchers moved to San Francisco.

A long-standing desire to go to Africa, renewed by the lectures of Rodney Wood, a British agricultural scientist in Nyasaland, British Central Africa, led Fletcher to raise the needed money by designing and managing a successful lecture series with Alice Seckles. In 1928 she toured British Africa, eventually traveling 40,000 miles in five months by herself. She commented about this trip, "There is a fascination about Africa impossible to describe that far exceeds that of any other country or continent." The material she collected on witchcraft, tribal rituals and customs, and colonialists' experiences found its way into her public lectures and articles; one contrasted a civilized, sophisticated African tribal society with "our" savage, childish one. Some tales told to her by Wood and oth-

ers were revised into her juvenile novel *The White Leopard* (1931). Fletcher's African experiences also provided her with material for a second, adult novel, *Red Jasmine* (1932), a love story of members of the British ruling class set against a savage native rebellion.

Returning to the southern (and British) roots of her family in North Carolina—her great-great-grandfather had had a shipyard near Albemarle Sound before the American Revolution—was, Fletcher says, "a call of the blood." She believed that "we are truly a part of the past." And the past that most interested Fletcher was the story of America's beginnings, from the first attempt in 1585 to found a colony at Roanoke to North Carolina's transition from colony to state. The first novel of what came to be known as the Carolina Series, *Raleigh's Eden* (1940), deals with both class and political struggles as the prominent Carolina landowners fight overtaxation during the years 1765 to 1782. The hero reflects Fletcher's abiding connection with the land: "For the land and the work of the land was Adam Rutledge's first interest. A deep, inherited feeling that had come to him from long generations. Since the early times in England, the Kentish Rutledges had held land and loved it above all, save one thing: freedom from unjust taxes" (p. 19).

A commercial success, *Raleigh's Eden* aroused controversy because many North Carolinians disputed its historical accuracy. However, believing that, as her article title put it, "Research Is Fun," Fletcher had fleshed out her plot and characters by extensive research into letters, wills, speeches, memoirs, and other historical records, using sources extending from California's State Library and the Library of Congress to North Carolina's many archival documents to provide, wherever possible, a historical character's own words. Her meticulous research—for each of the next eleven novels she spent a year researching and a year writing—allowed her to detail not only battles but scenes like the Blessing of the Hunt or Market Day in eighteenth-century Edenton. Vivid description is her gift: "The morning air vibrated with sound, the bustle and stir of the Market coming to life. Wagons were backed along the square to form booths where rosy-cheeked women sold their dairy products. Beyond the Inn, back of Town Hall, husbandmen were making ready for the horse and cattle auctions. Clouds of dust rose from the tramping hoofs and mingled with the acrid smell of closely packed cattle and damp wool" (p. 17). Scholars confirmed the historical accuracy of *Raleigh's Eden* even if local residents objected to departing from their family legends.

In 1944 the Fletchers bought Bandon Plantation near Edenton, North Carolina (a setting that appears in her novels). While offering warm hospitality to a steady stream of visitors, she also managed to travel, write, and still take active part in a variety of professional and historical associations. A longtime member of the International P.E.N. Club and a member of the California Writers Club, in 1950 and 1951 she helped establish the North Carolina Writers Conference. She also helped to make possible a formal Elizabethan garden near the site of the Lost Colony in Manteo, North Carolina.

Fletcher's imagination, stimulated both by family history and by her travels as an adult to the West Coast, Alaska, Africa, England, and the Carolinas, created the tales she converted into stories, articles, film scripts, opera librettos, and some fifteen published novels, including a serialized mystery, *Weeping Witch* (1939), written with Pauline Partridge. Her twelve Carolina novels, translated into eight languages, have sold millions of copies but received little critical attention. In 1949 the Woman's College of the University of North Carolina in Greensboro conferred on Inglis Fletcher the honorary degree of doctor of literature, and in 1953 her Carolina Series earned her the Sir Walter Raleigh Award.

A woman who revealed little of her personal feelings but took her writing seriously, Fletcher continued writing fiction well into her eighties. She died in Edenton, North Carolina. Historian Maurice C. York has termed her "a proud preserver of North Carolina history" and further commented that "her novels, despite their lack of literary recognition, constitute a significant contribution to North Carolina literature and history" (p. 179).

• About 15,000 of Fletcher's papers, including diaries, letters, and some draft manuscripts from the period 1883–1964, are in the East Carolina University Manuscript Collection at the Joyner Library, Greenville, N.C. The East Carolina University Library also has first editions of nearly all the Carolina novels as well as a number of autographed copies. Fletcher's published works not mentioned in the text include *Men of Albemarle* (1942), *Lusty Wind for Carolina* (1944), *Toil of the Brave* (1946), *Roanoke Hundred* (1948), *Bennett's Welcome* (1950), *Queen's Gift* (1952), *The Scotswoman* (1954), *Wind in the Forest* (1957), *Cormorant's Brood* (1959), *The Wicked Lady* (1962), and *Rogue's Harbor* (1964). A brief but thorough biographical and literary overview is Maurice C. York's "'The Land Always Calls to Its Own': The Inglis Fletcher Papers," *North Carolina Literary Review* (Spring 1993): 176–79. Two critical books are Richard Walser, *Inglis Fletcher of Bandon Plantation* (1952), and Erwin Hester and Douglas J. McMillan, eds., *Cultural Change in Eastern North Carolina as Reflected in Some of the Novels of Inglis Fletcher and Ovid Pierce* (1973). Sarah Jones Wooten, "Identification of African Ritual in the Writings of Inglis Fletcher" (M.A. thesis, East Carolina Univ., 1976), provides information on African influences on her work with maps of her African trip, and Jane W. Green, "Inglis Fletcher: A Personal Perspective" (M.A. thesis, East Carolina Univ., 1984), views her later life and career through the reminiscences of her friend and secretary Robert Gatling. See also Alice Caverly, "'Good Journeyings in This Our Land': Inglis Fletcher's African Adventure," *North Carolina Literary Review* 5 (1996). An obituary is in the *New York Times*, 31 May 1969.

MARIE T. FARR

FLETCHER, John Gould (3 Jan. 1886–10 May 1950), poet and writer, was born in Little Rock, Arkansas, the son of John G. Fletcher, a banker and politician, and Adolphine Krause. As the scion of a wealthy and prominent family, Fletcher's upbringing in Little Rock was sheltered and comfortable. His mother, with some help from tutors, directed his education until his enrollment in private school at the age of ten. He later attended a public high school in Little Rock. He entered Harvard in the fall of 1903.

Fletcher's father wanted him to study law, but Fletcher found the curriculum stifling. Rather than attend classes, he preferred to visit the Boston Museum of Fine Arts, attend Boston Symphony concerts, and engage in long, late-night discussions about the history and future of art. Influenced by his reading of Oscar Wilde, Arthur Symons, and the French Symbolist poets, Fletcher adopted the manner of an aesthete and began writing poetry. When his father died in 1906, Fletcher saw in his substantial inheritance an opportunity to reject Harvard's academic rigidity and pursue his newfound calling as a poet. Consequently, he withdrew from Harvard in 1907 and in the following year sailed to Europe, one of the first of a steady stream of American literary expatriates. After touring the Continent, Fletcher settled in London and formally commenced his literary career by publishing, at his own expense, no less than five books of poetry that appeared in May 1913. Though uneven in quality, these so-called "wild oats" volumes (*The Book of Nature*, *The Dominant City*, *Fire and Wine*, *Fool's Gold*, and *Visions of the Evening*) attracted enough favorable reviews to grant Fletcher legitimacy as a poet.

Shortly thereafter, Fletcher met another American expatriate, Ezra Pound, and was soon caught up in the fledgling modernist movement that had Pound at its center. Nevertheless, Fletcher was never able to trust Pound's motives, and when Amy Lowell arrived from Boston he was quick to support her effort to replace Pound as leader of the avant-garde Imagist poets. He subsequently joined the "Amygist" faction, consisting of H. D. (Hilda Doolittle), Richard Aldington, F. S. Flint, and D. H. Lawrence, and was amply represented in each of their annual *Some Imagist Poets* anthologies.

With the publication of his highly original and experimental *Irradiations: Sand and Spray* (1915), Fletcher achieved what he termed "scandalous success" and quickly became recognized as a leading Imagist poet, a reputation further enhanced by the appearance of *Goblins and Pagodas* (1916), *Japanese Prints* (1918), *The Tree of Life* (1918), and *Breakers and Granite* (1921). The latter volume contains some of the best examples of Fletcher's work in a form he invented and called "polyphonic prose."

During this time Fletcher met and carried on a love affair with Florence Emily "Daisy" Arbuthnot, a married woman who divorced her husband to marry Fletcher in 1916, but the stress of their tumultuous relationship exacerbated Fletcher's vulnerability to acute melancholia and mental breakdown. On several occasions Fletcher was hospitalized for treatment of his chronic depression.

Under the influence of William Blake's visionary poetry and a growing interest in Oriental art and religion, Fletcher's poetry assumed a distinctly religious cast, most notably in *Parables* (1925), *Branches of Adam* (1926), and *The Black Rock* (1928). He also wrote two biographical studies, *Paul Gauguin, His Life and Art* (1921) and *John Smith—Also Pocahontas* (1928), and a prescient comparison of Russia and the United States entitled *The Two Frontiers: A Study in Historical Psychology* (1930). By this time Fletcher was a widely published literary journalist with his work appearing in the leading magazines, and after befriending T. S. Eliot he became associated with the famed "*Criterion* gang."

While on a lecture tour in the United States in 1927, Fletcher spoke in Nashville, Tennessee, and there made the acquaintance of John Crowe Ransom and the Fugitive poets then clustered at Vanderbilt University. As a southern poet himself, Fletcher identified closely with the group and responded eagerly when they asked him to contribute an essay on education to the controversial Agrarian manifesto *I'll Take My Stand* (1930). Thereafter he remained a staunch advocate of the Agrarian agenda, which advocated the superiority of an agrarian economy over the economy of industrial capitalism, venerated southern culture and tradition, and in general asserted the superiority of the southern way of life over that of the Yankee North.

Fletcher returned to his native Arkansas permanently in 1933, and after divorcing Daisy, who had remained in England, he married the popular novelist Charlie May Simon in 1936. He reached the pinnacle of his fame when his *Selected Poems* won the 1938 Pulitzer Prize. The poetry of the final phase of his career—*XXIV Elegies* (1935), *South Star* (1941), and *The Burning Mountain* (1946)—is overtly regional in character and reflects Fletcher's increasing preoccupation with the South and southern themes. He also wrote his autobiography, *Life Is My Song* (1937), and a highly regarded history of his home state, *Arkansas* (1947). Nevertheless, Fletcher's bouts of depression became deeper and more frequent, and in 1950 he drowned himself in a small cattle pond near his home in Little Rock.

Although some of Fletcher's poetry seems today to be overly formal and flowery, at its best it is strikingly original and elegantly phrased. He is significant historically both as an Imagist and as a Fugitive-Agrarian; he was also the first southern writer involved in the modernist movement and the first important figure in the advent of the southern literary renaissance.

• Fletcher's correspondence, papers, and library are in the University of Arkansas Library. Charlie May Simon, *Johnswood* (1953), is an account of her life with Fletcher. A chronology of his life and a set of annotated bibliographies, primary and secondary, can be found in Bruce Morton, *John Gould Fletcher: A Bibliography* (1979). See also Lucas Carpenter, *John Gould Fletcher and Southern Modernism* (1990); Edmund S. de Chasca, *John Gould Fletcher and Imagism* (1978); Glenn Hughes, *Imagism and the Imagists* (1931); Amy Lowell, *Tendencies in Modern American Poetry* (1917); and Edna B. Stephens, *John Gould Fletcher* (1967).

LUCAS CARPENTER

FLEXNER, Abraham (13 Nov. 1866–21 Sept. 1959), educational reformer, was born in Louisville, Kentucky, the son of Moritz Flexner, a wholesale hat merchant who was ruined in the panic of 1873, and Esther Abraham. In 1884 a loan from his elder brother allowed Flexner to enroll at Johns Hopkins University, where he earned a B.A. in classics in two years, the most study he could afford. Flexner recalled his undergraduate study as "the decisive moment of my life." His subsequent career was an elaboration of the ideals of a new university (Hopkins was established in 1876) with very little formal administration and a zealous faculty training ambitious students.

Returning to Louisville, Flexner became a public high school teacher, a job he held until 1890 when he opened his own academy, "Mr. Flexner's School," with none of the conventional educational apparatus: no formal curriculum, no exams, no grades for classes taken. Flexner married a former student, Anne Laziere Crawford, after her graduation from Vassar; they subsequently had two daughters. The school's success in preparing students for admission to prestigious colleges brought some financial stability to Flexner and his extended family, but the production of one of his wife's plays on Broadway gave him financial independence.

In 1905 Flexner closed his school and enrolled in the psychology department at Harvard, earning an M.A. in 1906. He was soon dissatisfied with the focus on experimental psychology and left with his wife to spend a year at the universities of Berlin and Heidelberg, where he could study whatever and with whoever stimulated him. While in Germany, he wrote a caustic commentary on the deficiencies of most of American higher education that was published in 1908 as *The American College*. It caught the attention of Henry Smith Pritchett, the president of the new Carnegie Foundation for the Advancement of Teaching, who hoped that authoritative reports would help set the agenda for educational reform. He engaged Flexner to research and write the fourth report in this series, *Medical Education in the United States and Canada*, published in 1910 and later known as the "Flexner Report."

For two years, Flexner visited each of the 155 medical schools in the United States and Canada, contrasting their actual organization and facilities with the emerging ideals of university-based medical education. The report excoriated most schools and recommended closing 120 of them. Flexner cast himself in the report as exposing a "powerful and profitable vested interest [that] tenaciously resists criticism." These conclusions were not new to those active in medical education reform, but the comprehensive scope and investigatory style of the study brought it wide publicity and established Flexner as a tough-minded expert at just the moment such authority was highly prized. In 1910, Flexner returned to Europe to survey academic medicine for Bulletin no. 6 of the Carnegie Foundation for the Advancement of Teaching: *Medical Education in Europe*, a much more approving report.

At this time, Flexner also began working with the Rockefeller philanthropies. John D. Rockefeller, Jr., retained him in 1910 to research the regulation and suppression of prostitution in Europe. Flexner also prepared a special report for the Rockefeller Foundation on the Johns Hopkins Medical School, which resulted in a $1 million endowment grant. The thoroughness of both studies resulted in Flexner's appointment as assistant secretary to the Rockefeller-funded General Education Board in 1913.

During his tenure on the board from 1913 to 1928, Flexner became secretary and head of the Division of Studies and devoted most of his effort to primary education (laying the basis for the Lincoln School at Columbia Teachers College), the humanities, and, most important, medical education. He was determined that the future of medical education lie with universities and not with local medical elites. Flexner developed and oversaw a program of significant endowment grants to those universities which agreed to organize their medical schools on the basis of "the full-time plan," that is, paying salaries to clinical faculty rather than allowing them to earn fees for service. With practical command of Rockefeller medical philanthropy, Flexner directed more than $78 million to schools that adhered to his often quite detailed requirements, never hesitating to break old or to broker new relationships among medical schools, universities, hospitals, and local philanthropists. He specified the maximum salaries for different faculty ranks and dismissed all criticism because "the soundness of reform can never be left to a majority vote, else the human race would still be in the state of cave men." By restricting Rockefeller support to those schools, Flexner knit together a disjointed collection of institutionally weak medical schools into a fundamentally interrelated national system. Sometimes abrasive and always cocksure, he was for fifteen years the principal arbiter of the institutional development of American medical education.

The several Rockefeller philanthropies were reorganized in 1928, and the new leadership deliberately excluded Flexner from the new structure. His domineering style had become a threat to the public legitimacy of the foundations. Initially shocked, Flexner accepted a generous pension from John D. Rockefeller, Jr. Invited to Oxford to deliver the 1928 Rhodes Trust Memorial Lectures, Flexner used the opportunity to spend a year in England and Germany developing his lectures into an influential comparative study, *Universities: American, English, German* (1930), which proclaimed that unfettered research was the core function of the modern university. He particularly applauded the opportunities for postdoctoral study provided by German universities.

On his return to the United States, Flexner was approached by Felix Bamberger and Caroline Bamberger Fuld, sibling department store owners, who offered to support the development of a postdoctoral institution in New Jersey. Flexner agreed to guide the creation of a center where prominent scholars could pursue their research without distractions, including

that of teaching. The Institute for Advanced Study was founded in 1931 in Princeton with Flexner as director. In selecting subjects for the institute's "schools," Flexner focused first on mathematics as "both fundamental and severe." Together with Princeton mathematician Oswald Veblen, he selected and recruited its stellar initial faculty, including refugee scholars such as Albert Einstein and John Von Neumann. Flexner's leadership of the institute combined the great liberality of his vision with a contemptuous inflexibility in dealing with disagreements. He remained director of the institute until 1939, establishing a second school in economics and beginning the construction of an independent campus (the first offices of the institute were at Princeton University).

For the next twenty years, Flexner remained active writing books and maintaining an extensive and minatory correspondence with contemporary foundation executives, criticizing their emphasis on programs made up of small projects and their avoidance of the deep institutional support he had practiced. He died in Falls Church, Virginia.

Flexner's educational philosophy was grounded in highly particular, somewhat rarefied experiences—Johns Hopkins University in its early years and the glamorized German university—but his acerbic and direct rhetorical style made him one of the best-known educational reformers of his generation. His strategies for reform, though financially and politically costly, provided the new philanthropic foundations with the means to establish their visible role in American organizational life.

• Flexner's papers are in the Library of Congress. Other archival sources include the holdings of the Rockefeller Archive Center, Sleepy Hollow, N.Y.; the files of the Institute for Advanced Study at the Mudd Library, Princeton University; and the papers of Simon Flexner at the American Philosophical Society, Philadelphia. Flexner published two memoirs: *I Remember* (1940) and *Abraham Flexner: An Autobiography* (1960). During his retirement he wrote two biographies: *Henry S. Pritchett* (1940) and *Daniel Coit Gilman* (1946). His *Funds and Foundations* (1952) captures his distaste for all foundation methods but his own. Studies of his career include Steven C. Wheatley, *The Politics of Philanthropy: Abraham Flexner and Medical Education* (1988); Michael R. Harris, *Five Counter-Revolutionaries in Higher Education* (1970); Thomas Neville Bonner, "Searching for Abraham Flexner," *Academic Medicine* 73 (Feb. 1998): 160–66; Ronald F. Movrich, "Before the Gates of Excellence: Abraham Flexner and Education, 1866–1918" (Ph.D. diss., Univ. of Calif., Berkeley, 1981); and Laurie Smith Porter, "From Intellectual Sanctuary to Social Responsibility: The Founding of the Institute for Advanced Study, 1930–1933" (Ph.D. diss., Princeton Univ., 1988). The large literature on the "Flexner Report" and its implications is well summarized in Thomas Neville Bonner, "Abraham Flexner and the Historians," *Journal of the History of Medicine and Allied Sciences* 45 (1990): 3–10. See also Daniel M. Fox, "Abraham Flexner's Unpublished Report: Foundations and Medical Education, 1909–1928," *Bulletin of the History of Medicine* 54 (1980): 475–96.

STEVEN C. WHEATLEY

FLEXNER, Bernard (24 Feb. 1865–3 May 1945), lawyer, social welfare advocate, and Jewish community leader, was born in Louisville, Kentucky, the son of Morris (originally Moritz) Flexner and Esther Abraham. His parents, immigrants from Bohemia and the Rhineland, had settled in Louisville in the 1850s. Morris prospered as a hat merchant, but the panic of 1873 left his family of nine children impoverished. Bernard, who was the fifth child and fifth son, had two brothers who achieved eminence in American life. Abraham Flexner wrote the report that resulted in modernizing American medical education and was the first head of the Institute for Advanced Study at Princeton University. Simon Flexner was a distinguished pathologist who headed the Rockefeller Institute for Medical Research.

Bernard Flexner was educated in the Louisville public schools, received a law degree from the University of Louisville in 1898, and later studied law at the University of Virginia. He was admitted to the Kentucky bar in 1898, the Illinois bar in 1911, and the New York bar in 1919. He was prominent in Louisville's legal profession, serving as a partner in the firms of Bodley, Baskin and Flexner (1903–1905); Flexner, Campbell and Gordon (1908–1911); and Flexner and Gordon (1911–1914). Flexner's legal specialty was utilities law, and he was counsel to the companies organized by or associated with the wealthy Insull family in Chicago and New York.

While achieving prosperity as a lawyer, Flexner turned his attention to public service and devoted considerable time, energy, and thought to growing problems in social welfare. He was especially concerned with the growth of juvenile delinquency and advocated the establishment of juvenile courts. In Kentucky, he was chairman of Jefferson County's Juvenile Court Board (1906–1911) and helped draft the state's juvenile court law. He helped establish Chicago's first juvenile court and was appointed by the U.S. Attorney General in 1914 to chair a commission studying the need for legislation affecting children in Washington, D.C. In 1917 he moved to New York City, where he continued to practice law.

Flexner was interested in the whole range of social problems associated with the causes and treatment of crime and delinquency. He was active in the National Probation Association, serving as its president (1912–1913) and later as a member of its executive and advisory committees. One of his goals was to require professional education for social workers and probation officers. With Roger N. Baldwin, he wrote *Juvenile Courts and Probation* (1914); with Reuben Oppenheimer, *The Legal Aspect of the Juvenile Court* (1922); and with Oppenheimer and Katherine F. Lenroot, *The Child, the Family, and the Court* (1929).

Flexner achieved major prominence as a Jewish community leader who played a key role in the economic development of the Jewish settlements in Palestine, then under British mandatory control. In July 1917 he was a member of the American Red Cross commission to study relief needs in Romania. There he witnessed firsthand the plight of East European Jews. Spurred also by the November 1917 Balfour Declaration, Flexner was convinced the solution to the poverty and oppression he had seen lay in Jewish settlement in Palestine. He joined the Zionist Organization of America and quickly became part of the circle of American Zionist leaders associated with Supreme Court justice Louis D. Brandeis. In 1919 he went to the Paris Peace Conference as counsel to the American Jewish delegation headed by Louis Marshall. The following year he attended the World Zionist Congress in London, where he worked as Brandeis's lieutenant in internal political combat. The split between the Brandeis approach to Zionist policy, which stressed fiscally conservative development of Palestine, and that of Chaim Weizmann, the World Zionist Organization leader, who favored a broader, nationalistic approach, soon became irreconcilable. Brandeis and his friends, including Flexner, left the Zionist Organization of America in 1921.

Nevertheless, Flexner continued his efforts on behalf of the Jews of Palestine and Eastern Europe. As a member of the American Jewish Joint Distribution Committee, he worked to aid Polish Jews. Flexner was successful in bridging the gap between Zionists and wealthy non-Zionist philanthropists and community leaders. As a personal friend of Brandeis, his advice was frequently sought. In 1925, primarily at his initiative, the Palestine Economic Corporation was formed as a means of funneling investment funds and credit to the developing Jewish community in Palestine. Flexner succeeded in bringing together in the new entity such diverse figures as Louis Marshall, Herbert Lehman, Julian Mack, Louis Brandeis, and Felix Warburg. Flexner headed the corporation until 1931 and remained active in it until his death. By that time, the corporation had successfully fostered hydroelectric projects, rural cooperatives, urban housing, extraction of mineral resources, and irrigation. In 1929 Flexner again served as an intermediary between the Zionists and non-Zionists in the difficult negotiations to establish the Jewish Agency for Palestine.

After 1933 Flexner was active in assisting refugees from Hitler-dominated Germany and Europe. He was an organizer of the Emergency Committee in Aid of Displaced German Scholars and was an officer of the Refugee Economic Corporation. Among his other contributions was the 1928 publication and distribution to libraries of the complete six-volume record of the trial of Sacco and Vanzetti.

Flexner was not a magnetic or dynamic leader. Known as "Ben" to his associates, his qualities of integrity, thoughtfulness, loyalty, diligence, and moderation made him an asset to those who were more charismatic. A lifelong bachelor, Flexner lived with his sister Mary in New York City, where he died.

• Papers of the Palestine Economic Corporation are at the American Jewish Archives, Hebrew Union College, Cincinnati, Ohio. On the Flexner family, see Abraham Flexner, *An Autobiography* (1960). For Flexner's role in American Zionism, see Yonathan Shapiro, *Leadership of the American Zionist Organization, 1897–1930* (1971), and Melvin I. Urofsky, *American Zionism from Herzl to the Holocaust* (1975). On overseas aid, see Boris D. Bogen, *Born a Jew* (1930), and Joseph C. Hyman, *Twenty-Five Years of American Aid to Jews Overseas* (1939). Obituaries are in the *New York Times*, 4 May 1945, and *New Palestine*, 31 May 1945, and a memorial by Charles C. Burlingham is in the Association of the Bar of the City of New York, *Year Book* (1946).

MORTON ROSENSTOCK

FLEXNER, Helen Thomas (14 Aug. 1871–6 Apr. 1956), writer and educator, was born Helen Whitall Thomas in Baltimore, Maryland, the daughter of James Carey Thomas, a physician, and Mary Whitall, a reformer and Quaker leader. One of ten children, Nellie, as her family called her, grew up in an often chaotic, socially prominent, upper-middle-class Quaker household. The activities and beliefs of her siblings as well as her parents had a tremendous impact on Helen Flexner's life and frequently overshadowed her achievements.

Perhaps no event shaped Flexner's life course more than the death of her mother. Mary Thomas grew ill with breast cancer when Flexner was only sixteen. Convinced that she had a special relationship with God, Flexner's mother shunned all medical intervention, including her husband's efforts, and relied solely on faith to heal her. As her mother languished at home, Flexner skipped classes, ceased studying for the college entrance examinations, and took over the management of the large household. Flexner promised her dying mother that she would delay going to college and remain at home with her father for at least a year.

After her mother's death in 1888, Flexner became sickly and "morbid," and she lost her faith in God. Excruciating earaches, which plagued her for the rest of her life and caused a degree of deafness, began during Flexner's year of housekeeping, which she hated. On 30 September 1889 she left her family home for the first time and entered Bryn Mawr College; M. Carey Thomas, her sister, was then dean.

During her time at Bryn Mawr, Flexner matured socially and met Lucy Martin Donnelly, who became a lifelong friend. But her Bryn Mawr years were also troubled by bouts of sickness—the earaches returned, and she suffered from a series of winter "colds." Despite the interruptions caused by her illnesses, Flexner managed to graduate with an A.B. in 1893. After graduation, she joined Donnelly in Europe with the intention of studying for an advanced degree in English. Although she attended classes at the University of Leipzig, the Sorbonne, and the Collège de France between 1894 and 1895, Flexner lost interest in her studies and spent time on other more pleasurable pursuits. While abroad, she met her cousin Alys Pearsall Smith's future husband, the philosopher, mathematician, and writer Bertrand Russell. As her tour of Europe drew to a close, Flexner asked her sister M. Carey Thomas, now president of Bryn Mawr, if there were any jobs available for her and Donnelly. Thomas appointed the two women instructors in English composition.

In addition to teaching her students, Flexner decided to pursue her ambition of becoming a "distinguished writer of literary prose." Then, before classes met for the first time in the fall of 1896, she was struck by a new ailment—sciatica. The illness did not prevent her from fulfilling her teaching obligations, but she was unable to follow her writing ambitions. With the death of her father the following year, she became financially independent but continued to teach at Bryn Mawr.

During a Christmas vacation in Baltimore in 1898, she met Simon Flexner, her future husband, for the first time, and a friendship grew between the two. In 1900 she took a leave from Bryn Mawr to launch herself as a writer. She sailed to England and visited Bertrand and Alys Russell. Although the Russell marriage was breaking up, Helen Flexner and Bertrand Russell cemented their friendship. At the end of her year away from Bryn Mawr, Flexner had only one draft of a short story and a correspondence with Bertrand Russell to show for it.

In the fall of 1901 Flexner entered Johns Hopkins Hospital for treatment of her sciatica. Her treatment demanded complete muscle relaxation—of body and brain—and she was not allowed to read, write, or have visitors. In 1902 she was back at Bryn Mawr teaching. After her bout with sciatica Flexner's desire to write did not return, and she decided to resume her studies and become a professor of English. But in 1903 that goal was put aside permanently when she married Simon Flexner, physician, pathologist, and director of the Rockefeller Institute for Medical Research. Although quite upset by Flexner's engagement, Lucy Donnelly, after a brief period of estrangement, became a regular visitor in the Flexner home. She served on the Bryn Mawr faculty for decades before her death. During their marriage the couple had two sons, and Flexner tried to return to writing.

Flexner completed a novel in the first year of her marriage, but it was never published. She became a member of the Collegiate Equal Suffrage League, serving as vice president from 1905 to 1909, and as a representative of that organization she wrote the introduction to Helen L. Sumner's *Equal Suffrage: The Results of an Investigation in Colorado Made for the Collegiate Equal Suffrage League of New York State* (1909). She had her husband join her on at least one suffrage parade and encouraged him to contribute to a pamphlet that denied that women were intellectually inferior to men.

Flexner never became the literary giant she hoped to become; her writing portfolio contained few entries. In addition to the introduction to Sumner's book, she wrote several articles about suffrage. In 1905 Bryn Mawr College published her pamphlet *Bryn Mawr: A Characterisation*. Her autobiographical work, *A Quaker Childhood* (1940), recorded her reminiscences up to her mother's death and was her only book-length publication. Flexner did not publish in the last years of her life in New York City, where she died.

In many ways Helen Whitall Thomas Flexner's life reflects common conditions of women at the turn of the century: women often had to choose between marriage and a career, it was not uncommon for female ailments to be diagnosed as nervous conditions and treated with total bedrest, and family obligations often took precedence over women's personal desires. The most telling aspect of Flexner's life is that she is probably best remembered, not for her own accomplishments, but for her ties to prominent men and women of the time such as her husband, Simon Flexner; her sister, M. Carey Thomas; her aunt, Hannah Whitall Smith; and her friend, Bertrand Russell.

• The major archives of Helen Thomas Flexner and her husband, Simon Flexner, are in the Flexner papers at the American Philosophical Society in Philadelphia. Their son, James Thomas Flexner of New York City, also has a number of papers and artifacts that deal with the Thomas and Whitall families in his private collection. Helen Flexner's *A Quaker Childhood* (1940) is problematic as a source—it is a reminiscence and often glosses over unpleasant aspects of her early years. See also a biography by James Flexner, *An American Saga: The Story of Helen Thomas and Simon Flexner* (1984). An obituary is in the *New York Times*, 7 Apr. 1956.

GAYLE VERONICA FISCHER

FLEXNER, Jennie Maas (6 Nov. 1882–17 Nov. 1944), librarian and adult educator, was born in Louisville, Kentucky, the daughter of Jacob Aaron Flexner, a physician, and Rosa Maas. Flexner was educated first in the public schools of Louisville and then through private study. She worked for several years as a legal secretary and then as an administrative secretary before accepting a position at the Louisville Public Library in 1905. Her keen mind, love of reading, and intellectual curiosity led William F. Yust, chief librarian, to endorse her unqualifiedly for professional study at the Library School of Western Reserve University in Cleveland. She entered the class of 1908, was elected president of her class, and had close contact with library leaders on the faculty. Fourteen years later Flexner accepted the office of president of the library school's alumni association. Never married, Flexner was a dedicated career librarian typical of her generation.

Upon returning to the staff of the Louisville Public Library in 1909, Flexner soon supplemented her work in technical services with responsibilities for the library's training class. In 1912 Yust named her head of the circulation department, a position through which Flexner developed her concepts of reader services: open access to the collection for browsing, subject guides to reading choices, and professional advisory service.

Flexner's professional activity and leadership soon made themselves felt beyond Louisville. In 1923 and 1924 she served as president of the Kentucky Library Association. From this position she actively recruited Negroes to library education in order to strengthen library service to this community. In 1926 she served on the Council of the American Association for Adult Education.

While always committed to the fields of library education and adult education, Flexner was devoted above all to services for readers. As such, she prepared the first textbook on her specialty, *Circulation Work in Public Libraries* (1927), for the American Library Association (ALA). In this work she analyzed the duties and characteristics of circulation librarians at a time when the professional services of reading guidance and community contacts were an inherent part of circulation work. Field visits to some fifty outstanding U.S. public libraries, plus the intellectual stimulus of working under the guidance of W. W. Charters and Sarah C. N. Bogle, editors of the ALA textbook series, had provided Flexner with the broadened perspective that is reflected in her book. Reviewers were laudatory and saw the textbook as significant for both the novice librarian and the practitioner, replacing the rule of thumb with philosophically based service concepts. The work became the standard text in its specialty for the next two decades.

Having built the circulation services of the Louisville Public Library to an active open-shelf service over sixteen years, and having studied the advisory services in Chicago, Milwaukee, and elsewhere, Flexner was ready for new professional challenge. In 1928 she accepted an invitation to establish a readers' advisory service for the New York Public Library. The position in New York required organizing an advisory service for the users of both the great research collections of the library's reference department and the large branch library system of the circulation department. Flexner brought to the task her scholarly knowledge of books, ability to organize, skills in working with two well-differentiated departments, and enthusiasm. The modest, accessible Readers' Adviser's Office opened on 4 March 1929.

The public events of the next fifteen years, the depression and then World War II, dictated the emphases of the readers' advisory service. The personal needs of the unemployed, the displaced, and the distraught who sought help from books required precisely the personalized attention that the new service was designed to provide. Beyond developing this service for individual readers, Flexner worked extensively with groups, providing reading lists and materials to local and national organizations and using such study groups as channels to individual users.

The depression led Flexner to an intensive search for "readable books." She approached publishers, encouraging the production of "simple, well-written" introductions to new fields of knowledge to enhance background knowledge and employability of the vast numbers of undereducated unemployed during the period 1931 to 1939. In "Remarks at a Memorial for Jennie M. Flexner" in December 1944, Morse Cartwright, an eminent adult educator, commented, "Miss Flexner undoubtedly saved the lives of a few and the reason of many during the economic depression."

While close to half the users of Flexner's Readers' Adviser's Service in the late 1930s were unemployed, equally significant were the numbers of foreign-born refugees from Europe. Hundreds of well-educated refugees from Nazism turned to the New York Public Library for guidance in learning English and finding jobs. Flexner chaired national committees and organizations designed to meet the needs of foreign-born immigrants.

Staff training of librarians in the extensive branch library system became a major responsibility of Flexner and her office. In 1936 the first two branch system readers' advisers were appointed; by 1938 there were seventeen; by 1943, twenty-nine. Flexner published two reports on the service that became manuals not only for New York public librarians but also for libraries nationwide, *A Readers' Advisory Service* (1934) and *Readers' Advisers at Work* (1941). Flexner's final published monograph, *Making Books Work* (1943), was designed as a guide for the adult independent student. In 1938 the Joseph W. Lippincott Award Committee gave her a special citation for her "judgment and discrimination" in development of reader's advisory services and her publications in the field. She died at her home in New York City.

Given the cyclical nature of the emphases of public librarianship, from "reference" service to the library's "educational" function and back again, the influence of Flexner's concepts and service models has waxed and waned during the half century since her death. Recent surveys suggest, however, that her concepts have been integrated into professional practice (Kathleen M. Heim and Danny P. Wallace, *Adult Services: An Enduring Focus for Public Libraries* [1990]). As a reader's adviser, community librarian, and adult educator, Flexner consistently provided professional leadership by addressing basic social problems of her time. As the cycle of revived perspective continues, so Flexner's concepts and service models remain relevant into the twenty-first century.

• Letters, memos, and records related to Flexner are in the archives of the New York Public Library, the Louisville (Ky.) Public Library, and the School of Library Science of Case Western Reserve University in Cleveland, Ohio. Emily Miller Danton, *Pioneering Leaders in Librarianship* (1953), pp. 61–73, presents a personal and professional memoir of Flexner's life and career by Esther Johnson, chief of the New York Public Library Circulation Department. The prime professional source for this article is the *Dictionary of American Library Biography* (1975). An obituary is in the *New York Times*, 18 Nov. 1944.

MARGARET E. MONROE

FLEXNER, Simon (25 Mar. 1863–2 May 1946), pathologist and bacteriologist, was born in Louisville, Kentucky, the son of well-educated Jewish immigrants Morris Flexner, a merchant and salesman, and Esther Abraham, a seamstress. Simon Flexner had little formal education. As a child he was an indifferent student and a mischief maker. He quit school in the sixth grade and held a variety of menial jobs. At age sixteen

he nearly succumbed to typhoid fever, and after he recovered his attitude toward education changed. He became a pharmacy apprentice at Vincent Davis's drugstore for two years and attended two three-month courses of lectures at the Louisville College of Pharmacy, surprising his family by finishing first in his class in 1882. Upon graduating he clerked for eight years in the drugstore owned by his eldest brother, Jacob. Simon lived over the store, made up for his educational deficits by studying math and science from his brothers' school books, took up botanizing and microscopy, and organized the Louisville Microscopical Club. He taught himself histology and acquired an interest in pathology through local doctors, who gathered to converse in Jacob's store and brought him specimens to analyze. Simon Flexner hoped to open his own pathological laboratory in Louisville, so he entered the University of Louisville School of Medicine and earned an M.D. in 1889. At the urging of his younger brother Abraham, who later became known for writing the Carnegie Institution report on American medical schools, Flexner enrolled in the postgraduate course in pathology at the Johns Hopkins University.

Despite his meager medical education, Flexner's quickness and perseverance so impressed Johns Hopkins pathologist William H. Welch that he was made the fellow in pathology in 1891. When the Johns Hopkins Medical School opened in 1893, Welch hired him as his assistant and sent him to Europe for further study. By 1895 Flexner had gained promotion to associate professor of pathology and was the resident pathologist at the Johns Hopkins Hospital. He ran the daily operations of the pathological laboratory and assisted Welch with the pathology courses for the medical school. During his Johns Hopkins years, Flexner's research output was prodigious. Between 1893 and 1899 he published more than seventy articles, including collaborations with Welch on the bacteriology and pathology of diphtheria. He acquired valuable field experience in infectious disease in 1893 when Welch sent him and Lewellys Barker to investigate an outbreak of cerebrospinal meningitis for the Maryland State Board of Health. He further enlarged his research perspective by working in the laboratory of biologist Jacques Loeb at the Marine Biological Laboratory at Woods Hole, Massachusetts, in the summer of 1895. Shortly after the United States annexed the Philippines in 1899, Flexner chaired a Johns Hopkins University special commission to study Philippine tropical diseases, again accompanied by Lewellys Barker. This trip gave him more valuable experience in infectious disease research. In Tokyo he met Shibasaburo Kitasato, discoverer of the plague bacillus, and had the opportunity to autopsy cases of plague in Hong Kong. In Manila he studied leprosy and dysentery. He discovered a variety of *Bacillus* (now *Shigella*) *dysenteriae* that caused one of the most prevalent forms of dysentery. It was named *Shigella flexneri* in his honor.

In 1899 Flexner became professor of pathology at the University of Pennsylvania, one of the premier positions in the country. He also was appointed director of the university's Ayer Clinical Laboratory in 1901 and presided over the construction of a new building for the preclinical sciences. He remained active in research, expanding his work on the dysentery bacillus and developing research in immunology through his work on the toxic effects of snake venom with Hideyo Noguchi, who had come from Japan to study with him. His previous experience with plague led to his appointment by the U.S. secretary of the Treasury to head a federal commission to investigate an outbreak of plague in San Francisco in 1901.

Flexner's career took a new direction in 1901 when he was appointed to the Board of Scientific Directors of the newly formed Rockefeller Institute for Medical Research, endowed by oil baron John D. Rockefeller. In 1902 the board, headed by William H. Welch, invited Flexner to become the director of its laboratories and to organize their operations. He accepted, with some hesitation, since he considered it a gamble to leave his prestigious position at Pennsylvania to direct an institute that, at its founding, was assured of only modest funding for ten years. During 1903, the first year of his appointment, he visited research laboratories in Europe to plan, by comparison, the form and direction of the Rockefeller Institute. His new bride, Helen Whitall Thomas, whom he had married earlier that year, accompanied him (the couple eventually had two sons).

Flexner's rise in medical science was truly remarkable. In just ten years the impoverished, novice physician from Louisville had come to be entrusted by the most respected medical scientists in the country with the development of an important new research laboratory. Flexner created a research institution with unusual flexibility. In Europe he had realized that chemistry, physics, and experimental biology increasingly were the source of new knowledge in the medical sciences, and he purposely selected a scientific staff that had mastered research in the basic sciences. Flexner's choices for the new laboratory, which opened in 1906, proved especially astute. They included Samuel J. Meltzer, Phoebus A. Levene, Eugene L. Opie, Hideyo Noguchi, Alexis Carrel, Jacques Loeb, Rufus I. Cole, and Peyton Rous.

Flexner's own research won early public acclaim for the new institution and gained Rockefeller's confidence and continued philanthropy. In 1904 to 1905 New York City experienced a severe cerebrospinal meningitis epidemic that killed three of every four victims. Flexner studied the disease in monkeys and by 1907 had created an antiserum against the bacterial agent that reduced mortality by 50 percent. He produced the antiserum at the institute and distributed it free. Flexner's serum remained the best treatment for meningitis until the advent of sulpha drugs and antibiotics in the 1930s and 1940s. In 1907 he began a similar investigation after an outbreak of polio. At the time almost nothing was known about polio. Taking a lead from Karl Landsteiner, he successfully transferred polio from humans to monkeys, demonstrating that it was infectious, and determined that the agent was a virus. He believed that the virus affected only the nervous system and could not replicate in the intestine. He was proven wrong by younger Rockefeller scientists in the 1920s. Nonetheless, Flexner's work laid the basis for polio research and made the Rockefeller Institute a major center for research in virology.

John D. Rockefeller was so pleased with Flexner's accomplishments that he funded a fifty-bed research hospital at the institute. It opened in 1910 under the direction of Rufus Cole. A department of animal pathology, led by Theobald Smith, opened at Princeton, New Jersey, in 1916. During World War I, at Flexner's instigation, the institute set up a war demonstration hospital and laboratories for the training of medical officers and technicians. He was in charge of teaching bacteriology. He served in the Army Medical Corps from 1917 to 1919, attaining the rank of colonel, and was given the responsibility to inspect the expeditionary forces laboratories in Europe.

Initially, Flexner had been hired only to direct the laboratory at the Rockefeller Institute, but his administrative skill had made him, in effect, the head of the entire institute, a position that was formalized in 1924. One of his strengths as director was his personal involvement in research. He brought the *Journal of Experimental Medicine* to the institute in 1905 to support the publication of research and remained its editor until 1946. He recognized the need to free the investigative staff of the mundane so they could concentrate on their science, and he did everything he could to foster their initiative. His colleagues admired his logical skills and the ease with which he made clear, incisive decisions. Although he was a formal, reserved man, they found him to be generous and kind. As the institute grew and administration consumed more of his time, he stayed actively involved in research by advising or collaborating with scientists on the staff.

Flexner contributed substantially to public health and medical education worldwide as a charter member of the Rockefeller Foundation, the foremost international medical philanthropy. He served on the foundation's China Medical Board, which organized the Peking Union Medical College, and he helped the National Research Council secure foundation funding for postdoctoral fellowships in the physical, biological, and medical sciences, as well as mathematics. He had direct influence on the Johns Hopkins Medical School as a member of its board of trustees. He also chaired the Public Health Council of New York State for many years. Throughout his career he participated in numerous scientific organizations, serving as president of the Association of American Physicians in 1914, the American Association for the Advancement of Science in 1919, and the Congress of American Physicians and Surgeons in 1919. His work was acknowledged with membership in the National Academy of Sciences.

Flexner retired as director of the Rockefeller Institute in 1935. He spent 1937 to 1938 as Eastman Professor at Oxford University to advise on newly endowed medical professorships. While there he wrote a book,

The Evolution and Organization of the University Clinic (1939). In 1941 he and his son James Thomas Flexner coauthored a highly acclaimed biography of his teacher and friend, *William Henry Welch and the Heroic Age of American Medicine*. He died in New York City.

Simon Flexner made significant scientific discoveries in pathology, bacteriology, and immunology, but his greatest contribution to medical science was organizing the Rockefeller Institute. In his thirty-two years as its director, he created one of the world's most admired and imitated medical research institutes.

• Flexner's professional and family papers are located at the American Philosophical Society Library in Philadelphia. Large collections relating to the Rockefeller Institute that bear on Flexner's career are at the Rockefeller Archives Center, Pocantico Hills, Tarrytown, N.Y. James Thomas Flexner, *An American Saga: The Story of Helen Thomas and Simon Flexner* (1984), provides details about his parents' family history, Flexner's education, and his early career. The biography concludes in 1903 with their marriage. James Thomas Flexner reminisces in "My Father, Simon Flexner," in *Institute to University: A Seventy-fifth Anniversary Colloquium* (1977). Information about Flexner's scientific accomplishments is found in biographical accounts written by his Rockefeller Institute colleagues: Peyton Rous, "Simon Flexner, 1863–1946," *Obituary Notices of the Fellows of the Royal Society* 6, no. 17 (Nov. 1948): 409–45, which includes a complete bibliography of Flexner's nearly 400 research papers, articles, and lectures; Eugene L. Opie, "Simon Flexner, M.D.," *Archives of Pathology* 42 (1946): 234–42; Rufus Cole, "In Memoriam, Simon Flexner," *Bulletin of the New York Academy of Medicine* 22, no. 10 (1946): 546–52; and Rous, "Simon Flexner and Medical Discovery," *Science* 107 (1948): 611–13. Andrea K. Blumenthal, "Leadership in a Medical Philanthropy: Simon Flexner and the Rockefeller Institute for Medical Research" (Ph.D. diss., Drew Univ., 1991), analyzes his management style. Historical analysis of Flexner's career is found in George W. Corner, *A History of the Rockefeller Institute* (1964); John R. Paul, *A History of Poliomyelitis* (1971); Saul Benison, "Poliomyelitis and the Rockefeller Institute: Social Effects and Institutional Response," *Journal of the History of Medicine and Allied Sciences* 29 (1974): 74–93; and Benison, "Simon Flexner: The Evolution of a Career in Medical Science," in *Institute to University: A Seventy-fifth Anniversary Colloquium* (1977).

PATRICIA GOSSEL

FLICK, Elmer Harrison (11 Jan. 1876–9 Jan. 1971), baseball player, was born in Bedford, Ohio, the son of Zachary Taylor Flick, a farmer, and Mary Caine. After attending Bedford High School, Flick began his professional baseball career as an outfielder with Youngstown, Ohio, of the Inter-State League; there he played the last thirty-one games of the 1896 season and batted .438. The following year he played a full season with Dayton, Ohio, also of the Inter-State League, and proved that his previous success was no fluke by posting a .396 batting average in 126 games. After seeing Flick in action, the Philadelphia Phillies of the National League signed him to a contract.

Flick reported to the Phillies' training camp in Cape May, New Jersey, in April 1898. He brought with him a bat that was handmade; Flick had learned to use a lathe when he could not find bats with a thick enough handle (which, according to Flick, allowed him to hit inside pitches better). Flick's performance in training camp with his homemade bat was impressive, but the Phillies had a particularly strong set of outfielders: Ed Delahanty in left field, Dick Cooley in center field, and Sam Thompson in right field. Flick started the season figuring to serve primarily as a pinch hitter and backup fielder. But six games into the season, Thompson was sidelined with back problems, and on 26 April 1898 Flick started in right field. He made the most of the opportunity, hitting two singles against Boston's Fred Klobedanz. Thompson tried to return to the starting lineup but could not achieve a comeback, and Flick remained a starting right fielder his next thirteen seasons in the major leagues.

The 1898 season marked an auspicious beginning for Flick. In a 20 June game against St. Louis, Flick hit three triples with his 54-ounce bat in a 14–2 win. His season average was .302. The next season his average improved to .342, and in 1900 Flick batted a career-high .378. He narrowly lost the batting title that year to Honus Wagner, who batted .381. In 1900 Flick married Mary Ella Gates; they had five daughters.

In 1902 Flick jumped his contract and signed with the American League's Philadelphia Athletics. At that time, relations between the National and American leagues were hostile, as the upstart American League sought equal status as a major league. Flick's move outraged the owners of the Phillies, especially because Flick was admired by Fans and well liked in the organization by owners and players alike. The Phillies obtained a court injunction to prevent Flick from playing with any team in Pennsylvania other than the Phillies; and so, after only ten games with the Athletics, Flick signed with the Cleveland Indians.

Despite these turbulent events, Flick's career remained in high gear. In a 6 July game Flick became the first American League player to hit three triples in a game. He continued to prove adept at hitting triples, leading the American League in 1905, 1906, and 1907. In 1905 Flick won the batting championship, even though his .306 average was over seventy points lower than his career best. No player won a batting title with a lower average. The mark was the lowest until 1968, when Carl Yastrezemski won the American League title with a .301 average. Flick's low championship average was not a reflection of the ability of the league's players, who at that time included Flick, Ty Cobb, and Honus Wagner. Playing conditions in 1905 did not favor hitters, with the pitching mound height fluctuating as the league sought to lower scores and speed up games.

In 1907 Detroit Tigers manager Hugh Jennings attempted to trade Ty Cobb for Flick after he became fed up with the reckless and combative Cobb. Because Flick was very well liked by the Cleveland organization, however, Indians owner Charlie Somers resoundingly rejected the deal. Cobb would win the batting title that year (as he would eleven more times), batting .350. But Flick batted a solid .302 and stole forty-one bases, and thus Somers felt rewarded.

The 1907 season was essentially Flick's last great year in the American League, as he was plagued by an undiagnosable stomach ailment that took its toll quickly. He played only nine games in 1908, and in 1909 and 1910 Flick achieved only .255 and .265 averages, respectively. He retired from the Indians after the 1910 season.

The fact that Flick's lifetime batting average suffered during his final three seasons serves only as a tribute to what he achieved in the previous ten seasons. He retired with a .315 lifetime average in 1,484 games, with 1,767 hits, 170 triples, and 334 stolen bases. Flick was elected to the National Baseball Hall of Fame in 1963, at that time becoming the oldest living member at age eighty-seven. Although he had faded from popular memory, Flick retained his amiable personality and vivacity, and for the next eight years he served as a dignified ambassador from baseball's glory days of the early twentieth century to a generation that was born well after he had played his last game. Flick died in his hometown of Bedford.

• Documents relating to Flick's career are at the National Baseball Library, Cooperstown, N.Y. Flick is discussed in Mike Shatzkin, ed., *The Ballplayers: Baseball's Ultimate Biographical Reference* (1990); and Lee Allen and Tom Meany, *Kings of the Diamond: The Immortals in Baseball's Hall of Fame* (1965). The best-documented aspects of Flick's life are his baseball statistics, which are in Joseph L. Reichler, ed., *The Baseball Encyclopedia*, 6th ed. (1985); and James Charleton, ed., *The Baseball Chronology: The Complete History of the Most Important Events in the Game of Baseball* (1991).

PAUL WAYNE RODNEY

FLICK, Lawrence Francis (10 Aug. 1856–7 July 1938), physician, historian, and early leader in the campaign against tuberculosis, was born in Carroll Township, Cambria County, Pennsylvania, the son of John Flick, a mill owner and farmer, and Elizabeth Schabacher (changed to Sharbaugh). Flick grew up on the family farm, but poor health excused him from the usual chores. A bookish boy and a devout Roman Catholic, he first attended local schools. For most of his teenage years, he studied at St. Vincent's, a Benedictine college in Beatty (now Latrobe), Pennsylvania, but symptoms suggesting tuberculosis cut short his classwork, and he returned home. After a period of indecision and various jobs, he entered Jefferson Medical College in Philadelphia and graduated in 1879. He then completed an internship at Philadelphia Hospital and opened an office for the practice of medicine. His persisting illness, however, was finally diagnosed as tuberculosis and, following his physicians' advice, he traveled to the West for his health. By 1883, improvement allowed him to resume his practice, which soon included increasing numbers of patients with tuberculosis. "When I recovered from tuberculosis as a young man," he wrote, "I consecrated my life to the welfare of those afflicted with the disease and to the protection of those who had not yet contracted it" (*Beloved Crusader*, p. 225).

By the late 1880s, Flick began to express publicly two convictions that would become central themes of the campaign against tuberculosis: the disease was communicable, not hereditary, and it was preventable, not inevitable. He also argued that poor people with consumption (as tuberculosis was then called) should be helped through hospitalization. Institutionalization of the sick would be humane, and the resulting segregation would serve to stop the spread of infection to others. These ideas proved controversial in the medical profession more than a decade after Robert Koch's 1882 demonstration that tubercle bacilli transmitted the disease. Gradually, however, opinions changed. Flick was a good organizer with "a talent for . . . publicity" and "a capability of bearing responsibility not only easily, but aggressively" (Walsh, p. 114), and evidence of these qualities became abundant.

In 1890 Flick helped to found the Rush Hospital for Consumption and Allied Diseases. In 1892 he founded the Pennsylvania Society for the Prevention of Tuberculosis, the first voluntary organization of its kind in the United States. Among the society's goals were to teach consumptives and their families how to stop the spread of infection and to teach the public how to protect themselves. In 1895 Flick helped to found the Free Hospital for Poor Consumptives, an organization that arranged free hospital care for needy people with advanced tuberculosis. In 1901 the Free Hospital opened the White Haven Sanatorium, the first successful tuberculosis sanatorium in Pennsylvania. The industrialist Henry Phipps, who admired Flick's work at White Haven, established in 1903 the Henry Phipps Institute for the Study, Prevention, and Treatment of Tuberculosis—a research organization that included a hospital, a dispensary, and a laboratory. Flick became the institute's medical director. In 1904 he helped organize the National Association for the Study and Prevention of Tuberculosis, and through its auspices he succeeded in bringing the International Congress on Tuberculosis to the United States in 1908.

Flick had strong convictions about organizational methods, and frictions developed. By 1911, his relationships with all these organizations, except for the White Haven Sanatorium, had been severed. He remained active in medical practice, however, managing his own small private sanatorium in Philadelphia in 1913–1914 and seeing patients in his office into the 1930s. While the capacities of tuberculosis institutions for white patients were increasing in the early twentieth century, facilities for black patients were relatively few and often unacceptable to their intended clientele. In 1933 Flick helped organize a ward for such patients in the Frederick Douglass Memorial Hospital, Philadelphia's first hospital owned and managed by African Americans. This was the achievement of which he was most proud.

In addition to his productive medical career, Flick had a long and active interest in history. He was a founder in 1884 of the American Catholic Historical Society in Philadelphia and served as president in 1893–1896 and again in 1913–1914. In 1919 he was a founder of the American Catholic Historical Association in Washington, D.C., and served as president in 1920. His historical writings focused on tuberculosis and on Catholic topics, most notably *Development of Our Knowledge of Tuberculosis* (1925) and "The Study of History from a Christian Point of View" (*Records of American Catholic Historical Association* [1897]). In 1920 Notre Dame University awarded Flick the Laetare Medal, and in 1933 the Philadelphia County Medical Society gave him the Strittmatter Medal.

Family life was very important to Flick, who in 1885 had married Ella Mary Stone (previously Ella J. Stone); the couple had seven children. Flick "was domestic to a high degree, earnestly believ[ing] that children were given to parents to be personally cared for by them, and his only periods of relaxation were in their company" (Walsh, p. 119). He died at home in Philadelphia.

The results of Flick's efforts to combat tuberculosis cannot be easily assessed. Although he believed that the falling death rates from tuberculosis could be attributed to the institutionalization of infectious people, many other factors may have had an impact. His model of a voluntary association that brought together laypersons and professionals to cooperate in a fight against a specific disease, however, has been widely replicated. He created an organizational method of dealing with a complex medical and social problem at a time when medicine could give informed guidance to society even when it had no cure.

• Flick's extensive correspondence is in the Historical Collections of the College of Physicians of Philadelphia and the Department of Archives and Manuscripts, Catholic University of America, Washington, D.C. For his own writings, see Philip P. Jacobs, "Lawrence F. Flick, M.D.," in S. Adolphus Knopf, *A History of the National Tuberculosis Association* (1922), pp. 425–27. Useful accounts of his life by his daughter, Ella M. E. Flick, are *Dr. Lawrence F. Flick, 1856–1938* (1940) and *Beloved Crusader: Lawrence F. Flick, Physician* (1944). See also Joseph Walsh, "Memoir of Lawrence F. Flick, M.D.," *Transactions and Studies of the College of Physicians of Philadelphia* 7, no. 1 (1939): 114–19. For a social history of tuberculosis based largely on Flick's work and correspondence, see Barbara Bates, *Bargaining for Life* (1992).

BARBARA BATES

FLINT, Austin (20 Oct. 1812–13 Mar. 1886), physician and medical educator, was born in Petersham, Massachusetts, the son of Joseph Henshaw Flint, a physician, and Hannah Reed. Flint was the fourth generation of Massachusetts physicians of that surname, and his education was typical of medical education in antebellum America. He studied at Amherst College but entered Harvard Medical School before completing the arts curriculum. His preparation was among the best available in America of the 1830s; from James Jackson, Flint learned of the new medical ideas of the Paris school and from Jacob Bigelow he learned the

concept of self-limited diseases. Both physicians, as well as the surgeon John C. Warren, placed great emphasis on the new techniques of physical diagnosis—percussion and mediate auscultation. He attributed to the Harvard faculty his lifelong interest in clinical observation. He graduated from Harvard, after two courses of lectures and a three-year apprenticeship to his father, in 1833. Despite the encouragement of the Harvard faculty, Flint did not join the group of young Americans who went to Paris for postgraduate training. Instead, he entered practice in Boston and Northampton, establishing himself as a caring, personable, and gifted practitioner. In 1835 he married Anne Skillings; they had one child.

Flint's Harvard training as well as the realities of building a practice led him in 1840 to begin a career in medical publishing. It was considered unethical to advertise for patients, but medical articles often were reprinted and acknowledged in the lay press, bringing their authors to the attention of prospective patients. In 1841 Flint published an important article that contributed to a better understanding of quinine therapy for malaria, and in 1844 he was called to the chair of medicine at the new Rush Medical College in Chicago.

After teaching in Chicago for one term, Flint went to Buffalo, New York, where he resumed his practice and in 1846 founded the *Buffalo Medical Journal*. He attended the 1846 National Medical Convention in New York City and was appointed the chairman of its committee on medical education. In 1847 Flint, with Frank H. Hamilton and James P. White, founded the Buffalo Medical College. The new school did not meet the high standard Flint's committee recommended to the convention (which constituted itself as the American Medical Association) at its second meeting in Philadelphia in that same year.

In 1843, while Flint was serving as Erie County health officer, he was called in consultation to the village of North Boston, New York, where an epidemic of fever had occurred. This experience inspired his lifelong study of the diagnosis and epidemiology of continued fevers. In his 1843 report he alluded to the possibility that contagion had been introduced into the village by a passing stranger. He submitted suspect well water for analysis, but the analysis did not reveal anything helpful. In 1850 Flint would use the same experience, to which later cases were added, to help convince the American medical profession of the difference between the clinically similar but pathologically and epidemiologically distinct continued fevers—typhoid and typhus fever. Flint would use the data yet again in the 1870s to teach fecal-oral transmission of waterborne diseases.

In 1850 Flint made the suggestion, based on his experience as a medical teacher, that students might profitably attend to variations in pitch of auscultatory sounds as a means of better differentiating what they heard. In 1852 he synthesized his ideas on this subject for his first American Medical Association prize-winning essay. Later that year Flint accepted the chair in medicine at the medical department of the University of Louisville in Kentucky. There Flint began another valuable innovation in teaching auscultation—the teaching of the normal sounds in a physical diagnosis tutorial using members of the class as subjects.

Flint taught in Louisville for four years, and during that time his ideas on teaching physical diagnosis matured into his classic text, *Physical Exploration and Diagnosis of Diseases Affecting the Respiratory Organs* (1856). In 1856–1859 Flint again taught in Buffalo and served as president of the Buffalo Medical Society. In 1858 he joined the faculty of the new New Orleans School of Medicine. While wintering in New Orleans, Flint first described the Austin Flint murmur, a loud, presystolic murmur at the apex of the heart indicative of aortic regurgitation without a mitral valve lesion.

The coming of the Civil War made New Orleans uncongenial for Flint, and he accepted a position in New York at the new Long Island College and Hospital. In 1861 he was asked by Frank Hamilton to join a group of practitioners organizing a new medical school in association with Bellevue Hospital. The Bellevue Hospital Medical College merged with New York University after Flint's death, but for a generation it was one of the most successful and dynamic proprietary medical schools in the nation. In 1866 he published the first edition of his classic textbook of medicine, *Treatise on the Principles and Practice of Medicine*, which would go through five editions in his lifetime and become the most popular medical book of the English-speaking world. Flint used his position of prominence to encourage innovation supporting the new technique of clinical thermometry in the 1870s and the new science of bacteriology in the 1880s. Flint's leadership was important in the New York Code of Ethics fight in 1882; when the New York Medical Society adopted a new code permitting consultation with irregular practitioners, Flint resigned and helped found the New York State Medical Society to preserve the consultation restrictions of the American Medical Association.

Upon his death in New York, Flint was widely acknowledged as the dean of the American medical profession, having served as president of the American Medical Association in 1884 and president-elect of the International Medical Congress scheduled to meet in Washington, D.C., in 1887. He was called by Samuel D. Gross "The American Laennec" for his contributions to the study of auscultation.

• A bibliography of Flint's work may be found in *Medical Classics* 4 (1940): 843–61. There are several biographical articles about Austin Flint, including Norman Shaftel, "Austin Flint, Sr. (1812–1886): Educator of Physicians," *Journal of Medical Education* 35 (1960): 1122–35; Alfred S. Evans, "Austin Flint and His Contributions to Medicine," *Bulletin of the History of Medicine* 32 (1958): 224–41; and Dale C. Smith, "Austin Flint and Auscultation in America," *Journal of the History of Medicine and Allied Sciences* 33 (1978): 129–49. The best collection of remembrances is in "Addresses Delivered at the Memorial Meeting of the County Medical Association in Honor of the Late Austin Flint . . . ," *Gaillard's Medical Journal* 42 (1886): 579–614.

DALE C. SMITH

FLINT, Austin (28 Mar. 1836–22 Sept. 1915), physiologist, forensic psychiatrist, and specialist in mental disorders, was born in Northampton, Massachusetts, the son of Austin Flint, a prominent physician, and Anne Skillings. Early in Flint's life, his family resided briefly in Boston, and in 1836 they relocated to Buffalo, New York, where Flint obtained his early education. In subsequent years the father's highly peripatetic professional career took the family to numerous other cities, such as Chicago, Louisville, New Orleans, and New York City.

The younger Flint was an undergraduate student at Harvard University from 1852 to 1853 but left to pursue an interest in civil engineering. In less than a year he changed his mind in favor of medicine. He began his medical studies in Buffalo and continued at the University of Louisville from 1854 to 1856. During the summer of 1855 he was assistant in physiology to Dr. John Call Dalton at the Woodstock Medical College in Vermont. Flint received a degree in medicine from Jefferson Medical College in Philadelphia in 1857.

While in his second year of medical school, Flint first demonstrated his proclivity for writing. In 1855 he published in the *Buffalo Medical Journal* an analysis of 106 cases of felon (an acute, painful, pyogenic infection of tissues of the fingers or toes, usually near the nail), mostly from the practice of Professor Frank Hastings Hamilton, a well-known surgeon in Buffalo. His graduation thesis, published in the *American Journal of the Medical Sciences* in July 1857, was titled "Phenomena of Capillary Circulation."

After graduation Flint was appointed professor of physiology at Buffalo Medical College, where he was editor of the *Buffalo Medical Journal*. From 1857 to 1859 he maintained a private medical practice in Buffalo. In 1859 he moved with his father to New York Medical College. A year later he went to New Orleans Medical College, where, as professor of physiology, in a landmark study, he made physiological measurements on large alligators of such things as hepatic function, respiration, heart rate, and spinal nerve conduction. Then he moved back to New York City, where he and his father co-founded Bellevue Hospital Medical College in 1861. That year he spent several months in Paris, France, studying under Charles Robin and Claude Bernard. At this facility the younger Flint became the first professor of physiology, a position he kept for the next thirty years. In 1862 he married Elizabeth B. McMaster; they had four children, including a son named Austin, who also became a physician.

During the Civil War, Flint served as assistant surgeon at New York General Hospital. Between 1865 and 1868 he was department chair of physiology at Long Island College Hospital, while concurrently being deeply involved in setting up nutritionally balanced diets for inmates of state institutions. He was in constant demand as a teacher, consultant, and expert witness. Between 1898 and 1906, at the newly opened Cornell Medical College, he served as professor of physiology, professor emeritus, and consulting physician. Other appointments included visiting physician in the Insane Pavilion of Bellevue Hospital (1896) and president of the Consulting Board of the Manhattan Hospital for the Insane (1899).

Flint's interests gradually expanded beyond physiology to include criminology and forensic practice. By 1878 he was a member of the New York Lunatic Asylum. In 1887 he attended two courses on mental disease at Bellevue under Dr. Carlos F. MacDonald. These courses, along with his professional interest in physiology as it related to mental states, stimulated Flint to become a specialist in mental diseases. In his later years Flint served as an expert witness on mental disorders for the state of New York and testified in a number of famous criminal cases, including that of Harry K. Thaw.

Flint was appointed surgeon general of New York in 1874 and served in this post until 1878. He was a member of numerous professional organizations, including the Executive Committee of the New York State Prisoner Association in 1896, the American Medical Association, the Medical Societies of the State and County of New York, the American Academy of Medicine, the American Medico-Psychological Association, the Association of Military Surgeons, the American Philosophical Association, and as corresponding member of the American Academy of Natural Sciences in Philadelphia. Among the many honors he received was that of Third Class Order of Bolivar, Venezuela, in 1891.

Like his father, Flint was a prolific medical writer. His seminal work, *The Physiology of Man*, was published in five volumes between 1867 and 1873. Because of an enormous interest in and a demand for this work, there was an immediate second printing of the entire work. The volume on the nervous system, *Physiology of the Nervous System*, became a sought-after reference work on its own; it was published not only as part of the five-volume set, but also, beginning in 1872, as a separate standard reference work. After a few years all five volumes were consolidated into one massive volume and published as *A Textbook of Human Physiology* (1876; 4th ed., 1888). Flint died in New York City while putting on his coat in preparation for a speaking engagement.

Flint made many important contributions. He established physiology as an important medical specialty, and through his work he showed the close relationship between physiology and states of mental and physical health. He also collected and published all of the medically important physiological data known up until his time, and he was the first physiologist in the United States to perform surgery on the spinal cord and spinal nerves of a living animal.

• Other significant works by Flint include *Examination of the Urine in Disease*, published in six editions between 1870 and 1874; *On the Physiological Effects of Severe and Protracted Muscular Exercise* (1871), *Source of Muscular Power* (1878), *The Handbook of Physiology* (1905), and *Collected Essays and Articles on Physiology and Medicine* (1903). Obituaries are in the *British Medical Journal*, 16 Oct. 1915; *New York Medical Journal*, 25 Sept. 1915; and the *New York Times*, 23 Sept. 1915.

BILL SCOTT

FLINT, Charles Ranlett (24 Jan. 1850–12 Feb. 1934), merchant and company promoter, was born in Thomaston, Maine, the son of Benjamin Flint and Sarah Tobey, merchants. His mother died three years later and his father remarried in 1856. Charles attended schools in Maine and Brooklyn, graduating from the Polytechnic Institute in Brooklyn in 1868. His father and uncle operated a shipping business from 1837, which Flint eventually joined in 1885. In 1883 he married Emma Kate Simmons. He retained the occupational title of merchant throughout his life and his career reflected the expansion and changing character of the New York trading community during the late nineteenth century. In 1871 he and George W. Gilchrist, a shipbuilder and neighbor in Thomaston, established a ship chandlery firm. A year later Flint acquired a 25 percent stake in W. R. Grace & Co., a New York trading company with interests in Peru; George W. Gilchrist was the father-in-law of William Russell Grace, founder of the New York office. This connection involved Flint in considerable South American trade and periods of extensive travel in the region as W. R. Grace extended its interests outside Peru. Moreover, he acted as consul for Chile and Nicaragua in New York in the 1870s and at various stages he purchased warships and munitions for Peru and Brazil. His experiences, and domestic political links to the Democrats, led to his appointment by President Benjamin Harrison (1833–1901) to the U.S. delegation to the International Conference of American Republics in 1889–1890. The conference resulted in the formation of the Commercial Union of the United States, a further step in the development of U.S. economic and political links to Latin America.

Flint's overseas trading activities brought him into the orbit of the expanding New York financial houses. Although he was not a dominant figure, the most significant phase of Flint's business career came when the New York financial market shifted its attention from railroads to manufacturing investments. As one of the most active financial promoters of mergers during the 1890s, Flint earned the sobriquet "father of the trusts." The first involvement came with U.S. Electric Lighting Company, where Flint, as president, failed to achieve a merger of leading firms in the early 1880s; Thomas A. Edison refused to participate. In 1892 Flint organized the merger of the principal rubber footwear makers to create U.S. Rubber. In the same year the Belmont finance house, founded by August Belmont, persuaded Flint to arrange a merger of mechanical rubber goods firms. This company expanded in 1898 to include tire manufacturers and was renamed the Rubber Goods Manufacturing Company; in 1905 it was absorbed by U.S. Rubber. Flint was involved in around twenty further promotions during the turn of the century merger movement. As treasurer of U.S. Rubber, Flint appeared before the U.S. Industrial Commission in 1900 to proclaim the economic and organizational merits of industrial combinations. He argued that larger firms could obtain economies of scale, especially from centralized purchasing and direction, operate to maximum efficiency, attract the best management, and raise capital more readily and cheaply than smaller companies. Such advocacy, in response to critics of the merger movement, who feared a concentration of economic and political power, made Flint, along with lawyers such as Samuel C. T. Dodd, a significant defender of the consolidation of American business as a source of greater efficiency and lower prices. Flint generally left the duties of daily management to others; American Woolen failed and U.S. Rubber encountered vigorous competition as the automobile changed the nature of the rubber business. He moved on to acting as an agent in selling Wilbur Wright and Orville Wright's aircraft in Germany and establishing a Wright company in France. In 1911 he organized the merger of three machinery firms to create the Computing–Tabulating–Recording Company; three years later Flint hired Thomas J. Watson as general manager. The company was renamed International Business Machines (IBM) in 1924, with Watson as president. Flint retained a preference for overseas trading and travel. He purchased battleships for Japan in the 1890s. During 1905 he traveled widely in Europe acquiring vessels and munitions for the Russian government. During 1917 he chaired the American Committee for the Encouragement of Democratic Government in Russia.

Flint devoted considerable attention to his passions for yachting, hunting, and fishing, which he used to cultivate business and political contacts in the New York commercial, financial, and literary worlds. He was a founding member of the Automobile Club of America in 1899. After the death of his first wife in 1926, Flint married Charlotte Reeves the following year. They had no children. Flint's career symbolizes the growing international role of American business in the late nineteenth century and the manner in which the metropolitan banking and financial institutions contributed to the restructuring of American manufacturing. Flint died in Washington, D.C.

• Flint recalls his own career in vivid, if rather disjointed, fashion in *Memories of an Active Life* (1923). Four articles and addresses by Flint are in J. H. Bridge, *The Trust: Its Book* (1902), and he also gave evidence to the U.S. Industrial Commission, *Report of the Industrial Commission*, vol. 13 (1901), pp. 33–93, on the trust movement. The broader context of his activities is covered in V. P. Carosso, *The Morgans* (1987), and Harold Passer, *The Electrical Manufacturers, 1875–1900* (1953). An obituary is in the *New York Times*, 16 Feb. 1934.
MICHAEL FRENCH

FLINT, Timothy (11 July 1780–16 Aug. 1840), pastor, missionary, and author, was born in North Reading, Massachusetts, the son of William Flint and Martha Kimball, farmers. Flint attended the North Reading Grammar School and Phillips Academy at Andover

before entering Harvard, from which he graduated in 1800. Later he studied theology and, remaining in Massachusetts, he taught at Cohasset and preached at Marblehead, where he married Abigail Hubbard in 1802. He was ordained in 1802 as the pastor of the Congregational church at Lunenberg, at a salary of $400 per annum. He soon had disagreements with several parishioners. One townsman even accused him of counterfeiting. Flint, who was merely fond of conducting harmless chemical experiments, sued and was awarded damages. More serious matters were his laxity in Calvinist dogma and his being a Federalist in a Democratic parish. Becoming tactlessly unorthodox and evangelical, he requested and was granted his dismissal from the church in 1814.

In ill health and with his wife and their children—by that time three in number—Flint was hired by the Massachusetts Society for Promoting Christian Knowledge to do missionary work in New Hampshire, perhaps in Massachusetts, and in New York (1814–1815). Then in 1815 he was sent by the Missionary Society of Connecticut to Cincinnati. Getting there by horse-drawn wagon, flatboat, and keelboat was slow, dangerous, and not cheap. At $25, his weekly salary was higher, but the cost of living in the West kept the family poor. He augmented his income by missionary tours in Ohio, Indiana, and Kentucky. After a year of this drudgery, Flint obtained church work in St. Louis and then St. Charles, Missouri. Soon he was ill with fever, had offended his church members and his society officials, and was eager to resign. He accepted a teaching position near Natchez, Mississippi, but sickness forced the whole family to Arkansas (1819) and a year later to Jackson, Missouri, where in 1821 a fourth child was born, after which Flint became a farmer near St. Charles (1821–1822). This effort failing also, the Flints planned to return to New England via New Orleans. However, Flint turned to preaching and college administration at nearby Alexandria, Louisiana (1823–1825). Chronically ill, he sailed back to Salem, Massachusetts, in 1825, where he expected to die.

Instead, Flint got better and began to write *Recollections of the Last Ten Years, Passed in Occasional Residences and Journeyings in the Valley of the Mississippi, from Pittsburg and the Missouri to the Gulf of Mexico, and from Florida to the Spanish Frontier; in a Series of Letters to the Rev. James Flint, of Salem, Massachusetts* (1826). He returned to Alexandria in 1825, wrote his first novel, *Francis Berrian, or The Mexican Patriot* (2 vols., 1826), and settled into a literary career for the remainder of his life. Fearful of the hot, humid climate in Alexandria, he returned briefly to New England in 1826, established a residence in Cincinnati from 1827 to 1830, edited the *Western Magazine and Review* (soon retitled the *Western Monthly Review*) from 1827 to 1830, fathered a fifth and final child in 1828, and became a prolific man of letters.

Flint's major publications during this period, many of which grew out of magazine pieces, included *A Condensed Geography and History of the Western States, or the Mississippi Valley* (2 vols., 1828); *The Life and Adventures of Arthur Clenning* (2 vols., 1828); *The Personal Narrative of James O. Pattie, of Kentucky* (1831); *The History and Geography of the Mississippi Valley, to Which Is Appended a Condensed Physical Geography of the Atlantic United States, and the Whole American Continent* (2 vols., 1832); *Indian Wars of the West; Containing Biographical Sketches of Those Pioneers Who Headed the Western Settlers in Repelling the Attacks of the Savages, Together with a View of the Character, Manners, Monuments, and Antiquities of the Western Indians* (1833); *Biographical Memoir of Daniel Boone, the First Settler of Kentucky, Interspersed with Incidents in the Early Annals of the Country* (1833, often republished, sometimes as *The First White Man of the West*); and several novels, among them *George Mason, the Young Backwoodsman; or "Don't Give Up the Ship," a Story of the Mississippi* (1829); *The Lost Child* (1830); and *The Shoshonee Valley; a Romance* (2 vols., 1830). Most of these books were published in Boston and Philadelphia, but five were issued in Cincinnati by Flint's son Ebenezer Hubbard Flint, who by the late 1820s had become a publisher there.

Next, Flint, in poor health again, went to New York, where he edited one issue of the *Knickerbocker: or New-York Monthly Magazine* (Oct. 1833), after which he and his family moved back to Alexandria (1834–1840). He then traveled widely in a vain effort to regain his health, going to Cuba, New England, and Canada and writing very little. He returned to New England in 1840, where he died in the home of his brother back in North Reading.

Several of Flint's writings are of historical importance, especially *Recollections of the Last Ten Years, A Condensed Geography and History of the Western States,* and *Biographical Memoir of Daniel Boone.* His novels, beginning with *Francis Berrian,* however, now have value only in setting precedents for later frontier writing. *Recollections* is in the form of twenty-eight miscellaneous letters from Timothy Flint to his cousin James. They describe the Flint family moves to Cincinnati, Missouri, and Alexandria, Louisiana. More important than their autobiographical elements is Flint's presentation of historical, geographical, climatic, and demographic data. Flint's aims in this book are threefold: to tell Eastern readers about America's youthful West, to the end of encouraging migration; to trumpet the inevitable success of America's ever-westward progress; and to boast a little about his own adventures.

A Condensed Geography and History is Flint's ambitious, profitable effort not only to tell the history of colonization in Florida, Alabama, Mississippi, Louisiana, the Arkansas Territory, Tennessee, Missouri, Illinois, Indiana, Kentucky, Ohio, Michigan, the Northwest Territory, and Texas, but also to describe western geography, climates, and flora and fauna. The West as Flint presents it here is both a locus to be statistically reported and a reflection of the escapist romanticism of Jean Jacques Rousseau and François-René de Chateaubriand. Flint synthesizes data from more than thirty sources; depicts the West as a place of danger, disease, and challenge; and appeals to a wide range of readers, as he predicts that Yankee technological ingenuity will turn a resource-laden region into a democratic, agrarian, and bucolic utopia. Distressing today are sections of the book condoning slavery and picturing Native Americans as inept, cruel, and cowardly; perhaps sad is Flint's concentrating on the commercial potential of the West and ignoring its aesthetic appeal.

In his excellent *Daniel Boone,* Flint presents his hero, who was already the subject of legend, as a canny, uneasy, restless, avant-garde trailblazer after whom will come the bringers of civilization, with their instruments of progress, to tame the generous West.

Francis Berrian, memorable as the first novel in English set in the American Southwest, features a New Englander who fights in the Mexican Revolution of 1822, marries a Hispanic beauty in Santa Fe, and transports her back home. *Arthur Clenning* is an outlandish account of two people who are castaways on a South Sea island and who slowly decide to conduct a self-marriage but must first find a witness! Designed for juvenile readers are *George Mason,* a thinly disguised autobiography, and *The Lost Child,* a religious tract. *The Shoshonee Valley,* partly set in the Oregon territory, is the first novel with mountain men as characters.

Timothy Flint was a failed missionary who became a successful man of letters but wrote too much. Nevertheless, he deserves to be remembered for his descriptions of the West, which he observed carefully and for which he predicted greatness. His *Daniel Boone* has sparkling passages. Flint was an early western social historian and a literary pioneer who helped reveal the possibilities of the West as a subject for fiction. And when he writes about himself, best in his *Recollections,* he remains vividly alive.

• There are collections of Flint's papers at the American Antiquarian Society in Worcester, Mass., the Boston Public Library, the New-York Historical Society, and the Historical Society of Pennsylvania. The standard biography of Flint is John Ervin Kirkpatrick, *Timothy Flint: Pioneer, Missionary, Author, Editor* (1911). It contains bibliographies of Flint's writings and also of nineteenth-century studies devoted to Flint. Henry Nash Smith, *Virgin Land: The American West as Symbol and Myth* (1950), includes excellent comments in passing about several of Flint's works. James K. Folsom, *Timothy Flint* (1965), is the best critical study. The most thorough critics to consider Flint's novels in conjunction with those of other American novelists are the unsympathetic Arthur Hobson Quinn, *American Fiction, an Historical and Critical Survey* (1936), and the more favorably disposed Alexander Cowie, *The Rise of the American Novel* (1948). Edward Wagenknecht, *Cavalcade of the American Novel* (1952), dismisses Flint's novels in a note in an appendix. Bernard Rosenthal provides a splendid introduction to a facsimile reproduction of Flint's *A Condensed Geography and History of the Western States* (1970). Mary Lawlor, "The Fictions of Daniel Boone," in *Desert, Garden, Margin, Range: Literature on the American Frontier,* ed. Eric Heyne (1992), includes a profound discussion of Flint's biography of Daniel Boone. John

D. Seelye, "Timothy Flint's 'Wicked River' and *The Confidence-Man*," *PMLA* 78 (Mar. 1963): 75–79, theorizes that Herman Melville may have borrowed details from Flint's *Recollections* and *The History and Geography of the Mississippi Valley* for descriptions in *The Confidence-Man* of water, land, and people on and along the river.

ROBERT L. GALE

FLINT, Weston (4 July 1835–6 Apr. 1906), librarian, attorney, and government official, was born in Pike, Wyoming County, New York, the son of Nicholas Flint and Phebe Burt Willoughby, farmers. He grew up on the family farm in Cattaraugus County, New York, and was educated at the Chamberlain Institute, the Alfred Academy (later Alfred University) in Alfred, New York, and Union College in Schenectady, New York, from which he graduated in 1860.

Flint started teaching at the age of seventeen in New York. Between 1860 and 1863 he taught at various schools in New York State, Ohio, and Pennsylvania. He moved to St. Louis, Missouri, in 1863 to assist in caring for wounded Union soldiers and was appointed military agent for the states of Ohio, Michigan, and New York. After the Civil War, Flint remained in St. Louis as an attorney (1866–1869), as the editor and publisher of the *St. Louis Daily Tribune* (1869–1870), and as an organizer and a board member of the Second Geological Survey of Missouri (1868–1871). Flint was active in Republican politics, helping to organize the Radical, anti-Johnson Southern Loyalist Convention in Philadelphia (1866) and serving as a delegate to the 1868 Republican National Convention in Chicago. He was appointed U.S. consul to Chinkiang (Chenching), China, in 1871, a post he held until 1874 when he returned to the United States to lecture and write.

Flint received an LL.B. (1878) and an LL.M. (1879) from Columbian College (now George Washington University) Law School in Washington, D.C., and served as head of the scientific library of the U.S. Patent Office from 1877 to 1887. Under his direction the library was reorganized; two extensive catalogs of the library were published while he was the library's head: *Catalogue of the Library of the United States Patent Office* (1878) and *Catalogue of Additions to the Library of the U.S. Patent Office from 1878 to 1883* (1883). These achievements placed Flint in the forefront of the young profession of librarianship. He married Lucy Romilda Brown in 1883; they had one son.

Flint's service to the American Library Association in its formative years also earned him lasting regard. His contributions included participation as a member of its governing council (1881–1883), frequent appearances as a speaker on current library practices, and service on the Columbian Exposition Committee that oversaw the preparation of the exhibition at the World's Fair in Chicago in 1893. Flint's connection with the U.S. Bureau of Education led to the American Library Association's participation in that agency's display.

During his later years Flint continued his active involvement in both political and civic affairs in Washington, D.C. He assisted in organizing the newly formed U.S. Civil Service Commission and served as the acting chairman of the board of the U.S. Civil Service Examiners (1884–1887). In 1888 he also served on the U.S. Senate committee that investigated civil service operations. He was a statistician for the U.S. Bureau of Education from 1889 to 1895, preparing and publishing the book *Statistics of Public Libraries in the United States and Canada* (1893). Flint became the first librarian of the Washington Free Public Library (later the District of Columbia Public Library), holding that position from 1898 to 1904. He continued to serve the Washington Free Public Library as a trustee after his resignation, although his effective influence declined as his health deteriorated.

Flint was active in many civic and scholarly organizations in the Washington, D.C., area. He was the secretary of the Anthropological Society of Washington and a member of the American Historical Society, the American Association for the Advancement of Science, the American Folklore Society, the National Geographic Society, the Society for University Extension, the Washington Board of Trade's committee on libraries, the Freemasons (thirty-third degree), and the Presbyterian church. He was prominently associated with the Chautauqua movement and published numerous verses and newspaper articles under the nom de plume, "Ik Iopas." He died in Washington, D.C.

• Several references to Flint appear in Samuel Swett Green, *The Public Library Movement in the United States, 1853–1893* (1913), and Wayne A. Wiegand, *The Politics of an Emerging Profession* (1986). Obituaries are in the *Washington Evening Star*, 6 Apr. 1906, the *New York Times*, 7 Apr. 1906, and the *Library Journal* 31 (May 1906).

DONALD G. DAVIS, JR.

FLIPPER, Henry Ossian (21 Mar. 1856–3 May 1940), soldier and engineer, was born in Thomasville, Georgia, the son of Festus Flipper and Isabelle (maiden name unknown), slaves. During the Civil War and Reconstruction he was educated in American Missionary Association schools and in 1873 gained admission to Atlanta University. That year Flipper also obtained an appointment to the U.S. Military Academy through the auspices of Republican Representative James C. Freeman. He was not the first African American to attend West Point, as Michael Howard and James Webster Smith preceded him in 1870, but neither graduated. Flipper subsequently endured four years of grueling academic instruction and ostracism from white classmates before graduating fiftieth in a class of sixty-four on 14 June 1877. He was commissioned second lieutenant in the all-black Tenth U.S. Cavalry, and the following year recounted his academy experience in an autobiography, *The Colored Cadet at West Point* (1878).

Flipper enjoyed a brief but active military career. He was billeted at various frontier posts, including Forts Elliott, Concho, Davis, and Quitman in Texas, and Fort Sill, Indian Territory (now Okla.), and engaged in numerous engineering activities. This regimen included drainage of swamps at Fort Sill, building a wagon road from that post to Gainesville, Texas, and installing telegraph lines from Fort Elliott, Texas, to Camp Supply, Indian Territory. Flipper also distinguished himself in the 1880 war against the Apache Victorio and earned commendation from Colonel William H. Grierson. He was then posted as acting commissary of subsistence at Fort Davis in November 1881, when Colonel William R. Shafter accused him of embezzling $3,791.77 in missing commissary funds that were assumed to be stolen. A court-martial cleared Flipper of all charges but found him guilty of "conduct unbecoming an officer and a gentleman," and dismissed him from the service on 30 June 1882. For the rest of his life Flipper professed his innocence and ascribed the end of his military career to racial prejudice.

As a civilian, Flipper remained in the West for nearly half a century and distinguished himself in a variety of mining, engineering, and surveying work. Commencing in 1883, he functioned in northern Mexico as a cartographer for the Banco Minero and as chief engineer for several American mining concerns. Fluent in Spanish, Flipper became an authority on Spanish and Mexican land law, and in 1891 he represented Nogales, Arizona, in an important land grant case. His expertise convinced Justice Department officials to appoint him as a special agent in the court of private claims. In 1882 he published *Mexico Laws, Statutes, etc.*, which was long held as a definitive treatise on the subject.

Flipper returned to northern Mexico in 1901 and spent the next eleven years as resident engineer for a number of American mining companies. In this capacity he befriended Albert Fall, a future U.S. senator from New Mexico, with whom Flipper exchanged extensive correspondence during the Mexican Revolution. When Fall became secretary of the interior in 1921, he appointed Flipper as an assistant working on the commission tasked with locating, constructing, and operating railroads in Alaska. After Fall was implicated in the Teapot Dome scandal of 1923, Flipper left the Interior Department to work for an oil company in Venezuela and compiled another significant work, *Venezuela Laws, Statutes, etc.* (1925). He returned to Atlanta in 1930 to reside with his brother, Bishop Joseph Flipper of the African Methodist Episcopal church. Flipper died in Atlanta.

Flipper is best remembered as the first African-American graduate of West Point and for the controversy surrounding his dismissal. However, his 48-year career as an engineer established him as an important figure in western development. Furthermore, Flipper's impressive linguistic and legal credentials were valuable assets for the growth of mining industries in both the United States and Mexico. His civilian endeavors were all conspicuously marked by the high moral conduct and methodological problem solving imparted on him at West Point. Although he was denied vindication by the military while he was alive, in December 1976 the Department of the Army finally granted him a posthumous honorable discharge and a military reinterment. Furthermore, on 3 May 1977 a bust of Flipper was unveiled at West Point, signifying formal recognition from the institution that had so scorned him. Apparently, he never married.

• Flipper's military correspondence is in RG 94, Records of the Adjutant General, National Archives. Scattered personal materials are in the Benjamin H. Grierson Papers, Texas Tech University, Lubbock; and the Frank H. Edmund Papers, U.S. Military Academy. For published accounts, consult Theodore D. Harris, ed., *Negro Frontiersman: The Western Memoirs of Henry O. Flipper* (1963); and Charles M. Robinson, *The Court-martial of Lieutenant Flipper* (1994). Biographical treatments include Lowell D. Black, *An Officer and a Gentleman* (1985); Gary Wien, "The Military Career of Henry O. Flipper" (master's thesis, Univ. of Toledo, 1970); and Donald R. McLung, "Henry O. Flipper" (master's thesis, East Texas State Univ., 1970). Shorter, more popular accounts are Steve Wilson, "A Black Lieutenant in the Ranks," *American History Illustrated* 18, no. 3 (1983): 31–39; Bruce J. Dinges, "The Court-martial of Lieutenant Henry O. Flipper," *American West* 9 (Jan. 1972): 12–17; and Jane Eppinga, "Henry O. Flipper in the Court of Private Land Claims," *Journal of Arizona History* 36, no. 1 (1995): 33–54.

JOHN C. FREDRIKSEN

FLOCKS, Rubin Hyman (7 May 1906–17 May 1975), urologist, was born in New York City, the son of Morris Flocks, a tailor, and Rose Blackman. Flocks received his undergraduate degree from Johns Hopkins University in 1926 and a medical degree from the same institution in 1930. He was resident house officer at the Johns Hopkins Hospital in 1930–1931. In 1932 he joined the urology department at the University of Iowa College of Medicine in Iowa City. Flocks became full professor at Iowa in 1946 and chair of the Department of Urology in 1949. He was made professor emeritus in 1974.

Among Flocks's many contributions to the field of urology, five stand out as particularly significant. In 1933 he established the procedure for radiographic imaging of the prostatic urethra in an article published in the *Journal of Urology* (30:711–36). Urethography, as introduced by John H. Cunningham in 1910, allowed visualization of the anterior portion of the urethra but failed to present clear radiographic visualization of the prostatic urethra and the base of the bladder. Flocks resolved this problem by introducing a contrast medium of superior opacity and viscosity, by positioning the patient so that the entire course of the S-shaped urethra could be visualized during filming, and by the "principle of double contrast," that is, by filling the bladder with air at the same time the urethra was injected with medium, allowing urethra and prostate to be visualized simultaneously.

Perhaps Flocks's most important contribution to urologic literature was his 1937 article on the blood supply of the normal and enlarged prostate (*Journal of Urology* 37:524–48). Flocks distinguished two groups of arteries within the prostate: an external capsular group, which undergoes little change with age or hyperplasia (i.e., an abnormal increase in the number of cells in an organ or tissue); and an internal urethral group, which changes significantly with age and hyperplasia. With the advent of transurethral prostatic surgery, an understanding of the arrangement of these two groups of arteries became essential to solving the problems attending prostatic resection (excision of a portion of the organ).

In 1939 Flocks published, in the *Journal of the American Medical Association* (113:1466–71), an important quantitative study that related high levels of calcium in the urine to the formation of calculi. He also pointed out the importance of diet and liquid intake in the prevention and control of calcium urolithiasis (the formation of "stones" due to excessive levels of calcium in the urine).

Controversy attended the publication of Flocks's 1952 article in the *Journal of Urology* (68:510–22) on the treatment of carcinoma of the prostate gland with radioactive gold. Flocks noted that although malignancies of the prostate often showed reduction in mass following ordinary radiation therapy, the radiation sometimes caused complications in the surrounding tissues, particularly the bladder and rectum. He recommended the use of isotopes of radioactive gold (Au^{198}), which delivered intensive radiation in a very localized area. He described a procedure for suprapubic injection of the isotope, which, while acting on the prostate and regional lymph nodes, was compartmentalized by the layers of fascia (fibrous connective tissue) surrounding the prostate and seminal vesicles.

Twenty years later Flocks recommended another innovation in the treatment of prostatic cancer. In a 1972 article published in the *Journal of Urology* (108: 933–35), he recommended the use of cryosurgery (the application of subfreezing temperatures for the destruction of tissue) in the treatment of prostatic carcinomas. Flocks maintained that cryosurgery destroyed malignant lesions with minimal operative complications and without affecting adjacent tissues or the functioning of the lower urinary tract.

Flocks was the author of more than 150 journal articles, as well as several monographs. His most important books were *Surgical Urology*, which appeared in four editions between 1954 and 1975, and *Radiation Therapy of Early Prostatic Cancer* (1960); both were coauthored with David Culp, a colleague at Iowa.

Flocks served as a member of the National Advisory Cancer Council from 1965 to 1969 and was president of the American Urology Association in 1968–1969. He never married. He died in Iowa City.

• Very little has been written on Flocks's life and work, apart from H. J. Jewett, "Rubin H. Flocks and the Prostatic Disease Center," *Journal of the Iowa Medical Society* 62 (1972): 572, and R. E. Rakel's brief entry in the *Dictionary of American Medical Biography* (1984), vol. 1, pp. 255–56.

CHRISTOPHER HOOLIHAN

FLORA, William (fl. 1775–1818), war hero and businessman, was born probably in the vicinity of Portsmouth, Virginia, the son of free black parents, whose names are unknown. On the eve of the American Revolution fewer than 2,000 free blacks lived in Virginia. The colony's statutes forbade the manumission of slaves except those who exposed an incipient slave uprising. Consequently, Flora, who was known as "Billy," was probably descended from Africans who arrived in Virginia before 1640, when blacks were treated like indentured servants rather than slaves.

Nothing is known about Flora's life prior to 1775, when he joined Colonel William Woodford's Second Virginia Regiment as a private. He furnished his own musket, suggesting that he had already earned the esteem of his white neighbors, because the colony's statutes also barred free blacks from bearing arms and from serving in the militia. He fought against the British and Loyalist forces commanded by Lord Dunmore, Virginia's last royal governor, at the battle of Great Bridge in December 1775. On the morning of the battle Flora was one of several sentinels guarding the narrow bridge over the Elizabeth River, which separated the British and patriot positions, when the British attacked in force. While the other sentinels immediately retreated to the safety of the patriot barricade, Flora fired eight times as he withdrew and, still under enemy fire, removed the plank that afforded access over the barricade. His bravery in combat earned him the approbation of his superiors and a public commendation in the *Virginia Gazette*.

Nothing is known about Flora's activities during the rest of the American Revolution except that he fought at the battle of Yorktown in 1781. The suggestion that he fought against the British for the entire duration of the war is highly unlikely, since the vast majority of patriot soldiers fought for brief periods and then returned home. In addition, Woodford and virtually the entire Virginia Continental line were taken prisoner in 1780 after the successful British siege of Charleston, South Carolina. It is more likely that Flora left the army in mid-1776, following the departure of Dunmore's forces from Virginia, and returned to arms four years later, when a British force commanded by the traitor Benedict Arnold invaded Tidewater Virginia.

After the British surrender at Yorktown, Flora either began or continued to operate a cartage enterprise based in Portsmouth, hauling agricultural products and freight between the town's wharves and the farms in the surrounding countryside. He also operated a livery stable that rented out riding carriages. In 1784 he purchased two lots in Portsmouth and is believed to have been the first black to own land in that town. For a number of years thereafter he occasionally bought and sold houses and unimproved lots. Exploiting the opportunities made available to him as a consequence of his freedom while conducting himself in such a way as to avoid exciting the jealousies of his white neighbors, he acquired and retained considerable wealth. In 1810 he owned three large wagons, three two-wheeled carriages, and six horses, and when he died he willed two houses and one lot to his heirs. He married a slave woman, but her name and the date of the marriage are unknown. Flora purchased and freed his wife sometime after 1782, when Virginia's laws against manumission were liberalized considerably. They had two children.

In 1807, when the HMS *Leopard* attacked the USS *Chesapeake*, a wave of anti-British sentiment swept through Virginia and the rest of the United States. Caught up in this patriotic fervor, Flora, armed with his old musket, joined a number of local men who volunteered for service against the British once again. Their offer was courteously rejected by the local authorities. In recognition of his service during the American Revolution, Flora in 1818, along with other Virginia veterans, received a land grant of 100 acres in the Virginia Military District (now southwestern Ohio). He probably sold the grant to one of the large land companies attempting to settle the area. It is believed he died in 1820 in Portsmouth.

Flora was a hero of the Revolution in Virginia, a prosperous businessman, and a respected member of the Portsmouth community. Although these accomplishments may seem modest, they are significant in that they were achieved by a black man at a time when the vast majority of his white contemporaries regarded people of African descent as lazy and inferior and consequently afforded them second-class citizenship.

• Flora's papers have not been located. A biography is Luther Porter Jackson, "William Flora," in *Virginia Negro Soldiers and Seamen in the Revolutionary War* (1944). See also Benjamin Quarles, *The Negro in the American Revolution* (1961), Sidney Kaplan, *The Black Presence in the Era of the American Revolution 1770–1800* (1973), and Burke Davis, *Black Heroes of the American Revolution* (1976).

CHARLES W. CAREY, JR.

FLORY, Paul John (19 June 1910–8 Sept. 1985), Nobel Prize–winning polymer chemist, was born in Sterling, Illinois, the son of Ezra Flory, a Brethren minister and teacher, and Martha Brumbaugh, a schoolteacher. Flory's parents were the first in their families to go to college. In 1927 Flory entered Manchester College, a Brethren liberal arts college in North Manchester, Indiana. Carl Holl, who was the professor of chemistry at Manchester College, kindled Flory's interest in chemistry. After Flory completed his degree at Manchester in the summer of 1930, Holl encouraged him to go on to graduate work in chemistry at Ohio State University. Judging his preparation in mathematics to be inadequate, Flory decided to take his M.S. in organic chemistry, which requires less mathematics. Flory did his M.S. thesis in organic synthesis in Cecil Boord's laboratory. Flory's laboratory notebooks reveal that his interest in polymers was first aroused during that time. Told that polymers are "a nuisance to avoid," Flory discontinued his early attempts to understand polymers. Flory would later act to promote polymer education in American universities.

Flory's doctoral work at Ohio State University was in spectroscopy and photochemistry, which he did under the guidance of Herrick L. Johnston. He chose this subject because this was closest to chemical physics, which interested him most. After receiving his Ph.D. in 1934, in the midst of the depression, Flory was lucky to be offered a research position by Du Pont and so was able to continue his development as a scientist. He joined Wallace Hume Carothers's organic chemistry group, where his education in both organic and physical chemistry proved useful. Carothers was then engaged in fundamental research on polymers, which eventually led to the discovery of nylon. Carothers's research program played a leading role in establishing the revolutionary theory that polymers are ordinary molecules, distinguished solely by their large size. Carothers filled Flory with enthusiasm for polymer research, and he instilled in him the conviction that polymers could be understood through applying the same chemical and physical principles that obtained for the small molecules with which chemists were at that time familiar. Carothers enabled and encouraged Flory to engage in fundamental research on polymers and to apply to polymers mathematical analysis. This approach is manifest in Flory's first major breakthrough, his calculation of the statistical distribution of polymer chain lengths, which was indispensable for understanding the constitution of the polymers synthesized in the laboratory. Flory's calculations were based on the hypothesis that the reactivity of the molecule only depends on the local environment surrounding the active chemical group in the molecule, however big the rest of the molecule may be. Flory's theory was not based on any conclusive empirical evidence, and, furthermore, it challenged the prevailing view that molecules would be less reactive as they became larger.

Flory's principle of equal reactivity greatly simplified the application of kinetics to polymers. It soon received support on both theoretical grounds and experimental results. This first breakthrough characterizes Flory's style of work. He analyzed very complicated systems by inventing exceedingly simple models that isolated the essential features of the system. He broke new ground by applying relatively simple mathematical techniques and straightforward experimental procedures to polymer science.

In 1937 Flory made a fundamental contribution to the theory of addition polymerization. This process, which proceeds through a series of chain reactions, involves the creation of free radicals, atoms, or molecules with an unpaired, active electron. With little background in free radical chemistry, Flory introduced the powerful concept of chain transfer. He suggested that chain growth in chain reactions can be stopped by a transfer of activity from the growing polymer to another molecule. This introduced new perspectives on the role of controlling agents (or modifiers) in addition polymerization. During the Second World War, when the American synthetic rubber program was undertaken, chain transfer was widely used in controlling the production of synthetic rubber. Flory's four-stage mechanism for addition polymerization was still widely used late in the twentieth century.

Flory was among the first Americans whose entire career was exclusively devoted to polymer chemistry. Polymer chemistry was not established as an independent scientific discipline, nor was it an academically recognized field of research, in the late 1930s. Nevertheless, after Carothers's tragic death by suicide in 1937, Flory pursued his vision of a fundamental science of polymers and carved out a novel scientific career—that of the chemist who investigates the foundations of polymer science—years before polymer science became established academically. For a young scientist this was a risky undertaking. Flory's commitment to fundamental polymer research, however, was strong and unwavering. His move from industry to academe, eventually to the prominent academic institutions of Cornell and Stanford, and his winning the Nobel prize reflect not just his prescience and perseverance, but also his leadership in a general transformation of the field of polymer chemistry.

In 1938 Flory left Du Pont and joined the Basic Science Research Laboratory at the University of Cincinnati as a research associate. Although conditions at the Basic Science Laboratory were primitive, Flory appreciated the independence and freedom to pursue fundamental research on polymers. At Du Pont, especially after Carothers's departure, Flory had become more exposed to pressures to focus on applied research. At Cincinnati, Flory continued investigations initiated with Carothers on polymerization reactions that give rise to branched structures. He developed a mathematical theory of gelation, a process that transforms a polymer solution into an insoluble elastic material. Gelation takes place in polymers that, like vulcanized rubber, undergo cross-linking. Flory's theory predicted the point at which gelation takes place. This constituted a simple model for a phase transition, a fundamental problem in physics and chemistry on which eminent theoretical physicists and chemists were working at the time.

In 1940 Flory joined the laboratories of Standard Oil at Linden, New Jersey, where research on rubber polymers took place. There Flory began experimental and theoretical work on the thermodynamics of polymer solutions and the theory of rubberlike elasticity. In 1941 Flory and Maurice L. Huggins, a physical chemist working for Eastman Kodak, simultaneously and independently enunciated a general theory of polymer solutions, a theory that inspired much further research in the field of the theory of solutions. While working at Jersey Standard, Flory and John Rehner showed that the swelling of vulcanized rubber by solvents could be used to estimate the amount of cross-linking.

In 1943 Flory joined Goodyear Tire and Rubber Company at Akron, Ohio, where he was promoted to section head. At Goodyear Flory continued his studies on rubber constitution and elasticity. Although Flory worked within the framework of the American synthetic rubber research program, a crash program established by the U.S. government to help create a synthetic rubber industry, his work transcended the practical goals of the program by focusing on the foundations of the emergent polymer science. This earned Flory a reputation that led to his invitation in 1948 to give the prestigious annual George Fisher Baker Lectures at Cornell University. These gave rise to his classical textbook, *The Principles of Polymer Chemistry* (1953), which systematically expounded polymer chemistry as a self-contained body of knowledge closely based on physical theory. It influenced the transformation of polymer chemistry into a distinct academic discipline.

Flory remained on faculty at Cornell until 1957. At Cornell he and his coworkers showed that by varying the temperature of polymer solutions and their composition, a point is reached where polymer viscosity is directly proportional to the square root of the molecular weight. This marks the onset of conditions (called "theta conditions") analogous to those existing at the Boyle temperature for real gases, which then behave in certain respects as ideal gases. Thus, in theta conditions the osmotic pressure of polymer solutions obeys the law of ideal solutions (van't Hoff's law). By working at theta conditions, Flory and Thomas G. Fox showed that the intrinsic viscosity of a polymer molecule is related to the ratio of its effective volume to its molecular weight, the proportionality constant being essentially universal for flexible chain molecules.

By working in theta conditions, Flory and his collaborators Fox and William Krigbaum were further able to determine physical parameters that characterize the molecular chain itself. This is due to the balancing-out of the effect of long-range (excluded volume) forces by the polymer-solvent interactions when the polymer solution is in theta conditions and to the manifestation instead of short-range forces, which differentiate one polymer from another. Although Flory's derivation has been criticized as nonrigorous, it was in due course confirmed by computer simulations as well as neutron- and light-scattering experiments.

In 1957 Flory was appointed executive director of research at the Mellon Institute at Pittsburgh. Flory's appointment was meant to steer the Mellon Institute toward a stronger focus on fundamental research. By 1961 the program was not working out to Flory's expectations, and he left to take a position at Stanford University. In 1965 he was appointed J. G. Jackson–C. J. Wood professor of chemistry, and from 1969 to 1971 he served as the department's chairperson. At Stanford, Flory extended his study of the statistical thermodynamics of chain molecules, which was the subject of his second textbook, *Statistical Mechanics of Chain Molecules* (1969). He devised methods to calculate the configurations of polymer chains from physical properties of the units that make them up. Subsequently Flory addressed new research arenas, including theories of the structure of semicrystalline polymers, the formation of liquid crystals, and the rapidly evolving field of amorphous (or disordered) solids.

Flory was awarded the Nobel Prize for chemistry for 1974 for his wide-ranging contributions to the physical and theoretical chemistry of macromolecules. The first American polymer chemist, Flory was awarded many additional prizes including the National Medal of Science, the Priestley Medal, which is the American Chemical Society's highest award, and the Society of Chemical Industry's Perkin Medal. In addition to his two influential textbooks, Flory published more than 350 papers, and he held some twenty patents.

From the beginning of his career until his last day, Flory maintained close contacts with industry, serving as a consultant for Du Pont and IBM. He was likewise active as an educator and struggled to expand the teaching of polymer science, which was generally neglected in American universities. Flory chaired the National Research Council's Committee on Macromolecular Chemistry in 1955–1959. He served on the American Chemical Society's board of directors in 1959–1963 and the National Academy of Science policymaking council in 1967–1970.

Flory did not confine his activities to the ivory tower. He fought relentlessly for the human rights of oppressed scientists. He served on the NAS Committee on Human Rights in 1979–1984, and he participated in committees that discussed scientific exchange and human rights under the Helsinki Accords. Flory appeared at press conferences and protest demonstrations on the fate of Andrei Sakharov and other dissident Soviet scientists.

Flory had married Emily Catharine Tabor in 1936. They had three children. At the time he died, near his home in Big Sur, California, Flory was still at the peak of his creative powers, which had distinguished him as one of the major chemists of the twentieth century. His work has helped to demonstrate that macromolecules (or polymers), giant molecules that make up the most ubiquitous building blocks of nature, such as cellulose, rubber, protein, and DNA, are understandable through fundamental physical principles. His work further helped in developing synthetic polymers, which constitute much of our everyday environment.

• Flory's scientific manuscripts are deposited at the Chemical Heritage Foundation, Philadelphia, Pa. His early reports to Carothers are deposited at the Hagley Museum and Library, Wilmington, Del. Flory's papers on human rights are at the Hoover Institution on War, Revolution, and Peace at Stanford University. Flory's major papers are compiled in *Selected Works of Paul J. Flory*, ed. Leo Mandelkern et al. (3 vols., 1985). An interview of Paul Flory by Charles Overberger (American Chemical Society Eminent Chemists Videotape Series, 14 Feb. 1982) provides firsthand information on Flory's career, his personality, and his views on science policy, academe, and social issues. Further information about Flory's life is provided in Walter H. Stockmayer, "The 1974 Nobel Prize for Chemistry," *Science* 186 (1974): 724–26; Harold A. Scheraga, "Paul J. Flory on His 70th Birthday," *Macromolecules* 13, no. 3 (1980): 8A–10A; Robert Pecora, "Paul John Flory," *Physics Today* 39 (Nov. 1986): 116–17; Richard J. Seltzer, "Paul Flory: A Giant Who Excelled in Many Roles," *Chemical and Engineering News*, 23 Dec. 1985, pp. 27–30; and Peter J. T. Morris, "Paul Flory," in his *Polymer Pioneers* (1986), pp. 70–73. Flory's research in the context of the American synthetic rubber research program is described in Morris, *The American Synthetic Rubber Research Program* (1989). For a discussion of Flory's work with Carothers at Du Pont and his initiation into polymer science, see Michael Chayut, "New Sites for Scientific Change: The Case of Paul Flory's Initiation into Polymer Chemistry," *Historical Studies in the Physical and Biological Sciences* 23, no. 2 (1993): 193–218.

MICHAEL CHAYUT

FLOWER, Benjamin Orange (19 Oct. 1858–24 Dec. 1918), editor and social reformer, was born near Albion, Illinois, the son of Alfred Flower and Elizabeth Orange. Albion was founded in 1818 by Alfred Flower's father, George Flower, an immigrant from England. Benjamin Orange Flower studied at a private school near Albion on the farm of his father, a Disciples of Christ minister. At eleven he had already compiled a self-illustrated primary schoolbook and a long moral novel. Later, young Flower moved with his family to Evansville, Indiana, where he attended high school. Intending to become a minister like his father and an older brother, George Edward Flower, Benjamin Orange Flower attended the Disciples of Christ's School of the Bible at Kentucky University in Lexington. Changing theological perspectives, which ultimately led him to Unitarianism, sent Flower back to Albion, Illinois. There he won control of a local four-page newsletter, the *Egyptian Republican*, and transformed it into the *American Sentinel*, a weekly news magazine, which he edited in 1880–1881.

Benjamin Orange Flower sold the *American Sentinel* in 1881 and moved to Philadelphia. He moved to Boston, where he was a secretary in the mail order medical business of his brother, Dr. Richard C. Flower. In September 1885 Benjamin Flower married Hattie Cloud of Evansville, Indiana; they had no children. When Richard Flower opened a sanatorium-hospital with a sea-grotto swimming pool, Benjamin took charge of its house organ, the *American Spectator*. For three years he lectured and edited the journal; he was especially interested in revitalizing American drama and placing psychic research on a scientific basis. In 1889 Benjamin Orange Flower founded a monthly review, the *Arena*, and merged it with the *Spectator*.

With confidence in the progress that an enlightened and free democratic conscience would guarantee, Flower made the *Arena* a platform for advocates of direct democracy, populism, the single tax, and women's rights. He encouraged young writers of realist fiction with a moral purpose: Stephen Crane, Hamlin Garland, James A. Herne, Jack London, Frank Norris, Upton Sinclair, and others. Besides editing and publishing the *Arena*, Flower published books (many of them first serialized in the *Arena*) and contributed frequently to other periodicals. His most influential book of this period was *Civilization's Inferno; or, Studies in the Social Cellar* (1893). Its exposé of life in the city's slums did for Boston what Jacob Riis had done in New York. By 1894 Flower was organizing local groups of *Arena* readers into a national Union for Practical Progress, which had a mail order university and supplied its member units with lecturers and supplementary readings. Flower's critique of the moral corruption of concentrated wealth won for him a reputation as "father of the muckrakers," and he was proud that the *Arena* was the only major eastern journal to endorse William Jennings Bryan for president in 1896.

The most creative period of Flower's life ended when he had a nervous breakdown in 1895. Although he recovered by the end of the year, in 1896 Flower was forced out as editor of the *Arena*; the same year his wife was diagnosed as "completely insane" and hospitalized for the rest of her life. In June 1897 Flower joined Frederick U. Adams of Chicago to coedit *New Time*, "a magazine of social progress" once titled *New Occasions.* In December 1898 it merged with *Arena.* Flower founded and coedited the *Coming Age* with Anna C. E. Reifsnider in 1899 until it too merged with *Arena* in November 1900. He served on *Arena*'s editorial staff until 1904, when he became its editor again. When *Arena* collapsed in 1909, Flower founded and edited another reform journal, *Twentieth Century Magazine*, from October 1909 to November 1911. His most significant book of the period, *Progressive Men, Women, and Movements of the Past Twenty-five Years* (1914), is an important memoir of the progressive movement in American history.

Much interested in psychic research, Flower believed that the reality of a future life would ultimately be proven. He was national president of the National League for Medical Freedom and of the Free Press Defense League. In his last years Flower became convinced that a "monarchical" Roman Catholic church, which was "in effect a government within our Government," threatened American democracy. As president of the Menace Publishing Company of Aurora, Missouri, and editor of the *Menace*, he sought to arouse the public against the menace of Roman Catholicism. His *Patriot's Manual* (1915) was a handbook of facts "Showing Why Every Friend of Fundamental Democracy Must Oppose Politico-Ecclesiastical Romanism in Its Un-American Campaign to Make America 'Dominantly Catholic!'" A later work, *Righting the People's Wrongs* (1917), offered a similar warning. Flower died in Cambridge, Massachusetts, believing that the pope had instigated the wreckage of civilization in World War I.

• Benjamin Orange Flower apparently destroyed his personal papers, but a box of Howard F. Cline's correspondence about Flower's life is in Widener Library at Harvard University. A useful contemporary source is Edwin M. Bacon and Richard Herndon, *Men of Progress . . . in the Commonwealth of Massachusetts* (1896). Some important secondary sources are F. C. Mabee, "Benjamin Orange Flower and the *Arena*, 1889 to 1896" (master's thesis, Columbia Univ. 1938); Howard F. Cline, "The Mechanics of Dissent" (senior honors thesis, Harvard Univ., 1939); and Cline, "Benjamin Orange Flower and the *Arena*, 1889–1909," *Journalism Quarterly* 17 (June 1940): 139–50, 171. See also Cline, "Flower and the *Arena*: Purpose and Content," *Journalism Quarterly* 17 (Sept. 1940): 247–57; David Dickason, "Benjamin Orange Flower:

Patron of Realists," *American Literature* 14 (May 1942): 148–56; Roy P. Fairfield, "Benjamin Orange Flower: Father of the Muckrakers," *American Literature* 22 (1950): 272–82; Arthur Mann, *Yankee Reformers in the Urban Age: Social Reform in Boston, 1880–1900* (1954); Peter J. Frederick, *Knights of the Golden Rule: The Intellectual as Christian Social Reformer in the 1890s* (1976); and Roger Stoddard, "Vanity and Reform: B. O. Flower's Arena Publishing Company, Boston, 1890–1896," *Papers of the Bibliographical Society of America* 76 (1982): 275–337. An obituary is in the *New York Times*, 25 Dec. 1918.

RALPH E. LUKER

FLOWER, George (1788–15 Jan. 1862), Illinois pioneer, was born in Hertford, England, the son of Richard Flower, a brewery owner and farmer, and his wife, a daughter of the Fordham family (given name unknown). After protesting unsuccessfully against malt and beer taxes, Flower's father sold his brewery and devoted his energies to farming and sheep breeding. In 1814 he encouraged his son George to tour France in the company of prosperous sheep farmer Morris Birkbeck of Wanborough, Surrey, with an eye to emigrating there. The trip was memorialized by Birkbeck in *Notes on a Journey through France* (1814).

The influence of the clergy and the military in French life discouraged Birkbeck and Flower, both staunch republicans, from settling in France, and in 1816 Flower went to America to investigate the prospects for emigration there. Details are lacking, but it appears that Flower was married, with two small sons, by this time. The marriage was apparently an unhappy one, however, and part of the motive for emigration seems to have been to escape it. In America, Flower traveled west to Illinois, then back east through Tennessee, and spent the winter with Thomas Jefferson at Monticello.

In the spring of 1817 Flower met Birkbeck at Richmond, Virginia, with a party that consisted of four of the widowed Birkbeck's seven children and three other travelers. Among them was 25-year-old Eliza Julia Andrews, who traveled ostensibly as a friend of the Birkbeck girls but may have already become romantically involved with Flower. The party headed for Illinois with the intention of colonizing a tract of land on the Illinois prairie and setting up an English settlement there. Along the way the 53-year-old Birkbeck proposed marriage to Andrews but was rejected. The 29-year-old Flower then proposed and was accepted, and the couple was married in 1817 in Vincennes, Indiana; they had fourteen children, eight of whom survived to adulthood. That same year Flower and Birkbeck homesteaded a 26,400-acre tract of land on Long Prairie, in southeastern Illinois. Birkbeck remained on the homestead while Flower returned to England to arrange for the publication of Birkbeck's book promoting the settlement, to recruit settlers, and to raise money. Flower returned in the spring of 1818 with more than 100 emigrants, including his parents and sisters, who stayed in Lexington, Kentucky, while Flower readied a house for them on the "English Prairie."

When Flower reached the prospective settlement in Illinois, he found his partner Birkbeck mysteriously angry and embittered. After a brief confrontation, the two parted and never spoke again. Their division doomed the English settlement as it had been originally planned. Instead of one community, two sprang up: Flower's in Albion and, a few miles away, Birkbeck's in Wanborough.

Once the English settlement was founded it became the center of sharp controversy over the prospects of western settlement. From 1818 to the mid-1820s, more than fifty books, pamphlets, and long, polemical book reviews debating the wisdom of western emigration were published. Birkbeck, who died in 1825, was widely attacked for representing life in the settlement as better than it was; others angrily defended him. The settlement itself was a distinctly minor part of the westward movement, but perhaps because of their relatively high literacy rate, the settlers and their visitors were able to articulate issues in emigration that remained merely implicit elsewhere. Even today, the controversial literature of the English Prairie is a good compendium of the facts, ideology, and mythology of western settlement.

Flower and his wife remained in the English settlement for another quarter-century, not always happily. Financial difficulties pursued them and finally left them without any money. They were vehemently opposed to slavery, and their opposition led to persecution. Their oldest son, Richard, was murdered by a drunken ruffian who was acquitted of the crime. Finally, the couple left Albion in 1849 to settle in New Harmony, Indiana. During their last years, which were spent residing with various of their children, Flower wrote a history of the English settlement in Edwards County, Illinois, which was posthumously published by the Chicago Historical Society. In January 1862 the Flowers both fell ill while visiting their daughter in Grayville, Illinois. Eliza died on the morning of 15 January; on learning of his wife's death, Flower, who had been recovering, rapidly declined and died about sunset on the same day.

Flower is remembered, along with Birkbeck, not only for his ambitious and unusual plan for an English settlement in the American West but also for the book in which he described and interpreted their experiment and in the books of others that debated its success.

• The best, and almost the only, source of information about Flower is his own *History of the English Settlement in Edwards County, Illinois, Founded in 1817 and 1818, by Morris Birkbeck and George Flower* (1882). For Birkbeck's parallel accounts of the founding of the settlement, see his *Notes on a Journey in America, from the Coast of Virginia to the Territory of Illinois, with Proposals for the Establishment of a Colony of English* (1817) and *Letters from Illinois* (1818). The voluminous polemical literature of the settlement is usefully listed and excerpted in Charles Boewe, *Prairie Albion: An English Settlement in Pioneer Illinois* (1962).

JAMES HURT

FLOWER, Lucy Louisa Coues (10 May 1837–27 Apr. 1921), social reformer, was born in Boston, Massachusetts, the adopted daughter of Samuel Elliott Coues, a merchant and reformer, and Charlotte Haven Ladd. The locally prominent family, including eight children, resided in Portsmouth, New Hampshire, during Lucy's childhood. In 1853 President Franklin Pierce, a family friend, appointed Samuel Coues to the Patent Office, and the family moved to Washington, D.C.

Flower attended Packer Collegiate Institute in Brooklyn, New York, for the 1856–1857 academic year but left before graduation because of family illness. She drew plans in the Patent Office until 1859, when she left home to accept a teaching assignment in Madison, Wisconsin. She taught there for three years, first in the public high school and then in a private school that she founded and briefly ran. She married James Monroe Flower, a lawyer, in 1863, and the couple had three children. The Flowers moved to Chicago in 1873.

Flower was active in Chicago and Illinois philanthropic and reform efforts for almost thirty years and was instrumental in the establishment of the Cook County Juvenile Court. She began her charitable endeavors in Chicago as a member of a female committee of the St. James Episcopal Church, of which she remained a member throughout her residence in that city. Beginning in 1875, she served as a trustee of the Chicago Home for the Friendless and the Half-Orphan Asylum. She promoted the organization in 1880 of the Illinois Training School for Nurses, the first nursing school established west of Pennsylvania, and served on the board of trustees of that institution for twenty-eight years, eleven as its president. She was elected president in 1890 of the Chicago Woman's Club, the largest and most influential female service organization in Chicago during the late nineteenth and early twentieth centuries. In the early 1890s she founded the Every Day Club, a female discussion group concerned with civic affairs.

In 1891 Flower became the third woman appointed to the Chicago Board of Education, a position she held until a change in administrations forced her resignation in 1894. As a school board member, she supported public kindergartens, manual and practical training for girls and boys, reforms in deaf education, bathing facilities in schools, tenure-based pay increases for primary school teachers, and enforcement of compulsory attendance. In 1894 Flower won election as a trustee of the University of Illinois, thereby becoming the first woman to hold state elective office in Illinois.

Flower promoted the establishment of the first industrial school for dependent boys in Illinois, the Glenwood School, founded in 1889. She was active in efforts to found and maintain a manual training school at the Illinois State Reformatory (1891–1898) and spearheaded the campaign for effective compulsory education legislation, which became law in Chicago in 1898 after a decade of struggle. As part of her efforts to ameliorate the conditions of dependent and delinquent children, Flower advocated separate and distinct non-criminal legal proceedings for children, which culminated in the establishment of the Cook County Juvenile Court in 1899. She organized the Juvenile Court Committee shortly thereafter to coordinate private efforts to pay probation officers and erect separate facilities for the new court. The juvenile court represented a new style in child saving, which was replicated throughout the world in the early twentieth century.

In addition to Flower's numerous efforts on behalf of children, she also was concerned with welfare organizations and philanthropic endeavors generally. An advocate of scientific charity, she consistently opposed political involvement in welfare institutions and lobbied to reorganize the largest charitable organization in Cook County in 1891. Her reform activity occurred in the era before women won the right to general suffrage in Illinois. She therefore focused her efforts on lobbying, petitioning, and public campaigns in the press. She worked successfully with like-minded reformers, in particular Julia Lathrop from Hull-House, and was expert at influencing a wide range of organizations. One contemporary described her as "one of the most active and energetic workers" on behalf of children.

Politically conservative, Flower opposed universal female suffrage, believing that the vote should be limited to educated citizens of both sexes. She justified women's public roles, especially in education, on the insights and special skills they gained as mothers but cautioned young women to refrain from public involvement while their children were young. As the wife of a senior partner in a prestigious Chicago law firm who was a prominent figure in local Republican politics in the late nineteenth century, she enjoyed a comfortable upper-middle-class lifestyle and resided in a wealthy area of Chicago. Her career as a reformer ended in 1902 when she moved from Chicago to Coronado, California, with her ailing husband. He died there in 1909. She became ill shortly thereafter and passed the remainder of her life as an invalid in Coronado, where she died.

Reformer, educator, and pioneer female officeholder, Lucy Flower focused her energies on children's and educational issues and is best remembered for her efforts on behalf of the Cook County Juvenile Court, the first court in the world to treat children as noncriminals in need of saving rather than as adults to be punished. The Lucy Flower Technical High School for Girls, the first trade school for girls in Chicago, bears witness to her accomplishments.

• Five volumes of scrapbooks containing principally news clippings by or about Lucy Flower and other family members are at the Chicago Historical Society. Flower set forth her views on women's civic duty in "Women in Public Life," *Outlook* 56 (1897): 400–404. Harriet S. Farwell, Flower's daughter, wrote the only full-length biography, *Lucy Louisa Flower, 1837–1920: Her contribution to Education and Child Welfare in Chicago* (1924), which is both biased and factually inaccurate at times.

PATRICIA TAKAS NOZELL

FLOWER, Richard (1761–2 Sept. 1829), reformer and Illinois pioneer, was born in England, probably in Hertfordshire, the son of George Flower, a prosperous tradesman. His mother's name is unknown. Establishing himself in Hertford as a brewer, Flower did well in business for over twenty years. He married a daughter (name unknown) of Edward Fordham of Kelshall; they had five children. He joined in the activities of his brother Benjamin Flower, who had become involved in dissenting politics and pamphleteering, and wrote *Observations on Beer and Brewers, in Which the Inequality, Injustice, and Impolicy of the Malt and Beer Tax are Demonstrated* (1802). When it became clear that his agitation was not going to change the taxation laws that related to his business, he sold his prosperous brewery. He enthusiastically took up sheep breeding and other agricultural pursuits.

Although he produced a thriving herd of sheep and abundant crops, and purchased an estate, "Marden," near Hertford, Flower found it extremely difficult to remain profitable in the farming business. He also continued to become disenchanted with the government. In 1809 he wrote another antitax pamphlet, *Abolition of the Tithe Recommended, in an Address to the Agriculturalists of Great Britain*, which produced no greater effect on ministerial policy than had his first tract. As the Napoleonic wars dragged on, he suffered continuing distress over ever-lowering prices for agricultural products and ever-increasing taxes. In 1818 his eldest son, George Flower, and a friend, Morris Birkbeck, persuaded him to sell Marden for £23,000 and to emigrate with his family to the United States. He spent his first winter in America in Lexington, Kentucky, where he and his wife suffered the tragic loss of their son William. In the meantime, George Flower founded the English agricultural colony of Albion in Edwards County, Illinois, and constructed houses for himself and his father. In 1819 Flower moved his family to Albion, where he occupied "Park House." After becoming settled, he composed two pamphlets, *Letters from Lexington and the Illinois* (1819) and *Letters from the Illinois, 1820, 1821* (1822), in response to virulent attacks on efforts to found the Albion community by the critic William Cobbett, whose splenetic musings, according to one historian, were "seemingly motiveless" (Boewe, p. 169).

Flower spent his last years living happily at Park House in Albion, where he delighted in entertaining visitors from many parts of America and Britain with English hospitality. He and his son George conducted a vigorous letter-writing campaign in 1823 against attempts by proslavery citizens of Illinois to introduce black servitude into the state. Continuing to improve his colony, he caused numerous buildings to be constructed, including a capacious tavern. He also helped found a library and led weekly sabbath services for his community. In 1824 he and his youngest son, Edward Fordham Flower, returned to England, where the latter remained with the intention of becoming an author. There Flower acted as an agent for George Rapp in selling the community of Harmony, Indiana, to

Robert Owen. As soon as that task was accomplished, he returned to Albion, where he spent the remainder of his life working with son George to improve not only the sheep herds of his estates but agricultural production generally. He died at Albion.

• Information on the Flower family and the founding of Albion is in Benjamin Flower, *Statement of Facts, Relative to the Conduct of the Reverend John Clayton, Senior, the Reverend John Clayton, Junior, and the Reverend William Clayton: the Proceedings on the Trial of an Action Brought by Benjamin Flower against the Reverend John Clayton, Junior, for Defamation, with Remarks* (1808), and George Flower, *History of the English Settlement in Edwards County, Illinois, Founded in 1817 and 1818, by Morris Birkbeck and George Flower* (1882). Richard Flower's pamphlets on the Illinois colony are printed in Reuben G. Thwaites, *Early Western Travels, 1748–1846*, vol. 10 (1904). See also Charles Boewe, *Prairie Albion: An English Settlement in Pioneer Illinois* (1962), and E. E. Sparks, *The English Settlement in the Illinois* (1907).

PAUL DAVID NELSON

FLOWER, Roswell Pettibone (7 Aug. 1835–12 May 1899), governor and congressman, was born in Theresa, Jefferson County, New York, the son of Nathan Monroe Flower, a farmer and cloth manufacturer, and Mary Ann Boyle. His father died in 1843, and Flower worked successively in a brickyard, in a mill, in a store, and on the family's large farm. After graduating from Theresa High School in 1851, he took a job as a salesman in the Philadelphia dry goods store of E. D. Woodward, who declared bankruptcy two months after Flower's arrival. Flower thereupon taught in the country schools of Watertown, New York, where he also sold jewelry and clerked for a time in a hardware store. From 1854 to 1860 he was the assistant postmaster of Watertown, a patronage position that suggests he was already involved in local politics. In 1859 he married Sarah M. Woodruff; they raised three children.

Flower thereafter advanced in both business and politics. In 1869, four years after the Civil War, a conflict in which he played no military role, he relocated to New York City to become the administrator of the $4 million estate of Henry Keep, a former financier, banker, and railroad president who had been married to Flower's sister-in-law. The family retained their home and connections in Watertown, where Flower financed the building of a Presbyterian church. Admitted to the New York Stock Exchange in 1873, he formed a brokerage partnership with Elias Cornelius Benedict, a banker, that endured until Flower's death. These activities revealed his shrewd business acumen and made him wealthy, which aided his political career.

Flower reached political prominence in the 1880s. Having been a Democratic chairman of Jefferson County and a close friend of Governor Samuel J. Tilden, the 1876 Democratic presidential nominee, Flower had positioned himself for elective office. In 1881 he defeated his Republican challenger, William W. Astor, by 3,000 votes for a seat in the U.S. House

of Representatives, filling the vacancy occasioned by the resignation of Representative Levi P. Morton, who accepted a ministerial position in France. A product of Tammany Hall, the powerful Democratic political organization of New York City, Flower represented the city's Eleventh Congressional District for one term, from 1881 to 1883, using his position to advocate liberal pensions for Civil War veterans. Pledging not to seek renomination, he campaigned for his Democratic successor.

Flower's name surfaced in 1882 as a possible gubernatorial candidate. Opponents, however, assailed him as a wealthy spokesman for the railway and bondholding interests in the state. To avoid a conflict of interest, Flower relinquished his positions with railroads and sold his stock, but he lost the gubernatorial nomination to Grover Cleveland, an anti-Tammany candidate. In 1884 Tammany leaders proposed Flower for the presidency in an ill-conceived attempt to thwart Cleveland's presidential ambitions. Cleveland won the Democratic nomination and was elected president.

Flower's wealth and devotion to Democratic party principles made him an important figure in New York politics. In 1885 he was unanimously nominated as lieutenant governor on the ticket headed by David B. Hill. Citing personal and business reasons, Flower declined the nomination. Three years later he was elected to the U.S. House of Representatives, where he occupied his former seat from 1889 until his resignation in 1891. He chaired the Congressional Campaign Committee and was a member of the Ways and Means Committee.

Flower clearly articulated his views on various issues. He sought to reform the tariff laws by reducing duties. While opposed to the principle of high-tariff protectionism embedded in the McKinley Tariff of 1890, he saw political advantage for his party in not offering a Democratic alternative but simply attacking the Republican measure. In addition to denouncing high tariffs, he in 1890 castigated the Federal Elections Bill, sponsored by Representative Henry Cabot Lodge of Massachusetts, which would have provided for supervision of federal elections and the establishment of bipartisan boards to examine alleged voting irregularities. Designed to be a piece of national legislation to protect African-American voters in the South, the proposal encountered opposition not only from southern Democrats but also from northern city bosses, who abhorred the thought of federal inspectors in their wards. Accordingly Flower rejoiced when the bill was sidetracked in the Senate. His continuing advocacy of liberal pensions, in the meantime, made him a favorite among Civil War veterans.

With Tammany in control of the state's political apparatus in 1891, Flower, the machine's handpicked candidate, was nominated for governor of New York. He was elected by a margin of nearly 48,000 votes over his Republican opponent, Jacob S. Fassett, and served as governor from 1892 through the end of 1894. During the cholera epidemic of 1892, he ordered the purchase of Fire Island by the state to provide additional quarantine facilities. When people on the island threatened to oppose by force the establishment of such an institution, Flower directed the land and naval militia to assist in enforcing the state's authority. In 1893 he signed a bill legalizing timber cutting on forest preserve land in New York.

Flower opposed a third presidential nomination for Cleveland in 1892, preferring instead to have Senator Hill as the party's standard-bearer. He endorsed Cleveland only after Adlai E. Stevenson of Illinois, a former congressman and first assistant postmaster general, was nominated as Cleveland's running mate. Flower liked Stevenson because of the latter's endorsement of the spoils system, opposition to the McKinley Tariff, and denunciation of the Federal Elections Bill. He threw New York's delegation behind Stevenson, knowing that in Stevenson he would have a political ally in Washington, and the Cleveland-Stevenson ticket carried New York and the election. Two years later, in the midst of an economic depression and a resurgence of Republican strength, Flower chose not to seek a second term as governor.

After he left office in 1895, Flower spent the remainder of his life in private pursuits. When in 1896 the Democrats nominated William Jennings Bryan of Nebraska for the presidency on a platform calling for the free and unlimited coinage of silver, Flower led a delegation of New York Gold Democrats to Indianapolis, where sound money Democrats from across the nation convened to form the National Democratic party and nominate Senator John M. Palmer of Illinois for the presidency. Flower, as temporary chairman of this convention, declared, "This gathering is notice to the world that the Democratic party has not yet surrendered to Populism and Anarchy" (*New York Tribune*, 3 Sept. 1896).

Three years after William McKinley's presidential election on a sound money platform and Bryan's defeat for the White House, Flower died while on a fishing trip at Eastport, Long Island. Regarded as a powerbroker within the Democratic party, Flower's business acumen and his political career as governor and congressman earned him a national reputation.

• Flower left no personal papers. Genealogical information is in the New York Genealogical and Biographical Society Library and in the New-York Historical Society in New York City. His letters are scattered in various collections, including those of Grover Cleveland (Library of Congress), William Bourke Cockran (New York Public Library), Levi P. Morton (New York Public Library), and Whitelaw Reid (Library of Congress). Flower's speeches are in the *Congressional Record* from 1881 to 1883 and from 1889 to 1891. See also Roswell P. Flower, *Public Addresses of Governor Roswell P. Flower* (1894). A brief biographical sketch is in the *New York Herald*, 17 Sept. 1891. An obituary is in the *New York Times*, 13 May 1899.

LEONARD SCHLUP

FLOWERS, Tiger (5 Aug. 1895–16 Nov. 1927), African-American world middleweight boxer, was born Theodore Flowers in Camilla, Georgia, the son of Aar-

on Flowers, a railroad porter, and Lula Dawson. When he was a small child his family moved to Brunswick, Georgia, where he completed six school grades and afterward held various jobs. In 1915 he married Willie Mae Spellars, and in 1917 they moved to Philadelphia where he worked as a subway laborer, later taking a job in the Navy Yard when World War I began. While in Philadelphia he received his first instruction in boxing.

After the war ended, Flowers returned to Georgia and began to box professionally against the wishes of his parents. He won a few fights in the Savannah-Brunswick area, and rumors of his boxing ability reached Walk Miller, a gymnasium owner in Atlanta. Miller contacted Flowers and became his manager, and the two men established a close friendship. Fighting only on all-black programs in the South, Flowers won consistently until he was knocked out by Panama Joe Gans, a good middleweight, in Atlanta in late 1921.

Flowers's record in 1922 and 1923 was erratic. Taken out of the South for the first time by Miller, Flowers won 26 fights, including two victories over Gans. However, his chin proved to be fragile when exposed to the blows of heavy punchers. He was knocked out four times, by black light heavyweights Lee Anderson, Kid Norfolk, and Jamaica Kid and veteran heavyweight Sam Langford. Fighting in Mexico, he met white opponents for the first time.

In 1924 Flowers fought 35 times and won 33 of them, including rematches against Jamaica Kid and Anderson. The turning point in his career came in a close nontitle fight with the reigning middleweight champion, Harry Greb, in Fremont, Ohio, on 21 August, in which no official decision was given. Although reporters at ringside adjudged Greb the winner, Miller immediately mounted an effective propaganda campaign for his fighter, persistently claiming that Flowers actually had the better of the Greb fight, and succeeded in attracting attention to his man. On 9 December Flowers knocked out former middleweight champion Johnny Wilson in New York City and thus established himself as a leading contender.

On 16 January 1925 Flowers suffered a devastating knockout at the hands of future light heavyweight champion Jack Delaney in New York. Miller complained vociferously that Delaney had fought with metal objects in his gloves in order to give his punches greater force. In a rematch on 26 February, Delaney again scored a knockout and then removed his gloves in the ring to show that nothing was concealed. Despite these setbacks Flowers won 25 of 29 fights in 1925, including victories over such highly rated middleweights as Jock Malone, Lou Bogash, and Ted Moore. On 23 December Flowers lost a scandalously unfair decision to former light heavyweight champion Mike McTigue in New York City. According to noted boxing historian Nat Fleischer, who witnessed the fight, Flowers won nearly every round. The Flowers-McTigue bout occurred as part of a charity program, and the judges on this occasion were businessmen who evidently did not know how to fairly assess the outcome of a boxing contest. Despite his spotty record, Flowers was then matched with Greb for the middleweight title, probably in part because of his convincing performance against McTigue, and partly because of the effectiveness of Miller's claims that Flowers had once beaten Greb in a nontitle fight. Flowers and Greb met in New York on 26 February 1926, and Flowers won the decision after a close fight. They fought again for the middleweight title in New York on 19 August 1926, Flowers again winning the decision, although many spectators thought that Greb deserved the decision. On 3 December 1926 Flowers's short reign as middleweight champion ended when he lost a 10-round title fight to former welterweight champion Mickey Walker in Chicago. As with so many of Flowers's major fights, this one was controversial because nearly every newspaper reporter present thought that Flowers deserved to win.

Flowers was a colorful and unorthodox fighter. A pious Christian who was nicknamed "The Georgia Deacon," he read the Bible daily and prayed in his corner before each fight. When called to the center of the ring for the introductions, he would spring from his corner in a catlike manner, hence the nickname "Tiger." Once the fighting began he constantly threw punches from a left-handed stance. Although he could hit sharply, many of his blows were light taps landed with an open glove. He often overwhelmed his opponents with the number of his blows, which, combined with great speed and elusiveness, usually saved him from suffering serious punishment. His busy, colorful style made him a popular ring attraction and a difficult opponent.

In 1927 Flowers continued to fight successfully, winning 15 of 18 fights. He defeated highly rated light heavyweights Eddie Huffman and Chuck Wiggins and former welterweight champion Pete Latzo, lost only to Leo Lomski, and boxed two draws with future light heavyweight champion Maxie Rosenbloom. The last fight of his career occurred on 12 November in New York City; there, a few days afterward, he underwent an operation for removal of scar tissue from around his eyes. Anesthetized with ether, he failed to regain consciousness. Miller afterward claimed that Flowers had been murdered and had an autopsy performed, but no evidence of foul play was found.

Flowers saved his ring earnings and lived well during his few years of prominence. A friendly, quiet man who was widely liked, he served as a deacon of the Methodist church in Brunswick. His funeral in Atlanta was a large affair. Eulogies by sportswriters praised him, in the condescending manner of the time, as "white, clean white inside," no doubt in recognition of his gentlemanly demeanor.

Flowers was elected to the International Boxing Hall of Fame in 1993. The first African-American world middleweight champion, he was also the first black champion of any professional boxing division after Jack Johnson lost the heavyweight title to Jess Willard in 1915. There was little or no controversy when Flowers won the middleweight title, in part because of his unassuming personality, but mainly because the middleweight title was less prestigious than the heavyweight title. Also, the hostility to black boxing champions aroused by Johnson had subsided somewhat by 1926.

• Flowers's record may be found in Herbert G. Goldman, ed., *The Ring Record Book and Boxing Encyclopedia*, 1986–1987 ed. (1987). A brief biography by Nat Fleischer appeared in *Black Dynamite*, vol. 5: *Sockers in Sepia* (1947). A more obscure work is Henry Grady Edney, *Theodore (Tiger) Flowers: A Biography* (1928). Articles include Ed Van Every, "Tiger Flowers, Praying Fighter, Dies Under Knife," in *Everlast Boxing Record 1928* (1928), pp. 43–45; John L. Dorgan, "Tiger Flowers' Death Means Real Loss to Boxing in This Country," *The Ring*, Jan. 1928, pp. 24–25; and two articles by Jersey Jones: "Tiger Flowers' Mysterious Death Still Haunts Boxing World?," *The Ring*, May 1975, pp. 12–15, 40–41, and "Flowers for McTigue," *The Ring*, Feb. 1951, pp. 30–31, 41. A report of Flowers's untimely death and his obituary are in the *New York Times*, 17 Nov. 1927.

LUCKETT V. DAVIS

FLOWERS, Walter Winkler, Jr. (12 Apr. 1933–12 Apr. 1984), attorney and Alabama congressman, was born in Greenville, Alabama, the son of Walter Winkler Flowers, Sr., an attorney, and Ruth Swaim. He entered the University of Alabama in the class of 1955, graduating Phi Beta Kappa, and two years later earned the LL.B. He passed the Alabama bar in 1957 and commenced the practice of law in Tuscaloosa two years later—after a year abroad studying international law at the University of London, followed by a year of active duty as a reserve officer in the military intelligence branch of the U.S. Army. In August 1958 he married Margaret Pringle of Biloxi, Mississippi, with whom he had three children.

For a decade Flowers concentrated on building up his law practice, and apart from serving as chairman of the Tuscaloosa City Civil Service Board, he displayed little interest in politics. This changed in part because of the political ambitions of Governor George Wallace. In 1968 Flowers was elected as a Democrat to the Ninety-first Congress from Alabama's Seventh Congressional District. He ran as a strong supporter of Wallace, who carried 61 percent of the Seventh District in his bid for the presidency in 1968, appearing in advertisements arm-in-arm with the governor. Again, in 1972 Flowers served as a national campaign coordinator of an effort to get the governor on the ballot as the presidential candidate of the American Independent party. On 3 January 1969 Flowers began the first of five consecutive terms in the House of Representatives.

It was service on the House Judiciary Committee that brought Flowers to national prominence. His third term coincided with the crisis, known as "Watergate," that ended the presidency of Richard M. Nixon. What initially appeared to be a simple burglary of Democratic party headquarters during the 1972 presidential campaign took on wider significance with evidence of White House involvement. An investigation by a special committee of the Senate, broadcast live on network television over the spring and summer of 1973, revealed an array of illegal acts and other abuses of power by the executive branch, reaching back to midway of Nixon's first term.

Since the Department of Justice, and by strong implication the president himself, stood accused of illegal acts, Nixon was forced to acquiesce in the appointment of a special independent prosecutor, Archibald Cox. Cox was soon dismissed by presidential order because of his relentless pursuit of tapes of conversations recorded in the Oval Office, but not before Attorney General Elliot Richardson and his second-in-command at Justice resigned rather than comply with the order. Immediately dubbed the "Saturday Night Massacre," it led Peter Rodino, chairman of the House Judiciary Committee, to begin an inquiry into the impeachment of the president.

Flowers, an obscure figure little known outside his home state, was destined to play an important role in these proceedings. He was one of a group of seven (three southern Democrats and four Republicans), known as the "fragile coalition," who voted to impeach, though all were from congressional districts that gave Nixon resounding majorities in 1972. Flowers, formerly an ardent supporter of Nixon, became convinced after the Saturday Night Massacre that the president had guilty knowledge of the suppression of evidence. Skillfully, Flowers charted a course that enabled him to vote on national network television for two of the five articles of impeachment and still survive politically. Rightfully, he would remember this as "the single most important event I was involved in in Congress." During the hearings in July 1974 leading up to the impeachment votes, he and other members of the fragile coalition were, Flowers recalled, "newsmakers for awhile; it was pretty heady stuff." Nixon understood what the loss of Flowers's vote meant: "Well, Al, there goes the presidency," he said to his chief of staff, Alexander Haig, after a brief phone call to Wallace failed to gain his support in turning Flowers around.

For those who understood his dilemma, Flowers's ability to project before a national audience the agony of a former supporter, forced into opposition by the overwhelming weight of evidence, seemed to marry canny survival skills to surprising political courage. Survival seemed less an issue after the so-called "smoking gun"—the revelation shortly after the vote of an audiotape that conclusively proved Nixon's complicity in the cover-up. The tape seemed to justify Flowers's action even to the most diehard Nixon supporter.

A great comfort was his friendship with Andrew Young, a junior black congressman from Georgia, whom Flowers cultivated. Young endorsed Flowers in his bid for reelection in 1974, a year when blacks in Alabama were beginning to vote in large numbers. The Seventh District had the largest percentage of blacks in the state. In return, Flowers later voted for

extension of the voting rights act. The whole affair provided an instructive example of the changing nature of politics in Alabama.

Choosing not to stand for reelection in 1978, Flowers ran instead for the Senate seat of John Sparkman, losing to Howell Heflin, a former chief justice of the state supreme court, who denounced his opponent as "part and parcel of that Washington crowd," a tried and true formula on the Alabama political scene. Out of office, Flowers became a lobbyist for energy and fossil fuel companies. In April 1983 he was divorced from Margaret Flowers and seven months later married Beverly Burns. He suffered a fatal heart attack while playing tennis on his birthday in Falls Church, Virginia, near his home in McLean. He is buried in Arlington National Cemetery.

• Flowers's papers are deposited in the University of Alabama library. A biography has yet to be published. For the importance of Flowers's vote to Nixon see Richard Nixon, *RN: The Memoirs of Richard Nixon* (1978). The best overall history of Watergate, incorporating Flowers's role, is Stanley I. Kutler, *The Wars of Watergate: The Last Crisis of Richard Nixon* (1990). For obituaries see the *Birmingham News* and the *New York Times*, both 13 Apr. 1984.

JAMES L. PENICK

FLOYD, Charles Arthur (3 Feb. 1904–22 Oct. 1934), bank robber and killer, commonly known as Pretty Boy Floyd, was born in Bartow County, Georgia, the son of Walter Lee Floyd and Mamie Echols, farmers. The Floyd family lived in Georgia until 1911, when they moved to Sequoyah County, near the Cookson Hills, in the new state of Oklahoma. They settled first in Hanson and five years later relocated to Akins, near Sallisaw. Charles attended school and worked on the family cotton farm, earning the reputation of a prankster and the nickname "Choc," for illegal Choctaw beer. He was an athletic, friendly teenager who enjoyed hunting and fishing but had little interest in school.

In 1920 Floyd left home to find work in the harvests of the Great Plains. Soon attracted by the excitement of cities, he moved to Wichita, Kansas, and may have briefly attended barber college. Unfortunately the heavyset young man also became acquainted with the area's underworld. By 1922 Floyd was a bootlegger, gambler, and burglar. He often returned to visit family and friends in Akins and the Cookson Hills. In June 1924, in Sallisaw, Charles married Ruby Hardgraves, the attractive daughter of a tenant farmer. At the time of the marriage, she was three months pregnant, and a son was born in December.

Fatherhood did not slow Floyd's rapidly progressing criminal career. On 11 September 1925 Floyd participated in a payroll robbery in St. Louis, Missouri. Within days the ostentatious display of sudden wealth led to his arrest in Oklahoma. Floyd pleaded guilty and received a sentence of five years in the penitentiary at Jefferson City, Missouri. He proved to be an intelligent, average inmate who committed only minor infractions and became the eager student of experienced, older prisoners. In January 1929 his wife obtained an uncontested divorce; Floyd was discharged two months later.

During the next year Floyd was repeatedly arrested for armed robbery in Kansas City and served a brief jail sentence for vagrancy in Pueblo, Colorado. He also managed several visits back to Oklahoma, including one for the funeral of his father. According to legend, Floyd took revenge on Walter Lee Floyd's murderer. In fact, the killer was found to have acted in self-defense, moved to the West Coast, and died of natural causes.

On 5 February 1930 Floyd and four companions robbed the Farmers & Merchants Bank of Sylvania, Ohio, outside of Toledo. The following month alert police officers in Akron arrested the culprits. Floyd received a fifteen-year sentence in return for a plea of guilty. Then, on 10 December 1930, he made a daring escape from the train taking him to prison. He had been identified earlier as using the alias "Pretty Boy Smith," but after journalists made inquiries about the fugitive Floyd in Kansas City and a local madam volunteered the nickname "Pretty Boy," newspapers throughout the nation adopted and popularized the designation.

Floyd soon joined a gang of efficient bank robbers and killers. He was believed responsible for the murders of gangsters Wallace Ash and William Ash of Kansas City in March 1931. There followed numerous bank robberies in Kentucky, Ohio, Oklahoma, Missouri, and Mississippi. Floyd was also wanted for the killings of two local police officers, a federal prohibition agent, and an investigator for the Oklahoma Crime Bureau. During one five-month period the "Phantom of the Ozarks" robbed six small Oklahoma banks, only to vanish into the Cookson Hills where friends and family members remained sympathetic and supportive.

In the fall of 1931 Floyd located his former wife and his son. Ruby had remarried, but she promptly rejoined her first husband, bringing their child. The reunited Floyd family lived quietly under assumed names first in Fort Smith, Arkansas, and then in Tulsa, Oklahoma. Floyd proved to be a loving father and husband but continued his career of crimes and gunbattles.

On 17 June 1933 Floyd, together with Adam Richetti and Verne Miller, carried out the infamous Kansas City massacre. On that day, the three gunmen attacked a team of federal agents and local police officers who were transporting a prisoner to the federal penitentiary at Leavenworth. The fight they initiated at Union Station left five dead and two wounded. After several months the federal Bureau of Investigation identified Floyd, Richetti, and Miller as perpetrators of the massacre. Floyd always denied responsibility for the Union Station killings, however. Miller's mutilated corpse was discovered near Detroit in November 1933. Three months later a thousand lawmen and national guardsmen searched the Cookson Hills in one of the largest manhunts in U.S. history. Floyd and Richetti, however, had left the state several months before.

Floyd may have joined John Dillinger for a bank robbery at South Bend, Indiana, in June 1934. When that notorious bandit was killed the following month in Chicago, Floyd replaced him as the officially designated Public Enemy No. 1. Floyd and Richetti hid quietly in Buffalo, New York, until October 1934, when they determined to return to Oklahoma. On the way, they had an automobile accident near East Liverpool, Ohio. Police recognized Richetti and placed him in custody. Federal agents, led by Melvin Purvis, rushed to the scene and joined the hunt for Floyd. Eight lawmen located him hiding behind a corncrib; as the bandit ran up a hill, the officers opened fire, striking him twice. When Purvis reached the fugitive he said, "You're Pretty Boy Floyd." The man responded, "I am Charles Arthur Floyd," and died.

The man known as the Sagebrush Robin Hood was buried at Akins in a plot he had selected a year earlier. During the depression some people viewed Floyd as a hero, the enemy of the banks, and tens of thousands attended the funeral; dirt was stolen from the grave for decades. In 1938 Missouri executed Adam Richetti for his part in the Kansas City massacre. John Steinbeck portrayed Floyd sympathetically in *The Grapes of Wrath*, and fellow Oklahoman Woody Guthrie wrote a ballad in honor of the fallen Pretty Boy. Floyd's younger brother was elected sheriff of Sequoyah County and served with distinction for twenty years.

• Leading sources include Michael Wallis, *Pretty Boy* (1992); Merle Clayton, *Union Station Massacre* (1975); and Paul Wellman, *A Dynasty of Western Outlaws* (1961). An obituary is in the *New York Times*, 23 Oct. 1934.

FRANK R. PRASSEL

FLOYD, John (24 Apr. 1783–16 Aug. 1837), physician and politician, was born in Jefferson County, Virginia (now Ky.), the son of Colonel John Floyd and Jane Buchanan Preston. Among the first Virginians to settle in Kentucky during the Revolution, Colonel Floyd built a stockade fort near Louisville known as Floyd's Station and achieved prominence in the Kentucky settlements as a soldier, surveyor, legislator, and leading citizen. He was killed in a skirmish with American Indians just weeks before John was born.

After obtaining a rudimentary education at home, John enrolled in 1796 at Dickinson College in Carlisle, Pennsylvania. However, a combination of financial and health problems compelled him to drop out of school before completing his studies. In 1804 he married his second cousin, Laetitia Preston. Over the next twenty-two years the couple had twelve children, five of whom died in infancy or early childhood. The most famous of the children was John Buchanan Floyd, who was elected governor of Virginia in 1849 and served as secretary of war under President James Buchanan. Soon after marrying, John and Laetitia Floyd moved to Philadelphia, where John enrolled as a medical student at the University of Pennsylvania. Eighteen months later, in April 1806, he was awarded the M.D. degree.

Moving to Virginia, Floyd settled in the lower Shenandoah Valley in Christiansburg, Montgomery County. There he began a successful medical practice and became active in local government. His appointment as justice of the peace in June 1807 and his commission as major in the county militia a year later marked his entrance into public life. Rarely did one rise to high public office in Virginia without first serving a political apprenticeship as a justice on the county court, and this service was usually accompanied by a term as an officer in the militia. During the War of 1812 Floyd served with distinction in the Virginia Line, retaining his major's rank but rising subsequently to brigadier general of militia.

Floyd's growing public stature was attested by his election in the fall of 1814 to the Virginia House of Delegates. Because of the war with Britain, Virginia legislators were much more nationalistic at that time than they might otherwise have been, and Floyd joined them in supporting legislation and resolutions having a nationalist thrust. During his brief term in the assembly, which lasted only until 19 January 1815, Floyd accomplished nothing especially noteworthy, but he did make a favorable impression on fellow legislators and, more important, on his constituents.

The voters of Abingdon District rewarded Floyd in 1816 with election as a Republican to the Fifteenth Congress and reelection to five succeeding Congresses, a service that extended from 4 March 1817 until 3 March 1829. Although Floyd was never the leader of the Virginia congressional delegation, he effectively represented western and, for a short time, national interests. It was natural that he should be sympathetic to the needs of the frontier. His boyhood Kentucky home and his adopted home in southwestern Virginia were both parts of the frontier. He was a supporter of Henry Clay's nationalist program in the early postwar years, especially Clay's call to recognize the emerging Latin American republics. Floyd also supported Andrew Jackson when he invaded Florida in 1818 and opposed censoring the frontier general for his actions. He was one of a very few Virginia congressmen who voted for the Missouri Compromise, which he supported because he feared dissolution of the Union unless a compromise could be obtained. A strong advocate of westward expansion, in 1821 he introduced the first bill for organizing and occupying the Oregon country.

Following the Missouri debates, the political climate in Virginia became increasingly hostile to all nationalist legislation, and doctrinaire Republicans, led by John Randolph of Roanoke and John Taylor of Caroline, raised high the states' rights standard. Floyd rallied to that standard. Although he had supported some nationalist measures early in his career, he had remained, for the most part, true to his strict Republican principles. He now emerged as one of the main congressional defenders of the "Principles of '98," upholding strict construction of the Constitution, state

sovereignty, and minimal government. He was unrelenting in opposing the nationalist measures of John Quincy Adams's administration. Shifting his loyalty to the Democratic party, Floyd worked hard to secure Jackson's election to the presidency in 1828, believing that the general would be a strict-constructionist, states' rights president. He was disappointed when Jackson did not reward him with a cabinet post.

Declining to stand for reelection in 1828, Floyd retired from Congress in 1829 and returned to his medical practice in Christiansburg. His retirement from public life was brief, however, for in January 1830 the Virginia legislature elected him governor. Subsequently reelected to a second term, he served from 4 March 1830 to 31 March 1834. Elected by dominant states' rights Virginians, Floyd pursued policies as governor pleasing to that group. Nat Turner's slave insurrection, which occurred in Southampton County during Floyd's governorship, terrified slaveholders everywhere and made Floyd an even more vociferous defender of Thomas R. Dew's proslavery doctrines and of states' rights. He denounced President Jackson for threatening to use force against South Carolina nullifiers and abandoned both Jackson and the Democratic party over the nullification contest. A grateful South Carolina gave Floyd the state's presidential electoral votes in 1830. Thereafter Floyd joined with others in an unsuccessful attempt to bring Clay and John C. Calhoun together as leaders of a new anti-Jackson, states' rights party.

Suffering from poor health and prohibited by Virginia's new 1830 constitution from serving a third successive gubernatorial term, Floyd left public office permanently in March 1834. Not long afterward he fell ill and died of a stroke at Sweet Springs in Montgomery County, Virginia.

• Floyd's papers are scattered. The bulk of his letters are in the Preston Family Papers at the Virginia Historical Society, Richmond. The John Warfield Johnston Papers at Duke University contain 416 Floyd items; thirty items relating mainly to the presidential election of 1832 are in the John Floyd Papers, Library of Congress; and miscellaneous correspondence, business papers, and other items are in the Campbell-Preston-Floyd Family Papers, also in the Library of Congress. Charles H. Ambler, *The Life and Diary of John Floyd, Governor of Virginia, An Apostle of Secession, and the Father of the Oregon Country* (1918), is the best biography available, but it leaves much to be desired. Floyd's interest in Oregon is discussed in John H. Schroeder, "Rep. John Floyd, 1817–1829: Harbinger of Oregon Territory," *Oregon Historical Quarterly* 70 (Dec. 1969): 333–46. Historical context for Floyd's life and career is in Daniel P. Jordan, "Virginia Congressmen, 1801–1825" (Ph.D. diss., Univ. of Virginia, 1970); Harry Ammon, "The Richmond Junto, 1800–1824," *Virginia Magazine of History and Biography* 61 (Oct. 1953): 395–418; and Norman K. Risjord, *The Old Republicans: Southern Conservatives in the Age of Jefferson* (1965).

CHARLES D. LOWERY

FLOYD, John Buchanan (1 June 1806–26 Aug. 1863), governor of Virginia, secretary of war, and Confederate general, was born in Montgomery County, Virginia, the son of John Floyd, a planter and doctor who later served as governor of Virginia at the time of Nat Turner's rebellion, and Letitia Preston. He grew up in western Virginia and graduated from South Carolina College in 1829, where he was the protégé of the intellectual father of southern nationalism, Dr. Thomas Cooper. In 1830 he married his cousin, Sally Buchanan Preston, the sister of William C. Preston, later a senator from South Carolina and a leading advocate of southern rights. They adopted one child. Floyd established a law practice in Wytheville in southwestern Virginia but in 1836 moved to Arkansas, seeking a fortune in the cotton and land boom there. After this enterprise proved financially disastrous and physically debilitating, Floyd returned to Abingdon, Virginia, where he eventually repaid his debts and regained his health.

Well connected through family ties, Floyd entered politics and in 1847 was elected to the lower house of the Virginia General Assembly as a Democrat. In the House of Delegates he joined with the other western delegates in supporting constitutional reform and state-aided internal improvements and took a leading role in sustaining the resolutions of the general assembly that denied the constitutionality of congressional control over slavery and affirmed the rights of slaveholders in the territories.

In December 1848 Floyd was elected governor by a coalition of Democrats and Whigs, who supported his views on constitutional reform and internal improvements. As governor he advocated white manhood suffrage, a more equitable apportionment of the legislature on the basis of the white population, and an elective judiciary. He also pushed for an extensive program of turnpike, canal, and railroad construction. His administration stabilized the commonwealth's credit through a program of bond sales and oversaw an unprecedented expansion of appropriations for internal improvements.

Floyd continued to defend southern rights while governor. He sought to strengthen slavery by aiding the Virginia Colonization Society in the removal of the commonwealth's free black population. He attacked the "never ending aggression" of the northern abolitionists and proposed that the commonwealth tax the incoming goods from those free states that persisted in refusing to return fugitive slaves. Finally, Governor Floyd issued a call for a national convention to oppose "agitation of the slavery question" and aided the formation in Richmond of the Central Southern Rights Association. He warned that, if the South did not resist, the northern fanatics would eventually control Congress and eliminate slavery.

After leaving the governorship, Floyd served as a Democratic elector in 1852 and three years later joined forces with Henry Alexander Wise to resist the rise of nativism in the Old Dominion. Floyd campaigned vigorously against the Know Nothings and was elected to the general assembly. Although he and his brother-in-law, Preston, toyed with the idea of running John C. Frémont as the Democratic standard-bearer in 1856,

Floyd threw his influence behind James Buchanan and became his southern spokesman to the merchants of Philadelphia and New York City.

Buchanan, seeking a Virginian for his cabinet, brought Floyd in as secretary of war when Wise turned down the offer of a position as secretary of state. There Floyd acted with the "directory" of prosouthern advisers, repudiating Robert J. Walker's handling of the situation in Kansas and favoring the acceptance of the proslavery Lecompton constitution. Unfortunately, he became infamous for his slipshod administration of the War Department. Not only did Floyd favor his friends and relatives in awarding government contracts, but he also became increasingly involved in issuing "acceptances" that allowed contractors to borrow money against their promissory notes signed by the secretary of war. Although Buchanan had warned him against the practice, Floyd eventually became implicated in a scheme perpetrated by a western contractor, William Hepburn Russell, who used the "acceptances" to obtain $870,000 worth of negotiable bonds from the Indian Trust Fund. Russell was aided in this by a clerk in the Interior Department, a cousin of Floyd's wife named Godard Bailey, who owed his job to Floyd. When this was uncovered, even the other southern members of the cabinet—especially Secretary of the Interior Jacob Thompson—called for Floyd's resignation.

At this juncture, the crisis in Charleston Harbor consumed the administration. The secretary of war's verbal orders to Major Robert Anderson at Fort Moultrie instructed him to "exercise sound military discretion." When Anderson decided to move his entire force to Fort Sumter, Floyd joined a delegation of southern senators led by Jefferson Davis in demanding that Anderson return to Fort Moultrie. Anderson's action, they argued, had violated the "gentleman's agreement" with the sovereign state of South Carolina, which had seceded 20 December. The incident gave the embattled Floyd, who was also charged by Republicans with shipping ordnance to states he knew would secede, the opportunity to resign. This he did on 29 December 1860, as a matter of "patriotism" and "honor."

Throughout his political career, Floyd had been a states' rights Democrat and an outspoken defender of slavery and southern rights. On 3 December 1860 he asserted that he was "not for secession as long as any honorable effort can be made to preserve the Union . . . guaranteeing . . . protection to the negro property of the South." As southern states began to secede and the charges of misconduct mounted against him, Floyd increasingly embraced secession. Once Virginia had seceded, Floyd raised a brigade of volunteers and joined in the attempt to secure western Virginia for the Confederacy. Although he took part in the minor engagements at Cross Lanes and Carnifex Ferry, Floyd spent most of his energies in western Virginia bickering with his fellow officer Wise. His performance was generally inept and his troops were driven back.

Following his failure in western Virginia, Floyd was sent to Kentucky, where he assumed command of Fort Donelson, which was threatened by the southern thrust of the Union forces led by Ulysses S. Grant in February 1862. Although Floyd and his subordinates—Gideon J. Pillow, Simon B. Buckner (1823–1914), and Nathan Bedford Forrest—initially inflicted heavy damage on Commander Andrew Foote's flotilla and seemed about to break out toward Nashville, they hesitated and allowed Grant to regain a superior position. Over Pillow's objections, Buckner and Floyd decided to surrender. Fearing possible prosecution on charges of corruption and treason, Floyd turned over his command and escaped south with Pillow and 2,500 men aboard two commandeered steamboats, leaving Buckner to surrender the main force of 13,000 men to Grant. Despite his immediate removal from command by Davis, the Virginia legislature promoted Floyd to major general two months later. Meanwhile his health was failing rapidly, and he died of stomach cancer a year later near Abingdon.

A planter/lawyer born to political office, Floyd often proved to be out of his depth. Excessively self-centered and incapable of either acknowledging his own limitations or understanding his opponents, he consistently acted in a foolhardy fashion while insisting always that he was a man of honor, morally a notch above his fellows.

• Edward A. Pollard, *Lee and His Lieutenants* (1867), contains a typical nineteenth-century sketch by a pro-Confederate historian. Robert Hughes presents a defense of his grandfather in "Floyd's Resignation from Buchanan's Cabinet," *Tyler's Quarterly Historical and Genealogical Magazine* 5 (1923): 73–95. More modern (and hostile) evaluations can be found in the first five volumes of Allan Nevins's massive work, *Ordeal of the Union* (1947–1971), and in James M. McPherson, *The Battle Cry of Freedom: The Civil War Era* (1988). John M. Belohlavek, "John B. Floyd as Governor of Virginia, 1849–1852," *West Virginia History* 33 (1971): 14–26, treats his early career. Roy Franklin Nichols, *The Disruption of American Democracy* (1948), Philip S. Klein, *President James Buchanan* (1962), and Elbert B. Smith, *The Presidency of James Buchanan* (1975), provide the best discussions of Floyd as a member of the Buchanan administration. On corruption generally, see Mark W. Summers, *The Plundering Generation* (1987). Thomas Lawrence Connelly and Archer Jones, *The Politics of Command* (1973), is insightful on Floyd's military career.

WILLIAM G. SHADE

FLOYD, William (17 Dec. 1734–4 Aug. 1821), signer of the Declaration of Independence and congressman, was born in Brookhaven, on the south shore of Long Island, Suffolk County, New York, the son of Nicoll Floyd and Tabitha Smith. Nicoll Floyd's grandfather Richard Floyd had emigrated from Brenochshire, Wales, to Massachusetts about 1650 and had subsequently settled in Setauket, Long Island. Nicoll Floyd lived in Brookhaven, where he built the "Mastic" estate about 1724. William was sober and serious, a person of proper, respectable, and somewhat pretentious characteristics, who inspired confidence and respect,

if not affection. He married Hannah Jones in 1760; they had three children. Floyd lent money at interest and was one of Connecticut governor Jonathan Trumbull's (1710–1785) creditors. Mastic was tenanted and worked by free labor and, in 1795, by eleven slaves.

Floyd's first political office was as trustee of Brookhaven town in 1769; he was reelected in 1771. Brookhaven's Committee of Safety admitted that opinion among the townsfolk was divided and that some people, including some members of Floyd's extended family, were pro-British. Such division delayed the committee's active partisanship. On 22 April 1775 the Suffolk County committee elected him to the first Continental Congress, and on 5 September 1775 he was nominated to be a colonel of the Suffolk County militia's Western Regiment. In the next year, Floyd was the first of his congressional delegation to sign the Declaration of Independence after the New York state government allowed its representatives to vote for independence. He served until 1777 and again from 1778 to 1783. Not a floor or debate leader, he was deemed by Edward Rutledge in June 1776 to be one of the five New Yorkers who "tho' good men, never quit their chairs." Floyd served on the clothing committee and naval and treasury boards. Late in the war John Jay (1745–1829) considered Floyd an independent thinker who was not "a mere tool" of others. In the Arthur Lee–Silas Deane controversy (in which Lee accused Deane and Benjamin Franklin (1706–1790) of war profiteering during their negotiations for secret French aid to the American army) Floyd allied with the anti-Deane congressmen, although he did not share their antipathy to the French alliance and General George Washington. He supported New York's claim to Vermont and was critical of the peace treaty provision that sought restitution of Loyalist property.

Floyd absented himself from Congress when the British occupied eastern Long Island, and he helped evacuate his family to Middletown, Connecticut, although he could not bring out his property. For the rest of the war, when not attending government service, Floyd remained in exile in Connecticut. On 8 May 1777 the new government of New York appointed him state senator from the Southern District and a member of the Council of Safety. In 1778 Floyd returned to Congress. There he lamented the wartime increase in offices and factions. He favored additional congressional fiscal powers, especially after Rhode Island prevented adoption of the 5 percent impost in 1782, a rejection that to him was "a Convincing proof of a Defect in our Government."

In 1781 his wife died, and it was not until the spring of 1783 that Floyd returned home to rebuild his devastated estate. In the next year he married Joanna Strong. He invested in undeveloped land in northern and western New York and in a company that bought the Sadequeda Patent on the western Mohawk River. From 1784 to 1788 he was a founding trustee of a public educational academy and an honorary member of the Philadelphia Society for Promoting Agriculture.

As major general, Floyd continued his militia command until 1796.

Floyd continued in politics after the war, serving as a state senator until 1788. Even though Suffolk County was Antifederalist, he supported the federal Constitution and was elected to the first House of Representatives, serving from 4 March 1789 to 3 March 1791, when he failed to get reelected. In June 1791 he hosted Thomas Jefferson and James Madison (1751–1836) when they came to Long Island on their "botanizing excursion." Floyd also lost the election for lieutenant governor to Stephen Van Rensselaer in 1795. During the undeclared naval war he criticized French highhandedness but ardently supported Jefferson's candidacy in 1800. In 1800 and 1804 he served as a presidential elector, presumably for Jefferson. In 1801 he served as a delegate at the convention that rewrote New York's constitution.

In 1803 Floyd moved his family to his holding in the town of Western (called Westernville by some historians) on the Mohawk River. His reasons for such a move at an advanced age are uncertain. He oversaw the construction of a new estate, but when elected to represent his new district in the state senate in 1808, Floyd's attendance was limited because he could not travel during the winter. In 1820, at age eighty-six, he served in his last public office, as presidential elector. William Floyd died in Western, New York.

On the eve of the revolutionary war he had been a devoted anti-British committeeman in an area with a significant number of Loyalists. During the war he was an ardent but unspectacular revolutionary who served in several state offices and in the Continental Congress at least part of every year, except one, until 1783. It was on the shoulders of such ardent and trustworthy patriots as William Floyd that independence was achieved and that the new nation's political regimes were created.

• Letters of William Floyd appear in Paul H. Smith, ed., *Letters of the Delegates to Congress, 1772–1789* (20 vols., 1972–). Floyd appears in every volume of Smith's *Letters*, with the exception of vols. 8–10; his service on the Committee of Secret Correspondence appears in vol. 3. Floyd's participation in the Continental Congress is also noted in vol. 2 of the *Index of the Papers of the Continental Congress, 1774–1789*, comp. John P. Butler (1978). An early biographical sketch of Floyd appears in John Sanderson and Robert Waln, Jr., eds., *Biography of the Signers to the Declaration of Independence*, 2d ed., vol. 2 (1828), pp. 107–20. In the last half century, only William Quentin Maxwell's two essays have studied Floyd's life. Maxwell's booklet *Portrait of William Floyd, Long Islander* (1956) considers Floyd's life until he moved from Brookhaven; in "William Floyd at Western, New York," *Manuscripts* 9 (1957): 171–78, Maxwell reviews Floyd's early life but concentrates on his last eighteen years on the Mohawk. Many manuscripts that form the bases of Maxwell's works are privately held. Several are in the possession of Mrs. John Treadwell Nichols, while others are in the possession of Mr. Andrew Fiske. The footnotes and bibliography of *Portrait* and the footnotes in "Floyd at Western" offer further details and references.

Floyd appears briefly in Irving Brant, *James Madison: The Nationalist, 1780–1787* (1948); Edmund Cody Burnett, *The Continental Congress* (1941); and Robert East, *Business Enterprise in the American Revolutionary Era* (1938). Appreciative items appear in *Addresses Delivered on the Occasion of a Visit to the General William Floyd House at Mastic, Long Island, by Members and Friends of the Society for the Preservation of Long Island Antiquities . . .* (1950); information about the old house and the estate may be found here. Another brief sketch is Madelyn Kurth, "Mastic House," *D. A. R. Magazine* 69 (1935): 16–19.

EUGENE R. FINGERHUT

FLÜGGE-LOTZ, Irmgard (16 July 1903–22 May 1974), aeronautical engineer, was born in Hameln, Germany, the daughter of Oskar Lotz, a journalist with a fondness for mathematics, and Dora Grupe. She attended elementary school at Frankenthal and in Mönchen-Gladbach. Providing early encouragement for his daughter's interest in engineering and mathematics, Oskar Lotz enrolled Irmgard in a girl's Gymnasium in Hanover, shortly before he was drafted into World War I. This military service permanently ruined his health, thereby preventing him from resuming an active professional life. Irmgard consequently had to help support her family by tutoring younger students in mathematics and Latin.

The Technical University of Hanover admitted Lotz in 1923 as an applied mathematics major. She resolved her dilemma about whether to pursue mathematics or engineering by transferring to engineering mechanics. Gender discrimination discouraged her from seeking industrial employment after obtaining a Diplom-Ingenieur degree in 1927; she was virtually the only female engineering student at Hanover. Instead, she remained at the university for graduate studies. Lotz received a Doktor-Ingenieur degree in 1929; her dissertation involved a theoretical study of heat conduction in cylinders.

In spite of her unusual accomplishments, Lotz retained her character as a conventional German woman. She enjoyed exercising her domestic skills, being convivial and unpretentious, wearing simple clothing and jewelry, and never "shop talking" in nonacademic environments. Distant colleagues, therefore, were routinely shocked to discover that the woman they assumed was a modest housewife was actually the esteemed Dr. Lotz.

While the German industrial establishment may have questioned the appropriateness of her career choice, its need for mathematical talent outweighed its gender prejudices. In 1929 Lotz received a job offer from the steel industry but instead accepted a research position at Ludwig Prandtl's Aerodyamische Versuchsanstalt (Aerodynamic Research Institute, AVA) at the University of Göttingen. Initially assigned the "feminine" task of cataloging an extensive collection of reprints, Lotz found time to analyze span-wise pressure distribution on aircraft wings. Prandtl had already derived the integral equation describing this phenomenon for inviscid flow but had solved it only for wings with an ellipsoid planform. By 1931 Lotz had discovered an iterative numerical technique that provided a general solution to this basic aerodynamics problem. Its accuracy and convenience made it popular with aircraft designers; they dubbed it the "Lotz method." She continued to discover solutions to basic fluid-flow problems. These involved airships, wings with control surfaces, the wall effects of wind tunnels, propeller slipstreams, and turbine blades. An impressed Prandtl promoted her to head of the division of theoretical aerodynamics at the AVA. By the mid-1930s she was supervising Ph.D. students and managing a computing staff. Her approach to such authority was simple: "Make sure they don't confuse your office with a dance floor."

The Third Reich brought mixed blessings for Lotz. On the one hand, the AVA received generous financial support from the Luftwaffe. This allowed Prandtl and Albert Johann Betz to modernize their wind tunnels and increase their student and staff levels, benefiting Lotz. On the other hand, Lotz was distressed by the new political repression, vividly displayed by the destruction of Göttingen's famous mathematics department and the rabid pro-Nazi student unions. Such tension worsened when a young mechanics professor at Göttingen, Wilhelm Flügge, started courting her. Although Flügge was famous for his work in shell theory, his anti-Nazi sentiments would prevent him from getting tenure. After their marriage in 1938, the couple accepted positions in the Deutsche Versuchsanstalt für Luftfahrt (DVL) in Berlin, the Luftwaffe's research center. As Flügge-Lotz explained later at Stanford, "It was perfectly all right for non-Nazis to do research." Flügge became the director of structural research; Flügge-Lotz became a consultant in aerodynamics and flight dynamics. During World War II Flügge-Lotz worked to develop discontinuous control theory, a domain of nonlinear mathematics. It permitted the use of on-off switches for guidance purposes, especially in missile design where simple control hardware was desired. As she had in aerodynamics, Flügge-Lotz emphasized both mathematical rigor and engineering utility in this new field.

During the collapse of Nazi Germany, the Flügges were living in Saulgäu near Lake Constance, where Wilhelm had moved his DVL research group for safety. The French occupation authorities recruited the Flügges for the Centre Technique de Wasserburg after the war, and then for the Office national d'études et de recherches aérospatiales (ONERA), the French equivalent of the National Advisory Committee for Aeronautics (NACA), in 1946. Although they enjoyed Parisian culture, their status as German nationals prevented them from obtaining permanent positions. When Stephan Timoshenko, the famous Russian-American applied mechanics professor, discovered this situation, he sought faculty positions for them at Stanford University, where he was teaching. This proposal was opposed by Lydik Jacobsen, the chair of mechanical engineering. As a Danish national, he disliked Germans, especially those involved in the Axis war effort. Jacobsen eventually relented and gave Wil-

helm a faculty appointment but offered Irmgard only a lecturing job, citing an old policy prohibiting married couples from being professors in the same department as his formal excuse. Eager to leave wartorn Europe, Flügge-Lotz ignored this affront and accepted the offer.

Flügge-Lotz's graduate-level course in fluid mechanics at Stanford initially attracted students from NACA's Ames Research Center. Her intellectual and personal generosity also made her a popular dissertation adviser, especially in compressible boundary layer theory and finite-difference techniques. She simultaneously made much progress in her control-theory research, as demonstrated by her *Discontinuous Automatic Control* (1953), *Discontinuous and Optimal Control* (1968), and the numerous papers she coauthored with her Ph.D. students. In 1960 Flügge-Lotz finally received the formal recognition she deserved by becoming a full professor in the Department of Aeronautics and Astronautics, making her the first female engineering professor at Stanford. After retiring in 1968, Flügge-Lotz was honored in 1970 by the Society of Women Engineers with its Achievement Award and by the American Institute for Aeronautics and Astronautics, to which she delivered the prestigious von Kármán Lecture in 1972. She died in Palo Alto, California.

• Flügge-Lotz's papers do not appear to have survived, but she is represented in Wilhelm Flügge's papers at Stanford University. Biographical accounts include "A Life Full of Work—The Flügges," *Stanford Engineering News* 68 (May 1969); "Emerita Professor Flügge-Lotz (16 July 1903–22 May 1974)," *Automatica* (1975): i; and J. R. Spreiter et al., "In Memoriam Irmgard Flügge-Lotz, 1903–1974," *IEEE Transactions on Automatic Control*, AC-20 (Apr. 1975): 183a–183b. Interviews by the author with emeritus professors Nicholas Hoff and Walter Vincenti of Stanford University's Department of Aeronautics and Astronautics, Sept. 1995, provided personal recollections of Flügge-Lotz. See also W. Flügge and J. R. Spreiter, "Irmgard Flügge-Lotz (1903–1974)," in *Women of Mathematics: A Bibliographic Sourcebook*, ed. L. S. Grinstein and P. J. Campbell (1987), pp. 33–40. An obituary is in the *New York Times*, 23 May 1974.

BRETT D. STEELE

FLY, James Lawrence (22 Feb. 1898–6 Jan. 1966), lawyer and New Deal administrator, was born in Seagoville, Texas, the son of Joseph Lawrence Fly, a farmer, and Jane Ard. Fly attended the U.S. Naval Academy in Annapolis, Maryland, graduating in 1920. After serving in the Pacific, he married Mildred Marvin Jones in 1923; they had two children. He then went to Harvard Law School, and upon graduation in 1926 he entered private practice. After three years he left to become a special assistant to the attorney general of the United States. During his five years in this position, he represented the United States in antitrust cases and regulatory measures affecting interstate commerce.

In 1934, when private power companies began their systematic attacks on the Tennessee Valley Authority, Fly was brought in to the TVA as head of its legal department. Fly, like the TVA director David Lilienthal, had been a student of Felix Frankfurter at Harvard, and several younger former students of Frankfurter came to his staff for the legal battle. Over the next five years litigation twice went to the U.S. Supreme Court, and the Court first issued a narrow ruling on the legality of a single contract and then avoided the merits altogether. The power companies then settled with TVA. Through the litigation Fly established a reputation for toughness and energy. Wendell Willkie, as a spokesman for the private utilities, complimented Fly as "the most dangerous man in the United States—to have on the other side."

With TVA secure, President Franklin Roosevelt moved Fly over to chair the Federal Communications Commission in 1939. A year later he also was named chairman of the Defense Communications Board that directed efforts to coordinate the use of communications facilities during the Second World War.

With his arrival at the FCC, accompanied again by Frankfurter protégés, the heretofore lethargic agency began to bustle with activity, all seemingly reflecting a desire to increase competition. The FCC approved the engineering standards for commercial television and allocated the first spectrum to frequency modulation (FM) broadcasting. The FCC adopted the Chain Broadcasting Rules, which were principally designed to limit the ability of the networks to control their affiliates' programming. One of the rules also forced the National Broadcasting Company to divest itself of one of its two networks, thereby creating the American Broadcasting Company. A network challenge to the rules resulted in a Supreme Court opinion fully sustaining a broad theory of the FCC's regulatory authority.

There was another side to Fly's FCC, one that attempted to use regulatory power to harm those who opposed the president. This was most apparent when, following a Roosevelt directive, Fly initiated proceedings to preclude newspapers from owning radio stations. With newspapers decidedly anti-Roosevelt, the president wished to avoid similar opposition from broadcasters. Yet despite Roosevelt's desires and Fly's efforts, political pressures and a court defeat forced the FCC to drop the matter.

The FCC was successful, however, in preventing stations from taking partisan positions on the issues of the day. At a time when few stations editorialized, one anti-Roosevelt station did, and the FCC ruled that editorials were contrary to the public interest.

Fly was a highly controversial chairman: *Collier's* ran an article labeling his FCC "public enemy number one." The broadcast establishment held him in disdain which he reciprocated, likening it to "a dead mackerel in the moonlight—it both shines and stinks." Fly's willingness to take on the powerful, reluctance to back down, and outspoken nature resulted in a congressional buffeting ranging from attacks on his policies to budgetary threats and a Dies Committee investigation of supposed communist infiltration of the agency.

In 1944 Fly resigned and moved to Florida where he established a law firm and became active in the American Civil Liberties Union, becoming one of its directors. In 1950 he married Phyllis Beckman. He died at Daytona Beach, Florida. In an era that produced a number of exemplary administrators who performed well under difficult circumstances, Fly was one of the best.

• The records from Fly's periods with the Department of Justice and the FCC are in the National Archives, Washington, D.C.; those from the TVA period are at the Federal Records Center, East Point, Georgia. There is no biography of Fly, but there is a James Lawrence Fly Oral History Project at Columbia University. On his tenure at the TVA, see Thomas K. McCraw, *TVA and the Power Fight* (1971); on the TVA litigation, see Paul A. Freund, *The Supreme Court of the United States* (1961); and on the FCC, see Erik Barnouw, *The Golden Web* (1968), and Lucas A. Powe, Jr., *American Broadcasting and the First Amendment* (1987).

L. A. POWE, JR.

FLYNN, Edward Joseph (22 Sept. 1891–18 Aug. 1953), political leader and adviser, was born in New York City, the son of Henry T. Flynn and Sara Mellon. His Roman Catholic parents had immigrated from Ireland after his father graduated from Trinity College, Dublin; the family settled in the Bronx and was relatively well off, providing Flynn with a more comfortable and secure environment than was the case in most immigrant families of the time. Flynn graduated from Fordham University Law School in 1912 and began the practice of law. In 1924 he went into partnership with Monroe Goldwater, with whom he developed a profitable legal practice that continued for the rest of his life. In 1927 he married Helen Margaret Jones; the happy and successful marriage, centered in their Bronx home, produced three children.

Flynn's full-time involvement in politics was not really planned, but despite having an unusually reserved character for a politician he showed great skill in party affairs. (It was characteristic of Flynn throughout his career to work in the background, rarely calling attention to himself.) In 1917, having previously come to the attention of Charles Francis Murphy, the head of Tammany Hall, he was chosen by the Democratic organization to run for the state legislature. He served two terms and then in 1921 was elected sheriff of Bronx County, a lucrative sinecure that was followed in 1925 by his appointment as city chamberlain by Mayor James J. Walker. In 1929 then governor Franklin D. Roosevelt appointed him New York secretary of state, a post he held for ten years. None of these positions required much of Flynn's time or attention and thus permitted him to focus on politics as opposed to government.

In 1922, having become one of the Democratic party leaders of Bronx County, Flynn was selected by Murphy to be chairman of the Bronx County Democratic Executive Committee—in effect, the political "boss" of the county—a position he retained for more than thirty years. It was from this position that Flynn became an important leader of local and then national Democratic party affairs as well as an exponent of the idea of the "political machine" as a useful and creative agency of political control. Like Murphy, Flynn exemplified the ability of a strong political leader and tightly controlled machine to produce good candidates and good government; he was proud of his role in the success of people like Franklin Roosevelt, Alfred E. Smith, Herbert H. Lehman, and Harry S. Truman.

Flynn was an early supporter of Roosevelt and became an increasingly influential political adviser during his gubernatorial (1929–1933) and presidential (1933–1945) years. President Roosevelt appointed Flynn to positions as regional administrator of the National Recovery Administration public works program and as U.S. commissioner general to the New York World's Fair (1939–1940), but Flynn's political role was far more important. He provided a connection between the Roosevelt administration and the urban machines of New York, Chicago, and other cities. This was a part of his combined commitment to New Deal political and social liberalism and to a pragmatic emphasis on whatever would provide long-term benefit to the Democratic party. For the same reasons, he was one of the politicians who advised Roosevelt in the mid-1930s of the potential importance of the African-American vote and of the need to take action to bring black voters into the party.

A loyal proponent of Roosevelt's third-term candidacy, Flynn replaced James A. Farley, who broke with Roosevelt over the issue, as chairman of the Democratic National Committee in 1940 and thus became a principal Roosevelt confidant as well as political (as opposed to policy) adviser. He was among the close advisers who recognized the significance of Roosevelt's declining health in 1944, and he played a key role in the choice of Harry S. Truman as the vice-presidential candidate in that year's campaign. Flynn sometimes played a role in policy decisions in the Roosevelt administration, but political ramifications were never entirely absent. As a leading Roman Catholic layman, for example, Flynn went to the Yalta Conference (Feb. 1945) with the president to focus on the issue of postwar religious rights for Catholics in the Soviet Union and its satellites. After Yalta he went on to Moscow and Rome, where he discussed the issue with Soviet leaders and the pope.

Roosevelt had rewarded Flynn with nomination as minister to Australia and ambassador-at-large for the South Pacific in January 1943, but allegations of corruption associated with the paving of a parking area in Flynn's Carmel, New York, vacation home derailed the appointment. The expenditure of public money (about $750 total) apparently resulted from confusion rather than collusion, but Flynn ultimately withdrew from consideration to avoid the partisan strife. He also resigned from his national party chairmanship but remained an active player in New York and national politics into the early 1950s, remaining a strong supporter of President Truman. Flynn died while vacationing in Dublin, Ireland.

Flynn represents one of the best examples of the role that machine politicians played in the success of Roosevelt's New Deal and Truman's Fair Deal, and in the development of twentieth-century liberalism generally. While two generations of middle- and upper-class "reformers" constantly denigrated them, it was these professional politicians, along with officeholders and official policy makers, who shaped the modern liberal state. As Robert F. Wagner, later mayor of New York City, put it at the time of Flynn's death, he was "an honorable and decent gentleman who served the cause of liberal democracy."

• The best source of information on Flynn's public career is his autobiography, *You're the Boss* (1947); it reflects Flynn's own reticence relative to his private life but is frank and reasonably complete on his public career and ideas about politics. There is also a brief oral history interview, "The Reminiscences of Edward J. Flynn," in *The Oral History Collection of Columbia University*, ed. Elizabeth B. Mason and Louis M. Starr (1973). Useful information can also be found in Lyle W. Dorsett, *Franklin D. Roosevelt and the City Bosses* (1977), and in Unofficial Observer [John Franklin Carter?], *The New Dealers* (1934). Flynn's obituary in the *New York Times*, 19 Aug. 1953, provides a useful summary of his career.

JOHN M. ALLSWANG

FLYNN, Elizabeth Gurley (7 Aug. 1890–5 Sept. 1964), labor organizer and activist, was born in Concord, New Hampshire, the daughter of Thomas Flynn, a quarry worker and civil engineer, and Annie Gurley, a tailor. Both parents were descended from a long line of Irish rebels. During Elizabeth's childhood, the family was poor due to the hard times and her father's preference for political argumentation over earning a living. In 1900 the Flynns moved to a cold-water flat in the Bronx, which became a gathering place for Irish freedom fighters and prominent socialists. Impressed by Elizabeth's intelligence and militancy, they encouraged her activism.

Flynn's career as an orator began as early as elementary school, when she won a gold medal for a speech arguing that women should be given the vote. At the age of fifteen, she spoke on street corners, advocating government support of children to reduce women's financial dependence on men. She was arrested along with her father the following year for speaking without a permit. Fear of incarceration never prevented her from speaking, however. She was arrested ten times throughout her career and attained great notoriety in the press for her commitment to radicalism. In an era when street life and mass strikes were important in peoples' lives, Flynn's fame was like that given to media stars today.

In 1906 Flynn joined the newly founded Industrial Workers of the World (IWW), a militant union, and became a "jawsmith" or traveling agitator and organizer. In this capacity, the "Rebel Girl," as she was later christened, helped organize the major East Coast strikes of the day (Minersville, Pa., 1911; Lawrence, Lowell, and New Bedford, Mass., 1912; and Paterson, 1913–1914, and Passaic, N.J., 1926). Flynn mobilized workers, mostly low-paid immigrants, women, and children, through her fiery rhetoric and wrote articles for the IWW and the socialist press. Often IWW leaders and members were arrested and jailed for inciting riots, and Flynn helped secure lawyers for their defense and raised funds for support of their families.

Flynn was also involved in conflicts over free speech in Missoula, Montana (1908), and Spokane, Washington (1909–1910). She worked to gain public support for imprisoned anarchists Sacco and Vanzetti for seven arduous years (1919–1926). During this period she was also involved in organizing the Workers Defense Union to aid the victims of the Palmer Raids, a series of attacks against radicals precipitated by the post–World War I Red Scare, and helped establish the American Civil Liberties Union (ACLU). The ACLU later ousted her in 1940 because of her membership in the Communist party but reinstated her posthumously in 1976.

Flynn's personal life was stormy. After a brief marriage to Jack Archibald Jones (1908), she left him and returned home with her child, who was raised by her mother and sister. In 1926 her grueling work schedule led to her collapse from exhaustion, exacerbated by the strain of left-wing political faction fights and a tragic love affair with the anarchist organizer Carlo Tresca. She recuperated in Portland, Oregon, at the home of Dr. Marie Equi. Flynn was possibly romantically involved with Equi, an abortionist and IWW activist.

After finally regaining her health in 1936, Flynn returned to New York City, where she reentered left-wing politics. After such a long hiatus, she felt estranged, as the political world had changed. With the New Deal, labor organizers were no longer feared as outside agitators but were more accepted. They used legal methods and new technological devices such as the radio to organize unions. Flynn joined the Communist party in 1938 and rose quickly. After joining the party's National Board, in 1942 she ran for New York state representative-at-large on the Communist ticket. However, she was merely a figurehead and rarely dissented from the party line. Having no base of support, Flynn felt uncomfortable in the party, having entered at the top instead of rising through the ranks. Nevertheless, she was one of the most popular Communist speakers and columnists, writing two to four times a week for twenty-six years for the *Daily Worker*, the party's newspaper. Preferring direct organizing to bureaucratic reform work and internal party politics, she saw her constituency as immigrant workers and, in the late 1950s and the 1960s, civil rights workers and student activists.

Flynn was indicted with the top Communist party leadership in 1951 under the Smith Act, which made it illegal to be a member of any group that advocated the overthrow of the government. After defending herself eloquently during the nine-month trial, she was sentenced to a three-year term in the Alderson federal penitentiary in West Virginia. While awaiting her jail term, she wrote *I Speak My Own Piece* (1955; reprinted as *The Rebel Girl* in 1973), the autobiography of her early life. After her release in 1957, she published a prison memoir, *Alderson Story* (1963).

Flynn returned to political life exhausted but committed to reviving the Communist party, now in disarray. In 1961 she became the first female national chair of the Communist party. She ran unsuccessfully for the New York State General Assembly, headed the Women's Commission of the Communist party, and traveled abroad, attending conferences and giving speeches. She died in the Soviet Union, where she had traveled to write and rest, and was given an elaborate state funeral.

• Flynn's papers are in the Tamiment Library at New York University. The Workers Defense Union papers are in the State Historical Society at the University of Wisconsin, and the Industrial Workers of the World Papers are in the Labadie Collection, University of Michigan, Ann Arbor. The Archives of Labor History and Urban Affairs at Wayne State University, Detroit, includes a tape of Flynn's IWW recollections as well as some of her correspondence in the Mary Heaton Vorse Papers. Flynn's articles and columns appeared regularly in the *Daily Worker*, the *Sunday Worker*, and *Political Affairs*. The only biography is Rosalyn Baxandall, *Words on Fire: The Life and Writing of Elizabeth Gurley Flynn* (1987). Obituaries are in the *New York Times*, 6 Sept. 1964, and *Time*, 18 Sept. 1964.

ROSALYN FRAAD BAXANDALL

FLYNN, Errol (20 June 1909–14 Oct. 1959), film actor, was born Errol Leslie Thomson Flynn in Hobart, Tasmania, the son of Theodore Leslie Thomson Flynn, an Irish immigrant professor of marine biology, and Lily Mary Christian. Flynn's formal education, mainly in Tasmania and Australia but occasionally in England, was chaotic, though he completed a year (1927–1928) at the University of Tasmania. Always restless, Flynn preceded his university year by working as a wharf laborer, a beach lifeguard, and a clothing model. At times living in a cave, he boxed in the New South Wales championships in 1928.

Before he arrived in Hollywood in 1934, the man later called a "prince of liars" by his biographers essayed many adventures whose only common threads were twin lifelong loves: danger and the sea. Between 1928 and 1931 Flynn was mostly in New Guinea, running a coastal sloop, mining for gold, and growing tobacco and coconuts. In 1930 he made a seven-month, 3,000-mile jaunt with friends on a boat named the *Sirocco*, and in 1931 he wrote about the trip for the Australian weekly *The Bulletin*. Much doubt clings to other claims—slave trading, a murder trial, abandonment of a sinking ship. Biographer Lionel Godfrey wrote that Flynn was "learning . . . how to bluff, how you could always make things look a little better than they were."

At loose ends in Australia in 1932, Flynn was hired by a motion picture company to take a camera crew up New Guinea's Sepik River, shooting background footage for jungle films. In 1933 Flynn was hired as Fletcher Christian in Charles and Elsa Chauvel's Australian film *In the Wake of the Bounty*. By the time

Bounty opened (Flynn's performance was called "convincing and natural"), Flynn had abandoned a fiancée and a job on a sheep ranch and was on his circuitous way to London.

Visiting Hong Kong (he later claimed falsely to have been a soldier of fortune there), Saigon, Colombo, India, French Somaliland, and Marseilles, Flynn arrived in London in July 1933, determined to become an actor. For Warner Bros. Britain, an affiliate taking advantage of a law requiring at least 30 percent of films shown in the United Kingdom to be British-made, Flynn appeared, dancing in a hotel crowd, in *I Adore You* (1933). Later in 1933 he had a nonspeaking role in a London theatrical version of George Kaufman and Moss Hart's *Once in a Lifetime*, and after the show's provincial tour, which included Northampton, he joined that town's repertory theater, probably at the suggestion of Warner Bros.

Between October 1933 and June 1934 Flynn appeared in twenty-two Northampton productions. In one local newspaper Flynn claimed to have starred in six Australian films. He told another paper of the voyage up the Sepik, complete with barking crocodiles, guzzling leeches, and quickly dispatched headhunters. Onstage Flynn was basically a gorgeous ornament, though he collected moderately good notices in doublet and hose for a Christmas pantomime and as a "splendid villain" in *A Doll's House*. He achieved one lead, in Frederick Lonsdale's *The Fake*, a play dealing with the morality of murder.

After three small roles at the Malvern Festival, Flynn signed a Warner Bros. contract and played the newspaperman lead in *Murder at Monte Carlo* (1935) before coming to the United States in November 1934. He played a murder victim in a Perry Mason mystery, *The Case of the Curious Bride*, and a supporting role in *Don't Bet on Blondes* (both 1935). In the same year he married actress Lili Damita. They had one son. The settlement for their 1942 divorce raged through the courts for fifteen years and cost Flynn more than $1 million. Flynn's next film, *Captain Blood* (1935), which came his way after Robert Donat was sidelined with asthma, made him a star, the leading swashbuckler of the golden era of sound motion pictures.

Flynn eventually made sixty motion pictures, but his fame rests on two handsful made between 1935 and 1942. In *Captain Blood*, the first of six costarring the "perfect lady" Olivia DeHavilland, he blossomed as an astonishing sex symbol with flowing locks, a pencil-slim mustache, and a gently laughing voice that seemed to confirm his claim of being born Irish. Godfrey commented, "His love scenes are among the most chastely poetic ever shot . . . more spiritual than sexy. . . . [He was] the true flower of chivalry." Athletic, impudent, and reckless, Flynn was a perfect pirate. During the pinched depression, Flynn became, in biographer Charles Higham's words, a "symbol for men of everything they longed to be and could not be."

During the filming of *The Charge of the Light Brigade* (1936), a highly fanciful expansion of Alfred Tennyson's poem, Flynn began his career as an accomplished barroom brawler. The film's success allowed Flynn to buy another *Sirocco*. In late 1936 Flynn made a controversial trip to the Spanish Civil War with a friend, Dr. Hermann Erben, subsequently identified as a member of the Nazi party. Flynn wrote entertainingly of the junket for the newspapers and magazines of William Randolph Hearst.

Flynn appeared in two sentimental dramas and a flimsy light comedy before making *The Adventures of Robin Hood* (1938). Flynn's unabashed insolence, unbridled self-confidence, and what Earl Conrad later called "congenital democracy" made him an ideal choice to rob the rich and give to the poor. A grinning romantic dream walking and leaping, he made the role his own, displacing its previous owner, the jolly, athletic Douglas Fairbanks, largely because Flynn seemed more dangerous, hence sexier. The film's archery and dueling scenes helped make it a classic.

Flynn's first novel, *Beam Ends*, a youthfully exuberant and picaresque fictionalization of the original *Sirocco*'s journey, was published in 1937. On the new *Sirocco*, Flynn made his first voyages to the Caribbean. His performances in the remake of the World War I flying saga *The Dawn Patrol* (1938) and *Dodge City* (1939), the first of many westerns, further enhanced Flynn's drawing power and salary.

"In those careless days he was fun to be with. . . . You always knew exactly where you stood with him because he *always* let you down," wrote actor David Niven of Flynn, who, still beautiful, continued his relentless pursuit of dangerous experience. Niven also recorded Flynn's belief that the most beautiful girls in Hollywood went to the local high school. Flynn later wrote of himself, "My job is to defy the normal."

Flynn's run of success continued with *The Private Lives of Elizabeth and Essex* (1939) and *The Sea Hawk* (1940), probably the screen's best sea-adventure film. At thirty-one he was making $6,000 weekly, fishing for marlin, hunting boar, and introducing, so Niven claimed, waterskiing to the United States. Flynn became an American citizen in 1942 but was deferred from military service because a physical examination revealed malaria, a heart murmur, gonorrhea, emphysema, and tuberculosis.

In *They Died with Their Boots On* (1942), his last film with DeHavilland, Flynn seemed perfectly cast as the impetuous George Armstrong Custer. *Gentleman Jim* (1942), a rollicking fictionalization of the life of heavyweight champion James J. Corbett and Flynn's personal favorite among his films, was released in the same year, a turning point in Flynn's life.

In 1942 Flynn was tried for statutory rape of two teenaged girls. Although he was acquitted and his box office appeal temporarily increased, to the public he became a symbol of voracious sexuality. Flynn dated his own decline from the trial. "In like Flynn" replaced "As brave as Errol Flynn" in American parlance. Unsuccessful paternity suits dogged him for the next ten years. In *Thank Your Lucky Stars* (1943), an all-star film completed as the trial began, Flynn gave a lighthearted performance as a pseudo-Cockney, singing and dancing "That's What You Jolly Well Get." In 1943 Flynn married Nora Eddington, who had been running a tobacco stand in the courthouse where the rape trial was held. They had a son and a daughter. They were divorced in 1949.

Though Flynn was a noncombatant, during World War II he made one heroic battle film after another. There were later accusations of pro-Axis activity, even involving *Dive Bomber* (1941), shot on location at a naval base. British director Victor Savile described the 1942 Spencer Tracy film *Keeper of the Flame* as being about "someone like Errol—a national hero, the idol of boys' clubs, a Fascist." *Objective, Burma!* (1945), which Flynn called one of the rare films of which he was proud, was particularly offensive in Great Britain, as it seemed to suggest that Americans had liberated the former colony all by themselves.

In 1946 Flynn sold the *Sirocco* and bought the *Zaca*. His novel *Showdown*, another tale of the Sepik River adventure called by a reviewer a "parable of sacred and profane love," failed to sell. Flynn's 1936 script "The White Rajah" remained unproduced, as did another, "Jupiter Laughs," despite Flynn's willingness to produce it himself. Flynn never made another important or particularly popular film for Warner Bros., though *The Adventures of Don Juan* (1949) seemed to indicate a future in self-mockery. Warners released two home-made Flynn documentaries, *Deep Sea Fishing* and *The Cruise of the Zaca* (both 1952). In 1950 Flynn married costar Patrice Wymore (*Rocky Mountain* [1950]). They had one daughter. Wymore persuaded him to buy land in Jamaica, where he eventually owned a hotel and a copra plantation. On loan to Metro-Goldwyn-Mayer in 1951, Flynn briefly revived his career as Mahbub Ali, the Red Beard, in *Kim*, an adventurous tale based on one of Rudyard Kipling's Indian stories. On a visit to Northampton, England, he called his repertory years "the happiest days of my life."

Beset by legal costs and deteriorating health, Flynn suffered further financial reverse in 1953 when *William Tell*, intended as the second Cinemascope film, collapsed, taking his investment with it. Process servers cleaned out his Hollywood home. He lost the home itself in the final settlement of his divorce from his first wife. The U.S. government pursued him for nearly $1 million in back taxes, and he moved to Port Antonio, Jamaica. Flynn returned to England, making several films for producer Herbert Wilcox, including *Lilacs in the Spring* (1955), in which he sang and danced "Lily of Laguna" with Anna Neagle.

After further second-rate films, Flynn was cast as the drunken Mike Campbell, his savage despair lurking beneath a sophisticated surface, in *The Sun Also Rises*, a 1957 dramatization of Ernest Hemingway's novel of the Lost Generation. He repeated the characterization playing John Barrymore in *Too Much, Too Soon* (1958), then varied it slightly as a broken ex-army officer in *The Roots of Heaven* (1959). Flynn's only venture onto the American stage, *The Master of Thornfeld Hall*, Huntington Hartford's adaptation of *Jane Eyre*, did not survive Detroit. Fascinated by rev-olutionary Fidel Castro, Flynn traveled to Cuba for his freakish last film, *Cuban Rebel Girls* (1959), costarring his new "small companion," Beverly Aadland. In 1959 Flynn played a traveling peddler in a story on the anthology show "Goodyear Television Playhouse."

In 1956 Flynn had begun an autobiography; in 1958 his publisher sent Earl Conrad to Jamaica to collaborate. In Flynn's diaries Conrad found essays on faith and the meaning of life. Conrad found Flynn, suffering drug withdrawal pains, still risking, "living at the edge of life or death from instant to instant." *My Wicked, Wicked Ways*, later called Flynn's best work of fiction, was published in 1959. Suffering from cancer, Flynn had a heart attack in July 1959. He died in Vancouver, British Columbia, where he had gone to sell the *Zaca*.

• Aside from Flynn's own works, the following biographies, pamphlets, and memoirs are entertaining, if often contradictory: Nora Eddington, *Errol and Me* (1960); Florence Aadland, *The Big Love* (1961); Tony Thomas et al., *The Films of Errol Flynn* (1969); John Hammond Moore, *The Young Errol* (1975); David Niven, *Bring on the Empty Horses* (1975); Lionel Godfrey, *The Life and Crimes of Errol Flynn* (1977); Earl Conrad, *Errol Flynn: A Memoir* (1979); Charles Higham, *Errol Flynn: The Untold Story* (1980); and Gerry Connelly, *Errol Flynn in Northampton* (1995).

JAMES ROSS MOORE

FLYNT, Henry (5 May 1675–13 Feb. 1760), Harvard College tutor, was born in Dorchester, Massachusetts, the son of Josiah Flynt, the minister at Dorchester, and Esther Willet. He received his A.B. from Harvard College in 1693 and his M.A. in 1695. On receiving the latter degree he defended (prophetically it turned out) the lawfulness of receiving interest on loans. Four years later, after several unsuccessful attempts to secure a pulpit, he was appointed tutor at Harvard, a post previously held by recent graduates for a few years until securing a pastorate. Flynt was the first of the college's career tutors. He began with freshmen and moved up with them until graduation, teaching every subject (except divinity) in the curriculum, namely, Latin, Greek, Hebrew, logic, rhetoric, physics, ethics, metaphysics, geography, arithmetic, geometry, and astronomy. In 1722 a Hebrew instructor took charge of that subject as did a professor of science and mathematics for those subjects in 1727. From the almost 300 boys who spent most of their college days under Flynt's tutelage came two college presidents, two chief justices, fourteen councilors, thirty-four members of a lower house, and 107 ministers.

A lifelong bachelor, Flynt resided at Harvard and served as fellow of the corporation from 1700 until his death and as clerk of the overseers, a second governing body composed of councilors and ministers, from 1712 until 1758. He was the slowest speaking Harvard alumnus and clergyman Senator Paine Wingate of New Hampshire had ever heard, one who "hardly kept connected in his discourse so as to make progress." However, Wingate conceded that Flynt "made some amends for this defect by the weight and pertinency of his ideas." His numerous extant sermons make dull reading. They harp endlessly on man's duty to God and on the unreasonableness of sin, as if man could assure his own salvation simply by thinking things through before acting. As a tutor he saw himself as a minister of sorts and interested himself in the spiritual state of his charges, with most of whom he got along famously. He welcomed the Great Awakening, though with reservations, when it reached New England in the person of George Whitefield in September 1740 but quickly turned against it and signed the *Testimony* of the Harvard faculty against Whitefield in 1744.

Flynt counseled students who had become concerned about their salvation to avoid abstruse questions about human freedom and divine predestination. He thus revealed himself a thoroughgoing Old Light, detesting the New Lights for their extemporaneous preaching, shallow enthusiasm, and the divisions they had introduced into the churches of New England by claiming to know who was and who was not converted. He was also stung by Whitefield's published criticism of Harvard as a hotbed of religious indifferentism. Flynt was an admirer of John Tillotson, the tolerant (at least of all Protestants) archbishop of Canterbury, and was attracted by a low-church Anglicanism that espoused episcopacy but in other matters played down differences between dissenters and churchmen. A regular London correspondent was his cousin, Noah Newman, secretary of the Society for Promoting Christian Knowledge, the propaganda arm of the Church of England. Like many Harvard-trained eighteenth-century divines, Newman subscribed to Arminianism, which rejected John Calvin's supposedly harsh decrees of divine election and damnation and conceded to man a major role in working out his own salvation. It was commonly believed that Whitefield, in a company where Flynt was present, said that Tillotson was in hell for his heresy, to which Flynt replied, "It is my opinion that you will not meet him there." For put-downs like this Flynt became celebrated throughout New England.

"Father Flynt" cut a highly gregarious figure in provincial society, possessed as he was of an extensive and distinguished family network reinforced by numerous alumni. On his many summer trips he usually stayed over at night at the parsonages of former students. He mixed easily with royal governors and councilors as well as with those of lesser station, turned down an invitation to become president of Yale, claimed the rank of esquire, boasted of ancestral acres in Derbyshire, and saw himself as "a person of some interest [i.e., influence] in the province." He often visited Boston, and in Braintree in a two-story addition to the mansion of his brother-in-law, Edmund Quincy, he had a permanent home away from Harvard known as "Flynt's Study," still standing today with his portrait over the fireplace. He engaged in a vigorous and time-consuming campaign to supplement his regular salary by renting his farms in Grafton, Maine, and in western Massachusetts. He also lent large sums of money at interest, speculated in land, bought and sold imported goods, hoarded silver as a hedge against inflation, invested heavily in province bonds, and kept a meticulous record of his financial transactions.

With time, Flynt acquired the reputation of a character, and his harmless parsimony along with his put-downs became legendary. A contemporary, the stolid Charles Chauncy, pastor of the First Church, Boston, wrote that Flynt "was not contemptible for his learning; he might have excelled in it, considering his advantages, had he not been of an indolent temper to a great degree." He was content with his "Spher[e] and place" and wished only "to continue yet in my calling and abide therein." Actually, he had stayed on at Harvard too long. The inventory of his library was eighteen pages long and contained 572 titles, about 70 percent of which dated from the seventeenth century. He did not keep abreast of intellectual trends, especially in science, and apparently was unacquainted with the great men of English letters, such as Shakespeare, Milton, Dryden, Pope, Addison, or Steele. For light reading he turned to travel accounts and history from a Protestant perspective. He died and was buried in Cambridge. His pastor, Nathaniel Appleton, remarked in his funeral oration on Flynt that "any Foibles and Failings that were observable were owing in a great Measure to that single State in which he lived all his Days; which naturally begets in Man a Contractedness, with respect to their own private and personal Concern, and yet his Heart and Hands have often times opened in Acts of Piety and Charity to the Poor." On his retirement, the Harvard Corporation limited the term of his successor to three years.

• Two volumes of Flynt's diary are extant and contain financial accounts, reading notes, and pious reflections; vol. 1 (1712–1724) is at the Massachusetts Historical Society, and vol. 2 (1724–1727) is at the Houghton Library, Harvard. Also at Harvard are two copies of his manuscript textbook, "A Catechism Geographical, Historical and Chronological." Most of his correspondence and forty-one manuscript sermons are at the Massachusetts Historical Society. Flynt's published works are *The Doctrine of the Last Judgment* (1714); *An Appeal to the Consciences of a Degenerate People* (1729); *A Caution to Sinners* (1736); *Oratio Funebris in Obitum Reverendi Domini Benjaminis Wadsworth* (1737); *Twenty Sermons on Various Subjects* (1739); with others, *The Testimony of the President, Professors, Tutors, and Hebrew Instructor of Harvard College . . . against the Reverend Mr. George Whitefield* (1744); and the preface to Nathaniel Appleton, *Righteousness and Uprightness Recommended* (1728). Clifford K. Shipton, "Henry Flynt," in *Sibley's Harvard Graduates*, vol. 4 (1933), pp. 162–67, is a brief sketch. See also Edward T. Dunn, "Tutor Henry Flynt of Harvard College" (Ph.D. diss., Univ. of Rochester, 1968) and, also by Dunn, "The Diary of Henry Flynt of Harvard College, 1675–1760," three manuscript volumes in which the entire diary, Flynt's papers, and, in chronological order, all contemporary references to him are reproduced. These volumes are at the Canisius College Library, Buffalo, N.Y.

EDWARD T. DUNN

FODOR, Eugene (14 Oct. 1905–18 Feb. 1991), writer and publisher, was born in Leva, Hungary (now part of Slovakia), the son of Matthew Gyula Fodor, a businessman, and Malvine Kurti. After he received his primary education in Leva, Eugene Fodor earned a baccalaureate degree in 1924 from a school in Lucenec, Czechoslovakia, before attending the Sorbonne and the University of Grenoble in France. At Grenoble, he majored in political economics, graduating in 1927. He did postgraduate work at the University of Hamburg, Germany, but did not receive an advanced degree. After studying at Hamburg, Fodor took a job with a French shipping line, working as a shipboard interpreter. A lover of travel who spoke five languages, his new position seemed ideal. He traveled all over Europe and polished his language skills as well. Soon, he was writing articles about life aboard ship and his visits to interesting ports of call for an in-house magazine published by the company. He sold articles about exotic places to newspapers in Hungary and France, and from 1930 to 1933 he also served as travel correspondent for the *Prague Hungarian Journal*.

The year 1934 found Fodor in England, working for London's Aldor Publishing Company. He soon convinced company executives to publish a new kind of guidebook to foreign places; he would, he said, include the "human element" that was so glaringly absent from other travelogues of the day. He also used an upbeat, popular writing style.

Fodor's first effort was a guidebook for the European Continent, which was only modestly successful. However, when it was released in the United States in 1938, his book became a bestseller. By then Fodor had joined Britain's *Query* magazine as foreign editor, while still holding his position at Aldor. That same year he was in America on business when word came that Nazi Germany had annexed the Sudetenland in Czechoslovakia. Like many other people, Fodor recognized that European war was imminent; therefore, he remained in the United States. From 1939 to 1942 he served as an editor for Hyperion Press in New York. He joined the U.S. Army in 1942 and worked in its intelligence branch until 1947, when he ended his military career. Leaving with the rank of captain, he had earned six battle stars and other decorations. He married Vlasta Zobel the next year. The couple had one child.

By 1949 Fodor was associated with the David McKay Company, which began publishing the soon-to-be-famous Fodor guides for individual countries worldwide. Fodor returned to Paris to set up his headquarters; his first three guides, published in 1951, covered France, Switzerland, and Italy. All three were well received by consumers, and all three made a good profit. A fourth guide the same year proved impolitic: he published a travel book that combined Britain and Ireland. After hearing much from the dissatisfied Irish, he released new editions that treated the two countries separately. Eventually, Fodor had separate guides in print covering a score of countries, with more offerings appearing periodically. The public ap-

preciated his travelogues for sundry reasons, including their inexpensive price, their readability, and their thoroughness.

By 1964 Fodor was back in the United States, working out of his new home in Litchfield, Connecticut. That year he began writing guides about America itself. He held that the United States was much misunderstood by international tourists, who simply had too many misconceptions about the country and its people. Fodor hoped to correct such misunderstandings and also to promote the United States.

In his later years Fodor could not escape controversy. During the Watergate scandal of the early 1970s, he became the subject of ugly rumors and rather confused speculation. During the Watergate hearings, E. Howard Hunt alleged that Fodor was involved with the Central Intelligence Agency. Hunt charged that Fodor had been an agent for the CIA who had used his connections to "cover" other operating agents around the world (especially in Europe). Hunt testified that Fodor hired many CIA agents as researchers for his travel guides, thus allowing them to roam the world without attracting undue negative notice. Distraught, Fodor strongly denied the allegations verbally and in print. Hunt's charges were never proven, and Fodor's international reputation remained intact.

In his long career Fodor received many honors, especially from the travel industry. He won the Grand Prix de Littérature de Tourisme in Paris in 1959. Other awards came from the Caribbean Travel Association (1960); the Hong Kong Travel Association (1960); the Pacific Area Travel Association (1960–1962); and the British Tourist Authority (1972). He won the International Travel Book Contest in 1969. The Austrian government gave him a silver medal in 1970. He was inducted into the Travel Hall of Fame in 1978. Yet other awards came by the dozens, and he was still the recognized king of travel writers when he died in Torrington, Connecticut.

Fodor will be long remembered for his superior guidebooks and for his contribution to the growing awareness of the great diversity among all of the world's different nations.

• Little has been written on Fodor. Nevertheless, magazine articles include Amy Bernstein, "Epitaph: Fodor," *U.S. News and World Report*, 4 Mar. 1991, p. 20; and Michael Shnayerson, "America's Pathfinder," *Conde Nast's Traveler*, June 1989, pp. 74–80. Obituaries are in the *New York Times*, 19 Feb. 1991, and the *Los Angeles Times*, 20 Feb. 1991.

JAMES M. SMALLWOOD

FOERSTER, Norman (14 Apr. 1887–1 Aug. 1972), professor of literature and literary critic, was born in Pittsburgh, Pennsylvania, the son of Adolph Martin Foerster, a composer and musician, and Henrietta Reineman. Foerster graduated from Harvard College in 1910 and received an A.M. degree from the University of Wisconsin in 1912. In 1911 he married Dorothy Haskell, with whom he had two children. After teaching English at the University of Wisconsin (1911–1914) and the University of North Carolina (1914–

1930), he served as the first director of the School of Letters at the University of Iowa (1930–1944). He later taught at Duke University (1948–1951), and he held offices in the Modern Language Association and the College English Association.

Foerster's work was shaped by New Humanism (or Neohumanism), an informal movement growing from the ideas of Irving Babbitt and Paul Elmer More. New Humanism, and Foerster, promoted the restoration of classical ideals in American literature, criticism, education, and life. This school of thought stressed a philosophical dualism that disjoined man and nature and saw them as two discrete realms, two selves; and it opposed (in Foerster's word) "naturalism": Romanticism, realism, naturalism, humanitarianism, and other movements old and new that confused the human experience with the natural. Foerster presented these ideas most sharply in *Toward Standards: A Study of the Present Critical Movement in American Letters* (1930). In 1930 he edited a manifesto by various hands entitled *Humanism and America: Essays on the Outlook of Modern Civilization*. This book—and a rejoinder volume edited by C. Hartley Grattan, *The Critique of Humanism* (1930)—helped provoke public intellectual controversy about New Humanism (more than one hundred articles in 1930–1932), after which the movement waned.

Of more lasting influence was Foerster's service to American literature. At a time when that literature was scorned in many universities, Foerster argued that it was as worthy of serious study and rigorous critical judgment as English and European literature. Such attention, he insisted, was essential to move American literature, past and future, beyond provinciality, and the best form of attention would be criticism. *American Criticism: A Study in Literary Theory from Poe to the Present* (1928) proposed an American critical heritage, following New Humanist principles, that would provoke a more vital American criticism and, thus, a greater American literature. "In a word," Foerster argued, "America has no native tradition guiding her art and her criticism—no national background of ideas offering firm support to those who would rest upon the past, of firm resistance to those who would revolt. If our critics wish to be American, they must deploy in a vacuum." More mundane but probably more influential were Foerster's numerous classroom anthologies that stressed American writing. His *American Poetry and Prose* (1925) was, arguably, the first respectable classroom anthology of American literature; with revisions, it remained in print more than six decades. Among other labors, Foerster helped found the American Literature group of the Modern Language Association.

An outspoken critic of American higher education, Foerster in his later writings assailed it comprehensively as naturistic: vocational and materialist, shallow yet narrow, specialized yet superficial. It had, he insisted, betrayed its mission to create sound individuals who could guide a democracy and was largely responsible for the ills of the nation. Foerster's remedy emphasized the full development of the individual's humanity, using the liberal arts as the best vehicle to this end, in a largely common curriculum focusing on the great books. The key would be teachers devoted to teaching and the humanist ideal rather than to research and careers (some antihumanist teachers would be included for balance). College education would be absolutely free to qualified needy students. Foerster acknowledged that he had no ready scheme by which to reform the administrations and boards of trustees that would implement these proposals.

As director of the School of Letters at the University of Iowa, Foerster attempted with mixed success to implement his schemes for liberal education. The experiment ended when he resigned his directorship in the face of administrative opposition. He retired soon thereafter. Among the lasting contributions from his era at Iowa were the awarding of the doctorate for creative writing dissertations, the founding of the famed Writers' Workshop, and the recruitment of faculty members who made the University of Iowa a distinguished center of literary studies. He died in San Mateo County, California.

• The major collections of Foerster's papers are at the University of Iowa and Stanford University. Major works by Foerster other than those mentioned in the text include *Nature in American Literature: Studies in the Modern View of Nature* (1923), *The American Scholar: A Study in Litterae Inhumaniores* (1929), *The American State University: Its Relation to Democracy* (1937), *The Future of the Liberal College* (1938), *The Humanities and the Common Man: The Democratic Role of the State Universities* (1946), and "The Esthetic Judgment and the Ethical Judgment," in *The Intent of the Critic*, ed. Donald A. Stauffer (1941). There is no biography, but biographical details are in Mary Francis Flanagan, "The Educational Role of Norman Foerster" (Ed.D. diss., Univ. of Iowa, 1972), which is also the best study of Foerster's years at Iowa. The only modern study of Foerster's humanism is Gilbert Bruce Kelly, "Norman Foerster and American New Humanist Criticism" (Ph.D. diss., Univ. of Nebraska, 1982). The best study of New Humanism is J. David Hoeveler, Jr., *The New Humanism: A Critique of Modern America* (1977); useful also are Richard Ruland, *The Rediscovery of American Literature: Premises of Critical Taste, 1900–1940* (1967); John Stephen Lambert, "The Humanist Movement in American Criticism" (Ph.D. diss., Stanford Univ., 1967); and Glenn Sherman Weight, "The Humanist Controversy in American Literature, 1900–1932" (Ph.D. diss., Pennsylvania State Univ., 1956). An obituary by Robert Falk and Robert E. Lee, "In Memoriam: Norman Foerster[:] 1887–1972," is in *American Literature* 44 (1972–1973): 679–80.

GILBERT B. KELLY

FOGERTY, Tom (9 Nov. 1941–6 Sept. 1990), recording artist and songwriter, was born Thomas Richard Fogerty in Berkeley, California, the son of Galen Robert Fogerty and Edith Lucile Lytle Loosli. He attended high school in El Cerrito and by 1959 was performing in school shows and at parties as lead singer and songwriter for Tommy Fogerty and the Blue Velvets. The band included Doug Clifford on drums, Stuart Cook on bass guitar, and Fogerty's younger brother John, with whom he shared writing credits and lead vocals.

The band continued to play for local parties and fraternities, changing their name a number of times until 1963, when Fogerty's job as a packing and shipping clerk at Fantasy Records led to an audition for the band. Though the band emphasized its instrumentals, Fantasy signed them for their British-rock sound that echoed the Beatles. As a precondition to signing, Fantasy changed the band's name to the Golliwogs. The Golliwogs released a series of singles that were influenced by U.K. sensations the Beatles, the Rolling Stones, and the Kinks. Notable singles include "Don't Tell Me No Lies," "Where You Been," "You Can't Be True," "Fight Fire," and "Walking on the Water." "Brown Eyed Girl" was their biggest hit, selling more than 10,000 copies in 1965. Tom Fogerty dominated the group until 1965, after which his brother John took over the vocals and, ultimately, control of the band. A decade later in 1975, a compilation of Golliwog A and B sides was released.

Tom Fogerty achieved his greatest success as cofounder and rhythm guitarist for the San Francisco musical group Creedence Clearwater Revival (CCR). After drummer Doug Clifford and John Fogerty returned from army service in 1966, the band formed and recorded "Porterville," the first product of a new and distinct sound influenced by R&B artists, Delta bluesmen Howlin' Wolf and Muddy Waters, and early rock artists Elvis Presley, Jerry Lee Lewis, Carl Perkins and Chuck Berry. Fogerty was singer, songwriter, and rhythm guitarist, while John directed the band as songwriter and lead vocalist. Fantasy's new owner Saul Zaentz launched the group on the main label in 1968. The band became known for combining "political issues with rockabilly tunes" that featured hard guitar licks and John Fogerty's gruff vocals. Rather than promote antisocial behavior and exploit sex and drugs, the band advocated community and preferred a southern R&B sound to the experimental instrumentals of psychedelic music. Also unlike the rock bands of the time, Creedence members protected their privacy rather than engaging in behavior designed to gain attention or shock audiences.

Creedence was often erroneously considered a product of the bayou region because of their Louisiana sound and references to bayou dances, riverboats, and swamps in cover versions of Dale Hawkins's "Suzie Q," Screamin' Jay Hawkins's "I Put a Spell on You," and in John Fogerty originals, such as "Born on the Bayou." Their first album, *Creedence Clearwater Revival*, earned the band a gold record, and the single "Suzie Q" reached number twenty-two on *Billboard*'s Top 40 charts. Success brought them major venues, including Bill Graham's Fillmore West in San Francisco in 1968 and Woodstock in 1969. In 1969 and 1970 the band had ten songs on *Billboard*'s Top 40 chart: "Proud Mary," "Bad Moon Rising," "Green River," "Commotion," "Down on the Corner," "Fortunate Son," "Travelin' Band," "Who'll Stop the Rain," "Up around the Bend," and "Lookin' out My Back Door." The group's second album, *Bayou Country*, and the single "Proud Mary" became hits worldwide and earned Creedence another gold record. Two more gold records followed the same year, for *Green River* (1969) and *Willy and the Poorboys* (1969), each releasing two-sided hit singles. The band hit their peak with their fifth album, *Cosmo's Factory* (1970), selling more than 3 million copies.

Criticism of the music as one-dimensional led John Fogerty to experiment with the next album, *Pendulum*, recorded in 1970. The group changed the style of their music by using more keyboards, saxophone, and bass. The album was a hit, earning the band top album artists of the year for 1970 and the choice of England's *New Musical Express* as top international pop group. The change in style and John's increasing control led to Tom Fogerty's resignation from the band in 1971 to begin a solo career. Fogerty recorded five albums for Fantasy Records from 1972 to 1981: *Tom Fogerty* (1972), *Excalibur* (1973), *Zephyr National* (1974), *Myopia* (1975), and *Deal It Out* (1981). The Grateful Dead's Jerry Garcia contributed as lead guitar on *Excalibur*, while *Zephyr National* features all former Creedence musicians, including John Fogerty on guitar. Fogerty joined Merl Saunders, Jerry Garcia, and other musicians to produce the live album *Merl Saunders and Friends* between 1972 and 1973. In the late 1970s he launched his own band, Ruby, recording the albums *Ruby* in 1977 and *Rock and Roll Madness* in 1978. His last album, *Rainbow Carousel*, a collaboration with Randy Oda, has not been released.

Fogerty's marriage to Gail Skinner ended in divorce in 1977. They had four children. In 1980 Fogerty married Tricia Suzanne Clapper; they had two children. In the mid-1980s Fogerty moved to Scottsdale, Arizona, where he ran Wild Cherry Music from 1986 to 1990. Royalties from Creedence records supported him when his solo career failed. The four original members of Creedence took to the stage in 1980 for Fogerty's second wedding and for a final time at a school reunion three years later.

Creedence Clearwater Revival recorded eight Top 10 singles and six gold albums. The group sold more than 100 million records worldwide and by the late 1990s continued to sell approximately 2 million tapes and compact discs a year. CCR songs have been included on many hit movie soundtracks, including *The Big Chill* (1983) and *Forrest Gump* (1994). For its contribution to classic rock and roll, Creedence was inducted into the Rock 'n' Roll Hall of Fame in Cleveland, Ohio. In May 1997 *Rolling Stone* magazine chose Creedence's third album, *Willy and the Poor Boys*, as one of the 200 best albums ever made. Fogerty died at home in Scottsdale, Arizona, of respiratory failure due to tuberculosis.

• For a popular history of Creedence Clearwater Revival, see John Hallowell, *Inside Creedence* (1971). For details on Creedence Clearwater Revival following the band's breakup, see R. Gleason, "John Fogerty," in *The "Rolling Stone" Interviews* (1971), and Robert Christgau, "Creedence: Where Do You Go from the Top?" and "Whatever Happened to Creedence Clearwater Revival?" in *Any Old Way You Choose It: Rock and Other Pop Music, 1967–1973* (1973). A tribute to

Creedence's *Willy and the Poor Boys* appears in *Rolling Stone*, 15 May 1997, p. 57. An obituary is in *Rolling Stone*, 1 Nov. 1990, and the *New York Times*, 15 Sept. 1990.

BARBARA L. CICCARELLI

FOKINE, Michel (23 Apr. 1880–22 Aug. 1942), ballet dancer and choreographer, was born Mikhail Mikhailovich Fokin in Saint Petersburg, Russia, the son of a well-to-do businessman whose name is unknown and a German-born woman whose maiden name was Kind. Fokine was the youngest of five children, all of whom were exposed to the arts at an early age. He entered the ballet division of the Imperial Theater School in Saint Petersburg in 1889 and took first prize when he graduated in 1898, after studying with Platon Karsavin, Nikolai Volkov, Pavel Gerdt, and Nikolai Legat. He was immediately accepted into the ballet company at the Maryinsky Theater, at a salary and level considerably above that of the corps de ballet. In 1902 he was appointed an instructor in the girls' department of the Imperial Theater School, the youngest dancer ever asked to be on the faculty. He eventually taught the older girls and in 1908 began teaching the boys. In 1905 he married Vera Petrovna Antonova, a former pupil; they had one child.

Had he never choreographed or performed, Michel Fokine would still be remembered for his ideas for a "new ballet," which affected not only his own creations but also those of so many who followed him. He felt it was wrong that in a Greek ballet the costumes consisted of tutus, with, perhaps, a Greek key design on the skirt, or that in the middle of an Indian love story the male dancer performed bravura feats unrelated to the plot. His ideas were originally expressed in 1904 as part of a scenario submitted to the directorate of the Imperial Theater and were first published in the *Times* of London in 1914. His five basic principles of reform put ballet in the vanguard of changes occurring in twentieth-century theater by making it an expressive art that would mirror life. He felt that the technique of the ballet classroom was for training only, and that these steps need not appear on stage but should be replaced by those appropriate to the time, place, and theme of the work. Dramatic action should unfold in terms of movement. Sign language should be abandoned and the entire body made expressive. The corps de ballet should express the theme and not be merely decorative. Finally, music, decor, and dance should be unified around the theme. Although these ideas had been stated earlier in dance history, his reemphasis of them and the fact that his works illustrated them strongly affected dance and theater in the Western world.

Fokine started choreographing because he had to stage ballets for his senior students' graduation performances. As his work and ideas began to be known, he was asked by the dancers of the Imperial Theater to create pieces for them for charity performances outside the bureaucracy of the institution. (*The Dying Swan* for Anna Pavlova was one of these.) In 1907 he was asked to restage one of these works, *Le Pavillon d'Armide*, for the Maryinsky. Through this work he met Alexandre Benois, who introduced him to the *World of Art* clique, a group of men whose aim was to bring Western art into Russia and to introduce Russian art to the Western world, and who fervently believed in a unity of the arts. They met frequently and published a magazine called the *World of Art*, which familiarized the Russian avant-garde with the new ideas of the rest of the world. Among their members was Serge Diaghilev. When Benois persuaded Diaghilev to take Russian ballet to France (he had previously presented painting and opera), he also suggested that Michel Fokine would be the perfect collaborator.

When the Ballets Russes opened in Paris in May 1909, they presented four Fokine works: *Le Pavillon d'Armide*, the *Polovtsian Dances* from the opera *Prince Igor*, *Cléopâtre*, and *Les Sylphides*. The dance world and the art world were never the same again. Fokine remained with the company until 1912, when he left after an argument with Diaghilev, who Fokine felt was ignoring him in favor of Vaslav Nijinsky, and returned again for one season in 1914. The Ballets Russes presented seventeen works created by Fokine during this period and continued to present them until its demise in 1929, after which they were performed by ballet companies around the world. Among the many diverse individuals who have written about this influential artistic endeavor, all agree that without Michel Fokine's presence during its formative seasons there would have been no Ballets Russes. It was a partnership that matched a rebellious traditionalist with a group of creative dreamers, giving him an outlet for his creativity and allowing them to see the fruition of their ideas.

Les Sylphides, to music of Chopin, was the first abstract ballet of the twentieth century, with its single male in black velvet and sixteen females in ankle-length Romantic tutus. The constant, flowing movements through which the dancers enter, exit, and perform solos and duets give a seamless illusion of lightness and flight. For the first time a man danced alongside a woman as an equal, and the corps was integrated with the soloists. Fokine felt it was the perfect expression of his ideas. The *Polovtsian Dances* were also plotless and depicted the members of a primitive nomadic tribe in impetuous, ecstatic dances that were voluptuous for the women and swiftly hurtling airborne feats for the men.

In 1910 the company presented three new Fokine ballets. *Schéhérazade*, the story of the Shah's favorite wife who frees her lover, the Golden Slave, when she mistakenly thinks her husband has left, was an oriental spectacle to Rimsky-Korsakov's music, with lush decor by Léon Bakst, that catapulted Fokine to international fame. Its orgy and violent scene of slaughter portrayed uninhibited passion entirely through movement and positions of the body, marking the first application of these particular principles of Fokine. *Le Carnaval*, a gay *commedia dell'arte* work to Schumann's music, and *The Firebird*, the retelling of a Russian folktale to Stravinsky's first commissioned score, also were seen.

Le Spectre de la Rose, a short, ethereal pas de deux about a young girl's dream of the spirit of a rose she carries from her first ball, and *Petrouchka* were presented the following year. The idea for *Petrouchka*—the Russian Pierrot—came from its composer, Stravinsky, and in its final form it is often considered the supreme example of storytelling in ballet. Set in a large square during the Russian version of Mardi Gras, it contains dozens of diverse characters, centering on the tragicomic puppet with the human heart and soul who loves, is mocked, and finally killed. Fokine treated each character and vignette separately, with intellect and logic, as did the music. In its realization of discord and defeat and its sensitivity to the psychology of the individual, this ballet, which utilized all of Fokine's theories, truly belongs to the twentieth century.

Many mistakenly believe that Fokine's career effectively ended when he left the Ballets Russes. Although he never again worked in such an artistically exciting milieu or at such a highly productive pitch, he choreographed many more ballets during his lifetime, worked for several different companies, and continued to teach. After leaving Diaghilev, he returned to Russia briefly. Uneasy about living in the midst of a civil war, he left for Sweden, spent time in Denmark, and in November 1919 arrived in the United States to stage the ballets in the Broadway musical *Aphrodite*, produced by Morris Gest. In this and in *Mecca*, another oriental extravaganza produced by Gest, Fokine created many dances, including the inevitable bacchanale. By the time he settled permanently in New York in 1921, he had worked on three other Broadway musicals and had performed in the Metropolitan Opera House and on tour. He later was involved with three additional musicals, created works for various charity performances and individuals, and choreographed incidental dances for five dramas as well as for summer productions at Randalls Island and Jones Beach.

Fokine opened his first studio to teach ballet in New York in 1921, and in 1923 he rented a large house on Riverside Drive, which was his home and studio for fifteen years. His students included Patricia Bowman, Annabelle Lyon, John Taras, Paul Haakon, Nora Kaye, and others. Using many of his students as a nucleus, he formed a small classical company, the Fokine American Ballet, which first performed in 1924 at the Metropolitan Opera House. This group made sporadic appearances until 1938, including American tours under Sol Hurok and performances at Lewisohn Stadium in New York. The dancers also appeared on the movie house circuit, performing during intervals between films. At one point he moved to Hollywood, having been promised a rich and lucrative career, but the venture never materialized.

Fokine made frequent trips to Europe to perform, choreograph, and set works, and in the thirties, disillusioned with the United States, he began to direct his energies outside the country. In 1936 he joined René Blum's Ballets de Monte-Carlo. During the two seasons of this company's existence he created three new ballets: *L'Épreuve d'Amour*, *Don Juan*, and *Les Éléments*. He then went to work for Colonel Wassily de Basil's Ballet Russe, where he restaged many of his old ballets and created three more new works.

Fokine was the first choreographer signed by Ballet Theatre, and when this American company opened in New York in 1940 *Les Sylphides* began the program. He also restaged many works for them and created two new ones, *Bluebeard*, a satire that was a box-office hit, and *The Russian Soldier*. He had finished a rough version of *Helen of Troy* but died in New York City before he could polish and revise it. American Ballet Theatre still performs many of his dances.

Michel Fokine earned the title "The Father of Modern Ballet" owing to his principles of reform, which changed nineteenth-century ballet into a twentieth-century art. Nonetheless he did not consider himself avant-garde, and in many respects he was really an evolutionary who wished to change the artistic use of classical ballet, rather than a revolutionary who wished to overthrow it. Basically he was intent on pursuing his own beliefs and ideals. The early years of the Ballets Russes, sustained and dominated by such varied works as *Les Sylphides*, *Petrouchka*, *Le Spectre de la Rose*, *Firebird*, and *Schéhérazade*, gave to all the artists who saw them a renewed desire to pursue their own creations. Many of the most notable dance personalities in the United States, including George Balanchine, Jerome Robbins, William Dollar, Nora Kaye, and Pauline Koner, studied with or danced under Fokine. Through his stylistic and choreographic influence on them, and through the Fokine ballets presented to the American public by Ballet Theatre and the Ballet Russe de Monte Carlo, Fokine played a large role in shaping dance in this country. In addition, he left the world some remarkable ballets.

• The Dance Collection of the New York Public Library for the Performing Arts at Lincoln Center has clipping and program files for Fokine as well as for his many ballets and the Diaghilev Ballets Russes; the library also holds many articles written by him. Cyril Beaumont, *Michel Fokine and His Ballets* (1935) and *Supplement to the Complete Book of Ballets* (1942), give excellent descriptions of the actual ballets. Fokine's *Memoirs of a Ballet Master*, translated by his son Vitale Fokine and edited by Anatole Chujoy, was published posthumously (1961) and must be read with care, as it was incomplete at the time of his death. The Russian version, *Protiv Techeniia* (Against the Tide [1962]), was edited by Yuri Slonimsky and contains material the English version does not. Lincoln Kirstein, *Fokine* (1934), is a concise statement of his contributions; Lynn Garafola, *Diaghilev's Ballets Russes* (1989), presents some different and interesting interpretations; and Dawn Lille Horwitz, *Michel Fokine* (1985), covers the American years in great detail.

DAWN LILLE HORWITZ

FOLEY, Martha (21 Mar. 1897–5 Sept. 1977), editor and writer, was born in Boston, Massachusetts, the daughter of Irish-American parents, Walter Foley, a physician, and Millicent McCarty, a schoolteacher who had also written a novel and a book of verse.

When both of her parents fell ill, Foley was sent with her half-brother to stay with a family who, she later wrote, "either did not like or did not understand children." It was a harsh and brutal period in her life, mitigated only, she recalled, by the fact that her parents' library went with her. "Those books became home to me," she wrote, "the only home I was to know for a long time."

She attended Boston Girls' Latin School, where, at the age of eleven, she published her first story in the school magazine. She went on to Boston University in 1915 but left after two years and never received a college degree, though she later taught at many colleges, including Columbia University, New York University, Emory University, and the universities of Colorado, Utah, and Missouri.

After leaving Boston, where she was active in the women's rights movement, she worked for the next decade as a journalist and foreign correspondent for the *Boston Herald*, the *Newark Ledger*, the *Los Angeles Daily News*, the *San Francisco Record*, the *Glendale Evening News* (Calif.), the *New York Daily News*, the *Paris Herald*, and others.

She met Whit Burnett, essayist, short-story writer, and editor, in San Francisco, in 1925. They lived together in New York and Paris, and married in Vienna in 1930. They had one child. In 1931 they founded *STORY* magazine ("the only magazine devoted solely to the short story") and coedited it, first in Vienna (1931–1932), briefly in Majorca (1932), and then in New York City, until 1941. It became one of the most influential magazines of the period, publishing the first work of an extraordinary number of significant American writers, among them John Cheever, Norman Mailer, Erskine Caldwell, William Saroyan, Peter De Vries, J. D. Salinger, Tess Slesinger, Richard N. Wright, James T. Farrell, Tennessee Williams, Carson McCullers, and Nelson Algren. During these years she wrote and published her own fiction, and, with Burnett, she also edited several anthologies drawn from *STORY* and cofounded and coedited The Story Press.

Martha left *STORY* and her husband in 1941 (they were divorced the following year), and from 1942 until her death she edited the annual *Best American Short Stories*, replacing Edward J. O'Brien, who had edited the annual collection from its inception in 1915 until his death in 1941. "My own approach to the selection of the stories in this volume," she wrote in the foreword to the 1942 volume, "has been to follow as closely as possible what O'Brien himself sought: literary distinction, integrity on the part of the author and a freedom from hampering, artificial restrictions." She added, "All that any editor can say today is, 'These are the stories I myself liked best. I hope you will agree.'"

In her annual anthologies as well as in three special anthologies she edited (*The Best of the Best American Short Stories 1915 to 1950* [1952]; *Fifty Best American Short Stories, 1915–1965* [1965]; and *200 Years of Great American Short Stories* [1975]), she continued to emphasize the distinctions she often made while editing *STORY*: between unknown and established writers, and between the "little" magazines (our "richest source of fine short stories") and the large-circulation magazines. She recognized, in the *Best Stories* anthologies, long before they received wider acclaim, the talents of dozens of writers, including Saul Bellow, Bernard Malamud, Stanley Elkin, Flannery O'Connor, W. H. Gass, Vladimir Nabokov, Ray Bradbury, John Updike, and Eudora Welty.

Her son, David, coeditor of the *Best Stories* from 1958 to 1971, died in 1971. In 1973 she moved to Northampton, Massachusetts, where she worked on her own fiction, her memoirs (*The Story of STORY Magazine*), and continued to edit the annual *Best Stories* (for which task she read all the stories herself, in some years as many as 8,000). Throughout her life she remained friendly with many of the writers whom she had first published in *STORY*, and to many who remained grateful for having been chosen for one of the annual *Best American Short Stories* anthologies. Many of them acknowledged her help, by letter and in print. But Saroyan outdid them all: for having accepted his very first story, "The Daring Young Man on the Flying Trapeze," he thanked Martha by promising to send her a new story every day for a month, which he did. She accepted a few, and tried to sell the others for him. She died in Northampton. As the *New York Times* noted in its obituary, she was "a powerful force in the development" of the American short story. For a half century she had devoted herself, with singular and passionate dedication, to the discovery, nurturing, and protection of what she loved most: good stories and their writers.

• Martha Foley's papers are in the special collections of the Boston University Library, in Boston, and the American Heritage Center of the University of Wyoming, in Laramie. See also William Peden, *The American Short Story* (1964; rev. ed., 1975); William Jaspersohn, interview, *Harper's Bookletter*, 7 June 1976; and Juanita Taylor, "Martha Foley: The Plotless Duchess," in *Lost Generation Journal* 6, no. 3 (Winter 1981): 10–22. Her memoirs, *The Story of STORY Magazine: A Memoir*, edited, and with introduction and afterword by Jay Neugeboren, were published posthumously (1980). An obituary appears in the *New York Times*, 6 Sept. 1977.

JAY NEUGEBOREN

FOLEY, Red (17 June 1910–19 Sept. 1968), country music recording artist and television star, was born Clyde Julian Foley in Blue Lick, Kentucky, near the black community of Middletown, the son of Benjamin Harrison Foley, the proprietor of a Berea, Kentucky, general store, and Katherine Elizabeth (maiden name unknown). Foley's older brother Clarence nicknamed him "Red" because of his hair color. The Foleys attended a black Southern Baptist church, whose music influenced Red. Family members recalled him "entertaining almost as soon as he could walk." He began playing guitar in earnest when his father took one as trade for groceries. In grade school he was a prankster. At Berea High School (and briefly in college in 1928) he became a star basketball player. A teacher impressed by seventeen-year-old Foley's singing entered him in a classical competition at Georgetown College (Ky.). Though he forgot the song's words, he kept going and, said the contest administrator, "won not just for his voice but for his grit." In 1929, during Foley's first semester at Berea College, he frequently sang on WCKY radio in Covington, Kentucky, and on Cincinnati's WLW, where a WLS radio scout heard him and offered a job. Foley left college and borrowed $75 to join the Cumberland Ridge Runners vaudeville group as vocalist and clown on Chicago's "WLS National Barn Dance," carried on fifty NBC radio stations. In 1930 he gained a solo spot, dubbed "Ramblin' Red." His rich baritone and ease with "high hard" notes earned him instant popularity as "the Bing Crosby of the Hillbillies." He learned his "flat-top" guitar-playing style from southern blacks who migrated to Chicago.

In 1931 Foley met jewelry store clerk Axie Pauline Cox, originally of Berea, and after a whirlwind courtship they married that same year. In 1933 their daughter Elizabeth ("Betty") was born, but Axie Foley developed complications and died three days later. When Foley returned to work, he leaned toward musical comedy. Teamed with Myrtle Eleanor Cooper, a popular artist known as Lulu Belle, in a "fun 'n' fussin'" duo, they became a sensation.

In 1934 Foley began dating Eva Overstake, a fifteen-year-old singer from the Three Little Maids sister act. When he proposed marriage, her father objected because of the nine-year age difference and did not consider her old enough to raise a child. The couple eloped in 1934.

In 1935 Foley signed with the Conqueror label (owned by Sears-Roebuck) and recorded sixteen songs. As Red's career gained momentum, Eva had bouts of clinical depression. Because of her emotional state and his road schedule, he left his daughter with his parents. Eva and Red had three children, one of whom, Shirley, married singer Pat Boone.

In 1937 John Lair, formerly of WLS, began "Renfro Valley Barn Dance" on Cincinnati's WLW radio. With Foley as a partner and prime attraction, in 1939 he opened Renfro Valley Entertainment Center, a Mount Vernon, Kentucky, tourist complex. Its "barn dance" was fed to stations over telephone hookup, then syndicated. Also in 1939, "Avalon Time," a syndicated radio show from Chicago, starred "the two Reds," Red Skelton and Foley.

In December 1941 Foley attempted to enlist in the army but was rejected because of age and family. He used his popularity to sell war bonds and put on shows at Great Lakes Naval Training Station (Ill.). When Eva's mental condition grew worse, Red sold their Renfro Valley interests and built a popular entertainment attraction and dude ranch (later plagued by his lack of financial and administrative acumen) near Peoria, Illinois.

Foley is credited as one of the original innovators of contemporary country music. He signed with Decca in March 1941 and recorded eight songs in Chicago.

In April 1945 Foley became the first artist to record in Nashville, Tennessee, at WSM radio studios. These included "Tennessee Saturday Night"; "Blues in My Heart," which showed a rhythm and blues influence; and "Tennessee Border."

Until 1938 the Grand Ole Opry placed emphasis on instruments, but with the arrival of Roy Acuff and Eddy Arnold, singers took prominence. In 1946 Foley's hits and skill as emcee won him a spot as a prime headliner and host of the NBC radio network broadcast. He recorded "Old Shep" in 1947, a tearjerker poem he put to music about a dog, a tribute to his dog Hoover, whom he credited with saving his life in a childhood swimming incident. It was his first hit and sold more than a million copies. In 1949 he co-headlined the Opry's first overseas tour, appearing on U.S. military bases in Europe.

Eva Foley underwent heart surgery in 1951. During her recuperation, according to biographer Reta Spears-Stewart, Red Foley had an affair with Sally Kelton, a sophisticated, attractive former singer married to record producer Frank Kelton. Eva became despondent and took her life. Red went into a two-year bout of depression and alcoholism. Kelton's husband sued for divorce in 1952. In the midst of the scandal, Foley and Kelton married in 1952, causing bitterness among the Foley children. The couple had no children.

In 1954 Foley was hired away from the Grand Ole Opry by KWTO radio in Springfield, Missouri, to host the syndicated "Country Crossroads." For two years Foley tried to convince WSM radio and National Life & Casualty Insurance, then owners of the Opry, of the feasibility of broadcasting on TV. Worried that telecasting the show would cut attendance, they refused. Foley threatened to find a way to nationally televise a country variety show. According to Foley's son-in-law, his daughter urged him to meet with Ozark Jubilee producer Si Siman. The Jubilee offered Foley a $100,000 contract for 150 fifteen-minute radio shows to be done while the logistics of broadcasting on TV were worked out.

In January 1955 a landmark event in TV history took place. First from Columbia, Missouri, and then from Springfield after cables were installed in the Jewell Theatre, ABC-TV and local KYTV aired the "Ozark Jubilee," later titled on TV "Country Music Jubilee" and "Jubilee, USA," live on Saturday nights. This was the first national program to give country music long-term exposure. The variety show—with Foley as the easygoing host/star, cornball comedy, and local and Nashville stars—not only overshadowed the Grand Ole Opry but grew to attract an audience of 25 million.

Foley's alcoholism led to absences "due to illness." In 1957 he opened a program saying, "I've been hearing them tell you I've had a virus and I've been sick. That's not true. I've been in Four-North at St. John's hospital . . . the funny farm . . . drying out." Trials for income tax evasion in 1960 and 1961 (he was exonerated) and drinking problems led ABC to cancel his contract. Foley played Las Vegas in 1962 and toured the fair circuit. In the 1963–1964 season he costarred opposite Fess Parker on ABC's series "Mr. Smith Goes to Washington" as Cooter Smith, a guitar-playing philosopher.

Foley is perhaps country music's most complex artist. Interviews with friends and peers reveal him as a charismatic singer and intelligent, generous, religious gentleman and family man and, on a darker note, as stubborn, careless in money matters, cheap, an alcoholic, "a bit of a rounder," and capable of great highs and lows.

Foley recorded more than 500 songs. Many crossed from country to pop, such as his boogie-woogie version of "Chattanoogie Shoeshine Boy" (1950), another country and pop million-seller. He performed country music (including duets with Ernest Tubb and Kitty Wells), sacred music, and pop music with the Andrews Sisters. From 1944 to 1959 Foley was on the music trade charts with thirty-eight top-ten hits and six country number-one songs, including "Smoke on the Water" (1944), a World War II song supporting Allied victory; "Have I Told You Lately That I Love You?" (1946); "Satisfied Mind" (1951); "It's No Secret" (1951), a gospel song; "Don't Let the Stars Get in Your Eyes" (1952); "As Far As I'm Concerned" (1954), a duet with Betty Foley; "Beyond the Sunset" (1955); and "Crazy Little Guitar Man" (1958), a foray into rock and roll. The hymn "Peace in the Valley," his signature (and another million-seller), is a classic recording (1951), and he sang it at Hank Williams's 1953 funeral. Foley promoted many careers, especially those of Chet Atkins, Brenda Lee, and Charley Pride. Foley died of congestive heart failure in Fort Wayne, Indiana.

Red Foley was named to the Country Music Hall of Fame in 1967. His plaque reads, "One of the most versatile and moving performers of all time . . . A giant influence during the formative years of contemporary country music and today a timeless legend."

• Memorabilia on the Ozark Jubilee and Foley can be found in Springfield's KYTV Museum. A collection of Ozark Jubilee television programs is maintained by the Museum of Television and Radio, New York, and in Nashville's Country Music Foundation Library and Media Center. Reta Spears-Stewart chronicled Foley's career in *Remembering the Ozark Jubilee, Starring Red Foley* (1993), which contains recollections from peers, TV executives, and son-in-law Pat Boone. Spears-Stewart wrote an overview of his public and personal life in her series the Ozark Jubilee Saga, "Red Foley," *Springfield!* magazine, July 1996, pp. 24–29. Foley is prominently mentioned in Robert Shelton, *The Country Music Story* (1966), and *Country, the Music and the Musicians* (1988), by various contributors. His collaboration with Ernest Tubb is documented in Ronnie Pugh, *Ernest Tubb: Texas Troubadour* (1966). The definitive anthologies of Foley's recording career are *The Red Foley Story* (1969, MCA), and the compilation *Red Foley, Country Music Hall of Fame* (1991, MCA). Foley's association with Patsy Cline on the Ozark Jubilee is covered in Ellis Nassour, *Honky Tonk Angel: The Intimate Story of Patsy Cline* (1993). Obituaries are in the *Springfield Daily News* and the *Nashville Banner* and *Nashville Tennessean*, 20 Sept. 1968, and in the *New York Times*, 21 Sept. 1968. Hank Williams, Jr., wrote and recorded "I Was with Red Foley (the Night He Passed Away)" (1968), and the lyrics tell of their last conversation.

ELLIS NASSOUR

FOLGER, Charles James (16 Apr. 1818–4 Sept. 1884), jurist and secretary of the treasury, was born on Nantucket Island, Massachusetts, the son of Thomas Folger. (Neither the name of Folger's mother nor the occupation of either parent is known.) When Folger was twelve, his family moved to Geneva, New York. Folger attended Geneva (now Hobart) College, graduating in 1836 with high honors. He studied law at Canandaigua with a prominent local firm and in 1839 was admitted to the New York State bar. He practiced law a year in Lyons, Wayne County, then returned to Geneva, his lifetime home, where he resumed the legal profession. In 1844 he married Susan Rebecca Worth; the couple had three children.

In 1844 Folger's real juridical career began, for he was appointed judge of the Court of Common Pleas of Ontario County, then became master and examiner in chancery (similar to present-day equity courts). From 1851 to 1855 he was county judge, after which he returned to private law practice.

Originally an active Democrat, Folger supported Governor Silas Wright and backed the Barnburner faction of the state party. In 1854 he joined the newly formed Republican party, as he was sympathetic to its policies regarding slavery.

In 1861 Folger was elected to the New York State Senate, where he immediately became known as a strong Unionist. Serving until 1869, he chaired its judiciary committee and acted for four years as president pro tempore. Able to wield great political power, he blocked the confirmation of appointments proposed by Governor Reuben E. Fenton, a fellow Republican. When, in 1868, Cornelius Vanderbilt (1794–1877), owner of the New York Central Railroad, sought to buy out Jay Gould, who controlled the Erie Railroad, Folger backed Gould, saying it was against public policy for competing roads to be controlled by the same interest. In the New York State constitutional convention of 1867, he was chairman of the judiciary committee. He became known as the foremost public sponsor of the proposed constitution, which was rejected by the electorate in 1869.

All this time, Folger was becoming a protégé of the wealthy and unscrupulous Thomas Murphy, a New York hatter and politico, and U.S. senator Roscoe Conkling (R.-N.Y.), head of the Stalwart pro-Grant faction of the Republican party. In 1869 President Ulysses S. Grant appointed Folger as U.S. assistant treasurer in New York City, in which capacity he served a year. In 1870 Folger was elected an associate judge of the State Court of Appeals, the highest court in New York State. On the death of the court's chief justice in 1880, Governor Alonzo Cornell, another Stalwart, designated Folger to fill the unexpired term.

In November 1880 James A. Garfield was elected president. Realizing that he was under obligation to the Republican Stalwarts for support during the recent campaign, in February Garfield spoke to Conkling about the possibility of Folger joining the cabinet. Yet, when Garfield offered Folger the post of attorney general, Conkling was furious, for he wanted a far more powerful post for his faction, above all the patronage-rich Treasury Department. Folger's appointment was opposed by James G. Blaine, secretary of state designate, who headed the rival Half-Breed faction of the Republican party, outgoing president Rutherford B. Hayes, and Senator John Sherman (1823–1900) (R.-Ohio)—all of whom suspected the New Yorker's honesty, seeing him as the machine politician par excellence. Folger, out of his depth, could not face such varied opposition and, only ten days before Garfield's inauguration, declined the nomination.

In September 1881 Garfield died of an assassin's bullet and Chester A. Arthur became president. Arthur's longtime friend and fellow Stalwart, Folger was appointed secretary of the treasury on 27 October, assuming his duties on 14 November. Under Folger's administration, the public debt was reduced over $300 million, the largest reduction effected up to his time. Moreover, some reforms were instituted, such as placing certain offices in the classified service under civil service rules, alleviating some patronage abuse. At the same time, Folger assured a department employee that party "assessments" were quite legal. This practice, which involved tapping government employees for "voluntary contributions" to the party in power, had long been under fire from civil service reformers. In December 1881 the New York Civil Service Reform Association called Folger's attention to the fact that General Newton M. Curtis, a special Treasury Department agent, had received assessments from civil servants to help finance Republican campaigns. Folger sidestepped the issue by letting Curtis resign, then turned the case over to the U.S. district attorney. Curtis was later convicted.

In 1882, after a strong fight at the party convention, Folger received the Republican nomination for governor of New York State. Cornell, Folger's rival, had been a popular incumbent but had alienated the Stalwarts by allying himself with the Half-Breeds. Reformers claimed that the nomination was won by fraud, in the process greatly exaggerating the significance of a faulty proxy used in selecting the convention's temporary chairman. Several New York Stalwarts supposedly favored moving Folger from the Treasury to the governorship, as they believed he had been too slow in distributing jobs to his own faction, especially patronage slots in the strategic New York Customhouse. Folger found the gubernatorial race a hard one; neither the backers of Cornell nor the Half-Breed faction nor the reformers would support him. Some critics, such as Brooklyn minister Henry Ward Beecher and civil service reformer George W. Curtis, suspected that President Arthur had engaged in covert activity on Folger's behalf, but they were wrong. Indeed, privately Folger felt that Arthur, who was trying to shake the image of spoilsman, had let him down. Folger's Democratic opponent, Buffalo mayor Grover Cleveland, polled almost 200,000 votes more than Folger, the greatest margin in the Empire State's history up to that point.

After his humiliating defeat, Folger became a recluse. He was frequently ill, suffering spells of severe depression. In 1883 he had to seek complete rest, and the press carried daily reports on his health.

As much as his close friend Arthur, Folger epitomized the "gentleman boss" in politics. A man of distinguished bearing and superior education, he achieved respect as a highly competent jurist and administrator. Simultaneously, he was at the very core of a political machine that was crass in seeking power as an end in itself and not overly scrupulous about how this power was gained. No one ever accused Folger of outright corruption, but his position was difficult, walking a fine line indeed. He died in Geneva, New York.

• The papers of Charles James Folger are located in the New York Public Library. There is no comprehensive study of Folger. Valuable material is in Thomas C. Reeves, *Gentleman Boss: The Life of Chester Alan Arthur* (1975). Other scholarly mention of Folger can be found in George Frederick Howe, *Chester A. Arthur: A Quarter-Century of Machine Politics* (1935); Ari Hoogenboom, *Outlawing the Spoils: A History of the Civil Service Reform Movement, 1865–1883* (1968); David M. Jordan, *Roscoe Conkling of New York: A Voice in the Senate* (1971); and Justus D. Doenecke, *The Presidencies of James A. Garfield and Chester A. Arthur* (1981). Memoirs offering portraits of Folger include Mrs. Richard Crowley, *Echoes from Niagara: Historical, Political, Personal* (1890), and Louis J. Lang, comp. and ed., *The Autobiography of Thomas Collier Platt* (1910). For a valuable obituary, see the *New York Times*, 5 Sept. 1884.

JUSTUS D. DOENECKE

FOLGER, Emily Jordan (15 May 1858–21 Feb. 1936), student and collector of Shakespeareana, was born in Ironton, Ohio, the daughter of Augusta Woodbury Ricker and Edward Jordan, a newspaper editor, lawyer, and solicitor of the U.S. Treasury under Presidents Abraham Lincoln and Andrew Johnson. Emily Jordan's education at Vassar College was financed by her sister Mary Augusta, who had earned both a B.A. and an M.A. at that school and taught English at Smith College for more than forty years. At Vassar, Emily was president of the class of 1879 and joined several literary clubs. Following her graduation, she was an instructor in the collegiate department of Miss Hotchkiss's Nassau Institute in Brooklyn from 1879 to 1885.

In October 1885 Emily Jordan married Henry Clay Folger, who became the president of the Standard Oil Company of New York. They were a childless couple and rented a series of homes in Brooklyn, where they were active members of the Reverend S. Parkes Cadman's Central Congregational Church. Through the church, Emily supported the McAll evangelical mission in France. In 1928 the Folgers purchased an estate at Glen Cove, Long Island, near a golf course and the mansion of their good friend Charles Millard Pratt, whose father founded Pratt Institute.

As a couple the Folgers focused their energies on the collection of Shakespeareana. In 1894, to better inform their book-buying program, Emily Folger wrote to Horace Howard Furness, the Philadelphia lawyer and editor of a variorum edition of the plays of Shakespeare, for his recommendation on an advanced course of study in Shakespeare. At the same time, she contacted Vassar about the regulations governing graduate study. "How delightful is the glimpse that you give me in saying that your study aims at helping your husband," Furness responded, along with a list of critical works and editions to be consulted. "The work which Dr. Furness has laid out for you is enough, in amount and in scope, to earn the degree of A.M. at any American college or university," wrote her supervisor at Vassar, Elmer E. Wentworth. Folger's M.A., pursued in absentia, was awarded two years later from Vassar College. Her thesis, "The True Text of Shakespeare," largely ignores Wentworth's repeated suggestion that "your study, in order to prove satisfactory in the end to yourself, might well include the consideration of other Elizabethans as affecting Shakespeare or as affected by him." She was guided rather by Furness's growing conviction that the 1623 posthumous edition of Shakespeare's collected plays, known as the First Folio, is the authoritative edition, both in relation to the Second, Third, and Fourth Folios (or collected editions) and in relation to the earlier quarto (smaller-sized) editions of individual plays. As expected, Folger's thesis was a survey of the opinions of accepted authorities rather than the result of original investigation. She noted the existence of textual variation between individual copies of the First Folio. Whether or not the Folgers were already aware of that fact is unknown, but such variation does seem to have been the motivating factor behind their accumulation of more than a third of the extant copies of the First Folio.

In 1963 Charlton Hinman published a landmark study, *The Printing and Proof-Reading of the First Folio of Shakespeare*, which included the results of collating fifty-five of the Folger copies, the work that the Folgers envisioned their collection as facilitating. Although the cataloging of textual variants proved to be of minimal use to editors, the unexpected dividend of Hinman's analysis of printing-house procedures established a new direction for textual studies.

The Folgers luxuriated in the minutiae of collecting. During extended stays on Long Island or the Homestead resort in Virginia, they poured over booksellers' catalogs and their own growing catalog of purchases filed in customized chiffoniers. In a 1923 talk celebrating the tercentenary of the publication of the volume, Emily Folger indicated that the collection focused on First Folios "with the thought of a Shakespeare Library which may serve the students to come." Her familiarity with Washington no doubt influenced the location of the library there, as did her belief, stated in the preface to her thesis, that an English-speaking, though not necessarily English-national, person "is best qualified by that circumstance to learn what is his true text."

As the executor of Henry Clay Folger's estate, assisted by her nephew Edward Dimock, Emily Folger negotiated with the trustees of Amherst College regarding the administration of the library. The trustees and staff were surprised both by the bequest and by the need to accommodate Emily Folger's vision of the enterprise. When the endowment left by Henry Folger lost value in the stock market crash of 1929 and proved insufficient, Emily Folger contributed $3 million in Standard Oil securities and agreed to pay the salary of the library's director to ensure the library's opening. The increased endowment again proved inadequate after the library had been in operation for only a year. In 1933 Folger amended her gift, giving the trustees the right to use the principal of her fund, and the library's stockholdings were diversified. After her death, the bulk of her estate was added to the permanent endowment of the Folger Shakespeare Memorial Fund. In 1932 she received an honorary doctor of letters from Amherst, and dedication ceremonies for the $2 million library were held on 23 April, Shakespeare's birthday. President Herbert Hoover, as well as his wife, Lou Henry Hoover, and the ambassadors of Great Britain, France, and Germany were in attendance. Folger presented the key to the library to George Arthur Plimpton, president of the board of trustees of Amherst, with the words "Shakespeare says for Mr. Folger and me, 'I would you accept of grace and love' this key. It is the key to our hearts."

Emily Folger was greatly disappointed by her inability to appoint a director of speech to improve the elocution of Americans and to develop an active program of professional recitations of Shakespeare. She was also unsuccessful in convincing former president Hoover to become the second director of the library. She died at her home in Glen Cove. Emily Folger's ashes—like those of her husband—are in an urn in the library's reading room.

As a young woman, Folger had taken full advantage of the newly available opportunities of higher education for socially advantaged women. Her belief in the power of literature to form character, whether that of an individual or of a nation, was anchored by a progressive New England Protestantism. With her husband, she pursued a vision of an America—fully recovered from the Great Depression—as the proper place for the contemplative appreciation of England's literary treasures.

• Folger's papers are in the Folger Shakespeare Library. Details of her negotiations with the trustees of Amherst College are in Stanley King, *Recollections of the Folger Shakespeare Library* (1950). Obituaries are in the *New York Times* and the *New York Herald Tribune*, 22 Feb. 1936.

KATHLEEN LYNCH

FOLGER, Henry Clay (18 June 1857–11 June 1930), industrialist, book collector, and philanthropist, was born in New York City, the son of Henry Clay Folger, a dealer in wholesale millinery, and Eliza Jane Clark. After attending Brooklyn's Adelphi Academy on a scholarship, Folger entered Amherst College. When his father's business failed during his junior year, Folger briefly attended the City University of New York. He returned to Amherst after being guaranteed the necessary funds by patrons who included Charles M. Pratt, an oil merchant and the father of Folger's roommate. In March of his senior year Folger attended a lecture delivered by the aged poet and essayist Ralph Waldo Emerson entitled "Superlative or Mental Temperance." Folger dated his passionate devotion to Shakespeare to Emerson's address on the tercentenary of Shakespeare's birth. Following graduation from Amherst in the summer of 1879 he accepted a clerkship in Pratt's oil refinery, already aligned with Standard Oil. In 1881 Folger received a law degree from Columbia University, graduating cum laude because of extra work he had done in political science, which also earned him an M.A. from Amherst. He was admitted to the New York bar but never practiced as an attorney, remaining instead with Charles Pratt & Company. Folger married Emily Jordan in 1885. He bought for her a reduced facsimile of the 1623 First Folio edition of Shakespeare's works, edited by James O. Halliwell-Phillipps. (The designation "folio" refers to its large paper format.) "Here you may see Shakespeare's plays as they were actually given to the world," he told his bride. Emily Folger later described the volume as the cornerstone of the collection of Shakespeareana that was the shared avocation of the childless couple. Folger was not satisfied with the photographic facsimile because he believed that the sun distorted the images. Consequently, he bought a set of typographic reproductions of the complete works of Shakespeare, published by Lionel Booth (1862–1864).

In 1889 Folger made his first purchase of an early edition of the plays, a copy of the Fourth Folio, for $107.50 at Bangs New York auction rooms. Beginning in 1891 the Folgers made a series of eleven summer book-buying trips to England. Emily Folger pursued postgraduate study of the variations in Shakespeare's texts that are found from copy to copy as well as from edition to edition. She was awarded an M.A. from Vassar College in 1896. Of the numerous wealthy American collectors at the turn of the century, none were as focused as the Folgers. Henry "rather specialized in Folios," according to his wife. Horace Howard Furness, the noted American editor of Shakespeare, dubbed Folger "Forty Folio Folger" when his collection grew to that number (it was later surpassed). But in his collecting Folger did not neglect the smaller quartos containing individual plays, editions of poems, and even playbills, portraits, and relics. His most treasured purchase was the handsome copy of the First Folio that had been presented by publisher William Jaggard to Augustine Vincent, the herald who had prepared a coat of arms for Shakespeare. Perhaps the

highlight of Folger's career as a collector was his purchase for $10,000 of the unique 1594 quarto of *Titus Andronicus*, which had been discovered in Malmö, Sweden.

Folger was steadily promoted through the ranks of the Manufacturing Committee of Standard Oil. His "almost infinite capacity for detail" was well used by the committee responsible for analyzing refining processes. Folger also made a series of shrewd personal investments in the industry. In 1897 he and Calvin V. Payne financed the first commercial oil refinery in Texas in Corsicana. In 1909 Folger and Payne financed the Lone Star Gas Company to market natural gas from Texas's Red River region. By that time Folger was a newly elected member of the board of directors of the parent company, Standard Oil of New Jersey. When the Supreme Court granted six months for the dismemberment of the corporation because of a landmark federal antitrust suit against Standard Oil, Folger was secretary of the parent company. In February 1911 he assumed the vice presidency and, in December, the presidency of Standard Oil of New York, one of the newly independent companies. Charged to play by the rules of free enterprise, and facing an accelerated consumer demand for petroleum products together with increased competition from abroad, Folger oversaw many of the responsibilities dictated by the mandated dissolution. Folger's assessment of the efficacy of governmental oversight of business may be conveyed in his dour remark to the judge who had conducted Standard Oil's defense that the only "independent" oil operations after 1911 were those formerly in the Standard group. In 1923 Folger became chairman of the board of Standard Oil of New York. He resigned that post on 30 March 1928 to dedicate himself to the building of a Shakespeare memorial to house his collection of some 80,000 volumes stored in more than 2,000 Standard Oil cartons in several warehouses.

Several locations had been considered for the memorial, particularly Shakespeare's birthplace in Stratford-upon-Avon, England. Although the Folgers supported plans for a theatrical foundation there, they determined to build their own library in the capital of the United States. Folger had been quietly assembling plots of land for the building along what was known as Grant's Row, directly behind the Library of Congress. When the same land was eyed for an expansion of the Library of Congress, it was readily acceded to Folger, as his library accorded well with a larger vision of what one congressman called the Acropolis of America. Paul Philippe Cret, in consultation with Alexander B. Trowbridge, designed the building and deterred Folger from erecting a Tudoresque building among its monumental neighbors on Capitol Hill. The cornerstone of the library was laid on 28 May 1930. Folger died in Brooklyn. In his will, Folger named his wife executor and bequeathed the bulk of his estate to Amherst College in trust for the Folger Shakespeare Memorial. The estate must have had a large value when the will was prepared in 1927, but as a result of the shrinkage in value after the 1929 stock market crash, the trustees were left with about $1.5 million, an insufficient endowment with which to operate the library. Emily Folger's gift of Standard Oil securities with a market value of $3 million and her agreement to pay the salary of Joseph Quincy Adams, the library's first director, ensured the library's opening in 1932.

Known as a modest and retiring man, Folger was a trustee of the Central Congregational Church in Brooklyn. He established three annual prizes at Amherst College for the best essays by seniors on Shakespearean subjects and regularly presented favorite graduates with sets of the Booth reproductions. In later years he was an avid golfer and a frequent partner of John D. Rockefeller on the course. Folger's own assessment of his achievements, which he provided for a *History of the Class of 1879 in Amherst College, from 1904 to 1909* (1909), was astute: "By sticking closely to business with the Standard Oil Company, I have found the means for adding to my collection of Shakespeareana until it is probably the largest and finest in America and perhaps the world" (p. 14). His hopes of fostering the work of scholars were realized and surpassed by strategic additions to the collection made by successive directors of the library. Folger's project is singular for its institutional expression of a shared Anglo-American literary heritage.

• Folger's papers, as they relate to his book buying, are in the Folger Shakespeare Library. A sense of Folger's writing style and book-buying program is conveyed in his article "A Unique First Folio," *Outlook*, 23 Nov. 1907. He figures incidentally in Ralph Hidy and Muriel Hidy, eds., *Pioneering in Big Business, 1882–1911*, vol. 1 of *History of Standard Oil Company (New Jersey)* (1955); and George Sweet Gibb and Evelyn H. Knowlton, eds., *The Resurgent Years, 1911–1927*, vol. 2 of *History of Standard Oil Company (New Jersey)* (1956). He is also mentioned in Allen Nevins, *Study in Power: John D. Rockefeller* (2 vols., 1953). *Henry C. Folger* (1931), a privately printed volume, contains the funeral service delivered by S. Parkes Cadman, a biographical sketch by George E. Dimock, and an essay on the significance of the library by its first librarian, William Adams Slade. An appreciation is provided by George F. Whicher, "Henry Clay Folger and the Shakespeare Library," in *Amherst Graduates' Quarterly* (Nov. 1930). Stanley King, *Recollections of the Folger Shakespeare Library* (1950), is useful, as are Louis Wright, *The Folger Library: Two Decades of Growth* (1968); A. S. W. Rosenbach, *Henry C. Folger as a Collector* (n.d.), privately printed after Folger's death; and the unpublished, family-held recollections of Giles Dawson, longtime curator of manuscripts at the Folger Library. Peter W. M. Blayney, *The First Folio of Shakespeare* (1991), details the publication technology and historical significance of the book Folger so obsessively collected. Betty Ann Kane, *The Widening Circle: The Story of the Folger Shakespeare Library and Its Collections* (1976), provides an illustrated introduction to the Folger Shakespeare Library and its collections. Obituaries are in the *New York Times* and the *New York Herald Tribune*, 12 June 1930.

KATHLEEN LYNCH

FOLGER, Peter (1617–1690), translator and government official, was born in Norwich, England, the son of John Folger and Meriba Gibbs. Around 1635 Peter Folger immigrated to Massachusetts with his widower father. During the voyage to America on board the vessel *Abigail*, he met and fell in love with Mary Morrill, an indentured maidservant. Living at first in Dedham and Watertown, Folger worked as an artisan for nine years (he was variously skilled as a weaver, miller, surveyor, and shoemaker) to raise the sum of twenty pounds necessary to buy Morrill's freedom from Hugh Peters, a well-known Salem minister. The couple were married in 1644.

According to family tradition, Folger referred to his purchase of Morrill's indentures as "the best appropriation of money [he] had ever made." Together he and his wife had nine children who survived infancy, founding a family that generated several famous Americans with a flair for science and politics. Their daughter Abiah became the mother of Benjamin Franklin. Other lineal descendants of the Folger-Morrill union include whaling captain and marine geographer Timothy Folger, who charted the Gulf Stream; lawyer and congressman Walter Folger, who invented an astronomical clock; abolitionist and founder of the women's rights movement Lucretia Coffin Mott; and astronomer Maria Mitchell, discoverer of a comet and advocate of college education for women.

In the 1640s Folger moved with his growing family to the island of Martha's Vineyard, where he worked as a surveyor and became part of a Puritan mission to the Indians run by a father and son both named Thomas Mayhew. Quick to master the Algonquian language and described by Cotton Mather as "well learned in the scriptures," Folger acted as both schoolmaster and minister to the Vineyard Indians. In 1648 or 1649 Thomas Mayhew, Jr. extended the mission, including Folger's services, to nearby Nantucket Island. The mission's strategy favored the gradual replacement of the Indians' shamanistic religious leaders, called "powwows," with Indian pastor-preachers.

In 1659 Folger, who had radical spiritist tendencies, publicly declared himself a Baptist at a town meeting on Martha's Vineyard. That same year he aided a group of English settlers, led by Baptist Thomas Macy, in surveying Nantucket island, recently purchased from Thomas Mayhew, Jr. and populated by an estimated 2,000 to 3,000 Indian inhabitants. Folger, who may have quarreled with Mayhew about his declaration, then appears to have moved for a time to Rhode Island, a more tolerant colony created in the 1630s by religious exiles from Puritan Massachusetts.

Meanwhile, the Nantucket settlers, twenty in number, formed a "proprietorship"—owning and governing the island in common according to a system of purchased shares. Conflict with the Nantucket Indians over land use was inevitable. In 1663 the proprietorship voted to grant a half-share to Peter Folger provided that he settle on the island with his family and "atend the English in the way of an Interpreter between the Indians and them upon al necessary ocasions." Folger developed close ties with the Indian elders and was highly successful at his assigned task. In a letter of 1677 Folger recalled his early days on Nantucket: "[N]o Englishman but myselfe could speake scarse a Word of Indian. . . . I am sure some of these men [the English] . . . had felt Arrows in their Sides for reall Wrong that they did them [the Indians] . . . had I not stepped in between them and made peace."

In 1665 Folger helped defuse a particularly dangerous situation when the Pokanoket sachem Metacomet ("King Philip") and a war party arrived on Nantucket to capture and execute John Gibbs, a Harvard-educated Indian who had offended Metacomet by speaking the name of his dead father. Folger persuaded the English to back him in negotiating for Gibbs's life. Impressed that the English would take risks to protect an Indian, a substantial number of Nantucket Indians supported them in defying Metacomet, who left the island without incident after being paid a small ransom for his intended victim. Gibbs later established the island's first Indian church.

The mainland was not so lucky when in 1675 an Indian informer against Metacomet was murdered and Puritan judges had three Wampanoags executed for the crime. The incident torched an Indian uprising, known as King Philip's War, that involved most of New England, as Metacomet had already been at work organizing an alliance of tribes to try to halt English encroachment on Indian lands. Nantucket remained at peace. Folger, however, was moved by the tragedy of King Philip's War to compose a pamphlet, *A Looking-Glass for the Times, or The Former Spirit of New England Revived in This Generation* (1676). Written in ballad quatrains, the pamphlet treats the Indian war as God's punishment upon the Puritans for "the sin of persecution" and "crualty to brethren" both red and white. Folger calls on "magistrate and minester" to "heale the lande" by repealing "cruel lawes" and ceasing "to cheat and to oppress." In his autobiography Benjamin Franklin found his grandfather's work notable for being "in favour of Liberty of Conscience, and in behalf of the Baptists, Quakers, and other Sectaries, that had been under Persecution," and judged it "written with a good deal of Decent Plainness and manly Freedom."

In addition to acting as an interpreter on Nantucket, Folger also worked as a teacher, surveyor, and miller, and became the island's clerk of courts. Like many of the growing community of "half-share men" assembled to support the original proprietors' development of Nantucket, he was an indispensable citizen. In the 1670s Folger became caught up in an island political struggle known as the "Half-Share Revolt," an event that brought half-share men and Indians together against the original proprietors, who had reserved to themselves and their descendants all future distributions of land and decisions about its use and governance.

A half-share man himself and spokesman for the Indians, Folger was briefly jailed for contempt of court in 1676 when he refused to hand over records vital to the dispute. According to Folger, in a March 1677 letter of complaint to Governor Andros, his imprisonment "set a fire to the whole island, for I . . . was so well known and so well beloved of English and Indians." The Half-Share Revolt was waged in town meetings, legal actions, and petitions to the governor before settlements were reached in the early 1680s allowing half-share men to participate in future divisions of land and addressing Indian grievances about grazing rights.

Folger died on Nantucket. His importance resides not only in his role as biological sire of a great American family, but as an intellectual forefather whose early concern with religious liberty, racial tolerance, freedom of expression, and democratic government would, through his own work and that of his descendants, help to shape the nation.

• Biographical information on Folger can be found in Benjamin Franklin, *The Autobiography of Benjamin Franklin* (1771–1778); Franklin B. Hough, ed., *Papers Relating to the Islands of Nantucket, Martha's Vineyard, and Other Islands Adjacent* (1856); Lydia S. Hinchman, *Early Settlers of Nantucket: Their Associates and Descendants* (1896); Alexander Starbuck, *A History of Nantucket County, Island, and Town* (1924); Florence Bennett Anderson, *A Grandfather for Benjamin Franklin* (1940); Edward Byers, *The Nation of Nantucket: Society and Politics in an Early American Commercial Center, 1660–1820* (1987); and Nathaniel Philbrick, *Away Offshore: Nantucket Island and Its People, 1602–1890* (1994).

SUSAN F. BEEGEL

FOLIN, Otto (4 Apr. 1867–25 Oct. 1934), biochemist and professor, was born Otto Knut Olof Folin in Åseda (Småland), Sweden, the son of Nils Magnus Folin, a tanner, and Eva Olofsdotter, a midwife. Having completed elementary schooling and because of a stagnant economy, Otto, at age fifteen, was sent to join his older brother, Axel, in Stillwater, Minnesota. Determined to learn English, pay his way, and get an education, Folin graduated from the local high school at age twenty-one, and then in 1892 earned a bachelor's degree in chemistry from the University of Minnesota where he was managing editor of the university's journal, the *Ariel*. From 1892 to 1896 Folin worked on a doctorate in organic chemistry at the new University of Chicago, writing his thesis under Professor Julius Stieglitz. Interested in then-nascent biochemistry and encouraged by physiologist Jacques Loeb, Folin borrowed money and spent two years working in the laboratories of three eminent professors: Olof Hammarsten at the University of Uppsala (1896–1897); Ernst Salkowski at the Institute of Pathology, University of Berlin (1897); and Nobelist Albrecht Kossel at the Physiological Institute, Marburg (1897–1898). Four published papers resulted. He was initiated into clinical biochemistry during his short stay in Berlin by improving the analysis of urinary uric acid.

Returning to Chicago in 1898, Folin formally received his Ph.D. He worked locally for a year in a private laboratory and as a research assistant to a gastroenterologist. In 1899 Folin married a former fellow student at the University of Chicago, Laura Churchill Grant; they had three children. Folin then spent a year teaching chemistry at the University of West Virginia.

Folin's pioneering research as a clinical biochemist began in 1900 after he opened a new laboratory at the McLean Hospital in Waverley, Massachusetts. In seven years there, he published twenty-eight papers that nurtured biochemistry. Following vain attempts to detect published qualitative urinary differences between sane and insane patients, he shifted toward developing quantitative analytical methods. He introduced modern colorimetry via the Duboscq colorimeter and resurrected the Jaffé reaction using alkaline picrate for creatinine and creatine analysis. He devised and improved methods for quantifying nonprotein nitrogen via the Kjeldahl process, sulfur compounds, phosphate, uric acid, ammonia, and urea. Through studies of human protein catabolism and urinary composition, Folin found that urea output varied with protein intake, whereas creatinine output was constant. He proposed a theory of exogenous-endogenous protein metabolism that stood for four decades until Rudolf Schoenheimer introduced the concept of dynamic metabolism via radioisotopes. Folin also proposed creatine's special role in muscle. He published in and was a collaborating editor from its inception in 1905 of Christian Herter's *Journal of Biological Chemistry*. Earlier work appeared in the German *Zeitschrift für Physiologische Chemie* and in American journals. In 1906 Folin helped found the American Society of Biological Chemistry, serving on the first council and as its third president in 1909.

In 1907 Folin was appointed associate professor of biochemistry at Harvard Medical School, adding a new dimension to his career: teaching fundamentals of biochemistry to freshman medical students and establishing a program of research. In 1909 he was appointed Hamilton Kuhn Professor of Biological Chemistry. In this era few medical schools in the United States required more than a high school degree for entrance. Despite an early dearth of clinical facilities, Folin launched far-reaching studies introducing quantitative blood chemistry as a tool for investigating metabolism and for diagnosis. His success in facilitating blood and tissue testing was aided by two brilliant collaborators, Willey Denis, who joined him in 1910, and Hsien Wu, in 1917. His graduate students would make important research contributions: Walter R. Bloor, Edward A. Doisy, Philip A. Shaffer, Wu, and others. James B. Sumner and Doisy later earned a Nobel prize, an honor that eluded Folin though he was nominated six times.

Folin, who was elected to the National Academy of Sciences in 1916, published 151 journal articles, a monograph, and five editions of a laboratory manual. More than any individual, he provided the modern practical approach to the microanalysis of blood and other body fluids by introducing new or improved quantitative methods and using them to make systematic studies of metabolism, health, and disease. His knack for methods made specific testing feasible in the growing number of clinical laboratories in hospitals and clinics. He introduced as protein precipitants sulfosalicylic acid (1914), metaphosphoric acid (1916), and tungstic acid (1919). He transformed qualitative testing of uric acid with phosphotungstate into quantitative testing (1912) and introduced phosphomolybdate for detecting phenols (1912). He established methods for measuring tyrosine, cystine, and tryptohane in protein; the use of β-naphthaquinonesulfonic acid for determining amino acids (1922); and macro- (1920) and micromethods (1928) for determining blood sugar levels. Purification of standards and reagents, essential in this era, was a steady feature of his publications. He proposed "normal" values for blood and urinary constituents, particularly nonprotein nitrogen fractions.

In 1923 Folin was appointed director, with S. R. Benedict, and later a consultant of a new research laboratory at the Metropolitan Life Insurance Company of New York. As a result, improved qualitative tests of urinary sugar and protein, glucose tolerance testing, assessment of kidney function, and more standardization of measurements were developed for the insurance industry.

Although the place of death cannot be confirmed, it appears to have been either Brookline, Massachusetts, where the Folins chiefly resided, or the vicinity of Kearsarge, New Hampshire, where the family had a summer home and where Otto Folin was buried.

• Folin's books and manuscripts are in the Folin file at the Francis A. Countway Library of Medicine, Harvard Medical School. Samuel Meites, *Otto Folin: America's First Clinical Biochemist* (1989), provides further biographical information. Meites's "Otto Folin's Medical Legacy," *Clinical Chemistry* 31 (1986): 1402–4, and J. Buttner and C. Habrich, *Roots of Chemical Chemistry* (1988), pp. 99–102, trace Folin's career. Also, see a sketch by his former student Philip Schaffer, "Otto Folin (1967–1934)," National Academy of Sciences, *Biographical Memoirs* 27 (1952): 47–82. Obituaries are in the *Journal of Biological Chemistry* (Dec. 1934) and *Science* (Jan. 1935).

SAMUEL MEITES

FOLKS, Homer (18 Feb. 1867–13 Feb. 1963), pioneer in social welfare and public health reform, was born in Hanover, Michigan, the son of James Folks and Esther Woodliffe, farmers. After attending local schools, in 1885 he entered Albion, a nearby coeducational Methodist College.

An outstanding student, Folks had difficulty choosing between a ministerial and a teaching career when he received his bachelor's degree in 1889. He therefore enrolled at Harvard University for a year of further study. At Harvard he fell under the influence of Francis G. Peabody, Harvard's "theologian of the social gospel," and George Herbert Palmer, whose courses on ethics emphasized self-sacrifice and service to humanity. After leaving Harvard in 1890 with a second bachelor's degree, Folks decided upon a life of practical helpfulness to the needy and accepted a job as general superintendent of the Children's Aid Society of Pennsylvania.

Shortly after starting work with the CAS, located in Philadelphia, Folks helped to deinstitutionalize the care of needy children in the United States by developing, and successfully administering, a program for "boarding-out" dependent, neglected, and delinquent children that quickly gained national attention. In 1891 Folks married his college sweetheart, Maud Beard; they had three children.

In February 1893, Folks moved to New York City, where he became executive secretary of the New York State Charities Aid Association (SCAA). This private agency had been created some twenty years earlier by Louisa Lee Schuyler and other New Yorkers to keep an eye on the state's public welfare institutions and to promote various measures, public and private, to help the state's needy citizens of all ages. As head of that organization Folks was in the forefront of virtually every advance in social welfare over the following half-century.

At the outset Folks concentrated on furthering his earlier work with needy children, especially developing, implementing, and promoting sound techniques for foster home care for delinquents. Soon, however, he concentrated on studying the causes of child dependency (when children become wards of the state) and delinquency. Folks argued that in most cases child dependency and delinquency resulted from the breakdown of family life, which, in turn, usually was caused by poverty. He contended that poverty, contrary to popular belief, was rooted in social and economic conditions, especially sickness, invalidism, and death of the family breadwinner—not in personal failure. Convinced, therefore, that health and welfare were intimately related, he called for child welfare workers to concern themselves not only with the protection of children, but also with the safety of their parents, especially by preventing and eliminating distress and death resulting from the spread of avoidable disease. Folks turned his attention, and that of various agencies and associations with which he was affiliated, to that end, playing an important role in the early-twentieth-century public health movement. During a two-year leave of absence from the SCAA to serve as New York City's commissioner of public charities (1902–1903), Folks established the nation's first municipal tuberculosis hospital. He also served on the New York Charity Organization Society's Committee on the Prevention of Tuberculosis, which, in 1903, conducted the first comprehensive analysis of tuberculosis in the United States. A year later he helped to create the National Association for the Study and Prevention of Tuberculosis, served on its governing board for many years, and, in 1912, became the first layperson elected to its presidency.

Folks used the SCAA to organize and conduct a statewide antituberculosis campaign that led to the en-

actment of stringent laws governing the reporting and treatment of cases, including the building of public hospitals. This made New York a model in that regard and went a long way toward eliminating the disease from the state. He then did similar work with diphtheria and the venereal diseases.

At the same time, Folks, a man of great energy, played a leading role in numerous other efforts to promote social welfare. He was instrumental in the establishment of juvenile courts in New York and, in 1907, was responsible for the creation of the nation's first state Probation Commission, which he chaired for ten years. He was a founder, and later longtime chair, of the National Child Labor Committee, which for many years spearheaded the fight against child labor.

Folks also served as presiding officer of the first White House Conference on Dependent Children (1909), which led to the creation three years later of the U.S. Children's Bureau, whose work he greatly influenced. He was among the nation's first "private" social workers to support widows' pensions—now Aid to Families with Dependent Children—and played a prominent role in their introduction in 1915 in New York State. For these and other contributions, including helping to establish America's first "school" of social work, in 1911 Folks was elected president of the National Conference on Social Welfare—the highest tribute a social worker could receive—and was elected again in 1923 (its fiftieth-anniversary year, when it was known as the National Conference of Social Work), the only person in that organization's history to be so honored.

Meanwhile, Folks did not neglect his efforts in the field of health. In 1909 he was instrumental in launching the so-called baby-saving campaign by helping to create the American Association for the Study and Prevention of Infant Mortality, of which he served as president in 1915. In 1913 Folks drafted a measure that was hailed by C.-E. A. Winslow, a noted authority on public health, as "the most important landmark in the history of health administration in the United States" since the creation of the nation's first state health department in 1869. The most significant feature of that measure, which numerous other states quickly emulated, was the creation of the nation's first state Public Health Council (which he served as vice chair of from 1913–1955), a small body of appointed experts who had quasilegislative, or ordinance-making, power that, in effect, removed public health administration from politics in New York and other states.

Neither age nor honors slowed Folks down. In 1930 he served as secretary of a public health commission created by Governor Franklin D. Roosevelt to study ways to improve the state's health laws and institutions. A year later he played a leading role in the creation and work of the Joint Committee on Unemployment Relief, which shaped New York State's progressive response to the Great Depression—which in turn served as a model for the entire nation when Roosevelt entered the White House in 1933. In 1940

Roosevelt's successor as governor, Herbert H. Lehman, asked Folks to chair a state commission to study ways to curtail the rate of increase in the population of the state's mental institutions—a subject he had been interested in since 1906 when, as head of the SCAA, he had created the nation's first "aftercare committee" to provide assistance to persons discharged from such institutions.

In November 1946 Folks suffered a slight stroke and two months later, after some fifty-seven years of service with great distinction, this "statesman of the public good" finally retired as head of the New York State Charities Aid Association. He died in Riverdale, New York.

During his long career, Folks left his imprint on many areas of social service: child welfare and relief programs, child labor legislation and juvenile justice, baby-saving and maternity protection, mental hygiene and public health. Folks's greatest contribution to the struggle for health and welfare, however, was his ability to bring preventive medicine into the organized social welfare crusade. Convinced that the solution to social problems, especially poverty and dependency, involved the abandonment of the false dichotomy between health and welfare in favor of a vigorous and wholehearted cooperation among all citizens interested in the public welfare, Folks was one of the first social workers to recognize the vital importance of mobilizing the entire community—public officials and private citizens, health officers and social workers, physicians and laypersons—in the war against illness and insecurity. And while that concept may not have been his alone, few, if any, succeeded as Folks did in carrying it out. In the process he not only helped save thousands of lives each year, but also to extend the scope of social work, making it a valuable addition to the economic and political machinery organized for the improvement of the community.

• There are two major collections of papers essential for any study of the subject: the Homer Folks Collection at the Columbia University School of Social Work and the New York State Charities Aid Association Papers, located in the United Charities Building in New York City. Whereas the Folks papers are especially valuable for the development of his thought, the SCAA collection is indispensable for an understanding of Folks's influence on social reform and legislation in New York State and the nation. In addition, the Oral History Project at Columbia University is quite informative; the typescript copies made from recorded interviews with Folks and numerous others with whom he interacted provide a good deal of material on his varied activities and on social conditions and reform in general in New York throughout his career. Also useful are Folks's two published books, *The Care of Destitute, Neglected and Delinquent Children* (1902) and *The Human Costs of the War* (1920). See also Savel Zimand, ed., *Public Health and Welfare: The Citizens' Responsibility—Selected Papers of Homer Folks* (1958), a collection of forty-nine papers written by Folks between 1891 and 1946, most of them previously unpublished, which also contains a good brief biographical sketch (pp. xv–xxii) written by the editor, Folks's son-in-law. Readers also may wish to consult Anna Liebowitz, "Homer Folks: A Study of His Professional Growth in Terms of His Contributions to the Field of Social Work and the Milieu in Which He Developed" (master's thesis, New York [now Columbia Univ.] School of Social Work, 1950). Because of a newspaper strike, no New York City newspaper ran an obituary at the time of Folks's death; numerous newspapers throughout the country had lengthy ones, however, and in many cases separate articles on his death. See, for example, the Yonkers (N.Y.) *Herald Statesman*, 14 and 15 Feb. 1963.

WALTER I. TRATTNER

FOLLETT, Mary Parker (3 Sept. 1868–18 Dec. 1933), theorist of social organization and civic leader, was born in Quincy, Massachusetts, the daughter of Charles Allen Follett and Elizabeth Curtis Baxter. Follett's father attempted a variety of jobs and her mother took in boarders before the family finally moved in with Follett's wealthy maternal grandfather. In 1888 Follett enrolled at the Harvard Annex, the precursor of Radcliffe College, and graduated summa cum laude in 1898. During this ten-year period she also spent a year at Newnham College, Cambridge University, and worked for a few years as a schoolteacher at Mrs. Shaw's School in Boston. Follett's perceptiveness as an observer of social and political phenomena was evident even before her college graduation when Longmans, Green published her book *The Speaker of the House of Representatives* (1896), the first comprehensive historical study of the evolution of the Speakers' political and institutional power. Contemporaries favorably compared Follett's book with Woodrow Wilson's *Congressional Government*, and modern scholars have called it one of the best books ever written about the U.S. Congress.

In 1900, sustained by the devotion of Isobel Briggs, the English headmistress of Mrs. Shaw's School who became her lifelong partner, Follett began a career as a social and civic worker in Boston. She pursued this calling for eighteen years despite suffering periodically throughout adulthood from the debilitating effects of an incorrectly diagnosed kidney tumor. Throughout her work on behalf of woman suffrage, civic education, vocational guidance and placement, and the development of neighborhood community centers, Follett successfully enacted roles now variously ascribed to policy analysts, politicians, and management executives. She personally cultivated the support of public officials and neighborhood residents, negotiated conflicts of interest, orchestrated publicity favorable to her causes, championed the passage of enabling legislation, and raised and allocated funds. She also inspired her colleagues with a vision of the pioneering nature of their work, encouraging their creativity, proffering wise counsel, and liberally praising their accomplishments. Follett is remembered, however, not only for these accomplishments but also for the books and lectures in which she articulated her insightful and provocative conceptions of power, authority, leadership, conflict, coordination, and group process.

Follett's social and civic work began in 1900 at Children's House in Roxbury, one of eight Boston settlements originally founded as kindergarten-nurseries by philanthropist Pauline Agassiz Shaw. At Children's House, Follett established a club in which young men, many of whom were immigrants, debated contemporary political questions. She quickly saw, however, that these young men needed a variety of forms of stimulation and assistance if they were to realize their potential. Once again with Shaw's support, Follett founded the Highland Union, a social, athletic, and educational club for young men over the age of nineteen that was designed to "promote fellowship, civic co-operation, and to stimulate an intelligent interest in local economic questions."

About this same time, Follett also became active in the new Boston Equal Suffrage Association for Good Government (BESAGG). Founded in 1901 by Mary Hutcheson Page and Shaw, the BESAGG combined "efforts to secure suffrage for women with direct activities for civic betterment." It was through Follett's role as chairperson of the BESAGG Committee on Substitutes for the Saloon that she would make her first contributions to the school-and-community-centers movement in Boston. Under the auspices of the BESAGG, Follett applied to the Boston school board in 1902 for permission to use rooms in the Dearborn School for a new Roxbury Industrial League. The league, modeled in part on another of Shaw's successful projects, provided social, civic, and industrial training for boys aged fourteen to nineteen and thereby proved that public school buildings could be used for such purposes. By 1905 the league had become so successful that it required more work and money than the BESAGG could furnish. Follett responded by making the league independent of the suffrage association, but she continued her personal association with the BESAGG, exercising leadership on a variety of new projects: an analysis of bills pending in the Massachusetts legislature; an investigation of civic education in Boston; preparation of a civic primer for use in the evening schools; establishment of "school city" systems of student governance in schools; and the formation of "junior city councils" in Boston's neighborhoods.

In 1909, with BESAGG increasingly devoting its attention to suffrage rather than civic work, Follett decided to accept a major role in the newly established Women's Municipal League of Boston. For the next ten years, working as chairperson of the league's nonpartisan Committee on the Extended Use of School Buildings as well as chairperson of the Boston School Committee's Advisory Committee on Social Centres, Follett orchestrated a complex, multiorganization effort that by 1917 successfully established and secured stable financing for school-based community centers in eight Boston neighborhoods.

During the period 1910–1917, Follett also was a leader in the development of a program of vocational counseling and placement for Boston schools and for neighborhood school centers. The notion that school/community centers might profitably be married to a program of vocational guidance and placement almost certainly was inspired by Follett's experiences in Low-

er Roxbury, for she had seen there how ward bosses acquired and maintained political power by satisfying their constituents' needs for jobs. If vocational counseling and placement services could be extended beyond regular school hours and integrated with these neighborhood centers, Follett felt certain she could contribute to the liberation of grassroots political life. In 1909 Follett moved to secure a place on the executive board of a newly founded private organization dedicated to training one vocational counselor for each school in Boston. Two years later, frustrated by the Vocation Bureau's neglect of placement activities and follow-up counseling activities, Follett obtained the Boston school superintendent's approval to establish a privately financed Placement Bureau. This bureau provided vocational guidance, placement, and follow-up counseling to anyone, whether in neighborhood centers or the regular schools, who sought its services.

Over time, Boston school officials were so impressed with the projects Follett had implemented that the School Department assumed responsibility, first, for school-based community centers and, in 1917, for vocational guidance and placement as well. Follett then was free to concentrate on extending rather than merely defending these movements. Believing that the long-term accomplishment of her aims was heavily dependent on the quality of the personnel appointed to manage the new community centers, Follett turned her efforts, first, to defining the roles of these new community workers and, then, helping them learn how to develop local leadership and foster community control. Follett also emerged during this period as a major figure in the national-centers movement; she contributed her talents to the development of the National Community Centers Association and was elected in 1917 as national vice president.

During her years as a social and civic worker, Follett grappled with issues of contemporary concern: the origin and limits of leadership and authority, the struggle between individual freedom and collective control, the tensions of diversity in a pluralistic society, the proper use of expertise in a democracy, and the social responsibility of business. She was deeply concerned about whether democratic government was possible in light of the continuing waves of immigration, but she rejected many of the "solutions to popular government" then in vogue. Valuing difference over homogeneity, Follett was uneasy about efforts to achieve social order through assimilation, and she fiercely opposed the efforts of bosses, reformers, and professional experts to govern for others in "their best interest." Instead, she sought to empower those who heretofore had been excluded, working for woman suffrage and helping Boston's immigrants become skillful practitioners of self-government; eventually, however, she became persuaded that the future of democratic political life could be ensured only if practical methods were found for continuously creating the collective will. In 1918 she took up these issues in *The New State*, reflecting there on her social and civic experience and offering a critique of modern representative government.

Many of Follett's contemporaries sought a collective will through social control and the homogenization of culture; Follett herself, early in her career, had subscribed to the idealist tenet that individuals should subordinate themselves to the whole. In *The New State*, however, Follett firmly rejects this notion. Experience had taught her that Americans must overcome their conviction of separateness, not through domination, subordination, or imitation, but through the psychic interpenetration she had witnessed in effectively functioning groups. The "true group process"—a continual acting and reacting that brings out differences and integrates them into ever-larger unities—must, Follett argued, become the preeminent social process in a democracy. Arguing from her experience as well as from her study of philosophy and social psychology, Follett contends that the individual is not "separate," having rights prior to society, but instead is in a state of "continual relatings." And since the true self is a group-self, "then my only rights," Follett continues, "are those which membership in a group gives me." Further, following the English philosopher Thomas Hill Green, Follett believed that we are obeying ourselves and, therefore, are free only when we are obeying the group we have helped to make and of whose collective ideas, spirit, and will we are an integral part. Convinced of the importance for social organization of creating effective group processes, Follett confidently asserted that any new scheme of government is bound to fail, whether pluralist or socialist in nature, unless we first learn more through observation and experimentation about the functioning of groups and about productive intergroup relations.

Creative Experience (1924), Follett's final book, was written following almost two years of service on minimum wage boards in Massachusetts. Having heard that the procedures followed to determine an occupational group's minimum wage were based more on careful investigation of the facts than on political compromise, Follett was intrigued. These procedures reminded her of a process she was seeing with increasing frequency in the opinions of progressive jurists: cases were being decided, not in favor of one party at the expense of the other, but with appropriate regard for the complex, reciprocal relations of all parties concerned. Sensing that the new minimum wage boards, likewise, were seeking the "law of the situation," Follett was anxious to observe and study their methods. The richness of her experience on the wage boards whetted Follett's appetite for further group studies. Now, more than ever, she felt certain that the future of American social, political, and economic life depended on the working out of a new kind of group process.

Determined to make a contribution to finding these new modes of association, Follett embarked on a two-year collaboration with Eduard C. Lindeman, a young social scientist who later would be called the philosopher of social work. This collaboration would result in the publication of Follett's *Creative Experience* and

Lindeman's *Social Discovery* (1924). Surveying extant efforts to resolve conflict, Follett found jurists and economists too enamored of an "equilibrium" of interest, political scientists too enthralled with a "balance" of power, and ethicists too committed to "compromise" as the apex of ethical life. Follett firmly rejected compromise because it sacrificed the integrity of the individual, and she saw little to recommend the balancing interests and power as these tactics merely rearranged what already exists. A more promising route to "constructive" conflict seemed to Follett to lie in the eclectic reconceptualization of behaviorism offered by Harvard's neorealist philosopher and psychologist, Edwin B. Holt, and the emerging research and theorizing of the German Gestaltists.

The work of Holt and the Gestaltists, Follett argued, shows clearly that behavior is internally as well as externally conditioned and is a function of the interweaving activities of the organism and the environment; further, since both organism and environment are constantly changing and relating themselves anew, these interactions create a continually evolving situation. Seeing our ideas as a product of this dynamic interplay of behaviors, it seemed to her unrealistic to expect that differences can be harmonized solely by appeals to reason. The successful resolution of conflict, instead, depends on changing behaviors—on engaging conflicting parties in activities that, over time, create a new situation—a situation in which their differences actually can be integrated. If we were to adopt this sort of nonhierarchical integrating as our primary mode of human association, it would have profound implications, Follett argued, not only for our understanding of the origin and exercise of power, but also for the dynamics of governing expressed in "the will of the people," "the consent of the governed," and "representation," and for the functions served by the legal system in a democratic society. Follett's considerable contributions to early twentieth-century political thought remain to be fully explored by modern political theorists.

During the nine-year period preceding her death in Boston, Follett focused her attention on group processes as they occur in business organizations. She was drawn to such study by the enthusiasm of progressive business executives in England and the United States who wished to experiment with her ideas in their firms. The management theorists usually cited as exemplifying the era during which Follett wrote and lectured—the period of scientific management and classical theory—were concerned largely with efficiency and order. Follett shared these concerns, but she was equally committed to enhancing individual growth and development and fostering a capacity for organizational change. As a result, she sought to conserve and encourage difference when others preferred to eliminate it; she advocated shared forms of authority when others sought hierarchical domination and control; and she promoted a highly interactive concept of leadership, a "reciprocal relating" of leader and followers, at a time when leadership was considered largely a function of one's authority and position. Follett's rich legacy for theorists of organization and management may be found in *Dynamic Administration* ([1940?]; rev. ed. 1973) and *Freedom and Coordination* (1949), collections of lectures given in the United States and in England where Follett resided during the last five years of her life. These lectures, together with her earlier books on government, mark Follett as a preeminent contributor to organizational and management thought.

• Small collections of Follett's papers, most of which have been destroyed, are maintained at the Urwick Management Centre in Slough, England, and the Schlesinger Library at Radcliffe College. There are three large collections of letters by Follett; they are located in the Richard C. Cabot Papers at the Harvard University Archives, the Ella Lyman Cabot Papers at Schlesinger Library, and the Eduard C. Lindeman Papers at Columbia University. A partial bibliography appears in *Dynamic Administration* (1973). Many early speeches and reports are available in the *Bulletin: The Women's Municipal League of Boston* (1910–1917) and the annual reports of the Boston Equal Suffrage Association for Good Government (1900–1910).

Previously published biographical sketches, each of which contain errors, can be found in the first and second editions of *Dynamic Administration*; in Pauline Graham, *Dynamic Managing: The Follett Way* (1987); and in Tokiho Enomoto and Tadashi Mito, *Mary Parker Follett* (n.d., Japanese).

With the "rediscovery" of Follett's work in the mid-1960s, a series of authors sought to place her ideas within particular bodies of theory; see, for example, Joseph L. Massie, "Management Theory," in *Handbook of Organizations* (1965); R. E. Walton and R. B. McKersie, *A Behavioral Theory of Labor Negotiations* (1965); Elliot M. Fox, "Mary Parker Follett: The Enduring Contribution," in *Public Administration Review* 28 (Nov.–Dec. 1968): 520–29; Jean B. Quandt, *From the Small Town to the Great Community* (1970); Kenneth Thomas, "Conflict and Conflict Management," in *Handbook of Industrial and Organizational Psychology* (1976); and Dean G. Pruitt, *Negotiation Behavior* (1981).

For recent thinking in the field of management about Follett's work, see commentaries by Peter F. Drucker, Rosabeth Moss Kanter, and others in *Mary Parker Follett: Prophet of Management*, ed. Pauline Graham (1995); Joan C. Tonn, "Follett's Challenge for Us All," *Organization* 3 (Feb. 1996): 167–74; Lee D. Parker, "Control in Organizational Life: The Contribution of Mary Parker Follett," *Academy of Management Review* 9 (Oct. 1984): 736–45; Pauline Graham, *Dynamic Managing: The Follett Way* (1987); Peter Miller and Ted O'Leary, "Hierarchies and American Ideals, 1900–1940," *Academy of Management Review* 14 (Apr. 1989): 250–65; and Marlene G. Fine, "New Voices in the Workplace: Research Directions in Multicultural Communication," *Journal of Business Communication* 23 (1991): 259–74. Promising new analyses of Follett's ideas also have begun to appear in fields outside of management. In history, see Thomas A. Bender, *Community and Social Thought in America* (1978). In political science, see Roger H. Davidson and Walter J. Oleszek, *Congress against Itself* (1977); and Ronald M. Peters, Jr., *The American Speakership* (1990). In psychology, see Judith V. Jordan, "Courage in Connection: Conflict, Compassion, Creativity," *Work in Progress Papers*, no. 45, Stone Center for Developmental Services and Studies, Wellesley College (1990). In conflict and negotiation, see Deborah M. Kolb, Lisa Jensen, and Vonda L. Shannon, "She Said It All Before, or What Did We Miss about Ms. Follett in the Library?" *Organization* 3 (Feb. 1996): 153–60; Albie M. Davis, "An Interview with Mary Parker Follett," *Negotiation Journal* 5 (July 1989): 223–35; and Linda L. Putnam and Majia Holmer, "Framing, Reframing and Issue Development," in *Communication and Negotiation*, ed. Putnam and Michael E. Roloff (1992). In organizational communication, see Phillip K. Tompkins, "The Function of Human Communication in Organizations," in *Handbook of Rhetoric and Communication Theory*, ed. C. A. Arnold and J. W. Bowers (1984); and Marlene G. Fine, "New Voices in Organizational Communication," in *Transforming Visions: Feminist Critiques in Communication Studies*, ed. Sheryl P. Bowen and Nancy Wyatt (1993).

Obituaries are in the *New York Times* and the *Boston Evening Transcript*, 21 Dec. 1933, and the *Times* (London), 30 Dec. 1933 (first two editions).

JOAN C. TONN

FOLSOM, Charles (24 Dec. 1794–8 Nov. 1872), librarian and editor, was born in Exeter, New Hampshire, the son of James Folsom and Sarah Gilman (occupations unknown). After preparation at Phillips Exeter Academy, Folsom entered Harvard College as a sophomore in 1810. He taught school at Sudbury during winter vacations and graduated from Harvard in 1813. He then taught at the academy in Hallowell, Maine, and in the fall of 1814 returned to Cambridge to study divinity. After giving that up, he made arrangements to study medicine, but instead, on the recommendation of Harvard president John T. Kirkland, sailed in 1816 to the Mediterranean on the 74-gun ship of the line *Washington* as chaplain and teacher of mathematics. One of Folsom's pupils was David G. Farragut, the future admiral, who in later years acknowledged his debt to the "young Yankee Pastor" and visited him in his home. At European ports in the Mediterranean, "without letters and without acquaintance," Folsom came to bless librarians who, considering "the mere pursuit of knowledge as a bond of brotherhood, and a title to kindness," admitted him to their libraries (letter to Samuel A. Eliot, 27 Oct. 1845, quoted in Parson's "Memoir"). The experience shaped the nature of his subsequent work as a librarian, notable for his emphasis on admitting and assisting all qualified scholars.

In the fall of 1817, Folsom was appointed *chargé d'affaires* of the consulate at Tunis in the expectation that a successor would soon arrive, but the plague prevented that until late in 1819. After Tunis, he rejoined the naval squadron as private secretary to Commodore William Bainbridge.

Shortly after returning to Boston in 1821, Folsom began to serve as tutor in Latin at Harvard College. In 1823 he was appointed librarian. During 1825 and 1826 he was also instructor in Italian. The major duties of the librarian were to prepare catalogs and arrange for binding of materials, "besides the services required . . . in lending, receiving, & safe-keeping of books, waiting on those who resort to the library to consult books, and on those strangers visiting the University who may be entitled to special courtesy" (letter to President Kirkland, 22 Sept. 1825). He resigned from the librarianship in 1826 in order to devote himself to more lucrative duties at the University Press (privately owned after Sept. 1827) where, for a time at least, he was a partner and at the *United States Review and Literary Gazette* where, with William Cullen Bryant, he was an editor. The journal ran from October 1826 to September 1827, though Folsom apparently ended his editorial connection somewhat sooner. Some services to the library continued beyond 1826, and, in addition, Folsom served as acting librarian from 20 July to 5 September 1831. The multiple responsibilities of those years were increased by marriage in the fall of 1824 to Susannah Sarah McKean, daughter of Reverend Joseph McKean, professor of rhetoric and oratory at Harvard College. They had seven children, two of whom died in childhood.

At Harvard University Press, Folsom corrected and edited the more important works that it published, sometimes taking them apart and putting them back together again in much improved form. But his perfectionism was excessive and resulted in delays, even to the point of idling printers while he labored to verify an aspect of the work at hand. In 1835 he edited with Andrews Norton the short-lived *Select Journal of Foreign Periodical Literature*, drawn largely from British periodicals.

Folsom performed his careful editorial work for others, notably Norton, John Gorham Palfrey, Josiah Quincy, Jared Sparks, George Ticknor, and William Hickling Prescott. In 1838 he read each day ten pages of proof of Prescott's *Ferdinand and Isabella*. Folsom's perfectionism, though not pleasing to authors, was useful. As Prescott wrote, "Had I accepted half of my good friend Folsom's criticisms—what would have become of the style! Yet they had & will always have their value for accurate analysis of languages & thought—and for assessing of general facts." Editorial work helped support Folsom: in 1843 he received $50 per volume for the *Conquest of Mexico*.

In 1843 Folsom was also running a school for young women, which he had established in 1841 and continued until the winter of 1845, and before and after these dates he took young girls into his home to educate them.

Folsom's main activity from 1845 to 1856 was to serve as librarian of the Boston Athenaeum. He considered the major duty of a librarian, besides serving as custodian of the books, to be a "dispenser" of them. He defined that duty: "By *dispensing*, I am far from meaning only the finding of the particular volumes asked for, or the recording of the titles of such as are borrowed. I mean quite another ability in the Librarian,—an ability to 'bring forth, out of the treasure' committed to him, 'things new and old.'" He believed scholars should be "allured" to consult the library and that it should be proclaimed "not only that its stores are accessible for this purpose, but that a competent person stands ready, as the *organ of the liberal spirit of the Bostonians*, to aid in making them available for the promotion of knowledge throughout the land" (letter to Eliot, 27 Oct. 1845). Available, that is, to men. Folsom opposed admitting women to the library either as staff or as readers. (In 1857, after he had retired, women joined the staff of the Athenaeum.)

While librarian of the Boston Athenaeum, one of the country's largest libraries, Folsom's name was the first on a "Call for a convention of librarians," which met in New York in September 1853, the only such convention of librarians before 1876.

In addition to his editorial and library work, Folsom served the intellectual community of Boston and Cambridge as an active member of the Overseers Visiting Committee of the Harvard College Library. A member of the American Academy of Arts and Sciences and of the Massachusetts Historical Society, he also served on the council of the American Antiquarian Society. Folsom left no major writings or singular accomplishments, but he is one of those individuals whose labors underpin the achievements of others.

• Folsom's papers, including more than 1,600 letters to him, drafts of outgoing letters, and a memorandum book of letters written between March 1834 and May 1835, are in the Boston Public Library. The fullest account of Folsom's life is Theophilus Parsons, "Memoir of Charles Folsom," *Proceedings of the Massachusetts Historical Society, 1873–1875* 13 (1875): 26–42. Parsons had, as a fellow member of the Social Club, met regularly with Folsom from 1818. The memoir includes Folsom's letter of 27 Oct. 1845 to Samuel Atkins Eliot on the duties of the librarian of the Boston Athenaeum and the qualifications that the person should possess. The letter served as Folsom's paper at the librarians' conference of 1853; see George B. Utley, *The Librarians' Conference of 1853* (1951), on Folsom's role. Another member of the Social Club, John Gorham Palfrey, wrote a long letter on Folsom that was published in the *Proceedings of the Massachusetts Historical Society, 1871–1873* 12 (1873): 308–15. Another sketch that also focuses on the character of the man is A. P. Peabody's in his *Harvard Reminiscences* (1888). For microfiche copies of documents relating to Folsom's role in the Harvard Library, see *The Harvard University Library: A Documentary History*, ed. Kenneth E. Carpenter (1990). References to Folsom's library career are also in *The Librarians of Harvard College* (1897), *The Athenaeum Centenary* (1907), and Kenneth E. Carpenter, *The First 350 Years of the Harvard University Library* (1986). C. Harvey Gardiner, ed., *The Literary Memoranda of William Hickling Prescott* (1961), depicts Folsom in his editorial role; see also William Cullen Bryant II and Thomas G. Voss, eds., *The Letters of William Cullen Bryant*, especially vol. 1 (1975). Genealogical information is in Jacob Chapman, *A Genealogy of the Folsom Family* (1882).

KENNETH E. CARPENTER

FOLSOM, David (25 Jan. 1791–24 Sept. 1847), Choctaw political leader, was born near present-day Philadelphia, Mississippi, in the old Choctaw nation, the son of Nathaniel Folsom, an Anglo-American trader and innkeeper, and Ai-Ne-Chi-Hoyo, of the Choctaw "royal" clan. In matrilineal Choctaw society David Folsom enjoyed status as the kinsman of Chief Mosholatubbee of the Choctaw northeastern district. This family connection and his leadership abilities underpinned his political career during a critical phase of Choctaw national life.

Folsom, a Choctaw nationalist, typified the bicultural, biracial elite who increasingly dominated affairs of the Five Civilized Tribes during the nineteenth century. Childhood experiences in his father's inn on the Robinson Road and three years in the home of his brother-in-law, Choctaw Agent Samuel Mitchell, gave Folsom an understanding of Anglo-American/Choctaw dynamics. Although circumstances limited him to only six months' formal schooling, which he financed himself, he developed an enduring conviction that English education was a necessity for Choctaw young people. A Presbyterian convert and sincere Christian, he strongly supported the missionaries who offered literacy as well as religious teaching. Beginning in 1818 Folsom helped found the first mission schools for Choctaws and subsequently worked with missionaries Cyrus Byington and Alfred Wright to develop written Choctaw. His motive in supporting white-style education and religion was not assimilation of the Choctaws into Anglo-American culture, but strengthening of their nation to withstand an expanding, aggressive United States.

A trader and planter in private life, Folsom began his political career by age twenty. When the Choctaws rejected Shawnee Chief Tecumseh's recruitment to his anti-American confederacy in 1811, it is said that Folsom captained the warriors who escorted him out of their country. He then served three years with Choctaw allies of General Andrew Jackson in the Red Stick War (1813–1814) and concurrent War of 1812(–1815), attaining the rank of colonel at twenty-four. Despite Choctaw cooperation with the United States during the wars, federal officials then pressured them to yield parts of their homeland to white settlement. Folsom debuted as a Choctaw spokesman in 1816 during negotiations by which the nation exchanged land claims for funds to finance national development, particularly Choctaw education. Folsom, with most Choctaws, opposed federal insistence that they emigrate beyond the Mississippi River with all other eastern Indians. Nevertheless, they were compelled to sign treaties in 1820 and 1825, receiving roughly the southern third of today's Oklahoma in preparation for eventual removal.

Throughout the 1820s Folsom led Choctaw nationalists in transforming Choctaw society and government in an attempt to stave off exile to the West. Besides supporting Christian missionary activity and English education for both boys and girls, he encouraged Choctaws to substitute full-scale agriculture for their traditional hunting and farming economy and promoted the adoption of an Anglo-American style of government. Folsom and Greenwood LeFlore influenced the creation of the Choctaw lighthorse, a mounted police force serving as judge, jury, and sheriff under a new code of written law. The deaths of two of the hereditary chiefs of the three Choctaw districts created a power vacuum by 1824–1825 that allowed the rise of a new generation of bicultural leaders such as Folsom. In 1826 the Choctaws wrote the first of a series of constitutions, creating a republican government and installing elected officials, among them David Folsom as chief of the northeastern district.

This transition to Anglo-American ways was not always smooth, nor were Folsom's goals and leadership universally acceptable to traditional Choctaws, particularly his kinsman Mosholatubbee. The Pitchlynn family, which included Folsom's brother-in-law Peter, were also powerful political rivals. Concurrent federal and state pressure for emigration further exacerbated internal tensions. In 1830 Folsom resigned as chief after the state of Mississippi extended its laws over the Choctaw Nation and threatened to imprison its officials. Finally, with no acceptable options open, he agreed to sign the Treaty of Dancing Rabbit Creek (1830), by which Choctaws agreed to emigrate. Having led a party of emigrants west in 1832 over the Choctaw "Trail of Tears," he settled in Apuckshunnubbee District (in present-day southeastern Oklahoma).

In the new Choctaw Nation, Folsom continued his political career while he reestablished himself as a trader, planter, speculator, and proprietor of a salt works and a public house in Doaksville. He was elected to successive terms on the national council and helped write the constitutions that refined the Choctaws' republican government. A compelling, bilingual orator, Folsom worked untiringly to found the Choctaw national school system (1835) and opposed any encroachment on their sovereignty in the new homeland. On several occasions he traveled to Washington, D.C., as a delegate to state Choctaw views to the president.

Folsom loved the company of friends and family and playing the violin he crafted himself. He married Rhoda Nail and, after her death, Jane Hall (marriage dates unknown). His thirteen children continued Folsom's leadership of the Choctaws. Folsom died at Doaksville, Choctaw Nation, and was buried in the nearby Fort Towson cemetery.

Folsom's transitional role was demonstrated in that he was the first Choctaw to marry before a magistrate, establish a library, serve as a lay missionary, be elected chief in the evolving Choctaw republic, and lead immigrants into the Indian Territory. With many contemporary bicultural leaders of the Five Civilized Tribes, he chose a course that accommodated change in order to give his people the means to defend their nationhood. His legacy of literacy and a national development comparable to that of the larger American population helped the Choctaws maintain their independence until 1906.

• There is no single collection of Folsom's papers, but some correspondence may be found in the American State Papers and the records of the Choctaw Agency, Record Group 75, preserved in the National Archives. Other letters are available in the Western History Collection at the University of Oklahoma, Norman. Documents related to Folsom are found at the Oklahoma Historical Society, Oklahoma City, and the Gilcrease Institute Library, Tulsa. Horatio Bardwell Cushman quoted Folsom extensively in his *History of the Choctaw, Chickasaw, and Natchez Indians* (1899; repr. 1962), as did

Czarina C. Conlan, a Folsom descendant, in "David Folsom," *The Chronicles of Oklahoma* 4 (Dec. 1926): 340–55. Folsom's political career is analyzed in Barry Eugene Thorne, "David Folsom and the Emergence of Choctaw Nationalism" (master's thesis, Oklahoma State Univ., 1988). Folsom's career may best be understood in context from Angie Debo, *The Rise and Fall of the Choctaw Republic* (1934). See also W. David Baird, *Peter Pitchlyn: Chief of the Choctaws* (1972).

MARY JANE WARDE

FOLSOM, James Elisha (9 Oct. 1908–21 Nov. 1987), governor of Alabama, was born on a farm in Coffee County, Alabama, the son of Joshua Marion Folsom, a planter and county official, and Eulala Cornelia Dunnavant. Growing up in the wire grass region of southeastern Alabama, he spent hours with his father soaking up the rural political culture. After Folsom's father died of alcohol poisoning in 1919, the family endured economic hardship. Able to attend the University of Alabama and Howard College (later Samford University) only sporadically, Folsom joined the merchant marine and worked in Europe and Asia. He then returned to Alabama, and family connections helped him gain a Civil Works Administration post in 1933. He proved to be a creative administrator who responded to farmers' actual needs. From that Marshall County position he went to work in Washington, D.C., and attended night classes. In 1936 he returned to Alabama and married Sarah Carnley. They had two children before she died in 1944.

Folsom loved politics. He lost four early elections, but with each defeat he learned valuable lessons and gained important contacts. In 1933 he failed to gain a seat to a state Prohibition convention, in 1936 and 1938 he lost in congressional races against Representative Henry Steagall, and in 1942 he was defeated in the gubernatorial election. As Folsom became more experienced in campaigning, he emphasized his distinctive 6'8", 245-pound physique. Appearing in a white western hat and brogans, he often began a speech by taking off his size 15½ shoes to rub his feet. He effectively used rural symbols, such as corn-shuck mops, suds buckets, or the flavor of turnip greens, to stir emotions. String bands prepared the political rally just as a choir did at a religious service. An empty bucket was passed around for campaign contributions just as an offering plate was passed at church, making each contributor a part of the occasion.

Ignoring the courthouse clique that politicians usually sought, Folsom instead wooed the people of the rural hinterlands. "I am not afraid of too much democracy," he proclaimed. He would often lambast the power of the Big Mules, the large-scale planters and industrialists who he claimed controlled Alabama. Folsom was a populist, promising to help the masses with old-age pensions, better teacher pay, improved infrastructure, workmen's compensation, unemployment insurance, occupational disease compensation, repeal of the poll tax, and the one-man, one-vote principle.

It appeared that Folsom's fifth campaign, the 1946 governor's race, would be but another defeat. Starting in early January with less than $200, he tirelessly trekked the dirt roads of Alabama, talking and listening to small farmers and workers. His relationship with the people was symbiotic, with both energized by the contact. Startling the political establishment by polling a plurality of votes in the first phase of the Democratic primary, he defeated his opponent by 55,000 votes in the runoff.

In his first term as governor, from 1947 to 1951, Folsom promised much and delivered little. Although he successfully pushed a road improvement package through the legislature, he was humiliated at every attempt to enact his political agenda. His plans for better schools and hospitals for the people of Alabama evaporated in legislative committee rooms. Part of Folsom's legislative failure could be blamed on his lifelong battle with alcoholism. Often depressed by tragedies, such as the deaths of family members, by his second term as governor he was nearly paralyzed by his drinking. One aide remembered, "On any given day, you wouldn't know if he was going to be a genius or a fool." In 1948 he married Janelle Moore. They had no children.

Folsom demonstrated the ambivalence toward civil rights that was necessary for electoral success in the Deep South. Accepting the populist creed that class was far more important than race, he refused to use African Americans as scapegoats. At political rallies, he spoke of and treated blacks with respect and dignity, and he repeatedly tried to ensure blacks' voting rights. He opposed the 1948 Dixiecrat movement and supported President Harry Truman's civil rights initiatives. To deter the Ku Klux Klan, he banned the wearing of masks in public in 1949. Unable by law to succeed himself in 1950, Folsom easily won reelection in 1954 and served until 1959. Like other politicians in the South after World War II, he confronted the civil rights movement spawned by *Brown v. Board of Education* (1954). His civil rights record was flawed. In 1956 two black students tried to enter the University of Alabama graduate school, and three nights of racial violence and terror ensued. When a word from a moderate governor might have defused the situation, Folsom was in Florida on a week-long drunken binge. Although never openly racist, as was the later governor George Wallace, Folsom could be silent and absent at critical junctures.

Race was the key to Folsom's defeat by Wallace in 1962. In that campaign, Wallace brazenly courted white Alabamians' fears and fanned the hysteria of white separatism as Jim Crow cracked. Calling Folsom all the epithets found in the southern white demagogue's lexicon, Wallace preyed on anxieties and insecurities to defeat Folsom by 2,000 votes. An election eve fiasco added to Folsom's undoing. He appeared on television addled either by alcohol or personal problems, unable even to name his own children.

Folsom ran for governor four times after 1962, but he gained fewer and fewer votes with each attempt.

Debilitated by strokes and heart disease in his later life, he died in Cullman, Alabama. He was a rarity for a Deep South politician, able to connect emotionally with the people of Alabama while eschewing blatant racism. Politically, he fostered a New Deal liberal agenda to promote the working class. Although personal flaws prevented him from realizing all of his goals, many were achieved later, including a more integrated Alabama, more rights for women, better schools for all Alabama children, and safer working conditions for laborers.

• Folsom's papers are at the Alabama Department of Archives and History in Montgomery. The most perceptive biographies of Folsom are George Sims, *The Little Man's Big Friend: James E. Folsom in Alabama Politics, 1946–1958* (1985), and Carl Grafton and Anne Permaloff, *Big Mules and Branchheads: James E. Folsom and Political Power in Alabama* (1985). Good political analysis is in William Barnard, "The Old Order Changes," *Alabama Review* 28 (July 1975): 163–84; Grafton, "James E. Folsom and Civil Liberties in Alabama," *Alabama Review* 32 (Jan. 1979): 3–27; and Grafton, "James E. Folsom's 1946 Campaign," *Alabama Review* 35 (July 1982): 172–99. A good comparison of Folsom and George Wallace is in Dan T. Carter, *The Politics of Rage* (1995). Obituaries are in the *New York Times*, 22 Nov. 1987, and *Time*, 30 Nov. 1987.

RANDY FINLEY

FOLSOM, Nathaniel (18 Sept. 1726–26 May 1790), merchant and soldier, was born in Exeter, New Hampshire, the son of Jonathan Folsom and Anna Ladd Foster, farmers. When Folsom was fourteen his father died. He was apprenticed to a trade but later became a merchant and, with two partners, began his own trading firm. He had no formal or academic education.

Early on Folsom was drawn to military life. He was a member of the provincial militia for some years before his appointment as captain and commander of a company of Exeter militiamen in the Crown Point expedition of 1755 during the French and Indian War. Folsom and his men distinguished themselves in fighting against the French and Indians near Lake George. Folsom continued to be active in the militia in subsequent years, even as he built his fortune in the mercantile business.

With the outbreak of the revolutionary crisis, Folsom sided with the more radical colonists. As early as 1765 he signed a petition protesting the Stamp Act. With his colleague John Sullivan, he was chosen to New Hampshire's first delegation to the Continental Congress. When hostilities ensued, Folsom was put in command of three regiments of the New Hampshire militia. He assumed command in June 1775, three days after the battle of Bunker Hill. The militia was disorganized and ill equipped. After an acrimonious and public feud with a subordinate, John Stark, that resulted in both of them being passed over for an appointment to the Continental army in favor of John Sullivan, Folsom dedicated most of his time to organizational and quartermaster tasks. His experience as a merchant made this an ideal situation for him.

Folsom served in the Provincial Congress that drew up the New Hampshire Constitution. He also served on the twelve-member executive council that governed New Hampshire after the 1775 departure of the royal governor, John Wentworth, and on the committee of safety, and he was appointed a judge of the court of common pleas. In all instances his radical opinions were quite evident. In 1777 he supported an unsuccessful petition brought by the citizens of Portsmouth to banish or execute Tories living in New Hampshire.

Folsom had two more stints as a delegate to the Continental Congress (1777–1778 and 1779–1780). During his tenure he continually supported representation by state rather than by population. He accurately saw the weaknesses in the Articles of Confederation but was especially concerned that the southern states would gain commercial advantage over the more heavily burdened northern states, because slaves were exempted in counting population for taxation purposes.

Folsom was married twice, first to Dorothy Smith, with whom he had six children before her death in 1776, and then to the widow Mary Sprague Fisher, with whom he had one child. He died in Exeter, New Hampshire.

• The official record of Folsom's public life can be found in *New Hampshire Provincial Papers*, vols. 6 (1872) and 7 (1873); C. H. Bell, *History of Exeter, N.H.* (1970); Jere Daniell, *Experiment in Republicanism* (1970); and Richard F. Upton, *Revolutionary New Hampshire* (1936). Biographical information is in Henry M. Baker, "Nathaniel Folsom," New Hampshire Historical Society, *Proceedings* 4 (1899–1905); Cyrus P. Bradley, "Memoir of Nathaniel Folsom," New Hampshire Historical Society, *Collections* 5 (1837); and Rev. Nathaniel S. Folsom and Jacob Chapman, "The Folsom Family," *New England Historical and Genealogical Register* (Apr. 1876).

GREGORY C. COLATI

FOLTZ, Clara Shortridge (16 July 1849–2 Sept. 1934), first woman lawyer on the Pacific Coast, suffrage leader, and founder of the public defender movement, was born in Lafayette, Indiana, the only daughter of Elias Shortridge and Talitha Harwood. Trained as a lawyer, Elias Shortridge turned instead to preaching among the Disciples of Christ and in 1860 became pastor to a well-established church in Mt. Pleasant, Iowa. For a few years, Clara attended the progressive Howe's Academy until her father was expelled from his congregation for unorthodoxy. She then became a teacher herself in nearby Illinois before eloping—at the age of fifteen—with a handsome Union soldier, Jeremiah Foltz. During hard years on an Iowa farm, she bore four children.

In the early 1870s the Foltzes, Clara's parents, and her four brothers migrated first to Oregon and then to California, settling in San Jose, where Clara and Jeremiah had their fifth child. They arrived in the midst of a severe economic depression, and Jeremiah Foltz, a poor provider in the best of times, made matters worse by frequent trips to Portland to visit the woman who ultimately became his second wife. The Foltzes were divorced in 1879.

Realizing that she alone must soon support herself and her children and that her former occupations of boarding, sewing, and teaching would not suffice, Clara Foltz reached back to her girlhood dreams of "oratory, fame and political recognition." She embarked on a public speaking career, taking woman suffrage as her subject. Her dramatic gifts, passionate sincerity, and the still-novel sight of a woman lecturer all brought her some early success.

At the same time, she determined to become a lawyer and started studying with her father. Before she could even apply for bar admission, however, Foltz faced a California code provision that limited the practice of law to white males. Joined by a small band of sister suffragists, Foltz lobbied her Woman Lawyer's Bill through the legislature. On 4 September 1878 she was the first to take advantage of the new law, to the accompaniment of nationwide publicity dubbing her the "Portia of the Pacific."

In 1878–1879, at the end of an economically depressed decade, California held a constitutional convention, partly as a response to popular demand for legal curbs on the excesses of rich and unscrupulous businessmen. Extensive working-class protest centered on the importation of cheap Chinese labor but encompassed other causes as well. Led by Foltz and her friend Laura Gordon, soon to be the second woman lawyer in the state, woman suffragists came very close to winning a provision in the new constitution. What they achieved instead, with the help of the Workingmen's party delegates, were two clauses, unprecedented in any American constitution, guaranteeing women access to employment and education.

Foltz and Gordon demonstrated the need for the clauses not only by their lobbying efforts, but through their struggle, while the convention was in progress, to attend the newly established Hastings College of the Law. Denied admission by directors who apparently believed that women might practice, but should not learn, the law, the two women sued, representing themselves. They prevailed in the trial court and eventually in the California Supreme Court. The decision came too late for Foltz, however, who was already a busy lawyer supporting her family.

Foltz practiced law continuously for fifty years, but she always regretted her lack of formal training and worked to make the study of law easier for other women. In 1893 she started the Portia Law Club in San Francisco to prepare women for the bar, and over the years she often taught, in her office, law classes for women. In 1991, at the instigation of its women students, Hastings awarded Foltz a posthumous degree of doctor of laws.

Her greatest achievement as a law reformer was to conceive the idea of a public defender, which she presented compellingly as the representative of the California bar at the Congress of Jurisprudence and Law Reform held at the 1893 Chicago World's Fair. Her several law review articles on the subject are crisp and convincing in their formulation of the radical notion that the government should pay for the defense of the criminally accused. Foltz claimed to have lobbied for a public defender in thirty-two states; one clear success was California, which passed the "Foltz Defender Bill" in 1921.

Ever restless and adventurous, Foltz moved to San Diego in the late 1880s, where she practiced real estate law and started a daily newspaper. After returning to northern California for a few years, probably around 1890, she set out on a nationwide lecture tour ending in New York City, where in 1896 she joined the bar amid considerable press coverage. By some accounts, she was the first woman to argue in the city courts. She also lobbied for a public defender bill in Albany, started the Clara Foltz Gold Mining Company with a group of prominent businessmen, and sued a restaurant that refused service to her and Trella, her older daughter, because they had no male escort.

By the turn of the century she was back in San Francisco after a short period of practice in Denver. Specializing for a time in oil and gas law, she published *Oil Fields and Furnaces*, a trade and technical magazine. When she lost her home and office in the 1906 earthquake, she moved to Los Angeles for the last third of her life and was appointed the first woman deputy district attorney (1911–1913). During the same period she served on the state board of charities and corrections, the first woman in that important job. For a few years (1916–1918) she published her own magazine, *The New American Woman*.

In 1911, when California women won the vote, Foltz stood all night receiving congratulations as one of the few original suffragists who would live to cast a legal ballot. She yearned to add the U.S. Senate to her firsts but instead campaigned for her brother Samuel Shortridge, who was elected twice, serving from 1921–1932. Though she was mentioned for national posts and federal judgeships, her career was past its prime by the time women had even a remote chance for such offices. Foltz made a largely symbolic run for governor in 1930—politically too early and personally too late for election on her platform of equal rights for women.

At a time when juries were all male and she was often the only woman in the courtroom, Clara Foltz excelled as a trial lawyer, deftly turning the argument on anyone who tried to use her gender against her. Typical is this response, Foltz's professional credo:

I am a woman and I am a lawyer—and what of it? I came into the practice of my profession under the laws of this State, regularly and honestly, . . . and I have come to stay. I am neither to be bullied out nor worn out.

I ask no special privileges and expect no favors, but I think it only fair that those who have had better opportunities than I, who have had fewer obstacles to surmount and fewer difficulties to contend with should meet me on even ground, upon the merits of law and fact.

For almost five decades, whatever Foltz did and wherever she went, she was the "first woman." As lonely as it was to be first, she gloried in its towering advantage: there is no standard for comparison and thus little room for failure. For Clara Shortridge Foltz, being first was success itself.

• Letters from Foltz to other suffrage and political figures are indexed under her name at the Bancroft Library, University of California at Berkeley, and at the Huntington Library in San Marino, Calif. The text of her speech presented at the 1893 World's Fair is in *Chicago Legal News* 25 (12 Aug. 1893), and another article on public defenders, "Public Defenders for Criminals," is in *American Law Review* 31 (1897). A description of the public sources for writing a life when the subject's papers are lost or destroyed is in B. Babcock, "Reconstructing the Person: The Case of Clara Shortridge Foltz," in *Revealing Lives*, ed. Susan Bell and Marilyn Yalom (1990). Two contemporary summaries of her life work appear in *National Cyclopedia of American Biography*, vol. 1 (1930), and in Oscar T. Shuck, *History of the Bench and Bar of California* (1901). Many newspaper, periodical, and other contemporary articles are cited in Barbara Babcock, "Clara Shortridge Foltz: 'First Woman,'" *Arizona Law Review* 30 (1988), and "Clara Shortridge Foltz: Constitution-Maker," *Indiana Law Journal* 66 (1991). Events in Foltz's later career are well covered in Mortimer Schwartz, Susan Brandt, and Patience Milrod, "Clara Shortridge Foltz: Pioneer in the Law," *Hastings Law Journal* 27 (1976). See also Virginia Elwood-Akers, "Clara Shortridge Foltz: California's First Woman Lawyer," *Pacific Historian* 28 (1984), and Nicholas Polos, "San Diego's 'Portia of the Pacific,'" *Journal of San Diego History* (1980).

BARBARA ALLEN BABCOCK

FOLWELL, William Watts (14 Feb. 1833–18 Sept. 1929), historian and educator, was born in Romulus, Seneca County, New York, the son of Thomas Jefferson Folwell and Joanna Bainbridge, farmers. After receiving his early education in local district schools, he entered the Nunda Literary Institute in Nunda, New York, in the fall of 1848. He remained in Nunda for two years before moving to Geneva, New York, where he attended two different academies and continued to spend his summers doing farm work. Financial reverses suffered by his family ended his studies at Geneva after a year, and he spent the next two years teaching in district schools. He then completed his preparatory education at the academy in Ovid, New York, before entering the sophomore class at Hobart College in Geneva in the fall of 1854.

While at Hobart, Folwell achieved marked success in his studies. He also paid off accumulated debts by teaching Latin and Greek at Ovid Academy when a vacancy in the faculty ranks occurred. After graduating from Hobart as valedictorian in June 1857, he taught ancient languages and German at Seneca Collegiate Institute (formerly Ovid Academy) for the following academic year. Folwell returned to Hobart College in the fall of 1858 as adjunct professor of mathematics. He continued to teach Latin and Greek and also began to study law under Charles J. Folger, who later became a justice of the New York Supreme Court.

In 1859 Folwell prepared a paper on philology for delivery to a local literary society. Intrigued by the subject, he resolved to abandon legal studies and pursue further training in his new field of interest. He entered the University of Berlin in the fall of 1860 and continued his studies there until the outbreak of the American Civil War. Following a hasty tour of Western Europe and Greece, he returned home in October 1861 and accepted a commission in the Fiftieth New York Volunteer Infantry. After training in the field of engineering, the new first lieutenant served with his unit, later known as the Fiftieth New York Engineers, in the Army of the Potomac until the end of the war. His service, consisting mostly of building pontoon bridges and fortifications, was so exemplary that he left the army with the rank of major and brevet lieutenant colonel. During the war, in 1863, he married Sarah Hubbard Heywood; the couple had three children.

Following his discharge from the army, Folwell moved to the newly founded hamlet of Venice, Ohio, where for three years he ran a flour mill established by his father-in-law. He became dissatisfied, because his father-in-law refused to take him, or anyone else, as a partner, and returned to academia, spending a year at Kenyon College in Gambier, Ohio, as professor of mathematics and civil engineering. After turning down a faculty position at the new and struggling University of Minnesota, he was elected as the first president of the school on 23 August 1869.

Upon his arrival on campus, Folwell found that the school consisted of one dilapidated building. Established by the state legislature in 1851, the university had suffered from the effects of both the panic of 1857 and the Civil War. A preparatory department had opened in 1867, but under Folwell's administration college-level instruction finally became a reality.

The fifteen years of the Folwell administration provided a mixture of both success and frustration. Folwell entered his new position with very definite ideas regarding educational reform. He proposed a system that would include preparatory ("Latin") schools, collegiate education, and then professional schools. His main program, developing a junior college system, was at least fifty years ahead of its time and failed to gain the necessary support. He also chafed under the perceived restrictions of the campus location, arguing unsuccessfully for its removal from the site near the Falls of St. Anthony to a rural location that would allow physical expansion and agricultural instruction, which he felt must be practical in nature and meet the educational needs of both the student and the state. He did succeed in initiating a series of short winter courses for farmers so they could receive academic instruction at a convenient time of the year. Similar courses were also held at locations around the state to good effect. Perhaps Folwell's greatest achievement was convincing the state legislature in 1878 to establish a high school board, which, using state funds, encouraged certain select high schools to send their best students to the university. Long an advocate of increased funding for public schools, Folwell tirelessly backed the program, which was enormously successful and contributed greatly to the growth of the university.

Folwell's relations with the trustees, however, eventually proved to be his undoing. Although he was successful in changing the board's policy of hiring professors on a yearly basis, control of both the faculty and the direction of the university became a source of endless friction between Folwell and the trustees. His requests for funding the physical expansion of the campus were cut back, and his attempts to increase professional standards for both admission into and graduation from the university's medical school also met resistance. An incident in front of Folwell's home, during which his friend fired a gun at a group of unruly students, one of whom sustained a leg wound, was the final straw. Although Folwell himself was blameless in the incident, his resignation was accepted by the trustees. After leaving the presidency on 31 August 1884, Folwell remained at the university in the dual role of librarian and professor of political economy.

Folwell also served as a leading force in the establishment of the Minnesota Geological and Natural History Survey in 1872; assisted in the founding of the Minneapolis Society of Fine Arts, serving as president from 1883 to 1888; was a member of the Minneapolis Park Commission, serving as president from 1889 to 1907; and was a member of the state board of charities and corrections from 1896 to 1902. Following his retirement from the university in 1907, Folwell made numerous contributions to the field of local history, publishing *Minnesota, the North Star State* (1908) and the comprehensive *History of Minnesota* (1921–1930). A member of the Minnesota Historical Society since 1871, Folwell served as its president from 1924 until 1927. He died in Minneapolis, Minnesota.

Folwell's life and career in many ways typified progressive academics in the nineteenth century. Among the first group of American scholars to benefit from the superior graduate education available overseas, he rose through the ranks of academia, only to run afoul of reactionary university trustees and budgetary restrictions. Nevertheless, the University of Minnesota owes much to his pioneering efforts.

• The William Watts Folwell Papers are at the Minnesota Historical Society, St. Paul. The best source of information on his life and career is his own *William Watts Folwell: The Autobiography and Letters of a Pioneer of Culture*, ed. Solon J. Buck (1933). A collection of his *University Addresses* was published in 1909. James Gray, *The University of Minnesota, 1851–1951* (1951), is also useful. An obituary is in the *New York Times*, 19 Sept. 1929.

EDWARD L. LACH, JR.

FONDA, Henry (16 May 1905–12 Aug. 1982), actor, was born Henry Jaynes Fonda in Grand Island, Nebraska, the son of William Brace Fonda, a printer, and Herberta Jaynes. When Fonda was six months old, the family moved to Omaha, Nebraska, where his father set up a print shop. Fonda began working at the shop

at the age of twelve. After graduating from the local public high school in 1923, Fonda attended the University of Minnesota and prepared to follow a career in journalism. His father insisted that he work while attending school, but the hectic daily schedule that included five hours of classes and a full eight hours of work was too much for Fonda, and he flunked out in the middle of his sophomore year.

Back in Omaha, Fonda had difficulty finding a full-time position until Dorothy Brando (the mother of actor Marlon Brando and a family friend) suggested that he audition at the Omaha Community Playhouse, of which she was a founding member. With little else to do, Fonda agreed, but after getting the part of Ricky in Philip Barry's *You and I* Fonda admitted that "I was too self-conscious to say I didn't want to do it or didn't know how to do it" (*My Life*, p. 30). Despite his inexperience and a lack of confidence, Fonda fell in love with the theater and for the next year worked at the Omaha Community Playhouse building sets, ushering, and doing anything else that needed to be done. By the spring of 1926, however, Fonda's father had had enough of his son's "playing around," so Fonda got a job as a clerk at the Retail Credit Company of Omaha. The next season Gregory Foley, the director of the playhouse, cast Fonda in the title role in *Merton of the Movies*, and Fonda's love of the theater increased. In 1927 Fonda became an assistant director at the playhouse, where he soon met George Billings, an actor famous for his impersonation of Abraham Lincoln. Fonda wrote a sketch for Billings that included the role of Lincoln's private secretary, John Hay. Fonda got the part and began touring with Billings at $100 a week—the most Fonda had ever earned—but the venture lasted only three months because of Billings's alcoholism.

Fonda returned to Omaha but was determined to go to New York City. He got a free ride to the East Coast with a family friend who was driving to Cape Cod. Fonda joined a summer stock company in Dennis, Massachusetts, as a third assistant stage manager. He soon got a small juvenile role and later that summer joined the University Players Guild in Falmouth, Massachusetts. His first roles were bit parts, but, despite a critically unsuccessful performance as the dumb boxer in *Is Zat So?*, Fonda began playing bigger roles. When the season ended, Fonda finally moved to New York, where he soon learned how difficult it was to find an acting job. The next few years would be lean ones. That winter, he accepted a job at the National Junior Theatre in Washington, D.C., and acted in *Close Up* at Harvard with some of his University Players friends. In this production he met actress Margaret Sullivan.

For the next few years, Fonda spent his summers in Falmouth with the University Players, playing in *The Devil and the Cheese*, *The Firebrand*, *Juno and the Paycock*, and *The Masque of Venice* during the summer of 1929; *Paris Bound*, *Ghost Train*, *Silent House*, *A Kiss for Cinderella*, and *Merton of the Movies* during the summer of 1930; and *Hell Bent Fer Heaven*, *Holiday*,

The Watched Pot, The Constant Nymph, and *Crime* during the summer of 1931. Back in New York during the winter months, Fonda made an inauspicious Broadway debut on 25 November 1929 in a walk-on part in *The Game of Love and Death,* starring Claude Rains at the Guild Theatre; the play closed after six weeks. The following winter Fonda returned to the National Junior Theatre to play the Cowardly Lion in *The Wizard of Oz* and also appeared in *Penrod and Sam, Little Women, Tom Sawyer,* and *Treasure Island.* The next winter the University Players decided to produce a full year in Baltimore, with Fonda appearing in *Mr. Pim Passes By, The Second Man, Mary Rose,* and *The Dark Hours.* In 1931 Fonda married his costar Sullivan, but they separated shortly after and divorced in 1933.

For the next few years, Fonda was offered larger roles in New York, including Eustace in *I Loved You Wednesday* (opening at the Harris Theatre on 11 Oct. 1932) and a Gentleman in *Forsaking All Others* (opening at the Times Square Theater on 1 Mar. 1933). He worked at the Westchester Playhouse in Mount Kisco, New York, during the summer of 1933, but overall it was a difficult financial and professional time for Fonda. While appearing at the Westchester Playhouse, however, Fonda came to the attention of actress June Walker, who had just signed a contract to appear in Marc Connelly's *The Farmer Takes a Wife.* Walker thought Fonda would be ideal for the role of the farmer and arranged an audition with Connelly. Fonda got the part and the play opened to critical if not popular success on 30 October 1934 at the 46th Street Theatre in New York after playing successfully in Washington, D.C.

Fonda's success in the stage role led the producers of the film version to offer him the role opposite Janet Gaynor. Richard Watts, Jr., of the *New York Herald Tribune* called Fonda a "rarity of the drama, a young man who can present naive charm and ingratiating simplicity which will quickly make him one of our most attractive screen actors" (3 Oct. 1934). Watts was prophetic: the success of the film catapulted Fonda into stardom even though his next few films did not equal the acclaim of his first. He scored another hit in 1936 with *The Trail of the Lonesome Pine.* While filming *Wings of Morning* in 1936 in Europe, Fonda met Frances Seymour Brokaw, whom he married that year; they had two children, Jane and Peter, both of whom successfully followed their father into the movie business in the 1960s.

Fonda spent most of his career living on both coasts—performing in the movies but always returning to his first love, the live theater. He starred with Sylvia Sydney in Fritz Lang's *You Only Live Once* in 1937 then returned to New York to perform in *Blow Ye Winds* and *The Virginian,* both moderately successful, before going back to Hollywood to star opposite Bette Davis in William Wyler's *Jezebel.* Fonda's next film, *The Young Mr. Lincoln,* teamed him with renowned director John Ford and garnered critical praise; *Variety* called Fonda's performance "impres-

sively realistic" (7 June 1939). They worked together again in *The Grapes of Wrath* (1940). Fonda's portrayal of the dispossessed Okie Tom Joad was considered one of the best performances of his career and earned him his first Academy Award nomination for best actor. Frank Nugent of the *New York Times* said Fonda's portrayal "is precisely the hot-tempered resolute saturnine chap Mr. Steinbeck had in mind" (14 Dec. 1940). The role came at a high price for Fonda, though: Darryl Zanuck, the head of 20th Century–Fox studios, had required Fonda to sign a long-term contract with the studio in exchange for the opportunity to play Tom Joad. As a result, Fonda had to accept many roles he would not have chosen for himself over the next seven years. Nevertheless, Fonda took pride in his work in *The Lady Eve* (1940), *The Male Animal* (1942), *The Big Street* (1942), *The Return of Frank James* (1940), and *The Ox Bow Incident* (1943).

During World War II, Fonda tried to enlist in the navy, but Zanuck pulled strings so that Fonda could star in *The Immortal Sergeant* (1943). Zanuck's actions greatly angered Fonda, who enlisted as soon as the picture was completed. For the next three years, Fonda served in the navy, attaining the rank of senior lieutenant and being awarded the Bronze Star and a Presidential Citation. After the war, Fonda did not return to the studios for a year and then appeared in *My Darling Clementine* (1946), *Daisy Kenyon,* and *The Fugitive* (1947), the last movies to be made under his Fox contract. In 1948 Fonda teamed with Joshua Logan, whom he had first met during his University Players days, to play his most acclaimed theatrical role, Doug Roberts in *Mister Roberts.* The play was an unparalleled success; he played the role for more than three years, receiving a Tony Award and a Barter Theatre Award as best actor for his work. Brooks Atkinson of the *New York Times* called Fonda "lanky and unheroic, relaxed and genuine, he neatly skirts the maudlin when the play grows sentimental, and he skillfully underplays the bombastic scenes" (19 Feb. 1948). Ten days later Atkinson continued in the same vein, saying that Fonda "gives a perfect human performance. . . . It is difficult to define the perfection of Mr. Fonda's acting . . . simple and genuine" (29 Feb. 1948). On 14 April 1950, while Fonda was still playing Roberts, his wife, who had placed herself in a sanatorium, committed suicide after it became clear that Fonda was seeing another woman named Susan Blanchard. Less than a year later, Fonda and Blanchard were married, and Fonda adopted her daughter Amy.

Fonda had not acted on film for nearly seven years when he was lured back to Hollywood in 1955 to do the film version of *Mister Roberts,* but the filming was racked with trouble. Fonda sided against his longtime friend Logan, who had directed the stage version and had been slated to direct the film, in favor of John Ford, who according to those involved mishandled the film and had to be replaced by Mervyn LeRoy. Fonda, always the perfectionist regarding his own performances, was disappointed with the finished product. In 1956 Fonda went to Rome to film *War and Peace;*

there he became involved with Aferda Franchetti. Back in New York, his wife Susan filed for divorce after Fonda's affair became public. Fonda married Franchetti in March 1957 (they had no children) and returned to New York to play in *Two for the Seesaw*, which opened at the Booth Theatre on 18 January 1958. Over the next few years, Fonda also appeared in *Silent Night, Lonely Night*, which opened at the Morosco Theatre on 3 December 1959, and *Critic's Choice*, which opened at the Ethel Barrymore Theatre on 14 December 1960. During the late 1950s, Fonda took several breaks from New York to make films, including *The Wrong Man* (1957), *Stage Struck* (1958), *Warlock* (1959), and *The Man Who Understood Women* (1959). In 1957 Fonda was named as best foreign actor by the British Academy for his role in *Twelve Angry Men*. In 1962 his marriage to Franchetti ended in divorce, and in 1965 he married Shirlee Adams, a former model and stewardess. They had no children.

For the rest of his career, Fonda searched for challenging roles but often ended up in films like *Sex and the Single Girl* (1964) and *Welcome to Hard Times* (1967)—neither of the caliber Fonda had come to expect of himself. Fonda did continue to tackle challenging roles on the live stage, including the Stage Manager in *Our Town*, produced by American National Theatre and Academy and opening on 27 November 1969, and he toured in a one-man show titled *Fathers against Sons against Fathers* in 1970. His successful one-man show *Clarence Darrow* opened at the Helen Hayes Theatre in New York City on 26 March 1974 and the following year reopened at the Minskoff Theatre on 3 March. After its New York run, Fonda took the show on the road in the United States and England. Fonda received a Drama Desk Award for his portrayal of Darrow in 1974.

Fonda appeared in several short-lived television series. In 1959–1960 he coproduced and starred in "The Deputy" for NBC, and in 1971–1972 he appeared in "The Smith Family" for ABC. He appeared in two miniseries for television: "Captains and the Kings" (1976) and "Roots, the Next Generation" (1979); both received mediocre notices. Fonda also narrated the television special "John Steinbeck's America and Americans" (1967).

In 1978 Fonda was honored by the American Film Institute with a Lifetime Achievement Award—he had appeared in more than 100 films during his career. He continued to make films, appearing in *The Oldest Living Graduate* in 1980 and *Summer Solstice*, with Myrna Loy, in 1981. In 1979 Fonda received an honorary Tony Award for a lifetime of contribution to the theater; in 1980 he received an honorary Academy Award "in recognition of his brilliant accomplishments and enduring contribution to the art of the motion picture"; and in 1981 he received the Lifetime Achievement Award from the Los Angeles Drama Critics Circle. One of his greatest roles was also his last. In 1981 he starred opposite his daughter Jane and Katharine Hepburn in *On Golden Pond*. Fonda received the

Academy Award for best actor for this performance just months before his death in Los Angeles.

Throughout his career, Fonda personified for his audience decency, honesty, and integrity. According to Ephraim Katz, the author of the *Film Encyclopedia* (1994), "Fonda's engaging sincerity, natural style of delivery and characteristically 'American' personality proved ideal for the screen" (p. 466). Of his acting Fonda said: "My goal is that the audience must never see the wheels go around, not see the work that goes into this. It must seem effortless and real. I don't do anything very consciously except that my end results must never be obvious in any way" (*New York Times*, 13 Aug. 1982). John Steinbeck, the novelist whose character of Tom Joad Fonda brought to life in *The Grapes of Wrath*, said that Fonda "carries with him that excitement that can't be learned, but he backs up his gift with grueling, conscientious work and agony of self-doubt" (*New York Times*, 13 Aug. 1982). At the ceremony given by the American Film Institute that honored Fonda, actor Jack Lemmon called him "the definitive American actor," while actor Charlton Heston remarked that he "was one of the best actors America has produced this century. He proved it again and again both on stage and screen; the fact that he constantly divided his talent between the two, as few actors do, showed how much he cared about acting" (*New York Times*, 13 Aug. 1982).

• Fonda's autobiography *My Life* (1981), told to Howard Tiechmann, is informative. A number of biographies are also helpful, including Allen Roberts and Max Goldstein, *Henry Fonda: A Biography* (1984); Norma Goldstein, *Henry Fonda* (1982); and Michael Krebel, *Henry Fonda* (1975). Also of note, although incomplete, is John Springer, *The Fondas: The Films and Careers of Henry, Jane and Peter* (1970). A listing of the most important interviews and trade magazine articles regarding Fonda is included in the *International Dictionary of Film and Filmmakers*, vol. 3: *Actors and Actresses* (1986). Obituaries are in the *New York Times* and the *Los Angeles Times*, 13 Aug. 1982.

MELISSA VICKERY-BAREFORD

FONTANNE, Lynn. *See* Lunt, Alfred, and Lynn Fontanne.

FOOT, Samuel Augustus (8 Nov. 1780–15 Sept. 1846), congressman, U.S. senator, and governor of Connecticut, was born in Cheshire, Connecticut, the son of John Foot and Abigail Hall. His father was a graduate of Yale and a prominent Congregational minister in Cheshire. Samuel himself entered Yale at age thirteen (1793) and graduated four years later. He read law briefly in Washington, Connecticut, before going off to the Litchfield Law School. Debilitating headaches finally forced him to abandon legal training. In 1803 he married Eudocia Hull; they had three children.

As a young man, Foot looked for prosperity and adventure in the lucrative east coast carrying trade. From a base in New Haven, he organized a successful shipping business with the West Indies. Occasionally signing on his own vessels, Foot in these years ventured as far from his native New England as he would ever go. When financial reverses tied to Jefferson's embargo and the War of 1812 caused the firm to collapse in 1813, the disappointed proprietor sought the security of his father's Cheshire estate, but not without a New Englander's commercial expertise that would serve him well politically.

Foot's first immersion in politics came as a proponent of constitutional reform in Connecticut. A "Toleration-Republican," he parted company with the Congregational elite and joined those who advocated religious disestablishment, suffrage for all male taxpayers, fair representative apportionment, and annual elections for state officials. Foot's former business locale, New Haven, was the wellspring of this Jeffersonian surge. The new state constitution of 1818, replacing the 1662 Connecticut charter, embodied the "Tolerationist" program and effectively drove the Federalist party from the field. Involvement in this movement won Foot a Republican seat in the lower house of the Connecticut legislature in 1817 and again in 1818. Between 1819 and 1826, he alternated terms in the state assembly and the U.S. House of Representatives, serving in the Sixteenth and Eighteenth Congresses (1819–1821 and 1823–1825) and returning to the Connecticut statehouse in 1822–1823 and in 1825 as Speaker.

Thirty-nine years old upon entering Congress, Foot achieved recognition as an opponent of slavery expansion and an advocate of government frugality. In February 1820, after the compromise decision to admit Missouri as a slave state, he introduced a resolution to bar slavery from the remaining territories. He also insisted that the Missouri constitution be altered to allow the presence of free blacks and mulattoes, following the effort of the proslavery Missouri Constitutional Convention to ban those potentially disruptive groups from the state. Believing the military too expensive and not sufficiently accountable to the public, Foot focused his wrath on officer salaries. Escalation of these, he declared in February 1821, represented "a growing evil" inconsistent with the "republican simplicity" of an earlier era. Deaf to pleas of the more desperate westerners during the panic of 1819, Foot supported the Land Act of 1820, which repealed the credit system for public land purchases; voted in 1821 against the Relief Act that extended payment deadlines for indebted buyers; and urged restoration of the $1.64 per acre minimum price after its reduction in 1820 to $1.25.

During his second stint in the House, Foot added federally funded internal improvements and protective tariffs to his growing list of political targets. Apart from their cost and disproportionate benefit to westerners, he scorned transportation subsidies for stretching beyond powers expressly granted to the federal government. With traditional New England hostility to westward expansion, the Connecticut senator voted against extensions of the Cumberland Road. He gave equal intensity to the tariff, which most New Englanders in Congress treated as inimical to their sectional interest until the late 1820s. Though willing to consider "judicious" tariff revision, Foot warned against the "taxation of agriculture" and opposed Henry Clay's famous bill of 1824 on grounds that people can be "legislated into adversity" but not into prosperity. As the economic destiny of Connecticut came to lie with textile manufacturing, however, so did Foot's political sympathies. From 1828 on he supported major tariff bills.

In an election that reflected emerging ideological cleavage in Connecticut politics, Foot won a U.S. Senate seat in 1826, replacing Henry W. Edwards (1779–1847), who soon became an organizer of the Jacksonian movement in the state. Foot viewed Andrew Jackson and his party with contempt from the start. Though his view of federal spending resembled that of some Old Hickory boosters, Foot's consistently anti-western attitude helped to put him at odds with Jackson party organizers in Congress. At first a staunch "Adams man" with a stubborn New England bias, Foot moderated his sectional rigidity enough by 1833 to align with Clay and the new Whig party. As a senator, he condemned American Indian removal, voted for the Bank of the United States recharter, softened his earlier stand against internal improvements, supported Clay's Land Bill of 1832, and lamented the unrestrained cost and corruption of Jackson's "spoils system." Foot's greatest claim to fame occurred on 29 December 1829, when he introduced the resolution that triggered the "Great Debate" between senators Daniel Webster and Robert Y. Hayne (1791–1839).

"Foot's Resolution" was a seemingly innocuous proposal that public land sales be limited temporarily to tracts already surveyed and on the market. To promote government retrenchment, he also proposed abolition of the office of surveyor general. Because it came from a member who lacked firsthand knowledge of the West and had no record of concern for westerners, the resolution enraged colleagues from that section. Agrarians claimed that further restrictions on sales would stunt the agricultural growth of the West, strangling its fragile farm-based economy, while commercial-minded westerners feared that any halting of surveys and sales would threaten land investors thriving in frontier towns. The resolution elicited a bitter but calculated rebuttal from the Jacksonian Thomas Hart Benton (1782–1858) of Missouri. When Hayne of South Carolina, a protégé of John C. Calhoun, rose to speak in defense of Benton and the West, it was clear that the real issue was no longer the pace of frontier land sales. Caught by surprise, Webster's motivation was largely to nip a budding southern/western alliance that might alter the balance of power in Congress to the detriment of the Northeast. The Massachusetts senator reminded Foot's antagonists that public lands were reserved as a common fund to benefit all states, not the West alone, thus converting the focus of debate from a sectional issue to the nature of the Union as a whole.

The instigator of this famous drama, Foot, who probably did not anticipate its high political stakes, had quarreled with Benton before. His being the lone New Englander on Benton's Indian Affairs Committee strained their relationship during the 1827–1828 session. In 1828 Foot opposed the Missouri senator's Graduation Bill, which called for systematic reductions of price for public lands according to length of time on the market. In May of that year, he also refuted Benton's attack on New England for supporting the "tariff of abominations," which the South despised. Foot must have known that his resolution in 1829 would irritate his Missouri rival, among others.

As the tide of expansion surged westward, New England's influence in national politics declined, as did Foot's career. Defeated for reelection to the Senate in 1832 by Nathan Smith (1770–1835), another future Whig, Foot had to settle for a seat in the House of Representatives until 1834, when he became governor of Connecticut. He was installed by legislative vote (154 to 70) after failing to carry a clear popular majority over the incumbent Edwards, his old rival and now a leading Democrat. One year later, however, the depressed state economy unseated Foot in an electoral rematch with Edwards. In 1835 Foot retired from a formal role in politics until serving as a presidential elector for Clay in 1844.

Foot died in Cheshire. One of his sons, Andrew Hull Foote, a naval officer and Civil War hero, added the final *e* to the family name.

• No substantial collection of Foot papers exists. The Connecticut Historical Society in Hartford owns a few scattered letters. The best source on Foot's career in Congress is the *Register of Debates in Congress, 1825–1837*, comp. Joseph Gales and William W. Seaton. For valuable background on western issues in national politics, see Daniel Feller, *The Public Lands in Jacksonian Politics* (1984). On Connecticut politics during Foot's time, see Richard J. Purcell, *Connecticut in Transition, 1775–1818* (1918), and Jarvis M. Morse, *A Neglected Period of Connecticut's History, 1818–1850* (1933). An obituary notice for Foot appears in the *New Haven Daily Register*, 16 Sept. 1846.

JOHN R. VAN ATTA

FOOT, Solomon (19 Nov. 1802–28 Mar. 1866), attorney, U.S. representative, and U.S. senator, was born in Cornwall, Vermont, the son of Solomon Foot, a physician, and Betsey Crossett. After the death of his father in 1811, Solomon had a difficult childhood and was forced at times to reside with other families in Cornwall. Yet he graduated from Middlebury College in 1826, taught at Castleton Seminary, where he served as principal from 1828 to 1831, and was a tutor at the University of Vermont (1827). Studying law, he was admitted to the bar in 1831 and began practice in Rutland. From 1836 to 1842 he was the prosecuting attorney for Rutland County. In 1839 he married Emily Fay, who died, and in 1844 he married Mary Ann Hodges Dana. He had no children.

Foot quickly established himself in Whig politics, campaigning for Henry Clay's election in 1832 and, after Clay's defeat by Andrew Jackson, defending the Bank of the United States, then under attack by Jack-

son and the Democrats. Foot was elected several times to the Vermont legislature (1833, 1835, 1837, 1838, 1847) and served three times as Speaker of the house (1837, 1838, 1847). He also served in the Vermont constitutional convention in 1836. In 1842 he was elected to the first of two consecutive terms in the U.S. House of Representatives. In Congress, Foot gained some prominence, first in urging moderation in the dispute with Great Britain over Oregon and then in opposition to a declaration of war against Mexico in 1846. Joining other northern Whigs, he supported the Wilmot Proviso, which would have banned slavery in territory acquired from Mexico as a result of the war. He denounced James K. Polk's role in inciting the war, sarcastically paraphrasing the president's war message to suggest that "war exists by my acts and in consequence of my successful efforts to provoke it." Foot predicted that the seizing of new territory would prove fatal to the Union by triggering a war between the North and the South.

In October 1850 the Vermont legislature elected Foot to the Senate, where he served for the remaining fifteen years of his life. In the years preceding the Civil War, he adhered to the Whig and then the Republican philosophy opposing the extension of slavery into any new territory. He was especially critical of Stephen A. Douglas's Kansas-Nebraska Bill because of its repeal of the ban on slavery in the Louisiana Territory north of 36°30' and wrote an address condemning the bill. As a result of the bill's passage, he joined with many other northern Whigs and Democrats in 1854 in preliminary meetings leading to the formation of the Republican party. Although he chaired a meeting of anti-Nebraska congressmen in 1854, at that point he stopped short of calling for a new party. Nonetheless, as the Whigs disintegrated, he resisted the nativist American (Know Nothing) party and became an enthusiastic Republican. In the late 1850s he attacked what he called James Buchanan's deception in supporting the proslavery Lecompton constitution in Kansas, because of its violation of the principle of popular sovereignty, the right of territorial voters to decide the status of slavery. Foot also attacked the proslavery filibustering activities of William Walker in Nicaragua in the late 1850s. He, like Senator William H. Seward of New York, was critical of Great Britain's continuing efforts to remain in Central America as a threat to American dominance there. He favored Seward for the Republican presidential nomination in 1860.

During the Civil War Foot enthusiastically supported Abraham Lincoln's war and emancipation policies. On racial issues he was a moderate, as seen in his refusal to support Senator Charles Sumner's efforts to secure equal pay for black troops in 1864. During a large part of the Civil War he was president pro tempore of the Senate, where he maintained an evenhanded fairness amid emotional debates and exhibited his skill in parliamentary law. A moderate Republican during the early phases of Reconstruction, he could usually be counted on to support the program of the

Radicals in his party. Although he was not a noted speaker and did not greatly influence policy, he was well respected and well liked by his Senate colleagues. During the Civil War he chaired the Senate Committee on Public Buildings, which directed the completion of the Capitol even as the war raged on. At the time of his death he was the Senate's oldest member in continuous service. His death in Washington was followed by a funeral in the Senate chamber.

• Reflective of Foot's relative obscurity outside of his native Vermont little has been written about him. Foot left no papers, making him a difficult subject to research. Most studies of the years he served in Congress fail to mention him or note only the fact that he served and generally supported Whig and Republican policies. Foot's speeches in Congress are in the *Congressional Globe*, 28th–29th Congs. (1843–1846) and 32d–39th Congs. (1851–1867). See especially *Speech of Mr. Solomon Foot, of Vermont, on the Origin and Causes of the Mexican War* (1846) and *Speech of Mr. Solomon Foot of Vermont on the Character and Objects of the Mexican War* (1847). Additional information on his role in Congress is in U.S. Congress, "Proceedings on the Death of Hon. Solomon Foot, Including the Addresses Delivered in the Senate and House of Representatives on Thursday April 12, 1866," 39th Cong., 1st sess., 1866, and a eulogy delivered at his Rutland, Vt., funeral, Norman Seaver, "A Discourse Delivered at the Funeral of Hon. Solomon Foot" (1866), a copy of which is in the Cincinnati College of Law Library. Obituaries are in the *Rutland Daily Herald*, 29 Mar.–2 Apr. 1866, and the *Daily Morning Chronicle* (Washington, D.C.), 29, 30 Mar. and 2 Apr. 1866.

FREDERICK J. BLUE

FOOTE, Andrew Hull (12 Sept. 1806–26 June 1863), naval officer, was born in New Haven, Connecticut, the son of Samuel Augustus Foot, a merchant shipper, U.S. senator, and governor of Connecticut, and Eudocia Hull. Raised in a strict moral and religious environment and educated at schools in New Haven and Cheshire, Connecticut, and briefly at the U.S. Military Academy (1822), Foote (it is not known when he added the *e* to his name) entered the navy as an acting midshipman in December 1822. He was warranted midshipman in December 1823 and served in the West India Squadron, patrolling for pirates (1823–1824). He then served aboard the flagship *United States* in the Pacific Squadron (1825–1827) before returning to the West India Squadron aboard the sloop *Natchez* and as master aboard the sloop *Hornet* (1827).

Aboard *Natchez*, Foote's religious beliefs were transformed into a powerful faith that shaped his career and influenced the entire naval service. Lengthy religious discussions with one of the officers convinced Foote that the navy had to be manned with sailors of strong Christian principle. In 1828 he married Caroline Flagg; they had one child.

Promoted to passed midshipman in 1828 and to lieutenant in 1830, Foote served as sailing master aboard the sloop *St. Louis* in the Pacific Squadron (1829–1831) and as flag lieutenant in the Mediterranean Squadron aboard the ship of the line *Delaware* (1833–1836). In 1837 he sailed along the U.S. coast in the newly commissioned steamer *Fulton II*. He served as executive officer aboard the sloop of war *John Adams* on the East India Station from 1838 to 1840. His first wife having died in 1838, in 1842 he married Caroline Augusta Street; they had two children.

Foote applied his religious beliefs afloat and ashore. From 1841 to 1843 he served at the Naval Asylum, Philadelphia. While there, he concluded that alcohol was the source of moral and social evil and began to promote abstinence among the asylum's pensioners. As first lieutenant aboard the flagship *Cumberland*, Mediterranean Squadron (1843–1845), he conducted shipboard prayer meetings and organized a temperance society, in which the crew gave up their grog ration in return for extra pay. By transforming *Cumberland* into the navy's first temperance ship, Foote launched the movement that culminated in elimination of the grog ration throughout the service in 1862.

From 1846 to 1848 Foote served as executive officer at the Boston Navy Yard, thereby missing action during the Mexican War. Afterward, he commanded the brig *Perry* off the southwest African coast (1849–1851), striving to suppress the slave trade, to prevent British searches of American vessels, to stop the fraudulent flying of the American flag, and to engineer a voluntary ban on liquor aboard his ship.

During more than four years of shore duty that followed (1851–1856), Foote was promoted to commander (1852), served a second tour of duty at the Philadelphia Naval Asylum as executive officer (1854–1855), and was a member of the controversial Naval Efficiency Board (1855). He also wrote and lectured on the slave trade, temperance, and related topics. In *Africa and the American Flag* (1854), he expressed his outrage at the horrors of the middle passage and called on the United States to take the leading role in opening "vast regions" of Africa "to science and legal commerce" and "throwing wide the portals of the continent for the entrance of Christian civilization" (pp. 389–90).

Foote was commanding the sloop of war *Portsmouth* on the East India Station (1856–1858) when the Second Anglo-Chinese War broke out in October 1856. In November he landed a force of marines in Canton (Kuang-chou) to establish the American presence. When the four heavily fortified Chinese barrier forts between Canton and Whampoa (Huang-pu) fired on Foote's boats two weeks later, he moved swiftly to capture and destroy the forts. This example of "gunboat diplomacy" laid the groundwork for future American diplomatic contacts with China.

From 1858 until 1861 Foote served as executive officer of the Brooklyn Navy Yard. He instituted regular religious instruction for the yard's workers and neighborhood residents. When the Civil War broke out in April 1861, he participated in preparations for relieving Forts Sumter and Pickens.

Promoted to captain in June 1861, Foote took command of the western flotilla, headquartered at St. Louis, in September. The basic design and construction decisions had already been made, and much of the fleet was operational. However, Foote's administrative skills enabled construction to be completed and ordnance and crew to be assembled. He faced daunting administrative challenges, in part because the fleet was technically under army command.

On 6 February 1862 Foote commanded naval operations in the capture of Fort Henry on the Tennessee River. Using *Cincinnati* as his flagship, Foote led the gunboats, arranged in line of battle formation, in an assault on the fort, which surrendered after a two-hour bombardment. His daring strike, without the assistance of General Ulysses S. Grant's troops, demonstrated an overconfidence fostered by his experiences in China in 1856. His religious convictions, too, had spurred him on, as he saw victory as a sign from heaven. Although it was an easy victory, the capture of the fort bolstered sagging Union morale and helped to open western Tennessee to Federal troops. As a reward, Foote was promoted to flag officer.

Foote again demonstrated overconfidence a week later, on 14 February 1862, commanding a naval force at Fort Donelson on the Cumberland River. His gunboats engaged in vigorous shelling but were forced to withdraw in the face of heavy Confederate gunfire. The defeat made him realize that his gunboats were not invincible, and he became increasingly cautious. In operations against Island No. 10 (Mar. 1862), Foote postponed his vessels' arrival for more than a week and then maintained their distance from the enemy. Still crippled from wounds gained at Fort Donelson, he was now wary of risking his vessels. Although the April 1862 Confederate surrender of Island No. 10 was critical, Foote had lost enthusiasm for military action.

Thereafter, health problems increasingly impeded Foote's performance, and in May 1862 he surrendered command and went on sick leave. In July 1862 he was commissioned rear admiral and appointed chief of the new Bureau of Equipment and Recruiting. Secretary of the Navy Gideon Welles advised him to delay returning to active sea duty and privately lamented his old friend's growing petulance over administrative duties (*Diary*, 10 and 23 Aug. 1862). In June 1863 Foote accepted an appointment to succeed Samuel F. Du Pont as commander of the South Atlantic Blockading Squadron. Foote died of Bright's disease in New York City en route to his new post.

Foote was viewed during his lifetime as a brave, accomplished officer; quiet and unostentatious, yet determined; a devout Christian; and a fighting commander. Modern evaluations have acknowledged his technical and fighting abilities while also emphasizing his administrative skills and the importance of his reform efforts on behalf of temperance, the slave trade and colonization, and missionary activity.

• The Foote manuscripts are at the Library of Congress with additional papers at the New Haven Colony Historical Society Collections. Foote's official correspondence can be found in RG 45 and RG 92 of the National Archives. In addition to his book, Foote published two pamphlets, *Farewell Temperance Address* (1845) and *The African Squadron* (1855). Foote's Civil War career can be traced in *The Official Records of the Union and Confederate Navies in the War of the Rebellion* (30 vols., 1894–1922); Howard K. Beale, ed. (1960 ed.), *Diary of Gideon Welles* (1911; repr. 1960); and Robert Means Thompson and Richard Wainwright, eds., *Confidential Correspondence of Gustavus Vasa Fox* (1919). James Mason Hoppin, *Life of Andrew Hull Foote, Rear-Admiral, United States Navy* (1874), is generally reliable; it includes extensive excerpts from Foote's letters and journals. John D. Milligan, "Andrew Foote: Zealous Reformer, Administrator, Warrior," in his *Captains of the Old Steam Navy: Makers of the American Naval Tradition, 1840–1880* is judicious and thoroughly researched; a good bibliographical essay is included. Among other secondary accounts are the unsigned "Andrew Hull Foote," *Hours at Home: A Popular Monthly Devoted to Religious and Useful Literature* 1, no. 1 (May 1865): 83–92, an extensive sketch published two years after Foote's death emphasizing his religious and reform thinking; Edwin North McClellan, "The Capture of the Barrier Forts in the Canton River, China," *Marine Corps Gazette*, Sept. 1920, pp. 262–76; and Neville T. Kirk, "Commander Foote at the Barrier Forts," *U.S. Naval Institute Proceedings* 81 (1955): 126–27. His life and death are summarized in the *New York Herald*, 27 and 28 June 1863.

KENNETH J. BLUME

FOOTE, Arthur William (5 Mar. 1853–8 Apr. 1937), composer, was born in Salem, Massachusetts, the sixth child and youngest son of Caleb Foote, the editor of the *Salem Gazette*, and Mary Wilder White. His mother died four years after his birth, and he was reared by his older sister, Mary White Foote Tileston. His only other surviving sibling, his brother, Henry Wilder Foote, was a long-time minister of King's Chapel, Boston.

At age twelve Foote began piano studies in Salem with Fanny Paine, a student of Benjamin J. Lang; two years later he took a harmony class with Stephen Emery at the New England Conservatory of Music. Following his maternal grandfather's example, he entered Harvard College in 1870. He was director of the Harvard Glee Club for two years and graduated Phi Beta Kappa in 1874. His studies of counterpoint and fugue with John Knowles Paine continued into graduate school; at the same time he studied piano and organ with Lang. In 1875 Harvard granted Foote the first M.A. in music to be given by an American university. He was also the first American composer to receive his entire musical training in the United States; his only other formal instruction was a few lessons with Stephen Heller in France in 1883. Foote made eight summer trips to Europe over a twenty-year period, where he met many of the leading musicians of the day and attended the first Bayreuth Festival and the premiere of the complete *Ring des Nibelungen*. In 1880 he married Kate Grant Knowlton; they had one daughter.

A resident of Boston all his professional life, Foote had a long and active career as a teacher, church organist, and piano recitalist. Beginning in 1875 he taught piano and organ in his private studio; from 1921 until his death he also taught at the New England Conservatory of Music. In 1876 he became organist at the Church of the Disciples in Boston; two years later he was appointed organist and choirmaster of the First Church (Unitarian), a post he held until 1910. Foote made his piano recital debut in 1876 and continued performing regularly until 1895. In 1880 he instituted a series of chamber music concerts in Boston that featured not only new music from Europe but his own works and those of his American contemporaries; the series continued until 1895. Foote frequently played with the Kneisel Quartet and conducted the Boston Symphony and other orchestras in performances of his own compositions.

Foote began composing as a child, but his first extant composition dates from 1877, a gavotte for piano that was performed in Boston that same year by Annette Essipoff on the first all-American program in the United States. The first of Foote's works to be published, it came out in 1882 in the set *Trois morceaux de piano*, op. 3, under the imprint of the Boston publisher Arthur P. Schmidt. Virtually all of Foote's output was handled by Schmidt, whose international connections assured a ready market and numerous performance opportunities for Foote's compositions in Europe.

Foote wrote over two hundred compositions, primarily for voice, piano, organ, strings, or orchestra. A prolific songwriter, his strong melodic gift is best exemplified in "I'm Wearing Awa'" (1887) and "An Irish Folk Song" (1891), which has been published in many editions in the United States and abroad. In addition to numerous anthems and choruses for men's and women's voices, he wrote four cantatas for voices and orchestra. Although he composed many works for piano, Foote excelled in writing for strings, and much of his chamber music has been recorded. His first orchestral piece, the overture *In the Mountains*, op. 14 (1886), was performed at the Paris Exposition of 1889. Several works, including the Piano Quartet, op. 23 (1890), and the Serenade for Strings, op. 25 (1891), were featured at the World's Columbian Exposition in Chicago in 1893. His Suite in E major, op. 63, for string orchestra (1907–1908), is probably his most frequently performed work. Most of his symphonic works were premiered by the Boston Symphony Orchestra; the Cello Concerto, op. 33 (1893), and the *Four Character Pieces after the Rubaiyat of Omar Khayyam*, op. 48 (1907), which Foote considered to be his most successful work for orchestra, were premiered by the Chicago Symphony Orchestra. His last major work, *A Night Piece*, for flute and strings (1922), is his most famous.

The first American-born and -trained composer to achieve international recognition, Foote was one of the leading composers in Boston at the turn of the century. Grouped with Amy Beach, George Chadwick, Edward MacDowell, Horatio Parker, and John Knowles Paine as a member of the Boston Six or the Second New England School, he was strongly influenced by the predominant Germanic presence in the Boston musical scene during the second half of the nineteenth century. Firmly rooted in the romantic tradition, Foote's music is characterized by lyrical melodies, expressive phrasing, clear formal structure, colorful orchestration, and impassioned feeling.

Highly regarded as a pedagogue, Foote wrote numerous didactic articles for musical journals and two handbooks on modulation and piano playing. He translated Ernst F. E. Richter's *A Treatise on Fugue* (1878), edited Stephen A. Emery's *Elements of Harmony* (1924), and coauthored, with Walter R. Spalding, *Modern Harmony in Its Theory and Practice* (1905), which was for many years a popular theory text. Foote was dedicated to high standards and good repertoire, and he arranged and edited over one hundred piano pieces that introduced scores of students to the music of the classics. During the summer of 1911 Foote served as acting chairman of the music department and guest lecturer at the University of California at Berkeley, his only formal academic appointment.

Foote was an active member of the Harvard Musical Association, a life member of the Music Teachers' National Association, one of the founders and the national president (1909–1912) of the American Guild of Organists, and an honorary member of Phi Mu Alpha Sinfonia. He was elected to the National Institute of Arts and Letters, was a fellow of the American Academy of Arts and Sciences, and held honorary doctorates from Trinity College (1919) and Dartmouth College (1925).

Foote's editions of classical piano pieces and his theoretical writings probably had more influence on later generations than did his music, which, though solid and well crafted, was dependent on European traditions. His distinctive role was as a leader in establishing serious composition as a component of American musical life.

• The primary collections of Foote's musical manuscripts are in the Harvard Musical Association Library, the New England Conservatory of Music Library, and the Arthur P. Schmidt Company Archives in the Music Division of the Library of Congress. Personal scrapbooks are in the Music Department of the Boston Public Library, the Widener Library at Harvard University, the New England Conservatory of Music Library, and the Music Division of the Library of Congress. The major biographical source is *Arthur Foote, 1853–1937: An Autobiography*, privately printed in 1946 and reprinted with introduction and notes by Wilma Reid Cipolla (1979). A complete bibliography of his compositions and writings, along with a discography and listings of the secondary literature, is Cipolla's *A Catalog of the Works of Arthur Foote, 1853–1937* (1980). Analyses of his works are found in three unpublished dissertations: "Arthur Foote: American Composer and Theorist" by Frederick Kopp (Univ. of Rochester, 1957), Doric Alviani, "The Choral Church Music of Arthur William Foote" (Union Theological Seminary, 1962), and Douglas Moore, "The Cello Music of Arthur Foote, 1853–1937" (Catholic Univ., 1977). An obituary is in the *New York Times*, 10 Apr. 1937.

WILMA REID CIPOLLA

FOOTE, Edward Bliss (20 Feb. 1829–5 Oct. 1906), eclectic physician and birth-control pioneer, was born near Cleveland, Ohio, the son of Herschel Foote, a postmaster, and Pamelia Bliss. Foote left school at fifteen to pursue a career in journalism, first with the *Cleveland Herald* and then, over the next decade, with newspapers in Connecticut and New York. In September 1853 he married Catherine Goodenough Bond, a schoolteacher from Watertown, Massachusetts; they had three children.

After settling in New York, Foote devoted his leisure hours to reading medicine with a botanical practitioner. Later, while an associate editor of the *Brooklyn Morning Journal*, he resumed these studies in earnest with his old preceptor. Upon completing a two-year apprenticeship he left journalism for medicine; in 1860 he graduated from Penn Medical University in Philadelphia.

Foote started private practice in Saratoga Springs, New York, a resort town famous for its medicinal waters. Despite the alleged curative properties of these springs, he preferred the therapeutic effects of vegetable medicines and electricity. Although the majority of his patients suffered from consumption and rheumatism, he regularly encountered cases of leukorrhea, a whitish vaginal discharge, which he attributed to the custom of postcoital douching with caustics. This experience led to his life's work in birth-control reform.

Foote tackled the thorny issue of birth control in his popular work *Medical Common Sense* (1858). Married women, he maintained, were overtaxed by unwanted pregnancies and desperate for relief; however, getting sound contraceptive advice was difficult because the country was "flooded with quack nostrums, injurious and unreliable 'recipes.'" Foote exposed the shortcomings of douching, coitus interruptus, and the "prevention pills" peddled by charlatans. Induced abortion had become prevalent as a birth-control method among married, native-born, middle- and upper-class women (in 1860 20 percent of pregnancies ended in abortion). This custom could be curbed, Foote reasoned, by the availability of simple and reliable contraceptives. Nevertheless, he deliberately omitted explicit contraceptive advice from his book for fear of its misuse. Such delicate information would be provided, in strictest confidence, to married women who consulted him privately.

By 1864 Foote had settled in New York City, where he remained for the rest of his professional life. In advertising the opening of his Manhattan office he offered a phrenological evaluation by Orson Squire Fowler, the founder of "practical phrenology," as well as the usual testimonials from devoted patients. It is not clear if Foote embraced phrenology, but he obviously understood the value of its popular appeal to the success of his medical practice.

A revised edition of *Medical Common Sense* (1864) contained a comprehensive discussion of four dependable birth-control devices—the membraneous envelope (condoms made from animal ceca or fish bladders), the apex envelope (a rubber glans condom), an electromagnetic preventive machine, and the womb veil (a rubber cervical diaphragm). Foote favored the last because, he wrote, "It places conception entirely under the control of the wife." The condom, he noted, had the added advantage of protecting both partners against venereal infection. His claim that a weak current from the electromagnetic machine produced an electrical disparity between the male and female, causing the uterus to reject spermatozoa, perhaps derived from a faith in the therapeutic power of electricity presaged in his M.D. thesis, "Electricity in Relation to the Human Organism."

Continuing his birth-control crusade with *Plain Home Talk* (1871), Foote deleted discussion of contraceptives because they were treated fully in his tract *Words in Pearl* (c. 1870). Instead, he devoted considerable space to a criticism of "male continence" (coitus reservatus), a contraceptive practice that John Humphrey Noyes had introduced into his utopian community at Oneida, New York. Foote predicted that Noyes's technique, consisting of normal intromission and movements without ejaculation, would never gain widespread acceptance because it required extraordinary self-control.

Foote opposed male continence, but he approved wholeheartedly of Noyes's eugenic policy of stirpiculture, or the perfection of the human race by prohibiting the breeding of inferior individuals. In *Plain Home Talk* (1884) Foote's denunciation of coitus reservatus encompassed his own eugenic beliefs, which had hardened over the intervening years: "Indeed, the very ones who ought not to propagate their kind . . . will never listen to any advice requiring the exercise of self-denial or restraint. With mechanical means that would not interfere with their pleasures they might be induced to avoid the responsibilities of parentage." Contraceptive methods must be perfected, he argued, because "every community is infested with physical weaklings and natural-born sinners . . . who stand in the path of human progress."

Even though Foote continued to treat patients with various ailments, he concentrated on commercializing birth control. He published his own writings on the subject under the imprint of the Murray Hill Publishing Company (founded 1872) and created a large mail-order business in contraceptive literature and devices.

Foote's success proved costly. In June 1876 he was indicted under the federal Comstock Act (1873) for distributing birth-control information (*Words in Pearl*) through the mail. He was tried, found guilty, and fined $3,500; his total legal fees approached $5,000. A possible ten-year prison sentence was avoided through the intercession of influential friends, who convinced the judge that many patients would suffer if Foote were incarcerated. Foote had been entrapped by a decoy letter from Anthony Comstock, secretary of the New York Society for the Suppression of Vice, in retaliation for an attack on the federal and state Comstock laws in his pamphlet *A Step Backward* (1875). Foote's medical practice continued to flourish despite the affair.

In *Home Cyclopedia* (1902), his last major piece of popular writing, Foote lamented the existing legislation restricting the dissemination of contraceptive information and pleaded with his readers to help repeal those shortsighted statutes. He stressed the social benefits to be derived from a physician's freedom to counsel all who sought effective ways to prevent conception.

Worried that "bad stock" (Catholic immigrants) was outbreeding "good stock" (white, native-born Protestants), some leading physicians of the day opposed any means of family limitation and were responsible for the criminalization of abortion. Medical schools provided no contraceptive instruction; there were no textbooks on the subject, and medical journals were conspicuously silent until the *Medical and Surgical Reporter* (1888) published the first symposium on birth control. Amid this parochialism, Foote championed social reform by advocating the birth of fewer but healthier children. His books—unique in targeting female consumers—were bestsellers: total sales of *Medical Common Sense* and *Plain Home Talk* exceeded 500,000 copies. Foote pioneered a complete approach to the problem of reproductive control by explaining his philosophy, exposing faulty contraceptive devices and techniques, and providing explicit details of reliable methods. Skirting the Comstock laws, he wrote tirelessly about racial improvement through the rational use of birth control.

Little is known about Foote's private life. His personal papers were destroyed in a fire a few years before he died in Larchmont, New York.

• The most complete modern sources on birth control are Janet Farrell Brodie, *Contraception and Abortion in Nineteenth-Century America* (1994), and James Reed, *From Private Vice to Public Virtue: The Birth Control Movement and American Society since 1830* (1978). The best account of abortion is James C. Mohr, *Abortion in America: The Origins and Evolution of National Policy, 1800–1900* (1978). For an assessment of Noyes's ideas see Philip R. Wyatt, "John Humphrey Noyes and the Stirpicultural Experiment," *Journal of the History of Medicine and Allied Sciences* 31 (1976): 55–66. Focusing on Foote and the social and moral context of his work are three articles by Vincent J. Cirillo, "Edward Foote's *Medical Common Sense*: An Early American Comment on Birth Control," *Journal of the History of Medicine and Allied Sciences* 25 (1970): 341–45; "Edward Bliss Foote: Pioneer American Advocate of Birth Control," *Bulletin of the History of Medicine* 47 (1973): 471–79; and "Birth Control in Nineteenth-century America: A View from Three Contemporaries," *Yale Journal of Biology and Medicine* 47 (1974): 260–67. An obituary is in the *New York Tribune*, 6 Oct. 1906.

VINCENT J. CIRILLO

FOOTE, Henry Stuart (28 Feb. 1804–20 May 1880), U.S. senator and governor of Mississippi, was born in Fauquier County, Virginia, the son of Richard Helm Foote and Jane Stuart. After graduating from Washington College (now Washington and Lee University) in 1819, he was admitted to the bar in Richmond in 1823. Soon, he moved to Tuscumbia, Alabama, for a few years, where he edited a Democratic newspaper, and then to Mississippi, where he quickly became one of the leading criminal lawyers in the state.

After helping to found, and then editing, the Jackson *Mississippian*, Foote became involved in public affairs and ran for the constitutional convention of 1832 that gave the state perhaps the most democratic constitution in America at the time. Although not elected, Foote was nonetheless a leading advocate of the popular election of judges, the most controversial issue in the campaign, which the convention then enacted. During the 1830s he became a controversial and contentious figure in Mississippi politics, well known both for his flamboyant, vituperative rhetoric on the stump and for his personal combativeness. He fought three duels with political rivals—two with Sergeant S. Prentiss and one with Oswald Claiborne (another had taken place earlier in Alabama)—so the Mississippi legislature passed a special law to exempt him from the constitutional ban on duelists becoming officeholders. Simultaneously, he was known as "General Weathercock" because, although basically a Jacksonian Democrat, he had affiliated with the Whigs on several occasions. As a state legislator from Hinds County (where Jackson is located), he was an advocate of hard money, an opponent of banks, and a supporter of temperance who wrote the state's "gallon" law in 1839 outlawing the sale of liquor in amounts less than a gallon. That year, he visited Texas and was so intrigued by the region that he published *Texas and the Texans* (2 vols.) in 1841 and was a vigorous proponent of Texas annexation in 1844.

Between 1846 and 1854 Foote was at the center of the stormy politics in Mississippi. He was chosen to succeed Robert J. Walker in the U.S. Senate after initially being involved in the contest merely as the designated surrogate of the front-runner, John A. Quitman, who disliked and disdained campaigning. Foote later claimed that he had warned Quitman that the scheme might backfire. Once in the Senate, Foote played a major role in the furor over the 1850 Compromise. It was he who suggested to Henry Clay that the measures be packaged together as a single "omnibus" bill. Although this approach eventually failed, Foote nevertheless backed all the separate bills that constituted the final compromise except for California's admission as a free state. He was then confronted with opposition to the compromise from the rest of the Mississippi congressional delegation, Governor Quitman, and two-thirds of the state legislature. Leading the Unionist forces against Quitman's call for a state convention to consider secession, Foote resigned his Senate seat to run for governor. Ultimately, the Unionists prevailed. Not only did they control the convention but Foote himself became governor. By a mere 999 votes, he defeated Jefferson Davis, who had also resigned from the U.S. Senate to take on Foote after Quitman had withdrawn because of his opponent's verbally and physically threatening behavior on the stump.

Foote's term as governor (1852–1854) was not a success. The state legislature was divided into a "Davis senate" and a "Foote house" as a result of the elections, and the contests to fill the remainder of the two U.S.

Senate terms proved enormously contentious. In a typically impetuous and provocative fashion, Foote expressed his disgust by resigning five days before his term expired and moving to California.

Toward the end of the decade, he returned to Mississippi and became a leading opponent of secession. In 1859 he walked out of the Southern Commercial Convention at Vicksburg to protest its support of the reopening of the African slave trade, which he considered economically unwise and likely to disrupt the racial order and stability of the slave system with additional "thousands, and perhaps millions, of wild and savage Africans." In 1860 he campaigned for Stephen A. Douglas as the only hope for the Union and tore into the secessionists with his invective. When Mississippi seceded, he left for Tennessee. But in a dramatic shift of position after the war had begun, he decided to encourage eastern Tennessee to join the emergent Confederacy in May and June 1861, and soon he was running for the Confederate Congress from Nashville, where he now lived, a move he later regarded as the "most absurd blunder of my life."

Once in the Confederate lower house, however, Foote became its most vociferous and persistent opponent of Jefferson Davis and his administration. He was opposed to most of Davis's cabinet appointments—especially Judah P. Benjamin, but also Stephen Mallory and Christopher G. Memminger—and while he criticized the Confederate president's favorite generals, Foote allied himself with Davis's main foe, Joseph E. Johnston. At the heart of Foote's obstruction was an intense dislike for Davis that began with a fistfight on Christmas Day 1849 in the two senators' Washington boardinghouse and was intensified by the gubernatorial contest of 1851 and its immediate aftermath. Naturally, Foote also denounced Davis's policy initiatives such as the suspension of habeas corpus, the declaration of martial law, and the use of conscription. Meanwhile, he ferreted out corruption, especially in the commissary department. And he accused "Judas Iscariot" Benjamin of conspiring with other Jews to subvert the Confederacy. By 1863–1864, he was launching an all-out offensive against Davis and was insisting that overtures for peace be made to Washington. In January 1865 Confederate authorities arrested Foote and his wife as they were trying to cross the Potomac. After being censured for this by the Confederate House, he fled again hoping to meet with President Lincoln. But after being denied an interview, he went to England, where he published a pamphlet urging his Tennessee constituents to rejoin the Union, at which point the house finally expelled him. In August 1865, after a complicated series of negotiations, President Johnson allowed him to return to the United States. Except for a brief term as superintendent of the U.S. Mint in New Orleans, the bitter, intemperate politician lived the rest of his life in Nashville. During these years, he wrote *The War of the Rebellion, or Scylla and Charybdis* (1866); *Casket of Reminiscences* (1874), a miscellany of observations of people and events in his political career; and *Bench and Bar in the South and Southwest* (1876).

Foote was married twice, first to Elizabeth Winters in Tuscumbia, Alabama, and then, after her death in the mid-1850s, to Mrs. Rachel D. Smiley of Nashville. He had two sons and two daughters, one of whom married Senator William M. Stewart of Nevada, a prominent postwar Republican.

• Foote provides details about himself in his *Casket of Reminiscences*. Although there is no published biography, John E. Gonzales, "The Public Career of Henry Stuart Foote (1804–1880)" (Ph.D. diss., Univ. of North Carolina at Chapel Hill, 1957), is the most complete study available. Gonzales published parts of his research in three articles: "Henry Stuart Foote: A Forgotten Unionist of the Fifties," *Southern Quarterly* 1 (1963): 129–39; "Henry Stuart Foote: Confederate Congressman and Exile," *Civil War History* 40 (1965): 384–95; and "Henry Stuart Foote in Exile, 1865," *Journal of Mississippi History* 15 (1953): 90–98. See also the entry on Foote in Cecil L. Summers, *The Governors of Mississippi* (1980), and references to him in Richard A. McLemore, ed., *A History of Mississippi*, vol. 1 (1973). His prewar career can be followed in Edwin A. Miles, *Jacksonian Democracy in Mississippi* (1960), and Robert E. May, *John A. Quitman: Old South Crusader* (1985); his Confederate years are treated in Wilfred Buck Yearns, *The Confederate Congress* (1960), and Thomas B. Alexander and Richard E. Beringer, *The Anatomy of the Confederate Congress* (1972).

MICHAEL PERMAN

FOOTE, Lucius Harwood (10 Apr. 1826–4 June 1913), lawyer and diplomat, was born in Winfield, New York, the son of Lucius Foote, a Congregational minister, and Electa Harwood. In childhood Foote moved often, as his father received appointments in churches in New York, Ohio, Illinois, and Wisconsin. He attended Knox College and Western Reserve but did not graduate. In 1853 he traveled overland to California to seek his fortune.

In Sacramento he studied law, became active in Republican party politics, and held a series of elective and appointive offices. Admitted to the bar in 1856, he became a justice of the peace and later a municipal judge in Sacramento. He was collector of the port of Sacramento from 1861 to 1865. While there, in 1862, he married Rose Frost Carter; the couple did not have children. From 1872 to 1876 he served as adjutant general of California under Governor Newton Booth, a close friend. After holding this office, he was known as "General" Foote. He was a delegate to the Republican National Convention in 1876.

Foote is most noteworthy as a late nineteenth-century American diplomat in Latin America and Asia. Like most such figures, he obtained positions abroad as a result of patronage politics. He had no prior training or experience in diplomacy. He nonetheless served effectively in Valparaíso, Chile, during the War of the Pacific. He was named consul on 3 March 1879 and helped sort out tangled problems in protecting American neutral rights and property. When the American minister died, he served briefly from 22 March to 31 July 1882 in charge of the legation. While at home on leave, he was sent on 5 February 1883 to Aspinwall, Colombia, on a special consular mission. A more important assignment in Asia soon followed.

Foote became the first Western diplomat to reside in Seoul, Korea, after Commodore Robert W. Shufeldt's treaty negotiations in 1882 opened that country, which was previously closed to contact with the West. President Chester A. Arthur on 27 February 1883 appointed Foote to the highest American diplomatic rank of envoy extraordinary and minister plenipotentiary to establish this new post. When Foote and his wife arrived on 13 May, they entered a complicated diplomatic arena. Korea was a target of imperial rivalries, especially between China and Japan. Korean leaders disagreed over how to modernize their country and over which larger, more powerful state should serve as a model and possible protector. Both King Kojong and, separately, a "progressive" faction of young Koreans sought American support and tried to draw Foote into these international and internal conflicts.

The Department of State inadequately and infrequently instructed Foote. It remained generally indifferent to Korean affairs other than looking for commercial advantages. As a result, Foote engaged in a more activist diplomacy than American leaders, perhaps, intended or were prepared to support. He believed that successful commercial expansion would require more than aiding particular American businessmen; it would require broader and deeper involvement in Korea. He also sympathized with Korean efforts to establish independence from traditional Chinese suzerainty. Thus, Foote eagerly accepted a role as an "unofficial" adviser to the king. His encouraging words, however, caused the king to count too much on the United States.

Foote became better informed about internal Korean disputes after the arrival in early 1884 of U.S. naval attaché George C. Foulk. Foulk had escorted the first Korean diplomatic mission in visits to the United States and Europe in 1883–1884. His ability to speak Korean and his friendship with Korean leaders provided insights for Foote on the politics of court and society. Through Foulk, Foote learned of the progressive faction's plan, with the help of Japanese diplomats, to stage a coup against the conservative pro-Chinese Min faction then in control of the Korean government. Foote met with some of the young Koreans and cautioned against rash action.

Foote and his wife acted with great courage during the disorders that accompanied this unsuccessful coup in early December 1884. They opened the legation as a place of refuge, and Foote attempted to mediate among Korea, China, and Japan, all of whose military forces had clashed in Seoul. When he left Seoul temporarily to go to the coast on a mediation mission, Rose Foote stayed behind, at the king's request, despite the departure of many other Westerners, so that her presence might discourage further rioting. Later, the Japanese government paid special tribute to the Footes for giving sanctuary to Japanese threatened by Korean mobs during the chaotic days of the failed coup.

Foote eagerly sought to help American commerce in Korea but was less enthusiastic about assisting missionaries, whose activities he feared would offend Koreans. He nonetheless helped Dr. Horace N. Allen become established as the first resident missionary in Seoul. Foote named Allen physician to the American legation to assure Allen's status, since the right to evangelize was not then permitted. Allen became an influential figure in mission work and in American diplomacy in Korea, serving in the legation in several positions after Foote's departure.

Foote left Korea for the United States on 12 January 1885, after Congress, in a new appropriation for the State Department, reduced his diplomatic rank to that of minister resident and consul general. He believed that King Kojong, whom he had encouraged to hope for close ties with the United States, would perceive this change as a repudiation of Foote. Congress, in fact, was merely trying to economize and to equalize the rank of all missions to small countries in Asia and Europe. Rather than try to explain these purposes, Foote took a leave of absence to return home and then resigned. Foulk took over as acting chargé of the legation.

Foote held no other governmental offices after reaching San Francisco. Rose Foote, whose health had deteriorated while abroad, died within six months. In 1891 Foote became secretary and treasurer of the California Academy of Sciences, which was funded by the estate of the late philanthropist James Lick. Foote remained in that position until his death. In later years he also participated in the Bohemian Club, which he had helped found, and he published two volumes of poems, *On the Heights* (1897) and *The Wooing of the Rose and Other Poems* (1911). Foote died in San Francisco.

Foote's diplomatic career was not distinguished. However, he made no grave mistakes and on the whole performed satisfactorily, unlike some amateur political appointees of the era. The swirling imperial rivalries and domestic intrigues of Korea could easily have led a less prudent diplomat into error. His advice misled King Kojong about American intentions, but this did not create difficulties for American leaders or interests. Foote tried unsuccessfully to promote a larger role for the United States in Korea. That country, however, remained a modest post on the frontier of American commercial expansion, which Foote was able to do little to advance.

• Foote's papers were destroyed in the San Francisco earthquake and fire of 1906. There is no biography devoted solely to his career. Mention of his service in Chile is made in Herbert Millington, *American Diplomacy and the War of the Pacific* (1948). The most detailed account of his service in Korea is in Yur-Bok Lee, *Diplomatic Relations between the United States and Korea, 1866–1887* (1970). A more analytical study is Jongsuk Chay, *Diplomacy of Asymmetry: Korean-American Relations to 1910* (1990). An uncritical, privately published tribute to Rose Foote by a family friend, Mary V. Tingley

Lawrence's *A Diplomat's Helpmate* (1918), contains copies of photographs taken in Korea of the Footes, their staff and servants, the American legation, and other contemporary scenes. Other studies important for this era of U.S.-Korean relations and Foote's role include Martina Deuchler, *Confucian Gentlemen and Barbarian Envoys: The Opening of Korea, 1875–1883* (1977); Fred H. Harrington, *God, Mammon, and the Japanese: Dr. Horace N. Allen and Korean-American Relations, 1884–1905* (1944); and George A. Lensen, *Balance of Intrigue: International Rivalries in Korea and Manchuria, 1884–1899* (2 vols., 1982).

JAMES F. WILLIS

FOOTE, Mary Anna Hallock (19 Nov. 1847–25 June 1938), illustrator and author, was born on a farm near Milton, New York, the daughter of Nathaniel Hallock and Ann Burling, farmers. When Foote wrote her reminiscences (published posthumously in 1972 as *A Victorian Gentlewoman in the Far West*), she could still recall such antislavery and women's rights advocates as Frederick Douglass, Susan B. Anthony, and Ernestine L. Rose, who stayed at her parents' house after her activist aunt, Sarah H. Hallock, had invited the orators to lecture in the area. Foote's formal education began in a private Quaker school on the family property. For high school, she went to the Poughkeepsie Female Collegiate Seminary, and for her art education she attended the School of Design for Women at New York's Cooper Union.

By 1867, under the direction of such teachers as W. J. Linton, Foote had learned the techniques of woodcut illustration, and her work began appearing frequently in *Scribner's* and in books by such authors as Bret Harte and Henry Wadsworth Longfellow. A decade later when she began submitting her writing to literary journals, her illustrations would sometimes accompany her own prose in the *Century* magazine. Chosen as art juror for the World's Columbian Exposition in 1893 and as an exhibitor in the Armory Show of 1913, Foote was later praised by William Allen Rogers, who wrote in *A World Worth While* (1922), that "if Mrs. Foote were not so identified with her work as a novelist she would be better known as one of the most accomplished illustrators in America" (quoted in Johnson, p. 70). More recent art critics such as Robert Taft have confirmed the view of Foote's contemporaries that she ranks as one of the best illustrators of what is generally agreed to be the golden age of American woodcut illustration.

Foote began a second career after her marriage in 1876 to Arthur De Wint Foote, a cousin of Rev. Henry Ward Beecher. Arthur's job as a mining engineer took the young couple to New Almaden, California. The bride sent descriptions of the area to her friend Helena de Kay Gilder, wife of *Scribner's* editor Richard Watson Gilder. Enthusiastic about Foote's writing, the Gilders successfully encouraged her to revise her prose sketches for publication. More sketches followed when the Footes moved for a short time to Santa Cruz after the birth of their son, Arthur Burling, in 1877. When Arthur Foote landed a new mining job, the Footes moved to Leadville, Colorado, in 1879, and

in 1881 they traveled together on a business trip to Mexico. Foote's first novel, *The Led-Horse Claim*, appeared in 1883, a year after the birth of their daughter Elizabeth ("Betty") and a year before the Footes moved to Boise, Idaho. Their daughter Agnes was born in Boise in 1886. During their eleven-year residence in Boise and then while they lived in Grass Valley, California, Foote wrote eleven more novels, four collections of stories, and her reminiscences. In 1932 the Footes moved to Hingham, Massachusetts, to live with their daughter Betty. Mary Foote died in Hingham.

In *Selected American Prose: The Realistic Movement, 1841–1900* (1958), Wallace Stegner says of the mining camps in Foote's fiction that they "are almost the only real ones in local color fiction—very much more real than those of Bret Harte. By no means a major figure, she is too honest to be totally lost" (p. xi). Like *The Led-Horse Claim*, Foote's next two novels—*John Bodewin's Testimony* (1886) and *The Last Assembly Ball* (1889)—depict life in the mining town of Leadville. Limited to what her husband told her about the business of mining and to what, as a lady, she was allowed to see of frontier life, Foote organized her realistic material by means of melodramatic Romeo-and-Juliet plots. By the 1890s Foote had begun to write about Idaho, and her increasing skill as a novelist shows in *The Chosen Valley* (1892), a novel about early irrigation schemes in the West. When lean years forced her family to rely on her royalties, however, Foote resorted to writing what she privately admitted were potboilers, novels such as *Coeur d'Alene* (1894). After a hiatus in her writing following the death of her daughter Agnes in 1904, Foote turned her talents to historical fiction, writing *The Royal Americans* (1910), a romance about the American Revolution, and *A Picked Company* (1912), a wagon-train novel set in the 1840s.

As Lee Ann Johnson points out in *Mary Hallock Foote* (1980), the last fiction written by Foote is "intensely autobiographical . . . , three realistic novels in which domestic fireside matters unfold against a backdrop of war" (p. 139). *The Valley Road* (1915) partly parallels the Footes' experiences in Grass Valley; *Edith Bonham* (1917), her best work, recounts in fictional form the Footes' years in Boise; and *The Ground Swell* (1919) memorializes their daughter Agnes. As in much of Foote's earlier fiction, characters in these novels are tested by ordeals of nature and of the frontier community. In *Edith Bonham*, for example, Edith nurses Phoebe through a bout of scarlet fever in the isolation of the mesa. Harrowed by such ordeals, they nevertheless are aware of the sublimity in the land's power. As Edith Bonham says of that dangerous West, "I hated it, and so did Nanny. But it 'haunted' us both. It has tremendous force, concealed somehow; things may happen any time, but you don't know what, nor where to expect them" (p. 263).

Since 1970, renewed interest in Foote has been stimulated by several controversies. Wallace Stegner's *Angle of Repose* (1971; awarded the Pulitzer Prize for fiction in 1972) uses whole passages from Foote's novels and letters in a fictional re-creation, in part, of her life. Stegner's novel led to a debate over whether his borrowing is a matter of artistic license or plagiarism and whether his fictional portrait constitutes a defamation of character. Except for the last part of his novel, he followed the details of Foote's reminiscences, and their publication fueled the debate and created renewed interest in Foote because of her depiction of sustaining feminine communities in the late nineteenth-century West. Her letters, still in manuscript, have stirred more controversy, since late twentieth-century researchers do not agree on whether her early correspondence reveals a world for women superior to or worse than that of the present. Such controversy, as well as the eventual publication of Foote's letters, will undoubtedly keep alive, if not increase, interest in her work for decades to come.

• Foote's letters to Helena de Kay Gilder are in the Stanford University Library, along with three autobiographical fragments and the typescript of a short story. Locations of other letters are listed in the selected bibliography of Lee Ann Johnson's *Mary Hallock Foote* (1980), the only book-length study of Foote and her writing. James H. Maguire included an essay on Foote in *Fifty Western Writers: A Bio-Bibliographical Sourcebook*, ed. Fred Erisman and Richard W. Etulain (1982). Examples of her work as illustrator and as fiction writer have been reprinted in *The Idaho Stories and Far West Illustrations of Mary Hallock Foote*, ed. Barbara Cragg, Dennis M. Walsh, and Mary Ellen Walsh (1988), which includes an informative introduction by the editors. The case against Stegner's depiction of Foote and his use of her writing in *Angle of Repose* is set forth by Mary Ellen Williams Walsh in *Critical Essays on Wallace Stegner*, ed. Anthony Arthur (1982); Stegner responds in *Conversations with Wallace Stegner on Western History and Literature*, with Richard W. Etulain (1983). The controversy over Foote's early correspondence can be traced to two articles: Carroll Smith-Rosenberg, "The Female World of Love and Ritual: Relations between Women in Nineteenth-Century America," *Signs* 1, no. 1 (1975): 1–29, and Bari Watkins, "Woman's World in Nineteenth-Century America," *American Quarterly* 31, no. 1 (1979): 116–27. Although no complete study of Foote's work as an illustrator exists, the evaluative discussion in Robert Taft, *Artists and Illustrators of the Old West: 1850–1900* (1953), provides a context for understanding her achievement.

JAMES H. MAGUIRE

FOOTE, Paul Darwin (27 Mar. 1888–2 Aug. 1971), physicist, was born in Andover, Ohio, the son of Howard Spencer Foote, a school superintendent, and Abbie Lottie Tourgee. In 1893 he moved with his family to Chardon, Ohio, where he grew up. As a teenager he sold aluminum combs door-to-door to earn enough money to equip his basement electrical laboratory and to buy a two-way radio telegraph. He matriculated at Western Reserve University's Adelbert College in 1905 to study electrical engineering and supported himself by teaching algebra at night and collecting bad debts during the day. His early coursework in physics influenced him to pursue a career in that discipline instead; after receiving his A.B. in 1909 he became a graduate student and laboratory assistant at the University of Nebraska, where he received his A.M. degree in physics in 1911.

Later that year Foote accepted a position as a laboratory assistant with the U.S. National Bureau of Standards in Washington, D.C. In 1913 he married Bernice Claire Foote (her maiden name), with whom he had two children. In that same year he was promoted to assistant physicist and chief of the pyrometry section, which developed standards and equipment for measuring relatively high temperatures, such as those encountered in an industrial furnace. In 1916 he became assistant manager of Fisher Scientific Company in Pittsburgh, Pennsylvania, where he participated in the invention of several pieces of heat-measuring equipment, including the F & F optical pyrometer, a device that measures the temperature of an incandescent body by visually comparing its color with that of a calibrated incandescent filament whose temperature can be adjusted. A good portion of his work for Fisher was performed by correspondence from the University of Minnesota, where he was setting up a pyrometry section in that school's physics department and working toward the Ph.D. in physics that he received in 1917.

Foote returned to the Bureau's pyrometry section that same year as an associate physicist to contribute to the American effort during World War I. By developing and overseeing the heat-control processes used to manufacture optical glass for telescopic gun sights and binoculars, he also played a major role in stimulating the development of the optical glass industry in the United States. After the war he began experimenting with the spectra of electromagnetic radiation in an effort to apply the principles of quantum theory to the wave behavior of light. He and Fred L. Mohler published the results of much of this work in *The Origin of Spectra* (1922), the first book on quantum theory written by Americans. In that same year he was made chief of the Bureau's newly organized Section on Radium, X-Rays, and Atomic Structure and played an important role in developing the first standards and procedures for installing X-ray equipment in hospitals, standardizing X-ray dosages for therapy, measuring and certifying radium, and protecting radiology technicians from exposure to excessive doses of radiation. In 1926, two years after his promotion to senior physicist, he traveled to Europe on behalf of the U.S. Commerce Department to study new developments in X-ray technology and radioactivity.

In 1927 Foote became a senior industrial fellow in oil production technology at the Mellon Institute of Industrial Research in Pittsburgh. Because his fellowship was funded by Gulf Oil Corporation, he devoted most of his research to developing a method for locating large subterranean deposits of crude oil by using the principles of physics. Three years later his fellowship was subsumed into the new research department of Gulf Production Company, where he sought to apply physics to all aspects of oil field technology. In 1933 he was made director of research and executive vice president of Gulf Research and Development Corporation. In this capacity he was largely responsible for expanding physical research into the realms of refining and manufacturing and for overseeing the evolution of one of the world's foremost petroleum laboratories.

In 1940, the year after his first wife died, Foote married Sophie Miriam Shanks Sage, with whom he had no children. He became a vice president of Gulf Oil Corporation and Gulf Refining Corporation in 1945 and retired from Gulf in 1953. That same year he became an independent engineering consultant and undertook the task of coordinating the activities of the National Academy of Sciences' advisory services for the U.S. Office of Ordnance Research. In 1957 he was appointed assistant secretary of defense for research and engineering; in this position he was asked to enhance the performance of military research and development in general and the Defense Science Board in particular. In 1958 he retired to his home in Washington, where he died.

Foote served as president of the American Physical Society in 1933, vice president of the Washington (D.C.) Academy of Sciences in 1936, secretary of the American Philosophical Society (APS) from 1956 to 1959, chairman of the National Academy of Sciences' advisory committee to the Bureau of Standards from 1960 to 1965, and member of the APS Committee on Research from 1965 until 1971. In 1921 he founded *Review of Scientific Instruments*, and from that year until 1932 he served as its editor as well as editor in chief of *Journal of the Optical Society of America*. From 1924 to 1965 he served as associate editor of *Journal of the Franklin Institute*. In 1931 he played a prominent role in establishing the American Institute of Physics. He was elected to the National Academy of Sciences in 1943 and received the University of Minnesota's Outstanding Achievement Gold Medal in 1951, the Pittsburgh Junior Chamber of Commerce's Pittsburgh Man-of-the-Year in Science Award in 1953, the American Chemical Society's Pittsburgh Award in 1954, and the Department of Defense's Medal for Meritorious Civilian Service in 1958.

Foote contributed to the advance of physics in several ways. His work in theoretical physics led to a better understanding of pyrometry and quantum physics. His work in applied physics led to the development of several important heat-measuring devices and contributed to the growth of the optical glass and petroleum industries.

• A biography, including a bibliography, is Allen V. Astin, "Paul Darwin Foote," National Academy of Sciences, *Biographical Memoirs* 50 (1979): 175–94. An obituary is in *Physics Today* 24 (Nov. 1971): 73.

CHARLES W. CAREY, JR.

FORAKER, Joseph Benson (5 July 1846–10 May 1917), Ohio governor and U.S. senator, was born near Rainsboro, Ohio, the son of Henry Stacey Foraker, a farmer and miller, and Margaret Reece. In 1861 he moved to Hillsboro to become a clerk for his uncle, the county auditor. Serving in the Union army, he saw action in West Virginia, Tennessee, Georgia, and on Sherman's march, and he mustered out as a brevet captain in 1865.

Foraker attended Ohio Wesleyan University for two years and read law with a local attorney. After transferring to Cornell, he received a B.A. in 1869. He settled in Cincinnati, completed his legal studies, and passed the bar exam in October 1869. At Wesleyan, Foraker met Julia A. P. Bundy, and the two were married in 1870. They had five children.

With his law practice established, Foraker plunged into Republican politics and quickly emerged as a powerful stump speaker. He served as superior court judge in Cincinnati from 1879 until 1882. Although still relatively unknown in the state, he was nominated for governor in 1883, largely because party leaders hoped that his hailing from Cincinnati would attract that city's German-American voters disaffected by a Republican-sponsored law taxing saloons. Foraker lost to Democrat George Hoadly, but his vigorous campaign attracted admiration from Republicans throughout the state. In 1884 he stepped onto the national stage, placing Senator John Sherman in nomination for president at the national convention and campaigning in several states. The next year he defeated Hoadly and in 1887 won a second two-year term.

As governor, Foraker posted a record of moderate reform. At his urging the legislature passed a new saloon tax revising the previous act, which had been declared unconstitutional by the state supreme court. He endorsed voter registration and other election reforms. He created a state board of health to combat contagious diseases and a commission to inspect food and drink. His term also witnessed the repeal of laws mandating segregated schooling of black children.

This last action squared with Foraker's growing reputation as a champion of racial justice, especially for blacks in the South. While many Republicans espoused sectional reconciliation, partly to encourage New South economic interests to support the party's tariff protectionism, Foraker lashed out against the disfranchisement of southern blacks. He denied charges that he was "waving the bloody shirt" and insisted that he protested current, not past, behavior. Earning the sobriquet "Fire Alarm Joe" for his vehemence, he gained the most notoriety for damning President Grover Cleveland's attempt to return captured Confederate battle flags to their units.

Foraker's increasing visibility inspired speculation that he was angling for a position on the 1888 Republican national ticket and thus alarmed Sherman's Ohio backers. The governor's seemingly treacherous abandonment of Sherman in the midst of balloting at the national convention intensified a bitter factionalism among Ohio Republicans that damaged Foraker. Moreover, his rigorous enforcement of a state law barring Sunday liquor sales offended German Americans. In 1889 his campaign for a third term ended in defeat.

In 1892 Foraker made an unsuccessful attempt to unseat Sherman in the Senate. Determined to best his factional foes, he allied himself with Cincinnati "boss" George Cox, assiduously cultivated a statewide following, and finally won election to the Senate in 1896. At the national convention that year he chaired the Platform Committee that endorsed the gold standard, and he also gave a rousing speech nominating William McKinley. Foraker had little love for Marcus A. Hanna, McKinley's campaign manager, who soon joined Foraker in the Senate and battled him for control of the Ohio Republican party.

In the Senate Foraker advocated the McKinley administration's economic program, especially the protective tariff. He defended the interests of Ohio wool growers, for whom he secured favorable treatment in the Dingley Tariff Act of 1897.

As a member of the Foreign Relations Committee, Foraker deplored the deteriorating situation in the Cuban rebellion and called for U.S. recognition of Cuba's independence and for armed intervention against Spain. When war came, he engineered Senate approval of the annexation of Hawaii and also urged retention of the Philippines and Puerto Rico. He did not favor the Teller amendment abjuring annexation of Cuba but did consider it binding. In 1899 he sponsored the Foraker amendment barring the U.S. government from granting economic concessions in Cuba that might tend to prolong American intervention. The Foraker Act of 1900 outlined a colonial government for Puerto Rico, but the senator failed to win U.S. citizenship for the island's inhabitants.

Foraker easily won reelection in 1902 and afterward only selectively supported the foreign policy of McKinley's successor, Theodore Roosevelt. He stoutly defended acquisition of the Panama Canal Zone but opposed the Roosevelt Corollary to the Monroe Doctrine and a series of treaties for submitting international disputes to arbitration. On the domestic front as well Foraker frequently dissented, opposing, for instance, the Hepburn Act granting rate-making power to the Interstate Commerce Commission.

Foraker broke completely with Roosevelt over his handling of the Brownsville affair. When white citizens alleged that a few black soldiers stationed nearby had shot up that Texas town, the president sanctioned the dismissal of all 167 men in their unit. Foraker condemned Roosevelt's decision and labored in Congress to obtain justice for the soldiers. As a consequence, Roosevelt intensified his promotion of Foraker's new Ohio rival, Secretary of War William Howard Taft, as his likely successor and thus destroyed Foraker's own presidential ambitions for 1908. When evidence surfaced that year demonstrating Foraker's acceptance, while a senator, of large retainers from Standard Oil, Roosevelt labeled him a corrupt business stooge who insincerely criticized the Brownsville decision in order to discredit an administration trying to corral the trusts. Devastated by the revelations, Foraker withdrew his Senate reelection bid. In 1914 he lost a Senate

comeback effort to Warren G. Harding. Foraker died in Cincinnati.

As a ferocious campaigner and competent executive and legislator, Foraker achieved substantial success in politics, but with his contempt for compromise and his primal instinct for factional brawling, he also proved to be his own worst enemy.

• Large collections of Foraker's papers are housed in the Cincinnati Historical Society and in the Ohio Historical Society in Columbus. The Manuscript Division of the Library of Congress holds a medium-sized collection. Of course, the *Congressional Record* (1897–1909) is indispensable for any study of his Senate career. Foraker published his memoirs, *Notes of a Busy Life* (2 vols., 1916), and his wife published hers, Julia B. Foraker, *I Would Live It Again* (1932). A full-length biography is Everett Walters, *Joseph Benson Foraker: An Uncompromising Republican* (1948). Earl Ray Beck, "The Political Career of Joseph Benson Foraker" (Ph.D. diss., Ohio State Univ., 1943), chronicles Foraker's public life. John D. Weaver, *The Brownsville Raid* (1970; repr. 1992), extensively treats Foraker's involvement in the affair. An obituary is in the *New York Times*, 11 May 1917.

CHARLES W. CALHOUN

FORAN, Dick (18 June 1910–10 Aug. 1979), actor and singer, was born John Nicholas Foran in Flemington, New Jersey, the son of Arthur F. Foran, a state senator. (His mother's name is unknown.) He attended Princeton University where he was a star on the football team and a member of the glee club. His interest in acting was sparked while at Princeton, and he decided to spend a summer in Hollywood. While out West, his friend Lew Brown, a producer of musicals, encouraged him to take a screen test. After being signed to a contract at Fox Studios, he quit school never to return.

Foran's first screen appearance was in the 1934 Shirley Temple musical *Stand Up and Cheer* in which he sang to the popular child star under the name Nick Foran. He changed his name to Dick when he signed with Warner Bros. later in the decade. Early in his career he shared an apartment with Henry Fonda and James Stewart; Stewart often accompanied Foran on guitar at singing auditions.

Most of Foran's work in the 1930s was as a singing cowboy in a series of low-budget Warner westerns. He was the only singing cowboy employed by the studio. Foran came close to becoming filmdom's first singing western star with his film *Moonlight on the Prairie* (1935) but Gene Autry's *Tumbling Tumbleweeds* (1935) beat his film's release to theaters by two months. Foran's rugged, muscular physique and imposing height of 6'3" helped lend credence to his action sequences while his pleasant singing voice and friendly personality (accented by a mop of curly red hair) won him many fans, especially among children, who were his biggest admirers. Foran's Warner series was well produced and used great stock action footage. The other films in the series included *Treachery Rides the Range* (1936), *Song of the Saddle* (1936), *Trailin' West* (1936), *California Mail* (1937), *Guns of the Pecos* (1937), *Cherokee*

Strip (1937), *Blazing Sixes* (1937), *Land beyond the Law* (1937), *Empty Holsters* (1937), *Devil's Saddle Legion* (1937), and *Prairie Thunder* (1937). As the series developed, more and more children were added for Foran to mingle and sing with, and the forced sentimentality and artificial dialogue led to the downfall of the series.

Foran's popularity, however, prompted the Warners to offer him dramatic roles. He appeared with both Autry and Roy Rogers and proved perfect for the musical western genre. Not only was he an excellent horseman, but he also enjoyed using his musical talents and was not uncomfortable crooning to some rancher's daughter in his smooth Irish tenor. Among the songs he introduced to movie audiences were "I'll Remember April," "April in Paris," and "My Little Buckaroo," for which he helped write the music. Foran recorded two records in his lifetime, "Mexicali Rose/Moonlight Valley" and "Can't You Do a Friend a Favor?" with Vivienne Segal, both for Decca. He also sang on the George Burns and Gracie Allen radio show in 1937.

In 1936 Foran appeared in the thriller *The Petrified Forest* with Bette Davis, Humphrey Bogart, and Leslie Howard. He was nominated for a best supporting actor Academy Award but did not win. Some of his other films in the later half of the 1930s included *Cowboy from Brooklyn* (1938) and *Boy Meets Girl* (1938).

In the 1940s most of Foran's work was for Universal Studios, which used him in "B" westerns, horror films, and comedies. One of his busiest years was 1941, when he appeared in *Horror Island*, *The Kid from Kansas*, *Mob Town*, *Unfinished Business*, and the twelve-part western serial *Riders of Death Valley*. He was also in three comedy vehicles for the up-and-coming team of Bud Abbott and Lou Costello, *In the Navy*, *Keep 'Em Flying*, and 1942's *Ride 'Em Cowboy*. Foran is fine in the service comedy *In the Navy*, but he stands out even more in the two other Abbott and Costello comedies.

In *Keep 'Em Flying*, Foran soars as stunt pilot Jinx Roberts who romances lovely Carol Bruce. Bruce was originally supposed to sing the ballad "I'll Remember April" in the film (it was written for her), but the producers had Foran record it instead for *Ride 'Em Cowboy*. Bruce later recalled fondly that Foran had a romantic interest in her and invited her to his dressing room to play jacks. Although at first wary, she eventually accepted the invitation and found that the actor actually did want to play. She joined him in the game, delighting in the sight of the big man playing this children's game.

In *Ride 'Em Cowboy*, Foran was typecast as Bronco Bob Mitchell, an author of western novels and songs who had never actually been out West but seeks to become a true cowboy star. It recalled Foran's former roles as a singing cowpoke.

Other of Foran's films of the 1940s included *The Fighting 69th*, *The House of the Seven Gables*, *The Mummy's Hand*, and *My Little Chickadee* (all 1940), and *The Mummy's Tomb* (1942). He appeared with film legends such as W. C. Fields, Mae West, and Vincent Price. His most prestigious film of the decade was the 1948 John Ford western *Fort Apache*, in which he co-starred with John Wayne, Fonda, and the now grown-up Shirley Temple. Some film historians, however, consider his role in the 1945 light comedy *Guest Wife*, with Don Ameche and Claudette Colbert, to be the best of his career. In 1943 Foran spread his talents to the stage when he appeared in the Broadway revival of the musical *A Connecticut Yankee*.

In the 1950s Foran appeared in science fiction films, like *The Atomic Submarine* (1959), and even switched hats to play an outlaw in *Al Jennings of Oklahoma* (1951). In the 1960s he appeared in *Donovan's Reef* (1963) and made his last feature film appearance in the independently produced *Brighty of the Grand Canyon* (1967). After that he devoted his acting skills to television, appearing almost exclusively in commercials.

Foran was married three times. His first marriage was to Ruth Piper Hollingsworth in 1937, but it ended in divorce in 1940. He married Carole Gallagher in 1943 but divorced her one year later. In 1951 he married Susanne Rosser. Foran had four sons.

By the time Foran died in Panorama City, California, he had been an actor for forty-five years and had appeared in more than 200 films. According to a family friend, John Kubichan, "Dick always said he was the original singing cowboy. He liked to joke about his own talents and used to say he could outfight Gene Autry and outsing John Wayne. He did all his own stunts in movies." Foran referred to himself as "the good guy who doesn't get the girl."

Foran was a talented actor of many genres and media. Although he was never a major success as a Hollywood leading man, he merits favorable comparison to Gene Autry, Roy Rogers, and the other great singing cowboys.

• Little biographical information on Dick Foran exists, although he is included in *The Complete Encyclopedia of Popular Music and Jazz*, Halliwell's *Filmgoer's Companion*, and *The International Motion Picture Alamanac*. William K. Everson, *A Pictorial History of the Western Film* (1969), and David Rothel, *The Singing Cowboys* (1978), both contain short passages about Foran's appearances as a singing cowboy; Bob Furmanek and Ron Palumbo, *Abbott and Costello in Hollywood* (1991), contains some information about Foran's tenure at Universal. Informative obituaries are in the *Washington Post*, 12 Aug. 1979, and the *New York Times*, 13 Aug. 1979.

JEFFREY S. MILLER

FORBES, Alexander (14 May 1882–27 Mar. 1965), neurophysiologist, physician, and explorer, was born in Milton, Massachusetts, the son of William Hathaway Forbes, the first president of the Bell Telephone Company, and Edith Emerson, the daughter of Ralph Waldo Emerson. Forbes received his early education at the Milton Academy and in 1900 matriculated at Harvard College, after a year of travel in the western United States and then in Europe. In 1904 he received an A.B. from Harvard and the following year an M.A. Before undertaking medical training at Harvard,

Forbes spent another year in the western United States, living with his brother in a cabin in Wyoming. Forbes married Charlotte Irving Grinell in June 1910; the couple would have four children. That year Harvard awarded Forbes a medical doctorate, and he became a member of the American Physiological Society, which he later served as treasurer from 1927 to 1936. He did postgraduate studies in 1911–1912 with Charles S. Sherrington in Liverpool, England, investigating the reflexes of decerebrate animals. While in England, Forbes also visited Keith Lucas at Cambridge for several weeks. Returning to the United States, he worked with H. B. Williams, the Dalton Professor of Physiology at Columbia University, measuring reflex times with an Einthoven string galvanometer (a device invented by Willem Einthoven in 1902 to measure electrical currents in the heart).

In 1912 Forbes returned to Cambridge, Massachusetts, and took up duties as an instructor in the physiology department at Harvard Medical School. He was one of the first full-time neurophysiologists in the United States, implementing techniques developed by British scientists. In 1915 Forbes, in collaboration with Alan Gregg, reported on one of the first analyses of flexor reflexes in the United States, using a string galvanometer, in what fellow neurophysiologist John Eccles described as the first "skilled application of electrical recording to central reflex phenomena" (Eccles, p. 389). During the First World War, Forbes initially served in the U.S. Navy as radio officer on the scout cruiser *Salem*, and later he installed radio compasses on ships. Drawing on his acquaintance with electronic amplifiers during the war, Forbes used this technology in the spring of 1919 to study the conduction of an electrical impulse along a nerve. He also published anonymously an account of his war experiences in *Radio Gunner* (1924). In 1920 Forbes, in collaboration with Catharine Thacher, used an audion (an electron tube or thermionic amplifier) to measure nerve impulses that had been too small to detect with earlier equipment. In 1921 Harvard promoted Forbes to associate professor. That year he also worked with Edgar D. Adrian in England, and the two verified the "all-or-nothing" principle of conduction for sensory nerves, i.e., a nervous "impulse is normally conducted without any change in size" (*Adrian and Forbes*, p. 302).

In 1922 Forbes published his most influential paper "The Interpretation of Spinal Reflexes in Terms of Present Knowledge of Nerve Conduction," *Physiological Reviews* 2 (1922): 361–414, in which he interpreted the phenomenon of spinal cord reflex activity with respect to current understanding of the physiological activity of isolated nerves. Eccles viewed this work as a "remarkable synthesis" of the neurophysiological concepts of Sherrington on spinal reflexes and Adrian on nerve conduction, in that "Forbes came in quite clearly with the idea that the central nervous system is made of nerve fibers and that they have the same properties as the peripheral nerve fibers" (p. 395). According to Harvard colleague Hallowell Davis, Forbes's work influenced the development of Norbert Wiener's notion of cybernetics. During the 1920s and 1930s, Forbes maintained his connection with neurophysiologists in England and contributed to the scientific literature innovative concepts and terminology. Although Forbes was known for his clear and critical thinking, he fell prey to what Eccles calls the "apparent authority" of science, i.e., the acceptance of a scientific fact based on its reputation within the scientific community. In the late 1920s acceptance of recordings for muscle twitches by the scientific community required the Oxford "angle"—an inflection in the tracing at the start of the muscle's relaxation phase. Forbes and Davis designed an isometric myograph, but the recordings of muscle contraction and relaxation were smooth. Thinking that their equipment was flawed, the Harvard researchers ceased work with the apparatus until Eccles demonstrated that the "angle" was an artifact of Oxford equipment.

In 1936 Forbes became a full professor at Harvard and was elected to the National Academy of Sciences. At this time the electrically oriented Forbes began to incorporate the notion of chemical synaptic transmission (transmission of an electrical impulse from one nerve to another by neurohumors) into his understanding of neurophysiology, although he remained ambivalent about the role of chemical transmitters in synaptic transmission and referred to them as the "soup at the synapse." In his article "Problems of Synaptic Function," *Journal of Neurophysiology* 2 (1939): 465–72, he compared the controversy of neurophysiologists over synaptic transmission to that of physicists over the nature of light and suggested that "the electrical and chemical theories of synaptic conduction may also prove not to be mutually contradictory after all" (p. 470). During the Second World War, the U.S. Navy commissioned Forbes to map routes from the United States to England. By the end of the war he was promoted to captain, and he again wrote an account of his war adventures, in *Quest for a Northern Air Route* (1953). Forbes retired a few years after the war from Harvard Medical School, as an emeritus professor, but continued research, in Harvard's biology department, on vision in amphibians and reptiles. He maintained this research until the end of his life, with two papers appearing in the year of his death. He died in the town of his birth, Milton, Massachusetts.

In an article for the September 1951 issue of the *Christian Register*, Forbes, a self-confessed Unitarian, ascribed to science the task of "giving us a clearer, deeper understanding of man's place in the order of nature and the origins of his patterns of behavior, thus ultimately guiding us to a more harmonious way of living with one another." When not engaged in scientific work, Forbes was an active explorer. He earned a pilot's license in 1929 and flew a plane to many scientific meetings. In addition he enjoyed white-water canoeing and ski jumping. Forbes was also an accomplished sailor and navigator and wrote *Offshore Navigation in Its Simplest Form* (1935). In 1938 he received the Charles P. Daly Gold Medal of the American Geographic Society, for mapping the coast of Labrador. In assessing Forbes's career, Eccles quotes Adrian as observing that "if Alexander Forbes had been less adventurous, his many talents might have added an entirely new chapter to Neurophysiology, but his friends would have had fewer personal memories to enjoy" (p. 388).

• Forbes's papers are housed at the Francis A. Countway Library of Medicine at Harvard Medical School. For a comprehensive biographical account and an extensive list of Forbes's writings, see Wallace O. Fenn, "Alexander Forbes, 1882–1965," National Academy of Sciences *Biographical Memoires* 40 (1969): 113–41. Shorter biographical accounts include Hallowell Davis, "Alexander Forbes, 1882–1965," *Journal of Neurophysiology* 28 (1965): 986–88; and E. D. Adrian, "Prof. Alexander Forbes," *Nature* 206 (1965): 1095–96. For an analysis of Forbes's scientific research, as well as personal remembrances, see J. C. Eccles, "Alexander Forbes and His Achievement in Electrophysiology," *Perspectives in Biology and Medicine* 13 (1970): 388–404. For Forbes's contribution to the development of the "all-or-none" principle, see E. D. Adrian and A. Forbes, "The All-or-Nothing Response of Sensory Nerve Fibers," *Journal of Physiology* 56 (1921): 301–30, and Robert G. Frank, Jr., "Instruments, Nerve Action, and the All-or-None Principle," *Osiris* 9 (1994): 208–35. An obituary is in the *New York Times*, 30 Mar. 1965.

JAMES A. MARCUM

FORBES, Esther (28 Jan. 1891–12 Aug. 1967), historian and novelist, was born in Westborough, Massachusetts, the daughter of William Trowbridge Forbes, a judge, and Harriette Merrifield, an author of published studies of historical artifacts and documents. Harriette Forbes contributed greatly to background research for her daughter's writing. The Forbeses were a New England family with a long history, and Esther reputedly drew on that history for historical novels such as *A Mirror for Witches* (1928). Her writings reveal a care for historical background and detail gleaned partly from the old documents, artifacts, and books she loved to rifle through even as a child. Her love for history is apparent in her works, and she possessed a rare ability to bring it to life.

Forbes graduated from Bradford Academy in 1912 and, impelled by her interest in history, studied at the University of Wisconsin from 1916 to 1918 with some of the most noted American historians there before World War I intervened. Then she left college and worked as a farmhand in Harpers Ferry, West Virginia, as a way of contributing to the war effort.

After World War I Forbes returned home and found a job as an editor at Houghton Mifflin, where she worked from 1920 to 1926. At the publishing house, she learned the practical side of writing fiction. As editor, she discovered historical novelist Rafael Sabatini, best known today for his book *Captain Blood* (1922), the 1935 movie version of which starred Errol Flynn. Forbes herself began to write creatively while working at Houghton Mifflin, completing her first novel, *O Genteel Lady!* (1926), in her spare time. She also married Albert Learned Hoskins in 1926 and in the same year quit her job to become a full-time writer. The couple had no children.

Forbes's first four novels feature heroines who stand out from the crowd because of their passions. *O Genteel Lady!*, set in the mid-nineteenth century, is the story of Lanice Bardeen, who escapes Amherst for Boston and begins a career in publishing. Eventually she flees heartbreak by embarking on a European tour that involves her in the heady company of Alfred Tennyson, George Eliot, and Robert Browning. However, she finally returns to a life of domesticity in Boston. Forbes's first novel received very good reviews.

Forbes's second novel, *A Mirror for Witches* (1928), is a fascinating psychological thriller as well as a credible historical novel. Supposedly prompted by the fact that an ancestor of Forbes (also named Esther) was labeled a witch and thrown in jail, *A Mirror for Witches* tells the story of a girl who, rescued from a witch burning by an English sea captain named Bilby, becomes known as Bilby's Doll. She joins his family living near Salem, where, hated by her stepmother, she is branded as a witch. In the *New Republic*, Katherine Ann Porter called the book "a magic reflection of New England's past" (25 July 1928). Porter admired the quaint and archaic New England flavor of the style, but some other critics condemned precisely this feature of Forbes's language in the novel. A ballet based on *A Mirror for Witches* was performed by London's Sadler Wells Ballet.

Forbes divorced Hoskins in 1933, which may account for the gap in the publication of her novels. Her third book, *Miss Marvel*, did not appear until 1935. This is the story of an overly romantic young woman from a privileged family who cannot countenance a flesh-and-blood lover and so fantasizes one. Perhaps there is an autobiographical element to the novel. Forbes herself never married again but lived with her brother and sister, creating her works in Worcester, Massachusetts.

Her next novel, *Paradise* (1937), the story of the Parre family in seventeenth-century Massachusetts Bay, was praised for its realistic characterizations. Another novel, *The General's Lady* (1938), is set in the last years of the American Revolution. Forbes was credited with psychological insight in delineating this tale of the wife of an American general who falls in love with a British officer.

Perhaps the most notable of all of Forbes's works is her biography *Paul Revere and the World He Lived In* (1942), for which she won the Pulitzer Prize for history in 1943. (She would perhaps have won the prize for biography, but it went to Admiral Samuel Eliot Morison's biography of Christopher Columbus instead.) Forbes's biography of Revere was a departure from her novel writing, for which she had an interesting explanation. She said she had been working on a novel about a man who had remained neutral during the revolutionary war, but the outbreak of World War II exploded her notions about neutrality. Since she had labored on the book for two years, and her mother had done quite a bit of background research for her, she channeled it into the book on Revere.

After *Paul Revere*, honors flowed in steadily for Forbes. She was the first woman member of the American Antiquarian Society and was also a member of the Society of American Historians and the American Academy of Arts and Sciences. Shortly after completing the biography of Revere, she began the children's book *Johnny Tremain* (1943). Still steeped in the atmosphere of revolutionary Boston she had created for the earlier work, Forbes's imagination was easily engaged in the juvenile novel. The story of an orphaned apprentice silversmith who, after an accident maims his hand, finds his true vocation is espionage for the Sons of Liberty, *Johnny Tremain* won the 1943 Newbery Award. The book was lavishly praised in the *Saturday Review of Literature* as "almost uncanny in its 'aliveness'" (13 Nov. 1943); the *Horn Book* called it "the first classic story of Boston for young people" (Aug. 1944). The book remains a children's classic; Walt Disney even made a movie of it in 1957.

After Forbes published a picture book, *The Boston Book* (1947), with photographs of Boston by Arthur Griffin, her next effort was *The Running of the Tide* (1948), which won the Metro-Goldwyn-Mayer novel award and was also made into a film. The story of early nineteenth-century Salem and its inhabitants, it is a panoramic novel surveying ordinary and extraordinary citizens and includes a cameo of Nathaniel Hawthorne.

America's Paul Revere (1948), written with Lynd Ward, marked a return to children's literature. Like *Johnny Tremain*, the book was received as a splendid evocation of Boston around the time of the American Revolution as well as a biography of the revolutionary hero.

Forbes's last work was *Rainbow on the Road* (1955), a picaresque novel. Attesting to its hold on the popular imagination is the fact that the novel was the basis for a musical called *Come Summer*, staged and choreographed by Agnes DeMille, which opened on Broadway on 11 March 1969.

Forbes died in Worcester, Massachusetts. At the time of her death the *New York Times* praised her as "a novelist who wrote like a historian and a historian who wrote like a novelist" (13 Aug. 1967). Perhaps somewhat ironically, it seems that *Johnny Tremain*, which is still a children's classic, and not Forbes's Pulitzer Prize–winning biography of Paul Revere will establish her fame. Forbes's adult fiction, though, is perhaps overdue for a resurgence. Although *A Mirror for Witches* is still in print today, for a writer who was often compared to Hawthorne, Forbes's reputation seems sadly faded. Of all of Hawthorne's works, *The Scarlet Letter* seems the most resonant when compared to Forbes's novels, most of which deal with society's enforced repression of female sexuality and the tragedies that result when passion is thwarted. Praise for Forbes's books was almost universal, but the occasional critic faulted her for a too-tedious building up of details in her novels. However, most reviewers pointed

to the literary skill that enabled the reader to forget that he or she was reading history when reading Forbes's work.

Perhaps Forbes's biggest liability in the postmodern era is what has been perceived as her lack of sophistication as a historian. In an issue of the *Horn Book Magazine* devoted to old and new approaches to the American Revolution, Christopher Collier comments:

Such an event as a war involving the three major European nations, with implications for the western power structure of centuries to come, is bound to be a complex matter. To present history in simple, one-sided— almost moralistic—terms is to teach nothing worth learning and to falsify the past in such a way that provides worse than no help in understanding the present or in meeting the future. (repr. in *Cross-Currents of Criticism: Horn Book Essays, 1968–1977* [1977], p. 240)

However, Forbes was far from a Marxist and what her writings are perhaps most notable for is her psychological penetration. Forbes's own remarks about her craft reveal someone who was more interested in humanizing history than being entirely objective about it: "The historical novelist is like God himself so far as knowing his people is concerned. He knows the people in his book really better than he can actually know any one in life. He knows exactly why they fall in love or can't stand being snubbed. He works from the inside out."

• Some of Forbes's manuscripts are at the American Antiquarian Society in Worcester, Mass. An uncataloged collection (including manuscripts) of Forbes's papers from 1906 to 1967 is at the Richard Hutchings Goddard Library at Clark University, Worcester, Mass. Besides standard reference works, information about Forbes can be found in Alice M. Jordan, "Esther Forbes, Newbery Winner," in *Newbery Medal Books: 1922–1955* (1955), and Lee Kingman, "Esther Forbes, 1943 Newbery Winner," *Library Journal* 69 (1944): 448–49. More general articles about Forbes can be found in Robert van Gelder, "An Interview with Esther Forbes," in *Writers and Writing* (1946), and Dale Warren, "Esther Forbes and the World She Lives In," *Publisher's Weekly*, 13 May 1944, pp. 1844–45. Obituaries are in the *New York Times*, 13 Aug. 1967; *Time*, 25 Aug. 1967; and *Antiquarian Bookman*, 28 Aug. 1967.

JOSEPHINE MCQUAIL

FORBES, John (5 Sept. 1707–11 Mar. 1759), British army officer, was born in Fifeshire, England, the son of Colonel John Forbes of Pittencrieff estate. Neither his mother's name nor the details of his early life and formal education are known. He became surgeon of the Royal Regiment of North British Dragoons (Scots Grays) in 1729. Purchasing a cornetcy on 5 July 1735, he began an ascent to higher rank in both the regiment and the army, incurring heavy debts with each purchase. In the War of the Austrian Succession he served in the battles of Fontenoy (11 May 1745) and Laffeldt (2 July 1747). Forbes's reliability and ability to organize led Lieutenant-general John Ligonier to assign him to intelligence duties and eventually to a quartermaster general position. Perhaps he served at the battle of Culloden (16 Apr. 1746) against the Stuart uprising, although the Scots Grays were not there. The claim that he participated in the battle is based on the story that a farthing coin, preserved at the British Museum, deflected a bullet that struck him.

Although among the coterie of Scottish officers attached to William Augustus, Duke of Cumberland, second surviving son of George II, Forbes was unable to rise above lieutenant colonel for many years. Several attempts to advance himself at the beginning of the French and Indian War were blocked by creditors whose loans he had taken to acquire earlier commissions and had not repaid. Finally made colonel of the Seventeenth Regiment of Foot in February 1757, he joined the Earl of Loudoun's command in North America in July and served him as adjutant general. Despite his ties to Cumberland and Loudoun, both of whom sought to return to royal favor and did not like or trust William Pitt, he was promoted by Pitt in December to brigadier general with orders to conduct an offensive against the French in the colonies from Pennsylvania south to South Carolina. The objective was Fort Duquesne, the French stronghold at the site of what is now Pittsburgh. Forbes arrived in Philadelphia in April 1758 to assemble an expedition of nearly 7,000 troops, including Virginia and Pennsylvania provincial regiments, a North Carolina company, and redcoats, most of whom were Highlanders. In June he first acknowledged the impact of the illness that would disable him for his remaining months, although he believed it had begun two years before. Flux, constipation, and crippling pain were involved in his unclassified condition, made worse by purging and inability to eat. Unable to keep up with the main units of his westward moving command, he lingered weak and in pain in Shippensburg through August. His travel after that was in a litter borne by horses. Direct command in forward areas fell largely to Lieutenant Colonel Henry Bouquet of the Royal American Regiment.

Modifying army procedure to prevent ambush of the sort General Edward Braddock's ill-fated command had suffered in 1755, Forbes saw advantages in small tactical units and in soldiers positioned behind trees. He favored using reconnaissance in force and detailing elaborate lookout parties to surround the marching columns. In May 1758 he was briefly joined by about 700 Cherokee and Catawba allies. However, their demands for supplies and the British commitment to the Iroquois led the warriors to desert.

At the end of July Forbes made the critical decision to route his expedition through Pennsylvania's mountains rather than swing south to use the road cut by Braddock in 1755 as Virginians and other skeptics strongly advised. The reconnoitering of Ensign Charles Rohr detected an important shortcut across the Allegheny Ridge. The time saved would allow the army to reach the forks of the Ohio River before winter weather set in. The large units of the expedition moved in stages, cutting a road along a traditional route, the Old Traders' Path. Defensive posts were erected at intervals to store supplies and provide shelter in case of retreat. Wagons proved impractical be-

yond Fort Bedford, and packhorses were used thence westward. An artillery train appropriate for a siege accompanied the army.

Without Forbes's approval, Major James Grant undertook a precipitous and unsuccessful attack on Fort Duquesne on 14 September, but on 12 October a French and Indian attack on the British post on Loyalhanna Creek (later named Fort Ligonier) was repulsed. Forbes had encouraged the negotiations by Pennsylvania's government, the British Indian agency, and an independent association of Philadelphia Quakers with Iroquois, Shawnees, Delawares, and other tribes in the Ohio region that culminated in the Treaty of Easton (8–26 October). On 20 October Forbes learned that the Ohio Indian leaders had deserted the French. On 23 November a camp was established twelve miles east of Fort Duquesne, and Forbes considered an assault from there with 2,500 soldiers. He was spared the effort because the French, deserted by the Indians, abandoned and destroyed Fort Duquesne on 24 November. With his army Forbes occupied the site the next day.

Afterward, Forbes's litter returned him to Philadelphia, arriving on 11 January 1759. Despite his poor health, he continued to supervise posts along his army's route—later named the Forbes Road—and to influence diplomatic contacts with Indians. At Philadelphia on 9 February, Lieutenant James Grant, in Forbes's name, assured an Indian delegation that the English would not settle west of the Allegheny Mountains unless Indian leaders asked them to set up trading posts. Forbes died in Philadelphia, having barely survived the fall of Fort Duquesne. However, his triumph in western Pennsylvania helped to lay the groundwork for Anglo-American victory in the French and Indian War.

• The Papers of John Forbes, the principal source, are at the Tracy W. McGregor Library, University of Virginia, Charlottesville. Other original records are found in the Earl of Loudoun Papers, the James Abercromby Papers, and the Henry Bouquet orderly book, all at the Huntington Library, San Marino, Calif.; the Jeffery Amherst Papers (War Office 34 Series) and the Colonial Office 5 Series, both at the Public Record Office, Kew, England; and the Henry Bouquet Papers at the British Library, London. Forbes's papers from these and other collections are printed in *Writings of General John Forbes Relating to his Service in North America*, comp. and ed. Alfred Procter James (1938). Documents of the Forbes expedition for June through December 1758 are printed in *The Papers of Henry Bouquet, II: The Forbes Expedition*, ed. S. K. Stevens et al. (1951).

LOUIS M. WADDELL

FORBES, John (?1767–13 May 1823), merchant, was born in Gamrie, County of Banff, Scotland, the son of James Forbes and Sarah Gordon, occupations unknown. Although his exact birthdate is not known, sources indicate he was christened on 20 December 1767. No records have been found about his education in Scotland. Forbes came to St. Augustine, Spanish East Florida, in 1784. His brother Thomas had been in the colonies for some years and was engaged in the mercantile business with William Panton and others. Forbes remained in St. Augustine only a short time and soon departed for the Bahamas. In 1785 he accompanied Panton to Pensacola, Florida.

John Forbes impressed the owners of Panton, Leslie and Company, which controlled much of the Indian trade in the Spanish Floridas. In 1793 Panton described Forbes as "a young man of as much real ability and honour as I ever met with." The confidence seemed well placed as Forbes had already been named a junior partner and given charge of the company's Mobile (in present-day Alabama) branch. The Mobile trading post handled the Chickasaw and Choctaw trade.

Forbes first officially appears in the Mobile records on 12 June 1792, when he witnessed a deed. He became a landowner there in 1795, the year he purchased some small cabins on St. Charles Street. Panton, Leslie and Company owned several pieces of property in Mobile; the store and skinhouses were located on Royal Street and the stables and wagonyards on St. Michael's, all under Forbes's direction. Andrew Ellicott, the U.S. boundary commissioner, visited Forbes briefly in 1799 and described him as living in elegant style and as being "highly esteemed for his great hospitality & politeness."

Although the Indian fur trade represented the principal business of the Mobile branch of the company, Forbes did not restrict his activities to that: he also bought and sold slaves. Occasionally, he handled special orders for goods for high-ranking Spanish officers. But minding the Mobile store was only part of Forbes's responsibilities. He was constantly on the move on behalf of the company.

In the summer of 1795 Panton sent Forbes with a load of trade goods to open a store in San Fernando de las Barrancas (present-day Memphis, Tennessee). The new store gave the company a good site from which to strengthen trade with the Chickasaw and Cherokee. But within a few years the United States occupied the area, and the company, which was not licensed by the U.S. government, closed the trading post. In 1796 Forbes made a trip to the Knoxville area to secure the help of U.S. officials in collecting debts due the Panton company from the Cherokee. In 1798, during the Spanish-British war, he accompanied a load of furs destined for Charleston. Intercepted by a British privateer and forced to sail to the Island of New Providence (later Nassau), Forbes posted bond for the cargo and continued his journey. He sold the skins for a profit, handled other company business, returned to Nassau for the trial, and resolved the case to the company's satisfaction.

In 1803 Forbes attended a general Indian congress at the Hickory Ground in central Alabama to secure a land cession from the Indians for their unpaid debts and to capture the company's nemesis, the pro-British William Augustus Bowles, who had hoped to emerge from the conference as the new "king" of the southern Indians and to take the Indian trade away from Pan-

ton, Leslie and Company. The Upper Creeks, abetted by Forbes's supporters, seized Bowles, took him to Mobile in irons, and collected the $4,500 reward for his capture. Bowles's removal enabled Forbes to proceed with his plans to collect the Indian debts.

Around 1801 John Leslie and Company had officially replaced Panton, Leslie and Company in London. By 1805 John Forbes and Company was officially recognized in the Spanish Floridas as the successor firm to John Leslie and Company. Between 1804 and 1811, with pressure from Forbes and James and John Innerarity, Panton's nephews, the Indians ceded more than 1.4 million acres of land in Spanish West Florida to the company in payment of $181,243 of their debts. This area became popularly known as the "Forbes Purchase" (Forbes Grant I). In 1811, as a token of their appreciation for his services, the Indians gave Forbes a 9,811-acre island in the Apalachicola River, which has since been known as Forbes Island.

By 1808 all of the principal partners in Panton, Leslie and Company were dead. John Forbes served as one of the executors of the wills of William Panton, John Leslie, and Thomas Forbes. From their estates Forbes received some $62,000 that he promised to invest in public stocks and bonds in Great Britain. But Forbes never invested the money as promised.

During the War of 1812, John Forbes and Company sustained losses of some $100,000, and the Indian trade was greatly diminished. In December 1817 Forbes sold Forbes Grant I to the Savannah merchants Carnochan and Mitchel for $66,666 but reserved 16,680 acres and Forbes Island for himself.

By January 1818 Forbes had moved to Cuba, where he became a partner in the sugar plantation "La Reunion Deseada" in Matanzas Province. Shortly after his arrival, Forbes petitioned the captain general of Cuba for a grant of land in West Florida to compensate the company for losses during the War of 1812. Spain, which recognized it would soon lose the Floridas to the United States, gave the Forbes company a grant of more than 1.275 million acres (Forbes Grant II) adjacent to Forbes Grant I. Unfortunately for Forbes, after the United States acquired the Floridas in 1821, it protested the company's title to those lands. Finally, in 1830, the U.S. District Court in Pensacola denied the company's title to those lands on a technicality.

Forbes never married, but his will revealed that he had two daughters, Sophia and Juana, who accompanied him to Cuba. Forbes died of dysentery on board a ship bound for New York. His daughters inherited his estate, valued at about $150,000.

• The papers of Panton, Leslie and Company at the University of West Florida, Pensacola, include several documentary collections containing more than 200,000 pages. A large number of John Forbes and John Forbes and Company documents are in those collections. A 26-reel microfilm collection of selected documents with an accompanying 764-page guide, *The Papers of Panton, Leslie and Company*, was released in 1986. For the most complete biography and bibliography of John Forbes, see William S. Coker and Thomas D. Watson, *Indian Traders of the Southeastern Spanish Border-*

lands: Panton, Leslie & Company and John Forbes & Company, 1783–1847 (1986). See also Coker, "John Forbes and Company and the War of 1812 in the Spanish Borderlands," in *Hispanic-American Essays in Honor of Max Leon Moorhead,* ed. Coker (1979); House Committee on Private Land Claims, *Report on John Forbes and Company to Accompany Bill H. R. No. 747,* 24th Cong., 1st sess. (1836); Catharine V. C. Mathews, *Andrew Ellicott, His Life and Letters* (c. 1908); and Coker, "The Papers and History of Panton, Leslie and Company, and John Forbes and Company," *Florida Historical Quarterly* 73, no. 3 (Jan. 1995): 353–58.

WILLIAM S. COKER

FORBES, John Murray (23 Feb. 1813–12 Oct. 1898), merchant, capitalist, and railroad developer, was born in Bordeaux, France, and raised in Milton, Massachusetts, the son of Ralph Bennet Forbes, a merchant, and Margaret Perkins. Through the generosity of his elder brother, Thomas Tunno Forbes, young John enjoyed five years of schooling at the experimental Round Hill School in Northampton, Massachusetts, before taking up a place in 1828 as a clerk to his uncles in Boston, the China traders James and Thomas Handasyd Perkins. In 1830 Forbes sailed for Canton to replace his brother Thomas, who had recently died, as the Perkinses' resident agent in the Canton firm of Russell & Company. There the young apprentice also assumed an extraordinary role as confidential agent for Houqua, the leading Chinese export merchant. Situated fortuitously at the center of a risky but profitable commerce, Forbes quickly mastered the mercantile business and began accumulating his fortune.

After two years in China, Forbes returned to Boston to repair his health. In 1834 he married Sarah Hathaway of New Bedford (with whom he would have six children) and returned almost immediately to the isolation of the Canton factories alone. There he discovered that a partner's share in Russell & Company had been accruing for him since his first tour of service and also that Houqua wished to retain him on a 10 percent commission. Persuaded by such opportunities, the newlywed reluctantly exchanged domestic happiness for certain pecuniary gain by staying in China for three more years.

American firms such as Russell & Company traded opium on the fringes of a regulated Asian commerce controlled by the British East India Company. With the disestablishment of that monopoly in 1834, young Forbes endured at Canton a speculative free-for-all of cutthroat competition that by 1837 left him rich, exhausted, and forever disenchanted with the clash of raw market forces. He arrived home in Boston just as the panic of 1837 toppled the Atlantic financial establishment. He emerged from that crisis relatively secure but eager to find investments less vulnerable to wild fluctuations, chaos, and international intrigue. While his new firm, J. M. Forbes and Company, worked the China trade for many years, its founder turned in the 1840s toward domestic industrial investments, especially railroads.

Forbes entered the railroad business in 1846 through the invitation of James F. Joy and John W. Brooks, who solicited his help in purchasing the Central Railroad (renamed later the Michigan Central Railroad) from the bankrupt state of Michigan. The MC boasted 143 miles of primitive strap-iron line, a little traffic, a right-of-way to Lake Michigan, and a nominal selling price of $2 million payable in depreciated Michigan bonds. Assured by engineer Brooks that the property was salvageable and confident that Michigan's economic growth must inevitably repay the investment, Forbes accepted what he hoped would be a passive role as president of this new railroad company. However, he never could leave business to others, and soon Forbes found himself consumed with shaping the exciting new railway industry.

Pioneer railroads could be built and managed for their long-term developmental potential or for short-term speculative gain. From the beginning Forbes clung to the former, conservative strategy, imagining an orderly process of investment that would open the West systematically while yielding a comfortable, steady income to capitalist investors. Western consumers, however, desperate for transportation and impatient with monopolistic pricing, begged for new railroads, which eastern investors eagerly provided. Rival lines lunged into new territory, establishing at Chicago a center of cutthroat competition from which the next generation of western railroads would radiate. As president of the MC, Forbes found himself pressed to take extraordinary risks and meet conditions that reminded him (unpleasantly) of his days in Canton. No sooner had he piloted the Michigan line into Chicago in 1852 (over Indiana tracks he did not own and had a questionable right to build) than he faced a host of new promoters determined to drag his attention and his money inexorably westward.

In the decades that bracketed the Civil War, Forbes served as the financial wizard on a team of specialists in western railroading. Attorney Joy and engineer Brooks mastered the legal, political, and technical aspects while Forbes lined up investors, floated securities, and plotted commercial strategies. Forbes's team gathered together four small Illinois lines and in 1856 organized the Chicago, Burlington & Quincy (CB&Q), which became the flagship of their railroad empire in the post–Civil War era. To the west stretched the Hannibal & St. Joseph in Missouri and the Burlington & Missouri River in Iowa—both lines pushing ahead of demand, force-fed on government land grants—which Forbes picked up for the CB&Q to secure feeder traffic from the next tier of states. Forbes hated such defensive investments in hypothetical railroads because they flooded security markets, deranged settlement patterns, and prematurely introduced competition and rate distortions. Nevertheless, he learned to play an aggressive game of competitive railroad building that continued for decades after the Civil War.

The Civil War tested Forbes's energy and convictions in behalf of American liberty. Ideologically disposed to believe in a free entrepreneurial society, Forbes despised plutocrats as unproductive parasites;

accordingly, he saw black slavery as an evil tending to perpetuate an antimodern planter aristocracy that stifled ambition and opportunity for white Americans in the South. In the 1850s Forbes drifted into abolitionist circles, funneling money and arms through the New England Immigrant Aid Society, helping to organize the new Republican party in Massachusetts, and once sheltering the fugitive John Brown. Forbes served on President James Buchanan's last-minute Peace Commission in 1861; and when war finally came, he threw himself eagerly into the business of mobilizing Massachusetts and the Union for war.

Throughout the Civil War Forbes held no public office but labored unofficially to raise troops and supplies, outfit privateers, organize naval procurements, sell government securities, and promote enlistments. He took an early lead in urging Abraham Lincoln to emancipate the slaves and enlist black troops in the Union cause. In 1863 he helped organize and finance a free-labor demonstration plantation at Port Royal, South Carolina. That same year he traveled to England on a secret mission to prevent the ironclad "Laird rams" from being delivered to the Confederacy. By 1864 Forbes wished for a more ardent warrior to replace Lincoln; but once the president secured renomination, Forbes labored through the Loyal Publication Society and Union Leagues to promote total victory for the Union cause. One enduring artifact of his zeal for nationalistic propaganda was the *Nation*, a Republican political journal founded in part with Forbes's aid.

After the war, Forbes tried to retire to a life of genteel leisure—riding, sailing, and entertaining friends at home in Milton or at his retreat on Naushon Island (near Martha's Vineyard). He joined the intellectually fashionable Saturday Club of Boston (where he socialized with Ralph Waldo Emerson, among others) and cultivated a local reputation for wit and charm among men of letters as well as business. Western railroads, however, still claimed his entrepreneurial attention. In 1875, after a decade of what Forbes considered "loose" practices centered on Kansas City, Forbes seized control of the CB&Q from Joy and refocused the company's energies on developing Nebraska and the Far West. Threatened by Granger legislation in midwestern states, wild swings in the business cycle, Wall Street crashers such as Jay Gould, and competitive construction everywhere, Forbes struggled to keep the peace by pooling traffic west of Chicago and urging nonaggression among competitors he did not trust or respect. (To be fair, enemies such as Gould thought Forbes a dangerously aggressive competitor and a bit of a hypocrite besides!) Assuming the presidency of the CB&Q in 1878, he groomed both his company and a young successor, his cousin Charles E. Perkins, for the inevitable next round of wild expansion into the Rockies and beyond. In 1881 Forbes handed the CB&Q presidency to Perkins and settled into a barely-less-active role as chairman of the board and chief financial strategist for a firm that soon held Chicago, Minneapolis, and Denver in its regional embrace.

Like other developmental investors of his day, Forbes indulged in all sorts of ancillary enterprises alongside his railroad career. In the 1840s he tried his hand at iron making without success. In Michigan in the 1850s, he took part in building the ship canal at Sault Ste. Marie. With his brother Bennet Forbes he built oceangoing steamships, and with his fellow MC investors he briefly sponsored a line of steamers on Lake Erie. He shared in land speculations and town site promotions along the routes of his midwestern railroads. Spanning a creative age of general entrepreneurship, Forbes's multifaceted career never exhibited a narrow specialization or an obsessive focus on accumulating wealth and power.

As a transitional entrepreneur whose career helped transform the American agrarian republic into a modern industrial nation, John Murray Forbes perpetuated the habits and values of a leisured gentleman, a country squire, a man of cultivated manners into an age fast succumbing to rampant, monolithic materialism. Democratic ideals appealed to him even though the presumptions of class and character dominated his thinking. Advances in science and technology fascinated him even while he protested his commitment to old-fashioned tastes and views. A free trader in theory, Forbes never held government to be exclusively the enemy of business. With enduring faith in the possibilities of reform, he labored much of his life to rid both politics and business of corrupt adventurers, never recognizing the extent to which reckless competition and selfish interests typified the new industrial order. Forbes died at home in Milton, still fighting for the gold standard and the integrity of a gentleman's word in business. His family, friends, and Wall Street associates remembered his character more than anything, perhaps because it stood in shocking contrast to the new business culture he ironically had done so much to bring about.

• Major collections of Forbes's papers can be found in the John Murray Forbes Papers, Baker Library, Harvard Graduate School of Business Administration, Boston; the Forbes Family Papers (microform) of the Massachusetts Historical Society, Boston; the Burlington Archives, Newberry Library, Chicago; the Michigan Central Archives of the New York Central System, Detroit; and the James F. Joy Papers, Michigan Historical Collections, Ann Arbor, Michigan. Forbes's daughter has published several works: *Letters and Recollections of John Murray Forbes*, 2 vols., ed. Sarah Forbes Hughes (1899); *Reminiscences of John Murray Forbes*, 3 vols., ed. Sarah Forbes Hughes (1902); and *Letters of John Murray Forbes*, 3 vols., ed. Sarah Forbes Hughes (1905). For biographical treatments see John Lauritz Larson, *Bonds of Enterprise: John Murray Forbes and Western Development in America's Railway Age* (1984); Arthur M. Johnson and Barry E. Supple, *Boston Capitalists and Western Railroads* (1967); Thomas C. Cochran, *Railroad Leaders, 1845–1890* (1953); and Henry Greenleaf Pearson, *An American Railroad Builder: John Murray Forbes* (1911). For the Chicago, Burlington & Quincy Railroad, see Richard C. Overton, *Burlington Route* (1965). An obituary is in the *Atlantic Monthly*, September 1899.

JOHN LAURITZ LARSON

FORBES, Malcolm Stevenson (19 Aug. 1919–24 Feb. 1990), publisher, was born in New York City, the son of Bertie Charles Forbes, a newspaper columnist and publisher, and Adelaide Stevenson. Reared in a comfortable, upper-middle-class home in Englewood, New Jersey, Forbes attended private schools in Tarrytown, New York, and Lawrenceville, New Jersey. He graduated from Princeton University with a major in political science in 1941, and with the support of his father, the founder of *Forbes* magazine, he became the owner and publisher of two local weeklies, the *Fairfield Times* and the *Lancaster Tribune*, in Lancaster, Ohio. He had hoped to build on his experience as founder of the *Nassau Sovereign* while at Princeton, but the papers ceased operations after he enlisted in the U.S. Army in 1942. While in service, he rose to the rank of staff sergeant in a heavy machine gun section, was wounded while fighting in Germany in 1944, and spent the final months of World War II recuperating in an army hospital. In 1946 he joined the *Forbes* staff as an assistant publisher, became an associate publisher in 1947, and for a time, in 1948 and 1949, was also publisher of *Nation's Heritage*, an expensive bimonthly that failed after issuing only six numbers. In 1946 he married Roberta Remsen Laidlaw, with whom he had four sons and a daughter. The couple divorced in 1985.

From 1947 through 1957 Forbes combined his publishing activities with a strong interest in a political career. At *Forbes* he helped to launch a system for rating corporations, and after his father's death in 1954 he took over the journal's editorial side while his brother Bruce handled the business side. He was also instrumental in helping to convert the magazine from a financial emphasis to a broader business one, and he played a leading role in founding and directing the affiliated Investors Advisory Institute, which published *Forbes Investor*. Yet his real passion during the period was politics, in which he had hopes of rising to the highest level. In 1949 he was elected to the borough council of Bernardsville, New Jersey, and in 1951 he was successful in securing the Republican nomination for New Jersey state senator and winning election. He served as senator for six years (1952–1958) and became noted for his quarrels with the Republican Old Guard leadership. In 1952 he was an early supporter of Dwight D. Eisenhower for president and subsequently became chair of the New Jersey Ike-Nixon Clubs. The next year he was unsuccessful in a bid for the New Jersey Republican gubernatorial nomination, but in 1957 he mounted an unorthodox, door-to-door campaign that made his second bid for the nomination a success and gave him national prominence as the articulate challenger of Democratic governor Robert Meyner's fiscal and welfare policies. Commentators believed that he had a chance of upsetting Meyner. But he lost by a wide margin—"nosed out," he said, "by a landslide"—and after the defeat gave up his political ambitions and devoted himself to business and personal projects.

In the late 1950s and early 1960s Forbes helped to turn the enterprise he had inherited into an increasingly prosperous magazine directed especially to executives and investors who needed information about corporate worth. The real transformation, however, would come after his brother Bruce's death from cancer in 1964. Taking over as president of Forbes, Inc., Malcolm quickly became sole owner of the company and embarked upon a campaign of daring initiatives that in effect would recreate the magazine, this time as what Forbes biographer Arthur Jones called "a punchy, highly profitable, easy-to-read, mass-circulation business magazine devoted to money, wealth and success." One aspect of its new image was *Forbes* as a "capitalist tool" that businesspeople could use to find out how other businesses were run. Another was *Forbes* as an authoritative ranker, putting together a "Forbes 500" plus a 400-person ranking of the world's wealthiest individuals; and still another was *Forbes* as "interpreter of the corporate world" through a freewheeling journalism that combined aggressive exposés with a breezy style, opinionated commentary, and entertaining accounts of life among the rich and famous. From 1964 to 1975 *Forbes*'s circulation grew from 400,000 to 625,000, and by the end of the period its advertising revenues had overtaken those of its longstanding rivals, *Fortune* and *Business Week*.

In what turned out to be an effective way of promoting the magazine, Forbes also made himself a media personality increasingly celebrated as a lavish party giver and consummate world traveler, an ingenious public relations wizard, the last of the "fun millionaires," and an unabashed, insouciant, and exuberant reveler in the exotic consumer pleasures available to those at the top of an acquisitive society. The entertainment of corporate chieftains on the company's yacht or at its New York townhouse became legendary for its lavishness and the exquisiteness of the cuisine. The display of corporate and family collections, which had come to include fabulous assortments of Old Masters, Fabergé eggs, valuable historical documents, and toy boats and soldiers, made the company's New York headquarters a well-known landmark and generated publicity that could be turned into greater circulation and larger advertising revenues. And special events like the magazine's fiftieth anniversary party in 1967, held in huge tents on Forbes's New Jersey estate with Vice President Hubert Humphrey as the guest of honor, added to the fanfare. Some commentators saw Forbes's lifestyle as a throwback to the plutocratic excesses and "conspicuous consumption" of the Gilded Age. But for others it represented a deserved reward for American-style entrepreneurial success or an entertaining spectacle to be vicariously enjoyed.

By the 1970s Forbes's promotional display of the good life was also leading to investments that eventually created a diverse business empire deriving only about two-thirds of its revenue from the magazine. In 1969 Forbes purchased a 260-square-mile ranch in Colorado and, after being blocked from turning it into a commercial hunting preserve for rich patrons, proceeded to develop a portion of it into lots for vacation and retirement homes. Subsequently, he also acquired other real-estate holdings, among them a development in the Ozarks, ranches in Montana and Wyoming, a palace in Tangier, a château in France, an island plantation in the Fijis, and a fishing camp in Tahiti. In addition, he moved into other publishing ventures, including acquisition of *American Heritage*, purchase of a string of New Jersey weeklies, publication for a short period of a Forbes restaurant guide, and the launching in early 1990 of the magazine *Egg* as a guide to opulent living. He made sizable investments in art treasures and other collectibles and created for a time a special company for dealing in antiques. And in conjunction with his involvement in motorcycling and hot-air ballooning, he acquired a motorcycle dealership (Slegers-Forbes, Inc.) and had his company establish a balloon ascension division. Most of these new ventures, moreover, turned out to be moneymakers, leading *Newsweek* to describe Forbes as a "Walter Mitty dreamer with a solid Midas touch." By the 1980s his assets were conservatively estimated to be something in excess of $600 million.

During the 1970s Forbes also built up a considerable reputation as an international sportsman interested particularly in the promotion of motorcycling, yachting, and hot-air ballooning. His motorcycle feats and yachting trips were often in the news, and in 1973 he broke six ballooning records and became the first person to cross the United States from coast to coast in a single balloon. In 1974 and early 1975 his preparations for a transatlantic flight also became a major news story, but the project was finally abandoned after he nearly lost his life in an aborted takeoff. In 1975 he received the Harmon Trophy for his ballooning achievements and later received much publicity for his "friendship tours," with motorcycles and balloons, of Egypt, Russia, Thailand, Pakistan, Spain, and China. In China in 1982, he defied restrictions imposed on him by communist officials, cut his balloon loose, and became the first person to fly over Beijing in a free-flight balloon.

In the 1980s Forbes continued to stage numerous media events, the "splashiest" being his seventieth birthday party cohosted with the actress Elizabeth Taylor at his palace in Morocco. For the occasion he spent a reported $2 million on lavish entertainment, media spectacles, and "fly-ins" of illustrious guests. Articles about his private jet *The Capitalist Tool*, his yacht *The Highlander*, and the museums housing his fabled collections, especially the Museum of Military Miniatures in Tangier, also became media staples. And in more dignified settings, he continued to be honored with business and publishing awards and kept adding to a long list of honorary college degrees. In addition, he received some unwanted publicity, especially about his alleged involvement with young male homosexuals.

In his later years, Forbes published a number of books. Since the 1950s he had written a *Forbes* column, "Fact and Comment," which became noted for its sprightly style, outrageous opinions and puns, quotable epigrams, and a punchy humor that led Hubert Humphrey to label its author "the Bob Hope of business publications." In 1974 Forbes published the best of these columns in a book titled *Fact and Comment*, and when it succeeded he offered more of the same kind of commentary in *The Sayings of Chairman Malcolm* (1978) and *The Further Sayings of Chairman Malcolm* (1986). He also wrote two books about his personal exploits and interests—*Around the World on Hot Air and Two Wheels* (1985) and *More than I Dreamed* (1989)—and two odd books of popular biography, *They Went That-a-Way: How the Famous, the Infamous, and the Great Died* (1988) and *What Happened to Their Kids? Children of the Rich and Famous* (1990). In Forbes's view, these recovered history that had "slipped through the cracks," and at the time of his death he was working on a third such work, subsequently published as *Women Who Made a Difference* (1990).

In his personal relations with others, Forbes could be difficult. His critics found him arrogant and opinionated, excessively demanding, too inclined to treat his employees as family retainers, and loath to listen to anyone but himself. Yet at the same time he could be a man of considerable charm, geniality, and personal magnetism, able to put others at ease, artful as a host and raconteur, knowledgeable in worldly affairs and the social graces, and fascinating in his role of a "sparkling, naughty boy." Ruggedly handsome, with a solid build, ruddy face, energetic bearing, and jaunty air of venturesomeness, he became a memorable figure in the circles in which he moved. And despite practices that some employees found demeaning, he encouraged the rise of journalistic "stars" and succeeded in building an organization that benefited from the talents of some remarkably able editors, writers, and merchandisers. Of particular importance, his biographers have thought, was his elevation of and reliance on editor James Michaels in his remaking of the magazine.

For public consumption, Forbes often downplayed his business skills, saying that he got where he was "through sheer ability (spelled i-n-h-e-r-i-t-a-n-c-e)." But the skills and judgment that he brought to bear on business problems proved themselves at the bottom line; his transformation of the magazine he had inherited was a major achievement affecting business journalism as a whole; and his public relations artistry worked for the purposes intended and influenced what others undertook. In important ways, moreover, he became an inspiration to and model for a new generation of business leaders. Ahead of his time in the 1960s and 1970s, he became a mainstream symbol of the flamboyant consumerism, worship of moneymaking, and upbeat fantasizing that pervaded much of America's business and political culture in the 1980s, and during that decade he not only showed others how to spend their money but also became an even more outspoken defender of the capitalist system, minimal government and taxes, and entrepreneurial virtue. He died at his home in Far Hills, New Jersey, and was eulogized by President George Bush as "a giant of American business."

• The best biography, written by a former employee but generally well balanced, is Arthur Jones, *Malcolm Forbes: Peripatetic Millionaire* (1977). Another book-length treatment is the sensationalistic and gossipy Christopher Winans, *Malcolm Forbes: The Man Who Had Everything* (1990), focusing on Forbes's high living and alleged homosexual dalliances. Other biographical material can be found in Forbes's own writings (noted above), in periodic interviews published in *Forbes Magazine*, and in such articles as "Walter Mitty as King Midas," *Newsweek*, 20 Jan. 1975, pp. 70–71; Arthur Lubow, "Malcolm Forbes," *People Weekly*, 19 July 1982, pp. 48–59; Elizabeth Peer, "The High Life of Malcolm the Audacious," *New York*, 30 Jan. 1984, pp. 30–37; Ira Wolfman, "Just Another Thursday with Malcolm Forbes," *50 Plus*, Nov. 1988, pp. 52–59; and Harold Holzer, "Collecting's First Family," *Americana*, Mar.–Apr. 1983, pp. 41–47. An obituary is in the *New York Times*, 26 Feb. 1990.

ELLIS W. HAWLEY

FORBES, Stephen Alfred (29 May 1844–13 Mar. 1930), ecologist, state entomologist of Illinois, and chief of the Illinois Natural History Survey, was born in a log cabin in Silver Creek, Illinois, the son of Isaac Forbes, a farmer, and Agnes Van Hoesen. While enduring economic hardships common to pioneer families on the prairies, the Forbes family suffered further misfortune when Stephen was ten. With his mother already in poor health, Stephen's father died, forcing older brother Henry to assume responsibility for the farm and the rearing of Stephen and his younger sister, Nettie. Stephen attended the district school until he was fourteen, studied under Henry's instruction for two years, and briefly attended a college preparatory school until the family ran out of financial resources.

The Civil War would have interrupted Forbes's education anyway. Stephen was seventeen when he and Henry enlisted in the Seventh Illinois Volunteer Cavalry. Stephen saw extensive action, engaging in twenty-two separate battles against the Rebel army. By the time he was twenty, he had risen to the rank of captain. The war seemed to stimulate his ambition for learning as much as for military rank. He mastered Spanish and Italian, for example, during quiet moments by the light of a campfire. When he was captured and confined to Confederate prisons for four months, he used the time to learn Greek. Later, Forbes would make effective use of these language skills by keeping abreast of the latest European research in his field. Forbes credited the war with both kindling his passion for learning and pointing him toward a public-service career.

After the war, Forbes studied at Rush Medical College in Chicago for a year, grew strawberries for a season, and practiced medicine under a preceptor, before gaining a job as schoolmaster in Makanda, Illinois. He enjoyed teaching and set his sites on becoming a professor. He then taught school at two other towns in southern Illinois and briefly studied zoology at Illinois State Normal University between teaching appointments. Studying botany in his spare time, he became acquainted with some of the state's established naturalists, including George Vasey, who had left Illinois to become the curator of the Smithsonian Institution's National Herbarium. Impressed by an article Forbes had written for the *American Entomologist and Botanist*, Vasey helped Forbes become curator of the Illinois Natural History Society's museum at Normal— a position left vacant by John Wesley Powell's departure for a federal science post. Having attained reasonably secure employment, Forbes married Clara Shaw Gaston in 1873. The couple had five children.

Forbes spent the rest of his life building and shaping the institution that would evolve with his career; he progressed from curator of the Illinois Natural History Society Museum in 1872 to founder and director of the State Laboratory of Natural History in 1877, to chief of the State Natural History Survey in 1917. Appointed state entomologist in 1882, Forbes managed that office apart from the lab until both units were merged into the survey in 1917. In education he rose from zoology instructor at Illinois State Normal University in 1875 to professor of zoology and entomology at the University of Illinois in 1884 and then dean of the College of Science at the University of Illinois in 1888. In 1884 he received a Ph.D. in zoology from the University of Indiana. An active participant in professional groups, he served as president of a number of national organizations, including the Ecological Society of America and the American Association of Economic Entomologists.

Forbes did not permit his administrative, teaching, and public service responsibilities to displace his research. Early in his career he began to study the food of birds, fishes, and insects, investigations that laid the groundwork for his contributions to the burgeoning field of ecology. This research entailed the microscopic examination of the stomach contents of organisms to determine food relationships and habitat requirements. Although Forbes's publications grew to more than 400 titles over his lifetime, two articles summarizing conclusions from his food studies drew particular notice: "Interactions of Organisms" (1880) and "The Lake as a Microcosm" (1887). Both articles were extraordinary for their system-wide approach to the study of functional community relationships, with attention to nonliving as well as living components. In "The Lake as a Microcosm," Forbes explained how a lake could be studied as a scale model of nature to help investigators apprehend more general natural processes: "the lake," he wrote, "forms a little world within itself—a microcosm within which all the elemental forces are at work and the play of life goes on in full, but on so small a scale as to bring it easily within the mental grasp." This approach provided Forbes meaningful insights into predator-prey systems. He described, for example, how natural selection acted not just on predator and prey species individually, but on predator and prey as a unit. The populations of both must be well adjusted to each other "in a close community of interest." Forbes's one and only book, *The*

Fishes of Illinois (1908), a comprehensive volume written in collaboration with Robert E. Richardson, his colleague at the Illinois Biological Research Station, became a classic reference on freshwater ichthyology.

Throughout his career Forbes struck a balance between pure and applied science; his positions as director of the laboratory and state entomologist symbolized this dichotomy. In 1894 he founded the Biological Research Station, a floating laboratory on the Illinois River intended for both basic and applied research. In addition to conducting basic plankton studies aimed at determining the quantity of food available for fish, Forbes and his group collected baseline water quality data to study the ecological impacts of the Chicago sewage canal, which opened in 1900. The resulting research correlated various stages of river pollution with changes in the species of bottom-dwelling organisms. Forbes also documented changes in the character and abundance of fish whose loss of habitat had been caused by the construction of levees to expand agriculture on river bottomlands. Consequently, his years of basic research on the river yielded data that contributed to understanding of applied problems in conservation. Forbes died at Urbana, Illinois.

• Forbes's unpublished papers are spread over three different archives on the University of Illinois campus at Champaign-Urbana: the University of Illinois Archives, the Illinois Historical Survey, and the Illinois Natural History Survey Archives. Most of his scientific papers appear in issues of the *Bulletin of the Illinois State Laboratory of Natural History* and other state scientific periodicals. Frank Egerton has compiled some of Forbes's significant ecological articles in the volume *Ecological Investigations of Stephen Alfred Forbes* (1977). L. O. Howard's memoir in National Academy of Sciences, *Biographical Memoirs* 15 (1934), includes a brief account of Forbes's life and scientific work along with a comprehensive bibliography of his publications, compiled by H. C. Oesterling, a former editor of the Illinois Natural History Survey. Sharon Kingsland includes a brief discussion of the historical and philosophical context of Forbes's work in *Modeling Nature, Episodes in the History of Population Ecology* (1985). Stephen Bocking compares Forbes's work in aquatic ecology with that of Jacob Reighard in "Stephen Forbes, Jacob Reighard, and the Emergence of Aquatic Ecology in the Great Lakes Region," *Journal of the History of Biology* 23 (1990): 461–98. Two useful obituaries are H. B. Ward, "Stephen Alfred Forbes—A Tribute," *Science* 71 (1930): 378–81, and Frank Smith, "Stephen Alfred Forbes: An Appreciation," *Audubon Bulletin* 17 (1926): 19–25.

ROBERT A. LOVELY

FORBES, William Cameron (21 May 1870–24 Dec. 1959), businessman and diplomat, was born in Milton, Massachusetts, the son of William Hathaway Forbes, president of the American Bell Telephone Company, and Edith Emerson, daughter of Ralph Waldo Emerson. Forbes attended Milton (Mass.) Academy and Hopkinson's School in Boston and was graduated from Harvard University in 1892. Between 1894 and 1898 he traveled extensively, became a world-class polo player, and coached Harvard's football team. He joined Stone and Webster, a utilities holding company

and electrical engineering firm, in 1897. In 1899, after the death of his grandfather, John Murray Forbes, he became a partner in the private banking firm of J. M. Forbes and Co. of Boston.

In 1904 President Theodore Roosevelt appointed Forbes to the Philippine Commission, the governing body of the Philippine Islands, which was then a possession of the United States. Between 1904 and 1908 Forbes held the portfolio of secretary of commerce and police. As such he was responsible for public works programs, port improvement and construction, railroad construction, the development of a Philippine merchant marine, the coast and geodetic survey, supervision of corporations, and direction of police and prison affairs. Forbes also chaired a committee addressing the question of reorganization of the Insular government. Incorporating many of that committee's recommendations, the first Philippine Assembly was convened in 1907, at which time the Philippine Commission became the upper body of the Philippine legislature.

Forbes became vice governor in 1908. In 1909 President William Howard Taft appointed him governor general, a post he held until 1913. As governor he attempted to avoid partisan politics and to concentrate on the development of the Philippines. Toward that end he expanded primary and secondary education and founded the University of the Philippines. Forbes supported the improvement of road and railroad networks and developed an extensive irrigation program. He also promoted a major effort to eradicate rinderpest, a debilitating disease affecting draft animals, and authorized the employment of the constabulary to control plagues of locusts. Under Forbes's direction the government conducted large-scale land registration programs to establish title and to assure owners of their rights. Largely as a result of these efforts, agricultural production expanded and government revenues increased.

The economic gains were insufficient, however, to overcome simmering racial tensions between Americans and Filipinos and American anti-imperialist agitation at home. In addition, Forbes suffered from serious bouts of illness in 1911 and 1912, which hindered the effectiveness of his administration. The incoming administration of Woodrow Wilson requested Forbes's resignation in 1913, and upon his return to the United States he again took an active role in J. M. Forbes and Co. He accepted a number of directorships, and during the First World War he acted as receiver for the Brazil Railroad Company. In addition, in 1914 Forbes was elected overseer of Harvard University, a post he held until 1920.

Then, in 1921, President Warren G. Harding tapped Forbes to join General Leonard Wood to investigate conditions in the Philippines. Harding hoped for a report that would support his desire for retrenchment and a reverse of the Wilson administration's policies, which were aimed at a rapid move toward independence. The so-called Wood-Forbes Commission arrived in the Philippines in April 1921 and spent five months touring the countryside and holding hearings in numerous villages as well as in Manila. Wood, the primary author of the report, ignored the near-universal calls for independence. He was convinced that the past eight years had been a period of regression in all measurable areas of Filipino life—agriculture, commerce, education, health, transportation, and so on. Therefore the report concluded that the provisions of the Jones Act of 1916, which called for Philippine independence at the earliest possible moment, were far from being met and that the United States must continue its tutelage of the local population.

Forbes returned to private life until 1930, when President Herbert Hoover appointed him chairman of a commission to investigate conditions in Haiti, which had been occupied by American forces since 1915. Forbes was personally convinced that Haiti was not ready for self government, but the Hoover administration was committed to the Good Neighbor policy, so the Forbes Commission recommended that the United States begin to withdraw the marines; it also presented a plan for general elections, with the selection of a Haitian president by the popularly elected assembly.

Later that year Hoover named Forbes as ambassador to Japan, where he served until 1932. His tenure ended disastrously, however. He sailed for a planned leave to the United States the day after Japan and China began fighting in Manchuria. In addition, Forbes's thinking on the subject proved to be entirely different from that of Secretary of State Henry L. Stimson, who accepted Forbes's offer to resign.

Forbes never married. He was an avid yachtsman and the author of *As to Polo* (1911), *A Letter to an Undergraduate* (1900), *A Decade of American Rule in the Philippines* (1909), and the two-volume study *The Philippine Islands* (1929). Forbes received several honorary degrees; the Japanese government presented him with the Order of the Rising Sun, first class; and the Chinese government honored him with the Order of the Golden Grain and the Order of the Jade. He was active in a number of professional and scholarly societies, including the Massachusetts Historical Society and the China Society. Forbes was a trustee of the Carnegie Institution of Washington, D.C., the Massachusetts Institute of Technology Corporation, and Hampton Institute. He died in Boston.

• Forbes's papers are at Houghton Library, Harvard University. Copies of his annotated journal are at the Library of Congress. For additional information on Forbes's years in the Philippines, see Camillus Gott, "William Cameron Forbes and the Philippines, 1904–1946" (Ph.D. diss., Indiana Univ., 1974); Peter W. Stanley, *A Nation in the Making: The Philippines and the United States, 1899–1921* (1974); and Theodore Friend, *Between Two Empires: The Ordeal of the Philippines, 1929–1946* (1965). Also see Hans Schmidt, *The United States Occupation of Haiti, 1915–1934* (1971). An obituary is in the *New York Times*, 25 Dec. 1959.

ANNE CIPRIANO VENZON

FORBUSH, Edward Howe (24 Apr. 1858–8 Mar. 1929), ornithologist and conservationist, was born in Quincy, Massachusetts, the son of Leander Pomeroy Forbush, a school principal, and Ruth Hudson Carr. Soon after their son's birth, the parents moved their family to West Roxbury, Massachusetts, while Forbush's father went into business in nearby Worcester. In early childhood, Forbush developed a strong interest in birds, mammals, and nature in general; in his early teens, he taught himself to be a competent taxidermist. Forbush attended the public schools in West Roxbury and Worcester, but he left at age fifteen, to help his father in his business, and never graduated. All thought of college was soon abandoned. He assisted his father as a laborer, mechanic, and farmer for seven years, and studied natural history in such spare time as he could find. At age sixteen he became a member of the Worcester Natural History Society, and served as volunteer curator of ornithology for its museum. At age nineteen he became president of the society, and with like-minded friends, worked hard to develop local interest in the organization and in the nature study programs it offered. For several years he enjoyed the luxury of pursuing his natural history avocation with little thought for earning any independent income.

At the age of eighteen Forbush and a friend organized a nature exchange, offering animal specimens they had collected in their region, together with taxidermists' supplies. In about 1877 he participated in a modest private expedition along the eastern coast of Florida, both in order to collect needed specimens and to improve his state of health.

Forbush married Etta Hill in 1882, and the couple had four children. Determined to support his growing family from his natural history pursuits, he stepped up the work of his naturalists' exchange, taking trips to Florida in 1886 for more specimens and to Washington Territory, British Columbia, and Alaska in 1888 for the same purpose. In the summer of 1885, and for several years thereafter, Forbush directed a summer nature study camp for boys at Lake Quinsigamond, near Worcester, under the auspices of the Natural History Society. Some authorities consider this an important forerunner of the American summer camp movement that began early in the twentieth century.

When in 1891 Forbush was employed to take charge of the state Gypsy Moth Commission's moth control program, he worked diligently both to suppress the insect's activities and to educate the public about ways of dealing with the problem. With the assistance of the entomologist Charles H. Fernald, Forbush published a report titled *The Gypsy Moth* (1896), but the state legislature's stubborn refusal to appropriate sufficient sums for his program of control prompted him to resign in 1900.

In the meantime, Forbush had been appointed ornithologist to the Massachusetts State Board of Agriculture in 1893. In advancing the cause of ornithological conservation, he did valuable work in emphasizing the importance of birds to the Commonwealth and to agriculture. He lectured throughout the state and drafted reports concerning the life histories of birds and their preservation. In 1908 Forbush's title was changed to state ornithologist, and in 1920 he was named director of the Division of Ornithology in the Massachusetts Department of Agriculture, a post he held until his mandatory retirement in 1928.

Forbush was the author of over 170 articles and papers on various ornithological subjects. The three major works for which he is best known were published during the last several decades of his career. *Useful Birds and Their Protection* (1907) was a pioneering study during a period when Americans were first being made conscious of the importance of the nation's natural resources, and the National Audubon Societies and other organizations were trying to impress the American public with the importance of conserving wildlife. *A History of Game Birds, Wild Fowl and Shore Birds of Massachusetts and Adjacent States* (1912) was another pathbreaking study about an important group of birds which traced their "former abundance and later decrease," and described the "food species of New England which have been exterminated." Extensive coverage was given to most migratory species in the eastern part of the country. The book was published in a revised edition in 1916. Forbush's seminal work was *Birds of Massachusetts and Other New England States* (3 vols., 1925–1929), a classic account which was still consulted after nearly three-quarters of a century. Illustrated by the well-known contemporary artists Louis Agassiz Fuertes and Allan Brooks, these volumes constituted a detailed regional ornithology for much of the northeastern United States and Eastern Canada.

Forbush's considerable ornithological skills were honed over the years by dint of much active field work and familiarity with the literature of his subject. He became a member of the American Ornithologists' Union in 1903 and was elected a fellow of the union in 1912. For several years he served the organization as a member of its council. He was a founder and for twelve years president of the Massachusetts Audubon Society, and was active in the National Audubon organization as New England Field Agent for twenty-two years. In this latter capacity he strove for passage of a state law in Massachusetts that would terminate the sale of native wild game birds and animals, finally succeeding in 1912. His annual reports as field agent were published in *Bird Lore*, the predecessor of *Audubon* magazine. He was also president of the Northeastern Bird Banding Association, and of the Federation of Bird Clubs of New England.

Forbush vigorously lobbied in favor of strong game and conservation laws, which were eventually enacted by the legislatures of Massachusetts and the other New England states. In 1913 he was named a member of the advisory board of the U.S. Department of Agriculture, assisting in the implementation of the Migratory Bird Treaty between the United States and Canada. All of these activities did much to stimulate similar bird protection efforts in other parts of the nation. For a time, he produced monthly or semi-monthly articles which were printed in some fifty New England newspapers, informing the public about the importance of birds and their protection.

As state ornithologist, Forbush made valiant attempts over more than two decades to preserve the heath hen, an endangered species, on Martha's Vineyard. State and local authorities set aside land where the bird could receive absolute protection, and Forbush made efforts to propagate it. For a time these measures worked, and the number of birds rose to over 800. Fire destroyed many birds and much of their habitat in 1916, however, and their numbers were further decimated by an influx of goshawks in 1917, following which fewer than 100 heath hens survived. For several years, there was a heartening upsurge in the number of birds observed, but thereafter, despite continuing efforts by Forbush and others, their population steadily declined. Only thirty remained by 1927, when Forbush termed the survival of the species "problematical." The one remaining bird, an old male, was last observed in March 1932, three years following Forbush's death at his home in Westboro, Massachusetts.

• The most extensive biographical summary is by John B. May, "Edward Howe Forbush: A Biographical Sketch," in *Proceedings of the Boston Society of Natural History*, Apr. 1928. This was accompanied by a bibliography of Forbush's publications, prepared by the Reverend Robert F. Cheney. Other sketches include T. Gilbert Pearson, "In Memoriam: Edward Howe Forbush," *Auk*, Jan. 1930; Henry C. Tracy, *American Naturalists* (1930); Paul Brooks, "Birds and Men," *Audubon* (1980); and Richard Stroud, ed., *National Leaders of American Conservation* (1985). See also the obituary in the *Boston Transcript*, 8 Mar. 1929.

KEIR B. STERLING

FORBUSH, Scott Ellsworth (10 Apr. 1904–4 Apr. 1984), geophysicist and mathematician, was born near Hudson, Ohio, the son of E. A. Forbush, a farmer, and Grace (maiden name unknown), a former schoolteacher.

Forbush graduated second in his class in 1920 from Cleveland's Western Reserve Academy. He worked as a waiter before entering Case School of Applied Science in Cleveland in 1921. He graduated with a B.S. in physics and mathematics in 1925. He then began graduate studies in physics (optics, electronics, and thermodynamics) at Ohio State University in Columbus, also acting as a teaching assistant in general physics. Disappointed with the curriculum, however, he accepted a position as junior physicist with the National Bureau of Standards in Washington, D.C., in 1926. This, too, failed to satisfy him, and he applied in 1927 for a position with the Department of Terrestrial Magnetism (DTM) of the Carnegie Institution of Washington. He stayed with the DTM for forty-two years, until his retirement in 1969, except for a few leaves of absence in government and university service.

In 1930 Forbush married Clara Lundell, a pianist and teacher, often playing cello to her accompaniment. After she died in 1967, he married the science writer and artist Julie Daves in 1970. He had no children from either marriage.

When Forbush was employed by the DTM, he applied to be an observer at the Geomagnetic Observatory near Huancayo, Peru. He may have wanted adventure, but he aimed at a research career in physics. Within a year of beginning at Huancayo, he requested leave to begin work on an M.S. in mathematics and physics in the United States, hoping to return to Huancayo as observer-in-charge. Research in geomagnetism, the electrical properties of the atmosphere and ground, and radio transmission interested him intensely.

Instead, after two years at Huancayo, Forbush was reassigned to the Carnegie Institution's sailing yacht *Carnegie*. On board the nonmagnetic craft (no magnetic materials, such as iron, were used in its construction), he and the scientific crew measured geomagnetic variables, electrical conductivity of the atmosphere, and a range of oceanographic phenomena. Forbush gave special attention to gravimetric investigations, using a device developed by Felix Vening Meinesz. This seventh cruise of the *Carnegie* ended abruptly in November 1929, when its engine house exploded in harbor in Samoa. Forbush escaped, but two crew members died.

Forbush returned to Huancayo for a tour as observer-in-charge for 1930 and 1931; he then went to Johns Hopkins University for one year to work toward an M.S. After this leave, he resumed research at the DTM's Washington office, primarily analyzing gravimetric and geomagnetic variation data.

In the 1930s Forbush gradually shifted his research to cosmic rays. His first experience with this phenomenon had been on the *Carnegie*, where he helped with visual readings of a Kolhörster ionization chamber. In the 1920s the DTM began a collaboration with Arthur H. Compton of the University of Chicago, and by the mid-1930s this involved seven continuously-recording ionization chambers located worldwide. Forbush was responsible for an instrument at Cheltenham Observatory in Virginia.

An important influence on Forbush was the application of statistical analytical methods to geophysical data by the German geophysicist Julius Bartels. Bartels was a research associate at the DTM in the 1930s; there he wrote much of his portion of the two-volume classic *Geomagnetism*, the rest being the work of Sydney Chapman, another DTM research associate. Claims of statistical associations between solar and geomagnetic phenomena had long been made, and similar claims were being advanced regarding cosmic ray fluctuations and other phenomena.

Forbush decided to apply statistical methods systematically to cosmic ray data to test these claims. He announced the first success of this analysis in 1937: the well-known Forbush Effect or Decrease. With the help of his longtime assistant Isabelle Lange, he observed a worldwide decrease in the intensity of cosmic rays associated with solar magnetic storms. In 1946 he announced the solar-flare effect, demonstrating that the intensity of cosmic rays increases dramatically with some chromospheric events on the Sun. Later investigations indicated that this was due to increased solar ejections of protons and neutrons. He chaired the Cosmic Ray Committee for the International Geophysical Year (1957–1958). Forbush made many more discoveries about cosmic rays, continuing this research into the 1980s.

Other major areas of Forbush's research concerned currents flowing in the high atmosphere near Earth's equator—the equatorial electrojet—and the structure of the Van Allen radiation belts. Forbush determined the absolute field from the equatorial ring current and demonstrated its relation to solar activity. His work was crucial in establishing the investigation of solar-terrestrial relations.

During World War II and the Korean Conflict, Forbush turned his statistical expertise toward another arena, operational research. He headed the mathematical analysis section for the Naval Ordnance Laboratory (1940–1944); he was in the Office of Scientific Research and Development (1944–1945) and in the U.S. Army/Johns Hopkins University Operations Research Office (1951–1952).

Forbush was appointed chair of the DTM's section on analytical and statistical geophysics in 1957. His research successes gained him several invitations as visiting university professor. In 1959 he lectured at the University of San Marcos in Peru, where he was made honorary professor. He visited the University of Iowa in 1960–1961, teaching geomagnetism and statistics for geophysicists and researching the Van Allen radiation belts. He lectured in 1961 at the Royal Institute of Technology in Stockholm, at Uppsala University, and at Imperial College in London, England.

Forbush was elected a fellow of the American Association for the Advancement of Science in 1960. In 1961 he was awarded the Charles Chree Medal by the British Institute of Physics and Physical Society. In 1962 he was named a member of the National Academy of Sciences and a fellow of the American Geophysical Union, and was awarded an honorary D.Sc. by Case Institute of Technology. In 1965 the American Geophysical Union gave him the John Adam Fleming Award. He was a member of the Gauss Gesellschaft and distinguished professor with the Bartol Research Foundation of the Franklin Institute, Philadelphia.

Forbush contributed fundamentally to the use of statistics in geophysics and in solar-terrestrial relations. His studies of cosmic rays and of the near-space environment helped establish space science in the mid-twentieth century. He died in Charlottesville, Virginia.

• Some documents related to Forbush are in the archives of the Carnegie Institution, Washington, D.C. Among Forbush's nearly eighty publications is an important review essay, "Time Variations of Cosmic Rays," in *Handbuch der*

Physik, ed. J. Bartels, vol. 49, Geophysik III, pt. 1 (1966), pp. 159–247. With Mateo Casaverde, he wrote *The Equatorial Electrojet in Peru* (1961). A full bibliography is available at the Carnegie Institution. A review of his research by his colleague Martin A. Pomerantz appears in *EOS: The Transactions of the American Geophysical Union* 65 (1984): 473–74. An obituary is in the *Washington Post*, 6 Apr. 1984.

GREGORY A. GOOD

FORCE, Juliana Rieser (23 Dec. 1876–28 Aug. 1948), museum director and early champion of American art, was born in Doylestown, Pennsylvania, the daughter of Maximilian Rieser, a hatter and grocer, and Julianna Schmutz Kuster. As a girl she wanted to be a writer and hoped to go to college; when that proved financially impossible, she temporarily settled for teaching English and stenography at a business school in Hoboken, New Jersey, where the family had moved in 1886.

In about 1906 Force started working in New York City as a freelance stenographer and social secretary. A year later, she met and began assisting the sculptor and art patron Gertrude Vanderbilt Whitney. Force worked for Whitney off and on between 1907 and 1913 as a secretary and literary agent. She was then put in charge of negotiating Whitney's public sculpture commissions and ultimately became the manager of all her art activities. She married Willard Burdette Force, a dentist, in 1912; they had no children. In 1914, when she was busy with commissions yet wanted to open the Whitney Studio, which was to be a nonprofit gallery on 8 West Eighth Street for independent, uncredentialed artists to show their work, she employed Force full time to oversee the venture, and Force's career as an art impresario was launched. The partnership between Whitney and Force lasted until Whitney's death in 1942.

In the course of running the Whitney Studio, Force became familiar with the professional and financial difficulties facing American artists and began formulating ways to solve them. The chief means of patronage at the time was buying works of art, but owing to Force's imagination and Whitney's money, rents were met, hospital bills were paid, teaching positions were secured, and trips to Europe were guaranteed for hundreds of painters and sculptors who had nowhere to turn. The welfare of American artists and the significance of American art were Force's guiding concerns, and they permeated her stewardship of all the organizations she headed. The feeling that young artists were an endangered species greatly in need of care was the impetus behind the founding of the Whitney Studio Club, which any promising talent could join. Established in February 1918 in a townhouse at 147 West Fourth Street, the club, like the studio, held exhibitions—it was here that Edward Hopper was given his first solo show—but it was also a place to mingle and exchange ideas.

During the 1920s the studio and club (which moved in 1923 to 10 West Eighth Street, next door to the studio) grew in vitality and importance, with Force directing both. Notable exhibitions of art by Picasso, Henri Rousseau, Charles Sheeler, Reuben Nakian, Stuart Davis, Reginald Marsh, José Clemente Orozco, John Flannagan, and Isabel Bishop were mounted, as were members' annuals that allowed emerging artists to display their work before the public. The first exhibition of American folk art ever held in the United States took place at the Whitney Studio Club in February 1924. The event was a direct outgrowth of Force's interests: she was one of the earliest collectors of American folk art and played a crucial role in its discovery and promotion. Force's sympathies went beyond the visual arts. She persuaded Whitney to underwrite the work of composers Edgard Varèse and Carl Ruggles, and from 1923 to 1927 the International Composers Guild was headquartered in the Whitney Studio Club.

By 1928 the Whitney Studio was holding few shows and the Whitney Studio Club had outgrown itself—over 400 men and women had joined, and there was a long waiting list. To enlarge the club further was impossible, and to refuse worthwhile new artists would have been contrary to its principles. To streamline their operations, Whitney and Force disbanded the club and opened the Whitney Studio Galleries, but this move proved unsatisfactory. Although functioning effectively as a setting for artists to be noticed, the galleries were a stopgap measure, serving more as an escape from the cumbersome size of the club than as a fresh enterprise. In the autumn of 1929 Whitney deputized Force to offer her entire collection of American art, plus $5 million for a wing to house it, to the Metropolitan Museum of Art. When this gift was rejected, Whitney and Force decided to establish a museum that would collect, preserve, and interpret American art. The Whitney Museum of American Art, with Force as director, was announced in January 1930; when it opened its doors to the public on 18 November 1931, it became the first public institution devoted to twentieth-century American art. Along with biennial and annual exhibitions of contemporary art, the museum mounted pioneering survey shows that demonstrated the nation's largely unknown cultural heritage. Among the most important shows were those treating early abstract painting, Shaker handicrafts, and the Hudson River School. Retrospectives of Winslow Homer, Albert Pinkham Ryder, Thomas Eakins, Robert Feke, William Rimmer, Ralph Blakelock, Gaston Lachaise, Charles Demuth, and Maurice Prendergast were organized as well. The Whitney maintained a steady purchasing program, often spending up to $20,000 a year on acquisitions.

An activist and a scrapper, a woman of formidable temper balanced by a legendary solicitude toward artists, Force was a personality in the art world well before she became a museum director. Never afraid to involve herself in combat when she believed the cause to be just, she became the controversy-plagued chairman of the New York metropolitan region for the Public Works of Art Project (1933–1934), the first New Deal art program. In December 1933, within days of her announced appointment as chairman, Force was attacked by the Right as too modern and by the Left for showing favoritism. At the same time that unemployed artists were picketing her, she became a target of the *Herald Tribune*, a Republican newspaper eager to smear the Roosevelt administration, which ran a front-page exposé of alleged PWAP malfeasance. Force persevered, however, and by the end of her tenure in June 1934 she had employed between 800 and 850 artists of every aesthetic persuasion, or about 25 percent of all PWAP artists in the country. Furthermore, against the objections of her peers in the museum world, Force supported the artists who lobbied to receive rental fees from museums that loaned or sent their work out on prolonged exhibition tours. At the end of her life, Force labored long and hard on legislation that decades later would lead to the formation of the New York State Council on the Arts.

Force's most grueling battle was waged for the future of the Whitney Museum. At the time of Whitney's death, her family did not share her commitment to art patronage. In 1943 the Whitney children and the museum's other trustees decided to close the museum and give its collection to the Metropolitan—a decision that left Force aghast and enraged. The prevention of this merger—which Force believed would eradicate the Whitney's identity and raison d'être—became a consideration behind every move that she made, and the playing out of this professional drama coincided with her personal struggle against cancer. After enough indications by the Metropolitan that its policies were incompatible with those of the Whitney, the Whitney trustees agreed to call off the merger in June 1948. Force died two months later in New York City.

A lightning rod and an activist rather than a scholar or a connoisseur, Force was frequently criticized for valuing loyalty, friendship, and kindliness over strictly aesthetic judgments. Nevertheless, her unwavering advocacy was indispensable to a growing appreciation of American art. As the painter Alexander Brook remarked in 1949, "Juliana Force gave more of her time, her energies, her mind and her inexhaustible fighting spirit toward the realization of American art in the very broadest sense, far and away beyond the efforts of any other individual or group of individuals. . . . [I]n the memories of those of us who knew her she will ever remain a woman who worked hard, played magnificently, and fought recklessly for all artists worthy of the title" (*Juliana Force and American Art*). By furthering the careers of several generations of American artists, Force helped shape the social history of American painting and sculpture and to transform the pattern of American taste.

• Force's papers are in the Whitney Museum of American Art and in the Archives of American Art, Smithsonian Institution. The principal source of information on her life and work is Avis Berman, *Rebels on Eighth Street: Juliana Force and the Whitney Museum of American Art* (1990). Other useful publications are the Whitney Museum catalogs *Juliana Force and American Art* (1949) and *The Whitney Studio Club and American Art 1900–1932* (1975); Francis V. O'Connor, ed., *The New Deal Art Projects: An Anthology of Memoirs* (1972); and Berman, "Juliana Force and Folk Art," *Antiques* 136 (1989): 542–53. An obituary is in the *New York Times*, 29 Aug. 1948.

AVIS BERMAN

FORCE, Manning Ferguson (17 Dec. 1824–8 May 1899), soldier, jurist, and writer, was born in Washington, D.C., the son of Peter Force and Hannah Evans. His father was later mayor of Washington and was most famous as compiler of the "American Archives," a vast collection of rare books, pamphlets, newspapers, maps, and other documents dealing with the history of the American colonies. Manning Force attended Benjamin Hallowell's preparatory school in his mother's hometown, Alexandria, Virginia, preparing himself for appointment to the U.S. Military Academy at West Point. Instead, he went to Harvard, entering as a sophomore and graduating in 1845. He received a law degree after three years of further study, and in 1849 he moved to Cincinnati to practice law. He passed his bar examination in 1850, and the law firm he worked for made him a partner, changing its name to Walker, Kebler, and Force.

With the coming of the Civil War in 1861, Force joined the Federal forces. (Two of his brothers, Charles and Henry, joined the Confederate army, both serving in Alabama regiments.) He began his military career as major of the Twentieth Ohio Volunteer Regiment. He participated in Ulysses S. Grant's successful campaign against Fort Donelson and experienced the horror of Shiloh in April 1862, rising to colonel in the process. He remained with Grant as the general conducted campaigns in southwestern Tennessee and northern Mississippi. On 3 June 1863 Force became commander of the Second Brigade, Third Division, XVII Corps, Army of the Tennessee. He served with James B. McPherson during the Vicksburg campaign, providing security for supply routes while the Union army attacked Jackson, Mississippi. For his efforts at Vicksburg, Force received the XVII Corps Gold Medal. On 11 August 1863 he was made brigadier general of volunteers.

Force served in William T. Sherman's army during the Meridian campaign in early 1864. On 22 July 1864, during the Atlanta campaign, he led his brigade against a fortified hill before the city. He received a severe face wound; a bullet passing through his cheek left a scar that he would carry for the rest of his life. For his valor he was promoted to major general of volunteers in March 1865, and in 1892 he was awarded the Medal of Honor. He recuperated in his family home in Washington and returned to the army in time to lead his brigade in Sherman's March to the Sea during the late fall of 1864. He then commanded a division during Sherman's March through the Carolinas.

Force remained in the army after the war, commanding a military district in Mississippi until he was mustered out in early January 1866. He could have remained as a colonel in the regular army, but he returned to civilian life instead.

Force resumed his law practice in Cincinnati but was quickly elected to the Hamilton County Court of Common Pleas, a position he held until 1877. In 1876 he gained the Republican party nomination for Congress, but he lost the election. In 1874 he married Frances Dabney Horton; they had no children. He was elected to Cincinnati's superior court in 1877 and remained at that post until ill health forced him to retire in 1888. From 1878 to 1888 he was also professor of equity and criminal law at the Cincinnati Law School. Force was active in the Military Order of the Loyal Legion of the United States and was president of the Historical and Philosophical Society of Ohio. In 1888 he assumed the position of commandant of the Ohio Soldiers' and Sailors' Home in Sandusky, Ohio, remaining in that post until he died in Sandusky.

No doubt influenced by his historian father, with whom he maintained a regular correspondence, Force exhibited a deep interest in history and archaeology. He gathered material and published books, pamphlets, and articles, and he regularly gave speeches on historical topics. Among his books were *Pre-Historic Man, Darwinism and the Mound Builders* (1873) and *From Fort Henry to Corinth* (1881). He edited the eighth edition of Timothy Walker's *Introduction to American Law* (1882) and the third edition of Seymour F. Harris's *Principles of Criminal Law* (1885). His *General Sherman*, which was published the year he died, was partially written by another former Sherman general, historical writer, and Cincinnati legal educator, Jacob D. Cox. Among his many pamphlets were *Some Early Notices of the Indians of Ohio. To What Race Did the Mound Builders Belong?* (1879), *Marching across Carolina* (1883), *Memoirs of John McLean* (1885), *Some Observations on the Letters of Amerigo Vespucci* (1885), and an undated *John Pope, Major General, U.S.A. Some Personal Memoranda*. While never receiving the recognition of his more famous father, Force was a significant figure in the history of Ohio and a solid military commander during the Civil War, his Medal of Honor award a mark of his distinction.

• Force's papers contain material on all the various aspects of his life. The University of Washington Libraries collection has been microfilmed in five reels and contains incoming and outgoing correspondence for most of his life in addition to college and Civil War journals. At the Houghton Library, Harvard University, the six boxes of papers include mainly correspondence and Civil War diaries and photographs. The Cincinnati Historical Society's one box of material deals mostly with his life after 1870. Material on him is also in his father's papers at the Library of Congress. For wartime writings, see *The War of the Rebellion: A Compilation of the Official Records of the Union and Confederate Armies* (128 vols., 1880–1901). A biography has yet to be published. Some information is in Carolyn H. Sung, "Peter Force: Washington Printer and Creator of the *American Archives*" (Ph.D. diss., George Washington Univ., 1985). An obituary is in the *Cincinnati Commercial Tribune*, 9 May 1899.

JOHN F. MARSZALEK

FORD, Arnold Josiah (23 Apr. 1877–16 Sept. 1935), black Jewish leader, was born in Bridgetown on the island of Barbados, the son of the Reverend Edward Thomas Ford, a Methodist minister, and Elizabeth Augusta Braithwaite. Little is known about Ford's childhood. He was baptized in June 1877 in the Wesleyan Methodist Church on Barbados. After completing school, he took music lessons and became proficient on various string instruments. In 1899 he joined the British Royal Navy as a musician and spent twenty-one months aboard HMS *Alert*. At the end of the next year, at his request, he was stationed in Bermuda, where he worked for several years as a clerk at the Court of Federal Assize.

Around 1910 Ford surfaced in New York City, where he began to compose music. (Booker T. Washington was instrumental in finding a publisher for his compositions.) Ford settled in Harlem, where he met and married another West Indian, Olive Nurse, by whom he had two daughters. He provided for his family by giving music lessons, and he also performed with a number of well-known local orchestras.

In Harlem Ford became fascinated by the heady success of the Black Nationalist mass movement led by Marcus Garvey, and he soon became one of its leading lights, a much-loved and respected figure who was highly esteemed for his intelligence. In the summer of 1920 Garvey's Universal Negro Improvement Association (UNIA) organized its first big convention in New York, where the Declaration of Rights of Negro Peoples of the World was presented to enthusiastic supporters. Ford was one of the signers of the declaration.

It was in that same year, 1920, that Ford became the musical director of Liberty Hall, Garvey's headquarters in Harlem. At Liberty Hall he met Samuel Moshe Valentine, a West Indian from Jamaica. A common interest in Hebrew and the Jewish religion led Ford and Valentine, with a number of others, to set up a school at Liberty Hall, where lessons in Judaism were given each Sunday. Ford had studied Hebrew with a Jewish immigrant, and as a child on Barbados he had been sent by his parents to Hebrew and Talmud lessons. He had hoped that the Jewish religion would become the official faith of the Garvey movement, but by 1923 it was clear to him that this desire would not be realized, and he and Valentine gave up their active membership of the organization. After that, Ford's involvement was limited to attendance at the annual UNIA convention.

While in the UNIA Ford had become acquainted with Mordecai Herrmenz, a black spiritual leader who professed the Jewish faith and knew some Yiddish. At the time, Ford was looking around among the supporters of Garvey for someone to teach Hebrew. Herrmenz, a familiar figure in the Jewish neighborhoods of New York, where he peddled Jewish religious articles, was himself the leader of the Moorish Zionist Temple Inc. When Ford left the UNIA, he joined this group, which had been incorporated in 1921. Just when Ford had decided to set up a professional choir, however, he and Herrmenz fell out. Together with his choir and a number of adherents, Valentine among them, Ford left Herrmenz's temple in 1924 and founded his own synagogue, Beth B'nai Abraham, becoming its first rabbi.

Ford's synogogue prospered, ultimately developing into one of the largest congregations of Black Jews in Harlem. He had had a Christian upbringing, but he now turned into a rabid anti-Christian, viewing Christianity as the symbol of white domination, or at any rate the religion that whites had imposed on blacks during centuries of slavery. Ford rejected the word "Negro": "All I recognize by 'Negro' is an African or person of African descent whose mind is a by-product of European civilization, but has no traditions of its own. Hebrews are not 'Negroes.'" In his view, blacks were the only "true" Jews; white Jews were the European bastards of the original black African "Hebrews." Ford consistently used religion in advancing his political ideas regarding race pride and resettlement in Africa.

Despite his intense loathing of whites, whom he saw as oppressors, Ford did have a number of white visitors who came to the synagogue on 135th Street, and they pointed out to him certain inconsistencies with respect to the Jewish religion. The congregation also included a number of white members and sympathizers, and for circumcisions Ford was forced to call in a white mohel.

Services at Beth B'nai Abraham were generally held on Friday evening and Sunday evening. They were conducted partly in Hebrew and partly in English—prayers were said in Hebrew, the sermon in English—and were a mixture of Reform and Orthodox rites. The songs, both words and music, were largely the work of Ford himself and were published in a collection entitled *The Universal Ethiopian Hymnal*. "The Universal Ethiopian Anthem," composed by Benjamin E. Burrell and Ford, does not appear in this songbook.

Ford's Hebrew school conducted classes in mechanics, mathematics, Arabic, Hebrew, and Bible studies, courses designed to "prepare the members for the work which awaited them in Africa." Ford's view was that the members of his congregation needed to have a command of Hebrew and Arabic in order to study their history in the original languages, but he forbade classes in Yiddish because it was a European language. Around 1928 this led to a conflict between the members of the congregation who were from Jamaica and those who were from Barbados; the Jamaicans, including Valentine, left to found their own congregation. A more ideological bone of contention between Ford and Valentine was the latter's refusal to return to Africa. Moreover, accusations were directed against Ford, in-

cluding allegations of sexual misconduct with female members of his congregation and financial malfeasance.

In the midst of these controversies Ford continued his work; in 1928 he founded the B'nai Abraham Progressive Corporation, with the aim of financing a new building for his school. Shares were sold, and the school moved into the new premises, but in 1930 the corporation was declared bankrupt. This event heralded a rapid decline in the fortunes of Beth B'nai Abraham. Several members left the congregation, and Ford told his remaining followers that he wanted to go to Africa. Owing largely to their generosity he, together with three other members of the congregation, did so in December 1930. Once he was in Ethiopia, Ford exhorted his followers to join him there; attracted by the prospects of finding work on a dam being built in Lake Tana, more than fifty members of his congregation did make the move. However, because of the opposition of the local authorities and a number of whites, the entire enterprise failed, and most of Ford's people returned to their homeland.

Ford remained in Ethiopia and made a living by giving music lessons and repairing pianos. In the evenings he taught English and mathematics to well-to-do Ethiopians. In 1933 he remarried, he and his first wife having divorced in 1924. His new wife, Mignon Innis, who had emigrated with a second group of followers, bore him two sons. In September 1935, just before the Italians invaded Ethiopia, Ford suffered a fatal heart attack in Addis Ababa. His death was announced by the British Embassy.

• Biographical details and information on Ford's stay in Ethiopia are contained in the transcripts of his letters to his followers in Harlem and in some documents, such as his handwritten musical compositions, all of which are kept in a private collection in Holland. Most of Ford's musical compositions were published by his synagogue in *The Universal Ethiopian Hymnal* (c. 1922). The major sources on Ford's life are S. S. Kobre, "Rabbi Ford," *The Reflex* 4, no. 1 (1929): 25–29; A. Dobrin, "A History of the Negro Jews in America" (Unpublished paper, City College of the City University of New York, 1965), pp. 38–41; R. Landes, "Negro Jews in Harlem," *Journal of Jewish Social Studies* 9 (1967): 175–89; H. Waitzkin, "Black Judaism in New York," *Harvard Journal of Negro Affairs* 1, no. 3 (1967): 12–44; Howard M. Brotz, *The Black Jews of Harlem: Negro Nationalism and the Dilemmas of Negro Leadership*, 2d ed. (1970), pp. 11–12; William R. Scott, "A Study of Afro-American and Ethiopian Relations: 1896–1941" (Ph.D. diss., Princeton Univ., 1971), pp. 113–30, and *The Sons of Sheba's Race: African-Americans and the Italo-Ethiopian War, 1935–1941* (1993); K. J. King, "Some Notes on Arnold J. Ford and New World Black Attitudes to Ethiopia," *Journal of Ethiopian Studies* 10, no. 1 (1971): 81–87; R. K. Burkett, *Garveyism as a Religious Movement: The Institutionalization of a Black Civil Religion* (1975), pp. 178–82; and G. Berger, *Black Jews in America: A Documentary with Commentary* (1978), pp. 77–85. William R. Scott, "Rabbi Arnold Ford's Back-to-Ethiopia Movement: A Study of Black Emigration, 1930–1935," *Pan African Journal* 7 (1975): 191–202, is the most extensive article about his life.

J. F. HEIJBROEK

FORD, Barney Launcelot (1822–14 Dec. 1902), conductor on the Underground Railroad, Negro suffrage lobbyist, and real estate baron, was born in Stafford County, Virginia, the son of a Mr. Darington (given name unknown), a slaveholder and plantation owner, and Phoebe (surname unknown), one of Darington's slaves. Given simply the name "Barney" at birth, he adopted the name Barney Launcelot Ford as an adult to please his soon-to-be wife and to provide himself with a "complete" name.

Ford spent the first quarter-century of his life enslaved. His mother is reputed to have planted the seeds of education in him as a child by secreting him out of camp at night to meet with sympathetic people who taught him the basics of reading and writing. She may have put herself in mortal danger on many occasions by smuggling in a section of newspaper or a Bible page so that Barney could practice his studies. Upon the death of his mother (circa 1837), Barney was enslaved on a plantation in Kentucky, where, from age fifteen to eighteen he took advantage of any chance he had to read and practice the speech of people around him. At the age of eighteen he was sold again and lived on a plantation in Georgia. The mistress of the plantation allowed him to attend school with her own children, swearing her children to secrecy so that Ford would not be punished for pursuing an education. His self-education continued as he spent nearly five years as a slave on paddle-wheel boats along the Mississippi River. Ford always viewed his insatiable quest for education as his ticket out of captivity.

In 1847 Ford, with the aid of white sympathizers, escaped from slavery while serving on a riverboat in Quincy, Illinois. Using unusual disguises—he once dressed as a white female—and relying on his ability to mimic various manners of speech, Ford traveled by the Underground Railroad to Chicago, where he achieved his freedom. For the next four years, in gratitude for his escape and in honor of his mother's efforts toward his education, he became a "conductor" on the Underground Railroad, helping slaves travel from Chicago to Canada. During this time he apprenticed himself to a barber and soon became a barber in a Chicago hotel.

In 1849 Ford married Julia Lyoni, whose brother supervised the Chicago section of the Underground Railroad. That year Ford got word of the California gold rush. For two years he waited for the fares to drop so that he and his wife could make the trip west to try to make their fortune in the mines. When the ship that Ford and his wife took to San Francisco stopped in San Juan Bay, Nicaragua, Ford decided to take advantage of gold rush traffic by opening the United States Hotel and Restaurant. After losing the business to a fire three years later, he hired on as a steward on a local steamship. Within eight months he had bought the California Hotel at Virgin Bay, and five months later he sold it for a profit of $4,940. He sailed back to New York City in 1855. After traveling to Chicago, Ford was persuaded by his wife's family to take over the livery business of his brother-in-law. The livery was the main connection for the Underground Railroad in that area, and Ford again became deeply involved in helping enslaved people escape to freedom. During this time, Ford began building his contacts, reading everything he could find about abolitionists and corresponding with people who would later be influential in his political endeavors. He met with John Brown on several occasions and kept abreast of the increasing news about the possibility of war between the states.

In 1859 Ford was struck by gold fever again, although this time his goal was to reach Colorado. He took a circuitous route, avoiding proslavery states and hiring on as a cook and wrangler on a wagon train that took him to Denver in May 1860. As a rookie miner, Ford made several attempts at establishing claims, always to have someone take them away from him under threat of death. Eventually Ford became a partner in a Denver barber shop. He used this time to make contacts with the foremost citizens of the city and to help other blacks in town learn about their civil rights. His wife joined him in Denver with their young son (they later were to have two daughters) and elicited a promise from Ford that he would stick to the business he knew, that of being a hotelier and restaurant manager.

Beginning with a small barber shop and a "lean-to" lunch counter in 1861 and constantly beset by the fires that were common to mining towns with wooden buildings, Ford built a real estate empire. The opening of his People's Restaurant on 16 August 1863 rated notice in the *Rocky Mountain News*. The building included the restaurant on the ground floor, a bar on the second, and a basement with a barber shop and hairdressing salon. Fresh oysters and Havana cigars were two of the impressive attractions of the establishment. During this time, as Ford prospered, he never lost track of the Civil War and what it meant to blacks. He watched local and national legislation vigilantly, always wary that phrases might be slipped into pending bills that would endanger the freedom and civil rights of blacks. Vocally supporting the suffrage of black men, he fought to keep the territory from becoming a state until suffrage was given to all males. In 1865 the voters refused to make Colorado a state, but not over the issue of suffrage of black males; they felt it would simply be less expensive to run a territory than a state. Ford was bitterly disappointed over the lack of support from whites, whom he considered his friends. He sold the hotel, leased the building, hired a lawyer to supervise his improved and unimproved real estate holdings, and took his family to Chicago, along with approximately $23,000.

Ford soon began feeling guilty about giving up his fight for black male suffrage in Colorado. So when friends from Denver asked him to go to Washington, D.C., to lobby the president and Congress, he went gladly. Eventually his political ties paid off, and Colorado, although still a territory, granted full male suffrage. Ford immediately decided to return to Denver. There he opened a new restaurant in 1866 and threw himself into bettering segregated black schools. He remained active in local politics while opening yet another restaurant in Cheyenne, Wyoming, along the western railroad terminus. His next endeavor, Ford's House and People's Restaurant in Denver, was built across from the railroad station. Ford was asked to join the local bank as a trustee, and the city's most influential people were soon visiting his wife in the new Ford mansion. He was appointed a member of the Republican Party Central Committee and served as the first black member of a federal grand jury in Colorado. Inequities for blacks continued to occupy Ford's time, and when a new school was needed for the burgeoning city of Denver, he made sure there was no language in the school bond to keep his children and other blacks from attending.

Ford's empire building continued unabated. When he was worth about $250,000, he sold one restaurant in Denver and bought the four-story Sargent Hotel, renaming it Ford's Hotel. Determined to build the best hotel in Denver, in 1872 he spent over $50,000 on his newest treasure, the Inter-Ocean Hotel. When the depression of 1873 hit, Ford sold the Inter-Ocean for a profit of $25,000 and headed to Cheyenne. He built another restaurant and hotel, also named the Inter-Ocean, and drew praise for his operation from East Coast newspapers. For the next twenty years, Ford bought and sold many more properties, staying ahead of hard times but no longer living in a lavish style. In 1885, after two years of political fighting, Ford saw the passage of legislation in Colorado prohibiting discrimination in public facilities. He acknowledged that a law would not guarantee lawful actions by all citizens, but he was proud of his part in the fight for equality. Ford came full circle in his life when he bought two barber shops in Denver and returned to his first trade. Later, he hired managers to run the shops, while he sat and visited with political cronies and foes alike. Ford died in Denver.

• A general biography of Ford is Marian Talmadge and Iris Gilmore, *Barney Ford: Black Baron* (1973). The bibliography provided in that text is an important resource of secondary sources on his life. There are short references to Ford in Carl Abbott, *Colorado: A History of the Centennial State* (1982), and Stephen J. Leonard and Thomas J. Noel, *Denver: Mining Camp Metropolis* (1990). A tribute to Ford is in the *Denver Republican*, 22 Dec. 1902. A detailed report of his life appeared in the *Rocky Mountain News*, 20 May 1956.

MARIA ELENA RAYMOND

FORD, Daniel Sharp (5 Apr. 1822–24 Dec. 1899), editor and publisher, was born in Cambridge, Massachusetts, the son of Thomas Ford, a wallpaper manufacturer, and Elizabeth Lamson. A lifelong Baptist who might have become a preacher if his family's finances had been less precarious, Ford was the son of devout parents who are said to have named their child after the Reverend Daniel Sharp, pastor of the Charles Street Baptist Church of Boston, where Ford was later baptized as an adult. Ford's father died when his son was only six months old, leaving the family in straitened but not desperate circumstances. Educated in the public schools, Ford apprenticed himself in his teens to one of Boston's Baptist weeklies, probably the *Christian Watchman* (in 1848, the paper merged with the *Christian Reflector* to become the area's leading Baptist journal). Before he was thirty Ford secured a loan to purchase a share of the company that published the paper and formed a partnership with J. W. Olmstead.

When Ford and Olmstead bought the *Youth's Companion* in 1857, the paper had a solid thirty-year history as one of America's longest-lived children's periodicals. The journal was founded in 1827 by Nathaniel Willis, who decided that the popularity of the juvenile department in his weekly *Boston Recorder* warranted a sister publication devoted exclusively to children. Willis was retained as the nominal senior editor of the *Companion* until 1862, but Ford quickly became the driving force behind the paper's refurbished style. The *Companion*'s new direction was apparent from the first issue offered by Olmstead & Company. The old-fashioned logo, which had featured a simple woodcut of a nursery scene and Willis's famous motto "No Sectarianism, No Controversy," was replaced by a modernized one that depicted a couple cuddled intimately about the paper—implying that the *Companion* was now capable of pleasing young adults as well as children. Yet the changes initiated by the paper's new proprietors were not merely cosmetic; Ford replaced Willis's pious, Sunday-schoolish stories with more pungent, naturalistic fare. Though high moral tone prevailed, sermonizing gave way to fiction that grew less overtly didactic. Willis's staid departments (Biography, Morality, Religion) were replaced by chatty anecdotes, modernized illustrations, and puzzles and games. When Ford bought the *Companion*, the paper had a circulation of 4,800; by 1867 the paper boasted ten times that number.

To fund these changes without substantially raising prices, Ford departed from Willis's policies yet again: he allowed advertising into the *Companion*. By the early 1860s ads for carpets and Mrs. Allen's Hair Restorer appeared on page three; the last page typically contained advertisements as well. In the later 1860s, publishers began to use another method of self-promotion: the offer of premiums. This was a scheme by which a variety of valuable prizes were awarded to patrons who solicited new subscribers. In 1867 Olmstead broke with Ford, apparently over this issue; they drew lots, Ford found himself the sole owner of the *Companion* (Olmstead took the *Watchman*), and that year the *Companion* published the first of its Premiums Issues. In a gesture that speaks to Ford's modesty, Ford at this time renamed his firm the Perry Mason Company—though no such person existed. By 1885 Ford's *Companion* claimed a circulation of 385,000, the largest of any paper of its type.

While the offer of premiums boosted the *Companion*'s circulation, Ford revamped the magazine's content so that it appealed to the largest number of readers. By the late 1860s he relaxed policies that had prohibited writers from identifying themselves; soon famous names like Harriet Beecher Stowe appeared.

In 1870 he hired C. A. Stephens, whose realistic adventure stories gained a dedicated following; Louisa May Alcott and Rebecca Harding Davis also contributed. Ford published some of the most respected children's writers (Trowbridge and Aldrich), the poets Longfellow and Whittier, and serious, adult essays from a wide range of specialists—even Theodore Roosevelt wrote for the *Companion*. The *Companion* was so trusted that in 1892 the paper completed a successful campaign to add the Pledge of Allegiance—written by staff member James B. Upham—to America's schoolrooms. By the end of Ford's life, the *Companion* was the country's most popular family journal.

Though a shrewd businessman, Ford is also remembered as a generous yet unfailingly modest philanthropist who considered charitable giving a duty and an honor. During the last years of his life he is said to have given away close to $50,000 per year to church groups and charities. When Ford died in Boston, his will stipulated that nine-tenths of his fortune—estimated to be in excess of two million dollars—was to be divided among various benevolent associations, including his beloved Ruggles Street Church in Roxbury, Massachusetts. In his will Ford warned against the theory that "business men and capital" were the natural "enemies" of labor; he hoped that by funding the Boston Baptist Social Union he could posthumously forestall the potential "perils" of class conflict. He gave the Social Union money to build Boston's Ford Hall; Ford's gifts also endowed a series of public lectures called the Ford Hall Forum. The series, which was inaugurated to engage immigrants and workers in Christian and social issues, still exists. A forceful leader who is reputed to have suffered from painful shyness, Ford scrupulously guarded the details of his private life from public exposure. He married Sarah Upham in 1844; they had three children, one of whom, Ella Sarah, married the publisher William N. Hartshorn in 1875.

• For information on Ford and the *Youth's Companion*, see Louise Harris, *None but the Best* (1966), and Richard Cutts, *Index to the Youth's Companion, 1871–1929* (1972). Frank Luther Mott's sketch of the paper in *A History of American Magazines* (1938) is indispensable; another important source is David Reed's "Growing Up: The Evolution of Advertising in the Youth's Companion during the Second Half of the Nineteenth Century," *Journal of Advertising History* 10, no. 1 (1987): 20–33. For more on Ford's legacy, the *Watchman* (4 Jan. 1900) reprints portions of Ford's will; George Coleman's tribute to Ford Hall, *Democracy in the Making* (1915), is another valuable source. Obituaries of Ford appear in the *New York Times*, 25 Dec. 1899; the *Boston Transcript*, 26 Dec. 1899; the *Watchman*, 4 Jan. 1900; and the *Youth's Companion*, 1 Feb. 1900.

LESLEY GINSBERG

FORD, Edsel Bryant (6 Nov. 1893–26 May 1943), automobile manufacturer, was born in Detroit, Michigan, the only child of Henry Ford, then an employee of the Detroit Edison Illuminating Company, and Clara Bryant, a farmer's daughter. He inherited his father's sharp features and slight build and his mother's dark complexion.

Henry Ford completed his first experimental automobile when Edsel was three. After two false starts in automobile manufacturing, he formed the Ford Motor Company with new backers in 1903. The introduction in 1908 of the Model T, and the progressive lowering of its price through mass production techniques innovated at the Ford Highland Park plant in 1913–1914, made the Ford Motor Company the world's largest automobile producer and Henry Ford one of the most famous persons of his day.

With the Ford family's new affluence, Edsel transferred from public elementary school to Detroit University School, a private college preparatory academy. Henry equipped a workshop for him in the garage of their Detroit residence, and Edsel spent after-school hours and vacations with his father at the Ford factory. Edsel was driving by the age of ten and given his own car at fifteen. At the insistence of his father, who had received only a rudimentary education in one-room schools, and despite an excellent high school record, Edsel eschewed college to begin full-time work in 1912 at the Ford Motor Company.

After gaining a comprehensive knowledge of the company's operations by working in all of its chief departments, 22-year-old Edsel became company secretary and a member of the board of directors in 1915 when James Couzens resigned in protest against Henry Ford's pacifism. The Ford family bought out all minority stockholders in 1919, and Edsel became owner of 41.7 percent of Ford stock and was elected treasurer and president, positions that he would hold until his death. However, the real power in the company remained with his father, who not only controlled the majority of its stock, but whose egocentric personality dominated his self-effacing son. In his short biography in *Who's Who in America*, Edsel explained that he was "identified with father in mfg. of automobiles from the beginning of active career," and in 1929 he asserted, "I do not merely accept his beliefs. I feel as strongly about them as he does."

In fact, Henry and Edsel were temperamental opposites who disagreed about most company policies. Edsel was troubled by his father's arbitrary dismissal of executives and callous treatment of employees, slipshod management style, intransigent commitment to the utilitarian Model T long after it was outmoded, illegal opposition to unionization of the Ford plants after passage of the National Labor Relations Act in 1935, and reluctance to participate in the government's aircraft program set up in 1940 under former General Motors president William S. Knudsen. Henry thought his son too soft and held up Harry Bennett, an ex-pugilist with underworld connections, as a model worthy of emulation. For a time in the 1920s Edsel sought to sell his points of view to his father with the help of his brother-in-law, Ernest Kanzler, a Ford vice president and director. Yet Edsel typically raised no objection when he returned from a European trip in

1926 to find that Kanzler had been fired after sending Henry Ford a memo detailing why the Model T should be discontinued.

Always under his father's thumb at Ford, Edsel was allowed the freedom to implement his ideas about automobile design as president of the Lincoln Motor Company, which the Fords acquired from Henry and Wilfred Leland in 1922. Under Edsel's close personal supervision, the mechanically excellent but stodgy Lincoln car was progressively restyled to improve its appearance. And Edsel pioneered in formalizing the relationship between stylists and automobile manufacturers by moving a leading custom body designer, Raymond H. Dietrich, to Detroit from his New York City Le Baron studio in 1925 to do custom Lincoln bodywork and to act as a consultant on the styling of Lincoln production cars. At Edsel's prodding, the Ford Model A, which replaced the Model T in 1927, was designed to resemble the much higher-priced Lincoln in its overall styling. The 1936 Lincoln Zephyr, designed under Edsel's supervision by John Tjaarda and Eugene "Bob" Gregorie, was one of a handful of pathbreaking automotive designs of the pre–World War II period, featuring aerodynamically and structurally streamlined bodies. The Edsel-inspired 1940 Lincoln Continental ranks among car connoisseurs as one of the most beautiful classic automotive designs ever created.

Edsel amassed a large private art collection and was a generous patron of the arts. He commissioned Charles Sheeler to do a series of paintings of the Ford River Rouge plant and financed murals of the Rouge plant at the Detroit Institute of Arts done from a Marxist perspective by Mexican muralist Diego Rivera. These very different treatments of a common subject are today widely acclaimed by art critics.

In 1916 Edsel married Eleanor Clay, the niece of Joseph L. Hudson, a Detroit department store magnate who financed the Hudson Motor Car Company in 1909. Eleanor introduced Edsel into old-money Detroit society, which never had accepted Henry and Clara Ford. In the late 1920s he moved his wife and four children to the elite Detroit suburb of Grosse Pointe Shores rather than settle on property adjacent to his parents' Fair Lane estate. This further strained his relationship with his father, who turned to Bennett as a confidant and increasingly bullied Edsel.

Edsel developed stomach ulcers in the late 1930s. An operation on them in January 1942 revealed terminal cancer. Later that year, Edsel was hospitalized with undulant fever, contracted from drinking unpasteurized milk from the Ford farms, a practice advocated as a health measure by Henry Ford. He was not informed that his condition was terminal, and he carried on his heavy wartime duties at Ford until the spring of 1943, when he became bedridden. He died of cancer at his Grosse Pointe mansion.

• Edsel Ford's personal papers are in the Ford Archives, Henry Ford Museum and Greenfield Village, Dearborn, Mich., although in 1964 some of the papers were removed and destroyed on orders from Edsel's oldest son, Henry Ford II. The best short biographical sketch of Edsel is that by George S. May in May, ed., *The Automobile Industry, 1920–1980*, in *Encyclopedia of American Business History and Biography* gen. ed. William H. Becker (1989), pp. 138–44. Edsel is mentioned prominently in the enormous literature on Henry Ford and the Ford Motor Company. The most comprehensive work remains Allan Nevins and Frank E. Hill's trilogy *Ford: The Times, The Man, The Company* (1954); *Ford Expansion and Challenge* (1957); and *Ford: Decline and Rebirth* (1962). The best account of Edsel's contribution to styling probably is that in Richard Burns Carson, *The Olympian Cars: The Great American Luxury Automobiles of the Twenties and Thirties* (1976). There is as yet no full-length biography of Edsel Ford.

JAMES J. FLINK

FORD, Guy Stanton (9 May 1873–29 Dec. 1962), historian, editor, and academic administrator, was born in Liberty Corners, Salem Township, Wisconsin, the son of Thomas D. Ford, a medical doctor, and Helen E. Shumway, a teacher. During Guy's early childhood, his father's drinking and business failures forced his mother, with her two sons, to move in with a series of relatives, eventually leading them to Sutherland, Iowa, in 1883. Shortly thereafter his father moved to Plainfield, Iowa, a town of about 300 people. In 1884 the family reunited in Plainfield. Thomas Ford was an extremely impractical man and the family lived in relative poverty throughout Guy's years in Plainfield.

In 1888 Ford enrolled in Upper Iowa University, a small Methodist institution in Fayette. Frustrated with the school's limited curriculum, he left to spend the 1891–1892 academic year teaching school in Bremer County, Iowa. By the spring of 1882 he had accepted the principalship of a school in Janesville, Iowa, for the following year. But during the late spring or summer of 1892, Ford decided that he wanted to continue his education. He resigned his principalship and entered the University of Wisconsin as a sophomore in the fall of 1892.

The University of Wisconsin featured an extraordinary set of historians, including its new president, Charles Kendall Adams, professors Frederick Jackson Turner and Charles Homer Haskins, and Carl Becker, who was a student at the university with Ford. Ford studied extensively with Turner. Haskins became his undergraduate adviser, although he never assigned Ford to one of his own classes. In 1895 Ford received a B.Litt. from the University of Wisconsin. Although he had no definite career plans, Ford hoped to raise enough money to begin graduate work in history at Wisconsin. From the fall of 1895 to the spring of 1898 he served as superintendent of schools in Grand Rapids (now Wisconsin Rapids), Wisconsin, a position that consisted more of teaching high school and coaching football than of administration.

Returning to Wisconsin in the fall of 1898, Ford studied again with Turner and for the first time with Haskins and political scientist Paul Reisch. Ford became interested in the history of modern Germany. At

Haskins's suggestion, Ford departed for Germany in the summer of 1899. After spending a few weeks in Marburg, Ford arrived in Berlin, where he enrolled in the seminars of Max Lenz and Hans Delbrück. In the latter's seminar, Ford became interested in Hanover. Ford left Berlin after one semester for Göttingen and Hanover, where he began work on Hanoverian diplomacy during the age of Napoleon, a project that would eventually become his doctoral dissertation.

While in Germany Ford also applied, again at Haskins's suggestion, for scholarships to do doctoral work at a number of institutions in America. Upon returning to the United States in 1900 he began to pursue a doctorate in history at Columbia University. There his adviser was William Milligan Sloane, who took little interest in Ford and met with him only a handful of times. After a year of living in New York, and having completed his examinations, Ford decided to accept an instructorship at Yale.

In the fall of 1901, while working on his dissertation, Ford began to teach at Yale. Yale proved to be a disappointment for Ford, who was not impressed by the students, the faculty, or the administration. For most of his five years at Yale, Ford's teaching consisted of leading sections in the same large survey courses. Ford spent his summers conducting research in Germany. In the fall of 1903 he completed his dissertation and received his doctorate from Columbia. That same year his dissertation, *Hanover and Prussia, 1795–1803: A Study in Neutrality*, was published by Columbia University Press. By the summer of 1905, Ford had begun to suffer from the strain of nonstop, largely uninteresting work. He went again to Berlin but found himself incapable of working. While in New Haven in the fall of 1905, Ford suffered a complete nervous breakdown. After Christmas, he took a paid leave of absence and spent the winter and spring in Florida and Wisconsin.

Yale offered Ford an assistant professorship for the fall of 1906. However, Ford instead accepted the offer of a full professorship from the University of Illinois. Edmund James, the new president of the university, immediately put Ford on the faculty's graduate school committee and made him chair of its library committee. Ford's work on the library committee helped create a serious collection for the university and garnered Ford a reputation as a first-rate administrator. In 1907 Ford married Grace Ellis, daughter of a family friend; they had two children.

In 1913 Ford was asked by George E. Vincent, the president of the University of Minnesota, to become dean of the Graduate School and chair of the history department at Minnesota. Feeling constrained by life in Urbana, Illinois, and excited by the challenge of building a graduate school, Ford accepted the offer. Ford spent the next twenty-five years as dean of the Graduate School at Minnesota, a period of time he later characterized as the most constructive of his life. Ford was largely responsible for creating graduate education at the university, which had only 175 graduate students at the time of his arrival. From the beginning

of his appointment he insisted on taking part in all appointment decisions involving positions that included graduate teaching. By exercising this privilege, which he retained throughout his tenure as dean, Ford put his mark on the university. He soon developed a national reputation as an unusually sagacious judge of talent. Ford's single greatest accomplishment during the early years of his deanship was the establishment in 1915 of a formal relationship, unprecedented in American medical education, between the Mayo Clinic in Rochester, Minnesota, and the University of Minnesota's medical school. This arrangement, which for the first time allowed students at the university to receive training in clinical specialties, was made possible through a major donation to the university by William and Charles Mayo. In 1915 Ford also attained a position on the Executive Council of the American Historical Association (AHA).

In 1917 George Creel, director of the Committee on Public Information (CPI), the federal government's newly created wartime propaganda office, asked Ford to direct the CPI's Division of Civic and Educational Cooperation. Creel had become aware of Ford when he read the text of a patriotic address that Ford had recently given in Minnesota. "I have rarely read anything that made a more instant impression," wrote Creel after the war, "for it had beauty without sacrifice of force, simplicity, remarkable sequence, and obvious knowledge."

Upon his arrival in Washington, D.C., Ford discovered that Creel had only the roughest idea of what he wanted Ford's division to do. Assisted by Samuel B. Harding, a historian from Indiana University, Ford soon devoted his time to creating pamphlets, arranging informational speakers, and supervising the revision of school curricula. Ford himself went on the road as a speaker. Throughout his work for the CPI Ford had to navigate between scholarly responsibility and maintaining the government's official wartime line. The division came under considerable criticism. Historians occasionally attacked it for factual inaccuracies in its publications. Republicans in Congress accused Ford's division—and the CPI in general—of being a transparent use of federal money to promote Democratic, or perhaps even Socialist, causes. In fact Ford, who would later become a Democrat but had voted Democratic for the first time in 1916, considered himself a Republican. For the rest of his life Ford repeatedly averred that he never regretted any aspect of his work for the CPI. While Ford was finishing his work for the CPI in 1918, Frank E. Compton, who had attended the University of Wisconsin with Ford, asked him to become editor in chief of the revision of a reference work that was to become, under his guidance, *Compton's Pictured Encyclopedia* (1924).

As a result of his growing reputation as an administrator, Ford spent the next two decades serving on a variety of important professional committees. In 1918 he joined the AHA's Special Committee on History and Education for Citizenship in Schools. Ford was named to the Board of Editors of the AHA's journal, the *American Historical Review*, in 1920; from 1921 to 1927 he was its chairman. In 1923 he was among those who represented the AHA when historians were first invited to join the young Social Science Research Council; he continued to serve on the SSRC until 1940. In the midst of all this activity, he managed to complete his second monograph, *Stein and the Era of Reform in Prussia, 1807–1815* (1922).

In 1924 the Laura Spellman Foundation dispatched Ford to Germany to report on the condition of the universities and advise scholars there on ways of restoring these institutions to their prewar quality. From 1925 until his death he served on the advisory council of the John Simon Guggenheim Foundation. From 1929 to 1934 he sat on the AHA's Commission for Investigation of Social Studies in the Schools (more often known as the Krey commission after its chairman A. C. Krey). During the 1930s Ford played an instrumental role in the SSRC's Committee of Inquiry on National Policy in International Economic Relations. In 1937 he served as president of the AHA.

Meanwhile, Ford continued as dean of the Graduate School at the University of Minnesota. He oversaw an enormous expansion of the Graduate School, which by the time of his departure in 1938 had grown to 3,300 students. In 1925 Ford was responsible for creating the University of Minnesota Press, the faculty committee of which he chaired from its founding to his retirement as dean. Ford served two years, 1931–1932 and 1937–1938, as acting president of the University of Minnesota. Following the death of President Lotus D. Coffman in the summer of 1938, Ford became president of the university and remained in that post until reaching mandatory retirement age in 1941. Ford's years as president were uneventful.

In 1941 Ford moved to Washington, D.C., to become the first executive secretary of the AHA. This post encompassed both the role of editor in chief of the *American Historical Review* and responsibility for running the day-to-day operations of the association as a whole. In the next twelve years, he oversaw a redesign of the *American Historical Review* and a major expansion of the AHA's membership. During the years of America's involvement in World War II Ford participated in a wide variety of official war work, serving on more than twenty-five war-related committees and commissions. His most significant single contribution was the editing of the *G. I. Roundtable* pamphlet series. In 1951 the University of Minnesota honored Ford by naming its new social science building after him. Ford retired as executive secretary in 1953. He continued to live in Washington; it was there that he died.

Ford left his mark on American scholarship and education as few academic administrators have. He enjoyed the trust and admiration of almost everyone with whom he worked and gained a reputation for fairness, intelligence, and patience. His sober liberalism appealed to both educational reformers and traditionalists. "I can say truly," noted historian Charles Beard in 1937, "that I know no other scholar in America who

may be called more disinterested in the best sense of that word." In its obituary for Ford, the *American Historical Review* remembered his "quick awareness of the essentials of a situation or problem, a dislike of the grandiose or spectacular, [and] an ability to persuade people to work together for common ends." The *Review* concluded, "[I]f you are searching for monuments to his productivity, look around you—full circle."

• The bulk of Ford's voluminous personal papers are housed at the University of Minnesota. In addition to the works mentioned above, Ford edited numerous volumes, including the *Essays in American History Dedicated to Frederick Jackson Turner* (1910) and *Dictatorship in the Modern World* (1935; rev. ed., 1939). Upon Ford's retirement as dean, the University of Minnesota published a major collection of his writings from throughout his career, *On and Off the Campus* (1938); a good biographical sketch of Ford by George Vincent appears as the first chapter. In 1954 and 1955, as part of Columbia University's Oral History Project, Dean Albertson conducted extensive interviews with Ford, which have been preserved in typescript form and later reproduced on microfiche as *The Reminiscences of Guy Stanton Ford* (1956). His service with the CPI is covered extensively in CPI Director George Creel's *How We Advertised America* (1920); the chapters dealing with the work of historians in the CPI were drafted by Ford himself. The activities of Ford and other historians in the CPI are dealt with more critically in George T. Blakely, *Historians on the Homefront* (1970). An obituary is in the *American Historical Review* 68, no. 3 (1962): 908–10.

BENJAMIN L. ALPERS

FORD, Hannibal Choate (8 May 1877–12 Mar. 1955), engineer and inventor, was born in Dryden, New York, the son of Abram Millard Ford, a newspaper publisher, and Susan Augusta Giles. Ford was fascinated by clocks and watches as a child. After graduating from high school, he worked in the shops of the Crandall Typewriter Company in Groton, New York, from 1894 to 1896, the experimental department of Daugherty Typewriter Company in Kittaning, Pennsylvania, from 1896 to 1898, and Westinghouse Electric and Manufacturing Company in 1898. He entered Cornell University in 1899, graduating in 1903 as a "mechanical engineer in electrical engineering."

Ford then moved to New York City to work for J. G. White & Company, engineers designing subway systems in New York and the Philippines. While there, he devised methods to control the speed of a train on the basis of the position of preceding trains. These safety measures led to Ford's first two patents, awarded in 1906. Ford then returned to the office machine industry, working at the Smith-Premier Typewriter Company in Syracuse, New York, from 1905 to 1909. He assigned some of his inventions in this area to Smith-Premier, but he also took out patents on time recorders and typewriters, which he assigned to other companies.

In 1909 Ford's interests took a new turn when he began to assist Elmer A. Sperry in the development of the gyrocompass. This device determined the direction of motion of the ship on which it was installed and could be used on steel ships, where the traditional mariner's compass was deflected by the ship's magnetism. Instruments used in navigation and the control of gunfire from ships became the focus of Ford's inventive activity. He served as chief engineer at the newly established Sperry Gyroscope Company in New York City from 1910 to 1915 and then left to become vice president and manager of a firm producing products based on his own ideas, the Ford Marine Appliance Company of Long Island City, New York. This business soon was renamed the Ford Instrument Company, and Ford remained associated with it for the rest of his career.

In the late 1800s the range of guns fired from ships increased from about 100 yards to considerably over 10,000 yards. Hitting a target became much more complex. The target had more time to maneuver, and atmospheric conditions such as wind, temperature, and air pressure had a much greater effect on impact point. Changes in the condition of the gun barrel also had a perceptible influence on the path of the projectile. Ford and his associates at Ford Instrument Company designed and manufactured mechanical analog computing devices for gun control. His first product, the Range Keeper Mark I, computed the rate of change of the range of a gun on a ship, integrated this function over time to find the range, and computed the relative speed of the gun and target, at right angles to the line of sight. The Range Keeper Mark I was introduced into the U.S. Navy in 1917 on the battleship *Texas*. Drawing in part on ideas of the British inventor Arthur H. Pollen, Ford improved his instrument in the course of World War I so that it could compute the rate of change of a target's motion, and from this, its range and direction. Further additions to the device allowed for more precise aiming of guns and for corrections to the estimated target speed and course, made on the basis of observed bomb splash locations relative to the target. Ford incorporated his range keeper in a gun director, which also had an optical turret, elements to find the vertical on a rolling and pitching ship, and a device for pointing at the target.

Inspired, perhaps, by the success of his new business, Ford married Katherine Moyer in 1918 in Olive Bridge, New York. They would have no children.

During the 1920s Ford Instrument Company began work on systems to control guns aimed at airplanes flying over ships. American funding for antiaircraft gun control, and for the U.S. Navy more generally, was severely restricted. After the stock market crash of 1929, Ford Instrument Company and Sperry Gyroscope came to have common ownership as part of Sperry Corporation. Ford became president of Ford Instrument. At this time he also organized the Merrill Aircraft Company and developed an experimental airplane that was successfully demonstrated in Queens, New York, but the airplane never went into production.

The rearmament of the 1930s and 1940s brought a new demand for gun control devices. William H. Newell and others at Ford Instrument designed massive instruments that relied increasingly on automatic data collection. Like Ford's earlier products, they were mechanical systems packed with cams, ball and disc integrators, and gears. In the postwar years, these would be displaced by analog and then digital electronic computers.

Ford retired in 1943, when his company was approaching peak wartime production. He died in Kings Point, Rhode Island.

• Ford's work is assessed in A. Ben Clymer, "The Mechanical Analog Computers of Hannibal Ford and William Newell," *Annals of the History of Computing* 15 (1993): 19–34. An obituary is in the *New York Times*, 14 Mar. 1955.

PEGGY ALDRICH KIDWELL

FORD, Harriet French (1868?–12 Dec. 1949), playwright, was born in Seymour, Connecticut, the daughter of Samuel Cook Ford and Isabel Stoddard. Her parents' occupations are not known, but Ford once described her family background: "Generations and generations [of] forebears of theologians and college presidents, a long, grim, wonderful line of unusual men" (*Strand Magazine* [May 1915]). Although her strict Episcopalian parents, like many New Englanders, harbored a traditional prejudice against the stage, they took little Hattie to see a production of *Romeo and Juliet*, and that early childhood experience imbued her with a consuming passion for theater. Ford attended public schools in New Haven, graduating from Hillhouse High School in 1885. Her teachers regarded her as gifted in art, music, speaking, and writing, but she was bent on becoming an actress.

After brief enrollment at the Boston School of Oratory, Ford won her parents' permission to go to New York to study acting. Various sources report that she studied at the Sargent Dramatic School, Empire School of Acting, and American Academy of Dramatic Art. David Belasco was one of her teachers. Her verifiable New York stage appearances include *Called Back* (June 1888), *A Midsummer Night's Dream* (Oct. 1888), *She* (Nov. 1888), *The Clemenceau Case* (Sept. 1890), *Only a Farmer's Daughter* (Mar. 1891), *The Face in the Moonlight* (Aug. 1892), and *The Village Postmaster* (Apr. 1896). Ford's decade-long struggle to win recognition as an actress included a season with a stock company in Newfoundland, recitation programs performed at various local opera houses, a tour with Loie Fuller's Humorous Ballad Concerts, and perhaps as many as three seasons with Sol Smith Russell's touring company.

Ford saved her money, solicited letters of introduction from her famous friends (including actor-playwright William Gillette), and then in 1889 sailed for London in hopes of making greater headway as an actress, but her year there brought her only one role, an ingenue part for which she was unsuited. She did, however, win the five-guinea prize in a competition sponsored by the *New York Herald* for the best poem of welcome home to the African explorer Henry M. Stanley. As one of eleven finalist poems published in the newspaper, "Back from the Dead" by Harriet Ford, Hotel Victoria, Charing Cross W.C., had garnered 5,050 votes from readers. Returning to New York, she continued to support herself by acting but transferred to writing her hope of making a mark in the world. She wrote some dramatic monologues for Evelyne Hilliard, a successful platform reader, and by 1895 had published a book of dramatic episodes, *"Me an' Methusaler" and Other Episodes*. She then approached popular drawing-room reader Sarah Cowell LeMoyne with a blank verse monologue she had written for her. This led Ford to write a full-length play in collaboration with Beatrice De Mille (widow of Henry C. De Mille) for LeMoyne. *The Greatest Thing in the World* premiered in New Haven on 9 February 1900, then moved to Ford's Opera House in Washington, D.C., and reached Wallack's Theatre in New York in October. This turgid drama of self-sacrificing maternal love launched LeMoyne as a star of the legitimate stage.

Ford next honed her dramaturgical skills by adapting for the stage works by other authors—*A Gentleman of France* (1901; from the Stanley Weyman novel), *The Honour of the Humble* (1902; from a French play, *Danischeffs*), and *Audrey* (1902; from the Mary Johnston novel). These achieved minimal success despite the drawing power of performers Kyrle Bellew, James O'Neill, and Eleanor Robson, respectively. Meanwhile, Ford supported herself as a play reader for Liebler and Company, theatrical producers.

In collaboration with Joseph Medill Patterson, founder of the *New York Daily News*, Ford wrote *The Fourth Estate* (1909), a melodrama hailed for the effectiveness of the final act's setting in a newspaper composing room at presstime, with four Mergenthaler machines operating noisily. Their next collaboration, *A Little Brother of the Rich* (1909), appeared three months later, also at Wallack's Theatre, and was based on Patterson's novel of the same name. This "breezy and amusing . . . satire on modern society" (*New York Times*, 28 Dec. 1909) culminated in a scene set in a theater after the departure of the audience, which the reviewer saw as an equivalent of the previous play's composing-room scene. In 1910 Ford went to live in Denver while doing research for a play based on *The Beast and the Jungle* by Judge Ben Lindsey, but the work apparently did not reach the stage.

Ford next sought a collaboration with Harvey O'Higgins, who had written a series of magazine articles with the well-known detective William J. Burns. These became the basis for their first joint effort, *The Argyle Case* (1912). The play incorporated authentic crime-fighting techniques for getting admissions from a reluctant witness, operating a dictagraph, taking fingerprints, and so on. O'Higgins's "Detective Barney" stories served as the basis for a "crook comedy," *The Dummy* (1914), which achieved a run of 200 performances. Their most controversial effort, *Polygamy* (1914), purported to look "behind the scenes of Mormonism" (*Current Opinion*, Feb. 1915, p. 92), dramatizing a marital crisis in a Mormon household and fea-

turing a scene inside the Mormon Temple. Produced by Helen Tyler and starring Mary Shaw, it ran for 159 performances. Their comic curtain-raiser, *The Dickey Bird*, was added to the bill two months into the run, balancing the drama of *Polygamy* with a humorous look at the American "downtrodden husband" (*Evening World*, 22 Feb. 1915). *Mr. Lazarus* (1916), a "pleasant little comedy" of "a man who somewhat ruefully comes back from the dead" (*New York Times*, 6 Sept. 1916), provided excellent roles for the renowned Henry E. Dixey and rising star Eva LeGallienne. Ford's other collaborations with O'Higgins were *On the Hiring Line* (1919) and *Main Street* (1921), a dramatization of Sinclair Lewis's novel.

With Fannie Hurst, Ford adapted a portion of a Mary Antin novel as *Land of the Free* (1917). She and Eleanor Robson together wrote a melodrama, *In the Next Room* (1923). Ford's last professionally produced play, *Sweet Seventeen* (1924), a "rather decorous bedroom farce" (*New York Herald*, 18 Mar. 1924), credited O'Higgins and two others as coauthors.

Ford continued writing plays throughout the 1920s and 1930s, some as sole author, some with O'Higgins, some with other collaborators, including Caroline King Duer, Althea Sprague Tucker, and Eleanor Robson (the wife of August Belmont). These light comedies, mostly one acts, were published by Samuel French for amateur production. Although her work has largely been forgotten, Ford was widely recognized and respected in the 1910s. She was regarded within the profession as a highly competent script doctor, often called in on short notice by producers to save an ailing play before its opening. However, she never wanted credit for that aspect of her career. Remembering her early struggles, she took a special interest in helping aspiring young actresses.

In 1930 Ford married Fordé Morgan, a physician who was medical director of Sterling Products Company. She died at her home in the Bronx.

• The Billy Rose Theatre Collection at the New York Public Library for the Performing Arts, Lincoln Center, holds Ford's scrapbook and extensive clippings. She was the subject of numerous articles in the popular press, including *Green Book Magazine*, Aug. 1913, pp. 265–270; *Theatre*, July 1914, 19–20; *Current Opinion*, Feb. 1915, 92–95; *Theatre*, Apr. 1915, 188–89; *Strand Magazine*, May 1915, 553–64; and *Current Opinion*, Nov. 1916, pp. 317–20. The most complete listing of her plays may be found in Frances Diodato Bzowski, *American Women Playwrights, 1900–1930: A Checklist* (1992). Ford's obituary is in the *New York Times*, 14 Dec. 1949.

Felicia Hardison Londré

FORD, Henry (30 July 1863–7 Apr. 1947), automobile manufacturer, was born on a farm in Springwells (now Greenfield) Township, Wayne County, Michigan, the son of William Ford and Mary Litogot. After attending one-room public schools during the winter months from 1871 to 1879, Ford was barely proficient in reading and writing from the McGuffey readers, but he excelled in arithmetic. He was fascinated by machinery.

On 1 December 1879 Ford walked to Detroit to seek employment as a mechanic. Fired after only six days as a beginning apprentice engineer at the Michigan Car Company, he found employment at the Flower Brothers' Machine Shop. To supplement his $2.60 for a sixty-hour work week he took a part-time job at the Robert Magill Jewelry Shop repairing watches six hours a night and six days a week for $3 weekly. In August 1880 Ford moved from the Flower Brothers at a fifty-cent-a-week cut in pay to an apprenticeship at the Detroit Dry Dock Company, Detroit's largest ship-building firm. He was assigned to the engine shop, where he acquired excellent hands-on knowledge of various types of power plants.

After completing his apprenticeship in 1882 he returned to his father's farm. A neighbor, John Gleason, paid him $3 a day to operate a small portable steam engine that cut corn, ground feed, and sawed wood. Ford's ability came to the attention of the district representative of the Westinghouse Engine Company of Schenectady, New York, and he was hired late in the summer of 1882 to travel throughout southern Michigan setting up and servicing Westinghouse steam traction engines.

In 1888 Ford married Clara Bryant. As a wedding gift, Ford's father gave him forty acres that would become his legally when he had turned it into a productive farm. However, instead of beginning to farm the land, Ford cut down and sold the timber on the property. By the fall of 1891 all the timber had been cut, and Ford refused to farm.

So on 25 September 1891 Henry and Clara moved to a small apartment in Detroit, where he found employment as night engineer for the Edison Illuminating Company at a salary of $40 a month. On 6 November 1893 their only child, Edsel Bryant, was born. Three weeks after the birth of his son, Ford was promoted to chief engineer at Edison at a salary of $100 a month. The Fords moved to larger quarters in what became a pattern as their fortunes improved. They changed addresses eleven times between 1892 and 1915 before finally settling on their 2,000-acre "Fair Lane" estate in Dearborn, just two miles from Ford's birthplace.

In the early 1890s Ford began to work on an internal-combustion engine to power an experimental car, joining several thousand bicycle mechanics, machinists, and backyard inventors who hoped to build a commercially viable car.

Ford completed his experimental car at 1:30 A.M. on 4 June 1896. It had been built in a brick shed that he used as a workroom behind the duplex he was then renting. The car, which he called a Quadricycle, ran on four bicycle tires and weighed a mere 500 pounds.

With the backing of Detroit mayor William C. Maybury, Ford began to build a second experimental car. Completed by July 1899, it was larger, sturdier, and heavier than the Quadricycle. After the car's successful demonstration drive to Pontiac, Michigan, and back, William H. Murphy, a wealthy Detroit lumber merchant, agreed to help Ford form a company to manufacture motorcars. On 5 August 1899 the Detroit Automobile Company was formed with only $15,000 of its nominal $150,000 capitalization paid in by a dozen shareholders. Ford put up no money for his shares of stock. On 15 August he resigned from his position at Edison to become superintendent in charge of production at Detroit Automobile at a monthly salary of $150. The Detroit Automobile Company went out of business in November 1900 after turning out only about a dozen automobiles. The company was briefly revived on 30 November 1901 as the Henry Ford Company. (Ford later testified that from 1896 through 1901 he had built between seventeen and twenty-two cars.)

On 10 October 1901 Ford's newly designed racer defeated the vehicle of Cleveland auto manufacturer Alexander Winton, the nation's leading racing driver, at the Grosse Pointe, Michigan, track. This gave his backers new hope. But to their consternation Ford developed, in the words of his biographers Allan Nevins and Frank E. Hill, "an almost complete preoccupation with racing." On 10 March 1902 Ford was fired from his position as superintendent of production at the Henry Ford Company and began building racing cars with racing-driver Tom Cooper. Henry M. Leland and his son Wilfred, of the Detroit precision toolmaking firm of Leland & Faulconer, were brought in to manage the company, and the backers agreed to discontinue the use of Ford's name. On 22 August 1902 the Henry Ford Company became the Cadillac Motor Car Company, named after La Sieur Antoine de la Mothe Cadillac, the founder of Detroit.

Ford and Cooper constructed the most powerful racing cars then built in the United States, the 999 and the Arrow. The 999, driven by former bicycle racer Barney Oldfield, who had never before operated an automobile, surpassed Winton's car again at Grosse Pointe on 25 October 1902. Oldfield went on to establish several American speed records in the 999. Then on 12 January 1904 Henry Ford and "Spider" Huff in the four-cylinder, 24-horsepower Arrow broke all American records for cars of all weights for the one-mile straightaway, with a time of 39.4 seconds (91.4 miles per hour) on the ice of Lake St. Clair northeast of Detroit. With these victories Ford established himself as the foremost American designer of racing cars.

With new backers (principally Detroit coal dealer Alexander Y. Malcomson, who joined him in 1902), Ford reentered automobile manufacturing with the formation of the Ford Motor Company on 16 June 1903, with only $28,000 paid-in capital, a dozen workmen, and an assembly plant on Mack Avenue just 250 feet by 50 feet. Entry into the industry was easy because Ford, like just about all early auto manufacturers, was merely an assembler of components jobbed out to other small businesses. The first Ford engines and completed chassis, for example, were supplied by the machine shop of the Dodge Brothers, John and Horace, who became minority stockholders in Ford's company. John S. Gray, Malcomson's uncle and president of Detroit's German-American Bank, became nominal president of the new firm, and James Couzens, Malcomson's clerk, became its treasurer (unofficially until 1907) and business brains. Ford, who put up no cash, ran the manufacturing end as vice president and general manager.

A stumbling block to the new company was the patent on the gasoline automobile that had been awarded in 1895 to George B. Selden, a New York patent attorney. The rights to the patent were bought by the Electric Vehicle Company in 1899 as a hedge on its bet on the electric car. Some leading American makers of gasoline-powered cars, under the leadership of Henry B. Joy of Packard and Frederick L. Smith of Olds Motor, then negotiated an agreement with the Electric Vehicle Company to form a trade association, the Association of Licensed Automobile Manufacturers (ALAM), under the Selden patent to control entry into automobile manufacturing and competition.

In early 1903 Ford applied for but was denied a license by ALAM, which claimed that he lacked experience as an automobile manufacturer. Angered and assured of the support of his eastern agent, department store magnate John Wanamaker, Ford built cars without the requisite license and fiercely contested the lawsuit that was brought against him and other auto manufacturers by the ALAM in October 1903. Ford gained public sympathy by contrasting his own humble midwestern origins and status as a pioneer inventor and struggling small businessman with the image of the ALAM as a group of powerful and parasitical eastern monopolists.

ALAM won a fleeting victory when the U.S. Circuit Court of the Southern District of New York upheld its claim in 1909. But on 11 January 1911 the U.S. Circuit Court of Appeals declared the Selden patent valid only for cars that used Brayton two-cycle engines. Since almost all automobiles, including Fords, used Otto-type four-cycle engines, the decision made the Selden patent worthless. ALAM collapsed, and Ford was vindicated.

A controversy developed between Malcomson and Ford in 1905 over design and market philosophy. Malcomson wanted to move toward the production of heavier, more expensive cars. Ford, in contrast, was increasingly committed to the volume production of light, low-priced cars, exemplified by the 1906 Model N, an 800-pound runabout powered by a front-mounted, fifteen- to eighteen-horsepower, four-cylinder engine. Extensive use of vanadium steels in its construction made the $600 Model N a lighter, tougher, more reliable car than much higher-priced models. Ford boasted to reporters, "I believe that I have solved the problem of cheap as well as simple automobile construction."

The controversy between Ford and Malcomson was resolved when Ford bought out Malcomson on 12 July 1906. As his main strategy to get rid of Malcomson, Ford independently had formed the Ford Manufacturing Company on 22 November 1905 to manufacture his own engines and other chassis components for the popular Model N. This drained Model N profits from Malcomson and the smaller stockholders into Ford's

pocket. It was the first step toward the vertical integration of the Ford Motor Company that would in less than a decade make Ford largely independent of outside suppliers, except for auto bodies. On 1 May 1907 the Ford Manufacturing Company was absorbed into the Ford Motor Company. The acquisition in 1911 of the John R. Kiem Mills of Buffalo, New York, a leading producer of pressed- and drawn-steel parts, and the movement of Kiem machinery and key personnel to Detroit in late 1912 gave Ford the capacity to make its own crankcases, axles, housings, and bodies. Complete independence from the Dodge Brothers for engines and finished chassis came in 1913.

Even while deluged with orders for the Model N, work had begun on the Model T in an experimental room at the Ford Piquette Avenue plant some two years before the car was announced in a 19 March 1908 circular to dealers. It was the product of an engineering team of a dozen men headed by Ford, designer C. Harold Wills, and draftsman Joseph Galamb. The Model T was first made available to dealers on 1 October 1908 at initial prices ranging from $825 for the runabout to $1,000 for the landaulet, a design featuring an open driver's side and collapsible roof. By the time the last Model T rolled off the assembly line on 27 May 1927 the price for the coupe had reached a low of $290, and 15 million units had been sold. (Only the Volkswagen Beetle was to surpass this record output in a vastly expanded World War II market.) The Model T put the world on wheels.

Henry Ford designed the 22-horsepower, 100-inch wheelbase Model T to be "a farmer's car" for a nation of farmers. He advertised it as the "Universal Car," by which Ford meant that a number of body types serving different purposes could be fitted to a common chassis. As in the Model N, the Model T used lightweight vanadium steels. No other car in 1908 offered so many advanced features. Ford's advertising boast was essentially correct: "No car under $2,000 offers more, and no car over $2,000 offers more except in trimmings."

The Model T was the first mass-produced car. The term "mass production" dates from Ford's article of that title in the thirteenth edition (1926) of the *Encyclopaedia Britannica*. Until then the system of flow-production perfected at the Ford Highland Park plant in 1913–1914 was popularly referred to as "Fordism."

The 62-acre Highland Park plant, designed by Albert Kahn, that Ford opened in January 1910 possessed an unparalleled factory arrangement for the production of motorcars. Its well-lighted and well-ventilated buildings were a model of advanced industrial construction. Elementary time-and-motion studies begun at the Piquette Avenue plant were continued at Highland Park and led in 1912 to the installation of continuous conveyor belts to bring materials to the assembly lines. And with the move to Highland Park, manufacturing and assembling operations began to be arranged sequentially so that components traveled to completion over the shortest route possible with no unnecessary handling. This entailed the abandonment of grouping machine tools together by type in plant layout. Magnetos, motors, and transmissions were assembled on moving lines at the plant by the summer of 1913. After production from these subassembly lines threatened to flood the final assembly line, a moving chassis-assembly line was installed. It reduced the time of chassis assembly from twelve and a half hours in October to two hours and forty minutes by 30 December 1913. "Every piece of work in the shop moves," boasted Ford in 1922.

At Highland Park a new breed of semiskilled industrial workers was created. According to Ford, in his *My Life and Work*, mass production meant "the reduction of the necessity for thought on the part of the worker and the reduction of his thoughts to a minimum." Machines were closely spaced for optimal efficiency, and material was delivered to the worker at a waist-high level so that unnecessary motion was not expended in walking, reaching, stooping, or bending. The worker not only had to subordinate himself to the pace of the machine but also had to be able to withstand the boredom inevitable in repeating the same motions hour after hour. A fifteen-minute lunch break, which included time to use the restroom, was the only interruption in the fatiguing monotony of repetitive labor. Straw bosses and company "spotters"—another new element in the work force—enforced rules and regulations that forbade leaning against machines, sitting, squatting, talking, whistling, or smoking on the job. Workers learned to communicate clandestinely without moving their lips in the "Ford whisper" and wore frozen expressions known as "Fordization of the face."

On 5 January 1914 Ford announced the five-dollar, eight-hour day, which roughly doubled the going rate of pay for industrial workers while shortening the workday by two hours. The five-dollar minimum pay for a day's work was boldly conceived by Ford as a plan for sharing profits with his workers before the money was earned. Eligible workers were those who had been at Ford for six months or more and were married men living with and taking good care of their families, single men over twenty-two years of age of proved thrifty habits, men under twenty-two years of age, or women who were the sole support of some next of kin. Almost 60 percent of the Ford workers qualified immediately, and within two years about 75 percent were included in the profit-sharing plan.

A Sociological Department (after 1915, the Educational Department) was formed to check on the eligibility of employees and to ensure that the profits shared with them were put to uses approved by Henry Ford. A staff of investigators visited workers' homes gathering information and giving advice on the intimate details of the family budget, diet, living arrangements, recreation, social outlook, and morality. Americanization of the immigrant was enforced through mandatory classes in English. The worker who refused to learn English, rejected the advice of the investigator, gambled, drank excessively, or was found guilty of "any malicious practice derogatory to good physical manhood or moral character" was disqualified from the plan and put on probation. If a disqualified worker failed to reform within six months, he was discharged, and his profits accumulated under the plan were given to charity.

In the spring of 1915 Ford had begun buying up huge tracts of land along the River Rouge southeast of Detroit and announced plans for a great industrial complex there. The Dodge Brothers brought a lawsuit against Ford to stop his diversion of Ford profits into expanding the Rouge plant instead of distributing them as dividends, which the Dodge Brothers, who held a minority interest in Ford stock, were counting on to finance expansion at Dodge. On 6 January 1917 the courts permitted Ford to go ahead with the development of the Rouge facilities on the condition that he post a $10 million bond to safeguard the interests of minority stockholders. But on 7 February 1919 another court decision forced the Ford Motor Company to pay a special dividend of $19.275 million plus interest. Although Henry Ford, the principal Ford stockholder, received the bulk of this dividend, he resolved to buy out the minority stockholders, whom he had come to consider parasites.

Finally, on 11 July 1919 Ford managed to borrow $75 million from a syndicate of bankers to buy out his remaining stockholders, most importantly the Dodge Brothers. The reorganized Ford Motor Company was a wholly family-owned and family-managed business. Edsel became titular president, a position he held until his death from cancer in 1943. No one, however, doubted that the Ford Motor Company after its reorganization was an autocracy subject to the whims of its aging, egocentric founder.

By 1918 the inflation of the World War I years had reduced the $5 minimum daily pay to the equivalent of $2.80 in 1914 purchasing power, wiping out the workers' gains. The Educational Department folded, and its records were burned in 1921. Ford benevolent paternalism had ended earlier. Over the course of World War I the company's labor policies had undergone, as labor historian Stephen Meyer III put it, "a transition from a variant of welfare capitalism, which captured the mood of the Progressive Era, to a version of the American Plan, which typified the more recalcitrant employer attitudes of the twenties." Although all automobile manufacturers in the 1920s employed labor spies and informants to ferret out union organizers, the Ford Motor Company gained particular notoriety. Harry Bennett, an ex-pugilist with underworld connections, enforced discipline in the Ford plants as head of a gang of labor spies and thugs called the Ford Service Department. Bennett came to be Henry Ford's most trusted associate and comrade after the Model A replaced the Model T in 1928.

By American entry into World War I, Ford branch assembly plants had been set up at freight rate-breaking points in twenty-eight cities under the supervision of William S. Knudsen. By 1920 the Ford Motor Company owned, in addition to its main Highland Park and River Rouge plants, branch plants scattered across the globe, rubber plantations in Brazil, iron mines and lumber mills in Michigan, coal mines in Kentucky and West Virginia, glass plants in Pennsylvania and Minnesota, a railroad, and a fleet of ships. With the phenomenal success of the Model T and the consequent vertical integration and worldwide expansion of his giant enterprise, Henry Ford thus "wielded industrial power such as no man had ever possessed before." Outside the United States, assembly plants were built in Canada in 1904 and at Trafford Park, England, in 1911 under Percival Perry. This was the beginning of multinational expansion that would see Ford assembling cars in twenty-one countries on six continents by 1928. Control of these foreign subsidiaries remained tightly in Dearborn, which mandated policy through thick loose-leaf manuals called Ford Bibles.

With the inauguration of the five-dollar day in 1914, Henry Ford had begun to express his social views and to get involved in social causes. He donated $600,000 to build the Henry Ford Hospital in Detroit and assumed total responsibility for its administration. It became one of the best-publicized medical centers in the nation and contributed, as had the five-dollar day, to Ford's reputation as a humanitarian. Then in 1916 Ford formed the Henry Ford Trade School to train boys from poor families in a variety of trades. He later instituted a private school system at Greenfield Village in which the elementary pupils were taught in three one-room schools and the secondary students in a modern high school. Emphasis was on vocational training and learning by doing. Ironically for the innovator of mass production, Ford also set up a series of village industries for farmers to produce Ford parts part time using waterpower. He tried to revive square dancing and country fiddling. He championed drinking unpasteurized milk and substituting soybean meal for meat as health measures. He restored the farmhouse in which he was born, the Botsford Inn northeast of Dearborn, where the Fords had attended dances in the 1880s, and the Wayside Inn at South Sudbury, Massachusetts. On 21 October 1929, at a celebration of Edison's invention of the electric light, the Henry Ford Museum–Greenfield Village Complex was dedicated by President Herbert Hoover. It has become the most important historical preserve under nongovernmental operation in the United States.

Until U.S. entry into World War I, Henry Ford took an outspoken stand against conscription and preparedness. Couzens resigned in October 1915 in objection to Ford's mixing of his personal pacifism and opposition to American preparedness for World War I with company policy. Ford idealistically declared that he would spend half his fortune to shorten the war by one day and joined the American Peace Society, in which he came under the influence of Rosika Schwimmer, a Hungarian pacifist. Schwimmer wanted to stop the war before either side gained a complete victory and to establish a permanent organization for the mediation of international disputes. To implement these goals Ford sponsored a "Peace Ship," the *Oscar II*,

which set sail on 5 December 1915 on a planned fourteen-day voyage to Oslo, Norway, carrying an array of delegates, students, technical advisers, and reporters. Newspapers on both sides of the Atlantic stressed the idealistic naiveté of the Peace Ship and seized on bizarre details in an attempt to discredit "Ford's folly" as an exercise in futility and absurdity. After Ford became ill and left the delegation at Oslo, the peace party went on to Sweden and Denmark, ending up at The Hague in the Netherlands, where it disbanded on 15 January 1916, demoralized and dissension-ridden.

Once diplomatic ties between the United States and Germany were severed on 3 February 1917, Ford abruptly reversed his position, stating, "we must stand behind the President" and "in the event of war [I] will place our factory at the disposal of the United States government and will operate without one cent of profit." Tractors were desperately needed by the British to help alleviate grave food shortages caused by German U-boat attacks on ships importing foodstuffs and by the loss of 80,000 farmhands to the military services. Experiments with a number of makes of tractors conducted by the Royal Agricultural Society had left the British authorities most impressed with the Fordson, a 2,500-pound machine that Ford personally introduced in August 1915 at a plowing demonstration at Fremont, Nebraska. With a wheelbase of only sixty-three inches, the Fordson could turn in a 21-foot circle. It was cheap to operate because its four-cylinder, twenty-horsepower engine ran on kerosene. And, like the Model T, the Fordson was designed to be mass-produced at low cost. Henry Ford & Son was organized on 27 July 1917 to manufacture the Fordson as a corporation separate from the Ford Motor Company.

The Fordson tractor contributed little toward alleviating food shortages during the war. By 1 March 1918 only 3,600 of the 8,000 Fordsons ordered by the British government had been delivered, and privately owned steam tractors were plowing considerably more acres of British farmland than the government-owned Fordsons. It was 23 April 1918 before the first Fordson for domestic use came off the assembly line. Too late to have any significant impact on winning the war, mass production of the Fordson reached fantastic heights just as the market for American agricultural commodities rapidly evaporated in the postwar period. The proliferation of the Fordson farm tractor was a contributing factor in creating the ruinous combination of higher fixed costs and overproduction of staple commodities that plagued American farmers during the 1920s.

Even before Ford abandoned his pacifist neutrality, the Ford branch plants in Paris and Great Britain had disregarded Dearborn and turned out thousands of motor vehicles for the Allies. From an initial contract for 2,000 ambulances on 30 May 1917, Ford's American factories went on to produce about 39,000 motor vehicles for the war effort. They also made aircraft motors, armor plate, caissons, shells, steel helmets, submarine detectors, and torpedo tubes. Sixty Eagle Boats (submarine chasers) were completed by Ford too late to see action, and two tank prototypes developed by the company had just reached the point at which quantity production could begin when peace came. Although the manufacture of Model Ts for the civilian market never was stopped, automotive work was cut back significantly at Ford during the war. The production of Ford motor vehicles declined from a high of 734,800 units in 1916 to 438,800 units in 1918.

The abrupt termination of war contracts because of the armistice of 11 November 1918 caused little concern in the automobile industry. Automobile plants were quickly converted back to the production of passenger cars—at Highland Park it took only about three weeks—to fill the huge back orders for new cars that had accumulated during the war. Automobile manufacturers embarked on ambitious expansion programs, confident that the demand for motorcars was insatiable.

This illusion was shattered with the onset of the postwar recession. New-car sales slackened with the general decline in purchasing power. As the full impact of the recession began to be felt in the summer of 1920, Henry Ford still owed $25 million, due in April 1921, on the loan used to obtain control of his company in 1919. He also had pledged to distribute a $7 million bonus to employees in January, and he had to pay between $18 million and $30 million in taxes. Over the past three years he had spent $60.45 million on developing the River Rouge plant and between $15 million and $20 million on purchasing mines and timber tracts. Ford estimated that he needed $58 million, but he had only $20 million in cash on hand. He abandoned the thought of seeking another loan once it became apparent to him that the bankers would demand in return a voice in the management of his company.

The Ford Motor Company closed its plants "for inventory" on Christmas Eve 1920 and remained closed until 1 February 1921, while the company disposed of "stocks on hand." Unlike most of his competitors, Ford maintained full production up to the shutdown of his plants, curtailing only the purchase of raw materials. The strategy implemented at Ford was foremost to turn the huge inventory of raw materials that had been bought at inflated prices into a reservoir of finished cars, then to stop production until those cars were disposed of at a profit and raw-material prices had declined. Consignments of unordered cars were forced on more than 6,300 Ford dealers who had the unhappy choice of borrowing heavily from local banks to pay cash on delivery or forfeiting their Ford franchises.

The shutdown at Ford was accompanied by stringent economy measures that went beyond what was essential for survival and jeopardized the future well-being of the firm. The Ford plants were stripped of every nonessential tool and fixture, including every pencil sharpener, most desks and typewriters, and 600 extension telephones. The sale of this equipment netted $7 million. The company also benefited from replacing some equipment with improved machinery and methods that increased output per man-hour of labor.

These gains were canceled out, however, by a ruthless halving of the office force from 1,074 to 528 workers as most departments, including critical ones such as auditing, were overly simplified, merged, or eliminated. Many capable executives were discharged or resigned from the company. Although this critical loss of executive talent defies adequate summarizing, besides Couzens the most significant losses were probably William S. Knudsen and Norval A. Hawkins. (Knudsen left in disgust over Ford's callous treatment of employees and intransigent commitment to the Model T.) Both went to General Motors and were instrumental in Chevrolet's sales surpassing Ford's by 1927.

After stripping his business to the bone, Ford unaccountably undertook two new business ventures. On 4 February 1922 he bought the Lincoln Motor Company out of bankruptcy from Henry and Wilfred Leland for $8 million. After resigning from Cadillac in 1917 the Lelands had formed Lincoln to build Liberty aircraft engines. In 1919 they turned to building luxury cars, which were mechanically excellent but poorly styled. The Lelands lasted only four months as Ford managers; Henry Ford fired them on 10 June 1922 after the father-and-son team had altercations with the production men. Edsel was given control of Lincoln, and under his supervision the car became a style trend-setter. He and Eugene T. "Bob" Gregory created two of the outstanding classic cars of the 1930s, the Zephyr and the Continental. And Edsel was instrumental in encouraging leading custom coachbuilders, most important, Raymond H. Dietrich, to move from the East Coast to Detroit. Although the Lincoln did not set sales records, it set the main direction of American luxury-car design—great power combined with smooth performance and riding comfort—for the interwar decades and gave Ford visibility at the very top as well as at the bottom of the market.

It is less clear why Ford branched out into aviation by investing in late 1922 in a company formed by William Stout to build metal airplanes. The Stout Metal Airplane Company was incorporated into the Ford Motor Company in 1925. On 1 July 1925 Stout began a Detroit-Cleveland air service, and in 1926 the government awarded Stout the mail contracts between Detroit and Cleveland and between Detroit and Chicago. Ford hoped to develop a low-priced plane for the mass market, but the experiment ended when his forty-horsepower "flivver plane" crashed in 1926, killing its pilot. The most successful Ford aircraft venture was the Ford Tri-Motor, a three-engine plane that could carry eight passengers plus cargo. Some 198 Tri-Motors were built between 1926 and 1932, when production was halted because of the declining market for commercial aircraft. A monument to Ford's early aircraft ventures remains in the landmark Dearborn Inn, the world's first airport hotel, completed in 1931.

More was written about Henry Ford during his lifetime, and he was more often quoted, than any figure in American history. Theodore Roosevelt complained that Ford received more publicity than even the president of the United States. The people of what scholar

Reynold M. Wik calls "grassroots America" thought Ford a greater emancipator of the common man than Abraham Lincoln. From the early 1920s through the early 1930s Ford received several thousand letters a day, ranging from simple requests for help and advice to demands that he solve America's remaining social and economic problems.

Ford probably could have been elected president of the United States had he really wanted the office. In 1916 he spurned efforts to get him to head the tickets of the American party and the Prohibition party on a platform of peace and prohibition. And, even though he refused to campaign, he won the 1916 Michigan presidential primary of the Republican party by a comfortable margin.

President Woodrow Wilson, who sought a Senate favorable to the establishment of a League of Nations, urged Ford to run for U.S. senator from Michigan in 1918. He won the Democratic nomination, but the state was heavily Republican, and his opponent, Truman Newberry, spent lavishly and stooped to a mudslinging campaign that questioned Ford's patriotism at the outbreak of World War I and hammered away at the draft deferment that Ford had obtained for Edsel. Still, Ford only lost the election by the slim margin of 212,751 votes to Newberry's 217,088.

Ford-for-President clubs sprang up spontaneously across the nation from 1920 to 1923. In the summer of 1923 both a poll conducted by *Collier's Weekly* and the Autocaster nationwide survey found Ford far ahead of President Warren G. Harding. However, the Ford-for-President boom ended in October 1924 when Ford announced that he would support Calvin Coolidge, who had assumed the presidency after Harding's death in 1923, if Coolidge would enforce Prohibition. The evidence suggests that Ford supported Coolidge in exchange for the president's endorsement of Ford's bid to develop a government-owned nitrate plant at Muscle Shoals, Tennessee, a plan that was meeting stiff opposition in Congress.

Apart from Ford's increasing callousness toward his work force—from key executives to floor sweepers—the main blot on Ford's reputation was his blatant anti-Semitism. Ford's magazine, the *Dearborn Independent*, edited by William J. Cameron, began publishing anti-Semitic articles in 1920. Between 1920 and 1922 Ford reprinted them in four brochures and in a more comprehensive book, *The International Jew*, which was translated into most European languages and was widely circulated throughout the world. Among other things, Jews were accused of controlling the world's banks, starting World War I, and plotting the destruction of Christian civilization. In March 1927 Aaron Shapiro sued Ford for libelous material printed in the *Dearborn Independent*. The suit was settled out of court on 7 July, when Ford published an apology to Shapiro and a retraction of his attacks on the Jewish people.

But the damage could not be so easily undone. Ford was considered a "great man" in the Nazi pantheon of heroes. A picture of Ford was displayed in a place of honor at the National Socialist party headquarters, and he was the only American mentioned favorably in Adolf Hitler's *Mein Kampf*. By late 1933 the Nazis had published some twenty-nine German editions of *The International Jew*, with Ford's name on the title page and a preface praising Ford for the "great service" his anti-Semitism had done the world. At the post–World War II Nuremberg war crime trials, Balder Von Schirach, leader of the Hitler youth movement, testified that he had learned his anti-Semitism at age seventeen from reading Ford's book. On 30 July 1938, his seventy-fifth birthday, Ford accepted the Grand Cross of the Supreme Order of the German Eagle with Hitler's personal congratulations.

Except for minor face-liftings and the incorporation of basic improvements such as the closed body and the self-starter, the Model T remained basically unchanged long after it was outmoded. The popularity of the Model T declined in the 1920s as rural roads were improved, consumers became more style- and comfort-conscious, and the market for new cars shifted from a demand for low-cost, basic transportation by first-time owners to filling replacement demand.

In contrast with Ford's commitment to a single, static model at an ever-decreasing unit price, at General Motors Alfred P. Sloan, Jr., developed the counter-strategy of blanketing the market with "a car for every purse and purpose" at the top of every price bracket and by instituting the annual model change that called for an essentially new model every three years with minor face-liftings in between. Most important, GM's bottom-of-the-line Chevrolet was vastly improved mechanically and in appearance under the leadership of Knudsen (who had joined GM in 1922). The payoff was that the thirteen-to-one ratio by which the Model T had outsold Chevrolet in 1921 was cut to two-to-one by 1926, forcing even Henry Ford to recognize that the Model T era was over.

Model T production was halted on 27 May 1927, and the Ford plants were shut down while its successor, the Model A, was hastily designed. Some 400,000 orders were received before the Model A had been seen by the public. Following what was probably the most extensive changeover of an industrial plant in history, the assembly lines at River Rouge began to turn out limited numbers in November, and the Model A was introduced on 2 December. Unlike the revolutionary Model T, however, the Model A was a very conventional car for its time and was made obsolete even as it was introduced by further developments at Chevrolet, especially by the introduction of a six-cylinder engine as standard in the 1929 model year.

Ford took the radical step of going Chevrolet one better by introducing his 65-horsepower Model 18 V-8 on 2 March 1932. Casting its entire engine block as a single unit was perhaps the most significant manufacturing innovation of the 1930–1950 decades because it significantly reduced manufacturing costs, making a V-8 engine practical for low-priced cars. The 1932 V-8 engine remained the basic power plant of Ford cars for twenty-one years. V-8 styling followed that of the top-of-the-line Lincoln, and with the V-8 Ford began to emulate the annual model change innovated at GM.

Despite the V-8's excellence, Chevrolet outsold Ford in every year from 1931 through 1986 except 1935 and 1945, and the latter year was an exception only because Ford was the first automaker to return to civilian production after World War II. Plymouth also cut into Ford sales in the low-price field after it was introduced in 1929 by the Chrysler Corporation. Only in the sale of light trucks did the Ford Motor Company enjoy a slight lead over its competitors. In the oligopoly that had come to dominate the automobile industry, by 1936 Ford had dropped from undisputed leadership to third place in sales of passenger cars, with 22.44 percent of the market versus 43.12 percent for General Motors and 25.03 percent for Chrysler.

The Great Depression was an even more important impediment to the revival of the Ford Motor Company than competition from General Motors and Chrysler. Automobile registrations declined for the first time in the United States during the depression, and not until 1949 did the automobile industry equal its record 1929 output of 5.3 million units. Ford production collapsed from more than 1.5 million units in 1929 to a low of 232,000 units in 1932 and bounced back to only 600,000 units in 1941, the last full year of civilian automobile production before World War II. The number of Ford employees declined sharply from 170,502 in 1929 to 46,282 by 1932. Henry Ford, with the help of his Service Department, managed to resist unionization longer than General Motors or Chrysler. As a result the company's wages for 1937–1941 fell a few cents below the average for all industry in the United States and well below the average for the automobile industry.

A survey by *Fortune* magazine conducted in 1937 for the National Association of Manufacturers found that 47.2 percent of the respondents still approved of the policies of the Ford Motor Company, versus an insignificant 3.1 percent approval for General Motors and 1.2 percent approval for Chrysler. Yet the Ford myths were beginning to be shattered, and Henry Ford at least was no longer being deified. In 1932 critic Jonathan Leonard noted the paradox that Ford "is hated by nearly everyone who has ever worked for him, and at one time was worshipped by nearly everyone who had not. His story is certainly the most fascinating in all the gaudy tales of American business." Ford's rhetoric increasingly seemed irrelevant nonsense even to the grassroots Americans who had deified him for a generation as the depression wore on. Letters to the "Sage of Dearborn" dwindled and became bitter and resentful.

Ford refused to participate in the code drafted for the automobile industry by the National Automobile Chamber of Commerce (NACC), the industry trade association, under the National Industrial Recovery Act (NIRA). Section 7(a) of that act gave labor the right to collective bargaining. After Title I of the NIRA was declared unconstitutional by the U.S. Supreme Court, Section 7(a) was replaced on 5 July 1935 by the National Labor Relations Act (NLRA), which set up a National Labor Relations Board (NLRB), empowered to conduct elections to determine workers' bargaining agents. The American Federation of Labor then issued a charter to the International Union, United Automobile Workers of America (UAW).

By the end of 1936 the UAW had closed most General Motors plants through the new tactic of the sit-down strike. Michigan governor Frank Murphy refused to call out the National Guard to evict strikers from GM's Chevrolet and Fisher Body plants in Flint, which led GM to capitulate to the UAW on 11 February 1937. Following a sit-down strike at Chrysler in April, the automaker negotiated a similar agreement with the UAW.

These GM and Chrysler settlements left Ford the holdout against industry unionization and the main strike target of the UAW. Because the Roosevelt administration refused to enforce the law fully, the intransigent Ford Motor Company remained in violation of the National Labor Relations Act, even after the Supreme Court had upheld its constitutionality. Members of the Ford Service Department brutally beat Walter Reuther and several other UAW organizers in the notorious "battle of the overpass" at the River Rouge plant on 26 May 1937.

After the discharge of several union members on 1 April 1941, a spontaneous walkout of Ford workers closed down the River Rouge plant, initiating a UAW organizing strike. The UAW won about 70 percent of the votes in the NLRB election held at Ford on 21 May 1941. On 20 June Henry Ford finally signed a contract with the UAW—agreeing, ironically, to more generous terms than had either GM or Chrysler, including the deduction of union dues from workers' paychecks. With the signing of the Ford-UAW contract a new era of labor relations in the automobile industry had dawned as workers turned from dependence on Henry Ford's paternalism and fear of Bennett's Service Department to the union shop steward and the skills of UAW negotiators.

In 1938 Ford suffered a severe stroke, and his mental capacities eroded rapidly. He developed the hallucination that Franklin Delano Roosevelt was a warmonger controlled by General Motors and the Du Ponts and that U.S. involvement in World War II was part of a conspiracy to gain control of his company. "His memory was failing as rapidly as his obsessions and antipathies increased," Ford production head Charles E. Sorensen recalled. "His pet peeve was Franklin Roosevelt, but any mention of the war in Europe and the likelihood of this country's involvement upset him almost to incoherence. Edsel, who was suffering from stomach trouble, came in for unmerciful criticism."

With the rapid Nazi conquest of Europe, Hitler came to control Ford operations in eight countries on the Continent by late 1940. After the German declaration of war against the United States on 11 December 1941, Hitler seized these Ford European plants as "enemy property." Without the knowledge of Ford–U.S., the German management of Ford–Werke AG had been for some time "secretly engaged in the production of war materials" (*American Business Abroad*, p. 320). Despite proclamations of neutrality from Dearborn, Ford's British Commonwealth plants were quickly converted to war production during the fall of 1939.

In the United States President Roosevelt appointed Knudsen, who had risen to president of General Motors, to the chairmanship of the National Advisory Defense Committee (NADC). Knudsen left GM to assume his new duties at no salary on 28 May 1940. In late November, at a meeting in New York with more than one hundred auto-industry executives, he called on American automobile manufacturers to give their full cooperation to U.S. defense plans. His first priority was a program to produce aircraft engines and 35,000 aircraft.

Henry Ford already had reneged on an early June 1940 agreement with Knudsen to undertake the manufacture of Rolls-Royce aircraft engines for the British and was consequently under attack for his lack of patriotism by the press, especially in the United Kingdom. Edsel and Sorensen, however, managed to obtain his reluctant consent to participate in the aircraft engine program for the U.S. Air Force. Ford's failure to comply in this voluntarily, they knew, would invite the governmental takeover that his paranoia led him to fear.

On 1 November 1940 the Ford Motor Company signed a contract to make Pratt and Whitney aircraft engines for the U.S. Air Force, while Packard undertook production of the Rolls-Royce engines for the Royal Air Force. In February 1941 the government approved Ford plans for a vast bomber plant at Willow Run, near Ypsilanti, Michigan. Snags in getting "Will-It-Run" into production delayed acceptance of the first B-24 bombers completely assembled by Ford until September 1942. By then the Ford Motor Company, along with the rest of the American automobile industry, had completely converted to war production and was playing an indispensable role in producing a variety of other military items, including tanks, jeeps, trucks, armored cars, and gliders. Ford, who had suffered another stroke in 1941, feared that the military personnel at Willow Run were spies sent by Roosevelt to assassinate him and took to carrying an automatic pistol under the cowl of his car.

After Edsel's death in 1943, Ford reassumed the presidency of the Ford Motor Company. Aware of Ford's mental incompetence, Roosevelt toyed with the idea of removing him from the company and having the government operate it for the duration of the war. It took threats by Edsel's widow and Clara Ford that they would sell their shares of Ford stock outside the family to induce Ford finally to step down in favor of his grandson, Henry Ford II, who was granted a discharge from the navy to assume the Ford presidency a few weeks after the Japanese surrender in September 1945.

"During the last two years of his life," writes Ford biographer Richard B. Folsom, "Henry Ford resembled a blurred and faded photograph of his former self. Alert one moment, he was bewildered the next. . . . He tired easily and often did not feel well. Sometimes he wore a shawl and increasingly appeared to be an enfeebled old man." He died at his Fair Lane estate during a power outage caused by the flooding Rouge River.

Perhaps the ultimate irony of Ford's life was the Ford Foundation, a legal device conceived on 3 February 1936 as a means of avoiding Roosevelt's "soak-the-rich" taxes while maintaining family control of the Ford Motor Company. The foundation was given a 95 percent equity in the Ford Motor Company in nonvoting common stock. A 5 percent equity of all voting common stock was retained by the Ford family. Had it not been for the Ford Foundation, the heirs of Edsel and Henry Ford would have paid federal inheritance taxes estimated at $321 million and would have lost control of the company in selling the stock necessary to raise the money. But by the end of 1955 the foundation had disposed of some $875 million of the Ford fortune and had announced plans to diversify its investments; this involved selling nearly seven million reclassified shares of Ford common stock. Thus three-fifths of the Ford Motor Company voting common stock ended up in the hands of key Ford executives and the general public. The family control of the firm that the Ford Foundation was formed to preserve ended less than a decade after Henry Ford's death while the foundation had dispersed millions of the Ford fortune in ways that would not have pleased Henry Ford.

• So much has been written about Henry Ford that any Ford bibliography must be highly selective. The bulk of primary materials are on file at the Ford Archives, Henry Ford Museum and Greenfield Village in Dearborn, Mich. Researchers now are more handicapped than those of several decades ago because before his death Henry Ford II removed and destroyed a great amount of material on his grandfather and father from the archives as well as the family medical records from Detroit's Henry Ford Hospital. Henry Ford published three books, *My Life and Work* (1922) and *Today and Tomorrow* (1926), in collaboration with Samuel Crowther, and *My Philosophy of Industry* (1929), a series of authorized interviews with Fay L. Faurote. Although the writing in these volumes is undoubtedly Crowther's and Faurote's, there can be no doubt that the sentiments expressed either were made or approved by Ford. The major secondary work on Ford remains the monumental trilogy by Allan Nevins and Frank E. Hill, *Ford: The Times, the Man, the Company* (1954), *Ford: Expansion and Challenge* (1957), and *Ford: Decline and Rebirth* (1963). For the best account of Ford's career by a close associate, see Charles E. Sorensen with Samuel T. Williamson, *My Forty Years with Ford* (1956). The most informative single book on Ford is David L. Lewis, *The Public Image of Henry Ford* (1976). Lewis's book not only contains everything of value in the Nevins and Hill trilogy but also far more on some important aspects of Ford's life, and it is more objective and balanced in its interpretations. Probably the most informative short biographic article on Ford is Richard B. Folsom's "Henry Ford," in *The Automobile Industry, 1896–1920*, ed. George S. May (1990), pp. 192–222. For criticisms of

Ford and the Ford myth, see especially Keith Sward, *The Legend of Henry Ford* (1949); Jonathan N. Leonard, *The Tragedy of Henry Ford* (1932); and the material on Ford in John Kenneth Galbraith, *The Liberal Hour* (1960). For Ford's reputation among the common people of America and the world, see Reynold M. Wik, *Henry Ford and Grass-roots America* (1972). The definitive work on Henry Ford and the Selden patent is William Greenleaf, *Monopoly on Wheels* (1961); on the five-dollar, eight-hour day and Ford labor practices and relations from 1908 to 1921, see Stephen Meyer III, *The Five Dollar Day* (1981). Ford's attitude toward and treatment of blacks is covered in August Meier and Elliot Rudwick, *Black Detroit and the Rise of the UAW* (1979). By far the best exposition and assessment of Ford mass-production methods is David A. Hounshell, "The Ford Motor Company and the Rise of Mass Production in America," in his *From the American System to Mass Production* (1984). The most comprehensive study of Ford's overseas business empire is Mira Wilkins and Frank E. Hill, *American Business Abroad: Ford on Six Continents* (1964). The most informative book on the Model T remains Floyd Clymer, *Henry's Wonderful Model T* (1955). An obituary is in the *Detroit Free Press*, 9–10 Apr. 1947.

JAMES J. FLINK

FORD, Henry, II (4 Sept. 1917–29 Sept. 1987), automotive executive, was born in Detroit, Michigan, the son of Edsel Bryant Ford and Eleanor Clay and the grandson of Henry Ford, the founder of the Ford Motor Company. His father served as president of the Ford Motor Company from 1 January 1919 until his death on 26 May 1943; his mother was from a prominent merchant family. Henry Ford II attended Yale University but did not take a degree. In 1940 he married Anne McDonnell, with whom he would have three children. In August of that year he took his first job with Ford Motor as a mechanic in the dynamometer room. The U.S. Naval Reserve appointed him an ensign in April 1941, and during World War II he was on active duty. Although Ford volunteered for sea duty, he never served overseas. After Edsel Ford's death in 1943, the senior Henry Ford reassumed the presidency of the firm. Concerned that the elderly founder of the company was no longer competent to administer such an important manufacturing operation during the war mobilization emergency, Secretary of the Navy Frank Knox discharged the younger Ford from service so that he could return to the company as an executive.

Henry Ford II became vice president of Ford Motor Company on 15 December 1943 and was elected president on 21 September 1945. He served a leadership role in the company that bore his family's name until his death. In 1960 Ford became chairman of the board of directors as well as president. He remained in the position of president until 1963, except for a brief period in 1960 when Robert S. McNamara held the post. Ford retired as chairman of the board of directors in 1980 but retained considerable influence thereafter as chairman of the board's finance committee.

Henry Ford II had two principal accomplishments as an automobile manufacturer. First, he brought modern management techniques to the company, ensuring its success in the huge and expanding domestic American automobile and truck market; and, second, he gave Ford Motor a world vision. His grandfather, though a mechanical genius, had not adopted management structures and techniques suitable for the long-term success of Ford Motor in the American market. The elder Henry Ford had remained a paramount influence in the company even while his son Edsel was responsible for its day-to-day management. During the 1920s Ford Motor had lost its leading position in the American industry to General Motors, a well-led firm that pioneered systems for successfully running a very large and diversified manufacturing firm. Ford also had failed to adapt sufficiently to changes in customer preferences. During the 1930s Ford suffered from terrible labor relations; in fact, Henry Ford's resistance to the United Automobile Workers and collective bargaining had led him to turn power over to Harry Bennett, a man of doubtful character. The pistol-carrying Bennett used violence against the union and plotted to assume command of the company. The shambles of management at Ford Motor included a failure to use modern accounting techniques to know and control costs. In 1945 Ford Motor was losing $9 million each month and was rapidly failing.

These conditions prompted Knox and others in the Roosevelt administration to worry about the ability of Ford Motor to play a full role in mobilization for the war and caused them to recall Henry Ford II to the company's offices in Dearborn, Michigan. At war's end in 1945, in alliance with his mother, and with his grandmother's acquiescence, Henry II quickly took charge and began to correct his grandfather's mistakes. Soon after the war he employed a group of "whiz kids," so called because they were young men who had guided the air force's mobilization so successfully during the war. This group, along with Ernest R. Breech, formerly of General Motors and in 1946 executive vice president (and later chairman of the board of directors) at Ford, slowly changed the company's management and eventually ensured its competitive viability against the larger General Motors in the expanding American market. Henry Ford II thus is known primarily as a successful manufacturing executive. Under his leadership, Ford Motor developed successful new models of vehicles (with the notable exception of the ill-famed Edsel, which failed in the mid-priced market in the late 1950s, and the Pinto, which had an unsafe fuel tank but nevertheless survived in the marketplace). Ford improved its labor relations and worked with the United Automobile Workers to provide better, and more secure, wages and benefits.

Ford gave clear direction to his executives. "Personal mobility is our principal product," he stated in 1972, "and if we do not find ways of making better products, our competitors will. We must not become victims of change; we must capitalize on it." Although Ford Motor always faced stiff competition from General Motors in the American market, and after 1973 from Japanese manufacturers, Henry Ford II learned the importance of focusing on the development of products customers wanted. When in the 1970s competitive pressures, primarily from Japan, wounded the company's profitability in the American market, he oversaw policies of new product development that enabled the company to recapture market leadership a decade later.

Ford had assumed command of the company at a time when the American economy was supreme in the world, and American companies led the organization and development of economic activity across the globe. Very early in his career as an executive, Ford realized that the future expansion and well being of Ford Motor must include international manufacturing and distribution. Ford Motor increased its investments abroad and became a leading vehicle manufacturer outside the United States, especially in Europe. The company also had important plants elsewhere. In one important regard, however, Ford was less than prescient in his international vision: he failed to see, in the early stages, the aggressive efforts of Japanese manufacturers to penetrate the American automobile market. Eventually, however, Ford's investments included a substantial ownership share in Mazda, an important Japanese automobile manufacturer. Moreover, when energy crises in 1973 and 1979 caused profits in the domestic market to collapse, Ford Motor survived because of its successes abroad. In the 1980s and 1990s the company's resurgence in the American market was due in part to its ability to move funds and technologies from its worldwide operations to American factories in support of new product development. After Ford retired in 1980, executives who were not members of the family assumed the leadership of Ford Motor.

Henry Ford II was also deeply engaged in public service. He was a leader in the efforts of the Detroit business community to invest in local urban revitalization: Detroit's infrastructure had deteriorated as the inner-city economy declined and wealthier residents migrated to the suburbs. Ford served four U.S. presidents. Dwight D. Eisenhower named him an alternate U.S. delegate to the United Nations in 1953. In 1961 John F. Kennedy appointed him to his Advisory Committee on Labor-Management Policy. In 1968 Lyndon Johnson named him the first chairman of the National Alliance of Businessmen, and Ford became responsible for directing a program for the hard-core unemployed. (In 1969 Johnson awarded Ford the Medal of Freedom.) In 1970 Richard M. Nixon appointed Ford chairman of the National Center for Voluntary Action.

Henry Ford II was also an important philanthropist, able to draw upon the largest industrial fortune in history. In 1936 Henry and Edsel Ford had created the Ford Foundation, which under the grandson became the largest philanthropy in the world. Henry II and other family members continued to donate stock shares. In 1950 Henry II stepped down as president of the foundation but remained chairman of its board of trustees; that same year the foundation, which had focused exclusively on local Michigan affairs, turned toward the nation and the world. The foundation began selling shares of Ford Motor stock to the public, although the arrangements assured continued family control of the company. As Henry Ford II gradually withdrew from directing the foundation's strategy, he became disgusted with new programs that he considered radical. Under the leadership of McGeorge Bundy, the foundation took controversial positions on equal rights for minorities, making grants to overtly political organizations. In Ford's opinion, the funds should have been aimed at minority education and vocational training without getting the foundation involved in taking sides on certain issues. In 1977 he resigned from the foundation's board of trustees.

In his later years Ford suffered personal problems. His first marriage ended in divorce (in 1964), as did his second, to Maria Cristina Vettore Austin, whom he married in 1965 and from whom he was divorced in 1980. In October 1980 he married Kathleen Duross; he did not have children with either his second or his third wife. During this period he also abused alcohol. Before his death, however, he seemed to have recovered. Then, late in the summer of 1987, he contracted a strain of viral pneumonia known popularly as Legionnaires' disease and died in Detroit's Henry Ford Hospital, named after his grandfather.

Relatives remembered Henry Ford II as the successful patriarch of an extended family. Business associates knew him as a sometimes gruff and autocratic presence, a man determined to retain control of his company's affairs and always proud of his name, his heritage, and his accomplishments.

• Henry Ford II destroyed his office files and personal papers, but the Ford Motor Company Industrial Archives hold papers of business associates. Oral history interviews are in the Henry Ford Museum and Greenfield Village, both located in Dearborn, Mich. Walter Hayes, *Henry: A Life of Henry Ford II* (1990), is an informative biography written by a business associate and close friend. An obituary is in the *New York Times*, 30 Sept. 1987.

K. AUSTIN KERR

FORD, Henry Jones (25 Aug. 1851–29 Aug. 1925), journalist and historian, was born in Baltimore, Maryland, the son of Franklin Ford and Anne Elizabeth Jones. He graduated from Baltimore City College in 1868. Upon graduation he spent the next four years trying his hand at various trades, becoming in 1872 an editorial writer for the *Baltimore American*, the second largest paper in the state. In February 1875 he married Bertha Batory; they had four children.

In 1879 Ford accepted a position on the editorial staff of the *New York Sun* but missed the sophistication and elegance of Baltimore and returned in 1883 to become city editor of the *Baltimore Sun*. He remained in that position for three years, then decided to journey to Pittsburgh, Pennsylvania, to become an editorial writer on the *Commercial Gazette*, of which he was quickly made managing editor. From 1895 until 1901 he was managing editor of the *Pittsburgh Chronicle Tel-*

egraph, then served as editor of the *Pittsburgh Gazette* until 1905.

While in the newspaper business Ford began to write books and articles that brought him to the attention of academia. He became lecturer on political science at Johns Hopkins University in 1906. The following year he was appointed professor of politics and government at Princeton by the university's president, Woodrow Wilson. He remained at that position until 1923. When Wilson became governor of New Jersey he appointed Ford commissioner of banking and insurance (1912), and after he became president, Wilson appointed Ford as a member of the Interstate Commerce Commission.

Ford's first book, *The Rise and Growth of American Politics: A Sketch of Constitutional Development* (1898), was also his most important. In the late nineteenth century reformers were highly critical of the increasing scope of industrial and governmental structures, which they believed were overwhelming American society. Political parties, reformers reasoned, were justified only to the extent to which they served as vehicles for the dissemination of contrasting ideas. They insisted that modern political parties generally failed in this and degenerated into organizations devoted solely to the acquisition and maintenance of power and patronage.

Ford argued that political parties were incapable of carrying out idealistic programs because, at root, they were reflections of a human nature that is self-seeking and acquisitive. Had political parties not come into existence, the exigencies of human nature when coupled with representative government would have necessitated some other form of organization built around the pursuit of power. Any apparatus other than political parties, Ford reasoned, would have been less capable of balancing democracy and the geometrically expanding administrative structures.

Ford maintained that parties exist because they carry out political functions more effectively than any other organization in America. As the offices of government multiplied, the burdens of democracy upon the population became impossible to carry. Political parties, Ford reasoned, counteracted the centrifugal influences of an expanding democracy by providing a necessary degree of unity to government.

The era in which Ford wrote was marked by the influence of Herbert Spencer's concept that the healthiest and most efficient forms of social organization are those that survive, provided they are not permeated by corruption. Political parties, Ford wrote, engage in public affairs as a business pursuit, very much in the same way that individuals function in the marketplace. He viewed Adam Smith's "invisible hand" as promoting the general good in the political realm just as it did in economic affairs.

Ford illustrated the economy of political parties by tracing their connections to the massive immigration that occurred in the nineteenth century. Prior to Ford's work the standard imagery of the "melting pot" served to enclose discussion of immigration. Ford, however, drew attention to the fissured nature of ethnicity in America. Few American writers had even considered that the "Germans," for example, who flooded America after 1848, saw themselves not as Germans when they arrived, but as citizens of Bavaria, Prussia, or any one of seventy different principalities. Only later, after their arrival, did they see themselves as Germans and eventually as Americans. This held true, he argued, for nearly every other group that came to the United States in the nineteenth century.

One of Ford's most significant contributions to social history was studying how disparate peoples came to view themselves as unified by common interests. The party system, he wrote, was the mechanism by which immigrants were drawn into the political life of the nation. Ford neither ignored nor condemned the self-serving nature of the political process by which the immigrants used the party machines to better their lives and the parties exploited the immigrants for their votes. He simply described the processes by which the parties and immigrants interacted. The result, he demonstrated, was a political apparatus that became structurally cosmopolitan and composed of immigrant populations characterized by multiple layers of identity. These were expressed in varied allegiances: to the group, the neighborhood, communities of interest, and the party machines that, in turn, fused them into large-scale groups whose interests transcended ethnicity and locality and were, to a significant extent, national in scope.

Ford died in Blue Ridge Summit, Pennsylvania.

• Besides those works mentioned above, Ford also wrote *The Cost of Our National Government* (1909), *The Scotch-Irish in America* (1915), *The Natural History of the State* (1915), *Woodrow Wilson: The Man and His Work* (1916), *Washington and His Colleagues* (1918), *The Cleveland Era* (1919), *Alexander Hamilton* (1921), and *Representative Government* (1922). See also Richard S. Corwin, "Henry Jones Ford," *American Political Science Review* 14, no. 4 (1925): 813–16.

MICHAEL T. JOHNSON

FORD, Hugh (11 Jan. 1867–29 Dec. 1942), director and producer for theater and films, was born in Washington, D.C., the son of George Ford and Henrietta Price. He completed his education at the Van der Naillen School of Mines and Engineering.

Ford began his theatrical career as an actor; his appearance as a member of the cast of a melodrama, *The Ride For Life*, reviewed in the *New York Times* (9 Oct. 1894), may mark his first Broadway appearance. For several years he appeared in stock companies in New York and Pittsburgh. He married Jessie Weir Izett in 1898. The couple had one daughter.

From character comedian roles, Ford moved into directing stock company productions of established plays. He proved to have a tremendous capacity for enlivening familiar works. His friend Arthur Edwin Krows called him a "two-legged dynamo" who became "director-general of five stock companies in New York City for the Keith and Proctor interests," which were neighborhood theater troupes charging a top price of twenty-five cents per ticket in middle-class areas such as Harlem. Journalist David H. Wallace wrote in 1913 that a Broadway production firm, Liebler and Company, headed by producer George C. Tyler, "rescued [Ford] from the Harlem Opera House, giving him an outlet for his energies in their many big productions of the last ten years."

By 1907 Ford had become general stage director for the Liebler firm's productions. His method as director, says Krows, was to go gently, suppressing all impatience with the cast, never "bullying or brow beating," swallowing all his own frustrations "until the perspiration that starts out at such times over the tense muscles and veins of his face indicates only the triumph of an iron personal discipline." Among his major successes for Tyler's firm were *Salomy Jane* (1907), *The Man from Home* (1908), *The Melting Pot* (1909), *Alias Jimmy Valentine* (1910), *The Deep Purple* (1911), and *The Garden of Allah* (1911). Booth Tarkington, author of *The Man from Home* and other plays produced by Tyler, later wrote a novel about the theater of those years: *Presenting Lily Mars* (1933). The book's fictional producer is clearly modeled on George Tyler, and its hard-working, self-effacing, sallow-skinned director, "Pinkney Monk," may be a picture of Hugh Ford at this time.

In his autobiography, *Whatever Goes Up* (1934), Tyler says that Ford was "splendid," "the finest director alive," and he declares that without Ford's day-and-night supervision of rehearsals for *The Garden of Allah*, plagued with special effects and scenery problems, the play "would never have seen daylight at all." Ford also assisted Tyler by sketching out scenarios for plays and putting writers to work on them. In addition, he often functioned as the unacknowledged codirector and script doctor for plays in rehearsal. In 1910 playwright Louis N. Parker praised Ford's aid, patience, courtesy, and kindness to him during a new production, for which Ford received no program credit, and said in a letter to Ford that he should have been listed as "co-director" with Parker. Ford was not as successful with William Sydney Porter ("O. Henry"). Visiting the writer to persuade him to come up with a promised script, Ford had to leave after Porter, then in the last stages of alcoholism, brandished a gun at him.

Professional recognition of Ford's competent, skilled direction of plays grew. Even though his first loyalty remained with Liebler and Company, he accepted offers from other producers to stage new plays of all sorts. He was director of one of George Arliss's great successes, *Disraeli* (1911), and staged the tremendously successful garment-district comedy *Potash and Perlmutter* (1913). During this period Ford's consistent overwork and suppression of emotion contributed to periodic collapses and illnesses. A *New York Telegraph* article (30 Apr. 1912) noted that he might not get home for a week at a time during final rehearsals, just catching naps at the Lambs Club.

In the "show shop" atmosphere of the era's popular theater, Ford seemed to have directing nearly down to a science. He told Wallace: "The first thing to look for in a script is a real idea or motive. Then you decide what kind of treatment it ought to have. If it's a melodrama, you work for punches; if a farce, for snappy situations; and if you have a comedy you work for lines and situations. . . . But the important thing about every kind of play is to keep the characters human. Now let's talk about something else." Wallace noted Ford's interest in subjects outside the theater and his yearning for more time with his wife and daughter.

In 1914, Ford became director general for the East Coast studio of Famous Players Pictures, doing for movies the same kind of overseeing of scripts, direction, and productions he had done for Tyler in the theater. The credits on his forty-three films (1914–1921) list him, variously, as scenarist, codirector, and director. Many of the films were based on stage successes of the past. His principles of direction—going for "punches," "snappy situations," and so on, according to genre—were the same as in the theater. His eminence at the time was such that *Theatre Magazine* (Jan. 1918) profiled him as one of the three leading film directors of the day; the other two were D. W. Griffith and Cecil B. DeMille.

After 1916, when Famous Players merged with Lasky and Paramount, the studio's production work increasingly moved to Hollywood. Ford remained in New York to head the studio's play production department, known as Charles Frohman, Inc. In 1921 Ford left the film company and resumed stage work as director and coproducer for Tyler and others. Two of his successes in this later period were *Merton of the Movies* (1922) and *Aren't We All?* (1923). As the 1920s advanced and playgoers' tastes moved away from the formulas Ford had mastered, his successes became fewer. His final theatrical effort, *The Budget* (1932), on a depression-era theme, lasted only seven performances.

After 1932 Ford became inactive in the theater and led an increasingly secluded life pursuing other interests. He was rarely seen at the Lambs Club, a friend noted in a letter. Even during the period of his greatest success he had had an aversion to any personal publicity, especially about his private life. Now he became unresponsive to requests for biographical information. Upon his death in New York City, no obituaries were published to survey his career; there were brief death notices in the *New York Times* and *New York Herald Tribune*, both 30 December 1942. The latter lists his final occupation as "painter," a bare indication of surcease from theatrical frenzies and deadlines Ford at last allowed himself.

His enduring significance in theatrical history, despite the eclipse of his later years, is that he was one of the commercial theater's most skilled craftsmen, one whose instinct for what the public wanted in its entertainment was acute and prolonged. His significance in film history is that he was able to carry his gifts intact to the movies as they developed into feature productions, and he helped shape American film's story content and style during the formative years of the industry.

• The Hugh Ford Papers in the Manuscript Division, New York Public Library, include forty-seven letters to Ford. The Billy Rose Theatre Collection, New York Public Library for the Performing Arts, Lincoln Center, has some materials relating to his career. A list of his stage productions is in *Who Was Who in the Theatre . . . 1912–1976*. His films are listed in the *American Film Institute Catalog*, vol. 1 (1911–1920) and vol. 2 (1921–1930). Helpful contemporary articles, all with a portrait, include David H. Wallace, "Hugh Ford, A Maker of Plays," *New York Dramatic Mirror*, 3 Sept. 1913; "The Three Wise Men of the Movies," *Theatre Magazine*, Jan. 1918; Arthur Edwin Krows, "Hugh Ford—'Neverything,'" *Motion Picture Classic*, Dec. 1919. Death notices are in the *New York Times* and the *New York Herald Tribune*, both 30 Dec. 1942.

WILLIAM STEPHENSON

FORD, James William (22 Dec. 1893–21 June 1957), labor leader and Communist party official, was born James William Foursche in Pratt City, Alabama, the son of Lyman Foursche, steelworker, and Nancy Reynolds, a domestic. Not long after his birth, the family began to use a new surname when a white policeman questioning his father insisted that "Foursche" was too difficult to spell and changed the name to Ford. The most traumatic experience of Ford's boyhood was the lynching of his grandfather, a Georgia railroad worker. Ford started work at thirteen, joining his father at the Tennessee Coal, Iron and Railroad Company, where he worked as a water boy, mechanic's helper, and then steam-hammer operator. Nevertheless, he managed to complete high school.

Entering Fisk University at the age of twenty, Ford excelled in his studies and in athletics, but when America entered World War I in 1917, he withdrew from college to serve in France. He was a radio engineer in the Signal Corps and became a noncommissioned officer. He also organized a protest against the bigotry of a white captain; as a result, the officer lost his command. After his discharge in 1919, Ford returned to Fisk and graduated in 1920.

Moving to Chicago, Ford tried to get a federal job using the skills he had learned in the army, but he was rejected, apparently because of race. He played semiprofessional baseball for a time, and then in 1919 got a job as a parcel dispatcher at the post office. He soon joined the postal workers' union and served as its delegate in the Chicago branch of the American Federation of Labor. He also worked with A. Philip Randolph during the early years of the Brotherhood of Sleeping Car Porters. At his job Ford became known as a militant, quick to criticize his bosses and even the leaders of his own union. His aggressive style made enemies, and he was dismissed in 1927.

By this time Ford had abandoned his former conviction that blacks could make their way strictly through education and self-improvement. He had become interested in the left wing of the labor movement when white members of the Communist-backed Trade Union Educational League (TUEL) supported his accusations of racial discrimination in the Chicago Federation of Labor. He became a member of TUEL, helped

organize the American Negro Labor Congress in 1925, and joined the Communist party in 1926. The following year, attending the Fourth World Congress of the International Labor Union (ILU) in Moscow as a TUEL delegate, he was elected to the congress's executive committee. In 1928 Ford returned to Moscow for the Sixth World Congress of the Communist International, where he served on the party's Negro Commission. He was one of the first to identify the struggles of black Americans with those of colonized people around the world, and he pressed these views at one international conference after another during the late 1920s and early 1930s.

Moving to New York City, Ford threw himself into the activities of the party. He helped organize the Trade Union Unity League (an American affiliate of the ILU), and he directed the Negro Departments of both the TUUL and the TUEL. He was arrested in 1929 for leading a protest against the U.S. presence in Haiti, and again in 1932 during the Bonus March. In fall 1932 Ford was nominated by the Communist party for vice president of the United States. With the presidential nominee, William Z. Foster, he toured the nation's larger cities until he was disabled by a heart attack. The two received 100,000 votes. Resuming political activity in 1933, Ford became head of the Harlem section of the Communist party and also served on the party's political committee, national committee, and New York State committee.

During the early 1930s Ford was bitterly critical of black leaders, supporting his party's claim that they were "shamelessly aiding the white master class." But like many Communists, he became more amenable to cooperation once the party leadership called for a "Popular Front" against fascism in the summer of 1935. For the next several years he worked actively with black organizations like the National Association for the Advancement of Colored People, the National Negro Congress, and the Urban League. The new approach was evident during Ford's 1936 campaign for vice president. Running this time with Earl Browder, Ford called for coalitions among all progressive forces and advocated social legislation, relief for the unemployed, aid to farmers, and equal rights for blacks.

By 1940 Ford was the best-known black Communist in America. But by then the party was suffering from the country's anger over the recent pact between Stalin and Hitler—a pact that party members refused to disavow. When Browder and Ford headed the national ticket again that year, they faced investigations, arrests, and a hostile press. They received fewer than 50,000 votes, less than half their 1936 total. A year later the political winds changed again when Hitler invaded Russia. Ford, like most American Communists, then threw himself into the war effort. He now criticized other black leaders for launching the "Double V" campaign (aimed at a second victory, over racial injustice); he accused them of "aiding the Axis camp" by diverting attention from the main task of destroying Hitler.

Once the war ended and Soviet-American relations chilled again, Earl Browder was expelled from the party. Ford sided with Browder's critics, blaming his ally of twenty years for leading the party "into the swamp of revisionism." Ford was stripped of his offices but was allowed to stay in the party, and he remained a loyal member for the rest of his life. He was married twice. The name of his first wife, by whom he had three sons, is not known; his second wife was Reva. (Neither her maiden name nor the dates of his two marriages are known.) He died in New York City.

As a loyal Communist, Ford often changed his political tactics to conform to the dictates of party leadership. But Communism also provided Ford with a core of beliefs that allowed him to integrate his commitment to the labor movement, his experience as an African American, and his interest in liberation movements around the world. At his worst, he operated (in the words of one critic) as "the prototype of the pliable Stalinist functionary." At his best, he contributed to the country's dialogue on race relations by highlighting the economic and international context of the African-American experience.

• Ford left no papers, but the Schomburg Center for Research in Black Culture (New York City) has a file of clippings about his career. Ford contributed to the *Daily Worker* frequently during the 1930s and wrote a number of brochures and pamphlets, as well as *The Negro and the Democratic Front* (1938) and, with James Allen, *The Negroes in a Soviet America* (1935). Contemporary discussions of Ford's life and work include Benjamin Davis, *Communist Candidate for Vice-President of the United States, James W. Ford* (1936), William Z. Foster, *History of the Communist Party of the United States* (1952), and Wilson Record, *The Negro and the Communist Party* (1951). See also Irving Howe and Lewis Coser, *The American Communist Party: A Critical History* (1962), Philip Foner, *Organized Labor and the Black Worker, 1619–1973* (1974); Maurice Isserman, *Which Side Were You On? The American Communist Party during the Second World War* (1982), Philip S. Foner and James S. Allen, eds., *American Communism and Black Americans: A Documentary History, 1919–1929* (1987), and Fraser M. Ottanelli, *The Communist Party of the United States: From the Depression to World War II* (1991). Obituaries are in the *New York Times*, 22 June 1957, and the *Daily Worker*, 24 June 1957.

SANDRA OPDYCKE

FORD, John (1 Feb. 1895–31 Aug. 1973), motion picture director, was born Sean Aloysius O'Fearna in Cape Elizabeth, Maine, the son of Sean O'Fearna, a seaman and saloon keeper, and Barbara "Abbey" Curran. Both parents had emigrated to the United States from Galway, Ireland, and later changed their family name to O'Feeney.

Ford developed an early interest in drawing and sailing and worked as a seaman on merchant ships during his high school vacations. His application to the U.S. Naval Academy at Annapolis was rejected, and he briefly attended the University of Maine. He soon left school to travel to Hollywood, California, in July 1914. His elder brother, an actor who used the name Francis Ford, had established a film company

on the Universal Studio lots that produced westerns and serials. Ford adopted the name Jack Ford and learned the craft of filmmaking while working as a bit actor at several studios and as a general assistant for his brother. One of his first roles was riding as a Klansman in D. W. Griffith's *The Birth of a Nation* (1915).

Ford's first film as director was *The Tornado* (1917), which he also wrote and starred in. During the following six years Ford directed more than three dozen other films. In 1920 Ford married Mary McBryde Smith, a former officer in the U.S. Army Medical Corps. It was a marriage of opposites: Smith, a member of the Daughters of the American Revolution and a Protestant from the Deep South, disliked Ford's family, who considered the bride a haughty snob and were upset that the marriage had not been performed by a Catholic priest. Smith also complained that the clannish Hollywood community considered her an outsider, claiming that "there were a lot of sore heads when Jack married me. He had stepped outside the fold." The couple had two children.

In 1923 Ford moved to Fox Studios, where he began listing himself in movie credits as John Ford. *The Iron Horse* (1924), his movie about the building of the transcontinental railroad, won both critical acclaim and a hugh box office take of more than $2 million. In 1928 Ford directed *Hangman's House*, for which he first employed stunt man Marion Michael Morrison, whom Ford would later rename John Wayne.

Ford handled the transition from silent films to talkies without any difficulty and continued to turn out more hits. In 1930 he began a longtime collaboration with screenwriter Dudley Nichols on *Men without Women*, a film about submarine warfare. The pair won critical acclaim with *Arrowsmith* (1932) and *The Lost Patrol* (1934). The latter film's popularity persuaded studio executives to allow Ford to make *The Informer* (1935). This had been Ford's pet project, and he had spent several years planning it. Victor McLaughlin gave an unforgettable performance as a man who informs on the Irish revolutionaries and is subsequently hunted down and executed. The film won several Academy Awards, including one for Ford for best director, as well as his first New York Film Critics Award for best picture of the year.

Ford subsequently directed *Mary of Scotland* (1936), *The Plough and the Stars* (1936), *Young Mr. Lincoln* (1939), *Drums along the Mohawk* (1939), and *The Long Voyage Home* (1940). He received Oscars for *Stagecoach* (1939), *The Grapes of Wrath* (1940), and *How Green Was My Valley* (1941).

Prior to American entry into World War II, Ford made arrangements with the U.S. Navy to organize and train a documentary film unit. He joined the navy in 1941 with the rank of commander, and subsequently he became chief of the Field Photographic Branch of the Office of Strategic Services. Ford served in several naval battles, including the one at Midway Island, where he was wounded by machine gun bullets. He used the Midway footage to produce *The Battle of Midway* (1942), stating: "It's for the mothers of America.

It's to let them know that we're in a war and that we've been getting the shit kicked out of us for five months, and now we're starting to fight back." The film won an Oscar for best documentary of 1942.

Ford also went to Europe after the end of the war as head of an interservice group that collected photographic evidence of Nazi concentration camps for use at the Nuremberg trials. He received numerous military decorations, including the Purple Heart, the Legion of Merit, and the Air Medal. Ford retained his military connections as a naval reserve officer with the rank of rear admiral after he returned to Hollywood in 1946.

Ford's postwar western films included a trilogy based on the stories of James Wallah Bellah: *Fort Apache* (1948), *She Wore a Yellow Ribbon* (1949), and *Rio Grande* (1950). Other notable films were *My Darling Clementine* (1946); *Wagonmaster* (1950), which later inspired a television series; *The Searchers* (1956), which had immense influence on later filmmakers such as Stephen Spielberg; and *The Man Who Shot Liberty Valance* (1962). The latter contains one of the most famous lines in Ford's movies, spoken by newspaper editor Edmond O'Brien: "This is the West, sir. When the legend contradicts the facts, print the legend."

Most of Ford's westerns were filmed on location, principally in Arizona's Monument Valley. His employment of Navaho Indians from the nearby reservation as extras, bit players, and laborers (all paid, at his insistence, on the Hollywood scale) bolstered the economy of the impoverished region. He was inducted into the Navaho tribe and given the name Natani Nez, meaning "Tall Soldier."

Ford's later nonwestern films included *They Were Expendable* (1945), *What Price Glory* (1952), *Mogambo* (1953), *Mister Roberts* (1955), *The Last Hurrah* (1958), and *The Quiet Man* (1952), which won Ford his fourth Academy Award.

Ford's films were characterized by a strong artistic vision and frequently contained panoramas of magnificent outdoor settings that rendered the human actors almost insignificant. He once stated, "I think you can say that the real star of my Westerns has always been the land." His camera technique was dominated by head-high shots from a stationery camera. He used virtually no panning or any other camera movements, except for occasional tracking shots of cowboys, cavalry, or Indians during the chase scenes. Describing Ford's filmmaking, John Wayne noted, "When he pointed that camera, he was painting with it. He didn't just point it, he painted a picture each time. He didn't believe in keeping the camera in motion; he moved his people toward the camera and away from it."

Ford frequently focused on the tension between order (represented at times by the military, the cavalry, towns, and railroads) and disorder (the unsettled West, Indians, and lone gunslingers). His heroes were inarticulate, hard-drinking masculine archetypes, who frequently had ambivalent feelings about the inevitable triumph of civilization and order. The characters' strongest emotional bonds were to all-male groups such as the cattle drive team, the cavalry troop, the military squad, and the ship's crew. Female characters, with the exception of Maureen O'Hara in *The Quiet Man*, were undeveloped and had no important roles in any of the film plots. The dialogue in his films was kept sparse, since Ford relied primarily on visual scenes to convey his story. John Wayne recalled, "Ford had writers write the script, then he'd pull out three lines he'd use, lines that encapsulated what he wanted."

Throughout his career Ford tended to work with the same group of people again and again, as actors, writers, stagehands, and cameramen. He was known for his nonostentatious dress, and he frequently had both a drink and a cigar with him on the set. He wore thick glasses on account of his poor eyesight and a black patch over one eye, which had been injured in an accident during the 1940s. His later films contain an increasingly depressing outlook, owing in part to declining health aggravated by a lifelong addiction to alcohol.

Ford's films went out of fashion in the 1960s, when his conservative and rugged individualist outlook clashed with the more liberal and hedonistic spirit of the era. He was also known primarily as a director of westerns at a time when that genre was being superseded by science fiction films. His last commercial films, *Cheyenne Autumn* (1964) and *Seven Women* (1966), were not box office hits. In 1971 Ford made *Vietnam, Vietnam*, a documentary for the U.S. Information Agency, which went unreleased. A subsequent documentary, *Chesty* (1976), about U.S. Marine Corps general Lewis "Chesty" Fuller, was also never released.

Ironically, Ford's reputation among film critics began to revive at the time he was being shunned by audiences, sparked by the writings of French film theorists who developed the "auteur" theory of film direction, which regards every aspect of filmmaking as the conception of one mind—the director's. On 31 March 1973 the American Film Institute gave Ford its first lifetime achievement award for his outstanding work as a director. Ford had directed approximately 130 films over his half-century career. President Richard Nixon at the same time also awarded Ford the Medal of Freedom. Ford died at his home in Palm Desert, California.

• The John Ford Papers are at the Lilly Library, Indiana University, Bloomington. Also relevant are the production records of the 20th Century–Fox, Metro-Goldwyn-Mayer, and Warner Bros. studios at the Doheny Library, University of Southern California, Los Angeles. Ronald L. Davis, *John Ford: Hollywood's Old Master* (1995), is the best of the numerous biographies and critical studies of Ford and his films. Other useful works are Lee Lourdeaux. *Italian and Irish Filmmakers in America: Ford, Capra, Coppola, and Scorsese* (1990); Harry Carey, Jr., *Company of Heroes: My Life as an Actor in the John Ford Stock Company* (1994); Peter Bogdanovich, *John Ford* (1978); Joseph W. Reed, *Three American Originals* (1984); Dan Ford, *Pappy: The Life of John Ford*

(1979); Andrew Sinclair, *John Ford: A Biography* (1979); and Janey Ann Place, *The Western Films of John Ford* (1974) and *The Non-Western Films of John Ford* (1979). The French-inspired resurgence of Ford's reputation is examined in Peter Robert Lehman, "John Ford and the Auteur Theory" (Ph.D. diss., Univ. of Wisconsin, 1978). Helpful articles are Walter Lassally, "Ford Fever," *Sight and Sound* 61 (Nov. 1992); and Bertrand Tavernier, "Notes of a Press Attaché: John Ford in Paris, 1966," *Film Comment* 30 (July–Aug. 1994). An obituary is in the *New York Times*, 1 Sept. 1973.

STEPHEN G. MARSHALL

FORD, John Thomson (16 Apr. 1829–14 Mar. 1894), theater manager, was born in Baltimore, Maryland, the son of Elias Ford, a shoemaker, and Anna Greanor. After some education in Baltimore city schools, he left at the age of fifteen to become a clerk in his uncle William Greanor's tobacco factory in Richmond. When he found that work uncongenial, he became a bookseller. The young Ford also wrote a farce titled *Richmond As It Is*, produced with success by the Nightingale Serenaders, an established minstrel group. The manager of the Serenaders hired him to be advance agent and business manager for the troupe. From 1850 to 1854 Ford traveled the eastern seaboard and southern sections of the country with the Serenaders, gaining a personal knowledge of the theaters that would later serve him well.

Ford returned to Baltimore in 1854 and took control of the Holliday Street Theatre. He married Edith Branch Andrew (date of marriage unknown); they had eleven children. In 1856 he expanded his business by building a theater in Washington, D.C. When it burned in 1862, he rebuilt it. Ultimately he built three theaters in Washington, giving him an effective monopoly on theaters in the city. He likewise monopolized theatrical entertainment in Baltimore by building and managing theaters there, particularly the Grand Opera House (1871). At one time or another Ford provided management for seventeen theaters, among them show houses in Philadelphia, Alexandria, and Richmond.

At the time Ford began his rise to prominence as a businessman of the theater, the custom was to keep stock companies in each local theater to provide supporting actors for the popular vehicles of nationally known stars, who traveled alone or with a few leading actors for major roles. These local companies were training grounds for young aspiring actors, some of whom later became eminent themselves. For instance, when Ford took control of the Richmond theater in 1857, the company included Joseph Jefferson (as stage manager), John Wilkes Booth, and Oliver Doud Byron. In addition, over the years Ford built up a circuit of theaters extending as far south as New Orleans and booked traveling stars and some companies that he assembled himself over the entire route. Among his stars in the middle years of the nineteenth century were Edwin Forrest, Junius Brutus Booth, Charles Kean, Charlotte Cushman, Edwin Booth, and Mary Anderson. In a speech, Senator James G. Blaine once jokingly spoke of "my friend Ford, who has managed so well some theaters north of Mason and Dixon's line, and all of them south of it."

Ford is chiefly remembered today for his connection with the site of Abraham Lincoln's assassination in 1865, Ford's Theatre in Washington, D.C. He and his brother, Henry Clay Ford, were imprisoned for thirty-nine days after the assassination, as a frenzied investigation of possible conspirators began. Later both were completely exonerated. After the government seized the theater, declaring it should never be used for theatrical productions again, Ford was paid $100,000 for his loss of property. As a friend of the entire Booth family, in 1869 he arranged for the removal of John Wilkes Booth's body from its burial place in the federal prison in Washington, D.C., for reburial in the Booth family's cemetery plot. In an article for the *North American Review* (Apr. 1889), Ford wrote of his belief that Mary Surratt, whom he had met while imprisoned, was innocent of involvement in the conspiracy and—despite his attempt to save her by letters and personal appeals—was executed unjustly because favorable evidence was suppressed.

In his home city of Baltimore, Ford was an eminent civic dignitary for many years. He was a member of the city council, then its president, and for a time in 1858 the city's acting mayor. Ford fostered the organization of numerous municipal institutions, including the park system, the water works, a fire-alarm telegraph system, a salaried fire department, and a new city hall. He served as trustee for philanthropic organizations. At various times he was called on to arbitrate major business disputes. He was at one time president of the Union Railroad and was involved in numerous banking and financial concerns. As a theatrical businessman, Ford was viewed as both astute and honorable. He was said to have a gracious and ingratiating personality as well. A few sketch portraits in newspapers show him with a penetrating gaze and the full beard popular in the period. The astuteness of his honorable dealings was shown in 1878, when he was the only theater manager to pay Gilbert and Sullivan royalties on their much-pirated operetta success, *H.M.S. Pinafore*. The pair then gave Ford the North American rights to produce *The Pirates of Penzance* (1880). He leased the Fifth Avenue Theatre in New York City to showcase his production and toured it profitably for all involved.

By that time the American theater was much changed from what it was when Ford began his career. New York City had become the central point for booking road tours for companies. More and more, the rail network in place across the country made possible tours that went all over the nation, not just through a regional circuit such as Ford's. Also, producers increasingly mounted their plays and entertainments in New York City and sent out complete productions, both cast and scenery traveling by rail. As a result, local stock companies were quickly withering away. Reluctantly, Ford acceded to New York City's preeminence as the nation's theatrical capital. He discontinued stock companies in his theaters in 1881 and the same year reduced his direct control of theaters to his Grand Opera House in Baltimore. He did continue to organize repertory companies that played Shakespeare and classic comedies to tour his circuit. He also wrote a series of articles for the *Baltimore Sun* about the old English comedies. By the time of Ford's death in Baltimore, his son Charles E. Ford was manager of the Baltimore theater. One of his daughters, Martha Ford, became an actress.

In American theatrical history, Ford serves as an example of the evolution of the businessman of the nineteenth-century theater: starting out as advance man and business manager for a traveling group, rising to control theaters with resident local stock companies, managing the tours of star performers who acted with stock companies, mounting his own productions to tour a region, and at last giving way to the centralization of theater power in New York City and the rise of complete productions sent on national tours. Manager M. B. Leavitt remembered Ford as "one of the best known and one of the best liked of the old time managers."

• Materials on Ford are in the Billy Rose Theatre Collection at the New York Public Library for the Performing Arts, Lincoln Center. His business activities are detailed by his grandson in John Ford Sollers, "The Theatrical Career of John Thomson Ford" (Ph.D. diss., Stanford Univ., 1963). His professional esteem is noted in Michael Bennett Leavitt, *Fifty Years in Theatrical Management* (1912). His act of friendship for the Booth family is noted in Richard Lockridge, *Darling of Misfortune* (1932). An obituary is in the *New York Tribune*, 15 Mar. 1894.

WILLIAM STEPHENSON

FORD, Len (18 Feb. 1926–14 Mar. 1972), football player, was born Leonard Guy Ford, Jr., in Washington, D.C., the son of Leonard Guy Ford, a federal government employee. His mother's name is not known. Ford attended public schools in Washington and graduated from Armstrong High School, where as a senior he captained the football, baseball, and basketball teams and earned All-City honors in football in both 1942 and 1943. Ford recalled that his ambition was to play major league baseball, but since segregation prevented him from doing so he instead enrolled at Morgan State University, an all-black school in Baltimore, Maryland. There he played basketball and football, winning all-conference honors as a tackle his one year at Morgan. In 1944 Ford entered the U.S. Navy, where he met people who told him that at 6′5″ and over 220 pounds he should play at a higher competitive level.

As he neared his discharge in 1945, Ford wrote to schools in the Big Nine (later Big Ten) Conference regarding a transfer. He chose the University of Michigan, which under legendary coach Fritz Crisler had the type of successful program Ford sought. He was a fine end who played mainly on defense in 1946 and 1947, making major contributions to the undefeated 1947 team that trounced the University of Southern California in the 1948 Rose Bowl game. The season was marred only when Notre Dame edged out the Wolverines for the top spot in a controversial national poll. Ford did not make any of the most prestigious All-American teams, however, and attributed the slight to racism. Ford's view is understandable but not necessarily correct, for Michigan had two men who rated All-American status, the acclaimed tailback Bob Chappuis and offensive end Bob Mann, a black athlete who was selected to some of the postseason All-American squads. Other teammates also received national attention. Few blacks then played major college football in the North and none played in the South, and Ford was recognized by his selection to play in the College All-Star game in 1948.

Ford then joined the Los Angeles Dons of the short-lived All-America Football Conference (AAFC), playing end both on offense and defense during the 1948 and 1949 seasons. His speed, strength, and sure hands made him a standout receiver, and he was also known as a crushing blocker. When the league disbanded at the conclusion of the 1949 campaign, Ford was selected by the rival Cleveland Browns in a special dispersal draft. The Browns had been the most successful franchise in the AAFC and were one of a handful of teams from it absorbed by the National Football League (NFL). Already blessed with outstanding receivers, Cleveland coach Paul Brown believed Ford's greatest contribution to Cleveland would be as a defensive specialist. According to Browns' assistant Blanton Collier, Ford "had the speed and hands to be a fine tight end. But he was so devastating on defense that we knew this was his natural spot. Len was very aggressive and had that touch of meanness in him on the field that you find in most of the great defensive players. He certainly was the top defensive end of his time and maybe as good as any who played the game." In 1950 the Browns, who had several black regulars, entered the NFL, which had begun to integrate its personnel only in 1946. Ford's season was ruined, and his career was jeopardized, in a mid-October game against the Chicago Cardinals in which he was elbowed in the face by an opposing blocker and suffered a broken nose, two cheekbone fractures, and the loss of several teeth. Cleveland owner Mickey McBride charged the player with deliberate roughness, but Ford minimized the incident, saying he had forgotten to duck. After having plastic surgery, he rehabilitated more quickly than expected. Wearing a specially designed helmet, he rejoined the team in time to play an important role in the league championship game in which the Browns defeated the Los Angeles Rams.

Between 1951 and 1955 Ford reached his peak, winning All-Pro recognition each season and intercepting two passes in the Browns' 1954 championship victory over the Detroit Lions. As a mature athlete he weighed 265 pounds, and his size and quickness allowed him to dominate opposing players. He zealously shed blockers to keep runners from turning his corner and to harass opposing quarterbacks. Defensive coach Collier even recalled that the Browns, who had been using a standard six-man line, accommodated Ford's prowess as a pass rusher by dropping two men off the line so Ford at end would be positioned closer to the opposing quarterback. By allowing Ford to take a sharper angle when rushing the quarterback, this alignment made him more difficult to block. The Browns thus became one of the first teams to switch to the 4–3 defensive alignment that became increasingly popular in the 1950s. Six times the Browns defense led the league in fewest points allowed, and Ford's skill in rushing the passer was instrumental in the team's success.

Cleveland, which had begun to rebuild, sold Ford to the Green Bay Packers following the 1957 season, and Ford retired after one season there. With a career total of twenty fumbles recovered he held the league's lifetime record in that category at the time of his retirement, and he won recognition along with the Baltimore Colts' Gino Marchetti as one of the two dominant defensive ends of the 1950s. At Michigan and during his early years in the NFL, Ford also made a contribution as a pioneering black athlete. His task was especially difficult in the NFL, which had barred blacks from competition for nearly a generation prior to 1946, but in Paul Brown he had a coach who looked for talent first.

After his retirement Ford, who made Detroit his home, worked as a recreation director for the city and also sold real estate. He was married to an attorney and had two children, but the couple divorced. Ford died in Detroit. He was posthumously selected to the Professional Football Hall of Fame in 1976.

• A clipping file on Ford is at the Professional Football Hall of Fame, Canton, Ohio. Also helpful are Howard Roberts, *The Big Nine: The Story of Football in the Western Conference* (1948); Allison Dawzig, *The History of American Football* (1956); Murray Olderman, *The Defenders* (1973); Bill Levy, *Return to Glory: The Story of the Cleveland Browns* (1965); Bill Cromartie, *The Big One* (1994 ed.); Paul Brown with Jack T. Clary, *PB: The Paul Brown Story* (1979). An obituary is in the *New York Times*, 15 Mar. 1972.

LLOYD J. GRAYBAR

FORD, O'Neil (3 Dec. 1905–20 July 1982), architect, was born in Pink Hill, Texas, the son of Bert Ford, a railroad engineer, and Belle Sinclair. He attended elementary school in Sherman, Texas, from 1910 to 1918. His father's death in late 1917 in a railroad accident led to his family's move to Denton, Texas, where Ford attended Denton High School from 1918 until his graduation in 1924. Ford's only college education was at North Texas State Teacher's College in Denton from 1924 to 1926, with Ford receiving a manual training teaching certificate from the college. Simultaneously, Ford enrolled in the architecture course offered by the International Correspondence School, receiving their diploma in 1926.

Ford's first professional architectural training came as an assistant to the Dallas architect David R. Williams, for whom Ford worked from 1926 until 1932. Williams ran a small office, and he and Ford became lifelong friends. Perhaps of the most importance in terms of Ford's later development was Williams's interest in the indigenous architecture of Texas, the vernacular buildings of Spanish colonial settlers and early Anglo-American settlers. These structures, concentrated in the area around San Antonio and Fredericksburg, were the subject of several automobile tours by Williams and Ford. These tours were documented in photographs and sketches by the two architects, and the character of these buildings greatly influenced Williams and Ford's work. In 1929 Ford was given his first opportunity to design on his own. The commission was for a studio for the Dallas artist Jerry Bywaters. Ford's design reflected the architectural character of a German immigrant's house in New Braunfels, Texas, with the front porch sheltered by the leading edge of the roof. The following year he designed a new house for Bywaters, which, in contrast to the studio, reflected a more national interest in American colonial architecture.

In 1932 Ford left Williams's office to establish his own practice. During the early years of the Great Depression, Ford's practice was limited to private residences, the majority of which were in Dallas. In 1937 he received a major commission for a house in San Antonio for T. Frank Murchison, in which he again made use of regional elements such as numerous shaded porches to control the summer heat. This was the first of Ford's works to be published in an architectural journal. In 1939 Ford, in association with his partner, Arch Swank, won a juried competition for the chapel at Texas State College for Women in Denton. Now known as the Little Chapel in the Woods, the chapel was built of native stone, with the interior dominated by a series of brick parabolic arches. The combination of traditional and contemporary forms found in this design are hallmarks of Ford's style. That same year, Ford was given a significant appointment by Williams, his former employer, who was then the assistant administrator of the National Youth Administration in Texas. The NYA, in collaboration with the city of San Antonio, planned a restoration and building campaign for the area known as La Villita, a concentration of eighteenth- and early nineteenth-century vernacular structures just south of the city's downtown. This job led to Ford's moving to San Antonio from Dallas and to his marriage to Wanda Graham in August 1940. They had four children.

In 1946 Ford formed a partnership with Gerald Rogers, and in 1948 the firm was chosen to design the new campus of Trinity University in San Antonio, a continuing task that occupied Ford's career until his death. The Trinity project, which originally called for a dozen buildings to be built between 1950 and 1955, made use of a new, less costly structural system, the Youtz-Slick Lift-Slab process, which involved the pouring of structural floor slabs in concrete and then lifting them up the steel structural piers using hydraulic jacks. This new technology was coupled with Ford's interest in passive solar design and the use of tawny regional brick to produce a homogeneous campus, including major works such as the Taylor Music Center and Fine Arts Building (1958), Parker Chapel

(1966), and Laurie Auditorium (1971). In 1958 Ford's interest in new technology again manifested itself in his design for the Texas Instruments Semi-Conductor Components building, in Dallas. The building made use of a modular form covered by a hyperbolic paraboloid concrete roof designed and engineered by the Mexican engineer Felix Candela.

In the 1960s Ford's office continued to produce a large number of residential designs, and the growth of the firm led to the creation of Ford, Powell and Carson in January 1967. The new firm became involved in the design of HemisFair in San Antonio, contributing the theme structure, the Tower of the Americas, completed in 1968. The major project of the 1970s was the design of the new campus of the University of Texas at San Antonio, located north of the city. In spite of his deteriorating health, Ford remained active in the 1970s and 1980s, continuing to speak out in favor of the preservation of San Antonio's historic buildings, one of his favorite causes. He died in San Antonio.

Ford's significance as an architect stems from his ability to make use of both traditional eighteenth- and nineteenth-century architectural forms and materials as well as the building technology and forms of his own time. His sensitivity to the needs of building in the Southwest, with its severe summer climate, led him to adopt an inclusive approach to architectural design, making use of both historic and contemporary architecture for possible design solutions. He was also a leader in the field of historic preservation, especially in San Antonio. Lastly, he was an inspiring mentor to a number of architects who continue to practice in Texas.

• Ford's architectural drawings and other primary graphic materials are housed at the office of the architectural firm of Ford, Powell and Carson, Architects, located in San Antonio. Ford's most important published work, "Toward a New Architecture: II. Organic Building," appeared in *Southwest Review* 17 (Winter 1932): 215–29. In this article he discusses his design philosophy as well as his interest in regional architectural forms and their relevance to contemporary design. Ford's life is most fully discussed in Mary Carolyn Hollers George, *O'Neil Ford, Architect* (1992), which contains a nearly complete list of his architectural commissions and an extensive bibliography.

JOHN C. FERGUSON

FORD, Paul (2 Nov. 1901–2 Apr. 1976), actor, was born Paul Ford Weaver in Baltimore, Maryland, the son of Louis Weaver, a businessman, and Effie Ford. Ford graduated from public high school in Germantown, Pennsylvania, in 1918. In 1920–1921 he attended Dartmouth College, where he first appeared onstage with the Dartmouth Players as Sir Lucius O'Trigger in *The Rivals*. He left college at the end of the first year for financial reasons. Information concerning Ford's personal life before he became a professional actor is anecdotal and often ambiguous.

After leaving college, Ford sold newspaper advertising space and worked as a traveling magazine salesman throughout the Midwest and Pennsylvania. In 1924 he

married Nell Campbell; they had five children. By the early thirties Ford was living in Harlem. Hard-pressed to support his family during the Great Depression, Ford worked at whatever jobs came his way: adding machine salesman, proofreader, pulp fiction writer, caterer, night watchman, puppeteer, gas station attendant. His childhood adeptness at making and manipulating puppets served him well when, with a friend, he produced and acted in puppet shows at various sites at the 1939–1940 World's Fair. This activity rekindled his interest in acting, and at the age of thirty-eight he gave up a makeshift home catering business to take a $3-a-week job acting two roles in a long-lost summer theater production called *Skidding*. Soon thereafter he appeared in *Steel* (19 Dec. 1939, Provincetown Playhouse, N.Y.C.).

Starting in 1940 Ford sought work in radio, but he failed in his first audition. Taking his mother's maiden name (by dropping the surname Weaver), he successfully auditioned a second time as Paul Ford and spent the next year acting without pay on Sundays for a public radio station. In 1942, giving up a secure $112-a-month job as a gas station attendant, Ford concentrated on radio acting in an attempt to move closer to theater. He soon began to make his living exclusively in radio, playing sheriffs, neighbors, and politicians while acting in continuing series such as "Just Plain Bill," "The Goldbergs," and "Ma Perkins." Concerning his employment, Ford remarked, "When I began bringing home $225 a week, my wife was convinced that I wasn't just trying to escape from real work" (*New York Sunday News*, 7 June 1964, p. 4). Even though Ford did not think highly of his radio acting career, the work paid the bills and, supplemented by off-Broadway experience, helped to prepare him for his theatrical, film, and television career.

In February 1944 Ford traded in the then princely rewards of his radio career for a livable $86 a week to act in a very minor role in his first Broadway show, *Decision* (Belasco Theatre). Critics did not mention Ford's acting, but the production provided three months of valuable Broadway experience. Over the next three years, with critics continuing to ignore him, Ford took small roles in a series of brief productions: *The War President* (Apr. 1944, Shubert); *Lower North* (Aug. 1944, Belasco); *Kiss Them for Me* (Mar. 1945, Belasco); *Mr. Cooper's Left Hand* (Sept. 1945, Wilbur—Boston tryout; closed Oct. 1945); *Flamingo Road* (Mar. 1946, Belasco); *On Whitman Avenue* (July 1946, Cort); and *Another Part of the Forest* (Nov. 1946, Fulton).

The year 1947 was pivotal in Ford's legitimate theater career. He performed in *As We Forgive Our Debtors* in March at the Princess Theater and received welcome praise from critics. This warm acclaim brought Ford the role of Arthur Malcolm, a fatuous U.S. congressman in the hit production *Command Decision* (Oct. 1947, Fulton). Impressed with Ford's acting "an unctuous, bumptious Congressman so well he must have once been one" (New York *Sun*, 2 Oct. 1947), the critics en masse defined Ford's stage persona and established his career in comedy. The growing perception of Ford's talents as a character actor culminated in his being awarded the role of Charley in the prestigious 1949–1950 U.S. tour of Arthur Miller's *Death of a Salesman*. He returned to Broadway in the poorly received *The Brass Ring* in April 1952 (Lyceum) and was, for the most part, overlooked by critics. Ford opened to acclaim in *The Teahouse of the August Moon* (Oct. 1953, Martin Beck), in the part of Colonel Wainwright Purdy III, one of his best-known characters. The role established him as a leading comic actor who delighted audiences with his portrayal of a fuming, fulminating, fatuous, bumbling, sputtering army colonel. Ford took a hiatus from Broadway when the two-and-a-half-year run of *Teahouse* conflicted with his television commitment to the "Phil Silvers Sgt. Bilko Show." He returned in March 1957 in *Good as Gold* (Belasco) and followed with *Whoop-Up* (Dec. 1958, Shubert), two ill-received works. In June 1959 he replaced David Burns as Mayor Shinn in *The Music Man* (Majestic), making such a good impression that he was awarded the same role in the film version three years later. Two major hits followed: *A Thurber Carnival* (Feb. 1960, ANTA Theatre), a revue in which Ford beguiled the audience and critics by acting in various Thurberesque roles; and *Cradle and All* (July 1962, Dennis Playhouse, Dennis, Mass.) The latter, a pre-Broadway tryout, was retitled *Never Too Late* and opened in November 1962 at the Playhouse in New York. Ford played Harry Lambert, an unwilling older parent about to become a father again. He received critical and popular acclaim for his acting in these two productions, and he admitted that he had finally become a star when in *Never Too Late* his name appeared on the marquee above the title of the play. Four years later Ford entered the final leg of his theatrical career, a period during which he was able to pick and choose his roles. Noteworthy for the sheer volume of plays in which he performed, Ford was rather inept at selecting high-quality original works in which to star, but he astutely placed himself in the lead roles of successful revivals. In 1966 he appeared in the short-lived *3 Bags Full* (Mar. 1966, Henry Miller's Theatre), and later that year he acted in a stock tour of a revival of *You Can't Take It with You* and the lackluster *Send Us Your Boy*. Returning to Broadway, Ford performed in approximately one play a year until his retirement. Productions include the unsuccessful *What Did We Do Wrong?* (Oct. 1967, Helen Hayes) and revivals of *Harvey* (Summer tour, 1968), *Captain Brassbound's Conversion* (Fall 1968, Ahmanson, L.A.), *Three Men on a Horse* (Oct. 1969, Lyceum), *The Front Page* (Jan. 1970, Ethel Barrymore), and *Light Up the Sky* (1971 tour). *Fun City* (Jan. 1972, Morosco), a slight comedy, was Ford's last play on Broadway. After the 1972 summer revival tour of *Sabrina Fair*, he retired from the stage. During this period it was generally acknowledged that Ford was a hard-working major comedic figure on the American stage.

Ford's film work began in 1945. Paralleling his development in theater, he advanced from short character walk-ons to larger comedy parts and reprises of major roles he had made famous on Broadway. While acquiring valuable film experience, but no critical recognition, Ford took very small parts over the next five years: a sergeant in *The House on 92nd Street* (1945, Twentieth-Century-Fox); a detective in *Naked City* (1948, Universal); a sheriff in *Lust for Gold* (1949, Columbia); a lawmaker in *All the King's Men* (1949, Columbia); a judge in *Perfect Strangers* (1950, Warner Brothers); and a denizen of the Old West in *The Kid from Texas* (1950, Universal). In *The Teahouse of the August Moon* (1956, MGM), Ford reprised the part of Colonel Purdy. The reviews were mixed, with some critics feeling that the film had been directed as burlesque comedy. Critic Bosley Crowther described Ford as "a bag of windy clichés as the colonel whose command is being undermined," but he admitted that Ford fit the farcical pattern quite well (*New York Times*, 30 Nov. 1956). Ford was next relegated to the role of a bartender in *The Missouri Traveler* (1958, Buena Vista), a film that did not reach the New York critics. In *The Matchmaker* (1958, Paramount), the film version of the Broadway hit, Ford starred successfully as Horace Vandergelder, the only important film role of his career that he had not previously acted on Broadway. Though the Broadway charm of earlier days was missing, Ford's portrayal of a rich, miserly, cynical curmudgeon of a storeowner was the film's "outstanding job" (A. H. Weiler, *New York Times*, 13 Aug. 1958). Reprising the role of Mayor Shinn in *The Music Man* (1962, Warner Brothers), Ford was generally considered "outrageously comic as the chuckle-brained Mayor of the town" (Bosley Crowther, *New York Times*, 24 Aug. 1962). Earlier that year he had gone unnoticed as a senator in *Advise and Consent* (1962, Columbia) and as a judge in *Who's Got the Action* (1962, Paramount). Taking the cameo role of Colonel Wilberforce among numerous top-flight comedians in *It's a Mad, Mad, Mad, Mad World* (1963, United Artists), Ford was singled out for praise. The part of Harry Lambert in *Never Too Late* was one of Ford's favorite Broadway roles, and Ford was praised by critic Judith Crist when he redid the part in the film version (1965, Warner Brothers): "Paul Ford, anyone? Put that lumbering form and disillusioned-rooster face on film and ask for nothing more" (*New York Herald Tribune*, 5 Nov. 1965).

The conclusion of Ford's film career was disappointing. He did a competent job as the tight-fisted banker in the well-received western comedy *A Big Hand for the Little Lady* (1966, Warner Brothers), but his work in *Lola* (1973, American International) and the animated film *Journey Back to Oz* (1974, Filmation), were not reviewed by the New York critics. Ford received scant notice in the cameo roles of Fendal Hawkins in the successful *The Russians Are Coming, The Russians Are Coming* (1966, United Artists), an amorous American general in *The Spy with a Cold Nose* (1966, Embassy), and a presidential aspirant who had run on the Vegetarian party ticket in *The Comedians* (1967, MGM).

Ford debuted on television in 1948 during the medium's commercial infancy. He appeared frequently in television shows, but the extent of his television career seems to have been limited by the magnitude of his theater and film work. Even so, his face, voice, and mannerisms became well known nationally because of his exposure in the role of the irascible, furious, and fuming Colonel T. J. Hall on the "Phil Silvers Sgt. Bilko Show" (Sept. 1955–June 1959, CBS). Comparing his television persona to his work in theater and film, Ford noted, "It's a curious thing. I've worked in 14 plays and 9 movies, some important, too, and people don't know me. I play an incidental character in TV, and they approach me like I was a genius" (*New York Mirror*, 21 Aug. 1968). His television appearances included standard mild television fare such as "Bloomer Girl" (May 1956, NBC), "Junior Miss" (Dec. 1957, CBS), and "The Girls in 509" (Apr. 1960, WNTA). Ford reprised the role of Colonel Purdy in a television adaptation of *The Teahouse of the August Moon* (1962, NBC) and traveled to Hollywood to star in a short-lived series titled "The Baileys of Balboa" (1964–1965, CBS). He appeared in numerous rebroadcasts of his films, talk shows, and programs such as "Alfred Hitchcock Presents." Ford never seemed to care much for television work and summed up his feelings in a trenchant remark in an interview in the *New York Daily News*: "I imagine having the big part in 'The Baileys' will be tough, but they tell me you can get pretty rich doing a TV series, and that was the lure. I prefer to do my acting on stage" (7 June 1964, p. 4).

Ford's acting career began at the close of World War II and continued through the decades of the Cold War, the Korean War, the Vietnam War, and political assassination. The American people had been emotionally drained and wanted Ford to make them laugh. Ford, however, wished to be considered a "serious" actor and had worked assiduously at portraying his more important roles as fully realized characters. Nevertheless, his tall form, elongated face, and protuberant nose favored comedy. Critics likened him to one of James Thurber's cartoon dogs, and one interviewer observed, "Mr. Ford does indeed have the mournful mien, complete with dangling dewlaps, of a bassett, and his voice sounds appropriately forlorn" (*New Yorker*, 16 Apr. 1960, p. 34). He excelled as a bilious, fuming colonel, a bumbling small-town mayor, and a cantankerous, rich but miserly middle-aged widower. In these guises Ford built his career, made his fortune, and was well received by the public. His favorite parts were Colonel Purdy, Harry Lambert, and the roles in *A Thurber Carnival*. His retirement years were spent among family and with his friends at the Players' Club in New York City. Ford died in Mineola, Long Island, New York.

• Ford's work in films can be seen on videocassettes and discs. The Theatre Collection of the New York City Public Library for the Performing Arts at Lincoln Center houses a folder cataloged as *Paul Ford—Clippings*, which contains newspaper and magazine articles, theater reviews, playbills, and biographical press releases. Reviews of Ford's work by critics such as Howard Taubman, John Chapman, Brooks Atkinson, Ward Morehouse, Kay Gardella, and Robert Coleman are in the major New York City newspapers, including those that flourished during Ford's career and have ceased publishing—the *New York Mirror*, the *New York World Telegram and Sun*, the *New York Herald Tribune*, and the *New York Journal-American*. An obituary is in the *New York Times*, 14 Apr. 1976.

DAVID GILD

FORD, Paul Leicester (23 Mar. 1865–8 May 1902), historian and novelist, was born in Brooklyn, New York, the son of Gordon Lester Ford, a businessman and political figure, and Emily Ellsworth Fowler, a poet. As a baby Ford suffered a tragic fall that left him with a severely deformed spine, the pain from which would plague him all his life. Moreover, the nature of the injury dictated that Ford wear a special harness as a child. As a result he received very little formal schooling; instead, he was tutored at home and allowed the free run of his father's private library of more than 50,000 volumes, including perhaps the largest private collection of Americana in the world. At age eleven he acquired a small printing press, with which he began publishing compilations of historical material gleaned from his father's library.

Ford's first work, *Webster Genealogy* (1876), traced the family tree of Noah Webster, Ford's great-grandfather. In 1881 he edited and published an exchange of letters between Webster and George Washington, and the following year he published *Websteriana*, a bibliography of Webster's works. Although these early efforts were largely antiquarian, Ford's later projects were scholarly endeavors that focused on important figures of American history. These projects included *[Benjamin] Franklin Bibliography* (1889), *Writings of Christopher Columbus* (1892), the ten-volume *The Writings of Thomas Jefferson* (1892–1899), *The Writings of John Dickinson* (1895), *The True George Washington* (1896), *The Many-Sided [Benjamin] Franklin* (1899), and the two-volume *The Journals of Hugh Gaine, Printer* (1902). In between these major projects, Ford compiled dozens of minor bibliographies relating to early national American literature. He also edited and published an impressive number of obscure but significant historical documents. Some of these documents Ford found in his father's collection; others he rooted out of obscure resting places. In 1890, on one of his many extended visits to Europe, he spent a great deal of time and effort ferreting American historical documents out of the British Record Office. Most of his findings on this trip eventually found their way into print later that year and the next as part of a series known as Winnowings in American History. The series was published by the Historical Printing Club, a joint effort by Ford, his brother Worthington, their father, and occasionally Ford's sister Emily. This sort of historical detective work was a source of great delight to Ford, as these finds came at a time in American historiography when a newly discovered letter or manuscript could significantly alter the conventional interpretation of historical events. Ford was often criticized for his perceived shortcomings as a historian; he was accused of treating George Washington and the Puritans with excessive levity and occasionally crossed swords over factual matters, such as the authorship of certain issues of *The Federalist*. But he seemed unperturbed by negative reviews: "I shall not mind fair or unfair criticism till I find someone else making books without imperfections or errors. Till then I shall accept the first with thanks and the last with as good counter raps on the knuckles as I am capable of " (Du Bois, p. 128).

Ford also made important contributions as a journal editor. From 1890 to 1893 he coedited *Library Journal*, and in 1893 he briefly served as associate and managing editor of *Charities Review*. As editor of *Library Journal*, Ford embarked on a crusade of sorts to improve library service. He suggested that libraries specialize in only a few fields and acquire titles accordingly. He also proposed that libraries open the stacks to readers, form union catalogs, and offer interlibrary loan, all of which were revolutionary ideas at the time.

In 1894 Ford broadened his horizons as a man of letters by publishing his first novel, *The Honorable Peter Stirling*. Set in New York City, the novel portrays one man's rise to political power through the exercise of political flexibility and pragmatic compromise. Although Ford denied it, the novel's title character was almost certainly modeled after then president Grover Cleveland. As fiction *The Honorable Peter Stirling* is weak in several areas; its romantic plot is boring, and its political plot is too preachy. Nevertheless, the novel became a bestseller. By 1945 the book had gone into its seventy-sixth printing and had sold more than half a million copies. In 1899 Ford published his second novel, *Janice Meredith*, the story of a courtship amidst the swirl of the American Revolution. Although hackneyed by today's standards, *Janice Meredith* was well received because it neither portrayed Americans as dashing and flawless nor the British as vile and despicable. Within ten months of publication, the novel had sold more than 200,000 copies. By 1901 Ford had earned enough in royalties to build a fine mansion in Manhattan.

The success of these two novels benefited Ford greatly, for his scholarly works had brought him only marginal financial success and, at times, had been subsidized by his father.

The deaths of Ford's father in 1891 and his mother two years later left Ford and his brother Worthington in charge of sorting out the family estate. The elder Ford's will left his library to the two brothers, who donated the bulk of its contents to the New York Public Library in 1899. They divided the rest of the estate among six of the seven surviving Ford children. In 1894 Malcolm, the disinherited son, sued unsuccessfully to have himself included in the settlement of the estate. During the trial, Ford acted as principal spokesman for the family; while under oath, he blamed his father's demise on Malcolm, from whom his father had contracted the typhoid fever that led to his death. Apparently the public humiliation coupled with the financial loss played on Malcolm's mind to the point that, in 1902, he shot and killed Ford in his Manhattan study. Ford left behind a wife, Grace Kidder, whom he had married in 1900; their daughter was born shortly after Ford's death. At the time of his death, Ford had published fifty-four articles, forty-nine books and pamphlets, and fourteen works of fiction.

• Collections of Ford's papers are in more than a dozen libraries; the primary repositories are the Paul L. Ford Papers at the New York Public Library and the Paul Leicester Ford Collection in the Beinecke Rare Book and Manuscript Library at Yale University. The best account of Ford's life, as well as a complete list of his publications, is in Paul Z. Du Bois, *Paul Leicester Ford: An American Man of Letters, 1865–1902* (1977). The significance of Ford's historical endeavors is assessed in Lester J. Cappon, "A Rationale for Historical Editing Past and Present," *William and Mary Quarterly*, 3d ser., 23 (Jan. 1966): 56–75. An obituary is in the *Evening Post*, 9 May 1902.

CHARLES W. CAREY, JR.

FORD, Tennessee Ernie (13 Feb. 1919–17 Oct. 1991), country-music entertainer, was born Ernest Jennings Ford in Bristol, Tennessee, the son of Clarence Thomas Ford, a postal worker, and Maude Long. Ford grew up in a religious family that valued song as an expression of faith. He later said of music, "It was part of our religion, part of our way of life. . . . God and the Bible meant a lot to us, and hymns and spirituals and gospel songs seemed to us just about the best way of saying what was in our hearts and minds" (*This Is My Story, This Is My Song*, p. 75).

After graduating from high school in 1937, Ford briefly attended the Virginia Intermount College at Bristol as a music student but dropped out to work as an announcer for WOPI, a local radio station. Ford later attended the Cincinnati (Ohio) Conservatory of Music in 1939 and then moved to Atlanta, Georgia, to work as a disc jockey at WATL.

After the Japanese attack on Pearl Harbor in 1941, Ford enlisted in the Army Air Corps, where he rose to the rank of lieutenant. He trained as a bomber navigator and was an instructor at an air base in Victorville, California. Ford married Betty J. Heminger, a secretary at the air base, in 1942. The couple had two children.

After his discharge in 1945, Ford worked as a disc jockey on several radio stations in California and Nevada. At station KXLA in Pasadena, California, Ford invented the radio persona of "Tennessee Ernie," a naive and languid-voiced hillbilly with whom he conducted on-air interviews without his listeners realizing there was only one person speaking.

Ford also resumed his singing career in Pasadena, where he performed on country-western band leader Cliffie Stone's radio show "Hometown Jamboree." Stone, who would later become Ford's business manager, was impressed by Ford's deep baritone-bass voice and encouraged him to pursue his singing career. Stone also introduced Ford to guitarist Merle Travis, who later wrote Ford's most famous song, "Sixteen Tons."

Stone helped Ford obtain an audition with Capitol Records, and in 1948 he landed a recording contract. Ford produced a number of country music hits under the Capitol label, including "I'll Never Be Free," "Anticipation Blues," "Mule Train," "Smokey Mountain Boogie," which he wrote with Stone, and two of Ford's own compositions, "Shotgun Boogie" and "Blackberry Boogie."

The popular recordings led to a series of nightclub performances in 1950 and offers to host network radio shows for ABC and CBS. In 1953 he became the first country-music singer to perform at London's Palladium Theatre. The following year he made his television debut, appearing on several "I Love Lucy" shows and as a replacement host for Kay Kyser on NBC's "College of Musical Knowledge."

Ford carved a niche in American popular culture in 1955 with his song "The Ballad of Davy Crockett," which became the theme song of an immensely popular Walt Disney television program. But Ford had an even bigger recording hit that same year. "Sixteen Tons" was a single that sold more than 1 million copies within three weeks of its release, eventually selling 20 million copies worldwide. In 1957 Ford released *Hymns*, an album of spiritual music that by 1963 had become Capitol Records' most popular album up to that point.

In 1955 Ford also began hosting his own television program, "The Tennessee Ernie Ford Show," which began as a daytime show on NBC. Ford was so popular that the J. Walter Thompson advertising agency contracted with Ford to host a nighttime musical variety show sponsored by the Ford Motor Company. "The Ford Show" premiered on NBC in October 1956 and initially received low ratings. Public interest soon increased, however, and it eventually became one of the network's most popular shows. Viewers were won over by Ford's genial personality and low-key country approach. "Bless your little pea-picking hearts" became his signature address, and he would close each program with a hymn. In 1961 Ford left the show to spend more time with his family but returned to television a year later, hosting "The Tennessee Ernie Ford Show," which ran on ABC from April 1962 to March 1965.

Both during and after the period he hosted his own show, Ford made frequent guest appearances on other television programs and scheduled numerous nightclub performances with his own musical group. He also made many other recordings, particularly of spiritual and inspirational music. Ford was awarded a Grammy in 1964 for his album *Great Gospel Songs*. He later said, "Of all the singing I do, the hymns, spirituals, and gospel songs not only give me great pleasure but seem to be something that truly needs to be done. People may get all steamed up about big new love songs that come along, but let's not forget that hymns and spirituals are the finest love songs of them all."

Although his television show was still popular in 1965, Ford decided the task of producing a weekly series was too time-consuming. He limited himself to producing records, performing personal concerts, and working at his 540-acre cattle ranch in Clear Lake, California. Subsequent television work was limited to occasional guest appearances on musical variety shows and television specials. In 1968 Ford also provided the voice of an animated character in "Mouse on the Mayflower."

Ford hosted the annual awards show for the Country Music Association from 1969 to 1971. In 1974 he led the first American popular musical group to tour the Soviet Union, and in 1984 President Ronald Reagan awarded Ford the Medal of Freedom.

Ford's first wife died in 1989; later that same year he married Beverly Woodsmith. In 1990 the Country Music Association elected Ford to the Country Music Hall of Fame. He died in Reston, Virginia.

• No Ford papers are available, but Ford published an autobiography, *This Is My Story, This Is My Song* (1963). He is mentioned in George T. Simon, *The Best of the Music Makers* (1979), Patrick Carr, ed., *The Illustrated History of Country Music* (1979), and Minnie Pearl and Joan Dew, *Minnie Pearl: An Autobiography* (1980). Obituaries are in the *New York Times* and the *Washington Post*, both 18 Oct. 1991.

STEPHEN G. MARSHALL

FORD, Thomas (5 Dec. 1800–3 Nov. 1850), governor of Illinois and historian, was born near Uniontown, Pennsylvania, the son of Robert Ford and Elizabeth Logue, farmers. His father died in 1803, and Ford's remarkable mother moved her numerous family to Spanish Louisiana the next year, only to learn upon arrival at St. Louis that the free land she expected to find there was not available after the Louisiana Purchase. The Ford family located across the Mississippi at New Design, Illinois, where Thomas Ford received his first schooling and hired himself out to labor.

Through the influence of his devoted older half brother, George Forquer, who prospered first as a carpenter and later as a lawyer and politician in the new state of Illinois, Ford was able to attend Transylvania University for a year. He then studied law himself with Daniel Pope Cook, the son-in-law of Ninian Edwards, Illinois's territorial governor and one of its first U.S. senators. Duff Green invited Ford to help edit a Jacksonian campaign paper in St. Louis in 1824, and Ford practiced law between 1825 and 1829 with Forquer in Edwardsville, Illinois. His identification with the party of Andrew Jackson remained constant from this time. Ford married Frances Hambaugh in 1828, and they had five children.

In 1829, again through the intercession of Forquer, who was Illinois attorney general and influential in Edwards's powerful political faction, Ford was appointed state's attorney for Illinois's Fifth Judicial Circuit in the thinly settled western part of the state. For the next twelve years he served in the state's judiciary, being elected a circuit judge by the state legislature in 1835 and to the state supreme court in 1841. In this circuit duty Ford was constantly on the move, mostly in relatively remote sections of the state, where violence and vigilantism were not unknown, hardly having a chance either to establish a permanent residence or to become identified with any particular region. He was nonetheless able as a judge to meet and take the measure of many lawyers who would become Illinois's key legal and political figures, and he was invariably present, because of the concurrent term of the state supreme court, at the sessions of the general assembly. Thus, though no politician himself, he was well acquainted with politics and politicians, and on the bench he became known for honesty, ability, and legal learning. With such a positive and uncontroversial reputation, Ford was considered an ideal Democratic replacement for Adam W. Snyder in the 1842 Illinois gubernatorial campaign after Snyder died in May of that year. Though pressed into the campaign late, Ford prevailed in the August election against the Whig Joseph Duncan, and he entered the only popularly elective office that he was to hold.

As governor Ford came to office at the bottom of the depression following the panic of 1837. He had to deal most memorably with the anti-Mormon violence in Hancock County between 1844 and 1846 and with the financial problems created by failed banks and an unwise internal improvement program undertaken by the general assembly in the late 1830s. In the case of the Mormons, Ford had to contend with the assassination of Joseph Smith at Carthage, Illinois, in June 1844 and with the violence between Mormons and non-Mormons that continued until late 1846. He found himself utterly unable to protect the Mormons against the overwhelming antipathy of the majority of Illinoisians. Illinois militiamen, whose responsibility it was to deal with violence on so large a scale, were partisans themselves and could not be compelled to maintain order between the Mormons and their enemies. Ford saw, as eventually did the Mormon leaders themselves also, that the only solution would be for the Mormons to leave the state.

In straightening out the state's financial affairs, Ford urged that Illinois reduce its indebtedness by retiring bonds held by the failed state banks; that it negotiate a loan to complete the Illinois and Michigan Canal, which eventually connected Chicago with the Mississippi River; and that it guarantee to all internal improvements bondholders that they would be reimbursed with canal tolls at the end of the current hard times. His apolitical background insured that Ford had few political debts to pay and was a relatively free agent, hence he could and did actively direct the legislature. His financial program eventually came to pass, and Illinois's fiscal reputation was made secure.

Constitutionally Ford was unable to succeed himself as governor. Upon leaving office he and his family moved to Peoria, Illinois, where he unsuccessfully attempted to establish a law practice and became ill with tuberculosis. During 1847 and 1848 he wrote his *History of Illinois* (1854). This book should be considered the most enduring monument to Ford's life and servic-es. It covers the first thirty years of Illinois statehood, a period that Ford knew firsthand, and nearly half of it covers his gubernatorial administration. Ford wrote with an acerbic pen, and much of the book is defensive and somewhat self-serving, yet he also wrote with an unrivaled sensitivity to the problems of establishing new self-governing communities in frontier areas and to the social bases of politics. He was acutely aware of the strengths and weaknesses of democracy, and some of his observations compare well with those of Alexis de Tocqueville on the same topic. His book is a superior non-Mormon source on the Hancock County difficulties with which Ford had to contend. The scope and sophistication of the book is such that it is the major text for Illinois history during this period, and Ford's observations have a general relevance to the understanding of frontier political conditions in the Jacksonian Era. Ford died in Peoria.

• A thorough coverage of Ford's gubernatorial administration is in Evarts B. Greene and Charles M. Thompson, "Governors' Letter-Books, 1840–1853," in *Collections of the Illinois State Historical Library* (1911). David McCulloch, *Historical Encyclopedia of Illinois and History of Peoria County* (1902), contains a brief autobiography. A recent biographical sketch of Ford is in Robert P. Howard, *Mostly Good and Competent Men: Illinois Governors, 1818–1988* (1988). An earlier one is in Milo M. Quaife's introduction to the 1945–1946 edition of Ford's history. Biographical sketches by contemporaries are in John Reynolds, *My Own Times* (1855), and Charles Ballance, *The History of Peoria, Illinois* (1870). Evenhanded accounts of Ford's involvement with the Mormons are in Robert B. Flanders, *Nauvoo: Kingdom on the Mississippi* (1965), and Dallin H. Oaks and Marvin S. Hill, *Carthage Conspiracy* (1975). The most recent assessment of Ford's *History of Illinois* is by Rodney O. Davis in the introduction to the 1995 edition.

RODNEY O. DAVIS

FORD, Whitey (12 May 1901–20 June 1986), vaudeville and country musician and comedian, also known as the Duke of Paducah, was born in DeSoto, Missouri, fifty miles from St. Louis. The names and occupations of his parents are unknown. When he was one year old his mother died, and he was sent to Little Rock, Arkansas, to be reared by a grandmother. Ford attended Peabody Grammar School, acting in school plays and performing in talent shows. He ran away at age seventeen to join the navy during World War I and served four years. During this time he practiced on the tenor banjo, at that time a competitor with the guitar, until he became an accomplished performer. Jimmie Rodgers played the tenor banjo before he took up the guitar for his country material.

Ford's first foray into the musical field was in the genre of Dixieland, organizing Benny Ford and His Arkansas Travellers in 1922. Ford took this popular form of music (primarily performed by white musicians, distinguishing itself from the similar New Orleans jazz style that was played by blacks) on the road. Performing in small towns with his Dixieland band, as well as with other ensembles playing popular and country music, Ford made use of medicine shows, tent shows, burlesque, and vaudeville to earn a living. Ford first broadcast on KTHS, Hot Springs, Arkansas, in 1924, after which he played the Keith-Albee vaudeville circuit with Otto Gray's Oklahoma Cowboys. At this time the western swing of the territories had begun to make its impact on country music and was at the height of its popularity at this stage in his career.

In the 1930s Ford's comedic talents caught the attention of Gene Autry, who invited him to become part of his radio show on WLS in Chicago. WLS was one of the first radio stations to broadcast country music across the nation. Ford often had his wife (the details of his marriage are unknown) planted in the audience to answer his lines. These broadcasts capitalized on the homesickness and rustic tastes of the thousands of transplanted white ruralists—much as the country blues of the 1920s had appealed to the black populations living in cities; they proved immensely popular. Doing comedy, playing the banjo, and acting as master of ceremonies, Ford came into the three roles that would stay with him throughout his career.

Before 1937 Ford had joined the musical program "Showboat" on WLS, which became the "WLS Barn Dance." During this period of his performing career, Ford began to be known as the Duke of Paducah, capitalizing on his comic capabilities and assuming the role of a rube attempting sophistication: "They told me to read plenty of books in college so I went over to the library and they had a smart alec sissy behind the desk. I said, 'I'd like to have the life of Caesar.' He said, 'I'm sorry but Brutus beat you to it.'"

In 1937 Ford left WLS to act as master of ceremonies on "Plantation Party," which was broadcast over the NBC network. He was also the program's main comedian, writing the script and beginning a collection of jokes that later comprised more than half a million. He stayed with the show until 1939.

Ford was a partner with brothers Red and Cotton Foley in broadcasting the "Renfro Valley Barn Dance." The show originated from Renfro Valley, Kentucky, in 1939 and capitalized on the national appetite for country music. It was the first program to be broadcast from a rural region rather than from studios in Chicago or Cincinnati.

In 1942 Ford went overseas to perform for the men and women stationed abroad during World War II. After his return, on 19 September, he did his first show on the Grand Ole Opry, a venue that is generally recognized as the pinnacle of country music showcases. Ford found a home on the Opry for the next sixteen years. During this period he developed his coat of arms, which consisted of button shoes, two corn cobs, and a wagon. This capitalized on his famous closing line, "Take me back to the wagon boys, these shoes are killin' me."

During the 1950s and 1960s millions of Americans watched the Duke of Paducah perform on television shows such as "The Jimmy Dean Show," "Gary Moore," "The Red Foley Show," "The Porter Waggoner Show," and the Grand Ole Opry. Ford also

made up to 200 personal appearances a year, which were reminiscent of his career's beginnings in vaudeville and tent shows. He enjoyed playing to a live crowd in small towns and cities with country fans, doing a monologue as well as playing a number or two on his tenor banjo.

A look at Ford's material, available in recorded form on *Button Shoes, Belly Laughs and Monkey Business* (Starday, 1961) and *At the Fair* (Starday, 1963), as well as on transcribed 1953 Royal Crown Cola radio programs, gives a vision of rustic humor. He made use of what would later be considered offensive topics—jokes about his fat wife, for instance. Nonetheless, Ford's contributions to country music entertainment were substantial. Like many country comics—often a costumed musician in the band—Ford offered a relief from the hard times mirrored in the downhearted lyrics of country music. The sentimental and rousing qualities of the music were offset by his self-deprecating personage.

Ford was well thought of by his contemporaries. He became an after-dinner speaker in his later years and frequently chose self-fulfillment and happiness as topics. He retired to a chicken farm in Brentwood, Tennessee, near Nashville. Confined to a nursing home, Ford died of cancer.

• Ford donated his writings, more than 600 scripts, and a collection of 499 books to the Emory University library in 1985. His scrapbooks and other personal material are at the Country Music Foundation archives, Nashville, Tenn. Ford published two books, *These Shoes Are Killin' Me* (1947) and *Funneee* (1980). Douglas B. Green, *Country Roots: The Origins of Country Music* (1976), has some information on Ford. There is an entry on him in Barry McCloud, *Definitive Country* (1995).

PATRICK JOSEPH O'CONNOR

FORD, Worthington Chauncey (16 Feb. 1858–7 Mar. 1941), historical editor and bibliographer, was born in Brooklyn, New York, the son of Gordon Lester Ford, a businessman, civic and cultural leader, and bibliophile, and Emily Ellsworth Fowler, an author and a granddaughter of Noah Webster. In addition to five younger sisters, Ford had two younger brothers, Malcolm Webster Ford, a sporting-world habitué, and Paul Leicester Ford, a hunchback and prolific man of letters. Paul and Worthington edited and printed on their home press eighty or so bibliographical and documentary books and pamphlets between 1876 and 1899. They also helped their father create a library that contained 160,000 books, pamphlets, and manuscripts by 1891, the year of his death. Paul and Worthington donated the collection, valued at almost $200,000, to the New York Public Library in 1899. Three years later the greatest personal tragedy of Ford's life occurred. Malcolm, disinherited by their father, argued with Paul over money, shot him to death, and then immediately committed suicide in front of a witness.

After attending the Brooklyn Polytechnic Institute, Ford enrolled in the class of 1879 at Columbia College but withdrew short of graduation because of increasing deafness. He published his revision of David A. Wells's *Wells' Natural Philosophy: For the Use of Schools* (1879) and espoused Wells's theories concerning free trade and tax reform, became a cashier for a Long Island insurance company (1879–1882), and wrote columns on finance and economics for the *New York Evening Post* and the *New York Herald* (1882–1885). He also wrote *The American Citizen's Manual* (2 vols., 1882–1883), a pioneering civics text arguing for free trade, more liberal immigration, and civil service reform and against political bossism and exploitation of Native Americans. President Grover Cleveland appointed Ford chief of the Bureau of Statistics, State Department (1885–1889) and chief of the Bureau of Statistics, Treasury Department (1893–1898). Part of the time between these appointments, he engaged in private study in Washington, D.C. (1889–1891). Later, he was chief of the Statistical Department of the Boston Public Library (1898–1902). In 1899 he married Bettina Fillmore Quin, of Washington; they had two children. While serving as chief of the Division of Manuscripts at the Library of Congress, Ford wrote and did editorial work (1902–1909). In 1903 he inspected government records in Guam, Hawaii, and the Philippines, and an executive order issued by President Theodore Roosevelt that same year enabled Ford to gather into the Library of Congress historical documents from the State Department and other government agencies.

In 1909 Ford, already a successful scholar and editor, was named editor of publications at the Massachusetts Historical Society. He had to fight the entrenched indolence of Samuel Abbott Green, who was the society librarian and senior vice president, until Green's death in 1918. Intensely busy, Ford installed a photostat machine at the society office in 1914 and started a series called Photostat Americana. He edited more than fifty books for the society and did significant bibliographical work as well. His most fruitful friendship at the organization was with Charles Francis Adams, Jr., the son of President Abraham Lincoln's minister to England and the brother of Henry Adams. Through this contact, Ford helped open the Adams family treasure trove of documents. He was elected president of the American Historical Association in 1917. After resigning from his society post in 1929, he was appointed director of the European Mission of the Library of Congress (1929–1935). His charge was to seek out and order copies of materials that concerned American history and which were in European archives and libraries. He and his wife took up residence at Le Vésinet, outside Paris. She died there in 1931. Although funds for his project were cut off in 1933, Ford remained in France. He last visited the United States in 1937 to complete work on an edition of Henry Adams's letters. In 1938 Ford returned to France despite news that the German army had invaded Austria. When France fell in 1940, he escaped to the unoccupied Riviera, traveled early in 1941 over the Pyrenees into Spain and on to Lisbon. He headed home on a vessel owned by an American export line but died of exhaustion a week later at sea.

Ford, widely regarded as the most prolific editor in the field of American historiography who ever lived, published well over 250 separate works; these include reports, articles, and books he either wrote, edited, or compiled. In addition, he wrote many unsigned items and contributed indirectly to the production of other books. The following works he edited are indicative of his range and success: *Letters of William Lee* . . . (3 vols., 1891); *Historical Manuscripts in the Public Library of the City of Boston* (annually, 1900–1904); *Diary of George Washington, September–December 1785* (1902); *Journals of the Continental Congress, 1774–1789* (15 vols., 1904–1909); William Bradford, *History of Plymouth Plantation, 1620–1647* (2 vols., 1912; considered by some Ford's finest scholarly work); *Writings of John Quincy Adams* (7 vols., 1913–1917); *Letters of John Singleton Copley and Henry Pelham, 1739–1776* (1914); *Thomas Jefferson Correspondence* . . . (1916); *A Cycle of Adams Letters, 1861–1865* (2 vols., 1920); *War Letters, 1862–1865, of John Chipman Gray* . . . *and John Codman Ropes* . . . (1927); *Letters of Henry Adams* (2 vols., 1930, 1938). These titles represent only a sampling of Ford's various projects. Most are graced with his brief but cogent introductions and annotations. In addition, Ford saw several works by others through the press, notably C. F. Adams, Jr.'s autobiography (1916), *The Education of Henry Adams* (1918), and Albert J. Beveridge's unfinished biography of Lincoln (1928). One misfortune should be mentioned. Ford's edition of *Winthrop Papers* (1925) proved hasty and inaccurate, was recalled and destroyed (then redone by others), and occasioned Ford's resignation from the Massachusetts Historical Society. It was inevitable that Ford, who worked rapidly and for dangerously long hours, should display some weaknesses. His monumental strengths, however, included his grasp of American history, his ability to see value in neglected documents, and his professional generosity.

• Most of Ford's incredibly voluminous papers are at the New York Public Library and at the Massachusetts Historical Society in Boston. Many letters by Ford are also in the archives and administrative files of several historical offices and research libraries, notably the American Antiquarian Society, the Boston Public Library, the John Carter Brown Library, the William L. Clements Library, and the Library of Congress as well as in a few historical and state associations. The best sketch of Ford's life and survey of his career is L. H. Butterfield, "Worthington Chauncey Ford, Editor," *Proceedings of the Massachusetts Historical Society* 83 (1971): 46–82. Paul Z. DuBois, *Paul Leicester Ford: An American Man of Letters, 1865–1902* (1977), provides details of Ford's relationship with his brothers Paul and Malcolm and his joint activities with the former. Edward Chalfant, *Better in Darkness: A Biography of Henry Adams, His Second Life, 1862–1891* (1994), contains information on Ford's friendship with Henry Adams. Obituaries are in the *New York Times*, 8 Mar. 1941, and in the *Proceedings of the Massachusetts Historical Society* 51 (1941): 10–14.

ROBERT L. GALE

FORDNEY, Joseph Warren (5 Nov. 1853–8 Jan. 1932), lumberman and congressman, was born on a farm near Hartford City, in Blackford County, Indiana, the son of John Fordney, a farmer and mill owner, and Achsah Cotton. The youngest of ten children, Joseph Warren Fordney spent his childhood caring for his chronically ill mother and felling trees for his father's sawmill. At age thirteen he hired out as a farmhand, receiving ninety dollars a year and three months of schooling in return for his labor. Although Fordney had an affinity for mathematics, his formal education ended after a single summer. In 1867 he left the farm to serve as the water boy on a railroad construction crew.

In 1869 Fordney's father moved his family to Saginaw, Michigan, where he hoped to find employment in the rich pinelands of the Saginaw Valley. Joseph worked as a grocery clerk while learning to write and do arithmetic in his spare time, but he soon left home for a nearby lumber camp. After four years as a chore boy, teamster, and cook, Fordney started logging in the winter and assisting land locators during the summer off-season. Known as timber cruisers, these specialists sought out valuable tracts of timber and estimated the number of board feet they would produce. Cruising promised Fordney a substantially higher income, and in 1873 he married Catherine Haren. They had thirteen children, nine of whom survived infancy.

Despite his limited education, Fordney quickly became an expert cruiser. In 1879 he began working for Detroit lumberman Wilhelm Boeing and in 1883 became a partner with a one-third interest in the business. The two men pioneered logging operations in Michigan's Upper Peninsula, but Fordney's duties carried him throughout the prime forestlands of the Midwest, the South, and the Pacific Northwest. Along the way he not only amassed a sizable fortune but also developed an extensive knowledge of the nation's timber resources. These assets would serve Fordney well in his future positions as a legislator and business associate of timber magnates Frederick Weyerhaeuser and William Gilchrist.

In 1887 Fordney settled in Saginaw, which was struggling to recover from the collapse of the local lumber industry by broadening its economic base. When Boeing died three years later, Fordney became the city's preeminent businessman and the vice president of the Saginaw Board of Trade. In 1895 local Republicans persuaded him to run for city alderman. Fordney handily defeated his Democratic opponent and received the chairmanship of the Pavement and Sewer Committee. Although his ambitious program of civic improvement helped turn taxpayers against the Republicans, Fordney survived the electoral backlash and constructed the first bridge over the Saginaw River during his second term.

In 1898 Fordney's popularity prompted the Republican party to nominate him for U.S. representative. He faced a tough race because the loggers and millworkers of Saginaw favored silver coinage and generally voted Democratic, as did the city's large German population. Yet Fordney managed to beat Democrat Ferdinand Brucker, the prosilver incumbent, by a margin of 1,709 votes. Fordney confronted only one serious challenge in his eleven subsequent bids for reelection, and the Eighth Michigan District remained a secure Republican seat for the next twenty-four years.

During his freshman term in the House, Fordney received minor committee assignments that limited his influence on key legislation. However, in 1899 he distinguished himself during deliberations over the Cuban Reciprocity Treaty. Favored by coastal sugar refiners and their representatives, this measure proposed granting a preferential import duty to Cuban raw sugar. Fordney saw it as a threat to the American sugar beet industry, which had just taken off in Michigan, and his outspoken opposition helped defeat the treaty. Although the measure passed the following year, "Sugar Beet" Fordney had earned the respect of party leaders on both sides of the aisle and a reputation as a strong protectionist.

In recognition of his experience as a lumberman, Fordney received a seat on the Committee on Public Lands during his second term. In 1902 he also assumed the chairmanship of the Committee on Expenditures in the Navy Department. Fordney did not achieve his real goal until 1907, however, when Democratic Speaker Joseph G. Cannon appointed him to the Ways and Means Committee. Fordney used his seat to advocate the high timber and sugar tariffs desired by his fellow lumbermen, but in 1909 he had to compromise on the lower rates set by the Payne-Aldrich Act. Fordney vowed to avoid compromise in the future, and in 1911 he helped block a reciprocal tariff for Canadian agricultural products.

Fordney failed to alter the main provisions of the 1913 Underwood-Simmons Tariff, which reduced import duties on 958 items and placed both sugar and lumber on the free list. However, the outbreak of World War I soon disrupted foreign trade and distracted legislators from the issue of tariff reform. Fordney preferred to finance American military preparations through debt rather than taxation, but he cooperated with his Democratic colleagues in drafting several wartime revenue acts. After the armistice he supported legislation to relieve postwar distress in Europe and introduced a soldiers' bonus bill that drew heavy fire in the House.

The climax of Fordney's career came in 1920, when the Republicans regained control of Congress and the White House. Appointed chairman of the Ways and Means Committee, Fordney could finally craft his own tariff legislation. In 1922 he achieved his goal with passage of the Fordney-McCumber Tariff, which raised import duties to unprecedented levels. Satisfied with his handiwork, he retired the following year to pursue agricultural and oil development interests in Michigan. He died in Saginaw, which benefited from his charitable bequests and his previous service as chairman of the city planning commission.

Like many timber capitalists of his day, Fordney was a self-made man who espoused the philosophy of laissez-faire economics. As a legislator, however, he consistently supported federal intervention on behalf of business in the form of high tariffs. The Fordney-McCumber Tariff epitomized conservative protectionism, and by throttling trade it thwarted the prompt repayment of European war debts and prefigured the disastrous "beggar-thy-neighbor" policies of the 1930s.

• No single collection of Fordney's papers exists, but he is represented in the Michigan Historical Collections at the University of Michigan. John Andrew Russell's book-length biography, *Joseph Warren Fordney: An American Legislator* (1928), focuses heavily on Fordney's activities as a member of the House Ways and Means Committee. See also James Cooke Mills, *History of Saginaw County, Michigan* (1918). For a discussion of the role lumbermen like Fordney played in their communities, see Jeremy W. Kilar, *Michigan's Lumbertowns: Lumbermen and Laborers in Saginaw, Bay City, and Muskegon, 1870–1905* (1990), and Theodore J. Karamanski, *Deep Woods Frontier: A History of Logging in Northern Michigan* (1989). Obituaries are in the *Detroit News*, 8 Jan. 1932, and the *New York Times*, 9 Jan. 1932.

ANDREW H. FISHER

FOREMAN, Carl (23 July 1914–26 June 1984), producer and screenwriter, was born in Chicago, Illinois, the son of Isidore Foreman and Fannie Rozin, milliners. Foreman studied at the University of Illinois (1932–1933), Northwestern University (1935–1936), and the John Marshall Law School (1936–1937). During his schooling he supported himself as a newspaper reporter, press agent, radio writer, fiction writer, little theater director, and carnival barker. He dropped out of law school in 1938 to pursue a career in motion pictures and moved to Hollywood, where he found work as a story analyst and film laboratory technician while continuing to write. In 1940 he broke into the movies at Monogram Pictures, a low-budget studio, where he collaborated on a series of Bowery Boys pictures. He served as a writer-producer in the Army Signal Corps from 1942 to 1945, during which he worked for a while as a writer for Frank Capra's celebrated "Why We Fight" documentary series.

On his discharge from the service in 1945 Foreman went to work for Republic Pictures. Then, in 1948, he teamed up with producer Stanley Kramer and publicist George Glass to form Screen Plays Inc., an independent production company that specialized in inexpensive pictures based on social issues. The breakdown of Hollywood's venerable studio system beginning in 1948, the result of federal antitrust action that forced the major film companies to divorce their extensive theater chains; increasing public dissatisfaction with typical Hollywood fare; and the growing popularity of television opened the field to newcomers. Having greater access to theaters than ever before, independent producers like Screen Plays attempted to attract attention by targeting a segment of the audience largely ignored by Hollywood: literate, socially and politically aware adults.

Describing his objective as a filmmaker, Foreman told *Sight and Sound*: "I've only one thing to say really, one basic theme. I'm involved with the struggle of the individual against a society that for one reason or another is hostile . . . there *must* be such a struggle. Sometimes it's a struggle for dignity, sometimes for fulfilment, but a struggle continues. The mass can't help but move in on the individual." Following this tack, Foreman wrote a series of hard-hitting social problem pictures. *Champion* (1949), based on a Ring Lardner short story, was a gritty, realistic drama with a background of corruption in the boxing world; *Home of the Brave* (1949), based on the Broadway play by Arthur Laurents, attacked racism and bigotry in the armed forces; *The Men* (1950) dramatized the psychological and physical traumas of hospitalized World War II veterans; and *High Noon* (1952) presented a portrait of community cowardice in the American West. *Champion*, *The Men*, and *High Noon* all received Academy Award nominations for best screenplay. *High Noon*, which was interpreted by some as alluding to Hollywood during the Communist witch-hunt, also won the Writers Guild Award.

During the production of *High Noon* in 1951 Foreman was called to testify before the House Committee on Un-American Activities (HUAC). When asked the inevitable question, "Are you now or have you ever been a member of the Communist Party?," he invoked "the diminished fifth," a variation of the Fifth Amendment protection from self-incrimination. He testified that he was not a party member, but he declined to answer if he had been in the past. Moreover, he refused to name names of people who had been members of the party. Classified as an "uncooperative witness," Foreman was shunned by the industry. He severed his business relationship with Kramer and attempted to start his own independent production company with Gary Cooper, the star of *High Noon*, but *Los Angeles Times* columnist Hedda Hopper brought pressure on Cooper to dissociate himself from the venture.

Emigrating to London in 1952, Foreman worked as a screenwriter for British films and television. His work received no credits under his own name, including his screenplay for Joseph Losey's *The Sleeping Tiger* (1955), which he wrote as Derek Frey. In 1957 Foreman was hired by producer Sam Spiegel to ghostwrite the screenplay for *The Bridge on the River Kwai*. Columbia Pictures was financing the picture and would not have employed anyone on the blacklist, with the result that Foreman and Michael Wilson, a blacklisted writer who worked with him on the final draft of the screenplay, went uncredited. A masterpiece depicting the insanity of war, *The Bridge on the River Kwai* won five Academy Awards, including the Oscar for best screenplay. The writing laurel went to Pierre Boulle, a Frenchman who wrote the novel on which the film was based and who received official screen credit. (In a special ceremony in 1985 the Academy of Motion Picture Arts and Sciences changed the screen credit of the movie and awarded Oscars to Foreman and Wilson posthumously.)

As a result of Foreman's screenplay for *Kwai*, Columbia offered to finance a series of pictures produced and/or written by him in England, on the condition that he first clear himself before HUAC. Foreman did so through his attorney, Sidney Cohn, who arranged with HUAC chairman Francis E. Walter for Foreman to denounce himself as a former Communist party member in closed session but to indict no one else. As a result of this maneuver, Foreman broke the blacklist without becoming an informant.

Under the banner of his newly formed independent production company, Open Road Films, Ltd., Foreman produced and wrote *The Key* (1958), *The Guns of Navarone* (1961), *The Victors* (1963, his sole directorial effort), *Mackenna's Gold* (1969), and *Young Winston* (1972). His screenplays for *The Guns of Navarone*, a World War II epic based on an Alistair MacLean novel, and *Young Winston*, a film based on the early life of Winston Churchill, were nominated for Oscars. All were mainstream commercial efforts, but only *The Guns of Navarone* became a critical and box office hit. Foreman's other motion-picture work included serving as executive producer of *The Mouse That Roared* (1959), *Born Free* (1966), *The Virgin Soldiers* (1969), and *Otley* (1969).

During his years in England, Foreman was showered with honors and awards. According to *Variety*, Foreman "had more Royal premieres in Britain, 13, than any other filmmaker." His highest honor came in 1970, when Queen Elizabeth II made him a Commander of the Order of the British Empire (CBE).

After spending twenty-three years abroad, Foreman returned to the United States in 1975 to resume his career in Hollywood. He wrote and prepared TV projects for MCA-Universal and Warner Bros., few of which got off the ground. For the movies, he received story credit for *Force 10 from Navarone* (1978), a sequel to his earlier film. His final credit for the big screen was on Irwin Allen's *When Time Ran Out* (1980), a disaster film co-written with Stirling Silliphant.

Foreman died in Beverly Hills. He had been married twice, to Estelle Barr and Evelyn Smith, and had three children. Foreman is remembered today as one of the few Hollywood filmmakers during the fifties who attempted to create cinema of social commitment.

• Foreman's reminiscences were recorded in 1959 by the Columbia University Oral History Project. His published screenplays are found in *Young Winston: The Screenplay of the Film* (1972) and *Three Major Screenplays* (1972), ed. Malvin Wald and Michael Werner. Foreman's own ideas about screenwriting are found in Penelope Houston and Kenneth Cavander, "Interview with Carl Foreman," *Sight and Sound* 27 (Summer 1958): 220–23. The fullest treatment of his career is Malvin Wald, "Carl Foreman," *Dictionary of Literary Biography 26: American Screenwriters*, pp. 104–9. Production histories of the films Foreman wrote in partnership with Stanley Kramer are contained in Donald Spoto, *Stanley Kramer, Film Maker* (1978). Foreman's encounters with HUAC are described in Victor S. Navasky, *Naming Names* (1980).

See also Maurice Yacowar, "Cyrano de H.U.A.C.," *Journal of Popular Film* 5 (Jan. 1976): 68–75. Obituaries are in the *New York Times*, 27 June 1984, and *Variety*, 4 July 1984.

TINO BALIO

FOREPAUGH, Adam (28 Feb. 1831–22 Jan. 1890), circus owner, was born in Philadelphia, Pennsylvania, the son of John Forepaugh, a butcher and veterinary surgeon, and Susannah Heimer. After leaving Philadelphia at the age of sixteen, he worked his way westward to Cincinnati and eventually earned a small fortune as a livestock speculator. After returning to his hometown he began to invest in omnibus lines while buying and selling horses for horsecar lines in New York City, where he next set up business.

As an acknowledged expert in judging horseflesh, Forepaugh became one of the largest purveyors of horses in New York State, selling, according to estimates at the time, as many as 10,000 head in a single year. In the normal pursuit of his business Forepaugh often sold his animals to the owners of small circuses, an enterprise notoriously given to uncertainty. In 1862, when circus impresario John "Pogey" O'Brien proved unable to meet his financial obligations, Forepaugh accepted half ownership in the man's circus as payment on the debt.

To enlarge his circus menagerie Forepaugh began his practice of buying out other smaller shows. His first acquisition was the collection of animals belonging to the Mabie Brothers, who were about to retire from the business. Within two years, their circus much enlarged, Forepaugh and O'Brien decided to go their separate ways and split the show. Forepaugh remained in Philadelphia with his half; it featured Dan Rice, the most famous clown in America at the time. So great was the success of the show, which played under the name of Dan Rice's Circus and Menagerie, that Forepaugh reportedly paid his feature attraction the then unheard of amount of $1,000 a week.

In 1866 Forepaugh took his show on tour for the first time under his own name, the Great Forepaugh Show, Circus, Menagerie and Roman Hippodrome. His collection of animals having greatly expanded, Forepaugh hit on the idea of displaying the menagerie in a separate tent from the main performance, thus allowing many of his would-be patrons to visit the zoological display as an educational experience while avoiding what some considered the more morally objectionable main performance.

For the next ten years, despite its continued growth, the show traveled about the country by horse-drawn wagons. Then, in 1877, the Forepaugh Circus began traveling on its own railroad train, the Barnum and Bailey organization having by this time solved the difficulties of rail travel and demonstrated its usefulness to the circus. Forepaugh's only serious competition by then was Barnum and Bailey. The vituperative nature of the rivalry and the exaggerated claims of each were largely responsible for damaging public confidence in circus advertising. When P. T. Barnum began displaying a rare "white" elephant, Forepaugh retaliated in 1884 by advertising his own "sacred white elephant." While Barnum's was the genuine article, and therefore more pink than white, Forepaugh's was a whitewashed fake. Ironically the public preferred the fake. The circus rivals also clashed in their promotion of two other elephants—Jumbo and Bolivar—both of which were claimed to be the largest such animal in captivity. The deception and dishonesty that Forepaugh employed in promoting his attractions suggest a cavalier attitude toward the public that imitated the flimflammery Barnum often used in promoting the attractions of his museum.

Despite the damage he caused to be visited upon the reputation of all circuses, Forepaugh was universally considered to be an astute businessman. He stationed himself at the main entrance to the big top and, it was said, could tell within a few dollars how much money was in the till by the time the show began, thereby rendering himself immune from cheating employees. He could recite the exact receipts of his show in almost any town it ever played. His show had only one losing season and often earned a net profit of $250,000. His first chore each day, recalling his father's trade and the employment of his youth, was to drive directly to the local butcher shop of whatever town his circus was playing and purchase the daily supply of fresh meat, computing in his head the price of what he had purchased. Later he would butcher the meat himself.

When Barnum neglected to renegotiate his contract with New York City's Madison Square Garden for 1887, Forepaugh won the contract. His willingness to accede to a joint appearance of the two shows won him an agreement from his rivals to end their competition and divide the territory between them for the next four years. Although other circuses of the time might have been bigger, Forepaugh rightfully boasted that he "owned, controlled and exhibited more wild animals and individually possessed more show property than any other person in the world." In 1888 shortly before his death he presented the elephant Bolivar to his native city.

Forepaugh was twice married, first in 1861 to Mary Ann Blaker, with whom he had three children, including Adam Forepaugh, Jr., who became a noted elephant trainer in his father's and other circuses. His first wife died in 1878, and in 1884 Forepaugh married Mary Gertrude Tallman; his second marriage was childless.

Forepaugh died of pneumonia at his home in Philadelphia. After his death the Forepaugh circus and its title were bought by James Bailey. The title was finally retired in 1911.

Forepaugh made the display of rare and wild animals a standard part of the American circus. While his contributions to the reputation of the American circus were not always positive, his self-reliant management practices remain a model for any impresario who would be successful in this precarious field of entertainment.

• The Historical Society of Pennsylvania in Philadelphia houses a good deal of information on the Forepaugh family tree as well as the permutations of the family name from Vorbach to Forbach and finally to Forepaugh. Also on file there is Adam Forepaugh's obituary in the *Public Leger*, 24 Jan. 1890. The Billy Rose Theatre Collection at the New York Public Library for the Performing Arts, Lincoln Center, contains several pieces of contemporary anecdotal information. Various aspects of Forepaugh's circus career are noted in several books about the American circus, few of which, it should be noted, are in agreement about the dates of various episodes. The most extensive such discussion can be found in the 1963 Dover edition of Earl Chapin May's *The Circus from Rome to Ringling*. A briefer account appears in Charles Philip Fox and Tom Parkinson, *The Circus in America* (1969). Because much of Forepaugh's fame is derived from his rivalry with P. T. Barnum, the various biographies of his rival also offer some information on him. See in particular Irving Wallace, *The Fabulous Showman* (1959); Neil Harris, *Humbug: The Art of P. T. Barnum* (1973); and Arthur Saxon, *P. T. Barnum: The Legend and the Man* (1989).

ERNEST ALBRECHT

FORESTER, C. S. (27 Aug. 1899–2 Apr. 1966), writer, was born Cecil Lewis Troughton Smith in Cairo, Egypt, son of George Smith, British education official, and Sara Troughton. In 1901 Sara Smith moved back to London with her children so that they could have an English education. George Smith remained in Egypt for some years. Forester studied at Dulwich College, a prestigious British public school, until at age eighteen he attempted to enlist in the army to fight in World War I. Diagnosed as having a weak heart, he was rejected, but he evidently did not suffer from cardiac problems at this time. He then began medical studies at Guy's Hospital, London, in 1918. Lacking motivation, he failed a key exam and dropped out after a row with his family about his dissipated lifestyle and desire to be a writer. Changing his name to Cecil Scott Forester (he came to be known generally as C. S. Forester), he embarked on a literary career.

Forester trained himself as a writer by turning out lightweight biographies like *Napoleon and His Court* (1924), *Josephine, Napoleon's Empress* (1925), and *Victor Emmanuel II and the Union of Italy* (1927); and pot-boiler romances like *The Paid Piper* (1924) and *A Pawn among Kings* (1924). He barely earned enough for food and shelter. Nevertheless, in 1926 he was able to marry Kathleen Belcher, a star field hockey player; they had two sons.

Fortunately, his thriller *Payment Deferred* (1926) was successfully dramatized as a play (in London) and as a film, with Charles Laughton starring in both. Given a contract to write screenplays, Forester moved to Hollywood in 1932. He remained in California the rest of his life but never became an American citizen.

Living in Los Angeles and then Berkeley, Forester wrote historical novels as well as screenplays. He gradually developed a reputation as an entertaining, accurate, action-oriented storyteller with such novels as *Death to the French (Rifleman Dodd)* (1932); *The Gun* (1933); *The African Queen* (1934), later made into a highly regarded film starring Humphrey Bogart and

Katharine Hepburn; and *The General* (1936), a study of the World War I British military mind, which so impressed Hitler that he had copies of the novel distributed to his army commanders.

On a cruise to Central America in 1936, Forester conceived the idea for a series of novels about an English naval officer in the Napoleonic period who is both heroic and human. Based in part on Forester's study of Lord Nelson, Captain Horatio Hornblower emerged. Soon to become the author's best-known character, he battled Napoleon just as contemporary British naval officers began to fight Hitler. Starting with *Beat to Quarters* (1937), Forester wrote eleven Hornblower novels, including one that was left unfinished, and featured the hero in several short stories. Much of the saga was serialized in the *Saturday Evening Post* as Hornblower rose from midshipman to admiral. Whatever his rank, he remained shy, able, honest, brave, and prone to seasickness.

During the twenty-seven-year span of the Hornblower series (1937–1964), Forester wrote several novels that were not in the saga, the most successful being World War II stories like *The Good Shepherd* (1955), in which an intrepid American naval officer battles German U-boats in the North Atlantic. Forester's reading public, however, always clamored for more Hornblower, and the author obliged.

In 1944 Forester and his first wife were divorced; three years later he married Dorothy Ellen Foster. From 1943 on, the author was crippled with severe arteriosclerosis. Heart attacks befell him in 1948 and 1961, the latter one followed by a stroke and paralysis. He died in Fullerton, California.

Forester's forte was his ability to evoke a particular time and place. A prodigious reader and researcher, he always kept a volume of the *Encyclopaedia Britannica* at his bedside for nighttime reading. Forester knew what his large audience desired: broad, bold plots; strong, unambiguous, costumed characters; precise historical detail; exotic settings; and cinematic action. Despite carnage and the death of favorite characters, the endings of the Hornblower books are always happy, and good always triumphs. When Forester died, the *New York Times* highlighted his popularity by starting his obituary on page one. Thereafter, the Hornblower Saga remained in print and continued to be read avidly.

• The Hornblower books not mentioned in the text are *Flying Colours* (1938), *A Ship of the Line* (1938), *The Commodore* (1945), *Lord Hornblower* (1946), *Mr. Midshipman Hornblower* (1950), *Lieutenant Hornblower* (1952), *Hornblower and the Atropos* (1953), *Hornblower in the West Indies* (1958), *Hornblower and the Hotspur* (1962), *The Hornblower Companion* (1964), and the unfinished *Hornblower and the Crisis* (1967). Forester's other fiction includes *The Captain from Connecticut* (1941), *The Age of Fighting Sail* (1956), and *Hunting the Bismarck* (1959). See the autobiography of his early years, *Long Before Forty* (1968), and Sanford Sternlicht, *C. S. Forester* (1981). The obituary in the *New York Times* appeared on 3 Apr. 1966.

SANFORD STERNLICHT

FORMAN, David (3 Nov. 1745–12 Sept. 1797), soldier and landowner, was born near Englishtown, New Jersey, the son of Joseph Forman, a shipping merchant, and Elizabeth Lee. He was reared in an area of Monmouth County, New Jersey, populated by many of his relatives. His father had retired to a farm there from New York City. Nothing is known of David's formative years, but he may have spent part of them in Maryland, where there was evidently a long-standing family connection. An unsubstantiated family tradition asserts that he attended the College of New Jersey (later Princeton University) but did not graduate. In 1767 Forman was married in Princeton by the Reverend William Tennent to Ann Marsh of Maryland. They had eleven children, several of whom died in infancy.

The Forman family was in the forefront of revolutionary agitation in Monmouth County. In December 1774 Forman was elected a member of the county committee of observation. In 1775 he was lieutenant colonel of minutemen, and he may have commanded a company of militia who defiantly paraded past Governor William Franklin's door in Perth Amboy, New Jersey. That December he secured a British sloop and cargo stranded on the Monmouth coast.

In June 1776 the New Jersey Provincial Congress appointed Forman lieutenant colonel and, shortly thereafter, colonel of a state regiment in General Nathaniel Heard's brigade. Around the same time he apprehended without authorization several leading Monmouth Tories. During the summer his unit was stationed in the vicinity of New York City, and he participated in the battles of Long Island and White Plains. In late November General George Washington ordered him to suppress an insurrection of Tories in Monmouth. By war's end Forman's zeal against the disaffected earned him a reputation as "Black David, the most persecuting rebel in the country."

On 12 January 1777, in recognition of Forman's services, Washington commissioned him colonel of one of the additional Continental regiments. Largely because of state restrictions on recruiting, however, Forman's regiment was never completed, and its men were eventually merged into other units. On 5 March the state legislature elected Forman brigadier general of militia. During the spring and summer he was active in guarding the Monmouth coast, providing intelligence about enemy movements, and attempting to muster the militia.

In late September 1777 Forman took charge of New Jersey troops who joined the main army, and he led these troops at the battle of Germantown the following month. In the aftermath of the battle, Forman mustered troops for the defense of Fort Mercer (Red Bank), during which he clashed with General Silas Newcomb regarding priority of rank. When he attended the state assembly on 5 November to complain about Newcomb, Forman learned that two petitions had previously been introduced charging him with "undue and illegal proceedings" in the October county elections. Asked to attend the assembly session, Forman requested a delay because of his military duties, which was denied. Much to the consternation of both Washington and Governor William Livingston, Forman took umbrage and resigned his commission as brigadier general. For the rest of his life, nevertheless, he continued to be called "General."

In early January 1778 Forman rejoined the Continental army at Valley Forge. During the winter he sought a contract to provide the army with salt that was produced at his own works at Barnegat. He also stationed a Continental guard there, which was eventually opposed by the New Jersey Council. In June he was attached to General Charles Lee's staff in order to provide guides and local intelligence at the battle of Monmouth. A steadfast supporter of Washington, Forman gave damaging testimony against Lee at Lee's subsequent court-martial.

For the remainder of the war Forman's primary military role was to provide essential intelligence about movements of the British and French fleets in the vicinity of New York. He coordinated a network of lookouts along the Monmouth coast (principally at the Navesink Highlands opposite Sandy Hook), utilized "secret Intelligencers" who relayed information from New York City, and maintained a chain of express riders who conveyed accurate reports directly to Washington. In June 1780 the commander in chief recognized Forman's contribution: "He is intirely to be depended on."

Forman's concurrent political role was unremitting zeal in the suppression of dissent in Monmouth County. As early as 1777 he was compared to "some African tyrant." At the summary execution of a Tory that same year, Forman allegedly "assisted in pulling the Rope, hand over hand." He was also implicated in the fraudulent purchase of confiscated Loyalist estates, in which his relatives served as commissioners.

In response to frequent marauding raids, in the spring of 1780 hundreds of Monmouth patriots subscribed to "articles of agreement for the purposes of retaliation." The Monmouth County Association for Retaliation naturally chose Forman as its first chair. The Retaliators acted as a sort of parallel government to the duly constituted authorities. Their indiscriminateness in exacting reprisals, however, served to alienate neutral and moderate elements in the county. Moreover, in September 1781 Forman was appointed judge of the common pleas and justice of the peace. As judge, Continental officer, and chair of the Retaliators, Forman was instrumental during the spring of 1782 in gathering evidence and appealing to Washington for vengeance in the aftermath of the hanging of Retaliator Joshua Huddy, who had been captured by associated Loyalists.

After the war Forman concentrated on the management of his various farms. Eventually, he owned improved and unimproved lands in New Jersey, Maryland, Mississippi, and Maine. In 1783 he was elected to honorary membership in the Society of the Cincinnati and was admitted to hereditary membership in 1787; from 1791 to 1793 he served as the New Jersey

chapter's vice president. He was also a member of the Freehold lodge of Freemasons. Forman was elected to the New Jersey Legislative Council in 1785, but the election was contested, and in the runoff he was defeated.

In 1789 Forman negotiated with Spanish minister Diego de Gardoqui to acquire land in the Natchez District (later Mississippi Territory). The land was purchased under his older brother Ezekiel's name, who journeyed there with a party that included sixty of Forman's slaves. In May 1795 Ezekiel died. David, who had since relocated to Chestertown, Maryland, traveled to Natchez in September 1796 to attend to the property, and in March 1797 he suffered a stroke there. He was finally able to depart from New Orleans in August 1797, but his vessel was captured en route to New York by a British privateer. Forman died while the privateer was taking his vessel to New Providence in the Bahamas. He left a sizable estate, which was involved in a lengthy settlement among the heirs.

Forman undoubtedly made an important contribution to the American war effort by gathering and transmitting intelligence at critical junctures. On the other hand, he exhibited a propensity to use his public roles to gain private advantage and also to hatch self-aggrandizing schemes that, even by the standards of the day, exceeded the bounds of propriety. Forman's darkest side, the roots of which are unclear, revolve around his unrelenting vindictiveness against political dissenters. He seems to fit Benjamin Rush's categorization of "furious Whigs," those who "injure the cause of liberty . . . by their violence." On the local level, however, it was the kind of extremism that made a revolution succeed.

• There is no known collection of Forman's papers. Recipient's copies of letters relating to his military career, however, are found in the microfilm editions of the Papers of George Washington and the Papers of the Continental Congress. The best source of information is Charles Forman, *Three Revolutionary Solders: David Forman (1745–1797), Jonathan Forman (1755–1809), Thomas Marsh Forman (1758–1845)* (1902), which also contains the undated poem "Lines on General Forman" by Annis Boudinot Stockton. Local histories and genealogies contain inaccuracies, but useful information can be gleaned especially from Franklin Ellis, *History of Monmouth County, New Jersey* (1885); and Anne S. Dandridge, *Forman Genealogy* (1903). On his later life and estate settlement, see Samuel S. Forman, *Narrative of a Journey Down the Ohio and Mississippi, in 1789–90* (1888); *Princetonians, 1784–1790: A Biographical Dictionary* (1991); and Robert T. Thompson, *Colonel James Neilson* (1940).

DAVID J. FOWLER

FORNEY, John Wien (30 Sept. 1817–9 Dec. 1881), editor and publisher, was born in Lancaster, Pennsylvania, the son of Peter Forney and Margaret Wien. Forney left school when he was thirteen years old to become an apprentice to Hugh Maxwell of the *Lancaster Journal*, where he got the balance of his education and began a journalism career of more than fifty years. The *Journal* began publishing his editorials when he was only sixteen years old. He became, at age nineteen, joint owner and editor of a new publication, the *Lancaster Intelligencer*, where he served as editor, compositor, and pressman. He was so successful that within two years he was able to purchase the paper where he first worked and create the *Intelligencer and Journal*. Shortly thereafter, in 1840, he married Mathilda Reitzel; they had six children.

Politics particularly interested Forney, both as a journalist and as a participant. He was a man of strong but shifting loyalties, beginning and ending his career as a Democrat, with a twenty-year interruption as a devout Republican. He was first allied to the fortunes of Democrat James Buchanan, who became secretary of state in 1845 and arranged Forney's appointment as deputy surveyor of the port of Philadelphia. In the same year, he sold his Lancaster newspaper and became editor of the *Pennsylvanian*, a Democratic newspaper in Philadelphia. He held that position for seven years, even after being elected clerk of the House of Representatives in 1851 at the age of thirty-one and moving to Washington, D.C. He left the *Pennsylvanian* on his reelection to the clerkship in 1853 and joined the *Washington Daily Union*, the national Democratic organ. The following year he became a partner in the *Union* with A. O. P. Nicholson, and the two men prospered from House of Representatives printing contracts they arranged for the newspaper.

Forney left the *Union* and the clerkship in 1856 to return to Philadelphia. He became chairman of the Pennsylvania Democratic committee, working with determination for the election of his friend Buchanan to the presidency and hoping that his reward would be a cabinet post. Buchanan won but did not grant Forney the post he desired. Buchanan did, however, support Forney's candidacy for the U.S. Senate in 1857. He was defeated by Simon Cameron and returned to journalism, establishing a new newspaper, the *Philadelphia Press*, on 1 August 1857. Although described as a Democratic journal, the *Press* displayed decidedly Republican leanings, even opposing President Buchanan, who had declined to send political printing business to the newspaper.

A short time after the Republicans won Congress in 1858, Forney changed parties and again became clerk of the House of Representatives, serving until 1861. He then served as secretary of the Senate until 1868. A staunch supporter of Abraham Lincoln during the Civil War, he continued to edit the *Press* while in Washington and in 1861 started the *Washington Chronicle*, a weekly, moving it to daily publication in 1862. A woman subordinate of his during his House clerkship was Emily Pomona Edson Briggs, the wife of John R. Briggs, an adviser to President Lincoln and Forney's assistant clerk. Forney recognized her ability as a writer and offered her a regular column in the *Press*, thereby launching a career that made Mrs. Briggs one of the most prominent and best-paid women correspondents in the capital following the Civil War. She wrote about both Washington society and politics, joining Forney in opposing President Andrew Johnson's southern strategy.

Forney traveled to Europe in 1868, sending back letters on people and places that later were collected into a book, *Letters from Europe* (1869). He sold the *Chronicle* in 1870 and in 1873 and 1881 published two volumes, *Anecdotes of Public Men*, which were a collection of articles about prominent persons from the United States and abroad whom he had interviewed. He sold the *Press*, made a second visit to Europe, and was prominent in organizing the 1876 Centennial celebration in Philadelphia.

Forney returned to the Democratic party in 1880 after having started *Progress*, a weekly journal of political discussion, in 1878. In 1880 he published a campaign biography, *The Life and Military Career of Winfield Scott Hancock*. He died in Philadelphia. Forney's career is an example of how a self-made nineteenth-century American who took opportunities as he saw them could periodically exercise influence in government and journalism. But his temperament kept him from leaving a lasting mark on either field. John Russell Young, who worked for Forney in the early days of the *Philadelphia Press*, wrote some years after Forney's death:

The governing element in his character was intrepidity. He could see but one thing at a time, and what concerned him must concern the universe. While this gave him singular power and force, it was the force of the rifle ball. There was a Napoleonic genius in Forney, but he was Napoleon on the island of Elba. What would have done had he attained his empire, who can say? . . . He never came to his own. (Young, pp. 2–3)

• Forney's papers were not collected, but there are a number of his letters in the Jeremiah H. Black Papers at the Library of Congress and in the James Buchanan Papers at the Historical Society of Pennsylvania. A personal reminiscence about Forney by one who worked for him is in John Russell Young, *Men and Memories* (1901). For additional biographical information see H. O. Folker, *Sketches of the Forney Family* (1911). Obituaries are in the *Philadelphia Press*, 10, 12, 13 Dec. 1881; the *New York Times*, the *Philadelphia Record*, and the *Philadelphia Public Ledger*, all 10 Dec. 1881; the *Washington Sunday Chronicle*, 11 Dec. 1881; *Progress*, 17 Dec. 1881; and the *Printers' Circular*, Dec. 1881.

DANIEL W. PFAFF

FORREST, Edwin (9 Mar. 1806–12 Dec. 1872), first American-born star of the U.S. stage, was born in Philadelphia, Pennsylvania, the son of William Forrest, a Scottish-American bank messenger, and Rebecca Lauman. His father recognized Edwin's interest in oratory and provided him with elocution lessons. Edwin left school and took a series of odd jobs after his father's death in 1819. During his teen years, Edwin practiced acrobatic feats to train his weak body (a regimen he enhanced and continued throughout his life) and performed with an amateur thespian society. He made his stage debut as Young Norval, a conventional vehicle for aspiring juveniles, in 1820 at Philadelphia's Walnut Street Theatre. Accorded generous notices in the press, Forrest played a few minor roles for managers William Warren and William Wood and then in

1822 joined a company bound for the American frontier. At the end of their season, Forrest decamped for New Orleans, where he had been offered a higher salary by James H. Caldwell, manager of the American Theatre. Forrest thrived in New Orleans, befriending gamblers, duelists, a boat captain, and an Indian chief, with whom he later spent a summer. His passionate performances as Iago in *Othello* and Malcolm in *Macbeth* won him much praise from theatergoers and some jealousy from his manager, who was also Forrest's rival in love. The young actor quit the company during his second season and abruptly challenged Caldwell to a duel, which the older man refused to fight.

Returning to Philadelphia in 1825, Forrest accepted an offer from William Gilfert to join his company in Albany, New York. There he supported traveling stars William Conway, Thomas Hamblin, and Edmund Kean, the tempestuous reigning luminary of the London stage. Forrest had admired Kean's performances at the Walnut in 1821 and was already modeling his work on the charismatic Englishman's. Impressed by Forrest's energy and intelligence, Kean gave the young actor several pointers. Forrest would later swear that Kean was the most powerful influence on his acting style and professional career. Brimming with confidence, Forrest left Gilfert for his New York debut at the Park Theatre in 1826, but returned to his former manager in the fall for an extended run at the new Bowery Theatre. His Othello, shrewdly prepared for in the press by Gilfert, gained rave notices and catapulted the performer from stock actor to star. For the rest of the season, Gilfert hired out the young star to other managers for $400 per performance, paid Forrest $40 for his work, and pocketed the difference. By the 1827–1828 season, however, Forrest had learned how to work the new star system to his benefit; he demanded and received $200 per performance from Gilfert.

The young star was 5'10" tall, with such a herculean build that even taller performers looked insignificant beside him. Reviewers praised his resonant, melodious voice, which ranged easily from sotto voce to thunderous power, and his precise articulation. Forrest's mature style combined Kean's bursts of passion with the declamatory deliberateness of Conway, who had modeled his elocution on that of John Kemble. His performances thus tended to alternate between long passages of restrained power and moments of passionate emotion, all expressed with immense energy. The overall effect induced hero worship from many of his spectators. Awed by his larger-than-life stage presence and public image, many of his fans joined fire companies and militia units named in his honor or dubbed their steamboats, racehorses, and locomotives "Forrests."

In 1828 Forrest held the first play competition in the United States, a practice begun earlier in England. Until then, his major roles had been Damon in *Damon and Pythias*, Jaffier in *Venice Preserved*, Mark Antony in *Julius Caesar*, Macbeth, Othello, and King Lear.

Like other stars, Forrest was eager to perform characters who more closely reflected his public persona, in his case that of a primitive, muscular hero fighting for republican principles. His first contest, which promised $500 and a benefit to the author of a tragedy featuring an American Indian, netted him *Metamora, or The Last of the Wampanoags*, by John Augustus Stone. Eight more contests followed over the next nineteen years, resulting in three other plays made successful by the star: *The Gladiator* (1831), by Robert Montgomery Bird; *The Broker of Bogota* (1834), also by Bird; and *Jack Cade* (1841), by Robert T. Conrad. Although these vehicles became the backbone of Forrest's repertoire and earned him thousands of dollars, he paid the playwrights nothing beyond the initial prize money and the traditional third-night benefit. Nonetheless, performing these plays earned Forrest a reputation for supporting American playwrights.

In 1834 the 28-year-old star sailed for Europe, sent off by the elite of New York, who feted him as a symbol of American culture. Although repulsed by the decadence of Europe, the young bachelor nonetheless enjoyed its pleasures, including French royalty, Italian carnivals, and European women from Paris to Moscow. Following a brief return to the United States, Forrest made his London debut as Spartacus in *The Gladiator* at Drury Lane in 1836. The London press disliked the play but praised Forrest for his vigorous realism, sonorous voice, and sincere passion; one reviewer compared him favorably with Kean. While in England, Forrest also courted Catherine Norton Sinclair, the daughter of a professional singer and actress; they married in 1837. They had no children. Forrest's friends had trumpeted his London successes in the American press, ensuring him packed houses on his return. His three performances at the Park Theatre grossed $4,200, topping previous records.

Forrest lent his stentorian voice to Tammany Hall for a Fourth of July oration in 1838, leading many New York Democrats to urge him to run for Congress. Although he eventually declined, the incident cemented the star's identification with the Jacksonians. Forrest had many friends among New York Democrats, including ward captain Isaiah Rynders and William Leggett, the advocate of hard money and radical democracy. Indeed, by 1840 Forrest's public image mirrored the major attributes of Old Hickory's. To their hero-worshipping publics, both were self-made men, children of nature, artifacts of God's handiwork, and iron heroes of Napoleonic power. In 1844 Forrest visited the aging president at his home in Tennessee when on tour in the West. Now disdained by most elite playgoers, Forrest appealed primarily to male workers and the burgeoning middle class.

When Forrest made a second visit to England in 1845, his long-simmering rivalry with the English star William Charles Macready came to a boil. Forrest played Macbeth in London—not one of his better roles because of his difficulty in showing vulnerability—and was damned by the critics and hissed on stage. Believing that Macready was behind the affront, Forrest hissed his Hamlet in Edinburgh and followed up with a letter in the London *Times* justifying his petty vindictiveness. The actors' sparring continued when Macready toured in the United States in 1848–1849 and climaxed in the Astor Place Opera House riot. Following two days of public disturbances, on 10 May a mob of young working men claiming Forrest as their hero stopped Macready's performance of Macbeth and began setting fires and hurling rocks through the windows of the opera house. The militia fired over the heads of the rioters, killing twenty-two (most of them onlookers) and wounding scores of others. Crowds gathered the next day to protest the killings, but the presence of the militia prevented further rioting. Apparently Forrest took no part in the rioters' plans, but he clearly welcomed this chance to avenge his honor.

The Astor Place riot went far beyond a dispute between two actors and their advocates, however. It engaged nationalistic and class-based antagonisms that sharply divided the pro-English elite, who cheered for Macready, from Forrest's working-class fans living in the Bowery. For them, the opera house itself, with its high admission prices and dress codes, was a symbol of "aristocratic" oppression. The riot was also a watershed in the history of mob action in the United States. After Astor Place, most urban Americans came to view rioting as the deviant behavior of a dangerous underclass, rather than the semilegitimate expression of the public will.

Forrest's marriage to Catherine Sinclair began to fall apart in the spring of 1849. The star discovered a love letter addressed to his wife from a minor actor and assumed that they had shared the "bliss" spoken of in the note. Sinclair denied his accusations, but Forrest's suspicions led to their separation and finally to a scandalous divorce trial in 1851. While Sinclair looked on marriage as a private relationship involving mutual respect and affection, Forrest drew on more traditional notions of wedlock and saw his wife's possible infidelity as a threat to his honor. To defend his reputation, Forrest publicly caned a journalist friend of Sinclair's, N. P. Willis, who the star believed had encouraged his wife to question his patriarchal authority. Forrest and Sinclair sued each other, both on the grounds of infidelity. Sinclair's lawyers easily discredited Forrest's witnesses and allegations and produced compelling evidence that Forrest was a regular patron of a house of prostitution and that he had committed adultery with an actress while they toured together in the early 1840s. The press had a field day with the trial; thousands of New Yorkers jammed the streets near the courthouse in January to await the verdict. Sinclair beat Forrest on every count. Seeking vindication, Forrest performed his starring roles at the Broadway Theatre for a record-breaking sixty-nine performances, making copious curtain speeches to regain his honor. The star appealed his case against Sinclair five times but lost each trial.

After 1857 and nearly until his death in 1872, Forrest alternated occasional performances with long periods of rest at his cavernous home in Philadelphia. His performances of *Hamlet* in 1860 in New York and Boston drew vast houses but also some criticism from journalists who favored the spiritualized and idealized Dane of Edwin Booth to Forrest's increasingly ponderous bellowing. In 1865 Forrest suffered from several attacks of sciatica that left him with a limp and humbled his still-athletic body. With few friends but a still-adoring public, Forrest continued his occasional performances, pushing himself for thirty-five nights in San Francisco in 1866. He last appeared in 1872 as a platform reader of his favorite Shakespearean roles. Following his death in Philadelphia in the same year, it was discovered that his will established his former residence as the Edwin Forrest Home for superannuated actors, a retirement home that remained in use well into the twentieth century.

Forrest advanced a new system of national, capitalistic relations in the theater that shattered the traditional patron-artisan relationship. Unlike stock performers, stars such as Forrest became entrepreneurs of their own careers, appealed charismatically to a national audience, and wrested effective control of theatrical representation from local managers and elite theater owners. The new system rested on hero worship; Forrest's fans, like Andrew Jackson's, attributed exceptional, heroic powers to their star. Forrest's extensive use of the curtain speech and the play contest helped to institutionalize the star system in the United States. The hero worship induced by Forrest's performances contradicted the democratic rhetoric of many of his prize plays, pointing up a central tension in the culture of Jacksonian America.

• Most of Forrest's papers are at the University of Pennsylvania; a few items may also be found in the Harvard University Theatre Collection. Richard Moody, *Edwin Forrest, First Star of the American Stage* (1960), and Montrose Moses, *The Fabulous Forrest: The Record of an American Actor* (1929), are the most balanced biographies. William R. Alger's two-volume study, *Life of Edwin Forrest, the American Tragedian* (1877), is closer to hagiography but contains copious information. Other biographies include Lawrence Barrett, *Edwin Forrest* (1882), and James Rees, *The Life of Edwin Forrest, with Reminiscences and Personal Recollections* (1874). Recent interpretations of Forrest's significance may be found in David Grimsted, *Melodrama Unveiled: American Theater and Culture, 1800–1850* (1968), and Bruce A. McConachie, *Melodramatic Formations: American Theatre and Society, 1820–1870* (1992).

BRUCE A. McCONACHIE

FORREST, Jimmy (24 Jan. 1920–26 Aug. 1980), jazz and rhythm-and-blues tenor saxophonist, was born James Robert Forrest, Jr., in St. Louis, Missouri, the son of James Forrest and Eva Dowd, a pianist and church organist. His father's occupation is unknown, but he also played music. Forrest started on alto saxophone and switched to tenor about two years later. His first jobs were local, with his mother's trio and, at age fifteen, with Eddie Johnson and the St. Louis Crackerjacks. While still in high school he played with Fate

Marable's band during summer vacations (1935–1937). He was a member of the Jeter-Pillars big band, which included bassist Jimmy Blanton.

Leaving home, Forrest joined Don Albert's band early in 1938 for jobs in Houston, Fort Worth, and Dallas Texas, and a long tour of the South and the eastern seaboard. He left Albert by year's end. After a period of work with lesser-known bands, Forrest was working in Dallas in the summer of 1942 when Jay McShann's tenor saxophonist Bob Mabane was drafted. Forrest worked with McShann briefly before replacing Al Sears in Andy Kirk's orchestra, with which he remained until 1948. He replaced Ben Webster in Duke Ellington's band for about nine months in 1949–1950, during which time he performed in the film short *Salute to Duke Ellington* (1950). He returned home to St. Louis three days before the birth of one of his children. His wife's name and the marriage date are unknown; they had five children.

In St. Louis a small group under Forrest's leadership recorded "Night Train" (1951), an expansion of a blues theme from Ellington's "Happy Go Lucky Local." Now a classic tune, far better known than Ellington's original, "Night Train" became a nationwide rhythm-and-blues hit and the anthem of striptease dancers. It also flung Forrest out of jazz circles and onto the rhythm-and-blues touring circuit for about six years. Returning to jazz, he worked in small groups with trumpeter Harry "Sweets" Edison from 1958 to 1963, either man serving as leader; Joe Williams often sang with them. Forrest's recordings during this period include Edison's album *The Swinger* (1958), three tracks as a member of arranger Andy Gibson's band on the album *Mainstream Jazz* (1959), Forrest's own *All the Gin Is Gone* (1959), trombonist Bennie Green's *Hornful of Soul* (1960), and organist Jack McDuff's *Tough Duff* and *The Honeydripper* (both 1961).

After again returning to St. Louis, in 1966 Forrest moved to the West Coast, only to suffer a heart attack that summer. In December he played with tenor saxophonist Eddie "Lockjaw" Davis. He worked in the house band at Marty's in New York, and then he rejoined Edison. A second heart attack in 1969 forced him to retire temporarily in California. By 1972 he was keen to go on the road again. He substituted for Davis in Count Basie's big band on 2 June and replaced Davis in October. He left to lead his own band in December 1972 and exactly one year later began a long stay as the star tenor soloist with Basie. He toured internationally with Basie until October 1977, when he formed a quintet with trombonist Al Grey, but this new affiliation was repeatedly disrupted by Forrest's ill health. The two men performed in England in March 1980. Shortly after a two-week stand in Florida with Grey, Forrest died of a liver ailment in Grand Rapids, Michigan. In 1978 he had apparently married a second time, to Betty Tardy.

Forrest was never entirely comfortable with the hard-hitting simplicity of "Night Train," although naturally he had no complaints about its financial rewards. Like players such as Illinois Jacquet and Eddie Davis, he preferred to balance emotive outbursts with fast and heady improvised jazz melody. In this vein Forrest is heard to advantage on the aforementioned albums and even more so with Basie's band in the film documentary *Last of the Blue Devils* (in a segment from around 1976), where he almost steals the movie in his brief appearance.

• For more on Forrest, see Robert Reisner, ed., *Bird: The Legend of Charlie Parker* (1962; repr. 1975), pp. 92–93; Les Tomkins, "Jimmy Forrest," *Crescendo International* 14 (Jan. 1976): 12–13; and Bob Rusch, "Jimmy Forrest Interview," *Cadence* 2 (Apr. 1977): 3, 13. Bob Porter surveys "Jimmy Forrest on Record," in *Jazz Journal* 22 (Sept. 1969): 18–19. For details of his affiliations with big bands, see Ross Russell, *Jazz Style in Kansas City and the Southwest* (1971), pp. 57, 169; Albert McCarthy, *Big Band Jazz* (1974), pp. 107, 152; and Chris Sheridan, *Count Basie: A Bio-discography* (1986). A catalog of recordings is Don Tarrant, "Jimmy Forrest Discography," *Journal of Jazz Discography*, no. 3 (Mar. 1978): 8–21, and no. 4 (Jan. 1979): 2. Obituaries are in the *New York Times*, 28 Aug. 1980; *Melody Maker*, 13 Sept. 1980, p. 30; *Down Beat* 47 (Nov. 1980): 13; and *Jazz Journal International* 33 (Dec. 1980): 13.

BARRY KERNFELD

FORREST, Nathan Bedford (13 July 1821–29 Oct. 1877), Confederate general, was born in Marshall County, Tennessee, the son of William Forrest, a blacksmith, and Mariam Beck. When Forrest was sixteen, his father died, and Forrest supported his mother and five younger brothers by raising stock and crops until his mother remarried. No record or evidence indicates that he ever attended school. In 1841 Forrest volunteered to serve in Texas, but on arriving there he found that the Texas Republic was not recruiting. He earned his fare back to Tennessee by splitting rails. In 1845 he married Mary Montgomery, and they had one child who survived childhood.

As a young man, Forrest entered the plantation business in 1842 in Hernando, Tennessee, with an uncle. In 1857 he moved to Memphis, where he dealt in real estate and slaves, earning a fortune in a short time. Between 1857 and 1859 he invested in a cotton plantation, which he was successfully operating when the Civil War broke out in 1861. His annual plantation income exceeded $30,000, a vast sum in the period.

In June 1861 Forrest enlisted as a private in a mounted rifle company, which later became a unit in the Seventh Tennessee Cavalry Regiment. In July 1861 the governor of Tennessee authorized him to recruit his own battalion of cavalry. He was appointed lieutenant colonel and commanded a force of some 650 men. Over the next four years, he established a controversial reputation as the most brilliant cavalry officer on either side of the Civil War and, at the same time, as a ruthless and bloodthirsty officer with little regard for human life. His critics charged him with at least one major massacre, while his defenders claimed that such charges were based upon his reputation for success and his brilliant cavalry tactics.

Forrest's promotions to higher rank came quickly. He was promoted to colonel of the Third Tennessee Cavalry in March 1862; to brigadier general of the Confederate States Army (CSA) in July 1862; to major general, CSA, in December 1863; and to lieutenant general, CSA, in February 1865. The tally of his battles was extensive. He led a breakout of his troops from Fort Donelson on 13 February 1862, while the rest of the Confederate garrison surrendered to Ulysses S. Grant. At the battle of Shiloh he led a charge that captured a Federal battery. On 13 July 1862 he attacked a Federal encampment at Murfreesboro (Stones River), capturing the entire garrison of infantry and cavalry as well as four cannon.

Forrest had several disputes with his commanding officers, including General Joseph Wheeler. He participated with Wheeler in an unsuccessful attack on Fort Donelson and vowed never to serve under Wheeler again. Later, when army commander Braxton Bragg ordered Forrest to work under Wheeler, Forrest protested and was given an independent command in West Tennessee.

In the fall of 1862 Forrest organized a new brigade with local recruits and led them to several victories, the first near Lexington, Tennessee. He captured Trenton, Tennessee, along with a store of ammunition, then Union City, Tennessee. He destroyed the Mobile and Ohio Railroad near Jackson, Tennessee, preventing the Federal army from moving on Vicksburg. At Thompson's Station, Tennessee, on 5 March 1863, he defeated a Federal unit, capturing 1,500 prisoners, and at Brentwood, Tennessee, he captured another 700, including 35 officers. Forrest led the pursuit of General Abel Streight and captured him with his artillery and 1,200 men. Further successes at Chickamauga, Georgia, on 18 September 1863, at Okolona, Mississippi, in February 1864, and at Paducah, Kentucky, in March 1864 enhanced his reputation. The attack on Fort Pillow, 12 April 1864, was the battle that brought his name to the attention of the U.S. Congress and to the northern press.

The bare facts of that attack were that 221 defenders were killed, 130 were wounded, and the remainder were captured. An uncounted number of civilians who had taken refuge in the fort were also killed. The high military casualty rate stunned the North, and rumors spread that Forrest had ordered a "Black Flag" or "no quarter," which led to the massacre of many of the African-American defenders. His troops pursued men into the woods and continued to fire on the fleeing defenders, killing many as they sought to escape. Later, Forrest's supporters and friendly biographers collected evidence from both Confederate and Union veterans of the battle to offset the conviction that he was personally responsible for the massacre. Nevertheless, the casualty figures and the testimony of many suggested it was the worst incident of its kind during the war.

The congressional committee investigating the battle concluded that Forrest had taken advantage of a truce to reposition his forces and that he had allowed his troops to commit the slaughter. The committee heard testimony that some wounded Union troops were intentionally burned in their barracks, while other wounded were buried alive. Since Forrest was a slave trader before the war, his battle tactics were unconventional, rapid, and ruthless, and he had a personal reputation for certainty of purpose and strict discipline against any of his men charged with cowardice or violation of orders, he became a convenient symbol of the violence and sometimes explicit racism of the rebellion. On at least two occasions, he was reputed to have personally shot standard-bearers of his own men who were fleeing the front, thereby rallying his forces.

Nevertheless, Forrest's defenders argued, he always showed complete propriety in his dealing with prisoners, and at Fort Pillow, they claimed, he attempted to restrain his men. He punished those responsible for burning the barracks, and the burial detail, they claimed, was conducted by drunken Union troops. Forrest's troops continued the attack, they claimed, because the fort's defenders refused to lower their flag as a signal of surrender. Furthermore, Union forces violated the prebattle truce by moving gunboats to defend the fort.

The defending general of Fort Pillow, Major William F. Bradford, was, on his word he would return, given parole so that he could attend the funeral of his brother. Bradford, however, attempted to escape. On his recapture, Forrest's men quietly took him into the woods and murdered him, adding to Forrest's reputation for ruthlessness. On the other hand, some captured Union officers testified later that Forrest showed them every consideration, even punishing those of his own command responsible for their ill treatment.

In subsequent battles, Forrest continued to lead his troops to victory and to evade defeat or capture by Union forces. In August 1863, leading a surprise attack, he took Memphis with a group of 1,500 raiders and drove off a vastly superior force of 17,000 men, whom he had outflanked by his raid. He successfully interfered with the supplies flowing to William T. Sherman in Georgia. Sherman issued orders for Forrest's defeat or capture, even if it cost 10,000 men, but Forrest continued to elude the Federal forces dispatched to catch him. These efforts resulted in an embarrassing defeat for the Federals at Brice's Crossroads in Mississippi in June 1864. Sherman later commented that Forrest had a "genius for strategy that was original and to me, incomprehensible."

During the last months of the war, Forrest was put in charge of the Confederate cavalry in the whole district of Alabama, Mississippi, and eastern Louisiana. At this point he was promoted to lieutenant general. With a small command, he fought against an invasion of Alabama by Union forces, abandoning Selma and falling back to Gainesville. There, hearing of Robert E. Lee's surrender, Forrest ordered his men to surrender, which they did a few weeks later on 9 May 1865 to General Edward R. S. Canby. Despite suggestions from many of his officers to lead his troops across the

Mississippi River to continue the war, Forrest insisted on surrender.

Forrest's military victories were remarkable for several reasons. First of all, he was not a literate man, and his writing reflected the fact that he never mastered spelling or standard grammar. As a consequence, some of his reports and communiqués that survive have a distinctly illiterate flavor when published without editing or correction. However, he was reputed to be excellent in mathematics, and his personal business ventures demonstrated the truth of that observation. Furthermore, he had no military training whatsoever. Thus, his tactics were entirely based on his own thoughts about his own forces and the disposition of the enemy. He moved rapidly, perfecting the techniques of the surprise raid, the flanking and rear attack, and escape through unexpected routes. Military observers at the time and later concluded that Forrest was a natural military genius. He had few precepts but was quoted as saying that his rule of war was to "get there first with the most men," a motto that was often attached to his name. A tall and commanding figure, usually astride a horse, he was revered by his men. Forrest was wounded several times. By the careful count of one admiring biographer, he had twenty-nine horses shot while he was riding them and was personally responsible in hand to hand combat for the death or serious injury of thirty Union officers and men.

Following the war, Forrest returned to his life as a planter and later engaged in railway construction. He served briefly as president of the Selma, Marion and Memphis Railroad. He was active in politics, representing Tennessee at the Democratic National Convention of 1868. He was one of the organizers and leaders of the early Ku Klux Klan. Called before Congress to testify about the organization in 1870–1871, he claimed he knew little about it. He died in Memphis, perhaps of diabetes.

• Information on Forrest can be found in the Robert Selph Henry Papers at the Virginia Polytechnic Institute in Blacksburg. Sources on Forrest include John A. Wyeth, *Life of Lieutenant General Nathan Bedford Forrest* (1899), a generally laudatory account; Arlin Turner, "George W. Cable's Recollections of General Forrest," *Journal of Southern History* 21 (May 1955): 224–28; Robert Selph Henry, *As They Saw Forrest* (1956); Steven Woodcock, *Jefferson Davis and His Generals* (1990); Brian Steel Wills, *A Battle from the Start* (1992); and Jack Hurst, *Nathan Bedford Forrest: A Biography* (1993). An obituary is in the *New York Times*, 30 Oct. 1877.

RODNEY P. CARLISLE

FORREST, Sam (30 Nov. 1870–30 Apr. 1944), stage director, was born Simon Mordecai Lazarus in Richmond, Virginia, the son of two Jewish immigrants from Polish Russia. Raised in Texas, Forrest became interested in theater at an early age. He worked at various jobs, including as a bellhop in a Texas hotel, where he first came into contact with theatrical performers.

According to a story included in his *New York Times* obituary, Forrest broke his leg at age twenty and, capitalizing on his limp, went to New York City as a character actor to specialize in old men's roles. Whether or not this was true, he did achieve some success as a supporting performer. However, his acting career was minor.

Around the turn of the century, Forrest traveled to Chicago and became the stage director of the Dearborn Theatre's stock company, where he stayed for five years. In addition to gaining valuable theatrical experience, he also met Mary Ryan, a young actress in the company, whom he married in 1908; they had no children.

Although it is unclear when Forrest left Chicago, by January 1908 he was acting in a road company of George Broadhurst's *The Man of the Hour*, and by August of the same year he was performing in and stage-managing *All for a Girl*, by Rupert Hughes. (Since no director was acknowledged in the program, Forrest's stage-managing credit may have meant that he staged the show.) In 1909 he performed in and stage-managed *Springtime*, by Booth Tarkington and Harry Leon Wilson.

In 1910 Forrest's career took a major turn. Producers George M. Cohan and Sam Harris hired Forrest as their general stage director to help reduce Cohan's work load, and Forrest became an integral part of their organization. Harris initially sent Forrest to help Cohan with rehearsals for *Get-Rick-Quick Wallingford* (1910). Forrest assisted Cohan with the author's plays and also directed many of the firm's non-Cohan productions.

Cohan liked Forrest's personality (Forrest, Cohan, and Harris all shared an avid love of baseball) and appreciated the director's skill. While Cohan staged his own plays, Forrest won praise for his staging work on such Cohan and Harris productions as Elmer Rice's *On Trial* (1914); *Three Faces East*, by Anthony Paul Kelly (1918); and *The Acquittal*, by Rita Weiman (1920).

Cohan and Forrest had a similar approach to directing. In a review praising Forrest's direction of *The Acquittal* in the *New York Evening Mail* (6 Jan. 1920), Burns Mantle described the closeness between Forrest and Cohan: "I am willing to suspect, as most everyone does, that George Cohan helped a little, but Cohan and Forrest have worked together so much they are practically now of one mind in these matters."

After Cohan and Harris dissolved their partnership in 1919, Forrest staged productions for Harris. Among the shows he directed for Harris were *Honey Girl*, by Albert Von Tilzer, Neville Fleeson, and Edward Clark (1920); *Little Old New York*, by Rida Johnson Young (1920); *The Champion*, by Thomas Louden and A. E. Thomas (1921); *Six-Cylinder Love*, by William Anthony McGuire (1921); *Only 38*, by Thomas (1921); *The Varying Shore*, by Zoë Akins (1921); *Secrets*, by Rudolph Besier and May Edginton (1922); *Icebound*, by Owen Davis (1923); *New Toys*, by Milton Herbert Gropper and Oscar Hammerstein II (1924); *The Cradle Snatchers*, by Russell Medcraft and Norma Mitchell (1925); *We Americans*, by Milton

Herbert Gropper and Max Siegel (1926); and *Gentle Grafters*, by Owen Davis (1926). He also directed a revival of *Rain* starring Tallulah Bankhead for Harris in 1935. As this list makes clear, Forrest specialized in new and commercial comedies and dramas; while he was a skilled director, he did not stage new or innovative works.

Forrest also wrote a play of his own, *Paid* (1925), and co-wrote several others, including *Red-Light Annie*, with Norman Houston (1923), and *Thoroughbreds*, with Lewis B. Ely (1924).

In 1927 Forrest rejoined Cohan and staged all of Cohan's productions thereafter, including *The Baby Cyclone*, by Cohan (1927); *Elmer the Great*, by Ring Lardner (1928); *Vermont*, by Thomas (1929); and Cohan's *Gambling* (1929), *Friendship* (1931), *Pigeons and People* (1933), *Seven Keys to Baldpate* (1935), *Dear Old Darling* (1936), and *Fulton of Oak Falls* (1937). Forrest's last production was Cohan's last as well, *The Return of the Vagabond* (1940). Forrest died at his home in New York City.

Forrest was skillful at handling actors. His wife described him in a *New York Review* interview of 29 May 1915: "My husband is one of the most patient stage directors I have ever worked under. . . . And of course, he knows . . . how things should be done and he can tell how to do them." He could also recognize talent. In the 1921 production of Rachel Crothers's *Nice People*, on which he collaborated with Crothers, he introduced Tallulah Bankhead and Katharine Cornell in small roles.

Forrest was a successful, prolific commercial stage director who specialized in nonmusical dramas and comedies. As a commercial Broadway director, he did not follow a particular artistic or aesthetic approach. Instead, he was concerned with expressing the playwright's intentions and the dramatic content of the plays. He also approached directing as a craft. His prolific credits illustrate how quickly he worked. According to his *Variety* obituary, Forrest "is credited with having directed and staged more Broadway productions than any other three directors in his years in the theatre."

• Forrest's privately printed *Variety and Miscellanea* (1939) provides a glimpse of the sort of writing that attracted him but gives only a little biographical information. Informative articles about Forrest include "Sam Forrest, the Director, Likes to Loiter Backstage," *New York World-Telegram*, 7 Mar. 1936, and Leo Marsh, "New Plays of the Week—and Mr. Cohan," *New York Telegraph*, 26 May 1935. Mary B. Mullett, "What Happens to a Play Before You See It," *American*, Mar. 1923, pp. 34–35, 179–85, describes Forrest's working method. For biographical information, see the *Philadelphia Gazette*, 24 Aug. 1930. Obituaries are in *Variety*, 3 May 1944, and the *New York Times*, 1 May 1944.

STEPHEN M. VALLILLO

FORRESTAL, James Vincent (15 Feb. 1892–22 May 1949), secretary of the navy and first U.S. secretary of defense, was born in Matteawan, New York, the son of James Forrestal, a construction contractor, and Mary Ann Toohey, a schoolteacher. Raised in a small-town Irish-Catholic community, Forrestal attended Dartmouth College in 1911. In 1912 he transferred to Princeton University, where he developed social and business connections with the Protestant establishment. He withdrew before graduating with his class, possibly over a dispute with a professor. He held a number of sales jobs before a Princeton alumnus arranged for him to join the Wall Street investment firm of William A. Read and Company. The First World War interrupted Forrestal's rising career as a bond salesman. During the war he served as a lieutenant junior grade in the Aviation Division of the newly created Office of the Chief of Naval Operations in Washington, D.C. In 1926 he married Josephine Ogden, a *Vogue* magazine editor. They had two children.

During the postwar "New Era" of business expansion, Forrestal rose to social and economic prominence as top executive for Wall Street investment banker Clarence Dillon. Forrestal became president of Dillon, Read & Company in 1938. While he prospered in the unregulated, highly speculative bond market of the era, in October 1933 he also had to testify before the Senate Subcommittee on the Stock Exchange Investigation headed by Ferdinand Pecora. During the hearings, Forrestal revealed that he had created investment trusts to avoid paying taxes, a practice that Pecora's committee thought contributed to the stock market crash and economic depression in 1929. The unhappy experience with the Senate subcommittee probably convinced Forrestal to cooperate with William O. Douglas and other New Dealers who sought to bring order to and regulate the stability of the stock market. In 1940 Douglas recommended Forrestal to President Franklin D. Roosevelt for a position as a presidential assistant, maintaining that Forrestal was the New Deal's friend on Wall Street.

Roosevelt hired Forrestal as an assistant in June 1940. Forrestal set up for the president business and possibly espionage contacts in Latin America that could be activated if the United States were drawn into the world war that had broken out in 1939. On 22 August 1940 he became under secretary of the navy, a position created a few months earlier to coordinate the industrial expansion of the navy and the construction of a great fleet to fight a two-ocean war. Gradually Forrestal centralized all legal and administrative functions in the procurement and distribution of raw materials and contracts throughout a naval bureaucracy noted for jealously guarding its individual bureau interests. In 1941 he set up the Procurement Legal Division that bypassed the Judge Advocate General's Office in issuing contracts to private industry. In January 1942 he created an Office of Procurement and Material to define requirements, distribute materials, and coordinate the navy with the Army and Navy Munitions Board, War Production Board, and the other agencies established to facilitate wartime military production. Forrestal also developed public relations and information offices to ensure full national recognition of the navy's role during the Second World War. In the process, he asserted civilian control over the business of the navy, initiating a rivalry with Admiral Ernest J. King, the commander in chief of the U.S. Fleet (CO-MINCH). When Secretary of the Navy Frank Knox died in office in April 1944, Roosevelt selected Forrestal to replace him. Forrestal became secretary of the navy on 9 May 1944.

With the end of the Second World War, Forrestal adjusted the navy to postwar cutbacks and to a changing strategic role. His most difficult task was to defend the navy's interests in the face of a movement to unify the armed services under a single secretary and a single department of defense and to create an independent air force. Advised by his navy air admirals, he argued that unification meant the subordination of naval aircraft carrier defense to that of army air force strategic bombers carrying atomic weapons, which would, he claimed, result in the weakening of America's military position in the world. Harry S. Truman, who became president upon Roosevelt's death on 12 April 1945, sided with General George C. Marshall and other army and army air force generals who favored the single defense department and strategic air force doctrine. In response, Forrestal turned to Ferdinand Eberstadt, his only close friend and most intimate adviser since Princeton, to develop a counter proposal. Eberstadt constructed a plan for a national security establishment with coordinate agencies. The resultant National Security Act of 1947 created a compromise military establishment with one department, one secretary, and an independent department for the air force but also included a series of coordinate national security agencies and offices. Truman asked Forrestal to organize this compromise system, and Forrestal was sworn in as the first U.S. secretary of defense on 17 September 1947.

Forrestal soon discovered that he had helped create a nearly unmanageable organization. Though he was cabinet head of the national military establishment, he lacked adequate power over the subordinate secretaries of the navy, army, and air force. Moreover he found the Joint Chiefs of Staff structure torn by interservice rivalries. The National Security Council appeared of little value in assisting him in coordinating military and foreign policies or in developing estimates upon which to build a national defense budget adequate to provide for the national security. The latter was of most concern, since Truman insisted that Forrestal cut military spending. Forrestal tried desperately to balance service missions and budgets in the national interest. Thus he alienated both his former navy comrades, who revolted at the thought of giving up their aircraft carriers, and the air force, which saw the former navy secretary as overly sympathetic to the navy's interests.

Unable to organize the national military establishment smoothly or to maintain adequate force levels and defense budgets, Forrestal worried that the U.S. military could not defend American interests against growing postwar Soviet Communist expansionism. If the Soviet Union developed the atomic bomb, Forrestal worried that Soviet Russia and communism would pose the greatest threat in history. Thus he adamantly opposed sharing atomic secrets with the Soviets. Forrestal saw postwar signs of Soviet Communist intrigue in postwar Germany, Eastern Europe, the Balkans, the Mediterranean, and China. He advised Truman to develop military, foreign, and economic programs to contain this Communist menace. Convinced that neither the government nor the public understood the threat, Forrestal dabbled on his own in foreign policies, probably developing covert anti-Communist operations in Italy, France, and Greece. He worked for closer U.S. ties with the Arabs to ensure American access to critical Middle Eastern oil supplies and in the process seemed to oppose the development of an independent Jewish state. This drew vicious and entirely unfounded public accusations of anti-Semitism. Already exhausted by eight consecutive years of government service, the intense, dedicated Forrestal began to break down. When Truman asked for his resignation in 1949, Forrestal's health collapsed. He was hospitalized and committed suicide at Bethesda Naval Hospital in Bethesda, Maryland. Forrestal was buried in Arlington National Cemetery.

Forrestal held three vital governmental positions during one of the most critical wartime and postwar eras in American history, 1940–1949. He performed diligently at each post, particularly as under secretary of the navy, where he modernized navy supply, procurement, and industrial systems. He brought business management methods into government and developed public-private partnerships for national defense. Forrestal helped design and found the post–World War II American national security organization. He became a leading advocate for the containment of Soviet communism and can be seen as one of the architects of the Cold War. However, he never became an influential adviser to either President Roosevelt or President Truman and hence made no major impact on the direction of U.S. policies. In the end, Forrestal was one of the most prominent members of a dedicated legion of organizational experts from business and industry that helped to protect and preserve American capitalism and democracy from its many enemies between 1940 and 1949.

• The James V. Forrestal Papers and Unpublished Diaries are in the Seeley G. Mudd Manuscript Library, Princeton University. Important manuscript collections are in the Records of the Office of Secretary of the Navy (RG 80) and Secretary of Defense (RG 330), National Archives and Records Service; and in the Operational Archives, Navy Historical Center, Washington Navy Yard, Washington, D.C. The standard Forrestal biography is Townsend Hoopes and Douglas Brinkley, *Driven Patriot: The Life and Times of James Forrestal* (1992). The most important studies on Forrestal's place in American history are Jeffery M. Dorwart, *Eberstadt and Forrestal: A National Security Partnership, 1909–1949* (1992), and Robert Greenhalgh Albion and Robert Howe Connery, *Forrestal and the Navy* (1962).

JEFFERY M. DORWART

FORSTALL, Edmond Jean (7 Nov. 1794–16 Nov. 1873), merchant, banker, and sugar planter, was born in New Orleans, Louisiana, the son of Edouard Pierre Forstall and Celeste de la Villebeauve. The father's occupation is uncertain, but in Edmond's youth several members of the Forstall family, Edouard perhaps one of them, were active in Louisiana commerce. Record of Edmond's education is lacking, but at the age of twelve he went to work for a merchant. In his adulthood he was fluent in English as well as French and read and wrote widely in both languages. As early as 1818 he was named a director of the Louisiana State Bank. By 1819 he was associated with the New Orleans firm of Gordon, Grant & Company, and in 1823 when the firm reorganized as Gordon & Forstall, Forstall became managing partner. In July 1823 he married Clara Durel; the couple had eleven children, one of whom died in infancy.

Gordon & Forstall, with connections in England and Mexico, sold imported goods on commission, lent money on cotton shipments, were factors for sugar planters, and bought and sold produce on their own account. Active from an early age on the city's wharves, Forstall had a reputation throughout his life as a competent judge of cotton and tobacco. Through several changes of partners in the 1820s and 1830s, he remained the manager of the New Orleans firm, but the seasonal nature of the produce business, New Orleans's developing economy, and Forstall's exuberant energy afforded him time, opportunity, and desire for other endeavors as well.

In 1829 Forstall began his association with Louisiana's three property banks: the Consolidated Association of the Planters of Louisiana, the Union Bank of Louisiana, and the Citizens' Bank. The concept of Jean Baptiste Moussier, property banks were like other incorporated banks in that they issued currency, accepted deposits, and made loans; they differed only in their method of raising capital. Whereas other banks sold stock in order to raise capital, property banks sold bonds that were backed by mortgages on shareholders' real estate, slaves, and, ultimately, the faith and credit of the state. Forstall served as comptroller of the Consolidated Association in 1829, drafted the charter of the Union Bank in the early 1830s, and was president of the Citizens' Bank from March 1836 to August 1837. He lobbied tirelessly for the banks in the halls of the legislature, and he marketed their bonds in the North and in Europe, initially through his commercial contacts. Between 1828 and 1836 he was instrumental in placing at least $14 million of the banks' bonds with Prime, Ward, King & Company of New York City, Baring Brothers & Company of London, and Hope & Company of Amsterdam. Through the Barings he came to know their Boston agent, Thomas Wren Ward, who became his friend and mentor.

In 1835 Forstall expanded his New Orleans firm to include his brother, Placide, and Manuel de Lizardi, a member of an international merchant banking family, with branches in Paris, London, and Liverpool. The Lizardis also became European agents of the Citizens' Bank. This was the apex of Forstall's early career. He was head of his own flourishing business, president of one of the city's largest banks, and on familiar terms with international capitalists. Then came the panic of 1837. The Lizardis' misuse of the Citizens' Bank's funds in Paris, Forstall's own local reputation as an agent of European capitalists, his insistence on the bank's adherence to a tight credit policy, and the mingling of the affairs of the bank with those of his New Orleans firm all forced his resignation from the bank's presidency. At the same time his New Orleans partnership was dissolved. For reasons unknown Forstall was deeply indebted to the Lizardis, and in settling with them he became impoverished.

Ever resilient, Forstall reorganized his New Orleans firm as E. J. Forstall & Company and continued his interest in the city's banks. When the property banks and the state proposed to repudiate the banks' bonds, Forstall worked successfully to reverse the move. As a member of a joint committee of the House and Senate during a term in the state legislature from 1836 to 1838, he wrote the report that he later claimed was the basis of the Louisiana Bank Act of 1842, for which he took major credit, although he was no longer in the legislature.

The act indeed reflected the conservative principles that Forstall advocated and insisted on as president of Citizens' Bank. It included a requirement that every bank chartered by the state have specie reserves (gold and silver) equal to one-third the amount of its note-issue and deposits and that each institution hold short-term loans to the full extent of both. Concentrating on this clause of the law and convinced of the evils of "wildcat" banking, commentators long hailed the act as an important landmark on the road to responsible banking and were unstinting in their praise of Forstall. Later historians both downgraded Forstall's responsibility for the act and criticized the act itself as being unduly restrictive in a growing economy that required easy credit expansion.

In 1840–1841 Forstall was in Europe as agent of the Citizens' Bank, and when the bank's charter was forfeited in 1842, he served as president of the board of managers charged with the liquidation of the financial institution. From the latter 1840s to his death, Forstall was the New Orleans agent of both Baring Brothers & Company and Hope & Company. For them he bought large amounts of cotton, advanced money on produce shipments, managed exchange operations, and oversaw other interests in the city, including their investments in the property banks. As a condition of the agencies, he gave up commercial activities on his own account. With the death in 1845 of his aunt, Lise Poeyfarré, Forstall came into possession of her sugar plantation in St. James Parish, sixty-four miles upriver from New Orleans. From then on he divided his time between the city and his country place, relishing his position as a planter.

As Barings' agent Forstall traveled to Mexico City three times in the early 1850s, and in 1851 and 1852 he arranged the transfer of funds in payment of the indemnity that the United States owed to Mexico for the annexation of territory after the Mexican War. When the Union army occupied New Orleans during the Civil War, Forstall negotiated with General Benjamin F. Butler to protect $800,000 in silver that was awaiting transfer to his principals in Europe.

In 1865 Forstall took his sons, Oscar and Ernest, and his son-in-law, Adolph Schreiber, into his city firm. Gradually he turned the business over to the younger men and spent increasing periods of time on the plantation. In the late antebellum period he estimated his annual income from the estate at $30,000 to $40,000. At the same time he realized perhaps $20,000 to $30,000 yearly from his agencies. He lost heavily in the war, including his investment in more than 130 slaves, but the plantation remained productive. In 1867 he formally declared it his residence.

In addition to his primary commitments Forstall was active in other ways. He supported both the Louisiana Historical Society and local educational institutions, lobbied in Washington for a sugar tariff, and wrote on the agricultural production of Louisiana. Forstall also compiled an analytical index of the documents relative to Louisiana in the French colonial archives, the result of his own research. Throughout his career he contributed articles to newspapers and commercial journals, including the *New Orleans Bee*, the *National Intelligencer*, and *De Bow's Review*. In his old age Forstall was described as being "well crammed with facts and figures." He died in St. James Parish.

• The archives of Baring Brothers & Company, the Guildhall Library, London; the Baring Brothers & Company Papers in the Public Record Office, Ottawa, Canada; the National Archives, which contain microfilm copies; the Hope & Company Records in the archives of Hope & Mees, Amsterdam; and the Thomas Wren Ward Papers at the Massachusetts Historical Society, Boston, include many Forstall letters. His banking activities are documented in the Consolidated Association of the Planters of Louisiana, Department of Archives and Manuscripts, Louisiana State University, and the Canal Bank Collection (including the minute books of the Citizens' Bank), Tulane University. The Notarial Records of Louisiana, New Orleans, contain scattered information about Forstall. The most complete modern account of Forstall is Irene D. Neu, "Edmond J. Forstall," in the *Encyclopedia of American Business History and Biography: Banking and Finance to 1913*, ed. Larry Schweikart (1990). Emile Philippe Grenier, "Property Banks in Louisiana" (Ph.D. diss., Louisiana State Univ., 1942); Fritz Redlich, *The Molding of American Banking: Men and Ideas*, vol. 2 (1951); George D. Green, *Finance and Economic Development in the Old South: Louisiana Banking, 1804–1861* (1972); and Larry Schweikart, *Banking in the American South from the Age of Jackson to Reconstruction* (1987), assess Forstall as a banker and analyze his theories of banking. Ralph W. Hidy, *The House of Baring in American Trade and Finance: English Merchant Bankers at Work, 1763–1861* (1949) supplies context for Forstall's association with the company. Obituaries are in *L'Abeille de la Nouvelle-Orléans*, the *New Orleans Republican*, and the *Daily Picayune*, all 18 Nov. 1873.

IRENE D. NEU

FORSYTH, Jessie (29 Apr. 1847–18 Sept. 1937), temperance reformer, was born in London, England, the daughter of Andrew Forsyth, a baker, and Eliza Maria Kitteridge, both of Scottish origin. The caricaturist and illustrator George Cruikshank was her great-uncle. Ill health left her with a skimpy formal education. She was a devout, lifelong member of the Church of England. Orphaned in her teens, Forsyth found her sense of belonging in a fraternal temperance society, the militantly prohibitionist Independent (later International) Order of Good Templars. According to her memoirs, she had not been a teetotaler when her desire to make new friends and enjoy sociable weekly lodge meetings persuaded her to become a Good Templar in 1872. Late in 1874 she sailed to the United States to take a job as a bookkeeper for a printing company in Boston, Massachusetts. Within a few months she joined an American lodge of the Templar Order.

Organized in central New York in 1852, the IOGT endorsed the equality of women as members and officeholders. This universalist ideology embraced all teetotalers who advocated prohibition. In 1868 the Order claimed over 500,000 members in North America (a figure that quickly shrank) and later added hundreds of thousands in Britain (and its empire) and Scandinavia. Most members were young, often from working- or lower middle-class families, and, even when they remained abstainers, they tended to drift quickly out of the organization. Forsyth's lifelong commitment was exceptional.

In 1876, quarreling over the rights of blacks in the American South who wanted to become members, the Good Templars split into two rival international organizations. Americans and Canadians accused the British of seeking to take over the Order and made the retention of white Southern members their highest priority. At a time when the IOGT was losing members in most American states, membership was growing among Southern whites. Forsyth belonged to a small minority of Massachusetts Good Templars who supported the predominantly British party in condemning racism as contrary to the Good Templar principle of universal brotherhood and sisterhood. She was an admirer of William Wells Brown, a Boston physician, who was the leading African American in her Good Templar organization.

In 1883 Forsyth was elected Right Worthy Grand Vice Templar in her faction's international organization and was appointed the editor of its monthly newspaper, *Temperance Brotherhood*. She also became the American agent for the British committee that financed the campaign to recruit blacks. Once shy, she became an effective organizer and speaker and, in 1885–1886, traveled to Britain, Germany, and Scandinavia. She also wrote prolifically, including memoirs, didactic essays, biographical sketches, stories for children, and verse. After the Order reunited in 1887 on what amounted to a segregated basis, Forsyth remained Vice Templar until 1889.

At this time interested in socialism, Forsyth became a charter member and secretary of the Second Boston

Nationalist Club in 1889, inspired by Edward Bellamy's *Looking Backward* (1888). She was a staunch advocate of women's suffrage and occasionally criticized the Good Templars for failing to live up to their ideals of gender equality.

Beginning in 1893 Forsyth led the Good Templar international work for children. By the time that an Englishman defeated her for reelection, in 1908, Good Templar juvenile auxiliaries claimed nearly 240,000 members. The triumph of state prohibition contributed to the virtual disappearance of Good Templary in the United States, and the weakness of the Order in its birthplace helped explain Forsyth's defeat. Europeans dominated the membership, so Britons, Swedes, and Norwegians won election to most of the international offices. Forsyth's editorship of the monthly *International Good Templar*, begun in 1901, also ended in 1908, when a Scotsman defeated its American owner for reelection as international secretary. In 1911 she retired from the printing shop where she had worked all her American days, and which for the last eight or nine years she had owned. She then emigrated to Australia.

In January 1912 Forsyth arrived in Freemantle, Western Australia, where her sister lived. Although she briefly held office in the local Grand Lodge of the IOGT, she devoted most of her energy to the Woman's Christian Temperance Union, which she served as state president for Western Australia from 1913 to 1916. In 1917–1918 she was organizing secretary of the Australian National Prohibition League in Melbourne. She then returned to Western Australia where, in 1919, she founded the *Dawn*, a newspaper for women reformers, and resumed work for the state WCTU. In 1922 ill health forced her to curtail her service to temperance, although she continued to write, notably a newspaper column for children.

In her memoirs, published in Good Templar periodicals, Forsyth said almost nothing about her life outside the Order. She never married, although she loved children and cherished friendships with many men and women. She said that without the Good Templars her life would have been colorless and lonely.

Until her death in Leederville, a suburb of Perth, Western Australia, Forsyth remained committed to her Order. She regarded its program of total abstinence and prohibition, combined with universal brotherhood and sisterhood, as a moral crusade that offered a foundation for other social reforms, such as women's rights, racial justice, and the conquest of poverty.

• Letters from Forsyth are in the George F. Cotterill Papers in the University of Washington libraries and in the Grand Lodge of Wisconsin, IOGT, papers at the State Historical Society of Wisconsin. Her principal memoir, "Thirty Years of Good Templary," was published in the *International Good Templar* (1903–1904), reprinted in *The Collected Writings of Jessie Forsyth, 1847–1937: The Good Templars and Temperance Reform on Three Continents*, ed. David M. Fahey (1988),

with an editorial introduction, "One Woman's World." See also Ernest Hurst Cherrington, ed., *Standard Encyclopedia of the Alcohol Problem*, 6 vols. (1925–1930).

DAVID M. FAHEY

FORSYTH, John (22 Oct. 1780–21 Oct. 1841), politician and diplomat, was born in Fredericksburg, Virginia, the son of Robert Forsyth, a businessman and farmer, and Fanny Johnston Houston. John was reared in Augusta, Georgia, where the Forsyth family had made its home in 1785. In 1799 he graduated from the College of New Jersey (now Princeton University), returned to Augusta, studied law, and in 1802 started his practice. In May he married Clara Meigs, daughter of Josiah Meigs, the first president of Franklin College (now the University of Georgia). This union produced eight children.

Forsyth began his political career in 1808 as attorney general of Georgia. Although initially a Federalist, he entered the House of Representatives in 1813 as a Republican. There he acquired a reputation as a polished orator and a staunch supporter of presidential policies, advocating, for instance, aggressive prosecution of the War of 1812. In September 1814 he became chairman of the Committee of Foreign Relations, a post he held for four years. He also took an interest in banking and currency and backed the legislation that in 1816 created the Second Bank of the United States. In 1818 he urged forceful seizure of East Florida from Spain but, ironically, in the following year opposed the efforts of Henry Clay and others to accord recognition to the newly independent Latin American republics because it could lead to war with Spain.

Earlier, when the Georgia legislature appointed him to fill a short-term vacancy in the U.S. Senate, he reluctantly gave up his seat in the House. In February 1819, after serving less than three months in the Senate, he resigned to become minister to Spain. There he exchanged the ratifications, or the formal approval of each government, of the Adams-Onís Treaty that ceded Florida to the United States. His diplomatic mission ended in 1823 after he had offended the Spaniards with haughty behavior and a tactless lecture to the king on his international duties.

Before leaving Spain, Forsyth had again won election to the lower house of Congress. During the presidential campaign of 1824 he worked assiduously for the candidacy of his friend and political ally, Secretary of the Treasury William H. Crawford. When in the following year selection of the president was thrown into the House, Forsyth cast his vote for Crawford even though his fellow Georgian had suffered a paralytic stroke and stood no chance of being chosen. Although Forsyth owned slaves, he denounced the international slave trade as piracy, introduced a resolution calling for its suppression, and urged independent governmental action to help abolish it.

In October 1827, after winning a bitter campaign for governor of Georgia as the candidate of the aristocratic coastal faction of the state's Republicans, Forsyth resigned his congressional seat. As governor he worked to subordinate Cherokees and Creeks by law to whites, annul their land titles, and move them out of the state. He denounced protectionism, particularly the 1828 "tariff of abominations." In November 1829 he moved on to a vacancy in the Senate.

As a believer in states' rights, Forsyth at first acquaintance had not cared for the new president, Andrew Jackson. As the quarrel over states' rights reached a stage of crisis, the Georgian softened these convictions. Like Jackson, he opposed any course by extremists that could endanger the Union or wreck the Constitution. Forsyth thus changed into a broad nationalist who wanted to preserve the Union, who identified with Jackson's policies, and who devoted himself to defending them. In the Senate Forsyth continued his interest in removing American Indians from Georgia to the trans-Mississippi West. Disliking Vice President John C. Calhoun in part because he had attacked Crawford, Forsyth provided the president with a letter from Crawford revealing that Calhoun had recommended a presidential reprimand for Jackson's conduct in the Seminole War. This information turned Jackson against the South Carolinian.

Even though the tariff of July 1832 contained protectionist features, Forsyth voted for it because he regarded it as the best legislation the South could obtain from Congress. He and only one other southerner voted for the Force Bill of March 1833, designed to counter South Carolina's ordinance of nullification. Many Georgians condemned him as a traitor to his state and region. He also backed the compromise tariff bill of 1833. During the debate over the fate of the Bank of the United States, he reversed his previous support. On more than seventy occasions he defended the president's antibank position. As a reward, in June 1834 Jackson appointed him secretary of state.

Forsyth's most noted negotiation was with the French over spoliation claims based on their confiscation of neutral American property during the Napoleonic Wars. In a treaty of 4 July 1831, the French government agreed to pay 25 million francs ($5 million) in six annual installments. Since many in France regarded the indemnity as unnecessarily high, the legislature refused to appropriate the money.

Forsyth protested, but Jackson bristled. In December 1834 the president asked Congress for strong measures against France, but Whig leaders blocked reprisals. Angered by Jackson's harsh words, the French severed diplomatic relations. In January 1836 both countries accepted a British offer to mediate the dispute, which settled the matter. In March France paid her installments; in May Jackson sent France a gracious message; and soon the two countries resumed cordial relations. Throughout, the secretary tried to act as a moderating force on the president.

Forsyth also handled problems arising from the revolution in Texas in 1835–1836. The Mexican government protested American aid to the insurgents, but, because public sentiment favored such partisan assistance, the secretary did nothing about it. After Texas in March 1836 declared independence, he parried demands for recognition and annexation, fearing that the public's reaction, divided along sectional lines, might destroy the Democratic party. In March 1837 Jackson, who dominated the shaping of foreign policy, recognized Texas.

Jackson's action left the question of annexation up to his successor, Martin Van Buren, who retained Forsyth's services and permitted him more leeway in the conduct of foreign policy than had Jackson. In August, when Texas petitioned for annexation, even though the two men were sympathetic, they opposed it because they feared it would bring on war with Mexico, enrage abolitionists, and disrupt the Union.

Several other crises involved relations with Great Britain. The longstanding dispute over the boundary dividing New Brunswick from Maine became entangled in 1837 with problems of insurrection in Canada. With American help, the defeated rebel leaders seized a Canadian island in the Niagara River. Canadian militia retaliated by capturing the *Caroline*, a rebel supply ship, and killing one American. Forsyth demanded redress. Loose talk of war followed.

Late in 1838 Canadian lumberjacks exacerbated the crisis by cutting timber in a borderland valley, triggering the bloodless "Aroostook War." General Winfield Scott, whom Van Buren sent to the northern frontier in March 1839, worked out a truce along lines proposed by Forsyth. In June Forsyth himself visited Maine to ascertain the basis for a settlement. The New Englanders were disappointed that the administration would not resort to extreme measures against the British. Tension increased, nonetheless, when authorities in New York in November 1840 arrested a Canadian they accused of murder in the *Caroline* affair. Forsyth rebuffed British demands for his release. The dispute was not resolved until after the Georgian left the State Department.

Another incident that received international attention began in July 1839 when fifty-three blacks seized the Spanish slave schooner *Amistad* out of Havana and killed the captain. When the vessel reached Long Island waters, an American revenue cutter brought it to New London, Connecticut. Spain demanded its release along with the blacks. Forsyth was willing to comply on the basis of treaty obligations. Abolitionists, who accused him of antipathy toward the Africans, brought a politicized suit in federal courts to free them. The Supreme Court ruled in favor of the blacks after Forsyth left office.

In Forsyth's time no major crisis taxed the State Department. For this reason, and because he did not initiate policy, his diplomatic accomplishments were modest. He was a capable administrator who reduced bureaucracy, introduced efficiency, and tightened security. His reorganization of the department worked well enough to remain in force for over thirty years. Attractiveness, charm, a good mind, and an ability to survive political change through expedient shifts in his convictions marked much of his political career. He died in Washington shortly after his retirement.

• Manuscript sources are scattered. There are a few Forsyth papers in the Georgia Department of Archives and History, Atlanta, and in the Manuscript Division of the Princeton University Library, and official correspondence and letter books are in several divisions of the National Archives, Washington, D.C. The only full biography is Alvin L. Duckett, *John Forsyth: Political Tactician* (1962). See also Roberta F. Cason, "The Public Career of John Forsyth, 1813–1834" (master's thesis, Emory Univ., 1935); Eugene I. McCormac, "John Forsyth," in *The American Secretaries of State and Their Diplomacy*, vol. 4, ed. Samuel F. Bemis (10 vols., 1927–1929); Jennie Forsyth Jeffries, *A History of the Forsyth Family* (1920); and Lawton B. Evans, "John Forsyth," *Men of Mark in Georgia*, vol. 2, ed. William J. Northen (7 vols., 1907–1912; repr. 1974). Howard Jones, *Mutiny on the Amistad* (1987), is the best scholarly study of the incident.

ALEXANDER DeCONDE

FORSYTH, Thomas (5 Dec. 1771–29 Oct. 1833), fur trader and Indian agent, was born in what is now Detroit, Michigan, the son of William Forsyth, an innkeeper, and Ann Kinzie. Forsyth received such education as was available and was literate. His experiences in the multiethnic frontier world of Detroit, which even after the Revolution was dominated by British traders, completed his schooling. After the death of his father in 1790, Forsyth entered the fur trade as a clerk for George Sharp and spent several winters trading among the Ottawa on Saginaw Bay. By 1798 he was trading near what is now Quincy, Illinois. His first trading partner was a man named Richardson, and in 1802 he and his half-brother John Kinzie started a trading post at the present location of Chicago, Illinois. About 1804 Forsyth married Keziah Malotte, a former Indian captive, near Malden, Missouri, and they settled at Peoria, where he traded until the beginning of the War of 1812, when General William Clark secretly appointed him Indian subagent for the Illinois District at $600 per annum and three daily rations.

The Illinois country was a dangerous place in those years. Besides the conflict between British and American interests, the Indian peoples of the region were in constant turmoil because of continued white encroachment. Forsyth, having sent his wife and children to the safety of St. Louis, worked effectively to stymie British efforts among the Illinois River Potawatomi and other nearby peoples. He ransomed one soldier captured in the Potawatomi attack on Fort Dearborn. The British and their allies began to suspect that Forsyth was more than a trader. Robert Dickson, a British agent at Green Bay, dispatched a war party of Winnebago to kill or capture Forsyth, a plan that failed when the Potawatomi warned Forsyth. In November 1812 the commander of an American militia force concluded that Forsyth and the French citizens of Peoria were assisting the enemy. The militiamen torched the village and forced Forsyth and his neighbors downriver. The captives were released but many lost their homes and property. Years later Forsyth remained bitter over the episode.

After the Treaty of Ghent, Forsyth continued in the Indian service. In 1818 he was promoted to agent and

in 1819 Clark sent him up the Mississippi to distribute annuity goods and presents and report on conditions as far as the Falls of St. Anthony. Upon his return, Forsyth sent Clark a thorough report on the conditions he encountered.

Forsyth was next assigned to the Rock Island Agency for the Sauk and Fox located at Fort Armstrong on the Illinois River, a post he held until 1830. The United States was inclining toward a policy of removing Indian peoples beyond the Mississippi River. Forsyth had his hands full keeping track of events, stemming rumors and trying to maintain peace in the face of an increased flow of settlers, an escalation in the whiskey traffic, and even the presence of white lead miners in northwestern Illinois who were competing with the Sauk and Fox. Land cession treaties were concluded with increasing frequency. Tribes broke into factions over how best to deal with the white onslaught, meanwhile continuing to war with traditional enemies. Forsyth reported that the Sauk and Fox were amazed to learn that the goods they received annually were in part payment for lands ceded in an 1804 treaty of which most had no knowledge. Forsyth, who came to be called Mah-tah-win (the Corn) was successful in preventing serious trouble primarily by being forthright and open in his dealings and by doing what he could to argue on behalf of the Sauk and Fox to officials in the government. He seems to have been held in high regard by both Keokuk and Black Hawk, who represented opposing approaches to the tide of events, Keokuk favoring accommodation and Black Hawk calling for resistance.

Forsyth and three other capable, experienced agents were the first to fall prey to the "spoils system" policy of President Andrew Jackson's administration. By September 1831 half the Indian agents and subagents had been replaced. His dismissal in June 1830 removed a skilled and experienced agent at a delicate time. His continued presence might have prevented the outbreak of Black Hawk's War in 1832. A few weeks after his removal, his replacement negotiated another land cession by the Sauk and Fox. Forsyth moved to St. Louis but in 1833 traveled to a large treaty negotiation at Chicago, where he and many others sought compensation for losses sustained in conflicts with the British and the Indians. The Treaty of Chicago provided for an unusual number of payments to both Indians and whites. Forsyth died in St. Louis six weeks after the conclusion of the treaty negotiations. The U.S. Senate eventually approved the Treaty of Chicago, including the schedule of payees attached to the treaty. Forsyth's four children would have inherited whatever he was due, his wife having died in 1829.

Forsyth was a participant in and shaper of events in the Illinois country, a skilled and knowledgeable intermediary working at the intersection of Indian and white societies. His contributions during the War of 1812 are particularly important.

• The Forsyth manuscripts are located in the Missouri Historical Society and the Wisconsin Historical Society (Draper

Collection). His "Journal of a Voyage from St. Louis to the Falls of St. Anthony in 1819" appears in *Wisconsin Historical Collections*, vol. 6 (1872; repr. 1908), pp. 188–219. Additional Forsyth correspondence on the War of 1812 appears in *Wisconsin Historical Collections*, vol. 11 (1888; repr. 1908), pp. 316–52. Thomas Craig's explanation of the 1812 burning of Peoria and arrest of Forsyth appears in E. B. Washburne, ed., *The Edwards Papers* (1884), pp. 86–90.

Forsyth's ethnographic work remains well regarded (see *Handbook of North American Indians: Northeast* (1978), p. 646. His "An Account of the Manners and Customs of the Sauk and Fox Nations of Indians Tradition" (1827) appears in *The Indian Tribes of the Upper Mississippi Valley and Region of the Great Lakes*, ed. Emma Helen Blair, vol. 2 (1911), pp. 183–245; this work also includes Forsyth's "Shawnee Prophet," pp. 273–79, and "Kickapoo Prophet," pp. 280–81. Charles Kappler, ed., *Indian Affairs Laws and Treaties*, vol. 2 (1904) reprints the Treaty of Chicago. Juliette Kinzie (Mrs. John Kinzie) wrote *Wau Bun, The Early Days in the Northwest* (1844; repr. 1932), which is heavily based on hearsay. Useful modern studies are Roger Nichols, *Black Hawk and the Warrior's Path* (1992); Donald Jackson, ed., *Black Hawk: An Autobiography* (1964); R. David Edmunds, *Potawatomis: Keepers of the Fire* (1978). James Clifton is critical of Forsyth in "Chicago, September 14, 1833: The Last Great Indian Treaty in the Old Northwest," *Chicago History* 9 (Summer 1980): 86–97. More balanced is Francis Paul Prucha, *American Indian Treaties* (1994), pp. 189–90. For Forsyth's dismissal, see Herman J. Viola, *Thomas L. McKenney Architect of America's Early Indian Policy, 1816–1830* (1974), pp. 227–28.

DOUGLAS D. MARTIN

FORT, Charles Hoy (16 Aug. 1874–3 May 1932), writer, was born in Albany, New York, the son of Charles Nelson Fort, a grocery wholesaler, and Agnes Hoy. Both parents were descendants of old and prominent Albany merchant families. Fort was an indifferent student as a child but was intrigued by science and earnestly collected birds' eggs, insects, and rocks. When asked what he wanted to be when he grew up, he mystified his grandfather by answering, "a naturalist." At seventeen he became a reporter for the *Albany Democrat* and soon began to sell feature articles to the *Brooklyn (N.Y.) World*. When his grandfather died in 1891, Fort received a small legacy. He left high school without graduating and in 1892 went to New York and took a job on the *World*. The next year, with an allowance of $25 a month from his guardian, he set out to travel around the world, in order, as he later wrote, "to accumulate an experience and knowledge of life that would fit me to become a writer." After two years in Canada, Scotland, Wales, and South Africa, he returned to New York, where in 1896 he married Anna Filing, a childhood friend from Albany. The couple had no children.

Fort made a scant living as a writer, selling humorous stories to *Tom Watson's Magazine*, the *Popular Magazine*, and *Smith's Magazine*, edited by Theodore Dreiser, with whom he formed a close friendship. Although he is known to have written at least ten novels during this period, he published only one, *The Outcast Manufacturers* (1909), a comic fantasy of a poor family and the collapse of their shady business. None of his other long fiction has survived.

From his early thirties, Fort devoted much of his time to the pursuit that was to become the focus of his life: the collection of data he considered inexplicable by conventional science. He ransacked old newspapers and magazines for reports of mysterious appearances and disappearances, unexplained night lights, spontaneous combustion of human beings, and rainfalls of blood, frogs, and stones. In time he developed a series of explanations for these anomalous phenomena. Around 1912 he wrote a book called *X*, which suggested that the earth was controlled by Martians, and in 1916 followed it with another, titled *Y*, describing the influence on our civilization of a race living at the South Pole. Both books, now lost, greatly impressed Dreiser, who unsuccessfully tried to find a publisher for them.

Undeterred by failure, Fort continued his research and in 1919 produced a volume called *The Book of the Damned*, cataloging events dismissed (and thus "damned") by scientists, "upon no consideration for their individual merits or demerits, but in conformity with a general attempt to hold out for isolation of this earth." In it, Fort postulated a gelatinous Super-Sargasso Sea in space holding things that sometimes came unstuck and fell to earth. Dreiser compelled his publisher, Horace Liveright, to issue the volume by threatening to take his own future work elsewhere.

Fort and his wife lived from 1921 to 1929 in London, where the still-unknown writer devoted his full time to research at the British Museum. In 1923 he published *New Lands*, attacking astronomers as "led by a pillar of rubbish by day and a cloud of bosh by night." With an introduction by Booth Tarkington, the book had some success among writers, who were intrigued by Fort's elliptical, aphoristic style and his flashes of sardonic humor as well as by his bizarre theories. In 1931 Fort's most famous book, *Lo!*, appeared, with an introduction by novelist Tiffany Thayer ranking the author with Columbus, Galileo, Newton, Pasteur, and the Wright brothers. Embraced (though sometimes with tongue in cheek) by literary figures such as Dreiser, Tarkington, Alexander Woollcott, Ben Hecht, and John Cowper Powys, Fort generated something of a cult, and with the publication of *Lo!* a Fortean Society was formed by Dreiser and Thayer. The next year Fort's *Wild Talents*, describing such phenomena as precognition, extrasensory perception, and psychokinesis (for which Fort coined the term "teleportation," which was to become current in science fiction), appeared posthumously.

The reclusive Fort, described as "a shy bearlike man with a brown walrus mustache and thick glasses," refused to have anything to do with the society named for him. He spent his last years in the Bronx, where he died, working in his small, cluttered apartment surrounded by notes and clippings or haunting the New York Public Library reading room, culling further data from periodicals to support his theories. A skeptic to the end, he declined to see a doctor in his final illness. The Fortean Society lasted until Thayer's death in 1959 and was revived as the International Fortean Society in 1965. A bimonthly *Fortean Times* began publication in London in 1973.

Opinion on Charles Fort has been divided since his death. An engaging eccentric whose preposterous theories were at least half facetious, Fort mocked himself as shrewdly as he did the science he attacked and the system of logic on which it is based. "I go on with my yarns," he wrote. "I no more believe them than I believe that twice two are four." H. G. Wells described Fort in a letter to Dreiser as "one of the most damnable bores who ever cut scraps from out-of-the-way newspapers and thought they were facts. And he writes like a drunkard." H. L. Mencken was no less contemptuous; he wrote Dreiser that Fort was "enormously ignorant of elementary science" and "a quack of the most obvious sort." But many admired his courageous assault on what he called "scientific priestcraft," and Dreiser never lost his faith in Fort as an unappreciated genius. "To me," he wrote to Mencken, "he is simply stupendous & some day I really believe he will get full credit." If most of the literary people who celebrated Fort did so as a joke, his witty and often trenchant iconoclasm struck a responsive chord in an age increasingly suspicious of scientific dogma.

• Unpublished manuscripts of Fort are in the Tiffany Thayer Collection in the New York Public Library, and many letters between Fort and Theodore Dreiser are in the Dreiser collection of the University of Pennsylvania in Philadelphia. Selections from his journals and articles about his work were published in the *Fortean Society Magazine* 1 (Sept. 1937)–61 (Spring 1959), retitled *Doubt* from vol. 11 (Winter 1944–45). See also *INFO Journal*, the publication of the International Fortean Society (INFO), from 1965, and *Fortean Times: The Journal of Strange Phenomena*, from 1973. *The Book of the Damned, New Lands, Lo!*, and *Wild Talents* were issued in an omnibus volume with an introduction by Tiffany Thayer in 1941 as *The Books of Charles Fort*, republished with a new introduction by Damon Knight in 1975. Biographical information on Fort can be found in W. A. Swanberg, *Dreiser* (1969), and chapters are devoted to him in H. Allen Smith, *Low Man on a Totem Pole* (1941), and Martin Gardner, *In the Name of Science* (1952). A full-length biography of Fort is Damon Knight's respectful *Charles Fort: Prophet of the Unexplained* (1976). See also *Time*, 23 Feb. 1931, p. 63, and Miriam Allen deFord, "Charles Fort: Enfant Terrible of Science," *Magazine of Fantasy and Science Fiction*, Jan. 1954, pp. 105–16. An obituary of Fort is in the *New York Times*, 5 May 1932.

DENNIS WEPMAN

FORT, Syvilla (3 July 1917–8 Nov. 1975), dancer, choreographer, and dance teacher, was born in Seattle, Washington, the daughter of Mildred Dill. Her mother tried to enroll the four-year-old Fort in ballet classes, but teachers refused her entrance because they were afraid they would lose clientele by admitting an African-American student. Her mother then recruited a group of black children interested in learning dance and hired the advanced white ballet students to teach them. At nine Fort had private teachers and was on her way to becoming a pioneer African American in ballet and modern dance. Sensitive throughout her life to discrimination, Fort passed on what she learned to other black children. While still a high school freshman, she was teaching ballet, tap, and modern dance to as many as sixteen children under the age of thirteen for fifty cents a lesson.

In 1935 Fort received a scholarship to attend, as the first black student, the Nellie Cornish School of Allied Arts, known for experimental melding of dance, music, and drama. She was embraced by the city of Seattle for dance and choreography in which she blended modern dance with ballet. In 1938 she requested that John Cage compose a piano piece for a dance, *Bacchanal*. The result was his first prepared piano composition. Fort graduated from Cornish in 1938, moved to Los Angeles, and was recommended by William Grant Still, the black composer, to Katherine Dunham, the pioneer black concert dancer and teacher of the 1940s.

Fort toured with the all-black Dunham Dance Company as a soloist and joined Dunham in her mission to return the ceremonial meaning to imported dances—in the words of Dunham, "to take *our* dance out of the burlesque." Dunham accomplished this by imbuing modern dance with dance techniques from African-American cultural heritage. To classical ballet Dunham added isolated body movements that she discovered in her study of West Indian and African dance. Early productions in which Fort danced were characterized by theatrical lighting and lush costumes and scenery.

Fort was a solo sensation in Los Angeles after performing in the 1942 All-Negro Artists Concert for Russian war relief at the Wilshire-Ebell Theater. Reviewer Tom Cullen praised Fort as "incredibly graceful, with a beautifully-built body and the ease that comes with complete mastery of technique." Fort conducted research on the mixed folk dance of Native Americans, Mexicans, and African Americans off the Florida and Georgia coasts, then blended techniques to develop her own version of American dancing. She formed her own group of twelve dancers and "insist[ed] upon it remaining a mixed group. I know from the hard struggle I had to go through that this business of racial discrimination must be dragged out into the open and faced squarely."

Fort teamed up with Dunham because together they had a better chance of attaining their larger vision of getting African Americans recognized as performing artists. Fort appeared with the Dunham dancers in the film *Stormy Weather* (1943). The film's success gained the Dunham Dance Company national recognition. In September 1943 Dunham and her company opened to great success at New York's Martin Beck Theatre in a production titled *Tropical Revue*. The dance *Rites de Passage*, based on a fertility ritual, was banned in Boston for sexual content but hailed elsewhere. In 1945 Fort took the position of ballet mistress and supervising director at Dunham's newly established School of Arts and Research in New York City, teaching Dunham's dance technique and the cultural heritage from which it evolved. Included in the curriculum were philosophy, language, speech, and ethnology. Neglect of a knee injury ended Fort's dancing career, and it was as a teacher of adults and children at the Dunham school that she gained recognition.

After the Dunham school closed in 1955 owing to lack of funds, Fort taught at the Lee Strasberg Institute, Columbia University Teachers College, and New York City's Clark Center of Performing Arts. In 1955, with her husband, tap dancer Buddy Phillips, she opened the Phillips-Fort Studio in the theater district on West Forty-fourth Street, where she introduced her Afro-Modern technique. Fort drew on dance techniques from Africa, the West Indies, Haiti, and early American black jazz to create a technique freer than Dunham's with isolated upper-body movements backed by the roll of African drums. Like Dunham, Fort believed in dance as communication and so believed in training the mind as well as the body. If she imported a dance, she strove to provide an explanation of its original meaning.

Fort taught with an encouraging yet firm approach. Her list of students includes Butterfly McQueen, Alvin Ailey, Eartha Kitt, James Earl Jones, and a host of celebrities, including actors Marlon Brando and Jane Fonda. Harry Belafonte and the government of Guinea later recruited Fort to go to Africa to help establish a dance company. Fort served as choreographer for Langston Hughes's *The Prodigal Son* and composed many other works. After the death of her husband in 1963, Fort continued to run the small Manhattan studio, but her habit of teaching free of charge led to financial difficulties, and she was forced to close the studio. Before this, however, young filmmaker Ayoka Chenzira captured Fort on film teaching in her studio. In the documentary *Syvilla: They Dance to Her Drum* (1979), Chenzira recognized Fort as the important developmental link between Katherine Dunham and Alvin Ailey.

After Fort developed breast cancer (nine months before her death), she was honored at the Majestic Theater by the Black Theatre Alliance, formed in 1969 to provide central resources to the African-American theater community. The event exhibited Fort's contribution to the development of African-American modern dance and the success with which the African-American community could organize a benefit occasion. Proceeds from the event established the Syvilla Fort Fund to assist nonprofit dance and theater institutions with scholarships, aid a training school founded by Fort, and provide an emergency fund for dancers. Fort died in New York City.

• The Dance Collection of the New York Public Library for the Performing Arts at Lincoln Center possesses photographs, videotapes, films, programs, and clipping files, including a copy of *Syvilla: They Dance to Her Drum*. For information on Fort's childhood and early career, see Tom Cullen, "Young Negro Artist Talks of the Dance" in the daily California newspaper *People's World*, 2 May 1942. Fort's contribution to modern dance is mentioned in Lynne Fauley Emery, *Black Dance: From 1619 to Today* (1972), and Zita D. Allen, "Blacks and Ballet," *Dance Magazine*, July 1976, pp. 65–70. Ayoka Chenzira's interview with Fort for her film *Syvilla Fort: Spirit on the Dance Floor* is reproduced in part in *Dance Book Forum* (1981), pp. 5–6. The film is also discussed by Patricia Jones in the *Village Voice*, 27 Aug. 1980, p. 44. For tributes to Fort see *Dance Magazine*, Apr. 1980, pp. 51, 52, 98, 100; "BTA Honors Syvilla Fort," *Dance Herald* 1, no. 2 (1975): 1, 4; and J. B. Alexander, "Syvilla Fort: Mother to 3 Generations of Dance," *New York Post*, 28 Oct. 1975, p. 56. For a description of Dunham's vision and career highlights see Richard A. Long, *The Black Tradition in American Dance* (1989), Edward Thorpe, *Black Dance* (1990), pp. 124–30. An obituary is in *Dance News*, Dec. 1975, pp. 6–7, *Dance Magazine*, Jan. 1976, p. 100, and the *New York Times*, 9 Nov. 1975.

BARBARA L. CICCARELLI

FORTAS, Abe (19 June 1910–5 Apr. 1982), lawyer and associate justice of the Supreme Court, was born in Memphis, Tennessee, the son of Woolfe Fortas, a cabinetmaker, and Rachel Berzansky. Although Abe's father was born in Russia and his mother in Lithuania, the couple immigrated to the United States from England in 1905. Despite his father's attempts to assimilate by changing his name to William, his mother raised her children as Orthodox Jews in an overwhelmingly Protestant community. Neither well off nor poverty-stricken, young Fortas supplemented his family's income by working in a shoe store, giving violin lessons, and playing fiddle with local bands. His amateur violin skills helped finance Fortas's undergraduate studies at Southwestern College in Memphis, from which he received a bachelor's degree in 1930. At the age of twenty, he enrolled at Yale University Law School on scholarship, where he served as editor in chief of the law journal and graduated Phi Beta Kappa in 1933.

At Yale, Fortas established a close relationship with professor William O. Douglas, who persuaded the university to offer Fortas a teaching fellowship for the 1933–1934 school year. Before he could begin instruction, however, Fortas was summoned to Washington to work for the legal staff of the Agricultural Adjustment Administration under Jerome Frank. Although his position was temporary, his work made a striking impression on Frank; consequently, Fortas did not begin teaching until February 1934. In 1935 he married Carolyn Eugenia Agger, whom he persuaded to also study law at Yale. The couple had no children.

From 1934 to 1937 Fortas commuted between Yale and Washington, working on part-time assignments for the New Deal. In 1937 he was appointed assistant director of the public utilities division at the Securities and Exchange Commission (SEC), then under Douglas's leadership. When Douglas left the SEC in 1939 to accept an appointment to the Supreme Court, Fortas joined Secretary of the Interior Harold Ickes as general counsel to the Public Works Administration.

By the time Fortas was appointed under secretary of the interior in 1942, World War II was in full swing, and in September 1943 he left Ickes's staff to join the navy. Suffering from ocular tuberculosis, he was discharged within a month and returned to his former position just in time to help resettle Japanese Americans who had been sent to detention camps early in the war. Recalling Fortas's way of handling the matter, Adrian Fisher, a War Department representative, said: "Abe operated as a man of principle, but also with a certain deviousness. He was a very strong force for good. But he also cut a few close corners, and he laid on the political stuff a bit thick" (Shogan, p. 53).

In January 1946, after leaving government service, Fortas set up office with former professor Thurman Arnold. Paul Porter joined them a year later. Arnold, Fortas & Porter was one of the few firms willing to take on "loyalty cases" during the McCarthy era, defending various suspected security risks, including Owen Lattimore, a Johns Hopkins professor and Far Eastern affairs consultant who had been labeled as a top Russian espionage agent. Although such cases were financially and politically risky, Fortas insisted that the firm take them, saying, "If we don't do it, nobody else will" (Shogan, p. 59).

As evidenced in his oral arguments, Fortas was a phenomenal legal craftsman with a keen sensitivity to words and their meanings. Speaking of his tendency toward perfectionism, a friend of Fortas told the *New York Times* (29 July 1965), "He would rework the Lord's Prayer, if it came in a brief." Fortas's arguments in the famous and controversial *Durham* case eventually helped broaden the criminal insanity rule, thus setting a new precedent that "an accused is not criminally responsible if his unlawful act was the product of a mental disease or defect." However, the precedent applied only in federal cases in the District of Columbia, and ultimately it was rejected by Congress. In 1962 Fortas was appointed by the Supreme Court to handle the appeal of Clarence Earl Gideon, an indigent serving time in a Florida prison after a judge refused his request for a court-appointed counselor. Fortas's brilliant argument before the Court helped overturn a previous ruling, which held that the right to free counsel occurred only under "special circumstances." The Court's new ruling required that states provide free counsel for the poor in every serious criminal case.

As the firm flourished into one of the most prosperous in Washington, D.C., Fortas spent much of his time advising corporate clients such as Federated Department Stores and Greatamerica Corporation. His most important client was a nonpaying one, President Lyndon Johnson. Fortas's friendship with Johnson began during their New Deal days and was confirmed in 1948, when he persuaded Justice Hugo Black to reinstate Johnson's name to the general election ballot after it had been removed by a federal judge pending an investigation into voting irregularities in the Texas primary. As a result of Black's decision, Johnson won a Senate seat. After President John F. Kennedy's assassination in 1963, Fortas met Johnson at the airport in Washington and continued to be on hand for the rest of Johnson's first term as president, helping plan,

among other things, the Warren Commission. He was also, according to author Theodore H. White in *The Making of the President 1964* (1965), one of only three men Johnson "could trust with his own inner ruminative thinking" concerning particular problems of the 1964 election, which Johnson won.

In 1965 Johnson reportedly summoned Fortas to the White House and said, "I'm sending fifty thousand boys to Vietnam, and I'm sending you to the Supreme Court" (*New York Times*, 7 Apr. 1982). Although Fortas had declined Johnson's previous offer of the same appointment, he reluctantly accepted the nomination. On 4 October 1965 he was sworn in to the highest Court of the nation, a ceremony that solidified the liberal course of the Warren Court. As a justice, Fortas helped provide the margin of victory in several cases involving individual rights, including *Miranda v. Arizona* (1966), in which the Court ruled that police must advise a criminal suspect of his or her right to a lawyer and his or her right to remain silent. Fortas wrote the opinion in a 1966 case known as *In re Gault*, which held that children deserve the same constitutional protections as adults in court proceedings.

In 1968 Chief Justice Warren retired, and Johnson nominated Fortas to replace him. Criticisms immediately arose over Fortas's close relationship with the president, whom he continued to informally advise. Ultimately, Fortas's relationship with Johnson cost him the chief justiceship, even though he always denied any conflict of interest.

In 1969 Fortas found himself embroiled in another conflict, this one over his relationship with Louis Wolfson, a wealthy financier and philanthropist. In January 1966, only three months after he was sworn in as a Supreme Court justice and while Wolfson was under federal investigation, Fortas accepted $20,000 from the Wolfson Family Foundation, a fee that was to be paid yearly to Fortas for his efforts in shaping the foundation's program and that would continue to his wife in the event of his death. In June 1966, however, Fortas wrote to the foundation requesting that the work arrangement be canceled but citing only a heavy workload as the reason for his resignation. By September 1966 Wolfson was indicted on stock fraud charges. Fortas returned the entire sum of $20,000 in December. When the story was unearthed in *Life* magazine four years later, Wolfson was in prison, and many members of Congress clamored for Fortas's impeachment. Consequently, Fortas resigned from the Court on 14 May 1969, the first justice ever to do so under public criticism. Fortas maintained, however, that he had done nothing wrong since he had neither given Wolfson or the foundation any legal advice nor intervened on his friend's behalf regarding Wolfson's criminal behavior.

After leaving the Court, Fortas continued to practice law, although with a different firm. In 1982, just two weeks before his death, Fortas argued his first case before the Supreme Court since his resignation. Despite his association with Wolfson, he was remembered fondly by his associates. Justices William Brennan and Thurgood Marshall issued this joint statement upon his death: "He was not only an esteemed colleague but also a close friend. We shall miss him." Fortas's actions were paradoxical, and his peculiar combination of liberal idealism and political savvy was perplexing throughout a career viewed by many as that of a Washington insider. He loved music, which for him represented emotion. He also loved the law and viewed it as a model of discipline, a structured world in which he could safely operate. One biographer wrote: "As a government lawyer, private practitioner, and Supreme Court justice, he did subordinate process to substance, for he believed that the ends justified the means. But the means had to be legal, and if they were not, he devised a way of bringing them within the law" (Kalman, p. 1). Fortas died at his home in Washington, D.C.

• The Abe Fortas Supreme Court Papers are in the Yale University Archives, while the Abe Fortas Papers are privately held. Fortas's life and career are discussed extensively in Laura Kalman, *Abe Fortas: A Biography* (1990). See also Robert Shogan, *A Question of Judgment* (1972), which sheds particular light on the circumstances surrounding his resignation from the Supreme Court; and Bruce Allen Murphy, *Fortas: The Rise and Ruin of a Supreme Court Justice* (1988). Several other articles feature Fortas, including a flattering portrait printed in *Current Biography* in 1966, a year after Fortas was appointed to the high Court. A profile is Anthony Lewis, "A Tough Lawyer Goes to the Court," *New York Times Magazine*, 8 Aug. 1965, p. 11. See the *New York Times*, 29 July 1965, on Fortas's nomination to the Supreme Court. His obituary is in the *New York Times*, 7 Apr. 1982.

DONNA GREAR PARKER

FORTEN, Charlotte. *See* Grimké, Charlotte Forten.

FORTEN, James (2 Sept. 1766–4 Mar. 1842), businessman and social reformer, was born in Philadelphia, Pennsylvania, the son of Thomas Forten, a freeborn sailmaker, and Margaret (maiden name unknown). Forten's parents enrolled him in the African School of abolitionist Anthony Benezet. When Forten was seven, his father died. Margaret Forten struggled to keep her son in school, but he was eventually forced to leave at age nine and work full time to help support the family. His family remained in Philadelphia throughout the American Revolution, and Forten later recalled being in the crowd outside the Pennsylvania State House when the Declaration of Independence was read to the people for the first time.

In 1781, while serving on a privateer, Forten was captured by the British and spent seven months on the infamous prison ship *Jersey* in New York harbor.

After a voyage to England in 1784 as a merchant seaman, Forten returned to Philadelphia and apprenticed himself to Robert Bridges, a white sailmaker. Bridges taught Forten his trade, loaned him money to buy a house, and eventually sold him the business. Inheriting most of Bridges's customers and establishing a reputation as a master craftsman in his own right, Forten prospered. His profits were invested in real estate,

loans at interest, and eventually in bank, canal, and railroad stock.

In 1803 Forten married Martha Beatte, of Darby township, Delaware County, Pennsylvania. She died in 1804, and a year later he married Charlotte Vandine, a Philadelphian of European, African, and Native-American descent. They had eight children; Margaretta, Harriet, Sarah, and James were all active in the antislavery movement.

Forten's emergence as a leader in Philadelphia's black community coincided with his growing prosperity. Well-read and articulate, he was often called on to draft petitions and to chair meetings. In 1799 he joined other black citizens in petitioning for an end to the slave trade and for legislation to prevent the kidnapping of free people. When Congress refused to consider the petition, Forten wrote to thank the one man, George Thatcher of Massachusetts, who had spoken in its favor. The letter attracted considerable attention.

In 1813, responding to an attempt by the state legislature to restrict the rights of black Pennsylvanians, Forten published *Letters from a Man of Colour*. Attacking the proposed legislation, he cited Pennsylvania's reputation as a haven for the oppressed. He also objected strenuously to a law that would reduce all black people, including "men of property," to the status of felons.

Forten's role in the debate over African repatriation was pivotal. He was initially enthusiastic about the proposal of the African-American shipowner Paul Cuffe to take American free blacks to Britain's colony of Sierra Leone. Forten had no intention of relocating, but he agreed with Cuffe that less fortunate members of the community might benefit from emigrating.

With the formation of the American Colonization Society in 1816, Forten moved from support of African resettlement to outspoken opposition. At first, when approached by an officer of the ACS whom he knew to be a dedicated abolitionist, he gave the organization a qualified endorsement. When others in the ACS spoke of the need to deport free blacks to the new colony of Liberia because of their "pernicious" influence on the slaves, however, Forten expressed alarm. The leaders of the ACS repeatedly urged him to set an example by emigrating. They offered him incentives to begin a packet service between the United States and Liberia. Forten was unmoved, and for the rest of his life he remained one of the most vocal critics of the ACS.

Freeborn, Forten was a lifelong opponent of slavery, and he worked with two generations of white abolitionists. He had many contacts with the "gradualists" in the Pennsylvania Abolition Society. He hired servants recommended by the PAS, sent his four sons to the PAS school, and even took into his home an African prince the society was educating. However, neither he nor any other African American was invited to join the PAS.

The extent of Forten's involvement in the antislavery cause changed with the emergence of the "new school" abolitionists in the early 1830s. William Lloyd

Garrison became a close personal friend and often visited the Forten home. Forten advanced him money to begin publishing the *Liberator*. Thereafter he gave advice on sales and distribution and more money to tide Garrison over periodic crises. In 1832, when Garrison was preparing his *Thoughts on African Colonization*, Forten sent him his own collection of material on the ACS. He was elected a vice president of the new American Anti-Slavery Society and helped organize auxiliaries at the state and local levels.

Forten saw the abolition of slavery as one aspect of a moral crusade to transform society. Temperance, education, pacifism, and women's rights all had their place in his vision of America. In 1834 Forten and a group of like-minded black reformers founded the American Moral Reform Society, braving criticism from their own community that they were unrealistic, naive, and lacking in racial pride as they advocated the abandonment of terms of racial identification, promoted a sweeping reform agenda, and vowed to direct their efforts at all Americans, regardless of race.

In the last decade of his life Forten's faith in the power of reform to regenerate society was severely tested. As a wave of racial violence swept the country, he, his family, and the community institutions to which he belonged all came under attack, including mob violence and destruction of property. On several occasions he received death threats because of his opposition to colonization.

The violence was accompanied by an erosion of the civil rights of Pennsylvania's African Americans. In 1832 Forten and his son-in-law, Robert Purvis, protested a move by the state legislature to restrict the mobility of black Pennsylvanians. In 1838 Pennsylvania's constitution was revised. Blacks, regardless of wealth, were barred from voting, while most adult white men were enfranchised. On behalf of his community, Forten brought suit to establish his right to vote. After losing the case, he helped finance the printing of an appeal urging voters to reject the proposed constitution. Nevertheless, the constitution was ratified by a large majority.

In 1841 deteriorating health obliged Forten to curtail his business activities and his reform work. When he died in Philadelphia, the abolitionist press eulogized him, the local papers commented on the many prominent white merchants who attended his funeral, and the *African Repository*, the journal of the ACS, regretted that to the end he did not change his mind about colonization.

• Letters to and from Forten are in the Paul Cuffe Papers at the New Bedford Free Public Library, New Bedford, Mass.; the Antislavery Manuscripts at the Boston Public Library; and at the Historical Society of Pennsylvania, in the Cox, Parrish, Wharton Papers, the Samuel Breck Papers, and the manuscript collections of the Pennsylvania Abolition Society. See also the *Liberator*, *Freedom's Journal*, the *Colored American*, and the *Pennsylvania Freeman* for additional letters and accounts of his antislavery and reform work. Much of this material has been included in the microfilm edition of *The Black Abolitionist Papers, 1830–1865*. Two contemporaries

gave memorial addresses. See Robert Purvis, *Remarks on the Life and Character of James Forten* (1842), and Stephen Gloucester, *A Discourse Delivered upon the Occasion of the Death of Mr. James Forten, Sr.* (1842). More recent assessments of Forten's career are Ray Allen Billington's pioneering article, "James Forten—Forgotten Abolitionist," *Negro History Bulletin* 13 (Nov. 1949): 31–36, 45, and Esther M. Douty, *Forten the Sailmaker: Pioneer Champion of Negro Rights* (1968). On Forten and his community, see Gary Nash, *Forging Freedom: The Formation of Philadelphia's Black Community, 1720–1840* (1988), and Julie Winch, *Philadelphia's Black Elite: Activism, Accommodation, and the Struggle for Autonomy* (1988).

JULIE WINCH

FORTIER, Alcée (5 June 1856–14 Feb. 1914), linguist and historian, was born in St. James Parish, Louisiana, the son of Florent Fortier, a sugar planter, and Edwige Aime. Fortier came from distinguished Louisiana stock, the roots of the Fortier family tracing back to the founding of the French colony in the early eighteenth century. His mother belonged to one of the state's wealthiest sugar planting families.

Educated by private tutors and in A. V. Romain's classical school in New Orleans, Fortier showed an early aptitude for languages. He enrolled in the University of Virginia in 1872, but a serious illness terminated his studies there in 1873. Even so, his academic training in French continued on an informal basis under the tutelage of professors A. Marshall Elliott of Johns Hopkins and Paul Passy in Paris. Shortly after his return to Louisiana, Fortier began to study law, but with the family's fortune in ruins as a result of the Civil War, he was forced to work as a bank clerk, a French teacher in the Boys' High School of New Orleans, and as an instructor and principal of the preparatory department of the University of Louisiana, which became Tulane University in 1884. He remained there as a highly popular professor of French, then of Romance languages, for thirty-four years, until his death. He married Marie Lanauze, the daughter of a New Orleans merchant, in October 1881. The couple had eight children, five of whom survived into adulthood.

Despite his never having obtained the professional degrees later required for participation in academic life, Fortier's contributions to scholarship were varied and substantial. Fluent in at least six modern languages and a master of Greek, Latin, and Sanskrit, Fortier wrote numerous articles on philological subjects for literary and historical journals and magazines. Especially notable was his 1894 work, *Louisiana Studies*, which received high praise from his contemporaries and opened a new field in linguistics through its study of the various dialects developed in Louisiana among African Americans, Acadians, and Creoles. Equally important to Fortier was the preservation and promotion of the French language in Louisiana. As president of L'Athenée Louisianais from 1894 to 1914, a literary society formed in 1876 to perpetuate the French language in Louisiana, he advocated that every child in the state be taught French as well as English.

Consistent with this objective, he prepared several French textbooks for school and college use.

Closely related to his Francophile sympathies was Fortier's abiding passion for Creole culture. Defining the Creoles as a group comprised only of the white descendants of persons who had settled in Louisiana under the French and Spanish governments, Fortier overlooked those of partial African ancestry, as well as the native born *nouveaux* whose families had arrived after the Louisiana Purchase. This conception, reflecting his own aristocratic background and belief in the Creoles as an honorable and chivalric race, represented an attempt to restore the early glory of the Creole people at a time when the vestiges of French culture in Louisiana were rapidly fading amid growing American influence. Although Fortier's definition of Creole culture was highly restrictive, works such as *Louisiana Folklore* (1888) and *Louisiana Folktales* (1895) nevertheless succeeded in bolstering Creole identity, promoting general interest in colonial history, and helping to lay the foundation of a romantic tradition.

Fortier's linguistic and cultural interests led him quite naturally to consider the larger field of Louisiana history, and it was as a historian, not a philologist, that he secured his reputation. His most ambitious undertaking was the two-volume encyclopedia titled *Louisiana, Comprising Sketches of Counties, Towns, Events, Institutions, and Persons, Arranged in Cyclopedic Form* (1909). Other works, such as *Central America and Mexico*, written in collaboration with J. R. Ficklen for the *History of North America* series, showed his interest in history of a broader scope. However, it was Fortier's four-volume *History of Louisiana*, published in 1904, which became his most important and enduring work. Spanning the years from 1512 to 1904, the History was hailed as a monumental work at the time of its publication, and despite its cramped and sometimes pedantic style, it has continued to serve as a valuable reference, source book, and classic in Louisiana historiography.

For all of his scholarly accomplishments, Fortier was by no means a retiring academic. He was a president of the Modern Language Association of America in 1898, one of the organizers and later the president (1894) of the American Folklore Society, and, from 1894 to 1912, president of the Louisiana Historical Society, where he worked diligently to stimulate serious scholarship and general interest in Louisiana history. He also continued to have an abiding commitment to his native city and state and was a member of the Civil Service Commission of New Orleans, a member of the State Board of Education for many years, and a member of the board of curators of the Louisiana State Museum. As a tribute to his lifetime commitment to improving the educational standards of New Orleans's schools, Alcée Fortier High School bears his name. Fortier died in New Orleans and was buried in the city's St. Louis Cemetery.

Although a scholar and citizen of diverse accomplishments, Fortier is best remembered for his contributions to the study of Louisiana life and history. He was active in a period when scholars could still move freely across disciplines, and both his linguistic abilities and deep interest in his native state helped to open up new areas of research and historical inquiry, thereby offering a useful foundation for further studies in Louisiana scholarship.

• Many of Fortier's papers are located in the Fortier Collection of the Louisiana State Archives and Records Service. Additional materials can be found in the Archives and Louisiana Collection of Tulane University. The records of L'Athenée Louisianais also provide a good deal of information on Fortier, and some of his essays are published in *Comptes Rendus*, the journal of that organization. Biographical details can be found in Grace King, *Creole Families of New Orleans* (1921); Estelle M. Fortier Cochran, *The Fortier Family and Allied Families* (1963); the second edition of Fortier's *History of Louisiana*, ed. Jo Ann Carrigan (1966); the *Louisiana Historical Quarterly* 55, no. 1 (Winter–Spring 1972); and Glenn Conrad, ed., *A Dictionary of Louisiana Biography*, vol. 1 (1988). On Fortier's teaching career at Tulane, including a photo, see John P. Dyer, *Tulane: The Biography of a University* (1966). For a treatment of Creole society and Fortier's definition of it, see Joseph G. Tregle, Jr., "Creoles and Americans," in Arnold R. Hirsch and Joseph Logsdon, eds., *Creole New Orleans: Race and Americanization* (1992). An obituary is in the *New Orleans Times-Picayune*, 15 Feb. 1914.

JOHN DOUAHUE

FORTUNE, Amos (1710?–17 Nov. 1801), tanner and bookbinder, was born in Africa and brought to the colonies as a slave while very young. Nothing is known of Fortune's parentage, birth, or early years. It is estimated that he arrived in America around 1725, but little is known of his life in the colonies prior to the mid-1700s. Ichabod Richardson of Woburn, Massachusetts, purchased Fortune around 1740, kept him as a slave apprentice, and taught him the art of tanning. In December 1763 Richardson drafted a "freedom paper" granting Fortune's freedom but died without signing it. Fortune remained a slave of the Richardson family until 1770, when a valid article of manumission signed by Ichabod's sister-in-law, Hannah, secured his freedom.

Remaining in Woburn for several years, Fortune purchased a small homestead from Isaac Johnson in 1774 and continued to run the Richardson's tannery. During his Woburn years, Fortune married twice. He purchased the freedom of his first wife, Lydia Somerset, from Josiah Bowers on 23 June 1778, but the marriage was short-lived, ending with Lydia's death after only a few months. The couple had no children. In November 1779 he purchased and married another slave, Vilot, from James Baldwin. Vilot survived Fortune, but they had no children.

The most significant period of Fortune's life as a free man began in 1781 when he and Vilot moved to the town of Jaffrey, New Hampshire, where they established a home and a tannery on land set aside for the town's minister. There Fortune revealed his compassionate nature by taking in a young woman named Celyndia May. While Fortune's will refers to Celyndia as his "adopted daughter," leading some to conclude that she was Vilot's child from a previous relationship, other sources argue that Fortune brought her into the family after moving to Jaffrey. For many years, Fortune's Jaffrey tannery was located on the property belonging to Parson Laban Ainsworth, but Fortune relocated his operations after purchasing twenty-five acres, on which he also built a house and a barn. In 1789 Fortune indentured two apprentices to remain competitive with a second tannery in Jaffrey. That same year he again showed his kindness by taking in a second young woman, Polly Burdoo. Fortune remained in Jaffrey until his death there.

Fortune learned to read, write, and perform basic arithmetic, all skills attested to in his personal papers. He was a full member of the First Congregational Church of Woburn and the First Church of Christ in Jaffrey, as well as a subscriber to a newspaper and a charter member of the Jaffrey Social Library. His skill as a bookbinder is evident from a 1795 contract with the Jaffrey Social Library, which commissioned him to provide new leather bindings for its books. The fact that customers came from throughout New England to purchase his leather attests to his tanning expertise.

By all indications Fortune was a hard-working, sober individual. With its feather bed, writing desk, Windsor chair, six house chairs, and looking glass, Fortune's home likewise revealed his prosperity. His wardrobe, which included a great coat, a striped waistcoat, a black velvet jacket and breeches, a silver watch, and one pair of silver shoe buckles, showed he enjoyed some of life's finery. Affirming his valuation of religion and education, his will provided funds for the church and "School house No. eight." His dedication to the cost of freedom is proven in the prices he paid to establish his family. Fortune's name has been kept alive through the publication of *Amos Fortune: Free Man*, a children's book by Elizabeth Yates, but he deserves to be remembered for achieving what few African Americans of his day could: he established and ran a successful business during America's most oppressive period for African Americans. As the epitaph on his tombstone attests, "He purchased liberty, professed Christianity, lived reputably, & died hopefully."

• A collection of Fortune's personal papers, including his will, his estate inventory, and the signed and unsigned articles of manumission, is at the Jaffrey Public Library in Jaffrey, N.H. F. Alexander Magoun, *Amos Fortune's Choice: The Story of a Negro Slave's Struggle for Self-Fulfillment* (1964), provides a researched but fictionalized biography. Elizabeth Yates, *Amos Fortune: Free Man* (1950), is an interesting though highly speculative biography and the winner of the 1951 Newbery medal. For brief scholarly sources, see the chapter on Fortune in Albert Annett and Alice E. Lehtinen, *History of Jaffrey (Middle Monadnock) New Hampshire: An Average Country Town in the Heart of New England* (1937), and Ralph C. Williams's locally published pamphlet, *The Story of Amos Fortune*, which is reproduced in Lehtinen, *History of Jaffrey . . .* , vol. 3 (1971).

JEFFRY D. SCHANTZ

FORTUNE, Timothy Thomas (3 Oct. 1856–2 June 1928), militant newspaper editor, was born in Marianna, Florida, the son of Emanuel Fortune, a literate slave artisan, and Sarah Jane Moore, a slave. Fortune was raised amid tumultuous times in Reconstruction Florida. His father, one of two African Americans elected as delegates to the 1868 state's constitutional convention and a member of the Florida House of Representatives, was targeted by the Ku Klux Klan and had to flee the area for months in 1869. Thirteen-year-old Timothy became the man of the house in his father's absence. "The constant fear, the stories of outrage . . ., the sign of his once high-spirited mother gradually breaking under the strain of anxiety—all these had a lasting influence on the sensitive and imaginative boy" (Thornbrough, p. 17).

Despite less than three years of formal education, Fortune, an avid reader, enrolled at Howard University during the winter 1874 term. Inadequate finances forced him to leave after one year but not before he managed to complete a few law courses. His later writings would reflect an interest in constitutional law.

Fortune briefly taught school in Florida and worked for the *Jacksonville Daily Union*. Florida was then a degrading environment for an ambitious and proud African American. He migrated to New York City in 1881 with vivid memories of slavery and the exploitation of the postwar freedmen. Fortune never forgot them and spent his journalistic career supporting their political and economic rights.

During the 1880s, frustrated by the Democratic party's machinations and the inability of Republicans to protect their rights in the South, a number of African Americans called for political independence in party affiliation. Fortune articulated their grievances in editorials, articles, and several books. He militantly castigated both major parties for their mistreatment of the freedmen. In July 1881 Fortune, George Parker, and Walter Sampson launched the *New York Globe*. A few months later, Fortune became editor of the *Globe*, succeeding John F. Quarles. The *Globe* and its successors, the *New York Freeman* and the *New York Age*, would establish Fortune as the dean of black journalists. Under his leadership, they were rated by contemporaries as the most distinguished race papers in the nation.

As editor of the *Globe*, Fortune attacked the Republicans for not caring "a snap of the finger" for Negroes. He called upon blacks to form a "new honest party." In 1884 his *Black and White: Land, Labor and Politics in the South*, a study of contradictory threads, was published. In this study of race and the race problem, Fortune was influenced by the writings of Henry George (1839–1897), the proponent of the single-tax levy. Although Fortune criticized the United States for its brutal treatment of African Americans, he vigorously rejected back-to-Africa proposals. Fortune urged blacks and whites to reject established politics for independent voting and to understand that the future struggle in the South would be between "capital and labor, landlord and tenant." He informed both that their common enemy was the capitalist and that white workers who denied blacks union affiliation were tools of the ruling class.

In 1886 Fortune published *The Negro in Politics*, which accused the Republican party of contemptuous treatment of African Americans. He demanded that freedmen place race before party and stop following those leaders who "have swallowed without a grimace every insult to their manhood." Both *Black and White* and *The Negro in Politics received wide coverage in the African-American press, but few blacks were persuaded to desert the Republican party.*

Fortune's cry for political independence cost him control over the *Globe* on 8 November 1884, when Parker sold his interest and the purchaser, William Derrick, declared that the *Globe* would be a Republican paper. Fortune disagreed, and the Republican party refused to subsidize the paper until Fortune resigned. Fortune then established, on 23 November, the *Freeman* with himself as sole owner, editor, and chief printer. African Americans had considered the Democratic party the party of bigotry, treason, and mob rule. Fortune's warm praise of Democrat Grover Cleveland raised speculation that he was seeking a political appointment. Fortune denied this assumption and countered that Cleveland would check reactionary forces within his party. Cleveland's appointment of blacks, Fortune wrote, deserved credit, and he was ready to support him "if the Democratic party pursues a broad, liberal and honorable course toward us" (*Freeman*, 16 May 1885, p. 2). This political unorthodoxy forced him for financial reasons to sell the *Freeman* on 8 October 1887 to Jerome B. Peterson and Emanuel Fortune, Jr., his brother. A week later the new owners dissolved the paper and founded the *Age*. In 1889, after Emanuel Fortune's death, he accepted the editorship of the *Age*.

In 1884 Fortune had conceived the idea of a national organization that would fight for the civil and political rights of African Americans. He suggested in a 28 May 1887 *Freeman* editorial that an all-black organization modeled on the Irish National League was needed. Organized in January 1890, the Afro-American League had as its objectives the protection of black voters in the South; the end of the reign of lynch and mob rule; equal distribution of school funds to both races; eradication of chain gangs and convict leases that exploited blacks; the end of segregated public transportation vehicles; and the end of discrimination by race in hotels, inns, and theaters. Fortune urged African Americans to agitate for their rights, which would make each one "a new man in black . . . [who] bears no resemblance to a slave, or a coward, or an ignoramus" (*Freeman*, 28 May 1887). Although it had support from the black press and conventions that were held in 1890 and 1891, the league folded in 1893 because leading black politicians Frederick Douglass, John Mercer Langston, Blanche K. Bruce, and P. B. S. Pinchback refused to support its pointed attacks against the Republican party. The league's mili-

tant vision was later echoed in the modern civil rights movement.

Fortune's militancy was tempered in 1895 when he engaged in an alliance with *Booker T. Washington*. Both men were southerners who shared a common interest in self-reliance and manual education. After Washington's 1895 Atlanta Compromise speech, Fortune sent him a letter of praise. Frederick Douglass had died earlier that year, and Fortune informed Washington, "We must have a leader." For the next twelve years the two were close friends, and Fortune served as a ghost writer for Washington and editorially defended him from criticisms of younger militants. Fortune's financial dependency on Washington to publish the *Age* motivated W. E. B. Du Bois and William Monroe Trotter, editor of the *Boston Guardian*, to criticize him for being a mouthpiece for Washington. In 1901 Washington became an adviser to President Theodore Roosevelt (1858–1919) on racial matters. For the next six years Washington and Fortune would engage in an enigmatic relationship. At times Fortune would vigorously defend Washington from critics, but there were moments when he could not "reconcile his own views on race matters and politics with the accommodationist views of Washington" (Thornbrough, pp. 217–18). In 1902 his loyalty paid off when Washington arranged for him to receive an appointment as a special agent of the Treasury Department to study race and trade conditions in the Philippines. The seven-month trip cost Fortune dearly in health and finances and made him more dependent on Washington's support. The alliance between Fortune and Washington became strained when Fortune attacked Roosevelt for his indifference to the plight of mistreated southern blacks and particularly for the president's decision in 1906 to dishonorably discharge three companies of black soldiers of the Twenty-fifth Infantry stationed at Brownsville, Texas. On the night of 13 August a group of unidentified men killed one person and wounded two others in a shoot-out. The soldiers were blamed, but it was impossible to identify the culprits. None confessed, and not a single soldier offered to implicate his comrades. The black press, including the *Age*, criticized the president for his unprecedented action.

Since 1900 Fortune's drinking and depression had alarmed Washington. Concerned with Fortune's erratic personal and political behavior, Washington, who in early 1907 secretly became a major stockholder in the *Age*, removed Fortune from the editor's position. Out of frustration, Fortune wrote to William Monroe Trotter, "Don't let up on Roosevelt and Taft. Lay it on them thick, as usual." For the next three years Fortune drank heavily and suffered bouts of depression that caused his friends to worry about his mental stability. During this period his marriage to Carrie C. Smiley, whom he had wed in 1877, and with whom he had five children, ended in a separation that lasted until his death.

Fortune's health was restored by 1910, and Washington, believing that he had been sufficiently humbled, organized a testimonial for him and returned him to the *Age*'s editorship in 1911. Fortune left the *Age* in 1914 because debts kept him in dire financial straits. After Washington's death the next year, Fortune reflected that he had had more in common with the militancy of Frederick Douglass than with Washington and that he would have been better off if he had never developed an intimate relationship with the educator.

Fortune drifted in and out of writing assignments for the next nine years while he suffered from depression and alcoholism. In 1923 he assumed the editorship of Marcus Garvey's *Negro World*. Although he did not accept Garvey's emigration proposal, nor did he join the Universal Negro Improvement Association, he admired Garvey for his ability to mobilize the masses. For a time he returned to his earlier militancy, urging his readers to eschew political dependency. Later, after Garvey organized a Negro Political Union and instructed his followers to vote for Calvin Coolidge, Fortune, mindful that his anti-Roosevelt editorials had cost him favor, wrote no dissenting views about Coolidge's presidency.

Fortune died in Philadelphia. The *Negro World* (9 June 1928) eulogized him as one "who quite as much as Frederick Douglass, perhaps a little more than Booker T. Washington and less than Marcus Garvey, has been a healthful factor in the lives and fortunes of the Negro race in this generation." He was a visionary whose actions and writings in the 1880s predated the rhetoric of Malcolm X, Stokely Carmichael, and H. Rap Brown. Decades before the cries of "Black Power" and "Black is Beautiful," Fortune called for race love and unity. Years before the freedom rides, sit-ins, and demonstrations, Fortune called for organization and agitation.

• Fortune's correspondence with Washington is located in the Booker T. Washington Collection, Manuscript Division, Library of Congress. His editorials can be found in the *New York Globe*, the *Freeman*, the *Age*, and the *Negro World* on microfilm at the Schomburg Center for Research in Black Culture, New York Public Library. See also Emma Lou Thornbrough, *T. Thomas Fortune: Militant Journalist* (1972), and William Seraile, "The Political Views of Timothy Thomas Fortune: Father of Black Political Independence," *Afro-Americans in New York Life and History* 2 (July 1978): 15–28.
                                                           WILLIAM SERAILE

FORWARD, Walter (24 Jan. 1786–24 Nov. 1852), congressman, secretary of the treasury, and diplomat, was born in Old Granby (now East Granby), Connecticut, the son of Samuel Forward and Susannah Holcombe, farmers. In 1800 the family moved to a farm in Ohio. Forward left his parents' farm in 1803 for Pittsburgh, where despite having had little education he secured a job in the office of Henry Baldwin (1780–1844), a prominent Pennsylvania politician. Through Baldwin's efforts, Forward became editor of the Jeffersonian newspaper *Tree of Liberty* at the age of nineteen. He was admitted to the bar in 1806. He married Henrietta Barclay in 1808, with whom he had six children.

Forward's reputation as an orator, first gained as a trial lawyer, led to his election as a Jeffersonian Democrat to the Pennsylvania state legislature in 1817. When his mentor Baldwin left Congress in 1822 because of financial difficulties, Forward was elected to take his seat; reelected, he served until 1825. While in Congress, he supported a high protective tariff, a policy that he upheld throughout life. He was a delegate to the congressional caucus that nominated William H. Crawford for president in 1824, but then he voted for Andrew Jackson as a protest against the caucus system. In 1830 he was a delegate to the National Republican Convention at Baltimore and was influential in forming the Whig party in Pennsylvania in 1834. As a member of the state constitutional convention in 1837, Forward played a prominent part in reforming the public school system.

During the 1840 election, Forward presided at a huge Whig convention that John Tyler (1790–1862), the Whig candidate for vice president, declared to be the largest crowd he had spoken to during the campaign. In March 1841 President William Henry Harrison named Forward U.S. district attorney for the Western District of Pennsylvania, but Forward declined. He accepted appointment as comptroller of the currency in April. Following Harrison's death, the new president, Tyler, appointed Forward secretary of the treasury. Like many members of Tyler's cabinet, Forward had difficulty reconciling his ideas with those of the president. It is not clear whether his resignation in 1843 was a result of this friction—possibly stimulated and encouraged by Henry Clay—or because of questions raised about his competence.

Forward returned to his legal practice until November 1849, when he accepted Whig president Zachary Taylor's appointment as chargé d'affaires in Copenhagen. He remained at this post until 1851, when he resigned to assume the elected office of president judge of the district court of Allegheny County, Pennsylvania. It was at the bench that he was stricken and died.

• Still the most complete account of Forward's life is Robert M. Ewing, "Hon. Walter Forward," *Western Pennsylvania Historical Magazine*, Apr. 1925, pp. 76–89. See also J. N. Boucher, *A Century and a Half of Pittsburgh and Her People* (1908). For accounts of Forward's role in Tyler's cabinet, see Oliver P. Chitwood, *John Tyler: Champion of the Old South* (1939); Robert Seager, *And Tyler Too* (1963); and Norma Peterson, *The Presidencies of William Henry Harrison and John Tyler* (1989). Forward's obituary is in the *Pittsburgh Gazette*, 25 Nov. 1852.
                                                          LYNN H. PARSONS

FORWOOD, William Henry (7 Sept. 1838–11 May 1915), army medical officer, was born in Brandywine Hundred, Delaware, the son of Robert Forwood and Rachel Way Larkin (occupations unknown). He attended both private and public schools before entering the University of Pennsylvania, where he received his medical degree in 1861. He was commissioned as an assistant surgeon and first lieutenant in the Union Army Medical Department on 5 August of that year.

During the Civil War he served both in hospitals and in the field with the Army of the Potomac. His accomplishments while with the Army of the Potomac included a daring escape after he was captured by Confederate guerrillas led by John S. Mosby. Although often exposed to gunfire while serving in 1863 as regimental surgeon for the Sixth Cavalry Regiment, Stoneman's Division, he served through the battles of the spring and summer without injury; but in October of that year he was severely wounded in the chest during skirmishing north of the Rappahannock River in Virginia. His courage and devotion to duty during these campaigns drew the favorable attention of the medical director of the Army of the Potomac, Jonathan Letterman.

Forwood's assignments after his recovery from his wound included service as executive officer of the large Satterlee General Hospital in Philadelphia and commanding officer of the 2,000-bed Whitehall General Hospital at Bristol, Pennsylvania. On 13 March 1865 he was awarded the brevet ranks of both captain and major for his wartime service.

After the end of the Civil War, Forwood was given a series of assignments at posts in the West and South. During this period, he gained firsthand experience with two of the most feared diseases of the period, cholera and yellow fever. On 28 July 1866 he was promoted to captain. In 1870 he married Mary A. Y. Osborne; their marriage was childless. On 26 June 1876, when he was serving at Fort Richardson, Texas, he was promoted to major. In 1880 and 1881, he spent the summers serving as surgeon and naturalist with exploratory expeditions to the Yellowstone region organized by Lieutenant General Philip H. Sheridan. In the summer of 1883 he once again joined an expedition to Yellowstone, this time in the company of President Chester A. Arthur and other notables.

Forwood's final three years in the West were spent at Fort Snelling, Minnesota. In 1890 he returned to Washington, D.C., to serve as attending surgeon for the Soldiers' Home. He was promoted to lieutenant colonel on 15 June 1891. In the fall of 1893, while still attending surgeon at the Soldiers' Home, he joined the staff of the newly created Army Medical School in Washington for its first session. Because of efforts to reduce the size of the medical department, the session of 1894–1895 was canceled, but Forwood resumed teaching there when the school reopened in the fall of 1895 and he remained through the 1897–1898 session. Encouraged by his superiors, who wished to find a way to reduce the number of soldiers leaving the army because of physical disabilities, he became an authority on hernia surgery, performing many of the first operations of this type to be undertaken in the army. He also taught surgery and pathology from 1895 to 1897 and military surgery from 1897 to 1898 at the medical school of Georgetown University. He was promoted to colonel on 3 May 1897.

In July 1898 Forwood was ordered to establish a hospital and convalescent camp for Spanish-American War troops to be quarantined at Camp Wikoff, located at Montauk Point, Long Island, after exposure to yellow fever in the Caribbean. He was also required to serve as an adviser for line officers named to choose sites and water sources for the main camp. This assignment was arguably the most difficult of his career. Although he had little control over many of the problems that beset the hospital and its patients, he was heavily criticized in the press for shortages, delays, and confusion, criticism that did not seem to affect his reputation in the army.

On 8 September 1898 Forwood was relieved of his duties at Camp Wikoff and assigned to choose a site and to supervise construction of a 1,000-bed general hospital in Savannah, Georgia, to serve troops returning from service in the Caribbean. After being relieved on 12 December 1898 from the position he still held as attending surgeon at the Soldiers' Home, he was ordered to San Francisco to serve as chief surgeon of the Department of California, where he became responsible for the health of troops going to and returning from service in the Philippine Islands. In 1901 he returned to Washington, where he became president of the faculty of the Army Medical School.

On 8 June 1902 Forwood succeeded the retiring surgeon general, George Miller Sternberg, as head of the Medical Department, a promotion that brought with it the rank of brigadier general. He was able to serve in this position only three months before being forced to retire because of his age. During this brief period he was called upon to decide the difficult question of whether Major William C. Gorgas should be permitted to continue his attempts to develop a yellow fever vaccine after three of the volunteers involved died of the disease. Although the decision he reached after consultation with yellow fever expert Major Walter Reed did not actually ban further experimentation, the restrictions Forwood placed on the project had the effect of stopping all work on it.

On 7 September 1902 Forwood retired from the army; he remained in Washington, D.C., until his death there. Although he was a man of great physical courage and discipline and esteemed for his skills as a teacher, he served at a time of revolutionary change in the world of medical science, and the achievements of such men as Sternberg, Reed, and Gorgas outshone his relatively modest scientific accomplishments.

• As an author Forwood contributed both to journals and to edited collections by multiple authors. Representative of his work are "Remarks upon the Proper Form and the Advantages of a Diagnosis Tag for Use among the Sick and Wounded on the Battle-field," *Proceedings of the Association of Military Surgeons* 5 (1895): 456–60; "Military Surgery: Firearms and Projectiles," in *International Textbook of Surgery* ed. J. Collins Warren and A. Pearce Gould (1900); and his observations as a naturalist in Philip H. Sheridan, *Report . . . , Dated September 20, 1881, on His Expedition through the Big Horn Mountains, Yellowstone National Park, etc.* (1882), and *Report of an Exploration of Parts of Wyoming, Idaho, and Montana in Au-*

gust and September, 1882 (1882). Although they contain some minor inaccuracies, James M. Phalen, *Chiefs of the Medical Department United States Army 1775–1940: Army Medical Bulletin No. 52* (1940), and James Evelyn Pilcher, *The Surgeon Generals of the Army of the United States of America* (1905), contain biographical articles. A lengthy obituary is in *Military Surgeon* 36 (1915): 606–08.

MARY C. GILLETT

FOSDICK, Harry Emerson (24 May 1878–5 Oct. 1969), liberal Protestant minister, was born in Buffalo, New York, the son of Frank Sheldon Fosdick, a public schoolteacher and principal, and Amie Inez Weaver. Raised as a Baptist, Harry underwent a conversion experience at age seven, pledging his life to Christian service. His parents, though pious, were not narrow sectarians, and his father, especially, was salty, questioning, and open to the disturbing new intellectual currents of the late Victorian era. The major strains of Harry's youth seem to have been his family's relentlessly tight finances, his mother's periodic severe mental depressions, and, according to his later accounts, his own intense, persisting fears of divine wrath.

Fosdick graduated at the head of his high school class with myriad extracurricular honors. Five years later he received a B.A. from Colgate University, then a small Baptist school, again graduating first in his class and beribboned with prizes. Popular and cocky though he was, the Colgate period was not unshadowed. A serious break in his father's health forced Harry to drop out of school for a year. For a time, his religious faith unraveled; then he began having what G. K. Chesterton once termed "the first wild doubts of doubt." With his faith renewed he made a commitment to the ministry. Fosdick studied for a year at Hamilton Theological Seminary (associated with Colgate University), where Professor William Newton Clarke, the leading liberal Baptist theologian, made a profound impression on him. Hungry to know a wider world than Hamilton, Fosdick transferred to Union Theological Seminary in New York City. Having recently cut its official ties with the Presbyterian church, interdenominational Union was on the cutting edge of progressive theological thought and biblical scholarship. Within months of enrollment Fosdick was felled by a neurotic reactive depression so severe as to lead to an attempted suicide. Only after extended treatment in a sanitarium and a convalescent trip to England did his health permit a return to his studies. In 1904 he graduated from Union *summa cum laude* with a B.D. The terrifying mental smash-up fueled Fosdick's enduring interest in pastoral counseling, while the inspiration of his Union professors confirmed his commitment to the emerging theological liberalism. Marriage to Florence Allen Whitney in 1904 provided this intense, ambitious, self-contained, though not dour, man with sixty years of loving companionship and two cherished daughters.

Fosdick assumed his first major pastorate in 1904 at the First Baptist Church in the cosseted community of Montclair, New Jersey. For the next eleven years he

ministered successfully to this affluent church, involved himself deeply in civic concerns, received an M.A. in political science from Columbia University, taught part-time at Union, and rode the campus, student, and adult Bible conference circuits. Unquestionably, however, Fosdick's widening fame in the United States and abroad rested principally on six books published between 1908 and 1920: *The Second Mile, The Assurance of Immortality, The Manhood of the Master, The Meaning of Prayer, The Meaning of Faith,* and *The Meaning of Service.* Collectively these slim volumes enjoyed scores of reprintings, translation into over fifty languages, and millions of sales. Embodying both his hope that it was possible in the twentieth century to maintain faith and reason in creative tension, and his conviction that "though astronomies change the stars abide," these works merit for him a place in the pantheon of gifted Christian apologists. For Fosdick, secular humanism and scientific naturalism were even more formidable perils to Christian faith than a no longer credible orthodoxy.

Called to a professorship at Union in 1915, Fosdick interrupted his teaching for a half-year tour of duty overseas with American doughboys after America's intervention in the Great War, an intervention he had ardently advocated. The horrors of war witnessed in France converted him to a firm pacifism that remained unshaken even by Pearl Harbor. Returning from Europe, Fosdick accepted in late 1918 an invitation to become preaching minister of New York City's historic First Presbyterian Church. Because his duties were limited to preaching and counseling, he was able to continue to fulfill most of his teaching responsibilities at Union. The deliberate decision of the "Old First" leadership to invite a Baptist to occupy regularly a prestigious Presbyterian pulpit disturbed many conservatives nationwide. Yet even doubters could not deny that when Fosdick preached the sanctuary overflowed with worshipers, and hundreds waiting in lines outside were turned away. At the same time, Fosdick's international speaking engagements and his busy pen made his name as recognizable as any in American Protestantism.

When the long-simmering war within American Protestantism between fundamentalists and modernists exploded in 1919, no denomination was racked more desperately than the Presbyterian Church, U.S.A. Fundamentalists (or conservatives as many of them termed themselves) sought to fix as essential for all Presbyterians their cherished beliefs, including biblical inerrancy, Christ's virgin birth, his bodily resurrection, and (for some) his imminent premillennial return. Although not a doctrine, a total rejection of Darwinism was also a passionate article of conservative faith. Fosdick answered this challenge to his own creedless, experiential, yet profoundly evangelical, liberalism in his most famous and provocative sermon, "Shall the Fundamentalists Win?," preached in 1922 and distributed, thanks to the largess of John D. Rockefeller, Jr., to every ordained Protestant minister in the country. Fosdick immediately became the central symbolic figure in both the Presbyterian and Baptist denominational wars. When "Old First" refused to dismiss Fosdick, as conservatives demanded, a trap was set by his enemies in the Presbyterian national general assembly: he might remain if he became a Presbyterian and subscribed to the historic Westminster Confession. Yet if he did so he would surely be open to trial for heresy. Unwilling to be so snared and loyal to his liberal beliefs, Fosdick declined the "invitation"—though several liberal Presbyterians, including Union's president, Henry Sloane Coffin, urged him to accept. At this juncture in 1925 he accepted a call from the Park Avenue Baptist Church with the understanding that the congregation, led by Rockefeller, in time would erect a great, new interdenominational church. The Riverside Church on Morningside Heights was raised in all its Gothic splendor in 1931, and until Fosdick's retirement in 1946, the church and the man were unalterably linked.

Fosdick's voice from the Riverside pulpit and guest lecterns on both sides of the Atlantic reached thousands, while the airways, especially via the famed National Vespers Hour, beginning in 1927, carried his liberating, uplifting message to millions, marking him the "dean of radio preachers." The hymns he composed have endured, notably "God of Grace and God of Glory." His three major books of progressive biblical scholarship—drawn from his Union lectures—may be badly dated, but they were enormously influential in their day, especially to lay persons and "working" parsons who appreciated the accessibility of *The Modern Use of the Bible* (1924), *A Guide to Understanding the Bible* (1938), and *The Man from Nazareth* (1949). His pioneer work in psychological pastoral counseling, including collaboration with clinical psychotherapists, resulted in the bestselling *On Being a Real Person* (1943), a book more profound and gritty than is typical of that inspirational genre.

Seen by conservatives as a heretic, Fosdick was no radical in the realm of culture, and his late Victorian temperament was revealed in his disapproving, bewildered references to the seeming triumph of modernism in music, art, drama, literature, and film and the concomitant erosion of civility and sexual morality. He did, however, support the birth control movement and acknowledge the sad necessity, in rare cases, of divorce. Closely associated with Rockefeller since early in his career, due in part to his brother Raymond's leadership in the Rockefeller Foundation and in part to Rockefeller's own liberal religious beliefs, Fosdick did not permit this friendship to blunt his prophetic ministry, and in the areas of economic and racial justice he carried the Social Gospel banner into the midcentury. Never quite at the forefront of any social crusade, save pacifism, he was never far to the rear; he may be fairly characterized as a mainstream liberal in the tradition extending from Theodore Roosevelt (1858–1919) to Franklin Roosevelt. When death came to Fosdick in Bronxville, New York, his body was crippled by arthritis and other cruel infirmities,

but to the end his mind remained unclouded and his spirit undismayed.

Fosdick was American liberal Protestantism's most renowned leader in an era when he and his religious liberal companions knew their proudest hours. The stubborn refusal of their fundamentalist foes to be permanently routed, the stern critique leveled by neoorthodox challengers such as Reinhold Niebuhr, and the demoniac events of an increasingly calamitous century all ended the vaunted mainline liberal Protestant hegemony. Inevitably this has meant the dimming of Fosdick's once towering reputation. To the extent, however, that the Christian faith will always stand in need of persuasive apologists, gifted preachers, accessible scholars, concerned pastors, and courageous prophets, the life of Fosdick, termed by Albert C. Outler "the biopsy of an epoch," will long remain a model.

• Fosdick willed his papers to Union Theological Seminary; the resulting Fosdick Collection is massive. Major materials relating to his career are in the archives of the First Baptist Church, the First Presbyterian Church, and most crucially of all, the Riverside Church. The Rockefeller Family Archives also are rewarding. His autobiography, *The Living of These Days* (1956), is charming but veiled. *Riverside Sermons* is a collection ranging over his entire Riverside ministry. The only full biography is Robert Moats Miller, *Harry Emerson Fosdick: Preacher, Pastor, Prophet* (1985).

ROBERT MOATS MILLER

FOSS, Sam Walter (19 June 1858–26 Feb. 1911), poet and librarian, was born in Candia, New Hampshire, the son of Dyer Foss and Polly Hardy, farmers. Foss's mother died when he was four. He attended public or "common" schools, graduating from Portsmouth High School in 1877. He then matriculated at New Hampshire Conference Seminary and Female College in Tilton, which later became Tilton Academy, for one year. There he converted to Methodist Episcopalianism and earned a scholarship to attend Brown University. Because he worked to support himself, he was prevented from deep involvement in college life; nevertheless, he was elected class poet and a member of the *Brunonian* board in his senior year, 1881–1882. He received a bachelor's degree in 1882.

Rather than working on his father's farm after graduating from Brown, Foss sold subscription books for a year before entering journalism through the purchase of the Lynn, Massachusetts, *Union* (shortly renamed the *Saturday Union*) with William E. Smythe, becoming full owner in 1884. Because the paper lacked a promised comic column, he supplied material himself, was encouraged, and began writing humorous local-color and dialect verse. Wolcott Balestier of the comic magazine *Tid-Bits* began publishing his work, which appeared in the next few years in major comic periodicals, including *Puck* and *Judge*, as well as in the New York *Sun*, the *Christian Endeavor World*, and *Youth's Companion*. Typically, his poems showed Yankee characters and attitudes, emphasizing homespun cracker-barrel virtues over worldly and self-interested vices. In the poem "Odium Theologicum," reprinted in *Dreams in Homespun* (1897), he argued that men would differ smilingly on the merits of a horse but carry war in their hearts over theological arguments, a position he elaborated in his lectures by suggesting that once man had bombs big enough to destroy New York, he would fear to make war. His poems and speeches advocated hard work and optimism as life tenets, consistent with his own experience. From 1887 to 1894 he was editor of the (Boston, Mass.) *Yankee Blade* and contributed to the *Boston Globe* as well. In 1887 he married Carrie Conant of Providence, Rhode Island, a school principal, and settled in Somerville, Massachusetts; eventually the couple had two children. By 1893–1894 he was writing a poem a week for his own paper and a poem a day for syndication. From 1894 to 1897 he supported himself by freelance writing and by lecturing. His platform delivery of homely philosophy and local-color poems was bolstered by his farmerlike appearance, rapid speaking voice, and warm manner.

Five separate collections of Foss's poems began appearing in 1892 with *Back Country Poems*, which included "The Volunteer Organist" and "The Railroad through the Farm." *Whiffs from Wild Meadows* in 1895 included "The Confessions of a Lunkhead," advising, "we are all lunkheads. . . . Keep yer own selves in the dark; / Don't own or reckernize the fact, an' you will make yer mark"; "When We Worked Our Tax Out," describing the New England custom of working off taxes in place of cash payments; and "The Calf-path," which elaborated the legend that the streets of Boston were laid out by a calf, making the analogy with humans' foolish willingness to follow established precedent. Foss's most popular poem, "The House by the Side of the Road," which leaned on a figure in Homer, chanted,

Where the race of men go by—
They are good, they are bad, they are weak, they are strong,
Wise, foolish—so am I . . . .
Let me live in my house by the side of the road
And be a friend to man.

It was reprinted in *Dreams in Homespun* in 1897; despite the development of a New England cottage industry in search of the house, Foss denied any particular model for what became a folk landmark. *Songs of War and Peace* appeared in 1899. "The Song of the Library Staff," an immensely popular, humorously satiric description of public librarians, was printed alone in 1906 and reprinted in *Songs of the Average Man* in 1907. Foss's popularity as a poet of the common people is usually ascribed to his fluency in rhyme and meter, his use of the vernacular voice, and the simplicity and nostalgia of his optimistic message, which is also tolerant of misfits and underachievers. Foss attempted to generalize the tone of localist democratic goodwill to a muted mysticism in his later writings but died before undertaking longer and more ambitious epic poems

that might have elevated his reputation. His standing as a poet rests on his homespun Yankee New Hampshire voice and attitudes in humorous popular poetry.

In 1898 Foss became the librarian of the Somerville, Massachusetts, public library, although continuing his writing and speaking at a modified pace. He became a significant advocate in New England of the modern concept of the public library as an outreach and service institution with open shelves and multiple copies of popular books rather than being a repository of documents. He pioneered circulating and traveling collections in nursing homes, hospitals, public schools, and work and factory sites. He advocated his position through local activities as reflected in his annual reports for the town of Somerville and in speeches to library associations and in a column titled "The Library Alcove" in the *Christian Science Monitor* from 6 October 1909 through 1 March 1911. He retained the family home in Candia, vacationing there and remaining active locally, as he did as a Brown alumnus. The popularity of his broadly democratic philosophy of life and librarianship, as well as his personal warmth, is suggested by the overflowing attendance at his funeral in Somerville, where the number of mourners could not be accommodated at the church. Despite his immense popularity in his own time, and the ongoing references to "The House by the Side of the Road," Foss has received no attention since the late 1920s, probably due to the openness of his message and his genre painting and dramatic lyricism as opposed to the imagist obliqueness prevailing in American verse since his time.

• Papers of Sam Walter Foss are in the John Hay Library at Brown University, with a few items at the Somerville Public Library; scattered letters exist elsewhere. Various editions of his poems appeared around the turn of the century and as late as 1925. His writings on librarianship are collected in *The Library Alcove and Other Library Writings by Sam Walter Foss*, ed. Norman D. Stevens (1987). See also H. L. Koopman, "Poetry of Sam Walter Foss, Keen Humorist and Philosopher," *Providence Journal*, 7 July 1926, and "Sam Walter Foss/Literary Men of Brown, IV," *Brown Alumni Monthly*, Oct. 1908, pp. 54–57; B. O. Flower, "A New England Poet of the Common Life," the *Arena*, Oct. 1901, pp. 391–410; Mary S. Woodman, *Sam Walter Foss: Poet, Librarian and Friend to Man* (1922); Peter MacQueen, "Sam Walter Foss, 'Yankee Poet,'" *National Magazine*, May 1909, pp. 197–200; Richard Welton, "Sam Walter Foss—Librarian by the Side of the Road," *Bay State Librarian* 73 (Winter 1985): 8–9; and David E. E. Sloane, "'The Volunteer Organist,' an American Poem in Sussex," *Country Dance and Song* 20 (Mar. 1990): 40–41. Obituaries are in the *Boston Globe*, 27 Feb. 1911; W. E. Foster, *Brown Alumni Monthly*, Apr. 1911; *Somerville Journal*, 3 Mar. 1911; and *Library Journal* 36 (1911) 187–88.

DAVID E. E. SLOANE

FOSSE, Bob (23 June 1927–23 Sept. 1987), stage, film, and television dancer, director, and choreographer, was born Robert Louis Fosse in Chicago, Illinois, the son of Cyril Kingsley Fosse, a vaudeville entertainer turned salesman, and Sarah Alice Stanton. At nine years of age, Fosse began classes in jazz, tap, and ballet at Chicago's Academy of the Arts. Small and asthmatic, with a speech impediment that caused him to slur words, he later remarked that his early dance training stemmed from a need to overcompensate for his perceived "handicaps." He was still a child when he headlined his own act—Bobby Fosse's Le Petit Cabaret—tap dancing and telling jokes in local nightclubs.

Thus he began a schizophrenic adolescence: an honor roll student at Amundsen High School by day, a tap dancer in seedy nightclubs by night. From thirteen through sixteen, he was half of the Riff Bros. dance act, sharing billings with vaudeville and burlesque acts, including strippers. "The strippers were really something," Fosse told *Penthouse* in 1973. "Tough. Really tough. [W]hen these strippers discovered I was sixteen, they didn't believe it. . . . They'd walk out into the hallway with nothing on, or grab me and start playing with me." In his 1979 film *All That Jazz*, Fosse recreates this scene, which reveals as much about the inherent sexuality of his choreography as it does about his often-complex physical relationships with women.

At seventeen Fosse enlisted in the navy, where he performed in its special services entertainment division. When World War II ended, he moved to New York City and found his first job as a Broadway gypsy in *Call Me Mister* (1948), where he met his first wife, Mary Ann Niles, another dancer. They married in 1947 in Chicago and put together a dance act that performed in major hotels around the country; eventually, they were hired for Sid Caesar's television variety hour, "Your Show of Shows."

In 1950 Fosse and Niles were a featured act in the Broadway revue *Dance Me a Song*, which costarred Joan McCracken. He and McCracken began an affair that resulted in Fosse's divorce and his marriage to McCracken in 1951. He had no children from either marriage. Throughout his later career Fosse would remark that it was McCracken who encouraged him to study diction, ballet, acting, singing, and choreography at the American Theatre Wing. While performing a scene at the school, Fosse was spotted by a Metro-Goldwyn-Mayer talent scout, who flew him to Los Angeles for a screen test. The Hollywood film director Stanley Donen saw the test and signed Fosse to a contract with MGM in 1953.

The film musicals in which Fosse made his debut, *Give a Girl a Break* and *The Affairs of Dobie Gillis* (both 1953), are little remembered, but his performance that same year in *Kiss Me Kate*, a 3-D film adaptation of the Cole Porter Broadway musical, was pivotal to his career. Although Hermes Pan was credited as the film's dance director, Fosse choreographed his own dynamic jazz ballet, "From this Moment On," which attracted the attention of the Broadway director George Abbott and choreographer Jerome Robbins.

Abbott and Robbins hired Fosse to choreograph the 1954 musical *The Pajama Game*, which would forever define the "Fosse look": bowler hats, white gloves, turned-in or turned-out knees, low, slinky jazz pliés,

forward-thrust pelvises. Years later, Fosse confessed that the bowler hats were used to camouflage his own receding hairline, the gloves to hide inarticulate hands, and the bowed legs a result of his not being able to get himself into a proper ballet turnout. "I was always very bad in class," he admitted to *Dance Magazine* in 1975. To compensate for his shortcomings, "I used to work on other areas, such as rhythm, style of movement, and taking ordinary steps and giving them some little extra twist or turn. And I guess my 'style' came about mainly as a result of my own limitations as a dancer."

The Pajama Game, with numbers such as "Steam Heat" and "Hernando's Hideaway," became an enormous Broadway hit, leading to another Abbott–Robbins–Fosse collaboration, *Damn Yankees* (1955), and introducing Fosse to the show's star, Gwen Verdon, who would have a profound effect on his life and career. Verdon became his foremost interpreter in the musicals *New Girl in Town* (1957), *Redhead* (1959), *Sweet Charity* (1966), and *Chicago* (1975). In 1960 Fosse divorced McCracken and married Verdon; they had one child.

The successes of *Pajama Game* and *Damn Yankees* led to Hollywood film versions of both musicals, which Fosse choreographed. He returned to the stage to cochoreograph (with Jerome Robbins) *Bells Are Ringing* (1956), followed by *New Girl in Town*. Fosse made his directorial debut with *Redhead*, a musical whodunit set in a turn-of-the-century London waxworks, which won him Tony awards for outstanding direction and choreography.

With the exception of his choreography for the 1961 Pulitzer Prize–winning musical, *How to Succeed in Business without Really Trying*, the early 1960s were a troubling period for Fosse. He was dismissed as director-choreographer of *The Conquering Hero* (1961) while the show was still playing out-of-town tryouts. A year later, his critically well-received choreography for *Little Me* did not translate into a strong box office, and the show closed in the red. *Pleasures & Palaces* (1965), a musical about John Paul Jones's visit to Russia during the reign of Catherine the Great, closed out of town. But in 1966 Fosse's work galvanized in the Neil Simon–Cy Coleman musical *Sweet Charity*.

Considered to be Fosse's most enduring musical, *Sweet Charity* was based on Federico Fellini's film *Nights of Cabiria* (1957) and concerned the alternately tragic and comedic romantic exploits of a New York City taxi dancer named Charity Hope Valentine. Fosse's choreography in numbers such as "Big Spender" and "There's Gotta Be Something Better than This" forecast the direction his dances and subject matter would take through the rest of his career—more sexually explicit and unapologetically focused on marginal, if not illicit, subject matter such as prostitution, infidelity, murder, pornography, and drugs, to name a few. *Sweet Charity*'s Broadway success was not repeated when it was made into a $7.5 million film musical that was released in 1969. The film has since become a cult favorite. In 1986 Fosse again directed

Sweet Charity on Broadway, where it won a Tony award for outstanding revival.

In 1972 Fosse realized a major success with his film adaptation of the Broadway musical *Cabaret*, which used the comic vulgarity of a seedy Berlin nightclub called the Kit Kat Club to comment on the rise of the Third Reich in 1930s Germany. The film won nine Academy Awards, including best direction for Fosse. The same year his direction and choreography for the Broadway musical *Pippin* earned him more Tony awards, followed by an Emmy for his direction and choreography for Liza Minnelli's television special, "Liza with a Z."

Fosse's continued fascination with tragic heroes led to his 1974 film *Lenny*, based on the life and death of the comedian Lenny Bruce. Shot in stark black-and-white, the film was nominated for three Academy Awards, including best direction.

Fosse returned to Broadway in 1975 with the cynical "musical vaudeville" *Chicago*, which harked back to his beginnings on the burlesque circuit. Set in the 1920s, the show used vaudeville numbers to comment on a corrupt judicial system; some critics saw parallels to Watergate and the Nixon administration. The show also reunited Verdon and Fosse, legally separated since the early 1970s and was immensely popular with the public. In 1978 Fosse, notorious for his tempestuous relationships with composers and librettists, jettisoned score and plot in his Broadway revue, *Dancin'*, an all-dance show that played on Broadway for nearly four years.

Perhaps his most ambitious undertaking, *All That Jazz* (1979), revealed Fosse at his most introspective and audacious. In the film, a work-obsessed and women-obsessed director-choreographer named Joe Gideon attempts to reconcile his career with his obligations as a father and family man, opting ultimately for career. In the end, his peripatetic lifestyle, including a drug habit, leads to his "grand finale"—death, staged as an elaborate production number. *All That Jazz* won the 1980 best film award at the Cannes Film Festival and was nominated for nine Academy Awards but won only a handful of technical honors.

The 1980s were the apotheosis of Fosse's obsession with unsung heroes, resulting in projects that left him embittered with both Broadway and Hollywood. *Star 80* (1983), which portrayed a *Playboy* centerfold destined to die by the hands of her Svengali-like lover, was intended by Fosse as an indictment of Hollywood's ruthless star-making system; the film was a critical and financial failure.

In 1986 Fosse returned to Broadway, this time with his last musical, *Big Deal*, inspired by the 1956 Italian crime caper comedy *Big Deal on Madonna Street*. Opting to write the book himself and handpick the music from 1930s and 1940s standards, Fosse took total control of the production, which many of those associated with the show believe resulted in its failure. (It closed after seventy performances.) Nonetheless, Fosse's choreography won him another Tony award, his last,

in 1986. It was a bittersweet victory, overshadowed by the success of a revival of *Sweet Charity* the same year.

Fosse's death, foretold in *All That Jazz*, occurred following a final rehearsal for the opening of *Sweet Charity*'s Washington, D.C., company when he collapsed of a massive heart attack. A portion of his estate, valued at nearly $4 million, was bequeathed to sixty-six friends, "to have dinner on me. They all have at one time or another been very kind to me. I thank them."

• Two biographies of Fosse have been published, Martin Gottfried, *All His Jazz: The Life and Death of Bob Fosse* (1990), and Kevin Grubb, *Razzle Dazzle: The Life and Work of Bob Fosse* (1989). An obituary is in the *New York Times*, 24 Sept. 1987.

KEVIN GRUBB

FOSSEY, Dian (16 Jan. 1932–Dec. 1985), naturalist and zoologist, was born in San Francisco, California, the daughter of George Fossey, an insurance agent, and Kitty Kidd, a fashion model. Her alcoholic father left the family when Fossey was three years old, and her stepfather, Richard Price, was unloving and discouraging. Her uncle Albert Chapin helped take care of Fossey and financed her schooling.

Fossey first attended the University of California at Davis, where she planned to study veterinary medicine. After two years, however, her poor grades in chemistry and physics necessitated her transfer to San Jose State College, where she graduated in 1954 with a degree in occupational therapy. She completed clinical training by 1956 and accepted a position as director of the occupational therapy department at the Kosair Crippled Children's Hospital in Louisville, Kentucky. She devoted the next decade to serving as an occupational therapist for disabled children. Fossey enjoyed her career, friends, and animals, but felt unfulfilled.

In 1963 Fossey borrowed against three years of her salary to finance an African safari over the objections of her stepfather. Fossey had been interested in the rare mountain gorillas living in the Congo and wanted to study them. Her two-month vacation changed her life. At the Olduvai Gorge in Tanzania, Fossey met anthropologists Louis and Mary Leakey. She toured their excavation site, where they searched for fossils of prehuman ancestors, and announced that she wanted to see gorillas. Despite breaking her ankle during a fall at the Leakey's site, Fossey determinedly continued her safari to the Congo. "I had this great urge, this need to go to Africa," she later told a newspaper reporter. "I had it the day I was born. Some may call it destiny. My parents and friends called it dismaying" (*Current Biography 1985*, p. 121).

Fossey then returned to her work in Louisville, where Louis Leakey, impressed by her dedication, contacted her. He told Fossey that he needed people to observe gorilla behavior for his research, seeking a connection between ape behavior and the fossil remains that he was unearthing. He had already financed Jane Goodall's studies of chimpanzees in Tanzania and wanted Fossey to go to Rwanda, the Congo, and Uganda to observe mountain gorillas. Leakey traveled to Louisville in 1966 to initiate the program, and Fossey was in Africa by the end of the year.

Fossey visited Goodall's camp to learn how the latter collected information, and she studied the work of zoologist George B. Schaller, who had conducted the first reliable field study of gorillas. When Fossey moved to Africa, the remote region where she wanted to study was undergoing political upheaval while seeking independence from European colonial rulers. Congolese officials, viewing Fossey suspiciously, arrested her. She escaped and fled to Uganda, embellishing accounts of what had actually happened.

Because of the political turmoil in Africa, American officials attempted to persuade Leakey and Fossey's friends to convince her to abandon her study. The U.S. embassy renewed her visa, but the Department of State monitored her activities. When her Belgian friend Alyette de Munck's son was murdered by the Congolese, Fossey vowed to avenge his death. In an 8 October 1967 State Department cable, one consul stated that he had the "impression she's a resourceful, independent but highly emotional and erratic young woman." But when her friend, Alexie Forrester, visited her, "He found Fossey completely normal, rational and very much absorbed in her work" ("Dian Fossey's Early Days in Rwanda," pp. 28, 30).

By September 1967 Fossey had built the Karisoke Research Centre in the Rwandan rain forest. Her camp, 10,000 feet high in the Central African Virunga Volcanoes mountain range, was isolated and hazardous. The humid, hot climate, and thin oxygen made breathing difficult for the asthmatic Fossey. Her primitive and spartan cabin was flimsily constructed of corrugated tin. Wild animals and insects posed health threats, and the steep terrain resulted in falls and broken ribs and ankles and punctured lungs. Fossey refused medical treatment, splinting her legs and leaning on walking sticks.

Fossey hired natives to help her track the gorillas. The Africans considered her odd for wanting to live alone in the mountains. Fossey believed that they called her Nyiramacibili, meaning "Lady Who Lives Alone in the Forest," although some scholars have claimed that Fossey appropriated this nickname attributed to one of her colleagues. Contemporaries described Fossey as dedicated, single-minded, and strong-willed.

Fossey's immediate goal was to secure the gorilla's trust. She primarily studied three groups. Group Five, which consisted of fifteen gorillas on the southwest slope of the mountain, and Groups Four and Eight, two gorilla families on the western slope. She had discovered Group Four on the first day that she established her camp and watched them through binoculars as they interacted and played. Fossey imitated their vocalizations and behavior, especially how they walked and ate. She identified dominant male leaders and, despite scientific protocol requiring researchers not to become emotionally involved with animal sub-

jects, named individual gorillas based on unique features or personalities. Her favorite gorilla was a male she named Digit because he had an injured finger; she named another gorilla for her uncle who had supported her financially and emotionally.

Fossey observed the gorillas nurturing and protecting each other. She believed that only through interaction with them could she discover insights into their behavior. She watched the groups for two years, gradually getting closer to them. Peanuts, a Group Eight male, was the first gorilla that touched Fossey, while she was lying in foliage. A *National Geographic* photographer captured the moment on film, and Fossey named the site Fasi Ya Mkoni, "The Place of the Hands." After this initial contact, the gorillas welcomed Fossey into their groups. Delighted by the gorillas, Fossey stressed that "the gorillas are the reward and one should never ask for more than their trust and confidence after each working day" (Montgomery, p. 132).

Seeking professional legitimization for her work, in January 1970 Fossey enrolled at Cambridge University's Darwin College. Her primary professor, Robert Hinde, had also directed Goodall's doctoral work. Fossey disliked the male-dominated school, which emphasized "theoretical conservation," entailing monotonous data collection. Fossey refused to conform, insisting her observations were more valid than statistics, but managed to complete the degree. Her dissertation, "The Behaviour of the Mountain Gorilla," earned her a Ph.D. in zoology in 1976.

Returning to Africa, Fossey focused on "active conservation," wanting to protect the gorillas. A gorilla census revealed that the population had been halved between 1960 and 1980. The number of gorillas had decreased because of habitat destroyed for farming and poachers who killed adult gorillas to seize babies to sell to zoos and for trophies. In January 1978 Digit's body was found, and Fossey began an intense antipoaching program. She established the Digit Fund and urgently publicized the plight of the mountain gorillas worldwide.

Offering rewards for poachers, Fossey focused on avenging Digit's death. She alienated her graduate student workers and was hostile to lecture audiences, resulting in her funds being curtailed. Cultural conflicts with natives festered because Fossey failed to understand their language and traditions. Secretary of State Cyrus Vance and *National Geographic* officials pressured Fossey to leave Africa. She agreed to travel to New York in 1980 to receive medical care for calcium deficiencies of her bones and teeth and undergo back surgery. During this time, she taught at Cornell University and wrote her book, *Gorillas in the Mist*, published in 1983. She also lectured with Jane Goodall and Biruté Galdikes, an orangutan expert, throughout the United States, delivering her anti-poaching message.

Fossey returned to Africa in the summer of 1983, renewing her aggressive attack against poachers. She tortured poachers, kidnapped their children, and destroyed hunting equipment. Her militant, vigilante behavior may have triggered her murder. Fossey's machete-hacked corpse was discovered in her cabin on 27 December 1985. Although her murderer has never been identified, Rwandan government officials blamed her assistant, while other authors have suggested that poachers or even political leaders murdered her to prevent her from interfering in profitable gorilla smuggling. Fossey, who never married, was buried in the gorilla graveyard at the Karisoke Research Station. Although she bequeathed her money to primate research, her stepfather successfully contested her will. A 1988 movie, *Gorillas in the Mist*, depicted her life and her campaign to prevent the extinction of rare mountain gorillas and the destruction of their Central African habitat.

• Sy Montgomery, *Walking with the Great Apes: Jane Goodall, Dian Fossey, Biruté Galdikas* (1991), and Farley Mowat, *Woman in the Mists: The Story of Dian Fossey and the Mountain Gorillas of Africa* (1987), provide biographical information about Fossey. The article, "Dian Fossey's Early Days in Rwanda," *International Primate Protection League* 19 (Aug. 1992): 28–30, reprints primary documents, specifically government communications, concerning Fossey's activities in Africa. Fossey's *Gorillas in the Mist* (1983), Marianna Torgovnick, "A Passion for the Primitive: Dian Fossey Among the Animals," *Yale Review* 84 (Oct. 1996): 1–24, and Michael Nichols, *Gorilla: Struggle for Survival in the Virungas* (1989), are valuable sources about the gorillas that Fossey studied. Fossey's obituary is in the *New York Times*, 2 Jan. 1986. Books that discuss Fossey's murder and speculate about the reasons for her being killed and the identity of her murderer or murderers include Nicholas Gordon, *Murders in the Mist: Who Killed Dian Fossey?* (1993); Harold Hayes, *The Dark Romance of Dian Fossey* (1990); and Alex Shoumatoff, *African Madness* (1988).

ELIZABETH D. SCHAFER

FOSTER, Abby Kelley (15 Jan. 1811–14 Jan. 1887), abolitionist and feminist, was born Abigail Kelley in Pelham, Massachusetts, the daughter of Wing Kelley, a farmer and sawmill operator, and Diana Daniels. Her family moved to the Worcester area in 1811, and there Abby attended the common schools. In 1826 she finished her education at the Friends boarding school in Providence, Rhode Island. For five or six years thereafter she lived at home and taught in local schools.

In the early 1830s she became the principal teacher of the Friends School in Lynn, Massachusetts. A birthright Quaker, Kelley associated there with co-religionists committed to pacifism, diet reform, temperance, and antislavery. She joined the Lynn Female Anti-Slavery Society, founded in 1835, became its corresponding secretary in 1836, and in 1837 went to New York as one of its delegates to the Anti-Slavery Convention of American Women, where she helped draft its declaration. On returning to Lynn she took part in a campaign to gather signatures on antislavery petitions submitted to Congress and began her extended career as an abolitionist fundraiser.

A staunch Garrisonian, Abby was also influenced by fellow Quakers Angelina and Sarah Grimké, who

encouraged her to speak her reform views publicly. In 1838 she gave her first public speech at the women's antislavery convention in Philadelphia. Two weeks later she stirred controversy by speaking before the predominantly male New England Anti-Slavery Convention and by serving on a committee with men at the convention, thereby taking an active public role in organizations and meetings in which men also participated. After her father's death in 1836, Kelley gradually took over responsibility for the family and in 1838 gave up teaching and returned to Worcester to care for her mother. Guided by Quaker principle and practice, she began her career as an antislavery lecturer in 1838 and that same year took an active role in the pacifist convention that organized the New England Non-Resistance Society. Because the Society of Friends opposed a paid ministry, she rejected the salary offered her by the American Anti-Slavery Society for serving as its agent in 1839. But when her co-religionists objected to her platform style and her association with non-Quakers, and closed their doors to antislavery meetings, she left the sect.

Convinced that "whatever ways and means are right for men to adopt in reforming the world, are right also for women to adopt in pursuing the same object" (*Liberator*, 27 Mar. 1840), Kelley became the lightning rod for conservative clerics' opposition to women's active role in mixed-gender reform organizations. Many condemned her as a "Jezebel" on the lecture trail, and her appointment to a committee at the 1840 meeting of the American Anti-Slavery Society became the rock on which the society split. Undaunted, Kelley extended her organizational activity, lecturing and fundraising ever farther afield after her mother's death in 1842. Sometimes alone and sometimes with other agents, among them Frederick Douglass and Stephen Symonds Foster, she canvassed New England, New York, Pennsylvania, and the Old Northwest. In 1845 she married Foster, whose radical style and attacks on organized religion she adopted in part. Equally shocking to critics of "Abby Kelley" women, she continued to tour as a married woman and even after her daughter (their only child) was born in 1847. Although pressed by new domestic responsibilities and debts connected with the Tatnuck (now part of Worcester), Massachusetts, farm the Fosters had bought earlier that year, Abby continued to lecture, but for the first time she accepted an agent's salary. Sharing child care with Stephen and their numerous sisters, she found staying at home for long stretches "perfectly killing."

Nonetheless, by 1850 declining health sharply curtailed her ability to lecture, and in 1854 she became the American Anti-Slavery Society's general financial agent and chief fundraiser. Three years later she became its general agent, responsible for overseeing lecturers and convention schedules as well as soliciting funds from individual donors. None of this, however, dulled her reformer's radicalism. In 1850 she attended her first women's rights convention. In an address the following year, she asserted that women would never be free of their reliance on men until they became self-supporting. Simultaneously, the 1850 Fugitive Slave Law drove both Fosters to revolutionary rhetoric as they called for head-on confrontation with government not only to rescue the victims of slavecatchers, but also to bring down the slavery-tolerating federal Constitution. Necessarily remaining outside conventional politics, both Fosters opposed William Lloyd Garrison's increasing support for the Republican party. Although Stephen broke with Garrison in 1857, Abby remained as general agent of the American Anti-Slavery Society, dominated by Garrison, until in 1859 he made a public attack on her in which he questioned both her principles and personal rectitude.

During the Civil War internal organizational frictions multiplied. The Fosters opposed Garrison's determination to end the American Anti-Slavery Society should emancipation be achieved. At war's end, fearing that without "farther guarantees" going well beyond the Thirteenth Amendment freedmen and women would be "plunged into peonage, serfdom or even into chattel slavery" (Stanton, p. 216), Abby broke with suffragists Elizabeth Cady Stanton and Susan B. Anthony because she believed that tying woman suffrage to black suffrage imperiled the latter.

Nonetheless, after 1870 Abby rejoined the campaign for woman suffrage and, with Stephen, refused to pay taxes on the farm they owned jointly because she was politically unrepresented. She also was active in local temperance work.

Her activism curtailed by declining health, she shunned the conservatism of old age in correspondence that retained "the full flower of fanaticism" until her death in Worcester. Despite her early resignation from the Society of Friends, Abby Kelley Foster never abandoned the inner light that guided all her reform efforts.

• Primary material documenting Abby Kelley Foster's career can be found in the rich collection of Abby and Stephen Foster Papers at the American Antiquarian Society and the Worcester Historical Society, both in Worcester, Mass., and numerous letters from and about Abby are in the antislavery collections of the Boston Public Library, the Sydney Howard Gay Papers at Columbia University, and the Gerrit Smith Miller Papers at Syracuse University. The *Liberator*, *National Anti-Slavery Standard*, and *Anti-Slavery Bugle* contain reports of Abby's role in numerous conventions and reprint commentaries about her from other papers. The *Worcester Daily Spy* is the best source for her local public role. Elizabeth Cady Stanton et al., *History of Woman Suffrage*, vol. 2 (1881), documents feminists' clashes over support for the rights of freedmen. The most comprehensive secondary accounts are Jane H. Pease, "The Freshness of Fanaticism: Abby Kelley Foster" (Ph.D. diss., University of Rochester, 1969), and Dorothy Sterling, *Ahead of Her Time: Abby Kelley and the Politics of Antislavery* (1991).

Jane H. Pease
William H. Pease

FOSTER, Charles (12 Apr. 1828–9 Jan. 1904), politician, was born near Tiffin, Ohio, the son of Charles W. Foster, a merchant, and Laura Crocker. Although reared in a pioneer log cabin, he did not conform to the stereotypical frontier pattern of the self-made man. For one thing, the cabin doubled as his father's general store and real estate office, and the town, Fostoria, that grew up around it took his family name. Young Charles received no formal schooling beyond the age of fourteen, when he was withdrawn from classes and placed behind the counter. He proved adept at mercantile endeavors and by the age of nineteen was managing the family enterprise.

In 1853 he married Ann Olmstead and thereafter devoted his energies to their two daughters and his expanding business activities, which soon included banking, hardware, grain, and oil. At the outbreak of the Civil War Foster actively recruited troops for the Union army and was himself offered a commission as colonel of the 101st Ohio Volunteer Infantry, but he bowed to parental pressure and stayed home to mind the store, though offering aid and encouragement to soldiers and their families.

Foster watched politics, too, from the sidelines until 1870, when he was persuaded to run for the U.S. Congress as a Republican in a normally dependable Democratic district. Aided by his local prominence, his remarkably genial personality, and his willingness to spend money lavishly, Foster was successful in this and in three succeeding congressional contests. Speaker of the House James G. Blaine appraised the new member from Ohio's Ninth District as a man "distinguished by strong common sense, by a popular manner, by personal generosity, and by a quick instinct as to the expediency of political measures" and gave him a choice assignment to the powerful Ways and Means Committee. As chairman of the Subcommittee on Internal Revenue, Foster investigated the notorious Sanborn contracts, earning the wrath of spoilsman Benjamin Butler (1818–1893) but securing the repeal of the moiety system, the loophole that had allowed John A. Sanborn and others to skim off undeserved profits from the collection of customs duties.

In 1874 Foster again demonstrated his political independence as chairman of a committee investigating abuses by the Reconstruction legislature of Louisiana. His evenhanded report was criticized by many Republicans but won him the confidence of southern Democrats. That confidence was put to good use in the negotiations over the disputed election of 1876, when Foster served as a trusted intermediary between Rutherford B. Hayes and southern Democrats.

Gerrymandered into a heavily Democratic district, Foster made a gallant but unsuccessful run for a fourth congressional term in 1878. Undiscouraged by his setback, he secured his party's nomination for governor in 1879, pitted against Thomas Ewing (1829–1896), a popular Democrat, in one of the most exciting and strenuous state contests of the era. The campaign was marked by Foster's innovative application of business techniques to politics, featuring extensive preelection polling, meticulous statewide organization, and the hiring of a small army of paid agents. Democrats professed shock at this lavish use of money "to debauch the people, and corrupt the right of franchise" (Myers,

p. 121) and countered by accusing Foster of staying home to measure calico in his store while better men were fighting for their country. Foster's friends turned the tables by adopting the nickname "Calico Charlie" as a badge of honor, proudly wearing calico clothing and distributing pamphlets printed on calico scraps.

In 1880 Foster headed the Ohio delegation at the Republican National Convention. Ostensibly he was there to further the interests of John Sherman (1823–1900), but there were those who suspected he was playing a double game, hoping for a vice presidential slot if Blaine were nominated for president or, perhaps, to fill James A. Garfield's Senate seat should the convention turn to Garfield. After Garfield's nomination, Sherman was told that Foster had not given him "an hour of honest service" during the convention. Initially angry, Sherman subsequently forgave Foster, and the two worked hand in hand to control Ohio Republican politics for the next decade and a half.

In his two terms as Ohio governor, from 1880 to 1884, Foster brought to state administration the same efficiency and economy that had characterized his business practices. The tax system was streamlined, bipartisan boards were appointed to oversee public institutions, and humane reforms were instituted in mental hospitals. His chief effort, to regulate the liquor trade, proved his political undoing. In 1883 two constitutional amendments to that end were rejected by the voters, who also turned against the entire Republican ticket, including Foster.

In 1890 Foster was asked by President Benjamin Harrison (1833–1901) to lead a commission to negotiate the resettlement of the Sioux Indians. On 27 February 1891 Harrison appointed him to fill the cabinet vacancy created by the sudden death of Secretary of the Treasury William Windom. Foster's tenure at the Treasury Department was relatively lackluster and routine, although he did manage a successful refunding of a large issue of government bonds and maintained a substantial gold reserve in the Treasury.

That reserve melted away in the subsequent financial depression of 1893, as did Foster's own fortune. He held no further public office but remained a power behind the scenes in Ohio Republican affairs until his death in Springfield, Ohio, while visiting the home of General J. Warren Keifer.

• That no biography of Foster has been written is accountable, no doubt, to the absence of any significant collection of his papers other than his gubernatorial papers, which are on deposit at the Ohio Historical Society. There is also a collection of about one hundred letters, mostly to Hayes, at the Hayes Presidential Library, Fremont, Ohio, as well as some manuscripts at the Kaubish Memorial Library at Fostoria. An informative sketch of his life can be found in *A Centennial Biographical History of Seneca County* (1902), and some childhood reminiscences are included in Abraham J. Baugham, *History of Seneca County, Ohio . . .* (1911). Political colleagues who comment on Foster's career include James G. Blaine, *Twenty Years of Congress: From Lincoln to Garfield* (1884), and John Sherman, *Recollections of Forty Years*

(1895). A hostile contemporary view is expressed in Allen O. Myers, *Bosses and Boodle in Ohio Politics* (1895), but twentieth-century historians of Ohio have been more sympathetic, including Philip D. Jordan, *Ohio Comes of Age* (1943), and George W. Knepper, *Ohio and Its People* (1989). For obituaries see the *Ohio State Journal* and the Cincinnati *Commercial Tribune*, 10 Jan. 1904.

ALLAN PESKIN

FOSTER, Frank Hugh (18 June 1851–20 Oct. 1935), theologian and educator, was born in Springfield, Massachusetts, the son of William F. Foster and Mary Flagg Miller. He received a B.A. from Harvard in 1873 and graduated from Andover Theological Seminary in 1877, when he was ordained a Congregationalist minister. In 1881–1882 he was a Parker Fellow at Harvard; the fellowship allowed him to study in Germany, and he earned a Ph.D. from the University of Leipzig in 1882. He was married twice, first to Eliza Grout in 1877, who died in 1912; they had three children. In 1913 he married Margaret Tracy Algoe, who died in 1920; they had no children.

Foster's career as a theologian began in 1882–1884 at Middlebury College in Vermont, where he taught philosophy and German. In 1884 he moved to Oberlin Theological Seminary in Ohio for twelve years, taking the chair in church history. For ten years, 1892–1902, he taught systematic theology at Pacific Seminary in California, a Congregationalist school. Beginning in 1904 he served as the pastor of Olivet College and the Village Church in Olivet, Michigan, for three years. He also taught history (1907–1914) and philosophy (1914–1916) at Olivet. Two short-term positions concluded his teaching career: professor of biblical literature at Lake Erie College in Painesville, Ohio (1919), and instructor in Greek and Hebrew at Oberlin Graduate School of Theology (1926–1933).

Trained in classical theology and history, Foster became one of the leading historical theologians of his era. He was most heavily indebted to Edwards A. Park of Andover Theological Seminary for his theological perspectives and to Gottfried Thomasius of Erlangen for his conception of historical work. He prided himself as a "descendant of Puritan and Pilgrim . . . born and baptized in one of our most ancient Massachusetts churches, trained at our oldest university, and taught at the center of intensest interest in New England theology" (Foster, *A Genetic History of the New England Theology*, p. vi).

New England theology was Foster's lifelong preoccupation. As he defined it, New England theology was America's first indigenous theology and singularly identified the region as a microcosm of intellectual development. The school of thought, which included illustrious proponents such as Samuel Hopkins, Joseph Bellamy, Nathaniel W. Taylor, Charles G. Finney, Horace Bushnell, and Edwards A. Park, began in southwestern New England primarily around the epicenter of Yale College. Jonathan Edwards was the fountainhead and Park was the "ripest fruit," to use Foster's metaphor. Foster took what he called a "genetic" approach to writing historical theology to demonstrate that ideas develop and one writer is dependent upon another; he borrowed the "genetic" terminology from the emerging life sciences of the nineteenth century, which he sought energetically to relate to theological discourse. He held that the New England school of theology collapsed in his own lifetime because it focused too much on externals and paid little attention to the inner life of the spirit. Later New England theologians held little regard for human nature, the evolutionary nature of theological ideas, or an imminent God and were too deterministic. Foster rejected the old determinism and low estimate of the nature of human beings as taught by Calvin and New England theologians before 1850. He discussed his criticisms in *A Genetic History of the New England Theology*, published in 1907. That book became a methodological paradigm as well as the authority on the subject for many generations.

Early in his career Foster demonstrated the strength of his skills as a Reformation scholar. In a study of Hugo Grotius, he analyzed the theories of the atonement of Christ and concluded that the Grotian theory (the "governmental theory of the atonement," which held that God was the originator of the plan of salvation) was the only one that did justice to the freedom of the will. He provided exhaustive historical notes for his study of Grotius's original text. In 1899 he published *Fundamental Ideas of the Roman Catholic Church*, in which he sought to explain from a Protestant perspective the theological tenets of Catholicism. The book became a standard work in the anti-Catholic literature of the century, holding that the Protestant faith (which Foster fused into a unified system) more closely articulated the teachings of Christ. The machinery of the Catholic church he found "unnecessary, unwarranted, and injurious."

In the context of the turn of the century, Foster considered himself a progressive evangelical. The heir of a great tradition, he wanted to hand down to posterity an undiminished and perfected system of doctrinal truth. In the Stone Lectures at Princeton in 1900, he followed the trend of the "Chicago School" and called for a theology rooted in experience. For him, experience gave shape to doctrine; in theological assertions one must account for the new sciences. He wrote in *Christian Life and Theology; or, The Contribution of Christian Experience to the System of Evangelical Doctrine* (1900) that the history of doctrine should not be a "collection of learned lumber, but materials for ascertaining the mind of the Spirit and the truth of God." The Stone Lectures were repeated at Crozer Theological Seminary in Upland, Pennsylvania, and Hartford Theological Seminary, as well as Union College in Bradford, England. Foster's role as a bridge between more radical theologians and the evangelical community was seen in the choice of a publisher for this work, the Fleming H. Revell Company, which specialized in conservative evangelical doctrine.

Foster wrote two other important books. In 1930 he helped to introduce the German theologian Rudolf Otto to the American public by translating and annotating Otto's *India's Religion of Grace and Christianity, Compared and Contrasted*. With Otto he liked to think that the future would bring the unity of one faith and one communion through the recognition of common ideas like grace. In a sequel to his pioneering *Genetic History*, he gave the four Stephen Green Lectures at Andover Newton Theological School in 1934 in which he characterized the "new theology" as having emerged from forces like evolutionary theory, which caused pastors and church leaders to ask honestly what the truth was. He acknowledged several prominent American theologians including William Newton Clarke and George Burman Foster as exemplary of new theology. In the end, Foster believed that Congregationalists had always been in the vanguard of freedom and the introduction of new lines of thought, including missions, education, revivals, and associations. In his view, Congregationalists provided a more mainstream approach to the great issues of American Protestantism.

A committed Congregationalist and Protestant ecumenist, Foster was among the most articulate historical theologians of American Protestantism who tried to relate nineteenth-century classic Calvinism to the social and intellectual currents of the next century. He died in Oberlin, Ohio.

• Papers relating to Foster are in the Oberlin College Archives and in the alumni files of Harvard University. Besides those works mentioned, he wrote *The Modern Movement in American Theology: Sketches in the History of American Protestant Thought from the Civil War to the World War* (1939), which was largely autobiographical. He also edited *The Concise Dictionary of Religious Knowledge* (1891) and the theological journal *Bibliotheca Sacra*. An obituary is in the *New York Times*, 22 Oct. 1935.

WILLIAM H. BRACKNEY

FOSTER, George Burman (2 Apr. 1857–22 Dec. 1918), theologian and educator, was born in Alderson, West Virginia, the son of Oliver Harrison Foster and Helen Louise Skaggs. Foster entered Shelton College in 1876 and graduated from West Virginia University in 1883. He served as pastor of the Baptist church in Morgantown, West Virginia, from 1883 to 1884. While there he married Mary Lyon in 1884; they had three children, none of whom survived Foster. Also in 1884 Foster enrolled in the ministerial course at Rochester Theological Seminary, graduating in 1887. He then served at the Baptist church in Saratoga Springs, New York, until 1891.

Inclined toward academic interests, Foster left the pastoral ministry in 1891 to study theology at the universities in Göttingen and Berlin, Germany. Upon his return to the United States, he was awarded an honorary Ph.D. by Denison University in Granville, Ohio. His teaching career began at McMaster University in Toronto, Ontario, Canada, where he taught philosophy, psychology, and logic in the Faculty of Arts from 1892 to 1895. As a lecturer he was highly regarded, and his preaching in local Baptist churches in Ontario enhanced his reputation among Baptist churches in the convention. In 1895 William Rainey Harper invited him to a position at the University of Chicago, where Foster distinguished himself as professor of systematic theology and the philosophy of religion. He mentored important theologians of the next generation, including Douglas Clyde Macintosh and Albert E. Haydon. In addition to full-time teaching, Foster also served as interim minister of several Baptist congregations and a Unitarian church.

Foster was a liberal reinterpreter of Protestant theology. Influenced by Adolf von Harnack's understanding of the universality of Christianity and Jesus' teaching of the fatherhood of God, Foster moved beyond traditional doctrinal formulations to a theology grounded in human experience. In *The Finality of the Christian Religion* (1906), he argued that what was "final" were the moral values taught by Jesus of Nazareth. Eschewing the appeal to fear in religion, he asserted that the value of Western religious thought could be found in its ethical authority. In an acclaimed posthumous work, *Christianity in Its Modern Expression* (1921), he wrote that the Kingdom of God was realized when the economic order promoted righteousness and public welfare, rather than inconsiderate egoism. Partly in response to the new pragmatism fashionable in American thought and partly despairing over the loss of a son in World War I and two children before that, Foster turned ultimately to a functional interpretation of religion as one of the instruments humans use to adapt to their environment. In this his last and unfinished work, he displayed influences of Rochester theologian Walter Rauschenbusch and his theology of the social gospel, which emphasized the need of Christians to respond to the cultural crisis at the turn of the twentieth century.

Foster was a well-known controversialist who relished public debate. During the early days of Prohibition, he defended the brewer's trade in Chicago, Illinois, and in two classic public debates with Clarence Darrow in 1917 and 1918 he argued the positive side in "Is Life Worth Living?" and "Resolved: That the Human Will Is Free." Darrow said he esteemed Foster as one of the most learned men he had ever met. Foster's adversaries included Amzi C. Dixon, pastor of Moody Memorial Church in Chicago, who denounced him as the author of "Fosterism," by which Dixon meant that Foster was neither Roman Catholic nor evangelical because he rejected the supernaturalism in the Bible. In 1909 Johnston Myers, pastor of Immanuel Baptist Church in Chicago, led a drive to remove Foster from the Chicago Baptist Minister's Conference, a move that denominational editors across the country labeled "unbaptistic."

Tall and lanky in appearance, Foster was heedless and passionate in intellectual pursuits. In a kindly and gentle spirit, he raised honest and troubling questions for his era, without always proposing solutions and without regard for the impact of his assertions. Protected by a difficult writing style and abstruse expressions, Foster did not receive the kind of attention he deserved. The journalist and critic H. L. Mencken believed Foster could have been better known and more highly vilified than he was. Foster was best known through his many students at the University of Chicago, and he died in Chicago before the outbreak of extreme theological fundamentalism in the 1920s.

• Papers relating to Foster are at the University of Chicago, the American Baptist Historical Society in Rochester, N.Y., and the Canadian Baptist Archives in Hamilton, Ontario. His other major writings include *The Function of Religion in Man's Struggle for Existence* (1909), *The Function of Death in Human Experience* (1915), *The Contribution of Critical Scholarship to Ministerial Efficiency* (1916), and *A Guide to the Study of the Christian Religion* (1916). For works that interpret Foster's contribution, see W. Kenneth Cauthen, *The Impact of American Religious Liberalism* (1962), and William R. Hutchison, *The Modernist Impulse in American Protestantism* (1976). Foster's work is criticized as "modernistic" in Amzi C. Dixon, *Destructive Criticism versus Christianity* (1915), and affirmatively reviewed in Douglas Clyde Macintosh's preface to *Christianity in Its Modern Expression* (1921). Obituaries are in the *Chicago Daily Tribune*, 23 Dec. 1918, and the *Illinois Baptist Annual* (1919): 17–18.

WILLIAM H. BRACKNEY

FOSTER, Hannah Webster (10 Sept. 1758–17 Apr. 1840), writer, was born in Salisbury, Massachusetts, the daughter of Grant Webster, a merchant, and Hannah Wainwright. Details of her childhood and schooling are scarce. Following her mother's death in 1762, she was educated at boarding school, in a manner she was to praise and advocate for other young women in her novel *The Boarding School* (1798). Foster began publishing political pieces in Boston newspapers in the early 1780s. In 1785 she married the Reverend John Foster of Brighton, Massachusetts; they had six children.

Foster's first book, an epistolary novel titled *The Coquette; or, The History of Eliza Wharton*, was published anonymously in 1797 and became an instant bestseller. A second edition of the novel was printed in 1802, and other editions appeared steadily until 1874. Loosely based on the biography of Elizabeth Whitman, the novel recasts the story of this socially elite young woman whose elopement, abandonment, and solitary death from childbirth in a Connecticut inn had been a much publicized scandal in the New England papers nine years before. Most notably, *The Coquette* deemphasizes the sensational conclusion of its heroine's history (the narrative of her seduction and ruin comprises only the last quarter of the novel), in order to focus instead on the social conditions that impel her to this public disgrace.

Like Susanna Rowson, the other bestselling novelist of the 1790s, Foster labored under the contemporary social and literary establishment's suspicion of the novel. Timothy Dwight, among other notables of the period, contended that such fictions would poison the minds of young female readers; these impressionable women would find themselves inevitably attracted to the thrills rather than deterred from the dangers of the illicit romances such novels portrayed. By insisting on the factual basis of her novel, just as Rowson had insisted on the veracity of her novel, *Charlotte Temple* (1791), Foster sought to evade such condemnation. "A Novel founded on Fact," as the title page of the first edition proclaimed, *The Coquette* dealt in literal truths, Foster implied, not alluring fantasy.

Yet *The Coquette* is a far more subtle and polemical work than such a rationale suggests. In reshaping Elizabeth Whitman's history into the tale of the fictional Eliza Wharton, Foster contests the moral that the ostensibly factual newspaper accounts sought to impose on Whitman's life. "She was a great reader of romances," the *Massachusetts Centinel* of 20 September 1788 had intoned, "and having formed her notions of happiness from that corrupt source, became vain and coquetish." But Foster's Eliza Wharton is, quite to the contrary, a well-rounded and judicious reader, about whom even one of her most determined detractors in the novel concedes that "she discovers a fund of useful knowledge, and extensive reading, which render her peculiarly [i.e., particularly] entertaining."

Moreover, Foster's Eliza would seem to be a fully competent interpreter of her options as a single woman in early republican society. Having at the novel's outset narrowly escaped an arranged marriage to the aging Reverend Haly, who dies before their wedding, Eliza soon finds herself courted by two equally unpromising suitors, the sanctimonious Reverend Boyer, a younger incarnation of Haly, and the rakish Major Sanford, an unscrupulous man-about-town, patterned after the prototypical seducer Lovelace in Samuel Richardson's *Clarissa Harlowe*. Eliza reads both her suitors' words and intentions with considerable accuracy and deftly resists both Boyer's prim and petty standards of female good conduct and Sanford's duplicitous advances. But her determination to retain her freedom, to remain unattached in the face of these plainly inadequate choices, only serves to reveal that she has no freedom to retain, that, as the ironically named Lucy Freeman tells her, her "freedom" is a mere "play about words." When Boyer and Sanford renounce their respective campaigns to reform, or to corrupt, Eliza, she suddenly finds herself without options altogether, leading a reclusive, socially marginal existence in her mother's house, and prone to periods of extreme depression. In succumbing to Sanford's renewed advances (having married for money, he now lives respectably on a country estate in her vicinity), she indulges, less in coquetry, as critic Cathy Davidson tellingly observes, than in "an act of calculated self-destruction."

The Boarding School, Foster's second novel, promotes improved female education through its depiction of an exemplary boarding school teacher. Though equally concerned with the status of women in the early republic, it is a narrowly conceived, didactic work; less compelling and less successful than *The Coquette*, it was never reprinted.

Although Foster herself produced no other novels, two of her daughters, Eliza Lanesford Cushing and Harriet Vaughan Cheney, pursued literary careers.

Both women settled in Montreal, where Hannah Foster joined them and remained until her death there.

• Information on Hannah Foster may be found in Frederick C. Pierce, *The Foster Genealogy* (1889); Robert L. Shurter, "Mrs. Hannah Webster Foster and the Early American Novel," *American Literature* 4 (1932); and John P. C. Winship, *Historical Brighton* (1899). Discussions of historical context and critical assessments of *The Coquette* may be found in Charles K. Bolton, *The Elizabeth Whitman Mystery* (1912); Herbert Ross Brown, *The Sentimental Novel in America, 1889–1860* (1940); Caroline H. Dall, *The Romance of the Association* (1875); Cathy N. Davidson, *Revolution and the Word: The Rise of the Novel in America* (1986); Henri Petter, *The Early American Novel* (1971); Frank Shuffleton, "Mrs. Foster's *Coquette* and the Rise of the Brotherly Watch," *Studies in Eighteenth-Century Culture* 16 (1986); and Walter P. Wenska, Jr., "*The Coquette* and the American Dream of Freedom," *Early American Literature* 12 (1977–1978).

EVA CHERNIAVSKY

FOSTER, Harold Rudolf (16 Aug. 1892–25 July 1982), cartoonist, was born in Halifax, Nova Scotia, Canada, the son of Edward Lusher Foster and Janet Grace Rudolf. Foster's father died when he was four; his mother remarried a man named Cox, whose passion for hunting and fly fishing his stepson acquired. Bankrupt in 1906, Cox moved his family to Winnipeg, where Foster began working as an office boy, then learned shorthand and typing and became a stenographer. Disliking office work, in 1911 he found employment as an artist, illustrating mail-order catalogs. He worked for a succession of printing concerns and agencies in Winnipeg, establishing himself as a competent illustrator. During periods of low demand for artwork, he served as a professional guide for hunting expeditions and trapped for fur. In 1915 he married Helen Lucille Wells, an American from Kansas; they spent their honeymoon in a canoe, exploring unmapped lakes. They had two children.

Feeling he had reached a professional plateau in Winnipeg by 1921, Foster went to Chicago and found a position with Palenske-Yount, an advertising studio; he also freelanced for Jahn & Ollier Engraving Company. He began taking evening classes at the Chicago Art Institute in 1922, continuing, from 1925 to 1927, at the Chicago Academy of Fine Arts. In 1928 he illustrated the first volume in a projected series called Famous Books and Players—Edgar Rice Burroughs's *Tarzan of the Apes*. When the book did not fare well, Foster was asked to convert the material into newspaper comic strip format for Metropolitan Newspaper Service (soon to rename itself United Feature Syndicate). Foster's *Tarzan* ran six days a week for ten weeks, 7 January–16 March 1929, following the plot of the book faithfully. It was not a true comic strip: Foster's drawings merely illustrated the typeset narrative prose that ran beneath the pictures, and speech balloons were not used. The feature was popular enough to warrant continuing the Tarzan saga through Burroughs's other novels, but the art for these was handled by another artist, Rex Maxon; Foster stayed in advertising. However, soon after the full-page Sunday color *Tarzan* was launched on 15 March 1931, Foster was invited to do the weekly page. By then, the depression had reduced his income as an illustrator, so he accepted the offer; his inaugural *Tarzan* page appeared on 17 September 1931. At first, thinking that drawing for the funny papers was beneath his dignity as an artist, Foster illustrated the syndicate-furnished script somewhat perfunctorily, but as he began to receive fan mail, he realized he had an audience—faithful readers before whom he was performing every Sunday. With that realization, he started to take more care with his work. Unhappy with the quality of the scripts he was getting, he revised them; and he devoted more effort to the artwork, using cinematic techniques—close-ups, panoramic scenes, shifting camera angles—to intensify the drama of the stories. *Tarzan* soon emerged as the best-drawn feature in the comics, an inspiration to dozens of other artists in the medium.

By 1935 Foster began to feel the need for the kind of creative freedom that a character of his own would afford him. When he was approached by King Features, he already had an idea about the sort of strip he would like to do. Intrigued by knights in armor and medieval civilization, he considered a saga of the Crusades before deciding that he would have greater flexibility for storytelling if he focused on the legendary venue of King Arthur's Round Table. Despite the eagerness of King Features to begin, Foster took nearly two years to research and develop the feature.

An epic of the days when knighthood was in flower, *Prince Valiant* started on 13 February 1937. Foster deliberately moved the time of his story forward about five hundred years from the supposed reign of King Arthur: the costumes and pageantry of the later period were more in keeping with the popular idea of Arthurian knighthood. Within his chosen period, Foster was painstakingly accurate. His desire to create an authentic ambience for his new hero led him to study medieval history, art, and literature extensively. Since quitting school at age fourteen, Foster had been an avid reader and an enthusiastic devotee in the quest for knowledge, and he now indulged this passion in his work.

Writing as well as drawing the feature, Foster achieved an excellence in both story and illustration that would never be surpassed on the comics pages. *Prince Valiant* traces the life of its protagonist, beginning with his youth as a displaced Viking in the fens of England, where he grows to manhood, learning to hunt and fish and to be resourceful as a warrior. He journeys to Camelot and becomes squire to Sir Gawain, and the two embark on many action-packed quests. By his valor in battle, Val wins the legendary Singing Sword and, eventually, his knighthood. After a stormy courtship, he marries Aleta, the beautiful queen of the Misty Isles, and they have several children. Foster's stories demonstrated his hero's considerable ingenuity at all manner of enterprises as well as warfare; and Foster varied the focus, shifting from the battlefield to the hearth for interludes of marital bliss

(which usually resulted in Aleta's winning so many of her campaigns that Val left on another quest to find relief from domesticity). The stories were literate and suspenseful, by turns humorous and sentimental, violent and peaceful, romantic and pragmatic, and always realistic and tasteful.

An admirer of the classic illustrative styles of Howard Pyle and E. A. Abbey, Foster was a brilliant draftsman, and his art was realistic, confident, and masterful. Before long he began to vary the page layouts to give his story visual impact, producing magnificent vistas in spacious half-page panels—becalmed seascapes mirroring Viking vessels in the glassy surface, sprawling landscapes of fertile valleys dotted with medieval huts and castles, towering snowcapped mountain ranges, and teeming mob scenes with scores of people milling through the marketplace or manning siege machines outside walled cities. Like *Tarzan*, *Prince Valiant* was an illustrated narrative: Foster's luxuriantly detailed pictures appeared above blocks of his terse, languid prose, and speech balloons never intruded into the illustrations.

Foster produced for a brief time two other features—a daily strip, *The Song of Bernadette*, an adaptation of a novel by Franz Werfel (19 Apr.–22 May 1943); and, on his Sunday page, *Medieval Castle*, about life in the Middle Ages (Apr. 1944–Nov. 1945). He became a naturalized U.S. citizen in 1934, and in 1944 he purchased a six-acre farm in Redding, Connecticut, where he could hunt and fish on his own property. In 1971 he began to retire: he moved to Spring Hill, Florida, and hired John Cullen Murphy to draw the feature. Foster continued to write it until 1980 (his last page, 10 Feb.), when he relinquished the entire task to Murphy. He died at Spring Hill.

Although not strictly speaking a comic strip, *Prince Valiant*'s presence in the Sunday comics section gave the medium indisputable class, and Foster's illustrative style illuminated the possibilities for others, demonstrating on a grand scale what quality, realistic illustration can do to enhance the narrative of storytelling comic strips.

• Some original artwork and a complete file of color proofs for *Prince Valiant* are archived at Syracuse University. No biography of Harold Foster has been published in book form, but standard works on the history of newspaper cartooning contain some information about his life, Coulton Waugh's *The Comics* (1947) and *The World Encyclopedia of Comics* (1976). Arn Saba reviews the key developments in Foster's life and career in "Drawing upon History," *Comics Journal* 102 (Sept. 1985): 61–84, which includes a long interview with Foster. Robert R. Barrett adds a few more details in his introduction to *Tarzan in Color*, vol. 3 (1993). A synopsis of *Prince Valiant* and much information about peripheral works is supplied by Todd Goldberg and Carl Horak in *A Prince Valiant Companion* (1992). Foster's *Tarzan* is reprinted in eighteen volumes from NBM (four volumes a year beginning in 1992). Several publishers have attempted to reprint *Prince Valiant* in color, but only Manuscript Press has reproduced the feature satisfactorily in all its visual grandeur and nuance—and only the first two years of the feature in two expensive volumes. The most complete reprinting project in affordable form is by Fantagraphics Books, which began producing a series of volumes in 1987, one year of the feature to a volume. Hastings House published seven novelized versions of adventures of Prince Valiant in the 1950s, each liberally illustrated in black-and-white with pictures excerpted from the strip: *Prince Valiant in the Days of King Arthur* (1951), *Prince Valiant Fights Attila the Hun* (1952), *Prince Valiant on the Inland Sea* (1953), *Prince Valiant's Perilous Voyage* (1954), *Prince Valiant and the Golden Princess* (1955), *Prince Valiant and the New World* (1956), and *Prince Valiant and the Three Challenges* (1957). A version of Foster's *Medieval Castle*, called *The Young Knight: A Tale of Medieval Times*, also has been published (1945). A 1954 *Prince Valiant* motion picture starred Robert Wagner. An obituary is in the *New York Times*, 27 July 1982.

ROBERT C. HARVEY

FOSTER, John (1648–9 Sept. 1681), engraver and printer, was born in Dorchester, Massachusetts, the son of Hopestill Foster, a brewer, captain of militia, county commissioner, and member of the Massachusetts General Court, and Mary Bates. After he graduated from Harvard in 1667, he was employed by the town of Dorchester to teach Latin students at his father's house. By 1674 the town was paying him to teach English, Latin, and writing in the Dorchester schoolhouse. His avocations were wood engraving and medicine; he began engraving possibly as early as college.

Foster's career changed when the General Court of Massachusetts rescinded Cambridge's monopoly on printing in May 1674. He bought a printing press that Marmaduke Johnson had moved to Boston before his death on Christmas Day 1674. Foster had acquired printing skills by observing Samuel Green in Cambridge and possibly Johnson in Boston, and he taught himself the business of printing books and almanacs and produced the first wood engravings printed in the colonies. The impressive range of the approximately fifty pieces that he printed between 1675 and 1681 includes at least fifteen works by Increase Mather. Mather's sermon *The Wicked Man's Portion* (1675) was the first text printed in Boston. Other printing firsts for Foster included Anne Bradstreet's *Several Poems Compiled with a Great Variety of Wit and Learning* (1678), the first book by a woman published in America; Thomas Thatcher's *A Brief Rule to Guide the Common People of New England How to Order Themselves and Theirs in the Small Pocks, or Measles* (1677), the first medical treatise printed in the colonies; and the first map printed in America, a woodcut of New England included in William Hubbard's *A Narrative of the Troubles with the Indians in New-England* (1677).

Foster's first important woodcut was a portrait of his pastor Richard Mather used as a frontispiece in Increase Mather's *The Life and Death of That Reverend Man of God, Mr. Richard Mather* (1670), the earliest extant engraved portrait in the colonies. In 1671 he engraved an Indian ABC for John Eliot, the American Indian missionary. Circa 1672 Foster printed four cuts in *Divine Examples of God's Severe Judgements upon Sabbath Breakers*, which depicted playing football, gathering wood, spinning, and milling. The cuts of the seal of Massachusetts in *The General Laws and Liberties of the Massachusetts Colony* (1672) and the *Severall Lawes and Ordinances of War* (1675) are also attributed to him. His last engraving was a view of Boston and Charlestown from Noddles Island (1680).

Foster's woodcuts also appeared in the almanacs he compiled between 1675 and 1681. His first almanac, printed in Cambridge by Green, contained woodcuts of the Sun, the Moon, stars, and a lunar eclipse. The rest of his almanacs were printed in Boston and made a break with the colonial almanacs that had been published by the Harvard establishment since 1639. Harvard's almanacs were intended to popularize the scientific astronomical insights of Nicolaus Copernicus, and their compilers disdained the commercial astrology common in British almanacs. In 1676 Foster's competing almanac appealed to popular taste by including meteorological advice to assist farmers who wanted to plant by the signs of the zodiac. In 1678, as his confidence and independence grew, Foster added the Man of Signs, also known as *homo signorum*, the Moon's man, or anatomy. The Man of Signs (possibly invented by Petrus de Dacia, Danish astronomer and mathematician, for his own almanac printed around 1300) is the figure of a man surrounded by the twelve signs of the zodiac. A line is drawn from each sign to the part of the man's anatomy influenced when the Moon passes through the part of the sky containing that constellation. Rejected as unscientific by the almanac makers of Harvard, the Man of Signs was playfully included by Foster with the title "The Dominion of the Moon in Man's Body (According to Astronomers)." He also increased the importance of illustrations in his almanacs to make them more popular. Although he strove to outsell the almanacs produced by Harvard by including astrological information, practical advice, and copious illustrations, his primary focus remained, like theirs, scientific. In 1679 he concentrated on tides, in 1680 on planets, and in 1681 on comets. His last almanac, printed in 1681, went through two editions. It included his two scholarly essays, "Of Comets, Their Motion, Distance and Magnitude" and "Observations of a Comet Seen This Last Winter 1680," as well as his illustration of the Copernican system. He was unusual among colonial almanac producers in that he controlled every aspect of his almanacs himself, writing the text, doing the mathematical computations, engraving the woodcuts, and setting the type.

Foster died, unmarried, in Dorchester of tuberculosis. He requested in his will that his Boston printing house be sold to pay his debts and his funeral expenses and that his house be left to his widowed mother. He is remembered for his pioneering efforts in the fields of printing and engraving, for his innovations as a compiler of almanacs, and for his epitaph by Joseph Capen, which Benjamin Franklin reworked for the "Premature Epitaph" he wrote for himself in 1728:

The body, which no activeness did Lack,
Now's laid aside like an old Almanack;
But for the present only's out of date,
'Twill have at length a far more active state.
Yea, though with dust thy body soiled be,
Yet at the resurrection we shall see
A fair EDITION, and of matchless worth,
Free from ERRATAS, new in Heaven set forth;
'Tis but a word from God, the great Creator,
It shall be done when he saith IMPRIMATUR.

• Samuel A. Green, *John Foster: The Earliest American Engraver and the First Boston Printer* (1909), incorporates John L. Sibley's sketch in *Harvard Graduates*, vol. 2 (1881). Marion Barber Stowell, *Early American Almanacs* (1977), discusses Foster's importance in the development of colonial almanacs. Robb Sagendorph's *America and Her Almanacs: Wit, Wisdom, & Weather 1639–1970* (1970), includes the woodcut of Richard Mather.

SUSAN MCMICHAELS

FOSTER, John Gray (27 May 1823–2 Sept. 1874), soldier and engineer, was born in Whitefield Coos County, New Hampshire, the son of Perley Foster and Mary Gray. When Foster was very young, his family moved to Nashua, New Hampshire, where his father was major of the Nashua Light Artillery. Foster graduated fourth in his West Point class of 1846 and was commissioned in the Corps of Engineers. In 1851 he married Mary Moale (or Mole), with whom he had one child. After Mary's death in 1871, he married Anna Johnson in 1872; the number of their children, if any, is unknown.

Following his graduation from West Point, Foster, after serving briefly in Washington, D.C., saw extensive action in the war with Mexico. Serving with General Winfield Scott, he was at the siege of Veracruz and fought at Cerro Gordo, Contreras, Cherubusco, and Molino del Rey. At the end of the war he was breveted first lieutenant and captain for gallantry in leading General William Worth's storming column at the battle of Molino del Rey, where he was severely wounded in the hip. Between the war with Mexico and the Civil War, Foster served as assistant engineer in the Engineering Bureau in Washington and had several important engineering assignments, building coastal defenses and conducting coastal surveys. He spent 1848–1855 as assistant engineer in the building of Fort Caroll, Maryland, and in coastal survey work. He was assistant professor of engineering at West Point from 1855 to 1857. From 1858 to 1861 he was assigned to repairing Fort Moultrie and building Fort Sumter in Charleston harbor, throwing Foster into the inaugural fighting of the Civil War.

As engineer in charge of the fortifications in Charleston harbor and second in command at Fort Sumter when the Confederates shelled the fort to begin the Civil War, he successfully removed the garrison from Fort Moultrie to Fort Sumter. For his services in Charleston harbor Foster was breveted major of engineers. He was appointed brigadier general of volunteers 23 October 1861 and joined General Ambrose Burnside's North Carolina expedition.

Foster served with distinction as commander of the First Brigade in the Burnside expedition in North Carolina and was breveted lieutenant colonel in the regular army for his part in the capture of Roanoke Island. For services in the capture of New Berne (now New Bern), North Carolina, he was breveted colonel and was breveted major general of volunteers 18 July 1862. Over the next year and a half he commanded the XVIII Corps and the Department of North Carolina, the detachment of the XVIII Corps at St. Helena in the Department of the South, and the combined Department of Virginia and North Carolina from mid-July until 11 November 1863. Foster acquired a reputation as a fighting general in his vigorous conduct of several important expeditions, disrupting Confederate supply and diverting Confederate troops. In the most notable of these actions, he fought four battles in four days on an expedition to Goldsboro, North Carolina, where he destroyed a railroad bridge that was critical to Confederate supply.

Foster took part in operations to relieve Burnside during the siege of Knoxville and took command of the Department of Ohio on 11 December 1863. Injuries suffered in a fall from his horse forced him to resign this command 9 February 1864. He subsequently commanded the Department of the South from 26 May 1864 to 13 March 1865, cooperating with General William Tecumseh Sherman by opening communications with him during his march through Georgia and conducting raids against the Confederate railway between Savannah and Charleston. He concluded the war as major of engineers and brevet major general in the regular army.

Foster commanded the Department of Florida from 7 August 1865 to 5 December 1866. During 1867 Foster served on temporary duty with the Engineer Bureau and was promoted to lieutenant colonel in the Corps of Engineers. He distinguished himself as superintending engineer of various river and harbor improvements, including submarine engineering operations in Boston and Plymouth harbors. From 1871 until his death he served as assistant chief engineer in the U.S. Army.

Foster took his place among Civil War era graduates of West Point, especially from the Corps of Engineers, who distinguished themselves as scholars. He published extensively on engineering topics, including his authoritative *Submarine Blasting in Boston Harbor* (1869). His writings and his successful submarine blasting operations in Boston harbor and the harbor of Portsmouth, New Hampshire, gained him an international reputation.

Foster is one of the least visible officers of his rank and service of the Civil War, a fact attributable to his support role as a department commander for the major field armies, which he never led. He appears to have performed distinguished service as a departmental organizer and successful leader of small expeditions.

This service and his distinguished career as an engineer and scholar are deserving of more attention than Foster has received. He died in Nashua, New Hampshire.

• A small collection of Foster's papers is in the New Hampshire Historical Society. Foster's official report of his 1862 expedition while in command of the Department of North Carolina is in Frank Moore, ed., *The Rebellion Record*, vol. 6 (1863), pp. 253–56. Also see Foster, *Report to the Committee on the Conduct of the War* (1866). The best of the several brief synopses of Foster's life is the detailed account in Frederick Clifton Pierce, *Foster Genealogy* (1899), pp. 305, 394–96. See also Frank G. Noyes, "Biographical Sketch of Maj. Gen. John G. Foster," *Granite Monthly*, June 1899, pp. 331–44, based on Foster's papers. A limited compilation of documentary sources is David Hunter, *Correspondence, Orders, etc., between Maj. Gen. David Hunter, Maj. Gen. J. G. Foster, and Brig. Gen. Henry M. Naglee, and Others. February and March, 1863* (1863). The indispensable published documentary source is U.S. War Department, *The War of the Rebellion: A Compilation of the Official Records of the Union and Confederate Armies* (128 vols., 1880–1901). Foster's official reports as second in command at Fort Sumter are an especially valuable record of that period of the war.

EDWARD HAGERMAN

FOSTER, John Watson (2 Mar. 1836–15 Nov. 1917), diplomat and secretary of state, was born in Pike County, Indiana, the son of Matthew Watson Foster, a farmer, merchant, and local politician, and Eleanor Johnson. Following graduation from Indiana University in 1855, Foster studied for a year at Harvard Law School, then read law in a Cincinnati law office for an additional year before entering practice in Evansville, Indiana, with Conrad Baker, a prominent lawyer and politician. In 1859 Foster married Mary Parke McFerson, the daughter of a prominent Indiana family. The couple had three daughters, one of whom died before reaching adulthood. His strong antislavery feelings and Republican party loyalties led him to enlist in the Union army when the Civil War erupted in 1861. Completely lacking in military training, he was nevertheless commissioned a major in the Twenty-fifth Indiana Volunteer Infantry and saw action at Fort Donelson and Shiloh, where his gallantry under fire earned him a promotion to colonel. He saw further combat with the Army of the Ohio in East Tennessee, leading the Sixty-fifth Indiana Mounted Infantry into Knoxville, and in Kentucky he directed efforts to protect pro-Union elements from attacks by secessionists.

Following the war Foster became editor of the *Evansville Daily Journal* and continued his involvement in state politics, securing an appointment as postmaster of Evansville in 1869 and serving as chairman of the Republican state committee. His support in 1872 for the reelection of Oliver P. Morton to the U.S. Senate and Ulysses S. Grant to the presidency led to his appointment as minister to Mexico the following year.

Although he lacked experience in diplomacy, spoke no foreign language, and had never traveled abroad, Foster, a well-educated, astute, and pragmatic veteran of many partisan political battles, quickly proved to be well suited for foreign service. In Mexico during a time of revolution, he learned Spanish, traveled widely outside Mexico City, and established a friendly relationship with the nation's new dictatorial president, Porfirio Díaz, and engineered recognition of his regime by a skeptical U.S. administration in Washington. In 1880 Foster was appointed minister to Russia and served an uneventful year, during which he argued for better treatment of American Jews and became frustrated with the corruption of the government in St. Petersburg. Upon returning to the United States, he established a legal practice in Washington, D.C., specializing in international affairs. He served briefly as minister to Spain in 1883–1885.

The election to the presidency of Benjamin Harrison, a longtime political acquaintance from Indiana, brought Foster back into government service in 1889. On a mission to Madrid, Foster negotiated a reciprocity treaty facilitating U.S. trade with Cuba and Puerto Rico. He later negotiated agreements with Brazil, Austria-Hungary, and Germany, served as agent for the United States in international arbitration involving the harvesting of fur seals in the Bering Sea, and attended to issues related to Canadian-American relations. As Secretary of State James G. Blaine's health declined, Foster became increasingly involved in a myriad of diplomatic issues. Although still a private citizen and a lawyer whose clients included the governments of Mexico, China, and Chile, he enjoyed extraordinary privileges within the Department of State. He played a central, although clandestine, role in the diplomatic imbroglio with Chile known as the *Baltimore* Affair (1891–1982), urging the president to take a belligerent stand, a posture that brought the two nations to the brink of war. When Blaine resigned in June 1892, Foster was appointed to the post.

Foster's brief tenure in the cabinet was not without controversy. Critics questioned his role in the Chilean dispute and his legal work on behalf of numerous foreign clients while simultaneously advising the State Department and the president. In January 1893, following a coup against Queen Liliuokalani of Hawaii by planters with American ties who were openly supported by the U.S. minister in Honolulu and marines from the USS *Boston*, Foster attempted to rush a treaty of annexation through the Senate. The effort failed, in large measure because of the lame-duck status of the administration and the determination of President-elect Grover Cleveland and secretary of state designate Walter Q. Gresham to embarrass Harrison.

Upon leaving office, Foster returned to his legal practice. He continued preparations to represent the United States in the Bering Sea fur seal dispute that he had begun prior to his appointment as secretary of state. In the summer of 1893, following a fiasco in which he unknowingly submitted as evidence Russian documents fraudulently translated by a State Department employee, a tribunal in Paris ruled against the United States in its claim of jurisdiction over the seals' habitat.

Foster thereafter devoted himself to practicing law, carrying out sporadic diplomatic assignments, teaching at George Washington University, writing and lecturing on American diplomatic history, and participating in groups devoted to the advancement of world peace through international law. In 1895, at the urgent request of the Chinese government, Foster served as adviser to Viceroy Li Hung-Chang in the peace negotiations at Shimonoseki, Japan, that followed the Sino-Japanese War. In 1898 he advised the William McKinley administration on issues relating to the annexation of Hawaii and served on a ten-member Joint High Commission charged with resolving disputes among the United States, Canada, and Great Britain. In 1903 Foster prepared the U.S. case in the Alaska-Canada boundary dispute. In 1907 he accompanied the Chinese delegation to The Hague for the Second International Peace Conference to serve as their adviser. Foster participated in the founding of the American Society for International Law in 1906 and the Carnegie Endowment for International Peace in 1910. In speeches and articles he urged the United States to participate in the International Court of Justice and served four times as president of the Lake Mohonk (N.Y.) Arbitration Conference. His classroom lectures and frequent public addresses evolved into numerous publications, including such pioneering studies as *A Century of American Diplomacy, 1776–1876* (1900), *American Diplomacy in the Orient* (1903), *Arbitration and the Hague Court* (1904), and *The Practice of Diplomacy* (1906).

In retirement Foster continued to follow world affairs with interest and endeavored to advance the careers of his son-in-law Robert Lansing (secretary of state, 1915–1920) and his precocious grandson John Foster Dulles (secretary of state, 1953–1959). Foster died at his home in Washington, D.C.

• Foster's autobiography, *Diplomatic Memoirs* (2 vols., 1909), details his career and offers candid appraisals of his contemporaries. He destroyed his personal papers after completing this work. *War Stories for My Grandchildren* (1918) presents Foster's account of his Civil War experience. The volumes in the *Foreign Relations of the United States* covering the years Foster served in various diplomatic posts and as secretary of state contain much of his official correspondence. See also Michael J. Devine, *John W. Foster: Politics and Diplomacy in the Imperial Era, 1873–1917* (1981); William R. Castle, "John W. Foster" in *The American Secretaries of State and Their Diplomacy*, ed., Samuel F. Bemis (vol. 8, 1928); and Jack L. Hammersmith, "John W. Foster: A Pacifist after a Fashion," *Indiana Magazine of History* 84 (June 1988): 117–13. An obituary is in the *New York Times*, 16 Nov. 1917.

MICHAEL J. DEVINE

FOSTER, Judith Ellen Horton Avery (3 Nov. 1840–11 Aug. 1910), lawyer, temperance activist, and Republican party leader, was born in Lowell, Massachusetts, the daughter of Jotham Horton, a blacksmith and a Methodist minister, and Judith Delano. Both parents died when she was young, and Judith moved to Boston to live with her older married sister. She then lived with a relative in Lima, New York, where she attended the Genessee Wesleyan Seminary. After graduation she taught school until her first marriage to Addison Avery in 1860. They had two children, one of whom died in childhood. The marriage ended about 1866, and she moved to Chicago, supporting herself and her child by teaching music in a mission school. In Chicago she met Elijah Caleb Foster, a native of Canada and a recent graduate of the University of Michigan Law School. After their marriage in 1869, they moved to Clinton, Iowa. They had two children; one died at the age of five.

Foster's husband encouraged her to read law and supervised her education. In 1872 she became the first woman admitted to practice law before the Iowa State Supreme Court. The Fosters jointly practiced law in Clinton and became involved in Iowa temperance politics. In 1873 Judith Foster founded the Woman's Temperance Society of Clinton, Iowa. A year later the National Woman's Christian Temperance Union was formed, and Foster joined through the newly created Iowa WCTU. She quickly became an important voice in the National WCTU, holding the position of superintendent of the Office of Legislation and Petitions from 1874 until 1888. She participated in writing the first constitution of the WCTU.

In 1881 Judith Foster opposed National WCTU president Frances Willard's move to affiliate with the Prohibition party. Foster's opposition was based not only on her loyalty to the Republican party but also on her belief that there should be strong delineations between legal and political work for temperance. Foster saw the WCTU as directing legal efforts on behalf of temperance while leaving political questions to organizations such as political parties. Foster first protested Willard's endorsement of the Prohibition party in private, but the vote of the WCTU at the national conventions of 1884 and 1885 to "lend their influence to the Prohibition party" led her into open rebellion. With the Iowa WCTU solidly behind her, Foster entered official protests at the annual conventions of the National WCTU from 1885 until 1888, when the convention refused to hear the protest. At that point the Iowa Union left the national organization, and Foster formed the NonPartisan Woman's Christian Temperance Union in what she hoped would be a legitimate counter-organization. The NonPartisan WCTU held national conventions and published the *Temperance Tribune* and sixteen pamphlets.

The NonPartisan WCTU was but one political avenue Foster followed after her break with the National WCTU. In 1888 Foster used her connections to James Clarkson, co-owner of the *Des Moines (Iowa) Register* and president of the National Association of Republican Clubs, to gain entrance into the Republican party. She proposed to the National Republican Committee that the party recognize the establishment of her newly created Woman's Republican Association of the United States (later known as the Woman's National Republican Association). When it did so, she became its president. As president, she addressed the Republican

National Convention of 1892 and stated, "We are here to help you and we have come to stay." The object of the Woman's Republican Association was to unite women "in educational work and social influence for the maintenance of the principles of the Republican party in the home, in the state, and in the nation." Foster, with the financial backing of the National Republican Committee, traveled to all regions of the country during election years organizing women's Republican clubs. Her main coworker was the association's secretary, Mrs. Thomas W. Chace of Rhode Island. Helen Varick Boswell of New York City, appointed treasurer in 1892, would become president of the association upon Foster's death.

Foster was known for her excellent abilities as a public speaker and her persuasive written arguments for temperance and the Republican party. Her writings and published speeches include "The Republican Party and Temperance," a speech delivered at Roseland Park in Woodstock, Connecticut (1888); *The Saloon Must Go* (1889); a speech at the National Council of Women of the United States (1891); "The Influence of Women in American Politics," a speech to the World's Congress of Representative Women (1893); and "Woman's Political Evolution," *North American Review* (1897). All these works emphasize women's struggles for specific reforms such as temperance and woman suffrage, but they also concentrate on women's broader citizenship duties and the need for their participation in the political world at every level.

Foster's move into national Republican politics resulted in her relocation with her husband to Washington, D.C., where she opened a law office in 1889. Foster kept up a correspondence with Republican politicians to advance her political agenda and to secure patronage appointments for herself and her husband. In 1888 Elijah Foster was appointed by Benjamin Harrison to a post in the Justice Department. He became an assistant attorney in 1898, under William McKinley, a post he held until his death in 1906.

Judith Foster's major political appointments took her around the world. In 1898 McKinley appointed her to a delegation to inspect mobilization camps during the Spanish-American War. In 1900 she was appointed to the Taft Commission to the Philippines to study the conditions of women and children and to the U.S. delegation to the International Red Cross Conference in St. Petersburg, Russia. In 1906 she was asked by President Theodore Roosevelt to inspect and report on the condition of women and children in American industries. In 1908 she was appointed special agent of the Department of Justice to inspect conditions of criminals in federal and state prisons. During her years in Washington, Foster also continued to coordinate Republican women's campaign efforts through the Woman's National Republican Association. She died in Washington, D.C.

• There is no single collection of Foster's papers. Her political activities can be followed in *History of Woman Suffrage*, vols. 3–6 (6 vols., 1881–1922); the *Woman's Journal* and the *Union Signal* from the 1880s to 1910; and the papers of the National Woman's Christian Temperance Union in the Michigan Historical Collections and Ohio Historical Society. A few items of the NonPartisan Woman's Christian Temperance Union are located in the Sophia Smith Collection, Smith College. Correspondence to and from Foster are located in the Library of Congress collections of Presidents Benjamin Harrison, William McKinley, and Theodore Roosevelt. Biographical sketches include Ernest H. Cherrington, ed., *Standard Encyclopedia of the Alcohol Problem*, vol. 3 (1926); Elmer C. Adams and Warren D. Foster, *Heroines of Modern Progress* (1913); David C. Mott, *Annals of Iowa* (Oct. 1933); and Frances Willard and Mary Livermore, *A Woman of the Century* (1893). Foster's temperance and Republican party work are placed in a larger context in Ruth Bordin, *Women and Temperance* (1981), Melanie Gustafson, "Partisan Women" (Ph.D. diss, New York Univ., 1993), and Rebecca Edwards, "Gender and American Politics" (Ph.D. diss, Univ. of Virginia, 1995).

MELANIE GUSTAFSON

FOSTER, Pops (18 May 1892–30 Oct. 1969), musician, was born George Murphy Foster on a plantation near McCall, Louisiana, the son of Charles Foster, a butler, and Annie (maiden name unknown), a seamstress. Foster was African American, with considerable Cherokee Indian ancestry from his mother's family. As a boy he attended a Catholic elementary school and played the cello in plantation bands led by his father and uncle. His brother Willie excelled at the banjo and also became a professional musician. When Foster was ten his family moved to New Orleans, where he soon switched from the cello to the double bass. He enrolled at New Orleans University, a secondary school for blacks.

Foster did not complete his secondary education, however, because he was heavily involved in the exciting, working-class black musical scene in New Orleans that was giving birth to jazz. He played in pickup groups at lawn parties and fish fries, and he soon gained paid work with the Rozelle Orchestra and in bands led by Frankie Dusen, Kid Ory, Manuel Perez, Freddie Keppard, and John Robichaux. He also worked with such jazz pioneers as the cornetists Willie "Bunk" Johnson and Joe Oliver. Foster's posthumous autobiography, *Pops Foster: The Autobiography of a New Orleans Jazzman* (1971), is a uniquely colorful account of the vice and street life surrounding early New Orleans jazz. He married his first wife Bertha (maiden name unknown) in 1912, but they were soon estranged and obtained a divorce in the 1920s. They had no children. In 1918 Foster gained work on the Streckfus family's Mississippi riverboats, playing in Fate Marable's "colored" band for cruises between New Orleans and St. Louis.

During this time, New Orleans jazz musicians began to travel nationally to exploit the music's growing popularity. In 1921 Foster began the first of two residencies with the Charlie Creath Band in St. Louis, and the following year he traveled with Kid Ory to Los Angeles, where he may have taken part in the first purely instrumental recordings by a black jazz band—"Ory's Creole Trumbone" and "Society Blues" by Spike's

Seven Pods of Pepper (Sunshine Records, available on Nordskog 3009). In the late 1920s Foster toured the nation with a few groups, and in 1929 he moved to New York and joined the Luis Russell Orchestra, a popular ensemble that eventually became Louis Armstrong's backup band. Also in 1929 he made some of the first interracial jazz recordings with a white band, the Mound City Blue Blowers. Now living in Harlem, Foster married Annie Alma Gayle in 1936; they had no children.

In the 1930s Foster became widely known in the jazz community as the most rhythmically spirited double bassist, the "swinging" equivalent of his fellow New Orleans musicians Armstrong and Sidney Bechet. Foster's largely self-taught technique featured the application of strong pressure on the fingerboard by the left hand, as well as bowing, pizzicato, and string "slapping" by the right hand, which sounded sharply and resonated for many seconds—an effect that one analyst, bassist and teacher Bertram Turetzky, called "attack and decay." He also experimented with an aluminum instrument and other effects to amplify the bass sound in large dance halls. Foster usually filled each bar of music with "walking" (swinging notes that guided the entire ensemble rhythmically), and many critics consider him the musician most responsible for supplanting the tuba with the double bass as the jazz band's harmonic foundation. His recordings with the Luis Russell Orchestra, 1929–1934 (available on Gazell COCD-7, Classics 606, and other CDs), and Sidney Bechet, 1945 (on King Jazz CD-6101 and 6102), display his style. Dozens of young jazz bassists, including Milt Hinton, Jimmy Blanton, and Oscar Pettiford, eagerly emulated his style. Foster played at various times with most of the major jazz talents of the 1930s, including Duke Ellington, Fletcher Henderson, Fats Waller, Jelly Roll Morton, and Benny Goodman, while remaining with the Armstrong-Russell orchestra throughout the decade.

During World War II, as the orchestra was forced to limit its touring, Foster primarily worked as a New York subway employee and as a porter. He benefited from the growing popularity of early New Orleans or "Dixieland" jazz, though, and became a fixture in the jazz clubs of midtown Manhattan, playing in various pickup groups and participating in many recordings. Foster played with Sidney Bechet and the veteran pianist James P. Johnson, and on the radio program "This Is Jazz" in 1947–1948. In 1948, 1952, and 1955 he made tours of Europe with the Mezz Mezzrow, Jimmy Archey, and Sam Price bands. In 1956 Foster moved to San Francisco, a center of Dixieland activity, and played with Earl Hines's Small Band into the early 1960s. He continued to perform with other groups around the nation and toured Europe again in 1966 with the New Orleans All Stars. Despite increasing health problems, Foster remained an active player, and he was able to dictate his autobiography to Tom Stoddard up to the time of his death in San Francisco.

Foster was one of the best loved and most respected jazz musicians of his generation. His extraordinary sixty-year career was among the longest in jazz history. A quiet and modest man, his powerful and enthusiastic bass playing nevertheless set a high standard for emerging masters of the instrument in the 1920s and 1930s. Foster's longevity and versatility also helped to ensure that despite the advent of radically new jazz styles after 1940, the early New Orleans sound would remain popular with audiences around the world.

• For further information on Foster see Barry Kernfeld, ed., *The New Grove Dictionary of Jazz* (1988). An obituary is in the *New York Times*, 1 Nov. 1969.

BURTON W. PERETTI

FOSTER, Robert Sanford (27 Jan. 1834–3 Mar. 1903), soldier, was born in Vernon, Indiana, the son of Riley Foster and Sarah Wallace. After receiving a "fair business education," he learned the trade of tinner. At sixteen he went to Indianapolis to work in his uncle's mercantile store, where he remained until the outbreak of the Civil War. On 22 April 1861 he was mustered into volunteer service as a captain in the Eleventh Indiana Infantry, a ninety-day regiment that served in western Virginia. That year he married Margaret R. Foust; they had a son and a daughter.

In late June 1861 Foster transferred to the Thirteenth Indiana Volunteers. As major of the regiment, he fought under Brigadier General William S. Rosecrans in the battle of Rich Mountain. In his report of the fight, Rosecrans praised his subordinate for his "coolness and self-possession in forming a portion of his men under . . . fire" and leading an assault that drove the enemy from their breastworks. Foster's heroics won him promotion to lieutenant colonel in October and to colonel in April 1862. When the Thirteenth Indiana was transferred to the Shenandoah Valley as part of Brigadier General James Shields's division, Foster received favorable notice for his service at Kernstown, Virginia (23 Mar.), and at Somerville, Virginia (7 May).

Early in July Foster's outfit was ordered to the Virginia Peninsula, where it helped cover the retreat of the Army of the Potomac from Malvern Hill to Harrison's Landing. In September the colonel was dispatched to southside Virginia, where the following spring he withstood the siege imposed on Suffolk by Lieutenant General James Longstreet. Foster was conspicuous at several points in the Suffolk campaign, especially in attacking the rebel rear after Longstreet was recalled to Robert E. Lee's Army of Northern Virginia early in May. The following month Foster's brigade took part in Major General John Adams Dix's promising but ill-managed offensive against Richmond.

For his many accomplishments, Foster was promoted to brigadier general of volunteers to rank from 12 June 1863. Sent to South Carolina in early August to take part in the siege of Charleston, he commanded a three-regiment brigade in the X Corps, assigned to duty on Folly Island. In late February 1864 the peripatetic Foster accompanied an expedition to Florida, where he temporarily commanded a division. Two months later he led his brigade back to South Carolina, thence to southeastern Virginia, where for two months he served as chief of staff of the X Corps, now a part of Major General Benjamin F. Butler's Army of the James.

Returned to field service, Foster took a creditable part in Lieutenant General Ulysses S. Grant's operations against the Confederate capital. On 20 June 1864 he displayed what one observer called "wonderful celerity and precision" in leading 1,200 troops over the James River to capture and fortify the position known as Deep Bottom. The foray gave the Army of the James a strategic foothold on the doorstep to Richmond that it never relinquished. In subsequent months Foster expanded his lodgment while supporting two offensives above the James by elements of Butler's army and Major General George Gordon Meade's Army of the Potomac. Elevated to permanent divisional command, he took part in Butler's late-September advance on Chaffin's Bluff and New Market Heights. In attacking well-defended Fort Gilmer, a key point on Richmond's intermediate defense line, he lost about a third of the troops he took into action on 29 September.

During the balance of the 1864 campaign, Foster served conspicuously in numerous engagements, including those on the Darbytown Road on 7 and 27 October. Shifted to the Petersburg front as commander of the First Division in Major General John Gibbon's XXIV Corps, he spearheaded the 2 April 1865 assault that captured Fort Gregg, south of the Cockade City (Petersburg). Though his command suffered more than 700 casualties, Foster's effort, made in cooperation with the division of Brigadier General John W. Turner, not only left Petersburg untenable but precipitated the fall of Richmond. One week later Foster's troops teamed with Turner's in halting Lee's retreat near Appomattox Court House and persuading him to surrender his army to Grant.

In September 1865, fresh from serving on the tribunal that convicted the Abraham Lincoln assassination conspirators, Foster resigned his commission as brevet major general of volunteers. The following year he declined a lieutenant colonelcy in the Regular Army. Returning to Indiana, he resided in Indianapolis until his death there. He was city treasurer for five years (1867–1872), U.S. marshal for Indiana from 1881 to 1885, and for many years president of the Indianapolis Board of Trade. He also helped found the Union veterans' organization known as the Grand Army of the Republic in April 1866.

By all accounts, "Sandy" Foster was one of the ablest of the volunteer officers to attain high rank during the Civil War. He was a dutiful subordinate, an inspiring leader, dependable in a crisis, by nature a prudent and careful tactician, but willing to take chances when opportunities arose. One of his officers called him "deservedly popular, and beloved by all who knew him intimately." Another considered him "the model of an appealing officer. He attracted universal attention by his faultless military bearing; and

he was as brave in battle as he was imposing in appearance on review." An enlisted man whose regiment served apart from Foster wrote wistfully, "I wish he commanded our Division." The only stain on Foster's record was an occasional bout with the bottle. This vice, which he shared with many other Union commanders, does not appear to have adversely affected his tactical performances.

Despite lacking a military education, Foster sometimes outshone the professional soldiers with whom he served. On the morning of 9 April 1865, as the weary Federals made a final surge toward Appomattox, his was the only division in the XXIV Corps to break camp on time, most of his colleagues having overslept. Guilty of such a lapse, General Gibbon, a West Pointer and one of Grant's most respected lieutenants, shouted for all to hear: "Gen. Foster is a better soldier than I am!"

• No sizable body of Foster's personal papers has come to light. Foster is mentioned prominently in the letters of Joseph S. Bowler in the Minnesota Historical Society, St. Paul, and the diary of William A. Willoughby in the American Antiquarian Society, Worcester, Mass. *The War of the Rebellion: A Compilation of the Official Records of the Union and Confederate Armies* (128 vols., 1880–1901) contains several of his concise yet informative campaign reports. A brief biography is Charles W. Smith, *Life and Military Services of Brevet Major-General Robert S. Foster* (1915). Several regimental historians have characterized Foster's leadership, especially William L. Hyde, *History of the One Hundred and Twelfth Regiment N.Y. Volunteers* (1866), and George H. Stowits, *History of the One Hundredth Regiment of New York State Volunteers* (1870). Extensive obituaries are in the *Indianapolis Journal* and the *Indianapolis Sentinel*, 4 Mar. 1903.

EDWARD G. LONGACRE

FOSTER, Rube (17 Sept. 1879–9 Dec. 1930), baseball player and executive, was born Andrew Foster in Calvert, Texas, the son of the Reverend Andrew Foster, presiding elder of the African Methodist Episcopal churches in southern Texas. His mother's name is unknown. At age seventeen the six-footer pitched batting practice against white major league clubs doing spring training in Fort Worth, Texas. Foster played with the black Leland Giants of Chicago. In 1902 he joined the Cuban Giants, actually a misnamed Philadelphia team of American blacks. He recalled pitching for $40 a month, plus fifteen cents for meals, and confidently called himself "the best pitcher in the country." He reportedly won his nickname, Rube, by defeating the Philadelphia Athletics pitching ace Rube Waddell, probably in 1902, when he ranked among the best pitchers, black or white, in America.

John McGraw, manager of the New York Giants, is said to have hired Foster in 1903 to teach his star pitcher, Christy Mathewson, to throw the screwball. Mathewson called the pitch a "fadeaway." Although this story cannot be confirmed, Mathewson immediately improved his record from 14 to 34 wins.

In 1903 Foster joined the Cuban X-Giants of New York, an offshoot of the Cuban Giants, and the Cuban X-Giants challenged the Philadelphia team to the first black World Series. That same year the white major leagues played the first modern World Series. Foster won four games as the X-Giants claimed the championship, five games to two. The next year Foster signed with the Philadelphia Giants. In the World Series against his old club, he reported sick but won the first game with 18 strikeouts and the third game on a two-hitter, as Philadelphia took the title.

Foster pitched with his brain as much as his arm. Writing for Sol White's *Colored Baseball Guide* of 1906, he said that the real test of a pitcher comes when the bases are filled. "Do not worry," he counseled. "Try to appear jolly and unconcerned. I have smiled often with the bases full with two strikes and three balls on the batter. This seems to unnerve them."

Seeking more pay, Foster returned to his old team, the Lelands. Foster and Leland issued $100,000 worth of stock and began plans for a bowling alley, roller rink, and restaurant. In 1907 the team won 110 games and lost only ten. The next year, the Lelands became the first black team to hire its own Pullman car. In 1908 Foster married Sarah Watt; the couple had two children.

Wresting control of the team from Leland, Foster moved it in 1910 to a site four blocks from the White Sox park, changed its name to the American Giants, and challenged the major leaguers to an attendance war. One Sunday, when all three Chicago teams played home games, the Cubs drew 6,000 people, the White Sox 9,000, and the Giants 11,000. The Giants won 123 games that year and lost only six. Heavyweight boxing champion Jack Johnson handed souvenirs to the ladies at the games. Johnson later masqueraded as a Giants player in order to flee to Canada to escape prosecution under the Mann Act.

Foster was the manager as well as the owner. He built his teams around speed, using stars such as Elwood "Bingo" De Moss, Dave Malarcher, and Floyd "Jelly" Gardner. He was accused of raising the foul lines so bunts would stay fair and soaking the infield so they would roll slowly. It was also said that he gave his own pitchers frozen baseballs when the other teams were at bat.

Because the eastern teams were raiding the western squads for players, Foster established the Negro National League of eight teams. Among those attending the initial meeting at a Kansas City YMCA was Elisha Scott, who later argued the historic *Brown v. Board of Education* case before the Supreme Court.

Foster envisioned a completely black baseball league, keeping black money in black pockets. He admitted only one white owner, J. L. Wilkinson of the Kansas City Monarchs. Eventually he hoped that the black and white champions would play each other in a real World Series. This did not happen, but the league saved black baseball. Foster boasted that total players' salaries jumped from $30,000 a year to $275,000. Playing "inside baseball," he guided Chicago to pennants in 1920, 1921, and 1922.

New raids by the East threatened Foster's league, but peace was restored when he shook hands with his rivals in 1924 at the opening of the first modern black World Series. Kansas City competed against the Philadelphia Hilldales. The strain of running both the league and his team began surfacing, causing Foster to start acting irrationally. In 1926 he was committed to an asylum in Kankakee, Illinois. But his protégé, Dave Malarcher, guided the Giants to two more pennants.

Foster died in Kankakee. Three thousand mourners stood outside the church in a snowstorm as his casket was carried out to the strains of "Rock of Ages." The Negro National League died with him, a victim of the Great Depression, to be revived seven years later.

With Foster's election to the National Baseball Hall of Fame in 1981, Cooperstown opened its doors belatedly to one of the five or six truly towering figures in the history of North American baseball. White organized baseball has never known anyone quite like the versatile Foster, a great pitcher, manager, owner, league organizer, and czar. He has aptly been called "the father of black baseball."

Sportswriter Eric "Ric" Roberts of the *Pittsburgh Courier* summed up Foster's career: "Rube Foster was a creative personality. Way back in the darkest years he walked in and looked bankers in the eye and walked out with a $20,000 loan. . . . He tried to get black baseball respectability. Otherwise this reservoir of black talent, which is the backbone of the major leagues today, might not have been there."

• The National Baseball Hall of Fame has a file on Foster. For a full biography see Charles E. Whitehead, *A Man and His Diamonds* (1980). Additional information is in Robert Peterson, *Only the Ball Was White* (1970), John B. Holway, *Blackball Stars* (1988), and James Riley, *The Negro Leagues* (1996).

JOHN B. HOLWAY

FOSTER, Sidney (23 May 1917–7 Feb. 1977), concert pianist and teacher, was born in Florence, South Carolina, the son of Louis Foster, a jeweler, and Anne Diamond. Foster gave his first public performance at the age of five, and he soon became known as the marvel of Florence for his ability to compose music and to perform complete piano pieces based on just one hearing over the gramophone.

At the age of nine Foster was performing recitals in his new hometown, Miami, Florida, where his family had moved. In some of these recitals he would select pleasing titles to be printed on the program and then, on the night of the recital, improvise music appropriate to those titles. To ensure that no single composition lasted too long, his teacher would be stationed behind the curtain with a stick that he would press against young Foster to signal that the composition needed to be brought to an end. (Indeed, even much later in life Foster would sometimes improvise an encore and then invent a composer when asked backstage about the piece.)

At the age of ten he was admitted to the Curtis Institute of Music in Philadelphia, where, in addition to playing for the legendary pianist Josef Hofmann, he studied with Isabelle Vengerova and later with David Saperton. His studies at Curtis were interrupted when his family moved to New Orleans, where he studied with Walter Goldstein until he returned to Curtis in 1934. While studying at the Curtis Institute of Music, Foster met classmate Bronja Singer; they were married in 1939 and later had two sons, Lincoln and Justin.

In 1939 Foster won the MacDowell Award. One year later he became the first winner of the Edgar M. Leventritt Foundation Award and with it the prize of a debut performance with the New York Philharmonic. Playing Beethoven's Third Piano Concerto in C Minor with John Barbirolli conducting, Foster's Carnegie Hall debut on 16 March 1941 was a memorable one. Under the *New York Times* headline "Ovation to Foster," the reviewer wrote that "he proved himself an artist of first rank." After this stunning debut, record-breaking crowds attended his outdoor concerts at Lewisohn Stadium and Potomac Watergate as Foster embarked on a career that included appearances with the major orchestras, transcontinental tours, and regular recitals at Carnegie Hall.

His concert commitments took him to the major musical centers of the world. In 1964 during a "thaw" in the Cold War, Foster was invited to play in the Soviet Union, where he gave sixteen concerts in twenty-two days, including two recitals in Moscow and three in Leningrad. "One of the most impressive artists to play in this country," said the *Tass* dispatch. In Japan, as well as South America and Europe, his performances were greeted with accolades. The *Japan Times* said, "Tokyo was treated to magnificent playing."

In the 1940s Foster premiered the first and second sonatas of Norman Dello Joio in Carnegie Hall, and in 1965 he introduced and gave the first performance of Béla Bartók's Third Piano Concerto in Boston. His only release of commercial recordings were two Mozart concerti, the "Coronation" K. 537 and the C Major K. 246, and the complete Clementi sonatinas; Foster was not particularly interested in a recording career. The International Piano Archives has released a posthumous twin CD from tapes of live recitals.

From 1949 to 1951 Foster taught at Florida State University. In 1952 he joined the faculty at Indiana University School of Music in Bloomington, where he became one of the first artists to combine university teaching with a successful concert career. He was a unique teacher, with a singular knowledge of the mechanics of technique and an uncanny ability to communicate both the passion and intellectual understanding that is the essence of great art. Alberto Reyes, a Foster student and a winner himself of the Leventritt Prize and the Tchaikovsky and Van Cliburn competitions, said of his late mentor: "He was the ideal teacher . . . able to transmit with eloquence and precision the accumulated knowledge of a lifetime of thinking about music. His sympathetic awareness of the minefield that is the psychological relationship between artist and pupil made the process of studying with him an opportunity for emotional growth as well as musical

development" (brochure describing the CD "Ovation to Sidney Foster," International Piano Achives Maryland, p. 5).

For the last fourteen years of his life, Foster suffered from an increasingly virulent and incurable blood disease: myeloid metaplasia-fibrosis. However, he continued to teach full time and to perform throughout these years. "He is everything the connoisseurs claim he is: an interesting, original pianist, a master of tonal shading, an artist," wrote America's preeminent piano critic Harold C. Schonberg in a *New York Times* review of a 1963 Carnegie Hall recital. Foster played his last concert just a month before his untimely death in Boston at the New England Medical Center Hospital.

• Material relating to Foster's life and career is in the University of Indiana School of Music archives. An interview with Foster made for broadcast over the Voice of America c. 1965 is available at the Library of Congress, Washington, D.C. An obituary is in the *New York Times*, 8 Feb. 1977.

ROBERT KLOTMAN

FOSTER, Stephen (4 July 1826–13 Jan. 1864), songwriter, was born Stephen Collins Foster in Lawrenceville (now part of Pittsburgh), Pennsylvania, the son of William Barclay Foster and Eliza Clayland Tomlinson. His father, of Scots-Irish ancestry, had an early career as a merchant and trader. He owned, named, and subdivided the hillside town of Lawrenceville overlooking the Allegheny River; dedicated some of its land as a burial ground and memorial for the soldiers of the War of 1812; and with his own funds helped equip Colonel Andrew Jackson's soldiers for the Battle of New Orleans. Though he suffered financial reverses, lost his property, and the family was unable to maintain a comfortable middle-class household, he continued to fill politically appointed positions, served a term in the state legislature, and was mayor of Allegheny City (now Pittsburgh's north side).

Neither parent was musical, although his mother subscribed to literary magazines and his sisters received training in music and poetry. One of Foster's earliest influences was his sister, Charlotte Susanna, playing the piano and singing sensitive songs of love and loss; he picked out tunes on her guitar. When she died he was only three, and the loss of her music—and attendant happiness in the household—left a permanent imprint on his emotions. Foster was the tenth of eleven children in the family, and the youngest of seven to survive to adulthood.

Contrary to legend, though he chafed at his parents' proscriptions against practicing music, Foster received a solid education in English grammar, elocution, the classics, penmanship, Latin and Greek, and mathematics at private academies in Allegheny and in Athens and Towanda in northeastern Pennsylvania. He was especially adept in languages, and a sketchbook he kept from 1851 through 1860 includes his translations of song texts from German and French. His music tutor was Henry Kleber, Pittsburgh's foremost vocalist, conductor, composer, music dealer, impresario, and music teacher, who received his musical training in his native Germany.

Much has been made of Foster's performances in neighborhood children's blackface minstrel shows, but this was only one manifestation of his remarkable ear for language and style. He worked his impressions of professional performances into his own new songs, written for his circle of friends. His first reported composition was a waltz, performed by himself and two friends as a flute trio, for commencement exercises at Tioga Academy in northeastern Pennsylvania when he was fourteen. Three years later when he set to music the poem "Open Thy Lattice Love," by George Pope Morris, it was published by the Baltimore firm F. D. Benteen. As he matured, however, his parents insisted he pursue a useful life in commerce. His brothers made careers in engineering, trade, and commerce, and Foster started on that path in 1846 as bookkeeper for his brother Dunning's riverboat company in Cincinnati. Only after some of his songs found their way before the public and were snatched up by professional performers did he decide to pursue a career as a songwriter.

He left his bookkeeper's job in Cincinnati, returned to Pittsburgh, and in 1850 married Jane Denny McDowell. Their one child, Marion, born the following year, later earned a living as a piano teacher. The family never had a home of their own, living in lodgings or with relatives in Allegheny City, and for brief periods in or near New York City. Foster and Jane separated more than once; he lived his last three years alone in New York, and Jane supported herself as a telegraph operator for the Pennsylvania Railroad in Greensburg, Pennsylvania.

Foster was America's first professional songwriter, from 1850 until his death in 1864 earning his living solely through the sale of his music. He often spent weeks on a song, drafting the words first, then a melody and harmony, finally an accompaniment. While still in Cincinnati, he began selling songs outright to sheet-music publisher W. C. Peters who had music stores in Cincinnati and Louisville. These were parlor ballads for solo voice with piano accompaniment and characteristic piano pieces written for his circle of friends in Pittsburgh, or "Ethiopian melodies"—solos sometimes having a four-voice chorus—composed at first for his friends, later for local blackface minstrel performers. One of the minstrel songs was "Susanna" (1848), whose sudden and universal popularity was unprecedented. It became the "marching song of the '49ers" and the wagon trains, its tune known by members of all levels of society and all ethnic and racial groups on the continent, its melody and words "I come from Alabama, with my banjo on my knee" cherished as an enduring icon of American song. Foster's music was in demand, and minstrel leader E. P. Christy paid him for the right to perform new songs first.

Though his early comic minstrel songs used dialect and exaggerated imagery of nature to create their effect, Foster also wrote miniature tragedies modeled on popular ballads of Ireland, Scotland, and England.

"Nelly Was a Lady" (1849) was one of the first songs by a white author or composer to depict a black couple as faithful husband and wife and to use the term "lady" for a black woman nonsardonically. While he continued to produce frolicking tunes that also became popular instrumental numbers in oral tradition, such as "Nelly Bly," "Camptown Races," "Angelina Baker" (all 1850), and "Ring, Ring de Banjo" (1851), he increasingly portrayed sympathetic and compassionate black characters: "Uncle Ned" (1848); "Oh! Boys, Carry Me 'Long," "Old Folks at Home" ("Way down upon the Swanee River"), and "Farewell My Lilly Dear" (all 1851); "Massa's in de Cold Ground" (1852); "My Old Kentucky Home, Good-Night!" and "Old Dog Tray" (both 1853). Their themes of yearning for reunited family and home spoke to the conditions of an immigrant society.

During this first period of Foster's career, he seems to have followed unstated ethical principles for his racial imagery. The covers of his authorized sheet music lack the capering, denigrating cartoons of blackface performers common on his contemporaries' publications. The dialect is soft, more vernacular than condescending, and gradually disappears entirely. Moreover, in an 1852 letter to Christy, he stated his intention explicitly "to build up a taste for the Ethiopian songs among refined people by making the words suitable to their taste, instead of the trashy and really offensive words which belong to some songs of that order."

His output intermingled the minstrel songs with parlor ballads, most notably "Ah! May the Red Rose Live Alway!" (1850), but these were less remunerative. In 1854 he answered the demand for dance music with *The Social Orchestra*, a collection of seventy-three of his own and European composers' melodies arranged as solos, duets, trios, and quartets. The same year, minstrel melodies disappeared from his catalog. He began producing arrangements of his songs for guitar accompaniment and focusing on parlor ballads, including "Jeanie with the Light Brown Hair" and "Hard Times Come Again No More" (both 1854); the unaccompanied quartet "Come Where My Love Lies Dreaming," "Some Folks," and "Comrades Fill No Glass for Me" (all 1855); and "Gentle Annie" (1856).

In 1854 one of Foster's closest friends and sometime collaborator the abolitionist poet Charles Shiras died, and the following year after the loss of both his parents Foster stopped writing for a time. He produced only one published song annually in 1856 and 1857 and was borrowing heavily from his publisher against future profits. In March 1857, as royalties flagged (he had been receiving roughly 10 percent from the sale of each piece of his sheet music) and debts mounted, he cancelled his contracts and sold all rights to his previous work to his publishers Firth, Pond & Co. in New York and Benteen in Baltimore. He found his muse again in 1860 with a "plantation melody" "The Glendy Burk" and a ballad "Old Black Joe" and moved to New York to be near the publishers and theaters. The next three years, with ninety-eight titles including twenty-six Sunday school hymns, were his most fecund, many of his tunes written for the music halls to lyrics by George Cooper, including "If You've Only Got a Moustache" and "Mr. & Mrs. Brown" (issued posthumously in 1864). Forced to sell his creations to publishers for cash, he wrote hurriedly. His one enduringly popular ballad from this period is "Beautiful Dreamer" (written in 1862), which, like some fifteen other titles, was rushed out by the publisher after his death.

Within two months of his death, *Harper's New Monthly Magazine* proclaimed that "The air is full of his melodies. They are our national music." Other contemporary accounts affirm that his songs sounded distinctively American and were unprecedentedly popular: less than a year after "Old Folks at Home" appeared, the *Albany (New York) State Register* reported that it "is on everybody's tongue. . . . Pianos and guitars groan with it, night and day."

Contrary to romantic myth, Foster was not longing for a return to an idealized Old South nor did he snatch tunes from folk tradition. He realized the need to appeal to the widest possible audience, and he carefully crafted lyrics and melodies to appeal across ethnic lines. Musicologist Charles Hamm has documented the musical sources of Foster's style among the popular vocal music especially of the Irish, Scottish, Anglo, Italian, and German traditions, and William Austin similarly has discovered Foster's sources of poetic imagery and style.

Foster barely managed to survive in his self-created profession, without benefit of legal assistance or performing rights. Of his 286 known songs, hymns, arrangements, and piano pieces, most earned him very little, and his average annual income throughout his career was under $1,400. Even copyright provided scant protection: at least twenty-eight publishers issued "Susanna" during Foster's lifetime, only one of whom paid him. He tried to keep pace with the changing tastes and styles of American society during the Civil War, but seems gradually to have lost his determination, drifted away from his family, and in declining health resorted to alcohol. When he died at Bellevue Hospital in New York City, the result of a recurring, undiagnosed fever and a fall in his hotel room that gashed his head, he had only thirty-eight cents in his pocket. He was buried within a mile of his birthplace, after a funeral at Trinity Episcopal Church in Pittsburgh, which had also registered his birth and his marriage.

Foster's appraisal as a composer varies: his songs have been championed by recital vocalists including Jenny Lind, Adelina Patti, John McCormack, Paul Robeson, Marilyn Horne, and Thomas Hampson and have been arranged for performance by such musicians as violinist Fritz Kreisler and Czech composer Antonín Dvořák. And yet they have been excoriated by advocates of refined culture, such as John Sullivan Dwight who said that "they persecute and haunt the morbidly sensitive nerves of deeply musical persons," and "that such and such a melody *breaks out* every now and then, like a morbid irritation of the skin" (*Dwight's Journal of Music*, 19 Nov. 1853). He has been esteemed by songwriters, first of all George F. Root, who recognized Foster had created the "people's song," with seemingly simple words and music combined in such a way "that it will be received and live in the hearts of the people," a very difficult thing to achieve, and later by Irving Berlin and the founders of ASCAP who took pains to ensure that no future songwriters would suffer Foster's poverty and loss of control over his own works.

The general assessment of Foster has shifted with each generation, reflecting American social views. Around 1900, there was a post-Reconstructionist recasting of his music as "coon songs" and as having elevated and ennobled the crude material of a dark race. In early radio, Foster's songs—which were in the public domain and thus free—enjoyed unprecedented circulation; they were accorded "folksong" status and performed widely in schools. After the Civil Rights movement many schools banned them because of acquired racist connotations. Toward the end of the twentieth century they gained new currency, partly as a result of research into the original meanings and significance of the songs for positive racial relations, partly through their uninterrupted circulation among American country and folk-music musicians, partly because of worldwide interest in their idyllic imagery and beautiful melodies. Foster's songs remain among the best known American music throughout the world, having been recorded by ethnomusicologists in the most difficult to access regions of China along the Tibetan border, taught by black South Africans in their schools under Apartheid, used as emblematic melodies in the cartoon, film, and television industries, and universally taught to Japanese school children since the 1880s. They represent the United States to many of the world's peoples.

• The Foster Hall Collection, part of the Center for American Music in the University of Pittsburgh Library System, contains over 30,000 items of papers, photographs, musical instruments, artifacts, scores, editions, recordings, books and other writings from or relating to Foster, reflecting his life, career, music, themes, and influence. Calvin Elliker's *Stephen Collins Foster: A Guide to Research* (1988) offers lists of works, editions, bibliography, iconography, artifacts, correspondence, memorials, dramatic and literary tributes, and musical tributes and derivata. The first definitive biography is John Tasker Howard's *Stephen Foster: America's Troubadour* (1934, rev. ed., 1953), commissioned by Josiah Kirby Lilly; the composer's niece Evelyn Foster Morneweck provided documentation and genealogy unavailable elsewhere in print in *Chronicles of Stephen Foster's Family* (1944; repr. 1973); and Ken Emerson reassesses Foster's biography and the songs' social meanings in *Doo Dah!: Stephen Foster and the Rise of American Popular Culture* (1997). The first serious appraisal of the literary sources and reception history of Foster's songs is William Austin's *"Susanna," "Jeanie," and "The Old Folks at Home": The Songs of Stephen C. Foster from His Time to Ours* (1975; repr. 1987); the most extensive analysis of Foster's musical style is Charles Hamm's chapters devoted to the composer in *Yesterdays: Popular Song in America* (1979) and *Music in the New World* (1983). The authoritative version of the complete works is Steven Saunders and Deane L. Root, eds., *The Music of Stephen C. Foster: A Critical Edition* (1990).

DEANE L. ROOT

FOSTER, Stephen Symonds (17 Nov. 1809–8 Sept. 1881), abolitionist and reformer, was born in Canterbury, New Hampshire, the son of Asa Foster and Sarah Morrill, farmers. Foster worked as a carpenter for a number of years and then in his early twenties decided to seek a career in the ministry. Entering Dartmouth College, he joined the lively reform movement on campus, developing an interest in abolitionism, serving a jail sentence for refusing to join the local militia, and helping to launch a successful drive to humanize New England's prisons. He also began to question whether the church itself was living up to the highest standards of Christianity.

After graduating from Dartmouth in 1838, Foster attended Union Theological Seminary briefly, but he withdrew when the institution refused meeting space to a group of protesters. Not long afterward he ended all association with organized religion. He joined the American Anti-Slavery Society and became an itinerant lecturer for abolitionism, winning wide attention through the power of his voice and the vitriolic energy of his speeches. Enduring penury as well as verbal and physical attacks, Foster traveled through New England, excoriating not only slavery but the institutions that he believed perpetuated it—business, the political system, and the church.

After some years of traveling, Foster settled on a farm near Worcester, Massachusetts, but he continued to lecture widely. In addition, he wrote antislavery articles for newspapers and published one enormously successful pamphlet, *The Brotherhood of Thieves; or a True Picture of the American Church and Clergy* (1843), which was reprinted more than twenty times. Starting about 1841 Foster and his friend Parker Pillsbury also began visiting churches, where they would interrupt the services with speeches against slavery. Foster has sometimes been described as a leader of the "come-outer" movement, in which abolitionists left their established churches for new and more liberated forms of worship. But he seems to have seen the church primarily as a social institution whose acquiescence on slavery needed to be confronted. Parishioners were stunned when he condemned them for their complicity in the national sin and called them "thieves, blind guides, and reprobates, . . . a cage of unclean birds" (James Brewer Stewart, *Holy Warriors* [1976; rev. ed., 1996], p. 114). He was evicted, sometimes beaten, and several times arrested. Even William Lloyd Garrison—himself no stranger to confrontation—observed: "I could wish that bro. Foster would exercise more judgment and discretion in the presentation of his views" (Thomas, p. 321). But Foster's tactics did help to achieve the abolitionists' goal, which was to force public debate on the question of slavery.

In 1845 Foster married Abigail Kelley, a strong advocate for women's rights as well as an abolitionist lecturer in her own right. From then on, Foster had an enthusiastic partner in his crusades, which included not only antislavery, but also temperance, world peace, and the rights of labor. For his part, Foster enthusiastically endorsed his wife's feminism, several times risking the loss of his farm by refusing to pay taxes as long as women were denied the vote. Despite his happy marriage, he observed in 1858 that "every family is a little embryo plantation, and every woman is a slave breeder . . . and hence comes all the trouble." The couple had no children.

During the 1840s Foster supported "disunionism," arguing that northerners should no longer tolerate any political connection with the slaveholding South. He abandoned this idea within a few years, but he greeted the rise of the antislavery Republican party with little enthusiasm. To Foster the Republicans were no better than their political opponents, since they endorsed neither emancipation nor full racial equality. He wrote to Garrison: "Our business is to cry 'unclean, unclean—thief, robber, pirate, murderer'—to put the mark of Cain on every one of them" (Stewart, *Wendell Phillips*, p. 127). He tried unsuccessfully to organize a more militant abolitionist party; he even responded favorably when Lysander Spooner proposed encouraging slaves and nonslaveholding whites in the South to rise in armed rebellion. Some months later he praised John Brown for carrying out a similar undertaking. Though Foster was himself a pacifist, he insisted that "every man should act according to his own convictions, whether he believed in using moral or physical force."

Once Abraham Lincoln was elected president and the Civil War broke out, most abolitionists threw their full support to the Union, counting on their own rising influence within the Republican party to bring about emancipation and racial justice. But Foster and his wife resisted, interrupting several antislavery society meetings to demand that Lincoln be repudiated for his equivocation on these issues. As the war intensified, the couple found themselves accepted in communities where they had been attacked in the past, but this enhanced standing did nothing to soften their views. Foster condemned the Emancipation Proclamation of 1863 as too little too late, bitterly opposed the president's lenient plans for readmitting southern states, and helped organize John C. Frémont's unsuccessful campaign for the presidency in 1864.

After the slaves were freed, William Garrison proposed that the American Anti-Slavery Society be dissolved. In the bitter dispute that followed, the Fosters threw their support behind Wendell Phillips, who argued that until the freedmen were guaranteed equal rights, including suffrage, the work of the society was not finished. Five years later, when the Fourteenth and Fifteenth Amendments had fulfilled the society's agenda, at least in law, the organization did disband. But Foster resisted to the end. At the final meeting he argued that the group should continue its struggle until the freedmen had also been given a fair allotment of land, thus ensuring their economic as well as political security. His pleas went unheard, and he died a decade later.

Wendell Phillips said of Foster at his funeral: "It needed something to shake New England and stun it into listening. He was the man and offered himself for martyrdom" (*Dictionary of American Biography*, pp. 558–59). Another contemporary, Oliver Johnson, observed: "No saint of the middle ages ever surrendered himself more completely than he did to what he understood to be the service of God and humanity. . . . Sometimes those who best loved him dissented from his opinions and criticized his acts; but no one ever questioned his honesty or doubted his perfect candor" (Johnson, p. 331). Foster lived to see the cause to which he had devoted much of his life—the emancipation of the slaves—become the law of the land, and he could take some pride in having helped bring that victory about. Yet he also lived long enough to see his deeper fears confirmed and to recognize that the cause of racial justice would take much longer to achieve.

• The papers of Stephen and Abigail Foster are in the American Antiquarian Society in Worcester, Mass. Most histories of the abolition movement make some reference to him; see particularly James M. McPherson, *The Struggle for Equality: Abolitionists and the Negro in the Civil War and Reconstruction* (1964); James Brewer Steward, *Wendell Phillips: Liberty's Hero* (1986); Lewis Perry, *Radical Abolitionism: Anarchy and the Government of God in Antislavery Thought* (1973); John R. McKivigan, *The War against Proslavery Religion: Abolitionism and the Northern Churches, 1830–1865* (1984); Russel B. Nye, *William Lloyd Garrison and the Humanitarian Reformers* (1955); John L. Thomas, *The Liberator: William Lloyd Garrison* (1963); and Oliver Johnson, *W. L. Garrison and His Times* (1881). Additional recent sources include Stephen Lawrence Cox, "Power, Oppression, and Liberation: New Hampshire Abolitionism and the Radical Critique of Slavery, 1825–1850" (Ph.D. diss., Univ. New Hampshire, 1980); Jane H. Pease and William H. Pease, "The Perfectionist Radical: Stephen Symonds Foster," in *Bound with Them in Chains: A Biographical History of the Antislavery Movement* (1972); Joel Bernard, "Authority, Autonomy and Radical Commitment: Stephen and Abby Kelley Foster," *Proceedings of the American Antiquarian Society* 90 (Oct. 1980): 347–86; and Jane H. Pease and William H. Pease, "Confrontation and Abolition in the 1850s," *Journal of American History* 58, no. 4 (1972): 923–37. On Abby Kelley Foster, see Dorothy Sterling, *Ahead of Her Time: Abby Kelley and the Politics of Anti-Slavery* (1991). Obituaries are in the *Boston Daily Advertiser*, 9 and 10 Sept. 1881, and the *Worcester Daily Spy*, 9 Sept. 1881.

SANDRA OPDYCKE

FOSTER, William Hendrick (12 June 1904–16 Sept. 1978), African-American baseball player and college dean, was born in Calvert, Texas, the son of Andrew Foster, Sr., a United Methodist minister, and Sarah Lewis. At a young age Foster, his mother, and his sister Geneva joined relatives in Rodney, Mississippi. Foster attended nearby Alcorn College's lab school until 1917, when he developed an interest in playing baseball like his older half-brother Andrew "Rube" Foster, who founded the Negro National League in 1920. Disregarding his brother's advice to complete his education, Willie Foster made a youthful decision and joined the Memphis Red Sox in 1923, owned by his uncle Robert "Bubbles" Lewis.

To Rube's surprise the young pitcher defeated Foster's Chicago American Giants during a 1923 exhibition game in Memphis. Exercising his powers as league president, Rube demanded that Lewis allow Willie to split the next two seasons between the American Giants and the Red Sox. The American Giants had won pennants in 1920, 1921, and 1922, before the ascendancy of the Kansas City Monarchs. The American Giants needed an excellent left-handed pitcher to challenge the powerful Monarch hitters Hurley McNair, Oscar "Heavy" Johnson, Dobie Moore, and Wilber "Bullet" Rogan. The 6'1" Foster, who became known for his pinpoint control, hard-breaking slider, and sidearm curve that dropped like Niagara Falls, filled the requirement as the Giants' new ace.

In the winter of 1924–1925 the Negro National League was incorporated by Rube Foster and attorney Elisha Scott. Rube made Willie Foster plurality owner of the league with a 40-percent share, while the remaining shares were divided between Rube (20 percent), Monarchs owner J. L. Wilkinson (20 percent), and investors Russell Thompson (15 percent) and Walter Farmer (5 percent). Although the largest shareholder, Willie Foster did not play an active role in the league's operation, leaving administrative decisions to Rube.

Foster had perhaps his finest season in 1926, winning 29 games and leading the Giants to the league playoffs against the Kansas City Monarchs. The Monarchs had won the league championship the past two years and were favored to maintain their dominance in the best-of-nine game format. On the final day of the series, with the Monarchs leading four games to three, Foster pitched both games of the decisive doubleheader. He shut out the Monarchs in both games, 1–0 and 5–0, to help the American Giants earn the Negro National League title. He then pitched three complete games in the World Series against the Bacharach Giants of the Eastern Colored League to earn the American Giants their first black world series championship. Foster compiled an outstanding 1.27 ERA in the ten-game series.

In 1927 the American Giants repeated as pennant winners and again faced the Bacharach Giants in the Negro League World Series. Foster won the opening game 6–2 but lost the fifth game, called due to darkness after 6½ innings, and lost the eighth game behind four fielding errors. He came back in the ninth and deciding game to win, 11–4, for the Giants' second world series championship.

After the 1929 season Foster played in a two-game series against an American League all-star team led by future major leaguer Hank Greenberg and Art "The Great" Shires, who hit .312 that season. In the series Foster struck out Shires three times in the first game and twice in the second. Foster lost the first game but won the second, giving up no runs and no hits over eight innings and striking out nine major leaguers in the process. Detroit Tigers second baseman Charles Gehringer later testified, "If I could paint you white I could get $150,000 for you right now." In seven recorded games against major league opponents, Foster won six. He also won 11 out of 21 head-to-head encounters with the legendary Leroy "Satchel" Paige.

In July 1930 Foster was named player-manager of the Chicago American Giants, succeeding Jim Brown. The next season, he bounced between the Homestead Grays and the Kansas City Monarchs. In 1932 Foster returned to the Giants, which had joined the Negro Southern League, and guided them to another pennant. The following season the American Giants joined the reorganized Negro National League and won yet another pennant behind Foster's brilliant pitching. That year Chicago hosted the inaugural Negro League East-West All-Star game at Comiskey Park. The starting lineups were determined by the fans; with 40,637 votes, Foster received the highest total. He relished the honor by pitching the only complete game in all-star history. Foster gave up seven hits and two earned runs to capture the victory. He faced a star-studded lineup that included future Hall of Famers James "Cool Papa" Bell, Oscar Charleston, Josh Gibson, and William "Judy" Johnson, as well as other greats like Raleigh "Biz" Mackey, Jud Wilson, and Dick Lundy. Foster made his second and final all-star appearance in 1934, receiving a then-record 48,957 votes from the fans. In 1938 Foster closed out his 16-year career, pitching again for the Memphis Red Sox. He retired as the all-time Negro League leader in wins with 137, having lost only 62.

In 1933 Foster earned a degree in agriculture education from Alcorn College (later Alcorn State University) in Lorman, Mississippi. In 1960 he became dean of men and a coach at the college. In 1968 Foster married Audrey M. Davis; they had no children. He later sold insurance and managed the Harlem Globetrotters basketball team. Foster was a registered Democrat and followed the Baptist faith. He died in Lorman. Many consider Foster the finest left-handed pitcher to have played in the Negro Leagues.

• Foster is mentioned in John Holway, *Voices from the Great Black Baseball Leagues* (1975); Charles E. Whitehead, *A Man and His Diamonds* (1980); and Dick Clark and Larry Lester, *The Negro Leagues Book* (1994). Holway, "Historically Speaking: Bill Foster," *Black Sports* (1974); and Lester, "Bill Foster," *The Ballplayers,* ed. Mike Shatzkin et al. (1990). For Foster's career statistics, see *The Baseball Encyclopedia,* 10th ed. (1996).

LARRY LESTER

FOSTER, William Trufant (18 Jan. 1879–8 Oct. 1950), educator and economist, was born in Boston, Massachusetts, the son of William Henry Foster, formerly employed by a merchant but an invalid since the Civil War, and Sarah J. Trufant. His father's early death left the family poorly provided for, and Foster worked his way through Roxbury High School and Harvard University, where he was first in his class, receiving

his B.A., magna cum laude, in 1901. After teaching as an instructor in English at Bates College in his mother's hometown, Lewiston, Maine, from 1901 to 1903 Foster returned to Harvard for an A.M. in English (1904) and became an instructor in English and argumentation at Bowdoin College in Brunswick, Maine. On Christmas Day, 1905, he married Bessie Lucille Russell; they had four children.

Foster's great success as a teacher, reflected in his textbooks *Argumentation and Debating* (1908) and *Essentials of Exposition and Argument* (1911), led to his remarkably early promotion to full professor at Bowdoin in 1905. The vision of an "ideal college" discussed in *Administration of the College Curriculum* (1911), based on his Ph.D. dissertation at Teachers College of Columbia University, led to his selection in 1910 as first president of Reed College in Portland, Oregon. At Reed, Foster promoted a democratic spirit and serious intellectual pursuits, instituting seminars, theses, and comprehensive examinations, while excluding fraternities, sororities, and competitive intercollegiate sports. His educational experiment at Reed attracted national attention. He later returned to his early interest in rhetoric, publishing books on *Basic Principles of Speech* (with Lew Sarett, 1936) and *Speech* (1942).

A pacifist, Foster nevertheless went to France as an inspector for the American Red Cross after the United States entered World War I in 1917. Excessive work and controversies over his pacifism undermined Foster's health, and in December 1919 he resigned the presidency of Reed College. Although his formal training was not in economics, he then began a second career as director of the Pollak Foundation for Economic Research, established in Newton, Massachusetts, by Foster's Harvard classmate Waddill Catchings, of the investment bankers Goldman, Sachs and Company. The Pollak Foundation combined Catchings's financial resources and Foster's expository skill to promote their unorthodox ideas about the need for government demand stimulus to stabilize the economy.

Through Houghton Mifflin, the Pollak Foundation published books by Foster and Catchings: *Money* (1923), *Profits* (1925), *Business without a Buyer* (1927), *The Road to Plenty* (1928), and *Progress and Plenty* (1930). These books were widely read, especially *The Road to Plenty,* which was cast as a conversation aboard a train, and of which 58,000 copies were sold, primarily in a popular cloth edition priced at seventy-five cents a piece. Foster and Catchings also presented their ideas in periodicals such as the *American Economic Review,* the *Harvard Business Review,* and the *Atlantic Monthly. Progress and Plenty* (1930) reprinted 206 of the 400 two-minute talks on economic problems by Foster and Catchings that the McClure Newspaper Syndicate distributed in 1929 and 1930.

The Pollak Foundation also published major books on index numbers by Irving Fisher of Yale and on real wages by Paul Douglas of the University of Chicago, formerly Foster's student at Bowdoin and colleague at

Reed, as well as a shorter essay on cycles of unemployment by William Berridge of Brown University, winner of a Pollak Foundation prize competition. The Pollak Foundation's offer of a $5,000 prize for the best adverse criticism of *Profits* attracted 431 submissions, of which four winning essays were published in 1927 with a response by Foster and Catchings. The competition was judged by the two most recent presidents of the American Economic Association, Wesley Mitchell and Allyn Young, and by Owen Young of General Electric. The magazine *World's Work* offered a prize of $1,000 the same year for the best essay on a series of articles by Foster and Catchings in the magazine. The Pollak Foundation's publications and prize competitions won Foster and Catchings professional attention unprecedented for amateur economists of heterodox views.

Reflecting on the 1920–1921 recession, Foster and Catchings argued that recessions occur because a monetary economy does not automatically generate enough consumption to buy potential output. Thus, according to a Keynes-like "paradox of thrift," saving, which enriches an individual saver, contributes to recessions by reducing consumption and, through investment, by increasing the potential output to be bought. A steadily increasing rate of investment is needed for stability, an insight developed in later economic growth theory. Foster and Catchings proposed that monetary purchasing power be expanded by a steady 4 percent a year and that the government pursue this goal by varying public works spending, to be financed by money creation. In July 1929 Foster and Catchings presciently warned that the restrictive credit policy of the Federal Reserve Board had "created a state of mind which breeds business depression."

A scheme for countercyclical public works, closely resembling that proposed by Foster and Catchings, was presented to the Conference of State Governors in New Orleans in late November 1928 by Governor Ralph O. Brewster of Maine, with the blessing of President-elect Herbert Hoover and with Foster as an expert witness. The plan called for government bodies to have $3 billion of standby credit authorizations to be used for public works spending when a federal board decided that indexes of business conditions showed an impending business downturn. In the depression, however, President Hoover's support in principle for countercyclical public works was negated by his aversion to large budget deficits.

In 1932 Foster wrote *Medical Care for the American People*, the majority report of the Committee on the Costs of Medical Care (privately organized but chaired by the secretary of the interior), arguing for voluntary group medical insurance as a first step toward providing adequate medical care at tolerable cost. This proposal was opposed as excessive by the insurance industry and as inadequate by Walton Hamilton's minority report urging government-sponsored compulsory health insurance.

Although President Franklin D. Roosevelt did not act on Irving Fisher's suggestion that Foster be named to the Federal Reserve Board, Foster served on the Consumers Advisory Board of the National Recovery Administration (1933–1935) on the recommendation of Paul Douglas. This involvement led Foster to write a syndicated daily newspaper column on economics for laymen for three years, in succession to his earlier syndicated column with Catchings. He wrote extensively in the 1930s on consumer credit, sometimes jointly with his son LeBaron Russell Foster, and in 1935 chaired the Massachusetts Committee on Consumer Credit. Foster was a member of the Massachusetts State Planning Board and an economic adviser at the International Labor Conference in Geneva in 1938. He lived in Winter Park, Florida, in his last years and remained director of the Pollak Foundation until his death in Winter Park.

• Some of Foster's papers are in the Reed College Archives. *Writings of William Trufant Foster* (privately published, 1938) lists his publications up to that date. Joseph Dorfman, *The Economic Mind in American Civilization*, vols. 4–5: *1918–1933* (1959), pp. 339–52, 708–11, and William J. Barber, *From New Era to New Deal: Herbert Hoover, the Economists, and American Economic Policy, 1921–1933* (1985), pp. 54–58, 75–77, 100, discuss the economic views of Foster and Catchings. They are reconsidered as forerunners of later Keynesian macroeconomics and Harrod-Domar growth theory in Alan H. Gleason, "Foster and Catchings: A Reappraisal," *Journal of Political Economy* 67, no. 2 (Apr. 1959): 156–72, and John A. Carlson, "Foster and Catchings: A Mathematical Reappraisal," *Journal of Political Economy* 70, no. 4 (Aug. 1962): 400–402, and as forerunners of monetarism in George S. Tavlas, "Some Further Observations on the Monetary Economics of Chicagoans and Non-Chicagoans," *Southern Economic Journal* 42, no. 4 (Apr. 1976): 685–92, and in an exchange between J. Ronnie Davis, "The Last Remake of the New Economics and the Old Economists: Comment," and Tavlas, "The Last Remake of the New Economics and the Old Economists: Reply," both in *Southern Economic Journal* 45, no. 3 (Jan. 1979): 919–31.

ROBERT W. DIMAND

FOSTER, William Z. (15 Feb. 1881–1 Sept. 1961), American Communist party leader, was born in Taunton, Massachusetts, the son of James Foster, an Irish immigrant who worked as a carriage washer and livery stableman, and Elizabeth McLaughlin, an English immigrant. Foster grew up in poverty in Philadelphia's Irish-Catholic slums, where his family moved when he was six. His mother bore her husband twenty-three children, most of whom died in infancy. Elizabeth had hoped that Foster would grow up to become a priest. Instead, he dropped out of school at age ten to support himself with a series of menial jobs.

As a young man, Foster traveled across the country, working as an itinerant laborer in lumber camps, mines, foundries, and on the railroad. For a while he grew potatoes on a homestead claim in Oregon. He also saw a good portion of the world for several years as an able seaman.

Foster came of age in an era of bitter labor struggles and dynamic reform and revolutionary movements. He was converted to trade unionism after being clubbed by a policeman in a Philadelphia streetcar strike in 1895. Although briefly attracted to William Jennings Bryan's populism (he would entitle the first volume of his memoirs, published in 1937, *From Bryan to Stalin*), Foster joined the Socialist party (SP) in 1901. By 1909 he had grown disenchanted with what he regarded as the SP's reformism, including its commitment to work with the mainstream American Federation of Labor (AFL). After a brief attempt, with others, to form a separate group, the Wage Workers party, Foster joined the militant left-wing labor federation, the Industrial Workers of the World (IWW). He was arrested in 1909 for taking part in a famous IWW "free speech fight" in Spokane, Washington.

Traveling in Europe in 1910, Foster was converted by the syndicalist trade unionists he met there to the strategy of "boring from within" the existing trade unions. This attempt to radicalize the existing conservative labor organizations represented a break with the IWW's belief in independent and avowedly revolutionary unionism. Upon his return, Foster published a book entitled *Syndicalism* to spread his views. He also founded the Syndicalist League of North America in 1912; it lasted two years and was succeeded by the Independent Trade Union Educational League, which survived until 1917. In 1912 Foster married one of his comrades from the Syndicalist League, Esther Abramowitz, a Russian immigrant. She brought three children from an earlier marriage with her, but she and Foster had no children of their own.

In line with his new political views, Foster began working as an organizer for the Chicago Federation of Labor, proving himself a skillful unionist. During World War I Foster led a successful organizing drive among Chicago's meat-packing workers. As a result, he was appointed the head of the AFL's campaign to organize the steel industry, where employers had effectively barred unions from their mills. In September 1919 Foster led a strike of over 350,000 steel workers for union recognition. This strike represented an unprecedented attempt to create an industrial union in a mass industry characterized by a largely immigrant work force. It was Foster's finest moment; labor journalist Mary Heaton Vorse, who reported on the steel strike, later called him "the ablest labor organizer this country has ever known [with] the strategic sense of a great general."

In the fiercely antiradical and anti-union atmosphere of the postwar Red Scare, the steel strike went down to total defeat. Never comfortable without an organizational affiliation, Foster soon formed a new group, the Trade Union Education League (TUEL), which advocated industrial unionism, the formation of a labor party, and support for the Russian Revolution. In 1921 Foster traveled to Moscow in a delegation of left-wing unionists organized by his one-time lieutenant in the syndicalist movement, Earl Browder. In Moscow Foster was converted to the Communist cause. American Communists, initially committed to the IWW strategy of independent revolutionary unionism, switched to a boring-from-within strategy at

Moscow's behest. The Communists hoped that through Foster's TUEL they would be able to gain influence in the labor movement. But AFL leaders denounced TUEL as a Communist front organization. Foster would never again be able to play a direct role within the labor movement.

Foster initially kept his Communist membership a secret. When Communists, on orders from Moscow, abandoned efforts to establish a "Farmer-Labor party" in 1924, Foster ran for U.S. president as the candidate of the Workers party (as the American Communists were then known), attracting just over 33,000 votes. In 1928 he ran again, with equally unimpressive results. Increasingly, Foster's energy and organizing skills were devoted to the Communist movement's internal factional wars. Because of his unswerving obedience to the ever-shifting political demands placed upon American Communists by the Soviet leaders of the Communist International (including abandoning the boring-from-within strategy in 1929 in favor of organizing independent Communist-led "revolutionary" unions), Foster seemed well poised at the end of the decade to take over the leadership of the Communist party. Instead, at Moscow's behest, his longtime disciple Earl Browder was catapulted into the top spot. Foster was apparently regarded by Moscow as too compromised by the factional struggles of the preceding decade to be an effective leader.

This was a bitter blow to Foster, especially because the onset of the Great Depression in 1929 brought the Communists unprecedented opportunities. In the early 1930s Foster continued to play an important public role, as secretary of the Trade Union Unity League (TUUL). TUUL, unlike its predecessor TUEL, purported to be an independent revolutionary labor federation and represented a return to the "dual unionist" strategy that had long been anathema to Foster. Foster was one of the main speakers at the Communists' demonstration against unemployment in New York's Union Square in March 1930. The event, which attracted 100,000 demonstrators, resulted in a bloody riot and in Foster's sentence to six months in jail for "unlawful assembly." Foster also ran once again as the party's presidential candidate in 1932, attracting over 100,000 votes, a record for a Communist presidential candidate. In the later 1930s he was a behind-the-scenes senior adviser to Communist trade unionists but played no direct role in the upsurge of industrial unionism that led to the creation of the Congress of Industrial Organizations (CIO). The real power in the party lay with Browder, the general secretary, while Foster was relegated to the largely honorary post of chairman. Foster suffered a heart attack during the 1932 election campaign, and never fully regained his health.

Foster was one of the most prolific authors in the Communist leadership, contributing frequent articles to the party's newspaper, the *Daily Worker*, and to *The Communist*, its monthly theoretical journal. He wrote two memoirs in the 1930s, *From Stalin to Bryan* (1937) and *Pages from a Worker's Life* (1939). He also published *Toward Soviet America* (1932), which caused the Communists considerable embarrassment later in the decade as they embraced the more moderate policies and rhetoric of the Popular Front. Under the Popular Front, the Communists abandoned open calls for revolution and sought instead to forge alliances with any groups that opposed the growing threat of fascist aggression. It was the counterpart to the Soviet Union's quest in the later 1930s for collective security agreements with the Western democracies against Nazi Germany. Foster felt that the party, under Browder's enthusiastic embrace of the Popular Front, was abandoning its revolutionary purity and working-class identity. He made several trips to Moscow during this period in a fruitless effort to counter Browder's influence. With the signing of the Nazi-Soviet pact in 1939, Foster's influence grew (especially when Browder was imprisoned for passport fraud). But the party's return to Popular Front policies after the Nazi invasion of the Soviet Union in 1941 reestablished Browder's unquestioned primacy in the Communist leadership.

In 1944, at the height of Soviet-American cooperation in the war against the Nazis, Browder decided to disband the Communist party and replace it with a more loosely organized "political association." Along with his close political ally Sam Darcy, Foster wrote a letter to party leaders privately opposing the change. Darcy was expelled from the party, while the more senior Foster was reprimanded for his views, which he retracted. But Browder had overestimated the durability of the wartime coalition of the United States and the Soviet Union. With the end of the war in sight in early 1945, Soviet-American relations swiftly deteriorated. Browder was denounced within the international Communist movement for his wartime "revisionism" and soon driven out of the reconstituted American Communist party. Foster resumed his chairmanship and prepared to steer the party in a more militant direction, breaking many of the alliances that Browder had forged with mainstream political leaders and trade unionists in the 1930s. The Communist-backed Progressive party campaign in 1948 revealed the near-total political isolation of the Communists and their vulnerability to attack from hostile congressional investigating committees and federal prosecutors.

In 1948 Foster, along with eleven other top Communist leaders, was indicted by the federal government for violation of the Smith Act, a law that made it a crime to conspire to teach or advocate the overthrow of the government. Foster's eleven codefendants were convicted, and their appeal to the Supreme Court denied. Foster himself was spared imprisonment because he was severed from the case before it came to trial, due to ill health.

Foster contended that the legal attacks on the Communists were merely the prelude to full-scale fascism in the United States and that to protect itself the party should shift to a semi-underground stance; within the Communist movement this became known as the "five minutes to midnight" line. Foster's insistence that, at all costs, the party hew to an outspoken hard-line defense of Soviet policy led to the loss of much of its influence in the years following World War II. By 1955 the party had been reduced to about 20,000 members, a third of its membership ten years earlier.

The events of the next two years, the "de-Stalinization crisis" of 1956–1958, would further weaken the party. When Soviet premier Nikita Khrushchev denounced his predecessor Joseph Stalin for being a bloody tyrant in a "secret speech," the contents of which were leaked to the West by an unknown source, in February 1956, he inadvertently unleashed a wave of re-evaluation and self-criticism within the American Communist movement as well. Foster came under heavy attack for his hard-line views from factional opponents such as *Daily Worker* editor John Gates. But when Khrushchev sent Soviet troops to crush the Hungarian revolution in November 1956, his action strengthened the position of Foster and other hard-liners. Gates's followers poured out of the party, and Foster and his allies emerged the victorious leaders of a movement reduced to a few thousand aging members.

Foster did not have long to enjoy this final factional triumph. In January 1961 he flew to Moscow for medical treatment, so weak that he had to be carried off the plane on a stretcher. He died nine months later and was honored with a state funeral in Red Square. His ashes were returned to the United States and buried in Waldheim Cemetery in Chicago.

• Foster left no collection of papers. A starting point for any biographer should be his two volumes of memoirs. Foster also wrote *The Great Steel Strike and Its Lessons* (1920), *The Twilight of World Capitalism* (1949), *History of the Communist Party of the United States* (1952), and *History of the Three Internationals* (1955). Arthur Zipser, who worked as Foster's secretary and research assistant in the 1950s, has written an untrustworthy biography entitled *Workingclass Giant: The Life of William Z. Foster* (1981). Other works that consider various aspects of Foster's career include Theodore Draper, *The Roots of American Communism* (1957); Harvey Klehr, *The Heyday of American Communism: The Depression Decade* (1984); Joseph Starobin, *American Communism in Crisis* (1972); and Maurice Isserman, *Which Side Were You On? The American Communist Party during the Second World War* (1982). Foster's early life has been chronicled by Edward P. Johanningsmeier, "William Z. Foster: Labor Organizer and Communist" (Ph.D. diss., Univ. of Pennsylvania, 1988). An obituary can be found in the *New York Times*, 2 Sept. 1961.

MAURICE ISSERMAN

FOULOIS, Benjamin Delahauf (9 Dec. 1879–25 Apr. 1967), U.S. Army officer and aviation pioneer, was born in Washington, Connecticut, the son of Henry Foulois, a plumber, and Sara Augusta Williams. After only eleven years of schooling he entered an apprenticeship with his father. Learning of the sinking of the *Maine* in 1898, he ran away from home to enlist, using his brother's name as he was under age. Rejected by the navy, he enlisted as a private in the army, joining the First U.S. Volunteer Engineers. Displaying a natural aptitude for leadership, he was discharged at the end of the Spanish-American War as a sergeant, only to enlist again six months later under his own name. Foulois was assigned to the Philippines, where he displayed such exemplary qualities under fire that he was given a field promotion to second lieutenant in 1901. His professional education followed, with assignments to the Infantry and Cavalry School at Fort Leavenworth (1905) and the Army Signal School (1906).

The Signal School assignment changed the direction of Foulois's life. While a student there in 1907 he prepared a thesis entitled "The Tactical and Strategical Value of Dirigible Balloons and Aerodynamical Flying Machines," which impressed his superiors with his creative imagination and progressive outlook. Foulois then transferred from the infantry to the newly established Aeronautical Division of the Signal Corps and was directed to participate in the flight trials of the dirigible developed by lighter-than-air pioneer, Thomas S. Baldwin.

In September 1908 his fellow Signal Corps lieutenant, Tom Selfridge, was killed in the crash of the aircraft designed by Orville Wright and Wilbur Wright during acceptance trials. Ordered to take Selfridge's place in the rebuilt Wright plane, Foulois concluded on the basis of his experience with balloons and planes that the future lay with airplanes rather than lighter-than-air vehicles. When the army purchased the Wright machine in August 1909, Foulois was ordered to take the plane to Fort Sam Houston in San Antonio, Texas, and there teach himself to fly. This he did, with some help in the form of written instructions from the Wrights. Foulois also experimented with an airborne radio for reporting the results of aerial reconnaissance to command headquarters.

In April 1914 Foulois organized the First Aero Squadron, the U.S. Army's first aircraft tactical unit, at the Signal Corps Aviation School in San Diego. The squadron consisted of three of the five planes available at the school. When General John J. Pershing's Mexican punitive expedition set off in pursuit of the Mexican guerrilla Pancho Villa in 1916, Foulois joined the effort with eight frail training aircraft. These underpowered Curtiss JN2s performed badly and failed to achieve significant results, but the effort gave Foulois operational experience and dramatically highlighted the need for aircraft better suited to military requirements.

As a staff officer in the Aviation Section, Office of the Chief Signal Officer, Foulois drafted the aviation program to support the American Expeditionary Force (AEF) in France. When the United States joined the war in 1917, Foulois later regarded this effort, which conceptualized the whole aviation program, as the outstanding contribution of his career. Foulois testified before Congress in support of the aviation program, and four months after the United States declared war Congress appropriated some $640 million for aviation, the largest single appropriation ever made up to that time.

Promoted to brigadier general on 24 July 1917, Foulois was ordered to take command of the Air Service, AEF. This brought him into collision with the flamboyant brigadier general Billy Mitchell, who was already in the theater and resented the intrusion of a latecomer. Pershing resolved the difficulty by naming an experienced ground officer, Brigadier General Mason M. Patrick, chief with Foulois as his assistant to handle the rear area, while Mitchell took charge of aviation at the front.

After the war Foulois reverted to his permanent rank of major and served as air attaché in Berlin from 1920 to 1924. His first marriage ended in divorce in 1921, and in 1923 he married Elizabeth Shepperd-Grant. He had no children. After a year at the Command and General Staff School at Fort Leavenworth, he became a group commander with headquarters at Mitchel Field, New York. Given Foulois's wide-ranging experience, especially his frequent appearances on Capitol Hill in connection with the postwar spate of aviation bills, he was a logical choice as assistant chief of the Air Corps in 1927, when he was restored to his wartime rank as a brigadier general. In 1931 his performance in command of a test mobilization involving more than 600 airplanes won him the MacKay Trophy, and that same year he received another star when he became chief of the Air Corps.

During Foulois's tenure as chief, the depression brought drastic reductions in appropriations, keeping the Air Corps continually below authorized strength in aircraft and personnel, with slow promotions and little money for research and development. Despite these handicaps, the general consistently pressed for the development of strategic bombers using the pitifully small appropriations to fund experimental contracts, which eventually led to the Boeing B-17 Flying Fortress, as well as the creation of the General Headquarters Air Force, which gave the cause of air power greater organizational autonomy.

Unfortunately Foulois's feisty manner and lack of tact kept him embroiled with his service peers and superiors. His struggle for a greater air arm role in coast defense kept him in dispute with the navy, while his aggressive advocacy of autonomy and strategic bombardment alienated the general staff and many of the senior officers of the ground arms, who already resented the disproportionate share of scarce appropriations allocated to the air arm.

The climax in the general's career came in 1934, when he was asked by President Franklin D. Roosevelt's administration if the Air Corps could take over the air mail routes of the airlines accused of collusion or fraud. Without fully studying the problem, he gave a "can do" answer that proved disastrous. Air Corps pilots without adequate night flying skills or suitable navigational training, using aircraft that lacked appropriate instruments and radios, soon suffered a series of fatal crashes. When opposition congressmen accused the Roosevelt administration of "legalized murder" in sending ill-prepared airmen to their deaths, Foulois became the convenient scapegoat. Foulois promptly ordered increased training in navigation and instrument flying. Thereafter, all new Air Corps planes were required to have two-way radios, a crucial advance in preparing for the war soon to come.

The general retired in 1935 a deeply embittered man. He was energetic and often imaginative, but his limited education and irascible personality accentuated, if they did not actually bring on, many of his difficulties, such as his long-running feud with Billy Mitchell. Despite these drawbacks, his tenure as chief was marked by significant progress in the Air Corps, including greater autonomy, an enlarged procurement program, and a sharpened focus on strategic bombardment doctrine, all of which contributed to the successful mobilization of U.S. air power for World War II. He died at Andrews Air Force Base in Maryland.

• Foulois's personal papers are in the U.S. Air Force Historical Research Center, Maxwell Air Force Base, Ala.; the Air Force Academy Library at Colorado Springs; and the Manuscript Division of the Library of Congress. His memoirs are Foulois and Carroll V. Glines, *From the Wright Brothers to the Astronauts: The Memoirs of Major General Benjamin D. Foulois* (1968). Useful sources are John F. Shiner, *Foulois and the Army Air Corps, 1931–1935* (1983), which contains an exhaustive bibliography, and Robert F. Futrell, *Ideas, Concepts, Doctrine: A History of Basic Thinking in the United States Air Force,* vol. 1 (1989). An obituary is in the *New York Times,* 26 Apr. 1967.

I. B. HOLLEY, JR.

FOUR HORSEMEN OF NOTRE DAME, football players, formed the backfield of the 1924 Notre Dame University team, which received the Jack F. Rissman trophy awarded between 1924 and 1930 to the college football teams voted national champions by an informal group of "national" sportswriters. What set them apart from other successful players was their catchy nickname acquired in the 1920s, a time when college football players in particular and athletic heroes in general were riding the crest of popularity created by a nation hungry for heroes and a phalanx of talented sportswriters willing to create the heroes to fill that need. That combination vaulted the Four Horsemen into the status of a legend that transcended the confines of the sports world.

From varied backgrounds, each of the Four Horsemen arrived at Notre Dame as an outstanding midwestern high school football player. **Harry A. Stuhldreher** (14 Oct. 1901–26 Jan. 1965), the oldest of the four, was born in Massillon, Ohio, the son of William Stuhldreher and Flora Witt. Massillon was a football hotbed and supported a professional team in the early 1900s, well before the National Football League began in 1920. Stuhldreher was said to have first met Knute Rockne when the Notre Dame coach was moonlighting as a professional. Rockne supposedly let the young Stuhldreher carry his equipment into the Massillon stadium so he could gain free admission. Stuhldreher later became a standout halfback at Massillon High School and then spent a year as a player at Kiski, Pennsylvania, Preparatory School before enrolling at Notre Dame in the fall of 1921.

Donald C. Miller (29 Mar. 1902–28 July 1979) was born in Defiance, Ohio, the son of Martin Harold Miller and Ann Riley. He was the youngest of five boys, all of whom attended Notre Dame and played football. Miller had an excellent career as both a football and basketball player in high school before his 1921 enrollment as a Notre Dame freshman.

James H. Crowley (10 Sept. 1902–15 Jan. 1986) was born in Chicago, the son of Jeremiah Crowley and Agnes Sweeney. He graduated from Green Bay, Wisconsin, East High School where he played in the backfield on a state championship football team coached by Earl "Curly" Lambeau who in 1922 entered his Green Bay Packers in the National Football League. Crowley also began his Notre Dame career in 1921.

The youngest of the Four Horsemen, **Elmer F. Layden** (4 May 1903–30 June 1973), was born in Davenport, Iowa, the son of Thomas Layden and Rosemary (maiden name unknown). He was an excellent athlete at Davenport High School where he was an outstanding performer in football, basketball, and track. Like the other three, he enrolled at the South Bend school in 1921.

The four did not play together on Notre Dame's 1921 freshmen team. Only Stuhldreher, who was a good blocker and had an excellent understanding of the strategy of play selection, stood out on a poor freshmen team that was beaten by Lake Forest Academy and the Michigan State freshmen. It was not until the ninth game of the 1922 season that the group played in the same backfield. Early in that season Stuhldreher had been installed at quarterback, and Miller, who had developed quickly in spring practice, started at right halfback. Crowley and the speedy Layden alternated at left halfback, while a veteran, Paul Castner, played fullback. The four became a set piece when Layden moved to fullback to replace Castner, who suffered a broken hip in the Butler game. A scoreless tie with Army and a 14–6 loss to Nebraska were the only blemishes on Notre Dame's 8–1–1 record that season.

The 1923 Notre Dame team rolled over nine opponents while losing only one game. The backfield of Miller, Crowley, Layden, and Stuhldreher was small in size (between 5'7" and 6' and averaging about 160 pounds), but each man had excellent speed, and they worked exceptionally well as a unit. Coach Rockne designed an offense that took advantage of those qualities by emphasizing shifts, sleight of hand, and misdirection plays. For example, the backfield would often move as a unit in one direction immediately before the ball was snapped, or the offense would begin running a play in one direction and then quickly hand off to a ball carrier going the opposite way. An otherwise perfect record was marred by a 14–7 loss to a much larger Nebraska team on a muddy, slow field.

The Four Horsemen received their nickname following the third game of the 1924 season, when the Irish defeated Army 13–7 at the Polo Grounds in New York. In that Sunday's *New York Herald Tribune* the renowned sportswriter Grantland Rice began his game account: "Out from a cold gray October sky, Four Horsemen rode again. They are known in literature and dramatic lore as famine, fire, pestilence and sudden death, but these are only aliases. Their right names are Stuhldreher, Crowley, Miller and Layden."

The day after the team returned to South Bend, George Strickler, a student who worked in Notre Dame's sports publicity office, took a picture of the backfield stars in full uniform with footballs tucked under their arms, astride rented horses. That picture appeared in newspapers across the United States. The legend was complete when Notre Dame finished the season undefeated and agreed to a rare Rose Bowl appearance at which the team soundly defeated Stanford 27–10. Notre Dame was named as national champion and awarded the Rissman Trophy, and the Four Horsemen, along with Red Grange, were named to most All-America teams.

Following graduation, each of the Four Horsemen dabbled for a season or two with professional football, coached in college, and later went into business or law. Miller had the fewest years in coaching. He served as an assistant coach at both Georgia Tech and Ohio State before becoming a lawyer, U.S. district attorney, and judge in Cleveland, where he retired in 1977. He died in Cleveland.

Both Crowley and Stuhldreher became head coaches at major colleges. Crowley was successful in four seasons at Michigan State (22–8–3) before being promoted to Fordham, where he coached for nine seasons. The highlight of his Fordham career was the 1937 undefeated team, ranked third in the nation by an Associated Press poll. A commander in the navy during World War II, he became commissioner of the professional All-American Football Conference from 1945 through 1947 before moving to Scranton, Pennsylvania, as manager of a television station, then retiring in 1972. Crowley died in Scranton.

Stuhldreher revitalized the football program at Villanova before moving to Wisconsin, where he met with mixed success. In his thirteen seasons, Wisconsin had a poor record of 45 wins, 62 losses, and six ties, but his 1942 team was 8–1–1, beat Ohio State, tied Notre Dame, and was ranked third in the nation by an Associated Press poll. He resigned under pressure in 1948, and he later entered private business in Pittsburgh, where he died.

The most successful coach of the four was Layden, who, after rebuilding teams at Columbia College in Iowa and Duquesne in Pittsburgh, was called back to Notre Dame as head coach in 1934. The team immediately posted a 6–3 won-lost record, and during his seven years at South Bend he had a record of 47–13–3. He left Notre Dame to become commissioner of the National Football League (1941–1946). Layden later worked in private business in Chicago until he retired in 1968. He died in Chicago.

• The Notre Dame University Archives has holdings on each of the players. Elmer Layden, *It Was a Different Game* (1969), and Harry Stuhldreher, *Knute Rockne, Man Builder* (1931), discuss college football in the 1920s. See also Michael R. Steele, *Knute Rockne: A Bio-Bibliography* (1983); James Peterson, *The Four Horsemen of Notre Dame* (1959); Grantland Rice, "The Four Horsemen," *Esquire* (Nov. 1945); and David L. Porter, ed., *Biographical Dictionary of American Sports: Football* (1987). An obituary for each of the four is in the *New York Times*: Stuhldreher, 27 Jan. 1965; Layden, 1 July 1973; Miller, 30 July 1979; and Crowley, 16 Jan. 1986.

C. ROBERT BARNETT

FOURIER, Charles (7 Apr. 1772–10 Oct. 1837), utopian social theorist, was born Charles Fourrier in Besançon, Franche-Comté, France, the son of Charles Fourrier, a wealthy cloth merchant, and Marie Muguet. He received a solid classical but otherwise indifferent education at the Jesuit Collège de Besançon (1781–1787) and therefore was essentially an autodidact. It was expected that as the sole surviving son he would succeed his father as head of the family firm, and he began his apprenticeship in the cloth trade at age six. In temperament and sensibilities, however, he was unsuited to commercial life; he found its necessary chicanery morally repugnant. Nevertheless, with the death of his father (1781), and in accordance with the terms of his will, Charles was compelled to enter a commercial career by age twenty or forfeit a substantial patrimony of 42,932 livres. Since his writings remained largely unremarked until 1832, and generated, in any case, no reliable source of revenue, Fourier ironically relied on what he called "the jailhouse of commerce" for support throughout his life. He was by turns a mercantile clerk, a traveling salesman, and a *courtier marron* (unlicensed broker).

Fourier's life was played out on a grand historical stage. The events of the French Revolution, the Napoleonic Empire, the Bourbon Restoration, and the revolution of 1830 affected his personal life and fortunes, but seem to have little direct impact on the convoluted exposition of his ideas that found expression in his writings. He lost heavily in an ill-fated venture as a purveyor of colonial goods to Lyon, and he barely escaped execution by Jacobin forces when they purged that royalist stronghold in 1793. He was caught up in the *levée en masse* of the republic and served in the Army of the Rhine (1794–1796). By 1799, through a series of inauspicious investments, virtually all of his inheritance had been dissipated.

By 1799 as well, out of the chaos of revolutionary politics and the disappointments of his personal experience, Fourier had emerged with the fundamental insight that would provide the foundation for all of his later work—"the calculus of the mechanism of the passions." The calculus was an interactive system of three "distributive passions"—the cabalist or intriguing passion, the butterfly or alternating passion, and the composite or enthusiastic passion—that insured the gratification and equilibration of all other human passions, and made possible the formation of the "passionate series," which constituted the theoretical foundation of Fourier's utopian association, the phalanx.

Fourier had glimpsed a vision of a perfectly calibrated, harmonious world, one of "natural or attractive association." In this imagined world, the free pursuit of individual happiness and instinctual gratification would automatically subserve the commonweal. The conflict between work and desire would disappear through the social device of natural association within the "passionate" or "progressive series"—groups comprised of people with shared interests and personal characteristics that would provide both order and freedom through a perfectly balanced contrast of sex, age, wealth, temperaments, tastes, talents, and education. Fourier spent the rest of his life extending his critique of contemporary civilization, devising schematic outlines and systematic compendia of his ideas in order to reach a wider audience, and seeking a wealthy patron who would make it possible to establish a working model of his idealized community.

During much of his lifetime, Fourier's works were largely ignored or, occasionally, noticed with scorn and incredulity. As he himself was acutely aware, his lack of fortune and formal education meant that he was disparaged as a provincial philosophe manqué. Throughout his life he resented his treatment at the hands of the Parisian literati, who persistently ignored what they disdainfully termed his "inventive genius" and who saw in him only a "near illiterate" and a "scientific pariah." Contemporaries were troubled as much, however, by style and content as by Fourier's status. They found his work obscure (riddled with neologisms), unintelligible, and extravagantly fantastic—in his new order human beings would evolve to an improved physical state, attaining a height of seven feet, developing an *archibras* (a powerful tail tipped with a claw-like hand), and living for 144 years. His ideas of social change, especially his celebration of the instincts over reason, sexual liberation (he sought the emancipation of sexual expression—explicitly championing homosexuals, lesbians, sadomasochists, and fetishists—and the full integration of sexuality into collective life), and the emancipation of women (he argued that social progress could only occur in the context of an equitable treatment of the female population), scandalized many of his contemporaries.

It was not until the 1820s that Fourier had any substantial following, and then only among the provincial bourgeoisie. A schism among the followers of utopian socialist Henri Saint-Simon in the early 1830s drew adherents to Fourier and led to the establishment of the Fourierist movement in France. A journal, the *Phalanstère* (1832–1834), was established, and a model Fourierist community (a phalanx)—the Societary Colony—was established in Condé-sur-Vesgre (1833–1836). Fourier also had a following in Romania and, through the popularization of his ideas by Albert Brisbane (1809–1890), the social reformer, Fourierist disciple, and editor of the *Phalanx* (1843–1845), enjoyed the greatest practical trial of the phalanstery system in the United States, where some forty-odd phalanxes were established between 1843 and 1858.

The popularity of Fourierism in the United States was due chiefly to Brisbane's conversion of Horace Greeley, editor of the *New York Tribune*, to the cause. Greeley placed a regular column (entitled "Association") in his paper at the disposal of Brisbane for the promotion of Fourierism. The *Tribune* promoted the organization of associationists (as early American Fourierists were called) through editorials, announcements of meetings, and advertisements for publications.

The Fourierist movement grew rapidly in the United States through the organization of conventions of associationists. The growth of the movement was enhanced by its early advocacy of the abolition of slavery—both wage and chattel. But perhaps the greatest attractions of Fourierism were its seeming simplicity (as presented by Brisbane), its secular organization, and its relative moderation—avoiding the kind of socioeconomic organization that led contemporary historians of the utopian movement in the United States to describe these settlements as "communistic societies."

American phalanxes had an average lifespan of about two years; only two—the North American Phalanx (Red Bank, N.J., 1843–1855), and the Wisconsin Phalanx (Fond du Lac County, 1844–1850)—lasted more than five years. The most important Fourierist journal in the country was the *Harbinger*, published by Brook Farm, which functioned as a Fourierist community between 1844 and 1847. Like the overwhelming majority of the utopian communities founded in the United States in the nineteenth century, most phalanxes had collapsed by 1855.

Some selectivity was exercised in admitting members, since most American phalanxes required a probationary period of one year prior to acceptance to full membership. Life in most phalanxes centered around agricultural production, though all attempted to foster education and to cultivate the mind as well. Work was allotted according to preference, and wages were determined by a scale that awarded the highest pay for the most repulsive or exhausting jobs.

Though Fourierist communities are often categorized as utopian socialist experiments, they were really individualist, joint-stock ventures, often closer to anarchistic than communistic in operation. The egoistic dissentions and disgruntlement that surrounded the dissolution of Brook Farm were illustrative of the unrestrained individualism that overwhelmed the communal ideals of the Fourierist experiment in America.

As a social thinker, Fourier was a transitional figure, reacting to the ultrarationality of the Enlightenment and presaging the elevation of the instinctual in the Romantic age. He saw himself as the Newton of social law and the human passions, arguing that "the law of series is the unique rule of universal movement, the key to all the sciences because it balances the physical forces and the passionate energy of the soul" (*Théorie des quatre mouvements et des destinées générales* [1808]). In essence, this "law" required the division of the labor force into organized task groups or series—an office work series, for example—based on the "passional attractions" or instinctual preferences of the labor force for one or another task. Many modern communal societies employ this "law," which today might be better understood as a psychological insight, as the basis for their organization of collective work.

Aspirations to a universal system aside, however, Fourier can perhaps best be understood as a satiric moralist in the tradition of Jean de La Fontaine, Bernard de Mandeville, Jonathan Swift, Voltaire, Jean-Jacques Rousseau, and the marquis de Sade. His acute critique of contemporary society and his vision of a better world, like theirs, often grew out of a mordant sensibility to the foibles and vices of civilization. He divided human history into three stages, which he called savagery, barbarism, and civilization. The latter did not compare well with the earlier stages, being characterized by war, plunder, rapine, and duplicity. The world's sickness, he maintained, was graphically represented by 130 species of poisonous snakes, an "exact replica" of the "130 effects of calumny and perfidy" that comprised these "deceitful societies" (*Le Nouveau monde industriel et societaire*).

While Fourierism remains largely a historical curiosity, Fourier's attempt to legitimate desire and to reconcile the social order and instinctual life remains a fundamental preoccupation of social theorists. Fourier's monomaniacal absorption in his own theories, his paranoia about the threat of the theft of his social "invention," the opaqueness and hermetic nature of his prose, his bitter animosities arising out of his frustrations in life, and the personal jealousies and idiosyncrasies that even at the height of his popularity in France estranged him from his own disciples, certainly contributed to his relative obscurity among major social thinkers. Not surprisingly, Fourier died alone, apparently at his own desire, in a rented room in Paris. He was buried in Montmartre cemetery.

• Fourier's papers, comprising ninety-eight cahiers and correspondence, are in the Archives de l'École Sociétaire (Archives Nationales) in Paris. A collection of periodical and pamphlet literature by Fourier and about Fourierism may be found in the Fonds Fourieristes, Institut Française d'Histoire Sociale, Paris. Fourier's most important works include *Traité de l'association domestique-agricole* (2 vols., 1822), *La Fausse industrie morcellée, répugnante, mensongère, et l'antidote, l'industrie naturelle, combinée, attrayante, veridique, donnant quadruple produit* (2 vols., 1835–1836), *Le Nouveau monde amoureux* (1967), and *L'Ordre subversif: Trois textes sur la Civilization* (1972). Though the bulk of his work has not been translated, a rudimentary grounding in his thought for English readers may be derived from Albert Brisbane, *Social Destiny of Man; or, Association and Reorganization of Industry* (1840); Charles Fourier, *The Passions of the Human Soul and Their Influence on Society and Civilization*, trans. John Reynell (2 vols., 1851); and Jonathan Beecher, *The Utopian Vision of Charles Fourier: Selected Texts on Work, Love, and Passionate Attraction* (1971), the most extensive modern anthology. Charles Pellarin, *Charles Fourier, sa vie et sa théorie*, 2d ed. (1843), is an essential biographical source. Roland Barthes, *Sade, Fourier, Loyola* (1971), has a penetrating and insightful section on Fourier. The definitive modern biographical source, also offering acute critical insight, is Jonathan Beecher, *Charles Fourier, the Visionary and His World*

(1986). The most comprehensive treatment of Fourierism in the United States is Carl Guarneri, *The Utopian Alternative: Fourierism in Nineteenth-Century America* (1991).

LOUIS J. KERN

FOURNET, John Baptiste (27 July 1895–3 June 1984), jurist and state legislator, was born in St. Martinville, Louisiana, the son of Louis Michel Fournet, a wealthy sugar planter, and Marcélite Gauthier. The first of ten children, Fournet attended public schools in St. Martin Parish and after graduating from high school in 1913 became a teacher in a one-room schoolhouse in a rural part of southwestern Louisiana. In 1915 he graduated with honors from the Louisiana State Normal College in Natchitoches and returned to his teaching career. After teaching in Vernon, Jefferson Davis, and Pointe Coupée parishes, he became the principal of Morganza High School at the age of twenty-one.

Following service in World War I he received a bachelor of laws degree from Louisiana State University Law School in 1920. He was president of his law school class and was also considered one of the two best guards on the LSU football team from 1917 to 1919. After graduation he returned to St. Martinville to practice law. In 1921 he married Rose Dupuis, with whom he had two children. In 1928 he began what was to be the opening chapter of an amazing political career. He successively served as Speaker of the Louisiana House of Representatives, president of the Louisiana Senate, lieutenant governor of the state, and chief justice of the Louisiana Supreme Court.

Later in life Fournet stated that he had to fight for everything he obtained, but high office came rapidly to him. He first held public office in 1928, when as a freshman member of the Louisiana House of Representatives from Jefferson Davis Parish, he was elected Speaker of the house. During this term of office, he became a close friend and political ally of Governor Huey P. Long; he assisted in blocking an attempt to impeach Long in 1929. One year later Long himself went to the floor of the Louisiana House of Representatives to lobby successfully against an attempt to unseat Fournet as Speaker. By 1932 Long had been elected to the U.S. Senate, but he had no intention of abandoning his control of state politics. He saw to it that Oscar "O.K." Allen was nominated for governor (his nickname is self-explanatory), and he convinced Fournet to run on the ticket as lieutenant governor. Allen and Fournet won the election, and Fournet began his four-year term, presiding over the Louisiana Senate as part of his responsibilities.

In 1934 a vacancy occurred unexpectedly on the Louisiana Supreme Court bench, and Long persuaded Fournet to run for this office. Using sound trucks, Long campaigned for Fournet personally, and he won. Fournet took his seat as justice of the Supreme Court of Louisiana on 2 January 1935, became chief justice in 1949, and retired by constitutional mandate in 1970 after the longest tenure in office of any justice of that court.

In his thirty-five years of service to the Supreme Court of Louisiana, Fournet abandoned politics and dedicated himself to improving the administration of justice. Particularly, he spearheaded the reorganization of the appellate court system of the state. At the time he became chief justice the dockets of practically every court of the state had a heavy backlog of cases. He created the Louisiana Judicial Council and established the office of judicial administrator to implement the work of the council. He had hoped for a reorganization of the judiciary by means of a state constitutional convention. When such a convention failed to materialize, he resorted to restructuring the appellate court system, using constitutional amendments that moved much of the Louisiana Supreme Court's jurisdiction to a larger system of intermediary courts of appeal, thus freeing the supreme court to consider cases of greater importance through writ application. The creation of additional appellate judgeships effectively lessened court congestion throughout the judicial system of the state.

The chief justice often stated that the judiciary was not originally his ambition in life, but he made marked contributions as a jurist to almost every aspect of the substantive and procedural law of Louisiana. During his long tenure on the court Fournet participated in approximately 17,500 cases and wrote 1,239 opinions. Of these, 1,043 were majority opinions. Of the 525 rehearings sought from his opinions, only nineteen actually received a rehearing, and just seven were reversed. Of Fournet's majority opinions, only forty-one were appealed to the U.S. Supreme Court; only nine were granted, and of these, only four were reversed.

Fournet rendered several important opinions concerning freedom of speech and the privilege against self-incrimination. In *Kennedy v. Item Company* (1948) he asserted that although freedom of speech and of the press were foundations of American liberty, it was never intended for the press to be a vehicle for maliciously defaming a person's reputation. He also wrote a powerful decision protecting the rights of those accused from self-incrimination in *State v. Bentley* (1951). In other important criminal appeals he upheld the constitutionality of the Louisiana Criminal Code in *State v. Pete* (1944), defined the scope and applicability of the felony-murder doctrine of Article 30 of the criminal code in *State v. Bessar* (1948), upheld the constitutionality of the drunken-driving provision of the code in *State v. Hightower* (1960), and reaffirmed the validity of the definition of "public bribery" in *State v. Smith* (1968).

Fournet's decisions also streamlined criminal and civil procedure in Louisiana. He established the constitutionality of a simplified form of indictment in criminal matters and reduced technicalities in matters of civil procedure, including the executory process and the implementation of judgments. In *Voisin v. Luke* (1966) he wrote that the procedural rules of the civil code were intended to promote the administration of justice, not "for entrapping or tricking a litigant into admitting himself out of court without a trial on the merits."

Throughout his judicial career Fournet proved to be an advocate of civil law, relying on it in every possible instance. In *Humphreys v. Royal* (1949) he supported the sanctity of the Louisiana Civil Code. In *Succession of Lissa* (1941) he wrote a scholarly decision tracing the sources of Louisiana law to the Twelve Tables of the Romans, the Institutes of Gaius, the Novels of Justinian, the Custom of Paris, the Code Napoleon, and several Spanish legal sources.

Fournet married his cousin, Sylvia Ann Fournet, in 1953. (Details about the ending of his first marriage are unavailable.) He died in Jackson, Mississippi, where he had retired in 1978. His grave is in St. Michael's Cemetery in St. Martinville.

• Fournet's papers are at the Louisiana State University Archives, but he awaits a biographer. A sketch of his career can be found in *Biographies of Louisiana Judges* (1977), pp. 147–50. His colleagues on the court and other political luminaries wrote tributes that contain assessments of his tenure on the court on the occasion of his retirement in *Louisiana Reports* 256 (1971): 5–27. T. Harry Williams sketches Fournet's political career before taking the bench in *Huey Long: A Biography* (1969). An obituary is in the New Orleans *Times-Picayune*, 4 June 1984.

JUDITH SCHAFER

FOURNIER, Alexis Jean (4 July 1865–20 Jan. 1948), landscape painter, was born Alexis Jean Fournier de Prefontaine in St. Paul, Minnesota, the son of Isaie Fournier de Prefontaine and Anne Marie Mathilde, recent immigrants from French Canada. When Alexis was only one month old, the family moved to Fond du Lac, Wisconsin; there his father shortened the family name to Fournier. Little is known of Fournier's childhood, but apparently when he was twelve he was sent to a religious academy in Milwaukee, Wisconsin, where he was encouraged to carve wooden crucifixes as well as other images for the school's church altar.

Fournier's first paid work was as a painter of stage scenery, first in Chicago, Illinois, and then in Minneapolis, Minnesota, where he settled in 1879. This pursuit gave Fournier the opportunity to paint, in however broad a form, the landscapes that became his preferred subject throughout his life. In 1886, although he had begun to achieve modest success as a painter of Minnesota scenes on smaller canvases, Fournier felt that he needed professional instruction in art, so he arranged to be tutored privately by Douglas Volk, a Boston artist who had recently been appointed the first director of the newly founded Minneapolis School of Art (now the Minneapolis College of Art and Design).

The following year, Fournier married Emma Fricke of Pine Island, Minnesota; they had two children. Fournier established his first studio at about this time in some rooms above a tailor's shop on Nicollet Avenue, Minneapolis's main street. (The artist, who had a taste for fine clothing but not the income to afford it, exchanged some of his paintings for the tailor's well-cut suits.) Fournier was also acquiring a wider patronage: James J. Hill, for example, purchased a number of Fournier's paintings of Minneapolis and St. Paul scenes for the mansion he was building on St. Paul's fashionable Summit Avenue.

The years between 1886 and 1889 witnessed a remarkable progress in Fournier's development as a landscape artist. The dry, linear style of his early pictures gave way to a more painterly, broadly brushed style in which light was used to define form. He depicted local Twin Cities scenes such as *Mill Pond at Minneapolis* (1888), showing the tracks and recently completed stone arched bridge that carried Hill's railroad across the Mississippi River. The same year he also painted the *View of Fort Snelling*, still a St. Paul landmark. These paintings reveal a directness and lack of pretension that remained a characteristic of Fournier's work.

The dramatic possibilities of moonlit scenes also intrigued Fournier throughout his life, and even as early as 1889 he explored moonlight in paintings such as *Lake Harriet by Moonlight*. Though the picture endows nature with a hint of mystery and romance, it is still a genre scene, a straightforward image of the artist's world. The cool light of the moon contrasts with the warm glow of the lamplight in the lakeside pavilion, and ordinary people enjoy a summer breeze as they stroll along the shadowy path or sit at the pavilion tables.

In 1893, partly subsidized by a few local patrons including Hill, Fournier embarked on the first of several trips to France. His eagerness to go there was stimulated by his consciousness of his French ancestry and by his fluency in the French language. Indeed, throughout his life, Fournier cultivated a "French" appearance, occasionally even passing himself off as a French artist. In Paris he enrolled at the Académie Julian, which was run by two artists, Benjamin Constant and Jean Paul Laurent, who were much admired at the time for their polished academic style. While he was still at the Académie Julian, Fournier had one of his paintings, *Spring Morning on Minnehaha Creek*, depicting a familiar Minneapolis landmark, selected for exhibition at the prestigious Paris Salon of 1894. The painting excited the admiration of his teacher, Benjamin Constant: "Yes, it is a Spring morning and no mistake," he told Fournier. "You understand nature, I see that. Bon Courage." In 1895 Fournier had another painting, *Le Repos*, exhibited at the Paris Salon.

Fournier returned to the United States at the end of 1895 and began exhibiting widely, not only at the Minneapolis Society of Fine Arts but also at the Art Institute of Chicago, the National Academy of Design in New York City, and even in the Crystal Palace Exhibition in London, where his *Road to Calais* was shown in 1895. His style at this time was very much in the French Barbizon tradition, in which nature was described in an idyllic, poetic mood devoted to a nourishing, life-giving earth.

On 1 June 1903 Fournier moved to East Aurora, New York, following several invitations by Elbert Hubbard, a businessman, writer, utopianist, and eccentric, to join the Roycroft Arts and Crafts community Hubbard had established there. The two had met several years earlier, and Hubbard wanted to have Fournier as a sort of artist in residence with the Roycrofters. Inspired by William Morris's Kelmscott Press and the arts and crafts community that grew around it, Hubbard's Roycroft community also started off with a printing shop in East Aurora, a shop in which pride in individual craftsmanship was paramount. The Roycrofters soon expanded into bookbinding, metal work, furniture design, ceramics, and other crafts. Fournier had already been active in the arts and crafts movement in Minneapolis, and he agreed with Hubbard that an arts and crafts community could and should foster spiritual growth and at the same time encourage an artistic consciousness and personal pride in producing even objects of utilitarian purpose, aesthetically conceived, that would stand against the frequently shoddy products turned out by the factory system.

Fournier's full-time participation with the Roycrofters in East Aurora lasted until about 1921, when Emma Fournier died. During his time there, he had filled canvas after canvas with views of the picturesque and tranquil landscape of western New York, shifting gradually from a Barbizon mood to the more ebullient and light-filled impressionist style. He also produced, at this time, a series of canvases that he called *The Homes and Haunts of the Barbizon Masters* who had inspired him on his several trips to France. He even wrote a small book on the subject, titled *The Homes of the Men of 1830* (1910). In this endeavor he may well have been influenced by Elbert Hubbard's series of *Little Journeys to the Homes of the Great*, begun in 1894 and on which he worked for fourteen years.

In 1922 the widowed Fournier married Cora May Ball, the widow of a South Bend, Indiana, painter. In the preceding years, Fournier had become associated with a group of Hoosier impressionists who included T. C. Steele, William Forsyth, Otto Stark, and John Otis Adams. Brown County, Indiana, was their favorite locale, and Fournier painted the rural landscape there with an increasingly loose and impressionistic brush and with the broken color technique of the impressionist painters he had come in contact with in France. Cora May Fournier owned a house in South Bend, and after her marriage to Fournier, the couple divided their time between South Bend, where they spent the winters, and East Aurora, where they resided in the summer. Fournier, accompanied by his wife, continued his painting treks to Brown County, too, as well as to more far-flung artists' colonies like Woodstock, New York, and Provincetown, Massachusetts.

Cora Fournier died in 1937, and a year later Fournier moved permanently to East Aurora, where he continued to paint the western New York landscape. In 1944, at the age of seventy-nine, he married once again; his third wife, Coral Lawrence, was a writer for

Hubbard publications. She survived him when he died in East Aurora.

At the time of his death, Fournier had been recognized as an important artist in both France and the United States. In France his work was shown at five exhibitions of the Paris Salon, in 1894, 1895, 1899, 1900, and 1901. The Art Insitute of Chicago displayed his work periodically, including a special exhibition in 1902. The Albright Art Gallery in Buffalo, New York, and the Beard Art Gallery and Minneapolis Insitute of Arts, both in Minneapolis, also regularly exhibited his work. He won prizes and honors, including the Meek Memorial Prize in the tenth annual Hoosier Salon in Chicago in 1934 and the Frederick Nelson Vance Memorial Award of the Brown County Art Gallery Association in 1940. Because he maintained a respect for the natural, perceived image of the rural countryside, Fournier worked, in a sense, against the tide of his time, which witnessed the rise and spread of abstract art throughout the western world. His legacy lives on in the many fresh and intimate portraits of the rural scene in both France and the United States.

• A complete assessment of Fournier's work is Rena Neumann Coen, *In the Mainstream: The Art of Alexis Jean Fournier* (1985). References to Fournier are in an autobiography by Fournier's friend and fellow artist, Nicholas Brewer, *Trails of a Paintbrush* (1938). Fournier's own book, *The Homes of the Men of 1830* (1910), is an important source, as is Judy Oberhausen, *Impressionistic Trends in Hoosier Painting* (1979). Two books by William H. Gerdts can be profitably consulted, *American Impressionism* (1984) and *Art across America: Two Centuries of Regional Painting, 1710–1920* (1990). E. J. Rose, "Alexis Jean Fournier," *Brush and Pencil* 4 (Aug. 1899), is a good early source on Fournier. For the arts and crafts movement see Elizabeth Cumming and Wendy Kaplan, *The Arts and Crafts Movement* (1991), and Coy L. Ludwig, *The Arts and Crafts Movement in New York State, 1890s–1920s* (1983). Roger T. Dunn's essay for the Danforth Museum Catalog, *On the Threshold of Modern Design: The Arts and Crafts Movement in America* (1984), is a short but valuable work.

RENA COEN

FOWLE, Daniel (Oct. 1715–8 June 1787), printer, publisher, and author, was born in Charlestown, Massachusetts, the son of John Fowle, a tanner, and Mary Barrell. After both parents died in 1734, Fowle was placed under the guardianship of Boston printer Samuel Trumbull and, about the same time, was apprenticed to printer Samuel Kneeland. In 1740 Fowle left the apprenticeship and established a partnership with Gamaliel Rogers. Together they printed several sermons by Benjamin Colman, Thomas Foxcroft, and Charles Chauncy and three works by Jonathan Edwards: *The True Excellency of a Minister of the Gospel* (1744), *True Saints, When Absent from the Body, Are Present with the Lord* (1747), and *A Strong Rod Broken and Withered* (1748). They also reprinted John Locke's *A Letter Concerning Toleration* (1743) for members of Yale's senior class who had become disgruntled over the intolerant spirit of the college's president and governors, who would not let the students participate in nonconformist religious ceremonies. Fowle and Rogers's most notable imprint was William Douglass's *A Summary, Historical and Political, of the First Planting, Progressive Improvements, and Present State of the British Settlements in North America*, issued in parts from 1747 through 1752. In March 1743 Rogers and Fowle began printing the *Boston Weekly Magazine*, but it folded after three numbers. Their next periodical effort proved more successful. Starting with the first number in September 1743 (issued 20 Oct.), they printed Jeremiah Gridley's *American Magazine and Historical Chronicle* every month for three years and four months. They also printed Samuel Adams's *Independent Advertiser* from 4 January 1748 through 5 December 1749.

In April 1750 the partnership was dissolved, and Fowle continued printing on his own. He issued such popular works as James Hervey's *Meditations and Contemplations* (1750), Robert Dodsley's *Oeconomy of Human Life* (1752), John Huske's *Present State of North America* (1755), along with many theological works. In 1751 Fowle married Lydia Hall; the couple had no children. Fowle's political troubles began with *The Monster of Monsters*, a pamphlet published in 1754, under the pseudonym "Thomas Thumb," that wittily satirized the Massachusetts legislature's proposal to tax wine and other spirits in order to boost the rum traffic. Though the tract appeared with neither the name of the printer nor the place of publication, it is likely that Fowle's brother Zechariah printed it with the help of Daniel, who sold copies at his shop. The legislature ordered the pamphlet burned and Daniel Fowle imprisoned. He was apprehended on 24 October 1754, jailed, reprimanded, and assessed court costs. Fowle recounted the story of the trial in *A Total Eclipse of Liberty* (1755) and in *An Appendix to the Late Total Eclipse of Liberty* (1756). In the *Appendix*, Fowle expressed his disgust with the Massachusetts government and announced that he was taking his press away from Boston.

Fowle settled in New Hampshire in July 1756, established his press, and printed proposals for the *New-Hampshire Gazette*. In the unique Library of Congress copy of the Portsmouth edition of Nathaniel Ames's *Astronomical Diary; or, An Almanack for . . . 1757*, Fowle included the following statement: "The first Printing Press set up in Portsmouth, New Hampshire, was on August 1756; the Gazette publish'd the 7th of October; and this Almanack November following" (Wroth, *The Colonial Printer*, p. 24). Fowle was appointed printer to the New Hampshire government and printed many laws and statutes for the colony. Other imprints he published in Portsmouth include several sermons preached in New Hampshire, John Pringle's *Life of General James Wolfe* (1760), and George Cockings's *War: An Heroic Poem* (1762).

Fowle's *New-Hampshire Gazette* received his greatest attention. It began on 7 October 1756 as a quarto but was enlarged to a folio three months later. With the issue of 11 March 1763, the title was changed to the *New-Hampshire Gazette, and Historical Chronicle*.

In September 1764 Fowle established a partnership with his nephew Robert L. Fowle. In their publication, they tried to maintain the appearance of neutrality concerning the revolutionary cause, but such a stance was untenable during those volatile times. When in the 20 November 1772 issue they reprinted the opposing views of "Novanglus" and "Massachusettensis" in parallel columns, with the advice that people "read both Sides with an impartial Mind," Daniel was reprimanded for publishing an argument against independence (Botein, p. 35). Robert was eventually branded a Tory and forced to flee in April 1773; Daniel continued publishing the paper alone. The issue of 9 January 1776 contained a letter by "Junius" arguing against independence. One week later Fowle was summoned by the New Hampshire House of Representatives to explain who "Junius" was and why the letter had been printed. The *New-Hampshire Gazette* was suspended for the next four months.

On 25 May 1776 the weekly *Freeman's Journal; or, New-Hampshire Gazette* was established in Portsmouth. The paper was printed by Benjamin Dearborn, but Fowle was largely responsible for editing it. In January 1777 Dearborn transferred the paper to Fowle, although his name did not initially appear in the imprint. Starting on 16 June 1778, Fowle and his brother Zechariah began to print the paper with the title *New-Hampshire Gazette; or, State Journal, and General Advertiser*, using different imprints for Portsmouth and Exeter. Subsequent, though not all, numbers were issued for both towns from 1779 to 1781. On 24 December 1784 the title was changed to *Fowle's New-Hampshire Gazette, and General Advertiser*. The paper was by then being printed by Fowle's apprentices John Melcher and Jerry Osborne, but Fowle remained editor and proprietor until his death. He bequeathed to Melcher his property and business interests.

Fowle made worthy contributions to the history of American printing in both Boston and Portsmouth. *Total Eclipse* and its *Appendix* remain important documents in the establishment of freedom of the press. Fowle was New Hampshire's first printer, and the *New-Hampshire Gazette* its first newspaper. Continued after Fowle's death, the paper eventually became the longest running newspaper in American history.

• For Fowle's Massachusetts imprints see Charles Evans, *American Bibliography* (1903–1934). A source locating information concerning Fowle within Evans's work is Roger Pattrell Bristol, *Index of Printers, Publishers, and Booksellers Indicated by Charles Evans in His American Bibliography* (1961). See also Bristol, *Supplement to Charles Evans' American Bibliography* (1970). Other sources include Isaiah Thomas, *The History of Printing in America*, ed. Marcus A. McCorison (1970); Lawrence C. Wroth, *An American Bookshelf 1755* (1934); Wroth, *The Colonial Printer* (1938; repr. 1964); Robert W. Kidder, "The Contribution of Daniel Fowle to New Hampshire Printing, 1756–1787" (Ph.D. diss., Univ. of Illinois, 1960), which provides a bibliography of Fowle's New Hampshire imprints; Benjamin Franklin V, ed., *Boston Printers, Publishers, and Booksellers: 1640–1800* (1980); and Stephen Botein, "Printers and the American Revolution," in *The Press and the American Revolution*, eds. Bernard Bailyn and John B. Hench (1980). Fowle's newspapers are discussed in Clarence S. Brigham, *History and Bibliography of American Newspapers 1690–1820* (1947).

KEVIN J. HAYES

FOWLE, Elida Barker Rumsey (6 June 1842–17 June 1919), Civil War relief worker, was born in New York City, the daughter of John Wickliffe Rumsey, a businessman and banker, and Mary Agnes Underhill. At age nineteen, following a childhood spent in New York City and then in Tarrytown, New York, Elida moved with her parents to Washington, D.C., where the crisis of the Civil War and the swelling number of soldiers engaged her interest, and she soon began to consider her options for making a contribution to their welfare. Recognizing that the minimum age requirement of thirty-five precluded her from formal employment as an army nurse under Dorothea Dix, she took up the practice of hospital visitation and soon became a familiar face among the sick and wounded.

In her tours of the capital and its various military hospitals, Elida discovered that her love of singing provided a unique source of comfort to the battle-weary soldiers. According to Frank Moore's *Women of the War* (1866), Elida first recognized the power of song when she encountered a bedraggled contingent of Union soldiers returning from captivity in Libby Prison in Richmond. The men, "demoralized by disaster and suffering" and, temporarily at least, "indifferent to the glories and traditions of their country," asked her to sing. Elida's rendition of the national anthem generated such an enthusiastic response she became convinced that she had found her niche. Throughout the war, and often in the company of John Allen Fowle, a Navy Department clerk from Jamaica Plain, Massachusetts, whom she would later marry, Elida made regular visits to the soldiers in hospital and camp, "soothing, cheering, and sustaining" the sick and wounded in the course of some 200 different singing engagements; sometimes she combined her singing with prayer meetings and with the distribution of goods and stores gathered by various aid societies across the North. On at least one occasion, following the second battle of Manassas in August 1862, Elida also made her presence felt on the battlefield, where she carried food, bandages, and other supplies and offered her services as a nurse.

It was in connection with their visits to hospitals and camps around the capital that Elida Rumsey and John Fowle in 1862 conceived the idea of establishing a free library for the entertainment and edification of soldiers during periods of convalescence or while on sojourns in Washington. The library began to take shape in the fall of 1862 in a room at the Rumsey family home, but it soon became clear that a separate building was needed. Toward this goal, Elida and John organized in late 1862 and early 1863 a series of formal concerts, which, augmented by private donations, raised sufficient funds to construct a building on Judiciary Square. The Soldier's Free Library, dedicated on 1 March 1863, eventually held some 6,000 donated or purchased volumes as well as magazines, newspapers, pictures, and paper and ink for letter writing. Also, within the library was formed a nondenominational "soldier's church," whose attendees received signed certificates assuring their piety and temperance. Elida initially served as librarian, but before long she relinquished that post to a convalescent soldier, preferring to retain the freedom to circulate among the hospitals both to promote the library and to provide whatever other assistance and comfort she might to those who had been struck down by illness or gunfire. The library remained in operation until the end of the war.

That the persistent efforts of Elida and John Fowle on behalf of the Union army had caught the attention of both the citizens of Washington and the federal government is indicated by the fact that their marriage ceremony, which occurred the same day as the library's dedication, took place in the U.S. House of Representatives—where the couple had sung weekly in connection with Sunday services—and was attended by some 4,000 guests. (Records indicate that President Abraham Lincoln had expected to attend but that various delays prevented him from doing so.) In the fall of 1863, after honeymooning in the North and briefly returning to Washington to make sure that the library was in good order, the Fowles moved to Brooklyn, New York, where they remained until 1877, then settling in Dorchester, Massachusetts, with their four children, three of whom survived to adulthood, and an adopted war orphan.

Until the end of her life Elida Fowle pursued her philanthropic interests. Among her postwar activities in Boston she counted volunteer work at the Hanover Court Home for Aged Women, the Worcester Street Home for Intemperate Women, the New England Helping Hand Home for Working Girls, the Shawmut Avenue Home for Aged Couples, and the Chester Park Charity Hospital. She also retained memberships in such organizations as the Woman's Christian Temperance Union of Dorchester, the Massachusetts Army Nurses' Association, and the Bunker Hill chapter of the Daughters of the American Revolution. In 1898 she established a reading room and library for neighborhood children. She died in Dorchester.

When Elida Rumsey Fowle was born, her parents could never have anticipated that, twenty-four years later, when Frank Moore penned his commemoration of notable women in the Civil War, he would devote a chapter to their daughter, describing her as a "young lady" of "modest manner" who "gave herself unremittingly to labors for the good, the comfort, the social, moral, and mental well-being of the soldier." Neither could they have anticipated the praise that would be awarded to her by Julia Ward Howe in her *Representative Women of New England* (1904). To her contemporaries, Elida Rumsey Fowle was a model of Victorian womanhood, a woman destined to be "held in grateful remembrance by tens of thousands of soldiers" (Moore, p. 95), among other beneficiaries of her unfailing generosity.

• The current location of Fowle's wartime diaries and other personal papers is unknown, although most recently they were held by a granddaughter, Mrs. James G. Russell, of Milton, Mass. In addition to Frank Moore's *Women of the War*, Elida Fowle is the subject of a chapter in Mary A. Gardner Holland, *Our Army Nurses* (1895), pp. 67–78, which also focuses on her wartime activities. Robert W. Lovett, "The Soldiers' Free Library," *Civil War History* 8 (Mar. 1962): 54–63, provides further information. Lovett notes that the records of the Soldiers' Free Library are at the Dorchester, Mass., Historical Society and that an obituary is in the *Boston Transcript*, 18 June 1919.

ELIZABETH D. LEONARD

FOWLE, William Bentley (17 Oct. 1795–6 Feb. 1865), educator, was born in Boston, Massachusetts, the son of Henry Fowle, an educated mechanic and merchant prominent in Boston's literary circles, and Elizabeth Bentley. William began his education at the precocious age of three, completing the program in the Boston Latin School at the age of fifteen prepared to enter college. Family financial difficulties resulted in the end of his formal education at this point, but luckily Fowle was apprenticed to Caleb Bingham, one of Boston's most famous booksellers. Bingham was also active in education reform, and Boston schoolteachers often gathered at his bookshop to discuss the latest European educational theories.

In 1816 William became Bingham's partner and upon the latter's death continued to run the bookshop. In 1818 he married Antoinette Moulton, with whom he had seven children. In 1821 he was elected to the Boston Primary School Committee; finding that there were many children whom the schools were not reaching, he opened a temporary, experimental school for them. There he introduced the Lancasterian method of teaching with the aid of pupil monitors. Innovations in his school included blackboards, the teaching of geography with the aid of maps, written exercises in addition to recitations and rote memorization, and coeducation on a full-time basis. Most controversially, he abolished corporal punishment, instead offering financial payment for academic success and imposing fines for misbehavior. The experiment soon ended, but had so impressed some Boston citizens that they privately funded another school for Fowle to run.

In 1823 Fowle was placed in charge of the Female Monitorial School, which later became the first high school for girls in Boston. This institution had extensive scientific laboratories with specially imported apparatuses that introduced the pupils to the latest scientific knowledge from Europe. Fowle's science lectures were so popular that they were opened to the general public and became a foundation of the New England lyceum system of education. He also introduced daily physical exercise into the school curriculum and hired Lowell Mason to provide regular music instruction. Dorothea Dix was another of the school's early teachers. The monitorial system Fowle utilized in this school for seventeen years was so successful that it is sometimes described as the precursor of the American normal school. He continued the operation of this institution until his health failed in 1840.

In 1842 Fowle returned full time to the bookseller's business and became the publisher of Horace Mann's *Common School Journal*. A long-time Mann ally, he organized teachers' institutes throughout New England. From 1848 to 1852, with Mann in Washington, Fowle served as both editor and publisher of the journal. In addition to his practical work as an educator, lecturer, and lobbyest for educational reform, Fowle also authored more than fifty school texts. Among these were school spellers and grammars as well as instruction manuals for geography and French. Both his *Common School Speller* and his *Elementary Geography for Massachusetts Children* went through many editions. He participated in many arenas of Boston society, becoming an ardent abolitionist and a member of numerous societies, including the American Antiquarian Society and the New England Historic-Genealogical Society.

In 1852 Fowle opened another, much less successful private school. His wife died in 1859; the following year he married Mary Baxter Adams, with whom he had one more child. He died at his home in Medfield, Massachusetts.

William Fowle was one of the early experimenters in American education whose short-lived projects provided the inspiration upon which others would build. His most important contributions were in writing and publishing, for his textbooks and the *Common School Journal* spread the cause of educational reform to the nation.

• Upon his death William Fowle's extensive library was divided between Tufts College and the American Antiquarian Society. Biographical details may be found in "William Bentley Fowle," *American Journal of Education* 10 (June 1861): 597–610, and Elias Nason, "William Bentley Fowle," *New-England Historical and Genealogical Register* 23 (Apr. 1869): 109–17, which includes a list of his publications.

ROBERT T. BROWN

FOWLER, Bud (16 Mar. 1858–26 Feb. 1913), baseball player, was born John Jackson in Fort Plain, New York, the son of John W. Jackson, a barber, and Mary Lansing. By 1860 the family had moved to nearby Cooperstown, where Fowler grew up and, for reasons unknown, began calling himself John W. Fowler. Sol White, Fowler's contemporary and a pioneer historian of black baseball, claimed that Fowler began his playing career in 1869 with the black Mutuals of Washington, D.C.; in 1872 he joined the New Castle, Pennsylvania, club, thereby becoming "the first colored ball player of note playing on a white [professional] team." A staple of baseball folklore, White's unsubstantiated claim seems implausible given Fowler's age (fourteen).

Fowler's first documented appearance as a player is with a white team in Chelsea, Massachusetts, in April 1878. After pitching Chelsea to a 2–1 win over the National League champion Boston in an exhibition game,

he signed with the Live Oaks of Lynn, Massachusetts, a member of the International Association. On 17 May he became the first black to play in a professional baseball league. Released after two more games, Fowler for the next five years played as the lone black on several independent and semipro teams in the United States and Canada, his tenure typically abbreviated by the racism of teammates and spectators. In 1881 he signed with Guelph, Ontario, but he was soon released because, as the *Guelph Herald* explained, "some of the Maple Leafs are ill-natured enough to object to the colored pitcher."

Fowler resurfaced in organized professional baseball in 1884 with Stillwater, Minnesota, of the Northwestern League. He batted .320 and advanced the next season to Keokuk, Iowa. Unable to pitch because of arm problems, the versatile Fowler played several infield and outfield positions, chiefly second base. When the Western League disbanded in July, he considered becoming the player-manager of the black Orions of Philadelphia, but he decided instead to continue in white professional baseball despite mounting racial antipathy. In August he signed with Pueblo of the Colorado League, but he was "disengaged" after five games because "his skin [was] against him." In 1886, batting .309 with pennant-winning Topeka, Kansas, he was proclaimed the "best second baseman in the Western League."

The next season Fowler joined Binghamton, New York, in the International League. A .350 batting average as the cleanup hitter and more than 20 stolen bases in 34 games demonstrated an ability to excel at the highest level of minor league baseball, but he could not escape racism on the field or among the press. An opposing player admitted that pitchers deliberately tried to hit him (and the other six blacks in the league) when he was at bat, and he played second base "with the lower part of his legs encased in wooden guards" because, "about every player that came down to second base on a steal had it in for him and would, if possible, throw the spikes into him." (Frank Grant, Buffalo's black second baseman, also wore wooden guards; it is unclear which player first used them, but their example prompted all catchers to adopt "shin guards.") Racial animosity from his teammates led to Fowler's release on 30 June, just two weeks before league owners on 14 July agreed to stop signing blacks.

After playing briefly for Montpelier, Vermont, in the Northeastern League, Fowler considered entering the growing world of black baseball that emerged in the mid-1880s in response to the spread of racial segregation. He weighed the choices of joining one of the premier black clubs, the Cuban Giants or the New York Gothams, or of forming his own team to barnstorm through the South and Far West, but he opted instead to continue his odyssey through the lower minor leagues. In 1888 he played with clubs in Crawfordsville and Terre Haute, Indiana, in the Central Interstate League, Santa Fe in the New Mexico Territory, and a barnstorming team that traveled from California to Texas. He spent 1889 with Greenville of the Michigan State League, and in 1890 he played with Galesburg, Illinois, of the Central Interstate League, and Sterling, Illinois, and Burlington, Iowa, in the Illinois-Iowa League. In 1891 he joined a racially mixed independent club in Findlay, Ohio, returned to the minors in 1892 with Lincoln and Kearney of the Nebraska State League, and rejoined Findlay in 1893–1894.

Aided by two white businessmen, Fowler secured sponsorship in 1895 for a black team from the Page Woven Wire Fence Company of Adrian, Michigan, and from an unnamed bicycle manufacturer in Massachusetts. Based in Adrian and led by Fowler as player-manager, the Page Fence Giants traveled by custom-made railroad car throughout six midwestern states, announcing their arrival by riding into town on bicycles. The Giants enjoyed great success against independent and minor league teams, but for reasons unknown, Fowler bolted the team on 15 July and joined Lansing of the Michigan State League. He rejoined the Findlay club in 1896, remaining until 1899, when his white teammates drew the color line. To continue in professional ball and counter white racism, he returned to black baseball. In 1899 he founded the All-American Black Tourists, who for two years combined baseball with burlesque. Arriving in town, the Tourists paraded down the main street in formal dress suits with swallowtail coats, opera hats, and silk umbrellas. "By the request of any club," Fowler announced, "we will play the game in these suits." In 1901 he organized the Smoky City Giants of Pittsburgh, and in 1904 he managed the Kansas City Stars. Fowler's efforts to establish a Negro professional baseball league in 1904–1905 failed for want of adequate financial support, and his baseball career came to an end.

Fowler's career mirrored the experiences of blacks in the development of professional baseball after the Civil War. Partly because of the financial instability of franchises and leagues, but primarily because of racism, he played on at least seventeen different teams in at least nine different leagues and took the field in twenty-two states and Canada. The first black in organized professional baseball, he played longer (ten years) and in more games (465) than any other African American in the nineteenth century. He was almost always the lone black on an otherwise white team.

A superb athlete who conducted running and walking exhibitions during the off-season, Fowler began his baseball career as a pitcher and catcher, but his versatility led to his playing other positions, frequently more than one position in a game. He consistently batted above .300, possessed great speed as a base runner, and was an intelligent and exciting fielder. An itinerant ballplayer who supported himself by barbering during and after the playing season, Fowler saw his dream of reaching the major leagues thwarted by institutionalized racism. In 1885 *Sporting Life* declared: "He is one of the best general players in the country. . . . With his splendid abilities he would long ago have been on some good club had his color been white

instead of black. Those who know say there is no better second baseman in the country; he is besides a good batter and a fine base-runner." Called by Sol White "the celebrated promoter of colored ball clubs, and the sage of base ball," Fowler, who never married, died of pernicious anemia at a sister's home in Frankfort, New York.

• Biographical information on Fowler is incomplete, but L. Robert Davids has written two authoritative sketches, a commemorative pamphlet, *Memorial Observance for John (Bud) Fowler, Black Baseball Pioneer* (1987), and "Bud Fowler" in *Nineteenth Century Stars*, ed. Robert L. Tiemann and Mark Rucker (1989), p. 48. For details about Fowler's life and times, see Sol White, *Sol. White's Official Base Ball Guide* (1907); Robert W. Peterson, *Only the Ball Was White* (1970); Ocania Chalk, *Pioneers of Black Sport* (1975); James Delaney, Jr., "The 1887 Binghamton Bingos," *Society of American Baseball Research [SABR] Journal* 11 (1982): 109–14; Jerry Malloy, "Out at Home: Baseball Draws the Color Line, 1887," *National Pastime* 1 (1983): 14–28; Bob Tholkes, "Bud Fowler, Black Pioneer, and the 1884 Stillwaters," *SABR Journal* 15 (1986): 11–13; Richard White, "Baseball's John Fowler: The 1887 Season in Binghamton, New York," *Afro-Americans in New York Life and History* 16 (1992): 7–17; and Phil Dixon, with Patrick J. Hannigan, *The Negro Baseball Leagues, 1867–1955: A Photographic History* (1992).

LARRY R. GERLACH

FOWLER, Charles Henry (11 Aug. 1837–20 Mar. 1908), bishop of the Methodist Episcopal Church, was born in Burford (now Clarendon), Ontario, Canada, the son of Horatio Fowler and Harriet Ryan, farmers. In 1841, after his father suffered financial loss, Fowler was taken to live at a family farm near Newark, Illinois. Influenced by his Methodist family, he attended Rock River Seminary, Mount Morris, Illinois, from 1851, then the Genesee Wesleyan Seminary, Lima, New York, from spring 1855. He entered Genesee College in the fall of that year and graduated valedictorian in 1859. The same year he joined a law office in Chicago, and became known as "Whirlwind Fowler." A conversion to the Methodist faith on Christmas Eve 1859 caused him to leave law school and instead join the itinerant ministry. He entered the Garrett Biblical Institute, Evanston, Illinois, in March 1860, graduating valedictorian in 1861. He became a probationary member of the Rock River Conference of the Methodist Episcopal church in 1861, and he was ordained deacon in 1864 and elder in 1865. From 1861 to 1872 he was pastor in Chicago at the churches of Jefferson Street, Clark Street, and Wabash Avenue. From 1866 he supervised the building of the monumental Centenary Methodist Church in Chicago. After the Chicago fire of 1871, Fowler traveled throughout the United States giving lectures promoting the city in order to raise funds to rebuild its churches and schools. He raised $40,000 and in the process established himself as a talented orator. This reputation led to invitations to speak at occasions such as the Centennial Exposition in Philadelphia in 1876 and the Centennial of the

First Conference of American Methodism in Philadelphia, 1883. In 1868 Fowler married Myra A. Hitchcock of Chicago; they had one son.

In 1866 Fowler had been offered the presidency of Northwestern University, which was in need of reorganization and financial support. When he was approached a second time in 1872, he accepted and was elected 23 October. During his four years as president, he secured the sponsorship of Chicago businessmen and through his fundraising and restructuring, facilitated the transformation of the university. The exercise of his office was not without political and personal conflict, however. As part of his plan to aggrandize the university, a merger had been effected in 1873 with the Evanston College for Ladies. That college's dean was Frances Willard, who had broken off her engagement to Fowler in 1861. Fowler was successful in his aim to undermine her authority, reducing her role to that of an officer. This certainly contributed to her decision to resign in 1874.

As a delegate for the Genesee Conference, Fowler was chosen as one of the northern fraternal delegates to attend the General Conference of the Methodist Episcopal Church, South in Louisville, Kentucky, in 1874. This was the first step towards formal fraternity since the division in 1844, and Fowler was commended for his conciliatory address. In 1876 the General Conference elected him editor of *New York Christian Advocate*, then the leading organ of the Methodist Episcopal Church. A number of articles written by Fowler criticizing the southern Methodists provoked a retaliatory article with the caption "Fowl, Fowler, Fowlest," from the editor of the *Nashville Christian Advocate*. Circulation rose under Fowler's editorship, which he held until 1880.

From 1880 to 1884 Fowler was corresponding secretary of the Methodist Episcopal Missionary Society, his vigor fueling the society with a renewed vision. In 1884 Fowler was honored at his fourth General Conference with election to the episcopacy. Through his office he was able to continue his work in the expansion of foreign missions. He traveled to South America in 1885 and to Russia, Japan, Korea, and China in 1888. He organized the foundation of the Universities of Peking and Nanking in China and promoted and oversaw the establishment of the first Methodist Episcopal church in Russia at St. Petersburg. By the end of his life he had visited all the mission fields. He visited Europe, acting in 1898 as fraternal delegate at the Wesleyan Conference in Great Britain, and traveled to Malaysia and India. He established the Twentieth Century Forward Movement, a fund that raised $20 million. In the United States, he helped establish the Maclay College of Theology in San Fernando, California, and Nebraska Wesleyan University in Lincoln. His episcopal residences were San Francisco, 1884–1892; Minneapolis, 1892–1896; Buffalo, 1896–1904; and then New York City until his death.

In both ecclesiastical and state politics, he maintained a forceful presence. He devoted much energy to prohibition, and his support was highly valued by the temperance movement. He campaigned on behalf of the Methodist Republican William McKinley, who was elected president in 1900. He was also active in his opposition to female representation, at least in the governing bodies of the Methodist Episcopal Church. In 1888 controversy arose over the proposed seating in the New York General Conference of the five female lay delegates elected at the local level, one of whom was Willard. In May 1888 Fowler was placed on the board of bishops formed to determine their eligibility. His legal training made him a formidable opponent. This, combined with the sermon he delivered at the convention on 6 May, two days before the voting, certainly influenced the women's defeat, albeit by a narrow margin. Fowler's antagonism was felt with equal force by the Women's Foreign Missionary Society, which became aware in 1884 of his pre-General Conference campaign to have it dissolved.

Fowler was a figure of much influence in the Methodist Episcopal Church, a highly able administrator and fundraiser, an orator, and a determined ecclesiastical politician. His fundraising skills and unceasing energies (despite challenge from a physical illness) served the educational system, the foreign missionary enterprises of the Methodist Episcopal Church, and, not least, the city of Chicago, devastated after the fire. He died in New York City.

• Fowler's addresses are collected in *Missions and World Movements* (1903); *Missionary Addresses* (1906); *Addresses on Notable Occasions* (1908); and *Patriotic Orations* (1910). A bibliography listing Fowler's other publications is found in Frederick D. Leete, *Methodist Bishops* (1948). A memoir by W. F. Anderson can be found in *Minutes of the New York Conference of the Methodist Episcopal Church* (1908). His work for the *Christian Advocate*, and his attendance at the Conference of the Methodist Episcopal Church, South are discussed in Emory Stevens Bucke, ed., *History of American Methodism* vol. 3 (1964); the latter is also in Nolan B. Harmon, ed., *The Encyclopedia of World Methodism*, vol. 1 (1974). Reference to Fowler's political activity is found in Frederick A. Norwood *The Story of American Methodism* (1974). His advocation of Prohibition and his dealings with Willard are described in Mark Edward Lender, *Dictionary of American Temperance Biography* (1984). For additional information concerning his dealings with Willard, see also Mary Earhart Dillow, *Frances Willard: From Prayers to Politics* (1944); and Ruth Bordin, *Frances Willard: A Biography* (1986). His opposition to the representation of women is mentioned in Frederick A. Norwood, "Report on Seminar: Women in Methodism," *Methodist History* 10, vol. 1 (Oct. 1971): 56–57; Theodore L. Agnew, "Reflections on the Women's Foreign Missionary Movement in Late Nineteenth-Century American Methodism," *Methodist History* 6, vol. 2 (Jan. 1968): 3–16; and Wade Crawford Barclay, *Methodist Episcopal Church, 1845–1939*, vol. 3 (1957). Obituaries are in the *Christian Advocate*, 28 Mar. 1908, and the *Methodist Review*, Mar.–Apr. 1911.

JOANNA HAWKE

FOWLER, George Ryerson (25 Dec. 1848–6 Feb. 1906), surgeon, was born in New York City, the son of Thomas Wright Fowler, a master mechanic, and Sarah Jane Carman. In 1856 Fowler moved with his family to Jamaica, Long Island, where his father managed the Long Island Railroad repair shop, and Fowler received an elementary education. At the age of thirteen, with encouragement from his father, he took a junior position at the local office of the Long Island Railroad, learning telegraphy and other duties. After a year there, he became an apprentice in his father's machine shop; when a serious accident occurred in the shop, young Fowler was among those who came to the aid of the victims. Years later he would claim that this emergency awakened in him an interest in medicine. At the completion of his apprenticeship in 1866, he decided to follow his medical interests rather than his father's plans, resolving that he would become a surgeon.

After working for a year to gather the funds necessary for medical school, Fowler entered Bellevue Hospital Medical College in New York City, graduating with an M.D. in 1871. At the time most ambitious medical students attempted to secure a hospital internship after completing medical school. Fowler was ambitious, but his limited means did not allow further study before earning an income as a physician, so immediately following graduation he established a private practice in Brooklyn. The practice flourished and came to center increasingly on his area of greatest aptitude and interest, surgery. In 1872 he married Louise R. Wells. They had four children, one of whom died in infancy.

During the first dozen years of his medical career Fowler was hampered by a lack of official hospital affiliation. His first break into the prestigious ranks of New York hospital surgeons came in 1883, when he was appointed surgeon at the new St. Mary's Hospital in Jamaica. The doors of many other hospitals soon swung open to this talented, innovative, energetic surgeon. During his career he was appointed as an attending or consulting surgeon at eleven different New York hospitals, including the Methodist Episcopal Hospital, King's County, Nassau, and St. John's. He held most of these positions concurrently.

One of Fowler's colleagues, Lewis S. Pilcher, asserted in a memorial tribute that his friend was a nearly ideal surgeon "in possession of a tenacity of purpose; an inflexibility of will; a steadiness of nerve; a willingness to sacrifice ease and comfort; a devotion to labor and to research; a special knowledge that [was] certain, positive, and comprehensive; a readiness to assume great responsibilities, added to marked manipulative skill and aptitude in operative methods, together with fertility of resource and quickness of response in emergencies, self-control and coolness in the face of the most appalling conditions, and a judgment that [was] unerring and almost intuitive" (*Brooklyn Medical Journal*, p. 115). Fowler worked at the cutting edge of surgical innovation. He was among the early and most influential American proponents of the antiseptic surgical techniques pioneered by British surgeon Joseph Lister. He advocated a semi-sitting position for effective drainage during recovery from abdominal operations, which is still used and known as "Fowler's position." He was also among the early supporters of prompt surgical removal of the appendix in cases of appendicitis, publishing an important book, *A Treatise on Appendicitis* (1894).

In 1890 the state of New York organized the New York State Board of Medical Examiners under the auspices of the Board of Regents of the State University of New York. The regents chose Fowler as the state's official examiner in surgery, a capacity in which he served until his death. In the same year Fowler was also elected the first president of the Brooklyn Red Cross Society, reflecting his pioneering efforts to bring first-aid education to the American public. In 1884, during one of several trips to Europe he made during his career, he had attended a lecture in England on the significance of first-aid training for soldiers, police officers, and members of the general public; he carried this message with force to his fellow citizens when he returned home.

In addition to his book on appendicitis, Fowler published more than one hundred case histories and clinical reports. For twelve years he labored on a major synthetic treatment of surgery, published in 1906 as *A Treatise on Surgery*.

Shortly after correcting the final proof sheets of that work, Fowler departed Brooklyn by train to attend a meeting of the state medical examination board in Albany. During the trip he was stricken with intense abdominal pain. On his arrival in Albany, Fowler and his colleagues quickly agreed on a diagnosis of appendicitis and scheduled an emergency operation. A fellow surgeon (who might well have learned his techniques from Fowler's textbook) successfully removed a gangrenous appendix from the patient, but a paresis of the ileum set in after the operation, from which Fowler failed to recover. Fowler's death was in an almost eerie sense a recapitulation of his life: the fatal affliction began on a train and ended in the surgical ward of a hospital.

A Treatise on Surgery, which appeared several months after Fowler's death, stood as a legacy of a most impressive career. Pilcher wrote, "In its clearness of diction, comprehension of treatment, and the practical directions for resort to surgical relief, it was unsurpassed by any book of its day" (*Surgery, Gynecology and Obstetrics*, p. 567).

• A chronology of Fowler's life and a complete bibliography of his publications is in *Medical Classics* 4 (Feb. 1940): 531–48. Lewis S. Pilcher contributed a detailed and eloquent account, "George Ryerson Fowler," *Surgery, Gynecology and Obstetrics* 38 (1924): 564–67. Pilcher's eulogy at Fowler's memorial service was published in *Brooklyn Medical Journal* 20 (Mar. 1906): 114–17. Shorter tributes to Fowler appeared in the same issue, pp. 117–22.

JON M. HARKNESS

FOWLER, Joseph Smith (31 Aug. 1820–1 Apr. 1902), educator, lawyer, and senator, was born in Steubenville, Ohio, the son of James Fowler and Sarah Atkinson, farmers. He was brought up on their farm and attended local schools. After teaching for a time in Shelby County, Kentucky, to earn money for further schooling, he attended Franklin College in New Athens, Ohio, graduating in 1843. Returning to Kentucky, he taught school in Bowling Green and studied law.

In 1845 Fowler joined the first faculty of newly chartered Franklin College in Davidson County, Tennessee, as professor of mathematics, chemistry, and mechanic arts and as assistant professor of horticulture. He remained at Franklin for four years. In 1846 he married Maria Louisa Embry, daughter of a founding trustee of the college; they had two children. Fowler later assisted in the establishment of Washington Institute near Nashville, Tennessee, which had been chartered by the legislature in 1851. While with the Washington Institute, he opened a law office in Nashville and practiced there until 1857. From 1856 to 1861 Fowler was president of Howard Female Institute in Gallatin, Tennessee; during his presidency Howard's enrollment increased annually, and the student publication expressed the area's pro-Union, antisecession views.

When the Civil War broke out in 1861, Jefferson Davis issued his "forty-day" proclamation ordering Union sympathizers to leave the South. Although Fowler sympathized with the southern people, he opposed slavery and did not believe in the right of secession. Therefore, he resigned from Howard and took his family to Springfield, Illinois.

Since 1860 Fowler had corresponded with Andrew Johnson about efforts to hold Tennessee in the Union. In 1862, after federal troops took over Nashville, he returned with his family. Johnson was then military governor and appointed Fowler state comptroller. He worked hard on the reconstruction of Tennessee's state government and the abolition of slavery, while overseeing the state capitol, which served as a barracks.

Fowler organized political support in 1864 for the Union ticket of Abraham Lincoln and Andrew Johnson. He was a delegate to the Baltimore convention that nominated Lincoln and Johnson, acting as an effective floor leader for Johnson. In March 1865 Fowler was in the small party of Tennessee Union men who accompanied Vice President–elect Johnson to Washington, D.C., for the inauguration.

Returning home, Fowler decided to seek a seat in the U.S. Senate. On hearing of Lincoln's assassination, he wrote to Johnson of the crime "more startling than the rebellion," offering his support to the new president. Pro-Unionists in the state legislature were eager to restore Tennessee to the Union, and on 4 May 1865 they elected Fowler and David T. Patterson, President Johnson's son-in-law, to represent Tennessee in the Senate.

Congress, however, required more proof of loyalty before the Tennesseans could be seated. Tennessee had to ratify the Fourteenth Amendment to the U.S. Constitution, which included a profession of loyalty for officeholders. Thanks to intensive lobbying by Fowler, the state legislature ratified the amendment on 19 July 1866. Fowler was seated on 24 July, becoming the first senator from the former Confederacy to be ad-

mitted to the postwar Senate. The Nashville *Daily Press and Times* observed, "He is the first original antislavery and impartial suffrage advocate ever elected to the Senate from this state. He is no recent convert to the doctrines of the Republican Party, having defended them through good and evil."

Fowler entered the Senate at a time of extreme partisanship and political acrimony. Although he did not favor imposing military governments on the former Confederate states, he did vote for most of the Radicals' severe Reconstruction measures. This brought him into direct political conflict with President Johnson and strained the friendship of the two Tennesseans. Fowler was among those who called for a Southern Loyalists Convention to meet in Philadelphia in September 1866, and he attended as one of 390 delegates from border and southern states. They voiced their loyalty to the Union and their disapproval of Johnson's efforts to soften the Radicals' Reconstruction legislation.

As the president pursued his own agenda, Congress increased its vilification of him. When Johnson removed Secretary of War Edwin Stanton from the cabinet, the Radicals saw this violation of the controversial Tenure of Office Act as an impeachable high crime and misdemeanor. On 24 February 1868, climaxing the campaign against the president, the House voted to impeach. With the impeachment trial taking place in the Senate, Fowler was called on to judge a fellow Tennessean with whom he differed on how to restore the former Confederate states to the Union.

As Fowler carefully considered the charges against the president and his own reponsibility as a senator, he made it clear that the Radicals could not count on his vote. Although he was threatened, investigated, and even defamed by fellow Republicans, his decision was his own. It did not become public until 16 May 1868, when the chief justice of the Supreme Court, presiding over the impeachment trial, called the roll of the senators. Fowler quietly stated, "Not guilty." He was one of seven Republicans who broke with their party. The result for the president was acquittal; the accusers were one short of the two-thirds vote required for conviction. None of the seven who voted their conscience ever again held public office.

Fowler had concluded that the charges against Johnson were false and partisan, and he was horrified at the acrimony of the proceedings. He said, "Posterity will do justice to my judgment, if the present will not." He was rebuked by his party, replaced on the national committee, and stripped of Senate committee posts. Nevertheless, Fowler supported the 1868 presidential ticket of Ulysses S. Grant and Schuyler Colfax, and during the 1869–1870 Congress he worked hard to prevent Tennessee from being remanded to military goverment.

Fowler did not seek reelection in 1871. By 1872 he was disgusted with the Grant administration and joined liberal Republicans supporting Horace Greely for president, serving as an elector on the Greely-Brown ticket. After a brief return to Tennessee, he lived in Washington, practicing law and pursuing his scholarly interests. He was made an honorary member of the Tennessee Historical Society. Along with the other renegade Republicans he was hailed for his honor in the *Nation*, the Chicago *Tribune*, and the *New York Evening Post*, while historian James Ford Rhodes called them "seven tall men" who showed the highest possible degree of courage. Fowler died in Washington, D.C.

• There are Fowler papers at the Tennessee State Library and Archives and at the University of North Carolina. Some of Fowler's correspondence with Andrew Johnson is in Johnson's papers at the Library of Congress. His essays and commentaries on education appeared in *Naturalist, and Journal of Agriculture, Horticulture, Education, and Literature* (later *Naturalist and Journal of Natural History, Agriculture, Education and Literature*), published by the faculty of Franklin College, during 1846. The Manuscript Division of the Library of Congress contains a biographical sketch. Walter T. Durham, "How Say You, Senator Fowler?" *Tennessee Historical Quarterly* 42 (1983): 39–57, is the most thorough biographical account. Monographs on Johnson that contain references to Fowler include Milton Lomask, *Andrew Johnson: President on Trial* (1960); Fay W. Brabson, *Andrew Johnson: A Life in Pursuit of the Right Course, 1808–1875* (1972); and Hans L. Trefousse, *Impeachment of a President: Andrew Johnson, the Blacks, and Reconstruction* (1975), which includes an extensive bibliography. John F. Kennedy, *Profiles in Courage* (1956), chap. 6, on Edmund G. Ross (one of the seven voting against impeachment), includes praise of Fowler. An obituary is in the *New York Times*, 2 Apr. 1902.

SYLVIA B. LARSON

FOWLER, Lorenzo Niles (23 June 1811–2 Sept. 1896), phrenologist, was born in Cohocton, Steuben County, New York, the son of Horace Fowler and Martha Howe, farmers. He pursued studies that would lead to the ministry and also studied in the classical department of Amherst Academy, Amherst, Massachusetts. Deeply influenced by his older brother Orson Fowler, however, he devoted himself instead to phrenology, the science of mind developed by Franz Joseph Gall and popularized in the United States by Johann Gaspar Spurzheim in the 1820s and 1830s. Phrenology held that mental characteristics or faculties were indicated by the conformation of the skull and could not only be analyzed, but improved.

The two brothers lectured on phrenology along the eastern seaboard, examining heads and sizing "organs," or faculties, such as Amativeness, Ideality, Destructiveness, and Acquisitiveness, among others, to determine character and temperament. The phrenological examination included measuring the horizontal circumference of the subject's head with a tape in order to determine the size of the organs or faculties; placing the hands on the side of the subject's head to determine shape; applying the balls of the fingers to the subject's scalp to estimate distances between organs; and investigating individual organs: Amativeness at the base of the head, Philoprogenitiveness (parental love) nearby, and so on. The faculties were then graded, from 1 (very small) to 7 (very large). Lorenzo's examination in 1837 of the fifteen-year-old Clara Barton, whom he advised to seek responsibility, had a lasting effect on the future founder of the American Red Cross.

The Fowlers opened a temporary office in Washington, D.C., where Lorenzo developed an interest in the artistic aspects of phrenology, especially the manufacture of plastic casts, phrenological busts, and life masks. With Samuel Kirkham they published *Phrenology Proved, Illustrated and Applied* (c. 1836). In 1836 Lorenzo opened a phrenological office in New York, and in 1842 the firm of O. S. and L. N. Fowler was established in Clinton Hall, New York City. It offered a "Repository of Curiosities," including casts of heads, human and animal skulls, and phrenological busts. Insisting on the possibility of self-knowledge and self-improvement through phrenology, the brothers participated in such related reform movements as child guidance, vocational guidance, penal reform, sex education, and marriage counseling. They crusaded against alcohol, tobacco, and tight lacing (corsets) and endorsed water cure and vegetarianism.

Lorenzo published several phrenological manuals, including *The Principles of Phrenology and Physiology Applied to Man's Social Relations* (1842) and *Marriage: Its History and Ceremonies* (1847). The Fowlers added to their reputation as practicing phrenologists that of large-scale publishers in their specialty and in related reforms.

In 1844 Lorenzo married Lydia Folger of Nantucket Island, whom he had met while performing phrenological examinations there. In April 1844 he had examined his future wife's head, concluding that "she has a clear and original mind." She became the second woman to graduate from an American medical college (Central Medical College, Rochester, N.Y., in 1850) and the first woman professor of medicine in this country (Central Medical College). The author of a trilogy, *Familiar Lessons*, on astronomy, phrenology, and physiology (1847–1848), she also practiced medicine privately. Three daughters were born to them, the last of whom, Jessie Allen, would eventually continue the New York firm.

With the entry of Samuel Roberts Wells, brother-in-law of the Fowlers, the firm was reorganized as Fowlers & Wells in 1844, and Lorenzo devoted himself primarily to giving phrenological examinations. Among those he examined were Fanny Elssler, Elihu Burritt, Horace Greeley, Joseph Neal, Lydia Sigourney, Andrew Jackson Davis, Brigham Young, and Lucretia Mott. In 1849 Lorenzo examined Walt Whitman, detecting in him "a certain reckless swing of animal will," and producing an analysis that exerted some influence on the future poet of *Leaves of Grass*. Whitman kept his phrenological chart all his life and published it on several occasions.

Accompanied by his wife, Lorenzo made frequent lecture tours, and he served as vice president of the Phrenological Tract Society, established to furnish at cost tracts on the reforms of the age. He thus became an eloquent propagandist for phrenology. With the withdrawal of Orson Fowler, the company was restyled Fowler & Wells, moving to Broadway in 1854. Lorenzo's phrenological examinees now included Horace Mann, Oliver Wendell Holmes (1809–1894), Mathew Brady, and Allan Pinkerton.

Lecturing and examining, Lorenzo with his wife and Samuel Wells toured the United States and Canada between 1858 and 1860. In 1860 they journeyed to England. In 1863, perhaps motivated by a belief in pacifism during the Civil War, the Lorenzo Fowlers moved to England and established a British branch of the New York firm on London's Fleet Street. There in 1873 Lorenzo examined the head of Mark Twain, who scorned the phrenologist's analyses. Lecturing, examining, and traveling, Lorenzo and Lydia continued to stimulate a strong interest in phrenology in Britain. In 1879 Lydia died, and the youngest daughter, Jessie, assisted her father. At this time Lorenzo visited the United States briefly, and his sister Charlotte Wells arranged with him for a special London agency for Fowler publications.

Setting up offices in the Imperial Buildings, Ludgate Circus, London, Lorenzo also launched the *Phrenological Magazine* (1880), a British counterpart to the New York *Phrenological Journal*. The Fowler Phrenological Institute in London offered weekly classes, a library, a museum of casts and skulls, and circulated books published by the New York firm.

In 1893 Lorenzo suffered a paralytic stroke but recovered sufficiently to return to the United States with Jessie in 1896. Shortly thereafter, while visiting Charlotte in her home in West Orange, New Jersey, he had another stroke and died.

As a phrenologist Lorenzo Fowler examined a host of subjects, including two major literary figures—Whitman and Twain—both of whom, in different ways, were affected by his analyses. As a phrenologist Fowler displayed keen perception of character, and for many decades he was able to forward the cause of phrenology, offering convincing evidence to many that the mental faculties could be ascertained by an examination of the skull and, once ascertained, could also be developed and improved. He was a persuasive advocate of the belief that self-knowledge could lead to self-improvement. His phrenological analyses lent support to the optimistic affirmations and reform movements of his time.

• The Fowler Family Papers are in the Collection of Regional History in Cornell University Library. Details of Fowler's life and career are recorded in John D. Davies, *Phrenology: Fad and Science—A 19th-Century American Crusade* (1955), and in Madeleine B. Stern, *Heads & Headlines: The Phrenological Fowlers* (1971). See also "Fifty Years of Phrenology. A Review of Our Past and Our Work," *Phrenological Journal* 80 (Jan. 1885): 10–29; Stern, *A Phrenological Dictionary of Nineteenth-Century Americans* (1982) and "Lydia Folger Fowler, M.D.: First American Woman Professor of Medicine," *New York State Journal of Medicine* (June 1977): 1137–40. Death notices of Lorenzo Fowler are in the New York *Daily Tribune* and the *New York Times*, 4 Sept. 1896, as well as in the *Phrenological Journal* 102 (Oct. 1896): 113–15.

MADELEINE B. STERN

FOWLER, Orson Squire (11 Oct. 1809–18 Aug. 1887), phrenologist and publisher, was born in Cohocton, Steuben County, New York, the son of Horace Fowler, a farmer, and Martha Howe. He was graduated from Amherst College in 1834 and in 1835 married Eliza Brevoort Chevalier, a widow, by whom he had two children. Though educated for the ministry, he devoted himself to phrenology, the "science" of the mind that was formulated by Franz Joseph Gall and introduced to the United States by Johann Gaspar Spurzheim. Phrenology postulated that, because the brain was the organ of the mind and shaped the skull, there was an observable concomitance between the mind (talents, disposition, character) and the shape of the head. In an analysis, a phrenologist examined the latter to determine the former. Immediately after graduation Fowler started his professional career as itinerant practical phrenologist in New England. Using charts and a phrenological bust, he lectured on phrenology and analyzed heads, sizing "organs" or "faculties" such as amativeness, combativeness, firmness, and ideality to determine character. It was believed that each faculty manifested itself through its own cerebral organ, the size of which indicated its functional power. The size of the organ, it was believed, could be increased or decreased by exercise.

After briefly practicing phrenology with his younger brother Lorenzo Niles Fowler in Washington, D.C., he opened a Phrenological Museum at 210 Chestnut Street, Philadelphia, in 1838, with the assistance of his younger sister Charlotte. In October 1838 the *American Phrenological Journal*, which survived until 1911, was launched. The first editor, Nathan Allen, was followed by Fowler in 1842. With Lorenzo Fowler and Samuel Kirkham, he compiled a practical manual, *Phrenology Proved, Illustrated and Applied* (1836). In 1842 Fowler moved the phrenological office to Clinton Hall, Nassau and Beekman streets, New York City. In 1843 Samuel Roberts Wells, who married Charlotte the next year, joined the firm, which later was renamed Fowlers & Wells. Their office exhibited casts of skulls, phrenological busts, and animal heads. The phrenological injunction "Know Thyself" was applied in phrenological analyses, and since practitioners believed that the mental "organs" could be enlarged or shrunk at will, they also held that self-improvement and perfection were attainable. The Fowlers applied their phrenological doctrine to child guidance, vocational guidance, employment counseling, and marriage counseling. They advocated penal reform, dress reform, temperance, vegetarianism, and hydropathy. Among those examined during the 1840s were Horace Greeley, John Brown (1800–1859), and, in 1849, Walt Whitman, who later became a staff writer for the firm's periodical *Life Illustrated* and whose *Leaves of Grass* enlisted their support. Phrenology attracted a variety of patrons, writers, artists, reformers, performers, educators, politicians, merchants, people eager to learn more about themselves. The company continued to publish on a large scale, issuing manuals on water cure, phrenological almanacs, and treatises on temperance, vegetarianism, mesmerism, and psychology. Fowler continued to write and publish a succession of phrenology-related studies: *Fowler on Matrimony* (1842); *Love and Parentage, Applied to the Improvement of Offspring* (1844); *Memory and Intellectual Improvement* (1846); *Self-Culture and Perfection of Character* (1847); *Amativeness* (1848).

In 1848 Fowler turned his interest to architecture, writing *A Home for All; or, A New, Cheap, Convenient, and Superior Mode of Building*, which recommended the octagonal shape for domestic dwellings. Fowler saw the octagon as a shape that would allow more room than a square or rectangle, admit increased sunshine, eliminate square corners, and facilitate communication between rooms. Thus he believed it especially suitable for domestic dwellings. Between 1850 and 1853 he designed and built an octagonal edifice of sixty rooms in Fishkill, New York. In 1853 he issued a revised, enlarged edition of his book, *A Home for All; or, The Gravel Wall and Octagon Mode of Building*, which endorsed the gravel wall method of construction. His pioneer architectural treatise has a lasting place in American architectural history.

Preoccupied by his architectural pursuits and his writing, Fowler withdrew in September 1855 from the firm he had founded. As an independent itinerant lecturer and author he traveled through the West and South until in 1863 he set up business at 514 Tremont Street, Boston. After the death of his first wife, he married the widow Mary Aiken Poole in 1865. At his Boston office he gave phrenological examinations, but his practice was now concerned primarily with sex education. His preachments were based upon the dictates "Study and follow Nature" and "Sexual knowledge is sexual salvation." During the 1870s he wrote a number of tomes that elaborated his views: *Sexual Science* (1870); *Creative and Sexual Science* (1870); *Life: Its Science, Laws, Faculties* (1871); and *The Practical Phrenologist* (1876). His son-in-law Eugene W. Austin served as agent for his books, which were sold by subscription. In 1880 Fowler rejoined the Fowler firm, now headed by Charlotte Fowler Wells, and moved to Sharon Station, Dutchess County, New York. In 1882, at age seventy-two, he married his third wife, Abbie L. Ayres, by whom he had three children. Late in life Fowler was harassed by debts and charged by some with licentiousness for his pioneering work in sex education. He died at Sharon Station.

Patriarchal in appearance, with luxuriant beard, high forehead, and piercing eyes, Fowler had a magnetic personality. A successful practical phrenologist as well as an author and publisher of works in the field, he used the pseudoscience of the mind to advance the optimism and affirmations of his age. In his pioneering

work in domestic architecture, based upon the belief that form follows function, he was a precursor of Frank Lloyd Wright. As a pioneer in sex education who concentrated upon that subject and discussed sex freely in his books for the purpose of improving sexual relations, Fowler foreshadowed Sigmund Freud. His work in both fields was based upon his belief that self-knowledge, acquired from phrenological analysis, could lead to self-improvement.

• The Fowler Family Papers are in the Collection of Regional History in Cornell University Library. Details of Fowler's life and career are recorded in John D. Davies, *Phrenology: Fad and Science; a 19th-Century American Crusade* (1955), and in Madeleine B. Stern, *Heads & Headlines: The Phrenological Fowlers* (1971). See also "Fifty Years of Phrenology: A Review of Our Past and Our Work," *Phrenological Journal* (Jan. 1885); Orson S. Fowler, *The Octagon House: A Home for All*, with an introduction by Madeleine B. Stern (1973); and Madeleine B. Stern, *A Phrenological Dictionary of Nineteenth-Century Americans* (1982). Obituaries are in the *New York Times* and *New-York Daily Tribune*, 20 Aug. 1887.

MADELEINE B. STERN

FOWLER, Wally (15 Feb. 1917–3 June 1994), gospel music promoter, singer, and songwriter, was born John Wallace Fowler near Cartersville, Georgia, the son of Joseph Fletcher Fowler, a well-established cotton farmer; his mother's name is not known. By the time Wally Fowler was ready for school, the Great Depression had wrecked his father's fortunes, and he and his sisters grew up working as sharecroppers. The Fowler family, however, loved music; his mother played an old pump organ, and his father helped organize Saturday night gospel singings in the front rooms of neighborhood houses. "That's when I really learned gospel music," he recalled. What formal training the singers got came from J. M. Henson, an Atlanta publisher and singing school teacher, who came to the area to conduct singing schools, using the seven-shape note system that was popular throughout the South at that time.

When he was fourteen years old, Fowler had a religious experience at a local "protracted meeting" and became the choir director for the preacher who had "saved" him. By this time the family was living in Rome, Georgia, and Fowler received further musical training from a well-known teacher, Mack D. Weems. He learned harmony by sending for a book published by the Reubusch-Kieffer company. Soon after this, Fowler formed a gospel quartet called the Harmony Quartet, which began to appear on local radio stations and at local churches. This, in turn, led to his being hired, in 1936, to sing baritone with one of the more successful professional groups in the area, the John Daniel Quartet. Formed from the rich, complex singing tradition around the huge Sand Mountain in northern Alabama, the John Daniel Quartet was one of the first gospel quartets to break free from the support of specific churches or gospel publishing companies and to try to make it on its own. Fowler's tenure with Daniel lasted until 1944 and included a five-year stint on Nashville's famous country music radio show, the Grand Ole Opry.

After leaving Daniel, Fowler decided to keep a foot in both the secular and the gospel camps and organized two groups. His secular band he called the Georgia Clodhoppers, and they featured important young musicians such as Zeke Turner (electric guitar) and Joe Carrol (fiddle). The band backed up Fowler's lead vocals and soon landed a recording contract with Capitol; though they had no sensational bestsellers, they did have several modest hits, such as "Propaganda Papa" and "A Mother's Prayer." Fowler's songwriting ability began to develop in earnest, and he often penned songs with lyricist J. Graydon Hall. The band also began appearing on Knoxville radio station WNOX's popular program "Mid-Day Merry-Go-Round."

Fowler's gospel group came about when he began taking part of his band from Knoxville to Oak Ridge, the newly formed suburb where atomic bomb research was being conducted. In January 1945 he decided to name this gospel group the Oak Ridge Quartet, and it became a part of his regular radio act. By September 1945 Fowler had taken the whole group back to Nashville, where he rejoined the Grand Ole Opry and began to explore the developing music scene in Nashville. He soon organized his own publishing company—Wallace Fowler Publications, only the second publishing company to be founded in modern Nashville—and became a distributor for Mercury Records. In the meantime he developed a style for the Oak Ridge Quartet that featured spirituals such as "Dig a Little Deeper in the Well." He also started his own record label, Wally Fowler's Record of the Month Club, to sell by mail and at gospel concerts.

These concerts took a dramatic turn on 5 November 1948 when Fowler rented the Nashville Ryman auditorium, the home of the Grand Ole Opry, and staged his first "All-Night Sing." For years southern churches held all-night singings on New Year's Eve so they could break open the new year's songbook and try the new songs. In 1938 the Stamps-Baxter Music Company sponsored such a singing in Dallas, Texas, and had it broadcast locally. Fowler's purpose was not so much to introduce new songbooks but to stage a packaged gospel concert featuring a number of different gospel groups. It was, in some ways, a gospel music adaptation of the "package tour" that was becoming popular in country music. It was a commercial and aesthetic success, and he staged similar concerts in the Ryman for the next seventeen years. He also exported the idea to other southern cities, such as Birmingham, Alabama; Memphis, Tennessee; Miami, Florida; Fort Worth and Houston, Texas; Charlotte and Winston-Salem, North Carolina; and Oklahoma City, Oklahoma. Groups such as the Chuck Wagon Gang, the Blackwood Brothers, the Statesmen, the Speer Family, the Happy Goodman Family, the Harmoneers, and Martha Carson helped make national reputations through these concerts. They also influenced new generations of southern performers, such as Elvis Presley and Jerry Lee Lewis.

Though the all-night singing fad had run its course by the mid-1960s, Fowler continued to work in the field by creating his own syndicated television show, "The Wally Fowler Show," a gospel music anthology that was seen on ninety-six stations. In the 1970s he produced live stage shows in Nashville and in Branson, Missouri. During the last years of his life, Fowler lived in Nashville; he died suddenly on a fishing trip to nearby Clay County. Though his methods and techniques caused some controversy in the gospel music community, nobody could deny that he was one of the music's first great promoters, and that he showed that gospel music could be a viable commercial product.

• An article fully devoted to Fowler is Wayne W. Daniel, "The All Night Singing Man," *Precious Memories: Journal of Gospel Music*, Sept./Oct. 1991, pp. 21–27. For background on the all-night sings, see Charles K. Wolfe, "Gospel Boogie," in *Folk Music and Modern Sound*, ed. William Ferris and Mary Hart (1982). Other materials are from the author's oral interviews with Wally Fowler, Connor Hall, Harold Timmons, Wayne Daniel, Harlan Daniel, Sharon Gold, Ottis Knippers, and James D. Walbert.

CHARLES K. WOLFE

FOWLER, William Alfred (9 Aug. 1911–14 Mar. 1995), physicist, was born in Pittsburgh, Pennsylvania, the son of John McLeod Fowler, an accountant, and Jennie Summers Watson. When Fowler was two, his family moved to Lima, Ohio, where he attended the public schools and graduated in 1929 at the top of his class from Lima Central High School. He then entered Ohio State University from which he received his bachelor's degree in engineering physics in 1933. That same year he began his graduate studies in physics at the California Institute of Technology, where he became a research assistant of Charles C. Lauritsen (1892–1968), who was the head of Caltech's High Voltage and Kellogg Radiation Laboratories. Fowler was awarded his Ph.D. in 1936; his dissertation, "Radioactive Elements of Low Atomic Number," was written under Lauritsen's direction.

For the rest of his life Fowler's career was to be inextricably identified with that of Lauritsen (until his retirement in 1962), and together they were to propel Caltech into an international center of excellence in nuclear physics. Indeed, like his mentor, Fowler spent his entire life at Caltech: as a research fellow (1936–1939); assistant professor (1939–1942); associate professor (1942–1946); professor (1946–1970), and finally as the first Institute Professor of Physics (1970–1982). During the war years, together with much of the Kellogg lab staff, he followed Lauritsen to Washington, D.C. (1940–1941), where at the National Bureau of Standards and the Carnegie Institution for Terrestrial Magnetism they made noteworthy contributions to the development of proximity fuses for bombs, shells, and ordnance rockets.

When the National Defense Research Committee authorized the setup of Caltech's rocket project in

1941, Fowler returned to Pasadena as assistant director of the project (1941–1944). When this was subsequently taken over by the U.S. Navy, he was involved in the establishment of the Naval Ordnance Test Station at Inyokern (now China Lake). In 1944 he served for three months in the South Pacific as a technical observer, and with other Caltech scientists worked at Los Alamos in fabricating components of the atomic bomb. Concurrent with his Caltech duties, Fowler was a Fulbright Lecturer and Guggenheim Fellow at the University of Cambridge (1954–1955, 1961–1962), and a visiting professor at the Massachusetts Institute of Technology in 1966.

Fowler's many honors included sharing the 1983 Nobel Prize in Physics with Subrahmanyan Chandrasekhar, for his theoretical and experimental studies of nuclear reactions, which were important in forming the chemical elements in the universe. His other awards include the Naval Ordnance Development Award (1945); the Presidential Medal of Merit (1948); the Lamme Medal (1952); the Liège Medal (1955); the Barnard Medal (1965); the Apollo Achievement Award (1969); the Tom Bonnor Prize (1970); the G. Unger Vetlesen Prize (1973); the National Medal of Science, presented by President Ford (1974); the Eddington Medal (1978); the Bruce Gold Medal (1979); the Sullivant Medal (1985); and the French Légion d'Honneur, presented by President Mitterand (1989). Fowler was also elected a member of the National Academy of Sciences in 1956, was president of the American Physical Society (1976), and was a member of numerous governmental advisory boards and committees.

Fowler's main research was a bold attempt to determine and understand the nuclear reactions occurring in the birth, evolution, and death of stars and other objects in the universe. Although much of this work was a team effort, he was the acknowledged leader of a new area of physics, nuclear astrophysics, which included theories of nuclear synthesis and nuclear cosmochronology. These studies had their modern origin in 1937–1939 with the independent proposals of Hans Bethe in the United States and Carl Friedrich von Weizsäcker in Germany of a mechanism for supplying the energy required to keep stars shining for billions of years. This was known as the C-N cycle of reactions, and it employed carbon and nitrogen as catalysts to transmute four protons into a helium nucleus, plus two positrons and two neutrinos. Somewhat later Bethe and Charles Critchfield suggested a proton-proton chain of reactions that would yield the same result starting from hydrogen alone.

The first nuclear reaction in the C-N cycle was investigated at Caltech in 1933 and led to an intensive study of nuclear reactions involving light nuclei since they offered the possibility of a quantitative test of the proposed energy production processes. This work was interrupted by the onset of the war, but after the war Fowler and his associates renewed their work and showed that stars having masses up to about 1.2 solar masses derive their main energy from the proton-pro-

ton chain rather than the C-N cycle. Further experiments considered reactions that build carbon and oxygen from helium nuclei produced in stellar cores. Early in 1953 Fred Hoyle, who was visiting Caltech, suggested that this mechanism would not be adequate to supply the observed abundance of carbon unless there was an excited state of carbon-12 that would serve as a resonance.

Within days Fowler and members of his group, led by Ward Whaling, experimentally found this state and in doing so established the general feasibility of building elements in stars. Subsequently, during his first visit to Cambridge, Fowler began his historic active collaboration with Hoyle and Geoffrey and Margaret Burbidge. This work culminated in their seminal paper, "Synthesis of Elements in Stars," *Reviews of Modern Physics* 29 (Oct. 1957): 547–650, which outlined a series of processes taking place in successive generations of stars that produce the observed abundances of elements and nuclides in the universe. This paper was to be a key contribution leading to his Nobel prize. Later developments by Hoyle and Fowler in 1960 included the now standard mechanisms for type I and type II supernovae, and this was reprinted in their book, *Nucleosynthesis in Massive Stars and Supernovae* (1965). In the same year they extended the previous work with the Burbidges to date the synthesis of elements from their abundances in the isotopes of the radioactive nuclei of uranium, thorium, and their other transuranic ancestors (see *Annals of Physics* 10 [June 1960]: 280–302). Fowler coined the term nuclear cosmochronology for this theory.

Finally, in joint work with Hoyle and Robert V. Wagoner (*Astrophysical Journal* 148 [Apr. 1967]: 3–49), Fowler studied the dynamics of the expansion of the universe—the so-called Big Bang—and its implications for nucleosynthesis. This latter work continued until 1988, with a variety of coauthors, and has led to a comprehensive basis for modern research in the nuclear physics of stellar evolution and nucleosynthesis. Fowler's book *Nuclear Astrophysics* (1967), which was based on the text of his 1965 Jayne Lectures for the American Philosophical Society, gives a lucid overview of his research, which anticipates some of his subsequent work on supermassive stars, quasars, extragalactic radio sources, and galactic explosions.

Fowler was not only a distinguished scientist whose work has significantly contributed to our understanding of the nuclear processes governing the structure of the universe, but he was a rare individual who inspired others with his infectious optimism and seemingly boundless energy. He was devoted to Caltech and took great pride in his students and coworkers, whose work he freely praised. Upon being notified of his Nobel Prize, he commented that he considered it to be an award to the Kellogg Radiation Lab, and not just to him. He was known worldwide as simply "Willy" and had an unforgettable zest for life that never failed to brighten the world around him. Two awards that pleased him most were those bestowed by his Caltech colleagues and students: a "National Meddler" medal in 1974 and in 1983 a t–shirt bearing the inscription "Nuclear Alchemist 1."

In August 1940 he married Ardianne Foy Omsted; they had two daughters. After her death in May 1988, he married Mary Dutcher in December 1989. He died in Pasadena.

• Fowler's papers are held by the Institute Archives at Caltech and include an oral biography. A brief autobiographical note and portrait is in "From Steam to Stars to the Early Universe," *Annual Review of Astronomy and Astrophysics* 30 (1992): 1–9. In December 1995 a three-day symposium on nuclear astrophysics was held at Caltech in his memory, and excerpts of tributes presented there are in "A Celebration of Willy Fowler," *Engineering and Science* 49, no. 2 (1995): 34–43. Of special interest is his seventieth birthday volume, *Essays in Nuclear Astrophysics presented to William A. Fowler* (1982), ed. Charles A. Barnes et al. This contains a list of Fowler's publications through 1981 and a delightful paper, "Two Decades of Collaboration with Willy Fowler" (pp. 1–9) by Fred Hoyle. Fowler's early account, "The Origin of the Elements," *Scientific American* 195 (Sept. 1956): 82–91, contains a survey suitable for the general reader. Obituaries are in *Physics Today* 47 (Sept. 1995): 116–118; *Nature* 374 (30 Mar. 1995): 406; and the *New York Times*, 16 Mar. 1995.

JOSEPH D. ZUND

FOX, Catherine (1836?–2 July 1892), **Margaret Fox** (1833?–8 Mar. 1893), and **Ann Leah Fox** (1818?–1 Nov. 1890), spirit mediums whose experiences inaugurated modern Spiritualism, were the daughters of John D. Fox and Margaret Rutan, struggling farmers. There is conflicting information about the birth dates of all three, but Leah was probably the oldest and Catherine ("Kate") the youngest. Kate and Margaret were born following a ten-year separation between their parents caused by John Fox's alcoholism.

The origins of modern Spiritualism, the popular religious movement based on the belief that communication with the spirits of the dead provides empirical proof of the immortality of the soul, date to 1848, when mysterious noises began to be heard in the modest, rented farmhouse inhabited by John and Margaret Fox and their six children in the village of Hydesville, thirty miles east of Rochester. Inexplicable raps on walls and furniture occurred only in the presence of Kate and Margaret, the family's two adolescent daughters. The apparent intelligence of the mysterious sounds convinced the family—and neighbors—that the raps were being made by the spirit of a murdered peddler who was buried in the basement. The residents of Hydesville crowded the house to hear the supposed spirit demonstrate its superhuman knowledge by sounding the correct number of raps when asked the age or number of their children. The Fox family soon deserted the house, sending Kate and Margaret to live with their older, now married, sister, Ann Leah Fish, a music teacher in Rochester.

Unaccountable spiritual tidings were not unusual in the 1840s in the revival-minded "burned-over district" of upstate New York, the birth place of Mormonism and Adventism as well as Spiritualism. While many residents dismissed the raps as a bid for attention by two deceptive youngsters, others greeted them as providing long-awaited empirical proof of life after death. Two groups in particular found momentous religious significance in the new manifestations. For the first, disillusioned former members of the Society of Friends, direct communication with spirits promised a return to the Quaker doctrine of obedience to the promptings of God within each individual soul. For the second, exponents of the Harmonial Philosophy, it suggested confirmation of the spiritual experiences of Emanuel Swedenborg, as related during mesmeric trances by the prophet Andrew Jackson Davis.

Within a few days of their arrival in Rochester, one of the sisters visited family friends Amy and Isaac Post, respected ex-Quaker reformers whose home served as a stop on the Underground Railroad. The Posts accepted that the raps were made by spirits and became the Fox sisters' mentors and confidants. They gathered a small group to meet weekly in search of the truth that might be revealed by communicating with the dead through the girls' mediumship, and they spread word of the mysterious noises through Quaker and abolitionist networks. Because the raps could only communicate in response to questions, the inquirers, rather than the mediums, set the agenda for the first spirit communications. Persistent and repeated questions produced raps indicating the presence of spirits other than the dead peddler, in particular, the spirits of dead relatives of those present. Communications consisting of whole sentences began after Leah also proved to be a medium. Investigators used sessions with the Fox sisters to pursue relief from the host of anxieties that accompany separation at death—and many of them found it. The hunger for communion with the dead gave Spiritualism its content, transforming what may have been a teenage prank into a new religion.

After a year of these private communications, it was decided—allegedly by the spirits themselves—that public demonstrations would be held. Corinthian Hall, the largest auditorium in Rochester, was rented for three nights. On 14 November 1849 four hundred witnesses—each paying 75¢ admission—filled the hall. Before the actual demonstration began, Eliab Capron, another ex-Quaker, addressed the assembly, explaining the spiritual dimensions of what the audience was about to hear. A committee of skeptics was appointed to investigate the proceedings and report back at the next demonstration. After the committee members announced at the second meeting that no trickery had been discerned at the first, the crowd became boisterous.

In June 1850 Eliab Capron convinced Margaret Rutan Fox to accompany him, with her three daughters, to New York City, where he would serve as manager for public demonstrations of the sisters' mediumship. Capron rented rooms at Barnum's Hotel and invited the public to witness the raps, three times a day, $1 per admission. The popularity of these séances was great enough to warrant holding private sittings for select audiences. Among the many well-known personalities who attended these more intimate gatherings, held in the home of a local clergyman, were author James Fenimore Cooper, historian George Bancroft, and poets William Cullen Bryant and Nathaniel Parker Willis. Perhaps the most notable supporter was newspaper publisher Horace Greeley, editor of the *New York Tribune*. George Ripley, Greeley's head editorial writer and founder of the communitarian experiment known as Brook Farm, also attended. A series of séances was held at Greeley's home, where his wife, Molly, attempted to communicate with their recently deceased five-year-old son. Convinced that the sisters were honest, Greeley assured the readers of his paper that the women were not perpetrating a fraud. Kate Fox even lived with the Greeleys throughout the fall of 1850, and the grieving family took much comfort from the presence of their dead child at her séances.

Over the next few years Kate and Margaret gave demonstrations in New York City, Buffalo, Pittsburgh, Philadelphia, Washington, D.C., and at various sites in Ohio. Kate's letters to Amy Post reported numerous seemingly miraculous occurrences, such as instruments being played, bells being rung, and furniture being moved—all reportedly accomplished by the spirits. Thousands of Americans became sincere believers. But such notoriety also had its down side. The sisters had to live among strangers and could make few decisions for themselves. The isolation and long separations from friends and family took their toll. As adults both Kate and Margaret battled alcoholism.

Back in New York City, Leah received inquiring visitors to her séance room. At this time Rochester was a center of abolitionist activities, and many leaders in the antislavery movement, having heard about the sisters, went to visit Leah and through her were converted to Spiritualism. America's most-famous abolitionist, William Lloyd Garrison, reported his session with Leah in his antislavery paper, the *Liberator* (3 Mar. 1854). Not surprisingly, the spirits with whom Garrison communicated were reform-minded; among them were the spirit of a recently deceased member of the Hutchinson family singers and that of an antislavery pioneer who, rapping out by the alphabet, assured those in attendance that Spiritualism would "work miracles in the cause of reform."

Social reformers were not the only ones intrigued by the sisters. Noted explorer Elisha Kent Kane began an intimate correspondence with Margaret and, before leaving on his second Arctic expedition in 1853, arranged for her support and education. After his death in 1857, Margaret claimed that they had been secretly married and that Kane had left her an annuity. Kane's family denied Margaret's account of the relationship but promised her a small stipend on the condition that she relinquish his letters. After they stopped making the promised payments, she quoted the letters in *The Love-Life of Dr. Kane* (1866). Margaret converted to Roman Catholicism, claiming that that had been Kane's wish, but occasionally still functioned as a medium.

According to her own account, Leah was married at the age of fourteen to a man named Fish who abandoned her after she bore three children. In 1851 she married Calvin Brown, a foster brother who believed he was on his deathbed and hoped that the respectability of his name would afford Leah and her family some protection after his death. He did not die until two years later. Leah's seven-year-old son, who lived with her brother David, died the following week. In 1858 she married Daniel Underhill, a wealthy Spiritualist and insurance salesman. After her third marriage she continued to give private sittings but ceased to use her mediumship for profit.

As other mediums began to use writing and speaking to relay communications from the spirits of the dead, the rapping noises relayed by the Fox sisters lost their appeal. Within a decade of the advent of the Hydesville rappings, only Kate remained in public life. On account of her persistent problems with alcohol, Spiritualist supporters sponsored her residence at Dr. George Henry Taylor's Swedish Movement Cure in New York City for several months in 1865. She remained there after that at the Taylors' expense, eating in the kitchen with the servants. In 1869, following the death of Taylor's three-year-old son, Kate began conducting séances at their establishment. During intermittent residences with the Taylors, she continued these séances from 1869 until her death. The sessions attracted author Harriet Beecher Stowe and her sisters Catharine Beecher and Isabella Beecher Hooker, the last an ardent Spiritualist who maintained a long relationship with Kate. In 1871 Kate left for England, where her mediumship was well received. The following year she married the Spiritualist barrister Henry D. Jencken, with whom she had two sons. Margaret, then struggling to abstain from alcohol, joined Kate in England in 1876, but Henry Jencken's death in 1881 ended the brief respite of stability for both sisters.

In 1885 they returned to New York, where recurrent alcohol abuse prevented Kate from supporting her family. In 1888, during the furor over a celebrated exposé of another medium, an agent of the Society for the Prevention of Cruelty to Children arrested Kate for drunkenness and for failing to send her sons to school. A few months later Margaret attempted to publicly expose Spiritualism as a fraud perpetrated by Leah, who she claimed had manipulated her younger sisters. While Kate sat in the audience, Margaret demonstrated how she had faked the raps by using her big-toe joint. The public appeal of the demonstration failed to live up to the expectations of its promoter, however. Spiritualists, who by that time had survived more serious challenges, attributed this one to the medium's drunkenness. In 1889 Margaret recanted, saying she had been tricked into the exposé. Kate also resumed holding regular séances. Leah died in New York City, as did Kate. Margaret died in Brooklyn.

Whatever the source of their unusual talents, the Fox sisters converted many influential people to a belief in spirit presence and provided solace for bereaved persons hoping to communicate with departed loved ones. Because believers never viewed the Fox sisters as spiritual authorities but rather as passive vehicles being used for communication by external intelligences, neither recantation nor dissolution undermined the sisters' historic role in the Spiritualist movement. The toe-joint theory propounded by Margaret and accepted by many skeptics could not account for other manifestations, especially Kate's automatic writings produced during the Taylor sittings, which eventually were published by Taylor's grandson, William George Langworthy Taylor. Their youth, their lack of education, and their femininity became a model for other mediums, but the Fox sisters participated very little in the movement initiated by their experiences. They rarely appeared at conventions, contributed to publications, or cooperated with those interested in promoting the cause. Even the faithful viewed Kate and Margaret as victims, interpreting both their alcoholism and their mediumship as expressions of their extreme sensitivity to external stimuli.

• The Amy and Isaac Post Family Papers in the University of Rochester Library, Department of Rare Books and Special Collections, contain letters from Kate and Margaret as well as copies of letters from Isaac Post describing the first séances in Rochester. For early accounts of the Hydesville rappings see Eliab W. Capron, *Singular Revelations: Explanation and History of the Mysterious Communion with Spirits* (1850); Adelbert Cronise, *The Beginnings of Modern Spiritualism in and near Rochester* (1925); and J. B. Campbell, *Pittsburgh and Allegheny Spirit Rappings* (1851). Robert Dale Owen described his investigation of Spiritualism with Leah and Kate during the 1860s in *The Debatable Land between This World and the Next* (1872). Leah provided her account of the history of the raps in *The Missing Link in Modern Spiritualism* (1885). Other primary sources include Owen, *Footfalls on the Boundary of Another World* (1860), and William George Langworthy Taylor, *Katie Fox: Epoch Making Medium and the Making of the Fox-Taylor Record* (1933). In addition to entries in the standard biographical reference works, see Ernest Isaacs, "A History of Nineteenth-Century American Spiritualism as a Religious and Social Movement" (Ph.D. diss., Univ. of Wisconsin, 1975). Other secondary accounts include R. Laurence Moore, *In Search of White Crows: Spiritualism, Parapsychology, and American Culture* (1977), and Ann Braude, *Radical Spirits: Spiritualism and Women's Rights in Nineteenth-Century America* (1989).

ANN D. BRAUDE

FOX, Della May (13 Oct. 1870–15 June 1913), comic opera star, was born in St. Louis, Missouri, the daughter of Andrew J. Fox, a leading St. Louis photographer, and Harriet Swett. Della made her first appearance on stage as the Midshipmite in a St. Louis production of *H. M. S. Pinafore* at the age of seven. Precocious and cute, Della came to the attention of Augustus Thomas and the Dickson Sketch Club while playing the part of Adrienne in *A Celebrated Case* (1880) with James O'Neill and Marie Prescott. Her first professional engagement was on tour with Thomas's group as Editha in the short comedy *Editha's Burglar*, a dramatization of the story by Frances Hodgson Burnett. From 1883 to 1885 she toured the Midwest and Canada with the company, chaperoned by Nellie

Page, its leading lady, and tutored by Thomas. Della also played small roles in *His Last Legs* and *Combustion*, in which she sang and performed a sand jig that Thomas described as "up to the standard of the time." Despite her parents' desire that she continue her education at boarding school, Della was determined to become an actress and during her teens played leading roles with the Comley Barton and the Bennet and Moulton opera companies.

"A petite blond but of little experience," according to George C. D. Odell, Fox made her first New York appearance at Niblo's Garden as Yvonne, "the girl whom everyone tries to make a boy," in *The King's Fool* (17 Feb. 1890). Later that year, she secured the role of Blanche opposite the tall comedian De Wolf Hopper in Gustav Kerker's comic opera, *Castles in the Air*. The show opened on 5 May at the Broadway Theatre in New York and propelled both Fox and Hopper to stardom.

Hopper's Opera Bouffe Company next produced *Wang* with Fox as Prince Mataya opposite Hopper's title role. The operatic burletta opened at the Broadway Theatre on 4 May 1891 for 151 performances before traveling in elegant George Wagner Palace Cars for its two-season national tour. *Wang* was one of the most successful extravaganzas of its day, enhanced by the shocking and titillating spectacle of Fox in tightly fitting male attire, puffing on a cigarette and singing in a delicate voice. Along with the "curl in the center of her forehead," Fox's risqué appearance became the signet by which she was recognized and imitated from Maine to the Pacific.

Fox appeared in a brief revival of *The Lady or the Tiger?* (17 Oct. 1892) at the Broadway Theatre before Hopper's next major production, *Panjandrum*, opened there on 1 May 1893. She played the role of Paquita opposite Hopper's Pedro in this musical fantasy by J. Cheever Goodwin and Woolson Morse, the authors of *Wang*.

Breaking from Hopper in 1894, Fox made her first appearance as the star of her own company in *The Little Trooper*, which opened at the Casino Theatre in New York on 30 August. The *New York Times* review of the following day commented, "She is a young woman who has gone ahead on the stage on small capital, but she has made it pay her large interest." Her second starring vehicle was *Fleur de Lis*, an "old-fashioned comic opera" that opened at Palmer's Theatre on 29 August 1895 with Fox "charming to look upon" in the title role and Jefferson de Angelis as Count des Escarrbilles. Both shows were revived in the fall of 1896.

In 1897 she shared star billing with Lillian Russell and de Angelis in *The Wedding Day*, which opened at the Casino Theatre on 8 April. In the role of Willie Everdrop/Margery Dazzle, Fox once again masqueraded as a man in *The Little Host*, which opened on 26 December 1898 at Herald Square Theatre and subsequently toured the continent and the Pacific Coast.

It was while on tour in Vermont with *The Little Host* that Fox was stricken with peritonitis and was forced to abandon the show. In the fall of 1899 Fox returned home to New York, where her condition worsened and rumors of her imminent death circulated. She returned to the stage a few months later, only to suffer a recurring nervous condition that would haunt her the rest of her life. She reappeared briefly in the Rogers brothers' burlesque, *Central Park*, before leaving New York to tour vaudeville houses. On 26 December 1901, she married Jacob David "Jack" Levy, a New York jewelry broker and theatrical business manager, in Baltimore, Maryland. She was not featured in New York again until 1904, when she appeared in the dual role of Lillie and Billie in *The West Point Cadet* (Princess Theatre). Aside from tours on the vaudeville stage between 1908 and 1911, and a triumphant appearance as the maid in a revival of *Rosedale* that "brought the audience to its feet" at the Lyric Theatre in 1912, Fox's chronic ill health never allowed her fully to regain the ability to perform or to recapture the daring image she one emblematized. She died in a private sanitorium in New York City and was buried at Bellefontaine Cemetery in St. Louis.

Despite the brevity of her professional career, Fox was a popular sensation across the country. According to de Angelis, "It was not unusual to see 50 or 100 women and girls waiting at the stage door as she left the theatre." Though her singing and acting talents were often dismissed by drama critics, she was one of the highest-paid stars of her day, who appealed to audiences through her bouncy personality and saucy roles. According to the *New York Magazine Program*, "she tried to come back. . . . The world and the times had changed. . . . The public was no longer impressed at the sight of a girl in boy's clothing, nor shocked at her smoking a cigarette."

• No papers are known to exist. The Billy Rose Theatre Collection at the New York Public Library for the Performing Arts, Lincoln Center, maintains a clipping file that contains reviews, interviews, stories, and photographs. Additional photos are in the Roy Day Collection, also at the New York Public Library for the Performing Arts. Fox's New York career can be traced through George C. D. Odell, *Annals of the New York Stage*, vols. 14–16 (1949), and T. Allston Brown, *A History of the New York Stage*, vol. 3 (1964), as well as reviews in the *New York Times*, *New York Herald*, *Dramatic Mirror*, *World*, and *Boston Folio*. For anecdotal information, see Augustus Thomas, *The Print of My Remembrance*; Lewis C. Strang, *Prima Donnas and Soubrettes* (1900); M. B. Leavitt, *Fifty Years in Theatrical Management* (1912); Jefferson de Angelis and Alvin F. Harlow, *A Vagabond Trooper* (1931); and De Wolf Hopper, *Once a Clown, Always a Clown* (1927). Cecil Smith, *Musical Comedy in America* (1950), and David Ewen, *The Complete Book of the American Musical Theatre* (1958), provide additional information about particular productions. An obituary appears in the *New York Times*, 17 June 1913.

SUSAN F. CLARK

FOX, Dixon Ryan (7 Dec. 1887–30 Jan. 1945), historian and college president, was born in Potsdam, New York, the son of James Sylvester Fox, a seller of Vermont marble, and Julia Anna Dixon. He was graduated from Potsdam Normal School in 1907 and received an A.B. degree from Columbia University in 1911. He became teacher and principal at the Union District School in Thornwood, New York, while also enrolled in the master's program at Columbia and tutoring in the Department of History.

In 1915 Fox married Marian Stickney Osgood, daughter of Columbia history professor Herbert L. Osgood. They had two sons. The Foxes became members of the Hitchcock Presbyterian Church in Scarsdale, New York. Fox received an A.M. degree from Columbia in 1912 and a Ph.D. in history in 1917. His doctoral dissertation was published in 1919 as *The Decline of Aristocracy in the Politics of New York*. By then he was an assistant professor of history, and in 1927—following the publication of *Caleb Heathcote, Gentleman Colonist*, a study of colonial religion and society—he was appointed full professor. His scholarly writings included *An Historical Atlas of the United States* (1920), *An Outline of Early American History* (1922), and *Herbert L. Osgood, an American Scholar* (1923). He also established himself as a leader in the study of American social history with *Aspects of Social History* (1931) and as coeditor, with Arthur M. Schlesinger, Sr., of the thirteen-volume *A History of American Life* series (1927–1948).

Despite his strong Columbia University ties and his scholarly productivity—which included some thirty articles in learned journals and scores of papers presented to historical societies—Fox resigned in 1934 to become president of Union College in Schenectady, New York. In response to colleague Charles Beard's letter asking why he wanted to become a college president, Fox replied that he could never make the intellectual contributions of a scholar like Beard but that he could make important educational contributions as a college president. In addition, the trustees of Columbia University had indicated that when President Nicholas Murray Butler stepped down, Fox would be their choice to succeed him, particularly if he had gained experience at Union.

A stimulating public speaker and raconteur, and a sincere advocate of students and colleagues, Fox had a particular talent for encouraging businesses to contribute to college programs. Despite the depression, he raised funds for construction of a library, a chapel, an engineering building, and dormitories. Believing that the only way to attract and hold the loyalty of able teacher-scholars was "to offer them security in a certain kind of life," he increased faculty salaries substantially. To capitalize on the growth of civil service opportunities, Fox established a government-apprentice system that enabled students to coordinate their studies with practical experience in state and federal jobs. He joined with actor Charles Coburn to establish a major drama festival at Union and also inaugurated a concert series. He even became something of a radio personality with a weekly broadcast on Schenectady station WGY.

During his years at Columbia and at Union College, Fox was also an active member of the New York State

Historical Association. Founded at Lake George, New York, in 1899, the association's primary program was an annual meeting, held at various sites around the state. Fox attended the 1918 meeting, which was held in New York City. He became a member and almost immediately suggested that the association, whose only publication was an annual *Proceedings*, publish a quarterly journal. The society responded by launching the *Quarterly Journal of the New York State Historical Association* in 1919 (the title was changed to *New York History* in 1932) and by making Fox a trustee. He became president in 1929 and held the position for the rest of his life. His tenure was marked by innovation, a fecundity of practical ideas, growing membership, and Fox's ability to attract a talented staff and financial support.

His choices for the directorship of the association during the years 1932–1945—Julian Boyd, Edward Alexander, and Clifford Lord—all moved on to positions of eminence in the fields of history, museums, and education. He attracted philanthropist Stephen C. Clark, Sr., to membership in the association in 1933; in 1938 Clark offered the society a headquarters in Cooperstown, New York, and the financial support of the Clark Foundation, thus stimulating the association's most expansive decades.

Equally important were Fox's ideas, expressed in published papers or in the "President's Page," which appeared in each issue of *New York History*. Fox offered information and suggestions that eventually led to the creation of the Farmer's Museum, the New York Folklore Society, the association's pioneering seminars on American culture, and state programs in historic preservation. With state historian Alexander C. Flick, he initiated the association's magisterial ten-volume *History of the State of New York* (1933–1937) and found the means to have it published by Columbia University Press when the original publisher was forced by the depression to quit. He also edited and found publishing support for the New York State Historical Association Series (1932–1939), an eight-volume set of scholarly monographs.

At the same time Fox continued his own research and writing, producing *Sources of Culture in the Middle West* (1934), *Yankees and Yorkers* (1940), and *The Completion of Independence, 1790–1830* (1944), coauthored with John A. Krout. He also published seventy-four articles and editorials in *New York History*. His *Union College, an Unfinished History* (1945) was published posthumously. Fox died in Schenectady.

Fox's outstanding quality was his versatility: his scholarly works are still being cited decades after his death; his students became leaders in several fields; and he left Union College, its trustees have said, at an intellectual and financial high point. But his presidency of the New York State Historical Association was the seat of his most enduring contributions. His effort to join amateur and professional historians in the association's programs addressed a recurrent concern of twentieth-century historians. In a eulogy to Fox, Julian Boyd emphasized Fox's successful effort "to bring together, through the magic of his own personality, the layman and the professional on a meeting ground of mutual respect," while the association itself, Boyd said, "remains one of his greatest monuments as a teacher."

• Fox's personal papers are in Schaffer Library at Union College and in Special Collections at the New York State Historical Association. The Schaffer collection contains letters, drafts of speeches, and other material relating to his Union College presidency; the latter contains letters relating to his years at Columbia and to his historical association activities, and the notes and drafts for articles and papers. The archives of the New York State Historical Association include a large number of Fox's letters, dating from 1918 to 1945, which provide detailed information about his activities while a trustee and president of the association. Trustee resolutions and other accounts of Fox at Union College are in a "Dixon Ryan Fox" folder at Schaffer Library. For assessments of Fox's life and work see Julian Boyd, "Dixon Ryan Fox (1887–1945)," *Year Book of the American Philosophical Society, 1946* (1946): 297–302; [Berne A. Pyrke], "Dixon Ryan Fox," *New York History* 26 (Apr. 1945): 129–35. Fox's role in publishing and finances is included in Wendell Tripp, "Fifty Years of *New York History*," *New York History* 50 (Oct. 1969): 355–96. Obituaries are in *Concordiensis: The Student Newspaper and Wartime Log of Union College*, 2 Feb. 1945; the *New York Times*, 1 Feb. 1945; and *New York History* 26 (Apr. 1945): 257–58.

WENDELL TRIPP

FOX, Fontaine Talbot, Jr. (4 June 1884–9 Aug. 1964), cartoonist, was born in Louisville, Kentucky, the son of Fontaine Talbot Fox, a judge and author, and Mary Pitkin Barton. He was educated in the public schools of Louisville and then became a reporter and a part-time cartoonist for the *Louisville Herald*. He began to satirize, by means of unpretentious but graphic little cartoons, Louisville's Brook Street trolley service for its inability to maintain a reliable schedule, especially in bad weather. The drawings were popular at once.

Fox enrolled at Indiana University, in Bloomington, some eighty miles northwest of Louisville, in 1904. Even while he was a student there, he continued to draw cartoons for the *Herald*. He provided one a day for $12 a week, sending them by late-night train and thus reinforcing his awareness of rail transportation. Cartooning gradually assumed more importance to him than maintaining a good grade average; so in 1906 he withdrew from the university to work full time as an artist for the *Herald*. After a year, he transferred to the *Louisville Times* (1907–1911) and then became a cartoonist for the *Chicago Post* (1911–1915). He married Edith Elizabeth Hinz in 1915; the couple had two children. From 1915 until he retired forty years later, Fox was an independent cartoonist.

Fox is almost exclusively known for his humorous comic strip "Toonerville Folks." At its inception in 1915, it was a daily gag cartoon; it grew within a year into a comic strip and was distributed by the Wheeler Syndicate until 1920. Its narrative line was along the route of the make-believe "Toonerville Trolley That Meets All the Trains." Its tracks ran from its most rural station through suburbs and into a metropolis. It drew electrical current from an overhead wire along a twisted pole. Fox modeled his weird little trolley after lackadaisical streetcars not only on the Brook Street line in Louisville but also on Pelham Trolley Manor Line in Pelham, New York; Fox and his wife had ridden a Pelham Manor trolley car when they visited a fellow cartoonist there. In the days before radio and television soap operas, Fox's readers followed his ingeniously limned characters with an almost breathless interest. Members of his dramatis personae are neither rural nor urban but come from a kind of commuting circle. They include the Terrible Tempered Mr. Bang, said to be a dead ringer for Fox's father; Aunt Eppie Hogg, the most corpulent woman in three counties; Powerful Katrinka, a composite of two Fox family cooks, one strong and the other dumb, and so muscular that when necessary she can hoist the derailed trolley back onto its tracks by herself; a cigar-smoking dwarf, who was Katrinka's boyfriend; Flem Proddy, the inventor; Suitcase Simpson; the rickety, bouncing trolley's unnamed skipper; Tomboy Taylor; the Toonerville Cop; and Cy Wortle, who owned a laughing cow. Of special interest was another character, Mickey (Himself) McGuire, a feisty little runt who was the terror of the Scorpions' Club. He proved to be such a hit with Fox's clientele that Joe Ninian Yule, Jr., a child actor, called himself Mickey (Himself) McGuire and starred under that name from 1927 to 1934 in sixty-three two-reel movies. Fox took him to court and proved that since he owned the copyright on the character and his popular name, little Joe Yule must stop infringing. Yule thereafter called himself Mickey Rooney and became a famous actor.

In 1920 Fox moved with his family to Port Washington, on Long Island, New York, and worked in New York City. From that year until 1925 his Toonerville strip was distributed by the McNaught Syndicate. In 1926 Fox and his family moved to Roslyn Heights, still on Long Island, and he had an office in nearby Manhasset. Thereafter, his strip was distributed by the Bell Syndicate (1926–1942), McNaught again (1942–1949), and Bell again (until 1955). Meanwhile, the Foxes moved in 1940 to Greenwich, Connecticut.

The Toonerville comic strip enjoyed its greatest popularity in the 1920s and 1930s. It was so popular, in fact, that although trolleys in Louisville and Pelham were responsible, other cities actually advertised that their trolleys had inspired Fox's work. Miniature Toonerville trolleys were manufactured and sold as children's toys. In its heyday, the strip was syndicated in about 250 daily newspapers and was read by millions. When the Pelham trolley was replaced by a bus in 1937, 1,000 persons calling themselves pallbearers turned out to witness its final run. A similar mock ceremony occurred in 1950 when Westchester County's New Rochelle trolley was replaced by a bus. In 1953, in an attempt to revive diminished popularity, Fox drew his trolley getting smashed in an accident and replaced it with a bus. But his effort did not succeed with the public; so a few months later he had his skipper merrily running a vehicle made from salvaged parts of his old trolley's upper section atop the lower half of a bus. Soon thereafter Fox restored his same old trolley on its same old tracks—thus preparing it, as he explained, for its final journey. He retired in 1955.

Fox published *F. Fox's Funny Folk* (1917), *Cartoons, Second Book* (1918), and *Toonerville Trolley, and Other Cartoons* (1921). It has been estimated that by 1964 his cartoons had earned him in excess of $2 million. It is of incidental interest that in 1939 Fox was sent to the European theater of World War II and wrote a few humorous articles for the *New York Sun* concerning his escape from difficulties there. Once the United States entered the war he was active in the Division of Pictorial Publicity for the War Department. He was a member of the Society of Illustrators, the Authors' League of America, and several social and athletic clubs in the New York area, including the North Hempstead Country Club and the West Side Tennis Club. He won the Artists and Writers Golf Association title in 1934. Fox died in Greenwich, Connecticut.

• Minor Fox correspondence is in the Albert Charles Kiler Papers in the University of Illinois archives. A posthumously assembled collection of Fox's work is *Toonerville Folks* (1973). Everette E. Dennis and Melvin L. Dennis, "One Hundred Years of Political Cartooning," *Journalism History* 1 (Spring 1974): 6–10, cogently discuss American cartooning. William Murrell, *A History of American Graphic Humor (1865–1938)* (1938, repr. 1967), and Stephen Becker, *Comic Art in America: A Social History of the Funnies, the Political Cartoons, Magazine Humor, Sporting Cartoons and Animated Cartoons* (1959), praise Fox highly and place him in the context of comic-strip artists of the 1920s. Yolanda M. Simonelli, "America's Favorite Trolley," *Antiques & Collecting Magazine* 100 (June 1995): 38–43, discusses real trolley lines that inspired the popular Toonerville Trolley. In his autobiography *Life Is Too Short* (1991), Mickey Rooney discusses his use of the name Mickey (Himself) McGuire but makes light of the lawsuit. An obituary of Fox, with two illustrations, is in the *New York Times*, 10 Aug. 1964.

ROBERT L. GALE

FOX, George Washington Lafayette (3 July 1825–24 Oct. 1877), actor and pantomimist, was born in Boston, Massachusetts, the son of George Howe Fox, a stage carpenter at the Tremont Theatre, and Emily Cecilia Wyatt. "Laff," as the boy was known, and his four younger siblings were employed as child actors at the Tremont, National, and Federal theaters. Sources indicate that Laff's debut occurred at age five in William Dimond's *The Hunter of the Alps* during a benefit performance for Charles Kean, but Fox's name first appears in a playbill on 19 September 1832, where he is listed as Theodore in Henry Milner's *102, or The Veteran and his Progeny*. Evicted from their lodgings in the Federal Theatre in 1835, the Fox family joined Canadian-born actor George C. Howard on a tour of New England as "The Little Foxes," performing variety entertainments. Their domestic respectability and repertoire of such moral dramas as *The Drunkard* and *The Gambler* made them welcome in towns where the theater was usually considered the devil's chapel.

Fox picked up the rudiments of literacy at the Mayhew School but left school in 1838 to work as an errand boy at a department store and then as a clerk for the merchant-tailor Charles A. Smith, whom he served for about seven years. In 1845 Fox wed Caroline Gould; they had one child. In 1846 Fox left his clerking to reenter the family troupe, by then known as "Mr. Howard and the Foxes and the Company." The company took over Cleveland Hall in Providence, Rhode Island, where it played stock drama until 1850. After the company's star, James Fox, retired to attend law school in 1848, George Fox, who earlier had been relegated to minor comic roles, began to shine as an actor, especially in burlesques of Shakespeare and Sheridan. After a short and unpleasant stint in Worcester, Massachusetts, the company moved to Troy, New York.

Fox then accepted an engagement at the National Theatre on Chatham Street in New York City's Bowery, a proletarian playhouse where his funny antics rapidly gained the approval of the newsboy and bootblack component of the audience. Billed as Lafayette Fox, he made his debut at the National on 25 November 1850, and since Charles Burke had resigned the previous week, Fox was promoted to leading low comedian. His prominence was ensured when he imported his family from Troy to perform the adaptation of *Uncle Tom's Cabin* made by their cousin George Aiken. Opening at the National on 18 July 1853, the play enjoyed phenomenal success, running for 325 consecutive performances. Fox consolidated his success by following *Uncle Tom's Cabin* with burlesques and fairy tale extravaganzas, imitating the Franco-Italian mime troupe the Ravels. Fox shone as a physical comedian, less for his acrobatics and magic tricks than for his violent slapstick and expressive grimaces. During this period he also began a liaison with Fanny Herring, often his leading lady.

In partnership with English-born actor James W. Lingard, Fox took over and refurbished the Bowery Theatre in 1858; the following year the partners opened the New Bowery Theatre. Fox earned a reputation as an astute but coarse-grained manager. Despite productions of legitimate drama at the New Bowery (Fox was sued for pirating Boucicault's *The Octoroon* from the Winter Garden Theatre), the most popular genre was pantomime. Fox excelled as a clown and was considered "exceedingly quaint, and humorous, though scarcely ever smiling, and not once indulging in speech" (28 Mar. 1861 diary entry by Emilie Cowell, wife of English music hall singer Samuel Cowell, reprinted in *The Cowells in America*, ed. Maurice Willson Disher [1934]).

The outbreak of the Civil War led to Fox's joining the Eighth State Militia Infantry as a lieutenant and serving at the first battle of Manassas. Mustered out in August 1861, he returned to the New Bowery. Dissolving his partnership with Lingard in 1862, proba-

bly due to arguments over repertory, Fox reopened Wallack's Lyceum Theatre on Broome Street as G. L. Fox's Olympic Theatre but failed to attract an eastside audience. He returned to the Old Bowery, which was then under the management of G. C. Howard, and produced a series of lucrative pantomimes, *Jack and the Beanstalk* (1863), *The House That Jack Built* (1864), *Old Dame Trot and Her Comical Cat* (1865), *Jack and Gill Went Up the Hill* (1865–1866), and *Little Boy Blue and Hush-a-Bye Baby* (1867), whose profits were poured back into ever more lavish trickwork and stage effects. His lack of business acumen caused him to lose a fortune.

Unable to continue management, he allowed P. T. Barnum to transfer *Jack and Gill* to his Museum on Broadway, thus introducing Fox and his comedy to a more upscale, respectable audience. By this time, Fox was coming to be known, in John Oxenford's phrase, as the Grimaldi of America, referring to Joseph Grimaldi (1778–1837), an English clown who developed the role to be the leading feature of Regency pantomime and whose name, "Joey," became the generic term for a clown. Fox signed on as stage manager of the Olympic Theatre in September 1867 and staged a lavish *Midsummer Night's Dream*, with himself as Bottom. As part of his innovative advertising scheme, he had HAVE YOU SEEN FOX'S BOTTOM? painted all over New York's curbs and fences.

The pinnacle of Fox's success was *Humpty Dumpty* by Clifton W. Tayleure, which opened at the Olympic Theatre on 10 March 1868. It was the first time a pantomime had filled an entire bill in a Broadway playhouse, and the production was packed with in-jokes about New York politics and social life, and scenes of extravagant violence. The brick fight between Humpty, (played by Fox) and Old One-Two became legendary and may have later influenced George Herriman's *Krazy Kat*. Despite occasional complaints of vulgarity, *Humpty Dumpty* throve and eventually chalked up a record of 1,286 performances. Fox's first wife died in Providence on 30 September 1868, and less than three weeks later he married Mattie Temple, a ballet girl in the *Humpty Dumpty* cast, who soon gave birth to a daughter.

Over the next seven years, Fox played his clown character in variants of the original *Humpty Dumpty: The Second Volume (Bound to Please) of Humpty Dumpty* (1869), *Hiccory Diccory Dock* (1869), *Wee Willie Winkie* (1870), and *Humpty Dumpty Abroad* (1873). Gradually, however, interpolated variety acts, grandiose spectacle, and elaborate ballets eclipsed Fox's comic ingenuity. In 1870–1871 he was seen in a series of burlesques of tragedy: a *Hamlet* that parodied Edwin Booth and Charles Fechter, *Macbeth*, and *The Richelieu of the Period*. These ventures were not great box office hits, and in 1871 Fox, never an astute businessman, found himself a mere company member at the Olympic, working for Augustin Daly in a wide variety of plays that rarely capitalized on his peculiar talents.

Mistakenly confident of his financial acumen, and deceived by some shifty operators, Fox opened G. L. Fox's Broadway Theatre in 1874 to present *Humpty Dumpty at Home*. The enterprise quickly failed, however, and Fox was constrained to embark on a grueling tour of 400 performances of *Humpty* in twenty-six states and territories over the course of fourteen months. The tour enabled Fox to pay off his debts, but it undermined his health, and when he reopened the production at Booth's Theatre in Manhattan for a limited run of nine weeks, the strain soon showed. His behavior both on and off stage became erratic and violent, and he had to be replaced by a double in some scenes. On 27 November 1875, after pelting the occupants of a private box with a volley of bread, he was taken by relatives to Somerville, Massachusetts, where he was admitted to McLean's private asylum and declared legally insane.

Overexertion and financial worries played a role in Fox's insanity, possibly exacerbating syphilitic paresis, and rumors suggested that poison from the lead in his white clown makeup had weakened his mind. To the indignation of the Fox-Howard clan, who had never acknowledged Fox's second wife, Mattie Fox made public appeals for funds, and in September 1876 she had Fox released to live in her custody in Brooklyn. There he laid plans for a stupendous *Humpty Dumpty in Switzerland* that was to feature 400 rare songbirds, but in April 1877 he suffered a paralytic stroke and was returned to the asylum, where another stroke occurred in July. He was transferred to G. C. Howard's house in Cambridge, where he died.

"Old men have informed me that Fox was incontestably the funniest entertainer they ever saw," wrote the historian George C. D. Odell in his *Annals of the New York Stage*. Fox's distinction lay in the transformation of pantomime from a peripheral foreign import to a native genre of high quality and topical relevance, making it a relatively accurate mirror of the values and concerns of his audience. The physical violence and earthy ruthlessness of his comedy embodied the conflicts rampant in growing cities, but the unpleasantness was neutralized and rendered safely absurd by his comedy. "Humpty Dumpty" became a generic term for all such shows, and the image of Fox in the clown role entered folk iconography. As cigar box label, cigar store effigy, playing card joker, or baking powder advertisement, Humpty Dumpty distilled into one striking image the disarming innocence and the violent impetuosity of nineteenth-century America.

• The Howard family papers, collected by George P. Howard, are in the Hoblitzelle Theatre Collection, Humanities Research Center, University of Texas at Austin; however, a large number of Fox-Howard papers remain in private hands. Pantomime scripts and property lists of Fox's are in the McCaddon Collection at the Princeton University Library. The Harvard Theatre Collection contains Fox's promptbook for *The Irishman in Baghdad* (anonymous), some of his early playtexts, and account books for the Old Bowery and Tremont theaters. Laurence Senelick, *The Age and Stage of George L. Fox 1825–1877* (1988), is the only full-length study of the actor and contains a compendious bibliography. Obituaries are in the *New York Times*, 25 Oct. 1877, and the New York *Clipper*, 3 Nov. 1877.

LAURENCE SENELICK

FOX, Gustavus Vasa (13 June 1821–29 Oct. 1883), naval officer, assistant secretary of the navy, and business executive, was born in Saugus, Massachusetts, the son of Jesse Fox, a physician, inventor, and manufacturer, and Olivia Flint. Growing up in Lowell, Fox developed an "unconquerable desire" (Jesse Fox to Caleb Cushing, 5 Dec. 1837, Caleb Cushing Papers, Library of Congress) to be a naval officer, but his parents wanted him to become a minister or a lawyer. Beginning in April 1836 Fox studied at Phillips Academy in Andover for one year and then read law for the remainder of 1837 with Isaac O. Barnes before his parents at last supported his quest for a midshipman's commission. For that Fox had the necessary political connections: his father was a zealous Whig who had just been elected to the state legislature, and Barnes, a power in Massachusetts Democratic politics, was the brother-in-law of Secretary of the Treasury Levi Woodbury. On 12 January 1838 Fox, a sturdy sixteen-year-old, was appointed acting midshipman and ordered to the sloop of war *Cyane*.

Since the navy promoted only by seniority, Fox did not become a lieutenant until 1852. He had cruised the Mediterranean, had been stationed off West Africa and in the East Indies, had gone on the second expedition up the Tabasco (Grijalva) River in the Mexican War, and had participated in the U.S. Coast Survey. Anxious to study steam navigation, Fox was on detached service from 1851 to 1855, when he served as first officer and then commanded large mail passenger steamers, hobnobbing with business and political leaders on voyages to Liverpool and Panama. He then took a year's furlough and in 1856 resigned his naval commission.

For years Fox had been in love with Barnes's niece, Virginia Lafayette Woodbury, who refused to marry him unless he stayed on shore. Fox capitulated, and after he signed a wedding contract that enabled Virginia to retain her property, they married in 1855. Their childless marriage was happy despite Virginia's chronic ill health, for Fox, who possessed boundless energy, catered cheerfully to her needs. On land he started a new and successful career as "agent"—in effect plant manager—of the Bay State Mills at Lawrence, Massachusetts. As a captain he had commanded large numbers of men and administered a complex operation, and as his father's son he was no stranger to textile machines or mills. In June 1860, however, Fox resigned his position and, after a vacation, was casting about for a new job when the election of Abraham Lincoln to the presidency led to the secession of the Lower South.

Although Fox was a Democrat with little interest in the slavery issue, he was outraged by secession. He was a patriotic nationalist who believed it was the manifest destiny of the United States to expand, not to disintegrate. After South Carolina fired on the *Star of the West* and prevented the reinforcement of Fort Sumter in Charleston's harbor, Fox, as a civilian, planned an expedition for that fort's relief. Through his wife's brother-in-law, Montgomery Blair, the new postmaster general, Fox met Lincoln, who adopted his plan. As the expedition approached Charleston, the Confederacy attacked Sumter, but stormy weather and absent vessels prevented Fox from provisioning Sumter before it surrendered. He was chagrined, but Lincoln assured him that above all others he would select him for a similar "daring and dangerous enterprize" (Roy P. Basler, ed., *The Collected Works of Abraham Lincoln*, vol. 4 [1953–1955], p. 351).

On 8 May 1861 Lincoln urged that Fox, "a live man, whose services we cannot well dispense with" (Basler, vol. 4, p. 363), be given the crucial task of assisting Secretary of the Navy Gideon Welles. Initially as chief clerk and then as assistant secretary, Fox was the de facto chief of naval operations during the Civil War, eclipsing during his tenure the entrenched power and autonomy of the Navy Department bureaus. To blockade the Confederacy, the Union navy had to buy and arm or build sturdy, fast, shallow-draft vessels, and to supply and repair them, it had to capture (with army support) bases near southern ports. With his naval, merchant marine, and political connections, Fox was tailored for this work. He had the confidence of line officers, shipping magnates, and politicians, especially Lincoln and Senator James W. Grimes of the Committee on Naval Affairs. Personable and a lover of food and cigars, Fox was a boon dinner companion who could explain political imperatives to commanders and the navy's needs and limitations to politicians. Brimming with self-confidence, energy, and enthusiasm, he despised "old fogyism" and embraced innovative weapons and ships. He was decisive, but his seemingly impulsive faith in and enthusiasm for men and machines, strategies and tactics came only after reading pertinent articles, consulting specialists, conducting tests, and evaluating accomplishments.

Following the advice of Alexander Dallas Bache, superintendent of the Coast Survey, Fox successfully urged that Welles appoint a Blockade Strategy Board. Experts on this board came from the navy, Coast Survey, and Army Corps of Engineers, and its reports in the summer of 1861 guided Fox and Welles. To secure able and energetic commanders of expeditions and blockading squadrons, Fox, with an intimate firsthand knowledge of most naval officers and a secondhand acquaintance with the remainder, ignored the seniority system. He was guided by his extensive private correspondence with line officers, who conveyed to him how ships and guns, tactics and strategies were faring. From the start of the war, Fox advocated the construction of armored vessels to withstand shell fire, and by early 1862 three ironclads were under construction. Fortunately, John Ericsson's unique *Monitor*, with its low profile and its revolving turret, was completed in time to challenge the Confederate *Virginia* for the control of Hampton Roads, at the mouth of Chesapeake

Bay with access to Norfolk, Richmond, Washington, and Baltimore. Fox witnessed their engagement on 9 March 1862, and his consequent enthusiasm for monitors (although they were despised by many naval officers) armed with huge, fifteen-inch guns (developed at his insistence) accounts for their extensive use. Keeping up with the latest metallurgical developments, he hoped to construct monitors with Bessemer steel, but he was dissuaded by Abram S. Hewitt, who was planning to produce open-hearth steel for guns but not for armor plate. In planning and coordinating expeditions, Fox deserves much of the credit for the navy's successes at Hatteras, Port Royal, New Orleans, Mobile Bay, and Fort Fisher but also the blame for squandering naval resources in an obsessive attempt to capture Charleston. "The Fall of Charleston," he declared, "is the fall of Satan's Kingdom" (Thompson and Wainwright, eds., vol. 1, p. 128). By confusing symbolism with reality, Fox clouded his judgment. Assaults on Charleston's defenses revealed that he had exaggerated the power and invulnerability of the monitors and the capacity of the navy to succeed without army support. On the whole Fox learned from his mistakes and worked effectively with Welles. More than anyone else, Fox was responsible for the navy's success in the Civil War.

With peace, Fox crossed the Atlantic in a monitor (to advertise its virtues) on an 1866 mission to congratulate Czar Alexander II for escaping an attempted assassination. Upon his return, Fox resigned from the Navy Department and attempted unsuccessfully in 1867 and 1868 to take over the Southwest Pacific Railroad, the forerunner of the St. Louis–San Francisco. The next year he returned to textile manufacturing in Lowell, managing the Middlesex Mills, which his father had helped develop when Fox was an infant. In 1874 he moved to Boston and commuted to Lawrence, where he managed the Washington Mills for Mudge, Sawyer & Company. Four years later he retired to devote himself to his wife and nieces and nephews as well as to travel; to study, especially Christopher Columbus's landfall; and to reviewing the war with friends. He died in New York City.

• The voluminous Fox papers, the best unofficial source for the history of the Union navy, are in the New-York Historical Society. A generous selection of these letters have been published in Robert Means Thompson and Richard Wainwright, eds., *Confidential Correspondence of Gustavus Vasa Fox, Assistant Secretary of the Navy, 1861–1865* (2 vols., 1918–1919). See also the reactions to Fox in Howard K. Beale, ed., *Diary of Gideon Welles* (3 vols., 1960), and John D. Hayes, ed., *Samuel Francis Du Pont: A Selection from His Civil War Letters* (3 vols., 1969). William J. Sullivan, "Gustavus Vasa Fox and Naval Administration, 1861–1866" (Ph.D. diss., Catholic Univ. of America, 1977), also adds information about Fox before and after his service in the Navy Department. For a critical evaluation, see John D. Hayes, "Captain Fox—*He is the Navy Department*," *United States Naval Institute Proceedings* 91 (Sept. 1965): 64–71. For Fox's connection with the first shot in the Civil War, see Ari Hoogenboom, "Gustavus Fox and the Relief of Fort Sumter," *Civil War History* 9

(1963): 383–98; and for his role in planning joint expeditions, see Rowena Reed, *Combined Operations in the Civil War* (1978). An obituary is in the *New York Times*, 30 Oct. 1883.

ARI HOOGENBOOM

FOX, Harry (29 Sept. 1826–4 Sept. 1883), contractor, was born in Westfield, Massachusetts, the son of Hiram Fox, a mechanic (mother unknown). Little is known of his early life. Fox demonstrated his mechanical ability as a youth and, following his eighteenth birthday, was apprenticed to a machinist in Westfield. In 1846 he was sent to work dredging on the Northern New Hampshire Railroad, taking with him one of the first steam excavators. Fox's facility with the machine caused the railroad to use him as excavator operator rather than for shop work; his reputation grew. Over the next ten years, he performed similar work for several railroads, the last being the Grand Trunk Railway of Canada. He married Emeline Buxton Chamberlain, a daughter of Colonel M. Chamberlain of Newberry, Vermont, in 1852. The couple had two children.

Fox arrived in Chicago in 1856, shortly after the city had determined to raise its grade as part of sewer construction. The Illinois legislature empowered sewage commissioners to plan a coordinated sewage-and-drainage system and to install sewers in the most densely settled areas of Chicago. The plan, designed by E. S. Chesbrough, called for an intercepting combined sewer system that emptied into the Chicago River. Drainage was to be accomplished by gravity, but Chicago's flatness created problems. These were resolved by the simple, but costly, expedient of having the city raise its level. Chicago became the first North American city to construct a comprehensive sewer system.

Fox had brought a steam dredge with him and, shortly after arriving in Chicago, became partners with John P. Chapin, the mayor of the city, in a venture that was to dredge the Chicago River as part of the sewer project. The river channel had to become wider and deeper to accommodate the sewer outfall. According to the contract, the dredged earth was to be dumped into Lake Michigan, but Fox noticed that it was needed for fill around the new sewers. As construction progressed away from the river, the sewers were laid at the level necessary to accomplish gravity flow. New streets were constructed above the sewers, and Chicago became a city on two levels until the older buildings were raised higher or destroyed.

In 1860 Fox dissolved the partnership with Chapin and entered a new one with bridge and railroad builder William B. Howard, also a native of Massachusetts. Howard and his former partner, Newton Chapin, had constructed a wooden bridge across the Chicago River at Van Buren Street and were under contract to construct a railroad in Alabama when the Civil War began. After Alabama repudiated its promise to issue construction bonds, the work ceased, and Howard returned to Chicago. The firm of Fox & Howard constructed almost all of the twelve bridges that crossed

the Chicago River and did the vast majority of the city's dredging. As part of its river work, the firm straightened the banks of the north and south branches, as well as the main channel, and lined them with long rows of piling, creating dock lines along approximately fifteen miles of the river.

In these years, the river flowed east through the city and then turned south just before emptying into the lake. Sand, pushed by lake currents, created a bar at the river's mouth each year. The firm dredged a straight channel out into the lake, which came to be known as the north passage. The north pier was then extended out into the lake, into deeper water.

Inevitably the river became polluted, and the pollution spread into the lake until it reached the water-supply intake. In 1865 Chicago officials decided to reduce the summit level of the Illinois and Michigan Canal (which connected the Illinois and Chicago rivers) below the lake level. They hoped this would draw a sufficient quantity of lake water through the Chicago River to create a purifying current and to keep much of the sewage from the water-supply intake. The canal was to be deepened over the 26-mile stretch between Bridgeport and Lockport, and the dredging work was assigned to the firm of Fox & Howard. These new works, completed in 1871, reversed the flow of the river and transformed the Illinois and Michigan Canal into an open sewer.

Fox & Howard did not limit themselves to the Chicago area. Their dredges were employed at several other Lake Michigan ports; their railroad bridges could be found crossing the Illinois River at Pekin, Illinois, and the Fox River at Green Bay, Wisconsin. The town of Cairo, Illinois, located on a flat plain at the conjunction of the Ohio and Mississippi rivers hired the firm to bring its streets up to grade.

The Chicago fire of 1871 was extremely costly to the firm. It lost all its property, including the plant and docks, but it was quickly able to borrow the necessary funds to rebuild. The Howard partnership lasted until 1875. Afterward, Fox was associated with the firm of Fitz-Simons & Connell. Fox also was associated with the extension of the Chicago & Northwestern Railroad to Baraboo, Wisconsin, and with that of the Atchison, Topeka, and Santa Fe Railroad to the Grand Canyon of the Arkansas River in Colorado.

Harry Fox died of apoplexy in a Salt Lake City hotel en route back to Chicago from a pleasure trip to the West Coast. The Chicago *Tribune* obituary describes Fox as strong and as "an earnest man in his work and his friendships. He was companionable and generous." He understood each of his company's operations and always kept the promises he made. His skills were critical at a crucial time in Chicago's development; the straightened, reversed Chicago River still testifies to his contribution.

• The major source of information on Fox is an essay in *Biographical Sketches of the Leading Men of Chicago, Written by the Best Talent in the Northwest* (1868). Obituaries are in the Chicago *Tribune* and *Daily News*, 5 Sept. 1883, and in the Chicago *Times* on the following day.

LOUIS P. CAIN

FOX, John, Jr. (16 Dec. 1862 or 1863–8 July 1919), novelist, was born John William Fox, Jr., at Stony Point, Bourbon County, Kentucky, the son of John W. Fox, Sr., a schoolmaster, and his second wife, Minerva Carr. John Fox, Sr.'s first wife died in childbirth, leaving him three sons, but he soon wed again, and John was the first child of the second union; four more boys and two girls followed. The family was happy, closely knit, and socially prominent, living in the bluegrass section of Kentucky. Fox had an excellent education: he attended his father's school, Stony Point Academy, from 1867 to 1875; he was tutored in the classics by his half-brother James; he attended Transylvania University from 1878 to 1880; he was a student at Harvard from 1880 to 1883, graduating cum laude; and he attended Columbia University Law School for a few months in the latter part of 1883.

Fox had early experience as a journalist, working for the *New York Sun* in 1883 and the *New York Times* in 1884 on an assignment basis. In 1886, he was at Jellico, Kentucky, in mining engineering operations. Later, in 1889, he joined his half-brother James and his brother Horace in Big Stone Gap, Virginia, in the real estate business. This town, which had great mining possibilities, was being designated as a possible "Pittsburgh of the South." But the vast amount of money being poured into the town brought with it unpleasant elements: the sound of gunfire at night, occasional killings, widespread alcohol abuse, and family feuds. Fox joined the Home Guard, a local vigilante group and volunteer police force, which attempted to bring order to the area. John Fox, Sr., moved with the other members of the family to Big Stone Gap in 1890 and built the Fox home, which became the novelist's permanent residence during his lifetime.

Fox's first story, "A Mountain Europa," published serially in *Century* magazine in 1892, established a theme he was to use frequently: the conflict of mountaineer society with the culture of the outside world. In the story, a sophisticated outsider comes to the mountains because of new opportunities for exploiting the mineral-rich land. He falls in love with an innocent mountain girl, and they marry. But at the wedding celebration, the girl's father, who hates all "furriners," shoots at his new son-in-law, fatally wounding his own daughter. The story was so popular that Fox soon completed another, "A Cumberland Vendetta" (appearing serially in *Century* in 1894), based on an actual mountain feud that had taken place in Harlan County, Kentucky.

In the 1890s Fox went on the lyceum circuit, reading from his own works and the works of others, often in mountain dialect. In 1894 Theodore Roosevelt (1858–1919) heard one of Fox's performances. After Roosevelt became president, he invited Fox to the White House to read his stories. Fox delighted the audience by singing mountain songs as well, accompanying himself on the guitar. He was invited back to the White House on several other occasions. In 1899 Fox was elected to membership in the National Institute of Arts and Letters.

In 1898 Fox went to Cuba as a correspondent for *Harper's Weekly* during the Spanish-American War. In 1904 he traveled as a correspondent for *Scribner's* to Japan and Manchuria to report on the Russo-Japanese War, but government officials shielded him from combat.

Fox wrote two best-sellers: *The Little Shepherd of Kingdom Come* (1903) and *The Trail of the Lonesome Pine* (1908). The first of these focuses on the life of Chad Buford, a humble mountain man who thinks he is illegitimate. After working for a while as a shepherd in the valley of Kingdom Come Creek in the Cumberland Mountains, he visits the bluegrass country and discovers that he is related to the prominent Major Calvin Buford. In the latter part of the novel, Chad debates whether to join the Confederate or the Union forces during the Civil War; he finally decides to join the Union and proves to be a brave and honorable soldier. This novel enjoyed unusual popularity with old and young readers alike. It had a first edition of 30,000 copies and was reprinted frequently, becoming one of the first novels in the United States to sell a million copies. Fox said he was rescued from all his debts by "a shepherd's crook."

The Trail of the Lonesome Pine was even more popular, selling in advance 100,000 copies of the first edition. Numerous later editions appeared, and the total sales have reached two million. It too has been read and enjoyed by many juveniles as well as adults. In this novel, an engineer from the "outside world," Jack Hale, falls in love with a naïve but naturally intelligent mountain girl, June Tolliver. He persuades her to leave her mountain home to seek an education. After living in Big Stone Gap and Louisville, June goes to New York to study singing. Eventually she and Jack are married. The novel is of most interest for its local color, including various mountain entertainments like bean stringings, corn shuckings, and quilting parties; pipe-smoking women; entire families sleeping in one-room houses; mountain feuds; and the deceptive and fanatic Red Fox, a preacher and murderer (based on an actual personage) who eventually is hanged.

Both of these popular novels were adapted for the stage by Eugene Walter: *The Trail of the Lonesome Pine* (1912) was highly successful; *The Little Shepherd of Kingdom Come* (1916), however, was less popular. Movie versions, both silent and sound, have been made of the two novels. Notable are the sound version of *The Little Shepherd of Kingdom Come* (1961); the first silent version of *The Trail of the Lonesome Pine* (1916), directed by Cecil B. DeMille; and a sound version of this second work (1936), starring Fred MacMurray, Henry Fonda, and Sylvia Sidney. Earl Hobson Smith adapted the novel into an outdoor drama entitled *Trail of the Lonesome Pine* (1964).

In 1908 Fox married the beautiful, highly talented, volatile Fritzi Scheff, a former star of the Metropolitan Opera and some twenty years his junior. Although the marriage received much attention in the press, the two gradually drifted apart, and in 1913 they were divorced. In his later years, Fox wrote little but traveled extensively. He died of pneumonia at Big Stone Gap.

Fox is of some importance as a local colorist. Although he flourished toward the end of the period of intense enthusiasm for local color in this country, he does give accurate descriptions of social life in the mountains and of the scenic beauty of the surroundings. He is at his best when contrasting the mountaineers with the bluegrass aristocrats. Today, however, many view his mountaineers as stereotypes, and his sentimental appeals to love, loyalty, and hatred are annoying to some. In critical terms, Fox's most enduring works are probably not his two best-sellers but, rather, some of his local color short stories.

Fox felt at home with the mountaineers he wrote about; at the same time he moved comfortably among the most fashionable social circles in the country. In addition to Roosevelt, he counted as friends Thomas Nelson Page, Richard Harding Davis, Finley Peter Dunne, Booth Tarkington, and Jack London. Though his health was at times frail, he liked active sports such as fishing, hunting, and golf. He was a pleasant, jovial man noted for his humor and his devotion to family and country.

• There are important collections of Fox's papers at the University of Kentucky, Duke University, and the University of Virginia. The most important published biography is Warren I. Titus, *John Fox, Jr.* (1971). Other books by Fox are *A Cumberland Vendetta and Other Stories* (1895), *Hell-fer-Sartain and Other Stories* (1897), *The Kentuckians* (1897), *Crittenden* (1900), *Blue-grass and Rhododendron* (1901), *Christmas Eve on Lonesome and Other Stories* (1904), *Following the Sun Flag: A Vain Pursuit through Manchuria* (1905), *A Knight of the Cumberland* (1906), *The Heart of the Hills* (1913), *In Happy Valley* (1917), and *Erskine Dale, Pioneer* (1920). See the bibliographies in Titus and the *Dictionary of Literary Biography*, vol. 9, part 2. Recent articles are Marilyn DeEulis, "Primitivism and Exoticism in John Fox's Early Work," *Appalachian Journal* 4 (Winter 1977): 133–43; Alf H. Walle, "Devolution and Evolution: Hillbillies and Cowboys as American Savages," *Kentucky Folklore Record* 32 (Jan.-June 1986): 58–68; and Melissa McFarland Pennell, "Between Hell-fer-Sartain and Kingdom Come: John Fox, Jr.'s Preservation of the Masculine Ethos," *Kentucky Folklore Record* 32 (July-Dec. 1986): 130–36.

EDWARD L. TUCKER

FOX, Margaret. *See* Fox, Catherine, Margaret Fox, and Ann Leah Fox.

FOX, Richard Kyle (12 Aug. 1846–14 Nov. 1922), publisher, was born in Belfast, Ireland, the son of James Fox, a mason and carpenter, and Mary Kyle, the daughter of a Presbyterian minister. As a boy, Fox paid for his education by working at the *Banner of Ulster*, a religious newspaper. He then worked on the *Belfast News Letter*. He married Annie Scott in 1869; they had six children. They remained together until her death in 1890.

In 1874 the Foxes immigrated to New York City. According to one of Fox's many stories, he engaged in a fistfight on the dock the minute he landed in America. His opponent, who worked for the *Commercial Bulletin*, a business journal, escorted Fox to the newspaper office. Fox was hired to sell advertising at the *Bulletin*, but he also solicited advertising for other newspapers on the side.

In 1875 Fox was hired as business manager for a foundering weekly newspaper, the *National Police Gazette*. He became the owner two years later when the bankrupt owners gave Fox the paper in lieu of wages for selling advertisements. This vulgar little newspaper, known as a "storypaper" in the industry, had begun in 1845 and built its reputation by naming malingerers and criminals, especially during the Mexican War.

Fox's personality, however, matched the *Gazette*'s. He tightened and lightened the leaden style and added pictures and more bad taste. Fox detested nonwhites, and his headlines maligned every ethnic minority in America. He did not like foreigners, high-society dandies, or doctors; nor did he like members of the clergy, and he preferred to highlight their misdeeds over their good deeds. For example, the "Religious Notes" column for 11 March 1882 reported the arrest of a Methodist minister in Illinois for "attempting an outrage on a pretty choir singer." "Crimes of the Clergy" vied with "Homicidal Horrors" and "Glimpses of Gotham" for column inches.

In casting his dark view of the world over women, Fox violated society's rule that a woman's name appear in print only at birth, marriage, and death. He printed stories about prostitutes and hussies, Vassar students in a pillow fight ("a fierce and fiery combat"), "gay birds" who "sandbagged a sucker" and took his money, and the once-rich woman found drunk, "slowly starving to death, debauched and deserted."

Fox's *Police Gazette* added to the increasing mountain of myths of the "Wild West." Fox's reporters amalgamated "eye-witness" accounts of people like Billy the Kid and Belle Starr even though some of them had died before the writers were born. Imaginative writers, at Fox's encouragement and editing, developed a formula that included blue eyes that turned gray in anger, gentlemanly behavior toward women, and thieving from the rich, who deserved it. Heroes of the West in the *Police Gazette*'s tall tales rose from the dead in time for the next edition.

Fox considered bartenders and barbers his most loyal readers and discounted their subscription rates. In 1885 advertisements cost $1 an agate line, the same charged by the *Ladies' Home Journal*, the circulation leader of the day. Circulation of the *Police Gazette* rose to a high of 150,000 in the late 1880s.

Fox also changed the world of entertainment. Theater and sports had been left out of newspapers until Fox exploited them to boost circulation. Covering theater, especially the gossip, meant another jab at the clergy, who railed against plays and musicals and troupes.

Fox barely knew the rules to any game, but he knew that sports, like theater, brewed gossip, rancor, gambling, sin, and competition—all of which sold papers. Sports appeared in print as never before, beginning in 1879 with a report on a bareknuckle fight. Fox gave space to rowing, male and female rifle shooting, and running. He engineered contests such as hog butchering, water drinking, and drink mixing and promoted them through "advance dope" in the *Police Gazette*.

Chief among Fox's interests was heavyweight boxing. He lobbied to make the sport legal, if not respectable, and reportedly gave $1 million to support amateur and professional athletes. He sold promotional prints of boxers, such as John L. Sullivan and Jim Corbett. Pictures could be purchased from Fox's printing plant on Franklin Square in New York City. To the champions, he awarded belts; gems encrusted the $4,000 belt presented to Sullivan in 1882.

In the 1880s Fox changed the color of the *Gazette*'s newsprint from gray to pink. Columns in "The Pinky," as it became known, bore silly pseudonyms, if any names at all. "Paul Prowler," for example, was Samuel A. Mackeever, who produced ten columns a week under different names. Fox demanded tight, condensed writing and got it. His adjunct reporters were employed by other newspapers during the week, but they spent their weekends writing for Fox in exchange for food and drink and $10. However, Fox's illustrators drew full time, producing the woodcuts (opinions vary on their excellence) that accompanied the lurid stories almost from the beginning of Fox's ownership. Included in his stable of artists and cartoonists were George E. McEvoy, Charles Kendrick, and Philip G. Cusacha.

For twenty-five years Fox ruled, but for the last twenty years of his life his paper lost speed. The next generation of publishers, the Hearsts and Pulitzers, printed tabloids that owed a great debt to the *Police Gazette* even as they outsold the original scandal sheet. In 1913 Fox married Emma Louise Raven. He died at his home in Red Bank, New Jersey, a multimillionaire.

• Biographical information on Richard Kyle Fox, as well as facsimile pages of the *Police Gazette*, can be found in *American Heritage* 11, nos. 5 and 6 (1960). Gene Smith wrote an introduction to the *Police Gazette* (1972), which he and Jayne Barry Smith edited; the book reproduces articles as well as facsimile editions dating from 1878 to 1897. Frank Luther Mott, *A History of American Magazines*, vol. 2, *(1850–1865)* (5 vols., 1957–1968), includes a chapter on the *National Police Gazette*. See also Dan Schiller, *Objectivity and the News* (1981). Obituaries are in the *New York Times*, 15 and 21 Nov. 1922.

MARTHA K. BAKER

FOX, Virgil Keel (3 May 1912–25 Oct. 1980), organist, was born in Princeton, Illinois, the son of Miles S. Fox, a real estate promoter and theater operator, and Birdie E. Nichols. Both of his parents were musical: his father was in demand as a harmonica player at barn dances, and his mother was alto soloist in the church choir. Young Virgil switched from piano lessons to organ lessons a little reluctantly at first, but by the age of ten he was playing for services at the Princeton First Presbyterian Church, and at fourteen he gave his first public recital, at a high school in Cincinnati, for an audience of 3,000. Already he was performing his entire program from memory, a practice he would continue throughout his life. He took lessons from the Bach specialist Wilhelm Middelschulte in Chicago and then won a full scholarship to the Peabody Conservatory in Baltimore, where he spent 1931–1932 studying with Louis Robert and earning an artist's diploma in one year. In 1932–1933 he studied his instrument in Paris, with Marcel Dupré at St. Sulpice and Louis Vierne at Notre Dame.

On his return from France, Fox made his professional debut at Wanamaker's department store in New York and began a lifelong career as a touring recitalist. He eventually played concerts on nearly every important organ in the United States and Europe. In 1935 he settled in Baltimore as organist of the Brown Memorial Presbyterian Church, a post he held for ten years; during that period he also headed Peabody's organ department (1938–1942), succeeding his former teacher Louis Robert. Fox left Peabody to join the Army Air Force in 1942, rising quickly from private to staff sergeant at Bolling Field, where he played three recitals and five religious services per week, in addition to arranging other musical performances for the military.

In 1946 Fox took the post of organist at Riverside Church in New York City, where thousands of tourists annually came to hear him play the large organ, whose expansion (in 1955) to a five-manual, 10,561-pipe Aeolian-Skinner instrument he designed and superintended. He also maintained an extensive touring schedule, making between sixty and seventy appearances per year in addition to his recording sessions around the world.

Fox left Riverside in 1965 to devote himself exclusively to recitals, concerts, and recording. Soon, in collaboration with his manager, companion, and adopted son David Snyder, he developed and began to tour what was billed as a "Heavy Organ" concert format, traveling with his own specially built, highly amplified electronic organ, accompanied by a spectacular light show. His 1970 appearance at Fillmore East, a Lower East Side Manhattan rock-music emporium, made national headlines. These colorful events repelled some musical purists (a Boston critic called his 1973 recital there "the most unsavory show in town"), but they attracted huge crowds of young and enthusiastic members of the "psychedelic generation" to his performances.

Besides his astounding technical facility, Fox's greatest strength as a performer was his firm insistence on communicating as directly as possible with his audiences. Early on, he began the practice of speaking informally to them between pieces. "Years ago," he told an interviewer, "I was playing a concert at a church in Augusta, Georgia. The third piece was the Fantasy in G Minor of Bach, and I said to myself, 'My God, these 3,000 Georgia crackers won't have the slightest idea of what's going to happen. I have to tell them.' That was a milepost in my experience. I even played much better." Nor was he shy of articulating his strong religious beliefs in these talks.

Just as attractive to his fans were his flamboyant style of playing—flashy body motions and showy cross-handed changing of organ stops—and his concert dress. He often appeared on stage in an iridescent sports jacket, rhinestone-studded suede shoes, and a long black toreador's cape lined with red satin. He had little sympathy with the beginnings of the early music movement (the "Baroque boys," he called its partisans), which called for performance on "authentic" instruments; this seemed to him a regressive step.

Fox won many honors over his life, including the Distinguished Alumni award from Peabody. He was the first American to perform on J. S. Bach's organ at the Thomaskirche in Leipzig and the first to give a recital at Notre Dame in Paris. In 1962, with E. Power Biggs and Catherine Crozier, he inaugurated the organ in what is now Avery Fisher Hall at Lincoln Center in New York.

In the mid-1970s Fox, who never married, took up residence in Florida. He was diagnosed with terminal cancer in 1976 but continued to perform publicly. He gave his last concert (inaugurating the new concert hall in Dallas on 26 Sept. 1980) barely a month before he died in West Palm Beach.

• The Music Division of the New York Public Library for the Performing Arts has clippings, programs, and reviews on file. Fox recorded on the Capitol, RCA Victor, Columbia, and Command labels. Articles on his career appeared regularly in *The Diapason* beginning in the 1930s, including a long obituary in the Dec. 1980 issue. Vernon Gotwals wrote the article on Fox in *The New Grove Dictionary of American Music* (1986). An obituary is in the *New York Times*, 27 Oct. 1980.

BRUCE CARR

FOX, William (1 Jan. 1879–8 May 1952), motion picture executive and producer, was born Wilhelm Fried Fuchs in Tulchva, Hungary, the son of German-Jewish parents, Michael Fuchs, the operator of a general merchandising store, and Anna Fried. In 1880 the family emigrated to the United States, where the surname was Americanized to "Fox." They took up residence in a tenement on the Lower East Side of New York City, with Fox's father securing employment as a machinist in the garment industry. As a boy, Fox peddled newspapers, stove polish, and candy lozenges to help support his large family. At age eleven he quit school to work in a clothing firm. Ten years later, after

launching the Knickerbocker Cloth Examining and Shrinking Company with a friend, he married Eve Leo, a clothing manufacturer's daughter, with whom he had two children.

Over the next thirty years Fox parlayed this first, small business into a motion picture empire. In 1903 he sold his cloth-shrinking business for $50,000 and used $1,666 of his profits to purchase a Brooklyn nickelodeon from Vitagraph cofounder J. Stuart Blackton. A year later, Fox established the Greater New York Film Rental Company to distribute films to his own chain of theaters (which by 1910 had grown to fifteen) and to theaters owned by others. In 1908 the newly formed Motion Picture Patents Company (MPPC), which controlled the essential patents for movie cameras and projectors, began to expand its control over the industry, charging producers and exhibitors to use its equipment. In 1911, after obtaining damaging evidence of the MPPC's oligopolistic practices, Fox filed suit against the company and won a court judgment ordering its dissolution. The dismantling of the MPPC (which began in 1912 but was not completed until 1918) paved the way for the rise of independent film producers and distributors such as Carl Laemmle (whose Independent Motion Picture Company of America—known as IMP—became Universal), Adolph Zukor (whose Famous Players became Paramount), Marcus Loew (who founded Metro-Goldwyn Mayer), and Fox, all of whom gradually moved from exhibition and distribution into production. The defeat of the MPPC, spearheaded by the efforts of Fox and Laemmle, ultimately resulted in the installation of a new regime of producers, distributors, and exhibitors who would dominate the American film industry from the late 1910s to the end of the century.

In his new role as producer, Fox pioneered the film careers of William Farnum, Theda Bara, Tom Mix, Janet Gaynor, Charles Farrell, Will Rogers, Shirley Temple, and others. Starting in the late 1920s, he also increased the production budgets for his films and imported the famous German film director F. W. Murnau to add artistic prestige to the studio. Murnau's *Sunrise* (1927), along with Frank Borzage's *Seventh Heaven* (also 1927), won a string of Oscars (best director, actress, writing, cinematography, and "Artistic Quality of Production") for the studio at the first Academy Awards ceremony.

As studio head, Fox was instrumental in developing new motion picture technologies that he planned to use throughout his ever-growing cinema chain (in 1927 Fox had more than a thousand movie theaters). In 1926 he invested in Theodore Case's sound-on-film system, established the Fox-Case Corporation to produce sound motion pictures, and expanded the studio's newsreel division, which converted to sound and was renamed Fox Movietone News. At the same time, he acquired Western Hemisphere rights to crucial sound-on-film patents held by the Swiss Tri-Ergon Company. Sound-on-film technology similar to that employed by Fox eventually became an industry norm, eclipsing the Warner Bros. sound-on-disc Vitaphone system. In 1927 Fox bought patents and initiated the research and development of a 70mm wide-film process known as Fox Grandeur, which looked forward to the 70mm wide-film formats reintroduced in the 1950s and 1960s and still in use in the 1990s. Ironically, Fox's patent holdings provided him with a potential "patents trust" over the production and exhibition not only of sound film, but of wide film, putting him in a position similar to that of his former business rival—the MPPC. Fox's Tri-Ergon patents, however, were subsequently challenged in the U.S. Supreme Court, which in 1935 ruled that rival American sound recording and reproducing equipment did not infringe on them.

In 1929 Fox had dramatically expanded his empire through the acquisition of a controlling interest in the Loew's Corporation, the parent company of MGM; around the same time he bought a theater circuit in New England as well as a large block of stock in the Gaumont-British production-distribution-exhibition chain. These purchases resulted in the creation, virtually overnight, of the largest motion picture combine in the world. But they also put Fox in debt to the banking firm of Halsey, Stuart & Company and the American Telephone & Telegraph Company, from which he received short-term loans for $30 million that fell due in the fall of 1929.

Although Fox's discussions with the U.S. Attorney General's office had initially led him to believe that no legal problems would arise regarding his takeover of Loew's, the Department of Justice in June 1929 declared the sale invalid and instituted an antitrust suit against him, forcing him to sell his stock back to Loew's. When the stock market collapsed in October 1929, Fox was unable to secure financing to pay off his short-term obligations, and in the spring of 1930 his creditors forced him to sell his interests in Fox Film, seizing control of his $300 million empire. Subsequent management of Fox failed to achieve the prosperity it had enjoyed under its founder. In 1935 the Fox corporation was merged with Twentieth Century Pictures, headed by Darryl F. Zanuck and Joseph Schenck, who piloted the company—now named Twentieth Century–Fox—back to financial stability.

Fox encountered further financial setbacks. In 1932 a Senate committee investigated his dealings and accused him of selling Fox shares short on the stock market. His successors at Fox filed suit against him, and the IRS charged him with tax evasion, putting a $2 million lien on his assets. Ensuing lawsuits cost him $1 million in lawyers' fees and $1 million in out-of-court settlements, and by 1936 he was forced to declare bankruptcy. In 1941, having reportedly concealed $6 million in assets, he was convicted of bribing a judge in his bankruptcy hearings and sentenced to a year in prison. In May 1943, after serving more than five months, he was released from the federal penitentiary in Lewisburg, Pennsylvania. He died in New York City.

• Newspaper and magazine clippings on Fox are available in the Motion Picture Collection, Lincoln Center, Library of the Performing Arts, New York Public Library. For biographical information, see Glendon Allvine, *The Greatest Fox of Them All* (1969); Stephen Silverman, *The Fox That Got Away* (1988); Upton Sinclair, *Upton Sinclair Presents William Fox* (1933); Aubrey Solomon, *Twentieth Century–Fox: A Corporate and Financial History* (1988); Neal Gabler, *An Empire of Their Own* (1988); and Norman Zierold, *The Moguls* (1969). An obituary is in the *New York Times*, 9 May 1952.

JOHN BELTON

FOXCROFT, Thomas (26 Feb. 1697–18 June 1769), Congregationalist minister, was born in Boston, Massachusetts, the son of Colonel Francis Foxcroft and Elizabeth Danforth, merchants. The son of a wealthy and prominent Anglican family, Foxcroft's father was warden of King's Chapel in Boston. After moving into the Danforth family mansion in Cambridge, where there was no Church of England, the Foxcrofts attended the town's Congregational church led by William Brattle.

Foxcroft attended Harvard during a period when modern ideas and discipline were being merged with the values of the Puritan founders. Brattle, an influential figure in the lives of a generation of ministers who graduated from Harvard between 1686 and 1717, acted as unofficial chaplain to the college; one student of the era called him the "professor" of divinity at Harvard. Foxcroft's youth and college years were under Brattle's spiritual guidance, and in 1712 Foxcroft shared his spiritual relation with Brattle to become a full member of Brattle's Congregational church. Throughout his life, Foxcroft would share with Brattle the tension of standing for traditional Puritanism while at the same time endeavoring to be more "broad and catholick."

After converting to Congregationalism in college, Foxcroft graduated with the class of 1714. He then went to Roxbury to teach school and learn from the Reverend Nehemiah Walter, a prominent minister and brother-in-law of Cotton Mather. With the support of Brattle, Walter, and Mather, Foxcroft was called to serve with Benjamin Wadsworth at Boston's First Church—historically the city's most prominent pulpit and a bastion of Congregationalist orthodoxy. He received his A.M. from Harvard in 1716 and on 6 March 1717 was officially elected to the ministry at First Church. In 1719 he married Anna Coney; they had two children. Anna Foxcroft died in 1749, and he did not remarry.

In the pulpit of First Church, Foxcroft became a model of Puritan piety in the rising generation of ministers. Knowing that Foxcroft would be a model of virtue and piety, Cotton Mather sought the young minister's help with his incorrigibly sinful teenage son. In 1724 Foxcroft published a jeremiad sermon, *God's Face Set against Incorrigible People*, and in 1730 a call to Puritans to revive the values of their founders, *Observations Historical and Practical on the Rise and Primitive State of New-England*. With such sermons he gained a reputation as the rising successor to Cotton

Mather, who also had written on such subjects in the hope of maintaining a strong Puritan foundation in the increasingly cosmopolitan colony.

Such writings and his connection to Cotton Mather have led some historians to place Foxcroft among a conservative faction, but this is misleading. Foxcroft shared fully the values of his Boston colleagues Benjamin Colman, Joseph Sewall, Thomas Prince, and William Cooper, early eighteenth-century ministers who advocated a merger of old Puritanism with the new cosmopolitanism, Calvinist theology with more modern philosophy, and veneration of the early church with an understanding of the need for toleration. When Wadsworth left to become president of Harvard College in 1725, he was replaced in 1727 by Charles Chauncy, who became one of the most anti-Calvinist ministers of colonial Boston. The close, forty-year partnership of Foxcroft and Chauncy is a tribute to the "catholick" values held by that generation.

Foxcroft's published contributions to the attempts by ministers of his generation to create a strong but modern Congregational foundation in New England dealt primarily with reaching out to the young in such sermons as *Exhortations & Directions to Young People* (1721) and *Lessons of Caution to Young Sinners* (1733); advocating strong ministerial authority in such sermons as *A Practical Discourse Relating to the Gospel Ministry* (1718), *The Ruling & Ordaining Power of Congregational Bishops, or Presbyters, Defended* (1724), and *Ministers, Spiritual Parents, or Fathers in the Church of God* (1726); and modeling a careful rationalism that supported traditional orthodoxy and religious interpretations in scientific matters in such sermons as *The Voice of the Lord from Deep Places of the Earth* (1727), *The Earthquake, a Divine Visitation* (1756), and the long preface to Jonathan Dickinson's *The Reasonableness of Christianity* (1732). The extreme Calvinism he shared with his colleagues is evident in the title of *Divine Providence Adored & Justified in the Early Death of God's Children & Servants* (1727). William Cooper, assistant to Colman at the Brattle Street Church, wrote the preface to this work. Many of the works by the young ministers of Boston were prefaced or signed by fellow ministers. Through such works Foxcroft participated in a team effort by Boston ministers to try to lead New England into an urbane and tolerant Congregationalism that retained its pietistic fervor.

By the middle 1730s, Foxcroft at First Church and Colman at Fourth Church (Brattle Street Church) were the leading ministers of the generation who had been trained at Harvard by William Brattle and John Leverett. Colman was much older, and Foxcroft would eventually have been the recognized leader; in 1736, however, Foxcroft suffered a debilitating stroke. For the next thirty-three years he continued as a minister and sometimes published, but he necessarily took a lesser role in the religious affairs of his church and in Boston.

In 1740 Foxcroft once more shared with Colman a leading role, this time in the Great Awakening. Foxcroft's generation of ministers greatly emphasized order in worship services, in part because they wanted ministers to have the authority to keep the church on its traditional path even as the larger society became more diversified. Foxcroft wrote in *A Discourse Preparatory to the Choice of a Minister* (1727), before hiring Chauncy, that "The Lord is a God of Order, and not the Author of Confusion." But Foxcroft and his generation were also men of piety who could preach hell-fire sermons to encourage revival. In New England's Great Awakening, Colman invited the revivalist George Whitefield to preach in his pulpit and at Harvard. Controversy ensued from some of Whitefield's offensive and unknowledgeable remarks. Colman and Foxcroft both tried to mediate the controversy, and for his part Foxcroft published *An Apology in Behalf of the Revd Mr. Whitefield* (1745). An anonymous verse printed in the *Boston Evening Post* (3 June 1745) against Foxcroft aptly described the minister's intellectual abilities:

> With Grammar, Logick, and what not?
> With learned *Terms of Art* abounding,
> And Words of lofty Sense and sounding.
> And you can make as good *Distinction*,
> As any one wou'd ever think on.
> 'Twixt *Contradictions you can see*
> *A good intrinsick Harmony:*

Such was the intellectual strength of Foxcroft and the leaders of his generation of ministers. But the rising generation was not as committed to searching for logical harmonies between old and new religion. Foxcroft's final decades after the Great Awakening were full of theological discontent with what he considered to be the unorthodox, especially Arminian, tendencies of the time. He died in Boston.

• Foxcroft's notebooks are at the Congregational Library in Boston. *The Sermons of Thomas Foxcroft of Boston 1697–1769*, ed. and intro. Ronald A. Bosco (1982), offers a biographical sketch, a selection of sermons, and a complete bibliography. For a study of Foxcroft within the context of his generation, see John Corrigan, *The Prism of Piety: Catholick Congregational Clergy at the Beginning of the Enlightenment* (1991). See also biographical sketches in *American Writers before 1800: A Biographical and Critical Dictionary* (1983); Clifford Shipton, *Sibley's Harvard Graduates*, vol. 6 (1942), pp. 47–58; and Charles Chauncy, *Discourse Occasioned by the Death of the Reverend Thomas Foxcroft* (1769).

RICK KENNEDY

FOXX, Jimmie (22 Oct. 1907–21 July 1967), baseball player, was born James Emory Foxx near Sudlersville, Maryland, the son of Samuel Dell Foxx and Margaret S. "Mattie" Smith, farmers. At Sudlersville High School Foxx captained the basketball and soccer teams, starred in baseball, and dominated track meets. Baltimore sportswriters named him Maryland's best 1923 schoolboy athlete. Taught baseball by his father, a semiprofessional catcher, Foxx was given a tryout as a catcher in 1924 by the Easton club of the Eastern Shore League. That season he stepped in as the team's first-string catcher, batting .296 and hitting 10 home runs. Connie Mack, the Philadelphia Athletics manager, purchased Foxx's contract for a reputed $2,500 on the recommendation of Easton manager and former Athletics' third baseman Frank Baker. Mack took Foxx on Philadelphia's final 1924 road trip, during which Foxx had a pinch-hit single in an exhibition game at Cincinnati.

Foxx left school without graduating to attend Philadelphia's spring training in 1925, and he began his major league career with another pinch-hit single. At season's end he had six pinch hits in nine at bats, but during two midseason months at Providence in the International League he played regularly as catcher, outfielder, and first baseman and batted .327. From 1926 through 1928 Mack gradually broke Foxx in, experimenting with him as a catcher or infielder, and finally deciding to make him a first baseman. Immediately, Foxx, catcher Mickey Cochrane, outfielder Al Simmons, and pitchers Lefty Grove, George Earnshaw, and Rube Walberg formed the core of a team that won American League pennants in 1929, 1930, and 1931 two of three World Series. Foxx's 22 hits (.344 batting average) in 18 Series games included four home runs. The ninth-inning home run he drove deep into the left field stands at Sportsman's Park won the fifth game of the 1930 series, 2–0, over the St. Louis Cardinals and, he later said, gave him his greatest thrill.

When Philadelphia's fortunes declined, and hard times forced Mack to sell his stars, Foxx was the last to go, remaining through 1935. He led the league in home runs, slugging average, and runs batted in during 1932 and 1933 and received the league's Most Valuable Player award both years. His 58 homers in 1932 set a record for right-handed batters, equaled once but never exceeded into the 1990s. Several writers claimed he would have totaled 66 home runs had eight drives cleared outfield screens erected at St. Louis and Cleveland after the left-handed Babe Ruth hit 60 in 1927. Foxx also captured the 1933 batting championship with a .356 average after his .364 for 1932 finished second. In December 1935 Foxx and pitcher John Marcum were traded to the Boston Red Sox for two players and $150,000. Foxx continued his awesome hitting through 1941, favored by the short left field wall at Fenway Park. Again, in 1938, he won the league batting title, averaging .349, was again named Most Valuable Player, and drove in 175 runs, his best season total, while hitting 50 home runs.

By 1942 alcohol abuse had eroded Foxx's exceptional physical skills. Performing poorly before and after being waived to the National League Chicago Cubs, he quit baseball. During 1943 Helen M. (Heite) Foxx, his wife since 1928, divorced him and obtained custody of their two sons. He then married Dorothy Anderson Yard, by whom he had another son. He returned to the Cubs briefly in 1944, then managed their Portsmouth farm club in the Piedmont League. Signed by the Philadelphia Phillies for 1945, he batted .268 in 89 games, had seven home runs, and pitched as well. Later on, lesser baseball jobs came sparingly. He

managed St. Petersburg in the Florida International League in 1947; Bridgeport in the Colonial League in 1949; the Fort Wayne Daisies in the All-American Girls Baseball League in 1952; and he coached at Miami in the Florida State League in 1956–1957; at the University of Miami in those same two years; and at Minneapolis in the American Association in 1958 (where he was rumored to have been dismissed because of drinking problems).

Foxx was left to face his post-glory years with a family to support but no cash reserves or ability to earn. The $275,000 paid him as a player during his career had disappeared in bad investments, a prodigal style of living, and excessive generosity. He failed as a sports announcer, worked as salesman, store clerk, truck driver, continued drinking heavily, and drifted. In poor health, he suffered heart attacks during 1959 and 1963. While dining at his brother's home in Miami, he choked to death on a piece of meat lodged in his throat.

Although a dogged competitor, Foxx impressed people as gentle, amiable, placid, ever-smiling, and accessible to all, including ordinary fans. Almost 6' and 180 to 205 pounds in his prime, he had a physical stature that generated the upper body strength to drive baseballs hard, high, and far, frequently for extraordinary distances, and prompted his nickname "The Beast," affectionately bestowed. He batted from a closed stance, feet apart, a master of balance, timing, and controlled power. Although he was a dependable if unexceptional fielder at first base, his strong right arm mattered more when he caught or played third base.

Foxx's hitting skills through twenty major league seasons gained him election to the Baseball Hall of Fame in 1951. His most notable career statistics for 2,317 games played were 1,751 runs scored, 1,922 runs batted in, 534 home runs, a .325 batting average, and especially his .609 slugging average. In addition, Foxx ranks among the best with 4,956 total bases, a .428 on-base percentage, and about once in every fifteen times at bats—when not walked—he hit a home run. Ted Williams said of Foxx's power: "I never saw anyone hit a ball harder." Through twelve consecutive seasons (1929–1940) Foxx averaged 40 home runs and 137 runs batted in. Chosen by the *Sporting News* on its All-Star teams for 1929, 1932, 1933, 1938, and 1939, he ranks as one of the greatest first basemen in baseball history.

• A biography of Foxx is *Double X: The Story of Jimmie Foxx—Baseball's Forgotten Slugger* by Bob Gorman (1990). Profiles appear in Charles L. Johnston, *Famous American Athletes of Today, Fourth Series* (1934); Tom Meany, *Baseball's Greatest Hitters* (1950); Ira L. Smith, *Baseball's Famous First Basemen* (1956); Bob Broeg, *Super Stars of Baseball* (1971); and Donald Honig, *The Power Hitters* (1989). His career statistics appear in Craig Carter, ed., *Daguerreotypes*, 8th ed. (1990); *The Baseball Encyclopedia*, 9th ed. (1993); and *Total Baseball*, 3d ed. (1993). Foxx described his batting style in

"The Secret of Jimmy Foxx's Slugging Power" in *Baseball Magazine*, Aug. 1934. See also the Foxx file at the National Baseball Library in Cooperstown, N.Y.

FRANK VAN RENSSELAER PHELPS

FOXX, Redd (9 Dec. 1922–11 Nov. 1991), comedian, was born John Elroy Sanford in St. Louis, Missouri, the son of Fred Sanford, an electrician, and Mary Carson, a radio preacher and domestic worker. He spent his early childhood in St. Louis. After his father deserted the home in 1926, he and his mother moved to Chicago, where she worked for the vice president of the Chicago White Sox baseball team. While attending DuSable High School, he and two friends formed a washtub band, the Bon Bons. In 1939 the trio hopped a freight train to New York, where they met with sporadic success. Although they performed mostly on street corners and in subway stations, they occasionally appeared at the Apollo Theatre and on the "Major Bowes Amateur Hour."

Friends nicknamed Sanford "Chicago Red" because of his red hair. He then added the surname Foxx in admiration of the baseball star Jimmie Foxx. He devised a distinctive spelling of the name he would be known by for the rest of his life: Redd Foxx.

In the mid-1940s Foxx married Eleanor Killebrew; they divorced in 1951. He was married three more times, in 1955 to Betty Jean Harris (divorced in 1974); in the mid-1970s to Yun Chi Chong (divorced in the late 1980s); and in 1991 to Kahoe Cho. He had no children.

In 1942 Foxx got his first regular job as a solo entertainer at Gamby's, a nightclub in Baltimore. He returned to New York in 1945 with a unique, polished act. Two years later he teamed with Slappy White and saw his salary rise from $5 to $450 a week. In 1952 Dinah Washington invited the duo to open for her in California. Foxx and White split up soon after that, but Foxx remained on the West Coast at the end of the engagement.

Foxx found the club scene in California even more segregated than on the East Coast. Still, he persevered in finding progressively larger venues and contracts, while supplementing his income with work as a sign-painter. In 1955 Dootsie Williams, the owner of Dooto Records, caught Foxx's act and approached him with the revolutionary idea of recording an album consisting only of stand-up comic material and devoid of novelty songs. Foxx's sexually suggestive material prevented radio stations from broadcasting the albums. Nevertheless, the "party albums," as they would come to be known, were hugely popular in homes across the country. Foxx eventually recorded fifty-four party albums that together sold well over 10 million copies.

Owing to the popularity of the party albums, Foxx's salary and his acceptance at white nightclubs increased. In the early 1960s two famous patrons in these venues advanced Foxx's career. Frank Sinatra heard him perform, settled his Dooto contract, and signed him to LOMA, a subsidiary of the newly-formed Reprise label. In 1964 television host Hugh

Downs saw Foxx at a club in San Francisco. Although television producers had been leery of Foxx's blue reputation, Downs booked him as a guest on the "Today" show. Foxx was a smash, and this appearance led to regular spots on talk shows such as "The Tonight Show" and "The Joey Bishop Show," as well as appearances on television series such as "Mr. Ed," "Green Acres," and "The Addams Family."

Along with his television success, Foxx appeared regularly in Las Vegas throughout the 1960s. In 1968, when Aretha Franklin failed to appear for an opening-night show, Foxx, the opening act, entertained the crowd for one hour and forty minutes. Bookers from the Hilton International Hotel who saw this performance were impressed enough to offer him a year-long, $960,000 contract.

Foxx broke into motion pictures in 1970, portraying an aging junk dealer in the United Artists release *Cotton Comes to Harlem*. This led directly to his title role in Norman Lear's adaptation of the British comedy "Steptoe and Son," NBC's new television series "Sanford and Son." It was an immediate hit. Foxx created the main character, Fred Sanford, named after his late brother. Foxx's portrayal of the irascible junkman who faked heart attacks—crying out "I'm coming, Elizabeth!" with the arrival of each "big one"—elevated him to his highest popularity. During the show's 1972–1977 run, Foxx was nominated for six Emmy awards. Initially he had some degree of control over the show, but in 1977 he left it because of continual differences of opinion over the writing.

Although Foxx's talent was still bright, his luck was not. "The Redd Foxx Comedy Hour," which premiered an ABC after Foxx left NBC, ran only for the 1977–1978 season. A revival of the Fred Sanford character, "Sanford" (NBC, 1980–1981), was also short-lived, as was "The Redd Foxx Show" (1986). Throughout this period Foxx continued to entertain crowds in Las Vegas; however, his lavish spending habits caught up with him in 1989, when the Internal Revenue Service forced him to sell off houses and cars to cover back taxes. In 1991 Foxx's luck was finally turning good again with the early success of another situation comedy, CBS's "The Royal Family," but he died of a heart attack on the set, just weeks into the show's run.

Although Foxx will be remembered mainly for his work on "*Sanford and Son*," his most lasting contribution is the invention of the stand-up comedy album. In his party albums he pioneered not only an innovation in record marketing but also freedom of speech in comedy. As a result, the voices of many other comedians were heard more widely in the homes of America.

• The best narrative history of Redd Foxx in his own words is in *Redd Foxx B.S.* * (**Before Sanford*), ed. Joe X. Price (1979); the chapter "The Real Sanford," a serious reflection on his life, comes in the midst of reminiscences by famous friends such as Bill Cosby, Richard Pryor, and Norma Miller on Redd's Place, a club Foxx owned in the late 1960s. Foxx and Miller also coauthored *The Redd Foxx Encyclopedia of Black Humor* (1977), a serious history of blacks in American comedy; the chapter by Foxx on himself, however, is nothing more than a monologue in print. Foxx recorded party albums on many labels. The LOMA albums are representative examples of Foxx's masterful timing and use of double entendre. See also Mel Watkins, *On the Real Side: Laughing, Lying, and Signifying—The Underground Tradition of African-American Humor that Transformed American Culture from Slavery to Richard Pryor* (1994).

ALEXANDER BATTLES

FOY, Bryan (8 Dec. 1896–20 Apr. 1977), actor and film producer, and **Eddie Foy, Jr.** (4 Feb. 1910–15 July 1983), actor, were two of the eleven children born to vaudeville and Broadway comedian Eddie Foy (Edwin Fitzgerald Foy) and Madeline Morando, an ex-ballerina. Bryan was born in Chicago, Illinois, and Eddie (Edwin Fitzgerald) Jr. was born at the family home in New Rochelle, New York. The Foy children became part of their father's vaudeville act almost as soon as they could walk and talk; thus their public education was sporadic—both boys briefly attended St. Gabriel's School in New Rochelle, but the bulk of their education came from private tutors or from their mother's tutoring on the road.

Bryan entered his father's act at the age of four and Eddie Jr. at the age of five. Eventually billed as "Eddie Foy and the Seven Little Foys," the family toured the vaudeville circuit for more than a decade. *Variety* described the act as a "happy family and happy act" (23 Aug. 1912). Appearing in sketches entitled "Fun in the Foy Family" or "Slumwhere in New York," Eddie Foy, Sr., would often joke that if his large family lived in the town in which they were performing it would be a city. The family act usually included skits, jokes, and song and dance, and it would traditionally end with the nonperforming Madeline Morando taking a well-deserved bow with her progeny. Critic B. F. Keith, writing in *Theatre News*, observed that "The Foy family in vaudeville presents a simple problem in arithmetic. If one Foy is funny, how funny are eight Foys?" (15 Sept. 1919). The family act became the subject of a 1956 film called *The Seven Little Foys*, starring Bob Hope. A television version of the Foy family story, featuring Eddie Foy, Jr., as his father, was presented on "The Chrysler Theatre" during the mid-1960s.

In 1918, at the age of twenty-one, Bryan Foy left the family act and moved to Hollywood, where he began making two-reelers for Fox studios as well as working as a gag man for comedians Buster Keaton and Cecil B. De Mille. In 1927 Foy began working with Warner Brothers Studio as a producer and director of vitaphone shorts. This was some of the earliest work with sound in films, and in 1928 he directed *The Lights of New York*, the first all-talking picture. Although sound films still had a long way to go, as *Photoplay* magazine reported, *The Lights of New York* was a "landmark of the sound movie" (Sept. 1928). Produced and ready for public showing in eight days at a total cost of $18,000, the film grossed over $1 million as many movie theater managers scrambled to obtain sound equipment. Bryan Foy produced and directed low-budget B-films for Warner Brothers Studios for the next twenty years. Known as the "King of the B's," Foy made numerous films, including *Road Gang* (1936), *Murder in the Big House* (1936), and *Crime School* (1938). Foy disliked his reputation as a B-film maker, which implied that his work was of low quality, and instead referred to his films as "little pictures," differentiated from longer films solely on the basis of what it cost to produce them. (At the time, A-films cost $2 million-plus to produce, whereas Bryan Foy produced his B-films for less than $1 million each.) Foy disregarded critics and put more stock in the box office, where his work achieved great success. He said, "I string along at the box office. That's the best gauge" (*New York Times*, 2 Dec. 1945). *Crime School*, for example, cost Foy $210,000 to produce and brought in more than $1.5 million.

When Foy joined 20th Century–Fox studios as a producer in 1941, he moved up to producing A-films, among them, *Doll Face* (1945). In 1946 he became vice president of production at Eagle-Lion Studios, where he tested his faith in the box office by traveling to major cities across the country and soliciting comments and advice from theater managers who dealt with the theatergoing public on a daily basis. This research led Foy to believe that Hollywood had become "lax" and was churning out low-quality films. After two years at Eagle-Lion, he resigned his position to form Bryan Foy Productions with a contract to produce four pictures a year for three years for Eagle-Lion release. Foy's official statement asserted that he was venturing away from Eagle-Lion because his duties as vice president had left him no time to pursue his producing interests. However, the *New York Times* and others suggested that Foy's departure had more to do with friction between him and studio owner Robert Young and with Foy's desire to boost the capital gains of the studio, which would bring him additional income as a stockholder (*New York Times*, 11 Apr. 1948).

Elected to the Society of Motion Picture Pioneers in 1945 and always looking for innovative film technology, Foy helped to develop the three-dimensional (3-D) process and used it in producing the classic 3-D horror film *House of Wax*, starring Vincent Price, in 1953. *Variety* predicted that *House of Wax* would revolutionize film making in a way similar to the introduction of sound, but 3-D proved to be nothing more than a novelty. Foy's last film, *PT-109*, notable for its depiction of the World War II heroics of John F. Kennedy, was produced in 1963, while Kennedy occupied the White House. At some point Foy had married, but his wife's name is unknown; the couple had a daughter. Foy died in Los Angeles after having produced and/or directed more than twenty-one motion pictures.

Eddie Jr. continued as a performer after Bryan's departure from the family act in 1918. He performed in vaudeville as a song and dance man until 1929, when, on 2 July, he made his Broadway debut at the Ziegfeld Theater in the musical *Show Girl*. He subsequently appeared on Broadway as Corporal Jack Sterling in *Ripples*, which opened 11 February 1930 at the New

Amsterdam Theatre; as Gilbert Stone in *Smiles*, which opened at the Ziegfeld on 18 November 1930; and as Alexander Sheridan in *The Cat and the Fiddle*, which opened at the Globe Theatre on 15 October 1931.

In 1930 Foy married actress Barbara Newberry, whom he had met while performing in *Show Girl*. The couple had no children and were divorced in 1932. A year later Foy married Anne Marie McKenney, an actress who performed under the name Eleanor Bailey; they had one son, Edwin Fitzgerald Foy III, who followed his father onto the stage, making his debut at age ten. Anne Marie Foy died in 1952, and Foy never remarried.

In 1929 Foy began his film career, appearing in Bryan Foy's production of *Queen of the Night Clubs*, which he followed with *Leathernecking* (1930) and *Myrt and Marge* (1934). He portrayed his father in six films, including *Yankee Doodle Dandy* (1942) and *Wilson* (1944). Foy also starred with Alice Fay in *Lillian Russell* in 1940 and with Judy Holliday in *The Bells Are Ringing* in 1960. In addition to his success in film, Foy continued to star on Broadway, as Bubbles Wilson in *Orchids Preferred*, which opened at the Imperial Theatre on 11 May 1937; as Kid Conner in *The Red Mill*, which opened at the Ziegfeld Theater on 16 October 1945 (reviving his career after a dormant period of several years); and as Mikeen Flynn in *Donnybrook!*, which opened at the Forty-sixth Street Theatre on 18 May 1961. One of Foy's biggest hits was as Hines in the Richard Alder and Jerry Ross musical *The Pajama Game*, which opened 13 May 1954 at the St. James Theatre. Theater critic Brooks Atkinson called Foy a "true clown who can strut standing still" (*New York Times*, 16 May 1954). Foy reprised the role in the film version of *The Pajama Game* in 1957. With the success of *Pajama Game*, Foy finally came out of his father's shadow and stopped impersonating him on film. He furthered this independence in *Rumple*, which opened at the Alvin Theater on 6 November 1957, when Foy dropped the "Jr." from his billing. *Newsweek* said of his performance in the title role, "When he goes into a soft shoe routine, or merely when he trips over a chalk line he himself has drawn on stage, everything looks better" (18 Nov. 1957).

A frequent guest on television shows in the 1950s and 1960s, Foy starred in 1962–1963 in "Fair Exchange," a situation comedy about an English exchange student in the United States and his American counterpart in England. Foy's roles were almost exclusively comic character roles—his sense of comic timing and physical control allowed him to create diverse, yet distinctive, characters. In addition to his vaudeville tours, Foy appeared in more than twenty-four movies and thirteen Broadway productions. He died in Woodland Hills, California.

Although the Foy brothers contributed to the growth and success of vaudeville in their early years, it was as adults that they made their greatest mark, on stage and screen. In bringing sound to the screen and, later, in helping to implement such innovations as 3-D, Bryan Foy changed the film industry—developing his ideas as the fledgling industry was beginning to grow. Eddie Foy, Jr., as a featured performer on both stage and screen, perfected the comic genius that he had first displayed as a child in vaudeville. Although he was sometimes underappreciated in his own time, Eddie Foy, Jr., always conveyed in his work his lifelong love of entertaining.

• The Foy brothers' early life has been chronicled in their father's autobiography, *Clowning through Life* (1928). Additional information on Bryan Foy's career can be found in Evelyn Truitt, *Who Was Who on Screen* (1983). His obituary is in the *New York Times*, 22 Apr. 1977. Eddie Foy, Jr., is listed in the *Biographical Encyclopaedia and Who's Who in the Theatre* (1981). His obituary is in the *New York Times*, 16 July 1983.

MELISSA VICKERY-BAREFORD

FOY, Eddie (9 Mar. 1856–16 Feb. 1928), comedian, was born Edwin Fitzgerald in Greenwich Village, New York, the son of Richard Fitzgerald, a tailor, and Ellen Hennessy. Foy began his theatrical career at the age of eight busking on the sidewalks of Greenwich Village when his bootblacking business was slow. A fiddler noticed him one day and the two began to perform on the streets or in bars—anywhere that would allow them. As a youngster Foy spent hours hanging around the stage doors of local theaters watching performers in Emerson's or Manning's minstrel shows, learning the bits, dances, and songs of popular entertainment.

At age sixteen he changed his name from Fitzgerald to Foy (because the former sounded too Irish) and began a string of successful professional partnerships. Too young and unseasoned to play the big minstrel shows, Foy spent years playing in honky-tonks and beer halls that put together individual acts to form longer shows. His acts consisted of singing, dancing, and acrobatics, but Foy also worked as an acrobat in a circus and as a "super" in Edwin Booth's *Hamlet* in Chicago. In 1877 Foy teamed up with James Thompson in a partnership that would last the next six years and take them out west to Dodge City, Denver, Butte, San Francisco, and other western towns. The team became famous in the West as variety artists; they stayed six months or longer in some towns. In San Francisco they played at Emerson's Minstrels in 1882 and later performed with the Alcazar Stock Company. Foy, however, wanted success in the East. The team played for a short time at Carncross's Minstrels in Philadelphia in 1884, but when no other jobs were forthcoming Thompson wanted to return to the West. Foy stayed in the East waiting for his break.

After a few lean years Foy finally broke into musical comedy, eventually landing a comic part in one of David Henderson's huge extravaganzas based on nursery rhymes and fairy tales. Foy spent from 1888 to 1894 with Henderson's company and became immensely popular, starring first in *The Crystal Slipper* and then *Bluebeard*, *Sinbad*, and *Ali Baba*. A disagreement with Henderson caused Foy to leave the troupe in 1894, and for the next two years he toured off and on with a show in Europe. Henderson's company folded soon after Foy left.

Although he had not really considered himself a comic before, it was during this time that Foy's unique style of comedy took shape. Well known for his eccentric costumes and makeup, Foy had one of the funniest acts in vaudeville. His physical control became equally famous—his facial contortions and stage walk could get laughs by themselves. A reviewer in the *Indianapolis Journal* commented that "Foy, unadulterated and bubbling over with his original clownishness, is a show all in himself. . . . His stage face reminds one of the cat suffering with colic, and the more misery he puts into it, the more the people laugh."

In 1896 Foy headlined a show previously produced by Henderson called *Off the Earth*. It failed, but Foy's popularity grew and the show launched him into the next stage of his career—Broadway—and in 1900 he starred in *The Strollers*. He spent the next three years on Broadway, and then took the starring role in a new Klaw and Erlanger show called *Mr. Bluebeard*, which opened at the new Iroquois Theater in Chicago on 23 November 1903. One month later during a matinee performance the Iroquois was the site of the greatest theater fire in history. Until forced to leave when his own wig caught fire, Foy tried to calm down the terrified people as they attempted to flee the burning theater. More than 600 people died in the fire.

Foy then played the leading parts in *Piff! Paff! Pouf!* (1904), *The Earl and the Girl* (1905), *The Orchid* (1907), *Mr. Hamlet of Broadway* (1908), *Up and Down Broadway* (1910), and *Over the River* (1911). During these years on Broadway Foy spent his summers in vaudeville. In 1913 Foy took his children, the "Seven Little Foys," on the circuit, touring with them for the next ten years until some of the children formed their own act and others returned to civilian life. In 1923 he performed his last play, *That Casey Girl*, and retired. Although in his retirement Foy appeared in one motion picture, "the call of the footlights was too strong," and he decided to return to vaudeville. The Keith-Albee group picked up his sketch "The Fallen Star" in 1927 and scheduled it for a yearlong tour of the United States. Foy died in Kansas City during the tour.

Foy was married in 1878 to Rose Howland, who died in 1884. He married Lola Sefton in 1890 and the couple had one child before she died in 1894. He married Madeline Morando in 1896, with whom he had seven children before her death in 1918. He was survived by his fourth wife, Marie Combs, whom he married in 1923.

An obituary describes Foy as "a clown by choice." In his autobiography Foy writes, "I have never given the serious thinkers anything to discuss at their club meetings, but I have helped thousands to forget life's troubles for an evening—and that is something!" The hard knocks of theater life and his personal tragedies (he buried three wives and five children) did not dampen Foy's outlook on life or his profession. He concludes his autobiography by saying, "on the whole, life has been a pretty jolly affair. I have no complaints to make, and few regrets." Foy's contribution to a developing vaudeville is unquestionable. His inventiveness and popularity contributed to the building and sustaining of the vaudeville circuit.

• Foy's autobiography, *Clowning through Life* (1928), published just before his death and written with Alvin F. Harlow, is the primary source for information on his life and career. A special tribute to him is in the *New York Times*, 17 Feb. 1928.

MELISSA VICKERY-BAREFORD

FOY, Eddie, Jr. *See* Foy, Bryan, and Eddie Foy, Jr.

F.P.A. *See* Adams, Franklin P.

FRAENKEL, Osmond Kessler (17 Oct. 1888–16 May 1983), attorney, was born in New York City, the son of Jacob Kessler, a German-born mining engineer and businessman, and Emily (maiden name unknown). He received B.A. and M.A. degrees from Harvard University in 1908 and an LL.B. from Columbia University in 1911; that same year he was admitted to the bar. In 1913 he married Helene Esberg; they had three children.

As an undergraduate at Harvard, Fraenkel had organized the Socialist Club but dropped out when he found the party to be too doctrinaire. For nearly twenty-five years he gave only occasional attention to political and civil liberties issues. In 1921 he wrote a law review article on search and seizure, which was prompted by the federal government's violations of civil liberties during World War I. He did legal work for the Soviet Union and visited that country in 1925. These activities brought him into closer contact with the small civil liberties community.

His 1931 book on a major cause among civil libertarians, *The Sacco-Vanzetti Case*, marked the turning point in his career. As a result of his growing interest in civil liberties issues, he agreed in 1934 to assist with the Supreme Court appeal of one of the cases of the Scottsboro Boys, nine African Americans who were sentenced to death for raping a white woman. He and the American Civil Liberties Union lawyer Walter Pollak won a landmark decision in *Patterson v. Alabama* (1935), in which the Court held that the defendants had been denied a fair trial because African Americans were systematically excluded from jury service. From 1935 to 1955 he served as co-general counsel for the New York Civil Liberties Committee (later Union), the state affiliate of the ACLU. From 1935 to 1977 he served on the board of directors of the ACLU, and in 1954 he became their co-general counsel and served in that capacity also until 1977. He stated that his association with the ACLU was "the most rewarding part of my life." It was through the ACLU that Fraenkel came to handle the Supreme Court cases for which he is best known.

Fraenkel's second important Supreme Court case was *De Jonge v. Oregon* (1937), in which the Court reversed the conviction of a Communist party member who was prosecuted for his participation in a meeting organized by the Communist party. The decision was a landmark in extending First Amendment protection to the advocacy of unpopular political doctrine.

In 1940 Fraenkel represented the noted philosopher Bertrand Russell, who had been denied a teaching position at City College of New York because of his political beliefs. During World War II, Fraenkel was the principal author of the briefs filed by the ACLU in two unsuccessful Supreme Court cases challenging the evacuation and internment of the Japanese Americans, *Hirabayashi v. United States* (1943) and *Korematsu v. United States* (1944).

During the Cold War, Fraenkel was a staunch opponent of various anticommunist measures that he felt infringed on freedom of speech and association. In 1958 he argued and won the case of *Trop v. Dulles* (1958), in which the Supreme Court ruled that arbitrarily stripping a person of his U.S. citizenship violated the Eighth Amendment to the Constitution. In 1969, at the age of eighty-one, he argued and won the case of *Kramer v. Union Free School District* (1969), in which the Supreme Court ruled that a state could not bar people from voting in school board elections because they did not have children attending the public schools.

Fraenkel wrote a series of books for a general audience that summarized the current state of the law of civil liberties. *Our Civil Liberties* (1944) appeared in a revised version, *The Supreme Court and Civil Liberties*, in 1960. The final version was published as *The Rights You Have* in 1972. During a time of enormous change in the law of civil liberties Fraenkel's books provided a convenient and readable summary of the law for the general audience. Fraenkel also edited *The Curse of Bigness* (1935), a collection of essays by Supreme Court Justice Louis Brandeis on the problem of monopolies, and wrote more than 100 articles.

Fraenkel was an official in the National Lawyers Guild and served on committees of the National Association for the Advancement of Colored People and the Authors League. He refused to join the American Bar Association because it did not admit African Americans. He served on the board of directors of the ACLU from 1935 to 1977.

One of the most active and successful civil liberties lawyers in twentieth-century American history, Fraenkel argued twenty-six cases before the U.S. Supreme Court, and his name appeared on more than 100 briefs. Several of his cases established important precedents in constitutional law, and according to his obituary in the *New York Times*, "the 'Osmond Fraenkel brief' became synonymous with clarity and conciseness." Norman Dorsen, a former president of the ACLU, called him "one of the giants in contemporary life."

• Fraenkel's papers are located at the Harvard University Law School. His diary is closed to researchers until the year 2033. The portions of his diary that relate to the ACLU have been transcribed and are available in the ACLU Archives at Princeton University. (There is no way to verify the accuracy of the transcription.) Other correspondence is in the ACLU Archives. An interview with Fraenkel is in the Columbia Oral History Collection at Columbia University. His articles include "Concerning Searches and Seizures," *Harvard Law Review* 34 (1920–1921): 361–87; "What Can Be Done about the Constitution and the Supreme Court?" *Columbia Law Review* 37 (1937): 212–26; and "Law and Loyalty," *Iowa Law Review* 37 (1951–1952): 153–74. An obituary is in the Elizabeth Devine, ed., *The Annual Obituary 1983* (1984), pp. 237–38; see also Norman Dorsen, "An Appreciation of Osmond K. Fraenkel," *New York Law Journal*, 14 June 1983.

SAMUEL WALKER

FRAME, Alice Seymour Browne (29 Oct. 1878–16 Aug. 1941), missionary, was born in Harpoot, Turkey, the daughter of the Reverend John Kitteredge and Leila Kendall Browne, missionaries of the American Board of Commissioners for Foreign Missions (ABCFM). The eldest of six children, she was educated by her mother until 1892, when she enrolled at the Cambridge Latin School in Massachusetts, graduating in 1896. She graduated Phi Beta Kappa from Mount Holyoke College in 1900 and attended the Hartford Theological Seminary, finishing a course in religious pedagogy in 1903. (In the early twentieth century women were frequently permitted to attend the Hartford school as well as other professional schools but were not awarded degrees even though they might have completed all the course work required for men to obtain degrees.) Browne joined the Pilgrim Congregational Church in Cambridge, Massachusetts, in 1893. While in college she joined both the Young Women's Christian Association and the Student Volunteer Movement for Foreign Missions (SVMFM) and served as a leader of both groups.

Even though Browne had been born abroad into a missionary family, her career decision to become a missionary was made while in college where she was caught up in the SVMFM, so popular on American college campuses at the turn of the twentieth century. After completing her course of theological study she served as the junior secretary for young people's work of the Women's Board of Foreign Missions for the ABCFM from 1903 to 1905 and then was appointed as a missionary posted to Tungchow (Dongzhou), near Peking (Beijing), China.

Throughout her life in China, her work was supported by the students and alumnae of Mount Holyoke. At Tungchow she served as principal of the Goodrich Girls' School for six years while supervising Bible women (the native workers) and day schools, and then in 1912 she joined the faculty of the new North China Union Women's College. She spent the 1912–1913 year in the United States on furlough and married the Reverend Murray Scott Frame, of the North China Union College, in Kyoto, Japan, on her return to Asia in 1913. Of her marriage she wrote, "It will be a relief now not to have to be constantly explaining to bewildered Chinese why I am not married." Of their three children, only Rosamond, born in 1917, survived beyond infancy; the Reverend Frame died of typhus in China in 1918.

At the North China Union Women's College, Alice Frame taught both education and history, twice serving as head of the history department. She worked with Luella Miner on the reorganization of the college, which became a part of Yenching University. Frame headed the women's college while Miner was home on a fundraising trip in 1918–1920. Frame then returned to the United States in 1920 to raise money for seven women's Christian colleges in China, including Yenching. She frequently wrote articles for the *Congregationalist*, a church publication.

On her return to China in 1922 she served as principal of her mission's Bridgman Academy and as dean of the North China Women's College, assuming the latter post in June 1922 on the resignation of Miner. Frame supervised the architects and the construction of nine buildings on the Yenching campus, into which the women's college moved in 1926. She spent the summer of 1925 in the United States and then returned again to China. She journeyed homeward via the trans-Siberian railroad in 1928 for a year-long furlough, which she spent as acting dean of residence at Mount Holyoke. Again in China in 1930, student demonstrations over control of Yenching University by the Chinese forced her to resign as dean, but because a Chinese dean could not be found she continued to function in the post until 1931.

Typical of many bright young American women of the early twentieth century, she chose to escape the few career opportunities open to women in the United States by becoming a missionary in China. At Yenching she contributed to the growing interest in social studies and the changing views of education, as well as working for the emancipation of women and the end of discrimination against them within the university. Reassessing her career late in life, she wrote that she was "not easily satisfied" and "had not been sufficiently flexible," apparently acknowledging that the Chinese were capable of doing the work she had done in China.

After leaving Yenching she returned to the service of the ABCFM at Tungchow and served as secretary of religious education for the mission, then known as the North China Kung Li Hui. She also visited in the rural districts around Tungchow. After she contracted tuberculosis in 1932 she returned to the United States and lived near Boston with her father, who was then retired. She later moved to Laussane, Switzerland, to recuperate and to allow her daughter to attend school there. Frame returned to China in 1937, lived for a time at Paoting (Baoding), and then moved back to Tungchow, where she served until 1940. She was one of the few foreigners selected as a delegate of the China Christian Council to attend the International Missionary Council meeting in Madras, India, in 1938. In 1939 she was appointed general secretary of the Tungchow mission and co–general secretary of the North China Kung Li Hui. She contracted cancer in 1939 and returned to the United States. She died in West Newton, Massachusetts.

• Frame's papers, letters, pictures, and miscellaneous items are located in the archives of the American Board of Commissioners for Foreign Missions at Houghton Library, Harvard University. An obituary is in the *Chinese Recorder* 72 (1941): 609.

KATHLEEN L. LODWICK

FRANCIS, Convers (9 Nov. 1795–7 Apr. 1863), Unitarian clergyman and university professor, was born in West Cambridge, Massachusetts, the son of Convers Francis, a baker, and Susannah Rand. He was an older, and favorite, brother of Lydia Maria Child, the distinguished author and social reformer, who often acknowledged his salutary influence upon her. Francis entered Harvard College in 1811 and graduated with an A.B. degree in 1815. He remained at Harvard to complete a course of studies in divinity in 1818. That year he was licensed to preach by both the Boston and the Cambridge Association of Congregational Ministers. In June of the following year he was ordained and called as pastor to the First Parish Congregational Church in Watertown, Massachusetts, where he remained for twenty-three years, about one-half of his career. In 1822 he married Abby Bradford Allyn, daughter of Rev. John Allyn of Duxbury, Massachusetts; the couple had two children.

During his Watertown years Francis earned a reputation as an effective pulpit minister and an untiring shepherd of his flock, and his popularity extended beyond Watertown. At a time when pulpit exchanges constituted the ultimate test of fellowship, there was scarcely a Unitarian minister in the entire Boston area with whom he did not repeatedly exchange pulpits. His manner was simple and unaffected. Never known to preach extemporaneously, he invariably read his carefully written sermons, designed to inspire, not to frighten or intimidate. The subject matter of his sermons, about 2,000 of which are housed in booklet form in the Free Public Library at Watertown, generally concerned external nature, religious doctrine, civil responsibilities, reform, and youth. His achievements as a pastor and scholar were often recognized by Harvard College. In 1829 he delivered the annual Phi Beta Kappa address at Harvard and, in 1833, the annual Dudleian Lecture. In further recognition of his attainments, his alma mater honored him with a doctor of divinity degree in 1837.

One of Francis's most prominent traits was his erudition, especially in languages, literature, and theology. By the time he finished his studies at Harvard he had mastered Latin, Greek, and Hebrew; he soon became proficient in French, Spanish, Italian, and German. A lover of books since childhood, he systematically collected, from home and abroad, an impressive library of about 8,000 volumes, many of which were esoteric and rare. It was said that books were his only luxury. His seal depicted a book, under which was the motto: *Qui studet orat* (He who prays studies).

Francis also was a frequent and facile writer of sermons, tracts, civil discourses, biographies, and histories. Many of his articles appeared in the *Christian Dis-*

ciple, the *Christian Examiner*, the *American Monthly Review*, the *Unitarian Advocate*, and the *Liberal Preacher*. His best-known publication was *An Historical Sketch of Watertown, in Massachusetts, from the First Settlement of the Town to the Close of Its Second Century* (1830). On the merits of this history he was admitted in 1830 to the Massachusetts Historical Society.

Francis attracted people of learning to his home, in particular members of the Transcendental Club, founded in 1836. Francis was the club's oldest member as well as its moderator. He was especially a friend to, and an apologist for, the radicals Ralph Waldo Emerson and Theodore Parker in their controversies with Professor Andrews Norton and the conservative Boston Ministerial Association (essentially a Unitarian group) over the nature of miracles and the inspiration of the Scriptures.

In the summer of 1842 Francis was invited to replace Rev. Henry Ware (1794–1843) as Parkman Professor of Pulpit Eloquence and Pastoral Care at Harvard Divinity School. (Ware, who had been ill for some time, died in 1843.) Because of the wide doctrinal differences between the liberal Transcendentalist ministers and the more conservative Unitarian ministers in the Boston association and in the divinity school, the choice of a successor was not easy; Francis was chosen because he was free from dogmatism and had impeccable credentials as a scholar. He taught various courses in the divinity school, but his major responsibility was to give lectures to the senior class on ecclesiastical history and to the junior class on natural theology. Also, for one-half of each year he preached on Sundays and conducted a daily chapel program. Francis's teaching method was to present all points of view on a subject and then encourage his students to weigh and sift through these views in order to arrive at what they believed to be the truth. Because his approach was not dogmatic, some students and colleagues accused him of lacking a commitment to any one view; but most who knew him well appreciated his method. Francis was devoted to his students and to the classroom until the end of his life. During his last weeks, weakened by a debilitating disease (probably cancer), he had his students carry him to the lecture room in a chair; when he became unable to do this, he held classes in his home. He died at Cambridge.

• The majority of letters by and to Convers Francis are in the Boston Public Library, the Massachusetts Historical Society, and three libraries at Harvard University (the Harvard University Archives at the Pusey Library, the Andover-Harvard Theological Library, and the Houghton Library). The selected publications of Francis, most privately printed, include *Christianity as Purely an Internal Principle* (American Unitarian Association Tract, no. 105, 1836); *Experimental Religion* (1836); *Three Discourses Delivered before the Congregational Society in Watertown; Two upon Leaving the Old Meeting-House, and One at the Dedication of the New* (1836); "Life of John Eliot, the Apostle to the Indians," in *Library of American Biography*, vol. 5, ed. Jared Sparks (1836), pp. 1–357; *The Death of the Aged: A Discourse Occasioned by the Death of the Rev. Dr. Ripley, of Concord, 1841* (1841); "Life of Sebastian Rale, Missionary to the Indians," in *Library of American Biography*, vol. 7, ed. Jared Sparks, 2d ser. (1845), pp. 157–233; and *The Charge at the Ordination of Mr. Edwin M. Wheelock* (1857).

No complete biography of Francis has been written, but the most substantial sketch of his life is John Weiss, *Discourse Occasioned by the Death of Convers Francis, D.D.* (privately printed, 1863). Other studies that contribute much biographical information in the context of his milieu are Joel Myerson, "Convers Francis and Emerson," *American Literature* 50 (Mar. 1978): 17–36; and a pair of two-part overviews by Guy R. Woodall: "The Journals of Convers Francis (Part One)," in *Studies in the American Renaissance 1981*, ed. Joel Myerson (1981), pp. 265–343, "The Journals of Convers Francis (Part Two)," *Studies in the American Renaissance 1982*, ed. Joel Myerson (1982), pp. 227–384, "The Selected Sermons of Convers Francis (Part One)" in *Studies in the American Renaissance 1987*, ed. Joel Myerson (1987), pp. 73–129, and "The Selected Sermons of Convers Francis (Part Two)," *Studies in the American Renaissance 1988*, ed. Joel Myerson (1988), pp. 55–131. A good survey of the research on and criticism of Francis is Guy R. Woodall, "Convers Francis," in *The Transcendentalists: A Review of Research and Criticism*, ed. Joel Myerson (1984), pp. 167–70.

GUY R. WOODALL

FRANCIS, James Bicheno (18 May 1815–18 Sept. 1892), hydraulic engineer, was born at Southleigh, Oxfordshire, England, the son of John Francis, an engineer, and Eliza Frith Bicheno, a clergyman's daughter. Francis received the rudiments of a formal education at the Radley Hall and Wantage academies in Berkshire. However, in 1829, when his father was appointed superintendent of the Duffrynllyn and Port Cawl Railway and Harbor, he left school to work as his assistant. Two years later he took a position on the Great Western Canal in southwestern England.

In 1833 Francis emigrated to America, where he secured engineering employment through George Washington Whistler, a civil engineer then building the Stonington (Connecticut) & Boston Railroad. When Whistler was named chief engineer of the machine shop of the Proprietors of the Locks and Canals in Lowell, Massachusetts, in 1834, he took Francis with him and placed him in charge of dismembering, measuring, and making full-scale drawings of an imported British locomotive for duplication by the Boston and Lowell Railroad. The proprietors, however, soon shifted the focus of Whistler's and Francis's work. By 1834 Francis was deeply involved in the design and erection of the Boott Mill.

In 1837 Whistler left Lowell, and Francis succeeded him as the chief engineer of the Locks and Canals company, a position he was to hold for forty-eight years. Francis's primary responsibilities included maintaining, rebuilding, and expanding the system of dams, locks, and canals that tapped the waterpower of the Merrimack River for Lowell's mills and factories, monitoring water use to ensure that each mill received its proper share, and providing mill owners with engineering advice. The position required tact, evenhandedness, and honesty. Francis possessed these characteristics, along with exquisite organization, sound judgment, an unassuming manner, a cheerful temperament, and a quiet sense of humor. The stability offered by his new position enabled Francis to marry Sarah Wilbur Brownell, daughter of the superintendent of the Locks and Canals machine shop, in 1837. They had six children.

In 1845 the developers of a major waterpower complex at Lawrence, Massachusetts, attempted to lure Francis from Lowell. In response, the proprietors raised his salary, increased his authority, and made him their agent, or general manager, as well as chief engineer. Francis now undertook major enlargement of Lowell's waterpower system. In the mid-1840s, he supervised construction of a major new power canal (the Northern Canal), significantly increasing the number of waterpower sites and raising the waterpower available by around 50 percent. Simultaneously, Francis helped organize a system of upstream water storage dams and reservoirs to improve the reliability of the Merrimack's flow.

Francis's approach to problems was methodical and thorough. One of the best examples was the construction of the guard gate at the entrance to Lowell's Pawtucket Canal. Before designing the gates, Francis reviewed flood records along the Merrimack and designed the gates to withstand the worst flood on record (1785). The result seemed so grossly oversized that the gates were initially labeled "Francis's folly." But in 1852, two years after their completion, the Merrimack reached a flood stage higher than 1785, and Francis's gates saved Lowell and its mills from destruction.

As chief engineer for the manufacturing installations in Lowell, Francis was responsible for more than hydraulic power engineering. He studied the properties of wood and cast iron as structural materials and designed a firefighting system with a fire-service reservoir, a main and hydrant network, and sprinklers.

By the 1850s, in part as a result of Francis's oversight, Lowell had become the best-known waterpower complex in the world. Its system of storage reservoirs, dams, power canals, and waterwheels were capable of developing from 9,000 to 14,000 horsepower, and Lowell had become America's premier industrial city.

Francis contributed to engineering science as well as engineering practice and management. Because systematic and accurate measurement of water consumption by the mills was vital for managing the system, Francis was deeply involved in measuring water flow by the early 1840s. Finding existing methods insufficient, he conducted his own investigations and developed new and more accurate formulas for measuring the flow of water, both in open channels and over submerged weirs. Francis thus became one of the initiators of scientific research in American industry.

Francis's contributions to the development of the water turbine in America were equally significant. In 1844, after observing a turbine erected at Lowell by Uriah A. Boyden, a close friend and adviser, Francis became an enthusiastic advocate of turbines over traditional waterwheels. He persuaded the proprietors to purchase Boyden's patents and carried out an exten-sive turbine testing program. The work of Boyden and Francis at Lowell and that of other American inventors like Samuel Howd led to the development of the American mixed-flow turbine, commonly called the "Francis turbine." It combined the low cost of an inward flow turbine with the high efficiency of an outward flow turbine by reducing internal friction and turbulence. By the 1870s the Francis turbine had become (and still remains) the most widely used waterwheel in America.

Francis's exact contribution to the development of the turbine named after him is hotly disputed. He certainly worked with Boyden and on his own in improving the mixed-flow design and confirming its advantages through large-scale testing. More important, however, Francis encouraged its adoption by Lowell manufacturers and widely publicized its advantages, featuring it prominently in his best-known publication, *Lowell Hydraulic Experiments* (1855). Because this work, which outlines Francis's meticulous experiments on water flow and turbines, was long a standard engineering reference work, Francis's name, for better or worse, became permanently linked with the mixed-flow design.

As his career progressed, Francis was often called on to serve as a court expert, as a referee in suits involving water rights, and as a consultant. Although he did not seek them, Francis also held numerous public and corporate offices. He served a one-year term in the state legislature, five years on the Lowell city council, and twenty years as president of the Stony Brook Railroad. He also was elected president of the Boston Society of Civil Engineers (1874) and the American Society of Civil Engineers (1880).

In the 1870s Francis undertook the redesign and rebuilding of Lowell's Pawtucket dam and canal, completing this work before retiring in 1885. His second son, Colonel James Francis, succeeded him as chief engineer of Locks and Canals. He continued work as a consulting engineer until his death in Lowell, Massachusetts.

• The bulk of Francis's papers are contained in the records of the Proprietors of the Locks and Canals, Baker Library, Harvard University. There is also substantial correspondence between Francis and Boyden in the papers of Uriah A. Boyden at the National Museum of History and Technology of the Smithsonian Institution. Among the better biographical sketches of Francis are William E. Worthen, "Life and Works of James B. Francis," *Contributions of the Old Residents' Historical Association* [Lowell, Massachusetts] 5 (1892–1893): 227–42; Worthen, "James Bicheno Francis," *Proceedings of the American Academy of Arts and Sciences*, n.s., 20 (1893): 333–40; Desmond Fitz Gerald et al., "James Bicheno Francis: A Memoir," *Journal of the Association of Engineering Societies* 13 (1894): 1–9; and G. S. Greene et al., "James Bicheno Francis," American Society of Civil Engineers, *Proceedings* 19 (1893): 74–88. Edwin Layton, Jr.'s short book *From Rule of Thumb to Scientific Engineering: James B. Francis and The Invention of the Francis Turbine* (1992) puts Francis's career in a broader context. Layton's "Scientific Technology, 1845–1900: The Hydraulic Turbine and the Origins of American Industrial Research," *Technology and Culture* 20

(Jan. 1979): 64–89, deals with Francis's role in the emergence of scientific technology in the United States. For the debate on Francis's role in the development of the "Francis turbine," see Arthur T. Safford and Edwin Pierce Hamilton, "The American Mixed-Flow Turbine and Its Setting," American Society of Civil Engineers, *Transactions* 85 (1922): 1237–1356; Louis C. Hunter, *A History of Industrial Power in the United States, 1780–1930*, vol. 1: *Waterpower* (1979); and Layton, "James B. Francis and the Rise of Scientific Technology," in *Technology in America: A History of Individuals and Ideas*, ed. Carroll W. Pursell, Jr. (1981).

TERRY S. REYNOLDS

FRANCIS, Josiah (1770s–18 Apr. 1818), leading prophet of the Creek revolt against the United States in 1813, was likely born in Auttauge, an Indian town near the Alabama River, the son of a Koasati Indian woman and a blacksmith who may have been French. As the best biography of Francis states, his childhood "remains a mystery" (Owsley [1985], p. 273), but it is certain he participated in the deerskin trade and became fluent in English as well as Indian languages.

By 1811 Francis was a trader in his own right. Like many Creeks, he was indebted to the Pensacola firm of Forbes and Company, conscious of the steady flow of American settlers on the new federal road cut through Creek territory in 1806, angry that chiefs had ceded millions of acres to the United States, and fearful his people would lose all of their lands. In September 1811 Francis was among the 5,000 Creeks who welcomed a delegation of northern Indians led by the Shawnee Tecumseh.

Tecumseh promoted Indian solidarity, and his prophets declared that if Indian peoples purified themselves and united, cosmic forces would reverse the tide of the American invasion. Francis may have traveled with Tecumseh to promote this message among other Indian nations. Francis was a *hilishaya* (medicine maker), a person with esoteric knowledge, clairvoyant powers, and the ability to travel to secret realms of reality. Accordingly, Francis was known also by the names Hillis Hadjo or Hildis Hadjo. He reinterpreted Creek tradition so that the goal of restoring symbolic boundaries between Indians and whites became a sacred cause, and political revolt a religious duty. The great majority of Upper Creeks joined his and Tecumseh's movement until half of all Creeks, about 9,000 people, were involved in what became known as the Redstick movement. (Creeks used red sticks, distributed to villages in bundles, to count down the days before planned attacks.)

In the spring of 1813 Francis led a party of warriors that killed a chief, Captain Sam Isaacs, for the crimes of polluting a sanctuary town and murdering a prophet named Little Warrior. The Redsticks called for the execution of several other Upper and Lower Creek chiefs who were unsympathetic to their cause. Claiming the power to cause an earthquake, the Redsticks surrounded the town of Tuckabatchee, where many chiefs had sought refuge.

On this occasion, Francis claimed spiritual power, saying the Creek god, the master of Breath, had personally instructed him in all "the branches of writing and languages perfect enough to converse write and do his own business. . . . He wrote a lengthy letter in spanish (of which language he knew not a word) to the Govr. of Pensacola requesting him . . . to send arms and ammunition" (Nuñez, p. 151). Francis was behaving as a shaman, and later he would display powers of divination and declare that a village built on a site known as Ecunchattee, or the Holy Ground, was impenetrable by whites. Such actions made sense within the religious worldview of the Redsticks.

Francis helped lead a group of warriors to Pensacola to demand from the Spanish authorities many horseloads of arms, powder, and ammunition for every Redstick village. After receiving far less than they desired, the rebels headed north. They were attacked on 27 July 1813 at Burnt Corn (forty miles northeast of the Bigbe settlements above Mobile) by 180 militiamen of Washington County, Mississippi Territory. Although initially caught off guard, the Redsticks rallied, painted themselves for battle, gathered their forces, and prevailed.

Before Burnt Corn, the Redsticks had intended to wage a civil war in Creek country and to avoid war with the powerful neighboring nation-state, the United States. Redsticks had killed a handful of U.S. citizens, but they had killed far more of their fellow Creeks. After Burnt Corn, the Redsticks decided to avenge their losses by attacking a nearby fort harboring local métis, slaves, and settlers, among whom were many U.S. citizens. On 30 August 1813 700 Redsticks, led by another métis prophet named Paddy Walch, surrounded and after several hours took Fort Mims, killing at least 247 people and suffering substantial losses themselves. The battle of Fort Mims provided land-hungry U.S. leaders such as Andrew Jackson with the excuse they needed to justify a massive invasion of Creek country. In subsequent months, armies from Tennessee, Georgia, and the Mississippi Territory destroyed dozens of Creek villages. At the battle of Horseshoe Bend (27 Mar. 1814) at Tohopeka more Indians died than in any battle fought between the United States and Indians. As a result of the war, thousands of Creek men, women, and children perished from violence, starvation, or disease. Hundreds more fled to Florida as refugees. The forced and fraudulent treaty of Fort Jackson (Aug. 1814) transferred 14 million acres of land to the United States.

Francis had not been at the battle of Horseshoe Bend but on the Gulf Coast of Florida, and he continued to champion the Creek rebel cause for four more years, joining the British forces preparing to invade the South. In the summer and fall of 1814, on board British ships, he witnessed the failed British efforts to take Mobile and defend New Orleans. He then sailed, as a guest of Major Edward Nicolls, to England in hopes of persuading Britain to enforce the Treaty of Ghent (1814), which provided for the return of the lands that Britain's Creek allies possessed in 1811. The English procrastinated. Francis eventually left England, unsuccessful, at the end of 1816. He then spent several months in Nassau before moving close to St. Marks in Spanish Florida with his wife and two daughters. He is also known to have had two sons. This placed him near surviving Redsticks dwelling among the Seminoles. In April 1818 an American army under the command of Andrew Jackson attacked and destroyed Fowltown and St. Marks. Soon afterward Francis was captured when he boarded a schooner flying a British flag. The ship turned out to be an American vessel, and Josiah Francis was hanged.

• Information pertaining to Francis is sketchy and scattered. His activities are best documented during the latter part of his life when he provided prophetic leadership to the Redstick resistance movement. The fullest biography is Frank L. Owsley, Jr., "Prophet of War: Josiah Francis and the Creek War," *American Indian Quarterly* 9 (Summer 1985): 273–94. Valuable biographical insights are also provided by J. Leitch Wright, Jr., *Creeks and Seminoles: The Destruction and Regeneration of the Muscogulge People* (1986). For Francis's role as a prophet, consult George Stiggins, "A Historical Narration of the Genealogy, Traditions, and Downfall of the Ispocaga or Creek Tribe of Indians, Written by One of the Tribe," Draper Manuscripts, vol. 5, Georgia, Alabama, and South Carolina Papers at the Wisconsin Historical Society, which has been published as Theron A. Nuñez, Jr., ed., "Creek Nativism and the Creek War of 1813–14," *Ethnohistory* 5 (1958): 1–47, 131–75, 292–301. For the broader political, social, and cultural background of Francis's time and place, see David Tait, "Journal of David Taitt's Travels from Pensacola, West Florida, to, and through the Country of the Upper and Lower Creeks, 1772," in *Travels in the American Colonies*, ed. Newton D. Mereness (1916); Thomas Woodward, *Woodward's Reminiscences of the Creek, or Muscogee Indians, Contained in Letters to Friends in Georgia and Alabama* (1859; repr., 1939); Owsley, *Struggle for the Gulf Borderlands: The Creek War to the Battle of New Orleans* (1981); and Henry S. Halbert and T. H. Ball, *The Creek War of 1813–1814*, ed. Owsley (1969). The fullest treatment of the Muskogee resistance movement and its religious forms is Joel W. Martin, *Sacred Revolt: The Muskogees' Struggle for a New World* (1991).

JOEL W. MARTIN

FRANCIS, Thomas, Jr. (15 July 1900–1 Oct. 1969), physician, virologist, and epidemiologist, was born in Gas City, Indiana, the son of Thomas Francis, a Methodist lay preacher and steelworker, and Elizabeth Ann Cadogan, a Salvation Army worker. He graduated from Allegheny College in 1921 and from Yale University School of Medicine in 1925. He received his residence training under Francis G. Blake at the New Haven Hospital.

From 1928 until 1936 Francis worked at the hospital of the Rockefeller Institute. Blake and Rufus I. Cole, his supervisor there, were two inspiring teachers who taught him the principles of clinical medicine. He worked in the pneumonia unit, analyzing the chemical differences between various types of pneumococci, the bacteria that cause this disease. After the isolation of human influenza virus was reported by a group of British investigators in 1933, Francis started to study this respiratory disease and was the first to isolate the virus in North America ("Transmission of Influenza by a Filterable Virus," *Science* 80 [1934]: 457–59).

In 1933 Francis married Dorothy Packard Otton; they had two children. From 1936 to 1938 he was a staff member of the International Health Division of the Rockefeller Foundation, in charge of influenza research. From 1938 until 1941 he was professor of bacteriology and chair of the department at New York University College of Medicine. In 1940 he discovered influenza virus B, which differed from the known A strain ("A New Type of Virus from Epidemic Influenza," *Science* 92 [1940]: 405–8). In 1941 he was appointed professor of epidemiology at the University of Michigan in Ann Arbor. Early that year, at the invitation of Blake, who was then president of the U.S. Army Epidemiological Board, Francis was made director of the Commission on Influenza of that organization. In that capacity he was involved in the cultivation of influenza virus on artificial media and in the study of its antigenic properties during various epidemics. Under the auspices of the Commission on Influenza, he took part in the successful development, field trial, and evaluation of protective influenza vaccines—including the application of adjuvants, nonspecific enhancers of the immune response to antigens. Francis served on the Commission on Influenza and on the Armed Forces Epidemiological Board itself for more than twenty-five years.

It was after this wartime work that researchers discovered the rapid mutability of influenza viruses: a vaccine prepared for one year's virus would be unlikely to work on next year's strain. This led to the establishment of a worldwide network of laboratories to isolate and detect emerging new viral strains. Francis was one of the first to claim that these changes in the antigenic properties of the influenza virus follow a more or less orderly round of patterns, making the annual changes easier to anticipate if not fully predict. In 1950 a third type of influenza virus (the C strain) was reported by Francis and his collaborators ("Identification of Another Epidemic Respiratory Disease," *Science* 112: 495–97).

In the late 1940s Francis's studies of viral disease were extended to studies of enteric viruses, in particular the polio virus. In 1953 Francis was appointed to design, supervise, and evaluate the field trials of a vaccine prepared from inactivated polio virus. This vaccine had been developed by Jonas Salk, who was a former protégé of Francis and had worked with him on the influenza trials. In the latter, Francis had used a double-blind, placebo-controlled design to test the effectiveness of influenza virus vaccines. This meant the inclusion in the study of control subjects who received not the vaccine but a placebo, without either the volunteer or the doctor knowing which preparation was being administered. Despite resistance from experts of the National Foundation for Infantile Paralysis, the organization that was sponsoring the polio vaccine study, Francis insisted on this double-blind, placebo-controlled scheme. After statistical analysis and verification of the study, Francis was able to announce on

12 April 1955 that Salk's vaccine was safe, potent, and effective.

Francis's approach to analytic epidemiology was then applied in a study of the epidemiology of chronic disease and the understanding of the noninfectious factors involved. For this purpose, the community of Tecumseh, Michigan, was chosen as the object of biostatistical studies, and in 1961 Francis became the director of the newly established University of Michigan Center for the Study of Diseases of the Heart and Circulation and Related Disorders.

Francis's expertise on the science of epidemiology was sought again by the American government in the mid-1950s. In 1946 President Harry S. Truman had established the Atomic Bomb Casualty Commission (ABCC) to study the delayed effects of radiation on the survivors of the atomic bombs at Hiroshima and Nagasaki. In the mid-1950s the commission was at a dead end, without having reached a conclusion. Francis and others visited Japan in October 1955 to determine new objectives and a new strategy for the ABCC. This resulted in the "Unified Study Program" for ABCC, also known as the "Francis Report." It contained plans to investigate the natural history of a population over its lifespan (see, for example, R. W. Miller, "Delayed Radiation Effects in Atomic-Bomb Survivors: Major Observations by the Atomic Bomb Casualty Commission Are Evaluated," *Science* 166 [1969]: 569–74).

Francis received many honors and awards, notably the Medal of Freedom from the U.S. Army in 1946. His major contributions concern the rational application of epidemiological methods and their extension from infectious disease to noninfectious chronic disease, including environmental factors.

• A collection of Francis papers is in the Bentley Historical Library, University of Michigan, Ann Arbor. Among Francis's major publications are "A Clinical Evaluation of Vaccination against Influenza," *Journal of the American Medical Association* 124 (1944): 982–85; with R. F. Korns et al., "An Evaluation of the 1954 Poliomyelitis Vaccine Trials: Summary Report," *American Journal of Public Health* (special issue) 45 (May 1955); "Aspects of the Tecumseh Study," *Public Health Reports* 76 (1961): 963–65; and, with Frederick H. Epstein, "Tecumseh, Michigan," *Milbank Memorial Fund Quarterly* 43, supp. (1965): 333–42. Biographical details are in J. R. Paul, "Thomas Francis, Jr., July 15, 1900–October 1, 1969," National Academy of Sciences, *Biographical Memoirs* 44 (1974): 57–110; and Colin M. MacLeod, ed., "The Thomas Francis, Jr., Memorial Festschrift," *Archives of Environmental Health* 21 (1970): 225–474. The latter contains papers on various aspects of Francis's career and an extensive curriculum vitae and bibliography. A more literary description of Francis's work and its impact on the study and prevention of influenza and polio is in Richard Carter, *Breakthrough: The Saga of Jonas Salk* (1966); see also Naomi Rogers, "Thomas Francis, Jr.: From the Bench to the Field," in *Medical Lives and Scientific Medicine at Michigan, 1891–1969*, ed. Joel D. Howell (1993), pp. 161–87.

TON VAN HELVOORT

FRANCK, James (26 Aug. 1882–21 May 1964), physicist, was born in Hamburg, Germany, the son of Jacob Franck, a banker, and Rebecca Drucker. He graduat-ed from the Wilhelms Gymnasium in Hamburg and in 1901 entered the University of Heidelberg, where he studied mainly chemistry and met fellow student Max Born, who was to become a lifelong friend and scientific colleague. Finding physics more to his liking, he transferred in 1902 to the University of Berlin, where he was influenced by Max Planck, Heinrich Rubens, and Emil Warburg. There he received a Ph.D. in 1906 under the direction of Warburg with a dissertation, "Über die Beweglichkeit der Ladungsträger der Spitzenentladung," on ionic mobilities. Following a brief period at Frankfurt on Main, he returned to Berlin as an assistant in the laboratory of Rubens. In 1911 he became a privatdozent in Berlin in physics and, in 1916, an extraordinary professor. On the outbreak of World War I, Franck volunteered for service—out of a sense of duty—became an officer, and was awarded the Iron Cross, First Class. In 1918, however, he fell seriously ill with polyneuritis and was removed from combat duty and assigned to gas warfare research under Fritz Haber at the Kaiser Wilhelm Institut für Physikalische Chemie at Berlin-Dahlem. At the war's end he remained at this institute as head of the physics section. He was active in trying to reactivate postwar interest in physics, and while holding this position he met Danish physicist Niels Bohr in 1920.

Franck's friend Born was called to the University of Göttingen in 1921 as professor of theoretical physics, and, as a condition for accepting this post, he required that a chair in experimental physics be created for Franck. Accordingly, in 1921 Franck became professor of experimental physics at Göttingen and director of a new institute of experimental physics there. He held this position until 1933, when he was forced out by the Nazi accession to power. The Göttingen years were among the happiest and most productive of his life, and the close cooperation and free exchange of ideas with Born provided a unique environment for the development of the new quantum theory. After leaving Göttingen in 1933, Franck visited the United States, then returned to a temporary visiting professorship in Bohr's institute in Copenhagen (1934-1935). He then accepted a professorship of physics at Johns Hopkins University before moving to Chicago as professor of physical chemistry in 1938. The Chicago position was particularly attractive to him since by then he had developed an interest in photosynthesis and the Samuel Fels Foundation had offered to set up laboratory facilities for him. Franck became a naturalized citizen in 1941, and during the Second World War he headed the chemistry division of the Manhattan Project (the code name for the atomic bomb project) in the Metallurgical Laboratory at Chicago (1942–1945). He formally retired from his Chicago professorship in 1947 but remained actively involved in research (mostly dealing with photosynthesis) until his death.

In 1912 Franck and Berlin colleague Gustav Hertz began to conduct a series of experiments concerned with elastic collisions between electrons and atoms of mercury vapor, which they intended as tests of the quantum hypothesis. Bohr's theory of the atom appeared in 1913 but was not well received or understood in Germany, where, because of the meager evidence available, a model of the atom was regarded as highly speculative. In 1914, scarcely six months after this theory was published, Franck and Hertz obtained results that demonstrated the main tenets of the Bohr theory, i.e., the reality of quantized energy levels. Their results also confirmed Planck's quantum hypothesis and provided a direct method of measuring the value of Planck's constant. Bohr immediately saw that these results were confirmations of his theory, but Franck and Hertz did not share his view since their knowledge of his work was fragmentary. In particular, they interpreted their measurements in terms of an ionization potential rather than an excitation potential as required in the Bohr theory. In fact, in their view, their work seemed to contradict his theory. This confusion remained throughout the war years, and it was only in 1919 that they realized their error. Nevertheless, their measurements were correct, providing the first experimental confirmation of Bohr's atomic theory and the basis of Franck's and Hertz's joint award of the Nobel Prize in physics for 1925.

As Born related in his autobiography, this confirmation led Franck to view Bohr's theoretical insight as being almost infallible, and a warm relationship developed between them. Consequently, much of Franck's work focused on verifying quantum theory, and a mere suggestion from Bohr was sufficient to launch him into undertaking a series of experiments. For example, in 1925 Born's student Walter Elsasser, with Franck's encouragement, obtained the first experimental verification of Louis de Broglie's matter waves (1924), in an attempt to elucidate the Ramsauer effect. Likewise, Born's own statistical interpretation of the wave function (1926), which later won him the Nobel Prize in 1954, was partially stimulated by Franck's experiments on atomic and molecular collisions. Franck's publications are hardly a reliable guide to his influence during this period because he freely had discussions with everyone seeking his advice and—even with his own doctoral students—demurred from allowing his name to appear on their published theses. His collaboration with Born, however, produced two papers (1925), dealing with the basic ideas of molecule formation, triple collisions, the Franck-Condon principle, the theory of continuous molecular spectra, and adsorption catalysis. Also he coauthored an influential report on collision theory, "Anregung von Quantensprüngen durch Stösse," for the *Handbuch der Physik* (1926), with Pascual Jordan. During his Göttingen period, Franck's interests included collision between atoms, the formation of molecules and their dissociation, fluorescence, and chemical properties. The latter three topics ultimately led him into chemistry and biochemistry, the primary interests of his research in the United States, where he produced a basic paper in 1938 on exciton theory and the photographic process with American physicist Edward Teller and undertook a bold attempt to formulate a physical model of

photosynthesis. Although he was to devote almost thirty years of his life to this model, it involved him in much controversy and did not achieve either the acceptance or the recognition that was accorded his earlier work. In retrospect, his results were more important for the approach he took and the discussion that they generated than for their substantive content.

Not only a distinguished scientist whose work made a significant contribution to the understanding of quantum theory and photosynthesis, Franck was also one of the best loved and respected scientists of his time. He had two predominant qualities: his obsession with science and his kindness and generosity. The latter was extended not only to his family, friends, and co-workers, but to whomever he found in need. He was by nature a very gentle man, and Born was fond of relating the story that in World War I Franck's first order to his soldiers was "Platoon turn right—please." While this is probably apocryphal, it is perfectly consistent with his character. Possessing great moral courage, he was in 1933 one of the few who openly demonstrated against the Nazi laws of racial discrimination, even though his military record in World War I exempted him from the initial version of these decrees. On resigning his position in April, he published his resignation in the national press as a personal protest against the Nazi regime. This was a dangerous thing to do, and it was almost a miracle that later in the year he and his family were able to escape Germany unharmed. Some twelve years later, six days after the Alamogordo test of the atomic bomb, as chairman of a seven-man committee of concerned scientists, he sent a report to Secretary of War Henry Stimson urging a careful consideration of the social and political consequences of using the new weapon against Japan. This document became known as the Franck Report, and it urged an open demonstration of the bomb in an uninhabited locale as an alternative to dropping it without warning on the Japanese. It also advocated international control of the bomb and warned that its use could lead to an arms race. Whether one accepts these views or not, they stand as unmistakable symbols of the realization of the moral and social responsibility of scientists in the atomic age, and Franck proposed them in a rational and sincere manner. Later he became an advocate of the peaceful use of nuclear science in medical and biological research. He was one of the founding sponsors of the *Bulletin of the Atomic Scientists* in 1945.

In addition to sharing the 1925 Nobel Prize in physics (awarded in 1926) with his co-worker Gustav Hertz for their experimental verification of quantum theory, Franck became a member of the National Academy of Sciences (1944) and a foreign member of the Royal Society (1964). He was awarded the Max Planck Medal of the German Physical Society in 1951 and the Rumford Medal of the American Academy of Arts and Sciences in 1955. He had married the Swedish pianist Ingrid Josephson in 1907; they had two daughters. After his wife's death in 1942, he married in 1946 Hertha Sponer, a professor of physics at Duke University, who had been one of his former students and co-workers in Göttingen as well as a family friend. They had no children. Franck's health began to fail in the postwar years, but he remained active in his research activities. He was particularly gratified when upon returning to Göttingen in 1953 he was awarded Freedom of the City, and on a subsequent visit he died there.

• Of special interest are Franck's Nobel Prize lecture, "Transformation of Kinetic Energy of Free Electrons into Excitation Energy of Atomic Impacts," *Nobel Lectures in Physics*, vol. 1 (1965), pp. 98–111; and his memorial tributes, "Albert Einstein," *Bulletin of the Atomic Scientists* 11 (June 1955): 203, and "Niels Bohrs Persönlichkeit," *Die Naturwissenschaften* 50 (*Heft* 9, *Erstes Maiheft*, 1963): 341–43. The full text of the Franck Report has been published as "A Report to the Secretary of War," in *The Atomic Age—Scientists in National and World Affairs*, ed. Morton Grodzins and Eugene Rabinowitch (1963). An issue of *Reviews of Modern Physics* 24 (June 1952) was dedicated to him on the occasion of his seventieth birthday. There are numerous references to Franck in Max Born, *My Life—Recollections of a Nobel Laureate* (1978). A critical discussion of Franck's work on photosynthesis can be found in Roderick K. Clayton, *Molecular Physics in Photosynthesis* (1965), pp. 182–91. A most detailed, though not entirely reliable, obituary notice of Franck, which includes a portrait and a complete list of publications, is in the *Biographical Memoirs of Fellows of the Royal Society* 11 (1965): 52–74. Other obituaries are in the *New York Times*, 22 May 1964; and *Die Naturwissenschaften* 51 (*Heft* 18, *Zweites Septemberheft*, 1964): 421–23.

JOSEPH D. ZUND

FRANK, Jerome New (10 Sept. 1889–13 Jan. 1957), New Dealer, federal appeals judge, and legal philosopher, was born in New York City, the son of Herman Frank, a lawyer, and Clara New, a musician. The grandson of German Jews who immigrated to the United States around 1850, Frank moved with his parents to Chicago at the age of seven. A precocious child, he challenged his kindergarten teacher on such exotic subjects as Greek mythology. He attended Chicago public schools, graduated from Hyde Park High School at the age of sixteen, and then enrolled at the University of Chicago. By attending summer terms Frank graduated in three years. In the fall of 1909 Frank entered law school at the University of Chicago and in 1912 graduated with the highest grades ever achieved at the University of Chicago Law School. With characteristic humility, he shunned interview-seeking reporters. In 1914 he married Florence Kiper, a well-known poet and writer in Chicago literary circles.

For two decades Frank practiced law in Chicago and New York, concerning himself primarily with the complex legal and financial issues related to corporate reorganization. After Franklin D. Roosevelt was elected president in 1932, Frank began to play a major role in the New Deal. Offered the position of general counsel to the Agricultural Adjustment Administration (AAA), Frank accepted and put together an inspired legal staff, including Alger Hiss, Adlai Stevenson, Thurman Arnold, Telford Taylor, and Abe Fortas. Championing the interests of consumers, tenant farmers, and sharecroppers, Frank's advocacy eventually brought him into conflict with AAA administrator Chester Davis, which resulted in his being purged, along with other allies. Frank considered leaving the New Deal, but at Roosevelt's request he moved over to the Reconstruction Finance Corporation as special counsel. Then, in 1937, he was appointed to the Securities and Exchange Commission. Frank also provided the legal impetus for creating the Federal Surplus Relief Corporation, the first food program for needy Americans, and he was a principal founder of the National Lawyers Guild.

From 1941 until his death, Frank served on the U.S. Court of Appeals for the Second Circuit, where he rendered civil rights and civil liberties decisions that were to significantly influence the U.S. Supreme Court. Quick to denounce harsh police interrogations and the arbitrary deportation of foreigners, he was nevertheless slow to criticize the convictions of Julius and Ethel Rosenberg and the jail sentences given to lawyers who defended Communists in the early 1950s. He believed that music, art, philosophy, and politics shaped the law, and thus he enlivened his judicial opinions by quoting a variety of thinkers, such as Aristotle and Jonathan Swift.

In his opinions Frank frequently addressed the Supreme Court as an advocate—urging, persuading, coaxing, and cajoling the Court to move in desired directions. At the same time, he recognized the limits imposed by his subordinate position, and he gracefully accepted those bounds. Frank faithfully followed Supreme Court precedent, but if a rule seemed misguided he would criticize the doctrine and urge the Supreme Court to reexamine it. *United States v. Roth* (1956) illustrates Frank's technique. Although he considered a federal obscenity statute unconstitutional, several Supreme Court decisions had assumed the statute's validity without squarely facing the issue. In a new challenge to the law, Frank did not dodge these earlier rulings by describing them as obiter dicta. Rather, he followed them and voted to uphold the convictions. At the same time, in a concurrence, he analyzed the serious constitutional issues with a coherence and lucidity that has not yet been surpassed. Frank's seminal effort anticipated many later Supreme Court cases that, over the next two decades, relied on Frank's opinion and reasoning.

Protection for civil liberties was a persistent theme in Frank's judicial opinions. He believed that republican government maximized free choice and affirmed the dignity of the individual. On the Second Circuit he struggled to protect this vision. He regularly challenged the Supreme Court to expand the definition of, and protection for, civil liberties. For instance, he tried valiantly to humanize immigration and deportation law, which had treated aliens cavalierly. Frank wrote his most passionate opinions in the area of criminal law and procedure. He considered electronic eavesdropping a dangerous invasion of privacy that should be limited by the Fourth Amendment's prohibition on unreasonable searches and seizures. His skepticism about the accuracy of the law's fact-finding processes led him to believe that courts wrongly convicted many innocent persons. He thought that police investigation practices frequently degenerated into brutal "third degree" tactics that coerced confessions in violation of the Fifth and Sixth amendments. Following in Frank's path, the Supreme Court moved to curb prolonged police interrogations and to control offensive police practices. The progressive constitutionalization of American criminal process secured by the Vinson and Warren Courts reflected not merely the judgment of a majority of the Supreme Court, but rather a broader legal movement led prominently by Frank.

Best remembered for his legal philosophy, Frank pioneered American legal realism, a movement that began in the 1930s and remains influential. "Realism" drew on William James's pragmatism but was never a technical philosophical term. Instead, realism was used, as in art, to describe fidelity to nature or an accurate representation of things as they are, not as one wishes them to be. Frank's influence began with the publication in 1930 of *Law and the Modern Mind*, his first and most important book. Describing as a myth the concept that law is fixed and predictable, he attacked the conventional wisdom that judges discover preexisting law and use formal logic to reach the correct result. Frank reasoned that a syllogism provides only a logical structure, not the premises, and since courts select the premises judges may decide cases any way they choose and camouflage their preferences behind flawless logic. To Frank, legal rules played a limited role in determining judicial decisions. Instead, judges begin with the desired conclusion and then rationalize their decisions by finding facts and selecting rules that justify the desired conclusion. Frank thought that "the personality of the judge is the pivotal factor in law administration." He thus identified unfettered judicial discretion, rather than legal rules and *stare decisis*, as the real explanation for court decisions.

Law and the Modern Mind attempted both to expose the basic myth of legal predictability and to explain its remarkable persistence. For a partial explanation of the source of this widespread illusion, Frank turned to the nascent discipline of psychology. In early life each child comes to rely on a seemingly omniscient and omnipotent father who personifies certainty and infallibility. As evidence of the father's fallibility slowly accumulates, however, the child becomes disillusioned. Yet the urge to find certainty and security continues. The law "inevitably becomes a partial substitute for the Father-as-Infallible-Judge." To overcome the blindness of legal uncertainty, adults must relinquish their childish need for an authoritative father. Frank's "modern mind is a mind free of childish emotional drags, a mature mind."

A hallmark of Frank's legal realism was his bold and innovative use of sources outside the law. He sought to understand how law works by looking beyond narrow legal rules and drawing creatively on the insights of other disciplines. Psychology had special utility as the best instrument available for the study of human nature: Freudian concepts permeate Frank's father-substitute theory, and Jean Piaget's child psychology also influenced him. In addition, Frank relied on the philosophical writings of Plato and Aristotle, the work in logic of F. C. S. Schiller and John Dewey, the linguistic theories of Charles K. Ogden and I. A. Richards, and the anthropology of Bronislaw Malinowski.

Frank pioneered the introduction of social science analysis in the law, but his effort never took hold. A problem in interdisciplinary study is to select among competing methodologies from the companion field. Frank's eclectic style led him to borrow from conflicting approaches, such as Freudian and gestalt psychology, without appreciating that each theory had its own coherence and demands. His effort to engage in social science analysis was primitive and incomplete. Yet he lent credibility to psychology as a serious discipline at an early critical stage in its development, and he generally encouraged the subsequent use of social science methodology to analyze legal problems.

Law and the Modern Mind exaggerated the degree of judicial discretion and unpredictability in the legal system. By concentrating only on court-made law, Frank slighted the role of the legislature in enacting statutes and thereby circumscribing judicial discretion. Because he could demonstrate that rules do not translate into absolutely predictable court decisions, Frank assumed that the legal rules had negligible value. He did not take into account how probability guides human behavior as men and women adapt their behavior to comply with legal rules. The law affects people not merely by the litigation that produces a court order, but also by shaping their expectations of what will probably, or even possibly, occur if a rule is violated.

Law and the Modern Mind nonetheless challenged central tenets of the American legal system. Conventional wisdom portrays the common law system as one of slow growth guided by *stare decisis*; reasoning from past experience to present problems, judges apply the law. The democratic system prides itself on being a government of laws not of men, remembering the maxim that "where law ends, tyranny begins." Under the American system of separation of powers the legislature makes the law, and the judiciary applies it. In rejecting these ideas, *Law and the Modern Mind* presented a potentially explosive attack on the political status quo. By exploding the myth of the role of *stare decisis* and by exposing judicial power and discretion, Frank tried to disabuse both the profession and the public of the idea that judges follow the law, thereby raising a serious challenge to the legitimacy not only of court decisions, but of law generally. By exposing the political aspect of law, Frank revealed the law's inevitable role in distributing wealth and power.

Frank died in New Haven, Connecticut.

• The principal collection of Frank papers is in the Sterling Library at Yale University. A biography of Frank is Robert Jerome Glennon, *The Iconoclast as Reformer: Jerome Frank's Impact on American Law* (1985).

ROBERT JEROME GLENNON

FRANK, Leo Max (17 Apr. 1884–17 Aug. 1915), lynching victim, was born in Paris, Texas, the son of Rudolph Frank and Rae (maiden name unknown). Frank is known for the events that occurred during the last two years of his life rather than for anything that he did before that time. And he is remembered more as victim than as activist, for he did not order the incidents of his life during that period—malevolent forces dictated their course.

Until he entered the limelight in April 1913, Frank had led an ordinary life. A few months after his birth his parents had taken him from Texas to Brooklyn, New York, where he attended the public schools and Pratt Institute. He received a degree in mechanical engineering from Cornell University in 1906. His first job was with the B. F. Sturtevant Company of Hyde Park, Massachusetts, a suburb of Boston, and then in 1908 he moved to Atlanta, Georgia, where his uncle, Moses Frank, asked him to help establish the National Pencil Factory, which he agreed to do. The younger Frank also invested in the factory and served as its superintendent and manager. In 1910 he married Lucille Selig, daughter of a prosperous Atlanta family. (The marriage was childless.) That year he also joined the B'nai B'rith, a Jewish fraternal organization of which he was elected president in 1912.

Frank's demise began with the rape and murder of a thirteen-year-old girl, Mary Phagan, in his factory on Confederate Memorial Day, 26 April 1913, a Saturday. Phagan had gone to the office to collect her pay, which Frank gave to her. Early the next morning the night watchman found the girl's body and summoned the police, who found two scrawled notes (referred to thereafter as the "murder notes") next to her body, allegedly indicating how the murderer committed the deed. At 7:00 A.M. they went to Frank's home and took him first to the morgue and then to the factory. By that time the sister-in-law of one of the policemen had identified the body and given the name; Frank checked his records and saw that he had paid Phagan the previous afternoon.

When Phagan's body had first been found, clear fingerprints were discovered on her jacket, and later in the morning bloody fingerprints were noted on the back door of the factory's basement. No record indicates, however, that the prints were ever tested. On the other hand, reporters as well as the police observed that Frank had appeared nervous when summoned by the police, and alleged blood stains (later discovered to have been drops of paint) led from an upstairs workroom to Frank's office. With no witnesses attesting to having seen the girl after Frank had paid her, the police arrested him on suspicion of murder. The chief of police claimed that because the townspeople were upset this seemed the best course of action at the time.

During the next two months the inept police arrested other people, including two blacks: the night watchman who had found the body and a janitor, Jim Conley, who was seen washing blood from a shirt. The police confiscated the shirt and then lost it before the blood could be tested. Assuming that the notes found near the body had been written by the murderer, the police tested the handwriting of various people. By chance, Frank indicated that Conley knew how to write (the janitor had previously denied it), and the police got him to copy the notes. The handwriting matched and the police began more serious questioning of Conley. The janitor ultimately gave four different affidavits alleging that Frank had been alone with the girl and had summoned him to assist in disposing of the body. Because of the contradictions and illogical sequences described in them, the first three affidavits made no sense, and although newspaper reporters pointed that out, the prosecuting attorney relied on the fourth one as the basis for the state's case against Frank.

Unfortunately for Frank he hired lawyers with excellent reputations who failed to perform at the level of their presumed courtroom capabilities. They interrogated Conley, who had been kept in seclusion by the district attorney's office for sixteen hours, since signing the fourth affidavit. Frank's lawyers assumed that the janitor was lying, but they were unable to convince the jury of that. Conley claimed to have assisted Frank in removing the girl's body from the factory manager's office and to have taken it to the basement after the deed had been done. Despite repeated questioning, the attorneys could not get the janitor to change his tale. They also encouraged him to speak about other occasions when he had allegedly "watched out" for the factory manager who he claimed was alone with young women. Finally, failing to prove that Conley was lying, Frank's attorneys petitioned the judge to remove the testimony from the record. The prosecution objected, noting that although the line of questioning by the defense had been inappropriate it could not now plead to have the janitor's words expunged. The presiding judge agreed, noting that while the testimony "may be extracted from the record . . . it is an impossibility to withdraw it from the jury's mind."

When the defense presented its case, Frank spoke for four hours, and his words, according to the *Atlanta Constitution*, "carried the ring of truth in every sentence." In his summation for the prosecution, however, the chief prosecuting attorney focused on the fact that "two of the ablest lawyers in the country" had been unsuccessful in their attempt to discredit the janitor's testimony. The jury accepted this conclusion as well. Thus the failure of the defense attorneys to discredit the state's main witness ultimately led to Frank's conviction, and the judge sentenced him to hang.

Frank's trial did not take place in a neutral atmosphere. The populace had been worked up by the brutal crime against the child. The people were also upset because they believed that Frank, a northerner and a Jew, was a factory manager who exploited the youth and workers of the South. And because the newspapers had given so much attention to the case—front-page headlines daily for four months—everyone knew that Frank was the state's target. Nothing occurred during the trial to lead the citizenry to doubt the verdict. Indeed, their assumption of Frank's guilt was demonstrated by the applause that greeted the prosecuting attorneys as they left the court each day and by shouts from the street warning the twelve male jurors: "hang the Jew or we'll hang you."

Appeals made on Frank's behalf—three to the Georgia Supreme Court and two to the U.S. Supreme Court—were all turned down on legal technicalities rather than on a review of the evidence. A plea for clemency went to Governor John Slaton, who, after carefully reviewing the case records in June 1915, commuted the death sentence to life imprisonment. That decision provoked Georgians into a rampage, and thousands marched on the governor's mansion with the intention of lynching him. They would have accomplished their task had not an entire battalion of the National Guard been on hand to protect Slaton.

Two months later "the best citizens" of Marietta, Georgia, Phagan's hometown, took the law into their own hands. They stormed the prison farm where Frank was being held, removed him, and took him to Marietta, where they lynched him from a tree.

The Leo Frank case has come down in American Jewish lore as one in which the victim suffered because of anti-Semitism. And barely three weeks after the trial ended, B'nai B'rith established its Anti-Defamation League, partially on the ground that prejudice toward a Jew influenced the Atlanta jury. To be sure, anti-Semitism did affect the course of the trial. But it is also important to recognize the difficulty of obtaining a jury verdict that goes against the temper of the community. Moreover, the ineptness of Frank's attorneys combined with the skillful use of witnesses by the prosecution led most Atlantans to conclude that the state had a foolproof case. Only afterward, when careful examinations were made by those who wanted Frank to be given a new trial, did the full nature of the defense's incompetence become apparent.

• An important essay on Leo Frank is Steve Oney, "The Lynching of Leo Frank," *Esquire*, Sept. 1985, pp. 90–94ff. Harry Golden, *A Little Girl Is Dead* (1965), focuses on the trial and events leading to it. Leonard Dinnerstein, *The Leo Frank Case* (1966), gives less attention to those aspects of the case but much more detail on the subsequent appeals and the reaction of the American Jewish community.

LEONARD DINNERSTEIN

FRANK, Philipp G. (20 Mar. 1884–21 July 1966), scholar of physics and philosophy of science, was born in Vienna, Austria, the son of Hans Frank, a chemist, and Marta Hoffmann. Frank received his doctorate in theoretical physics from the University of Vienna in 1907, having studied under Ludwig Boltzmann. During that year he published the essay "Kausalgesetz und Erfahrung" (*Causal Law and Experience*), written under the influence of the scientist-philosophers Henri Poincaré and Ernst Mach; with the latter he soon became closely associated. By its analysis of the limits of causality in science, and its base in convention, this paper attracted the attention both of Albert Einstein, who became a lifelong friend, and of V. I. Lenin, who condemned it in his *Materialism and Empirio-Criticism* (1909). Frank's influential book, *Das Kausalgesetz und seine Grenzen* (1932), was a further development of the 1907 paper.

At the end of his student years, Frank began to meet regularly with a small group on Thursday nights in one of the old Viennese coffeehouses, the Café Central. The group consisted of students as well as Hans Hahn (later professor of mathematics at the University of Vienna) and the political economist and sociologist Otto Neurath. Others, such as the scientist Richard von Mises, joined them occasionally. Their lively, informal discussions on current problems of philosophy and science, and particularly on the relation between reason and experience, aimed, according to Frank, to "bring about the closest possible *rapprochement* between philosophy and science" and also "to avoid the traditional ambiguity and obscurity of philosophy." This group eventually transformed itself in the 1920s, under Moritz Schlick, into the Vienna Circle, the antimetaphysical movement of scientific philosophy identified with logical positivism, or logical empiricism.

In 1912 Einstein recommended Frank as his choice as successor to the professorship of theoretical physics at the German University of Prague. There he taught classes in classical physics, relativity theory, and the philosophy of science and eventually became an active, commuting member of the Vienna Circle. In 1917 he was promoted to full professorship and became director of the university's Institute for Theoretical Physics. In 1920 he married his student Hanna Gerson; they had no children. As a physicist his main research interests were relativity and quantum theory, variational calculus, Hamiltonian geometrical optics, and wave mechanics. He published widely on these topics and had great skill as an expositor as well. Frank's early papers on relativity demonstrate a masterful presenter of the elements of special relativity theory—but also a conciliator who stressed the continuities with pre-Minkowskian sensibilities. In the 1920s and 1930s, Frank collaborated with Richard von Mises on *Die Differential- und Integralgleichungen der Mechanik und Physik* (1925, rev. 1935), which benefited the mathematics training of a whole generation of physicists.

Throughout his career, Frank published constantly on the philosophy of science, essentially in the spirit of Ernst Mach. In 1931 he succeeded in having the author of the seminal book *Logical Structure of the World*, Rudolf Carnap, appointed to a special chair at the

University of Prague. Of Frank's work in the philosophy of science it has been said by Herbert Feigl, a philosopher of science and one of the earliest members of the Vienna Circle to emigrate to the United States, that it "combines informal *logical* analysis of the sciences with a vivid awareness of the *psychological* and *social-cultural* factors operating in the selection of problems, and in the acceptance or rejection of hypotheses, and which contribute to the shaping of styles of scientific theorizing."

In 1938 Frank left Prague with his wife, having accepted an invitation for an extensive lecture tour of American universities. When Czechoslovakia was invaded by the Germans, he could not return there. The Harvard physicists P. W. Bridgman and E. C. Kemble, who had admired Frank's work, spearheaded a drive to help Frank obtain permission to stay in the United States at their university. Starting at Harvard in 1939, he lectured on physics and philosophy of science on various term appointments until his retirement in 1954. Once settled in Cambridge, Frank became the admired center of groups with an interest in scientific philosophy. He organized interdisciplinary discussion groups that were similar in spirit to that of the Vienna Circle. Frank was an energetic organizer of the Institute for the Unity of Science (serving as founder and as president from 1948 to 1965); the *International Encyclopedia of Unified Science*; the Philosophy of Science Association (the publisher of the journal *Philosophy of Science*); *Synthèse*; and the Boston Colloquium for Philosophy of Science.

Frank's lifelong motivation, like Mach's, was to achieve an evolutionary, demystified view of both science and philosophy, and he regarded both fields as congruous, related pursuits. It was his conviction that the breach between a scientific and a humanistic orientation toward life, which characterized the modern age, could be largely overcome by an adequate philosophy of science. In this spirit he wrote, for example, a book on ethics, which he titled *Relativity: A Richer Truth* (1950). In the 1940s and 1950s, Frank published a number of influential books, among them the authoritative biography, *Einstein: His Life and Times* (1947), and the textbook *Philosophy of Science: The Link between Science and Philosophy* (1957). As a teacher in Prague and at Harvard he was widely admired in the classroom by large numbers of students. He also argued energetically and effectively for his philosophic point of view before large audiences on the lecture circuit of academe. He died in Cambridge, Massachusetts.

• The papers of Philipp Frank are in the Harvard University Archives, Pusey Library. Additional information regarding Frank may be found in the Harlow Shapley Papers and the Richard von Mises Papers in the same location. Among Frank's publications not already mentioned in the text is *Between Physics and Philosophy* (1941), which was enlarged and reprinted as *Modern Science and Its Philosophy* (1949). A full listing is in the *Dictionary of Scientific Biography*, vol. 5 (1972), pp. 122–23. A festschrift for Frank is R. S. Cohen and M. W. Wartofsky, eds., *Boston Studies in the Philosophy of Science*, vol. 2 (1965). See also Frank's interview by Thomas S. Kuhn, 16 July 1962 Transcript, in the Archive for the History of Quantum Physics; Gerald Holton, et. al., "In Memory of Philipp Frank," *Philosophy of Science* 35 (1968): 1–5; and Gerald Holton, "Ernst Mach's Heritage in America," *Isis* 83 (1992): 27–60.

GERALD HOLTON

FRANK, Ray (1861–10 Oct. 1948), journalist and preacher, was born in San Francisco, California, the daughter of Bernard Frank, a peddler and fruit vendor, and Leah (maiden name unknown). She was brought up in a deeply religious home. Her mother was an unassuming, pious woman who was fond of reading the Bible, while her father, an Orthodox Jew, was the great-grandson of Rabbi Elijah ben Solomon, the renowned Vilna Gaon, a great eighteenth-century Lithuanian rabbi. After attending public schools in San Francisco, she graduated from Sacramento High School in 1879 and subsequently moved to Ruby Hill, Nevada, where she taught for six years. She then rejoined her family in Oakland, California. To support herself, she offered private lessons in literature and elocution and began to write for periodicals. She also taught Sabbath school classes at First Hebrew Congregation and soon after became superintendent of its religious school.

During the 1890s she also served as a correspondent for several San Francisco and Oakland newspapers. In this capacity, she traveled throughout the Pacific Northwest. In 1890 she happened to be in Spokane, Washington (then known as Spokane Falls), on the eve of Rosh Hashanah (the Jewish New Year) and was interested in attending religious services. After learning that no service was planned, as the Jewish community was quite small and fraught with religious dissension, she offered to preach at such a service if a *minyan* (prayer quorum) could be gathered. At her suggestion, and with the encouragement of one of the community's leaders, to whom she had letters of introduction, a special edition of the *Spokane Falls Gazette* was printed announcing that a young woman would be preaching to the Jews of the community at the Opera House that evening.

According to local newspaper reports, the worship service was attended by 1,000 Jews and Christians. Frank's sermon, an appeal to her co-religionists to resolve their differences and form a permanent congregation, apparently was well received. She preached the next morning and again, less than ten days later, on the evening of Yom Kippur (the Day of Atonement), the holiest day of the Jewish year. She reiterated her plea that members of the Jewish community drop their religious differences and "join hands in one glorious cause." A Christian who had heard her preach was so impressed that he offered to present the ground for a synagogue, and by the end of the holidays members of the Jewish community agreed to form themselves into a permanent congregation.

While supporting herself as a journalist throughout the 1890s, Frank began to preach and lecture in synagogues as well as in churches throughout the western and northwestern parts of the United States. Although she herself had become religiously liberal, she helped to establish both Orthodox and Reform congregations and to heal congregational squabbles. Local newspapers quickly heralded her as a "latter-day Deborah," referring to the biblical judge and religious leader, and erroneously identified her as a "Lady Rabbi." She later maintained that she had no intention of studying for the rabbinate, but during the spring semester of 1893 she attended classes at Hebrew Union College, the Reform movement's rabbinical seminary in Cincinnati. She apparently did so at the invitation of Isaac Mayer Wise, the college's president and founder. She accepted his invitation, she later wrote, "in order to learn more of the philosophy of Judaism." Subsequently, she was asked by at least one Reform congregation in Chicago to serve as its full-time spiritual leader, an invitation that she declined. As she wrote to a friend (in 1896), she felt that she could work best "unfettered by boards of trustees and salary stipulations." Among the invitations she did accept was one from an Orthodox congregation in Victoria, British Columbia, to officiate at their Rosh Hashanah and Yom Kippur services in 1895. The officers of the congregation subsequently presented her with a scroll in which they expressed admiration for "her masterly eloquence and learning."

Frank's understanding of Judaism, revealed in numerous published sermons and addresses, was both practical and simple. She believed that true piety was direct and earnest and that it involved opening one's heart to God and singing God's praises. Further, it involved recognizing that, while moral laws are from God, external forms of worship (that is, religious ceremonies and observances) are human creations that must be altered "to suit the times" if they are to retain their meaning.

She delivered the opening prayer at the first Jewish Women's Congress, held in Chicago in conjunction with the World Parliament of Religions, which met during the 1893 world's fair. The following day, she gave an address titled "Women in the Synagogue" in which she spoke of what she believed to be women's spiritual superiority and their consequent responsibility as mothers, wives, sweethearts, and sisters to serve as religious teachers and to lead others to God. Although she believed that women had the right and that many had the natural ability to serve as either rabbis or congregational presidents, she reiterated the more conventional view that a woman's "noblest work will be at home."

Her two careers, as journalist and preacher, ended with her marriage to Simon Litman, a professor of economics, in August 1901. As she once remarked to a journalist, Frank did not believe that a woman could "properly fulfil her home duties and be out in the world too." She and her husband did not have children, however.

After teaching at the University of California, Berkeley, for seven years after their marriage, Simon Litman accepted a teaching position in the Department of Economics at the University of Illinois, Champaign-Urbana. During her husband's long association with the university, Ray Frank took a great interest in Jewish student life on campus and became an active supporter of what became the first campus Hillel organization established in the United States. Regularly attending its on-campus activities, in 1915 she also created and led a student study circle that met in her home. The study circle, which focused on Jewish postbiblical history, continued to meet for many years until supplanted by courses established by the Hillel Foundation. She was also active in local Jewish communal affairs and was an active member of a Reform congregation, whose Sisterhood (women's auxiliary) she established. Occasionally she lectured in the community and elsewhere in the Midwest. She died in a private sanatorium in Peoria, Illinois, and was buried in Urbana.

Ray Frank remains significant as the first Jewish woman to preach from a pulpit in the United States and the first to be seen as a Jewish religious leader.

• Frank's papers, including personal correspondence and scrapbooks highlighting her preaching career, are in the American Jewish Historical Society, Waltham, Mass. Excerpts from many of her sermons, public addresses, and newspaper articles, as well as a lengthy biographical sketch, can be found in Simon Litman, *Ray Frank Litman: A Memoir* (1957). For a more critical evaluation of her career see Reva Clar and William M. Kramer, "The Girl Rabbi of the Golden West," *Western States Jewish History* 18 (1986): 91–111, 223–36, 336–51.

ELLEN M. UMANSKY

FRANK, Tenney (19 May 1876–3 Apr. 1939), historian of ancient Rome and philologist, was born in Clay Center, Kansas, the son of Oliver Frank and Caroline Danielson, farmers. He received his A.B. in classics and geology (1898) and his M.A. in classics (1899) from the University of Kansas and his Ph.D. in classics (1903) from the University of Chicago. In 1907 he married Grace Edith Mayer, who became a noted scholar in Romance philology. They had no children. He pursued his studies on a sabbatical at the Universities of Göttingen and Berlin in 1910–1911.

Frank's professional career led him from Chicago (instructor in Latin, 1901–1904) through Bryn Mawr College (associate in Latin, 1904–1909; associate professor, 1909–1913; professor, 1913–1919) to Johns Hopkins University (professor in Latin, 1919–1939). In 1916–1917 he served as Annual Professor and in 1922–1923 and 1924–1925 as professor in charge of the American School of Classical Studies in Rome. He received numerous academic distinctions: he was a member of the Swedish Royal Society of Letters in Lund (1933), the American Philosophical Society (1927), corresponding fellow of the British Academy (1934), and fellow of the American Academy of Arts and Sciences (1935). In 1928–1929 he was president of the American Philological Association. In 1934 he was elected honorary member of the Society for the Promotion of Roman Studies (London), the first American so honored, and in 1938–1939 was Eastman Visiting Professor at Oxford. From 1936 to 1939 he was editor of the *American Journal of Philology*. He died in Oxford, England.

Famous for his dry wit, Frank provided a powerful stimulus for his students, two of whom, Lily Ross Taylor and Thomas Robert S. Broughton, achieved fame matching his own. His scholarly output comprises twelve books, some 150 articles, and numerous reviews. His early publications were in the field of philology and linguistics (also Germanic and Scandinavian), as exemplified by his dissertation "Attraction of Mood in Early Latin" (1904), and he continued to publish in this field throughout his life. Several books dealt with Latin literature; the title of *Life and Literature in the Roman Republic* (1930; originally the Sather lectures at the University of California, 1929–1930) spelled out Frank's program: that to understand literature one must study the social and economic setting in which it is produced, and to illuminate history one must keep a constant eye on literature.

But it was his expertise in Roman history that propelled Frank to international fame. The remarkable *Roman Imperialism* (1914), *An Economic History of Rome to the End of Republic* (1920; revised and extended in 1927 to cover the empire), and *Aspects of Social Behavior in Rome* (1932) established him as a leading scholar in the field. *A History of Rome* (1923) was for a time a successful textbook. Nor did he neglect archaeology: in *Roman Buildings of the Republic: An Attempt to Date Them from Their Materials* (1924) he put to use his early geological training. His major project was to compile, with a group of American and European scholars, the information on Roman provinces published in *An Economic Survey of Ancient Rome* (5 vols., 1933–1940). Frank wrote the first volume, *Rome and Italy of the Republic* (1933), but died before completing the fifth, *Rome and Italy of the Empire* (1940).

As a collection and elucidation of sources Frank's volumes continue to be indispensable, for his goal was to present evidence and eschew grand theories. This was in sharp contrast to Michael I. Rostovtzeff's imposing *The Social and Economic History of the Roman Empire* (1926), which was written under the influence of the Bolshevik Revolution and espoused the idea of a fatal conflict between the city bourgeoisie, the rural proletariat, and the increasingly despotic state. But no work of vast scope is devoid of a thesis. As Frank's colleague W. F. Albright observed in the obituary he wrote for the *Year Book of the American Philosophical Society* (1939), Frank was "proud of his rural beginnings, of his Scandinavian origin, and of the acquaintance with the manual labor. . . . His American heritage was his most prized possession." Frank's American identity (although his father had come from Sweden, and Swedish was the language of his parental household) influenced to an uncommon degree his perception of Rome as an ancient America and of America as a new Rome.

On the eve of World War I he argued in his *Roman Imperialism* against "Old-world political traditions . . .

[that] accept territorial expansion as a matter of course"; in an agricultural republic, such as Rome, there existed "cross-currents to neutralize . . . the blind instinct to acquire." If Rome had become mistress of the world, argued Frank, it was because after defensive wars law and order had to be imposed on unruly tribes. Thus "the free Roman people stumbled on falteringly and unwittingly into ever increasing dominion" until the burden of the empire "leveled the whole state to the condition of servitude" (pp. vii–viii, 358).

In *A History of Rome* he reiterates that "Rome's rapid and ill-considered expansion" was a prime cause of its decline, along with slavery and "the thorough-going displacement of Romans through non-Romans" (pp. 566–67, 574). Darwinian and Mendelian principles permeated Frank's work, beginning with his famous article, "Race Mixture in the Roman Empire" (*American Historical Review* 21 [1916]: 689–708). To Frank, the pervasive admixture of an Oriental "brood" with the Roman "melting-pot" proved fatal, producing people "soft of fiber, weak of will, mentally fatigued." He caps his *Survey* (vol. 5, p. 304) with an explanation for Rome's downfall—and a warning for America: the decline of Rome began with a betrayal of "the free yeomanry" by the selfish "landed gentry." Unlike his detailed articles, Frank's books (with the exception of the *Survey* volumes) have scant documentation: they are works of ideology driven by the belief that there exists an American way to ancient Rome. As such they remain an important part of the American intellectual tradition.

• A small collection of Frank's letters is in the Special Collection of the Milton S. Eisenhower Library of the Johns Hopkins University. A full bibliography of his books and articles (but not of his reviews) is in the *American Journal of Philology* 60 (1939): 280–87. Books not mentioned in the text are *Vergil: A Biography* (1922), *Catullus and Horace: Two Poets in Their Environment* (1928), and an English translation of eighteenth-century Dutch jurist Cornelius van Bynkershoek's *Quaestionum juris publici libri duo* (1930). For specific points, see J. Linderski, "*Si vis pacem para bellum*: Concepts of Defensive Imperialism," in *The Imperialism in Mid-Republican Rome*, ed. W. V. Harris (1984). Among numerous obituaries are those in the London *Times*, 4 and 6 Apr. 1939, and the *American Journal of Philology* 60 (1939): 273–80.

J. LINDERSKI

FRANK, Waldo David (25 Aug. 1889–9 Jan. 1967), author and cultural critic, was born in Long Branch, New Jersey, the son of Julius J. Frank, a successful Wall Street attorney, and Helene Rosenberg. Growing up on the Upper West Side of Manhattan, Frank took an early interest in writing, finishing his first novel at age sixteen. After spending a year at a private prep school in Lausanne, Switzerland, Frank entered Yale University in 1907. While at Yale, he served as drama critic for the New Haven *Courier-Journal* and completed another unpublished manuscript. Frank graduated Phi Beta Kappa in 1911, receiving his bachelor's and master's degrees concurrently. He then worked briefly as a reporter for the New York *Evening Post* and the *New York Times* before leaving for Paris in early 1913. There Frank began to formulate a personal philosophy based on his belief in the interconnectedness of all things. Influenced by the works of Sigmund Freud, Spinoza, Friedrich Nietzsche, and in particular the romantic organicism of Walt Whitman, Frank held that recovery of a "consciousness of the Whole" could be the catalyst for a regeneration of American democratic culture.

Convinced that writers and artists had a vital role to play in fueling a cultural renewal, Frank returned to the United States determined to do his part. Initially unsuccessful in having his plays and short stories published, in September 1916 he joined James Oppenheim, Van Wyck Brooks, Randolph Bourne, and Paul Rosenfeld in founding the *Seven Arts*, a highly regarded literary journal that fused political radicalism and cultural criticism. In its pages, Frank argued that excessive individualism and a materialistic business culture had blinded Americans to the "sensitive reaction between ourselves and the whole." He called for a new, authentically American literature that, he believed, would revive the communal spirituality that industrial modernization had dissolved. Having achieved "that sense of unity . . . with an exterior world which saves [us] from becoming a mere pathetic feature of it," Frank asserted, Americans might then replace the cruelty and sterility of capitalist culture "with a true community of vision and experience." Subject to government harassment because of its pacifist stance during World War I, *Seven Arts* folded after only twelve issues. Frank, however, continued to explore similar themes in many of his later books, including the semiautobiographical novel *The Unwelcome Man* (1917) and *Our America* (1919), hailed at the time as the "Manifesto of the Twenties" and perhaps his most influential work of cultural criticism. He married Margaret Naumburg in 1916. They had one child and were divorced in 1926.

During the early 1920s Frank published a series of innovative "lyric novels"—*The Dark Mother* (1920), *City Block* (1922), *Rahab* (1922), *Holiday* (1923), and *Chalk Face* (1924)—that blended poetry with prose and employed an experimental stream of consciousness technique. Though addressing different topics, each reflects the author's preoccupation with the unity of all life. In 1923 Frank's colleague Gorham Munson proclaimed him "the most exciting figure in contemporary American letters." Other critics were less enthusiastic, finding his style impenetrable, a cross of "James Joyce and the Hebrew prophets," Edmund Wilson cracked.

By 1925, when Frank joined the editorial board of the *New Republic*, his literary focus had returned to nonfiction. The following year he finished *Virgin Spain*, the first of several admiring studies of Spanish culture he would publish during his career. Frank saw in Spanish culture the organicism and devotion to premodern values he hoped to cultivate in America. He also wrote frequently for the *New Yorker* and *New Masses*, serving as contributing editor for the latter magazine from 1926 to 1930. In 1927 he married Alma Magoon, with whom he had two children. They divorced in 1943. *The Rediscovery of America*, Frank's sequel to *Our America*, appeared in 1929. Elaborating on many of his earlier ideas, the author again argued that "consciousness of the Whole" was central to precipitating radical change. Frank maintained that the prerequisite for the new order was a religious transformation of each individual. "We cannot transfigure the world while each of us is in the state of the world," he wrote. There had to be "a revolution of the inward man" before the nation's problems could be solved.

The economic crisis of the 1930s changed Frank's outlook. Horrified by the mass unemployment and rampant poverty brought on by the Great Depression, he abandoned contemplation for direct political action. Along with many other left-leaning writers and artists of the period, Frank embraced Soviet Marxism and moved into the orbit of the Communist party. Hoping to find in the Soviet Union a model for a better society, he embarked on a four-month tour of the country in 1931. Upon his return, Frank recorded his observations in *Dawn in Russia* (1932), a sympathetic though not entirely uncritical account. In 1932 he traveled to Harlan County, Kentucky, with a group of intellectuals to take part in a Communist-inspired demonstration against mining conditions there. After receiving a beating from the mine owners' mercenaries, Frank returned to New York a hero in the party press. His experience inspired his 1934 novel, *The Death and Birth of David Markand*. As a leading member of the League of Professional Writers for Foster and Ford, Frank actively supported the Communist ticket in the 1932 presidential election. Four years later he accompanied Communist candidate Earl Browder on the campaign trail. During 1935–1936 Frank served as the first chairman of the League of American Writers, one of the party's most successful front organizations. Still, his relationship with the Communists was always ambivalent. Too independent-minded to accept the role of "artist in uniform," Frank nonetheless declared that "I must serve and understand [the revolutionists]; and part of my service is to let them exploit me." When he expressed doubt about Leon Trotsky's guilt during the purge trials of 1937, however, the party chastised him harshly, and he severed all connections.

With the outbreak of World War II, Frank became an ardent interventionist. He ended his long association with the *New Republic* in 1940 when the editors refused to support aid to Great Britain. In *A Chart for Rough Water* (1940), he called on the United States to "make ourselves non-belligerent allies of the Allies." The book received decidedly mixed reviews. Indeed, Frank's reputation had declined significantly by the 1940s. Although he continued to publish novels and cultural criticism, most notably *The Rediscovery of Man* in 1958, his American audience had virtually disappeared. Frank's continuing praise for Hispanic culture and his frequent lecture tours of Latin America did help him retain a loyal following in the Spanish-speaking world, however. An early admirer of Fidel Castro, Frank expressed support for his Communist regime in *Cuba: Prophetic Island* (1961) but later became disillusioned. Frank married his third wife, Jean Klempner, in 1943. They had two sons.

Though an innovative novelist and penetrating cultural critic, Frank never achieved the literary greatness many expected from him during the 1920s. Politically, his fascination with mysticism and spiritual renewal placed him outside the more pragmatic, materialist tradition of American radicalism, while his rejection of capitalist individualism barred him from the American mainstream. Late in life Frank compared himself to Don Quixote, a rejected and ridiculed dreamer. He died in White Plains, New York.

• Waldo Frank's papers are in the Rare Book and Manuscript Collection of the University of Pennsylvania. Frank's autobiography, *Memoirs of Waldo Frank*, ed. Alan Trachtenberg (1973), was published posthumously. Gorham Munson, *Waldo Frank, a Study* (1923), provides a positive assessment of Frank's early work. For a concise overview of Frank's literary career, see Paul J. Carter, *Waldo Frank* (1967). William Bittner, *The Novels of Waldo Frank* (1958); Jerome W. Kloucek, "Waldo Frank: The Ground of His Mind and Art" (Ph.D. diss., Northwestern Univ., 1958); and Michael A. Ogorzaly, *Waldo Frank, Prophet of Hispanic Regeneration* (1994), address Frank's fiction, his philosophy, and his relationship with Latin America, respectively. Henry May, *The End of American Innocence* (1959); Daniel Aaron, *Writers on the Left* (1961); R. Alan Lawson, *The Failure of Independent Liberalism, 1930–1941* (1971); Richard Pells, *Radical Visions and American Dreams: Culture and Social Thought in the Depression Years* (1973); and Judy Kutulas, *The Long War: The Intellectual People's Front and Anti-Stalinism, 1930–1940* (1995), discuss Frank and his work within the larger contexts of American literary, political, and intellectual history. Casey Nelson Blake, *Beloved Community: The Cultural Criticism of Randolph Bourne, Van Wyck Brooks, Waldo Frank, and Lewis Mumford* (1990), offers a compelling case for reexamining the cultural criticism of Frank and the other "Young Americans." An obituary is in the *New York Times*, 10 Jan. 1967.

THOMAS W. DEVINE

FRANKEL, Charles (13 Dec. 1917–10 May 1979), philosopher, was born in New York City, the son of Abraham Philip Frankel, an executive with a motion-picture theater chain, and Estelle Cohen. Frankel grew up in the Washington Heights section of Manhattan and attended local public schools. He was an excellent student and graduated from high school at the age of fourteen. Frankel attended high school for an additional year to take advanced courses in mathematics and foreign languages and then enrolled at Columbia University in the fall of 1933.

At Columbia, Frankel majored in English and philosophy while pursuing extracurricular activities in swimming and dramatics. He belonged briefly to a socialist political group, the Student League for Industrial Democracy, but resigned his membership when the organization merged with a pro-Communist group. Frankel was elected to Phi Beta Kappa and received a B.A. with honors in 1937. He then spent the

1937–1938 academic year as a graduate student in philosophy at Cornell University before returning to Columbia on a graduate fellowship. While at Cornell, Frankel met his future wife, Helen Lehman; the couple were married in 1941 and later had two children.

While working on his Ph.D., Frankel taught for three years in the philosophy department at Columbia (1939–1942). During this period he also edited a textbook, *Introduction to Contemporary Civilization in the West* (1941). Having completed all requirements for the doctorate except his dissertation, Frankel enlisted in the U.S. Navy in 1942. During the war, he worked for Naval Intelligence in the Far East and spent a year on the Marianas Islands of the South Pacific. After the surrender of Japan in 1945, Frankel served in the U.S. military government of that country. He was discharged from the navy in 1946 with the rank of lieutenant senior grade.

Frankel returned to Columbia and received his doctorate later that year. His dissertation, on the idea of progress during the French Enlightenment, was awarded Columbia's Woodbridge Prize in 1947 and published a year later under the title *The Faith of Reason*. Frankel was named an assistant professor at the university in 1947 and promoted to an associate professorship three years later. In 1953 he received a Guggenheim fellowship for research at the University of Paris, and a Fulbright award enabled him to serve as a research professor at that university during the 1953–1954 academic year. In 1954 he also lectured at the University of Dublin.

Frankel became a full professor at Columbia in 1956. In addition to offering courses in the philosophy department, he taught one day a week at the university's School of Social Work as a means of keeping himself informed about current social issues. Frankel was now focusing his academic research on contemporary politics, and he became increasingly concerned that traditional liberalism, the backbone of American democracy, was being threatened and undermined by what he called "the creation of a metaphysics which makes anguish and sin, mystery and frustration, the plan of the universe and the keys to history."

In *The Case for Modern Man*, published in 1956, Frankel attacked four prominent twentieth-century intellectuals whom he singled out as the principal authors of this new metaphysics: British historian Arnold Toynbee, American theologian Reinhold Niebuhr, French philosopher Jacques Maritain, and Austro-Hungarian sociologist Karl Mannheim. Liberalism, Frankel asserted, could survive only if it re-created itself to address the major problems of the modern age, in particular the loss of individuality in the face of bureaucratization and technological revolution. Frankel's polemic attracted wide attention and earned favorable commentary from both liberal and conservative critics.

While *The Case for Modern Man* was making its author something of a media celebrity, Frankel was turning his attention to issues in American higher education. In 1956 he served as chair of the Committee on

Professional Ethics of the American Association of University Professors, and that same year he became a fellow of the Conference on Science, Philosophy, and Religion. Also in 1956 he served as chair of the Conference on Higher Education in the United States, an organization that brought together visiting Fulbright scholars from abroad. He was an active participant in the conference the following year and edited its publication *Issues of Higher Education* (1959), a collection of essays addressed to foreign scholars.

Frankel became widely known outside academia in the late 1950s, when he began appearing on television. In 1958 he moderated the first program in a public-affairs series called "Concept," broadcast on CBS-TV, and the following year he hosted the network's "World of Ideas" series. Later he served occasionally as moderator of the CBS-Radio program "Invitation to Learning" and subsequently made numerous appearances on cultural and educational programs broadcast by FM radio stations.

In 1959 Frankel became a director of the New York State Civil Liberties Union and chief editorial consultant to the organization's magazine, *Current*. He served as the principal author of a study for the Rockefeller Brothers Fund, *The Power of the Democratic Idea* (1960), which considered the theory and practice of democracy around the world. As a consequence of this study, Frankel was awarded a grant from the Carnegie Foundation to study the development of democracy in countries undergoing rapid social change, and he spent nearly two years doing research in Mexico, Japan, and Turkey.

From 1962 to 1965 Frankel served as co-chair of the National Assembly for the Teaching of the Principles of the Bill of Rights, later renamed the Center for Education and Research in American Liberties, at Columbia University. During the 1960s he also served as a consultant to the Ford Foundation and to the U.S. Department of State. Over a two-year period (1963–1965), Frankel made a study of the State Department's educational and cultural affairs bureau for the Brookings Institution; this study was later published as *The Neglected Aspect of Foreign Affairs* (1966). In 1965, aware of Frankel's study of the bureau, President Lyndon B. Johnson appointed Frankel its director. Frankel took office on 15 September of that year with the title of assistant secretary of state for educational and cultural affairs.

Frankel served in this post until 1967, when he resigned to protest the escalation of U.S. involvement in the Vietnam War. The government's preoccupation with the war, Frankel argued, had caused it to neglect cultural exchange programs, which he believed were essential to the establishment of international understanding. Two years later, he published *High on Foggy Bottom*, a memoir of his tenure in the State Department, in which he not only criticized the war effort but also expressed dismay over the stultifying effects of the Washington bureaucracy.

Frankel, who had taken a leave of absence from Columbia when he accepted the presidential appointment, returned to the university after his resignation. There he continued to teach classes and to write scholarly articles and books on democratic social thought, and in 1970 he received the Mark Van Doren Award for distinguished teaching from Columbia. That same year he was named Old Dominion Professor of Philosophy and Public Affairs at the university, and three years later he also became chair of the International Council on the Future of the University; he held both posts until his death.

In the mid-1970s Frankel took a leave of absence from Columbia to become the founder of the National Humanities Center near Raleigh, North Carolina. Funded by grants from the federal government, businesses, and private foundations, the center was created as an institute for advanced study in the humanities—history, literature, philosophy, and the arts. Although Frankel believed that insights gleaned from these fields should be applied to political and social problems, he made clear his belief that scholarship in the humanities should be free "to follow crooked paths to unexpected conclusions" and should not be directed toward political goals. The Humanities Center opened in September 1978, with Frankel serving as its first president.

In the months after the opening of the center, Frankel divided his time between North Carolina and Bedford Hills, a suburb of New York City in Westchester County. On the night of 10 May 1979, Frankel and his wife were asleep at their home in Bedford Hills when it was broken into by burglars, and in the course of the robbery the couple was murdered.

In the aftermath of his untimely death, Charles Frankel was praised by scholars for his work on behalf of the preservation of fundamental liberties—including freedom of speech, religion, and the press—in the Western world. He was also remembered by many former and current students for his dynamic performances in the classroom. For relaxation, the six-foot-tall Frankel smoked cigarettes and a pipe and enjoyed swimming, fishing, and tennis. In addition to his essays published in scholarly journals, Frankel wrote for popular periodicals, including the *New Yorker* and *Harper's*. His thirteen books include a novel, *A Stubborn Case* (1972); a fable for children, *The Bear and the Beaver* (1951); and a collection of essays, *The Love of Anxiety* (1965). Frankel edited ten additional books, including a translation of Jean Jacques Rousseau's *The Social Contract* (1947) and a collection of essays, *The Uses of Philosophy* (1955).

• Biographical information about Charles Frankel can be found in Brand Blanshard, "The Case for Modern Man," *Saturday Review*, 17 Mar. 1956, p. 12; *Current Biography 1966*; "Charles Frankel Will Be Rusk Aide," *New York Times*, 23 Aug. 1965; and *Contemporary Authors, New Revision Series*, vol. 4 (1981), which also includes a bibliography of his publications. An obituary is in the *New York Times*, 11 May 1979.

ANN T. KEENE

FRÄNKEL, Hermann Ferdinand (7 May 1888–8 Apr. 1977), classical scholar, was born in Berlin, Germany, the son of Maximilian Fränkel, an archaeologist, epigraphist, and librarian, and Johanna Benary, daughter of Berlin orientalist Ferdinand Benary. Fränkel studied classical philology at the universities in Bonn, Berlin, and Göttingen. Among his teachers were the greatest scholars in the history of the discipline: the Hellenists Max Pohlenz and Ulrich von Wilamowitz-Moellendorff, a friend and correspondent of his father, and the Latinists Franz Buecheler and Friedrich Leo. Fränkel's Göttingen dissertation of 1915 on the Hellenistic poet Simias of Rhodes remains authoritative. That year he married Lilli Fraenkel, the sister of his brilliant fellow student Eduard Fraenkel (not related), who would later transform Oxford classics. Fränkel and his wife had one child. In 1921, after four years of military service in World War I, Fränkel published his Göttingen Habilitationsschrift on the similes of Homer. The study emphasized the content of the simile rather than the point of comparison and so deepened understanding of the Homeric poems that Kurt Riezler in 1936 argued the origin of Greek philosophy from the Homeric simile. But most German philologists with the singular exception of Wilamowitz considered the book overly subtle and therefore unconvincing. Fränkel became Privatdozent in classical philology at Göttingen in 1920, assistant in 1923, and Extraordinarius (associate professor) there in 1925. Despite Wilamowitz's support, however, Fränkel never was offered a chair at a German university, although in 1922 he was granted a research fellowship at the German Archaeological Institute in Athens. Fränkel's greatest student, Bruno Snell, called this neglect a scandal.

In 1933 Fränkel was forbidden to teach because he was a Jew. Two years later he emigrated with his family to the United States, where he became a naturalized citizen. He accepted a temporary post as acting professor of classics at Stanford University, became a tenured professor there in 1937, and remained at Stanford until his retirement in 1953. In later years he was occasionally offered a graduate course. His teaching was long remembered because of his conscientious preparation, his thorough mastery of the primary and secondary sources, his lucid exposition of complex problems, and his encouragement of student discussion. In 1942 during war with Germany he was elected president of the Pacific Coast Philological Association. The next year he became the only Californian ever appointed Sather Classical Lecturer at Berkeley, an honor testifying to the affection in which he was held by American colleagues. Although a Hellenist, he delivered his lectures on Ovid. He held no grudge against defeated Germany and from 1955 to 1960 was Fulbright visiting lecturer at the University of Freiburg. Fränkel also served as guest professor at Beloit College and Cornell University. In 1972 he moved with his wife to Santa Cruz, where their daughter lived, and died there.

Fränkel was one of some twenty great classical scholars driven from Germany in the 1930s who transformed and broadened classical studies in the United States. He was unusual in that, unlike Werner Jaeger, Friedrich Solmsen, and others, he had no doctoral students to transmit his ideas since Stanford had no doctoral program in classics at that time. It was rather through his books and numerous articles that Fränkel influenced classical studies. His American period was his most productive. His books from this period include *Ovid: A Poet between Two Worlds* (1945); *Dichtung und Philosophie des frühen Griechentums: Eine Geschichte der griechischen Epik, Lyrik, Prosa bis zur Mitte des fünften Jahrhunderts* (1951; English trans. by Moses Hadas and James Willis, *Early Greek Poetry and Philosophy: A History of Greek Epic, Lyric, and Prose to the Middle of the Fifth Century*, 1975); *Apollonii Rhodii Argonautica* (1961); and *Noten zu den Argonautika des Apollonios* (1968). These were decisive in reviving interest in two neglected ancient epic poets, Ovid and Apollonius. His studies of early Greek literature reveal a reflective, analytical intelligence more interested in texts as documents in the intellectual history of the West than in literary criticism. He was a modest, thoughtful man, fully devoted to scholarship and without an enemy. Bruno Snell said of his books: "Classical studies are not really dead when they can still produce such works as his."

• The published sources for Fränkel's life are William M. Calder III, "The Refugee Classical Scholars in the USA: An Evaluation of Their Contribution," *Illinois Classical Studies* 17 (1992): 153–73; Calder, "Fränkel, Hermann Ferdinand," in *Biographical Dictionary of North American Classicists*, ed. Ward W. Briggs, Jr. (1994); Andrew R. Dyck, "Wilamowitz to Paul Friedländer on the Career of Hermann Fränkel," *Philologus* 136 (1992): 136–39; Kurt von Fritz, *Gnomon* 50 (1978): 618–21; and Bruno Snell, *Gesammelte Schriften* (1960): 211–12.

WILLIAM M. CALDER III

FRANKEN, Rose Dorothy (28 Dec. 1898–22 June 1988), author and stage director, was born in Gainesville, Texas, the daughter of Michael Lewin (occupation unknown) and Hannah Younker. When Rose was young, her parents separated, and her mother took her four children to New York to live with her family in Harlem. According to Rose Franken's autobiography, she was originally named Rosebud Dougherty (the middle name after her father's best friend), but possibly because of tensions resulting from her parents' separation, the name caused her "deep bitterness" and she soon "nipped the 'bud'" and changed her middle name to Dorothy. After attending the School for Ethical Culture, Rose was scheduled to enter Barnard College in September 1915, but she decided instead to marry Dr. Sigmund Walter Anthony Franken, an oral surgeon. Shortly after the wedding, Dr. Franken was diagnosed as having tuberculosis, and the couple spent the first ten months of their marriage at the Trudeau Sanatorium on Saranac Lake in New York. Three boys were born to the couple over the next thirteen years.

In spite of his recurrent illness, Dr. Franken became the mainstay of Rose Franken's life, and he encouraged her to write as an escape from her worries about his health. While managing a household and bringing up a family, she began to write short stories. Several of them appeared in women's magazines, and in 1925 her first novel, *Pattern*, was accepted for publication by Maxwell Perkins of Scribner's, who became her editor and friend. It was a story with autobiographical overtones, about a young, married woman who finds it difficult to loosen the ties to her mother. This theme recurred frequently in Franken's writing, particularly in the eight highly successful *Claudia* novels, which began as magazine stories in 1939 and were adapted by Franken into a play, two movies, and a radio series, as well as being translated abroad.

After the favorable reception of *Pattern*, her husband suggested that Franken also try writing plays. Her first effort, *Fortnight*, was never produced, but her second play, *Another Language* (1932), became a Broadway hit and was followed by a successful tour and a London production. Underneath its bright dialogue, *Another Language* is a critical examination of the narrow, materialistic values of middle-class family life, as exemplified by a domineering mother who rules the lives of her sons and their wives.

Dr. Franken died in December 1933 of bronchial pneumonia. Early in 1934 Franken took her three sons to Hollywood, where *Another Language* was being produced as a film. Soon after arriving in California, she was hired by Fox Studios to polish and revise scripts prepared by others; this taught her discipline and facility in adapting material for the movies. She then went to Universal Studios, where she collaborated with other writers and received her first screen credit, for *Beloved Enemy* (1936). Her collaborator on the script was William Brown Meloney, an attorney and former English professor as well as a writer, whom she had met soon after arriving in California. After their marriage in 1937, they continued to work together on films for various studios (*The Secret Heart* for MGM and *Claudia and David* for 20th Century–Fox, both released in 1946), and they also wrote fiction under the pseudonym of Franken Meloney.

The couple returned to New York, where they divided their time between the city and a farm in Lyme, Connecticut. Franken wrote and directed the stage version of *Claudia*, produced by John Golden, in 1941. It ran for 453 performances and then had a second run of 269 performances in New York in 1942–1943. Dorothy McGuire, who played the title role, also starred in the film version, *Claudia* (1943), and its sequel, *Claudia and David* (1946).

Franken continued to direct her plays, and her husband began to produce them. *Outrageous Fortune* (1943) was a serious drama that generated considerable controversy because it dealt openly with such subjects as anti-Semitism, suicide, homosexuality, and sexual frigidity in marriage. Although the play closed after seventy-seven performances, critic Burns Mantle called it one of "the most intelligently written" dramas of the season, and L. A. Sloper of the *Christian Science Monitor* characterized it as a "brilliant, subtle, moving . . . social study." Later that year, Franken offered *Doctors Disagree*, a play about a woman doctor trying to balance home life with a competitive career among her male colleagues. It fared poorly at the box office and was criticized for its stereotyped plot and characters. *Soldier's Wife* (1944) dealt with the problems of a returning veteran and his wife, who has matured in his absence and begun to think about a career. Franken kept the dialogue light, and the play ends with the wife deciding that she would rather have a baby than a job. This pleased both critics and audience, and the play ran for 253 performances. Franken's next play was a sequel to *Another Language* called *The Hallams* (1948), in which the matriarch begins to lose her grip on the family; it closed after twelve performances. Disappointed at its failure, Franken stopped writing for the stage. However, she continued to turn out novels and short stories, and she wrote an autobiography, *When All Is Said and Done* (1963). She and Meloney took several trips abroad during these years, but they divorced after twenty-five years of marriage. Toward the end of her life, Franken moved to Tucson, Arizona, where she died.

With very little formal training, Franken learned to write in many genres with facility and insight, becoming one of the highest paid short-story writers in the country. She was also a competent director of her own works, and four of her six produced plays were cited in Burns Mantle's *Best Plays* series. While Franken had serious things to say about women and their changing place in the family and in society, she realized that she could say them most effectively in a lighthearted domestic setting. This caused many critics to take a condescending attitude toward her work and may be one reason why she never achieved the reputation of some of her more solemn colleagues.

• Franken's papers, approximately 1,000 items covering the years 1925 to 1966, are in Butler Library, Columbia University. The Billy Rose Theatre Collection of the New York Public Library has files of material on the author and her plays, including scripts, programs, photographs and reviews. Biographical articles appear in *Current Biography* (1947) and *Notable Women in the American Theatre* (1989). Biobibliographies are in *American Women Writers: A Critical Reference Guide from Colonial Times to the Present* (1980) and *Dictionary of Literary Biography Yearbook* (1984).

Judith Olauson discusses several of Franken's plays in *The American Woman Playwright: A View of Criticism and Characterization* (1981), and Pamela J. Bongas examines *Another Language* in "The Woman's Woman on the American Stage in the 1930's" (Ph.D. diss., Univ. of Missouri-Columbia, 1980). Joan McGrath considers the *Claudia* novels of the 1940s from the perspective of the 1980s in *Twentieth-Century Romance and Gothic Writers*, ed. James Vinson (1982). An obituary is in the *New York Times*, 24 June 1988.

DOROTHY L. SWERDLOVE

FRANKENA, William (21 June 1908–22 Oct. 1994), philosopher, was born Wibe Klaas Frankena in Manhattan, Montana, the son of Nicholas A. Frankena and

Gertie Vander Schaaf, farmers. Frankena was raised in Zeeland, a Dutch Reformed community in western Michigan, where his family moved shortly after he was born. He went to Calvin College, receiving his B.A. in 1930, and began graduate work in philosophy at the University of Michigan. He continued doctoral study at Harvard, where he studied with Clarence Irving Lewis, Ralph Barton Perry, and Alfred North Whitehead. In 1934 Frankena wed Sadie Roelfs, to whom he was happily married until her death in 1978. They had two sons.

Frankena spent a year at Cambridge University in 1935–1936, working with G. E. Moore, and completed his Ph.D. at Harvard in 1937. His dissertation, "Recent Intuitionism in British Ethics," formed the basis for his first published paper, "The Naturalistic Fallacy," which appeared in *Mind* in 1939 and instantly earned him a significant place in analytical moral philosophy. Moore had famously and influentially argued in *Principia Ethica* (1903) that ethical naturalism was guilty of a fundamental logical error. However, with the analytical rigor that would characterize his entire philosophical career, Frankena was able to show that nothing deserving to be called a "fallacy" was involved. What the intuitionist critics of naturalism such as Moore should have charged it with, he argued, was a sort of moral blindness. Where intuitionists claim to perceive sui generis ethical properties in addition to natural properties, the naturalists claim to see only the latter.

In 1937 Frankena began teaching at the University of Michigan, where he remained until his retirement in 1978. There he received virtually every honor the university could bestow and was, when Charles Stevenson and Richard Brandt arrived, a member of one of the most formidable faculties in moral philosophy in the country. He served as chair of the philosophy department from 1947 to 1961, received the university's Distinguished Faculty Achievement Award, and was named Roy Wood Sellars and Distinguished Collegiate Professor of Philosophy in 1974. In 1978 he was honored as the first Distinguished Senior Faculty Lecturer in the College of Literature, Science, and the Arts. He also held visiting positions at Harvard, Columbia, Princeton, the University of Washington, and the University of Tokyo.

Frankena was elected president of the Western Division of the American Philosophical Association in 1965–1966 and delivered the prestigious Carus Lectures to the association in 1974. He was also chair of the Council for Philosophical Studies from 1964 to 1972, a member of the American Academy of Arts and Sciences, and a recipient of a Guggenheim fellowship and a fellowship from the Center for Advanced Study of Behavioral Science.

As a philosopher, Frankena was known for clarity, penetrating analysis, and the ability to structure philosophical issues and theoretical approaches in ways that achieved new insights. He brought these virtues to metaethics, the history of ethics, normative ethical theory, moral education, moral psychology, applied ethics, and other topics. And he also seriously engaged the philosophy of education and religious ethics, doing work that was highly respected by scholars in those fields. The sweep and quality of his philosophizing about ethics was extraordinary.

Among Frankena's best-known essays in fundamental moral philosophy were, in addition to "The Naturalistic Fallacy," "Obligation and Motivation in Recent Moral Philosophy" (1958), a classic treatment of whether motivation is intrinsic to morality or moral judgment, and two essays on the nature of morality, "Recent Conceptions of Morality" (1963) and "The Concept of Morality" (1966). Many of these articles were collected in an anthology, *Perspectives on Morality* (1976), and their themes were further developed in his monograph *Thinking about Morality* (1980).

No doubt the widest recognition Frankena enjoyed came from his text *Ethics* (1963), which was translated into eight languages. It is unique as an introduction to the subject, as useful in a first undergraduate course as it is to graduate students and professional philosophers looking for perspicuous ways to frame issues and categorize alternative solutions. Frankena's formulation of the distinction between teleological and deontological ethical theories—between theories that base their standard of right conduct on the promotion of nonmoral value and those that do not—became a paradigm during the "great expansion" of normative ethical theory in the 1960s and 1970s.

Frankena was also known as the preeminent historian of ethics of his generation, even though relatively little of his published writing was explicitly devoted to it. The exceptions were essays on Hutcheson and Spinoza and editions of Jonathan Edwards's *On the Nature of True Virtue* (1960) and *Freedom of the Will* (1969). Usually Frankena's learning and scholarship provided the background against which he engaged issues of contemporary interest.

Ranging well beyond the usual scope of academic moral philosophy, Frankena also made significant contributions to the philosophy of education, including moral education, and to religious ethics. The former included *Three Historical Philosophies of Education* (1965), and the latter, "The Ethics of Love Conceived as an Ethics of Virtue," which appeared in the *Journal of Religious Ethics* in 1973.

If there was a figure before Frankena who most closely shared his philosophical temper, it would have been Henry Sidgwick, who also combined a sharply analytical insight, a systematic sensibility, and a well-informed appreciation for the history of ethics. Appropriately, Frankena's last published essay was "Sidgwick and the History of Ethical Dualism" (*Essays on Henry Sidgwick*, ed. Bart Schultz [1992]).

Frankena died in Ann Arbor, Michigan.

• An overview of the significance of Frankena's work is in Alvin I. Goldman and Jaegwon Kim, *Value and Morals: Es-*

says in Honor of William Frankena, Charles Stevenson, and Richard Brandt (1978). An obituary is in the *New York Times,* 27 Oct. 1994.

STEPHEN DARWALL

FRANKFURTER, Felix (15 Nov. 1882–22 Feb. 1965), associate justice of the U.S. Supreme Court, was born in Vienna, Austria, the son of Leopold Frankfurter, a rabbinical student turned petty businessman, and Emma Winter. Like other Jews who faced mounting anti-Semitism in the twilight of the Hapsburg Empire, the Frankfurters immigrated to the United States in 1894 and took up residence on New York City's Lower East Side. From the example of a father whose entrepreneurial dreams always outpaced his achievements and a mother whose expectations for her children never waned, Frankfurter developed a blinding ambition to scale the ramparts of the American establishment, not noted at the dawn of the twentieth century for its openness to either immigrants or Jews. By virtue of brains, boundless energy, and a knack for cultivating older, influential men throughout his life, he succeeded.

From his experiences in the public schools of New York City, where teachers insisted that he speak only English, Frankfurter imbibed a deep and simple patriotism, a love for his second language, and an affection for public education that shaped the remainder of his professional life. Combining both high school and college degrees in a single set of courses, he graduated from the College of the City of New York in 1902. After a one-year tenure in the city's tenement house commission, Frankfurter entered the Harvard Law School, where, despite an initial shyness and lack of social polish, he impressed the faculty with his analytical powers, debating skills, and flair for writing.

At Harvard in this era before the arrival of Dean Roscoe Pound and sociological jurisprudence, Frankfurter could not escape from the dominant legal orthodoxy of law as a science, a rationalistic enterprise best dominated by a skilled elite. Despite the later impact of Pound and the legal realists in the 1920s, he never entirely severed his intellectual ties to this older, more conservative tradition of thinking about law and judges. He absorbed as well the ideas of James Bradley Thayer, who taught that judges should seldom overturn the will of popularly elected legislatures.

But at Harvard he also heard an inspiring talk by a famous graduate, Boston attorney Louis Brandeis, also the child of Jewish immigrants from Central Europe, who urged law students to devote themselves to public service and to defend the weak against giant corporations and their allies on Wall Street. Frankfurter's dedication to assorted progressive causes began at that moment.

Frankfurter secured a position after graduation in 1906 with the prominent New York firm of Hornblower, Byrne, Miller and Potter. He became the firm's first Jewish lawyer, but to advance farther, a senior partner advised, it would be desirable if he changed his name. Frankfurter politely declined. He left the Hornblower firm shortly thereafter and, taking up Brandeis's call to serve the public, joined the staff of Henry Lewis Stimson, whom President Theodore Roosevelt had persuaded to become a U.S. attorney for the Southern District of New York.

As Stimson's assistant, Frankfurter helped to clean up fraudulent activities in the customs office and the immigration service. When Stimson ran unsuccessfully for governor of New York in 1910 on a Progressive-Republican ticket, Frankfurter managed his campaign, drove his car, and wrote his speeches. When President William Howard Taft named Stimson secretary of war a year later, Stimson brought Frankfurter to Washington as his special assistant and put him in charge of the Bureau of Insular Affairs, with jurisdiction over the nation's new imperial domain. Stimson also helped raise the funds that permitted Harvard to hire Frankfurter as an assistant professor of law in 1914, the first Jew on its law faculty.

By the time Frankfurter returned to Harvard as a professor on the eve of World War I, he had already argued a series of territorial cases before the U.S. Supreme Court, deepened his relationship with Brandeis, cultivated a friendship with Justice Oliver Wendell Holmes, Jr. (1841–1935), and helped Herbert Croly, Walter Lippmann, and Learned Hand found the *New Republic.* Although a passionate supporter of Roosevelt and the Progressive party in the 1912 presidential contest, Frankfurter swallowed his doubts and, along with the rest of the *New Republic* intellectuals, supported both Woodrow Wilson's domestic programs and his call to arms in 1917.

Frankfurter returned to Washington after the declaration of war against Germany as a special assistant to the new secretary of war, Newton D. Baker. He soon found himself in the middle of the first of a series of war-related controversies that earned him the enmity of conservatives and an undeserved reputation for radicalism. At Baker's urging he became secretary and legal counsel to the president's Mediation Commission, a combined labor-management-government effort to repair tattered relations between workers and employers in key defense industries.

The most violent confrontation had come in 1917 in the tiny Arizona copper town of Bisbee near the Mexican border. There, officials of the Phelps Dodge Corporation, working hand-in-glove with local law enforcement personnel, broke a strike by herding workers at gunpoint into railroad boxcars and shipping them into the New Mexico desert, where they were abandoned without food or water. The employers and their allies justified the Bisbee deportations by noting that some strike leaders belonged to the militant antiwar Industrial Workers of the World (IWW) and that many of the rank-and-file miners were immigrants who did not support America's war aims.

The Mediation Commission's public report on Bisbee, drafted almost entirely by Frankfurter, condemned the company's behavior and urged federal prosecution of those individuals responsible, including the county sheriff, a former Rough Rider and friend of Theodore Roosevelt. The former president blasted Frankfurter's document and accused the commission and its secretary of coddling anarchists and sabotaging the war effort. The final terms of the agreement that reopened Arizona's copper mines was not all that favorable to the miners, however. It created local grievance machinery but rejected union recognition for the copper miners and curbed the influence of the IWW.

At Wilson's command Frankfurter also investigated the 1916 San Francisco murder trial of Tom Mooney and Warren Billings, labor organizers who had been sentenced to death for detonating a bomb that killed ten people during a Preparedness Day parade. The verdicts in the Mooney-Billings case had stirred great protest among trade unionists who believed the pair had been framed as part of a capitalist conspiracy to destroy organized labor.

Frankfurter argued that Mooney and Billings should receive a new trial because the first had been flawed by warrantless searches, coercive interrogations, prejudicial newspaper publicity, and perhaps perjured testimony. Once again his report came under hysterical attack by San Francisco and California authorities, but Wilson was sufficiently impressed to urge the state's governor to commute both death sentences, which the governor did. Frankfurter continued to believe they were entitled to a new trial. Finally, in 1935 the Supreme Court reversed Mooney's conviction on the grounds that prosecutors had indeed used perjured testimony. Billings, however, languished in a California prison for another thirty years.

In 1919, after a long and somewhat turbulent courtship that had begun before the war, Frankfurter married Marion A. Denman, a Congregational minister's daughter. High-strung, intelligent, and very attractive, Marion Frankfurter would preside empress-like over her husband's frequent social and intellectual gatherings during the next four decades and suffer several mental breakdowns during the course of their marriage. The Frankfurters had no children. Frankfurter's continued legal and political activities during the 1920s did not endear him to conservatives. He chaired a large meeting in Boston where speakers urged the Wilson administration to accord diplomatic recognition to the Bolsheviks. With other Boston attorneys he successfully defended immigrant members of the Communist Labor party threatened with deportation solely on account of their political beliefs. Representing the National Consumers' League, he argued for the constitutionality of a minimum-wage law passed by Congress for the District of Columbia. At Harvard he led the faculty charge against President A. Lawrence Lowell's effort to enforce a quota against Jewish undergraduates.

Frankfurter's efforts in 1927 to secure a new trial for Nicola Sacco and Bartolomeo Vanzetti, two Italian anarchists sentenced to death for murder and robbery in Massachusetts, made him a still more controversial figure. In the pages of the *Atlantic Monthly*, Frankfurter exposed the glaring weaknesses in the commonwealth's case against the two condemned men and the prejudice of the trial judge. Sacco and Vanzetti were executed despite worldwide protests, but the verdict of historians has vindicated Frankfurter's position.

After World War I Frankfurter taught innovative courses at the Harvard Law School, produced important legal treatises, and trained scores of young attorneys. He became the first member of the Harvard law faculty to treat seriously in class and in his writings the areas of administrative law, federal jurisdiction, and public utility regulation.

Frankfurter's students, many of whom he sent on to become law clerks to Brandeis, Holmes, Benjamin Cardozo, and Hand, began to play important roles in national and state government beginning in the late twenties. They included James M. Landis, later chairman of the Securities and Exchange Commission and dean of the Harvard Law School; Thomas G. Corcoran and Benjamin V. Cohen, two of the New Deal's ablest legal minds; David Lilienthal, head of the Tennessee Valley Authority; and Joseph L. Rauh, Jr., the prominent civil rights–civil liberties attorney.

During his World War I service, as chairman of the War Labor Polices Board Frankfurter worked closely with Assistant Secretary of the Navy Franklin D. Roosevelt. When Roosevelt became governor of New York in 1929 and president of the United States four years later, he turned often to Frankfurter for advice about proposed legislation and for legal talent with which to staff his administrations.

Although not an official member of Roosevelt's Brain's Trust, Frankfurter and his protégés, especially Landis, Corcoran, and Cohen, played key roles in drafting early New Deal reforms, notably the Securities Act of 1933 and the Securities Exchange Act of 1934. Frankfurter himself crafted the legislative compromise over the so-called "death sentence" in the 1935 Public Utilities Holding Company Act, a provision that permitted a few geographically compact firms to escape eventual dismemberment by the Securities and Exchange Commission. The measure could not have passed Congress without such a compromise, but Frankfurter was denounced by some New Dealers as a tool of big business, while the utilities' allies in the House of Representatives still labeled him a communist.

Frankfurter's influence grew larger as Roosevelt lost support among business groups and advocated more sweeping reform measures in 1935–1936. Major statutes, including the Social Security Act, the Revenue Act of 1935, and the Fair Labor Standards Act, all bore the imprint of Frankfurter and his legions from the Harvard Law School. General Hugh Johnson, a disillusioned New Dealer, called him the most powerful single individual in the administration. George Peek, a spokesman for traditional agricultural interests, denounced Frankfurter and his acolytes as "a plague of young lawyers."

Roosevelt, however, failed to consult Frankfurter on the most controversial proposal of his presidency: the Judicial Procedures Reform Act of 1937, a plan that would have permitted the president to add additional judges to the Supreme Court. Frankfurter had been among the sharpest critics of the Court's performance under Chief Justice Charles Evans Hughes between 1935 and 1936, when a majority of the justices invalidated numerous federal and state laws aimed at economic recovery and reform.

Without publicly endorsing the "court-packing" plan, Frankfurter provided Roosevelt with advice to be used against the justices. The strategy put great strain on his relationship with Brandeis. When Hughes and four of his brethren began to sustain New Deal measures in 1937, however, it doomed Roosevelt's already flawed plan. The retirement of several conservative justices in 1937 and the death of Cardozo in 1938 gave Roosevelt for the first time a number of vacancies to fill on the high court. He rewarded Frankfurter with nomination to the Cardozo seat.

Closely identified with the reforms of the New Deal and long associated with liberal causes, Frankfurter generated paranoia among conservatives when the Senate considered his nomination in 1939. Elizabeth Dilling, author of *The Red Network* (1934), a volume highly recommended by the American Legion, warned members of the Senate Judiciary Committee that the nominee had "long been one of the principal aids of the 'red' revolutionary movement in the United States." The national director of the Constitutional Crusaders wondered why the president had not chosen "an American from Revolutionary times instead of a Jew from Austria just naturalized."

New Dealers and liberals, on the other hand, greeted Frankfurter's nomination and confirmation with euphoria. Secretary of the Interior Harold Ickes pronounced it "the most significant and worth-while thing the President has done." In 1939 the *Nation* believed "no other appointee in our history has gone to the Court so fully prepared for its great tasks. . . . There will be no Dred Scott decisions from a Supreme Court on which he sits." That same year *Newsweek* predicted the newest justice would be "a magnificent champion of the underdog."

Supreme Court justices have a habit of disappointing, amazing, and confounding the presidents who select them as well as the groups who support and oppose their appointment. There are few better examples of this situation than Frankfurter. Over the next quarter century on the Court Frankfurter seldom wavered in his support for the economic reforms of the Roosevelt years. He proved a bitter disappointment to those who expected him to be equally vigorous in defense of civil liberties, especially those touching freedom of speech and political association. But in this regard he may have faithfully reflected the values of the president.

From 1939 until his retirement in 1962, Frankfurter served on a Supreme Court led by four different chief justices—Charles Evans Hughes, Harlan Fiske Stone, Fred Vinson, and Earl Warren. It is a supreme irony that only under Hughes, a figure whom he had bitterly criticized in the past, did Frankfurter feel truly at home on the Court and exercised a decisive influence over its constitutional development. While often providing the crucial swing vote in close cases, especially during the Vinson years from 1945 to 1954, he more usually found himself in the role of dissenter against a liberal bloc of justices who from his perspective practiced a brand of judicial activism as dangerous as the discredited jurisprudence of the Taft era.

Frankfurter's heroes, Holmes and Brandeis, also had dissented against the orthodoxies of their time with respect to economic regulation, freedom of speech, and criminal procedure, but their dissents had forecast the future and had become mainstream. Frankfurter's dissents, on the contrary, blazed no fresh trails and failed to inspire a later generation. They were jeremiads to a vanishing and ultimately discredited interpretation of the Court's constitutional role.

Frankfurter is most remembered for two dissents, one at the beginning and one at the end of his career—the second flag salute case, *West Virginia State Board of Education v. Barnette* (1943), and the first reapportionment decision, *Baker v. Carr* (1962). Restating the views he had expressed in *Minersville School District v. Gobitis* (1940), Frankfurter rejected the view that the Constitution's guarantee of religious liberty barred mandatory flag salutes and larded his dissent with gratuitous references to his own religion and minority status. His dissent in *Baker*, rejecting any judicial remedy for malapportioned legislatures, struck even some of his most fervent admirers as excessive and wrongheaded.

Of all the justices who have served on the Court, it can be argued that Frankfurter was both the least and the most influenced by his ethnocultural heritage. He displayed an almost Enlightenment faith in the powers of Reason. But he was also, in the shrewd assessment of one recent scholar, "first and foremost a teacher in the rabbinic style," who relished "complexities, balanced truths, entertained questions, and understood puzzles." Instead of the Torah, however, he quoted endlessly from the opinions of Holmes and Brandeis, much to the annoyance of his brethren. "We would have been inclined to agree with Felix more often in conference," Justice William Brennan once remarked, "if he quoted Holmes less frequently to us."

A Jew and a naturalized citizen, Frankfurter never attempted to conceal these attributes, but his own journey from New York's Lower East Side to the Supreme Court shaped his almost mystical faith in assimilation—in the transforming powers of American culture, especially public education. His robust belief in cultural assimilation, in the melting pot, in the ideal of a meritocratic social order where talent, brains, and energy counted far more than race, religion, or class led him in 1948 to employ the Court's first black law clerk, William Coleman, Jr. And it inspired perhaps his greatest contribution to American law: helping

Warren forge a unanimous Court to strike down segregated public schools in *Brown v. Board of Education* in 1954.

In addition to Coleman, Frankfurter actively promoted the careers of other black lawyers, notably Charles H. Houston, his student at Harvard who later became the chief legal strategist of the National Association for the Advancement of Colored People (NAACP), and William Hastie, the first black named to the federal bench by Roosevelt and later dean of the Howard University Law School. But Frankfurter also wrote the Court's 1950 opinion in *Hughes v. Superior Court of California*, which upheld an injunction prohibiting blacks from picketing at a supermarket in order to secure for themselves a certain percentage of its jobs.

A supporter of the NAACP's original program of nondiscrimination and the ideal of a "color-blind" legal order, Frankfurter never moved beyond that position. When the civil-rights struggle escalated in the South, Frankfurter expressed grave doubts about the militant tactics of black college students and the Court's response to the first sit-in demonstrations.

In Louisiana and elsewhere, black protestors in department stores, theaters, amusement parks, and restaurants had been jailed for trespassing on private property. Following a heated conference about one of these cases, he told Justice Hugo Black, another skeptic, "It will not advance the cause of constitutional equality for Negroes for the court to be taking short cuts to discriminate as partisans in favor of Negroes or even to appear to do so." Aside from *Hughes*, Frankfurter never faced the dilemma of affirmative action programs, but it does seem likely that his views would have been closer to Antonin Scalia's than to Thurgood Marshall's.

Frankfurter was a person of paradox and contradiction. He acted and thought in ways that were not always consistent. Warm, charming, and supportive with his law clerks, he could be rude, abrasive, and petty with his brethren on the Court. Because of his intimate relationship with Brandeis, probably no person came to the Court with greater inside information about how that institution functioned and about the importance of collegial relations among its members. Yet Frankfurter failed to put what he knew into practice.

The diary Frankfurter kept sporadically during the 1940s reveals a justice filled with bitterness when he failed to carry the Court with him, attributing only the blackest motives to his opponents. His letters to Hand in the 1950s likewise boil with indignation against Chief Justice Warren, William O. Douglas, and Black. Over a quarter century he appears to have remained close to and respected only three colleagues—Owen Roberts, Robert Jackson, and John M. Harlan. Others he dismissed as intellectual lightweights (Stanley Reed, Sherman Minton, Vinson) or conniving demagogues (Black and Douglas).

Frankfurter usually lacked self-awareness, introspection, and a sense of irony. Always critical of those

like Black who read constitutional provisions in absolute terms, he could be a strict constructionist himself when it came to issues of church and state or the Fourth Amendment. In cases such as *Everson v. Board of Education* (1947) and *Zorach v. Clauson* (1952), no justice spoke more fervently against the growing entanglement of government with religion. He took literally the commands of the Fourth Amendment and regularly quoted one of his heroes, James Otis, on the abuses of search and seizure. No one denounced with more zeal the extrajudicial activities of his colleagues, such as Douglas, while engaging himself in off-the-bench politics and policy making.

An almost universal scholarly consensus prevails that Frankfurter, the justice, was a failure; a jurist who, in Joseph Lash's memorable phrase, became "uncoupled from the locomotive of history" during the flag salute cases and left little in the way of an enduring doctrinal legacy. Frankfurter would have made a superb contribution to the Court in an earlier era when its rampant activism often thwarted the creation of the modern welfare state, but his brand of judicial restraint became an anachronism when the nation's agenda shifted to the expansion of civil rights and civil liberties. Like the judicial conservatives of the New Deal years, Frankfurter saw many of his cherished constitutional structures demolished during his own lifetime—notably in the case of the exclusionary rule and legislative reapportionment.

Frankfurter's appointment in 1939 simply confirmed the triumph of New Deal jurisprudence, especially its deference to social and economic legislation. His retirement in 1962, however, fundamentally altered the course of constitutional development. When Arthur Goldberg took Frankfurter's seat, he gave Chief Justice Warren a dependable fifth vote and opened the most expansive era in the Court's defense of civil rights and civil liberties. Frankfurter had been prepared to sustain the government in pending cases that challenged portions of the Immigration and Nationality Act (*Kennedy v. Mendoz-Martinez* and *Rusk v. Cort*), the contempt powers of the House Un–American Activities Committee (*Russell v. United States*), and the authority of Florida to compel certain disclosures by the NAACP (*Gibson v. Florida Legislative Investigation Committee*). Goldberg tipped the balance in the other direction.

In the following decade, a majority of the justices spurned virtually all of Frankfurter's views on justiciability, political questions, and the speech clause of the First Amendment. He suffered perhaps his greatest defeat by Black in their long battle over the relationship of the Bill of Rights to the Fourteenth Amendment's Due Process Clause.

Beginning with *Betts v. Brady* (1942) and continuing in *Adamson v. California* (1947), Black held to the view first advanced by Justice Harlan after the Civil War that the framers of the Fourteenth Amendment intended the specific guarantees of the Bill of Rights to apply to the states as well as against the federal government. Only in this fashion, Black argued, could the "vague contours of due process" be given defined content that would both protect individual rights and guard against judicial subjectivity.

Frankfurter, more confident than Black about judicial self-restraint, rejected the incorporation thesis. He wrote in 1949:

Due Process of law conveys neither formal nor fixed nor narrow requirements. It is the compendious expression for all those rights which the courts must enforce because they are basic to our free society. But basic rights do not become petrified as of any one time, even though, as a matter of human experience, some may not too rhetorically be called eternal verities. It is of the very nature of a free society to advance in its standards of what is deemed reasonable and right. Representing as it does a living principle, due process is not confined within a permanent catalogue of what may at a given time be deemed the limits or the essentials of fundamental rights. (*Adamson v. California*)

Black ultimately won the great incorporation debate. In *Gideon v. Wainwright* (1963), decided a year after Frankfurter retired, the Warren Court unanimously overruled *Betts v. Brady* and extended the Sixth Amendment guarantee of counsel in all state felony prosecutions. By the late 1970s, the Court had applied almost all guarantees of the Bill of Rights to the states.

Frankfurter's more open-ended, evolutionary approach to due process had several virtues, however. It permitted him to strike down racial segregation in the District of Columbia, even though the Fifth Amendment did not contain an Equal Protection Clause. And it did not run aground when the Court was called on to protect individual rights, such as privacy, not explicitly cataloged in the Bill of Rights. In these situations, Frankfurter's approach to due process, carried on by Justices Harlan and Harry Blackmun, advanced the revolution in civil liberties.

Although they made an effort to do so, post-Frankfurter conservatives on the Supreme Court had difficulty adopting him as one of their own. Frankfurter practiced judicial restraint, but not always in areas they endorsed, such as economic regulation. Unlike them, he abhorred the death penalty and took every opportunity to overturn capital convictions. He remained an absolutist when it came to the Fourth Amendment and the Establishment Clause. He became almost a jurist without jurisprudential progeny, except for pragmatic centrists such as Lewis Powell or David Souter.

Time and again over the course of his judicial career, Frankfurter spoke out in capital cases where criminal defendants faced execution under circumstances that suggested to him that their accusers had played fast and loose with the basic rules of criminal justice—notably in the cases of Julius and Ethel Rosenberg, convicted atomic spies, and Caryl Chessman, California's alleged "red light" bandit.

During the 1920s Brandeis, himself a towering figure in both law and social reform, once referred to

Frankfurter, his close friend and ally in the early Zionist movement, as "the most useful lawyer in America." Certainly few Americans in the era from Theodore Roosevelt to John Kennedy made greater contributions to public policy than this diminutive, fiesty son of Austrian immigrants who excelled as a law professor, intellectual gadfly, presidential adviser, and Supreme Court justice. He sent generations of Harvard Law School graduates into public service and influenced numerous judicial and academic appointments in Washington and Cambridge.

While virtually all of his important constitutional decisions failed to survive the judicial revolution of the 1960s and 1970s, Frankfurter left a number of critical legacies—the importance of judicial restraint in a democratic society, the value of federalism, the necessity for the Court to articulate an evolving conception of due process, and a passionate belief in the role of the courts and in something called the Rule of Law.

Courts, Frankfurter held, are not the only or the primary institutions of government in this society. They could not, he often repeated, guarantee toleration where that spirit had withered among the people at large. If his greatest failing on the Court was an all-too-eager deference to majorities, it sprang from a unique historical context in which the judiciary had for decades thwarted the popular will and from a passionate belief in the virtues of self-education through the trial-and-error of messy democratic politics.

The pre–New Deal judiciary often confused disputes over policy with debates over constitutional fundamentals. Reacting to those judicial excesses, Frankfurter sometimes forgot that the Constitution does articulate basic values and that it is the duty of the Court to give preference to them over the competing policy choices of transitory majorities. He died in Washington, D.C.

• Frankfurter's pre-judicial papers are maintained at the Library of Congress. His Supreme Court papers are in the library of the Harvard Law School. Each institution also has microfilm copies of the other's collections as well as copies of some Zionist materials housed in Tel Aviv, Israel. Frankfurter's major writings include *The Business of the Supreme Court* (1927), with James Landis; *The Case of Sacco and Vanzetti* (1927); *The Labor Injunction* (1930), with Nathan Greene; *The Public and Its Government* (1932); *The Commerce Clause under Marshall and Taney* (1937); and *Mr. Justice Holmes and the Supreme Court* (1938). With Harlan Phillips, Frankfurter published *Felix Frankfurter Reminiscences* (1960). His relationship with Roosevelt can be traced in Max Freedman, ed., *Roosevelt and Frankfurter: Their Correspondence 1928–1945* (1967). The rich correspondence between Frankfurter and Brandeis has been collected in David W. Levy and Melvin I. Urofsky, *"Half-Son, Half-Brother": The Letters of Louis D. Brandeis to Felix Frankfurter* (1991). The best short biography is Urofsky, *Felix Frankfurter: Judicial Restraint and Individual Liberties* (1991). Other interpretative accounts that examine both his pre-judicial career and tenure on the Supreme Court include Michael E. Parrish, *Felix Frankfurter and His Times: The Reform Years* (1982); Harry N. Hirsch, *The Enig-*

ma of Felix Frankfurter (1981); and Bruce Allen Murphy, *The Brandeis/Frankfurter Connection* (1982). An obituary is in the *New York Times*, 23 Feb. 1965.

MICHAEL E. PARRISH

FRANKLAND, Agnes Surriage, Lady (bap. 17 Apr. 1726–23 Apr. 1783), prominent Boston socialite and wife of Sir Charles Henry "Harry" Frankland, Baronet, was born in Marblehead, Massachusetts, the daughter of Edward Surriage, a fisherman, and Mary Pierce. She began life in poverty in a family of eight children. In the summer of 1742 sixteen-year-old Agnes worked as a servant at the Fountain Inn in Marblehead, owned and operated by Nathaniel and Jane Bartlett.

One day while scrubbing the floor, she caught the eye of Sir Harry Frankland, an English aristocrat some ten years her senior and the great-great-grandson of Oliver Cromwell. George II had offered Frankland the governorship of Massachusetts, but he decided on the more lucrative post of collector of the port of Boston. Contemporaries describe Agnes as having beautiful dark eyes and hair, a lively wit, charm, and a good singing voice, which sounded "musical, birdlike." After a second meeting, with her parents' permission, Frankland took her to Boston as his ward. Here she took classes at Peter Pelham's private school in reading, writing, music, dancing, needlework, and other social skills to make her a refined lady.

In 1746, upon the death of his uncle, Frankland inherited the family title, becoming the fourth baronet of Thirsk, with estates in Thirkleby, York, and Mattersea, England. Shortly after this good fortune, Agnes agreed to become his mistress. This affair scandalized Boston society, and so in the summer of 1752 Frankland bought 482 acres in Hopkinton, some twenty-five miles southwest of Boston, built a mansion, and purchased twelve slaves. Here the couple, along with twelve-year-old Henry Cromwell, Sir Harry's illegitimate son, enjoyed the leisurely life of the English landed gentry. More important, they lived away from prying eyes. One would anticipate that all the gossip and criticism would have prompted Frankland to marry Agnes, but their vastly different social backgrounds and the class-conscious views of the British aristocracy doomed any such idea.

In 1754 Harry returned to England with Agnes. Finding that his family and friends disapproved of his colonial mistress, he took Agnes on a tour of the Continent. During the couple's stay in Lisbon, Portugal, on 1 November 1755, an earthquake destroyed a large part of the city, killing some 30,000 people. Frankland was buried in his carriage under a collapsed building. Miraculously Agnes found him and hired men to dig for an hour to free her beloved Harry. In his diary Frankland recorded that he was "providentially saved," and he immediately married Agnes in a Roman Catholic church. Later, on the voyage back to England, he had a second, shipboard wedding solemnized by a clergyman from Frankland's own Church of England.

Surprisingly, Sir Harry's British family and the British nobility now welcomed Agnes as Lady Frankland. From 1756 to 1758 the couple again lived in Massachusetts, where their legal marriage made all the difference in proper Boston social circles. Now they lived on fashionable Garden Court Street, next door to the wealthy Thomas Hutchinson, later governor of Massachusetts. Agnes graciously forgave her former detractors and entertained the best of colonial society in her elegant mansion of twenty-six rooms.

In 1757 Sir Harry's health declined, primarily because of gout, and so in 1758 he secured an appointment as British consul general to Lisbon. Here they lived until 1764, when the couple retired to Bath, England, with its famous mineral springs. Sir Harry died there in January 1768.

After her husband's death, Lady Frankland returned to Massachusetts and resided on her Hopkinton estate. As a widow she was a frequent guest for dinner in the homes of such future Loyalists as John Rowe, Solomon Davis, Ralph Inman, David Phipps, and Robert Temple and British officials such as Admiral Montagu. When the American Revolution came, patriots suspected that as the widow of a former Crown officer who remained devoted to the Anglican church and hobnobbed with Tories, she was a Tory herself. In May 1775 she asked permission from the Hopkinton Committee of Safety to travel into British-occupied Boston. In this letter Lady Frankland stated that she was not leaving because of any "disaffection," but remained a "warm friend to all the Constitutional Rights of the Country." She claimed her motive was a fear of "Civil war" and personal business in England and promised to return to Massachusetts after the war. Although granted a pass, Lady Frankland was arrested on her way into Boston, and the provincial Congress had to send six soldiers to escort her safely to Boston. From the window of her Boston mansion she witnessed the battle of Bunker Hill and ministered to wounded British soldiers. When the British evacuated Boston, she cleverly turned over her properties to family members (her sister Mary Swain and her niece Sally Dupee) and thus saved them from confiscation.

Choosing exile in England, in 1782 Lady Frankland married John Drew, a wealthy banker of Chichester, England, but became ill with an inflammation of the lungs. She died at home in Little London, parish of St. Andrew Oxmarket. Her inscription on Sir Harry Frankland's crypt states that he died "without issue."

Lady Agnes Frankland's main legacy is as a romantic figure, an eighteenth-century "Cinderella," who went from a barefoot servant scrubbing floors to the wife of "Prince Charming," an English aristocrat. Their love story has inspired many literary efforts, ranging from a 1774 British publication of their romance, to the ballad "Agnes" by Oliver Wendell Holmes (1809–1894), to a section in James Fenimore Cooper's *Lionel Lincoln* (1825), to three twentieth-century novels.

• Sir Charles Henry Frankland's diary is in the Massachusetts Historical Society. For two short biographies see James H. Stark, *The Loyalists of Massachusetts and the Other Side of the American Revolution* (1907), and E. Alfred Jones, *The Loyalists of Massachusetts: Their Memorials, Petitions and Claims* (1930). For the love story of Sir Harry and Lady Agnes Frankland see Diana Ross McCain, "A Fine Romance: An Eighteenth-Century American Cinderella Story," *Early American Life* 21 (1990): 10–13. The best accounts of her life are in Elias Nason, *Sir Charles Henry Frankland, Baronet; or, Boston in the Colonial Times* (1865), and Stella Palmer, *Dame Agnes Frankland, 1726–1783, and Some Chichester Contemporaries* (1964). For a detailed description and re-creation of the Fountain Inn and its history see Nathan Sanborn, *The Fountain Inn, Agnes Surriage and Sir Harry Frankland* (1905).

DAVID E. MAAS

FRANKLIN, Ann Smith (2 Oct. 1696–19 Apr. 1763), printer and editor, was born in Boston, Massachusetts, the daughter of Samuel Smith and Anna (or Ann; maiden name unknown). She grew up in Boston.

In light of her later successful career, it is reasonable to conclude that she was at least as well educated as most girls of her era. In 1723 she married James Franklin, Benjamin Franklin's older brother. The couple had five children. Earlier, James Franklin had been apprenticed as a printer in England, from which he had returned to Boston in 1717 with a press, types, and other supplies. He printed and published the *New-England Courant*, in which he grew so critical of ecclesiastical and civil authorities that in 1722 he was taken into custody, publicly censured, and jailed for four weeks—for printing "scandalous libel." When the Massachusetts assembly ordered James Franklin to cease publishing the *Courant*, his brother Benjamin took over as its official publisher for a few months before leaving for New York and then Philadelphia. James Franklin then resumed printing and publishing the *Courant* in a more chastened style until it discontinued in 1726.

James and Ann Smith Franklin soon moved to Newport, Rhode Island, a busy commercial center, in which he set up the colony's first printing press. Among other business ventures, he printed the *Rhode-Island Almanack*, beginning in 1727; it was also known as *Poor Robin's Almanack*. In 1730 he received the first of several government contracts. Beginning in September 1732 he also issued the *Rhode-Island Gazette*, but it died eight months later. The Franklins also sold books.

Ann Franklin helped her husband in the printing shop and bookstore early on and was coprinter of the *Gazette*. While in England her husband had learned to print on calico. In Newport the two advertised that they were able to print on linens, silks, calicoes, and other textiles in figures of vivid and durable colors and without the unpleasant odors often associated with linen prints.

After a lingering illness of at least two years, James Franklin died in 1735, and Ann Franklin took over management of their printing business. Later that year she issued *A Brief Essay on the Number Seven* in 350 pages. She thus became in all likelihood the first woman printer in New England and the second in all of British North America. In 1736 she became the official printer for the general assembly of colonial Rhode Island. Her first order was a 284-page supplement to the *Acts and Laws*, for which she was paid ten pounds. She continued as assembly printer until the year of her death. Between 1735 and 1748 Franklin printed at least forty-seven items, including government, literary, and religious pieces, legal forms and broadsides, and the *Rhode-Island Almanack for the Year 1737*. As "the Widow Franklin," printer, and using "Poor Robin," her husband's pseudonym, as author, she issued this almanac from 1736 until its demise in 1741. At first she engaged Joseph Stafford to prepare almanac numbers, but when he left her shop in 1738 she prepared successive issues herself and thus became a very early woman almanac writer in colonial America. Franklin was kept immensely busy, one government order being for 500 copies of *Acts and Laws of 1745*, which came to more than 300 pages in folio. When she illegally ran off a number of copies for herself, to sell privately because she needed the money for her children, she was charged with breach of contract and forbidden to sell any of her copies for a year.

Franklin trained her two surviving daughters, Elizabeth and Mary, to set type and otherwise help in the shop. The daughters were said by contemporaries to be sensible and amiable young women and correct and quick compositors. In 1748 Franklin's surviving son (and youngest surviving child), James Franklin, Jr., returned to Newport from Philadelphia, where he had been an apprentice printer for Benjamin Franklin, his uncle. Franklin made her son her partner, and beginning in 1748 the firm was known as "Ann & James Franklin." In September 1758 Franklin and her son established the *Newport Mercury*, which was the first newspaper in Rhode Island. Published on Mondays, it was of crown size, folio, but generally half sheet only, and with a large cut of Mercury on its title. Franklin may have written copy for it and done editorial work on it as well. When the aging woman, probably retired by this time, let her son print the legislative schedules by himself, he did the work inefficiently and orders for printing two of the 1759 legislative sessions went to a Boston firm. In 1760, however, he was again entrusted with the assignment.

Evidently sometime before 1762 Franklin's daughters Elizabeth and Mary had both died. When her son died in April 1762, Franklin, though in failing health, prepared the newspaper by herself and without missing a single issue. She thus became the fourth woman to publish a newspaper in colonial America—after Elizabeth Timothy of Charleston, South Carolina (from 1739), Cornelia Bradford of Philadelphia (1742), and Catherine Zenger of New York City (1746). In August 1762 Franklin made Samuel Hall her business partner, and the two continued to print legislative documents and run the bookstore. Franklin died the following year in Newport, and her printing firm was legally dissolved.

• Collections of Franklin's printings are in the Rhode Island Historical Society, Providence; the Newport Historical Society, Newport, R.I.; and the American Antiquarian Society, Worcester, Mass. An early source of information about Franklin is Isaiah Thomas, *The History of Printing in America: With a Biography of Printers and an Account of Newspapers* (2 vols., 1810; repr. 1 vol., 1970). Comprehensive discussions of Franklin are Ellen M. Oldham, "Early Women Printers of America," *Boston Public Library Quarterly* (Jan. 1958): 6–26, and especially Susan Henry, "Ann Franklin: Rhode Island's Woman Printer," in *Newsletters to Newspapers: Eighteenth-Century Journalism*, ed. Donovan H. Bond and W. Reynolds McLeod (1977). Placing Franklin in the context of eighteenth-century American newspapers is Clarence S. Brigham, *Journals and Journeymen: A Contribution to the History of Early American Newspapers* (1950). An obituary is in the *Newport Mercury*, 25 Apr. 1763.

ROBERT L. GALE

FRANKLIN, Benjamin (6 Jan. 1706–17 Apr. 1790), natural philosopher and writer, was born in Boston, Massachusetts, opposite the Congregational Old South Church, where the Reverend Samuel Willard baptized him the same day. The youngest son and fifteenth child of Josiah Franklin, a tallow chandler and soap maker who emigrated from England in 1683 to practice his Puritan faith, Benjamin had eleven living brothers and sisters. Five were Josiah's children by his first wife, Anne Child, and six were by his second wife, Abiah Folger, Benjamin's mother. Two sisters were born later.

At age eight Franklin studied at the South Grammar School (later Boston Latin), his father intending him as "the tithe of his sons" for the ministry. But the expense and the subsequent poor living of many ministers made his father withdraw him at the school year's end. The following year, 1715–1716, he attended George Brownell's English school, completing his only formal education. He worked in his father's hot, pungent shop, boiling fats and making candles and soap, but hated the trade and wanted to become a sailor. His father had lost one son to the sea and kept Franklin home. Josiah took him to watch various artisans at work, but none of the trades interested him. In March 1717 his brother James, a printer, returned from England and by the fall of 1718 set up his own printing shop. Since Franklin loved to read and since he wrote poetry as a child, his father apprenticed him to James. In 1718, at the age of twelve, Franklin signed a nine-year indenture.

Franklin read everything in his father's small library and made friends with booksellers' apprentices in order to borrow books from them. He became a vegetarian partly to save money to buy books. Having purchased an odd volume of the *Spectator*, Franklin taught himself prose style by outlining the essays and later composing them in his own words. He compared the originals with his versions and corrected them.

In 1721 James Franklin started his own newspaper, the *New England Courant*. Benjamin set the type for the paper, printed it, delivered it to the customers, and heard their comments. Aged sixteen, he emulated his brother's friends, the Couranteers, and wrote for the paper. "But being still a Boy, and suspecting that my Brother would object to printing any Thing of mine in his Paper if he knew it to be mine, I contriv'd to disguise my Hand, and writing an anonymous Paper I put it in at Night under the Door of the Printing-House" (*Benjamin Franklin's Autobiography: A Norton Critical Edition* [hereafter *Autobiography*], ed. Lemay and Zall, p. 15). Franklin's pseudonym "Silence Dogood" alluded to the Reverend Cotton Mather's *Bonifacius; or, Essays to Do Good* and his recent sermon, *Silentarius*. The first essay series in American literature, Silence Dogood opened with two numbers depicting a vain, opinionated minister's widow; number four satirized Harvard College; and number seven travestied the typical New England funeral elegy.

While the fourteen Silence Dogood essays were appearing, the Massachusetts general assembly imprisoned James for suggesting that the local officials deliberately delayed sailing out to battle pirates. The sixteen-year-old Benjamin therefore managed the paper for four weeks, 12 June to 7 July 1722. When James again offended the authorities in January 1723, the Massachusetts assembly (by one vote) prohibited him from publishing the newspaper without prior review. James defied the order, printed the *Courant*, and went into hiding from 24 January to 12 February 1723, leaving Benjamin again in charge. The adolescent "made bold to give our Rulers some Rubs in it" (*Autobiography*, p. 16). Since only James Franklin was forbidden to print the paper without prior review, the *Courant* appeared under the name Benjamin Franklin beginning 11 February 1723. In case the authorities should question the artifice, Benjamin's indenture was returned to him with a full discharge, though he signed another, secret one.

The siblings quarreled, and James, who "was otherwise not an ill-natur'd Man," often beat his apprentice. Franklin reflected in his *Autobiography*, "Perhaps I was too saucy and provoking" (p. 17). When a fresh argument between the two broke out in September 1723, Benjamin left the shop, believing his brother could not prosecute him with the secret indenture. Warned off by James, no other Boston printer would hire Benjamin; so he ran away, sailing on 25 September 1723 for the nearest printing establishment, New York. Failing to find work there, the seventeen-year-old went on to the only other town in English-speaking North America with a printing press, Philadelphia, arriving about eight or nine o'clock Sunday morning, 6 October, with one Dutch dollar and about twenty pence in copper. The *Autobiography*'s description of his journey, arrival, and first hours in Philadelphia is a touchstone of American literature.

Franklin found work with Samuel Keimer, who was just setting up a printing shop, and lodged next door with John and Sarah Read and their children, one of whom, Deborah, was to be his future wife. Seven months later, befriended by Pennsylvania governor William Keith, who promised to award him the public printing, the eighteen-year-old returned to Boston to ask his father for a loan to start a printing shop. Josiah turned him down. Back in Philadelphia, Governor Keith pledged to lend Franklin the money to buy the press and types but suggested he go to London to make the purchases and to arrange for supplies from the stationers, booksellers, and printers. Franklin and Deborah courted and planned to marry, but after the death of her father, on 3 July, her mother insisted the youngsters wait until Franklin's return. He sailed for London on 5 November 1724 with his friend James Ralph and a Quaker merchant, Thomas Denham.

Arriving in London on Christmas Eve 1724, Franklin learned that Governor Keith, with "no credit to give," had duped him. The youth had neither money nor prospects. He found employment at Samuel Palmer's printing shop, 54 Bartholomew Close, where in February 1725 Franklin set in type the third edition of William Wollaston's *Religion of Nature Delineated*. He then wrote an ironic rejoinder, *A Dissertation on Liberty and Necessity, Pleasure and Pain*, burlesquing the arguments for the existence of God. With no publisher, no author, and no bookseller indicated, the pamphlet was archetypal clandestine literature. *A Dissertation* won him notoriety among London libertines, and William Lyons, who had spent six months languishing in jail for his own freethinking book, befriended him, introducing him to the notorious Bernard Mandeville, author of *The Fable of the Bees*, and to Henry Pemberton, a friend and popularizer of Isaac Newton. In the fall of 1725 Franklin left Palmer's printing house for John Watts's larger establishment near Lincoln Inn Fields. Denham proposed the next spring that Franklin return with him to Philadelphia to work as his clerk and shopkeeper while learning the mercantile business. Franklin agreed and sailed with Denham on 23 July 1726.

Denham rented a store on Water Street. Franklin "attended the Business diligently, studied Accounts, and grew in a little Time expert at selling" (*Autobiography*, p. 41). In February 1727 he fell ill with pleurisy and nearly died. Denham too fell ill, lingered on, and finally died on 4 July 1728. About the end of March 1727 Franklin recovered and returned to work as the manager of Keimer's printing shop, while Keimer ran the stationery store. That fall Franklin formed the Junto, a society for mutual improvement that met every Friday night and included his friends Joseph Breintnall, William Coleman, Robert Grace, and Hugh Meredith. In the late spring of 1728 Meredith and he borrowed money from Meredith's father to set up their own printing shop. They did so on 1 June 1728. Before winter, Keimer learned that Franklin and Meredith intended to start a newspaper to challenge Andrew Bradford's *American Weekly Mercury*. Keimer immediately announced plans for his own paper, the *Pennsylvania Gazette*. In resentment, Franklin began, on 4 February 1729, writing an essay series, the "Busy Body," to popularize Bradford's paper and to ensure Keimer's failure. The last "Busy Body" Franklin wrote (suppressed after a few newspapers came off the press) demanded the assembly pass a pa-

per currency issue and threatened uprisings if it did not. He continued the campaign by writing, on 10 April 1729, *A Modest Inquiry into the Nature and Necessity of a Paper Currency*, the first highly successful printing from his own press. Though Franklin said the "Rich Men dislik'd it," the pamphlet influenced public opinion, and the Pennsylvania assembly passed a paper currency bill.

That fall the partners bought the failing *Pennsylvania Gazette* "for a Trifle" from Keimer. Franklin immediately made it famous by writing an editorial analysis of the vicious controversy between Governor William Burnet and the Massachusetts assembly. Franklin and Meredith petitioned the Pennsylvania assembly on 18 February 1729 to print for the province, but the lucrative contract was again awarded to Bradford. On 14 October 1729 Andrew Hamilton, a distinguished lawyer who had become Franklin's friend and patron, was elected Speaker of the Pennsylvania assembly, and on 30 January 1730 the assembly chose Franklin and Meredith as the province's official printers. Nevertheless, in the spring of 1730, Meredith's father found he could not pay for the printing press and types. Suit was brought against him and the young partners. Since Meredith wanted to return to farming, Franklin borrowed money from his Junto friends Grace and Coleman to buy out Meredith and pay off the debt.

Franklin's former betrothed, Deborah Read, had married John Rogers in August 1725, exactly nine months after Franklin sailed from Philadelphia. Rogers proved to be a poor husband who, rumor reported, had another wife elsewhere. Deborah soon left him and returned to live with her mother. Rogers absconded in December 1727. William, Franklin's illegitimate son, was born in 1728 or 1729. His mother is unknown. On 1 September 1730 Franklin and Deborah Read Rogers joined together in a common-law marriage because John Rogers might still be alive. They took William into their home and brought him up as their son. Two years later Francis Folger Franklin was born, only to die of smallpox at age four. Eleven years after the birth of Francis, Franklin's third and last child, Sarah, was born. Deborah and the children attended Philadelphia's Anglican Christ Church.

Admitted a Freemason in January 1731, Franklin attended his first meeting in February. In June 1734 he was elected grand master, a sign of his local rise to prominence and the respect he enjoyed. Franklin remained active in the Philadelphia Freemasons until 1757 and attended Masonic meetings on his travels in the colonies and in various countries.

On 1 July 1731 Franklin drafted an "Instrument of Association" for the Library Company of Philadelphia, America's first subscription library. He served as its president, acted for a time as its librarian and for years as its secretary, contributed books to it, printed its first extant catalog (1741) for free, and nurtured it throughout his life. In the fall of 1731 Franklin sponsored his journeyman Thomas Whitemarsh as his printing partner in Charleston, South Carolina. The act was revolutionary in the closed circuit of colonial American printers. Previous patrons of independent printers were family members, helping their sons or close relatives to start printing businesses. Franklin's system of partnerships was generous—and, he hoped, would be profitable. He gradually established more than half a dozen printing partnerships.

By 1732 the indefatigable Franklin had taught himself to read, write, and translate German fluently. He gradually studied French, Spanish, Italian, and Latin, attaining a reading knowledge of them all. In the fall of 1732, finding that Bradford had arranged to print all the local almanacs, Franklin started his own, *Poor Richard*, predicting in the preface the death of Titan Leeds, the best-known almanac maker of the Middle Colonies. *Poor Richard* instantly became famous and soon sold almost 10,000 copies annually. The prefaces were more entertaining, the rustic, naive astrologer persona more engaging, the proverbs (often revised by Franklin) more memorable, and the contents more valuable than those of other almanacs. *Poor Richard* and the *Pennsylvania Gazette* became the mainstays of Franklin's successful publishing business. Even after he retired from printing in 1748, he continued to supply the copy for *Poor Richard* until 1757, when he wrote the last almanac, *Poor Richard Improved . . . 1758*, on his voyage to England. Reprinted under the title *The Way to Wealth* (at first as *Father Abraham's Speech*), the prefatory skit in the last almanac became his best-known writing before the *Autobiography*.

By 1 July 1733 Franklin had devised a scheme of thirteen useful virtues and a chart recording the violations that he recorded in part two of the *Autobiography*. Franklin's "virtues" were intended to correct his particular faults. Two virtues were directed at his tendency to be overweight and to prattle, pun, and joke too often (p. 68). He included the list and the chart in the *Autobiography* because he thought the method could be valuable for others. Franklin commonsensically concluded that though he fell far short of the ideal envisioned, "yet I was by the Endeavour made a better and a happier Man than I otherwise should have been" (p. 73).

Franklin proposed a fire protection society in the Junto, publicized the necessity of being prepared to fight fires in the *Pennsylvania Gazette* (4 Feb. 1735), and organized the Union Fire Company, Philadelphia's first, on 7 December 1736. He suggested in the Junto about 1735 reforming the night watch and hiring regular watchmen, but this reform was not adopted until 9 February 1751. To hinder counterfeiting of paper currency, he devised a new printing technique (reproducing images of plant leaves) and used it on the New Jersey paper currency of 1736. On 21 October 1743 Franklin intended to observe an eclipse of the moon, but a hurricane prevented it. Reprinting news of the eclipse, he found that it was observed in Boston and that the hurricane had struck there the next day. That observation led him to theorize that though the winds in "all our great Storms" blew from the northeast, the storm itself moved up from the south. Typi-

cally, he did not publish the theory at the time but waited until he had confirmed it by repeated observations. Fascinated by the whirling winds in the great storms, he analyzed the nature of whirlwinds and waterspouts, correctly theorizing that they had vacuums at the center and ingeniously comparing their motion to the circular motion in draining a tub of water. During the winter of 1740–1741 he designed the Pennsylvania fireplace and in 1744 wrote a pamphlet to popularize an improved version. Its purpose was part conservation and part efficiency: "My common Room, I know, is made twice as warm as it used to be, with a quarter of the Wood I formerly consum'd" (*Papers of Benjamin Franklin* [hereafter *Papers*], ed. Labaree et al., vol. 2, p. 437).

On 15 October 1736 the Pennsylvania assembly elected Franklin its clerk. Besides taking the minutes, the clerk was the legislature's historian and record keeper. The position allowed him to keep up his interest "among the Members, which secur'd to me the Business of Printing the Votes, Laws, Paper Money, and other occasional Jobs for the Public, that on the whole were very profitable" (*Autobiography*, p. 84). On 5 October 1737 he was appointed postmaster of Philadelphia. That office too helped his printing business. "Tho' the Salary was small," the postmastership "facilitated the Correspondence that improv'd my Newspaper, increas'd the Number demanded, as well as the Advertisements to be inserted, so that it came to afford me a very considerable Income" (*Autobiography*, p. 85).

Other projects failed. Franklin started America's first German-language newspaper, *Philadelphische Zeitung* (6 May 1732), which soon languished. In partnership with Johann Böhm, he published the *Philadelphier Teutsche Fama* in 1749 and 1750, but Böhm died in July 1751. The next month Franklin started America's first bilingual newspaper, *Hoch Teutsche und Englische Zeitung*, which was discontinued after thirteen issues. He projected the first American magazine in 1740, but his would-be editor, John Webbe, took the idea to his printing rival Bradford, and they produced the *American Magazine* three days before Franklin's *General Magazine* appeared. The times were premature for any American magazine, however, and both folded.

The Great Awakening came to Philadelphia with the arrival of George Whitefield on 2 November 1739. "It was wonderful to see the Change soon made in the Manners of our Inhabitants; from being thoughtless or indifferent about Religion, it seem'd as if all the World were growing Religious; so that one could not walk thro' the Town in an Evening without hearing Psalms sung in different Families of every Street" (*Autobiography*, p. 87). Franklin admired Whitefield because he sponsored humanitarian causes.

Franklin organized and publicized, on 17 March 1742, a project to sponsor botanist John Bartram's exploratory trips throughout the colonies and the frontiers to collect American plants, but the funds raised were insufficient. The following year Franklin wrote *A*

Proposal for Promoting Useful Knowledge, the founding document of the precursor of America's first scientific society, the American Philosophical Society. In April 1745 the London merchant Peter Collinson, a member of the Royal Society, sent the Library Company a pamphlet describing the new German investigations in electricity. Franklin and his friends Ebenezer Kinnersley, Philip Syng, and Thomas Hopkinson practiced the experiments with the Leyden jar (an early capacitor) and designed their own experiments for the next two years. On 25 May 1747 Franklin sent Collinson a letter describing the revolutionary research. He proved that there were not two kinds of electricity (the current theory) but only one; to explain the seemingly two kinds, he applied the terms *plus* and *minus*, or *positive* and *negative*, to electricity. Franklin demonstrated that in electrifying objects nothing new was created or lost but that the electricity was rearranged. The Nobel Prize–winning physicist Robert A. Millikan called Franklin's law of the conservation of charge "the most fundamental thing ever done in the field of electricity" (Lokken, p. 38).

People flocked to Franklin's house to see the experiments. He suggested that Kinnersley tour the colonies giving lectures on electricity and wrote out two lectures for him, "in which the Experiments were rang'd in such Order and accompanied with Explanations in such Method, as that the foregoing should assist in Comprehending the following" (*Autobiography*, p. 131). On 29 April 1749 Franklin wrote a letter to Kinnersley theorizing that clouds became electrified and that lightning was electrical in nature. On 2 March 1750 Franklin proposed lightning rods to the scientific community. Several months later, 29 July, he devised a sentry box experiment to prove that lightning is electrical and therefore that lightning rods could protect actual houses. Since the sentry box experiment needed to be performed on a tall tower, Franklin intended to wait until the steeple on Philadelphia's Christ Church was constructed.

Franklin's letters on electricity were gathered and published in London as *Experiments and Observations on Electricity* (1751). The brief book was translated into French by Thomas François D'Alibard, who set up the sentry box apparatus atop a tall tower at Marly, France, where on 10 May 1752 electricity from the air charged the Leyden jar (as Franklin had hypothesized). Before learning of the French proof, Franklin imagined that he might be able to obtain the same evidence by flying a kite at the approach of a thunderstorm. In June 1752, as dark clouds came up, he tried the kite experiment. He knew the hemp string attached to the kite would conduct electricity. Franklin ran the string from the kite to a Leyden jar, insulating himself by holding a silk ribbon to the string. When he observed the fibers on the hemp string stand out, he realized the experiment had succeeded. It must have been one of the most satisfying moments of his life. Franklin had proven electricity to be a basic element of nature. In late July he learned of the sentry box experiment's success in France. "This engag'd the public At-

tention everywhere" (*Autobiography*, p. 133). Franklin became the most famous natural philosopher since Isaac Newton, and, in the popular mind, more so, since Newton's theories were not generally understood nor their profound significance widely recognized. In 1756 Immanuel Kant dubbed Franklin the "Prometheus of modern time" (*Papers*, vol. 20, p. 490).

Franklin had to abandon his electrical experiments in late 1747 when French and Spanish privateers attacked ships and settlements on the Delaware River and the French and Indians assaulted Pennsylvania's frontiers. Because the Quakers, many of whom were pacifists, controlled the Pennsylvania assembly, the authorities could not raise a militia to defend the colony. Franklin therefore wrote *Plain Truth* (17 Nov. 1747), setting forth the province's defenseless and alarming situation and urging that private citizens take steps if the government would not. On the verso of the title page, he printed America's first cartoon used in a political situation, with the moral that God helps those who help themselves. He proposed and raised a militia association in which the volunteers elected their own company officers and the company officers elected the higher officers. The association proved immediately successful. When the company officers met, on 1 January 1748, they elected Franklin colonel, but he refused, pleading military inexperience, and served instead as a common soldier. The association made him a popular local hero, thus provoking the jealousy of Thomas Penn, Pennsylvania's main proprietor. He wrote that Franklin "is a dangerous Man and I should be very Glad he inhabited any other Country, as I believe him of a very uneasy Spirit. However as he is a Sort of Tribune of the People, he must be treated with regard" (*Papers*, vol. 3, p. 186). With the conclusion of King George's War (1740–1748) by the treaty of Aix-la-Chapelle on 18 October 1748, the association gradually dissolved.

On 1 January 1748 Franklin formed a partnership with David Hall and retired from printing. The poor boy from Boston had become the best-known and most prosperous printer, editor, and publisher of colonial America, but Franklin did not care to amass a fortune. The idealist wanted to devote his time to scientific research and civic affairs. The partnership with Hall was to last eighteen years, at which time the business would become Hall's. As the 1 October 1748 election approached, Franklin's friends urged him to run for the assembly, but he said he would not serve if chosen. The common council of Philadelphia, however, which elected its own members, chose Franklin a councilman on 4 October. On 30 June 1749 he was named a justice of the peace for Philadelphia, and on 9 May 1751, in a special election to replace William Clymer, who had died, he was elected from Philadelphia to the Pennsylvania assembly. Because Franklin had been the clerk of the Pennsylvania assembly since 1736, he was intimately familiar with its workings and was immediately assigned to the most important committees. Known as a superior writer, he chaired the committees that replied to the governor's messages. His public offices culminated in his being appointed joint deputy postmaster general of North America on 10 August 1753. As postmaster of Philadelphia from 5 October 1737, he had been permitted to receive mail free and had helped friends like John Bartram by having their mail directed to himself. Now he could send and receive mail free throughout the colonies. In the prerevolutionary period, he used this privilege and at the same time propagandized American principles by endorsing the covers of his letters "B. FREE Franklin."

In 1749 he wrote *Proposals Relating to the Education of Youth in Pennsylvania*, distributed it gratis, and "set on foot a Subscription for Opening and Supporting an Academy. . . . The Care and Trouble of agreeing with the Workmen, purchasing Materials, and superintending the Work fell upon me" (*Autobiography*, pp. 98–100). The academy became the Academy and College of Philadelphia and later the University of Pennsylvania. In 1751 Franklin's friend Dr. Thomas Bond decided to establish a hospital in Philadelphia and enlisted Franklin. He wrote two essays on the subject in the *Pennsylvania Gazette* (8 and 15 Aug. 1751) and helped raise subscriptions for the hospital. When they began to flag, he petitioned the legislature for additional funds. The county legislators objected that it would only benefit the city and claimed that even the Philadelphians were not really supporting the plan. Franklin then devised the first matching grant. He proposed a bill making the grant conditional: when the hospital's subscribers had raised £2,000, then the legislature would add 2,000 more. The Pennsylvania Hospital, America's first, opened 6 February 1752.

On 26 July 1751 Franklin proposed that the members of the several fire companies then existing join together in an insurance company. They did so and on 7 September 1751 formed the Philadelphia Contributionship. On a post office tour through New England, mid-June through September 1753, he received an honorary master of arts degree from Harvard (25 July) and Yale (12 Sept.). On 30 November he was awarded the Copley Medal of the Royal Society, at that time the most distinguished prize for scientific achievement in the world. The Royal Society unanimously elected him to membership 29 April 1756. On another post office tour to Virginia, William and Mary College granted him its first honorary master's degree, 20 April 1756. The Society (later Royal Society) of Arts elected him a corresponding member 1 September 1756.

Though for his contemporaries his scientific achievements eclipsed his literary achievements, Franklin nevertheless by the mid-eighteenth century had an international reputation as a writer of hoaxes, satires, essays, and letters. His salacious "Old Mistresses Apologue" (or "Reasons for Preferring an Old Mistress to a Young One"), written 25 June 1745, was considered too risqué for publication in nineteenth-century America. "The Speech of Miss Polly Baker, before a Court of Judicature, at Connecticut in New England, where she was prosecuted the fifth Time for

having a Bastard Child; which influenced the Court to dispense with her Punishment, and induced one of her Judges to marry her the next Day" (17 Apr. 1747) was among the most popular hoaxes or satires of the eighteenth century. The *American Weekly Mercury* published "An Apology for the young Man in Goal, and in Shackles, for ravishing an old Woman of 85 at Whitemarsh, who had only one Eye, and that a red one" (15 Sept. 1743), and the *New York Gazette* printed his poetic travesty of Sir William Gooch's speech on the burning of Virginia's capital (1 June 1747). All these pieces, like Franklin's mock biblical parables (1755), circulated widely in manuscript copies in England and America before some printer (never Franklin) published them.

In addition to belletristic writings satirizing such topics as the double standard for men and women, Franklin also wrote the best American propaganda objecting to England's treatment of the colonies. His outraged hoax "Rattlesnakes for Felons" (9 May 1751) proposed sending rattlesnakes to Great Britain in return for the transported convicts dumped in America. His great 1751 essay "Observations Concerning the Increase of Mankind, Peopling of Countries, &c." replied to Great Britain's Acts of Trade and Navigation. It roused young John Adams to contemplate the future independence of the United States and influenced the theories of both Adam Smith on capitalism and Thomas Malthus on population.

Inspired by the union of the Iroquois or Six Indian Nations that had "subsisted Ages, and appears indissoluble" (*Papers*, vol. 4, p. 119), Franklin optimistically thought that the colonies would unify. Three years later, alarmed by the French incursions into the Ohio Valley and along the Pennsylvania and Virginia frontiers, Franklin wrote an editorial (4 May 1754) urging unification of the colonies and printed it under a cartoon showing a snake cut into pieces, with the caption underneath reading "JOIN OR DIE." The first political American cartoon in a newspaper, it was the first symbol of the unified American colonies. That summer, representing Pennsylvania, he attended the Albany Conference, called by the British authorities, to urge the Six Nations to remain with the English and to arrange a common defense of the frontier against the French troops and their Indian allies. Franklin drafted a plan of union as he journeyed to the conference. On 2 July the conference voted to form a union of the colonies, and on 10 July it adopted, with revisions, Franklin's plan (see *Papers*, vol. 5, pp. 374–87, for a masterly discussion). But the colonies rejected it because they thought it had too much prerogative, and the Board of Trade rejected it because its members feared a union of the colonies might lead to their independence.

The following winter, when Franklin was in Boston on post office business, Governor William Shirley showed him a tentative plan of union proposed by the Board of Trade. Franklin objected that the British plan did not give the colonists the right to choose their own representatives and also protested the proposal to have Parliament tax Americans. The following day, 4

December 1754, he wrote that it was "an undoubted Right of Englishmen not to be taxed but by their own Consent given thro' their Representatives." On 22 December, in reply to Governor Shirley's suggestion that the colonists elect members of Parliament, Franklin said that if all the past Acts of Trade and Navigation were repealed and if the colonies were given "a reasonable number of Representatives," then the colonists might be satisfied. But Franklin and Shirley both knew that Great Britain would never take either step. Franklin argued that if there were any difference between the merits of the English and the colonists, then "those who have most contributed to enlarge Britain's empire and commerce, encrease her strength, her wealth, and the numbers of her people, at the risque of their own lives and private fortunes in new and strange countries, methinks ought rather to expect some preference" (*Papers*, vol. 5, p. 451). Franklin's patriotic Americanism was a new, bold note in the political discourse of the eighteenth century.

After the rout of General Edward Braddock by the French and Indians near Pittsburgh on 9 July 1755, the English troops fled to Philadelphia. With the Pennsylvania frontier defenseless and the Indians raiding the borders, Franklin drew up a bill for establishing a voluntary militia, which the Pennsylvania assembly quickly passed. Because Governor Robert Hunter Morris knew that Franklin was popular and that volunteers would join if he commanded, Morris made Franklin the military and civilian commander of the frontier on 5 January 1756. Franklin led 500 soldiers out to the frontier and built a fort before he was summoned to Philadelphia for a special assembly meeting. The company officers elected him colonel on 12 February; this time he accepted the command. Governor Morris commissioned him on 24 February, but the Board of Trade and Privy Council vetoed the militia bill (7 July 1756) as too democratic. As a result of the proprietors' continuing refusal to tax the proprietary lands in common with other Pennsylvania property, the assembly resolved to petition the king. On 3 February 1757 the assembly appointed Franklin its agent. Fearing the sea, Deborah refused to sail with him to England, but Franklin accepted. In London, on 27 July 1757, Franklin met Lord Granville, president of the Privy Council, who told him that the king's instructions to the governors were law and that "the King is the Legislator of the Colonies" (*Autobiography*, p. 143). Franklin, however, knew that the colonial legislatures made their own laws, though these had to be approved by the king. Franklin found the British public and the authorities ignorant about America. He thereupon began a campaign to enlighten them. His first major attempt, "A Defense of the Americans," appeared in the *London Chronicle* (12 May 1759). It was the grandest statement of Americanism in the colonial period. Franklin wrote a constant stream of American propaganda throughout his years in England, 1757–1762 and 1764–1775. In this first mission, his pamphlet arguing the economic and strategic importance of Canada to the colonies and to Great Britain (*The In-*

terest of Great Britain Considered [1760]) was his longest and most influential writing.

Franklin's mission to England changed when he consulted the famous London physician and friend of Pennsylvania's Quaker leaders Dr. John Fothergill, whose advice the assembly had directed him to ask. Fothergill and other prominent English Quakers said he should first try for an accommodation with the proprietors. That negotiation dragged on inconclusively, but in Pennsylvania Governor William Denny passed an act, 17 April 1759, taxing the proprietors' estates. The Penns tried to have the act disallowed. Despite the arguments of lawyers hired by Franklin, the Board of Trade on 24 June 1760 recommended the act be annulled. Franklin appealed to the king in council, and, after personally guaranteeing that the proprietary estates would be taxed with perfect equity, he won the case for the assembly. Thus Franklin's first mission to England had some success, though the Penns continued to oppose acts taxing their lands.

In England Franklin became close friends with William Strahan, a member of Parliament, with Margaret Stevenson (Franklin's landlady), her daughter Mary (Polly) Stevenson, and their circle of friends and relatives. He spoofed himself, "Dr. Fatsides . . . the Great One," and the activities of the Stevenson circle in a wonderful parody of court gossip, "The Craven Street Gazette" (22 Sept. 1770). Franklin also joined two informal clubs. One, consisting primarily of scientists, philanthropists, and explorers (the future captain James Cook occasionally attended), met on Mondays. The other, dubbed the Club of Honest Whigs, met on Thursdays and included dissenting ministers like Joseph Priestley and Richard Price, as well as James Boswell, who recorded in his *Life of Johnson* (1791) Franklin's definition of humankind: "Man is a tool-making animal."

Occasionally, instead of attending the Honest Whigs, Franklin went to the Club of the Royal Philosophers (later called the Royal Society Club). The official organizations that Franklin frequented were the Royal Society of London, the Associates of Dr. Bray (a small philanthropic organization that Dr. Samuel Johnson visited, 1 May 1760, while Franklin was its chairman), and the Society of Arts (which promoted new crops and improved farming techniques).

When time permitted, he continued his scientific interests, inventing a clock with only three wheels; designing a damper for stoves and chimneys, 2 December 1758; and gradually improving his new musical instrument, the glass armonica. After Franklin received the honorary degree of doctor of laws from the University of St. Andrews in Scotland, 12 February 1759, his contemporaries usually called him Dr. Franklin. Oxford conferred on him the honorary degree of doctor of civil law, 30 April 1762. During his years in England, Franklin tried to take an annual vacation. In 1759 he toured northern England and Scotland, meeting David Hume, Adam Smith, William Robertson, and Lord Kames. In 1761 he toured the Austrian Netherlands and the Dutch Republic.

During his first English mission, Franklin was elected annually to the Pennsylvania assembly. He left England in the late summer of 1762 and arrived back in Philadelphia on 1 November. Just after Franklin left England, his son William was appointed governor of New Jersey and then married. Some scholars have believed that Franklin, when asked by Lord Bute if he could render Franklin a service in reply for influencing government policy with *The Interest of Great Britain Considered*, asked that Bute reward his son. Franklin found troubles at home. In the fall of 1763 the proprietary party gained strength from an alliance of Scotch-Irish and Germans on the frontiers. When a frontier mob (the "Paxton Boys") massacred a group of friendly Christian Indians in Lancaster, Franklin scathingly denounced the action in *A Narrative of the Late Massacres* (30 Jan. 1764). When the Paxton Boys marched on Philadelphia to kill the Christian Indians there, the government floundered. Franklin organized Philadelphia's defense, met with the leaders of the rioters, and persuaded them to present a list of their grievances and to disperse. In this crisis he again demonstrated dramatic leadership and personal bravery.

Throughout the early eighteenth century, some Pennsylvania assemblymen, disgusted with proprietary government, favored petitioning for royal government. In the spring of 1764 Franklin and the assembly majority adopted that policy. On 24 March 1764, after Pennsylvania governor John Penn again refused to pass an act taxing proprietary lands, the assembly passed twenty-six resolves condemning the proprietors and proprietary government. Franklin publicized the resolves with his *Explanatory Remarks* (29 Mar.) and urged the people to petition for a royal government in *Cool Thoughts* (12 Apr.). On 26 May Isaac Norris resigned as the assembly's Speaker, pleading illness, and Franklin was elected Speaker of the Pennsylvania House. The proposed change to a royal colony frightened the electorate. The secular Franklin paid little attention to the religious apprehensions and prejudices of his contemporaries, but many dissenters (Quakers, Moravians, Presbyterians, and Baptists) in Philadelphia and Pennsylvania feared that a change to a royal government would eliminate religious freedom and lead to establishing Anglicanism as Pennsylvania's official religion. Franklin's political opponents claimed that he favored royal government because he coveted the governorship; that he had bilked the public monies while he was the assembly's agent in England; that William Franklin's mother was his maidservant Barbara whom he had mistreated and buried in an unmarked grave; that he was prejudiced against the Germans; and that he was an Indian-lover. The most bitterly contested assembly election in colonial Pennsylvania began at 10 A.M. on 1 October 1764 and continued until 3 P.M. on 2 October. Franklin lost by eighteen votes.

The anti-proprietary party retained its majority, however. It appointed Franklin on 26 October 1764 to join Richard Jackson as the assembly's agent to England. The purpose of Franklin's second English mission (1764–1775) was to petition the king for a change from proprietary to royal government in Pennsylvania. But British imperial politics intervened. During Franklin's brief tenure as Speaker of the Pennsylvania House, 26 May to 1 October 1764, news of the impending Stamp Act reached the colonies. The Massachusetts House of Representatives requested the speakers of the other colonial assemblies to oppose the act. On 12 September Franklin presented the request to the Pennsylvania assembly. It promptly instructed Jackson, Pennsylvania's agent, to oppose the Stamp Act and to argue that only the Pennsylvania legislature had the right to impose taxes in Pennsylvania. When Franklin arrived in London on 10 December 1764, the Stamp Act demanded attention. On 2 February 1765 he and the other colonial agents met Minister George Grenville to protest the proposed duties. Grenville said that the colonies must bear some expense for Britain's defending them and challenged the agents to present a more equitable tax. Since Franklin knew the colonies needed a paper currency, he suggested that the British government issue an American paper currency and use the low interest rate charged for borrowing the money to pay Britain. He and Thomas Pownall met Grenville on 12 February and proposed the plan, but Grenville, "besotted with his Stamp Scheme," ignored them (*Papers*, vol. 13, p. 449).

The Stamp Act passed the House of Commons on 27 February 1765 and received the royal assent on 22 March, to take effect on 1 November. Franklin had lost. But he supposed the Stamp Act could be tolerated. He wrote the young Philadelphia patriot Charles Thomson (11 July 1765), "I took every Step in my Power, to prevent the Passing of the Stamp Act," but "We might as well have hinder'd the Suns setting." Out of touch with the mounting American resentment, Franklin accepted defeat. When asked by Grenville to nominate some local person of integrity to be stamp distributor for Pennsylvania, Franklin suggested his friend John Hughes. That compounded his mistake. Virginia's House of Burgesses passed a series of anti–Stamp Act Resolves on 30 May 1765 denying that the British had the right to tax Virginians. Emboldened by the Virginia Resolves, other colonies followed. Mobs threatened the stamp distributors. Because of rumors that Franklin had supported the Stamp Act, his Philadelphia home was threatened the night of 16 September. Deborah armed herself, ready to fight, causing numerous friends to show up in her support. On 1 November, the day the Stamp Act was to take effect, courts throughout the colonies refused to convene. American colonial administration collapsed.

Galvanized by American resistance, Franklin became a one-man propaganda machine, writing dozens of pieces against the Stamp Act. He designed an anti–Stamp Act cartoon, gave copies to every member of Parliament, and sent his messages on cards bearing the design. On 13 February 1766 he testified before a committee of the whole of the House of Commons against the Stamp Act, leading to its repeal on 22 February. His answers to the questions posed by the members of Parliament constituted a triumphant display of political knowledge and of Americanism. To the suggestion that military forces should be sent to America, he boldly answered, "They will not find a rebellion; they may indeed make one" (*Papers*, vol. 13, p. 142). Publication of his *Examination* established him as the preeminent spokesman for the American colonies.

In late 1765 Franklin had petitioned the Privy Council for Pennsylvania's change from a proprietary to a royal government, but the reply was continually postponed. On 10 June 1766 he requested permission to return home, but the Pennsylvania assembly instead reappointed him joint agent with Jackson. On 11 April 1768 the Georgia assembly appointed him its agent; on 8 November 1769 the New Jersey assembly did the same; and on 24 October 1770 the Massachusetts assembly followed suit. Throughout his second agency, Franklin continued writing superb American propaganda: the "Grand Leap of the Whale" (3 May 1765); "Causes of the American Discontents before 1768" (7 Jan. 1768); "Rules by Which a Great Empire May Be Reduced to a Small One" (11 Sept. 1773); and "An Edict by the King of Prussia" (22 Sept. 1773).

Franklin predicted American independence, but he also said that every year brought America increasing strength, and if there must be war, it was best to postpone it as long as possible. In the summer of 1766 Franklin traveled to Germany, where he was elected to its Academy of Sciences. In 1767 he visited France and was presented to Louis XV at Versailles (6 Sept.). In 1769 Franklin revisited France, making further acquaintances among the physiocrats. In the fall of 1771 he toured Ireland and Scotland with Richard Jackson, staying with David Hume in Edinburgh and with Lord Kames at Blair-Drummond. In Ireland especially, the great difference between the few rich "Landlords, great Noblemen and Gentlemen, extremely opulent, living in the highest Affluence and Magnificence," and the overwhelming majority of the people "extremely poor, living in the most sordid Wretchedness in dirty Hovels of Mud and Straw, and cloathed only in Rags," disgusted him. He wrote (13 Jan. 1772), "That in the Possession and Enjoyment of the various Comforts of Life, compar'd to these People every Indian is a Gentleman: And the Effect of this kind of Civil Society seems only to be, the depressing Multitudes below the Savage State that a few may be rais'd above it."

Whenever he had time, Franklin continued his intellectual interests. He described a series of experiments, 10 May 1768, on the relationship between canal water depths and the speed of canal boats. He devised a phonetic alphabet, taught it to Mary Stevenson, and corresponded, 20 July 1768, with her in it. That fall (29 Oct.), he had maps of the Atlantic engraved that contained the course of the "river in the ocean," the Gulf Stream. In Philadelphia, the renewed American Philosophical Society elected him its president on 2 January 1769, reelecting him annually until his death. He supervised the publication of the revised and enlarged fourth English edition of his *Experiments and Observations on Electricity* (1769). The Batavian Society of Experimental Science, Rotterdam, elected him to membership on 11 June 1771. The Académie royale des sciences, Paris, elected him a foreign associate on 16 August 1772. Later that year he produced a list of forty-five human emotions that could be expressed in music. He repeatedly experimented with the interaction of oil and water. The modern scientist Charles Tanford said that in his experiments Franklin "actually correctly determined the scale of magnitude of molecular dimensions, the first person ever to do so, but he did not recognize it" (*Ben Franklin Stilled the Waves* [1989], p. 80). Franklin suggested that John Viny manufacture wheels made of one piece of wood and gave him suggestions for improving the design, which Viny patented.

In Philadelphia, Franklin's daughter Sarah married Richard Bache in 1767. In 1769 the first of the eight Bache grandchildren, Benjamin Franklin Bache, the future Jeffersonian publisher of the Philadelphia *Aurora*, was born. Deborah Franklin had suffered a stroke that previous winter, partially recovered, became worse, and died on 19 December 1774. From the time of his return to England in 1764, Franklin had been overseeing the education and care of his son's illegitimate child, William Temple Franklin.

Learning that England's repressive measures toward Massachusetts had been urged by Massachusetts governor Thomas Hutchinson and Lieutenant Governor Andrew Oliver, Franklin obtained their correspondence with Thomas Whately, undersecretary of state, and sent the letters to the Speaker of the Massachusetts House of Representatives, Thomas Cushing. Franklin believed that the correspondence would lessen the rage of the Massachusetts radicals against the British authorities. Instead, the letters exacerbated the strife between the governor and the assembly, which resolved to petition for Hutchinson's and Oliver's removal. At the same time, Hutchinson surreptitiously obtained a copy of Franklin's 7 July 1773 letter to Cushing in which he urged the colonial assemblies to resolve never to "grant aids to the Crown in any General War till" the rights of the Americans "are recogniz'd by the King and both Houses of Parliament. . . . Such a Step I imagine will bring the Dispute to a Crisis; and whether our Demands are immediately comply'd with, or compulsory Means are thought of to make us Rescind them, our Ends will finally be obtain'd" (*Papers*, vol. 20, p. 282). Hutchinson sent this letter to Lord Dartmouth, the colonial secretary, who judged it treasonable. Dartmouth asked General Thomas Gage, military commander in chief in America, to obtain the original so that Franklin could be prosecuted, but Gage could not. The Hutchinson-Oliver letters were published in Boston in June 1773. It has never been determined how Franklin obtained them. William Whately (John Whately's brother), however, accused John Temple of purloining the letters. The two dueled on 11 December 1773. As Whately recovered from the minor wounds he received, it appeared that the two would fight again. To prevent it, on 25 December 1773 Franklin published a statement that he knew must bring down upon him the British authorities' wrath: "I alone am the person who obtained and transmitted to Boston the letters in question."

Franklin forwarded to Lord Dartmouth the Massachusetts petition to remove Hutchinson and Oliver. A preliminary hearing took place 11 January 1774. News of the Boston Tea Party reached London on 20 January. The British authorities became furious with Massachusetts and its agent. The hearing on the Massachusetts petition before the Privy Council took place in the Cockpit (a room at Whitehall, the site of which had formerly been used for cockfighting) on 29 January. British solicitor general Alexander Wedderburn excoriated and denounced Franklin in an hour-long diatribe, demanding that he be marked and branded as a criminal and calling him not *"a man of letters"* but (in a well-known classical allusion) *"homo* trium *literarum"* i.e., a man of three letters, *fur,* or thief. "The muscles of " Franklin's "face had been previously composed, so as to afford a placid tranquil expression of countenance, and he did not suffer the slightest alteration of it to appear during the continuance of the speech" (*Papers*, vol. 21, pp. 49, 41). Britain's greatest officials, many of whom, like Wedderburn, Franklin knew well, sneered and snickered while he stood silent, America's scapegoat. It was the most dramatic ignominy of Franklin's life.

Two days later Franklin was dismissed as deputy postmaster general for North America. The American post office had never been profitable before Franklin took it over and it has never been since. During 1774 and early 1775, even as he petitioned against the Boston Port Bill (which became law 31 Jan., closing Boston's port), he wrote increasingly bitter satires against England while still attempting to reconcile Great Britain with the colonists. In an effort to forestall the Boston Port Bill, he personally guaranteed payment of the cost of the tea dumped in the Boston harbor. All his efforts failed, including his collaboration with William Pitt, earl of Chatham, in January 1775. He left England, his second mission officially an abysmal failure.

While Franklin was at sea, the battles of Lexington and Concord (17 and 18 Apr. 1775) ignited the war. He arrived at Philadelphia on 5 May. The next day the Pennsylvania assembly unanimously chose him a delegate to the Second Continental Congress. He immediately became Congress's most radical leader, drafting articles of confederation by 21 July 1775 that asserted America's sovereignty and gave greater powers to the central government than the U.S. Constitution did in 1787. But Congress was not yet ready for such bold action. John Adams reported to his wife Abigail on 23 July that Franklin "does not hesitate at our boldest Measures, but rather seems to think us, too irresolute, and backward" (Adams, *Family Correspondence*, vol. 1 [1963–], p. 253). Congress appointed him in the fall to a committee to confer with General George Washington in Massachusetts and, on 29 November, chair of a standing committee of secret correspondence to deal with foreign affairs. His propagandistic writings of the period include an "Account of the Devices on the Continental Bills of Credit" (20 Sept. 1775), the popular satiric song "The King's Own Regulars" (27 Nov. 1775), and the hoax "Bradshaw's Epitaph" (14 Dec. 1775), which concluded with the words that Thomas Jefferson adopted as his personal motto: "rebellion to tyrants is obedience to God."

On 16 January 1776 Franklin again argued for an "instrument of confederation" in Congress but was defeated. On 19 February 1776 he urged the four New England colonies to enter into a confederation, which they would subsequently offer the other colonies an opportunity to join, but the New England colonies decided to wait. Appointed commissioner to Canada by Congress with Charles Carroll of Carrollton, Samuel Chase, and John Carroll, S.J., he undertook the mission at age seventy, though sick with large boils, swollen legs, and frequent dizziness. The mission (26 Mar. to 30 May) to convince the Canadian colonists to join with the Americans failed. On his return, Franklin served on the committee to draft the Declaration of Independence. Since Thomas Jefferson was named first, he chaired the committee and decided to draft the document himself, though Franklin added to and revised it. Congress voted for independence on 2 July and then debated, altered, and finally adopted the Declaration of Independence on 4 July 1776. Elected to the Pennsylvania state convention on 8 July, Franklin was chosen its president, 16 July. Under his guidance, Pennsylvania enacted the most egalitarian of all state constitutions, with a unicameral legislature elected annually.

In a draft for Pennsylvania of a Declaration of Rights, Franklin asserted that the state had the right to discourage large concentrations of property and wealth in single individuals as a danger to the happiness of the majority. The Pennsylvania convention rejected his radical suggestion. During congressional debates on the Articles of Confederation, 30 July to 1 August 1776, he unsuccessfully advocated proportional rather than equal representation of states in Congress. Congress appointed Franklin, Adams, and Edward Rutledge a committee to confer with Lord Howe on Staten Island (11 Sept.), but they failed to reconcile English and American differences. In the fall, Franklin drafted a "Sketch of Propositions for a Peace," suggesting that Britain cede Canada to an independent United States. Elected by Congress a commissioner to France with Silas Deane and Arthur Lee, Franklin sailed from Philadelphia on 27 October 1776, taking his grandsons William Temple Franklin and Benjamin Franklin Bache with him.

Franklin landed at Auray, France, on 3 December 1776 and proceeded to Paris where on 28 December he met secretly with the comte de Vergennes, French foreign minister. The American commissioners formally requested French aid on 5 January 1777, and on 13 January they received a verbal promise of two million livres. At the end of February, Franklin moved to the nearby village of Passy where he lived throughout the French mission.

Franklin had a scalp irritation that was exacerbated by wearing a wig, so he rarely wore one. He knew that since Voltaire's *Lettres philosophiques* (1734) and Montesquieu's *L'esprit des lois* (1748), the French associated virtue and simplicity with Pennsylvania and Quakerism. Accordingly, he dressed plainly, partly because it reflected his homespun taste. On 8 February 1777 he wrote to his flirtatious friend Emma Thompson: "Figure me . . . very plainly dress'd, wearing my thin grey strait Hair, that peeps out under my only Coiffure, a fine Fur Cap, which comes down my Forehead almost to my Spectacles. Think how this must appear among the Powder'd Heads of Paris."

Franklin was idolized. John Adams wrote: "His name was familiar to government and people, to kings, courtiers, nobility, clergy, and philosophers, as well as plebeians, to such a degree that there was scarcely a peasant or a citizen, a *valet de chambre*, coachman or footman, a lady's chambermaid or a scullion in a kitchen, who was not familiar with it, and who did not consider him as a friend to human kind" (*Autobiography*, p. 245).

On 4 December the American commissioners learned of the British defeat at Saratoga, giving impetus to the negotiations for a loan and for an alliance. On 28 January 1778 they reported that France had granted the Americans six million livres. And on 6 February they signed treaties of "alliance for mutual defense" and of amity and commerce with France. The treaty shocked Great Britain, for now it would have to wage war against a major European power with a great navy as well as against its rebellious colonies. To the treaty signing, Franklin wore the same brown velvet suit he had worn 29 January 1774 when denounced by Wedderburn before the Privy Council. Thus he symbolically declared the treaty his revenge. The American commissioners were formally received and presented to Louis XVI on 20 March.

Franklin escorted Voltaire to the Masonic Lodge of the Nine Sisters on 7 April 1778, was inducted to the Lodge shortly thereafter, and served as its grand master in 1779 and 1780. At the demand of the members present for a meeting of the French Academy, 29 April 1778, Franklin and Voltaire embraced and kissed one another. The jealous Adams recorded the French exclaiming: "Oh! it was enchanting to see Solon and Sophocles embracing!" (Adams, *Diary and Autobiography*, vol. 4 [1961], p. 81).

Having three American commissioners in Paris was a mistake. Lee and Adams resented Franklin's fame. Fortunately, France sent a minister plenipotentiary to the United States; Congress, obliged by protocol to choose a similar diplomatic officer for France, elected Franklin (21 Oct. 1778) minister plenipotentiary. To facilitate the production of passports, loan certificates, promissory notes, and other documents, he purchased type and a press and printed such items (the earliest so far found is dated 2 Aug. 1779), as well as his bagatelles, himself. Franklin borrowed another three mil-

lion livres for war supplies from France. Despite Franklin's being minister plenipotentiary, Adams deluged Vergennes with officious letters. Exasperated, the French foreign minister gave copies to Franklin, demanded that Franklin send them to Congress, and declared that he would no longer receive communications from Adams. Franklin had to comply. Adams thereupon became bitterly hostile to Franklin and to France.

As minister plenipotentiary, Franklin borrowed funds from France for the confederation of states, issued letters of marque for American privateers, managed the interests of the Continental navy overseas, and negotiated for humane treatment and exchanges of American prisoners of war. He often attended court on Tuesdays with the other ministers, entertained Americans at dinner most Sundays, helped numerous American prisoners of war who had escaped (including Israel Potter, 14 Feb. 1777, whom Herman Melville later memorialized), cashed hundreds of American loan office certificates, oversaw the purchase and shipping of arms and other supplies for the Continental army, coordinated and often wrote American propaganda for English and European distribution, acted as head of American intelligence in Europe, and cultivated friendly relations with a host of influential French intellectuals and politicians. He was the most essential and successful American diplomat of all time.

Too busy to carry out many scientific experiments, Franklin nevertheless suggested experiments to others. Learning that ships used in the salt trade lasted longer than others, he conceived a method for prolonging the life of lumber by seasoning it in salt. He devised a method to test the conductivity of different metals. A magnificent display of the aurora borealis (3 Dec. 1778) prompted him to write a series of "Suppositions and Conjectures" on the phenomenon. He described his new invention, bifocal glasses, on 23 May 1784.

Congress, on 11, 14, and 15 June 1781, appointed Franklin, Henry Laurens, and Thomas Jefferson to join John Jay and John Adams as commissioners to negotiate peace, with instructions requiring them to act only with the knowledge and concurrence of France. After the surrender of General Charles Cornwallis to Washington at Yorktown (19 Oct. 1781), Britain lost hope of defeating the colonies in a land war. When the marquis of Rockingham became prime minister in 1782, he initiated peace talks. From March to June, Richard Oswald, a London merchant with American sympathies and an old friend of Franklin, negotiated with Franklin who suggested, on 18 April, that Britain should cede Canada to the United States. Had Franklin been the only commissioner, he might have been able to settle the peace in June 1782, securing Canada. But when Jay arrived in Paris on 23 June, he insisted on prior recognition of American independence as a condition for formal peace negotiations, thus delaying the talks while the war at sea slowly changed to favor the British.

On 10 July Franklin proposed to Oswald the "necessary" terms for peace, ignoring Congress's instructions to communicate them first to Vergennes. Oswald's new commission from Britain (21 Sept. 1782) effectively recognized the United States and overcame Jay's hesitation. A draft of the articles for the treaty was prepared and sent to England, again without informing Vergennes. Adams arrived in Paris 26 October and joined the negotiations. British envoy Oswald and the American commissioners signed the preliminary articles of peace on 30 November 1782. When Vergennes complained in December of the American failure to consult the French, Franklin, on 17 December, diplomatically admitted the impropriety, expressed gratitude to France, and asked for another loan. Vergennes assured him of a further six million livres. On behalf of Congress, Franklin, Adams, and Jay signed the definitive treaty of peace on 3 September 1783.

During the war, Franklin issued documents asking American vessels to give safe passage to English humanitarians, explorers, and scientists, the most famous of whom was Captain James Cook (10 Mar. 1779). At the conclusion of the war, when consulted by the papal Nuncio in Paris about organizing the Roman Catholic church in the United States, Franklin suggested Maryland's John Carroll, S.J., as its head. Fascinated by the early balloon ascensions, Franklin reported them in great detail to the Royal Society. Asked by a scoffing observer, "What use is it?" Franklin gave the greatest defense ever made of pure research, "What use is a new-born baby?" (Van Doren, p. 700). On 12 May 1784 the formal ratification of the peace treaty with Great Britain was exchanged, and the next day Franklin requested to be relieved from his post to return home. Jefferson arrived in Paris on 30 August 1784 to join Franklin and Adams in attempting to make treaties with the European nations and Barbary States. On 2 May 1785 Franklin received permission to leave France. "I shall now be free of Politicks for the Rest of my Life. Welcome again my dear Philosophical Amusements." Franklin left Passy 12 July 1785. He had begun to suffer from a bladder stone in August 1782, and by now it was large and painful. He spent most of the voyage delighting in his "philosophical amusements," writing the extraordinary *Maritime Observations*, which suggested dozens of reasonable improvements for convenience, safety (two kinds of floating anchors, watertight separate compartments), and swiftness in sailing; composing an essay "On the Causes and Cure of Smoky Chimneys"; and drafting his "Description of a New Stove."

Franklin arrived at Philadelphia on 14 September 1785, was elected to the supreme executive council of Pennsylvania on 11 October, chosen its president on 18 October, and served in that position (in effect, governor) for three years. In January 1786 he fashioned an instrument for taking down books from high shelves. He designed a chair with a seat that unfolded to become a ladder, another chair that had a writing arm on one side (the common school seats imitated it), and a rocking chair with an automatic fan. He was named president of the Pennsylvania Society for Promoting the Abolition of Slavery (23 Apr. 1787). From 28 May to 17 September Franklin served as a Pennsylvania delegate to the Constitutional Convention. Though he early on argued that representation should be proportional to population, on 3 July he moved the "Great Compromise," whereby representation was proportional in the House of Delegates but equal by state in the Senate. He argued, on 7 and 10 August, for extending the right to vote as widely as possible, specifically condemning property qualification as necessary either for the franchise or for office holding. His closing speech supporting the Constitution was the most effective propaganda for its ratification. Franklin's presence and argument contributed more than any other element to harmonize the delegates and to persuade thirty-nine of the forty-two members present to sign the formal document.

On 14 October 1788 Franklin ended his service as president of the supreme executive council of Pennsylvania, terminating his career in public office. Despite his gout and bladder stone, he still, as of 25 November 1788, enjoyed "many comfortable Intervals, in which I forget all my Ills, and amuse myself in Reading or Writing, or in Conversation with Friends, joking, laughing, and telling merry Stories" (*The Writings of Benjamin Franklin* [hereafter *Writings*], ed. Smyth, vol. 9, p. 683). He wrote and signed the first remonstrance against slavery addressed to the American Congress (12 Feb. 1789), but Congress said it had no authority to interfere in the internal affairs of the states. He observed to Jean Baptiste Le Roy (13 Nov. 1789) that "In this world, nothing can be said to be certain except death and taxes." On 23 March 1790 he brilliantly satirized a defense of slavery. He died at his home in Philadelphia of pleurisy. He was buried in Christ Church burial ground, Philadelphia, beside his wife Deborah and their son Francis. The French assembly voted to wear mourning for three days. The U.S. House of Representatives passed but the Senate defeated the motion to wear mourning for a month (for an analysis of the politics involved, see *The Papers of Thomas Jefferson*, ed. Julian P. Boyd, vol. 19 [1950–], pp. 78–108).

Metamorphoses marked Franklin's life. The runaway Boston Puritan (1706–1723) became the London libertine (1725); the impecunious apprentice became the most successful printer, publisher, and editor of colonial America (1728–1748); the prosperous businessman became the world's most famous scientist (1748–1757); the scientist became the world's best-known American (1757–1775); the American became the revolutionary and, simultaneously, the most cosmopolitan European (1775–1785); and finally, the shape-shifter was nearly universally regarded as the sage (1785–1790).

Yet these changing identities do not begin to do Franklin justice. Nor can his hundred pseudonyms (each brilliantly chosen for the specific occasion), from "Silence Dogood" and "Old Janus" to "Poor Richard" and "Homespun," to "FART-HING" and "Samuel Gerrish," begin to capture the range of his writings. As a young man, he wanted to become a great writer. David Hume believed (10 May 1762) that Franklin had achieved that stature and called him a "Great Man of Letters." But most of his popular writings came later. He wrote the most delightful bagatelles in the English and French languages. And though his *Autobiography* is the most popular autobiography of the modern world and among the greatest works in the genre, it does not begin to reveal all the complexities of his literary genius. Franklin was the greatest letter writer of the eighteenth century, with more variety, tones, and moods than anyone else. He is the only major American writer whose achievements are more diverse than his fictional creations. Nor can the numerous epithets that his contemporaries and later scholars gave him quite sum him up, though each has an element of truth. And yet there is something archetypically American about Franklin, the self-made man, the fix-it-yourself person, the gadgeteer, the creator and joiner of clubs and associations, the friendly stranger, and the person who, more than any other great American, thoroughly identified with the common man.

Franklin adopted the traditional Whig beliefs as a youth, but he became more politically radical as he grew older. There was always something subversive about him, partly because he viewed ultimate values as a continuously shifting set of hypotheses, partly because he saw all sides of a question, partly because he was supremely conscious of life's ironies, and partly because he was uncannily aware of humans' ultimate vanity. No man burlesqued himself more than Franklin: "a *Boo bee* he may be allow'd to be, namely *B.F.*" (*Papers*, vol. 1, p. 219).

Franklin had even more paradoxes than metamorphoses. A shrewd businessman, Franklin nevertheless allowed hundreds of people to owe him small debts (and scores to owe him large ones); yet there is no evidence that he ever prosecuted anyone for debt. Though offered a patent for the Franklin stove, he declined it and never sought to patent the lightning rod, bifocals, armonica, or any of his numerous successful designs—though, in some cases, others did. Max Weber found that some of Franklin's writings contained the spirit of capitalism "in almost classical purity," but he cared little about personal wealth. He came to distrust large accumulations of wealth by individuals, believing great capital in the hands of a single person injured society as a whole. He despised trade and avarice, he respected agriculture and the ordinary person, and he loved natural philosophy and those who did good for others.

When young, Franklin wrote prolifically on theology, ethics, and morality but gradually abandoned them for what we now call science. By 1743 he found "What is True?" an inadequate question. Instead, he asked "*How a Thing is true?*" Truth had different natures: the *verum physicum, metaphysicum*, and *morale*. He wrote of deism, "This doctrine, tho' it might be

true, was not very useful" (*Autobiography*, p. 46). From the late 1740s to his death, Franklin spent most of his spare time pursuing science. In the opinions of the early nineteenth-century scientist Sir Humphrey Davy and the modern philosopher of science Thomas S. Kuhn, Franklin created electricity as a science. The Harvard scientist John Winthrop said that Franklin was good "at starting Game for Philosophers" (*Writings*, vol. 9, p. 652). He instigated scientific research by his early American friends like Joseph Breintnall, by his English friends like Joseph Priestley, and by his European friends like Jan Ingenhousz.

Franklin was a patriotic American from at least the early 1750s, well before the nation existed. Writing of the genesis of the U.S. Constitution at the end of his life, James Madison observed that Franklin's 1754 letters to Massachusetts governor William Shirley "repelled with the greatest possible force, within the smallest possible compass" Britain's claim to govern America. He said that "volumes" of all succeeding arguments on American rights to self-governance were here expressed "within the compass of a nut shell" (*Records of the Federal Convention*, vol. 3, p. 540n). Franklin was the oldest revolutionary. On 5 October 1775 Edmund Burke marveled: "What say you to your friend and brother Philosopher Franklin, who at upwards of seventy years of age [he was sixty-nine], quits the Study of the Laws of Nature, in order to give Laws to new Commonwealths; and has crossed the Atlantick ocean at that time of life, not to seek repose, but to plunge into the midst of the most laborious and most arduous affairs that ever were. Few things more extraordinary have happened in the history of mankind" (*The Correspondence of Edmund Burke*, vol. 3 [1958–1978], p. 228).

The following year, 4 July 1776, when Congress adopted the Declaration of Independence, Franklin was seventy, by far the oldest signer; Adams was forty; and Jefferson, thirty-three. Even Washington was only forty-four. Except for Franklin, young men led the American Revolution. At a time when his childhood friends, like the poet Joseph Green, were attempting to provide for a financially secure old age in England, he loaned Congress all the money at his disposal, more than £3,000 and sailed to France on a leaky ship that foundered and sank on its return. When the marquis of Rockingham (6 Jan. 1777) thought of the recent British victories in America, he declared with chagrin that "Franklyn at *Versailles*" was "much more than a balance for the few additional acres" that "the arms of Great Britain" had won (*The Correspondence of Edmund Burke*, vol. 3, p. 315).

Rockingham was right. After the Revolution, that master diplomat Vergennes testified in a confidential letter to Luzerne (French minister to the United States) on 15 February 1784 that the "calmness and prudence" of Franklin had inspired him "with confidence. I do not believe that the superior services which this minister has rendered his country will be requited; I can say that it will be very difficult for Congress to replace him" (Francis Wharton, *Diplomatic Corre-*

spondence, vol. 1 (1889), p. 490). Jefferson testified that "the succession to Doctor Franklin, at the court of France, was an excellent school of humility. On being presented to anyone as the minister of America, the commonplace question used in such cases was 'It is you, sir, who replace Doctor Franklin?' I generally answered, 'no one can replace him, sir; I am only his successor" (19 Feb. 1791). Only Franklin signed all three basic documents of the nation: the Declaration of Independence, the peace treaty with Great Britain, and the Constitution of the United States.

Injustice of all kinds rankled Franklin (see "A Petition," signed "The Left Hand," 1785). He was a feminist before feminism. "Women . . . ought to be fix'd in Revolution Principles" (8 Feb. 1777). John Updike (*Odd Jobs* [1991], p. 258) found "the androgyny of Franklin's imagination" surprising. Though Franklin was not optimistic by nature, he had great common sense and so acted as if he could make a difference in his world (see "The Handsome and the Deformed Leg," Nov. 1780). He loved his friends and wanted to believe well of people. He had great curiosity, amazing versatility, astonishing genius, and, above all, an enormous capacity for self-discipline and sustained work. As he grew older, he grew more humanitarian and idealistic. In a worldwide slave society, Franklin owned, at various times, five slaves, but he gradually came to regard slavery as "an atrocious debasement of human nature" (*Writings*, vol. 10, p. 67). He wrote against the practice in the 1770s and became a leading abolitionist in the 1780s. At age eighty-one he was the most egalitarian member of the Constitutional Convention. In his last years he advocated reform of the criminal laws and roused others to the cause (14 Mar. 1785). He called for an end to the Spanish inquisition and inspired Ruiz de Padron to carry out its demise.

Poor Richard said: "If you would not be forgotten / As soon as you are dead and rotten, / Either write things worth reading, / Or do things worth the writing" (*Papers*, vol. 2, p. 194). Franklin did both. After he had become a world-renowned scientist, writer, and statesman, he returned to his early and favorite goal of doing good for mankind. Many contemporaries came to believe that he succeeded. William Pitt, earl of Chatham, said he was "an Honour not to the English Nation only but to Human Nature" (*Papers*, vol. 21, p. 582). Edmund Burke (28 Feb. 1782) called him the "Friend of Mankind." Franklin spent his first forty-two years as a tradesman and businessman and his second forty-two years as a natural philosopher, public servant, and statesman. He was the most practical and perhaps the sanest of all the idealistic visionaries who have committed their lives to doing good for humankind. In his forties he wrote, "The only Thanks I should desire is, that you would always be equally ready to serve any other Person that may need your Assistance, and so let good Offices go round, for Mankind are all of a Family" (*Papers*, vol. 4, p. 504). And at the end of his life, he said, "God grant, that not only the Love of Liberty, but a thorough Knowledge of the Rights of Man, may pervade all the Nations of the Earth, so that a Philosopher may set his Foot anywhere on its Surface, and say, 'This is my Country'" (*Writings*, vol. 10, p. 72).

• The greatest collection of Franklin manuscripts is at the American Philosophical Society, Philadelphia. Other major collections are at the Library of Congress; the Historical Society of Pennsylvania; the University of Pennsylvania; Yale University; the Clements Library, Ann Arbor, Mich.; and the Huntington Library, San Marino, Calif. The best edition of Franklin's writings is the multivolume *Papers of Benjamin Franklin*, ed. Leonard W. Labaree (1959–), which locates the depositories of all materials printed. *The Papers of Benjamin Franklin*, through vol. 29, plus the unpublished papers for the remainder of Franklin's life, are also available on CD ROM (1994). A number of additions to the *Papers* have been made by J. A. Leo Lemay, *The Canon of Benjamin Franklin, 1722–1776: New Attributions and Reconsiderations* (1986). Formerly, the most complete edition of Franklin was *The Writings of Benjamin Franklin*, ed. Albert Henry Smyth (10 vols., 1905–1907). The *Papers*, the CD ROM, and Smyth's *Writings* are arranged chronologically. Textually, the best edition of Franklin's autobiography is *The Autobiography of Benjamin Franklin: A Genetic Text*, ed. Lemay and P. M. Zall (1981). Excellent annotated editions are *The Autobiography of Benjamin Franklin*, ed. Labaree et al. (1964), and *Benjamin Franklin's Autobiography: A Norton Critical Edition*, ed. Lemay and Zall (1986). The most complete selected edition is *Benjamin Franklin: Writings*, ed. Lemay (1987).

Of the biographies, the best are James Parton, *Life of Benjamin Franklin* (2 vols., 1864), and Carl Van Doren, *Benjamin Franklin* (1938). Shorter biographies that make significant contributions include Alfred Owen Aldridge, *Benjamin Franklin: Philosopher and Man* (1965); Ronald W. Clark, *Benjamin Franklin* (1983); Thomas Fleming, *The Man Who Dared the Lightning* (1971); David Freeman Hawke, *Franklin* (1976); Ralph L. Ketcham, *Benjamin Franklin* (1965); and Esmond Wright, *Franklin of Philadelphia* (1986). Specialized biographical studies include Claude-Anne Lopez, *Mon Cher Papa: Franklin and the Ladies of Paris* (1966); Lopez and Eugenia W. Herbert, *The Private Franklin: The Man and His Family* (1975); David Schoenbrun, *Triumph in Paris* (1976); and Arthur Bernon Tourtellot, *Benjamin Franklin: The Shaping of Genius: The Boston Years* (1977).

There are more excellent studies of special topics than can be listed here, but see especially Alfred Owen Aldridge, *Benjamin Franklin and Nature's God* (1967) and *Franklin and His French Contemporaries* (1957); Verner Crane, *Benjamin Franklin and a Rising People* (1954); Jonathan Dull, *Franklin the Diplomat: the French Mission* (1982); Bruce I. Granger, *Benjamin Franklin: An American Man of Letters* (1964); Max Hall, *Benjamin Franklin and Polly Baker* (1960); William Hanna, *Benjamin Franklin and Pennsylvania Politics* (1964); James H. Hutson, *Pennsylvania Politics, 1746–1770* (1972); Lemay, *Benjamin Franklin: Optimist or Pessimist?* (1990); Luther S. Livingston, *Franklin and His Press at Passy* (1914); Robert Middlekauff, *Benjamin Franklin and His Enemies* (1996); C. William Miller, *Benjamin Franklin's Philadelphia Printing* (1974); Charles Coleman Sellers, *Benjamin Franklin in Portraiture* (1962); and Zall, *Ben Franklin Laughing* (1980). For science, see I. Bernard Cohen, *Benjamin Franklin's Science* (1990) and *Franklin and Newton* (1956); Humphrey Davy's appreciation appeared in his *Works*, vol. 8 (1840), pp. 263–65; John L. Heilbron, *Electricity in the Seventeenth and Eighteenth Centuries* (1979); and Thomas S. Kuhn, *The Structure of Scientific Revolutions* (1970), pp. 13–22.

Volumes of essays devoted to Franklin include Roy N. Lokken, ed., *Meet Dr. Franklin*, rev. ed. (1981), and Lemay, ed., *Reappraising Benjamin Franklin: A Bicentennial Perspective* (1993).

Franklin's primary bibliography and the secondary scholarship to 1889 is in P. L. Ford, *Franklin Bibliography* (1889). For the secondary scholarship to 1983, see Melvin Buxbaum, *Benjamin Franklin: A Reference Guide* (2 vols., 1983, 1988).

J. A. LEO LEMAY

FRANKLIN, Benjamin (1 Feb. 1812–22 Oct. 1878), editor and itinerant preacher, was born in Belmont County, Ohio, the son of Joseph Franklin and Isabella Devold, farmers and millers. Apprenticed as a carpenter, Franklin moved in 1832 to Henry County, Indiana, where he married Mary Personnett in 1833 and built and operated a sawmill. Although baptized and raised by his parents as a Methodist, Franklin had experienced no particular religious convictions until he came under the preaching of Samuel Rogers, the pioneer itinerant preacher of the Disciples of Christ in Indiana, and Elijah Martindale, another noted Disciples itinerant. Rogers later rebaptized Franklin by immersion in 1836.

The Disciples of Christ were a product of the Restorationist movement, which sought to impose a strict New Testament primitivism (forsaking any church practice or belief that could not be expressly tied to the New Testament church), including believer's baptism, baptismal regeneration, and strict congregationalism. The Disciples represented the merger in 1831 of two streams of Restorationist thinking, as represented by Barton W. Stone and Alexander Campbell. Franklin soon left his milling business to become an intinerant preacher for the Disciples in eastern Indiana, Ohio, and Kentucky. He was a formidable preacher, and "under his personal ministry, about eight thousand persons have obeyed the Gospel."

Part of the deep impression Franklin made on his hearers was due to his imposing physique: standing at just under six feet, Franklin had been "in his youth a leader in feats of strength and skill," and "his feats of strength at log-rolling bees were marvelous." He was also a direct and talented communicator in open-air preaching and debate. "There is no hesitating, no doubting in his manner," wrote one observer. "He does not depend upon either elocution or rhetoric for effect, but upon the *power of the truth*, which he presents to the people." Franklin was particularly noted for his pugnacity in a favorite genre of Disciples preachers, the two- or three-day open-air debate with representatives of rival denominations. Franklin engaged in thirty such debates in his career; the transcripts of six of them were later published in full.

It was not in preaching, however, that Franklin made his greatest mark on the development of the Disciples in the West, but as editor and publisher of a series of periodicals that took a purist position regarding Disciples' discipline and that tended to be prone to argument and controversy. In 1843 Franklin began publishing and editing the *Reformer*, a sixteen-page

monthly, for the Disciples in New Paris, Ohio. He moved the *Reformer* to Centerville, Indiana, in 1845 and from there in 1847 to Milton, Indiana, where he renamed it the *Western Reformer*. Franklin then merged it with another publication, the *Gospel Proclamation*, in 1850 to produce the *Proclamation and Reformer*, which he then headquartered in Loydsville, Ohio. Franklin briefly published an unsuccessful weekly newspaper for the Disciples, the *Christian Age*, and then in 1856 launched his most successful endeavor, a monthly called the *American Christian Review* (it became a weekly in 1858). During the same period (the 1850s), he also was an early supporter and trustee of the North Western Christian University (Butler University), even though he had enjoyed no formal education of his own.

Franklin made his publications the platform for articulating the severest brands of pure Campbellism and strict primitivism. Franklin was driven by the conviction that the Christian church was bound strictly to the express statements of the New Testament; he would not tolerate the suggestion that practices or procedures in the church could be sanctioned merely because nothing in the New Testament expressly spoke *against* them. "The brethren," he wrote in 1875, "have not received the supplement to the last commission, to 'observe all things whatsoever I have not forbidden,' but are simply under the old commission, 'all things whatsoever I have commanded.'" So, even though he opposed slavery on the pages of the *American Christian Review* from 1856 onward, he refused to endorse the Civil War on the grounds of scriptural pacifism. In 1861 he editorialized, "We doubt the whole business of Christians taking up arms and fighting, even if *drafted*. This is not *our country*. We are only pilgrims and sojourners here." And even though he qualified his pacifism so far as to join other Ohio civilians in digging fortifications for the defense of Cincinnati and "blistered his hands with shovel and pick, slept on the ground, and declared himself attached to the Government," Franklin insisted that he "would not shoot his brethren whom he had brought into the church." Franklin was even more trenchant in his primitivism when specific church controversies came in view. He opposed any form of permanent, settled ministry among the Disciples, editorializing vehemently against "the building up of a new or older order of *clergy*, as a class, distinct from all other members of the Church" and all "clerical conventions . . . or associations for their own government . . . or any other purpose not taught in Scripture." He even opposed the use of organs or other instrumental music in Disciples' congregations and criticized the use of terms of address such as "reverend," "doctor," or even "pastor."

Franklin's primitivism found its most sensational target in the increasing appearance among the Disciples of voluntary "societies" independent of local congregations. Franklin was convinced that many of these societies were being organized to carry on work that belonged, by right, to local congregations alone. Franklin's opposition was put to its severest test over the American Christian Missionary Society (ACMS), which had been formed by the Disciples in 1849 to carry on evangelism. Although Franklin initially supported the ACMS, and even served as its corresponding secretary in 1856–1857, he gradually came to doubt the legitimacy of the ACMS mission, apart from the authority of local congregations. His reservations deepened in 1863 when the ACMS unilaterally endorsed the Union war effort, an action that Franklin interpreted as a usurpation of the missionary society's place as a mere auxiliary agency, especially because the Disciples as a whole had adopted no such political position. The death in 1866 of Alexander Campbell (who had remained favorable to the ACMS) was the opening for Franklin to launch a campaign against the ACMS and other auxiliary societies; and within a year, the ACMS staggered into decline and then into virtual eclipse as an active evangelistic organization. Franklin's popularity as a preacher was underscored by the eagerness with which his printed sermons were read among the Disciples. In the years before his death he published two volumes of collected sermons titled *The Gospel Preacher*: the first, which appeared in 1869, went through thirty-one printings over the next three decades, and the second, published in 1877, went through nineteen printings. In addition, he published a number of devotional tracts that also were widely read among the Disciples. Franklin remained active as a Disciples evangelist until 1875 and edited the *American Christian Review* until his death in Anderson, Indiana.

• Franklin's surviving papers and manuscripts are housed at the Christian Theological Seminary in Indianapolis; a complete collection of his publications and periodicals is located at the Disciples of Christ Historical Society in Nashville. His most unusual publications were the transcripts of six of the public debates he conducted against various theological opponents. These include his encounters with Erasmus Manford, a Universalist, in *An Oral Debate on the Coming of the Son of Man, Endless Punishment and Universal Salvation* (1848); with James Mathews, a Presbyterian, in *Predestination and the Foreknowledge of God: A Discussion* (1852); with Joel Hume, a Baptist, in *A Debate on Total Hereditary Depravity* (1854); with T. J. Fisher, a Baptist, in *Debate on Some of the Distinctive Differences between the Reformers and Baptists* (1858); with S. W. Merrill, a Methodist, in *An Oral Discussion on Justification* (1858); and with J. A. Thompson, a Baptist, in *An Oral Debate, between Benjamin Franklin of Anderson, Indiana, and John A. Thompson, of Lebanon, Ohio, . . . Held at Reynoldsburg, Ohio* (1874).

Franklin has been the subject of several biographical studies, beginning with Joseph Franklin and J. A. Headington, *The Life and Times of Benjamin Franklin* (1879), and including the more recent work of Ottis L. Castleberry, *They Heard Him Gladly: A Critical Study of Benjamin Franklin's Preaching* (1963), and Earl Irvin West, *Elder Benjamin Franklin: Eve of the Storm* (1983). Franklin's place in the overall history of the Disciples is discussed in Winfred E. Garrison and Alfred T. DeGroot, *The Disciples of Christ: A History*, rev. ed. (1958); Lester G. McAllister and William E. Tucker, *Journey in Faith: A History of the Christian Church (Christian Church)* (1975); Henry K. Shaw, *Hoosier Disciples: A Comprehensive*

History of the Christian Church (Disciples of Christ) in Indiana (1966); and Alanson Wilcox, *A History of the Disciples of Christ in Ohio* (1918).

ALLEN C. GUELZO

FRANKLIN, Deborah Read (1704?–19 Dec. 1774), wife of Benjamin Franklin (1706–1790), was the daughter of John Read, a carpenter, and Sarah White. It is not certain whether Deborah Read was born in Birmingham, England, where her family originated, or in Philadelphia, to which they emigrated. Nothing is known about her youth. She entered American lore on 9 October 1723 as she stood in front of her father's shop on Market Street in Philadelphia and first caught sight of Franklin, a tall, broad-shouldered youth passing by, his pockets bulging with socks, a puffy roll held under each arm while he munched on a third, and she giggled at his awkwardness—a moment to be immortalized some fifty years later in his memoirs.

He was seventeen at the time, a tired and disheveled runaway from Boston, in great fear of being caught and punished for breach of his apprenticeship contract. Two years later he asked Deborah to marry him. He had lodged with the Reads and done so well in his new life that the governor of Pennsylvania proposed to send him to England to buy equipment and become the colony's printer. Although promises were exchanged between the young people, the marriage, at the insistence of Deborah's recently widowed mother, was postponed until Franklin's return.

But when Franklin discovered in London that the governor's promises were so many empty words and that he could not even afford the voyage home, he informed Deborah that he was not likely to return soon, never wrote again, and proceeded to forget their engagement. While he was sowing his wild oats in London, she was prevailed upon by her mother in 1725 to marry John Rogers, a potter, who soon dissipated her dowry and whom she suspected of having another wife in England. Deborah obtained a separation, and when Franklin came back in 1726 after eighteen months, she was in limbo, neither married nor free, and utterly miserable. Franklin felt guilty at the sight of the distress caused by what he would call, in the *Autobiography*, his giddiness and inconstancy. He too was to experience some difficult years, unable as he was to start a business for lack of capital or to convince future in-laws that he was a good prospect. Rogers meanwhile absconded to the West Indies, and rumor had it that he had been killed in a brawl.

After four years of false starts and disappointments, Franklin decided, at twenty-four, to take Deborah as his common-law wife. She simply came to live in his house on 1 September 1730 and called herself Mrs. Franklin without benefit of a religious ceremony or record. Had they made their relationship official and Rogers reappeared, the couple could have been charged with bigamy. Deborah compensated for her lack of dowry by accepting to raise as her own the baby, fathered by Benjamin, that some hitherto unidentified woman was about to deliver: William

Franklin (1731–1813), future governor of New Jersey.

In spite of its dispiriting beginning, the marriage, while never romantic, worked well, especially during the first half of their lives. "She prov'd a good and faithful Helpmate . . . we throve together, and have ever mutually endeavor'd to make each other happy." Thrive they did. Within two years of their union, his debts were paid off. Under a single roof on Market Street flourished their printing shop, a newspaper, and a general store. The store was Debbie's special preserve. It carried a wide range of merchandise, from the salves and ointments concocted by her mother "sufficient to remove the most inveterate itch" to the "crown soap" made in Boston according to a secret Franklin family recipe. She sold bills of lading, servants' indentures, powers of attorney, quills, ink horns, slates, parchment, sealing wax, spectacles, Bibles, primers, maps, dictionaries, ballads, almanacs—including of course the highly popular *Poor Dick*, as she called it. The shop's inventory eventually reflected Philadelphia's cosmopolitan commerce: chocolate, tea, palm oil, saffron, mustard powder. Patent medicines were for sale, along with homemade lampblack, scarlet cloth, feathers plucked from live geese, iron stoves, lottery tickets, bookbinding services, and occasionally even a slave.

Having in mind *Poor Richard*'s precept to keep one's eyes well open before marriage and half-closed afterward, Franklin had only good things to say about a wife whose industry and frugality matched his own: "She assisted me cheerfully in my Business, folding and stitching Pamphlets, tending Shop, purchasing old Linen Rags for the Papermakers. We kept no idle Servants." Years after Debbie's death, her husband, reminiscing with French friends in the salon of Madame Helvétius, paid tribute to Debbie's part in his success. Young Dr. Pierre-Jean-Georges Cabanis was there, listening intently:

Their age was not exactly the same; that excellent woman was a few years older than him. Her wisdom helped him shape his plans of conduct and work. He told us more than once that a great part of his achievements was due to her . . . His printing shops, his newspapers and the almanacs of America, his enterprises in bookselling and papermaking were almost as much his wife's work as his own, he said. She also helped him with her advice, for she was full of common sense and experience. To quote Franklin: "I always discovered that she knew what I did not know; and if something had escaped me, I could be certain that this was precisely what she had grasped." (Cabanis, pp. 233–34).

As it turned out, Deborah's greatest contribution to her husband's fame was unwitting and unappreciated: she did not saddle him with the numerous offspring he would have liked. At a time when the average was eight children per colonial family, this robust woman produced only two, one of whom died in early childhood, thus affording Franklin the luxury of winding up his private business in his early forties and devoting himself to the pursuit of knowledge and to public life.

Initially, she adjusted to their new life. As of 1737, she helped him run the post office that was installed right in their house. She kept track of the addressees who could not pay postage and fulfilled the duties of postmistress during his many absences. Electricity, too, blossomed under the domestic roof. The neighbors came in to watch the new game, Deborah's household goods became the tools of experiment, and bells rang in her house whenever electrically charged clouds passed overhead.

When Benjamin Franklin entered political life, she lost him. He went off to England for five years the first time (1757–1762), for ten the second (1764–1775), with eighteen months in between, during which they started building the house that they would never live in together. But even far away, he was thrilled by the sense of self-sufficiency, so vital to his nature, that she had given him. Standing before the House of Commons at the time of the Stamp Act debate, and threatening America's nonimportation of English goods, he remembered how in his young days he had been dressed from head to toe in clothes of his wife's weaving and "never felt prouder in my life."

The Stamp Act also provided Deborah with her hour of glory. On 16 September 1765 she kept cool in the face of a threatened mob attack against her house by those who felt her husband was not fighting the act vigorously enough in London: she enlisted the help of a few relatives armed with guns, turned one room into a magazine, and "ordered sum sorte of defens up Stairs such as I cold manaig my self." She declared that she would not stir and would be much "afrunted" if anybody disturbed her. The would-be rioters had second thoughts, and the night ended quietly. "The Woman deserves a good House that is determined to defend it," exclaimed her proud husband upon reading her account.

So brave that night, but not brave enough to cross the ocean and join Franklin in England, she spent fifteen years separated from him. More than the voyage, she surely feared the perils of transplantation, the prospect of being a source of embarrassment to him in the exalted circles he now frequented. She remained what she was, a woman of the working class, plain, stocky, sometimes noisy in her disputes with neighbors, more often giving of herself, tirelessly, to the sick and afflicted, intensely loyal to the man she addressed as her "dear Child" (as he did her) or as "Pappy," not asking questions about his private life, indeed maintaining a cordial relationship with his London landlady, keeping him informed of all the happenings, big and small, of their circle, in a stream of unpunctuated letters invariably signed "your a feck shonet wife." He responded in kind for a long time. Only in the last few years of his second mission did his letters become brief and perfunctory. He chose to ignore the repeated warnings of her illness and never even mentioned the existence of an important new person in his life: his grandson Temple, the illegitimate child left in

London by William when he became governor of New Jersey. When he broke the pattern one day and called her "my dear Love," she was too enfeebled by strokes to rejoice or respond. She died in Philadelphia, not having seen her husband in nine years.

• Letters and account books left by Deborah Franklin are housed at the American Philosophical Society in Philadelphia. Information about Franklin can be gleaned from works devoted to the life and writings of her husband, including Leonard Labaree et al., eds., *The Papers of Benjamin Franklin* (30 vols., 1955–), and Claude-Anne Lopez and Eugenia W. Herbert, *The Private Franklin: The Man and His Family* (1975). Also see Pierre-Jean-Georges Cabanis, "Notice sur Benjamin Franklin," in *Oeuvres posthumes de Cabanis*, vol. 5 (1825), pp. 219–74.

CLAUDE-ANNE LOPEZ

FRANKLIN, Irene (13 June 1876–16 June 1941), vaudeville singer and actress, was born in St. Louis, Missouri. Very little is known of her childhood, but she claimed to have made her theatrical debut at the age of six months and by age three was being hired out by Minnie Palmer, a theatrical agent. A popular feature by the time she was six, Franklin was cast in the famous children's roles of the time, appearing in *Shore Acres*, *The Prodigal Father*, *Editha's Burglar*, *Chris and Lena*, *The Emigrant*, and *Fire Patrol*, although the exact date of these itinerant performances is unknown. At the age of fifteen she spent three years abroad under the management of J. C. Williamson both in the London variety theaters and in Australia. Little is known of Franklin's parents, but her mother accompanied her to Australia and died there during the tour; her father died shortly afterward in New York. When she returned to the United States in 1894, Franklin made her American vaudeville debut and established herself as a headliner by the time she was twenty.

Franklin's vaudeville act, billed as "Original and Exclusive Character Songs," consisted of singing characterizations that were both witty and topical. Some of her early material included a kiddy song, "I'm Nobody's Baby Now"; a satire of the feminist movement, "The Woman Policeman"; and a satire on Prohibition, "What Have You Got on Your Hip? You Don't Seem to Bulge Where A Gentleman Ought To." A regular performer at Tony Pastor's, Franklin frequently worked with Pastor's pianist, Burt Green, and a strong friendship grew between them. In 1898 Green divorced his wife, and he and Franklin became a couple both on and off the stage.

As a professional team, Franklin and Green were popular, and Green's orchestrations of Franklin's songs enhanced her characterizations. Together they wrote some of Franklin's most popular songs, including "Expression," in which she impersonated all the human emotions through her facial expressions, and "The Red Head," where a little girl tells of the names other children call her. In *Variety*, critic Sime Silverman wrote that "Red Head" "is a work of art in character study, and Miss Franklin's delivery of the selection could not be improved upon" (10 Oct. 1908). In like adoration, Frederick James Smith of the *New York Dramatic Mirror* wrote that Franklin "is quite as invigorating as a breeze from the sea" (26 May 1915). Similarly, Jack Lait of *Variety* reviewed Green and Franklin's performance at the Majestic Theatre in Chicago and said Franklin "is original and has the soul of the true comedienne, seasoning with a dash of quaint pathos her commentaries on contemporary life viewed from indulgently satiric angles" (8 Oct. 1919). Although Franklin had tried to make the jump from vaudeville to Broadway as early as 1907 when she played Josephine Zaccary in *The Orchid* at the Herald Square Theatre, she felt more at ease when she had greater control over the production and consequently always returned to vaudeville. She did, however, play Claribel Clews in *The Summer Widowers* (1910) at the Broadway Theatre; Violet Lavender in *Hands Up* (1915) at the Forty-fourth Street Theatre; *The Passing Show of 1917* (1917) at the Winter Garden; and Lulu Ward in *Sweet Adeline* (1929) at the Hammerstein Theater, in between vaudeville appearances.

In 1908 Franklin won the title of "Most Popular Woman Vaudeville Artist" in a popularity contest organized by promoter Percy Williams, defeating Eva Tanguay, Vesta Victoria, and Marie Dressler. Franklin and Green were also the first vaudeville artists to have a paid advertisement on the cover of *Variety* (19 Dec. 1913), and their popularity followed them overseas as they entertained the troops in France during the First World War. After returning from France, Franklin and Green remained on the vaudeville circuit until Green died of Bright's disease in November 1922, leaving Franklin with two daughters.

In 1925 Franklin married Jeremiah Jarnagan, who also became her accompanist; they had no children. In 1934 Jarnagan died in their Hollywood home, and although Franklin insisted he had been murdered, his death was ruled a suicide; afterward Franklin seemed to lose interest in performing. *Variety* commented that "vaudeville was her medium and when vaudeville died Irene Franklin as an entertainer died with it" (17 June 1941). Franklin tried to make the move to film and played minor roles in *Lazy River* (1934), *Change of Heart* (1934), *The President Vanishes* (1934), *Timothy's Quest* (1936), *The Song and Dance Man* (1936), *Midnight Madonna* (1937), *Married before Breakfast* (1937), and *Fixer Dugan* (1939). Her film roles were not successful, however, and in 1940 Franklin was forced by poverty to enter the Actors Fund Home in Englewood, New Jersey, where she later died. According to columnist Louis Sobol, three days before her death Franklin wrote to him saying, "Irene Franklin speaking. Perhaps you remember her. . . . She was born on June 13, Friday, and her name is spelled with 13 letters. Now another Friday, June 13 is near. Do you think anyone remembers or cares?" (quoted in *Variety*, 17 June 1941).

Franklin's artistic style led *Variety* to say that "she lifted the varieties out of the broad and slapstick metier into the era of sophistication. . . . She was satirical and subtle, witty and beautiful" (17 June 1941). Earlier in her career *Variety* described Franklin as having "a style that is smooth and quiet but which baffles accurate description" (9 Feb. 1907). Franklin's unique contribution to vaudeville was that her characterizations and impersonations resembled the ordinary man or woman who came to see her perform, rather than following the vogue of impersonating other performers. Consequently the audience could identify with her characters and, in turn, laugh at themselves.

• Franklin's personality may best be seen in her own writing. She published "How Not to Write Lyrics—Being an Exposition of Curious Phenomena, as Observed by a Collector of Crippled and Destitute Story Compositions," *Variety*, 14 Dec. 1907, pp. 20, 65, and Making Songs Tell a Story," *New York Dramatic Mirror*, 16 Dec. 1914, pp. 19. Franklin is also included in Douglas Gilbert, *American Vaudeville: Its Life and Times* (1940), and Anthony Slide, *The Encyclopedia of Vaudeville* (1994). Obituaries are in the *New York Times*, 17 June 1941; *Time*, 23 June 1941, p. 69; and *Variety*, 18 June 1941, pp. 43–44.

MELISSA VICKERY-BAREFORD

FRANKLIN, James (4 Feb. 1697–4 Feb. 1735), printer, was born in Boston, Massachusetts, the son of Josiah Franklin, a candle and soap maker, and Abiah Folger. He was apprenticed to a printer in London but returned to Boston in 1717 to establish a print shop on Queen Street. Franklin turned out books, pamphlets, and broadsides and was eventually assisted by an apprentice, his brother Benjamin Franklin, who was nine years his junior. James Franklin was hired in December 1719 to print the *Boston Gazette* for William Brooker, but when the paper changed hands the following year, Franklin lost the job. This inspired him to found his own newspaper. The *New-England Courant* first appeared in August 1721, only the fourth newspaper in Britain's American colonies.

Without access to government patronage, but also likely inspired by the Whig periodicals Franklin had surely encountered in England, most particularly Joseph Addison and Richard Steele's the *Spectator*, Franklin through the *New-England Courant* offered readers an alternative to the warmed-over English news and official pronouncements featured in rival papers. The paper carried essays and doggerel penned by a circle of "ingenious men" (or so Benjamin Franklin termed them) that included a doctor, a leather dresser, an apothecary, and James Franklin himself. The *Courant* also reprinted contemporary commentary from England, including merciless attacks on the allegedly corrupt government of Robert Walpole. Franklin began to publish portions of John Trenchard's *Cato's Letters*, termed by some the "textbook of revolution," less than a year after the first appeared in London. The local material often consisted of rather strained attempts at wit, including pseudonymous gibes at competing newspapers, Harvard College, local swells, frivolous women, political candidates, and assorted officials. For instance, the postmaster was labeled a "Butter-headed Churl" (Smith, p. 97). But the *Courant* also featured the teenaged Benjamin Frank-

lin's first significant literary efforts, the "Silence Dogood" essays.

Whatever its literary merits, James Franklin's *New-England Courant* is chiefly remembered for the enemies it made. Indeed, some have termed it America's first "opposition" newspaper. The *Courant* premiered in the midst of a local controversy over inoculation, an unfamiliar practice being promoted by Cotton Mather. Many Bostonians suspected Mather of abusing his influence as a Puritan divine to encourage measures that might actually be spreading the smallpox then besetting the city. The *Courant* came down firmly against inoculation. Contributors not only attacked the practice and the doctor who employed it but also mocked the clerics who promoted it "without any weight of Argument, by meer importunity, and reiterated Praying, Preaching, and Scribling" (Ford, p. 346). The divines responded in kind. Increase Mather denounced Franklin and his "Wicked *Paper*," warning subscribers that they were "*Partakers in other Mens Sins*" (Thomas, p. 236). Although the Mathers ultimately had science on their side, the resistance to inoculation that the *Courant* helped cultivate came to be seen as an important example of the declining authority of Puritan clerics in Massachusetts. Through the *Courant*, Perry Miller noted, "an accumulated store of antiministerial sentiment found a long sought vent" (Miller, p. 333).

However, it was not the *Courant*'s brawls with the Mathers that first got Franklin into trouble with colonial authorities. Instead, it was the paper's suggestion that officials had been slow to combat piracy that led the General Court in 1722 to jail Franklin for the duration of the legislative session. In the meantime, his talented apprentice saw to it that the paper continued. The discipline seems not to have tamed the *Courant*. Franklin protested the injustice of his arrest and published material in support of freedom of expression. The following year he ran pieces presuming to instruct legislators in how to deal with the governor and attacking hypocrisy among the conspicuously pious, who "dissemble and lie, shuffle and whiffle, and . . . defraud all who deal with them" (Miller, p. 339). At that point the legislature, finding that the paper demeaned religion and insulted officialdom, forbade Franklin to publish the *Courant*. He did so nonetheless, but the paper listed Benjamin Franklin, who was still an apprentice, as its publisher. Authorities were inclined to prosecute James Franklin again, and he was forced into hiding for a time. But a grand jury refused to indict him, marking the end of official attempts to restrain the press in colonial Massachusetts.

As vital as each had become to the other's livelihood, James and Benjamin Franklin were hardly the picture of fraternal devotion. A half-century later Benjamin still seemed to smart at the "harsh and tyrannical treatment," including beatings, that James had dealt out. "Though a brother," Benjamin wrote in his autobiography, "he considered himself as my master, and me as his apprentice, and accordingly expected the same services from me as he would from another, while I thought he demeaned me too much in some he required of me, who from a brother expected more indulgence." Benjamin, in fact, attributed his lifelong "aversion to arbitrary power" to his brother's conduct toward him. In late 1723 Benjamin Franklin slipped off to the city of brotherly love. Earlier that same year James Franklin had married Ann Smith. The couple had six children, one of whom, also named James, was, in an ironic coda, apprenticed to Benjamin Franklin after the elder James Franklin's death.

Even in Benjamin Franklin's absence, the *Courant* was published under his name. The paper continued on occasion to chide the government and clergy, engage in personal controversies, and advance freedom of the press. Original material appeared less frequently, however, and advertisers were scarce. In June 1726 the paper folded with its 255th number. After publishing an apologia attributing the paper's failure to its exposure of "the gainful Secrets of the cheating trade" (Dean, p. 13), James Franklin moved to Newport, where he set up Rhode Island's first press. His publications there included religious tracts, official material, and an annual, *Poor Robin's Almanack*, which some suspect inspired his brother's *Poor Richard's Almanack*. In September 1732 Franklin established the *Rhode Island Gazette*, which like the *Courant* mixed wit and political opinion. The paper went under the following May. Franklin reconciled with Benjamin but died less than two years later in Newport. His wife and several children continued to work as printers.

• Runs of Franklin's *New-England Courant* have been microfilmed and are available at various libraries, including Butler Library at Columbia University and the University of Texas Library, Austin (see *Newspapers in Microform*). An elegant, brief discussion of Franklin and the *Courant* is in Perry Miller, *The New England Mind: From Colony to Province* (1953). See also Jeffery A. Smith, *Printers and Press Freedom: The Ideology of Early American Journalism* (1988); Isaiah Thomas, *The History of Printing in America* (1810); Benjamin Franklin V, *Boston Printers, Publishers, and Booksellers: 1640–1800* (1980); Worthington Ford, "Franklin's *New England Courant*," *Proceedings of the Massachusetts Historical Society* 57 (Apr. 1924): 336–53; H. L. Dean, "The *New-England Courant* against the Ministers," *New-England Galaxy* 5, no. 3 (1964): 3–13; C. Edward Wilson, "The Boston Inoculation Controversy: A Revisionist Interpretation," *Journalism History* 7, no. 1 (1980): 16–19, 40; Clyde Duniway, *The Development of Freedom of the Press in Massachusetts* (1906); and any of the many editions of Benjamin Franklin's autobiography.

PATRICK G. WILLIAMS

FRANKLIN, Martha Minerva (29 Oct. 1870–26 Sept. 1968), nursing leader, was born in New Milford, Connecticut, the daughter of Henry J. Franklin, a laborer and a private in the Twenty-ninth Connecticut Volunteer Division during the Civil War, and Mary E. Gauson. Reared in Meriden, Connecticut, during the post–Civil War period, Franklin lived in a town that had very few African Americans. She graduated from Meriden Public High School in 1890. In 1895, choosing nursing as a career, Franklin entered the Women's Hospital Training School for Nurses in Philadelphia.

She graduated in December 1897, the only black graduate in the class. After graduation, she worked as a private-duty nurse in Meriden and thereafter in New Haven, to which she relocated.

Franklin's interest in organizing the National Association of Colored Graduate Nurses (NACGN) was prompted by the difficult challenges black women encountered. During the Reconstruction era, rigid practices of discrimination and segregation developed. Black women were rarely accepted into schools of nursing, which motivated the formation of black hospitals and schools of nursing. Although fully qualified, black nurses were denied membership in their state nurses association, the only avenue to the American Nurses Association, thus precluding their membership in the national organization of nurses. In addition, black nurses received little respect and less pay than their white cohorts and, as women, faced the inequality all women experienced in American society.

In 1906 Franklin launched a handwritten survey to analyze the status of the black nurse in American society because she believed that many black nurses shared her concerns. She concluded that only through collective action initiated by black nurses would their problems be recognized and gain the national attention that would in time make it possible to practice nursing without racial bias. Armed with this belief and commitment, Franklin sent out 1,500 letters for two years asking black nurses to consider a meeting in the near future.

Adah Belle Samuels Thoms, a nursing leader and president of the Lincoln Hospital School of Nursing Alumnae Association, invited Franklin and interested nurses to hold their first meeting in New York as guests of the association. Thoms was an immediate supporter of Franklin and the NACGN. On August 25–27 1908 fifty-two nurses attended the first meeting of the National Association of Colored Graduate Nurses in New York. Franklin's leadership and organizational skills emerged as she presided over the meetings using a democratic process and what appeared to be Robert's Rules of Order.

Franklin set forth her ideas and goals for an organization that became the goals of the association: advance the standards and best interests of trained nurses, break down discrimination in the nursing profession, develop leadership within the ranks of Negro nurses. Franklin also believed that an organized group would gain the attention, cooperation, and support of nursing leaders. She was elected president of the NACGN by acclamation. At the 1908 meeting the National Medical Association (NMA), the black physicians association whose convention was in New York at the same time, lent its enthusiastic support to the NACGN.

Franklin worked toward building the newly founded organization. In 1909 the NACGN met in Boston, Massachusetts, where it acquired a strong source of support from Mary Eliza Mahoney, America's first black registered nurse. Franklin, Thoms, and Mahoney developed a professional bond of mutual respect and friendship; they were the pillars and major supporters of the NACGN, and in 1976 they were posthumously admitted to the Nursing Hall of Fame.

The NACGN grew to 2,000 members during World War I and to more than 12,000 by 1940, with members from nearly every state. As the organization grew, a national registry was established to assist black nurses in securing positions. The NACGN gained community and national support systems by organizing local citizens committees in New York and an advisory council on the national level. The NMA helped the organization greatly by allowing and encouraging it to publish all of its news and announcements in the *Journal of the National Medical Association* until the NACGN obtained its own journal, the *National News Bulletin*, in 1928.

Franklin was a slender, light-complexioned African American, and as she rose to national prominence she was mistakenly characterized by nursing leaders as a white nurse who had befriended colored nurses.

In about 1920 Franklin relocated to New York City, completed a postgraduate course at Lincoln Hospital in the Bronx, and became a registered nurse in New York State. She worked in the New York City public school system as a school nurse. Committed to continuing her education, at fifty-eight years of age she was admitted to Teachers College, Columbia University, and during 1928–1930 she was enrolled in the Department of Practical Arts, today known as the Department of Nursing Education.

Franklin never married; however, she had friends who were like her family. In addition to Thoms and Mahoney, Franklin had many friends in Connecticut; of special note was Dr. Ernest Saunders, who was like a grandson to her. Franklin returned home to New Haven, Connecticut, to retire. She resided with her sister Florence, who also never married. Franklin attended the Dixwell Congregational Church of Christ in Connecticut regularly until advancing age precluded her weekly attendance.

Martha Minerva Franklin devoted many years of service to the NACGN. The organization dissolved in 1950 when black nurses were granted direct membership into the American Nurses Association, a moment that was made possible in large part because of Franklin's stamina, focus, and persistence.

• For Franklin's contributions to the founding of the National Association of Colored Graduate Nurses, see the organization's minutes of 25–27 August 1908, Schomburg Center for Research in Black Culture, New York City. Other discussions of her contributions to nursing are in the American Nurses Association, *Nursing Hall of Fame* (1976); Althea T. Davis, "Architects for Integration and Equality: Early Black American Leaders in Nursing" (Ed.D. diss., Teachers College, Columbia Univ., 1987); Mabel K. Staupers, *No Time for Prejudice: The Story of the Integration of Negroes in Nursing in the United States* (1961); Isabel Stewart and Annie Austin, *A History of Nursing: From Ancient to Modern Times, a World View*, 5th ed. (1962); and Adah B. Thoms, *Pathfinders: A History of the Progress of Colored Graduate Nurses* (1929).

ALTHEA T. DAVIS

FRANKLIN, William (1731–16 Nov. 1813), Loyalist leader and last royal governor of New Jersey, was the son of Benjamin Franklin, a printer and later statesman and diplomat, who addressed his autobiography to "My Dear Son." Born out of wedlock in Philadelphia, William always referred to Deborah Read, Benjamin's common-law wife, as his mother, but the real identity of his mother is unknown. A close friend of Benjamin's said William was born of a disagreeable woman "not of good circumstances" who did not want her maternity known. As a boy William liked to read books from his father's and uncle's bookstores and had his own race horse, a rarity for the son of a tradesman. Years later, Benjamin wrote about childrearing to a young mother, "Pray let him have everything he likes: I think it of great consequence, while the features of the countenance are forming." He was tutored by mathematician Theophilus Grew before attending Alexander Annand's classical academy for two years. His father put him to work in his print shop. "As to going on petty errands, no boy loves it, but all must do it." William tried to stow away on a ship during King George's War. "My only son left my house unknown to us all and got on board a privateer, from whence I fetched him. No one imagined it was hard usage at home that made him do this." When recruiters for the American Regiment came to Philadelphia, William enlisted. Commissioned an ensign, he served for two years on the New York frontier, distinguishing himself for bravery by leading dangerous patrols near Fort Ticonderoga. He emerged a captain of grenadiers. During a furlough in 1747, he helped his father organize the Philadelphia Associators, Quaker Philadelphia's first defensive militia. At war's end, Captain Franklin became official courier for the Pennsylvania Land Office at the Treaty of Lancaster in July 1748. Conrad Weiser, leader of a trade mission to Delaware and Shawnee Indians in the Ohio Valley, invited William to accompany him to Logstown.

Away during his father's early electrical experiments, William became Benjamin's assistant, first describing the path of lightning, installing lightning rods, and taking part in the famous kite and key experiment. William designed the silken kite and three times raced across a cow pasture in an electrical storm to get it aloft. When Oxford University awarded Benjamin an honorary doctorate in 1762, the rectors conferred an honorary master's degree on William for his electrical contributions. In 1802 Joseph Priestley acknowledged William's role in a London newspaper. Father and son together also raised funds to build Freemasons Hall in Philadelphia (the first Masonic hall in America), a belltower for Christ Church, and the Academy of Philadelphia (later the University of Pennsylvania). Over the pseudonym "Humphrey Scourge," William attacked his father's political enemies. Benjamin passed on to him a succession of minor offices: clerk of the Pennsylvania Assembly, postmaster of Philadelphia, and comptroller-general of the British-American postal system. When French-led natives attacked Pennsylvania's undefended frontier in

1755, Captain Franklin accompanied Benjamin, chairman of the Assembly's defense committee, on a fort-building expedition. As the commission's secretary, William led a 130-man militia escort on the three-month mission. In his autobiography, Benjamin acknowledged that "my son was of much use to me."

Shunning his father's commercial enterprises, William read law with Joseph Galloway. In 1757, when Benjamin was appointed the Assembly's London lobbyist to seek an end to the Penns' proprietorship and obtain royal government for Pennsylvania, William was appointed delegation clerk. Benjamin enrolled William as a law student at the Middle Temple, where he read law with Richard Jackson. He compiled a legislative history of Pennsylvania, *An Historical Review of the Constitutional History of Pennsylvania*; Benjamin wrote the preface.

Described by publisher William Strahan as "one of the prettiest gentlemen I ever knew," the handsome William moved easily in Northumberland House society. He represented the Pennsylvania mission before the Board of Trade, whose secretary, John Pownall, already knew his antiproprietary pamphleteering, as some of it had been in defense of Pownall's brother, former governor of New Jersey.

Pownall probably recommended William for office when the new prime minister, the Earl of Bute, clashed with the New Jersey Assembly. Bute insisted that all royal officials be appointed "at pleasure" instead of "during good behavior." The New Jersey Assembly refused to pay the chief justice's salary. When Governor Hardy ignored Bute's instructions and sided with the assembly, the Board of Trade recalled him. Bute recommended the appointment of William Franklin as royal governor in August 1762. William's son, William Temple Franklin, later wrote unequivocally that his father "was appointed through the influence of Lord Bute and without any solicitation on the part of his father." William Franklin was the first royal governor invested by George III.

Franklin proved an able governor; avoiding quarrels with the assembly, he put forth effort to bring about popular reforms, such as the improvement of roads and construction of bridges. He also worked to secure crop subsidies from England and founded the colony's chancery courts. He encouraged the assembly to grant a charter to Rutgers, the state university, and curtailed imprisonment for debt. He pardoned 105 women sentenced to jail for adultery during his fourteen-year term. The Delaware Indians nicknamed him "Dispenser of Justice" after he hanged two Sussex County men for beheading a prisoner during the Pontiac Rebellion. He also established the first Indian reservation in America at Brotherton in Burlington County.

After the Stamp Act crisis, Governor Franklin strictly upheld the Crown's prerogatives. His father denounced him as "a thorough government man." William relocated his home from Burlington to Perth Amboy, taking up residence in the opulent Proprietary House. When most royal governors fled after Lex-

ington, he stayed on, convening the assembly and warning against "all the horrors of a civil war," even as he gleaned intelligence about revolutionary activities and forwarded it to London. He broke with his father after a meeting at Joseph Galloway's estate in Trevose, Pennsylvania, in May 1775. When he summoned the assembly in June 1776, the New Jersey Provincial Congress declared him "an enemy to the liberties of this country," and the Continental Congress voted to order his arrest (his father, a delegate, was absent when the vote was taken). He was taken "like a bear" to house arrest in Wallingford, Connecticut. There he violated his parole by issuing written "protections" for thousands of Loyalists. He considered himself a prisoner-of-war, not obliged to honor an oath taken under duress. On 21 April 1777 the Continental Congress ordered him placed "into close confinement," prohibiting him "the use of pen, ink and paper or the access of any person or persons." He was held in solitary confinement in Litchfield Jail for 250 days. Exchanged on 1 November 1778, "considerably reduced in flesh," he was embittered that during horrible confinement, his wife, the former Elizabeth Downes, whom he had married in 1762, had died "of a broken heart occasioned by our long separation and ill-treatment."

Franklin helped organize the Refugees Club in New York City and obtained its headquarters building from Sir Henry Clinton. He helped to form the Board of Associated Loyalists and was its first president. This part-military, part-civilian organization provided protection for thousands of Loyalists in camps on Long Island. Urging guerrilla warfare tactics, he drew up a plan, approved by Lord George Germain, to establish Loyalists bases on Long Island, Staten Island and at Sandy Hook. The Associated Loyalists were authorized to pay themselves from booty and take their own prisoners. On one of their raids, they burned the privateer base at Tom's River, New Jersey, and in reprisal for the killing of a Loyalist hanged its commanding officer, Captain Joshua Huddy. Richard Lippincott, the Loyalist officer accused of hanging Huddy, was court-martialed and acquitted, but George Washington believed William Franklin had verbally ordered the execution. He demanded that Lippincott be turned over to him. When Sir Henry Clinton, the British commander in chief, refused, Washington had thirteen British officers taken at Yorktown draw lots: Captain Asgill of the Grenadier Guards was selected to be hanged. Asgill's mother appealed to the king and queen of France, who intervened diplomatically. After a bitter three-day debate in Congress, Washington released Asgill. William Franklin emerged as the most notorious Loyalist after Benedict Arnold.

He left America in August 1782. For the loss of his considerable estate, which included lands in New Jersey and New York, he received £1,800 from the Commissioners of Loyalist Claims, only the value of his furniture. He also received a brigadier's half-pay pension of £800 per annum. Reconciled briefly with his father, he met Benjamin one last time on shipboard in 1785 to settle accounts. His father subsequently disinherited him. William married a wealthy Irish widow, Mary D'Evelyn, and acted as agent for Loyalist claims in London. An 1802 article in *Public Characters*, a London magazine, described him as a "martyr to his principles and an honor to the country." He died in London.

• Studies of various aspects of Franklin's life and career include Willard Sterne Randall, *A Little Revenge: Benjamin Franklin and His Son* (1984); Randall, *The Proprietary House at Amboy* (1975); Randall, "William Franklin," in Randall and Nancy Nahra, *American Lives* (1996); and Randall, "William Franklin: The Making of a Conservative," in *The Loyalist Americans: A Focus on Greater New York*, ed. Robert A. East and Jacob Judd (1975). Other biographical studies include Larry R. Gerlach, *William Franklin: New Jersey's Last Royal Governor* (1976); William H. Mariboe, "The Life of William Franklin, 1730–1813: Pro Rege et Patria" (Ph.D. diss., Univ. of Pennsylvania, 1962); Catherine Fennelly, "William Franklin of New Jersey," *William and Mary Quarterly*, 3d ser. (July 1949): 362–82; and Edward H. Tebbenhoff, "The Associated Loyalists: An Aspect of Militant Loyalism," *New-York Historical Society Quarterly* 63 (1979): 115–44. Benjamin Franklin, *Papers*, ed. Leonard W. Labaree et al. (1960), includes references of William. See also Esmond Wright, *Franklin of Philadelphia* (1985).

WILLARD STERNE RANDALL

FRANKLIN, William Buel (27 Feb. 1823–8 Mar. 1903), soldier and engineer, was born in York, Pennsylvania, the son of Walter S. Franklin, a clerk of the U.S. House of Representatives, and Sarah Buel. As a young man Franklin showed great promise as an engineer and a soldier. He gained admission to the U.S. Military Academy at West Point at the age of sixteen and graduated four years later first in the class of 1843, whose members included Ulysses S. Grant. Commissioned in the Corps of Topographical Engineers, Franklin had several important assignments before the Mexican War that utilized his technical expertise in topographical survey. In his first tour of duty he assisted in the completion of the survey of the Great Lakes. He then accompanied Philip Kearny's expedition to the South Pass to analyze routes to California. During the Mexican War he served in General John E. Wool's command, which marched overland from San Antonio in late 1846 and fought at the battle of Buena Vista on 22–23 February 1847.

After the Mexican War Franklin was assigned to civil engineering duties in Washington, D.C., where he served until the outbreak of the Civil War. Promotion was slow in the peacetime army (he was not promoted to captain until 1857), but his responsibilities were considerable for one so junior in rank. While in Washington, he was responsible for overseeing the construction of the iron dome over the rotunda of the U.S. Capitol, additions to the U.S. Treasury Building, and other minor projects. In 1852 he married Annie L. Clark.

With the outbreak of hostilities in the Civil War, Franklin was marked by his prior service and West Point training for rapid promotion in rank and command. He was appointed in 1861 to the rank of colonel and command of one of the new regular regiments, the Twelfth Infantry, and shortly thereafter to command of a brigade. While in charge of his new command, he saw action at the battle of Manassas on 21 July 1861. His performance there, while not particularly noteworthy, was solid enough to earn him a division command in the reorganization of the Army of the Potomac under Major General George B. McClellan. Franklin soon became one of McClellan's most devoted subordinates, which further propelled his rapid rise in rank.

Under McClellan Franklin took part in the 1862 Peninsula campaign, McClellan's ponderous attempt to take the Confederate capital of Richmond, Virginia. In May 1862 McClellan appointed him commander of the VI Corps, and in July 1862 he was promoted to major general. With the failure of the campaign to take Richmond, Franklin's command was evacuated from Virginia and returned to Washington. In late 1862 he was again in the field, commanding an attack through Crampton's Gap in Maryland on 14 September 1862 that took the VI Corps within a day's march of General Thomas "Stonewall" Jackson's troops attacking Harpers Ferry. Without positive orders, however, Franklin failed to press forward and lost the opportunity of blunting Robert E. Lee's invasion of Maryland. Three days later he took part in the battle of Antietam, then the costliest battle in U.S. history. Franklin's VI Corps stood in a critical part of the Army of the Potomac's right wing. With the Confederates outnumbered and their center weakened by Union assaults, Franklin requested that McClellan issue orders for him to attack. McClellan, ever hesitant in battle, replied, "It would not be prudent to make the attack" (James McPherson, *Ordeal by Fire: The Civil War and Reconstruction* [1982], p. 285), and the best opportunity of the day to destroy the Confederate army evaporated.

Franklin's cautious competence was again rewarded in late 1862, when Abraham Lincoln replaced McClellan with Major General Ambrose E. Burnside. In preparation for another campaign in Virginia, Burnside created three "grand divisions" composed of two corps of infantry and supporting arms. He awarded Franklin command of the "Left Grand Division." On 13 December 1862 Franklin commanded more than 50,000 troops in the Union disaster at Fredericksburg. Under Franklin the left wing of the army was supposed to attack across the Rappahannock River south of the town and roll up Lee's flank. Burnside's orders of the day had changed and were ambiguous, but Franklin could not escape the charge that he got only half of his soldiers into the fight and failed to reinforce the only breach of the Confederate line opened by one of his subordinates, Major General George G. Meade.

Franklin was a vigorous participant in the recriminations that followed the defeat at Fredericksburg. He openly disparaged Burnside's incompetence among his own officers; signed a letter to President Lincoln complaining about Burnside's new plans in December 1862; and permitted two of his generals to visit Washington to criticize Burnside. In January 1863 Burnside angrily struck back, blaming Franklin (among others) for the defeat and ordering him cashiered. On 25 January 1863 Lincoln took matters into his own hands, dismissing Burnside from command and transferring Franklin out of the Army of the Potomac.

Reassigned to General Nathaniel Banks's Department of the Gulf in New Orleans, Franklin fared no better in Louisiana than he had in Virginia. In September 1863 he was ordered to command an amphibious expedition to Sabine Pass on the Texas-Louisiana border to demonstrate Union resolve to establish a presence in Texas in the face of Napoleon III's invasion of Mexico. Franklin failed to take the lightly held port city, ordering a hasty retreat to Louisiana after Confederates shelled his fleet and disabled two ships. In 1864 he took part in Banks's campaign up the Red River to take the Confederate capital of Shreveport. He was wounded at Sabine Crossroads on 8 April 1864 but participated in the Union victory at Pleasant Hill. Aggravation of his wounds forced him to turn over the command of the XIX Corps to Major General William Emory during the retreat. While on leave from the army in Virginia in July 1864, he was captured by troops from Jubal Early's army, who were raiding railroads near Washington. He escaped on his own the next day but took no further part in the remainder of the war.

After the war Franklin resigned his regular commission in the army and pursued a civilian career in engineering. In 1866 he became general manager of the famous Colt's Fire Arms Company in Hartford, Connecticut, where he lived for the rest of his life. From 1872 to 1880 he presided over the construction of the new capitol for the state of Connecticut in Hartford. He also served as adjutant general of the Connecticut state militia for two years and held a number of honorary positions connected with civil engineering. In the bitterly disputed presidential election between Rutherford B. Hayes and Samuel J. Tilden in 1876, he was an elector for Tilden. Franklin died in Hartford.

One Civil War historian has described Franklin as a "McClellanite general" (McPherson, *Ordeal by Fire*, p. 317), a description that fits not only his professional career but his personality as well. Franklin's early accomplishments marked him for high rank in the Union army, but like McClellan his rapid rise probably made him excessively attached to conservative approaches and cautious actions when the situation demanded boldness. When his military operations failed, he was inclined to blame his superiors. He was unquestionably a gifted civil engineer, and this field, rather than the military, is where his accomplishments will be longest and best remembered.

• For Franklin's record during the Civil War, see *The War of the Rebellion: A Compilation of the Official Records of the Union and Confederate Armies* (128 vols., 1880–1901), esp. vols. 2, 11 (pts. 1 and 2), 19 (pt. 1), 21, 26 (pt. 1), 34 (pts. 1, 2, and 3), and 51 (pt. 1). Franklin is the subject of two works by J. L. Greene, *In Memoriam: William Buel Franklin* (1903),

which is biographical, and *General William B. Franklin, and the Operations of the Left Wing at the Battle of Fredericksburg* (1900), a detailed apologia of Franklin's actions in that battle. Franklin's role in the Union high command and his personality emerge distinctly through the first half of Bruce Catton, *Glory Road: The Bloody Route from Fredericksburg to Gettysburg* (1952), which traces the fortunes of the Army of the Potomac in 1862 and 1863. See also Stephen Sears, *Landscape Turned Red* (1983); James F. Murfin, *The Gleam of Bayonets: The Battle of Antietam and Robert E. Lee's Maryland Campaign* (1965); and Kenneth P. Williams, *Lincoln Finds a General* (5 vols., 1949–1959). An obituary is in the *Thirty-fourth Annual Reunion of the Association of Graduates, U.S. Military Academy* (1903), pp. 203–20.

JAMES K. HOGUE

FRANTZ, Virginia Kneeland (13 Nov. 1896–23 Aug. 1967), surgeon and medical pathologist, was born in New York City, the daughter of Yale Kneeland, a wheat merchant, and Anna Ilsley Ball. She attended Brearley School in New York City and entered Bryn Mawr College in 1914, intending to prepare for a career in medicine. Toward that end she was encouraged by college president M. Carey Thomas. An excellent student, Kneeland was also involved in undergraduate activities, managing dramatic productions and editing publications. She was elected president of the undergraduate association, and during World War I she was a participant in the College War Council, which directed activities toward the war effort. Her "maturity in dealing with people of all ages and her perceptive and sound judgment contributed largely to the success of this council," said a classmate later (quoted in letter, Bryn Mawr College Archives). The organization became the College Council and continued after the war as a useful liaison among faculty, staff, and students. Kneeland received an A.B. in chemistry and biology in 1918, graduating second in her class and receiving the Mary Helena Ritchie Memorial Prize for "qualities of character and of spirit."

In 1918 she entered the College of Physicians and Surgeons of Columbia University, from which she received the M.D. in 1922. In 1920 she married fellow student Angus Macdonald Frantz; they had three children and were divorced in 1935.

Virginia Frantz was accepted in 1922 as a surgical intern at Presbyterian Hospital in New York City, the first woman to serve in its surgical department. In 1924 she received two appointments—instructor in surgery at the College of Physicians and Surgeons and assistant surgeon in the outpatient department of Presbyterian Hospital. Her advancement in both positions was steady for the rest of her career. At the college, she was promoted to associate in surgery in 1929, assistant professor of surgery in 1936, associate professor in 1948, and professor of surgery in 1951. At the hospital, she advanced to assistant attending surgical pathologist in 1931, associate attending surgical pathologist in 1948, and attending surgical pathologist in 1951.

Frantz and Allen O. Whipple, chief of the hospital's Department of Surgery, in 1935 first described insulin-producing tumors of the pancreas ("Adenoma of Islet Cells with Hyperinsulinism," *Annals of Surgery* 101: 1299–1335). They summarized the history of studies of secretions of the pancreas, listed seventy-five cases in the literature of hyperinsulinism of tumors of the pancreas, described case histories of eight of their own patients, and outlined a surgical procedure. Frantz also studied and published on breast cancer. With Harold D. Harvey she coauthored the textbook *Introduction to Surgery* (1943, revised several times), which was used in many medical schools.

During World War II Frantz was on a committee on medical research of the Office of Scientific Research and Development. For that office in 1941 she conducted research on controlling bleeding during surgery by using absorbent oxidized cellulose in place of gauze and cotton. Her preliminary report was published in 1943 ("Absorbable Cotton, Paper, and Gauze (Oxidized Cellulose)," *Annals of Surgery* 118: 116–26). She and her coworkers then determined that such material was absorbed over varying lengths of time in body tissue, so that ligature stitches and gauze packing did not have to be removed later. This was summarized as "Hemostasis with Absorbable Gauze" (Virginia Kneeland Frantz, Hans T. Clarke, and Raffaele Lattes, *Annals of Surgery* 120 [1944]: 181–98). The procedure was put into use in military hospitals during the war and soon came into more general use. For this development Frantz was awarded the Army-Navy Certificate of Appreciation for Civilian Service in 1948.

Noted for her studies of the thyroid gland, Frantz was one of the first to use radioactive iodine, which became available for medical use in 1948, to demonstrate and treat thyroid cancer. She contributed a chapter, "Tumors of the Pancreas," to the widely used *Atlas of Tumor Pathology* (1959) of the Armed Forces Institute of Pathology. Through the years she published a number of articles in medical journals, especially on thyroid research.

Frantz retired from her positions in 1962 but continued as a consultant in surgery at Presbyterian Hospital and as a special lecturer in surgery at Columbia for three years. At times she was a consultant surgical pathologist at St. Luke's Hospital in New York City, at Sharon Hospital in Connecticut, and at Roswell Park Memorial Institute in Buffalo, New York. She was president of the New York Pathological Association from 1949 to 1951 and of the American Thyroid Association in 1961–1962. She was awarded the Elizabeth Taylor Blackwell award of the New York Infirmary in 1957 and the Janeway Medal of the American Radium Society in 1962. In 1960 Bryn Mawr College gave her a Distinguished Service Award at its seventy-fifth anniversary convocation; the citation described her as "dynamic, witty, generous, always a leader." Members of her college class contributed funds toward a new research laboratory in the Bryn Mawr biology building.

For some years Frantz owned and maintained a herd of about ninety dairy cattle in Clarendon, Vermont, on property that had been farmed for about two centuries by her family. She died in New York City.

• Bryn Mawr College and Columbia University archives have some professional and employment records concerning Frantz but do not possess her personal papers. An obituary is in the *New York Times*, 24 Aug. 1967.

ELIZABETH NOBLE SHOR

FRANZ, Shepherd Ivory (27 May 1874–14 Oct. 1933), psychologist and administrator, was born in Jersey City, New Jersey, the son of D. W. William Franz and Frances Elvira Stoddard, occupations unknown. In 1890 he entered Columbia University, from which he earned an A.B. in 1894 and a Ph.D. in 1899. His principal supervisor was James McKeen Cattell, who had been a doctoral student of Wilhelm Wundt, the founder of scientific psychology. Franz studied for one semester with Wundt in 1896 but reported that Wundt had little influence on him.

Franz served from 1899 to 1904 as an instructor in physiology at the Harvard Medical School followed by three years of similar service at the Dartmouth Medical School. During this time he was influenced by H. P. Bowditch, the "father of American physiology," and by W. T. Porter. In 1902 Franz married Lucy (or Lucie) Mary Niven of London, Ontario, with whom he had three children. Also in 1902 Franz published the first experiment ever to combine brain extirpation and animal training (*American Journal of Physiology*). When a German scholar later claimed priority, Franz protested in several publications, concluding that "I could see no reason why the method, if of any worth, should be labeled 'made in Berlin.' Kalischer's article was, however, as complimentary as is all plagiarism."

Beginning with his 1902 paper, Franz addressed the long-debated question of whether functions are localized in the brain or whether the brain functions as a whole. His findings revived the theory of the nineteenth-century physiologist Pierre Flourens that "unity is the grand principle that reigns." As the title for his 1911 presidential address to the Southern Society for Philosophy and Psychology, Franz chose "New Phrenology," his term of derision for the postphrenological localizationists. Published in *Science* in 1912, "New Phrenology" established Franz as the leading advocate of the mass function view. His research also contributed to his belief that the brain could be "re-educated" following damage and loss of function, a view that influenced his human clinical neuropsychological work.

In 1904 Franz accepted the position of research psychologist at McLean Hospital of the Harvard Medical School, where he established the first psychological laboratory in a hospital; Franz credited Edward Cowles, but Cowles had hired Franz to develop the psychology laboratory. At McLean, Franz became an expert in abnormal psychology, and his research on diagnosis and treatment of human psychological and neurological disorders continued throughout his career in tandem with his basic neuropsychological research. In 1906 Franz was appointed professor of physiology and professor of experimental psychology at George Washington University, affiliations that he retained until 1924. In 1907 Franz was also hired to be the hospital psychologist by Superintendent William Alanson White of Saint Elizabeths Hospital in Washington, D.C., which was known formally until 1917 as the Government Hospital for the Insane.

In 1907 Franz established at St. Elizabeths a psychological laboratory and implemented, for the first time at a hospital, routine psychological testing of all patients. As a result, Franz contributed a chapter to White's *Outlines of Psychiatry* (1908) that Franz later enlarged to the *Handbook of Mental Examination Methods* (1912), which may have been the first such manual for clinical psychology in the United States. Franz also appears to have been the first American experimental neuropsychologist and clinical neuropsychologist. Beginning in his years at McLean Hospital, Franz wrote articles and gave addresses that gained him recognition for his effort to bring about a rapprochement between psychology and psychiatry, and in 1908 he was made an honorary member of the American Medico-Psychological Association (later the American Psychiatric Association), a rare occurrence for a non-physician.

In 1910 Franz was appointed scientific director at St. Elizabeths and in 1919 its director of laboratories. From 1915 to 1917 Franz was a postdoctoral mentor to Karl Spencer Lashley, now widely considered to be one of the greatest neuropsychologists of the twentieth century. Lashley included Franz as one of his three most influential mentors. At St. Elizabeths, Franz published steadily in experimental and clinical psychology, including a second book *Nervous and Mental Reeducation* (1923). In 1920 he served as president of the American Psychological Association, and from 1912 to 1924 he edited the highly prestigious *Psychological Bulletin*.

Although Franz and White (perhaps the most prominent American psychiatrist at this time) had begun working together amicably and enthusiastically, personnel records from St. Elizabeths reflect clashes between them. In May 1924 White reduced Franz's title and salary after another employee left a door unlocked and a bunsen burner aflame in a building under Franz's supervision. Franz quickly submitted his resignation effective 1 June 1924. Although Franz did not address the circumstances of his resignation directly, he noted in his autobiography that "during the last fifteen years of my St. Elizabeths service there was a volcanic rise of psychoanalytic belief. Tedious laboratory studies were looked upon as unfruitful, if not entirely useless."

In the fall of 1924 Franz moved to Los Angeles, where he soon became professor and head of the psychology department at the University of California at Los Angeles. Also in 1924 he began serving as chief of the psychological and Educational Clinic of the Children's Hospital in Hollywood. At UCLA, Franz contributed significantly to the development of the uni-

versity and of the psychology department, and in 1940 UCLA's Franz Hall, named in his honor, was opened for use. He continued to be academically productive and published two books, *Psychology* (1933; with Kate Gordon), and *Persons One and Three: A Study in Multiple Personalities* (1933). He edited *Psychological Monographs* from 1924 to 1927, served as associate editor for the *Journal of General Psychology* from 1927 until his death, and served as president of the Western Psychological Association in 1927–1928. Franz was also elected a fellow of the American Medical Association and of the American Association for the Advancement of Science, and he received the Butler Medal from Columbia University in 1924. Franz died in Los Angeles a few months after having been diagnosed with amyotrophic lateral sclerosis.

• Unpublished letters, memoranda, annual reports, and miscellaneous records from files that pertain to St. Elizabeths Hospital are maintained by the National Archives and by the U.S. Office of Personnel Management. Franz's autobiography is included in Carl Murchison, ed., *A History of Psychology in Autobiography*, vol. 2 (1932). Franz's list of publications until 1929 is included in Murchison, ed., *The Psychological Register* (1929). See also Darryl Bruce, "Lashley's Shift from Bacteriology to Neuropsychology, 1910–1917, and the Influence of Jennings, Watson, and Franz," *Journal of the History of the Behavioral Sciences* 22 (1986): 27–44; and Samuel W. Fernberger, "Shepherd Ivory Franz 1874–1933," *Psychological Bulletin* 30 (1933): 741–42. Information regarding the cause of Franz's death was provided by Eran Zaidel of UCLA's Department of Psychology, and information regarding Franz Hall was provided by UCLA's campus architect Charles W. Oakley. An obituary is in the *New York Times*, 15 Oct. 1933.

ROGER K. THOMAS

FRARY, Francis Cowles (9 July 1884–4 Feb. 1970), chemical engineer, was born in Minneapolis, Minnesota, the son of Francis Lee Frary, a merchant, and Jeanette Cowles. Frary was educated at the University of Minnesota, where he earned an A.C. degree (1905) and an M.S. (1906) in chemistry. He studied in Berlin in 1906–1907, then returned to Minnesota to complete a Ph.D. in chemistry (1912). He married Alice Hall Wingate in 1908; they had two children.

While at Minnesota, Frary taught and conducted research in electrochemistry and metallurgy. His work there reflected a breadth of interests and a practical bent that would characterize his approach to research throughout a long career. In one two-year period, he taught fifteen courses in nine different subject areas, including glass blowing, which he had learned in order to be able to keep his experimental equipment in good repair. Frary also developed a safe process for making phosphorous sesquisulfide, used on matches, and an electrolytic process for making age-hardenable lead alloys. The latter became significant during World War I, when lead-hardening antimony was in short supply. His patented alloys were then produced by the National Lead Company, one under the trade name Frary Metal.

These accomplishments, reflecting Frary's commitment to and capacity for work of practical significance, virtually assured him a place in the world of industrial research that was opening up in that era, as U.S. corporations in significant numbers began to establish in-house research programs aimed at acquiring the knowledge they needed to master their processes and develop new products. In 1915 he accepted an offer from Oldbury Electrochemical Company in Niagara—the sole U.S. producer of phosphorous sesquisulfide—to become director of its new research laboratory. Two years later, Frary was recruited for a similar position by Aluminum Company of America (Alcoa). Alcoa had been struggling for some years to meet competition from European competitors, who by 1914 had captured one third of the United States market for aluminum with a product that was both lower priced and higher in quality than its own. In addition, in 1916 the U.S. Navy had enlisted the company in an effort to develop an alloy comparable to Duralumin, the high-strength, heat-treatable aluminum alloy that Germany was then using in its dreaded Zeppelin airships. That proved to be a difficult challenge. By 1917 Alcoa's leaders had become convinced of the need for an independent research department that could address those problems in a systematic, fundamental way. World War I intervened: Frary was drafted into the army, but this afforded him the opportunity to set up and manage a state-of-the-art chemical research and production facility, at Edgewood Arsenal, in Maryland. When he joined Alcoa, in 1919, he brought with him not only this valuable experience but also a handful of chemists from Edgewood, who became central to the company's new research activities.

In recruiting Frary, Alcoa executives promised to build and equip a research facility at a centralized location and to support his determination to pursue work "of an original nature," not driven by the short-term concerns of the plants. It would be a decade before his organization, the Research Bureau, got its laboratory building; but from the beginning, Frary enjoyed nearly complete independence in setting the research agenda and determining how it would be pursued. The company was well rewarded for its faith in his judgment, as the Research Bureau mounted systematic investigations on a broad front, through which Alcoa gained control of its basic refining and smelting processes, improved key products such as electrical transmission wire, and developed new applications, such as aluminum powder for paint. Other research programs advanced understanding of aluminum alloys, laying the groundwork for discoveries that very quickly made aluminum the basic structural material of modern aircraft. In 1928 the company recognized these achievements, pulling together its research and development organizations into a single, centralized unit—renamed Aluminum Research Laboratories—and placing it under Frary's direction. The next year, Alcoa provided ARL with a brand new laboratory building in New Kensington, Pennsylvania, equipped with the most up-to-date experimental equipment then available.

During the depression, Frary focused ARL's program more tightly than ever on bench-scale work aimed at establishing the fundamentals of refining, smelting, and aluminum metallurgy. He organized his research staff into divisions by disciplines—metallurgy, physical testing, analytical chemistry, physical chemistry, and chemical development—and nurtured an academy-like environment, encouraging publication of results and active participation in technical and professional societies. Three areas of particular importance in which ARL's work and publications contributed essential data and understanding were aluminum alloys (microstructure, behavior, properties), corrosion in aluminum, and design and properties of aluminum structures. In addition, ARL in this period contributed to the improvement of Alcoa's proprietary processes, in particular with the development of direct-chill ingot casting. By the late 1930s Alcoa's technical community felt itself to be sitting on a great storehouse of knowledge that begged application. Indeed, much of it was applied with striking rapidity during World War II, as the company developed essential processes for refining low-grade domestic bauxite and casting large-scale ingots required for aircraft production and brought forth improved high-strength alloys, the super-Duralumins, which became the basic structural materials of the nation's wartime air fleet.

In the postwar era, which brought the loss of Alcoa's monopoly, the push for applications continued with numerous incremental process improvements and the roll-out of a myriad of new aluminum products. Frary retired from ARL at the end of 1951. Largely in response to the threat of competition, his successors redirected the research agenda away from fundamental investigations, but it would be decades before his legacy of applicable knowledge was exhausted.

Frary was widely recognized in the scientific community of his day. At Alcoa, his research centered mainly on primary processes. In the early 1920s, he played a critical part in developing an electrolytic process for refining aluminum to near-100-percent purity, an essential step in understanding the basic characteristics of the metal. In 1930 Frary, Junius D. Edwards, and Zay Jeffries jointly edited *The Aluminum Industry*, which for decades served as the definitive source book on the production and properties of aluminum. Frary served as president of the Electrochemical Society in 1929–1930 and of the American Institute of Chemical Engineers in 1941. He received many awards, including the Electrochemical Society's Acheson Medal (1939), the prestigious Perkin Medal of the joint British and American Section of the Society of Chemical Industry (1946), and the Legion of Honor award of the American Institute of Mining, Metallurgical, and Petroleum Engineers (1969). Frary remained active as an adviser and consulting engineer to Alcoa until 1967. He died in Oakmont, Pennsylvania.

Frary launched his career at a time when the United States lagged well behind Europe in both chemistry and metallurgy, and he began his work at Alcoa just as

American industry was setting out to remedy that situation. During the 1920s, when research became firmly established as an industrial function, companies in the chemical and metallurgical industries that Alcoa considered its technical community were spending substantial sums to master their basic processes and materials. Within that community, Frary was among a group of research directors, including Charles Stine of DuPont and C. E. K. Mees of Eastman Kodak, who were outspoken in advocating the value of fundamental research in corporate programs. For most of Frary's tenure, Alcoa was the only producer of primary aluminum in the United States, and its research program was the principal source of knowledge about the metal, its production and fabrication. The prodigious contributions of science-based companies like Alcoa to the Allied victory in World War II focused national attention on the value of industrial research, which, through the investment of billions of dollars of federal funding, became a big business in the postwar era.

• Manuscript sources are maintained in Alcoa Corporate Archives, Pittsburgh, Pa., and the information department of Alcoa Technical Center, Alcoa Center, Pa. Frary published extensively in chemical and metallurgical journals. See in particular *Industrial and Engineering Chemistry* 38 (Feb. 1946), which includes articles by and about him. For further consideration of his career and its significance, see Margaret B. W. Graham and Bettye H. Pruitt, *R&D for Industry: A Century of Technical Innovation at Alcoa* (1990). An obituary is in the *New York Times*, 5 Feb. 1970.

BETTYE H. PRUITT

FRASCH, Herman (25 Dec. 1851–1 May 1914), chemist, chemical engineer, and inventor, was born in Gaildorf, Wuerttemberg, Germany, the son of Johannes Frasch, a prosperous pharmacist and burgomaster of the town; his mother's name is not recorded. Frasch was educated at the Gymnasium and then apprenticed to a pharmacist but decided to come to the United States at age seventeen. He settled in Philadelphia, Pennsylvania, where he became an assistant in the laboratory of Professor John M. Maisch at the Philadelphia College of Pharmacy. He studied chemistry on his own, becoming interested in industrial applications, and in 1873, at age twenty-two, he felt confident enough to open his own laboratory, where he established a small clientele among Philadelphia manufacturers. Around 1873 he married Romalda Berks; the couple had two children. Meanwhile he followed his own experimental program, resulting in 1876 in a patent for a process for refining paraffin wax, which he sold to the Cleveland (Ohio) Petroleum Company, a subsidiary of John D. Rockefeller's Standard Oil Company.

Standard retained Frasch as consultant chief chemist, apparently associated with the head corporation and various subsidiaries, at an aggregate salary reputed to be the highest paid in the industry. During his years there Frasch worked out new methods for refining petroleum and for making wax (paraffined) paper,

but he also produced many inventions outside the petroleum industry. Among these were an oil lamp greatly improved in brightness; carbon adapted for arc lighting; elements for electric generators; and a series of chemical processes. These included a method for producing white lead pigment directly from the ore galena (lead sulfide), production of salt, and synthesis of soda ash (sodium carbonate) by a method patented despite its similarity to the Solvay process.

In 1885 Frasch's contracts with Standard and its subsidiaries expired, and he had accumulated enough capital to purchase an oil field and form the Empire Oil Company in London, Ontario, Canada. He acquired the field at distress-sale price, for the crude oil it produced, even when refined, had such a high sulfur content that locals called it "skunk oil"; the gases emitted by the oil blackened house paint and table silver and rendered foods stored near it inedible. A successful lawsuit, in fact, by a shipper whose bacon and flour were tainted by the oil was the reason why Frasch was able to acquire the oil fields so cheaply. In addition to the unpleasant side effects, the oil was nearly useless for its basic purpose: it blackened the chimneys of lamps, gummed up wicks, and produced corrosive sulfuric acid on oxidation (burning). It was useful only as the lowest grade fuel oil. Frasch set about solving this problem with his characteristic energy and between 1887 and 1894 accumulated twenty-one U.S. patents for desulfurization methods. In general, his process was based on heating the crude oil with heavy metal oxides, principally copper oxide; the metal combined with the sulfur compounds, and the oil, thus purified to the standard of the day, was distilled away, stored, and sold. The copper sulfide produced could be roasted to convert it to the oxide for reuse.

In 1886 Standard Oil brought Frasch back to the United States to deal with high-sulfur oil newly discovered in fields in Ohio, Indiana, and later, Illinois. He scaled up his Canadian methods by many multiples of ten, solving problems of scale by his own inventions. For example, the stirring arms that kept the copper oxide in suspension in the heated crude tended to overheat. To prevent this, water-cooling ducts within the arms, provided a cooling system, and the resulting steam was used to heat the incoming stream of new crude and to drive the engines used in the refining operation. In 1888 Frasch sold his desulfurization and refining patents to Standard Oil, which also purchased Empire Oil. Payment was in rapidly growing Standard Oil stock, which made Frasch a rich man.

To focus only on Frasch's engineering innovations, however, would be to neglect the achievement for which he would be remembered and celebrated, the Frasch process for recovery of underground sulfur deposits. Extensive beds of essentially pure sulfur were known to exist across Louisiana and eastern Texas, trapped by limestone domes, which were, unfortunately, overlain by shale, clay, gravel, and, at the surface, swamp. Conventional shaft mining was impossible, and company after company had failed in the effort to get the sulfur out of the ground for sale (sulfuric acid made from raw sulfur was and is today the largest-volume chemical produced in the United States). Frasch discovered the method of drilling to the sulfur layers and installing concentric pipes. Superheated water at 335° F (about 170° C) and about seven atmospheres pressure was pumped into the outer pipe to melt the sulfur (all crystal forms of sulfur melt at 120 degrees Celsius or less). After enough time had elapsed for the sulfur to melt, the liquid sulfur was pumped out through the central pipe. The resulting product was about 99.5 percent pure. Frasch received his first U.S. patent on the process in 1891 and organized the Union Sulfur Company in 1892, with himself as president. Also in 1892, after the death of his first wife (in 1889), Frasch married Elizabeth Blee. The next decade saw heroic efforts to improve and stabilize the sulfur production process and ensure the financial future of the company. By 1900 the world monopoly held by the English-Sicilian and the French producers was broken; Frasch, in fact, became president of the International Sulfur Refineries of Marseilles. By his own estimate, however, the American company was not on safe ground financially until about 1903. Thereafter, although the company eventually dissolved because of patent infringement, Frasch's process gave the United States world leadership in sulfur production.

In 1912 Frasch received the Perkin Medal of the Society of Chemical Industry for his work in both sulfur mining and oil refining. His award address gives the best single account in print of his lifetime achievements. Frasch retired to France in his final years, dividing his time between St. Jean, on the Riviera, and Paris, where he died. In 1928 his widow established the Herman Frasch Foundation for Research in Agricultural Chemistry, with the American Chemical Society as technical adviser and the U.S. Trust Company of New York as trustee.

• Frasch's Perkin Medal account of his discoveries is found in *Journal of the Society of Chemical Industry* 31 (1912): 168–76, which discusses economic and production figures and includes a biographical sketch by Professor C. F. Chandler. It also appears in *Journal of Industrial and Engineering Chemistry* 4 (1912): 131–40 and in *Metallurgical and Chemical Engineering* 10 (1912): 73–82, as well as in a condensed version with illustrations in *Journal of Chemical Education* 6 (1929): 129–38. Detailed accounts of the Frasch process of sulfur recovery are in Williams Haynes, *The Stone That Burns: The Story of the American Sulphur Industry* (1942), and in William R. Sutton, "Herman Frasch" (Ph.D. diss., Louisiana State Univ., 1984). Economic maneuverings in Ohio oil refining are treated in Charles G. Moseley, "The Capitalist, the Chemist, and Lima Sour Crude Oil," *Journal of Chemical Education* 56 (1979): 657–58. Obituaries are in the *New York Times*, 2 May 1914, as well as "Herman Frasch," *Journal of the Society of Chemical Industry* 33 (1914): 539, and "Herman Frasch," *Journal of Industrial and Engineering Chemistry* 6 (1914): 505–6.

ROBERT M. HAWTHORNE JR.

FRASER, Charles (20 Aug. 1782–5 Oct. 1860), miniature portraitist and painter, was born in Charleston, South Carolina, the son of Alexander Fraser and Mary Grimké. He attended the College of Charleston in 1792 (at that time more a grammar school than a college) and studied art privately for a short period with Thomas Coram, an engraver and painter of small views. He studied law from 1798 to 1801 and from 1804 to 1807 in the office of John Julius Pringle and was admitted to the South Carolina bar in 1807. He practiced law until 1818, at which time he had earned enough money to devote himself to painting full time. He never married and for his entire life resided in Charleston, where he died.

Through his miniature portraits Fraser provides a pictorial social register of Charleston during the antebellum period. In small-format likenesses painted in watercolor on ivory he captured the faces of the city's elite, including members of the Rutledge and Pinckney families, among many others, as well as the marquis de Lafayette (City Hall, Charleston), a distinguished visitor to Charleston in 1825. Over an active career of almost thirty years, Fraser's output numbered approximately 400 portraits, many of which remain in Charleston in the hands of descendants or are in the collection at the Gibbes Museum of Art.

In addition to Coram, the other important artistic influences on the young Fraser were Thomas Sully, a schoolmate who had immigrated to Charleston as a child, Washington Allston, and Edward Greene Malbone, a distinguished miniature painter. Although Fraser never had formal lessons from Malbone, he may have learned from examining and making copies of Malbone's portraits of Charlestonians. Fraser's skill at capturing likenesses was acknowledged during his lifetime by the dean of American portraiture, Gilbert Stuart. In a letter Fraser describes Stuart's response to viewing his *Self-Portrait*: "I showed him my picture and he appeared delighted with it. Indeed he said that he scarcely or never had seen a head on ivory which he preferred to it. If he had said nothing I would still have been much flattered, for he held it in his hands a half hour, looking at it" (Severens, *Fraser*, p. 2). Fraser's miniatures are meticulously rendered characterizations; his depictions of older men are insightful and perceptive, while his likenesses of young ladies and matrons are stylish and less discerning. His stylistic hallmark consists of delicately stippled pinkish-blue backgrounds.

Fraser maintained an account book, begun in 1818, that records his sitters as well as his income from painting. In his prime he typically received forty or fifty dollars for each ivory he painted. By the late 1830s Fraser had diversified his output by painting still lifes and landscapes. These reflect the artist's failing eyesight as well as a shift in his patrons' taste away from portraiture. With the invention of the daguerreotype in the late 1830s, miniatures suffered a further decline in popularity. The late landscapes are a return to an earlier interest; as Coram's student in the mid-1790s Fraser filled several sketchbooks with landscape views, many copied from illustrations in European travel books of places that Fraser would never visit.

He also did small (3 x 6 inches) watercolor views of Charleston-area plantations.

Although Fraser never traveled abroad, he made several trips north, primarily to New England (Boston and Newport, 1806; New York, 1816; Boston and New York, 1824; Hartford, 1831; and New Hampshire, 1833). He painted several watercolors showing views of the Hudson River and Niagara Falls, although a trip to the latter location has never been documented. For the *Analectic Magazine* he provided illustrations of American scenes, including Richmond, Boston, and Passaic Falls, New Jersey, that were engraved and published. Late in his career he painted landscape scenes in oil on canvas, many of which are his artistic inventions, while others are derived from engravings.

In 1857 the city of Charleston saluted the talents and contributions of their native artist by mounting an ambitious exhibition of his work called *The Fraser Gallery*. For two months 313 miniatures and 139 "landscapes and other pieces" were displayed in a local hall. Such retrospective exhibitions were rare occurrences in nineteenth-century America. In the accompanying biographical sketch, Robert W. Gibbes acclaimed Fraser's accomplishments: "not only in the life-like miniature is Mr. Fraser's ability and skill evidenced, but in the higher rank of landscape, his pencil has been eminently engaged, and equally successful." Other accolades at the time described Fraser as a pillar of his community, alluding to his roles as a trustee of the College of Charleston, 1817–1860; as a director of the South Carolina Academy of Fine Arts, 1821–1828; and as an orator who spoke at the dedication of the main building of the college and at the inauguration of Magnolia Cemetery. In 1853 he delivered his recollections to the Conversation Club, which were subsequently published as his *Reminiscences of Charleston*. They provide an insightful historical description of postrevolutionary and antebellum Charleston.

• The Gibbes Museum of Art remains the single largest repository of Fraser's work, with one of his youthful sketchbooks, over sixty miniatures, and about ten oil paintings. Other collections with examples of his work are the Metropolitan Museum of Art; the Museum of Fine Arts in Boston; the National Museum of American Art, Smithsonian Institution; and the Greenville County Museum of Art, Greenville, S.C. A short sketch of Fraser appears in William Dunlap, *History of the Rise and Progress of the Arts of Design in the United States* (1834; repr. 1965); Fraser was also a frequent contributor to Dunlap's history. The catalog of *The Fraser Gallery* (1857) includes a biography, tributes, a checklist for the exhibition, and a selection of Fraser's poems. The standard monograph on Fraser is Alice R. Huger Smith and D. E. Huger Smith, *Charles Fraser* (1924; repr. 1967). Alice R. Huger Smith, *A Charleston Sketchbook, 1796–1806* (1940), is an annotated facsimile of one of Fraser's juvenile sketchbooks. Martha R. Severens and Charles L. Wyrick, Jr., eds., *Charles Fraser of Charleston: Essays on the Man, His Art and His Times* (1983), consists of six essays about various aspects of the artist and an appendix featuring his account book. In Severens, *The Miniature Portrait Collection of the Carolina Art Association* (1984), fifty-eight miniatures are illustrated and described.

MARTHA R. SEVERENS

FRASER, James Earle (4 Nov. 1876–11 Oct. 1953), sculptor, was born in Winona, Minnesota, the son of Thomas Alexander Fraser, a civil engineer, and Cora West. The first four years of Fraser's life were nomadic. At that time his father supervised construction for the Northern Pacific Railroad. About 1880 the family bought a ranch near Mitchell, South Dakota, where Fraser grew up with the Native Americans, wild animals, and expansive prairie that would affect his art for years to come. As a child he modeled sculpture from a native chalky clay that hardened naturally over time.

After a few years of school in Minneapolis, Fraser lived briefly in Chicago, where he began his formal study of art at the Art Institute. He also worked in the studio of Chicago sculptor Richard Bock. At nineteen he traveled to Paris, where he studied at the École des Beaux-Arts under Jean A. J. Falguière and at the académie Julian and the Atelier Colarossi.

In 1898 the American Art Association of Paris voted one of his sculptures the best work at the salon by an American. Among the jurors was Augustus Saint-Gaudens, the most respected American sculptor of the day. Saint-Gaudens soon put Fraser to work in his Paris studio on the Sherman monument he was making for New York City. Fraser returned to the United States with Saint-Gaudens in 1900 and worked on the Sherman equestrian in Saint-Gaudens's Cornish, New Hampshire, studio. From Saint-Gaudens he acquired a controlled discipline in sculptural form and a lively naturalism in his modeling.

In 1902 Fraser moved to New York City, opened a studio, and quickly earned renown for his sensitive portrait reliefs and busts. In 1907 he became one of the first of many important artists and writers to take a studio in MacDougal Alley in Greenwich Village. He taught at the Art Students League from 1907 until 1911 and in 1913 married Laura Gardin, one of his students and thirteen years his junior, who became a well-known sculptor. They had no children. That same year he purchased a summer home in Westport, Connecticut. The couple continued to winter in New York until 1935, when they moved to Westport permanently. Throughout their forty years of marriage the Frasers worked prodigiously, collaborating freely on many of their larger projects.

Fraser's first public notice in the United States came in 1901. He was asked to make the portrait medallion to be presented to Saint-Gaudens by the Pan-American Exposition in Buffalo, New York. Commissions for other portraits soon followed. His portraits of children were especially popular, but he also depicted many important people. On Saint-Gaudens's recommendation he made the official vice presidential bust of Theodore Roosevelt in 1910. He also made Roosevelt's death mask and in 1940 completed a monumental equestrian bronze of Roosevelt for the American Museum of Natural History in New York.

Like Roosevelt, Fraser was an enthusiastic outdoorsman. His early life on the northern plains instilled in him a respect for nature and Native Americans. At the age of seventeen he modeled a sculpture of a gaunt, downcast Indian astride a weary war pony that he titled *End of the Trail*. Fraser's heroic-scale plaster model of it won a gold medal at the Panama-Pacific International Exposition in San Francisco in 1915 and became an instant icon of the cruel fate of American Indians at the hands of the advancing white peoples. The uncopyrighted image proliferated on exposition souvenir items, but the full-size sculpture was not put into bronze until 1929 when Waupon, Wisconsin, commissioned a cast. The plaster original stood outdoors in Visalia, California, until about 1970, when it was replaced by a bronze and moved to the Cowboy Hall of Fame in Oklahoma City to join a large collection of James and Laura Gardin Fraser's artwork.

In 1911 Secretary of the Treasury Franklin MacVeagh asked Fraser to design a coin to replace the Liberty Head nickel. The sculptor's goal was "to achieve a coin which would be truly American, that could not be confused with the currency of any other country." The result was the Indian head and buffalo nickel. Fraser also created several other medallic designs, including the Victory Medal (1919), which was distributed to more than four million World War I veterans, and the Navy Cross, which in prestige is second only to the Congressional Medal of Honor.

Among Fraser's best-known architectural sculptures and monumental statuary are the pediments of the National Archives (1935) and Commerce (1934) buildings, two statues flanking the entrance of the Supreme Court (1935), the *Second Division Memorial* (1936), and two colossal gilded bronze equestrian groups for the Arlington Memorial Bridge (1951), all in Washington, D.C. He created monuments to Harvey Firestone (1950) for Akron, Ohio, to John Hay (c. 1917) for Cleveland, Ohio, to Benjamin Franklin (1935) for the Franklin Institute in Philadelphia, and to George Patton (1950) for West Point, New York.

Fraser became an associate of the National Academy of Design in 1912 and an academician in 1917. He served on its council from 1930 to 1933. He was president of the National Sculpture Society from 1924 to 1927 and honorary president later in life. He won medals of honor from the National Sculpture Society, the National Arts Club, and the Century Association. The American Numismatic Society gave him the Saltus Medal in 1919, and the American Academy of Arts and Letters awarded him a gold medal in 1951.

Fraser was stocky, five feet, ten inches tall, athletic as a youth, and clean shaven. Malvina Hoffman said he had "the squarest jaw" she ever saw, and Barry Faulkner likened his character to "a good piece of Scotch tweed, handsome, durable, and warm" (Wilkinson, p. 304). In his *History of American Sculpture* (1924), Lorado Taft indicated that Fraser's talent, in-

dustry, and fairmindedness had won him the esteem of his colleagues. Fraser died in Westport, Connecticut.

Fraser's early career was noted for his sensitive portrait reliefs and busts. His monumental period lasted from 1915 until his death. Fraser was an important and influential member of the New York art world who steadfastly maintained his allegiance to traditional figurative sculpture despite the increasing popularity of abstract and nonrepresentational art in the United States after about 1910.

• Typescripts for Fraser's unpublished autobiography are in the Saint-Gaudens Collection of the Baker Library, Dartmouth College, Hanover, N.H., and the George Arents Research Library for Special Collections, Syracuse University. The James Earle and Laura Gardin Fraser Papers in the Archives of American Art at the Smithsonian Institution document their varied careers with about 900 photographs of the Frasers' artwork, numerous clippings, correspondence, and unpublished manuscripts, including "Indian Prairie," a record of his childhood memories in the Dakota territory in the 1880s. Another group of eleven letters is at the Archives of American Art. Additional archival material is at the National Cowboy Hall of Fame in Oklahoma City and the American Academy of Arts and Letters in New York City. Wayne Craven, *Sculpture in America* (1968; rev. ed. 1984), provides the most complete published summary of Fraser's career. Dean Krakel, *End of the Trail: The Odyssey of a Statue* (1973), documents one of Fraser's most important sculptures in detail and lists most of his work. George Gurney, *Sculpture and the Federal Triangle* (1985), discusses his important work for the federal government in Washington in the 1930s. J. Walker McSpadden, *Famous Sculptors in America* (1924), and Beatrice Proske, *Brookgreen Gardens Sculpture* (1943), are insightful assessments of his achievements. Burke Wilkinson, *Uncommon Clay* (1985), provides biographical insights. Obituaries are in the *New York Times* and *New York Herald-Tribune*, both 12 Oct. 1953.

MICHAEL W. PANHORST

FRASER, John (1750–26 Apr. 1811), botanical explorer and collector, was born in Tomnacross near Kiltarlity, Inverness-shire, Scotland, the son of Donald Fraser, a farmer and grounds officer of the Jacobite leader Simon Fraser, thirteenth Lord Lovat. John Fraser's mother was probably one Mary McLean of Cragganmore, Inverness-shire. Nothing is known of his childhood and education. In the 1770s, Fraser moved to London and established himself as a draper and hosier in Paradise Row, Chelsea, where he married Francis Shaw in 1778. The Frasers had two sons, John (baptized 1780), who accompanied his father on two collecting trips to North America, and James Thomas (baptized 1782), who helped manage the family's botanical nursery in England in the 1800s.

Soon after arriving in London, Fraser developed an enthusiasm for botany as a result of visits to the Physic Garden of the Worshipful Society of Apothecaries, which was located close to his home in Chelsea. William Forsyth, curator of the garden, strongly encouraged Fraser, who received further support from William Aiton, manager of King George III's royal botanical garden at Kew, and from Sir James Edward Smith, President of the Linnean Society. By the early

1780s, Fraser's deteriorating health, attributed to consumption, prompted a recommendation that he travel to North America in the hope of regaining his strength. When his friend Vice Admiral John Campbell was appointed governor of Newfoundland in 1782, Fraser accepted Campbell's invitation to accompany him to St. Johns on what was to be the first of Fraser's seven major botanical collecting ventures in eastern North America.

Based on the dates given to his plant specimens, Fraser was apparently in Newfoundland between 1783 and 1786. After returning to England with his Newfoundland collections, Fraser sailed to Charleston, South Carolina, and from September 1786 until January 1788 he explored South Carolina and Georgia, extending his searches into the Cherokee lands northwest of the Blue Ridge mountain escarpment. Fraser briefly accompanied the French botanist Andre Michaux in the spring of 1787 and subsequently provided more than 400 plants to Thomas Walter, who used the collection to describe many new species and genera in his *Flora Caroliniana* (1788). Fraser returned to England in March 1788, taking with him more than 30,000 American plant specimens, the manuscript of Walter's *Flora*, and plans to market a new grass that he and Walter had discovered. In London, Fraser financed the publication of Walter's *Flora Caroliniana*, the first regional flora from eastern North America to use the Linnean binomial Latin system for scientific nomenclature. The grass scheme was a business failure in England; but, at the invitation of comte d'Angiviller, minister to Louis XVI, Fraser in January 1789 visited Paris, where he sold plants and seeds to Thomas Jefferson, the duc D'Orleans, the marquis de Lafayette, the comte d'Provence, and the botanist Charles L'Heritier. Unfortunately, Fraser's hopes for a continuing market in France fell victim to the events of the French Revolution, and his American partner, Walter, died of a fever in January 1789.

After returning from France to England, Fraser established a commercial garden, known as the "American Nursery," on the King's Road at the corner of Sloane Square in Chelsea. He visited South Carolina in 1790 and again in 1791 in search of new plant species. From 1791 until the early 1800s, he and his brother James Fraser shipped large numbers of North American plants from their growing garden at Charleston and from their plantation on nearby Johns Island to Chelsea for wholesale and public purchase in England. According to Liverpool historian and botanist William Roscoe, it was through these nurseries that John Fraser "brought more plants into this kingdom [England] than any other person" (P. Smith, *Memoir and Correspondence of the Late Sir James Edward Smith, M.D.*, vol. 2 [1832], p. 362).

From 1796 until 1803, Fraser's activities involved the Romanov court of Russia. In 1796 he visited Petersburg and sold a large botanical collection to Catherine II. In 1797 and 1798 he returned bringing plants for the royal gardens at Pavlovsk and Gatchina, and in August 1798 he was appointed royal botanical collec-

tor by Czar Paul I. Believing he had been authorized to undertake an expedition for the czar, Fraser returned to Charleston and, in company with his son John, collected plants in Virginia, Kentucky, Tennessee, and the Carolinas in late 1800. In early 1801, father and son were shipwrecked and nearly died on a remote islet off the Cuban coast. Following their rescue by fishermen, they proceeded to Havana, where they were befriended by the German naturalist Alexander von Humboldt, who entrusted the younger Fraser to transport a large plant collection back to London and on to Berlin. When Fraser arrived in Russia, he found that Alexander I, who had succeeded his father Paul I as czar, would not pay for the Frasers' American expedition. After petitions and intervention by the British ambassadorial corps, Fraser finally received 6,000 rubles from the czar in April 1803 for his American plants.

By 1807 Fraser and his son John had returned to Charleston for their final joint botanical venture in America. During this visit they discovered Catawba rhododendron in bloom on the summit of Roan Mountain, along the North Carolina–Tennessee border. Although described earlier by Michaux, Catawba rhododendron had not been imported into England until the Frasers began shipping their plants in 1808. British horticulturists immediately used the handsome shrub as the basis for a variety of important hybrid rhododendrons.

A few months before Fraser's departure for England in 1810, he was thrown from his horse and broke several ribs while returning to Charleston from the mountains. He never recovered from this injury, and he died at his home in Chelsea the following year, complaining that "Providence had cut him off in the midst of his labours." He was interred at the Old Burial Grounds at St. Lukes, Chelsea, but the gravesite is not presently identifiable. His plant nursery was continued for some years by his two sons, although he was declared to have been bankrupt at the time of his death. Through much of his life, Fraser had been so "ardently attached" to botanical exploration that he neglected the business management of his enterprise, and he was often under financial duress and in serious debt.

Described as energetic, affable, and garrulous, Fraser was held in high regard by the botanical community of his day. Loudon (1838) praised Fraser as "one of the most enterprising, indefatigable, and perservering men who ever embarked in the cause of botany and natural science," and Sargent (1889) asserted that "the value of his contributions to English gardens has, perhaps, never been surpassed." Fraser's name is commemorated in a number of American plants, including the Fraser magnolia and the Fraser fir, the latter species an important commercial Christmas tree in the eastern United States. Many of Fraser's discoveries and introductions were delineated in Curtis's *Botanical Magazine* and in Edwards's *Botanical Register*; and his collections were extensively used by Frederick Pursh, Alexander von Humboldt, Carl Ludwig

Willdenow, Jean Baptiste Lamarck, Alphonse deCandolle, Asa Gray, and other nineteenth-century botanists. Fraser's scientific specimens are currently housed in the Natural History Museum and the Linnean Society in London, the Conservatoire et Jardin botaniques in Geneva, the Museum national d'Histoire naturelle in Paris, the Academy of Natural Sciences in Philadelphia, and the Russian Academy of Science in St. Petersburg.

• No Fraser manuscript collections are in public archives, except for some of his son John's letters in the John Lindley Papers at Kew, England, and in the Joseph Banks Papers at the Sutro Library, San Francisco. Documents published by Fraser include his *A Short History of the Agrostis Cornucopiae; or, The New American Grass* (1789) and several annotated catalogs of plants offered for sale at his American Nursery. One such catalog is in *Journal of Botany* 43 (1905): 330. Most articles on Fraser are entirely derived from three sources: John C. Loudon, *Arboretum et Fruticetum Britannicum* 1 (1838): 119–22; William J. Hooker, *Companion to the Botanical Magazine* 1 (1836): 300–305; and Robert Hogg, *The Cottage Gardener* 8 (1852): 250–52. Marcus B. Simpson, Jr., et al., "Biographical Notes on John Fraser (1750–1811): Plant Nurseryman, Explorer and Royal Botanical Collector to the Czar of Russia," *Archives of Natural History* 24, no. 1 (1997): 1–18, provides new information and corrections of errors by earlier writers. Additional resources include David H. Rembert, *Thomas Walter: Carolina Botanist. Museum Bulletin No. 5, South Carolina Museum Commission* (1980); Charles S. Sargent, "The Journal of Andre Michaux," *Proceedings of the American Philosophical Society* 26 (1889): 1–145; William T. Aiton, *Hortus Kewensis*, vols. 1–5 (1810–1813); and Frans A. Stafleu and Richard S. Cowan, *Taxonomic Literature* 1 (1976): 873.

MARCUS B. SIMPSON, JR.

FRASER, Laura Gardin (14 Sept. 1889–13 Aug. 1966), medalist and sculptor, was born in Chicago, Illinois, the daughter of John Emil Gardin, a bank executive, and Alice Tilton, a painter. She attended elementary school in Morton Park, Illinois, and spent the summers with her family in New Jersey, where Laura had her first horse. It was there that she developed the lifelong love of animals that shows in her sculpture. She also studied in Rye, New York, and graduated from Horace Mann High School in New York City in 1907. That same year she attended Columbia University briefly before entering the Art Students' League, where she matriculated for four years. There she studied with James Earle Fraser and taught from 1910 through 1912 under his supervision. On Thanksgiving Day in 1913 they were married. Her art received early recognition when her *Nymph and Satyr* was awarded the Barnett Prize at the National Academy of Design in 1916. She served as a captain in the ambulance corps in World War I.

The Frasers shared a studio in New York and summered at a studio they built in Westport, Connecticut. Both were hard-working, successful artists. They collaborated freely on each other's commissions, often working as a team. Laura was James's most capable and trusted collaborator. Her contributions to his de-

signs for the pediments of the Department of Commerce (1934) and National Archives (1935) buildings in Washington were especially significant. She executed the preliminary sketch models for four pediments for the Commerce building from his drawings and developed his design for the important Constitution Avenue pediment of the Archives Building through three scale models into the finished limestone sculpture. He had her name inscribed on the pediment with his own without telling her, yet she insisted it should not be there since she was "merely carrying out his design." Collaborations such as this helped make the Frasers one of the most successful husband-and-wife teams in American sculpture.

Fraser's greatest fame was as a medalist. She was commissioned to make commemorative coinage for the centennials of Alabama (1919), the Oregon Trail (1926), and Fort Vancouver, the Congressional medals honoring Charles Lindbergh (1928), the National Geographic Society medal for Admiral Richard Byrd (1930), the George Washington Bicentennial medal (1932), and the Congressional medal honoring Benjamin Franklin (1956). Her Ulysses S. Grant gold dollar and half dollar were the first coins designed for the U.S. Treasury by a woman. She also executed the Morse Medal for the American Geographical Society and a medal for the National Institute of Social Sciences. In 1947 she designed the coinage for the Philippines. Proske characterized her medals as "notable for fidelity to the subject combined with distinction of design."

Although best known as a medalist, Fraser's favorite subjects were animals. She modeled the portrait of Fair Play, sire of Man o' War, for the Joseph Widener estate outside Lexington, Kentucky. Her *Baby Goat* (1919) stands in Brookgreen Gardens, and her *Reclining Elks* (1928) flank the entrance to the National Elk Memorial in Chicago. She made numerous small animals for the United States Polo Association as well as sketches of the Army mule and the Navy goat. Fraser's largest public sculpture is the double equestrian bronze portrait of Robert E. Lee and Stonewall Jackson in Wyman Park in Baltimore. Six sculptors were invited to submit designs; she was the only woman. The monument was commissioned in 1936 and dedicated in 1948.

Fraser joined the National Academy of Design in 1916, becoming an associate in 1924 and an academician in 1931. She was a fellow of the National Sculpture Society and a member of the National Academy of Women Painters and Sculptors. For the National Sculpture Society she was asked to design a special medal honoring Daniel Chester French.

Fraser received numerous awards. The NAD awarded her the Shaw Memorial Prize in 1919 for her *Baby Goat*. The academy also gave her the Saltus Medal in 1924 and the Watrous Gold Medal in 1930. She considered her greatest accolade to be the Saltus Gold Medal of the American Numismatic Society—the highest honor for medallic art in the United States—which was awarded to her in 1926.

• The James Earle and Laura Gardin Fraser Papers in the Archives of American Art document their varied careers with about nine hundred photographs of the Frasers' artwork, numerous clippings, correspondence, and unpublished manuscripts. Laura's diaries (1931–1934) and additional material on the couple are in the George Arents Research Library for Special Collections, Syracuse University. Dean Krakel, *End of the Trail* (1973), provides the best published account of Fraser's career with a single chapter and a list of her major works. George Gurney, *Sculpture and the Federal Triangle* (1985), discusses her collaboration with her husband. Charlotte Rubinstein, *American Women Artists* (1982), and Beatrice Proske, *Brookgreen Gardens* (1943), supply brief coverage.

MICHAEL W. PANHORST

FRAUNCES, Samuel (1722 or 1723–10 Oct. 1795), innkeeper, was born in the West Indies of unknown parentage. Little is known about his life before his arrival in New York City sometime in the mid-1750s. Though he was often referred to by contemporaries as "Black Sam," surviving census records and other sources indicate that he was white. He first appeared in official city records in 1755 as an "innholder," and a year later he acquired a tavern license. From 1759 to 1762 he maintained Masons' Arms, the first of several taverns he would own or lease in New York and later in Philadelphia. Little is known about his first wife, Mary Carlile, except that she died shortly after he established himself as a tavern owner in New York City. He soon married again, and his second wife, Elizabeth Dailey, played a crucial role in his business operations, especially in the 1790s. They raised two sons and five daughters in a household that at various times contained several slaves and indentured servants.

In 1762 Fraunces established his most famous tavern in Lower Manhattan in the former Delancy mansion at the corner of Pearl and Broad streets. He purchased it for £2,000 and named this tavern the Queen Charlotte's Head (soon shortened to Queen's Head). Catering to the high-end trade and noted for its excellent food, the tavern hosted some of the most prestigious visitors and residents of the city, including the first meeting of the New York Chamber of Commerce. In 1765 Fraunces leased this tavern for several years to different individuals and moved to Philadelphia, where he briefly operated a tavern from 1766 to 1768. He returned to New York City in 1770 and resumed direct control of the Queen's Head Tavern.

In addition to his substantial investments in taverns, Fraunces in 1765 leased from Trinity Church the Old Bowling Green Gardens fronting the North River. Renaming them the Vauxhall Gardens, he modeled them after the more famous outdoor gardens in London bearing that name. Until 1774, when Fraunces relinquished control, Vauxhall was noted for fine food and entertainment, including a series of wax statues designed by Fraunces that featured representations of the Roman general Publius Scipio and other famous figures.

Fraunces's Lower Manhattan tavern served as an important center of revolutionary activity during the late 1760s and the 1770s, and for a time it hosted meetings of the New York Sons of Liberty. It was renamed Fraunces Tavern with the outbreak of war, and during the battle for New York several Continental army courts-martial were convened there. George Washington ate several meals at the tavern, initiating a long-term relationship with Fraunces. In a petition to Congress in 1785, Fraunces claimed he had discovered a plot against the life of Washington in 1776. At best only circumstantial evidence exists suggesting that Thomas Hickey and other members of the Headquarters Guard sought to assassinate Washington. Nonetheless, Fraunces and his family fled to New Jersey to escape the British occupation of New York City in 1776.

Captured by the British in 1778, Fraunces returned to New York City and became a household cook for a British general, most likely James Robertson. In his 1785 petition to Congress, Fraunces claimed he smuggled food and clothing to American prisoners of war and aided them in their escapes. In oblique terms, Fraunces recounted his services as a spy for the American cause and noted that he passed confidential information through British lines. It is clear from a letter of recommendation Washington sent to Fraunces in 1783 that he had earned Washington's trust and gratitude. In 1783, after the British evacuation, Fraunces reestablished his New York City tavern, which served as the site of Washington's famous farewell to his senior officer corps prior to his departure from the city. After Washington returned to Virginia, he corresponded on several occasions with Fraunces regarding household affairs and solicited recommendations for a household steward for "Mount Vernon."

Fraunces was buffeted by the economic dislocations produced by the Revolution and the postwar period. To recoup some of his fortune, he unsuccessfully brought suit against the estate of General Charles Lee. In 1785 he convinced Congress to provide, as compensation for his services rendered during the war, more favorable terms of rental payments owed to him for use of his tavern as executive offices. In addition, Congress provided the early redemption of a loan certificate he owned. After selling his Lower Manhattan tavern in 1785, he moved to New Jersey for a brief time to farm, but he quickly abandoned this pursuit and returned to Manhattan to resume his career as an innkeeper.

Upon Washington's inauguration to the presidency in May 1789, Washington hired Fraunces as a household steward in New York City. Supervising a household staff that numbered between twelve and fourteen, Fraunces was noted for creating lavish meals. Evidence suggests that his extravagance, which included providing the household staff with wine at their meals, led to his replacement in February 1790. He returned to this post later in the year, after Washington and the federal government relocated to Philadelphia. Fraunces remained with the presidential household until 1794, when he left on good terms and reestablished himself as a tavern keeper in Philadelphia.

Fraunces's fame rests with his taverns and his association with Washington. Nonetheless, it is clear from the documentation that survives that he was a superior businessman who by the time of his death in Philadelphia had recouped much of the fortune he lost in the upheavals of the Revolution. In 1904 the Sons of the Revolution in the State of New York purchased Fraunces's Lower Manhattan tavern and restored it as a public museum.

• Little Fraunces correspondence survives, but scattered letters are in the New-York Historical Society, the Historical Society of Pennsylvania, and the papers of George Washington in the Library of Congress. The papers of the Continental Congress, located in the National Archives and available on microfilm, contain Fraunces's 1785 petition and other documentation related to his revolutionary war claims. Some of Washington's correspondence with Fraunces is published in *The Writings of George Washington from the Original Manuscript Sources, 1745–1799*, ed. John C. Fitzpatrick (39 vols., 1931–1944), and *The Papers of George Washington* (Revolutionary War Series, Confederation Series, and Presidential Series). For a definitive and well-documented biography of Fraunces, see Kym S. Rice, *Early American Taverns: For the Entertainment of Friends and Strangers* (1983). Information on Vauxhall Gardens is in Harold Donaldson Eberlein and Cortlandt Van Dyke Hubbard, "The American 'Vauxhall' of the Federal Era," *Pennsylvania Magazine of History and Biography* 68 (1944). The plot against Washington is discussed in John E. Ferling, *The First of Men: A Life of George Washington* (1988). Useful for documenting the role of Fraunces as Washington's steward is Stephen Decatur, Jr., *Private Affairs of George Washington* (1933). A notice of Fraunces's death is in the *Gazette of the United States*, 13 Oct. 1795.

G. KURT PIEHLER

FRAZEE, John (18 July 1790–25 Feb. 1852), sculptor, was born in Rahway, New Jersey, the son of Reuben Frazee, a carpenter, and Jane Brookfield. His father was an undependable provider, subject to heavy drinking and abusive behavior, and soon after Frazee's birth his family's precarious economic state worsened dramatically when his parents parted company and his father eventually disappeared. At age five Frazee went to live on the nearby farm of his maternal grandparents, where he assisted in the fieldwork and where he was able to attend school for only two brief periods. Instead, he obtained his basic knowledge in reading, writing, and math through instruction from his grandmother and a program of self-education that he pursued into his teens.

Except for two years spent indentured to another farmer, Frazee resided with his grandparents until his fourteenth year, when he began a seven-year apprenticeship with builder William Lawrence. While working for Lawrence, he took his first steps toward becoming a sculptor, for it was his employer's request for an inscribed stone tablet naming him as the builder of a local bridge that led to Frazee's first crude attempt at stone carving in 1808. Later, while working on the construction of the First Bank of New Brunswick, he advanced his carver's skills under the tutelage of a veteran New York City stonecutter, brought in to do the bank's ornamental stonework, and on his last job as an apprentice he was chief cutter for a house near Haverstraw, New York.

With the end of his apprenticeship in 1811, Frazee had difficulty finding steady work in building, and he was soon trying to supplement his uncertain income by operating a singing school. At the same time he set himself up as a carver of cemetery tablets and in that endeavor quickly exhibited an unusually strong drive for originality of design. In July 1813 he was sure enough of his future to marry Jane Probasco, with whom he had ten children. In 1814 the couple moved to New Brunswick, New Jersey, where Frazee became coproprietor of a stonecutting business.

After some initial setbacks, including confinement to debtor's prison, Frazee eventually thrived in the new venue. With prosperity, he became ever more ambitious and proficient in his carving endeavors, and in the spring of 1818, not long after fashioning his first composition in marble, he moved to New York City to establish himself as a marblecutter in partnership with his brother William.

In general Frazee developed his carving proficiency through self-instruction. Nevertheless, according to Frazee's self-promoting "Autobiography" (1835), his talents inspired "discomfiture" among his fellow New York marblecutters. Although that may have overstated the case, the evidence suggests that by now his carving technique and sense of design had advanced considerably. Perhaps the most compelling testimony to that fact was his richly ornamented cenotaph memorial to Sarah Haynes, completed about 1821 (Trinity Church, New York City).

By the mid-1820s that ambition had turned into a drive to graduate from artisan marblecutter to fullfledged sculptor. The transition was achieved in part upon his admission to membership in the American Academy of Fine Arts in mid-1824, but not until later that year did he produce a piece that legitimately belonged in the fine arts category: a plaster bust, fashioned from a life mask, of the visiting marquis de Lafayette. The success of that portrait led to the commission for a landmark work in American sculpture, a memorial to John Wells (St. Paul's Chapel, New York), featuring a three-dimensional portrait of Wells. In creating this work, Frazee became the first nativeborn American artist to execute a likeness in marble. Doubtless in recognition of that achievement, he was invited to become a charter member of the National Academy of Design in 1826, and by the time he submitted his remarkably vibrant neoclassical self-portrait to the NAD's annual exhibition the following year, Frazee clearly felt that he had proven himself as an artist.

In 1829 Frazee dissolved his partnership with his brother William to establish his own marble business. Coinciding with this split was the arrival of Robert Launitz, a European sculptor who started with Frazee as a journeyman carver and became his partner in 1831.

In the early 1830s Frazee's sculpture career reached its high-water mark. In 1831 Congress designated him to do a bust of John Jay for the Capitol's Supreme Court chamber. Within America's young artistic community out to prove itself, this was cause for special celebration, since it was the first time that Congress had not given a sculpture commission for the Capitol to a European artist.

Unfortunately Frazee's pleasure over this and several other portrait commissions was overshadowed by the death of his wife in mid-1832. His bereavement did not last long, however; in March 1833 he married Lydia Place, with whom he had ten children.

Meanwhile demand for Frazee's talents was growing. In 1833, just as he completed an elaborate monument to the Episcopal bishop John Hobart (St. Peter's Church, Auburn, N.Y.), the Boston Athenaeum asked him to model a marble likeness of Nathaniel Bowditch. On the strength of that likeness, the Athenaeum requested six other portraits of notable figures, including Daniel Webster and Chief Justice John Marshall.

Frazee's hope that his Athenaeum pieces would generate other significant commissions was never realized. In need of a steady income to support his large brood of children, he felt compelled in 1835 to accept appointment as superintending architect for New York City's new Custom House. Although he did not intend to give up sculpture altogether, continual failure to obtain patronage discouraged him, and after the dissolution of his partnership with Launitz in 1837, he devoted most of his time to the Custom House until its completion in 1842.

Frazee's final ten years were marked by declining health and financial difficulties that began with an investigation into irregularities regarding construction of the Custom House, which led, in turn, to Frazee's loss of a year of his architect's salary. To support his family he worked as a customs inspector from 1843 to 1847 and picked up random sculpture commissions. In late 1851, while working on a marble version of the plaster portrait of Andrew Jackson he had made in Washington in 1834, he collapsed. He never recovered his strength and died in Compton Mills, Rhode Island.

• The largest collection of Frazee papers is in the Archives of American Art, Smithsonian Institution. Frazee's "The Autobiography of Frazee, the Sculptor," *North American Quarterly Magazine* 1, no. 2 (Apr.–July 1835): 395–403, 1–22, is highly useful but should be used cautiously since it is so clearly an exercise in self-promotion. The most comprehensive study of Frazee is Frederick S. Voss, *John Frazee, 1790–1852, Sculptor* (1986). The best account of Frazee's work as architect of the Custom House is Louis Torres, "John Frazee and the New York Custom House," *Journal of the Society of Architectural Historians* 23 (Oct. 1964): 143–50.

FREDERICK S. VOSS

FRAZER, John Fries (8 July 1812–12 Oct. 1872), scientist and educator, was born in Philadelphia, Pennsylvania, the son of Robert Frazer, a lawyer, and Elizabeth Fries. By the time he was eight, both Frazer's mother and father had died, and he spent the rest of his childhood in the care of guardians, including his maternal grandfather, John Fries, a Captain Partridge at his Connecticut military academy, and finally the family of the Reverend Samuel B. Wylie, who trained him in classics and mathematics and prepared him for the University of Pennsylvania.

Frazer spent his undergraduate years as Alexander Dallas Bache's laboratory assistant and graduated as valedictorian of his class in 1830. Continuing his studies and his assistantship to Bache, Frazer received his M.A. in 1833. Joseph Henry recalled that during this period Frazer helped to determine "with accuracy, for the first time in this country, the periods of the daily variations of the magnetic needle" (LeConte, p. 2) and the relationship between the aurora borealis and magnetic forces.

While beginning preparation for a medical career, Frazer briefly readjusted his career goals away from science and studied law. After being admitted to the bar and beginning practice in the firm of John M. Scott, the lure of scientific investigation enticed him to change career paths once again.

In 1836 Frazer accepted a position as first assistant geologist to Henry D. Rogers, who was performing the first geological survey of Pennsylvania. The Pennsylvania Geological Survey was an attempt to raise the level of geological science in the United States to the current European standard and resulted in numerous important geological discoveries, including the location of anthracite coal deposits in Pennsylvania. Frazer resigned this position after one year to teach chemistry and natural philosophy at Philadelphia High School. In 1838 he married Charlotte Jeffers Cave; they had three children. Frazer continued to teach at the high school until 1844, when he was offered Bache's chair at the University of Pennsylvania. Entering the university as the youngest faculty member, he held the professorship of chemistry and natural philosophy until his death. Other administrative duties at the University of Pennsylvania included a vice provost position he held from 1855 to 1868.

Frazer was also active in scholarly activities outside his university life. In 1842 he was elected a member of the American Philosophical Society, becoming secretary in 1845 and a vice president in 1855. In 1863 he became one of the original fifty members of the National Academy of Sciences, which formed to become the government's official scientific advisory agency. Some of Frazer's most important work was done at the Franklin Institute, which was the central technical organization in the United States from 1824 to 1865. He served as a lecturer to the institute and as editor from 1850 to 1866 of the *Journal of the Franklin Institute*, which helped to prove that the specialization and professionalization of technology were as important as science. Frazer devoted his editorial career to reading the European scientific journals, selecting the best articles, and translating them for reproduction. Because of the time required for the editorship and academic teaching, he made no significant, original literary contributions of his own. Louis Agassiz praised Frazer for his educational and editorial work and claimed that he was "the first of American physicists of his time" (*National Cyclopedia of American Biography* [1895], p. 349). John L. LeConte, a medical doctor and close friend of Frazer, described him as having a "quickness of thought, great power of conversation, . . . and brilliancy of wit, [that] made him a most attractive member of society" (LeConte, p. 5).

In a city such as Philadelphia where status was so important, Frazer's family wealth and position allowed him early access to the elite intellectual society. He cultivated this opportunity by opening his house once a week to a circle of friends from Philadelphia. This became such a well-known occurrence that rarely would a visiting scientific dignitary fail to attend one of Frazer's gatherings. He took great care and pride in disseminating the advanced scientific concepts of his day to his colleagues, students, and the lay audience. At home he maintained a large personal library of more than 2,500 books, where he enjoyed reading Latin and Greek classics and stayed current with both French and English literature.

Frazer died unexpectedly in the University of Pennsylvania's physics laboratory. His son Persifor succeeded him as the chair of chemistry at the university. Frazer is best remembered as a deep inquisitor of scientific and technical knowledge, with a lifelong passion for educating as a lecturer, editor, and friend to the scientific intelligentsia of the nineteenth century.

• Frazer's papers are in the archives of the University of Pennsylvania, the American Philosophical Society, and the National Academy of Sciences. The best survey of his life is John L. LeConte, "Obituary Notice of John F. Frazer," *Proceedings of the American Philosophical Society* 13 (1872): 183–90. Bruce Sinclair, *Philadelphia's Philosopher Mechanics: A History of the Franklin Institute, 1824–1865* (1974), provides an extended treatment of the Franklin Institute and Frazer's role as editor.

MARK D. BOWLES

FRAZER, Joseph Washington (4 Mar. 1892–7 Aug. 1971), automobile industry executive, was born in Nashville, Tennessee, the son of James S. Frazer, an attorney for the Louisville-Nashville Railroad, and Mary Washington. Frazer's father died when the boy was six weeks old. Joseph attended the Nashville Day School, the Hotchkiss Preparatory School in Connecticut, and the Sheffield Scientific School of Yale University, from which he graduated in 1913. In 1914 Frazer married Lucille Foster Frost of Chicago, whom he had met at Yale; they had one daughter. After graduating Frazer struck out for Detroit, where he apprenticed as a mechanic at the Packard Motor Car Company's factory. This was grueling work: he was paid just sixteen cents an hour for six twelve-hour days. These oppressive working conditions made Frazer support a liberal and enlightened labor policy for the rest of his career. He eventually became an instructor in the Packard factory school but soon moved to New York,

where he sold automobiles for a Packard agency. He returned to Nashville to become a partner in his brother's automobile dealership, and in 1916 he acquired his own dealership in Cleveland, Ohio.

In 1919 Frazer joined the export division of General Motors (GM). He later became assistant treasurer of the GM Acceptance Corporation (GMAC), where he helped to pioneer auto installment buying. In 1923 he became vice president and general sales manager of the Pierce-Arrow Finance Corporation, and the following year he began work for the Maxwell-Chalmers Motor Company, which had a product that was "about as poor a vehicle as was ever sold as an automobile," Frazer once recalled. The Chrysler Motor Company absorbed Maxwell-Chalmers in 1927, and Frazer served as vice president of the Chrysler Sales Division and of its Plymouth and DeSoto divisions.

It was Frazer who had originally suggested to Walter P. Chrysler the name "Plymouth" for the new, low-priced car that Chrysler was planning to introduce; the name came from the legendary Massachusetts site where the Pilgrims had landed in 1620. Under Frazer's direction, the Plymouth Division enjoyed spectacular growth. In 1930 Plymouth accounted for 28 percent of Chrysler's sales; by 1933 it represented 72 percent. By the end of the decade Plymouth had established itself as America's third bestselling car model, behind Ford and Chevrolet. Plymouth had the unusual distinction of prospering during the Great Depression, in large part due to the car's low price, good workmanship, and appealing style.

In 1939 Frazer left Chrysler to become president of the financially troubled Willys-Overland Company of Toledo, Ohio. Taking with him several Chrysler executives, Frazer helped to transform Willys-Overland into a thriving, profitable business. Under Frazer's leadership, the company paid off all its debts, increased production and sales, and showed a profit for the first time in almost two years. When he became president of Willys-Overland, the company employed 1,100 workers, and annual business hovered around $9 million. When he left the company, it had 14,000 workers and boasted annual business of $170 million. In particular, Willys-Overland prospered under the production demands of World War II, and Frazer quickly converted all of its factories to wartime production within a few months after the United States entered the war. The *American Machinist* reported that Frazer was the first automobile manufacturer to effect wartime conversion. He also led Willys-Overland's production of the Jeep, the workhorse of World War II; he was later called "the father of the Jeep." While he was not involved with the original development of the Jeep, Frazer did generate publicity for the vehicle and increased the country's awareness of its utility. During the war Frazer also served the government without pay on a committee of eleven leading truck and automobile manufacturers assisting the Office of Production Management (later the War Production Board). Although the company thrived during Frazer's tenure, his postwar plans clashed with those of board chair Ward Canaday, and in September 1943 Frazer resigned from Willys-Overland, marking the first time he was out of the automobile business in three decades.

In January 1944 Frazer became head of the Warren City (Ohio) Tank and Boiler Company, which made landing barges and other equipment for the U.S. Navy and which was experiencing production problems. Using the assets of this corporation, Frazer formed the Warren City Manufacturing Company. Frazer served as president of this new concern, which merged with the Graham-Paige Motor Company, an automaker that had stopped production in 1941 but still had considerable capabilities to produce cars.

Frazer, who had become chair of the board of directors of Graham-Paige after the merger, sought to expand the company and resume automobile production. These plans led him to meet with Henry Kaiser, a millionaire sand-and-gravel entrepreneur and automobile enthusiast. On 23 July 1945, only eight days after the two men first met, they formed the Kaiser-Frazer (K-F) Corporation, with Frazer as president and Kaiser as chair. Frazer wanted larger manufacturing facilities than those that Graham-Paige owned, so he took out a five-year lease on the gigantic, million-square-foot Willow Run Aviation Plant in Ypsilanti, Michigan, where the Ford Motor Company had produced Liberator bombers during World War II. At this plant the K-F Corporation produced two cars, the Kaiser and the Frazer, both of which were unveiled at a sensational public event at New York's Waldorf-Astoria Hotel in January 1946, during which people waited outside in long lines in the snow for a chance to see the vehicles.

The Kaiser and the Frazer models both featured smooth, rounded styling and a peculiarly high nose on the hood. The Frazer was the slightly more luxurious and expensive of the two cars, featuring a special trim, overdrive, and a dual-choke carburetor. The cars hit dealers' showrooms in June 1936, and though they were relatively expensive, they sold well in the postwar market, where demand for cars was high. But the cars had notable liabilities that led to a steady decline in sales. Their six-cylinder engines, although providing good fuel economy, could not deliver the high performance that most drivers found in the eight-cylinder engines available in other cars. The K-F models did not offer automatic transmissions, another liability that, along with their high price and stiff competition from the all-new postwar models that the "Big Three" automakers, General Motors, Ford, and Chrysler, offered, made the make increasingly unattractive.

In a race with the Big Three to provide consumers with new models, Frazer recommended slashing production for the 1949 model year and instead concentrating on an all-new model for 1950. Kaiser refused, and Frazer responded by resigning the presidency in protest in 1949, allowing Kaiser's son to succeed him. Although Frazer remained as vice chair of the board and director of K-F, his relationship with the corporation was effectively finished. From 1951 to 1954 he be-

came involved in another venture, the Sterling Engine Company, serving as chair. In 1954 he formally resigned from K-F, which was renamed the Kaiser Motors Company. The company stopped production the same year. For a brief time K-F had been the fourth largest automaker in the country, and it represented the last credible attempt by an independent to challenge the supremacy of the Big Three American automakers.

After leaving the company he had helped to found, Frazer entered the uranium mining business with uranium geologist Charles Steen. Frazer became a major stockholder and president of the Standard Uranium Company, which he formed and financed with a group of businessmen. His other notable business venture was the Frazer-Walker Aircraft Corporation, which he served as chair of the board. During this stage of his business career Frazer maintained an office in Manhattan.

During his retirement Frazer spent considerable time at his summer home, "High Tide," located in Newport, Rhode Island. He died in Newport.

• The National Automotive History Collection of the Detroit Public Library maintains a file on Frazer. Articles on Frazer and the formation of the Kaiser-Frazer Corporation are "Adventures of Henry and Joe in Autoland," *Fortune*, Mar. 1946, pp. 96–103ff.; "Joe and Henry," *Time*, 6 Aug. 1945, p. 79; and W. C. White, "Kaiser-Frazer," *Life*, 31 Dec. 1945, pp. 72–79. Obituaries appear in the *Newport* (R.I.) *Daily News*, 7 Aug. 1971, and in the *Detroit Free-Press*, the *Detroit News*, and the *New York Times*, all 8 Aug. 1971.

YANEK MIECZKOWSKI

FRAZIER, Brenda Diana Duff (9 Mar. 1921–6 May 1982), socialite, was born in New York City, the daughter of Frank Duff Frazier, a millionaire broker, and Brenda Taylor, a native of England. Frazier's maternal grandfather, Sir Frederick Williams-Taylor, a banker, was knighted by King George V. She attended finishing school in Munich, Germany, in 1937 and, a year later, made her debut at the Ritz-Carlton Hotel in New York City. The social event of the season, her debut launched Frazier into a glistening and giddy whirlwind life. This was not the first time, however, that she had been in the spotlight. When she was three years old, her parents had separated, and she became the focus of a highly public custody battle. Then, at age eleven, she was again in the limelight when her divorced parents had a financial row. Her father, whose family had gotten rich before the depression by cornering the western wheat market, put a proviso in his will that he would leave his money to Yale University if his daughter elected to live with her mother. A court later overrode this proviso, but the controversy kept Frazier in the public eye until her father's death in 1933. When she turned twenty-one, she inherited $4 million.

In the 1930s and 1940s, Frazier, called Diana by her friends, was the reigning princess of high society. Very photogenic with long black hair, hazel eyes, and a splendid figure, she also had a vivacious personality.

Her picture appeared almost daily in New York newspapers as she was photographed having lunch at the Stork Club or dancing at the nightclub El Morocco, always in the company of an eligible bachelor, such as Howard Hughes, John F. Kennedy, and Douglas Fairbanks, Jr. Her name became a household word when comedian Bob Hope, referring to Frazier, dubbed one of the shop-girl comediennes on his radio show "Brenda." Columnist Walter Winchell coined the word "celebutante" to describe her.

The captivating aura of that era, with its debutante balls and social whirl, which helped offset the gloom of the depression, ended with Pearl Harbor, and in 1941 Frazier married John Sims "Shipwreck" Kelly, a professional football player turned stockbroker. They separated a decade later, after producing a daughter, Brenda Victoria Kelly. In 1956 John Kelly filed for divorce, and within a year Frazier had married Robert F. Chatfield-Taylor, a New York sales executive from whom she separated a few years later. In a harsh memoir published in *Life* magazine in 1963, Frazier spoke of the "confining and meaningless life that had frozen a smile on her face." Although she had been compared with the movie stars Hedy Lamarr and Bette Davis and paired with fashionable escorts such as Anthony Eden and the Duke of Windsor, Frazier had only bitter memories of the time when her life epitomized the glamour of high society.

Following her two failed marriages, Frazier settled in Massachusetts where, after a suicide attempt and with the help of psychotherapy, she lived a quiet life until her death in Boston from cancer.

• Bits and pieces of Frazier's life are recorded in Louise Tanner, *Here Today . . .* (1959), pp. 143–64, and "Best Years of Their Lives," *Coronet*, Mar. 1960, pp. 85–87; and in B. Weintraub, "Girl of the Year," *Esquire*, July 1966, pp. 73–75. Frazier is also mentioned in Richard Lamparski, *Whatever Became Of . . . ?*, 2d ser. (1968), pp. 50–51. An obituary is in the *New York Times*, 6 May 1982.

PATRICIA FOX-SHEINWOLD

FRAZIER, Charles Harrison (19 Apr. 1870–26 July 1936), neurosurgeon, was born in Philadelphia, Pennsylvania, the son of William W. Frazier, a prominent businessman, and Harriet Morgan Harrison. After graduating from the Episcopal Academy in Philadelphia in 1886, Charles Frazier began a long association with the University of Pennsylvania. He received an A.B. in 1889, an M.D. in 1892, and an Sc.D. in 1925. He was elected a trustee of the university in 1934.

Following his graduation from medical school in 1892, Frazier served internships in University and Episcopal hospitals. He became interested in surgery and surgical pathology and spent 1895 in Berlin studying with Rudolf Virchow, the "father of cellular pathology," and Ernst von Bergmann, a famous surgeon who introduced aseptic technique to surgery and who was an early pioneer in the surgical treatment of disorders of the nervous system. On his return to Philadelphia, Frazier was appointed to the surgical staff of University Hospital and to the teaching staff of the medical school. In 1901 he was named professor of clinical surgery at the University of Pennsylvania; from 1922 until his death he was John Rhea Barton Professor of Surgery and chief of the surgical service of the Hospital of the University of Pennsylvania.

Frazier treated a variety of surgical conditions but concentrated on brain surgery and thyroid surgery. He was among the few surgeons who advanced neurosurgery in the beginning of the twentieth century, largely because of his association with a medical school classmate, the brilliant neurologist William G. Spiller. Together they developed the operation of subtemporal retrogasserian trigeminal neurotomy (surgical sectioning of the trunk of the trigeminal nerve at the base of the skull, beneath the temporal lobe of the brain), which they first described in 1901; it became the standard surgical treatment for a certain type of facial pain (trigeminal neuralgia) for almost seventy years. The two men were also pioneers in the development of the operation of spinothalamic cordotomy (surgical sectioning of the main fibers transmitting pain sensation in the spinal cord) for the treatment of pain in the trunk and limbs; this procedure, first introduced by Spiller and Edward Martin at the University of Pennsylvania in 1911, remained a standard neurosurgical operation for more than sixty years.

During World War I Frazier, with the rank of lieutenant colonel, was in charge of the neurosurgical services in Base Hospital 11 at Cape May, New Jersey, and Base Hospital 41 at Staten Island, New York, where he gained extensive experience in the surgical treatment of peripheral nerve injuries. Frazier was a founding member and second president (1921–1923) of the Society of Neurological Surgeons, a founding member and president (1925–1927) of the Society for Clinical Surgery, and a member and president of the American Neurological Association (1928–1929). Among other organizational activities, he was a fellow of the American College of Surgeons and a member of the American Surgical Association and the American Society for the Study of Goiter.

Frazier pursued two other careers along with that of surgeon. With his uncle, he was directly involved in structuring medical education; with his wife, he was involved in social welfare organizations.

Frazier's uncle and namesake, Charles Harrison, was a man of great wealth who retired from business at the age of forty-eight and devoted himself to the University of Pennsylvania. As provost, starting in 1894, he was able to attract funds from the business world to expand the university. He then became interested in upgrading the medical school. In 1903 Harrison fired the dean of the School of Medicine and installed his young nephew as dean. The following year, at the age of thirty-four, Frazier became one of the charter members of the newly-established Council on Medical Education of the American Medical Association. During his tenure as dean (1903–1909) Frazier was responsible for tightening admission requirements and reorganizing and strengthening the medical faculty.

In 1901 Frazier married Mary Spring Gardiner of Albany, New York, daughter of a mining engineer. She became his partner in many civic undertakings until her death in 1920, including the establishment in 1910 of a social service department in the University Hospital, and in 1914 of the Public Charities Association of Pennsylvania. Frazier was president of the latter association for many years and gradually developed it into a statewide organization for the betterment of handicapped and mentally-impaired individuals and prisoners.

Frazier is best remembered as a pioneer in neurosurgery, especially for the development of two operations for the treatment of certain pain syndromes, and in thyroid surgery. He also was influential in improving medical education, especially at the University of Pennsylvania, and in advocating for disadvantaged citizens of that state. Frazier made more than 200 contributions to medical literature, including two monographs and a textbook on spinal surgery. He died at his summer home in North Haven, Maine.

• Assessments of Frazier's life and achievements by his associates, students, and successors include Francis Grant, "Charles Harrison Frazier," *Surgery, Gynecology, and Obstetrics* 63 (1936): 531–33, and "Charles Harrison Frazier, M.D., 1870–1936," *Archives of Neurology and Psychiatry* 36 (1936): 1330–2; Jonathan Rhoades and Thomas Langfitt, "Charles Harrison Frazier: His Influence on the Development of Early Neurosurgery in America and on the Development of the University of Pennsylvania School of Medicine," *Surgical Neurology* 34 (1990): 129–31; and Pendleton Tompkins, "Recollections of Charles H. Frazier," *Transactions and Studies of the College of Physicians of Philadelphia* 12 (1990): 491–97. His role in the development of subtemporal retrogasserian neurotomy and cordotomy is reviewed by Robert H. Wilkins in *Journal of Neurosurgery* 19 (1962): 1007–13, and 20 (1963): 1009–22 and 1090–99. An obituary is in the *New York Times*, 27 July 1936.

ROBERT H. WILKINS

FRAZIER, E. Franklin (24 Sept. 1894–17 May 1962), sociologist, was born Edward Franklin Frazier in Baltimore, Maryland, the son of James Edward Frazier, a bank messenger, and Mary E. Clark. Frazier's father had taught himself to read and write and until his death in 1904, stressed the usefulness of a formal education as a means of escaping poverty.

Young Frazier's interest in sociology began at an early age. It can be partly traced to James Frazier's attempt to make his children aware of the volatile atmosphere of race relations in Atlanta, Georgia, and Baltimore with daily discussions of articles and editorials from local newspapers. Despite the death of his father when Frazier was eleven years old, it appears that this process had a profound effect on Frazier's intellectual growth. He attended elementary and secondary school in Baltimore, and after graduating from Baltimore Colored High School in 1912, he attended, on scholarship, Howard University in Washington, D.C., graduating with honors in 1916. At Howard he subscribed to a vague socialist philosophy but more importantly, demonstrated his mastery in languages, literature, and

mathematics. He later taught these subjects at successive institutions: mathematics at Tuskegee Institute (1916–1917), English, French, and history at St. Paul's Normal and Industrial School in Lawrenceville, Virginia (1917–1918), and French and mathematics at Baltimore High School (1918–1919).

In 1919 Frazier entered the graduate program in sociology at Clark University (Worcester, Mass.), where, under the tutelage of Frank Hankins, he became skilled in the use of sociological methods and theories as objective tools in the examination of racial problems in American Society. After receiving his M.A. in 1920, Frazier spent a year as a researcher at the New York School of Social Work (1920–1921) followed by a year at the University of Copenhagen in Denmark (1921–1922), where as a research fellow of the American Scandinavian Foundation, he studied that nation's rural folk high schools.

In 1922, back in the United States, Frazier married Marie Brown. Their union was childless. Earlier that same year he became director of the summer school session at Livingstone College in Salisbury, North Carolina. Until 1927 he also held a combined appointment as director of the Atlanta University School of Social Work and as instructor of sociology at Morehouse College in Atlanta. During these years Frazier published often and widely, more than thirty articles on such topics as the African-American family, the activities of black business leaders, and the development of the African-American middle class, until the appearance of "The Pathology of Race Prejudice" in the June 1927 issue of *Forum*. Frazier's analysis of racial discrimination as a social pathology manifested in societal norms was highly controversial. Locals discovered the article with the appearance of several editorials in the *Atlanta Constitution* and the Atlanta *Independence* that condemned the findings revealed in the article. Not only did these editorials criticize Frazier's analysis, but they also questioned his intellectual abilities. Soon thereafter, the Fraziers began to receive harassing phone calls, death threats, and threats of being lynched. As a result of this violent atmosphere, and at the urging of friends, the Fraziers soon left the city.

From Atlanta Frazier went to the University of Chicago as a graduate student and as a research fellow in the Department of Sociology. In 1929 he accepted a position as a lecturer in the sociology department at Fisk University in Nashville. After earning a Ph.D. in 1931, Frazier remained at Fisk, where he subsequently became a research professor of sociology in the Department of Social Science. In 1934 he became professor and head of the Department of Sociology at Howard University. He retired as professor emeritus of sociology in 1959 but continued to teach through both the African Studies Program at Howard and the School of Advanced International Studies Program at the Johns Hopkins University until his death.

The black family, which Frazier viewed as a social unit that helped integrate its members into American society, and race relations in the United States, especially its negative impact on the development of the

African-American family, as well as the effects of urbanization on black family structure were all explored in Frazier's dissertation, published as *The Negro Family in Chicago* (1932). This pathbreaking book, which has been compared to W. E. B. Du Bois's classic study *The Philadelphia Negro* (1899), was followed by his book *The Negro Family in the United States* (1939). This book, which won the Anisfield Award in 1939 for the most significant work in the field of race relations, expanded on Frazier's earlier findings in Chicago and analyzed the various cultural and historical forces that influenced the development of the African-American family from the time of slavery until the 1920s.

Frazier's most controversial book was *Black Bourgeoisie* (1957), an examination of the economic, political, and social behavior of the African-American middle class as shaped by the experience of slavery and the forces of racial prejudice and discrimination. Frazier argued that the African-American middle class had developed a hybrid group. Lacking a solid economic base and subject to the same social marginality and isolation suffered by the African-American population as a whole, the African-American middle class tended to adhere to a set of values that differed from that of middle-class whites. More interested in high levels of consumption and status than in production and savings, the black bourgeoisie, Frazier concluded, tended to share the values and mirror the behavior of the white upper class rather than the white middle class. A Guggenheim Fellowship awarded in 1939 enabled Frazier to extend his study of race relations and black family life to Brazil and the Caribbean. An ancillary interest in European and African relations was the focus of his *Race and Culture Contacts in the Modern World* (1957).

Frazier served as president of the District of Columbia Sociological Society and the Eastern Sociology Society and as vice president of the African Studies Association and the American Sociological Society (now the American Sociological Association). His election in 1948 as president of the American Sociological Society marked the first time that an African American had served as chief presiding officer of a national professional association. In 1955 he became an honorary member of the Gamma chapter of Phi Beta Kappa at Howard University. He died in Washington, D.C.

• Franklin's papers are in the Moorland-Spingarn Research Center, Howard University. His other writings include "The Co-operative Movement in Denmark," *Southern Workman* 52 (Oct. 1923): 479–84; "Some Aspects of Negro Business," *Opportunity* 2 (Oct. 1924): 293–97; "Durham: Capital of the Black Middle Class," in *The New Negro*, ed. Alain Locke (1925); *The Free Negro Family* (1932); "Graduate Education in Negro Colleges and Universities," *Journal of Negro Education* 2 (1933): 329–41; "Some Effects of the Depression on the Negro in Northern Cities," *Science and Society* 2 (Fall 1938): 489–99; *Negro Youth at the Crossways* (1940); *The Economic Future of the Caribbean* (1944); *The Integration of the Negro into American Life* (1945); "Sociological Theory and Race Relations," *American Sociological Review* 12 (June 1947): 265–71; "What Can the American Negro Contribute to the Social Development of Africa?" in *Africa: Seen by American Negroes*,

ed. John Davis (1959); and *The Negro Church in America* (1963). The most complete assessment of his life is Anthony M. Platt, *E. Franklin Frazier Reconsidered* (1991). See also G. Franklin Edwards, "E. Franklin Frazier: Race, Education, and Community," in *Sociological Traditions from Generation to Generation*, ed. Robert K. Merton and Matilda White Riley (1980), and "E. Franklin Frazier," in *Black Sociologists*, ed. James E. Blackwell and Morris Janowitz (1974), on his early educational and academic career. Howard Odum, *American Sociology* (1951), documents the educational factors that influenced Frazier's decision to become a sociologist. Also see Dale R. Vlasek, "E. Franklin Frazier and the Problem of Assimilation," in *Ideas in America's Cultures from Republic to Mass Society*, ed. Hamilton Cravens (1982). An obituary is in the *New York Times*, 22 May 1962.

ERIC R. JACKSON

FRAZIER, Lynn Joseph (21 Dec. 1874–11 Jan. 1947), governor of North Dakota and U.S. senator, was born in Steele County, Minnesota, the son of Thomas Frazier and Lois Nile, farmers. When Frazier was a boy his parents moved to Pembina County, North Dakota, to farm. Frazier received a teaching degree from Mayville Normal School in 1895 and a bachelor's degree from the University of North Dakota in 1901. Despite his extraordinary formal education, Frazier continued to farm near Hoople, North Dakota. In 1903 he married Lottie Stafford; they had five children. Frazier's first wife died in 1935, and in 1937 he married Catherine Paulson.

Frazier was an early supporter of the Nonpartisan League, a farmers' organization founded in North Dakota. The league's program promised farmers freedom from the exactions of railroads, bankers, millers, and other middlemen, making it attractive to hard-pressed agriculturalists on the Northern Plains.

Attracted by the unusual combination of farming and advanced education embodied in Frazier, the league nominated him for governor in 1916. In an exciting campaign featuring league attacks on big business oppression of farmers, Frazier won the Republican primary by a 16,000-vote margin and swamped his Democratic opponent in November by 4 to 1. He was reelected in 1918 by a narrower but still comfortable margin.

Frazier's years as executive were characterized by a high level of governmental activity and divisive political controversy. The United States entered World War I shortly after Frazier's inauguration, and he supervised a difficult and sometimes chaotic mobilization process made especially sensitive by the state's strong opposition to involvement in the conflict. At the same time, Frazier worked with other league leaders to translate the organization's platform principles into policy. That effort was crowned with some success. Especially noteworthy was the creation of a state-owned bank and a state-owned flour-milling and grain elevator complex. Both of these institutions, unique in the United States, still exist.

In 1920 Frazier was narrowly reelected, but a scandal in the state-owned Bank of North Dakota and rising opposition to the socialistic aspects of the league program, fanned by the conservative Independent Voters Association, resulted in his defeat in a close recall election in 1921.

Frazier was without public office only briefly. In 1922 he defeated four-term incumbent Porter J. McCumber for the Republican nomination for U.S. senator and was victorious in the general election in November. He was reelected in 1928 and 1934.

Frazier's senate career was generally undistinguished. Quiet, awkward, and ill at ease, he was easily overshadowed by his more flamboyant North Dakota colleague, Gerald P. Nye. As a legislator Frazier generally eschewed the limelight and exerted little legislative leadership. His committee assignments and votes reflected his constituents' interest in farm relief, Indian affairs, and maintaining the isolation of the United States from European problems. The most important piece of legislation with which he was closely associated was the Frazier-Lemke Act of 1935, which gave farmers who received judicial approval a three-year moratorium on seizure of their farms for debt.

In his 1940 reelection bid, Frazier was defeated by the colorful and popular demagogue William Langer, a former league colleague with whom he had parted. Frazier's further attempts to gain public office were unavailing. He died in Riverdale, Maryland.

• There is no complete collection of Lynn Frazier's papers. Small and fragmentary collections are housed at the North Dakota Institute for Regional Studies, North Dakota State University; the Libby Library, University of North Dakota; and the State Historical Society of North Dakota. Frazier has not been the subject of a scholarly biography. His gubernatorial activities are well covered by Robert L. Morlan, *Political Prairie Fire: The Nonpartisan League, 1915–1922* (1955). Frazier also plays a significant role in Elwyn B. Robinson, *History of North Dakota* (1966), and in Robert P. Wilkins and Wynona H. Wilkins, *North Dakota: A Bicentennial History* (1977). An obituary is in the *New York Times*, 12 Jan. 1947.

DAVID B. DANBOM

FRAZIER, Maude (4 Apr. 1881–20 June 1963), educator and state legislator, was born in Sauk County near the town of Baraboo, Wisconsin, the daughter of William Henry Frazier and Mary Emma Presnall, farmers. Frazier began teaching as soon as she graduated from high school, having received a teaching credential through examination. Her determination to attain a higher education led her to attend college over her father's objections, and she worked her way through the two-year course at the State Teachers College in Stevens Point, Wisconsin. She then accepted a teaching job in a small Wisconsin mining town, where she heard stories about opportunities for teachers in the West. The challenge of new experiences appealed to Frazier, who accepted a position in Nevada.

In 1906 Frazier began fifteen years of teaching in small Nevada schools. At her first job in Genoa she taught in a two-room schoolhouse, and the following summer she was a ranch teacher in a two-family school in Lovelock. The next year she began a new school in the Seven Troughs mining district. As Frazier rode into the developing mining town, a passenger on the stage coach pointed to a pile of lumber and told her that it would be her new school. She followed the mining rush into the southern part of the state and worked in the boom town of Beatty between 1909 and 1912 and then in Goldfield and Sparks.

By 1921 Frazier had gained considerable experience and had served as a principal at Sparks. She applied for the position of deputy state superintendent of public instruction for the southern part of the state when it became vacant that year, competing with several men for the post. When it looked as though she might be offered the job, several of her competitors attempted to dissuade her from taking it by telling her about the difficulties of the desert—the rough terrain and the hostile treatment she could expect from outlaws and farmers alike. "I was well aware that when a woman takes over work done by a man," she wrote of this period, "she has to do it better, has more of it to do, and usually for less pay" ("Autobiography," p. 104). Frazier landed the job and began a segment of her career that led to her major influence in the reorganization of education in the state.

When Frazier assumed the position, sixty-three districts existed in southern Nevada, and only one-third had regular funding through a special school tax. She needed to find teachers for the remote schools and supervise them as well as assist schools to develop their budgets and raise revenues. These challenges were exacerbated by the physical characteristics of the region. It covered about one-third of the state's total area and had few developed roads. She learned to drive and to repair her Dodge roadster, which she called "Teddy the Rough Rider," so she could visit schools in her vast area. These years strengthened Frazier's commitment to provide the best education possible to Nevada's youth. In addition to teacher training, she promoted greater benefits for rural schools to enhance their development and attract better teachers.

In 1927 Frazier became the superintendent of the Las Vegas Union School District, a position she held for nearly twenty years. She had the vision to see the area through its rapid growth and became a persistent advocate for public education funding. Construction on Hoover Dam in the early 1930s and the influx during the 1940s of workers into the area's war-production plants, military bases, and new Las Vegas casinos placed greater pressure on the area's schools. Frazier took the lead in building new schools, securing public funds, and promoting revenue equalization for schoolchildren in the southern part of the state.

Frazier retired from her post in 1946 to work for better education through state politics. She entered politics herself to remedy what she believed were the two greatest obstacles to public education: unequal funding for southern schools and an apparent lack of understanding by legislators about the importance of education to community life. She lost her first campaign for state legislator in 1948 but won her second campaign in 1950 due to strong local support, particularly among professional women. Frazier's long-standing involvement in organizations such as the Business and Professional Women's Club, the Soroptimist Club, the Clark County Democratic Women's Club, and the Chamber of Commerce helped draw attention to her record and support for her campaign. Her legislative career in the assembly spanned the next twelve years. As chair of the Education Committee for her entire term and a member of the Ways and Means and Social Welfare committees, Frazier supported legislation that reorganized the state's fragmented school system.

One of Frazier's most popular campaign issues focused on the need for a junior college in southern Nevada, where youths were without access to college courses. Beginning in 1950 Frazier built a solid base of support among community leaders, public officials, and university administrators to create in Las Vegas a branch of the Reno-based University of Nevada. In 1954 she succeeded in getting a bill passed in the state legislature for the branch and matched state funds with private donations to build the first buildings. Later renamed the University of Nevada, Las Vegas, the school honored its early supporter by naming its first building after Frazier in 1957.

In 1962 Governor Grant Sawyer appointed Maude Frazier interim lieutenant governor. At the age of eighty-one she occupied the highest state-level position ever held by a woman in Nevada. Responding to press queries that her age might prevent her from assuming the duties of governor should the need arise, Frazier responded characteristically that she had held other positions generally reserved for men "and got by all right" (*Las Vegas Review-Journal*, 21 June 1963, p. 1). Her tenure as lieutenant governor lasted approximately six months; she died in Las Vegas the next year.

Maude Frazier, who never married, spent most of her life working to improve public education in Nevada. As a teacher, administrator, and state legislator she improved the quality of schools and teachers in this sparsely populated western state. Although her most notable achievement may be the creation of a university in the south, to Frazier this was all part of a plan for better public education in Nevada. An independent woman who walked around career obstacles designed to truncate the efforts of women, Frazier used her experience and her organizational network to move into areas of even greater public service to the state.

• Maude Frazier's papers are located in Special Collections, James R. Dickinson Library, University of Nevada, Las Vegas. This small manuscript collection contains two important sources, Frazier's unpublished autobiography and an unpublished synopsis of that work written by Elbert B. Edwards, "Maude Frazier—Nevadan" (1970). Her efforts to establish the University of Nevada, Las Vegas, are covered in Robert W. Davenport, "Early Years, Early Workers: The Genesis of the University of Nevada, Las Vegas," *Nevada Historical Society Quarterly* 35, no. 1 (Spring 1992): 1–19. A survey of her work in the state legislature can be found in Mary Ellen Glass, "Nevada's Lady Lawmakers: Women in the Nevada Legislature," *Nevada Public Affairs Report* (Oct. 1975):

12–14. The most complete sources available on her political and education careers are the Nevada State Legislature, *Journals of the Assembly* (1951–1961), and newspaper articles in the *Las Vegas Review-Journal*. Obituaries are in the *Las Vegas Review-Journal*, 20 June 1963, and the *Las Vegas Sun*, 21 June 1963.

JOANNE L. GOODWIN

FRECHETTE, James George (22 Aug. 1900–9 Feb. 1980), leader of the Menominee of Wisconsin, was born in Keshena, Wisconsin, the son of Charles Frechette, a forester and political leader, and Josephine Dixon. Reared on the 230,000-acre heavily forested Menominee Reservation in northeastern Wisconsin when the traditional life of the Algonquian-speaking tribe still flourished, he grew to maturity as it evolved a modern structure and political system, with a self-sustaining forest based on advanced harvesting principles and a lumber mill. The oldest of ten children, he attended reservation schools. He graduated in 1919 from St. Norbert's College in DePere, having studied business administration.

As a young Menominee who had completed higher education, Frechette left the reservation for Chicago, where he worked as a mechanic, bookkeeper, and clerk. There he met and, in 1922, married Marie Waukechon, the granddaughter of the last traditional principal chief of the Menominee. She had attended the federal Indian school at Carlisle Barracks, Pennsylvania, which, she later recalled, provided her with an excellent education and worthwhile experience.

In 1928 James G. Frechette returned to the reservation to stay, a move motivated as much by love of Menominee life as for the hope embodied in the singular accomplishment of the tribe that year of adopting an innovative new constitutional government designed to block federal efforts to dismember the tribe. The year before, the Bureau of Indian Affairs had strongly tried to appoint a bureau-controlled government, turn a large portion of the reservation into a national park, damn and flood the central part to generate electric power for Chicago, and allot the remaining poor-soil lands to the tribal members in fee simple absolute, a process clearly designed to destroy the tribe under the proclaimed euphemism of progress.

In 1928 the tribe assumed responsibilities for some aspects of its tribal structures, including minor parts of the forest and lumber system. It struggled to create an infrastructure, preserve the forest and mill, and maintain the tribe. It faced, however, inimical federal policy and sustained bureaucratic pressures coupled with Bureau of Indian Affairs autocratic control.

Menominee Indian Mills employed Frechette on its forestry staff, where he had several responsibilities, including the management of fire fighting, a hard task in that era of primitive tools. Fires often took a week of difficult crew work to extinguish. In the 1930s he became a member of the elected Advisory Council, roughly equivalent to a legislature, and slowly earned the trust and respect of the tribal members, which led to important committee assignments and special appointments. For over seventeen years he served as chairman of the Advisory Council, the principal political office of the tribe. Noted for his dispassionate judgments, clear definition of the principles involved in issues, and faithful adherence to the tribal general will, he was often sent as a delegate to Washington, D.C., to testify for the tribe before various congressional committees and government departments.

As one of the group of Menominee who led the tribe in these tumultuous years, Frechette played a major role in pursuing two complex legal suits against the federal government. Successful prosecution meant the survival of the tribe itself. The swamp land case involved 33,000 acres scattered across the reservation and claimed by the state of Wisconsin. After four generations of difficult litigation, from 1865 to 1945, the tribe regained title to the land. The second suit, from 1930 to 1951, for damages inflicted on tribal property and forest by federal mismanagement, was also successful. It preserved the principle of forestry conservation and resulted in a large monetary award.

In 1954 the federal government redefined its relationship to tribes. Under the doctrines of the new termination policy, it ended recognition of the Menominee, withdrew services, and ceased support. After a planning period the actions took effect in 1961.

Although Frechette had stoutly resisted termination as inimical to tribal interests, the responsibility for preparing a plan of transition into the dominant white community fell on the shoulders of tribal leaders, among whom he played a major role. He had no models to follow, found no federal guidelines to assist him, and lacked expert assistance. The tribe possessed few resources, owned a lumber mill that required modernization, and lacked an adequate tax base.

The central focus of Frechette's numerous actions was to preserve the land base and protect the forest until enlightened federal policy returned and the tribe could rise again. In meetings with state and federal officials, Frechette consistently argued for preservation policies. He spoke extensively statewide to public and private audiences in order to generate public support for positive state decisions, and he wrote on the Menominee, their forest, and its history. Particularly important was his full-page "Menominee Indian Reservation," in the *Shawano Evening Leader* (10 Sept. 1958), where he cogently traced the unusual history of the forest and mill.

Ultimately the former reservation became a Wisconsin county, with the forest, mill, and other assets held intact by the tribal members in a corporation with restricted shares. In 1973 the federal government restored the Menominee tribe, but by then Frechette had retired.

Frechette was deeply interested in Indian history and the history of the Menominee. To this end he kept a large library of books and articles. Believing with the traditional Menominee that their history helped to define them as a tribe, Frechette spoke and wrote extensively on it; most of his published work appeared in newspapers and Menominee tribal publications. As

chairman of the Advisory Council, he actively supported and participated in the pageant the tribe developed in 1935 to depict historical and cultural aspects of the Menominee. As a citizen he avidly participated in the dramas, playing numerous roles in the celebrated popular annual event that continued until the hammer of termination crushed it. He belonged to numerous civic and professional organizations, labored on the board of directors of several Menominee institutions, and served the Menominee Nation Band in many ways, including drum major.

When he died in Keshena on the Menominee reservation, Frechette left a wife, five daughters, and four sons. Two daughters had preceded him in death.

• Almost every congressional committee hearing on the Menominee from 1931 to 1960 contains his testimony. Minutes of the Menominee Advisory Council meetings over the same years include numerous addresses, oral reports, and comments. The papers of the Wisconsin Legislative Council Menominee Indian Study Committee in the state historical society hold references to him for the years 1957–1960. On the swamp lands, see *Menominee Tribe of Indians v. The United States*, 101 C. Cls. 22 (1944). On the mismanagement suit, see *Menominee Tribe of Indians v. The United States*, 119 C. Cls. 832 (1951). Gary Orfield, *A Study of Termination Policy* (1965), is best on termination, while the unreadiness of the Menominee for this profound political shift can be found in Melvin Laird, "The Status of the Termination of the Menominee Indian Tribe," *Congressional Record*, 30 Mar. 1965, pp. 6312–17.

DAVID R. WRONE

FRED, Edwin Broun (22 Mar. 1887–16 Jan. 1981), bacteriologist and university president, was born in Middleburg, Virginia, the son of Samuel Rogers Fred, a landowner, and Catherine "Kate" Conway Broun. Fred's interest in science began as a boy in Virginia. Having completed his B.S. at the Virginia Polytechnic Institute (VPI) in 1907, Fred stayed on to complete his M.S. at the same institution in 1908. While pursuing this first phase of graduate work, he held an appointment as an assistant in bacteriology. For his doctoral work Fred went abroad in 1909, getting his Ph.D. from the University of Göttingen in Germany in 1911. This was a natural decision given that the virtues of German graduate education were extolled by many at VPI, including bacteriology professor Meade Ferguson, who himself received a Ph.D. at Göttingen. Fred studied under some of the leading scientists of the day, including bacteriologist Alfred Koch.

Fred returned to VPI in 1912. The following year he joined the faculty of the University of Wisconsin and quickly rose from assistant professor of bacteriology (1913–1914) to associate professor (1914–1918). In 1913 he married Rosa Helen, the daughter of VPI professor John Robert Parrott; they had two daughters. During World War I Fred was a first lieutenant in the U.S. Army, serving in the Chemical Warfare Branch in 1918.

Having returned to the University of Wisconsin from the war, Fred held the rank of professor from 1918 to 1958, after which he was emeritus professor.

Fred's pioneering research centered around fermentation, soil bacteriology, and nitrogen-fixing bacteria. In 1922 his work with W. H. Peterson made the newspapers. It was reported that they had discovered a valuable new resource in corncobs, often regarded as merely a waste product of farming. In their laboratory, the scientists found that each ton of corncobs, partially water soaked and inoculated with the bacteria *Lactobacillus pentoaceticus*, could yield as much as 320 pounds of lactic acid and more than 300 pounds of acetic acid. Lactic acid is an important ingredient in the leather industry, and acetic acid is a crucial component of the dye industry. Other bacteriological research work with Peterson yielded further practical applications benefiting agriculture and industry, including how to reduce spoilage in sauerkraut cabbage and silage. Fred was the author or coauthor of four books, *A Laboratory Manual of Soil Bacteriology* (1916); *Textbook of Agricultural Bacteriology* (1923), with Felix Lohnis; *Laboratory Manual of General Microbiology, with Special Reference to the Microorganisms of the Soil* (1928), with Selman A. Waksman; and *Root Nodule Bacteria and Leguminous Plants* (1932), with Ira L. Baldwin and Elizabeth McCoy. He was also a consulting editor to the academic journals *Soil Science* and *Archiv für Mikrobiologie*.

In 1934 Fred was appointed dean of the graduate school at Wisconsin, a position he held until 1943, at which point he became dean of the College of Agriculture and director of the Agricultural Experimental Station for two years. In February 1945 Fred succeeded Clarence A. Dykstra as president of the University of Wisconsin. During his thirteen-year tenure Fred saw student enrollment triple and research spending grow to almost eight times the level of the mid-1940s. Believing that the university should serve the whole state, Fred oversaw the growth of a statewide liberal arts extension program, part of which eventually led to the founding of the University of Wisconsin, Milwaukee. All of this was done, according to long-time associate Ira L. Baldwin, with a fierce belief that academic freedom was a fundamental cornerstone of a worthwhile institution of higher learning, even during the restrictive, anti-communist McCarthy era.

In addition to his academic career, Fred spent a number of years serving on government committees, many of which held the mandate of encouraging basic research and education in the sciences. In May 1950 he was named by the U.S. Senate to the U.S. Advisory Commission on Educational Exchange. In December of the same year the National Science Board, which oversees the National Science Foundation in Washington, D.C., elected Fred its first vice chair. He was reelected to that position in 1951 and continued his work with the NSB until 1956. Afterward he was a member of the National Institutes of Health Advisory Commission for Biology and Infectious Diseases and a member of the Advisory Committee for Biology and Medicine of the Atomic Energy Commission, both from 1956 to 1957. His interest in education was revived with his involvement from 1958 to 1961 with the American Council on Education's Commission on Education and International Affairs.

In 1958 Fred retired from his post as university president but continued his work on government projects. In 1959 President Dwight Eisenhower named him to one of twelve places on the International Development Advisory Board of the International Cooperation Administration, where he held a two-year term. Fred counted among his memberships those in the American Association for the Advancement of Science, the Society of American Bacteriologists (where he served as president in 1932), and the National Academy of Sciences. He died in Madison, Wisconsin.

Fred's career took two roads, and he achieved success as both a bacteriologist and an administrator. The prologue to Diane Johnson's biography of Fred is an excerpt of the *Laudatio* that was given to Fred along with the Golden Diploma from the University of Göttingen in 1961. Part of that accolade states, "He earned the reputation of being one of the leading bacteriologists of the States, and as President of the University of Wisconsin entered the ranks of those men who bear the responsibility for the guidance of scientific development in their nation." The award recognized "his extraordinary merits as an outstanding scientist and far-sighted administrator."

• Fred participated in the University of Wisconsin Oral History Project in 1976, and his autobiographical interview is part of its collection. Diane Johnson, *Edwin Broun Fred: Scientist, Administrator, Gentleman* (1974), concentrates on his career as a scientist up until the mid-1930s, offering relatively little on his administrative career; she includes a listing of Fred's scientific publications as well as a list of his graduate students. Ira L. Baldwin, National Academy of Sciences, *Biographical Memoirs* 55 (1985), includes a bibliography of Fred's writings and a list of his degrees, honors, and service on various boards and committees. Much of his administrative career is reported throughout the 1940s and 1950s in the *New York Times*.

MARIANNE FEDUNKIW STEVENS

FREDERIC, Harold (19 Aug. 1856–19 Oct. 1898), journalist and novelist, was born Harold Henry Frederick in Utica, New York, the son of Henry De Motte Frederick, a freight conductor on the New York Central Railway, and Frances Ramsdell, a boardinghouse proprietor. His father died in 1858, and in 1860 his mother married William De Motte, a cousin. He was educated in local schools between 1861 and 1871. From 1871 to 1875 he held numerous jobs in Utica and Boston, mainly in photography studios. In 1875, after a period of ill health forced him to leave Boston for Utica, he began to work as a proofreader for the *Utica Herald*. Later that year he moved to the *Utica Daily Observer*, where he carried out a wide range of reporting and editing tasks. Frederic dropped the final *k* from his surname at some point in his early years, in order to invent himself as a writer. He began publishing stories in journals and newspapers in 1876, several in imitation of the French collaborative writers Erckmann-Chatrian, who were enjoying great popularity at that time. Frederic would often cite his literary "parentage" as being a combination of Nathaniel Hawthorne and the two French writers.

In October 1877 Frederic married Grace Williams, the daughter of a neighbor. The couple had six children, only four of whom survived infancy. In May 1880 he became editor of the *Utica Daily Observer* when the previous editor became ill, and he soon began the astonishing rise that characterized his early years as a journalist. His ability, ambition, and breadth of experience made him ideally suited for the job, despite his youth. In August 1882 he moved to Albany, New York, where he became editor of the *Albany Evening Journal*, a Republican paper, although he remained a Democrat. The following month the paper bolted the Republican ticket and supported the Democratic gubernatorial candidate, Grover Cleveland. By the following year he still openly supported Cleveland in the paper's columns, and when the paper was sold in March 1884 Frederic resigned rather than change his allegiances to suit the politics of the paper's new owner.

With this action Frederic made his name as a principled and individualistic journalist. Later, with more panache than accuracy, he called himself "pretty much the first Mugwump." He rapidly obtained an appointment as London correspondent of the *New York Times*, a position he held until his death. Soon after his arrival in London, Frederic traveled to France and produced a series of articles on the cholera epidemic that was raging through the country. His vivid accounts of the disease were based on firsthand observations of infected towns and villages, and his factual and gripping articles were widely copied.

Despite his early successes in journalism, however, Frederic claimed that his chief ambition was to be a successful novelist. Ultimately, he managed to successfully combine the two forms of writing. Frederic's early fiction centers on the historical past and the present economic and political realities of upstate New York. He was a keen admirer of Walter Scott, Mark Twain, and W. D. Howells, and their influence is clearly seen in his early work. His first novel, the cumbersomely titled *Seth's Brother's Wife* (1887), was a combination of grim, rural comic realism, melodrama, and political pastiche. He had great ambitions for it and reworked it as a play. His second novel, *In the Valley* (1890), was an account of the events leading up to the battle of Oriskany in 1777. With characteristic self-confidence, Frederic thought very highly of this text, even stating, whimsically, that every American school child should have a copy. Yet neither this, nor any of his early novels, attracted the interest or the sales he anticipated. *The Lawton Girl* (1890) was an attack on corruption, an investigation of industrial relations set within the "human interest" framework he had learned from his newspaper work. This novel shows the redemption of a former prostitute, Jessica Lawton. Frederic had not yet developed the courage to counter convention in his writing, and he ended the novel with Jessica Lawton's death, a censorious conclusion he later described as "false and cowardly." In his own life, however, he was more bold. Previously, around 1889, he had met Kate Lyon, an American living in London. Since his wife would not give him a divorce, he began a complex and ultimately unhappy domestic existence after 1891, when he began spending part of the week with Kate, with whom he would later have three children, and the other part with his wife.

At this stage in his life, Frederic remained ambitious about both journalism and fiction, although he publicly continued to proclaim his allegiance to his novels rather than his journalism. Still, he was financially dependent on newspaper work. By the early 1890s his financial situation was precarious because of the demands of his domestic life, so he collected and published several extended pieces of journalism in book form. *The Young Emperor, William II of Germany: A Study of Character Development on a Throne* (1891) and *The New Exodus: A Story of Israel in Russia* (1892) were both developed from articles written for the *New York Times* after visits to Germany and Russia. The latter, an investigation of anti-Semitism in Russia, caused him to be barred permanently from that country. Two frolicsome books followed, although much like his later fiction, they reveal a degree of desperation. Both feature worldly, cynical, middle-aged men who comment shrewdly on the world. *The Return of The O'Mahony* (1892) is a fantastical and farcical Irish novel, and *Mrs. Albert Grundy: Observations in Philistia* (1896) is a collection of satirical journalistic writings.

Two substantial stories also appeared during this period. "The Copperhead" (1893) was published in *Scribner's Magazine*, and "Marsena" (1894) was published in the *New York Times*. Both were subsequently published in separate collections in 1894. Other collected stories also appeared over the years. Frederic's best-known work, *The Damnation of Theron Ware* (1896), published in England as *Illumination*, was a bestseller in the year of its publication and the most successful of all Frederic's works. It was widely acclaimed. Set in a small town in New York state, it centers on a naive young Methodist minister's attempts at self-education and social advancement among a group of people who represent and embody a range of differing and sometimes conflicting ethical positions. It is a puzzling and challenging novel, not least because of the way in which Theron's own self-deception seeps into the narrative, making his motivation continually unclear. Although always ironic and often funny, it is ultimately a bleak and pessimistic novel. Owing to its success, Frederic's next novel, *March Hares* (1896), was a light-hearted exercise in what the *Yellow Book* called "cat literature." The text was published under the pseudonym George Forth in order not to challenge the sales of the other novel. Frederic's growing reputation was recognized when Charles Scribner's Sons published a "uniform edition" of his work in 1897. Frederic contributed a preface to the collection, the only piece that he ever wrote about his own writing, which gives an account of the genesis and trajectory of his career as a writer of fiction. In 1898 another collection of stories appeared, as did *Gloria Mundi* (1898), the last book published in his lifetime in which Frederic considers the social institutions of England from the perspective of an outsider.

In April 1898 Frederic fell ill and had a stroke in late summer at "Homefield" in Kenley, Surrey, the house he shared with Kate Lyon. He remained there until his death that fall. His ill health was complicated by his antipathy toward doctors and Lyon's belief in Christian Science. After his death Lyon and Athalie Mills, a Christian Science healer, were tried for manslaughter in a sensational case that attracted international press attention. The two women were eventually acquitted. Frederic's *The Market-Place* (1899), a fine novel about an amoral financial buccaneer, appeared posthumously.

Frederic's significance is twofold. As a foreign correspondent for the *New York Times* for fourteen years, he shaped British and European news for an American readership, acting as a guide and commentator to a large audience. As a writer of fiction, he acted as a chronicler and interpreter of his birthplace, New York state, while also investigating the promise and the failure, as he saw it, of the new republic. In his later writings, he began to experiment with innovative forms of narrative perspective that challenged the conventions of literary realism.

• The main library holdings are the Harold Frederic Papers in the Library of Congress; for details of the collection see Noel Polk, *The Literary Manuscripts of Harold Frederic: A Catalogue* (1979). Frederic's correspondence has been published as *The Correspondence of Harold Frederic*, ed. George E. Fortenberry et al. (1977) and is an invaluable source of reference. The pioneering (though dated) study of Frederic, on which many other works draw, is Paul Haines, "Harold Frederic" (Ph.D. diss., New York Univ., 1945). See Thomas F. O'Donnell and Hoyt C. Franchere, *Harold Frederic* (1961); Austin Briggs, Jr., *The Novels of Harold Frederic* (1969); Stanton Garner, *Harold Frederic* (1969); and Robert M. Myers, *Reluctant Expatriate: The Life of Harold Frederic* (1995), all of which combine biography with literary criticism. For details concerning Frederic's final illness and death, as well as facts surrounding the manslaughter trial, see C. W. E. Bigsby, "The 'Christian Science Case': An Account of the Death of Harold Frederic and the Subsequent Inquest and Court Proceedings," *American Literary Realism, 1890–1910* 1 (Spring 1968): 77–83, and Stanley Weintraub, *The London Yankees: Portraits of American Writers and Artists in England, 1894–1914* (1979). For information about Frederic's writing, see Robert H. Woodward, "Harold Frederic (1856–1898): A Critical Bibliography of Secondary Comment," *American Literary Realism, 1890–1910* 1 (Spring 1968): 1–70, and O'Donnell et al., eds., *A Bibliography of Writing by and about Harold Frederic* (1975). For a wealth of eccentric and useful information, see issues of the *Frederic Herald* (Apr. 1967–Jan. 1970), all of which are entirely devoted to Frederic. Obituaries, which are often inaccurate, include *The Times* (London), 22 Oct. 1898, and the *New York Times*, 20 Oct. 1898.

BRIDGET BENNETT

FREDERICK, Pauline Annabel (13 Feb. 1908–9 May 1990), journalist, was born in Gallitzin, Pennsylvania, the daughter of Matthew Phillip Frederick, a postmaster, and Susan Catharine Stanley. The family later settled in Harrisburg, where her father worked for the state in jobs ranging from factory inspector to director of the Bureau of Industrial Relations.

As a student, Frederick won essay contests, occasionally wrote school news bulletins or articles for local newspapers, and became class valedictorian. At eighteen she had a complete hysterectomy. Bitterly disappointed that she would never bear children, Frederick vowed, according to her niece, that if she could not be "a complete woman/mother," she would prove that she was as good as any man.

She earned bachelor and master of arts degrees in political science at American University and wrote the school's alma mater. After graduation she taught school and wrote articles, and within four years she began to receive invitations to White House press events.

At about this time Frederick accepted a clerical job, but she also auditioned for NBC news and conducted a news interview on the air. After this experience she wanted only to work in broadcast news. For some time, however, she continued to work as a clerk in federal agencies and to write articles; in 1941 she also collaborated on a book about America's preparations for war, infusing it with her idealism and patriotism.

During a shortage of silk stockings in 1941, Frederick conducted an interview for NBC with Myrlie Henderson, the wife of the nation's price control chief. Fifteen seconds into the program, Frederick asked if the interviewee's husband had thrown out a hint about the shortage in advance. Indeed he had not, Henderson responded, and she didn't wear stockings in the summer anyway. Frederick said, "So there were no runs in the Henderson family!" The interview was a hit at NBC, and Frederick became secretary/editorial assistant in the network's Washington bureau soon thereafter.

In 1945 she went with other journalists to the Far East, selling articles to newspapers and becoming the first woman journalist to broadcast from China. About six months later, while covering the Nuremberg trials, she interviewed Nazi prisoner Hermann Goering for ABC. She wrote prolifically but received disappointing pay vouchers as well as many rejections. Discouraged and homesick, Frederick wrote, "I guess I'm not too good at this writing thing." She went to Poland, where she wrote about the machine-gunning of civilians in Cracow. Back home, legislators introduced Frederick's reports and analyses in the *Congressional Record*.

Returning to the United States in 1946, Frederick made New York her home, worked as a freelance journalist, and tried to break into broadcasting. Finally, after rejections elsewhere, she freelanced for ABC.

According to Frederick, women had few opportunities in radio because male news directors said the female voice was not suited for the microphone. More often than she liked, male newscasters read her reports over the air, so she searched for exclusives, interviews that she alone could conduct, while covering the United Nations. The world peace organization was a glamorous beat at that time to some correspondents. Frederick likened her work there to covering world summit meetings, one after the other. But, more important, she enjoyed working in the area of international affairs. Her big break came when ABC assigned her to cover a six-week session of the Council of Foreign Ministers. Afterward, ABC asked Frederick to cover other stories concerning foreign affairs.

In 1948 she and a few other radio journalists showed up at a national political convention to participate in an experiment—the first serious attempt by network television to broadcast news. Within weeks after the last vote was in, Frederick worked full time for ABC. She flew to Europe to cover the Berlin Blockade. Then, returning to the states, in 1949 she launched a weekday news show, "Pauline Frederick Reports." Soon thereafter she helped develop and launch other programs of her own, and ABC billed her as the only female news commentator on network radio or television. She covered the Korean crisis, winning several important tributes for her work. In 1954 she had the distinction of being the first woman to win the prestigious Alfred I. Du Pont Award. She won a second in 1956.

With each award, Frederick received national publicity and became better known. She joined NBC, where she had her own news programs, lectured, and made frequent guest appearances on pioneering television programs like "Today" and "Meet the Press." As a *journalist*, she was a pioneer in network television news. As a *woman correspondent*, however, her contribution to the birth of this new medium for news took on added significance: she was the only woman of any duration handling hard news on network television until 1960, twelve full years after her debut in the medium.

Frederick had entered college less than a decade after the ratification of woman suffrage. She was not a central activist in the women's movement, but she sympathized with it and quietly worked for the cause. She said she had been discriminated against, and as the years passed the inequities mounted. Frederick's career was at its zenith before female journalists began to collectively demand equal treatment on the job. In the 1950s and 1960s she was as well known in the United States as Barbara Walters became two decades later, and, like Walters, she had an international reputation. Then in the 1970s, when the efforts of women to change the policies of news organizations peaked, Frederick, according to several sources, was a casualty of personnel policies that favored young female faces in front of the cameras.

During her twenty-year career at NBC, the United Nations remained her beat, and she gave comprehensive daily reports on the world's most important stories—stories that could last for weeks, months, or years. She was a master at broadcasting several hours a day or even around the clock, as demonstrated during the Congo war, the Cuban missile conflict, and other world crises.

After leaving NBC, Frederick commented on foreign affairs for National Public Radio. She retired in 1980 and lived quietly in Connecticut with her husband, Charles Robbins, earlier the vice president and executive manager of the Atomic Industrial Forum, whom she had married in 1969. Even in retirement, Frederick continued to lecture about the mission of the United Nations and about international affairs. She died in Lake Forest, Illinois.

Frederick received honors too numerous to list here. She was the first woman to take home the prestigious Peabody Award as well as the Paul White Award, the first to anchor national political conventions for network radio and to be elected president of the United Nations Correspondents Association, and, in 1976, the first to moderate a presidential debate on national network radio and television. She received at least twenty-four honorary doctoral degrees, and Americans listed her among the ten most admired women in the world in Gallup Polls conducted in 1961 and 1962.

Many of Frederick's significant awards were for "the contribution she made to international understanding," partially based on the clarity and depth of her analyses. Her commentary was usually shaped by her belief that the world's fate depended on a rethinking of and a focus on the word *understanding*.

After the first idealism, the high expectations of the United Nations, faded, Frederick still believed that this forum was the world's best hope for world peace, and she was often outspoken about her views. She did not shrink from criticizing members—including the United States after the Bay of Pigs invasion—who acted unilaterally. And almost from the first U.N. challenge, she had sharply criticized its members for using the forum to promote national interests instead of world peace.

Frederick was an ambitious small-town girl who became famous because of her tremendous drive and dedication. Her standards were high. She did not want to make a mark as a woman journalist, but as a journalist. She disapproved of the "star" image that came to be associated with herself and her colleagues, thinking that stardom and professionalism did not mix. A purist, she believed that news was a serious business and that reporters should not be entertainers. Perhaps an idealist, she wanted the United Nations—prodded by journalism's intense scrutiny, trenchant investigation, and power of critique—to make a positive difference. She had left the small town far behind, but she wanted to preserve its peace.

• Frederick's papers are at Smith College. Her writings include *Ten First Ladies of the World* (1967) and four chapters in W. D. Boutwell et al., *America Prepares for Tomorrow: The Story of Our Total Defense Effort* (1941). See Marion Marzolf, *Up from the Footnote: A History of Women Journalists* (1977), and Marlene Sanders and Marcia Rock, *Waiting for Prime*

Time (1988), on Frederick's contribution to the history of women in broadcast journalism. Obituaries are in the *New York Times* and the *Washington Post*, 11 May 1990.

CAROLYN D. TOZIER

FREED, Alan (15 Dec. 1921–20 Jan. 1965), disc jockey, was born Aldon James Freed in Johnstown, Pennsylvania, the son of Charles Freed, a clothing store clerk, and Maude Palmer. Freed graduated from Salem (Ohio) High School in 1940 and then briefly attended Ohio State University until the spring of 1941, when he enlisted in the U.S. Army. He was issued a medical discharge in the fall of that year.

Freed's broadcasting career was intertwined with the birth and growth of rock 'n' roll, one of the most important cultural developments in post–World War II America. Freed began his radio career in 1942 playing classical music on WKST in New Castle, Pennsylvania. He moved to Akron's WAKR in the late 1940s and by 1951 was hosting a classical music show over Cleveland's WJW. That year, Leo Mintz, owner of one of Cleveland's largest record stores, convinced him to stop by to witness the many white teenagers who were purchasing black rhythm and blues records. The experience caused the white disc jockey to ask his station manager to allow him to follow his classical music show with a rhythm and blues program. To avoid the racial stigma attached to the term *rhythm and blues*, Freed substituted the name *rock 'n' roll*.

The self-proclaimed "Father of Rock 'n' Roll" later insisted that he had invented the phrase rock 'n' roll, which he even tried (unsuccessfully) to copyright. Actually, the term had been used by black rhythm and blues singers since at least the 1930s as a euphemism for sexual intercourse. Most evidence suggests that Freed did not pay much attention to rhythm and blues until 1951, by which time many whites, including Bill Haley and His Comets, were already listening to and playing the music. But if Freed did not coin the phrase rock 'n' roll, he certainly helped popularize it.

Numerous white and black fans throughout the Cleveland area tuned in nightly to WJW to hear Freed's program, "The Moon Dog Rock 'n' Roll Party," which featured Todd Rhodes's rhythm and blues classic "Blues for the Red Boy" (which Freed insisted on calling "Blues for the Moondog") as its theme song. Freed's raspy voice, jive talk, frenetic delivery, and habit of pounding on a telephone book to the beat of the music added to the excitement of the new, hot sound.

Freed's tremendous success as a disc jockey opened the door to other ventures, establishing him as the chief promoter of early rock 'n' roll. He staged live concerts featuring both black and white performers. He also syndicated his radio program nationally and even sold it to Radio Luxembourg, which beamed Freed and rock 'n' roll throughout Central Europe and into England. He became involved in record production and promotion and was credited (for commercial reasons) with coauthoring at least fifteen hit records, including Chuck Berry's "Maybellene" and the Moon-

glows' "Sincerely." In 1954 he moved to New York City's WINS. Two years later, he appeared on Eric Sevareid's CBS television show to defend rock 'n' roll against charges that it encouraged immorality and juvenile delinquency. Freed also hosted dance shows on television as well as an ABC-TV summer replacement show, "The Big Beat," which featured many of the top rock acts of 1957. He compiled albums of greatest rock 'n' roll hits, and he appeared as himself in movies such as *Rock around the Clock* (1956) and *Mr. Rock 'n' Roll* (1957). The latter title aptly described Freed, who by the late 1950s had emerged as a leading spokesman for rock 'n' roll. Freed was married three times: to Betty Lou Greene, with whom he had two children; Marjorie "Jackie" McCoy, having two children with her as well; and Inga Boling.

Freed's high profile made him an obvious target for various critics of early rock 'n' roll. In 1958 he was indicted for inciting a riot in Boston during a rock concert. The unfavorable publicity caused Freed to leave WINS radio for WABC. The following year he was investigated by a House of Representatives subcommittee looking into alleged corruption in the music industry. The payola scandal all but finished Freed's career. After being dismissed from WABC for refusing "on principle" to sign a statement that he had never taken payola, Freed caught on for a brief time at KDAY and KNOB in Los Angeles and WQAM in Miami. In 1960 he was indicted on payola charges in New York City. Two years later, he was convicted, fined $300, and given a six-month suspended sentence. In March 1964 he was again indicted, this time by the Internal Revenue Service for failure to pay taxes on unreported income. His energy and financial resources drained, Freed was hospitalized for uremia. Shortly thereafter he died in Palm Springs, California.

Alan Freed played an important role in American social and cultural history of the 1950s. Although he certainly did not invent either rock 'n' roll or its name, Freed did as much if not more than any other individual to publicize and promote the new sound. In the process, he established a model for a new style of disc jockey—a folk performer in his own right, spinning records and preaching the message of a new youth cult. Freed and his imitators became gatekeepers and promoters of a new youth culture built in part on rock 'n' roll. The rise of Alan Freed reflected the growing importance of mass media in the 1950s as well as the emergence of African-American culture. Freed's integrated rock concerts brought together black and white performers and audiences, reflecting and perhaps reinforcing the era's movement toward desegregation.

In the 1980s the music industry officially recognized Alan Freed's significant place in music history when it named Cleveland, Ohio, which had served as the launching pad for Alan Freed and rock 'n' roll, as the site for the Rock 'n' Roll Hall of Fame.

• The definitive biography of Alan Freed is John A. Jackson's *Big Beat Heat: Alan Freed and the Early Years of Rock and Roll* (1991). Other information about Freed and early rock 'n' roll can be found in Richard Aquila, *That Old Time Rock & Roll: A Chronicle of an Era, 1954–63*; Ed Ward et al., *Rock of Ages: The Rolling Stone History of Rock & Roll* (1986); David Szatmary, *Rockin' in Time: A Social History of Rock and Roll* (1987); Carl Belz, *The Story of Rock* (1969); and Arnold Shaw, *The Rockin' 50s* (1974). Obituaries are in the *New York Times*, 21 Jan. 1965, and *Billboard*, 30 Jan. 1965.

RICHARD AQUILA

FREED, Arthur (9 Sept. 1894–12 Apr. 1973), film producer and popular song lyricist, was born in Charleston, South Carolina, the son of Max Grossman, an international art dealer, and Rosa (maiden name unknown). His father's job as an art dealer led the family all over the world. But the family eventually settled in Seattle, in a large house filled with antiques. Freed grew up there in a musical family. His father sold zithers as a sideline and was said to have a strong tenor voice. While a student at Phillips Academy in Exeter, New Hampshire, where he graduated in 1914, Freed began writing poetry. From prep school he went into show business, starting out as a piano player for a Chicago music publisher. During World War I, while in the army, he wrote shows with his partner, Louis Silvers. Then, after the war, he went back to Seattle.

During the mid-1920s Freed moved to California and became a theater manager in Los Angeles, where he began to produce his own shows with some of his own songs. In 1923 he married Renee Klein; they had one child. Also in that year he was the author of lyrics to "I Cried for You (Now It's Your Turn to Cry over Me)," his first hit song. Six years later, Freed wrote the lyrics for the songs of Nacio Herb Brown on a new film musical for Metro-Goldwyn-Mayer, *The Broadway Melody* (1929). A landmark picture, the first musical to win an Academy Award for best picture, the film's best-known song was "You Were Meant for Me."

Also that year, Freed and Brown wrote "Singin' in the Rain," first sung by Cliff "Ukelele Ike" Edwards in the film, *The Hollywood Revue of 1929*. Freed and Brown's most famous song, it was featured in several musicals, including *Little Nellie Kelly* (1940) and *Singin' in the Rain* (1952). Freed's collaboration with Brown lasted for more than twenty years, producing such memorable songs as "Pagan Love Song" (1929), "Temptation" (1933), "All I Do Is Dream of You" (1934), "Broadway Rhythm" (1935), "You Are My Lucky Star" (1935), and "Make 'Em Laugh" (1952).

From 1938 until 1970 Freed was a associate producer at MGM. His first assignment as an associate producer was on *The Wizard of Oz* (1939). That year he formed his own production unit at MGM, where he produced forty musicals, from *Babes in Arms* (1939) to *Bells Are Ringing* (1960). Among the most notable were *Babes in Arms*, *Strike up the Band* (1940), *For Me and My Gal* (1942), *Cabin in the Sky* (1943), *Meet Me in St. Louis* (1944), *The Harvey Girls* (1946), *Easter Parade* (1948), *On the Town* (1949), *Annie Get Your Gun* (1950), *An American in Paris* (1951), *Singin' in the Rain* (1952), *The Band Wagon* (1953), *Brigadoon* (1954), *Gigi*

(1958), and *Bells are Ringing*. His last film production was a nonmusical, *The Light in the Piazza* (1962).

He remained at MGM until 1970 but was inactive as a producer. During these years he encouraged the studio to purchase rights to such Broadway shows as *My Fair Lady* and *Camelot*, but both were made at Warner Bros. In 1963 Freed and Roger Edens, his associate producer, conceived an idea for a musical of Irving Berlin songs, to be titled *Say It with Music*. A screenplay was written by Arthur Laurents, but the film was never made.

Freed served as president of the Academy of Motion Picture Arts and Sciences from 1963 through 1967. At ceremonies for the 1968 Academy Awards he received a special Oscar for producing six telecasts. He retired from MGM in December 1970, three years before his death in Hollywood.

Freed's 32-year career as a producer at MGM was one of the most distinguished in film history. His productions received twenty-one Oscars, including two musicals named as best picture, *An American in Paris* and *Gigi*. In 1951 he received the Irving G. Thalberg Memorial Award.

Freed is recognized for the high quality of his musicals at MGM and for cultivating such performers as June Allyson, Cyd Charisse, Judy Garland, Eleanor Powell, Howard Keel, and Gene Kelly, as well as encouraging such directors as Busby Berkeley, Stanley Donen, Vincente Minnelli, and Charles Walters. Freed always tried to "hire the best possible talent" and "to get important stories" for his musicals. Irving Berlin said of him: "His greatest talent was to know talent, to recognize talent and to surround himself with it. . . . After all, all you have to do is look at the record."

• Freed's papers are located in the Arthur Freed Archive at the University of Southern California, Los Angeles. The best source for his years at MGM is Hugh Fordin's *The Movies' Greatest Musicals—Produced in Hollywood USA by the Freed Unit* (1984). Also see Ephraim Katz, *The Film Encyclopedia* (1979). For a list of Freed's songs, see Dick Jacobs, *Who Wrote That Song?* (1988). His Academy Awards are discussed and listed in Mason Wiley and Damien Bona, *Inside Oscar* (1986). An obituary is in the *New York Times*, 13 Apr. 1973.

ROGER L. HALL

FREEDLEY, George (5 Sept. 1904–11 Sept. 1967), curator of the New York Public Library theater collection, drama critic, and author, was born George Reynolds Freedley in Richmond, Virginia, the son of George Washington Jacoby Freedley, a manufacturing executive, and Maude Reynolds. He grew up in Richmond, where his grandfather and father were prominent in the city's commercial life; he attended Richmond Academy and John Marshall High School, from which he graduated in 1920. He received a B.A. from the University of Richmond in 1925 and studied with George Pierce Baker in Yale University's drama department from 1926 to 1928.

In 1928 Freedley began his professional career as stage designer and technical director with the Stillington Players in Gloucester, Massachusetts. That fall he began working for the Theatre Guild of New York and held a series of progressively more responsible technical positions until 1931. During these years he also made his New York acting debut in *The Gray Fox* at the Playhouse (1928) and played small roles in some productions of the New York Theatre Assembly.

In April 1931 Freedley joined the New York Public Library as an assistant in the picture collection. Shortly thereafter, the executors of David Belasco's estate offered his unique theatrical holdings to the library, on the condition that the materials, which included manuscripts, scrapbooks, prompt books, photographs and scenic and costume designs, be cataloged and made accessible to the public. Freedley was made librarian in charge of the newly designated theater collection.

While working on the library's formidable project, Freedley also helped lay the groundwork for the Yale-Rockefeller Theatre Collection. He went abroad to examine the theatrical resources of libraries, museums, and theaters in thirteen countries on an American Library Association–Carnegie Traveling Fellowship. The results of this research were published in 1936 as *Theatre Collections in Libraries and Museums: An International Handbook*, written by Freedley and Rosamond Gilder. That same year Freedley received his M.F.A. from Yale, and in 1938 he was named curator of the library's growing and increasingly acclaimed theater collection, a position he held for twenty-nine years.

Over the course of those years, Freedley engaged in many theater-related activities while continuing to build the library's collection, which he described in a 1945 *New York Times* article as the "hub of dramatic information in the theatrical capital of the country . . . at its tables gather the country's celebrities in search of theater lore or glamour." He wrote *A History of the Theatre* with John A. Reeves in 1941, a text well known to students of theater. Other books include *The Lunts: An Illustrated Study of Their Work* (1958) and *Theatrical Designs from the Baroque through Neoclassicism* (1940). He was coeditor and coauthor, with Barrett H. Clark, of *A History of Modern Drama* (1947). In addition to writing on theater, he reviewed books on theater and was drama critic for New York's *Morning Telegraph* from 1940 through 1949 and theater editor of the *Library Journal* from 1940 through 1967. His outspoken criticism of the theater in an article in the *Saturday Review* (14 Aug. 1943) created controversy but also attested to his passionate commitment to the profession. Titled "The Theatre Has Swallowed a Tapeworm," the piece denounced the commercialism and greed that he claimed were choking the theater and criticized the skyrocketing production costs, union featherbedding, and everyone-out-for-himself attitudes. "The theatre must come to terms with itself, must forget its absurd quarrels, its internecine strife, its bigotry and hostility to new ideas, its public-be-damned policy," he wrote.

With his prodigious knowledge of theater history and current theater issues, Freedley was a popular speaker at colleges, organizations, and professional conferences around the country, as well as on radio. He also participated actively as a member and officer in theater organizations throughout his career, including the Theatre Library Association, of which he was cofounder and served as president; the New York Drama Critics Circle; the American National Theatre and Academy; the Players Club; the Equity Library Theatre; the National Board of Review of Motion Pictures; and the Societe Universelle du Theatre. Among the honors he received over his long, successful career were the Antoinette Perry Award, the Kelcey Allen Award, the American Theatre Wing Award, the Theta Alpha Phi Educational Award, the Outer Circle Award, and the American Educational Theatre Association Citation for Distinguished Service to the Theatre.

Freedley stepped down from his curatorship at the New York Public Library on 1 May 1967, but he remained consulting curator. On 5 May *Washington Post* columnist Richard Coe wrote, "George Freedley, critic and historian, is the man New York has to thank for the nation's largest and finest theater collection. During his long curatorship the Theatre Collection of the New York Public Library has become unrivaled in the land." Freedley died in Bay Shore, Long Island. In 1968 the Theatre Library Association created the George Freedley Memorial Award in his honor.

• The Billy Rose Theatre Collection at the New York Public Library for the Performing Arts, Lincoln Center, is the major resource for information about Freedley's career and activities. It also holds the magazine and newspaper articles written by him. *Contemporary Authors*, new rev. ser., vol. 4 (1981) provides facts on his writings, awards, and activities for theatrical organizations. An informative obituary is in the *New York Times*, 12 Sept. 1967.

ADELE S. PARONI

FREEDLEY, Vinton (5 Nov. 1891–5 June 1969), theatrical producer, was born in Philadelphia, Pennsylvania, the son of Angelo Freedley, a lawyer, and Ida Vinton. Educated at Groton School and Harvard College (1914), where he engaged in dramatics, Freedley took his LL.B. from the University of Pennsylvania in 1917, the year in which he married Mary Mitchell. They had two children.

Freedley joined the musical comedy stage almost immediately, appearing in several shows between 1917 and 1920, with time out in 1918 for service in the marines. In 1920, while playing in *Oui Madame*, Freedley met Alex Aarons, then producing his first musical comedy. For Aarons's third musical comedy, *For Goodness' Sakes* (1922), Freedley played the lead, and in 1923 Aarons and Freedley became partners.

Guy Bolton and P. G. Wodehouse, who subsequently wrote many librettos for Aarons and Freedley, noted the team's advantages: Freedley was wealthy by inheritance and marriage, while Aarons, via his producer-manager father, knew practically everybody in town. Bolton and Wodehouse called the partners "the best dressed managers who had ever been in New York."

Nevertheless, the first Aarons-Freedley show, *The New Poor* (1923), played for only six weeks. The second, *Lady, Be Good!* (1924), introduced them as the decade's leading musical producers, at home and abroad. Starring Fred and Adele Astaire, from *For Goodness' Sakes*, the show marked the first Broadway score for George and Ira Gershwin.

The Gershwins' talents were perfectly suited to enable Aarons and Freedley to achieve one of their goals, the creation of a series of "smart" musical comedies along the lines—only on a larger scale—of the literate, contemporary Princess Theatre shows (1915–1920), largely by Wodehouse and Bolton, usually composed by Jerome Kern. The Gershwins, Aarons, and Freedley eventually collaborated on *Tip-Toes* (1925), *Oh, Kay!* (1926), *Funny Face* (1927), *Treasure Girl* (1928), *Girl Crazy* (1930), and *Pardon My English* (1933).

Aarons generally handled the aesthetic side of the partners' shows, leaving practical decisions largely to Freedley, who eventually became known for his "million dollar instinct" during a show's evolution. However, one of the Gershwins' most enduring songs, "The Man I Love," was cut from *Lady, Be Good!* because Freedley thought it slowed the action.

Freedley and Aarons proved excellent at drafting into their bright, snappy Gershwin musicals talent from other genres, including Gertrude Lawrence from revue into *Oh, Kay!* and *Treasure Girl* (1928), and insecure comic Victor Moore from comedy and film into a host of shows beginning with *Oh, Kay!* All these shows, excepting *Treasure Girl*, were so successful that in 1927 Aarons and Freedley opened a new theater named for them (the Alvin) and designed specifically for musical comedy.

After *Treasure Girl* Freedley and Aarons produced four non-Gershwin musical comedies. *Hold Everything!* (1928) starred low comedian Bert Lahr, whom Freedley had signed to a five-year contract after seeing him in a revue. In the rush for Broadway musicals engendered by the advent of sound motion pictures, Lahr was wanted for the Hollywood version of *Hold Everything!* but Freedley chose to hold him to his contract. The partners were successfully sued by producer George White, and Lahr was freed.

Here's Howe (1928) and two moderately successful 1929 musicals by Richard Rodgers and Lorenz Hart, *Heads Up!* and *Spring Is Here*, preceded *Girl Crazy*, in which another Freedley discovery, the brassy Ethel Merman, became a major star and ingenue Ginger Rogers caught the attention of motion picture producers. Though *Girl Crazy* ran for nearly a year and proved the most durable of the entire series, the gloom of the Great Depression caused the partners to play it safe, concentrating on *Girl Crazy* rather than developing new properties. The Gershwins moved to producer Sam H. Harris for *Of Thee I Sing* (1931), the first musical to win a Pulitzer Prize. Aarons eventually found *Pardon My English* for the Gershwins; Freedley thought the weak book merited only an intimate pro-

duction, but Aarons went lavish. Freedley took over when Aarons, $30,000 in debt, gave up. The show lost another $50,000, and the partnership was dissolved in February 1933. A pending production, *Singin' the Blues*, was taken over by the cast.

Although Aarons never produced again, Freedley went into exile from creditors and planned another show, deciding to rehire Merman, Bolton, and Wodehouse as well as the stars of *Of Thee I Sing*, Victor Moore and William Gaxton. The composer was Cole Porter, whose 1927 audition had brought Freedley's verdict that his songs were "too unusual and esoteric to fit into a book musical." Freedley helped Porter's score by buying the American rights to background music Porter had written for his 1933 London show *Nymph Errant*; it became "I Get a Kick out of You," a standard.

The new show, *Anything Goes* (1934), was one of the last great hits in its carefree, wisecracking tradition and was regularly revived in subsequent decades. It also introduced Howard Lindsay and Russell Crouse as major librettists; in hiring them to revise the book, Freedley used the excuse that Bolton and Wodehouse's original version was unusable because its central plot device, a shipwreck, had been rendered tasteless when the real-life *Morro Castle* sank in 1934.

Freedley and Porter eventually collaborated four times, next in *Red, Hot and Blue!* (1936), a Lindsay-Crouse musical satire for Merman. The many arguments between Freedley and Porter (Freedley wrote Porter's agent, "Why can't he take it like a man?") were resolved in Freedley's favor when tryout audiences, as Freedley had predicted, did not like the original songs. New songs helped the show succeed, but seven years later Porter complained that Freedley still treated him like a neophyte.

Although revues were now the era's most popular form, Freedley continued to produce book musicals. After abandoning production of another Porter show, Freedley produced *Leave It to Me!* (1938), involving Porter, Freedley, Gaxton, and Moore and introducing another star, Mary Martin. Freedley's musical fantasy *Cabin in the Sky* (1940), with music by Vernon Duke and lyrics by the socially conscious John LaTouche, featured an all-African-American cast, including Ethel Waters, lured from revue. For Porter's *Let's Face It!* (1941) Freedley stole singing comedian Danny Kaye from *Lady in the Dark* with a huge salary and a starring role. The show was Freedley's last success. Porter took his next show to Michael Todd.

A 1943 Freedley venture, *Dancing in the Streets*, closed out of town. Freedley's *Jackpot* (1944) was unsuccessful. His only directorial effort came in *Memphis Bound* (1945), a failed revision of *HMS Pinafore*. In 1948 Freedley negotiated briefly with British producers Robert Nesbitt and Jack Buchanan for a revue reuniting Buchanan, Gertrude Lawrence, and Beatrice Lillie, the stars of the 1924 *Charlot's London Revue*, but nothing came of it. Freedley's last production, in association with Anderson Lawler and Russell Markert, was *Great to Be Alive* (1950).

In his later years Freedley became director of the League of New York Theaters and president of the Actors Fund of America, the Episcopal Actors Guild of America, and ANTA, the American National Theatre and Academy. He died in New York City.

• Freedley is glimpsed in histories, biographies, and autobiographies such as P. G. Wodehouse and Guy Bolton, *Bring on the Girls* (1953); Ira Gershwin, *Lyrics on Several Occasions* (1959); Fred Astaire, *Steps in Time* (1960); George Eells, *Cole Porter: The Life That Late He Led* (1967); John Lahr, *Notes on a Cowardly Lion* (1969); Robert Kimball and Alfred Simon, *The Gershwins* (1973); Richard Rodgers, *Musical Stages* (1975); Michael Marshall, *Top Hat and Tails* (1978); and Stanley Green, *The Great Clowns of Broadway* (1984). An obituary in the *New York Times*, 6 June 1969, is useful.

JAMES ROSS MOORE

FREEHOF, Solomon Bennett (8 Aug. 1892–12 June 1990), rabbi, scholar, and author, was born in London, England, the son of Isaac Freehof and Golda Blonstein. Freehof came to the United States with his mother in 1903, a year and a half after his father and older brother Morris emigrated from England. His family settled in Baltimore where Freehof attended the German-English School, the Talmud Torah, and Baltimore City College. He also studied with Rabbi William Rosenau of Congregation Oheb Shalom, who influenced his decision to enter the Hebrew Union College (HUC) in 1910. Freehof earned his baccalaureate degree from the University of Cincinnati in 1914 and, after his ordination as rabbi in 1915, he joined the HUC faculty. From October 1918 to July 1919 he was given a leave of absence to serve as a chaplain with the American Expeditionary Force in Europe. At the conclusion of his military service, Freehof resumed his academic career at HUC where he became Professor of Rabbinics and Liturgy. He earned a Doctor of Divinity degree from HUC in 1922.

Freehof left the college in 1924 to become the rabbi of Congregation Kehillath Anshe Maariv in Chicago, Illinois. In 1934 he moved to Pittsburgh, Pennsylvania, where he assumed the pulpit of Rodef Shalom Temple. Freehof spent the rest of his life at Rodef Shalom, first as rabbi for over thirty years, then as rabbi emeritus. He was highly regarded for his intellectual capacities and profound erudition in both the Jewish and general communities of Pittsburgh. At the height of his career, 1,500 people would regularly file into Rodef Shalom to attend Freehof's classes in modern literature.

Throughout his years in the pulpit Freehof was a prominent figure in Reform Jewish life. In 1939 he became chairman of the Committee on Liturgy for the Central Conference of American Rabbis (CCAR). In this capacity he supervised the writing and editing of *The Union Prayer Book*, volumes 1 (*Siddur*) and 2 (*Makhzor*). He was president of the CCAR from 1943 to 1945, and from 1959 to 1964 he served as the first North American president of the World Union for Progressive Judaism, the international organization of Reform Jews.

Freehof won acclaim as a speaker of preeminent distinction. Possessed of a rich, sonorous voice, his preaching was accentuated by a range of impressive gestures, expressions, tones, and mannerisms that left his listeners rapt. Freehof committed his meticulously constructed sermons to memory, yet in delivery he conveyed the impression that his ideas were emerging extemporaneously. Having memorized large sections of Scripture, classic prose, and poetry, Freehof astounded his audience by effortlessly quoting these sources verbatim. In a personal reflection written for the *Detroit Jewish News* (6 July 1990), David Breakstone recalled how Freehof's "entire being was fully at the service of what he wanted to say." Many of his sermons and lectures were subsequently published in separate volumes such as *Modern Jewish Preaching* (1941), *Spoken and Heard* (1972), *Bible Sermons for Today* (1973), and *The Sermon Continues* (1982).

A prolific scholar, Freehof published works on diverse areas of Jewish interest. In addition to *Preface to Scripture* (1950), his commentary on the Hebrew Scriptures, Freehof also wrote commentaries on the Books of Job, Isaiah, Jeremiah, Ezekiel, and the Psalms. Through these Scriptural commentaries Freehof hoped to bring the Bible into the everyday life of contemporary Jews who had lost touch with these ancient writings. Freehof believed that the teachings of the prophets embodied the essential spirit of Judaism. He understood the prophetic message to be the cornerstone upon which Jewish law had been established.

The primary focus of Freehof's scholarly work, however, was the development of Jewish law through the literature of Responsa—annotated answers to a rich array of complex questions pertaining to matters of Jewish life and practice. Freehof's research in this area began during World War II, while he was a member of the Chaplaincy Commission of the National Jewish Welfare Board. When the Chaplaincy Commission began receiving questions about the nature of Jewish religious practice during the exigencies of wartime, Freehof researched traditional Jewish sources and prepared the response. This experience led him to write the first of many volumes that address the relationship of Jewish law (*Halakha*) and Reform Judaism: *Reform Jewish Practice and Its Rabbinic Background*, vol. 1 (1944).

Afterward Freehof remained steadfastly devoted to the formulation of Reform Responsa. In 1960 *Reform Responsa*—the first collection of Freehof's Responsa to questions addressed to him by Reform rabbis, congregations, and laity—was published. Over the following two decades eight additional volumes followed: *Treasury of Responsa* (1963), *Recent Reform Responsa* (1963), *Current Reform Responsa* (1969), *Modern Reform Responsa* (1971), *Contemporary Reform Responsa* (1974), *Reform Responsa for Our Time* (1977), *New Reform Responsa* (1980), and *Today's Reform Responsa* (1990). By the sheer magnitude and depth of his writings, Freehof influenced the direction of Reform Jewish thought by advancing a lesson that he himself had already learned: "there cannot be any authentic Judaism of any kind which does not achieve some positive relationship to . . . the legal literature" (*Reform Revaluation of Jewish Law*, 18 Apr. 1972).

Freehof remained active after retiring from Rodef Shalom's pulpit. In addition to continuing his research, teaching, and publication, Freehof spent many hours "saving" old books, many of which had been rescued from the Nazi Holocaust. Finding many of these volumes in a state of disrepair, Freehof learned to bind books by hand. He restored these works to usefulness and, as he was fond of saying, "gave them a home" in Jewish libraries around the world.

Freehof had married Lillian Simon on 29 October 1934. They had no children. He died at Montefiore Hospital in Pittsburgh. By virtue of his prodigious scholarship, his grand oratorical style, and his preeminence among rabbinic colleagues, Freehof became one of the foremost rabbis of the twentieth century. Through his research in the field of Reform Responsa, Freehof contributed significantly to a revival of interest in *Halakha* and traditional Jewish studies within a Reform Judaism which had, years earlier, formally dissociated itself from the authority of rabbinic law.

• The Freehof Collection at the Jacob Rader Marcus Center, The American Jewish Archives, Cincinnati, Ohio, is an excellent resource. Helpful sources include Walter Jacob, "Solomon B. Freehof," *Central Conference of American Rabbis Yearbook* 100 (1990): 190–91. For biographical data as well as an analysis of Freehof's contributions to Reform Jewish thought in the twentieth century, see Kenneth J. Weiss, "Solomon B. Freehof—Reforging the Links: An Approach to the Authenticity of the Reform Rabbi in the Modern World" (D.H.L. dissertation, Hebrew Union College–Jewish Institute of Religion, 1980). For a comprehensive bibliography of Freehof's publications through 1964 and some helpful biographical information, see Walter Jacob et al., eds., *Essays in Honor of Solomon B. Freehof* (1964). A topical index of Freehof's Reform Responsa in the *Central Conference of American Rabbis Yearbook*, vols. 1–90, is compiled in Steven R. Chatinover, *A Topical Index of Reform Responsa* (1982). For an analysis of Freehof's approach to theological ethics based on his Responsa, see Alan H. Henkin, *The Moral Argumentation of Four Reform Rabbis: A Study in the Logic of Moral Discourse* (Ph.D. diss., Univ. of Southern California, 1985). Obituaries are in the *New York Times* and the *Pittsburgh Post-Gazette*, both 13 June 1990; and the *Detroit Jewish News*, 6 July 1990.

GARY P. ZOLA

FREEMAN, Bernardus (c. 1660–1741 or 1743), Dutch Reformed minister, was born in the Netherlands; nothing is known about his parents. With very little schooling, he first earned his living as a tailor, but his real ambition was to become a Reformed minister. After the Dutch Reformed church in Albany, New York, petitioned the Classis of Amsterdam for a minister in 1699, Willem Bancker, an Amsterdam merchant and patron to pietistic clergy, took it upon himself to commission Freeman for the vacancy, even though Bancker knew full well that the Classis, which claimed responsibility for the colonial churches, had already designated Johannes Lydius for the post. The Classis of Amsterdam refused to ordain Freeman, ridiculing the young tailor as someone "who had neither ability for his own craft, much less that demanded of a pastor."

With the intercession of Bancker, Freeman was ordained by the Classis of Lingen, and both Freeman and Lydius sailed for the New World and toward a confrontation. Because of a chronic shortage of clergy in the colony, however, an agreement was reached: Albany reaffirmed the legitimacy of Lydius's call, and the neighboring church at Schenectady, without a pastor for a number of years, gladly accepted Freeman. The erstwhile tailor, however, refused to submit to the jurisdiction of the Classis of Amsterdam, a circumstance that worried the ecclesiastical authorities and portended further disruptions.

Freeman was remarkably effective both as a pastor in Schenectady and as a missionary to the Indians in the Mohawk Valley. He learned the Mohawk language, translated a number of religious texts, and baptized the Indians in large numbers. In 1705 he married Margareta Van Schaick, a resident of Long Island; they had one child. Despite his success Freeman sought, apparently at the insistence of his wife, to improve his station by insinuating himself into the churches on Long Island. Those congregations had already applied to the Classis of Amsterdam for a new minister, but Freeman managed to secure an appointment at New Utrecht, with the understanding that he served that congregation alone and not the other Long Island churches. Freeman then persuaded Edward Hyde, viscount Cornbury, the colony's governor, to allow him to expand his charge to the other churches, thereby violating the longstanding arrangement between the Dutch and the English whereby the Dutch Reformed church retained autonomy in its ecclesiastical affairs.

The Classis of Amsterdam, in the meanwhile, had commissioned Vincentius Antonides for the Long Island churches, and when the minister arrived in January 1706 Cornbury denied him access to his congregations, claiming that a Dutch Reformed minister—Freeman—already served there. For the next eight years Freeman and Antonides remained at odds, with rival consistories and rival congregations. Antonides, with the support of the orthodox Dutch clergy in the Middle Colonies, claimed his authority from the Classis of Amsterdam. Freeman relied on his civil licensure from the English governor and betrayed his pietistic sympathies by refusing to observe traditional church-order rubrics in the conduct of worship services.

Despite the interventions of successive English governors, the schism on Long Island festered until 1714, when the two parties finally reached a compromise. However, the fault line between pietist and orthodox within the colonial Dutch Reformed church continued to widen. When Theodorus Jacobus Frelinghuysen, another pietist preacher supported by Bancker, arrived in the Middle Colonies in 1720, he enjoyed Freeman's support in his efforts to bring a warm-hearted piety to the Raritan Valley of New Jersey. When the orthodox clergy tried to block the ordination of another young pietist, John Henry Goetschius, Freeman and Frelinghuysen, together with a Dutch pietist, Peter Henry Dorsius, and a New Light Presbyterian, Gilbert Tennent, ordained him. Freeman published three books, all of them elaborations on pietistic themes: *De Spiegel der Zelfs-kennis* (1720), *De Weegschaale der Genade Gods* (1721), and *Verdeediging van D. Bernardus Freeman* (1726). Freeman died in Flatbush, Long Island, New York.

Freeman's challenge to the Dutch ecclesiastical authorities on both sides of the Atlantic set in motion larger changes in the configuration of the Dutch Reformed church in the Middle Colonies. His appeal to Cornbury had disrupted the cozy relationship between the Dutch clergy and the English magistrates. His pietistic leanings and his refusal to submit to the Classis of Amsterdam and to the orthodox clergy placed Freeman in league with other pietists such as Guiliam Bertholf, Dorsius, and Frelinghuysen. Having broken the hold of tradition and orthodoxy, Dutch pietists pushed the Dutch Reformed church out of its ethnic particularity and into cooperation with other evangelicals during the Great Awakening.

• Most of the documents surrounding Freeman's career and the schism on Long Island have been reprinted in Edward T. Corwin, *Ecclesiastical Records: State of New York* (1901–1916). For a summary of the Long Island schism and Freeman's role in the colonial Dutch Reformed church, see Randall Balmer, *A Perfect Babel of Confusion: Dutch Religion and English Culture in the Middle Colonies* (1989).

RANDALL BALMER

FREEMAN, Bud (13 Apr. 1906–15 Mar. 1991), jazz tenor saxophonist, was born Lawrence Freeman in Chicago, Illinois, the son of a Jewish garment cutter and a French-Canadian Catholic. His parents' names are unknown. Freeman did not enjoy or do well in school, though he was an avid reader. He recalled that he graduated from Nash Grammar School only because of his athletic ability.

Freeman's mother and siblings played piano, and he heard lots of music at home. During his sophomore year he became involved in the Austin High School Gang, a group of jazz-crazy teenagers devoted above all to the sounds of the New Orleans Rhythm Kings. (Not all of the members of the Austin High School Gang actually attended that school; also, historian William Kenney reports that Freeman was born in Chicago, but not in the Austin suburb, as he claims in his autobiography.) Soon after Freeman purchased a C-melody saxophone, his mother died, and his father encouraged him to do whatever he wanted. Thus his musical career began.

Among the members of the Austin High School Gang, drummer Dave Tough had a maturity, worldliness, and artistic and literary intellectuality that was especially influential on Freeman. In 1923 the Gang switched their foremost allegiance to King Oliver's Creole Jazz Band, then at the Lincoln Gardens in Chicago. Freeman remembered, "The big, black doorman weighed about 350 pounds, and every time he saw us he would say, 'I see you boys are here for your music lessons tonight.' He knew. That was rather a sage thing for him to say because hardly any whites knew about this music" (*Crazeology*, p. 6).

Freeman took a few lessons from the father of a fellow Austin High student, cornetist Jimmy McPartland. He first played professionally in the summer of 1924, but he did not learn to read music until the following year, when he studied clarinet for six months with Duke Riehl before settling permanently on tenor saxophone. During this period he regularly heard all of the leading African-American musicians in Chicago, including cornetist and trumpeter Louis Armstrong, pianist Earl Hines, clarinetist Jimmie Noone, and singer Bessie Smith; he also idolized the white cornetist Bix Beiderbecke.

Freeman worked with his Austin High colleagues, including clarinetist Frank Teschemacher, McPartland, and Tough, as the Blue Friars, the Red Dragons, and Husk O'Hare's Wolverines, this last group name dating from about 1925 to 1926. In 1927 he played in obscure dance bands and, far more significantly, in jam sessions with Beiderbecke, the Dorsey Brothers, clarinetist Benny Goodman, and guitarist and banjoist Eddie Condon at Chicago's Three Deuces club. This experience led to his participation in a seminal recording session by Red McKenzie and Condon's Chicagoans in December 1927. Their four titles, including "Nobody's Sweetheart" and especially "China Boy," defined a fervent amalgam of Dixieland jazz and swing that came to be known as Chicago jazz.

At that point Freeman joined Ben Pollack's dance band and traveled with it to New York City in February 1928. He left Pollack in the summer, visited Paris, and then returned to Chicago. Until 1933 he freelanced in Chicago and New York City, playing in theaters, dance halls, and nightclubs. Recordings from this period include "Craze-o-logy" (Dec. 1928), from his first session as a leader; cornetist Red Nichols's "Rose of Washington Square" (1929); and Condon's "The Eel" and "Home Cookin'" (1933). "The Eel" is an aptly named piece featuring a slithering melody that Freeman composed. It brought him some modest fame, and for this reason he continued to perform the piece throughout his career, even though its ornate and etude-like qualities are not at all characteristic of his playing.

In 1933 Freeman joined Roger Wolfe Kahn's society band. From the spring of 1934 he spent eighteen months in Joe Haymes's band. He was with Ray Noble's band from 1935 to 1936, and then, after a brief period with Paul Whiteman's dance orchestra, he became a soloist in trombonist Tommy Dorsey's big band (Apr. 1936–Mar. 1938). Dorsey's "At the Codfish Ball," recorded in 1936, is one of many pieces on which he was featured. Apart from Dorsey, Freeman participated, in January 1938, in an outstanding session by Condon's group, to which he contributed an unaccompanied introduction to "Love Is Just around the Corner," a polite blues solo on "Carnegie Drag," a simple and rhythmic (in jazz parlance, "booting") blues solo on "Carnegie Jump," and numerous examples of his ability to help energize collectively improvised ensemble passages.

Freeman joined Goodman's big band in late March 1938 but found few opportunities to solo, and he left the band at the end of November. He established his own group and then took over Condon's. Renamed Bud Freeman's Summa Cum Laude Orchestra, its eight instrumentalists included trumpeter Max Kaminsky, clarinetist Pee Wee Russell, and Condon, who remained under Freeman's leadership. They recorded a new version of "China Boy" (July 1939) and performed at Kelly's Stable in New York City (Nov. 1939). In July 1940, as the Summa Cum Laude Orchestra disbanded, Freeman recorded "Jack Hits the Road" with key members of the group, plus Tough on drums and trombonist and singer Jack Teagarden.

After working with clarinetist Joe Marsala in October 1940, Freeman returned to Chicago to lead a jazz band at the Brass Rail and then to lead a succession of society orchestras. Drafted into the army in June 1943, he married Estilita (maiden name unknown) late that year. He was stationed in the Aleutian Islands, where he led a service band until his discharge in the summer of 1945. Returning to New York City, he studied briefly with bop pianist Lennie Tristano to get his playing back into shape. He worked in small groups on Fifty-second Street and then led a band for the opening of Eddie Condon's club in Greenwich Village in 1946. He played in Rio de Janiero (Feb. to late 1947), returned to Condon's, and then took that band to the Blue Note in Chicago, staying on to play at that same club with Jimmy McPartland and pianist Marian McPartland.

Freeman separated from Estilita in 1949; they had no children. After further work in Chicago, he went with Margo (surname unknown) to live in Viña del Mar in Chile for ten months, but Freeman was ill suited to a life away from jazz. He resumed touring North America as a freelancer. He finally divorced Estilita in 1955, and in 1958 he married Faye (maiden name unknown).

Freeman studied Zen Buddhism and underwent psychoanalysis in the early 1960s as an aid to dealing with criticism and playing with different styles of bands. An ardent anglophile, he first performed in England in 1962. He recorded the album *Something Tender* in 1963, the same year he separated from Faye. During the 1960s he increasingly found work playing in Europe, and in 1964 he toured Japan with Condon.

In 1967 Freeman was one of the Nine Greats of Jazz at an annual party in Denver. After suffering an auto accident in which he broke his ribs and was unable to play for seven months, he rejoined the Nine Greats, now reorganized as the World's Greatest Jazz Band of Yank Lawson and Bob Haggart. He toured with the group from 1968 to 1974, when he decided to work as a soloist based in London. He kept up a grueling schedule, mainly touring Europe, but in 1975 he returned to the United States specifically to record the album *Bucky and Bud* with guitarist Bucky Pizzarelli. Finally in 1980, while continuing to play at festivals in the United States and Europe, he moved his base of operations back to Chicago, where he died.

Freeman had a delightful, low-key sense of humor that is well documented in his writings. Reed player Bob Wilber recalled their years together in the World's Greatest Jazz Band:

Bud Freeman always roomed by himself because he was such an individualist and so set in his own ways. Bud liked living in hotels. Our road manager, Gerry Finningley . . . used to see Bud leaving his clothes in the hotel rooms and finally said, "Look, Bud. If you don't need those things, I sure could use them." Gradually Gerry built up a complete wardrobe of Bud's cast-offs. Bud always dressed immaculately, but hated to be burdened with material possessions. The rest of us in the band used to say that all Bud needed to keep him happy was his saxophone, a room with a mirror, someone to pay his rent and an occasional grateful widow. (*Music Was Not Enough*, p. 143)

Freeman was one of the pioneering musicians who defined a place in jazz for the tenor saxophone. Unlike his peers in this area, Freeman loved to play within the controlled chaos of Dixieland collective improvisation, in which he took over the trombone's subsidiary role in the characteristic combination of trumpet, clarinet, and trombone, or perhaps added a fourth part, together with a trombone. For most of his career Freeman's solo style was angular, pointedly rhythmic, and somewhat harsh. But in his last two decades, he became interested in a more conventionally tuneful and beautiful approach to melody, as the album with Pizzarelli testifies.

• Freeman and Robert Wolf coauthored *Crazeology: The Autobiography of a Chicago Jazzman* (1989). Freeman also published "Hoagy," *Saturday Review*, 28 June 1969, pp. 43–45, 59; and two collections of anecdotes, *You Don't Look Like a Musician* (1974) and *If You Know of a Better Life, Please Tell Me* (1976). The autobiography draws closely from surveys and interviews, including George Hoefer, "Freeman Big Influence on Saxists," *Down Beat*, 21 Mar. 1952, pp. 2, 6, 19; Ira Gitler, "Saga of a Saxophone Sage," *Down Beat*, 24 May 1962, pp. 20–22, 40; Steve Voce, "It Don't Mean a Thing," *Jazz Journal* 28 (June 1975): 18–20 and (July 1975): 20–21; John Lucas, "You Hafta Hanid ta Bud: Half a Century of Freeman," *Mississippi Rag* 6 (Nov. 1978): 9–10; John Bainbridge, "Our Far-Flung Correspondents: The Diamond-Studded Saxophone," *New Yorker*, 2 Apr. 1979, pp. 98–102, 105–8, and Martin Richards, "Bud Freeman," *Jazz Journal International* 37 (Sept. 1984): 8–9 and (Oct. 1984): 14. See also Bill Moody, *The Jazz Exiles: American Musicians Abroad* (1992); Eddie Condon and Thomas Sugrue, *We Called It Music: A Generation of Jazz* (1947; repr. 1985); Herb Sanford, *Tommy and Jimmy: The Dorsey Years* (1972); Condon and Hank O'Neal, *The Eddie Condon Scrapbook of Jazz* (1973); Bob Wilber, *Music Was Not Enough*, ed. Derek Webster (1987); Robert Hilbert, *Pee Wee Russell: The Life of a Jazzman* (1993); and William Howland Kenney, *Chicago Jazz: A Cultural History, 1904–1930* (1993). An obituary is in the *New York Times*, 16 Mar. 1991.

Barry Kernfeld

FREEMAN, Cynthia (?1915–22 Oct. 1988), author, was born Beatrice Cynthia Freeman in New York City, the daughter of Albert C. Freeman and Sylvia Jeannette Hack. When Freeman was six months old, her German immigrant parents relocated from the Lower East Side of Manhattan to San Francisco, California, where she remained for the balance of her life.

Citing her boredom with the public school system, Cynthia Freeman dropped out of school during the sixth grade and was educated at home by tutors and her mother. At fifteen, she considered herself ready for higher education and audited only the classes she found of interest at the University of California at Berkeley. She never entered a formal degree program. In 1933, at the age of eighteen, she married Dr. Herman Feinberg, who was fifteen years her senior and her grandmother's physician. She gave birth to two children, a daughter who was killed in an automobile accident in 1985, and a son.

Although it was not customary for women of her day and social stratum to work outside the home, Cynthia Freeman expressed a desire to be, as she later recalled, "a person, not just a doctor's wife." In the late 1940s, with her husband's approval, she propelled her love of beautiful things into a career in interior design, an occupation in which she enjoyed a respected following for twenty-five years. Around 1965 Freeman was diagnosed with a rare intestinal disorder, resulting in five years of intermittent hospitalization. Because of the critical nature of the disease, she was forced to give up her interior design business and to pursue a more sedentary lifestyle.

In order to amuse herself during her confinement, Freeman began to write, initially by reworking a short story she had created some twenty years earlier. The story grew until, four years later, it chronicled multiple generations of a Jewish family and their immigration to the United States and assimilation into American Society. Published as *A World Full of Strangers* in 1975 by Arbor House and introducing the pseudonym Cynthia Freeman (her middle and maiden names), the novel sold 20,000 hard-cover copies and more than two million copies in paperback. When interviewed about her unusual change of profession and becoming a first-time novelist at the age of fifty-five, Freeman told the reporter that she had never thought of herself as a writer, "but the simplest thing seemed to be to put a piece of paper in the roller and start typing" (*New York Times*, 26 Oct. 1988).

During a thirteen-year period, Cynthia Freeman wrote nine novels, which were subsequently translated into thirty-three languages. Other titles include *Fairytales* (1977), *Come Pour the Wine* (1981), *No Time for Tears* (1981), *Illusions of Love* (1984), *Seasons of the Heart* (1986), and *The Last Princess* (1988). Each addressed the same essential theme—that of the attempt of Jewish immigrants to adjust to life in the United States while maintaining their own traditions and cultural heritage. In spite of the fact that many reviewers classed the works as romance novels, Freeman insisted that she was addressing the "human dilemma" (*Los Angeles Times*, 12 June 1986), particularly displacement and the search for racial identity and cultural roots. She insisted that her writings were not autobiographical, even though she herself was Jewish and the child of immigrant parents.

Although the critical evaluation of her work was far from favorable, ranging from comments like "burdened with stock characters and heavy predictability" (*Publishers Weekly*, 30 May 1977) to "Jewish soap opera" (*New York Times Book Review*, 14 Nov. 1976) to "written in tenth-grade English for simple minds" (*Washington Post Book World*, 3 Apr. 1980), her books, nevertheless, sold more than twenty million copies worldwide during her lifetime. In response to critics, who cited her as never having taken a writing course, Freeman said, in an interview with the *Los Angeles Times*, "I just do what's comfortable for me. I don't believe there are any rules—that's why it is called creative writing" (12 June 1986).

In 1986, after the death of her husband, Freeman was contemplating embarking on a new career, the lecture circuit, but those plans were curtailed by cancer. She died two years later in San Francisco. Although it is improbable that her fiction will ever be anthologized as literature, Cynthia Freeman will be remembered, at least by those who study the lives of women, as one who was not afraid to defy convention. She began a new career at a time when many glance fondly toward retirement.

• Critical appraisals of Freeman's work are available in the *New York Times Book Review*, 14 Nov. 1976; *Publishers Weekly*, 30 May 1977; and the *Washington Post Book World*, 3 Apr. 1980. An interview in the *Los Angeles Times*, 12 June 1986, adds insight. Obituaries are in the *New York Times*, 26 Oct. 1988, and the *Los Angeles Times*, 27 Oct. 1988.

JOYCE DUNCAN

FREEMAN, Douglas Southall (16 May 1886–13 June 1953), newspaper editor and military historian, was born in Lynchburg, Virginia, the son of Walker Burford Freeman, a general agent for the New York Life Insurance Company, and Bettie Allen Hamner. He was not yet six years old when the family moved to Richmond, the former capital of the Confederacy and a center of Confederate memorials and gatherings. He earned a B.A. from Richmond College (now the University of Richmond) in 1904 and a Ph.D. in history from Johns Hopkins University in 1908 at the age of twenty-two. Freeman never published his dissertation, on secession in Virginia, but he published an edited volume in 1908, *A Calendar of Confederate Papers*. The dissertation ended with the appointment of Robert E. Lee to the command of Virginia's army, and thus it supplied a beginning for much of Freeman's subsequent work—as he had intended when he began his graduate study. His keen interest in the Civil War in general and the military history of the Confederacy in particular can be traced to his father, a Civil War veteran whom young Freeman accompanied to Confederate reunions.

Freeman almost always followed two vocations at the same time, newspaper work and historical research and writing. Even as an undergraduate he had begun a newspaper career as a college correspondent for the *Richmond News Leader*. After graduate school he worked on the editorial staff of the *Richmond Times-Dispatch* in 1909 and 1910, served on the Virginia State Tax Commission from 1910 to 1912, and then returned to journalism. He became editor of the *News Leader* in 1915, a position he held until he retired in 1949 to gain what he called "freedom to follow my first love," historical research and writing (Armour, pp. 23–24). Beginning with an edited collection, *Lee's Dispatches* (1915), he wrote many volumes in American military history, including a Pulitzer Prize–winning, four-volume biography of Robert E. Lee. He married Inez Virginia Goddin in 1914, and they had three children.

Freeman's career as a historian had many dimensions. He embraced the scientific approach to history that he encountered at Johns Hopkins but only as it related to reliance on original documents and not as it related to taking a dispassionate approach to his subject. Focusing until the mid-1940s on the Army of Northern Virginia, Freeman took a biographical approach and wrote through the eyes of his subject, particularly his hero Robert E. Lee. He published the four-volume *R. E. Lee: A Biography* (1934–1935) and a three-volume work, *Lee's Lieutenants: A Study in Command* (1942–1944). Taking a "fog of war" approach, according to which the reader learns things only as the subject does, Freeman said about his Lee biography that he "endeavored to give the reader no information beyond that which Lee possessed at any particular moment regarding the strength, movements and plans of his adversary" (*Lee*, vol. 1, p. ix).

Freeman then embarked on the seven-volume *George Washington: A Biography* (1948–1957). At his death he had published the fifth volume and had largely completed the sixth; his research assistant Mary Wells Ashworth coauthored the seventh volume with John Alexander Carroll. Lesser works included *The South to Posterity: An Introduction to the Writing of Confederate History* (1939) and a number of lectures later edited by Stuart W. Smith as *Douglas Southall Freeman on Leadership* (1993). In addition, Freeman chaired the advisory committee for *The Papers of Thomas Jefferson*, a multivolume collection published by Princeton University Press, from 1943 until his death.

Freeman's work as a journalist, too, had many dimensions. His daily editorials on the Federal Reserve Act, as it was being framed, on the political and military events of World Wars I and II, and on all manner of affairs across four decades gained him a wide hearing. Beginning in 1925 and continuing to the day of his death he discussed the news in a regular fifteen-minute program on the radio, typically twice a day until his retirement and once a day thereafter. Between 1934 and 1941, moreover, he lectured at the Columbia University Graduate School of Journalism.

Freeman had wide influence on political and military affairs, though his views on policy were not always adopted. Political and military leaders read his books as primers on leadership. He lectured at the Army War College (1936–1940); corresponded with Admiral Chester Nimitz, General George C. Marshall, and various other American military leaders; made a recommendation in 1942 to Secretary of War Robert Patterson that pointed toward the education benefits incorporated in what became the G.I. Bill of Rights; and successfully urged in a 1944 editorial that the forthcoming "invasion" of Europe be termed instead the "liberation" of Europe. After World War II he circled the globe by air in a three-month tour in 1945 as an adviser to Assistant Secretary of War John J. McCloy, and he urged Congress in 1945 to maintain a system of compulsory military service rather than the traditional boom-and-bust of rapid wartime mobilization and then postwar demobilization. Though a Democrat, he urged General Dwight D. Eisenhower to consider going into politics, and in 1952 he helped organize Virginians for Eisenhower.

Freeman's other activities included scores of public speaking engagements in a typical year. He served as rector (president) of the board of trustees of the University of Richmond, and he was a member and trustee of the Carnegie Endowment for International Peace, the General Education Board, and the Rockefeller Foundation.

Two things permitted Freeman's strenuous schedule and extraordinary productivity. One was his ability to write rapidly and clearly; in his early years at the *News Leader* he actually set his editorials in type as he wrote them. The other was his faithful commitment to the motto "Time alone is irreplaceable; waste it not." For many years his schedule had him rising at 3:15 A.M. and going to the office; reading the news dispatches that had come in overnight; writing an editorial; and by 8:00 A.M. preparing for his first radio broadcast of the day. The major difference in his schedule after his retirement from the newspaper was that he worked out of his home, even receiving dispatches there and broadcasting his radio show from there. He thus no longer had occasion, each day on his way to work, to salute the statue of Robert E. Lee on Monument Avenue. Freeman died at his home in Richmond.

• The Douglas Southall Freeman Papers—including annual diaries, voluminous correspondence, manuscripts of his books, and a damaged copy of his dissertation that was singed in a fire at Johns Hopkins—are at the Library of Congress, and a smaller collection of Freeman Family Papers is at Johns Hopkins. John L. Gignilliat, "The Thought of Douglas Southall Freeman" (Ph.D. diss., Univ. of Wisconsin at Madison, 1968), supplies a full account that mostly ends, however, in 1935. Other significant assessments of his work appear in Dumas Malone, "The Pen of Douglas Southall Freeman," a foreword to vol. 6 of Freeman's *George Washington* (1954); T. Harry Williams, "Freeman, Historian of the Civil War," *Journal of Southern History* 21 (Feb. 1955): 91–100; John L. Gignilliat, "Douglas Southall Freeman," in *Dictionary of Lit-*

erary Biography, vol. 17, *Twentieth-Century American Historians*, ed. Clyde N. Wilson (1983), 157–69; Robert A. Armour, ed., *Douglas Southall Freeman: Reflections by His Daughter, His Research Assistant, and a Historian* (1986); William Harris Bragg, "'Our Joint Labor': W. J. De Renne, Douglas Southall Freeman, and *Lee's Dispatches*, 1910–1915," *Virginia Magazine of History and Biography* 97 (Jan. 1989): 3–32; and Part 1 of Stuart W. Smith, ed., *Douglas Southall Freeman on Leadership*. Obituaries are in the *New York Times*, the *Richmond Times-Dispatch*, and the *Richmond News Leader*, all 14 June 1953.

PETER WALLENSTEIN

FREEMAN, Elizabeth (c. 1742–28 Dec. 1829), slave, nurse, and slavery lawsuit plaintiff, was born either in New York or Massachusetts, the daughter of parents probably born in Africa. She apparently became the slave of Pieter Hogeboom of New York quite early. The only trace of her parents is Freeman's bequest to her daughter of two articles of clothing—a black silk gown given to Freeman by her father as a gift, and another gown that supposedly belonged to Freeman's mother. During her lifetime and even after her death, she was known as "Mum Bett" or "Mumbet," a name derived from "Elizabeth." Lacking a surname for most of her life, she sued for freedom under the name "Bett" and adopted the name "Elizabeth Freeman" after winning her lawsuit in 1781.

The proposed dates for her birth, which range from 1732 to 1744, are derived from an estimate carved on her tombstone suggesting that she was about eighty-five when she died. The tombstone also states that she was a slave "for nearly thirty years," which could place her birth year as late as 1751. Clearly, she did not know exactly how old she was.

Hogeboom died in 1758, and Freeman and her sister were transferred, presumably by purchase, to the Sheffield, Massachusetts, estate of John Ashley, who had married Hogeboom's youngest daughter, Hannah, in 1735. Ashley was a prominent citizen and eventually a cautious revolutionary. From 1761 until 1781, when he resigned his position because Freeman's suit was to come before him, he was a judge of the court of common pleas, and he held other state and local positions.

In 1773 Ashley chaired the committee that drew up the Sheffield Declaration, which resolved that "Mankind in a State of Nature are equal, free and independent of each other, and have a right to the undisturbed Enjoyment of their lives, their Liberty and Property." The committee probably met at Ashley's house; its clerk was a 26-year-old lawyer, Theodore Sedgwick, who also played an important role in Freeman's life. Freeman later claimed to have overheard a conversation about a proposed Bill of Rights, claiming that "all people were born free and equal." Such overheard comments were apparently the source of Freeman's resolve to sue for her freedom, although she did not do so until 1781, a year after Massachusetts approved its new constitution.

The triggering incident occurred when Hannah Ashley attempted to strike Freeman's sister with a heated kitchen shovel. Freeman intervened, receiving a blow that left a scar she carried to her death, then left the house immediately and never returned. She sought legal help from Sedgwick, who argued her case in Great Barrington on 21 August 1781 in *Brom and Bett v. J. Ashley Esq* (Brom was a laborer in Sheffield; Bett was identified as a spinster). The plaintiffs alleged that they were illegally detained in bondage. The jury found for them and fined Ashley thirty shillings damages and court costs. Ashley's appeal was dropped after the Massachusetts Supreme Court ruled in another case that slavery was unconstitutional under the state constitution.

At that point, Freeman became a paid servant for the Sedgwick family, who moved from Sheffield to Stockbridge in 1785. Most of what we know of Freeman's subsequent life comes from members of two generations of the Sedgwick family, who spoke of her nursing skill, her personal courage, and her eventual retirement and purchase of a house of her own. Sedgwick's son reported that Freeman married at an early age and her husband died in the Continental service in the revolutionary war. Her will, signed with a cross on 18 October 1829, indicates that she had a daughter, grandchildren, and great-grandchildren. Freeman's nursing skill was exemplified in her care for the ten children of Thomas Sedgwick and for his wife, who suffered from severe depression, possibly insanity, before her death in 1807.

Freeman's personal courage, demonstrated by her court case, was further illustrated by her behavior during Shays's Rebellion in 1786. Theodore Sedgwick was away from home when men invaded the house. It is said that Freeman hid the family silver among her own possessions and threatened the invaders with a large kitchen shovel. When they started to search her possessions, she shamed them into leaving.

When Freeman retired, she purchased a small house in Stockbridge, where she lived until her death there. She was buried in the Sedgwick family plot in the Stockbridge Cemetery, the only African American and the only non-Sedgwick interred there. Her epitaph, written by Thomas Sedgwick, reads:

ELIZABETH FREEMAN, known by the name of MUMBET died Dec. 28, 1829. Her supposed age was 85 years. She was born a slave and remained a slave for nearly thirty years. She could neither read nor write, yet in her own sphere she had no superior or equal. She neither wasted time nor property. She never violated a trust, nor failed to perform a duty. In every situation of domestic trial, she was the most efficient helper, and the tenderest friend. Good mother fare well.

Freeman is universally regarded as an exemplary model of courage, wit, and charity. Her dignity and intelligence are a matter of record. Catherine Sedgwick recollected this sentence from Freeman's conversation: "Anytime, anytime while I was a slave, if one minute's freedom had been offered to me, and I had been told that I must die at the end of that minute, I would have taken it—just to stand one minute on

God's earth as a free woman—I would" (Swan, p. 54). W. E. B. Du Bois claimed that she was a cousin of his grandmother (Du Bois *Darkwater*, p. 173) and, in another instance, that she was the second wife of his great-grandfather, Jacob Burghardt (Du Bois, *Dusk of Dawn*, pp. 110–14). The direct line of descent was through Jacob's wife Violet. Freeman's legal case played a major role in the abolition of slavery in the state of Massachusetts.

• Information on Freeman is in William C. Nell, *The Colored Patriots of the American Revolution* (1855; repr. 1968), and Harriet Martineau, *Retrospect of Western Travel*, vol. 2 (1838). W. E. B. Du Bois's family claims are in his *Darkwater: Voices from within the Veil* (1920) and *Dusk of Dawn: An Essay toward an Autobiography of a Race Concept* (1940). Jon Swan, "The Slave Who Sued for Freedom," *American Heritage* 42 (Mar. 1990): 51–52, 54–55, includes a portrait and a photograph of the tombstone.

BETHANY K. DUMAS

FREEMAN, Frederick Kemper (15 June 1841–9 Sept. 1928), frontier journalist, was born in Culpeper County, Virginia, the son of Arthur Freeman, a railroad agent, and Mary Allison Kemper. Freeman attended schools associated with his mother's family; between the ages of ten and about fourteen, Freeman attended Kemper Family School, later known as Kemper Military School, in Boonville, Missouri. After returning to Virginia, he attended Kemper College in Gordonsville. On 9 May 1861 he enlisted in the Confederate army, in which he participated in the battle of Manassas and rose to the rank of lieutenant in the Signal Corps.

Freeman's career in frontier journalism, for which he is principally known, began in the spring of 1866 when his brother Legh Richmond Freeman asked him to take over the *Kearney Herald*. Legh had founded the newspaper in December 1865 at Fort Kearny, Nebraska Territory, a site on the construction route of the Union Pacific railroad. While Legh traveled around the West and sent dispatches to his brother, Freeman managed the daily activities of the newspaper, which he initially published on an old hand-roller press. Shortly after taking over the paper, he moved operations out of Fort Kearny and into Kearny City. Moving, it turns out, was Freeman's specialty. In the fall of 1866, when railroad construction proceeded beyond Kearny City, Freeman loaded his printing equipment on three wagons and traveled a hundred miles to the next railhead, North Platte, Nebraska Territory, whose rowdy population earned it the nickname "Hell on Wheels." The Freemans' newspaper, which they had renamed the *Frontier Index*, also quickly earned a nickname, the "Press on Wheels." Between 1866 and 1868 the paper rolled through Fort Sanders, Laramie City, Benton, and Green River City in Dakota Territory and Bear River City in Wyoming Territory. During one of these moves, a wagon and equipment weighing close to 7,000 pounds ran over Freeman, causing spinal and internal injuries and hospitalizing him for two months at Fort Sanders.

As much businessman as journalist, Freeman also printed fliers for rail workers and miners. His commercial interests were obvious in the *Frontier Index* as well. Thomas H. Heuterman, biographer of Legh Richmond Freeman, has calculated that about two-thirds of the space in the forty-five extant issues of the paper was devoted to advertising. Advertisers included a bakery, a saloon, and a saddlery. The two brothers combined to fill the remaining one-third of the newspaper's space. Roving reporter Legh, often writing under the pseudonym "General Horatio Vattel, Lightning Scout of the Mountains," contributed witty sayings, travel narratives, and tall tales about an enormous buck sheep and a petrified forest. Freeman handled more mundane matters, such as news about railroad construction, Indians, stage schedules, and the weather. Both brothers, however, were capable of producing incendiary material. Legh regularly blasted Ulysses Grant, whom he called a "whisky bloated, squaw ravishing adulterer," and Freeman accused a Fort Sanders general of being a southern sympathizer who supported Grant in order to advance his own career. However, Freeman, who also owned hotels and speculated on real estate, used editorial space to criticize western rowdiness as well. In an article published on 29 May 1868, he wrote, "Our citizens should support a strong police force and help them to put down crime and rowdyism. We were told yesterday of two bands of horse thieves and highwaymen that have their dens on Crow and Dale creeks, each numbering thirty or forty men. They are circling around Laramie, playing Indian. We say go for 'em."

The Freemans' controversial reporting may have contributed to the dramatic end of their enterprise in Bear River City in November 1868. A mob, reportedly led by a relative of a man imprisoned or killed by vigilantes, destroyed the Freemans' equipment and burned their office. The riot, in which more than a dozen people may have died, has been blamed on various factors, including the Freemans' association with vigilantes and the paper's harsh treatment of Grant and Mormons. Legh himself blamed the Credit Mobilier ring, which the Freemans supposedly had angered. Freeman, on the other hand, claimed that railroad owners arranged the riot to remove the brothers from land holding huge coal supplies.

Whatever the reason for the riot, both brothers returned to Virginia. Freeman left behind careers in not only journalism and business but politics. He had sat on the Nebraska Territorial Council in 1867, served as a Nebraska state senator in 1867 and 1868, and traveled to New York in 1868 as a delegate for the Dakota Territory to the Democratic National Convention.

Again following the lead of his brother, who had returned to the West in the 1870s, Freeman became a frontier journalist again in 1892. This time, the Freemans operated an agricultural paper, the *Washington Farmer*, in Anacortes, Washington. Freeman again left journalism, however, and moved to Georgia, where he grew pecans and ran a wholesale grocery business. In 1896 he married Mary Julia Roper. He died in Albany, Georgia.

During its brief existence under Freeman's leadership, the *Frontier Index* became more than a novelty. First, its readership extended well beyond the rail workers, business people, and speculators in the boomtowns where it was published. In 1868 Legh claimed a circulation of 15,000 and said 2,000 editors wished to publish the paper's news. A reference to the *Frontier Index* in a New Hampshire newspaper shows that the paper was recognized in the East. Its major impact, however, was in the West, where it exerted economic, social, and cultural influence. Legh wrote, "After the Union Pacific Railroad came along, our print became the advertising medium which built up ten of the terminal towns of that national artery of commerce." While emphasizing the Freemans' economic motives, Heuterman points out that their newspaper helped to shape its communities, particularly in the area of law and order. Finally, James R. Dow credits the *Frontier Index* with helping to spread folklore in the Wyoming Territory.

• Extant copies of the *Frontier Index* are stored at the Bancroft Library at the University of California, Berkeley. Letters of the Freeman family are in the James Lawson Kemper File at the Alderman Library Manuscripts Department, University of Virginia, Charlottesville. Almost all the published information relating to Frederick Freeman concerns his role in publishing the *Frontier Index*. One particularly thorough source on the Freemans and their newspaper is Thomas Heuterman, *Movable Type: Biography of Legh R. Freeman* (1979). Brief descriptions of the *Frontier Index* also appear in James Melvin Lee, *History of American Journalism* (1923); Robert F. Karolevitz, *Newspapering in the Old West: A Pictorial History of Journalism and Printing on the Frontier* (1965); and John Myers Myers, *Print in a Wild Land* (1967). Legh Freeman wrote his own account of the newspaper, *The History of the Frontier-Index (the "Press on Wheels"), the Ogden Freeman, the Inter-Mountains Freeman and the Union Freeman*, which Douglas C. McMurtrie edited and published in 1943.

MARK CANADA

FREEMAN, Harry Lawrence (9 Oct. 1869–21 Mar. 1954), composer and conductor, was born in Cleveland, Ohio, the son of Agnes Sims (father's name unknown). Freeman studied piano as a child with Edwin Schonert and later with Carlos Sobrino. He engaged in the study of theory, composition, and orchestration with Johann Beck, founder and first conductor of the Cleveland Symphony Orchestra. By age ten Freeman had organized a boys' quartet, for which he arranged most of the music, was accompanying pianist, and sang soprano. By age twelve he was assistant organist and later became organist for his family church. While in his early twenties Freeman moved to Denver, Colorado, where he began composing salon pieces, dances, and marches.

The motivation behind his attraction to composition on a larger scale was his attendance at a performance of Richard Wagner's opera *Tannhäuser* by the Emma Juch grand opera company. The result was a composition almost daily from the pen of Freeman for about

six months. An avid student of "history, the great poets, romances, and the tragic dramas" (Hipsher, p. 190), his first large work was an opera, *The Martyr*, composed in 1893, about Platonus, an Egyptian nobleman who is condemned to death for accepting the faith of Jehovah instead of that of his ancestors. He formed the Freeman Grand Opera Company, which presented *The Martyr* at the Deutches Theater in Denver and, later, in Chicago, Cleveland, and Wilberforce, Ohio. The performance at Wilberforce is explained by his membership on the Wilberforce University faculty (1902–1904). Under the leadership of Beck the Cleveland Symphony performed scenes from *Zuluki* (1898), Freeman's second opera (originally known as *Nada*), in 1900.

Around Freeman's composing of "serious" larger works he spent several years composing (either individually or collectively) and conducting works in a lighter vein. His most notable activities in this area took place in the first decade of the twentieth century, during which he served for a brief period as music director of Chicago's Pekin Theater and was also music director of the road show John Larkins Musical Comedy. Freeman was music director for the noted entertainer Ernest Hogan's *Rufus Rastus* company (1906), composed the music for *Captain Rufus* (1907), and with James "Tim" Brymn composed the music for *Panama* (1908).

Freeman married singer/actress Carlotta Thomas from Charleston, South Carolina (year unknown). They had one child, Valdo Lee. Both mother and son starred in several of Freeman's operas, and Valdo produced and/or directed many of them.

As the 1910s approached, Freeman and his family moved to New York City. There, Freeman worked with the Bob Cole/Johnson Brothers' (J. Rosamond and James Weldon) *Red Moon* company. When *Red Moon* closed in 1910, Freeman moved on to other activities. He established the Freeman School of Music and the Freeman School of Grand Opera, served as choral conductor with the Negro Choral Society, organized the Negro Grand Opera Company, engaged in music criticism, and taught at the Salem School of Music.

Freeman received a William E. Harmon Foundation first-place award in 1930, resulting in a gold medal and $400 as "the composer of the first Negro grand opera." (Musicologist Eileen Southern, however, points out that this distinction belongs to John Thomas Douglass for *Virginia's Ball* in the 1860s.) Also in 1930 excerpts from nine of Freeman's fourteen operas were presented in concert at Steinway Hall in New York City.

Freeman himself was the librettist for most of his operas. Synopses of several appeared in historian Benjamin Brawley's essay "A Composer of Fourteen Operas," published in *Southern Workman* (July 1933). Brawley wrote, "Anyone who has opportunity to study his work at close range is amazed at his achievement and overwhelmed by the sheer power exhibited. His creative faculty is just now at its height. What he may yet produce in the years to come is beyond all estimate." Although the number of operas remained at fourteen, Freeman did many revisions of earlier ones.

Much of his recognition stemmed from the 1928 production of his opera *Voodoo* (1923), produced by Freeman himself at the Palm Garden in New York City, though he did not attain financial success from it or any of his other compositions. Performed by an "all-Negro cast of thirty" and an all-black orchestra, the presentation was reviewed by the *New York Times* (11 Sept. 1928). The reviewer said of the musical character of the work: "The composer utilizes themes from spirituals, Southern melodies and jazz rhythms which, combined with traditional Italian operatic forms, produces a curiously naive mélange of varied styles." An abridged version of *Voodoo* was presented on WCBS radio. In her 1936 publication *Negro Musicians and Their Music*, music historian Maud Cuney-Hare reported that Paramount Film Company "purchased 'Voodoo,' to be presented on the screen in a condensed version." There is no evidence that filming took place or that a film was released.

Other titles of Freeman's known operas are *An African Kraal* (1903), *The Octoroon* (1904), *Valdo* (1905), *The Tryst* (1909), *The Plantation* (1915), *Athalia* (1916), and *Vendetta* (1924). Brawley indicated that at the time of his *Southern Workman* article, Freeman was working on his fourteenth opera, *Uzziah*. Other works by Freeman include ballet music, a symphonic poem for chorus and orchestra, two cantatas, songs, and instrumental pieces. Freeman was guest conductor and music director of the pageant *O Sing a New Song* at the Chicago World's Fair in 1934. *The Martyr* was presented in concert at Carnegie Hall in 1947. Freeman died in his home in New York City.

Not only is Freeman important to the history of African-American music, but his work demands recognition in the annals of American music. As the first African American to attain any type of recognition and respectability as a composer of operatic compositions, he was an American pioneer. With little formal instruction, his accomplishments were all the more remarkable. To stage his productions, it was necessary to establish his own opera companies and schools; to finance the productions, it was necessary for him to teach and engage in less demanding theatrical activities. But Freeman never lost faith in himself and his many abilities, nor did he lose faith in the eventual eradication of a segregated system.

• Edward Ellsworth Hipsher, *American Opera and Its Composers* (1927), is an invaluable source on Freeman, containing much information by way of correspondence from Freeman himself. Eileen Southern, *The Music of Black Americans: A History* (1983), is an important source not only for information on Freeman but also for placing his contributions in historical context. Henry Sampson, *Blacks in Blackface: A Source Book on Early Black Musical Shows* (1980), treats Freeman's involvements in American musical theater. Benjamin Brawley's *Southern Workman* article offers a good overview of Freeman's "forty years . . . [of] earnest work in the field of opera." Celia Davidson, "Operas by Afro-American

Composers: A Critical Survey and Analysis of Selected Works" (Ph.D. diss., Catholic Univ., 1980), offers a valuable discourse on blacks in opera, including information on Freeman. An obituary is in the *New York Times*, 26 Mar. 1954.

D. ANTOINETTE HANDY

FREEMAN, James (22 Apr. 1759–14 Nov. 1835), minister, was born in Charlestown, Massachusetts, the son of Constant Freeman, a merchant, and Lois Cobb. Soon after his birth, the family moved to Boston and sent James to the prestigious Latin School and then to Harvard College, where he earned his A.B. in 1777. The following year he spent reading theology, for he had developed, along with a fascination for languages and mathematics, an abiding interest in religion.

By now Freeman had decided to become a minister, but the American Revolution postponed his seeking ordination. While he favored the colonial cause, he did not play an active role in the war. In 1780, when he was escorting his sister and brother to Quebec, where the family now lived, he was arrested when the ship reached port and was treated by the British as a prisoner of war. Eventually, however, he was paroled. He used this Quebec period to further his religious studies until June 1782, when he was able to return to Boston. That September the wardens of King's Chapel invited him to officiate as the chapel's reader for six months until he could be ordained as their minister. He immediately accepted the appointment.

King's Chapel was one of Boston's oldest and most important churches. Founded in 1686 as the first Episcopal church in New England, its congregation included royal governors and wealthy merchants. The American Revolution deeply affected the chapel. Because of their Loyalist views, many of its communicants and the minister had to flee Boston when the British evacuated the town. Those few who remained continued to worship, but after the war they and other Episcopal churches were forced to consider an American organization to replace the old Anglican administrative hierarchy. Thus, Freeman became the chapel's reader at a propitious time for change.

Freeman's own religious upbringing had been within Congregationalism, and he had sought a parish in that tradition. Obviously, however, the opportunity offered to a young man at King's Chapel was too good to ignore. His ministry was popular from its start, and by the end of the year he was writing his father that the church had grown from forty to eighty families. The satisfactory relationship that always existed between Freeman and his congregation helps to explain the ease with which Freeman was able to alter the liturgy used at the chapel. Yet his ministry had two trouble spots: his lack of ordination and his developing objections to the Trinity.

As his doubts about the validity of the Trinity became pressing, Freeman wondered about his future at the chapel. He considered resigning, but friends urged him to deliver a series of sermons explaining his problems with the doctrine. He did so, and on 19 June 1785 the Proprietors of the Pews voted to revise their

Book of Common Prayer, eliminating such items as the Nicene Creed, the Thirty-nine Articles, and references to the Trinity in the prayers and collects. In his changes Freeman had been especially influenced by the liturgical ideas of the English Unitarian minister Theophilus Lindsey and the English philosopher and theologian Samuel Clarke.

Freeman's ordination was particularly necessary for his performing the sacraments. The proprietors had voted on 21 April 1783 to call him as their pastor. For good reasons the American Episcopal church leadership was reluctant to authorize his ordination. Therefore, King's Chapel itself ordained him on 18 November 1787. So it was a lay ordination that, in the words of the ordination service, gave Freeman the right

to preach the Word of God, and to dispense lessons and instruction in piety, religion and morality, and to minister the holy sacraments in the congregation; and to do, perform and discharge all the other duties and offices which of right belong to any other rector, minister, public Teacher, Pastor, teaching Elder or Priest in orders.

This was an important act, and one thoroughly consistent with his Congregational background.

If King's Chapel was not the first Unitarian church in America as has been claimed, in 1785 it was the first parish to revise its prayer book and publicly adopt the Unitarian position on the Trinity. Throughout his career Freeman endorsed "liberal Christian" views (a contemporary Unitarian phrase) and was associated with those of similar opinion. He maintained for years an intimate friendship with the Reverend William Bentley, the noted Salem diarist, and with the British Unitarian William Hazlitt, with whom Freeman promoted the religious ideas of Joseph Priestly. In 1788 he married Martha Curtis Clarke, a widow. They had no children, but Freeman adopted Martha's one child from her first marriage. Their grandson James Freeman Clarke was a notable nineteenth-century Unitarian minister. Freeman continued as minister at King's Chapel until 1826, when ill health forced him to move to the country town of Newton, Massachusetts, where he died.

Even though Freeman's religious activities were many, he was still active in community affairs. He served on the Boston School Committee, helped to establish the Massachusetts Historical Society and was its recording secretary from 1798 to 1812, and was a member of the American Academy of Arts and Sciences and of the Massachusetts Constitutional Convention in 1820–1821.

Freeman lived in an age of growing political and religious liberalism, which was characterized by the rejection of the orthodox beliefs of earlier generations (in New England, the rejection of the older Puritanism). Early in his ministerial career he abandoned Trinitarianism in favor of Unitarianism, and he was the first to openly preach this view in New England. Yet his Socinian Christology (the view of Christ as simply a human being) was very different from the Arian Christology (the view of Christ as a supernatural being but below the Father) held by his contemporary liberal ministers in Boston, especially as reflected in the ministries of Charles Chauncy, Jonathan Mayhew, and William Ellery Channing. American Unitarianism developed from the Arian view, but eventually that position was abandoned by the Unitarians as they came more and more to emphasize the human Jesus. Clearly Freeman's position and example helped to make that possible.

• Manuscript material is at Dr. Williams' Library, London; Houghton Library, Harvard University; and the Massachusetts Historical Society. The records of King's Chapel for 1686 to 1899 are also housed at the Massachusetts Historical Society; they may be accessed through Deborah A. Cozort et al., comps., *Guide to the Archives of King's Chapel* (1979). Freeman's books are *Sermons on Particular Occasions* (1812) and *Eighteen Sermons and a Charge* (1829). The best assessment, if succinct, is Conrad Wright, *The Beginnings of Unitarianism in America* (1955), pp. 210–17. Respectful sketches of Freeman are F. W. P. Greenwood, *Massachusetts Historical Society Collections*, 3d. ser., 5 (1836). pp. 255–71; Samuel A. Eliot, *Heralds of a Liberal Faith*, vol. 1 (1910), pp. 1–19; William Ware, *American Unitarian Biography*, vol. 1 (1850), pp. 139–56; and William B. Sprague, *Annals of the American Unitarian Pulpit*, vol. 8 (1865), pp. 162–76. See also Greenwood, *A History of King's Chapel* (1833); Henry Wilder Foote, *Annals of King's Chapel from the Puritan Age of New England to the Present Day* (2 vols., 1882); and Foote, "The Historical Background of the Present King's Chapel," *Proceedings of the Unitarian Historical Society* 8, pt. 2 (1950): 34–46.

ALAN SEABURG

FREEMAN, John Ripley (27 July 1855–6 Oct. 1932), civil engineer, was born in West Bridgton, Maine, the son of Nathaniel Dyer Freeman and Mary Elizabeth Morse, farmers. He completed his secondary education at the public school in Lawrence, Massachusetts, where he worked during the summer as the assistant to Hiram F. Mills, a consulting engineer who designed factories and water power projects while also working as the chief engineer of the Essex Water Power Company. Freeman continued to spend his summers in this way while studying civil engineering at the Massachusetts Institute of Technology (MIT). After receiving his B.S. in 1876, he became both the assistant engineer at Essex and Mills's full-time assistant in his consulting firm.

In 1886 Freeman moved to Winchester, Massachusetts, to start his own consulting firm and to become the engineer and special inspector of factories for the Associated Factory Mutual Fire Insurance Companies. In 1887 he married Elizabeth Farwell Clark; they had seven children. As a consultant he specialized in projects involving water power, municipal water supply, and mill construction. In 1892 he determined the flow rate of water through the various sizes of pipes and pipe fittings, and these data were used by hydraulic engineers for planning purposes for a number of years afterward. In 1895 he was appointed to the Metropolitan Water Board of Massachusetts, a regional body whose task was to provide sufficient water for twenty-two cities in the Boston Vicinity by developing a plan to divert water from the Nashua River. As special inspector for Associated, he reorganized, trained, and supervised the companies' fire inspectors and conducted a number of experiments to determine the causes of industrial fires and prevent their outbreak. He also invented and patented a number of fire prevention devices, including a valve operating and indicator post, an automatic fire extinguisher, a hose nozzle, and a valve-controlling mechanism for sprinkler systems.

In 1896 Freeman moved to Providence, Rhode Island, to become the president and treasurer of the Manufacturers, Rhode Island, and Mechanics Mutual Fire Insurance Companies. In 1903 he also became the president and treasurer of the State, Enterprise, and American Fire Insurance Companies. He oversaw the consolidation of all six companies into the Manufacturers Mutual Fire Insurance Company. By 1932 he had developed a unique system of inspection and protection that resulted in a 93 percent reduction in the number of fires at Manufacturers-insured properties, a significant reduction in insurance rates, and a fivefold increase in the dollar value of the company's insurance in force. Meanwhile he continued to devote about half of his professional time to the Freeman Engineering Corporation, his growing consulting business. In 1899 he completed a survey of New York City's water supply. In 1903 he served as the chief engineer of the Charles River Dam Commission, which implemented the conversion of that river's lower estuary into a freshwater lake and park in Boston. That same year he became a member of the Commission on Additional Water Supply of New York City, commonly known as the Burr-Hering-Freeman Commission, which designed a system to bring water to the city from the Catskill Mountains. He also served as a consulting engineer during the system's construction.

From 1904 to 1905 Freeman designed waterpower development projects on the Feather River in California and on the St. Lawrence River in Canada. From 1905 to 1932 he was retained as a consultant by the New York State Board of Water Supply. From 1905 to 1908 he served on a federal advisory board to determine the location and type of canal to be built across the Isthmus of Panama, and in 1915 he advised the government concerning the general design of the locks and dams that would constitute the Panama Canal. He was one of three consultants in 1906 who developed plans to supply Los Angeles, California, with water and power that would be provided by the Owens River, located over 240 miles from the city. Freeman served as the senior consulting engineer in charge of the waterpower investigations of the New York State Board of Water Supply Commission in 1907–1908. He was a consultant between 1909 and 1912 to projects designed to increase the water supplies of seven cities in the United States and Mexico.

In 1910 Freeman designed the Hetch-Hetchy Valley water supply project for San Francisco, California,

and began consulting for the Canadian government on waterpower conservation. From 1917 to 1920 he was a member of the Chinese government's Grand Canal Improvement Board and in this capacity helped design the reconstruction of 400 miles of canal as well as flood prevention projects along the Yellow and Hwai rivers. From 1924 to 1926 he was a member of the Sanitary District of Chicago's Engineering Board of Review, which settled the controversy concerning the effect on the level of Lake Michigan that resulted from flushing the city's sanitary canal with lake water.

Freeman's work with water supply and flood control convinced him that a national hydraulic laboratory was essential to the development of a better understanding of river hydraulics, so in 1922 he began to campaign for its establishment. To this end he published four scholarly articles describing the need for a more scientific approach to these problems and made several trips to Germany and neighboring countries to examine existing laboratories. In 1929 he edited *Hydraulic Laboratory Practice*, a collection of articles by European hydraulic engineers that outlined the important work done in the field of hydraulic science in European laboratories. This work became a standard reference for hydraulic engineers in the United States. The result of his campaign was the construction in 1932 of the National Hydraulic Laboratory at the U.S. Bureau of Standards in Washington, D.C., and of two River Hydraulic Laboratories, one at MIT and one in Vicksburg, Mississippi—the latter under the auspices of the U.S. Army Corps of Engineers.

In 1930 Freeman, interested in earthquakes from an insurance point of view, issued a call to seismologists and geophysicists to disseminate data on the motion of earthquakes to civil engineers so that they could design quake-resistant buildings. As a result of his own studies on the subject, he concluded that the structural damage caused by an earthquake rarely exceeded 5 percent of a building's construction cost; by increasing this cost by 15 percent, a quake-resistant building could be constructed. In 1932 he brought Kyoji Suyehiro, the noted Japanese seismologist, to the United States for a lecture tour. That same year he published *Earthquake Damage and Earthquake Insurance*, a massive volume that came to be known as the "Encyclopedia of Seismology."

In 1890 and 1891 Freeman received the Norman Medal of the American Society of Civil Engineers (ASCE) for the best engineering article to appear in its *Transactions* for those years. He also received the Gold Medal of the American Society of Mechanical Engineers (ASME) in 1923 and the ASCE's J. James R. Croes Medal in 1931. He was awarded the United Engineering Society's John Fritz Medal in 1934 after his death. He served as the president of the Boston Society of Civil Engineering in 1893, the ASME in 1904–1905, and the ASCE in 1922–1923. He was the chairman of the National Advisory Committee for Aeronautics in 1918–1919. Freeman was elected to fellowship in the American Academy of Arts and Sciences and, in

1918, to membership in the National Academy of Sciences.

Freeman devoted much of his time to civic and professional organizations. From 1893 until his death he was a member of the Corporation of MIT and served on a number of visiting and advisory committees. In 1904 he was a member of the Rhode Island Metropolitan Park Commission and in 1911 prepared a study for improving the highways and parks on the east side of Providence. From 1917 to 1919 he was the president of the Providence Gas Company; he also served on the board of directors of that city's National Bank of Commerce from 1901 to 1922 and on the board of directors of the Rhode Island Hospital Trust Company from 1904 to 1916. He was a civilian member of the U.S. Army Gun Carriage Testing Commission and served as a member of the visiting committee of the Bureau of Standards for a number of years. He died in Providence.

Freeman made several important contributions to the development of American technology. He was one of the first engineers to recognize the critical importance of geological formations and to take them into consideration during the design phase of a construction project. He was also one of the first engineers to recognize the complexity of river hydraulics and to predict the ways in which a river would interact with an engineered structure by using scale models. He strove to educate other engineers regarding the importance of these factors through his publications and by promoting the establishment of a national hydraulic laboratory. He also made significant contributions to the field of fire prevention and control by inventing several pieces of firefighting apparatus and shedding light on the causes of many different types of industrial fires.

• Freeman's papers are located in the MIT Archives. A biography, which includes a complete bibliography, is Vannevar Bush, National Academy of Sciences, *Biographical Memoirs* 17 (1936): 171–87. An obituary is in the *New York Times*, 7 Oct. 1932.

CHARLES W. CAREY, JR.

FREEMAN, Joseph (7 Oct. 1897–9 Aug. 1965), writer, was born Joseph Lvovovitch in Ukraine, Russia, the son of Isaac Lvovovitch, a merchant, and Stella (maiden name unknown). After experiencing poverty and brutal anti-Semitism in Ukraine as a child, Freeman came to the United States in 1904 and grew up in Brooklyn, where he faced anti-Semitism from other immigrant groups and teachers. His father changed the family name after they immigrated. Growing up in a world where his father rose to become a prosperous builder, Freeman found himself combining aspirations for higher educational and professional status with a mix of socialist and labor Zionist beliefs. Influenced by this background, Freeman considered himself a socialist when he entered Columbia College in 1916 to study literature.

After graduating Phi Beta Kappa from Columbia in 1919, Freeman struggled, as he would for the next two decades, to integrate his political ideals and cultural aspirations with his desire for professional success. In 1920 he became a U.S. citizen and went to work for the conservative *Chicago Tribune/New York Daily News* press group, working on the *Tribune*'s Paris edition in 1920 and becoming correspondent for the group in London in 1921. However, he soon became a freelance writer, lecturer, and active member of the political wing of the "Lost Generation." In the early 1920s he worked as an editor for a radical cultural journal, the *Liberator*, and helped to found the *New Masses* (1926), which continued the tradition of the Socialist journal, the *Masses*, under Communist party USA (CPUSA) leadership and was to become very influential in the 1930s.

Freeman became part of the Lost Generation's cultural and political scene in New York, in which poets, writers, and artists fought furiously over questions of artistic and personal freedom, social liberation, and personal pleasure, a world he would chronicle in his memoir *American Testament* (1936). At the same time, he had his first major political breakthrough as a writer when he cowrote, with the well-known radical scholar and former Columbia professor Scott Nearing, a critique of U.S. foreign policy. Widely translated at the time, *Dollar Diplomacy* (1925) is still regarded as a classic expression of the economic interpretation of U.S. foreign policy.

Freeman also wrote literary criticism and poetry, became very involved with the cultural side of the Russian revolution, served briefly in 1924 as the publicity director of the then five-year-old American Civil Liberties Union (ACLU) and worked intermittently for the Soviet news agency Tass from 1925 to 1931. In 1926 he signed on as a seaman on the first U.S. ship to visit Russia after the revolution and served as Moscow correspondent for the *New Masses* for a year. Deeply involved in the movement for both socialism and the development of revolutionary aesthetics, Freeman coedited, with Joshua Kunitz, *Voices of October* (1930), the first complete treatment of the arts and the Russian revolution published by Americans. In 1931 he worked in Hollywood with the Soviet novelist Boris Pilnyak on *Soviet*, a screenplay for MGM that was never produced. Freeman believed political reasons stymied the film. In 1932 he married Charmion von Wiegand, an abstract artist; they did not have children.

As the depression radicalized many of his Lost Generation friends, Freeman intensified his work as an organizer, editor, and writer for the radical cultural movement of the 1930s. The CPUSA played a leading but complex role in this movement, seeking to achieve unity of action and to build trade unions among artists, while opposing both political and aesthetic defenders of its rivals on the left and all who championed art for arts sake. Freeman was active in the CPUSA-led cultural organization, the John Reed Clubs, and served as a founder and editor of the clubs' theoretical journal, *Partisan Review* (1934–1936), before it fell into the hands of leftist opponents of the CPUSA's cultural policies.

The publication of *American Testament* was initially greeted with critical acclaim; however, Soviet criticisms, which centered on both the work's romanticism and its failure to denounce Leon Trotsky, led both the CPUSA and Freeman himself to distance themselves from the work. In essence, Freeman's work captured the sensibility of popular front politics in the United States, which the CPUSA was leading, but ran afoul of the siege mentality of the Soviet purges, which the CPUSA was also supporting.

Critical of Soviet policies, but seeing the Communist movement as the only practical force for socialism, Freeman maintained his political commitments against the background of the Soviet purge trials and the Spanish Civil War. However, he left New York City to live, study, and write in the Catskill mountains near the writers colony of Woodstock, New York, believing that his political organizing and polemical writing had detracted from his aspirations to write literary history and major fiction.

Following renewed criticisms of his work from Soviet and CPUSA cultural figures and, more importantly, the German-Soviet pact nonaggression treaty of August 1939, Freeman broke with activist left politics. "That fall," he wrote a few years later, "all my connections with left publications and groups of every kind were completely severed." However, Freeman's influence with the left and work declined as he drifted away from the attempt to marry art to politics and came to concentrate on art and commerce.

During World War II, Freeman wrote articles for *Fortune* and *Reader's Digest* and fiction for *Harper's Magazine*, turning down a position as an aide to ambassador Joseph E. Davies, who respected his writing on the Soviet Union. Henry Luce also admired Freeman's writing; however, his hope to obtain a position with *Time* was dashed by *Time* editor Whittaker Chambers, a former associate on the *New Masses* who screened ex-Communists for the magazine. Freeman also returned to the ACLU to become its publicity director for another brief stint and served as a member of the editorial board of *Information Please* in 1944–1945.

In the 1940s Freeman's hopes to write important fiction were disappointed. His wartime *Never Call Retreat* (1943), chronicling the struggle throughout history between democracy and repressive authority, gained critical praise but had little impact. His postwar novel, *The Long Pursuit* (1947), was unsuccessful both commercially and critically. Yet, throughout his life Freeman maintained his interest in the arts, wrote poetry, and found positions in public relations to support himself, working for the public relations firm of Edward L. Bernay (1948–1952) and for Executive Research (1953–1961) and the American Pulp and Paper Association. Ironically, Freeman found himself doing the sort of advertising and organizational work for establishment commercial organizations that he had done for the radical cultural movement in the 1920s and 1930s.

While he survived the postwar anti-Communist repression without having to make ritualistic confessions before congressional committees (perhaps his lack of either political involvement or much success limited his value as a target), Freeman showed the effects of the Cold War more subtly. In the 1955 edition of *Contemporary Authors*, he wrote "I now feel that my experience in rhetoric, sociology, politics and journalism was something that I passed through on my way to my present view of the world. This is primarily mystical, with a complete acceptance of science."

Freeman died in New York City, while working on a satirical novel and other literary projects, just as another great upheaval, centered on civil rights and antiwar movements rather than on labor and antifascism, was taking shape and influencing the world of politics and culture. Malcolm Cowley, a colleague and peer in the 1930s, captured Freeman's role in the pre-Cold War U.S. cultural history perfectly when he wrote that Freeman was "a citizen of two worlds, the bohemian and the revolutionary [whose] essential position has always been that of a translator and an intermediary."

A prominent left literary intellectual and cultural activist of the 1930s, Joseph Freeman, like many others of his generation was largely forgotten in the postwar period, except in orthodox anti-Communist histories and remembrances, most prominently Daniel Aaron's *Writers on the Left* (1961), as an example of both Soviet domination of all aspects of the Communist movement and Communist exploitation of intellectuals.

• For those interested in Freeman, his *American Testament* (1936) is the best place to begin. Freeman's entries in the 1942 and 1935 editions of *Contemporary Authors* are also useful, as is Daniel Aaron's portrayal of him in *Writers on the Left* (1961). Obituaries are in the *New York Times*, 11 Aug. 1965, and *Publishers Weekly*, 6 Sept. 1965.

NORMAN MARKOWITZ

FREEMAN, Mary Eleanor Wilkins (31 Oct. 1852–13 Mar. 1930), author, was born in Randolph, Massachusetts, the daughter of Warren Wilkins, a carpenter, and Eleanor Lothrop. Until Freeman (the name she would adopt when she married in 1902) was fifteen, she and her family lived in Randolph, a rural town fourteen miles south of Boston. Her education and upbringing, with a strong religious emphasis, were conventional for the time and place. In 1867 the family moved to Brattleboro, Vermont, where Warren Wilkins became a partner in a dry goods store. In 1870 Freeman enrolled in Mt. Holyoke Female Seminary. The regimen there did not agree with her, however, and, in ill health, she withdrew after a year and settled down in Brattleboro, taking courses for another year at Glenwood Seminary in West Brattleboro. Although this ended her formal schooling, she continued her education through extensive reading of such authors as J. W. von Goethe, Ralph Waldo Emerson, Henry David Thoreau, and Sarah Orne Jewett.

Brattleboro, which had been a fashionable spa, retained a cultural atmosphere unusual in a town of its size. Among its natives were painters William Morris

Hunt and Robert G. Hardie, sculptor John Larkin Mead, Jr., and architect Richard Hunt. Though Freeman did not associate with these persons—most of them lived elsewhere at the time—she did benefit from the townspeople's respect for literature and the arts. She found others who shared her enthusiasm for reading, and she received local recognition when one of her earliest literary efforts, a short poem, was published in the *Century Magazine*. Among her friends were members of Brattleboro's most distinguished family, the Tylers. With one of them, Hanson Tyler, a young naval officer, she fell in love, but he did not reciprocate.

In 1873 Warren Wilkins's business failed. He returned to carpentry, and his wife became housekeeper for the Reverend Thomas Pickman Tyler, Hanson Tyler's father. With her husband and daughter, Mrs. Wilkins lived in her employer's house until her death in 1880. Meanwhile, Freeman did some schoolteaching, for which she soon found herself temperamentally unsuited. Trying her hand at writing, she slowly began to publish, first children's poems, some of which appeared in *St. Nicholas*. Though throughout her life she wrote and published poetry, her forte was prose fiction. In 1882 the *Boston Sunday Budget* published her first story for adults, "A Shadow Family," no copy of which exists, and the next year *Harper's Bazar (sic)* accepted her story "Two Old Lovers." That year her father died in Florida, where he was working on a construction job.

In 1884 the prestigious *Harper's New Monthly* printed Freeman's story "A Humble Romance." With her career as an author now well launched, she permanently returned that same year to her native Randolph, where she lived on a farm with the family of a childhood friend, Mary Wales. Here she had comfortable quarters in which to work and soon was sharing in the life of the villagers, many of whom were old acquaintances or relatives. The country and village folk here became models for those in her most successful fiction. Though neurasthenic and plagued by nightmares, she found security in sharing a household with intimate friends.

The arrangement with the Wales family lasted until Freeman's marriage in 1902. During this time Freeman produced volume after volume of short stories and several novels, most of them published by Harper & Brothers and its periodicals. Mary Louise Booth, editor of the *Bazar*, and Henry Alden, editor of *Harper's New Monthly*, became her close friends and, especially Booth, were helpful to her as literary advisors. Freeman's connection of almost fifty years with a major publisher was mutually advantageous. Her popularity grew in both the United States and Great Britain until she was one of the most widely read writers in English. Her critical reception, too, was highly favorable. William Dean Howells, advocate of literary realism, ranked her writings with "the best modern work everywhere in their directness and simplicity." He placed her best work on a level of excellence with that of Sarah Orne Jewett and Ivan Turgenev. Henry James admired her writing.

Though Freeman had a surprisingly shrewd business sense, she was somewhat retiring, shy, and unassertive. She had a number of close friends, but she shunned public appearances and moved only peripherally and somewhat uncomfortably in literary circles in Boston and New York. She refused to make pronouncements on public issues. She was extremely conscious of her personal appearance, especially of her clothes, and she cultivated a rather childlike, graceful beauty that earned her among her friends the sobriquet "Dolly."

Freeman's first two published volumes of fiction for adults—*A Humble Romance and Other Stories* (1887) and *A New England Nun and Other Stories* (1891)—are typical of her work and contain much of her best writing. Portraying people and places she had known in Vermont and rural Massachusetts, she wrote with direct, concrete language and convincing psychological insight.

The New England countryside and villages of which Freeman wrote were in severe economic decline. Many farmers had left for less sterile land in the West; the more ambitious young men and women had been lured to more lucrative jobs and more exciting lives in the cities. The population remaining on run-out farms and in decaying villages lived in varying degrees of material poverty and spiritual bleakness. Yet these people still retained, often in stunted or warped form, certain Puritan traits, especially the famed New England conscience and unyielding will and a conviction that poverty was a punishment decreed by God. These "exaggerations" or "abnormalities," to use Freeman's words, motivate the characters in much of her fiction. Graphic examples appear in "A Conflict Ended," "An Honest Soul," and "Gentian," all in *A Humble Romance*, and "A Solitary" in *A New England Nun*. Yet in some of her characters the Puritan traits have faded into a general impotence, as is the case with Louisa Ellis, the single woman in "A New England Nun," one of Freeman's finest stories in its delicate symbolism and evocation of setting. In other stories the will, far from being diseased or stunted, is alive and vigorous, as is the case in "A Taste of Honey" (*A Humble Romance*) and "The Revolt of Mother" (*A New England Nun*); here, determined women prevail against formidable odds. Among Freeman's male characters, strength of will is almost always expressed as an unproductive stubbornness or "setness." An exception is the title character in her play *Giles Corey, Yeoman*, who suffers death rather than admit to witchcraft in colonial Salem.

Freeman deals repeatedly with the conscience and will in overdeveloped or diseased forms, and she does so in depth in her three best novels—*Jane Field* (1893), *Pembroke* (1894), and *Madelon* (1896). *Pembroke* is particularly noteworthy for its literary merit as well as for its insights into the residual Puritanism in individuals and in a village community at large.

Two later novels—*Jerome: A Poor Man* (1897) and *The Portion of Labor* (1901)—focus on industrial strife in a mill town like those Freeman knew in eastern Massachusetts. But while the settings and most of the characters are convincing, Freeman seems unwilling or unable to analyze the root causes of the problems she describes or to suggest any feasible remedy for them.

During visits in the 1890s with the Alden family at their home in Metuchen, New Jersey, Freeman became engaged to Dr. Charles Manning Freeman, an intelligent and charming but rather fast-living and heavy-drinking bachelor seven years her junior. He held a degree from Columbia University's College of Physicians and Surgeons but no longer practiced medicine. The two were married on 1 January 1902, and thenceforth Freeman's home was in Metuchen. The marriage started auspiciously enough. Freeman continued to write, encouraged by her husband, who welcomed the added income her work brought in. But soon her husband's drinking worsened, and he required treatment in a sanatorium and later in the New Jersey State Hospital for the Insane. In 1921 the Freemans legally separated. He died in Metuchen in 1923. In his will, which was later successfully contested, Dr. Freeman left his wife one dollar.

During the first twelve years of her marriage, Freeman's prolific writing continued, although, with occasional exceptions, its quality was far below that of her earlier work. Among her later story collections, *Six Trees* (1903) and *The Winning Lady and Others* (1909) deserve attention. Among her late novels, *By the Light of the Soul* (1906) and *The Shoulders of Atlas* (1908) are the most interesting. In the former, the central character is guided through her life by recurring experiences of ecstasy and mystical insight. Some consider this work to be in part Freeman's spiritual autobiography. The novel is flawed, however, by a preposterous plot. *The Shoulders of Atlas* dramatizes various psychological stresses and abnormalities in a New England village and deals (rather daringly for the time) with the lesbianism of two of its characters. The novel was first published serially in the *New York Herald* as the American entry in an Anglo-American literary contest, in which Freeman would be pitted against British romance writer Max Pemberton. Freeman won the contest. Another literary stunt in which Freeman took part was a "cooperative novel" in which each of twelve well-known authors—among them William Dean Howells and Henry James—would contribute a chapter. The project was completed with the publication of *The Whole Family: A Novel by Twelve Authors* in 1908, but it contributed nothing to the participants' reputations.

In 1918 Freeman published her last book, *Edgewater People*, an undistinguished collection of short fiction. However, she still wrote occasionally for periodicals. But two honors awaited her: in 1926 the American Academy of Letters presented her with the William Dean Howells Gold Medal for Fiction, and the National Institute of Arts and Letters elected her to membership. She died in Metuchen.

At the time of her death Freeman's reputation was steadily declining. A few of her short stories were still being read, mainly in anthologies. Her fourteen novels, three dramas, and three volumes of poetry were virtually ignored. One problem was her prolixity: there was too much second-rate material from which to cull the first-rate. A more significant reason was the literary taste of the postwar period, which favored such authors as Sinclair Lewis, Ernest Hemingway, and F. Scott Fitzgerald and rejected what readers considered the sentimentality in much of Freeman's writing. Finally, "local color," which was wrongly taken to be Freeman's chief concern, had gone out of fashion.

Since World War II there has been a renewed interest in Freeman. Critics, increasingly recognizing that "local color" is mainly incidental to her work, have pointed to her psychological and sociological insights. In addition, her sympathetic understanding of the problems faced by rural and village women and of their determination in living with and overcoming them has attracted the attention of feminist critics, though Freeman herself denied being a feminist. New studies of her life and works have appeared, as have new collections and editions of her fiction.

• The most extensive collections of Freeman's letters and other papers are in the Butler Library, Columbia University, New York City, and in the Barrett Library at the University of Virginia. The only full-length biography of Freeman is Edward Foster, *Mary E. Wilkins Freeman* (1956). *The Infant Sphinx: Collected Letters of Mary E. Wilkins Freeman* (1985), edited by Brent L. Kendrick, contains all of Freeman's letters extant at the time of the book's publication. Perry D. Westbrook, *Mary Wilkins Freeman* (rev. ed., 1988), discusses Freeman's development and reception as a writer.

PERRY D. WESTBROOK

FREEMAN, Robert Tanner (c. 1846–10 June 1873), dentist, was born in Washington, D.C., the son of Waller Freeman. His mother's name is not known. His father, a carpenter in Raleigh, North Carolina, purchased his freedom from slavery in 1830. After purchasing his wife's freedom, he moved with her to Washington, D.C., where Robert T. Freeman was born, raised, and educated.

Freeman's early interest in medicine after high school led him to apply for a position as a dental assistant in the office of Dr. Henry Bliss Noble on Pennsylvania Avenue. Impressed by Freeman's determination and earnestness, Noble hired him and tutored him privately in the "art and science of the practice of dentistry." In light of strained race relations and rigid segregation in the nation's capital following the Civil War, it was unusual to have a "person of color" working in such close proximity to white patients in a dental office. Noble nevertheless encouraged Freeman to pursue a dental career through formal training.

When Harvard University established its School of Dental Medicine in 1867, Freeman applied. Harvard was the first nonproprietary dental school in America attached to a university. Freeman entered with the initial class of sixteen matriculants in 1868. In early

March 1869 he was one of only six who passed the first examination. On 10 March 1869 Freeman received the Doctor of Dental Medicine degree. In speaking of the school's first group of graduates, Dean Henry M. S. Miner of the Dental School noted that "Robert Tanner Freeman, a colored man who has been rejected by two other dental schools on account of his race, was another successful candidate. The dental faculty maintained that right and justice should be placed above expediency and insisted that intolerance must not be permitted. Dr. Freeman was the first of his race to receive in America a dental school education and dental degree."

After graduating from Harvard, Dr. Freeman moved back to Washington, D.C., and started his own dental practice on Pennsylvania Avenue. He developed a thriving practice, which lasted until his early death some fourteen years later.

The first dental society composed of African Americans, the Washington Society of Colored Dentists, was founded in 1900. In 1909 this society changed its name to honor America's first African American in dentistry. The Robert Tanner Freeman Dental Society has reached a membership of more than 600 dentists in the metropolitan Washington, D.C., area, becoming an active chapter of the National Dental Association established by African Americans in dentistry in 1913—forty years after the death of Robert Tanner Freeman.

• Biographical information can be found in two accounts by Clifton Orrin Dummett: *The Growth and Development of the Negro in Dentistry in the United States* (1952) and "Courage and Grace in Dentistry: The Noble-Freeman Connection," *Journal of the Massachusetts Dental Society* 44, no. 3 (Fall 1995): 23–26, 31.

ROBERT C. HAYDEN

FREEMAN, Thomas (?–8 Nov. 1821), surveyor, civil engineer, and explorer, was born in Ireland and immigrated in 1784 to America. Nothing is known of his parents, early life, or formal training, but he apparently had a background in the sciences. He may have acquired employment at Plymouth, Massachusetts, as an inspector and surveyor. In 1794 George Washington named him one of the surveyors of the site for Washington, the new capital city on the Potomac. Nothing is known about why Washington selected Freeman for this task. He served in the position for two years, although he did not actually complete the survey himself.

In 1796 Freeman became the U.S. surveyor of the boundary between Spanish Florida and the United States. He and Andrew Ellicott, a mathematician, arrived at Natchez—then part of Spanish Louisiana—on 24 February 1797. There Freeman met Philip Nolan, William Dunbar, and General James Wilkinson, all somewhat notorious for their exploration in the Southwest and their schemes to alienate territory from Spain. During the survey Freeman and Ellicott became bitter enemies, for Freeman claimed Ellicott's dalliance with a woman of questionable morals and past delayed the survey. Ellicott dismissed Freeman in November 1798 as a consequence of Freeman's open

criticism of his procrastination. Ellicott evidently feared that Freeman would inform Ellicott's wife of the episode, and thus he wrote to her saying that Freeman was "one of the greatest rascals and liars in existence." Ellicott preferred charges against Freeman presumably for insubordination and other irritations. Since the survey was being conducted in General Wilkinson's jurisdiction, Wilkinson presumably heard the charges and determined to dismiss them. No concrete evidence on this matter survives.

During 1798–1800 Freeman was at General Wilkinson's headquarters as supervising engineer during the construction of Fort Adams, located on the lower Mississippi River. Between 1800 and 1804, no specifics are known about Freeman's activities. Some sources indicate that he may have done some surveying in Tennessee and North Carolina and somewhat later journeyed up the Wabash River with Indiana territorial governor William Henry Harrison to parlay with Native Americans.

On 14 April 1804 President Thomas Jefferson appointed Freeman to explore the Red and Arkansas rivers in the newly acquired Louisiana Territory. The expedition did not immediately get under way, for in November 1805 Freeman journeyed to Washington to receive instructions from Jefferson on the work. Freeman chose a young naturalist, Peter Custis, who was pursuing medical studies at the University of Pennsylvania, to accompany him. Custis, although not officially a leader of the expedition, shared with Freeman the duties of keeping the expedition's journals. Jefferson named Captain Richard Sparks commander of the military contingent. Lieutenant Enoch Humphres, like Sparks serving at Fort Adams, was made second in command of the military group and was to take separate celestial readings to correlate with those of Freeman.

Freeman's original instructions from Jefferson included exploration of both the Red and Arkansas rivers, but Jefferson later reduced the scope of the expedition to the Red River only before it departed. The expedition was to make astronomical observations and accurate measurements of distance as it followed the Red River from its mouth to the remotest source of the main branch of the river. Members of the group were also to keep records on the soil, the appearance of the country, the animals and plants endemic to it, descriptions of minerals, and a meteorological chart.

Freeman led his expedition to the Red River during April 1806. With two flatboats, and with the assistance of twenty-four soldiers, Freeman headed up the Red River for three months, reaching approximately where the Oklahoma, Texas, and Arkansas boundaries would later meet. There several hundred Spanish soldiers, perhaps warned of Freeman's approach by the nefarious General James Wilkinson, known later as agent 13 in the Spanish secret service. Freeman was able to convince the Spaniards that he and the United States were not then a threat, and the Spanish commandant allowed Freeman to return to the United

States with his documents containing the information Jefferson had requested.

The Spanish government had evidently received information about several conspiracies originating in the United States that had as their purpose the separation of this area explored from Spanish control. In fact, the Spaniards were confused about U.S. intentions toward Texas and other regions. When Spanish authorities learned of Freeman's presence, they believed that the scientific exploration could simply be a euphemism for surveying a boundary that later allowed the United States to claim Spanish territory. Freeman's expedition was scientific only, however. Spanish interruption of his trip cut short his aim of following the Red River farther, and the party returned to Alabama, but the expedition provided new information about the river and the region.

In 1807 Jefferson appointed Freeman to survey the boundary between Alabama and Tennessee, surveying in the process the boundaries for the new Chickasaw treaty. On 10 January 1811 President James Madison appointed Freeman surveyor of public lands south of Tennessee. Government officials reviewed his work later and pronounced it "generally very correct." He died in Huntsville, Alabama.

Freeman was an ethical individual who throughout his career fought against the schemes of land speculators and others seeking personal profit. His explorations contributed to the growing knowledge of the region, and he deserves to be remembered as a significant frontier explorer and surveyor.

• An adaptation of Freeman and Custis's records of their expedition was published by Nicholas King in 1806 (or 1807) as *An Account of the Red River in Louisiana, Drawn Up from the Returns of Messrs. Freeman & Custis.* The original of this is in the Manuscripts Division of the Library of Congress. Custis's reports are in the records of the War Department at the National Archives and the Benjamin Smith Barton Papers at the Library of the American Philosophical Society in Philadelphia. Freeman's expedition journal seems to have been lost. An expanded version of the accounts, together with a lengthy introduction and epilogue by Dan L. Flores, has been published as Flores, ed., *Jefferson and Southwestern Exploration: The Freeman and Custis Accounts of the Red River Expedition of 1806* (1984). See also Joseph A. Stout, Jr., *Frontier Adventurers, American Exploration in Oklahoma* (1976). An obituary is in the (Huntsville) *Alabama Republican,* 9 Nov. 1821.

JOSEPH A. STOUT, JR.

FREER, Charles Lang (25 Feb. 1854–25 Sept. 1919), art collector and museum founder, was born in Kingston, New York, the son of Jacob R. Freer, variously a horseman, innkeeper, and farmer, and Phoebe Jane Townsend. At age fourteen, Freer left school to work in a cement factory; he later became an office clerk for Frank J. Hecker, the director of a local railway. In 1876 Freer followed Hecker to Logansport, Indiana, to work for the Detroit, Eel River and Illinois Railroad, and in 1880 they went together to Detroit to incorporate a company that manufactured rolling stock. In 1892 the Peninsular Car Works merged with its Detroit competition, and in 1899 Freer engineered the consolidation of thirteen car-building companies, including his own, to create the American Car and Foundry Company. At the age of forty-five, he retired from active business to pursue a career in connoisseurship.

Freer began collecting books and European prints during his early years in Detroit, and through his work for the art committee of the Detroit Club became acquainted with several leading American artists. In 1889 he bought his first oil paintings and the following year commissioned Philadelphia architect Wilson Eyre to design a house for him on Ferry Avenue. He would live alone—he never married—for the rest of his life. By 1893 Freer had assembled a small but important collection of contemporary American paintings, largely by Dwight William Tryon, Thomas Wilmer Dewing, Abbott Handerson Thayer, and James McNeill Whistler. After visiting the World's Columbian Exposition in Chicago, he concluded that the work of those four artists was "the most refined in spirit, poetical in design and deepest in artistic truth of this century," a conviction that set the course for much of his future collecting.

Of those artists, to Freer's mind, Whistler ranked supreme. Freer bought his first Whistler etchings from a New York dealer in 1887; three years later, in London on business, he sought out the artist himself to forge a "mutually advantageous" arrangement, wherein he agreed to purchase at least one impression of every new print that Whistler produced. Freer's holdings of Whistler etchings and lithographs eventually exceeded 900 impressions. In 1892 Freer acquired *Variations in Flesh Colour and Green: The Balcony*, thus making it the first of Whistler's major works to be held in an American collection. Seven years later Whistler proposed that Freer build "a fine collection of Whistlers!!—perhaps *the* collection." Consequently, Freer assembled some 1,200 examples from every phase of Whistler's career, including the artist's only surviving interior decoration, *Harmony in Blue and Gold: The Peacock Room.*

Whistler played another role in Freer's life by encouraging his interest in the art of China and Japan. On his first trip to Asia in 1894, Freer traveled as a tourist and bought little of lasting importance. But in 1901 he met Ernest F. Fenollosa, an authority on the art of Japan, who guided him through the largely unexplored realm of Asian art. Consequently, by the time Freer made his second Asian tour in 1906–1907, he was equipped with specialized knowledge and the tools of connoisseurship and was well prepared to make significant acquisitions of Japanese art, largely from private collections. In Egypt, depending entirely on his instincts, Freer purchased the biblical text now known as the Washington Manuscript of the Gospels. His holdings expanded to include Korean porcelain and Indian paintings, and in 1908 he traveled to West Asia specifically to study the eleventh and twelfth-century Syrian pottery known as Rakka ware, which in his opinion was possibly Babylonian. The next year he spent two months in China as the first westerner to search "scientifically and determinedly," as he phrased it, for early Chinese paintings. "The result," he wrote from China, "carries me off my feet and almost out of my head." By the time he made his final trip to China in 1910, Freer had become an internationally recognized connoisseur of Asian art, with a collection that outranked in size and quality any other private holding in the United States.

Freer's idea of presenting his art collections to the nation probably arose from discussions with Whistler, who would have had ideas of his own about preserving "*the* collection" for posterity. In 1904, the year after Whistler's death, Freer formally offered his holdings to the Smithsonian Institution. "My great desire," he wrote, "has been to unite modern work with masterpieces of certain periods of high civilization harmonious in spiritual and physical suggestion, having the power to broaden aesthetic culture and the grace to elevate the human mind." His gift, which included funds for a building, was accepted on 24 January 1906; it was the largest single art donation ever made by a private citizen. Freer, however, retained possession of his collection and spent the remaining thirteen years of his life "refining" it; because he considered his holdings "harmonious and allied in many ways," Freer stipulated that the collection as he composed it should never be altered.

In 1913 Freer commissioned architect Charles Adams Platt to design the gallery in Washington, D.C., that was to house his collections. Construction began in 1916 but slowed down during the First World War, and Freer did not live to see its completion. In failing health in 1916, he took up residence in a New York hotel but continued to collect, primarily ancient Chinese jades and bronzes. Three months before he died, Freer appended a codicil to his will making provisions for occasional acquisitions of Asian and Near Eastern art. The restriction on the American collection remained intact, as did two other conditions originally imposed on his gift to the nation: that nothing in the collection ever be lent for exhibition elsewhere and that nothing but works in the collection ever be exhibited in the Freer building. When Freer died in New York City, he left some 9,000 works of Asian and American art. The Freer Gallery opened to the public on 2 May 1923 as the first national museum devoted exclusively to the fine arts.

• Freer's personal and business correspondence, collection inventories, invoices, pocket diaries, press cuttings, and vintage photographs are preserved in the Charles Lang Freer Papers, Freer Gallery of Art, and Arthur M. Sackler Gallery Archives, Smithsonian Institution, Washington, D.C. Thomas Lawton and Linda Merrill, *Freer: A Legacy of Art* (1993), provides a comprehensive account of Freer's life as a collector. *With Kindest Regards: The Correspondence of Charles Lang Freer and James McNeill Whistler, 1890–1903*, ed. Linda Merrill (1995), traces Freer's relationship with Whistler and its consequences. A special issue of *Apollo* (Aug. 1983), "Charles Lang Freer as a Connoisseur," contains articles on Freer's holdings of Chinese, Japanese, Korean, Indian, Egyptian, Byzantine, and American art. Impor-

tant assessments of the collection by Freer's contemporaries include Ernest F. Fenollosa, "The Collection of Mr. Charles L. Freer," *Pacific Era*, Nov. 1907, pp. 57–66; Louisine Havemeyer, "The Freer Museum of Oriental Art," *Scribner's Magazine*, May 1923, pp. 529–40; Leila Mechlin, "The Freer Collection of Art: Mr. Charles L. Freer's Gift to the Nation," *Century Magazine*, Jan. 1907, pp. 357–70; and Agnes E. Meyer, "The Charles Lang Freer Collection," *Arts* (Aug. 1927): 65–82. An obituary is in the *New York Times*, 26 Sept. 1919.

LINDA MERRILL

FREETH, George Douglas (8 Nov. 1883–7 Apr. 1919), surfer, was born in Honolulu, Hawaii, the son of an English sea captain and a Hawaiian princess whose names are unknown. At the time of his birth, New England missionaries had succeeded in banishing surfing from most of the local island population. A noticeable exception to the surfing ban were members of the royal Hawaiian family. Given his royal status (Freeth's mother was raised by Queen Liliuokalani, the last of the Hawaiian royal rulers), and inspired by ancient paintings of Hawaiian royals surfing the waves of Waikiki Beach, Freeth took up the sport at an early age.

While the sport of surfing itself bordered on extinction at the turn of the century, Freeth's extraordinary surfing skills became internationally known through the colorful writings of Jack London. Describing the beauty and bliss of watching Freeth, whom he called the "Brown Mercury," London helped to foment worldwide interest in the sport. Another island visitor, railroad magnate and southern California land developer Henry E. Huntington, was so impressed with Freeth's prowess in the water that in 1907 he invited the "King of the Surfers" to southern California to demonstrate his surfing skills in front of large crowds. In addition, Freeth was guaranteed additional employment as a lifeguard and swimming instructor at Huntington's massive new saltwater plunge in Redondo Beach, California.

Freeth's arrival in southern California in 1907 would turn the course of American aquatic history. Not only would Freeth be the first to popularize the sport of surfing for Americans, he also would gain fame as the preeminent water polo player of his time and develop a reputation as one of the era's greatest swimmers. Surfing legend and swimming gold medalist Duke Kahanamoku, who was once coached by Freeth, called his mentor "the greatest swimmer of his day." Freeth's greatest calling, however, was the protection of human life against drowning, and he was a tireless educator on behalf of water safety. Besides promoting water safety through hands-on instruction, such as teaching hundreds of American swimmers the speedy Australian (freestyle) crawl, Freeth worked tirelessly to create well-trained and disciplined professional lifeguards who would patrol popular swimming beaches.

It was as a working ocean lifeguard that Freeth again attracted national attention. On the afternoon of 16 December 1908 a sudden and violent storm hit Santa

Monica Bay. Stationed at the Venice Pier with other members of the U.S. Volunteer Lifesaving Corps, Freeth spotted several fishing vessels in distress. According to eyewitnesses and newspaper accounts, Freeth, without concern to the odds against him, jumped into the raging sea and swam against massive waves and gale-force winds in an attempt to rescue members of the doomed boats. As fellow lifesavers aided his efforts, Freeth repeatedly swam out from shore to rescue a total of eleven fishermen. For his actions, Freeth was awarded a congressional gold medal for valor.

Despite public acclaim for his surfing and lifesaving skills, Freeth was known to be humble. Rather than rest on his laurels, he seemed driven to share his water expertise wherever he went. In the Los Angeles area alone, Freeth served as a swimming instructor at both the Redondo and Venice Beach Plunges, as well as the Los Angeles Athletic Club. Under his tutelage several swimmers became American record holders. In addition, Freeth coached fellow Hawaiian Kahanamoku and young Redondo Beach protégé Ludy Langer to several world record swims. While proud of his swimmers' accomplishments, Freeth seemed more intent on encouraging his swimmers to use their aquatic skills in public service as ocean lifeguards. Many of those who learned to swim under Freeth would later become the nuclei of well-trained, year-round, professional ocean lifeguard services.

Sadly, much like the life of an ancient Greek hero, Freeth would die an early but heroic death. At age thirty-five, after performing numerous ocean rescues in chilly springtime waters off San Diego, Freeth succumbed to pneumonia. He had never married. The ashes of America's first surfer and California's first professional ocean lifeguard were returned to his native Hawaii.

Freeth was once popularly billed as the "man who can walk on water," and his contributions to the sport of surfing and to the profession of ocean lifesaving earned him legendary status among surfers and ocean lifeguards worldwide. In remembrance of his public service and his many aquatic accomplishments, a bust of Freeth was placed on the Redondo Beach pier, very near the site of where the sport of surfing first came to the shores of the United States.

• Legendary surf historian John Heath "Doc" Ball once wrote of Freeth, "Too little is known today about this great and colorful figure." Freeth himself wrote several brief articles for the Los Angeles Athletic Club magazine *Mercury*; these appear in the magazine's volumes for the years 1913, 1914, 1915, and 1919, along with other stories written about Freeth. Accounts of Freeth's legendary rescue of 16 Dec. 1908 can be found in both the *Los Angeles Times* and *Daily* (now *Evening*) *Outlook*, 17 and 18 Dec. 1908. Secondary sources regarding Freeth include Leonard Lueras, *Surfing: The Ultimate Pleasure* (1984); Dennis Shanahan, *Old Redondo* (1982); and Ball, *California Surfriders* (1979).

ARTHUR C. VERGE

FREI, Hans Wilhelm (29 Apr. 1922–12 Sept. 1988), theologian and intellectual historian, was born in Breslau, Germany, the son of Wilhelm Sigmund Frei, a venereologist, and Magda Frankfurther, a pediatrician. The family had become nominally Lutheran, and Frei was baptized in infancy, but they were Jewish by ancestry and thus fled to the United States in 1938.

Difficult financial circumstances, exacerbated by the illness and death of his father, forced Frei to choose the only college that offered him a scholarship, improbably to study textile engineering at North Carolina State University, where he received his B.S. in 1942. While at North Carolina State, he had become involved in a Baptist youth group, and at one of their meetings he heard a speech by H. Richard Niebuhr, then teaching theology at Yale. At Niebuhr's urging, Frei entered Yale Divinity School, from which he received his B.D. in 1945. After two years as minister of a Baptist church in North Stratford, New Hampshire, he decided to return to Yale to get a Ph.D. and to change his denominational affiliation to the Episcopal church.

He married Geraldine Frost Nye in 1948 (they had three children), was ordained an Episcopal priest in 1952, and received his Ph.D. in 1956, with a dissertation titled "The Doctrine of Revelation in the Thought of Karl Barth, 1909–1922: The Nature of Barth's Break with Liberalism," written under Niebuhr's direction. While working on his doctorate he taught at Wabash College (1950–1953) and the Episcopal Seminary of the Southwest (1953–1956) and then joined the faculty of Yale, where he remained until his death. Frei soon established himself as both a popular undergraduate teacher and a superb adviser of dissertations, and he served seven years as master of Ezra Stiles College and three years (1983–1986) as chair of the Yale religious studies department. His death, in New Haven, was sudden and unexpected.

Just after finishing his dissertation, Frei wrote two long chapters for *Faith and Ethics* (1957), the festschrift for Niebuhr edited by Paul Ramsey. But then he published virtually nothing for ten years, until *The Mystery of the Presence of Jesus Christ* appeared in 1967 as a series of articles in *Crossroads*, a Presbyterian adult education magazine. *The Eclipse of Biblical Narrative*, published in 1974, traced developments in biblical hermeneutics through the eighteenth and nineteenth centuries and was quickly recognized as a masterpiece of sensitive historical scholarship. Its historical analysis set a clearer context for *The Mystery*, which was republished in book form as *The Identity of Jesus Christ* in 1975.

The preface to *The Eclipse* mentions Erich Auerbach and Karl Barth as among the important influences on Frei's work. Auerbach was a literary critic whose masterpiece, *Mimesis*, published in 1946, surveys "the representation of reality in Western literature." His chapters on the Bible argue that the Scriptures present realistic narratives, which, unlike a novel, make the startling claim that the world they narrate is "the only real world. . . . All other scenes, issues, and ordinances have no right to appear independently of it" (p. 15). Auerbach draws no conclusions about the *truth* of the biblical claims; he simply asserts that this is their central *meaning*: the literal sense of the narratives and the claim that those narratives define the framework of all reality.

In the theological context of the 1960s, this was a challenging idea. Most biblical interpreters sought the meaning of the biblical narratives either in the moral or religious lessons they offered or in the historical information one could retrieve from them, but either way the narrative shape of the stories themselves got lost. In *The Eclipse*, Frei traces the history of how this had happened. Around the eighteenth century, Christian writers had begun to think of the world of their daily experience as the primary world, into which the world of the biblical narratives had somehow to be fit, rather than the other way round. That implied apologetics as a key theological task: one had to argue for the truth of the Bible by connecting its world to "ours," either by showing that its moral lessons applied to our lives or by defending some of its claims in terms of the canons of critical history.

Karl Barth, the great early twentieth-century Swiss theologian, had rejected apologetics as the starting point for theology. A Christian theologian, he said, should describe how the world looks from a Christian perspective, not begin with some other framework into which Christian claims need to be fit. In his multivolume *Church Dogmatics*, Barth does what Frei called "ad hoc apologetics"—he connects the world of the biblical narratives with all sorts of contemporary issues and experiences—but he does not let some other worldview serve as the foundation for his theological project. Therefore, Frei said, Barth can respect the integrity of the narrative character of Scripture because he is not trying to redefine its meaning in order to be able to argue on some extra-Christian grounds for its truth.

In a series of lectures delivered in the 1980s but not published until after his death in *Types of Christian Theology* (1992), Frei distinguishes two ways of thinking about theology: either as an academic discipline, subject to the academy's canons of rationality, or as an activity of the Christian community, whose rules emerge from its functions within that community. Among the five types of theology he defines across a spectrum from pure academic discipline to pure activity of the Christian community, Frei locates Barth and himself in the fourth, where the internal norms of the community have methodological precedence but where, in contrast to the purely internal description of the fifth type, theology keeps making ad hoc connections with philosophy, contemporary concerns, and all sorts of cultural phenomena.

Frei's work drew early attention to the importance of narrative, which, by the time of his death, had become a major theme in theology and biblical studies. His interpretation of Barth helped make that theologian again a creative influence in American theology. In 1984 Frei's longtime Yale colleague George Lindbeck published *The Nature of Doctrine*, in which Frei's work served as the prime example of a new "post-liberal" theological paradigm, though the increasing references to "narrative theology" or "the new Yale school" in the late 1980s made Frei nervous, particularly when he was identified as the founder of such a movement. He was conscious of his own differences from various colleagues at Yale, and he worried that much discussion of "narrative" in theology privileged it as *the* key category for understanding Scripture and indeed human experience. While Frei thought that realistic narratives have a central place in the Bible, he mistrusted the use of any category as a general hermeneutical principle.

• Frei's papers are collected in the Yale University Library. In addition to the books and essays already mentioned, a number of Frei's articles and lectures are collected in George Hunsinger and William C. Placher, eds., *Theology and Narrative* (1993), which also includes introductory and concluding essays on his life and work. An important piece on German critical scholar D. F. Strauss appears in vol. 1 of *Nineteenth-Century Religious Thought in the West*, ed. N. Smart et al. (1985). Garrett Green, ed., *Scriptural Authority and Narrative Interpretation* (1987), includes essays on Frei's works and a partial bibliography of them. An obituary is in the *New York Times*, 14 Sept. 1988.

WILLIAM C. PLACHER

FRELENG, Friz (21 Aug. 1906–26 May 1995), animator and producer of animated films, was born Isadore Freleng in Kansas City, Missouri. He developed his artistic skills without formal training and earned a living in his native Kansas City as a freelance artist. He married and had two daughters with his wife, Lilly. After moving to Hollywood in 1928, he joined the Walt Disney Studios, where many of the innovators of animation began their careers and honed their skills. The following year, he left Disney for a position with the Charles Mintz studios, where he worked on the Krazy Kat series. Freleng worked there for a year and then left Mintz studios to assist Hugh Harman and Rudolph Ising in creating the Warner Brothers Animation Studio in 1930. He remained with Warner Brothers as a pioneering animator, writer, producer, and director, ultimately running the animation studio.

Freleng's career developed and matured in tandem with the genre of animation itself. Early in his career he helped in the creation of the first talking-sync cartoon (1928). In his first years with Warner Brothers he was an animator for silent black and white cartoon shorts that played before feature films. In the early 1930s Freleng worked long hours to help produce the Looney Tunes and Merrie Melodies series, efforts that imitated the Mickey Mouse cartoons, which were the rage at the time. In 1933 Hugh Harman and Rudolph Ising left Warner Brothers, and Leon Schlesinger, the Warner studio executive responsible for cartoons, made Freleng the new head of the animation studio.

Within a few years the Warner Brothers studio, located in a building known as "Termite Terrace," combined the creative talents of Tex Avery, Chuck Jones,

Mel Blanc, Robert Clampett, Michael Maltese, Robert McKimson, and Frank Tashlin. Led by Freleng, the Warner Brothers team broke new ground and created a group of animated characters known throughout the world. Freleng personally created Yosemite Sam (whom Freleng resembled, with his red hair, mustache, and blustery personality) and directed the debut of Porky Pig. Along with the other artists of Termite Terrace he helped to create the most loved Warner Brothers character, the clever gray rabbit, Bugs Bunny.

The critical accolades earned by Freleng and the studio resulted from the bilevel perspective of many Warner films. For example, on one level, "Birds Anonymous," one of Freleng's Oscar-winning cartoons, is filled with the slapstick action of Sylvester, a cat attempting to quit eating birds. This level appealed especially to the younger part of the audience. On another level, the cartoon is a satire on humans trying to stop drinking alcohol, adding an adult-oriented and subtler humor to the feature.

The years of work in Warner Brothers Termite Terrace animation studio were not always harmonious. Freleng left Warner Brothers for a brief position with Quimby studios around 1939, but he returned in 1940 and stayed until the animation studio closed in 1963. The creative artists found themselves at odds with one another. Freleng, Chuck Jones, and Robert McKimson would all direct and produce, in a given year, films starring the studio's most popular character, Bugs Bunny. Freleng's temperament and role as a manager, in addition to the competition among creative teams, brought him into conflict with his collaborators. Despite the tension and close quarters in the studio, Chuck Jones and other artists maintained an admiration and respect for Freleng as a mentor.

After 1963 Freleng joined with David DePatie. DePatie-Freleng is best known for producing the Pink Panther, an animated cartoon that aired on Saturday mornings in the 1960s and 1970s. Freleng hired Robert McKimson to help produce this new creation. The studio had high hopes for its new character and its experienced animator. At the time of this new endeavor Freleng had to contend with an industry quite different from that of his early days with Warner Brothers. The animation industry changed to accommodate the demands of television and as a result cartoons had to be done in volume with less attention to detail and lower visual quality. Despite the lowering of quality in animation, DePatie-Freleng's Pink Panther remained one of the most creative products of its time. Freleng died in Los Angeles.

Friz Freleng's fame stems from his role in producing animated films and developing a style that revolutionized cartoons. He was at the forefront of the use of music with animation, and he developed a uniquely explosive slapstick style, aiming his gags and stories at children and adults simultaneously. Moreover, he managed a team of talents that set the new standards of animation in the color, talking era of cartoons, especially in their move from cinema to television. By the conclusion of his career he had worked on more than three hundred cartoons and had won five Oscars, three Emmys, and awards from the Motion Picture Screen Actors Guild and the International Animated Film Society. Through his ground-breaking work with Warner Brothers and at the close of his career with DePatie-Freleng, he helped to set the artistic standard of animation during a half-century of change in television and media communication. His cultural impact has less to do with his many awards than with the timeless animated characters he helped bring to life. He has also served as mentor to a younger generation of animation artists. One could fault Freleng's work for its violence and for some characters that were stereotypes of Africans and Asians, but most of his film catalog is critically valuable and continues to entertain audiences of various ages years after it was produced.

• An oral history from Freleng is held at the University of California at Los Angeles. Some examinations of his working life are Joe Adamson, *Bugs Bunny: Fifty Years and Only One Grey Hare* (1990); Warren Spector, "The Warner Brothers Cartoon: A Critical History" (M.A. thesis, Univ. of Texas at Austin, 1980); Greg Ford, "Warner Brothers," *Film Comment* 11, no. 1 (1975): 10–16, 93. There are also interviews with Freleng's coworkers in that issue: Joe Adamson, "Well, for Heaven's Sake! Grown Men!" pp. 18–20, and Greg Ford and Richard Thompson, "Chuck Jones," pp. 21–38. See also Chuck Jones, "Friz Freleng and How I Grew," *Millimeter* 4, no. 1 (1976). On the development of the cartoon during Freleng's career, see Gerald Peary and Danny Peary, eds., *The American Animated Cartoon* (1980).

JAMES H. TUTEN

FRELINGHUYSEN, Frederick Theodore (4 Aug. 1817–20 May 1885), senator and secretary of state, was born in Millstone, New Jersey, the son of Frederick Frelinghuysen, a lawyer, and Jane Dumont. Only three years old when his father died, he was sent to Newark to live with his distinguished uncle, Theodore Frelinghuysen, then attorney general of New Jersey. Frederick graduated from Rutgers in 1836, studied law with his uncle, and launched his legal career in 1839. He married Matilda Griswold in 1842; they had six children.

The combination of Frederick Frelinghuysen's own abilities and his family's influence—the Frelinghuysens have been described as the "aristocracy of New Jersey"—led him to public office on the local level. In the 1850s, while he continued to represent such major corporate clients as the New Jersey Central Railroad and the Morris Canal and Banking Company, he served as Newark city prosecutor and as a member of the city council. His party allegiances reflected the rapidly changing political situation of that decade. Along with many of his contemporaries, he quit the Whig party, as it disintegrated in the early 1850s, and eventually moved into the new Republican party. Frelinghuysen did not participate as a "founding father" of the new party, however, because he agonized for several years over his decision to abandon the Whigs.

His family felt a unique attachment to the party, which had offered the nation the ticket of Henry Clay for president and Theodore Frelinghuysen for vice president in the election of 1844. By 1860, however, Frederick Frelinghuysen enthusiastically supported the Republicans and endorsed Abraham Lincoln in his bid for the presidential nomination.

In February 1861, as civil war threatened, Frelinghuysen served as one of New Jersey's representatives at an ill-fated "peace conference" in Washington. Prominent statesmen from some twenty states, determined to arrive at a position that would satisfy both sides and somehow avoid hostilities, found little support in either the North or the South. At the same time, Frelinghuysen began to follow closely in his uncle's political footsteps. First, he agreed to serve as attorney general of New Jersey, remaining in that office through the Civil War. (Theodore Frelinghuysen had used the same position as a springboard for national office, representing New Jersey in the Senate between 1829 and 1835.) Frederick Frelinghuysen moved onto the national political scene as well in 1866. The governor of New Jersey appointed him to fill out an unexpired term in the U.S. Senate; the state legislature endorsed him.

Over the next two decades, Frelinghuysen's political fortunes reflected the struggle between Democrats and Republicans in New Jersey, one of only four "swing" states—along with Connecticut, Indiana, and New York—which could be carried by either party in the late nineteenth century. He played a prominent role in the continuing struggle for control of the Republican party at the national level and in the ongoing effort to keep the Democrats out of the White House. Establishing his credentials as a Radical Republican, those in Congress who demanded civil rights and voting rights for former slaves, Frelinghuysen supported the bill that granted voting rights to African Americans in Washington, D.C., in December 1866. He participated in the impeachment trial of President Andrew Johnson in 1868 and, along with all but a handful of Republican senators, voted to convict the president. When his interim term in the Senate expired in 1869, the Democrats were in control of the New Jersey legislature and selected one of their own to replace Frelinghuysen.

The following year President Ulysses S. Grant asked Frelinghuysen to accept the nation's most prestigious diplomatic post—to serve as minister to Great Britain. He refused, apparently because he wanted to remain in New Jersey and make himself available in 1871 for the opportunity to return to the Senate. Indeed, the Republicans regained control of the legislature and awarded Frelinghuysen his own term in the Senate. Frelinghuysen continued to identify with the Radical Republicans and supported the Civil Rights Act of 1875. He also served as one of five senators—along with five members of the House of Representatives and five justices of the Supreme Court—on the Electoral Commission that determined that Republican Rutherford B. Hayes had won the disputed presidential election of 1876. Once again, when Frelinghuysen's term expired in 1877, the Democrats controlled the legislature. Frelinghuysen, about to turn sixty, seemed to have no further political ambitions; he returned to New Jersey to practice law.

Once President Hayes made it clear that he would not seek a second term, the jockeying for the Republican presidential nomination in 1880 saw the party split into two factions in the late 1870s. The "Stalwarts" favored the nomination of Grant for an unprecedented third term as president. The "Half Breeds" were convinced that the nomination of Grant had to be prevented. Frelinghuysen supported the Stalwarts, joining Americans from all walks of life who chose to ignore Grant's failures as president and maintained faith in the man who had led the nation to victory in the Civil War. Frelinghuysen could not have known that his Stalwart credentials—and fate—would soon lead him back to Washington to serve as secretary of state in a Stalwart administration.

The Republican National Convention of 1880 was deadlocked through thirty-five ballots, until Half Breed candidate James G. Blaine threw his support to James A. Garfield. When the Half Breed Garfield won the nomination on the next ballot, the delegates tried to heal the wounds in the party by selecting the Stalwart Chester A. Arthur as his running mate. As president-elect, Garfield then solidified ties to the Half Breeds by appointing Blaine secretary of state.

The assassination of President Garfield put Arthur in the White House on 20 September 1881. Arthur knew that if he were to seek the presidential nomination in 1884, Blaine would be his most serious rival, but Arthur allowed Blaine to remain on as secretary of state for another three months. In that period, Blaine established his reputation as "Jingo Jim," launching a spirited foreign policy that became part of the struggle between Half Breeds and Stalwarts before the Republican National Convention of 1884. In any case Blaine clearly placed new emphasis on increasing American commerce and prestige in the hemisphere, while he moved toward control of any Central American canal. Blaine informed the British government that the United States wished to terminate the Clayton-Bulwer Treaty of 1850, which stipulated that the two nations would cooperate on building a canal in Central America. Shortly thereafter he extended invitations for the first Pan-American Conference. Finally, Blaine declared Hawaii "essentially part of the American system."

The Stalwart Frelinghuysen took over the State Department on 19 December 1881 and moved quickly to deal with the Blaine legacy. While both Arthur and Frelinghuysen may have supported some of Blaine's initiatives, they did not want to boost his reputation. In Frelinghuysen's case, it is clear that he intended to put his own stamp on American foreign policy. In 1882–1883, he withdrew the invitations for the Pan-American Conference while he systematically reviewed all aspects of Blaine's policies. At the same time Frelinghuysen took his own approach toward increasing American influence in the hemisphere. Clearly, he agreed with Blaine on the importance of a Central American canal. Thus he began negotiations with Mexico and Spain on behalf of Cuba and Puerto Rico for what he hoped would be the first two in a series of treaties establishing commercial reciprocity with the nations ringing any future canal in the Caribbean.

At the Republican National Convention of 1884, Blaine led President Arthur from the first ballot. The Half Breeds finally secured a presidential nomination for Blaine, only to see a deeply divided Republican party then lose the White House for the first time since the Civil War. In the aftermath of the presidential election, Frelinghuysen, now officially a lame duck, launched his own version of a vigorous foreign policy. Building on Senate ratification in March of the reciprocity treaty with Mexico, the Arthur administration signed similar treaties with Spain and the Dominican Republic and agreed to renew an existing reciprocity treaty with Hawaii. At the same time Frelinghuysen moved beyond Blaine in his determination to obtain a Central American canal. Ignoring the Clayton-Bulwer Treaty, he negotiated the Frelinghuysen-Zavala Treaty with Nicaragua, acquiring for the United States control of a strip of land two and a half miles wide. All four treaties were signed in a period of less than three weeks, between 18 November and 6 December.

It was too late, however, for Frelinghuysen to establish a reputation as an architect of the "new empire" that the United States began to create in the late nineteenth century. While the treaty with Hawaii would be renewed in 1887, the Senate never considered the agreements with Spain and the Dominican Republic, and the House of Representatives never approved enabling legislation to implement the treaty with Mexico. When the Senate voted on the Frelinghuysen-Zavala Treaty in January 1885, a majority approved—but the treaty did not receive the two-thirds vote required. Frelinghuysen did not get to participate in the heated national debate over expansion into the Caribbean and the Pacific. He died in Newark within three months of the end of the Arthur administration.

• The Manuscript Division of the Library of Congress holds some 700 items relating to Frelinghuysen's service as secretary of state. John William Rollins, "Frederick T. Frelinghuysen, 1817–1885: The Politics and Diplomacy of Stewardship" (Ph.D. diss., Univ. of Wisconsin, 1974), is the only study of Frelinghuysen's life. On his contributions as secretary of state, see Justus D. Doenecke, *The Presidencies of James A. Garfield and Chester A. Arthur* (1981); Walter LaFeber, *The New Empire: An Interpretation of American Expansion, 1860–1896* (1963); and David M. Pletcher, *The Awkward Years: American Foreign Relations under Garfield and Arthur* (1962).

ALLAN BURTON SPETTER

FRELINGHUYSEN, Theodore (28 Mar. 1787–12 Apr. 1862), lawyer, politician, and educator, was born in Franklin Township, Somerset County, New Jersey, into one of New Jersey's most prominent families. His great-grandfather, Theodorus Jacobus Frelinghuy-

sen, participated prominently in the eighteenth-century religious movement known as the "Great Awakening"; his father, Frederick Frelinghuysen, served as a captain of artillery at the battles of Trenton and Monmouth and later was a Federalist U.S. senator. His mother, Gertrude Schenck, died when he was a boy, and the chief feminine influences in young Theodore's life were his stepmother, Ann Yard, and his paternal grandmother, Dinah Frelinghuysen, both women of strong Christian convictions. His education prepared him for the kind of leadership expected of his social class: the Reverend Robert Finley's Academy at Basking Ridge, College of New Jersey (now Princeton University) class of 1804, and law study with Richard Stockton (1764–1828). He began practicing law in Newark in 1808 and the following year married Charlotte Mercer. Although their marriage would last until her death in 1854, they had no children other than adopted nieces and nephews (among whom was Frederick T. Frelinghuysen, future secretary of state).

Well connected, ambitious, and able, Frelinghuysen began a successful political career in his late twenties. In a politically confusing time, he steered an ideologically consistent course, from Federalist to National Republican to Whig. A legislative alliance of Federalists and dissident Jeffersonian Republicans elected him attorney general of New Jersey in 1817, a post he held until 1829, when a National Republican legislature sent him to the U.S. Senate for one term. As a senator, he was not a front-rank leader, but he gained the respect of members of both parties. His six-hour speech against the Jackson administration's plan to uproot the Cherokee Indians from their ancestral lands in northern Georgia earned him national fame and the nickname "Christian Statesman" as well as a laudatory poem by William Lloyd Garrison. Typical for one of his political persuasion, he attacked Sunday mail delivery and refused to obey instructions from a Democratic New Jersey legislature to vote for removal of federal funds from the Bank of the United States. Such independence, along with the enmity of the Hicksite Quakers of West Jersey, cost him his Senate seat. He returned to New Jersey and held his last political office in the late 1830s as mayor of the newly incorporated city of Newark.

A man of deep Christian piety, Frelinghuysen was forever active in Presbyterian church affairs and the benevolent societies that played such an important role in antebellum American life. At various times he was president of the American Board of Commissioners for Foreign Missions, the American Bible Society, and the American Tract Society; vice president of the American Sunday School Union; and an officer of the American Colonization Society and the American Temperance Union. While in the Senate, he founded the Congressional Temperance Union. One cause he never took up was that of the abolitionists. Although there is abundant evidence of Frelinghuysen's hatred of slavery, as a former pupil of Robert Finley he remained convinced that colonization, accompanied by emancipation, was the only morally acceptable solution to the evil.

In 1844, after Frelinghuysen had been out of politics for six years, the Whig nominating committee chose him as Henry Clay's running mate in the presidential election. His unblemished moral reputation was considered attractive to the Christian reform wing of the party, and his eastern background provided the obligatory regional balance. The Democrats campaigned for the Irish vote by portraying Frelinghuysen as an extreme Protestant whose leadership in benevolent societies was aimed at destroying Hibernian devotion to Catholicism and liquor. In a postelection letter to Clay, Frelinghuysen attributed James K. Polk's victory to immigrant bloc voting and confusion caused by the abolitionist Liberty party.

The vice presidential candidacy notwithstanding, in 1839 Frelinghuysen had effectively abandoned law and politics. He gave serious thought to studying for the ministry but instead accepted an appointment as chancellor of New York University. He remained there until 1850, at which time he became president of Rutgers College in New Brunswick, New Jersey. He was not as successful in those positions as in his previous careers. His educational philosophy was old-fashioned, and his fundraising objectives at both institutions were only partially achieved. Nonetheless, his last years were happy, largely owing to his marriage to Harriet Pumpely in 1857. He died in New Brunswick, New Jersey, while still president of Rutgers.

• There are several collections of papers pertaining to Frelinghuysen's personal and professional affairs in the New Jersey Historical Society in Newark and the Alexander Library at Rutgers University. A chronological listing of published speeches may be found in the bibliography of Robert J. Eells, *Forgotten Saint: The Life of Theodore Frelinghuysen; A Case Study of Christian Leadership* (1987). Talbot W. Chambers, *Memoir of the Life and Character of the Late Hon. Theo. Frelinghuysen, L.L.D.* (1863), should also be consulted, as well as Joseph Folsom, ed., *The Municipalities of Essex County, New Jersey*, vol. 3 (1925). Frelinghuysen is mentioned frequently in Herbert Ershkowitz, *The Origin of the Whig and Democratic Parties; New Jersey Politics, 1820–1837* (1982). The most detailed treatment of his vice presidential candidacy is William S. Hunt, "Theodore Frelinghuysen: A Discussion of His Vice Presidential Candidacy in the Clay-Polk Campaign in 1844, and Its Reasons," *Proceedings of the New Jersey Historical Society* 56 (1938): 30–40. An up-to-date account of Frelinghuysen's educational career is in Richard P. McCormick, *Rutgers: A Bicentennial History* (1966), but Joshua L. Chamberlain, ed., *New York University: Its History, Influence, Equipment and Characteristics* (1901), and William H. S. Demarest, *A History of Rutgers College, 1766–1924* (1924), are also enlightening.

HERMANN K. PLATT

FRELINGHUYSEN, Theodorus Jacobus (1691–c. 1747), Dutch Reformed minister, was born in Lingen, Germany, near the Netherlands border, the son of Johan Henrich Frelinghaus, a Reformed pastor, and Anna Margaretha Brüggemann. Frelinghuysen received his early education from his father, from Otto Verbrugge, later a professor at Groningen, and at the Reformed Gymnasium in Hamm. In 1711 Frelinghuysen matriculated at the University of Lingen, at that time a hotbed of pietism, which emphasized religious fervor and godly living over theological scholasticism. At Lingen Frelinghuysen fell under the influence of teachers who styled themselves Voetians, pietistic followers of Gysbertus Voetius; Frelinghuysen retained his pietistic sympathies throughout his career.

Ordained in Westphalia in 1715, Frelinghuysen assumed his first pastorate at Loegumer Voorwerk in East Friesland and in 1718 was made subrector at the Latin School in Enkhuizen, West Friesland. Shortly thereafter Frelinghuysen received a call to become pastor of the fledgling Dutch churches in the Raritan Valley of central New Jersey: North Branch, Raritan, Six-Mile Run, Three-Mile Run, and New Brunswick. He accepted, under the mistaken impression that the congregations were located somewhere in Flanders or Brabant. Frelinghuysen, however, made good on his promise, and he was reordained by the Classis of Amsterdam on 5 June 1719, at which time he promised to maintain a correspondence with the classis.

Frelinghuysen sailed for the New World with Jacobus Schuurman, a schoolmaster who was to be Frelinghuysen's partner in the Raritan Valley. Upon Frelinghuysen's arrival in New York in January 1720, he began immediately to challenge the orthodox, traditionalist Dutch clergy in the middle colonies, accusing them of theological and moral lassitude. Invited to the home of Gualtherus Du Bois, the venerable minister of New York City's Dutch Reformed church, for instance, Frelinghuysen immediately noticed a large wall mirror and remarked that "even by the most farfetched necessity" it could not be justified. When he preached in New York he pointedly omitted the Lord's Prayer as too formalistic. Frelinghuysen took his censorious preaching to New Jersey, where he proceeded to restrict access to Holy Communion to those who showed visible signs of regeneration. He angered the more affluent members of his congregations when he suggested that "the largest portion of the faithful have been poor and of little account in the world."

When Frelinghuysen began excommunicating his opponents the battle between orthodoxy and pietism was joined. In 1725 the objects of Frelinghuysen's execrations published an extensive bill of particulars, called the *Klagte* (Complaint), against Frelinghuysen and sought to enlist the aid of the more traditionalist Dutch Reformed clergy. Frelinghuysen and his pietist allies, however, refused to submit to such authorities, invoking instead the principle of congregational polity, which vests all authority in the individual congregation. The Classis of Amsterdam, which claimed jurisdiction over the colonial Dutch Reformed churches, sought to dampen Frelinghuysen's pietistic fervor in the interests of ecclesiastical peace—but to no avail.

Although plagued by recurrent, debilitating bouts of mental illness and dogged by allegations of homosexual relations with Schuurman, his schoolmaster,

Frelinghuysen continued to demand high standards of probity from his congregants. (Frelinghuysen eventually married Eva Terhune, in part to silence his critics, and they had seven children; Schuurman married Eva's sister, Autje.) To his enemies Frelinghuysen was contumacious and imperious. Shortly after his arrival in the Raritan Valley he had the following sentiment painted on the back of his sleigh:

> No one's tongue, and no one's pen
> Can make me other than I am.
> Speak slanderers! Speak without end;
> In vain, you, all your slanders send.

Frelinghuysen's partisans, on the other hand, looked to him as the champion of true religion and warmhearted piety against those who had fallen into a cold orthodoxy.

Frelinghuysen's evangelical fervor and his itinerancy contributed significantly to the onset of the Great Awakening in the middle colonies. Gilbert Tennent, the Presbyterian revivalist, who often shared Frelinghuysen's pulpits, declared that Frelinghuysen had taught him a great deal about piety and revival. Both Jonathan Edwards and Heinrich Melchior Mühlenberg spoke highly of Frelinghuysen's ministry. During his swing through the middle colonies, George Whitefield acknowledged Frelinghuysen as "a worthy old soldier of Jesus Christ, and the beginner of the great work which I trust the Lord is carrying on in these parts."

Frelinghuysen's traditionalist Dutch Reformed colleagues, however, did not offer such encomiums. As he and other pietists pressed for greater autonomy from the Classis of Amsterdam so that they could press their evangelical agenda, the orthodox clergy resisted. The pietists eventually prevailed, however, gaveling the Coetus, an autonomous ecclesiastical body, to order on 8 September 1747. Frelinghuysen, however, did not live to see the fruit of his labors. The time and place of his death, possibly following one of his occasional bouts of insanity, which according to a contemporary "robbed him of his reason," is shrouded in mystery.

• Frelinghuysen's papers are no longer extant, although a collection of sermons was published in 1856, *Sermons by Theodorus Jacobus Frelinghuysen*, trans. William Demarest. Frelinghuysen's biographer, James R. Tanis, has included one additional sermon as an appendix to his biography, *Dutch Calvinistic Pietism in the Middle Colonies: A Study in the Life and Theology of Theodorus Jacobus Frelinghuysen* (1967). For a treatment of Frelinghuysen in the context of the struggles between pietism and orthodoxy in the middle colonies, see Randall Balmer, *A Perfect Babel of Confusion: Dutch Religion and English Culture in the Middle Colonies* (1989).

RANDALL BALMER

FRÉMONT, Jessie Benton (31 May 1824–27 Dec. 1902), writer, was born at "Cherry Grove" in Rockbridge County, Virginia, the daughter of Thomas Hart Benton, a U.S. senator from Missouri, and Elizabeth Preston McDowell. High-spirited and precocious, she was her father's favorite: "We were a succession of girls at first, with the boys coming last, and my father gave me early the place a son would have had" (*A Year of American Travel*, p. 25). Raised mainly in Washington, D.C., she was educated at home until adolescence, when she reluctantly attended Miss English's Female Seminary in Georgetown. More informally, she acquired an intimate knowledge of Washington politics under her father's shrewd tutelage, and in frontier St. Louis, his political base, she developed an enduring interest in the West and a taste for adventure.

In 1841 seventeen-year-old Jessie defied her family and scandalized Washington society when she secretly married John Charles Frémont, a mercurial army explorer who was born illegitimate. Over the course of their nearly fifty-year marriage, she would use her considerable political, managerial, and literary skills to play an active though often hidden role in her husband's controversial career, serving as adviser and aide, collaborating on writing projects, penning much of his correspondence, and defending him against critics. The couple would have five children, two of whom died in infancy.

Jessie Frémont discovered her "most happy life work" in late 1842, when her new husband returned from his first important exploring expedition and she served as an essential partner in writing the required government report. However, it was the Frémonts' second report, written when John returned from Oregon and Mexican-held California in 1844, that captured the nation's imagination. Combining scientific accuracy with narrative verve, it made John Frémont famous and induced thousands to go west.

When John Frémont's third expedition ended in a controversial court-martial, he bitterly resigned from the army, and the Frémonts resolved to settle in California. In 1849, while John traveled overland on a privately financed fourth expedition, Jessie and their young daughter journeyed west via Panama, crossing the isthmus by dugout canoe and muleback, and nearly succumbing to tropical fever. In California, in one of the dramatic reversals that punctuated the Frémonts' lives, their Las Mariposas gold mines brought them a sudden fortune and John was elected the new state's first senator.

In 1856, when John Frémont was nominated for the presidency by the new Republican party on a platform opposing the extension of slavery, Jessie became the first national candidate's wife to play an active although necessarily discreet role in what became known as the "Frémont and Jessie" campaign. Long opposed to slavery, she wrote abolitionist Lydia Maria Child during the campaign, "I would as soon place my children in the midst of small pox, as rear them under the influences of slavery" (*Letters*, pp. 122–23). Inspired in part by her prominence, women attended political rallies in increasing numbers, while at the 1856 National Woman's Rights Convention, Lucy Stone asserted that the enthusiasm for Jessie Frémont represented "a recognition of woman's right to participate in politics" (Elizabeth Cady Stanton et al., *History of Woman Suffrage*, vol. 1 [1881], p. 633).

When her husband lost the election, Jessie Frémont suffered a period of depression, possibly augmented by rumors of her husband's infidelity. She spent six months in Europe with their three children, but in March 1858 the reunited family journeyed to California, settling first on their gold-mining property near Yosemite and then in San Francisco, where Jessie encouraged the gifted Unitarian minister Thomas Starr King and the struggling writer Bret Harte.

When the Civil War began and John Frémont was named commander of the Western Department of the Union army, Jessie became his chief assistant, virtually running his St. Louis headquarters while he was in the field. Critics condemned her as "General Jessie," and Abraham Lincoln himself branded her a "female politician" when, in a dramatic meeting with the president in September 1861, she urged immediate emancipation of the slaves. Six weeks later, amid charges of corruption and incompetence, Frémont was removed from his command. Angry at the Lincoln administration's treatment of her husband as well as its "tenderness toward slavery," Jessie Frémont wrote *The Story of the Guard* (1863), an artfully indirect defense of her husband's Missouri tenure.

Jessie Frémont spent the next decade in domestic retreat at the Frémonts' Hudson River, New York, estate, but when their wealth evaporated in the panic of 1873, she began to write professionally. Over the next two decades, she turned out a stream of reminiscences and children's stories that became the family's most reliable source of income. Published mainly in Robert Bonner's *New York Ledger*, *Harper's*, and the children's magazine *Wide Awake*, her work was later collected as *A Year of American Travel* (1878), *Souvenirs of My Time* (1887), *Far West Sketches* (1890), and *The Will and the Way Stories* (1891).

Jessie Frémont accompanied her husband to Arizona in 1878, when he was appointed territorial governor, but a year later she returned east to act as his agent in several ill-fated mining and land ventures. Subsequently she collaborated on the first volume of his *Memoirs of My Life* (1887), but sales were disappointing.

The Frémonts journeyed to Los Angeles in late 1887, hoping to bolster John's failing health and to profit from the southern California real estate boom. When the boom collapsed, John returned east to seek a military pension while Jessie and their unmarried daughter remained in Los Angeles. In 1890 John Frémont unexpectedly died in New York City. A year later, as a final defense of her husband's career, Jessie and a son completed the second volume of his memoirs, but the lengthy manuscript was never published. Meanwhile Congress granted her a widow's pension, and a group of California women, spearheaded by her friend Caroline Severance, the suffragist and civic leader, purchased a house for her. With additional income from her writing, Jessie Frémont lived in Los Angeles in modest comfort for the remaining twelve years of her life. She died in Los Angeles.

Witty, shrewd, vigorous, and fiercely devoted to the causes in which she believed, Jessie Frémont was one of the most well-known and controversial women of her time. Caroline Severance called her "brilliant, spontaneous, original," yet in an era of few options for women, she achieved significance as a promoter of western expansion, as an opponent of slavery, and even as a writer primarily in connection with her husband's often erratic career. Ambivalent about such issues as woman suffrage, she remained partially trapped in the role of celebrated wife, promoting and defending a career that in reality was not her own.

• Jessie Benton Frémont's papers are widely scattered. Important material can be found in the Blair-Lee Papers, Princeton University; the Jeremiah S. Black, John Gutzon Borglum, Francis Preston Blair Family, and Theodore Talbot papers, Library of Congress; the William King Rogers, William J. Morton, and Frémont papers (which include her unpublished memoirs), Bancroft Library, University of California, Berkeley; the Billings Mansion Archives, Woodstock, Vt.; the James T. Fields Papers, Huntington Library, San Marino, Calif.; the Thomas Starr King Papers, Society of California Pioneers, San Francisco; and the Frémont Papers, James S. Copley Library, La Jolla, Calif. Her most significant correspondence is collected in *The Letters of Jessie Benton Frémont*, ed. Pamela Herr and Mary Lee Spence (1993). Herr, *Jessie Benton Frémont* (1987), is a comprehensive biography.

PAMELA HERR

FRÉMONT, John Charles (21 Jan. 1813–13 July 1890), explorer and presidential candidate, was born in Savannah, Georgia, the son of Jean Charles Fremon, a French émigré teacher, and Anne Beverley Whiting Pryor, a Virginia woman of patrician birth who left her elderly husband in 1811 to run away with Fremon. The couple, who apparently never married, moved frequently, living for a period in Savannah, where Jean Charles gave French and dancing lessons, and Anne took in boarders. In 1818 Jean Charles Fremon died, and the family, which by then included several younger children, eventually settled in Charleston, South Carolina, to a life of genteel poverty. The social and economic insecurity of his situation profoundly influenced Frémont. He grew up an outsider—proud, reserved, cautious in sharing his feelings, skeptical of rules and authority, and eager, at times to the point of recklessness, to prove himself.

As a youth, Frémont (who added the *t* and accent sometime after his father's death) worked in the law office of John W. Mitchell, who sponsored his preparatory education. In 1829 he entered the College of Charleston. Although he excelled in mathematics, in time he began to neglect his studies (he had fallen in love, he explained in *Memoirs of My Life* [1887]), and in 1831, a few months before graduation, he was expelled for "incorrigible negligence." He applied for and was granted a B.A. some five years later. In 1833 the influential South Carolina politician Joel R. Poinsett secured him a place as a civilian mathematics instructor on the USS *Natchez*, bound for a two-year South American voyage. When Frémont returned, Poinsett arranged for a position with a topographical survey of a projected Charleston, Louisville and Cincinnati Railroad route through the Carolina and Tennessee mountains and, in 1837–1838, with a reconnaissance of Cherokee lands, principally in Georgia. Frémont relished this wilderness work and in it discovered "the path which I was 'destined to walk.' Through many of the years to come the occupation of my prime of life was to be among Indians and in waste places" (*Memoirs*, p. 50).

In 1838 Poinsett, who had become U.S. secretary of war, assigned the French-speaking Frémont to assist Joseph N. Nicollet, a French scientist-explorer, in surveying the region between the upper Mississippi and Missouri rivers. Several months later Frémont received his commission as a second lieutenant in the U.S. Army Corps of Topographical Engineers.

During two successive expeditions (1838 and 1839), Nicollet gave Frémont an invaluable education in both the scientific and practical aspects of a wilderness survey. While in Washington, D.C., assisting Nicollet with the expedition map and report, he met advocates of westward expansion, including Missouri senator Thomas Hart Benton (1782–1858). Frémont's elopement with Benton's gifted seventeen-year-old daughter Jessie Benton in 1841 provided him with both a devoted collaborator and, through her father, a powerful advocate in the halls of government. The couple had five children, three of whom lived to adulthood.

The following year, with the aging Nicollet too ill to travel, Benton arranged for his son-in-law to head a 25-man, four-month expedition to survey and map the region of the emerging Oregon Trail through South Pass on the Continental Divide. *A Report of an Exploration . . . between the Missouri River and the Rocky Mountains . . .* (1843), the lively, factually detailed government report that Frémont and his wife produced after the journey caught the public imagination: images of Frémont's guide, the then little-known Christopher "Kit" Carson, riding bareback across the prairie, and Frémont himself, raising a flag on a Rocky Mountain peak, entered the national mythology.

In 1843 Frémont set out on a far more ambitious journey to the Oregon region. Disregarding government orders to return by the same route, he went south to Nevada and, in a dangerous midwinter journey, over the snow-covered Sierra Nevada into Mexican-held California. By the time the expedition returned east across the southern rim of what Frémont defined as the Great Basin, they had completed a bold fourteen-month circuit of the West, traveling 6,475 miles by their own calculations. The Frémonts' account of the journey, *A Report of the Exploring Expedition to Oregon and California . . .* (1845), enthralled the nation. Skillfully combining adventure, scientific data, and detailed practical information for emigrants, supplemented by a valuable map prepared by expedition cartographer Charles Preuss, it was "monumental in its breadth—a classic of exploring literature" (Wil-

liam H. Goetzmann, *Exploration and Empire* [1966], p. 248). Powerful propaganda, it stirred Americans to head west, guided, as pioneer Sarah Royce stated, "only by the light of Frémont's *Travels*."

Initial instructions for Frémont's third expedition (1845–1847) limited him to a brief journey to the Rocky Mountains, but when expansionist James Polk assumed office in March 1845, Frémont was given more funds and men, and his destination again became the Pacific Coast. Though the expedition was a scientific survey, the new administration doubtless thought it would be useful to have Frémont in California should war with Mexico occur, particularly since Polk and Benton feared that Great Britain might attempt to occupy the province.

When Frémont reached the Monterey, California, region in February 1846, the Mexican authorities were highly suspicious of his sixty-man armed expedition and ordered them to leave the country. Reacting defiantly, Frémont raised the American flag on a nearby mountain but, with the prudent American consul Thomas Larkin as intermediary, was persuaded to retreat. He moved north to Klamath Lake in southern Oregon, where, on 8 May, Polk's secret agent, Archibald Gillespie, reached him with messages, the contents of which historians have long debated, as well as news that war with Mexico was imminent. Frémont returned to the Sacramento Valley, where he encouraged and then joined American settlers in the Bear Flag Revolt, action, he told a congressional committee in 1848, that was "without expressed authority from the United States, and revolutionary in its character" (Jackson and Spence, vol. 2, p. 469).

When confirmed reports of war with Mexico reached the Pacific, the U.S. Navy seized California ports. Commodore Robert F. Stockton named Frémont commander of the California Battalion, which helped to occupy the province. In the winter of 1846–1847, during a revolt centered in Los Angeles, Frémont became entangled in a quarrel between Stockton and late-arriving General Stephen Watts Kearny of the army, both of whom claimed supreme authority in California. When Frémont, an army officer, rashly sided with Stockton, who had named him governor, Kearny marched him east in disgrace to face a court-martial. Despite widespread public support and Benton's personal defense of him during the long, rancorous trial, Frémont was found guilty and dismissed from the army. Although President Polk reinstated him for "meritorious and valuable services," Frémont bitterly resigned.

In October 1848 Frémont set out on his ill-fated fourth expedition, partially financed by St. Louis businessmen eager to locate a central, all-weather railroad route through the Rockies. During the unusually severe winter, the expedition lost its way in the rugged mountains of southern Colorado, and ten men, a third of the expedition, perished in the snow. While Frémont and several reliable men in his party blamed the guide, William S. "Old Bill" Williams, other members blamed Frémont himself.

Despite the tragedy, Frémont pushed on to California, where gold had been discovered at Las Mariposas, a seventy-square-mile tract near Yosemite Valley that he had purchased sight unseen in 1847 for $3,000. Las Mariposas made Frémont rich, but he was not a shrewd businessman. Until he sold it in 1864, its legal entanglements and escalating costs diminished both his profits and his energy.

In December 1849 Frémont was elected California's first senator and began his term in 1850. During his brief tenure (he drew the short term), he voted for abolition of the slave trade in the District of Columbia and against stiff penalties for those who aided runaway slaves. When he ran for reelection in 1851, the state legislature deadlocked over his candidacy and eventually chose a proslavery Democrat.

In the winter of 1853–1854, Frémont headed his fifth and final expedition, again a privately financed journey to find an all-weather railroad route through the Rockies. Although he believed he had found a suitable pass, he and his men, starving and pounded by blizzards, escaped disaster only when they stumbled to safety in the village of Parowan in southwestern Utah.

Frémont reentered politics in 1856. With crucial early support from Nathaniel Banks and Francis Blair, Sr. (1791–1876), he became the first presidential candidate of the newly formed Republican party on a platform opposing the extension of slavery. Chosen more for his heroic image than his political skills, he nonetheless inspired great enthusiasm in the North, while in the South he was branded a "Frenchman's bastard" and, incorrectly, a secret Roman Catholic. Although Frémont gained the majority of northern votes, he was defeated nationwide by the Democratic candidate, James Buchanan (1.8 to 1.34 million, with an electoral vote of 174 to 114). Despite the loss, his candidacy established the Republican party's dominance in the North and set the stage for Abraham Lincoln's victory in 1860.

For the next four years, Frémont eschewed politics as he attempted to manage his increasingly debt-ridden gold mines. When the Civil War began, President Lincoln appointed him major general commanding the Department of the West with headquarters in St. Louis. Arriving in late July 1861, Frémont faced a chaotic and divided state, inadequate troops and arms, and within two weeks, the disastrous battle of Wilson's Creek, when southwest Missouri fell under Confederate control. On 30 August 1861, without consulting Lincoln, Frémont issued a limited emancipation decree, freeing the slaves of Missouri rebels, but the president, concerned with Border State loyalty, ordered him to rescind it. Over the next two months, continued military defeats, corruption and war profiteering among his staff, and the unexpected enmity of the powerful Blair family weakened Frémont's position. Although he personally led troops through southern Missouri in pursuit of the Confederate army, effectively driving them from the state, on 2 November, just before, Frémont claimed, he was about to face the enemy in battle, Lincoln relieved him of his command.

Frémont's emancipation decree gained him a large following, particularly among radical Republicans critical of Lincoln's management of the war. Bowing to their pressure, the president placed Frémont in command of Union troops in western Virginia in the spring of 1862. When Frémont fell victim to Thomas "Stonewall" Jackson's brilliant tactics, Lincoln reorganized his command, and Frémont resigned. He never received another command, and by 1864, when he was nominated for the presidency by a group of radical Republicans and other dissidents, his ineffective leadership along with rumors of business and personal scandal weakened his appeal. Nonetheless Lincoln viewed him as a threat. A bargain was struck, and on 22 September Frémont withdrew from the race; the next day, Lincoln dismissed Frémont's enemy Montgomery Blair from the cabinet.

During and after the war, Frémont pursued railroad and other investments with no lasting success. His Memphis, El Paso, and Pacific Railroad venture ended in a financial scandal, for which he was at least partly responsible, and in the panic of 1873, he was reduced to near poverty. Appointed governor of Arizona Territory (1878–1881) by President Rutherford B. Hayes, Frémont used his position in a futile attempt to recoup his fortune through mining and land schemes and was eventually forced to resign. His *Memoirs*, the first of a planned two volumes, brought little remuneration. In 1890 Congress granted him a long-sought $6,000-a-year pension. A few months later he died suddenly in a New York City boardinghouse.

Frémont remains a controversial and somewhat elusive figure. While many were inspired by his stand against the extension of slavery during the 1856 election campaign and for immediate emancipation during the early Civil War, others suspected he was an ambitious poseur, more self-promoting than idealistic. Similarly, evaluations of his role in the conquest of California have ranged from hero to the fraud depicted by Josiah Royce in *California . . . A Study in American Character* (1886). A restless loner, Frémont disliked politics, found administrative work tedious, and lacked business acumen. He was at his best as the daring and resourceful leader of his early expeditions. The knowledge of the West and impetus to the westward movement that these journeys inspired remain a remarkable and enduring achievement.

• Major collections of Frémont's papers are at the Bancroft Library, University of California, Berkeley; at the Huntington Library, San Marino, Calif.; at the James S. Copley Library, La Jolla, Calif.; in the Allan Nevins Papers at Columbia University; in the Jeremiah S. Black, Nathaniel Banks, and Francis Preston Blair Family Papers at the Library of Congress; and in the Billings Mansion Archives, Woodstock, Vt. The essential source for Frémont's career as a western explorer is Donald Jackson and Mary Lee Spence, eds., *The Expeditions of John Charles Frémont* (1970–1984), a multivolume compendium of documents, including the expedition reports. For Frémont's later career, particularly his 1856 presidential campaign, Civil War activities, and business ventures, Allan Nevins's classic biography, *Frémont: Pathmarker of the West* (1955), while too uncritical, remains the most comprehensive.

PAMELA HERR

FRENCH, Alice (19 Mar. 1850–9 Jan. 1934), short-story writer and novelist, was born in Andover, Massachusetts, the daughter of George Henry French, a manufacturer of leather, and Frances Wood Morton. Both parents came from prominent New England families. On the mother's side, George Morton, an original pilgrim, authored *"Mourt's" Relation* (1622). Marcus Morton (1784–1864), whom Alice knew in her childhood, was a former Massachusetts governor and politician. In 1856 health reasons prompted George French to move the family to Davenport, Iowa, where his principal investments included a lumber mill, bank, railroad, and plow factory. The family supported the local Unitarian church, and Bronson Alcott once stayed with the family for a week.

French was sent east to school. After an unsuccessful stay at Female College (later called Vassar), she completed her education at Abbot Academy in Andover, Massachusetts, before returning to Davenport in 1868. Marriage did not materialize, although at age thirty-one she accompanied Andrew Carnegie and ten others on a walking tour of England. Bored with Davenport, she authored her first story, "Hugo's Waiting," in 1871 for a local newspaper. In the years that followed French embraced a tame version of realism. Her first stories were about labor unrest in the 1870s and 1880s. She later developed an interest, again marked by realism, in local history.

In 1883 she accompanied her friend and lifelong companion, Jane Allen Crawford, on a visit to the Clover Bend plantation in Lawrence County, Arkansas. This visit began an annual routine, lasting until 1909. During her Arkansas visits, French made a thorough study of local dialect, incorporating it into her stories. She published a nonfiction study of folklore in 1892 in the *Journal of American Folklore*. Her nonfiction essays on American character types appeared in *Scribner's* magazine, and essays on southern town life and plantation life appeared in the *Atlantic Monthly*.

Early in her career French adopted the sexually ambiguous pen name of Octave Thanet. In the late nineteenth century she was one of the most popular American writers, commanding good prices for her stories, most of which were later collected and printed in book form. In general, four themes predominated in her work. Her first theme was labor. Writing in an age of labor unrest, she studied labor conditions, and, although she sympathized with the workers' plight, she showed scant sympathy for labor unions and distrusted new immigrant groups. Six of her labor stories were collected in *The Heart of Toil* (1898). Second, after 1883 she undertook to study the common people of the South, both whites and blacks. She attacked the notorious convict lease system prevalent in the South in the controversial story, "Trusty, No. 49" (1890). Both

"river rats" and farmers figured prominently in her writing. Although originally scattered over several books, most of these stories were collected in *By the Cypress Swamp: The Arkansas Stories of Octave Thanet* (1980). Her third interest was in the West, and *The Missionary Sheriff* (1897) contained a number of her western stories. Some were set in the Davenport of her youth, others in the Far West. Finally, she wrote sympathetically of women. The story, "The Mortgage on Jeffy," dealt with a migrant cotton picker; "Why Abbylonia Surrendered" with a hardworking minister's wife; and "Sist' Chaney's Black Silk" with a black domestic at Hot Springs. Her stories of women not specifically relating to the South were collected in *A Slave to Duty and Other Women* (1898).

Early in the twentieth century French began to produce novels. The most popular was *The Man of the Hour* (1905), a book that combined two of her favorite themes, labor management relations and local history. All of her Republican prejudices in favor of an Anglo-Saxon ruling elite were displayed, and its hero, a clean young man, won out with enlightened management.

Her novel *By Inheritance* (1910) examined southern race relations. French had studied and appreciated the writing of W. E. B. Du Bois, opposed racial demaguery, and endorsed Booker T. Washington's self-help doctrine. Nevertheless, she continued to hold white supremacist views. She believed that blacks should be subservient to the ruling white elite, who would protect their servants from lynching and perhaps even let them drive cars.

Although largely forgotten after 1911, French was well remembered by her contemporaries. A famous gourmand, she was over six feet tall and, as William Allen White recalled, a "great marshmallow of a woman." Her contemporary, novelist Opie Read, cast her as a character in his last novel, *The Gold Gauze Veil* (1927). At "Thanford," as she and Jane named their Clover Bend, Arkansas, retreat, she engaged in carpentry, plumbing, and specialized in entertaining guests. She interested herself in photography, writing a book for amateurs, *An Adventure in Photography* (1893). She opposed woman suffrage but interested herself in the activities of the Colonial Dames and the Daughters of the American Revolution. A friend of Andrew Carnegie, she corresponded regularly on Arkansas Republican party matters with President Theodore Roosevelt, who called her "a trump in every way." Although French in her early writings had dared to offer sympathy to labor and expressed compassion for the southern underclasses, she became increasingly conservative politically after 1900 and published nothing of importance after 1911. Her physical and mental deterioration accelerated as her income declined. Diabetic infection led to the amputation of her right leg. Jane Allen Crawford, her "sweetest, noblest, truest friend and sister," died in 1932. The Great Depression completed her financial ruin, reducing her to living in two rented rooms. "My work is done," she told a local reporter. "What I have written already must stand for me in literature." She died in poverty in Davenport.

During her lifetime French was highly regarded by such critics as William Dean Howells, but in the twentieth century she was dismissed as a mere local-color storyteller. Reevaluation began with the publication of her biography in 1965 and the collection and re-publication of her Arkansas stories. Although not a major figure, she did play an important role in introducing the underside of American life into literature. Modern critic Lawrence I. Berkove, noting the "unexpected power" of her Arkansas stories, has called for a reassessment of her work.

• French's papers can be found at the Newberry Library in Chicago. George McMichael wrote an admirable biography, *Journey to Obscurity: The Life of Octave Thanet* (1965), which also contains a complete bibliography of her writings. Additional material relating to her Arkansas years can be found in the introduction to Michael B. Dougan and Carol W. Dougan, *By the Cypress Swamp: The Arkansas Stories of Octave Thanet* (1980). Two analyses of her writings are by Michael B. Dougan, "When Fiction Is Reality: Arkansas Fiction of Octave Thanet," *Publications of the Arkansas Philological Association* 2 (Summer 1976): 29–36, and "Local Colorists and the Race Question: Opie Read and Octave Thanet," *Publications of the Arkansas Philological Association* 9 (Fall 1983): 26–34. Lawrence I. Berkove's reassessment is in "New Old Additions to the American Canon," *American Periodicals: A Journal of History, Criticism, and Bibliography* 1 (Fall 1991): 25–33.

MICHAEL B. DOUGAN

FRENCH, Anne Warner. *See* Warner, Anne Richmond.

FRENCH, Daniel Chester (20 Apr. 1850–7 Oct. 1931), sculptor, was born in Exeter, New Hampshire, the son of Henry Flagg French, a lawyer, judge, and later assistant secretary of the U.S. Treasury, and Anne Richardson. Henry French moved his law practice to Boston when Daniel was six years old, and the family settled in Cambridge, Massachusetts. Daniel's mother had died some years before, and Henry French married Pamela M. Prentiss in 1859. The family moved to Concord, Massachusetts, shortly thereafter, establishing its long-time home.

At a young age French demonstrated artistic qualities that were encouraged by his stepmother and by family friends including Louisa May Alcott, a Concord resident. She had studied art in Paris and was able to help him learn basic sculpture techniques. He spent one year at the Massachusetts Institute of Technology in Cambridge, where he learned drawing. French is usually described as being "largely self-taught," but he had learned from many teachers by observing them in their studios. Early influences were William Morris Hunt on drawing and color, John Quincy Adams Ward on sculpture, and William Rimmer on anatomy.

French's first big commission came with the help of a family friend, Ralph Waldo Emerson, a resident of Concord. That town and Lexington commissioned a sculpture to celebrate the one-hundredth anniversary of the American Revolution's first battle. French's studio was in Boston at the time, and he produced a model slightly over two feet tall that was accepted without dissent. The statue became the *Minute Man*, with a musket in one hand and the other hand resting on a plow. This image of the citizen-farmer-soldier became famous and was used to sell U.S. war bonds during World War I. The *Minute Man* was unveiled one day before French's twenty-fifth birthday, on 19 April 1875, before a crowd of 10,000. President Ulysses S. Grant, Speaker of the House James G. Blaine, and several cabinet members were there. James Russell Lowell and Henry Wadsworth Longfellow were in the crowd, and Emerson read a poem, the lines of which were cut into the granite pedestal of the statue. French, however, was not present at the unveiling, since he had moved in 1874 to Florence, Italy. French lived there in the home of the sculptor Preston Powers for two years, working alongside Powers and under the guidance of Thomas Ball.

On his return to America French proceeded to establish a studio in Washington, D.C., on the site of the current Library of Congress. Here he turned his attention to sculptural groups on new public buildings. His first three commissions were for the St. Louis Custom House (1877), the Court House in Philadelphia (1883), and the Boston Post Office (1885), all of which were in marble. Around the same time he also executed the seated bronze statue of John Harvard, placed in the Harvard Yard.

Completed in 1888, French's standing statue of General Lewis Cass in marble stands in National Statuary Hall in the U.S. Capitol, Washington, D.C., representing the state of Michigan. This statue is French's only work in the hall, and according to critics, it is one of the best. Lorado Taft in *History of American Sculpture* said it had "an individuality, an equipoise, and a technical perfection undreamed of by the earlier generation of American sculptors."

About this time French went to Paris, where he worked with Augustus Saint-Gaudens and others, including the sculptor Edward Potter. He enrolled for Antonin Mercié's sculpture class, and his modeling grew more crisp and definite. On his return to the U.S., French used the style of the École des Beaux-Arts, but he emerged as an "American" sculptor as the influences of European sculpture (e.g. romantic interpretations of nature and classic echoes) weakened.

French postponed marriage until age thirty-eight, then even postponed his wedding so that he could finish his statue of Thomas Hopkins Gallaudet (at Gallaudet College, Washington, D.C.). His bride was his cousin Mary Adams French; they had one daughter and settled in lower Manhattan. French maintained a studio in New York City for the remaining forty-two years of his life.

The friendship of French and Saint-Gaudens paid dividends when the latter was chosen director of sculpture at the 1893 World's Columbian Exposition in

Chicago. Saint-Gaudens selected his friend French to design a massive statue, which was seventy-five feet tall when complete. A twenty-foot model of this statue, *The Republic*, was later permanently installed in the city of Chicago.

Death Staying the Hand of the Young Sculptor was fashioned by French as a tribute to Martin Milmore, a younger, less well-known sculptor who died a premature death in 1883. The bronze original was erected at Milmore's grave in Roxbury, Massachusetts, at Forest Hills Cemetery in 1893, and a marble replica is in the Metropolitan Museum of Art.

Among the many equestrian statues French designed with the help of Edward Clark Potter are *General Grant* in Philadelphia (1899); *Washington* (1900), a gift from the women of America to France placed in the Place d'Iéna in Paris; and *General Joseph Hooker* in Boston (1903). The breadth of his work is seen in the bronze doors of the Boston Public Library, the fountain in Dupont Circle, Washington, D.C., and various war memorials.

For all this diversity, French is best remembered for his portrayal of Abraham Lincoln in the massive seated statue in the Lincoln Memorial in Washington, D.C. At the dedication on Memorial Day 1922, President Warren G. Harding said that the Lincoln statue "will be a national shrine forever." Designing the memorial itself was French's friend Henry Bacon, a noted architect. French is quoted as saying that Bacon was created for the sole purpose of making the memorial.

The colossal statue required approximately twenty blocks of Georgia marble, cut and reassembled on site so skillfully that the seams are almost invisible. The seated Lincoln is about eighteen feet high, a dimension French arrived at by painstakingly constructing models and testing them until he was satisfied with the proportions relative to the interior space of Bacon's temple. (The pedestal adds another eleven feet to the piece.) Lord Charnwood, a Lincoln biographer whose work French studied during his preparation, saw a photograph of the completed statue and proclaimed it the finest Lincoln he had ever seen, citing specifically its stability, repose, and natural majesty. He went on to say that the only one approaching it was in the state house in Lincoln, Nebraska. A friend of French's wrote to Lord Charnwood to inform him that French had also created that one.

Examples of French's sculpture are now found in more than thirty-five cities, both in the U.S. and abroad. His work in Washington, D.C., alone requires a map of the city for its presentation. Although he lived there but a few years (1876–1878), French had a fondness for the American capital, demonstrated by his work on the national Commission of Fine Arts. He and others had sought such a group since the mid-1890s, but it was not until 1910 that congress approved the legislation. The duty of the commission was "to advise upon the location of statues, fountains, and monuments in the public squares, streets, and parks in the District of Columbia." This commission brought artistic input and continuity to the congressional decision-making process, which had previously appointed a different committee to advise on each project under consideration. French served as a member of the commission from 1910 to 1915, the last three years as chairman.

About 1896 French and his wife bought a farm in the town of Stockbridge, Massachusetts, to serve as a summer home and studio. Bacon began construction of a summer studio for French in 1898, and in 1900 he also designed the large (seventeen main rooms) residence French built on the property. French named the estate "Chesterwood" after Chester, New Hampshire, where he had spent some childhood summers with his grandparents. It is said that his affection for the town caused him to adopt its name as his middle name. About the estate, he said "I spend six months of the year up there. That is heaven. New York is—well, New York."

The gardens, modeled after English and Italian gardens, were French's pride and joy. He spent much time designing them and working in them. Chesterwood was used by the family for many years, and in 1969 French's daughter Margaret gave the 120-acre estate to the National Trust for Historic Preservation. It is now open to the public, and his studio remains as it was when he was active. The doors are some twenty-two feet high, and one can see the railroad track French used to wheel models in and out of the sunlight so that he could oversee the effect of natural light on his work. The largest collection of French's work is there in the Berkshires at Chesterwood.

French was a founder of the American Academy at Rome in 1905 as part of his effort to encourage young sculptors. He supported the fledgling school with labor and money during its early years, in part undoubtedly because of his own training in Italy. He belonged to many artistic organizations, including the National Sculpture Society and the Metropolitan Museum of Art, of which he was a trustee from 1904 until his death. He was a fellow of the American Academy of Arts and Sciences.

French's awards were numerous, including medals of honor from the Paris Exposition, 1900; from the New York Architectural League in 1912; from the Panama-Pacific exposition at San Francisco in 1915 and from the National Institute of Arts and Letters in 1918. France honored him twice: he became a chevalier of the Legion of Honor in 1910, and ten years later he became one of only nineteen foreign associate members of the fine arts class of the French Academy.

When French died at Chesterwood, funeral services were held in his studio at Chesterwood. He is remembered for using his European training and influences in developing American sculpture and in particular for his seated *Lincoln* in the Lincoln Memorial. This monument, seen by millions each year, conveys the power and dignity of its subject in a way demonstrated by few, if any, other pieces.

• French's papers are in the Library of Congress. Biographies of French written by family members are *Journey into*

Fame: the Life of Daniel Chester French (1947), by French's daughter Margaret French Cresson (a sculptress herself), and *Memories of a Sculptor's Wife* (1928), by his wife Mary French, published three years before his death. Cresson's work has a particularly complete list of French's work and an extensive bibliography. Michael Richman has written two works about French: an exhibit catalog, *Daniel Chester French, an American Sculptor/Washington, D.C.* (1976 and 1983 editions), and "The Early Career of Daniel Chester French, 1869–1891" (Ph.D. diss., Univ. of Delaware, 1974). Works that discuss French while dealing with specific statuary include Roland Wells Robbins, *The Story of the Minute Man* (1945); New York (State) Sheridan Monument Commission, *Unveiling of the Equestrian Statue of General Philip H. Sheridan, Capitol Park, Albany, New York, October 7, 1916* (1916); Georgia Historical Society, *A History of the Erection and Dedication of the Monument to Gen'l James Edward Oglethorpe, Savannah, Ga.* (1911); Robert Henry Myers, *Beneficence; the Statue on the Campus of Ball State University, Muncie, Indiana* (1972); and Lorado Taft, *History of American Sculpture* (1903).

PHILIP H. VILES, JR.

FRENCH, Lucy Virginia Smith (16 Mar. 1825–31 Mar. 1881), writer and editor, was born in Accomac County, Virginia, the daughter of Mease W. Smith, a lawyer and educator, and Elizabeth Parker. French's wealthy and cultured family—dating to the revolutionary war—provided her with a solid education for her extensive writing career. After their mother's death in 1826, French and her younger sister, Lide, were educated at Miss Foster's Presbyterian boarding school in Washington, Pennsylvania (her maternal grandmother's hometown), from which Lucy graduated with honors in 1846. In 1848 she and her sister returned to Virginia, only to leave within the same year because they were unhappy with their father's remarriage. They moved to Memphis, Tennessee, where both were able to secure teaching jobs. Their self-willed exodus from Virginia strengthened the bond between the sisters, who remained close all their lives.

Soon after arriving in Memphis in 1848, French launched her writing career by submitting pieces to the *Louisville Journal* under the pen name "L'Inconnue" or "the unknown." She did not remain unknown to the writing community, however. In 1852 French edited the *Southern Ladies' Book*, a magazine "dedicated to Woman, as the symbol of progress" and to "the promotion and establishment of a great Southern literature" (Peck, p. 5). Four years later she published a book of poems, *Wind Whispers* (1856), and a five-act tragedy in blank verse, *Istalilxo: The Lady of Tula* (1856), which is set in Mexico. Even though French's poetry tended to be sentimental, both books share genuine concern for the plight of women victimized by an unforgiving set of double standards. The girl with "The Sullied Name" in *Wind Whispers* is ostracized by her own society (because she gave up her virginity, and thus her honor, to her inconstant lover), but "God, in mercy, did not strike / Thine image from His Book away."

Likewise, the narrator of "Pariah" accuses an inconstant lover of murder and the aristocratic society to which he belongs as hypocritical when a girl he had seduced kills herself. Although French wrote poems on subjects such as insanity, maternity, historical events, and folklore (her third book of poetry was titled *Legends of the South* [1867]), her poems on women's rights, education, and victimization set a foundation for the remainder of her writing career.

French's reputation as a writer was the catalyst in a courtship that was just as romantic in the popular sense as her poetry was in its melodramatic and impressionistic style. In 1852 Colonel John H. French, on a boat trip that had a layover in Memphis, visited a bookstore in search of something to relieve the tedium of the trip. He had already developed an admiration for the poetry of "L'Inconnue" when a chance meeting with her in the bookstore determined his fate. The boat left Memphis without him. She left Memphis as Lucy Virginia Smith French (after the wedding on 12 January 1853) for her husband's hometown of McMinnville, Tennessee. From "Forest Home," the colonel's family estate, French juggled her career as a writer and editor with being the mother of three children.

After the Civil War, French began to write historical novels instead of poetry, although her style remained sentimental. Her *Kernwood; or, After Many Days* (1867) is a moralistic romance loosely based on the events of the Civil War. Nonetheless, *Kernwood* explores what French called "The monster, Custom" as it held its power over women and slaves in the South. Although various methods of escaping custom are explored in the novel, it eventually sides with the traditions governing both women and slaves—marriage and servitude. *Kernwood* is a serious exploration of how the Civil War affected women and the various possibilities open to women during Reconstruction. Thus, the heroine Amanda Douglas adopts the guise of a man and becomes one of the South's best spies. Another woman in the novel who escapes custom is Corrine Houghton, who, after being jilted by a lover, becomes a doctor of women's diseases and states, "That man has a right to arrogate to himself all the higher instruments of learning I deny; woman shares with him the common school of life, why should she be excluded from the college?" Another character in *Kernwood*, Eloise Courie, challenges the custom of prearranged marriages. She eventually does marry the cousin to whom she had been betrothed since birth, but not until after she becomes engaged to someone else.

Portraying prostitution as another type of slavery, French argues that prostitution is the most entrenched economic opportunity in *My Roses* (1872), a novel about prostitution. In spite of the economic opportunities for women after the Civil War—marriage, as well as careers in writing, teaching, and nursing—French argues that prostitution remained the most entrenched economic opportunity for women. As in her *Wind Whispers*, French again shows genuine sympathy for prostitutes in *My Roses*. Furthermore, a basic tenet of this book is that women are obligated to help one another escape this ancient form of slavery. Like

Amanda Douglas, the heroine Henriette de Hauterive disguises herself as a man to save two women whose hardships forced them into prostitution.

Although French is primarily remembered as a fiction writer, from 1858 to 1861 she was also the literary editor of three magazines, the *Southern Homestead* of Nashville, the *Georgia Literary and Temperance Crusader* of Atlanta, and, in her later years, *Ladies' Home*. Her final book, *Darlingtonia: The Eaters and the Eaten* (1879), is a collage of sketches taken from French's diaries added to historical facts and local stories about Civil War events at Beersheba Springs, Tennessee. A collaborative collection of poems *One or Two?* by French and her sister Lide Smith Meriwether was published in 1883, although French did not live to see its publication. She died in McMinnville.

• Two standard but dated sources on French are Mary T. Tardy, ed., *The Living Female Writers of the South* (1872), and James Wood Davidson, *The Living Writers of the South* (1869). See also *American Illustrated Methodist Magazine* (July 1900). Virginia Lewis Peck's dissertation, "Life and Works of L. Virginia French" (Ph.D. diss., Vanderbilt Univ., 1939), remains the only comprehensive study of French's writings. The most modern assessments of French are Herschel Gower's introduction in *The Beersheba Springs Diaries of L. Virginia French* (1986), and his article "Beersheba Springs and L. Virginia French: The Novelist as Historian," *Tennessee Historical Quarterly* 42 (1983): 115–37. An obituary is in the *Nashville Daily American*, 3 Apr. 1881.

TAMARA HORN

FRENCH, William Henry (13 Jan. 1815–20 May 1881), army officer, was born in Baltimore, Maryland, the son of William French, a post office worker (mother's name unknown). Little is known of French's early life until he entered the U.S. Military Academy in 1833. He graduated in 1837, twenty-second in a class of fifty. Commissioned second lieutenant in the First Artillery, French served in the Second Seminole War and the Cherokee removals in 1837–1838. Promoted to first lieutenant in 1838, French spent the next several years along the Canadian border during periods of heightened tension there. During the Mexican War, French served in diverse capacities, including aide-de-camp to Brigadier General (later president) Franklin Pierce, winning brevets to captain and major during actions at Cerro Gordo, Contreras, and Churubusco. French became a captain in 1848 and spent the next thirteen years in routine duties on the frontier, in Florida during the Third Seminole War, and on a three-officer board revising the army's manual for light artillery tactics.

The secession of Texas in February 1861 found French at Fort Duncan (Eagle Pass) with five companies of the First Artillery. The rapid collapse of Federal authority in Texas left French in a precarious position, but despite numerous difficulties, he led a combined battalion of artillery and infantry on a long march to the Gulf of Mexico and sailed for Fort Taylor at Key West, Florida, in March 1861. He vigorously suppressed secessionist stirrings there in the spring of 1861, attracting favorable notice from his superiors.

French accepted an appointment as brigadier general of U.S. volunteers in September 1861 and two months later assumed command of the Third Brigade, Sumner's Division, Army of the Potomac. A capable brigade commander during George B. McClellan's (1826–1885) Peninsular campaign in the spring and summer of 1862, French distinguished himself at Fair Oaks and the Seven Days battles. His success led to command of the Third Division of the II Corps at Antietam in September 1862. In the fighting around the "Bloody Lane," French's division suffered heavy casualties but earned distinction by restoring the Federal line at the Sunken Road during a critical portion of the fight and holding it for four hours under heavy fire.

Promoted to major general of volunteers in November 1862, French served at Fredericksburg in December, where his division was one of the first to assault Robert E. Lee's position on Marye's Heights. French continued in division command at Chancellorsville in May 1863, but his best professional moment came during the Gettysburg campaign in June-July 1863. Ordered by Major General Joseph Hooker (and subsequently by Major General George G. Meade, Hooker's successor as commander of the Army of the Potomac) to command field troops in the Frederick, Maryland/Harpers Ferry, West Virginia area, French demonstrated notable independent initiative by destroying Confederate pontoon bridges during Lee's retreat after the Union victory at Gettysburg, even before receiving Meade's orders to do so.

Consequently, on 7 July 1863 Meade appointed French to command the III Corps of the Army of the Potomac. Over the ensuing several months, French experienced reasonable success, but the lull in the eastern campaign after Gettysburg proved to be no true test of his suitability for corps command. There is no extant record of French ever having married, but it is likely, considering his name and given that Civil War generals often had their sons of military age serve as aides, that the William Henry French, Jr., who served in the army during the Civil War, frequently as General French's aide-de-camp, was in fact the general's son. The record offers no other indication that French had a family.

In early November 1863 Meade commenced his Rappahannock/Mine Run campaign, hoping to take Lee by surprise. Meade's goal, to isolate and defeat a portion of Lee's army, required the Army of the Potomac to execute well-planned movements in an area of Virginia notorious for poor roads and dense forests. French began capably, directing the move of the I, II, and III Corps columns across the Rappahannock River at Kelly's Ford on 7 November. Several weeks later, however, on 26 November, French fared poorly from the very beginning of a new operation when Meade commenced the Mine Run phase of the campaign. The III Corps began its march that morning several hours late, causing increasing problems for other corps. French finally got most of the III Corps across the Rapidan River, but on 27 November he became badly confused over the line of march his corps needed to take in order to link up with G. K. Warren's I Corps at nearby Robertson's Tavern. Consequently, III Corps spent the day halted, allowing a Confederate division to get into position to block French's advance as well as that of the VI Corps. Nearly frantic messages from Meade did not spur French onward, and with the element of surprise slipping from Union hands, Lee had time to prepare formidable fieldworks that the Federals dared not assault. Within days, Meade canceled the campaign, retired across the Rapidan and the Rappahannock, and settled into winter quarters, the hope of defeating Lee vanished.

Throughout the army, blame for the failure fell squarely on French, characterized by one soldier as "that master of 'how not to do it'" (Goss, p. 242). Rumors and even a newspaper account attributed French's failure to drunkenness, but no definitive proof of this charge exists. French denied any errors or wrongdoing, largely blaming circumstances and subordinates for the III Corps's performance. The consensus of historians is that French himself was to blame. Possibly as a result, in March 1864 Meade consolidated the corps of the Army of the Potomac, disbanding the III Corps and ordering French to Philadelphia to await assignment in his regular army rank of lieutenant colonel.

Aside from a few days of service at Havre de Grace, Maryland, during the Confederate raid on Washington in July 1864, French rendered no further significant service during the Civil War. Brevetted major general in March 1865 for war service, French spent subsequent years in a variety of routine posts and boards. Promoted to colonel of the Fourth Artillery at Washington, D.C., in July 1877, French commanded the first regular army troops sent to suppress the great railroad strike that erupted that month. While he quelled trouble in the area of Martinsburg, West Virginia, and its environs, clashes with civilian authorities again inspired rumors of drunkenness.

French retired in July 1880 and died in Washington, D.C., less than a year later. Winning Civil War brevets for his conduct at Fair Oaks, Antietam, and Chancellorsville, French was a competent brigade and division commander. However, like a number of other general officers on both sides during the Civil War, he clearly lacked the exceptional degree of military skill needed for success at higher levels of command.

• No professional biography of French has been published; however, adequate primary and secondary sources are available. Foremost among these for general information on French's career are George W. Cullum, *Biographical Register of the Officers and Graduates of the U.S. Military Academy* (3 vols. 1891); an obituary by General O. O. Howard in the *Twelfth Annual Reunion of the Association of the Graduates of the U.S. Military Academy* (1881); Francis B. Heitman, *Historical Register and Dictionary of the United States Army* (1903); and obituaries in the *New York Times* and *Washington Post*, 21 May 1881. Details of French's Civil War years are best found in many different volumes of *The War of the Rebellion: A Compilation of the Official Records of the Union and Confederate Armies* (128 vols., 1880–1901), most significantly in ser. 1, vols. 1 (Tex./Fla. operations), 27 (Gettysburg), and 29 (Mine Run). Other primary source materials with helpful information on French's Civil War career and his character include Robert U. Johnson and Clarence C. Buel, eds., *Battles and Leaders of the Civil War* (1887–1888); George T. Stevens, *Three Years in the Sixth Corps* (1866); Warren Lee Goss, *Recollections of a Private* (1890); and Allan J. Nevins, ed., *A Diary of Battle: The Personal Journals of Colonel Charles S. Wainwright, 1861–1865* (1962). Sources critical of French's conduct in the Mine Run campaign include Bruce Catton, *Never Call Retreat* (1965); Shelby Foote, *The Civil War: A Narrative*, vol. 2, *Fredericksburg to Meridian* (1963); and Herman Hattaway and Archer Jones, *How the North Won* (1983). See also Edwin B. Coddington's classic, *The Gettysburg Campaign: A Study in Command* (1968). For French's involvement in the railroad strike of 1877, reference should be made to various reports in the *New York Times*, July 1877.

BROECK N. ODER

FRENEAU, Philip Morin (2 Jan. 1752–19 Dec. 1832), poet and polemicist, was born in New York City, the son of Pierre Freneau, a successful wine factor and land speculator, and Agnes Watson, the daughter of a New Jersey planter. Shortly after Philip's birth, Pierre moved his growing family to the hamlet of Mount Pleasant, in Monmouth County, New Jersey. Although a devout man of Huguenot ancestry, Pierre purchased a large library well stocked with secular literature, which he encouraged his four children to study. Following a private education at the hands of his mother, at the age of fifteen Philip began to prepare for a life in the clergy. A brief period of study at the Mattisonia Grammar School in Manalapan allowed the boy to enter the sophomore class at the College of New Jersey (Princeton) in 1768. During the next year James Madison of Virginia joined Freneau as both his classmate and—according to college tradition—his roommate.

The death of Pierre Freneau plunged the family into a period of financial uncertainty, and one such crisis, the auction of portions of the family estate, caused Philip Freneau to be "necessarily absent" from his 1771 graduation ceremony. As a result, he missed the public reading of his first major poem, "The Rising Glory of America." For the next several years, family responsibilities kept the young writer away from his pen. The clergy paid little enough, and the wages of a poet could not support his mother and three younger siblings. For a time he tried his hand at teaching school. "The old hag Necessity," he informed Madison, has "a prodigious gripe of me." But with the coming of the Revolution, the 23-year-old Freneau was inspired anew. *American Liberty* was published in July 1775; two Swiftian satires, *General Gage's Soliloquy* and *General Gage's Confession*, in which the British general was lampooned as an ambitious puppet, quickly followed. The pamphlets were widely reprinted and found an audience among moderate Whigs, who, like Freneau, aimed their fire not at Britain or even the monarchy but rather at individuals and royal advisers who stood accused of corrupting the English political system.

Growing fame as a patriotic poet, however, was small recompense. When a chance encounter in Philadelphia with a Captain Hanson led to an offer to serve as the captain's private secretary on a plantation in Santa Cruz in the Danish West Indies, Freneau found it impossible to refuse. Hard as it was to leave his family and growing fame, the Caribbean promised adventure and solvency. For two years Freneau resided in Santa Cruz. He found the island to be as "inexpressibly beautiful" as he found Caribbean slavery to be barbarous. "No class of mankind in the known world," observed Freneau, "undergoes so complete a servitude." Although familiar enough with unfree labor— New Jersey passed a gradual emancipation act only in 1804—the condition of slaves on the captain's sugar plantation left Freneau "melancholy and disconsolate." Although some critics date it as early as 1775, most scholars believe that Freneau's gloomy "The House of Night" reflects the dreamy atmosphere of the Caribbean.

After returning home in July 1778, Freneau promptly enlisted as a private in the First Regiment of the New Jersey militia. Although his service as a scout won him promotion to the rank of sergeant, Freneau found time to publish *American Independence*, a passionate indictment of British rule. Only days after the pamphlet appeared, Freneau decided to combine his duties as a militiaman with the somewhat more lucrative career of a coastal privateer. While ferrying tobacco to St. Eustacia in May 1780, Freneau was captured by a British man-of-war and incarcerated on the prison ship *Scorpion*, which anchored in the Hudson River. After six weeks of ill treatment he was released; his friends found him a "perfect skeleton." Bitter about his inhumane handling, Freneau wrote "The British Prison Ship."

Although Freneau slowly regained his health, his career as a soldier was over. In April 1781 Freneau took residence in Philadelphia with Francis Bailey and worked as a writer and occasional coeditor of the *Freeman's Journal*. Over the next three years nearly one hundred of his poems and essays appeared in the journal. Most of the poems satirized Tories and British generals, but others ignored imperial concerns and instead advanced an egalitarian view of the Revolution as a movement that should benefit all Americans, and not merely the old merchant elite. Many of his essays were reprinted in newspapers from New York to South Carolina, which served to earn him the title "Poet of the Revolution."

When the war at long last ended, so evidently did Freneau's source of inspiration. His contributions to the *Freeman's Journal* grew scarce, and once again in need of money, Freneau was forced to take a position as a postal clerk. Although his new occupation offered ample time for writing, Freneau grew restless. In 1784 he returned to the Caribbean, this time as the captain of his own brig. His romantic adventures provided his pen with inspiration but did little for his purse. Nearly

broke after six years at sea, Freneau determined to return to Monmouth County and marry Eleanor Forman, the daughter of a prosperous farmer. At age twenty-eight, Eleanor was considered a spinster with few options. Although she accepted Philip's proposal she nonetheless demanded that he put the sea behind him. They were married in 1790; they had four children.

His wife's dowry allowed Freneau to return to journalism. The year 1791 found Freneau editing the *Daily Advertiser*, an underfinanced New York sheet dedicated to upholding the ideals of the French Revolution and criticizing the fiscal policies of Treasury Secretary Alexander Hamilton. When the federal government moved to Philadelphia later that year, Congressman Madison sought an editor able enough to counter the labors of John Fenno, whose aristocratic *Gazette of the United States*, like the majority of urban newspapers, supported Hamilton's programs. Madison urged his former roommate to move south, and after Secretary of State Thomas Jefferson agreed to pay him an annual salary of $250 to translate documents, Freneau agreed to relocate. The first edition of the *National Gazette*, spewing invective at the "stock-jobbers and monarchy-jobbers," appeared on 31 October. Freneau's political responsibilities left him little time for his art; although the *National Gazette* carried many of his poems, most were reprinted works that had first appeared in the *Daily Advertiser*.

Although Freneau's pen required little assistance, the anonymous writings of Congressman Madison and other opposition leaders soon found their way into the pages of the journal. Madison in particular frequently contributed editorials advocating the economic visions of Jefferson's Democratic Republicans. When Hamilton, a Federalist writing under the pseudonym "Civis," began to return fire, President George Washington labored to effect a reconciliation between Hamilton and Jefferson, his two chief cabinet members. Jefferson responded with a long missive asserting he had never published "a syllable" in the *National Gazette*. But without naming Madison he defended Freneau's habit of providing editorial space to anonymous essays "written against the aristocratical & monarchial principles" allegedly advanced by Federalist writers.

If Freneau accepted Republican money, he was no mere puppet. His rigid dedication to principle, as well as his staunch support for French minister Edmond Genet, even after the Virginians abandoned the blundering "madman," occasionally caused Jefferson political embarrassment. When Freneau, against Jefferson's advice, denounced Washington's "monarchial pettiness," the president demanded the secretary of state fire "that rascal Freneau." Jefferson deferred a decision owing to his own impending retirement at the end of 1793. With no patron or defender in the cabinet, Freneau once more found himself "in want of money." On 27 October, Freneau sadly informed his subscribers that the paper would be discontinued.

At the age of forty-one, the most active and exciting period of his life was at an end. Returning to Mount Pleasant to the New Jersey home built by his father decades before, Philip tried his hand at publishing several rural papers, the *Monmouth Gazette* (1794) and the *Jersey Chronicle* (1795–1796). Neither proved successful. His attempt to edit a Manhattan literary journal, the *Time-Piece*, also ended in failure after but one year. Philip's disinclination to pursue a more lucrative career damaged his marriage, and the couple was already estranged when Freneau decided to return to the sea. The remainder of his life was spent aboard the *John*, a schooner that carried salt and cider to southern ports, and at a small farm on the outskirts of Freehold, New Jersey. Freneau's battle with poverty occupied his days and left little time for poetry; between 1816 and 1821 he produced no publications of any sort. In late 1832 Freneau applied for the pension of $35 a year due him as a revolutionary veteran. The application was approved, but Freneau did not live to enjoy it. On 18 December, while on the way home from a country store, Freneau lost his way and perished in a howling blizzard.

• The core collection of Freneau papers is in the Rutgers and Princeton University libraries. Letters written by Freneau may be found in the Historical Society of Pennsylvania, Philadelphia, and in the yet-unfinished *Papers of Thomas Jefferson*, ed. Julian P. Boyd et al. (1950–) and *Papers of James Madison*, ed. Robert A. Rutland et al. (1962–). The New-York Historical Society has a nearly complete set of the last four newspapers published by Freneau, and the New Jersey Historical Society owns copies of the *Freeman's Journal*. Virtually all of Freneau's poems and essays were published during his lifetime. One can consult *The Miscellaneous Works of Philip Freneau* (1788), *Poems Written and Published During the American Revolutionary War* (2 vols., 1809), and *A Collection of Poems on American Affairs* (2 vols., 1815). The best modern edition is F. L. Pattee, *The Poems of Philip Freneau* (3 vols., 1902). Freneau is the subject of several able biographies. Lewis Leary, *That Rascal Freneau: A Study in Literary Failure* (1941), focuses on the poet, whereas Jacob Axelrad, *Philip Freneau: Champion of Democracy* (1967), emphasizes Freneau's political career. Both supersede Mary S. Austin, *Philip Freneau: The Poet of the Revolution* (1901). Philip Marsh has also written widely on the poet. See his "Madison's Defense of Freneau," *William and Mary Quarterly* 2 (1946): 269–74; "Jefferson and Freneau," *American Scholar* 16 (1947): 201–10; and "Philip Freneau and His Circle," *Pennsylvania Magazine of History and Biography* 63 (1939): 37–59.

DOUGLAS R. EGERTON

FRENKEL-BRUNSWIK, Else (18 Aug. 1908–31 Mar. 1958), psychologist, was born in Lemberg, a Polish town in the Austro-Hungarian empire (and later Lvov in Russia), the daughter of Abraham Frenkel, a banker, and Helene Gelernter. The family moved to Vienna in 1914 to escape a pogrom.

Frenkel-Brunswik would later attribute her professional achievements to her relationship with her two sisters—one older, whose beauty was a source of great pride for their mother, and one younger, whom the mother babied. Else, plain and in the middle, maintained her closest relationship with her father, who would have welcomed a son and valued her academic accomplishments. The two remained close even after her marriage to a gentile, an event that estranged her from the other members of her strict Jewish family. Her later psychoanalysis revealed what she referred to as a "Cordelia complex" stemming from these familial experiences (Heiman and Grant, pp. 36–57).

Frenkel-Brunswik was educated in Vienna, graduating from the Gymnasium in 1926 and receiving a doctorate in psychology at the University of Vienna in 1930. She remained at its Psychological Institute for a decade with an appointment equivalent to an assistant professorship. The institute was then directed by Karl and Charlotte Bühler; Frenkel-Brunswik assisted Charlotte Bühler in her biographical research, the qualitative study of lives that was later regarded as a forerunner of life-span developmental psychology. A severe attack of rheumatic fever in 1932 interrupted Frenkel-Brunswik's first venture into personal psychoanalysis.

Two intellectual currents of interwar Vienna, psychoanalysis and logical positivism, were central to Frenkel-Brunswik's career. She resumed psychoanalysis in 1937 with Ernest Kris, the eminent psychoanalytic ego psychologist. She and Egon Brunswik, her former teacher at the University of Vienna and later her colleague at the Psychological Institute, both participated in the logical positivist "Vienna Circle." These two influences, combined with her experiences living as a Jew under the Nazi regime, shaped the focus of her psychological investigations throughout the following decades.

Egon Brunswik accepted a professorship at the University of California at Berkeley in 1937. After the *Anschluss* that incorporated Austria into Nazi Germany, Else followed him to Berkeley. They were married in 1938; they had no children. She was unable to gain a tenured appointment in psychology because of the university's nepotism rules. Instead she joined the Institute of Child Welfare (later the Institute of Human Development) at Berkeley as a research psychologist, remaining there for the rest of her career.

With her credentials in psychoanalysis and logical positivism, Frenkel-Brunswik's arrival in the United States was well timed. A new self-conscious psychology of personality was developing, as was a new profession of clinical psychology. Both were greatly influenced by psychoanalysis, which was then approaching its apogee in American psychology and psychiatry. Her dual credentials enabled her to defend psychoanalytic constructions effectively on scientific grounds against the criticism of behaviorism, which was then also at the peak of its influence (Heiman and Grant, pp. 161–231).

In her most enduring contribution, Frenkel-Brunswik worked with Nevitt Sanford and Daniel Levinson (then one of their students) to design and implement major studies of the psychological components of anti-Semitism. In these studies anti-Semitism was found to be an aspect of a more general pattern of personality regarded as underlying German vulnerability to Nazism, including a readiness to reject all "out groups." The book, *The Authoritarian Personality*, was published in 1950. A significant aspect of Frenkel-Brunswik's contribution to the collaborative research was her shedding light on the characteristics of personality of highly prejudiced and unprejudiced persons, the data for which she had gathered through the careful analysis of numerous clinical interviews with members of both groups.

The book received wide acclaim for its deft insights on prejudice and proto-fascist attitudes—achieved through a brilliant blending of the empiricism of social psychology and the clinical explorations of psychoanalysis—and for its presentation of a significant model of how child rearing, character structure, and ideology are interconnected. Criticism of the book focused on its tendency to ignore the cultural and environmental influences on prejudice in favor of its characterological roots, its emphasis on right-wing authoritarianism while ignoring similar tendencies in the left, and its various technical flaws. During the 1950s psychological journals were filled with studies preoccupied with these technical matters—none of which involved Frenkel-Brunswik's analysis of her interviews.

The important substantive claims of *The Authoritarian Personality* received appropriate research attention only decades later with the work of Bob Altemeyer, which resolved the methodological problems of the earlier work. His work essentially confirmed the authoritarian pattern of conventionality, submission to the strong, and readiness to act with hostility toward the weak and socially marginal, especially when sanctioned by legitimate authority; the psychoanalytically based conceptions advanced by Frenkel-Brunswik and her colleagues about its origins in child rearing do not fare as well.

After publication of *The Authoritarian Personality*, Frenkel-Brunswik researched the development of prejudice in children and wrote on the cognitive style of personality that she labeled "intolerance of ambiguity" (Heiman and Grant, pp. 58–91), which had become apparent through her researches on prejudice. She had also begun a major study on aging when her personal life fell into ruin.

On 7 July 1955 Frenkel-Brunswik's husband committed suicide after suffering for years with severe hypertension. Frenkel-Brunswik was devastated. The tragedy unfortunately coincided with her growing dissatisfaction with psychoanalysis and logical positivism—once her intellectual foundations. Her colleagues attempted to reward her for her achievements in child and developmental psychology, personality and cognition theory, and psychoanalytic theory through an appointment as full professor at Berkeley, which was possible since the nepotism barrier had been removed. However, Frenkel-Brunswik's emotional anguish was not lessened by this gesture, and she died in Berkeley of an overdose of barbitol before the promotion could take effect.

Frenkel-Brunswik was a major contributor to American psychology. Her contributions in research and theory depended on her command of the perspectives of psychoanalysis and logical positivism, both of which have since suffered loss of force and credibility. *The Authoritarian Personality* remains a landmark of continuing significance. The concept of intolerance of ambiguity is part of the enduring vocabulary of personality psychology.

• Nanette Heiman and Joan Grant, eds., *Else Frenkel-Brunswik: Selected Papers*, Psychological Issues, vol. 8, no. 31 (1974), contains a biographical essay and an annotated bibliography of Frenkel-Brunswik's publications in German and English. A major contribution of Frenkel-Brunswik not included is *Motivation and Behavior*, Genetic Psychology Monographs, vol. 26 (1942). Dietmar Paier, ed., *Else Frenkel-Brunswik: Studien zur autoritären Persönlichkeit* (1996), a German translation of her selected works, contains a full scholarly biography. Also see Bob Altemeyer, *Right-Wing Authoritarianism* (1981), *Enemies of Freedom: Understanding Right-Wing Authoritarianism* (1988), and *The Authoritarian Spectre* (1996). A judicious appraisal of the status of authoritarianism after four decades is contained in William F. Stone et al., eds., *Strength and Weakness: The Authoritarian Personality Today* (1993). For information on Egon Brunswik see Kenneth R. Hammond, ed., *Psychology of Egon Brunswik* (1966). An obituary is in the *American Sociological Review* 33 (Oct. 1958): 585–86.

M. BREWSTER SMITH

FREUND, Ernst (30 Jan. 1864–20 Oct. 1932), professor of law and political science, was born in New York City, the son of Ludwig A. Freund and Nannie Bayer. His parents were natives of Berlin, Germany; before 1875 they returned to that city, and Freund was educated there. He was awarded a doctorate (J.U.D.) in canon and civil law at Heidelberg in 1884, and in that year he elected to return to New York as a native citizen. There he studied law and politics at Columbia University, where his mentor was Frank J. Goodnow, earning a Ph.D. in public law for his dissertation entitled *The Legal Nature of Corporations*. He assisted in writing Goodnow's most noted work, a treatise on comparative administrative law published in 1893. Freund also practiced law in New York from 1886 to 1894.

In 1894 Freund was appointed to the political science department of the new University of Chicago and was the person on whom President William Rainey Harper chiefly relied in the founding of the university's Law School in 1902. Freund retained his ties to the political science department, helping to found the American Political Science Association in 1903 and serving as its president in 1916, but he was also the intellectual leader of the law school for its first three decades. He was responsible for its decision to extend its curriculum into law-related fields at a time when many university law schools, notably Harvard's, were narrowing their focuses on technocratic aspects of their discipline. Although his intellectual interests were broader than most, they were also practical; one contemporary attributed to him the lawyer's "natural revulsion against the nebulous speculation that often passes as legal philosophy" (Cohen, p. 316). In 1916 he married Harriet Woodworth Walton; they adopted two children.

Freund's scholarship was notably prescient. As early as 1893 he published an article presaging the virtual abolition of the doctrine of sovereign immunity in all states and the enactment of the Federal Tort Claims Act, reforms that took effect a half-century later. His doctoral dissertation, published in 1897, foretold the extension of jurisdiction of state courts over corporations responsible for consequences in the states, a development upheld by the Supreme Court in 1945. In 1904 he published a treatise on the police power of state legislatures that was widely cited by progressive state courts; that treatise was later reckoned a more accurate forecast of future Supreme Court decisions than were the opinions of the Court published at the time of his writing. He was also among the first to declare the growing practice of racial segregation by law to be a violation of state and federal constitutions, and he was perhaps the first to contend that the Equal Protection Clause of the Fourteenth Amendment to the Constitution of the United States obligated the states to assure women of equal pay for equal work.

From the beginning of his academic career, Freund was politically active. Some of his views identified him with the radical left of his time. He was in 1898 an outspoken critic of the war with Spain and of the acquisition of a colonial empire. He questioned the newly invented zoning boards as institutions likely to advance the interests of wealthy citizens at the expense of others. He supported the embattled Eugene Debs's right to oppose the war effort in 1918, and he was among the leading critics of Attorney General Alexander M. Palmer's "Red Raids" in 1919. In 1921 he helped to organize the defense of Nicola Sacco and Bartolomeo Vanzetti, outspoken anarchists who were convicted and executed for a homicide that many believed they had not committed.

These involvements were minor episodes in a long series of political efforts, most of which were devoted to sundry reforms of the laws of Illinois and other states and of federal laws. For example, in 1905 Freund drafted Illinois legislation on compensation of workers for job-related injuries. He joined with Louis Brandeis, then a Boston lawyer, in founding the American Association for Labor Legislation, an organization to secure state and federal legislation protective of workers. He advocated legislative protection of the right to bargain collectively and was among the first to urge the need for compulsory health insurance. In 1906 he drafted a new charter for the city of Chicago and became an advocate for the Progressive doctrine of municipal home rule. In 1920 he drafted provisions of the Illinois constitution bearing on that issue. In 1908 he was cofounder of the Immigrant Protection League, and for over two decades he was a leading advocate of the civil rights of immigrants. Also that year he was appointed to represent Illinois in the National Conference of Commissioners on Uniform State Laws, which

he served as chairman and also as draftsman of numerous statues enacted by state legislatures, taking particular interest in the rights of illegitimate children and in the enforcement of child support obligations. In response to these efforts, Jane Addams said of Freund that "he never once failed to be sensitive to injustice and preventable suffering" (Addams, p. 44). These activities also served to inform his later scholarship.

Freund's books constitute one of the most important accounts of the formation of American public law. He perceived the limitations of law made by judges in the course of resolving particular disputes and favored the use of the legislative process as the democratic method of law reform, a position that placed him at odds with the prevailing view among academic lawyers of his time. He explained:

Most of the common law has developed in that atmosphere of indifferent neutrality [to social consequences] which has enabled courts to be impartial, but also keeps them out of touch with vital needs. When interests are litigated in particular cases, they not only appear as scattered and isolated interests, but their social incidence is obscured by the adventitious personal factor which colors every controversy. If policy means the conscious favoring of social above particular interests, the common law must be charged with having too much justice and too little policy. (Freund, *Standards of American Legislation*, p. 48)

Freund offered extensive guidance to those responsible for the drafting, enactment, interpretation, and enforcement of legislative texts. He proposed rules to assure that legislative procedures are open to broad public participation. He was among the first to advocate empirical study of the social and economic consequences of legislative enactments and to call attention to the law of unintended consequences. He urged judicial review of administrative action to assure the fidelity of administrators to legislative commands. On the latter point, he stood in opposition to the views of early New Dealers such as Felix Frankfurter and James Landis, who advocated administrative discretion as the most effective means of regulation. Experience with New Deal agencies tended to confirm the wisdom of Freund's cautions, leading Frankfurter in 1954 to acknowledge that Freund had been a "voice crying in the wilderness" (Frankfurter, p. 1). By then, however, the views expressed by that lonely voice had formed the basis for the Administrative Procedure Act of 1950. That act is a major feature of the American legal landscape.

Freund died in Chicago. Within decades after his death, almost every position that he had taken was vindicated and almost every cause he had advocated prevailed. The extent to which he influenced those events is uncertain, but his intuition and practical judgment regarding the moral values underlying twentieth-century American public law were proven to be virtually flawless.

• Freund's papers reside in the Special Collections of the Joseph Regenstein Library of the University of Chicago. His major writings include *The Police Power: Public Policy and Constitutional Rights* (1904), *Standards of American Legislation: An Estimate of Restrictive and Constructive Factors* (1917), *Administrative Powers over Persons and Property: A Comparative Survey* (1928), and *Legislative Regulation: A Study of the Ways and Means of Written Law* (1932). A biography is Oscar Kraines, *The World and Ideas of Ernst Freund* (1974). The formation of American administrative law, in which Freund played a prominent role, is recounted in William C. Chase, *The American Law School and the Rise of the Administrative Government* (1982). An account of the founding of the University of Chicago Law School is Frank L. Ellsworth, *Law on the Midway: The Founding of the University of Chicago Law School* (1977). Evaluations of Freund include Jane Addams, "The Friend and Guide of Social Workers," *University Record* 19 (1933): 43–45; Francis A. Allen, "Preface" in Freund, *Standards of American Legislation*, 2d ed. (1965); Morris R. Cohen, "A Critical Sketch of Legal Philosophy in America" in *Law: A Century of Progress, 1835–1935*, vol. 2, ed. Alison Reppy (1937); Felix Frankfurter, *The Ernst Freund Lecture: Some Observations on Supreme Court Litigation and Legal Education* (1954); Arthur H. Kent, "Ernst Freund (1864–1932)—Jurist and Social Scientist," *Journal of Political Economy* 41 (1933): 145–51; Maurice T. Van Hecke, "Ernst Freund as a Teacher of Legislation," *University of Chicago Law Review* 1 (1933): 92–94. Obituaries are in the *New York Times*, the *Chicago News*, and the *Chicago Tribune*, 21 Oct. 1932.

PAUL D. CARRINGTON

FREY, John Philip (24 Feb. 1871–29 Nov. 1957), labor leader, was born in Mankato, Minnesota, the son of Leopold Frey, a small manufacturer, and Julia Philomen Beaudry. At the age of fourteen Frey started working in a lumber camp near Ottawa, Canada, then after eighteen months moved on to a clerk's job in a Worcester, Massachusetts, grocery store. In 1888 he became an apprentice iron molder, and when his training was finished in 1891 he went to work at a local foundry. That same year he married Nellie Josephine Higgins; they had three children.

Frey joined the Iron Molders Union (IMU, later the International Molders and Foundry Workers Union of North America) in 1893 and was elected president of the Worcester local only three months later; at the age of twenty-two he was one of the youngest men in the country to hold such an office. Rising rapidly through the union hierarchy, he became treasurer of the New England IMU conference board in 1898, vice president of the Massachusetts Federation of Labor in 1899, and in 1900 vice president of the IMU, a position he would hold for the next fifty years. In 1903 Frey moved his family to Cincinnati, the IMU headquarters, and began a 24-year stint as the editor of the *Iron Molders' Journal*. He also served as a special lecturer on economics and trade unions at the University of Chicago in 1908.

Seeking wider opportunity than his own union could provide, Frey became active in the American Federation of Labor (AFL), where he rose to importance as one of Samuel Gompers's closest aides. Under Gompers's sponsorship he served as secretary of the AFL's Committee on Resolutions 1909–1927, helping to ensure that debate at the annual conventions was structured according to Gompers's wishes; he also attended the 1909 British Trades Union Congress as an AFL delegate. During World War I, Frey worked actively at Gompers's side to support the entry of the United States into the war and to promote the Allied cause among trade unionists in Europe. At the Inter-Allied Labor and Socialist Conference in London in 1918 the two men helped to silence proposals for a negotiated peace and to block the idea of an international labor conference involving workers from both sides. They also visited areas near the front in France and toured Italy to rally union leaders there to the Allied cause. The following year Frey chaired the AFL European Reconstruction Committee; he also served as an AFL delegate to two Pan American Federation of Labor meetings in Mexico City in 1921 and 1924 and joined the American delegation to the International Economic Conference in Geneva in 1927.

Shortly before Gompers died in 1924, he helped Frey win election as president of the Ohio Federation of Labor, a position Frey held until 1928. He was active in many other organizations as well; he was president of the Norwood, Ohio, Board of Education 1918–1922; chairman of the board of the National Bureau of Economic Research 1918–1927; and a member of the Workers Education Bureau executive board 1923–1927. Serving on a number of government advisory committees and doing extensive lecturing and writing, Frey led labor's fight against scientific management during the 1920s and vigorously protested the use of the injunction in the 1930s. In 1928 he was given the rank of lieutenant colonel for presenting a series of lectures at the army industrial college; he used the title "Colonel" for the rest of his life. Although he joined the labor advisory board of the National Recovery Administration in 1933, Frey remained a committed Republican and opposed most New Deal programs, maintaining the AFL's traditional "voluntarist" position that workers should count on their unions, not the government, for social change. He was one of the few within the AFL who opposed state-run unemployment insurance in 1932.

Frey's adherence to Gompers's conservative principles won him support among other like-minded men in the AFL leadership, including Daniel Tobin and Arthur Wharton. With their backing Frey was named secretary of the AFL's Metal Trades Department in 1927 and became president of the department in 1934. During these years the AFL became increasingly polarized between those like Frey and his allies, who favored the traditional separate unions for each craft, and industrial unionists like John L. Lewis, who advocated mass organizing across entire industries. Frey threw himself into the fight, reiterating the failure of earlier industrial unions like the Knights of Labor and the Industrial Workers of the World, and insisting that as new mass production workers were organized they should be assigned within the existing craft structure.

Any other course, he argued, would "completely demoralize, if not actually destroy" the right of established unions. The bitter debates climaxed in 1935, when the AFL voted to reject industrial unionism and Lewis established the Committee of Industrial Organizations (CIO, later the Congress of Industrial Organizations).

In subsequent years Frey used both fair means and foul to combat the CIO, which he saw as a mortal threat to the AFL and to the labor movement as a whole. Besides spearheading the final eviction of the CIO unions from the AFL, he used public statements, separate agreements covering only craft union members, and secret collaboration with employers to undermine the CIO's organizing efforts. He repeatedly accused the CIO of being a Communist front and testified to that effect before the newly formed House Un-American Activities Committee in 1938. He continued these efforts during World War II, when he served as a labor member of the War Production Board's Shipbuilding Stabilization Committee and headed the Federal Commission on Apprentice Training. According to some historians, it was only his retirement in 1950 that made it possible for the AFL and CIO to initiate serious discussions of reunification; the merger took place in 1955. Frey died in Washington, D.C.

Frey was often spoken of as a labor movement intellectual. Others called him a pedant who delighted—as one critic observed—in "blear-eyed researches" that perpetuated "the ancient and honorable dogmas of craft unionism." In any case he was known for his extensive writing, his elaborate vocabulary, and his encyclopedic knowledge of labor history. The craft union tradition was indeed central to his life, giving shape and meaning to his early career. Unfortunately, his inability to move beyond that tradition embittered his later years, leading him to concentrate his energies on destroying rival unions rather than helping to extend union rights to more American workers.

• Frey's papers in the Library of Congress contain information on his life as well as his unpublished history of the labor movement. Frey's reminiscences are in the Oral History Collection at Columbia University; this collection also holds references to his career by other labor figures. His published works include *An American Molder in Europe* (1911), *The Labor Injunction* (1922), *Calamity of Prosperity* (1930), *Bakers Domination* (1933), *Calamity of Recovery* (1934), and *Craft Unions of Ancient and Modern Times* (1944). Frey's activities during World War I are described in Samuel Gompers, *Seventy Years of Life and Labor* (1925), and Bernard Mandel, *Samuel Gompers: A Biography* (1963). Most histories of organized labor discuss his battles against industrial unionism; see Walter Galenson, *The CIO Challenge to the AFL: A History of the American Labor Movement, 1935–1941* (1960); Sidney Lens, *The Labor Wars: From the Molly Maguires to the Sitdowns* (1974); Edward Levinson, *Labor on the March* (1938); Bruce Minton and John Stuart, *Men Who Lead Labor* (1937); and Milton Derber and Edwin Young, eds., *Labor and the New Deal* (1957). An obituary is in the *New York Times*, 30 Nov. 1957.

SANDRA OPDYCKE

FRICK, Ford Christopher (19 Dec. 1894–8 Apr. 1978), sportswriter and baseball executive, was born on a farm near Wawaka, Indiana, the son of Jacob Frick and Emma Prickett. Determined to become a sportswriter, Frick took typing and stenography courses at the International Business College in Fort Wayne before entering DePauw University in 1912. At DePauw he lettered in baseball and track and worked his way through school by serving as a sports correspondent for newspapers in Chicago, Indianapolis, and Terre Haute.

On graduating in 1915, he moved to Colorado Springs, Colorado, where he played first base for the semiprofessional Walsenburg club and taught "business English" in high school and at Colorado College. In 1916 he married Eleanor Cowing, with whom he had one child. Frick left teaching in 1917 to work full time as a reporter for the Colorado Springs *Gazette*, but a year later he became a supervisor of rehabilitation workers for the War Department. In 1919 he joined the *Rocky Mountain News* in Denver as a sports reporter. Within the year he returned to Colorado Springs, opened an advertising agency, and also wrote feature articles and editorials for the *Gazette* and the *Evening Telegraph*. His writing came to the attention of Arthur Brisbane, chief editor of William Randolph Hearst's New York *American*, who offered him a job.

Frick began as a baseball writer covering the 1922 New York Giants. A year later he switched papers and leagues, reporting on the New York Yankees for the Hearst-owned *New York Journal*. A proponent of Grantland Rice's "gee-whiz" school of sportswriting, Frick wrote about a variety of sports and received prestigious special assignments. But baseball was his passion, and he soon became more than a beat writer. A trusted confidant of the Yankees, he was the "ghostwriter" for star players Lou Gehrig and Babe Ruth as well as for manager Miller Huggins. From 1924 to 1933 he produced thrice-weekly newspaper columns under Ruth's byline, often without collaboration; he also wrote *Babe Ruth's Own Book of Baseball* (1928). In addition to his sports reporting and regular column, "Ford Frick's Comments," he gained recognition and popularity as the host of a pioneering radio sports show in 1930 and by participating in the first radio broadcast of Brooklyn Dodgers home games in 1931. His decision to take part in teletype re-creations of Dodgers and Giants games during the pennant race of 1933 earned him the staunch friendship of Giants manager John McGraw and proved pivotal in determining his future career. In February 1934 Frick was appointed director of the National League's Service Bureau, largely because of McGraw's influence, and when John A. Heydler retired nine months later, Frick, with strong support from the New York teams and press, was elected National League president.

Frick served as league president for seventeen years. During his tenure, the league faced unprecedented difficulties from the depression, World War II, racial integration, and player challenges to lifetime restrictions in their contracts. By means of financial arrangements involving new capital, Frick assisted the Boston, Brooklyn, and Philadelphia clubs to survive economic hard times in the mid-1930s. He strongly advocated night baseball as a means of increasing attendance revenues. When Commissioner Kenesaw Mountain Landis was preparing to shut down major league baseball after the Japanese attack on Pearl Harbor in 1941, Frick led the move to request an exemption from President Franklin D. Roosevelt. The result was the February 1942 "green light" letter in which Roosevelt declared that baseball should continue being played to bolster public morale. Frick resolutely supported the reserve clause binding players to their teams, opposed collective bargaining efforts, and favored banning players who jumped to the Mexican League in 1946. But he did endorse higher salaries for players and expanded rosters; during his presidency team rosters increased from twenty-three to twenty-five and then to thirty players.

A dedicated history buff, Frick was sensitive to the game's past and its future. His 1935 innovation of providing lifetime game passes to major league veterans was a prelude to what he considered to be his greatest contribution to baseball—the Hall of Fame in Cooperstown, New York. When community leaders in 1938 called on major league baseball to help celebrate the supposed centennial of the game's creation in the town, Frick suggested the idea of a baseball museum and library. Over Landis's persistent opposition, Frick played a key role in the creation of the Hall of Fame by providing financial support, donating documents and memorabilia, and underwriting a motion picture, *The National Game* (1938), that depicted baseball's development over the past century.

Perhaps Frick's finest hour as league president came in 1947 when Jackie Robinson broke the modern-era color line. Frick had not publicly questioned the traditional exclusion of blacks from major league baseball, but he now endorsed the correctness and inevitability of racial integration. Reacting generally to the verbal threats and epithets directed toward Robinson as well as specifically to rumors of a players' strike led by the St. Louis Cardinals, Frick announced in May that any player who boycotted the Dodgers would be suspended. "I don't care if it wrecks the National League for five years," he declared. "This is the United States of America, and one citizen has as much right to play as another. The National League will go down the line with Robinson whatever the consequence." Frick's forthright statement did much to mitigate overt hostilities and facilitate baseball's racial integration.

Because he served as league president in a dignified, dedicated, and gracious manner and, more important, confined himself to administrative matters that did not encroach on teams' self-interest, Frick was the choice of many owners to become commissioner after Landis's death in 1944. However, those who favored an appointment from outside the baseball establishment carried the day, and in March 1945 U.S. Senator Albert B. "Happy" Chandler of Kentucky was selected. Chandler's independence and candor aroused the ire of the owners and led to his resignation in 1951. This time Frick found himself deadlocked with Warren Giles, president of the Cincinnati Reds; when Giles withdrew after the twentieth ballot, Frick became the third commissioner of baseball.

Frick was the first commissioner elected from within baseball's administrative hierarchy. In contrast to the independent-minded Landis and Chandler, he announced on his election: "I am the commissioner of the owners who elected me." He disliked controversy and was content to serve as a ceremonial functionary, to use his office as a public relations instrument, and to allow the owners to reassert their power. Consequently, Frick adopted a low-key profile, avoiding hard decisions on controversial issues. "It's a league matter, not for the commissioner's office," was his persistent refrain.

During Frick's fourteen years as commissioner (1951–1965), major league baseball was transformed from a business to a nationwide industry. Six franchises relocated to new cities, including the pivotal move of the Dodgers and Giants in 1957 to Los Angeles and San Francisco; also four teams were added in 1961–1962, two to each league. Frick avoided addressing the negative aspects of relocation and expansion or their dire consequences for the minor leagues. Neither did he speak to the persistence of racism on the field and in front offices or the meager compensation of umpires. He focused more on urging the construction of new multipurpose, all-weather stadiums to increase profits, and, recognizing the lucrative potential of television, he negotiated contracts with networks to televise the All-Star Game, the World Series, and, beginning in 1955, a Saturday "Game of the Week." Frick also fought challenges to the owners' vested economic interests. He testified seventeen times before congressional committees in support of baseball's unique antitrust exemption, opposed the efforts of players to establish collective bargaining, and defended the reserve clause binding players to clubs.

In contrast to the favorable press he received as National League president, Frick as commissioner was roundly criticized by sportswriters for kowtowing to the club owners, thereby devaluing the authority of his office. Criticism turned to ridicule when Frick, allowing personal feelings for Babe Ruth to cloud professional judgment, denigrated Roger Maris's breaking of Ruth's single-season home run mark in 1961 by declaring that the record books contain dual entries crediting Maris with hitting 61 homers during a 162-game season and Ruth with 60 in 154 games. The Maris-Ruth fiasco aside, the criticism of Frick as a figurehead was understandable at the time but misplaced historically. As the selection and performance of subsequent commissioners demonstrated, Frick's tenure marked the transition of the position from a disinterested protector of the game's "best interests" to a hired advocate of the owner's economic interests. His aptly subtitled reminiscence, *Games, Asterisks, and People: Memoirs of a Lucky Fan* (1973), is a bland defense of his role as commissioner and a preview of the essential qualities and attitudes of his successors.

In the end, Frick proved himself a master of self-assessment. On his election to the Hall of Fame in 1970 for administrative contributions to baseball, he remarked: "I've always been a lucky guy. I've always been at the right place at the right time." And thirteen years after his retirement, just before his death in Bronxville, New York, he confessed to fellow sportswriter Jerome Holtzman: "I'm a newspaperman at heart. I still think of myself basically as a baseball writer." Hence, his frequent lament that his job as commissioner, being close to the game but removed from players and fans, was "a lonely one."

• An extensive collection of material is in the Ford Frick file, National Baseball Library, Cooperstown, N.Y. Frick's autobiography is episodic and sentimental. A brief but revealing reflection on his career is in Jerome Holtzman, ed., *No Cheering in the Press Box* (1973), pp. 198–214. For important information and context regarding Frick and baseball, see Lee Allen, *The National League Story* (1961); Lee Lowenfish and Tony Lupien, *The Imperfect Diamond: The Story of Baseball's Reserve System and the Men Who Fought to Change It* (1980); and David Quentin Voigt, *American Baseball*, vol. 3: *From Postwar Expansion to the Electronic Age* (1983). For his role in creating the Hall of Fame, see James A. Vlasich, *A Legend for the Legendary: The Origin of the Baseball Hall of Fame* (1990). Valuable contemporary accounts are Robert H. Boyle, "The Perfect Man for the Job," *Sports Illustrated*, 9 Apr. 1962, pp. 36–38ff; Daniel M. Daniel, "The Wise Leadership of Ford Frick," *Baseball Magazine*, Apr. 1949, pp. 373–75, and "Ford Frick Speaks Out," *Baseball Magazine*, Mar. 1965, pp. 12–17; and Joe Williams, "What They Think about Ford Frick," *Sport*, Aug. 1956, pp. 12–13ff. Important obituaries are in the *New York Times*, 10 Apr. 1978, and the *Sporting News*, 22 Apr. 1978.

LARRY R. GERLACH

FRICK, Henry Clay (19 Dec. 1849–2 Dec. 1919), industrialist, was born in West Overton, Pennsylvania, the son of John W. Frick, a farmer, and Elizabeth Overholt, the daughter of Abraham Overholt, a successful distiller of whiskey and the wealthiest citizen in Westmoreland County. Other than providing a small cottage and a few acres of poor land on his estate, Overholt shared none of his wealth with his daughter and her family. He did, however, serve as a role model for his grandson. From early childhood, Clay, as his family called him, was eager to escape the poverty with which his unambitious father seemed content and was determined that before he reached the age of thirty he would acquire a larger fortune than his grandfather's.

In 1864 Frick enrolled in nearby Westmoreland College and from there transferred to Otterbein College in Ohio. Having early set his goal on becoming a millionaire, Frick had little interest in the classical curriculum of a liberal arts college; after only ten weeks at Otterbein, at the age of seventeen he left college to take a job as a clerk in an uncle's store in Mount Pleasant, Pennsylvania.

Finding salesmanship a congenial occupation, in 1868 Frick accepted a position in a Pittsburgh department store. He quickly demonstrated his talents both in knowing and properly displaying the store's merchandise. His employer commended him particularly on his success in "waiting upon lady customers." A severe case of typhoid fever, however, necessitated Frick's returning home. Upon his recovery his grandfather employed him as his chief bookkeeper. This position held out the possibility that he might eventually take over the management of the Overholt distillery, but Frick was a young man in a hurry, eager to find his own road to wealth.

Frick's cousin, Abraham O. Tintsman, in 1869 had entered into a partnership with Joseph Rist and A. S. M. Morgan to buy up some 600 acres of coal land in the nearby Connellsville area. The soft bituminous coal in which the region abounded apparently had little industrial use except for the manufacture of coke. In 1870 only twenty-five coke plants were in operation in the country, but even that limited production exceeded the demand; iron manufacturers wanted anthracite coal and the few steel mills used charcoal.

Tintsman and his partners soon regretted their venture. Frick, however, aware of recent technological innovations in the manufacture of steel, had the vision to foresee that the new Bessemer process would provide an expanded market for coke. When Morgan dropped out, Frick asked to join the enterprise. He then persuaded the others to expand their operations. On borrowed money they bought up 123 more acres of coal land, and in 1871 they formed a company bearing the name Henry C. Frick Coke Company.

From that moment on, Frick was obsessed with buying up all the Connellsville coal lands and building as many coke ovens as he could finance. Driven by his vision, Frick approached Pittsburgh's leading and most conservative banker, Thomas Mellon, to ask for a loan of $10,000. Undoubtedly to the surprise of Frick and even of Mellon himself, the banker provided the loan. It was the beginning of a long and profitable association between the Mellon family and Frick.

By 1872 Frick's company had built 200 ovens and was selling all the coke it could produce. The depression of 1873 caused the price of coke to drop to 90 cents a ton, and there were few purchasers even at that price. Frick's partners, who had only reluctantly acceded to his expansion policies, were now thoroughly frightened and eagerly accepted Frick's offer to buy their interests. Frick never wavered in his belief that steel was the key product in industrial development, and coke was the key ingredient for the manufacture of steel. He kept a sharp watch as Andrew Carnegie, also undeterred by economic depression, was building the J. Edgar Thomson steel plant. Like his future partner, Frick saw bad times as a good time for expansion. Again with money borrowed from Mellon, he acquired more land and ovens by buying out timid competitors. When the steel mills were again in full production by 1877, Frick was ready to furnish coke at an ever-increasing price—up to $4 a ton. In 1879, on his thirtieth birthday, he had a fortune of $1 million, twice that of his grandfather's estate.

In 1881 he married Adelaide Childs of Pittsburgh. While in New York on their wedding trip, the Fricks were invited to a dinner given by Carnegie and his mother. Frick quickly sensed that America's Steel King had something more in mind than simply extending best wishes to the newlyweds, but he was not prepared for Carnegie's sudden proposal of a toast to the success of the Frick-Carnegie partnership. Even if caught off guard by this surprise announcement, Frick was not displeased. He knew what Carnegie wanted—an assured source of the best coke made in America. Frick also knew what he wanted—access to Carnegie's capital to expand his coke empire further. Carnegie's toast was acknowledged with one of Frick's rare smiles.

Within a month after Frick returned home to Pittsburgh, the partnership was effected. The Frick Coke Company in 1882 was reorganized and capitalized at $2 million. Carnegie initially received 11 percent of the company, which through a generous use of capital he increased to over 50 percent. Frick now had the funds for which he previously had had to beg.

Carnegie and Frick held the same views on the proper management of a business, which augured well for this partnership. The reduction of the cost of production was what mattered. Profits would then result, but the gains made in the marketplace were not to be distributed as dividends but rather used for larger and more efficient production. Both men believed in expanding in those times when their competitors were cutting back, and both held fast to the limited partnership organizational structure so as to ensure control of company policy. Each admired the other's insatiable appetite for more money and his shrewdness in satisfying this greed.

In personality and temperament, however, the two were poles apart. Neither man ever understood or particularly liked the other as a person. Carnegie's love of the limelight, his sanctimonious preaching of the Gospel of Wealth, and his foolish prattling about the "rights of labor" were all anathema to Frick. Frick's total absorption in business, his lack of humor, and his apparent ignorance of literature, science, or of any region outside the narrow confines of the Monongahela valley made him in Carnegie's eyes the prototypic American businessman and socially uninteresting.

Carnegie concurred with the opinion of another partner whom he did find interesting, Charles M. Schwab, that Frick was "a curious and puzzling man. No man on earth could get close to him or fathom him. He seemed more like a machine, without emotion or impulse. Absolutely cold-blooded" (Hessen, p. 106). Yet Frick was a far more complex person than his business associates ever appreciated. Cold-blooded he indeed was in his office, but in his home he was a devoted family man and a loving father to the two of his four children who survived infancy. Carnegie saw no evidence that his partner ever read anything except trade journals and business reports, but Frick was to amass one of the finest private collections of European art in America. The story of a business associate who in calling on Frick at home found him seated regally on a fifteenth-century papal throne reading the *Wall Street Journal* is undoubtedly apochryphal but nevertheless illustrative of Frick's contradictory attributes.

So impressive were Frick's managerial skills in directing the affairs of the coke company that in January 1887 Carnegie decided to bring Frick directly into the steel business by selling him a 2 percent interest in Carnegie Brothers Steel Company that entitled him to a seat on the board of managers. Two years later Frick's interest was increased to 11 percent, and he was made chairman of the board. Carnegie wrote to Frick, "Take supreme care of that head of yours. It is wanted. Again expressing my thankfulness that I have found THE MAN, I am always yours, A. C" (Harvey, p. 90).

Over the next few years Carnegie found many occasions to reaffirm his judgment that he had found the right man. Frick took as masterful a leadership of Carnegie's steel business as he had of the coke industry. He acquired Duquesne Steel at the bargain price of $1 million, and he built the Union railroad to tie the many separate Carnegie steel operations in the Pittsburgh area into an integrated unit. Over Carnegie's initial opposition, Frick also acquired through lease and purchase the rich Mesabi iron ore reserves of northern Minnesota. He pursued cost reduction with as much insistence as Carnegie himself, and it was he who in 1892 consolidated the two separate Carnegie Brothers and Carnegie Phipps steel companies into one giant concern, the Carnegie Steel Company, Ltd., to achieve administrative efficiency. Frick's management paid off handsomely. In 1889, when he took the chairmanship of Carnegie Brothers, the net profit for all of Carnegie's steel operations amounted to $3.5 million. In 1899 the net annual profits reached $21 million—a 600 percent increase in one decade.

With such rich returns, there should have been no threat of disruption to this successful alliance. Differences in temperament as well as over means by which to achieve commonly held goals, however, resulted at the end of this same decade in a particularly acrimonious divorce. The responsibility for this break lay with both men. Frick in his eagerness to acquire capital had allowed Carnegie to grab a controlling interest in the Frick Coke Company, but quite understandably Frick continued to regard the company he had founded as his special province. He fiercely defended it even at the expense of Carnegie Steel, in which he was a major shareholder. Carnegie, on the other hand, treated the coke company as a mere auxiliary support, existing only to serve the needs of steel manufacturing in whatever way Carnegie desired. For the first time since he had entered the industry in 1865, however, Carnegie now encountered a partner who refused to bow in humble obeisance to his command. A single enterprise with two commanders giving contradictory orders was destined to run aground.

The first serious disagreement came in 1887 when the coke workers of western Pennsylvania went on strike. Frick had entered into agreements with the other coke owners to hold firm against labor's demands, but Carnegie needed coke. He went over Frick's head and ordered the company to break its pledge and to end the strike on the workers' terms. An embarrassed and angry Frick promptly resigned as president of the company that bore his name.

A strike at Homestead provided a further rift in their relationship. Homestead was one of the few plants in the Carnegie organization that had unionized labor. Carnegie was determined to break that union when its contract came up for renewal in the summer of 1892; in this decision Frick was in complete agreement. Before leaving for his annual summer vacation in Scotland, Carnegie had given Frick carte blanche to destroy the union by any means he saw fit. Frick's means entailed breaking off contract negotiations, locking the workers out of the plant at the moment they called a strike, and then deploying 300 Pinkerton guards to Homestead to protect the scab labor Frick intended to import.

The result was the bloody battle on 6 July 1892 between the people of Homestead and the Pinkerton guards—one of the most violent episodes in American labor history. With the aid of the state militia, Frick was able to reopen the plant and break the union. He delivered what Carnegie had ordered, but Carnegie in far-off Scotland was not pleased. He attempted to shift the blame for the violence at Homestead onto Frick, claiming that if only he, Carnegie himself, had been present, the fiasco would not have occurred. General public sentiment held that Frick was at least honest in his antilabor stand, while Carnegie had played the role of coward and hypocrite. After surviving an attempted assassination by the anarchist Alexander Berkman, Frick even emerged as a public hero. Neither Frick nor Carnegie would ever forget the other's response to the Homestead strike.

The final incident to rupture the men's strained relationship occurred in 1899 when the Frick Coke Company raised the price on the coke it sold to Carnegie Steel without Carnegie's permission. Carnegie forced the maintenance of the former price, but not content with that tactic he sought to punish Frick for insubordination by removing him as chairman of the steel company. Carnegie then demanded that Frick sell his 11 percent interest in the company at the book value of $5 million—far below its actual worth.

Frick's response was to take the matter to court. The attention that this sensational suit generated forced Carnegie to seek an out-of-court settlement. At a meeting in Atlantic City on 12 March 1900 a compromise satisfactory to Frick was effected. The Carnegie Steel Company was reorganized as the Carnegie Company, capitalized at $320 million. Frick was allowed to keep his 11 percent interest, which under the new organization was now worth $31-plus million instead of the paltry $5 million for which Carnegie had sought to obtain it. The only concession Frick made to Carnegie was to agree never again to hold office in the company.

When Carnegie sold his company to a syndicate headed by J. P. Morgan the following year, Frick's interest in the resulting billion-dollar United States Steel Corporation again more than doubled in value, and much to Carnegie's chagrin, Frick was invited to serve on the board of the new corporation. Frick had no difficulty in finding other outlets for his managerial talents. Soon after his ouster from Carnegie Steel, Frick and Andrew Mellon in 1900 built a small but highly efficient concern, Union Steel, for the manufacture of finished steel products; it was later sold to U.S. Steel at a considerable profit. Again with Mellon, Frick founded the Union Trust Company of Pittsburgh. He was also instrumental in the reorganization of the Equitable Life Assurance Society of New York and served as director of the Cerro de Pasco Corporation for the mining of copper in Peru.

In 1905 the Frick family moved from Pittsburgh to a mansion on Fifth Avenue in New York City, especially designed to house his art collection. Here Frick died a few days short of his seventieth birthday and was buried in Pittsburgh.

Frick was a major protagonist in America's industrial development. In the business world he was regarded as a demanding employer who successfully fought off unionization, a tough competitor, and a manager par excellence. Of Carnegie's several partners in the steel industry, Frick contributed the most in the building of the industrial empire Carnegie envisioned.

Frick left an estate worth $142 million, of which $117 million was designated for philanthropic purposes. Included among his gifts were his New York home and his art collection (valued at $50 million), to be given to the city of New York after the death of his wife, and a large public park in Pittsburgh.

• Frick's papers are in the Helen Clay Frick Foundation Archives in Pittsburgh. The Andrew Carnegie Papers in the Library of Congress also provide a valuable source of primary material. A major biography—George Harvey, *Henry Clay Frick, the Man* (1936)—was authorized by the family and is entirely commendatory in interpretation. Other secondary sources of value are Robert Hessen, *Steel Titan: The Life of Charles M. Schwab* (1975); James Howard Bridge, *The Inside History of the Carnegie Company* (1903; repr. 1991); Joseph Frazier Wall, *Andrew Carnegie* (1970; repr. 1989); Kenneth Warren, "The Business Career of Henry Clay Frick," *Pittsburgh History* 73 (1990): 4–15; and Jill Connors, "The Fricks at Home," *Americana* 20 (1992): 24–31. Obituaries are in the *New York Times*, 3 and 7 Dec. 1919.

JOSEPH FRAZIER WALL

FRIEDHOFER, Hugo Wilhelm (3 May 1901–17 May 1981), composer, was born in San Francisco, California, the son of Paul Mathias Friedhofer, a cellist, and Eva Koenig, a pianist. Friedhofer grew up in a musical home. He began cello lessons with his father when he was thirteen, and by nineteen he played professionally in the People's Symphony Orchestra, a rival of the San Francisco Symphony Orchestra. In the 1920s he worked in various theater orchestras playing for silent films and the shows between features. During this time he studied composition with Italian composer Domenico Brescia, head of the music department at Mills College. Friedhofer began writing arrangements and sequences to accompany the films, and by the end of the decade he gave up the cello in favor of composing and arranging. Friedhofer married Elizabeth Barrett, a pianist, in 1920; they had two daughters. In 1929 Friedhofer moved his family to Los Angeles to take a job as an arranger and orchestrator of film music at the Fox Studio.

Friedhofer worked for Fox until 1935, when he was fired along with most of the music department after the studio merged with Twentieth Century Pictures. Warner Bros. offered him a position as an orchestrator for the prestigious Austrian composer Erich Wolfgang Korngold, who was about to embark on his first film score, *Captain Blood* (1935). Korngold was so impressed with Friedhofer's talents that he insisted on Friedhofer as his orchestrator on nearly all of his sixteen scores. When composer Max Steiner came to Warners from RKO in 1935, Friedhofer orchestrated Steiner's first Warner film, *The Charge of the Light Brigade* (1936); he went on to orchestrate over fifty films for Steiner. Friedhofer remained at Warner Bros. studio for eleven years, taking occasional freelance jobs with other studios. He finally left in 1943 to become a composer in his own right.

Friedhofer also worked for Alfred Newman, head of the music department at 20th Century–Fox. Newman had given Friedhofer his first opportunity to score a film in 1937, *The Adventures of Marco Polo*, starring Gary Cooper. Newman appreciated Friedhofer's talent and gave him fifteen films to score over the next three years. When Samuel Goldwyn was looking for a composer for his 1946 feature, *The Best Years of Our Lives*, Newman recommended Friedhofer, for which he won an Academy Award for his brilliant musical score. He composed music for over sixty films after that, winning a total of nine Oscar nominations.

Friedhofer diverged from the prevailing influence of nineteenth-century romanticism that was popular in Hollywood film scoring during the 1930s and 1940s. He drew from the styles of Hindemith, Copland, and Stravinsky, striving, as he put it in a letter to film music critic Page Cook, for a "simplicity of line, clarity of texture and an avoidance of over-lush chromaticism. In short, something that didn't sound as if it had just gotten off the boat from Europe (no disrespect intended)" (Friedhofer/Cook Correspondence, Harold B. Lee Library, Brigham Young Univ.).

His other well known film scores include *The Bishop's Wife* (1947), *Joan of Arc* (1948), *Broken Arrow* (1950), *Vera Cruz* (1954), *An Affair to Remember* (1957), *Boy on a Dolphin* (1957), *The Sun Also Rises* (1957), *The Young Lions* (1958), and *One-Eyed Jacks* (1961).

Friedhofer had a near photographic memory and astonished his peers with his musical recall. He had a passion for literature and art and possessed a quick wit ("a proper score for *The Hunchback of Notre Dame* should be quasi-modal").

After 1960 Friedhofer composed music for only seven more films, turning his musical talents to television. He scored over a hundred episodes of various television shows, including *Night Gallery*, *The Danny Thomas Show*, *The Dick Van Dyke Show*, *The Guns of Will Sonnett*, *Lancer*, *Voyage to the Bottom of the Sea*, *The Outlaws* and *I Spy*, with co-composer and master of television scoring Earle Hagen. Hagen praised Friedhofer's talent: "Hugo had the ability that I think separates men from the boys and that is, it's easy to make an 80 piece orchestra sound pretty good . . . when you're down to 12 or 14 or 10, you've got to know what you're doing. And Hugo was absolutely a master orchestrator. He could make anything sound good. I don't think there was a better orchestrator who ever lived."

Eventually, the demanding pace and limited amount of time to turn out television scores took a toll on Friedhofer. He suffered from eye infections, nervous exhaustion, and the general deterioration of his health. He stopped composing for television by 1973 and wrote his last film score in 1976 at the age of seventy-five. He turned to teaching and held classes in his home for aspiring film composers. His music for *The Best Years of Our Lives* was recorded by The London Philharmonic Orchestra and packaged into a long-playing record album in 1979. A souvenir booklet accompanied the recording with written tributes to the composer by several of his colleagues, honoring Friedhofer's fifty-year career in Hollywood. Composer Lalo Schifrin wrote, "Exuberant sonorities, a delicate balance in the melodic contours, unpredictable harmonies, a keen sense of timing, a labyrinth of orchestral colors—Hugo Friedhofer's music reflects his humanity, his sharp sense of humor, his compassion, the complexity of his mind in the search for knowledge, his sophisticated simplicity, and above all, his joy of life (in B Major)."

Hugo Friedhofer devoted his life to writing music for motion pictures and television. His score to *The Best Years of Our Lives* has become a textbook example of an outstanding film score. Friedhofer died in Los Angeles.

• A large collection consisting of loose and bound original musical sketches and complete conductor scores of Hugo Friedhofer's film and television music is housed in the Harold B. Lee Library at Brigham Young University. William Darby and Jack DuBois devote a chapter to Friedhofer, including musical analyses and a filmography, in *American Film Music* (1990). See also Tony Thomas, *Film Score, The Art and Craft of Movie Music* (1991). An analysis of the score to *The Best Years of Our Lives* by Louis Applebaum appears in *Film Music Notes*, vol. 8, no. 3 (Jan.–Feb. 1954). Lengthy liner notes by Royal S. Brown and Page Cook are included in the CD recording of *The Best Years of Our Lives*, on the Preamble label. An obituary is in the *New York Times*, 18 May 1981.

LINDA DANLY

FRIEDLAENDER, Israel (8 Sept. 1876–5 July 1920), professor and Semitics scholar was born in Włodawa, Poland, the son of Pinḥas Friedlaender, a cattle dealer, and Gittel Ehrlich. He was raised in Praga, a suburb of Warsaw, in comfortable circumstances in a traditional yet enlightened Jewish household. In early childhood Friedlaender acquired an almost verbatim knowledge of the Hebrew Bible as well as of the corpus of rabbinic literature. Studying with a private tutor, he also mastered the German language and its literary classics.

At age eighteen Friedlaender emigrated to Berlin. As a student at the Hildesheimer Rabbinical Seminary, he took classes with David Hoffmann, the articulate Jewish opponent of the new "higher" biblical criticism. The documentary hypothesis promoted by German scholars discovered various strands of literature in the Pentateuch and reconstructed the history of ancient Israel along new lines. At the same time, Friedlaender enrolled in the University of Berlin, where he studied Semitics and philosophy with leading scholars in the field: Julius Wellhausen, who synthesized the documentary hypothesis, Frederich Delitzsch, an early Assyriologist, and Wilhem Windelband, a philosopher and historian of philosophy. Later he transferred to the new German University of Strassburg, where he completed a Ph.D. in medieval Islamic studies with the noted Semitist Theodor Noeldeke. Upon graduation in 1901, Friedlaender became an untenured instructor at Strassburg. Realizing the near impossibility of a Jew securing a professorship of Semitics at a European university, he accepted the invitation of Solomon Schechter to assume a chair as professor of biblical literature and exegesis at the Jewish Theological Seminary of America in New York City, a traditionalist yet modern graduate school for rabbis. He held that position for the remainder of his life. He also taught Jewish history in the seminary's Teachers Institute, established in 1909. In 1905 he married Lilian Bentwich, eldest daughter of the noted British Zionist Herbert Bentwich. They had six children.

In the United States Friedlaender was a fierce opponent of the higher critics, who, in his opinion, jumped to conclusions that were not warranted by the biblical text or context and were informed by anti-Semitism. He himself was a competent lower critic who posed radical questions then responded with moderate answers. As a teacher, he demonstrated how archaeology and philology are essential tools for an understanding of ancient Israel in its Near Eastern matrix. At the same time he argued that medieval rabbinic exegesis must be studied for its essential insights.

Friedlaender's excellent scholarly reputation rests not on his biblical scholarship, but in the field of medieval Semitic philology and history. His dissertation on Maimonides' *Guide for the Perplexed* was the first of several important studies of Jewish and Moslem heterodoxy and messianic movements; the most noteworthy is *The Heterodoxies of the Shiites according to Ibn Hazm* (1909). Among Friedlaender's pioneering studies in the field of comparative religion were "Shiitic El-

ements in Jewish Sectarianism" (appearing in three consecutive issues of the *Jewish Quarterly Review*, 1910–1913) and *Die Chadhirlegende und der Alexanderroman*, (1913). *The Chadhirlegende* traced many versions of the legend of Eternal Life, from the Babylonian and Greek epics through Jewish, Christian, and Moslem myths.

Unlike many of his academic colleagues, Friedlaender was also a communal activist. He supported many Jewish organizations, such as The Intercollegiate Menorah Society, which sought to raise the Jewish consciousness of college students, and Young Israel, a religious organization. He helped establish Zionist organizations for children and college youth and suggested the motto ("the healing of the daughter of my people") for Hadassah, the important woman's Zionist organization founded by his friend Henrietta Szold. With his friend Judah Magnes he organized the New York Kehillah (1909–1922), an ambitious but ultimately futile attempt to unify the burgeoning New York Jewish community. Friedlaender headed its most enduring constituent body, the Bureau of Jewish Education.

In pursuit of his overarching objective of Jewish renewal, Friedlaender wrote many essays that appeared in the Jewish and general press and lectured before lay audiences. He was a popular speaker in New York and enjoyed traveling by overnight train to address audiences in other cities. Because of his proven expertise, mild and pleasant accent, and a felicitous style of speaking English rare in an immigrant speaker and writer, he attracted an enthusiastic following. At a time when a third of East European Jewry was transplanting itself onto American soil, Friedlaender was an important conduit of European ideas to American Jewry. He was one of the first explicators of the philosophy of Conservative Judaism, tracing the new American religious movement to its roots in nineteenth-century German Jewish historical scholarship and sensibility.

Friedlaender also popularized the ideas of two Russian Jewish contemporaries. For public audiences he explicated Simon Dubnow's cultural nationalism; for the reading public he translated the great historian's essays (1903) and his *History of the Jews in Russia and Poland* (1916–1920). It was the philosophy of Aḥad Haʿam (Asher Ginzberg), the noted Jewish philosopher, essayist, and Hebrew stylist, that formed the basis of Friedlaender's Zionism. For him, as for his mentor, Zionism was "the material agency for the consummation of the great [biblical] ideas of justice and righteousness." A diligent guardian of the Zionist faith, Friedlaender also produced a corpus of writings defending Zionist principles against the young movement's Jewish and non-Jewish critics. Friedlaender was not only a Zionist philosopher and apologist, but also an active leader of the Federation of American Zionists and the Provisional Executive Committee for General Zionist Affairs. For his Zionist activity he was rewarded with an appointment to the American Red Cross wartime commission to Palestine in 1918. On the eve of his departure, however, he was compelled to resign after two Zionist associates, Rabbi Stephen Wise and Professor Richard Gottheil, wrote scurrilous letters to the New York press impugning his loyalty to the Allied cause during World War I.

To compensate Friedlaender for this deep disappointment, the leaders of the American Jewish Joint Distribution Committee, a relief organization formed during the war, invited him to join a postwar mission to Eastern Europe. Though assigned to dispense funds for the restoration of Jewish cultural and religious facilities, he was soon caught up in the civil wars raging in Poland. Friedlaender was murdered near Kamenets-Podolsk in the Ukraine, in all likelihood in an effort by thieves to steal funds that he was transporting.

In his own lifetime, Friedlaender often complained that he squandered his energies on too many diverse activities. A letter to his wife on the fatal last journey promised that, upon his return, he would concentrate on scholarship. The bitter disappointment of 1918 left him with the impression that his efforts on behalf of the Jewish community were not appreciated. It was only through a martyr's death that Friedlaender acquired the universal acclaim that had eluded him in life.

• The Friedlaender papers are in the archives of the Jewish Theological Seminary Library. They contain letters, published and unpublished manuscripts, minutes of organizations, and Seminary memoranda. Some letters remain in the hands of Friedlaender's daughter Carmel Agranat in Jerusalem. Friedlaender's most enduring work is *Past and Present: Selected Essays* (1919; repr. 1961), a collection of essays on historical and contemporary issues. Friedlaender's biography is by Baila R. Shargel, *Practical Dreamer: Israel Friedlaender and the Shaping of American Judaism* (1985). Earlier biographical sketches are by Jacob Kohn in *The American Jewish Yearbook*, vol. 23 (1921–1922); Alexander Marx, *Essays in Jewish Bibliography* (1947); and Herbert Parzen in *Architects of Conservative Judaism* (1964). See also Margery Bentwich, *Lilian Ruth Friedlaender* (1957), a biography of Friedlaender's wife. Boaz Cohen systematized Friedlaender's writings in *Israel Friedlaender: A Bibliography of His Writings, with an Appreciation* (1936).

BAILA R. SHARGEL

FRIEDLAENDER, Walter Ferdinand (10 Mar. 1873–6 Sept. 1966), art historian, was born in Glogau, Germany (now Poland), the son of Sigismund Friedlaender, a merchant, and Anna Joachimsthal, both of whom died when Walter was young. Though their background was Jewish, he was brought up a Lutheran, like nearly everyone in Glogau. From age thirteen on he lived with an older sister in Berlin, where he was nicknamed "Fridolin" and was a member of a club called the Sharp Tongues. He received a Ph.D. in Sanskrit from Berlin University in 1898, studying under Albrecht Weber, generally held to have been the leading Sanskrit scholar of the time. Unusual for his generation in Germany, he did not travel among universities, except for one semester in Geneva studying with the linguist Ferdinand Saussure.

A postdoctoral fellowship in 1900 enabled Friedlaender to travel to London to edit a manuscript of medicinal recipes at the British Museum, but, soon bored, he spent time at the National Gallery and decided to pursue a career in art history. Berlin University did not permit him to obtain a second Ph.D., but he studied with Heinrich Wölfflin and, beginning in 1904, wrote exhibition reviews for newspapers and magazines, at first under the pseudonym Dr. Friedrich Walter. After having spent some years in Italy, in 1912 Friedlaender wrote a book on a sixteenth-century building with frescoes by Federico Barocci; the book served as a second thesis. A stay in Paris produced a fascination with Cézanne and a substantial monograph, *Nicolas Poussin*, that was published in 1914. That same year he married Emma Cardin. They divorced in 1943, having had no children. Also in 1914 he became Privatdozent, or unpaid instructor (the normal initial appointment), at the University of Freiburg. The art history seminar there had been inaugurated only in 1908, by the distinguished medievalist Wilhelm Voege. Voege was reported to have found all of his colleagues dull, except for a few, including Friedlaender, whom he described as "out of the ordinary, cosmopolitan, unstuffy." Friedlaender's courses ranged from those covering the Middle Ages to German nineteenth-century painting. His formal inaugural lecture on the "Anti-classical Style" of 1520 offered a positive view of artists then thought to represent the decline of the Italian Renaissance; they are now admired as the Mannerists, a label Friedlaender vainly rejected. Erwin Panofsky, who took his degree with Voege in 1914, was among Friedlaender's first students.

Friedlaender was not extremely successful in Germany. Though he was promoted to *Nichtbeamtete Professor extraordinarius*, he never became a full professor, at Freiburg or elsewhere. His German reputation appears to have been tied to his Poussin book; indeed, many of the essays contained in the 1965 Festschrift published in Friedlaender's honor deal with Poussin and related artists. But Friedlaender's book was always overshadowed by Otto Grautoff's *Nicolas Poussin*, unluckily published the same year. Additionally, Friedlaender's five-volume catalog of Poussin drawings (1939–1974) was much altered by editors, starting with Rudolf Wittkower, who disagreed with his judgments about authenticity. The second volume of the catalog was coedited by Anthony Blunt, whose subsequent book on Poussin became the standard for a generation.

Friedlaender's stronger, if initially narrow, repute stemmed from the "Anti-classical" article (not published until 1925), a matching article on the anti-Mannerist style of 1590 (1929), and a small book, *Von David bis Delacroix* (1932). In all three works he championed artists who had previously been called weak and, echoing Wölfflin, sought to define whole eras of style. The articles also present a criticism of Wölfflin's *Classic Art* (1901) for his failure to discuss the phase between the Renaissance and Baroque periods. Friedlaender's article on the anti-Mannerist style was published by the Warburg Library in Hamburg, at which Panofsky played a central role. The article's approach is entirely unlike the Warburg's usual focus on iconography and cultural history, but mutual respect for superior scholarship overcame the discrepancy. Panofsky soon cited the 1520 article, and contributions by authors from the Warburg dominated the Festschrift offered to Friedlaender in 1933. He was in the process of retiring when the Nazis intervened and forced his dismissal. They also forbade the Festschrift's publication; two copies survive at the Warburg Institute (London) and New York University.

Following his dismissal from the university in April 1933, he was rescued by Panofsky, already well connected in America. It took two years, while Friedlaender traveled widely in Europe, always returning home to Freiburg and to studying. In 1935 he received two part-time appointments, at the University of Pennsylvania and at New York University's new Institute of Fine Arts. He soon obtained a full-time position at the latter, remaining in that capacity until his death in New York City. The institute is often described as one that assembled many refugee art historians, but just two, Friedlaender and archaeologist Karl Lehmann, were chosen as mentors by many students. Although Panofsky and art historian Mayer Schapiro are often credited with the establishment of art history as a major research area in the United States, Friedlaender led in teaching the next generation. Students of his translated *From David to Delacroix* (1952) and the 1520 and 1590 articles (the latter published in 1957, after wide circulation in manuscript), which remain in print. He was "possessive" and "meddlesome" in the personal lives of his favorite students, who "adored" him, but his own life was firmly out of bounds. Friedlaender dedicated his last major book, *Caravaggio Studies* (1955), to all his New York University students, but he explicitly omitted credits for their offered materials. The book had been begun in Freiburg as a monograph but ultimately took a more modest form. It remains influential for its underlining of Caravaggio's religious seriousness rather than his Bohemian crudity, which had been the focus previously. Friedlaender's presentation, again demanding respect for what had been viewed negatively, was his nearest approach to social and contextual art history. His thought shows little evolution, but he remained active into his nineties. His Wölfflinian model may have had its most meaningful effect on students such as Robert Goldwater, Milton Brown, and Robert Rosenblum, who applied it to the definition of other, briefer eras, chiefly the modern age. The majority of theses written under him, however, focused on Friedlaender's own areas of scholarship.

• The Walter Friedlaender Collection at the Leo Baeck Institute, N.Y., includes diaries of forty years, early exhibition reviews, drafts of lectures and papers, and many letters to Friedlaender (some with reminiscences of his youth). His published dissertation, *Der Mahavrata-Abschnitt des Cank-hayana-Aranaka* (1900), includes a one-page autobiography. Reminiscences of Voege by Panofsky in *Wilhelm Voege, Bildhauer des Mittelalters* (1958), p. xxv, and of Panofsky by William Hecksher in *Record of the Art Museum, Princeton University* 28 (1969): 8, are useful for information about his activity in Germany. See also *Deutscher Universitäts-Kalender*, Leipzig, 85th to 113th eds. (1914–1933), which shows his appointment at Freiburg, as well as his promotion and dismissal, and includes the title of every course he taught. Colin Eisler, "Kunstgeschichte American Style," in *The Intellectual Migration*, ed. Fleming and Bailyn (1969), places Friedlaender in context. The Festschrift *Walter Friedlaender zum 90. Geburtstag*, ed. Georg Kaufmann and Willibald Sauerlaender (1965) includes a bibliography of his writings, complete except for early exhibition reviews. *Essays in Honor of Walter Friedlaender*, ed. Dora Wiebenson (1965), includes a full list of American theses written under his supervision. See also the review by Francis Haskell in *Art Bulletin* 48 (1966): 116. Anthony Blunt's introduction to vol. 5 of Friedlaender and Blunt, *The Drawings of Nicholas Poussin* (1974), gives an account of the evolution of the project. An obituary, unreliable on a number of points, is in the *New York Times*, 8 Sept. 1966.

CREIGHTON GILBERT

FRIEDLANDER, Leo William (6 July 1888–24 Oct. 1966), sculptor, was born in New York City, the son of German immigrants David Friedlander, who worked in the real estate business, and Margaretha Koenig, an opera singer. He studied at the Art Students' League before being apprenticed, in 1902, to Klee Brothers, a shop that specialized in architectural ornamentation. In 1908 he left Klee Brothers to attend the École des Beaux-Arts in Brussels and, later, Paris. Returning to New York in 1911, he won his first sculptural commission the following year, creating granite spandrels for the Memorial Arch (designed by architect Paul Cret) at Valley Forge, Pennsylvania. In 1913 Friedlander won the Prix de Rome, entitling him to three years of study at the American Academy in Rome. In 1917 he married painter and sculptor Rhoda Liechter; they had two children.

During World War I, Friedlander worked in Washington, D.C., on the design of navy aircraft and ships. In New York City after the war, he served as an assistant to sculptors Hermon A. MacNeil and Paul Manship. Friedlander's earliest sculptures were smaller pieces for private homes and gardens. In the 1920s he began receiving commissions for architectural sculpture, creating ornamentation for several churches in the Midwest designed by architect Bertram Grovesnor Goodhue.

Friedlander's major monumental civic works date mostly from the 1930s. He executed relief panels for banks, courthouses, and office buildings; sculpture for expositions, including the 33-foot-high panels depicting the Four Freedoms for the 1939 New York World's Fair; and large commemorative statues, such as *Roger Williams* in Providence, Rhode Island, and *The Pioneer Woman of Texas* in Denton, Texas. He designed the reliefs in the entrance hall and council chamber of the U.S. Chamber of Commerce building in Washington, D.C., and the sculptured clock over the speaker's rostrum in the U.S. House of Representatives in the U.S. Capitol.

In the early 1930s Friedlander was one of the team of artists commissioned to provide ornamentation for New York's Rockefeller Center complex. He designed two pairs of panels symbolizing Radio and Television, which terminate the piers flanking the north and south entrances to the RCA Building, respectively. The panels celebrate the new technologies through the depiction of nude human figures shown in the act of conducting and performing, listening and observing. Set thirty-four feet above ground level, the panels are meant to be clearly visible to pedestrians approaching from any direction.

In 1929 Friedlander was awarded the most significant commission of his career when the architectural firm of McKim, Mead and White selected him in competition to execute a pair of equestrian sculptures exemplifying the theme "the Arts of War" to stand at the entrance to Arlington Memorial Bridge in Washington, D.C. Friedlander adapted his 1916 bronze equestrian statue, *Valor*, and created a companion piece, *Sacrifice*. Numerous obstacles plagued the project over the next twenty-two years, including federal government regulations that stipulated that study models in various sizes be prepared. Originally to be made of granite, in 1941 the material was changed to bronze; however, after the war the cost of bronze production soared, making it impossible to have the sculptures cast in the United States. In 1949 the government of Italy offered to cast and gild the pieces as a gesture of gratitude for the Marshall Plan. Friedlander traveled to Italy to oversee the casting. Finally dedicated in 1951, the two nineteen-foot-tall statues portray nude male figures astride massive horses flanked by the figure of a nude woman. Friedlander was awarded a special Gold Medal of Honor for *Valor* and *Sacrifice* from the National Sculpture Society in 1951.

Though he received few commissions in the 1940s, Friedlander's career revived in the following decade, and he remained active until his death. In 1951, with architect Richard E. Collins, he won the commission to design the Virginia World War II and Korean War Memorial in Richmond. Friedlander's seventeen-foot-high marble figure, *Memory*, is a stylized woman, her chin lowered and her hand resting on her chest, which stands within a modern temple structure; it represents the mingled sorrow and pride of Virginia women contemplating the names of their dead.

Early in his career Friedlander taught at the Cooper Union and the Beaux-Arts Institute of Design. He was a professor and head of the Department of Sculpture at New York University from about 1935 to 1937 and later offered private instruction at his home. President of the National Sculpture Society from 1954 to 1957, Friedlander was also a member of the Architectural League of New York, the National Academy of Design, and the National Institute of Arts and Letters.

Friedlander believed that architecture is the mother of the arts, and he required the skillful integration of sculpture and mural painting. Writing in the *Journal of the American Institute of Architects* (23 [May 1955]), he condemned the work of modernist extremists who reduced art's "emotional appeal to an automaton-like, technological barrenness, devoid of human feeling, sentiment or warmth" (p. 201). However, he also rejected historicism, advocating instead an art of "true conservatism"—the "dynamic force that advances on the thesis of sound and progressive moderation" (p. 201). He recommended returning to the Renaissance and Beaux-Arts ideal of collaboration among artists and emphasized that designers should acquire craft skills and rely on intuition.

Friedlander worked most frequently in stone. As discussed by Joel Rosenkranz in his 1984 catalog, *Sculpture on a Grand Scale: Works from the Studio of Leo Friedlander*, Friedlander emphasized the weight and solidity of figures by pulling limbs close to the body. His conventionalized, largely static forms are typically enlivened by a significant gesture, made with hands, arms, or gaze. For all their massiveness, most of Friedlander's statues exhibit a linear quality and frontal orientation, resulting from his method of working from drawings projected photographically onto stone. His sculpture often embodies patriotic or idealistic themes; his plaques for the chapel door at the World War II American Cemetery in Luxembourg (1960) symbolize such virtues as faith, fortitude, and family ties. Friedlander's focus on realistic, if abstracted, depictions of the human form have led him to be viewed as a reactionary figure within twentieth-century sculpture. He died in White Plains, New York.

• Friedlander's papers are in the Smithsonian Institution's Archives of American Art. He wrote several articles for the *Journal of the American Institute of Architects*, including: "The American Academy in Rome: What Is Its Educational Value Today?" 18 (July 1952): 27–28; "Architecture and Sculpture," 23 (May 1955): 200–202; "Modern—and All Too Modern," 24 (Aug. 1955): 81–84; "Government and the Arts," 28 (June 1957): 111–13; and "Dexterous Hands," 29 (June 1958): 297–98. He also wrote "Line Drawing in Three Dimensions," *Pencil Points* 7 (Jan. 1926): 45–47, and "The New Architecture and the Master Sculptor," *Architectural Forum* 46 (Jan. 1927): 1–8. The Rockefeller Center project and the equestrian statues for Arlington Memorial Bridge received much attention in the contemporary press; see, for example, Eugene Clutz, "The Story of Rockefeller Center, XI: The Allied Arts," *Architectural Forum* 58 (Feb. 1933): 128–32, and "Italians Will Ship Gift Statues Here," *New York Times*, 13 May 1951. Friedlander frequently collaborated with architect Ralph T. Walker, who published "Architectural Sculpture by Leo Friedlander," *Architectural Forum* 65 (Dec. 1936): 533–38. An obituary is in the *New York Times*, 25 Oct. 1966; see also *National Sculpture Review* 17 (Winter 1968–1969): 22, 27. In 1984 the Hudson River Museum organized a retrospective exhibition and published a catalog, Joel Rosenkranz, *Sculpture on a Grand Scale: Works from the Studio of Leo Friedlander*.

KAY FANNING

FRIEDLÄNDER, Paul (21 Mar. 1882–10 Dec. 1968), classicist, was born in Berlin, the son of Maximilian Friedländer, a businessman, and Clara Schidlower. He attended school at the Friedrichs-Gymnasium and in 1900 began study at the Friedrich-Wilhelms-Universität, both in his native city. There he first met his mentor and patron, Ulrich von Wilamowitz-Moellendorff, the greatest Hellenist of modern times. He studied for two semesters in 1902 at Bonn under the Latinist Franz Buecheler and the Hellenist and historian of religion Hermann Usener as well as the archaeologist Georg Loeschcke. He hesitated between archaeology and philology, dedicating his Berlin dissertation, *Argolica* (1905), to both Wilamowitz and Loeschcke. A year's stipend for travel in Greece and Asia Minor followed. In 1911 he completed his Berlin *Habilitationsschrift* (1912), a second, larger dissertation required for qualification to teach in German universities, publishing an edition of a Greek text with an exegetical commentary, *Johannes von Gaza und Paulus Silentiarius: Kunstbeschreibungen Justinianischer Zeit* (1912). He was *Dozent* (lecturer) in classical philology at Berlin until 1914, when he volunteered for service in World War I. Because of the intervention of Wilamowitz at the top, he became one of the few Jewish officers in the German army. He served valiantly on the eastern front and received the iron cross for heroism. He returned as *Extraordinarius* (associate professor) to Berlin in 1918.

In 1920 he was appointed *Ordinarius* (full professor) of classical philology at Marburg, where he soon joined the circle that included the great New Testament scholar Rudolf Bultmann, the comparatist Ernst Robert Curtius, the philosophers Hans-Georg Gadamer and Martin Heidegger, and the Romanist Leo Spitzer. His twelve years there are rightly called by Winfried Buehler "the most fruitful of Friedländer's life." That year he married Charlotte Friedländer (her maiden name), with whom he had two children (one died in infancy). In 1932 he accepted an appointment at Halle. Three years later, on racist grounds, he was removed from his chair and lived three more years in Berlin without any position. He was then imprisoned six weeks in the concentration camp Sachsenhausen, but through the intercession of Rudolf Bultmann he was released. His war decoration caused the Germans to grant him privileges denied other Jews, and in 1939 he was allowed to emigrate with wife and daughter to Baltimore. He taught briefly at Johns Hopkins but was desperate for a permanent post. In 1940, at age fifty-eight, he was made instructor at UCLA but deserved better: only in 1945 did one of the greatest Hellenists of his generation become full professor at UCLA. He retired with the title emeritus four years later with a pension of $58 a month. He lamented in old age how far removed he felt in remote California from any sort of exchange of ideas in classics, especially after retirement when association with students and colleagues practically ceased. He died in Los Angeles.

His writings before 1938 reveal extraordinary breadth, with publications in mythology, Greek literature from Homer to Nonnos, Latin, ancient music and metrics, archaeology, and even German literature and philosophy. They are characterized by great learning, a mastery of the sources, seriousness, and an ability to see problems. His two English books have made him well known to American scholars. The first, *Epigrammata: Greek Inscriptions in Verse from the Beginnings to the Persian Wars* (1948), contains text, translation, and commentary for 178 important archaic Greek metrical inscriptions. But his masterpiece is his *Plato* (3 vols., 1958–1968), an English translation of his revised German publication *Platon* (2 vols., 1928–1930). Friedländer was torn between the biographical approach of Wilamowitz, who lacked interest in philosophy, and the treatment of Plato as a gestalt (a timeless figure) by the circle of the poet Stefan George, to whom Friedländer was drawn through his wife. He sought, not entirely successfully, to bridge the gap, and neither side has been satisfied. The historian of Platonic scholarship E. N. Tigerstedt concludes that ". . . from a methodological point of view, Friedländer's *Platon* must be called a mistake. It falls between two stools; it does not achieve its aim." The great value of the book for Americans remains its mastery of the earlier German hermeneutic tradition presented in English and his penetrating analysis of individual dialogues. No one since George Grote a century before had attempted in English such a detailed portrait of Plato and his work. Though one might not agree with all that Friedländer says, his work must be cited and his opinion respected.

Friedländer belonged to the diaspora of the 1930s that did so much to rejuvenate American humanities and make it world class. His breadth, with competence in archaeology, art history, philology, and philosophy, set him far above any American classical scholar of his time. His lucid style and his carefully documented writings have won him readers in classics and philosophy. Behind the books there was a gentle, patient, introspective man, unembittered by an unjust exile. The pity is that he could have achieved so much more if things had been different.

• Friedländer's papers are located in Special Collections, Library of the University of California at Los Angeles. For a full bibliography see Paul Friedländer, *Studien zur antiken Literatur und Kunst* (1969). For his life see Winfried Buehler, "Paul Friedländer," *Gnomon* 41 (1969): 619–23 (with portrait); William M. Calder III, "The Credo of a New Generation: Paul Friedländer to Ulrich von Wilamowitz-Moellendorff," *Antike und Abendland* 26 (1980): 90–102; A. R. Dyck, "Wilamowitz to Paul Friedländer on the Career of Hermann Fränkel," *Philologus* 136 (1992): 136–39; and Rudolf Bultmann, "Paul Friedländer," *Marburger Gelehrte in der ersten Hälfte des 20. Jahrhunderts*, ed. Ingeborg Schnack (1977), pp. 91–92 (with portrait), followed by the UCLA departmental obituary, pp. 93–94. The authoritative summary of his contribution to Plato is E. N. Tigerstedt, *Interpreting Plato* (1977), pp. 49–50, 126.

WILLIAM M. CALDER III

FRIEDMAN, Benny (18 Mar. 1905–23 Nov. 1982), football player and coach, was born Benjamin Friedman in Cleveland, Ohio, the son of Lewis Friedman, a tailor, and Mimi Levy. Of Jewish origin, Friedman grew up in a middle-class neighborhood in Cleveland. Attracted to football, as a senior quarterback he led Glenville High School to Cleveland's city championship in 1922.

After graduating from high school in 1923, Friedman enrolled at the University of Michigan, influenced by athletic director Fielding Yost's offer of help in finding him a job. Friedman's first two years at Ann Arbor were disappointing. As part of a freshman football team that scrimmaged against the varsity but did not schedule games of its own, he played intermittently at several positions. As a sophomore halfback, Friedman, the only Jew on the 1924 varsity, endured anti-Semitic treatment from head coach George Little. The next season, however, Yost, having fired Little, returned to coaching. In 1925 and 1926 the 5′10″, 172-pound Friedman emerged as one of the best collegiate football players of the interwar era.

During his junior and senior years, Friedman was Michigan's starting quarterback and a safety, a "sixty-minute man" (one who played both defense and offense), notable for his remarkable passing, broken-field running, and place kicking. As a quarterback Friedman had an uncanny ability to read the opposition's defense, move laterally, and take advantage of an adversary out of position. Friedman led the Wolverines to consecutive Big Ten championships with identical 7–1–0 won-lost-tied records in 1925 and 1926, and he received All-American honors both years. The American Jewish community also took notice of his successes; thousands of Jews telegraphed their congratulations when Friedman was elected team captain for the 1926 season.

After his 1927 graduation from the University of Michigan, Friedman spent seven seasons (1927–1933) as a National Football League quarterback and defensive back. Friedman's exploits significantly increased attendance, and, like running back Red Grange, he helped give the fledgling professional game legitimacy. At a time when franchise and personnel changes were common in the National Football League, Friedman played for the Cleveland Bulldogs (1927), Detroit Wolverines (1928), New York Giants (1929–1931), and Brooklyn Dodgers (1932–1933). While playing for the Giants, Friedman was also an assistant coach at Yale. From 1927 to 1931 he was an All-Pro selection. Friedman, asserted Grange, "was the first quarterback to recognize the potentialities of the pass as a touchdown weapon on par with the running game."

In 1931 Friedman married Shirley Immerman, who was also Jewish. They had no children. During much of their fifty-one years of married life, the Friedmans made their home in New York City.

Friedman retired from the professional game after the 1933 season, and in 1934 New York City mayor Fiorello La Guardia persuaded him to become varsity football coach at City College of New York. The CCNY team had just finished the worst season it had experienced in ten years, with a record of 1–5–1. Friedman faced a difficult task. Some of his players lacked previous football experience, and CCNY did not award athletic scholarships. CCNY's record during Friedman's coaching stint (1934–1941) was 27–32–0.

World War II terminated Friedman's association with CCNY. At the age of thirty-seven, he enlisted in the navy, serving from 1942 to 1945. Friedman was backfield coach of the famed football team at Great Lakes Naval Training Station. He later served aboard the aircraft carrier *Shangri-la*, participating in the Okinawa campaign and rising to the rank of lieutenant commander.

After the war, Friedman briefly operated an automobile sales agency in Detroit before becoming, in 1949, the first athletic director at Brandeis University. Friedman, who aspired to coach an established football power, accepted the position with ambivalence. Brandeis, newly established in 1948, was America's first Jewish-sponsored liberal arts university. Abram Sachar, the university's president, persuaded Friedman that Brandeis's survival depended on quality in all areas and that a viable athletic program would distinguish Brandeis from yeshivas (rabbinical seminaries). In convincing Friedman that he had a responsibility to the American-Jewish community, a reluctant Sachar agreed to include football—a sport he felt potentially uncongenial to an academic environment—in the athletic program, with Friedman as coach.

Despite Brandeis's modest enrollment and rigorous academic standards, Friedman assembled a freshman football team in 1950 and a varsity squad the next year. Brandeis football and the athletic program as a whole was successful through much of that decade. Friedman's 1957 team had a 6–1–0 record. Friedman's name recognition and numerous connections in the sport facilitated recruiting. Nonetheless, a number of Brandeis faculty were concerned that the burgeoning athletic program could be harmful to the academic climate of the university. Athletic scholarships were eliminated, and Friedman's 1959 team ended the season with a 0–7–1 record. Then, despite Friedman's protests, the board of trustees, citing the need to reallocate resources, terminated Brandeis football on 16 May 1960. During its nine-year existence at Brandeis, Friedman's football program had a record of 34–33–4. An embittered Friedman resigned as athletic director in 1963.

Although Friedman operated successful summer camps for aspiring quarterbacks in subsequent years, a resentment that his achievements were not adequately appreciated festered. Neither Brandeis nor the National Football League, he believed, acknowledged his contributions. Following loss of a leg to surgery in 1979, Friedman experienced severe depression. He died in New York City of a self-inflicted gunshot wound.

Friedman's career in football as a player and coach reflects the public relations role of sport in American society. At Michigan his football exploits enhanced the university's prestige and generated revenue. Likewise, his success in the National Football League contributed to the emergence of professional football as a profitable business enterprise. Possessed of intelligence and verve, Friedman was an eloquent public speaker and wrote several magazine articles. During its early years, Brandeis used Friedman's athletic reputation and acumen to emphasize the university's American identity, setting it apart from parochial institutions established by the Jewish community.

• A transcript of a comprehensive interview with Friedman conducted by Elli Wohlgelernter under the auspices of the American Jewish Committee (1980) is in the Jewish Division of the New York Public Library. Although largely uncritical toward their subject matter, Bernard Postal et al., *The Encyclopedia of Jews in Sports* (1965), and Harold Ribalow and Meir Ribalow, *The Jew in American Sports* (1985), provide significant information about Friedman as a collegiate and professional football player. See Peter Levine, *Ellis Island to Ebbets Field: Sport and the American Jewish Experience* (1992), on Friedman's ethnic identity. Abram Sachar, *Brandeis University: A Host at Last* (1976; rev. ed., 1995), and William Simons, "Brandeis: Athletics at a Jewish-Sponsored University," *American Jewish History* 83 (1995): 65–81, examine Friedman's tenure as Brandeis athletic director and football coach. An obituary is in the *New York Times*, 24 Nov. 1982.

WILLIAM M. SIMONS

FRIEDMAN, William Frederic (24 Sept. 1891–2 Nov. 1969), cryptologist, was born Wolfe Frederic Friedman in Kishinev, Russia, the son of Frederic Friedman, a postal clerk, and Rosa Trust. **Elizebeth Smith Friedman** (24 Aug. 1893–31 Oct. 1980), cryptanalyst, was born in Huntington, Indiana, the daughter of John Marion Smith and Sophia Strock, dairy farmers.

Two years after Wolfe Friedman's birth, his family emigrated to Pittsburgh, Pennsylvania. In 1896 Friedman's parents became naturalized citizens and renamed him William. Friedman spent one year at Michigan Agricultural College before transferring to Cornell University in 1920. He earned the B.S. and M.S. degrees in plant genetics at Cornell. From 1915 to 1918 he directed the department of genetics at Riverbank Laboratories, near Chicago, owned by eccentric millionaire George Fabyan.

After graduating from Hillsdale College, Michigan, in 1915, Elizebeth Smith also began her career as a code and cipher breaker when hired by Colonel Fabyan. Fabyan hired scholars to research projects ranging from agriculture to literature. Among them was Elizabeth Wells Gallup, who attempted to prove that the original folios of Shakespeare's works contained a bilateral cipher showing that Francis Bacon was both the true author of the sonnets and the illegitimate son of Queen Elizabeth I. Originally assigned to the Bacon project because of his skills as a photographer, Friedman discovered his true calling in life, cryptology. He also met Elizebeth Smith. They married in 1917 and had two children.

Although the Friedmans abandoned working with Gallup on the Bacon project in 1917, they intermittently studied the alleged cipher over the next several decades. Their conclusions, which demolished Gallup's thesis, received the Folger Shakespeare Library literary prize in 1955 and were published as *The Shakespearian Ciphers Examined* (1957).

In winter 1916–1917 the Friedmans improved their cryptology by examining the scant literature available. After America's entry into World War I, Colonel Fabyan offered the talents of Riverbank personnel to the federal government. Riverbank remained the primary source of American cryptological expertise until the creation of the Army Cipher Bureau in 1918. The Friedmans checked the reliability of Allied ciphers and codes and taught courses to U.S. Army officers at Riverbank. They also tested the security of a prototype British wheel enciphering machine, managing in a mere five hours to break five British messages, one of which began, "This cipher is absolutely indecipherable" (Clark, p. 59).

In 1917 the Friedmans assisted a joint U.S.–Scotland Yard investigation of secret ties between the German government and radical Hindu nationalists living in America and India. While successfully breaking intercepted messages of the Germans to Hindu nationalists, the Friedmans uncovered one of the cornerstones of cracking many ciphers and codes—the frequency of use of key letters in messages. After the war, they jointly published *The Index of Coincidence and Its Applications in Cryptography*, which expounded on this principle. This was a volume of the groundbreaking series, the *Riverbank Publications on Cryptography and Cryptanalysis* (1917–1922), that became primers for U.S. cryptological students.

From July to November 1918 William served as an army first lieutenant in France, where he worked on German codes and ciphers. Elizabeth remained at Riverbank. Demobilized in 1919, William returned to Riverbank, where he became a civilian cryptologist at Army Signal Corps Headquarters in Washington. In December 1919 he joined the War Department as its chief cryptanalyst. Elizebeth's skills as a codebreaker also became increasingly in demand during the 1920s and 1930s, especially when government departments failed to hire her husband. She served as a cryptanalyst for the War Department during 1921–1922 and continued in this capacity, working part time for the Department of the Navy in 1923.

During Prohibition, the U.S. Coast Guard, an arm of the Department of the Treasury, sought her expertise to attack the increasingly sophisticated coded radio messages of rumrunners off the Atlantic Coast and in the Gulf of Mexico. She provided expert testimony in federal court trials and traveled to coast guard bases, giving seminars on cryptography. Eventually Elizebeth became the head of a cryptologic unit based in Washington serving all law enforcement bureaus of the Treasury Department. She remained a member of the unit until the navy absorbed it in 1941.

The most famous of her numerous court appearances concerned the liquor-carrying ship *I'm Alone*. Allegedly registered in Canada, it had been sunk in the Gulf of Mexico by the U.S. Coast Guard after a warning shot went awry. By cracking a large number of coded radio interceptions, Elizebeth proved that the ship was actually owned by an American. This ended a $250,000 damage suit the Canadian government had filed against the United States.

During the 1920s William Friedman wrote a number of articles and books on cryptology, including the seminal *Elements of Cryptanalysis* (1926) and *The History and the Use of Codes and Code Language* (1928).

During the late 1920s refinement in electronic enciphering machines increased the difficulty of breaking messages and became the basis for Japanese and German machine ciphers of the Second World War. Friedman's writings were important keys to their eventual decryption. In 1930 he became chief of the Army Signal Corps' Signal Intelligence Service (SIS). The SIS built a global network of radio listening stations that sent raw data to Washington. It also developed improved codes and ciphers. Friedman trained the young scholars who teamed to break the Japanese "Purple" code.

The SIS began to attack Purple in 1937 but had little success. Therefore, in early 1939 Friedman was relieved of administrative duties in order to devote all of his efforts to Purple. After eighteen months of work, his team calculated how the Japanese device worked, built a mock-up of the Japanese *Angooki Taipu A* machine out of $684.85 worth of spare parts, and broke Purple.

While William was involved in breaking Purple, Elizabeth acted as a consultant for various governmental agencies. In 1941 her coast guard staff created secure codes and ciphers for communications between Washington and London for General William Donovan's Office of the Coordination of Information, the forerunner of the Office of Strategic Service (OSS). Elizabeth Friedman also recruited and instructed cryptographers for the OSS. In August 1942 she aided the Federal Bureau of Investigation in the successful prosecution of the "doll woman," who was found guilty of sending naval intelligence to Japan via coded orders for dolls from South America. For the rest of the war, Elizabeth Friedman continued to break the codes of suspected Axis agents operating in the United States.

The emotional and mental strain of attacking Purple caused William Friedman to have a nervous breakdown in January 1941. He was discharged from the army but continued to suffer intermittently from depression and other psychiatric illnesses. But in the spring of 1941 he returned to the SIS as civilian director of communication research. He attacked various Japanese codes and ciphers and improved American ciphering machines.

During and after the war, William Friedman invented a number of electronic enciphering devices but was unable to profit because of security concerns. In 1958 Congress appropriated a $100,000 payment in lieu of profits he could have made. For his wartime efforts, Friedman received three of the highest civilian decorations—the War Department's Commendation for Exceptional Civilian Service (1944), the National Security Medal (1955), and the Medal for Merit

(1946). Chief of Staff General George C. Marshall wrote that Friedman's work "contributed greatly to victory and tremendously to the saving of American lives" (Kahn obituary, p. 47).

After the war, William Friedman helped reorganize American cryptological activities and aided the formation of the National Security Agency (NSA), where he became the special assistant to the director, in 1952. He also undertook a number of secret missions to Europe to coordinate American and allied cryptological efforts during the Cold War. In the 1950s he became somewhat disenchanted over what he perceived to be the overzealous security efforts of the NSA. This concern, combined with nervous strain and two heart attacks in 1955, contributed to his retirement that year.

After William's retirement, he and Elizabeth returned to the Bacon cipher project and attempted to use their cryptological skills to read Mayan hieroglyphs. William also served as a consultant for the NSA. He died in Washington, D.C. Elizabeth spent her retirement creating a bibliography of her and William's work for the George C. Marshall Research Library in Lexington, Virginia. She died in Plainfield, New Jersey.

• William and Elizabeth Friedman's papers are in the George C. Marshall Library, Lexington, Va. Many remained classified until the mid-1980s, when the National Security Agency declassified a large number of documents pertaining to Second World War cryptology. Copies of most of these documents, including many written by William Friedman, are in the National Archives, Washington, D.C., and *A Cryptologist Looks at Literature* (1945). Other selections are located in *Signal Corps Bulletin* and *Philological Quarterly*. There is a distinct possibility that many of the documents solely attributed to William Friedman were the result of a collaborative effort with Elizabeth. This was confirmed by their daughter Barbara Friedman Atchison in fall 1993. The only book-length biography of William Friedman is Ronald Clark, *The Man Who Broke Purple* (1977). There is no biography of Elizabeth Friedman, but Clark's biography provides a fair amount of detail about her life and career. James R. Chile, "Breaking Codes Was This Couple's Lifetime Career," *Smithsonian*, June 1987, pp. 128–44, provides a brief overview of the lives of both of the Friedmans. Readers seeking a more detailed explanation into the complexities of cryptology should examine Cipher A. Deavours and Louis Kruh, *Machine Cryptography and Modern Cryptanalysis* (1985); David Kahn, *The Codebreakers: The Story of Secret Writing* (1967); and Ronald Lewin, *The American Magic* (1982). Kahn wrote William Friedman's obituary in the *New York Times*, 3 Nov. 1969. Elizabeth's obituary is in the *New York Times*, 3 Nov. 1980.

FREDRICK M. GLENWRIGHT

FRIEDMANN, Herbert (22 Apr. 1900–14 May 1987), ornithologist and museum director, was born in Brooklyn, New York, the son of Uriah M. Friedmann, a druggist, and Mary Behrmann, a teacher. Growing up in New York City, he developed an interest in nature and art through frequent visits to the American Museum of Natural History and the Metropolitan Museum of Art. During high school Friedmann joined a bird club and began making observations of the local avifauna. Friedmann graduated from the City College of New York with a B.Sc. in biology in 1920. Shortly thereafter he published his first ornithological paper, "The Weaving of the Red-billed Weaver Bird in Captivity" (*Zoologica* 2, no. 16: 355–72), based on observations made at the New York Zoological Society's Bronx Zoo.

Friedmann received his Ph.D. in ornithology from Cornell University in 1923. His dissertation was a study of brood parasitism by cowbirds. After serving as a summer instructor of zoology at the University of Virginia in 1923, Friedmann was awarded a National Research Council postdoctoral fellowship at Harvard University to work under William Morton Wheeler on the parasitic breeding habits of birds. During 1923–1924 he was in Argentina studying three species of indigenous cowbirds and in 1924–1925 conducted investigations of honeyguides, weaverbirds, and cuckoos in Africa. He made extensive collections for Harvard's Museum of Comparative Zoology (MCZ) on these trips. Friedmann's postdoctoral work was followed by teaching assignments at Brown University (1925–1926) and Amherst College (1927–1929). While at Amherst, he continued his association with the MCZ, working on his own and other collections of African birds.

Friedmann joined the Smithsonian Institution in 1929, when he was appointed curator of the Division of Birds, United States National Museum (USNM), replacing the veteran ornithologist Robert Ridgway, who had recently died. Two months after Friedmann arrived in Washington, D.C., the stock market crashed, and his plans to change the scope of the division's research from straight taxonomy to studies based on bird behavior and biology were for the most part abandoned due to lack of funds. The depression also played havoc with Friedmann's personal research program as money to publish larger monographs could not be found. Nevertheless, he managed to publish hundreds of papers and several books during his tenure in the Division of Birds, as well as overseeing a steady growth of ornithological collections and playing a central role in the modernization of exhibits at the USNM. In 1937 he married Karen Juul Vejlo; they had one daughter.

The 1930s and 1940s saw Friedmann become increasingly interested in art, especially the symbolic use of animals in works of medieval and Renaissance artists. The opening of the National Gallery of Art on the National Mall in 1941 intensified the interest, and, even though his boss, ornithologist Alexander Wetmore, was skeptical, Friedmann continued to work on the subject in his spare time. The result was the publication in 1946 of *The Symbolic Goldfinch*, in which he analyzed the use of the European goldfinch as an amulet during the era of the bubonic plague in Europe. He published another book, *A Bestiary for St. Jerome: Animal Symbolism in European Religious Art* (1980), as well as several papers on the subject.

After serving as head curator of zoology at the USNM from 1958 to 1961, Friedmann left the Smithsonian to accept the position of director of the Los Angeles County Museum of Science, History and Art. One of his first duties after moving west was to oversee the completion of plans to separate the natural history and art divisions into two museums. After that plan was completed, Friedmann served as director of the newly named Los Angeles County Museum of Natural History from 1961 to 1970. An interesting challenge awaited him in Los Angeles, a challenge he saw as threefold: building collections, promoting research, and planning exhibitions. According to Friedmann his job at the Smithsonian "was primarily making great collections meaningful and useful in as many ways as possible. There [Los Angeles] it was a matter of building them up." The museum's holdings grew by three to four million during Friedmann's tenure, primarily through expeditions and the transfer of university specimen collections. He secured grants from the National Science Foundation and other agencies to fund collecting trips and to strengthen the museum's research program. Drawing on his experience at the USNM, Friedmann directed a major program of exhibition construction and renovation. New halls of pre-Columbian, South Pacific, and African ethnology were completed during his directorship. During this period Friedmann began an association with the University of California at Los Angeles, serving as professor in residence in the Department of Zoology (1963–1970) and in the Department of Art (1968). Shortly after his retirement in 1970, Friedmann spent several weeks in the Antarctic evaluating biological programs for the National Science Foundation.

Described by S. Dillon Ripley as "one of this country's most scholarly ornithologists," Friedmann is probably best known for his research on the evolution of brood parasitism in birds. In several books and scholarly papers, Friedmann described the morphological adaptations and specialized behavior that allowed brood parasites (cuckoos, cowbirds, honeyguides, and weaverbirds) to build no nests of their own but instead to lay their eggs in the nests of other species. He also conducted extensive studies of the honeyguides, analyzing their habit of leading humans to beehives and their ability to digest beeswax. His body of work comprises more than 300 scholarly papers and seventeen books, including *The Cowbirds: A Study in the Biology of Social Parasitism* (1929), *Birds Collected by the Childs Frick Expedition to Ethiopia and Kenya Colony* (2 parts, 1930, 1937), *Notes on the Ornithology of Tropical East Africa*, with Arthur Loveridge (1937), *The Parasitic Cuckoos of Africa* (1949), *The Honeyguides* (1955), and *The Parasitic Weaverbirds* (1960).

Friedmann was a member and officer of numerous organizations and was the recipient of several awards for his professional achievements. He served as president of the American Ornithologists' Union (1937–1939); of section F (Zoology) of the American Association for the Advancement of Science (1939); and of the Biological Society of Washington (1957–1958). Friedmann's honors included a Guggenheim Fellowship (1950); the Leidy Medal of the Academy of Natural

Sciences, Philadelphia (1955); the Elliot Medal of the National Academy of Sciences (1959); and the Brewster Medal of the American Ornithologists' Union (1964). He was elected a member of the National Academy of Sciences in 1962. He died in Laguna Hills, California, and his ashes were placed in a memorial step at the Oak Hill Cemetery in Washington, D.C.

During nearly sixty years of active ornithological research, Friedmann contributed much to our understanding of nest parasitism, the behavior and wax digestion of the honeyguides, the avifaunas of Africa and South America, and animal symbolism in the art of the Renaissance and Middle Ages. Ripley stated in 1993 that *The Cowbirds: A Study in the Biology of Social Parasitism* continued to be a key reference on the subject six decades after its publication. Friedmann was an effective museum administrator contributing to the increase of collections and the modernization of exhibits at the USNM during an era of fiscal restraint. As director of the Los Angeles County Museum of Natural History he helped to establish a world-class organization, increasing collections, developing research potential, and creating new exhibitions.

• Correspondence documenting Friedmann's curatorial and administrative careers at the United States National Museum, as well as his ornithological research, is maintained in the Office of Smithsonian Institution Archives (OSIA). OSIA also has a series of oral history interviews with Friedmann, which cover his education, careers at the USNM and Los Angeles County Museum of Natural History, and research interests. Some of Friedmann's field catalogs and an unpublished manuscript on the birds of the Smithsonian-Roosevelt African Expedition are housed in the Division of Birds, National Museum of Natural History. Records documenting his directorship of the Los Angeles County Museum of Natural History are located in the museum's library. The most complete biographical articles are S. Dillon Ripley, "Herbert Friedmann, April 22, 1900–May 14, 1987," National Academy of Sciences, *Biographical Memoirs* 62 (1993): 143–65, which gives an overall assessment of his career and provides insights to his personality and private life; and Stephen I. Rothstein et al., "In Memoriam: Herbert Friedmann," *Auk* 105 (Apr. 1988): 365–68, which provides a complete evaluation of his contributions to ornithology. An obituary is in the *New York Times*, 20 May 1987.

WILLIAM COX

FRIEND, Charlotte (11 Mar. 1921–7 Jan. 1987), immunologist and cell biologist, was born in New York City, the daughter of Russian-Jewish immigrants Morris Friend, a businessman, and Cecelia Wolpin, a pharmacist. Friend's father died when she was three years old, and her mother was left with four young children to raise during the depression. Friend took advantage of the many free cultural and educational advantages that New York offered and developed a wide-ranging, lifelong interest in art, music, and science. Following graduation from Hunter College of the City of New York in 1944, she enlisted in the U.S. Navy and served as an officer in hematology laboratories in California and Florida. When World War II

ended, she enrolled as a graduate student at Yale University with the financial assistance of the G.I. Bill. She received her Ph.D. in bacteriology in 1950.

Friend then returned to New York and joined the staff of the Sloan-Kettering Institute for Cancer Research, which had recently been founded under the directorship of Cornelius P. Rhoads. Here she had the freedom to pursue her research interests in a strongly supportive atmosphere. She and a colleague designed experiments to determine if a transplantable cancer of mice (the Ehrlich carcinoma) could be transmitted with cell-free extracts containing no intact cells, which would suggest that the cancer was caused by a virus. In carrying out these experiments, Friend fortuitously discovered a virus-like agent that induced a transmissible, malignant disease of red blood cells. At that time, theories of the viral, and possibly infectious, etiology of cancer were not viewed favorably, and the scientific community initially evinced great skepticism, on the one hand, that the disease observed was a cancer and, on the other hand, that the causative agent of the disease was a virus. However, Friend's solid data, published in the *Journal of Experimental Medicine* (105 [1957]: 307–18), soon convinced others that she did have a bona fide virus and that that virus produced a leukemia-like disease that could be transmitted serially from mouse to mouse.

For the experimentalist, Friend's virus had two major advantages: first, it was active when inoculated into adult non-inbred mice and did not require special mice for its transmissibility, and second, the latent period was short, with symptoms of the disease appearing within two to three weeks after virus inoculation. Consequently, Friend received numerous requests for the virus from scientists all over the world. She generously fulfilled these requests, providing detailed instructions on how to handle the material. Soon the Friend leukemia virus (FLV) became one of the most widely used model systems for studying tumor virology and cancer pathogenesis.

Within a short time, however, other investigators discovered a second agent in FLV preparations, one that had either gone undetected in the original virus stocks or had arisen through genetic recombination during multiple passages in other laboratories or perhaps even in Friend's laboratory. This new agent differed from the original prototype FLV in both the pathogenesis of the disease it induced and in its mode of replication. Unlike FLV, it produced small foci of tumor cells in the spleen and was named "spleen focus-forming virus" (SFFV). In addition, the virus was defective, requiring interaction with FLV or a similar virus to complete its replication cycle. Because of these unique features, SFFV and the FLV/SFFV complex also became important and fascinating tools for those doing cancer research. Although no exact human equivalents of these murine viruses have been found, the unraveling of their mechanism of action and mode of replication has greatly aided our understanding of virus-induced human diseases and cancer.

In 1966 Friend became director of the Center for Experimental Cell Biology at a new medical school established by New York's Mount Sinai Hospital. It was here that she made another important, seminal observation. Using in vitro cultures of Friend leukemia cells she had developed, she showed that the chemical dimethyl sulfoxide could stimulate these cancer cells to differentiate: the treated cells acquired many of the characteristics of normal red blood cells, including hemoglobin production and loss of the ability to multiply (Friend et al., *Proceedings of National Academy of Sciences USA* 68 [1971]: 378–82). This was one of the first demonstrations that expression of the malignant phenotype could be reversed, and Friend cells became a widely used model for analyzing gene expression during cell proliferation and differentiation. Cell cultures of Friend leukemia cells joined FLV and the SFFV/FLV complex as powerful research tools for cell and molecular biologists. The Friend Cell Workshop held in West Germany in 1975 (summarized in *Nature* 257 [1975]: 741–43) was typical of the many meetings held to discuss work on the Friend virus–Friend cell system.

Friend was a warm and social person, a good conversationalist with extensive knowledge of music and the arts and a droll sense of humor. She received international recognition for her achievements and contributions and enjoyed the opportunities this gave her to travel. She particularly liked to visit other scientists in their own laboratories and discuss their work with her cells and virus. Among her many honors were the Alfred P. Sloan Award for Cancer Research (1962), the Prix Griffuel (1979), and the Papanicolaou Award (1982), and several honorary degrees. She was elected a member of the National Academy of Sciences in 1976, at a time when less than 2 percent of the academy's members were women.

Friend was an active participant in the women's movement in the 1970s and considered it her responsibility to encourage and support other women in science. Consequently, when women of achievement were called on to head major scientific organizations, Friend always agreed to run for election when asked. From 1975 to 1979 she found herself serving as president of three large societies (the Harvey Society, the American Association for Cancer Research, and the New York Academy of Sciences). These responsibilities, however, together with those she had as director of her own laboratory, kept her from her favorite activities—peering through her microscope and working at the laboratory bench.

Friend, who never married, was diagnosed with lymphoma on her sixtieth birthday and succumbed to the disease six years later in New York City.

• The papers of Charlotte Friend are in the archives of the Mount Sinai Medical Center; a guide to the collection was prepared in 1993. Friend's own history of her discoveries can be found in her presidential address to the American Association for Cancer Research, "The Coming of Age of Tumor Virology," published in *Cancer Research* 37 (1977): 1255–63.

Friend's complete bibliography of more than 160 publications is published in Leila Diamond and Sandra R. Wolman, eds., "Viral Oncogenesis and Cell Differentiation: The Contributions of Charlotte Friend," *Annals of the New York Academy of Sciences* 567 (1989): 5–13. A more extensive biography of Charlotte Friend, by Diamond, is in the National Academy of Sciences, *Biographical Memoirs* 63 (1994): 126–48. An obituary is in the *New York Times*, 16 Jan. 1987.

LEILA DIAMOND

FRIENDLY, Henry Jacob (3 July 1903–11 Mar. 1986), judge, was born in Elmira, New York, the son of Myer H. Friendly, the president of the Friendly Boot and Shoe Company, and Leah Hallo. The Friendly family was active in the local Jewish community of Elmira. Henry J. Friendly attended the local public schools, graduating from the Elmira Free Academy in 1919.

Friendly graduated summa cum laude both from Harvard University in 1923 and from the Harvard Law School in 1927. He performed so brilliantly at the law school that he attracted the attention of Felix Frankfurter, then a professor at the school. During the 1920s and 1930s Frankfurter, working in close cooperation with Supreme Court Justice Louis D. Brandeis, acted as a recruiting agent, encouraging promising young scholars to enter public service. Following Friendly's graduation, Brandeis, on Frankfurter's recommendation, made him his law clerk for the 1927–1928 court term. In 1928 Friendly published an article on diversity jurisdiction in the *Harvard Law Review*. In 1930 he married Sophie Stern, daughter of Horace Stern, who was a justice of the Pennsylvania Supreme Court. They had a son and two daughters.

After his clerkship with Brandeis, Friendly entered private practice. Brandeis expressed some disappointment at this decision but remained confident that Friendly would someday enter public service. His hope, however, was deferred for some years as Friendly launched a successful career as an expert in railroad law, having passed the bar in 1928. He worked as an associate for the prestigious firm of Root, Clark, Butler & Ballantine in New York City from 1928 to 1936 and then as a partner in the firm from 1937 to 1945 before starting his own firm of Clary, Gottlieb, Friendly & Hamilton, which he headed from 1946 to 1959. He also served as general counsel and vice president for Pan American World Airways.

Friendly, a Republican, was appointed to the United States Court of Appeals for the Second Circuit in 1959 and was chief judge of this court from 1971 to 1973. He served with distinction on the U.S. Court of Appeals, and his reputation, both as a judge and as a legal scholar, steadily grew during these years. In the late 1960s there was speculation that he would be nominated for the U.S. Supreme Court, but Republican president Richard Nixon did not select him.

While serving as a judge, Friendly, in addition to many journal articles, wrote *The Need for Better Definition of Standards* (1962), *Federal Administrative Agencies* (1962), *Benchmarks* (1967), *The Dartmouth College Case and the Public* (1969), and *Federal Juris-*

diction: *A General View* (1973). In addition, in 1974 he was appointed presiding judge of a special court that dealt with the reorganization or bankruptcy of several U.S. railroads.

Over the years Friendly found himself increasingly at odds with the judicial activism of the Warren Court, particularly in its application to police work. He expressed concern over the implications of the Supreme Court's decisions in *Escobedo v. Illinois* (1964), which affirmed the right of suspects to have their lawyers present during questioning, and *Miranda v. Arizona* (1966), which required the police to inform suspects of their right to remain silent. Friendly believed that these decisions tilted the scale too much in favor of criminals.

Despite the fact that Friendly was out of sympathy with much of the contemporary legal climate of opinion, his reputation remained high. He was the recipient of numerous honorary degrees and delivered prestigious law lectures, including the Oliver Wendell Holmes Lecture at Harvard University in 1962 and the James S. Carpenter Lecture at Columbia University in 1973. Indeed, he was regarded by many, along with Learned Hand, "as one of the greatest U.S. jurists never to sit on the Supreme Court" (*Time*, 24 Mar. 1986, p. 84).

Friendly died at his Park Avenue apartment in New York City. His death, due to a drug overdose, was an apparent suicide. In three notes found in his apartment, Friendly expressed distress over the loss of his wife, who had died on 7 March 1985, his failing eyesight, and poor health.

• There is no collection of Friendly's papers. The details of his life can be found in standard biographical reference sources. There is a historical folder on Friendly and his family at the Chemung County Historical Society in Elmira, N.Y. Friendly's oral history interview for the Columbia Oral History Research Office (1962) is brief and focuses on the aviation industry. For a brief but glowing tribute to his legal scholarship, see Michael I. Sovern's foreword to *Federal Jurisdiction: A General View* (1973). An obituary is in the *New York Times*, 12 Mar. 1986.

NELSON L. DAWSON

FRIES, John (1750–Feb. 1818), vendue crier and leader of the Fries Rebellion of 1799, was born in Hatfield Township, Montgomery County, Pennsylvania, the son of Simon Fries, a Welsh immigrant to Maryland whose occupation is unknown. Nothing is known of his mother. Fries was apprenticed to the coopering trade as a youth. During that time he learned to read, write, and perform simple arithmetic. Living in a predominantly German region, Fries, an English speaker, acquired the German language as well. In 1770 he married Margaret Brunner; they had ten children. In 1775 he and his family moved to Lower Milford Township, Bucks County, Pennsylvania, where they rented a log cabin and a small piece of land. There Fries left the coopering trade and began calling public auctions for a living. He was a natural for this position as a literate, bilingual man living in a region dominated politically by English speakers and populated mostly by Pennsylvania Dutch. He quickly gained the respect of the Anglo and German-American communities in his own township and in the bordering counties of Northampton and Montgomery.

During the American Revolution, Fries increased his local popularity and fame with his service to the patriot cause. During the British occupation of Philadelphia, as local legend holds, a foraging party of British Light Horse swept through Bucks County confiscating milk and beef cattle. Upon hearing the ruckus in the middle of the night, Fries left his house and assembled the local militia, led them to the British party, and liberated the livestock. Whether truth or fiction, the popular conception of this episode elevated Fries's reputation, and he was given command of a company of Bucks County militia. In the fall of 1777 his company was called to reinforce General George Washington's Continentals at Whitemarsh and Camp Hill, Pennsylvania. The following spring Fries commanded the same company in the patriot's defeat at Crooked Billet in Montgomery County, Pennsylvania.

By 1794 Fries's reputation as a patriot and an auctioneer along with his middle-aged years brought him a promotion in the militia from lieutenant to captain. In that capacity he led troops under President Washington and General Alexander Hamilton into western Pennsylvania to quell the Whiskey Rebellion. By 1798 Fries and his family moved to a log cabin on a twelve-acre tract of land they bought in Charlestown (now Trumbaursville), Lower Milford Township, Bucks County. That same year spawned the events that led to Fries's fame and infamy.

In 1798 the Federalist-controlled Fifth U.S. Congress passed a body of legislation to provide for national security in light of recent French actions. In the XYZ affair of that spring, French officials had demanded a payment of tribute before receiving American ministers, and in addition France had openly attacked American commercial shipping since the Washington administration's negotiation of the Jay Treaty with Britain, France's military enemy, in 1795. With the new laws, Congress provided for fortification of ports and harbors, commissioned the construction of three warships, augmented the navy and the army, restricted naturalization, and curbed First Amendment rights with the so-called Alien and Sedition Acts. To fund these military measures, Congress passed a Stamp Act to raise revenue from various legal transactions on paper and the Direct Tax Act, the first national "direct" tax on "lands, dwelling houses, and slaves." Fries and his German-American neighbors, hitherto members of the Federalist party out of patriotic respect for General Washington, objected to this draconian and seemingly monarchical body of legislation. In the fall of 1798 Democratic-Republicans from regional districts in Bucks, Northampton, Montgomery, and Berks counties were swept into local and national offices. Stoked by the fires of election year politics, the Pennsylvania Germans of the Lehigh Valley region flooded Congress with petitions to repeal much of the national security legislation, including the taxes. When tax assessors made their way into Bucks County in December, they were met by obstinate citizens who obstructed the valuation of their homes. Fries held meetings in his home and led his neighbors in signing "associations," in which they pledged to one another that they would not allow their homes to be assessed because, in Fries's words, the laws were "unconstitutional." What Fries and his neighbors meant by this charge was that the laws did not conform to their conception of acceptable behavior by a republican government bound by a republican constitution. By the end of February 1799 William Nichols, a federal marshal, had swept through neighboring Northampton County, arresting tax resisters on orders from U.S. judge Richard Peters. When word spread of the arrests and the marshal's intent to transport the prisoners to Philadelphia for trial, militia units from Northampton and Bucks counties marched to the Sun Tavern in Bethlehem, where the accused were jailed on 6 March. The two contingents met outside the Moravian town at midday on 7 March, and Fries assumed command of the combined force, which totaled nearly 140 men, some armed and some not. Fries first tried to secure the prisoners' release on bail, stating that he and his neighbors did not want to prevent a trial. He appealed for their Sixth Amendment right to a local trial by a jury of their peers, but the marshal refused to respond. Fries then warned that he was not sure he could restrain his troops, and the marshal quickly surrendered the prisoners to the "rebels." The "Fries Rebellion" concluded without the firing of a single shot.

In the months that ensued, the Federalist president John Adams's administration sent federal troops into the region under the command of General William MacPherson to apprehend Fries and thirty others. They were taken to Philadelphia and charged with crimes ranging from obstruction of process to treason. Fries and two of his neighbors, William Getman and Frederick Heaney, were charged with treason, tried, and convicted with considerable public attention in April and May 1799. The convictions were thrown out with the revelation of a biased juror. A yellow fever epidemic delayed their subsequent trials for treason for another year, but once again they were convicted and sentenced to hang by Judge Samuel Chase, who was later a Supreme Court justice. President Adams had used the preceding year to inquire into the matter for himself and was convinced that, while illegal, Fries's actions did not amount to treason. On 21 May 1800, forty-eight hours before the scheduled execution, Adams pardoned the three condemned men. The Federalist party was already disintegrating, but the president's leniency so outraged the followers of Hamilton that the pardon completed the split just months prior to Adams's bid for reelection.

After his eleventh-hour reprieve, Fries returned to Lower Milford and continued to call public auctions until his death there. Yet he and his cause were not forgotten. He was resurrected as a martyred figure decades later by the Pennsylvania Dutch of the Lehigh Valley, who colored the Whig party as Federalist aristocratic militarists and warned the people that to put the Whigs in the White House in 1836 would bring back "the Times of '99."

• No known collection of Fries's papers exists, though the William Rawle Papers at the Historical Society of Pennsylvania in Philadelphia include extensive depositions and affirmations taken from participants in and eye witnesses to the Fries Rebellion. For the impression of the rebellion upon the popular memory of the Pennsylvania Dutch of the Lehigh Valley region, see newspaper clippings in the Ray A. Weaver Collection, Henry Snyder Manuscripts, in the Lehigh County Historical Society. The best source for the trial testimony of Fries and other resisters is the stenographer's account, John Carpenter, *Two Trials of John Fries* (1800). W. W. H. Davis, *The Fries Rebellion* (1899), provides a monographic treatment of the insurrection. More modern treatment of the affair and bits of biographical information on Fries are in Dwight F. Henderson, "Treason, Sedition, and Fries Rebellion," *Journal of Legal History* 14 (1970): 308–17; Peter Levine, "The Fries Rebellion: Social Violence and the Politics of the New Nation," *Pennsylvania History* 40 (1973): 241–58; Jane Shaffer Elsmere, "The Trials of John Fries," *Pennsylvania Magazine of History and Biography* 103 (1979): 432–35; Paul Douglas Newman, "Fries's Rebellion and American Political Culture, 1798–1800," *Pennsylvania Magazine of History and Biography* 119 (1995): 37–74; and Newman, "The Fries Rebellion of 1799: Pennsylvania Germans, the Federalist Party, and American Political Culture" (Ph.D. diss., Univ. of Kentucky, 1996).

PAUL DOUGLAS NEWMAN

FRIETSCHIE, Barbara Hauer (3 Dec. 1766–18 Dec. 1862), the inspiration for John Greenleaf Whittier's poem "Barbara Frietchie," was born in Lancaster, Pennsylvania, the daughter of Johann Niklaus Hauer, a hatter, and Catherine Zeiler (or Ziegler). Barbara Hauer's parents were both German immigrants, arriving in the American colonies in the middle of the eighteenth century. When Barbara was a child, the Hauer family moved from Lancaster to Frederick, Maryland, where Johann Hauer established his haberdashery. In Frederick, Barbara Hauer met and married John Casper Frietschie, a glover whose father had been hanged for his involvement with a Tory plot in the American Revolution. In stark contrast to her father-in-law's disloyalty, Barbara Frietschie gained a reputation for exuberant patriotism. It was the legend of her patriotic defiance of Confederate troops that caught the attention of Whittier and became the subject of his 1863 poem published in the *Atlantic Monthly*.

Barbara Frietschie lived most of her life in relative obscurity. Her education was minimal, although she was apparently able to sign her name. In 1806, nearly forty, she wed a man fourteen years her junior. She had no children and survived her husband by thirteen years. Although records indicate that the Frietschies, like the Hauers, owned slaves, Barbara Frietschie was not a secessionist. In 1862, when one year of fighting had passed between Union and Confederate troops and Robert E. Lee's army took the offensive and entered Maryland, Barbara Frietschie was ninety-six years old. According to some reports, she was in failing health at the time of the Confederate occupation of her city.

In Whittier's tribute, Barbara Frietschie hung an American flag prominently from her window during the Confederate march through Frederick. When Stonewall Jackson passed Frietschie's home he was angered by the sight of the Union banner and ordered his men to shoot the flag down. But "quick, as it fell, from the broken staff, / Dame Barbara snatched the silken scarf" and uttered these immortal words: "Shoot, if you must, this old gray head, / But spare your country's flag." Frietschie's remark, as imagined by Whittier, "stirred" Jackson's "nobler nature," prompting him to order each soldier to cease his firing or to die "like a dog."

At the time of its publication, and in the years since its appearance, many have disputed the accuracy of the Whittier poem. Following Lee's famous decision to divide his army into four parts, General Jackson did lead one unit through Frederick on 10 September 1862 on his way to Harpers Ferry. Still, most contemporary and historical accounts suggest that Frietschie had no encounter with Jackson and that the Confederate leader seems to have bypassed the elderly woman's home on his way through town. There were, however, flag-waving episodes involving some of the many Unionist residents of Frederick. Reports circulated of Union women who defiantly displayed their flag to the rebel soldiers or hid them out of fear of confiscation. Moreover, many townspeople waved Union banners when Federal troops entered Frederick three days after the Confederates, and it is believed that Frietschie was among this group. Indeed, evidence exists that connects Frietschie to one specific patriotic incident, albeit with Union and not Confederate forces. When Union soldiers arrived in Frederick, Barbara Frietschie apparently met with Union general Jesse Reno and gave him the flag that had flown from her window. This same flag was draped on General Reno's coffin following his death at the battle of South Mountain. Such visible support for the northern effort gave Frietschie a local reputation as an avid supporter of the Union cause.

Soon after Frietschie's death at her home, an account of her devotion to the Union, now embellished with the story of a defiant meeting with Stonewall Jackson, was picked up by the novelist E. D. E. N. Southworth and passed on to Whittier, who composed and published his tribute to the elderly woman of Frederick in the year following her death. Whittier's work, in depicting Jackson's bullying of an aged woman, proved to be humiliating to the Confederate leadership. The authenticity of the incident was strenuously denied by southerners, who responded angrily to the poem's unsavory depiction of Jackson, recently killed at Chancellorsville and often celebrated as a symbol of southern chivalry. Seeking to defend their sense of honor, southern whites challenged the whole notion of Jackson's encounter with Frietschie; subse-

quent scholars have done likewise. Yet, despite the doubtful nature of the story, Whittier's poem ultimately made the elderly woman a symbol of patriotism on the Union home front and a legendary figure in American history. So widespread did the Frietschie legend become that even Winston Churchill, stopping at a replica of Frietschie's home in Frederick during a 1942 visit with President Franklin D. Roosevelt, was able to recite the poem from memory.

• Informative studies of Barbara Frietschie and the Frietschie legend include Adelaide Cole, "Of Dame Barbara and Her Legend," *Indiana Social Studies Quarterly* 37 (1984): 54–57; Dorothy M. and William R. Quyunn, "Barbara Frietschie," *Maryland Historical Magazine* 37 (Sept. and Dec. 1942): 227–54 and 400–413; and George O. Seilheimer, "The Historical Basis of Whittier's 'Barbara Frietchie,'" in *Battles and Leaders of the Civil War*, vol. 2, ed. Robert U. Johnson and Clarence C. Buel (1887).

NINA SILBER

FRIGANZA, Trixie (29 Nov. 1870–27 Feb. 1955), actress and singer, was born Brigid O'Callaghan (sometimes listed as Delia O'Callahan) in Grenola, Kansas, the daughter of Cornelius O'Callaghan and Margaret Friganza, occupations unknown. She revealed little about her parentage except that they were Spanish and Irish. She made her stage debut in 1889 as a chorus girl in a touring production of *The Pearl of Pekin*. For the next few years, she continued touring with the Carlton Opera Company, singing minor roles, until 1894 when she appeared in a nonmusical dramatic production, *One Christmas Night*. Later that year she turned to musical comedy, appearing in *The Little Trooper*, and it was in this theatrical genre that Friganza became a star, known for her light comedic touch. Through the remainder of the century she appeared—often in touring companies—in a series of musical comedies: *Fleur de Lys* (1895), *A Trip to Chinatown* (1896–1897), *La Poupée* (1897), *The Casino Girl* (1900), and *The Belle of Bohemia* (1900), a production that went to London in 1901 where Friganza stayed to play in *The Whirl of the Town* with Henry Dixey.

Friganza returned to the United States and appeared as Julie Bon-Bon in *The Girl from Paris* (1902) and as Aramanthe Dedincourt in *The Chaperones* (1902). She also began performing in vaudeville, continuing until 1910, and became known as "Broadway's Favorite Champagne Girl," earning success with songs such as "The Sweetest Story Ever Told" and "No Wedding Bells for Me." Her most successful musical comedy came in 1903 as Sally in *Sally in Our Alley*, which she followed with the role of Mrs. Madison Crocker in *The Prince of Pilsen* (1903), a production that moved to London in 1904. Also in that year she played Omee Omi in *The Shogun* at Wallack's in New York. In 1906 she revived the role of Julie Bon-Bon in New York, then went on tour in *Twiddle-Twaddle*, a musical revue with Joe Weber and Marie Dressler. Back in New York in 1907, Friganza played Caroline Vokins in *The Orchid* with Eddie Foy, touring late in the year in *His Honor the Mayor* and *The Girl from Yama*. Also in New York she portrayed Mrs. Waxtapper in *The American Idea* in 1908 with George Beban. Friganza began her career tall and sylphlike but quickly gained weight, often being compared to fellow comediennes May Irwin and Marie Dressler. However, as she grew heavier, the lightness of her comedy increased. She became known for her delicate, bright comedic style.

Friganza became politically active in 1908 when she led a march of militant suffragettes to New York's City Hall, from the steps of which they lectured Mayor George McClellan and a crowd of several thousand on women's rights in pursuing a career. Much of the crowd was unsympathetic, and it was the only time Friganza was ever jeered by an audience. She continued performing on the stage for the next couple of years, opening *The Sweetest Girl in Paris* in 1910 in Chicago. She performed in the all-star musical revue *Passing Show of 1912* that played at the Winter Garden before touring the country. In 1912 Friganza married Charles A. Goettler, a dramatic agent in New York, but she divorced him two years later. They had no children.

Remaining on the stage through World War I in musical comedies such as *Ned Wayburn's Town Topics* (1915) and *Canary Cottage* (1917), Friganza then made the move to films, becoming a silent screen comedienne and repeating many of her stage and vaudeville successes. Quite popular in silent films, she appeared with major stars such as Buster Keaton and Noah Beery. Her films included *The Charmer*, *The Road to Yesterday*, *Free and Easy*, *Myrt and Marge*, and *Proud Flesh*. Because of progressively severe arthritis, she retired from acting in 1939, selling her Hollywood home along with her jewelry and furs and living in seclusion at Sacred Heart Academy in Flintridge, California, where she died sixteen years later. During World War II she performed at veterans' hospitals, and each year on her birthday she would pose for photographers and blow out the candles on her cake. Throughout her life she was known for her charitable spirit, always helping out a stagehand or a chorus girl and in her retirement supporting several needy families.

Because of her generosity of spirit, Friganza enjoyed the esteem of both colleagues and audiences. Her comedy was usually self-deprecating, and she began a tradition among comediennes of deriding their own flaws. Her vaudeville act, "My Little Bag o' Trix," was filled with songs and jokes lamenting a loveless life and poking fun at her own large size.

• There is no known repository of Friganza's papers. Surveys of her stage career can be found in *Who's Who in Music and Drama* (1914) and Daniel Blum's *A Pictorial History of the American Theatre* (1950). A brief description of her career appears in Mary Unterbrink, *Funny Women* (1987). Her political involvements are mentioned in Benjamin McArthur, *Actors and American Culture* (1984). Obituaries are in the *New York Times*, 28 Feb. 1955, and *Time*, 14 Mar. 1955.

PATTY S. DERRICK

FRIIS, Harald Trap (22 Feb. 1893–15 June 1976), electrical engineer, was born in Naestved, Denmark, the son of a Danish brewer and a Norwegian mother. He studied at the Royal Technical College in Copenhagen, where he earned a degree in electrical engineering in 1916. Then inducted into the Danish Signal Corps, he served as a radio laboratory assistant in Copenhagen in 1916–1917 and as technical director of the Royal Gun Factory in that city in 1917–1918. With the aid of a grant from the American-Scandinavian Foundation, he came to the United States to study for a year at Columbia University in 1919 and decided to stay. He became a U.S. citizen six years later. He married Harriet Inger Lindhard in 1927; they had no children. He earned a D.Sc. in 1938 from his undergraduate institution.

Friis began work as a radio research engineer with Western Electric (the American Telephone and Telegraph Company manufacturing subsidiary) in 1919 and transferred to the Bell Telephone Laboratories on its formation in 1925. His research work at Bell Labs over the next three decades focused on radio reception techniques, including improvements and innovations in vacuum tube technology, ship-to-shore reception techniques, and radio-telephone transatlantic links. Much of Friis's research took place at a modest, wooden research facility in Holmdel, New Jersey, where he directed small teams working on a variety of radio projects. Increasingly the work was mathematical and involved taking numerous quantitative measures of radio equipment or antenna performance in an attempt, as Friis put it, "to demystify radio." He served as director of radio research at the labs from 1946 to 1951, and as director of research into high frequencies and electronics from 1952 to 1957.

Friis is credited with designing the first commercial version of the "double-detection, superheterodyne" tuning device used in virtually all radio receivers. He initiated and supervised early research by Karl Jansky and others concerning static in shortwaves. The research team was seeking the causes of signal fading in commercial transatlantic radio telephone service. The results helped lay the groundwork for the field of radio astronomy, including the 1933 discovery that radio waves were emitted by distant stars.

With Bell Labs colleagues, Friis developed two important types of antenna, one for shortwave radio, and the other for microwave transmission and reception. With Edmond Bruce, he developed in 1931 what became known as a rhombic antenna. This simple diamond-shaped antenna allowed directional shortwave reception from great distances, while rejecting spurious noise from other directions. The rhombic antenna design was unrivaled for twenty-five years. In 1936 Friis and his associates combined six to twelve rhombic antennas in a huge linear array to create the Multiple Unit Steerable Antenna, the world's first electronically steerable antenna. This greatly reduced signal distortion in shortwave reception. A horn reflector antenna was developed in the late 1930s by Friis and

A. C. Beck. It was soon widely used for microwave radio links, being simple, relatively inexpensive, and highly efficient.

Friis held thirty-one patents, granted between 1926 and 1967. Unlike some in his field, he did not seek the limelight. As the official history of the Bell Labs later put it, "Friis, an outstanding researcher and radio engineer, in addition to innumerable personal contributions, served as a mentor to a generation of Bell Laboratories radio scientists and engineers. He was as much loved and respected for his human qualities as for his technical acumen. To those who knew him, the enormous microwave-radio network is a fitting monument to his memory" (quoted in O'Neill, p. 171). Friis's approach to designing large complex systems—partitioning the research into a number of smaller and more easily understood portions—reflected his belief in decentralized research where possible to encourage individual initiative and innovation. His autobiography summed up his positive approach: "One must be an optimist to work in research [as] research is really a gamble" (p. 48).

After retiring from Bell Labs in 1958, Friis remained in New Jersey and served as a consultant for many companies for another dozen years. His clients included the microwave division of Hewlett-Packard Company in Palo Alto, California, a town to which he moved in 1973, and where he died.

• Friis published nearly two dozen technical papers and co-authored, with S. A. Schelkunoff, *Antennas: Theory and Practice* (1952). Friis authored a brief autobiographical sketch, *Seventy-five Years in an Exciting World* (1971). His Bell Labs colleague John Pierce edited the privately published *The Wisdom of Harald Friis* (1957), a collection—with commentary—of Friis's notes about the research process issued just before he retired from Bell Labs. Context for his career with the labs is found in two volumes of *A History of Engineering and Science in the Bell System*, specifically vol. 5, *Communication Sciences (1925–1980)*, ed. S. Millman (1984), which notes that he "made fundamental contributions to the understanding of the role of noise in radio receivers"; and vol. 7, *Transmission Technology (1925–1975)*, ed. E. F. O'Neill (1985). An obituary is in the *New York Times*, 17 June 1976.

CHRISTOPHER STERLING

FRIML, Rudolf (7 Dec. 1879–12 Nov. 1972), composer and pianist, was born Charles Rudolf Friml in Prague, Bohemia (later Czech Republic), the son of Frantisek Friml, a baker, and Maria Kremenak. Encouraged by his father, who played the zither and accordion, Rudolf began studying the piano and, at age ten, published his first composition, a "Barcarolle." With financial assistance from his poor family and neighbors, he attended the Prague Conservatory beginning in 1893, won a scholarship, and studied piano with Josef Jiránek and composition with Josef Foerster and Antonín Dvořák, completing the normal six-year course of study in three years.

Following his graduation, Friml toured as piano accompanist for violinist Jan Kubelik, first through Europe, then to the United States in 1901 and 1906. Between these tours, he made his American solo debut in 1904. After the second tour, he settled in New York, where he performed his first piano concerto with the New York Symphony Society under Walter Damrosch, improvising sections of the uncompleted work. He concertized around the country, appearing with the Philadelphia Orchestra and Boston Symphony, and published compositions with G. Schirmer, some under the pseudonym Roderick Freeman. He became an American citizen in 1925.

It was Friml's association with publishers Rudolph Schirmer and Max Dreyfus that launched his career and provided an entree into the American musical theater. The publishers recommended Friml to producer Arthur Hammerstein as a replacement for Victor Herbert, who had refused to compose a second operetta featuring soprano Emma Trentini, after the prima donna ignored Herbert's request to sing an encore during a performance of his *Naughty Marietta* in 1912. With no Broadway experience, Friml created the music for *The Firefly*, with lyrics by Otto Harbach, in less than one month. The romantic story of a disguised Italian street singer opened at the Lyric Theatre on 2 December 1912 and was a huge success. Among its hit songs were "Giannina Mia," "Love Is Like a Firefly," "Sympathy," and "When a Maid Comes Knocking at Your Heart."

Friml quickly followed his first show with *High Jinks*, whose title referred to a perfume that was sprayed on the audience and included the hit song "Something Seems Tingle-ing-eling," in 1913. He continued to create new shows throughout the next decade. Among them, *The Peasant Girl* and *Katinka*, which included "Allah's Holiday," in 1915; *You're in Love* and *Kitty Darling* in 1917; *Glorianna* and *Sometime*, featuring Ed Wynn, Francine Larrimore, and Mae West as a vamp dancing the shimmy, in 1918; *Tumble In* and *The Little Whopper* in 1919; *June Love* in 1921; *The Blue Kitten* in 1922; *Cinders* in 1923; and music for the Ziegfeld *Follies* of 1921 and 1923.

But it was Friml's 1924 collaboration with Harbach, Oscar Hammerstein II, and Herbert Stothart in *Rose-Marie* that was the biggest hit of the decade. Set in the Canadian Rockies, the melodramatic tale of romance and murder mingled with Indians and Canadian Mounties was one of the earliest attempts to integrate the plot and music in an American musical. Highlights included the title song "Rose-Marie," "Indian Love Call," "Song of the Mounties," "Why Shouldn't We?" "The Door of My Dreams," and the production number "Totem Tom-Tom," which featured one hundred dancers costumed as totem poles. It ran for 557 performances at the Imperial Theatre in New York, 851 performances at Drury Lane in London, and 1,250 performances in Paris, and it made more money than any Broadway musical until *Oklahoma!* nearly two decades later.

Friml's next hit followed immediately, an action adventure *The Vagabond King*, based on the life of fifteenth-century poet and scoundrel François Villon, starring Dennis King. Among the memorable songs of this picaresque musical, which opened at the Casino Theatre on 21 September 1925, were "The Song of the Vagabonds," "Only a Rose," "Someday," "Love for Sale," "A Flagon of Wine," "Huguette's Waltz," and "Love Me Tonight." Another success, Friml's musical adaptation of Alexandre Dumas's swashbuckling *Three Musketeers*, again starring King, opened on 13 March 1928, at the Lyric Theatre, and included "The March of the Musketeers," "Ma Belle," "Your Eyes," and "Heart of Mine."

Friml's *The Wild Rose* (1926), *The White Eagle* (1927), *Luana* (1930), and *Music Hath Charms* (1935) were all commercial failures. The public taste had obviously changed, and, as David Ewen put it, "Friml was a voice out of tune with the chorus of the times."

Friml relocated to Hollywood, California, where several of his stage works were transformed into movies. Three different versions of *Rose-Marie* were made by Metro Goldwyn Mayer, with Joan Crawford in a 1928 silent version, Jeanette MacDonald and Nelson Eddy starring in W. S. Van Dyke's classic 1936 release, and Howard Keel, Ann Blyth, and Bert Lahr appearing in Mervyn LeRoy's 1954 remake.

For the 1937 film version of *The Firefly*, Friml created "The Donkey Serenade," which became one of his most enduring hits. It was adapted from his "Chansonette," published for piano in 1920, used in the 1923 Ziegfeld *Follies*, and performed on the 1924 Paul Whiteman concert, which included the premiere of George Gershwin's *Rhapsody in Blue*. A recording by Allan Jones sold over a million copies.

Friml composed the music for other films, including *The Lottery Bride* (1930), *Music for Madame* (1937), and *Northwest Outpost* (1947). Movie versions of *The Vagabond King* were made by Paramount in 1930 and 1956. Ironically, Friml's "Indian Love Call" and "Rose-Marie" were recorded by country singer Slim Whitman in the 1950s, both ranking high on the popular music charts in America and the United Kingdom. A 1959 off-Broadway musical, *Little Mary Sunshine*, parodied Friml's *Rose-Marie* and other operettas of a bygone era.

In his later years, Friml continued to compose and concertize, and he frequently traveled to the Orient. A young Chinese woman, Kay Ling, who had served as his secretary, became his fourth wife in 1957. He was first married in 1909 to Mathilde Baruch; they had one son and one daughter and divorced in 1915. He and his second wife, Blanche Betters, divorced in 1918. In 1919 he married Elsie Lawson, with whom he had one son; they also divorced.

A gala concert, hosted by the American Society of Composers, Authors, and Publishers (ASCAP), an organization of which Friml was a founding member in 1914, was held at the Shubert Theatre in New York City with over a thousand invited guests, to celebrate his ninetieth birthday. The evening included tributes from the greatest names in show business and a congratulatory message from President Richard Nixon and featured Friml at the keyboard. In 1971 Friml was one of the first ten composers inducted into the American Songwriters Hall of Fame. He died the next year in Hollywood, survived by his wife, two sons, daughter, and six grandchildren.

Although Friml's theatrical works were successful for a time, he, along with immigrant composers Sigmund Romberg and Victor Herbert, was unable to make the transition from operetta to musical comedy. Stanley Green concludes that

his European background, his classical training, and his basically Old World outlook combined to give most of his scores—even his earliest ones—a fundamentally old-fashioned quality . . . Though most of the musical comedies of the Twenties and Thirties can no longer be performed as originally written, the rich emotional music of Rudolf Friml continues to provide occasions of melodic pleasure whenever his operettas are revived. (Green, p. 39)

• The Rudolf Friml collection is among the special collections in the music library at the University of California at Los Angeles. Performance materials for his musical theater works are available from the Tams-Witmark Music Library and Samuel French, Inc. Recordings of Friml's Broadway musicals are listed in Jack Raymond, *Show Music on Record: The First 100 Years* (1992). An interview with Friml, "The Mystery of Musical Inspiration," is in *The Etude* 41 (1923): 229–30. A later interview is in Gene Lees, "In Love with Life," *High Fidelity* 22 (1972): 19ff., and a tribute is in John Aquino, "The Friml Legacy," *Music Educator's Journal* 66 (1979): 64–65. See also David Ewen, *Composers for the American Musical Theatre* (1968); Ewen, *American Songwriters* (1987); Stanley Green, *The World of Musical Comedy* (1980); Gerald Bordman, *American Operetta from H.M.S. Pinafore to Sweeney Todd* (1981); and Richard Traubner, *Operetta: A Theatrical History* (1983). An obituary is in *The New York Times*, 14 Nov. 1972.

H. G. YOUNG III

FRINGS, Ketti (1915?–11 Feb. 1981), writer, was born Katharine Hartley in Columbus, Ohio, the daughter of Guy Herbert Hartley, a paper box salesman, and Pauline Sparks. Frings later claimed that she remembered little of her childhood because the family moved so often. "No matter where we lived, my father was always commuting somewhere else" (Amory). The Hartleys had lived in thirteen cities by the time Frings was thirteen, when her mother died. Sent with her two sisters to live with an aunt in Milwaukee, she attended Lake School for Girls and wrote daily "letters" to her mother via her diary for several years.

During her one year at Principia College, a St. Louis boarding school, Frings dreamed of becoming an actress and wrote plays in order to create good roles for herself. Her best, she later recalled, was *Babs, the Sub-Deb*. At eighteen, she found herself at a crossroad: to act or to write. She chose writing as a profession in which she could improve with age. "What is writing anyway—but the study of life?" she commented in 1959 (Smith). She left school to take a job as advertising copywriter for Bamberger's, a Newark department store.

Frings supported herself easily with a steady flow of periodical columns such as "Feminifties," publicity materials, radio scripts, and magazine stories. Throughout her career she used a number of bylines, her favorite being Anita Kilore.

She met her husband, Kurt Frings, a German-born lightweight boxer working in France and Belgium, when she went to France for a year with the intention of writing a novel. "Ketti" was his nickname for her, and she took it as her writer's name. They were married in 1938, but it took two years to get him into the United States because of immigration quota restrictions. During that time he lived in Tijuana on the Mexican border, while she did ghostwriting for movie stars for the fan magazines. Her experience of commuting between the immigrant colony and a one-room Hollywood apartment became the basis for Frings's well-received first novel, *Hold Back the Dawn* (1940), and the 1941 film of that title, starring Charles Boyer, Olivia DeHaviland, and Paulette Goddard. Frings's second novel, *God's Front Porch* (1944), a wartime fantasy of the afterlife, was dismissed by critics as "slight" and "sentimental."

In Los Angeles, Kurt Frings became an agent whose clients included Elizabeth Taylor and Audrey Hepburn, while Ketti Frings devoted herself more and more to screenwriting. They had two children and moved into an ultramodern house with a Japanese garden and swimming pool on Ladera Drive in Beverly Hills. In the elegantly designed home, with its expanses of glass to create an outdoor feeling indoors, Frings worked in a windowless (except for a skylight), white-carpeted room, explaining that "you can't look out. You have to look in. It's a darn good thing too, not only for writing, but for everything else" (Amory). She regularly spent ten to twelve hours a day at her typewriter.

Among Frings's many screenplays were *Guest in the House* (1944), *The Accursed* (1949), *File on Thelma Jordan* (1949), *The Company She Keeps* (1951), *Because of You* (1952), *Come Back, Little Sheba* (1952), *About Mrs. Leslie* (1954), *Foxfire* (1955), and—her best-known—*The Shrike* (1955), on which she assisted director Jose Ferrer. In 1950 she was a feature writer for United Press International. Her short stories were published in *Collier's*, *Good Housekeeping*, *McCall's*, *Saturday Evening Post*, and *Woman's Home Companion*.

In 1957, with her dramatization of Thomas Wolfe's *Look Homeward, Angel*, Frings attained the success in theater to which she had always aspired. It won the Pulitzer Prize and the New York Drama Critics' Circle Award for best play of 1958, and it remains her best-known work. Her only previous play to reach Broadway was *Mr. Sycamore* (1942), which starred Stuart Erwin and Lillian Gish but ran for only nineteen performances. *Look Homeward, Angel*, in contrast, ran for 564 performances. Frings had worked for two years to condense the 626-page novel into two hours of stage time with only nineteen characters. She recalled, "The play enabled me to write about my own family relationships as well as his. I made Wolfe in my own mind my collaborator" (Amory). "And a strange thing—the

more I worked with Wolfe and his memories of his childhood, his mother, his sisters, his brother Ben, the family—the more I began to remember my own childhood" (Smith). *Angel*, a 1978 musical version of her play, with book by Frings and Peter Udell and music by Gary Geld, was panned by critics and closed in four days.

Frings's dramatization of Richard Wright's novel *The Long Dream* opened on Broadway on 17 February 1960 to generally unfavorable reviews. According to Robert Coleman (*New York Mirror*, 18 Feb. 1960), "What it has to say is more important than the way it says it. It doesn't quite come off." Her next Broadway show, *Walking Happy*, (1966), a musical version of *Hobson's Choice* by Harold Brighouse, starring British comic Norman Wisdom, was more successful, with mixed reviews from the critics. Other plays by Frings are *Judgment at Nuremberg* (1970), based on the movie, and *My Genius, My Child* (1981), about Eugene O'Neill.

In 1958 Frings was named *Los Angeles Times* Woman of the Year for playwriting. Other prizes include the 1958 Martha Kinney Cooper Ohiana Award from the Library Association, the 1959 Theta Sigma Phi distinguished achievement award, and the 1981 Harold C. Crain Award for playwriting. She died in Los Angeles.

• Frings's papers, works, and manuscripts are in the Ketti Frings Collection, University of Wisconsin. *Current Biography 1960* offers the fullest treatment of her life, well supplemented by personality profiles by Cleveland Amory, "First of the Month," *Saturday Review*, 6 Sept. 1958, pp. 6–7, and Cecil Smith, "Ketti Frings Studies Life," *Los Angeles Times*, 22 Feb. 1959. In Henry Hewes, "Broadway Postscript," *Saturday Review*, 23 Nov. 1957, pp. 27–28, Frings discusses her strategy in dramatizing Wolfe's novel. Further comments on the subject are found in *Theatre Arts*, Feb. 1958. An obituary is in the *New York Times*, 13 Feb. 1981.

FELICIA HARDISON LONDRÉ

FRISCH, Frank Francis (9 Sept. 1898–12 Mar. 1973), baseball player and manager, was born in either Queens or Bronx, New York, the son of Franz Frisch, a German immigrant, and Katherine Stahl. Franz Frisch climbed from store clerk to successful linen merchant. Frank excelled in baseball, football, and basketball at Fordham Jesuit Preparatory School and captained teams in the same sports at Fordham University until the New York Giants signed him to a baseball contract after his junior year for $400 per month and a $200 signing bonus.

Frisch joined the New York Giants in June 1919 without playing a single minor league game. At 5'11" and 165 pounds, he played second and third base but batted only .226. However, John McGraw, the Giants' authoritarian and short-tempered manager, was impressed with Frisch's aggressive charge on ground balls, strong arm, and lateral range. Frisch was a switch-hitter but cross-handed from the right side. McGraw reversed Frisch's right-handed grip, enabling him to drive the ball much harder. Frisch matured into the premier switch-hitter of his era. The Fordham Flash lived up to his nickname as a constant threat to steal and take the extra base. McGraw taught him the hook slide.

In the 1920s Frisch was second only to Rogers Hornsby among major league second basemen and was recognized as the best switch in baseball up to that time. From 1921 to 1924 Frisch averaged .337 at bat, scored more than 100 runs three times, and batted .363 in four World Series with the Giants. In 1923 he signed for $12,500, reportedly, at the time, the largest contract the Giants had ever given. Frisch planned to marry during spring 1923, but McGraw pressured him to wait until after the season, because a honeymoon would distract a ballplayer. Frisch married Ada Lucy in November 1923. They had no children.

In 1926 "McGraw's boy" reported late for spring training, demanding more money. As the season progressed, the Giants slipped in the standings, and McGraw used Frisch as his scapegoat even though his team captain was building a sixth straight .300 season. In August Frisch left the team due to McGraw's constant criticism. When he returned, his days in New York were numbered.

On 20 December 1926 Frisch was part of one of the most celebrated trades in baseball history. Frisch was swapped with journeyman hurler Jimmy Ring to St. Louis for Rogers Hornsby, the Cardinals' second baseman and field manager. Frisch, while extremely popular in New York, had to replace Hornsby, the winner of six batting titles, including three seasons over .400. Hornsby had piloted the Cardinals to their first world championship, and St. Louis renamed a street for him. The St. Louis Chamber of Commerce denounced the Cardinals for the deal. Frisch contemplated retiring but reported to St. Louis. As St. Louis sportswriter Bob Broeg wrote, Frisch "didn't make them forget Hornsby, but rather remember Frisch."

In 1927 Frisch finished second in the most valuable player voting; Hornsby finished third. With the Cardinals from 1927 to 1934, Frisch batted over .300 six times, twice led the National League in stolen bases, scored over 100 runs three times, and in 1927 handled 1,059 chances at second base with 641 assists, all longstanding major league records. In 1931 Frisch had a good, but not great, season statistically. However, the Baseball Writers Association of America voted Frisch most valuable player because they recognized that he was the soul of the team and the catalyst that drove the Cardinals to 101 victories and a pennant that year. With Frisch the Cardinals won four National League pennants. Frisch played in the first two major league All Star games in 1933 and 1934. He hit a solo home run in each contest. In midseason 1933 he was named Cards' field boss and managed Hornsby before Hornsby moved over to the St. Louis Browns as player-manager. In 1934 as player-manager of the famous St. Louis Gas House Gang, which included such notables as Dizzy and Paul Dean, Pepper Martin, Ripper Collins, Joe Medwick, and Leo Durocher, Frisch employed principles of team baseball learned from McGraw. Working the gang hard, he knew just how far to let the Gas House pranksters go in their mischief. The result was a Cardinal world championship over the Detroit Tigers in 1934. After two second place finishes the Gas House Gang sputtered in 1937 and 1938. Dizzy and Paul Dean's careers were ruined by injuries. The bottom dropped out of Durocher's batting average. Frisch played only 17 games in 1937. With the Cardinals mired in sixth place in September 1938, a tearful owner, Sam Breadon, fired his favorite manager and player.

Frisch managed the Pittsburgh Pirates from 1940 to 1946, only once finishing higher than fourth place. He assumed the reins of a weak Chicago Cubs team in 1949, staying through midseason 1951. The Flash did baseball play-by-play for the Boston Braves in 1939 and the Giants from 1947 to 1949. Frisch made 2,880 hits in 2,311 games for a .316 batting average, scored 1,532 runs, drove in 1,244, and stole 419 bases. He fanned on average only 15 times a year over 17 full seasons. As a manager he won 1,138 and lost 1,078. In 1947 Frisch was elected to the National Baseball Hall of Fame. In 1972 he married Augusta Kass; they had no children. He died in Wilmington, Delaware.

• The National Baseball Hall of Fame Library in Cooperstown, N.Y., has an extensive file on Frisch. Bob Broeg, *The Pilot Light and the Gas House Gang* (1980), is a biography of Frisch. See also Broeg, *Redbirds: A Century of Cardinals' Baseball* (1981); Broeg, *Super Stars of Baseball* (1971); David Porter, ed., *Biographical Dictionary of American Sports* (1987); and Ken Smith, *Baseball's Hall of Fame*, rev. ed. (1970). For complete statistical information on Frisch's baseball career, see MacMillan's *Baseball Encyclopedia*, 8th ed. (1990). Obituaries are in the *New York Times* and the *St. Louis Post-Dispatch*, both 13 Mar. 1973.

FRANK J. OLMSTED

FRISHMUTH, Harriet Whitney (17 Sept. 1880–1 Jan. 1980), sculptor, was born in Philadelphia, Pennsylvania, the daughter of Frank Benoni Frishmuth, a physician, and Louise Otto Berens. At nineteen, after attending private schools in Paris, Dresden, and Philadelphia, Frishmuth, intent on becoming a sculptor, returned to Paris and enrolled in the modeling classes of Auguste Rodin. Although her studies with him were brief, his attention to the surface quality of a figure caught in transitional movement left a lasting effect on her work. She later studied with Henri Gauquié and Jean Injalbert at the Académie Colorossi. After exhibiting in the Paris Salon of 1903, Frishmuth went to Berlin where she spent two years assisting Cuno von Euchtritz on several large commissions. She returned to the United States and took classes with Hermon MacNeil and Gutzon Borglum at the Art Students League in New York. There she was awarded the Augustus Saint-Gaudens Prize. Frishmuth thereafter became an assistant to the sculptor Karl Bitter while attending weekly dissections at Columbia University's College of Physicians and Surgeons in New York.

Frishmuth's initial studio was in the home of her uncle, Dr. T. Pasmore Berens, where she received her first commissions in 1910, a bas-relief portrait of Dr. Abraham Jacobi and a medal for the New York County Medical Society. In 1913 she opened her own studio at Sniffen Court near Thirty-sixth Street and began her more than sixty-year affiliation with the Gorham Company's Bronze Foundry in Providence, Rhode Island. Her early productions were small decorative and functional pieces ranging from five to thirteen inches: ashtrays, paperweights, doorstops, and bookends depicting both male and female nudes and such garden subjects as frogs, dolphins, and lily pads. In 1913 she created the almost four-foot *Saki Sun Dial*, a kneeling nude female holding a globe in her hands, a work that earned her an honorable mention at the Panama-Pacific International Exposition in San Francisco. Her *Girl with Fish Fountain* (1913) marked the beginning of her many depictions of nude women and girls frolicking in natural aquatic settings. Although this work reveals the influence of Rodin, it has classical characteristics, still present in her *Morning, Noon, and Night Sundial* (1916).

A major shift took place in Frishmuth's work in 1916. She met Desha Delteil, a spirited young Yugoslavian dancer from the Fokine Ballet troupe who had the ability to strike and hold any pose for long periods. What Frishmuth saw in Desha and her dancing colleagues was caught in the life-size *Joy of the Waters* (1917), which she cast in an edition of sixty-five. (In 1920 she remodeled the figure in a 45-inch size in an edition of forty-five.) *Joy of the Waters* is a realistic, lean athletic nude with muscles taut and arms reaching high above her head. The figure stands on the tiptoes of one foot in the act of jumping in the air, an expression of exalted female liberation. The upward thrust of her body, like those in *Extase* (1920), *Bubble* (1921), and *Crest of the Wave* (1925), boldly proclaims the vertical forces becoming manifest in the skyline of New York. In 1922 Frishmuth yielded to the Art Deco style with her stylized and streamlined figure entitled *Speed*, created first as a carhood ornament and later enlarged for the Telephone Building in Erie, Pennsylvania.

In 1921 Frishmuth created her masterpiece, *The Vine*, a sensuous female nude standing on her toes with her back arched like a taut bow and swinging a grapevine behind her in complete Bacchanalian revelry. *The Vine* was first cast in a 12½-inch size, which became an immediate success; more than three hundred copies were sold before the figure was taken out of production. In 1923, in preparation for an exhibit at the American Sculpture Society, Frishmuth remodeled *The Vine* into a six-foot version that she cast in five copies. This statue brought her serious attention and the Julia A. Shaw Memorial Prize at the National Academy of Design.

From the start of her career Frishmuth also depicted athletic men. Her model for *Slavonic Dancer* (1921) was Leon Barté, one of Anna Pavlova's dancing partners. Depictions of Desha and Barté together in *The Dancers* (1921), *Fantasie* (1922), and *Rhapsody* (1925) exhibit a vigorous sensuality and eroticism restrained by an underlying geometric structure. *Fantasie* won the Elizabeth N. Watrous Gold Medal at the National Academy of Design in 1922; all three pieces were exhibited at the Pennsylvania Academy of the Fine Arts in 1923.

Frishmuth's statues and statuettes were in great demand during the 1920s, as noted in the records of the Gorham Company's catalogs. Her works sold well in such leading franchises as Tiffany & Co. in New York, J. E. Caldwell in Philadelphia, and the Marshall Field department store in Chicago and were collected by wealthy businessmen for their offices and gardens. In 1928 Grand Central Gallery, her leading dealer in New York, gave Frishmuth her first one-woman exhibit.

Frishmuth's fame brought her commissions for several memorials: the *Roses of Yesterday* (1923) in Hackensack, New Jersey; *Aspiration* (1926) in Windsorville, Connecticut; a statue entitled *Christ* (1927) in Denver; and *The Beyond* (1929) in Bridgewater, Massachusetts. She also received portrait commissions. Her most famous was *Woodrow Wilson* (1924), created in marble for the Virginia State Capitol in Richmond.

With the onset of the depression and war in Europe, and with a growing interest in nonfigurative sculpture, Frishmuth's icons of gay abandon no longer seemed relevant. The women in her later works, *Reflection* (1930) and *Revery* (1939), are introverted and preoccupied. In 1937 she left New York and settled first near Philadelphia and then in Connecticut, where she continued to handle the sale of her works with the help of her devoted companion, Ruth Tàlcott. By the late 1960s she closed the editions of her work at Gorham. In 1966 *Sweet Grapes* (1922) was awarded first prize by the Council of American Artist Societies, and in 1971 *Laughing Waters* (1929) won a silver medal at the National Sculpture Society. Frishmuth died in a nursing home in Waterbury, Connecticut, during her hundredth year.

Frishmuth's work is represented in the Metropolitan Museum of Art, New York City; at Brookgreen Gardens, South Carolina; in the Cincinnati Art Museum; the Los Angeles County Museum of Art; the Dallas Museum of Art; the Reading Public Museum and Art Gallery, Pennsylvania; the Dayton Art Institute, Ohio; the Allentown Art Museum, Pennsylvania; the Fine Arts Museum of San Francisco; the Frank H. McClung Museum, University of Tennessee; and the Elvehjem Museum of Art, University of Wisconsin.

• In 1964 Frishmuth gave several private papers, plaster casts, photographs, clippings, account books, and a tape-recorded interview to the George Arents Research Library, Syracuse University. Gorham Company Bronze Foundry records have been filmed by the Archives of American Art, Smithsonian Institution (Roll 3680). Gorham Company records are also in the John Hay Library, Brown University. The most recent and thorough account of Frishmuth's biography, with an excellent bibliography, is in Janis Conner and Joel Rosenkranz, *Rediscoveries in American Sculpture: Studio*

Works, 1893–1939 (1989). An interpretive account of her life is in Charlotte Streifer Rubinstein, *American Women Sculptors* (1990). See also Charles N. Aronson, *Sculptured Hyacinths* (1973), an unscholarly but useful reference on the artist that Frishmuth found offensive and never endorsed; Loring Holmes Dodd, *The Golden Age of American Sculpture* (1936); Beatrice Gilman Proske, *Catalog of Brookgreen Gardens* (1968); and Ruth Talcott, ed., "Harriet Whitney Frishmuth, 1880–1980," *National Sculpture Review* 29 (Summer 1980): 22–25, and "Harriet Whitney Frishmuth, American Sculptor," *Courier* 9 (Oct. 1971): 21–35. An obituary is in the *New York Times*, 4 Jan. 1980.

SYLVIA LEISTYNA LAHVIS

FRITCHMAN, Stephen Hole (12 May 1902–31 May 1981), Unitarian minister and social activist, was born in Cleveland, Ohio, the son of Addison Hutton Fritchman, a salesman, and Esther Hole. He graduated from Ohio Wesleyan College in 1924 and entered Union Theological Seminary in preparation for the Methodist ministry, graduating in 1927. That same year he married Frances Putnam. A gradually accumulating uneasiness with what he would later call "institutionalized piety" resulted in his conversion to Unitarianism in 1930, after which he held pastorates at Petersham, Massachusetts (1930–1932), and Bangor, Maine (1932–1938). During his Bangor pastorate, Fritchman distinguished himself in his work with high-school age youth and in 1938 was invited by American Unitarian Association (AUA) president Frederick May Eliot to become director of American Unitarian Youth. Fritchman encouraged the participation of the organization in "broader, more inclusive sections of America's life," recognizing that the experience of the depression had made many middle-class Unitarian youths "more and more sensitive to the social issues we discussed in our conferences, leadership meetings, summer institutes."

By the time Fritchman began his work at the AUA, he had become humanist in his theology, and, affected deeply by the Spanish civil war, he had come to see progressive political activity as a fundamental element of his role as a minister. In 1942 Fritchman was also appointed editor of the Unitarian journal, the *Christian Register*. He made it a more visible organ for dissenting political opinion, devoting the first issue under his direct control to race relations and giving extensive coverage to the emerging shape of the world as the Second World War ended. Fritchman's editorship revitalized the journal but also made it a focus of controversy within the Unitarian denomination. The controversy reached a crisis when, in a May 1946 letter to the AUA board of directors, former board member Larry S. Davidow accused Fritchman of pro-Communist sympathies. As a result, Fritchman was investigated by the executive committee of the AUA board; he was exonerated of the charges and retained as editor of the *Christian Register* and director of American Unitarian Youth. However, the board decided to turn over the documents of the investigation to the AUA divisions of publication and education for further study, thus continuing the controversy.

Fritchman became a target of the House Un-American Activities Committee because of his political stands and associations and was called before the committee in October 1946, increasing the pressure against him within the Unitarian denomination. His editorship of the journal was placed under the control of an editorial advisory board in December 1946. In a dispute over an editorial in which Fritchman criticized the American intervention in Greece, he was removed from his editorship after a stormy AUA annual meeting in May 1947.

Although he was dismissed from the editorship of the *Christian Register*, a painful episode in American Unitarian history, Fritchman did not leave the Unitarian denomination. With the help of a supporting letter from Eliot, he assumed the pastorate of the First Unitarian Church of Los Angeles, where for twenty-two years (1947–1969) he conducted a vital ministry to the rapidly expanding region of southern California. Fritchman conducted the church with a policy of open inclusiveness, and his ministry was characterized by a persistent commitment to social reform and political activism. He was active in the movement for world peace, criticizing in his sermons the beginnings of the postwar arms race in the early 1950s. Within the Unitarian denomination, he supported the movement for African-American autonomy and power represented by the Black Unitarian Caucus. As part of his pastorate, he conducted extensive counseling, terming his third-floor study a "free thinkers' 'confessional,'" where he served as "a one-man clinic for people who felt turned down at the reception desk of psychiatric hospitals or the offices of public social-services agencies." He also revived the "Unitarian Public Forum" series, which sponsored dissenting and controversial speakers. In 1976 the Unitarian Universalist Association presented Fritchman its Award for Distinguished Service. He died in Los Angeles.

Fritchman's career exemplified the movement of the clergy, in the Unitarian and other denominations as well, to regard social and political involvement as an essential element of the modern ministry. In his autobiography, he described himself as "an agitator-preacher in a turbulent century." His commitment required a courageous willingness to take public positions on highly controversial political issues. "As an American dissenter I know the value of freedom of speech," Fritchman wrote. "I wish it for every living creature."

• Material about Fritchman is available in the Papers of Melvin Arnold, 1945–1956, and in the Presidential Papers of Frederick May Eliot at the Andover-Harvard Theological Library, Harvard Divinity School. A collection of his printed and mimeographed sermons and addresses also is held at the Andover-Harvard Theological Library and is available on microfiche. A complete listing of the titles and dates of these works is included in "Addresses by Stephen H. Fritchman," in *For the Sake of Clarity: Selected Sermons and Addresses*, ed. Betty Rottger and John Schaffer (1992), pp. 415–31. Fritchman was the author of *Men of Liberty* (1944), a series of biographical portraits of Unitarian leaders. Biographical information on Fritchman can be found in his autobiography, *Heretic: A Partisan Autobiography* (1977), and in Carl Seaburg's obituary, "Stephen Hole Fritchman," *Unitarian Universalist Association Directory 1981/82* (1981). Accounts of Fritchman's removal as editor of the *Christian Register* can be found in Carol Morris, "It Was Noontime Here . . . ," in *A Stream of Light: A Sesquicentennial History of American Unitarianism*, ed. Conrad Wright (1975), and Philip Zwerling, *Rituals of Repression: The 1985 Minns Lectures* (1985). Zwerling's account is based on both documentary study and interviews with those who had a part in the incident and includes an extensive bibliography.

DAVID M. ROBINSON

FRITSCHEL, Conrad Sigmund (2 Dec. 1833–26 Apr. 1900), Lutheran pastor, educator, and church leader, was born in Nürnberg, Germany, the son of Martin Heinrich Fritschel, a merchant, and Katharine Esther Kässler. In 1850 he enrolled in the Missionary Institute at Nürnberg, and when the school moved to Neuendettelsau in 1853, he followed, completing his work in 1854. At the Missionary Institute he was strongly influenced by teachers Friedrich Bauer and Wilhelm Löhe, and under their direction he prepared for ministry among the German immigrants in America. On 23 April 1854 Fritschel was ordained in Hamburg as pastor for an immigrant group. He arrived in Dubuque, Iowa, on 28 July 1854, where he began his ministry.

In Dubuque, Fritschel taught with Georg Martin Grossmann at a theological seminary supported by Wilhelm Löhe's Home Missionary Society of Bavaria, and also ministered to the local German-American population. On 24 August 1854 Fritschel, Grossmann, Johannes Deindorfer, and Michael Schüller organized the Evangelical Lutheran Synod of Iowa at St. Sebald, Iowa, which eventually grew into a national denomination for German-American Lutherans.

Soon after the formation of the Iowa Synod, the Bavarian Home Mission Society was forced to cut back its support, turning over control of the seminary in Dubuque to the Iowa Synod. Since the synod had no funds to support its teachers, Fritschel moved to Platteville, Wisconsin, in 1855, where he organized several congregations in that area. In 1856 he accepted a call from St. Matthew Lutheran Church in Detroit, Michigan, from which he also started several congregations in southern Michigan. That same year he married Margarethe Prottengeier; they had eleven children.

In August 1858 Fritschel joined his younger brother, Gottfried Leonard Wilhelm Fritschel, who had taken a position at the reestablished Iowa Synod seminary, called the Wartburg Seminary. The seminary, which led a precarious existence for its first years, had moved in 1857 to St. Sebald, Iowa, then in 1874 it would relocate in Mendota, Illinois, finally moving in 1889 to Dubuque, where it remained. The synod sent Fritschel to Europe in 1860 to canvass for funding for the beleaguered school; he won many supporters for the synod in Germany and among German-speaking Russians. He returned to Europe a number of times

(1866, 1870, and 1891) as a representative of the Wartburg Seminary and the Iowa Synod, establishing important ties with confessional Lutherans in Europe and recruiting students for the seminary.

Fritschel strengthened the seminary and also established and defined the Iowa Synod as one of several German-American Lutheran denominations. He espoused a conservative Lutheranism that appealed to the Lutheran confessional documents of the sixteenth century, but he differed with other confessional Lutherans over the meaning of allegiance to the confessions. He allowed that some doctrinal issues could remain "open questions," that is, points of theological debate that need not disrupt church fellowship. Other confessional Lutherans, especially Carl Ferdinand Wilhelm Walther of the Missouri Synod, along with the theologians of the Ohio Synod, rejected the belief that questions could be left "open" in this way, insisting on total doctrinal agreement before church fellowship. Fritschel was involved in a series of long-running disputes from the 1860s to the 1880s, especially with Walther, over differing positions on the doctrine of election (predestination). Much of this polemic was carried on in the synod's theology journal, *Kirchliche Zeitschrift*, which he and his brother began editing in 1876. He was also involved with another confessional Lutheran group, the General Council of the Evangelical Lutheran church. He was part of the Iowa Synod delegation at the constituting convention of the General Council in 1867, and although the Iowa Synod never formally joined the General Council, Fritschel attended many of its annual meetings. In 1899 he contracted Bright's disease; he died in Dubuque.

The Wartburg Seminary and the Iowa Synod were Fritschel's life. He and his brother were the guiding forces that built these institutions and established them as an integral part of American Lutheranism. Fritschel stood firm in his support of a confessional Lutheranism, but not one that was so closed as to be divisive.

• Fritschel's papers are in the Archives of Wartburg Seminary, Dubuque, Iowa. A biography is Herman L. Fritschel, *Biography of Professor Dr. Sigmund and Professor Dr. Gottfried Fritschel* (1951). *Reden und Ansprachen gehalten bei der Trauerfeier für Professor D. Sigmund Fritschel . . .* is a collection of remembrances. Adolph Spaeth, *S. Fritschel: A Short Biography* (1901), has a list of his writings. Selections of his work, with an introduction to the theological disputes, is found in Theodore Tappert, *Lutheran Confessional Theology in America, 1840–1880* (1972). Johannes Deindorfer, *Geschichte der Evangel.-Luth. Synode von Iowa* (1897), and Gerhard Ottersberg, "The Ev. Lutheran Synod of Iowa and Other States, 1854–1904" (Ph.D. diss., Univ. of Nebraska, 1949), are histories of the Iowa Synod.

MARK GRANQUIST

FRITSCHEL, Gottfried Leonhard Wilhelm (19 Dec. 1836–13 July 1889), pastor, educator, and church leader, was born in Nürnberg, now in Germany, the son of Martin Heinrich Fritschel, a merchant, and Katharina Esther Kässler. At his father's request, Fritschel first prepared for a career in business, but he eventually followed his older brother Conrad Sigmund Fritschel to the Lutheran Missionary Institute at Neuendettelsau. Studying at the institute from 1853 to 1856, Fritschel was deeply influenced by the director of the school, Wilhelm Löhe. After completing his work at Neuendettelsau, Fritschel attended the University of Erlangen for a year, 1856–1857, where he studied with J. K. C. von Hofmann, Theodosius Harnack, Gottfried Thomasius, and others and received his certificate of theology. Fritschel immigrated to the United States in 1857 and was ordained in the ministry of the Lutheran Iowa Synod by Georg Martin Grossmann in Dubuque on Pentecost Sunday, 31 May 1857.

Fritschel's first call in 1857 was as pastor at St. Sebald, Iowa, and as teacher in the newly reestablished Iowa Synod seminary (eventually Wartburg Seminary), which had been moved to St. Sebald in 1857 for financial reasons. After his first year his brother Conrad joined him at the seminary, and they taught together for the next thirty-one years. In 1858 Fritschel married Elisabeth Eleanor Köberle in St. Sebald, Iowa, and together they had ten children. Five of their sons entered the ministry of the Iowa Synod, two of whom also taught at Wartburg Seminary.

In 1866 Fritschel attended the preliminary meeting of synods that were to form the General Council of the Evangelical Lutheran Church in North America in 1867. Although he had reservations about some of the denominations involved, and the Iowa Synod never officially joined the General Council, Fritschel frequently represented the Iowa Synod at its meetings.

In 1874 Fritschel accepted a call to a congregation in Mendota, Illinois, and the seminary moved with him. As seminary professors, he and his brother Conrad worked to build Wartburg Seminary and the Iowa Synod as a distinctive force within German-American Lutheranism. University trained, and of a scholarly disposition, Fritschel was the more learned of the two and published a large number of theological writings, especially in theological journals. He edited the Iowa Synod periodicals *Kirchenblatt* (1858–1873) and *Kirchliches Zeitschrift* (1876–1889).

Although Fritschel's Lutheranism was based on a strict interpretation of the sixteenth-century Lutheran confessions, he did not go as far as some strict Confessionalists and suggest that church fellowship must be preceded by absolute and complete doctrinal agreement. During the 1870s Fritschel and the Iowa Synod came to believe that the church should allow for "open questions," theological differences that would not hinder fellowship. On this issue the Iowa Synod was fiercely attacked by other German-American confessional Lutherans, most notably C. F. W. Walther of the Missouri Synod. Fritschel was not slow to return fire and was constantly defending the Iowa Synod in church periodicals.

Fritschel was also interested in areas outside the world of German-American Lutheranism. He studied and became fluent in English and strongly urged his students to do the same. He also learned to speak Swedish and Norwegian so that he could communicate with these immigrants and their denominations as they moved into the Upper Midwest. In 1871 Fritschel entered a debate that was raging among Swedish- and Norwegian-American Lutherans over the question of justification. The Norwegian Synod held to objective justification (that salvation is outside the human person), while the Swedes and other Norwegians held to subjective justification (that salvation is subject to human responses). Fritschel was opposed to the "objective" position held by the Norwegian Synod and entered into a literary debate with its partisans.

The debate over justification was soon eclipsed by another theological controversy over the question of predestination (or election). By 1881 theologians of the Ohio and Norwegian Synods had concluded that Walther held to a non-Lutheran understanding of predestination. Walther argued that one is predestined to faith before any subjective elements of that faith can be determined. Walther's opponents, on the other hand, suggested that God had foreseen one's faith in advance, and thus the person was predestined "in view" of that faith. Fritschel sided with Walther's opponents, and entered the debate in support of the Ohio Synod's position.

Because of Ohio's break with Missouri, in 1883 Fritschel and the Iowa Synod made overtures to Ohio for a closer relationship between the two synods. Fritschel pushed for a meeting of delegates from the two groups in Richmond, Indiana, and prepared a document for that meeting, the "Richmond theses." But intersynodal relations were tortuous, and it would not be until 1930 that the two groups merged. Fritschel continued to teach at Wartburg seminary and direct the course of the Iowa Synod until he fell ill during a summer missionary tour through the Dakotas in 1888. He returned to Mendota but never recovered.

Together with his brother, Fritschel was a main force behind the development of Wartburg Seminary and the Iowa Synod. On a wider scale, Fritschel was an important theological voice outside his denomination, participating in and contributing to major disputes within nineteenth-century American Lutheranism, especially the justification and predestination controversies. In developing the idea of the "open questions," Fritschel represented a confessional Lutheran position that stressed agreement on essential theological questions without calling for complete doctrinal agreement. This position, though battered by his opponents, eventually led to the union of the Iowa and Ohio synods.

• Fritschel's papers can be found at the Archives of Wartburg Seminary, Dubuque, Iowa. Principal works include *Geschichte der Christliche unter der Indianern Nordamerikas in 17 und 18 Jahrhundert* (1870), *Die Lehre der Missouri Synode von der Praedestination* (n.d.), and *Passionsbetrachtungen* (1868). The standard biography is Herman L. Fritschel, *Biography of Drs. Sigmund and Gottfried Fritschel* (1951). *In Memoriam: Zum Gedächtnis des selig entschlafenen G. L. W. Fritschel* (1889) is a memorial tribute, with a list of his writings. Selections of his work, with an introduction to the theological disputes, are in Theodore Tappert, *Lutheran Confessional Theology in America, 1840–1880* (1972). G. J. Fritschel, *Quelle und Dokumente zur Geschichte und Lehrstellung der Iowa Synod* (1916), is a collection of primary documents.

MARK GRANQUIST

FRITZ, John (21 Aug. 1822–13 Feb. 1913), mechanical engineer, was born in Chester County, southeastern Pennsylvania, the son of George Fritz, a farmer, mechanic, and millwright, and Mary Meharg. As a boy he helped his father in farming and repairing machinery and for several years attended local schools, three months in winter and three in summer, as was then customary for farmboys in Pennsylvania. In 1838 he became an apprentice in blacksmithing and country machine work in nearby Parkersburg, where he saw mechanical developments that whetted his ambition. Parkersburg was on the line of the Philadelphia and Camden Railroad, later part of the Pennsylvania Railroad, and transportation by railroad was in an initial stage of growth. The industry needed iron, and southeastern Pennsylvania was the center of the nation's iron industry. Fritz remained in Parkersburg for five years, then returned for a brief stay on his father's farm, and in 1844 moved to Norristown, Pennsylvania, for employment in the ironworks of Moore and Hooven. There he mastered the art of puddling, the process by which pig iron is changed into wrought iron; learned to operate a rolling mill; and became successively night foreman and general manager of Moore and Hooven's mill. In 1849 he resigned and over the next five years held various positions in which he learned other aspects of the iron industry, including rolling T rails at Safe Harbor, Lancaster County, Pennsylvania; remodeling the Kunzie Furnace from the use of charcoal as a fuel to anthracite coal at the Schuylkill; and superintending the construction of a shop and foundry at Catasauqua, Pennsylvania, on the Lehigh River. In 1851 Fritz married Ellen W. Maxwell; they had one child who did not reach adulthood.

In 1854 Fritz became superintendent and chief engineer of the Cambria Iron Company's plant at Johnstown, Pennsylvania. The plant was large for the times, consisting of three blast furnaces, a rolling mill, and puddling furnaces. His equally talented brother George accompanied him. Together they made Cambria a model engineering plant for the industry. Their most notable achievement was a set of three-high rolls for making iron rails. This allowed a rail to be passed continuously back and forth between rollers, thus eliminating the excessive cooling that had occurred when rails had to be returned to the point of origin for re-rolling in the conventional two-high mill. The Fritzes' three-high rolls were extensively copied in the United States and England.

In 1860 Fritz accepted the position of general superintendent and chief engineer of the newly organized Bethlehem Iron Company at South Bethlehem on the bank of the Lehigh River, opposite the borough of Bethlehem, Pennsylvania. Asa Packer, founder of the Lehigh Valley Railroad (which needed a reliable source of rails), and several of his assistants had bought a controlling interest in a local company, which they renamed Bethlehem Iron. Fritz's first tasks for this company were building a blast furnace and a rolling mill. In spite of the severe economic depression preceding the outbreak of the Civil War and the shortages occasioned by the conflict, he succeeded in putting the company's first furnace into blast on 4 June 1863 and rolling the first rails in September of that year.

For the next twenty-eight years Fritz worked for the Bethlehem Iron Company and was instrumental in making it one of the nation's leading manufacturers of iron and steel. He was not, however, responsible for all of its important decisions. The directors were wary of Fritz's tendency to innovate in matters not yet approved by company policy and in 1874 created the position of general manager with oversight of operations, leaving Fritz in charge of "designing and erecting all new works and constructions and all modifications of existing works, buildings, and machinery." Although he was no longer his own master and was often harshly criticized by his superiors, he generously credited colleagues and subordinates, of whom, he wrote in his autobiography, "All that needed to be said was 'Come, boys,' but never 'Go, boys,' and if the difficulties were not insurmountable they were sure to be overcome."

Fritz, in collaboration with Alexander Lyman Holley, who had spearheaded in the United States the use of the Bessemer-Kelly process of making steel, in 1873 made the initial blow of steel in the company's first converter. Fritz's Bessemer mill, wrote B. F. Fackenthal, Jr., "was acknowledged to be the best and most economical that had up to that time been built" (Fackenthal, p. 105). Fritz revised the design of the company's anthracite furnaces to keep them competitive with those in western districts using coke; built rail and pipe mills; and introduced into the works the open-hearth process for making steel. In the mid-1880s he cooperated with the board in a venture to modernize vessels of the U.S. Navy by means of armor plate and large guns. Both the steel manufacturer Andrew Carnegie and the Midvale Steel Company, the latter with considerable experience in making guns to the standards set by the U.S. government, had refused to undertake this project because of the technical difficulties involved. Although no company in the United States had ever made heavy forgings such as were needed for modern naval vessels, the Bethlehem Iron Company agreed to do it.

In 1887 Fritz and others from Bethlehem Iron went to England and France to secure licenses and plans, make purchases, and become familiar with the heavy-forging processes used there. As a result, Bethlehem Iron purchased two gun and forging presses from Sir Joseph Whitworth in England and set them up in South Bethlehem in 1888–1889, and Fritz made a decision to harden armor plate with a hammer as was done at the Creusot works of Schneider and Company in France, rather than use an alternate process employing hydraulic presses. From 1889 to 1891 he designed and built a 125-ton steam hammer, the largest of its kind in the world, which was widely publicized. During the same period he designed and built three presses having a capacity of 14,000 gross tons pressure, which within a few years proved to be more effective than the hammer and served the Bethlehem Iron Company until the outbreak of the Second World War. In conjunction with these and related projects, he designed a machine shop, described by the trade journal *Iron Age* (26 Mar. 1891, p. 577) as "the largest building of its kind under one roof in the country, and possibly in the world. . . . Heavy forgings, for which we were dependent upon Krupp and the other foreign makers, are now produced at Bethlehem of unequalled quality." In 1890 the directors of Bethlehem Iron co-opted Fritz onto the board.

Fritz's accomplishments had been achieved without formal education, but this fact did not prevent him from supporting higher learning. When in 1865 Packer founded Lehigh University, he made Fritz a trustee, a position that Fritz held until he retired in 1892 from the Bethlehem Iron Company. After resigning as company superintendent, Fritz remained as chief engineer and a member of the board for most of 1893, and he was the recipient of many honors. In 1893 the Iron and Steel Institute of Great Britain awarded him the Bessemer Gold Medal. He served as president in 1894 of the American Institute of Mining Engineers and in 1895–1896 of the American Society of Mechanical Engineers. These, the leading professional societies in their respective fields, together with the top professional associations in civil and electrical engineering, the American Society of Civil Engineers and the American Institute of Electrical Engineers, in 1902 established in his honor the John Fritz Gold Medal to be awarded for notable scientific or industrial achievement and made him the first recipient. From 1907 until his death Fritz served for a second time as a trustee of Lehigh University. During the last several years of his life he wrote an autobiography and designed and built for Lehigh University a laboratory for testing materials, the Fritz Engineering Laboratory. He died in Bethlehem.

Fritz's long life coincided with the spanning of the continent by railroads, the emergence of the United States as a major producer of iron and steel, and the beginning of the nation's modern defense establishment. Although not an inventor himself, he was celebrated for bringing engineering standards of economy and safety to bear in improving many of the inventions instrumental in these developments. Frank B. Copley, writing in *Frederick W. Taylor, Father of Scientific Management* (vol. 2 [1923], p. 5), characterized Fritz as "beloved of all engineers, hailed throughout his latter years as the dean of the American Engineering fraternity, and intensely admired by Taylor as probably the finest product of the old empirical school."

• The *Autobiography of John Fritz* (1912) is the principal source, but it should be read with discrimination for two reasons. First, Fritz was poorly educated and had Natt W. Emery, assistant to the president of Lehigh University, correct and stylize the manuscript. Parts of Fritz's original draft exist in the archives of the Linderman Library, Lehigh University, and include comments omitted from the final version. Second, Fritz wrote his autobiography after his principal critics at Bethlehem Iron were dead. Their views on his accomplishments can in part be obtained from many of the entries in the fifty-six years of (unpublished) diaries kept by Robert H. Sayre, who brought Fritz to Bethlehem and was general manager of Bethlehem Iron from 1886 to 1897. The diaries are in the Library of the Canal Museum, Easton, Pa. Another source of views on interactions between Fritz and other principals in Bethlehem Iron is the collected papers of board member Joseph Wharton, Friends Historical Library, Swarthmore College, Swarthmore, Pa. An excellent survey of Fritz's life by one who knew him personally is that of B. F. Fackenthal, Jr., "John Fritz," *Proceedings of the Pennsylvania German Society* 34 (1923): 97–112. See also *John Fritz, His Role in the Development of the American Iron and Steel Industry* (1987) by Lance E. Metz, director of the Canal Museum at Easton. Obituaries are in *Transactions of the American Society of Mechanical Engineers, 1913* (1914), and *Transactions of the American Institute of Mining Engineers* (Aug., Oct. 1913).

W. ROSS YATES

FRIZZELL, Lefty (31 Mar. 1928–19 July 1975), country music singer and composer, was born William Orville Frizzell in Corsicana, Texas, the son of Naamon Frizzell, an oil field worker, and A. D. Cox. He grew up, in his own words, "in an oil field behind an oil well" in the rough boomtown in north Texas. He was one of eight children, three of whom, David, Billy, and Allen, later joined him in the music industry. Though the family always called him "Sonny," by the time he was fourteen Frizzell had acquired the nickname "Lefty." Though a popular publicity story later insisted that Lefty got his nickname through Golden Gloves boxing, it came about through a schoolyard fight. His early musical influences included Jimmie Rodgers, and he spent hours with his head next to the Victrola listening to Rodgers's old records. By the time he was twelve, Frizzell knew he wanted to become a yodeling cowboy singer and had started making his first public appearances.

During the 1940s Frizzell spent his teenage years playing local radio shows in the Southwest and traveling to talent contests and jobs as far west as Las Vegas. By 1947 he had married Alice Lee Harper, with whom he would have three children, and the young couple had settled in Roswell, New Mexico, where Lefty had his own radio show. This career collapsed, though, when the singer was convicted of statutory rape and was sentenced to a six-month jail term. Though he used the time to write songs, when he got out he temporarily gave up music and returned to Texas to work with his father in the oil fields. But he was soon attracted back into music and was caught up in a dramatic revolution in country music. During the late 1940s a new type of music was replacing the familiar cowboy and mountain-styled songs of an earlier day. This was "honky-tonk" music, a more modern music designed for the Texas roadhouses and jukeboxes and which dealt with the problems of modern blue-collar workers: drinking, divorce, broken homes, and job problems. Texas was the center for this new music, and young Frizzell found himself on the cutting edge.

While performing at the Ace of Clubs in Big Spring, Texas, Frizzell attracted the attention of Jim Beck, who owned a recording studio in Dallas and worked as a talent spotter for several major record companies. In April 1950 Frizzell drove to Dallas and made demo recordings of several original songs, including "If You've Got the Money, I've Got the Time." Beck took the results to Columbia producer Don Law hoping to get him interested in the song; instead, Law was interested in the singer and at once offered Frizzell a contract. That summer Frizzell was back in the studio, recording a master for a major label. On 4 September 1950 the first sides were released: "If You've Got the Money" backed with another original, "I Love You a Thousand Ways." The results were spectacular; both songs shot to the top of the bestseller charts, and soon other singers, both pop and country, were falling over themselves to record their own versions of "Money."

Columbia rushed their new star back into the studio for more records and hastily set up a tour and back-up band. For the next two years Frizzell's music dominated the charts. His 1951 recording of his own song "Always Late (with Your Kisses)" became a model for hundreds of later singers who wanted to copy the unique "Frizzell style." This was a manner of singing softer and closer to the microphone, and in which words were broken into long, complex syllables. "When I sing," Frizzell explained, "to me every word has a feeling about it. I had to linger, had to hold it. I didn't want to let go of it. I want to hold one word through a whole line of melody, to linger with it all the way down." Later singers such as Merle Haggard, Willie Nelson, Keith Whitley, Randy Travis, and Vince Gill openly admitted their debt to Frizzell for this style, which came to be the dominant singing style in modern country music.

Bad management decisions plagued the early years of Frizzell's career, and he was unable to capitalize fully on his immense fame. He stayed for a short time on the Grand Ole Opry, experimented with working out of Beaumont, Texas, and flying to dates, and spent some time in a partnership with harmonica star Wayne Raney. By the mid-1950s he was no longer having hit records and had relocated to California, where he appeared on the TV show "Town Hall Party." But in 1959 he began to work with Nashville producers and bookers and soon had another impressive hit with "Long Black Veil," a song that became so pervasive that many assumed it was an old folk ballad. "Long Black Veil" was actually a contemporary Nashville song written by veteran songsmiths Danny Dill and Marijohn Wilkin. He then moved to Nashville and had an even bigger hit in 1964 with "Saginaw, Michigan." During the next two decades he continued to work in Nashville, writing songs with partners such as Whitey Shaeffer and Doodle Owen and occasionally doing albums that were more respected by critics than bought by the public. He eventually amassed a total of some 240 individual commercial recordings for Columbia and ABC during his career.

Later songs included "I Never Go around Mirrors," which dealt with growing old and became an informal Nashville anthem. Frizzell died in Nashville from a stroke. In 1982 he was inducted into the country music hall of fame.

• The earliest and most detailed account of Frizzell's career is found in Charles K. Wolfe's *Life's Like Poetry* (1991), which was issued with the singer's complete works released on LP and then CD by Bear Family Records of Bremen, Germany. This book contains a complete discography of all the records, along with personnel and composer credits, as well as extensive illustrations. A later, even more detailed account of the singer's colorful life is Daniel Cooper's popular book *Lefty Frizzell* (1995).

CHARLES K. WOLFE

FROELICH, William (1 Mar. 1901–5 Feb. 1980), lawyer, was born in Stromsburg, Nebraska, the son of William Froelich and Nellie Morgan. He grew up in O'Neill, Nebraska, and attended the local public schools. In 1920 he went to study at the University of Nebraska; two years later he transferred to Georgetown University in Washington, D.C., earning an A.B. and then his law degree in 1926. He worked in the Justice Department while attending law school at night. In July 1926 he married Irma Frances Stout; they had five children.

Soon after he finished his studies, Froelich returned to Nebraska, where he was admitted to the bar and appointed an assistant U.S. attorney in Omaha. He was assigned to handle narcotics and liquor cases, winning most of the cases he prosecuted. He then joined the U.S. attorney general's office in Washington. He became part of a special task force, the "Secret Six" lawyers whose purpose was to oversee the investigation and prosecution of high-profile federal cases. As a member of the task force, Froelich investigated organized crime around the country, focusing on violators of the Volstead Act, the federal statute designed to implement the Eighteenth Amendment (Prohibition).

In December 1927 federal agents raided Chez Morgan, a nightclub on West Fifty-second Street in New York City. The club was owned by Helen Morgan, a singer and actress who had achieved national fame for her performance in the Broadway musical *Show Boat*. Morgan, only twenty-seven years old, was arrested. At her arraignment, however, she was not charged with violating the Volstead Act but rather with tax evasion. In the meantime, Morgan opened a new club, the Summer House, which was raided in June 1928. The *New York Times* headlined the crackdown as the "War on the Night Clubs."

Froelich charged Morgan with conspiracy and "maintenance of a nuisance," which carried the possibility of a one-year jail sentence and a $1,000 fine. Mabel Walker Willebrandt, an assistant U.S. attorney, handled the trial in 1929 but failed to convince the jury of Morgan's guilt.

Froelich also represented the federal government in its prosecution of Sydney J. Catts, the governor of Florida from 1918 to 1922. A former Baptist preacher turned insurance salesman, Catts was elected governor in 1917 on an anti-Catholic platform supporting Prohibition and antigambling laws. Throughout the 1920s, the irascible and controversial populist tried to regain office, losing his 1928 bid for governor. In April 1929 a federal grand jury indicted him on charges of counterfeiting. The case was tried in October. The jury in its short deliberations was deadlocked, and after only twenty-four hours the judge declared a mistrial. A retrial a year later ended in Catts's acquittal.

Froelich's most celebrated case brought him to Chicago, Illinois. Chicago had become known as a place where criminal syndicates pervaded economic life, and where as many as 20,000 people might attend the funeral of a gunned-down mobster. Chicago's civic and financial leaders feared that the continued bad publicity would hurt the city economically, and they requested federal help in investigating and prosecuting the most flagrant and notorious of all the underworld figures: Al Capone, known as "Scarface." Capone, born in Naples, Italy, had become the personification of crime and gangsterism not only in Chicago but throughout America. In the autumn of 1928, Frank J. Loesch, the president of the Chicago Crime Commission, wrote to U.S. Vice President Charles Dawes and asked him to lobby President Calvin Coolidge for federal help. In October 1928 Coolidge responded by creating a special unit of the U.S. Bureau of Internal Revenue to investigate Capone's income tax history.

After taking office in 1929, President Herbert Hoover personally instructed Attorney General William Mitchell to assign Froelich as a special assistant to the attorney general to oversee the investigation of Capone, by then dubbed "Public Enemy Number One" by the press. Froelich made his home at the Blackstone Hotel in Chicago and thereafter commuted on weekends to his family and 7,000-acre farm in O'Neill, Nebraska. He hired Eliot Ness as one of his investigators.

In June 1931 Froelich obtained a 21-count indictment against Capone for tax evasion. Capone was confident that his henchmen had tampered with the jury, but a new judge assigned to the case at the last minute, James H. Wilkerson, assembled a new jury. Along with three other government prosecutors, Dwight H. Green, Jacob I. Grossman, and Samuel G. Clawson, Froelich questioned Capone about his finances. Over the years, Capone had used cash for all of his financial transactions, and he had kept no records, books, or accounts or filed an income-tax return. Froelich's investigators, however, had found a record book in the Ship, a gambling house, in Cicero, Illinois. The handwriting in it matched that of Lou Shumay, a bookkeeper at the club and a known Capone associate. Shumay agreed to talk, and others came forward with details of Capone's expenditures and lavish spending. Froelich later explained that he was to show Capone's income "on the basis of what he spent in certain periods of time."

Relying on the evidence Froelich presented about Capone's spending to establish Capone's income, the jury convicted the gangster on five counts, including willful evasion of payment of income taxes. In October 1931 the court sentenced him to eleven years in prison and fined him $70,000. The *Chicago Tribune* called Capone's trial the "most famous of all prosecutions of gang chieftains."

Froelich remained in government service for several more years. He helped write the charter for the Federal Deposit Insurance Corporation (FDIC), serving later as its first chairman. The FDIC, created by the Banking Act of 1933, was one of the early initiatives of President Franklin D. Roosevelt's New Deal. In 1934 Froelich retired from the Justice Department. In Chicago he practiced law, specializing in corporate and tax law. A Roman Catholic, he served on the board of directors of the University of Notre Dame and was a director of several corporations and banks, including the Wisconsin Public Service Corporation and the First National Bank of Atkinson, Nebraska.

A lawyer of exceptional ability, Froelich was a dedicated public servant who held many high positions yet never exploited his status for personal gain—unlike his top investigator Eliot Ness, whose name is better known in popular legend. Froelich died in O'Neill, Nebraska.

• Books that deal with the cases in which Froelich was involved include Gilbert Maxwell, *Helen Morgan: Her Life and Legend* (1977), a rather glib and facile biography; Wayne Flynt, *Cracker Messiah: Governor Sydney J. Catts of Florida* (1977), a scholarly work on Catts; Francis X. Busch, *Enemies of the State* (1954); Laurence Bergen, *Capone: The Man and the Era* (1994); and Dennis Hoffman, *Scarface Al and the Crime Crusaders* (1993).

GEOFFREY B. GNEUHS

FROHMAN, Charles (17 June 1860–7 May 1915), theatrical producer, was born in Sandusky, Ohio, the son of Henry Frohman, an itinerant peddler from Darmstadt, Germany, who emigrated to the United States in 1845, and Barbara Straus. In 1864 Frohman was taken by his parents to New York City, where family friends found Frohman's father employment in a cigar store on Broadway, within easy reach of the theaters. Frohman attributed his love of the theater to his father, who read dramas to him and his brothers, frequently acting out the parts. In return for displaying posters for shows in his shop, Henry Frohman received free tickets, which further abetted his own and his family's passion for all things theatrical.

Frohman left school at age fourteen to work alongside his brother Daniel in the business office of the New York *Daily Graphic*. By night he sold tickets at Hooley's Theatre in Brooklyn, which his brother Gustave had rented for the presentation of Charles Callender's Georgia Minstrels during the summer months. Gustave Frohman had begun by hawking souvenir programs at the theaters and had eventually obtained the position of traveling advance agent for the ever-popular touring minstrel shows; he introduced his brothers to the world of show business. In 1877 he telegraphed Frohman that he had found a job for him as advance man for John Dillon's touring stock company. With Gustave's help—and later Daniel's—he continued his apprenticeship in theatrical management for several years, traveling as advance man or road manager for several companies, including Haverly's Mastodon Minstrels and the *Hazel Kirke* company from the Madison Square Theatre.

In 1883 Frohman struck out on his own by producing his first play, *The Stranglers of Paris*, which had been adapted by David Belasco from a French story by Adolphe Belot. Frohman had seen the play in San Francisco, where he had first met Belasco, and had recognized its dramatic possibilities. The melodrama opened on 10 November 1883 and closed a month later. Although the production was somewhat successful on tour, Frohman lost money on the enterprise. Undaunted, he felt that he had found his niche and in 1883 opened his own production and business office at 1215 Broadway in New York. He acted as an agent for promising performers and sent productions on the road, while keeping a sharp eye out for potential projects. Many actors, playwrights, and managers were attracted by his enthusiasm and eternal optimism and were willing to help forward his projects. In 1885 he managed the first road tour of the famed Wallack's Company, which had never before played outside of New York. Frohman acquired an associate, W. W. Randall, to whom he could entrust the booking of tours while he devoted himself to producing plays. (The partnership was later dissolved when Frohman began producing his own productions exclusively.)

Although he had produced several plays by 1889, Frohman's first real triumph was his production of Bronson Howard's *Shenandoah*, a Civil War melodrama, which he opened at the Star Theatre (formerly Wallack's) on 9 September 1889. The play's success engendered the formation of a road company even before the conclusion of its run of 250 performances at Proctor's Twenty-third Street Theatre. Frohman, now established as a producer, stepped up his activities for the next few years, relying on the talents of Howard, Augustus Thomas, William Gillette, Belasco, and Henry C. de Mille to supply him with plays for the stock company he was assembling, which was eventually to include Maude Adams, John Drew, Ethel Barrymore, Arnold Daly, Margaret Anglin, and many others, all of whom got their start with Frohman before moving on to stardom on Broadway. In 1893, not content with producing his plays in other people's theaters, Frohman built the Empire Theatre at 1430 Broadway to house his productions and his offices. Its location just below Fortieth Street, more than any other factor, launched the northward shift of the theater district from Fourteenth Street to the area around Longacre (later Times) Square. Three years later, in 1896, Frohman and five of his colleagues established the infamous Theatrical Syndicate, which sought to wrest control of show business from independent managers, producers, performers, and agents through the use of tactics learned from the burgeoning industrial trusts of the late nineteenth century. With a nucleus of only thirty or so theaters throughout the country, the syndicate was able to squeeze out all competition by manipulating the products (the shows) and the market outlets (the theaters) throughout the country. Despite the hostility of actors and independent producers and the condemnation by the press and the public, the syndicate held sway over the American theater for almost two decades, until the rise of the Shuberts, who mimicked the syndicate's methods. The very popular Frohman alone appeared to be untouched by the excoriations heaped on the syndicate. The actor John Drew considered him "one of the fairest and squarest men I ever met." That sentiment was shared by many others under his management, all of whose contracts with Frohman consisted of only a handshake or a verbal agreement.

Frohman concerned himself almost exclusively with the productions rather than the business of the syndicate and once remarked that his association with the organization brought him nothing but trouble. He did, however, benefit financially, and he became in time the most active producer in the United States, credited with bringing more than 600 premieres of plays to the public as well as with introducing scores of talented playwrights and players. He was the first to present the plays of Sir James M. Barrie in the United States, the most important of which, *Peter Pan*, became a long-running starring vehicle for Maude Adams and many actresses to follow. Not only did he produce plays, he often directed them himself. Helen Hayes recalled that Frohman directed the actors almost wordlessly, using gestures, facial expressions, hands and shoulders, and short grunts to convey his meanings. He expanded his activities to England and the Continent, leasing theaters in London and Paris for his productions. In order to negotiate some of his English theatrical interests, he booked passage on the SS *Lusitania*, which was sunk off the Irish coast by a German torpedo on 7 May 1915. Although many notable figures went down with the ship, it was Frohman's death that garnered the headlines in the American press. According to a survivor of the tragedy, Frohman's last words were a paraphrase of a line from *Peter Pan*: "Why fear death? It is the most beautiful adventure of life."

Just over five feet in height and nearly as round as he was tall, Frohman was characterized in one lengthy obituary as a man "who went through the world always looking on life through the proscenium arch of a theatre." Dedicated only to the theater, Frohman never married. He left only his legend, which has become dimmed by time and the rapidly changing conditions in the greater world of entertainment.

• The Frohman file at the New York Performing Arts Library contains the Robinson Locke scrapbook, with information about Frohman, along with clippings and obituaries.

The most complete source of information on Frohman is Isaac F. Marcosson and Daniel Frohman, *Charles Frohman: Manager and Man* (1916); see also John D. Williams, "C. F.," *Century Magazine*, Dec. 1915, pp. 173–88.

MARY C. HENDERSON

FROHMAN, Daniel (22 Aug. 1851–26 Dec. 1940), producer and theater manager, was born in Sandusky, Ohio, the son of Henry Frohman, an itinerant peddler, and Barbara Straus. His father, an immigrant from Darmstead, Germany, and a cigar maker, sold his wares by traveling from town to town with his horse and buggy. An amateur actor, Henry Frohman joined the Little German Theatrical Company in Sandusky, exposing Daniel and his brothers Gustave and Charles Frohman to the theater and dramatic literature. When he was ten, Daniel was sent to New York to live with friends of his parents to further his education. (His family followed in 1864.) When he was thirteen, Daniel began work as personal errand boy for Albert D. Richardson, chief Civil War correspondent for the *New York Tribune*. Richardson subsequently procured a job for Frohman with the *Tribune*, where he sold papers over the counter, deciphered editor Horace Greeley's illegible handwriting, and did other odd jobs. He left the *Tribune* in 1870 to work in the business offices of the *New York Standard* and, later, the *New York Graphic*.

In 1874, on the basis of his business experience, Frohman followed his brother Gustave into the theater world and for four years traveled throughout the country as an advance agent for Callender's Georgia Minstrels, one of the leading all-black performing groups. All three Frohman brothers received invaluable training in the theater business by working as advance men. Arriving in towns in advance of the performers, the Frohmans provided local newspapers with information and pictures, posted bills, distributed free tickets in exchange for favors and services given, checked on box office procedures, made arrangements for the company's accommodations, and acted as general troubleshooters. The first of the Frohmans to enter the business was Gustave, who had begun his career hawking souvenir programs in front of theaters and later posting placards for performers. When an advance man was needed for the 1872 southern tour of the Callender Minstrels, Gustave was chosen for the job. Two years later Daniel took his place as advance agent for the minstrel show and remained with the group for four years.

Having demonstrated his business acumen, Frohman was hired in 1879 by Steele MacKaye as business manager of the Madison Square Theatre on Twenty-fourth Street, near Broadway. The company included David Belasco as stage manager and, for a brief period, Frohman's brothers Gustave and Charles as advance agents for touring companies of MacKaye's productions. In 1881 Frohman managed the Fifth Avenue Theatre Company. He returned to the Madison Square in 1882, after MacKaye had left to form the Lyceum Theatre Company in a theater that he equipped with an innovative mechanized stage for efficient play production. Frohman joined MacKaye in the management of the Lyceum in 1885, and he took over as sole producer-manager in 1887, when the mercurial MacKaye departed after a dispute with the owners. From then until 1902, Frohman developed a stock company of young and talented performers, including Georgia Cayvan, Henry Miller, Maude Adams, E. H. Sothern, and Annie Russell, many of whom later achieved stardom under different producers. In 1903 Frohman married actress Margaret Illington. They had no children and were divorced six years later.

In 1903, following the exodus of theaters and managers to the then upper reaches of Broadway, Frohman oversaw construction of a new theater, also called the Lyceum on West Forty-fifth Street, equipped with such typically nineteenth-century appointments as a green room for the actors and an office-apartment for himself, as well as scene, costume, and prop shops within the building. Such amenities quickly became obsolete with the demise of the stock company system, which was supplanted by a new era in the theater that regarded the theater building as merely the site for a transient production. After struggling briefly against the tide, Frohman dissolved his stock company and began to function as a theater landlord, leasing the Lyceum to other producers. In 1912 Frohman received a five-year contract from Adolph Zukor, eventual founder of Paramount Pictures, to produce movies for the Famous Players Film Company, known for its motion picture adaptation of successful stage plays. Under Frohman's aegis, between 1913 and 1918 the company produced such films as *The Count of Monte Cristo* with James O'Neill, *The Prisoner of Zenda* with James K. Hackett, *Tess of the D'Urbervilles* with Mrs. Fiske, and *The Good Little Devil* with Mary Pickford. When his contract expired, Frohman remained as director of the company, which later became Paramount. Among other professional activities, Frohman managed the American tours of the great Polish actress Helena Modjeska and the English stars Mr. and Mrs. Kendal.

The Lyceum occupied the center of Frohman's life during his later years, even though his official connection with the theater ended long before his death. As had happened to so many other theater owners, the depression robbed Frohman of his investment in the theater building, which was taken over by the mortgage bank. When Frohman was threatened with eviction from his apartment in the theater, the theatrical community rallied around him; he was ultimately permitted to occupy his studio for the rest of his life. Frohman was a charter member of the Players, a club founded by Edwin Booth as a place where professionals in the theater could mingle with leaders in other walks of life. Frohman's most cherished position was as president of the Actors' Fund of America, a philanthropic organization founded in 1882 to aid members of the theatrical community who found themselves in financial distress. He served as the organization's fifth president from 1903 to 1940.

Never as successful as his brother Charles, Frohman nonetheless achieved a rare standing in the theatrical community as a hardworking and supremely competent businessman in a raffish, often wildly unbusinesslike industry. When his more famous brother went down with the SS *Lusitania* in 1915, Frohman ruefully remarked that Charles died at the right moment in history, because the theater that both of them had known throughout their lives had vanished. Frohman died in New York City.

• Three autobiographical works by Daniel Frohman are *Memories of a Manager* (1911), *Daniel Frohman Presents* (1935), and *Encore* (1937). The New York Performing Arts Library has information on Frohman in the Robinson Locke Scrapbook, ser. 2, vol. 187, and in clipping files. An obituary is in *Variety*, 1 Jan. 1941.

MARY C. HENDERSON

FROMM, Erich Pinchas (23 Mar. 1900–18 Mar. 1980), psychoanalyst, social psychologist, and author, was born in Frankfurt, Germany, the son of Naphtali Fromm, a wine merchant, and Rosa Krause. The marriage was unhappy, and Fromm was, in his words, an "unbearable, neurotic child" (Burston, p. 8). When he was twelve, a gifted, beautiful young woman close to his family committed suicide. The event impressed on him the irrationalities of human behavior, as did the First World War. When the war ended in German defeat in 1918, Fromm "was a deeply troubled young man who was obsessed with the question of how war was possible, by the wish to understand the irrationality of human mass behavior, by a passionate desire for peace and international understanding" (Burston, p. 10).

Fromm attended secondary school in Frankfurt and entered the University of Heidelberg. In 1922 he received his doctorate in sociology under the supervision of Alfred Weber. He was trained as a lay (not medically trained) psychoanalyst at the University of Munich in 1923–1924 and later at the Berlin Psychoanalytic Institute. At first he accepted orthodox Freudian concepts of the importance of sexuality on human emotional development. Fromm opened his psychoanalytic practice in 1925. The next year he married the psychoanalyst Frieda Reichmann (thereafter Fromm Reichmann); they had no children. About the same time he stopped observing Jewish religious rituals and rejected a cause he had once embraced, Zionism. He "just didn't want to participate in any division of the human race, whether religious or political," he explained decades later (Wershba, p. 12), by which time he was a confirmed atheist. Fromm, beginning in 1927, also helped to organize the Frankfurt Psychoanalytic Institute.

During the 1920s, before Hitler took power, Weimar Germany was bitterly polarized between forces of the far left and right. Fromm, like many German intellectuals, was inspired by Marx's critique of capitalism and vision of future socialism. Fromm concluded that Freud underestimated the importance of socioeconomic forces in molding individuals and their societies and overstated the role of the libido and patriarchalism. To Fromm, Freud's view of human nature—that it was biologically rooted, and that the price of civilization was neuroses caused by the repression of dangerous instincts—was too pessimistic. It seemed to encourage bland acceptance of the social status quo and to discourage hopes for overthrowing capitalist forces that alienate humans from their true selves and potential. Instead, Fromm and other leftist psychoanalysts, such as Otto Fenichel and Wilhelm Reich, hoped to merge the best aspects of Marx and Freud. In particular, they hoped to answer a question then haunting the left: why had workers outside Soviet Russia failed to take power and establish socialist governments? What factors in the average individual's unconscious, family upbringing, and social roles drove him to accept the status quo instead of to challenge it? According to one contested account, Fromm was a passionate Trotskyist in the late 1920s.

Fromm grew familiar with a fledgling group of leftist scholars called the Frankfurt Institute of Social Research. Funded by a leftist millionaire, it has become known to history as the Frankfurt School. Frankfurt School members aimed to develop a "critical theory" of society that would update Marxism and provide intellectual guidance for future revolutionary practice. Key members included Max Horkheimer, Theodor Adorno, Herbert Marcuse, Leo Lowenthal, Friedrich Pollock, and, in its early years, Fromm. Fromm was appointed head of the institute's social psychology division. He and Ernst Schachtel conducted a pioneering survey of "authoritarian" or protofascist traits among blue-collar German workers. The survey revealed that the workers' support for the left was weakened by their conformism and, in some cases, by "sadomasochistic" tendencies that predisposed them to support a dictatorship. In a sense, the study prophesied the fascist takeover of Germany in the early 1930s. As Hitler rose to power, the Frankfurt Institute moved its main headquarters to Columbia University in New York City.

Fromm came to the United States in 1933 to help Karen Horney and Franz Alexander at the fledgling Chicago Psychoanalytic Institute. After a brief time there, he moved to New York City, entered private practice, and resumed his work for the Frankfurt Institute. He taught at the International Institute for Social Research at Columbia University from 1934 to 1939. He also participated in scholarly discussions of the Zodiac Club, an informal group that included Harry Stack Sullivan and Horney. Horney influenced Fromm's notions on sexuality, while he guided her thinking about cultural sources of neurosis; he also psychoanalyzed her daughter. Fromm and Horney had a romantic liaison for a time. It ended sourly when she tried to limit his responsibilities as a lay analyst. She may also have been jealous of his influence on her daughter and his popularity with students.

In 1938 Fromm also split angrily with the Frankfurt Institute. The apparent causes included personal conflicts and disagreements over Freudian ideas. Fromm remained a guest lecturer at Columbia for three years. In 1940 he became a U.S. citizen and was divorced from his first wife, although they remained lifelong friends. As the world again clashed in war, he produced a work that would bring him national fame.

Fromm's *Escape from Freedom* (1941) painted a bleak picture of the historical and societal forces that herd individuals into mass conformity. The most brutal examples were European fascism and Stalinist-style dictatorship in the Soviet Union. Most Frankfurt School scholars wrote in a dense, forbidding style, but Fromm's prose was clear and eloquent. To clarify nebulous concepts such as alienation and the loss of "self," he used mundane analogies; for example, he discussed soap advertising and the popularity of "personalized" goods that bear the owner's initials. *Escape* sold well and went through twenty-five printings over the next quarter of a century.

Fromm asserts in *Escape* that, as traditional religion and society lose influence, the typical individual is stranded without emotional anchors amidst the political chaos of democracy and the economic mayhem of industrial capitalism. He seeks security in conformity, just as animals change their color to camouflage themselves. He settles for a societally approved role—an orthodox job, marriage, political philosophy, and value system—like an actor who "is only playing a role that has been handed over to him." For economic protection, he disguises his true feelings on the job; for emotional protection, he pretends to enjoy people whom he despises. A true, secret "self" may survive within him, but its existence is constantly in peril. In time he can no longer distinguish between his acting and his authentic feelings. He is easily manipulated by business and political propaganda, as well as by the invisible edicts of "anonymous authority." The latter comes "disguised as common sense, science, psychic health, normality, public opinion." Lacking an internal moral or aesthetic compass, he reacts to everything, whether a commercial product or a Rembrandt, as anonymous authority advises him to react. Eventually he becomes a "pseudo character" who no longer knows his own soul; he recalls it only intermittently, perhaps during dreams or drunkenness. He has become a robot.

Fromm traced spreading global violence to "the thwarting of the whole of life, the blockage of spontaneity of the growth and expression of man's sensuous, emotional, and intellectual capacities." Hence "the individual overcomes the feeling of insignificance in comparison with the overwhelming power of the world outside of himself either by renouncing his individual integrity, or by destroying others so that the world ceases to be threatening." While Freud blamed human destructiveness on a "death instinct," Fromm, as a Freudian-Marxist, attributed it to social conditions that starve psychological needs. The inhabitants of fascist Germany manifested what Fromm called "authoritarian characters": they both worshiped and resented the primacy of power in their society. They prostrated themselves before the powerful (as does a masochist who submits to the cruelties of a sadist) while compensating for their weakness by assaulting those even more helpless.

In 1944 Fromm married Henny Gurland Schonstadt. She developed rheumatoid arthritis, and the couple moved to Mexico in 1949, where Fromm started the Mexican Institute of Psychoanalysis at the National Autonomous University of Mexico. After Henny died in 1952, Fromm married Anis Freeman of Alabama the following year. Neither marriage produced children.

During the early Cold War, McCarthyism paralyzed much social dissent. Fromm was one of a number of widely read social critics—ranging from the scholar C. Wright Mills to the journalist Vance Packard—who continued to assail fundamental features of American society. In the pages of *Dissent* (Summer 1955, Autumn 1955, and Winter 1956), Fromm tangled with Marcuse, who insisted that Freudianism, far from being reactionary, contained a covert attack on modern culture and offered hope for future emancipation. Fromm's *The Sane Society* (1955) confronted the "pathology of normalcy," the belief that most persons' behavior and beliefs, being "normal," are desirable. He argued that social psychologists were "the apologist for the status quo" because they championed the "American way of life" in the false conviction that it "corresponds to the deepest needs of human nature." Fromm lobbed similar accusations at psychotherapists.

Fromm was terrified by the possibility of nuclear war. In 1957 he helped launch the peace group SANE (National Committee for a Sane Nuclear Policy), which took its name from the title of his 1955 book. He joined the American Socialist party in 1960 and wrote its election platform for that year. He traveled to Eastern Europe to befriend Marxists and discussed U.S. foreign policy and misperceptions of Soviet intentions in *May Man Prevail? An Inquiry into the Facts and Fictions of Foreign Policy* (1961). He and sociologist David Riesman often met with U.S. senators such as J. William Fulbright and Philip Hart to discuss Cold War issues. In *Marx's Concept of Man* (1961), Fromm accused Western scholars and political leaders of slurring Marx's reputation for Cold War propagandistic purposes.

As a writer, Fromm remained prolific and popular through the 1960s and early 1970s, a time of social unrest in American society. The so-called counterculture, particularly the young, rebelled against conformity by opposing the Vietnam War, rejecting the materialistic lifestyles of their parents, marching for the rights of blacks and immigrant farm workers, assailing capitalism and militarism, and experimenting with sexual roles, drugs, and alternative social visions such as "communal" living. Much of Fromm's "conformist" society had, it seemed, become radically nonconformist. His writings attained what some observers regarded as a near-cult following. Critics complained that as he grew more popular, his prose became less analytical and more homiletic, less scathing and more Pollyannaish. He defended his hopes for the future in

The Anatomy of Human Destructiveness (1973): "Most people are quite ready to denounce faith in man's improvement as unrealistic, but they do not recognize that despair is often just as unrealistic. . . . The spreading of irrational despair is in itself destructive, as all untruth is; it discourages and confuses." In 1974 Fromm ended his clinical practice and moved with his wife to Locarno, Switzerland, where he died.

• Among Fromm's many other books are *Man for Himself* (1947); *The Forgotten Language: An Introduction to the Understanding of Dreams, Fairy Tales, and Myths* (1951); *The Art of Loving* (1956); *Sigmund Freud's Mission: An Analysis of His Personality and Influence* (1959); *Zen Buddhism and Psychoanalysis* (1960), with D. T. Suzuki and R. DeMartino; *Beyond the Chains of Illusion: My Encounter with Marx and Freud* (1962); *The Dogma of Christ and Other Essays* (1963); *The Crisis of Psychoanalysis* (1970); *To Have or to Be?* (1976); *Greatness and Limitations of Freud's Thought* (1980); and *On Disobedience and Other Essays* (1981). Fromm's early work is described in Martin Jay, *The Dialectical Imagination* (1973), a standard history of the Frankfurt School. A detailed study of Fromm's thought, intellectual debts, and scholarly milieu is Daniel Burston, *The Legacy of Erich Fromm* (1991). See also John H. Schaar, *Escape from Authority: The Perspectives of Erich Fromm* (1961), which scolded Fromm for occasional "superficiality." Fromm and Horney's influence on each other is discussed in Jack L. Rubins, *Karen Horney: Gentle Rebel of Psychoanalysis* (1978). Fromm's *Escape from Freedom* influenced the concept of "totalitarianism" accepted by the anti-Stalinist left in the early Cold War; see Arthur M. Schlesinger, Jr., *The Vital Center: The Politics of Freedom* (1949). For profiles of Fromm near the height of his popularity, see C. Brossard, "Visit with Dr. Erich Fromm," *Look*, 5 May 1964, pp. 50ff, and Joseph Wershba, *New York Post Magazine*, 22 Apr. 1962, p. 12. Fromm's impact on an important congressional critic of U.S. foreign policy is clear in J. William Fulbright, *The Pentagon Propaganda Machine* (1970). Fromm is depicted as "next to Horkheimer . . . the most important theoretical talent in the early phase of what was later called the Frankfurt School" in Rolf Wiggershaus, *The Frankfurt School—Its History, Theories, and Political Significance* (1994). The role of Fromm and fourteen other figures in laying the basis for the dissident intellectual discourse of the 1960s is scrutinized in Andrew Jamison and Ron Eyerman, *Seeds of the Sixties* (1994). An obituary is in the *New York Times*, 19 Mar. 1980.

KEAY DAVIDSON

FROMM-REICHMANN, Frieda (23 Oct. 1889–28 Apr. 1957), psychoanalyst and psychiatrist, was born in Karlsruhe, Germany, the daughter of Adolf Reichmann, a merchant and banker, and Klara Simon, a teacher. Believing that young women should be educated and able to support themselves, Klara Reichmann directed the education of her daughters in the arts and sciences and encouraged their professional training. Frieda Reichmann entered the medical school at Albertus University in Könisberg, Germany, in 1908, receiving her medical degree in 1913.

During the next seven years, she completed internships and worked and taught in psychiatric hospitals in Könisberg and Berlin. Her tutelage under Kurt Goldstein and work with brain-injured soldiers not only schooled her in the physiology and pathology of

brain functions but also led her to study the soldiers' panic states. Her probing of their anxieties and her ability to apply this understanding to her later schizophrenic patients would become the hallmark of her life's work.

She became increasingly interested in psychotherapy in the early 1920s, worked at a sanitarium near Dresden, and served as a visiting physician for awhile at the psychiatric clinic of Emil Kraepelin in Munich. In the writings of Sigmund Freud she found intellectual challenge and answers to many of her therapeutic questions. Undergoing personal analysis with Wilhelm Wittenberg and, then, Hans Sachs, she practiced in Heidelberg and in 1926, with Eric Fromm (whom she had married that same year), established the Psychoanalytic Training Institute of Southwestern Germany. (She and Fromm did not have children.) At the same time, Georg Groddeck, experimenting with using psychoanalysis with patients suffering from physical disorders, captured her interest in symbolic communication, another approach she would use effectively with schizophrenic patients.

In 1933, as Germany became increasingly under the control of the National Socialist party, Fromm-Reichmann moved across the border to France, where she could continue the analysis of her German patients. Her attempt to remain in Europe, however, was short-lived. Having practiced Orthodox Judaism in her youth, she traveled briefly to Israel although she had abandoned her earlier religious beliefs. In 1935 she immigrated to the United States, where she found a receptive community of psychoanalysts. Taking a position at Chestnut Lodge, a private psychoanalytic sanitarium in Rockville, Maryland, Fromm-Reichmann worked closely with Harry Stack Sullivan. Because she both possessed an ability to listen patiently through the fears and anxieties of even the psychotic patient and held a conviction that a therapist should measure a patient's progress as an individual rather than against a theoretical norm, Sullivan's theories of interpersonal psychoanalysis especially appealed to her.

Fromm-Reichmann was a therapist of outstanding skill and personal charisma. She used what she called "psychoanalytically oriented psychotherapy" with psychotic patients, especially schizophrenics. According to colleagues who knew her well, she excelled in what one has called the "communication of understanding." She understood the nature of the anxieties of her schizophrenic patients, respected their "vigilant caution" against "intrusion," and left ample room for a variety of interpretations, even (and especially) those of the patients (Weigert, P. 93). Both her technique and success are portrayed in Hannah Green's novel, *I Never Promised You a Rose Garden*, in which Dr. Fried is based on Frieda Fromm-Reichmann.

For more than two decades Fromm-Reichmann worked at Chestnut Lodge, gaining renown for her clinical successes, offering training opportunities to analysands and colleagues, and intriguing professional audiences with descriptions of her therapeutic approaches. She was an active member of professional organizations such as the William Alanson White Institute, the American Psychiatric Association, the American Medical Association, the Women's Southern Medical Society, the American Psychoanalytic Association, and the Washington Psychoanalytic Society. During the 1940s the American psychoanalytic community experienced numerous schisms. Dissension abounded around definitions of orthodoxy, the appropriate role of lay analysis, and personal and professional power struggles. In 1943 Fromm-Reichmann was part of the schism in the Washington Psychoanalytic Society that, with Clara Thompson and others, formed the New York Division of the Washington School of Psychiatry.

Fromm-Reichmann was the author of two books, *Principles of Psychotherapy* (1950; repr. 1974) and *Psychoanalysis and Psychotherapy* (1959), a selection of her papers in English published posthumously. She wrote twenty-seven papers in German. She also coauthored articles, among them "An Intensive Study of Twelve Cases of Manic-Depressive Psychosis," with Kurt Goldstein (1954). In 1952 she received the Adolf Meyer Award for her contributions in the area of using psychotherapy with psychotic patients; she delivered an invited lecture to the annual meeting of the American Psychiatric Association in 1954; and she was awarded a prestigious fellowship at the Stanford Center for Advanced Study in the Behavioral Sciences in 1955–1956.

Frieda Fromm-Reichmann was a woman of untiring curiosity. She maintained her spirit of intellectual inquiry and therapeutic advancement throughout her life. At the Stanford Center for Advanced Study in the Behavioral Sciences she crossed disciplines to seek out a deeper understanding of what happens in therapy even after having been one of the most successful practitioners for forty years; in the process she became the "shaman" of the other forty-nine Fellows and their families. Older and younger colleagues sought her advice and reveled in her presence. She was "courageous as a therapist," held large audiences spellbound, and practiced her profession and lived her life with "humor, empathy, indignation, intuition, a first-rate intellect, linguistic sensitivity, and the endearing quality of not exploiting her patients to prove herself or her theories."

In 1957 she was invited to deliver a paper, "Basic Problems in the Psychotherapy of Schizophrenia," at the Second International Congress for Psychiatry in Zurich. She died of a heart attack at Chestnut Lodge before she had the opportunity to deliver the paper to that assemblage.

• Fromm-Reichmann's papers are in the private collection of Virginia Gunst. A complete bibliography of Fromm-Reichmann's writings is included in Albert Grinstein, *The Index of Psychoanalytic Writings* (1956; repr. 1967). Helpful biographical sources include Gregory Bateson, "Language and Psychotherapy—Frieda Fromm-Reichmann's Last Project," *Psychiatry* 21 (1957): 96–100; Marianne Marschak, "One Year among the Behavioral Scientists: In Memory of Frieda Fromm-Reichmann," *Psychiatry* 23 (Aug. 1960): 303–11; and Edith Weigert, "In Memoriam: Frieda Fromm-Reichmann, 1889–1957," *Psychiatry* 21 (Feb. 1958): 91–95. An obituary is in the *New York Times*, 30 Apr. 1957.

CONSTANCE M. McGOVERN

FRONTENAC, Comte de. *See* Buade, Louis de.

FROST, Arthur Burdett (17 Jan. 1851–22 June 1928), illustrator, painter, and author, was born in Philadelphia, Pennsylvania, the son of John Frost, a bibliographer, and Sarah Ann Burdett, a painter. He was eight years old when his father died, and by the time he was fifteen he was working, first for a wood engraver and then for a lithographer. During these early years he took evening classes at the Philadelphia Academy of the Fine Arts, working briefly under Thomas Eakins, but he was primarily a self-taught artist with an inclination toward the humorous.

In 1874 William J. Clark, a friend of Frost's who took a fatherly interest in the talented artist, arranged for him to draw some illustrations for a book by his brother, Charles (pseud. Max Adeler). *Out of the Hurly Burly* (1874) sold more than a million copies, including foreign translations, and launched Frost's career as an illustrator. At first he worked at New York Graphic, and then he worked for ten years at Harper and Brothers. At Harper's, Charles Parsons, the head of the art department, encouraged him with illustration assignments for *Harper's Weekly* and for books the company published by the leading authors of the day. Frost's earliest pen-and-ink drawings were done on wood, cut by an engraver, and then the printing was done from the original wood block. This tedious woodcut process was superseded by improved technology during the last quarter of the century. About 1876 Frost began working in watercolor and gouache, an opaque medium, primarily in black and white, grey, and sepia, as did most illustrators, because reproduction technology at the time was limited to those colors. Frost was color-blind, but he had a strong sense of light and shade, so this was particularly appropriate. Whatever the medium, his art fell into two categories, finished individual illustrations and comic line sketches in story sequence that were precursors of comics.

In 1877 Frost illustrated *Almost a Man*, written by his sister, Sarah Annie, and in 1884 his brother, Charles, the owner of *Godey's Ladies Book*, wrote jingles for one of Arthur's books. The same year Parsons sent him to Europe, where many artists went to learn and be inspired by art unavailable even in reproduction in the United States. Within a year he returned, having learned that he preferred living in the United States drawing American subjects. It was the right choice, because during the last quarter of the nineteenth century continuously improving technology made increasing titles and copies of illustrated publications possible. The audience for them grew, and A. B. Frost, with his talent for depicting humorous situations and sporting scenes, became one of the most sought-after American illustrators.

Through his work for Harper's Frost met many illustrators, among them Edwin Abbey, George Boughton (with whom he had worked in London), Charles Stanley Reinhart, and F. Hopkinson Smith. As members of the Tile Club (1877–1887), they and others met weekly when in New York City, painted on tiles, and went on sketching trips together. The group promoted admiration for American scenery and American characters in their art, subjects that were also important to Frost. They were fun-loving people who frequently wrote about their adventures using their club names; Frost's sobriquet was Icicle.

In 1883 Frost married Philadelphian Emily Louise Phillips, an accomplished painter and illustrator; they had two children. For the next few years they lived in Huntington, Long Island, so that Frost could easily commute to New York City on the Long Island Railroad. As their family grew the Frosts moved first to a small farm at West Conshohocken near Philadelphia, Pennsylvania, in 1887. Then in 1890 they purchased a 120-acre estate at Convent Station near Morristown, New Jersey, which with characteristic humor was named "Moneysunk." He had always loved outdoor life, especially hunting, rowing, and fishing, but now he took up sports that were new in the United States: golf and bicycling. All these activities became a part of his portfolio of subjects to illustrate; his drawings were the unglamorized record of the ideas and manners of country folk. While other artists depicted the western United States, Frost pictorially reproduced the eastern story with charm and matchless humor.

Like many illustrators, Frost wanted also to be a painter, so in 1884 he attempted his first oil paintings. In 1891 he took a few painting lessons from William Merritt Chase, and he exhibited two paintings at the Paris Exposition of 1900. His illustrations, however, were what popular magazine and book publishers of his day wanted and what brought him lasting fame.

With two sons who became painters and his wife, Frost spent eight years in Europe, mostly in a house at Giverny, France, near Claude Monet, whom he admired. When he returned to the United States in October 1914, 300 members of the Society of Illustrators attended a dinner in his honor that included a skit with costumed characters from his illustrations. Frost moved to Pasadena, California, in 1920, continuing to work at his illustrations until he died there in his son's home.

For more than fifty years Frost was one of the best illustrators of the American country scene, admired and appreciated by both artists and the public. His work appeared in *Harper's Weekly*, *Scribner's*, *Collier's*, *Century*, *Puck*, and *Life*. As a humorist, he knew how to blend both the real and the ridiculous to create visual images for the forms he and others wrote about. In more than ninety books and countless articles written by Lewis Carroll, Charles Dickens, Joel Chandler Harris, Theodore Roosevelt, Sir Walter Scott, Frank R. Stockton, Mark Twain, and many others he created the picture worth a thousand words.

• The Archives of American Art at the Smithsonian Institution has some of Frost's personal correspondence. F. Hopkinson Smith and Edward Strahan, *A Book of the Tile Club* (1886), and "A Night at the Tile Club" in Smith, *American Illustrators* (1892), are replete with drawings and comments by and about Frost. An article by H. C. Bunner, "A. B. Frost," *Harper's Monthly*, Oct. 1892, pp. 699–706, includes family history and a portrait of Frost by John Alexander. *A Book of Drawings by A. B. Frost* (1904), contains some of his best work and an introduction by Joel Chandler Harris. For a biography written by an admirer and collector, which includes a list of books illustrated by Frost, see Henry M. Reed, *The A. B. Frost Book* (1967). An obituary is in the *New York Times*, 24 June 1928.

CONSTANCE KOPPELMAN

FROST, Edwin Brant (14 July 1866–14 May 1935), astronomer, was born in Brattleboro, Vermont, the son of Carlton Pennington Frost, a physician, and Eliza Ann DuBois. In December 1871 the family moved to Hanover, New Hampshire, where Frost's father became professor of medicine at Dartmouth College and developed a successful private practice. Frost was educated at home until the age of eleven, after which he enrolled in the local public school. In the fall of 1882 he entered Dartmouth, where he pursued a traditional classical curriculum but also increasingly concentrated on science courses and learned to use the telescope and spectroscope in the small campus observatory. He graduated in 1886 with honors in physics.

The following fall, Frost began taking graduate courses in chemistry at Dartmouth. He served as an assistant in several chemistry courses and, after the fall term ended, taught briefly at a nearby public school. Frost journeyed to Princeton University in the spring of 1887 to study with noted astronomer Charles Augustus Young, who had been close friends with the Frosts as a Dartmouth faculty member during the 1870s. Following his return to Hanover in the summer, Frost was appointed instructor in physics and astronomy, with responsibility for the campus observatory. For the next three years, he combined a heavy teaching load with his initial astronomical research. Although hampered by inadequate equipment, Frost observed solar prominences with a visual spectroscope and recorded sunspot positions. He also satisfied the requirements for an A.M., which he received in 1889.

Advanced work in astronomy, Frost realized, would require European study. Provided by Dartmouth with a two-year leave of absence, he left the United States in the summer of 1890. After visiting various astronomical facilities, he took courses at the University of Strasbourg and then secured an appointment in 1891 as a voluntary assistant at Potsdam Observatory, one of the premier research facilities in Europe. Frost's most important work at Potsdam was with the noted spectroscopist Julius Scheiner. In addition to learning advanced spectroscopic techniques and assisting in research projects, Frost arranged to translate Scheiner's recent book on celestial spectroscopy. Published in 1894 as *A Treatise on Astronomical Spectroscopy*, Frost's translation merged the most recent results of spectroscopic research with Scheiner's earlier contributions. Although he had originally intended to return to Strasbourg to pursue a doctorate in astronomy, Frost decided to remain at Potsdam for another year of research and training before returning to the United States in the summer of 1892.

Frost rejected the offer of a faculty position at the University of Minnesota to accept appointment as assistant professor of astronomy at Dartmouth in the fall of 1892. He devoted himself to the revitalization of astronomy on campus, tapping the growing Dartmouth endowment to upgrade observatory equipment and reworking courses to increase student interest. He also became increasingly involved with the national astronomical community. He attended the astronomy congress held at the Columbian Exposition in Chicago (1893) and reported on the complicated spectrum of the variable star Beta Lyrae to the Brooklyn meeting of the American Association for the Advancement of Science in 1894. Promoted to professor the following year, Frost married Mary Elizabeth Hazard of Dorchester, Massachusetts, in 1896; they had three children.

Frost was presented with an unexpected opportunity in the spring of 1898. His astronomer friend George Ellery Hale, who had recently established the Yerkes Observatory of the University of Chicago, offered Frost a position at this new facility in Williams Bay, Wisconsin. Made possible by a grant from the philanthropist Catherine Bruce, this five-year appointment allowed Frost to pursue various research activities. His first major project at Yerkes was the determination of radial velocities of stars through spectroscopic observations with the observatory's forty-inch refracting telescope. The existing Yerkes equipment proved inadequate to the task, compelling Frost to design and supervise construction of a new spectroscope. With the new equipment, Frost and his colleagues were able to expand the number of known radial velocities by several hundred over the next few decades. Frost's own work led to several important advances, including the discovery that stars of different spectral classes displayed characteristic radial velocities. In 1901–1903 Frost and his assistant Walter S. Adams, a former astronomy student at Dartmouth on a graduate fellowship at Yerkes, studied B-type stars in similar fashion, determining that many of these stars were binary systems. Frost also continued to pursue his interest in solar astronomy. A member of the Yerkes solar eclipse expedition to Wadesboro, North Carolina, in May 1900, he took photographs of the spectrum at the edge of the solar disk and published an extensive report, "Spectroscopic Results Obtained at the Solar Eclipse of May 28, 1900," in the *Astrophysical Journal* (12 [1900]: 307–51).

Frost's active research career was abbreviated by administrative demands. In 1903 Frost's position at Yerkes became permanent as Hale began to be increasingly involved with the survey, plans, and establishment of Mount Wilson Observatory in southern California. During Hale's frequent absences, Frost served as acting director of the Yerkes Observatory, a position that became permanent in 1905 when Hale moved to California to direct the new observatory. While directing observatory affairs and overseeing an extensive publication program, Frost remained active in other areas of astronomy. He had been managing editor of the *Astrophysical Journal* since its founding in 1895 and became its editor in 1902. In addition to coordinating the review and publication of manuscripts, Frost translated reports from French and German astronomers for inclusion in the journal. Frost chaired two sessions of the International Solar Union meeting at Mount Wilson in 1910 and chaired the astronomy section of the American Association for the Advancement of Science in 1911. He also served on various committees of the National Academy of Sciences, including several that distributed funds for astronomy projects.

Despite his administrative duties, Frost continued his observational work as time permitted. In mid-December 1915, while photographing stellar spectra, he noticed impaired vision in his right eye. Caused by a detached retina, Frost's condition progressively worsened and led to complete blindness in the eye by late 1916. A few years later, the vision in his left eye also began to deteriorate through the growth of a cataract and, in 1921, an extensive hemorrhage. Reading became impossible and ordinary visual work was greatly restricted as surgical correction of the cataract proved impossible. Frost was soon virtually blind, although in his autobiography, *An Astronomer's Life* (1933), he remarked that the remaining 3 to 4 percent vision "served me in good stead for several years."

Frost's blindness failed to restrict his activity. With assistance from his colleagues, he continued to direct the Yerkes Observatory and to edit the *Astrophysical Journal*. His extraordinary and well-developed memory was of great use during these years. In 1918 he led an expedition to Wyoming to observe a solar eclipse. Five years later, he traveled to Catalina Island as part of another Yerkes eclipse expedition. Although foggy conditions made observations impossible, Frost's role in the organization and supervision of the expedition remained significant. In 1925 he chaired a committee of the International Astronomical Union to select a new list of standard velocity stars that would provide a precise set of stellar radial velocities.

Frost also contributed to science in other ways. During the winter of 1922–1923 he organized a Yerkes committee to coordinate the relief of Russian astronomers and their families during that nation's famine. He wrote a chapter entitled "The Structure of the Cosmos" for University of Chicago divinity school dean Shailer Mathews's *Contributions of Science to Religion* (1924) and continued to give public addresses throughout the United States to colleges and universities, civic groups, and other organizations. As Yerkes director, he frequently opened the observatory to the various groups that summered in the area and coordinated lectures and tours for church groups, youth organizations, and other visitors. Frost remained active in community affairs as well, serving as a member of the town council of Williams Bay, director of the country Young Men's Christian Association, member of the Walworth County Park Commission, and trustee of the local Congregational church.

Following his retirement in the summer of 1932, Frost and his wife remained in Williams Bay. They traveled to Maine for the August 1932 solar eclipse, whose line of totality passed near their son's home in Portland. Following the eclipse, Frost attended the Harvard meeting of the International Astronomical Union. He spent much of the next year dictating his autobiography to his wife and continued to give occasional public addresses. Frost's health, however, slowly deteriorated after retirement. Gallbladder surgery in the fall of 1932 appeared successful, but his health remained fragile. He died at the Billings Hospital of the University of Chicago.

Frost received significant recognition during his career, including honorary doctorates and election to the National Academy of Sciences (1908), the American Philosophical Society (1909), and the American Academy of Arts and Sciences (1913). Frost was made a foreign associate of the Royal Astronomical Society in 1908 and was an honorary member of the Royal Astronomical Society of Canada, the Astronomical Society of Mexico, and the Russian Astronomical Society.

• Frost's papers from his directorship are filed in the Director's Correspondence Collection at Yerkes Observatory, Williams Bay, Wis. The Yerkes Archives also contain a small collection of miscellaneous manuscripts and selected items of correspondence. Among Frost's most significant publications are "On the Classification of Stellar Spectra," *Astrophysical Journal* 33 (1911): 273–77; "Results of Observations of the Eclipse by the Expedition from Yerkes Observatory," *Proceedings of the American Philosophical Society* 58 (1919): 282–88; "The Expedition from the Yerkes Observatory for Observing the Total Eclipse of September 10, 1923, at Camp Wrigley," *Popular Astronomy* 32 (1924): 205–17; and, with Storrs B. Barrett and Otto Struve, "Radial Velocities of 368 Helium Stars," *Astrophysical Journal* 64 (1926): 1–77. A survey of Frost's career, written by a Yerkes colleague and including a list of publications, is Otto Struve, "Biographical Memoir of Edwin Brant Frost," National Academy of Sciences, *Biographical Memoirs* 19 (1938): 22–51. Obituaries are in *Astrophysical Journal* 83 (Jan. 1936): 1–9 and *Science* 81 (21 June 1935): 605–7.

GEORGE E. WEBB

FROST, Holloway Halstead (11 Apr. 1889–26 Jan. 1935), naval officer, was born in Brooklyn, New York, the son of Halstead H. Frost, a lawyer, and Mary Louise Downing. In 1910 he graduated from the U.S. Naval Academy and was assigned to the battleship *Michigan*. Two years later he was commissioned an ensign. In 1912 Frost married Helen M. Prentice; they had two children. After completing his tour on the *Michigan* in 1914, Frost served on the submarine *Ozark* for one year and in 1915 was promoted to lieutenant, junior grade. In 1916–1917 he was a student at the Naval War College, and after the United States entered World War I in the spring of 1917, he was assigned as senior aide and operations officer for the commander of Squadron One of the U.S. Atlantic Fleet Patrol Force.

After World War I, Frost, who was promoted to lieutenant in 1917 and lieutenant commander in 1921, served in a variety of school, sea, and staff assignments. From 1919 to 1921 he was assigned to the Office of the Chief of Naval Operations in the Navy Department, and after commanding the destroyer *Breck* in 1921–1922, he served on the staff of Admiral Edwin A. Anderson, commander of American naval forces in Europe and later commander of the U.S. Asiatic Fleet. While on duty with the Asiatic Fleet, Frost was given temporary command of the destroyer *John D. Ford*, and in the spring of 1924 he took his ship and the destroyer *Pope* to the Kuril Islands to establish a refueling base for U.S. Army Air Service flyers engaged in a round-the-world flight. From 1924 to 1927 Frost was assigned to the Planning Division of the Bureau of Navigation in Washington, and from 1927 to 1929 he commanded the destroyer *Toucey*. He also was a technical adviser for the American naval delegation to the Geneva, Switzerland, conference on naval limitations in 1927. In 1929–1930 Frost, now holding his final rank of commander, was a student at the U.S. Army War College, and from 1930 to 1932 he was a faculty member at the college. He then served as navigation officer for the battleship *California*, and in 1933–1934 he was operations officer for the the U.S. Fleet. Following this assignment, he was appointed a faculty member at the U.S. Army Command and General Staff School at Fort Leavenworth, Kansas, a post he occupied until his death.

Early in his naval career, Frost became a prolific writer on naval affairs, history, strategy, and tactics, and over a twenty-year span he published numerous articles in the *Proceedings of the U.S. Naval Institute* and other publications. In "National Strategy," a prize-winning article that appeared in the *Proceedings* in August 1925, Frost provided a cogent analysis of the strategy of World War I. Calling for naval officers to expand their view of strategy to include nonmilitary elements, he argued that the short decisive wars that were typical of the nineteenth century had been the result of unique circumstances. The experience of World War I, which saw Germany defeated only after the will of the German army had been undermined by the collapse of the home front, showed that in the future it was unlikely that a rapid and purely military decision could be achieved when nations with approximately equal strength were at war. Rather, victory could only come by breaking the enemy's strength through severe pressure applied to all aspects of its national life over a period of time. He also published several books, including *Some Famous Sea Fights* (1927), coauthored with Fitzhugh Green; *We Build a Navy* (1929), a study of early American naval history; and *On a Destroyer's Bridge* (1930), which deals with the handling of destroyers and was adopted by the Japanese and Argentine navies as a textbook.

Frost's most important writings dealt with the battle of Jutland, the only major fleet engagement in World War I. He began his study shortly after it occurred in 1916, and for eighteen years he examined every aspect of the battle, gathering data and interviewing participants. He published his findings in four articles in the *Proceedings* between 1919 and 1925 and in *The Battle of Jutland* (1936), a scholarly work that appeared after his death. Frost believed that the British could have won a decisive victory at Jutland if the commander of the British Grand Fleet, Sir John Jellicoe, had been more aggressive in seeking the destruction of the German High Seas Fleet instead of adopting a negative strategy based on the proposition that nothing must be left to chance. To Frost, a willingness to assume risks was the foundation of naval greatness, and in his opinion Jellicoe's cautiousness cost him the opportunity for a victorious fleet action that could have altered the course of the war.

During the 1920s and 1930s, as naval officers everywhere examined Jutland in minute detail to draw lessons for a future war, American naval officers, in line with Frost's interpretation of Jellicoe, adopted the view that a successful commander must be willing to accept risks and compel the enemy battle fleet to engage in a decisive clash. Thus, during World War II they developed a strategy in the Pacific designed to bring the Japanese fleet to battle through an aggressive advance by the American fleet across the Central Pacific.

A tough-minded officer who impressed his colleagues with his commitment to professionalism and his intellectual acumen, Frost was the leading American naval writer of his generation. He died in the prime of his career in Kansas City, Missouri, from meningitis following an operation for an ear infection.

• Frost's naval career is traced in the *U.S. Navy Register* (1907–1934). For references to Frost's writings see Peter Karsten, *The Naval Aristocracy: The Golden Age of Annapolis and the Emergence of Modern American Navalism* (1972), and Russell F. Weigley, *The American Way of War: A History of United States Military Strategy and Policy* (1973). An obituary is in the *New York Times*, 28 Jan. 1935.

JOHN KENNEDY OHL

FROST, Robert (26 Mar. 1874–29 Jan. 1963), poet, was born Robert Lee Frost in San Francisco to Isabelle Moodie, of Scottish birth, and William Prescott Frost, Jr., a descendant of a Devonshire Frost who had sailed to New Hampshire in 1634. The father was a former teacher turned newspaper man, a hard drinker, a gambler, and a harsh disciplinarian, who fought in politics for as long as his health allowed. In the wake of his death (as a consumptive) in his thirty-sixth year, his impoverished widow, with the help of funds from her father-in-law, moved east. She resumed her teaching career in the fall of 1885 in Salem, New Hampshire, where Robert and his younger sister were enrolled in the fifth-grade class. Soon he was playing baseball, trapping animals, climbing birches. And his mother, who had filled his early years with Shakespeare, Bible stories, and myths, was reading aloud from *Tom Brown's School Days*, Burns, Emerson, Wordsworth, and Percy's *Reliques*. Before long he was memorizing poetry and reading books on his own.

Frost's high school years in Lawrence, Massachusetts, marked a further change. Greek and Latin delighted him; at the end of the first year he was head of his class. An older student, Carl Burell, introduced him to botany and astronomy. More important, Frost became a promising writer: his poem "La Noche Triste," inspired by William H. Prescott's *History of the Conquest of Mexico* (1843), appeared in the April 1890 issue of the high school *Bulletin*, of which he was soon made editor. He joined the debating society, played on the football team, and again was head of his class. At the beginning of his senior year he fell in love with Elinor White, who had also published poetry in the *Bulletin*. On commencement day (1892) they shared valedictory honors and, before summer ended, pledged themselves to each other in a secret ritual.

In the fall they went their separate ways: Elinor to St. Lawrence University in Canton, New York, Frost to Dartmouth on a scholarship and with his grandfather's aid. Though he relished his courses in Latin and Greek and his own wide reading of English verse, in particular Francis Turner Palgrave's *Golden Treasury of the Best Songs and Lyrical Poems in the English Language*, the campus life dismayed him. Isolated and restless, he quit at the end of December, being needed, he said, to take over his mother's unruly eighth-grade class. He was nursing the hope that Elinor might give up school to marry him, but when she returned in April his attempts to persuade her failed.

After working for months as a trimmer of lamps in a woolen mill in Lawrence, Frost turned to teaching in grade school, while also writing poetry. At the end of the term, startling news greeted him: the New York *Independent* had accepted "My Butterfly: An Elegy," with a stipend of $15. His first professionally published poem would appear in November—he could earn his living as a writer! Once again he implored Elinor to marry him; once again she refused. Convinced there was now another suitor, he engaged a printer to make two leather-bound, gold-stamped copies of *Twilight*, each containing five of his poems. He took the train to Canton, knocked at her door, and handed her his gift. The inimically cool reception hurled him into despair. Pained and distraught, he destroyed his copy and went home. Still distraught, on 6 November he set out for the Dismal Swamp in Virginia—to throw his life away? punish Elinor? make her relent? On 30 November 1894, frightened and worn, he was back in Lawrence. Before long he became a reporter, then returned to teaching. Elinor, having finished college, also taught in his mother's private school. Then at long last, on 19 December 1895, they were married by a Swedenborgian pastor. Nine months later, Elliot, a son, was born.

They both kept working as teachers, and Frost kept publishing poems. In the fall of 1897, thanks to his grandfather's loan, Frost, at age twenty-three, entered Harvard in the hope of becoming a high school teacher of Latin and Greek. Certain courses proved meaningful, most of all in the classics and geology, but also in philosophy with Hugo Munsterberg, who assigned *Psychology: Briefer Course* by William James, Frost's "greatest inspiration," then absent on leave. In March 1899, however, severe chest and stomach pains combined with worries about his ailing mother and pregnant wife forced him to leave Harvard.

Medical warnings—the threat of tuberculosis—drove Frost from the indoor life of teaching. In May 1900, with his grandfather's help, he rented a poultry farm in Methuen. Two months later, Elliot, the Frosts' three-year-old, became gravely ill with *cholera infantum*; on 8 July he died. Frost flailed himself for not having summoned a doctor in time, believing that God was punishing him by taking his child away. Elinor, silent for days, at last let fly at him for his "self-centered senselessness" in believing that any such thing as a god's benevolent concern for human affairs could exist; life was hateful and the world evil, but with a fourteen-month-old daughter, Lesley, to care for, they would have to go on. And when their landlord ordered them to leave by fall, Elinor took matters in hand. She persuaded Grandfather Frost to buy for their use the thirty-acre farm that her mother had found in Derry, New Hampshire, and to arrange, in addition, for Carl Burell, Frost's high school friend, to move in to help with the chores.

The "Derry Years" (1900–1911) were especially creative ones, bringing forth—complete or in draft—nearly all of *A Boy's Will* (1913), much, if not most, of *North of Boston* (1914), many poems of *Mountain Interval* (1916), as well as some that appeared in each of his later books. Yet at times in the first two years he was deeply depressed: in November 1900 his mother died; in July 1901, his other firm supporter, Grandfather Frost. But the latter's will bequeathed to his grandson an immediate annuity of $500 and after ten years an annuity of $800 and the deed to the Derry property.

Frost continued to write at night: poems and articles for poultry journals. He enjoyed working the farm by day and learning about the countryside and the lives of its people. By 1906, though fairly well off compared to his neighbors, yet with four children under seven, he was pressed for money. With the aid of a pastor-friend and a school trustee who admired his poems, he obtained a position at the nearby Pinkerton Academy, which he held with outstanding success. A pedagogic original, he introduced a conversational classroom style. He directed students in plays he adapted from Marlowe, Milton, Sheridan, and Yeats. He revised the English curriculum. And besides teaching seven classes a day, he helped with athletics, the student paper, and the debating team. At the end of five years, utterly exhausted, he resigned.

In the fall of 1911 he was teaching again, part time in the Plymouth, New Hampshire, Normal School.

But in December he announced to his editor-friend at the *Independent*, Susan Ward, that "the long deferred forward movement you have been living in wait for is to begin next year." In July 1912 he started making plans for a radical change of scene. When he suggested England to Elinor as "the place to be poor and to write poems, 'Yes,' she cried, 'let's go over and live under thatch.'"

On 2 September 1912 the Frosts arrived in London. They stayed there briefly before moving into "The Bungalow" in Beaconsfield, where they would live for eighteen months. Elinor, charmed by the "dear little cottage" and its long grassy yard, strolled the countryside with the children; Frost traveled at will to London—forty minutes by train—roaming the streets, the bookshops, "everywhere." Before long he was finishing the manuscript of *A Boy's Will* that he had brought to England and adding a few new poems. In October the book was accepted by David Nutt for publication the following March.

Through the next few months Frost was seized by a powerful surge of creativity, producing twelve or more lengthy poems, each strikingly different from the brooding narratives of *A Boy's Will*: dialog-narratives in a style of "living" speech new to the language, exploring the inward lives of ordinary people in the New England countryside. By April 1913, most of (if not all) the poems that would constitute *North of Boston* had been written.

At the January 1913 opening of Monro's Poetry Bookshop Frost was urged by the poet Frank Flint to call on Ezra Pound (whom he had never heard of), a reviewer for various journals. Frost waited until 13 March, about a week before *A Boy's Will* was to appear. At Pound's insistence, they walked to the publisher's office for a copy. On their return, Pound started reading at once, then told his guest to "run along home" so he could write his review for *Poetry*, a new American monthly. In the next few weeks, thanks to Pound and Flint, Frost came to meet some of the best-known writers then living in England, including Yeats, H.D., Richard Aldington, and Ford Madox Ford.

A Boy's Will, finally issued on 1 April 1913, elicited favorable but qualified reviews. Chronicling the growth of a youth from self-centered idealism to maturity and acceptance of loss, the thirty-two lyrics offered few hints of the masterful volumes to come, except for those in "Mowing," "Storm Fear," and scattered passages. Yeats pronounced the poetry "the best written in America for some time," leading Elinor to "hope"—in vain—that "he would say so publicly." Happily, in the fall, on his return from a family vacation in Scotland, Frost was greeted by two extraordinary tributes in the *Nation* and the Chicago *Dial* and a superb review in the *Academy*.

During the next few months, Frost came to know the writers Robert Bridges, Walter de la Mare, W. H. Davies, and Ralph Hodgson; the Georgian poets Rupert Brooke, Wilfred Gibson, Lascelles Abercrombie; and the essayist and poet Edward Thomas, who would become his bosom friend. With Flint and T. E. Hulme he discussed poetics, having spoken in letters to his Pinkerton friends John Bartlett and Sidney Cox of "the sounds of sense with all their irregularity of accent across the regular beat of the metre" and "the sentence sound [that] often says more than the words." He also wrote that he wanted not "a success with the critical few" but "to get outside to the general reader who buys books by the thousands."

In April, badly strained for funds, Frost moved his family 100 miles northwest of London to an ancient cottage, not far from Abercrombie's and Gibson's, in the rolling Gloucestershire farmland near Dymock. On 15 May *North of Boston* appeared, to be hailed in June by important reviews, particularly those by Abercrombie ("there will never be," said Frost, "any other just like it"), Ford Madox Ford ("an achievement much finer than Whitman's"), Richard Aldington ("it would be very difficult to overpraise it"), and Edward Thomas ("Only at the end of the best pieces, such as 'The Death of the Hired Man,' 'Home Burial,' 'The Black Cottage,' and 'The Wood-pile,' do we realize that they are masterpieces of a deep and mysterious tenderness"). By August, Frost's reputation as a leading poet had been firmly established in England, and Henry Holt of New York had agreed to publish his books in America. By the end of 1914, however, financial need forced him to leave Britain.

When Frost and his family returned to the United States in February, he was hailed as a leading voice of the "new poetry" movement. Holt's editor introduced him to the staff of the *New Republic*, which had just published a favorable review of *North of Boston*, and Tufts College invited him to be its Phi Beta Kappa poet. Before the year's end, he had met with Edwin Arlington Robinson, William Dean Howells, Louis Untermeyer (who would become his intimate friend), Ellery Sedgwick of the *Atlantic Monthly*, and other literary figures. In the following year he was made Phi Beta Kappa poet at Harvard and elected to the National Institute of Arts and Letters. *Mountain Interval*, which appeared in November 1916, offered readers some of his finest poems, such as "Birches," "Out, Out—," "The Hill Wife," and "An Old Man's Winter Night."

Frost's move to Amherst in 1917 launched him on the twofold career he would lead for the rest of his life: teaching whatever "subjects" he pleased at a congenial college (Amherst, 1917–1963, with interruptions; the University of Michigan, 1921–1923, 1925–1926; Harvard, 1939–1943; Dartmouth, 1943–1949) and "barding around," his term for "saying" poems in a conversational performance. Audiences flocked to listen to the "gentle farmer-poet" whose platform manner concealed the ever-troubled, agitated private man who sought through each of his poems "a momentary stay against confusion." In the great short lyrics of *New Hampshire* (1923) and *West-Running Brook* (1928)—such as "Fire and Ice," "Stopping by Woods on a Snowy Evening," and the title poem of the latter book—a bleak outlook on life persuasively emerges

from the combination of dramatic tension and nature imagery freighted with ambiguity. Only the will to create form, the poet in effect says, can stave off the nothingness that confronts us as mortal beings.

In 1930 Frost won a second Pulitzer Prize for *Collected Poems*—the first had been won by *New Hampshire*—and in the next few years, other prizes and honors, including the Charles Eliot Norton Professorship of Poetry at Harvard. However, when *A Further Range* appeared in 1936, several influential leftist critics, unaware that Frost had "twice been approached" by the *New Masses* "to be their proletarian poet," attacked him for his conservative political views, ignoring the bitter meanings in "Provide, Provide" and such master poems as "Desert Places," "Design," and "Neither Out Far nor In Deep." *A Further Range* earned him a third Pulitzer Prize in May 1937. Ten months later, on 26 March 1938, Elinor died and his world collapsed. Four years before, in the wake of their daughter Marjorie's death, they had helped each other bear the grief. Alone now, wracked in misery and guilty over his sometimes insensitive behavior toward Elinor, he hoped to find calm through his children, but Lesley's ragings only deepened his pain. For some time he continued to teach, then resigned his position, sold his Amherst house, and returned to his farm. In July Theodore Morrison invited him to speak at the Breadloaf Writers' Conference in August. Frost's lectures enthralled his listeners, but at times his erratic public behavior drew worried attention. To the great relief of his friends, Kathleen Morrison, the director's wife, stepped in to offer him help with his affairs. He accepted at once and made her his official secretary-manager.

Weeks before, however, Kathleen had called at his farm to invite him to visit her at a nearby summer house. Before long he proposed marriage, but she insisted on secrecy, on maintaining appearances. "We wanted to marry," he told Stanley Burnshaw, his editor in the 1960s. "It was all decided. But you know how matters seem at times—others to think of . . . It was thought best," he repeated, "It was thought best"—marriage without benefit of clergy, an altered way of life. He continued to bard around and to teach, residing from January through March at "Pencil Pines," his newly built Miami retreat; at his Cambridge house until late May; then in Ripton, near Breadloaf, for the summer; and in Cambridge again through December.

During the 1940s Frost published four new books: *A Witness Tree* (1942), inscribed "To K.M./For Her Part in It," containing some of his finest poems, among them "The Most of It" and "The Silken Tent," and for which he received his fourth Pulitzer Prize; two deceptively playful blank verse dialogs, *A Masque of Reason* (1945) and *A Masque of Mercy* (1947), on the relationship between God and man, to be "taken" in light of his statements on "irony . . . a kind of guardedness" and "style . . . the way the man takes himself . . . If it is with outer humor, it must be with inner seriousness"; and fourth, *Steeple Bush* (1947), his weakest volume, although it included "Directive," one of Frost's major poems. None but his intimates knew of the decade's griefs: his son Carol's suicide in 1940, his daughter Irma's placement in a mental hospital in 1947.

In the last fourteen years of his life Frost was the most highly esteemed American poet of the twentieth century, having received forty-four honorary degrees and a host of government tributes, including birthday greetings from the Senate, a congressional medal, an appointment as honorary consultant to the Library of Congress, and an invitation from John F. Kennedy to recite a poem at his presidential inauguration. Thrice, at the State Department's request, he traveled on good-will missions: to Brazil (1954), to Britain (1957), and to Greece (1961, on his return from Israel, where he had lectured at the Hebrew University).

More important for Frost as an artist and for his readers were the changed perceptions of his works, which began with Randall Jarrell's 1947 essay "The Other Frost." Jarrell saw him as "the subtlest and saddest of poets" whose "extraordinary strange poems express an attitude that, at its most extreme, makes pessimism a hopeful evasion." Twelve years later Lionel Trilling hailed Frost at his eighty-fifth birthday dinner for his "representation of the terrible actualities of life in a new way," for though "the manifest America of [his] poems may be pastoral, the actual America is tragic." And two years earlier, in London at the English-Speaking Union, T. S. Eliot (who in 1922 had dismissed Frost's verse as "unreadable") toasted him as "perhaps *the* most eminent, the most distinguished Anglo-American poet now living," whose "kind of local feeling in poetry . . . can go without universality: the relation of Dante to Florence, . . . of Robert Frost to New England."

In the Clearing, Frost's ninth and last collection of poems, appeared on 26 March 1962, the date of his eighty-eighth birthday dinner in Washington, attended by some 200 guests who heard Justices Earl Warren and Felix Frankfurter, Adlai Stevenson, Mark Van Doren, and Robert Penn Warren speak in his honor. Five months later, at the president's request, Frost made a twelve-day trip to the USSR, where he met with fellow writers and with Premier Nikita Khrushchev. On his return, "bone tired" and exhausted after eighteen sleepless hours, he made some ill-considered public remark, which was taken as a slur on both Khrushchev and President Kennedy. To Frost's deep dismay, the president did not receive him.

On 2 December at the Ford Forum Hall in Boston Frost made his last address and, though admitting he felt a bit tired, he stayed the evening through. In the morning he felt much too ill to keep his doctor's appointment. After considerable wrangling, he agreed to enter a hospital "for observation and tests." He remained in its care until his death in the early hours of 29 January 1963. Tributes poured in from all over the land and from abroad. A small private service on the 31st at Harvard's Memorial Church for family members and friends was followed by a public one on 17

February at the Amherst College Chapel, where 700 guests listened to Mark Van Doren's recital of eleven Frost poems he had chosen for the occasion. Eight months later, at the October dedication of the Robert Frost Library at Amherst, President Kennedy paid tribute to the poetry, to "its tide that lifts all spirits," and to the poet "whose sense of the human tragedy fortified him against self-deception and easy consolation."

Within a decade, however, the poet's public image was shattered by the appearance of the second volume of Lawrance Thompson's authorized biography, *Robert Frost: The Years of Triumph, 1915–1937* (1970), which reviewers took at face value to be an accurate account of a man whom Helen Vendler deemed a "monster of egotism" (*New York Times Book Review*, 9 Aug. 1970). Although Frost later came to have grave misgivings about his choice, he had designated Thompson his official biographer in 1939. For whatever reason, the poet felt unable to renounce that decision despite his awareness of Thompson's frequently unsympathetic, even hostile constructions of his attitudes and conduct. Although reviewers perceived in Thompson, as Vendler put it, "an affectation of fairness," they tended to subscribe, nevertheless, to the "monster-myth" that poisoned Frost's reputation. Evidence that he was not a wrecker of others' lives was soon at hand in the form of *The Family Letters of Robert and Elinor Frost*, edited by Arnold Grade (1972). More than a decade would pass before the tide was turned: first by W. H. Pritchard's *Frost: A Literary Life Reconsidered* (1984) and then by Stanley Burnshaw's *Robert Frost Himself* (1986), which enabled *Publishers' Weekly* to state that "the unfortunately influential 'monster-myth' stands here convincingly corrected."

• Significant collections of Frost materials are in the Jones Library in Amherst, Mass., Amherst College Library, Dartmouth College Library, University of Virginia Library, and University of Texas Library, Austin. In addition to the volumes by Frost cited in the text above, editions of his writings include *Collected Poems, Prose & Plays*, ed. Richard Poirier and Mark S. Richardson (1995), and "The Collected Prose of Robert Frost," ed. M. S. Richardson (Ph.D. diss., Rutgers Univ., 1993). Additional correspondence appears in *Letters of Robert Frost to Louis Untermeyer*, ed. Louis Untermeyer (1963), and *Selected Letters of Robert Frost*, ed. Lawrance Thompson, 1964. Frost's spoken words are transcribed in *Robert Frost Speaks*, ed. Daniel Smythe (1964); *Robert Frost, Life and Talks-Walking*, ed. Louis Mertins (1965); *Interviews with Robert Frost*, ed. E. C. Lathem (1966); *Robert Frost: A Living Voice*, ed. Reginald Cook (1974); and *Newdick's Season of Frost*, ed. William Sutton (1976).
Biographical materials include L. Thompson's typescript "Notes on Robert Frost" (1962; Alderman Library, Univ. of Virginia); Sidney Cox, *A Swinger of Birches*, with an introduction by Robert Frost (1957); Elizabeth Shepley Sergeant, *Robert Frost: The Trial by Existence* (1960); Margaret Bartlett Anderson, *Robert Frost and John Bartlett: The Record of a Friendship* (1963); F. D. Reeve, *Robert Frost in Russia* (1964); Wade Van Dore, *Robert Frost and Wade Van Dore*, rev. and ed. Thomas Wetmore (1987); John E. Walsh, *Into My Own:*

The English Years of Robert Frost (1988); and Lesley Lee Francis (his granddaughter), *The Frost Family's Adventure in Poetry* (1994). In addition to *The Years of Triumph* volume discussed above, L. Thompson's official biography comprises *Robert Frost: The Early Years, 1874–1915* (1966) and *Robert Frost: The Later Years, 1938–1963*, with R. H. Winnick (1976). Assessments and criticism of note include Richard Thornton, ed., *Recognition of Robert Frost* (1937); Reuben Brower, *The Poetry of Robert Frost* (1963); Jac Tharpe, ed., *Frost: Centennial Essays* (3 vols., 1974–1978); R. Poirier, *Robert Frost: The Work of Knowing* (1977); and M. S. Richardson, *The Ordeal of Robert Frost: The Poet and His Poetics* (1997).

STANLEY BURNSHAW

FROST, Wade Hampton (3 Mar. 1880–30 Apr. 1938), epidemiologist and physician, was born in Marshall, Virginia, the son of Henry Frost, a physician and Sabra J. Walker. Frost was brought up in the rural setting of Marshall, near the Blue Ridge Mountains. His days as a boy were generally spent doing chores, accompanying his father on rounds to see patients throughout the countryside, and studying. Frost was schooled at home by his mother until the age of fifteen, when he was sent for a year to a military school in nearby Danville. He completed his college preparatory education at the Randolph Macon Academy, graduating in 1897. After working in a local store for a year, Frost entered the University of Virginia in Charlottesville. He received his undergraduate degree three years later in the spring of 1901. That fall he enrolled in the University of Virginia's Medical School, and he earned the degree of Doctor of Medicine in June 1903.

During the summer of 1903 Frost served as a substitute intern accompanying the ambulance drivers at Bellevue Hospital in New York City and at St. John's Hospital in Yonkers. He moved back to Virginia in the fall to complete a year's internship at St. Vincent's Hospital in Norfolk. Although there may have been a time when Frost had considered joining his father in private practice, he decided after his internship to pursue a career in public health as a medical scientist.

In 1905 Frost joined the U.S. Public Health Service in which he served as a commissioned medical officer until his resignation in 1928. During his first two years Frost's assignments were varied. He acted as an assistant surgeon at the Marine Hospital in Baltimore, as a member of surgeon Joseph E. White's team combating the 1905 yellow fever epidemic in New Orleans, as a medical inspector of immigrants at New York's Ellis Island, and as a surgeon at the Revenue Cutter Service's Training School, based in Curtis Bay, Maryland. Frost was finally given the opportunity to devote his full attention to the epidemiological investigation of infectious human diseases in the fall of 1908, when he was assigned to duty at the recently created Hygienic Laboratory in Washington, D.C.

Frost's work at the Hygienic Laboratory introduced him to such pioneer epidemiologists as Milton J. Rosenau, John F. Anderson, M. Goldberger, and Claude H. Lavinder. His investigations focused in particular on the cause, spread, and control of typhoid fever,

septic sore throat, cerebrospinal meningitis, and poliomyelitis. Although Frost's analysis of typhoid fever was not unique, his study of the disease focused great attention on the potential menace of polluted water systems and the importance of maintaining municipal reservoirs of clean drinking water. In the summer of 1913 Frost was selected to direct an independent field study of problems associated with stream pollution as well as water purification methods in Cincinnati, Ohio. His organization and analysis of information collected by staff epidemiologists, microbiologists, sanitary engineers, and biologists proved significant in public health efforts to prevent the spread of typhoid fever through contaminated public water supplies. He married Susan Noland Haxall in 1915; they had one daughter.

Frost's work on poliomyelitis engaged him in an ongoing debate with leading microbiologists about the etiology and pathogenesis of the disease. The 1916 epidemic offered Frost an opportunity to confirm his theory that healthy carriers and mild cases of the disease that escaped recognition played an extensive and important role in the dissemination of the virus. His epidemiological understanding of poliomyelitis eventually proved correct. Frost, however, did not receive due credit until participants in the poliovirus controversy reached a resolution in the late 1930s.

When the United States became involved in World War I Frost suspended his disease investigations and joined the American Red Cross detail at its national headquarters in Washington, D.C. There he organized and directed the Bureau of Sanitary Services. In November 1917 Frost discovered that he had incipient pulmonary tuberculosis. Consequently, he was forced to leave work and chose to convalesce in a sanitarium near Asheville, North Carolina. He was not able to actively serve again until the end of 1918. Upon his return, he faced the worst outbreak of influenza in recorded history.

Frost's assignments during the great influenza pandemic included several collaborative efforts with statistical economist Edgar Sydenstricker. As they worked to piece together a comprehensive epidemiological picture of influenza in the United States and various foreign countries, Frost and Sydenstricker developed new techniques and methods that eventually enhanced the scientific scope of their disciplines. Frost firmly believed that direct personal observation of social and environmental conditions in relation to disease occurrence would reveal the most accurate picture of human infection. In order to best ascertain the incidence and distribution of a particular ailment, Frost advocated house-to-house canvassing making the family the unit of study. Traditionally field studies were concerned with large populations, but Frost believed the family was the most useful unit in determining the tendency of disease to spread. He applied the life table analysis to his understanding of tuberculosis, as well as other diseases, after realizing that observation of the exposed group had to extend over a number of years to adequately define rates of morbidity and mortality.

Frost integrated his new techniques and methods into American medical curriculum beginning in 1919 as a resident lecturer, then in 1921 as professor, and in 1928 as head of the department of epidemiology at the School of Hygiene and Public Health at Johns Hopkins University. He then served as dean of the school in the years between 1931 and 1934. During his nineteen-year-academic tenure in Baltimore, Frost set the trend for future training of medical students in the epidemiological approach to infectious disease.

Frost's untimely death from cancer took his family, friends, and colleagues by surprise. He was remembered as a "fine and rare spirit [who] made living a noble adventure" (*Baltimore Sun*, 1 May 1938).

• Frost's papers are divided between the archives at the University of Virginia in Charlottesville and the Chesney Medical Archives at Johns Hopkins University in Baltimore. For a thorough biographical account of Frost see Kenneth F. Maxcy's *Papers of Wade Hampton Frost* (1941). To understand Frost's participation in the debate over the etiology and pathogenesis of poliomyelitis see Margaret L. Grimshaw's work on *The Poliovirus Controversy in the Years before World War II* (1996), and Naomi Rogers's *Dirt and Disease: Polio Before FDR* (1992). For more information on Frost's personal life see obituaries in the *Baltimore Sun*, 1 May 1938, *New York Times*, 2 May 1938, *Lancet*, 28 May 1938.

MARGARET L. GRIMSHAW

FROTHINGHAM, Arthur Lincoln (21 June 1859–28 July 1923), archaeologist and historian of art and architecture, was born in Boston, Massachusetts, the son of Arthur Lincoln Frothingham, an author and amateur art collector, and Jessie Peabody. The Frothinghams enjoyed a certain degree of prosperity, moving to Italy when Arthur was five years old in order to protect his delicate health. Living first in Florence, the family later moved to Rome, where Frothingham spoke and wrote Italian as his first language. He attended the Academy of the Christian Brothers from 1868 to 1873 and the Catholic seminary of St. Apollinare and the Royal University from 1875 to 1881. In 1883 he received a Ph.D. from the University of Leipzig in Germany. Having become a fellow in Semitic languages at Johns Hopkins University in 1882, Frothingham remained there as lecturer until 1887, when he accepted a position at Princeton University. He was appointed full professor at Princeton, first of archaeology and the history of art (1896–1898), and then, of ancient history and archaeology (1898–1905). He remained at Princeton until retiring in 1906. In January 1897 he married Helen Bulkley Post; the couple had no children.

A scholar of remarkable diversity and learning, Frothingham was equally at home with the Gothic architecture of England and France as he was among the ruins of ancient Rome. Among his classical pursuits, he was especially interested in Christian Rome, having already joined the Società dei Cultori di Archeologia Cristiana, an academic association devoted to the study of Christian archaeology, by age nineteen. His 1908 work, *The Monuments of Christian Rome*, marked the culmination of his research on the topic. Another important focus, the history and significance of Roman memorial and triumphal arches, resulted in his "De la véritable signification des monuments Romans qu'on appelle 'Arcs de Triomphe'" (*Revue Archéologique* 4th ser., 6 [1905]: 216–30) and "Who Built the Arch of Constantine?" (*American Journal of Archaeology* 16 [1912]: 368–86; 17 [1913]: 487–503; and 19 [1915]: 1–23, 367–84). Frothingham was planning a significant work on the topic at the time of his death.

Frothingham's depth of learning and industry resonated in other areas as well. He not only completed the second volume of Russell Sturgis's *A History of Architecture* (1917) following the death of the author, but in 1915 he went on to publish two additional volumes under his own name on European Gothic architecture and its later forms. His mastery of Semitic languages found expression in various writings, among them "A Historical Sketch of Syriac Literature and Culture" (*American Journal of Philology* 5 [1884]: 200–20) and *Stephen Bar Sudaili, the Syrian Mystic, and the Book of Hierotheos* (1886).

Frothingham's most enduring achievement was his founding of the *American Journal of Archaeology* in 1885. Contributing more than fifty articles and abstracts to this publication during his career, he also served as its owner and managing editor until it was taken over by the American Institute of Archaeology in 1896. The *Journal* remains one of the premier publications in the world of classical archaeology. In addition, Frothingham was associate director of the American School of Classical Studies at Rome in 1895–1896 and a delegate to the International Congress of Art and Archaeology at Rome in 1912.

Earnest in whatever he undertook, Frothingham continued his scholarly pursuits following his retirement from Princeton, leaving more than twenty works unfinished at the time of his death. During these years he also became a zealous spokesman against radicalism and other movements that he considered dangerous. In the years after World War I, the Joint Legislative Committee of the State of New York Investigating Seditious Activities, also known as the Lusk Committee, had been formed to investigate such activities. Frothingham testified before this committee in 1920, emphasizing the critical role of public schools in acculturating aliens into American culture as a means of preventing seditious activity. In 1921 he coauthored a four-volume, 4,000-page report on the history and current state of revolutionary radicalism in the United States for the committee. Also during this period he traveled to Italy to study fascism in the wake of Benito Mussolini's rise to power in the early 1920s. His many years spent living in Rome as a youth and the subsequent time he spent in the country as a scholar made Frothingham an ideal candidate for the mission. He later reported his findings to the National Civic Federation, an American group organized to promote national unity, to which he belonged. Frothingham died in a New York sanitarium, where he was receiving treatment for heart trouble.

An exacting scholar and a man of diverse interests, Frothingham was a central figure in the emergence of classical archaeology in early twentieth-century America. His almost exclusively European education and knowledge of Semitic languages put him in a unique position among classical scholars of the day, allowing him to undertake studies that few others were equipped to handle. Moreover, his active participation in and devotion to the Archaeological Institute of America, along with his founding of the *American Journal of Archaeology*, helped to establish the discipline on a firm footing in the United States for years to come.

• Various letters and papers of Frothingham are in the Johns Hopkins University Archives. A faculty file, including bibliographies of his works, obituary notices, and newspaper clippings, is located in the Seeley G. Mudd Manuscript Library at Princeton University. In addition to the works cited above, many of Frothingham's writings are accessible in various issues of the *American Journal of Archaeology*. Tributes can be found in *Revue Archéologique* 5th ser., 19 (1924): 393–94, and the *American Journal of Archaeology* 27 (1923): 381–82. An obituary is in the *New York Times*, 29 July 1923.

JOHN DONAHUE

FROTHINGHAM, Nathaniel Langdon (23 July 1793–4 Apr. 1870), Unitarian minister, was born in Boston, Massachusetts, the son of Ebenezer Frothingham, a merchant, and Joanna Langdon. He graduated from Harvard in 1811. He read theology in preparation for the ministry, at the same time serving as an instructor in rhetoric and oratory at Harvard. He was ordained at First Church in Boston on 18 March 1815. In 1818 he married Ann Gorham Brooks (two of whose sisters married Charles Francis Adams and Edward Everett); they had five children, one of them being Octavius Brooks Frothingham, New York minister and advocate of "free religion" after the Civil War.

Frothingham's thirty-five years at Boston's First Church spanned the most important phase of the Unitarian controversy and the rise of Transcendentalism. He stood apart from both, deploring controversy and sectarian division. He was Unitarian in theology but never preached a polemical sermon and took no part in denominational concerns. It is said that when the denomination met each May for its annual meetings, he commonly found occasion to be in New York. He was a firm believer in Christianity as a revealed religion, and recognized the authority of Jesus Christ as a divine messenger, but rejected as essentially deism the basic principle of the Transcendentalists in grounding religion on personal religious experience rather than the historical proofs of the Christian revelation. In 1843, when the Boston Association of Ministers discussed these issues with Theodore Parker, Frothingham characterized Parker's position as "vehemently deistical" and declared that he could have "no ministerial intercourse" with him. He added, however, that he still hoped to have "a friendly and social intercourse,"

shook Parker's hand cordially as he left in tears, and expressed the hope that he would come to see him soon.

Frothingham was not a popular preacher, though his literary style was regarded as notably polished and elegant. His ministry was traditional. He devoted his time to preaching and pastoral duties, rejected the tendency of the times to organize Sunday schools for children and groups for social intercourse among members of the congregation, and eschewed agitation for social reform. His interests were literary as well as theological: he was well read in the classics and modern literature and had the reputation of being preeminent among the clergy in the richness and extent of his intellectual culture. He produced no major contribution to literature, most of his publications being occasional sermons. He did publish a volume of "sacred songs" or poems entitled *Metrical Pieces* (1855), once thought to have some merit. In *Boston Unitarianism* (1890), his son Octavius, who rejected much of what his father had stood for, took him as typical of the simple rationalism of the Unitarianism of his generation, to be distinguished from the spiritual Christianity of William Ellery Channing on the one hand and the naturalism of Parker on the other.

Failing health led to retirement in 1850, eased by the fact that his wife had inherited from her father, Peter Chardon Brooks, the wealthy merchant. In the 1860s, Frothingham's eyesight was increasingly affected by glaucoma, and for the last six years of his life he was completely blind. He died in Boston. In his own day Frothingham was one of the prominent exponents in Boston of liberal religion. But his conservative Unitarianism was challenged in his late years by the Transcendentalism of a younger generation, and his reputation diminished with the obsolescence of his theology.

• Scattered letters may be found in the Andover-Harvard Library and the Houghton Library in Cambridge as well as the Massachusetts Historical Society in Boston, but there is no major collection of papers. The chief biographical source is Octavius Brooks Frothingham, *Boston Unitarianism* (1890), which is colored by the author's ambivalence toward his father. See also the memoir by Frederic Henry Hedge in the *Proceedings* of the Massachusetts Historical Society, vol. 2 (1869–1870), pp. 371–86.

CONRAD WRIGHT

FROTHINGHAM, Octavius Brooks (26 Nov. 1822–27 Nov. 1895), minister and author, was born in Boston, Massachusetts, the son of Nathaniel Langdon Frothingham, a Unitarian minister, and Ann Gorham Brooks. Frothingham graduated from Harvard College in 1843 and from Harvard Divinity School in 1846. Within two weeks of his ordination as minister of Salem's North Church in 1847, he married Caroline E. Curtis of Boston; the couple had two children, one of whom died in infancy. Although Frothingham described himself as having been a rather conservative divinity student, some of his lectures from that period reveal the beginnings of his later religious radicalism. While in Salem he departed significantly from the tenets of mainstream Unitarianism and developed strong antislavery views, at least in part as a result of his friendship with Theodore Parker, the Transcendentalist minister and abolitionist. Frothingham's decision to leave Salem in 1855 owes much to a controversy that had erupted the previous year over his response to the Anthony Burns affair. Incensed by Burns's reenslavement under the Fugitive Slave Act, Frothingham preached a sermon attacking Christianity for its sectarianism and complicity with proslavery forces. He also refused to administer communion because he felt "that the larger part of his congregation were in sympathy with the government" (*Recollections and Impressions* [1891]). The ensuing conflict exacerbated Frothingham's sense of constraint in Salem; he desired a post "where he could exercise his independence without check or limit" (*Recollections*). After leaving Salem, he no longer administered communion at all because he considered the ritual to be divisive and productive of self-righteousness.

After several years in Jersey City, New Jersey, as minister of a newly formed Unitarian congregation, Frothingham moved to New York in 1859 to form that city's third Unitarian society (eventually renamed the Independent Liberal Church). His New York congregation was large and diverse, made up, he later wrote, of "Unitarians, Universalists, 'come-outers,' spiritualists, unbelievers of all kinds, anti-slavery people, [and] reformers generally" (*Recollections*). He earned a reputation as an engaging speaker, able to command the attention of several hundred listeners without relying on notes or a written text. During the years of his New York ministry, he and other radical Unitarians formed the Free Religious Association (FRA), largely in response to the 1865 founding of the National Conference of Unitarian Churches, an organization that proved insensitive to the radical faction's distaste for centralized authority and articulated creeds. The FRA was not a sect in its own right but instead sought to eliminate all sectarianism. Frothingham wrote in the *North American Review* (July 1887) that Free Religion allowed him "absolute freedom of thought in the study of religious literature . . . [and] a frank confession of the superiority of practical morality to dogma even of the most liberal description." He served as the FRA's first president (1867–1878) and eventually broke with Unitarianism altogether.

In addition to publishing numerous sermons, Frothingham disseminated his religious views in a variety of periodicals, including the *Christian Examiner*, the *Index*, and the *Radical*. His most influential theological work, *The Religion of Humanity* (1873), was, according to the historian William R. Hutchison, "an attempt to recast theistic and Christian ideas in universal and mainly naturalistic terms" (p. 4n). Frothingham also produced a body of secular writing while living in New York, including book reviews, literary and social commentaries, and criticism of art and drama. His *Theodore Parker: A Biography* (1874) and *Transcendentalism in New England* (1876), a study of the move-

ment's philosophies, implications, and key figures, inaugurated his career as a biographer and historian.

Poor health contributed to Frothingham's decision in 1879 to retire from the ministry; after an extended stay in Europe he settled once again in Boston, where he continued to write while enjoying a more tranquil existence than he had known in New York. Among the most important of his postretirement works are *Boston Unitarianism, 1820–1850* (1890), a study—both historical and personal—of his father's generation of ministers, and *Recollections and Impressions, 1822–1891*, a memoir of his own professional and intellectual life. He continued to publish on religious subjects as well, including the essays "The Philosophy of Conversion" (Oct. 1884) and "Why Am I a Free Religionist?" (July 1887), both of which appeared in the *North American Review*.

Frothingham's strong tendency toward self-questioning led him over time to reconsider and refine many of his positions. Clearly, his enthusiasm for Transcendentalism faded; he wrote that "absolute faith in that form of philosophy grew weak and passed away," yielding to what he called a more "scientific" view, inflected by rationalism and the theory of evolution (*Recollections*). Many of Frothingham's contemporaries accused him of retreating after his retirement from his prior religious radicalism, but these accusations seem overblown, given his continued support of Free Religion in a number of late writings. While he clearly took a conciliatory stance after his return to Boston toward his old opponents in the Unitarian establishment, and while he even attended the First Unitarian Church where his father had been minister, the Unitarianism with which he made peace had liberalized considerably since the 1860s, due in part to the influence of dissenters like himself. Perhaps commentators were simply confronting the conservatism that, while more obvious late in his life, had been present in Frothingham's personality and thought all along. In terms of religious belief, he never departed as radically from mainstream Unitarianism as did some of his FRA colleagues, such as Francis Ellingwood Abbot, and he had always been rather conservative on political and social issues, investing little in reform movements (except for abolition) and even opposing certain progressive causes, such as woman suffrage. In some sense he was, as the historian Sydney E. Ahlstrom wrote, a "born traditionalist" (p. xvi).

Nevertheless, Frothingham was thoroughly committed to combating the traditions of religious dogmatism and divisiveness; he looked forward to a time when "no forms of truth . . . will be honored with more respect than is due to equally well meant endeavors in the same direction. There will be no more . . . claim to authority, no more conceit of final discovery" (*The Religion of Humanity*). His most important contribution to American culture was his advocacy of a degree of religious freedom that, to many, seemed radical indeed. He died in Boston.

• Frothingham's personal papers are not available to scholars, having been either destroyed or lost after his death. His letters and manuscripts are scattered; the largest collections of letters can be found at the Library of Congress, Harvard's Houghton Library, the Massachusetts Historical Society, and Princeton University. For the locations of manuscripts and other letters, see *American Literary Manuscripts* and J. Wade Caruthers's biography, *Octavius Brooks Frothingham, Gentle Radical* (1977). Frothingham's published works include a number of biographies and memoirs, including *Gerrit Smith: A Biography* (1877); *George Ripley* (1882); *Memoir of William Henry Channing* (1886); "Memoir" (of Wasson) in *Essays: Religious, Social, Political*, ed. David A. Wasson (1889); and the rather critical *Theodore Parker: A Sermon Preached in New York, June 10* (1860). Several collections of Frothingham's sermons are available, including *Sermons of O. B. Frothingham* (3 vols., 1871–75). Among Frothingham's political writings are *Colonization* (1855), in which he argues against sending freed slaves to Africa, and a brief antisuffrage essay included in the tract *Woman Suffrage: Unnatural and Inexpedient* (1894). See also his collections for juveniles, *Stories from the Lips of the Teacher, Retold by a Disciple* (1863) and *Stories of the Patriarchs* (1864), each of which went through several editions. For contemporaries' assessments of Frothingham, see his nephew Paul Revere Frothingham's biographical essay, "Octavius Brooks Frothingham," in *Heralds of a Liberal Faith*, ed. Samuel A. Eliot, vol. 3 (1910); Edmund C. Stedman's *Octavius Brooks Frothingham and the New Faith* (1876); and Josiah P. Quincy's "Memoir of Octavius Brooks Frothingham," *Proceedings of the Massachusetts Historical Society* 10 (Mar. 1896), which includes, in addition to much praise, a judiciously phrased catalog of its subject's shortcomings.

The most extensive critical study of Frothingham is Caruthers's biography, cited above; see also his bibliographical essay in *The Transcendentalists: A Review of Research and Criticism*, ed. Joel Myerson (1984). For useful commentary on Frothingham's works, see William R. Hutchison's introduction to *The Religion of Humanity* (repr. ed. 1975) and Sydney E. Ahlstrom's introduction to *Transcendentalism in New England* (1959). See also Stow Persons, *Free Religion: An American Faith* (1947), on Frothingham's involvement in the Free Religious Association; and David Robinson, *The Unitarians and the Universalists* (1985), on his role in the development of Unitarianism.

SUSAN M. RYAN

FRY, Birkett Davenport (24 June 1822–21 Jan. 1891), Confederate general, was born in Kanawha County, Virginia (now W.Va.), the son of Thornton Fry, a substantial landowner, and Eliza Thompson. Fry attended the Virginia Military Institute and Washington College in Pennsylvania before being appointed to West Point in 1842. Failing to master mathematics, he withdrew two years later. Unable to pursue a military career, Fry read law instead and in 1846 was admitted to the Virginia bar. When the war with Mexico began shortly thereafter, Fry offered his services and, because of his earlier military training, was commissioned a first lieutenant in the U.S. Voltiguers. He fought at the battle of Chapultepec and was subsequently praised by his commander for his courage. On 31 August 1848 he was discharged.

The following year Fry journeyed west to Sacramento, California, where he opened a law office. He married Martha Micou Baker in 1853. No record of any children exists. Two years later he joined William Walker's filibuster expedition to Nicaragua. Fortunately for Fry, he was back in California on recruiting duty when Walker's venture fell apart. Fry remained in Sacramento until 1859, when he moved to Tallassee, Alabama, where he managed a cotton mill.

After Alabama seceded from the Union, Fry volunteered his services to the state and received a commission as colonel of the Thirteenth Alabama Infantry, which was sent to Virginia. He was severely wounded at Seven Pines in the spring of 1862 and returned to service only to have his arm shattered at Antietam the following September. Spurning doctors' insistence that the arm be amputated, Fry recovered but was wounded yet again at Chancellorsville in May 1863. Less than two months later he assumed command of General James J. Archer's brigade at Gettysburg after Archer was captured on 1 July. On 3 July, during the Pickett-Pettigrew charge, Fry's brigade was the unit of direction. Displaying his typical gallantry, Fry led his unit nearly to the Union line. Shot in the thigh, he urged his men forward, believing victory was in reach. "Go on; it will not last five minutes longer!" he cried. He was captured as the Union soldiers turned back the Confederate tide. Exchanged nine months later, Fry commanded a Virginia brigade in the fighting at Drewry's Bluff in May 1864 during the Bermuda Hundred campaign. On 24 May he was commissioned brigadier general and assigned to command Archer's and Walker's brigades of the Army of Northern Virginia. Shortly after taking part in the battle of Cold Harbor, Fry was selected by Braxton Bragg, then acting as military adviser to Jefferson Davis, to command the military district of Augusta, Georgia, and he served in this capacity until the war ended.

Fry subsequently moved to Cuba, where he was employed in the tobacco business. He returned to Alabama in 1868. A memorial account stated that he subsequently served as superintendent of the state's public schools, but no official record of him having done so exists. Following the death of his wife, he moved to Tallahassee, Florida, where he had interests in a cotton mill. In 1880 or 1881 he relocated to Richmond, Virginia, and took the position of secretary and treasurer of the Marshall Manufacturing Company, of which his brother-in-law, John L. Bacon, was president. Upon Bacon's death, Fry succeeded him as president, retaining the position until his death in Richmond. Fry was described by R. A. Brock, the secretary of the Southern Historical Society as a man "of slight physique and medium height, and of mien so modest and gentle that a stranger would never have suspected that a form so frail held the lion spirit of so redoubtable a warrior."

• Some of Fry's battle reports were published in *The War of the Rebellion: A Compilation of the Official Records of the Union and Confederate Armies* (128 vols., 1880–1901). Fry recalled the fighting at Gettysburg in Birkett D. Fry, "Pettigrew's Charge at Gettysburg," *Southern Historical Society*

Papers 7 (1879): 91–93. For sketches of Fry see E. F. Barker, *Frye Genealogy* (1920), and R. A. Brock, "General Burkett Davenport Fry," *Southern Historical Society Papers* 18 (1890): 286–88. See also William Walker, *The War in Nicaragua* (1860); George Stewart, *Pickett's Charge* (1980); and Herbert Schiller, *The Bermuda Hundred Campaign* (1988). An obituary is in the *Richmond Dispatch*, 22 Jan. 1891.

D. SCOTT HARTWIG

FRY, Franklin Clark (30 Aug. 1900–6 June 1968), Lutheran pastor, church executive, and ecumenist, was born in Bethlehem, Pennsylvania, the son of Franklin Foster Fry and Minnie Clark McKeown. Both his father and his grandfather Jacob Fry were nationally prominent pastors and church statesmen.

Fry was an excellent student at Hamilton College, from which he received an A.B. in 1921. He continued his education with a year at the American School for Classical Studies in Athens, Greece. Upon graduating from the Lutheran seminary at Philadelphia in 1925, he was ordained to become pastor of Redeemer Lutheran Church in Yonkers, New York. Fry married Hilda A. Drewes in 1927; they had three children. In 1929 he was called to Holy Trinity Lutheran Church in Akron, Ohio, where he served for the next fifteen years. After serving the United Lutheran Church in America (ULCA) as secretary of its Commission on Evangelism (1930–1938) and as a member of the Board of American Missions (1934–1942) and the church's executive board (1942–1944), Fry was elected president of the denomination in 1944.

Fry's aggressive leadership helped accelerate the transition of American Lutheranism from an isolationist, immigrant mentality to a self-assured participation in the mainstream of American Christianity and American culture. Already in 1945 he began to show himself a leader in efforts to repair relations among the alienated European churches and to open opportunities for American relief and reconstruction on the war-ravaged continent. Beginning in 1947 he served as president of Lutheran World Relief, the humanitarian enterprise launched cooperatively by American Lutherans. He was a leader in the founding of the Lutheran World Federation at Lund, Sweden, in 1947, serving as its president from 1957 to 1963. When the World Council of Churches (WCC) was established at Amsterdam in 1948, Fry was chosen vice chair of both the powerful Central Committee and the Executive Committee; he served as chair of both committees from 1954 to 1968. In these roles he became, along with general secretary W. A. Visser 't Hooft, the leading spokesman of the ecumenical movement.

American Lutherans had declined, chiefly for confessional reasons, to affiliate with the Federal Council of the Churches of Christ in America, the leading agency of Protestant cooperation, formed in 1908. In the movement during the 1940s to enlarge and reconstitute the agency, Fry influenced the revision of the constitution that formed the new National Council of the Churches of Christ in the U.S.A. (1950); the changes he proposed induced some Lutheran bodies to become members and in due time helped make it possible for Eastern Orthodox Christian churches to join. He served for several years on its General Board, and from 1954 to 1960 he was the chair of its Policy and Strategy Committee. From 1950 to 1954 Fry was the first vice chair of American Relief for Korea. In 1951 he made a world-circling flight in behalf of the "One Great Hour of Sharing" appeal of Church World Service, reporting to America on the persisting plight of displaced persons and war refugees.

In the mid-1950s Fry became the foremost leader in designing the merger of four Lutheran churches of German, Swedish, Finnish, and Danish background to form the Lutheran Church in America (1962), a communion of more than 3 million members. He drafted its constitution and was elected its first president. He played a leading role in negotiations to replace the National Lutheran Council with another agency that the Lutheran Church–Missouri Synod, until that time remaining aloof on confessional grounds, might join. The plans succeeded, and the Lutheran Council in the U.S.A. (1967), with a constitution drafted by Fry, brought into effective (though short-lived) cooperation four church bodies representing more than 95 percent of the nearly 9 million Lutherans in America.

Fry's peers acknowledged him as "a superb presiding officer," a master of parliamentary procedure, and a genius at analyzing complex issues. He delighted in designing constitutions that endowed organizations with stability, clarity of purpose, and orderly procedure. As an administrator, he was an astute strategist and diplomat who kept long-range goals in mind while working realistically toward attainable ends.

Legendary in World Council circles were his addresses to host dignitaries in India and in Communist Hungary and Russia, speeches felicitously worded for the ceremonial occasions but forthrightly witnessing to the council's Christian faith. Some European and Asian church leaders at first saw him as an "American ecclesiastical tycoon"; others resented his occasionally caustic words; eventually all came to respect his talents and his deep commitment to the Christian ecumenical vision as well as to his Lutheran tradition. Proper ecumenism, Fry insisted, is "a movement back toward the center of the Christian faith." He believed that Lutherans belong in the ecumenical movement because their confessions proclaim a Christ-centered faith.

Although Fry was not a professional theologian, he had a keen theological instinct. In particular he helped clarify and promote the twin principles of church relationships that had been drafted in the 1930s by his older colleagues F. H. Knubel and A. R. Wentz and their German associate Hanns Lilje. The "evangelical principle" maintains that progress toward church unity rests "a discovery of what the Scriptures teach." A "Christocentric concern," therefore, regulates "the proper relationship between the twin imperatives of truth and unity." The "representative (or confessional) principle" insists that the WCC and the National Council are councils of *churches*—not of autonomous *churchmen*. Neither is a "super-church": each remains a "servant and instrument" directly responsible to the churches that compose it.

Evidence of Fry's concern for sound theology includes his ULCA presidential report on church unity in 1956 and the "Minneapolis Theses," a document on freedom and unity in Christ composed by a committee of theologians under Fry's chairmanship at the Lutheran World Federation Assembly in Minneapolis (1957). He took a keen interest in the national and international "bilateral dialogues" that began in the 1960s, such as Reformed/Lutheran, Roman Catholic/Lutheran, and Orthodox/Lutheran. His theological acumen also helped him encourage churches to address social issues such as civil rights and poverty without becoming merely political pressure groups.

Fry was one of the most influential American Protestant churchmen of the twentieth century. He had not yet reached the height of his career when *Time* magazine (7 Apr. 1958) featured him in its cover story as "Mr. Protestant." Decorations from the governments of West Germany and Austria, as well as several foreign universities, and honorary citizenship of South Korea attest to his eminence. He died in New Rochelle, New York.

• Fry's presidential and ecumenical papers are preserved in the Archives of the Evangelical Lutheran Church in America in Chicago, as are the files of journalistic releases by the News Bureau of the National Lutheran Council and its successor, the LCUSA. Important sources for understanding Fry's churchmanship are his ULCA (1946–1962) and LCA (1964–1968) presidential reports, printed in the biennial convention minutes; his reports as chair of the WCC Central Committee in the *New Delhi Report* (1961) and the *Uppsala Report* (1968); and his reports as president of the Lutheran World Federation in *Proceedings of the Fourth Assembly* (1963). Also see his remarkable "Dear Partners" letters to ULCA/LCA pastors (under the heading "State of the Church") in the monthly mailings from church headquarters titled *Pastor's Desk Book* (1947–1962) and *Ministers Information Service* (1963–1968). Albert P. Stauderman edited a small book, *Mr. Protestant: An Informal Biography of Franklin Clark Fry* (1960), which consists of topical chapters by eight of Fry's colleagues, a reprint of the *Time* feature article of 7 Apr. 1958, and a four-page curriculum vitae. Robert H. Fischer, ed., *Franklin Clark Fry: A Palette for a Portrait*, a supplementary number of *Lutheran Quarterly* 24 (1972), assembles ninety-two essays by colleagues and close acquaintances, a lengthy obituary by Erik Modean, and a comprehensive listing of sources by and about Fry. See also E. Theodore Bachmann, "'So Deep Is My Commitment . . . ,'" *Lutheran World* 22 (1975): 258–60; and William H. Lazareth, "Franklin Clark Fry," in *Ecumenical Pilgrims*, ed. I. Bria and D. Heller (1995).

ROBERT H. FISCHER

FRY, James Barnet (22 Feb. 1827–11 July 1894), Union army general, was born in Carrollton, Illinois, the son of Jacob Fry, a general, and Emily Turney. Little is known of Fry's life until he entered West Point when he was sixteen. He graduated fourteenth in the class of 1847 and was assigned to garrison duty in Mexico City. In the interim between Mexico and his assignment to the U.S. Military Academy in 1853, he served at various posts in the southern and western United States. In addition to instructional duties during his six-year tenure at West Point, he acquired valuable administrative experience when the academy's superintendent, Robert E. Lee, appointed Fry as adjutant. Ordered to Fort Monroe in 1859, he participated in the arrest of John Brown (1800–1859). For a brief period in 1860, he returned to West Point to assist in revising the curriculum.

At the beginning of the Civil War, Fry served as General Irvin McDowell's chief of staff and was present at First Manassas. Appointed as Major General Don Carlos Buell's chief of staff in November 1861, he served at Shiloh and Perryville before being ordered to the adjutant general's office a year later. While in Washington, Fry encountered difficulty with Generals Ulysses S. Grant and William T. Sherman because of his defense of Buell's actions at Shiloh. Although Buell had taken his time in moving toward Shiloh, the arrival of the first of his three divisions on 6 April 1862 proved important in stemming the attack of Confederate general Braxton Bragg. Buell was subsequently criticized for failing to pursue Bragg's forces and encountered difficulty when he unjustly claimed that he had saved Grant's army from destruction at Shiloh. Despite Fry's deep loyalty to Buell, Grant nevertheless endorsed Fry as the best officer to administer the provost marshal general's bureau. On 17 March 1863 Colonel Fry was appointed to this post and on 21 April 1864 was promoted to brigadier general of volunteers. He served as the provost marshal general until the bureau was dissolved on 28 August 1866. In February 1868 he received a belated promotion to major general by brevet for his meritorious service during the Civil War.

As the individual directly responsible for the implementation of the North's first national conscription system, Fry bore the brunt of the criticism for the several defects that existed in the enabling legislation. Although he and several of his subordinates brought some of this antagonism on themselves, a large portion of their difficulties resulted from having to interpret a law that was confusing, subject to constant change, and that demonstrated little regard for local conditions. Moreover, Fry had to implement an enrollment process and administer four major troop calls within a two-year period, which required an additional 1.4 million new soldiers from a total pool of approximately three million enrolled men. To compound the problem of seemingly large troop quotas, the federal draft had to operate concomitantly with a bounty system that was rife with abuses. Not only did Fry need to wait for localities to fill levies with bounties to recruits, but these delays prevented Fry from setting exact quotas. Partially as a result of this indirect approach, a perception arose that the government's demands for men were excessive and unrelenting, even though there was less than one chance in a hundred of a northern man being drafted. Indeed, much of the potential burden of the draft became mitigated through the heavy reliance on volunteering and the existence of various liberal exemption policies.

Considering that some 185 district enrollment boards had to be established and given the inherent deficiencies in the legislation, Fry performed no small achievement in implementing the system in 1863. In addition to conscription, his agency was responsible for other diverse activities, such as arresting deserters and conducting the medical examination process. Moreover, the system sparked numerous challenges to federal authority, which ranged from overt resistance in the July 1863 New York City draft riots to more subtle attempts at subverting the conscription process as communities attempted to fill quotas with unfit recruits. Throughout this two-year period, with varying degrees of success, Fry constantly addressed numerous complaints from powerful officials and ordinary citizens. Although he was accused of incompetence and inefficiency because of the way in which he had to assign troop quotas in accordance with continuous changes in the law, his integrity was never seriously called into question. However, charges of ineptitude, dishonesty, partisanship, and immorality were lodged against a number of officials who were part of the vast bureaucratic machinery he directed. By the winter of 1864–1865, discontent with his bureau became so pervasive that it even transcended party lines, which in turn led to a public demand for his removal. With the prestige of his bureau at its lowest ebb of the war, only the intervention of President Abraham Lincoln and the approaching end of the war saved him from this ignominious fate.

Fry's problems with the draft did not come to an end with the close of hostilities in 1865. In the spring and summer of 1868 he became the focal point of a controversy between Congressmen James G. Blaine and Roscoe Conkling. At issue was whether western New York had been assigned excessive troop quotas during the war. The matter escalated largely because Fry chose to refute the charges publicly instead of ignoring the allegations.

Between bouts of extended illness in the 1870s, Fry served in the adjutant general's office and as an adjutant general in various military departments as a full colonel, his permanent rank in the regular army. During this period, he completed three works on official aspects of the U.S. Army. On 1 July 1881 he retired from active service to devote more time to his literary interests. Fry apparently never married or had children. Before his death in Newport, Rhode Island, and his subsequent interment in Philadelphia, he contributed to the *North American Review* and the multivolume *Battles and Leaders of the Civil War* (1884–1887). Also, he published five other works including *New York and the Conscription of 1863; A Chapter in the History of the Civil War* (1885).

An appreciation of Fry's administrative talents and an awareness of the difficulties he encountered in implementing a federal conscription system eluded him during his lifetime. Such accolades would need to wait for the more detached judgments of later generations.

Through the voluminous documents and reports created during his tenure, Fry left a legacy that enabled future draft administrators to avoid the mistakes that had plagued him as the North's provost marshal general. Despite some occasional lapses in judgment, he more than any other person demonstrated the necessary qualities of leadership that helped to establish the principle of a citizen's liability to national service.

• Fry's personal papers were destroyed in a fire before his death, but there is ample official source material on the day-to-day work of the agency whose operations Fry oversaw. In addition to almost fifteen hundred feet of original documents in the provost marshal general's bureau (Record Group 110) at the National Archives, most of series 3 in *The War of the Rebellion: A Compilation of the Official Records of the Union and Confederate Armies* (128 vols., 1880–1901), concerns his bureau. Secondary sources on General Fry are not as plentiful. For a dated but still useful biographical overview of his life, see Ezra J. Warner, *Generals in Blue: Lives of the Union Commanders* (1964). The most detailed description of the Blaine-Conkling controversy is Eugene Converse Murdock, *Patriotism Limited, 1862–1865: The Civil War Draft and the Bounty System* (1967), and the best discussion of the abuses inherent in the Civil War bounty system can be found in Murdock, *One Million Men: The Civil War Draft in the North* (1971). Murdock is also among Fry's greatest defenders. For a critical appraisal that casts part of the blame on Fry for creating discontent with the system, see James W. Geary, *We Need Men: The Union Draft in the Civil War* (1991). There are numerous accounts that criticize the competence and character of some of Fry's subordinates. See, for example, Phillip Shaw Paludan, *'A People's Contest': The Union and the Civil War, 1861–1865* (1988).

JAMES W. GEARY

FRY, Joshua (c. 1700–31 May 1754), professor and surveyor, was born in Crewkerne, Somersetshire, England, the son of Joseph Fry. His mother's name and his parents' occupations are unknown. He graduated from Wadham College at Oxford University and moved to the colony of Virginia, where the first record of his presence is his service as a vestryman in Essex County. He married Mary Micou Hill; they had five children. Fry became master of the grammar school connected with the College of William and Mary in 1729, and he became a professor of natural philosophy and mathematics at the college in 1731. His Oxford education paved the way for these important positions, since English-educated gentlemen were rare in early eighteenth-century Virginia.

Fry remained in his professorship until 1737. Feeling a need to increase his income to provide for his large family, he moved to the frontier of Northwest Virginia in the late 1730s. The next definite record of his presence is 1744, when he lived on the Hardware River, between present-day Charlottesville and Scottsville in Goochland County. In the following year Albermarle County was formed out of Goochland County, and Fry became the first presiding justice of the new county. In 1745 he became the county lieutenant, the county surveyor, and one of the two representatives from Albermarle County to the Virginia House of Burgesses.

In his career as a surveyor, Fry served in 1746 as the representative of King George II in defining the boundaries of Lord Fairfax's grant, and with Peter Jefferson, the father of Thomas Jefferson, he worked on a joint commission to survey and define the Virginia–North Carolina boundary in 1749. The commissioners ran the boundary ninety miles further west to Steep Rock Creek, near the present-day northwest corner of North Carolina. Fry and Jefferson also cooperated on the *Map of the Inhabited Parts of Virginia . . .* , which was first printed around 1751 and remained the best map produced in Virginia until the end of the eighteenth century. Fry was also well acquainted with Dr. Thomas Walker, chief agent of the Loyal Company of Virginia, and he had access to maps and materials that laid out the French claim to the Ohio River valley area, allowing him to make his map more complete.

In 1752 Virginia governor Robert Dinwiddie named Fry as one of the three Virginia commissioners to treat with the Iroquois, Shawnee, Mingo, and Delaware Indians at Logstown, eighteen miles north of present-day Pittsburgh, Pennsylvania. Fry and his two fellow commissioners, Colonel James Patton and Lunsford Lomax, negotiated with the tribal leaders between 1 June and 13 June 1752. The negotiations have generally been viewed as a success for the Virginians and for the Ohio Company, but recent research has indicated that the parties who negotiated most skillfully were in fact the Iroquois, who granted rights to the colonists and ignored the needs of fellow Indian tribes, especially the Delawares. The negotiations concluded with a promise by the Indians not to attack any English settlers south of the Ohio River. This agreement, however, was contingent upon the approval of the Iroquois council fire at Onondaga.

Circumstances in the Ohio, Pennsylvania, and Virginia regions moved ominously toward warfare during the early 1750s. In March 1754 Governor Dinwiddie named Fry as colonel of the militia being raised in Virginia to resist any French incursion into the Ohio area. Fry's second in command was Lieutenant Colonel George Washington. Fry mustered troops and brought them to Wills's Creek (now Cumberland, Md.), while Washington moved ahead with a small advance guard. On 28 May 1754 Washington fought a skirmish against a French column led by Ensign Coulon de Jumonville. This small wilderness engagement ignited the final French and Indian War in America. One day after the skirmish, in ignorance of the events that had transpired, Colonel Fry was badly injured when he fell from his horse. He died two days later at Wills's Creek.

Fry was a fine teacher, a devoted family man, and an active public servant. He distinguished himself amid the rival claims of the French, English, American colonists, and American Indians. Fry's surveying and mapmaking made him one of the most knowledgeable men on the frontier during the early 1750s. One of his contemporaries declared at the time of Fry's death, "He was a man of so clear a head, so mild a temper, and so good a heart, that he never failed to engage the love and esteem of all who knew, or were concerned with him, and he died universally lamented" (Brock, p. 8). Fry was an excellent example for the 22-year-old Washington, who succeeded him in command of the Virginia militia.

• Information about Fry is in Philip Slaughter, *Memoirs of Colonel Joshua Fry* (1880); Richard L. Morton, *Colonial Virginia*, vol. 2 (1960); Walter O'Meara, *Guns at the Forks* (1965); and Francis Jennings, *Empire of Fortune: Crowns, Colonies & Tribes in the Seven Years War in America* (1988). See also R. A. Brock, ed., *The Official Records of Robert Dinwiddie* (1883–1884); P. L. Phillips, "Some Early Maps of Virginia," *Virginia Magazine of History and Biography*, July 1907; and Alfred P. James, *The Ohio Company: Its Inner History* (1959).

SAMUEL WILLARD CROMPTON

FRY, Sherry Edmundson (29 Sept. 1879–9 June 1966), sculptor, was born in Creston, Iowa, the son of John Wesley Fry and Ellen Green, farmers. He may have had early art training, for he placed directly into advanced classes at the Art Institute of Chicago. For the year 1900–1901 he studied sculpture with Lorado Taft and Charles J. Mulligan in day and evening courses. In 1902–1903 he studied sculpture in Paris at the Académie Julian and the École des Beaux-Arts with Louis Ernest Barrias and Charles Raoul Verlet. He received an honorable mention at the 1902 Paris Salon. Fry went on to study in Florence in 1904, and from 1905 to 1907 he studied at the new studio school of American sculptor Frederick MacMonnies in Giverny, France. There Fry probably worked on garden and architectural sculptures.

Two years later Fry won a third-class medal at the Paris Salon for *Indian Chief*, a realistic model for the bronze monument to Chief Mahaska that was dedicated on 12 May 1909 at the City Park in Oskaloosa, Iowa. Fry received the commission at the recommendation of sculptor George Bissell.

The success of *Indian Chief* led to Fry being awarded a fellowship to the American Academy in Rome in 1908. He spent three years studying in Italy, Greece, and Germany, stating in 1909 that "a man should not be sent [on a fellowship] until he no longer has need of a master, and has, or is able to map out, work which he will greatly desire to do. In this case the Scholarship is a wonderful aid to him to start his career and prove whether or not he is a sculptor" (Valentine and Valentine, p. 47).

Fry was elected an associate sculpture member of the National Sculpture Society in New York in 1908 and a member of the Architectural League of New York in 1911. Back in New York in 1912 he completed a bronze boy and turtle for the Burnside Memorial Fountain at the Common in Worcester, Massachusetts, that was begun by sculptor Charles Y. Harvey before his death. Architect Henry Bacon designed the sculpture's granite pedestal.

Prior to the celebrated international art display at the 1913 Armory Show in New York, Fry was selected in 1912 as a member of the Association of American

Painters and Sculptors, which organized the show. He had a bronze bust chosen for display (number 171), but for unknown reasons it was not received. He resigned from the group that same year.

In 1914 Fry bought a home in Roxbury, Connecticut, but kept a New York studio. That year he was elected associate national academician of the National Academy of Design; he presented an oil portrait by Edmond T. Quinn as a membership requirement. Fry's *Maidenhood* (1914), derivative of archaic Greek sculpture, was awarded a silver medal at the Panama-Pacific Exposition in San Francisco in 1915. (A cast is in Brookgreen Gardens in South Carolina.) Fry also produced symbolic decorations for the entrance to the exposition's Festival Hall. He received the commission for the Civil War major Clarence T. Barrett Memorial Fountain (Staten Island, N.Y.), and the life-size bronze figure of a Greek warrior holding a spear and shield was dedicated on 11 November 1915.

Fry executed a stone memorial to revolutionary war captain Thomas Abbey at Enfield Congregational Church in Connecticut, with the architectural firm of McKim, Mead and White of New York. The memorial was dedicated on 4 November 1916, and it features a realistic standing figure in a colonial costume that sculptor Daniel Chester French had loaned to Fry.

In 1917 Taft spoke of Fry as "another of our western men whose career the Art Institute follows with gratified interest" in his Scammon Lecture on the "Modern Tendencies in Sculpture." He praised Fry's use of Apollo's pose from the Parthenon pediment for the Barrett memorial as "a stroke of genius," *Indian Chief* as "a handsome figure most skillfully modeled," *Unfinished Figure* as graceful and simple as a "Tanagra figurine enlarged to life-size without addition of detail," and *Captain Abbey*, although less successful, as "very decorative."

Fry won the Elizabeth N. Watrous gold medal in 1917 at the National Academy for *Unfinished Figure*. He enlisted in the U.S. Army in 1917 as a private in the Camouflage Corps during World War I, and he served as liaison officer with the camouflage section of the French army. He returned to the United States in 1919. The Detroit Institute of Arts owns *Spartan Mother*, created that year.

In 1920–1921 Fry produced a bronze monument to revolutionary war soldier and university founder Ira Allen for the University of Vermont in Burlington. The sculpture, unveiled on 18 June 1921, shows a contemplative figure in a simplified realistic style. It was commissioned by James Benjamin Wilbur, a businessman, benefactor, and author of a 1928 biography of Allen.

Fry modeled reliefs of *The Infantry* for the pedestal of the General Ulysses S. Grant Memorial in Washington, D.C., which was dedicated on 27 April 1922. The memorial was a collaborative effort with architect Edward Pearce Casey and sculptors Henry Mervin Shrady and Edmond Amateis.

In 1923 Fry was awarded the William M. R. French gold medal by the Art Institute of Chicago for *Fortuna,* *Fountain Figure*, also shown that year at the Pennsylvania Academy, the National Sculpture Society, and in the latter's traveling exhibition. Fry was elected national academician of the National Academy in 1930, and his diploma portrait, a bronze bust of sculptor Gerome Brush completed some twenty years earlier, was presented in 1931.

One of Fry's last projects was a pediment for the Department of Labor and Interstate Commerce Building (now the U.S. Customs Building) in Washington, D.C. In 1935 Fry completed the model for *Abundance and Industry*, a classical female figure pouring fruit from an urn and flanked by rams, which was carved in limestone in 1936 by the John Donnelly company.

Other projects included a bronze figure of the Greek goddess Ceres for the dome of the Missouri State Capitol in Jefferson City; a pediment for the Clark Mausoleum in Los Angeles; and privately owned fountains such as *The Dolphin* in Mount Kisco, New York, and *Au Soleil*, unlocated.

After a distinguished and promising career as an academic sculptor in the first three decades of the twentieth century, little is known of Fry's later years. He apparently did not marry, and he lived for a time with sculptor Albert Piouffle in Roxbury, Connecticut. Fry died in Kent, Connecticut.

• Illustrations of three of Fry's works are in Lorado Taft, *Modern Tendencies in Sculpture* (1921), figs. 416, 418, 419, pp. 142–43. See also Lucia Valentine and Alan Valentine, *The American Academy in Rome 1894–1969* (1973). The best comprehensive biographical source on Fry is Beatrice Gilman Proske, *Brookgreen Gardens Sculpture* (1968). For information and illustrations of Fry's pediment for the Department of Labor and Interstate Commerce Building, see George Gurney, *Sculpture and the Federal Triangle* (1985), figs. 154, 156, 158, 160, 161, pp. 256, 263–64. An obituary is in the *New Milford* (Conn.) *Times*, 16 June 1966.

SUSAN JAMES-GADZINSKI

FRY, William Henry (10 Aug. 1813–21 Dec. 1864), composer, journalist, and music critic, was born in Philadelphia, Pennsylvania, the son of William Fry, publisher of the *National Gazette*, and Ann Fleeson. Fry began his musical education by listening to his older brother's piano lessons. He composed an overture while a student at Mount St. Mary's School in Emmitsburg, Maryland, and afterward studied theory and composition in Philadelphia with Leopold Meignen, a graduate of the Paris Conservatory. Fry was eager to make his musical mark early, and he composed three more overtures before his twentieth birthday.

His first major work was the opera *Aurelia the Vestal* (1841), which failed to find a producer. He then composed *Leonora* with a libretto by his brother Joseph based on Edward Bulwer-Lytton's play *The Lady of Lyons*. This work was first performed in Philadelphia's Chestnut Street Theater on 4 June 1845 by the Seguin troupe in what is considered the first performance of a grand opera by an American-born composer. It ran for sixteen performances. A revival with an Italian translation was performed in New York in 1858. Fry collaborated with his brother again in 1863 on a grand opera, *Notre Dame de Paris*, which was performed in Philadelphia the following year under the baton of Theodore Thomas. Fry's compositions also include four symphonies, *The Breaking Heart, Santa Claus, or the Christmas Symphony, A Day in the Country*, and *Childe Harold*, some chamber pieces, and a *Stabat Mater* (1855). Although his work was closely derived from popular French, Italian, and German operatic and symphonic models, Fry is notable as the first American to compose extended works in a Romantic musical idiom.

Fry was also known as a journalist, beginning his career in his father's office and becoming editor of the Philadelphia *Public Ledger* in 1844. He served as a correspondent to the *New York Tribune* from London and Paris between 1846 and 1852, returning to New York in that year to become the *Tribune*'s music editor. In addition to his musical interests, Fry was active as a writer on political and economic topics, and he served as secretary to the American legation in Turin from 1861. During his years in Europe, Fry tried unsuccessfully to stage *Leonora*, the opera that had achieved moderate notice in Philadelphia.

As a champion of works by American composers, Fry wrote and lectured extensively, encouraging American creative artists to eschew European models and create their own national style. Although Fry argued that the creation of an independent American music free from European influences was a cultural imperative, his own works were more derivative than original. He did not turn to folk, popular, or patriotic music for national or regional inspiration, although his columns and lectures inspired many nineteenth- and early twentieth-century American composers to do so. He died in Santa Cruz, West Indies.

• The *New York Tribune* and *Dwight's Journal of Music* both contain many of Fry's columns and the texts of his 1852–1853 lecture series in New York. Dwight himself wrote about Fry's contribution to American culture in "Mr. Fry and His Critics," *Dwight's Journal of Music* 4, no. 18 (1854). William Treat Upton, *William Henry Fry: American Journalist and Composer-Critic* (1954; repr. 1974), contains a complete listing of Fry's works. See also Thomas Ridgeway, "William Henry Fry," *Publications of the Genealogical Society of Pennsylvania* 14 (1943): 129; Irving Lowens, "William Henry Fry: Fighter for American Music," *Musicology* 2 (1948): 162, and "William Henry Fry: American Musical Nationalist," in *Music and Musicians in Early America*, ed. Irving Lowens (1964); Betty E. Chmaj, "Fry versus Dwight: American Music's Debate over Nationality," *American Music* 3, no. 1 (1985); and Barbara L. Tischler, *An American Music: The Search for an American Musical Identity* (1986).

BARBARA L. TISCHLER

FRYE, William John (18 Mar. 1904–1 Feb. 1959), airline executive, was born near Sweetwater, Oklahoma, but grew up in Wheeler, Texas, the son of William Henry Frye and Nellie Cooley, ranchers. Frye did not complete a public high school education, dropping out at age fourteen to join the U.S. Army and fight in World War I. He never saw action but spent a year in the Army Corps of Engineers. By 1923 he had drifted to southern California, where he worked at a series of menial jobs including dishwasher and soda jerk.

While working in the Los Angeles area, Frye (who was known as "Jack") became interested in aeronautics and took flying lessons at the local airfield. Before the end of 1923 he had borrowed money from a brother and bought a half interest in the Burdett Flying School. He and his partner, William Burdett, built the school into a successful enterprise, adding a second "Jenny" trainer and working in the emerging film industry as stunt flyers. On 3 February 1926 Frye and two other partners—Paul Richter, Jr., and Walter Hamilton—bought out Burdett and renamed the school the Aero Corporation of California. At the same time, Frye, the driving force in the company, expanded activities by selling aircraft in the area. The Aero Corporation became the regional distributor for Fokker aircraft and made a reputation selling its F-10 trimotor, one of the first comfortable airliners.

Frye also took the Aero Corporation of California directly into the airline industry. On 28 November 1927 Aero's newly created subsidiary, Standard Air Lines, began regularly scheduled service between Los Angeles and Tucson, Arizona, via Phoenix. In 1928 Frye extended the flights to El Paso, Texas, and on 4 February 1929 Standard announced the inauguration of "America's First Trans-Continental Air-Rail Travel Route" through the extension of its air route eastward to El Paso and linkage to the Texas and Pacific Railroad. Passengers could now make a trip from New York to Los Angeles via rail and air connections in less than forty-four hours.

The Great Depression took its toll on the Aero Corporation. On 1 April 1930 Frye and his partners sold out to Western Air Express (WAE), a Los Angeles–based airline under the energetic leadership of Harris M. Hanshue that was trying to develop into a transcontinental carrier. Frye joined WAE, accepting the post of vice president for operations. Taking other failing airlines and their routes that had been acquired by Hanshue at about the same time, Frye created, during the spring and summer of 1930, a western air transport structure that ran from Los Angeles to Kansas City and linked the region's major cities.

Also in 1930, the federal government intervened to affect Frye's plans. Postmaster General Walter Folger Brown, who had worked for years to establish three transcontinental air routes, each with hubs and smaller regional routes operating to the north and south, viewed WAE as being ripe for merger with another airline to create a fourth route across the southwest. Brown directed WAE to merge with Transcontinental Air Transport before either company would receive highly prized airmail contracts. Known as the "Shotgun Marriage," the result was the creation, on 24 July 1930, of Transcontinental and Western Air (TWA). Hanshue became president; Frye, vice president for operations.

As heavy-handed as Brown had been in forcing the creation of TWA, Frye later admitted that the merger had been good for both the airline industry and the nation. For the first time Frye could really build a transcontinental air route. He wasted little time, and on 25 October 1930 TWA announced coast-to-coast service in thirty-six hours, with an overnight stop in Kansas City. Two years later TWA began overnight transcontinental service, inaugurating on 5 November 1932 a daily flight between New York and Los Angeles. During the same period Frye developed a feeder air service linking many smaller cities with the major stops on the TWA transcontinental route.

Frye was also instrumental in bringing about the technological revolution in air transport that took place in the 1930s. After the 1931 crash of a TWA Fokker trimotor, Frye decided to replace the aging fleet of Fokkers with modern airliners. In August 1932 he wrote to the major manufacturers asking for proposals to build a new aircraft of all-metal construction, three engines, a capacity of twelve passengers, and a cruising speed of 146 mph over a distance of 1,060 miles. Only Donald W. Douglas responded, offering TWA the DC-1 then under development, a twin-engine, all-metal, mono-winged airliner. Frye was concerned that the DC-1 was a twin-engine rather than a trimotor, but Douglas demonstrated that it could perform on one engine if necessary. The DC-1 prototype of 1932 became the DC-2 that filled the TWA order in 1934, carrying fourteen passengers and reducing transcontinental flying time to sixteen hours. TWA also purchased DC-3s from Douglas in 1937. The DC-3, with its efficient engines, favorable lift/drag ratio, high payload capability, relative comfort, and ease of operation, helped make passenger aviation profitable without government airmail contracts. It became a mainstay of the airline for more than a decade.

Frye also played a key role in resolving the 1934 airmail controversy. On 9 February Roosevelt canceled the airmail contracts of commercial carriers, charging that the contracts had been obtained through collusion and fraud, and directed the Army Air Corps to carry out domestic airmail operations until the issue could be resolved. The result was a complete fiasco. Army aircraft were obsolete, its pilots poorly trained; soon there were sixty-six crashes and twelve deaths. Aware that airmail contracts were critical to the financial welfare of the airlines, Frye and World War I ace Eddie Rickenbacker, then vice president of Eastern Air Transport, flew TWA's DC-1 from Los Angeles to Newark, New Jersey, in thirteen hours and four minutes on 18–19 February to demonstrate the capability of the commercial carriers. The following month Frye worked with Washington lawyer Max O. Gardner, who had entree to Roosevelt, to settle the crisis. After a series of reorganizations to distinguish the airline companies from those that had been charged with illegal activities—TWA simply added an "Inc." to its name—on 20 April 1934 the government awarded new airmail contracts to TWA and the other major carriers. Frye ended 1934, a year that had begun with a crisis, with a great success, being named on 27 December president of TWA, Inc.

Frye presided over TWA for the next thirteen years. Under his direction the airline became known as a pilot's company. He pushed safety and reliability while watching the bottom line. He pioneered in the use of high-performance, all-weather transports, purchasing the Boeing 307, the first pressurized passenger transport, in July 1940. This bold move gave TWA a competitive edge over other airlines, but it got him into trouble with John D. Hertz, who controlled the TWA board of directors. Hertz thought that the costs involved were too great to warrant the move, and the two battled for control of the corporation. The matter was resolved in 1941 when Frye persuaded Howard Hughes to acquire a controlling interest in the company and to oust Hertz.

Frye and Hughes made a powerful combination at TWA, expanding operations during the war years, moving into international routes, contracting with the military, and pushing aeronautical technology. TWA began flying to Europe and onward to India in July 1945 and to Shanghai in August 1946. In addition, it took delivery of the first Lockheed-049 Constellation, and in April 1944 Frye and Hughes flew it from Burbank, California, to Washington, D.C., in a record six hours, fifty-eight minutes.

Although on good terms with Hughes, Frye found himself in a constant power struggle with Hughes's chief assistant, Noah Dietrich. In 1946 a pilot's strike, an economic downturn, and a grounding of the Lockheed Constellations gave Dietrich the pretext he needed to get rid of Frye. In February 1947 Frye resigned from TWA, Inc., and took a position as president of the General Aniline and Film Corporation, which supported the movie industry, and remained there until 1955. He then formed his own company, the Northrop Aircraft Corporation, to develop a trimotor aircraft for use in underdeveloped countries. Northrop built a prototype, the Pioneer, but before much could be done with mass-producing and marketing the airplane, Frye was killed by a drunk driver in Tucson, Arizona, where the Pioneer factory was to be located.

Jack Frye's career reads like a Horatio Alger tale. A high school dropout and onetime soda jerk, he ambitiously rose in the emerging airline industry during the interwar period. Aviation writer Robert J. Serling characterized Frye as "Brash, energetic and fiercely competitive, he was the quintessential airline leader at the crossroads in aviation history." His success in business was equaled by the storm of his personal life. Married four times—information about the first two wives is unavailable—his third wife was Helen Varner Vanderbilt, former wife of Cornelius Vanderbilt, Jr. They were married in 1941 and divorced in 1950. His last wife was Nevada Smith, a former Las Vegas showgirl, whom Frye married in 1950 and with whom he had one child.

• There is no formal collection of Frye's papers. Material by and about him can be found in scattered collections at the National Air and Space Museum, Smithsonian Institution, Washington, D.C., and at the Trans World Airlines Archives in Kansas City, Mo. For more information on his career see R. E. G. Davies, *Delta: The Illustrated History of a Major U.S. Airline and the People Who Made It* (1990); Robert W. Rummel, *Howard Hughes and TWA* (1991); Robert J. Serling, *Howard Hughes' Airline: An Informal History of TWA* (1983); Paul Tillett, *The Army Flies the Mails* (1956); and Douglas J. Ingells, *The Plane That Changed the World: A Biography of the DC-3* (1966). A discussion of his work at TWA is in "Chest Expansion of an Airline," *Fortune*, Apr. 1945, pp. 132–38, 192, 195–96, 199. An obituary is in the *New York Times*, 4 Feb. 1959.

ROGER D. LAUNIUS

FRYE, William Pierce (2 Sept. 1831–8 Aug. 1911), U.S. representative and senator, was born in Lewiston, Maine, the son of Colonel John M. Frye and Alice M. Davis. He entered Bowdoin College at fifteen and graduated in 1850. He studied law with the influential Republican leader William Pitt Fessenden and then practiced in Lewiston and Rockland. Frye married Caroline Francis Spear in 1853; they had three children. In 1861 Frye won election to the state legislature, where he served three terms. He became mayor of Lewiston in 1866–1867 and then attorney general of Maine from 1867 to 1869.

Frye was elected to the U.S. House of Representatives in 1871. "His rank as a debater was soon established," former Speaker of the House and close political ally James G. Blaine recalled (*Twenty Years of Congress*, p. 510). James A. Garfield heard him speak to an Ohio audience in 1875 and observed that Frye had "a very pleasing address, and soon gets a vigorous hold on the sympathies of his hearers" (Brown and Williams, vol. 3, p. 51). He became a favorite speaker to Republican audiences across the country. He emerged as a leader of the Republicans in the House, and, after five terms, seemed on the verge of becoming Speaker in 1881.

When Blaine left the Senate to join President Garfield's cabinet in March 1881, the Maine legislature chose Frye to succeed him. Frye benefited from the political truism that "Maine retains its Congressmen" (Alexander, p. 1503). He was reelected four times in the years that followed. In the Senate, Frye was popular with members of both parties. He was a staunch advocate of the protective tariff and a force in the periodic debates over the level of customs duties. "He made the dry questions of rates of duty glow with interest as he went from one topic to another," said his Republican colleague Henry Cabot Lodge (Hatch, vol. 2, p. 621).

The encouragement of the American shipping industry was Frye's favorite cause. He sponsored legislation to provide a government subsidy to the merchant marine; the Hanna-Frye shipping bill of 1902 came closest to success. The defeat of the subsidy proposal was his most painful setback as a lawmaker. Although he took a conservative position against regulating railroads and controlling corporations, he told a fellow senator that the Constitution "is a thing made for the benefit of the United States of America and can be stretched to any extent provided only that the stretch-

ing covers a benefit to the country" (Frye to William E. Chandler, 6 Sept. 1898, Chandler papers). Frye was a proponent of the Bureau of American Republics (organized to build economic and cultural links in the hemisphere) and introduced the law creating the Department of Commerce and Labor. He also pushed for the annexation of the Hawaiian Islands in 1897–1898.

Frye became president pro tem of the Senate in 1896, and he was the presiding officer after the death of Vice President Garret A. Hobart in 1899 and the assassination of President William McKinley in 1901. As leader he used "as little show of force as if he were presiding over a company of guests at his own table" (Alexander, p. 1502). Democrats praised his fairness and impartiality.

In 1898 McKinley asked Frye to serve on the commission to negotiate peace with Spain after the war over Cuba. Frye tried to decline the assignment, "but the President insisted that I should give a good excuse" (Frye to Chandler, 6 Sept. 1898). Since the best Frye could say was that he wanted to hunt and fish, McKinley persuaded him to go to Paris.

Frye believed that the United States should obtain the Philippines. When McKinley asked him what he wanted as far as the islands were concerned, Frye responded, "To take everything in sight" (Alexander, p. 1505). In 1899 he commented about the Philippines: "We will hold them as our own, for the good of the people who inhabit them, and for the immense advantage, commercially, they promise us" (New York *Sun*, 27 Apr. 1899). At the Paris peace negotiations, Frye suggested that a monetary payment to Spain of up to $20 million might secure Spanish approval of the proposed treaty. The idea helped to produce Madrid's agreement with what became the Treaty of Paris.

Frye lived for his legislative work. He served on the Foreign Relations Committee and chaired the Committee on Rules and the Committee on Commerce. On the Commerce panel, he took a strong interest in issues relating to the nation's inland waterways. Aware of the passionate views of his Maine constituents about the state's prohibition laws, he drank Poland Springs water on all occasions. His health deteriorated after 1908 and brought about his resignation from the Senate in April 1911; he died four months later in Lewiston. Frye has receded into Senate history, but in his time he was one of the important leaders of the upper house. He belonged to the Republican "Old Guard" that set the legislative agenda and opposed the progressive legislation of Theodore Roosevelt. His influence on the public policy of the McKinley-Roosevelt era has yet to be measured.

• Small collections of Frye papers are at the Maine Historical Society and at Bowdoin College. The papers of Benjamin Harrison, William McKinley, Theodore Roosevelt, and William Howard Taft at the Library of Congress as well as the William E. Chandler Papers at the New Hampshire Historical Society contain Frye letters. For examples of Frye's own writings, see his *The White League in Louisiana* (1875), reprinting one of his speeches; "Fishing," *Independent*, 2 June 1904, pp. 1235–37; and "The Meaning and Necessity of Ship

Subsidy," *Independent*, 21 June 1906, pp. 1459–63. No biography of Frye has been published. Contemporary sketches include David S. Alexander, "Senator Frye of Maine," *Independent*, 30 Dec. 1909, and (no author), "A Statesman of the Old School," *Outlook*, 19 Aug. 1911, p. 857. See also James G. Blaine, *Twenty Years of Congress* (1884); Winthrop L. Marvin et al., "The Frye Shipping Bill," *American Monthly Review of Reviews* 23 (Feb. 1901): 197–202; E. N. Dingley, *The Life and Times of Nelson Dingley, Jr.* (1902); "William Pierce Frye, Memorial Addresses Delivered in the Senate and the House of Representatives," U.S. Senate, Sen. Doc. 1145, 62d Cong., 3d sess. (1912); Louis Clinton Hatch, ed., *Maine: A History*, vol. 2 (1919); Harry James Brown and Frederick D. Williams, eds., *The Diary of James A. Garfield*, vol. 3, *1875–1877* (1973); and H. Wayne Morgan, ed., *Making Peace with Spain: The Diary of Whitelaw Reid* (1965). The *New York Times*, 9 Aug. 1911, and the *Lewiston* (Maine) *Evening Journal*, 11 Aug. 1911, have very full obituaries.

LEWIS L. GOULD

FUCHS, Klaus Emil Julius (29 Dec. 1911–28 Jan. 1988), physicist and spy, was born in Russelheim, near Frankfurt, Germany, the son of Emil Fuchs, a Lutheran minister, and Else Wagner. Klaus Fuchs studied mathematics and physics at Leipzig University (1928–1931) and continued his undergraduate studies in physics at Kiel University (1931–1933). As a student at Kiel University, he joined, first, the Social Democratic party and, in 1932, the German Communist party. After the Reichstag fire in February 1933, and the attendant Nazi reprisals against the political Left, Fuchs went into hiding in Berlin for a few months, then migrated to Britain in September 1933. He continued his studies in physics at Bristol University, where he secured a position as a research assistant to Neville Mott. In his research Fuchs applied quantum physics to questions of the electrical resistance of metallic films, working with Bernard Lovell, who was later knighted for his achievements in physics. In 1937 Fuchs was granted a Ph.D. in physics at Bristol. A paper that resulted from his doctoral research, "A Quantum Mechanical Calculation of the Elastic Constants of Monovalent Metals," appeared in the *Proceedings of the Royal Society* in 1936 and won him a teaching position at Edinburgh University in the fall of 1937.

Because of classification restrictions in Britain and the United States and because Fuchs's later confession of espionage may have contained deliberate disinformation, the currently available biographical and historical literature is inconsistent on exactly when he began spying. Nonetheless, by 1939 his political sympathies had made him a willing member of the Soviet Union's international espionage apparatus operated by the GRU (Army Intelligence). He established contact with that network through Jurgen Kuczynsky, a Polish Communist who had migrated to Britain in 1936. In June 1940, ten months after the outbreak of World War II and at the time of the abortive German-Soviet alliance, Fuchs was taken into custody by British authorities as an enemy alien and was transferred to internment camps, first on the Isle of Man and then at Quebec City, Canada. There he met and worked with others in the Communist party network. He gave lectures in physics at the camp university and attended meetings of an open cell of the Communist party headed by Hans Kahle, a famous German veteran of the Loyalist forces in the Spanish Civil War. After several months Fuchs was allowed to return to Edinburgh to resume his teaching position, having been cleared of suspicion of pro-Nazi sentiments.

In 1941 he was invited by British physicist Rudolf Peierls to join him at Birmingham, where Peierls headed the British MAUD project, the code name for nuclear weapons research. Fuchs was cleared by British internal security (MI-5) for this post, which some scholars have cited as evidence of the early penetration of MI-5 by Soviet agents. At this time Fuchs began passing information about the classified project to the Soviets through Kuczynski. Fuchs applied for British citizenship, and it was granted on 7 August 1942. As a member of the Peierls team, Fuchs moved to the United States in November 1943. He then worked at Los Alamos, New Mexico, on the design of the atomic weapon.

As a senior scientist Fuchs had full access to information about the atomic bomb project and, it was later revealed, transmitted detailed reports via the American-born Soviet agent Harry Gold, whom he knew by the code name "Raymond." Fuchs remained at Los Alamos after the war, then transferred to Britain's Atomic Energy Research Establishment at Harwell in August 1946. Ironically, he participated in a crucial postwar conference in 1947 with American scientists on how to maintain nuclear secrecy while at the same time continuing to file reports from Harwell via contacts in Britain to the Soviet espionage network. In 1949, as a result of a series of revelations springing from delayed decryption of intercepted Soviet communications, the American Federal Bureau of Investigation requested that the British security agencies interview Fuchs to determine if he had spied while at Los Alamos. After prolonged but gentlemanly inquiry by the experienced MI-5 officer William Skardon, Fuchs made a detailed confession of his espionage work. Convicted in Britain of violation of the Official Secrets Act, he was sentenced in 1950 to the maximum prison term of fourteen years.

In June 1959, however, he was repatriated to the Soviet-satellite German Democratic Republic and accepted an appointment at the Institute for Nuclear Research in Berlin. At that time he married Margarite Keilson, whom he knew from student days at Kiel University. He continued his work in theoretical physics, was elected to the German Democratic Republic's Academy of Sciences, and received the Order of Merit of the Fatherland and the Order of Karl Marx. Fuchs retired from active research in 1979. After his retirement he resided near Dresden.

Although a physicist of some accomplishment, Fuchs is remembered for his espionage work, which advanced Soviet progress toward nuclear weaponry. The revelation of his spying spread political shock waves through Britain and the United States in 1950. He died near Dresden.

• As of the mid-1990s Fuchs's personal papers have not been made available. He has been the subject of several studies of Soviet espionage, which vary from sensationalist to scholarly. Two reliable studies are Robert Chadwell Williams, *Klaus Fuchs: Atom Spy* (1987), and Norman Moss, *Klaus Fuchs, A Biography* (1987). The place of Fuchs in the British espionage scandals is treated well in Chapman Pincher, *Too Secret, Too Long* (1984). Some 5,000 pages of heavily redacted FBI files have been released in response to Freedom of Information Act requests and were used by both Williams and Moss. A useful obituary is in the *New York Times*, 29 Jan. 1988.

RODNEY P. CARLISLE

FUERTES, Louis Agassiz (7 Feb. 1874–22 Aug. 1927), artist, naturalist, and scientific illustrator, was born in Ithaca, New York, the son of Estevan Antonio Fuertes of Puerto Rico, a professor of civil engineering at Cornell University, and Mary Perry of Troy, New York. Named after but unrelated to the great nineteenth-century naturalist Louis Agassiz of Harvard, Fuertes was the youngest in a family of six. He traveled widely throughout the world but always considered Ithaca his home.

At age fourteen Fuertes's lifelong interest in wildlife took tangible form with his first crude drawings of native birds. Over the next few years his artistic ability and ornithological knowledge were honed by self-directed study that included frequent visits to the Ithaca Library to examine a copy of John James Audubon's double elephant folio of *The Birds of America* (1827–1838). In a letter written in 1916 he described the book as "my daily bread" and "the most potent influence that was ever exerted upon my youthful longings to do justice to the singular beauty of birds."

After he traveled to France with his family in the summer of 1892 and attended school in Zurich in the winter of 1892–1893, Fuertes returned to Ithaca and entered the College of Architecture at Cornell with the intention of following his father's career as an engineer. Halfway through his sophomore year, however, a college friend introduced Fuertes to Elliott Coues, one of America's most highly respected and influential ornithologists. Coues convinced Fuertes that his talent was sufficient to support a career as a painter of birds. "Ever since that first interview with Coues," wrote Fuertes, "[I] never thought of adopting any other profession." It was, at least in part, thanks to Coues that he would never have to.

Coues's promotion of Fuertes's talent within the scientific community resulted in a series of commissions that launched Fuertes's career before he had even graduated from college. A series of pen-and-ink drawings for Florence A. Merriam's *A-Birding on a Bronco* (1896); four plates for *The Osprey*, a new ornithological magazine (1897); and 111 illustrations for Coues's *Citizen Bird* were followed by other important commissions soon after his graduation in 1897. Among these were eighteen illustrations for *Song Birds and Water Fowl* (1897), by H. E. Parkhurst; a color frontispiece for *On the Birds' Highway* (1899), by R. Heber Howe, Jr.; and a series of illustrations for *The Auk*, the professional journal of the American Ornithologists' Union. Fuertes's success in launching a full-time career in bird painting without the security of an independent income was unprecedented in the United States.

Fuertes attributed much of his early success to Coues's encouragement, sponsorship, and support. He acknowledged as his other great mentor the American artist Abbott H. Thayer, who pioneered a number of interesting theories on the optical properties of color and light. Thayer, who first met Fuertes at an American Ornithologists' Union meeting in Cambridge, Massachusetts, in 1896, provided Fuertes with the formal art training he lacked, beginning with several months of intensive study at the artist's summer home in Dublin, New Hampshire, in 1897. Fuertes later described this summer and subsequent visits to the Thayers as "my happiest and most uplifting days. . . . Where would I be—and what—if I had not had them," he mused.

Fuertes's knowledge of natural history, his artistic abilities, and his genial personality made him a welcome companion in the field. Beginning with a trip to Florida with the Thayers in 1898 and an expedition to Alaska with railroad magnate Edward H. Harriman in 1899, he spent part of almost every year away from home in search of birds. He developed close relationships with most of the professional ornithologists of his day, most notably Frank M. Chapman, curator of birds at the American Museum of Natural History, with whom he traveled widely on behalf of the museum. In between—or as part of—major illustrative commissions, Fuertes enthusiastically participated in research expeditions to the Bahamas (1902), Mexico (1910), Colombia (1911 and 1913), and Abyssinia (now Ethiopia) (1926–1927), as well as countless shorter trips throughout North America.

His paintings, which were praised by scientists for their accurate depiction of anatomy and pose, were admired by others for their strength of composition and effective use of color and light. They appeared as illustrations in scores of books and in virtually every major magazine in the United States.

At the heart of Fuertes's success was his innate ability to observe and re-create from memory every aspect of a bird's appearance and behavior. "His pictures are instinct with life, and differ from the work of the inexperienced or unsympathetic artist as a living bird differs from a stuffed one," wrote one of his contemporaries. So lifelike were his depictions of birds that many bird-watchers, raised on Fuertes illustrations, saw birds more as Fuertes painted them than as they appeared in life. His influence on the field of wildlife painting in America was to become as great as Audubon's. A series of collecting cards on the birds of North America that he created for the Arm & Hammer Baking Soda company did much to popularize bird-watching and gain public support for conservation.

Louis Fuertes married Margaret Sumner of Ithaca in 1904. They had two children.

The artist's career was cut short by a fatal automobile accident near his home in Ithaca. At his memorial service, Frank Chapman paid tribute to his friend and field companion by describing his personality:

It was one of the marvels of Fuertes' nature that, much as he loved birds, he loved man more. No one could resist the charm of his enthusiasm, his ready wit and whole-souled genuineness, his sympathetic consideration and generosity of thought and deed. Everywhere he made new friends and everywhere he found old ones. . . . If the birds of the world had met to select a human being who could best express to mankind the beauty and charm of their forms, their songs, their rhythmic flight, their manners for the heart's delight, they would unquestionably have chosen Louis Fuertes.

Fuertes himself could not have asked for a finer tribute.

• The largest single collection of Fuertes's papers is in the Department of Manuscripts and Archives at Olin Library, Cornell University. The largest collections of original paintings by Fuertes are at the Academy of Natural Sciences of Philadelphia (220+ watercolors from the U.S. Fish and Wildlife Service), the American Museum of Natural History (400+ drawings and paintings), Cornell University (1,000+ pencil and watercolor studies at Olin Library and 100+ paintings at the Laboratory of Ornithology), and the Field Museum of Natural History (100+ watercolor studies, most from Fuertes's 1926–1927 expedition to Abyssinia). For a description of major institutional collections of Fuertes's art, see Appendix I in Peck. The best-known series of Fuertes's paintings were published in *National Geographic* (various dates, 1913–1920); Elon Howard Eaton, *Birds of New York* (1910); and Edward Howe Forbush, *Birds of Massachusetts and Other New England States* (1925). Fuertes was an excellent letter writer and memorable raconteur, but he rarely wrote for publication. Two notable exceptions are "Impressions of the Voices of Tropical Birds," *Bird Lore*, 1913 and 1914; and, with Wilfred H. Osgood, *Artist and Naturalist in Ethiopia* (1936). Comprehensive biographical sources are Mary Fuertes Boynton, ed., *Louis Agassiz Fuertes, His Life Briefly Told and His Correspondence* (1956); Frederick George Marcham, *Louis Agassiz Fuertes and the Singular Beauty of Birds* (1971); and Robert McCracken Peck, *A Celebration of Birds; The Life and Art of Louis Agassiz Fuertes* (1982). See also works by Fuertes's friend and student George Miksch Sutton: *To a Young Bird Artist: Letters from Louis Agassiz Fuertes to George Miksch Sutton* (1979) and *Bird Student, an Autobiography* (1980).

ROBERT MCCRACKEN PECK

FULBRIGHT, J. William (9 Apr. 1905–9 Feb. 1995), educator, U.S. senator, and Vietnam-era dissenter, was born James William Fulbright in Sumner, Missouri, the son of Jay Fulbright, a banker, and Roberta Waugh. When he was three years of age, the family moved to Fayetteville, Arkansas. In the years that followed Jay Fulbright became one of the community's leading bankers, while Roberta Fulbright attended to family affairs and built a network of friends centering on the University of Arkansas. Her parlor became a salon that included economists, historians, literary critics, local lawyers, physicians, and politicians. "Bill" Fulbright enjoyed a secure if somewhat sheltered childhood amid the foothills of the Ozark Mountains. He attended the University of Arkansas from the time he enrolled in the experimental kindergarten run by the College of Education until his graduation with a bachelor of arts degree in 1924. His father died suddenly in 1923, and his mother took over management of the family businesses.

In the fall of 1924 Fulbright, having won a Rhodes Scholarship, departed for Oxford University, where for the next four years he studied modern history; he also traveled throughout Europe. On graduating from Oxford in 1928 he spent a year with journalist and bon vivant Mikhail Fodor, who was based in Vienna, Austria. Acting as Fodor's assistant, Fulbright toured Southeastern and Central Europe and met the leading political figures of the day. In 1929 the former Rhodes scholar returned to Fayetteville to join his mother in running the family business empire, which included a bank, a bottling company, a lumberyard, and the local newspaper. During a business trip to Washington, Fulbright met Elizabeth Kremer Williams, and they married in 1932. The couple had two daughters.

In 1939 Fulbright was named president of the University of Arkansas. At thirty-four, he was then the youngest college head in the United States. Other than brief teaching stints in the law schools of George Washington University and the University of Arkansas, he was unqualified for the job. Indeed, his selection had more to do with his mother's substantial political clout than with his academic and administrative record. Fulbright served as the university's chief executive until 1941, when Homer Adkins, the newly elected governor and a bitter enemy of Roberta Fulbright, summarily dismissed him from the post.

In 1942 Fulbright began his career in public service by successfully running for Congress from the district comprising Northwest Arkansas. His time at Oxford studying modern European history and his travels in Europe had generated in him a deep interest in international affairs. During his thirty-two years in Congress, he appealed to the peoples of the world but especially his countrymen to appreciate and tolerate other cultures and political systems without condoning armed aggression or human rights violation.

In the House Fulbright made a name for himself by cosponsoring the Fulbright-Connally Resolution, which placed Congress on record as favoring membership in a postwar collective security organization (subsequently, the United Nations). In 1944 Fulbright captured the U.S. Senate seat held by Hattie Caraway, beating the incumbent and two other candidates, including his nemesis Adkins. In 1946 the junior senator from Arkansas sponsored legislation creating the international exchange program in graduate studies and scholarly research that bears his name. The program has subsidized hundreds of thousands of "Fulbright scholars" from the United States and some sixty other countries.

At the close of World War II and the dawn of the Cold War, Fulbright perceived the central problem of U.S. foreign policy to be how to preserve Anglo-American civilization from destruction. Appalled by the bombing of Hiroshima and Nagasaki, he decided that the world was far too dangerous a place for each member of the Atlantic community simply to go its own way. His dedication to internationalism generally and the United Nations specifically and his passionate support of the Fulbright Exchange Program followed logically. He was convinced that the exchange of students and scholars would increase understanding generally and breed political elites capable of pursuing enlightened foreign policies. They would act as counterweights to the xenophobia and nationalism that had bred wars since the beginning of history.

Confronted with the reality that neither his country nor its wartime allies were willing to relinquish their freedom of action within the context of the United Nations, Fulbright turned his attention to rehabilitating Western Europe and defending the Atlantic community from the scourge of Stalinism. Thus he championed the Truman Doctrine, the Marshall Plan, and the North Atlantic Treaty Organization (NATO), and he defended executive branch prerogatives in foreign policy against isolationists in Congress who wanted to retreat within "Fortress America." With his support, the Truman administration formulated and implemented the policy of containment, intervening on the side of the pro-Western monarch in the Greek civil war and helping both Turkey and Iran fend off Soviet efforts to convert them into protectorates.

For Fulbright the greatest threat to America's republican form of government and its civic culture came not from the political left but from the right. He understood that the confrontation with the Soviet Union coupled with the dawn of the atomic age had bred in the United States a virulent anticommunism that threatened civil liberties at home and peace abroad. This realization prompted him to participate in the movement to censure Senator Joseph McCarthy in 1954. Later, in the early 1960s, he challenged and denounced the John Birch Society, the Christian Crusade, H. L. Hunt, Strom Thurmond, and the other organizations and personalities that made up the radical right.

In 1959 Fulbright assumed the chair of the powerful Senate Foreign Relations Committee and served in that capacity until his departure from the Senate in 1975, longer than any previous head of the committee. When Soviet leader Nikita Khrushchev visited the United States in 1959 and proved to be conciliatory, Fulbright was greatly impressed, even as he was fearful of the resurgence of the American radical right. In these circumstances compounded of sober hope and somber uneasiness, he felt that the policy of competitive coexistence, with each side of the Cold War ready to take advantage of its enemy, should be replaced with the concept of détente. The Kennedy administration's flexible response to the Communist threat, as in the measures taken to defuse the Berlin Wall crisis and

the Cuban missile crisis, heartened Fulbright. During the 1964 presidential campaign, Fulbright took the lead in responding to the virulent anticommunism of the Republican candidate, Senator Barry Goldwater, and his vanguard of "true believers," who were inflexible in their hostility toward anything that smacked of compromise with the Soviet Union and its client states. A devoted advocate of liberal internationalism, Fulbright was initially sympathetic to Lyndon Johnson's views on foreign policy. Both the senator and the president believed that the United States should deter Sino-Soviet aggression through rational military preparedness and combat Communist-inspired wars of liberation in the Third World through foreign aid and support of counterinsurgency movements. In essence, Fulbright saw no good alternative to peaceful coexistence, to the extent that it could be maintained, and he believed that the Communist world would eventually collapse of its own internal contradictions.

Fulbright parted company with President Johnson because he believed that his longtime political comrade in arms had sold out to the very forces that Johnson had defeated in 1964. The decision to intervene in the Dominican Republic and to escalate the war in Vietnam signaled to the Arkansan the triumph of the nationalist, xenophobic, imperialist tendencies that had always lurked beneath the surface of American society. He had supported the Gulf of Tonkin Resolution of 1964, which was precipitated by the alleged firing on American ships by North Vietnamese torpedo boats, because he believed it was necessary to protect Johnson's right flank in the upcoming presidential contest with Goldwater and because he was assured it would not lead to a wider war. After reading Bernard Fall and George Kahin on recent Vietnamese history and talking with newspeople and diplomats involved in the Vietnam conflict, Fulbright came to the conclusion that the war was not a case of northern aggression against the south. Rather, North Vietnamese leader Ho Chi Minh represented the forces of an authentic nationalism, and the war in the south pitted an American-supported puppet government in Saigon against indigenous revolutionaries who were seeking social justice and national self-determination.

In February 1966 the Senate Foreign Relations Committee, under Fulbright's leadership, held televised hearings on Vietnam. The misgivings expressed there began the national debate on the wisdom of U.S. policy toward Southeast Asia. From then until Johnson's departure from the presidency, Fulbright labored to undermine the consensus that supported the war in Vietnam. In 1967 he published *The Arrogance of Power*, a sweeping critique of American foreign policy that eventually sold 400,000 copies.

Only months after Richard Nixon's election in November 1968, Fulbright concluded that, like Johnson, the new president had become a prisoner of the radical right, the military-industrial complex, his own psyche, and other forces of which he was only dimly aware and which he could not control. Using the Constitution as a rallying point, the Arkansan aligned conservatives and liberals behind a national commitments resolution that required explicit congressional approval for any executive commitment of aid or troops to a foreign power. Passage of that measure paved the way for additional resolutions limiting presidential prerogatives in taking military action and led to the War Powers Act in 1973.

Two primary aspects of Fulbright's public career are enigmatic—his civil rights record and his about-face on congressional executive prerogatives in foreign policy. In 1956 he signed the Southern Manifesto, a call by southern members of Congress for resistance to court-ordered school integration, and he did not vote for a civil rights bill until 1970. His racism had much more to do with class than skin color, however. In the milieus where he lived in Fayetteville and Washington, he escaped contact with sharecroppers and ghetto dwellers. Yet he had played a key role in toning down the Southern Manifesto, and he was deeply affected by the killing of four African-American girls in the Birmingham church bombing of 1963. He even provided behind-the-scenes help on behalf of civil rights measures to both the Kennedy and the Johnson administrations. During Nixon's presidency, Fulbright led the way in defeating the nomination of G. Harold Carswell, an outspoken opponent of the civil rights movement, to fill a Supreme Court vacancy.

In regard to the foreign policy powers of the executive versus those of Congress, Fulbright's concern was not with a particular interpretation of the Constitution. In the aftermath of World War II, with the tide of isolationism still running strong, an assertive, active executive was needed to advance the cause of internationalism and keep the peace. But over the years the stresses and strains of fighting the Cold War under the shadow of a nuclear holocaust had taken their toll. With its power to act sometimes circumscribed and sometimes dictated by a fanatical anticommunism, the executive had embarked on an imperial foreign policy that led to the quagmire in Vietnam and the country's longest war, while it also created a maze of international commitments and overseas bases not seen since the British empire was in full bloom. The only way to check this trend, Fulbright believed, was to restore congressional prerogatives in the making of foreign policy.

Fulbright lost his Senate seat to Arkansas governor Dale Bumpers in 1974. For the next twenty years he played the role of elder statesman, addressing the world from his office in the prestigious Washington law firm of Hogan and Hartson. In 1981 the College of Arts and Sciences at the University of Arkansas was named for him, and in 1993 President Bill Clinton, one of Fulbright's protégés, presented him with the Medal of Freedom. "Betty" Fulbright lived to witness the first event but not the second, having died in 1985. In 1990 Fulbright married Harriet Mayor, then the executive director of the Fulbright Alumni Association. Fulbright died at his home in Washington, D.C.

Like his Oxford tutor, R. B. McCallum, Fulbright believed that a "parliament of man" was possible, that educated, enlightened human beings were able to recognize that their individual interests were inextricably bound up with the well-being of the community. The crux of that education was knowledge about and appreciation of other cultures. Tolerance, peaceful coexistence, respect for human rights, and collective security were Fulbright's bequests to the nation and the world.

• Fulbright's papers are in Special Collections, Mullins Library, University of Arkansas, Fayetteville. Several books have been written on Fulbright's life and his opposition to the Vietnam War, including Haynes Johnson and Bernard M. Gwertzman, *Fulbright: The Dissenter* (1968); William C. Berman, *William Fulbright and the Vietnam War* (1988); and Randall Bennett Woods, *Fulbright: A Biography* (1995). Melvin Small, *Johnson, Nixon, and the Doves* (1988), and Charles De Benedetti and Charles Chatfield, *An American Ordeal: The Antiwar Movement of the Vietnam Era* (1990), discuss Fulbright's place in the antiwar movement. Also helpful is William Conrad Gibbons, *The U.S. Government and the Vietnam War: Executive and Legislative Roles and Relationships* (1984). Obituaries are in the *New York Times* and the *Washington Post*, 10 Feb. 1995.

RANDALL BENNETT WOODS

FULD, Caroline Bamberger Frank (16 Mar. 1864–18 July 1944), philanthropist and cofounder of the Institute for Advanced Study, known as "Carrie," was born in Baltimore, Maryland, the daughter of Elkan Bamberger, a merchant, and Theresa Hutzler. One of eight children, Caroline was raised in an extended German Jewish family in Baltimore. Her father and two brothers operated E. Bamberger & Sons, a wholesaler's business in notions, small wares, laces, and embroideries, and her mother's family owned Hutzler Bros., one of Baltimore's leading mercantile establishments. Her upbringing was, according to her sister, Lavinia, governed by her father, a "stern disciplinarian who believed in a strict regimen for his daughters" (letter to Abraham Flexner, Flexner papers, 8 Nov. 1944). In 1882 Caroline Bamberger married Louis M. Frank and left Baltimore for Philadelphia, where her new husband had a successful business. When Frank lost his livelihood during the panic of 1892, Caroline "gave up wealth with the same grace that she showed later when she acquired it again" (Flexner papers, 8 Nov. 1944). They joined her brother, Louis, in Newark, New Jersey, where he was preparing to open his own store. Bamberger, Frank, and Felix Fuld, a friend from New York, became equal partners in L. Bamberger & Co., which rapidly emerged as Newark's premier department store. When Bamberger sold the store to R. H. Macy's of New York in 1929 for $25 million, the company employed between 4,000 and 5,000 persons and grossed $35 million annually.

After Louis Frank died in 1910, Caroline Frank married her brother's second partner, Felix Fuld, in 1913; both marriages were childless. The Fulds and Bamberger lived together in South Orange, New Jersey, on a small estate owned in common and belonged to Congregation B'nai Jeshurun, Newark's Reform synagogue. The three were deeply committed to charity and community service. Until Felix Fuld's death in 1929, they were a philanthropic triumverate, remembered by their adviser, attorney Herbert H. Maass, for "the close unity of thought that existed amongst the three, both in relation to the high standard of ethics they maintained in connection with the business of L. Bamberger & Co., their outstanding philanthropies, and their great ambition to devote their accumulated fortunes to some philanthropic purpose." The Fulds typically insisted upon anonymity in their benefactions, which, at Felix Fuld's death, amounted to approximately $2,500,000. Primarily targeting Jewish welfare, their contributions included a gift of $500,000, which helped to build and sustain Beth Israel Hospital in Newark. They founded and supported the Newark chapters of the Young Men's and Young Women's Hebrew Associations. During World War I, they supported the American Jewish Relief Committee with substantial contributions; in 1918, Caroline Fuld purchased $50,000 in liberty bonds, the largest subscription purchased by a woman in Newark. In the 1920s the Fulds made generous contributions to the American Jewish Joint Agricultural Corporation (AgroJoint) to aid Jewish farm settlements in Russia.

In addition to the gifts that she and her husband made in common, Caroline Fuld had her own charitable interests, particularly the Jewish Day Nursery and Neighborhood House in Newark. She participated in local charity drives, was a patron of the New York Philharmonic Orchestra, and supported the Newark Museum. She belonged to the Newark chapter of Hadassah and, with her husband, was a board member of the Child Welfare Commission of America. In 1931 she was elected president of the National Council of Jewish Women.

Her greatest contribution, made with her brother in 1930, was $5 million for the endowment and development of the Institute for Advanced Study. In 1929 the brother and sister were introduced to Abraham Flexner, an expert on American medical education. Flexner convinced them that "the time was ripe for the creation in America of an institute in the field of general scholarship and science, resembling the Rockefeller Institute in the field of medicine." The Institute for Advanced Study–Louis Bamberger and Mrs. Felix Fuld Foundation was incorporated on 20 May 1930. It was, from the start, strictly a postdoctoral research institution. Its faculty consisted of carefully selected professors, who were appointed for life and freed from teaching and administrative responsibilities in order to concentrate exclusively on scholarship. The founders assumed no responsibility for the administration of the Institute but insisted that Abraham Flexner become the first director and that the new institution be located in New Jersey. Their stipulation that "no account shall be taken, directly or indirectly, of race, religion, or sex" in the appointment of faculty, staff and fellows expressed their continued commitment to social welfare.

In October 1933 the Institute opened in Princeton with a small full-time faculty in mathematics that included Albert Einstein, John von Neumann and Hermann Weyl. In its first decade, the Institute emerged as an acknowledged leader in mathematics and theoretical physics; and since then, as an intellectual retreat for outstanding scholars in a variety of fields it has been an authoritative symbol of excellence in research. During the 1930s, Fuld and Bamberger contributed an additional $3 million to finance the Institute's building of a campus and its expansion into the fields of the humanities and social sciences. At their deaths they left the Institute an estimated $18 million. Fuld died at her summer cottage in Lake Placid, New York.

• There are no known papers for Fuld, although the Abraham Flexner Papers at the Library of Congress contain some letters pertaining to her life in Baltimore and Newark. An obituary is in the *New York Times*, 19 and 27 July 1944. Discussion of the Bamberger-Fuld role in the founding and early development of the Institute for Advanced Study can be found in Laura Smith Porter, "From Intellectual Sanctuary to Social Responsibility: The Founding of the Institute for Advanced Study, 1930–1933" (Ph.D. diss., Princeton Univ., 1988); and Abraham Flexner's *I Remember: The Autobiography of Abraham Flexner* (1940), and "Louis Bamberger and Mrs. Felix Fuld," *Publications of the American Jewish Historical Society*, no. 37 (1947): 455–57. In the Archives of the Institute for Advanced Study, the *Bulletin of the Institute for Advanced Study* 1–12 (1930 to 1945–1946), and the *Minutes of the Regular Meeting of the Institute for Advanced Study* (10 Oct. 1930–10 Oct. 1938) are quite useful. Records of Fuld's philanthropic contributions are found in the *Jewish Chronicle* (Newark, New Jersey), 24 Apr. 1930; the *New York Times*, 21 Jan. 1929, 7 May 1931, 23 Mar. 1934, and 22 Nov. 1941; and the *Princeton* (N.J.) *Herald*, 21 July 1944.

LAURA SMITH PORTER

FULKS, Joseph (26 Oct. 1921–21 Mar. 1976), professional basketball player, was born in Birmingham, Kentucky, the son of Leonard Fulks and Mattie Estes, farmers. Later Leonard Fulks served as a prison guard. When a dam was built, covering the area with water, the family moved to Kuttawa, Kentucky. Joseph Fulks attended school in Marshall County and Kuttawa, where he gained recognition for his basketball abilities. In 1941 he went on to nearby Murray State Teachers College. At 6'5" and 190 pounds he averaged more than 13 points per game, winning selection to conference all-star teams after his freshman and sophomore seasons. The National Association of Intercollegiate Athletics (NAIA) named him to its 1943 All-America team. That year he married Mary Sue Gillespie; they had four children.

Fulks served in the U.S. Marine Corps and played service basketball from 1943 to 1946. Competing against other service players who had played at major colleges, he was not unduly impressed with their abilities and gained confidence in his own. A professional scout spotted him in Hawaii, and in 1946 Eddie Gottlieb signed him to a contract with the Philadelphia

Warriors of the Basketball Association of America (BAA), a newly organizing professional league.

Fulks as a Warrior fulfilled his basketball potential. Relying on his leaping ability (sportswriters quickly nicknamed him "Jumpin' Joe"), his ambidexterity, and a quickly lofted one-handed jump shot, he became a prodigious scorer. At a time when 20-point performances in any game still astonished fans, he also frustrated opposing players by consistently topping that mark. In his first professional game he scored 25 points. Twelve different times during the BAA's initial season he finished a game with more than 30 points (once totaling 41)—a feat unheard of before him. He led the league by averaging 23.2 points per game and at season's end was the BAA's only unanimous all-star first-team choice. Led by his contributions, the Warriors won the BAA's first championship.

Fulks maintained his scoring pace over the next two seasons. He averaged 22.1 points per game in 1947–1948 and 26.0 in 1948–1949; each year he was named to the all-league first team. Then on 10 February 1949 he topped even himself with a record 63 points against the Indianapolis Jets, a single-game total that would stand for ten seasons.

Generating sports news coverage with his offensive displays, Fulks assumed a major role in promoting fan interest in the exciting, fast-paced style of basketball that the pros introduced. Competition between the BAA and the rival National Basketball League ended with their merger to form the National Basketball Association (NBA) in 1949. With the new, seventeen-team league came larger numbers of highly capable, experienced players and a greater emphasis on such facets of the game as better rebounding and ball-handling, stronger defense and court mobility, and increased reliance on the tall center (or "big man") for point production. Fulks's onetime dominance was over. Although he turned in four more creditable seasons, surging back to an 18.7 scoring average and all-NBA second-team selection in 1950–1951, his career was clearly over by the spring of 1954.

Still, his first three precedent-setting seasons were crucial to the NBA's early development and significant in the transition to later styles of basketball offense.

Fulks scouted for the Warriors into the 1970s, and he continued to win athletic honors. In 1952 the NAIA and in 1965 Murray State University elected him to their halls of fame. In 1977, a year after an argument resulted in his death by a gunshot wound in Eddyville, Kentucky, where he had served as athletic director for the Kentucky State Correctional Institution, Fulks was inducted into the Basketball Hall of Fame.

• Biographical information on Fulks can be found in Dwain McIntosh, "Fulks Named to NBA's All-Time Team," *Murray State University Alumnus Magazine*, Mar. 1971, pp. 5 and 27, and the Fulks file at the Naismith Memorial Basketball Hall of Fame in Springfield, Mass. For statistical information on Fulks's career, see David S. Neft, *Sports Encyclopedia: Pro Basketball* (1975), and David L. Porter, ed., *Biographical Dictionary of American Sports: Basketball and Other Indoor Sports* (1989).

GERALD R. GEMS

FULLER, Alfred Carl (13 Jan. 1885–4 Dec. 1973), brush manufacturer and door-to-door marketer, was born in Welsford, Kings County, Nova Scotia, the son of Leander Joseph Fuller and Phebe Jane Collins, farmers. The eleventh of twelve children, Fuller grew up in an extended family of New England émigrés on Acadian land settled following the French and Indian War. The farm relied on oxen rather than horses, the family worshiped with the local Methodist congregation, and the children studied at the common school. As he came of age Fuller joined most of his generation in migrating to cities to find work. In January 1903 he left from the port at Yarmouth, Nova Scotia, for Boston, where three brothers and two sisters already lived. A sister in Somerville provided him a room, while a brother got him a job as a streetcar conductor. He was discharged after eighteen months for derailing a car. Then failing as a groom and a teamster, Fuller sought a job with the Somerville Brush and Mop Company, a business begun by another brother who had subsequently died, and started work there on 7 January 1905 as a salesman.

Fuller proved extraordinarily adept at direct sales, gaining housewives' confidences and learning about their household cleaning needs. During his first year in the field, he proposed several modifications for brush designs to increase customer appeal, only to be rejected by his boss. But he recognized that the market for cleaning aids was much deeper than currently developed. With the blessings of his landlady-sister, Fuller converted his savings and her basement into a brush-making workshop and went into business himself early in 1906. He made house calls during the day for brush orders and twisted wire brushes during the evening to fill those orders. This pattern of getting orders and then making the brushes became the key to his success.

Since the technology of brush making was simple and widely known, Fuller concentrated on refining the process of getting orders. Independent peddlers were common in American marketing, but at the time only a few producers relied on direct house sales, such as the Stark Brothers Nursery, J. R. Watkins, Avon Products, and Wear-Ever Aluminum. Fuller's experience had taught him that some products were best suited to direct sales, where women bought from household budgets and could directly see the benefits of the product demonstrated in their homes. Confidence in a salesman with products designed with the user in mind would expand demand.

Fuller moved his operation from Somerville to Hartford, Connecticut, in April 1906, with a sense of mission, confident that he was "a benefactor to the housewives, a crusader against unsanitary kitchens and inadequately cleaned homes." He moved his equipment into rented quarters and began calling on area housewives, continuing a cycle of getting orders during the week and delivering brushes on the weekends when husbands were home with their week's pay. As his business grew, he hired a man to make brushes and a woman to keep books. He continued selling, ranging outside Hartford and filling orders COD. Then he began to recruit and train college men to sell part time, renting them a sample case and requiring a deposit on all their orders. Gradually his sales and production force expanded as he pushed into New York and Pennsylvania to open new markets.

In 1908 he married a fellow Nova Scotian, Evelyn W. Ells, whose background was similar to Fuller's and who had been working as a clerk in a Boston department store. After they settled into an apartment near the workshop in Hartford, she tried direct sales and proved successful. Her commissions paid for their first vacation trip back to Nova Scotia. But her pioneering efforts at direct sales ended when she had the first of their two sons, and their lives diverged more because of Fuller's preoccupation with work and insistence on the separation of work and home. Although married in the Somerville Methodist parsonage, Fuller shortly thereafter became intrigued with Christian Science and became a faithful practitioner following an illness in 1921 for which he was successfully treated by a Christian Science practitioner.

As his business grew Fuller's major difficulty was in keeping salesmen. Each time he opened a new market he would look for a salesman to take over for him, but men proved difficult to find and few lasted very long. While working Syracuse in 1909, Fuller decided to advertise for help in the local paper and repeated the ad in the nationally distributed magazine *Everybody's*. The response was overwhelming, even with the requirement of a $17 deposit for the sample case and a dealer's account. By March 1910 Fuller had 260 dealers and a nationwide business.

Setting up an organization that would maintain and develop this network proved to be Fuller's full-time challenge. It involved moving into mass production and purchasing, and necessitated creating a system of recruiting and training a sales force in a field that was particularly susceptible to high turnover rates. He fought high turnover by building a pyramid organization that promoted supervisors from among the more successful salesmen, and intensively trained his personnel through psychological emphasis on positive thinking. Fuller perfected his sales organization by 1915, and annual sales that topped $30,000 in 1910 grew to over $1 million by 1919 and was run out of 100 branch offices. In 1921 Fuller consolidated his various workshops scattered around Hartford into a new plant employing 800 workers. By 1923 sales skyrocketed to $15 million.

Indeed, Fuller's reputation as an innovative marketer became so great that in 1921 he was featured in the *American Magazine* and invited the next year to write about his experiences for readers of *System: The Magazine of Business*. The *Saturday Evening Post* coined the term "Fuller Brush Man" in 1921, introducing an American icon, which became the subject of cartoons in the national press and study in trade magazines. Like Henry Ford, Fuller received considerable correspondence from customers, singing his praises and offering suggestions for brush designs.

Yet with explosive growth came many problems, reflected in company sales falling by half in 1924 because of vacancies in sales territories. Fuller experimented with pricing and commission structures, established a system of bonuses and incentives for dealers, and contained losses in the sales force and volume. By the time the nation entered the depression in 1930, Fuller was able to expand his force, and annual sales, which were only $5 million in 1932, rose by $1 million a year for the balance of the decade. By the outbreak of World War II, sales had returned to the 1923 peak.

In 1930 Fuller and his first wife divorced. Two years later he met and married another Nova Scotian, Mary Primrose Pelton; they had no children together. By the end of the thirties both sons from his first marriage had graduated from college and entered the company, each starting out with a sales kit and a territory. With the world at war, markets for brushes shifted from direct sales to military supply, and the oldest son, Howard, took charge of the company in 1942. The company continued to prosper and expand under Howard's leadership, though the father-son relationship contained many of the classic conflicts occurring between founding entrepreneurs and children who replace them and change operations. The founder remained chairman of the board, but devoted increasing time to volunteer work, such as heading the Connecticut Manufacturers Association and representing New England producers in wartime mobilization efforts. When Howard died unexpectedly in 1959, his other son, Avand, took over the company. Alfred Fuller remained company board chairman until 1968, when the Fuller Brush Company was sold to Consolidated Food Corporation.

Fuller, who had become an American citizen in 1918, voted Republican and maintained a residence at West Hartford, Connecticut. He contributed to several charitable and educational institutions, particularly the Hartt College of Music at the University of Hartford. He founded Hartford's Junior Achievement organization, seeing himself as a model in the Horatio Alger mold, without advantages save perseverance, whose accomplishments could be duplicated by anyone. He died at the Hartford Hospital.

• No collection of Fuller papers exists, and there are no Fuller Brush Company archives. Fuller proves to be both comprehensive and introspective about himself and his company in his memoir, *A Foot in the Door: The Life Appraisal of the Original Fuller Brush Man*, as told to Hartzell Spence (1960). An excellent analysis of the Fuller marketing system is "The Fuller Brush Company," *Fortune*, Oct. 1938, pp. 68–73ff. A popular treatment of him is by John Bainbridge, "May I Just Step Inside?" *New Yorker* 13 Nov. 1948, pp. 36–56. An extensive obituary is in the *New York Times,* 5 Dec. 1973.

WILLIAM O. WAGNON

FULLER, Alvan Tufts (27 Feb. 1878–30 Apr. 1958), automobile dealer, congressman, and governor of Massachusetts, was born in Boston, Massachusetts, the son of Alvan Bond Fuller, a Civil War veteran who worked in the composing room of the *Boston Globe,* and Flora Arabella Tufts. He grew up in an old New England family of modest means in the Boston suburb of Malden, where he attended public schools. A champion bicycle racer, he went to work in the shipping department of the Boston Rubber Shoe Company factory and sold rubber boots evenings and weekends to earn money to build his own bike shop. After Fuller opened the shop in Malden in 1895 his ebullient personality and flair for salesmanship made it an immediate success. A notable Fuller innovation was his Washington's Birthday open house, which gave customers an opportunity to view new models on a winter holiday and to plan their spring purchases. He moved his business to Boston in 1898.

By 1899 Fuller had become convinced that the horseless carriage was the wave of the future in transportation. He subsequently traveled to Europe to investigate the flourishing automobile industry there and returned from France with two de Dion Voiturettes, the first motor vehicles to enter the port of Boston. He convinced the executives of the Packard Motor Car Company of Detroit to make him the exclusive dealer for their product in Boston in 1903, and a year later he also opened a Cadillac agency. In 1908 Fuller purchased a sizable tract of pasture land on the outskirts of Boston, in Brighton, where he constructed the first combination motorcar salesroom and service station in Massachusetts. Though detractors labeled the venture "Fuller's Folly," he was hailed as a visionary when the automobile became popular, his agency prospered, and other dealers followed him out to Brighton. His rivals even adopted his Washington's Birthday open house and helped to make it a Boston and New England tradition. In 1910 he married Viola Theresa Davenport, an operatic singer from Medford, Massachusetts; they had four children.

Having established himself in the automotive business, Fuller turned to politics. Brash, fiercely independent, and contemptuous of professional politicians, he began as an avid supporter of the unsuccessful third-party bid of former president Theodore Roosevelt (1858–1919) in 1912. Under the banner of Roosevelt's Progressive party, Fuller was elected to a state legislative seat from Malden by sixteen votes in 1914. After serving a single one-year term in the Massachusetts House of Representatives he ran in 1916 for the U.S. House as an independent candidate against nine-term Republican incumbent Ernest W. Roberts. He defeated Roberts by 314 votes and was reelected as a Republican by a better than 2 to 1 margin in 1918. A strong advocate of preparedness, Fuller served as a member of the Committee on Military Affairs and voted in favor of American entry into World War I. He also opposed the seating of Victor Berger, an antiwar socialist who had been elected to Congress from Wisconsin in 1918. Fuller shared his hero Theodore Roosevelt's dim view of wartime dissent, believing, he told the House, that the American people had "paid too dearly for their Government to see it thrown to the wolves of anarchy." At the same time, he was outspoken in behalf of efforts to bring about institutional reform in a Congress he characterized as a "kind of political stock exchange, gambling in pork and patronage." In this vein, Fuller eschewed the congressional franking privilege during his four years in the House and never cashed a paycheck in fourteen years of public service. (The checks were left to his sons as a "souvenir.")

Bored with Washington, Fuller returned home to challenge Joseph E. Warner, Speaker of the Massachusetts House of Representatives, in the Republican primary for lieutenant governor in 1920. Fuller won the contest by 854 votes and easily outdistanced a Democratic opponent in the general election. He bested Warner more decisively in a primary rematch in 1922 on his way to a second term. Two years later, Fuller captured the Republican nomination for governor and went on to defeat Democrat James Michael Curley, the mayor of Boston, by more than 160,000 votes after a bitter campaign that featured the Catholic Curley's sensational charge that his candidacy had been actively opposed by the Ku Klux Klan. The effort to link Fuller, a Baptist, even indirectly to the Klan failed because his wife was a devout Catholic and he was well known for his generous donations to Boston archdiocesan charities. In 1926 Fuller waged a populistic campaign against Democrat William A. Gaston, a Boston lawyer closely tied to railway and utility interests, and handily won reelection.

Fuller's governorship was a modest blend of fiscal conservatism and reform. He continued the "pay-as-you-go" budgetary policies instituted by Republican predecessors Samuel Walker McCall, Calvin Coolidge, and Channing H. Cox. In addition to reducing the state debt significantly, Fuller signed legislation requiring compulsory personal liability motor vehicle insurance and authorizing the first state-sponsored cancer hospital in the United States, and he intervened personally with utility companies to keep electricity and telephone rates low for consumers. Fuller also was applauded for high-quality appointments to judgeships and important posts in his administration. In making such appointments he usually ignored the patronage recommendations of the Republican State Committee, which he regarded as a "corrupt outfit" whose members "should be fired bag and baggage and the premises fumigated."

Another keynote of Fuller's gubernatorial administration was a hard line on crime and punishment. In his first term penalties were increased for persons convicted of carrying concealed weapons, prompt trials were required for violent offenders, and nightclubs and roadhouses were tightly regulated. A believer in the "strict enforcement of the law of capital punishment for those who have taken human life," Fuller refused to commute the death sentences of three young World War I veterans convicted of killing a night watchman at a Boston-area carbarn in 1925 and, far more notably, of Nicola Sacco and Bartolomeo Vanzetti, Italian immigrants and militant anarchists who had been found guilty after a controversial trial of having murdered two men during a payroll robbery at a shoe factory in 1920.

After seven years of appeals and much agitation by the radical left, respectable opinion leaders backed the request of Sacco and Vanzetti for a review of the evidence, which was circumstantial, and of the trial, presided over by Judge Webster Thayer, whom they charged with bias against immigrants and political radicals. Acceding to this request in the spring of 1927, Fuller and his staff set aside much state business to conduct an extensive inquiry into the case before the condemned men were sent to the electric chair. The governor pored over transcripts, interviewed witnesses at his home and office, and even visited Vanzetti at the Charlestown Prison. He also appointed a blue-ribbon panel consisting of A. Lawrence Lowell, the president of Harvard University; Samuel Stratton, the president of the Massachusetts Institute of Technology; and Robert Grant, a retired probate judge, to study the evidence and the trial proceedings. In August 1927 both Fuller and his advisory committee concluded that the trial had been fair and just. The governor then heard pleas for mercy until an hour before the execution but ultimately refused to intervene. Subsequently, the Sacco-Vanzetti case became America's Dreyfus affair, and Fuller, Lowell, and Thayer were vilified by liberals and radicals at home and abroad as symbols of American provincialism and intolerance in the 1920s.

The case took its toll on Fuller and probably ended his promising political career. After receiving numerous threats prior to his decision in 1927, Fuller's home was placed under police guard for two years and then again for a time after Thayer's home was bombed in 1932. Though he was touted for the Republican national ticket in 1928, Fuller was dropped from consideration for vice president after party leaders expressed concern that his candidacy would be anathema to the burgeoning immigrant vote. At the 1932 convention his name was put in nomination for the vice presidency, but he received only fifty-seven votes (thirty-four from Mass.) and finished far behind incumbent Charles Curtis (634 votes). Fuller was also considered for but did not receive President Herbert Hoover's (1874–1964) appointment as ambassador to France in 1929, apparently because the French government felt unable to protect him adequately in a country that had experienced violent demonstrations following the execution of Sacco and Vanzetti. Even in Massachusetts Fuller abruptly withdrew from primary races for the U.S. Senate (1930) and for governor (1934). His last significant position in government came in 1933 when Secretary of the Interior Harold Ickes appointed him chairman of a federal board charged with supervising the distribution of Public Works Administration funds in Massachusetts.

Returning to his automobile business, Fuller divested himself of his Packard agencies and sold only Cadillacs and Oldsmobiles after 1949. He also devoted considerable time and much of his estimated $40-million fortune to philanthropy. Boston-area hospitals, universities, and especially Baptist and Catholic causes benefited from his largesse. In addition, Fuller and his wife were noted art collectors. Works by Thomas Gainsborough, Rembrandt, Joseph Mallord William Turner, and other masters adorned their Renaissance mansion in Boston's Back Bay, and many of them were eventually donated to the Museum of Fine Arts, where Fuller had served as a trustee. He died in Boston.

• Fuller's papers are in private hands. A collection of his speeches and addresses, 1925–1929, is in the Fingold Library in the Massachusetts State House in Boston. *Addresses and Messages to the General Court, Proclamations, Official Addresses, Correspondence and Statements of . . . Governor Alvan T. Fuller* (1928) is the published official record of Fuller's governorship. An important interview with Fuller is Alvan T. Fuller and Schuyler Patterson, "Why I Believe in Capital Punishment," *Success Magazine*, Dec. 1926, pp. 15–16, 94. Fuller's political career is discussed in the *New York Times*, 29 Jan. 1928; the Boston *Post*, 8 Dec. 1930; Michael E. Hennessy, *Four Decades of Massachusetts Politics, 1890–1935* (1935); and J. Joseph Huthmacher, *Massachusetts People and Politics, 1919–1933* (1959). See "Governor Fuller in Berlin," *Living Age*, Nov. 1930, p. 330; G. Louis Joughin and Edmund M. Morgan, *The Legacy of Sacco and Vanzetti* (1948); Francis Russell, *Tragedy in Dedham* (1962); David Felix, *Protest* (1965); and Roberta Strauss Feuerlicht, *Justice Crucified* (1977), concerning Fuller's role in the Sacco-Vanzetti case. Obituaries are in the *Boston Globe* and the *Boston Herald Traveler*, 1 May 1958.

RICHARD H. GENTILE

FULLER, Blind Boy (10 July 1907?–13 Feb. 1941), blues singer and guitarist, was born Fulton Allen in Wadesboro, North Carolina, the son of Calvin Allen and Mary Jane Walker. The exact date of his birth remains debatable because two different years are listed on official documents. Little is known of his early life except that he attended school through the fourth grade in Wadesboro and began learning to play guitar in his teens. After his mother's death in the mid-1920s, he moved with his father and the rest of his family to Rockingham, North Carolina; there he met Cora Mae Martin, whom he married around 1926. They married in Bennettsville, South Carolina, possibly for legal reasons: she was only fourteen, and he was either nineteen or seventeen (depending on his actual birthdate). It is believed that they raised one adopted child.

By this time Allen was developing eye problems and was diagnosed as having ulcers behind his eyes. In 1927 Allen and his wife moved to Winston-Salem, North Carolina. He worked in a coal yard for a short time, but his failing vision caused him to quit, and by 1928 he was totally blind. At this point he turned to music to make a living. He and Cora Mae settled in Durham, North Carolina, and by the early 1930s he was an established street musician. It was during the 1930s that he also picked up the name Blind Boy Fuller—possibly a street corruption of his real first name or, in some accounts, a name he was given after he started recording.

Although Fuller's repertoire and guitar technique derived mainly from phonograph records, he also learned from Gary Davis, a blind street singer and gifted guitarist who had come to Durham from Greenville, South Carolina. Fuller also kept company with washboard player George Washington, better known as Bull City Red, who doubled as Fuller's guide. In 1935 Fuller encountered James Baxter "J. B." Long, a scout for ARC records and manager of the Durham United Dollar Store. After writing to ARC in New York, Long used his family's 1935 summer vacation to drive Fuller, Davis, and Bull City Red to ARC's New York studio. The resulting sessions, presided over by race-record veteran Art Satherly, took place over four days, beginning 23 July. Fuller recorded a dozen issued sides, playing solo on some and accompanied by Davis and Red on others. The session produced a substantial hit, "Rag, Mama, Rag," a typical Piedmont ragtime dance blues.

Nine months later, in April 1936, Long again used his vacation time to record Fuller in New York. Apparently Long had a falling out with Davis, so Fuller recorded ten solo sides, including another classic Piedmont dance piece, "Truckin' My Blues Away." By this time his recordings had made him something of a celebrity, and other musicians, including blues guitarists Willie and Richard Trice, who lived outside Durham, sought him out. Fuller used his connections to the recording studio to act as a scout, supposedly charging a ten-dollar fee to musicians he helped record.

Willie Trice later told biographer Bruce Bastin that Fuller had been an ardent poker player, using a sighted person to tell him what cards he was holding. Hot-tempered and suspicious, Fuller always carried a pistol and would brandish it to discourage cheating. "People didn't know what to do when a blind man began waving a pistol in their faces," Trice told Bastin.

The year 1937 was by far Fuller's most productive recording year. He cut an astonishing forty-nine titles. His first session in February was a three-day affair, yielding fourteen sides. Reunited with Bull City Red, he also brought along a new protégé, Chapel Hill, North Carolina, truck driver Floyd "Dipper Boy" Council, who played guitar. The session produced more dance tunes, a fine version of the traditional Piedmont blues "Mamie," and a tune called "Boots and Shoes," a reprise of Amon Easton's hit "Meet Me in the Bottom."

Along with artistic success, 1937 also brought difficulties—first a contract squabble, then a criminal charge. The contract matter started after Fuller went to New York and recorded a dozen sides for Decca.

When Decca released two of the tunes, Long bluffed Decca into withdrawing the releases and issuing no further sides by implying that he had an exclusive recording contract with Fuller, when in fact he did not. Long and Fuller then came to terms on an exclusive lifetime contract.

The criminal charge stemmed from a shooting in which Fuller's wife was wounded in the leg. The shooting may have been an accident, but Cora Mae's uncle swore out a warrant, and Fuller was jailed. When his wife did not press charges, the case was dropped. Fuller later commemorated his experience in the song "Big House Bound."

Taking advantage of his new contract, Long set up two more ARC sessions in 1937, one in September and one in December. The sessions produced thirty sides. The December session paired Fuller with Sonny Terry, a harmonica player who had come to Durham from Georgia and who had worked the streets with Fuller as early as 1930.

An October 1938 session in Columbia, South Carolina, included Terry and Bull City Red and produced the expected dozen sides. The same group was in Memphis, Tennessee, on 12 July 1939 for a two-day session. Along with Fuller's dozen solo cuts, they formed a trio for an additional six religious sides, issued as performed by Brother George and His Sanctified Singers. In March 1940 another two-day session with Terry and Red yielded Fuller's bestseller, a two-sided hit, "Step It Up and Go," supposedly written by Long, and "Little Woman You're So Sweet," a tune influenced by traditional field hollers. Four of the dozen issued sides from this session were "Brother George" gospel tunes.

Although Fuller's health was beginning to decline, he traveled to Chicago in July 1940 for what would be his last session, accompanied by guitarist Brownie McGhee as well as Terry and Red.

The next month he underwent an operation related to kidney problems. He was in and out of the hospital several times in subsequent months and finally went home to die. He died in Durham of a bladder infection and blood poisoning.

By any measure, Blind Boy Fuller was one of the most popular and prolific blues artists of his time, recording 135 titles in a mere six years. A highly versatile guitarist, he was at ease with several styles—bottleneck, ragtime, dance tunes, and deep blues—and had a gift for reworking the hits of other artists. In this sense, he was a synthesizer of styles, parallel in many ways to Mississippi's Robert Johnson, his contemporary. Like Johnson, Fuller died young.

Much of Fuller's output was good-time house-party music, often with risqué double-entendre lyrics. But his more serious music, such as "Lost Lover Blues," "Mamie," or "Big House Bound," was as emotionally charged as any on record.

According to Richard Trice, quoted in Bastin's biography of Fuller, Fuller renounced the blues on his deathbed—an act also attributed to Robert Johnson. However, his influence and many of his songs lived on in the styles and repertoires of blues and country musicians who followed him, including John Jackson, John Cephas, and Merle Travis. In sum, Fuller was probably the Southeast's most important and influential blues artist.

• For additional details about Fuller's life see Bruce Bastin, *Red River Blues* (1986) and *Crying for the Carolines* (1971); Samuel Charters, *The Blues Makers* (1991); Paul Oliver, *Blues Off the Record: Thirty Years of Blues Commentary* (1984); Sheldon Harris, *Blues Who's Who: A Biographical Dictionary of Blues Singers* (1989); and Bill Phillips, "Piedmont Country Blues," *Southern Exposure* 2, no. 1 (n.d.): 56–62. For an interview with Long, see Kip Lornell, "J. B. Long," *Living Blues* 29 (Sept.–Oct. 1976): 13–22. Discographical information is given in Robert M. W. Dixon and John Godrich, *Blues and Gospel Records: 1902–1943* (1982), and Paul Oliver, ed., *The Blackwell Guide to Blues Records* (1989). For a sample of his recorded music, try *Blind Boy Fuller: Truckin' My Blues Away* (Yazoo 1060) and *Blind Boy Fuller: East Coast Piedmont Style* (Roots 'n' Blues, Columbia Legacy, CK 46777).

BARRY LEE PEARSON
BILL MCCULLOCH

FULLER, Charles Edward (25 Apr. 1887–18 Mar. 1968), radio evangelist, was born in Los Angeles, California, the son of Henry Fuller, a furniture store owner, and Helen Maria Day. When Fuller was a child his mother's asthma forced a move to the drier climate of Redlands, California, where the family ran a profitable orange grove. After high school Fuller attended Pomona College, where he majored in chemistry and captained the football team. Fuller graduated in 1910 and, in keeping with his father's plans for him, returned home to work on the farm. In 1911 he married his high school sweetheart, Grace Leone Payton. Two years later, after a disastrous frost, the young couple decided to leave farming; they moved to Placentia, California, where Fuller managed a packinghouse.

Fuller's parents were devout Christians, and Fuller became an active member of the Presbyterian church in Placentia. But in 1916 he underwent what he later saw as his true conversion experience. In July of that year he attended services led by revivalist Paul Rader; as Fuller informed his wife afterward, "There has come a complete change into my life. . . . I feel now that I want to serve God if He can use me instead of making the goal of my life the making of money" (D. Fuller, pp. 34–35). In 1919 Fuller resigned his packinghouse position in order to train for the ministry at the Bible Institute of Los Angeles (BIOLA). There he was taught by such conservative stalwarts as Reuben Torrey, who inculcated Fuller with a fundamentalist theology, including emphases on inerrancy and dispensational premillennialism, and a burning desire to evangelize.

After graduation in 1921 Fuller became president of the Orange County Christian Endeavor. He also continued to teach a Sunday-morning Bible class at Placentia Presbyterian Church, a class that was more popular than the workship service itself. The class's success, combined with the fundamentalist theology

Fuller was aggressively promoting, created serious tensions in the church, and in 1924 Placentia Presbyterian withdrew its sponsorship. In response, Fuller organized his Bible class into an independent, fundamentalist church. Unsurprisingly, Fuller was chosen as minister; he received ordination through the Baptist Bible Union, a fundamentalist association. Under his leadership Calvary Church emphasized soul winning and eschatology and grew from fifty to 370 members.

Pastoring a church could not satisfy Fuller's evangelistic fervor. During these years he also held revival meetings throughout the West. But then he discovered his true medium: radio. He had preached on BIOLA's radio station in the mid-1920s, but it was not until 1929, when listeners responded enthusiastically to a sermon he delivered over an Indianapolis station, that he grasped radio's potential. In 1930 he began broadcasting Calvary Church services over a Long Beach station; this arrangement lasted until 1933, when congregational unhappiness over his preoccupation with radio work forced him to resign. It seemed like a bad time for him to leave the church, as the depression had wiped out the Fullers' financial reserves. Nevertheless, in 1933 he formed the Gospel Broadcasting Association, an enterprise totally dependent on listeners' contributions. After experimenting with various formats, in 1934 he began the show that would catapult him to national prominence: the Old Fashioned Revival Hour (OFRH). In three years OFRH was broadcasting coast to coast over thirty stations of the Mutual Network. By 1939 the show was on all 152 Mutual stations; by 1942 OFRH was broadcast on 456 stations, including many not affiliated with Mutual. It was probably the most popular radio program in the United States.

Certainly some of the success was due to Fuller's promotional efforts: when he was not in front of the microphone, Fuller was appearing at revival meetings all over the United States, building his radio audience. More important, his show conveyed the feel of a down-home, Sunday evening church service: a quartet sang familiar gospel songs; Grace Fuller, whom her husband referred to on the air as "Honey," read a few testimonials from viewers; and Fuller, unpretentious and sincere, delivered a message that focused on God's love, human sinfulness, and the need for personal conversion. As Fuller explained the show: "Each Sunday . . . we endeavor by God's grace to beseech men and women to be reconciled to God in Christ Jesus, never closing a broadcast but what we give every one an opportunity to accept Christ as their personal Savior— this is truly an old-fashioned Revival Hour" (D. Fuller, p. 122).

OFRH reached its peak during World War II, with an estimated audience of twenty million. But in 1944 the Mutual network, following the lead of other networks, and responding to antifundamentalist pressure, eliminated all paid religious broadcasts. Fuller reacted by putting together a chain of independent stations that would broadcast OFRH. Fortunately for Fuller, in 1949 the American Broadcasting network agreed to air the show. But in the 1950s radio began to lose out to television, a medium Fuller did not master, so Fuller's audience began to shrink. In 1958 ABC cut OFRH to thirty minutes and in 1963 dropped it. Even though he was in his seventies, Fuller continued to broadcast messages on independent stations.

Fuller's evangelistic efforts were not limited to radio preaching. In the 1940s Fuller had begun plans to establish a school that would train ministers and missionaries as well as serve as a center of conservative Protestant scholarship; his goal, he often told his son, was to create "a Cal Tech of the evangelical world" (D. Fuller, p. 211). Toward that end, in 1947 he founded Fuller Theological Seminary, in Pasadena, California. Within a few years a number of prominent scholars had joined the faculty. Fuller's institution soon became the largest interdenominational evangelical seminary in the world, with schools of psychology and missions added in the 1960s. But there were problems. Many on the faculty consciously sought to go beyond fundamentalism toward a more open-minded, intellectually defensible form of the Christian faith. As a result, the seminary, and Fuller himself, became the target of attacks by fundamentalists who in the past had warmly supported Fuller's evangelistic efforts. Fuller winced at the criticism and the withdrawal of support for the OFRH but continued to support the seminary, one reason being that his only child, Dan, who was appointed dean in 1962, was a major supporter of "progressive" faculty members.

Fuller died in Pasadena. He should be remembered as a pioneer in broadcast evangelism, probably the greatest radio preacher of his time, and as the founder of an influential evangelical seminary.

• Some of Charles Fuller's papers and sermons are in the archives of Fuller Theological Seminary, Pasadena, Calif. The most important among secondary sources is the well-researched biography written by Fuller's son, Daniel Fuller, *The Story of Charles E. Fuller: Give the Winds a Mighty Voice* (1972). Despite the author's obvious affection and admiration for his father, this work is a solid treatment of Charles Fuller's life. A less helpful work, written two decades before Fuller's death, is Wilbur M. Smith, *A Voice for God: The Life of Charles E. Fuller, Originator of the Old-Fashioned Revival Hour* (1949). Ben Armstrong, *The Electric Church* (1979), locates Fuller and the Old-Fashioned Revival Hour in the history of radio evangelism, which Armstrong uncritically celebrates. Also see Barry Siedell, *Gospel Radio* (1971). Finally, for an excellent study of Fuller and his seminary and the school's place in American Protestantism, see George Marsden, *Reforming Fundamentalism: Fuller Seminary and the New Evangelicalism* (1987).

WILLIAM VANCE TROLLINGER, JR.

FULLER, George (17 Jan. 1822–21 Mar. 1884), artist, was born in Deerfield, Massachusetts, the son of Aaron Fuller, a farmer, and Fanny Negus. He attended Deerfield Academy and had his first artistic training in 1841 when he embarked on a tour with his half-brother Augustus, an itinerant portrait painter. In 1842 he studied drawing in Albany, New York, with the sculptor Henry Kirke Brown, and later that year moved to Boston, where he joined the Boston Artists' Association, continued to work on his draftsmanship, and painted portraits both in the city and on the road. During his years in Boston, he admired the art of Washington Allston, whose romantic, tonally complex works remained an inspiration throughout Fuller's life. In 1847, hoping to improve his training and professional prospects, Fuller moved to New York City. Enrolling in the drawing curriculum at the National Academy of Design, he again sought to make a living through portraits, even though he longed to branch out into landscape or genre painting. In 1857, he was elected an associate member of the National Academy of Design.

In the winter of 1857–1858, Fuller journeyed with his painter friend Edwin Billings to Montgomery, Alabama, where he hoped to secure lucrative commissions for portraits of wealthy townspeople and planters. Although he had gone to the South twice before, to Augusta, Georgia, in 1849 and Mobile, Alabama, in 1856, it was only during this third visit that Fuller developed an interest in slave life. In and around Montgomery, he made dozens of precisely observed sketches showing blacks, mostly women and children, laboring outside or resting in their shanties. Fuller hoped that his picturesque images of slaves, which he called "real prizes in an artistic way," would mark the start of a new direction in his art.

Fuller's painting career, however, was interrupted when he was obliged to take over the management of the family farm after the death of his father in 1859. Before moving back there, he spent the first six months of 1860 in Europe, where he engrossed himself in the study of modern French painters of the Barbizon school in addition to the old masters. In 1861 he married Agnes Gordon Higginson, with whom he had five children, and for some fifteen years cultivated tobacco and cranberries on the Deerfield farm. Throughout this time, he continued to paint but exhibited very little. An impending financial crisis brought Fuller out of seclusion in 1876 to exhibit in Boston at Doll and Richards' Gallery, in the hopes of raising some cash to rescue the farm from bankruptcy. The paintings he displayed there, rendered in a completely new style developed during the preceding decade, brought him immediate acclaim.

After 1876, admiration for Fuller, expressed in glowing reviews and rising prices, increased every year. Until his sudden illness and death in Brookline, he followed a pattern of spending winters in his Boston studio and summers on the Deerfield farm. He exhibited regularly at the Boston Art Club and the St. Botolph Club, and showed several important paintings in New York at the National Academy of Design and the newly formed Society of American Artists. This new organization, composed chiefly of young, cosmopolitan artists in revolt against the authority and conservatism of the National Academy of Design, unanimously elected Fuller to membership in 1880. Among his most ardent supporters were the novelist William

Dean Howells and the prominent critic Mariana Griswold van Rensselaer.

No longer tight and linear, Fuller's late paintings were broadly brushed and suffused with atmosphere that cast a veil of muted tone over his images, softening outlines, blurring details, and creating a dreamy, moody effect. The chief stimulus to Fuller's transformation was French Barbizon painting, especially the broadly rendered, emotionally charged landscapes of Camille Corot and the works of Jean-François Millet, who celebrated the enduring nobility and simplicity of peasant life. Considered supremely poetic, Barbizon painters were greatly admired in late nineteenth-century America, nowhere more than in Boston. Fuller's adaptation of this mode effectively positioned him in the mainstream of modern, poetic painting, which rejected the scrupulous detail and tight finish of midcentury Hudson River school landscapes in favor of broader effects that signified a subjective response to nature. Although Fuller continued to produce portraits, he became especially well known for several other subjects: delicate, pensive young female figures such as the 1881 *Winifred Dysart* in the Worcester Art Museum; poetically idealized depictions of rural blacks, notably *The Quadroon* of 1880 in the Metropolitan Museum of Art; and dark scenes featuring mysterious events or characters and vaguely hinting of old New England witchcraft, such as *And She Was a Witch* (1877–1883) in the Metropolitan Museum of Art, and *The Gatherer of Simples* (1878–1883), in the Art Institute of Chicago.

Considered at the time of his death to be one of America's foremost painters, Fuller achieved his late success because his works represented a form of idealism thought to be increasingly threatened by the materialism and commercialism of modern America. Critics invariably described him as an idealist, a poet, and a dreamer, who painted spiritual realities rather than material facts. As Fuller himself said, "The main thing is to get ourselves above our matter. . . . The great thing is to have an idea—to eliminate and clear away the obstructions that surround it. It is more what is left out than what is left in." Fuller was also associated with the spirit of New England before the Civil War, and particularly with the Romantic writer Nathaniel Hawthorne. Mariana van Rensselaer in *Six Portraits* (1890) compared Fuller's art to Hawthorne's prose, sensing the same uncanny, witch-like atmosphere in both, and describing Fuller's art as "a painter's version of the vague, transcendental New England poesy that is fast dying out of this generation." While his reputation was strong in New York, Fuller found his most devoted audience in Boston, where, amidst anxieties brought on by a perceived cultural decline and the strains of modernization, his rise to fame symbolized the continuing vitality of the city and region identified with the era of Hawthorne and Ralph Waldo Emerson. His subjects answered a need for nostalgic evocations of a Romantic past, a need expressed on a broader scale by the contemporaneous colonial revival movement. In the art world of the time, he ranked

with his contemporary George Inness and younger peers such as Thomas Wilmer Dewing and Dwight Tryon as a creator of the tonalist style, an important mode of poetic pictorial expression in late nineteenth-century America.

• Fuller's papers are in the Memorial Library, Deerfield, Massachusetts. The most important nineteenth-century source is Frank D. Millet, ed., *George Fuller: Life and Works* (1890), which includes a detailed biography by William Dean Howells. Several articles by Sarah Burns address various aspects of Fuller's art: "A Study of the Life and Poetic Vision of George Fuller," *American Art Journal* 13 (Fall 1981): 11–37; "Images of Slavery: George Fuller's Depictions of the Antebellum South," *American Art Journal* 15 (Summer 1983): 35–60; "George Fuller: 'The Hawthorne of Our Art,'" *Winterthur Portfolio* 18 (Summer/Fall 1983): 125–45; and "Black, Quadroon, Gypsy: Women in the Art of George Fuller," *Massachusetts Review* 26 (Summer/Fall 1985): 405–24.

SARAH BURNS

FULLER, George Warren (21 Dec. 1868–15 June 1934), sanitary engineer, was born in Franklin, Massachusetts, the son of George Newell Fuller and Harriet Craig, farmers. At age sixteen he passed the entrance examination for the Massachusetts Institute of Technology, where he graduated at the head of his class in 1890 with a degree in chemistry. While at MIT he came under the influence of William T. Sedgwick, Ellen Swallow Richards, and Hiram F. Mills, leaders in the fields of public health and water pollution control. After graduation he spent a year at the Hygienic Institute of the University of Berlin and worked in the office of C. Piefke, engineer of the Berlin waterworks.

When Fuller returned to the United States, he began to specialize in engineering. He was best known for his accomplishments in sanitary engineering but was in demand as a consultant in related areas. From 1890 to 1895 he was employed by the Massachusetts State Board of Health. Fuller devoted much of his time to the immensely significant water and sewage investigations conducted at the Lawrence Experiment Station, where he extended the work of engineer and chemist Allen Hazen. The Lawrence Experiment Station was the leading research laboratory in the country on water purification and sewage treatment. During this period Fuller also lectured on biology and bacteriology at MIT.

In 1895 Fuller traveled with a team of engineers to Louisville, Kentucky, to conduct extensive inquiries into the city's water purification problem. The project lasted until 1897. His *Report on the Investigations into the Purification of the Ohio River Water at Louisville, Kentucky* (1898) is a classic. It provided a model for future water purification systems. This work was largely instrumental in introducing the rapid-sand—or American—filter and emphasized the importance of preparing river water by coagulation and settling before filtering. While more conservative engineers had reservations about this process, Fuller was instrumental in defining the place of mechanical filtration in water purification for the first time. The investigation of clay-bearing Ohio River water established the precedent for using mechanical filters to purify municipal water supplies.

At the end of the Louisville project, Fuller began a similar study in Cincinnati, Ohio. In 1899 he established an independent engineering practice in New York City. In 1901 he joined forces with the celebrated sanitary engineer Rudolph Hering, a professional relationship that lasted until 1911. The first major municipal rapid-sand plant was established at Little Falls, New Jersey, in 1902 to treat Passaic River water. Fuller designed this precedent-setting filtration plant for the East Jersey Water Company. He received the Rowland Prize of the American Society of Civil Engineers for "The Filtration Works of the East Jersey Water Company," published in the society's *Transactions* in 1903.

Fuller advised more than 150 cities and commissions on water supply and sewerage issues. He also served as an expert witness on many court cases and was sought out for advice in several rate cases. Some of his engineering projects included filtration plant planning (with Hazen) for Baltimore in 1910, a series of comprehensive reports on sewerage for the New York Metropolitan Sewage Commission from 1910 to 1914, and development of a plan for treating raw sewage discharged into the Harlem and East rivers in New York City.

Fuller was deeply involved in the development of plans for a modern sewerage treatment facility in Chicago, and in 1924–1925 he served as the chair of the Engineering Board of Review of the Sanitary District of Chicago on the Lake Lowering Controversy and Program of Remedial Measures. He worked with several other experts on the value of installing large new works for disposing sanitary district sewage to decrease the quantity of water diverted from Lake Michigan into the Mississippi Valley, which was used for sewage disposal. During World War I he served on a national committee that dealt with engineering, planning, and sanitation at army camps, which resulted in remarkably low rates of typhoid fever. He also served as an adviser to the Council of National Defense.

After the war Fuller kept abreast of national and international developments in sanitary engineering; he traveled to Europe on a regular basis to visit water and sewer plants and to meet with other experts. For many years he urged the development of an international standard of water and sewage analysis to provide a common technical language for practitioners. Following the war he attended the Franco-American Engineering Congress held in Paris in 1918 to consider reconstruction and economic problems in France.

Early in the Great Depression Fuller returned from a trip to England convinced that the United States should follow the British example and develop a program of nationally subsidized public works projects. He disagreed with the approach of the Herbert Hoover administration and became a Roosevelt Democrat. The public programs of FDR's New Deal administration were more in line with his own thinking about the promotion of public works projects.

Fuller also played a central role in many professional organizations. He served as president of the American Water Works Association (AWWA) at a time when its constitution and bylaws were being revised. He is credited with the initiative that led to the publication of *Water Works Practice: A Manual Issued by the American Water Works Association* (1925). At times he was president of the American Public Health Association (APHA); vice president, chair of the Committee on Publications, and chair of the Special Committee on Technical Expansion of the American Society of Civil Engineers (ASCE); council member of the American Institute of Consulting Engineers; and chair of the Engineering Foundation. At the time of his death he served on the coordination committees of the four major engineering societies.

Active in the field of engineering education, aside from his courses at MIT, Fuller was on the advisory committee of New York University's Council for the School of Engineering and assisted in developing a course on sanitary engineering. He frequently lectured at colleges throughout the country, including an annual series on sewage disposal at Yale University. He also published *Sewage Disposal* in 1912 and *Solving Sewage Problems* (with James McClintock) in 1926.

In 1937 the board of directors of the AWWA established the George Warren Fuller Award to recognize advancements in waterworks practices by members of the association. Fuller was among the first five engineers elected in 1970 to AWWA's Water Utility Hall of Fame.

Outside of his profession, Fuller had a rich social life. He was associated with the arts and theater, especially as an "angel" for Broadway shows such as *No No Nanette*. He was a silent partner in a Wall Street brokerage firm and a not particularly successful investor in real estate ventures.

Fuller was married four times. In 1888 he married his first wife, Lucy Hunter, with whom he had a son; it is not known how the marriage ended. In 1899 he married Caroline Goodloe, with whom he had a second son, but she died in 1907. In 1913 he married Charlotte Bell Todd, with whom he also had a son; they were divorced in 1918. He married Eleanor Todd Burt that same year and later adopted her three sons. Fuller died at his residence on Fifth Avenue in New York City.

According to the *American Journal of Public Health*, Fuller "probably [had] more to do with the technical development and the public stimulation in the installation of municipal sanitary devices than almost any man in this country." George Warren Fuller was part of an elite group of municipal engineers who designed and implemented much of the sanitation infrastructure of American cities in the late nineteenth and early twentieth centuries.

• Biographical material on Fuller is rather limited. Abel Wolman has provided some valuable recollections, however, in

George Warren Fuller: A Reminiscence (1976) and "George Warren Fuller," APWA Reporter 51 (Oct. 1984): 14–15. See also American Public Works Association, History of Public Works in the United States (1976). Some additional biographical information on Fuller is in "Who's Who in Municipal Sanitation," Municipal Sanitation 1 (Jan. 1930): 13; "The George Warren Fuller Award," Journal of the American Water Works Association (Mar. 1949): 284–88; James C. Harding, "Personal Reminiscences of George Warren Fuller," Journal of the American Water Works Association 53 (Dec. 1961): 1523–27; C. E. A. Winslow, "There Were Giants in These Days," American Journal of Public Health 43 (June 1953): 15–19; and "George W. Fuller," Engineering News-Record 112 (21 June 1934): 816. Obituaries are in the New York Times, 16 and 19 June 1934.

MARTIN V. MELOSI

FULLER, Henry Blake (9 Jan. 1857–28 July 1929), writer, was born in Chicago, Illinois, the son of George Wood Fuller, a railroad executive and banker, and Mary Josephine Sanford. The family were numbered among the "old settlers" of Chicago and were substantial citizens of the city. Educated in the public schools of Chicago and the Allison Classical Academy, Oconomowoc, Wisconsin, Fuller early showed no desire for a business career. Instead he was interested in the arts, especially literature and architecture. In 1879 he made the first of many pilgrimages to Europe. Out of his Italian journeys came his first books, The Chevalier of Pensieri-Vani (1890) and The Chatelaine of La Trinité (1892), thinly veiled comparisons between the culture and beauty of Italy and the rawness and ugliness of Chicago, themes that were to dominate his entire artistic life.

In 1885 Fuller wrote an important essay, "Howells or James?," in which he stated the choice that many American writers felt at the time. Should a writer resist the appeal of Europe, return to the United States, and write about American characters and subjects as William Dean Howells had done; or should one enjoy European culture as an expatriate, the choice made by Henry James (1843–1916)? Fuller's career was to swing between these two poles.

The Cliff-Dwellers (1893) was Fuller's first assault on the money-based society of Chicago, where the artist had no place. Fuller's sarcastic advice to the young men of the city was to shun the arts and "go in for mining or dredging, or build bridges, or put up railway sheds." The great World's Columbian Exposition, designed to show Chicago both as a culturally and materially progressive city, had, in Fuller's eyes, done little to improve its physical or spiritual life.

Fuller followed The Cliff-Dwellers with an even stronger attack, With the Procession (1895). Whereas the former book had been a harsh assault, heated by Fuller's anger and somewhat blunted by hasty composition, the latter was just as sweeping but more artistically conceived. Fuller himself sympathized with many of his characters, who were based on members of his own family. Class competition through social climbing is the controlling idea of the novel. Fuller presents the Marshall family as typical of Chicago.

The parents belong to the "old settlers," conservative, moral, hard working, and unimaginative. Jane, their eldest daughter, determines to bring her parents up to date. Her brother, Truesdale, who finds Chicago dull and drab, abandons his studies at Yale to seek culture and adventure in Europe. A crisis occurs when the young people urge their parents to move to a new house in a fashionable part of town. The children succeed, and as the novel closes the parents move to a chilly, inhospitable, unfinished, and mostly unfurnished home. Reviewing With the Procession, Howells wrote, "we have no one to compare with him [Fuller] in the East, in scale and quality of work."

In The Cliff-Dwellers and With the Procession, Fuller's career reached a peak that he would not again attain. His themes would remain much the same, but the characters would not be as sympathetically drawn or as realistically portrayed. From the Other Side (1898), The Last Refuge (1900), and Gardens of This World (1929) added little to his reputation. Bertram Cope's Year (1919) may well be the first American novel to deal openly with homosexual material. Of his later works, On the Stairs (1918), an autobiographical novel that is excellently plotted and more sympathetically presented, is probably the best.

From the very beginning, Fuller had been drawn to satire. The Cliff-Dwellers and With the Procession contain many splendid satirical passages. Among his finest satires are the novelettes in Under the Skylights (1901), in which Hamlin Garland, Lorado Taft, Mrs. Potter Palmer (Bertha Honoré Palmer), and Henry George (1839–1897) are used to illustrate Fuller's own ideas about the place of art in America. As Fuller aged, his predictions of the future of the American artist and art in America steadily became more gloomy. The humor of these pieces, however, saves them from bitterness.

For many years Fuller was an almost constant companion of Hamlin Garland. Fuller's wit, personal charm, and passion for art are apparent in many of the forty-odd volumes of Garland's diary and in Garland's autobiographical books. Fuller was also a close friend of Harriet Monroe, whom he assisted in editing Poetry: A Magazine of Verse. Throughout much of his creative life, he associated with such members of the Little Room as Anna Morgan, Ralph Clarkson, Bessie Potter, Charles Francis Browne, Ralph Fletcher Seymour, Lorado Taft, and Hamlin Garland. The Little Room was a loosely organized and informal gathering of Chicago artists founded around 1893. Its name derived from a story by Madeline Yale Wynne about a room that intermittently appeared and disappeared. The club met on Friday afternoons in Bessie Potter's studio. Although Fuller was never an official member, rarely did the group meet without him. Fuller was well liked by the group, most of whom referred to him as "Henry B." Although he enjoyed the company of his friends and often sought them out, Fuller was essentially a lonely, diffident, self-effacing figure. Almost no one even knew where he lived. In artistic matters he was a perfectionist; he demanded a high standard of achievement not only for himself, but for his associates.

During the last years of his life, Fuller resolved the dilemma that had inspired most of his work. His final journey to Europe in 1924 convinced him that he belonged in the United States. As he said, he "crossed over" for good and thus came to terms with Chicago. Shortly before Fuller's death, when Hamlin Garland predicted that Fuller would rank next to Howells, Fuller replied that he would "fall in somewhere behind Howells, and be glad to." Theodore Dreiser placed him with Stephen Crane and credited Fuller with leading the movement of realism and naturalism in American literature. Fuller's reputation has not continued to be as high as Dreiser thought it would, but Fuller, for his realism, his satire, and his literary craftsmanship, still retains a respectable position in American letters. Fuller died in Chicago.

• The largest single repository of Fuller's papers is in the Henry B. Fuller Collection of the Newberry Library, Chicago. Other manuscript material may be found in the library of the University of Southern California; the Henry E. Huntington Library, San Marino, Calif.; the Houghton Library of Harvard University; and the Chicago Historical Society library. Bibliographies of Fuller's work may be found in Bradford Fuller Swan, *A Bibliography of Henry Blake Fuller* (1930), and Jacob Blanck, ed., *Bibliography of American Literature* (1959). The First effort at a Fuller critical biography is Constance M. Griffin, *Henry Blake Fuller: A Critical Biography* (1939). A modern assessment of Fuller's life and work appears in John Pilkington, *Henry Blake Fuller* (1970). Other evaluations of Fuller's life and work appear in Anna Morgan, ed., *Tributes to Henry B.* (1929); Bernard Duffey, *The Chicago Renaissance in American Literature* (1956); Blanche Housman Gelfant, *The American City Novel* (1954); Donald M. Murray, "Henry B. Fuller, Friend of Howells," *South Atlantic Quarterly* 52 (1953): 431–44; and Victor Schultz, "Henry Blake Fuller: Civilized Chicagoan," *Bookman* 70 (Sept. 1929): 34–38.

JOHN PILKINGTON

FULLER, Hoyt William (10 Sept. 1927–11 May 1981), editor and literary critic, was born in Atlanta, Georgia, the son of Thomas Fuller and Lillie Beatrice Ellafair Thomas. A member of the African-American middle class, Fuller was raised in Detroit, Michigan, and came of age against the backdrop of the violent race riots in that city in 1943.

Fuller attended Wayne State University in Detroit, where he received his B.A. in 1950. As a student, he was deeply influenced by Fred Hart Williams, a historian who specialized in the experiences of blacks in the Michigan-Ontario area and who founded what is now known as the Hackley Memorial Collection of Black Arts at the Detroit Public Library. Williams introduced Fuller to regional black history and to African history, beginning Fuller's deep and abiding commitment to African affairs.

Fuller worked as a reporter for the *Detroit Tribune* from 1949 to 1951 and as feature editor for the *Michigan Chronicle* from 1951 to 1954. In 1954 he became associate editor of *Ebony* magazine, a position he held until 1957. In that year he left the United States, choosing—like an earlier generation of black writers and intellectuals—voluntary exile in Europe. As he later commented in *Journey to Africa* (1971): "I had quit *Ebony* magazine, for the magazine did not seem to be moving in any direction that it seemed important for me to go. . . . I had left the United States in 1957 because, quite literally, I could not live there. That was the year of Little Rock." For the next three years, Fuller lived on the Spanish island of Mallorca, supporting himself by working as the West African correspondent for the Amsterdam *Haagse Post*. During that time he traveled to North Africa and West Africa and spent three months in Guinea shortly after Sékou Touré proclaimed its independence in 1958. His experiences in Africa became the basis of *Journey to Africa*. In 1960 he returned to the United States, where he worked as assistant editor at *Collier's Encyclopedia* before joining *Negro Digest* as managing editor in 1961.

Created in 1942 by Chicago-based publisher John H. Johnson, *Negro Digest* was initially closely modeled after *Reader's Digest*, but instead of focusing primarily on white America it reprinted generally upbeat articles about African-American life. The original *Negro Digest* ceased publication in 1951; Fuller's appointment represented an attempt to resurrect the magazine after a ten-year hiatus. When he assumed its helm, he brought to his task a sensibility shaped and nurtured by years of experience as a journalist and a passionate commitment to the cause of black freedom in the United States. During the next fifteen years, he turned *Negro Digest* into the most influential journal of its kind in the country.

Initially, the revived *Negro Digest* continued the practices and policies of its predecessor, reprinting articles from other magazines and journals and expressing a generally optimistic outlook in its editorial column. Beginning in August 1962, however, when Fuller assumed sole authorship of the editorial column, he charted a course that steered *Negro Digest* from the ethos of the civil rights movement through the black power/black arts movement into its Pan-Africanist position as *Black World* magazine (1970–1976). In a broad sense, the shifts and turns of Fuller's ideological perspective corresponded to shifts in the mood and outlook of black activists in the United States, which Fuller helped to shape by his uncompromising editorial positions. Beginning with his June 1964 essay "Ivory Towerist vs. Activist: The Role of the Negro Writer in an Era of Struggle" Fuller insisted that there was an inextricable connection between politics and literature and that the black writer had a critical role to play in shaping the social and political consciousness of the black community. By the mid-1960s he was directing his verbal attacks at two targets: white literary critics and anthologists, such as David Littlejohn, whom he saw as cultural interlopers lacking the requisite understanding to interpret black literature, and African-American writers—most notably Ralph Ellison—who emphasized craft and technique over political commitment.

After another trip to the African continent on a John Hay Whitney Opportunity Fellowship in 1965–1966, Fuller became even more outspoken in his views. He spurred on the debate about the "black aesthetic," an attempt to define the fundamental characteristics of African-American cultural expression, establishing himself as one of the key spokesmen for the black arts movement. By the late 1960s *Negro Digest* had become the national forum for established and emerging black writers and intellectuals, the key arena in which many of the debates about black literature, culture, and politics occurred. LeRoi Jones/Amiri Baraka, Larry Neal, Carolyn Gerald, Sonia Sanchez, Addison Gayle, Jr., Harold Cruse, Mari Evans, Gwendolyn Brooks, and Ishmael Reed were among the writers who appeared in its pages.

Fuller's role as an editor was complemented by his organizational efforts in other arenas. Although he later became sharply critical of the organization, he was actively involved in the American Society for African Culture and participated in the first World Festival of Negro Arts in Dakar, Senegal, in 1966. In 1967 he was a founding member of the influential Organization of Black American Culture in Chicago, where he conducted a weekly writer's workshop. He taught African-American literature at Northwestern University in 1969–1970, at Indiana University in 1970–1971, and at Wayne State University in 1974. After he moved to Atlanta in 1976, he taught at Emory University and traveled back and forth to Ithaca, New York, to teach in the Africana Studies Program at Cornell University. A tireless speaker, Fuller was a frequent participant in the black writers' conferences and gatherings that flourished, nationally and internationally, from the late 1960s through the mid-1970s. In 1977 he served as the North American vice chair of the second World Black and African Festival of Arts and Culture in Lagos, Nigeria.

In April 1976 John Johnson ceased publication of *Black World*, a decision that signaled a radical shift in the cultural, economic, and political climate within which the magazine had flourished. In a post–civil rights, post–black power era, many of the issues with which Fuller and *Black World* had been identified seemed out of step with the mood of the times. Fuller returned to his native Atlanta where, with a number of supporters, he launched a new journal, *First World*, which he edited until his sudden death in Atlanta by heart attack. At the time of his death he was working on a novel, "An Hour of Breath," and two literary histories, "History and Analysis of the Black Arts Movement" and "The New Black Renaissance." He never married.

Hoyt Fuller's significance rests primarily in the central role that he played as an editor during a historical moment when the relationships between blacks and whites in the United States were being sharply contested and actively renegotiated. Through the pages of *Negro Digest*, *Black World*, and *First World*, his influential essays and editorials, and his public statements, Fuller helped to shape the context in which many of these cultural and political issues were raised and debated.

• The Hoyt W. Fuller Papers are in the Atlanta University Library. For an account of Fuller's influence, see Carole A. Parks, ed., *Nommo: A Literary Legacy of Black Chicago, 1967–1987* (1987), which includes essays and tributes by Pamela Cash-Menzies, Robert L. Harris, Mari Evans, George E. Kent, Gwendolyn Brooks, Kalamu ya Salaam, Addison Gayle, Jr., Houston A. Baker, Jr., Eugenia Collier, Richard A. Long, and Carole A. Parks. An obituary appears in the *New York Times*, 13 May 1981.

JAMES A. MILLER

FULLER, Jesse (12 Mar. 1896–29 Jan. 1976), songster and one-man band, was born in Jonesboro, Georgia, near Atlanta. Raised by a succession of foster families, he never knew his father and barely knew his mother. "My mother used to give me away to different people and they were so darn mean to me I used to run away," Fuller told interviewer Richard Noblett many years later. Fuller showed early aptitude for making musical instruments, constructing a mouth bow at age seven or eight. He was eight and still being cared for by a foster family when his mother died. He dropped out of third grade and spent the next year or two working various jobs, including tending cattle outside Atlanta and carrying water at a grading camp. At age ten he ran away from foster care for good, staying briefly with his sister and her husband in the Atlanta area, where he learned to play banjo and harmonica. Fuller then spent the next ten years moving from job to job, mostly in northern Georgia.

In his early teens, Fuller heard guitarists around the town of McDonough and was inspired to make a guitar. Later, around the age of eighteen, he was taught to play guitar by Debbie Fletcher, a woman who lived in Stockbridge. He studied with her until her husband put an end to the lessons. Having absorbed local musical traditions from the house-party circuit and from traveling shows, as well as from his teacher, Fuller began to play square dances, earning twenty cents a set. In 1916 he married Curley Mae (maiden name unknown), but the couple soon separated.

While working for a junk dealer during World War I, Fuller was arrested and accused of receiving stolen goods, but he supposedly escaped from jail. Around 1918 he moved to Cincinnati, where he worked for a streetcar company. Still footloose, Fuller joined the Hagenbeck Wallace Circus, traveling with it for six to eight months as a tent stretcher and roustabout. In Big Rapids, Michigan, he played music for a group of soldiers and, by his own account, earned a substantial sum of money. From there he hoboed around the country, supporting himself by playing in stores or on streets and taking odd jobs. In the early 1920s he slowly made his way to California, where he lived for the rest of his life.

In Los Angeles around 1923 Fuller carved wooden snakes and sold them on the streets; he later shined shoes across from United Artists Studios. There he met various film personalities, including actor Douglas Fairbanks and director Raoul Walsh, who helped him set up a hot dog stand on the studio lot and get work as a film extra. In 1927 Fuller also tried to reconcile with Curley Mae, but shortly after they moved to Bakersfield, California, around 1928, the marriage ended for good. She later committed suicide.

In the early 1930s Fuller worked as a yard hand with the Southern Pacific Railroad. Using his railroad pass—good for "self and wife"—he traveled to Atlanta in search of a bride, and in 1935 he married Gertrude Johnson, a much younger woman who had known his sister.

By 1938 Fuller and his wife were living in Oakland. As the country mobilized for war, Fuller left the railroad for more lucrative work as a shipyard welder, earning enough to buy a house for his family. He and Gertrude eventually had three daughters. Following the war, Fuller resumed work as a laborer, playing his twelve-string guitar at parties or clubs to earn extra money.

In 1944 Fuller met fellow songster and twelve-string guitar player Leadbelly. They played together several times, doubtless inspiring Fuller to become a more active performer, but it wasn't until 1951 that he dreamed up the one-man-band format that became his trademark. He put together an ensemble that, at various times, included amplified twelve-string guitar, harmonica, kazoo, vocal microphone, foot cymbal, washboard, and an instrument of his own invention: a double bass that was played with a foot pedal. His wife referred to the creation as a "foot diller," a term later dignified to "fotdella."

Playing as a one-man band, Fuller worked local clubs and made several television appearances in the early 1950s. In 1954 he recorded for World Song, the label's only release. The record included his "San Francisco Bay Blues," which would go on to become one of the anthems of the folk revival in the 1960s. Through the 1950s into the 1960s Fuller recorded several more times in the San Francisco area and also picked up bookings at festivals and clubs, working mainly jazz venues in the 1950s and folk clubs in the 1960s. He toured England and Europe in 1960–1961 and helped spark a fleeting interest in American skiffle—a term for music played by small street ensembles employing washboards, jugs, or other unorthodox instruments. Admired and promoted by such folk revival stars as Jack Elliott and Bob Dylan, he did well on the folk circuit in the 1960s. He recorded for Folk-Lyric, Prestige, and Fontana; worked top folk clubs like Gerdes Folk City in New York; and appeared at Newport and other major festivals. In 1968 Fuller appeared in a short film, *Jesse "Lone Cat" Fuller*, and also was heard on the soundtrack of the major motion picture *The Great White Hope* (1970).

Despite health problems in the early 1970s, Fuller continued to perform, although less frequently, finding yet another comfortable venue: blues festivals. In 1976 he entered Dowling Convalescent Hospital, where he died.

Nicknamed "Lone Cat" because of his one-man band format, Fuller was a songster with an electric repertoire and a singular style. As a guitarist he employed a northern Georgia/Piedmont picking style and could play in open-tuned slide style as well. While there were other songsters, from Leadbelly to Henry Thomas, and other one-man bands, from Joe Hill Louis to Doctor Ross, Fuller was an original. His music, heavily flavored by years of rambling and street playing, combined traditions of the Old South with those of the San Francisco Bay area. His material was drawn from blues, ragtime, religious songs, folk ballads, work songs, novelty tunes, pop tunes, and even jazz.

One of the few traditional African-American artists who began playing mostly to white audiences as early as the mid-1950s, Fuller reached the peak of his influence during the folk revival. His accessible, good-time sound, combined with his wit, charm, hustling ability, and penchant for philosophizing, endeared him to revival audiences and musicians alike.

• For additional biographical information on Fuller, see Sheldon Harris, *Blues Who's Who: A Biographical Dictionary of Blues Singers* (1989); Richard Noblett and John Offord, "I Got a Mind to Ramble and I Don't Want to Settle Down," *Blues World* 25 (Oct. 1969): 10–12, and 26 (June 1970): 21–22; and Barbara Dane, "Lone Cat Jesse Fuller," *Sing Out* 16, no. 1 (Feb.–Mar. 1966): 5–11. For a discography, see Mike Leadbitter and Neil Slaven, *Blues Records, 1943–1966* (1968). For a sample of Fuller's music, try *Jesse Fuller: Frisco Bound*, Arhoolie 360; and *Jesse Fuller: Jazz, Folk Songs, Spirituals and Blues*, Good Time Jazz, OBCCD-564-2 S-10031.

BARRY LEE PEARSON
BILL MCCULLOCH

FULLER, Loie (15 Jan. 1862–1 Jan. 1928), dancer and choreographer, was born Marie Louise Fuller in Fullersburg, Illinois, the daughter of Reuben Fuller, a fiddler, farmer, and tavernkeeper, and Delilah (maiden name unknown). Little is known of her education, though she claimed to have given a recitation to a "freethinking" Sunday school class at age two-and-a-half.

Progressively known as Marie Louise Fuller, Marie Louise, Louise Fuller, Lois Fuller, and Loie Fuller, she enjoyed an early and varied career not untypical of the show business era during which she lived. By age fifteen Fuller had lectured in the Midwest on temperance, sung in opera, and produced her own play. Her New York acting debut came in Dion Boucicault's *The Shaughraun* (1878). In the 1885 Boston production of *Our Irish Visitors* Fuller performed a "sensational dance with . . . no corsets." She took male roles in such burlesques as *Arabian Nights* and *Little Jack Sheppard* (1886), appeared with Buffalo Bill, and learned the voguish skirt dance, skillfully maneuvering inside a large skirt. Notorious for leaving bills unpaid, Fuller never left the theaters' confines in some towns for fear of the sheriffs. A West Indies tour in 1888 led to a brief, disastrous contract marriage the next year to backer William Hayes (a nephew of President Rutherford B. Hayes). The childless marriage was dissolved in 1892 because of Hayes's "bigamy," and she never remarried.

After her first visit to London in 1889 Fuller returned there in 1890 to rent the Globe Theatre, at which she unsuccessfully produced her play *Caprice*. Later that year, signed by the Gaiety's impresario George Edwardes, she appeared in the "operettas" *His Last Chance* and *Carmen Up-to-Date*, becoming Edwardes's skirt dancer. Returning to New York in 1891 with no reputation as a lighting technician, she created the Serpentine Dance for *Quack, M.D.* The quack hypnotist and Fuller, his subject, swooped to and fro under "carefully arranged [by Fuller] red, blue and yellow lights." She performed the same dance in *A Trip to Chinatown*, which set a Broadway long-run record of 657 performances. She later wrote that, garbed in a fluttering, transparent voluminous skirt of thin China silk (she had so increased its size that it became "draperies"), she swept the audience "into an emotional frenzy requiring 20 encores."

Fuller had presumably discovered the play of light upon silk alongside a sunlit window in New England: she recalled, "As I shook the silk, I saw a thousand movements unknown to that moment. . . . The silk itself created a movement vocabulary." (She later told a similar story about Paris, where the effect was created by light falling from Notre Dame's rose windows.) Fuller was hired for the 1892 extravaganza *Uncle Celestin*, performed in New York, and was soon doing her Serpentine in three theaters. In London Fuller interpolated the dance into the Gaiety's 1892 *In Town*, usually called the first "musical comedy."

Although Fuller occasionally returned to London and the United States thereafter, her life changed once she had performed in Paris. Though a rival serpentine dancer was already appearing there, Fuller's 1892 debut at the Folies Bergère created an immediate sensation. She added evocatively lit dances called "Violet," "Butterfly," and "White" to the Serpentine original. In 1893 she created "Clouds," about which the symbolist poet Stephen Mallarmé wrote, "Her performance . . . an artistic intoxication and an industrial achievement . . . blends with the rapidly changing colors which vary their limelit phantasmagori of twilight and grotto . . . the dizziness of soul made visible by an artifice." Fuller later boasted that she had made the Folies Bergère respectable, since there came such a demand from women and children for matinees. Soon there were Loie Fuller hats, ribbons, shoes, and petticoats for sale.

In her 1895 "Lily," Fuller used 500 yards of gossamer thin silk (it was close to 100 yards around the hem) that could radiate ten feet from her body in every direction and could be thrown up higher than twenty feet. A journalist wrote that in order to keep the kinetic sculpture of a "lily" aloft Fuller had to "run all the while as fast as she can." That same year she created a ballet of *Salome* and a program of *Ballets Lumineuses*.

Also in 1895 came "Fire," Fuller's greatest solo, performed to Wagner's "Ride of the Valkyries." On a stage completely darkened by draping and carpeting, she seemed isolated and suspended in space, dancing atop a pane of glass lit fierily from below. She had patented this "underlighting" in 1893. Other patents include a series of onstage mirrors, forming "an octagonal room bisected by the front edge of the stage . . . giving an impression of many figures whirling in all directions," and long wands sewn into the sleeves of her garments, helping to create a lily, butterfly, or rose.

Eventually a member of the French Academy of Sciences and the French Astronomical Society, Fuller perfected electrical lighting effects well in advance of contemporary stage technicians. Though Fuller said of her art and craft, "It is a matter of intuition, of instinct, and nothing else," she developed the secret formulas for her magic lantern slides, colored glasses, and gelatins. She wrote, "The scientific admixture of chemically composed colors, heretofore unknown, fills me with admiration, and I stand before them like a miner who has discovered a vein of gold, and who completely forgets himself as he contemplates the wealth of the world before him."

Lauded for what Felicien deMenil (in *Histoire de La Danse a Travers Les Ages* [1904]) calls her "starry and luminous path of hashishien dreams," Fuller commented, "I SEE the colors just as you SEE them in a kaleidoscope." She was first to use luminous phosphorescent material on a darkened stage. Fuller was introduced to the laboratory study of color and light by the astronomer Camille Flammarion, and she met chemists Pierre and Marie Curie and created a radium dance, which may have led to the near blindness of her later life. Between 1892 and 1908 Fuller choreographed more than 130 dances.

In Paris, Fuller, who never learned to speak French well, became a favored subject of posters, an art form that came into its own during the art nouveau period. In 1893 artist Henri Toulouse-Lautrec made fifty "spatter" lithographs of Fuller, varying color to illustrate her lighting range. In 1896 François-Rupert Carabin's seven small sculptures caught the flowing serial movements of her dance. At the 1900 Paris Exhibition, which highlighted new uses of electric light, a Loie Fuller Theatre designed by Henri Sauvage and featuring an "immense veil of pleated plaster caught in mid-flight" was built to house her performances. The building won a gold medal; Fuller danced amid dark draperies within a kaleidoscope of colors radiating from the stained glass entrance. Choreographer Ruth St. Denis's later use of lighting and draperies stems from seeing Fuller there. In 1902 Fuller sponsored Isadora Duncan's first European dance tour, and in 1904 Fuller appeared in her first film for the Pathe film production company.

In 1908 Fuller founded a dance school for girls between the ages of four and twelve. Her companion and lover, Gabrielle Bloch, whom she had known since 1900, became her lieutenant. Fuller's girls, dressed in Grecian gowns, developed—often in such "found spaces" as the Bois de Boulogne and the staircase of the Grand Palais—dances "of natural movements." Fuller encouraged her girls' "idiosyncrasy" because in real life "no two persons do the same thing at the same time." During the Russo-Japanese war (1904–1905) her troupe toured Europe. In 1907 she produced a new version of *Salome*, which was performed in Paris.

In group works such as *The Bottom of the Sea* (1906) and *Ballet of Light* (1908) Fuller's dances, accompanied by images suggesting water and the Aurora Borealis, became more abstract. In 1911 and 1913 she created dances to Claude Debussy's *Petite Suite*. For entertaining troops during World War I, Fuller was decorated by France, Belgium, and Rumania, whose Queen Marie became her lifelong friend. In 1919 Fuller began to make her own art films, including one based on a fairy tale by Marie.

Fuller's 1921 shadow dances were optic plays in black and white, evoking witches and dreams. In an effect soon copied in musical theater, as the dancers moved away from the screen their shadows loomed larger. In "La Mere" (1925) unseen dancers controlled the movement of "a boundless sea of silk." Fuller's last London stage appearance, in 1927, involved a shadow ballet interweaving live performers and shadows. That same year Loie Fuller troupes played at the Moulin Rouge in Paris and in Morocco and Egypt. Journalist Jules Claretie called her work "feministic theatre" and mistakenly predicted that her work would change the course of drama.

In her earlier Paris years Fuller had met sculptor Auguste Rodin, of whom she wrote, "In his rather unwieldly body and his features . . . great kindliness and sweetness of disposition are evident." Though insisting that she had never been inside an art museum before coming to Europe, as self-appointed agent for Rodin she joined with American industrialist Sam Hill (a co-worker of Fuller's and the queen in Rumanian war relief) and philanthropist Alma Spreckels to found two museums in the United States, the California Museum of the Legion of Honor in San Francisco and the Maryhill Museum. In 1926 Fuller toured the United States with Queen Marie, who dedicated the Maryhill, which was located atop a Washington bluff overlooking the Columbia River. The collection featured a Marie of Rumania Room, Loie Fuller Room, seventy Rodin sculptures, and a French miniature fashion theater.

Fuller's aesthetic brilliance contrasted her undancerly looks: barely over five feet tall, she was described by Anatole France as "rather plump," with a pug nose and dark, curly hair. In later years Fuller recalled a child who visited her dressing room at the Folies Bergère and complained to her mother, "This one is a fat lady, and it was a fairy I saw dancing." It required athleticism and strength to create her evanescent kinetic sculptures. Revue producer Andre Charlot noted that her muscular arms made her look like a charwoman—until she began dancing. He called Fuller "an artist of the first rank without effort," while to him Duncan was "an artist of high rank with considerable effort."

Although Fuller's art had flowered amidst the fin de siècle symbolists and practitioners of art nouveau, in the course of her thirty-five years in Paris Fuller continued to develop, influencing such later innovators as Alvin Nikolais. She absorbed the influences of Japanese dancers (who for years formed part of her huge household). Her choreography, which stresses constant evolution from the concrete to the abstract, freed the form from its reliance on music. Fuller's biographer Sally Sommer called Fuller "the first American dancer honored as the originator of a modern dance form."

Despite huge earnings, Fuller was not an able money manager (Charlot recalled that she would order the most elaborate electrical equipment to test a theory, though "there might be . . . nothing at all to her credit in the bank") and paid her troupe whether or not they worked. At the time of her death in her private Paris hotel ("within calling distance of Prince Carol of Rumania and in constant telegraphic communication with Queen Marie") she was, though penniless, working on a film based on E. T. W. Hoffmann's tale of a man walking on the sky. The French press wrote, "a magician is dead . . . a butterfly has folded its wings." Loie Fuller dance troupes continued to tour Europe as late as 1938.

• The Robinson Locke Scrapbooks and Players' Collection are among the large Fuller holdings at the New York Public Library for the Performing Arts, Lincoln Center. Material particularly relevant to Fuller's British career is found in the archives of the Theatre Museum, London. In Paris Fuller published *Fifteen Years of My Life* (1908), enlarged to *Fifteen Years of A Dancer's Life* (1913). The standard biography is Sally R. Sommer and Margaret Haile Harris, *La Loie: The Life and Art of Loie Fuller* (1986). Sommer's monograph, "Loie Fuller," in the *Drama Review* 19 (Mar. 1975): 53–67 is highly useful, as is Harris's "Loie Fuller: Magician of Light" in the catalog for an exhibition on Fuller at the Virginia Museum in Richmond (12 Mar.–22 Apr. 1979).

JAMES ROSS MOORE

FULLER, Margaret (23 May 1810–19 July 1850), author and feminist, was born Sarah Margaret Fuller in Cambridgeport, Massachusetts, the daughter of Timothy Fuller, a lawyer, and Margaret Crane. Her father taught his oldest child reading at age three and Latin at age six, but Fuller's education grew eclectic in later childhood when she was left largely to her own resources. "To excel in all things should be your constant aim; mediocrity is obscurity," her father wrote to Margaret when she was ten. Under such pressures, Fuller suffered periodically throughout her life from depression and headaches. Timothy Fuller was often away, serving four terms in Congress (1817–1825). Margaret's mother, a devout Unitarian, was subdued by sickly health. In Fuller's fictional *Autobiographical Romance* (1852), she portrays an authoritarian father in his study and a poetic mother in her garden.

At home Margaret was charged with educating the children. She attended Port School alongside Richard Dana and Oliver Wendell Holmes, who was to model the title character of *Elsie Venner* after her, and then the Boston Lyceum for Young Ladies. Young Margaret was uneasy around her peers. Acute but plain, with eyes blinking nervously from nearsightedness, she countered teasing with formidable wit; she "made up [her] mind to be bright and ugly" (*Memoirs*, vol. 1 p. 228).

Timothy Fuller moved the family to Groton in 1833 to reside as a farmer-scholar, an exile Margaret resented. Nevertheless, she knew Unitarian preacher William Ellery Channing from the family's Boston days, met English writer Harriet Martineau, who visited Cambridge in 1834 and encouraged Fuller to write a biography of Goethe, and two years later was invited to stay at Ralph Waldo Emerson's home in Concord. Fuller taught German pronunciation to Emerson, and he reciprocated by writing Thomas Carlyle for assistance on her Goethe project. By age twenty-four, she was under the sway of philosophers soon to be known as Transcendentalists, whose philosophical and social idealism, with its Unitarian center, was applied especially to religious doubts.

Fuller's energy was drained by having to raise her siblings while reading voraciously. Excursions to New York only reminded her how isolated farm life was. She ran a home school and submitted didactic literary critiques to *Western Messenger* (June 1835) and a short romance, "Lost and Won," to *Galaxy* (Aug. 1835). She taught at Bronson Alcott's school in Boston until it foundered over his antireligious views and then in Providence for one and a half years.

After her father died in 1835, Fuller's complex of resentment and admiration emerged, prompting her to write that children "should not through books antedate their actual experiences" (*Memoirs*, vol. 1, p. 31). She recognized the fragile female position: "You know we women have no profession except marriage, mantua-making and school-keeping" (*Letters*, Feb. 1836). In reviewing *The Life of James Mackintosh* in the *American Monthly Magazine* (June 1836), she analyzed a statesman who failed for insufficient "earnestness of purpose," which she blamed on "the want of systematic training in early life" and "uncommon talents for conversation," both reflections on herself.

In 1837 Fuller attended Emerson's Phi Beta Kappa address at Harvard and was inducted into the Transcendentalist movement, in which she was recognized as an equal by men and shared the gibes hurled at Transcendentalism, as even Unitarian churches closed their doors to these freethinkers. Her professional watershed occurred in 1839, when she published translations of Johann Eckermann's *Conversations with Goethe* and German poetry and moved back to Boston. In October Fuller accepted the editorship of *The Dial*, a new quarterly for Transcendentalism, and a month later opened the first of her "Conversations," at which Boston women, and some invited men, met to discuss society and women's roles in society.

The first issue of *The Dial* appeared in July 1840. Fuller emphasized literature more than religion, which was just as well because dissenting Unitarian ministers were scarcely unified or eager to publish under a single masthead. During her two-year tenure as editor Fuller supplied numerous articles, including "Short Essay on Critics" and a re-evaluation of Goethe at a time when he was considered a moral renegade. Her analyses employed a conversation technique to allow opposing viewpoints, a manner that mirrored Goethe's concept that truth can occupy grounds in both camps of an argument.

Fuller also contributed a series of four mystical sketches on women, which dramatized both maternal strength and the female quest into the self, a search for woman's power and buried creativity that, in Fuller's own time and country at least, had to emerge outside patriarchal law. Her language posited a mythology of the female realm akin to imagery seen later in the female selfhood generated by twentieth-century artists Georgia O'Keeffe and Judy Chicago.

Most important, Fuller followed these sketches with "The Great Lawsuit: Man *versus* Men, Woman *versus* Women," a feminist tract that coupled mysticism with her own reading and admiration for feminist predecessors Martineau (*Society in America*, 1837) and Anna Jameson (*Winter Studies and Summer Rambles in Canada*, 1838). Fuller emphasized women's intellect as well as sensibility and proclaimed that "the restraints upon the sex were insuperable only to those who think them so," but pragmatically added "or who noisily strive to break them." Her articles appeared without a byline and without remuneration. With strained nerves aggravated by the withdrawal of a promised $75 per quarterly, Fuller departed from *The Dial* in 1842, to be succeeded as editor by Emerson.

For five years Fuller's Conversations, however, continued to attract Boston's leading lights and show off her star qualities, for as Emerson recorded in his journal, "Her powers of speech throw her writing into the shade." More than her writing, they established her reputation and enhanced her income. The 1841 series of Conversations was titled "The Ethical Influences of Women on the Family, the School, the Church, Society and Literature." Her 1842 Conversations, titled simply "Woman," stretched Emerson's philosophy on the infinitude of the individual to include women. The sessions ended with Fuller in a trancelike state, uttering Delphic wisdom. For Emerson, "She rose before me at times into heroical and godlike regions, and I could remember no superior woman, but thought of Ceres, Minerva, Proserpine" (*The Journals and Miscellaneous Notebooks of Ralph Waldo Emerson*, ed. William Gilman et al., vol. 8 [1960], pp. 368–69), but in truth the two were often irreconcilable in philosophy as well as personality. She never stayed in Emerson's home after 1842.

Fuller's visit to Chicago and Niagara resulted in *Summer on the Lakes, in 1843*, a potpourri of frontier scenes and contrived poetic flights. She fretted over the rapacity of white settlers, notably their treatment of Native Americans, and saw lost opportunities to secure a fresh start for civilization and for women. For her research on westward expansion, the Harvard library allowed her in as its first woman scholar.

By 1844, when Horace Greeley offered her the literary editorship of his *New-York Daily Tribune*, making her the first woman in the working press, Fuller's private life was at a crossroads. Her family no longer needed tending, and her web of friendships was strained. Emerson remained cordial but grew distant. She stayed at Nathaniel Hawthorne's Old Manse, but it was his wife who admired Fuller; Hawthorne considered her brash and intellectually pretentious, a "great humbug."

In 1845 Fuller expanded "The Great Lawsuit" into *Woman in the Nineteenth Century*, which celebrated both the creative and intellectual sides of woman's nature, her muse and her Minerva. She combined Charles Fourier's critique that woman must be entirely equal to man with Goethe's pragmatic "as the man, so the institutions," meaning to Fuller that society at large, namely "unready men," must be reformed in order for woman to achieve her "radiant sovereign self." Her poem at the end of the volume stresses the equality of the sexes, "So shalt thou see what few have seen, / The palace home of King and Queen."

Although her disruptive prose style only loosely associated the rush of inspirations (again, from Emerson, "She ought not to write because she talked so well"), the first edition of *Woman in the Nineteenth Century* sold out in two weeks. Greeley trumpeted its success, and *Knickerbocker Magazine* called it "a well-reasoned and well-written treatise." Conservative critics in the *Quarterly Review* and the *Southern Quarterly* were appalled that she encouraged women to pursue knowledge as men did; they also noted that an unmarried woman should not presume to "truly represent the female character."

For most of her tenure at the *Tribune*, Fuller lived with Greeley and his wife (Mary Greeley had attended the Conversations in Boston). Greeley's air was one of "friendly antagonism" (*Memoirs*, vol. 2, p. 153), and he often hailed her by her signature remark on women: "Let them be sea-captains if you will" (*Woman*, p. 191). Fuller's reputation was such that *Woman in the Nineteenth Century* was pirated in England by December and her *Tribune* column placed on the front page. During her rise to prominence in 1845, Fuller fell in love with James Nathan, a prosperous businessman in New York City (only her letters survive, and her nineteenth-century biographers made no mention of this romance). The affair was a passing interlude, ending when Nathan left the country that same year.

For eighteen months Fuller's 250 newspaper articles influenced culture in a populist way that Emerson avoided—and even worse, in that Babylon, New York City. She praised Herman Melville's *Typee*, chastised Henry Wadsworth Longfellow's Euro-poetic elegance, and belittled James Russell Lowell, who later lampooned her in *A Fable for Critics* (1864). Her columns also directed public attention to slums, immigrants, and working women. In *Papers on Literature*

and Art (1846) she neglected Edgar Allan Poe, for which he rescinded his earlier praise of "high genius" and called her "an ill-tempered and very inconsistent old maid" (letter to George W. Eveleth dated 4 Jan. 1848, *The Letters of Edgar Allan Poe*, ed. John Ward Ostrom, vol. 2 [1966], p. 355).

In 1846, as Fuller was about to go to Europe as Greeley's foreign correspondent, Emerson journeyed from Concord to see her off. In England, she met Martineau, William Wordsworth, Matthew Arnold, and Carlyle, then departed accompanied by the exiled Italian patriot Giuseppe Mazzini, who traveled incognito. In Paris she adored woman novelist George Sand, whom she had singled out in "The Great Lawsuit." She traveled to Genoa, Naples, and finally Rome, where in 1847 she met Giovanni Angelo, marchese d'Ossoli, the handsome, youngest son of fallen aristocrats. Ten years younger and casually educated, Ossoli was scarcely a match for Fuller, but by June he offered marriage and by December she was pregnant. Whether she ever officially married has not been determined (April or May 1848 is a suggested date); Ossoli, a Roman Catholic, could not marry a Protestant.

In love, Fuller wrote cryptic letters, sounding miserable but desiring to stay in Italy for three years. Twice, Emerson, in London, urged her to Paris so he could escort her home to Concord, but she remained to fulfill her destiny: "to be free and absolutely true to my nature" (*Letters*, Apr. 1847). A year after her son's birth, Fuller broke her silence to family and friends back home: "You may address me in future as Marchioness Ossoli" (Aug. 1849).

Meanwhile, democratic uprisings were occurring across Europe in 1848, and Fuller was on the scene to chronicle the Roman republic's birth and ultimate demise when French troops retook Rome in the name of the pope. As war broke out, Fuller identified with the Italian people: "What shall I write of Rome in these sad but glorious days? If Rome falls, if Venice falls, there is no spot of Italian earth where they can abide more" (*Tribune*, 24 July 1849). With Ossoli fighting bravely in the civic guard, Fuller staffed the hospital during the two-month siege and fall of Rome, writing home to remind Americans of the marquis de Lafayette's intervention in their own fight for freedom and the current "holocaust of broken hearts" (*Tribune*, 16 May 1849).

Fuller and her husband escaped to Florence, where she wrote a history of the Roman struggles at the home of Robert and Elizabeth Barrett Browning, and Robert then accompanied them to Leghorn for their voyage to America. On 19 July 1850, in a diminishing gale, only four hundred yards off Fire Island, New York, their ship foundered on a sand dune and sank ten hours later. The Ossoli family drowned; only the baby's body was recovered. Emerson sent Henry David Thoreau to scour the beaches, but all was lost, including Fuller's Roman revolution manuscript.

Emerson and William Henry Channing undertook a biography, although Fuller's family stifled much concerning her religious views and dubious marriage. The sanitized two-volume *Memoirs of Margaret Fuller Ossoli* (1852), with little mention of the romantic final years, sold 1,000 copies its first day; thirteen editions were printed by the century's end. Fuller's correspondence for the *Tribune* was published in *At Home and Abroad* (1856). *Woman in the Nineteenth Century* was reissued in 1855, and Greeley published a six-volume edition of Fuller's works in 1869. Thomas Wentworth Higginson's biography in 1884 de-emphasized her Transcendentalism by saying that Fuller desired "a career of mingled thought and action, such as she finally found," because she was not framed by nature for a mystic, a dreamer, or a bookworm (p. 4).

Fuller's writings never achieved the landmark status of Mary Wollstonecraft's *A Vindication of the Rights of Woman* (1792), for they were pontifical and mystical as well as imaginative. Hence her life was more influential than her works. Emerson's letters reveal his great indebtedness to Fuller, which ironically is often neglected as feminists strive to show Fuller's independence. Critics speculate that Hawthorne, in spite of his hostility, refigured her as characters in all his major novels. Certainly Fuller inspired women writers, including Emily Dickinson, Louisa May Alcott, and Edith Wharton. Her influences on Walt Whitman, Poe, Melville, and Henry James are documented but have not been fully explored.

In the twentieth century, Fuller is a puzzling icon in American feminism because early feminists came to recover her "experience" as a woman but stayed to find only her intense theoretical emphasis. Her modern biographer Joan von Mehren touted Fuller as a major figure in American Romanticism whose "original experiments with symbolism and mysticism, misunderstood by her contemporaries as expressions of morbid self-absorption, extended her insight into feminine psychology and the boundaries of religious experience" (*Minerva and the Muse*, p. 351). Fuller's other enduring contribution was the national dimension she brought to the role of literary critic.

• Fuller's manuscripts are at the Houghton Library, Harvard University, and the Boston Public Library. See *The Letters of Margaret Fuller*, ed. Robert Hudspeth (6 vols., 1983–1994), and *Memoirs of Margaret Fuller Ossoli*, ed. R. W. Emerson et al. (2 vols., 1852). Early biographies are Julia Ward Howe, *Margaret Fuller (Marchesa Ossoli)* (1883; repr. 1970), and Thomas Wentworth Higginson, *Margaret Fuller Ossoli* (1884; repr. 1968). Perry Miller's introduction to his *Margaret Fuller, American Revolutionary* (1963) and Jeffrey Steele's introduction to his *Essential Margaret Fuller* (1992) are excellent, although Miller's analyses were frequently hostile toward Fuller. *The Woman and the Myth: Margaret Fuller's Life and Writings*, ed. Bell Gale Chevigny (1976; rev. ed., 1994), collects commentary by contemporaries for each period of Fuller's writings. Charles Capper, *Margaret Fuller: An American Romantic Life*, vol. 1 (1992), is rich in historical and social context. Joan von Mehren, *Minerva and the Muse: A Life of Margaret Fuller* (1994), is based on her writings. Christina Zwarg, *Feminist Conversations: Fuller, Emerson and the Play of Reading* (1995), provides a feminist reading. Catherine

Mitchell, ed., *Margaret Fuller's New York Journalism* (1995), covers Fuller's *Tribune* activities. Horace Greeley's obituary is in the *New-York Daily Tribune*, 23 July 1850.

JOEL ATHEY

FULLER, Melville Weston (11 Feb. 1833–4 July 1910), chief justice of the U.S. Supreme Court, was born in Augusta, Maine, the son of Frederick Augustus Fuller, a lawyer, and Catherine Martin Weston, daughter of Nathan Weston, chief justice of the Maine Supreme Judicial Court. Within months of his birth, Fuller's mother sued his father for divorce on the ground of adultery. Fuller's father did not contest the suit and played no further role in his son's life. Mother and son moved into the home of Judge Weston, where young Fuller remained even after his mother's remarriage in 1844. From his grandfather, a Jacksonian Democrat, Fuller acquired a political faith that remained with him for the rest of his life.

Fuller matriculated at Bowdoin College in 1849, graduating in 1853. He read law for a year in the law office of a maternal uncle, George Melville Weston, in Bangor, Maine, then attended Harvard Law School for six months. Although he came too soon to experience the reforms in legal education begun at Harvard in 1871 by Dean Christopher Columbus Langdell, Fuller later played a prominent role in the Harvard Law School Alumni Association and lent the prestige of the chief justiceship to the new style of legal education by casebook and Socratic dialogue.

Admitted to the Maine bar in 1855, Fuller engaged briefly in law practice in Augusta and was elected to the Augusta City Council, promptly becoming president of the council and city solicitor. Despite this promising beginning, he soon decided to leave Maine and try his fortune in the West, perhaps influenced by a broken marriage engagement. In May 1856 the 23-year-old Fuller arrived in Chicago, which was to remain his base of operations until he moved to Washington, D.C., thirty-two years later. At first his law practice, in a series of short-lived partnerships, was modest, and his finances strapped. In 1858 he married Calista Ophelia Reynolds. A seemingly unhappy match, the marriage ended in his wife's death in 1864, after the birth of two daughters. From his wife Fuller inherited valuable downtown Chicago real estate on which he erected a large office building, housing his own law offices and considerable rental space. In 1866 Fuller married Mary Ellen Coolbaugh, with whom he enjoyed a lifelong relationship that resulted in eight children. This marriage, too, produced significant economic advantage since the bride's father was president of Chicago's largest bank, a source of lucrative contacts for the aspiring attorney, and also a generous benefactor to the young couple.

As early as 1858 Fuller had begun an active role in Illinois Democratic politics as an operative for Stephen Douglas in his bid for reelection to the U.S. Senate against the challenge from Abraham Lincoln, the contest that included the celebrated Lincoln-Douglas debates. In 1860 Fuller again campaigned for Douglas against Lincoln, this time in the Democrat's unsuccessful race for the presidency. The outbreak of the Civil War put Fuller and all Northern Democrats in a difficult position. Generally supportive of the Union but zealous for states' rights, Fuller avoided military service and harshly criticized many of the policies of the Lincoln administration. In 1862 Fuller served as a delegate to the Illinois constitutional convention, which was called to draft a new state constitution but was inevitably overshadowed by the politics of national crisis. In 1863 he was narrowly elected to the Illinois House of Representatives, his first and only state office. His term was marked by a series of biting attacks on the Republican war effort, notably the Emancipation Proclamation, which he denounced as an unconstitutional usurpation of power by the president. Although never again holding elective office, Fuller remained active in Democratic politics in Illinois, regularly serving as a delegate to Democratic national conventions.

Despite his outspoken partisanship, Fuller was able to maintain cordial personal relations even with his political opponents. Short of stature, only 5'6", sporting a distinctive mustache reminiscent of that later popularized by Mark Twain, whom he resembled, Fuller cultivated an open and genial manner. In Chicago society he was known for his avoidance of political or legal topics and his preference for composing conventional verse, some of which was published. His law practice profited from his easygoing style, his economic and political contacts, his oratorical skill, and his legal acumen. By the mid-1880s Fuller was much sought after, particularly as an appellate advocate, frequently arguing cases in state and federal courts, including the U.S. Supreme Court. On the eve of his appointment as chief justice, he was earning about $30,000 annually from his law practice and considerable sums from his real estate investments.

The sudden death of Chief Justice Morrison R. Waite on 23 March 1888, during the presidency of Democrat Grover Cleveland, created a vacancy at the top of the national judiciary and a political opportunity for the president. Confirmation by the Senate would be a challenge because of a small but determined Republican majority, so the nominee had to be able to attract some opposition support. Seeking to make an appointment from Illinois, Cleveland first selected Judge John Scholfield of the state supreme court, who declined because of an unwillingness to relocate. Fuller, lacking national prominence but known to the president for his good nature, Democratic credentials, and fiscal conservatism, was nominated on 30 April 1888. Republican concerns about Fuller's war record or lack thereof slowed consideration by the Senate Judiciary Committee. Despite a valuable endorsement by Robert T. Lincoln, President Lincoln's son and an active member of the Chicago bar, Fuller's nomination was reported to the full Senate without recommendation. On 20 July 1888 Fuller was confirmed. Regional loyalties were still important, as shown by the affirmative votes cast by the Republican senators not only of Illinois but also of Maine.

On 8 October 1888, at the opening of the new term of the Supreme Court, Fuller took the oath of office. Pursuant to recent legislation, he was the first person to be formally commissioned "chief justice of the United States," as opposed to the former title "chief justice of the United States Supreme Court." Fuller was called to preside over a bench of independent-minded and experienced judges, including Stephen J. Field, Samuel F. Miller, Joseph P. Bradley, and Horace Gray. Fuller's personal charm, his considerable organizational skills, and perhaps even his lack of many strong jurisprudential convictions made his task more manageable than it first appeared. Within a few years of his appointment, the personnel on the Court changed as older justices died and were replaced, but the chief justice made no sustained effort to claim intellectual leadership. Instead, the initiative passed to newer justices like David J. Brewer, Justice Field's nephew, appointed to the Court in 1889, and Rufus W. Peckham, appointed in 1895. Throughout Fuller's chief justiceship the Court was staffed by a Republican majority, but partisan allegiance was not a defining factor in judicial divisions; instead, a broad conservative consensus united Democratic and Republican judges. While not offering the Court leadership, Fuller was unexcelled as its administrator. He earned unqualified praise in this regard from Justice Oliver Wendell Holmes, who came to the Court in 1902 from the chief justiceship of the Massachusetts Supreme Judicial Court.

On the great constitutional issues concerning civil rights that came to the Supreme Court during his tenure, the key to Fuller's decisions can be found in his belief, publicly avowed in an extraordinary address to a joint session of Congress on 11 December 1889, marking the centennial of the inauguration of President George Washington, that the Fourteenth Amendment had worked "no revolutionary change" in American federalism. The Jacksonian faith of Fuller's youth remained intact despite the constitutional and social upheaval wrought by the Civil War. In consequence, Fuller rejected the contention, vigorously advocated by Justice John Marshall Harlan, that the Fourteenth Amendment incorporated the Bill of Rights and made its guarantees binding on the states, a view progressively accepted in the mid-twentieth century. He also joined the majority in the leading case of *Hans v. Louisiana* (1890), authored by Justice Bradley, citing the Eleventh Amendment as authority for denying federal jurisdiction over suits against states brought by state citizens to remedy constitutional violations, a decision that was limited in practice before the end of Fuller's chief justiceship by *Ex parte Young* (1908), authored by Justice Peckham, in which he also joined. Fuller, too, participated in the decision of *Plessy v. Ferguson* (1896), accepting the separate-but-equal doctrine of racial segregation, finally overturned by the Supreme Court's desegregation decision in 1954.

On the pressing economic question of the day, Fuller joined the majority in developing the doctrine of substantive due process as a constitutional limitation on government power to regulate the market. In his Washington memorial address Fuller had repeated the cliché that "it is the duty of the people to support the government and not of the government to support the people." He joined the majority in *Lochner v. New York* (1908), written by Peckham, holding unconstitutional a state statute limiting working hours in the baking trade, thereby inaugurating the "Lochner Era" that lasted until 1938. In commercial law, Fuller's speciality while in law practice, the chief justice led the Court in *Leisy v. Hardin* (1890) to adopt his version of the "original package" doctrine, holding that goods shipped in interstate commerce were not subject to state regulation so long as they remained in their original package. As applied in *Leisy*, this invalidated a key provision of Iowa's law prohibiting the sale of alcoholic beverages. The doctrine survived, but its specific application was promptly eliminated by a federal statute permitting state regulation of alcohol "upon arrival." Fuller also wrote the Court's opinion in *In re Rahrer* (1891), upholding the constitutionality of that statute.

Fuller also wrote the opinion in *United States v. E.C. Knight Co.* (1895), finding the monopolistic Sugar Trust not in violation of the Sherman Antitrust Act on the ground that manufacture for sale is not commerce. "Commerce succeeds to manufacture," he wrote, "and is not a part of it," a specious distinction speedily eroded in later decisions. The same term he also authored the two opinions in the *Income Tax Cases* (1895), holding invalid a federal income tax on the dubious ground that the Constitution prohibited direct taxes unless proportioned to state population; this decision prompted the adoption of the Sixteenth Amendment two decades later. Himself a millionaire, Fuller often appeared as the arch-defender of property in decisions such as these.

On legal questions generated by late nineteenth-century Anglo-Saxon imperialism, Fuller was seemingly inconsistent, dissenting from the holding in *United States v. Wong Kim Ark* (1898) that the children of Chinese immigrants born in this country were American citizens, but also dissenting from the holding in *Downes v. Bidwell* (1901), one of the Insular Cases, that the newly acquired island territories of the United States were not covered by the U.S. Constitution. On the legal issues concerning labor, Fuller in part confounded expectations. Although before his appointment to the Court he had often appeared as counsel for Illinois corporations arguing in favor of the fellow-servant rule that insulated employers from liability for many workers' on-the-job injuries, as chief justice he routinely ruled against application of the doctrine. In his opposition to labor unions, however, Fuller proved quite consistent. He joined the opinion of the Court authored by Brewer in *In re Debs* (1895), upholding a sweeping federal injunction against a strike in the railway industry led by Eugene V. Debs,

the labor leader and later socialist. In *Loewe v. Lawlor* (1908), the Danbury Hatters' Case, Fuller personally confounded the labor unions with an opinion holding them subject to the Sherman Antitrust Act. His categorical assertion that every combination in restraint of trade had been outlawed seemed hardly consistent with his opinion on the Sugar Trust and was reversed by subsequent legislation and judicial decision.

Other than the Washington memorial address, Fuller authored no significant off-the-bench statements concerning his legal philosophy. In 1892 he declined President Cleveland's invitation to resign from the Court to become secretary of state, writing the president that departure under such circumstances from "the highest judicial office in the world" would be "distinctly injurious to the court." He generally avoided extrajudicial assignments, although he did serve on the international Venezuelan Boundary Commission from 1897 to 1899 and on the Permanent Court of Arbitration at The Hague from 1900 until his death. By virtue of his position as chief justice, Fuller was an ex officio member of the board of regents of the Smithsonian Institution, and from 1899 until his death he served as its chancellor. At his last board meeting in 1910 he presented a Smithsonian medal to Orville and Wilbur Wright.

In 1902, as Fuller neared seventy years of age, President Theodore Roosevelt was eager to fill his place with the ambitious William Howard Taft, former circuit court judge, then serving as governor of the Philippines. In hopes of nudging Fuller into retirement, the president arranged for a news story to include a paragraph suggesting the possibility. Repeatedly over the next few years similar paragraphs appeared until an exasperated Fuller insisted to Justice Holmes that "I am not to be 'paragraphed' out of my place." By the 1909 term the chief justice was clearly failing, and even friends and colleagues began to consider the advisability of urging retirement after twenty-two years of service. The move was forestalled, however, by Fuller's death from a heart attack while vacationing at his summer home in Sorrento, Maine.

Fuller is best remembered as a gifted judicial administrator. His jurisprudential contribution was limited, however, as many of his own and his Court's most famous decisions have failed the test of time.

• Fuller's judicial decisions and those of his Court are found in vols. 128–218 of the *United States Reports*. His "Address in Commemoration of the Inauguration of George Washington" (1889) appears in vol. 132, pp. 705–34. The standard full-length biography is Willard L. King, *Melville Weston Fuller* (1950), an almost affectionate account. A tart short chapter, dated but still valuable, is in Kenneth Bernard Umbreit, *Our Eleven Chief Justices* (1938). A modern summary by Irving Schiffman is in vol. 2 of *The Justices of the United States Supreme Court: Their Lives and Major Opinions* (1969). The Fuller Court is chronicled extensively in the Oliver Wendell Holmes Devise History of the Supreme Court of the United States, vol. 8, *Troubled Beginnings of the Modern State, 1888–1910* (1993), by Owen Fiss. Shorter but no less estimable is James W. Ely, Jr., *The Chief Justiceship of Melville W. Fuller,*

1888–1910 (1995). For a term-by-term review that places the Fuller Court in a larger context, see John E. Semonche, *Charting the Future: The Supreme Court Responds to a Changing Society, 1890–1920* (1978). A provocative examination of the central years of the Fuller Court is Arnold M. Paul, *Conservative Crisis and the Rule of Law: Attitudes of Bar and Bench, 1887–1895* (1960). An influential article is Walter F. Pratt, "Rhetorical Styles on the Fuller Court," *American Journal of Legal History* 24 (1980): 189–220. The Fuller memorial proceedings in the Supreme Court are reported in vol. 219 of the *United States Reports* (1910), pp. vii–xxviii.

JOHN V. ORTH

FULLER, Minnie Rutherford (25 Jan. 1868–15 Oct. 1946), reformer and suffragist, was born Minnie Ursula Oliver in Ozark, Arkansas, the daughter of James M. Oliver, a planter, and Mattie A. Hale. She received her A.B. degree from Sullins College in Virginia. She also studied music, languages, and law at the University of Chicago, the University of Leipzig, Harvard University, the University of California, and in France and Italy. Having sufficient legal training, she was admitted to the bar. It is unknown whether she ever practiced law, but she did teach voice and piano following her first husband's death.

Minnie was married at age fourteen to Omer H. Scott, age twenty. Upon his father's death in 1886, Scott is reputed to have inherited $50,000 in gold coins and his father's properties of land tracts and a store near Magazine, Arkansas, where Minnie had been raised. Omer Scott died in 1887, leaving his fortune to his wife and infant daughter. In 1889 Minnie wed William B. Rutherford, a Little Rock lawyer. In 1909, after twenty years, their childless marriage was to end in divorce. In 1915 Minnie married Dr. Seabron Jennings Fuller, a physician and surgeon at Magazine, who died in 1932.

A devout Methodist and fervent prohibitionist, Minnie Fuller was initially involved with the Woman's Christian Temperance Union (WCTU), particularly in its work on behalf of children. Beginning in 1907 and continuing for more than a decade, she was the WCTU national superintendent of the Department of Juvenile Courts. She spent much of her life crusading for legislation regulating child labor and worked as a state organizer and lecturer for the Arkansas WCTU.

Between 1907 and the 1930s Fuller attended many conferences across the country working for the rights of children. These conferences included the National Conference of Charities and Correction at Buffalo, New York, in 1909 and the Conference for Education in the South at Little Rock, Arkansas, in 1910. In 1911, with the support of the WCTU and the Arkansas Federation of Women's Clubs, she persuaded the state legislature to pass the Juvenile Court Law. In 1912 she helped found and became the first vice president of the Arkansas Conference of Charities and Correction, which later became the Conference on Social Welfare. In 1913, 1914, 1922, and 1923 she was the president of this conference. As part of her efforts to promote child labor and other reform legislation, she joined the Southern Sociological Congress in 1913 and chaired an

Arkansas Inter-racial Committee. Before and after World War I she traveled extensively to Hungary, Germany, Switzerland, Italy, and England to investigate the social service methods of other countries.

Besides her efforts on behalf of children, Fuller fought for women's right to vote. In March 1911 she and Alice Gaitlin were the chief speakers lobbying for the passage of the woman suffrage resolution before the Arkansas Committee on Constitutional Amendments. To persuade the committee, Fuller cited the many reforms achieved in Colorado, where women had received the vote in 1893. The same year she was involved in the formation of the Woman's Political Equality League of Little Rock. This group, later known as the Arkansas Woman Suffrage Association, was formed in Little Rock, Arkansas, by members of the WCTU and the College Women's Club. She was appointed chair of the legislative committee. In October 1914, a state convention was held in Little Rock and the organization became statewide. Mrs. O. F. Ellington of Little Rock was elected as president and Fuller was elected its first vice president. In January 1915 the resolution to enfranchise women through a state constitutional amendment was passed by the Arkansas Senate by a vote of twenty-three to twelve. The resolution was then referred to the House Committee on Constitutional Amendments. This committee called a hearing at which Fuller spoke for passage of the amendment. She lobbied for woman suffrage and supported Governor Charles H. Brough, under whose administration Arkansas ratified the Nineteenth Amendment.

Her other legislative causes included fighting for the formation of a girls' industrial school and a state prison farm for women. These institutions were established, largely due to her efforts, in 1917 and 1919, respectively. She was involved in the passage of state laws related to school consolidation, property rights for women, guardianship of children, and prohibition, a topic on which she wrote numerous articles for publications both in the United States and abroad. Other legislation that she sponsored includes a white-slave law, a mother's pension bill, a minimum-wage act, and probation and parole statutes.

During World War I, Fuller was secretary of the Arkansas Division of the Woman's Committee, U.S. Council of National Defense. Later, she stayed politically active as a member of the Arkansas Women's Democratic Club, serving as Fourth District chair in 1933. From 1913 through 1925, she was president of the state WCTU and editor and publisher of its journal, the *Arkansas White Ribboner*. She was also an associate editor of *Twentieth Century Church* and treasurer of the Woman's Southwestern Bar Association. She died in Brookline, Massachusetts, at the home of her daughter.

• On Minnie Rutherford Fuller's work with the Southern Sociological Congress, see two works edited by James E. McCulloch, *The South Mobilizing for Social Service* (1913) and *Battling for Social Betterment* (1914). See also Elizabeth Putnam Gordon, *Women Torch-Bearers: The Story of the Woman's Christian Temperance Union* (1924); David Yancey Thomas, *Arkansas and Its People: A History, 1541–1930*, vol. 2 (1930); and Ida Husted Harper, ed., *History of Woman Suffrage, 1900–1920*, vol. 6 (1922; repr. 1969). An obituary appears in the *Arkansas Historical Quarterly* 6 (1947): 92.

KAREN VENTURELLA

FULLER, R. Buckminster (12 July 1895–1 July 1983), inventor, designer, and environmentalist, often referred to as "Bucky," was born Richard Buckminster Fuller, Jr., in Milton, Massachusetts, the son of Richard Buckminster Fuller, an importer of leather and tea, who died in 1910, and Caroline Wolcott Andrews. He was the grandnephew of author and literary critic Margaret Fuller. Crossed eyes and poor vision kept Fuller from seeing objects clearly during his youth, but he perceived and etched on his mind the large designs and patterns of nature, especially those he encountered in summers on Bear Island, eleven miles off of Camden, Maine. After graduating from Milton Academy in 1913, he attended Harvard University but was expelled in his first year, after he skipped an examination to date a show girl in New York and used his tuition money to take her entire chorus line to dinner.

After his mother consulted his uncles, Fuller was sent to Sherbrooke, Quebec, Canada, to be an apprentice mechanic in a cotton mill–machinery factory run by a distant relative. Impressed by Fuller's mechanical ability, the chief engineer convinced him to keep a notebook of his design sketches. Harvard reinstated Fuller in 1914, only to expel him again in 1915, officially for cutting classes but actually, Fuller later stated, "for general irresponsibility" (*Ideas and Integrities*, p. 11). Securing a job in New York City with Armour and Company, he thrived while learning the meatpacking business. In 1917 he married Anne Hewlett; they had two children.

Poor eyesight kept Fuller out of the army in World War I, but the navy, when offered the use of his family's cabin cruiser *Wego*, accepted him. He was soon patrolling the Maine coast at the head of the Bar Harbor flotilla. Later, while located at Newport News, Virginia, he designed a combined winch, mast, and boom for rescue boats, which, by speedily pulling overturned aircraft out of the water, ultimately kept hundreds of pilots from drowning. Impressed by this invention, the navy in 1918 sent Fuller to its academy at Annapolis for three months of intensive officers' training.

That same year Fuller worked with Atlantic troop transport operations and compiled their official statistics. Then as the communications officer on the *George Washington*, which carried President Woodrow Wilson to the Paris Peace Conference, Fuller helped install the radiotelephonic equipment for the world's first wireless transatlantic telephone conversation. When he returned to New York in 1919, he resigned from the navy to be with his young daughter who had contracted both infantile paralysis and spinal meningi-tis. Fuller blamed her subsequent death partly on drafty houses and vowed to improve housing conditions. His first venture, the manufacturing of a lightweight, innovative building material, invented by his father-in-law, the architect James Monroe Hewlett, taught him how difficult it was to introduce new ideas and materials. Fuller and Hewlett lost control of their Stockade Corporation in 1927.

Despite the birth of his second daughter, Fuller, unemployed in Chicago and drinking heavily, contemplated suicide in 1927. He was saved by an experience on the shore of Lake Michigan. "You belong to Universe," a mystical voice said, before telling him he had no right to kill himself and insisting that he use his talents to help others (Sieden, p. 88). Deeply moved, he spent the next two years in libraries (refusing to speak unless he had something important to say), formulating general ideas on serving humanity and searching for local and immediate ways to implement them. As a result, he helped introduce the concept "that every aspect of man's physical environment was connected to every other" (*New York Times*, 3 July 1983). Working to express this interconnectedness mathematically in what he would later call synergetic geometry, he adopted the term "fourth dimension" (4D), used in physics and mathematics, in addition to length, width, and depth, to discuss phenomena that depended on four variables (for instance, time is a fourth dimension for locating points in space). He founded the 4D research company; distributed his essays "4D" and "4D Timeline" (published as *4D* in 1930), outlining his design philosophy; and used aircraft technology to plan large multi-deck apartment houses and single-family dwellings. His job, Fuller decided, was to identify a problem, develop a way to solve it, and wait—perhaps as long as twenty-five years—for public awareness to catch up.

Fuller's first creative period, roughly 1927 to 1946, concentrated on housing and transportation. In 1929 he acquired "Dymaxion" as a trademark when a wordsmith, hired by Chicago's Marshall Field Department Store, renamed Fuller's futuristic 4D House, which the store was displaying. The word combined dynamic, maximum, and tension, and expressed Fuller's "maximum gain of advantage from minimal energy input" (McHale, p. 17). Enclosed by six aluminum and glass walls and divided into a living room, library, utility room, two bedrooms, and a covered patio, Fuller's newly named Dymaxion House was suspended by six cables from a central mast that contained a staircase, electric power cables, and plumbing. Seen by more people than his housing prototypes, Fuller's three Dymaxion cars (the first was built in 1933) caused excitement and foretold changes in car design. He used high-strength, lightweight materials for his streamlined, high-speed, three-wheeled, eleven-passenger Dymaxion cars (with rear motors, front-wheel drive, and single rear-wheel steering). The design of these extremely maneuverable vehicles—which were interim models of a design planned for both air and land travel—was based on the "maximum efficiency and low resistance in motion" of birds and fish (Sieden, p. 146).

Although industry sometimes backed his research, Fuller learned that he could not count on it to mass produce his inventions. Working first for the American Standard Sanitary Manufacturing Company (1930–1932) and later for the Phelps-Dodge Corporation (1936), he refined his fully equipped, dye-stamped bathroom units until they could be plugged into a home like a refrigerator. Fearful of losing jobs, the plumbing establishment kept these units from being mass produced. To finance the development of his inventions, to continue his studies of structural principles, and to explore world economic planning, Fuller supplemented his uneven cash flow with inherited funds and even cashed insurance policies. In 1940, however, he realized a substantial profit when he utilized circular metal grain bins for his inexpensive Dymaxion Deployment Units, which the U.S. government bought to house troops and protect radar equipment in remote areas.

Fuller was eager to utilize resources efficiently. To popularize ecology and emphasize the dangers of pollution, he purchased in 1930 and edited anonymously for two years an architectural magazine called *T-Square*, which he renamed *Shelter*. During his tenure from 1938 to 1940 as *Fortune* magazine's science and technology consultant, its tenth-anniversary issue, featuring Fuller's charts and graphs comparing the resources of the United States with those of the world, was so successful that it sold out three printings. In his visual designs, he strove to make complex relations understandable, creating new formulations, such as using "energy" units rather than tonnage or man-hours. Despite the recognition he had gained, Fuller was not always taken seriously. Blaming that fact partly on his habits of drinking and partying, he gave up alcohol and tobacco in 1941. During World War II, from 1942 to 1944, while directing mechanical engineering for the U.S. Board (later Office) of Economic Warfare, he perfected his Dymaxion World Map. Published in 1943 by *Life* magazine in a huge 3,000,000-copy issue, it eliminated the distortions of the common Mercator projection by dividing the world into a regular spherical icosahedron of twenty equilateral triangles, then transforming it into a planar icosahedron, and finally cutting it apart to produce a flat map that could be centered on any point.

Fuller's first creative period closed with the development of his Wichita House. Its prototype was built in 1945 and 1946 at the Beech Aircraft plant, where it was to be produced by assembly-line techniques. The project put into practice his plan, worked out while in the Office of Economic Warfare, to convert the aircraft industry into a postwar housing industry. A circular structure of aluminum, steel, and plexiglass—with a ventilator in its low-slung roof giving ten complete changes of air per hour—the house was an updated version of his earlier Dymaxion House. Of those viewing its spacious furnished prototype, 3,700 registered to buy it. In limited production each house would retail for $6,500; in full production (500,000 per year) that cost would be cut nearly in half. The financial backers of the Wichita House were satisfied with its prototype and, to cash in on the postwar housing boom, wanted to rush into production. Fuller, however, insisted on two more prototypes; when his backers refused, the plan was abandoned, and Fuller vowed never again to work on a project dependent on speculative capital.

The abrupt ending of Fuller's Wichita project freed him to focus on his geodesic/tensegrity domes, which dominated his next creative period, 1947 to 1969. They were modeled on patterns he had long discerned in nature, and for two years he explored the mathematics (primarily spherical geometry) and the techniques involved in their construction. Fuller called his domes geodesics, the Greek name for the arcs of great circles, since they utilized the strength of the tetrahedron (a three-sided pyramid with a base) by creating a hemisphere of triangular struts forming trusses held in place by tension. Although a prototype—made from venetian blinds in the summer of 1948 with the help of students at North Carolina's Black Mountain College—collapsed, the next summer's dome of aluminum aircraft tubing stayed upright. That summer Kenneth Snelson, a sculpture student, illustrated the engineering principles of the geodesic dome with a model, which, held in place by taut wires, balanced tension to produce maximum strength. Fuller named the phenomenon "tensegrity" from the words "tension" and "integrity." In 1958 biologists and physicists confirmed that geodesic/tensegrity domes replicated structural patterns occurring naturally at the most fundamental level in viruses and atomic nuclei. Nearly four decades later, in 1996, three chemists—Robert F. Curl, Jr., and Richard E. Smalley of Rice University and Harold W. Kroto of the University of Sussex, England—won the Nobel Prize for their 1985 discovery of spherical molecular forms of carbon, which they called "fullerenes" or "buckyballs."

In the 1950s Fuller's geodesic domes inspired students on campuses all over the world and spread rapidly. They appeared at the Ford Motor Company River Rouge headquarters, at U.S. Marine Corps bases, and at radar installations (where they were called radomes). For a U.S. display at a 1956 International Trade Fair in Kabul, Afghanistan, a 100-foot-diameter geodesic dome was delivered by one cargo plane and erected in forty-eight hours. In assembling his domes, which exceeded 300,000 in his lifetime, Fuller used the innovative, efficient, and safe top-down construction method he had devised for his Dymaxion Deployment Units (always working at ground level, the top was hoisted on a mast to add lower sections). To manufacture his domes, Fuller in 1955 set up Synergetics, Inc., and Geodesics, Inc., but by 1966 he had licensed, for a 5 percent royalty under his patents, approximately 200 companies to build 3,000 geodesic domes.

Fuller's most impressive geodesic design was the 250-foot-diameter, twenty-story, three-quarter sphere

U.S. Pavilion at Montreal's Expo in 1967. With a monorail entering its glimmering shell (composed of thousands of triangular plexiglass panels programmed by a computer to open or shut, according to the weather), the pavilion was a "totally dynamic" structure. Attracting and delighting 5.3 million fairgoers in six months, it won Fuller worldwide acclaim. He also created models of even grander schemes, including a floating city for Japan in the early 1960s; a revamped version of it for Baltimore later in that decade; in 1971, a model of Old Man River City, with a geodesic dome one mile in diameter, which he hoped would revitalize East St. Louis, Illinois; and a two-mile diameter dome for midtown Manhattan, which by eliminating snow removal costs would pay for itself in a decade. None of these was built, but their creativity and his outstanding versatility led contemporaries to compare Fuller to Leonardo da Vinci.

Using games, lectures, and writings, Fuller devoted his last period to saving "Spaceship Earth," a term he coined in 1951 to encourage people to view themselves as passengers on a single-system planet with a common interest in its survival. Rejecting Malthusian notions that growing population threatened finite resources, he optimistically preached that the problem was not supply but maldistribution and waste of resources. In 1969, hoping to present to the public a dramatic summary of the material he had collected and the insights he had formed, he developed "World Game," contrasting it with war games and concentrating on "livingry" rather than weaponry. His goal was to convince players, and through them the public, that what had become a "One-Town World" could support all its people if technology were employed on a worldwide basis. Divided into competing yet cooperative research and design teams, players in World Game seminars used Fuller's archives on the world's resources (dating back to his days at *Fortune*). The task of these players was to find ways to better conserve and allocate resources. Twenty-six students played a "pilot" World Game in early 1969 at the New York Studio School, but later that year Fuller conducted with the help of Edwin Schlossberg, who was then a young Ph.D. candidate, a full-fledged, two-week World Game seminar at Southern Illinois University. Other World Game seminars, with graduate students the chief participants, were held at various university campuses. These games exposed waste and inspired efforts to eliminate starvation, disease, homelessness, and poverty.

Fuller's lectures were as famous as his geodesic domes. In these packed "thinking-out-loud" sessions, sometimes lasting six or more hours, he was energized by eye-to-eye contact with the very students whose radicalism frightened his generation. To give these lectures—whose number per year often topped 100 and reached 150 in 1974—he engaged in what he called "toing and froing," rounding the globe fifty-seven times. He visited and revisited 544 different universities and colleges, and on these campuses he was the hero of those in the counterculture, who discovered

that his concerns coincided with many of their own. Focusing in these encounters on the future, Fuller shared his faith that rational technological planning could solve its problems.

A prolific and versatile author and poet, Fuller received an appointment as Charles Eliot Norton Professor of Poetry at Harvard from 1961 to 1962. Although his score or more books (many written with collaborators) sold more than a million copies, they were often complex and difficult to understand. His last books were not exceptions. In *Synergetics: Explorations in the Geometry of Thinking* (1975) and *Synergetics 2: Further Explorations in the Geometry of Thinking* (1979), Fuller fused his geometric-mathematical concepts with his understanding of the fundamental coordination of nature. His *Critical Path* (1980) and *Grunch of Giants* (1983) summed up his personal philosophy, observations, and solutions for future problems.

By focusing his great energy and intellect on promoting "the total use of total technology for total population" at the fastest possible pace, Fuller captured the attention of his contemporaries and completed numerous inventions for which he secured more than 2,000 world patents (Marks and Fuller, p. 9). He was on the cover of *Time* magazine in 1964; received more than 100 awards, including the Presidential Medal of Freedom (1983); held at least twenty-five academic appointments (the most lengthy one was at Southern Illinois University, where he and his wife lived in a geodesic dome); and was awarded forty-seven honorary degrees. Fuller died in Los Angeles, California. Throughout his life Fuller drew sustenance from the memory of his great aunt Margaret Fuller. Because, like him, she grappled with the Universe, a contemporary admirer used her celebrated statement to pair them across the generations:

> "I'll accept it,"
>   Said the famous spinster.
> "I'll explain it,"
>   Said the bold Buckminster.
>   (quoted in Applewhite, p. 146)

• Fuller's voluminous papers are at the Buckminster Fuller Institute in Santa Barbara, Calif. They include his "Chronofile," with his life's correspondence, starting with his "earliest childhood," and the printed collection he started on the wonders of modern technology and later used to document his reactions and those of others to technology. Also in his papers is the collected public record since 1917 of "Guinea Pig B" (Fuller's name for himself in his life's experiment), as portrayed in over 100,000 books, newspaper and magazine articles, and radio and television broadcasts. The institute also holds a thirteen-page "Introduction to R. Buckminster Fuller" (containing a "Glossary" to the words he coined or used in a new way, recommended books and videos for further information on Fuller, and the listing of computer access to additional information on him), as well as his 72-page "Basic Biography" (a listing of his well-known geodesic domes, patents, awards, honorary degrees, and publications). See also Fuller's *Ideas and Integrities: A Spontaneous Autobiographical Disclosure*, ed. Robert W. Marks (1963).

For Fuller's design projects, see James Ward, ed., *The Artifacts of R. Buckminster Fuller: A Comprehensive Collection of*

His Designs and Drawings (4 vols., 1985). Biographical accounts include Lloyd Steven Sieden, *Buckminster Fuller's Universe: An Appreciation* (1989); Edgar J. Applewhite, *Cosmic Fishing: An Account of Writing Synergetics with Buckminster Fuller* (1977); Alden Hatch, *Buckminster Fuller: At Home in the Universe* (1974); John McHale, *R. Buckminster Fuller* (1962); Robert Marks and R. Buckminster Fuller, *The Dymaxion World of Buckminster Fuller* (1960, 1973); *Buckminster Fuller: An Autobiographic Monologue/Scenario*, compiled by Robert Snyder (1980), an account of Fuller's life and work in his own words, by his son-in-law, a documentary filmmaker; Calvin Tomkins, "Profiles: In the Outlaw Area," and "Talk of the Town," *New Yorker*, 8 Jan. 1966, pp. 35–97; 10 Oct. 1959, pp. 34–36; and Paul Goldberger, "An Apostle of Technology: R. Buckminster Fuller Preached a Religion of Simple Principles and Rational Planning," *New York Times*, 3 July 1983. An obituary is in the *New York Times*, 2 July 1983, and is reprinted the following day with additional information.

OLIVE HOOGENBOOM

FULLER, Richard (22 Apr. 1804–20 Oct. 1876), Baptist theologian and pastor, was born in Beaufort, South Carolina, the son of Thomas Fuller and Elizabeth Middleton, cotton planters. He was educated at Beaufort College, a Baptist preparatory school, under William T. Brantley, a distinguished southern Baptist clergyman. In 1822 he suffered from a pulmonary infection that nearly cost his life. He graduated from Harvard College in 1824 with an A.B.

Fuller returned to South Carolina where he read law. He was admitted to the bar in 1825. In 1831 he married Charlotte Bull; they had three children. He was converted to the Christian faith by an itinerant evangelist, Daniel Baker, and was ordained a minister without any theological studies. In 1832 he became pastor of the Beaufort Baptist Church, for a salary of $1,000, which he gave to charity. He preached to slaves as part of his ministry at Beaufort and was admired in the black community. He temporarily lost his voice in 1836. Having to abstain from preaching, he traveled in Europe, returning after a year's absence to his congregation at Beaufort.

Fuller preached the annual sermon at the Ninth Baptist Triennial Convention in 1841 in Baltimore, Maryland. He delivered the keynote address and was considered at that time a key figure in the future of the national Baptist movement. He regretted deeply the irreconcilable differences dividing the Baptist denomination in 1845, when he became one of the founders of the Southern Baptist Convention, delivering its first annual address in 1846. In 1847 he became pastor at the Seventh Baptist Church in Baltimore, where he served until 1871. During his tenure the congregation increased in membership from less than 100 to 1,200 members. He also supervised the erection of a new edifice and the constitution of a new congregation, the Eutaw Place Baptist Church in Baltimore. He served as president of the state Baptist Union of Maryland in 1850 and later as president of the Southern Baptist Convention (1859 and 1861).

Fuller was considered a well-informed speaker and addressed a wide variety of issues. In 1854, in response to the denial of American citizens in Europe the right to conduct religious services and build churches, he called upon the U.S. Congress to support comprehensive religious liberty. In a debate in Baltimore with Archbishop John Hughes of New York, who pointed out that Catholic Maryland was the only colony that allowed freedom of religion in the colonial period, Fuller maintained it was the Baptists of Rhode Island who first advocated religious liberty.

In a series of sermons published in 1854, Fuller traced the history and theology of baptism and made a cogent case for believer's baptism by immersion as a requisite for church membership and admission to the ordinance of the Lord's Supper. His Lutheran ministerial colleague in Baltimore, Joseph A. Seiss, controverted Fuller's book as "arrogant and full of dexterous evasions." The published Fuller-Seiss exchanges represent a major American Protestant theological debate on the sacraments at mid-nineteenth century.

In 1844 Fuller engaged in published correspondence in the *Christian Reflector* of Philadelphia, Pennsylvania, with Francis Wayland of Providence, Rhode Island, on the morality of slaveholding. This debate, later published in book form in 1845, became a classic statement of southern Christian culture. Fuller argued that the Old and New Testaments sanctioned and recognized slavery. Slavery was not to be confused with its abuses, and the southern states were not accountable for American slavery, since it was the British who introduced slavery to the colonies. Moreover, he held that Africans were greatly improved by their transport to the new world. He believed that southern ministers, not northern missionaries, were appropriate to serve the slave population.

During the Civil War, Fuller remained a nationalist and supported President Abraham Lincoln's calls for days of prayer and fasting. He held war to be an unacceptable answer to the sectional differences and scrupulously avoided taking political sides. However, his signature on the Savannah Resolutions, accusing the North of fanaticism and approving the formation of the Confederate States of America, caused bitter criticism among northerners who thought him to be a rebel. Once convinced of separate nations, North and South, he called in 1861 for a peaceful separation. Four years later, he called for an end to animosities and a rapid postwar reconciliation.

Following the Civil War, Fuller's reputation as a national leader in his denomination was quickly recovered. He was widely renowned as a preacher and published several volumes of sermons. He was a practical Calvinist, who, while holding to predestination, exhorted a life of faith and discipleship. Christological in tone and biblical in scope, he frequently emphasized evangelistic themes and advocated a doctrine of Christian social egalitarianism. He favored a somewhat formal liturgy and supervised the preparation of a Baptist praise book for congregational use. He died in Baltimore.

• A small collection of manuscripts and published material relating to Fuller is at the American Baptist Historical Society, Rochester, N.Y. Fuller's writings are extensive. His debates with Francis Wayland were published as *Domestic Slavery Considered As a Scriptural Institution in a Correspondence between the Rev. Richard Fuller and the Rev. Francis Wayland* (1845). He published three volumes of sermons (1860, 1877) on topics ranging from predestination to personal religion, and "Our Duty to the African Race." His theological positions are found in Joseph Seiss, *The Baptist System Examined: A Review of Dr. Richard Fuller and Others on "Baptism and the Terms of Communion"* (1883), and Fuller, "Religious Freedom," *Baptist Memorial and Monthly Chronicle* (1854): 225–34. Biographical details are in *Baptist Memorial and Monthly Chronicle* 8, no. 6 (1849): 173–77, and James H. Cuthbert, *Life of Richard Fuller D. D.* (1879). See also Anne Loveland, *Southern Evangelicals and the Social Order* (1980).

WILLIAM H. BRACKNEY

FULLER, Sarah (15 Feb. 1836–1 Aug. 1927), educator and advocate for deaf children, was born in Weston, Massachusetts, the daughter of Hervey Fuller and Celynda Fiske, farmers. After receiving her early education in Newton Lower Falls, Massachusetts, Fuller attended the Allan English and Classical School of West Newton. Cyrus Pierce, founder and president of Framingham State College in Massachusetts, one of the first normal schools in the United States, encouraged Fuller to become a teacher after having observed her intelligence and talent with teaching materials. Fuller entered the teaching profession in 1855 and taught for fourteen years in the public intermediate school of Newton, at the Boylston School on Fort Hill, and at the Bowditch School in Boston.

Fuller's career in deaf education began with the Reverend Dexter King, who had participated in creating the Clarke School for the Deaf in Northhampton, Massachusetts, and wished to open a similar school in Boston. Fuller, recognized for her patience and talent as an exceptional educator, was transferred from the Bowditch School in 1869 and was chosen by King to teach and preside as the school's principal, primarily because of her bearing and manner. King requested that the principal be able to supervise the interests of the school, secure the affection of the pupils, gain the confidence and respect of the school community, and instruct the deaf in oral language techniques, which the Clarke School for the Deaf employed as opposed to the use of sign or manual language. Fuller, after having completed three months of training at the Clarke School for the Deaf in Northhampton, was fully instructed in articulation or oral language and believed strongly that this method was more beneficial to the deaf child than the use of sign language. These three months when she had been instructed in both articulation and lip reading methods were the foundation for Fuller's oralist philosophy. During these years, the debate continued between educators of the deaf who believed in the combined use of sign language and articulation and those, such as Fuller, who firmly believed in the sole use of oral methods.

On 10 November 1869 the Boston School Board oversaw the opening of the Boston School for Deaf-Mutes, located on East Street in Boston, Massachusetts. Nine students originally enrolled in what became the first public day school for the deaf in the United States (earlier schools had been residential). The Boston School for Deaf-Mutes functioned as a primary school, and upon graduation its students were expected to attend the board's regular grammar schools. The school was renamed the Horace Mann School for the Deaf in 1877, and its enrollment grew to approximately sixty-five. Fuller, who never married, dedicated herself to the school and served as principal until 1910, overseeing the curriculum, which was among the first to include woodworking and printmaking. Fuller secured the money for both of these programs from friends and acquaintances.

After attending two of his lecture series in 1869 and 1870 at the Lowell Institute in Boston, Fuller became intrigued by the theories of Alexander Melville Bell, a distinguished British elocutionist and author of *Visible Speech: The Science of Universal Alphabetics*, published in 1867. Visible speech was a method of teaching speech to the deaf using a physiological alphabet that provided a visual guide to the production of oral sounds. This alphabet demonstrated the position of the tongue and lips when they produced a specified sound. The method was considered very scientific and modern at the time, and, convinced of its worth, Fuller asked the Boston School Board to request that Bell instruct her and her staff in the methods of visible speech. When Bell subsequently declined, Fuller, undaunted, sought out his son, Alexander Graham Bell, who had employed his father's theories and methods in teaching speech to the deaf in a small school in London.

In 1871 Alexander Graham Bell was living in Canada when Fuller arranged for him to provide demonstration lessons to the thirty students in residence at the school and to train both herself and her assistant Mary True. Bell resided at the home of Fuller's sister and spent his days teaching and his evenings working with electrical equipment that eventually resulted in the invention of the telephone. During the summer of 1871, Fuller arranged for Bell to address a meeting in Flint, Michigan, of the principals of deaf schools. In his speech, Bell promoted visible speech to teach speech to the deaf, correct speech defects, teach literacy to adults, and provide missionaries with a method for recording unwritten languages. Impressed with Fuller's fluency in visible speech, Bell declared her one of the best speech teachers in the country.

The Horace Mann School for the Deaf became the first school to adopt visible speech as an aid in articulation teaching, and the school's mission provided that every child be taught to speak and to lip read the speech of others. In 1855 the state of Massachusetts gave Boston property in the Back Bay area to build a new facility to house the school, which opened 10 November 1890. In 1888 Fuller wrote an *Illustrated Primer* to educate and train teachers in the methods necessary to teach oral language to deaf students. Within the professional deaf education associations at this time, a debate raged between the pure oralists, represented by Alexander Graham Bell, and those who called for a combined system of sign and speech, represented by Thomas Gallaudet. At the 1890 convention of the American Instructors of the Deaf, Fuller became a cofounder with Bell and Caroline Yale, among others, of the American Association to Promote the Teaching of Speech to the Deaf (Fuller later served on its board of directors). This represented a political move that splintered the American Instructors of the Deaf into two opposing camps.

On 26 March 1890 Fuller taught her method of oral language instruction to her most famous pupil, a deaf and blind girl named Helen Keller. Keller remembered her as a lovely and sweet-natured woman. After receiving eleven lessons under Fuller's tutelage, Keller uttered her first sentence. In August of 1865 Fuller founded one of the first parents' associations in Boston. She supported the construction of public playgrounds and was one of the first educators to employ departmental teaching of specific curriculum areas, such as science and math, at the elementary school level. With Alice Porter and Sarah Jordan Monro, community members and teachers at the school, Fuller established and taught afternoon classes for stammerers.

Committed to the belief that deaf infants should be treated in the same manner as hearing infants, Fuller maintained that the education of deaf children should begin in the family circle. Fuller firmly believed that deaf infants had the right to live in their own homes, under the care of their parents, while receiving a common school education. Her conviction inspired Mr. and Mrs. Francis Books, Boston parents of a deaf daughter, to establish a home school for deaf children of nursery school age. The Sarah Fuller Home for Little Children Who Cannot Hear opened in 1888 in West Medford, Massachusetts. The first institution to undertake the preschool education of deaf children, the school operated for thirty-seven years, until lack of financial resources forced its closing.

Fuller dedicated her life to the needs of the deaf student population. When she retired from the Horace Mann School in 1910, the student population had grown substantially from nine to 150 pupils. She was succeeded by her niece, Ella Celynda Jordan, who had been assistant principal at the school for many years. Following her retirement, Fuller remained committed and active in her efforts to educate the deaf. She continued to write letters and have students visit her home in Newton Lower Falls, until her death. Fuller stipulated that no music be played at her funeral, because her beloved pupils would be unable to hear it. As a testimony to her efforts to teach speech, one of Fuller's former deaf students from the Horace Mann School for the Deaf spoke aloud the words of the burial service.

Fuller is remembered primarily as an oralist in the debate between those supporting the appropriateness of sign language and those favoring oral language instruction. Although Fuller's career can be linked to the visible speech movement, her advocacy of early speech education and day instruction of deaf children and her innovation in the area of departmental elementary school teaching were her most noteworthy accomplishments.

• Fuller's own account of the history of the Horace Mann School for the Deaf is recorded in Edward A. Fay, ed., *Histories of the American Schools for the Deaf, 1817–1893*, vol. 2 (1893). Information on Fuller's professional life and the history of the Horace Mann School for the Deaf can be found in the published proceedings of the *American Instructors of the Deaf and Dumb* 35 (1890), *American Annals of the Deaf and Dumb* 55 and 56 (1910), and in the *American Association to Promote the Teaching of Speech to the Deaf*. Mabel Ellery Adams wrote of Fuller's professional accomplishments in the *American Annals of the Deaf* (Nov. 1927), as did Fred Deland in the *Volta Review* (Jan. and Nov. 1927). Fuller is also included in Julia Ward Howe, ed., *Representative Women of New England* (1904). A tribute to Fuller is presented in Anna P. Butler, "Her Smile Was a Benediction," published by the Delta Gamma Society of Boston (1958). Her biography is listed in *Woman's Who's Who of America, 1914–1915*. Additional accounts can be found in the *Volta Review* (Nov. 1912); the *American Annals of the Deaf* (Jan. 1945), and in the Boston School Committee's special reports of 1873 and 1874 on the "School for Deaf-Mutes." See also Hugo F. Schunhoff, *The Teaching of Speech and by Speech in Public Residential Schools for the Deaf in the U.S. 1815–1955* (1957). Fuller's involvement with Alexander Graham Bell is noted in Catherine Mackenzie, *Alexander Graham Bell* (1928). Fuller's instruction of Helen Keller is mentioned by Keller in *The Story of My Life* (1903), and in *Teacher: Anne Sullivan Macy* (1955). See Harlan Lane's *When the Mind Hears: A History of the Deaf* (1984) for an account of Fuller's impact on the education of the deaf. Obituary notices are in the *American Annals of the Deaf* (Sep. 1927).

KAREN I. CASE

FULLER, Solomon Carter (11 Aug. 1872–16 Jan. 1953), neuropathologist and psychiatrist, was born in Monrovia, Liberia, the son of Solomon Carter Fuller, a coffee planter and Liberian government official, and Anna Ursala James. His father, son of a repatriated former American slave, was able to provide a private education for his children at a school he established on his prosperous plantation. In the summer of 1889 young Solomon Fuller left home to return to the country where his grandfather had once been held in bondage. He sought higher education at Livingstone College in Salisbury, North Carolina, a college for black students founded ten years earlier.

Fuller graduated from Livingstone in 1893 with an A.B. and proceeded to pursue a medical degree at Long Island College Hospital in Brooklyn, New York. After one year he transferred to Boston University School of Medicine, where he received an M.D. in 1897. Although he was deeply disturbed by the racism he found in America, Fuller decided that he would not return to Liberia. Shortly after graduating he accepted an appointment as an intern at the Westborough State Hospital for the Insane, west of Boston. Two years later he was promoted to become the institution's chief pathologist, beginning a 45-year tenure at Westborough—twenty-two years as a pathologist and twenty-three as a consultant. In 1899 he also accepted a part-time instructorship in pathology at Boston University, where he quickly established a reputation as a talented teacher.

During these early years as a pathologist, Fuller took his room and board on the grounds of the Westborough State Hospital, which allowed him to spend long hours in the laboratory he directed. He concentrated on photography of extremely thin sections of brain tissue, employing great technical skill with microtome, microscope, and camera to search for connections between mental disorder and organic disease.

During the 1904–1905 academic year Fuller took a leave from his positions at Westborough and Boston and traveled overseas. At the University of Munich he studied under several prominent German medical scientists, including Alois Alzheimer, who would soon identify Alzheimer's disease. On a sightseeing trip to Berlin in 1905, Fuller worked up the courage to introduce himself to the famed immunologist Paul Ehrlich. Much to Fuller's surprise, Ehrlich was happy to have the company of the young American pathologist for the afternoon, and the two continued their friendship by correspondence for years.

A few years after Fuller's return to Massachusetts, he had another brush with greatness. In 1909 Sigmund Freud was invited to give a series of five lectures at Clark University in Worcester, Massachusetts, not far from Westborough. Those lectures stand as a landmark in the history of American psychiatry, and Fuller was among the invited members of the audience. In the same year Fuller married Meta Vaux Warrick, a woman of exceptional artistic talent whom he met when she happened to visit Westborough State Hospital. Meta's special gift was sculpture, and her works were often dramatic renderings of the black experience in America. In the years immediately surrounding the turn of the century, she had spent time in Paris and emerged briefly as an artistic sensation in the French capital when she won the admiration of Auguste Rodin, who said to her on their initial meeting, "My child, you are a sculptor; you have the sense of form in your fingers" (quoted in Hoover, p. 678). However, after returning home to Philadelphia, racial discrimination—and the traditional expectations of her upper-class black family—sapped much of the energy from Meta's artistic rise. When she met and married Fuller, Meta continued with her sculpture as an avocation and found some significant but limited success; she gave up the pursuit of her art as an all-consuming passion.

The newlyweds bought a house in Framingham, Massachusetts, roughly halfway between Boston University and Westborough State Hospital. Their initial welcome was not warm in the predominantly white community: some of the citizens circulated a petition in an unsuccessful attempt to prevent the black doctor and his wife from purchasing a house there. The Fullers managed to overcome—or at least to ignore—this insult and less overt manifestations of racism and went on to establish a comfortable home in Framingham, where they would raise three children and live out

their days. Soon after their arrival in Framingham, Solomon Fuller began a private psychotherapy practice out of an office in his home, which added another layer of responsibility. Fuller's practice became large and included both white and black patients. His son recalled, "My father had great spiritual qualities. People came to him for a spiritual communion that was a refreshing, inspiring, and motivating experience. . . . My father had such a gracious, loving, radiant, and quieting personality that it had a great calming effect on his patients' problems" (quoted in Hayden and Harris, p. 27).

Although Fuller's private practice focused on psychiatric counseling, his research and teaching continued to center on neurology. He published a number of papers, including several on the disease named for his German mentor Alzheimer (Fuller is credited as having identified the ninth case of Alzheimer's disease in a 1911 publication). He also served for many years as the editor of the *Westborough State Hospital Papers*, an outlet for the publication of scientific work carried out by members of the hospital staff.

After twenty years of service at Boston University, in 1919 Fuller was named an associate professor of neuropathology; in 1921 his title was revised to associate professor of neurology. From 1928 until 1933 he functioned as the effective chair of the university's Department of Neurology. He retired in 1933, when a white assistant professor was promoted over him to a full professorship and officially named head of the department. Through his long years as a popular and respected teacher at Boston University, Fuller had never been placed officially on the school's payroll, although he had been paid for his services. The promotion of the junior colleague over him in 1933 was the final blow in a series of institutional indignities. On the occasion of his resignation, he stated with characteristic grace, "I regard life as a battle in which we win or lose. As far as I am concerned, to be vanquished, if not ingloriously, is not so bad after all." But he added, with understatement, "With the sort of work that I have done, I might have gone farther and reached a higher plane had it not been for the color of my skin" (quoted in Hayden and Harris, p. 22).

Soon after his retirement from Boston University, Fuller began to suffer increasingly from diabetes. By 1944 his eyesight had failed entirely as a result of the disease, and he was forced to end his long association with Westborough State Hospital. Although he lived his final decade in darkness, he continued to meet with a limited number of patients in his private psychiatric practice nearly until the time of his death in Framingham.

Fuller had returned to the country where his grandfather had begun life as a slave, and there he had won a high degree of professional success. His attainments might have been greater if his skin had been white, but in the place of some unrealized aspirations we are left with an impressive legacy of patience and perseverance.

• A valuable biographical piece on Fuller is by W. Montague Cobb, *Journal of the National Medical Association* 46 (1954): 370–72; it includes a bibliography of Fuller's publications. An informative chapter on Fuller appears in a book for young readers, Robert C. Hayden and Jacqueline Harris, *Nine Black American Doctors* (1976), pp. 14–29. Information on Fuller's artist wife (and her life with Fuller) is in Velma J. Hoover, "Meta Vaux Fuller: Her Life and Art," *Negro History Bulletin* 40 (Mar.–Apr. 1977): 678–81.

JON M. HARKNESS

FULLER, Thomas (1710–1790), calculator, was born in West Africa. Nothing is known of his parents or other family. At the age of fourteen he was brought as a slave to British North America and apparently lived the remainder of his life in Virginia. In his old age he was owned by Elizabeth Coxe of Alexandria, Virginia.

Fuller led the typical life of a slave and never learned to read or write but was widely noted late in his life for his extraordinary ability to perform rapid and complicated mathematical calculations in his head. He was often visited by travelers wanting to witness his skill. One of them was Benjamin Rush of Philadelphia, the noted physician and educator. Rush quizzed him and verified the accuracy of his answers. Fuller could multiply nine figures by nine, give the number of seconds in a year, calculate how many seconds anyone had lived, determine the number of yards, feet, and inches in any huge distance, and perform other such feats. His legendary abilities earned him the sobriquet the "Virginia Calculator." Told that it was regrettable that he had not had a formal education commensurate with his abilities, Fuller replied, "It is best I got no learning; for many learned men be great fools."

It is impossible to determine the source of Fuller's talent from a medical or psychological point of view. There is no doubt that in the area of arithmetic calculations he was a prodigy. He seems to have been otherwise normal and displayed none of the idiot savant symptoms of mental retardation accompanied by extraordinary skill in one particular area.

• Fuller was publicized by Rush in the *American Museum or Repository of Ancient and Modern Fugitive Pieces* (1789). Vivian Sammons, *Blacks in Science and Medicine* (1990), has a brief reference to him. The fullest account of his life is in George Washington Williams, *History of the Negro Race in America*, vol. 1 (1883). Rayford W. Logan and Michael R. Winston, eds., *Dictionary of American Negro Biography* (1982), has a useful but shorter summary. Henri Grégoire, *An Enquiry Concerning the Intellectual and Moral Faculties and Literature of Negroes* (1810; repr. 1967), summarizes Rush's account. *Needles's History Memoir of the Pennsylvania Society for Promoting the Abolition of Slavery* (n.d.) also mentions Fuller. An obituary appears in the *Columbia Centinel*, 29 Dec. 1790.

WILLIAM F. MUGLESTON

FULLER, Thomas Oscar (25 Oct. 1867–21 June 1942), educator, clergyman, and politician, was born in Franklinton, North Carolina, the son of J. Henderson Fuller and Mary Elizabeth (maiden name unknown).

Fuller's father was a former slave who had purchased his freedom and later his wife's with money earned as a skilled wheelwright and carpenter. While a slave, the elder Fuller taught himself to read, and after the Civil War he became active in Republican politics. During Reconstruction he served as a delegate to the 1868 state Republican convention and as a local magistrate.

Fuller completed his primary education in local schools and subsequently attended the Franklinton Normal School, an institution founded to educate black teachers. He graduated from Shaw University in 1890 and received a Master of Arts from the same institution in 1893. After graduation, Fuller simultaneously pursued careers in education and the ministry. Raised in a devoutly religious family, he was ordained as a Baptist minister, and in 1893 he was called to the pulpit of Benton Creek Church in Oxford, North Carolina. As the church paid Fuller only fifty dollars per year, the young minister derived most of his livelihood from teaching public school in Granville County. In 1892 he returned to Franklinton to organize a primary school for local black women, called the Girls' Training School, and in 1895 he was appointed to the principalship of the Shiloh Institute in Warrenton.

Fuller served in this position for three years and became a respected leader of the black community. He was also active in local Republican politics. In 1898 he reluctantly accepted the party nomination for the state senate, representing the Eleventh District, comprised of Vance and Warren counties. He won election easily.

Fuller, the last black to serve in the North Carolina legislature until 1968, was one of several black North Carolinians elected to state and national offices between 1894 and 1901 as a result of a shaky political alliance between Republicans and Populists. When this fusion alliance provoked a violent white supremacy campaign, first in Wilmington and later across the state, Fuller called on blacks to avoid confrontation and suppress the temptation to riot. Nevertheless, he could not escape the prevailing racial sentiments of the day. In his memoirs, when reflecting on his reception as a newly elected state senator, Fuller recalled that he was seated last, after white senators who were seated alphabetically. Furthermore, such prejudice prevented him from being appointed to any senate committee. Nevertheless, he lobbied for legislation that benefited both races in North Carolina. His belief in temperance, derived undoubtably from his staunch Baptist faith, led Fuller to lobby for a law that closed an open bar in Warrenton. He also introduced a bill to allow the criminal court to meet every four months and to give the state superior court concurrent jurisdiction with country courts, a measure that decreased docket loads and led to speedier trials. Two of his legislative triumphs directly aided blacks. One act incorporated the North Carolina Mutual and Provident Association, forerunner to the North Carolina Mutual Life Insurance Company, a model for black businesses of the period. He also sponsored a bill to allow outside labor agents to recruit black workers in North Carolina, a practice previously forbidden by law and custom. In

1899 the legislature began debating measures to disfranchise blacks through literacy tests, a poll tax, and a grandfather clause. Fuller was in the center of these debates, arguing that whites had nothing to fear from a black electorate. Despite his eloquent oratory, the resolution passed, and the constitutional amendment took effect in 1900.

Fuller's passionate defense of black voting rights was his last shining moment in the legislature. In 1900 he went to Memphis to pastor the First Baptist Church, a post he held until 1941. In 1902 he also became principal of the Howe Institute, a coeducational normal school, where he taught theology and law, among other subjects. He served as president of the institute until 1912, when it merged with Roger Williams College.

Fuller's abilities and character were well recognized in the black community. He remained active in the National Baptist Convention, serving as a secretary for twenty-five years. President Theodore Roosevelt briefly considered appointing Fuller ambassador to Liberia in 1906, but much to Fuller's relief, the appointment never materialized.

An author of note, Fuller wrote on a variety of subjects, but race was an important theme in most of his works. His memoir, *Twenty Years in Public Life: 1890–1910, North Carolina–Tennessee* (1910), provides an excellent overview of his political, educational, and ministerial careers. Furthermore, it is an excellent case study of the triumphs and tribulations of a black leader in the Jim Crow South. In *Banks and Banking* (1920) Fuller outlined the steps necessary in organizing and managing a bank, an attempt to stimulate the growth of a black financial community. *Pictorial History of the American Negro* (1933), *Negro Baptists in Tennessee* (1936), and *Story of Church Life among Negroes* (1938) contain useful biographical information about black leaders and insight into the social life of blacks in the early twentieth century. Other works include *Flashes and Gems of Thought and Eloquence* (1920), *Bridging the Racial Chasms: A Brief Survey of Inter-Racial Attitudes and Relations* (1937), and *Notes on Parliamentary Law* (1940).

Although Fuller married four times, little is known of his spouses or the dates of his marriages. His first wife was Lucy G. Davis. With his second wife, Laura Faulkner, he had two sons, only one of whom survived childhood. Little is known of his third wife, Rosa, and his fourth wife, Dixie Williams. His first three marriages ended with the death of each wife.

After his death in Memphis, Fuller was eulogized as a great minister, teacher, and leader of the black community. Through his educational, religious, and political efforts, he attempted to better the lives of his fellow blacks during a tumultuous time in American history. Although not as well known as many contemporaries, Fuller's drive, eloquence, and example helped pave the way for future black leaders in the quest for civil rights.

• No known collection of Fuller's personal or professional correspondence exists. The most accessible sources of information about his career are his own writings. A scholarly assessment of Fuller's political career is in Helen G. Edmonds, *The Negro and Fusion Politics in North Carolina, 1894–1901* (1951). An obituary emphasizing Fuller's importance as a black minister and community leader is in the *National Baptist Voice*, 15 July 1942.

RICHARD D. STARNES

FULTON, John Farquhar (1 Nov. 1899–29 May 1960), neurophysiologist and medical historian, was born in St. Paul, Minnesota, son of John Farquhar Fulton, a physician, and Edith Stanley Wheaton. After spending the 1917–1918 academic year at the University of Minnesota, Fulton entered Harvard University, from which he received a B.S., magna cum laude, in 1921. As a recipient of a Rhodes Scholarship, Fulton attended Magdalen College at Oxford University for two years, followed by an additional two years at Oxford as a Christopher Welch Scholar and demonstrator in physiology. He received a B.A. from Oxford with first-class honors in 1923, and an M.A. and D.Phil. in 1925. Returning to the United States, he studied medicine at Harvard, receiving his M.D., again magna cum laude, in 1927. He married Lucia Pickering Wheatland, of Salem, Massachusetts, in 1923; they had no children.

At Oxford Fulton pursued neurophysiological experiments under the tutelage of Charles Scott Sherrington. He incorporated these experimental findings in his *Muscular Contraction and the Reflex Control of Movement* (1926). Fulton spent much of 1927 and 1928 in the service of Harvey Cushing as an associate neurological fellow at Peter Bent Brigham Hospital, Boston. It was while working with Cushing that Fulton and Jaime Pi-Suñer distinguished the parallel arrangement of muscle spindles and the series arrangement of tendon organs that are now classic concepts of muscle contraction physiology. Fulton recounted the life of his neurosurgical mentor, and later colleague and friend, in his most enduring historical work, *Harvey Cushing: A Biography* (1946).

Fulton returned to Oxford for two years as a fellow of Magdalen College, where he continued work with Sherrington and compiled *Readings in the History of Physiology* (1930). In this work Fulton emphasized the ways in which human experimentation had contributed to new physiological discoveries. This book has remained a standard resource in the field.

Fulton returned to the United States and was appointed Sterling Professor of Physiology at Yale University in 1929, a position he held until 1951; after that he served as Yale's Sterling Professor of the History of Medicine until his death. As a physiology professor Fulton established the first primate laboratory in America and dedicated his time to discerning correlations between ape and human cerebral physiology and pathology.

During clinical studies at Harvard, Fulton began to discern similarities between the work of neurophysiologists and neurosurgeons while working with the renowned neurosurgeon Harvey Cushing. Fulton continued investigations in each of these areas. Among his most noted contributions was the study of the ways in which the cranial cerebrum controlled particular segments along the spinal cord. Fulton turned particular attention to the production of spasticity in animals and to distinguishing the motor and premotor control areas of the brain. Key papers describing this work include "Forced Grasping and Groping in Relation to the Syndrome of the Premotor Area" (*Archives of Neurology and Psychiatry* 31 [1934]: 221–34), "A Note on the Definition of the 'Motor' and 'Premotor' Areas" (*Brain* 58 [1935]: 311–16), and "Spasticity and the Frontal Lobes" (*New England Journal of Medicine* 217 [1937]: 1017–24). Fulton's early work prompted Antonio Egas Moniz to attempt to relieve psychotic mental patients with prefrontal lobotomies; the results earned Moniz the Nobel Prize in medicine and physiology in 1949. Fulton summarized his own research and that of his contemporaries in *Physiology of the Nervous System* (1938). This work went through three editions, was translated into French, German, Portuguese, Spanish, Japanese, and Russian, and it became the standard source on the subject. Demonstrative of his own directions in research, it served to bridge the gaps between neurophysiology, neurology, and neurosurgery. During World War II Fulton placed a decompression chamber in his primate laboratory in order to study the applications of physiological research to aviation. Many of these research findings were published in *Aviation Medicine in Its Preventive Aspects* (1948).

Fulton fostered many experimental disciples in his laboratory, an environment that contemporaries described as yielding a "maximum of stimulation and a minimum of direction." Given this credo, it is not surprising to find that many future discoverers in neurophysiology owed their experimental approach to Fulton. Several of Fulton's students who later gained renown contributed their accounts of Fulton's influence in a special issue of the *Yale Journal of Biology and Medicine* (1955–1956).

In 1938 Fulton cofounded, with J. G. Dusser de Barenne, the *Journal of Neurophysiology*, for which he served as editor until 1960. He also served on the editorial board of the *New England Journal of Medicine* from 1936 to 1943, and as editor of the *Journal of the History of Medicine* from 1951 to 1960. Fulton edited and made significant contributions to *Howell's Textbook of Physiology* from its fourteenth through seventeenth editions (1942–1955).

Fulton maintained active membership in many national scholarly and professional societies, including the American Philosophical Society, as well as international societies, including the Royal Society of Medicine (London); he was a fellow of the Royal College of Physicians (London) and of the Deutsche Gesellschaft für Neurologie. He held many leadership positions, including serving as a trustee of the Institute for Advanced Study at Princeton. For the National Research Council, Fulton served as chairman of the Committee on Historical Records (1940–1946) and the Committee on Aviation Medicine (1940–1946), and in 1943 was vice chairman of the Division of Medical Sciences. He received many honors and awards, including the Order of Cultural Merit (Rumania, 1932), Honorary Order of the British Empire (1948), President's Certificate of Merit (U.S.A., 1948), Officer of the Legion of Honor (France, 1949), Gold Medal, University of Liège (1951), Commander of the Order of Leopold II (Belgium, 1951), Orden de Mérito (Cuba, 1954), and the Sarton Medal from the History of Science Society (1958).

After Fulton's death in Hamden, Connecticut, much of his massive collection of rare medical and science books was donated to the Historical Library of Yale University's Medical School. In the words of one Fulton memorialist, Lloyd G. Stevenson, it was "as a contributor to the domain of medical history, in which [Fulton] gave so much encouragement and opportunity to others," and it was through this lifelong contribution that he "deserves a lasting name." Fulton's donation joined those of Harvey Cushing and Arnold Klebs to comprise one of the world's stellar collections on the history of science and medicine. A seminar room at Yale University School of Medicine also bears his name.

• Fulton's correspondence and memorabilia, including forty-six volumes of unpublished diaries, are held in the Fulton Papers at the Yale Medical Library. In addition to works cited in the text, his key book-length writings include *The Sign of Babinski: A Study of the Evolution of Cortical Dominance in Primates* (1932), written with Allen D. Keller, which contributed to the understanding of the pyramidal and extrapyramidal motor systems; a philosophical work, *Humanism in an Age of Science* (1950); and the medical biographies *Sir Kenelm Digby* (1937), and *Michael Servetus, Humanist and Martyr* (1953), written with Madeline E. Stanton. The most complete account of Fulton's life is Elizabeth H. Thomson, "John Farquhar Fulton," an unpublished manuscript in the section of the History of Medicine at Yale University School of Medicine. Published biographical accounts include Hebbel E. Hoff, "The Laboratory of Physiology," *Yale Journal of Biology and Medicine* 28 (1955–1956): 165–76, with Fulton's bibliography to that date; and Lloyd G. Stevenson, "John Farquhar Fulton," *Bulletin of the History of Medicine* 34 (1961): 81–87. The editors of the *Journal of the History of Medicine and Allied Sciences* issued a special memorial volume 17 (1962), including Arnold Muirhead, "John Fulton—Book Collector, Humanist, and Friend," pp. 2–15; Hebbel E. Hoff, "John Fulton's Contribution to Neurophysiology," pp. 16–37; William LeFanu, "John Fulton's Historical and Bibliographical Work," pp. 38–50; and M. E. S. and E. H. T., "Bibliography of John Farquhar Fulton, 1921–1962," pp. 51–71.

PHILIP K. WILSON

FULTON, Robert (14 Nov. 1765–23 Feb. 1815), artist, engineer, and entrepreneur, was born on a farm in Little Britain (later Fulton) Township, south of Lancaster, Pennsylvania, the son of Robert Fulton, a Scotch-Irish tailor and tradesman, and Mary Smith. Fulton's father had left the prosperous market town of Lancaster to establish his family on the land, but like so many others with the same goal, he failed. The farm and the dwelling were sold at sheriff's sale in 1772, and he took his family back to Lancaster. He died two years later.

According to family accounts, young Fulton received his earliest education from his mother, then studied with a Quaker schoolmaster in Lancaster. At about the age of fourteen he was apprenticed to Jeremiah Andrews, an English jeweler who had established a business in Philadelphia. Andrews permitted his charge to work at portraiture, a necessary adjunct to the jeweler's trade, and Fulton became sufficiently proficient at rendering likenesses (and the associated hair working) to warrant his own separate listing as a miniature painter in the Philadelphia directory of 1785. The following spring, apparently suffering from the early stages of tuberculosis, he was able to travel to the warm springs resort at Bath, Virginia. Along the way or on his return, Fulton, "yeoman" and "miniature painter of the city of Philadelphia," purchased land in Washington County, Pennsylvania, and, as if to replace what his father had lost, soon settled his mother on a small farm there.

In late 1786 or 1787 Fulton sailed for London, intending to study and perfect his art. He carried letters of recommendation, notably one to the famous Benjamin West (1783–1820), who was well known for his interest and support for aspiring American artists and who had been, for a brief time at the outset of his career, a resident of Lancaster, Pennsylvania. With West as his mentor, Fulton improved a little as a painter, exhibiting two canvases at the Royal Academy in 1791 and four in 1793. More importantly, he developed the social skills essential to success in the world of power and privilege. He learned to use his good looks and enthusiasm to advantage in securing patrons and retaining their interest. The firmness of West's friendship, as well as the proximity of superior talent, also made it easier for Fulton to recognize his artistic limitations and to seize other opportunities.

The artist's transition to engineer began during the years 1791–1794, much of which time he spent at or near Powderham, Devonshire, the estate of William Courtenay, third viscount of Powderham (later ninth earl of Devon). The young viscount's patronage brought several portrait commissions, but because Courtenay had been the subject of scandal only a few years earlier, Fulton was fortunate to gain the attention of his patron's weightier colleague on the Bude Canal Committee, the political radical and inventor Charles Mahon, third earl Stanhope. Stanhope's interest in Fulton's ideas, albeit condescending, encouraged the artist to direct his full energies to canal design and construction. While in Devon he also contrived machinery for "sawing marble or other stone." In June 1794 "Robert Fulton late of the City of Exeter, but now of the City of London, Gentleman" received royal patent number 1988 for "a machine or engine for conveying boats and vessels and their cargoes to and from the different levels . . . without the assistance of locks." He then went to Manchester, the industrial

center of England's expanding network of inland waterways, to gain "practical knowledge" (Dickinson, pp. 29–30). There he shared lodgings with the cotton manufacturer (later utopian reformer) Robert Owen, who, in the capacity of investor in his canal projects, advanced him much needed money.

Fulton established himself as a "civil engineer" with the publication of his *Treatise on the Improvement of Canal Navigation* by I. and J. Taylor of London in 1796. Elaborating on the idea of his patent, he boldly argued that his "small canal system" (that is, system of canals designed for small boats) would prove so much cheaper and more efficient to construct and operate that it would render large canals with traditional locks obsolete. The boats would move to higher and lower levels along railed inclines, carried in wheeled carts or frames attached to an endless chain, or by means of a lift, the power to be gained by lowering a preponderating weight (a container of water) in a vertical shaft or, alternatively, by the action of a waterwheel. Critics judged Fulton's *Treatise* more visionary than practical and pointed out that his components derived from the innovations of others, which he admitted, claiming, as he would later, that the "genius" lay in his new combinations. However, the "ingenuity" of his small canals and their suitability for less accessible regions and difficult terrains, especially in America and Europe, were acknowledged (Chapman, p. 2). Indeed, Fulton had published his designs for inclines, related machinery, and compatible wood and iron bridges and aqueducts (which he expertly illustrated in seventeen handsome plates) with opportunities in those regions uppermost in his mind. Hoping to profit from his notoriety, he renewed his pleas for support to Lord Stanhope, petitioned President George Washington and the elected officials of his native Pennsylvania to support extensive canal projects, and even urged West and his patrons to invest in such ventures. In April 1797 he succeeded in selling a portion of his patent rights to the wealthy Anglo-American John Barker Church, Alexander Hamilton's brother-in-law.

Fulton went to Paris in mid-1797, intending to promote his ideas for canals (for which he received a French patent in Feb. 1798) but also to exploit other opportunities. He fell in with the community of Americans there, among whom were the poet, diplomat, and mercantile agent Joel Barlow and his wife Ruth Baldwin Barlow. The Barlows and Fulton soon formed a ménage à trois, based on "dearest friendship" as well as a chemistry of affection and passion, living in four rooms of a large hotel adjacent to the Luxembourg Gardens (Philip, p. 227). Such a relationship was dangerous but perhaps never less so than in the indulgent society of Directoire Paris.

The Barlow's friendship and patronage were crucial to Fulton in his career as well as in his personal life. In their company he expanded his education, especially in mathematics and the sciences, and transformed himself into the poised and slightly arrogant figure captured in the portraits of him that date from this period. Joel Barlow was the perfect mentor in living by one's wits. A man of some influence in Paris, he enjoyed French citizenship and had access to official circles. Barlow's assistance enabled Fulton to promote and sell two moneymaking schemes—his rights to an improved cording device (much like that of the Reverend Dr. Edmund Cartwright, which Fulton had seen in London) and to a series of popular exhibits of cityscapes or "panoramas."

Encouraged and largely financed by Barlow, Fulton enlisted his engineering skills in Barlow's (and by now his) political causes—republicanism, free trade, and the liberty of the seas. He devoted most of his energies to what he first called the "Mechanical Nautulus [sic]," later the *Nautilus*, a weapon to defeat the all-powerful British navy and to break up its blockade of the French Republic. Fulton presented proposals for constructing his "plunging boat" to the Directory in December 1797. The design derived from the earlier "diving boat" of David Bushnell, a Yale graduate from Connecticut, with which Barlow was familiar. Fulton's experiments, however, went well beyond anything previously contemplated and demonstrated for the first time the seaworthiness of submersible vessels and their value as instruments of naval warfare.

The Directory nevertheless could not decide whether to embrace or to abandon Fulton's plan for submarine attack; scientific panels endorsed it, while the politicians vacillated. Following Napoléon Bonaparte's coup of 18 brumaire (9–10 Nov.) 1799, however, work on the submersible boat was permitted to proceed in secret. The small sailing craft, elliptical in shape, some twenty feet in length, was constructed by the firm of Périer frères et cie. and tried out on the Seine on 13 June 1800. After further trials Fulton and the *Nautilus* went into action against the British fleet off Le Havre on 12 September 1800. The British ships, apparently alerted by spies, evaded each of his efforts to attach a "torpedo" or contact mine to one of their hulls.

Fulton continued to experiment with the *Nautilus* the following year, but, just as Napoléon's interest in the weapon appeared to warm, the boat began to fall apart from wear and tear. Fulton sold its parts for cash in September 1801 then refused to display his drawings to the First Consul's committee of engineers. The invention was his private property, he explained, and "ought to secure to me an ample independence" (Hutcheon, p. 49). Although he previously had asked only for prize money and bounties, he now demanded that the government contract for his services in advance.

Fulton turned his attention to steamboats in the summer of 1802, which he spent with Ruth Barlow at Plombières, a fashionable spa in the Vosges Mountains. There he sketched a steamboat moved by an endless chain of float boards to run "from New York to Albany in 12 hours" and experimented with a working model that had probably been constructed to such a design. His interest in the Hudson River was not theoretical—President Thomas Jefferson's new minister to France, Robert R. Livingston of New York, had arrived in Paris the preceding winter, and the two men were exploring a collaboration. One of the wealthiest men in the United States at this time, Livingston had a "passion" for steamboats and held exclusive rights to operate them in New York State, although he had failed thus far to make one that would work.

With prospects for his naval weapons diminishing, Fulton seized opportunity anew. In characteristic fashion he gathered any information he could of previous efforts then tried to find a better working design. He knew of Stanhope's experimental steamboat "ambi-navigator" and something of Cartwright's attempts to improve steam engines, and with Joel Barlow's help he learned of the work of the Americans James Rumsey and John Fitch and of advances made by French inventors. Fitch alone had enjoyed significant, if brief, practical success with working steamboats, when in 1790 his *Experiment* had made regular, publicly advertised runs from Philadelphia along the Delaware River. Fulton made no claim to originality in the invention at this point, touting only his engineering skill. In October 1802 he and Livingston entered into a partnership to put a steamboat on the Hudson River. His first working boat, roughly 74 by 8 feet, employed side waterwheels, one of Périer's double-acting steam engines, and a pipe boiler based on a design patented in France by Barlow. It was tried out successfully on the Seine the following August but at speeds of less than three miles per hour.

Events now directed Fulton to Great Britain. War resumed in Europe in the spring of 1803, and the British government, after initiating secret negotiations with him, indicated a willingness to meet his financial demands to secure his services. Fulton had another reason for crossing the Channel: further progress with the steamboat depended on his ability to obtain one of the larger and more powerful steam engines manufactured by the firm of Matthew Boulton and James Watt, the export of which had heretofore been prohibited. Fulton arrived in Britain in May 1804 and, using the name Robert Francis, spent the next three years experimenting with explosive devices and various methods for their delivery. His plan to build a successor to the *Nautilus*, however, was not approved. The British government seemed content merely to keep him beyond the reach of Napoléon; following the battle of Trafalgar in October 1805, it ceased payments for Fulton's support. In the end it paid him only a small portion of the enormous sums he demanded as compensation (£60,000 for agreeing not to use a submarine boat against the British!). His steam engine, however, was cleared for export.

Fulton returned to the United States in December 1806, still determined to make his fortune. With Barlow's help he energetically promoted his "torpedo [mine] system of defense and attack" to a government that was particularly eager, after the *Chesapeake* incident of June 1807, to believe that he could disarm the British navy. The naval establishment was dubious. President Jefferson, while receptive, wondered how Fulton could succeed without submarines to deliver his mines (the question was ignored). Congress eventually appropriated $5,000 for a public demonstration, and one took place in New York Harbor in September 1810. However, Fulton was unable there and in other demonstrations to stage a sufficiently convincing display of his methods to justify government support.

Lacking a dramatic success with his naval weapons, Fulton increasingly directed his attention and energies to the commercial development of the steamboat. He pushed ahead, as Livingston urged, with the construction of a flat-bottomed craft, 146 feet by a narrow 12 feet, with side wheels, powered by his imported low-pressure, coal-fired steam engine. The *North River Steam Boat*, as he registered it (writers later celebrated it as the *Clermont*), made a successful if not much publicized trial run from New York to Albany in August 1807. Fulton gained more notice the following year, when the rebuilt boat (with wider hull) made regular weekly runs between the two cities. He built a second boat in 1809 and began to expand his operations. Five years later the Fulton-Livingston partnership and related stock companies controlled steamboats on the Hudson, Delaware, Potomac, James, Ohio, and Mississippi rivers and the Chesapeake Bay as well as other steamboats, steam ferries, and a dry dock and workshop in the vicinity of New York City. In 1813–1815 Fulton adapted the steam ferry, a catamaran, into the first steam warship or "steam battery." The War of 1812 concluded before it was put into service.

This extraordinary activity roused several rival steamboat operators (notably Livingston's brother-in-law John Stevens) and also led to a series of challenges to the monopolies the partnership enjoyed in New York State and Louisiana. After first hesitating to do so, Fulton applied for U.S. patents in 1809 and 1811, claiming originality in the "scientific principles" and "mathematical proportions" of his steamboats and, more practically, in his use of side paddle wheels and other components. In the opinion of the superintendent of the Patent Office, Dr. William Thornton, who reluctantly issued the patents, patent law offered no protection for Fulton's claims. Still, the U.S. patents helped to further intimidate rivals, although the patent issue also earned the monopolists the enmity of Superintendent Thornton, who had been active in Fitch's steamboat company and had taken out several related patents of his own.

Thornton continued to oppose Fulton and Livingston's claims and went so far as to encourage their opponents. Thornton's view that their state monopolies (and those of their rivals) conflicted with provisions of the federal Constitution eventually prevailed, but only after the U.S. Supreme Court ruled in the case of *Gibbons v. Ogden* (1824), in which a license granted by the Fulton-Livingston interest was at issue.

Despite its rapid expansion, Fulton's steamboat business remained fragile. The death of his wealthy and influential partner in February 1813 not only put the New York monopoly in jeopardy but also, because Livingston had not made adequate provision, divided his share of the partnership among less farsighted heirs. Fulton inflicted a serious wound upon himself

in January 1815, when he appeared before an extraordinary session of the New Jersey legislature to defend his monopoly and patent rights. To document a priority in the use of side-mounted paddle wheels, he submitted a copy of a letter to Lord Stanhope that he had dated 1793; on examination it was discovered to be written on paper bearing a 1796 watermark (Dickinson, pp. 24–25). Fulton withstood the immediate challenge, but the episode dramatically advertised the weakness of his legal position. The following month he died of pneumonia in New York City. His widow, Harriet Livingston Fulton (whom he had married in 1808), a second cousin of his partner, sold off her husband's holdings in pieces; their four children would inherit nothing of their father's business.

Fulton's place in history was secure even before his early death. He was proclaimed a genius by a nation eager to boast of its intellectual accomplishments and increasingly receptive to the idea of steam navigation. Whatever the dispute over patent rights, the public, as one opponent put it, considered Fulton the "*establisher*" of the steamboat. In death, largely owing to the efforts of New York City commercial interests, his fame and reputation as an inventor reached mythic proportions, his complex character refashioned to meet the requirements of inspirational and patriotic literature.

Fulton deserved his reputation for imagination, daring, and mechanical skill. His real genius, however, was for implementation and promotion—he was able to improve on the first ideas of others, to translate them in several instances into real working devices, and in the case of the steamboat, to capture the popular mind and change everyday expectations. He is perhaps best understood as the prototype of the nineteenth-century entrepreneur. His concept of an expansive continental (transcontinental if one takes into account his interest in operating steamboats in Russia and India) transportation enterprise was visionary, although based, to be sure, on a realistic assessment of the economic reordering demanded by the country's vast distances. In the underwater realm, which he considered the more important, Fulton was a futurist, too far ahead of his times to effect technological change. His career fell short of his ambitions, but it continued to influence and inspire, by fact and by myth, the ongoing transportation revolution and the creed of progress, which accompanied it.

• The New-York Historical Society and the New York Public Library hold the largest collections of Fulton's papers; other important holdings are in the New Jersey Historical Society, the Library of Congress, the National Archives, and the Archives Nationales (Paris). In addition to his *Treatise on the Improvement of Canal Navigation*, Fulton published another technical (but also promotional) work on *Torpedo War and Submarine Explosions* (1810).

Fulton mythmaking began with Cadwallader D. Colden, *The Life of Robert Fulton* (1817), written by his friend and personal attorney. Alice Crary Sutcliffe, Fulton's great-granddaughter, elaborated the heroic theme in *Robert Fulton and the "Clermont"* (1909) and *Robert Fulton* (1915), in which she published several family-held manuscripts but also undocumented anecdotes. The first scholarly treatments, G.-L. Pesce, *La navigation sous-marine* (1906), and H. W. Dickinson, *Robert Fulton, Engineer and Artist: His Life and Works* (1913), reproduced important documents and drawings from British and French archives. Modern biographical studies, Wallace Hutcheon, Jr., *Robert Fulton: Pioneer of Undersea Warfare* (1981), which has an annotated bibliography on pp. 170–87; and Cynthia Owen Philip, *Robert Fulton* (1985), have expanded the corpus of known primary sources. See also James Thomas Flexner, *Steamboats Come True: American Inventors in Action* (1944; rev. ed. 1978); James Woodress, *A Yankee's Odyssey: The Life of Joel Barlow* (1958); and George Dangerfield, *Chancellor Robert R. Livingston . . .* (1960). The steamboat patent controversy is documented in *Papers of William Thornton*, ed. C. M. Harris (2 vols., 1995); its legal outcome is the subject of Maurice G. Baxter, *The Steamboat Monopoly: "Gibbons v. Ogden," 1824* (1972).

Special scholarly treatments of note appear in Dorinda Evans, *Benjamin West and His American Students* (1980); Brooke Hindle, *Emulation and Invention* (1985); Jacques Payen, "Capital et machine à vapeur au XVIIIe siècle: Les frères Périer et l'introduction en France de la machine à vapeur de Watt," *Histoire des Sciences des Techniques* 1 (1969): 198–202; and canal engineer William Chapman's *Observations on the Various Systems of Canal Navigation, with Inferences Practical and Mathematical; in which Mr. Fulton's Plan of Wheelboats, and the Utility of Subterraneous and of Small Canals are Practically Investigated . . .* (1797).

C. M. HARRIS

FULTON, Robert Burwell (8 Apr. 1849–29 May 1919), professor and college president, was born in Sumter County, Alabama, the son of William Fulton and Elizabeth K. Frierson, farmers. His parents were deeply interested in their children's educations. After receiving instruction at home until the age of thirteen, Fulton enrolled at the Pleasant Ridge Academy in Greene County, Alabama. He completed his preparatory training in 1865 and in the fall of 1866 entered the University of Mississippi in Oxford as a sophomore. He graduated in 1869 ranked first in his class of twenty-one, then returned to Pleasant Ridge, where he taught in a local high school. After a brief teaching stint at a high school in New Orleans, he returned to the University of Mississippi on 5 March 1871 as a tutor in the Department of Physics and Astronomy.

In 1871, having achieved a degree of professional stature, Fulton married Annie Rose Garland, the daughter of fellow faculty member and former University of Alabama president Landon C. Garland. They had five children before she died in 1893. Fulton received the M.A. from the university in 1873 and advanced to full professor of physics and astronomy in 1875, replacing his father-in-law, who resigned to accept the chancellorship of Vanderbilt University. When University of Mississippi president Edward Mayes resigned his post in December 1891, Fulton was named acting president. His election in June 1892 as Mayes's permanent successor launched Fulton into the final and most auspicious period of his career at the school.

Fulton's fourteen-year administration was one of remarkable growth and progress at the university. His first major policy decision was to close the university's preparatory department in 1892. The preparatory students had swelled the university's enrollment figures but drained the school's limited resources, and Fulton had a different vision of the future of Mississippi's secondary education system. To facilitate teacher training, Peabody Normal Institute courses, short summer sessions, were initiated to provide continuing training for active teachers in 1893. More than 450 teachers attended the first such institute, and while the teachers benefited from the additional instruction, Fulton also made many valuable contacts within the state's teaching profession. In that same year Fulton took the lead in creating the School of Education at the university, thus greatly facilitating the training of new teachers for the state. The associations formed during the Normal Institute courses paid off in 1894, when Fulton initiated a pioneering program that resulted in the direct affiliation of many of the state's high schools, which grew to nearly fifty in number, with the university. The high schools profited from the fresh stimulus of contact with the university, and the university, by permitting students from the affiliated schools to bypass the usual entrance examinations, was soon assured a steady stream of better-qualified students.

Growth and development within the university, of course, required funding. Fulton noted in his 1892 report to the trustees that the university had received only one tract of land, provided by the U.S. Congress through the Ordinance of 1787, while other state universities had received two parcels. Responding to his lobbying efforts, Congress granted an additional plot of land, the so-called Naval Reserve Lands, 23,040 acres in Harrison and Jackson counties, which soon provided important additional revenue for the school. Money from the land was used for a campus power house, a women's dormitory (by 1896 the school had gone coed), a hospital, and a complete renovation and beautification of the campus, including the addition of sewer, electrical, water, and telephone services.

Under Fulton's leadership the University of Mississippi assumed many of the characteristics of modern comprehensive universities. Instruction in engineering was revived in 1900 with the founding of the School of Engineering, and the School of Medicine made its debut in 1903. Student numbers grew from 165 in 1892–1893 to 361 in 1905–1906, and the school initiated intercollegiate football in 1893, a student-edited *University of Mississippi Magazine* in 1894, the Alumni Loan Fund for needy students in 1895, and the student annual, the *Ole Miss*, in 1897. The name "Ole Miss" soon became associated with the university, and the designation has lasted to the present.

A firm believer in the benefits of professional association, Fulton was a charter member of the Mississippi Historical Society in 1890. He served on the executive committee of the society and as its archivist, and when society records were turned over to the newly created Mississippi Department of Archives and History in 1902, he served on the first board of trustees of the department. Fulton also took a leading role in the formation of professional associations for higher education, most notably in the case of the National Association of State Universities, which he served as president from its founding in 1896 until 1903. He was president of the Southern Educational Association (now the Southern Association of Colleges and Secondary Schools) in 1899 and helped to ensure the success of that organization by including Ole Miss as one of the six charter member institutions. In 1903 he married Florence Thompson; they had no children.

Unfortunately, trouble within the student body eventually led to Fulton's resignation. Tensions between fraternity and nonfraternity students simmered for years and were exacerbated by the election of populist governor James K. Vardaman. As governor, Vardaman possessed the power to appoint the university trustees, and he stacked the board against Fulton, who had opposed Vardaman's election. Through Vardaman's efforts and to Fulton's frustration, the board in 1905 turned down a $25,000 library grant from the Carnegie Foundation and rejected Fulton's request for foundation assistance in setting up a faculty retirement plan. Matters came to a head when a law student wrote a pamphlet resurrecting an earlier incident in which Fulton suspended a poor student who had been in a fight with a fraternity member. The fraternity member's family had donated generously to the university, and charges of favoritism flew back and forth until Fulton resigned the presidency in the summer of 1906. Refusing to stay on as a member of the faculty, he moved to the Miller School, a technical school for poor boys near Charlottesville, Virginia, and served as superintendent until his retirement in 1918. Fulton spent his last months in New York City, where he died.

A true educational pioneer, Fulton is remembered for his role in building the University of Mississippi into a modern institution and for his tireless efforts in the establishment of two national educational associations as well as the Mississippi state archives.

• The Robert Burwell Fulton Papers are at the University of Mississippi Archives, Oxford. The best secondary sources on his life and career are James B. Lloyd, *The Formative Years: The University of Mississippi, 1848–1906* (1979), and Allen Cabaniss, *A History of the University of Mississippi* (1950). The dispute with Vardaman is given extensive coverage in William F. Holmes, *The White Chief: James Kimble Vardaman* (1970). An obituary is in the *New York Times*, 31 May 1919.

EDWARD L. LACH, JR.

FUNK, Casimir (23 Feb. 1884–20 Nov. 1967), biochemist, was born in Warsaw (then a Polish enclave of Russia), the son of Jacques Funk, a dermatologist, and Gustawa Zysan. Because of political conditions in Poland at that time, educational opportunities were marginal. Casimir was tutored at intervals to prepare him for studies in the Warsaw Gymnasium. After graduation in 1900, he was sent to Switzerland, where he spent a year at Geneva before transferring to the University at Bern. There he completed a Ph.D. in 1904, working in the organic chemistry laboratory of Stanis-

law Kostanecki. His dissertation dealt with the preparation of Brasilin and Hämatoxylin, two dyes of the stilbene family.

Funk was then accepted by Gabriel Bertrand at the Pasteur Institute to pursue studies on organic bases and amino acids. Bertrand, who was interested in pharmaceutical chemistry, offered an introductory biochemistry course to new students but had little interest in guiding research students. At Bertrand's suggestion, Funk studied laccol, a phenol, which caused him to suffer intense irritation and swelling. After he stopped work on the compound and recovered, he spent the rest of the term repeating studies of German chemists on the building blocks of sugars and proteins. In 1906 Funk moved to Emil Fischer's organic chemistry laboratory in Berlin. Under Emil Abderhalden, Fischer's laboratory director, Funk conducted studies on protein metabolism, which led to several publications. Abderhalden then sent Funk to the Municipal Hospital in Wiesbaden, where, in addition to undertaking routine hospital chemistry, Funk fed dogs purified proteins or amino acids and observed that they lost weight. When Funk fed the dogs dried horse meat and milk powder, weight was regained. Abderhalden, who had been working on a related problem, was critical of the experiments, and his personal relations with Funk became strained. The two nevertheless continued to work on similar problems and had a cool respect for each other.

In 1910 Funk left Germany and became associated with the Lister Institute of Preventive Medicine in London, England. He soon published a paper on the synthesis of dihydroxyphenylalanine, or DOPA. Charles Martin, head of the institute, then suggested that Funk explore the beriberi problem. For centuries beriberi had been endemic in the Orient, where the population ate rice that had been polished to remove the dark outer coat before cooking. Martin urged Funk to study the disease from a dietary perspective. Beriberi, now known to be caused by a lack of vitamin B_1, is a disease of the peripheral nerves that results in pain and paralysis.

Funk read medical accounts of the disease, procured some pigeons, and fed them polished rice. The birds soon lost weight and showed signs of poor health. Because they were eating abundant proteins, Funk dropped the idea that the disease was a protein or amino acid problem. The addition of the extracted rice polishings to the diet of some of the birds caused them to recover, while those still on polished rice were dying. He also fed small amounts of yeast to some of the sick birds, who then quickly recovered their vitality. Funk concluded that the extracted polishings and the yeast still contained the substance that kept the birds healthy even though the concentration of the protective compound was very low. In a publication dealing with essential substances in food, Funk suggested that diseases such as beriberi, scurvy, pellagra, and possibly rickets could be cured by supplying certain organic compounds that supplied traces of a chemical substance that supported good nutrition. He concluded that these chemicals kept the animal healthy, or could restore health. He proposed that such nutrients might be called "vitamines," "vita" representing vitality or life and "amines" representing a chemical unit containing nitrogen. When such compounds were finally purified it became apparent that most were not amines. The "e" was then dropped from the title, producing the term "vitamins."

With the outbreak of World War I, Funk worried that England might be attacked by Germany, and he had no desire to return to Germany or Poland. He decided to move to New York with his new bride, Alix Denise Schneidesch of Belgium, whom he had married in June 1914; they had two children. Funk accepted a job offer from the Harriman Research Laboratory in New York City. On arrival, however, he found that no laboratory existed and there was no provision for research funds. The worries of having no position led to serious health problems, but he soon accepted a position with the Calco Company in Bound Brook, New Jersey. In 1917 he moved to Metz and Co. in New York City, a dealer in pharmaceuticals. He also held an appointment with Columbia University's College of Physicians and Surgeons. He became a U.S. citizen in 1920.

In 1923 the Rockefeller Foundation, which had supported some of his work in New York, sent Funk back to Poland as chief of the biochemistry department at the State Institute of Hygiene in Warsaw. There his main responsibility was production of insulin, a hormone used in treatment of diabetes. The political problems of the Pilsudski government, however, caused Funk to move his family to Paris in 1928, where he was offered a position with Grémy, a pharmaceutical house. In Paris he also founded a private laboratory, the Casa Biochemica, where medicinal products were produced with the help of his family. The Roussel Company used him as a consultant for a decade, and in 1936 he became a research consultant with the U.S. Vitamin Corporation. When the German army invaded Poland in 1939, Funk returned with his family to New York, where he resumed his connection with the U.S. Vitamin Corporation. In 1947 he became chief of the Funk Foundation for Medical Research, founded with the support of the Vitamin Corporation. He retired from active research in 1963 and died in New York City.

Funk contributed extensively in opening up the study of vitamins during the first half of the twentieth century. Although he never isolated a fully pure vitamin, he prepared concentrates of several vitamins and had a strong influence on early vitamin research. A lone investigator who recognized the significance of various biological problems, he is also noted for early studies on hormones, particularly sex hormones; on cancer; and on diabetes.

• Funk published more than 140 papers on vitamins, hormones, nutrition, and the biochemistry of cancer, diabetes, and ulcers, but his most influential papers were those between 1911 and 1920 that dealt principally with vitamins and nutrition. Two of these early publications of major importance are, with E. A. Cooper, "Experiments on the Causation of Beriberi," *Lancet* 11 (1911): 1226; and "Studies on Pellagra: The Influence of the Milling of Maize on the Chemical Composition and the Nutritive Value of Maize-Meal," *Journal of Physiology* 47 (1913): 389. Funk published *Die Vitamine* (1914), a treatise that summarized the work done up to that year; an English translation, *The Vitamins*, was prepared in collaboration with his student Harry E. Durbin in 1922. In 1955 Benjamin Harrow published a biography of Funk that includes a listing of 141 research papers and 31 books, reviews, and articles. Also see Paul Griminger, *Journal of Nutrition* 102 (1972): 1106–13, which has good coverage of Funk's entire career. There is an anonymous sketch in *Current Biography* 6 (1945): 22–24. An obituary is in the *New York Times*, 21 Nov. 1967.

AARON J. IHDE

FUNK, Isaac Kauffman (10 Sept. 1839–4 Apr. 1912), publisher and reformer, was born near Clifton, Ohio, the son of John Funk and Martha Kauffman, farmers. Funk graduated from Wittenberg College in 1860 and from its theological seminary the following year. He subsequently held pastorates at Lutheran churches near Moreshill, Indiana, and in Carey, Ohio, before moving to St. Matthews' English Lutheran Church in Brooklyn, New York, where he remained the longest. In 1863 he married Eliza Thompson; they had two children. The year after his wife's death in 1868 he married her sister, Helen G. Thompson. The couple had one son.

In 1872 Funk left Brooklyn to travel for several months in Europe, Egypt, and Palestine. He returned to the United States and took up religious journalism, first becoming associate editor of the *Christian Radical*, published in Pittsburgh, and moving to New York in 1873 to accept a similar position with the *Advocate*. Aware of the clergy's need for a regular supply of printed matter, Funk opened his own business in New York in 1876 to provide clerics with books and pictures. He also established the *Metropolitan Pulpit*, a journal that specialized in biblical exegesis and in developing themes for sermons. The periodical underwent various name changes over the years but after a merger with another publication took the title *Homiletic Review*, the name by which it was best known.

Although he continued to address the needs of the clergy, Funk soon began expanding into general publishing, taking in as an associate and then partner a lawyer and college friend, Adam Willis Wagnalls. In 1891 they incorporated the enterprise as the Funk & Wagnalls Company. Funk, who made most editorial decisions, served as president. Much of Funk's early success in publishing came from reprinting English-language materials, including a low-priced edition of the *Encyclopaedia Britannica* and books that Funk regarded as uplifting such as Charles Haddon Spurgeon's *John Ploughman's Talks* and Canon Frederic William Farrar's *The Life of Christ*. Many of these were offered in low-cost series such as the "Standard Series" (1884) or, later that year, the well-promoted "Standard Library" that cost subscribers who paid in advance only $4 for the set of twenty-six volumes published over the course of a year. The company also published novels.

International copyright had not yet been established, but an increasing number of prominent publishers had committed themselves to its advocacy by the 1880s. Funk, however, made liberal use of works whose rights were owned by other publishers. By no means the only publisher to engage in literary piracy, Funk resented the way E. L. Godkin, editor of the *New York Evening Post* and a firm advocate of copyright, appeared to single him out for criticism. Funk was probably right, for Godkin seems to have thought that Funk, the model of rectitude in denominational and temperance circles, made an excellent target for his crusade against literary piracy. In 1891 Funk sued Godkin for libel after a spirited attack Godkin made on him in the *Evening Post*. Calling several prominent publishers to testify on trade practices, attorney Joseph Choate defended Godkin, also arguing that Funk's numerous honors from various churches and temperance groups showed that Godkin's criticism of Funk had not caused him any real injury. Godkin was acquitted and Funk ordered to pay court costs. Ironically, by the time the case was decided in 1893, Congress had long since enacted an international copyright law.

The controversy over Funk's literary piracy should not obscure the fact that his successes included many original undertakings. Funk & Wagnalls invested a large sum in the production of *A Standard Dictionary of the English Language*. Beginning work on the project in 1890, Funk made the plans, served as editor in chief, hired the staff (which with definers numbered several hundred), and for over three years, even as the litigation with Godkin was proceeding, labored tirelessly on the 2,000-page manuscript, which marked a major advance over previous works in that it stressed what users would find most helpful: the correct spellings of words, their most common meanings, and their pronunciation. He reversed the practice of most previous dictionaries by placing the etymology of a word after its definition. In 1899 Funk & Wagnalls published the 39-volume *Columbian Encyclopedia*, which was a predecessor of the firm's *Standard Encyclopedia of the World's Knowledge* (1913). Funk & Wagnalls also published the twelve-volume *Jewish Encyclopedia* (1901–6).

Funk was deeply committed to the temperance movement. He and Wagnalls were both investors in the model community of Harriman, Tennessee, established in 1890 to provide for its residents an alcohol-free setting and decent jobs. Harriman became home to the American Temperance University. But the community did not become the utopia its founders envisioned, and Funk and the original investors lost money during the depression of the 1890s. Funk was also involved in the establishment of the residential area of Prohibition Park on Staten Island, New York.

In 1880 Funk had published on a trial basis the *Voice*, a campaign journal that served as the de facto organ of the Prohibition party after it began regular publication in 1885. Under the editorship of Edward Jewitt Wheeler, the *Voice* moved by 1894 onto the broad-gauge reform track, espousing not only prohibition but such other causes as the free coinage of silver, woman suffrage, and government ownership of railroads and telegraphs. The *Voice* peaked in circulation in 1888 at 700,000. However, numerous controversies rent the prohibition movement. Dismayed by continuing disputes over the range of issues and such questions as local option or federal regulation of the liquor trade, Funk removed Wheeler as editor of the *Voice* in 1896, temporarily took over the editorship himself, and committed the publication to the narrow-gauge camp. Funk & Wagnalls eventually sold it to Samuel Dickie, leader of the narrow-gauge faction.

The best known of Funk's journalistic endeavors was the *Literary Digest*, a ten-cent weekly magazine he founded in 1890 in open imitation of *Current Literature* and William T. Stead's new English publication, the *Review of Reviews*. The *Literary Digest* offered readers a variety of appealing features. Perhaps half the magazine was at first given over to a section called "The Reviews," containing some two dozen condensations of articles drawn from nearly 200 other journals published in the United States, Canada, and Western Europe. In its early years the *Literary Digest* also featured book reviews and a section on the contents of American newspapers categorized by topic. Over the years this section, originally titled "Questions of the Day," and later "Topics of the Day," grew in importance and eclipsed "The Reviews."

Assisted by his office staff, Funk edited the *Literary Digest* for some five years before appointing Edward Wheeler editor. Wheeler made the publication more appealing and by 1900 circulation had climbed to more than 60,000 an issue. In his sixties Funk still came to his firm's offices regularly but was content to name William Seaver Woods editor when Wheeler resigned in 1905. For several years Funk & Wagnalls had placed financial management of the magazine in the hands of Robert J. Cuddihy, a long-time employee of the firm who had played a major part in several of its other projects. Funk preferred to concentrate on a campaign for simplified spelling and on his own studies of psychic and religious phenomena. Several books, including *The Next Step in Evolution* (1902) and *The Psychic Riddle* (1907), resulted from these investigations. Lexicography remained of great interest to him, and at the time of his death in Montclair, New Jersey, he was nearing completion of work on the manuscript for a revised and enlarged edition of the *Standard Dictionary*.

A man of enterprise and great energy—rather like a "steam engine," an acquaintance observed—Funk was a major figure in the temperance movement of the late nineteenth century and in publishing. He had what historian Frank Luther Mott described as "an acute perception of the demands of middle-class culture in America." Many of his successful publications, especially the *Literary Digest* and Funk & Wagnalls reference works, were built on the growth of the new middle class, which created a potentially large market for a magazine like the *Literary Digest* and for the conveniently packaged knowledge that Funk & Wagnalls's many dictionaries and encyclopedias offered. *A New Standard Dictionary* stands out for the new and useful avenues in lexicography it opened and for its continuing success.

• Funk's scrapbook containing letters and clippings from the 1860s is in the Thomas Library at Wittenberg University in Springfield, Ohio. No biography of Funk has yet been written. Some information is available in Alden Whitman, ed., *American Reformers* (1985). Funk's many interests are described in Frank Luther Mott, *A History of American Magazines*, vol. 4: *1885–1905* (1957); Jack S. Blocker, Jr., *Retreat from Reform: The Prohibition Movement in the United States, 1890–1913* (1976); Frank H. Vizetelly, *The Development of the Dictionary of the English Language* (1915); Louise Davis, "Town Built for Teetotalers," *Tennessean Magazine*, 19 Nov. 1972, pp. 14–18; and Walter T. Pulliam, *The Town That Temperance Built* (1978). The dispute with Godkin is discussed in George Haven Putnam, *Memories of a Publisher, 1865–1915* (1916), and John Tebbel, *A History of Book Publishing in the United States*, vol. 2: *The Expansion of an Industry, 1865–1919* (1975). Tebbel also provides additional information about Funk's place in the publishing industry. Obituaries are in the *New York Times*, 5 Apr. 1912, and the *Literary Digest*, 13 Apr. 1912.

LLOYD J. GRAYBAR

FUNK, Wilfred John (20 Mar. 1883–1 June 1965), publisher and writer, was born in Brooklyn, New York, the son of Isaac Kauffman Funk, a Lutheran minister turned publisher, and Helen Gertrude Thompson. His father was one of the founders of the Funk and Wagnalls publishing firm, a business he would later pass on to his son.

Wilfred Funk received a B.L. from Princeton University in 1909. He then joined Funk and Wagnalls, where he sold subscriptions to the *Jewish Encyclopedia*, wrote advertising and direct mail copy, and headed the firm's education department. Following his father's death in April 1912, he was named secretary of Funk and Wagnalls. Two years later he became vice president. In 1925 he became president of the firm, a position he held until 1940. Funk married Eleanor McNeal Hawkins in 1915. They had four children.

At Princeton, Funk had been class poet. After graduation he had continued writing light verse, some of which appeared frequently in magazines after 1927. His first volume of poems, *Manhattans, Bronxes and Queens*, was published in 1931. Five other books of his poetry appeared in subsequent years. In 1933 his poem "The Surgeon" won the Cora Smith Gould Poetry Prize from *Bozart and Contemporary Verse*, a magazine published at Oglethorpe University in Atlanta, Georgia.

In the latter years of his presidency of Funk and Wagnalls, Funk took on the additional job of editor in chief at *Literary Digest* in March 1936, hoping to revive the failing magazine. Funk and Wagnalls had founded the weekly in 1890; Isaac K. Funk had served as editor

in its first five years. Pressed by competition from the newer weeklies *Time* and *News-Week* and by the economic pressures of the depression years, *Literary Digest* had been losing circulation and advertising for several years. By 1936 its circulation had dropped below 700,000. During Funk's tenure as editor, the *Digest* published the results of its presidential straw poll reporting that Republican Alfred M. Landon was leading incumbent President Franklin D. Roosevelt in an election that ended in a Roosevelt landslide. (Later, in 1948, when professional pollsters missed the Truman victory, Funk was asked to comment on the inaccurate prediction. He said, "I do not want to seem to be malicious, but I can't help but get a good chuckle out of this" [*Time*, 11 June 1965, p. 53].)

Although the Roosevelt-Landon poll was an embarrassment and damaged the *Digest*'s image, it did not immediately bring about the magazine's demise. However, Funk's efforts to modernize the *Digest* did not succeed. In June 1937 it was sold and merged with the *Review of Reviews* but lasted only eight months longer. Funk, using proceeds from the *Digest*'s sale, began several new magazine publishing firms, including Kingsway Press, Yourself Publications, Your Health Publications, and Publications Management. As president and director of each firm, Funk acted as editorial director of their publications, all of which emphasized self-improvement. They included *Your Life: A Popular Guide to Desirable Living* (1937), *Your Personality* (1938), *Your Health* (1939), and *Success Today* (1946). After resigning as president of Funk and Wagnalls, Funk formed his own book publishing house, Wilfred Funk Incorporated. Its first book was Funk's *If You Drink*, a text about the effects of alcohol on the body and a plea for moderation. Another of his new firm's early works was John F. Kennedy's *Why England Slept* (1940). In 1954 Funk sold the publishing house to Funk and Wagnalls. Seven years later he sold his other publishing enterprises.

Funk gained wide recognition and readership over the years for articles and books on vocabulary-building, words and word origins, and other results of his "whimsical research," as one reviewer noted in 1937 of his first published prose volume, *So You Think It's New*. From time to time, he produced lists about words, which, the *New York Times* wrote, "became cultural conversation pieces" (2 June 1965). Among them were lists of the ten most beautiful words (*dawn, hush, lullaby, murmuring, tranquil, mist, luminous, chimes, golden, melody*); the ten most overused words (*okay, terrific, lousy, racket, definitely, gal, honey, swell, contact, impact*); modern Americans who had done the most to keep American jargon alive (including, H. L. Mencken, Walter Winchell, Ring Lardner, and Damon Runyon); and the 204-word vocabulary of a pet dog. With Norman Lewis, he wrote *30 Days to a More Powerful Vocabulary* (1942), a book on vocabulary improvement that for many years remained a leading seller among works of its type. He also was a contributor to various magazines and for several years wrote a feature for *American Weekly*, "What's the Good Word?"

From 1946 until his death in Montclair, New Jersey, Funk also wrote a popular *Reader's Digest* monthly feature, "It Pays to Increase Your Word Power," which appeared under his name through September 1965, when it was taken up by his son, Peter V. K. Funk. "Wilfred J. Funk was born to words," *Time* (11 June 1965) wrote after his death. "He reveled in them, ranked them and made a small fortune from them." His work, *Time* observed, "made the entire nation self-conscious about its vocabulary," and he was "a tireless missionary for the English language," who converted many readers to the belief expressed in the title of his *Reader's Digest* feature. Funk's enthusiasm for words and his eagerness to share that feeling with readers shows in his statement of intent in *Word Origins and Their Romantic Stories* (1950): "I can only wish that the reader might be encouraged to walk among words as I do, like Alice in Wonderland, amazed at the marvels they hold" (p. 4).

• Funk's papers have not been collected. In addition to those mentioned in the text, his books include *When the Merry-Go-Round Breaks Down* (1938); *The Way to Vocabulary Power and Culture* (1946); *Six Weeks to Words of Power* (1953); and *25 Magic Steps to Word Power* (1959). See also the unsigned article, "Rimes and Dictionaries," *Publishers Weekly*, 25 July 1931, pp. 324–25, and Frank Luther Mott, *A History of American Magazines 1885–1905* (1957), for information on *Literary Digest* and Funk and Wagnalls. An obituary is in the *New York Times*, 2 June 1965.

RONALD S. MARMARELLI

FUNSTON, Frederick (9 Nov. 1865–19 Feb. 1917), major general in the U.S. Army, was born in New Carlisle, Ohio, the son of Edward Hogue Funston, a politician and farmer, and Anna Mitchell, a farmer. The family moved to Iola, Kansas, when Frederick was two years old. Although the son of a Civil War hero and congressman, Funston was turned down by West Point because of his short height (five ft. five in.) and lackluster academic record. He attended the University of Kansas for three years before wandering off to a succession of odd jobs.

In 1896, he acquired a commission in the Cuban revolutionary army as a captain. After distinguishing himself as a daring artillerist, he returned to Kansas to recover from wounds and malaria in 1897. In 1898, he married Edna Blankart; they had four children.

Once war was declared against Spain in 1898, Funston was given command of the Twentieth Kansas Volunteer Infantry with the rank of colonel. Arriving in Manila after the armistice with Spain, his regiment guarded that city until warfare broke out with the Filipino nationalists commanded by General Emilio Aguinaldo.

At Calumpit, Funston planned and personally led a daring river crossing to outflank General Antonio Luna, who retreated before completely dismantling a railroad bridge coveted by the U.S. division commander, General Arthur MacArthur. For this, Funston was awarded the Congressional Medal of Honor and promoted to brigadier general of volunteers.

Not long afterward, a soldier's letter claiming that Funston had ordered his regiment to take no prisoners fell into the hands of an anti-imperialist editor. In spite of one soldier testifying that he shot two prisoners under orders and a number of affidavits to that effect, the matter was dropped. After his return to the United States in 1899, this charge came back to haunt Funston, along with additional ones that he ran his own "advertising bureau" for personal aggrandizement and that he looted and desecrated Catholic churches to amuse his soldiers from the Bible belt.

Under clouds of suspicion, Funston returned to the Philippines to command a brigade of three new national volunteer regiments just as the Filipinos began the guerrilla phase of the war, a type of conflict not entirely suited to Funston's impetuous temperament. In March 1900, he informed reporters that he had summarily executed two prisoners in retaliation for their guerrilla activities. This seemed to confirm the worst rumors that he had left behind, but when anti-imperialists demanded his court-martial, Funston claimed that he had been misquoted.

In March 1901, Funston carried off the most brilliant and daring maneuver of his career, capturing Aguinaldo at his remote headquarters near Luzon's rugged northeastern coast. He was rewarded with a regular commission as brigadier. His name dominated national headlines for weeks, and a Republican ticket of Theodore Roosevelt and Funston in 1904 was predicted. Critics labeled this possibility "a militaristic nightmare."

Funston returned to San Francisco on medical leave early in 1902, receiving an almost hysterical reception. Ecstatic crowds and hordes of reporters dogged his every step. He soon embarked on a cross-country speaking tour that proved to be his undoing. He mocked Governor William Howard Taft's "naive" attempts to establish home rule in the Philippines, advocating instead "bayonet rule," and he bragged about an increasing number of prisoners he had summarily executed, even suggesting a similar fate for prominent Americans who had signed a peace petition to Congress. President Roosevelt, who had been Funston's champion, sent a warning to him through their mutual friend, William Allen White, the publisher, presidential confidant, and Funston's fraternity brother in college. When Funston attacked Senator George Frisbee Hoar in his next speech, he was silenced with a presidential reprimand. Although he was denounced on the floor of the Senate, and calls for his court-martial multiplied, he escaped with no further punishment.

Funston was temporarily in command of the Department of the Pacific when the San Francisco earthquake of 1906 thrust him once again into the national limelight. He declared martial law and was accused of many rash actions, which have never been proven, but he was quickly transferred to Cuba. In 1907, he returned to his former command and was soon embroiled in another controversy with labor leaders. Taft, now the secretary of war, had to caution him that he could not use federal troops to "discipline strikers," as he had publicly threatened, without the president's "express approval."

Roosevelt and then Taft continually denied a promotion for Funston, but when in 1914 he performed credibly in command of the forces of occupation in Veracruz during the Mexican Revolution, President Woodrow Wilson rewarded him with his long-awaited second star. Given command of the Mexican border, Funston supervised Brigadier General John J. Pershing's pursuit of Pancho Villa after Villa's raid into Texas. Funston died suddenly of a heart attack in San Antonio only months before his country entered the First World War. The watch officer at the White House that night, Major Douglas MacArthur, carried the news to the president, who was dining with his secretary of war, Newton Baker. MacArthur inferred from their comments that Funston had already been selected to lead an American Expeditionary Force to France should war be declared.

General Funston was a daring and imaginative military leader, but he was also impetuous and recklessly outspoken. He frequently violated army regulations that he remain at all times with the bulk of his command. His memoirs describe him swimming a river with two soldiers to take an already-deserted redoubt, leading a company-sized charge into Malolos, and as a general, riding all night with a cavalry company to surprise a guerrilla encampment. Such unorthodoxy earned him many critics in the War Department through much of his career. His jingoism and nativism must be placed in the context of his era, particularly those aspects of progressivism. In many ways, he resembled Theodore Roosevelt, but he chose to remain in the army rather than to convert his martial glory into political victories.

• Funston's memoirs are Frederick Funston, *Memories of Two Wars: Cuban and Philippine Experiences* (1911). More information is in Thomas W. Crouch, *A Yankee Guerrillero: Frederick Funston and the Cuban Insurrection, 1896–1897* (1975); Stuart Creighton Miller, *"Benevolent Assimilation": The American Conquest of the Philippines* (1982); and William Allen White, *The Autobiography of William Allen White* (1946). References to Funston can be found in the collection of letters and diaries of soldiers in the Philippines, U.S. Army Military History Institute, Carlisle Barracks, Pa.; and U.S. Congress, *Senate Document 331*, 57th Congress, 1st session, pp. 1428–47.

STUART CREIGHTON MILLER

FUNSTON, George Keith (12 Oct. 1910–15 May 1992), president of the New York Stock Exchange, was born in Waterloo, Iowa, the son of George E. Funston, a banker and insurance executive, and Genevieve Keith. He relocated with his family to Sioux Falls, South Dakota, during childhood and completed high school there in 1927. Following graduation he traveled east to attend Trinity College in Hartford, Connecticut, and received a B.A. degree in economics

and history in 1932. Funston then entered the Harvard University Graduate School of Business Administration. He earned an M.B.A. cum laude in 1934 and spent the year following graduation as a research assistant at the school.

Funston entered the business world in 1935, when he joined the American Radiator and Standard Sanitary Corporation in New York City. Initially serving as an assistant to the vice president, he became assistant to the treasurer in 1938. He married Elizabeth Kennedy in 1939; they had three children. Funston remained at American Radiator until 1940, when he moved across town to Sylvania Electric Products, Inc. After initially serving as sales planning director for Sylvania, he became director of purchases. With war clouds looming, he took a leave of absence from Sylvania in September 1941 to become special assistant to deputy chairman Sidney J. Weinberg of the War Production Board. Funston then served as special assistant to chairman of the board Donald M. Nelson until 1944, when he entered the U.S. Naval Reserve as a lieutenant commander. Ordered to Washington, D.C., he had just joined the Industrial Readjustment Branch of the Office of Procurement and Material when he received notification of his election in June 1944 to the presidency of Trinity College.

Unable to immediately fulfill his new duties, Funston obtained a leave of absence from the college. With the end of hostilities, he was released from his wartime duties and formally took office in November 1945. Although he turned down several lucrative offers from private industry in order to serve his alma mater, he did maintain memberships on the boards of several national corporations. Funston's administration was marked by successful fundraising (the combined endowment and physical plant value rose from $4 million to $6 million in value), the creation of both public relations and student placement offices, and a near doubling of enrollment.

Funston remained at Trinity until 10 September 1951, when he assumed the presidency of the New York Stock Exchange. As the third salaried president to serve in the position, he entered the job with little practical knowledge of the exchange's inner workings. Established in 1792, the exchange was the largest financial market in the world when Funston assumed its presidency. Dominated by large institutional investors, including banks, insurance companies, and pension funds, the exchange was still suspect in the eyes of small investors, who remembered the crash of 1929 all too well. Funston set out to change this perception, and in the charged Cold War atmosphere of the time managed to tie individual stock ownership to patriotism. He proclaimed himself a "salesman of shares in America" and presided over a massive increase in the overall number of investors in corporate stocks—from a little over six million in 1951 to more than twenty-two million by 1967. Some of his innovations flopped; a 1954 plan to allow small investors to purchase a minimum of $40 per month in stocks proved cumbersome and never caught on. Nevertheless, his efforts benefited from a growing national economy as well as prevalent optimism among the American public regarding the future.

Although Funston occasionally struggled to make an impact in a job that was viewed by some as a figurehead position, he did lobby aggressively for greater investor access to information and also sought to introduce new technologies—most notably in the area of computers—that would increase the speed and accuracy of stock transactions. Funston's leadership proved critical on several occasions. He did much to calm investor fears when stock prices threatened to collapse in the spring of 1962, and in the following year he convinced member firms to cover $12 million in debt owed by Ira Haupt & Company and Williston & Beane, two fellow member firms whose major client, Allied Crude Oil Refining Corporation, had filed for bankruptcy. Within hours of reaching an agreement that saved the investments of some 30,000 securities clients, Funston faced still another crisis. Having successfully avoided an embarrassing scandal that might have incurred increased government scrutiny, he upheld disciplinary actions against trading specialists who had failed to follow established procedures in the panic-stricken aftermath of President John Kennedy's assassination.

Although generally well liked on Wall Street, Funston was far from immune to criticism in a job that President Franklin D. Roosevelt once described as the second worst in America (the American presidency took first place). He frequently feuded with Securities and Exchange Commission chairman William Cary over the New York Stock Exchange's alleged exclusiveness and lax self-regulation. Funston also unsuccessfully sought to exempt the exchange from the "Special Study of the Securities Market" that was undertaken by Milton Cohen. The Chicago attorney's massive study (released in 1963) criticized several aspects of exchange operations, including excessive brokerage commissions on "odd lots"—blocks of less than 100 shares per trade—and floor trading by exchange members for their own accounts. However, no sweeping changes took place in the exchange's methods of business.

After leaving the exchange in April 1967, Funston served as chairman of the Olin Mathieson Chemical Corporation until 1972. He died in Greenwich, Connecticut. His efforts to bring small investors back into the stock market and his promotion of computer technology helped to create the modern New York Stock Exchange.

• An oral history interview with Funston regarding his service on the board of B. F. Goodrich is in the Goodrich Collection at the University of Akron library. *Current Biography 1951* provides an extensive look at Funston's life and career up until his appointment as New York Stock Exchange president. Numerous secondary sources mention his work at the exchange, including Robert Sobel, *The Big Board: A History of the New York Stock Market* (1965); Sobel, *Inside Wall Street: Continuity and Change in the Financial District* (1977); and Martin Mayer, *Wall Street: Men and Money* (1959). An obituary is in the *New York Times*, 16 May 1992.

EDWARD L. LACH, JR.

FURBISH, Kate (19 May 1834–6 Dec. 1931), botanist and watercolorist, was born in Exeter, New Hampshire, the daughter of Benjamin Furbish, a hardware merchant and civic leader, and Mary A. Lane. The family moved to Brunswick, Maine, when Furbish was an infant, and she was educated in the Brunswick schools. Her public school education was supplemented by art courses in Portland and Boston, botanical study in Boston, and the study of French literature in Paris. In 1870 she began to focus on the Maine flora, and for the next sixty-one years she devoted herself to its study. She did not marry, and on her father's death in 1873 she inherited enough money to live comfortably on her own for the remainder of her life.

Throughout the last quarter of the nineteenth century, Furbish traveled extensively through Maine, large parts of which were wilderness, to collect specimens. Her accounts of these trips are full of anecdotes about adventures and behavior that defied the norms set for women of the time. In a letter to the prominent botanist Asa Gray, dated 28 June 1882, she apologized for the condition of some accompanying specimens: "I could not carry a vasculum up the mountain, it was a two miles' climb over rocks and fallen trees. And the air was warm and the black flies thick" (Gray Herbarium, Historical Letter File). Her best-known account of her rough-and-ready botanizing is in a letter to Bowdoin College's president, William D. Hyde, written at the time when she donated her folios of watercolors of the Maine flora to the college: "I have wandered alone for the most part, on the highways and in the hedges, on foot, in Hayracks, on country mail stages, (often in Aroostoock Co., with a revolver on the seat) on improvised rafts, . . . in row-boats, on logs, crawling on hands and knees on the surface of bogs, and backing out, when I dared not walk, in order to procure a coveted treasure. Called 'crazy,' a 'Fool'—and *this is the way* that my work has been done" (5 May 1909, Bowdoin College Library). Furbish was no ordinary Victorian woman.

The result of this spirit and energy was a vast collection that included a number of newly discovered plants. Furbish's personal herbarium of nearly 4,000 specimens has been incorporated into the Gray Herbarium at Harvard as part of a collection of the New England Botanical Club. She corresponded regularly with Gray and with a younger colleague of his at Harvard, George Goodale, both of whom had a high respect for her. In her honor, the Harvard naturalists named two plants for her. One of them, the Furbish lousewort (*Pedicularis furbishiae*), was the object of great controversy in the mid-1970s when a proposed dam in Maine threatened its extinction.

Furbish combined her scientific skills to great effect. Her watercolor series of the Maine flora, contained in sixteen folio volumes, is full of paintings that are both beautiful and scientifically accurate. She was a founding member of the Josselyn Botanical Society of Maine and was active in it until her death. Furbish's botanical activities brought her both great respect and great ridicule. Since she defied the codes of acceptable female behavior in the pursuit of plant specimens, many thought her unladylike at best and crazy at worst. While this perception does not appear to have altered her behavior, her frequent mention of it in letters to botanist friends suggests that it did sting. For example, in another letter to Gray, dated 25 June 1862, she reported having caused great concern among those she was staying with because she had returned very late one evening from a botanical expedition; the delay was due to her having spent three hours constructing a raft in order to procure samples of an aquatic plant that she spotted (Gray Herbarium, Historical Letter File). She died in Brunswick, Maine, active until the last.

• Furbish's letters can be found in the Bowdoin College Library and the Historical Letter File of the Gray Herbarium, Harvard University. Furbish did not publish widely, and no bibliography exists. The best of her limited work is the series on her collecting of the early 1880s, published in the *American Naturalist* 15 (1881): 469–70 and 16 (1882): 397–99, 1004. The most detailed biographical source is Ada Graham and Frank Graham, Jr., *Kate Furbish and the Flora of Maine* (1995). The sketch of her in *Notable American Women* is a good overview of her career and life; also useful is Louise H. Coburn, "Kate Furbish, Botanist," *Maine Naturalist* 4 (1924): 106–8. On the Furbish lousewort controversy, see Richard Saltinstall, Jr., "Of Dams and Kate Furbish," *Living Wilderness* 40 (1977): 42–43, and Sally Aldrich Adams, "The Rare Flower That Challenged a Dam: It All Started with Plucky Kate Furbish," *Christian Science Monitor*, 13 Apr. 1977.

LIZ KEENEY

FURER, Julius Augustus (9 Oct. 1880–5 June 1963), naval officer and inventor, was born in the rural township of Mosel, Wisconsin, the son of Rev. Edmund F. Furer and Caroline Louis Wedemeyer. He was appointed to the U.S. Naval Academy in 1897 and graduated at the top of his class in 1901. After sea duty on the USS *Indiana* and USS *Shubrick* he transferred to the U.S. Navy Construction Corps. Furer subsequently pursued three years of graduate study in naval architecture at the Massachusetts Institute of Technology and graduated with a master of science degree in 1905.

Furer's first assignment was to the Brooklyn Navy Yard as assistant naval constructor. He had only two years to acquire practical experience there before being transferred to the newly organized navy yard at Charleston, South Carolina. At Charleston Furer was assigned the responsibility of installing ship machinery and getting ship repair work initiated. He was designated industrial manager at Charleston in 1909.

In late 1910 Furer was transferred to the Hull Division of the Philadelphia Navy Yard. At Philadelphia he became acquainted with the ideas on scientific management of native Philadelphian Frederick W. Taylor. Furer subsequently became a disciple of Taylor

and an ardent proponent of applying Taylorian principles to the management of navy industrial facilities.

In 1913 he was detached from the Philadelphia Navy Yard and ordered to duty as inspector of hull material for the eastern Pennsylvania district. Furer had acquired extensive experience at Charleston and Philadelphia in laying out and equipping navy yard shops. As a consequence he was ordered to Honolulu in late 1913 to serve as construction officer at the Hull Division shops of the Pearl Harbor Naval Station, then under construction.

In preparation for the commissioning of the new naval station four recently completed submarines of the F-Class had been sent to Honolulu in late 1914. On 25 March 1915 one of the submarines, the F-4, did not return from a training run. A search subsequently located the vessel on the bottom in over 300 feet of water two miles from the Honolulu harbor entrance. Furer argued that an attempt should be made to learn the cause of the accident and, as a consequence, was placed in technical charge of the salvage attempt. He designed specially built windlasses for lifting and towing the submarine into shallower water and invented submersible pontoons to raise the vessel and bring it into harbor. The recovery of a vessel from such a depth was unprecedented.

After serving on the F-4 Board of Inquiry, Furer was assigned to the Bureau of Construction and Repair in the fall of 1915 as head of its Supply Division. His most important contribution in this position, which lasted throughout World War I, was his design for the wooden-hulled, 110-foot submarine chasers, which were used for antisubmarine operations in the Mediterranean and Adriatic during the latter part of the conflict. He received the Navy Cross in recognition of his wartime accomplishments.

Following the war Furer received many assignments with various divisions of the navy, rising in rank, ultimately, to rear admiral. His many prewar assignments provided him with an extensive knowledge of the navy's technical base and needs. Additionally, work with the U.S. Naval Mission to Brazil and then with the naval attaché in London provided him with the diplomatic skills that proved critical to his subsequent duties during World War II. A highly skilled naval architect, thoroughly conversant with the principles of scientific engineering, Furer took a leading role in helping to upgrade the materiel base of the navy's fighting ships and port facilities during the 1920s and 1930s.

In November 1941, now a rear admiral, Furer was appointed coordinator of research and development of the Navy Department and senior member of the Naval Research and Development Board. As coordinator and navy member of the Office of Scientific Research and Development advisory council, Furer served as an intermediary between the operational and shore navy and the civilian scientific community involved in war-related research and development. It was a role Furer filled with great success. Well trained technically and fully sympathetic to the needs and interests of the civilian scientific community, he was also a decorated and well-known officer in the navy's shore establishment. Thus he was able to smooth the often bumpy relations between a proud and prickly navy establishment and its sometimes supercilious civilian scientific counterpart. In the process Furer became a leading proponent of maintaining postwar relations between the navy and civilian scientists. He advanced the idea for a postwar "Bureau of Naval Research," which served as a template for the Office of Naval Research, established in 1946. He was awarded the Legion of Merit for his World War II service.

Furer retired from active service in 1945 but wrote frequently on technical and historical subjects. His *Administration of the Navy Department in World War II* was published in 1960. He married twice, the second time to Helen C. Emery, and had one child by his first marriage. He died at Bethesda Naval Hospital in Maryland.

Julius Furer was a leading member of the navy's small but increasingly influential, scientifically and technically trained officer corps. His most lasting achievement was to play a central role in bridging the gap between civilian science and the operational navy in order to mold the best of both into a new whole.

• The Furer papers are in the Manuscript Division of the Library of Congress and include a diary covering his World War II service. Furer wrote several articles on naval topics in the *Encyclopedia Americana*, from the early 1940s on, and is the author of contributions dating from the 1940s to early 1950s in the U.S. Naval Institute *Proceedings*, the *Army and Navy Journal*, and the *Journal of the American Society of Naval Engineers*. Secondary biographical sources are in short supply. An official, five-page biography is at the Operational Archives of the Naval Historical Center, Washington, D.C. An obituary is in the *New York Times*, 8 June 1963.

DAVID K. VAN KEUREN

FURMAN, Bess (2 Dec. 1894–12 May 1969), journalist, was born in Danbury, Nebraska, the daughter of Mattie Ann Van Pelt and Archie Charles Furman, editor and publisher of the *Danbury News*. Bess Furman's training began almost at birth, since her father published the local newspaper in their home. By the time she was ten, Bess was helping report local news, setting type, and inking and folding papers for distribution. As she put it, "I learned to set type as I learned to read."

Like many women, Furman prepared for a "safe" teaching career. As a student at Kearney (Neb.) State Teachers College, she served as the first woman editor of the school newspaper, the *Antelope*. After her graduation in 1918, she was happy to abandon teaching when her reporting of Armistice Day, 11 November 1918, in the *Kearney Daily Hub* landed her a job offer at the *Omaha Daily News*. For ten years she was a street reporter, sometimes using the tomboyish pen name Bobbie O'Dare for its symbolic value. One biographer notes:

Every day there was something doing—red-blooded tales of Fred Brown the Manacle Man; the Deadly Sniper; the thrice-terrible Axe Murderer; the *crime passionnel* in Little Italy; Louise, the Bootleg Queen; Margaret, the Cigarette Heiress. . . . She talked to all the visiting celebrities, did re-write on police-court stories, and took a whack at fashions. She was sent to the Black Hills to do special features . . . when President Coolidge established his summer home there. (Ross, p. 346)

In 1928 Democrat Al Smith (1873–1944) swung through Omaha in his campaign for the presidency. Furman, who had already worked two shifts without sleep, jumped at the chance to cover his appearance, capturing the spirit of his visit in her prizewinning story, "We Want Al! Crowd Shouts." Since Smith was anti-Prohibition, Furman used a cocktail simile to recreate the excitement. Smith, she told her readers, "had flavored his drink with that mint called humor, added the faintest tang of satiric vermouth, had given it body with logical lime, and had brought it to rosy perfection with the big red maraschino cherry of his own personality."

When her story led to an offer to work for the Associated Press, Furman insisted on being assigned to Washington, D.C.; as she later put it, "Washington I wanted, Washington I got, and Washington has been wonderful to me." In her autobiography, *Washington By-Line* (1949), she refers to it as "our great, gay, glittering, fey, embittering national capital." For two years she covered the House of Representatives, and it was thus that she met her future husband, Robert B. Armstrong, Jr., a photographer and correspondent for the *Los Angeles Times* (and later for the *San Francisco Chronicle*) who was nine years her junior. They were married in 1932. The Franklin D. Roosevelt White House was her special beat from 1933 to 1936. In her study of presidential families, *White House Profile* (1951), she referred to the election of Franklin D. Roosevelt as a "peaceful revolution." Furman was invited to lunch, the first of many such occasions, by Eleanor Roosevelt just before the inauguration through Lorena Hickok of the AP New York staff, who had covered Mrs. Roosevelt in New York State. Furman commented, "Here was an outstanding woman reporter who . . . was handing the subject over with a gesture more than generous to another woman reporter who just happened to be 'geographically right.'"

Furman and Armstrong were frequently nine-to-five companions as they covered the same Washington stories and went on many of the same road trips, including several to Hyde Park. One place, though, that Armstrong was not permitted to accompany his wife was to Eleanor Roosevelt's Monday morning press conferences, which differed from her husband's in one outstanding way: they were limited to the forty to fifty women reporters in Washington. There Mrs. Roosevelt "taught" them, Furman said, on subjects close to her heart, including Works Projects Administration projects and work camps for single women. On her own, with her husband, or as one of several women reporters, Furman covered receptions, teas, committee reports, press conferences, House sessions, party conventions, and candidates on the campaign trail.

When she discovered she was pregnant in 1936, Furman decided she was "ready to quit" work. She resolved to have her baby on the plains, where it would acquire "grassroots" and "adaptability to the variable winds of life." The next February, her husband escorted her to her family in Nebraska and returned to his press relations job with the Interior Department in D.C. Two months later, to her "utter amazement," the 42-year-old Furman gave birth to twins. Until they were in school, her work was mostly limited to what she could do at home, although she did miss seeing them take their first steps while she was in St. Louis doing publicity for the Voters League.

From 1937 to 1941 Furman worked with her sister Lucile, with whom she had begun Furman Features in the fall of 1936. They wrote freelance for various national women's organizations, including the Women's Division of the Democratic party, in their homes until they could afford an office. They also produced a "Know Your Government" feature for the *Democratic Digest*, a magazine "originated by and for women party workers." During the 1940 campaign they wrote a series of "Rainbow Fliers," handbills presenting the Roosevelt position on various issues, under the direct guidance of the president.

Eager to contribute after Pearl Harbor, Furman joined the scramble for war jobs in Washington, but her job at the Office of Facts and Figures was soon abolished. Once again, women's networking saved Furman; Dorothy Ducas, a reporter whom Furman had met when they both accompanied Eleanor Roosevelt to Puerto Rico in 1934, offered her a job in the Office of War Information. This job was later abolished by Congress, but Furman again found work in the private sector in 1943 when Kathleen McLaughlin of the *New York Times* recommended her to replace Eleanor Darnton as the "woman-interest" *Times* reporter in Washington. While she held that job she also produced her two books. Her husband, whose government job had also been abolished, found work first with the *Washington Post* and then as a correspondent for the *St. Louis Globe-Democrat*. In April 1945, they attended together as reporters the swearing-in ceremonies for President Harry S. Truman after the sudden death of FDR.

Later in 1945 Furman was lent by the *Times* to the United Nations Relief and Rehabilitation Agency, interviewing officials and gathering facts of aid in postwar reconstruction. As president of the Women's National Press Club in 1946, she centered the speaker's table at the annual banquet in the Mayflower Hotel, flanked by President Truman and Lord Halifax, ambassador of Great Britain. She brought her eight-year-old twins as guests "so that they'd remember Mamma." Widowed in 1955, Furman remained in her *Times* job until 1961, preferring the "more measured and sustained" pace there to that at the AP, where "the news ran staccato the clock around." In 1961 she joined the Department of Health, Education, and Welfare as an assistant in public affairs; in 1962 she became head of its Press Information Section and accepted a special three-year assignment to do a history of the Public Health Service for dissemination to the working press.

Bess Furman died in Woodacres, Maryland. Her legacy, aside from a successful career combined with marriage and motherhood, is her clear-sighted assessment of the need for feminine power in national politics. Throughout her autobiography, she notes women in important jobs and always comments on advances that women pushed for, such as alternate representation (affording a chance to sit without vote at least some of the time) on the all-male Democratic Party Platform Committee in 1936 rather than lowly roles on the Women's Advisory Committee. In a 1953 essay, "Women Have Learned to Count in Public Life," she noted that there was hope, not in the election results of 1952 themselves, which left only one woman in the Senate, but in a "little cloud . . . no bigger than a woman's hand" on the horizon—the realization of women that they have political strength. "Yes," she concluded, "women have indeed learned to count in politics. Now all they need do is multiply." Bess Furman's life was as influential as she could make it; she used her talent for writing in the largest possible political sphere.

• Bess Furman's papers and clippings, including her diaries and correspondence, are in the Library of Congress. The major source of information about her life is her autobiography, *Washington By-Line* (1949), although there is also an interesting segment about her in Ishbel Ross's *Ladies of the Press: The Story of Women in Journalism by an Insider* (1936; repr. 1974) and in an October 1953 article by Doris Minney in *Independent Woman* entitled "She Meets Such Interesting People." The one essay with which she is credited is "Women Have Learned to Count in Public Life," to be found in Elizabeth Bragdon's *Women Today: Their Conflicts, Their Frustrations and Their Fulfillments* (1953). Furman has never been the subject of a full-length biography, although she appears in several standard reference works. Obituaries appeared in the *New York Times* and in the *Omaha World-Herald* on 13 May 1969.

KATHLEEN ROUT

FURMAN, Richard (9 Oct. 1755–25 Aug. 1825), Baptist minister and educator, was born in Esopus, New York, to Wood Furman and Rachel Brodhead. Shortly after Richard's birth his father, a farmer, decided to move the family south, where the royal governor of South Carolina offered land grants to entice settlers. The family chose land near Charleston, South Carolina.

Richard's education was almost entirely in the hands of his father. As a child he learned to read from the family Bible. By persistent study he learned Latin, Greek, Hebrew, French, German, metaphysics, history, and theology.

In May 1770 the Furmans moved inland to the High Hills of Santee, near the fork of the Congaree and Wateree rivers. The next year Richard experienced a religious conversion under the ministry of Joseph Reese.

This brought him under the influence of evangelistic Calvinism in Baptist circles. He soon began to preach. Before his nineteenth birthday, he was ordained pastor of the newly formed Baptist church at High Hills. The following year he married Elizabeth Haynesworth. Two years after Elizabeth's death in 1787, Furman married Dorothea Maria Burn. From the two marriages came fifteen children.

From the beginning of his adult years Furman's fortunes were intertwined with the political and religious life of South Carolina. He identified with the colonial cause during the Revolution. He volunteered to fight, but Governor John Rutledge persuaded him to work among the Tories of western South Carolina to convince them that the patriot's cause was just. Furman was apparently highly successful. When Charleston fell to the British, Cornwallis tried to make an example of Furman. Reports circulated that the British leader offered a thousand pounds for his capture. The young pastor fled to North Carolina and Virginia until the war ended.

Upon his return to the infant state in 1782, Furman emerged as the most influential leader among Baptists of the South. In 1787 he assumed the pastoral responsibilities of the Baptist church in Charleston, the first church of the denomination established in the South (1696). Under Furman's predecessor, Oliver Hart, the church had gained both religious and social status in the city. Furman's leadership of the church enhanced his influence in denominational and civic circles. For example, his friendship with Dr. James Manning of Rhode Island College led to the school's conferring of the master's degree on Furman in 1792 and the doctor of divinity in 1800. He served the church until his death in the port city.

In 1790 Furman was a prominent delegate to the constitutional convention for South Carolina. He pressed, successfully, for an end to the special privileges of the Episcopal church and for the right of incorporation for all religious denominations. In 1821 he demonstrated similar leadership when the South Carolina convention for Baptists was organized. He became its first president. Though a staunch defender of religious liberty, Furman was also an aristocratic slave owner. Early in his ministry he called slavery "undoubtedly an evil," but in 1822, after plans for a slave uprising in Charleston were uncovered, Furman wrote, in a communication to the governor of South Carolina, the classic southern biblical defense of slavery, "Exposition of the Views of the Baptists Relative to the Coloured Population of the United States." In this piece he argued that the Bible supported slavery by example and precept.

Furman maintained a lifelong interest in education. Since Baptists at that time had no schools for formal ministerial education, he often took into his home young men who were committed to preparation for the ministry. When the proposal arose among Baptists to establish a school for ministerial training, Furman was one of the leading advocates. Although Furman died before he saw the plans realized, the founders gave his name to the academy established in Edgefield, South Carolina, in 1826, that later became Furman University.

Furman was also dedicated to Christian missions. When Congregationalists Adoniram Judson and Luther Rice, early American missionaries to Burma, adopted Baptist views and appealed to Baptists for support for their work, Furman assumed leadership of the cause. The first meeting of the Baptist Triennial Convention in Philadelphia in 1814 chose Furman as its first president. The new organization was the first national body created for Baptist denominational life. He was reelected to the presidency in 1817.

Upon Furman's death in Charleston, South Carolina, religious and civic leaders alike spoke in glowing terms of his role in the early history of South Carolina. His classic defense of slavery provided biblical and Christian support for slavery in wide circles of the South.

• The Furman papers, part of the South Carolina Baptist Historical Society Collection, are located at the James B. Duke Library, Furman University. J. A. Rogers, *Richard Furman: Life and Legacy* (1985), probably the best biography, contains an extensive bibliography as well as archival locations. Other studies include H. T. Cook, *Biography of Richard Furman* (1913); E. C. Dargan, "Richard Furman and His Place in American Baptist History," *Bulletin of Furman University* (July 1914): 1–25; H. C. Haynesworth, *Haynesworth-Furman and Allied Families* (1942); H. M. Kinlaw, "Richard Furman as a Leader in Baptist Higher Education" (Ph.D. diss., George Peabody College, 1960); and J. Alvin Reynolds, "A Critical Study of the Life and Work of Richard Furman" (Ph.D. diss., New Orleans Baptist Theological Seminary, 1962).

BRUCE L. SHELLEY

FURNAS, Robert Wilkinson (5 May 1824–1 June 1905), governor and agriculturist, was born near Troy, Ohio, the son of William Furnas and Martha Jenkins, farmers. Orphaned at the age of eight, Robert lived with his paternal grandfather until he was twelve and then went to work in a general store in Troy. At fourteen he began an apprenticeship with a Troy tinsmith, followed by four years as a printer's apprentice in Covington, Kentucky. During his childhood, Robert attended school only irregularly, accumulating no more than twelve months of formal schooling.

After his apprenticeship as a printer, Furnas operated a book and job printing office in Cincinnati. In 1845, during his Cincinnati sojourn, he married Mary E. McComas. They were to become the parents of eight children. In 1847 Furnas returned to Troy, where he became editor of the *Times*, a local Whig newspaper. After five years in this position, he had a succession of jobs, including jewelry and notions merchant, railroad ticket agent, railroad conductor, and insurance agent.

Unable to establish himself successfully in any business, in 1856 Furnas abandoned Ohio and moved to the frontier territory of Nebraska. There he settled in the Missouri River community of Brownville and began publishing the *Nebraska Advertiser*, one of the territory's earliest newspapers. From 1856 to 1860 he also published the *Nebraska Farmer*, the first agricultural periodical in the territory. Furnas quickly established himself as a leading citizen of the fledgling community, and in the fall of 1856 he was elected to the territorial legislature, serving in that body through 1859. As a legislator he wrote the first school law for Nebraska as well as legislation creating a territorial board of agriculture. Furnas was the first president of that board, thus beginning his career as Nebraska's greatest agricultural booster. Throughout the remainder of his life, he expressed a boundless faith in the agricultural bounty of his adopted home, and no one was more active in promoting the advantages of Nebraska for farming.

During the Civil War President Abraham Lincoln commissioned Furnas a colonel in the army, and he was charged with organizing regiments of Indians to fight on the side of the Union. After some skirmishes with Confederate soldiers in the Indian Territory, Furnas returned to Nebraska and led a troop of Nebraskans against the hostile Sioux tribe. Then from 1864 through 1866 he served as agent for the Omaha Indian Reservation, losing this position because of differences over Reconstruction policy with President Andrew Johnson.

Appointed to the newly revived Nebraska board of agriculture in 1867, Furnas remained a member until his death. From 1869 through 1873 he was president of the board, and from 1884 to 1905 he served as its secretary. As secretary he was responsible for overseeing the Nebraska State Fair. Moreover, he became known for his interest in scientific farming and horticulture, especially fruit growing. In recognition of his knowledge of apple raising, he was chosen vice president of the American Pomological Society. He also was dedicated to transforming the treeless Nebraska prairies through an ambitious tree-planting initiative and was one of the progenitors of Arbor Day.

In 1870 Furnas was a candidate for the Republican nomination for governor but was defeated at the party convention by incumbent governor David Butler. Two years later, however, Furnas was the party's choice for chief executive, and on election day he handily defeated his Democratic foe. During the election campaign the Democratic *Omaha Herald* accused Furnas of having accepted a $3,000 bribe while serving in the territorial legislature. Furnas supposedly had been paid money after agreeing to change his vote on the removal of the territorial capital from Omaha. Following his election as governor, the outraged Furnas brought a well-publicized libel suit against the newspaper. The jury split, with ten jury members supporting the newspaper and two siding with the governor. Dissatisfied with this outcome, Furnas published a lengthy newspaper article, which he distributed throughout the state in a fairly successful effort to exonerate himself. But the trial and surrounding publicity cast a shadow over his short tenure as governor and soured Furnas on the idea of further pursuing a political career. In 1874 he was not a candidate for reelection.

Furnas spent the remaining years of his life boosting Nebraska and promoting its institutions and industries. He was a member of the Board of Regents of the University of Nebraska and was a founder of the Nebraska Historical Society, serving as its first president from 1878 through 1890. His first wife died in 1897, and two years later he married Susannah Emswiler Jamison. At the time of his death in Lincoln, Nebraska, he remained active in the promotion of agriculture and was making arrangements for the upcoming state fair.

Though not a notable national leader, Furnas was a significant figure in the formative years of the state of Nebraska. He was representative of state builders across the nation, men and women who were among the first white settlers of their respective states and devoted their lives to transforming their new homes in accord with nineteenth-century notions of civilization. Furnas sought to make over Nebraska so that it would resemble his more civilized birthplace in Ohio, complete with trees, apple orchards, and bountiful croplands. Moreover, he sponsored legislation creating public schools, nurtured the state university, and founded a historical society for a state that had little history. Like pioneering leaders in other states, he sought to replicate the world he had known in the East while convincing all who would listen that his new homeland had greater potential than the world he had left behind.

• Furnas's papers are in the Nebraska Historical Society. For information on Furnas's activities during the 1860s, see Robert C. Farb's articles in *Nebraska History* 32 (1951): "The Military Career of Robert W. Furnas," pp. 18–41, and "Robert W. Furnas as Omaha Indian Agent, 1864–1866," pp. 186–203, 268–83. Short sketches of Furnas's life and political career appear in Thomas W. Tipton, *Forty Years of Nebraska at Home and in Congress* (1902), and J. Sterling Morton and Albert Watkins, *Illustrated History of Nebraska* (1911). A memorial tribute appears in *Proceedings and Collections of the Nebraska State Historical Society* (1907).

JON C. TEAFORD

FURNESS, Frank (12 Nov. 1839–27 June 1912), architect, was born in Philadelphia, Pennsylvania, the son of William Henry Furness, the pastor of Philadelphia's First Congregational Unitarian Church, and Annis Pulling Jenks. Originally from Boston and educated at both Harvard College and Harvard Divinity School, his father turned the family home at 1426 Pine Street into a Philadelphia outpost for Bostonian intellectual and social ferment. Reverend Furness counted Ralph Waldo Emerson among his closest friends. During the 1840s and 1850s, Reverend Furness used his pulpit repeatedly to preach abolitionism, used his parlor to entertain abolitionists William Lloyd Garrison and Wendell Phillips, and used the family basement as a stop on the underground railroad.

Frank was the youngest of four children, and his siblings included William Henry Jr., Annis Lee, and

Horace Howard. The eldest child embarked on a career as an artist, but died prematurely. Annis followed her father's love of German literature and became a translator of some reputation. Horace, too, pursued a career in the newly emerging world of professional scholarship. After the Civil War he began work on the *New Variorum Shakespeare*, the first volume of which appeared in 1871. He went on to enjoy a distinguished career as a Shakespearean scholar at the University of Pennsylvania.

Though Emerson assumed that his friend's youngest son would attend Harvard, he did not. Instead, filled with the liberal education provided by his intellectually vital family, Furness chose a career in the arts. By choosing architecture specifically, he entered a field that was in the mid-nineteenth century being transformed from a craft into a profession. Though there already existed a handful of art academies in the United States, architecture remained the preserve of master builders and carpenters through the first half of the century. That changed in the 1850s when Richard Morris Hunt opened his atelier in New York City. Hunt had gone to Paris to study architecture at the École des Beaux-Arts, and when he returned to the United States his studio became the birthplace of American professional architecture.

Hunt had met Furness's oldest brother William in Paris, and it was through this family connection that Frank Furness entered the atelier in 1859. The outbreak of war in 1861 abruptly interrupted his training; he enlisted in the Union cavalry in October 1861 and served for almost three years, discharged at the rank of captain. Congress recognized his service, though not until 1899, by awarding him the Congressional Medal of Honor for his bravery at Trevilian Station, Virginia. On his return to civilian life Furness went back to work for Hunt in New York, but only briefly. By 1866 he had married Fannie Fassitt and begun his career as an architect in Philadelphia.

The city to which Furness returned after the Civil War had already begun its transformation from a commercial entrepot centered around a river port into a thriving industrial city that would by the early twentieth century boast the widest manufacturing diversity and highest industrial concentration of any city in the country. This maturing industrial city of Philadelphia, nicknamed the "Workshop of the World," supported Furness's career; and Furness, more than any other architect, gave shape and form to this new metropolis. Working for clients made prosperous by Philadelphia's burgeoning industrial economy, Furness designed many banks, railroad stations, institutional buildings, townhouses, and suburban estates.

One of Furness's first commissions was a new church for the Unitarian congregation of the Germantown section of the city. Done in 1866, the church seems to be wholly Furness's design. By the next year, however, Furness had joined with John Fraser and George Hewitt to form an architectural partnership. That partnership lasted until 1871, when Fraser re-

moved to Washington, D.C., to supervise work on the Treasury Department.

In the early 1870s Furness and Hewitt received the commission to design a new home for the Pennsylvania Academy of the Fine Arts. The building was dedicated in April 1876 in time for Philadelphia's Centennial. Visitors to the Exposition could also view Furness and Hewitt's work closer to the fairgrounds at the Philadelphia Zoological Gardens, where the firm had designed several buildings. The Academy building, however, located in the heart of Philadelphia's new downtown, established Furness as one of the major architects of his generation.

As Furness worked on the Pennsylvania Academy, a building destined to become his first masterpiece, a young architect named Louis Sullivan came from Boston to train in Furness's office. Sullivan stayed only a short while, moving on to Chicago, where he later helped shape the development of twentieth-century American architecture. Sullivan described his time with Furness as crucially formative, writing in his autobiography that he was dazzled to watch Furness "making buildings out of his head."

Hewitt left Furness in 1875, shortly before the academy was completed, and Furness worked without a partner until 1881, when his assistant Allen Evans became his partner in a collaboration that lasted until 1895. During his solo years Furness designed a number of banks and several churches. He also executed one of his most important domestic buildings for the banker William H. Rhawn. "Knowlton" was one of a series of large suburban houses Furness designed for Philadelphia's industrial and financial elite. But as Furness's architectural vision matured and became even more distinctive, American architectural tastes began to move in other directions.

Drawing increasingly from European sources, American architects in the last quarter of the nineteenth century produced historicizing designs in a series of revival styles. Furness, on the other hand, imbued with Emersonian notions of what a distinctively American architecture should be, wrestled to create buildings that were wholly original and gave expression not to some vague sense of a European past but to the American present. It had become increasingly popular for American architects to study in Europe and for their patrons to vacation there. Furness, tellingly, preferred instead to visit the American West. The year 1878 marks symbolically Furness's official divergence from the rest of the American architectural profession: it was the last time an article taking Furness's work seriously appeared in an architectural journal.

If the rest of the nation preferred historically based European revival styles, Philadelphians at least recognized the dynamic originality of Furness's architecture. When Furness celebrated his fiftieth birthday in 1889 he could survey a city dotted with more than three hundred of his buildings. He had designed several of the city's major landmarks. As he celebrated his half century Furness was in the midst of another of his most important projects, in 1888 the University of Pennsylvania had announced it would build the finest collegiate library in the world. With his brother Horace Howard in charge of the library committee, Furness was chosen to design the building. The cornerstone was laid in October 1888, and the library was dedicated in 1891.

The University Library remains a spectacular demonstration of Furness's architectural principles. Designed in conjunction with several of the country's leading library experts, including Melvil Dewey, the creator of the Dewey Decimal System, the building was intended first and foremost to function as a library. From the exterior the building expresses both that the library serves as a protective vault for books—and Furness designed stacks that could be rearranged as the collection grew—and that the library is a place of illumination, metaphorically and literally. The building is covered with leaded glass windows, and the centerpiece of the design is a four-story sky-lit reading room.

As he was perhaps the seminal architect of a distinctly American modernity, it is not surprising that Furness did considerable work for the greatest symbol of the modern industrial age: the railroad. He began a long association with the Reading Railroad Company as early as 1879. He would go on to provide designs for the Baltimore and Ohio and for the Pennsylvania Railroad. He began work on a Philadelphia station for the former in 1886. Between 1892 and 1894 he completed an extensive renovation for the latter's Broad Street depot. In both of these stations Furness had to provide monuments commensurate with the importance of the railroad in modern life and functional buildings that would handle the growing traffic of vehicles and people. By all accounts he achieved both goals remarkably.

With these architectural triumphs of the 1880s and early 1890s, Furness's creative powers seem to have been spent. His work after 1895 stands as less powerful and less confident than his earlier buildings. Though he continued to produce significant numbers of designs, he no longer received the major commissions he had earlier. In part, Furness's notorious and cantankerous personality may have become too much for many potential clients. Perhaps more significantly, under the influence of the 1893 Chicago World's Fair, American tastes in public and ceremonial architecture turned increasingly to the neo-classical. When Philadelphia's Girard Bank commissioned a new building from the firm of Furness, Evans and Company in 1904, bank president E. B. Morris wrote specifically to Evans requesting that Furness be excluded from the project. Furness died in a curious obscurity. The few obituaries he received barely mentioned his career as an architect.

The last few years of Furness's life foreshadowed the trajectory of his reputation for the next half century. Architectural critics had begun to turn with some savagery on Furness's work in the 1890s, and this treatment continued apace through the first half of the

twentieth century. For this generation of writers and architects Furness came to stand for everything that was wrong with what they labeled, inappropriately perhaps, "Victorian Gothic" architecture. If Furness had lost the debate with the historicist and neo-classical architects during his own lifetime, then he lost it again posthumously with those who searched in American architecture for the origins of the International Modern style, which came to prominence in the 1930s. They didn't find it in Furness's buildings and they condemned them and him for this lack. However, Louis Sullivan pointed to Furness as important, and Lewis Mumford, writing in 1931, grudgingly acceded that Furness's work was "bold, unabashed, ugly, and yet somehow healthily pregnant." These, however, were exceptional comments, and throughout the middle of this century the wrecking ball did physically to dozens of his buildings what the critics had already done to Furness's reputation.

When in the 1950s Frank Lloyd Wright came to Philadelphia, he probably surprised many by expressing interest and enthusiasm for Furness. Furness's reputation had reached its lowest ebb, but Wright insisted that his was the "work of an artist." Wright's visit might be seen as the beginning of Furness's resuscitation, and his comments may have also helped save the University Library from destruction as well. Several writers began to re-evaluate Furness's achievements. Mumford became more generous in his assessment, calling Furness's Provident Building "nothing less than a second Declaration of Independence."

This revival was helped even more in 1966 with the publication of *Complexity and Contradiction in Architecture* by Robert Venturi. Venturi's book gave expression to a growing dissatisfaction with the numbing sameness of International Modern buildings. Venturi, not coincidentally from Philadelphia, saw in Furness's buildings expressions of the "messy vitality" he called for in contemporary architecture. With *Complexity and Contradiction in Architecture* Furness moved beyond being a figure of historic importance to become one who could perhaps provide useful lessons to a new generation of postmodern designers.

Though at the end of the twentieth century interest in Furness may be higher than at any point since the 1890s, his legacy has been badly handled. Scholars will always be hampered by the sorry fact that all of the records from Furness's office were unceremoniously destroyed. Lovers of streetscapes must mourn the loss of dozens of Furness buildings, including some of his greatest. However, both the Pennsylvania Academy and the University of Pennsylvania successfully undertook major restorations of their Furness treasures (the university's project fittingly supervised by Venturi), and the results remind us of how stunningly original Frank Furness's architecture remains.

• The most sophisticated and authoritative critical assessment of Furness's work is George E. Thomas et al., *Frank Furness: The Complete Works* (1991). In addition, the catalog that accompanied a 1973 museum exhibition, James F.

O'Gorman et al., *The Architecture of Frank Furness* (1973, 2d ed. 1987), remains a useful source. References to Furness and his buildings appear in a number of architectural guide books and reference books. Among them are Edward Teitelman and Richard Longstreth, *Architecture in Philadelphia: A Guide* (1974); Richard J. Webster, *Philadelphia Preserved: Catalogue of the Historic American Buildings Survey* (1976); and Sandra L. Tatman and Roger W. Moss, *Biographical Dictionary of Philadelphia Architects, 1700–1930* (1985). Several articles have appeared discussing restoration projects on Furness buildings, including Avis Berman, "Two Masterworks by Frank Furness: Pennsylvania Academy of the Fine Arts, Philadelphia, 1871 and the Furness Building, the First Library at the University of Pennsylvania," *Architectural Digest* 46, no. 10 (Oct. 1989); Vincent Scully, "Emlen Physick House, Cape May, NJ," *Architectural Digest* 46 (Mar. 1989); and "Pennsylvania Academy of the Fine Arts Restoration: Furness Unfettered," *Progressive Architecture* 57, no. 11 (Nov. 1976). Two sources that provide the most complete bibliographies to date about Furness and his architecture are Lamia Doumato, *Frank Furness, 1839–1912* (1980), and Mark Orlowski, "Frank Furness and the Heroic Ideal" (Ph.D. diss., Univ. of Michigan, 1986).

STEVE CONN

FURNESS, Horace Howard (2 Nov. 1833–13 Aug. 1912), Shakespearean scholar and man of letters, was born in Philadelphia, Pennsylvania, the son of the Reverend William Henry Furness, a Unitarian clergyman, and Annis Pulling Jenks. His early love of Shakespeare was stimulated by actress Fanny Kemble, a family friend whose public readings of the plays Furness admired at age fifteen and whose example as a reader he imitated in later life to great acclaim. Like his father, Furness attended Harvard from 1850 to 1854, tutoring younger students in Greek while still an undergraduate and ranking fifth in his class of ninety-one; his revered mentor at Harvard was Francis J. Child, later the editor of the collection *English and Scottish Ballads* (8 vols., 1857–1859).

Following his graduation, Furness traveled for two years in Europe and the Near East with his classmate Atherton Blight; while there he learned German and French. Abandoning plans to teach, Furness studied law in Philadelphia, passed the Pennsylvania bar in 1859, and opened practice as an attorney. In 1860 he married Helen Kate Rogers, the daughter of Evans Rogers, an affluent hardware merchant and a trustee of his father's church. They had four children.

Furness shared his father's fervent abolitionist sentiments and witnessed the mob scene in 1859 when the corpse of the hanged martyr John Brown arrived by train in Philadelphia, and rioting by a hostile crowd at the station was narrowly averted. Shortly thereafter he communicated his hatred of slavery to Scottish writer Thomas Carlyle (who was pro-South) by sending him a photograph of a Negro's flogged back. Unfit for military service in the Civil War on account of deafness (caused by scarlet fever), Furness was appointed by President Abraham Lincoln to reorganize the U.S. Sanitary Commission and raise funds for the Organization, which inspected drainage in the field and supplied food, clothing, and medical supplies for the war

effort. Financially secure and limited in his legal career by his poor hearing (he invariably used a silver ear trumpet), Furness increasingly turned to editing and writing, correcting proofs of his father's theological writings and his sister's translations of German fiction and recasting major sections of a two-volume reference work, *The Practice in Civil Actions and Proceedings in the Supreme Court of Pennsylvania* (1867–1868). Such experience paved the way for his major accomplishment, the successive volumes of the New Variorum Shakespeare.

In 1860 Furness had been admitted to the fledgling Shakspeare [*sic*] Society of Philadelphia (composed mainly of legal friends), which devoted itself to detailed and systematic study of the playwright, trying to assimilate the burgeoning scholarship produced since the so-called variorum editions of 1803, 1813, and 1821. An early experiment of pasting up the notes of several editions of *Hamlet* in a notebook "with a little rivulet of [the 1821 Boswell-Malone] text" (*Letters*, vol. 2, p. 55) helped Furness to formulate the ambitious concept of a new variorum, which he contracted to publish with the local firm of J. P. Lippincott. Befriending leading scholars at home and abroad, he made a fresh collation of the important editions of *Romeo and Juliet*, recording all the variants, creating an eclectic independent text (he jettisoned an original plan to use the Clark and Wright Cambridge text), assembling source materials, and extracting and impartially summarizing (in English) all the critical opinions (even on minute points) thus far advanced. The volume, partly subsidized by Furness, came out in 1871 and was well received. Thus was launched the monumental project forever linked with his name.

With wealth acquired through his wife's inheritance, Furness gradually assembled an extensive Shakespeare library to aid him in the preparation of succeeding volumes—*Macbeth* (1873), *Hamlet* (1877), *King Lear* (1880), *Othello* (1886), *The Merchant of Venice* (1888), *As You Like It* (1890), *The Tempest* (1892), *A Midsummer Night's Dream* (1895), *The Winter's Tale* (1898), *Much Ado about Nothing* (1899), *Twelfth Night* (1901), *Love's Labour's Lost* (1904), *Antony and Cleopatra* (1907), and finally *Cymbeline* (posthumously issued in 1913). His wife often worked with him, and in 1874 she published a concordance of Shakespeare's poems to supplement Mary Cowden-Clarke's concordance of the dramatic works. Blessed with leisure time and a memory for detail, along with being energetic, careful, proficient in languages, and indefatigable (his habit was to work after dinner until the early hours of the next day), Furness rapidly established himself as the leading American expert on Shakespeare. No mere arid philologist-collator, he maintained an active interest in the theater, often consulting the leading Shakespearean actors of his time, especially Edwin Booth, whom he knew well.

Working before Walter W. Greg, Ronald B. McKerrow, and Alfred W. Pollard (the pioneers of modern bibliographical criticism) had demonstrated the importance of the quartos, Furness abandoned modernized spelling in *King Lear* and adopted the principle (as in *Othello*) of relying almost wholly—even for accidentals—on the unemended text of the 1623 Folio. He also became increasingly less hesitant to interject his own critical views and to evaluate the commentary of others (often facetiously), usually from the perspective of a conservative who distrusted attempts, like those of Edward Dowden, to read Shakespeare's works as unconscious autobiography or revelations of an interior life. Largely indifferent to the chronology of the plays, Furness became ever more impatient of speculative interpretation and subjective theorizing. In his Phi Beta Kappa address of 1908 at Harvard, for instance, he insisted that if his closest friend were dying and "could be saved by permitting him to divulge his theory of Hamlet, [he] would instantly say, 'Let him die!'" (Gibson, p. 220). Among contemporary aesthetic critics of Shakespeare, Furness particularly admired A. C. Bradley; to Samuel Chew, the Byron Scholar, he once observed, "I hear no voice but his [Bradley's]" (*Letters*, vol. 2, p. 191). Furness can hardly be regarded today as an unusually creative or permanently significant figure in the transmission of Shakespeare's text; his chief service was to make available the complete editorial history of the plays addressed, to epitomize the arguments and interpretations of his predecessors, and to bring together all the materials necessary for forming an independent judgment.

Apart from his eminence as a Shakespearean Scholar, Furness was a prominent public servant and a patrician member of numerous distinguished clubs and societies. Among the many writers whom he knew were Walt Whitman, the linguist-explorer Richard Burton, Edmund Gosse, Oliver Wendell Holmes, William Dean Howells, Mark Twain, and the theater manager and playwright Augustin Daly. He served for many years as a trustee of the University of Pennsylvania, interesting himself in the squalid lodgings of students and chairing (as well as writing the *Preliminary Report* [1887]) the Seybert Commission on spiritualism, a subject to which grief for the loss of his wife in 1883 inclined him but which he ultimately dismissed as fraudulent; he also oversaw the administration of the expanding university hospital, supervised the cataloging of the university library as well as planning a new building to house it, reformed the structure and curriculum of the English Department, and even lectured in 1888 as an honorary professor. His popular readings of Shakespeare, in a voice unimpaired by his deafness, revealed genuine histrionic capacity and raised funds for various charities; one listener claimed that "Furness gave . . . a better idea of 'Hamlet' in a quarter of an hour than [Henry] Irving did in the whole evening" (Gibson, p. 202). His valuable library, housed first at his town house in West Washington Square and later at "Lindenshade," his country estate in the Philadelphia suburb of Wallingford, became a shrine to Shakespeare, containing treasured memorabilia such as gloves believed to have been Shakespeare's (once owned by actors David Garrick and

Mrs. Siddons and bequeathed to Furness by Fanny Kemble) and a skull used by Charles Kean, William Charles Macready, Booth, and other actors in performances of *Hamlet*. Furness died at Lindenshade.

• The Furness Memorial Library of Shakespeariana at the University of Pennsylvania contains his famous collection of books and memorabilia as well as numerous family papers. *The Letters of Horace Howard Furness* (2 vols., 1922), edited with a memoir by his grandson Horace H. F. Jayne, is the primary source apart from Furness's addresses and published writings. See also Francis N. Thorpe, "Letters of H. H. Furness," *Lippincott's Monthly Magazine*, Apr. 1914, p. 449. Sara Norton and M. A. DeWolfe Howe, eds., *Letters of Charles Eliot Norton* (2 vols., 1913), contains important information about Furness by one of his closest friends. The standard biography is James M. Gibson, *The Philadelphia Shakespeare Story: Horace Howard Furness and the New Variorum Shakespeare* (1990), a volume that quotes generously from unpublished letters and other materials scattered in various libraries. Frances Anne Kemble, *Further Records, 1848–1883* (2 vols., 1891), is significant for Furness's early relationship with Fanny Kemble. The periodical *Old Penn: Weekly Review of the University of Pennsylvania*, dedicated one of its issues (1 Feb. 1913) to memorializing Furness. For other tributes by friends, occasioned by his death, see articles by Felix E. Schelling, *Nation* 95 (22 Aug. 1912): 165–67; Samuel C. Chew, *Nation* 95 (29 Aug. 1912): 188–89; Talcott Williams, *Century Magazine* 85 (Nov. 1912): 109–13; and Agnes Repplier, *Atlantic Monthly*, Nov. 1912, pp. 624–28. John Russell Hayes contributed verses titled "Gentlest and Kindliest: In Memory of Dr. Furness," *Lippincott's Monthly Magazine*, Dec. 1912, pp. 762–63. An obituary is in the *New York Times*, 14 Aug. 1912.

CHARLES R. FORKER

FURNESS, William Henry (20 Apr. 1802–30 Jan. 1896), Unitarian minister, was born in Boston, Massachusetts, the son of William Furness, a clerk, and Rebekah Thwing. He prepared for college at the Boston Latin School, graduated from Harvard in 1820, and completed Harvard Divinity School in 1823. Among friends made during his school years were Ralph Waldo Emerson and Ezra Stiles Gannett, later key spokesmen of radical and conservative positions, respectively, that emerged within Unitarianism. Furness's longtime friendship with both was a sign of his disinclination to enter denominational struggles and of his intellectual eclecticism. Perhaps his distance from Boston as an adult contributed to his independence. In 1825 Furness was ordained minister of the First Unitarian Church of Philadelphia. He became pastor emeritus of the congregation in 1875 and continued to preach occasionally until his death.

Furness epitomized the pastor-scholar whose writing depended on the growth of a literary market and yet preceded the domination of intellectual affairs by academic thinkers of the late nineteenth-century universities. Influenced by German biblical criticism, Furness published numerous books on the New Testament. Among works spanning almost sixty years were *Remarks on the Four Gospels* (1836), *Jesus and His Biographers* (1838), *A History of Jesus* (1850), *Thoughts on the Life and Character of Jesus of Nazareth* (1859), *The*

Veil Partly Lifted and Jesus Becoming Visible (1864), and *The Gospels Historical, and Other Sermons* (1895). In all these writings, Furness's basic position remained unchanged. He presented the gospel narratives as historically reliable on the whole, a conclusion that strengthened the authority of Jesus and his teachings through their basis in fact. The biblical accounts were not "romances," he wrote in *Remarks on the Four Gospels*, "but true histories of real persons and real events." Along with his empirical concern with authenticity, Furness incorporated aspects of Transcendentalist philosophy and a broader sentimentalism. Transcendentalists such as Emerson held that the supernatural was immanent in nature, and Furness argued that the miracles performed by Jesus were valuable not for their violation of natural law, but for their revelation of the unsuspected wonders of the physical world. Furness saw the limitations of rationalism and professed to study the historical Jesus in order to bring Jesus closer to the sensibility of modern Christians. He did not probe the gospels simply to find proofs of Jesus's authority, but to stir the affections of what Furness saw as a skeptical generation through the image of a human Jesus.

Furness's practical and occasional writings were informed, like his gospel commentaries, by his pastoral concern with the spiritual well-being of his contemporaries. Throughout his life Furness translated German poetry and wrote original hymns to enhance the aesthetic and emotional satisfaction of both private and public worship. *Verses: Translations from the German and Hymns* (1886) contained exemplary selections composed over a long career. In the years before the Civil War Furness tried to comprehend a Christian's duty toward slavery without turning his pulpit into a partisan forum. Between *A Discourse Occasioned by the Fugitive Slave Case* (1851) and *A Discourse Delivered on the Occasion of the National Fast* (1861), Furness moved from cautious advocacy of civil disobedience to a profession that war making was consistent with righteousness. His intellectual transformation was not unique among Christian thinkers who probed religion for guidance on the troubling issue of slavery.

The same year Furness became minister in Philadelphia, he married Annis Pulling Jenks of Salem, Massachusetts. Of their four children, one son, Horace Howard Furness (1833–1912), became an authority on Shakespeare. Annis Furness died in 1884. William Henry Furness died in Philadelphia.

As a man whose life and thought spanned the awesome changes of the nineteenth century, Furness occupied an intellectual middle ground between traditional liberal Christian rationalism and the experimentation with non-Christian forms of theism that emerged as a radical and growing philosophical strain within the Unitarian community. Sensitive to the intellectual claims of biblical criticism and Transcendentalism, Furness nonetheless used innovative thinking to reinforce the authority and influence of Christianity as a unique revelation.

• There is no single collection of Furness's papers, but collections that contain some of his manuscripts are the American Unitarian Association Letter Books, Andover-Harvard Theological Library, Harvard Divinity School (letters to the American Unitarian Association), and the John Vaughan Papers, American Philosophical Society Library, Philadelphia (poems and songs). Biographical information on Furness may be found in Elizabeth M. Geffen, *Philadelphia Unitarianism, 1796–1861* (1961), and Samuel A. Eliot, ed., *Heralds of a Liberal Faith*, vol. 3 (1910), which also includes the most complete list of his published works. The correspondence between Furness and Emerson has been published as *Records of a Lifelong Friendship, 1807–1882: Ralph Waldo Emerson and William Henry Furness* (1910), ed. H. H. F. [Horace Howard Furness]. On Furness's biblical criticism, see R. Joseph Hoffman, "William Henry Furness: The Transcendentalist Defense of the Gospels," *New England Quarterly* 56 (1983): 238–60.

ANNE C. ROSE

FURTHMAN, Jules G. (5 Mar. 1888–22 Sept. 1966), screenwriter, was born in Chicago, Illinois, the son of Edmund Furthmann, a lawyer, and Sara Ford. Furthman was often ill as a boy and read widely, including the classics, from which he later borrowed for his films. Bad grades caused him to drop out of Northwestern University preparatory school after only two semesters. He began selling stories to the movies in 1915, but he did not get scenario credits until 1917. His earliest films are signed by his full original name, Julius Grinnell Furthmann. In 1918, probably as a result of the public's anti-German feelings during World War I, he began signing his films Steven Fox, and in 1920 his name on the credits became Jules Furthman.

In 1921 he married Sybil Travilla, an actress; they had no children.

Furthman's earliest silent films, nearly all of which have been lost, were often adventure stories. Those scripts included several for such later well-known directors as Henry King (1886–1982), Clarence Brown, and John Ford. In 1920 and 1921 Furthman directed three films, but after those efforts he never directed again. After writing for the Fox Film Corporation in the early twenties, he began to work for Paramount in 1926. There, he wrote star vehicles for Pola Negri, among others. In 1927 he wrote *The Way of All Flesh*, the story of the downfall of a married bank cashier seduced by another woman. At the first Academy Award ceremonies the film won Emil Jannings, who played the cashier, the initial Oscar for best actor.

One skill Furthman learned in silent films was how to write for performance: to create scenes that show characters primarily through their actions. In director Josef von Sternberg's 1928 silent film, *The Docks of New York*, Furthman's script tells the story of a steamship stoker who marries a prostitute; for all the director's renowned visual style, what remains most vivid are the moments between the stoker and the girl, especially their scene the morning after the wedding.

Part of Furthman's reputation as a screenwriter rests on the nine films he did with von Sternberg. His script for the sound film *Morocco* (1930) was Marlene

Dietrich's first American picture. The story of a love triangle between a nightclub singer, a wealthy man, and a Foreign Legionnaire, *Morocco* was a commercial success. Furthman followed with *Shanghai Express* (1932). Both movies have tightly drawn narrative structures, a skill that came from Furthman's experience in developing stories for silent films.

Like many other silent film writers, Furthman made the transition to talkies easily. He had a gift for tough, funny dialogue, as in Dietrich's famous line in *Shanghai Express*, "It took more than one man to change my name to Shanghai Lily." Furthman's script helped shape Dietrich's star persona as a "good-bad girl," a type that he created in his silent films and returned to often. The "good-bad girl" is a woman who usually does not follow conventional morality or behavior but has great strength of character.

Von Sternberg eventually felt constrained by the strict narrative lines of Furthman's scripts. In *Blonde Venus* (1932), a screenplay Furthman co-wrote with S. K. Lauren, the story rambles over several years and incidents. Probably only Furthman's sense of structure makes it hang together at all, since many of von Sternberg's films without his contribution look good but make little sense.

Furthman moved from Paramount to Metro-Goldwyn-Mayer in 1932. One of his first credits there was *Bombshell* (1933), a comedy co-written with John Lee Mahin. A satire on Hollywood, *Bombshell* constantly doubles back on itself and its connections to reality. While Mahin was more of a comedy specialist than Furthman, the dizzy narrative intrigues of the film are more likely to have been Furthman's.

For MGM, Furthman wrote *China Seas* (1935), another of his full-blooded, exotic adventure stories, and the same year he had his most prestigious credit on *Mutiny on the Bounty*, for which he received his only Academy Award nomination. While the film received the Best Picture award, Furthman (and his two credited co-writers) did not win.

Another major part of Furthman's reputation comes from his work with director Howard Hawks. Furthman worked for the first time with Hawks on *Come and Get It!* (1936). Their collaboration, *Only Angels Have Wings* (1939), is set at a small South American airport, the home of a modest airline running dangerous mail flights. While some critics have complained that the film presents an adolescent view of male adventure, Furthman's brilliant screen dialogue, often seemingly lighthearted on the surface, reveals deeper emotions and well-realized characters underneath.

In 1944 Furthman and Hawks collaborated again (along with co-writer William Faulkner), this time on an adaptation of Ernest Hemingway's novel *To Have and Have Not*. The story was shifted from Cuba of the late thirties to Martinique during World War II in an effort to make it more like the studio's recent hit *Casablanca* (1942). Furthman's dialogue, particularly the famous exchange between Humphrey Bogart and the young Lauren Bacall, culminating with the lines "You

know how to whistle, don't you? You just pucker yr lips & blow," was the highlight of the film.

Hawks again called on Furthman, along with Faulkner and Leigh Brackett, to work on the film of Raymond Chandler's *The Big Sleep* (1946). Furthman structured the last part of the script, and he added dialogue to build up the scenes between Bogart and Bacall, hoping to repeat their earlier success together. Furthman borrowed again, this time not from the classics, but from a horse race comedy, *Straight, Place and Show* (1938), and what had been an innocent conversation about horses and jockeys became pure sexual innuendo.

In 1947 one of the best films Furthman wrote, *Nightmare Alley*, was released. Directed by Edmund Goulding, the screenplay was an adaptation of William Lindsay Gresham's novel about a carnival con man, Stanton Carlisle, who pretends to be a spiritualist and is destroyed when his honest wife cannot go along with his deception and gives him away. Furthman managed to select exactly the right scenes to move the story forward, without unnecessarily repeating seances and tricks, and his characters are richly complex. One female character, an intelligent, corrupt psychologist who helps Carlisle deceive rich clients, was an interesting 1940s' variation on Furthman's traditional "good-bad girl."

Furthman's last produced screenplay, *Rio Bravo* (1959), co-written with Brackett, has become one of his most highly acclaimed. Directed by Hawks, the film's plot and dramatic tension are minimal, as a sheriff and his friends wait for the villains to come to break a killer out of jail. The film was later seen as an influential departure from the conventional Hollywood western narrative, since Furthman spends more time on character development and relations than on plot. However, Furthman had been playing around with film structure since at least the early thirties in scripts such as those for *Blonde Venus* and *Bombshell*, so perhaps *Rio Bravo* should be seen as the last in a long line of his playfully innovative screenplays.

After retiring from films in 1960, Furthman grew orchids and collected first editions. While on a book-buying trip to England, he died in Oxford.

In 1967 film critic Pauline Kael wrote that Furthman had "written about half of the most entertaining movies to come out of Hollywood." Among many film historians, however, Furthman is often seen as merely an adjunct to von Sternberg and Hawks; but Furthman got his first screenplay credit in 1917, which was (1) eight years before von Sternberg directed his first film and (2) nine years before Hawks directed his first film. Perhaps Furthman is as much responsible for von Sternberg and Hawks as they are for him.

• No biography of Furthman has yet been published nor did he write his autobiography. There also is no known collection of his papers, although his scripts can be found in the Warner Bros. collections at the University of Wisconsin and the University of Southern California (USC), the MGM collection at USC, and the Twentieth Century-Fox collection at the University of California at Los Angeles. The most detailed look at Furthman's overall career is by Renee D. Pennington in the American screenwriters' volume of the *Dictionary of Literary Biography* (1984). Richard Koszarski, "The Golden Years: Jules Furthman," in *The Hollywood Screenwriters*, ed. Richard Corliss (1972), discusses in some detail Furthman's scripts for the von Sternberg films. References to working with Furthman can be found in interviews in various sources with Howard Hawks, John Lee Mahin, and Leigh Brackett. Josef von Sternberg did not bother to mention Furthman at all in his autobiography.

TOM STEMPEL

FURUSETH, Andrew (12 Mar. 1854–22 Jan. 1938), labor leader, was born Anders Andreassen in Romedal, Hedmark, Norway, the son of Andreas Nilsen and Marthe Jensdatter, farmers. "Furuseth," which he adopted as his surname at some point, was the name of the cottage in which he was born. As the family was poor, Furuseth went to work at the age of eight on a nearby farm in Ostby, where he began his schooling. At sixteen, he left Ostby to work in Christiania (later Oslo). In 1873 Furuseth left Norway as a seaman aboard the *Marie* out of Draman.

Furuseth sailed around the world until 1880, when he made San Francisco his home port. He joined the Coast Seamen's Union (CSU) in 1885, which had been founded that year by deck seamen. Furuseth became secretary in 1887 after a bitter and unsuccessful strike. Furuseth rebuilt the CSU and rid it of members of the socialist International Workingmen's Association who had helped found the union.

In 1891 Furuseth helped establish and became secretary of the Sailors' Union of the Pacific (SUP), which combined the CSU with the Steamshipmen's Protective Union, whose members the CSU earlier had refused to organize because they, Furuseth included, looked down on steamship seamen as inferior. His attitude was typical of older sailors who thought steamship seamen were second-class sailors, while sailors were highly skilled workers, whose craft prerogatives and union must be jealously protected. Nevertheless, as the industry switched from sailing to steam ships, the seamen's unions adapted.

Furuseth's role as a labor leader continued to grow in the 1890s. The SUP became very important in the San Francisco labor scene as a part of the city's Federated Trades Council. In 1899 he helped establish the International Seamen's Union of America (ISU), a federation of relatively autonomous seamen's unions of various crafts and regions. From 1908 until 1936 he was president of the ISU. Furuseth attended every American Federation of Labor (AFL) convention, except for three, from 1891 to 1936 as a representative of the seamen. From 1894 to 1901 he served as the legislative representative of the AFL in Washington, D.C. During this time, Furuseth became good friends with the AFL head, Samuel Gompers. Furuseth and Gompers had much in common: both were fierce craft unionists and antisocialists.

In 1894 Furuseth went to Washington, D.C., for the first time to lobby Congress on the Maguire bill, which passed the following year and abolished the imprisonment of sailors for desertion in the coastwide trade. However, the Maguire Act was effectively circumvented when the Supreme Court ruled in the *Arago* case, which sailors labeled the second Dred Scott decision because the Court ruled that the Thirteenth Amendment did not apply to seamen.

Once it became apparent that the Maguire Act was a failure, Furuseth began a twenty-year quest that would define his career. Having sailed aboard ships for close to twenty years and knowing literally thousands of other sailors, Furuseth was well aware of the brutal life the sailor led. They were among the lowest-paid workers, faced long periods of unemployment between voyages (when they were "on the beach"), lived in unsanitary and overcrowded conditions (Furuseth described the forecastle where the sailor lived as "too large for a coffin and too small for a grave"), sailed unsafe ships that were undermanned, were subject to oppressive hiring conditions through the crimp (a land-based shipping agent), and suffered tremendous cruelties from ship officers without legal recourse.

In 1915 the Seamen's Act passed thanks to the leadership of Furuseth and Senator Robert LaFollette. Among its most important provisions, the Seamen's Act abolished imprisonment for deserting ship, allowed seamen to get half the pay owed to them in any port of call, increased the amount of forecastle space, improved food provisions, and prohibited the payment of an advance to crimps. The law also called for the United States to abrogate all treaties that provided for the return of seamen deserting in U.S. ports. The rationale was that if foreign seamen could desert in U.S. ports, then shipowners would be forced to hire crews at U.S. wage scales.

When the bill passed, Furuseth rushed from the gallery where he watched the three days of deliberation and cried, "This finished the work Lincoln began" by freeing the seamen. LaFollette said that the "Fourth of March, 1915, is your emancipation day" and praised Furuseth, saying, "Whatever I happen to know about this subject, I have acquired from talking with him." The law was often referred to as Andy's Bill, or as "Andy's Pill" by his detractors in the Industrial Workers of the World (IWW), who argued that only industrial unionism would help seamen, not legislation.

From 1906 until 1921 the ISU had peaceful relations with employers. Like the rest of organized labor, the ISU emerged from World War I stronger than ever, with a membership of 115,000 in 1920. However, in 1921, an ISU strike was crushed as part of a nationwide effort to undermine the increasing power of the labor movement, and by 1923 the ISU was barely 15,000 strong.

The ISU remained a shadow of its former self throughout the 1920s and into the depression. Furuseth continued to defend the Seamen's Act in Congress and the courts. In the early 1930s the ISU faced serious challenges from the IWW and the Communist Party's Marine Workers Industrial Union. Furuseth bitterly fought these far more left-wing industrial unions. In fact, Furuseth worked against his own union's rank and file, which grew more militant in the 1930s.

To those who admired him, Furuseth was Lincolnesque, "the emancipator of the seamen." He was widely respected by labor leaders, employers, and politicians for his sincerity and total dedication to the deck sailor's cause. His frugal lifestyle was well known: he worked long days; drew a salary no larger than that paid an able-bodied seaman; never married; showed no interest in material goods; and wore simple, often wrinkled suits, which he supposedly ironed "sailor style" by placing them under his mattress when he slept. He was the most widely recognized maritime labor leader of his time prior to the emergence of Harry Bridges and Joe Curran in the 1930s. When Furuseth died in Washington, D.C., his body was placed in the Department of Labor auditorium, the first labor leader to receive such an honor.

• Although no collection of Furuseth's papers exists, letters written by him are in the Woodrow Wilson Papers at the Library of Congress and in the LaFollette papers at the Wisconsin State Historical Society in Madison and the Library of Congress. The best biography of Furuseth is Hyman Weintraub, *Andrew Furuseth: Emancipator of the Seamen* (1959). A less scholarly approach is Arnold Berwick, *The Abraham Lincoln of the Sea: The Life of Andrew Furuseth* (1993). Also see Arthur Emil Albrecht, *International Seamen's Union of America: A Study of Its History and Problems* (1923), and Silas B. Axtell, ed., *A Symposium on Andrew Furuseth* (1945). For a more critical look at Furuseth and the ISU, see Bruce Nelson, *Workers on the Waterfront: Seamen, Longshoremen, and Unionism in the 1930s* (1988). Obituaries are in the *New York Times* and the *Washington Post*, both 23 Jan. 1938.

PETER COLE

G

GABB, William More (20 Jan. 1839–30 May 1878), paleontologist and naturalist, was born in Philadelphia, Pennsylvania, the son of Joseph Gabb and Christiana (name unverified) More. Gabb's father was a "salesman in mercantile affairs," whose name disappeared from the city directory in 1853. His mother then apparently became a milliner. As a boy, Gabb was interested in natural history, bought books in its subjects, collected mineral specimens, and frequented the museum of the Academy of Natural Sciences. He attended public schools through Central High School in Philadelphia, which awarded him the A.B. in 1857.

Gabb wrote to James Hall, then probably the most widely known geologist in the United States and director of the New York State Museum in Albany. As a result, Gabb worked for Hall from about 1857 as an assistant, presumably on invertebrate fossils. He returned to Philadelphia by 1860, became a member of the Academy of Natural Sciences, and from 1859 to 1862 published more than twenty papers on the museum's invertebrate fossils in its *Proceedings*. A major publication was the 200-page *Synopsis of the Mollusca of the Cretaceous Formation, Including the Geographic and Stratigraphic Range and Synonymy* (1861). Perhaps at the suggestion of naturalist Spencer Fullerton Baird, then assistant secretary of the Smithsonian Institution, Gabb spent some time at that institution in about 1860. His biographer William Healey Dall described Gabb as a "young, eager, ambitious, able, and self-confident student."

In late 1861 Josiah Dwight Whitney hired Gabb for the California State Geological Survey that had begun a year before. According to botanist William Henry Brewer, Gabb "had been recommended to [Whitney] by competent judges as the best authority in America on Cretaceous paleontology, and as one possessing a good general knowledge of the science in its broader relations" (quoted in Dall). The Cretaceous fossils were chiefly marine invertebrates, widespread in California deposits.

Gabb was elected a member of the California Academy of Sciences and its honorary curator of paleontology on the day that he arrived in California in January 1862. He studied fossils that had been accumulated previously by the survey, and he then went into the field. From 1862 to 1866, with others, he traveled the eastern slope of the Diablo Range east of San Francisco, the area of Fort Tejon north of Los Angeles, some of the Mojave Desert, the southern part of the Sierra Nevada, the Coast Ranges, the White Mountains of California, and the northern part of the state. For that survey he also traveled to Oregon, Washington Territory, and Vancouver Island for three months to study Cretaceous fossils. Gabb's reports for the survey were illustrated by his own careful drawings. Late in 1867 he participated in an exploration of Baja California, Mexico, with approval by Whitney and with permission from Mexican authorities, under the command of J. Ross Browne. The group produced the first geologic map of the peninsula in 1868 and a report by Browne, "Geographical and Physical Features of Lower California." Gabb published on the Cretaceous fossils in the survey's report in 1868, and his "Notes on the Geology of Lower California" was published as an appendix of the Geological Survey of California (1882).

When the reports on California and Baja California were completed, Gabb resigned from the California survey. In 1869 he became chief of a survey to study the topography and geology of Santo Domingo for a New York corporation. From the three years of work, Gabb completed a report in 1872, contributed to a geological map, and published papers on the geology, petroleum, fossils, vegetation, and an aurora.

In 1873 the government of Costa Rica hired Gabb to conduct a similar survey of its province of Talamanca, for planning a railway route. While carrying out the survey over three years, Gabb also made extensive collections of biological and geological specimens for the Smithsonian Institution, and he gathered material on ethnology. He published several papers on the geology of Costa Rica and one "On the Indian Tribes and Languages of Costa Rica" (*Proceedings of the American Philosophical Society* 14 [1876]: 483–602). In Costa Rica he suffered from a severe form of malaria that permanently injured his lungs.

When herpetologist Jay Mathers Savage visited the same region of Costa Rica in 1964, he learned that Gabb had married a local Indian woman, Victoria, in about 1874 and that they had one child; descendants of this marriage were still living in the area.

Back in the United States in 1876, Gabb prepared a report on the mineralogy of the exhibits at the Centennial Exposition in Philadelphia for the *New York Herald*. He went back to Santo Domingo to develop a mining claim but became ill in the spring of 1878 and returned to the United States. He died a few weeks later in Philadelphia.

Gabb was excellent at identifying invertebrate fossils and was a competent field geologist. Well liked by colleagues, he was said to have a "peculiarly even disposition." He was elected to the National Academy of Sciences in 1876. His valuable collections of fossils from Santo Domingo and Costa Rica were left to the Academy of Natural Sciences. Many of the reptiles and amphibians that he collected in Costa Rica for the Smithsonian Institution became type specimens.

• According to Gabb's biographer William H. Dall, most of Gabb's books and papers were sold. He published about ninety scientific papers, chiefly in paleontology and geology. The work in Baja California, Mexico, was published in J. Ross Browne's *Report on Mineral Resources of the States and Territories West of the Mississippi* (1869), pp. 630–39. The primary biography of Gabb is in Dall, National Academy of Sciences, *Biographical Memoirs* 6 (1909): 347–61. A discussion of Gabb's collecting sites in Costa Rica and on his descendants is in Jay M. Savage, "On the Trail of the Golden Frog: With Warszewicz and Gabb in Central America," *Proceedings of the California Academy of Sciences*, 4th ser., 38, no. 14 (1970): 273–88.

ELIZABETH NOBLE SHOR

GABLE, Clark (1 Feb. 1901–16 Nov. 1960), movie actor, was born William Clark Gable in Cadiz, Ohio, the only son of William H. Gable, an oil driller and farmer, and Adeline Hershelman. Ten months after his birth, his mother died. His father remarried in 1903, and Clark's stepmother, Jennie Dunlap, introduced him to ideas of culture and gentility. In his maturity Gable was a big man who dominated a crowded room, but even at age fourteen he was six feet tall and weighed 150 pounds. He was not, however, good-looking: his ears were big and his front teeth widely spaced. Later, after his teeth were capped and then finally replaced with dentures and his broadened features reduced the appearance of his ears, he was considered the essence of masculine handsomeness.

Against his father's wishes, Gable dropped out of high school and moved to Akron, where he worked in a tire factory and discovered the excitement of the theater. For a time he became a drifter, working when he could in little theater groups, stock companies, and traveling theater companies, and at other times in oil fields, lumberyards, and eventually a department store in Portland, Oregon, where he was briefly engaged to a young actress, Franz Dorfler, who introduced him to drama coach Josephine Dillon. Young Gable had heretofore displayed an eagerness to become, but no innate ability to be, a stage actor. Dillon, who taught Gable basic stage techniques such as voice projection, transformed him into a competent player. After Dillon moved to Los Angeles in order to secure Gable work in the film industry, he followed, and they were married in 1924. She was fourteen years older than he, and the marriage was essentially one of convenience. Gable worked as an extra in five silent films and acted on West Coast stages in productions (1926–1928): with Jane Cowl in *Romeo and Juliet* and with Pauline Frederick in *Madame X*, gossip allowing that his major contributions to them were pleasing his leading ladies after the performances, but he earned good notices as a journalist in *Chicago*. He next acted briefly with a company in Houston, where he became a local celebrity, before moving to New York where Josephine Gable had secured him a leading role in *Machinal* (1928). In New York he met Houston socialite Ria Langham who, like his wife, instructed him, but this time in good manners, stylish clothes, and elegant living. In 1929 Josephine filed for divorce, and Gable

and Ria, who was seventeen years his senior, were married a year later. Clearly Gable had used his wives (with their approval) to advance himself professionally and socially.

A turning point in Gable's career came in 1930 when he played Killer Mears in a Los Angeles production of *The Last Mile*, a prison drama in which Spencer Tracy had created a sensation in New York. Gable, too, was critically acclaimed, his performance being the culmination of his years of apprenticeship in the theater. Paradoxically, his performance also earned him a movie contract, and, like many stage actors who brought their expertise to the lucrative medium of sound film, he became thereafter exclusively a movie actor. Gable appeared in twelve films in 1931, mostly in supporting roles. The first was *The Painted Desert*, a western for which he learned to ride. In the second, *The Easiest Way*, his first under contract to Metro-Goldwyn-Mayer, to which audiences responded strongly, he was a working man married to the sister of the leading lady, Constance Bennett (who would star opposite Gable four years later in *After Office Hours*). After playing a bootlegger, a newspaper reporter, and a gangland leader, Gable was cast as a gambler and underworld figure who seduces and then shoves around Norma Shearer as the spoiled daughter of a wealthy lawyer. Audience response to Gable's rough masculinity indicated to the studio that it had a new star, and within a year he established himself as a leading man, starring opposite Jean Harlow in *Red Dust*, even becoming a household word because of the phrase "Who do you think you are? Clark Gable?"

In the decade that followed MGM paired its major box office attraction—always in the top ten, usually second or third—with its best leading ladies: in addition to Shearer (*Strange Interlude* [1932] and *Idiots Delight* [1939]) and Harlow (*Hold Your Man* [1933], *China Seas* [1935], *Wife Versus Secretary* [1936], and *Saratoga* [1937]), Marion Davies (*Polly of the Circus* [1932] and *Cain and Mabel* [1936]), Joan Crawford (*Dancing Lady* [1933], *Chained* and *Forsaking All Others* [both 1934], *Love on the Run* [1936], and *Strange Cargo* [1940]), and Myrna Loy (*Manhattan Melodrama* and *Men in White* [both 1934], *Wife Versus Secretary*, *Parnell* [1937], and *Test Pilot* and *Too Hot to Handle* [both 1938]). MGM, which boasted of having "more stars than there are in heaven," was thus able to package its male star with most of its major female stars. An exception was Greta Garbo, with whom the young Gable appeared awkwardly in *Susan Lennox—Her Fall and Rise* (1931). Whether as a gambler, ship's captain, flier, prize fighter, saloon keeper, or, most often, as a news reporter, Gable projected a sexual magnetism that stirred women and a roguish masculinity that appealed to men. Gable sometimes practiced self-deception, claiming that he was "no actor," but his struggle to become an accomplished stage actor belies such a claim. He was more than a personality who in general played himself, as some critics have asserted. Within a certain range he was very good, the notable exception in his career being *Parnell*, a costume drama dealing with love and politics in Ireland in which both he and Loy were miscast.

Gable's deftness at comedy was first exploited in *It Happened One Night* (1934), completed on loanout to Columbia, where he was exiled briefly by MGM as punishment for refusing various roles. He played a newspaperman who befriends an heiress (Claudette Colbert) fleeing her tyrannical father. Gable, brashly impertinent and extremely likable, won an Academy Award (his only Oscar), as did Colbert, the director Frank Capra, and the film itself, a record sweep that remained unmatched until 1975. Often cited as an indication of the influence of movies on society is that Gable's appearance in the film without an undershirt in one scene caused sales of undershirts to plunge.

A year later Gable was bare-chested again as Fletcher Christian, the virile opponent of injustice represented by Charles Laughton as Captain Bligh in *Mutiny on the Bounty*. In *San Francisco* (1936) as Blackie Norton (a typical name for a Gable character), the owner of a saloon on the Barbary Coast, he tries to seduce Mary Blake (played by Jeanette MacDonald) but is reformed after the 1906 earthquake and its aftermath. A popularity poll in 1937 named Gable The King, a lasting sobriquet that was reinforced when Judy Garland sang "You Made Me Love You" to Gable's photograph ("Dear Mr. Gable") in *The Broadway Melody of 1938* and that reached its zenith in 1939 when he appeared as Rhett Butler in *Gone with the Wind*, a role that audiences insisted had been written for him. He failed to win an Academy Award in 1939, but the enduring popularity of the film and of his film image as Rhett ("Terrific in Ascot ties," said Dwight MacDonald) is due in no small part to his performance. Although he was in awe of Spencer Tracy, with whom he costarred three times—*San Francisco*, *Test Pilot* (1938), and *Boom Town* (1940)—and whose acting ability far outshone his, the fact is that Tracy could never have portrayed Rhett Butler as Gable did.

His personal life also reached its peak in 1939 when, after Ria Gable's agreement to a divorce, Gable married Carole Lombard, one of the great beauties in movies, with whom he had begun a love affair in 1936. For moviegoers, theirs was a marriage made in heaven, and indeed it brought Gable his greatest domestic happiness. The newlyweds bought a ranch in the San Fernando Valley and effectively dropped out of the Hollywood world of parties and nightclubs. Lombard became Gable's good companion, accompanying him on hunting and fishing trips, the kinds of activities that he enjoyed most. When they did dress formally, as at the Atlanta premiere of *Gone with the Wind*, they were Hollywood glamour personified. They nicknamed each other "Ma" and "Pa," although the marriage remained childless. It ended abruptly and tragically in January 1942, when Lombard was killed in an airplane crash as she was returning from a hugely successful trip to her home state of Indiana to sell war bonds. Inconsolable, Gable enlisted in the army as a private at the age of forty-one and completed the rigorous training at Officer Candidate School. He became a tail gunner on a bomber in England, and, as a result of his wartime assignment to make a recruiting film for the air force, he flew several dangerous missions over Germany, causing some to suspect that after Lombard's death he cared little whether he lived or died. He served with distinction and returned to Hollywood in 1944.

Gable's career divides neatly between the prewar and postwar periods. Audiences were pleased by the return of The King and remained loyal, but few, if any, of his films after 1945 were equal to those of the 1930s. "Gable's Back and Garson's Got Him" was the famous advertising slogan for *Adventure* (1945), costarring Greer Garson, MGM's Queen of the Studio at that time, but her genteel manner was ill suited to Gable's roguish image. The ladylike Deborah Kerr, who eventually became Garson's replacement, fared better opposite Gable in *The Hucksters* (1947), a satire on radio advertising. As he grew older, Gable remained a virile figure on screen with leading ladies of his own generation—Loretta Young in *Key to the City* and Barbara Stanwyck in *To Please a Lady* (both 1950)—but he was also a believable love interest with younger actresses like Ava Gardner and Grace Kelly in a remake of *Red Dust* titled *Mogambo* (1953). His riding skills enabled him to make several westerns: *Across the Wide Missouri* (1951), *The Tall Men* (1955), and *The King and Four Queens* (1956). He earned the respect of his fellow players and took pride in his performance as an aging cowboy in his final film, *The Misfits* (1961). This view was shared by Arthur Miller, who dedicated the printed script to him, and by the critics, who gave him the best reviews of his career.

In his later years Gable remained very much a ladies' man, his name being linked with several women. He was married disastrously for a fourth time in 1949 to Lady Sylvia Ashley, who tried to turn him into an English gentleman and his ranch house into an English manor house. They were divorced in 1952. His final years were brightened by his fifth marriage, in 1955, to Kay Spreckles, who resembled Lombard and with whom he revived the nicknames Ma and Pa.

Gable died of a massive heart attack believed to have been induced by the exertions of the riding and roping scenes in *The Misfits*, which he performed without a double in the heat of a Nevada summer. His son John was born posthumously, but he knew before his death that he would be a father. Gable is buried next to Carole Lombard in a grave on which only his name is inscribed.

• Book-length biographies of Gable, in chronological order, include Charles Samuels, *The King* (1961); Gabe Essoe, *The Films of Clark Gable* (1970); Rene Jordan, *Clark Gable* (1973); Warren G. Harris, *Gable and Lombard* (1974); Lyn Tornabene, *Long Live the King* (1976); Joe Morella and Edward Z. Epstein, *Gable and Lombard and Powell and Harlow* (1976); and Jane E. Wayne, *Clark Gable: Portrait of a Misfit* (1993). Much of the material from Wayne's book appears in the same words in her earlier *Gable's Women* (1987). Tornabene's study of Gable is the most balanced, while Wayne is the most interested in Gable's sexual activities. A knowledgeable review of Gable's career is in David Shipman, *The Great Movie Stars: The Golden Years* (1979). An assessment of his star quality is in Richard Griffith, *The Movie Stars* (1970).

JAMES VAN DYCK CARD

GABO, Naum (5 Aug. 1890–23 Aug. 1977), constructivist sculptor, was born Naum Neemia Pevsner in the village of Kilmovich, near Bryansk, Russia, an industrial town southwest of Moscow, the son of Boris Pevsner, a successful factory owner, and Agrippine Osersky. Although his father was a Jewish mystic, Gabo and his siblings—including his older brother, constructivist sculptor Antoine Pevsner—were brought up in the Christian tradition, owing largely to a Russian Orthodox nanny. The two icons that he saw morning and night in his childhood nursery reportedly made a deep impression on him, and he claimed to have made his first sculpture when he was six. During the 1905 revolution Gabo was inadvertently caught in, and narrowly escaped, a massacre of Jews and progressive Christians by the Cossacks. At the end of his long life he wrote, "I saw a lot that day, but I do not know if I can convey in words the horror that oppressed me and seized my soul for many years. I was fifteen years old, and that day and that night I became a revolutionary."

By the time he graduated from the Kursk Gymnasium in 1910, with a prize for an essay on Russian writer Nikolay Gogol, Gabo had been drawing and painting for at least three years. His father nonetheless decided that he would study medicine, and he was enrolled at the University of Munich in the fall of 1910. Two years later he switched to the study of engineering at a technical college and then, in 1912–1913, changed his university registration to philosophy and devoted himself to the study of Immanuel Kant's *Critique of Pure Reason*. He also attended the lectures of the art historian Heinrich Wöfflin, who strongly urged him to take a tour of Italy, which, lacking funds, he did as a six-week walking tour in the summer of 1913.

Apparently Gabo met none of the Italian futurists on this trip; nor did he see their work, as his "task was to study mainly the classics." During earlier visits with his brother Antoine in Paris in 1912–1913, however, he had seen the work of Picasso, Braque, Gris, Lipchitz, Archipenko, and Delaunay. He read Wassily Kandinsky's *Concerning the Spiritual in Art* (1910) in 1913, though there is no record of his having seen Der Blaue Reiter exhibitions of German expressionist art in Munich in 1911 and 1912. In a letter to Ronald Johnson, he claimed to have met Kandinsky in 1917 when they both were in Russia. In letters to Herbert Read, however, Gabo discussed the artistic ferment in Munich as well as new ideas of nonobjective art on a "deeper, more philosophical level." He also mentioned his membership in a Russian student society through which he heard revolutionary speakers such as Leon Trotsky, as well as a professor "talking of Einstein's theory [when] I myself was studying physics."

Following the outbreak of World War I in 1914, Gabo and his brother Antoine spent the next three years in Norway. During this period, to avoid confusion caused by their shared surname, Naum Pevsner changed his name to Naum Gabo. The brothers returned to Russia with the outbreak of the Revolution in 1917. Gabo had modeled the *Head of a Negro* in 1913, but he created his first constructivist sculpture, *Constructed Head No. 1*, from plywood in Norway in 1915 and his *Constructed Head No. 2* in galvanized iron, also in Norway, in 1916. He nonetheless told American nonobjective artists Ibram Lassaw and Ilya Bolotowsky in 1956 that "there was no constructivism until 1920 . . . and it was a term given by critics." As opposed to the old art of carving and modeling, he said, "we built art up into space out of our imaginations in the same way as an engineer builds a construction."

One of the seminal sculptors of the Russian constructivist movement (1915–1922), Gabo is regarded, along with the suprematist painter Kasimir Malevich, as the most rigorous of the utopian and philosophically idealist artists of the early modern tradition of nonobjective art. This pioneering group of men and women included among its painters Natalia Goncharova, Mikhail Larionov and Liubov Popova. Along with Gabo and Antoine Pevsner, the most influential sculptors among the constructivists were Vladimir Tatlin and Alexander Rodchenko.

Fully cognizant of major developments in contemporary European abstract art from cubism to Italian futurism and their offshoots, and championing the new materials of the Industrial Revolution, the artists of the Russian avant-garde were considerably more radical in pushing abstraction to complete nonobjectivity. Several explanations for their radical perspective can be found in Russian culture of the early twentieth century. The visionary religious mysticism promulgated by the Orthodox church was one such element; another was the drive, from the mid-nineteenth century onward, toward a purely Russian art based on Russian cultural sources, a campaign that paralleled the growing quest for a national identity. These forces produced an ambitious intellectual ferment that transformed everything "from the forms of art to the structure of the state," as Hilton Kramer phrased it. The art and thought of Naum Gabo was one of the significant forces in the radical shift that took place in Russian art. Gabo's *Realist Manifesto*, published in Moscow in 1920, proclaimed that "art has its absolute, independent value and a function to perform in society whether capitalist, socialist or communistic."

Like the futurists, the Russian constructivists initially affirmed the aesthetic of the machine, whose spare structures the latter regarded as a metaphorical blueprint for objectivity, suggestive of the absolute structures of the universe. Like both the cubists and the futurists, the constructivists embraced the concepts of time and space, not only as the subject matter of their art but also as a concrete factor in it. The highest form of artistic expression was to make metaphysical structures real. Gabo wrote in his *Realistic Manifes-*

to that art should not only embrace concepts of time and space but should also "include a new element, a kinetic rhythm as the basis of our perceptions of the world." In Gabo's view, the representation of kinetic reality was "the only aim of our pictorial and plastic art."

In 1920, at the end of the Russian Revolution, Tatlin and Rodchenko broke with Gabo and Pevsner over Tatlin's conviction that art must adapt to the demands of the new Soviet age and become primarily social in its purpose and function. The design of furniture, topography, stage sets, workers' clothing, and architecture (mostly unbuilt) replaced the adventurous autonomous abstractions initially produced by Tatlin and Rodchenko. By 1922 their utilitarian and productivist program dominated the new Soviet art, which rapidly evolved into the banalities of state-supported social realism. This domination also led to the exit from Russia of those artists who were to become the most internationally influential. In addition to Gabo and Pevsner this group included El Lissitzky and Wassily Kandinsky, who, along with Hungarian László Moholy-Nagy, propagated the absolute nonobjectivity of constructivist theory through their teaching at the German Bauhaus (from 1923 to 1931) and beyond. The work of American painters Ad Reinhardt and Barnett Newman was a direct outgrowth of Malevich and suprematist ideas, whereas the sculpture of Alexander Calder and George Rickey and kinetic sculpture in general were legacies both of Gabo and of constructivist influences.

Gabo's early experiments in motion culminated in his paradigmatic *Kinetic Construction* (1920), a metal-and-plastic sculpture measuring eighteen inches in height and consisting of a single vibrating rod propelled by a motor. He did not, however, pursue his experiments in motion to their logical conclusion. In Germany, where from 1922 to 1932 he occasionally lectured at the Bauhaus, Gabo contributed significantly to Moholy-Nagy's ideas on light, space, and movement. Moholy-Nagy's *Light-Space Modulator* (1921–1930) was the first electrically powered sculpture to emit light. Gabo became known for his intensive explorations of the possibilities of new materials, such as plastics, and for his creation of monumental architectural designs through constructed sculpture. Of his *Column* (1923), forty-one inches high and made of plastic, metal, and wood, Gabo wrote, "My works of this time are all in search for an image which would fuse the sculptural element with the architectural element . . . I consider my *Column* the culmination of that search." Other such examples include a *Monument for a Physics Observatory* (1922), *Monument for an Institute of Physics and Mathematics* (1925), and *Monument for an Airport* (1924–1932).

After Nazi storm troopers entered his studio in Berlin in 1932, Gabo left for Paris, where Antoine had been working productively for a decade. In Paris Gabo joined the Abstraction-Création group and contributed to its journal. Through this group he met British artists Ben Nicholson and his wife, Barbara Hep-

worth, and the poet-critic Herbert Read, who became both his friend and a lifelong supporter of his work. After settling in London in 1936 (Antoine remained in Paris), Gabo, with Nicholson, edited the journal *Circle*, to which he also contributed essays. Beginning with the important exhibition Erste Russische Kunstausstellung, which Gabo had helped to organize in Berlin in 1922, his sculpture had continued to be shown in international exhibitions in Germany, Paris, London, and New York. In 1936 Gabo married Miriam Israels; they had one daughter.

In 1938 Gabo made his first trip to the United States with his one-man exhibition Constructions in Space, which was shown at the Wadsworth Atheneum in Hartford, Connecticut, the Julien Levy Gallery in New York City, and at Vassar College in Poughkeepsie, New York. With his wife and daughter, Nina, Gabo left England to settle in Woodbury, Connecticut, in 1946. In 1953, the year after becoming a U.S. citizen, he moved to Middlebury, Connecticut. Gabo's sculpture making continued unabated until the last years of his life. His *Linear Constructions in Space*, dating from the 1940s and 1950s and made of perspex with nylon monofilaments, are among his best-known American sculptures.

Gabo's years in the United States were marked by numerous exhibitions and honors of impressive scope. These included an exhibition with Pevsner at the Museum of Modern Art in New York City and one-man exhibitions at the Massachusetts Institute of Technology, the Philadelphia Museum of Art, the Tate Gallery in London, and others in Rotterdam, Amsterdam, and Stockholm. Lecturing widely, at Yale, the Chicago Institute of Design, the Chicago Art Institute, the Baltimore Museum of Art, and the Museum of Modern Art, Gabo also delivered the A. W. Mellon Lectures at the National Gallery of Art in Washington, D.C., in 1959. At the invitation of Bauhaus founder Walter Gropius, he taught at the Harvard University Graduate School of Architecture in 1953–1954, and he was awarded a Guggenheim Fellowship in 1954. He was elected to the National Institute of Art and Letters (1965), the Royal Academy of Art in Sweden (1966), the American Academy of Arts and Sciences (1969), and the American Academy of Arts and Letters (1975) and was made an Honorary Knight Commander, Order of the British Empire (1971).

Major examples of Gabo's public sculpture are his large *Construction* for the stairwell of the Young People's Art Center at the Baltimore Museum of Art (1951) and the famous monumental *Construction* for the Bijenkorf Department Store in Rotterdam (1954–1957); eighty-five feet high, it is made up of steel and bronze wire and was constructed by a Dutch ship building company under Gabo's guidance. Gabo's last public work was his large *Revolving Torsion Fountain* (1974–1975). Produced by Stainless Metalcraft of London, the sculpture remains on long-term loan at St. Thomas Hospital in London.

The study of engineering, idealist philosophy, art history, and physics provided the conceptual basis from which Gabo's sculpture developed. Combining elements of the Orthodox mysticism of his youth, the idealizing tendencies of the new Western art all over Europe, and the messianic zeal of the Russian Revolution, his work is a remarkable, rigorous achievement that is both explicable and elusive.

• Gabo gives his views of constructivist art in Naum Gabo and Herbert Read, "Constructive Art: An Exchange of Letters," *Horizon*, July 1944. For additional biographical information see Ruth Olson and Abraham Chanin, "Naum Gabo," in *Constructivism: The Art of Naum Gabo and Antoine Pevsner*, ed. Herbert Read (exhibition catalog, Museum of Modern Art, 1948); Alexei Pevsner, *A Biographical Sketch of My Brothers, Naum Gabo and Antoine Pevsner* (1964); and George Rickey, "Naum Gabo: 1890–1977," *Artforum*, Nov. 1977. For more on Gabo and his impact on constructivism see Christina Lodder, "Gabo in Russia and Germany, 1890–1922: A Biographical Study," Jorn Merkert, "Conceptions of Sculpture: Gabo and Paris in 1937," and Steven Nash, "Naum Gabo: Sculptures of Purity and Possibility," all in *Naum Gabo: Sixty Years of Constructivism*, ed. Steven A. Nash and Jorn Merkert (exhibition catalog, Dallas Museum of Art, 1985); C. E. Buckley, "Mobiles and Constructions—Alexander Calder and Naum Gabo," *Wadsworth Atheneum Bulletin* 42 (Oct. 1953); Graham Williams, ed., *Naum Gabo Monoprints* (1987); and Herbert Read and Leslie Martin, *GABO: Constructions, Sculpture, Paintings, Drawings, Engravings* (1957). Also see Sam Hunter et al., *Modern Art: Painting, Sculpture, Architecture*, 3d ed. (1992), chaps. 10 and 15. An obituary is in the *New York Times*, 24 Aug. 1977.

ANN GLENN CROWE

GABRIEL (1776–10 Oct. 1800), slave and revolutionary, was born near Richmond, Virginia, at "Brookfield," the Henrico County plantation of Thomas Prosser. The identity of Gabriel's parents is lost to history, but it is known that he had two older brothers, Martin and Solomon. Most likely, Gabriel's father was a blacksmith, the craft chosen for Gabriel and Solomon; in Virginia, the offspring of skilled bondpersons frequently inherited their parent's profession.

Status as an apprentice artisan provided the young craftsman with considerable standing in the slave community, as did his ability to read and write (a skill perhaps taught to him by plantation mistress Ann Prosser). As Gabriel developed into an unusually tall young man, even older slaves looked to him for leadership. By the mid-1790s, as he approached the age of twenty, Gabriel stood "six feet two or three inches high," and the muscles in his arms and chest betrayed nearly a decade in Brookfield's forge. A long and "bony face, well made," was marred by the loss of two front teeth and "two or three scars on his head." His hair was cut short and was as dark as his complexion. Blacks and whites alike regarded him as "a fellow of courage and intellect above his rank in life."

During these years Gabriel married a young slave named Nanny. Little is known about her, including the identity of her owner and whether she had any children with Gabriel. It is likely that she lived on a nearby farm or tobacco plantation.

In the fall of 1798 Gabriel's old master died, and ownership of Brookfield fell to 22-year-old Thomas

Henry Prosser. An ambitious young man with a Richmond townhouse and a lucrative auction business, Prosser increasingly maximized his profits by hiring out his surplus slaves. Even the most efficient planters could not find enough tasks to keep their slave artisans occupied year-round, and many masters routinely hired out their craftsmen to neighboring farms and urban businessmen. Despite all of the work to be done at Brookfield, Gabriel doubtless spent a considerable part of each month smithing in and around Richmond. Though no less a slave under Virginia law, Gabriel enjoyed a rough form of freedom as his ties to young Prosser became ever more tenuous.

Emboldened by this quasi-liberty, in September 1799 Gabriel moved toward overt rebellion. Caught in the act of stealing a pig, a delicacy slaves used to supplement their meager diet, Gabriel refused to suffer his white neighbor's verbal abuse. Instead, he wrestled his tormentor to the ground and bit off the better "part of his left Ear." Under Virginia law, slaves were not tried as whites; instead they were prosecuted under a 1692 statute that established special segregated county tribunals known as courts of oyer and terminer. Composed of five justices of the peace, there was no jury and no route for appeal except to the governor. On 7 October Gabriel was formally charged with attacking a white man, a capital crime in Virginia. Although he was found guilty, Gabriel escaped the gallows through an ancient clause that, ironically, was now denied to white defendants. Slaves possessed the right of "benefit of clergy," which allowed them to escape hanging in favor of being branded on the thumb by a small cross if they were able to recite a verse from the Bible, an option available to Gabriel thanks to the Afro-Baptist faith of his parents. (There is no truth, however, to the Gilded Age myth that Gabriel was a messianic figure who wore his hair long in imitation of his hero Samson.)

Gabriel's branding and incarceration was the final indignity. By the early spring of 1800, his fury began to turn into a carefully considered plan to bring about his freedom—and the end of slavery in Virginia. As he explained it to his brothers Solomon and Martin, slaves from Henrico County would gather at the blacksmith shop at Brookfield on the evening of 30 August. As the small but determined band of insurgents—armed with crude swords fashioned from scythes—neared Richmond, it would split into three groups. The center column planned to swarm into Capitol Square and seize the guns stored in the building. Governor James Monroe, slumbering in the adjacent executive mansion, was to be taken as a hostage but otherwise left unharmed. The other columns would set fire to Rocketts Landing, the warehouse district, as a diversion and then fortify the town. A small number of town leaders were to die, while most would live as hostages in order to force the Virginia elite to grant the rebels' demands, which included their freedom and an equitable division of city property. "Quakers, Methodists and French people," three groups who had earned a sometimes undeserved reputation as foes of slavery, were not to be harmed. The "poor white people," who had no more political power than did the slaves, "would also join" the rebels. If the town leaders agreed to Gabriel's demands, the slave general intended to "hoist a white flag" and drink a toast "with the merchants of the city."

Using their ability to hire their time away from their owners, Gabriel and his chief lieutenants contacted only those slaves whose talents and skills meant they had little contact with their owners. Recruiters moved north into Hanover, Goochland, and Caroline counties, while black mariners ferried word of the uprising down the James River to Petersburg, Norfolk, and Gloucester County.

The uprising, set to begin on the night of Saturday, 30 August, collapsed just before sunset on the appointed day when a severe thunderstorm hit southern Henrico. Creeks rose, washing away fragile wooden bridges and cutting off communications between Brookfield plantation and the city. Perhaps only a dozen slaves reached the blacksmith shop. The chaos of the storm convinced two Henrico house slaves, Tom and Pharoah, that the revolt could not succeed. They informed their owner of the conspiracy, and he hurried word to Governor Monroe in Richmond. As the militia closed in, Gabriel escaped south by way of the swampy Chickahominy River. After hiding along the James River for nearly two weeks, Gabriel decided to risk boarding the schooner *Mary*. Captain Richardson Taylor, a former overseer who had recently converted to Methodism, willingly spirited Gabriel downriver to Norfolk. There Gabriel was betrayed by Billy, a slave crewman who had heard of Monroe's $300 reward for Gabriel's capture. Returned to Richmond under heavy guard, Gabriel was found guilty of "conspiracy and insurrection." On 10 October 1800 the slave general died with quiet composure at the town gallows near Fifteenth and Broad. He was twenty-four. In all, twenty-six slaves, including Gabriel, were hanged for their part in the conspiracy. Another bondman allegedly hanged himself while in custody. Eight more rebels were transported to Spanish New Orleans; at least thirty-two others were found not guilty. Reliable sources placed the number of slaves who knew of the plot to be between five and six hundred.

Although the abortive uprising failed in its goals, southern whites were painfully aware that it was the most extensive and carefully planned slave plot yet devised in North America. In the aftermath, Virginia legislators labored to ensure that it would not be repeated. Intent on crushing black autonomy, the general assembly passed a number of laws abolishing black liberties, including the right to congregate on Sunday for religious services. After 1806 all manumitted slaves had twelve months to leave the state or be "apprehended and sold" back into bondage.

• The trial records for Gabriel and his fellow conspirators are located in the Library of Virginia (Richmond). State newspapers covered the trials in great detail; the Richmond *Virginia Argus* and Fredericksburg *Virginia Herald* are especially use-

ful. The papers of Thomas Jefferson and James Monroe, both in the Library of Congress, discuss the plot, as do the Tucker-Coleman Papers at the College of William and Mary; see also George Tucker's anonymous pamphlet, *Letter to a Member of the General Assembly of Virginia, on the Subject of the Late Conspiracy of the Slaves* (1801).

Douglas R. Egerton, *Gabriel's Rebellion: The Virginia Slave Conspiracies of 1800 and 1802* (1993), and James Sidbury, "Gabriel's World: Race Relations in Richmond, Virginia, 1750–1810" (Ph.D. diss., Johns Hopkins Univ., 1991) are full-length accounts of the plot. Herbert Aptheker, who has done more than any other scholar to rescue slave rebels from the insidious myth of docility, has an excellent pioneering chapter on the conspiracy in *American Negro Slave Revolts* (1943). Gabriel has also received chapter-length treatment in Gerald Mullin, *Flight and Rebellion: Slave Resistance in Eighteenth-Century Virginia* (1972), and Virginius Dabney, *Richmond: The Story of a City* (1976). Philip J. Schwarz, *Twice Condemned: Slaves and the Criminal Law of Virginia, 1705–1865* (1988), discusses Gabriel and other rebels in the context of white law; see also Schwarz's "Gabriel's Challenge: Slaves and Crime in Late Eighteenth-Century Virginia," *Virginia Magazine of History and Biography* 90 (1982): 283–309.

DOUGLAS R. EGERTON

GABRIELSON, Ira Noel (27 Sept. 1889–7 Sept. 1977), wildlife biologist and first director of the U.S. Fish and Wildlife Service, was born in Sioux Rapids, Iowa, the son of Frank August Gabrielson, a partner in a hardware store and later a farmer, and Ida Jansen. During a boyhood spent hunting, fishing, and exploring the countryside, Gabrielson developed a love of nature, photographed and studied birds, and became particularly interested in waterfowl. He graduated from Morningside College, Sioux City, Iowa, with a B.A. in biology in 1912 and spent the next three years teaching high school biology in Marshalltown, Iowa. Just as he was about to enter the University of Iowa on a graduate fellowship, he was offered and accepted a position he had coveted with the Bureau of Biological Survey.

The survey bureau had its origins in the Division of Economic Ornithology established by Congress in the Department of Agriculture in 1885. Mammalogy was added to the duties of the division, and by 1905 its name had been changed to the Bureau of Biological Survey. Under its first director, C. Hart Merriam, it had evolved into a scientific and research-oriented agency. Although Gabrielson dreamed of being sent to the West to carry out field work, he was ordered to Washington, D.C., and set to identifying seeds and insects found in bird stomachs. There he met the stalwarts of the early bureau, including Albert K. Fisher, Edward W. Nelson, E. R. Kalmbach, Hartley H. T. Jackson, and Vernon Orlando Bailey. He was assigned a desk facing that of Alexander Wetmore, future secretary of the Smithsonian Institution, with whom he became lifelong friends. Later Gabrielson said that he learned more practical biology at this time than at any other in his life.

By 1918 the bureau was becoming heavily involved in a program of predator control and extermination through poisoning, a mission partially financed and influenced by western ranchers. Over the next thirty years, the span of Gabrielson's career in the federal government, first controversy and then public outrage erupted over the policy, followed by the growth of scientific data defining the role of predators in the judicious control of wildlife and the laying of foundations for modern federal wildlife management.

Sent to South Dakota and Oregon in 1918, Gabrielson learned every facet of the bureau's work: predator control, game management, food habits, and wildlife research. He quickly rose to supervisory positions and in 1935 was called to Washington to become assistant chief of the bureau's Division of Wildlife Research. Later that year he was named chief of the bureau. He made an important contribution in the first year when he was the guiding force in the establishment of the Patuxent Wildlife Refuge Center in Laurel, Maryland. In 1940 the survey bureau was combined with the Bureau of Fisheries, transferred to the Department of the Interior, and renamed the U.S. Fish and Wildlife Service, with Gabrielson as its first director.

Gabrielson worked closely with conservation-minded interior secretary Harold Ickes, and New Deal legislation resulted in gains for wildlife in every area. Millions of acres were set aside for wildlife refuges, legislation assured that fishing and hunting license funds would be spent for wildlife land acquisition, the first North American Wildlife Conference was held, and wildlife preservation was incorporated into the missions of the Civilian Conservation Corps and the Soil Conservation Service.

During World War II Gabrielson served as deputy coordinator of fisheries and as a U.S. delegate to the International Whaling Conference. He retired from federal service in 1946 to join the Wildlife Management Institute, a private organization dedicated to wildlife research, where he was president until 1970, when he became chair of the board of directors. He was responsible for the establishment of a nationwide network of wildlife research units and was called on by the governors of thirty-eight states and four Canadian provinces for analysis and recommendation of conservation programs.

By virtue of his experience and reputation, "Gabe," as he was often called, assumed a position of national prominence in the field of wildlife management. In 1948 he helped found the International Union for the Conservation of Nature and in 1961 became president of the World Wildlife Fund (United States). He was also a trustee of the World Wildlife Fund (International) and the National Wildlife Federation and had memberships in the Wilderness Society, the Izaak Walton League, the American Society of Mammalogists, the American Ornithologists' Union, the Audubon Society, the Washington Biologists' Field Club, the Washington Academy of Sciences, and the Cosmos Club. He served on the Virginia Outdoor Study Commission (1966–1974), helped to found the Northern Virginia Regional Park Authority, and served as its chair from 1959 to 1976 and as chairman emeritus until his death in Washington, D.C.

Gabrielson was the author of four books, *Western American Alpines* (1932), *Wildlife Conservation* (1941), *Wildlife Refuges* (1943), and *Wildlife Management* (1951), and was coauthor of two others, *Birds of Oregon*, with S. G. Jewett (1940), and *The Birds of Alaska*, with Frederick C. Lincoln (1959). His many articles and speeches served to popularize the principles of wildlife management.

Gabrielson received every major award in the wildlife conservation field: the Audubon Conservation Award, the Distinguished Service Award of the Interior Department, the Leopold Medal of the Wildlife Society, the Hugh Bennett Award of Friends of the Land, and the Distinguished Service Award of the American Forestry Association. He also received several honorary degrees. Posthumously, he was named to the National Wildlife Federation's Conservation Hall of Fame.

As the last chief of the Bureau of Biological Survey and the first director of the U.S. Fish and Wildlife Service, Gabrielson played a key role in shaping both the modern agency and federal wildlife policy. His early years working with western state legislators provided useful experience for dealing with Congress, and his forthright manner and personal style made him successful at all levels. His strength lay not in the conceptualizing of wildlife principles but in ensuring that the federal government built the machinery and carried out a national program to preserve animals and their habitats. As president of the Wildlife Management Institute, he was able to work for national and international acceptance of wildlife conservation.

Gabrielson was married in 1912 to Clara Speer; they had four children. Industrious and energetic in his domestic pursuits, he wrote in his journal, built his first house in eight days, kept a vegetable garden each year, continued a lifetime of bird watching, and participated in the Audubon Society's annual Christmas bird count.

Asked to summarize the conservation achievements of the last fifty years, he wrote in 1951, "The understanding of the repercussions of human actions is perhaps the greatest advance made in the philosophy of [wildlife] management during this period. It will have a major effect for many years."

• Most of the professional correspondence of Gabrielson as chief of the Bureau of Biological Survey and director of the U.S. Fish and Wildlife Service is located in RG 22, Records of the U.S. Fish and Wildlife Service, at the National Archives and Records Administration. Gabrielson's official correspondence as president of the Wildlife Management Institute has not survived. The Smithsonian Institution Archives contains a small collection of Gabrielson material in record unit 7319, including his diaries, a chronological memoir of his life, which he had completed up to 1966, copies of his speeches and articles, and records created during the writing of *The Birds of Alaska*. Also included in the collection are copies of published obituaries and statements from friends and colleagues collected by Robert A. Nesbitt. The archives also has a small number of "Special Reports," sent in by Gabrielson from the field in his early years with the Bureau of

Biological Survey; these are located in record unit 7176, Field Reports of the U.S. Fish and Wildlife Service. In addition, the archives contains some correspondence, scattered through a number of collections, between Gabrielson and Smithsonian officials and curators, including Alexander Wetmore.

SUSAN GLENN

GABRILOWITSCH, Ossip (7 Feb. 1878–14 Sept. 1936), pianist and conductor, was born in St. Petersburg, Russia, the son of Salomon Gabrilowitsch, a successful member of the bar, and Rosa Segal, who was German-Russian. (According to modern conventions of transliteration from the Cyrillic, the surname would be rendered Gabrilovich.) When Gabrilowitsch was four, his oldest brother, George, gave him piano lessons for a short time, but soon a professional teacher, Olga Theodorowitsch, took over the lessons. She also arranged for Anton Rubinstein to hear the ten-year-old Ossip play. Rubinstein was very impressed and insisted that the boy enter the St. Petersburg Conservatory. Rubinstein oversaw Gabrilowitsch's music education, which consisted of piano lessons with Victor Tolstoff and composition with Glazunov, Liadov, and Navratil.

Graduating at age sixteen, in 1894 Gabrilowitsch was the first winner of the Rubinstein Prize. On the advice of Anna Essipoff, Theodor Leschetizky's former student and ex-wife, he went to Vienna for lessons with the master teacher Leschetizky. He made his formal debut in October 1896 in Berlin and was enthusiastically received. In 1905 he went to Berlin for study with the great Arthur Nikisch, one of the few conductors who taught the art of conducting.

In 1898 Gabrilowitsch had met Clara Clemens, daughter of Samuel L. Clemens (Mark Twain). Clara was in Vienna studying piano with Leschetizky, and Gabrilowitsch was in the city to visit his former teacher. After a prolonged friendship and courtship, they were married in 1909 at her father's home in West Redding, Connecticut. They had one child.

The couple returned to Europe where from 1910 to 1914 Gabrilowitsch was conductor with the Munich Konzertverein, while continuing to perform in concerts. In 1914 they returned to the United States where he applied for American citizenship, which he gained in 1921. Gabrilowitsch continued playing recitals and appearing as soloist with orchestras, and in the 1917–1918 season he conducted a successful series of concerts in New York City with an orchestra assembled for the occasion. This led to his appointment as music director of the Detroit Symphony Orchestra in 1918. He retained the post until his death (caused by intestinal cancer) in Detroit.

Gabrilowitsch was a brilliant and sensitive artist at the piano. He revered his teacher Leschetizky, saying that he taught his students not only about piano playing, but about life and living. He maintained that his own playing relied not on a Leschetizky "method," but on the individualism encouraged by his teacher. Gabrilowitsch said it was useless to imitate and that tradi-

tion needed to be looked into and verified. Those who heard him commented on Gabrilowitsch's poetic playing, beautiful tone, and exquisite taste. He gained much renown for a series of six historical concerts illustrating the concerto from Bach through Sergei Rachmaninoff. These concerts included three or four concertos in each concert, a feat seldom repeated by other pianists. In addition to these concerts, he also performed a series of solo recitals along the same lines. Both series were repeated through the years, lasting from 1912 until his declining health finally halted all musical activity in 1935. His repertoire included not only the standard literature (Beethoven, Schumann, Chopin, Liszt, and Brahms), but also lighter works of his time as well as several of his own pieces.

In addition to his solo playing, Gabrilowitsch played many two-piano recitals with Harold Bauer and occasionally accompanied singers in recital (including his wife, who was a contralto).

Gabrilowitsch was the soloist in the initial concert of the Philadelphia Symphony Orchestra in 1900 during the year of his first tour of the United States. More than a quarter-century later he shared the podium of this orchestra with Stokowski for two seasons, 1929–1931.

As conductor of the Detroit Symphony Orchestra, Gabrilowitsch achieved great success. After only one year in the position, he was able to bring about the building of a new hall for the orchestra. The musicianship he had learned and practiced as a pianist was evident in his conducting. The tonal quality of the orchestra was always a central concern. He conducted from memory for two reasons: his imperfect eyesight made it difficult for him to follow the small notes in a score; perhaps more important, he maintained that knowing the score from memory freed one to make more beautiful music.

In addition to the standard symphonies, overtures, and concertos, Gabrilowitsch also included vocal masterworks in his concerts. The most outstanding of these were the superlative performances of Bach's *St. Matthew Passion* given in Detroit and in New York. To his credit, Gabrilowitsch did not forget the composers of his adopted country, conducting works by John Alden Carpenter and his good friend Daniel Gregory Mason, among others.

As was true of so many performers of his time, Gabrilowitsch also composed a small body of works, including piano pieces, a few songs, a duo for cello and piano, and one orchestral work. When he assumed serious conducting responsibilities he stated that he was giving up composing because he could serve two masters, but not three.

A gentle man, Gabrilowitsch held strong convictions on human justice, personal responsibility, and fairness, and he did not hesitate to make his feelings known. Whether it was protesting the Pascist treatment of Arturo Toscanini or condemning lynching in Georgia, he spoke out eloquently for his beliefs. He was described as generous (he once conducted the Detroit Symphony Orchestra for a whole season without pay in order to save the orchestra from financial failure), kind, and considerate, full of fun and wit, and possessed of the utmost integrity. His 25-year marriage was the center of his life, and this happy union balanced his inclination to pessimism and depression.

Although he never achieved the fame of Rubinstein or Leschetizky, or indeed, of many of his contemporaries, Gabrilowitsch was highly respected and admired by his colleagues and by all who heard him in concert.

• The principal collections of Gabrilowitsch papers are in the Detroit Public Library and the Library of Congress. His personal collection of orchestra scores and parts was given to the New York Public Library. Items in this collection are scattered through the Music Division collection at the Lincoln Center Library of Performing Arts. Although it lacks scholarly documentation, much information may be gleaned from Clara Clemens, *My Husband Gabrilowitsch* (1938). See also Daniel G. Mason, "A Conversation on Music with Ossip Gabrilowitsch," *Century Magazine* 78 (May 1909): 112–19, and William Armstrong, "Individualism in Music," *The Musician* 22 (Sept. 1917): 652–53, for earlier assessments of the artist. Daniel G. Mason, *Music in My Time* (1938), is an important source especially for information about Gabrilowitsch's conducting. An obituary is in *Musical America*, 10 Oct. 1936.

DALE L. HUDSON

GADSDEN, Christopher (16 Feb. 1724–28 Aug. 1805), merchant and patriot, was born in Charleston, South Carolina, the son of Thomas Gadsden, the British collector of customs in that port, and his wife Elizabeth, the daughter of indentured servants whose names are unknown. Between the ages of eight and sixteen, young Christopher, nicknamed "Kittie," lived with relatives in England and went to school there. He returned to British North America in 1740, passed five years in a mercantile apprenticeship in Philadelphia, and from 1745 to 1746 served during King George's War as a purser on the British man-of-war *Aldborough*.

Gadsden's parents died in 1741, leaving him a large fortune. In 1748 young Gadsden returned to Charleston to establish his family and business. He began his business career modestly as a "country factor" who bought rice, indigo, and furs from planters and resold them to large merchants engaged in the transatlantic trade. He was not involved in the slave trade. He owned warehouses, two plantations, a fleet of small boats, and, after 1767, a large wharf on the Cooper River. He owned property in Georgetown and developed a residential district known as "Gadsdenboro" in Charleston, but he was always primarily a merchant.

Gadsden was married three times: on 28 August 1746, to Jane Godfrey (d. 1755); on 29 December 1755, to Mary Hasell (d. 1769); and on 14 April 1776, to Anne Wragg (d. 1805). His second marriage produced four children. He was fiercely loyal to his family. He participated fully in the social and political life of Charleston. He was a member of the Winyah Indigo Society, the South Carolina Society, the Charleston Library Society, and St. Philip's Anglican Church.

In 1757, when he was elected from St. Philip's Parish to the Commons House of Assembly, Gadsden began his twenty-seven years of service in the lower house of assembly. At the center of the dramatic political debates of the revolutionary era, he embraced the radical whig ideology that American revolutionaries used to condemn the reign of King George III of England. Given to furious outbursts of temper and sometimes profane language, he spoke and wrote to support causes he thought were right. In 1774, responding to the coercive measures that Parliament imposed on Massachusetts, he wrote to Samuel Adams that he would rather see his own family "reduced to the utmost extremity and cut to pieces" than submit to the "damned Machinations" of Parliament (5 June 1774). Near the end of the Revolution, Gadsden declared that "Our case may, therefore, be called the cause of God also" (to Morton Wilkinson, Sept. 1782).

From 1759 through 1783, Gadsden was intensely involved in the American Revolution. His first defiance of British authority came during the French and Indian War when he vigorously and publicly condemned the British authorities on three issues: the royal governor's interference with the Commons House of Assembly's right to raise local troops; the House's authority to determine the election of its own members; and the debate between the Royal Council and the Assembly over control of money bills. When Gadsden was reelected to the Commons House of Assembly in 1762, Governor Thomas Boone, who had identified Gadsden as a troublemaker, thought the election improper because the churchwardens who were in charge of the election had not been first administered an oath by a magistrate of the county. Boone refused to allow Gadsden to be seated. New elections were held, with the wardens properly certified, and Gadsden was easily elected. When he took his seat on 25 October 1762, Gadsden became the principal actor in a furious struggle between the Commons and the governor, known as the Gadsden Election Controversy. The Commons contended that the royal governor had illegally interfered in the assembly's election of its own members. They argued their case for two years in the press and through appeals to the Lords of Trade until June 1764, when the Lords ordered Boone to return to England. The Gadsden Election Controversy was one of only two times in the colonies that a local assembly forced the recall of a royal governor.

When the Stamp Act crisis erupted in 1765, Gadsden organized the Sons of Liberty in South Carolina and actively participated in the Stamp Act Congress in New York. He triumphantly attended the meeting under the Liberty Tree in Charleston where the repeal of the Stamp Act was celebrated, but he somberly warned the celebrants that the mother country had only begun to fight.

Known as "the Sam Adams of the South," Gadsden was in the forefront of every succeeding dispute with Great Britain until the colonies won their independence. He helped organize the nonimportation of British goods after the passage of the Townshend Duties in 1767; and he openly supported the whig journalist and politician John Wilkes, who had publicly declared that young King George III and his ministers were denying the British people the rights they had won in their Glorious Revolution of 1688. He served in both the first and second sessions of the Continental Congress. At its first meeting in 1774, Gadsden won the respect and friendship of John Adams (1735–1826). During the second meeting of the Continental Congress in 1775, he served on the Navy Committee. He designed the famous yellow flag depicting the coiled rattlesnake with the words "DON'T TREAD ON ME" as the personal flag of Commodore Esek Hopkins.

In January 1776 Gadsden left Philadelphia to assume command of the First South Carolina Regiment and to serve in the Provincial Congress. On 10 February 1776, in a speech that William Henry Drayton said fell upon the congress "like an explosion of thunder," he declared that he was in favor of independence, a sentiment not yet shared by many in his audience. He recruited men for the Provincial Regiment, assisted William Moultrie in turning back a British invasion at Charleston in the summer of 1776, and designed and constructed a remarkable bridge as part of the colony's fortifications. The Continental Congress rewarded him on 17 September 1776, by appointing him a brigadier general in the Continental army.

Gadsden was elected vice president of the province under the constitution of 1778, but he lost much of his popular support when he condemned rioting over the deadline for taking an oath of allegiance to the state. Nevertheless, he remained loyal to the state and to the war for independence, stubbornly refusing to flee to a safe location in 1780 when the British invaded Charleston. The British held him prisoner for forty-two weeks in a dungeon in their fort at St. Augustine, Florida.

After the war, Gadsden returned to Charleston, determined to preserve the victory he had helped to win. Because of his advanced age, declining health, and the changing political climate, he rejected the offer by the assembly to serve as governor. A Federalist, he endorsed the new Constitution of the United States and supported both George Washington and John Adams for the presidency. With the help of his sons, he recouped the fortune he had lost during the war by rebuilding and expanding his wharf, his real estate district in Charleston, his factorage business, and his planting operations. He died in Charleston.

• The biography of Christopher Gadsden is E. Stanly Godbold, Jr., and Robert H. Woody, *Christopher Gadsden and the American Revolution* (1982). It contains comprehensive bibliographical information and notes. The majority of Gadsden's writings are published in Richard Walsh, ed., *The Writings of Christopher Gadsden, 1746–1805* (1966). Secondary works include Jack P. Greene, *The Quest for Power: The Lower Houses of Assembly in the Southern Royal Colonies, 1689–1776* (1963); Pauline Maier, *From Resistance to Revolution: Colonial Radicals and the Opposition to Great Britain, 1765–1776* (1972); Je-

rome J. Nadelhaft, *The Disorders of War: The Revolution in South Carolina* (1981); David D. Wallace, *The Life of Henry Laurens* (1915); and Richard Walsh, *Charleston's Sons of Liberty: A Study of the Artisans, 1763–1789* (1959).

E. STANLY GODBOLD, JR.

GADSDEN, James (15 May 1788–26 Dec. 1858), soldier, politician, and railroad executive, was born in Charleston, South Carolina, the son of Philip Gadsden, and Catherine Edwards. He was the grandson of Christopher Gadsden, a merchant and revolutionary leader. Like his older brothers, he attended Yale, from which he was graduated in 1806. After leaving Yale he returned to Charleston and became a merchant. Gadsden married Susanne Gibbs Hort; the couple had no children.

With the outbreak of the War of 1812, Gadsden entered the military as a lieutenant of engineers and saw service on the Canadian border. After the war he accompanied General Andrew Jackson on an expedition to inspect the military fortifications of the Gulf Coast and the Southwest. He also served under Jackson during the First Seminole War in Florida. Through the efforts of Gadsden papers were seized, which led to the capture, trial, and execution of Alexander Arbuthnot and Robert Ambrister, British subjects who were accused of inciting the Indians against the United States. In 1818, in the rank of captain, he was placed in charge of constructing works of defense in the area. One small fort located near the mouth of the Apalachicola River in West Florida was named Fort Gadsden in his honor. In 1820, with the endorsement of Jackson, he was promoted to colonel and appointed inspector general of the Southern District of the U.S. Army. In 1821 President James Monroe, at Jackson's suggestion, appointed Gadsden Adjutant General of the Army. Gadsden served for several months in this position, but the U.S. Senate refused to confirm his nomination for political reasons. Thus rejected, Gadsden retired from the army and moved to Florida. His warm friendship with Jackson continued, and Gadsden was a strong supporter of Jackson's campaign for the presidency. Later, Gadsden's support of the right of states to nullify federal laws at will greatly cooled their friendship.

Gadsden's sixteen years in Florida, from 1823 to 1839, were marked by successful efforts to consolidate it as a state but failure in politics. In 1823 President Monroe appointed Gadsden commissioner to negotiate with the Seminole Indians concerning the sale of their lands in northern Florida and their removal to reservations in southern Florida. Later Monroe assigned him the tasks of making a survey of the new Seminole reservations and overseeing the building of the first government roads in the territory. In 1824 he was named a member of the first territorial legislative council by Monroe. Gadsden found the fertile lands of Florida attractive, and in 1825 he sold his Tennessee property, which he had obtained between 1819 and 1822 when he was closely associated with Jackson, and became a Florida rice planter. The former soldier soon tired of the agrarian life, however, and turned to Florida politics. In nearly every year of the next dozen, he ran as a candidate for some political office in the territory of Florida. He ran several times for the office of territorial delegate to Congress but was always defeated by his rival, Joseph M. White, a Kentucky lawyer who moved in 1821 to Pensacola. In his closest race with White, Gadsden lost by only eighty votes out of 4,000 that were cast. His distaste for farming, his numerous failures in politics, and the devastation of the Second Seminole War convinced Gadsden that he should leave Florida, and in 1839 he returned to Charleston.

Back in Charleston Gadsden again became a merchant, and in 1840 he was elected president of the Louisville, Cincinnati, & Charleston Railroad. This railroad had been projected in 1836 as an extension of the earlier Charleston & Hamburg by Robert Y. Hayne, former U.S. senator and South Carolina governor. Hayne's sudden, early death in 1839 left Gadsden, his successor, with a dream of a railroad, a $3 million debt, and only 136 miles of track. In 1842 the line was reorganized as the South Carolina Railroad, a line with more limited ambitions. Gadsden completed a 68-mile branch to Columbia by 1841 and a 38-mile line to Camden in 1848. By midcentury the 242-mile South Carolina was the longest railroad in the southern Atlantic states, as it remained on the eve of the Civil War. Under the management of Gadsden, gross revenues on the line increased from $388,000 in 1840 to $913,000 in 1850, and dividends were paid from 1843 to 1850, averaging about 4.5 percent a year on the par value of the stock. In 1850 the equipment roster of the railroad listed 37 locomotives and 455 passenger and freight cars, but by the late 1840s Gadsden's main ambition had become the extension of the railroad west of the state on toward the Mississippi River. The stockholders, however, were more interested in larger dividends and thus Gadsden lost the presidency of the South Carolina Railroad in 1850.

For several years Gadsden had been interested in southern commercial conventions, attending such meetings in Augusta in 1837 and Charleston in 1839. He was a major promoter of the Memphis Commercial Convention in July 1845. Delegations from sixteen states attended and quickly selected John C. Calhoun as the chairman. Calhoun appointed Gadsden to chair the committee on railroads, which strongly urged the building of a southern railroad to the Pacific, probably hoping for some state and federal aid. During the next few years Gadsden worked diligently, but unsuccessfully, for the completion of a southern line to the Mississippi and then on through Texas to the Pacific. At midcentury Gadsden favored not only a southern railroad to the West but also the extension of slavery, states' rights, and if need be, even secession.

In 1853 Gadsden's friend, Jefferson Davis, became Franklin Pierce's secretary of war and chief adviser and was soon directing U.S. Army surveys of four rather parallel routes across the western plains and mountains for a projected railroad to the Pacific. As the surveys progressed, Davis, Gadsden, and other southern rail promoters pressed for the southern route along the thirty-second parallel from Texas to San Diego. This route was not only shorter than those farther north, but the estimated cost of construction was lower. However, this favored southern route dipped well below the Gila River, which then formed a portion of the American–Mexican border established after the end of the Mexican War. President Pierce, largely through the influence of Davis, appointed Gadsden minister to Mexico in May 1853, instructing him to settle Indian claims and other disputes. Gadsden also was to obtain a portion of Mexican land sufficient to allow the building of the proposed railroad south of the Gila River. Gadsden found the Mexican president, Antonio Santa Anna, in some financial difficulty and thus willing to consider the sale of Mexican land. After weeks of negotiation a treaty was concluded in December 1853, by which Mexico would cede an area south of the Gila River for $15 million. The proposed agreement caused a violent sectional debate (many in the North wanted a northern route and saw the treaty as aiding slavery), but an amended treaty, providing for a purchase price of $10 million for a reduced area, was finally approved by the U.S. Senate in a close vote on 25 April 1854. Known as the Gadsden Purchase, the acquired territory consisted of 29,640 square miles located south of the Gila River and extending from the Rio Grande west to the Colorado River, in what are now southern New Mexico and Arizona. Gadsden remained as minister in Mexico until he was recalled late in 1856. He returned to Charleston, where he died two years later. In the 1870s and 1880s a Southern Pacific line went through the Gadsden Purchase.

• Material on the life of Gadsden is found in Paul N. Garber, *The Gadsden Treaty* (1923). Gadsden's railroad years are reviewed in Ulrich B. Phillips, *A History of Transportation in the Eastern Cotton Belt to 1860* (1908). J. Fred Rippy, *The United States and Mexico* (1931), covers the Gadsden Treaty and its background. The antebellum 1850s are detailed in Allan Nevins, *Ordeal of the Union: A House Dividing, 1852–1857* (1947). John F. Stover, *Iron Road to the West: American Railroads in the 1850s* (1978), surveys railroad development during the 1850s. An obituary is in the *Charleston Daily Courier*, 28 Dec. 1858.

JOHN F. STOVER

GÁG, Wanda (11 Mar. 1893–27 June 1946), artist and children's book writer, was born Wanda Hazel Gág in New Ulm, Minnesota, the daughter of Anton Gág and Elisabeth Biebl. Gág (which rhymes with "cog") grew up in a heavily European culture. Her father was born in Bohemia, as were her mother's parents. New Ulm was settled largely by German and Bohemian and Hungarian immigrants, and Gág grew up surrounded by Old World customs and legends and Bavarian and Bohemian folk songs, an upbringing that would heavily influence her artistic style and choice of subject matter.

Gág's father was a painter who decorated houses and churches, and he taught each of his seven children how to draw and paint. But in 1908 Anton died of tuberculosis, telling Gág on his deathbed, "Was der Papa nicht tun könt', müss die Wanda halt fertig machen." (What papa couldn't do, Wanda will have to finish.) At fifteen, with her mother weakened by the stress of caring for her husband, Gág became the sole financial and emotional support for the family. Despite the advice of family friends, who urged her to stop drawing and take any job to support the family, she pressed on with her ambition to become an artist. She took any art jobs she could find and began selling stories and sketches to the childrens' newspaper supplement in Minneapolis. She drew greeting cards, designed place cards and calendars, and wrote and illustrated stories for magazines. She kept the family together until her younger siblings were old enough to work and contribute to the household. She was befriended financially by Herschel V. Jones, the editor of the *Minneapolis Journal*, who bought her illustrations and later paid her fees to attend the Art Students' League in New York. Charles Weschcke, a St. Paul businessman, also helped her financially.

Gág attended the St. Paul Art School during the 1913–1914 school year and the Minneapolis Art School from 1914 to 1917. Her mother died in 1917, and that same year she won a year's scholarship to the Art Students' League in New York. During the next decade, she worked hard, saved her money, and moved her family to New York as she could afford it. In 1923 she lived in Connecticut for a year, then moved to an old farmhouse near Glen Gardner, New Jersey. In addition to her commercial work, she produced a number of prints, drawings, and watercolors.

In 1928 Gág began a new career when her second one-woman show at the Weyhe Gallery in New York City attracted the attention of Ernestine Evans, childrens' book editor at Coward-McCann. Evans asked her to submit a story, and she responded with one that publishers had rejected years before. *Millions of Cats* began life as a tale she made up to amuse her friends' children. Published in 1928, the story of a lonely old couple's search for a feline companion was a popular success and became a Newbery Honor Book. *Millions of Cats* was the first to use a hand-lettered text and to integrate the copy with the illustrations, resulting in a unified page design. Gág wrote four more picture books in this fashion, each a popular success: *The Funny Thing* (1929), *Snippy and Snappy* (1931), *ABC Bunny* (1933), and *Nothing at All* (1942). In 1930 she married her longtime friend Earle Humphreys and bought a farm near Milford, New Jersey, where she lived for the rest of her life with her husband, her brother Howard, and her sister Flavia.

A commission to illustrate the story of Hansel and Gretel for the *New York Herald-Tribune* rekindled her interest in the fairy tales she heard in her youth. In 1936 she translated and illustrated sixteen stories by the Grimm brothers and published *Tales from Grimm*. *Snow White and the Seven Dwarfs* followed in 1938,

then *Three Gay Tales from Grimm* in 1943. *More Tales from Grimm* was published in 1947, a year after her death from lung cancer in New York City.

Wanda Gág was a successful illustrator and popular children's book author in her day, but now she is considered an artist of minor significance, and her illustrations have dated considerably. Although she was talented in a number of media, including woodcutting and lithography, her financial needs prevented her from creating more noncommercial art, a goal toward which she was working before her early death.

• Gág's notebooks and diaries are at the University of Pennsylvania Library. The New York Public Library, the Free Library of Philadelphia, the Kerlan Collection at the Walter Library of the University of Minnesota, and the Minneapolis Institute of Art house major collections of prints, drawings, and watercolors; the most complete collection is at the Philadelphia Museum of Art. Her diary, published as *Growing Pains* (1940), covers her years until she moved to New York City. See also Alma Scott, *Wanda Gág: The Story of an Artist* (1949). An obituary appears in the *New York Times*, 28 June 1946.

BILL PESCHEL

GAGE, Frances Dana Barker (12 Oct. 1808–10 Nov. 1884), reformer, lecturer, and author, was born on a farm in Union Township, Washington County, Ohio, the daughter of Joseph Barker and Elizabeth Dana, farmers. The rugged conditions of farm life bred in her a hardiness and resourcefulness that served her well as an adult.

From her mother and her maternal grandmother, who urged her to assist runaway slaves, the young Frances developed a social consciousness as well as an impatience for being told to stay in woman's sphere. When she was ten, her father admonished her for helping a cooper make a barrel and remarked, "What a pity she was not a boy!" She bristled, and, as she said later, "Then and there sprang up my hatred to the limitations of sex. . . . I was outspoken forever afterward."

In 1829 she married James L. Gage of McConnelsville, Ohio, a lawyer. While rearing eight children, Frances Gage supplemented her meager formal education by reading voraciously. Imbued by the spirit of reform that suffused the antebellum years, she ardently supported the three great causes of her day, abolition, women's rights, and temperance. She began writing letters to the newspapers in support of these causes and also published poetry. By 1850 Gage was regularly published in the *Ladies' Repository* of Connecticut.

Around that time, Gage started to write letters to the *Ohio Cultivator*, a bimonthly farm paper, under the pen name "Aunt Fanny." These missives, which were printed in the "Ladies Department," offered practical advice about health, dress reform, and other domestic matters, but they also reflected her interest in social reform.

Gage was unable to attend the first Ohio women's rights convention, held in Salem in April 1850. But she sent a letter registering her support, and in May 1850, at a local meeting in McConnelsville, she drafted a petition to the state legislature urging that the words *white* and *male* be stricken from the new state constitution being drafted.

In 1851 Gage was chosen to lead the second state women's rights convention at Akron, Ohio; it was there that African-American women's rights advocate Sojourner Truth gave her stirring, eloquent response to a minister's denunciation of women's rights. Despite the audience's protestations, Gage let Truth speak—and later recorded for all time her ringing words and the crowd's emotional support.

In 1853 Gage presided at the third national women's rights convention in Cleveland, Ohio. Her days were now filled with appearances at temperance and women's rights conventions and with public speaking. She was a witty, engaging speaker who charmed her crowds as she won them over.

However, that same year she and her family left McConnelsville and moved to St. Louis, Missouri, a less hospitable community to abolitionists and women's rights advocates such as Gage. She contributed letters and articles to two St. Louis newspapers, but her radical ideas alienated the editors, and they stopped printing her writings. Undiscouraged, she worked in the burgeoning women's rights movement with Elizabeth Cady Stanton and Susan B. Anthony and contributed poems and articles to two pro–women's rights newspapers, the *Lily*, edited by Amelia Bloomer, and Jane Grey Swisshelm's *Saturday Visiter*.

In 1860, owing to business reverses, the Gages returned to Ohio and settled in Columbus. Frances Dana Gage became associate editor of the *Ohio Cultivator* and of *Field Notes*, a new weekly farm journal. She also continued to lecture, though only in Ohio, to remain near her ailing husband.

When the Civil War erupted, Gage stopped her editorial work to do volunteer relief work. All four of her sons fought for the Union. In October 1862 she and her daughter Mary sailed from New York to the Union-captured Sea Islands of South Carolina. There, with no official title or salary, she was appointed to supervise the welfare of 500 former slaves on Parris Island. Her staff consisted of three white people, including her daughter. She returned home in June 1863 to care for her husband and remained in Columbus several weeks before returning to the Sea Islands.

But the following November she returned north and embarked on a lecture tour to publicize the plight of the freedpeople. Almost every day she appeared in Pennsylvania, New York, Ohio, Illinois, and Missouri, lecturing to soldiers' aid societies. Beyond covering her expenses, all proceeds from her lectures went to support relief for former soldiers and slaves. During the summer of 1864, she briefly did relief work in Memphis, Vicksburg, and Natchez for the Western Sanitary Commission and then returned to lecturing. The following September she was severely injured when her carriage overturned in Galesburg, Illinois, and she was forced to end her speaking tour.

After recuperating from her accident, Gage worked as a lecturer for temperance organizations and renewed her involvement in the women's rights movement. In May 1866 she lectured at the New York meeting of the Equal Rights Association, a national organization devoted to securing equal rights for all American women and for African-American men and women. The following year she published a volume of poetry, *Poems*, and a temperance novel, *Elsie Magoon*. Although a stroke in the summer of 1867 severely paralyzed her, she bravely continued to write. She died in Greenwich, Connecticut, from paralysis.

Unlike Elizabeth Cady Stanton, Susan B. Anthony, and several other women's rights leaders, Gage had little formal education. But she parlayed a love of knowledge and a reformer's zeal into a vocation as a writer and lecturer, using her pen and her tongue to do battle for the causes that rocked American society in the nineteenth century: abolition, temperance, and women's rights.

• Gage's correspondence and miscellaneous papers are located in the Lilly (Martin) Spencer Papers, Smithsonian Institution, Archives of American Art; the collection of her sister Catherine Barker, Iowa State Historical Department, Division of Historical Museums and Archives, Historical Library; the Anti-slavery Manuscripts Division, Boston Public Library; and the Schlesinger Library, Radcliffe College (which holds one letter from Gage to Anthony). Her major publications not mentioned above include *Christmas Stories* (1849), *The Man in the Well: A Temperance Tale* (1850), *Fanny's Journey* (1866), *Gertie's Sacrifice; or, Glimpses at Two Lives* (1869), and *Steps Upward* (1870). Elizabeth Cady Stanton et al., *History of Woman Suffrage*, vol. 1 and 2 (1881–1882), includes information on Gage's role in the women's rights movement, and Lillian O'Connor, *Pioneer Woman Orators* (1954), offers a brief profile. Gage's obituary is in the *New York Tribune*, 13 Nov. 1884.

HARRIET SIGERMAN

GAGE, Lyman Judson (28 June 1836–26 Jan. 1927), banker and secretary of the treasury, was born in Deruyter, New York, the son of Eli A. Gage and Mary Judson, farmers. He received an elementary education in Madison County, New York, and Rome, New York, and at the age of fourteen he became a mail clerk on the Rome & Watertown Railroad. Three years later he took a job as an office boy in a bank in Rome, New York. He worked in this position until he moved to Chicago in 1855. He took a job as a night watchman in a lumberyard, where he remained for three years until reentering banking as a clerk and bookkeeper at the Merchants' Savings, Loan & Trust Company in Chicago, Illinois. By 1861 Gage had become a cashier and was wealthy enough to buy a substitute during the Civil War. In 1864 he married Sara Etheridge; they had four children before her death in 1874. In 1868 he moved to the First National Bank, the institution he helped make into the largest bank in the city. Because of his hard work and diligence, within two years he was named a director, and by 1882 he became a vice president. Nine years later he became president of First National. In 1887 he married his brother's widow, Cornelia Washburne Gage.

Always a supporter of the gold standard, Gage helped build "The Honest Money League of the North West" and worked hard in the fight against any kind of paper money. His work in this area helped him become president of the American Banker's Association in 1883, the major lobbying group for the industry. His popularity with the nation's banking leaders helped him get reelected twice to this position. Although he was a leader in the banking profession, Gage also managed to earn the respect of such labor groups as the Knights of Labor because of his work to save seven men convicted of murder and sentenced to death after the Haymarket Riot of 1886. He rejected the popularly held view that the men who made speeches or helped organize the labor rally were responsible for the deaths of eight policemen from a bomb thrown by an unknown person. Gage held that the men sentenced to death were guilty of nothing more than making unpopular speeches. He brought critics of the verdict together in a petition drive, but their calls for executive clemency failed and three of the defendants were hanged. Gage continued to meet with opponents of the verdict and launched a series of public meetings to discuss other problems dividing capital and labor. These meetings, called Economic Conferences, were presided over by Gage every Sunday evening and continued into the early 1890s. They brought together labor radicals, conservative business leaders, and Republican and Democratic political leaders. Participants talked, read papers, asked questions of each other, and engaged in open debate.

In 1890 Gage was elected president of the Chicago Board of Directors of the World's Columbian Exposition. In this capacity he helped raise $10 million in private contributions before the fair opened in 1893. The following year Gage became head of the Civic Federation of Chicago, a major reform group and enemy of corruption and machine politics. Though Gage felt he had failed at cleaning out the "boodlers," the federation exposed the worst areas of corruption and elected honest candidates to the city council.

In 1892 Gage declined President Grover Cleveland's offer to become secretary of the treasury. Gage opposed "free silver" as fervently as he had fought greenbacks, a position shared by the president. He had always been a Republican, however, and did not wish to serve in a Democratic administration. Four years later he led efforts in Chicago to raise money for the Republican ticket and helped defeat William Jennings Bryan. President William McKinley offered him the Treasury position and Gage accepted. In the Treasury Department he proved to be a responsible, hardworking leader. He became a favorite of McKinley's during cabinet meetings by reading Peter Finley Dunne's "Mister Dooley" columns in an Irish brogue. He managed the successful sale of bonds used to pay for the Spanish-American War and helped get the Gold Standard Act through Congress in 1900. Although the nation had resumed specie payments twenty-one years earlier, the act more definitively enforced the gold standard, making all money redeemable in gold and establishing a gold dollar of 25.8 grains, nine-tenths pure. This seemed to seal the fate of free silver, and although increased supplies of gold made the money issue one of less concern, Gage felt that the act was the most important contribution of his career in public service.

Gage continued to head the Treasury Department after the presidential election of 1900. Theodore Roosevelt kept him in his cabinet when he assumed office after McKinley's assassination. Gage resigned in 1902, however, after the death of his second wife. He accepted the presidency of the United States Trust Company of New York a short time later because it was less time-consuming than the job in Washington. After four years he resigned from the trust company and moved to Point Loma, California. He met his third wife, Frances Ada Ballou, at a Theosophical Society meeting in San Diego. They were married in 1909. Gage turned to theosophy and mysticism in the latter part of his life especially after the suicide of his alcoholic son. He spent his remaining time writing his memoirs and died in Point Loma.

As a leader of Chicago's banking community, Gage gained the accolades of his colleagues for his hard work and diligence, but it was his recognition of the problems of labor, as acknowledged in his Economic Conferences and his call for clemency in the Haymarket affair, that made him stand out among the city's business elite. He witnessed tragedy in his life, especially in the deaths of his first wife and later his eldest son, which seemed to increase his sensitivity to the problems of others. In his memoirs he listed one of his goals in life as "moderating conflict" among social classes.

• The *Memoirs of Lyman Gage* (1937), published by his daughter, contain some details on his private life, including his relationship with his son. There is surprisingly little, however, on his activities as secretary of the treasury. No manuscript collections relating to his career exist. There is a brief description of his early career in A. T. Andreas, *History of Chicago* (1886). Henry C. Morris, *History of the First National Bank* (1902), focuses on Gage's contributions to building that bank into a major financial institution. For his role in the McKinley administration, see Margaret K. Leech, *In the Days of William McKinley* (1959), and Robert Dallek, *McKinley's Decision: War on Spain* (1970). Obituaries are in the *New York Times* and the *Chicago Tribune*, both 28 Jan. 1927.

LESLIE V. TISCHAUSER

GAGE, Matilda Joslyn (24 Mar. 1826–18 Mar. 1898), suffragist and writer, was born in Cicero, New York, the only child of Hezekiah Joslyn, a physician, and Helen Leslie. Hezekiah Joslyn supported woman suffrage, abolition, and temperance and made his family's home a gathering place for activists and intellectuals. It was also a stop on the underground railroad. Gage's father provided her early education, which included mathematics, Greek, and biology, after which she attended the Clinton Liberal Institute in New York. She married Henry H. Gage, a merchant, in 1845; they had five children, although one son died in infancy. The couple later moved to Syracuse and Manlius before finally settling in Fayetteville, New York. The first years of Gage's marriage were ones of financial prosperity because of her husband's successful dry goods business, but also ones of strain because of the burden of child care and the handicap of Gage's recurrent invalidism.

Gage's activism in women's rights began at the National Woman's Rights Convention in Syracuse in September 1852. Her speech, though loud in its criticism of women's inferior place in society and lack of legal rights, was delivered in such a soft voice that most of the audience could not hear her. But Gage grew stronger in her public advocacy and speaking skills. Becoming close friends with Elizabeth Cady Stanton, she began lecturing and organizing in support of women's rights. During the Civil War, a general moratorium was declared within the movement for women's rights so that women could devote their efforts to the war efforts. An original member of the National Woman Suffrage Association (NWSA) and the New York State Woman Suffrage Association in 1869, she was elected vice president and secretary of the latter organization in 1869. She campaigned for Ulysses S. Grant in the 1872 presidential election and tried unsuccessfully to vote for him. In 1875 Gage was elected president of both the state and national suffrage associations. She contributed to the NWSA's newspaper, *The Revolution*, and testified before several House and Senate committees that debated woman suffrage.

Gage became more and more convinced that the misogynist elements of Christian doctrine were major causes of women's lower social status. She argued that many churches taught that woman was inferior to man and blamed women for the introduction of sin into the world. From 1878 to 1890 Gage lobbied within the NWSA to make opposition to misogynist religious teachings a priority. Her efforts met with strong resistance from the moderate and conservative party elements, and in 1890 she left the organization to found the Woman's National Liberal Union. The WNLU's objectives included woman suffrage, but the organization also sought to expose the religious denigration of women and to fight for a constitutional amendment guaranteeing the separation of church and state.

Perhaps Gage's greatest contribution to the suffrage movement was her writings. One early pamphlet, *Woman as Inventor* (1870), credits women with, among other things, the invention of the cotton gin, medical science, and bread. With Elizabeth Cady Stanton and Susan B. Anthony, she authored the Woman's Declaration of Rights, which was read at the 1876 Independence Day celebration in Philadelphia. Between 1878 and 1881 she edited and published the *National Citizen and Ballot Box*, the monthly newspaper of the NWSA. Her 1881 essay *Preceding Causes* places the nineteenth-century women's rights movement within the larger historical context of Western

civilization. The church and the state, she argued, have been twin barriers to human rights because both conspire to limit freedoms. Women are most vulnerable to their limitations because they are socially more helpless than men and because they are more prone to superstition. One surprising pamphlet, *Who Planned the Tennessee Campaign of 1862? or, Anna Ella Carroll vs. Ulysses S. Grant* (1880), makes the claim that Carroll deserves the credit for masterminding the Union military campaign in Tennessee during the Civil War. Gage's second collaboration with Stanton and Anthony resulted in the first three volumes of the exhaustive six-volume *History of Woman Suffrage* (1881–1922). In the final chapter of the first volume, Gage asserts that "the most grievous wound ever inflicted upon woman has been in the teaching that she was not created equal with man, and the consequent denial of her rightful place and position in Church and State" (p. 754). The scholarly *Woman, Church and State* (1893), which Gage considered her most important work, continues in this vein, expounding her controversial views on the relationship between Christianity and women's status.

Gage spent her final years in Chicago with her daughter, Maud Baum, wife of L. Frank Baum, who later wrote *The Wizard of Oz*. Her later writings concentrated on religious and metaphysical questions. In her last months she wrote a paper for the National American Woman Suffrage Association's celebration of the fiftieth anniversary of the first women's rights convention. She died in Chicago.

Along with Stanton and Anthony, Gage was one of the foremost leaders of the woman suffrage movement. An intellectual rather than a public speaker, Gage's contribution to the movement lies in her scholarship and historical work. Her range of interests in women's studies was broad—blending history with contemporary politics and also examining educational, economic, legal, and religious issues—continuous, and courageous.

• The Matilda Josyln Gage Woman Suffrage Scrapbooks are housed in the Library of Congress. Biographical information is in W. Leach, *True Love and Perfect Union: The Feminist Reform of Sex and Society* (1980), and Frances E. Willard and Mary A. Livermore, eds., *A Woman of the Century* (1893). Obituaries are in the *New York Times* and the *Chicago Tribune*, 19 Mar. 1898.

ELIZABETH ZOE VICARY

GAGE, Thomas (1719 or 1720–2 Apr. 1787), soldier and the last royal governor of Massachusetts, was born in Firle, Sussex, England, the son of Thomas Gage, first Viscount Gage of the Irish peerage, who had for political reasons abandoned his family's traditional Roman Catholicism and joined the Church of England, and Benedicta or Beata Maria Theresa Hall, an heiress who gained notoriety for her alleged promiscuity. The year of Gage's birth traditionally has been given as 1721, but the fact that he entered school in 1728 suggests that he was actually born in 1719 or early 1720. Gage spent much of his early childhood at his mother's family seat in Gloucestershire. During his eight years at the Westminster school (1728–1736), Gage associated with a number of youths who would later achieve military and political prominence.

Being a younger brother and thus barred from inheriting his father's estates or titles, Gage chose a career in the military. In 1741 he purchased a lieutenancy in a new regiment, later known as the Forty-eighth Foot. In May 1742 he transferred as captain lieutenant to Battereau's Foot, an Irish corps of two battalions. In the hopes of advancing his career Gage also served as aide-de-camp to the second earl of Albemarle against the French at Fontenoy (1745), the Scots at Culloden (1746), and again against the French in Flanders (1747–1748). By 1751 he held the rank of lieutenant colonel in the Forty-fourth Foot.

In January 1755, Gage's regiment sailed from Cork, Ireland, to join Major General Edward Braddock's ill-fated campaign to drive the French from the forks of the Ohio River. He led the advance guard in Braddock's disastrous attempt to seize Fort Duquesne in July 1755. Although he displayed great bravery and determination, he was unable to respond quickly and effectively to the tactics of the French and Indians. During this period, Gage formed a brief friendship with his future adversary, George Washington, who had commanded Braddock's rear guard at Duquesne.

The following year Gage took part in Major General Daniel Webb's failed attempt to relieve the British garrison at Oswego. In May 1758, drawing upon his hard-earned experience in frontier warfare, Gage took the initiative in raising a new type of British regiment, the Eightieth Foot, a combined British and colonial force of physically fit, lightly armed, and highly mobile soldiers well suited to warfare in the American forests. His efforts earned him the long-desired command of a regiment. Later that year, Gage found himself in another military disaster when Major General James Abercromby made a doomed frontal assault on Montcalm's breastworks at Ticonderoga. Following this incident, Gage was raised to the rank of brigadier general on the American establishment and placed in command of the troops and forts of the Albany region.

In December 1758 Gage married Margaret Kemble, the popular daughter of Peter Kemble, president of the Council of New Jersey. They had eleven children, of whom the eldest surviving son, Henry, became a major general and third Viscount Gage. The youngest, William, became an admiral and was knighted. Margaret Kemble Gage died in 1824.

In 1759 Gage's failure to drive the French from La Galette, at the head of the Saint Lawrence River, earned him a rebuke from his friend and superior General Sir Jeffrey Amherst. The following year he was assigned the less demanding role of commanding Amherst's rear guard in the successful assault on Montreal, the last French stronghold in Canada. After this victory, Amherst appointed Gage military governor of the Montreal region, a post he held until October 1763. He carried out the duties of this office with tact and ability.

Gage was next appointed acting commander in chief of the British forces in North America (comprising about five thousand men in the eastern half of the continent, except New Orleans and the Hudson Bay region, plus Bermuda and the Bahamas, with headquarters in New York) pending Amherst's return from England. In November 1764 Gage replaced Amherst in this post when the latter declined to return.

Between 1763 and his return to England in 1773, Gage played an important role in the imperial administration's attempts to find satisfactory solutions to four pressing and interrelated problems. These included the suppression of the Indian uprising known as Pontiac's Rebellion (1763–1766), the need to develop an effective policy concerning the fur trade and the westward expansion of colonial settlement, how best to deploy troops to meet the needs of external security and internal order, and how to distribute the costs of maintaining these troops. As commander in chief, Gage not only oversaw British forces in his assigned area but also served as advisor to the home government and to royal governors. The solution of the first of these objectives was achieved but no effective solutions were reached for the others. Given the lack of a serious external threat and the widely differing goals and needs of the older colonies and the imperial government, perhaps none could have been. Gage favored British sovereignty over the colonies but was moderate, diplomatic, and legalistic in carrying out imperial policy.

From July 1773 until April 1774, Gage took a leave of absence in England to visit family and old friends, to attend to his private affairs, and to consult with the king and various officials on conditions in the colonies. At this time the British government became deeply angered over the destruction of East India Company tea in the Boston harbor. They were determined to punish the unruly Bay Colony and to place it under greater royal authority. In keeping with these goals, the government passed the so-called Intolerable Acts and sent Gage to Massachusetts to replace Thomas Hutchinson as royal governor. This post was added to his duties as commander in chief of British forces in North America.

Although Gage was personally well received when he arrived in Boston in May 1774, he found himself in a virtually impossible position. The colonists feared his civil and military powers, and he had enough soldiers in Boston to antagonize the residents but not to compel obedience. Furthermore, he was forced to try to enforce the detested Intolerable Acts in the colony that was the best organized, most experienced, and most skilled in resisting unwanted British policy. To make matters worse, the other colonies had rallied to support Massachusetts. While in England, Gage had greatly underestimated the threat to British rule in the colonies, especially in New England. Now he tried unsuccessfully to alert the lethargic and overconfident home government to the realities he had encountered, requesting a force of twenty thousand men to subdue New England.

On 19 April 1775, fighting broke out when Gage, under orders from home, sent out a detachment of troops to seize the patriot military stores at Concord and to apprehend Samuel Adams and John Hancock (1737–1793). The Revolution had begun. Gage, who until then had proved himself a reliable subordinate, an excellent administrator and camp commander, and an effective military diplomat, was now faced for the first time with assuming a large-scale wartime command under unfavorable conditions. He was outnumbered by better than three to one in a hostile region and besieged in an overcrowded city where many of the inhabitants sympathized with the besiegers. The sporadic reinforcements and supplies he received barely enabled him to hold his position. The battle of Bunker Hill, Gage's only major engagement after Lexington and Concord, attained its objective of dislodging a force of Americans, but at the staggering cost of a near 40 percent British casualty rate. Unable to meet the unrealistic expectations of the home government or of his own forces, Gage was recalled to London for "consultations," a face-saving gesture insisted upon by George III. He left Boston on 10 October 1775.

In England, Gage remained interested in American affairs. In April 1781, amid the threat of a French invasion, he was placed on Amherst's staff and assigned to prepare for the defense of Kent. In November 1782 he was raised to the rank of full general. He died at his home in Portland Place, London.

Hard working, devoted to duty, and anxious to do what he thought was right, Gage represented the best in British imperial administration on the eve of the American Revolution. Unfortunately, his position required him either to reconcile the colonists to the British government or to suppress rebellion with inadequate forces.

• The largest collection of Gage's papers is located in the William L. Clements Library at the University of Michigan. Gage's official correspondence with various departments of the British government is in the British Public Record Office, London. Transcripts of much of this material are in the Library of Congress, and some are in the Bancroft Transcripts in the New York Public Library. Most of what is left of Gage's private papers is located in the Gage family seat in Firle, Sussex. The most important published collection of Gage's documents is *The Correspondence of General Thomas Gage with the Secretaries of State and with the War Office and the Treasury, 1763–1775*, ed. Clarence E. Carter (2 vols., 1931–1933).

The basic biographical work on Gage is John R. Alden's sympathetic *General Gage in America* (1948). An important, if overly critical, essay on Gage as a military commander is John Shy, "Thomas Gage: Weak Link of Empire," in *George Washington's Opponents*, ed. George A. Billias (1969). Still the most vivid account of the military side of the Seven Years' War or the French and Indian War is Francis Parkman's epic *Montcalm and Wolfe* (2 vols., 1884). More recent and important accounts are Edward P. Hamilton, *The French and Indian Wars* (1962), and Howard H. Peckham, *The Colonial Wars, 1689–1762* (1964); see also Francis Jennings, *Empire of Fortune: Crown, Colonies, and Tribes in the Seven Years War in America* (1988), and Lawrence Henry Gipson, *The British Empire before the American Revolution* (15 vols., 1939–1970). Excellent accounts of Gage as commander in chief of British forces in North America are in Don Higginbotham, *The War of American Independence* (1961), and John Shy, *Toward Lexington* (1965). Important sources for Gage's role as royal governor and military commander in Massachusetts are Allen French, *The First Year of the American Revolution* (1934), and Justin Winsor, *Memorial History of Boston, 1630–1880*, vols. 2 and 3 (1880–1881).

PHILIP CASH

GAIGE, Crosby (26 July 1882–8 Mar. 1949), theatrical producer and writer, was born Roscoe Conkling Crosby Gaige in Nelson, New York, the son of George Edward Gaige, a postmaster, and Jane DeMaine. Gaige was descended from Enoch Crosby, a confidential emissary for General George Washington during the revolutionary war whose exploits James Fenimore Cooper drew upon in his novel *The Spy*. Early interested in classics and drama, Gaige attended his first theatrical show during a boyhood visit to Richmond, Virginia, where he saw the nineteenth-century melodrama *The Black Crook*. To earn money for college, during the summer following his high school graduation Gaige peddled a book composed of sermons on Christ's life titled *Our Elder Brother*. He entered Columbia University in 1899 but left in 1903 without a degree, having studied drama with Brander Matthews, poetry with George Edward Woodberry (through whom he met poet William Butler Yeats), and Latin with Harry Thurston Peck. While at Columbia he operated the University Commons with classmate Roi Megrue; served as editor in chief of the college newspaper; was campus correspondent for the *New York Times*; and with Megrue wrote the 1903 Columbia varsity show, "The Isles of Illusia." During his senior year Gaige began work for the play agent Elisabeth Marbury, reading manuscripts and writing digests of them. He also frequented Delmonico's and the Lyric Theatre, where Richard Mansfield's performances especially impressed him. Later in 1903 Gaige switched to Marbury's rival, Alice Kauser, from whom he received a much higher salary. Kauser sent him by bus to Denver on business, and Gaige later wrote in his autobiography *Footlights and Highlights*: "I was astounded by the richness and variety of the country . . . that many Americans lived in horizon-bounded worlds all their lives and had neither opportunity nor desire to peer over the rim."

Gaige became the American representative of the English playwright Henry Arthur Jones, and in 1905 he became associated with Selwyn & Company, Inc., a group of theatrical playbrokers and producers who sold the performance rights for melodramas to theater companies. Gaige headed the department that handled more serious dramas, and he worked with playwrights such as Eugene Walter and Bayard Veiller. Until 1923 he served as vice president and financial adviser of the company, directing the financing and building of the Times Square, Selwyn, and Apollo theaters in New York and the Selwyn and Harris theaters in Chicago, and he operated the monumental Hanna Theater in

Cleveland with Lee Shubert. In 1907 he married Hilda Wilson; they adopted a child.

During his tenure at Selwyn & Company Gaige co-produced commercial successes such as Veiller's *Within the Law* (1912), which brought prominence to actress Jane Cowl and made more than $1 million; Megrue's *Under Cover* (1914); Salisbury Field and Margaret Mayo's *Twin Beds* (1914); Avery Hopwood's *Fair and Warmer* (1915); Jesse Lynch Williams's *Why Marry?* (1917), the first play to win a Pulitzer Prize; Cowl and Jane Murfin's *Smilin' Through* (1919); W. Somerset Maugham's *The Circle* (1921); and *Charlot's Revue* (1924), which marked the American debuts of Beatrice Lillie, Jack Buchanan, and Gertrude Lawrence. Not all of Gaige's efforts were similarly successful; in the autumn of 1918 he had ready sterling silver tickets for some opening night critics for Cowl and Murfin's *Information Please*, but the show ran a mere forty-six performances. Gaige also produced plays in association with director-producer Jed Harris, including successes such as Philip Dunning and George Abbott's *Broadway* (1926); Abbott and Ann Preston Bridgers's *Coquette* (1927), starring Helen Hayes; and Samson Raphaelson's *Accent on Youth* (1934).

During his career Gaige was connected with the production of more than 150 plays, many of them after 1923, when he became an independent producer. Among his most successful productions were Max Marcin's *Silence* (1924); George S. Kaufman's *The Butter and Egg Man* (1925); Floyd Dell and Thomas Mitchell's *The Little Accident* (1928); and Shakespeare's *Othello* and *Macbeth* (both 1935). Gaige's less successful efforts included Eugene O'Neill's *Welded* (1924), which he referred to as among his "flops d'estime." Well before his retirement from theatrical production in 1938 Gaige sensed the innate fragility of his profession: "I always had an inner feeling of the impermanence of show business. If ever there was a career deserving of the here-today-and-gone-tomorrow stigma, it is the occupation which stems from devising entertainments behind the footlights. . . . I knew that I was making more money than I was entitled to. . . . Most current successful theatre is as dated as a newspaper; the thrills of yesterday are the boredom of today."

Long a collector of first editions, Gaige pursued a second career from 1927 to 1930 as a printer and maker of beautiful limited editions of works by such writers as Siegfried Sassoon, Liam O'Flaherty, Lytton Strachey, James Joyce, John Galsworthy, Virginia Woolf, Thomas Hardy, and Arnold Bennett. In the 1930s, on his farm in Peekskill, New York, Gaige bred cattle; experimented with inventions such as expanding rail joints and coupling devices for railroad cars; and installed a collection of 200,000 invention models submitted to the U.S. Patent Office from 1820 and 1890, including the original dentist's chair (1855) and the first egg beater (1866).

Gaige's most successful enterprise in his later life grew out of his longtime interest in food and wine. Conducting extensive research in his own laboratory,

Gaige furthered the science of food dehydration; during World War II his firm, Dry-Pack Corporation (established 1937), produced dehydrated foodstuffs for the armed forces. Also during the final twelve years of life, Gaige earned a reputation as a writer and editor on gourmet foods, spices, and seasonings. He once said, "I consider myself the greatest cook in the world yet unhanged. I may have a certain . . . reticence as a theatrical producer, but as a cook I am brazen." Having been divorced from his first wife in 1928, Gaige married Cecilia Bauer in 1945. They had no children.

Despite his other achievements, Gaige is primarily remembered for his role in the advancement of American drama beyond the sensational melodrama typical of the turn of the century toward a somewhat more serious and literary enterprise after 1915. Though not a theatrical revolutionary and very much a man of commerce, Gaige moderated the "show shop" mentality, the production of commercial, nonartistic drama, railed against by Eugene O'Neill. While absorbed in classical scholarship at the height of the 1929 Crash, Gaige wrote in his autobiography, "I have always believed that the making or losing of money is only an incident of life. . . . The important thing is not to lose your sense of humor nor lose sight of the irreplaceable things." He died in Peekskill, New York.

• The best source of information about Gaige is his autobiography, *Footlights and Highlights* (1948). His major works on cooking include the *New York World's Fair Cook Book* (1939), *Crosby Gaige's Cocktail Guide and Ladies' Companion* (1941), *The Standard Cocktail Guide* (1944), *Crosby Gaige's Macaroni Manual* (1947), and *Dining with My Friends* (1949); he also edited the American edition of *Madame Prunier's Fish Cookery Book* (1939). Also important, given the paucity of secondary material about Gaige, are the entries in *Who Was Who in America*, vol. 2 (1950), p. 202; and in *The National Cyclopaedia of American Biography*, vol. 38 (1953), pp. 555–56. An obituary is in the *New York Times*, 9 Mar. 1949.

FRANK R. CUNNINGHAM

GAILLARD, David Du Bose (4 Sept. 1859–5 Dec. 1913), soldier and engineer, was born in Fulton, Sumter County, South Carolina, the son of Samuel Isaac Gaillard (pronounced Ge-*yard*), a planter, and Susan Richardson Du Bose. He received an appointment to the U.S. Military Academy in 1880. His high standing in the graduating class of 1884 entitled him to a commission in the Corps of Engineers as a second lieutenant and admission to the army's Engineer School of Application, Willets Point, New York. He completed the course in 1887 and was promoted to first lieutenant. That year he married Katherine Ross Davis; they had one child.

From 1887 to 1891 Gaillard was assistant to the officer in charge of river and harbor improvements in Florida. As a member of the international commission for establishing the boundary between the United States and Mexico from 1891 to 1896, he spent much of that period in the field leading a resurvey of the boundary line from El Paso, Texas, to the Pacific Coast. In 1895 he was given supervision of defensive works at Fort Monroe, Virginia. Later that year he was promoted to captain and put in charge of the Washington Aqueduct with responsibility for increasing the water supply of Washington, D.C. He served in that capacity until 1898. Meanwhile, in 1896 he conducted a survey of the Portland Channel in Alaska.

With the outbreak of the Spanish-American War in 1898, Gaillard became the engineer officer on the staff of Major General James F. Wade, commander of volunteer troops. Soon, however, Gaillard was commissioned as colonel of the Third Regiment of U.S. Volunteer Engineers. The regiment served in the United States and the Cuban cities of Matanzas, Cienfuegos, and Pinar del Rio and earned a good reputation for its work in improving sanitation. Early in 1899 Gaillard became chief engineer of the Department of Santa Clara, Cuba. In the spring of that year he was honorably mustered out of the volunteer service and reverted to his regular rank of captain.

Gaillard's first peacetime duties were again with the Washington Aqueduct and the water supply of Washington and as assistant to the engineer commissioner of the District of Columbia. In 1901 he was given charge of river and harbor improvements on Lake Superior, being stationed at Duluth until 1903. He published a well-regarded paper on *Wave Action in Relation to Engineering Structures* (1904), based on his observations at the lake and on the Florida Coast. After special duty at Headquarters, Department of the Columbia, at Vancouver Barracks, Washington, he became assistant to the department's chief of staff and, from 1903 to 1904, its chief of staff. During this period he also was a member of the General Staff Corps. At St. Louis, in 1904, he was assistant to the chief of staff of the Northern Division and the division's engineer officer. That year he was promoted to major. He returned to Washington, D.C., and studied at the Army War College, 1904–1905, following which he was once again a member of the General Staff Corps. Unrest in Cuba brought American forces to the island again, and Gaillard's principal duty there was as chief of Military Information, Army of Cuban Pacification, 1906–1907.

In the spring of 1907 Gaillard received the assignments that were to crown his already successful career as a military engineer: member of the Isthmian Canal Commission, director of the Panama Railroad, and supervisory engineer in charge of dredging harbors, building breakwaters, and all excavation in the canal prism except that which was incidental to lock and dam construction. From 1908 to 1913 he was the division engineer of the canal's Central Division, which ran from Gatun to Pedro Miguel, Panama. Within the division, along the Continental Divide, was the nine-mile section known as the Culebra Cut. One of his colleagues described it as "the most trying, discouraging and difficult feature connected with the building of the Panama Canal" (W. L. Sibert, in *David Du Bose Gaillard: A Memorial*, pp. 84–85). It was Gaillard's responsibility to dig the cut, and much of it was solid rock. Complicating the task were the massive slides, resulting from heavy rains and unstable rock formations, that fell into the cut, burying or destroying structures and equipment.

Gaillard was made a lieutenant colonel in 1909. In the summer of 1913 he suffered what was thought to be a nervous breakdown brought on by overwork and was sent back to the United States. The fatal illness was actually a brain tumor. Nevertheless, his family believed the cause had been the heavy workload imposed by the canal's chief engineer, George W. Goethals. Gaillard died in Baltimore and was interred at Arlington National Cemetery.

Gaillard was one of America's most talented and industrious military engineers of the late nineteenth and early twentieth centuries. Following his death, Congress passed a joint resolution expressing the nation's appreciation for his efforts and accomplishments in Panama, and President Woodrow Wilson issued an executive order changing the name of the Culebra Cut to the Gaillard Cut.

• Articles by Gaillard relating to some of his major activities are "The Washington Aqueduct and Cabin John Bridge," *National Geographic* 8 (1897): 337–44; "The Perils and Wonders of a True Desert," *Cosmopolitan* 21 (1896): 592–605; and "Culebra Cut and the Problem of the Slides," *Scientific American* 107 (1912): 388–90. Third U.S. Volunteer Engineers, *David Du Bose Gaillard: A Memorial* (1916), contains much biographical material and many tributes. David McCullough, *The Path between the Seas: The Creation of the Panama Canal* (1977), provides information on Gaillard's role in the construction of the canal. Obituaries are in *Engineering News*, 11 Dec. 1913, and *Army and Navy Journal*, 13 Dec. 1913.

MICHAEL J. BRODHEAD

GAILLARD, Edwin Samuel (16 Jan. 1827–2 Feb. 1885), medical educator and editor, was born near Charleston, South Carolina, the son of Edwin Gaillard and Mary White. He received a B.A. from South Carolina College (later the University of South Carolina) in 1845 and an M.D. from the Medical College of the State of South Carolina (now part of the University of South Carolina) in 1854. He then moved to Florida, where he opened a general medical practice. In 1856 he married Jane Marshall Thomas, with whom he had no children. He relocated his practice to New York City the following year but closed it in 1860 after his wife's death. He then studied medicine for a year in Europe and in 1861 settled in Baltimore, Maryland.

When the Civil War broke out that same year, Gaillard became an assistant surgeon in the First Maryland Regiment, which fought as part of the Confederate Army of Northern Virginia. Over the next twelve months he served successively as brigade surgeon, army medical inspector, medical director of half the army, member of the army medical examining board, and medical director of the Aquia District before becoming in mid-1862 the medical director for all Confederate forces defending Richmond, Virginia. During the Peninsular Campaign he performed a daring operation on General Wade Hampton, who had been shot in the foot but refused to dismount or retire from the front while the battle ensued. Making his way to

Hampton under heavy fire—his horse was shot out from under him moments before reaching the general—Gaillard removed Hampton's boot, then dug the bullet out of his foot with a knife while the general remained in the saddle. Four days later Gaillard lost his right arm in a similar situation during the fighting leading up to the battle of Seven Pines, thus ending his career as a surgeon. After recuperating for three months in Montgomery County, Virginia, he returned to active duty in Richmond, first as medical director and then as medical inspector of military hospitals in Virginia and North Carolina. In 1863 he was appointed medical inspector of the Confederacy's more than 150 military hospitals, a position he held for the war's duration. One of his greatest challenges in this position involved determining the cause of a number of cases of spinal meningitis that broke out sporadically throughout the entire system, a determination he was never able to make.

In 1865 Gaillard married Mary Elizabeth Gibson, with whom he had six children, and accepted a position as professor of the principles and practice of medicine and general pathology at the Medical College of Virginia in Richmond. The following year he and William S. McChesney began publishing and editing the *Richmond Medical Journal*. Unlike most medical journal editors of the day, he and McChesney paid for accepted manuscripts, and, after a year, they claimed to have the largest circulation of any medical journal in the United States. Gaillard's editorials stressed the importance of raising the standards of medical education and advocated lengthening each seasonal course of study from four months to five and toughening the entrance and graduation requirements. He also insisted that students be trained in dissection and that they receive clinical as well as classroom instruction.

In 1868 Gaillard moved to Louisville, Kentucky, where he became a dean and professor of general pathology and pathological anatomy at the Kentucky School of Medicine (later a part of the University of Louisville) and changed his journal's name to *Richmond and Louisville Medical Journal*. The following year he helped to found Louisville Medical College and served as its first dean and professor of general medicine and pathology. In 1874 he established the *American Medical Weekly*, perhaps the first weekly publication devoted to medicine in the United States, and served as its editor for the next nine years. In 1879 he moved to New York City, where he continued to publish his monthly journal, now known as *Gaillard's Medical Journal*, which he published with the assistance of a staff of assistant editors.

Gaillard served as president of the Medico-Chirurgical Society of Louisville and the Richmond Academy of Medicine. He was awarded the Fiske Fund Prize in 1861 for an article about ozone's effect on health and disease and the Georgia Medical Association Prize in 1866 for an article on the causes and treatment of diphtheria. Illness forced him to retire in 1883 to his home in Ocean Grove, New Jersey, where he died.

Gaillard was one of the Confederacy's most competent executive medical officers. He contributed to the advance of American medicine as a teacher of medicine and as editor of two important medical journals.

• Gaillard's papers are in the National Archives in Washington, D.C. Several of his letters are in Peter W. Houck, ed., *Chapter VI, Vol. 416, Medical Department, Confederate Records, Letters Sent and Received, Medical Director's Office, Richmond, Va., 1862–1863, National Archives, Wash. D.C.* (1991). His contributions are discussed in Horace Herndon Cunningham, *Doctors in Gray: The Confederate Medical Service* (1958), and Wyndham Blanton, *Medicine in Virginia in the Nineteenth Century* (1933). An obituary is in the *Virginia Medical Monthly* 11 (Feb. 1885): 648–50.

CHARLES W. CAREY, JR.

GAILLARD, Slim (3 Jan. 1906, 1911, or 1916–26 Feb. 1991), jazz musician and composer, was born Bulee Gaillard probably in Santa Clara, Cuba (although a birth certificate shows Claiborne, Ala.), the son of Theophilus Rothschild, a ship's steward, and Mary Gaillard. He apparently was always known by his mother's name. Any formal education may have come in Pensacola, Florida, which Gaillard apparently left at age twelve in order to travel the world with his father. Gaillard—a lifelong embellisher of his own legend—later claimed that, en route, he was accidentally left on Crete and that he lived there for at least four years, taking up various occupations and learning to speak Greek. He subsequently traveled the Mediterranean as a ship's cook, learning the languages, including Armenian and Arabic dialects, he later worked into his compositions, written as well as improvised.

In 1932 Gaillard surfaced in Detroit, where he lived with an Armenian family. During the next few years he worked for morticians, slaughterers, hatters, shoemakers, and gangsters. Crediting his redemption from a life of crime to a resourceful judge and a tough policeman, Gaillard took up boxing and music, learning vibraphone, guitar, and piano, an instrument from which he soon could coax music with the backs of his hands.

By the mid-1930s Gaillard was playing in small jazz groups in towns as far east as Pennsylvania. His first recording was as a singer with Frankie Newton's band in New York City in 1937. He met Slam Stewart, a bassist whose specialty was humming—an octave higher—the tune he was bowing. They became a duo, appearing regularly on radio on the "Original Amateur Hour" (Slim occasionally tap dancing) and in breakfast shows at the Criterion Theater, where master of ceremonies Martin Block christened them Slim and Slam. Soon they were regulars on New York radio station WNEW.

Slim and Slam's eccentric composition "Flat Foot Floogie" (originally either "Flat Fleet Floogie" or "Flat Foot Floosie") became a hit in May 1938, when it was recorded by Benny Goodman's swing band, then America's favorite. Having recorded it themselves that January, Slim and Slam soon became famous. (Their version was buried in the 1939 New York World's Fair time capsule.) The song surpassed contemporary nonsense novelties such as "Hold Tight" ("foodley yacky sacky, want some seafood, Mama") largely because of its authentic jazz underpinning. Gaillard called it "mostly a riff with jive lyrics." These lyrics stemmed from scat singing, the vocal attempt to mimic instrumental music. Gaillard's subsequent variation on scat, a playful, multicultural, and highly personal language he called "vout," became his trademark.

Slim and Slam's partnership, which lasted until 1942, produced memorable odes to food such as "Tutti Frutti." At the beginning of a nightclub set Gaillard might begin baking a cake in the kitchen and at the end invite everyone to eat it. On one occasion he stopped the music and joined the conversation taking place at a table of Greeks. Turning to the audience, he said, "It's okay. We just talkin' 'bout cheeseburgers."

In 1941 Gaillard and Stewart moved to Hollywood and appeared in the film *Hellzapoppin'*, released the next year. They helped form the Lee and Lester Young and Slim and Slam Orchestra, whose shows were broadcast with Gaillard as the supremely "hip" master of ceremonies. In 1942 Gaillard appeared as a musician in the films *Almost Married* and *Star Spangled Rhythm*.

Drafted in 1942 or 1943, Gaillard served as a pilot in the South Pacific. Wounded, he suffered a nervous breakdown and was discharged in 1944. He returned to Los Angeles, replaced Stewart with "Bam" Brown, with whom he recorded "Dunkin' Bagels," and opened at Billy Berg's club in Hollywood, where his affably entertaining form of jazz quickly made him popular. In 1945 Dizzy Gillespie and Charlie Parker, proponents of be-bop, appeared at Berg's with Gaillard, recording "Slim's Jam" and "Dizzy's Boogie" with Slim introducing the solos.

It was during these years that Los Angeles newspapers, reporting on Gaillard's romantic involvements among the film set, dubbed him "The Dark Gable." Gaillard lived with many women in his lifetime and fathered at least four children. In 1946 "Cement Mixer (Put-ti, Put-ti)," another "vout" song, written with Lee Ricks, was America's favorite for eight weeks; that same year Gaillard and Brown recorded the lengthy "Opera in Vout," a jam session in jive, Gaillard's *Vout-o-Renee Dictionary* was published, and he appeared in the film *The Sweetheart of Sigma Chi*. Gaillard became a radio regular, and his song "Laguna O Vouty" (1947) earned him the key to the city of Laguna Beach.

Between 1947 and 1949 Gaillard was often in New York, playing clubs such as Birdland. Also in those years he recorded "Yep Roc Heresay," whose lyrics were an Armenian restaurant's menu; "Laughin' in Rhythm" (1951), which had no lyrics, just laughter; "Down by the Station" (1947), a hit children's song that Gaillard later claimed caused the Reverend W. V. Awdrey to write a series of British children's books about Thomas the Tank Engine (Awdrey firmly denied the claim).

In 1950 Gaillard moved to San Francisco, where he married Nettie Walker; they had one child. In 1952

the Gaillard Trio, which usually included drummer Zutty Singleton, made two short films. Gaillard appeared at San Francisco's Say When club, where he met writer Jack Kerouac, a "good listener," friend, and fellow cook. *On the Road*, Kerouac's novel of the outsider "beat generation," was published in 1957, with Gaillard and pianist George Shearing serving as symbols of the inner freedom that Kerouac believed jazzmen embodied. In it, Gaillard is described as a "tall, thin Negro with big sad eyes who's always saying 'Right-orooni.' . . . Great eager crowds of young semi-intellectuals sat at his feet and listened to him on the piano, guitar and bongo drums." Kerouac added, "He'll join *any*body, but he won't guarantee to be there with you in spirit." Kerouac's comment seems to have prefigured one of Slim's later reflections: "From time to time I used to get lost."

Gaillard remained popular throughout the jazz boom of the 1950s, playing clubs and concerts throughout the United States and aiding the rise of Afro-Cuban jazz, but in 1959, divorced, he returned to Los Angeles. As rock music ascended, Gaillard's popularity waned. He moved around the western states, working as a disc jockey, managing clubs, and buying and selling farms and businesses.

After a reunion with Stewart at the 1970 Monterey Jazz Festival, Gaillard dropped out of music, finding his way as an actor in nonmusical films and television series, such as "Roots: The Next Generation" (1978). Then, in 1982, Gaillard's hand clapping was featured in a recording by his son-in-law, Marvin Gaye, and in the same year Gaillard's son (with Frances Miller) Mark persuaded him to perform again in public. That September Gaillard reportedly caused "hysteria in the audience" at a jazz festival in Nice, France. Gaillard moved to London, and for the next nine years the white-bearded performer became, in the words of jazz critic Paul Bradshaw, a new generation's embodiment of "the hipster and Fifty-second Street, a bebop Santa Claus." In 1985 Gaillard married Angela Mary Gorman in London.

The Gaillard revival was an international phenomenon. His recordings were reissued in Europe and Asia, and he became a clothing model in Japan. British critics likened his humor to surreal, anarchic contemporaries such as Peter Sellers. Gaillard traveled to the United States, playing in jazz clubs while the British Broadcasting Corporation prepared a four-part television series (1989). A new song, "Easy to Put Together but Hard to Take Apart," was recorded by the American rap group the Dream Warriors in 1990. At the time of his death in London an autobiography and a screenplay about his Birdland days remained incomplete.

A genuinely able pianist with a mellow, beguiling voice, a natural entertainer who sometimes played the vibraphone with swizzle sticks and coaxed tunes from snare drums, Slim Gaillard carved a career as a jazz cartoon character; his only rival as a humorous jazzman was Thomas "Fats" Waller. His verbal fantasies—"How High the Moon" conjured moon potatoes as large as the Hollywood Bowl, diggable only by bull-dozers—outweighed his instrumental improvisations. His lyrics were often doggerel, but also (as on the night at Birdland when he created the impromptu "Billie Holiday, I Love You" in order to restore the haggard Lady Day's confidence) typically playful, human, and kind.

• Some of Gaillard's papers and other memorabilia are held by family members in California; others are privately held in Japan. Although Gaillard is sometimes credited with writing an autobiography, the book was never finished. He is mentioned in numerous other autobiographies and critical works, including Arnold Shaw, *The Street That Never Slept: New York's Fabled Fifty-second Street* (1971); Lewis Porter, *A Lester Young Reader* (1991); Bill Crow, *From Birdland to Broadway* (1992); and David Ritz, *Divided Soul: The Life of Marvin Gaye* (1985). The Viking critical edition of Kerouac's *On The Road* (1979) includes useful critical commentary. Gaillard was regularly covered by British periodicals in his final ten years. A Gaillard discography appears in *Discographical Forum*, nos. 49 and 50 (1985). The best obituary is Burt Folkart's in the *Los Angeles Times*, 27 Feb. 1991.

JAMES ROSS MOORE

GAILOR, Thomas Frank (17 Sept. 1856–3 Oct. 1935), Episcopal bishop, was born in Jackson, Mississippi, the son of Frank Melancthon Gailor, a journalist, and Charlotte Moffett, originally of Belfast, Ireland. In 1858 Frank Gailor became editor of the *Memphis Avalanche*. Thomas and his younger sister, Hattie, remained in Memphis with their mother after the death of their father, a Confederate major, at the battle of Perryville in 1862. At St. Mary's Elementary School Thomas was profoundly influenced by the rector and at "Captain Anderson's" high school by a former Confederate officer, both excellent teachers. He took city-wide examinations, graduating as valedictorian from Captain Anderson's high school in 1872, and then worked for a year in the crockery business. After recovering from yellow fever, he set out in 1873 for Racine College in Wisconsin with enough money to pay his first year's expenses. Skipping the freshman year because of his thorough grounding in Latin and Greek, he again was named valedictorian and entered General Theological Seminary in New York City in 1876, graduating in 1879. He formed a firm friendship with young William Crawford Gorgas, who had graduated from the University of the South the year before and was studying medicine at Bellevue Hospital. In later years, as Gorgas rose to international fame for conquering yellow fever in Havana and Panama, the two men, each at the pinnacle of his calling, were mutually supportive. Almost anyone would give an audience to one or the other. Gailor continuously sought support for religion and education, Gorgas for science and medicine.

Ordained to the Episcopal ministry in 1879 at Columbia, Tennessee, Gailor began his pastoral work in the same year at the Church of the Messiah in Pulaski, Tennessee; from there he went in 1882 to the University of the South, where he was professor of ecclesiastical history and English literature. The next year he became chaplain, and Sewanee, Tennessee, henceforth became his home, although he also presided at the diocesan office in Memphis (1893–1935) and had a second home there. In 1885, the imposing six-foot young chaplain married Ellen Douglas Cunningham of a prominent Nashville family, a union approved by his ever-watchful mentor, the bishop of Tennessee, Charles Todd Quintard. The Gailors had four children; their only son became a justice of the Tennessee Supreme Court.

Gailor, who referred to his Sewanee chaplaincy (1883–1891) as "my happiest years," was elected in 1890 as administrative head of the institution; at thirty-three, he was the youngest vice-chancellor (Oxford terminology) in its history. In 1908 he became chancellor (chairman of the board), a post he held until 1935, longest in the history of the university. In 1893 Quintard arranged the election of his favorite protégé as bishop coadjutor of Tennessee. On Quintard's death in 1898, Gailor became diocesan bishop. Having overcome what he considered inadequacies as a speaker, he shortly became the most powerful preacher in the Episcopal church. To have him on a program ensured a record audience. For example, he spoke to 4,000 people in Chattanooga on Near East relief and to 5,000 in New York at a chamber of commerce convention. He wrote in his journal that he had been paid only two guineas for preaching to 2,000 people at Westminster Abbey. As arbitrator in 1919 for a Memphis street railway strike, he was able to resolve the dispute to the satisfaction of both sides in only two weeks. In England in 1920 to see his friend Gorgas be knighted, he had a private audience with King George V and recorded in his diary the names of the archbishops and bishops from all over the world with whom he had conversations, or luncheons, or dinners. Four Sewanee graduates, besides Gorgas, provided entrée for him in Washington and New York. They were Silas McBee, editor of the *Churchman* and a close friend of Theodore Roosevelt (1858–1919); Archibald Butt, military aide to Roosevelt and President William Howard Taft; Admiral Cary T. Grayson, personal physician to Woodrow Wilson; and Gailor's former student William T. Manning, bishop of New York. His daughter's marriage to the son of Grover Cleveland opened other doors for him, and his talents as an enchanting raconteur attracted such prominent figures as J. P. Morgan, Marshall Field, Andrew Carnegie, Elihu Root, and Franklin Delano Roosevelt.

Gailor never held the title of presiding bishop of the Episcopal church because the office was automatically held by the senior bishop, but when the Episcopal church was restructured in 1919, he became the first president of the national council, the executive committee for the ruling body, the General Convention. Therefore, at gatherings of international church figures, he was seated with the archbishops as the highest-ranking American bishop. He found himself at home in England, where he was a prominent figure at the Lambeth Conferences held every ten years after

1867, except during World War I. Speeches at the Lord Mayor's dinner and St. Paul's Cathedral drew capacity audiences.

In his four decades of ministry Gailor firmly faced major issues, no matter how controversial. He was against Prohibition, communism, fascism, isolationism, and anti-Semitism. He favored the League of Nations and the New Deal, earning the gratitude of Presidents Wilson and Roosevelt. In 1922 Gailor convened and presided over the first national meeting of Episcopal social workers in Milwaukee. A majority of American dioceses sent representatives to this gathering, after which the Episcopal church turned its efforts toward social service and outreach.

Throughout his life Gailor maintained a scholarly interest in Latin, Hebrew, history, and philosophy. One notation in his diary states, "Read my Greek New Testament and a detective story." He was a scholar's scholar who never lost his popularity with the broad spectrum of laity. Gailor also maintained Tennessee's influential position in the Episcopal church, which had been gained by his two predecessors, James H. Otey and Quintard. Together these three strong bishops with Catholic leanings led the Episcopal church in Tennessee for more than a century. Gailor was considered by his peers among the southern bishops as their ranking prelate and spokesman. He died in Sewanee, Tennessee, and is one of nine bishops buried in the university cemetery.

• The four major repositories of research material on Thomas Frank Gailor are the National Archives of the Episcopal Church in Austin, Tex.; the office of the Diocese of Tennessee in Memphis; the library of General Theological Seminary in New York City; and the archives of the University of the South, Sewanee, Tenn. In the latter collection, placed by his daughter, are his diaries and correspondence. The *Journals* of the Diocese of Tennessee and the *Journals* of the General Convention of the Episcopal Church in the appropriate years are invaluable. Gailor's most important published work is *Some Memories* (1937), edited by his daughter Charlotte Moffett Gailor and Tudor Seymour Long. Other publications include *The Christian Church and Education* (1910), *The Episcopal Church* (1914), *The Church, the Bible, and the Creed* (1924), and *A Manual of Devotion* (1897). Numerous sermons and addresses appear in Episcopal publications. Donald S. Armentrout, *The Quest for the Informed Priest* (1979), a history of the School of Theology of the University of the South, contains information on Gailor as professor, chaplain, fourth vice-chancellor, and eighth chancellor of the University of the South, the only man to hold all four of these positions. A biography of Gailor appears in Moultrie Guerry, Arthur Chitty, and Elizabeth Chitty, *Men Who Made Sewanee* (1981).

ARTHUR BEN CHITTY

GAINE, Hugh (1726–25 Apr. 1807), printer-editor and bookseller, was born in Portglenone in the parish of Ahoghill, Ireland, the son of Hugh Gaine and his wife (name unknown). At age fourteen he began his apprenticeship to Samuel Wilson and James Magee, Belfast printers. When the partnership split in 1744, Gaine left Ireland for America and settled in New York City, where he became a printer's journeyman for James Parker (1714–1770) in 1745. In 1752 he was managing his own printing company, which in 1755 he named the Bible & Crown; by 1760 it had become the leading publishing company in New York. Gaine printed his first newspaper, the *New-York Mercury*, in August 1752. He began printing almanacs in 1753 and was printing three different ones by 1754, the most popular being that of John Nathan Hutchins. Gaine also printed other forms of almanacs, such as the sheet, the register, and the pocket almanac.

Gaine, an Episcopalian, became involved in a bitter religious conflict in 1753 when he was criticized by Presbyterians for refusing two of their articles refuting some of the attacks on their sect that Gaine had printed. The Presbyterians vehemently opposed the strong political influence that Episcopalians exerted on the colony's affairs and were especially concerned at this time that their influence would result in Protestant Episcopal church domination of the proposed King's College (founded in 1754; later, Columbia University). Gaine eventually published both sides, but when another controversy erupted fifteen years later between the two sects regarding the establishment of an American bishopric, he printed only the Episcopalian side.

In 1759 he married Sarah Robbins; they had three children. Gaine renamed the newspaper the *New-York Gazette; and the Weekly Mercury* on 1 February 1768 and became the official printer for the colony; from 1769 through 1775 he was official printer for both the colony and the city of New York. In 1776 he printed a proclamation for the colony; in 1789, laws for the state of New York; and, in 1793, the laws for New York City. His first wife having died in 1764 or 1765, he married Mrs. Cornelia Wallace in 1769; they had two children.

Gaine is best known as a printer who, during the revolutionary war, espoused both Whig and Loyalist causes. He was always against violence and mobs, no matter which side he chose. He had good reason to fear mobs, for he was not only much too objective to satisfy the Whigs, but was also becoming a wealthy man. Gaine tried desperately to avoid political alliances and actually took a stand later than any other printer. In 1773 he seemed to side with the Whigs, advertising Thomas Paine's *Common Sense* for sale, supporting the nonimportation agreement, and printing announcements for the Sons of Liberty, essays for the rebels, Philip Freneau's poems, and the Declaration of Independence (a broadside). Apparently he had convinced the Whigs that he was a patriot, for the Whigs destroyed competitor James Rivington's press in 1775 but not Gaine's. When he heard that the British were to occupy New York, Gaine fled with some printing equipment to Newark, New Jersey, in September 1776. He published seven issues of his newspaper through 2 November 1776.

In September 1776 the British appointed Sir Ambrose Serle to print their own newspaper beginning 30 September, appropriating Gaine's press, title, and imprint. When switching allegiances seemed politic, Gaine returned to his press in New York and printed the 11 November 1776 issue of his newspaper for the British, but his press was still supervised by Serle. Not until mid-1777 did Gaine regain complete control. The British did not trust him, and the Whigs hated him. Although Rivington, who had returned in 1777 from his two-year exile in England, was immediately made the Royal printer after Serle left New York, Gaine remained a Loyalist and even delayed printing the news of Burgoyne's surrender and the deaths of both Burgoyne and Cornwallis. Thomas Paine openly criticized Gaine in the second of the *Crisis* essays. After the British left, Gaine dropped the "Crown" from the title of his printshop, leaving only the "Bible." After he ceased to publish his newspaper in November 1783, he continued printing books, pamphlets, and almanacs. At this time Philip Freneau immortalized Gaine in a lighthearted satire called "Hugh Gaine's Petition to the New York Assembly" or "Hugh Gaine's Life." First printed in Freneau's the *Freeman's Journal* (Jan. and Feb. 1783) and reprinted frequently in Freneau's *Works*, the ten-stanza poem stressed Gaine's acquisitiveness, his ambition, and his ability to shift his views expediently "to the party that's like to be strongest . . . who'er are his masters, or monarchs, or regents. / For the future he's ready to swear them allegiance . . . [even] If the Turk with his turban should set up at last here / While he gives him protection, he'll own him his master."

After Gaine discontinued his newspaper he printed other works until 1800 and continued bookselling until at least 1802. Throughout his life his primary interest appeared to be accumulating wealth and social position, yet be contributed much to the literary fabric of the nation. In 1802 he was a founder and first president of the American Booksellers Association. Active in civic affairs, he was a vestryman at Trinity Church (Episcopal), a Mason, a charter member and trustee of the New York Society Library, a supporter of the theater, vice president of the New York Hospital, and a member of the St. Patrick Society (then Protestant). Gaine left a large estate when he died in New York.

Huge Gaine's output as printer and almanac-maker was prodigious. As official government printer his work greatly surpassed in quality and quantity the work of previous printers. Also important are his journals, which include detailed information on the French and Indian War (two years), the Revolution (five years), and John Adams's (1735–1826) presidency (two years). The journals also reveal that Gaine's sympathies with the British may have been sincere. Serle's influence during the months he continued to supervise the newspaper after Gaine's return was negligible, for Gaine's private comments expressed genuine anxiety about the English troops and his hopes for their success. The effusions over British triumphs and patriot failures in newspaper accounts were apparently his real feelings. Not at all embittered because Rivington was public printer, Gaine continued to support the Loyalist cause, despite his being distrusted by the English. A comparison of the newspaper accounts and concurrent journal entries shows that Gaine frequently modified the truth to strengthen the morale of his readers and occasionally, even withheld information, as in the case of Burgoyne's surrender. His colorful career in printing is noteworthy not only because he was exceedingly industrious and prolific, but also because he documented one of the most crucial periods in American history.

• The New York Public Library is the repository for files of the *Mercury* and some of Gaine's manuscripts. The American Antiquarian Society has many of Gaine's original almanacs. Facsimiles of original newspapers and almanacs are found on microprint in *Early American Imprints* (American Antiquarian Society), which is keyed by entry number to Charles Evans, *American Bibliography*, ed. Clifford K. Shipton (14 vols., 1941–1959). The chief secondary source is Alfred Lawrence Lorenz, *Hugh Gaine: A Colonial Printer-Editor's Odyssey to Loyalism* (1972). Paul Leicester Ford, ed., *The Journals of Hugh Gaine* (2 vols., 1902; repr. 1970), contains in vol. 1 a biography and bibliography; vol. 2 consists of Gaine's journals and seventeen letters (1768–1806). See also Clarence S. Brigham, "Bibliography of American Newspapers, 1690–1820," *Proceedings of the American Antiquarian Society* 27 (1917): 423, 456–58. An obituary is in the *New York Evening Post*, 27 Apr. 1807.

MARION BARBER STOWELL

GAINES, Edmund Pendleton (20 Mar. 1777–6 June 1849), army officer, was born in Culpepper County, Virginia, the son of James Gaines and Elizabeth Strother. His father, a revolutionary war veteran, was a nephew of the noted jurist Edmund Pendleton. Gaines was raised in North Carolina and in Sullivan County, Tennessee, and in 1795, at the age of eighteen, he was elected lieutenant of a volunteer rifle company. Gaines joined the army as an ensign on 10 June 1797, rose to lieutenant on 3 March 1799, and was mustered out on 15 June 1800. He reentered the military as a second lieutenant, Fourth Infantry, on 16 February 1801 and spent three years surveying a road from Nashville to Natchez. Gaines transferred to the Second Infantry on 1 April 1802 and advanced to first lieutenant three weeks later. In 1804 he was billeted at Fort Stoddert (Alabama Territory) and within two years functioned as both commanding officer and collector of the port of Mobile. Gaines attracted national attention in February 1807 by arresting Aaron Burr; he subsequently testified against him at his trial. He rose to captain on 28 February 1807. Gaines apparently considered pursuing a legal career. During a long furlough in 1811 he read law and briefly served as a judge in Pascagoula Parish, Mississippi Territory.

Impending hostilities with England prompted Gaines to rejoin the army as a major in the Eighth Infantry on 14 March 1812. On 6 July of that year he was promoted to lieutenant colonel, Twenty-fourth Infantry, and performed recruiting duty at Nashville. Several months later Gaines was assigned to the Northwestern Army of General William Henry Harrison, where he functioned as adjutant general. He became a colonel of the Twenty-fifth Infantry on 12 March 1813 and participated in the recapture of Detroit. Soon after, Gaines transferred to the army of General James Wilkinson during the ill-fated St. Lawrence expedition. He served as brigade adjutant under General Leonard Covington, and during the 11 November 1813 battle of Crysler's Farm he skillfully covered the American withdrawal. Gaines wintered with his regiment at the infamous cantonment of French Mills, New York, where on 9 March 1814 the rank of brigadier general was conferred upon him.

For several months into 1814 Gaines commanded garrisons at the strategic port of Sackets Harbor, New York. In late July he was summoned to Fort Erie, Upper Canada, by General Jacob J. Brown to assume control of the Left Division. He arrived there on 4 August, relieved the controversial General Eleazer W. Ripley, and further consolidated the fort's defenses. This paid immediate dividends when, on the night of 14 August 1814, a British attack was bloodily repulsed, the British losing 900 men to an American loss of 84. The siege continued with little interruption until 28 August when a shell exploded in Gaines's headquarters, seriously wounding him. He was evacuated and spent a long convalescence on the East Coast before assuming command of the Fourth Military District (Md., Pa., and N.Y.). Gaines was then ordered to New Orleans but arrived too late to participate in Andrew Jackson's decisive victory of 8 January 1815. Nonetheless, for his role in the defense of Fort Erie, Gaines received a congressional gold medal, the Thanks of Congress, and brevet promotion to major general. The legislatures of New York, Tennessee, and Virginia also voted him ceremonial swords.

Gaines's postwar career was as lengthy and varied as it was controversial. He was retained as one of three brigadiers in Jackson's Division of the South and accompanied that general throughout the 1818 Seminole War in Florida. After the military reductions of 1821, Gaines took control of the newly created Western Division, where he capably built forts, conducted Indian treaties, and facilitated frontier settlement. He also became embroiled in a bitter contretemps with General Winfield Scott over the issue of seniority. Their public bickering proved so embarrassing to the War Department that in 1828 both men were passed over for the position of commanding general in favor of Alexander Macomb. Gaines subsequently fought in the 1832 Black Hawk War and in the initial stages of the Second Seminole War. Disregarding orders to remain in Louisiana, he mounted an expedition against Indians concentrated at Tampa Bay, Florida. Gaines attacked and defeated them at Withlacoochee River on 29 February 1836 but sustained a mouth injury. He was summarily relieved by General Scott and ordered back to his jurisdiction in Louisiana. He arrived just as the Texas Revolution was commencing, and, without orders, he crossed the Sabine River and garrisoned Nacogdoches for several months. The following year both Gaines and Scott weathered courts of inquiry regarding their recent activities. The verdicts were critical but exonerated them of serious charges.

Gaines was married three times: first to Frances Toulmin at an unknown date; then to Barbara Blount of Tennessee who died in 1836; and finally to youthful socialite Myra Clark of New York in 1839. He continued to rankle superiors in Washington, who viewed his increasing belligerence with unease. When the Mexican War commenced in 1846, Gaines recruited several thousand volunteers in Louisiana, Alabama, Mississippi, and Missouri without authorization. Gaines was summarily ordered to cease. When he refused, the War Department relieved him and initiated court-martial proceedings. During his trial at Fort Monroe, Virginia, the old general forcefully defended his actions, was acquitted, and was restored to command of the Eastern Division. In 1848 he resumed control of his old jurisdiction at New Orleans, where he died the following year.

Gaines was part of an important army cadre who distinguished themselves in the War of 1812 and facilitated the growth of professionalism in the years that followed. A stubborn fighter, he was nonetheless a gifted administrator and a far-sighted military planner. In 1838 Gaines penned a memorial to Congress wherein he outlined a scheme for frontier fortifications, railroad construction, and the pioneering use of steam batteries for harbor defense. The government balked on account of the expense, but Gaines's vision presaged by two decades the very measures that materialized during the Civil War. He also evinced great empathy for the Indians and opposed the policy of removal, preferring education and assimilation in its stead. Despite many fine qualities, Gaines's garrulous disposition remained that of a rough-hewn frontier officer. Blunt, insubordinate, and outspoken to the point of shrillness, he never avoided antagonizing superiors if he believed he was right. These confrontations notwithstanding, Gaines successfully concluded fifty years of useful service to his country. He, like many senior officers of his generation, proved instrumental in guiding the nascent U.S. Army toward institutional maturity and military professionalism. His memory is perpetuated by the city of Gainesville, Florida, founded in 1856.

• Gaines's official correspondence is in RG 98, Records of Army Frontier Commands, and RG 107, Records of the Secretary of War, National Archives. Transcripts of his various courts-martial are in RG 153, Records of the Judge Advocate General's Office. Large collections of personal papers are in the Clements Library, University of Michigan; the Historical Society of Pennsylvania; the Andrew Jackson and Jacob Brown papers, Manuscript Division, Library of Congress; the New-York Historical Society; and the U.S. Military Academy Library, West Point. Smaller caches include the Jacob Brown Papers, Massachusetts Historical Society; the Butler Family Papers, Historic New Orleans Collection; the Southern Historical Collection, University of North Carolina Library; and the Manuscript Division, Tennessee State Library. See also *The Papers of John C. Calhoun*, ed. Edwin Hemphill (8 vols., 1969), and Clarence E. Carter, ed., *Territorial Papers of the United States* (25 vols., 1935–1965). A thorough listing of congressional publications relative to Gaines's dismissal is in the index to Norman E. Tuturow,

The Mexican-American War (1981). An objective biography is James W. Silver, *Edmund Pendleton Gaines* (1935), although an informative panegyrical sketch is Sarah M. Maury, *Statesman of America* (1846). For greater historical context see Francis P. Prucha, *The Sword of the Republic* (1969), and William B. Skelton, *An American Profession of Arms* (1992). For a detailed discussion of Gaines's role in the defense of Fort Erie consult John C. Fredriksen, "Niagara, 1814: The American Quest for Tactical Parity in the War of 1812 and Its Legacy" (Ph.D. diss., Providence College, 1993).

JOHN C. FREDRIKSEN

GAINES, George Strother (c. 1784–21 Jan. 1873), frontier trader and Alabama businessman, was born in Stokes County, North Carolina, the son of James Gaines, a revolutionary war captain, and Elizabeth Strother, farmers. Major General Edmund Pendleton Gaines, who was a prominent army officer on the western and southern frontiers between 1797 and the Mexican War, was his brother. At age ten Gaines moved with his family to Tennessee, where he later gained employment in a Gallatin general store. In 1804, Joseph Chambers, the factor of the U.S. Choctaw Trading House, invited Gaines to become his assistant. Subsequently Gaines relocated to St. Stephens on the Tombigbee River in the Mississippi Territory. In 1806 he succeeded Chambers as factor.

Although others served as the government's official contacts with the Native Americans, the Choctaw came to respect Gaines for his fairness in dealing with them. Gaines annually bartered as much as $40,000 in manufactured goods for furs, hides, and deerskins. His liberality in pricing, in discounting damaged goods, in extending credit, and in accepting surplus deerskins produced at best a minimal profit and, at times, such as from 1808 to 1811, an annual operating loss of almost $3,000. Between 1810 and 1813 Gaines directed pack trains along Indian paths connecting the Tennessee and the Tombigbee rivers, a route that became known as Gaines Trace. About 1812 he married Ann Gaines; they had seven children.

During the Creek war of 1813–1814, the wide range of Gaines's contacts propelled him into organizing the defense of the scattered American settlements of southwest Alabama. The massacre of 500 civilians at Fort Mims in August 1813 had spread panic throughout the region. Gaines, who had known Andrew Jackson from his years in Tennessee, wrote the letter and arranged the relay of horses that summoned General Jackson and his Tennessee Mounted Volunteers to the Alabamians' assistance. While the frontier was endangered by the Creeks, Chief Pushmataha offered the services of his Choctaw warriors in defense of the Tombigbee settlements. Gaines understood the necessity of engaging the Choctaw, many of whom "were desirous" of fighting on the "right side in the war." It was due to his influence that the military accepted the Choctaw offer.

During the winter of 1815–1816, on orders from the War Department, Gaines supervised the relocation of the trading house upriver to Fort Confederation Bluff. The formation of a separate Alabama Territory was ac-

companied by the creation of the region's first bank. In October 1818 Gaines's resignation as factor was accepted. Thereafter he returned to St. Stephens to become the secretary and cashier of the Tombeckbee Bank. St. Stephens, however, quickly withered as the appearance of the steamboat stimulated the economic development of the interior. In 1821 Gaines moved his family to Demopolis and entered into a mercantile partnership with Allen Glover. After the U.S. government abolished its Indian factory system in 1822, Glover and Gaines bought the Choctaw trading house and privately continued the Choctaw trade. The town of Gainesville, ten miles to the north, was named for Gaines, and twice during the 1820s he was elected to the state senate as a Democrat.

Although the Choctaw had made two previous cessions of their Mississippi lands (in 1805 and 1820), in 1830 they still possessed almost a third of the state. Because of the size and value of their holdings, both Mississippi and the federal government were determined to remove them to what is today southeastern Oklahoma. When the U.S. commissioners, led by Secretary of War John H. Eaton, met with Choctaw leaders to conclude the Treaty of Dancing Rabbit Creek (1830), Gaines served as an unofficial adviser and facilitator to both sides. Because indignant factions among the Choctaw threatened violence to those who had signed the treaty, the widely esteemed Gaines was prevailed upon to lead a party of Choctaw elders in exploring their new Oklahoma territories. The four-month exploration, begun in October 1830, satisfied the Choctaw as to the suitability of their new property.

In May 1831 a War Department agent sought to determine the readiness of the Choctaw to depart from Mississippi. He was informed by the Native Americans that "when Mr. Gaines is ready [to lead us] we will be ready." Since the Choctaw would not willingly cooperate with anyone but Gaines, he was appointed to superintend their removal. From September 1831 until June 1832 he supervised several assistants in arranging transportation, opening roads, stockpiling supplies, and in "hastening the Indians in their preparations." A portion of the Choctaw removed that fall. Before the removal resumed in the following summer, Gaines, who was apparently thought by the War Department to be too protective of the Native Americans, was replaced. By 1833 Gaines had resettled in Mobile, Alabama, where he and a partner operated a store until 1856. From 1832 until 1838 he served as president of the Mobile branch of the Bank of Alabama. He was also a prominent promoter of the Mobile & Ohio Railroad. At seventy-two he retired to his farm in State Line, Mississippi, where he died. Near the end of his life the *Mobile Register* bestowed upon him the title of "patriarch of two States."

• In retirement Gaines penned several reminiscences. These have been published as "Notes on the Early Days of South Alabama," *Alabama Historical Quarterly* 26 (1964): 133–228, and "Dancing Rabbit Creek Treaty," [Alabama] *State Department of Archives and History, Historical and Patriotic Series* no. 10 (1928): 8–31. See also "Letters from George Strother Gaines Relating to Events in South Alabama, 1805–1814," *Transactions of the Alabama Historical Society* 3 (1899): 184–92; Fr. Aloysius Plaisance, "The Choctaw Trading House—1803–1822," *Alabama Historical Quarterly* 16 (1954): 393–423; and Grant Foreman, *Indian Removal* (1932; repr. 1972), pp. 27–50.

ALAN V. BRICELAND

GAINES, Irene McCoy (25 Oct. 1892–30 Mar. 1964), social worker and clubwoman, was born in Ocala, Florida, the daughter of Charles McCoy and Mamie Ellis. She grew up in Chicago where her mother moved after her parents divorced in 1903. From 1905 she attended the Fisk University Normal School in Nashville, Tennessee, from which she graduated in 1910.

Returning to Chicago after her graduation, McCoy could not find work as a teacher because of racism. She engaged in the kind of drudgery work most black women were able to find at that time: laundry and cleaning, earning as little as $5 per week. In 1914 she married Harris B. Gaines, a Chicago lawyer; they had two sons. She returned to school in 1918, studying social work at the University of Chicago until 1921. She eventually did further study at Loyola University's School of Social Administration from 1935 to 1937.

Gaines's social service career began in 1917 when she was the county organizer for War Camp Community Services, directing the Girls' Work Division. From there she began a fifteen-year career as a social worker with the Cook County Bureau of Public Welfare. She initially worked as a typist in Chicago's Juvenile Court. She was assigned to the complaint department where she was exposed more fully to the problems blacks faced, particularly women and children. She also worked as a caseworker for the Bureau of Public Welfare where she started clubs for young people.

Gaines worked with the Urban League, serving as a recruiter and director of its women's division. She was industrial secretary of the first black branch of the YWCA from 1920 to 1922. Her last official position was that of executive director of a recreational program for teenagers at the Parkway Community House from 1945 to 1947. She retired in 1947.

In 1936 Gaines was one of the founders and president of the Chicago Council of Negro Organizations. This group served as a central coordinating body of nearly one hundred social, civic, labor, educational, and religious organizations in the city of Chicago. She used it to launch attacks against social problems that plagued the black community, such as teenage pregnancy, problems facing domestic workers, and employment discrimination.

Active in Republican party politics as well, Gaines worked in several campaigns, including that of her husband, who served in the Illinois legislature from 1928 to 1936. She was the Republican state central committeewoman for the First Congressional District of Illinois from 1928 to 1930 and was a member of the Second Ward Republican Organization. In 1940 she ran for public office, the first black woman to seek the position of Illinois state representative. Although she was unsuccessful in her bid, she was victorious in her run for the Republican nomination for the Board of County Commissioners from Chicago in 1948 and led the ticket of candidates for that position.

Gaines was an outspoken critic of inequality and segregation. In 1941 she led a group of fifty Chicagoans on a march on Washington to protest employment discrimination. She investigated and protested the working conditions for domestics and testified before congressional committees for fair employment practices and legislation.

An active clubwoman whose advocacy for social reform earned her a national reputation, Gaines served as president of the Illinois Federation of Republican Colored Women's Clubs from 1924 to 1935. This was the first federation of Republican clubs in the state. She was also president of the Chicago and Northern District Federation of Colored Women's Clubs and the Illinois Association of Colored Women. Through the Northern District Federation she created a program called Negro in Art Week, designed to promote artistic and cultural development in young black men and women.

From 1952 to 1958 Gaines served as president of the National Association of Colored Women's Clubs [NACW], a position in which she focused on promoting international peace and human rights. As president of the NACW, she continued the organization's efforts to restore the home of Frederick Douglass in the Anacostia area of Washington, D.C. She directed the members to center their attention on the organization's motto "to lift as we climb" and to focus on solving problems that affected the black community. She felt it was their responsibility to enhance the quality of life for black Americans.

Gaines worked through NACW and as vice president of the Chicago chapter of the Congress of American Women to address issues of global sisterhood. In this capacity she spoke before the secretary general of the United Nations, Trygve Lie, expressing concern over the inferior status of black women in the United States and throughout the world.

Gaines was active in a number of other organizations, including Sigma Gamma Rho Sorority and the African Methodist Episcopal [AME] church. She was a steward of the Bethel AME Church and often used biblical themes and phrases in her speeches and lectures. For her years of outstanding service, Gaines was named "Woman of the Year" by Sigma Gamma Rho, the Women's Division of the AME church and the Northern District of Colored Women's Clubs. She died in Chicago.

• Gaines's papers are in the Chicago Historical Society. Jessie Carney Smith's *Notable Black American Women* [1991] contains a biographical sketch, as does *Lifting as They Climb*, comp. Elizabeth L. Davis (1933). There is a short sketch in the *Negro History Bulletin* 17 (May 1954), along with a story on the National Association of Colored Women's Clubs.

MAMIE E. LOCKE

GAINES, Matthew (4 Aug. 1842–11 June 1900), politician and Texas state senator, was born in Alexandria, Louisiana. His parents (names unknown) were slaves on the plantation of Martin G. Despallier, where Gaines learned to read and write. In 1858, after Despallier's death, Gaines was sold to an owner in New Orleans who hired him out to work on a steamboat. He left the boat on a trip up the Ouachita River and lived in Camden, Arkansas, for six months. He later went back to New Orleans, where he was captured and returned to his master, who subsequently sold him in 1859 to C. C. Hearne, a planter in Robertson County, Texas.

In 1863 Gaines ran away from the Hearne plantation hoping to escape to Mexico. He was captured by a frontier ranger company near Fort McKavitt in western Texas. The company did not send him back to Hearne but left him in Fredericksburg, where he worked as a blacksmith. He ran away again and worked as a shepherd in nearby Texas hill country until the end of the Civil War.

After the war, Gaines moved to Burton in Washington County, Texas, where he farmed and also was the preacher for a local Baptist church. He became involved in politics as a member of the Republican party and in 1869 was elected to the state senate from Washington County. During the Twelfth Legislature (1870–1871), he was an outspoken advocate of the interests of his black constituents and a strong proponent of measures to secure their civil rights. To those ends Gaines supported most measures of Republican governor Edmund J. Davis, including the organization of a state police, creation of the state militia, providing frontier protection, and legislation to encourage both public and private education. He antagonized many whites with his support of integrated public schools. As a state senator, he gained a reputation as an excellent speaker and a shrewd politician.

During the Thirteenth Legislature, in 1873, Gaines became increasingly radical on racial issues. He introduced legislation to prohibit racial discrimination on the state's railroads. He also sponsored a bill to give farm tenants, primarily blacks, a lien upon their crops to be held against damages by landlords or landowners. Both measures encountered strong opposition from white Democrats and Republicans and were defeated. Gaines had also been increasingly critical of Governor Davis and his party for blocking efforts by blacks to run for public office. In 1871 the senator broke with Davis over the renomination of white congressman William T. Clark in the state's Third Congressional District. Gaines bolted the regular party to back Richard Nelson, a black justice of the peace from Galveston, who lost to Clark.

Thwarted by white leaders, Gaines continued to push for more black recognition and to that end en-

couraged blacks to take more control over local Republican organizations. In 1872, at his urging, blacks in his senatorial district put forward a slate of black officers and seized control over the party's local machinery. In July 1873 Gaines was prominent in the organization of Texas's first Colored Men's Convention, which sought to give blacks a greater role in state politics. That convention endorsed the national Republican party and the civil rights bill being considered in the U.S. Senate but refused to endorse the Republican state administration.

Controversial from the beginning of his career, Gaines attracted the hostility of whites, who assaulted his character in efforts to undermine his political strength. In 1871 James G. Tracy, secretary of the Republican state executive committee, to undercut the senator's attack on Clark, promoted rumors that Gaines had been indicted for rape. On 9 December 1871 the district court of Fayette County, Texas, under the control of white Democrats, indicted Gaines for bigamy. He had in fact married Elizabeth Harrison in 1870, after being informed by the minister who had performed his first marriage, to Fanny Sutton in 1867, that this marriage was illegal. After failing in repeated appeals to have his case transferred to federal court, Gaines was found guilty by the court in Fayette County on 15 July 1873, and he was sentenced to one year in prison. Gaines appealed that decision, and on 24 November 1873 the state supreme court reversed the district court decision. By such measures, however, his enemies hampered his political effectiveness severely, forcing him to defend himself in the courts for some two years.

In 1874 Gaines again ran for the state senate. He appeared to have been elected, but the results were contested by Seth Shepard, a white Democrat. The legislature, controlled at this time by Democrats, seated his opponent, citing Gaines's conviction for bigamy as a reason.

Gaines never held state office again, but he continued to be active in local politics in Giddings, Texas, and an outspoken advocate of black rights. At Giddings, he was a prominent Baptist preacher until his death there.

• For an early biography of Gaines, see J. Mason Brewer, *Negro Legislators and Their Descendants* (1935). More recent studies of Gaines may be found in Ann P. Malone, "Matthew Gaines: Reconstruction Politics," in *Negro Legislators of Texas and Their Descendants*, ed. Alwyn Barr and Robert Calvert (1981), and Merline Pitre, *Through Many Dangers Trials and Snares: Black Leadership in Texas, 1868–1900* (1985).

CARL H. MONEYHON

GAINES, Myra Clark (June 1805–9 Jan. 1885), celebrated litigant, was born in New Orleans, Louisiana, the daughter of Daniel Clark, a prominent merchant, real estate speculator, and first territorial representative from Louisiana to the U.S. Congress, and Marie Julie "Zulime" Carrière. Born in Sligo, Ireland, Daniel Clark emigrated to New Orleans, where he inherited his uncle's extensive property holdings in Louisiana in 1799. A reputed bachelor, it is unclear whether Clark was ever legally married to Zulime Carrière, who was married to another man, but the couple did have two daughters, the second of whom was Myra. Clark failed to acknowledge his children publicly, and he placed Myra in the home of his close friend, Samuel Boyer Davis. She became known as Myra Davis and in 1812 moved with the Davises from New Orleans to Lewes, Delaware. She was educated at a selective female academy in Philadelphia.

In 1830 Myra made a discovery that changed her life and drew her into a half-century–long legal struggle over her legitimacy and inheritance. When Samuel Davis, away after having been elected to the state legislature, asked Myra to search his files for certain papers that he needed, she stumbled on letters disclosing her true parentage. Davis later revealed to her the full details surrounding her birth, and Myra, learning that her wealthy father had died in 1813, became convinced that she had been unfairly deprived of a fortune. Clark's estate, after all, included a number of plantations in Mississippi and Louisiana as well as extensive property in New Orleans. After marrying William Wallace Whitney of Binghamton, New York, on 13 September 1832, with whom she eventually had three children, Myra and her husband continued looking for more information about her father and his death.

Their search soon proved successful. In an old letter to Davis, Whitney discovered a reference to an 1813 will made by Clark in which Myra was deemed the sole heir of Clark's vast landholdings. Myra and her husband tracked down the writer of the letter, an intimate friend of Clark's who had moved to Cuba, who swore that Clark had indeed bequeathed his entire estate to his youngest daughter. From there they traveled to New Orleans, where they gained further confirmation of the existence of this will. The document itself, however, was never found, and much to their dismay, Myra and her husband soon discovered that two of Clark's business associates, Richard Relf and Beverly Chew, had presented for probate another will, dated 1811, in which Clark left his entire estate to his widowed mother, Mary Clark. In 1836 Myra and her husband filed a claim in a federal district court against the executors Relf and Chew, the heirs of Mary Clark, and all the purchasers and occupants of what had been Clark's estate. Under Louisiana's civil code, if Myra was able to establish herself as the legitimate daughter of Clark, she was entitled to recover four-fifths of her father's estate, the 1811 will notwithstanding. (Myra's older sister was definitely illegitimate, as the marriage between Clark and Carrière was alleged to have occurred between the births of the two daughters.)

As Myra's case worked its way through the courts, in 1837 her husband died of yellow fever. Two years later, after her cause had begun to attract national attention, she married the flamboyant military hero General Edward Pendleton Gaines, a widower who was thirty years her senior. Gaines fully supported his wife in her legal struggle and often added color to court proceedings by appearing in full military dress. Known for his highly visible feuds with his War Department superiors, Gaines and his wife went on several speaking tours during the 1840s to promote the general's plan for a strengthened national defense. Myra frequently joined her husband on the platform to speak on his behalf, and though her "unfeminine" outspokenness drew much criticism, huge crowds always turned out to hear the famous couple, and popular opinion was in her favor.

In 1848 the U.S. Supreme Court rendered a decision in an appeal filed by Charles Patterson, one of the occupants of what had been Clark's estate and a defendant in the 1836 suit. The Court held that a lawful marriage had indeed taken place between Myra's parents and that Myra was the legitimate heir of Daniel Clark. Under the civil code she was entitled to four-fifths of the property held by Patterson; however, the decision was limited to Patterson's claim and did not grant to her any other portion of the Clark estate. After this initial triumph, the following few years proved difficult for Myra. Edward Gaines died of cholera in 1849, and two years later, when the whole of Myra's original suit reached the Supreme Court for a decision, the Court ruled against her. Reversing itself on further review of evidence regarding the marital status of Myra's parents, the Court rejected Myra's claim to legitimacy and to her inheritance.

Even though her husband's death had rendered her penniless, Myra had no difficulty securing competent legal counsel to pursue her now nationally known cause, and she thus continued her struggle. Having failed to establish her legitimacy, Myra began to stress another aspect of her case—her rights of inheritance under Clark's "lost will" of 1813. Myra had never been able to produce the will, which she believed had been fraudulently suppressed by Relf and Chew, but in 1855 she made a bold move: she drew up such a will herself, based on the testimony of witnesses, and filed it for probate. In 1857 the Louisiana Supreme Court surprisingly upheld the validity of the will—a will many believed had never even been written. Boosted by her victory, Myra filed another suit to recover her father's estate, and in 1861 the U.S. Supreme Court upheld her claim based on the second will. During her hour of triumph, dime novels and the national press recounted her story and hailed the decision as a victory for justice.

Myra instituted a final round of legal proceedings after the Civil War. She sued the city of New Orleans, which had built a large waterworks on part of what had been the Clark estate, and in 1867 the U.S. Supreme Court again ruled in her favor and ordered a master in chancery to compute the sum owed her. Unfortunately, more legal delays prevented Myra from ever receiving payment from the city. She died of a bronchial condition in New Orleans and was buried there in the Clark vault at St. Louis Cemetery. In 1891 her heirs finally received compensation, a total of $576,707.92, thus bringing to an end a 55-year-long legal battle.

The case of Myra Clark Gaines was, as the U.S. Supreme Court referred to it, "one of the most remarkable in the records of its courts." Over the years Myra employed more than thirty different lawyers, including notables Daniel Webster, John A. Campbell, Caleb Cushing, Reverdy Johnson, and Francis Scott Key, and the records of the case became so bulky that they were said to have filled two large trunks. The exceptional length and complexity of Myra's case reveal the depth of her personal determination and make the struggle of this nineteenth-century woman to achieve her rights all the more extraordinary.

• About seventy-five of Myra Clark Gaines's personal letters have been published as *Supreme Court, King's County— General Term. Second Judicial Department. In the Matter of the Probate of the Last Will and Testament of Myra Clark Gaines, Deceased. Julietta Perkins and Marie P. Evans, Appellants. Record of Appeal* (4 vols., 1896). The standard work on the Myra Clark Gaines case is Nolan B. Harmon, Jr., *The Famous Case of Myra Clark Gaines* (1946), which includes an extensive bibliographical essay. See also John S. Kendall, "The Strange Case of Myra Clark Gaines," *Louisiana Historical Quarterly* 20 (1937): 5–42, and Perry Scott Rader, "The Romance of American Courts: *Gaines v. New Orleans*," *Louisiana Historical Quarterly* 27 (1944): 5–322. The most complete statement of the facts of the Gaines case by the U.S. Supreme Court can be found in *Gaines v. New Orleans*, *U.S. Reports*, vol. 73, pp. 642–719. An obituary is in the *New York Times*, 10 Jan. 1885.

TIMOTHY S. HUEBNER

GAITHER, Horace Rowan, Jr. (23 Nov. 1909–7 Apr. 1961), lawyer and foundation officer, was born in Natchez, Mississippi, the son of Horace Rowan Gaither, a banker, and Marguerite Chamberlain. After growing up in Portland, Oregon, Kansas City, Missouri, and San Francisco, Gaither earned his B.A. from the University of California at Berkeley in 1929 and his law degree from the University of California Law School in 1933. He married Charlotte Cameron Castle in 1931; they had two children.

From 1933 to 1936 Gaither worked in Washington, D.C., with the Farm Credit Administration of the New Deal. He then returned to San Francisco and joined the law firm of Cooley, Crowley and Supple, where he acquired a specialized knowledge of private nonprofit organizations. Through teaching a course in "war law" at Berkeley after Pearl Harbor, he was proposed by a Berkeley dean as assistant director of the Massachusetts Institute of Technology Radiation Laboratory, a planning and administrative post he held from 1942 to 1945. This wartime experience had a critical formative influence on Gaither and his career. It gave him an opportunity to develop his talents for planning and building good working relationships; nourished his immense regard for the value and potential of scientific research, bringing him close and lasting personal ties with leading American scientists like Lee DuBridge, Karl Compton, Ernest O. Lawrence, and Vannevar Bush; and introduced him to the national defense establishment, with which he was associated throughout his career.

After the war Gaither served as a consultant to the National Defense Research Council and played a vital role in establishing the RAND Corporation as an independent nonprofit organization to carry out defense studies, initially for the U.S. Air Force. Gaither provided the necessary legal briefs and used his personal connections, first with San Francisco banks and then with Karl Compton and Donald David as trustees of the Ford Foundation, to secure the initial capital funds. After RAND was formally launched, he served as chairman of the board of trustees from 1948 until his death.

When Henry Ford II assumed leadership of the Ford enterprises in 1945, he sought to have the Ford Foundation, which since its establishment in 1936 had managed Ford family interests largely in Michigan, broaden its interests and leadership. He brought to the foundation board national figures like Gordon Rentschler, Karl Compton, and Donald David, who felt that a serious study should be undertaken on the most productive uses of the funds the foundation would control after the settlement of the estates of Henry Ford, Sr., and Edsel Ford, which would make it the largest foundation in the world. Compton proposed that Gaither head such a study, and after assuring himself that Henry Ford II was ready to allow the Ford Foundation to be controlled by an independent board and to be separated financially from the Ford Motor Company, Gaither accepted. He assembled a distinguished committee, strongly academic in background, and a competent staff. They began work in November 1948 and completed their report a year later. It was accepted without substantial change by the trustees and became a kind of sacred text guiding the foundation's program choices and organization over its first decades.

Although Gaither had proposed that neither he nor other members of the study group play any further role in the governance of the foundation, tensions between the first president, Paul Hoffman, and the trustees soon led to his return on a part-time basis. After the trustees forced Hoffman to resign, Gaither became acting president in February 1953 and was confirmed as president later that year.

Gaither assumed the Ford Foundation presidency at a difficult time. A congressional investigation of foundations (under Congressman Edward Eugene Cox) had preceded his presidency, and another, more hostile one (under Congressman B. Carroll Reece) followed within a year of his assuming office. In this era of McCarthyism, a steady stream of criticism of the foundation as a dangerously liberal institution was generated by conservative commentators such as Fulton Lewis, Jr., Westbrook Pegler, and George Sokolsky, troubling and dividing the foundation's trustees. The legacy of the actions of Hoffman and his associate director, Robert M. Hutchins, also brought continuing troubles. The trustees had been more displeased with Hutchins than with Hoffman, and after offering what they had considered a generous terminal settlement to Hutchins, the trustees were dismayed when he reappeared as the head of the Fund for the Republic, an organization concerned with civil rights that had been funded with a $15 million grant by the foundation. While the foundation tried to treat this fund as what Hutchins characteristically called a "wholly disowned subsidiary," the fact that it was enveloped in ideological controversy added to the foundation's political discomforts. Hutchins had also been the prime mover in the foundation's establishment of two other quasi-independent organizations, the Fund for the Advancement of Education and the Fund for Adult Education, whose ambiguous connections with the foundation required clarification. Gaither also had the difficult tasks of moving the foundation's headquarters from Pasadena, California to New York City, instituting more orderly procedures after the freewheeling practices of the Hoffman era and loosening relations with the Ford Motor Company at a time when many of its dealers and officers were nervously critical of the foundation's actions.

Gaither did not prove to be able to cope readily with this array of problems and demands. His talents in conciliation and consensus building were not complemented by decisiveness when disagreements could not be resolved. His accomplishments as president included the beginning of financial separation from the motor company, the resolution of trustees' doubts about the overseas development programs Hoffman had started, the establishment of National Merit Scholarships, and the initiation of a major effort to promote the raising of academic salaries. But as dissatisfaction with his leadership grew, power and initiative moved toward Donald David, chairman of the board's executive committee, and in 1956 Gaither was replaced as president and elevated to the position of chairman of the board.

In 1957 Gaither received the opportunity that has given his name a prominent and lasting place in the history of the United States during the Cold War era. A report recommending the expenditure of $40 billion on bomb shelters led President Dwight Eisenhower to appoint an independent committee to study the nation's defense and alternate uses of the large sums proposed. James Killian, then Eisenhower's special assistant for science and technology, persuaded his old friend Gaither to be cochair of the committee with Robert C. Sprague. Gaither unfortunately fell ill with cancer at the very beginning of the committee's work and was not able to participate in the preparation of its famous report or to sign it. The committee nevertheless became known as the "Gaither Committee" and its findings as the "Gaither Report." Its fame came in part from its authoritativeness and its alarming conclusions stressing the vulnerability of the United States to the rising Soviet strength in intercontinental ballistic missiles and the overriding need to develop an invulnerable second-strike force. Its timing was also critical: the report was released shortly after the first Russian satellite, Sputnik, was launched on 4 October 1957. Although it was a highly secret document, parts of it were leaked to the press, and a clamor ensued for its full release. Gaither was able to participate in the presentation of the report to the president, and in publicly supporting Eisenhower's refusal to release it to the public he undoubtedly strengthened the attachment of his name to the document.

Increasingly debilitated by cancer, Gaither resigned as chairman of the Ford Foundation board in 1958 but continued as a member until his death in Boston. During the last year of his life he was also intermittently engaged in venture capital activities as a partner in the San Francisco firm of Draper, Gaither, and Anderson.

Rowan Gaither was a man of his time in his loyal attachment to the nation's interests and security and in his optimistic faith in the possibility of finding solutions to the nation's and the world's problems through objective analysis and scientific research. Shaped by the experience of World War II, he sought to continue to serve the national security, and in the successes of the RAND Corporation he could claim an important achievement. His 1949 report for the Ford Foundation remains an outstanding example of philanthropic planning; its emphasis on the central importance of American strength and democracy for world peace bore the marks of Gaither's beliefs. His positivistic belief (or perhaps hope) that right courses of action would emerge clearly if only the facts were set forth and dealt with in an orderly way was evident in his work. His faith in science extended to the social and behavioral sciences, which he fostered at RAND and the Ford Foundation. He was above all a facilitator seeking to influence the course of decision making and action without intruding his own views or will. Dwight Macdonald once wrote that he was a man "not easy to pick out in a crowd." With his amiable and undisturbing ways, Gaither seemed to want not to impose or stand out. He was not a strong executive and often relied on those with more forceful personalities to get things done. Nevertheless, his achievements at MIT and RAND and his ability to set directions and ease conflicts at the Ford Foundation prove that gentler human qualities, which are not often allowed to surface in the rarified world in which Gaither made his mark, can achieve much greater success than their unobtrusiveness would suggest.

• Gaither's Ford Foundation papers are in the foundation archives in New York City. On his career there, see Dwight Macdonald, *The Ford Foundation: The Men and the Millions* (1956; repr. 1990), and Francis X. Sutton, "The Ford Foundation: The Early Years," *Daedalus* 116 (Winter 1987): 41–91. On Gaither's role at RAND, see Bruce L. R. Smith, *The Rand Corporation* (1966). The "Gaither Committee Report," entitled "Deterrence and Survival in the Nuclear Age," is reprinted in Morton H. Halperin, *National Security Policy-Making: Analysis, Cases, and Proposals* (1975), which contains Halperin's classic 1960 paper, "The Gaither Study and the Policy Process." On this report, see also J. R. Killian, Jr., *Sputnik, Scientists, and Eisenhower: A Memoir of the First Special Assistant to the President for Science and Technology* (1977).

FRANCIS X. SUTTON

GALAMIAN, Ivan (5 Feb. 1903–14 Apr. 1981), violin pedagogue, was born in Tabriz, Persia, the son of Alexander J. Galamian and Sarah Khounoutz, merchants. The family moved to Russia in 1904, and he began playing violin at an early age. He studied at the Moscow Philharmonia School with Konstantin Mostras from 1916 to 1918. In 1919, at the precocious age of sixteen, he joined the Bolshoi Theatre Orchestra. After numerous unpleasant incidents with the new leadership in Russia, Galamian escaped the Bolshevik rule and joined the Russian refugee community in Paris in 1922. Shortly after his arrival, he continued advanced violin studies with the great violinist and teacher Lucien Capet. Capet was the author of *La Technique Supérieure de l'Archet*, the most exhaustive study of violin bowing in history. During this period Galamian developed the groundwork of his teaching method, which later became known internationally as "the Galamian Bow Arm." After his studies with Capet, he commenced a solo career that included many concerts in Parisian concert halls and salons as well as tours in France, Germany, and Holland.

By 1926 Galamian began the career shift that would influence thousands of musicians for the remainder of the century. The first step of the transition from performer to teacher began when Capet made Galamian his assistant. The second step was the formation of the Conservatoire Russe de Paris. With such luminaries as Rachmaninoff, Medtner, and Glazounov listed as faculty members there, Galamian was honored to be named professor of violin. The final step was the appearance of the four-year-old prodigy Paul Makanowitzky in his studio. Makanowitzky was the first world-class talent that Galamian had the opportunity to teach. In four short years the pupil was advanced enough to be presented in an official Paris debut, which received outstanding press and launched not only a solo career for the child but a lifetime teaching career for the professor. Galamian's years in Paris also included work with Roland Gundry, who made a sensational debut in New York at the age of fifteen, and with Veda Reynolds, who won the Kreisler Competition, also at the age of fifteen, and went on to become the first female member of the Philadelphia Orchestra. By the early 1930s Galamian was increasingly sought after by American students, so he decided to spend half of each year in Paris and the other half in New York. After five years of this dual residency, the political instability in Western Europe and his own career success convinced him that his future was best served on American soil.

In 1937 (the year of Roland Gundry's New York debut), Galamian settled permanently in New York, teaching both privately and at the Henry Street Settlement School. In the following decade he worked with major American talents Berl Senofsky, who won first prize in the Queen Elisabeth Competition; Charles Libove, concertmaster of the Rochester Philharmonic; Stuart Canin, concertmaster of the San Francisco Symphony; and Fredell Lack, Esther Glazer, Gerald and Wilfried Beal, Toshiya Eto, Sylvia Rosenberg, Caroll Glenn, and Helen Kwalwasser, international soloists.

By 1940 he began plans for a summer academy patterned after the famous Stolyarski School in Odessa. Since Stolyarski had produced such major international violinists as Nathan Milstein and David Oistrakh, Galamian felt very strongly about the necessity of such a project. At the suggestion of his friend, Gregor Piatigorsky, he decided to locate the school in upstate New York. In 1941 Galamian married Judith Johnson, who turned out to be a brilliant leader of young people, even though she was not musically trained. By 1944 the couple established the Meadowmount School of Music in Essex County, New York, which has become the model for the increasing number of summer music schools in the United States.

The international career of Ivan Galamian was securely established with the phenomenon of child star Michael Rabin. Rabin performed with all major American orchestras by the time of his twelfth birthday and recorded the Paganini Caprices for Columbia Records at the age of thirteen. He went on to a performing, recording, television, and motion picture career of the highest international level. After this meteoric success Galamian was invited to join the faculty of the Curtis Institute of Music in 1944 and the faculty of the Juilliard School in 1945. The success of Rabin was followed quickly by that of Erick Friedman, Jaime Laredo, Arnold Steinhardt, Paul Zukovsky, Pinchas Zukerman, Miriam Fried, Kyung-Wha Chung, Young-Uck Kim, Eugene Fodor, James Oliver Buswell IV, Charles Treger, Ida and Ani Kavafian, and Itzhak Perlman.

The elite international chamber ensembles that feature Galamian students include the Juilliard, Guarneri, New Music, Curtis, Orion, Cleveland, and LaSalle String Quartets; the Beaux Arts, Meadowmount, Amadeus Kalichstein-Laredo-Robinson, and Kaplan-Golub-Carr Piano Trios; the Los Angeles, Cantilena, and Amabile Piano Quartets; the Chamber Music Society of Lincoln Center; and Music from Marlboro. Galamian students also occupy the concertmaster positions of many major orchestras, including New York, Cleveland, Philadelphia, Boston, San Francisco, Montreal, Atlanta, Minnesota, Detroit, and Los Angeles. His students continue his pedagogical legacy in such prestigious international music schools as Juilliard, Curtis, New England Conservatory, Oberlin College, Cincinnati Conservatory, Cleveland Institute of Music, and the Universities of Michigan, Indiana, and Southern California, as well as the Toho School of Tokyo and the Cologne and Berlin Hochschule für Musik.

His most important publications are *Principles of Violin Playing and Teaching* (1962) and *Contemporary Violin Technique*, vols. 1 and 2 (1966), as well as editions of most of the standard violin solo repertoire. His influence is remarkable in its universality, for every major school of violin playing has been influenced by his work.

• Galamian's bow technique developed from the treatise of Lucien Capet, *La Technique Supérieure de l'Archet* (1916). Elizabeth Green's monograph, *The Miraculous Teacher Ivan Galamian and The Meadowmount Experience* (1993), describes his teaching methods. Edgar Koob's "The Violin Pedagogy of Ivan Galamian" (Ph.D. diss., Univ. of Illinois, Urbana, 1986) draws on interviews with Galamian's students and videotapes of lessons to illustrate the teacher's style. The *Cambridge Companion to the Violin* (1992) includes several articles about Galamian's career and his prominent students.

STEPHEN B. SHIPPS

GALARZA, Ernesto (7 Aug. 1905–22 June 1984), scholar and union activist, was born in Jalcocotán in the state of Nayarit, Mexico. His parents, about whom few details are known, were farm workers. In 1911 Galarza went to the United States with his mother and two uncles to escape the dangerous conditions of the Madero revolution in Mexico. Galarza began his formal education in 1911 in Mazatlán, Sinaloa, and continued his schooling in Sacramento, where his family eventually settled. As a child, Galarza held a number of jobs, including positions as a messenger, drugstore clerk, court interpreter, and cannery and field worker, but with the aid of his uncle he was also able to continue his education. Even as a young boy Galarza became something of an activist. As he was fond of recalling in later years, he became a leader and negotiator for the adult workers in his Mexican community at age eight because he knew perhaps two dozen words of English. Galarza's mother died when he was only twelve years old. Encouraged by his uncle, Galarza entered Occidental College in Los Angeles on scholarship in 1923.

In a pattern that was to characterize the rest of his life, Galarza combined scholarship with activism as he attended college and graduate school. At Occidental, he joined the debate team, wrote for the school newspaper, did field work in Mexico during his senior year, and earned a membership in Phi Beta Kappa. In 1927, a year after he completed college, Galarza began graduate study in Latin American history. He completed an M.A. at Stanford University in 1929; that same year he entered doctoral studies at Columbia University. While at Stanford he married Mae Taylor, a teacher from Sacramento, with whom he had two daughters. While working on his Ph.D., Galarza taught, lectured, and did research on Latin America for the Foreign Policy Association in New York. He and his wife also created an experimental elementary school program on Long Island, the Year-long School, where students spent the summer working on a farm. From 1936 to 1947 he served first as a specialist in education and then the chief of the labor section of the Pan American Union (PAU) in Washington, D.C. While in Washington, Galarza also worked as an adviser to the Bolivian government on labor and economic conditions. He completed his doctoral dissertation, "*La industria Eléctrica en México*," a study of the electrical industry in Mexico that was based on extensive field work, and received his doctorate in 1944. In the same year he completed a report for the PAU on the problems of discrimination and labor conditions among

Mexicans in the United States, which received broad circulation and appeared as testimony before the House Labor Committee. Thus Galarza, now a naturalized U.S. citizen, became a widely recognized spokesperson for Chicanos in the United States.

From 1947 to 1955 Galarza was the director of research and education and field organizer for the National Farm Labor Union (NFLU), the successor to the Southern Tenant Farmers Union. As a leader in the NFLU, Galarza was involved in several important farm workers' strikes, including the 1947 strike against the DiGiorgio Fruit Company, which was one of the earliest and longest strikes of farm workers in California's San Joaquin Valley. Galarza also helped organize sugar cane workers and strawberry pickers in Louisiana. From 1955 to 1960 he worked in a similar capacity for the renamed National Agriculture Workers Union (NAWU), an affiliate of the AFL-CIO. As an organizer he was particularly interested in eliminating abuses of the *bracero* (day laborer) system, a program created by the U.S. and Mexican governments during World War II to import Mexican farm labor to the United States. Although Galarza was sympathetic to Mexican immigrants, he also realized that growers abused the *bracero* system in order to depress wages, replace American workers, and ultimately undermine the efforts of farm-labor unions. Based on his research among farm workers as an organizer and later as a counsel to the House of Representatives Committee on Education and Labor, Galarza wrote two pioneering investigations of the abuses of the *bracero* system, *Strangers in Our Fields* (1955) and *Merchants of Labor: The Mexican Bracero Story* (1964).

After 1960 Galarza left the labor movement, but he continued his advocacy of farm workers as an activist, consultant, and scholar. In 1963 he led a grass roots movement in the San Jose, California, Mexican-American community to demand a Congressional investigation of the Chualar disaster, a collision between an overloaded bus of workers and a train which killed thirty-two *braceros*. Appointed chief labor counsel in the subsequent investigation, Galarza wrote a report later published as *Tragedy at Chualar: Elcrucero do las treinta y dos cruces* (1977). As a widely recognized Mexican-American leader, Galarza served as a consultant for numerous government agencies, charitable foundations, and political organizations, including positions as program analyst for the Economic and Youth Opportunities Agency in Los Angeles, consultant for the Ford Foundation, chairman of the La Raza Unida Unity Conference in 1967, and member of the Board of Directors of the Mexican American Legal Defense and Educational Fund. In the 1960s and 1970s Galarza authored several books and held a series of academic appointments in sociology at Notre Dame, in the Department of Education and Mexican-American graduate studies program at San Jose State University, and a regents professorship at the University of California, San Diego. In the early 1970s he published several books based on his personal experiences of working and organizing in the Mexican-American community, including *Spiders in the House and Workers in the Field* (1970), his autobiography *Barrio Boy* (1971), and a final scholarly book on agricultural workers, *Farm Workers and Agribusiness in California, 1947–1960* (1977). Bicultural and bilingual education became a consuming interest of Galarza's later life. In the 1970s he created a resource center of Spanish teaching materials for the San Jose Unified School District at San Jose State and also wrote several short stories and poems for children, including "Zoo Risa," "La Mula No Nacio Arisca," and "Rimas Tontas," for use in bilingual education programs. In 1979 he was nominated for consideration for the Nobel Prize in literature. Though Galarza's health began failing him in his final years, as one of the most prominent Mexican-American leaders of his generation, he remained an important symbolic and intellectual mentor, who was still sought out by young scholars and activists. A leader for sixty of his seventy-eight years, Galarza died in his San Jose home.

• Galarza's papers are held in the Department of Special Collections at Stanford University. Although Galarza's personal papers provide few biographical details about his family background, *Barrio Boy* (1971) recreates the texture of his childhood experiences in Mexico and the barrios of Mazatlán and Sacramento in moving and vivid detail. Interviews with Galarza conducted in 1977, 1978, and 1981—published as *The Burning Light: Action and Organizing in the Mexican Community in California* (1982)—provide insight into Galarza's organizing career as well as his ideas about bilingual education and university teaching. An introduction to the interviews by Mary Anna Colwell and a biographical sketch published in the *Guide to the Papers of Ernesto Garlarza* (1984) are also helpful biographical sources. For a discussion of Galarza as an ethnic leader of the Mexican-American community, see Laura Gomez, *From Barrio Boys to College Boys: Ethnic Identity, Ethnic Organizations, and the Mexican American Elite: The Cases of Ernesto Galarza and Manuel Ruiz, Jr.* (1989), published by the Stanford Center for Chicano Research Working Paper Series. Another helpful source on Galarza's career as an organizer is Joan London and Henry Anderson, *So Shall Ye Reap: The Story of Cesar Chavez and the Farm Workers' Movement* (1970).

MICHELLE BRATTAIN

GALBREATH, Charles Burleigh (25 Feb. 1858–23 Feb. 1934), librarian, historian, and teacher, was born on a farm in Columbiana County, Ohio, near the town of Leetonia, the son of Edward Paxson Galbreath and Jane Minerva Shaw. His parents were Quakers of Scotch-Irish heritage who moved to Ohio from North Carolina due to their antislavery stand. They instilled in their son an appreciation and interest in the antislavery cause that probably influenced his research on John Brown, the Underground Railroad, and his lifetime association with the Republican party. Galbreath graduated from New Lisbon High School in 1879 and continued his education at Mount Union College in Alliance, Ohio, where he earned the bachelor of philosophy degree in 1882, bachelor of commercial science and bachelor of arts in 1883, and master of arts in 1894. In 1882 he married Ida Kelley of Salem, Ohio; they had one son.

After leaving Mount Union College in 1883 Galbreath worked in two administrative positions as superintendent of the Wilmont (Ohio) public schools (1884–1886) and the East Palestine (Ohio) public schools (1886–1893). He was also school examiner of Columbiana County during the latter period. From 1893 to 1896 Galbreath taught history and literature and also served as vice principal at Mount Hope Academy in Rogers, Ohio. He became the school's principal in early 1896. This new position ended within months when Galbreath accepted an appointment on 25 May as librarian of the Ohio State Library in Columbus.

Galbreath held the position of state librarian during three separate periods, 1896–1911, 1915–1918, and 1927–1928. He was appointed as the first librarian to work in a reorganized state library in compliance with the "Garfield Library Law," which established a new board of commissioners to oversee the policies and activities of the library. The board sought to develop a state library that would be more responsive to the needs of all Ohio citizens, not just the legislature and state agencies. Because of his extensive education and administrative experience, Galbreath was viewed as the perfect choice to lead the state library into a new era of service. In *The Library Movement in Ohio* (1909) he wrote that "the State Library is the public library of the state and citizens are entitled to the best service it can give."

During his administration Galbreath introduced modern methods of librarianship and emphasized the preservation of archival materials. He directed a thorough cleaning of the library, the rearrangement of newspapers and U.S. government documents, the classification of the general collection, and the organization of a legislative reference service. Galbreath was particularly interested in building the library collection on Ohio history through the acquisition of gifts and the purchase of important Ohio newspapers and periodicals. The public was given greater access to the library, and this included Ohioans throughout the state. The state library extended services to many people in small towns and rural areas by way of traveling libraries patterned after a similar service in New York. Beginning in 1896 collections of two or three dozen books were sent to small communities for the purpose of providing books where few existed and to encourage reading and education that would promote the development of libraries statewide. By 1909 1,031 traveling libraries had been sent to 832 communities.

Despite Galbreath's achievements as state librarian, his first term in office came to an end in 1911 after the political party in control of the governor's office changed from Republican to Democratic. The position of librarian was supposed to be apolitical, but during most of the period from 1896 to 1921, when the governor was a Republican, Galbreath was librarian, and when the governor was a Democrat (1911–1915,

1918–1921), John Henry Newman was librarian. Ever since his days in East Palestine, Galbreath had closely identified with and worked for the state Republican party. He edited the Republican newspaper *Reveille* for two years and supported U.S. intervention in Cuba in 1897 to bring freedom and independence to the island. After leaving the state library in 1911 he used his organizational skills in state politics. He was elected to serve as secretary of the fourth Ohio constitutional convention from 1912 to 1913, and after a second term as state librarian he worked, from 1918 to 1920, with legislative committees, including the Joint Legislative Committee on Survey and Reorganization of State Administrative Agencies.

In 1920 Galbreath accepted an appointment as secretary, librarian, and editor of publications of the Ohio State Archaeological and Historical Society in Columbus. Throughout his thirteen-year career with the society, Galbreath sought to increase its revenues from the state general assembly and from private sources, to increase the library collection of books, periodicals, manuscripts, and newspapers related to Ohio without duplicating the state library, and find funding for adequate facilities and publications. He also edited and contributed articles to the quarterly *Ohio Archaeological and Historical Society Publications* and to the monthly newsletter published by the society, *Museum Echoes*. Galbreath acquired a photostat machine in 1923 to make copies of manuscripts owned by other institutions, and he helped initiate the state archives through the transfer of state agency documents to the library in accordance with an act passed by the general assembly in 1927. His achievements at the society were also illustrated by the addition of two new wings to the main building on the campus of Ohio State University in 1926 and 1929 and the expansion of the newspaper collection to approximately 25,000 bound volumes by 1933. The newspaper collection was named for him after his death in Columbus.

Throughout his life Galbreath was a prolific author of historical essays, biographical sketches, and articles related to Ohio and his lifelong interest in antislavery issues. His antislavery interests led to the publication of a long biographical article on the life and Ohio connections of antislavery activist John Brown and an article on the antislavery movement in Galbreath's home county of Columbiana. Both articles appeared with related works by other authors in the *Ohio Archaeological and Historical Society Publications*, vol. 30 (1921). He also wrote poems and several books, including the compilation *Sketches of Ohio Libraries* (1902), which includes information about activities at the state library, and a five-volume *History of Ohio* (1925). He also compiled and edited the two-volume *Proceedings and Debates of the Fourth Constitutional Convention of the State of Ohio* (1912–1913). He was noted for both his elegant writing style and his skills as a public speaker. Galbreath held membership in a variety of local and national organizations, including the American Library Association, American Historical Association, National Association of State Librarians (serving

as its first president in 1900), Ohio Library Association, and local literary organizations—the Kit Kat Club of Columbus and the Columbus Verse-Writers Guild.

• The Ohio Historical Society in Columbus houses many of Galbreath's professional papers, including a large collection related to his work at the society. For general biographical information consult *Ohio Archaeological and Historical Society Quarterly* 43 (1934): 115–29; *Museum Echoes* 2 (Jan.–Feb. 1929): 1, 3; and *Museum Echoes* 7 (Apr. 1934): 13–16. See also James K. Mercer, *Representative Men of Ohio, 1896–1897* (1896), including editions for 1900–1903 (1903) and 1904–1908 (1909). For more information about his work at the state library consult Sidney Cohen, "Biographical Data on the Librarians of the Ohio State Library, 1817–1960" (M.A. thesis, Kent State Univ., 1961); for additional information on his work at the historical society see "Report of the Secretary, Minutes of the Annual Meeting of the O.A.H.S." in annual volumes of *Ohio Archaeological and Historical Society Publications* (1920–1933). An obituary is in the *New York Times*, 24 Feb. 1934.

DAVID ALAN LINCOVE

GALE, Benjamin (14 Dec. 1715–6 May 1790), physician, scientist, and political polemicist, was born in Jamaica, New York, the son of John Gale, a miller, and Mary (maiden name unknown). The family moved to Goshen, New York, in 1721. Gale prepared for college with Connecticut Anglican Samuel Johnson and graduated from Yale in 1733. He moved to Killingworth, Connecticut, where he studied medicine under the Reverend Jared Eliot, the most distinguished physician in the colony and a renowned agricultural scientist. In 1739 Gale married Eliot's only daughter Hannah Eliot; the couple had eight children.

Gale was considered a man of "great Skill in the medical Profession—& a successful Practitioner" (Dexter, *The Literary Diary of Ezra Stiles*, vol. 3, p. 393). He experimented with mercurial inoculation against smallpox and in 1765 published "Historical Memoirs, Relating to the Practice of Inoculation for the Small Pox" in *Philosophical Transactions of the Royal Society of London*, to which group he was elected a corresponding member. Controversy always followed Gale, and in 1769 he had to respond publicly to accusations that he had sent the Royal Society false and exaggerated accounts of his success in order to magnify his own importance. A strong believer in smallpox inoculation, he three times unsuccessfully petitioned the Connecticut General Assembly for the right to erect an inoculation hospital. Gale published notes in 1765 on "the successful Application of Salt to Wounds made by the Biting of Rattle Snakes" and in 1787 on the value of the same treatment for bites from a mad dog.

Gale was also a businessman and, like his father-in-law, interested in agricultural improvement. In 1744 Gale and his Eliot relatives built a steel mill in Killingworth, which they successfully operated until the 1780s. In July 1766 he noted, "We carry on our Steel Manufacture very Brisk." The Royal Society of Arts and Sciences in London awarded Gale a gold medal in 1770 for his invention of the drill plow, a tool designed to deliver seed and manure into the ground at the same time. Gale helped publicize the type-founding experiments of Abel Buell and encouraged David Bushnell in his submarine experiments. His agricultural interests found expression in the natural history and uses of "Black Grass" (Newport *Mercury*, 7 July 1766) and "Observations on the Culture of Smyrna Wheat" (*Memoirs of the American Academy of Arts and Sciences* 1 [1785]). He also experimented with growing Tartarian rhubarb, made molasses from cornstalks, and was an amateur vintner and distiller.

The freemen of Killingworth elected Gale to represent them in the general assembly twenty-three times between May 1747 and October 1770. He also served as a justice of the peace from 1746 to 1755 and 1759 to 1773. Gale was best known in Connecticut, however, as a virulent partisan of the Old Light political cause, which represented the establishment and was opposed to awakened religion, westward expansion, and ardent protests against the British government. Gale burst on the political stage with his savage 1755 attack on Yale president and New Light luminary Thomas Clap in *The Present State of the Colony of Connecticut Considered*, calling Clap "an Assuming, Arbitrary, Designing Man; who under a Cloak of Zeal for Orthodoxy, design'd to govern both Church and State and Damn all who would not worship the Beast" (Bushman, p. 248). This publication marked a new departure in colony politics by its assault on a prominent leader and Gale's attempt to mobilize public opinion in a legislative controversy over college funding. As a result of this pamphlet, the general assembly voted to cancel its annual appropriation to the college and stripped Gale of his justice of the peace commission.

Gale's successful attack on President Clap led to a significant decline in standards of political decorum, increased political bitterness in the colony, and launched a pamphlet war that lasted for fifteen years. The doctor renewed his assault in 1759 with *A Letter to a Member of the Lower House of Assembly of the Colony of Connecticut: Shewing, That the Taxes at Yale-College, Are Stated Higher Than Necessary to Defray the Annual Expences*. In two additional tracts, Gale broadened his attacks to charge that New Lights were engaged in an election plot to overthrow the Old Light majority in the upper house. Passage of the Stamp Act in 1765 provided New Lights with the opportunity to do so. Although Gale did not support the Stamp Act, in October 1765 he was one of five deputies to the general assembly who voted against a resolution condemning the act as a violation of the charter and destructive of the colony's liberties. He condemned efforts of the Sons of Liberty, New Lights in another guise, to defeat Old Lights, upholders of parliamentary authority, in the 1766 election. He referred to the Sons of Liberty as people who in "Rage & Folly" intended to carry out a "wicked Sceem [*sic*] . . . to destroy us." After the Old Light defeat, Gale strove unsuccessfully to reverse the 1766 election results. In pamphlets published in 1769 and 1770 he castigated New Light members of the Susquehannah Company, established to promote ter-

ritorial expansion in northeastern Pennsylvania. Shortly thereafter Gale withdrew from politics.

When the revolutionary crisis came, Gale claimed that he was "firmly attach'd to the cause of Liberty," yet he was never entirely trusted by patriots. Ezra Stiles believed that Gale "was always against the Amer. Revolution" (Dexter, *The Literary Diary of Ezra Stiles*, vol. 3, p. 393). Gale accused the local committee of inspection of intercepting and publishing his private letters and complained that the "Cry of Heresy or even of Toryism" was directed at him. During the war, therefore, he devoted himself to agricultural and religious pursuits, served on a committee to examine military surgeons, and testified to the good character of several Long Island refugees. Gale returned to the political fray in 1782 with *Brief, Decent, but Free Remarks, and Observations on Several Laws Passed by the Honorable Legislature of the State of Connecticut, since the Year 1775*, in which he condemned the assembly's revolutionary leadership as self-seeking men who had taken control of the government and through maladministration had led it into bankruptcy.

Gale opposed the French alliance, railed against privileges sought by officers in the Continental army, and criticized Connecticut's decision not to write a new constitution but to continue governing itself under the charter of 1662. He strongly opposed the movement to draft a new federal Constitution, however, arguing in February 1787 against what he called "a fixed and Settled Design to Alter The Form of our *Republican* Government . . . and to Convert It into An *Aristocracy*" (Jordan, p. 18).

Gale devoted a great deal of attention in his last twenty years to studies of and correspondence on Old Testament "Prophecies & the speedy Second Appea[nce] of the Messiah" (Dexter, *The Literary Diary of Ezra Stiles*, vol. 1, p. 324), the results of which were published in 1788 in *A Brief Essay; or, An Attempt to Prove, from the Prophetick Writings of Old and New Testament, What Period of Prophecy the Church of God Is Now Under*. Gale never joined any church, yet he was an enemy of both deists and Anglicans. He died in Killingworth believing that the Second Coming was close at hand.

Stiles termed Gale "a singular Character . . . of an acrimonious Temper." Gale was a zealous defender of the old order and a man who resolutely opposed all the major trends of his era. A versatile and fascinating figure, he was a prominent physician and scientist, a person of considerable political influence, and the individual most responsible for the contentious character of Connecticut politics in the twenty years before the American Revolution. Even in death Gale did not escape controversy, as his 1788 will was "Judged Illegal" by probate court because of doubts about his mental competence.

• Gale's correspondence is in the Ezra Stiles Papers, Yale University, and the William Samuel Johnson Papers, Connecticut Historical Society. Gale published some two dozen pamphlets and essays, some under his own name and others under the pseudonyms "A. Z.," "Plain Facts," and "A Connecticut Farmer." A partial list is in Franklin Bowditch Dexter, *Biographical Sketches of the Graduates of Yale College*, vol. 1 (1885). Gale letters are published in Dexter, ed., *Extracts from the Itineraries and Other Miscellanies of Ezra Stiles . . . with a Selection from his Correspondence* (1916); Dexter, ed., "A Selection from the Correspondence and Miscellaneous Papers of Jared Ingersoll," *Papers of the New Haven Colony Historical Society* 9 (1918); "Correspondence of Silas Deane," *Collections of the Connecticut Historical Society* 2 (1870); and "The Wyllys Papers," *Collections of the Connecticut Historical Society* 21 (1924). Articles on Gale include George C. Groce, Jr., "Benjamin Gale," *New England Quarterly* 10 (1937): 697–716; E. H. Jenkins, "Benjamin Gale," *Yale Journal of Biology and Medicine* 2 (1930): 257–68; and Philip H. Jordan, Jr., "Connecticut Anti-Federalism on the Eve of the Constitutional Convention: A Letter from Benjamin Gale to Erastus Wolcott, February 10, 1787," *Connecticut Historical Society Bulletin* 28 (1963): 14–21. Additional information is in Dexter, "Notes on Some New Haven Loyalists, Including Those Graduated at Yale," *Papers of the New Haven Colony Historical Society* 9 (1918): 29–45; and Dexter, ed., *The Literary Diary of Ezra Stiles* (3 vols., 1901). Gale is featured in Richard L. Bushman, *From Puritan to Yankee: Character and the Social Order in Connecticut, 1690–1765* (1967); Christopher Collier, *Roger Sherman's Connecticut: Yankee Politics and the American Revolution* (1971); Lawrence Henry Gipson, *American Loyalist: Jared Ingersoll* (1920; repr. 1971); Louis Leonard Tucker, *Puritan Protagonist: President Thomas Clap of Yale College* (1962); and Oscar Zeichner, *Connecticut's Years of Controversy, 1750–1776* (1949).

BRUCE P. STARK

GALE, George Washington (3 Dec. 1789–13 Sept. 1861), Presbyterian clergyman and educator, was born at Stanford, Dutchess County, New York, the son of Josiah Gale, a farmer, and Rachel Mead. Gale's mother died in 1797, and his father died in 1798. Until 1808, when he went to Middlebury Academy in Middlebury, Vermont, Gale lived with several of his older sisters and spent short terms teaching common school. He entered the junior class of Union College, Schenectady, New York, in 1812 and graduated in 1814. Gale studied theology at Princeton Seminary, beginning in late fall 1814. In 1816 he received a ministerial license from the Hudson Presbytery and began preaching in several small churches in Dutchess County, New York. In 1817 he went to Schenectady to study theology privately. Gale worked for six months on behalf of the Female Missionary Society of Western New York but went back to Princeton in 1818. He left without graduating in 1819 when he received an invitation to preach from Presbyterians at Adams, Jefferson County, New York. Gale was ordained and installed as the minister of the Presbyterian Church of Adams on 27 October 1819. Gale married Harriet Selden in 1820. Due to poor health, Gale announced his resignation in 1823 and left Adams in 1824. While at Adams, Gale had given theological instruction to Charles G. Finney, the famed evangelist who sparked the great religious revivals that were known collectively as the Great Revival, which swept central and western New York in the 1820s.

In 1825 Gale settled on a farm in Oneida County, New York, and began to give theological instruction to young men who were Finney converts and who were anxious to enter the ministry without having to complete the traditional Presbyterian seminary curriculum. Gale emphasized the practical aspects of ministry in order that his students might join in the campaign to evangelize the West. The students offset the cost of their educations by performing manual labor on Gale's farm. As their number grew, Gale began a search for a site to organize a school.

Gale moved to a farm of about 115 acres in Whitesboro, just west of Utica, New York, and in May 1827 opened Oneida Academy in the old Hugh White farmhouse. The school was chartered in 1829 as the Oneida Institute of Science and Industry. Students were given a classical education along with opportunities for manual labor in the fields and shops. Oneida Institute was then the most widely known American version of the social regeneration idea of education, combining learning and labor, pioneered in Europe for poor youth by Phillip Emmanuel von Fellenberg, the Swiss educator and philanthropist, in the early 1800s.

With support from the Presbyterian Education Society, Gale sought to strengthen theological studies at Oneida Institute and attempted unsuccessfully to recruit Finney and others as theological faculty. Some of the more zealous students, strong Finney admirers, began to complain that Gale was not providing the school with aggressive enough leadership. This discontent increased after July 1832 when a group of students organized New York State's first antislavery society and announced their support for William Lloyd Garrison's call for immediate emancipation. Feeling that new leadership was essential to the welfare of Oneida Institute, Gale resigned as principal. On his Oneida years, Gale later wrote, "I had done enough, expanded means and labor enough to bring the Institution to its maturity and tested the practicability of combining labor and study, and the carrying forward of the enterprise might now devolve on someone else."

While still in Whitesboro, Gale began to talk with a number of families who were interested in migrating to Illinois. In 1836 he and his family and about thirty others from the Whitestown area journeyed to Knox County, Illinois, where the company purchased 20,000 acres of federal land. The settlers named their new community Galesburg in honor of Gale. A staunch advocate of The Society for Promoting Manual Labor in Literary Institutions, Gale led in the formation of Knox Manual Labor College, later known as Knox College, at Galesburg. A preparatory school was erected in 1838, and the college opened in 1841. Hiram Huntington Kellogg became president, but Gale, as one of the trustees and the principal founder of the college, was intimately connected with the development of Knox College.

Harriet Gale died in 1840 as the result of a difficult childbirth; seven of her ten children survived her. Gale married Esther Williams of Galesburg in 1841. She and her infant son died in 1842. Gale's third wife was Lucy Merriam, whom he married in 1847 at New Haven, Connecticut.

Gale served as professor of moral philosophy and rhetoric until 1857 when he resigned after a heated controversy with Jonathan Blanchard, Kellogg's successor as president in 1845. Personal rivalry, denominational differences, and political disagreements separated Gale and Blanchard. Gale led the Presbyterian faction that opposed Blanchard's efforts to entangle Knox College in abolitionist politics, and he resented Blanchard's promotion of Congregationalist influence over the school. Gale and his supporters among the trustees forced Blanchard's resignation, leaving the more conservative Gale faction in control of Knox College. Settlement of the dispute, however, included the provision that Gale resign from the college faculty. He died in Galesburg, Illinois.

As founder and first principal of Oneida Institute and principal organizer of Knox College, Gale was an important American pioneer in the movement to establish educational institutions based on the manual labor philosophy. As an educator and theologian, he also influenced many young men to become involved in Christian revivalism and social reform, chief of whom was the famed American evangelist Charles G. Finney.

• A collection of Gale papers does not exist, though there are letters from Gale to Finney in the Finney papers, Oberlin College, Oberlin, Ohio. For further documentation see George W. Gale, *The Gale Family Records in England and the United States* (1866). Gale's daughter, Margaret Gale Hitchcock, transcribed an unfinished autobiography that covers the pre-Illinois period of his life, *Autobiography (to 1834) of George Washington Gale (1789–1861)* (1964). Gale describes the goals and program of Oneida Institute in "Oneida Institute," *Quarterly of the American Education Society* 1 (Nov. 1829): 112–15, and in *First Report of the Trustees of Oneida Academy, March 1828* (1828). On the founding of Knox College, see his *A Brief History of Knox College* (1845). Secondary sources include Wallace G. Lamb, "George Washington Gale: Theologian and Educator" (Ph.D. diss., Syracuse Univ., 1949); Charles P. Coates, "From George Gale to Arthur Morgan," *Educational Review* 81 (1926): 53–55; Milton C. Sernett, *Abolition's Axe: Beriah Green, Oneida Institute, and the Black Freedom Struggle* (1986); and Hermann R. Muelder, *Fighters for Freedom: The History of the Anti-Slavery Activities of Men and Women Associated with Knox College* (1959).

MILTON C. SERNETT

GALE, Henry Gordon (12 Sept. 1874–16 Nov. 1942), physicist, was born in Aurora, Illinois, the son of Eli Holbrook Gale, a physician, and Adelaide Parker. Gale's mother died when he was only six weeks old, after which he was raised by his maternal grandparents. He graduated from high school in Lacon, Illinois, and completed college preparatory studies in Aurora in 1892. That fall he enrolled with the first undergraduate class at the new University of Chicago. He excelled in student activities, especially football, and his studies, earning his A.B. in 1896. Three years later, Gale was awarded a Ph.D. in physics, summa

cum laude, for his experiments (under the direction of Albert A. Michelson) on the relation between the density and refractive index of air using a pressure gauge of his own invention. Except for seventeen months of military service, Gale would spend the next forty-one years of his life associated with his alma mater. In 1901 he married Agnes Spofford Cook, whom he had met at the university; they had one child.

Gale made many beneficial contributions to physics and to his beloved university as a teacher, researcher, and administrator. After receiving his doctorate, Gale was appointed an assistant in the physics department to teach introductory college physics courses. There he began a long partnership with Robert A. Millikan, who had joined the department three years earlier. Based on their teaching experiences, they coauthored an introductory text for secondary schools and colleges, which emphasized coordinated laboratory experiments and practical applications. This highly regarded *First Course in Physics* (1906) went through four revisions by 1938 and sold more than two million copies. Over the next thirty-five years, Millikan and Gale wrote ten college and high school physics textbooks. Many of these books proved successful because their authors were able to address the different educational backgrounds and changing needs of the growing numbers of physics students and teachers.

Like his educational publications, Gale's experimental researches in various aspects of spectroscopy were usually collaborative efforts with highly respected colleagues from the University of Chicago. Gale excelled at resolving difficult problems with apparatus and making careful observations. His first investigation, on solar spectra, was done in alliance with George E. Hale and Walter S. Adams between 1906 and 1915 at the Mount Wilson Observatory in California. Adams and Gale convincingly demonstrated that changes in the spectra of sunspots, like those for light sources in the laboratory, could be explained by differing physical conditions (such as temperature or pressure).

Gale's career was interrupted in 1917 by voluntary service as an officer in the meteorological section of the Signal Corps in France. Returning home in 1918 decorated with the Legion of Honor, Gale resumed a second joint effort he had begun in 1910 with Michelson. Together they determined the rigidity of the Earth to be greater than steel. Gale made all the meticulous measurements of tides in the Earth, simulated by water-filled pipes buried in the ground, with a sensitive optical instrument (an interferometer Michelson had perfected). They joined forces a second time, in the early 1920s, to measure the effect of the Earth's rotation on the velocity of light as a test of Albert Einstein's general theory of relativity. Because Michelson was ill, Gale supervised the construction and use of an elaborate apparatus of mile-long evacuated piping containing two colliding light beams. The resulting shift in interference fringes agreed with Einstein's predictions, but Michelson and Gale were reluctant to adopt Einstein's ideas. These and several other scientific achievements earned Gale the respect of the American physics community. He was elected president of the American Physical Society (1929–1931), chairman of the Division of Physics of the National Research Council (1920–1921), vice president of the American Association for the Advancement of Science (1934), and he coedited the *Astrophysical Journal* for twenty-eight years.

Unlike most of his academic colleagues, Gale embraced administrative duties of growing responsibility at the University of Chicago. He served as a dean of the college from 1908 to 1922 and of the Ogden Graduate School of Science (later the Division of Physical Science) from 1922 until his retirement in 1940. As a dean and chairman of the physics department from 1925 to 1940, Gale was a strong advocate for research as the primary pursuit of the university, at a time when its president, Robert M. Hutchins, was refocusing its aims on undergraduate education in the classics. A year after his retirement, Gale died in the University of Chicago hospital.

Gale devoted his entire academic career to the advancement of science at the University of Chicago. He is remembered less for his individual talents or accomplishments and more for the contributions he made in concert with other eminent scientists in teaching, research, and administration.

• Many of Gale's papers, including correspondence, notebooks, manuscripts, reprints of articles, and photographs, are located in the University of Chicago Department of Special Collections. His friend Henry Crew wrote a well-informed obituary in the *Astrophysical Journal* 97 (Mar. 1943): 85–88. A commemorative issue, *Henry Gordan Gale, 1874–1942: A Record of the Memorial Services Conducted by Members of the Faculty of the University of Chicago on November 18, 1942 at the Joseph Bond Chapel, Illinois* (1943), contains a complete bibliography of his research publications. Alfred Romer discusses the Millikan-Gale collaboration in "Robert A. Millikan, Physics Teacher," *Physics Teacher* 16 (Feb. 1978): 78–85. Loyd Swenson, Jr., describes the Michelson-Gale joint research efforts in *The Ethereal Aether* (1972). An obituary is in the *New York Times*, 17 November 1942.

JOHN L. MICHEL

GALE, Zona (26 Aug. 1874–27 Dec. 1938), novelist and playwright, was born in Portage, Wisconsin, the daughter of Charles Franklin Gale, a railroad worker, and Eliza Beers. Gale's father introduced her to the intellectual life through diverse writings by Plato, Ralph Waldo Emerson, Charles Darwin, and others, but she had a particularly intense relationship with her mother, a possessive and deeply religious woman who contributed to Gale's notion of an all-encompassing female life-force. Gale's bond with her mother also seems to have been instrumental in preventing her from marrying the love of her life, poet Ridgely Torrence, following a two-year courtship, although she intermittently corresponded with Torrence for the remainder of her life. Only in 1928, after the death of her mother, did Gale marry William L. Breese, a stocking manufacturer from Portage, with whom she adopted a daughter. (Breese also had a daughter from a previous marriage.)

Following her graduation from the University of Wisconsin with a B.A. in 1895 and an M.A. in literature in 1899, Gale worked for a year and a half on the editorial staff of the Milwaukee *Evening Wisconsin* before beginning a six-year stint as a reporter with the Milwaukee *Journal*. She also worked for a while for the New York *Evening World* but resigned to pursue a career in creative writing. Her first novel, *Romance Island* (1906), is an improbable adventure tale framed by a sentimental love story, but it won a $2,000 prize for short fiction, after which Gale began a prolific output of novels, short stories and plays. Her first collections of short stories, *The Loves of Pelleas and Etarre* (1907), *Friendship Village* (1908), and *Friendship Village Love Stories* (1909), exemplify Gale's earliest themes of love and community in small-town, folksy settings based on Portage. Pressure from her mother led Gale to return there on a permanent basis most likely in late 1909, though she continued to spend long periods in New York City. Her novels from this era include *Mothers to Men* (1911), *Christmas* (1912), *Heart's Kindred* (1915), *A Daughter of the Morning* (1917), and *Birth* (1918). Like her earlier short stories, these were drawn from characters and situations suggested by Portage and evoke the wholesome sentiments of simple family lives and loves in a rural, middle-class small town.

It was the wedding of her two literary interests, fiction and drama, that produced her quintessential work, *Miss Lulu Bett* (1920), the novel and play for which she is best remembered. Produced and directed by Brock Pemberton, *Miss Lulu Bett* opened on 27 December 1920 and ran for 201 performances. Although some critics wrote that Gale lacked the theatrical experience and background to write a great play, most found it to be among the best of its time. Gale was favorably compared with Eugene O'Neill and other important contemporary dramatists. Frank Harris, writing in the *New Republic* (12 Jan. 1921), asserted that Gale "has done authentically what perhaps only a feminist and certainly what only an artist could do. She has shown, in perfect American terms, the serious comedy of an emancipation—the sort of emancipation that no national optimism can set aside." The play was awarded the Pulitzer Prize for drama in 1921, but it was a controversial selection. Burns Mantle's annual "Best Plays" volume had failed even to list it.

Miss Lulu Bett is set in the arid small-town Wisconsin home of Ina and Dwight Deacon, where Ina's spiritless sister Lulu also resides, living off the charity of the Deacons by doing menial household chores. When Dwight and his brother Ninian force her to endure a humiliating mock civil wedding ceremony that turns out to be legal (despite the fact that Ninian already has a wife), Lulu undergoes a significant feminist awakening and a subsequent revolt against the middle-class values that have victimized her. Controversy was generated over Gale's decision to rewrite the ending of the play after it opened, changing the ending to a more conventional, happy one by bringing Ninian back to Lulu with news of his first wife's death. In the *Nation* (2 Feb. 1921), Ludwig Lewisohn noted of the change that Lulu's "act of liberation is thus stultified and with it the significance and strength of the dramatic action sacrificed at one blow." Gale defended the change on the grounds that life does not always end unhappily, and the softening of Lulu's feminist revolt may well have contributed to the play's long run and the subsequent Pulitzer Prize, awarded by a conservative selection panel. Gale's few other plays, most of which were adaptations of her novels and short stories, include *The Neighbors* (1914), *Uncle Jimmy* (1922), *Mister Pitt* (1925), *The Clouds* (1932), *Evening Clothes* (1932), and *Faint Perfume* (1934), but none achieved the acclaim of *Miss Lulu Bett*.

The financial success provided by her early writings allowed Gale to devote considerable time in support of pacifist activities during World War I (some of her Portage neighbors suspected her of being a German sympathizer), labor unions, woman suffrage, and Progressive party politics. In 1924 she actively campaigned for Wisconsin's third party presidential candidate Robert La Follette, although she subsequently became disenchanted with him, and she worked actively in the movement to free Italian anarchists Nicola Sacco and Bartolomeo Vanzetti. Although Gale subsequently became best known as a prolific writer of fiction and drama, her commitment to a number of causes and civic projects led to several works of nonfiction, including *Civic Improvement in Little Towns* (1913), *What Women Won in Wisconsin* (1922), *Portage, Wisconsin and Other Essays* (1928), and *Frank Miller of Mission Inn* (1938). In general, all of these are sentimentalized yet earnest polemical tracts of little interest except as historical documentation of a bygone era.

Following the success of *Miss Lulu Bett*, Gale continued to write short stories, which were collected under the titles *Peace in Friendship Village* (1919), *Yellow Gentians and Blue* (1927), *Bridal Pond* (1930), and *Old Fashioned Tales* (1933). These collections, along with her later novels, from *Faint Perfume* (1923) to *Magna* (published posthumously in 1939), continue to focus on middle-class existence and provincial attitudes. However, Gale's later fiction demonstrates an evolution away from her earlier romanticized views toward a darker impressionistic realism that led many critics to compare her with Sinclair Lewis. Although Lewis, Sherwood Anderson, and Willa Cather found similarly potent themes and characters in small-town life (Cather wrote to Gale in 1928: "I am haunted by Portage"), Gale's uniqueness lay in her ability to hear small-town voices even in the big city where, as she stated in a May 1921 Janet Flanner interview in *Shadowland*, "I overheard them, as perfect in their provincialism as the day they left Main street and the village store." Writing of Gale's major works in *Our American Theatre*, Oliver Sayler has noted that, in examining provincial small-town life, "Zona Gale has penetrated

to the exciting significance beneath that same smug exterior."

After a visit to Japan in 1937 at the invitation of the Japanese government, Gale began her autobiography but became ill and died suddenly of pneumonia in a Chicago hospital. As a result of her flowery verbiage and sentimental mysticism, the latter based on equal parts Theosophy and transcendental pantheism, Gale tends to be overlooked today; her novels and short stories are rarely read, and the plays are seldom staged. However, in her time she was an influential feminist writer and a leader among the so-called small-town novelists of the post–World War I era. At her finest, in *Miss Lulu Bett* and some of her later fiction, Gale succeeds in moving the reader through her impressively consistent characterizations of women who, trapped in the confines of middle-class provinciality, know that "life is something more than that which we believe it to be."

• Substantial collections of Gale's papers can be found at the State Historical Society of Wisconsin and the University of Wisconsin, both in Madison, and in the Ridgely Torrence Collection in the Princeton University Library. A useful clipping file is in the Billy Rose Theatre Collection of the New York Public Library at Lincoln Center. Among the available sources, August Derleth's biography, *Still Small Voice* (1940), and Harold P. Simonson's study, *Zona Gale* (1962), are the most reliable. Gale is examined in Robert Gard, *Grassroots Theater: A Search for Regional Arts in America* (1955); Ima H. Herron, *The Small Town in American Literature* (1939); and June Sochen, *Movers and Shakers: American Women Thinkers and Activists, 1900–1970* (1974). Useful sketches are in the *American Magazine*, June 1921; the *Bookman*, Apr. 1923; *Capital Times*, 29–31 May and 3–4 June 1974; and the *Wisconsin Magazine of History*, Autumn 1962. Gale's work is also surveyed in two fine documentary films, *Some Will Be Apples* (1974) and *Zona Gale: Her Life and Writings* (1989).

JAMES FISHER

GALES, Joseph (10 Apr. 1786–21 July 1860), journalist and publisher, was born in Eckington, England, the son of Joseph Gales, a printer, and Winifred Marshall. The elder Gales was a political refugee who brought his family in 1795 to Philadelphia, where he published the *Independent Gazette*. The younger Gales was taught to read Latin by his mother. He also attended a private school in Raleigh, North Carolina, where the family moved after 1797. He attended the University of North Carolina for a short time but was expelled for disciplinary reasons.

Gales returned home to work on his father's newspaper, the *Raleigh Register*, but the elder Gales, who feared that his son would become indolent, sent him to Philadelphia as an apprentice printer. In 1807, after receiving a diploma from the Typographical Society of Philadelphia, Gales became a reporter for the *National Intelligencer* in Washington, D.C. Its owner Samuel Harrison Smith had been approached to hire Gales on a trial basis by the elder Gales, who wanted to buy the paper for his son. Gales was taught shorthand by his father, and he was assigned to report the daily proceedings in the Senate for the triweekly *Intelligencer*.

In 1809 Gales became Smith's partner; the following year he became the sole proprietor when Smith retired. In 1812 Gales's brother-in-law William Winston Seaton became an equal partner in the business. Both men shared the work and the profits. In 1813 Gales married Sarah Juliana Maria Lee.

Under Gales and Seaton the *National Intelligencer* was the most extensive printing business in the United States, remaining so until Congress reduced appropriations for official printing prior to the Civil War. The two personally reported the proceedings of both houses of Congress, with Gales covering the Senate and Seaton the House. Both were liked by the members of Congress and were even invited to dip from the official snuff boxes. Gales wrote most of the editorials, which were usually short and compact. Most of the space in the newspaper, which became a daily in 1813, was devoted to running condensed versions of the previous day's proceedings in Congress.

The *Intelligencer* under Smith had been the semiofficial organ of the Jefferson administration. Under Gales and Seaton it maintained a similar role in the administration of John Quincy Adams. The newspaper warmly supported James Madison in the War of 1812, and Gales enlisted in the infantry stationed around the capital to demonstrate his loyalty to his adopted country. He and Seaton took turns supervising the newspaper's operations on alternate days until the British attacked Washington in 1813 and destroyed the presses and type.

Gales and Seaton enjoyed their greatest period of success and influence while the old Jeffersonian political coalition, known as the Republicans, controlled the federal government. From 1819 to 1827 Gales and Seaton served as the official printers of Congress and they profited handsomely. The *National Intelligencer* was the medium through which government declarations, decrees, and laws were announced to the American public. The *Intelligencer* was distributed free in the mail to all newspaper editors in the country, who clipped and reprinted its contents. Thus it served as a national clearinghouse for government news.

With the election of Andrew Jackson in 1828 (an event that Gales viewed as a national calamity) and the decline of the Republicans, the influence of the paper began to wane. Gales turned his political support to the Whigs, and later to the Constitutional Democrats. He served as mayor of Washington, D.C., from 1827 to 1830. Despite the financial success of the *National Intelligencer*, Gales and Seaton incurred significant debt that forced them to obtain loans from the Bank of the United States. This compromised their position opposing Jackson's war on the bank, which aimed at eliminating the Second Bank of the United States. Gales did not believe that government by the masses could succeed, but he encouraged liberalism in religion and was a member of the Unitarian Church. Under Gales the *National Intelligencer* supported free education and Henry Clay's "American System." The paper

opposed war with Mexico in 1846, but it supported continued compromise on slavery. Gales also gave material support to the American Colonization Society.

The role of the *National Intelligencer* as a national disseminator of government news was challenged in the 1820s by the appearance of "letter writers" sent by newspapers outside of Washington. From this would blossom the Washington press corps of modern times. The influx of editors during the Jackson administration meant competition for government printing contracts, as well as competition for newspaper readership. One of these new papers, the *Washington Globe*, and its subsidiary the *Congressional Globe*, replaced the *Intelligencer* as the official printer of government policies and recorder of congressional debates by 1851.

Nevertheless, Gales's efforts in recording the daily affairs of Congress left an invaluable record of the functioning of the nation's government in its formative years. The files of the daily edition of the *Intelligencer* provide an illuminating running account of government at work. These accounts were compiled and published in twenty volumes as the *Register of Debates* (1825–1837), covering the period between 1825 and 1837. A second series, the *Annals of Congress* (1834, 1849–1856), covers the period between 1789 and 1824. Also valuable are the *American State Papers* (1832–1861), a compilation of government documents dating before 1832 and published in thirty-eight volumes. Gales died at his home estate, "Eckington," in Washington, D.C.

• Gales's letters are in the Martin Van Buren Collection in the Library of Congress. A definitive study of Gales and the *Intelligencer* is William E. Ames, *A History of the National Intelligencer* (1972). The *Intelligencer*'s role as a disseminator of government news is examined in Culver H. Smith, *The Press, Politics, and Patronage: The American Government's Use of Newspapers, 1789–1875* (1977). Two comprehensive studies of the history of government news reporting are F. B. Marbut, *News from the Capital: The Story of Washington Reporting* (1971), and Donald A. Ritchie, *Press Gallery: Congress and the Washington Correspondents* (1991).

JOSEPH P. McKERNS

GALL (1840–5 Dec. 1894), Lakota Sioux warrior and leader, was born into the Hunkpapa band near the Moreau River in present-day South Dakota. His parents' names are not known. He earned the name Pizi from his mother, who watched him eat the gallbladder of an animal. Gall is the English translation of the Sioux word *pizi*, which means gallbladder. Gall also earned other names—Walks-in-Red-Clothing and The-Man-Who-Goes-in-the-Middle. While Gall preferred the latter name, it was Gall that stuck. Among his playmates, Gall admired and followed the leadership of an older youth who would later be known as Sitting Bull. Gall spent his early adult life along the Missouri River, where he and other Sioux generally made life miserable for the Mandans, Arikaras, and Hidatasas, all long-standing enemies of the Sioux. During the winter of 1865–1866, Gall's attacks on the Arikaras, who had submitted to reservation life and

U.S. protection, intensified to the point that soldiers from nearby Fort Berthold were summoned to arrest him. Captured, he bolted only to be knocked to the ground and pinned to the earth with a bayonet thrust. A soldier's last-minute intervention saved Gall from a muzzle blast to the head by an angry Arikara named Bloody Knife, who sought retribution for Gall having killed his two brothers. Left for dead, he recovered with the nursing of a Sioux woman. Although it is known that Gall had wives and children, his wives' names and the number of their children are unknown.

Gall allied with Sitting Bull's faction over the refusal to sign the 1868 Fort Laramie Treaty, which established a Sioux reserve in western Nebraska. The reservation split the Sioux into two camps of nontreaty and treaty Sioux. As a disciple of Sitting Bull's nontreaty policy, Gall gained status within the Hunkpapas, and he became one of Sitting Bull's emissaries to Fort Rice in 1868, where he told peace commissioners there could be no peace until all the Missouri River forts were burned. The next day, however, Gall was the first to place his mark on the Fort Laramie Treaty. Always the consummate pragmatist, Gall simply accepted the government bribes of food and presents while personally attaching no significance or binding position to his mark on a piece of paper.

Gall spent much of the next six years living along the Yellowstone River or in the Powder River country. In 1872 Sioux anger turned to hostility when railroad surveyors entered the Yellowstone valley, which the Sioux adamantly claimed as their land. Gall played a prominent role as he and other warriors attacked General David S. Stanley's escort along the Yellowstone. The next year Gall engaged elements of Lieutenant Colonel George A. Custer's Seventh Cavalry along the Yellowstone. In two firefights, 4 and 11 August, Gall and other warriors gave warning that the Sioux intended to keep the whites and other interlopers out of their domain.

In December 1875 the U.S. government issued an edict declaring that all American Indians including the nontreaty Sioux must report to a reservation or face military reprisals. The followers of Sitting Bull ignored the ultimatum and began the summer of 1876 by congregating in large numbers for common defense along the tributaries of the Yellowstone River. Custer discovered a great Sioux and Cheyenne encampment on 25 June 1876 on the Little Bighorn. Custer ordered Major Marcus Reno to attack the village. Gall was prominent in spearheading an American-Indian defense that halted Reno's charge and forced him to retreat across the stream in disarray. After turning back Reno, Gall received word that other soldiers were observed downstream. Collecting warriors, Gall led his forces against Custer's men spotted one-half mile east of camp. According to Gall, whose account of the battle was incorporated into Edward S. Godfrey's classic, "Custer's Last Battle," he fought with a hatchet, stating that in the earlier fight with Reno, stray bullets had killed two of his wives and three children, which "made my heart bad" (*Century Magazine*, Jan. 1892,

pp. 358–87). Gall's warriors trapped Custer's command against other American Indians led by Crazy Horse circling from the north. The battle with Custer lasted about one-half hour, according to Gall. Custer and his five companies of Seventh U.S. Cavalry, totaling about 210 soldiers, were wiped out.

While the battle of the Little Bighorn marked the zenith of Sioux struggle to resist encroachment on their lands, it also hastened their demise. Because of constant military patrols, Sitting Bull and Gall were forced to take their people into Canada. Facing starvation and the strain of five years of exile, Gall was persuaded to surrender. Breaking with Sitting Bull, Gall surrendered his followers at Camp Poplar, Montana, on 2 January 1881. Gall settled onto the Standing Rock Reservation along Oak Creek, South Dakota. He became an Episcopalian, sent his daughters to the Standing Rock Missionary School, and was appointed an American-Indian judge in Standing Rock. Many of Gall's detractors argued that he owed his political and tribal status to Indian agent James McLaughlin. In reality, both men used each other. McLaughlin played Gall against the nonprogressives like Sitting Bull. Gall used McLaughlin to establish himself as one of the influential statesmen in Standing Rock. While Gall in many ways became a "white man's Indian," he fought for American-Indian rights on many issues. Together with Sitting Bull he opposed the sale of surplus Sioux lands known as the Sioux Act of 1889. When informed that the government might take the land anyway, Gall reluctantly signed after negotiating a higher price per acre.

A nonbeliever in the Ghost Dance religion, which was sweeping the Sioux reservation in 1889, Gall urged his people to refrain from the religious teachings, which if followed would restore the glory of lost Sioux culture. To his credit, Gall's followers did not become involved in the tragedy that occurred at Wounded Knee, South Dakota, in December 1890 where more than 200 Sioux of Big Foot's band, many of them women and children, were killed when the military attempted to disarm them. Gall's last years were anticlimactic. He died of heart failure at his home on Oak Creek. Before his death, Gall donated 160 acres to St. Elizabeth Mission and Church. Interment followed at St. Elizabeth Mission Cemetery in Wakpala.

Prior to his surrender in 1881, Gall symbolized a fearlessness in battle. Defiant and haughty, he is best remembered for his historical account of the battle of the Little Bighorn, which is still a standard reference for students of the battle. In recent times Gall has been seen as a pawn of white culture who sold out the reservation Sioux for personal gain. This perception is not entirely accurate. Gall was a visionary who understood that survival of American-Indian culture meant adaptation to white values. Gall accepted reservation confinement because to resist meant defeat and death. Using the infrastructure of the U.S. government, Gall became a Sioux leader who helped prepare his people to meet the challenges of an alien world in the twentieth century.

• A full-length biography of Gall has yet to be written. Two monographs that provide biographical treatment are Thomas B. Marquis, *Sitting Bull and Gall, the Warrior* (1934), and Neil C. Mangum, "Gall: Sioux Gladiator or White Man's Pawn," paper presented at the fifth annual symposium of the Custer Battlefield Historical and Museum Association, 21 June 1991. Fragmentary information on Gall is contained in James McLaughlin, *My Friend the Indian* (1910), and De-Lorme W. Robinson, "Pi-zi (Gall)," *South Dakota Historical Collections* 1 (1902): 151. Robert M. Utley, *The Lance and the Shield: The Life and Times of Sitting Bull* (1993), offers a more recent assessment of Gall. For treatment of the Wounded Knee Massacre and the Ghost Dance religion, see Utley, *The Last Days of the Sioux Nation* (1963) and Rex A. Smith, *Moon of Popping Trees* (1975).

NEIL C. MANGUM

GALLAGHER, Edward Francis (1873–28 May 1929), comic actor, was born in San Leandro, California, the son of Edward Francis Gallagher and Catherine Byrne. His education and other whereabouts before 1894 are obscure, but in 1923 he claimed to have had twenty-nine years in show business, specifying "concert hall, burlesque, vaudeville and extravaganza," adding that at one time he had managed and booked a burlesque company. In 1895 he formed a successful vaudeville song-and-dance act with Joe Barrett. By 1900 Gallagher and Barrett's sketches on the military, particularly "The Battle of Too Soon," had made them a top act and Gallagher one of the medium's best "straight men." Vaudeville historian Joe Laurie noted, "A good straight man had to make a good appearance, dress well, have sex appeal, and have a good speaking and singing voice. They were usually fairly well-educated guys who had a good vocabulary (for an actor) and handled the business for the act. The comic just had to be funny and was the mixer of the team."

In Chicago in 1910 Gallagher met and joined forces with "Dutch" comic Al Shean, who spoke in fractured English, supposedly imitating immigrant Germans, and for four years the new team was successful, their partnership including one musical comedy appearance, *The Rose Maid* (1912). But in 1914 came the first of the rifts between Gallagher and Shean that became as legendary as their act; according to Shean, Gallagher did not speak to him for the next six years. Gallagher played solo with decreasing success. Early in 1920 he appeared in Bronco Billy Anderson's *Frivolities*, a revue featuring low comedy more typical of burlesque than the musical stage.

The reconciliation of Gallagher and the equally unemployed Shean later in 1920 came through the intervention of Minnie Marx, Shean's sister and the mother of the Marx Brothers. Gallagher had played an actors' benefit with Harpo Marx, and one day at the Marx home he told Minnie, "Al and I could do a great act together only he won't talk to me." She invited Gallagher to dinner at their home on Riverside Drive in New York, an invitation seconded by Shean himself. Gallagher and Shean re-formed their act, with Shean as a frock-coated, be-fezzed ethnic comic and Gallagher as a genial, nonchalant wisecracker who sometimes affected a monocle and cigarette holder. They achieved a memorable nonsense. Their new act, "Mr. Gallagher and Mr. Shean in Egypt," opened at the Fox Crotona Theatre on Long Island in April 1920. At its heart was the song "Oh! Mr. Gallagher and Mr. Shean," which was, according to vaudeville historian Douglas Gilbert, "probably known to every adult man and woman in America." Gallagher and Shean left the Keith circuit, vaudeville's long-established monopoly, in 1921, signing with producers Lee and Jacob Shubert, who were attempting to add vaudeville to their own growing theatrical empire. In 1922 "Oh! Mr. Gallagher and Mr. Shean" was published by Jack Mills, Inc. The sheet music carried the words "about themselves by themselves," and Gallagher, Shean, and Mills were consequently sued (unsuccessfully) by Bryan Foy (Brian Fitzgerald). Foy claimed the song was his; Gallagher and Shean contended that the idea had been theirs and that Foy had provided "only the verses."

By 1922 Gallagher and Shean had taken their act into that year's *Ziegfeld Follies*, generally regarded as the series' last great edition. Their salary climbed to $1,500 a week, then to $2,500. In 1923 the Shuberts sued them for breach of contract for appearing in the *Follies*, contending that Gallagher and Shean's services were "unique and extraordinary" (though the key words did not appear in the contract itself). The partners argued that they had signed with the Shuberts because they had been promised a Broadway musical comedy (which never materialized) that would have allowed them to live at home. Despite their phenomenal success, Gallagher and Shean argued that they were only ordinary vaudevillians and that anyone could do their act.

The trial featured testimony from many of the era's major producers and performers. Supporting the partners in their ordinariness, cowboy folk humorist Will Rogers called their act so good that "Volstad [author of the Prohibition act] and Bryan [William Jennings Bryan, defender of the Bible] would make as much of a hit." Gallagher testified that he could be replaced for $75 a week and in fact had once hired a replacement for Shean at $50. The New York Supreme Court judge ruled in favor of Gallagher and Shean, noting, "They are ordinary performers—good, clever performers, who by chance or luck got a clever skit and have made a hit. There are other men who with the same skit provoke just as much hilarity."

Although the ruling was overturned in November 1923, and "unique and extraordinary" clauses became universal in contracts, events eventually proved the judge right. Aside from other stars such as Harry Lauder, Charlie Chaplin, and Jimmy Durante, Gallagher and Shean soon became "the most imitated men in the world," notes Laurie, "there were so many imitations of Gallagher and Shean that the Keith office had to issue a rule that there would be only one on a bill."

Gallagher's decline came swiftly. According to Eddie Cantor, who replaced Rogers midway through the 67-week *Follies* run, "Their sudden rise unbalanced Gallagher's perspective, and he tried to dominate the show." Gallagher threatened to quit because Cantor was ad-libbing during rehearsals. Ziegfeld intervened, however, and Gallagher remained with the production until it closed in 1923.

In 1923 Gallagher's wife Helen (maiden name and year of marriage unknown) divorced him, and later the same year he married Anne Luther, a film actress who specialized in "other woman" roles. Their marriage ended within two months. These were Gallagher's third and fourth marriages, but the names of his other wives and dates of the marriages are unknown. He had one child, probably with Helen.

In 1924, after the litigation with the Shuberts had been settled and Gallagher and Shean had joined the Shubert *Greenwich Village Follies*, Gallagher cowrote (with James McHugh and lyricist Al Dubin) a song called "You Know Me Al, You Know Me Ed." The title reflects an attempt to capitalize on a contemporary catchphrase derived from the baseball stories of Ring Lardner, but the song did not succeed. Soon the partnership of Gallagher and Shean dissolved permanently.

In 1925 Gallagher, an alcoholic, suffered a breakdown and was confined to a sanitarium on Long Island. In 1927 a second breakdown led to permanent confinement. In 1928 Shean sued Gallagher for $10,672.40, asserting that he had lent the money on notes and paid sums in Gallagher's behalf and that Gallagher had withheld Shean's share of song royalties; the suit was denied. At the time of Gallagher's death in the sanitarium, Shean was doing their song in a new act, "Business Is Business," and Shean hired other actors to be "Gallagher."

"Gallagher and Shean" lived on even past Shean's death in 1949. In the musical *The Golden Apple* (1953), the Homeric Scylla and Charybdis, portrayed as unethical stockbrokers, parodied "Mr. Gallagher and Mr. Shean." In 1972 Neil Simon focused his comic play *The Sunshine Boys* on the reconciliation of two aged former vaudeville partners who had stopped speaking to each other years earlier.

• An envelope of clippings regarding Gallagher and Shean is in the Robinson Locke Collection of the Performing Arts Library, New York Public Library. There is no biography of Gallagher, but he features prominently in Joe Laurie, *Vaudeville: From the Honky Tonks to the Palace* (1953); Douglas Gilbert, *American Vaudeville: Its Life and Times* (1940); and Eddie Cantor and David Freedman, *Ziegfeld, The Great Glorifier* (1934). The litigations concerning the song "Oh! Mr. Gallagher and Mr. Shean" are well covered in contemporary issues of the *New York Times* from 27 Feb. 1923 through 2 Mar. 1923. A photograph of Gallagher and Shean is in Stanley Appelbaum and James Camner, *Stars of the American Musical Theater* (1981).

JAMES ROSS MOORE

GALLAGHER, Ralph W. (27 May 1881–31 July 1952), oil industry executive, was born in Salamanca, New York, the son of Charles Edward Gallagher and Catherine Lanning. He attended local schools until his father's death forced him to drop out of high school at the age of sixteen. In order to help support his family, he oiled machinery and swept floors at a pumping station in nearby Olean, New York. While working at the station, which was owned by the New York Transit Company, a subsidiary of industry giant Standard Oil, Gallagher completed his education by studying engineering and related subjects at night. Details of the next several years of Gallagher's life remain murky; he at some point moved to the United Pipe Lines Company and the National Transit Company, where he held a variety of positions, including fireman, relief telegrapher, tank gauger, and construction foreman. He also married Mary (maiden name unknown) and had four children; the date of his marriage is unknown.

In 1900 Gallagher moved to Akron, Ohio, where he became paymaster and assistant superintendent of the East Ohio Gas Company. The company, another Standard Oil affiliate, was then heavily involved in the construction of pipelines from its supply fields in West Virginia. Gallagher rose steadily through the ranks and by 1906 was supervising all trunk line construction work as well as the firm's distribution activities. In 1908 Gallagher relocated to Cleveland and was placed in charge of all company properties. By 1923 Gallagher had risen to the positions of director, general manager, and vice president of the firm, and his standing within the industry was confirmed by his election as president of the American Gas Association that same year. Three years later, in 1926, Gallagher became president of East Ohio and in the years that followed established his reputation as a friend of the working man, with his emphasis on workplace safety, and as an effective spokesperson for the industry, which was heavily involved in direct consumer sales.

Gallagher's astute management at East Ohio did not go unnoticed by his superiors at Standard Oil of New Jersey, and in November 1933 he was rewarded with a directorship in the parent company and took charge of Standard Oil's natural gas production as well. In 1937 he became a vice president at Standard and helped the firm meet the increasing consumer demand for natural gas in the years prior to World War II. With the outbreak of hostilities in 1939 Standard Oil faced many difficult decisions, none more vexing than the status of I. G. Farbenindustrie (IGF), a German-owned company with which Standard had conducted joint research in a number of areas, including synthetic rubber production. Although Standard managed to negotiate a September 1939 settlement with IGF shortly after the outbreak of hostilities—one that seemingly met the needs of both parties—the firm faced additional challenges, such as supplying the petroleum needs of the Allies without violating neutrality laws. Upon the entry of the United States into the conflict in December 1941, Standard Oil threw itself into the production of oil for America's wartime needs, only to face censure at the hands of both the Justice Department and the U.S. Senate. In the face of American military setbacks early in the war, Standard became a convenient scapegoat for America's general state of unpreparedness. Assistant Attorney General Thurman W. Arnold charged Standard with near-treasonous activity in light of its arrangement with IFG, one that he claimed delayed the onset of synthetic rubber production, which became increasingly important after Japanese advances in the Pacific cut off American supplies of natural rubber. The firm also faced the wrath of Senator Harry S. Truman's committee investigating U.S. military preparedness, and the strain of answering public charges wore heavily on Standard president William S. Farish. Although Standard successfully defended itself against the charges, Farish's sudden death in November 1942, coupled with the resignation of other key management figures, left the company in precarious straits.

Having risen to the chairmanship of Standard's board only a week before Farish died, Gallagher quickly stepped up to fill the leadership void. He assumed Farish's duties as Standard's president and in that role moved quickly to stem the damage resulting from the firm's adverse publicity. Drawing on his long years of experience in the consumer-oriented natural gas industry, he guided Standard through its first real efforts at public relations and also streamlined the firm's decision making, which had become concentrated in the Executive Committee to the detriment of overall efficiency. During his brief tenure as president, Gallagher also gained industrywide notice for his work in both employee benefit programs and personnel selection. Under his direction, Standard Oil produced items such as toluene (an ingredient in TNT), 100-octane aviation fuel, and synthetic rubber that contributed greatly to the Allied war effort. Faced with horrific losses among its tanker fleet to German submarines, he led the firm in developing additional pipeline capacity. Perhaps his greatest achievement as president, however, came in his renegotiation of oil leases with Venezuela. In the face of increasing nationalistic discontent in South America, Gallagher successfully mollified the Venezuelans and thereby preserved an important source of oil for the Allies.

Seeking to devote more time to long-range planning, Gallagher turned over Standard's presidency to Eugene Holman in June 1944. He retained the position of board chairman until 1 January 1946, after which he retired. Having suffered the loss of his wife in 1938, he died at his home in New York City following a long illness.

Although largely forgotten today, Ralph Gallagher deserves to be remembered for his brief but crucial stint as president of Standard Oil. His experience and leadership filled a void during a critical period in company history and helped to assure that Standard Oil would contribute to an eventual Allied victory in World War II.

• Gallagher's actions within Standard Oil are documented within company records. His life and career receive attention in several secondary sources, including Charles Sterling Popple, *Standard Oil Company (New Jersey) in World War II* (1952), Henrietta M. Larson et al., *History of Standard Oil Company (New Jersey): New Horizons, 1927–1950* (1971), and Bennett H Wall et al., *Growth in a Changing Environment: A History of Standard Oil (New Jersey)–Exxon Corporation, 1950–1975* (1988). An obituary is in the *New York Times*, 1 Aug. 1952.

EDWARD L. LACH, JR.

GALLAGHER, William Davis (21 Aug. 1808–27 June 1894), poet, journalist, and government official, was born in Philadelphia, Pennsylvania, the son of Bernard Gallagher, apparently a printer or journalist, and Abigail Davis. At the age of eight Gallagher headed west with his three brothers and mother (a widow since 1814) and settled in Mount Pleasant, Ohio. There he attended the Lancastrian Seminary and learned the printing trade through an apprenticeship.

Gallagher launched his career in Cincinnati. From 1826 to 1828 he edited, wrote for, or helped manage the short-lived *Western Tiller, Cincinnati Emporium, Western Minerva, Literary Gazette,* and *Saturday Evening Chronicle.* Meanwhile, he also became known as a Whig partisan. In 1830 party leaders of Green County, Ohio, appointed him editor of the *Xenia Backwoodsman,* an anti-Jackson campaign paper. With its demise in 1831 Gallagher returned to Cincinnati and entered into several unsuccessful efforts to establish a western literary journal. His first endeavor, as editor of the *Cincinnati Mirror,* ended in April 1836 when he defied the publisher, who wished to endorse the free-thinking views of Thomas Paine. In June he became editor of the *Western Literary Journal and Monthly Review,* which folded one year later. Gallagher then moved to Columbus and in May 1838, after a brief term as literary editor of the *Ohio State Journal,* started the *Hesperian,* another literary paper, only to see it too expire eighteen months later.

In 1839 Gallagher's fortunes improved after he accepted a position offered by Charles Hammond, editor of the *Cincinnati Gazette.* For the next decade Gallagher served on the paper's editorial staff, wrote poetry on the side, and remained active in Whig politics. In addition, he became increasingly committed to the antislavery movement.

According to criticism levied by John C. Wright, one of Hammond's successors, Gallagher was at this time "forever treading upon somebody's toes" (Venable, *Ohio Archaeological and Historical Quarterly* 2: 311). Chastened, Gallagher resigned from the *Cincinnati Gazette* in 1850 to accept a post as assistant to Thomas Corwin, an Ohio Whig and newly appointed Treasury secretary under Millard Fillmore. Late in 1852 he left this position as well and acquired a controlling interest in the *Louisville Courier* to promote Corwin as a presidential candidate, only to discover the unpopularity of his own antislavery views in Kentucky. Gallagher responded in 1854 by selling his interest in the paper and retiring to a farm near Louisville, where for the next six years he planted orchards, edited the *Western Farmer's Journal*, and wrote poetry and antislavery articles.

As Whiggism died in the 1850s, Gallagher shifted his political allegiance to the Republican party. In 1860 he attended the Republican convention in Chicago as a delegate from Kentucky and a supporter of former Ohio governor and U.S. senator Salmon P. Chase, a literary aspirant and fellow antislavery activist from Cincinnati. In the ensuing election, Gallagher supported Abraham Lincoln and was rewarded after the party's victory with a series of positions under Chase, who became Treasury secretary. From 1861 to 1865 Gallagher served as Chase's assistant, special collector of customs, commercial agent for the upper Mississippi Valley, and surveyor of customs at Louisville. He also received an appointment as pension agent around the end of the Civil War. After the war, he returned to his farm, where he wrote articles and poetry and for an unknown time worked as a clerk for the Kentucky Land Company. Gallagher's wife of thirty-seven years, Emma Anderson, died in 1867. Gallagher died at his home in Louisville. Four of his nine children survived him.

Two major themes appear in Gallagher's writing. His earliest poetry, represented in *Erato No. I* (1835), *Erato No. II* (1835), and *Erato No. III* (1837), is notable for graphic imagery wielded to describe nature and the trials and accomplishments of the pioneers of the West. Most famous is his description of a hot summer afternoon, which appears in "August," a poem published in *Erato No. II*:

> Flame-like, the long mid-day—
> with not so much of sweet air as hath stirr'd
> The down upon the spray,
> Where rests the panting bird,
> Dozing away the hot and tedious noon,
> With fitful twitter, sadly out of tune.

According to one modern critic, Gallagher's early volumes contain "almost, if not quite, the best verses written on the frontier" (Rusk, vol. 1, p. 339). Similar celebrations of the West and nature reappear in *Selections from the Poetical Literature of the West* (1841), a volume edited by Gallagher to preserve notable verse written by thirty-eight western writers, and, to a lesser degree, in *The Area of Subsistence, and Its Natural Outlet to the Ocean and the World* (1879). In his final book, *Miami Woods: A Golden Wedding and Other Poems* (1881), which includes poetry written from 1839 to 1856, Gallagher's vision expanded to encompass concern for humanitarian causes characteristic of his political activities.

Gallagher left a literary legacy far more enduring than his accomplishments as a politician and government official. According to one eulogist, Gallagher was "preeminent among the early poets of Ohio," comparable in his talents to John Greenleaf Whittier and William Cullen Bryant (Emerson Venable, pp.

16–17). Gallagher can justly claim membership in the circle of notable founders of middle western literature such as Timothy Flint, James Hall, and George Dennison Prentice.

• There is no known collection of Gallagher's papers. For his biography see W. H. Venable, "William Davis Gallagher," *Ohio Archaeological and Historical Quarterly* 1 (Mar. 1888): 358–75, and 2 (Sept. 1888): 309–26, repr. in 1889 as a separate volume, *William Davis Gallagher*, and in Venable, *Beginnings of Literary Culture in the Ohio Valley: Historical and Biographical Sketches* (1891), pp. 436–70. William T. Coggeshall, *The Poets and Poetry of the West, with Biographical and Critical Notices* (1861), includes many of Gallagher's minor poems, while sections from *Miami Woods* have been republished in Emerson Venable, ed., *Poets of Ohio* (1909). For analyses of Gallagher's literary efforts, see Ralph Leslie Rusk, *The Literature of the Middle Western Frontier* (2 vols., 1925), and James A. Tague, "William D. Gallagher, Champion of Western Literary Periodicals," *Ohio Historical Quarterly* 69 (July 1960): 257–71. Obituaries are in the *Louisville Commercial*, *Louisville Courier-Journal*, and *Louisville Times*, all 28 June 1894.

LEIGH JOHNSEN

GALLATIN, Albert (29 Jan. 1761–13 Aug. 1849), fourth secretary of the treasury and diplomat, was born Abraham Alfonse Albert Gallatin in Geneva, Switzerland, the son of Jean Gallatin, a merchant, and Sophie Albertine Rolaz du Rosey. Albert, as he preferred to be known, traced his ancestry to thirteenth-century Savoy, where the Gallatins (or Gallatinis) were a noble family holding fiefs along the upper Rhône. Enrolled as citizens of Geneva by the late fifteenth century, the Gallatins became so prominent in the republic's affairs that by the eighteenth century they would be permitted to use the title "Noble" and to prefix the family name with a *de*. Albert's parents were not wealthy, however, and both died by the time he was nine, leaving him in the care of a distant relative, Mlle. Catherine Pictet. At the age of thirteen he entered the Academy of Geneva, where his precocious intelligence brought him to the attention of such renowned scholars as the historian Johannes von Müller, the physicist George Louis Le Sage, and the naturalist Horace Benedict de Saussure. In 1780, a year after graduating from the academy, Gallatin slipped out of Geneva on a pretext and ran away to America. Henry Adams, his first biographer, believed that the young Gallatin, inspired by the Declaration of Independence, wanted to escape the stifling conservatism of upper-class Geneva. The truth is rather more prosaic. Gallatin had discovered that his inheritance barely covered the expenses of his education, and he could not bear the thought of relying on his family connections to find employment. What drew him to the United States was simply the hope of making enough money, through trade and land speculation, to achieve the personal independence that seemed impossible in Geneva. Initially, he in fact regarded the American Revolution as a tragic mistake and deplored the "depredations" committed by "men of the People" who knew nothing of "honor, manners & integrity."

Gallatin's first several years in the United States improved neither his fortune nor his attitude toward the new nation. Boston, where he arrived in July 1780, was dispiritingly provincial, and its narrow-minded residents refused to buy a shipment of tea on which he had expected to turn a large profit. He then sank his remaining capital in a wagonload of sugar, tobacco, and rum and went up to Machias, Maine, where he spent the next year dickering with the local Indians and a handful of American soldiers stationed nearby. In October 1781, having barely broken even, Gallatin returned to Boston and struggled to make ends meet by giving French lessons to Harvard students. Chastened by his lack of progress in commerce, he also began fleshing out a land-development project that would settle European farmers and craftsmen in frontier communities. Early in 1783 he broached his ideas to Jean Savary de Valcoulon, an agent for French purchasers of American real estate and public securities. Savary agreed to underwrite Gallatin's project on the understanding that Gallatin would tend to the details. The two left Boston in July 1783 and traveled down to Baltimore, where they purchased Virginia and Pennsylvania warrants for more than 120,000 acres of land along the Ohio River. The following April, after hurried preparations in Richmond and Philadelphia, Gallatin set out for the Virginia-Pennsylvania backcountry to survey and register his holdings. A chance encounter with George Washington in the Monongalia, Virginia, surveyor's office alerted him that plans were afoot to canalize the Potomac and link it with one or another of the Ohio's tributaries. Betting on the Monongahela, Gallatin leased a farm near its confluence with George's Creek in Fayette County, Pennsylvania. There, only a few miles above the Virginia line, he built a small store and office in preparation for the settlers that he envisioned streaming by his front door. But Indian troubles and delays on the Potomac canal soon dashed those hopes, and over the next several years he labored to keep the George's Creek operation going. By 1788, despite the arrival of a former schoolmate, Jean Badollet, and despite the acquisition of a lovely 400-acre tract overlooking the Monongahela that he called "Friendship Hill," Gallatin was ready to give up. After the sudden death of his wife Sophie Allegre in the autumn of 1789—they had been married only a matter of months—he grew so depressed that for a long time he would not go outside or even put on clothes. His original disdain for the United States was nonetheless giving way to real enthusiasm for its republican principles and institutions. One reason for the change was his relationship with Savary, an outspoken advocate of the American cause. Another was his exposure to the more cosmopolitan societies of Virginia and Pennsylvania, where he would always feel much more at home than in New England. Still another was an outbreak of political violence in Geneva that dissuaded him from returning and forced him to question, for the first time, the values of his class and connections.

Against this background, in September 1788, Gallatin made his political debut as a delegate from Fayette County to the Antifederalist convention at Harrisburg. His thoughtful criticism of the proposed federal Constitution earned him a seat the following year in the convention that rewrote the Pennsylvania state constitution. In October 1790 he was elected to the first of three one-year terms in the state house of representatives, where he made a name for himself as a spokesman for the small farmers and entrepreneurs with whom he shared a desire for equal opportunity and economic development. His brilliant reports for that body's committee of ways and means established him as an authority in the field of public finance, and no sooner had the legislature elected him to the U.S. Senate in February 1793 than he called for an investigation into Alexander Hamilton's management of the U.S. Treasury. Although the Federalist Senate denied him his seat on the dubious theory that he had not been a citizen for the required nine years, two events ensured him a continuing role in the nascent Democratic-Republican opposition. In November 1793 he married Hannah Nicholson, with whom he had two sons and four daughters. Hannah's father, Commodore James Nicholson of New York City, was one of Hamilton's most influential and distinguished critics. The following year western Pennsylvania was convulsed by the so-called Whiskey Insurrection, brought on by discontent over the imposition of a federal excise on distilled spirits. Although Gallatin figured importantly in restoring law and order, Federalist attempts to blame him for the violence virtually guaranteed that western Republicans would put his name forward in that year's congressional elections. His victory marked the beginning of a spectacular six-year career in the House (1795–1801), during which his painstaking critiques of Federalist financial policy swept him to the forefront of the Democratic-Republican party alongside James Madison and Thomas Jefferson.

Nothing alarmed Gallatin more than the Federalists' seeming reluctance to reduce the public debt incurred during the Revolution. His own fears of personal dependency and his small-shopkeeper's sense of integrity, both reinforced by a strain of radical republican thought that originated in England a century earlier, convinced him that public debts were a nursery of multiple public evils—corruption, legislative impotence, executive tyranny, social inequality, financial speculation, and personal indolence. Not only was it necessary to extinguish the existing debt as rapidly as possible, he argued, but Congress would have to ensure against the accumulation of future debts by more diligently supervising government expenditures (it was in fact his idea to set up a permanent Ways and Means Committee in the House). These ideas reached a national audience through the publication of Gallatin's numerous speeches, reports, and pamphlets, among them *A Sketch of the Finances of the United States* (1796) and *Views of the Public Debt, Receipts, and Expenditures of the United States* (1800). After Jefferson was sworn in as president in 1801 it surprised no one that he tapped Gallatin to be his secretary of the treasury.

At first it seemed that Gallatin would succeed in freeing his adopted country from the shackles of debt. He set aside about three-fourths of the government's revenue every year to pay the interest and principle. At that rate, he said, the United States would be out of debt entirely by 1817. His zealous cost cutting, despite a war with the Barbary states of North Africa (1801–1805) and the purchase of Louisiana (1803), meanwhile left the Treasury with a growing surplus. During Jefferson's second term, buoyed by these signs of fiscal stability, Gallatin turned his attention to internal improvements, which he, like the president, regarded as vital to the expanding nation's prosperity and unity. Early in 1808 he sent Congress a bold proposal to spend $20 million on the construction of turnpikes and canals in every section of the country. "No other single operation, within the power of government," he declared, "can more effectively tend to strengthen and perpetuate that Union which secures external independence, domestic peace, and internal liberty." Already, however, Gallatin's financial program had begun to unravel. In 1807 the British ministry brought new pressure to bear on Napoleon by closing continental ports to neutral shipping and impressing British subjects from neutral vessels. Over the next five years, Jefferson and then Madison tried in vain to defend American rights against both belligerents by using economic coercion rather than armed force, a strategy that Gallatin regretted but did not publicly oppose. Its failure caused federal revenues to plummet and forced him to raise taxes and increase rather than reduce government borrowing. By 1812, when continued British depredations against American ships and crews finally compelled Madison to ask Congress for a declaration of war, the national debt was higher than ever and Gallatin's ambitious program of internal improvements lay in ruins.

In the spring of 1813, with palpable relief, the 52-year-old Gallatin left the Treasury to help negotiate an end to the conflict with Great Britain. The Anglo-American accord signed at Ghent in December 1814 was largely a product of his perseverance, his aptitude for detail, and the good-humored patience with which he mediated sectional and personal tensions between two of his fellow commissioners, Henry Clay and John Quincy Adams (the latter of whom praised Gallatin as unrivaled "for extent and copiousness of information, for sagacity and shrewdness of comprehension, for vivacity of intellect, and fertility of resource"). In the wake of his success at Ghent, Gallatin considered returning to Congress or going into partnership with his old friend John Jacob Astor. President Madison persuaded him to accept an appointment as American ambassador to France, however, and in 1816 Gallatin began what would be a seven-year sojourn with his family on the Continent. It was the least productive period of his career. The social duties of a diplomat in Paris were exhausting, besides which the government of Louis XVIII rebuffed his repeated attempts to win compensation for losses to American shipping caused by the Napoleonic decrees. His principal achievement, perhaps ironically, was to go to London in 1818 to help settle the boundary between Canada and the United States, paving the way for American occupation of the Pacific Northwest.

In 1824, soon after returning to the United States, Gallatin agreed to have his name put forward as candidate for vice president on the Republican ticket behind William H. Crawford of Georgia. But Crawford fell ill, and when it became apparent that the rank and file preferred Andrew Jackson—a man Gallatin believed "altogether unfit" for the White House—party leaders pressured him to step aside. He did so, saddened by the realization that the principles he had cherished during his thirty-five years in public life were fast becoming anachronisms. Hoping for a quiet retirement, Gallatin moved his family out to Friendship Hill on the Monongahela, then again to Baltimore when his wife wearied of life in the "Siberia" of western Pennsylvania. In 1826 President Adams lured him out of retirement with an offer to serve as the American minister to Great Britain. He remained at the court of St. James little more than a year, during which time he successfully negotiated with the British for the renewal of the 1818 commercial treaty and for continued joint occupation of the Oregon Territory.

Back home again by the end of 1827, Gallatin settled his family in New York City. He was not poor, but decades of underpaid public service and the bad luck in business that dogged him throughout his life had drained his resources. In 1831, now seventy, he accepted Astor's offer to become president of the new National Bank of New York at the comfortable salary of $2,500 per year. It was no sinecure, and in addition to playing an active role in the bank's affairs Gallatin became a vigorous advocate of free trade, hard money, and fiscal responsibility. His *Considerations on the Currency and Banking System of the United States* (1831) brought him new renown as a proponent of the Bank of the United States in its ill-fated struggle against President Jackson. After the panic of 1837, which he attributed to the bank's misguided suspension of specie payments, Gallatin labored tirelessly to extricate New York's financial community from the crisis. Although he eventually stepped down as president of the National Bank in 1839, his concern for the nation's financial integrity continued undiminished. In a pamphlet entitled *Suggestions on the Banks and Currency of the Several United States* (1841), published shortly after his eightieth birthday, he rang again the old republican warnings against speculation, improvidence, and debt. Five years later, in *The Oregon Question* (1846), he cautioned that armed confrontation with Great Britain would have "calamitous" fiscal and social consequences. Then, toward the end of the Mexican War, he composed *Peace with Mexico* (1847) to protest the "iniquitous aggression" of the United States and warn that greed, national chauvinism, and racism were endangering the "political morality" of the republic. "But I do not despair," he added with Jeffersonian optimism, "for I have faith in our institutions and in the people."

While a resident of New York, Gallatin helped found New York University in 1830, led a gathering of prominent businessmen known simply as "The Club," and served as president of the New-York Historical Society in 1842. Somehow, he also managed to conduct extensive research on Native American languages, culture, and history—subjects that had fascinated him for years, at least partly because of their bearing on the rise and future of American republicanism. The first fruit of his labors was a paper published in 1836 by the American Antiquarian Society as "A Synopsis of the Indian Tribes within the United States East of the Rocky Mountains, and in the British and Russian Possessions of North America." Gratified by the praise it received, Gallatin spearheaded the organization of the American Ethnological Society in 1842. He became the society's first president, and over the next half-dozen years it acknowledged his reputation in the field by publishing several more of his papers, including "Notes on the Semi-Civilized Nations of Mexico, Yucatan, and Central America" (1845). This pioneering body of work, which was not superseded for another half-century, gave him even deeper satisfaction than the financial writing for which he would be much more widely known.

Old age at last began to catch up with Gallatin in the summer of 1848. Bedridden for nearly a year thereafter, he died at his daughter's summer home in Astoria, Long Island. At age eighty-eight, he was, as one newspaper put it, "the last patriarch of the Republican party."

• Gallatin's extensive private papers, the bulk of which is held by the New-York Historical Society, are available on microfilm through Scholarly Resources, Inc., of Wilmington, Del. *Writings of Albert Gallatin*, ed. Henry Adams (3 vols., 1879), remains useful as a judicious selection of Gallatin's private correspondence and important publications. The standard modern biography is Raymond Walters, Jr., *Albert Gallatin: Jeffersonian Financier and Diplomat* (1957), although Adams's own *Life of Albert Gallatin* (1879), magisterial in scope and style, is arguably a superior work. More specialized studies include Chien Tseng Mai, *The Fiscal Policies of Albert Gallatin* (1930); Alexander Balinky, *Albert Gallatin: Fiscal Theories and Policies* (1958); and Edwin G. Burrows, *Albert Gallatin and the Political Economy of Republicanism, 1761–1800* (1986), which presents much new material on Gallatin's early life and career. Gallatin's initial opinions of the United States are available in Burrows, " 'Notes on Settling America': Albert Gallatin, New England, and the American Revolution," *New England Quarterly* 58 (1985): 442–53.

EDWIN G. BURROWS

GALLATIN, Albert Eugene (23 July 1881–15 June 1952), art museum founder, critic, and painter, was born in Villanova, Pennsylvania, the son of Albert Horatio Gallatin, a professor of analytical chemistry at New York University, and Louisa Belford Ewing. He was the proud namesake of his great-grandfather, Albert Gallatin, secretary of the treasury under Presidents Thomas Jefferson and James Madison who had posed for portraits by such illustrious artists as Gilbert Stuart and Rembrandt Peale.

Other than a brief stint at the University of the State of New York Law School from 1901 to 1903, Gallatin had little education beyond high school. As the heir in 1902 to a family fortune made in banking, among other ventures, Gallatin soon established his reputation as an art connoisseur and critic. Collecting and writing extensively from 1897 to 1920 about James McNeill Whistler, Aubrey Beardsley, Max Beerbohm, the French and American impressionists, as well as the Ash Can school, Gallatin during this time virtually ignored more avant-garde art.

During World War I and the 1920s, Gallatin embarked on a program of self-education. As a result, he began to support modernism enthusiastically and vociferously. Between 1921 and 1938 he traveled frequently to Paris, where most of the works in his collection were acquired. By 1922 Gallatin, a benefactor of the Brooklyn Museum and the Metropolitan Museum of Art, already was beginning to confront the problem of the neglect of modern art by art institutions and to articulate the importance of the enlightened private collector in remedying the situation. Demand for a museum of modern art in America increased, and Gallatin, sensitive to this need, opened his collection to the public on 13 December 1927 as the first museum in America dedicated to modern art alone. Located in the country's major art center, Gallatin's Gallery of Living Art was in the South Study Hall of the main building at New York University, cofounded by his great-grandfather and for which he served as a trustee.

The small core of cubist works by Pablo Picasso, Georges Braque, Juan Gris, and Fernand Léger on view in the opening installation established the Gallery of Living Art's preeminence as a museum of modern art. In 1931 the gallery won the admiration of the critic James Johnson Sweeney for exhibiting the fullest representation of cubism in America. New York's Museum of Modern Art, founded two years after Gallatin's institution, did not possess a comparable collection until the late 1930s.

Gallatin's catalogs of 1928, 1929, 1930, 1933, 1936, and 1940 chart the considerable growth and refinement of his museum, which was a one-man operation whose reputed annual budget was just fifteen dollars. With no board of trustees, staff, or major operating expenses, Gallatin was free to use his own judgment, informed by advice from artists and critics, in discovering important painters and sculptors. From 1928 to 1933 he purchased the first works by Joan Miró, André Masson, Robert Delaunay, Piet Mondrian, and Jean Arp to enter a public collection in America.

Gallatin adhered strictly to cubism's formal principles; he deplored narrative or symbolic content and rejected expressionism, futurism, dada, and verist surrealism. During the 1930s he expanded his collection to encompass not only cubism but its offshoots—constructivism, De Stijl, neoplasticism, and abstract surrealism. Still dominating the collection were representative works by Picasso, Braque, Gris, and Léger. According to Gallatin, these artists "helped revive the great traditions of design and form one finds in such painters as Giotto, Francesca, and Uccello."

In 1936 Gallatin announced his purchase of Picasso's *Three Musicians* (1921, Philadelphia Museum of Art) and renamed his institution the Museum of Living Art. He also launched a second career as a self-taught painter, having experimented briefly ten years earlier. Gallatin's own collection played a formative role in the evolution of his synthetic cubist style. In 1937 he joined the American Abstract Artists group (AAA).

During the museum's last years from 1937 to 1943, Gallatin acquired and exhibited work by such fellow AAA members as Ilya Bolotowsky and George L. K. Morris, whose paintings were mostly unappreciated by other New York institutions promoting the American Scene. In turn, these artists and others such as Arshile Gorky and Willem de Kooning warmly acknowledged Gallatin's informal museum as an accessible, influential resource.

In January 1943 the Museum of Living Art was closed by the officials of New York University, who wanted to use the space for a library processing facility (now the site of the Grey Art Gallery and Study Center). Gallatin then transferred the majority of his works to the Philadelphia Museum of Art, which in May 1943 provided the most complete presentation of his collection to date. The collection of 168 works of art was expanded through Gallatin's continued acquisitions and bequeathed to the museum in 1952.

After Gallatin's death in New York City, his close friend and fellow abstract painter Charles Shaw wrote: "In his paintings, both those by [him] and those he collected, in his writings . . . taste par excellence played a leading role. . . . As few men I have known, he had a veritable horror of all that was vulgar, cheap, or common." Gallatin's patrician demeanor belied his progressive decision to found New York's first modern art museum and to become an artist himself. As a unique resource to many artists and critics, Gallatin's institution played a vital role in the development of American modernism and the emergence of New York as the center of the international art world. He never married.

• Gallatin's archives are in the Manuscript Division of the New-York Historical Society. Additional papers and materials are in the Philadelphia Museum of Art and the New York University Archives. For a complete bibliography of Gallatin's many articles and books, see Alexander D. Wainwright, "A Checklist of the Writings of Albert Eugene Gallatin," *Princeton University Library Chronicle* 14 (Spring 1953): 141–51. The most complete modern assessment is Gail Stavitsky, "The Development, Institutionalization, and Impact of the A. E. Gallatin Collection of Modern Art" (Ph.D. diss., New York Univ., 1990). See also Stavitsky, "A. E. Gallatin's Gallery and Museum of Living Art (1927–1943)," *American Art* 7 (Spring 1993): 47–63; and Stavitsky, "The A. E. Gallatin Collection: An Early Adventure in Modern Art," *Bulletin of the Philadelphia Museum of Art* 89 (1994). An obituary is "Who's News—Albert Eugene Gallatin," *Art Digest* 26 (July 1952): 12.

GAIL STAVITSKY

GALLAUDET, Edward Miner (5 Feb. 1837–26 Sept. 1917), educator, was born in Hartford, Connecticut, the son of Thomas Hopkins Gallaudet, noted educator of the deaf and principal of the Connecticut Asylum for the Education and Instruction of Deaf and Dumb Persons (now the American School for the Deaf), and Sophia Fowler, a deaf graduate of the Connecticut Asylum. Edward attended Trinity College in Hartford, supporting himself by teaching part time at the Connecticut Asylum, where he continued to work full time after leaving Trinity College.

At college, Gallaudet had considered becoming a missionary, and he was still uncertain about his career when, in 1857, Amos Kendall, a wealthy philanthropist, offered him the post of superintendent of the newly established Columbia Institution for the Instruction of the Deaf and Dumb and Blind in Washington, D.C. Gallaudet accepted the position and devoted the remainder of his life to this institution, which became the first college for the deaf in the world when the U.S. Congress authorized it to grant degrees in 1864. Renamed Gallaudet College in 1894 after Gallaudet's father, the college became the single most important institution in the maintenance and development of the deaf community in the United States.

In 1858 Gallaudet married Jane M. Fessenden, a childhood friend, and they had three children. After her death in 1866, Edward married Susan Denison in 1868; they had five children.

During his career, Gallaudet published over one hundred articles on various aspects of deaf education as well as a biography of his father, *Life of Thomas Hopkins Gallaudet* (1888). Indicative of his importance in deaf education was his election as president of the newly created Convention of American Instructors of the Deaf in 1895, a post he held until his death. He was also made a chevalier of the French Legion of Honor in 1912. He died in Hartford.

Gallaudet is well remembered for his advocacy of manualism (the use of sign language) in the education of deaf children. While stressing the need for instruction in speech and lip-reading for the deaf, Gallaudet also strongly advocated the value of sign language, in preference to the growing oralist movement in the United States. As Gallaudet wrote, "As a means of developing and stimulating thought, and of explaining the meaning of words and phrases new to a pupil, signs often serve a purpose that nothing else can." Gallaudet's advocacy of manualism led to his rivalry with Alexander Graham Bell, the leading oralist of the time. At the heart of the rivalry were different conceptions of the social meaning of deafness, competing views of the deaf community, and radically divergent goals for the education of the deaf.

• Letters from Gallaudet are in the Gallaudet papers in the Library of Congress; additional materials can be found in the Gallaudet collection in the Gallaudet University Archives. Biographical treatments are provided in Maxine Boatner, *Voice of the Deaf: A Biography of Edward Miner Gallaudet* (1959); John Vickrey van Cleve and Barry A. Crouch, *A Place of Their Own: Creating the Deaf Community in America* (1989); Harlan Lane, *When the Mind Hears: A History of the Deaf* (1984); and Richard Winefield, *Never the Twain Shall Meet: Bell, Gallaudet and the Communications Debate* (1987). The best bibliography of Gallaudet's own writings is in Lane's *When the Mind Hears.*

TIMOTHY REAGAN

GALLAUDET, Thomas (3 June 1822–27 Aug. 1902), Episcopal minister to the deaf, was born in Hartford, Connecticut, the son of Thomas Hopkins Gallaudet, educator of the deaf, and Sophia Fowler. Thomas Hopkins had founded the Connecticut Asylum, a school for the deaf in Hartford in 1817, and Sophia was one of its first graduates. They had little money but their work was well known and brought them into contact with the highest echelons of society. Growing up in these surroundings, Thomas early became interested in education for the deaf and particularly in communication through sign language.

At his father's insistence, Gallaudet attended Hartford's Washington College (later renamed Trinity College), graduating in 1842. While there, he became interested in a career in the ministry of the Protestant Episcopal church. His father, a Congregationalist minister, encouraged Gallaudet to reconsider his vocation while teaching in the public schools of Glastonbury and Meriden. After a year of reflection, the younger Gallaudet remained concerned about the legitimacy of the Congregationalist ministry and convinced of the need to join the Episcopal church. Accordingly, he moved to New York City, sought baptism at Saint Luke's Episcopal Church, and began studying for the Episcopal ministry. To cover his expenses, he took a job teaching at the New York Institution of the Deaf and Dumb (later New York Institute for the Deaf) where Elizabeth R. Budd was a student. The two fell in love and were married in 1845. They had seven children over the course of their 57-year union. The young couple lived with Elizabeth's parents in New York, and Gallaudet shelved his plans for the ministry for the next few years.

A chance meeting with a priest in 1849 inspired Gallaudet to renew his studies for the ministry, leading to his ordination as deacon in 1850 and then as priest a year later. At this stage, he did not plan to devote his ministry to work with the deaf, but he continued to teach at the New York Institution of the Deaf and Dumb. While working with a dying student, Cornelia Lathrop, Thomas recognized the failure of the churches to provide for the unfilled spiritual needs of deaf people. Even before his ordination to the priesthood, he had begun Bible study classes for deaf people at Saint Stephens, but his work with Cornelia inspired him to more ambitious plans. On the first Sunday in October 1852, Gallaudet held a service for the deaf in the chapel of New York University, initiating Saint Ann's Church for Deaf-Mutes. He remained connected to Saint Ann's for the rest of his life.

Under Gallaudet's leadership Saint Ann's grew until it had to move to the building of the New-York Historical Society in 1857. The following year Gallaudet resigned his work at the New York Institute for the Deaf in order to devote himself to Saint Ann's full time, and the parish moved into its own building in 1859. Gallaudet served as rector of Saint Ann's until 1892 when he retired from his full responsibilities and became rector emeritus. The parish sold its building in 1895 and worshiped at the Church of Saint John the Evangelist, then consolidated with Saint Matthew's Church. With a new building on West 148th Street, Saint Ann's became independent once again in 1898. From this location, Saint Ann's continued to serve as the spiritual center for deaf Episcopalians in New York long after Gallaudet's death. The *New York Tribune* described a typical service at Saint Ann's in its 11 April 1897 issue. While a minister spoke, Gallaudet interpreted his words in sign language. Four young women interpreted the hymns for the benefit of the deaf congregants. In a memorial tribute to Gallaudet, Bishop Horatio Potter of New York later described "the singular grace and beauty and eloquence of Dr. Gallaudet's actions as a preacher with the hands."

Saint Ann's was only the first parish of the Episcopal church devoted to the spiritual welfare of the deaf. Gallaudet worked diligently to expand this ministry, establishing missions for the deaf in Albany, Baltimore, Philadelphia, Boston, Washington, D.C., and other cities on his many missionary trips throughout the country. As the work of the Episcopal church with deaf people grew, he supported the ordination of deaf ministers and encouraged hearing ministers to learn sign language. He was the first general manager of the Church Mission to Deaf Mutes, begun in 1872, and the first president of the Conference of Church Workers among the Deaf, begun in 1881. The Church Mission was designed to serve as an umbrella organization for all of the work of the Episcopal church with the deaf, but after 1885 it concentrated its resources on running the newly formed Gallaudet Home for the Aged and Infirm Deaf in Poughkeepsie, New York. Through this type of work, as well as through his personal example, Gallaudet made the ministry to the deaf an important concern of the Episcopal church.

Not all of Gallaudet's work with the deaf was so closely connected to the Episcopal church. He also helped to establish schools for the deaf in Rome, New York, Rochester, New York, and Beverly, Massachusetts, as well as in other places. But his fame rests primarily on his role in establishing the first church missions to the deaf. He died at home in New York City surrounded by his family. The deaf community throughout the nation mourned his passing.

• Gallaudet University Archives in Washington, D.C., has an unpublished autobiographical work by Gallaudet entitled "A Sketch of My Life" as well as papers from Saint Ann's.

Few published sources treat Gallaudet's career in any detail. The only full-length biography is Otto Benjamin Berg and Henry L. Buzzard, *Thomas Gallaudet: Apostle to the Deaf* (1989), which includes a good bibliography. For shorter biographies, see Amos G. Draper's "Thomas Gallaudet," *American Annals of the Deaf* 47 (Nov. 1902): 393–403, and John H. Kent's "Rev. Thomas Gallaudet," *American Annals of the Deaf* 67 (Sept. 1922): 326–33. The most complete account of Gallaudet's work among the deaf as an Episcopal minister is Otto Benjamin Berg, *A Missionary Chronicle: Being a History of the Ministry to the Deaf in the Episcopal Church (1850–1980)* (1984). Berg quotes contemporary reports of some of Gallaudet's activities. An obituary is in the *New York Times*, 28 Aug. 1902.

HARVEY HILL

GALLAUDET, Thomas Hopkins (10 Dec. 1787–10 Sept. 1851), educator of the deaf, was born in Philadelphia, Pennsylvania, the son of Peter W. Gallaudet, a merchant, and Jane Hopkins. Gallaudet was a gifted and successful student, graduating from Yale University in 1805. He entered Andover Theological Seminary in January 1812 and graduated in 1814. As a result of health problems that would continue throughout his life, Gallaudet returned to Hartford, Connecticut, where his parents had moved when he was thirteen, rather than accepting a ministerial position.

Shortly after returning to Hartford, Gallaudet met a young deaf girl, Alice Cogswell, who was the daughter of the noted surgeon Dr. Mason Cogswell. At that time, no formal facilities for the education of the deaf existed in the United States. Gallaudet attempted to teach Alice himself, and, although he did have some limited success teaching her to spell a few words, he recognized the need for more effective education for Alice and other deaf children. Cogswell and several friends raised a small sum of money to send a person to Europe to study methods of teaching the deaf, and they ultimately prevailed upon Gallaudet to make the trip. Despite serious misgivings about both his health and his aptitude for such a mission, Gallaudet left for Britain in 1815.

Gallaudet's original intention had been to study the British methods of educating the deaf and to return home as quickly as possible. He discovered, however, that the oralist methods used and promoted by the Braidwood family (who essentially held a monopoly on deaf education in Britain) were utilized only as a profit-making endeavor and hence were a closely guarded family secret. Gallaudet could only be given access to these techniques by remaining in Britain as an apprentice for a number of years and by promising not to make the Braidwoods' system public. Such conditions were unacceptable to Gallaudet, and he was nearly ready to return to the United States when he met the abbé Roch-Ambroise Sicard, the head of the French Royal Institute for the Deaf (Institut Royal des Sourds-Muets), who was visiting London. At Sicard's invitation, Gallaudet spent several months at the Institut Royal in Paris, studying and observing. He returned to Hartford in 1816 with an understanding of French methods for educating the deaf, which involved the use of sign language. Of greater importance, a gifted young French deaf man, Laurent Clerc, who had himself been a student at the Institut Royal, agreed to go to Connecticut with Gallaudet as a teacher of the deaf.

Shortly after his return, and with the help of Cogswell and others, Gallaudet successfully established the Connecticut Asylum for the Education and Instruction of Deaf and Dumb Persons, which began operating in 1817. The Connecticut Asylum—later renamed the American School for the Deaf—was the first free school for the deaf in the United States, made possible by private donations and a $5,000 grant from the Connecticut legislature.

Gallaudet was made the principal of the Connecticut Asylum and served in that capacity, despite ongoing health problems, until 1830. As principal, Gallaudet made a number of noteworthy contributions to the education of the deaf, not the least of which was his continuing advocacy of the use of sign language. In fact, to a considerable degree modern American Sign Language can be traced to the Connecticut Asylum, and especially to the French Sign Language brought to this country by Laurent Clerc. Since the asylum also served as a training ground for those who would establish other residential schools for the deaf in various parts of the United States, Gallaudet played a vital role in the expansion of educational opportunities for deaf children throughout the country.

Guided to a significant extent by his deep religious convictions, Gallaudet also participated in a number of other educational and social reform movements. These included programs promoting the establishment of normal schools for the training of teachers in Connecticut, the acceptance of women as teachers, and better educational opportunities for African Americans.

In 1821, Gallaudet married a former pupil at the Connecticut Asylum, Sophia Fowler, shortly after her graduation. She became a noteworthy figure in the American deaf community, especially after she accompanied her son Edward Gallaudet to Washington, D.C., to the Columbia Institution for the Instruction of the Deaf and Dumb and Blind (later renamed Gallaudet College). T. H. and Sophia Gallaudet had a total of eight children. The oldest son, Thomas, founded St. Ann's Episcopal Church for the deaf in New York and served as its rector, while the youngest son, Edward, became the first superintendent of what was to become Gallaudet College.

After leaving the Connecticut Asylum, Gallaudet devoted the remainder of his life to various educational, social, and religious activities, as well as to writing on educational topics. He died in Hartford, Connecticut.

• Letters from Gallaudet are in the Gallaudet papers in the Library of Congress. Classic works on his life are E. M. Gallaudet, *Life of Thomas Hopkins Gallaudet* (1888), written by his son; H. Humphrey, *The Life and Labors of Rev. T. H.*

Gallaudet (1857); and Henry Barnard, *Tribute to Gallaudet* (1852). Also useful are Harlan Lane, *When the Mind Hears: A History of the Deaf* (1984), and John Vickrey van Cleve and Barry A. Couch, *A Place of Their Own: Creating the Deaf Community in America* (1989). Gallaudet himself wrote several articles on the education of the deaf that were published in the *American Annals of the Deaf*, the *American Annals of Education*, and the *Christian Observer*. He also wrote several religious works including *Discourses on Various Points of the Christian Faith* (1818). The best bibliography of Gallaudet's works is in Lane's *When the Mind Hears*.

TIMOTHY REAGAN

GALLEANI, Luigi (12 Aug. 1861–4 Nov. 1931), anarchist, was born in Vercelli, Piedmont, Italy, the son of Clemente Galleani, an elementary school teacher, and Olimpia Borini. Raised in a bourgeois family, he studied in the faculty of law at the University of Turin. He did not receive a degree since he soon became involved in the social ferment that was sweeping Italy. Although his father was a religious monarchist, Galleani quickly moved from republicanism to democratic socialism to anarchist communism. During the 1880s he wrote for several labor papers, organized workers' circles, and gave numerous speeches. His police dossier commented that he had given himself "body and soul to the revolutionary movement."

Fleeing arrest for his role in strikes in Turin in 1889, Galleani spent two years in France and Switzerland, where his activities soon made him persona non grata. Returning to Italy in 1891, he plunged into the labor and political struggles of the day. In the bitter conflicts among socialists and anarchists, Galleani became a leading exponent of intransigent, antiparliamentary anarchism, an ideological stance that he vigorously maintained throughout his life.

During the reaction following the *fasci siciliani* (uprisings in Sicily) of the early 1890s, Galleani was sentenced to prison for three years and then condemned to confinement on Pantelleria, a penal island, for five years. In his police dossier he is described as "endowed with a vast, if superficial, culture; elegant and facile of speech; strong and vibrant of voice; with a pleasing appearance; he knows how to insinuate himself in the souls of the workers."

In 1900 Galleani escaped from Pantelleria, making his way to Egypt, where he remained for a year. Upon the invitation of comrades, he arrived in Paterson, New Jersey, in October 1901. This city had gained notoriety as a center of Italian anarchism following the assassination of King Umberto I of Italy by Gaetano Bresci, who had returned from Paterson for that purpose. Galleani resumed his agitation through speeches and articles in *La Questione Sociale*, an anarchist journal of which he soon became editor. Not one to be cowed, Galleani extolled Bresci as an "apostle of absolute liberty" and referred to Leon Czolgosz, who had killed President William McKinley, as an "instrument of justice."

When a strike erupted in April 1902 among the silk mill workers, Galleani emerged as their tribune, inciting them to a general strike. In violent clashes with the police, he was shot in the mouth, but he managed to escape to Montreal. Entering the United States under an assumed name, he went to Barre, Vermont, a granite center with a large number of Italian stone workers. The workers were divided between socialists and anarchists, and Galleani's intolerant orthodoxy exacerbated their conflicts, resulting in bloodshed.

Galleani began publication of *Cronaca Sovversiva* (Subversive chronicle) in Barre on 6 June 1903; he moved the paper and himself to Lynn, Massachusetts, in 1912. In this journal he expounded his uncompromising brand of antiorganizational anarchism until he was deported in 1919. Given Galleani's international connections, the paper published original pieces by Pyotr Kropotkin, Errico Malatesta, and other leading anarchists. Despite a modest circulation of some 5,000, the paper was read by Italian workers throughout the United States as well as in Europe and South America. Through *Cronaca Sovversiva* and extensive speaking tours, Galleani converted thousands to his militant creed.

Influenced by Mikhail Bakunin and Kropotkin, Galleani espoused anarchist communism. He was primarily an activist and propagandist rather than a theorist, and his writings appeared in newspapers or pamphlets, only later to be collected in volumes. The most fully developed statement of his ideas was a series of articles published in 1925 as *La fine dell'anarchismo?* (The end of anarchism?). Responding to a work that asserted that anarchism was dead, Galleani proclaimed that the social revolution was inevitable. Parliamentary politics, reform socialism, and bourgeois society were all corrupt and exploitative. The workers through unrelenting class war would destroy the existing social order. While embracing all forms of direct action, including assassination and terrorism, Galleani believed the social revolution would be realized through insurrection and the general strike. With the abolition of private property and all forms of authority, "natural harmony" would prevail based on human solidarity and mutual aid.

Since Galleani opposed all forms of organization, the movement of *Galleanisti* took the form of local autonomous groups, often called *Circoli di Studi Sociali* (social studies circles), bound together only by his charismatic leadership. Although strikes were to be exploited as episodes in the class war, *Galleanisti* rejected labor unions, even the Industrial Workers of the World. Despite their numbers and militancy, Galleani's followers played at best a disruptive role in the American labor movement.

Viewing nationalism and militarism as mere rhetorical facades for bourgeois mercenary interests, Galleani condemned the war in Europe, urging immigrants not to respond to Italy's call for arms. When the United States entered the war, he advocated resistance; an article of 26 May 1917 in *Cronaca Sovversiva* denounced military conscription as a form of slavery. Regarded by the federal government as "the most dangerous anarchist in the United States," Galleani and his associates were subjected to repeated detentions, sequestrations, and raids. *Galleanisti* were arrested by the hundreds. Despite tough measures to suppress *Cronaca Sovversiva*, the paper continued to be published regularly until 18 July 1918 (two additional issues appeared clandestinely in 1919).

From 1917 on the *Galleanisti* responded with a campaign of terror. Dynamite was their explosive of choice. In 1905 Galleani had published a bomb-making manual, *La salute è in voi!* (Health is in you!). A series of bombings from 1914 on have been attributed to the *Galleanisti*, and in the spring of 1919 thirty letter bombs were sent to leading congressmen, public officials, and businessmen. On 2 June bombings took place in eight cities. On 16 September 1920 a bomb exploded on Wall Street, killing thirty-three persons. While Galleani appears not to have been directly involved in the conspiracy, there is no doubt that the bombers were inspired by his teachings and that he approved of their actions.

Meanwhile Galleani was deported with eight of his followers on the *Duca degli Abruzzi* on 24 June 1919. He left behind his wife, Maria Rallo (they formally married in May 1919), and their five children. Although suffering from diabetes, Galleani threw himself into the maelstrom of postwar Italy, reviving *Cronaca Sovversiva* in Turin in 1920. He was soon arrested, imprisoned, and once again confined to a penal island. Mussolini had reason to fear Galleani and his followers, since anarchists made several assassination attempts in the 1920s. Aged and ill, Galleani was finally allowed to return to a small village on the mainland, Caprigliola, where he died.

Galleani left behind a troubled legacy in America. Among his most dedicated followers were Nicola Sacco and Bartolomeo Vanzetti, who were involved in the terrorist conspiracy. Arrested on 5 May 1920 for a robbery and murder in South Braintree, Massachusetts, they were convicted and finally executed on 23 August 1927. The question of their innocence or guilt has never been conclusively established, but there is no doubt that they were victims of the "Red Scare" to which Galleani had given substance.

Once feared as the most dangerous radical in America, Galleani has been largely ignored by history. Yet he ranks with Emma Goldman and Alexander Berkman in the heroic age of American anarchism. The *Galleanisti* carried out the most extensive terrorist campaign conducted in the United States to that time. Following Galleani's deportation and severe government repression, Italian anarchism in America became a mere shadow of its former self. Yet the *Galleanisti* maintained a presence for another half-century. Their organ, *L'Adunata dei Refrattari* (The gathering on the refractories), published until 1971, continued to disseminate Galleani's ideas. The movement, however, failed to attract a second generation, and as the faithful gradually died, there were no replacements.

• No body of Galleani's papers has survived, but scattered correspondence is in the Jacques Gross, Max Nettlau, and Ugo Fedeli archives of the International Institute of Social History, Amsterdam. The institute holds extensive files of the Italian-American anarchist press. The Aldino Felicani Papers at the Boston Public Library are an important source for the *Galleanisti*. Rich documentation on Galleani is in the Archivio Centrale dello Stato (Rome) and in the National Archives, Washington, D.C.

Collected writings by Galleani are *Faccia a faccia col nemico* (1914); *Figure e figuri* (1930); *Aneliti e singulti* (1935); *Il pensiero di Galleani* (1950); and *Methodi della lotta socialista* (1972). A major work translated into English is *The End of Anarchism?* trans. Max Sartin and Robert D'Atillio (1982). A full-length, if uncritical, biography is Ugo Fedeli, *Luigi Galleani: Quarant'anni di lotte rivoluzionarie, 1891–1931* (1956). The most thorough history of the *Galleanisti* movement is Paul Avrich, *Sacco and Vanzetti: The Anarchist Background* (1991). For a brief biography see Franco Andreucci and Tommaso Detti, eds., *Il movimento operaio italiano: Dizionario biografico, 1853–1943*, vol. 2 (1976), pp. 418–24. On the *Galleanisti*'s bombing campaign, Nunzio Pernicone, "Luigi Galleani and Italian Anarchist Terrorism in the United States," *Studi Emigrazione* 30 (1993): 469–89, is useful. For bibliographies of Galleani's writings see Fedeli, pp. 199–206, and Andreucci and Detti, pp. 213–14. Obituary notices are in *L'Adunata dei Refrattari*, 14 Nov. and 19 Dec. 1931.

RUDOLPH J. VECOLI

GALLERY, Daniel Vincent (10 July 1901–16 Jan. 1977), naval officer and author, was born in Chicago, Illinois, the son of Daniel V. Gallery, a lawyer, and Mary Josephine Onahan. In 1917, at the age of sixteen, Daniel was appointed to the U.S. Naval Academy. He graduated 47th in his class of 285 in 1920. After wrestling in the 1920 Antwerp Olympic Games, Gallery went to sea as an engineering specialist. In 1927 he elected flight training at Pensacola. Winning his wings, he engaged in many aspects of naval aviation over the next decade by piloting torpedo, observation, and scouting planes; by commanding the carrier *Langley* in 1936; by returning to Pensacola as a flight instructor; and by studying aviation ordnance at the navy's Post Graduate School. During this period, in 1929, Gallery married Vera Lee Dunn. The couple adopted two boys and a girl.

The outbreak of World War II found Gallery commanding the Aviation Ordnance Section of the Bureau of Aeronautics. In January 1941 he assumed the post of assistant naval attaché for air in London. With the U.S. declaration of war on Germany, Gallery took command of the Fleet Air Base in Iceland, where he organized long-range antisubmarine patrols in the North Atlantic until May 1943. For the able performance of his unit in the face of adverse weather and spartan living conditions, Gallery won the Bronze Star.

In July 1943 Gallery returned to sea duty as commanding officer of the new escort carrier *Guadalcanal*, the flagship of a submarine hunter-killer task group. Enjoying marked success, Gallery's force sank *U-544* on 16 January 1944 and *U-515* and *U-68* in April 1944. Because of these victories, Gallery became convinced that his force, with adequate preparation, might capture a submarine. He therefore ordered his ships to organize and exercise boarding parties. In the face of widespread skepticism, their hard work paid dividends on 4 June 1944, when Gallery's sailors forced *U-505* to the surface off Cape Blanco, French West Africa, boarded the sinking submarine, and towed the prize to Bermuda. This was the first U.S. Navy capture of an enemy warship at sea since 1815. More significant, the submarine yielded extremely valuable code information as well as new German electric torpedoes. After the war, the *U-505* was moved to the Chicago Museum of Science and Industry.

In September 1944 Gallery began a stint in the Bureau of Aeronautics, then he took command of the carrier *Hancock* in the last days of the war. Promoted to rear admiral in December 1945, Gallery next commanded Escort Carrier Division Fifteen. In June 1947 he reported to the Pentagon as the first assistant chief of naval operations for guided missiles. Over the next two years he figured prominently in laying the groundwork for what would become the navy's first operational guided missiles, the Regulus cruise missile and the Talos, Terrier, and Tartar antiaircraft missiles.

However, Gallery soon became embroiled in the controversies surrounding defense unification and force structure. With the newly independent air force consuming most of the defense budget, top navy officers (in the so-called "Revolt of the Admirals") protested cuts in key navy programs. Writing articles with titles like "If This Be Treason—," Gallery mounted an especially outspoken defense of his service. Narrowly escaping court-martial, he left Washington in November 1949 to take the post of deputy commander of the Operational Development Force, Atlantic Fleet. Following an administrative assignment at Quonset Point, Rhode Island, in March 1951, he enjoyed his last sea command as flag officer of Carrier Division Six. During 1952 he headed up the Hunter-Killer Force, Atlantic Fleet, and held, over the next eight years, various shore assignments with training and district commands. Gallery retired on 1 October 1960 with the rank of rear admiral.

By this point Gallery had embarked on a second career as a writer of both fact and fiction. He possessed a gift for descriptive narrative and a fine sense of humor; most of his work was based on his personal experience. Among his better-known publications were *Clear the Decks!* (1951), describing his experiences on the *Guadalcanal*, and *Twenty Million Tons under the Sea* (1956), tracing the German submarine depredations in World War II. Among his other works were books of fiction, *The Brink* (1968) and *"Away Boarders"* (1971); *The Pueblo Incident* (1970); and pieces in the *Saturday Evening Post* and *Collier's*. His article "We Can Baffle the Brainwashers" in the *Saturday Evening Post* (22 Jan. 1955) created a storm of controversy by advocating that prisoners of war be allowed to sign confessions, thereby robbing such statements of their propaganda value for the enemy.

Gallery died at the Bethesda Naval Medical Center in Maryland. Over the course of his career, he had won the Distinguished Service Medal for his successful command of antisubmarine forces during the first half of 1944 and the Order of the Commander of the British Empire. Two of his brothers, William D. Gallery and Philip D. Gallery, also retired as rear admirals, and another brother, John I. Gallery, became a Naval Reserve chaplain.

During his career Gallery flew more than 6,000 hours in a wide variety of naval aircraft from bi-wing torpedo bombers to single-engine jet fighters. Through his ordnance expertise, he helped shepherd the navy into the missile age, and through his pen, he helped publicize its place in the defense establishment to a sometimes skeptical nation. But above all, he is remembered for his remarkable combat exploit in capturing a German submarine intact on the high seas.

• Gallery's autobiography is entitled *Eight Bells and All's Well* (1965). A biographical sketch is in Clark G. Reynolds, *Famous American Admirals* (1978). Gallery's obituary is in the *New York Times*, 20 Jan. 1977.

MALCOLM MUIR, JR.

GALLI, Rosina (1896–30 Apr. 1940), ballerina and ballet mistress of the Metropolitan Opera, was born in Milan, Italy. Little is known of her parents or early life. Trained at the Scuola di Ballo of the Teatro alla Scala, Milan, Galli distinguished herself early as an unusually precocious and popular child performer. By the age of fourteen she was dancing prima ballerina roles at La Scala and by fifteen was a guest ballerina at the San Carlo Opera House in Naples.

Galli's Italian career was short, however. During her only season at San Carlo in the winter of 1911, she signed a contract to dance as première danseuse étoile with the Chicago Grand Opera. She made her American debut with that company on 11 October 1911 during a performance of *Carmen* in Philadelphia. Galli remained in Chicago until the end of the 1913–1914 season when the Chicago Grand Opera disbanded. Immediately afterward she was hired by Giulio Gatti-Casazza, general director of the Metropolitan Opera in New York.

Traditionally, ballet had been a decidedly minor part of the Metropolitan Opera's endeavors. Although custom dictated the inclusion of ballet in the nineteenth-century operatic repertory, no part of the season was devoted entirely to ballet as was commonplace in Europe. Nevertheless, in her prime and at the height of her technical power, Galli was compared favorably by critics to Anna Pavlova and the ballerinas of Serge Diaghilev's Ballets Russes. Galli's most important and popular roles included the Warrior Princess in the "Polovtsian Dances" from Borodin's *Prince Igor*; the Queen in Rimsky-Korsakov's *Le Coq d'Or*, in which the dancers took center stage and the singers sat at the sides; and the Doll in *Petroushka*, staged by Adolf Dolm after Michel Fokine.

Beginning with the 1919 season, Galli became the Metropolitan's ballet mistress while continuing to dance leading roles. Her new responsibilities were "to compose dances" as well as to "supervise" the ballet school. Throughout the early twenties, Galli danced in and choreographed a remarkable array of divertissements. America's taste in dance was not yet sophisticated. The reigning ballet aesthetic in the American opera house combined qualities of the old grand opera and the new musical revue: lavish spectacle replete with ornate costumes and stage designs, pageantry that featured the gracious deployment of pretty girls, and, on occasion, the excitement of acrobatic virtuosity. More than once reviewers compared the opera's sensationalism with Broadway.

Through all kinds of grand balletic displays, Galli herself continued to make the most striking impression. In his review of *Le Prophète* in the *New York World*, 5 February, 1920, James Huneker gushed, "Miss Galli is a lyric dancer. She trills with her toes. Such coloratura! . . . Such dancing as hers, brilliantly technical or dramatically characteristic, is rare enough in this period of freak contortionists."

As a choreographer Galli was not an innovator. She employed the prevailing opera-house style, often merely rearranging the dances of former productions. But according to Rita De Leporte—who danced with the Metropolitan during the twenties and succeeded Galli as première danseuse—Galli was quite skilled at her craft, able to work with great facility and in a manner that kept her public quite happy.

In 1925 Galli became seriously ill with appendicitis and stopped dancing for a year and a half. According to the dance historian Lillian Moore, who was in the Metropolitan corps de ballet at that time, after her illness Galli "made no attempt to regain the spectacular technique which had made her dancing so remarkable, although she continued to dance with superb finesse until her retirement." Galli's last decade at the Met was a period of general decline for the opera house. With the spread of modernism in music and dance, Americans had become more sophisticated in their tastes. But like the opera stagings of Gatti-Casazza, whose reign at the Metropolitan lasted twenty-seven years, the ballets were becoming moribund. Reviewing a 1927 production of *La Giara*, a one-act comic ballet based on a novel by Pirandello, Olin Downes, the critic of the *New York Times*, asserted, "The characters on stage were dressed as peasants, but acted like accomplished manikins . . . with the formality of the dance as it was half a century ago, and as it is no longer for those with any realization of its evolution since the coming of America of the great Russian ballet."

In 1930 Galli and Gatti-Casazza married and she retired from the stage. However, she retained her title as ballet mistress until June 1935 when her husband quit the opera house and she retired to Italy with him. Nearly thirty years younger than her husband, Galli was against the move but finally relented. She died in Milan, Italy, of pneumonia five years later.

Galli presided over the most illustrious period of dance in the Metropolitan Opera's history. Long before dance performances were widespread in New York, Galli, an excellent technician of the Italian school, was showing an important segment of the cultured public, the opera audience, what good classical dancing could be and helping to pave the way for the new American ballet. Her success was made possible by the fortuitous coming together of her own talents, the prosperity of the opera house during the 1920s and the interest in ballet sparked by the touring Ballets Russes of Diaghilev. The prestige and accolades accorded to Galli at her peak also reflected on the Metropolitan Opera Ballet School, which attracted many pupils who later became important figures in American ballet including Nora Kay, Maria Karnilova, and Ruthanna Boris.

• The Dance Collection at the New York Public Library for the Performing Arts, Lincoln Center contains clipping files of magazine and newspaper articles about Galli's career in the United States and photograph files of her in costume and in publicity shots. The dance collection also houses the Walter Toscanini Collection of Research Materials in Dance, which refers to Galli's Italian career. The library's music division houses the Metropolitan Opera Scrapbook, vols. 16–56 (May 1914–Dec. 1935), which contains many reviews of Galli's performances in New York and the *Metropolitan Opera Annals*, which chronicle performances and cast members by season.

Behind the Scenes at the Opera, a 1925 book by Mary Watkins, music and dance critic of the *New York Herald Tribune*, contains a chapter devoted to Galli.

TULLIA LIMARZI

GALLICO, Paul William (26 July 1897–15 July 1976), writer, was born in New York City, the son of Paolo Gallico, an Italian concert pianist and music teacher, and Hortense Erlich, an Austrian. Although he was educated in New York City's public school system, Gallico spent much of his childhood accompanying his parents while his father toured the United States and Europe giving concerts. Gallico grew to be a large, athletic man, standing 6′3″. His interest in sport, an enthusiasm his European father did not understand, developed along with his interest in writing. Gallico wrote his first story in Brussels at the age of ten. Though his father prevented him from playing high school football, Gallico lettered four years in crew at Columbia University, serving as captain his senior year.

Gallico entered Columbia in 1916, intending to be a physician and to use his professional income to support his writing. He worked his way through school as a gymnastics instructor, an usher, and at other odd jobs. At the end of his sophomore year, however, he decided against medical school, believing that it would be cowardly for him to go into medicine because his true desire was to write. Without informing his parents, Gallico began studying literature. After serving in the U.S. Navy as a gunner during World War I, Gallico completed a B.S. at Columbia in 1921.

Following college, Gallico worked for one year as a review secretary with the National Board of Motion Picture Review before becoming a journalist and sportswriter. In 1922 Gallico joined the staff of the New York *Daily News* as a motion picture critic. One year later he moved into the sports department and in 1924 was promoted to sports editor. Over the next twelve years Gallico earned a reputation as one of America's finest sportswriters. Believing that in order to understand sport one must experience it, Gallico boxed with Jack Dempsey, golfed with Bobby Jones, Gene Sarazen, and Tommy Armour, swam against Johnny Weissmuller, caught and hit with pitchers Dizzy Dean, Dazzy Vance, and Herb Pennock, skied an Olympic run at Garmisch-Partenkirchen, and received passes from NFL quarterback Benny Friedman. In 1927 Gallico organized the Golden Gloves amateur boxing tournament, and in 1932 he learned to fly.

By 1936 Gallico had become one of the highest-paid sportswriters in New York. In addition, he had written fourteen short stories, most of which were published in the *Saturday Evening Post*. Gallico decided to give up regular newspaper sportswriting in order to become a freelance writer, and he rented a cottage on the Devonshire coast in England. Between 1936 and 1943 he spent his summers writing in Devonshire. When not in Devonshire or on assignment for *Cosmopolitan*, Gallico lived on his farm in Hunterdon County, New Jersey. In 1944 he served as *Cosmopolitan*'s European editor and war correspondent. He returned to Columbia later in 1944 to teach a short-story course. In 1950 Gallico moved to Europe permanently, living in London, Lichtenstein, and, from 1963 on, in Monaco, where he died.

A prolific writer, Gallico produced forty-one books and several screenplays during his career. Among his most important works are *Farewell to Sport* (1938), in which he denounced racial discrimination in sport and the hypocrisy of amateurism, and *The Snow Goose* (1941), a sentimental romance about a crippled artist and a young girl in wartime England. The latter work received an honorable mention as an O. Henry Memorial Prize story in 1941. Gallico also wrote a number of children's stories and animal tales. Gallico's works *Lou Gehrig: Pride of the Yankees* (1942) and *The Poseidon Adventure* (1969) were made into feature films. Gallico's popular novel *The Adventures of Hiram Holiday* (1939) inspired a sequel, *The Secret Front* (1940), and a television series starring Wally Cox. The popularity of *Mrs. 'Arris Goes to Paris* (1958) also prompted several sequels.

Gallico married the first of his four wives, Alva Thoits Taylor, daughter of columnist Bert Leston Taylor of the Chicago *Tribune*, in 1921. This marriage produced his only two children before ending in divorce in 1934. In 1935 he married Elaine St. Johns, daughter of writer Adela Rogers St. Johns; they were divorced the next year. His third marriage, to Baroness Pauline Garibaldi, lasted from 1939 until their divorce in 1954. In 1963 Gallico married his fourth wife, Baroness Virginia von Falz-Fein.

Never abandoning his interest in athletics, Gallico took pleasure in deep-sea fishing, skiing, horseback riding, and dancing. Gallico was a world-class fencer, serving as a master to the French army up to the year before his death. And though he wrote *Golf Is a Friendly Game* (1942), Gallico is reported to have sometimes broken clubs in mid-course.

With a sizable body of work in various genres to his credit, it is difficult to categorize Gallico's efforts as a writer. Willing to accept challenges—in journalism, athletics, or fiction—the ambitious Gallico was not content with being only a sportswriter. Gallico's varied interests and numerous wives brought him additional public attention. His two marriages to baronesses brought him into the social circle of European nobility, and by midlife he had become a cosmopolitan known throughout Europe and the United States. Having given up a lucrative career in journalism, Gallico turned his attention to short stories and novels and proved to be a gifted and successful storyteller.

• Gallico's papers are at Columbia University. A short autobiography is included in Gallico, *Confessions of a Story Writer* (1946) and *Further Confessions of a Story Writer: Stories Old and New* (1961). See also David L. Porter, ed., *Biographical Dictionary of American Sports: Outdoor Sports* (1988). An obituary is in the *New York Times*, 17 July 1976.

BRIAN S. BUTLER

GALLI-CURCI, Amelita (18 Nov. 1882–26 Nov. 1963), opera singer, was born Amelita Galli in Milan, Italy, the daughter of Enrico Galli, a banker and businessman, and Enrichetta Bellisoni. There were musicians on both sides of the family, and Amelita was encouraged to develop her musical gifts at an early age. At the age of five, she began studying the piano, and her lessons continued at the Milan Conservatory while she completed primary and secondary education at private schools in Milan, where she became fluent in German, French, Spanish, and English.

Galli graduated from the Milan Conservatory at the age of sixteen, receiving a gold medal for her proficiency at the piano. When a family friend, the composer Pietro Mascagni, heard her sing at a private gathering, he praised her coloratura and advised her to prepare for a career in opera. Amelita, who had never taken voice lessons and claimed that she had learned to vocalize by listening to birds, decided that instead of finding an instructor she would teach herself. She used the techniques described in *Traité complet de l'art du chant* (1840) by the Spanish baritone and pedagogue Manuel Patricio Rodriguez Garcia, who had taught the Swedish soprano Jenny Lind, and those of the contemporary German soprano and teacher Lilli Lehmann. She employed these techniques in daily practice, learning several operatic roles.

In 1906, hearing about an opening for a low-budget production of *Rigoletto* at the opera house in Trani, Galli traveled from Milan to the small southern seaport and successfully auditioned for the role of Gilda. She made her operatic debut on 26 December to local acclaim and remained with the company until the three-month season ended. During her stay in Trani, she met Gennaro Curci, an operatic basso, and his brother Luigi, a painter, who later became the marchese di Simeri. In February 1908 Amelita Galli married the marchese, and two months later, on 20 April, she made her official debut as Amelita Galli-Curci in Rome at the Teatro Costanzi in Bizet's *Don Procopio*.

During the next eight years, Galli-Curci's career grew, albeit slowly. She sang in various Italian opera houses, performed in Madrid and Barcelona, and twice in Buenos Aires, where in 1915 she appeared with Enrico Caruso, and toured in the Caribbean and Central America. Not until her American debut, however, did she emerge as a star.

In 1916, during a stopover in New York City, Galli-Curci auditioned for several American opera directors, including Cleofonte Campanini of the Chicago Opera Association, who hired her to sing the role of Gilda in two performances of *Rigoletto* at $300 each. She made her American debut at the Chicago Opera House on 18 November 1916 to tremendous acclaim and was hailed by local critics as the equal of Jenny Lind and the nineteenth-century Italian soprano Adelina Patti. Campanini immediately extended her contract through the remainder of the season at a salary of $1,500 for each performance.

Galli-Curci continued under contract with the Chicago Opera Association during the next few years, performing both in Chicago and on tour. In 1917 she began making records for the Victor Talking Machine Company, which enhanced her career. Her recordings of "The Bell Song" from *Lakmé* and "Caro Nome" from *Rigoletto* were especially popular and sold thousands of copies, making her a recording artist as successful as Caruso.

Galli-Curci made her New York debut with the Chicago company on 28 January 1918, singing the title role in *Dinorah*, a popular nineteenth-century opera by Giacomo Meyerbeer that had frequently starred Adelina Patti. This time the reviewers were not unanimous in their praise. Writing in the *New York Times*, Richard Aldrich was adulatory, but other critics found fault with aspects of her performance and some accused her of singing off-key.

American audiences, however, were uniformly enthusiastic about Galli-Curci, and in 1921 the tiny soprano was finally engaged by the Metropolitan Opera. She made her Met debut on 14 November of that year, singing the role of Violetta in *La Traviata*. Again, the critics were divided about her performance, but Galli-Curci delighted the audience. During the 1920s she was one of the Metropolitan Opera's most popular leading ladies in such operas as *The Barber of Seville*, *Romeo and Juliet*, *Rigoletto*, *La Bohème*, *La Traviata*, and *Lakmé*. She also sang with the Chicago Opera Association until 1924.

In the late 1920s Galli-Curci developed an enlarged goiter that increasingly impaired her breathing. In 1930 she announced that she was abandoning her operatic career but did not give illness as the reason: it was opera, she claimed, that was ailing, losing audiences because it was out of date. Galli-Curci made her last performance at the Metropolitan Opera on 24 January 1930 as Rosina in *The Barber of Seville*. During the next few years, she made concert tours in Europe,

South America, South Africa, and India, interrupted at intervals by goiter attacks.

Finally, in 1936, Galli-Curci underwent surgery for treatment of the goiter, and in November of that year she returned to opera as Mimi in *La Bohème* at the Chicago Civic Opera. She received a tremendous ovation from the audience, but reviewers criticized her performance, claiming that she had lost her earlier range and clarity. Following several more appearances on the operatic and concert stages, Galli-Curci retired in 1937. An American citizen since 1921, she moved to southern California with her accompanist and second husband, Homer Samuels, whom she had married in 1921, a year after divorcing Luigi Curci. She had no children from either marriage.

In her nearly thirty years of retirement, Galli-Curci took up oil painting, became a devotee of Swedenborgian and Indian philosophies, and enjoyed nature. Following her husband's death in 1956, Galli-Curci moved from their home in Rancho Santa Fe to La Jolla, where she died.

Although Galli-Curci had not sung in public for nearly thirty years, her death was front-page news in the United States as well as abroad—notable in view of the fact that President John F. Kennedy's assassination only three days earlier continued to dominate the headlines. Music historians paid tribute to her as the reigning coloratura of the operatic stage for nearly two decades, and they praised her clear, unaffected voice that, at its peak, extended over a range of two and one half octaves. Galli-Curci was also remembered for her gracious stage manner and personal attractiveness.

Galli-Curci left an estate valued at $285,000, most of which was given to the Amelita Galli-Curci Foundation, which she had created to provide grants and scholarships for music students.

• For biographical information on Galli-Curci, see her article "My Career as a Prima Donna and How It Developed," *Musical Observer*, May 1919, pp. 9–10; C. E. Le Massena, *Galli-Curci's Life of Song* (1945); Rupert Christiansen, *Prima Donna: A History* (1984); and "Diva's Will Aids Students," *New York Times*, 7 Dec. 1963. An obituary and an appreciative essay by music critic Harold Schonberg appear in the *New York Times*, 27 Nov. 1963.

ANN T. KEENE

GALLIER, James, Sr. (24 July 1798–10 Mar. 1866), architect, was born in Ravensdale, County Louth, Ireland, the son of Thaddeus Gallier, a builder, and Margaret Taylor. Gallier seemed destined to follow his father in terms of his profession, for he studied architectural drawing at the School of Fine Arts in Dublin before leaving for Liverpool in 1816 to seek work as a builder. In 1820 he returned to Ireland but two years later moved to London, where he worked for Cover and Lawrence, Builders. In 1823 he married Elizabeth Tyler; they had one child. In 1826 he was appointed to superintend the construction of the Huntingdon County Gaol by its architect, William Wilkins. By 1828 he was back in London, where he remained until his departure for New York City in 1832. Upon arrival in New York, he associated himself first with architect James H. Dakin and then with Minard Lafever, an architect and the author of several significant architectural pattern books. In October 1834 Gallier left for New Orleans, Louisiana, accompanied by James Dakin's younger brother Charles. The two stayed briefly in Mobile, Alabama, where they received the commission for Barton Academy, a large academic building in the Greek revival style.

In early 1835 Dakin and Gallier arrived in New Orleans, where they met with immediate success, designing the St. Charles Hotel and the Merchants Exchange, two large and complex public buildings, both in the Greek revival style. The St. Charles Hotel, with its dome supported on a ring of columns, was the largest building in the city until it was destroyed by fire in 1855. By late 1835 James Dakin had arrived in New Orleans and formed a partnership with his brother, while Gallier continued to practice individually. In 1839 Gallier was hired to complete St. Patrick's Church. It had been begun by the Dakins, but they were dismissed on account of structural problems with the building. The church, designed in the gothic revival style, is Gallier's most important religious work and features elaborate plaster fan vaulting, with stained glass set into the vault above the main altar. It was restored in the 1980s.

In the 1840s Gallier continued to work in New Orleans, receiving numerous commissions for private residences, including one for William Newton Mercer, built in 1844, now the home of the Boston Club. The Mercer house, while larger than most of Gallier's domestic designs, is typical in terms of its style—Greek revival—and its plan, which is oriented around an entry hall set to one side. Gallier also designed numerous townhouses, most of which have been demolished, including a fine trio of houses with identical giant order columnar portico facades. In 1845 Gallier received the commission for the Municipal Hall, without doubt his masterpiece in the Greek revival style. Designed to house government offices as well as a library and lecture hall, the Municipal Hall's multifunction plan was dictated by the city council. The Lyceum Hall, once located on the second floor of the building, featured a coffered, arched ceiling and must have been one of Gallier's finest interiors. Municipal Hall was completed in 1851 and, on the dedication of a new city hall in 1955, was renamed Gallier Hall in his honor. By 1849 Gallier's eyesight had begun to fail him, and he retired, turning over the firm to his son, James, Jr. Following his first wife's death in 1843, Gallier married Catherine Robinson in 1850. Gallier and his wife perished when the steamship *Evening Star* sank off the coast of North Carolina.

Gallier is significant in the context of American architecture for his English architectural training, which placed him among the top of his profession on his arrival in the United States in 1832. While he acted as a builder as well as an architect for many of his own designs, he clearly saw himself as a skilled professional designer, a fact that is evident from the quality of his extant works. He was also active as an author, writing and publishing *The American Builders Price Book and Estimator* in 1833 and completing his *Autobiography of James Gallier, Architect*, which was published in Paris in 1864. His impact was perhaps greatest on the architecture of New Orleans, where his most noted designs were built and where many survive today.

• Gallier's surviving architectural drawings are housed at the Southeastern Architectural Archive of Tulane University, New Orleans, La. Modern scholarly references to his work can be found in Arthur Scully, Jr., *James Dakin, Architect* (1973), which focuses on the relationship between Gallier and Dakin. Talbot Hamlin, *Greek Revival Architecture in America* (1944), discusses Gallier's career in the context of the development of the Greek revival style. Discussion of Gallier's work in New Orleans can be found in the Friends of the Cabildo series New Orleans Architecture, vol. 1: *The Lower Garden District* (1971) and vol. 2: *The American Sector* (1972), and in S. Frederick Starr, *Southern Comfort: The Garden District of New Orleans, 1800–1900* (1989).

JOHN C. FERGUSON

GALLINGER, Jacob Harold (28 Mar. 1837–17 Aug. 1918), U.S. senator, was born in Cornwall, Ontario, Canada, the son of Jacob Gallinger and Catharine Cook, farmers. At age twelve Gallinger served as an apprentice to a Cornwall printer, remaining there for four years. He then worked a year in a printing office at Ogdensburg, New York, before returning to Cornwall for another year of general newspaper work. In 1855 he relocated to Cincinnati, Ohio, where he found employment on the staff of the *Cincinnati Gazette* while studying medicine at the Cincinnati Medical Institute, from which he graduated in 1858. Gallinger studied in Europe for two years before beginning his medical and surgical practice in association with Dr. W. B. Chamberlain at Keene, New Hampshire, in 1860, the year he married Mary Anna Bailey. They moved to Concord, New Hampshire, in 1862, and raised two children. While practicing in Concord, Gallinger continued his studies, receiving a medical degree from the New York Homeopathic Medical College in 1868. A frequent contributor to medical journals, he became surgeon general of the state in 1879 and 1880 on the staff of Governor Natt Head and maintained his practice in Concord.

Gallinger developed strong interests in local Republican politics. He held a seat in the New Hampshire House of Representatives in 1872 and 1873 and again in 1891. He also participated in the state's constitutional convention in 1876. Elected to the state senate in 1878, Gallinger served as president of that legislative body during his last two terms, leaving the New Hampshire Senate in 1881. The following year Gallinger became chairman of the Republican State Committee, a position he maintained intermittently for a total of eighteen years. In 1884 he won a seat in the U.S. House of Representatives, serving from 1885 to 1889. Noted for his ability as a debater, Gallinger forced the House to conduct an investigation into the conduct of the Government Printing Office. As chairman of the New Hampshire delegation to the Republican National Convention in 1888, Gallinger seconded the presidential nomination of Benjamin Harrison, who won the election. He later quarreled with the chief executive over patronage and continued a long personal and political feud with his Republican colleague, Senator William E. Chandler of New Hampshire, who had defeated Gallinger in a U.S. Senate election in 1888.

In 1891 Gallinger began his career in the U.S. Senate, which lasted twenty-seven years. A strong partisan and orthodox politician known for his political adroitness, oratorical skills, attention to detail, and a determination to uphold senatorial prerogatives, Gallinger supported high tariff legislation, sound money measures, and other policies favorable to eastern financial and industrial interests. Fervently conservative, Gallinger exemplified the standpattism of the "Old Guard" of his generation. He was contemptuous of most reforms, including civil service, though he supported prohibition and woman suffrage.

Gallinger's choice for the presidency in 1896 was Congressman Thomas B. Reed of Maine, the crusty Speaker of the House of Representatives. Gallinger considered Reed to be more able than former governor William McKinley of Ohio, but he grudgingly reconciled himself to McKinley's nomination. "I quite agree with you," Gallinger wrote to an editor, "that Reed is a great man and that McKinley is not a great man, and yet we must keep in mind the fact that the great men of the country have not been nominated for the Presidency." After McKinley's election, Gallinger supported the president's foreign and domestic policies.

During his long tenure in the Senate, Gallinger weathered various political storms and became one of the most powerful political leaders in New Hampshire history. Because of his political ability and personal popularity, he was never seriously challenged for his Senate seat. Self-confident and pugnacious, he melded individual independence with devotion to his party. His committee assignments included Appropriations, Finance, Pensions, Rules, and Printing. Gallinger's most important role revolved around his chairmanship of the Committee on the Affairs of the District of Columbia, a position he held from 1901 to 1913. His approval was necessary before any law could be passed relating to the federal district. Although interested especially in the beautification of the city, the senator also authored an act to reform the district's medical practices. From 1904 to 1905 he was chairman of the Merchant Marine Commission.

Gallinger's espousal of political conservatism and belief in party loyalty crystalized during the presidential campaign of 1912, when he steadfastly endorsed the renomination and reelection of President William Howard Taft. Appalled that former president Theodore Roosevelt had decided to challenge Taft for the White House and cognizant of the hazards of a divided party, Gallinger led the movement for Taft in New Hampshire. He was among those who engineered to retain conservative control of the party machinery in the state. Fearful of a Democratic sweep of local and state offices, Gallinger blamed Roosevelt for the turmoil, peppering his speeches with criticism and hostility that seemed vindictive. He referred to the former chief executive as "a rabid and unreasoning advocate of civil service reform" determined to cling to "office with the tenacity of grim death." According to Gallinger, Roosevelt's departure from the Republican fold necessitated a concerted effort to defeat him as much as the Democratic contender. Following Taft's success at the Republican National Convention, which Gallinger attended, the senator wholeheartedly maneuvered to put New Hampshire in Taft's column. He addressed rallies, coordinated efforts with national groups, and informed Republican officials of their chances for success. Taft's devastating defeat in 1912 perturbed Gallinger, who emerged as an outspoken critic of President Woodrow Wilson's administration.

From 1913 to 1918 Gallinger served as the Republican caucus chairman. He was president pro tempore of the Senate during the Sixty-second Congress. At the time of his death in Franklin, New Hampshire, he was the senior member of the Senate in years of continuous service. Though he upheld the status quo during a transitional era, Gallinger refused to back down from controversy. Instead, he stated his views forthrightly, articulated his perception of established American values, and worked tirelessly for the people of New Hampshire.

• Gallinger's papers are in the New Hampshire Historical Society at Concord. The most thorough accounts of Gallinger's life and career are Leonard Schlup, "Consistent Conservative: Jacob Harold Gallinger and the Presidential Campaign of 1912 in New Hampshire," *International Review of History and Political Science* 21 (1984): 49–57, and Schlup, "The Presidential Election of 1896 and the Gallinger-Marseilles Correspondence," *Manuscripts* 46 (Summer 1994): 205–17. Obituaries are in the *New York Times*, 18 Aug. 1918, *Boston Evening Transcript*, 17 Aug. 1918, *Granite Monthly*, July–Sept. 1918; *Manchester Union*, 19 Aug. 1918; and *Washington Post*, 18 Aug. 1918.

LEONARD SCHLUP

GALLITZIN, Demetrius Augustine (22 Dec. 1770–6 May 1840), Russian prince and Catholic missionary, was born into a royal Russian family in The Hague, Holland, the son of Prince Demetrius Alexejewitsch Gallitzin, the Russian ambassador to Holland, and the German countess Amalia von Schmettau. His father had been, prior to his ambassadorship to The Hague, ambassador to Paris, where he was closely associated with the French philosophers. A rationalist, Demetrius Alexejewitsch's relationship with the Russian Orthodox church was purely nominal, and although his son was baptized in that church he was not educated in it. The Countess Amalia, although born into a German Catholic family, was also a devotee of Enlightenment rationalism. In 1772 the countess separated from her husband and moved to Münster in 1779, where she became the center of a Romantic intellectual and religious movement known as the Münster circle. She eventually rejected rationalism and returned to Catholicism. Demetrius, whom she had educated in the best Gymnasiums of Holland and Germany, became a Catholic at the age of seventeen. After finishing his education in a Münster school established by his mother, Demetrius was appointed an aide-de-camp to the Austrian general von Lillien. There was no opportunity for him in the military, however, so in 1792, when he was twenty-two, his mother sent him to tour America and the West Indies to broaden his education.

Against the objections of his friends and relatives in Europe, in 1792 Gallitzin entered the Baltimore, Maryland, Sulpician seminary, drawn to the priesthood because he saw the need for missionary clergy in the newly organized American Catholic church. In 1795 he was ordained, the first Catholic to receive all his education for the priesthood within the United States. From 1795 to 1799, he served as pastor to various Catholic communities in Maryland and Pennsylvania.

In 1799 Gallitzin founded a small Catholic colony at Loretto, Pennsylvania, in the Allegheny Mountains. For the next forty years he served as a pioneer missionary to Catholics within a hundred-mile radius of this western Pennsylvania town. Using his considerable fortune, he purchased large tracts of land and invited Catholic immigrants to settle in the area. He built saw mills, grist mills, tanneries, schools, and other institutions and businesses to make Loretto a hub of Catholic activity in the Pennsylvania frontier.

Throughout his early years in the United States, Gallitzin was known as Augustine Smith, having changed his name to conceal his royal Russian heritage. To protect his property and to secure his inheritance, however, he returned to his family name in 1809. This did not ultimately protect his patrimony; after his father's death, the Russian government refused to honor his claims to his father's fortune.

Gallitzin gained national attention in 1816 when he published a *Defense of Catholic Principles* in response to a Pennsylvania Protestant minister's attack on "popery." This pamphlet, the first widely distributed American Catholic apologetical tract, went through many editions, and Catholics throughout the country referred to it to clarify their beliefs, religious practices, and customs and to demonstrate the compatibility of Catholic and American principles. Gallitzin's *An Appeal to the Protestant Public* (1819) and *A Letter to a Protestant Friend on the Holy Scriptures* (1820) also gave Catholics and Protestants a basic outline of Catholic beliefs and practices.

His defense of the Catholic faith and his development of Catholicism in western Pennsylvania earned Gallitzin high reputation among American Catholic bishops, who nominated him twice for the episcopacy (once for Cincinnati and once for Detroit), but he declined to be considered. Gallitzin was a horseback-riding missionary whose princely background and theological education made him a strong authoritarian figure on the frontier who was not always accepting of the free aspirations and democratic inclinations of the

pioneer Catholics of the area. Before the late 1820s he was periodically in conflict with leading lay members of his congregation, but eventually he won over his opponents and ran his church like a priestly prince.

When he died he was a poor man, disinherited by the Russian government and bereft of his family fortune. Yet he had seen significant growth in the settlement of western Pennsylvania, had helped develop numerous parishes in the area, and had encouraged other priests to join his missionary endeavors. The planning, financing, establishment, and construction of Loretto, however, remained his lasting monument to fame. He died in the town he had founded.

• Gallitzin's letters and other unpublished papers are located primarily in the archives of the archdioceses of Baltimore and Philadelphia. Many of his apologetical tracts are found in Grace Murphy, *Gallitzin's Letters: A Collection of Polemical Works of the Very Reverend Prince Demetrius Augustine Gallitzin, 1770–1840* (1940). The most recent biography is Stasys Maziliauskas, *Pioneer Prince in USA: An Historical Account of Prince Demetrius Augustine Gallitzin and His Eminent Relatives* (1982). Robert Gorman, *Catholic Apologetical Literature in the United States, 1784–1858* (1939), provides a critical assessment of his place in the history of American Catholic apologetics.

PATRICK W. CAREY

GALLO, Fortune (9 May 1878–28 Mar. 1970), opera impresario, was born Fortunato Gallo in Torre Maggiore, Italy, a town located a hundred miles east of Naples, the son of Tommaso Gallo and Zelinda Accetturo. He was encouraged as a boy by his father to become a musician, although his mother had hoped he would enter the priesthood. He learned to play the harmonica at age eight and at age fourteen became an apprentice drummer in the town band. When Gallo was seventeen the visit to Torre Maggiore of a man who had gone to the United States and prospered in the produce business suggested similar possibilities for the youth. At the visitor's urging his family agreed to let him seek his own fortune in the New World.

Gallo obtained his first job with one of a number of small banking institutions in the Italian section of New York City's Lower East Side. The appearance in New York in November 1898 of the Banda Rossa, a famous Italian concert band, and the opening performance of its American tour at the Metropolitan Opera House revealed to young Gallo an entirely different type of career opportunity. Recognizing a band member from his hometown, he quickly made friends with the rest of the ensemble and served as their guide to the pleasures of the city.

During this period Gallo shortened his first name to Fortune, and he became an American citizen in 1900. He was sought out by Channing Ellery, a music magazine publisher who was interested in organizing a concert band similar to the Banda Rossa since some of the band members had become attracted to the American way of life and didn't want to return to Italy. Ellery recruited other talented musicians from Europe, named his new aggregation the Royal Italian Band,

and started it on a nationwide tour in 1901. He made Gallo his advance man who went out ahead of the band to lay the groundwork for its appearances, arranging the publicity and making the contacts that would help ensure its success.

Gallo was in San Francisco in April 1906 when the Metropolitan Opera Company, with Enrico Caruso as its most celebrated star, was in the city as part of a Pacific Coast tour. At a reception for the company he was introduced to a young singer named Sofia Charlebois Wood, the daughter of an affluent local family, who sought his advice on furthering her vocal education in New York. In December 1907 he was sent by Ellery to Italy to recruit new talent for the band. After visiting his home in Torre Maggiore, he proceeded to Rome, where he again encountered Sofia, who was enjoying a holiday respite from her vocal studies. A romantic attachment developed but was not immediately pursued.

Returning to New York, Gallo shared with his employer his impressions of ragtime, a new type of music that was sweeping Western Europe. Ellery, however, was firmly committed to traditional content for his concerts, and in frustration Gallo began managing other groups more attuned to the new style, including the band of Giuseppe Creatore, one of Sousa's chief rivals.

The decisive break in Gallo's career came in March 1910, when he received a request from Mario Lambardi, an Italian architect who had organized an opera company to occupy the state opera house he had designed for Bogota, Colombia, and had then encountered serious difficulties in maintaining it. Gallo helped revive the fortunes of the troupe. In May 1912 he married Sofia in San Francisco, and in December he organized his own San Carlo Opera Company, naming it for the resident company of Naples's famed opera house.

Gallo's central idea was to present opera at popular prices in order to attract the widest possible audiences. The San Carlo company closed its second season with a deficit of $700, a trifling amount for enterprises of this nature. In its 1911–1912 season, during which he took the company to Hawaii, it cleared a profit of $25,000 and thereafter operated solidly in the black, in sharp contrast to major American opera companies, which either accumulated large deficits or were sustained by private subsidies.

Gallo's success was partly attributable to his popular price scale and partly to his no-frills operation of the company. He served as his own advance man and managing director, and only after the business of the organization had become complicated by the addition of other enterprises did he move his activities from a hotel suite to a Broadway office building. Gallo selected relatively unknown singers for leading roles, although some, such as Dorothy Kirsten, Richard Bonelli, and Queena Mario, as well as Helen Traubel, who sang in a locally augmented chorus in St. Louis during one San Carlo season, later went on to important careers with the Metropolitan Opera Company. The effectiveness of the San Carlo operation was also attributed to the careful groundwork Gallo laid in each community to which he took his company, building on his previous experience with the Royal Italian Band. He identified local social leaders to whom he was able to stress the value of the performances as social events, while reaching out to the general public through sponsorships of the engagements by service clubs and other nonprofit groups. He also sought to broaden his audiences by donating many seats to charitable organizations. Finally, he kept carefully to the standard repertoire; seven of his mainstay operas, *Aïda*, *Carmen*, *Faust*, *La Bohème*, *Rigoletto*, *La Traviata*, and *Il Trovatore*, were performed more than a thousand times.

The San Carlo Opera Company made its New York debut at the historic Thalia Theatre, formerly the Bowery, in the Bowery section of the Lower East Side. In 1920 Gallo took over the Manhattan Opera House, and in 1936 he made a further move to the Center Theatre in Rockefeller Center, where he succeeded in filling the large house for every performance in his two- to three-week engagements there each season until 1950.

From time to time he was able to enlist the services of major guest stars like Maria Jeritza and Giovanni Martinelli outside the Met season. During the 1940–1942 seasons he served as managing director of the Chicago Opera with Martinelli as artistic director, a partnership that achieved a substantial reduction in the company's annual deficit.

Following World War I Gallo presented a spectacular production of Verdi's *Aïda* at the Sheepshead Bay Speedway in Brooklyn to aid the victims of an earthquake in the Florence area of Italy and a production of Mascagni's *Cavalleria Rusticana* and Leoncavallo's *I Pagliacci*, featuring Metropolitan Opera stars at Madison Square Garden in a benefit for Italian orphan babies.

He brought Anna Pavlova and her ballet company to the United States for an extended tour in 1920 and three years later managed Eleanora Duse's final American tour in collaboration with the Selwyn Brothers. He also directed tours of the original Ballet Russe and Leonide Massine's Ballet Russe Highlights. At the time of Pavlova's tour he was managing three companies at once, the third being the Gallo English Opera Company, which performed Gilbert and Sullivan operettas.

In addition to his live presentations Gallo became a pioneer in the production of opera films and was responsible for the first full-length grand opera sound film, *I Pagliacci*, produced in 1930. During the summers of 1936 through 1938, he introduced the highly popular seasons of opera and operetta at Jones Beach State Park on Long Island. Other opera spectacles were offered at Soldier Field in Chicago and the Orange Bowl in Miami.

Sofia died in 1948, and Gallo terminated the activities of his company seven years later, reviving it briefly in Boston in 1963. Looking back on his long career, he could reflect that no one had done more to bring the beauties of live productions of opera to mass audiences in his adopted country. He died in New York City.

• Gallo's *Lucky Rooster: The Autobiography of an Impresario* (1967) is an ebullient account of his career. Other sources of information are "An Immigrant Boy Who Made Grand Opera Popular," *American Magazine*, July 1923, p. 72, and "Opera in the Black," *Time*, 25 May 1942, pp. 55–56. An obituary is in the *New York Times*, 29 Mar. 1970.

ALBERT O. WEISSBERG

GALLO, Julio (21 Mar. 1910–2 May 1993), vintner and wine industrialist, was born in Oakland, California, the son of Joseph "Giuseppe" Gallo, Sr., a tavern owner and winemaker from the Piedmont region of northern Italy, a noted wine-producing area, and Assunta Bianco. Gallo spent most of his teenage years on his father's vineyards near Modesto, California, graduating from Modesto High School in 1929. Before, during, and after school, he worked for his father, as did his older brother Ernest and his younger brother Joseph. Giuseppe began his winemaking career during Prohibition because a legislative "loophole" allowed home winemakers to produce 200 gallons per year for home consumption. After the repeal of Prohibition in 1933, Giuseppe Gallo increased the family's production, founded the Gallo Wine Company, and soon became a major supplier of grapes for the national markets.

In their early twenties, the Gallo brothers suffered a major tragedy when in 1933, their father murdered their mother just before committing suicide. Forced to take over the family business, the two older brothers turned it into the E. & J. Gallo Winery. By 1940 they had made a noticeable advance after purchasing bottling works in Los Angeles, California, and New Orleans, Louisiana, which allowed them to begin national distribution. By the 1950s the Gallos were having great success with low-priced wines, and within approximately a decade more success came with their low-cost "pop" wines that were aimed at the mass market.

In managing their business, each of the older Gallo brothers had definite spheres of interest. Ernest was largely responsible for sales and marketing while Julio oversaw the actual winemaking, paying particular attention to the wine's taste and overall quality. Julio was also responsible for production cost control and the department of research. The Gallos "secret" to success was simply the production of inexpensive wines that appealed to the palates of the working and the middle classes. Julio practiced vertical blending, the mixing of varied vintage years with each other, in order to better control overall taste. In an effort to establish consistency while simultaneously living up to customers' expectations, Julio made sure that the company hired chemists, viticulturists, and other scientists to maintain and improve quality control. Julio also adapted the latest technology to his winemaking operation, pioneering experiments using stainless steel winemaking vats. Years ahead of other winemakers, he also used computers to help with consistent blend-

ing. For those who wanted inexpensive wines with an alcoholic "kick," the company also marketed Thunderbird, Ripple, Spañada, and Boone's Farm for the mass market. Later, the company diversified somewhat, also marketing some vintage middle-priced wines, as well as its Bartles & Jaymes wine coolers.

By the mid-1970s Ernest and Julio Gallo were selling approximately 28 percent of all the wines bought in the United States, and their wineries were fully automated. The company continued to expand. Despite growing competition and a declining market for its inexpensive wines, the Gallo winery still held 26 percent of the American wine market by the 1990s and had annual revenues of approximately one billion dollars.

The Gallo winery did not escape controversies of one kind or another, however, despite its financial successes. In the 1970s the United Farm Workers (UFW), led by Cesar Chavez, conducted a protracted boycott when the winery signed a contract with the Teamsters' Union. But Chavez and the UFW refused to stop its anti-Gallo campaign even after workers' votes presumably settled the question. Instead a bitter "undeclared war" continued with Chavez alleging that the winery used child labor, that it had paid workers only seventy-seven cents an hour before signing the first United Farm Workers contract in 1967, that it did not protect its workers from pesticides, and that it provided no drinking water for field laborers. The Gallo brothers disputed each charge made by Chavez, but the winery had a public relations nightmare that continued for years after the boycott faded.

That same decade an investigation by the Federal Trade Commission found that the Gallos had been pressuring wholesalers. The company signed a consent decree in 1976 that was not rescinded until 1983. Three years later the company sued Joseph Gallo, Jr.—the youngest of the three brothers—over trademark usage after Joseph founded a cheese factory. A messy trial resulted wherein Joseph alleged that he had been cheated out of his rightful one-third interest in the winery, worth at least $200 million. Nevertheless, the older brothers prevailed, and Joseph was forced to drop the disputed trademark.

In a controversy of another kind, in January 1990 San Francisco authorities investigated Julio Gallo and his wife, Pauline Biederman, after a car crash that took the life of a young 27-year-old mother. The Gallo car had veered into an oncoming traffic lane on a city thoroughfare. That crash foreshadowed Julio Gallo's death; he was killed three years later in an automobile wreck after the vehicle he was driving went out of control and plunged down a San Joaquin Valley embankment on the family ranch near Tracy, California.

• Shortly before Gallo died, he and his brother Ernest coauthored a company autobiography (with Bruce B. Henderson) that was released after Julio's death, *Ernest and Julio: Our Story* (1994). See also Ellen Hawkes, *Blood and Wine: The Unauthorized Story of the Gallo Wine Empire* (1993). Numerous magazine articles reveal much about Julio's life: Jaclyn Fierman, "How Gallo Crushes the Competition," *Fortune*, 1 Sept. 1986, pp. 24–31; Johnny Dodd, "Grapes of Wrath,"

People, 14 June 1993, pp. 121–24; and Marvin Shanken, "The Gallos Dream," *Wine Spectator*, 39 June 1993, p. 5. For the conflict the two older Gallos had with their younger brother Joseph, see the *New York Times*, 21 June 1989 and 14 Apr. 1993, and the *Los Angeles Times*, 21 June 1989. An obituary is in the *New York Times*, 4 May 1993; also see the brief article in the *New York Times*, 5 May 1993.

JAMES M. SMALLWOOD

GALLOWAY, Beverly Thomas (16 Oct. 1863–13 June 1938), plant pathologist, was born in Millersburg, Missouri, the son of Robert McCauley Galloway, a farmer and miller, and Jane McCray. He became a registered pharmacist, passing the state examination in 1878. Soon, however, he decided to study agricultural science, especially horticulture and botany. He went to the University of Missouri, graduating with his Bachelor of Agricultural Science degree in 1884. He continued his graduate studies after spending parts of 1884 and 1885 exhibiting horticultural materials at the New Orleans Exposition. Galloway studied plant diseases at a time when plant pathology was a very young science. He left Missouri in 1887 to work at the U.S. Department of Agriculture (USDA) and never finished an advanced degree.

While undertaking his graduate studies, Galloway was an assistant in the horticulture department at the University of Missouri, in charge of the greenhouse at the agricultural college. During these years he also presented papers on plant diseases and their prevention at the State Horticultural Society and disseminated them to farmers through agricultural newspapers. In 1887 he accepted an offer from Norman Colman, commissioner of agriculture and editor of *Colman's Rural World*, to work at the USDA as an assistant in the section of vegetable pathology. When Galloway left Missouri, he continued to pursue his interest in understanding and controlling plant diseases. He intended his work to have practical benefits for farmers, and he demonstrated his techniques to growers directly in the field. He also pursued experimental work on the nature of plant disease.

Galloway moved quickly through the ranks in the federal agricultural establishment. He became the chief of the section of vegetable pathology in 1888. In 1895 the section changed its name to the division of vegetable physiology and pathology, and Galloway remained its chief. He had married Agnes Stewart Rankin of Kansas City, Missouri, in 1888; they had three children.

One of Galloway's most important goals was to put plant studies on a par with animal work in the Bureau of Animal Industry. In 1901 Galloway made a substantial move toward that goal when he helped to establish the Bureau of Plant Industry within the Department of Agriculture. Galloway himself headed the new bureau, and under his direction the USDA made substantial improvements in plant breeding and in introducing foreign varieties and also used field demonstrations to help farmers overcome attacks of various pests, including the boll weevil in the South. In 1913

Galloway was appointed assistant secretary of agriculture. He helped to pass the Smith-Lever Agricultural Extension Act of 1914, drawing on his many positive experiences in demonstration work to encourage farmers and others in the USDA to support the measure.

In 1914 Galloway left government service to become dean of the College of Agriculture at Cornell University, succeeding Liberty Hyde Bailey. His tenure there was brief, and he resigned in 1916, returning to the Bureau of Plant Industry and taking on the role of advisory plant pathologist. He then focused on pathological problems and quarantine work associated with introducing foreign seeds and plants into the United States. He retired in 1933. Suffering from medical problems, he committed suicide in Washington, D.C.

Galloway began research in plant pathology when the field itself was barely recognized by most scientists and farmers. By the end of the nineteenth century he had helped to establish plant pathology as an important science and an important aid to the practical farmer. He made significant scientific contributions to the understanding of plant disease and prevention and important recommendations for practical farming practice. He also organized the Bureau of Plant Industry in the USDA, raising the profile and the importance of plant studies in the federal agricultural establishment.

• Most of Galloway's papers are held at the National Agricultural Library, Beltsville, Md.; a small collection also exists at Cornell University. Paul D. Peterson and C. Lee Campbell have written a useful biography, "Beverly T. Galloway—Visionary Administrator," *Annual Review of Phytopathology* (1996). See also Wilbur Powell, *The Bureau of Plant Industry* (1927), and J. A. Stevenson, "Plants, Problems, and Personalities: The Genesis of the Bureau of Plant Industry," *Agricultural History* 28, no. 4 (Oct. 1954): 155–62. The *Yearbook of the USDA* is an important source for Galloway's writings and the workings of the USDA. For examples of his papers devoted to topics of particular interest to farmers, "Work of the Bureau of Plant Industry in Meeting the Ravages of the Boll Weevil and Some Diseases of Cotton," *Yearbook of Agriculture 1904* (1905), pp. 497–508; and "Industrial Progress in Plant Work," *Yearbook of Agriculture 1902* (1903), pp. 219–30. Galloway also published USDA circulars, including "Distribution of Seeds and Plants by the Department of Agriculture," Bureau of Plant Industry Circular 100 (1912). Obituaries are in *Science*, n.s. 88, no. 2270 (1938): 6; *Mycologia* 30 (Oct. 1938); and the (*Washington, D.C.*) *Evening Star*, 14 June 1938.

KATHY J. COOKE

GALLOWAY, Joseph (c. 1731–29 Aug. 1803), colonial statesman and Loyalist, was born in West River, Anne Arundel County, Maryland, the son of Peter Bines Galloway and Elizabeth Rigbie. The family owned large estates in Maryland and Pennsylvania. After the early death of his father, Joseph Galloway moved to Philadelphia, where as a precocious teenager he began to practice law in 1747. In 1748 he was welcomed as the forty-sixth member of the city's most exclusive club, "The Colony in Schuylkill" (known after the Declaration of Independence as "The Schuylkill Fishing Company of the State of Schuylkill"). Fishing company members, about sixty gentlemen in 1748, hunted and fished in the wilderness west of the city along the Schuylkill River, an area known for its abundant fish and game. They socialized and conducted society business in a meetinghouse near the river. Galloway's election to this company indicates his position within the elite of the city's aristocracy. He relinquished his former select status as a leading Quaker in 1753 when he married Grace Growdon, the daughter of Lawrence Growdon, an Episcopalian, a social coup fostering Galloway's own wealth and influence. Joseph Galloway was a highly self-educated man, familiar with the classics and greatly interested in science; from 1769 to 1775 he served as vice president of the American Philosophical Society. He was recognized as an authority on land titles and thereby accumulated much land for himself. Gradually, though, his political ambition took precedence.

In 1756, with the help of Benjamin Franklin, Galloway was elected to the Provincial Assembly of Pennsylvania. In 1757 the Pennsylvania Assembly sent Franklin on a fruitless five-year mission to London to require the Penn proprietors to pay taxes during the French and Indian War, leaving Galloway in legislative charge. In 1764 Galloway won the support of the Pennsylvania Assembly for a petition to King George III pleading that the proprietary (mainly Quaker) governors should be replaced by direct royal government. Franklin was chosen to deliver the petition.

In the assembly's election on 1–2 Oct. 1764, both Galloway and Franklin were defeated. The following year Galloway forestalled mob violence against the threat of a compulsory British Stamp Act and managed to persuade the Pennsylvanians that although the Stamp Act should be repealed (as it was), it was wise to retain British help through willing American participation in some form of taxation offered "in a constitutional manner" (Kuntzleman, p. 55). On 21 September 1765 Galloway regained his lost seat in the assembly, gleefully unseating his main proprietary opponent, John Dickinson. In spite of a printed broadside opposing Galloway's reelection in 1766, he was not only elected but chosen Speaker, though not unanimously, and reelected to that powerful position annually until 1775.

Joseph Galloway had come to believe, after much serious thought and many literary arguments, that a viable government for the separate American states must rest solidly on a stable imperial policy. All of the colonial charters had already "expressly retain[ed] the submission of the subject to the British laws. . . . The dictates of sovereignty required either American subordination to Parliament or an American proclamation of independence." His main problem, however, "was to discover a settlement which would provide an adequate representation of America while preserving the imperial sovereignty of Parliament" (Ferling, pp. 85, 94).

Over the years Galloway tinkered with various plans to secure an amicable union between the colonies and the mother country. His somewhat reluctant agreement to join the First Continental Congress in 1774 gave him an opportunity to present one of his plans. Galloway also had his way in naming conservative delegates to represent Pennsylvania at the initial meeting of the Congress, which officially convened on 5 September 1774. On 28 September Galloway proposed an American Congress that would serve as a separate branch, though subsidiary, of the original Houses of Parliament. The idea gained some cordial support but was tabled after a full day's debate by six colonies against five; the proposal was expunged from the minutes on 22 October. The Congress ended on 26 October 1774, agreeing to spurn Galloway's attempts at reconciliation, instead forming the Continental Association and agreeing not to import or consume any British goods. On 10 December 1774 the Pennsylvania Assembly, led by John Dickinson, was the first to ratify these acts of the Congress. On 15 January 1775 Galloway refused to serve in the Second Continental Congress and spent the interval before his official resignation from the Pennsylvania Assembly in preparing an account of his own scheme and its rejection, *A Candid Examination of the Mutual Claims of Great Britain and the Colonies, with a Plan of Accommodation, on Constitutional Principles*.

On 12 May 1775 the Pennsylvania Assembly officially released Galloway from his service in the Continental Congress, thus ending for him "the distressing and ungrateful drudgery of public life." Franklin's tireless attempts to draw him back were unsuccessful, and in December 1776 he joined the British army, then encamped around New York. During the winter of 1777–1778 General William Howe occupied Philadelphia and employed Galloway there as superintendent general for the maintenance of civic peace in the occupied city, as well as an intelligence officer, until Howe's evacuation of Philadelphia in June 1778. General Henry Clinton, Howe's successor, provided transportation to New York for the Pennsylvania Loyalists, including Galloway and his daughter Elizabeth, while his wife Grace fruitlessly tried to salvage their confiscated family property, valued at £40,000. She was dispossessed on 18 March 1779.

The Galloways landed in London in December 1778, and Galloway became a spokesman for the Loyalists in Britain; he challenged the military tactics of their generals and offered his services for maintaining a united empire. From 29 March until June 1779 the House of Commons held an inquiry into the conduct of the war, during which Galloway gave damaging testimony against General Howe. In 1780, concurrent with discussions in Parliament of the American rebellion, Galloway published the pamphlet *Historical and Political Reflections on the Rise and Progress of the American Rebellion*, in which he offered a plan of union to reconcile differences and restore the American colonies to the British Empire. His claim to be compensated for his losses was eventually settled in 1790, when Galloway himself was awarded an annual pension of £500 pounds. After his death his daughter recalled:

"His morning room for twenty years was often crowded, and seldom empty of Americans who received from him his best services in their own affairs" (Ferling, p. 63; Boyd, pp. 77–78).

Galloway first met John Wesley in London on 13 November 1779. It is quite clear that Galloway found Wesley a sympathetic listener, as is witnessed by Wesley's speedy reprints of Galloway's *An Account of the Conduct of the War in the Middle Colonies. Extracted from a Late Author* (1779). Wesley followed that with *Reflections on the Rise and Progress of the American Rebellion*, based on Galloway's *Historical and Political Reflections . . .* (1780). Wesley's press continued to produce editions of Galloway's many accounts of the war. Galloway also remained in close touch with Charles Wesley. As is evidenced by his friendship with Wesley, Galloway's thoughts turned from politics to religion and some annotations on biblical prophecies. He died in Watford, Hertfordshire, where he was quietly buried without pomp or ceremony in Watford churchyard.

• In seeking to discover the mind of Galloway, "a prolific writer . . . who reached the pinnacle of power in his colony only to be toppled and driven into exile," John E. Ferling, *The Loyalist Mind* (1977), furnishes a voluminous essay on the sources, and massive documentation of his pamphlets, essays, broadsides, and letters. To this should be added Julian P. Boyd, *Anglo-American Union: Joseph Galloway's Plans to Preserve the British Empire, 1774–1788* (1941). Much useful material, from a different angle and arranged in a chronological rather than a topical order, is furnished by Oliver C. Kuntzleman, *Joseph Galloway, Loyalist* (1941). His life in exile can be seen through the friendly eyes of John Wesley, in his *Letters*, ed. John Telford, vol. 7 (1931).

FRANK BAKER

GALLUP, George Horace (18 Nov. 1901–26 Jul. 1984), public opinion polling expert, was born in Jefferson, Iowa, the son of George Henry Gallup, a land speculator, and Nettie Davenport. In high school he founded the school newspaper with money he earned managing a small dairy farm. At the State University of Iowa he was editor of the college newspaper and founder of Quill and Scroll, the national high school journalism honor society. After completing his B.A. in 1923, he became an instructor in the university's newly formed school of journalism. He earned a master's degree in 1925 and a Ph.D. in 1928, in applied psychology. Gallup married Ophelia Smith Miller in 1925; they had three children.

Gallup headed the journalism department at Drake University from 1929 to 1931 and taught journalism and advertising at Northwestern University in 1931–1932. In 1932 he applied his journalistic and research skills to the successful campaign of his mother-in-law, Ola Babcock Miller, for lieutenant governor of Iowa. As he noted in later years, this was the last political campaign in which he took a side, although he did advise President Franklin D. Roosevelt on public reactions to policy proposals.

Also in 1932, Gallup left teaching in order to head the first advertising agency research department to test product appeal and radio impact, established by Young & Rubicam in New York City. He was made vice president in 1937 and remained with Y&R at least part-time until 1947 while building up his polling business on the side.

Gallup, who often called polling "a new field of journalism," began conducting survey research in his university days. His dissertation, "An Objective Method for Determining Reader-Interest in the Content of a Newspaper," was based on his experimentation with systematic methods of gathering data for client newspapers. He introduced the interview procedure of sitting with a respondent and asking, article by article, how much of each story the reader had read in the previous day's edition. He outlined the methods he was developing in a 1930 *Journalism Quarterly* article, the first quantitative audience analysis published in that journal.

In New York Gallup set up a part-time polling business with a marketing specialist, Harold Anderson. With a clientele of forty newspapers, the fledgling firm, popularly known as the Gallup Poll, produced a regular column based on survey results (originally called "America Speaks"). In his first attempt at nationwide sampling, Gallup earned recognition by correctly predicting that the Democrats would gain congressional seats in the 1934 elections. Although Gallup was not literally the inventor of opinion surveys, early on his became the best known, along with Elmo Roper's Fortune Quarterly Poll (1935).

In 1935 Gallup established his survey research headquarters, the American Institute of Public Opinion (AIPO), in Princeton, New Jersey; the marketing office remained in New York City. The Poll's reputation was firmly established in 1936 when Gallup correctly predicted the reelection of President Roosevelt—in contrast to the famous *Literary Digest* poll, which predicted a Republican victory. Gallup relied on "only" 125,000 interviews, a sample size that was less than 6 percent of the *Digest*'s less representative data base, although far larger than later Gallup samples.

Buoyed by this public success, Gallup in the late 1930s set up similar polls in Great Britain, Canada, Australia, and Sweden. During World War II these overseas agencies studied public sentiment on policy issues such as rationing and conscription, and by the end of the war newspapers in all four countries were subscribing to the Gallup column.

Gallup polls in newspapers were the most visible component of an interlocking set of applied social science enterprises. At Y&R he continued to test-market advertisements and product names and to measure mass-media audiences. He developed the "coincidental" method of measuring the radio audience by contacting people at home to ask what they were listening to at the moment. In 1939 Gallup founded the Audience Research Institute (ARI) for radio and motion picture clients. In the 1940s, ARI studies affected film titles, promotion strategies, casting, and plotlines, leading writers and actors to complain about Gallup's predictable advice. To "do an ARI" became Hollywood slang for any sort of market-testing.

AIPO asked questions about a wide variety of topics, such as religion, alcoholism, and attitudes toward women, though politics was a mainstay. Gallup was the first to ask people their opinions about "the job the president is doing," and responses to that question became a standard by which journalists and historians judged presidential performance. Gallup recognized the value of keeping question wording constant over the years so that results could be compared. "We know our era," he reflected, "in a manner not available to any society that has preceded us."

In 1948 Gallup experienced the great crisis of his career: the presidential election in which Harry S. Truman defeated Thomas E. Dewey. Gallup and others had predicted that Dewey would win, and the popular cry became, "Why were the polls wrong?" Gallup attributed the error primarily to ending his polling three weeks before election day. The Gallup staff overhauled its sampling and survey questions and in future elections continued interviews through the final weekend of the campaign. Despite increased accuracy of the poll, however, Gallup's business fell off severely after the 1948 debacle. Film studio contracts were not renewed. AIPO became dependent on earnings from other market research enterprises, which from 1958 on were run by The Gallup Organization, Inc.

Gallup interviewed elites, such as government officials and journalists, about polls and based *The Sophisticated Poll Watcher's Guide* (1972) on their criticisms. In this book he drew back from promoting his services on the basis of prediction, asserting instead that his purpose in comparing polls with election results was merely to validate the sample-survey method. Originally an advocate of huge quota samples and of tracking "barometer counties" that had voted like the nation as a whole, Gallup now held that the validity of a survey depends upon random sampling of individuals. Precision, he noted, is almost entirely a function of sample size, regardless of the size of the total population in question.

Gallup's greatest professional strengths lay in his ability to formulate questions, his journalistic sense, and his capacity to speak broadly on behalf of the polling field. He advocated full reporting of survey methods and outlined his own sampling and interviewing techniques as part of each Gallup Poll release; there were no "secret formulas." In 1947 Gallup helped organize the American Association for Public Opinion Research (AAPOR), and served as its president in 1954–1955. Through AAPOR and kindred professional organizations he pressed for self-policing and reporting standards in the polling field.

Gallup was characterized by contemporaries as "an ardent Jeffersonian" who was "deeply rooted in agrarian America" and had "boundless faith" in the "good sense" of the majority. He argued for electoral reforms that would counteract the influence of special interests

against majority opinion. He wrote after the Vietnam War that "the collective judgment of the people is amazingly sound, even in the complex area of foreign policy," echoing a view he had expressed on the eve of World War II.

Gallup never fully retired from professional activity. He held the titles of chairman of the board and chief executive officer of the Gallup Organization when he died, while on vacation in Switzerland. At his death, Gallup Polls were being published in some fifty countries. In 1988, the year the Gallup Organization was sold to Selection Research, Inc., of Lincoln, Nebraska, the first annual Gallup Memorial Survey was conducted; it was an international study of people's knowledge, perceptions, and behaviors related to acquired immune deficiency syndrome (AIDS).

• Some of Gallup's papers are in special collections at the University of Iowa libraries and at the Gallup Organization in Princeton, N.J.; transcripts of his reminiscences are at the Oral History Research Office at Columbia University. Gallup Poll data are archived by the Roper Center at the University of Connecticut, Storrs. Gallup's published works include *The Best Creative Work in American High Schools* (1926–1927), *Public Opinion in a Democracy* (1939), *The Pulse of Democracy* (1940), *A Guide to Public Opinion Polls* (1944), *The Miracle Ahead* (1964), *The Sophisticated Poll Watcher's Guide* (1972), *America Wants to Know* (1983), and the *Phi Delta Kappa Gallup Polls of Attitudes toward Education, 1969–1984* (1984); numerous volumes presenting poll results in various countries over a period of nearly fifty years; and frequent articles in academic journals, including: "What Shall We Do about High School Journalism?," *Journalism Quarterly* 5, no. 2 (1928): 33–36; "A Scientific Method for Determining Reader-Interest," *Journalism Quarterly* 7, no. 1 (1930): 1–13; "Reporting Public Opinion in Five Nations," *Public Opinion Quarterly* 6, no. 3 (1942): 429–36; "Impact: A New Method for Evaluating Advertising," *Journalism Quarterly* 27, no. 4 (1950): 378–82; and "Polls and the Political Process—Past, Present, and Future," *Public Opinion Quarterly* 29, no. 4 (1965–1966): 544–49. An obituary is in the *New York Times*, 28 July 1984.

STEVEN H. CHAFFEE

GALLUP, Joseph Adam (30 Mar. 1769–12 Oct. 1849), physician and medical educator, was born Joadam Gallup in Stonington, Connecticut, the son of William Gallup, a prominent legislator, and Lucy Denison. When Gallup was six years old he moved with his family to Hertford, New Hampshire Grants (later Hartland), Vermont. No record of his early education has been found, but his writings show evidence of a good classical background. He studied medicine, presumably in Hartland, with a preceptor and attended the first series of medical lectures at Dartmouth College, where in 1798 he was the first recipient of its bachelor of medicine degree. Practicing medicine in Hartland, then Bethel, and by 1800 in Woodstock (all in Windsor County, Vermont), he soon became a busy and well-respected physician. In 1814 Dartmouth awarded him an M.D., for which, according to the custom of the time, he qualified by having engaged in successful practice for several years and by submitting a thesis and passing an examination. In 1792 he married Abigail Willard; they had three children.

Gallup had begun to take students into his office soon after setting up practice in Woodstock, Vermont. In 1820 he accepted a professorship at the Castleton Medical Academy (after 1822 the Vermont Academy of Medicine) and later that year assumed the academy's presidency in addition to his teaching duties. In 1823, possibly because of a dispute over fees, he left Castleton and joined the newly organized medical department of the University of Vermont as lecturer in theory and practice of medicine. Although this appointment would ordinarily have led to a professorship, Gallup returned after one year to Woodstock, where he had maintained his residence, and probably continued to attend to patients.

In 1827 Gallup opened the Clinical School of Medicine in his office. Although additional professors are mentioned in the early advertisements of the school, it remained essentially a one-man operation. Gallup conducted most of the lectures, which were given for twelve weeks in the spring of the year; students also gained practical instruction by working for several years with a practitioner. Anticipating the need to correlate theory with practice, Gallup was a pioneer in presenting patients with his lectures. He invited the sick to be treated gratis if they presented themselves as subjects for demonstration during the school term. As medical education advanced during the first part of the nineteenth century, students found didactic lectures alone unsatisfying and instead chose schools in larger cities, where hospital patients were readily available. Consequently, most country schools such as the one in Woodstock went out of business by mid-century (Woodstock closed in 1856).

Gallup was one of the organizing members of the Vermont Medical Society in 1813. Its first piece of business after setting up its bylaws was a discussion of the shortcomings of the current system of medical education. Gallup took an active interest in this and other matters and was elected president of the society in 1817, a position to which he was reelected each year until 1827. In 1825 he joined a committee to prepare a circular to be sent to other societies proposing new, and for the time, radical changes in schools of medicine. According to the proposals, each student applying for the medical degree should have either a bachelor's degree or enough preliminary education to qualify for admission to a college; three or four years of preceptorship with a licensed practitioner; receipt of a bachelor of medicine degree after at least one course of lectures, and the M.D. be conferred only after seven years of meritorious practice. The circular attracted wide attention throughout New England and New York and later was adopted by other state societies. Most societies suggested modifications, and general acceptance was slowly achieved. Led by Gallup, the Vermont Medical Society continued to press for reforms; its regional conferences eventually culminated in 1846 in a national conference in New York, which was the precursor of the American Medical Association.

In addition to his educational and organizational efforts, Gallup was a prolific and influential medical writer. In the winter of 1811–1812 a devastating epidemic of spotted fever (probably meningitis), begun in an army barracks, spread widely over northern Vermont, causing high mortality. At a subsequent meeting of the medical society, Gallup requested that members communicate their experiences of treating epidemic patients. Urged at a professional visit to Philadelphia to share his knowledge, he wrote *Sketches of Epidemic Disease in the State of Vermont . . . to Which Is Added Remarks on Pulmonary Consumption* (1815). The book became a definitive text on infectious diseases and a second edition was printed in 1822. Gallup's writings include a report of a visit to a popular watering place in Clarendon, Vermont, in which he discusses chemical analysis of the water, reports conversations with enthusiastic participants in the water cure, and gives a personal evaluation of its value. He also wrote papers on various clinical problems and made scientific addresses to the state medical society. In 1839 he published the two-volume *Outlines of the Institutes of Medicine, Founded on the Philosophy of the Human Economy in Health and Disease*, a major compendium of theory and practice of the day filled with personal observations and evaluation. In places the work has a modern flavor: Gallup offers an opinion on the limitations of clinical trials (then in their infancy), uses terms such as "molecule," and discusses brain experiments recently done on pigeons by physiologist Pierre Flourens in Paris. Gallup strived to make his publications comprehensible and his literary style attractive. He wrote "Acute affections of the thorax are quite managable . . . the tokens of suffering organs are always present and ought to be read, even if they are not always legible" ("Remarks on Paracentesis of the Chest for Empyema," *Medical Magazine* [June 1835], p. 699).

Gallup, who died in Woodstock, was well respected in his time as a competent physician and an innovative educator and administrator. He was a leader of the state medical society, founder of one medical school and teacher in others, and was known nationally for his contributions to medical literature.

• The manuscript minute book of the Vermont Medical Society from 1814 to 1846 is in Special Collections of the University of Vermont library in Burlington. The Dana Medical Library of the University has copies of Gallup's major writings. Gallup's *Observations Made during a Visit to Clarendon Springs* was published in Windsor, Vermont, in 1840, and two of his clinical papers appeared in the *Medical Magazine* in 1835. A biographical account of Gallup is in Frederick C. Waite, *The Story of a Country Medical College—A History of the Clinical School of Medicine and the Vermont Medical College—Woodstock, Vermont, 1827–1856* (1945), which contains a portrait of Gallup. The library of the Vermont Historical Society in Montpelier has John D. Gallup, *The Genealogical History of the Gallup Family* (1893). For the story of Vermont Medical Society's circular on medical education, see Byron

Stookey, "Origins of the First National Medical Convention, 1826–1846," *Journal of the American Medical Association* 177, no. 2 (15 July 1961): 33–140.

LESTER J. WALLMAN

GALT, Alexander (26 June 1827–19 Jan. 1863), sculptor, was born in Norfolk, Virginia, the son of Alexander Galt, Sr., a postmaster, and Mary Silvester Jeffery. Except for some youthful drawing lessons, Galt was largely self-taught. He began his sculptural career modestly, cutting small cameo portraits for Norfolk friends and relations, the first of which date from about 1845. During this period he made several visits to Washington, D.C., and while there met Samuel F. B. Morse and Clark Mills, who encouraged him in his aim of a career in sculpture.

To work in Italy was the goal of most sculptors of Galt's generation, as that country held the multiple allures of superb art collections, famed marble quarries, and skilled Italian workmen who could be hired as carving assistants. Galt sailed for Italy in September 1848, arriving in Florence in late January 1849. He found himself part of a large expatriate community of sculptors, led by Hiram Powers, and his new acquaintances also included Chauncey Bradley Ives, Joel Tanner Hart, Randolph Rogers, Horatio Greenough, and Joseph Mozier. A visit to Rome enabled him to meet Thomas Crawford. Unfortunately he soon discovered that his fellow Americans were intensely competitive for scarce patronage, and artistic jealousy was rampant, a situation Galt later found accurately delineated in *The Marble Faun* (1860) by Nathaniel Hawthorne.

Galt arrived in Italy ignorant of the most basic tools and techniques of his chosen profession. He began an intensive program of art studies, an effort that took place against the exciting backdrop of the Italian Risorgimento, the nineteenth-century movement that led to the unification of the modern Italian nation. It was several years before he felt ready to begin his first piece, an ideal neoclassic female bust embodying his native state, *Virginia* (1850–1851, unlocated), a work he sent back to New York to be exhibited at the American Art-Union. This was followed by *Psyche* (1851–1852, private collection) and *Christopher Columbus* (1852–1853, Chrysler Museum, Norfolk). His *Bacchante* (1851–1852, Corcoran Museum of Art), a marble neoclassical bust, proved to be his most popular work. Its beautiful Grecian profile, following the model of Powers's *Greek Slave*, was favored as the ideal of feminine beauty during this period. About a dozen versions were made, the last in 1862.

He returned to Virginia in the spring of 1853, establishing his studio in Richmond that fall. In 1854 he received his first major public commission when the State of Virginia selected him to execute a statue of Thomas Jefferson (1854–1860) to be installed on the campus of the University of Virginia in Charlottesville. He commenced work on preliminary studies for the statue he hoped would secure his reputation. He also worked on some portrait busts, the economic staple of the nineteenth-century sculptor. He modeled

busts of his father (1853, private collection) and of his cousin, Dr. John Minson Galt II (1854–1857, Eastern State Hospital, Williamsburg). It was while he was at work on the latter that he learned that his father had become one of the many victims of Norfolk's deadly yellow fever epidemic, which raged during the summer of 1855. Galt absorbed his grief in his work, for which his father had always given him strong support.

Galt realized that to be a success he would need to secure patronage from Virginia's aristocratic plantation families. He was therefore pleased when he received a commission from one of the state's wealthiest men for a bust of his wife, Mrs. Charles Bruce (Sarah Alexander Seddon) (1854–1857, private collection). Other orders followed for portraits of Mrs. Joseph Reid Anderson (Sarah Eliza Archer) (1855, Valentine Museum, Richmond), Mrs. James Marion Morson (Ellen Carter Bruce) (1855–1857, Virginia Historical Society, Richmond), and Justice Robert Craig Stanard (1855–1859, The Supreme Court of Virginia).

With the statue of Jefferson well along and several orders in hand, Galt was finally able to return to Italy during the summer of 1856. Once back in Florence he would put into marble those works he had already executed in plaster and continue work on his *Jefferson*. The state of South Carolina gave him another important commission for a bust of Chief Justice John Rutledge (1858, U.S. Capitol) to be displayed in the state supreme court, though Galt's hopes for extensive patronage from this state remained largely unrealized. He was further gratified when a prominent Virginia congregation gave him an order for a baptismal font (1859, St. Paul's Episcopal Church, Richmond). Although he would receive few additional commissions while in Italy, he commenced several subject pieces, including *Aurora* (1858–1860, Tudor Gallery, Richmond), for which his friend Isabelle Hinckley, a young opera singer from Albany, New York, served as the model. He also executed *Hope* (1859–1860, Robert M. Hicklin, Jr., Spartanburg, S.C.) and *Sappho* (1859–1860, Tudor Gallery, Richmond).

When Galt completed the *Jefferson*, statue in October 1860, he returned to Virginia and once again established his studio in Richmond. Unfortunately, historical events intruded on his career. Increasing political instability resulted in the cancellation of the dedication ceremonies of his new statue. When the Civil War commenced, Galt, who was proslavery, joined the cause and was soon at work drawing maps and helping with the design of fortifications and protective batteries. He continued to work in his studio when he could, but commissions were scarce in the Confederate capital, and his wartime duties kept him busy. Among the few works from this period are portraits of Jefferson Davis (1862, Museum of the Confederacy, Richmond; Department of Archives and History, Montgomery, Ala.) and the state's Civil War governor, John Letcher (1862, Virginia State Library and Archives, Richmond; Virginia Military Institute, Lexington). Left unfinished at his death was an ideal bust titled *Spirit of the South* (1862, Museum of the

Confederacy, Richmond). His last work was a small pencil sketch of Thomas Jonathan "Stonewall" Jackson (15 Dec. 1862, Galt Family papers), of whom he had hoped to execute a statue. Unfortunately he contracted smallpox and died in Richmond early in 1863.

During his brief career, Galt established himself as one of the leading nineteenth-century southern sculptors. That he was both a southerner and a Virginian remained fundamental to his character and personal views. His patronage was almost entirely southern, and his sense of regional identity strengthened throughout the 1850s. The state of his birth had a particularly rich sculptural history, and several other carvers were his contemporaries, including William Randolph Barbee and William James Hubard. Galt was fortunate to have as his mentors several notable Virginians, including Hugh Blair Grigsby, Joseph Reid Anderson, and John Young Mason.

• The Galt Family Papers, which are extensive, are in the Swem Library at the College of William and Mary in Williamsburg. The sculptor was included in important pioneering histories of American sculpture, notably those by Wayne Craven, *Sculpture in America* (1968), and William H. Gerdts, *American Neo-Classic Sculpture, the Marble Resurrection* (1973). The first scholarly study of the artist was by William B. O'Neal, "Chiselled Lyrics," *Arts in Virginia* 7 (Fall 1966): 4–19. Galt was placed in the general historical context of the city of his birth in Betsy Fahlman et al., *A Tricentennial Celebration: Norfolk, 1682–1982* (1982). The most definitive study is an exhibition catalog by Betsy Fahlman, *The Spirit of the South: The Sculpture of Alexander Galt (1827–1863)* (1992).

BETSY FAHLMAN

GALT, John (2 May 1779–11 Apr. 1839), author, lobbyist, and businessman, was born in Irvine, Scotland, the son of John Galt, a shipmaster and trader, and Jean Thomson. Galt left school to begin a career as a merchant at about age sixteen (one of his schoolmates was Henry Eckford), but he continued his studies in his spare time and was much affected by the ideas and achievements of the Scottish Enlightenment. Galt left Scotland for London in 1804, and although often described as a Scottish novelist or as a Canadian colonizer, he was based in London for most of his adult life. He toured the Mediterranean in 1809–1811, meeting Lord Byron, and returned to the region in 1812–1813 to continue his earlier attempts to outflank the Napoleonic blockade by setting up new trade routes. In 1813 he married Elizabeth Tilloch, with whom he had three children.

Galt's first publication had appeared in 1801 in the London version of William Cobbett's *Porcupine*, but his literary reputation only became fully established after 1820, when he published his first important Scottish fiction, *Ayrshire Legatees*. It was followed by *Annals of the Parish* (1821), *The Provost* (1822), and *The Entail* (1823).

In 1820 Galt became actively involved in helping a group of Canadians get compensation for damages suffered in the American invasion of Canada in 1812.

This work led to the creation of the Canada Land Company in 1826. Galt first traveled to the United States in 1825, made at least seven trips through New York State and one to Philadelphia, and resided in Canada as superintendent of the Canada Company until recalled to England in 1829. Poverty and ill health forced him from London back to Scotland in 1834.

Traces of Galt's interest in the New World are in most of his writings, including the earliest ones. He was not only intrigued by factual details about North America but by the possibility it offered of creating a new and better society, one that would supplant what he saw as the "foredoomed" social systems of Europe. Galt's play *The Apostate* (1814), nominally set in Atlantis, chronicles the arrival of a shipwrecked Christian sailor in the New World, from the point of view of the indigenous inhabitants. The sailor converts the natives to Christianity and founds a city, but his moral corruption and importation of the "civilized" crimes of adultery and suicide leads to his death and the rejection of European culture by the Atlantines. The play deals with the moment of contact between the hemispheres in an unusual way, and Galt's conviction at the close of his career that the play was of value led him to direct attention to it in his autobiographies. He published a reworking of part of it in the *Knickerbocker Magazine* in July 1838.

One of Galt's essays on the fine arts earned the approval of the American painter Benjamin West, and Galt wrote a two-volume biography (1816, 1820) of his friend West that is an irreplaceable source of information about West's extraordinary career. The biography also reveals much about the depth of Galt's effort to understand the two-way process of cultural transference between the mother country and the new nation. Many of Galt's compilations of voyages and travels include passages on America, and his interest in American autobiographies is apparent from his 1822 London edition of the autobiography of Alexander Graydon of Philadelphia, which Galt dedicated to Richard Rush. Galt's farce "An Aunt in Virginia" was written and performed while he was in New York in 1828, and on his return to England his "Letters from New York" began to appear in the *New Monthly Magazine*; they contain a witty and detailed account of his travels in New England.

In January 1830 Galt published his most important "American" work, a fictional autobiography that he had constructed in the solitude of the forests of North America. Called *Lawrie Todd; or, The Settlers in the Woods*, it is perhaps the first novel by a British author of any stature that takes the United States as its setting and is based on firsthand observation. Because of this surprising fact, because *Lawrie Todd* was popular and acclaimed for its authenticity on both sides of the Atlantic, and because it was published at a crucial moment in the development of the American sense of self, the novel holds much for those who wish to understand a vital phase of the cultural and human migration that is the most important event in the modern history of the English-speaking peoples.

Galt hit on the idea for his reworking of the Robinson Crusoe story on one of his visits to New York. He was introduced to the deeply religious and eccentric Grant Thorburn, and discovered he had written an account of his experiences as pauper immigrant made good. Aiming to write a book that would speak to readers on both sides of the Atlantic, Galt instantly bought the manuscript and copyright of Thorburn's life.

The use of Thorburn's actual autobiography, and common knowledge of Galt's exploits in the forests, added weight to Galt's statement in his *Literary Life* (1834) that he was "not aware that any book existed prior to [*Lawrie Todd*] which gave a just account of backwood operations . . . it will thus increase in value as it becomes obsolete . . . I say this with a perfect recollection of Mr. Cooper's descriptions applicable to settlers, which are as little like reality as his sea pictures are inimitable." (The reference is to James Fenimore Cooper.)

Lawrie Todd went through some twenty editions in its first twenty years, and though it faded from view as the frontier moved west and as the Civil War overshadowed the events of the 1820s and 1830s, it had had a profound effect on the imaginations of many in Britain and America. As a reviewer observed in *Fraser's Magazine* (Mar. 1830, p. 239), in "works formerly written upon the subject of making a settlement in the woods, we have learned something of how men did, but could seldom find any thing to please us as to how they *thought* and *felt* in circumstances so new to most, and therefore so interesting."

The *North American Review* concurred, and Willard Phillips's critique, published in October 1830, begins by making lightly veiled comparisons between Galt's and Cooper's works, at Cooper's expense. Phillips suggests that Galt "can without the help of moving incidents by sea . . . invest with a moral and philosophical dignity, and a poetical interest, the passions, motives . . . and endeavours, that from day to day move and trouble the veritable world. Fictions so written are more true than history."

Galt's dissatisfaction with the authenticity of the productions of Cooper and others played a part in his supremely self-confident but well-intentioned attempts to demonstrate how American authors might use the opportunities offered by the "newness" of their environment. While in America he had begun to collect ephemeral chapbooks and stories concerning the conflicts of the settlers with the American Indians as well as accounts of early pioneer life. In 1830, before Henry Schoolcraft, Galt began to publish his own versions of these tales in *Blackwood's Magazine, Fraser's Magazine*, the *Lady's Magazine and Museum*, and the literary annuals. In the introductions to his versions of these traditional tales he argues that the collection of such stories would not only assist the creation of a shared national folklore (which he saw as necessary to the creation of a genuinely American literature), but he also thought it would be "a boon to English literature, in which we need an infusion of new mind" ("American Traditions," *Fraser's*, Oct. 1830, p. 322).

Galt featured more that twenty-five nationalities or countries in his writings, but few relationships mattered to him as much as the special relationship he tried to foster between Britain and the United States. In 1833 he began a series of articles on national characters in *Lady's Magazine* with one titled "The British and Americans." He argues that "Adverse, [the British and Americans] can only injure one another; united in sentiments and language, they may become the arbiters of the destiny of the world" (Feb. 1833, pp. 47–53). He sustained his contacts with America in his final years, corresponding with Lewis Gaylord Clark and Willis Gaylord Clark, editors of the *Knickerbocker*. Galt supported the magazine's plan of encouraging specifically American literature and sent money and contributions, including a revised portion of *The Apostate* called "The Atlantines, a Romance of America" (*Knickerbocker*, July 1838). In the preface to "The Atlantines" (inscribed to New York City mayor Philip Hone) Galt draws attention to a saying of George Washington's about the unity of the English and American peoples, and says Washington's statement took possession of his mind from the day of his arrival in America in 1825, influencing all of his later writings on the United States.

Galt died in Greenock, Scotland, less than a year after "The Atlantines" was published. His wife and children made Canada their home after his death.

Although Galt's American writings passed into obscurity after the Civil War, *Lawrie Todd* alone is enough to secure Galt a niche in American literary history. His works were read by almost all of his contemporaries and fellow authors in Britain and the United States, including Edgar Allan Poe, Nathaniel Hawthorne, Philip Hone, Lewis Gaylord Clark, DeWitt Clinton, William Leete Stone, and other literary and commercial figures in upstate New York.

• Galt's papers are scattered among at least forty-five different repositories in North America and Britain. Important collections are in the U.K. Public Record Office, the British Library, the National Library of Scotland, the National Archives of Canada, the Archives of Ontario, the University of Guelph Library (Ontario), and the New York Public Library. Galt published over 300 separate items, and the most easily available guide to many of them (and to other works on Galt) is Ian A. Gordon's excellent *John Galt: The Life of a Writer* (1972). Jennie Aberdein, *John Galt* (1936), provides the most rounded account of the whole of Galt's career, and P. H. Scott, *John Galt* (1985), is a brief but useful summary of his activities. The American *National Union Catalogue* includes entries on the many American editions of Galt's books, and the most detailed account of Galt's "American" interests is in Nicholas McCarthy Whistler, "John Galt and the New World" (Ph.D. diss., Univ. of Cambridge, 1993). The entry for Galt in vol. 7 of the *Dictionary of Canadian Biography* (1988) is another source of information on Galt's links with North America.

NICHOLAS MCCARTHY WHISTLER

GALT, John Minson, II (19 Mar. 1819–18 May 1862), physician, was born in Williamsburg, Virginia, the son of Alexander D. Galt, a physician, and Mary Dorothea Galt (his parents were third cousins). He was the namesake of, and later successor to, his paternal grandfather, John Minson Galt I, who in 1793 was appointed attending physician to the Public Hospital for Persons of Insane and Disordered Minds, in Williamsburg. This institution, renamed the Eastern Lunatic Asylum in 1841 (later the Eastern State Hospital), was the first public hospital in the United States founded exclusively for the care of the mentally ill.

John Galt the younger was educated at home by his parents before entering a preparatory school. From an early age he was an avid reader, with botany his first, and lifelong, interest. Like his father and grandfather, he attended the College of William and Mary in Williamsburg, from which he received an A.B. in 1838. After reading medicine with his father—who had succeeded the first John Galt as attending physician at the hospital—he entered the University of Pennsylvania Medical School, where he earned an M.D. in 1841. On the death of Alexander Galt that same year, and with the Virginia state legislature's creation of the new office of medical superintendent of the asylum, John Galt II was called to fill the post; he was then twenty-two years old. According to Dr. P. G. Hamlin, in a memorial tribute to Galt in the *Virginia Medical Monthly* (Sept. 1941), the choice was made not only because of the Galt family's long association with the institution but because their descendant demonstrated great promise.

In 1844 Galt, a member of the Virginia Medical Association, was one of the thirteen physicians who met in Philadelphia to found the Association of Medical Superintendents of American Institutions for the Insane (the forerunner of the American Psychiatric Association). He also began to contribute to their new publication, the *American Journal of Insanity*; his first article, "Fragments on Insanity" (Oct. 1844), gives reports on thirty of his cases.

By the end of his life, Galt had written several hundred papers on medical matters and on botany for various publications. In addition to these and his annual hospital reports, he published two series of *Essays on Asylums for Persons of Unsound Mind* (1850 and 1853). Revealed in these writings is Galt's ongoing concern with the legal ramifications of insanity, the question of when and by what standards a plea of insanity justifies acquittal in a criminal case; and his awareness of the dangers in administration of public mental institutions by political appointees.

Well read, and proficient in modern and classical languages (he also studied Hebrew and Arabic), Galt eventually amassed a sizable private library in his Williamsburg home. With his knowledge of French, especially, he was able to keep up with the latest work being done in Europe on the diagnosis and treatment of the insane. For the benefit of English-reading medical students, he compiled a series of his own translations and précis of French writings on the subject from the seventeenth century on, published as *The Treatment of Insanity* in 1846 (and reprinted in 1973 in the Arno Press series *Mental Illness and Social Policy: The American Experience*). He also edited a textbook begun by his father, *Practical Medicine: Illustrated by Cases of the Most Important Diseases* (1843).

Acquainted with the latest psychiatric theory, Galt recommended—and in some instances was able to implement—changes in the care of mental patients, as set forth in his annual reports. His guiding belief was that "kindness" was the key component. (Galt family anecdotes mention that he often fed his patients himself and waived any increase in his salary.) In 1848 he wrote to the Virginia General Assembly that the Eastern Lunatic Asylum would continue, so far as space allowed, to make provisions for all who needed care, including slaves (the asylum had been the first such public institution in the nation to accept freed slaves). His 1853 annual report advocates passing a law requiring female guards to accompany women patients being taken to the hospital. Other aspects of his humanitarianism included his recommendations that violent patients be housed apart from the less severely disturbed; and that—despite his conviction that postmortems were justified on the ground of scientific advance—no autopsy should be performed without the legal consent of a patient's family or friends.

Above all, Galt was one of the first American physicians to perceive the benefits of training the mentally ill to do some meaningful work and of providing them with learning opportunities, books, games, and musical instruments. To this end, in 1843 he set up shops at the hospital for sewing, carpentry, and making shoes and brooms. He also provided games and a library for the patients' use (with the idea that biographies and works on travel and history would be particularly helpful). Contrary to accepted psychiatric opinion, Galt encouraged, whenever possible, visits from patients' relatives and allowing patients to leave the confines of the hospital during the day. An advocate of the "cottage plan" that, already existing in parts of Europe, let certain patients live in small, supervised groups, in a home-like, preferably rural, environment outside the hospital, he found no support for this proposal from his peers.

Galt's reports make clear his scientific approach to the general function of a mental hospital. His meticulous records contain patients' physiological data, including data on the attendants as well, as a control; daily temperature and barometric records, kept to assess the possible relationship between illness and atmospheric fluctuations; and tests on the use of chloroform and ether, supposed to control mania but found to be ineffective.

Galt, who never married, died suddenly at the age of forty-three in Williamsburg. Family lore hints at opium addiction and death from an accidental overdose; Dr. Hamlin states that he died "possibly of angina" (p. 508). Both sources agree that a contributing cause was anxiety over the fate of his patients when in

May 1862 the Union army occupied Williamsburg, took over the hospital, and forbade him entrance.

Galt's annual reports as medical superintendent of the hospital demonstrate his enthusiasm for his work. His *Treatment of Insanity*, much acclaimed in its day in America and England, was to Dr. Hamlin, writing almost a century later, still "full of interest to the student of psychiatric history" (p. 505). Both idealist and pragmatist, Galt combined humane concern with emphasis on the most advanced treatment; and in so doing, his recommendations for improved care anticipate modern occupational and recreational therapy programs and systems of integrating patients into the outside community.

• Archival material on Galt is available in the Library Special Collections at Eastern State Hospital, which contains the originals of his medical papers, as well as at the John D. Rockefeller, Jr., Library at the Colonial Williamsburg Foundation. The Swem Library of the College of William and Mary maintains the Galt Family Papers collection. Some other material on the Galts is in the library of the Virginia Historical Society in Richmond. Biographical accounts include an entry in *Institutional Care of the Insane in the United States and Canada*, ed. Henry W. Hurd, vol. 4 (1917); and P. G. Hamlin, "Dr. John Minson Galt and the Williamsburg Asylum," *Virginia Medical Monthly* 68 (Sept. 1941): 502–9. Howard Spilman Galt, *The Galt Families: Notes on Their Origin and Their History . . .* (1938), provides some anecdotal family history. Information on the early years of the Galts's hospital and the younger John Galt's contributions is found in vol. 3 of *Institutional Care . . .* (1916), and in two Colonial Williamsburg Foundation publications: Shomer S. Zwelling, *Quest for a Cure: The Public Hospital in Williamsburg, 1773–1885* (1985); and Norman Dain, *Disordered Minds: The First Century of Eastern State Hospital in Williamsburg, Virginia* (1971).

ELEANOR F. WEDGE

GALT, William Craig (8 Apr. 1777–22 Oct. 1853), physician, was born in Williamsburg, Virginia, the son of John Minson Galt, a physician, and Judith Craig. In Williamsburg, he served an apprenticeship with his father, who had been surgeon general of the Virginia troops during the revolutionary war. He may have moved to Louisville as early as 1799, but it was in Virginia that Galt married Matilda Booth (Aylett?) Beall in 1802. Their only child was born in Louisville in 1805 and later became a physician in the city. In addition to practicing general medicine, for several years William Galt also owned a dry goods and apothecary shop. After his first wife's death, in 1826 he married Elizabeth Mildred Thompson Gray in Louisville; they had ten children.

Because he lacked the appropriate training and experience, Galt did not perform major operations. Recognizing the community's need for another doctor with specialized surgical skills, he persuaded his cousin, Richard Ferguson, a surgeon in Virginia, to move to Louisville in 1802 or 1803. Thereafter, Galt and Ferguson referred patients to each other. For example, as personal physician to General George Rogers Clark, Galt served as attending physician when Fergu-

son and Dr. John Collins amputated Clark's right leg in 1809.

Like countless physicians and others around the nation, Galt endorsed self-improvement and the expansion of knowledge, and in 1816 he became one of the incorporators of the Louisville Library Company. In 1819 he was a founding member of the Louisville Medical Society, and in 1822 the city appointed him to its board of health. He may also have been a preceptor to a number of private pupils.

Thriving Louisville was only a day's ride from the smaller community of Lexington, Kentucky, where Transylvania University's medical department enjoyed regional dominance in medical education. Interested in enhancing the appeal of his city, the status of his profession, and his own business opportunities, and because of his well-established community leadership, Galt was chosen president of a group of eleven physician-incorporators who obtained a state charter for the Louisville Medical Institute on 3 February 1833. Destined to become an academic unit of the University of Louisville a decade later, the institute began as a proprietary medical school, with those incorporators who served as faculty receiving a portion of the student fees. However, when the institute began accepting students in 1837, Galt was not a member of the faculty. Age alone probably did not preclude his appointment; more likely his lack of a medical degree stood in the way.

Galt continued to work long hours even late in life. He sold his city residence, replete with hanging gardens, to land developers who razed the property to construct a grand hotel. Honoring his contributions to improving the quality of community life in Louisville, the hotel was named the Galt House. In 1835 he bought a farm near Louisville that he named "Repton." There he soon acquired the reputation of a successful horticulturalist, specializing in the cultivation of fruit trees and flowers suitable for the region. He died at Repton.

Without a medical degree, Galt was a typical doctor on the expanding urban frontier. Yet he earned the respect of the city's inhabitants through his dedicated practice, charity, and general involvement in the life of the community. His most enduring contribution to Louisville was his participation in the creation of what became one of the most popular medical schools in the nation during the nineteenth century.

• No collection of private papers, manuscripts, or publications is available to date. The most credible source for basic vital data on Galt is Howard Spilman Galt, *The Galt Families: Notes on Their Origin and Their History with Genealogical Lists* (1938). Additional information can be found in C. B. VanArsdall, *Kentucky Pioneer Doctors* (1934), and Medical Historical Research Project of the Works Progress Administration, *Medicine and Its Development in Kentucky* (1940). Emmet Field Horine, "A History of the Louisville Medical Institute and of the Establishment of the University of Louisville and Its School of Medicine, 1833–1846," *Filson Club Historical Quarterly* 7 (1933): 133–47, assesses Galt's role.

Though full of amusing anecdotes, his obituary notice in the *Louisville Weekly Courier*, 29 Oct. 1853, also provides useful details not found elsewhere.

ERIC HOWARD CHRISTIANSON

GÁLVEZ, Bernardo de (23 July 1746–30 Nov. 1786), colonial governor of Spanish Louisiana and viceroy of New Spain, was born in Macharaviaya, Spain, the son of Matías de Gálvez, a prominent court official, and Josefa Gallardo Madrid. After distinguished service as a lieutenant in the Spanish campaigns against the Portuguese in 1762, which won him promotion to the rank of captain, Gálvez traveled to Mexico in 1765 with his uncle, José de Gálvez, visitor general of New Spain. In that posting he engaged in a series of campaigns against the Apaches along the Rio Grande (1769–1770) and became commander of Nueva Vizcaya and Sonora in northwestern Mexico. Returning to Spain in 1775 he joined the invasion of Algiers and after being wounded and promoted to lieutenant colonel served briefly in the military academy at Avila.

Gálvez became acting governor and intendant of Louisiana on 1 January 1777, beginning what was to become the most brilliant and successful administration of that colony under Spanish rule. Reinforcing his own unmistakable talents, his marriage in November 1777 to Felicité Destréhan, the young widowed daughter of the prominent creole St. Maxent family, won him the abiding loyalty and affection of the colonial population.

Success seemed to mark his every effort. He reduced export duties to encourage trade with the neighboring British in Florida, expanded agricultural production by increasing the importation of slaves, and gave particular encouragement to immigration into the colony. New arrivals from the Canary Islands, so-called *islenos*, were granted lands below New Orleans, where their descendants still comprise a distinct community; Germans from Maryland and Europe received places along the Mississippi above the city; Loyalist refugees from the American Revolution formed a settlement along Bayou Manchac that they gratefully named Galveztown; and a major portion of the continuing Acadian migration to the colony was provided for along the bayous of southwestern Louisiana.

From the very beginning of his governorship Gálvez lent growing support to the efforts of the United States to win its independence from Britain, working closely with Oliver Pollock in New Orleans to funnel money and supplies to George Rogers Clark in his Old Northwest campaign and providing sanctuary for James Willing and his raiders after their incursion into British West Florida in 1778. When Spain declared war on Great Britain in May 1779, the English had already strengthened their forts along the Mississippi at Natchez (Fort Panmure), Baton Rouge (Fort New Richmond), and at the mouth of Bayou Manchac (Fort Bute), and Gálvez sensed the imminence of attack on his colony. Newly commissioned as governor in his own right, he immediately planned a preemptive

strike for 23 August 1779 against British positions along the Mississippi, but a hurricane on 18 August destroyed most of the ships that he had gathered for the campaign. Undeterred, he rallied his forces and moved against the British by land on 27 August. In an impressive display of strategic skill, he quickly reduced Forts Bute, New Richmond, and Panmure to break the British hold on the lower Mississippi and then turned toward British positions along the Gulf Coast at Mobile and Pensacola.

After a brief siege Gálvez occupied Mobile on 14 March 1780, for which he was rewarded by promotion to major general. The superior forces and defensive position of Pensacola provided greater challenge, leading Gálvez to shift his base to Havana. Yet another fierce hurricane in October 1780 scattered the fleet gathered for his first move against Pensacola, but he persisted with accustomed tenacity and launched a second effort in February 1781, supported by a contingent of the Spanish navy. When the dangers of entering Pensacola Bay under the guns of the British caused the commander of the royal fleet to hold back, Gálvez, on the brig *Galveztown*, led the smaller ships of his colonial contingent through the pass, shaming the royal vessels into following, and Pensacola fell on 10 May 1781. All of British West Florida now lay in Spanish hands. In recognition of his triumphs Carlos III raised Gálvez to the rank of lieutenant general, appointed him captain general of Cuba and governor of Louisiana and West Florida, and named him viscount with a coat of arms bearing the motto "Yo Solo" (I Alone).

After months spent in Spain during 1783–1784 consulting with colonial officers on Louisiana affairs, Gálvez in 1785 received appointment as viceroy of New Spain, with authority as well over Cuba, Louisiana, and the Floridas. His immediate predecessor in that position had been his father, who had held the office from 1783 until his death in 1784. Gálvez and his wife, with their three children, arrived in Mexico early in 1786, but his career was cut tragically short in Tacubaya by a mysterious fatal fever in the fall of that year. He is buried in the Church of San Fernando, Mexico City. Galveston Bay (and thus the city of Galveston, Texas) was named for Gálvez.

• The standard study of Gálvez's career is John W. Caughey, *Bernardo de Gálvez in Louisiana, 1776–1783* (1934). Other biographies are Jose Rodulfo Boeta, *Bernardo de Gálvez* (1976), and Jack D. Holmes, *Gálvez* (1980). Gálvez figures prominently in the voluminous manuscript archives of the Council of the Indies, and documentary materials on his military campaigns may be found in the Archivo General de Simancas.

JOSEPH G. TREGLE, JR.

GALVIN, James Francis (25 Dec. 1856–7 Mar. 1902), major league baseball player, was born in St. Louis, Missouri. (The names of his parents and other details of his early life are unknown.) He grew up in the city's Irish-American Kerry Patch section, where he learned to play baseball at an early age. Galvin began his professional career in 1875 with the St. Louis Brown Stockings in the loosely organized National Association. After pitching just one game, he switched to the rival St. Louis Red Stockings, but the club dropped out of the association before the season ended. In 1876 Galvin remained with the Red Stockings as they played an independent schedule throughout the East and Midwest. He is reputed to have thrown two no-hitters that year, one against Philadelphia on 4 July and another, probably professional baseball's first perfect game, against the Cass Club of Detroit on 17 August.

Galvin played for Allegheny of the International Association, baseball's first minor league, in 1877 and pitched four shutouts in nineteen games. The following season he played for Buffalo, a remarkable team that captured the International Association pennant and won eleven of seventeen exhibition games against National League competition. Buffalo fielded a lineup of ten future major leaguers and compiled a record of 85 wins, 28 losses, and 3 ties. Galvin started 99 games, completed 96, won 72, and lost 25. He finished the season with back-to-back victories over the famed Chicago White Stockings of the National League. That same year he married Bridget Griffin; they had eleven children.

Galvin earned the nickname "Gentle Jeems" for his modest manner. Later he was called "the Little Steam Engine" because he stood 5′8″ and weighed 200 pounds, and then "Pud" because he made pudding of opposing batters. A devoted father, Galvin laughingly boasted that he could use his own offspring to start his own baseball team, the "Galvanized Nine."

In 1879 the Buffalo club was admitted to the National League. Galvin started 66 games for the Bisons, pitched 593 innings, and was credited with 37 of the team's 46 victories. Refused a raise from his $900 salary, he headed to San Francisco early in 1880, only to return in May when the Buffalo club's directors agreed to negotiate. The Bisons won only 24 games that year against 58 losses, but Galvin won 20 of them, including a 1–0 no-hitter against Worcester on 20 August.

After winning 29 games in 1881 and 28 in 1882, Galvin put together his two best seasons in consecutive years. He pitched 656 innings in 1883 and 636 innings in 1884, winning 46 games each season. During one week in August 1884 he pitched a one-hitter, a no-hitter two days later, a shutout three days after that, and 11 scoreless innings the following day in a game that he lost in the twelfth inning, 1–0. On 9 September he shut out Providence, 2–0, thereby stopping Charles "Hoss" Radbourne's string of 18 consecutive victories.

Galvin began the 1885 season as Buffalo's captain, or playing manager, but in June he collided with Chicago first baseman Adrian "Cap" Anson and injured his leg. His pitching suffered, as did the team's overall performance, and he was sold in July to the Pittsburgh Alleghenys of the American Association. Galvin received $750 of the $2,500 sale price and a $1,000 raise to $3,000. He finished poorly at 3–7 but bounced back in 1886 to win 29 games. He stayed with the Alleghenys as they moved to the National League in 1887 and won 28, 23, and 23 games over the next three seasons.

In 1890 Galvin, along with many other National League players seeking higher salaries, jumped to the ill-fated Players' League. He won 12 games for the Pittsburgh Burghers, but when the league collapsed after just one season, he returned to Pittsburgh's National League club, newly named the Pirates. He found his salary cut in half and two younger pitchers handling the bulk of the work.

Early in 1892, Galvin injured his finger, and the Pirates released him. He caught on with the St. Louis Browns of the American Association, thereby finishing his playing career in the same city where it began. He retired from major league baseball at the end of the season with a record of 360 wins and 308 losses and an earned run average of 2.87.

Galvin became a National League umpire for two seasons; he then opened the largest saloon in Pittsburgh. The business failed, and he was wiped out financially. He took a construction job and moved into a rooming house. His weight ballooned to more than 300 pounds. He contracted a stomach ailment on Thanksgiving Day in 1901 and died destitute in Pittsburgh. Friends held a benefit to pay for his funeral.

On baseball's all-time lists, Galvin stands seventh in wins, second in losses, second in complete games, and second in innings pitched. Year after year, he compiled exceptional statistical totals using a fine fastball and excellent control. Yet the teams on which he played never won a major league pennant, and his stature as one of nineteenth-century baseball's best pitchers gradually eroded. He was inducted into the National Baseball Hall of Fame in 1965, more than sixty years after his death.

• There is no full-scale biography of Galvin. Clipping files on him can be found at the National Baseball Library, Cooperstown, N.Y., and at the *Sporting News*, St. Louis, Mo. An obituary is in *Sporting Life*, 15 Mar. 1902.

STEVEN P. GIETSCHIER

GAMBINO, Carlo (24 Aug. 1902–15 Oct. 1976), organized crime boss, was born in Palermo, Sicily, Italy. His parents' names are unknown, but his mother's maiden name was Castellano. (The date of his birth is uncertain; the *New York Times* obituary gives it as 1 Sept. 1902.) Gambino, who grew up during a time in which the Mafia was gaining prominence in Sicily, came to revere the suave, well-dressed men who controlled the section of Palermo where he lived, especially Don Vito Cascio Ferro, the leader of the so-called Sicilian Honored Society. By the time he left Sicily, Gambino had been initiated into organized crime. Joining the large numbers of Italians immigrating to the United States, Gambino in November 1921 stowed away on a freighter bound for Norfolk, Virginia. He soon moved on to Brooklyn, New York, where some of his mother's family lived. He resided for the balance of his life in the United States, although he never became an American citizen.

Upon his arrival in New York, Gambino's cousin, future crime boss Paul Castellano, offered Gambino a position at a garage he owned. Soon, however, the profitable world of organized crime took precedence over his day job, as he began defying Prohibition by selling liquor for Brooklyn's Giuseppe "Joe the Boss" Masseria. Gambino was a successful bootlegger, making money for both himself and Masseria by satisfying the public's craving for spirits.

By 1932 Gambino had switched loyalties to join with the ambitious Salvatore Maranzano, who aspired to become *càpo di tùtti I càpi* (boss of all bosses). Maranzano's objective was achieved in 1931, after directing Lucky Luciano to execute Masseria. After becoming boss, Maranzano set about the task of organizing the somewhat disordered American Mafia, fashioning the concept of La Cosa Nostra (this thing of ours) and creating five New York "families." Gambino was named a *caporegime* (captain) in the family run by Vincent Mangano. Maranzano's rule was short lived, however, as Luciano had him murdered just a few months later. Luciano ostensibly did away with the position of boss of all bosses and created a more democratic twelve-member commission to run the Mafia in the United States.

Luciano's reconstruction did not affect Gambino's standing in the family, as the quiet, affable Gambino assisted Mangano in governing the waterfront district, extorting money from shipping companies, shipowners, and dockworkers and stealing cargo. In addition, Gambino continued to market illegal liquor, even after the repeal of Prohibition, by providing a product that was economical and quite fortified. During World War II he made millions procuring and reselling ration stamps obtained either from bribable federal employees or by theft. He also held assorted business interests, both legal and illegal, investing in bakeries, nightclubs, restaurants, and meat markets, among other ventures. Becoming very wealthy, Gambino married his first cousin Kathryn Castellano in 1932; they had one daughter and three sons.

Since few resign or retire willingly from the Mafia, attrition usually occurs by assassination. In 1951 Albert Anastasia, the head of Murder, Inc., a group officially unconnected to La Cosa Nostra that carried out contract killings, had Mangano killed, and he ascended to boss of the family, promoting Gambino to underboss. Gambino ran the waterfront with the occasionally unstable Anastasia until 1957, when the latter was shot in the head as he sat in a barbershop chair at the Park Sheraton Hotel in New York City. Though no one claimed responsibility for the murder, many believe that the shrewd and enterprising Gambino, who was soon named boss of the family, played a role in the shooting. He would be known for the rest of his life as "Don Carlo."

During Gambino's successful reign as boss, he made money for himself and the organization by retaining control of the waterfront, by assuming command of the unions that moved cargo out of Idlewild (in 1963 John F. Kennedy) International Airport in New York City, and by running gambling rackets. Some allege that he also was immersed heavily in hero-

in smuggling. Under Gambino's guidance the Mafia took control of trucking in the garment districts of New York and the private garbage disposal industry in the city, among other activities. He also retained his legitimate holdings, making a fortune with interests in supermarkets, meat-packing companies, and furniture retail. He even united with two partners to form a labor relations consulting firm, Saltzstein, Gambino & Schiller, charging $40,000 a consultation. By the late 1960s more than 1,000 persons worked for Gambino; 400 were initiated members of the crime family, and the rest were businesspersons and union officials.

Gambino's style contrasted with that of other notorious organized crime figures such as Luciano, Joseph Colombo, and John Gotti. Never gaudy or ostentatious, he was dedicated to his wife and children, well mannered, charitable, and seemingly passive. He is said to be the archetype for Don Vito Corleone in Mario Puzo's bestselling novel *The Godfather* (1969; three years later made into an Oscar-winning film by Francis Ford Coppola), as he was known for holding court in Little Italy, greeting the people and dispensing favors as he saw fit. Gambino never acquired a good command of the English language and spoke in a Sicilian dialect. Though possessing a reputation for being nonaggressive, he punished when the circumstances called for it, but, unlike the public hits ordered by some Mafiosi, in most cases Gambino's enemies just "disappeared."

The 1970s marked a personal and professional decline for Gambino. In 1970 he was charged in connection with the theft of several million dollars from an armored car, though he was never brought to trial because of ill health. In 1967 the Justice Department had failed in an attempt to force Gambino, an illegal alien, to leave the country. A few years later they tried again, but when Gambino learned the order had been issued, he was rushed to the hospital for treatment of a heart attack. In 1971 his wife died. Realizing the fragile state of his health, Gambino chose his cousin and brother-in-law Paul Castellano as his successor in 1975. He died at his summer home in Massapequa, Long Island. During his long, prominent career in crime, he had spent less than two years in prison.

Gambino's management style emphasized control and discretion. Until the end of his life he discouraged initiating new soldiers into the family, especially non-Italians, as he felt that increasing membership would make organized crime more vulnerable to authorities. His success must be attributed in part to his longevity, and his conservative approach doubtless played a key role in keeping him alive and out of jail for most of his seventy-four years. Gambino's legacy in organized crime is immense. Under his control, the New York Mafia became larger, wealthier, and more powerful than at any time in the twentieth century.

• As is true with most organized crime figures, reliable information on Gambino is limited. See John H. Davis, *Mafia Dynasty: The Rise and Fall of the Gambino Crime Family* (1993), and Carl Sifakis, *The Mafia Encyclopedia* (1987). An obituary is in the *New York Times*, 16 Oct. 1976. An account of his funeral is in the same newspaper, 19 Oct. 1976. An analysis of the effect of Gambino's death on organized crime is in the *New York Times*, 18 Oct. 1976.

STACEY HAMILTON

GAMBLE, Hamilton Rowan (29 Nov. 1798–31 Jan. 1864), judge and provisional governor of Missouri, was born in Winchester, Virginia, the son of Joseph Gamble and Ann Hamilton, Irish immigrants. Although self-educated, the father wrote extensively on various political and historical topics and, being a staunch Presbyterian, reared his family in the Calvinist tradition. Educated at Hampden-Sydney College (1812–1816), Hamilton studied law and was admitted to the Virginia bar at age eighteen. He left Virginia in 1818 to join his brother Archibald, who was serving as clerk of the St. Louis Circuit Court. After a short time as his brother's deputy, Gamble moved to the thriving frontier town of Franklin, Missouri, in the heart of the Boonslick Country, to establish his law practice.

Gamble relocated to St. Louis in 1823 and shortly thereafter established what would be a lifelong friendship with Edward Bates, who recommended him the following year for appointment as secretary of state by his brother, Governor Frederick Bates. Gamble served in this post until 1826. He married Caroline J. Coalter in 1827. Of their seven children, only three survived infancy. Although active in establishing the Whig party in Missouri, Gamble devoted himself primarily to his law practice during the next two decades.

Gamble was elected to the legislature as a Whig in 1846, but he declined a second term because of the press of his legal business. When Missouri moved to an elected supreme court in 1851, a change that Gamble had championed for some time, he secured an easy election, serving until 1854. In the most noted case to come before the court during his term, Gamble, in a lone dissenting vote, asserted that Dred Scott was entitled to his freedom because his master had taken him into free territory—a view in accord with eight previous decisions by the Missouri Supreme Court but now unpopular with his two fellow justices, who were proslavery Democrats.

Retiring from political and professional life in 1854 because of ill health and his wife's failing eyesight, Gamble moved to Norristown, Pennsylvania, where he remained until called back to Missouri by his friends in 1861 in the midst of the secession crisis. Elected in February to the state convention called to determine Missouri's course, Gamble chaired the committee on federal relations and dominated its proceedings, bringing in a report that rejected secession. Thereafter he worked through his brother-in-law Edward Bates, Abraham Lincoln's attorney general, to try to assure Missouri's neutrality. This worked temporarily as Brigadier General William S. Harney, commanding Union forces at St. Louis, and Major General Sterling Price, commanding the Missouri State Guard, worked out an arrangement for the latter to keep peace in the interior of the state. This failed,

however, when Congressman Frank Blair (1821–1875), receiving reports of pro-Unionists having difficulties in the interior, persuaded Lincoln to remove Harney and replace him with Brigadier General Nathaniel Lyon. Neutrality broke down, and Missouri's pro-Confederate constitutional government was driven from Jefferson City by Lyon. Missouri was now plunged into the Civil War. Price, Governor Claiborne F. Jackson, and the Missouri State Guard retreated to southwest Missouri after losing to Lyon at the battle of Boonville. Jackson maintained a shadow government thereafter, cooperating with the Confederate government.

In the aftermath of this action, Gamble and others reconvened the state convention in late July 1861. It deposed the legislature and all elected state officials and named Gamble as provisional governor to serve until a new election could be held. Because of Missouri's turbulent condition, Gamble continued as governor until his death. He worked closely with the Lincoln administration and its various military commanders in Missouri to organize local militia to keep order within the state. Many of the militia were willing to serve on the homefront but not elsewhere. Their presence, however, relieved regular federal troops for service on other fronts. The militia proved moderately successful, but Missouri continued to be racked by partisan and guerrilla warfare throughout the war.

Although Gamble insisted that slavery should not be jeopardized by the war, more radical voices calling for an end to that institution became increasingly insistent by 1862. When the state convention, which had been meeting periodically, called for the election of a new legislature that fall, it quickly became obvious that the slavery issue would have to be addressed. Gamble now announced his support for gradual, compensated emancipation, but a badly divided legislature failed to agree on a specific plan. Consequently Gamble called the state convention into one last session in June 1863 and secured its adoption of his proposal to end slavery by 4 July 1870.

The emancipation controversy led to the creation of the Radical Union party, which demanded a quicker resolution of the slavery issue. Gamble provided some leadership to the Conservative Union party, which emerged in support of his program, but he was to be spared most of the political turmoil that followed. While traveling by train from Philadelphia to Washington in late summer 1863, he extended his arm out an open window. It was hit by a bridge timber, shattering his elbow. He did not return to Missouri for six weeks. In early January 1864 Gamble fell on the icy steps of the capitol in Jefferson City, reinjuring his arm. Pneumonia ensued, and he died at his home in St. Louis later that same month.

Gamble inherited an exceedingly difficult situation in 1861 and dealt with it quite credibly. He determined from the outset to let Missourians retain as much control of their internal situation as the establishment of martial law would allow, hence his concern to have local militia cooperating with federal military authorities to try to keep order. While Gamble's relationship with the federal military commanders at St. Louis was not always harmonious because of their jealous guardianship of authority, the militia worked fairly effectively given the turbulent condition of the state. Gamble's insistence on the militia's use allowed many Missourians who would not have volunteered beyond the state's boundaries to participate in the war effort. Although determined to protect slavery at the beginning of the war, Gamble moderated that stand as it became obvious that sentiment was shifting toward some form of emancipation. He effectively steered a middle course on that issue. Throughout the war his was the voice of local control and moderation, and his leadership did much to hold Missourians together during the four years of internecine strife.

• Gamble's papers are in the Missouri Historical Society, St. Louis. The only biography is Wilbert H. Rosin, "Hamilton Rowan Gamble, Missouri's Civil War Governor" (Ph.D. diss., Univ. of Missouri–Columbia, 1960). The best brief sketch is Marguerite Potter, "Hamilton R. Gamble, Missouri's War Governor," *Missouri Historical Review* 35 (Oct. 1940): 25–71. His record as provisional governor is covered in William E. Parrish, *Turbulent Partnership: Missouri and the Union, 1861–1865* (1963). At the time of Gamble's death, his staff prepared a memorial booklet, *In Memoriam, Hamilton Rowan Gamble, Governor of Missouri, a Memorial* (1864).

WILLIAM E. PARRISH

GAMBLE, James Lawder (18 July 1883–28 May 1959), physician and clinical investigator, was born in Millersburg, Kentucky, the son of Edward Gamble, a prosperous farmer, and Elizabeth Lawder. Gamble began his education at the Millersburg Female College, where he remained until age twelve. He was then transferred to the Millersburg Military Institute, where he received an education grounded in the classics. He was accepted at Harvard, but because his parents were concerned that the frigid Cambridge climate would be harmful to his health, in 1901 he entered the premed program at Stanford University. Ironically, in warm California he lost an entire year of studies as a result of being struck with typhoid fever. After receiving his A.B. from Stanford in 1906, he entered Harvard Medical School, from which he was graduated in 1910. In 1913, after a two-year medical internship at Massachusetts General Hospital of Boston, Gamble went abroad to observe the work being conducted in the prominent medical clinics of Europe. Researchers there were using quantitative methods to study human disease, and this experience guided his future work in medicine.

After his return from Europe, Gamble went to work in the laboratory of Otto Folin, who trained him in basic chemical procedures that could be adapted to the study of metabolic processes in humans. In 1914 Gamble returned to clinical work at Massachusetts General Hospital, where he used the simple procedures he had learned from Folin to investigate diseases in the patients of Fritz Talbot. Initially he studied the effect of varying an infant's protein intake on the partition of

nitrogen and end products in the urine, repeating an experiment that Folin had carried out in adults. The results of these studies, with J. Howard Means and Walter W. Palmer as collaborators, resulted in Gamble's first publication, "Basal Metabolism and Creatinine Elimination" (*Journal of Biological Chemistry* 19 [1914]: 239). Through Palmer, Gamble was introduced to L. J. Henderson, who encouraged Gamble to undergo additional training in biochemistry, which eventually led to his interest in electrolyte chemistry and physiology.

In 1915 Gamble accepted the invitation of John Howland to become an associate in the pediatrics department at the Johns Hopkins Hospital. Within six months of his arrival in Baltimore, Gamble had decided to abandon clinical medicine and work full time in the laboratory. In 1916 he married Elizabeth Cahfee, with whom he would have five children. The following year, after the United States entered World War I, Gamble became a Red Cross physician, serving in a small American hospital in France. In 1919, after returning from France, he embarked on his first significant undertaking at Hopkins, a study of the ketosis produced by the starvation therapy then being used by Howland for the treatment of epilepsy. The data that he and his collaborators, S. Graham Ross and F. F. Tisdall, collected showed that the kidney maintained acid-base balance in the body by exchanging ammonia for sodium. They also found that osmolality (the concentration of a solution in osmolal units) of both the plasma and urine was regulated by the kidney. These studies, published in the classic paper "The Metabolism of Fixed Base during Fasting" (*Journal of Biological Chemistry* 57 [1923]: 633), were highly significant, for they signaled the introduction of experimental design in clinical investigation. Another development of this work was the "Gambelian diagram" or "Gamblegram" (a graphic presentation of quantitative data) describing electrolyte balance and electrolyte changes in various clinical conditions as well as in the healthy person; it has since become a mainstay in teaching the chemistry of electrolyte balance.

In 1922 Oscar Schloss, professor of pediatrics at Harvard, asked Gamble to return to Boston as assistant professor of pediatrics. Gamble accepted the offer because it gave him the opportunity to form his own laboratory for the study of electrolyte balance. He became an associate professor in 1925 and in 1932 was appointed a full professor. He was chairman of the department from 1946 to 1950, when he became an emeritus professor. During his tenure at Harvard, from 1933 to 1953, Gamble also served as director of the Metabolic Laboratory at Children's Hospital in Boston. During the Second World War he and Allen Butler undertook research to determine the minimal amounts of food and potable water that were necessary for an individual to survive while abandoned at sea. This work, elicited by the realities of war, has since been categorized as the "life raft" studies.

Gamble enjoyed leisure as much as he enjoyed science, and he and his wife liked to entertain at their various residences, a home in Brookline, a farm in Taunton, and a summer home in Maine. His best-known hobby was the filming of legendary stories adapted from the historical novels of Sir Walter Scott in which his children acted out the various roles. Among his numerous honors, Gamble was a recipient of the Borden Award (American Academy of Pediatrics, 1946), the Kober Medal (Association of American Physicians, 1951), the Moxon Medal (Royal College of Physicians, London, 1954), and the John Howland Medal and Award (American Pediatric Society, 1955). He died in Boston.

• Gamble's papers are at Harvard University. For more details on Gamble's research, see Robert F. Loeb's memoir in National Academy of Sciences, *Biographical Memoirs* 36 [1962]: 145–60. Obituaries are in the *Journal of Pediatrics* 56 (1960): 701, and the *Boston Herald*, 29 May 1959.

DAVID Y. COOPER

GAMOW, George (4 Mar. 1904–20 Aug. 1968), theoretical physicist and science popularizer, was born Georgy Antonovich Gamov in Odessa, Russia, the son of Anton Michailovich Gamov and Alexandra Arsenievia Lebedinzeva, high school teachers. During his first three decades, Gamow survived the Russian Revolution; graduated from the Odessa Normal School in 1920; learned and did theoretical physics in Leningrad and such centers as Göttingen, Copenhagen, and Cambridge; got married in 1931 to optical engineer Lyubov "Rho" Vokhminzeva, with whom he had his only child; and—eager for a better life—attended in 1933 a prestigious conference in Belgium from which he never returned to the Soviet Union. His years in Europe are vividly recounted in his posthumous autobiography, *My World Line* (1970).

In 1934 Gamow came to the United States in order to teach at the famed summer school for theoretical physics at the University of Michigan and, if at all possible, to find a permanent position. Although the depression was far from over and he was but thirty, Gamow had reason to be optimistic about his prospects. He had become a familiar, and welcome, figure on the conference circuit as a result of his original quantum theory of radioactive alpha decay (1928), his pioneering monograph *Constitution of Atomic Nuclei and Radioactivity* (1931), and his fun-loving, irreverent approach to physics. Accomplished theoretical physicists were much sought after then by American universities. Before the summer was over, Gamow was offered a professorship at George Washington University in Washington, D.C.

In accepting this position, Gamow used his experiences in Niels Bohr's circle in Copenhagen to persuade the university that his success would depend on the institution's willingness to foster an environment where discussion would flourish. In 1935 he arranged for the appointment of another theorist, his ebullient Hungarian-born friend, Edward Teller. That same year he started the Washington Conference on Theoretical Physics, which soon became a significant annual forum for the discussion of current theoretical problems. American work on nuclear fission was, in fact, initiated by the fifth Washington Conference (1939) when Bohr reported the latest German and Scandinavian research on neutron bombardment of uranium.

Gamow's own research in America focused initially on nuclear theory. Among other things, he and Teller collaborated on the problem of radioactive beta decay, announcing in 1936 what have since been called the "Gamow-Teller selection rules." Soon thereafter, however, Gamow abandoned pure nuclear theory because he did not enjoy competing with more and more theorists to explain increasingly subtle effects. He turned to the then-outstanding problem in stellar theory—identifying the nuclear processes that generate stellar energies for billions of years. Hoping to stimulate interest in this interdisciplinary question, Gamow devoted the fourth Washington Conference (1938) to stars and atomic nuclei. Indeed, shortly after attending, his friend Hans Bethe identified the thermonuclear reactions powering ordinary stars.

Gamow rapidly followed up on Bethe's breakthrough with studies of giant stars, supernovae, and the primordial origin of the elements. He continued working along these lines throughout World War II because, despite being naturalized in 1940, he was wrongly regarded as too great a security risk for the Manhattan Project. After the war, he, his student Ralph Alpher, and Alpher's friend Robert Herman concentrated on the question of how elements might have been created in the very early stages of an expanding universe. Although he became the leading champion for what rival proponents of the steady-state universe dubbed the "big bang" model, Gamow remained an irrepressible jokester. He insisted, for instance, that his first paper with Alpher include Bethe (in absentia) as a collaborator so that the authors' names would mimic the first three letters in the Greek alphabet, alpha, beta, and gamma. Gamow's light-hearted style and his incapacity to develop a convincing account of the origins of the heavier elements help explain why Alpher and Herman's prediction of a low-temperature residual cosmic background radiation from the big bang was not taken seriously until Arno Penzias and Robert Wilson, working in ignorance of the prediction, established the existence of this phenomenon in the mid-1960s.

Well before this gratifying confirmation, however, Gamow had moved on to another interdisciplinary research front: the emergent specialty of molecular biology. Soon after learning in June 1953 about the recent work of Francis Crick and James Watson in England on the structure of DNA, he wrote them to propose that DNA serves as a template for the synthesis of proteins. Although they saw many faults with the idea, Crick later credited Gamow with leading him and others to think about the next stage in DNA research. For the next year or so, Gamow played an active role in the burgeoning field both by forcefully advocating his template proposal and by founding the "RNA Tie Club" for the circulation of informal papers.

Gamow was also active as an author of popular and semipopular books on science. His first ventures in science popularization were occasional columns that he wrote for *Pravda* before his defection. Later in the United States, he tried without success to get major American monthlies to accept an article describing the physics of "a toy universe" only five miles in diameter. Turning to England, he persuaded C. P. Snow in 1937 to publish it and some companion pieces in *Discovery*. Then, on the invitation of Cambridge University Press, he gathered the material together in *Mr. Tompkins in Wonderland* (1939). Over the next decade and a half, he wrote another eight books for lay readers, including most notably *The Birth and Death of the Sun* (1940), *Mr. Tompkins Explores the Atom* (1944), *One, Two, Three . . . Infinity* (1947), and *The Creation of the Universe* (1952). His achievements as a science popularizer were recognized by UNESCO, which awarded him the Kalinga Prize in 1956.

That same year Gamow got divorced and relocated to the University of Colorado in Boulder. In 1958 he married Barbara Perkins, the American publicity manager for Cambridge University Press. He remained active as a lecturer and science writer during his last decade. He died in Boulder.

Gamow made three main contributions to science during his American period. He wrote or collaborated on important papers dealing with beta decay, giant stars, supernovae, the big bang, and DNA. He nurtured interdisciplinary research both by his own example and by promoting informal communications among specialists in different fields. And perhaps most important of all he conveyed the idea that science could be fun and exciting to legions of young writers.

• Gamow's scientific correspondence from the mid-1950s is in the Library of Congress. An excellent oral interview (25 Apr. 1968) and much further information are in the Niels Bohr Library of the American Institute of Physics. In addition to his autobiography, the best general sources on Gamow's life are *Current Biography* (1951), pp. 228–30; *Contemporary Authors* 102 (1981): 208–9; and George Greenstein, "The Magician," *American Scholar* 59 (1990): 118–25. Several former colleagues gave their recollections of Gamow in *Cosmology, Fusion and Other Matters: George Gamow Memorial Volume*, ed. Frederick Reines (1972). See also Yu. I. Lisnevsky, "Georgy Antonovich Gamov: Zhizn'v Rosii i SSSR," *Voprosy Istorii Estestvoznaniia i Tekhniki* (1989), an archivally based study of his first three decades; Roger Stuewer, "Gamow's Theory of Alpha-Decay," in *The Kaleidoscope of Science*, ed. Edna Ullmann-Margalit (1986), on the background, development, and reception of his theory; Ralph Alpher and Robert Herman, "Reflections on Early Work on 'Big Bang' Cosmology," *Physics Today* 41 (Aug. 1988): 24–34, on his collaboration with them in cosmological research; and Horace Judson, *The Eighth Day of Creation: The Makers of the Revolution in Biology* (1979), on his brief yet intense involvement in early molecular biology.

KARL HUFBAUER

GANNETT, Deborah Sampson. *See* Sampson, Deborah.

GANNETT, Ezra Stiles (4 May 1801–26 Aug. 1871), Unitarian minister, was born in Cambridge, Massachusetts, the son of Caleb Gannett and his second wife, Ruth Stiles, the daughter of Ezra Stiles, a president of Yale College. Caleb Gannett had once been a minister, but for nearly forty years he served as steward of Harvard College. Gannett's mother died when he was seven, and his father died while he was a student at Harvard. He graduated from Harvard in 1820 and from Harvard Divinity School in 1823. Coming of age at a time when Unitarians were still distinguishing themselves from orthodox Congregationalists, Gannett experienced uncertainty about his religious commitments and vocation. Before entering the divinity school, he was troubled by his lack of heartfelt conviction and contemplated becoming a lawyer. Gannett apparently resolved his doubts during his theological education. He signed the covenant of the Harvard College church in 1822 and accepted a call to be assistant minister to William Ellery Channing (1780–1842) at the Federal Street Church in Boston in 1824. He was ordained in Boston on 30 June 1824. He became minister of the church after Channing's death in 1842 and held that position until his own death. In 1861 he presided over the congregation's move to Arlington Street in Boston.

Gannett's principal public contribution was as an organizer of the Unitarian denomination. Because early nineteenth-century Unitarians embraced the principle of freedom of conscience, many ministers were reluctant to adopt a formal statement of beliefs and an organizational structure sufficient to unite congregations and to propagate Unitarian views. Gannett was aware of the challenge to Unitarianism posed by well-organized evangelical denominations, and he became a leading figure in the founding of the American Unitarian Association in 1825, serving as its first secretary. In 1834 he headed a committee to establish the Benevolent Fraternity of Christian Churches to support the Unitarian ministry-at-large to the urban working classes. Beyond his institutional efforts, Gannett believed that Unitarian ideas needed to be voiced clearly in order to gain adherents. He edited a number of denominational periodicals, including the *Scriptural Interpreter* from 1831 to 1835 and the *Christian Examiner* from 1844 to 1849.

Gannett's work was centered in the conviction that Unitarianism was not simply a critique of Calvinist orthodoxy, but was a positive system of beliefs. In an early series of sermons, including "The Unitarian Belief" (1830) and "Unitarianism Not a Negative System" (1833), Gannett emphasized the unity of God, the saving example of Christ, the importance of moral growth, and the necessity of freedom of conscience. Around 1840 the still fragile Unitarian denomination was divided over Transcendentalist ideas, particularly those of Theodore Parker. As editor of the *Christian Examiner*, Gannett strenuously contested Transcendentalist philosophy and condemned its divisive impact on the denomination. In articles such as "Mr. Parker and His Views" (1845) and "The Unitarian Denomination" (1846), he rejected the Transcendentalist belief in intuitive revelation, reaffirmed the sole authority of historical Christianity, and professed the right of Unitarians to exclude from their fellowship those who differed with these views. Gannett admitted that he walked a thin line between protecting denominational integrity and violating freedom of thought, but he willingly risked compromising principles to protect the faith of the people. Gannett probably knew that his efforts did not quell dissent in the denomination. His polemical writings helped to define the theological position of conservative Unitarians, but Gannett played little role in public controversy after 1850.

Gannett experienced substantial difficulties in his private life. Pushing himself to overwork, his health was poor. He had a nervous breakdown in 1836. A stroke in 1840 left him partly paralyzed. He married Anna Tilden in 1835, and the couple had three children. After she died in 1846, he did not remarry. Gannett died in a railroad accident on his way from Boston to Lynn, Massachusetts, to preach.

Ezra Stiles Gannett's work was a significant part of the organizational initiative in nineteenth-century Unitarianism. Following the pioneering intellectual efforts of such liberal Protestant thinkers as William Ellery Channing, Gannett helped to ground Unitarian convictions in denominational institutions. Ill prepared for the radical challenge to historical Christianity posed by the Transcendentalists, Gannett was nonetheless instrumental in creating a liberal alternative to mainstream evangelical Protestantism.

• The most significant collection of Gannett's papers is located in the Massachusetts Historical Society, Boston. Other manuscripts are found in the papers of his son, William Channing Gannett, at the University of Rochester, and of his grandson, Lewis Gannett, in Houghton Library, Harvard University. The principal biography of Gannett is William C. Gannett, *Ezra Stiles Gannett: Unitarian Minister in Boston, 1824–1871* (1875). The biography contains substantial extracts from letters, sermons, and essays as well as a complete list of Gannett's published sermons, addresses, and essays. Supplemental biographical information may be found in Samuel A. Eliot, ed., *Heralds of a Liberal Faith*, vol. 3 (1910). Obituaries are in the *Boston Transcript*, 28 Aug. 1871, and the *Christian Register*, 2 Sept. 1871.

ANNE C. ROSE

GANNETT, Frank Ernest (15 Sept. 1876–3 Dec. 1957), newspaper publisher, was born in Bristol, New York, near Rochester, the son of Joseph Charles Gannett, a farmer and later hotelier, and Maria Brooks. Gannett began his first reporting for the *Buffalo News* while attending high school. As a student at Cornell University in Ithaca (1894–1898), he worked for the school paper, the *Cornell Sun*. He also served as a correspondent for the *Ithaca Journal* and the *Syracuse Herald* in his junior year. He was named secretary to the first Philippine Commission (1899–1900) headed by Cornell president Jacob Gould Schurman, who had known Gannett at Ithaca. Upon completion of that task, he returned to New York to become city editor and later

business manager for the *Ithaca News* (1900–1905). He left that position after a quarrel with the owner and worked as a subeditor of *Frank Leslie's Illustrated Weekly* (1905–1906) and contributed to the *Pittsburgh Index*.

Gannett's first chance for ownership came in 1906 when he and Erwin Davenport paid $20,000 for the *Elmira* (N.Y.) *Gazette*, an evening daily that backed the Democratic party. Gannett took on the responsibilities of editor and supervisor of news. Some of the Gannett trademarks appeared immediately in the *Gazette*—editorial conciseness and a refusal to accept liquor advertising. Gannett tried to maintain a separation between the news and editorial functions of the paper. Within a year, the *Gazette* merged with its afternoon rival, the *Evening Star*, to create the *Star-Gazette*, making Gannett a one-fourth owner of the new property. After working as managing editor at the *Star-Gazette* for six years, he seized an opportunity to become part owner of the *Ithaca Journal* in 1912. Despite his personal attraction to the Democratic party, he maintained the *Journal*'s Republican editorial position. The *Journal* merged with the *Ithaca News* in 1919 to form the *Journal-News*.

In 1918 Gannett and his partner Davenport gained financial backing from auto manufacturer John Willys to purchase two Rochester afternoon dailies: the Republican *Times* and the Democratic *Union and Advertiser*. The two papers were combined into one, the *Times-Union*, which became politically independent. Later, in 1922, the *Times-Union* launched a radio station in Rochester. In 1920 Gannett married Caroline Werner and the couple had a natural daughter, Sarah, and an adopted son, Dixon. In 1921 Gannett and his partners purchased the two afternoon papers in Utica and combined them into the *Observer-Dispatch*.

In 1923 Gannett's group purchased two faltering Elmira papers, the daily *Advertiser* and Sunday *Telegram*, giving them a monopoly there. The owners formed the Empire State Group corporation of newspaper holdings, but Gannett soon bought out his partners' shares and formed the Gannett Company, Inc., with six newspapers in Rochester, Utica, Elmira, and Ithaca.

Gannett attempted unsuccessfully on two occasions to negotiate the purchase of the *Chicago Daily News*, in 1925 and 1931, and also failed in a bid to buy the *Kansas City Star*. In 1927 he bought the *Winston-Salem Sentinel*, contemplating moving into the South, but he decided within six months to sell and remain concentrated in New York. By purchasing the morning *Rochester Democrat and Chronicle* in 1928 for $3.5 million, Gannett gained membership in the Associated Press. Also in 1928 he paid $5.5. million for the *Hartford* (Conn.) *Times*, $2 million for the *Albany* (N.Y.) *Knickerbocker Press* (morning) and *Evening News*, and $4 million for the *Brooklyn Daily Eagle*. In 1929, after allegations that Gannett's creditor, International Paper Company, sought favorable editorial backing for International's campaign for private power companies, Gannett not only denied any such arrangements but also paid off his debt and severed ties with International.

During the New Deal era, Gannett papers criticized many of President Franklin Roosevelt's programs. Gannett founded the National Committee to Uphold Constitutional Government in 1937 to fight Roosevelt's Supreme Court packing plan and the 1938 Government Reorganization Bill. Nonetheless, the Gannett papers maintained editorial independence by allowing local boards to make editorial policy. Gannett got the political bug after the 1936 presidential election. He unsuccessfully sought the Republican nomination for governor of New York in 1938 and the Republican presidential nomination in 1940.

During World War II Gannett wrote a number of articles that were published separately by the company: *Britain Sees It Through* (1944) and *The Fuse Sputters in Europe* (1946). He was a great promoter of commercial aviation and wrote a series of articles about a world flying tour, *Winging round the World* (1947). Gannett continued to maintain editorial independence for the papers he owned through individual editorial boards. When he retired as president in 1957, his company owned twenty-three newspapers in sixteen cities as well as four radio and two television stations. All the properties were situated in New York, Connecticut, New Jersey, and Illinois.

Frank Gannett's philosophy of seizing opportunities to acquire newspaper properties and then allowing local papers to develop their own editorial policy was a winning conbination. It permitted the Gannett chain to develop gradually and maintain financial solvency while remaining responsive to local community concerns. Good stewardship by Gannett positioned the chain to expand even more after his death in Rochester and become the largest newspaper chain in the United States.

• The Gannett papers (1859–1958) are housed at Cornell University. There are also some Gannett letters in the Paul Miller Papers at Oklahoma State University in Stillwater. Samuel T. Williamson, *Imprint of a Publisher: The Story of Frank Gannett and His Independent Newspapers* (1948), is an authorized yet competent biography. See also T. A. Govert, A. C. Lipsky, and E. D. Engst, eds., *Guide to the Frank E. Gannett and Caroline Werner Gannett Papers* (1987), and "Frank E. Gannett," *Editor and Publisher*, 7 Dec. 1957, pp. 11, 66, 68, 70. Obituaries are in the *Rochester Democrat and Chronicle* and the *New York Times*, both 4 Dec. 1957.

DANIEL WEBSTER HOLLIS III

GANNETT, Henry (24 Aug. 1846–5 Nov. 1914), geographer, was born in Bath, Maine, the son of Michael Farley Gannett and Hannah Church. He studied first at local schools and then at Harvard University, where he earned a B.S. (1869) from the Lawrence Scientific School and an M.E. (1870) from the short-lived Hooper Mining School. Trained in astronomy as well as in the earth sciences, Gannett was employed at the Harvard Observatory before taking a position in 1871 as topographer on Ferdinand V. Hayden's U.S. Geological and Geographical Survey of the Territories. In 1874 he married Mary E. Chase; they had three children.

Gannett worked on the Hayden Survey until its incorporation in 1879 into the new U.S. Geological Survey. He methodically collected and organized data on large and previously little-known regions of the American West. Among his field expeditions were important surveys of the Yellowstone country. His precision and thoroughness won him the regard of the USGS's second director, John Wesley Powell, and appointment as the survey's chief geographer in 1882. In that position, Gannett supervised the progress of the most ambitious project of Powell's directorship: the detailed topographical mapping of the entire United States. The work proceeded rapidly, and the maps released soon proved their usefulness for many purposes ranging from geologic mapping to land and water resource development. Haste made them uneven in quality, however, and it was alleged that some topographic appointments were used as patronage to secure congressional support for the survey. When Powell's successor, Charles D. Walcott, reorganized the topographic work on a more professional basis upon assuming the directorship, Gannett, who was held responsible for the problems that had arisen, was removed in 1896 as chief geographer (although outside of the survey, he continued to identify himself by that title). He remained affiliated with the USGS until his death, assuming charge of its Forestry Division in 1897.

Gannett's outside activities were numerous. Between 1880 and 1882 he served on assignment as geographer to the Tenth Census, for which he demarcated the enumeration districts and aided the superintendent, Francis A. Walker, in advancing the cartographic display of data. With Fletcher Hewes, Gannett coedited a statistical atlas of the United States that appeared in 1885. He played a similar role in the Eleventh and Twelfth censuses and took part in the U.S. censuses of Cuba (1899 and 1907), Puerto Rico (1899 and 1907), and the Philippine Islands (1903). His announcement following the 1890 census that the frontier had ceased to exist as a distinct line of settlement prompted the historian Frederick Jackson Turner to formulate his frontier thesis of American development. He was a founding member and later president (1910–1914) of the National Geographic Society, a founder (1904) of the Association of American Geographers, and an active participant in many other scholarly organizations. He took part in the 1899 Harriman Expedition to Alaska and chaired the National Geographic Society committee that endorsed Robert A. Peary's claim to have reached the North Pole. Instrumental in establishing the U.S. Board on Geographic Names, he served for twenty years as its chairman and published gazetteers of many of the states and territories. He also wrote a standard manual on topographic methods and compiled dictionaries of altitudes, boundaries, magnetic declinations, and positions in the United States. Addressed to a wider audience were

The Building of a Nation (1895), *The United States* (1898), and *Commercial Geography*, with C. L. Garrison and E. J. Houston (1905), along with many articles in popular periodicals.

Gannett's most important services to American science were institutional. His government and organizational activities did much to promote professional interchange and the diffusion of geographical information to scholars and the public. Aside from a few of his early geomorphological papers, he contributed to no important conceptual advances. His writings emphasized description and enumeration over analysis. When he did seek to interpret the data, the results reflected the received notions of his milieu, demonstrating strains of geographical and racial determinism, a conviction in the superiority of American political institutions to all others, and a strong inclination toward laissez-faire in economic matters. To the last-named principle, however, Gannett made several exceptions. He supported government restriction of foreign immigration, support of scientific research, and protection of forests. Though cautious and measured in his claims for forest influences, he allied himself with the conservation movement and edited the influential 1908 report of President Theodore Roosevelt's National Conservation Commission. Gifford Pinchot, a close associate in the cause, would recall Gannett as "a vigorous, forthright, competent man of wide knowledge and varied experience" and personally as "a man of decided opinions and strong antagonisms, brusque in manner but with a golden heart." Gannett died in Washington, D.C.

• Gannett's correspondence is in institutional archives in Washington, particularly those of the National Geographic Society and the U.S. Geological Survey. The best account of Gannett's life and work is Robert H. Block, "Henry Gannett, 1846–1914," *Geographers: Biobibliographical Studies*, vol. 8 (1984), pp. 45–49. A valuable background source on Gannett's Hayden Survey years is Richard C. Bartlett, *Great Surveys of the American West* (1962). On his service with the U.S. Geological Survey, see Thomas G. Manning, *Government in Science: The U.S. Geological Survey, 1867–1894* (1967). Obituaries are in the *National Geographic Magazine* 26 (1914): 609–13, and the *Annals of the Association of American Geographers* 7 (1917): 68–70.

WILLIAM B. MEYER

GANNON, Mary (8 Oct. 1829–22 Feb. 1868), actress, was born in New York City of Irish descent; however, no details of her parentage, childhood, or education are known. Her early career is shrouded in uncertainty. Historian T. Allston Brown says she appeared for the first time at the age of three at the Richmond Hill Theatre in *The Daughters of the Regiment*; historian Joseph Norton Ireland places her first performance at the Bowery Theatre in 1835, while chronicler George C. Odell records her first performance at the Franklin Theatre in *The Wonder*, starring Mary Ann Duff. While it is certain Gannon played the Bowery in 1835, her earlier performance recorded by Brown is uncorroborated.

As a child star Gannon played in *Cupid in London* in 1836 and in *The Young Widow* in 1837. Odell continually praised the young actress, and in 1838 she appeared as Lady Flennap in *Lilliputt* at the Walnut Street Theatre in Philadelphia, opening on 18 January; her success in the role led to her nickname, the "Lilliputian Wonder." In 1839 Gannon worked at the Park Theatre, and in 1840 she began playing the vaudeville sketch "The Actress of All Work," assuming all seven roles and playing at the American Museum. As part of the sketch Gannon performed an imitation of dancer Fanny Elssler in *La Bayadere*, for which she gained the nickname "La Petite Elssler."

Over the next few years Gannon worked at theaters in New York and Philadelphia, and by 1844 she had graduated from entr'acte song and dance routines to regular drama. She appeared as the Fairy of the Lake in *Kate Kearney*, which opened 10 March 1846 at the Masonic Hall in Philadelphia. In 1848 she joined the company of William Mitchell at the Olympic Theatre and remained there for several seasons. Among her roles at the Olympic were Sarah Bunt in *Poor Piddcoddy*, Katherine Kloper in *The Catching of Governor*, Theseus in *Theseus and Ariadne*, and Esmerelda in *The Hunchback of Notre Dame*. She also took on the role of wife at this time by marrying George Stevenson, a lawyer. Brown notes that Gannon was "in those days a beauty, fresh and plump, with a foot that Titania might have envied, eyes that sparkled . . . a sweet, ever-ready laugh, and a vivacious nature" (*Oxford Companion*, p. 282).

In 1854 George Stevenson died suddenly, leaving no children. Gannon in that year was on the verge of stardom. In 1855 Gannon became a member of James Wallack Sr.'s company at the Broadway Theatre and, with periodic appearances at other theaters, remained with the company until her death. Soon after joining the company, her comedic talents made her a favorite of the audience. During the 1857–1858 season at the Broadway, she appeared as Pert in *London Assurance*, earning thirty-five dollars a week plus a clear benefit—a sum comparable to that earned by the other leading players of the company and indicative of her growing popularity. That same season she appeared briefly in Philadelphia at the Walnut Street Theatre as Katryn in *Captain of the Watch*, which opened on 21 September. Back in Wallack's company for the 1858–1859 season, Gannon played Tommy Titmous in *The Lady of Bidehober*, Bella Dashwood in *Going to the Band*, and Rose in *Blue and Cherry*. The 1859–1860 season proved the most successful for Gannon, and Wallack's company came to be considered one of the best in the country. During this season she played Betty in *The Clandestine Marriage*, Mrs. Swansdown in *Everybody's Friend*, and Mrs. Pru in Congreve's *Love for Love* as her benefit. Gannon's other notable performances for Wallack's company included Jenny in *The Provoked Husband*, Atalanta Cruiser in *How She Loves Him*, Mary Netley in *Ours*, and Laura St. Leger in *The Fox Hunt*, a performance that George C. Odell called "especially good." In January 1868, during a remount of

Ours, in which she reprised her role of Mary Netley, Gannon became ill and barely managed to complete the performance before collapsing. She did not return to the stage and died a month later in New York City.

Although records regarding her performances and style are scant, the *New York Times* said "probably no other comedienne on the modern American stage enjoyed a better reputation for natural ability and acquired talent. . . . her demise deprives the stage of the most efficient general comic actress known to its patrons and critics" (23 Feb. 1868). Ireland likewise placed Gannon at the forefront of the comedic craft, calling her "literally perfection" and further describing her as "entirely original in style, with a truthfulness to nature almost unparalleled, and a fund of quiet humor apparently inexhaustible, she has in some characters never been approached in merit, is in none surpassed, and is now universally acknowledged to be the best general comic actress in the city" (p. 416). As one of the foremost actresses of her day, Gannon's reputation and ability paved the way for talented comediennes who followed, and her good-natured sense of humor and personality raised the level of the theater of her day, both in quality and in the opinion of the public.

• Information on Gannon is scarce. Brief biographical sketches appear in T. Allston Brown, *History of the American Stage* (1870), Joseph Norton Ireland, *Records of the New York Stage from 1750–1860* (1866–1867), and *The Oxford Companion to the American Theatre* (1984). Scattered references also appear in George C. Odell's *Annals of the New York Stage*, vol. 4–7 (1937–1942). Her obituary is in the *New York Times*, 23 Feb. 1868.

MELISSA VICKERY-BAREFORD

GANO, John (22 July 1727–10 Aug. 1804), Baptist minister, was born in Hopewell, New Jersey, the son of Daniel Gano and Sarah Britton, farmers. A farm boy, John Gano became caught up in the Great Awakening and gradually settled on the ministry as a vocation. He was at first attracted to the Presbyterianism of his father, whose own French Huguenot grandfather had fled Guernsey after the revocation of the Edict of Nantes in 1685. Troubled over the issue of infant baptism, Gano ultimately tilted toward his mother's Baptist faith but retained many Presbyterian ties and traits. A Calvinist throughout his life, Gano audited classes at Princeton, where, though never officially enrolled, he was a favorite of college president Aaron Burr.

While still studying in preparation for the ministry, Gano in 1754 was one of three men that the Philadelphia Baptist Association sent to the great valley of western Virginia at the request of Baptists there. Gano returned to New Jersey within a short time to find himself accused of preaching without proper permission from his church. He answered the charge satisfactorily, was ordained that same year, and began to preach at a number of churches in the vicinity of Morristown. In 1756 the Virginia Baptists again petitioned the Philadelphia Association for a preacher, and Gano was again dispatched southward. He did not remain long in Virginia, instead traveling as far south as Charleston, where he preached with great success. In North Carolina Gano preached to large crowds in the Tar River valley near the Virginia line and also further west in the Yadkin River valley. Within a year he returned to New Jersey and acquired a farm near Morristown. Probably in 1757 he married Sarah Stites, the daughter of John Stites, mayor of Elizabethtown (now Elizabeth). The couple had at least eleven children. Gano continued to preach at a number of local churches, settling on the Baptist church at Morristown as his base of operations.

Repeated petitions from Carolina Baptists drew Gano south for a third time in 1758. Upon his return to the Yadkin River valley of North Carolina, his old friends there sent messengers to the Morristown church to seek permission from that congregation for Gano to relocate permanently to the "Jersey Settlement." In a journey of about five weeks, Gano moved his family the 800 miles between New Jersey and the North Carolina frontier, where he purchased several tracts of land. Although he was wildly popular in North Carolina, Gano moved back to New Jersey by 1760 because he feared for his family's safety during the French and Indian War. In 1762 he became the pastor at the new First Baptist Church in New York City, where he enjoyed a very successful career for many years. For a time he also provided pastoral care for the Baptists of Philadelphia.

When the revolutionary war began, American forces sought Gano's services as chaplain. At first he declined, but eventually he did become a Continental army chaplain. He served from 1776 through the end of the war in 1783; he was in General James Clinton's brigade during most of the fighting in the middle Atlantic region and was present during the Yorktown campaign in Virginia.

At the end of the war Gano returned to his New York City church, but factional infighting within the congregation of 200 eventually ended his ministry there. Active in the founding of Rhode Island College (now Brown University), Gano became a regent of the State University of New York in 1786 and was named trustee of King's College (now Columbia University) in 1787. In 1786 he answered the call of Kentucky Baptists to again relocate to the frontier. Not long after arriving in Kentucky the following year, his wife suffered a fall from a horse and died. Shortly afterward Gano returned to North Carolina to settle business affairs and to preach among the Yadkin River valley settlers he had known before the Revolution. There, probably in 1788, he married Sarah Hunt Bryant, a widow. They had no children. After traveling on to Charleston, Gano returned to Kentucky, where his new wife joined him some months later. Although now past sixty years of age, he continued a vigorous preaching schedule, but a fall from a horse followed by a stroke in 1798 greatly reduced his public ministry. Gano died in Frankfort, Kentucky.

• While no set of Gano's personal papers exists, his son Stephen Gano, a Baptist minister of note in his own right, published *Biographical Memoirs of the Late Rev. John Gano of Frankfort (Kentucky), Formerly of the City of New York, Written Principally by Himself* (1806). Most of what is known of John Gano's career comes from this short autobiography, which is alternately frustrating in its lack of precise chronology and fascinating for its insights into the eras of the Great Awakening and the American Revolution. A sketch of Gano's life in J. H. Spencer, *A History of Kentucky Baptists, from 1769 to 1886, Including More Than 800 Biographical Sketches*, vol. 1 (1885), is largely based on Gano's memoir but adds some additional information. See also George Washington Paschal, *History of North Carolina Baptists* (2 vols., 1930; repr. 1955).

JAMES P. WHITTENBURG

GANS, Joseph (25 Nov. 1874–10 Aug. 1910), professional boxer, was born in Baltimore, Maryland. He reputedly was the son of an African-American baseball player, Joseph Butts. His mother's name is unknown. He was adopted at age four by Maria Gant and her husband. It is not known why he altered his name from Gant to Gans or if in fact previously printed sources had misspelled his adopted mother's surname. Gans began fighting in 1890 in battle royales, brawls in which several African Americans fought each other for money, with the last one standing declared the winner. These free-for-alls taught him to block, dodge, and lead with his punches. His first real fight was for a $2 side bet; in addition, he collected $5.40 in change from the crowd.

A fishmarket clerk, the 5′6″ Gans turned professional in 1891, fighting almost exclusively in Baltimore at 133 pounds. He won all of his early bouts, gaining a reputation for ingenuity in the ring, excellent timing, and knockout ability with either hand. He went undefeated until his thirty-third fight, which he lost to left-hander Dal Hawkins in fifteen rounds in October 1896. Four years later, on 31 August, Gans evened the score with a third-round knockout of Hawkins in the last legal fight held in New York under the Horton Act.

A deadly puncher and counterpuncher, Gans fought for the lightweight championship on 23 March 1900 in New York City, but he was knocked out by titleholder Frank Erne in the twelfth round. After winning his next several bouts, Gans was matched in December 1900 in Chicago against featherweight champion Terry McGovern, who outweighed him by ten pounds; the fight was attended by 17,000 spectators, a record local crowd. Gans was a 3–1 favorite, but he agreed to fix the result. Many fighters in that era were known to prearrange the outcomes of their fights. African-American boxers often had to throw fights because they had a difficult time getting matches and needed the money. Prominent African-American gamblers were forewarned that Gans was not in top shape, but his loyal fans were left in the dark. Gans hardly defended himself against McGovern and lost by a second-round knockout. The fix was so obvious that disgruntled spectators started a riot that nearly ended prizefighting in Chicago.

Gans won his next nineteen fights, including eleven straight knockouts, and he secured a rematch with lightweight champion Erne in May 1902 in Fort Erie, Canada. With his first and only punch, Gans knocked out the champion, the first time that had happened in a title fight. Gans had a hard time getting fights while he was champion because ranking contenders, who were afraid of losing to him, drew the color line as an excuse. He occasionally fought at higher weights, taking on physically stronger boxers like middleweight black Canadian Sam Langford, one of the great fighters of all time, who defeated him in December 1903 in fifteen rounds, and welterweight champion Joe Walcott from Bermuda whom Gans met in 1904 in a nontitle fight that ended in a draw. Gans fought only twice in 1905, having contracted tuberculosis. Because his manager, the astute Al Herford, is said to have taken advantage of him, they split up in 1905, Gans having concluded, probably because he was broke, that it was a mistake to have a white manager.

Gans married twice. (His wives' maiden names and pertinent marital dates are unknown.) His first marriage was to Madge, a Chicago actress, with whom he had two children. They divorced. His second wife was Margaret, a teacher.

Gans's most memorable defense of his championship occurred on 3 September 1906 in the obscure mining town of Goldfield, Nevada. The match was the first major fight promoted by Tex Richard, who, working for a saloon and gambling casino, hoped to entertain the miners, boost the town's fame, and make a lot of money. Gans signed for $11,000, although white challenger O. M. "Battling" Nelson was guaranteed $23,000. A prohibitive 6–1 favorite, Gans had to limit himself before the fight to beef tea to make the 133-pound limit at the ringside weigh-in. Seven thousand spectators, including 500 women, attended the contest, paying nearly $70,000. After forty-two rounds of vicious brawling, during which Nelson repeatedly fouled the champion with head butts, referee George Siler halted the bout, disqualifying Nelson for a punch to the champion's groin. Experts of that era regarded it as one of the greatest fights of its time.

Rickard promoted another outdoors lightweight championship fight for Gans four months later, on New Year's Day 1907, at the Tonopah Casino A.C. in Reno, Nevada, pitting him against Kid Herman, who, like Nelson, was from Chicago. The match took place in zero-degree weather, and the 3,000 fans who watched it wore overcoats and gloves. The champion was a 4–1 favorite and won an uninteresting eight-rounder. Gans received $12,000 of the $31,000 gate, and Herman got $8,000. On 4 July 1908 Gans defended his crown for the second time against Nelson in Colma, California, outside San Francisco, then the national boxing center. Gans had physically deteriorated from tuberculosis and was further worn down by the dreadful conditions of the Herman fight. He lost the championship, knocked out in the seventeenth round.

A rematch was staged on 9 September, and Gans was again knocked out, this time in the twenty-first round.

The "Old Master," as some sportswriters called him, fought just once more in March 1909 before he retired, moving to Arizona for the benefits of its climate. It was too late to stem his TB, however and he died in Baltimore. The *Baltimore Sun* reported that he was worth $70,000, primarily invested in the heavily mortgaged Hotel Goldfield in Baltimore and in two adjoining homes. It is unclear how much he actually had saved during his career because of crooked management and an addiction to dice.

Gans had 156 professional fights, with a record of 120 wins, 8 losses, 10 draws, and 18 no decisions; nearly half of his victories (55) came from knockouts. Many boxing experts consider him the greatest lightweight fighter of his time. He was elected to the *Ring* magazine Hall of Fame in 1954.

• On Gans's life, see Nat Fleischer, *Black Dynamite: The Story of the Negro in the Prize Ring*, vol. 3 (1938), and Bill Doherty, "The Old Master," *Ring* 18 (Nov. 1939): 31, 44. For contemporary reports of his career, see *National Police Gazette*, 16 Dec. 1900, 5 Jan. 1901, 9 Dec. 1905, 10 Mar. 1906. On the McGovern fake, see *Chicago Tribune*, 14 Dec. 1900; Dan Daniel, "Was McGovern-Gans Fight a Fake?" *Ring* 39 (June 1960): 8–9, 43. For detailed narratives of his most famous fight, see James Chinello, "The Great Goldfield Foul," *Westways* 68 (Sept. 1976): 27–30, 88; "Old Timers Hold the Fort," *Ring* 27 (Mar. 1948): 44–45; Dan Daniel, "Gans at His Peak," *Ring* 26 (Apr. 1947): 30–31; and Jim Tully, "The Dark Shadow," *Ring* 15 (Aug. 1936): 10–11, 48. His career and death were closely followed by the African-American press. See the *Chicago Defender*, 13, 20 Aug. 1910; (Chicago) *Broadax*, 10 Aug. 1910; and the *Baltimore African American*, 13 Aug. 1910. For Gans's record, see *The* Ring *Record Book and Boxing Encyclopedia* (1984). For obituaries, see the *Baltimore Sun*, the *New York Times*, and the *Chicago Defender*, all 11 Aug. 1910.

STEVEN A. RIESS

GANTT, Henry Laurence (20 May 1861–23 Nov. 1919), management consultant, was born near Prince Fredericktown, Maryland, the son of Virgil Gantt and Mary Jane Steuart, farmers. The Gantts had been influential tobacco planters along Maryland's Patuxent River for generations. However, the Civil War and the shift to a free labor system created large and ultimately insuperable challenges for Gantt's father. By the late 1860s the family was deeply indebted. Bankrupt by 1871, the Gantts abandoned the family plantation and moved to Baltimore, where Gantt's mother ran a boardinghouse. Gantt always bore the imprint of these struggles and his family's downward mobility.

Gantt attended public schools in Baltimore until 1873, when he was admitted to the McDonogh School, a free private school for poor boys. Excelling in mathematics and science, he won a scholarship to the new Johns Hopkins University in 1878. He graduated from Johns Hopkins two years later and returned to McDonogh to teach science and mechanics. In 1883 Gantt enrolled at the Stevens Institute of Technology in Hoboken, New Jersey, to study mechanical engineering,

graduating with an M.E. in 1884. He worked as a draftsman for two years and returned to McDonogh for another year to introduce courses in woodworking, ironworking, and mechanical drawing. Although Gantt remained close to his mother (his father had died in 1880), McDonogh had taken the place of his family in his early development. For most of the rest of his life a close association with the prominent engineer Frederick W. Taylor would serve a similar function.

In 1887 Gantt formally entered the new world of the college-educated engineer, a milieu that would shape his career thereafter. That world had several poles: it prized technical competence and versatility, emphasized the necessity of an independent but conservative outlook, and cast the engineer as a scientist in industry, a participant observer. Gantt would henceforth exemplify the possibilities of the engineering professional.

At the Midvale Steel Company, which Gantt joined in 1887, he was reunited with Taylor, a Stevens classmate who had become Midvale's chief engineer. For two years Gantt served as Taylor's assistant. During that period Gantt and Taylor cemented an intellectual and professional relationship that would last for the rest of their lives. Gantt followed Taylor's lead as an inventor, patenting numerous inventions for improved foundry machinery. He also became active in the American Society of Mechanical Engineers and like Taylor presented most of his ideas first to that group. Most important, Gantt joined Taylor in developing his new "scientific" system of factory management, a system that included careful organization of machinery and operations, meticulous scheduling and maintenance, wage-rate setting through stopwatch time study, and an incentive wage. By 1889, when Taylor left Midvale, they had made substantial progress in reorganizing the Midvale plant.

After Taylor's departure, Gantt's influence at Midvale declined. In 1893 he accepted the superintendency of the American Car Wheel plant at Garwood, New Jersey, only to lose that position when the plant closed because of the depression of the mid-1890s. He then held other short-term jobs until the economy improved and Taylor, engaged in applying his new methods at Simonds Rolling Machine Company of Fitchburg, Massachusetts, summoned him to Fitchburg.

At Simonds and at the Bethlehem Iron Company (later Bethlehem Steel Company) between 1898 and 1901, Taylor and Gantt applied Taylor's managerial methods. Gantt's role was that of a trusted and proficient lieutenant, first in rank among the coterie of men who worked for Taylor. He contributed to Taylor's technical experiments, particularly the effort to improve metal-cutting tools, and prepared special slide rules to guide their use. He also participated in the introduction of Taylor's managerial techniques and in the management of the reorganized operations. However, Gantt's single most notable contribution came in 1901, when he devised an incentive wage for the Bethlehem machine shop. Since the Bethlehem plant was not completely reorganized, and accurate time studies were impossible, Gantt devised an expedient, called the "task and bonus," that anticipated many incentive plans of the following years. Under Gantt's plan, workers who met the manager's goals received a "bonus"; those who failed merely received their usual wage. The task and bonus gradually became the basis for a modified management system that increasingly occupied Gantt's time. Together with time study, it gave him a claim to a scientific yet humane approach that would satisfy everyone.

After Taylor's dismissal by the Bethlehem managers in early 1901, Gantt left Bethlehem and developed his own consulting practice in close cooperation with Taylor. He served approximately fifty clients over the next decade and a half, appeared frequently at professional meetings, and wrote a popular guide to his managerial ideas, *Work, Wages, and Profits* (1910). His best-known assignments were at the Sayles Bleachery between 1904 and 1908, at Remington Typewriter between 1910 and 1917, and at Cheney Brothers between 1912 and 1917. In general he followed Taylor's prescriptions. But he also devoted increasing attention to the task and bonus and to the issue of worker motivation. By 1910 his interest in personnel issues and his increasingly independent consulting practice had strained his relationship with Taylor. Though Gantt remained an engineer and a critic of contemporary personnel management, he sensed the appeal of his ideas on worker motivation and shop floor harmony.

During World War I Gantt developed the most enduring feature of his work. As a consultant to the army's Ordnance Department, the War Industries Board, and the Shipping Board, he devised a series of charts that enabled managers to compare actual with scheduled production, follow the movement of ships, and monitor other activities. Gantt's charts soon became popular management tools in private industry as well. They also whetted his interest in economic and social planning. In 1916 Gantt briefly became the head of a group of politically active engineers, the New Machine, that attacked the role of financiers in production and advocated economic planning.

Gantt had married Mary Eliza Snow in 1899; they had one daughter. The Gantts had a home in Montclair, New Jersey, and a large farm near Myrtle Beach, South Carolina, where Gantt attempted to apply management principles to agriculture. But Gantt's incessant travels and growing prominence left little time for family life. Worn by his busy schedule, he suffered a fatal heart attack and died in Montclair. His death came at the height of his career, when his ideas and techniques had at last brought wealth, fame, and a promising, independent future.

• There is no single collection of Gantt papers, though his correspondence appears in the collections of his colleagues and professional contemporaries such as Taylor and Frank B. Gilbreth. The best source on Gantt's life is L. P. Alford, *Henry Laurence Gantt: Leader in Industry* (1934), an official biography that includes much laudatory commentary collected after Gantt's death as well as important information on his life and work. Gantt's work is described in most works on the rise of scientific management, including Milton Nadworny, *Scientific Management and the Unions, 1900–1932* (1955); Daniel Nelson, *Frederick W. Taylor and the Rise of Scientific Management* (1980); and Edwin T. Layton, Jr., *The Revolt of the Engineers: Social Responsibility and the American Engineering Profession* (1971). Gantt's charts are described and explained in Wallace Clark, *The Gantt Chart: A Working Tool of Management* (1922).

DANIEL NELSON

GANTT, Love Rosa Hirschmann (29 Dec. 1875–16 Nov. 1935), physician, was born in Camden, South Carolina, the daughter of Solomon Hirschmann, a wholesale grocer and leading Jewish citizen who emigrated from Austria in 1815, and Lena Debhrina. In 1883 the family moved to Charleston, South Carolina, where Rosa received her education. When Rosa, as she preferred to be called, was fourteen her mother died of cancer (a disease that would eventually claim the lives of all her children), leaving Rosa with the responsibility of caring for her father and siblings.

In 1901 Hirschmann became one of the two first women graduates of the Medical College of the State of South Carolina (now the Medical University of South Carolina). After doing postgraduate work in the Eye and Ear Clinic of New York University and the New York Ophthalmic and Aural Institute, she returned to South Carolina as resident physician at Winthrop College in Rock Hill. She left Winthrop to marry in March 1905 Colonel Robert Joseph Gantt, a Spartanburg attorney. The couple made a fine team. It was said of him that his life was "dedicated to the unfortunate, the poor, and the troubled." The same could be said of hers. The Gantts had a beautiful home and their door was always open, especially to servicemen and young women in the medical profession.

Gantt began a private practice in diseases of the eye, ear, nose, and throat. She was the first woman physician in Spartanburg and served as secretary of the Spartanburg Medical Society from 1909 to 1918. One of the first women to be a member of the Southern Medical Association, she presented papers at its annual meetings in 1915 and 1916 and by her achievements did much to strengthen the position of women in medicine.

With the outbreak of World War I, Gantt became the director of recreational activities for the soldiers at Camp Wadsworth. She was the only woman to serve on a draft board in the United States, was acting surgeon in the U.S. Public Health Service, and held a commission from the Department of Commerce as a medical examiner of pilots. Her personal interest in the soldiers was shown by her warm hospitality in her home to the young recruits. She played a leading role in numerous "war drives" for causes such as the Red Cross, Liberty Loan bonds, and U.S. savings bonds.

Although the Gantts had no children of their own, Rosa's concern for children was great. She established the first playground program in Spartanburg and was instrumental in founding in 1918 a state reformatory for delinquent girls. She served on its board of trustees for ten years. She would later be a prime mover in legislation enacted in 1920 to provide medical examinations for schoolchildren. Gantt also had a very active religious life. She organized and served as the first president of the Temple Sisterhood of Congregation B'nai Israel in Spartanburg.

Like many of the young, idealistic doctors in the South of the 1930s, Gantt found herself drawn to the area of public health. Surrounded by poverty and disease in the mill villages hard hit by the Great Depression, she ran a free clinic for a time, even employing a nurse with her own funds. It was in the depth of the depression that Gantt's most lasting contribution to her profession and her community would come. In 1930 Spartanburg County reported 3,000 cases of pellagra, a disease of malnutrition that claimed the health and often the sanity and life of its victims. In 1930 Gantt was president-elect of the Medical Women's Hospitals, a service arm of the association that had been formed during the war for medical relief work in Europe, decided to start its first "home service" in Spartanburg County to combat pellagra.

In cooperation with the Spartanburg County Health Department and the Department of Education, a massive project of "Bringing Health to the Country" was begun. A trailer was furnished with medical and dental equipment and staffed by a physician, a nurse, a nutrition worker, and, at times, a dentist. This "healthmobile" made the rounds in the mountainous areas, drawing a curious crowd at each stop. At that time little was known about vitamins, and, had they been available in the Piedmont South, few would have been able to purchase them. Education and nutrition were the keys to the prevention and treatment of pellagra. These the healthmobile provided. The typical diet of the population was fatback, corn bread, and molasses. The turnip tops and dandelion greens so readily available and so filled with pellagra-preventing vitamins were not considered fit food for humans.

Hilla Sheriff, another graduate of the Medical College of the State of South Carolina, worked with Gantt and headed the healthmobile team that covered the county, "preaching the gospel of health" to the people. In addition to pellagra education, the team provided immunizations, general examinations, prenatal care, family planning, and dental care. In 1931 the service was extended across the state line into Polk County, North Carolina, where Gantt had her home and where she directed the public health activities. Because of the terrain of Polk County, the healthmobile could not be used, so a series of "health houses" was established to carry out the lifesaving work. In just two years the number of deaths from pellagra was cut by more than half. The people knew pellagra when they saw it, and they knew what to do about it.

When Gantt's health began to fail in 1927, she moved to her summer home in Tryon, North Carolina, seeking to regain her strength. In November 1935 she was taken by her husband to the Women's College Hospital in Philadelphia for treatment of uterine can-

cer. She died there of an embolism following a hysterectomy.

Throughout her active career Gantt was a champion not so much of women's rights as of their potential. In her address to the Medical Women's National Association as incoming president in 1931 she said:

I call you to the labor of building upon the foundation laid by those who have gone before. Bring your best scientific knowledge, your best medical thought, your most skilled touch of scalpel, your clearest clinical foresight, and in the light of deepest sympathy for humanity build up the pioneer work of those who have gone. . . . There is work in the field for which we are especially fitted and suited. . . . In giving to our patients the best that is in us, and in reducing sickness and delaying death . . . I bespeak your united effort. (*Bulletin of the Medical Women's National Association*, July 1931)

Gantt's life was filled with meaning for all with whom she came in contact: lonely soldiers away from home for the first time; young medical students struggling in financially difficult times; countless victims of pellagra, diphtheria, and malnutrition; impoverished mothers with unhealthy babies; troubled teens; her community, her state, and her nation. Her life personified all the ideals of her chosen profession.

• Biographical information on Gantt is available in the Waring Historical Library, Medical University of South Carolina, Charleston. Among Gantt's own articles the following are useful: "Medical Inspection of Schools in South Carolina," *Southern Medical Journal* 6 (Apr. 1913): 239–42, "A New Year's Greeting from the President," *Bulletin of the Medical Women's National Association* 35 (Jan. 1932): 8–9, and "President's Address," *Bulletin of the Medical Women's National Association* 33 (July 1931): 10–11. Secondary sources include Irma Henderson-Smathers, ed., "History of Women in Medicine: Medical Women of North Carolina," *Medical Women's Journal* 58, no. 2 (Mar.–Apr. 1951): 33–35; and Elizabeth Bass, "Past Presidents of the AMWA: L. Rosa Hirschmann Gantt, M.D.," *Journal of the American Medical Women's Association* 11, no. 3 (Mar. 1956): 109. Information on the work of the American Women's Hospitals in North Carolina and South Carolina is in the *Annual Report of the Spartanburg General Hospital* (1931) and Esther Phol Lovejoy, *Women Physicians and Surgeons* (1939) and *Women Doctors of the World* (1957). An obituary is in the *Spartanburg (S.C.) Herald*, 17 Nov. 1935.

ELIZABETH YOUNG NEWSOM

GANTT, W. Horsley (24 Oct. 1892–26 Feb. 1980), psychophysiologist, was born William Andrew Horsley Gantt in Wingina, Virginia, the son of Thomas Perkins Gantt, a farmer, and Ann Maria Horsley, a schoolteacher. Although his father died in 1895, leaving the family impoverished, Horsley (as he was known) grew up as a member of the gentry: both of his grandfathers were physicians, and he lived on a farm that had been deeded to his father's family in the mid-eighteenth century.

Gantt received a B.S. from the University of North Carolina in 1917 and an M.D. from the University of Virginia in 1920. He interned at Church Home and Hospital and at Union Protestant (now Union Memorial) Hospital in Baltimore, Maryland. He remained in Baltimore to begin a residency in gastroenterology at University Hospital (the teaching hospital of the University of Maryland) but soon took a leave of absence to join the Russian Unit of the American Relief Administration (ARA), a private charity providing food and medical care to famine-ravaged and wartorn Soviet Russia. In 1922, while serving as the ARA's district physician in Petrograd (later Leningrad and now St. Petersburg), Gantt experienced what he deemed "an event . . . from which I can date my whole subsequent professional life" (Gantt papers, Johns Hopkins): he met Ivan Pavlov, the Nobel prize–winning physiologist, and toured his laboratory at the Institute of Experimental Medicine in Petrograd. Gantt soon left Russia with the other members of the ARA, but in 1925 he returned to Petrograd and worked in Pavlov's laboratory for the next four years.

In 1929 Gantt accepted an invitation from Adolf Meyer, chair of the Department of Psychiatry at the Johns Hopkins University School of Medicine, to establish a Pavlovian laboratory at Johns Hopkins. In 1948 he helped to found a second research base, the Psychophysiological Research Laboratory at the Veterans Administration Hospital in Perry Point, Maryland. Gantt married Mary Gould Richardson in 1934; they had a son and a daughter. In 1965, a year after his first wife's death, he married Rebecca Esler Bromiley; they had no children.

For fifty years Gantt's laboratory investigations extended those of Pavlov, striving to establish the conditional (learned) reflex as the primary basis of behavior and to elucidate the principles governing conditioning. Gantt applied what he termed "objective" principles to the study of neuroses and psychoses and challenged the Freudian (or "subjective") interpretations of psychiatric conditions. Like Pavlov, Gantt experimented mainly on dogs; his long-term work with the dog Nick, the subject of his book *The Experimental Basis for Neurotic Behavior* (1944), earned him the Lasker Award in 1946 for contributions to the field of mental hygiene. In addition to investigating "nervous breakdown" due to stress, Gantt studied the conditional reflex in a variety of organs, most notably the heart, and received an award from the American Heart Association in 1950.

Among Gantt's most useful contributions to behavioral biology was his development of several terms, including "schizokinesis" (the idea that different organ systems acquire and maintain conditional responses at different rates); "autokinesis" (the concept that symptoms and signs—especially cardiovascular ones—may persist and intensify without any obvious reinforcement from the external environment); "effect of person" (the influence of one individual on another, which emerged from his observation that the heart rate of laboratory dogs slowed in response to petting by laboratory personnel); and "organ responsibility" (an explanation for the inability to elicit conditional responses from some organs owing to the "responsibility" of that organ to maintain the body's internal equilibrium, or homeostasis). Scientists in other fields drew on his investigations of the conditioning of ingestive behavior and sexual function and of the influence of drugs, hormones, and vitamins on the conditional response. Gantt's work attracted public attention because it could be applied to contemporary concerns such as the mental health of soldiers during and after World War II and an analysis of brainwashing in the 1950s.

A collegial proponent of Pavlovian principles, Gantt founded the Pavlovian Society of North America in 1955, serving as its first president until 1964. He was simultaneously president of the Society of Biological Psychiatry (1959) and of the American Psychopathological Association (1960). Gantt's enthusiasm for promoting Soviet medicine and science complemented his scientific work. Several of his publications concerned the problems and practice of medicine in Soviet Russia. He translated Pavlov's two-volume *Lectures on Conditioned Reflexes* (1928, 1941) as well as works by Pavlov's students, and he was a devoted popularizer of Pavlov's ideas in the United States. Gantt venerated Pavlov as a scientist and a philosopher: "Like a beacon on a hill on a dark night," Gantt wrote, "to the lost traveler in the storm, Pavlov is a torch for the human beset with the gloom, confusion, and ambivalence of our twentieth century" (Gantt papers, Johns Hopkins). In speeches, translations, manuscripts, notes, diaries, articles, and book chapters directed at other scientists and the lay public, Gantt continually paid tribute to his teacher.

Gantt was an active member of the Foreign Policy Association from the 1930s through the 1950s. His interest in the Soviet Union—maintained through contacts with scientists and membership in organizations such as the National Council of American-Soviet Friendship—brought him under governmental scrutiny; in late 1953, in the era of McCarthyism, the Veterans Administration pronounced him a threat to national security and suspended him from his position as consultant at Perry Point. By rebutting the charges of membership in Communist organizations and producing character references, he was exonerated of the charge against him and reinstated four months later.

Upon his retirement from Johns Hopkins in 1958, Gantt became chief investigator of an expanded Pavlovian laboratory at Perry Point. Stepping down from this position in 1973, he remained a senior scientist at Perry Point and was appointed a clinical professor of psychiatry at the University of Maryland. In 1966 Gantt founded the journal *Conditional Reflex* (renamed the *Pavlovian Journal of Biological Science* and later *Integrative Physiological and Behavioral Science*) as the official organ of the Pavlovian Society, and he was its editor until his death. In 1976 he also took on an adjunct professorship at the University of Louisville. Physically hardy and energetic, courtly in demeanor (especially to women and small children), Gantt remained active professionally and socially until his death in Baltimore.

• Gantt's collected papers are in the Alan Mason Chesney Medical Archives at the Johns Hopkins Medical Institutions, Baltimore, Md. Nancy A. Heaton, *The W. Horsley Gantt Papers* (1986), catalogs the collection and offers perceptive commentaries on the man and his work. Among Gantt's most-cited articles are "Principles of Nervous Breakdown in Schizokinesis and Autokinesis," *Annals of the New York Academy of Science* 56 (1953): 143–63; "Cardiovascular Component of the Conditional Reflex to Pain, Food, and Other Stimuli," *Physiology Reviews* 40 (1960): 266–91; and Gantt et al., "Effect of Person," *Conditional Reflexes* 1 (1966): 18–35. His books about the Soviet Union include *A Medical Review of Soviet Russia* (1928) and *Russian Medicine* (1937). Gantt summarized his life's work in his last published article, "Proflex, Schizokinesis, and the Internal Universe," *Johns Hopkins Medical Journal* 146 (1980): 55–70. Appreciations are A. McGehee Harvey, "W. Horsley Gantt: A Legend in His Own Time," *Johns Hopkins Medical Journal* 139 (1976): 121–26, and F. J. McGuigan, "In Memoriam: W. Horsley Gantt, M.D., 1892–1980," *Pavlovian Journal of Biological Science* 15 (1980): 1–4. A celebratory volume is F. J. McGuigan and Thomas A. Ban, eds., *Critical Issues in Psychology, Psychiatry, and Physiology: A Memorial to W. Horsley Gantt* (1987). One of Gantt's ancillary facilities, a basement in East Baltimore, is the subject of Nancy McCall, "Ionizing Radiation as an Exterminant: A Case Study," *Conservation Administration News* 23 (Oct. 1985): 1–2, 20–21. An obituary is in the *New York Times*, 28 Feb. 1980.

SUSAN L. ABRAMS

GARACONTIÉ, Daniel (fl. 1654–1677), Onondaga Bear Clan sachem, presiding lord of the Iroquois League (Hotinonhsioni), negotiator of a thirty-year peace with New France (1654–1684) and the Covenant Chain Treaties with the English Crown and colonies (1675–1982), and Christian convert. Garacontié first appears in the historical record as the Sagochiendagehté ("He the Name Bearer," the ritual name of the Onondagas, or their representative) in May 1654 at Montreal. As the head of an Iroquois delegation, he exchanged prisoners for peace, ending a decade of war with New France. Instead, Garacontié announced a League policy of accelerated acculturation with European colonists and extended enmity toward indigenous rivals. In August Garacontié welcomed Father Simon Le Moyne, Jesuit missionary and French ambassador, to the League capital, Onnontagé (now Indian Hill, Onondaga County, N.Y.) where Le Moyne ratified the Treaty of 1654. The "jealousy almost verging on fury" of the Mohawk (Ganienkeh) Iroquois at the Onondagas' French connection was excited by the mission station of Ste. Marie that the French built on the bluffs overlooking Onondaga Lake. The presence of French priests, soldiers, and traders authenticated Onondaga's position as the capital of the Iroquois League. The mission provided the Onondagas with hostages for the peace with New France (which was rejected by the Mohawks); agents for a direct European trade for the Onondagas and their Iroquoian clients, the Cayugas and the Oneidas (without paying tribute to the Mohawks, who controlled access to Dutch goods at Fort Orange); and valued services from blacksmiths and, increasingly, religious instruc-

tors. But by February 1658 Mohawk poison, ambush, and threats of worse to come forced the League council to decree the mission's destruction. Garacontié delayed the attack and warned the French, permitting their escape in the early hours of 20 March 1658.

Periodically, Garacontié was able to restore the mission. In between times he labored to quench "the secret sparks in hearts which breathe only pillage and war," the hearts of the Ongweoweh, the "Real People," the Iroquois. At last, in July 1670 Garacontié carried his alliance with the French to the point of accepting Christian baptism, "renouncing Polygamy, the vanity of dreams, and all kinds of sins." In the cathedral of Quebec, Garacontié took the name of his godfather "Daniel" (Daniel de Rémy de Courcelle, the governor-general). The bishop, François de Montmorency de Laval, performed the ceremony. Daniel Garacontié, the ritual head of the Iroquois, had placed Christian teaching in competition with traditional spirituality at the very center of the Great League of Peace and Power.

Garacontié sought peace with the French so that the Onondagas could lead the League's expansion of its sphere of influence south from Onondaga down the valleys of the Delaware and the Susquehanna rivers and west along the shores of the lower Great Lakes and down the Allegheny. Everywhere, the "western" Iroquois (the Cayugas, the Oneidas, and both divisions of the Senecas, as well as the Onondagas) would take prisoners to eat or to adopt into Iroquois nations reduced and traumatized by European disease and Amerindian warfare. From these victims the Iroquois would take beaver, or hunting grounds, or trade routes, to facilitate Iroquois exchanges for iron-age technology: the needle and the stew pot, the axe and the musket.

Increasingly that technology was Anglo-Dutch rather than French. It was obtained from Albany, Maryland, and the Delaware settlements. From August 1671 Garacontié began to take the lead in negotiations at Albany, in the Mohawk towns, and finally in Onondaga itself. All of these discussions were designed to stabilize the frontier between the Iroquoian sphere of influence and the English colonies and to build a relationship with the English imperial authorities to counterbalance the increasingly aggressive French, who, in the New World as in the Old, enacted the totalitarian ambitions of Louis XIV.

In 1672 the Sun King commissioned a new governor-general of New France, Louis de Buade, comte de Frontenac. In July 1673 he fortified Cataraqui (now Kingston, Ontario), formerly the site of an Onondaga settlement, in an effort to overawe the western Iroquois. The Englishman who would become Frontenac's great rival for American empire and Iroquoian alliance arrived on the scene in October 1674 when New York was retaken from the Dutch by Major Edmund Andros, lieutenant of the duke of York. English "New York" bordered the Iroquoian sphere for much of the distance from Maine to Maryland along the fall line of the rivers. The destruction of the indigenous peoples of the fall line, caught between the Iroquois and the English, reached its final phase in the general Algonquin uprising that broke out in the spring of 1675 and in the subsequent conflict between the Chesapeake colonists and the Susquehanna Iroquoians.

In August 1675 Andros met Garacontié at the upper Mohawk town of Tinontougen to negotiate the first of the Covenant Chain Treaties, which linked the Iroquois to the English until 1982, the oldest and longest-lived alliance of the Crown. Following this initial agreement, Andros facilitated the resettlement of the Susquehannas among the Western Iroquois, the Delawares along the river of that name, and the Mahican and other Algonquin refugees from New England at the eastern door of the Iroquois Longhouse. The achievement of a southern Iroquoian sphere, extending from Onondaga to the English frontiers, and of an operating alliance with New York's imperial executive confirmed the ascendancy of Garacontié in Iroquois councils. He was no longer named personally but rather referred to honorifically as "the Old Man, "the Elder," or "the Man of Note."

On 21 July 1677 in the statehouse at Albany, the Man of Note opened the fundamental Covenant Chain Treaty negotiation. He spoke for the Onondagas and for the League. Garacontié employed the condolence council form that served to bind the League together spiritually and politically. So Garacontié shaped Euro-Iroquoian diplomacy in an indigenous mold. The Longhouse lord announced that the League would suspend hostilities between its peoples (the Susquehannas now included) and the inhabitants, red and white, of the Chesapeake colonies. He agreed that the League would forgo all revenge for past injuries done to the Iroquois on the Chesapeake frontiers, and he arranged that for the future the practice of reparations, the founding principle of the League, would prevail in Iroquois-English relations: "we might give one another satisfaction and not immediately fall in war."

Most important, the Elder proclaimed that "we doe make now an Absolute Covenant of Peace, which we shall bind with a Chain" between the Western Iroquois (the Mohawks insisted on ratifying for themselves) and all the participating parties: New England and New York, Maryland and Virginia. Periodically "brightened" until 1794 this Covenant Chain defined the first American frontier, the boundary between the Iroquoian sphere and the European settlements. The Old Man added that he had arranged a model peace with New France. On the Covenant Chain too, he said, "we desire that God Almighty who dwells in heaven may give his blessing." In the feasting that followed, Garacontié was overcome with wine, perhaps poisoned by Jacob Young, the Maryland-Susquehanna trader whose livelihood Garacontié's people had destroyed and whom he had denounced as a warmonger at the Albany conference. The Old Man was carried home to Onondaga. In six weeks he was dead. He was buried as a Christian. He was succeeded by his brother, who took up the name, policies, and character of "Garacontié."

This succession in the maternal lineage is the final evidence that Garacontié had been "Prince and Orator" of the Onondagas and the League, rather than simply a spokesman for the Grand Council, "a man to do business." Garacontié's own elevated name, "Moving Sun"; his use of the senatorial "Sagochentaghé"; his position among the five senior lineage leaders of Onondaga; his appellation as "Roksten Goa," meaning "the Old Man," or the "Ancient par Excellence"; and his ritual leadership of the calendrical ceremonies of his people, all marked Garacontié as the senior clan chief of the Onondaga, and so of the League. He was the Iroquois architect of a thirty-year peace with the French and of the three-hundred-year alliance with the English that first defined the American frontier and that finally was the makeweight of the English empire in America.

• The primary sources for the life of Daniel Garacontié are Ruben Gold Thwaites, ed., *The Jesuit Relations and Allied Documents: Travels and Explorations of the Jesuit Missionaries in New France 1616–1791* (1896–1901). Early use of these sources appears in Father Joseph Francois Lafitau, *Customs of the American Indians Compared with the Customs of Primitive Times*, ed. William N. Fenton and trans. Elizabeth L. Moore (1974). Other printed primary sources are John Romelyn Brodhead et al., eds., *Documents Relative to the Colonial History of the State of New York* (1853–1887). A printed text of the Covenant Chain Treaties is in Lawrence H. Leder, ed., "The Livingston Indian Records," *Pennsylvania History* 23 (1956): 43–44; and see Francis Jennings et al., eds., *The History and Culture of Iroquois Diplomacy* (1985). Recent studies of the Onondagas include James A. Tuck, *Onondaga Iroquois Prehistory* (1971), and James W. Bradley, *Evolution of the Onondaga Iroquois* (1987). The standard study of the Iroquois in this period remains George T. Hunt, *The Wars of the Iroquois: A Study in Intertribal Trade Relations* (1940), but many modifications appear in two collections: Bruce G. Trigger, ed., *Northeast*, vol. 15 of *Handbook of North American Indians*, ed. William C. Sturdevant (1978); and Daniel K. Richter and James H. Merrell, eds., *Beyond the Covenant Chain* (1987). See also Richter's *The Ordeal Of the Longhouse* (1992), and Stephen Saunders Webb's study of Garacontié and his times, *1676: The End of American Independence* (1984; repr. 1995).

STEPHEN SAUNDERS WEBB

GARAND, John C. (1 Jan. 1883–16 Feb. 1967), inventor, was born on a farm near St. Remi, Quebec, Canada, a village near Montreal. His father was a farmer. At age eight his mother died, and three years later the family moved to Connecticut. There Garand dropped out of school and worked as a floor sweeper and bobbin boy in a textile mill. He spent his free time in the machine repair shop, watching the mechanics at work. By age fourteen, Garand had filed for his first patent, on a new type of jack screw.

By the age of eighteen Garand had become a machinist at the mill. He also helped his father and a brother tend a shooting gallery one summer in Norwich, Connecticut, but his enthusiasm for target practice interfered with his work. He moved to Providence, Rhode Island, to take a job in the Federal Screw Corporation tool factory. In providence he took up motorcycling and designed a motorcycle engine with which he won several races at local tracks. His main interest, however, remained firearms.

After the outbreak of the First World War, Garand moved to New York City to work in a micrometer plant, and took up correspondence courses to continue his education. He spent his Saturdays at Coney Island at the shooting galleries, studying the rifles. The practice became expensive, but he found a gallery near Times Square that allowed him to shoot for free, as his expert marksmanship would draw a crowd to the gallery.

Reading in a newspaper that the U.S. government was having trouble finding a satisfactory machine gun, Garand began in either 1916 or 1917 to design an improved machine gun. He sent his plans to the Bureau of Standards in Washington, D.C., and was invited to present his ideas in person. As a result, he was taken on as a master gauge and gun experimenter at the Bureau of Standards, to develop a model of the machine gun he had designed. At the end of eighteen months, he had completed a model, but the war was over.

The U.S. Army, which was searching for a new semiautomatic rifle that would combine the best features of a light machine gun and the bolt-operated Springfield rifle, in 1919 hired Garand as a consulting engineer at the Springfield, Massachusetts, Armory. There he began two decades of work that contributed to the rifle which bore his name. He became a U.S. citizen in 1920. He married Nellie (maiden name unknown), with whom he had two children.

Garand's basic design used the expanding-gas pressure from the firing of a round to propel the bullet, to eject the empty cartridge, and to throw the next cartridge into firing position. This would not only increase the speed and accuracy of firing, but would reduce the heavy kick characteristic of the Springfield. He submitted his first model for testing to the Bureau of Standards in 1923. It took the next eleven years to bring the rifle to the point at which it met the army's standards for lightness, strength, and simplicity. In 1929 Garand submitted an improved model, which allowed a man to fire eight times without taking his eyes from the target. Furthermore, the weapon could be disassembled in the field, using a cartridge as a tool. The weapon performed well in heat or cold, and could be immersed in water and still be fired.

The central problem for Garand was getting the rifle to the desired light weight. He worked on this problem day and night, on the weekends or at recreation, often thinking of new shortcuts that could reduce weight. He tried over fifty plans for the rear sight. The final gun contained nineteen different types of steel, which had been selected in consultation with metallurgists. He was able to save a whole pound in weight by using only one hammer spring to replace five separate springs. Other changes would save an ounce or two. In 1932 Springfield Armory built eighty Garand .30 caliber rifles on a semiproduction basis, which involved building jigs and gauges to insure uniformity and interchangeability. Garand did most of the design work

on the fixtures, tools, and jigs himself. The finishing of the eighty guns took more than two years, since every production tool had to be designed, produced, and tested itself before the gun part for which it was intended could be produced.

The guns were finished in May 1934, and fifty of them were sent to the infantry for testing. Another twenty-five were sent to the cavalry for extended service tests under field conditions. The guns were issued to all groups of soldiers, from recruits through experienced marksmen. Reactions and suggestions were taken from the men and were carefully studied, leading to a number of minor changes. The test guns developed a weakness in the operating rod in service. The guns were then collected and returned to the Springfield Armory to incorporate the changes. After reworking under Garand's personal supervision, the guns were returned and field testing continued through 1935. Assistant Secretary of War Harry K. Woodring cleared the weapon for procurement on 7 November 1935.

The rifle was standardized on 9 January 1936. A total of over four million were manufactured during World War II. Another 600,000 were made between 1945 and 1948. The weapon weighed 9.5 pounds, with an overall length of 43.6 inches. It had a muzzle velocity of 2,805 feet per second, with an effective range of 500 yards. Called the Garand Rifle or the M-1, it became the main weapon of U.S. infantrymen of the World War II era. During the war, the marines and navy also adopted the weapon. The weapon fired about three times as fast as the 1903 Springfield model it had replaced.

The last of six million Garands came off the production line in 1957, when the army moved to the M-14. Garand served on the team that had developed this new rifle. Garand himself received little financial compensation for the weapons, and this issue became somewhat controversial in the years before his death, as many believed the government's failure to amply reward Garand himself constituted an injustice. He retired from government service in 1953, with the rank of chief ordnance engineer. Several bills were introduced into Congress to award Garand a $100,000 grant in recognition of his work, but they were not passed. He was granted the Government Medal of Merit in 1944. He died in Springfield, Massachusetts.

• Further information on Garand's life and work is contained in the following: "Garand's Gun: Modest Inventor Bewildered by Fame His Gun Has Drawn," *Newsweek*, 4 Dec. 1939, p. 18; "He Invented the World's Deadliest Rifle," *Popular Science*, Dec. 1940, pp. 68–71; D. Wilhelm, "What an Order Means: Graphic Story of the Garand Rifle Typifies the Problem of Getting into Production," *Reader's Digest*, Oct. 1940, pp. 33–36; and Julian S. Hatcher, *The Book of the Garand* (1948). An obituary is in the *New York Times*, 17 Feb. 1967.

RODNEY P. CARLISLE

GARBO, Greta (18 Sept. 1905–15 Apr. 1990), film actress, was born Greta Lovisa Gustafsson in Stockholm, Sweden, the daughter of Karl Alfred Gustafsson, a peasant laborer, and Anna Lovisa Karlsson. Garbo's early life was spent in straitened circumstances. In August 1912 her formal schooling began. She left school in 1919 to attend to her seriously ill father until he died the following year, while her family eked out a bare living.

The mature-looking teenager went to work as a barber's assistant (lathering faces) and then as a salesgirl at PUB, one of Stockholm's largest department stores. Because of her looks she was chosen to model hats for a PUB catalog, and in 1921–1922 she appeared in several short films advertising the store's products.

Ambitious and determined, Garbo left PUB in mid-1922 to play the female lead in a poorly received, low-budget comedy film, *Luffar-Pettar* (Peter the tramp). In August 1922 Stockholm's Royal Dramatic Theatre Academy accepted her as a scholarship student. While she was enrolled there, Sweden's foremost film director, Mauritz Stiller, a forty-year-old Russian Jew, cast her as the female lead in his epic movie, *Gosta Berling's Saga* (1924).

Stiller took over Garbo's life, personally and professionally: he coached her as an actress, bullied the shy, plump teenager into losing weight, taught her how to dress and what to think, and arranged (Dec. 1923) for a new surname—Garbo (whose origins are lost in conflicting stories). They went everywhere together. The enormous success of *Gosta Berling's Saga* in Germany enabled him to find financing there for a movie to be shot in Turkey. It was never completed, and Stiller and Garbo went to Berlin, where Garbo played a lead in *Die Freudlose Gasse* (The street of sorrow), director G. W. Pabst's stark view (1925) of post–World War I Vienna. Garbo, "advised" by Stiller, effectively portrayed a girl from a respectable but impoverished family who is faced with becoming a prostitute.

MGM production chief Louis B. Mayer, on a European talent tour, signed Stiller and, at Stiller's insistence, Garbo. They reached Hollywood in September 1925. Stiller foundered, being fired from their only American film together, and after a brief stint at Paramount he returned in 1927 to Europe, where he died the next year. Garbo flourished, making twenty-four films (ten silent) before retiring in 1941. In her first MGM picture, *The Torrent* (1926), she was cast as a passionate and seductive but insecure woman, and she played variations on that role over and over again. She won critical acclaim for her beauty, poise, and acting ability. Always shy, Garbo became an aloof figure who, in her own words, "became a hermit" with "a trousered attitude to life," believing that "my private affairs are strictly private."

Flesh and the Devil (1927), her third MGM film, was what *Variety* called her "breakthrough hit," partly because of the seemingly uninhibited romantic scenes with costar John Gilbert, with whom she was having a well-publicized affair. Gilbert wanted to get married; she did not; the affair effectively ended in 1928. The androgynous Garbo never married, but she was linked romantically in the press with various men, including the conductor Leopold Stowkowski, the nutritionist Gaylord Hauser, and the businessman George Schlee (a relationship lasting nearly twenty years until his death in 1964). The bisexual photographer Cecil Beaton claimed to have had an affair with her as did various lesbians, both during her movie-making days and afterward.

Garbo's silent films generally succeeded at the box office. *The Kiss*, completed in September 1929, was MGM's final silent production. The studio carefully packaged her first sound film, a version of the Eugene O'Neill play *Anna Christie*, with Garbo as the eponymous central character whose background would explain her Swedish accent. MGM advertised "Garbo Talks," and she did well enough to win the first of four Oscar nominations as best actress, the others being for *Romance* (1930), *Camille* (1937), and *Ninotchka* (1939). For *Camille* and *Anna Karenina* (1935) she won the New York Film Critics best actress award. She received an honorary Oscar in 1954 for "her unforgettable screen performances."

Garbo's box-office peak came in 1931–1932, and MGM took advantage of her popularity, releasing five films (*Inspiration, Susan Lenox—Her Fall and Rise*, and *Mata Hari*, 1931; *Grand Hotel* and *As You Desire Me*, 1932). Increasingly, however, the profitability of her films depended on overseas earnings. World War II's outbreak in 1939 adversely affected her career as American films were steadily shut out of overseas markets.

At this point MGM attempted to change her screen persona, from a poetic, doomed, tragic personality to a more light-hearted and less serious one. The studio had some success with *Ninotchka*, an anticommunist satire advertised as "Garbo Laughs." But *Two-Faced Woman* (1941), a witless comedy, was a debacle. Condemned by the Legion of Decency on its initial release, the film was altered and rereleased, but "the new Garbo" failed critically and commercially. Garbo never made another movie. Attempts to lure her back failed. Among the projects she spurned were portrayals of Madame Bovary, George Sand, Sarah Bernhardt, and Saint Francis of Assisi.

Having earned more than $250,000 a film in the 1930s and having invested wisely, the frugal Garbo had a comfortable if ever more reclusive retirement. She died in New York City.

Garbo lit up the screen; she often transcended her material; she was a star like few others. Her retreat into seclusion kept her luminescent screen image indelible. An icon from the Golden Age of American movies, she retained her following and won new admirers as her films were shown on television and at festivals and became available on videotape and laser disc. According to the critic David Robinson, "other legends . . . crumble and fade," but Garbo is "the true immortal."

• A useful overview on Garbo is Michael Conway, Dion McGregor, and Mark Ricci, *The Films of Greta Garbo* (1963), which contains a provocative introductory essay by Parker Tyler on "the Garbo image." Useful biographies are John

Bainbridge, *Garbo* (1971), and Frederick Sands and Sven Broman, *The Divine Garbo* (1979). A fascinating curiosity is Raymond W. Daum and Vance Muse, *Walking with Garbo: Conversations and Recollections* (1991). Interesting if anecdotal is Michael Gross, "Garbo's Last Days," *New York*, 21 May 1990. Obituaries and appreciations of Garbo are in the *New York Times*, 16 Apr. 1990, *Financial Times*, 17 Apr. 1990, *Variety*, 18 Apr. 1990, and *Time* and *Newsweek*, both 30 Apr. 1990.

DANIEL J. LEAB

GARCÉS, Francisco Tomás Hermenegildo (12 Apr. 1738–19 July 1781), Franciscan missionary, explorer, and martyr, was born in Morata del Conde (Aragón), Spain, the son of Juan Garcés and Antonia Maestro, occupations unknown. Educated by his uncle Moisés Garcés, the local parish priest, in 1753 he entered the Franciscan order of the province of Aragón and studied theology and philosophy at the monastery of Calatayud, where he was ordained a priest in 1762. The following year at Madrid, Garcés presented himself to the commissary of the college of Santa Cruz of Querétaro, Fray Juan Crisóstomo Gil, and volunteered as a missionary in New Spain. In 1766 Garcés reached the college, where he held the post of confessor.

After the Jesuits were expelled from Spanish domains in 1767, the college of Santa Cruz was assigned to occupy vacated Sonora missions, and in January 1768 Garcés with his co-religious sailed from San Blas, Nayarit, for Guaymas. After reaching Guaymas in April, the group moved inland to Horcasitas, where Garcés was assigned to go to San Xavier del Bac, near Tucson, a Pima village in present-day Arizona, the most northerly and most dangerous post in the region.

After reaching his mission on 30 June, Garcés quickly achieved the respect and affection of his neophytes and began to expand his ministry. In August he followed the Gila River westward to Pápago villages, and in his absence hostile Apaches raided his mission. Undaunted, in 1769 he sought contact with the Apaches, and in 1770 he returned to the Gila, baptizing Pápago children and initiating contact with Opas further west. A three-month expedition along the Gila enabled Garcés to reach the mission of Caborca and the Colorado River, which he followed to its mouth. Garcés's report of this reconnaissance, submitted to Viceroy Antonio María Bucareli y Ursúa, aroused new interest in overland contact between Sonora and California, and in 1773, supported by California mission superior Fray Junípero Serra, the appointment of commandant Juan Bautista de Anza of Tubac presidio near San Xavier del Bac, exploration for a route from there to southern California was commenced.

After a visit to Casa Grande in present-day Arizona and the Gila River with Fray Pedro Font, Garcés, accompanied by Fray Juan Díaz, joined the Anza party on 2 January 1774 and reached Mission San Gabriel on 22 March, thus opening a route following the Gila to the Colorado River, across the barren Colorado Desert near present-day Palm Springs, and over the mountains into the San Gabriel valley. After traveling to San Diego and meeting with Serra, Garcés returned to San Xavier del Bac in May and ministered to his neophytes. On 21 October 1775 he left for Tubac with fathers Tomás Eixarch and Pedro Font to accompany Anza on his return westward with settlers destined for California.

After exploration of the Colorado flood plains in December, in January 1776 Garcés left Anza and worked among Yumans at the village he named La Concepción near the confluence of the Gila and the Colorado. There he performed baptisms and gained the apparent friendship of the Yuman headman, Palma. On 14 February, with two neophytes, Garcés explored the Colorado to present-day Needles, struck out across the Mojave Desert, and through Cajon Pass reached San Gabriel on 24 March. On 9 April he continued exploration through the modern San Fernando and Antelope valleys, across the Tehachapi range to the Kern and San Joaquín rivers, and, retracing his route, reached Needles on 4 June. He then proceeded eastward across the Coconino Plateau Oraibe pueblos, returned westward along the Grand Canyon, and, following the east bank of the Colorado to La Concepción, reached San Xavier on 17 September. Virtually alone, Garcés had achieved the incredible feat of exploring some of the most arid, rugged, and desolate regions of North America.

Although initial success at La Concepción had declined on his return from Oraibe, Garcés was appointed to establish missions on the Colorado in 1780. With Fray Juan Antonio Barreneche, Garcés founded La Purísima Concepción in the fall of that year while his companions, fathers Juan Díaz and José Matías Moreno, opened San Pedro y San Pablo de Bicuñer a few miles upriver. As planned, the missions became central stopovers for parties bound for California, and when the party of Captain Fernando de Rivera y Moncada bound for Monterey devastated Yuman crops in July 1781, followers of Palma rose in revolt on 17 July, massacring the settlers. Fathers Díaz and Moreno were decapitated the same day, and Garcés and Barreneche were clubbed to death two days later. Their remains were recovered in December 1781 and ceremoniously reinterred at the college of Santa Cruz on 19 July 1794.

• Contemporary chronicles of Garcés's exploits are Juan Domingo Arricivita, *Crónica Seráfica y Apostólica del Colegio de Propaganda Fide de la Santa Cruz de Querétaro en la Nueva España* (1792), and Diego Miguel Bringas de Manzaneda y Encinas, *Sermon que en las Solemnes Honras Celebradas en Obsequio de los VV.PP. Predicadores Apostólicos Fr. Francisco Tomas Hermenegildo Garcés . . .* (1819). Modern historical works include Elliott Coues, trans. and ed., *On the Trail of a Spanish Pioneer: The Diary and Itinerary of Francisco Garces (Missionary Priest) in His Travels through Sonora, Arizona, California, 1775–1776* (2 vols., 1900); Herbert E. Bolton, *Anza's California Expeditions: An Outpost of Empire* (1930); Francisco Tomás Hermenegildo Garcés, *A Record of Travel in Arizona and California, 1775–1776: A New Translation*, trans. Sean Galvin (1965); Maynard Geiger, *Franciscan Missionaries in Hispanic California, 1769–1840* (1969); John L. Kessell, *Friars, Soldiers, and Reformers: Hispanic Arizona and the Sonora Mission Frontier, 1767–1856* (1976); and Kieran

McCarty, *Desert Documentary, the Spanish Years, 1767–1821* (1976) and *A Spanish Frontier in the Enlightened Age, Franciscan Beginnings in Sonora and Arizona, 1767–1770* (1981).

W. MICHAEL MATHES

GARCIA, Céline Léonie Frémaux (21 Mar. 1850–23 Nov. 1935), author of a memoir, was born in Donaldsonville, Louisiana, the daughter of Napoléon (Léon) Joseph Frémaux, a civil engineer, and Caroline Flore Marion de Montilly. Céline Frémaux grew up in a family of French immigrants. Her mother, Caroline, had been raised in aristocratic circles in France and in Russia, but Caroline's father had dissipated his wealth and that of his wife. Caroline dominated the Frémaux household, focusing her energies on educating her six children and raising them in the French cultural tradition to which she was deeply attached. During the Civil War, Céline's father served as captain in the Confederate Corps of Engineers. The family joined him in Port Hudson, Louisiana, and then moved to nearby Jackson, Louisiana, until the end of the war.

After the war the Frémaux family moved briefly to Mobile, Alabama, and Céline attended the Judson Institute in Marion, Alabama. In 1866 the family moved to New Orleans, where Céline taught for a time at the Bayou Bridge school. In 1871 she married Joseph Garcia, a young printer who was a friend of her father's and, like him, a leader in Company C of the Crescent City White League. Joseph Garcia eventually bought the printing firm in which he had worked and developed it into a successful business. In time the family became socially prominent in New Orleans. Céline Garcia was particularly active in Confederate memorial organizations. Four of her five children survived to adulthood.

Garcia kept a diary for many years and wrote several historical reminiscences and slightly fictionalized accounts of her youth. Sometime after the death of her father in 1898, she began writing her memoirs, which covered the period from 1850 until her marriage. This memoir, found only after her death, is a revealing portrait of the conflicts within a middle-class immigrant family. Even fifty years later, Garcia still resented her domineering and demanding mother, her lively but duplicitous sister, and her morose sister-in-law, while worshiping the memory of her father. She describes her gradual emergence from the sheltered world of French Louisiana into the wider arena of Anglo-American society and evokes the rigors of civilian life between Confederate and Union lines in Jackson during the Civil War. Her social and political values are those of the dominant white New Orleans society to which she belonged in later life, and her memories of her childhood and adolescence are filtered through and transformed by this perspective. While not always accurate in details and although colored by her long-smoldering anger and frustrations, the memoir is a valuable document exposing the inner life of middle-class southern whites during her lifetime.

In addition to her memoir, Garcia wrote many unpublished works, including accounts of travel to Washington, D.C., North Carolina, and Virginia, written between 1906 and 1926. Also extant are three vignettes from her childhood and young adulthood and a slightly fictionalized account of her courtship with Scott Worthy, a Confederate veteran from Jackson.

• Céline Frémaux Garcia's manuscripts are in the possession of her descendants. Her memoir was published in Patrick J. Geary, ed., *Céline: Remembering Louisiana, 1860–71* (1987), with a historical introduction and annotations.

PATRICK J. GEARY

GARCIA, Jerry (1 Aug. 1942–9 Aug. 1995), rock band leader, guitarist, and singer, was born Jerome John Garcia in San Francisco, California, the son of Joe Garcia, a ballroom jazz musician and bartender, and Ruth (maiden name unknown), a nurse. Garcia was raised in a home filled with Spanish relatives and music. An active boy, he lost the third finger of his right hand in a childhood accident. Although he sang at an early age, he first aspired to become a painter.

At the age of five Garcia saw his father drown. After his mother remarried, the family moved to Menlo Park, California. At age thirteen, after being influenced by George Orwell's novel *1984*, Garcia rebelled, left school and his family, and went back to San Francisco, where he learned to play the piano. He idolized the rocking sound of Chuck Berry and in 1957 bought a Danelectro guitar and a small Fender amplifier upon which he learned to play rhythm and blues. Inducted into the U.S. Army in 1958, Garcia practiced acoustic guitar in his San Francisco barracks. He was dishonorably discharged in 1959.

In 1960, after he survived a car accident that took one life, Garcia concluded he was put on earth for a specific purpose. He quickly formed a bay-area bohemian band named the Thunder Mountain Tub Thumpers. He learned to play a five-string banjo proficiently, and with Ron "Pigpen" McKernan, a harmonica player, keyboardist, and vocalist; Phil Lesh, a trumpeter, bassist, and composer; and Bill Kreutzmann, a drummer, Garcia formed a short-lived jug band called the Zodiacs and concentrated on bluegrass, blues, and northern California folk music. In 1963 he was briefly married to Sarah Katz, with whom he had one daughter. Garcia then married Carolyn Adams, with whom he had two daughters. They divorced in 1987.

In December 1964 Garcia joined guitarist and songwriter Robert Hunter and guitarist Bob Weir in Palo Alto, California, and formed the cover band Mother McCree's Uptown Jug Champions. Playing Rolling Stones hits and the blues, the band rejected acoustic instruments for electric and combined rock music with rhythm and blues. They added Dan Morgan on bass and renamed the group the Warlocks.

In 1965 the Warlocks joined Ken Kesey (author of *One Flew over the Cuckoo's Nest*) and his band of Merry Pranksters to live communally in La Honda, California, and experiment with the hallucinogenic drug

LSD during parties called "acid tests." Garcia's drug problems escalated during these parties, and the music of his band changed from jug-folk-blues to psychedelic rock.

Renamed the Grateful Dead in 1965, the band's long performances were free-form events with improvisory, intense, highly amplified sound. While fans flocked from the new drug culture to hear the Grateful Dead, chemist Stanley Owsley (a manufacturer of LSD) became the band's financial benefactor.

The Grateful Dead and the Jefferson Airplane performed at San Francisco's Fillmore Auditorium in 1965. That same year the group moved to the Haight-Ashbury section of San Francisco, where a distinct counterculture was thriving. Playing hybrid music of rhythm and blues, jazz, and rock, Garcia performed on a pedal-steel guitar, dressed in blue jeans and a T-shirt, and always wore sunglasses. He expressed his feelings through music without inhibition. He and the Grateful Dead rejected advertising, promotional videos, and media attention, and they performed without elaborate light or stage shows to a growing crowd of fanatical fans.

Garcia's nonconformist, utopian vision of total independence and freedom (in mind and body) appealed to "hippies" and other young people who denounced the Vietnam war, monogamy, parental or authoritarian guidance, formal education, and conformist jobs. Because fans believed the band's music brought listeners to a psychedelic state of mind, John Tobler observed in *Guitar Heroes* (1978) that the Grateful Dead originated "a soundtrack for the drug experiments of a generation."

Giving long, free concerts at a local bar called the Family Dog, the band refused numerous record deals until Warner Bros. guaranteed it artistic control in 1967. The first album, *The Grateful Dead*, was released in March, and the group rose to national attention as the sovereigns of psychedelic groupies (named "Deadheads") when they performed at the Monterey Pop Festival (Aug. 1968); the North California Rock Festival, with the Doors (May 1968); and at Woodstock (summer 1969).

The band refused to cut single records to increase their popularity or earn more money. Warners released the LP *Aoxomoxoa* in 1969 and their first non-studio album, *Live/Dead*, in 1970, but by that time the band was deeply in debt. While Lenny Hart managed the group, his son Mickey joined it as a second drummer, and Tom Constanten played keyboards for a season.

The band was near financial ruin because of drug addictions, police arrests, poor management, and unorganized concert tours. *Workingman's Dead* and *American Beauty* (with "Sugar Magnolia" and "Truckin'") were also released in 1970 to help pay bills, but the band and Garcia were still close to bankruptcy. When McKernan became ill in 1971 (and died of a liver ailment in March 1973), he was replaced by Keith Godchaux, whose wife Donna became a vocalist for the Grateful Dead. Garcia cut the solo album *Hooteroll*

in 1971 on the Douglas label and the LP *Garcia* in 1972. After touring Europe in 1972, the band released a triple album, *Europe '72*, and members of the group dispersed to do individual projects.

In 1973 Garcia's group left Warner Bros. and formed Grateful Dead Records and Round Records (both of which folded by 1977) and released *Wake of the Flood*, which featured improvisational jazz. By the end of 1974 the band, exhausted by drug abuse and overwork, gave a farewell concert at San Francisco's Winterland to an over-capacity crowd that had come to experience the band's famous ten-hour concerts of continuous, spontaneous rock music. Unable to stay in retirement, the band signed with Arista records in 1977 and premiered a documentary film, *The Grateful Dead*. Garcia released two solo albums, *Cat under the Stars* and *Run for the Roses*.

For the next five years, a group called the Jerry Garcia Band performed in the United States, the United Kingdom, and Egypt. Musicians came and left, and drug arrests were common. Garcia and bassist John Kahn were the only constant players in the band, and Garcia became recognized as the "father" of the hippie generation. From 1982 to 1987 the group stopped recording and touring.

Garcia encouraged audiences to record live concerts, from which many bootleg albums were produced. When Bob Dylan toured with the band in 1987, free taping sessions at concerts ended. *Dylan and the Dead* peaked on the charts at no. 37 in the United States in 1989.

By 1983 fans feared Garcia, a diabetic, would die from drug overdose and that the "Dead culture" would perish with him. In 1985 Garcia was arrested and entered a drug rehabilitation program, but its effects were short lived. In 1986 he lapsed into a five-day diabetic coma. Garcia recovered, but the band's problems continued. In 1987 a drug-addicted fan and a police officer were shot to death during the Grateful Dead's twentieth-anniversary "Summer of Love" concert at San Francisco's Golden Gate Park. The incident received so much media attention that it initially overshadowed the release of the band's comeback/first platinum LP, *In the Dark*. It would take three years for the band to have another LP success with *Without a Net* (1990) and *Deadicated* (1991).

Thousands of Deadheads followed the band and Garcia wherever they went, mostly because of the freedom of their music; the concerts' liberal, party-like atmospheres; and Garcia and Weir's socially conscious focus on performing benefit concerts to help charitable organizations. They gave hundreds of thousands of dollars to causes such as the Vietnam Veterans Project, Cultural Survival, Greenpeace, Rainforest Action Network (the band's major preoccupation), AIDS research, the Egyptian Department of Antiquities, and the Faith and Hope Society for the Handicapped.

As their fame grew, so did the band's wealth. After a nine-concert series at New York's Madison Square Garden in June 1988, the gross receipts totaled

$3,768,244, and by the end of 1989 *Forbes* estimated the band earned $12.5 million annually.

Garcia's emancipated, communal approach to family, music, and life endeared him as "Captain Trips" to fans, many of whom thought of him as a divine being. When Garcia died at a drug treatment center in Forest Knoll, California, he was survived by his third wife, Deborah Koons, whom he had married in 1994, and four daughters (he had one illegitimate child), was mourned by millions as a liberating guru of the hippie generation.

• For overviews of Garcia's life, see Sandy Troy, *Captain Trips: A Biography of Jerry Garcia* (1994); Robert Greenfield, *Dark Star: An Oral Biography of Jerry Garcia* (1996); and Rock Scully, *Living with the Dead: Twenty Years on the Bus with Garcia* (1996). For the early years of the Grateful Dead, see Hank Harrison, *The Dead Book: A Social History of the Grateful Dead* (1973), and Michael Uslan and Bruce Solomon, *Dick Clark's the First 25 Years of Rock and Roll* (1981). For the family lifestyle of Deadheads, see Sandy Troy, *One More Saturday Night: Reflections with the Grateful Dead* (1991). For chronology, see Dafydd Rees and Luke Crampton, comps., *Rock Movers and Shakers* (1991), and John Tobler, ed., *Who's Who in Rock and Roll* (1991). For fans' reactions to Garcia's death, see Richard Folkers, "The Band for the Eternally Young," *U.S. News and World Report*, 21 Aug. 1995, pp. 6–7. Obituaries include William F. Buckley, *National Review*, 25 Sept. 1995, pp. 102–3; H. Espen, *New Yorker*, 21–28 Aug. 1995, pp. 11–12; and D. K. Garcia, "He Faced His Demon," *Rolling Stone*, 21 Sept. 1995, pp. 30–31. Articles on the ramifications of Garcia's death include D. Gates, "Requiem for the Dead," *Newsweek*, 21 Aug. 1995, pp. 46–48, and "The Trip Ends," *Time*, 21 Aug. 1995, pp. 60–62.

PATRICIA JOBE PIERCE

GARCÍA DIEGO Y MORENO, Francisco (17 Sept. 1785–30 Apr. 1846), first bishop of Ambas (Both) Californias, was born in Lagos, Jalisco, Mexico, the son of Francisco García Diego and Ana Maria Moreno. In 1795 he enrolled in the Seminario Conciliar de San Jose in Guadalajara, Mexico, to study for the priesthood for the archdiocese of Guadalajara. In 1801 he entered the Franciscan Order (OFM) and made his solemn profession on 21 December 1802. He studied at the Apostolic College of Nuestra Senora de Guadalupe in Zacatecas and was ordained a priest on 14 November 1808 by Bishop Primo Feliciano Marín de Porras of Linares at Saltillo's Convent of San Estevan. García Diego initially labored in the home missions of central Mexico, from which he later compiled a handbook for missionaries entitled *Metodo de Misionar* (Method of giving missions) (1841). From 1816 until 1819 he served as novice master for the Franciscans at Zacatecas. In 1819 he was made a lecturer at his alma mater, the Apostolic College of Nuestra Senora de Guadalupe in Zacatecas, and gave his first lecture in January 1820.

During this turbulent era of Mexico's struggle for independence from Spain, Mexican-born García Diego was an ardent patriot and advocate for an independent Mexico. His sympathies were clearly displayed in a lengthy oration on 11 November 1821 to celebrate Mexico's newly achieved independence, which García Diego suggested heralded a revival of the Catholic faith in Mexico.

On 21 July 1828 García Diego was appointed commissary prefect for the Apostolic College at Zacatecas with a mandate to supply Mexican friars to the Alta California missions to replace the Spanish missionaries from the Apostolic College of San Fernando in Mexico City, who had served the missions since their inception in 1769. In 1831 he sent four Zacatecan friars to assess the situation in the Alta California missions. In 1832 he and nine other Franciscans set out for Alta California, and after a grueling journey of more than six months García Diego arrived in California on 15 January 1833. At that time, there were still twenty Spanish missionaries left in the missions of Alta California. García Diego engaged the president of the missions, Father Narciso Durán, in negotiations to cede certain missions to the Mexican Zacatecan friars. On 13 February an agreement was reached ceding the eight missions north of Monterey to the care of García Diego and his Mexican friars. He established his headquarters at Mission Santa Clara.

Within a short time García Diego was consumed with the problems surrounding the secularization of the missions as mandated by the Mexican government. In theory, secularization was to reduce the missions to the status of ordinary parishes, strip them of their temporal power, and replace the Franciscans with secular clergy. The mission lands and holdings were to be distributed to the American Indians, who were to become productive citizens in the new Mexican order. This policy was never accomplished—the missions were stripped of their lands and authority, but few Indians benefited. For the most part the native peoples were simply released from the mission to a worse life outside. García Diego opposed secularization and sought to modify its harshness, but he counseled his friars to submit to the new regulations. In 1835 he traveled to Mexico City to present the missions' concerns.

Though unsuccessful in halting the secularization of the missions, his recommendation that a new diocese of the Californias be created was ultimately accepted. On 27 April 1840 Pope Gregory XVI erected the diocese of Both (Ambas) Californias, separating it from the diocese of Sonora, Mexico. On 4 October 1840 García Diego was ordained the first bishop of the new diocese at the National Shrine of Nuestra Senora de Guadalupe, near Mexico City, by the Right Reverend Antonio María de Jesús Campos, mitered abbot of the national shrine.

On 10 December 1841 García Diego returned to California to the proposed seat of his diocese, San Diego, but, unimpressed with San Diego, he soon transferred his headquarters to Santa Barbara. There he set about solidifying the Catholic foundations in Alta California. He left Baja California to the care of the Dominican Order, appointing the Dominican president of the missions, Gabriel Ramírez, O.P., as vicar forane.

The church García Diego encountered was in great disarray. His immediate concerns were to place his new diocese on a firm financial basis and to establish a diocesan seminary to provide a native clergy for Alta California. In theory, funds for the new diocese should have been provided by the Pious Fund, a trust fund held by the government of Mexico to fund missionary labors in Alta California; the government, however, confiscated the fund and provided virtually no money to the new diocese. García Diego attempted to establish a system of tithing in Alta California, in which the laity would donate one-tenth of their earnings for the operating expenses of the church. This program met with little success and damaged García Diego's popularity.

Equally as pressing was the need to provide additional priests for the diocese. In 1842 García Diego opened a seminary at Mission Santa Barbara; two years later the seminary was transferred to property at Mission Santa Ynez, provided by the governor of California, Manuel Micheltorena. On 4 May 1844 the new seminary was dedicated to Nuestra Senora de Guadalupe. The first three priests for the diocese were ordained 1 January 1846, but the seminary never provided an adequate number of new clergy.

García Diego's difficult episcopate came to an end as the bishop contracted tuberculosis and died in Santa Barbara. Shortly after his death, the Mexican War broke out, resulting in the cession of California to the United States. During the years 1846 to 1850, the church in California was directed by García Diego's able assistant, Jose González Rubio, who was replaced by the first American bishop, Joseph Sadoc Alemany, O.P., in 1850.

• García Diego's papers are housed in the Archives of the Archdiocese of San Francisco in Menlo Park, Calif., and in the Archives of the Archdiocese of Los Angeles in Mission Hills, Calif. For further information on García Diego, see Maynard Geiger, "Francisco García Diego y Moreno," in *Franciscan Missionaries in Hispanic California, 1769–1848: A Biographical Dictionary* (1969); Francis Weber, *The Writings of Francisco García Diego y Moreno: Obispo de Ambas Californias* (1976); and Weber, *A Biographical Sketch of the Right Reverend Francisco García Diego y Moreno* (1961).

JEFFREY M. BURNS

GARDEN, Alexander (Jan. 1730–15 Apr. 1791), physician and naturalist, was born in Birse, Scotland, the son of the Reverend Alexander Garden, a clergyman in the Church of Scotland. The details of Garden's early education are not known, but from around 1743 to 1746 he was apprenticed to James Gordon, professor of medicine at Marischal College, Aberdeen. Garden studied medicine, philosophy, classics, Latin, Greek, French, and Italian at Marischal, and during this time Gordon sparked Garden's initial interest in natural history. In 1746 Garden was qualified as a surgeon's second mate in the British navy, but, failing to receive an appointment, he returned from London and re-

sumed his work with Gordon until 1748. From 1748 to 1750 he was a surgeon's first mate in the navy, serving on three ships. In 1750 he resumed his medical education at the University of Edinburgh, where he studied under John Gregory and Charles Alston. Alston was the King's Botanist, Keeper of the Garden at Holyrood, and professor of botany and medicine at the university, and under his influence, Garden acquired a passion for botany that continued for the rest of his life. Completing his formal training, Garden was awarded the A.M. degree in 1753 from Marischal College, which also granted him the M.D. degree in 1754.

By 1751 Garden had begun to fear that he might have consumption. Hoping to protect his health and improve his financial situation, he accepted an invitation to join a medical practice with William Rose in Prince William Parish near Charles Town, South Carolina. Garden arrived in April 1752 and was soon devoting much of his spare time to natural history. To maintain his connections with the scientific world, he began corresponding with prominent naturalists and physicians in Britain and Europe, including John Ellis, Charles Alston, Stephen Hales, and John Huxham. Garden acquired a copy of *Flora Virginica* (1739, 1743), by John Clayton and John F. Gronovius, a book that was essential to him in identifying American plants. He borrowed copies of two key works by Linnaeus, *Classes plantarum* (1747) and *Fundamenta botanica* (1741), to enhance his skills in describing and classifying new plants. Among his first contributions was the description of the vermicidal properties of "pink root" or Indian pink (*Spigelia marilandica*), which he sent to Dr. Rutherford, lecturer in physic at Edinburgh, in 1752. Garden extended his botanical research south into Florida in the spring of 1754, but illness in July of that year prompted him to take a recuperative trip north; he visited leading American naturalists, including Cadwallader Colden, botanist and lieutenant governor of New York, as well as John Bartram and Benjamin Franklin in Philadelphia.

In 1755 Garden relocated to Charles Town, where he acquired one of the largest medical practices in the city. During the summer of 1755 he accompanied South Carolina's governor, James Glen, on an expedition to the Saluda area of the Cherokee Indian territory in the Blue Ridge Mountains. Garden's report on the natural history of this trip was sent to England but never published. In the same year he first wrote to Carolus Linnaeus, the beginning of a voluminous correspondence and transit of specimens across the Atlantic. Garden sent plants to Ellis in 1756, including the Loblolly Bay, later named *Gordonia* in honor of James Gordon, a plant nurseryman of London. Shipments from Garden to Linnaeus included large collections of fish in 1760 and 1761, the latter set including some twenty-nine type specimens and co-types for new species. Garden also sent Linnaeus large shipments of plants, insects, and reptiles in 1761, and plants forwarded in 1765 enabled Linnaeus to establish four new genera. Other valuable specimens included the mud iguana (*Siren lacertina*), which required Linnaeus to describe a new class of amphibian, the Sirenidae. Garden's colleague Ellis read a paper on the iguana before the Royal Society in 1766 and published an account the same year in the *Philosophical Transactions*. Garden sent zoological material to the British naturalist Thomas Pennant in 1770 and 1771, including birds described in *Arctic Zoology* (1784), and a soft-shelled turtle reported in 1771 in the *Philosophical Transactions*. Garden enlarged his list of correspondents to include Peter Collinson in England, John F. Gronovius in Holland, and John Clayton in Virginia.

Garden was soon recognized for his contributions in describing the flora and fauna of America. He was elected the first corresponding member of the Royal Society of Arts of London in 1755 and subsequently elected to membership in the Philosophical Society of Edinburgh (1760) and the Royal Society of London (1773). In 1763 Linnaeus successfully nominated Garden for membership in the Royal Society of Uppsala. Ellis named the genus *Gardenia* in his honor in 1760; *Fothergilla gardenii* also commemorates him. In 1768 Garden was elected a corresponding member of the American Society for Promoting and Propagating Useful Knowledge, the Philadelphia Medical Society, and the American Philosophical Society. Although he managed to find time for his natural history research, he remained one of the busiest physicians in Charleston during these years, particularly from 1762 to 1765, when his health suffered from the intensity of his practice and the strain of combating an epidemic of smallpox.

With the coming of the American Revolution, Garden was torn between his strong loyalty to the British crown and his devotion to his friends and adopted land. Although he attempted to avoid involvement with the conflict by remaining occupied with his medical practice, his loyalist sentiments were clearly manifest in such incidents as his congratulating Cornwallis after the battle of Camden. Under the Act of 26 February 1782, his property was confiscated, and he was ordered banished. His health had deteriorated significantly during the 1770s, and after departing South Carolina in December 1782, he experienced debilitating seasickness during the long voyage back to England. Suffering from consumption by the time he arrived in England, Garden nevertheless continued his natural history activities, serving as vice president of the Royal Society and preparing a series of papers on the natural history of South Carolina, which were never published. He maintained his contact with Pennant, who used Garden's data in *Arctic Zoology* (1784) and its *Supplement* (1788).

In a futile attempt to restore his health, Garden traveled to France and Switzerland in 1788 and to Scotland in 1789. In 1755 Garden had married Elizabeth Peronneau, daughter of a prominent Huguenot merchant, Henry Peronneau of Charleston. Garden's son Alexander rose to the rank of major with the American forces during the Revolution, and the doctor never forgave his son for fighting against England. He fought to regain his American properties, but they were turned over to his son in 1784. Eventually confined to his home on Cecil Street, London, Garden lived out his remaining time there with his wife and two daughters.

• Papers by Garden include "An Account of the *Gymnotus electricus*," *Philosophical Transactions* 65 (1775): 102, which was read by Ellis before the Royal Society, and "An Account of the Indian Pink, by Alexander Garden, M.D., F.R.S., to John Ellis, Esq., F.R.S.," *Essays and Observations, Physical & Literary* 3 (1771): 145–53. The major study on Garden is Edmund Berkeley and Dorothy S. Berkeley, *Dr. Alexander Garden of Charles Town* (1969), which lists his publications and manuscript collections. Other important sources include Clark A. Elliott, *Biographical Dictionary of American Science* (1979), p. 99; Frans A. Stafleu and Richard S. Cowan, *Taxonomic Literature* 1 (1976): 914; Margaret Denny, "Linnaeus and His Disciple in Carolina: Alexander Garden," *Isis* 38 (1948): 161–74; and J. E. Smith, *A Selection of the Correspondence of Linnaeus and Other Naturalists* (1821). Plant specimens collected by Garden are held at the Linnean Society in London.

MARCUS B. SIMPSON, JR.

GARDEN, Alexander (4 Dec. 1757–24 Feb. 1829), soldier and scholar, was born in Charleston, South Carolina, the son of Alexander Garden, a famous naturalist, and Elizabeth Peronneau. Growing up in the long shadow of his father, Garden's life was carefully monitored, and he received his early education at home. In 1771 he was enrolled at Westminster School in England and after four years there matriculated at the University of Glasgow. He received an M.A. in 1779 and then began the study of law at Lincoln's Inn. Garden did not long pursue his legal education for in 1780, despite the vehement protests of his Loyalist father, who had fled to London as a refugee, he returned to America to assist his fellow countrymen in their struggle against Britain. For this act of filial defiance he was never forgiven by his father, who died in 1791.

Entering patriot military service, young Garden enrolled as a cornet in "Lee's Legion," a famous cavalry force commanded by Lieutenant Colonel Henry "Light-Horse Harry" Lee, a swashbuckling officer. In 1781 he was promoted to the rank of major and selected by General Nathanael Greene to act as an aide-de-camp, a duty he fulfilled for the remainder of the war. In 1784 the state of South Carolina rewarded Garden for his services by allowing him to take possession of his father's abandoned plantation, "Goose Creek," near Charleston, which had been confiscated in a general sequestration of Loyalists' estates in 1782. It had not been sold probably because of the younger Garden's intervention.

Also in 1784 Garden married Mary Anna Gibbes; although the couple had no children, they adopted her nephew, Alester Gibbes, who took Garden's name and became his heir. In the same year Garden was elected to a term in the South Carolina Assembly, which duty he fulfilled with no particular distinction. In subsequent years he traveled widely, visiting Pennsylvania and New Jersey on a number of occasions and Virginia and England once.

Garden's overwhelming interest after 1783 was in celebrating the American Revolution, which he saw as a glorious chapter in his own life and in human history. Although he had only served the cause of American liberty for two years, he had paid a high price in the loss of his father's approval. He compensated by romanticizing that time as the highlight of his career. He joined the South Carolina Society of the Cincinnati in 1808 and became famous for eulogizing before the society dead patriots such as Charles Cotesworth Pinckney and William Moultrie. In 1825 his eulogy of Pinckney was published in Charleston. He served the Cincinnati from 1814 to 1826 as vice president, then as president until his death. In 1826 Garden attempted, with other members of the society such as Thomas Pinckney and William Read, to put an end to dueling in his state.

Garden expressed his interest in the Revolution most strongly by amassing and editing *Anecdotes of the Revolutionary War in America, with Sketches of Character of Persons the Most Distinguished in the Southern States, for Civil and Military Services . . .* (1822), which he revised and updated in 1828. In these works, which he sold by subscription in Charleston, Garden concentrated on South Carolina history spiced with stories, newspaper accounts, and other pieces of information accumulated during his various excursions outside the state. Garden admitted that his anecdotes were didactic and intended to arouse patriotic feelings in his readers, particularly the young. He filled them with accounts of his informants' firsthand experiences of political and military episodes, such as the defense of Fort Moultrie in 1776 and passage of the Confiscation Act in 1782.

Garden also wrote sharply etched character portraits, such as his description of Francis Marion as a man "wedded to the cause of liberty" with an "ermine character" unsoiled by anything selfish or mercenary (Ravenel, pp. 376–77). Although Garden sold only 1,000 copies of the first edition and 700 of the second, his work was appreciated by its original readers for its humor and verisimilitude and by historians for its value as a source on the Revolution. In 1865 Thomas Warren Field edited and reissued both volumes in an abridged—and, said some critics, a less valuable—form. Garden died probably at Goose Creek.

• Edward Alfred Jones, *American Members of the Inns of Court* (1924), provides biographical information on Garden, as does Mrs. St. Julien (Harriott Horry Rutledge) Ravenel, *Charleston: The Place and the People* (1925). Garden's early dedication to the Revolution is revealed in A. S. Salley, ed., *Journal of the House of Representatives of South Carolina, 1782* (1916). Useful background on Garden, his father, and other matters are David Ramsay, *History of South Carolina: From Its First Settlement in 1670 to the Year 1808* (1809) and *The History of the American Revolution* (2 vols., 1791).

PAUL DAVID NELSON

GARDEN, Mary (20 Feb. 1874–3 Jan. 1967), operatic soprano, was born in Aberdeen, Scotland, the daughter of Robert Davidson Garden and Mary Joss. Mary Garden came to the United States as a child after her father established his career as an engineer in this country. The family lived in Brooklyn, New York, and Chicopee, Massachusetts, before settling in Chicago. Garden studied violin and piano and began taking voice lessons at age sixteen. In 1897 she traveled to Paris with her teacher, Sarah Robinson-Duff, who had arranged the trip with the financial assistance of a local patron. In Paris Garden studied with voice teacher Antonio Trabadello and baritone Lucien Fugère.

While in Paris, Garden met the American singer Sibyl Sanderson, who introduced her to the director of the Opéra-Comique, Albert Carré. Garden made her operatic debut on 13 April 1900 in Gustave Charpentier's *Louise*, replacing soprano Marthe Rioton, who became ill after the second act. She was an immediate success with the audience, who found her red hair and American accent exotic, and she sang with the Opéra-Comique for eight years. Carré and composer Claude Debussy chose Garden to create the role of Mélisande in *Pelléas et Mélisande*, which opened on 30 April 1902. The production had been controversial from the start: dramatist Maurice Maeterlinck had objected to the choice of the American soprano for the leading role, and the public dress rehearsal seemed to signal critical disaster. In spite of apprehension about this Impressionist work, critics and audiences were won over by the end of the season, and *Pelléas et Mélisande* became a success.

Garden made her New York debut with Oscar Hammerstein's Manhattan Opera House on 25 November 1907 in the American premiere of Jules Massenet's *Thaïs*. Her Mélisande, first performed in New York with a Parisian cast on 9 February 1908, brought her wide popular and critical acclaim. Although some writers found fault with the details of her vocal production, specifically the quality of her tone, none criticized her acting or remarkable stage presence. The sensuality of her portrayal of Salome triggered controversy at a time when most operatic divas simply sang and eschewed any sexual implications in their acting or dancing, and Richard Strauss's opera was pulled from the repertoire twice in Chicago. Garden was renowned for her theatricality and adventurous artistic spirit. She declined opportunities to sing traditional lyric soprano roles, making her reputation instead as an interpreter of modern French opera.

Garden made her debut with the Chicago Grand Opera as Mélisande in 1910 and sang leading roles there for twenty years. She served as the company's director during the 1921–1922 season. Although her artistic direction was innovative, including the staging of the American premiere of Prokofiev's *The Love for Three Oranges*, she had difficulty in her relationships with singers and proved unable to keep within the company's budget.

On 24 January 1931, after her last performance with the Chicago Grand Opera as Jean in Massenet's *Le Jongleur de Notre Dame* (a role usually sung by a tenor), Garden moved to Paris, where she performed only occasionally. She returned to Scotland during World

War II. After the war, Garden lectured on the vocal works of Debussy in the United States and auditioned singers for the National Arts Foundation between 1949 and 1954. In 1951 she published her autobiography, *Mary Garden's Story*, with Louis Biancolli. She died in retirement in Aberdeen.

Garden's legacy was her striking stage presence and her acting ability as much as her vocal production. She helped to create a new image of the operatic diva in the twentieth century.

• Press clippings and pictures from the beginning of Garden's career to October 1923 can be found in the Robinson Locke Collection of Dramatic Scrap Books in the Billy Rose Theatre Collection at the New York Public Library at Lincoln Center. In addition to Garden's autobiography, see James Gibbons Huneker, *Bedouins* (1920); a profile of Garden in the *New Yorker*, 11 Dec. 1926; Edward C. Moore, *Forty Years of Opera in Chicago* (1930); Oscar Thompson, *The American Singer* (1937; rev. ed., 1969); G. Whelan, "The Recorded Art of Mary Garden," *Gramophone* 29 (1951–1952): 248–91; R. D. Fletcher, "The Mary Garden of Record," *Saturday Review*, 27 Feb. 1954, p. 47; Edward Wagenknecht, *Seven Daughters of the Theater* (1964); H. Cuenod, "Remembrances of an Enchantress," *HiFi* 14, no. 7 (1964): 36; C. Williams, "Garden, Mary" in *Le grandi voci*, ed. R. Celletti (1964); Quaintance Eaton, *The Boston Opera Company* (1965); Ronald L. Davis, *Opera in Chicago* (1966); and Henry Pleasants, *The Great Singers* (1966). An obituary is in the *New York Times*, 5 Jan. 1967.

BARBARA L. TISCHLER

GARDENER, Helen Hamilton (21 Jan. 1853–26 July 1925), author, suffragist, and U.S. Civil Service commissioner, was born Alice Chenoweth in Winchester, Virginia, the daughter of the Reverend Alfred Griffith Chenoweth and Katherine A. Peel. A Methodist minister, Chenoweth freed his inherited slaves in 1854 and transplanted the family to Washington, D.C., so that his children would not grow up tarnished by slavery. In 1855 the family moved to Greencastle, Indiana, where Gardener went to local schools and was tutored at home. In her late teens she moved by herself to Cincinnati, Ohio, where she attended high school. She later was a student at Ohio State Normal School, where she served as a teacher and principal after her graduation in 1873.

At age twenty-two Gardener married her first husband, Charles Selden Smart, and they settled in New York City. (She remained childless during both of her marriages.) In addition to taking biology classes at Columbia University, she began writing short stories and essays using various pseudonyms before settling on the pen name Helen Hamilton Gardener, which she legally adopted. The agnostic Gardener affiliated with the Freethinkers, a group devoted to secularism, the separation of church and state, and challenging authority in general. In the 1880s, with the Freethinker Colonel Robert Ingersoll as a mentor, Gardener began questioning religion in her writing. In *Men, Women and Gods, and Other Lectures* (1885) she concluded that "all religions have been made by men, for men, and through men." She also accused religious institutions

of degrading women and condemned the use of Christian theology to prohibit women's education or careers.

Gardener applied the freethinking model of examination to social problems relating to women, emphasizing scientific issues. Growing up with her father's scientific library, she had developed a fascination with heredity, especially the contemporary debate regarding the biological inferiority of women and women's education. Gardener's feminism seems to have blossomed from her early interest in science and the discrepancies she observed between scientific theories on women and her own life. Her scientific curiosity eventually developed into the relation of women to heredity and other issues of social evolution. In her article "Sex in Brain" (1888), she disputed the popular scientific claim that female brains were inferior because they were smaller, asserting that women had the same capacity for education and achievement as men despite brain size. This article caused a stir in the scientific community and was reprinted in journals in eight languages.

The issues of heredity and eugenics appeared as a theme in several of Gardener's fictional and nonfictional essays. She argued the submissiveness that nineteenth-century society idealized as a female trait created weak women who bore inferior children and undermined social stability. Her views reflected the scientific theories of Jean Lamarck, who believed that acquired characteristics were biologically passed on to children. To improve the caliber of children, Gardener supported educational opportunities for women. Moreover, she argued that women who were not willing to demand greater personal liberty and education should not procreate. To Gardener, female education and voluntary motherhood were essential to social evolution, regardless of the woman's race or class.

Gardener was an editor of the *Arena*, a reform magazine to which she frequently contributed. She also wrote novels. *Is This Your Son, My Lord?* (1890), a novel dramatizing the plight of a young girl drawn into prostitution, became Gardener's most popular work, quickly selling over 25,000 copies. Continuing to fight for better conditions for women, Gardener intended the novel as a challenge to the double standard of morality, in support of campaigns to raise the legal consent age for girls. Her greatest literary work, though, may have been *An Unofficial Patriot* (1894), a semibiographical novel about her father. A critical success, the novel was adapted into the play *The Reverend Griffith Davenport* (1899).

In 1901 Charles Smart died, and the following year Gardener married Colonel Selden Allen Day, embarking with him on a tour of the world. They returned in 1907 to Washington, D.C., where suffrage leaders, familiar with Gardener through her writing on women's issues, persuaded her to join the National American Woman Suffrage Association (NAWSA). On suffrage, Gardener echoed the ideas of Progressive reformers who claimed that women as "social housekeepers" would bring a woman's touch to politics and help reform society. She used the rhetoric of democracy to champion women's rights, questioning how the government could claim to support the principle of "consent of the governed" when half of its population did not enjoy this right.

In 1913 Gardener was appointed to NAWSA's Congressional Committee, serving as an important liaison between the organization and the federal government. She cultivated a strong working relationship with President Woodrow Wilson, influencing some of Wilson's suffrage proclamations, and Speaker of the House Champ Clark, her next-door neighbor. Gardener was later promoted to vice chairman of the Congressional Committee and vice president of NAWSA. A NAWSA leader declared that Gardener's work as "our diplomatic corps" was "as essential to our success in Washington as Mrs. [Carrie Chapman] Catt was to the country-wide campaign" (Park, p. 93). In reward for her work on suffrage, NAWSA presented Gardener with the pen used to sign the nineteenth amendment into law.

President Wilson appointed Gardener to the U.S. Civil Service Commission in 1920, at that time the highest federal position ever awarded to a woman. Her appointment and unanimous confirmation illustrate the strength of her political connections. She served as a commissioner until her death and was noted for efforts to increase opportunities for women in civil service.

Upon her death in Washington, D.C., Gardener willed her brain to Cornell University for research on sex differences in brains. Dedicated to expanding opportunities for women in public life, as author, freethinker, suffragist, and civil servant, Gardener fought for the equality for women in scientific thought and practical politics.

• There is a small collection of Helen Hamilton Gardener's papers at the Schlesinger Library, Radcliffe College. Gardener's own works include *A Thoughtless Yes* (1890); *Pulpit, Pew and Cradle* (1891); *Pushed by Unseen Hands* (1892); *Pray You, Sir, Whose Daughter?* (1892); an 1895 speech at the National Purity Congress in *Papers, Addresses, Portraits*, ed. Aaron M. Powell (1896); *Plain Talk, a Pamphlet on the Population Question and the Moral Responsibility of Woman in Maternity* (1900); and "Woman Suffrage, Which Way?" (n.d.) "Sex in Brain" was originally presented before the International Council of Women in Washington, D.C., in 1888 and then published in a collection of Gardener's essays, *Facts and Fictions of Life* (1893). Several of these works are available on the Schlesinger Library's *History of Women* microfilm series. Biographical sources include the memorial booklet *Helen Hamilton Gardener (Alice Chenoweth Day), 1853–1925* (1925?) in the NAWSA Collection at the Library of Congress; James W. Papez, "The Brain of Helen H. Gardener," *American Journal of Physical Anthropology* (Oct.–Dec. 1927): 29–88; Frances E. Willard and Mary A. Livermore, eds., *A Woman of the Century* (1893); and John William Leonard, ed., *Woman's Who's Who of America, 1914–1915* (1914). On her freethinking period, see Samuel P. Putnam, *400 Years of Freethought* (1894). On her eugenics writing, see Linda Gordon, *Woman's Body, Woman's Right: Birth Control in America* (1974). For suffrage material, see Maud Wood Park, *Front Door Lobby* (1960),

and Elizabeth Cady Stanton et al., *History of Woman Suffrage*, vols. 4 and 5 (1902, 1922). For her civil service history, see U.S. Civil Service Commission, 42d *Annual Report* (1925). An obituary is in the *New York Times*, 27 July 1925.

ELISA MILLER

GARDINER, Sir Christopher (c. 1596–c. Feb. 1662), early settler of Massachusetts, was born in England, the son of Christopher Gardyner and Judith Sackville, members of the English gentry. The family was related to Bishop Stephen Gardiner, who persecuted Protestants at the behest of Queen Mary (1553–1558). Christopher Gardiner entered Cambridge University in 1613 but abandoned the school by the next year. He then pursued a legal education at the Inner Temple. Abandoning that potential career as well, in 1615 he received official permission to travel in Europe. After Gardiner's return to England, he married Elizabeth Onslow about the year 1620; they had three children.

Apparently, after his wife died in 1624, Gardiner traveled to continental Europe again and became a Roman Catholic. He served in the army of the Holy Roman Empire, most likely as a military engineer. Such service would have employed his skills in the sciences and mathematics. It must have been his brief military career that earned him his knighthood. Gardiner claimed to have more than one order of knighthood, which was probably empty boasting, but he does seem to have been a Knight of the Golden Melice, a lesser title given by the pope. During his time on the Continent, Gardiner cohabited with a woman in France.

Gardiner's European jaunt was over by 1626, for in that year he purchased an estate in Surrey. He appears to have cohabited with another woman on trips to London. There is no record that he legally married either woman. With his smattering of legal training, Gardiner may have convinced each one in turn that she was his wife according to English common law.

As Gardiner had many connections at the English court, he made the acquaintance of Sir Ferdinando Gorges, who controlled the Council for New England. Gorges may have inspired Gardiner, who had reconverted to Protestantism, to settle in what became the Massachusetts Bay colony. Arriving there about May 1630 Gardiner was accompanied by his new mistress, Mary Grove, who had been told that his wife was dead and kept in ignorance about the other women. He passed his mistress off as his cousin to any who inquired about her and claimed that he only wanted to find peace in the wilderness. He lived in what is now North Quincy.

During 1630 the two women Gardiner had spurned in Europe learned of each other's existence. Infuriated, they tracked him down in America. Letters from the angry women (one even accused Gardiner of stealing her jewelry) were received by Governor John Winthrop of Massachusetts. On 1 March 1631 authorities there ordered his seizure and deportation to England, but Gardiner learned what was happening and escaped.

Fleeing into the Plymouth colony, Gardiner was noticed by some Indians interested in the reward that had been announced for his apprehension. Fearful of the armed Gardiner, they would have preferred to have killed him, but Governor William Bradford insisted that he be taken alive. When Gardiner fell out of a canoe, losing most of his weapons, the Indians beat him with long sticks until he surrendered. After he recovered from his beating, he was returned to Boston in early May 1631.

Governor Winthrop jailed Gardiner. When letters arrived for him from Sir Ferdinando Gorges, Winthrop opened them and learned that Gorges "reposed much trust" (Hosmer, vol. 1, p. 64) in the captive. Now convinced that Gardiner was an important man, Winthrop released him from jail. In June 1631 an Anglican, Philip Ratcliffe, was to be punished for speaking disrespectfully about a Puritan church. Gardiner interceded in Ratcliffe's behalf and his punishment was reduced to, among other things, the cutting off of his ears.

Meanwhile, Mary Grove had married a colonist, Thomas Purchase, who lived in Brunswick, Maine. In August 1631 Gardiner was allowed to leave Massachusetts. He stayed with the Purchases at their home in Maine until his departure from America and was back in England as of 15 August 1632.

Gardiner joined forces with Gorges in his campaign against the charter of the Massachusetts Bay Company. Gaining the support of Ratcliffe and Thomas Morton, another determined foe of Massachusetts, Gorges's forces submitted a petition to the Privy Council during December 1632 that called for the revocation of the charter. On 19 January 1633 the Privy Council totally rejected the petition, but the campaign against Massachusetts continued. Morton, whose book *New English Canaan* (1637) attacked the colony, had a chapter on Gardiner's complaints, which also included a sonnet by Gardiner.

Afterward, Gardiner busied himself on his estate and in conducting chemical experiments. When the English Civil War began in 1642, Gardiner took the king's side and probably became a royalist colonel. After the king's eventual defeat, Gardiner remained in England. When the monarchy was restored in 1660, Gardiner sought office, unsuccessfully, although he did receive a land lease from the king that year. The exact date and place of his death are unknown.

Gardiner's brief sojourn in America became a popular subject in American literature. the most well known account is "The Landlord's Tale: The Rhyme of Sir Christopher," which Henry Wadsworth Longfellow wrote in 1873.

• Sources for Gardiner include William Bradford, *Of Plymouth Plantation, 1620–1647*, ed. Samuel Eliot Morison (1952); John Winthrop, *Winthrop's Journal: "History of New England," 1630–1649*, ed. James Kendall Hosmer (2 vols., 1908); and Thomas Dudley's letter to the countess of Lincoln, March 1631, in *Letters from New England: The Massachusetts Bay Colony, 1629–1638*, ed. Everett Emerson (1976), pp. 80–81. Puritan Thomas Wiggin wrote two letters referring to Gardiner that are reprinted in Massachusetts Historical Society, *Collections*, 3d ser., 8 (1843): 320–24. The best biography is Louis Dow Scisco, "Sir Christopher Gardyner," Colonial Society of Massachusetts, *Transactions* 38 (1947–1951), pp. 3–15. Charles Francis Adams, Jr., "Sir Christopher Gardiner," Massachusetts Historical Society, *Proceedings* 20 (1882–1883): 60–88, still has value. Longfellow's poem is part of *Tales of a Wayside Inn*, of which there are many editions.

PHILIP RANLET

GARDINER, John (Dec. 1733?–8 Aug. 1793), attorney, political radical, and legal reformer, was born in Boston, Massachusetts, the son of Silvester Gardiner, a physician, and Anne Gibbins. He attended local schools and in 1745 was sent to the office of attorney Benjamin Prat to be tutored in law. For his advanced education Gardiner studied in Great Britain where he matriculated at the University of Glasgow in 1752 and completed his master's degree in 1755. Admitted to the Middle Temple in 1758, he studied law under Charles Pratt, the future Lord Camden and later the Lord Chancellor. Called to the bar in 1761, Gardiner started his legal career on the Welsh circuit where in 1763 he married Margaret Harries of Wales.

A successful attorney, Gardiner moved his practice to London and developed an interest in the English radical politics of the 1760s. He associated with radical leaders such as John Wilkes and was retained as junior counsel for Wilkes's 1764 trial on *The North Briton*. Gardiner defended him successfully against charges of libel. An ardent Whig, Gardiner defended other radicals although his politics alienated him from his conservative father. He also embraced radical religious tenets that would lead to Unitarianism, which further estranged him from his staunchly Anglican father.

Appointed the attorney general for St. Christopher's Island in 1768, Gardiner sailed to the Caribbean to begin his political career. His radical politics, however, angered local planters and led to his removal from office in 1770. Undeterred, he opened a law practice on the island, befriended the French in his Caribbean travels, and supported the Whig principles of the American Revolution. In letters to his Tory father he boldly stated his radical creed: "I'm a staunch, thorough revolution[ary] Whig, you know—and abhor all Kingcraft and all Priestcraft. Such have been my Principles since I could judge for myself, and such I trust will be the Principles I shall carry with me to the Grave."

With the end of the revolutionary war in 1783, Gardiner returned to the colonies after an absence of thirty years. As a radical Whig, he enjoyed the acclaim of George Washington and Samuel Adams. He established a successful law practice in Boston and became known as a forceful man in court as well as a leader of the Massachusetts bar. Gardiner petitioned the state for the return of his property, which was confiscated with his father's Loyalist estate, and secured the return of some of the family's vast lands in Maine. He obtained his father's pew in King's Chapel and led the old Anglican church in its transition to the Unitarian faith. He was appointed a justice of the peace and, as one mark of local approval, in 1785 delivered Boston's Fourth of July oration.

Upon his father's death in 1786, John Gardiner inherited the family land in Maine and moved to the district of Pownalborough. An affable and popular man, he was elected moderator of the town meeting and in 1789 was elected to the Massachusetts House of Representatives. In the legislature he earned the reputation of a "law reformer" for his successful efforts to repeal old colonial statutes, particularly those relating to entail and primogeniture. In 1792 his dramatic speech in the Massachusetts House helped win repeal of the state's antitheater laws. His book on the controversy, *Gardiner on the Theatre* (1792), was a learned survey of the history of drama. In other reform efforts he tried to establish a college in Maine and advocated statehood for the region. For his legal reforms and his public service, Harvard College awarded him an honorary degree in 1791.

Tenacious in his convictions and eloquent in his speeches, Gardiner enjoyed a fine reputation. He was an accomplished lawyer noted for his wit, and he delighted colleagues at the bar and visitors to his Maine home. But the death of his wife in 1789 grieved him deeply, and he never remarried, which was unusual for a man of his social status. He was devoted to his four children, especially his son John Sylvester John Gardiner, who would become a prominent rector of Trinity Church in Boston. Gardiner was at the peak of his political career and a man of exceptional promise when he boarded the passenger ship *Londoner* to attend the legislature in Boston. He had a premonition of disaster yet did not change ships and drowned when the *Londoner* capsized in a gale off Cape Ann.

• Manuscripts on John Gardiner are scattered, and an important source, with some very pungent letters to his father, is the Whipple-Gardiner Letters at the Massachusetts Historical Society in Boston; his legal efforts to reclaim the family lands in Maine are in the Silvester Gardiner Papers at the Maine Historical Society in Portland; and the family correspondence is in the Gardiner papers at the Historical Society of Pennsylvania in Philadelphia.

Among the old biographical sources are Bertram E. Packard, *John Gardiner, Barrister* (1923); Caroline E. Robinson, *The Gardiners of Narragansett* (1919); E. Alfred Jones, *American Members of the Inns of Court* (1924); and Henry W. Foote, *Annals of King's Chapel* (3 vols., 1882–1896).

More recent information is available in Clifford K. Shipton, *Biographical Sketches of Those Who Attended Harvard College*, vol. 13 (1965), pp. 593–603. On the radicalism of English politics see Colin Bonwick, *English Radicals and the American Revolution* (1977). For the legal profession in early Massachusetts see William E. Nelson, *The Americanization of the Common Law* (1975), and the Colonial Society of Massachusetts, *Law in Colonial Massachusetts 1630–1800* (1984).

PETER R. VIRGADAMO

GARDINER, Leon (25 Nov. 1892–5 Mar. 1945), African-American bibliophile, researcher, and photographer, was born in Atlantic City, New Jersey, the son of Jacob Gardiner and Martha (maiden name unknown).

In 1902 he and his family moved to Philadelphia, Pennsylvania. From childhood he was interested in reading, cross-country running, hiking, camping, and bicycling. Later he developed an interest in music, choir singing, and photography. Blatant racial discrimination kept him from attending the photography school of his choice in Philadelphia, to his great disappointment. In the very early 1900s he began to collect material of various kinds concerning the achievements of blacks, black institutions, and lynchings of blacks.

From 1908 to 1923 or so, Gardiner attended meetings held by Philadelphia's Afro-American Historical Society (later the American Negro Historical Society), expressed his ideas and described his findings in what he called "race literature," and was encouraged by fellow members in various ways. He kept adding to his collection of black memorabilia, and he and others formed a group of bibliophiles. His nighttime job at a post office in Philadelphia left him free during daylight hours to read books and articles on black history, to collect black oral history, to seek the advice of rare-book dealers, and to continue assembling books, memorabilia, and manuscripts pertaining to his absorbing interest. He sought out survivors and descendants of Philadelphia's black families and strenuously urged them to ferret out old correspondence and printed matter from their cellars and attics. He was instrumental in securing the collections of deceased bibliophiles Jacob C. White and Robert Mara Adger from their separate estates. Materials therein included rare books and pamphlets, brochures, letters, and autographs.

After the American Negro Historical Society became inactive in 1923 or soon thereafter, Gardiner and some other members joined the Association for the Study of Negro Life and History, which had been formed in Philadelphia by Carter Godwin Woodson in the late 1920s. Gardiner was later credited as being the only member to keep the association's collection intact. Heirs of several other prominent collectors unfortunately did not do so. Gardiner was also a member of the Philadelphia Society for Negro Records and Research, which was active from 1937 until 1952.

In the 1930s and early 1940s Gardiner wrote articles for the *Philadelphia Tribune* and the *Philadelphia Independent*. Some of these pieces were cowritten with his friend Arthur Huff Fauset, author of *Sojourner Truth, God's Faithful Pilgrim* (1938) and *Black Gods of the Metropolis: Negro Religious Cults of the Urban North* (1944). Gardiner's popular essay "One Hundred Years Have Passed since Garrison Handed This Promise to the World" (*Philadelphia Tribune*, 7 Dec. 1933) advanced his reputation. Over the years Gardiner was frequently called upon to answer queries from fellow African-American scholars throughout the United States. His knowledge and experience as a researcher made him a valued resource, and he was well known for cooperating generously. His most enduring work, however, was the result of his fixed belief that individual publications would be insufficient and that permanent, free-standing collections of black historical materials of all sorts should be gathered and maintained. To this end, he acquired and carefully preserved the collection of the Afro-American Historical Society and added other materials that he had been gathering for years. In 1933 he deposited his collections in the Historical Society of Pennsylvania and in the Berean Institute, both in Philadelphia. The collections include books and documents from as early as 1766, much nineteenth-century material, varied correspondence from often highly prominent blacks, and documents relating to black history, political efforts, charitable organizations, literary organizations, and church, educational, and athletic activities.

Gardiner was married twice. His first wife was Bernice Modeste; the couple had three children. After her death, he married another woman named Bernice in 1940; she was the niece of the prominent African-American novelist Charles Waddell Chesnutt. The couple had no children. Each of his wives enthusiastically aided Gardiner in his efforts. He worked so energetically that he severely impaired his health. When he was advised to schedule more time for leisure or rest, he insisted that his desire to accomplish his goals was more important to him than life itself. He died suddenly of a heart attack in Philadelphia.

• Gardiner's papers and related materials are in the Berean Institute, the Historical Society of Pennsylvania, and the Moorland-Spingarn Research Center, all in Philadelphia. Other materials are at Howard University, Washington, D.C. Dorothy Porter, "Documentation on the Afro-American: Familiar and Less Familiar Sources," *African Studies Bulletin* 12 (Dec. 1969): 293–303, praises Gardiner for collecting and preserving American Negro Historical Society records. James G. Spady, "The Afro-American Historical Society: The Nucleus of Black Bibliophiles (1897–1923)," *Negro History Bulletin* 37 (June–July 1974): 254–57, describes Gardiner's contributions to the development of Afro-American studies. Charles L. Blockson, *African Americans in Pennsylvania: A History and Guide* (1994), praises Gardiner for keeping his collections intact.

ROBERT L. GALE

GARDINER, Lion (1599–1663), military engineer and colonist, was born in England. His birthplace and parentage are uncertain. He served in the English army and went to the Netherlands, where he became a "Master of Works of Fortification" in the armies of the prince of Orange. In 1625 he married a Dutch woman, Mary Wilemson (or Duereant) of Woerden, Holland. They eventually had three children, of whom David Gardiner (born in 1636) was the first white child born in Connecticut, and Elizabeth (born in 1641) was the first English child born in New Netherland (present-day New York State). In 1635 Gardiner made contact with Hugh Peter and John Davenport—two eminent Puritan ministers living in Rotterdam. After discussions and negotiations, Gardiner signed a contract for four years—at one hundred pounds a year—to work as an engineer in the New World, especially to build a fort at the mouth of the Connecticut River for a projected new colony. This agreement was loosely un-der the umbrella of the so-called Warwick Patent (1632–1644), a tract of land that included most of present-day Connecticut.

Gardiner sailed to London and then to the New World aboard the *Batchelor*, arriving in Boston on 28 November 1635. Greeted by John Winthrop (1588–1649) and other Massachusetts Bay leaders, Gardiner examined the environs of Salem and stated that a fortification there was unnecessary since "it was Capt. Hunger that threatened them most." He helped the people of Boston to build a fort on Breed's Hill and then sailed in the spring of 1636 for the mouth of the Connecticut River, where twenty Bostonians had already begun to create a settlement. Gardiner directed them in building a fort and developing Saybrook, Connecticut. Gardiner arrived just in time, for the Dutch in New Netherland were planning to lay claim to the mouth of the river as well.

Gardiner understood the danger of the fort's location, exposed both to possible Dutch incursions and to the hostility of the local Native Americans, the Pequot tribe. When events led toward a full-scale conflict between white settlers and the Pequots, Gardiner chastised Massachusetts Bay leader John Endecott, who was leaving on a punitive raid against the Pequots. Gardiner claimed that "you come hither to raise these wasps about my ears, and then you will take wing and flee away." Indeed, members of the Saybrook garrison were attacked during the winter of 1636–1637, and Gardiner was wounded in the leg. In the spring of 1637 Gardiner sent twenty of his men along with the expedition of Captains John Mason (1600–1672) and John Underhill against the Pequots. The Puritan expedition burned Fort Mystic and 700 Pequots were either killed, captured, or burned to death. Although he had opposed the start of the Pequot War, Gardiner now hailed this "victory to the glory of God and honour of our nation." In the immediate aftermath of the Pequot War, Gardiner became friendly with and a protector of the sachem Waiandance (now Wyandanch) of the Montauk tribe, which was located on eastern and central Long Island and which formerly had paid tribute to the Pequots.

When his contract with the Puritans expired in 1639, Gardiner moved his family to the island at the eastern end of Long Island that the Indians called Montauk. Gardiner called it the Isle of Wight, but it eventually became known as Gardiner's Island, the name it still bears. Gardiner purchased it from the Indians for ten coats of trading cloth. He also secured a patent from James Farrett, the deputy of Lord Stirling on Long Island. The Gardiner family lived peacefully on the island in near self-sufficiency, nearly independent of both the new Connecticut colony and New Netherland. Gardiner's privately held island was something of an anomaly—a colony set up not for religious motives or for expansion of the claims of a mother country, but for personal enjoyment. Politically his island was almost a neutral zone in the midst of several conflicting spheres of influence: the Massachusetts Bay Colony, the Connecticut Colony, New Netherland, the Montauk tribe, the Narragansett tribe, and others. All of these groups knew of Gardiner, and most of them recognized him as the lord and proprietor of the island.

Gardiner maintained his strong friendship with Waiandance and helped the Montauks to defend themselves against the Narragansett Indians, who made raids across Long Island Sound. At Gardiner's request the Massachusetts Bay authorities sent a vessel to patrol the sound. In 1653 Gardiner moved to Easthampton, Long Island, and became a leading member of that community. In later life he wrote his history of the Pequot War (1660). Disappointed in the behavior of his son, David, Gardiner left his property to his wife in his will. Gardiner died on his island. His wife survived him by two years, after which the property reverted to David. In 1686 New York governor Thomas Dongan raised Gardiner's Island to the level of an English manor, with the Gardiner family holding full manorial rights. The island entered into history at least twice more: Captain Kidd (William Kidd) buried treasure there in 1699, and Julia Gardiner left her ancestral home to marry President John Tyler (1790–1862) in 1844.

Perhaps Gardiner's largest claim to historical note is that he created a personal fiefdom, later raised to a manor, that remained in the family's hands; as of 1993 the sixteenth generation of Gardiners still owned the island.

• Documentary sources on Lion Gardiner's life are not plentiful. Gardiner's *Relation of the Pequot Warres* is in Charles Orr, ed., *History of the Pequot War: The Contemporary Accounts of Mason, Underhill, Vincent and Gardener [sic]* (1897). Robert Payne, *The Island* (1958), contains in-depth information on Gardiner and Gardiner's Island. To understand the Pequot War and Gardiner's place in it, one should turn to Herbert Milton Sylvester, *Indian Wars of New England*, vol. 1 (1910), and Francis Jennings, *The Invasion of America: Indians, Colonialism, and the Cant of Conquest* (1975).

SAMUEL WILLARD CROMPTON

GARDINER, Robert Hallowell, III (9 Sept. 1855–15 June 1924), lawyer, social gospeler, and Episcopal ecumenical leader, was born in Fort Tejon, California, the son of Major John William Tudor Gardiner and Anna Elizabeth West Hays. While Gardiner was a child, the family moved to Boston where his father, who suffered from crippling arthritis, was a recruiting officer for the Union armies. Sometime after 1865 the family moved to Montreal, Canada, where Gardiner attended high school. He took an extra year at the Roxbury Latin School from 1871 to 1872 and then distinguished himself at Harvard College. He was appointed Latin orator at his graduation in 1876. Throughout his life, Gardiner maintained a keen interest in languages and spoke French, modern Greek, Italian, German, and ecclesiastical Latin. In 1877 he spent a year as an assistant teacher at Roxbury Latin, where he taught French.

Gardiner attended Harvard Law School until 1879, when the death of his father forced him to drop out in order to help support his widowed mother, an unmarried sister, and his adolescent twin brothers. At the same time, he continued the study of law under the brilliant James J. Storrow and William Minot, a tax and trust attorney. Gardiner was admitted to the Massachusetts bar in 1880. From his Boston office, he managed six private real estate trusts and was the director of an equal number of companies.

In June 1881 Gardiner married Alice Outram Bangs of Boston; they had five children. In 1886 Gardiner inherited the family estate in Gardiner, Maine—"Oaklands"—from a childless uncle. As a boy he had been forced by circumstances to live frugally, but by his early thirties he was a wealthy and successful man. In 1900 he moved his legal residence from Massachusetts to Maine, where he and his wife kept an elaborate home.

But it was as a leader, first in the Episcopal church and then in international Christian circles that Gardiner made his greatest contribution. He was active in parish and diocesan affairs his entire adult life. He was a trustee of the Christian Social Union and of the Episcopal City Mission. During the 1880s and then from 1904 to 1922 he was a lay deputy to the Episcopal church's General Convention, first from Massachusetts and then Maine. From 1904 to 1910 he acted as the president of a national Episcopal society for men and boys, the Brotherhood of St. Andrew. Gardiner also served on executive and administrative committees of the Federal Council of Churches. An early champion of women's rights in the church, he proposed in 1916 that they be elected deputies to the denomination's General Convention. After the World Missionary Conference in Edinburgh, Scotland, in 1910, he became secretary to a commission that was financially backed by J. P. Morgan and was also appointed by the church's General Convention to bring about a world conference on faith and order.

Through his scholarly reading of church history, Gardiner came to believe that individual, personal conversion emphasized by evangelicals must be completed by a corporate understanding of the church derived from the Oxford Movement, the high church revival emanating from the University of Oxford in the 1830s that emphasized apostolic succession, a romantic view of medieval Christianity, and the immanence and continuity of Christ in church, ministry, and sacraments. That understanding, he believed, would ultimately lead to a larger church unity. Gardiner believed that both democratic government and Christian unity needed each other, would inevitably influence each other, and would bring about each other's triumph. While his awareness of both religious and political pluralism was limited, Gardiner took the Gospel of John to be the means of achieving this triumph. In it Jesus had spoken of his oneness with the Father (John 14:6) and had gone on to mandate for his followers unity with himself and also with each other (John 15:9–17). According to Gardiner, self-giving love as seen in the incarnation of Jesus Christ and in his cross and resurrection provided the guiding principle for unity in both church and world. By commitment to prayer and to local, national, and international conferences, unity would be realized. "As the world grows smaller," he wrote, "[an understanding of the] corporate aspect of our religion is the special need." By the networks he created, he sought to make corporateness a reality.

Tirelessly and practically, Gardiner undertook a vast correspondence to world Christian leaders of every denomination—11,000 pages of letters. No detail or nuance of language escaped him. He was not above criticizing one Roman Catholic scholar as "perhaps a little careless" and declared humorously that he was unaware that "in using Latin you must have a perfectly clear meaning in mind. I thought ecclesiastical Latin was especially arranged to conceal thought." He remarked, "All my business training has been in the direction of getting things to move faster than the Church is accustomed to," and pointedly reminded a heedless bishop in his own denomination that a great deal more "was needed . . . [than] to write polite letters to the other Communions asking them to join us in the Conference." At the same time he had great respect for the women of the Episcopal Society of the Companions of the Holy Cross, whom he felt were "accustomed to getting things done, and not trained as we men have been in ecclesiastical procrastination." He wanted "no infringement of the principles of any Church"; the only condition to participation in the worldwide conference was belief in the Incarnation—and prayer for the oneness of the church. Gardiner was the single most important figure in the movement toward church unity in the early twentieth century and was acknowledged as such posthumously by the Lausanne Conference, held in Lausanne, Switzerland, in 1927. There more than 400 delegates from 108 churches honored the man about whom it can be said, "There is not a church in Christendom . . . that does not know his name."

Gardiner was also a founder of the Republican Club of Massachusetts, treasurer of the Foreign Policy Association, and eventually president of the board of trustees of the Roxbury Latin School from 1917 to 1924. A quiet, self-possessed, decisive man, Gardiner gave full attention to whatever task he undertook. His ability to analyze situations and to coordinate them with larger ends was noteworthy. Occasionally he showed impatience with those whose thoughts were less clear than his, but he was extraordinarily kind. On his first day as a school teacher he had all the students stand and recite the Lord's Prayer; that done he took out the switch with which teachers were supposed to keep order in the classroom, broke it into pieces, and threw the lot into the waste basket. In similar fashion, as a world leader for Christian unity he declared that he was against ultimatums to other churches, "a relic of the age of brute force." Gardiner died in Boston, Massachusetts.

• The bulk of Gardiner's papers are with the World Council of Churches in Geneva. Microfilm copies of the faith and order correspondence and other letters are at the General Theological Seminary in New York City. Gardiner wrote a number of articles and book reviews, including "A Lawyer's View of the Function of the Church," *Publications of the Christian Social Union*, no. 37 (15 May 1897): 1–20; "Address," *St. Andrew's Cross* (Nov.–Dec. 1904): 38–40; "The Church and the Federal Council," *The Living Church* 48, no. 9 (28 Dec. 1912): 290–93; "Creed, Life, and Unity," *Christian Union Quarterly* 3, no. 12 (Apr. 1914): 111–18; "The American Council for Organic Union," *The Churchman* (21 Feb. 1920): 2–3; and "Address of Welcome," in *One Hundredth Anniversary of the Diocese of Maine* (1920).

JOHN F. WOOLVERTON

GARDINER, Silvester (29 June 1708–8 Aug. 1786), physician and land magnate, was born in South Kingston, Rhode Island, the son of William Gardiner and Abigail Remington, members of a prominent New England family. Frail and bookish as a child, he roamed the nearby fields and learned the medicinal value of local plants. His brother-in-law, the Anglican missionary Rev. James MacSparran, recognized his intelligence and tutored him in the classics. MacSparran encouraged Gardiner's aptitude for medicine and persuaded his father to send him to Boston as a physician's apprentice.

In the mid-1720s, young Gardiner studied in Boston under Dr. John Gibbins, a noted practitioner. He went to London in 1727 to complete his medical education under Dr. William Cheselden at St. Thomas's Hospital. There he learned Cheselden's new "lateral" method for the lithotomy operation to remove various "stones." He also studied medicine in Paris, where he was shocked by what he believed was the immoral behavior of the inhabitants and developed a lifelong hatred of the French.

Upon his return to New England, Gardiner established his medical practice in Boston, and in 1732 he married Anne Gibbins, the daughter of his mentor, at King's Chapel. Within a decade he emerged as the foremost surgeon of the city and demonstrated his skill in several operations that received extensive publicity. Swiftly and without anesthesia, he removed various "stones" that threatened the lives of his patients. These celebrated lithomy operations confirmed the benefits of a European medical education and created a lucrative practice for him.

Gardiner joined the Boston Medical Society, founded in 1736 by William Douglass, and enriched the profession with lectures, anatomy lessons, and plate illustrations from Europe. Also, he revolutionized the apothecary business when he opened a shop that sold prepared packages of drugs to be distributed to doctors throughout New England. It was a profitable venture, and he opened two other shops, which he entrusted to business colleagues. Gardiner dominated the apothecary trade in New England and enjoyed an excellent reputation among physicians. However, he accused his business partners of embezzlement; protracted lawsuits in the 1760s, with numerous pamphlets, ended with judgments in his favor.

Like many colonial men who accumulated great wealth, Gardiner invested in land. He concentrated his investments with the Kennebeck Company, a speculative venture along the Kennebec River in the Maine district, which attracted wealthy proprietors like James Bowdoin (1726–1790) and Thomas Hancock. Gardiner joined the proprietors in 1751 and emerged as the dominant figure. He acquired nearly 100,000 acres and with his vast capital developed the new towns of Pittson and Dresden, encouraging German immigration to the latter. Also he founded the town of Gardiner, where he built houses, wharfs, dams, and sawmills, manufactured potash, and endowed an Anglican chapel. Disputes over land titles, with lawsuits that reached the Privy Council, tended to slow the region's development; these lawsuits ended with the Revolution.

As the leader of Boston's medical community, Gardiner worked industriously in various aspects of the profession. He trained medical apprentices to be physicians, proposed a smallpox hospital for Boston (it was rejected by the selectmen), and treated the wealthy citizens of the town. The colonial wars brought him additional work as he dispensed medical supplies for the military, built a hospital for the English wounded, and prepared surgical chests for their warships.

When John Singleton Copley painted Gardiner's portrait in 1772, he captured the assurance and strength of an urbane colonial, typical of the Anglican elite in Boston. His mansion was a lively place with six children, most of whom married prominent members of the seaboard establishment. Gardiner and his wife entertained a vast array of celebrated individuals that included royal officials and elite members of the British officer corps. Anne Gardiner was an accomplished chef and over the years compiled a rare colonial cookbook, *Mrs. Gardiner's Recipes*. She died in 1771, and a year later Gardiner married Abigail (Pickman) Eppes of Salem.

A deeply religious Anglican, Gardiner was singular in his devotion to King's Chapel. For many years he served as a lay officer, was a generous benefactor, and hosted the church's Christmas parties for the poor. Indulgent to the Anglican poor of Boston, his humanitarian services included forty years of work with the Episcopal Charitable Society, and he wrote a book of prayers for the poor, which disappeared during the Revolution.

An avid supporter of royal government, his Tory views were well known at the start of the American Revolution, especially his support of Governor Thomas Hutchinson. Gardiner's politics antagonized the populace, and he remained in town with the British military during the siege of Boston. He tended to their wounded after the battle of Bunker Hill, an act that many Americans never forgave. When the English evacuated Boston in 1776, a bitter Gardiner was forced to leave behind his vast medical supplies to "that thief Washington."

His loyalty to the Crown cost him dearly. Bereft of home and fortune, Gardiner and his family fled with the English fleet to Halifax and then to New York. In 1778 they sailed to Poole, England, and awaited the outcome of the Revolution. As a consequence of his Loyalism, the state of Massachusetts confiscated his Boston home, sold his magnificent library, distributed his Maine lands to various speculators, and banished him for life.

As a Loyalist in exile, he struggled to rebuild his life at the age of seventy. Gardiner's losses in the Revolution exceeded £40,000, and the English government compensated him with an annual stipend of £150. His second wife died in 1780. Chastened by a decade of exile, he petitioned the state of Massachusetts to return home to Boston, but the petition was denied.

Helped by his eldest son, John Gardiner, the old doctor returned quietly to Rhode Island in 1785 and married Catherine Goldthwaite, who was nearly fifty years younger than he. They settled in Newport, where he resumed his medical practice and his activities in the Anglican faith. Kindly and popular, he enjoyed a sedate existence and earned the respect of local inhabitants. At his funeral, ships in the harbor lowered their flags to half-mast, an unusual mark of respect for a former Loyalist.

• Important manuscripts include the Gardiner-Whipple Papers and the King's Chapel Archives at the Massachusetts Historical Society in Boston; the diary of John Denison Hartshorne at the Francis A. Countway Medical Library in Boston; the Silvester Gardiner Papers at the Maine Historical Library in Portland; and the Gardiner papers at the Historical Society of Pennsylvania in Philadelphia.

For biographical information see Henry S. Webster, *Silvester Gardiner* (1913), and Caroline E. Robinson, *The Gardiners of Narragansett* (1919). On his medical career see Robert F. Seybolt, "Lithomies Performed by Dr. Gardiner, 1738 and 1741," *New England Journal of Medicine* 202 (1930): 109, and Eric H. Christianson, "The Colonial Surgeon's Rise to Prominence: Dr. Silvester Gardiner," *New England Historical and Genealogical Register* 136 (1982): 104–14.

For Gardiner's interest in land development see John W. Hanson, *History of Gardiner, Pittson and West Gardiner* (1852); William S. Bartlett, *The Frontier Missionary: A Memoir of the Life of the Rev. Jacob Bailey* (1853); and Gordon E. Kershaw, *The Kennebeck Proprietors 1749–1775* (1975).

Gardiner's life in Boston is noted in Lyman H. Butterfield, ed., *Diary and Autobiography of John Adams* (4 vols., 1962); L. Kinvin Wroth and Hiller B. Zobel, eds., *The Legal Papers of John Adams* (4 vols., 1965); and Henry W. Foote, *Annals of King's Chapel* (3 vols., 1882–1896).

PETER R. VIRGADAMO

GARDNER, Ava (24 Dec. 1922–25 Jan. 1990), actress, was born Ava Lavinia Gardner in Brogdon, a Johnston County, North Carolina, tobacco-growing community known locally as Grabtown, the daughter of Jonas Bailey Gardner, a sharecropper, and Mary Elizabeth Balcer, the proprietor of a boardinghouse. The youngest of seven children, Ava enjoyed a sheltered, pampered childhood, avoiding school and running barefoot through the country. After her father's death in

1938, Ava took a commercial course at a secretarial school in Wilson, North Carolina. A brother paid the tuition. When her sister Beatrice went to New York in 1940 with her husband, photographer Larry Tarr, Ava went along. A publicity photo led to a silent screen test designed to highlight her striking good looks but also hide her Tar Heel accent and the fact that she could not act. Pleasing an executive at Metro-Goldwyn-Mayer (MGM), Gardner was signed to the standard seven-year studio contract, which guaranteed her a starting salary of $50 a week. Joined by Bea, who had divorced Tarr, Ava moved to Hollywood; she was only nineteen.

Gardner posed for cheesecake and publicity stills while simultaneously learning how to look and act the part of a star. She was certain stardom would come quickly and later said she was surprised when it did not. Studio workers remember her as having been alternately indifferent and determined. In January 1942 she married Mickey Rooney, then Hollywood's number-one box office star. Studio chief Louis B. Mayer at first opposed the match and sent a press agent on the couple's honeymoon to control the publicity that was created by their marriage. Rooney helped the young actress through a series of unbilled bit roles in *We Were Dancing*, *Joe Smith, American*, *Sunday Punch*, and *This Time for Keeps*, all in 1942. By the time the two divorced sixteen months later, she had appeared in a series of walk-ons, as a cashier in an Our Gang short, a car hop in *Kid Glove Killer* (1942), a salesgirl in *Reunion in France* (1942), and as a heroine in a Bela Lugosi–Bowery Boys Monogram programmer called *Ghosts on the Loose* (1943).

Gardner later admitted that she was "no actress, just good to look at," and she struggled to gain the respect of her studio. That tension marked much of her forty-four years as an actress, including a decade-long build-up at MGM during which she was cast in small parts in important films and larger parts in smaller films. Her yearlong marriage to band leader Artie Shaw, beginning in October 1945, introduced her to the world of art, music, and literature and kept her name in the headlines. The following year she earned critical notices for her leading role in the breakthrough film *The Killers* (1946), made on loan out to Universal-International, in which she played Kitty Collins, the amoral vixen who leads Swede (played by Burt Lancaster) to destruction and death. She now appeared to be an actress with a future. Her divorce from Shaw in 1946, followed by flashy parts alongside Clark Gable in *The Hucksters* (1947), Fred MacMurray in *Singapore* (1947), Robert Walker in *One Touch of Venus* (1948), and Gregory Peck in *The Great Sinner* (1949), furthered her growing reputation as the most beautiful woman in film, the cinema's ultimate sex goddess between the reigns of Rita Hayworth and Marilyn Monroe. Highly public love affairs with Howard Duff, Howard Hughes, and finally Frank Sinatra led to numerous cover stories in the glamour magazines.

Between 1949 and 1954 Gardner made twelve films, enjoyed her greatest critical success, and became financially independent. Headlines chronicled her marriage to Sinatra in 1951, their stormy separation and subsequent divorce in 1957, her friendships with writers Ernest Hemingway and Robert Graves, and her widely publicized involvements with Spanish bullfighters. She was nominated for an Academy Award for her role opposite Gable in John Ford's *Mogambo* (1953). Gardner's performance as Eloise "Honey Bear" Kelly, under Ford's deft direction, displayed her capacities as a comedian. Her partly improvisational performance showed she could be sexy in the context of a more fully developed character. Her part in *Mogambo* followed a series of typically sultry roles opposite Robert Taylor in *The Bribe* (1949), Robert Mitchum in *My Forbidden Past* (1951), and as the half-caste singer Julie in *Showboat* (1951). She did little more than pose beautifully for the camera opposite James Mason in *Pandora and the Flying Dutchman* (1951), beside Gable again in *Lone Star* (1952), and in a reteaming with Peck in Hemingway's *The Snows of Kilimanjaro* (1952). Her billing as "the most beautiful animal in the world" opposite Humphrey Bogart in *The Barefoot Contessa* (1954) pushed Gardner's carefully crafted screen persona of ineluctable temptress to its limits. By her middle thirties, years of being "the perfect party girl" had taken their toll; she looked her age and then some. Her short stint as Hollywood's reigning beauty queen was behind her. Claiming a need for privacy, in 1954 she left Hollywood for Madrid.

Bhowani Junction (1956) and *The Little Hut* (1957) both failed at the box office, and her sixteen-year association with MGM ended. The breakup of the Hollywood studio system forced Gardner and other graduates of the dream factory to fend for themselves. Apart from *The Sun Also Rises* (1957), *On the Beach* (1959), and *The Night of the Iguana* (1964), in all of which Gardner played her standard role of a woman with a past, her last two decades in film were largely unremarkable. Supporting roles in *The Bible* (1966) and *The Life and Times of Judge Roy Bean* (1972) teamed her again with Huston. *The Blue Bird* (1976), directed by George Cukor, reunited her with Elizabeth Taylor, another product of the MGM stock company.

Gardner resented being treated "a little like merchandise" as a contract player and bitterly blamed MGM for "neglecting" her career, but she had achieved her lasting fame within the Hollywood studio system and began to fade from view after it. As an independent actress she initially commanded $400,000 per picture, but the roles soon became fewer and fewer and the pay smaller and smaller. She settled into an increasingly reclusive life following her move to London in 1968, emerging only for an occasional supporting part in such films as *Earthquake* (1974) and *The Cassandra Crossing* (1977). She also made guest appearances on television shows, including the popular prime time soap opera "Knots Landing" and "A.D." She got good reviews, but fellow actors remember her as "a lonesome lady" who desperately needed reassurance.

When she turned sixty Gardner told interviewers that she would have gladly exchanged her career for "a long and happy marriage." To her Hyde Park neighbors, who saw her leave her apartment only to walk her dogs, she seemed to like to hibernate. A stroke suffered in 1986 slowed her further, and she began to dictate her memoirs. Early one morning in mid-January 1990 she called former costar Stewart Granger on the telephone. She had been watching *Bhowani Junction* on television and drinking. "Weren't we beautiful," she told him sadly. A week later she was dead in London after a bout of pneumonia. The press noted the passing of "the most irresistible woman in the world," a "farmer's daughter" who became a "movie goddess." Some recalled a fundamental ambivalence that had made her screen sensuality all the more enigmatic. To those critics, Ava Gardner was a "breathtaking beauty" who seemed "proud, prowling" and "sure of her powers." Yet in her best work she evoked an unaffected vulnerability that suggested the distracted, self-conscious air of a woman who was in search of something she could never quite define.

• The Ava Gardner Museum in Smithfield, N.C., which is open to the public, places her in the context of her rural N.C. upbringing and contains items that belonged to Gardner. Her memoirs, *Ava: My Story* (1990), were compiled from tape recordings made before her death. She is featured in most of the standard movie industry reference works. Full biographies include David Hanna, *Ava: A Portrait of a Star* (1960); Charles Higham, *Ava: A Life Story* (1974); and Judith M. Kass, *Ava Gardner* (1977). See also James Robert Parish and Ronald L. Bowers, *The MGM Stock Company* (1973). A nationally televised appreciation of her life, titled *Ava Gardner*, premiered in 1992 on Home Box Office.

BRUCE J. EVENSEN

GARDNER, Erle Stanley (17 July 1889–11 Mar. 1970), lawyer and popular author, was born in Malden, Massachusetts, the son of Charles Walter Gardner, a civil engineer, and Grace Adelma Waugh. When Gardner was ten, his family moved to Oregon and then to Oroville in northern California. After graduating from high school in Palo Alto, California in 1909, he studied law briefly at Valparaiso University in Indiana. He returned to California to study with local attorneys and was admitted to the California bar in 1911. He practiced criminal law actively for twenty years in Oxnard and Ventura, exercising a flair for courtroom dramatics that he later magnified and assigned to his most famous character, Perry Mason. Gardner married Natalie Frances Beatrice Talbert in 1912. The couple had one child; they separated in 1935, but Gardner did not remarry until after Natalie's death in 1968, when he married his longtime secretary, Agnes Jean Bethell.

From 1918 to 1921 Gardner served as an executive with the Consolidated Sales Company. In 1921 he began to supplement his legal practice by composing stories for the pulp magazine markets. He published formulaic short stories and serials in such subgenres of popular fiction as action, western, mystery, fantasy, war, and Klondike tale. By 1925 he had sold nearly a half-million words. In the early 1930s he was setting himself a goal of selling 100,000 words a month. In 1933 he finally ended his practice of law altogether and published his first novel, *The Case of the Velvet Claws*, featuring the lawyer-hero Perry Mason. As Mason's success became assured, Gardner decreased (though he never eliminated) his production of magazine fiction and articles. Over the next forty years he composed eighty-one additional Mason novels (and three Mason short stories). He also developed other series protagonists in the mystery genre: Doug Selby, D.A. (nine novels, 1937–1949), and, under the pen name A. A. Fair, the detectives Donald Lam and Bertha Cool (twenty-nine novels, 1939–1970). He also published eight more mystery novels, six volumes of short stories, and sixteen volumes of nonfiction (primarily travelogues describing the landscapes of California and Baja California).

The profits from his fiction enabled Gardner to live well in his desert retreat, "Rancho del Paisano," near Temecula, southeast of Los Angeles. Though he continued to issue three to four novels a year, in the late 1940s Gardner became the prime mover behind Court of Last Resort, an informal committee of professional criminologists who investigated possible miscarriages of justice. Between 1948 and 1958 Gardner publicized their conclusions in a series of articles for *Argosy* magazine. Through Paisano Productions he was also actively involved in producing the popular Perry Mason television series (1957–1966; revived in 1974 and again in 1986) and other television and film projects.

Gardner was, in his own phrase, a "fiction factory." An early advocate of the dictaphone, he occupied up to seven secretaries at one time in the transcription of his fiction and his correspondence. He was one of three prominent California writers who in the 1930s established hard-boiled detective fiction as a significant subgenre in popular American literature. All three began their writing careers in *Black Mask* magazine. The other two, Dashiell Hammett and Raymond Chandler, have since been recognized as literary craftsmen; Gardner's importance has derived more from the impressive statistics of his production and of his popularity. By the time of his death, the Mason novels alone had sold more than 300 million copies worldwide, and in a listing of the fifty-five bestselling crime and mystery novels between 1895 and 1975 (those selling more than two million copies), Gardner is represented by twenty-five titles.

Gardner's novels have been admired for the pace of their action and for their complex and inventive plots. His prose is simple and efficient, characterized by short sentences and paragraphs and much dialogue. His characters are usually stereotypical and almost always drawn from middle-class life, from the young working woman to the successful entrepreneur. Moral judgments are conventional, and little effort is made to supply psychological nuance. Though his travel books suggest he was fascinated by the landscapes of California, in his fiction he rarely supplies more than the background details necessary to make the action credible and the plot possible. Gardner's peers admired his facility at plotting his narratives, and his early novels especially are often impressive in this respect. The basic structure of a Mason novel was defined early: Mason acquires a client; a murder occurs; numerous red herrings are drawn across the track of the investigation; the authorities—most often Sgt. Holcomb and Lt. Tragg of the police and Hamilton Burger of the district attorney's office—reconstruct a false scenario that assigns guilt to Mason's client; and Mason, through his dramatic courtroom cross-examinations, vindicates his client and discovers the villain.

The Bertha Cool/Donald Lam detective series may be somewhat more entertaining and less mechanical than the Mason series, but in Perry Mason, the combative defense attorney who manipulates the legal system to vindicate the innocent, Gardner created one of the most widely recognized figures in American literature. Supported by his loyal secretary, Della Street, and his efficient investigator, Paul Drake, Mason came to embody the ideal American lawyer. Gardner saw Mason essentially as a tough fighter for victims of misfortune, a figure of obvious appeal in the depression. After 1946 the Mason novels began to lose some of their extraordinary popularity, but Gardner continued to publish at least two books a year until his death at Rancho del Paisano.

• Gardner's papers have been collected by the Humanities Research Center at the University of Texas, Austin. His bibliography consists of over 150 books and over 800 stories, scripts, and articles, often written under pen names, such as Charles M. Green, Kyle Corning, Grant Holiday, Robert Parr, Carleton Kendrake, and Charles Kenny. His first stories, "The Police of the House" and "Nellie's Naughty Nighty," were published in *Breezy Stories* in June and Aug. 1921. His first *Black Mask* story, "The Shrieking Skeleton," appeared in Dec. 1923. The first two Mason novels, *The Case of the Velvet Claws* and *The Case of the Sulky Girl*, were published in 1933; the last two, *The Case of the Fenced-In Woman* (1972) and *The Case of the Postponed Murder* (1973), were published posthumously. The Cool/Lam series ran from *The Bigger They Come* (1939) to *All Grass Isn't Green* (1970); the D.A. series ran from *The D.A. Calls It Murder* (1937) to *The D.A. Breaks an Egg* (1949). Gardner also experimented with other detectives in novel-length works: Sam Moraine (*This Is Murder* [1935]), Terry Clane (*Murder up My Sleeve* [1938]; *The Case of the Backward Mule* [1946]), Gramp Wiggins (*The Case of the Turning Tide* [1941]; *The Case of the Smoking Chimney* [1943]), Sheriff Bill Eldon (*Two Clues* [1947]), and Rob Trenton (*The Case of the Musical Cow* [1950]). His travel books began with *The Land of Shorter Shadows* (1948) and ended with *Host with the Big Hat* (1970). In 1952 he collected his *Argosy* articles on miscarriages of justice in *The Court of Last Resort* (rev. ed., 1954); in 1970 he published a volume of social commentary, *Cops on Campus and Crime in the Streets*. Some of Gardner's early pulp fiction has been reprinted, including novels such as *The Adventures of Paul Pry* (1989) and *Dead Men's Letters* (1990) and short-story collections such as *The Amazing Adventures of Lester Leith*, ed. Ellery Queen (1980); *The Human Zero: The Science Fiction Stories*, ed. M. H. Greenberg and C. G. Waugh (1981); and *Whispering Sands: Stories of Gold Fever and the Western Desert* (1981) and *Pay Dirt and Other Whispering Sands Stories*, ed. C. G. Waugh and M. H. Greenberg (1983).

Dorothy B. Hughes, *The Case of the Real Perry Mason* (1978), provides an uncritical but comprehensive account of Gardner's life; Alva Johnson, *The Case of Erle Stanley Gardner* (1947), provides a friendly early view. The two major critical treatments of his fiction are Francis L. and Robert B. Fugate, *Secrets of the World's Best-Selling Writer* (1980), which draws upon his papers and describes the mechanisms of the fiction factory, and J. K. Van Dover, *Murder in the Millions: Erle Stanley Gardner, Mickey Spillane, and Ian Fleming* (1984).

J. K. VAN DOVER

GARDNER, Helen (17 Mar. 1878–4 June 1946), art historian and art history textbook author, was born in Manchester, New Hampshire, the daughter of Charles Frederick Gardner, a merchant tailor and Baptist deacon, and Martha W. Cunningham. In 1891 her family moved to Chicago, where her father set up a successful shop downtown. Helen attended Hyde Park High School and later the University of Chicago. She was elected to Phi Beta Kappa in 1900 and graduated with a B.A. with honors in Latin and Greek in 1901. After earning the degree Gardner taught at Brooks Classical school in Chicago, where her sister was principal. She herself served as assistant principal from 1905 to 1910. Like most other professional women of her era, she never married.

Building on her classical training and probably influenced by the strong art focus of the women's community in Chicago, Gardner became interested in the study of art history and returned to the University of Chicago as a graduate student in 1915. She received a university fellowship in 1917 and was awarded an M.A. in 1918, for which she submitted a thesis called "A Critical Chart of Florentine Painting of the Fifteenth Century." Although she never earned a doctorate, Gardner continued to take art history courses at the university through 1922.

Gardner was appointed head of the photograph and (lantern) slide department of the Ryerson Library of the Art Institute of Chicago about 1919. The following year she established a lecture course at the School of the Art Institute of Chicago called "Survey of Art." By 1922 she had resigned from the library to devote herself to developing a comprehensive art history curriculum and a single-volume survey textbook. *Art Through the Ages: An introduction to Its History and Significance* was published in 1926, while Gardner was active as a lecturer, and it quickly brought her ideas to national attention. In 1927 she was invited to serve as a guest lecturer at the University of California at Los Angeles for two terms. In 1928 she lectured for two terms at the University of Chicago. Gardner then returned to the School of the Art Institute, where she continued to teach until 1944. For the last ten years of her tenure there she was a full professor and the department chair.

Art Through the Ages was the first succinct, well-illustrated, and comprehensive art history textbook published in the United States. Many of the photographs were Gardner's own, taken while on her travels in Europe, Egypt, and the United States. Others had been culled from the resources of the Ryerson Library. The book was clearly written, well organized, and easily understood, and it was adopted at schools throughout the country. Primarily a college text, the work was also intended to be useful for the general reader and traveler. Its very existence stimulated the development of art history courses at the high school level.

Gardner's approach was inclusive and holistic. She covered the arts of Europe, the Orient, the Near East, and the United States. For each area she included a thorough discussion of the "minor" arts (jewelry, textiles, ceramics, books, furniture, etc.) as well as painting, sculpture, and architecture. Gardner believed all the arts were interrelated and equally important and, taken together, expressed the character and ethos of their culture.

To help extend the appreciation of art to an even wider audience, Gardner published *Understanding the Arts* in 1932. Her goal was to enrich everyday life through an increased sensitivity to design principles and aesthetic meaning in all aspects of the material environment—in clothing, interiors, gardens, and urban planning, for example, as much as in painting and the "fine" arts. The book was particularly utilized by art educators during the 1930s.

Gardner revised and expanded *Art Through the Ages* in 1936, incorporating more illustrations and, for the first time, material on modern art. The book went through four more printings in the depression years, and during World War II it was adopted as a text by the armed service schools. More than 260,000 copies of the first two editions were sold. Gardner hoped to expand her coverage of the art of the Western Hemisphere and to sharpen her discussion of the interconnections among cultures. Despite the fact that she was so ill with breast cancer that she found it necessary to retire from the Art Institute in 1944, Gardner completed a third edition that more closely approximated her ideal. She continued working on the book until the final days of her life; she was reviewing page proofs when she died of bronchopneumonia in Chicago. The third edition of *Art Through the Ages* was published posthumously in 1948. Left unfinished at Gardner's death was a book on the arts of the Americas, which would have provided extensive coverage of the pre-Columbian and American-Indian arts she particularly admired.

In later years *Art Through the Ages* went through several more editions, the last of which was published in 1980. Hundreds of thousands of students and general readers were introduced to the study of art history through this famous work, for it was the most popular and successful art history text from the 1930s into the 1960s. Ironically, however, the later editions changed the structure and even-handed emphasis of the original work, largely eliminating the integration and thorough treatment of the "minor" arts and the cultural-historical approach that treated each civilization in a

holistic fashion. Gardner's book was eclipsed in the 1960s by H. W. Janson's *History of Art*, which limited its discussion to Western art and focused more closely on "great" works of "fine" art.

Gardner's personal mission was to extend a deep appreciation of all forms of art to as many people as possible, in order that their lives be perpetually enriched with aesthetic experience. As Andrene Kauffman, one of Gardner's students, recalled, "she had an uncanny ability to give you the essentials so you could see what made art the core of human expression" (1983 letter to Roger Gilmore, dean of the School of the Art Institute of Chicago). Gardner's approach was essentially democratic and inclusive, embracing all forms of creative endeavor in the visual arts. She was able to integrate her classical training with the kind of "feminine" training in the "decorative" and "minor" arts that was considered suitable for women at the turn of the century, and she looked beyond arbitrary definitions and hierarchies. Gardner's legacy may be best assessed from the works that she wrote, rather than those that were substantially rewritten after her death. It appears particularly rich, forward-looking, and full of loving appreciation.

• In addition to the works mentioned in the text, Gardner contributed an entry titled "Mediaeval Art" to the *Encyclopaedia of the Social Sciences* (1930). There are few sources of information on Gardner outside of her own books and entries in biographical dictionaries; no studies or articles focus on her or her work. Slight though it is, the most comprehensive biographical information is found in Harold Allen's entry in *Notable American Women* (1971). (Allen worked at the School of the Art Institute of Chicago and gathered his data in part from school records.) Also see Allen, "Helen Gardner: Quiet Rebel," in *Sacred Spaces and Other Places: A Guide to Grottos and Sculptural Environments in the Upper Midwest*, ed. Lisa Stone and Jim Zanzi (1993).

BEVERLY GORDON

GARDNER, Horod Long Hicks (1623?–c. 1670s), wife or companion to several early colonists, was born in England to unknown parents. At the age of thirteen or fourteen she married John Hicks in March 1637 in St. Faith's underchapel of St. Paul's Cathedral in London. Hicks was some eighteen years older. Alone in London, separated from her family, and without means of support, Horod married Hicks out of desperation. Shortly after the wedding, the couple migrated to Massachusetts, settling in Weymouth. By 1639 they had moved to Newport, Rhode Island, joining William Coddington, erstwhile assistant in Massachusetts and leading antinomian, who had just established that town.

After six years of marriage and two children, Horod's marriage to Hicks broke down irretrievably. When Hicks beat her severely in December 1643, perhaps for having an affair with a man, the fledgling government of Rhode Island (which was also known as Aquidneck) separated them by an apparent divorce decree, and Hicks left for Flushing and later Hempstead, Long Island, there to reestablish himself as a leading member of the community. The decision to grant a complete divorce came at a time when the fledgling government did not have a charter and flew in the face of established English law that permitted separation of bed and board, not remarriage, unless the couple was divorced by act of Parliament.

Horod moved in with another Newport freeman, George Gardner, the man with whom she may have had relations before Hicks's departure. With Gardner, she had six children. When their living arrangements received a court challenge in 1655 shortly after John Hicks received a Dutch divorce from New Netherland, the Rhode Island court found that her original divorce was valid and that she and George Gardner were not involved in a bigamous relationship. Shortly after, she converted briefly to Quakerism when Quaker missionaries came to New England and returned to Weymouth in 1658 to berate that town and Massachusetts for persecuting Quakers and other dissenters. She was whipped for her efforts, and Quaker critics of Massachusetts in the seventeenth and subsequent centuries publicized her punishment.

By March 1665, she had tired of Gardner and also no longer retained her association with the Quakers. That year, when she petitioned visiting royal commissioners to request relief from her living arrangements with Gardner, Rhode Island leaders who knew of the divorce and subsequent cohabitation, having already ruled on both matters, were appalled. At the time the commission was investigating several issues in New England, a number of them vital to Rhode Island and including the extent of the colony and its boundaries with its neighbors. The commissioners turned Horod's case over to colony officials. Rhode Island leaders moved quickly to defuse the issue, no doubt worried that unfavorable royal decisions might follow. They decided that she and Gardner had not had even the benefit of a common law marriage and fined them for fornication.

Shortly after Horod discarded her second consort, she took up housekeeping with her third, John Porter, a prominent Rhode Islander. Hitherto a resident of Portsmouth, Porter had moved in 1664 to the Pettaquamscut Purchase, of which he was one of the proprietors, across Narragansett Bay from Aquidneck. He had left his wife Margaret in Portsmouth when he moved. She appealed to the same assembly that had separated George and Horod Gardner for assistance to compel Porter to support her. The colony forced him to provide. While Horod may have moved across the bay to keep house for him in 1665, by 1666 it was clear that she had. In October 1666, he faced charges of incontinency (a failure to restrain sexual appetite), charges subsequently extended to Horod. They answered the charges to the satisfaction of the colony (the jury must have accepted the argument that she was merely keeping house not cohabiting with him). After Margaret's death, they married, probably by 1670. Horod's children by George Gardner followed their mother when she took up housekeeping with Porter. Eventually, they received Porter lands in the Pet-

taquamscut Purchase, no doubt a contributing factor in Horod's original decision to move. The date of her death is uncertain as there is no record—perhaps it was as early as the 1670s or as late as 1692.

Horod (also cited as Herodias, Harwood, and Harriet, presumably in efforts to avoid her given name) is noteworthy for being one of the first colonists to divorce. Her life has a curiously modern ring to it, replete with one instance of religious protest, divorce, and remarriage. While she could not as a woman serve in a major political role, she did surface in rather significant ways beyond those expected of colonial New England good wives.

• Primary sources are John Russell Bartlett, ed., *Records of the Colony of Rhode Island and Providence Plantations in New England*, vol. 2 (1857), and Howard M. Chapin, ed., *Documentary History of Rhode Island*, vol. 2 (1919). Both sources should be supplemented by the original records in the Rhode Island Archives in Providence. Secondary works that deal with Horod Gardner include G. Andrews Moriarty, "Herodias (Long) Hicks-Gardiner-Porter: A Tale of Old Newport," *Rhode Island History* 11 (1952): 84–92; Clara Gardner Miller and John Milton Stanton, *Gardiner-Gardner Genealogy Including the English Ancestry of George Gardner . . .* (1937); and Lyle Koehler, *A Search for Power: The "Weaker Sex" in Seventeenth-Century New England* (1980).

ARTHUR J. WORRALL

GARDNER, Isabella Stewart (14 Apr. 1840–17 July 1924), patron of the arts and museum founder, was born in New York City, the daughter of David Stewart, an importer and businessman, and Adelia Smith. Educated at a series of private girls' schools in New York, Gardner (known as "Belle" from early childhood) was sent to a French Protestant school in Paris at age sixteen. Her parents soon joined her in Paris, where the Stewarts befriended the family of John L. Gardner, a Boston businessman involved in shipping. Belle Stewart and Julia Gardner, a girl of her own age, quickly became close friends.

The Stewart family returned to New York in 1857. Visiting her friend Julia Gardner in Boston soon after, Belle Stewart met John Lowell "Jack" Gardner, Jr. The vivacious but not conventionally beautiful Belle was a dramatic change from the small circle of Boston society women Jack Gardner had known. Belle was equally taken by the quiet young man, and the two were soon engaged and married in 1860. After a honeymoon in Washington, D.C., the couple moved into an apartment house—then a "European" novelty—in Boston while their new home, a gift from Belle's father, was being constructed on the newly reclaimed land of Back Bay. The couple moved into the house in 1862.

Holding with the strong anti-Lincoln feelings common among many merchants, Isabella Gardner was ambivalent about the Civil War and in later life refused to comment on the era, claiming she was "too young to remember" it. Jack Gardner, like many of his class and station, avoided service by purchasing a substitute. Despite the war, the Gardners' shipping, and later railroad, business prospered. For the young bride, however, her "crass" New York origins excluded her from the decorous circles of young Boston matrons, and she escaped into a series of convenient illnesses. In 1863 Gardner gave birth to a son, but the couple's happiness was short-lived when the boy died in 1865. Gardner soon after suffered a miscarriage, and the couple were to have no more children.

Depressed and convalescing from her miscarriage, Gardner was cared for by the noted Boston physician Henry J. Bigelow. After nearly two years in which she showed no sign of recovering her lively personality, Bigelow prescribed a European trip. Carried on board a ship in New York, Gardner disembarked under her own power in Hamburg, and she and her husband began a grand tour of seven countries, including Germany, Norway, Sweden, Austria, Russia, and France. While in Paris on this first trip, Gardner became a customer of the transplanted English fashion designer Charles Worth, who clothed her with the new off-the-shoulder, tight-fitting gowns that would raise eyebrows in Boston when she returned in 1868.

After the great Boston fire of 1872, Jack Gardner and his father began an insurance company, and the fortune of the families increased dramatically. In 1873 Isabella Gardner's art collection began modestly with the acquisition of a small painting from the Barbizon School by Emile Jacque. The next year the couple took an extended tour of Egypt, Palestine, Greece, and Turkey. When Isabella Gardner's brother-in-law and his wife died suddenly in 1874, the Gardners became guardians of their three nephews.

On a trip to London in 1879, the Gardners met James McNeill Whistler, who painted a portrait of Belle Gardner. Also on this trip, she met Henry James. Though James and Gardner had grown up within blocks of each other in New York, they had never before met. The two became close friends and frequent correspondents for the remainder of James's life. By the end of the 1870s Gardner also formed a close friendship with the young novelist Francis Marion Crawford. The relationship attained the status of scandal in 1881 when Crawford became a neighbor of the Gardners. Boston society felt there was more than mere friendship between Gardner and the novelist and gossiped about the "improper" nature of the relationship. Partially to defuse the growing scandal, the Gardners embarked on an around-the-world voyage in 1883.

After first crossing the United States, the Gardners continued on to China, Japan, and Indochina, where they became among the first Americans to visit the temple complex of Ankor Wat. Traversing India, they made their way to Europe, stopping in Venice, where they took up residence at the Palazzo Barbaro, which became their home whenever they visited Venice. Upon her return to Boston, Gardner became an active patron of music, supporting local musicians and sending others to Europe for study.

Gardner first met John Singer Sargent in 1886. When Sargent visited Boston again the following year, he painted a portrait of Gardner. This portrait was exhibited at the St. Botolph Club in Boston, and the stunning work, showing Gardner in a low-cut gown gazing directly at the viewer, was a controversial sensation. Gardner's husband had the painting withdrawn from the exhibition and refused to allow it to be shown publicly during his life, denying even Sargent's request to show it at the Paris Salon.

On their 1888 visit to Europe, the Gardners visited Spain, at that time slightly off the usual tourist trails. Gardner became enamored of the art and crafts of Spain. Thus, when in 1890 Sargent returned to the United States from his own stay in Spain, Gardner was interested in acquiring his masterpiece of frenzied motion, *El Jaleo*. The painting had already been sold to Thomas Jefferson Coolidge, a relation to Gardner by marriage. In 1915 Coolidge gave Gardner *El Jaleo* after seeing the "Spanish Cloister" space in the museum she had created for it.

Though Gardner had been acquiring art works on a small scale since 1873, it was jewels, particularly pearls and rubies, that commanded her collecting zeal until the early 1890s. During their visit to the Palazzo Barbaro in 1892, however, the couple began to actively collect both fine and decorative arts. That same year, while in Paris, Gardner acquired Vermeer's *The Concert*, a work that united her two loves of music and painting. In 1893 at the World's Columbian Exposition in Chicago, Gardner admired the work of the Swedish-born artist Anders Zorn. She purchased one of his paintings and introduced him to Boston society.

Earlier in 1887 Gardner helped send the young art critic Bernard Berenson to Europe to study and to partake in a general course of self-improvement. She would continue to contribute to Berenson's European education for a number of years. After falling out of touch, Berenson contacted his patron with an offer to help her acquire Botticelli's *The Tragedy of Lucretia*. Berenson acted as Gardner's agent and adviser for the remainder of her life. Berenson often exercised undue influence on those he advised. With Gardner, however, he met his match. "Do bear my purse in mind," Gardner wrote to Berenson on 1 January 1897, "and beat down the people who have what I want; for I *must* have the picture!"

Acquiring the unique Rembrandt, *Storm and Sea*, in early 1898, Gardner's pleasure in this acquisition was eclipsed by the death of her husband on 10 December 1898. Jack Gardner left a significant fortune of more than $2 million to his widow. The Gardners had planned to remodel their Beacon Street house as a museum. Soon after her husband's death, however, Gardner contacted the architect, Willard T. Sears, and ordered him to start afresh with plans for a new structure to be built on a site in Boston's Fenway.

Gardner was intimately involved in the design and construction of Fenway Court, exasperating both the architect and workers with her imperious orders. Construction began in 1899 and continued for the next four years with Gardner not only supervising but also taking part in the "mason-work, the plastering, the carpentry, and in the carrying out of multitudinous details." On 5 December 1900 the Isabella Stewart Gardner Museum was chartered.

The opening of the museum on 1 January 1903 was a major social event with music by members of the Boston Symphony Orchestra and all of Boston society present. It opened to the general public on 23 February. Though Gardner had to weather some early controversy surrounding the museum and her policy of charging a small admission fee, the museum, which doubled as her residence, was soon a popular tourist attraction. On her last trip to Italy in 1906, Gardner saw a number of works that would complete her museum. Over the next few years, she acquired, among others, a number of the Barberini tapestries and Piero della Francesca's *Hercules*.

On Christmas Eve in 1919, Gardner suffered an embolism that paralyzed her right side. Only her friends and family knew about her condition for nearly two years until it was announced in the Boston papers. When John Singer Sargent visited her in 1922, he painted her last portrait, a delicate watercolor of the collector swathed in white. Gardner died in Boston.

To maintain her vision of her museum, Gardner stipulated in her will that Morris Carter should continue as director for life. Gardner's vision of a complete, aesthetically unified exhibition space that included decorative arts, architecture, literature, and music as well as the fine arts would be her legacy to the world. Unlike the many eclectic collections formed in the late nineteenth and early twentieth centuries, the works in the Isabella Stewart Gardner Museum have stood up to rigorous academic reevaluation.

• Extensive manuscript sources for Gardner and her museum, including travel diaries, letters, and guest books, are held in the archives of the Isabella Stewart Gardner Museum, Boston. The correspondence of Gardner and Bernard Berenson is collected in *The Letters of Bernard Berenson and Isabella Stewart Gardner, 1887–1924, with Correspondence by Mary Berenson,* ed. Rollin van N. Hadley (1987). Morris Carter's *Isabella Stewart Gardner and Fenway Court* (1925) provides firsthand details of Gardner's life by one who knew her and is extensively documented with quotations from family papers. A primary biography is Louise Hall Tharp, *Mrs. Jack: A Biography of Isabella Stewart* (1965). *Town Topics* covered Gardner's active social life from 1885 forward. Sylvester Baxter, "An American Palace of Art," *Century Magazine,* Jan. 1904, pp. 362–82, gives numerous details on the building of the Gardner Museum. Eleanor Palffy, *The Lady and the Painter* (1951), is a fictionalized account of Gardner and John Singer Sargent. An obituary is in the *New York Times,* 18 July 1924.

MARTIN R. KALFATOVIC

GARDNER, John (21 July 1933–14 Sept. 1982), writer and teacher, was born John Champlin Gardner, Jr., in Batavia, New York, the son of John Champlin Gardner, a farmer, and Priscilla Jones, a teacher. Gardner's father could recite Shakespeare by the page. While milking his cows, he would listen to his wife read from the plays and would speak his favorite parts from memory. Priscilla Gardner was of Welsh stock, and her son took pride in this heritage. Gardner was keenly interested in music. His father would give him and the other farmhands Saturday afternoons off to listen to the Metropolitan Opera, and in time Gardner took French horn lessons in nearby Rochester. He became a good musician.

Gardner's childhood, however, was not wholly idyllic. When he was eleven, his six-year-old brother died in a farming accident for which Gardner held himself responsible. Gardner had been pulling a two-ton cultipacker behind a tractor, and his brother, riding behind, fell off and was crushed. Gardner's story "Redemption," which appears in *The Art of Living and Other Stories* (1981), is a largely unaltered account of the accident and its aftermath, and Gardner's lifelong sense of guilt might even have shaped his depiction of that "spawn of Cain," the *Beowulf* monster, in *Grendel* (1971).

Gardner attended DePauw University (1951–1953), where at first he studied chemistry. Presently he turned to English and philosophy. On completion of his sophomore year (1953) he married Joan Louise Patterson, a second cousin, and transferred to Washington University in St. Louis, where he received his A.B. in 1955. With a Woodrow Wilson fellowship, he began graduate work at the University of Iowa (1955–1958), where he studied medieval literature and creative writing. Gardner's dissertation novel, *The Old Men,* has not been published, but part of his M.A. thesis, a set of four short fictions, would later be reshaped as one of his most popular novels, *Nickel Mountain* (1973).

On taking his doctorate in 1958, Gardner was still years from success as a writer. Before the appearance of *The Resurrection* in 1966, he held academic posts at several colleges and universities, including Oberlin, Chico State College, San Francisco State, and Southern Illinois University. He taught creative writing and medieval literature, and he produced some substantial scholarly publications, notably a 1962 textbook *The Forms of Fiction,* on which he collaborated with Lennis Dunlap, and *The Complete Works of the Gawain-Poet* (1965). After his career as a novelist began to go well (*The Wreckage of Agathon* appeared in 1970; *Grendel,* a succès d'estime, the following year; and *The Sunlight Dialogues,* his first popular success, in 1972), he continued his existence as increasingly distinguished academic gypsy, teaching at the University of Detroit, Northwestern, Bennington, Williams, Skidmore, and George Mason. He also taught regularly at the Bread Loaf Writers' Conference. By this time, he was winning an impressive array of fellowships and other honors: in addition to the Woodrow Wilson, he won a Danforth (1970), a National Endowment for the Arts grant (1972), and a Guggenheim (1973) before becoming a member of the American Academy of Arts and Letters (1975). His novel *October Light,* published in 1976, received the National Book Critics Circle Award the following year. In 1978 his academic odyssey ended when he accepted a position as director of creative writing at the State University of New York at Binghamton.

Gardner was a bundle of energetic contradictions. His friend Nicholas Delbanco recalls him at their first meeting as "a short, pot-bellied, pipe-smoking man" who "emptied a quart of vodka before he sat to eat." He worked hard, loved hard, drank hard—yet never seemed the cliché of the artistic temperament these phrases imply. "John was an extremely complex personality," novelist Joyce Carol Oates has observed, "like a character out of a Dostoyevski novel." He projected himself into his works as both hero and outlaw, for he simultaneously respected order and bohemian excess: "I am on the one hand a kind of New York State Republican, conservative," he once remarked. "On the other hand, I am a kind of bohemian type. I really don't obey the laws. I mean to, but if I am in a hurry and there is no parking here, I park." Occasionally suicidal, he maintained an extraordinary discipline that allowed him to produce a large body of good work in virtually every genre: short stories, novels, children's books, opera libretti, lyric and epic poetry, film scenarios, and radio and stage plays. He was by all accounts a fine and generous teacher, even after he no longer had to teach.

Gardner's last years were troubled. Though he battled successfully against colon cancer, he could not prevail against the Internal Revenue Service, which charged him $500,000 in back taxes and penalties. He also suffered indifferent or hostile reviews of his last major novels, *Freddy's Book* (1980) and *Mickelsson's Ghosts* (1982). The critical contumely may have derived in part from Gardner's incautious attacks on the entire literary establishment in the highly polemical *On Moral Fiction* (1978). In this still controversial book, Gardner took his most widely respected contemporaries to task for what he construed as their literary gamesmanship, their modish despair, and their failure to create myths by which their readers might live, rather than die. For Gardner, throughout his career, "moral fiction" was that which produced models of heroism and virtue, not that which endlessly rehearsed existential negativism.

After four years of separation from his wife, he divorced her in 1980 to marry Liz Rosenberg. This union lasted—legally—until shortly before his death. He died in a motorcycle accident near Susquehanna, Pennsylvania, only days before he was to have married Susan Thornton. Work in press at the time of his death continued to appear for about four years: *On Becoming a Novelist* in 1983, *The Art of Fiction* the following year, and finally, as a single volume, a fictional record of the author's first marriage, *Stillness,* and an unfinished novel, *Shadows* (1986). Also posthumously published were collaborative translations of stories by Kikuo Itaya (*Tengu Child,* with Nobuko Tsukui, in 1983) and, with John Maier, of the Babylonian epic *Gilgamesh* (1984).

American literary life is replete with careers that prove inconsequential in retrospect. But if, in the years since his death, Gardner has registered less robustly on our critical instruments than he did during his life, he may yet demonstrate the kind of staying power reserved to writers who eschew the literary fashions of their times, writers who strive to engage not narrow political or ideological ends but what William Faulkner called "the old verities and truths of the heart." Gardner left a large and varied body of carefully crafted work. As his own Beowulf says, he will "burn green" again.

• Published works not mentioned above include *Jason and Medeia* (1973), *The Construction of the Wakefield Cycle* (1974), *The King's Indian: Stories and Tales* (1974), *Dragon, Dragon and Other Tales* (1975), *Gudgekin the Thistle Girl and Other Tales* (1976), *A Child's Bestiary* (1977), *In the Suicide Mountains* (1977), *The King of the Hummingbirds and Other Tales* (1977), *The Life and Times of Chaucer* (1977), *Poems* (1978), *The Poetry of Chaucer* (1977), *Rumpelstiltskin* (1978), *Death and the Maiden* (1979), *Frankenstein* (1979), *William Wilson* (1979), and *The Temptation Game* (1980). Gardner's papers are in the John Gardner Collection at the University of Rochester Library, Department of Rare Books and Special Collections, Rochester, N.Y. Useful chronologies appear in John M. Howell, *John Gardner: A Bibliographical Profile* (1980); Jeff Henderson, *John Gardner: A Study of the Short Fiction* (1990); and Allan Chavkin, ed., *Conversations with John Gardner* (1990), which also features abundant biographical detail in its twenty interviews and articles based on interviews. Major critical studies include David Cowart, *Arches and Light: The Fiction of John Gardner* (1983); Gregory L. Morris, *A World of Order and Light: The Fiction of John Gardner* (1984); and Leonard Butts, *The Novels of John Gardner* (1988). There are also three collections of critical essays: Robert A. Morace and Kathryn VanSpanckeren, eds., *John Gardner: Critical Perspectives* (1982); Beatrice Mendez-Egle, ed., *John Gardner: True Art, Moral Art* (1983); and Jeff Henderson, ed., *Thor's Hammer: Essays on John Gardner* (1985). For bibliography, in addition to Howell, see Robert A. Morace, *John Gardner: An Annotated Secondary Bibliography* (1984). An obituary appears in the *New York Times,* 15 Sept. 1982.

DAVID COWART

GARDNER, Julia Anna (26 Jan. 1882–15 Nov. 1960), geologist, paleoecologist, and fossil mollusc taxonomist, was born in Chamberlain, South Dakota, the daughter of Charles Henry Gardner, a physician, and Julia M. Brackett, a schoolteacher. She had seven half siblings through her father's first marriage but was the only child of his second marriage. When Gardner was four months old, her father died. She and her mother lived in Chamberlain until 1895, then moved to her mother's family home in Dixon, Illinois. In 1898 they moved to Massachusetts, then later to Vermont.

With the support of an inheritance from her grandmother, Gardner studied geology and paleontology at Bryn Mawr College. She was greatly encouraged to continue her studies by her teachers and was inspired by her fellow students, many of whom she worked with throughout her life. She graduated from Bryn Mawr College in 1905, received her A.M. there in 1907, and received her Ph.D. in geology from Johns Hopkins University in 1911. She was a member of Phi Beta Kappa. Gardner's work focused on detailed studies of the interpretation of Tertiary molluscs of the Atlantic and Gulf coasts. Her doctoral thesis was titled, "On Certain Families of Gasteropoda from the Miocene and Pliocene of Virginia and North Carolina." She remained until 1915 as a research assistant in paleontology at Johns Hopkins University, where she launched her career as an expert taxonomist and paleoecologist focusing on several groups of molluscs from the Paleocene to the Eocene.

Gardner provided service during both world wars. During the first, following the death of her mother, she assisted in the war effort as an ambulance driver with the American Red Cross American Hospitals Unit in France from 1917 to 1919. After the war, she continued with the American Friends Service Committee until she was injured on the job in an accident in 1919. Her service during World War II was in the provision of strategic and tactical information as a member of the Military Geology Unit of the United States Geological Survey (USGS), supported by the Army Corps of Engineers. She was able to contribute knowledge of precisely which beaches in Japan were being used by the Japanese to send balloon bombs that were designed to set fires in the forests of the Pacific Northwest of the United States. She did this by identifying the shells within the sand of the ballast of the balloons.

Following her injury in World War I, Gardner returned to the United States and was immediately hired, in 1920, as a paleontologist by the USGS. In 1920–1924 she worked on a mapping project in the lower part of Texas, the Rio Grande area, providing information on Eocene invertebrates. She was considered a leading paleontologist, was highly regarded by her colleagues, and was promoted to associate geologist with the USGS in 1924, then geologist in 1928.

As a result of her work during World War II, Gardner was invited by the Office of the Chief of Engineers to engage with a team mapping the geology of many of the islands of the Western Pacific. Her work, once again focused on the Cenozoic mollusc, was enhanced by studies of living animals in the area. Her research on the biotas, paleoecology, and sedimentary rocks of the Atlantic Coastal Plain area through Texas and north of Mexico proved of economic importance as petroleum geologists looked for markers of large-scale stratigraphic sections containing rocks from the Tertiary. Her work on molluscan faunas from the Paleocene and Eocene had significant impact internationally. It was valuable to petroleum geologists in setting standard sections for Tertiary rocks in the southern Caribbean. Gardner was a renowned mentor, who generously encouraged and aided many geologists throughout her life.

Gardner was a coauthor of the major work, *Correlation of the Cenozoic Formations of the Atlantic and Gulf Coastal Plain and the Caribbean Region* (1943), with C. Wythe Cooke and Wendell Woodring. Between 1915 and 1957, she was the author or coauthor of five major reports and more than forty government reports and articles in scientific journals.

Gardner was the recipient of many honors and awards. The Department of the Interior awarded her its Distinguished Service Honor Award in 1952. She was elected president of the Paleontological Society in 1952 and was vice president of the Geological Society of America in 1953. She was a member of numerous professional organizations, including the American Association for the Advancement of Science. Gardner, who never married, died of a major stroke at her home in Bethesda, Maryland, having suffered several previous minor strokes and artheriosclerosis for many years.

• Some of Gardner's papers (many were destroyed after her death) are in the following collections: Bryn Mawr College Archives; Ferdinand Hamburger, Jr., Archives, Johns Hopkins University; Florence Bascom Papers, Sophia Smith Collection, Smith College; and Tasker Howard Bliss (Additional) Papers, Library of Congress. Gardner's *The Mollusca of the Tertiary Formations of Northeast Mexico* was published as Memoir 11 of the Geological Society of America in 1945. Gardner recalled events in her field work for the USGS in "Notes on Travel and Life," *Johns Hopkins University Alumni Magazine* (Apr. 1940). Her life and work are discussed in Margaret W. Rossiter, *Women Scientists in America: Struggles and Strategies to 1940* (1982), and Lois Barber Arnold, *Four Lives in Science: Women's Education in the Nineteenth Century* (1984). See also the biography by H. S. Ladd in the *Geological Society of America Proceedings* (1960). An obituary is in the *New York Times*, 16 Nov. 1960.

BONNIE SHAPIRO

GARDNER, Leroy Upson (9 Dec. 1888–24 Oct. 1946), physician, was born in New Britain, Connecticut, the son of Irving Isaac Gardner, a real estate and insurance broker, and Inez Baldwin Upson. As a boy, Gardner attended the public schools of Meriden, Connecticut. He then went to Yale University in nearby New Haven, receiving a B.A. in 1912. He proceeded to the Yale School of Medicine and graduated in 1914 with an M.D. Gardner pursued an interest in pathology by accepting a three-year internship at Boston City Hospital, where he worked under the guidance of Frank B. Mallory, professor of pathology at Harvard Medical School. During Gardner's final year there, 1916–1917, Mallory secured a concurrent appointment for him as instructor in pathology at Harvard Medical School.

In the fall of 1917 Gardner was invited back to Yale as an assistant professor of pathology. His first year on the faculty was interrupted by the military mobilization that accompanied America's entry into World War I. Late in 1917 Gardner was commissioned a first lieutenant in the Army Medical Corps and assigned to duty at Camp Devens in Massachusetts, but after only a short time there he was diagnosed with pulmonary tuberculosis and discharged from military service. Gardner sought therapy for his condition at the Trudeau Sanatorium near Saranac Lake, New York, which had become famous as a model for the fresh-air treatment of tuberculosis pioneered by its founder, Edward L. Trudeau.

By the spring of 1918 Gardner began to regain his health and was eager to join in the exciting investigations taking place in Saranac Laboratory, the tuberculosis research branch of Trudeau's medical establishment. While still a patient, Gardner won a Trudeau Foundation Fellowship in April 1918. Within a year Gardner's medical condition had shown sufficient improvement—and Gardner himself had demonstrated ample research talent—that he earned a position as a staff pathologist at the Saranac Laboratory. He would maintain his association with the Trudeau Foundation until his death almost three decades later. In coming to Saranac Lake first as a tuberculosis patient and remaining there as a physician, Gardner was following the path of several prominent predecessors, including Trudeau himself, Edward R. Baldwin, and Lawrason Brown.

Soon after Gardner began working at the Saranac Laboratory, he became interested in the sharp contrast between the high tuberculosis death rate among Vermont granite cutters, and the much lower incidence of tuberculosis among marble cutters. He carried out ingenious experiments with guinea pigs that clearly pointed to the presence of silica in granite dust as the culprit in activating the latent tuberculosis prevalent in the population. Gardner's first report on this research, published in the *American Review of Tuberculosis* in 1920, quickly established him as an expert on the medical dangers associated with the inhalation of silica. Gardner continued to build on this research throughout his career and gained a worldwide reputation as an authority on the hazards faced by workers in dusty places of employment.

As David Rosner and Gerald Markowitz explain in their historical examination of silicosis, *Deadly Dust*, the workplace hazards of dust became an issue in the labor strife of the 1930s. Gardner viewed himself as a neutral expert in struggles between managers and workers, but he and Saranac Laboratory, which sought research funding from industrial patrons, were viewed as less than neutral by some contemporaries. Rosner and Markowitz place Gardner squarely in the management corner in these battles; however, a posthumous tribute published in the *Labor Union* suggests that Gardner was more sympathetic to the labor position in struggles over the dusty dangers of the workplace. Gardner was referred to as "a man who never carried a union card, but who nevertheless was one of the unsung heroes of the labor movement" (quoted in *Occupational Medicine* 4 [1947]: 6–7).

Gardner's reputation soon extended beyond his laboratory, and his level of responsibility at the Trudeau complex increased as well. In 1927 he was named director of the Saranac Laboratory, and in 1938 he became director of the Trudeau Foundation and a trustee of the Trudeau Sanatorium. His bibliography included more than fifty publications, including a major textbook written with Edward R. Baldwin and S. A. Petroff, *Tuberculosis: Bacteriology, Pathology, and Laboratory Diagnosis* (1927). He won a number of awards and honors for his work, including the Trudeau Medal from the National Tuberculosis Association in 1935 for his investigations on dust-induced disease, and the

Knudson Award of the American Association of Industrial Physicians and Surgeons in 1940 for outstanding achievement in industrial medicine.

Gardner died suddenly of a heart attack in Saranac Lake at the height of his professional influence. He was survived by his wife, Carabelle McKenzie, whom he had married in 1915, and their two children.

• A number of biographical tributes to Gardner by colleagues appeared on the occasion of his death, including a piece by Edward R. Baldwin in *American Review of Tuberculosis* 54 (1946): 585–87, and several published together in *Occupational Medicine* 4 (1947): 1–12, with a complete bibliography of Gardner's publications, pp. 13–16. Gardner is also given attention in David Rosner and Gerald Markowitz, *Deadly Dust: Silicosis and the Politics of Occupational Disease in Twentieth-century America* (1991). Obituaries are in the *New York Times*, 25 Oct. 1946, and the *Journal of the American Medical Association* 132 (1946): 532.

JON M. HARKNESS

GARDNER, Mary Sewall (5 Feb. 1871–20 Feb. 1961), pioneer of public health nursing, was born in Newton, Massachusetts, the daughter of William Sewall Gardner and Mary Thornton, a descendant of Matthew Thornton, who had signed the Declaration of Independence. Gardner graduated from Miss Porter's School in Farmington, Connecticut, in 1890. Years later, she attended Newport Hospital Training School for Nurses, in Rhode Island, and graduated cum laude in 1905.

Immediately after graduation, Gardner became the director of the Providence District Nursing Association, a small public health nursing agency in Providence, Rhode Island. She held the position from 1905 until her retirement in 1931, with a leave of absence during and after World War I. The expanding agency made numerous contributions to the field of public health nursing and Gardner became a national and international adviser on public health nursing administration and techniques.

In her book *Public Health Nursing* (1916), Gardner estimated that there were only 300 public health (also called district or visiting) nurses in the country in 1900 but that they had become popular figures and their numbers had expanded dramatically by 1910. Nursing care provided to patients at home was sufficiently different from that given in hospitals that the two national nursing organizations, the American Nurses' Association (ANA) and the American Society of Superintendents of Training Schools (which became the National League of Nursing Education [NLNE] in 1912), began to push for national standards for public health nursing. In 1911 the two organizations appointed a joint committee, with Gardner as secretary, to examine whether a new organization for nurses was needed. Some nursing leaders were opposed, but Gardner obtained support for a new organization from M. Adelaide Nutting, the most prominent leader in nursing at the time.

Gardner invited 800 agencies that employed public health nurses to send representatives to a meeting at the joint convention of ANA and NLNE in Chicago in 1912. At the meeting, Gardner issued an appeal for a new national organization, and, after two days of heated discussion, the new National Organization of Public Health Nursing was founded with Lillian Wald as president. Gardner served as the organization's first secretary and was on the board of directors. In 1913 she became president of NOPHN, a position she held until 1916.

NOPHN not only established national standards for public health nurses but also developed instructional courses and recruited more nurses into the public health nursing field. It also organized voluntary and official agencies to make better use of visiting nurses. According to Isabel M. Stewart, another prominent nursing figure, NOPHN's influence on the expansion of the nursing profession cannot be overestimated (Stewart and Austin, p. 210).

When Gardner's *Public Health Nursing* appeared in 1916, it represented the first and only text in the field for many years. The work became a classic and was translated into French, Chinese, Spanish, and Japanese, influencing public health nurses around the world. Gardner's second revised edition appeared in 1924 and the third and final edition was published in 1936. Gardner adapted a regional nursing journal, *Cleveland Visiting Nurses' Quarterly*, into *Public Health Nurse*, the monthly journal of NOPHN, and over her career wrote more than fifty articles for numerous professional journals.

Not all physicians believed that public health nurses contributed positively to health care; many perceived them to be interfering. To counter this negative attitude, Gardner urged public health nurses to support the physician's authority and not usurp his or her responsibilities. She advised that public health nurses "should not diagnose, should not prescribe, should not recommend a particular doctor or a change of doctors, should not suggest a hospital to a patient without the concurrence of the doctor, and should never criticize, by word or unspoken action, any member of the medical profession" (Kalisch and Kalisch, p. 414).

In 1917 Gardner took a leave of absence from the Providence District Nursing Association to assist the American Red Cross in developing its public health nursing service, Town and Country Nursing Service, and served as its temporary director. She was released early from this assignment to serve with the American Red Cross commission on tuberculosis in Italy as director of its nursing department from 1917 to 1919.

In 1920 Gardner worked for the American Red Cross as a special adviser on child health programs and visited many European countries. She advocated three separate phases in schoolchildren's health: periodic examinations to determine who needed medical care; periodic examinations to identify vision or dental defects and heart murmurs; and a policy of prevention. In addition, Gardner served as chairperson of the public health nursing section of the International Council of Nurses and on numerous other national and international public health nursing committees, including NLNE's public health education subcommittee, representing NOPHN.

Upon retirement in 1931, Gardner was made honorary director of the Providence District Nurse Association, honorary president of NOPHN, and was awarded the Walter Burns Saunders Medal for distinguished nursing service. She was a fellow of the American Public Health Association (which succeeded NOPHN) and a member of the board and executive committee of the American Social Hygiene Association. Gardner continued to write, publishing *So Build We* (1942), a book on public health nursing administration, and *Katharine Kent* (1946), a book that includes many of her own experiences. In 1986 she was elected to the American Nurses' Association Nursing Hall of Fame, a tribute to the exemplary career of one of the nation's foremost nursing leaders, particularly in the field of public health nursing. Gardner, who never married, died in Providence, Rhode Island.

• Gardner's papers are located at the Schlesinger Library, Radcliffe College, Cambridge, Mass. In addition to her books, Gardner wrote articles for *Public Health Nurse*, *American Journal of Nursing*, *Modern Hospital*, *Pacific Coast Journal of Nursing*, and *Visiting Nurse Quarterly* from 1912 to 1937, as well as for *National League of Nursing Education: Biographic Sketches, 1937–1940* (1940). No biography or autobiography of Gardner exists, although Sophie Nelson provides a cursory look at Gardner's life and work in "Mary Sewall Gardner," *Nursing Outlook* (1953): 54. Secondary sources that touch on Gardner are M. Louise Fitzpatrick, *The National Organization for Public Health Nursing* (1975); Grace L. Deloughery, *History and Trends of Professional Nursing* (1977); and Ellen Condliffe Lagemann, ed., *Nursing History: New Perspectives, New Possibilities* (1983). See also M. Patricia Donahue, *Nursing, the Finest Art: An Illustrated History* (1985); Minnie Goodnow, *Outlines of Nursing History* (1939); Philip A. Kalisch and Beatrice J. Kalisch, *The Advance of American Nursing* (1986); Susan M. Reverby, *Ordered to Care: The Dilemma of American Nursing, 1850–1945* (1987); Mary M. Roberts, *American Nursing: History and Interpretation* (1954); and Isabel M. Stewart and Anne L. Austin, *A History of Nursing: From Ancient to Modern Times, a World View* (1962), for briefer mentions.

CONNIE L. REEVES

GAREY, Thomas Andrew (7 July 1830–20 Aug. 1909), citriculturist and land developer, was born in Cincinnati, Ohio, the son of Samuel Garey, a physician, and Margaret Wringer. Little is known about his childhood, except that his family lived in Hagerstown, Maryland, for several years, eventually moving to Iowa in 1847. By age twenty Garey was living in Independence, Missouri, at which time he left with a group of travelers bound for California. In the fall of 1850, however, Garey abandoned the group in Albuquerque, New Mexico, when he met Louise Josephine Smith, whom he married on 27 October 1850. The couple had seven children who survived infancy.

In July 1852 the Gareys journeyed to California. After spending several weeks in San Diego, they moved north to the sparsely populated valleys east of the then small town of Los Angeles, where between 1852 and

1865 they unsuccessfully attempted to farm several different lots in the region. Garey finally achieved success in farming in 1865 when the state of California voted to subsidize the production of silk and mulberry trees. Consequently, he quickly turned a 65-acre ranch in Los Angeles into a thriving nursery business.

Although Garey promptly emerged as the region's leading grower of mulberry trees and silk, his interests soon turned to the development of citrus products. The switch was fortuitous, for in 1869 the California legislature ended its support of silk and mulberry farming, effectively collapsing the industry. By 1870 Garey had become a noted local citriculturist and would soon introduce several new citrus products including the St. Michael's orange, the Mediterranean Sweet, and the Eureka lemon, the latter product quickly becoming one of the state's most significant agricultural commodities. Garey's nursery empire rapidly enlarged to encompass several different nurseries including a 210-acre venture called the Cooperative Nursery and Fruit Company of Los Angeles, and by the early 1870s his annual income had reached a high of $80,000.

Garey's interest in his citrus ventures quickly expanded to California agriculture in general. He helped to establish the Southern California Horticultural Society and was an instrumental figure in the Los Angeles Pomological Society, a group concerned with the development of the fruit industry. Garey also played a pivotal role in the formation of the California Grange, serving as Los Angeles's representative at its founding in 1873 and later launching several Grange chapters throughout Los Angeles County.

Garey's involvement in agricultural development meshed well with land development, another local industry coming to life in the early 1870s. As southern Californians awaited the establishment of a transcontinental railroad link, which was finally completed in 1876, land speculation dominated the interests of local residents with capital. Garey used his nursery profits to buy land and in 1874 helped to found the Los Angeles Immigration and Land Cooperative Association, also serving as the organization's first president. The group's initial project was the development of a parcel of land in southeastern California County. The resulting creation and subsequent success of the community of Artesia led Garey and his associates to turn to another venture in eastern Los Angeles County, named after the Roman goddess of fruit, Pomona. Garey lavishly helped to cultivate the tract by planting thousands of trees along its primary thoroughfare, which became known as "Garey Avenue."

The mid-1870s proved to be the zenith of Garey's entrepreneurial successes. His citrus ventures fell on hard times during the late 1870s after repeated freezes decimated his orchards. In 1880 he also lost control of his nurseries, although he continued to dabble in the business for many years in various associations with others.

Just as the citrus industry began to collapse, Garey's Pomona venture also fell through. In 1876 one of the banks involved in the deal failed in a chain reaction set off by the now legendary Comstock Lode mining scandal in Nevada. The following year a fire destroyed much of the town, and in 1881 Garey's land association lost control of the property.

While struggling to free himself from these financial setbacks, Garey returned to prominence in 1882 within the agricultural industry with the publication of his *Orange Culture in California* (1882). In the text Garey laid out the fundamentals of citrus farming, writing, "A lover by nature of the beautiful in horticulture, I have applied myself assiduously to assist in developing the latent interests of the business of citrus culture" (p. 5). The 227-page practical guide to citrus farming offered aspiring growers detailed instruction in the selection, planting, and care of citrus.

Garey spent his remaining years in different land and nursery ventures in various parts of southern California. Many of his later activities were in Santa Barbara County, where a town bearing his name was founded in 1877. Although none of his later ventures succeeded in a significant way (even the town of Garey itself ultimately failed), Garey spent his final years in comfort. Having been a pioneer nurseryman in the region, the developer of several critical local agricultural products, and the author of one of the first texts on citrus farming, Garey played an important role in founding what would be two of southern California's most pivotal early industries.

• Primary materials related to Garey's life can be found at the Huntington Library, San Marino, Calif., and the Pomona Public Library. For further information on Garey and his activities, see Gloria Ricci Lothrop, *Pomona: A Centennial History* (1988); James M. Jensen, "Thomas Andrew Garey," *Pomona Valley Historian* 5 (July 1969): 115–19; Christine Holt, "The Los Angeles Immigration and Land Cooperative Association," *Pomona Valley Historian* 9 (Winter 1973): 1–30.

CLARK DAVIS

GARFIELD, Harry Augustus (11 Oct. 1863–12 Dec. 1942), lawyer, educator, and public official, was born in Hiram, Ohio, the son of James A. Garfield, the twentieth president of the United States, and Lucretia Rudolph. A witness to the fatal shooting of his father in 1881, Garfield grappled with the implications of that tragedy for the rest of his life. He earned a B.A. at Williams College, 1881–1885, and after teaching briefly at St. Paul's, a private school for boys, he studied law at Columbia University, 1886–1887, and in England at Oxford University and the Inns of Court, 1887–1888. In the latter year he married Belle H. Mason; they had four children.

In 1888 Garfield established in Cleveland a law partnership with his younger brother, James Rudolph Garfield. He immersed himself in local business affairs, organized the Cleveland Trust Company, invested in railroads and coal properties in southeastern Ohio, and taught contracts at Western Reserve University Law School, 1892–1895. A founding member of both the Cleveland Chamber of Commerce (1893) and the Cleveland Municipal Association (1896), he supported the cause of civil service reform, including reorganization of the nation's consular service.

During his late thirties, Garfield began to lose interest in business and legal activities. He rejected a career in national party politics, despite his family heritage, yet wanted a role in public affairs. In 1903 Woodrow Wilson opened a path by inviting him to join Princeton University as a professor of government. Garfield shared Wilson's patrician belief in training privileged young men in the liberal arts for leadership in community and national affairs. Five years later Garfield became president of Williams College, a position he held until his retirement in 1934.

Garfield also shared Wilson's hopes for the power of education to create a better society. In his public philosophy, however, Garfield aimed less to increase entrepreneurial opportunity and economic competition than to discover new forms of economic cooperation and institutional coordination. The outbreak of the European war in August 1914 reinforced this quest. Garfield regarded the crisis as a turning point in U.S. and European history and as conclusive proof of the destructive force of individualism and competition in modern life. "We have come to the parting of the ways," Garfield told the Economic Club of Boston in January 1917. "We have come to the time when the old individualistic principle of competition must be set aside and we must boldly embark upon the new principle of cooperation and combination."

Although Garfield was ambivalent about the U.S. declaration of war on 7 April 1917, he retained his faith in Wilson and responded to the call. In July 1917 he joined a committee affiliated with Herbert Hoover's (1874–1964) proposed Food Administration to recommend a government-guaranteed price for wheat production. In August 1917 he accepted Wilson's personal request to head the U.S. Fuel Administration.

Throughout his tenure as fuel administrator (Aug. 1917–Jan. 1919), Garfield championed the values of cooperation and coordination among coal mine owners and workers and between the coal industry and government. As a key administrator in the sudden expansion of emergency government in wartime Washington, he encountered bitter criticism from congressmen who resented administrative disruption of traditional political and economic relationships. He also bore the brunt of public outrage over the administration's decision, announced on 17 January 1918, to close down all factory production east of the Mississippi for a week and for a specified number of Mondays thereafter as a way to free transport for coal supplies.

Garfield and his organization did facilitate coal distribution, and they did bring order to the nation's coalfields. Rising fuel demand provided a congenial environment for negotiations among business, labor, and government, as did Garfield's recruitment to Washington of coal trade association personnel and of representatives of the United Mine Workers. Wartime made him optimistic about the permanent application to industrial affairs of labor-management and business-government cooperation.

Garfield advocated cooperation after the armistice, 11 November 1918. He lobbied successfully to have the fuel administration retained until June 1919. More ambitious still, he urged Wilson to reorganize the federal branch and, on the model of the fuel administration, create supervisory commissions for key commodities led by management and labor representatives and a presidentially appointed director. Garfield had no success with this initiative nor with a subsequent effort to have the fuel administration revived as a way to defuse accelerating tension between the federal government and the United Mine Workers. In the fall of 1919 fraying wartime wage agreements gave way to bitter strikes, and in December 1919 Garfield, having rejoined the administration in late October, officially resigned from the Wilson administration.

Unlike many of his wartime administrative colleagues, Garfield received no invitation to accompany the president to Paris for postwar negotiations, but his commitment to Wilson and to Wilsonian ideals remained. He kept the internationalist faith both during the unsuccessful fight for Senate passage of the Versailles treaty and throughout the interwar years.

In 1921 Garfield combined his international views with his long-standing belief in education to found the Institute of Politics at Williams College. With funding from fellow Wilsonians and the Carnegie Corporation, the institute met over twelve summers and provided a forum for academics, editors, and government officials from the United States and abroad to discuss the issues of the day. In 1923 Garfield expanded his role in an interwar network of internationalist organizations by becoming president of the American Society of International Law. In 1930 he joined the board of trustees of the World Peace Federation and subsequently chaired its Committee on Implementation of the Kellogg-Briand Pact.

An idealistic, even utopian, quality pervaded Garfield's views. He exemplified the genteel reformer's hope that enlightened leadership by people of goodwill could resolve domestic and international conflict. He underestimated the limits set on good intentions by class conflict, interest group politics, and national calculations of competitive advantage. Yet he never succumbed to postwar disillusionment. His willingness to consider experiments in voluntary economic planning separated him from more traditional individualists among his generation of reformers, and he continued to hope for the application of cooperative principles to domestic and foreign affairs. He died in Williamstown, Massachusetts.

• Garfield's papers are in the Manuscript Division, Library of Congress, Washington, D.C. For appreciative biographical accounts by Garfield's daughter, see Lucretia G. Comer, *Strands from the Weaving* (1959) and *Harry Garfield's First Forty Years: Man of Action in a Troubled World* (1965). Useful studies of Garfield and the U.S. Fuel Administration include Robert Cuff, "Harry Garfield, the Fuel Administration, and the Search for a Cooperative Order during World War I," *American Quarterly* 30 (1978): 39–53; James P. Johnson, "The Wilsonians as War Managers: Coal and the 1917–18

Winter Crisis," *Prologue* 9 (1977): 193–208, and *The Politics of Soft Coal: The Bituminous Industry from World War I through the New Deal* (1979), chaps. 2–4; and John G. Clark, *Energy and the Federal Government: Fossil Fuel Policies, 1900–1946* (1987), chap. 3. See also Warren F. Kuehl, *Biographical Dictionary of Internationalists* (1983).

ROBERT D. CUFF

GARFIELD, James Abram (19 Nov. 1831–19 Sept. 1881), twentieth president of the United States, was born in Orange township (now Moreland Hills) in the Western Reserve region of northern Ohio, the son of Abram Garfield and Eliza Ballou, farmers. After his father's death in 1833, James was brought up amid rural poverty by his strong-willed mother. The hardships of those early years would later provide grist for campaign biographers, including Horatio Alger, who transformed Garfield's log-cabin birth and his brief stint as a canal boy into political legend.

Conversion, at age eighteen, to the Disciples of Christ gave young Garfield a sense of self-worth; education, especially in classical languages, gave him his first vocation. In 1851 he entered the Western Reserve Eclectic Institute (now Hiram College), and three years later he enrolled at Williams College in Massachusetts, receiving his A.B. in 1856.

After graduation, Garfield returned to Hiram as professor of ancient languages, and in 1857 he was named president of the tiny school. In 1858 he married Lucretia Rudolph. They had seven children, five of whom survived infancy. He was ordained a minister in the Disciples church and studied law but found himself strongly drawn to politics, even though his church frowned on such "carnal" activity. Elected as a Republican to the Ohio legislature in 1859, he expressed antislavery views in the heated debates during the secession crisis. When that crisis exploded into the Civil War, he helped recruit the Forty-second Ohio Volunteer Infantry and was commissioned colonel of the regiment.

His first assignment was in eastern Kentucky to counter a small Confederate force led by Brigadier General Humphrey Marshall. Marshall's invasion was already floundering, and after an inconclusive skirmish at Middle Creek on 10 January 1862, the Confederates withdrew, leaving Garfield in control of eastern Kentucky. It was a modest triumph, but at this stage of the Civil War even small victories were welcome. Garfield was rewarded with considerable acclaim as well as a promotion to brigadier general. In April 1862 he was given command of a brigade, just in time to participate in the last stage of the battle of Shiloh.

These military laurels helped boost Garfield's political stock. Although he had a lifelong aversion to "place-seeking" and consistently refused to promote his own advancement, his friends had no such scruples. In September 1862 they engineered his nomination for Congress from Ohio's Nineteenth District. In such a solidly Republican district, nomination was tantamount to election, and Garfield won a lopsided triumph, the first of nine consecutive victories.

While waiting for the Thirty-eighth Congress to assemble, Garfield served in the Army of the Cumberland as chief of staff to Major General William S. Rosecrans. In that capacity he planned the skillfully designed Tullahoma campaign of June 1863, which led to the capture of the vital railroad center of Chattanooga, Tennessee. His role in the subsequent Union defeat at Chickamauga on 19–20 September 1863 was ambiguous, but Garfield salvaged his military reputation by leaving the retreating Rosecrans to join General George H. Thomas in his memorable stand at Chickamauga, an act that gave him the aura of a hero and helped earn him a major general's stars.

In December 1863 Garfield resigned his commission to take his seat in Congress. He initially joined the ranks of Republicans who were impatient with President Abraham Lincoln's seemingly cautious moves toward full emancipation, but after the war Garfield's radicalism moderated. Although in 1868 he supported the impeachment of President Andrew Johnson, he felt increasingly uncomfortable in the role of firebrand. His interests shifted to matters of financial policy. He advocated lower tariffs (except for items produced in his district) and was an avid crusader for hard money. He worked tenaciously for these policies on the House Ways and Means Committee and as chairman of the Appropriations Committee during the Forty-second and Forty-third Congresses. In that chairmanship, his capacity for sustained intellectual effort and his ability to form generalized principles from a mass of detail enabled him to exert some congressional control over the previously unchecked spending process and brought him into the inner circle of congressional leadership.

He was assisted in this rise to prominence by a number of personal assets. One was his eloquence, honed by years in the classroom and on the pulpit, which he developed into a crisp, modern style of oratory. Another was his unique blend of amiability and intellectuality. Over six feet tall, fun-loving, and warm-hearted, Garfield was, he ruefully admitted, "a poor hater," unlike his friend James G. Blaine and his rival Roscoe Conkling. At the same time, Garfield retained the scholarly habits he had cultivated as a college professor. Even in the midst of political battles he could find time to study ancient history or translate Goethe and Horace. His judicious temperament, which enabled him to see all sides of a question, was sometimes mistaken for indecisiveness. Ulysses S. Grant scoffed that Garfield lacked "the backbone of an angleworm."

In 1873 Garfield's political career was threatened by a series of scandals. The most damaging was the accusation that he had once accepted stock in the notorious Crédit Mobilier corporation. Although he received only $329 from the transaction and no corrupt intention was firmly established, his reputation was marred by the charge. It was further darkened by his vote in favor of the unpopular retroactive increase of congressional pay (dubbed the "Salary Grab") and by a rumored linkage with the DeGolyer paving contract scandal. After a hard-fought reelection battle in 1874, Garfield was returned to his congressional seat.

Many other Republicans were not so fortunate. For the first time since the Civil War, the Republicans lost control of the House of Representatives. Garfield spent the rest of the decade in the legislative minority while becoming a leading spokesman for his party. In that capacity he was one of the "visiting statesmen" who investigated the disputed Louisiana returns in the election of 1876, and he then sat on the electoral commission that awarded that presidential election to Rutherford B. Hayes. During the Hayes administration, Garfield helped preserve harmony among the fractious congressional Republicans and kept the majority Democrats off balance by skillfully waving the "bloody shirt" of Civil War memories. It was a virtuoso performance but not one congenial to a man who preferred dealing with ideas and issues rather than with personalities.

In January 1880 the Ohio legislature elected Garfield to the U.S. Senate. To smooth his path to the Senate, Garfield had to agree to support Treasury Secretary John Sherman's presidential bid and put aside, for the time being, his own presidential ambitions. At the 1880 Republican National Convention Garfield served as floor manager for Sherman's campaign and even placed his name in nomination.

The convention was sharply divided, reflecting the divisions within the party itself. The "Stalwart" element, led by Roscoe Conkling of New York, looked back with nostalgia to the days of Grant. Appropriately enough, their candidate was Grant himself, now back from his world travels and ready for an unprecedented third term. He was opposed by an assortment of rivals, most notably Sherman and Blaine, who feared that another round of Grant would sink the Republican party. The clear leader on the first ballot, Grant would very likely have been nominated if Garfield had not blocked a Stalwart attempt to impose the unit rule.

For thirty-three ballots the convention remained deadlocked, with Grant unable to secure a majority and his rivals equally unable to unite on an acceptable alternative. On the next ballot, however, the Wisconsin delegation unexpectedly cast sixteen votes for Garfield, who had not even been nominated. Despite Garfield's attempt to withdraw his name, the convention impulsively elected him on the thirty-sixth ballot in an emotional frenzy seldom matched in U.S. politics. Three hundred and six Stalwarts stubbornly stood by Grant to the end and were only partially placated by the selection of one of their number, Chester Alan Arthur of New York, as Garfield's running mate.

Garfield began the presidential campaign as an underdog. Not only was his party deeply divided, but the Democratic candidate, General Winfield Scott Hancock, a hero of Gettysburg, was likely to neutralize the reliable Republican issue of the "bloody shirt." Republican party unity was established by making further concessions to Conkling and by sidestepping the explosive issue of civil service reform. Hancock was attacked at his most vulnerable point: his lack of civilian experience. An unfortunate interview in which Hancock dismissed the tariff as "purely a local question" gave Republicans an opening to exploit their own support for tariff protection. In so doing, they helped reorient Republicans from the party of the Union to the party of prosperity.

Nineteenth-century presidential candidates were not expected to campaign on their own behalf, a convention Garfield evaded by delivering little talks to visiting delegations on the front porch of his Mentor, Ohio, home, "Lawnfield." The candidate's conciliatory personality helped bring Republican factions together, and his inspirational life story provided a text for Republican orators and pamphleteers. Garfield was "the ideal candidate," said outgoing president Hayes, "because he is the ideal self-made man."

By October the tide had turned in Garfield's favor and not even the forged Morey letter, which alleged that Garfield supported importation of Chinese laborers, could prevent his victory in November. Garfield's popular majority over Hancock was less than 0.1 percent of the total votes cast, but he secured 214 electoral votes to Hancock's 155. Except for New Jersey, Nevada, and California, Democratic strength was confined to the former slave-holding states.

Between his election and his inauguration on 4 March 1881, Garfield was occupied with constructing a cabinet that would balance all Republican factions. Blaine was rewarded with the State Department. William Windom of Minnesota was named secretary of the Treasury. The Navy Department was headed by William H. Hunt of Louisiana; the War Department by Robert Todd Lincoln, the martyred president's son; and the Interior Department by Iowa's Samuel J. Kirkwood. Wayne MacVeagh of Pennsylvania was asked to be attorney general, and New York was represented by Postmaster General Thomas James. This last appointment infuriated Conkling, who demanded nothing less for his faction and his state than the Treasury Department. He was so insulted that he, in effect, declared war on the administration.

This unedifying squabble would consume the energies of the brief Garfield presidency. It overshadowed promising activities such as Blaine's efforts to build closer ties with Latin America, Postmaster General James's investigation of the "star route" postal frauds, and Windom's successful refinancing of the federal debt.

The feud with Conkling reached a climax when the president, at Blaine's instigation, nominated Conkling's enemy, Judge William H. Robertson, to be collector of the port of New York. Conkling raised the time-honored principle of senatorial courtesy in attempting to defeat the nomination but to no avail. Finally he and his junior colleague, Thomas Platt, resigned their Senate seats to seek vindication, but they found only further humiliation. Garfield's victory was complete. He had routed his foes, weakened the principle of senatorial courtesy, and revitalized the presidential office.

He had little time to savor his triumph. On 2 July 1881, as Garfield was waiting at the Baltimore and Potomac station for a train to carry him to his summer vacation, a shabby, unhinged religious fanatic named Charles J. Guiteau pumped two .44-caliber bullets into his back. Mortally wounded, the president was carried back to the White House where he slowly wasted away, as an anxious nation hung on the daily medical bulletins from his sick room. In September he was transferred to Elberon, New Jersey, to escape the Washington heat, and there he died.

After a massive funeral in Cleveland, Ohio, Garfield was buried in Lake View Cemetery. Over his tomb a 165-foot-high monument was constructed at a cost of $225,000. This might seem an excessive memorial for a president who served only six months, two of which were spent as a helpless invalid. But in mourning Garfield, Americans were not only honoring a president; they were paying tribute to a man whose life story embodied their own most cherished aspirations.

• The majority of Garfield's papers are at the Library of Congress and are also available on 177 reels of microfilm as part of the Presidents' Papers series. Smaller collections can be found at the Ohio Historical Society in Columbus and the Western Reserve Historical Society in Cleveland. A meticulously annotated edition of Garfield's diaries has been prepared by Harry James Brown and Frederick D. Williams: *The Diary of James A. Garfield* (4 vols., 1967–1981). His most significant speeches and essays can be found in *The Works of James Abram Garfield* (2 vols., 1883), edited by his friend Burke Aaron Hinsdale. Among modern biographies, the most thorough are Margaret Leech and Harry J. Brown, *The Garfield Orbit* (1978), and Allan Peskin, *Garfield* (1978). An intensive look at Garfield's adolescence, placed within the social context of the Western Reserve, can be found in Hendrik Booraem, *The Road to Respectability: James A. Garfield and His World, 1844–1852* (1988). The brief presidential administration receives a thorough review in Justus D. Doenecke, *The Presidencies of James A. Garfield and Chester A. Arthur* (1981). H. Wayne Morgan, *From Hayes to McKinley: National Party Politics, 1877–1896* (1969), provides insight into the politics of Garfield's era.

ALLAN PESKIN

GARFIELD, James Rudolph (17 Oct. 1865–24 Mar. 1950), lawyer and secretary of the interior, was born in Hiram, Ohio, the son of James Abram Garfield, U.S. congressman and, later, twentieth president of the United States, and Lucretia Rudolph. Because his father was dissatisfied with Garfield's educational progress and because the family resided in both Ohio and Washington, D.C., where the elder Garfield served in the House of Representatives, "Jim" Garfield had a variety of educational experiences. In addition to attending public and private schools, he was tutored at home. Although intelligent, he was not intellectually inclined, preferring physical activity to his studies.

The Garfields were a close-knit family with an active social life. Jim and his brother Harry Augustus Garfield, who served many years as president of Williams College and was U.S. fuel administrator during World War I, often accompanied their father during his political travels. In fact, they were with him when Charles Julius Guiteau shot President Garfield in Washington's Baltimore and Potomac Railroad depot on 2 July 1881. That evening Jim Garfield confided in his journal that Harry "was very brave and helped. I was frightened and could do nothing but cry."

Although President Garfield was not wealthy, the residual of his estate, his wife's pension from Congress, and about $500,000 raised by private subscription made it possible for the family to continue their upper-middle-class existence. After his father's death in September, Garfield entered Williams College with his brother Harry. Once again he excelled in social and physical activities, but his studies were uninspired.

After graduation from Williams in 1885, Garfield took more than a year to decide whether to pursue a career in medicine or law. In 1886 he entered Columbia University Law School, attending classes in the afternoons and working in the law offices of Bangs and Stetson in the mornings. Believing that he had learned all that was necessary by January 1888, he left New York and returned to Ohio, where he passed the state bar examination in March. Garfield spent one month as an apprentice lawyer with the firm of Hotze and Adams but left because of a scarcity of work. With his brother Harry, who had also studied law at Columbia and then at Oxford University in England, he formed a law partnership in Cleveland.

At first Garfield handled mostly divorce and criminal cases, which he found repugnant. In time the brothers developed a modest practice in corporate law, often representing insurance and railroad companies. Frederic C. Howe joined the firm in 1898. In 1890 Garfield married Helen Newell, the daughter of the president of the Lake Shore Railroad. They had four children. Garfield settled in Mentor, Ohio, where he began his political career by winning a position on the town council in 1889. The next year he was a delegate to his father's old Nineteenth Congressional District convention, and in 1891 and 1892 he represented Lake County at the Republican State Convention.

Garfield, who said he was a Republican by "birth, association, and principle," was a supporter of "gentlemen reformers," those men derisively called "goo-goos" or "man milliners" by many regulars. He believed that, if decent and upright men were allowed to administer government, most problems in the existing system would disappear. In 1895, despite being ill suited as a campaigner, he was elected to the Ohio State Senate, where he spent two terms allying himself with the Hanna-McKinley wing of the party. While there he authored the Corrupt Practices Act (1896), which passed. He was unsuccessful in efforts to revamp higher education, create a merit system for cities, establish municipal home rule, and pass moderate temperance legislation.

Because of trouble with Mark Hanna over party regularity in 1900, Garfield temporarily faded from the political scene. Midway through the 1890s he had become acquainted with Theodore Roosevelt, and although it was not a frequent relationship, the pair kept in touch. Roosevelt noted in October 1899 that he had "taken a great fancy to young Jim Garfield" (Morison, ed., vol. 2, p. 1089). Thus it was not a complete surprise when President Roosevelt appointed Garfield to the U.S. Civil Service Commission in 1902.

As a commissioner, Garfield helped rewrite civil service rules in a way that made government employees a separate caste, insulated from party and Congress and beholden to executive branch officers. The commission cooperated so successfully with the various agencies of government that, for the first time in U.S. history, the commission's nineteenth annual report pointed to "the spirit of friendly cooperation which exists in all the departments of the government in the enforcement both of the letter and spirit of the civil-service act." The most important thing that Garfield did while a civil service commissioner was cement a lifelong friendship with Roosevelt and become one of his closest confidants, a member of the "tennis cabinet."

In 1903 Roosevelt named Garfield to head the newly created Bureau of Corporations. Garfield's first important investigation was an examination of the so-called "beef trust," and while he was criticized by some for being too lax, his work contributed to legislation providing for meat and factory inspection and tagging. He next responded to a congressional resolution to investigate Standard Oil. During his inquiry he found that the company received secret, lower railroad rates for oil shipments. His efforts began the famous antitrust suit that ultimately led to Standard's dissolution in 1911. But like Roosevelt, Garfield favored regulation of big business over "trust busting," causing the president to describe him as one of "the honest, brave, decent fellows who are trying in practical fashion to realize ideals of good government" (Morison, ed., vol. 5, p. 517).

Soon after the 1904 presidential election, Roosevelt appointed Garfield to the Committee on Department Methods, called the Keep Commission in honor of its chairman, Charles Keep. In fact Garfield and his close associate, Chief Forester Gifford Pinchot, another tennis cabinet member, were the group's driving force. Designated to look into ways to coordinate administrative activities and improve performance in the executive branch, the committee made a variety of recommendations that Congress refused to implement, even though all the suggestions eventually became governmental policy. The Keep Commission also investigated the Department of the Interior and played a role in the transfer of the chief forester's office from Interior to the Department of Agriculture.

In 1907 Roosevelt appointed Garfield secretary of the interior, which department he thoroughly reorganized. The president had appointed him so that with Pinchot he could begin implementing the administration's conservation policies of rational use. Over the next two years the duo developed what they believed was a program that provided orderly and efficient use of natural resources based on scientific planning by trained professionals. They promoted arid land reclamation, waterway improvements, and leasing of na-

tional forest and public domain land for range cattle; withdrew coal, oil, and phosphate lands for classification and investigation; and established national parks. They also worked to protect potential hydroelectric sites until ready for use. To gain public support they held the White House Conservation Conference in May 1908.

Nevertheless, the program was not always popular. Garfield and Pinchot's support for San Francisco's efforts to develop a water reservoir in the Hetch Hetchy Valley of Yosemite National Park caused problems with John Muir and other preservationists. A more strident group of Garfield-Pinchot opponents included western leaders in Congress and other cabinet members, such as Secretary of War William Howard Taft, who disliked the pair's high-handedness. This opposition ultimately proved the most formidable.

In 1909 President-elect Taft replaced Garfield with Richard A. Ballinger as secretary of the interior. Ironically, Garfield had brought Ballinger, a former classmate at Williams College, into government in 1907 as commissioner of the General Land Office, where Ballinger served for one year. Following the general election of 1908, Roosevelt had told Garfield that Taft intended to reappoint him, but in 1910 Taft said, "The reason why I kept Garfield out of the Cabinet was because I knew him" (Pringle, vol. 1, p. 386). By then Garfield, Pinchot, Ballinger, and Taft were involved in a bitter struggle over Alaska coal lands known as the Ballinger-Pinchot affair. Although Taft removed Pinchot as chief forester because of insubordination, the affair was an important factor in bringing Roosevelt into the Republican presidential race in 1912.

Garfield returned to Cleveland as a member of the law firm of Garfield, MacGregor, and Baldwin and remained a senior partner through the firm's various expansions and reorganizations. He tried to secure the Republican nomination for governor in 1910 as leader of the party's progressive wing, but his efforts failed. In 1911 he joined Senator Robert M. La Follette's National Progressive Republican League to oppose Taft's renomination and became a leader of the Progressive-Republican bolt from the GOP following Taft's renomination in 1912.

In 1912 Garfield helped organize the national Progressive party, which nominated Roosevelt for president in Chicago. Garfield created its Ohio branch, chairing the state convention and giving the keynote address. He ran as its candidate for governor in 1914 but failed to carry a single county. In 1916 he advocated reunification with the old party and later served on a special committee to elect Charles Evans Hughes, the Republican presidential nominee. He was a proponent of military preparedness and a critic of Woodrow Wilson's policy in dealing with German provocations prior to America's entry into World War I.

Rejoining the Republicans in 1916, Garfield never left that party again. On several occasions Republican administrations appointed him to special committees. In 1923 Secretary of the Interior Hubert Work appointed Garfield to a committee of advisers on reclamation known as "the Fact Finders Committee." Many of the changes it recommended were carried out by Commissioner of Reclamation Elwood Mead, who was also on the committee. In 1926 President Calvin Coolidge named Garfield to an emergency board to investigate railroad labor disputes in the southwestern United States.

After Congress authorized the Committee on the Conservation and Administration of the Public Domain in 1930, President Herbert Hoover made Garfield its chair. A year later the committee recommended that the national government keep jurisdiction over reclamation projects, national forests, national parks and monuments, wildlife refuges, and areas important to national defense. Remaining public lands, largely grazing lands, were to be granted to states if they wanted them. The titles to public mineral lands were also to be given to the states, with mineral rights to remain with appropriate federal agencies. This recommendation was opposed by the Pinchot conservationists and had no chance of passage.

Garfield's thinking had undergone considerable change by then. In 1924 he supported Coolidge against Robert M. La Follette, presidential candidate of the Progressive Party of 1924. He worked for Hoover's election in 1928 and 1932, chairing the party's Resolutions Committee in the latter year. During the 1930s he attacked the Democrat Franklin D. Roosevelt's usurpation of judicial and legislative power, maintaining that "the wise balance of legislative, executive and judicial powers must be preserved" (*New York Times*, 25 July 1938).

As a political leader Garfield was typical of business-oriented, moderate progressives who were uninterested in, if not opposed to, many of the movement's social ideas. He was a reformer of the Theodore Roosevelt mold, seeking governmental efficiency through scientific planning and administration. He made important contributions as an initiator of the American version of the modern bureaucratic state and as a conservationist. Of him Theodore Roosevelt wrote, "I think that he has been the best Secretary we have ever had in the Interior Department" (Morison, ed., vol. 6, pp. 1535–36).

Until the mid-1940s Garfield was extremely active in educational, civic, and charitable institutions. In 1919 he was a founder of the Roosevelt Memorial Association (later the Theodore Roosevelt Association) of New York and served as its president from 1924 to 1950. After his wife's death in 1930, he lived with his brother Abram Garfield in Cleveland until his final illness. He died in a Cleveland nursing home.

• The James R. Garfield Papers, which include his journal, are at the Library of Congress. Government documents related to Garfield include *Annual Report of the United States Civil Service Commission* (1903), *Report of the Commissioner of Corporations on the Beef Industry* (1905), *Report of the Commissioner of Corporations on the Transportation of Petroleum* (1906), and *Annual Reports of the Secretary of the Interior* (1907– 1909). Garfield's articles include "A Review of President Roosevelt's Administration: III. Economic and Industrial Influences," *Outlook*, 20 Feb. 1909, pp. 389–93; "How President Taft Pledged Himself to Follow the Roosevelt Policies—and Failed," *Outlook*, 18 May 1912, pp. 116–22; and "Publicity in Affairs of Industrial Combinations," *Annals of the American Academy of Political and Social Science* 42 (1912): 140–46. A biographical treatment of Garfield is Jack M. Thompson, "James R. Garfield: The Career of a Rooseveltian Progressive, 1895–1916" (Ph.D. diss., Univ. of South Carolina, 1958). He appears frequently in the pages of his father's journal, *The Diary of James A. Garfield*, ed. Harry James Brown and Frederick D. Williams (4 vols., 1967– 1981), and *The Letters of Theodore Roosevelt*, ed. Elting E. Morison (8 vols., 1951–1954). Gifford Pinchot, *Breaking New Ground* (1947), often mentions Garfield. His childhood is discussed in Margaret Leech and Harry James Brown, *The Garfield Orbit* (1978), and Joseph Jerry Perling, *Presidents' Sons* (1947). For his role in Ohio politics see Hoyt Landon Warner, *Progressivism in Ohio, 1897–1917* (1964). Sources that provide insight into his activities as a government executive include Joseph Carver Edwards, "Herbert Hoover's Public Lands Policy: A Struggle for Control," *Pacific Historian* 20 (1976): 34–45; Oscar Kraines, "The President versus Congress: The Keep Commission, 1905–1909," *Western Political Quarterly* 23 (1970): 5–54; Samuel P. Hays, *Conservation and the Gospel of Efficiency* (1959); Stephen Skowronek, *Building a New American State* (1982); Donald C. Swain, *Federal Conservation Policy, 1921–1933* (1963); and Paul P. Van Riper, *History of the United States Civil Service* (1958). For his relations with Taft see Henry F. Pringle, *The Life and Times of William Howard Taft, a Biography* (2 vols., 1939). Garfield's obituary is in the *New York Times*, 25 Mar. 1950.

ROBERT S. LA FORTE

GARFIELD, John (4 Mar. 1913–21 May 1952), actor, was born Jacob Julius Garfinkle in New York City, the son of David Garfinkle, a presser in the garment industry, and Hannah (maiden name unknown). After the death of his mother in 1920, John fell in with a rough crowd and in 1923 was enrolled in a public school with a reputation for reforming juvenile delinquents. There he took up boxing, debate, and drama, eventually qualifying as a semifinalist in a Golden Gloves tournament and placing second in a citywide debate competition.

While attending high school he joined the drama workshop of the Heckscher Foundation in 1928, and shortly thereafter he studied under Maria Ouspenskaya at the American Laboratory Theater. Calling himself Jules Garfield, the actor made his first credited Broadway appearance in a bit role in *Lost Boy* in January 1932. That year he married Roberta Seidman; they would have three children. He also began a long association with the Group Theater, whose founding members included playwright Clifford Odets; actor-turned-director Elia Kazan; and acting coaches Lee Strasberg and Stella Adler. The Group staged productions with liberal political messages and became the most important Left influence in American theater during the 1930s. Garfield got his first big break in the spring of 1932 playing "Henry the office boy" in the company's Chicago production of *Counsellor at Law*, a role he repeated when the production moved to Broadway that fall. Because he considered himself a stage actor, Garfield turned down an invitation from Universal Studios to play Henry in the film version of *Counsellor at Law* (1933) and refused requests from Warner Bros. for a screen test, although he did accept a day's work in that studio's *Footlight Parade* (1933), shot in New York City.

During the height of the Group Theater's success, Garfield appeared in productions of *Peace on Earth* (1933); *Gold Eagle Guy* (1934); Odets's revolutionary *Waiting for Lefty* and the depression drama *Awake and Sing* (both 1935); and *Johnny Johnson* (1936). In 1937 he starred in Marc Connelly's production of the comedy *Having a Wonderful Time*. Though its success promised a long run, Garfield left to join the ailing Group Theater's production of Odets's *Golden Boy*. The story of a talented prizefighter had been written for Garfield, but he was crushed to learn that Luther Adler would play the lead, while Garfield was given the minor role of "Siggie."

In 1938 Garfield signed a contract with Warner Bros., who renamed him John Garfield. That year he appeared in the smash hit *Four Daughters*, in which he developed the charming, rebellious, hard-luck persona for which he would become famous. His performance earned him an Academy Award nomination, a New York Film Critics' nomination for best supporting actor, and the D. W. Griffith Award for Acting. His critical success was accompanied by the birth of a daughter in the fall of 1938. In 1939 Garfield joined the executive board of the Screen Actors Guild, on which he served six years, nonconsecutively, before resigning in 1947.

In 1939–1940 Garfield played streetwise toughs in *They Made Me a Criminal, Blackwell's Island, Daughters Courageous, Dust Be My Destiny*, and *Castle on the Hudson*. Garfield protested loudly against such predictable roles and was enraged by Warner Bros.' failure to loan him to Columbia Studios for the film version of *Golden Boy*. The studio responded with the first of several suspensions for the actor, yet his protests led to better opportunities, including *Saturday's Children* (1940), *The Sea Wolf* (1941), and *Tortilla Flat* (1942).

Though heart trouble kept him from fighting in World War II, Garfield made several enormously popular war films and entertained troops overseas. In 1942 he cofounded with Bette Davis the Hollywood Canteen, where Hollywood stars served drinks to American soldiers. He joined the Hollywood Anti-Nazi League and supported numerous fundraising campaigns and liberal causes.

After the war Garfield did some of his finest acting in such films as *The Postman Always Rings Twice* (1946), based on James M. Cain's novel; *Humoresque* (1946); *Gentleman's Agreement* (1947), which criticized anti-Semitism; *Force of Evil* (1948), directed by Abraham Polonsky, who later would be blacklisted; *We Were Strangers* (1949), about the Cuban revolution; and *He Ran All the Way* (1951), his last film. In *Body and Soul* (1947), the first project from Garfield's own production company, Enterprise Productions, he starred as a boxer who trades love and honor for mate-

rial success. His performance earned best actor nominations from the Academy of Motion Picture Arts and Sciences and the New York Critics's Circle.

Garfield's career included occasional Broadway appearances, including the 1949 production of Clifford Odets's *The Big Knife*, in which Garfield starred as an actor struggling to break free of Hollywood's grasp. In 1951 he appeared in a production of Henrik Ibsen's *Peer Gynt*, and he appeared on stage for the last time on 12 March 1952 in a stage revival of *Golden Boy*, playing the role of the prizefighter that had been written for him years before.

The House Committee on Un-American Activities subpoenaed Garfield in 1951. He was accused of nothing in particular and had never actually been a member of the Communist party, but his lifelong support of liberal causes made him a prime target. His friends and associates had included many people suspected of political subversion, and as a Screen Actors Guild board member he had supported the newly formed Conference of Studio Unions in a 1946 labor dispute, to the consternation of many studio executives and conservatives. Garfield answered the committee's questions but refused to "name names" of those with whom he associated. He was subsequently blacklisted, suffering a deterioration of mental and physical health as a result. He died of a heart attack in New York City.

Art imitated life for John Garfield. Amidst the glitz and glamour of Hollywood, he sustained a distinctive edge, born of poverty and politics. He invented the soulful, streetwise underdog suffering from a never-ending bout with tough luck, a persona later taken up by James Dean, Montgomery Clift, and Robert DeNiro. Garfield's legacy has been imprinted on the faces of young actors in the decades since his death.

• For further information on Garfield, see James Beaver, *John Garfield: His Life and Films* (1978); George Morris, *John Garfield* (1977); Larry Swindell, *Body and Soul: The Story of John Garfield* (1975); and Patrick J. McGrath, *John Garfield: The Illustrated Career in Films and on Stage* (1993). An obituary is in *Variety*, 28 May 1952.

JENNIFER M. BARKER

GARFIELD, Lucretia Rudolph (19 Apr. 1832–13 Mar. 1918), first lady, was born in Garrettsville, Ohio, the daughter of Zebulon Rudolph and Arabella Mason, farmers. Sickly as a child, demure as an adolescent, and reared in a dutiful but unaffectionate family, Lucretia (or "Crete" as friends called her) grew into a bright, attractive but solemn young woman. At the Western Reserve Eclectic Institute in nearby Hiram, Ohio, a semicollegiate Disciples of Christ institution that her father had helped found, she pursued a formal education somewhat beyond that customary for her time and gender. She also displayed a surprising degree of intellectual independence, not only by obtaining a job as a schoolteacher but by asking, in a college essay, "Is it equitable that a woman who teaches school equally well should receive a smaller compensation than man?"

At the institute Lucretia also caught the eye of a fellow student and sometime teacher, James Abram Garfield, only six months her senior but the school's most promising student. They had known each other casually for a number of years but, in November 1853, while she was a student in Garfield's Greek class, their relationship blossomed after they began to correspond. Initially concerned with "the Study of Dead Languages," their correspondence became, by degrees, more personal and intimate. These two high-minded young people proceeded warily, since each had recently recovered from an unhappy infatuation. Nonetheless, by the spring of 1854, Garfield's diary recorded: "We love each other and have declared it," even though inwardly he harbored some reservations about his apparent lack of passion.

Passion was important to Garfield. An impoverished, fatherless farm boy, he was consumed by ambition to transcend his humble origins, which lent a heightened intensity to his studies, his work, and his emotions. These emotions became more fully engaged by another young woman, Rebecca N. Selleck, whom he met while he was completing his education at Williams College in Massachusetts. Yet when he returned to Hiram, to assume the presidency of the school, Lucretia was still waiting. On 11 November 1858 they were married, but the reluctant groom would not even tell his diary all his thoughts "on this sorrowful theme." He did tell his wife, a few years later, that their marriage was "a great mistake," but the birth of a daughter, Eliza, in 1860 brought them somewhat closer.

Yet not even his daughter, his beloved "Little Trot," could keep Garfield long at home. From 1859 to 1861 he spent much of his time at Columbus in his new career as state senator, and in 1861 he volunteered for service in the Union army, rising rapidly to major general. A year after enlisting, he returned to Ohio, near death from camp disease. As Lucretia nursed him back to health a stronger bond was forged between them that the grateful Garfield hailed as "a baptism into new life." That bond almost snapped after Garfield, resigning from the army in December 1863 to begin his long tenure as a U.S. congressman, was apparently burned by "the fires of . . . lawless passion" sparked by Lucia G. Calhoun, a New York widow. Lucretia's forgiveness, her husband's repentance, and the shared tragedy of the death of their daughter finally brought the couple together on a firm and lasting basis.

The Garfields remained together in a physical sense as well. In the fall of 1864 Lucretia handed her husband a note on which she had made some calculations showing that in the past 4¾ years they had lived together for only twenty weeks. From that time on, the Garfields would live as a family: in Washington, D.C., when Congress was in session and, during recess, at their various Ohio homes in Hiram, Little Mountain, and Mentor. Their Washington house, at the corner of Thirteenth and I streets, became a hive of middle-class domesticity, a model Victorian-era haven where Lu-

cretia's husband could rest from the cares of the masculine world. While her mother-in-law, Eliza, sat quietly knitting, Lucretia and her husband would read together from Dickens or Tennyson to their steadily growing circle of children. From 1863 to 1874 six children were born to the Garfields, and all survived but the youngest one. Presiding over this expanding brood was Lucretia, whose no-longer-roving husband now hailed as "the best woman I have ever known." "The tyranny of our love is sweet," he belatedly acknowledged. "We waited long for his coming, but he has come to stay." The duties of her domestic domain kept Lucretia from sharing in much of her husband's social life. Nonetheless, she promoted the political career of "the General" (as she invariably referred to her husband) in countless ways, both small and large.

When a stunning and unexpected series of events led James Garfield to the Republican nomination for the presidency in 1880 and victory in the subsequent election, Lucretia Garfield's position gave her considerable opportunity to exercise behind-the-scenes influence on the new administration. She served as a sort of moral policewoman, scrutinizing the character of potential appointees. She vetoed a cabinet post for Wisconsin's Thaddeus Pound because of a scandal that had once involved his wife but approved of the appointment of James G. Blaine as secretary of state despite rumors that Mrs. Blaine's first child had arrived embarrassingly soon after their marriage. She advised the president not to deal with Roscoe Conkling, leader of the rival Republican "Stalwart" faction, partly because of her disapproval of his well-publicized affair with Kate Chase Sprague, the wife of a former senator.

Little in her previous stay-at-home experience had prepared Lucretia to assume the complex social responsibilities of a first lady (as president's wives were only recently coming to be called). Her most pressing social dilemma was the politically loaded question of whether the new administration would follow the precedent set by Lucy Hayes (Mrs. Rutherford Hayes) of banning wine and spirits from White House functions. Taking the advice of James Blaine's wife, Harriet Blaine, on whom she increasingly leaned, Lucretia decided to reintroduce alcoholic refreshments quietly at the proper time.

That time never arrived. On 4 May 1881, two months to the day after her husband's inauguration, Lucretia Garfield was stricken with a fever similar to malaria. She was sent to Long Branch, New Jersey, to recuperate. She was still there when, on 2 July 1881, her husband was shot by Charles J. Guiteau, a demented religious fanatic and political hanger-on. Shaking off her own illness, she swiftly returned to Washington to nurse the wounded president. When he spoke of his impending death she briskly countered, "Well, my dear, you are not going to die as I am here to nurse you back to life; so please do not speak again of death."

Despite Lucretia's heroic efforts and those of a small army of physicians her husband steadily weakened from blood poisoning and other complications. During an eighty-day ordeal the president wasted away, first at the White House, where the sultry Washington summer heat could not be relieved even with the installation of a primitive precursor of air conditioning, and then at the seaside resort of Elberon, New Jersey. When her husband died at Elberon at 10:35 P.M. on 15 September 1881, Lucretia Garfield cried out, "Oh! why am I made to suffer this cruel wrong?"

After personally supervising her husband's funeral and helping to select the design of the massive monument that would rise over his tomb in Cleveland's Lake View Cemetery, Lucretia Garfield withdrew to "Lawnfield," her farm at Mentor, Ohio. There, supported by the income from a $300,000 trust fund raised by popular subscription, she conducted her correspondence on black-bordered stationery, organized her husband's papers for posterity, and took pride in the successful careers of her children and grandchildren. Her oldest son Harry became a lawyer, a professor of political science at Princeton, fuel administrator during World War I, and president of Williams College. Her second son James at first entered law, in partnership with Harry, then went his own way to the Ohio Senate and the U.S. Civil Service Commission; he was later appointed secretary of the interior by Theodore Roosevelt. The younger boys also did well: Irvin was a Boston lawyer and Abram a Cleveland architect. When her daughter Mary ("Mollie") came of age, she married Joseph Stanley-Brown, her father's private secretary.

Lucretia Garfield died at her winter home in South Pasadena, California. She was buried in the basement crypt of the Garfield Monument beside her husband.

• Lucretia Garfield's papers are at the Library of Congress, alongside other relevant collections such as those of Harry Garfield, the Garfield family, James R. Garfield, and James A. Garfield. The last-named collection, which also contains much by and about Lucretia, is available on 177 reels of microfilm as part of the Presidential Papers series. Lucretia Garfield's White House diary, which she kept from 1 March to 20 April 1881, can be found as an appendix to *The Diary of James A. Garfield*, vol. 4, ed. Harry J. Brown and Frederick D. Williams (1981). Biographies of her husband, especially Allan Peskin, *Garfield* (1978), and Margaret Leech and Harry J. Brown, *The Garfield Orbit* (1978), deal, perforce, with family matters. Paul Boller, *Presidential Wives* (1980), and Betty Boyd Caroli, *First Ladies* (1987), place Lucretia Garfield's activities as first lady within the context of the other women who have held that responsibility.

ALLAN PESKIN

GARIS, Howard Roger (25 Apr. 1873–5 Nov. 1962), writer, was born in Binghamton, New York, the son of Simeon Harris Garis, a railroad telegrapher/dispatcher, and Ellen A. Kimball. The family moved to Syracuse, New York, when Garis was about five. Garis loved Syracuse, especially the Erie Canal, but Simeon Garis's job required frequent moves along the Delaware, Lackawanna, and Western system. Formal or regular education was not something that young Garis got much chance to experience. He did manage to graduate from high school, however, and at the age of

sixteen he began work in the baggage office of the Erie Lackawanna Railroad in Newark, New Jersey. In between the tedium of examining, tagging, and loading bags, Garis wrote poems and stories. In 1894, to prepare him for a more lucrative career as an engineer, however, Garis's father sent him to the Stevens Institute of Technology, across the bridge in Hoboken. Garis promptly failed every subject but English and elocution and was asked to leave. His father next sent him to a printer's school in New York City, but that brief endeavor was cut short by Simeon Garis's death.

In the meantime, Garis had kept up his writing. His first novel, "A World without Women," his response to an unsuccessful teenage romance, was fortunately never published; but some short stories and poems began to be published locally, and in 1896 he landed a job as a reporter on the *Newark Evening News*. Garis proved to be a very good reporter, if sometimes overly colorful and imaginative, and frequently pounded the police beat. And it was at the *News* that he met Lilian McNamara, the first woman reporter in the state of New Jersey. The two were married in 1900 and eventually had two children, a son and a daughter. While Lilian began writing freelance, Garis continued at the *News*, making only $18 a week at the paper, but this did not seem to worry him. Contrary to his booming voice, he had a preternaturally calm disposition; constantly fascinated by what was going on around him, he was absolutely secure that things would work out the way he intended. This was a useful attribute, as his bride possessed an apprehensive nature.

Garis continued to write his stories—at night, away from the *News*—and in 1902 his first published novel, *With Force and Arms: A Tale of Love and Salem Witchcraft*, appeared. Not a juvenile adventure story, it was a critical and financial disaster. But, in 1904, *Isle of Black Fire*, a children's adventure story about an expedition to find a radium deposit, was published, and it did modestly well. It was followed that same year by *The White Crystals*, wherein the discovery of salt saves the family farm from being mortgaged. Garis had hit upon his adventure story formula, which he would use to good and clever effect in all of his books and stories. Part of this formula, which he described as "laying pipes," was the placing, early on in the story, of an integral paragraph or short section that later would bring the story together. This process later became known in the series book world as the "Garis formula."

In 1898 Edward L. Stratemeyer—taking his cue from Horatio Alger, Jr., father of series books, and Edward Judson, inventor of the "dime novel"—began to build an extremely successful dynasty of adventure series books, hardcover works that read like lightning and had recurring heroes. Initially, Stratemeyer wrote all of the books himself, starting with the Rover Boys, but using pseudonyms so that, should he die suddenly, his publisher could find someone else to step in and finish the job. By 1905 the number of different Stratemeyer series had expanded and public demand was so great that he decided to organize a syndicate that employed and promoted young writers who could write in his style. Stratemeyer had read Garis's books and admired his ability to write children's stories. After some persuading, Garis signed on for the Motor Boys series, writing under the name "Clarence Young," at a starting rate of $100 per book. Garis was not too keen about writing under a pseudonym, but everything else about the job was appealing, so long as he could keep his day job at the *Newark Evening News* (he stayed with the *News*, as a special writer, until 1947). In addition, Lilian Garis was recruited to write, as "Margaret Penrose," the Motor Girls series. The "Motor" stories, about the dangers and thrills of crossing the continent in an automobile, were very popular with the reading public.

Garis found that he could put out a 35,000-word book in a few weeks without tiring or losing plot interest. The fictional formula he had devised, and which became the Syndicate standard—problem-suspense-climax-solution—became even more effective when Stratemeyer's elements were entered in: plots were built upon outlines designed only by Stratemeyer, books were to comprise 30 chapters, and each chapter was seven pages or fewer. In 1908 Stratemeyer suggested a series about a young creative genius who invented amazing gadgets. Garis loved the idea, and the character Tom Swift was born. Another cultural touchstone was created around this time, a series of books featuring the Bobbsey Twins, written by Lilian Garis as "Laura Lee Hope."

Their income from the Stratemeyer Syndicate enabled the Garises to move to East Orange and summer at Belmar on the Jersey shore. Garis continued to commute two hours to his job at the *News*, which he loved and which provided material for his Larry Dexter, Boy Reporter series. Garis's family life was another great source of material. He had been writing a variety of stories involving animal characters in a series for the *News* called "Bedtime Stories"—he is credited with coming up with the term "bedtime" (Jordan, p. 163)—when, in 1910, he unveiled Uncle Wiggily Longears, a sweet-natured, top-hatted, arthritic, somewhat obtuse gentleman rabbit who manages to get into and out of improbable and hilarious adventures. The rabbit was a hit. By 1912 Mr. Longears had accumulated enough experiences to have them gathered together in *Uncle Wiggily's Adventures*. The book took off across the country like one of the Rocket Riders' gizmos (another of Garis's Stratemeyer series).

Although Garis was now being published under his own name, he did not end his association with Stratemeyer (he stayed with the Syndicate until 1962), or with the newspaper. In 1917 he invented the Uncle Wiggily board game, which became the largest-selling children's game in the world. Not only that, by the 1920s the entire Garis family was in on the act together, turning out hundreds of juvenile adventure stories. Garis's son Roger later noted that there was a good chance that any juvenile books popular between 1905 and 1935 had been written by a Garis (Roger Garis, p. 8).

In 1950 Howard and Lilian moved to Amherst, Massachusetts, to live with their son Roger and his family. Robert Frost was living in Amherst at the time, and he and Garis became great friends. After several years of deteriorating health, Lilian McNamara Garis, Girl Reporter for the *Newark Evening News*, died on 14 April 1954. Howard bore the loss stoically. He and Lilian had been married for fifty-four years and had been writers together for all that time. And Garis continued to write, six days a week. Fame did not greatly interest him, but he thoroughly enjoyed the attention he drew as "Uncle Wiggily," for that was who he had become. The popularity of the series had never diminished; Wiggily was an original, more singular and idiosyncratic than the Syndicate serial heroes and heroines. High-toned literary honors were never bestowed on Garis, but he knew his audience, their smiles and laughter were his honors; he wrote for children, period.

Although he had asked his daughter-in-law Mabel to continue the Uncle Wiggily tradition after he was gone, Garis was still writing when one morning in early November 1962 he did not join the family after his breakfast. His son and daughter-in-law went to check on him; he said he was fine, just tired, but the family doctor was called nevertheless. Garis was taken to Cooley Dickinson Hospital in Northampton, where he died a few days later. The physician on call telephoned Roger Garis and quietly told him, "Uncle Wiggily has gone." Family, friends, and countless children attended his funeral, at which the priest offered a simple epitaph, "This was a man who was blessed of all. He made children happy."

Garis wrote more than 15,000 Uncle Wiggily stories and nearly 700 other stories and books between 1902 and his death. His writing was popular almost the minute he put pen to paper, but with Uncle Wiggily his fans became legion and international. When he organized the Uncle Wiggily Hollow Stump Club in 1949, he received 1,500 fan letters in just three weeks. There was even an Uncle Wiggily Radio Hour. Luckily for those around him, he was as kind and fun and funny in person as in print. (Garis would time his strolls so that he would pass Amherst's elementary schools during recess, on the "off" chance that some children might like to hear some stories.) The appeal of his series books has since waned, but Uncle Wiggily seems eternal. A little adventure, a little silliness, a little common sense, a little mystery, a little quirky perspective, a little lesson—not bad ingredients for a good kid's story, and Garis knew how to mix them for enduring and entertaining effect. If there is a moral to the story of Howard Garis and Uncle Wiggily, it is "never underestimate the power of a rabbit, or of your own imagination." Some may consider Garis a writing machine, his style a bit rough, but he was no hack. His memorable characters, his sly but gentle humor, and his digressive approach to storytelling let his readers know there was more going on than just one word following another.

• Garis's papers are at Syracuse University in New York, including his unpublished autobiography, "Chain in the Road." Some minor material is in Special Collections at the Jones Library in Amherst, Mass., and some letters are with the Milton Bradley Company in Springfield, Mass. For a bibliography of his work with Stratemeyer, see Deirdre Johnson, ed. and comp., *Stratemeyer Pseudonymous and Series Books: An Annotated Checklist of Stratemeyer and Stratemeyer Syndicate Publications* (1982). Under his own name, in addition to works already mentioned, Garis wrote the "Great Newspaper" series, the Dick Hamilton series, the Smith Boys series, the Three Little Trippertrots series, the "Daddy" series, the Curlytops series, the Venture Boys series, the Rick and Ruddy series, the Two Wild Cherries/Dick and Janet Cherry series, the Tom Cardiff series, the Buddy series, the Mystery Boys series, and the Teddy series. Listings in *Contemporary Authors* and the *Dictionary of Literary Biography* mistakenly attribute to Howard Garis several series that Lilian Garis authored. Howard Garis's other works include *The King of Unadilla: Stories of Court Secrets Concerning His Majesty* (1903), *The Island Boys; or, Fun and Adventures on Lake Modok* (1912), *The Adventures of the Sailing Sofa* (1926), *Tam of the Fire Cave* (1927), *Tuftoo the Clown* (1928), *Chad of Nob Hill* (1929), *The Bear Hunt* (1929), *The Face in the Dismal Cavern* (1930), *The Gypsy Camp* (1930), *The Mystery of the Brass Bound Trunk* (1930), *On the Showman's Trail* (1930), *Saving the Old Mill* (1930), *The Secret of Lost River* (1930), *Shipwrecked on Christmas Island* (1930), and *Swept from the Storm* (1930). The fullest biographical account is by his son Roger Garis, *My Father Was Uncle Wiggily: The Remarkable Story of the Garis Family* (1966). See also Howard R. Garis, "Uncle Wiggily Comes to Amherst," *The Pioneer: A Magazine for New England*, 4 Mar. 1949; John T. Dizer, "Other Than Uncle Wiggily; or, The Lesser-known Works of Howard R. Garis," *Newsboy*, Nov./Dec. 1996; and J. D. Salinger's *Uncle Wiggily in Connecticut*. For brief assessments see Sam Castan, "The Wonderful World of Uncle Wiggily," *Look*, 3 July 1962; Charles J. Jordan, "So Who Wrote Poppy Ott and the Pedigreed Pickle?" *Yankee*, May 1971; F. K. Kelly, "Uncle Wiggily Hops Merrily Along," *Better Homes and Gardens*, Apr. 1947; and S. K. Oberbeck, "Longears & Co.," *Newsweek*, 7 Nov. 1966. Obituaries are in the *New York Times*, 6 Nov. 1962; *Publishers Weekly*, 19 Nov. 1962; and the Northampton/Amherst paper, the *Daily Hampshire Gazette*, 5 Nov. 1962.

E. D. LLOYD-KIMBREL

GARLAND, Augustus Hill (11 June 1832–26 Jan. 1899), governor, U.S. senator, and attorney general, was born in Covington, Tennessee, the son of Rufus Garland and Barbara Hill, farmers. When he was less than a year old, his family moved to Lost Prairie, Arkansas, on the Red River, where his father opened a store. Shortly after his father's death in 1833, his mother moved the family to Spring Hill, Arkansas. When she married Judge Thomas Hubbard in 1836, the family settled in Washington, Arkansas. Garland began his education in a private school and later attended St. Mary's College in Lebanon, Kentucky. He graduated from another Catholic college, St. Joseph's, in Bardstown, Kentucky, in 1849. Following a year as a rural school teacher in Arkansas, he read law and was admitted to the bar in 1853, joining his stepfather's firm in Washington, Arkansas. He married Sarah Virginia Sanders in 1853; they had eight children.

In 1856 Garland moved to Little Rock to become a law partner with Ebenezer Cummins, who died less than a year later. Thus Garland became the head of a lucrative law office in the state capital. He was admitted to the bar of the U.S. Supreme Court in 1860.

Though earlier an Arkansas Whig, in 1860 Garland campaigned for John Bell and the Constitutional Union party and was chosen as a presidential elector. Elected in 1861 to the convention considering whether Arkansas should secede from the Union, he was initially opposed, but after the firing on Fort Sumter he joined the majority in voting for secession. Rising to political prominence, he was elected in 1861 to the Confederate House of Representatives, a position that he occupied for the next three years. Elevated to the Confederate Senate in 1864, he remained there until the end of the Civil War. Described by his contemporaries as a conservative constitutionalist, he generally supported President Jefferson Davis, but he opposed him on the question of suspending the writ of habeas corpus.

Pardoned by President Andrew Johnson on 15 July 1865, Garland returned to the practice of law in Little Rock. Although his legal services were in great demand, his most important case involved his own effort to resume practice before the U.S. Supreme Court. Congress passed a law requiring attorneys who appeared before the Court to take an oath that they had never borne arms against the United States nor held office in a government hostile to the nation. In the case of *Ex Parte Garland* he argued that, because such a requirement was an ex post facto law, it was unconstitutional. The Court agreed.

During the presidential phase of Reconstruction, the Arkansas General Assembly elected Garland to the U.S. Senate in 1867. Denied a seat because Arkansas had not been readmitted to the Union, he returned to his law practice in Little Rock. During the Congressional or Radical phase of Reconstruction when the state was under Republican control, Garland emerged as an articulate and forceful Democratic-conservative spokesman. He figured, either directly or indirectly, in various activities contributing to the collapse of the Republican regime, primarily by galvanizing conservative Democrats and by articulating Republican Corruption. As the Democratic nominee for governor in 1874, he spearheaded the campaign for a new state constitution. Not only did the voters approve the new constitution that year, but they also elected Garland as governor.

Inaugurated on 12 November 1874, Governor Garland confronted an array of complicated problems, not the least of which were an empty state treasury and a large debt. Unalterably opposed to debt repudiation, he instituted a series of measures to reduce the debt, among them the creation of a sinking fund and the creation of a finance board with powers to negotiate loans for current expenses, restored the state's credit, and kept the state government solvent. At the same time he promoted education and labored to improve the state's image. At the end of his two-year term he refused to be a candidate for reelection.

In 1877 the state legislature chose Garland to succeed Powell Clayton, a Republican, as U.S. senator. During his tenure in the Senate (1877–1885) he proved a persistent advocate of tariff revision (he supported lowering the tariff) and sound money. He also strongly supported civil service reform, federal aid to education, and federally funded internal improvements for Arkansas. Skilled in the handling of constituent relations, Garland enjoyed the respect of his Senate colleagues, acquired a reputation as a knowledgeable student of the Constitution, and earned a seat on the important Senate Judiciary Committee.

Garland resigned his Senate seat on 5 March 1885 to become attorney general in the cabinet of President Grover Cleveland. During his tenure the Justice Department was involved in much litigation, notably cases concerning the exclusion of Chinese immigrants, abuse of railroad land grants, and limitations on foreign investors. A trusted legal adviser to the president on pension fraud and various other controversial issues, he urged Cleveland to support federal regulation of interstate commerce and to establish a federal prison system. Despite his reputation as an honest and responsible public official, the so-called Pan-Electric Telephone Company affair cast a shadow over his performance as attorney general. Garland owned stock in Pan-Electric, which challenged the patent owned by Alexander Graham Bell. Without Garland's knowledge, a subordinate in the Justice Department initiated legal action to test the validity of the Bell patent, which if successful would have enhanced the value of his stock. Garland flatly denied exercising any influence on behalf of Pan-Electric. Even after the suit was dropped, however, a congressional committee investigated the matter for some months.

The Republicans recaptured the White House in 1888, and Garland established a law practice in Washington, D.C. There he became highly successful and influential, appearing frequently before the Supreme Court. He maintained his interest in legal studies and published three works: *Third Term Presidential* (pamphlet, 1896), *Experience in the Supreme Court of the United States* (1898), and *A Treatise on the Constitution and Jurisdiction of the United States Courts* (2 vols., 1898), which he coauthored with Robert Ralston. Garland died suddenly from a stroke while addressing the U.S. Supreme Court in the case of *Towsen v. Moore*. Garland was buried beside his wife in Mount Holly Cemetery in Little Rock.

• There is no sizable collection of Garland papers, but the Arkansas History Commission (Little Rock) possesses a small collection, including some of his official correspondence as governor. The Grover Cleveland Papers in the Library of Congress contain numerous letters from Garland. For brief biographical accounts see Farrar Newberry, *A Life of Mr. Garland of Arkansas* (1908); Beverly Watkins, "Augustus Hill Garland," in *Governors of Arkansas: Essays in Political Biography*, ed. Timothy P. Donovan and Willard B. Gatewood (1981); and Leonard Schluys, "Augustus Hill Garland: Gild-ed Age Democrat," *Arkansas Historical Quarterly* 40 (Winter 1981): 338–46. For a full-length biography see Watkins, "Augustus Hill Garland, 1832–1899: Arkansas Lawyer to United States Attorney General" (Ph.D. diss., Auburn Univ., 1985). An obituary is in the *New York Times*, 27 Jan. 1899.

WILLARD B. GATEWOOD

GARLAND, Hamlin (14 Sept. 1860–4 Mar. 1940), writer, was born Hannibal Hamlin Garland near West Salem, Wisconsin, the son of Richard Garland and Isabelle McClintock, farmers. He spent his early years moving with his family from farm to farm, in Wisconsin, Minnesota, Iowa, and finally the Dakota Territory. After rudimentary schooling at a rural school in Iowa, he attended Cedar Valley Seminary in nearby Osage from 1876 through June 1881. His early semi-autobiographical sketches, published in the *American Magazine* (1885) and later collected as *Boy Life on the Prairie* (1899), recount his work on the farm. In them he examines the hardships of farm life and describes being torn by an attraction to the natural beauty of the newly settled "Middle Border," as he called it, and his desire to escape the monotony and drudgery of the farm.

Before leaving the West for Boston, where he hoped to pursue a literary life, Garland, in 1883, located a claim near his father's farm. He then mortgaged it, and with the money he moved to Boston. By diligence, confidence, and boldness he made the contacts necessary to become a student, a lecturer, a teacher, and finally a writer, breaking into Boston's literary circles by publishing early pieces in such journals as the *Arena*, *Century*, *Harper's Weekly*, and *American Magazine*.

Garland acquired a thorough education by haunting the public library in Boston, where he read, by his own account, from opening to closing, schooling himself in such authors as Walt Whitman, Herbert Spencer, and Henry George (1839–1897). At the invitation of Moses True Brown (1742–1827), Garland became a student at Brown's Boston School of Oratory, where he attended formal lectures and later began himself to lecture in American literature.

By 1887, when he went to the Dakota Territory to visit his family, Garland had already achieved modest success in Boston. He had published, was known in lecture circles, and had made friendships with people in the literary field, most prominent among whom stood William Dean Howells. Despite this success, his return to the West marked a major turning point in his career. Stopping in Chicago on his way, he met and befriended the realist Joseph Kirkland, who advised him about his writing. This meeting, combined with a depressing but eye-opening return to the places of his boyhood, provided the stimulus and material for his first fiction. With the perspective distance had given him, he sensed the "tragic futility" of the farmers' existence and resolved, as he wrote in retrospect, to put the "stern facts" of the rural American West into literature.

The result was the realistic, local-color stories that made up *Main-Travelled Roads* (1891). In the collection's six original stories, Garland narrates episodes in the grueling life of middle-border farming. In "A Branch Road," for example, the youthful Will runs from the woman he loves and from farming. He returns seven years later to discover that the love of his youth has grown "worn and wasted incredibly." His mission becomes to rescue her from the plight of life as a farmer's wife. In a story with a similar theme, "Up the Coulee," Howard, who has become a successful actor, visits his family on their farm. Guilt motivates him to ask his brother's forgiveness for ten years of neglect and to buy back the old homestead. In these stories, as in much of his Middle Border fiction, Garland describes realistically the "sorrow, resignation, and a sort of dumb despair" of the farmers and members of their families.

Although he lived in Boston, Garland's interests and material were of the West, and he became an advocate of farmers in their political and economic struggles. Influenced by his reading of Henry George, he supported the Single Tax Law, which was meant to alleviate the problems caused by landlords' greed and by farmers not profiting despite the increase in the value of their land. Contributing to the populist movement, in 1890 Garland wrote the play *Under the Wheel* (rewritten and published as the novel *Jason Edwards* [1892]). The play tells the story of an immigrant in Boston who, because of the poverty of his life as a mechanic, migrates to the West with his wife and daughter in hopes of prosperity. But here, too, he is the victim of landowners, fluctuating prices, and bad weather. The once-hopeful immigrant is forced to move back to the East; his American dream has failed. In *A Member of the Third House* (1892), Garland exposes the political corruption involving a railroad monopoly. Also in 1892 he published *A Spoil of Office*, a novel treating political movements—the Grange, the Farmer's Alliance, and the Populist party—as they related to a young western politician who sees and tries to rectify the injustice caused by monopolistic landowners against farmers.

With his literary career fairly launched, Garland moved to Chicago in 1893, living there intermittently until 1916. In Chicago he saw the potential for an aesthetic awakening and thought the new metropolis to be on the verge of taking "its place among the literary capitals of the world." Also appealing to him was the city's proximity to the West, where his literary interests lay and where his family lived. Of special importance to him was his responsibility toward his mother, whose ill health had brought him west before. Garland's biographers argue that the successful writer felt guilty about leaving his mother to the hard life of the farm. He bought his parents a home in West Salem, Wisconsin, only eight hours by train from Chicago. Thus he was able to visit his mother regularly.

At this point in his career Garland gathered and wove together earlier literary essays and published them in his only collection of literary theory, *Crumbling Idols* (1894), which was influenced by Howells's *Criticism and Fiction*. Garland argued that the conservative traditions crumbled before contemporary regional art, local color, and "veritism," the word he coined to describe his own kind of realism, a truthful but impressionistic reaction to fact.

In his fiction, Garland also took a liberal stand on issues of women's rights. In "The Land of the Straddle Bug" (published serially in the *Chap-Book* [1894–1895], later issued as a novel, *The Moccasin Ranch* [1909]), he portrays sympathetically a married farm woman who defies societal norms by running away with her lover. In a crucial scene, Garland describes a character coming to terms with the notion that a woman has the right to make choices for herself, that she need not be bound by the decisions a husband has made for her. In *Rose of Dutcher's Coolly* (1895), perhaps his best novel, Garland creates another autonomous and strong woman who leaves her father's Wisconsin farm to live and work in Chicago. There she makes important friends, establishes a viable career, and meets and marries a man who accepts and complements her independence and autonomy.

In December 1896 Garland published the first of several pieces in *McClure's* magazine, which had commissioned him to write a serial biography of Ulysses S. Grant. He later published the book, *Ulysses S. Grant: His Life and Character* (1898). In Chicago Garland became active as the president of the city's Central Art Association and a charter member and first president of the Cliff-Dwellers Club.

Besides his insightful and authentic depictions of the plight of farmers and the social and economic oppression of women, Garland wrote sympathetic accounts of the problems the Plains Indians faced. Basing his descriptions on actual experience and tales told by his Indian agent friends John Seger and George Stouch, Garland treated the Plains Indians realistically. As he reports in retrospect, his "one underlying motive" was "to show the Indian as a human being, a neighbor." The most noteworthy instances of this motive at work are the novel *The Captain of the Grey Horse Troop* (1902) and several stories, much later published in *The Book of the American Indian* (1923).

Though the depictions of the Indians are somber, sometimes even gruesome in their realistic depiction, Garland advocates throughout the stories the need for the Indians to accept the irretrievable loss of land and culture and to allow themselves to be assimilated as quickly and painlessly as possible. In "Rising Wolf—Ghost Dancer" he describes the purpose of the late nineteenth-century ghost dancing among Plains Indians and suggests that it borrowed from Christian ritual. The story also emphasizes Garland's belief that the Indians would be better off being assimilated into the white culture than starving and dying without the resources to live in traditional ways. His fictionalized biography of Sitting Bull, "The Silent Eaters," may well be the best of Garland's Indian narratives. Told by a member of Sitting Bull's bodyguard (The Silent Eaters), the novella describes as lamentable but inevitable the decline of the Sioux between the 1850s and the end of the century. Ironically, while gathering material for his Indian stories by night, Garland himself was buying Oklahoma farm land by day, thus dispossessing the Indians in deed as he lamented their plight in theory.

Garland's Far West fiction coincides with his change from the mode of realism to that of more popular romance. Though romance had always been a part of his work, after the turn of the century he published numerous contemporary romances set in the Far West. Besides the Indian books already mentioned, he published *The Spirit of Sweetwater* (1898), *The Eagle's Heart* (1900), *Her Mountain Lover* (1901), *Hesper* (1903), *The Light of the Star* (1904), *Money Magic* (1907), *Cavanaugh, Forest Ranger* (1910), and *The Forester's Daughter* (1914). Although critics have seen Garland's turn to western romance as a decline, this fiction does retain his characteristic vivid and realistic descriptions of people and places.

Garland's move to New York from Chicago in 1916 marked another major turning point in his career. Garland essentially abandoned fiction and turned to autobiography. In *A Son of the Middle Border* (1917) he recounts his boyhood days and move to Boston, covering much of the same material he recounted in *Boy Life on the Prairie*. In *A Son*, however, he also describes his move to Boston and his return to the West to see his family in West Salem, Wisconsin. The book ends with a sentimental account of a family Thanksgiving in which he sits at head of table and promises his mother a daughter.

The promised new daughter of *A Daughter of the Middle Border* (1921) is Garland's wife, the artist Zulime Taft (1870–1942), whom he met through his friendship with her brother, the sculptor Lorado Taft, and married in 1899. Garland's mother also represents a daughter of the Middle Border. Despite the importance of literal daughters, the sequel primarily recounts Garland's literary life as he recreated it from his journals from 1899 through about 1915. In 1922 Garland won the Pulitzer Prize for *A Daughter*, but evidently it was awarded more in recognition of *A Son of the Middle Border* than for its less successful sequel. Of the two volumes that followed, *Trail Makers of the Middle Border* (1926) describes Garland's father's early life, and *Back-Trailers from the Middle Border* (1928) describes Garland's own return to New York and his life with his wife and two daughters.

To these autobiographical accounts, Garland added four volumes of literary memoirs, *Roadside Meetings* (1930), *Companions on the Trail* (1931), *My Friendly Contemporaries* (1932), and *Afternoon Neighbors* (1934). Besides being of interest to Garland scholars, this autobiographical material is interesting for the light it sheds on the farming and literary culture of Garland's era. In this sense, Garland remains a realist.

In 1930 Garland moved to California, where he lived near Hollywood until his death. In the last few years of his life he returned to writing about spiritualism, a subject that had interested him some thirty years earlier. *Forty Years of Psychic Research* (1936) reviews the earlier work on which his psychic novels were grounded: *The Tyranny of the Dark* (1905), *The Shadow World* (1908), and *Victor Ollnee's Discipline* (1911). Garland's last book was also about spiritualism, *The Mystery of the Buried Crosses* (1939).

Garland was famous primarily for two works, a collection of local color stories, *Main-Travelled Roads*, and the autobiographical account of his childhood and early years as a writer, *A Son of the Middle Border*. In *A Son* he articulates the literary precepts "that truth was a higher quality than beauty, and that to spread the reign of justice should everywhere be the design and intent of the artist." In that he followed these precepts throughout his career as a writer, Garland deserves recognition for several other works: he challenged the myth of bucolic farm life, advocated the responsibility of the literary artist to challenge the establishment, and provided insightful depictions not only of farmers', but also of women's rights and the plight of American Indians in the face of Manifest Destiny and capitalistic imperialism. One of the earliest realists and the first to bring authentic, firsthand accounts of midwestern farm life to American literature, Garland was also a social critic and human rights advocate.

• The Doheny Library, University of Southern California, houses the Hamlin Garland Collection, which, besides records, memorabilia, and Garland's personal library, contains letters, notebooks, journals, and manuscripts. The Huntington Library in San Marino, Calif., houses Garland's annual diaries, 1898–1940. Jean Holloway, *Hamlin Garland* (1960; repr. 1971), remains the best biography; Donald Pizer discusses the early literature in *Hamlin Garland's Early Work and Career* (1960). Joseph B. McCullough, *Hamlin Garland* (1978), provides a critical and biographical overview, and James Nagel, ed., *Critical Essays on Hamlin Garland* (1982), makes accessible several recent articles. Several more good critical essays are collected in Charles Silet et al., eds., *The Critical Reception of Hamlin Garland, 1891–1978* (1985).

LEE SCHWENINGER

GARLAND, Judy (10 June 1922–22 June 1969), movie star and singer, was born Frances Ethel Gumm in Grand Rapids, Minnesota, the daughter of Frank Avent Gumm and Ethel Marian Milne. Her parents were vaudevillians during the period when vaudeville shared theaters with film presentations. Frank Gumm managed a theater in Grand Rapids and sang, accompanied on the piano by his wife. Later their daughters Mary Jane and Dorothy Virginia (born 1915 and 1917, respectively) became part of the act, joined in December 1924 by Baby Frances.

For the next ten years the Gumm Sisters, with Ethel Gumm at the piano, performed in the Grand Rapids area. In 1926 the family, lured by the idea of Hollywood, moved to California, where the sisters appeared primarily in Lancaster in another theater managed by their father. A stage mother ambitious for her children, Ethel Gumm enrolled the girls in a theatrical school in nearby Los Angeles, and the sisters slowly developed as a singing team, dominated by Frances. In 1934 they performed in Chicago at the Exposition and at the Oriental Theater, where George Jessel, perhaps mistakenly, introduced them as the Garland Sisters, a name change that stuck.

In 1935, during performances in several large theaters in Los Angeles, Frances, a thirteen-year-old with a voice that could fill the largest auditorium, demonstrated that she would be the family's meal ticket. After an audition in September at Metro-Goldwyn-Mayer at which her accompanist was Roger Edens, who became her lifelong mentor, she was awarded a contract and subsequently renamed Judy. The achievement of landing the contract was negated somewhat by the shock of her father's untimely death. While the studio made plans for her, she became active in radio and signed a contract with Decca records. Her first film was a two-reel short subject, *Every Sunday* (1936), which she shared with another teenage singer, Deanna Durbin, who, before the year was over, moved to Universal where she immediately became a major star, whereas Garland struggled for three more years to establish herself. She was loaned to 20th Century–Fox for a minor musical, *Pigskin Parade* (1936), followed by *Broadway Melody of 1938* (1937), in which she sang "Dear Mr. Gable," written by Edens, the first of her memorable screen moments. Later that year she made *Thoroughbreds Don't Cry*, the first of her films with Mickey Rooney, whom she had known earlier at theatrical school. Two more films in 1938, *Everybody Sing*, with Fanny Brice, and *Listen, Darling*, led to her first appearance with Rooney in the popular Andy Hardy series *Love Finds Andy Hardy*, as Andy's friend and neighbor Betsy Booth, in which she sang "In Between," an Edens song that expressed indirectly what became her lifelong feeling of inferiority about her appearance. She added two other Hardy films in 1940 and 1941, by which time she was too important to the studio to be wasted in the series.

The turning point in Garland's career was *The Wizard of Oz* (1939), one of the most popular films ever made, in which she was permanently associated with the character of Dorothy and with the song "Over the Rainbow." In addition to the Hardy series, her musical films with Rooney, who was number one at the box office, included *Babes in Arms* (1939), *Strike up the Band* (1940), *Babes on Broadway* (1941), and *Girl Crazy* (1943). On her own, she was the title character in *Little Nelly Kelly* (1940) and *Presenting Lily Mars* (1943). She wowed audiences in the extravagant production number "Minnie from Trinidad" (again by Edens) in *Ziegfeld Girl* (1941) and shared honors as a dancer with Gene Kelly in *For Me and My Gal* (1942).

As the dates of these films suggest, Garland was making two or three major films a year. Her hyperactive nature and resultant insomnia led doctors to prescribe barbiturates to induce sleep and amphetamines to counteract sedative effects. Furthermore, because she tended to be plump and therefore unglamorous by the standards of the day, she took diet pills. As a consequence, probably by the age of twenty-one she was addicted to pills commonly called "uppers" and "downers."

A round-faced young Garland is the sign of a healthy Garland in her best form. In the late 1940s, however, the slim and glamorously gowned Garland can be understood, in retrospect, as working under stress, her prominent cheekbones cosmetized to create an illusion of health, although she did some of her best work in that period. Garland seems pretty and fresh in her second great success, *Meet Me in St. Louis* (1944). With a blonde rinse she becomes Marilyn Miller in *Till the Clouds Roll By* (1946), but in the same year she again is the girl-next-door (and in good voice) in *The Harvey Girls*.

MGM seemed determined to maintain an image of Judy Garland at first as a little girl and then as an immature woman, when she was long past adolescence. In later life she blamed Louis B. Mayer and her mother for controlling and ultimately ruining her life. She married composer-arranger David Rose in 1941, in great part as an attempt to escape her mother's influence. Within two years, the marriage failed. In 1943 Mayer broke up her affair with producer Joseph L. Mankiewicz, but not before, on Mankiewicz's advice, she began to see a psychiatrist. Vincente Minnelli, who drew out her best work in *Meet Me in St. Louis* and *The Clock* (1945), in which she had a nonsinging role, became her second husband in June 1945. They had one daughter, Liza, born in 1946.

Under Minnelli's influence, Garland performed more sophisticated material, not always suitable for her, such as "A Great Lady Has an Interview" in *Ziegfeld Follies* (1946) and *The Pirate* (1947), released in 1948, in which her voice sounds strained. Her erratic behavior on the set—lateness, refusing to leave her dressing room—which had begun with *Meet Me in St. Louis*, manifested itself distressingly during filming of *The Pirate*. When shooting ended, she entered a mental institution in California, followed by a second confinement in Massachusetts. Still thin but in good spirits, Garland returned to film, with Fred Astaire, in *Easter Parade* (1948), considered one of her best. She later adapted the tramp costume of "A Couple of Swells" for stage appearances.

The studio promised Garland a long rest, but after *Easter Parade* reaped huge profits she was announced for *The Barkleys of Broadway* with Astaire. In the meantime, she played herself in *Words and Music* (1948), performing with Rooney, the final teaming of the MGM superkids. When the filming of *Barkleys* began, the studio had to replace her with Ginger Rogers. After a rest Garland returned for *In the Good Old Summertime* (1949), in which Baby Liza, like Baby Frances before her, made an early debut. She separated from Minnelli soon after. The studio's extensive plans for her—the lead in *Annie Get Your Gun* and the role of Julie in a remake of *Show Boat*, the rights for both bought specifically for her—were never fulfilled because of her health. After she underwent another hospitalization, Garland made *Summer Stock* (1950) with Gene Kelly, looking plump and cheerful and performing as its final number an exuberant "Get Happy." However, on her next film, *Royal Wedding* with

Astaire, she evidenced more problems, and the studio summarily fired her. She had worked at MGM since age fifteen; now, at twenty-eight, she was considered washed up.

Disconsolate, Garland attempted "suicide," inflicting a scratch on her throat with a broken glass, an act more rightly identified as a cry for help although it would not be the last attempt. Even though *Summer Stock* was a hit, there were no more film offers. Consequently, she turned to radio, where she had sung often in wartime, and to a recording contract with Capitol, moving to New York, where she met Sid Luft, a theatrical agent who in the long run was responsible for revitalizing her career.

Garland divorced Minnelli in 1951, and with Luft as negotiator signed a contract to perform at London's Palladium in April 1951. The result was an overwhelming success. Having worked out her stage performance with Edens, she took "her first step toward becoming one of the greatest stage performers of the century." The British, who remembered her affectionately from her wartime films, roared their approval, which was echoed by the critics. She was "as plump as a peach," Kenneth Tynan noted approvingly. The following fall, under Luft's management, she brought vaudeville back to the Palace Theater in New York for nineteen weeks, establishing an unequaled house record. She was creating the "Garland legend" and establishing the "Garland cult," cheering fans who followed her performances for years. Something of her stage manner can be seen in the "Born in a Trunk" sequence of her next film, *A Star Is Born* (1954).

Garland married Luft in June 1952, and he subsequently set up a production company to operate through Warner Bros. *A Star Is Born*, a musical remake of the 1937 film, is often described as a commercial failure when actually it was one of the most popular of the year. However, its huge cost (for the time), for which Garland was unfairly blamed, reduced its profits, and the film's running time of three hours, suitable for an epic (even one about Hollywood), was detrimentally cut by the studio by forty minutes. *Time* magazine called Garland's performance "just about the finest one-woman show in modern movie history." She was nominated for an Academy Award but was denied the Oscar by Hollywood, an action Groucho Marx termed "the greatest robbery since Brinks." Indeed, even though she was again nominated as a supporting actress in 1961 for a nonsinging role in *Judgment at Nuremberg*, Garland was seen in only two more films, *A Child Is Waiting* and *I Could Go on Singing* (both 1963). She devoted the remainder of her career to the concert stage, where her rapport with live audiences was unparalleled. In effect, as David Dahl and Barry Kehoe assert in *Young Judy*, the mature Garland was simply a fulfillment of Baby Frances, a grown-up counterpart of the little girl who loved to sing. Certainly, the Palace and Palladium evenings indicate why some critics maintain that Garland is more important as a singer than as a movie star.

The last fifteen years of Garland's life were a series of personal and professional triumphs and tragedies. She had two children with Luft, Lorna and Joey, who with Liza constituted for a time a stage family. Her health jeopardized by alcohol and even more by amphetamines, she reached a nadir in 1959 when she became a semi-invalid because of liver damage and was judged unable to work again. Amazingly, she made a comeback once more, giving for some the performances of a lifetime at the Palladium in the fall of 1960 and following them on 23 April 1961 with an evening at Carnegie Hall, sometimes described as the greatest night in show business history. The recording of this performance, which sold 2 million copies and won five Grammy Awards, attests that although the wistful sweetness and shimmering tone of her voice had vanished, it was replaced with a vibrant, luscious fullness.

The passing of time, of course, frayed that wonderful sound, but she recovered it periodically. "The Judy Garland Show" (1963–1964), her major endeavor on television, was a failure in the ratings even though it had undeniable moments of quality. Unfortunately, the series and its residuals were designed to provide financial stability for Garland, whose large earnings throughout her life had not been managed decently. After the cancellation of the program, she was forced to keep working to pay her bills, in spite of declining physical and emotional resources. She divorced Luft in 1965 and, after a disastrous tour of Australia that same year, married Mark Herron, her "traveling companion." The marriage lasted two years. Her fifth husband, Mickey Deans, whom she married in 1969, took care of her in her final months, spent in England and on a tour of Scandinavia. She died in London of an apparent accidental overdose of barbiturates, and Deans brought her body back to New York. Her funeral was bigger than Rudolph Valentino's: 21,000 people filed past the bier of a beloved entertainer.

• Much has been written about Judy Garland. Selected biographies include Gerold Frank, *Judy* (1975), 600 pages filled with conversations "as told to" the author; Anne Edwards, *Judy Garland: A Mortgaged Life* (1975), in which the monsters are Ethel Gumm and Louis B. Mayer; David Dahl and Barry Kehoe, *Young Judy* (1975), which explores the family history up to the MGM contract of 1935, intercut with scenes from later years; and David Shipman, *Judy Garland: The Secret Life of an American Legend* (1993), by an admirer, an eminent British film historian. Joe Morella and Edward Epstein, *Judy: The Films and Career of Judy Garland* (1969), is a dutiful chronicle in the Citadel "Films of " series. As their titles indicate, Thomas J. Watson and Bill Chapman, *Judy, Portrait of an American Legend* (1986), and John Fricke, *Judy Garland, World's Greatest Entertainer: A Pictorial History of Her Career* (1992), are written by idolaters in fan magazine language; both essentially are coffee table books and have superb illustrations. Al DiOrio, *Little Girl Lost: The Life and Hard Times of Judy Garland* (1973), is more of the same but without the illustrations. Mel Torme, *The Other Side of the Rainbow* (1970), is a mean-spirited account of his days with the Judy Garland television show. Mickey Deans and Ann Pinchot, *Weep No More, My Lady* (1972), is a self-serving account of her fifth husband's experience with the star. In

James Spada, *Judy and Liza* (1983), Judy is the monster. Ronald Haver, A Star Is Born: *The Making of the 1954 Movie and Its 1983 Reconstruction* (1988), is a fascinating record of the film's production and of its preservation. Ethan Mordden, "I Got a Song," *New Yorker*, 22 Oct. 1990, perceptively discusses Garland's place as a singer in American popular music. Emily Coleman, *The Complete Judy Garland* (1990), is the ultimate bibliography.

JAMES VAN DYCK CARD

GARLAND, Red (13 May 1923–23 Apr. 1984), jazz pianist, was born William McKinley Garland, Jr., in Dallas, Texas, the son of William Garland, Sr., an elevator operator. His mother's name is unknown. Garland played clarinet and then alto saxophone in high school during which time he received lessons from renowned jazz saxophonist Buster Smith, who took a disciplined approach to Garland's learning to read music. Before settling into music, Garland had thirty-five fights as a lightweight professional boxer, at one point losing to Sugar Ray Robinson.

While serving in the army, Garland switched from alto sax to piano. At Fort Huachuca in Arizona he demonstrated his ability to read music and received informal lessons from pianist John Lewis, who cofounded the Modern Jazz Quartet. He later studied with pianist Lee Barnes. Discharged in 1944, Garland performed in Fort Worth, Texas, in 1945, when visiting trumpeter Hot Lips Page hired him for a tour to New York City. He arrived in New York around March 1946 and during that year joined singer Billy Eckstine's bop big band for about six weeks.

From 1947 to 1949 Garland performed at the Down Beat Club in Philadelphia as the house pianist. In that capacity he accompanied all-star guest soloists such as alto saxophonist Charlie Parker and trumpeters Miles Davis and Fats Navarro. He toured with tenor saxophonist Coleman Hawkins and trumpeter Roy Eldridge at some point early in the 1950s, worked as a soloist, and then rejoined Hawkins. He led a trio in Boston, Massachusetts, and also worked with tenor saxophonist Lester Young.

Garland's fame derives from his position as pianist in Miles Davis's hard bop combos. In the summer of 1955 Davis formed a quintet with Garland, tenor saxophonist Sonny Rollins, bassist Paul Chambers, and drummer Philly Joe Jones for a residency at the Café Bohemia in New York. The group began touring in the fall with John Coltrane replacing Rollins, and in this form they recorded the acclaimed Columbia album *'Round about Midnight* (1955–1956) and numerous sessions for the Prestige label. Garland also made albums without Davis as a leader on Prestige, introducing in a trio session on the album *Red Garland's Piano* (1956–1957) a version of "If I Were a Bell" that Davis soon made his own. Garland also headed a quintet that included Coltrane and trumpeter Donald Byrd for *All Mornin' Long* and *Soul Junction* (both 1957). Also in 1957, with Chambers, Jones, and alto saxophonist Art Pepper, Garland made the album *Art Pepper Meets the Rhythm Section* for the Contemporary label.

While working with Davis, Garland became addicted to heroin, as did Chambers, Coltrane, and Jones. Despite great success, as measured in the modest world of jazz finance, he was often broke, being compelled to spend nearly all his money on drugs. Because of associated personal problems, Garland was replaced by pianist Tommy Flanagan in fall 1957. After Davis's solo tour of Europe, Garland rejoined him in December 1957. At the same time, Coltrane, who had been in and out of the group, overcame his addiction and rejoined the group, making Davis the leader of a sextet with alto saxophonist Cannonball Adderley, Chambers, and Jones.

Garland was featured in a swinging trio version of "Billy Boy" on the sextet album *Milestones*, and the fresh, punching, chordal patterns at the opening of that album's title track, "Milestones," contribute to one of the most exhilarating moments in recorded jazz. But Garland was dissatisfied with his lack of opportunity to take solos on *Milestones*, and he quit the sextet in 1958. His replacement was Bill Evans. Garland began to lead his own trio, and he worked with Jones, who left Davis soon thereafter. In late November 1958, after Evans, suffering from exhaustion, resigned, Garland returned to the sextet. He remained until February 1959, when Davis hired pianist Wynton Kelly.

Garland performed in Philadelphia during the early 1960s. In 1965, when his mother died, he returned to Dallas to live with his father. At some point he married Lillie (maiden name unknown); they had two children. Debilitated by drug addiction and having lost his youthful zeal for the peripatetic jazz life, Garland devoted himself to his family and showed no interest in pursuing a potentially international career. From 1969 onward he usually worked with saxophonist Marchel Ivery, and they appeared at local clubs such as the Rounders, Wellington's Arandas, and the Texas Magic Asylum.

Garland did leave Dallas to perform in New York in May 1971 at which time he recorded two albums, including *The Quota*, for the German MPS label, and in March 1974 he had a brief stand at the Keystone Korner in San Francisco, leading a trio with local bassist James Leary and drummer Eddie Marshall. But in 1975–1976 he stopped playing altogether for eighteen months. He resumed his career at the aptly named Recovery Room in Dallas.

From 1977, when he recorded *Red Alert*, into the early 1980s Garland was once again making records regularly. He returned to the Keystone Korner in May 1977, with Jones in his trio, and again in May 1978 with a quartet featuring alto saxophonist Leo Wright. He performed briefly with bassist Bob Cunningham and drummer Ben Riley at Salt Peanuts in New York in midsummer 1980. Details of a European and a Japanese tour are unknown. In June 1982 he spent a week at Lush Life in New York with bassist George Mraz, drummer Al Foster, and Ivery as his sidemen. He died of heart disease in Dallas.

According to jazz educator Jerry Coker, Garland

omitted the root from the bottom, if not altogether, placing instead a seventh or third (usually) on the bottom, and played the voicings more in the middle and upper rather than the lower portions of the keyboard. Within a very short time, virtually all jazz pianists made a similar change, sometimes modifying Garland's exact voicings. It was plain to see that we were not going to be hearing many root-oriented voicings again, except perhaps in ballads or at important cadence points in faster selections. (Chambers, p. 220)

This innovative musical detail may be evident only to expert listeners. More generally, Garland was not an innovator but a keeper of the flame. He is remembered as a soloist for utilizing block chords (two-handed melody and harmony locked in rhythmic unison) after the manner of Milt Buckner and George Shearing. As an accompanist he formed, with Chambers and Jones, one of the most swinging and fiery rhythm sections in jazz history.

• For information about and interviews with Garland, see Mike Hawker, "Jazz from Carnegie Hall," *Melody Maker*, 6 Sept. 1958, pp. 2–3, 11; Gary Giddins, "Red Garland's Texas Cocktail," *Village Voice*, 3 Apr. 1978, pp. 49–50; Robert Palmer, "Jazz Pianist Makes a Rare Appearance," *New York Times*, 1 Aug. 1980; Mitch Albom, "Red Garland," *Jazz Times*, Oct. 1982, pp. 8–9; Len Lyons, *The Great Jazz Pianists: Speaking of Their Lives and Music* (1983); and Douglas K. Ramsey, *Jazz Matters* (1989). For details of Garland's affiliation with Miles Davis, see Jack Chambers, *Milestones 1: The Music and Times of Miles Davis to 1960* (1983). See also Leonard Feather, *The Encyclopedia of Jazz*, rev. ed. (1960), Feather, *The Encyclopedia of Jazz in the Sixties* (1966), and Feather and Ira Gitler, *The Encyclopedia of Jazz in the Seventies* (1976). For a brief musical analysis, see Feather, "Piano Giants of Jazz," *Contemporary Keyboard* 6 (Feb. 1980): 78–79, and Thomas Owens, *Bebop: The Music and Its Players* (1995). A catalog of Garland's recordings is in *Swing Journal* 33 (May 1979): 220–25. An obituary is in *New York Times*, 26 Apr. 1984.

BARRY KERNFELD

GARMAN, Charles Edward (18 Dec. 1850–9 Feb. 1907), professor, was born in Limington, Maine, the son of John Harper Garman, a Congregational minister and a founder of Limington Academy, and Elizabeth Bullard, a former public school teacher. Garman grew up in a home where religious values were taught and education was prized. In 1872 he graduated from Amherst College, where he impressed his teachers with his academic scholarship, his probing questioning mind, and his remarkable memory. After graduation, he became principal of Ware (Mass.) High School. While at Ware he introduced college preparatory courses and expanded the existing programs in natural science and the social sciences.

In 1876 he left Ware and entered the Yale Divinity School to study philosophy. At Yale he was again recognized as an exceptional scholar by such noted professors as Timothy Dwight (1752–1817) (later president of the university), Samuel Harris, and George Park Fisher. After graduation in 1879, Garman was awarded the Hooker Fellowship, which assured him

two more years of graduate study. Having refused the offer of President Julius H. Seelye (one of his former teachers) to return to Amherst College in 1878, Garman accepted his second offer in 1880 and became the Walker Instructor in Mathematics. The following year he was appointed instructor in philosophy and in 1882 became an associate professor. That same year he married Eliza Nancy Miner, the daughter of a Ware High School colleague; they had no children. By 1892 Garman had been awarded a full professorship in mental and moral philosophy by the college.

During his twenty-six years at Amherst College, Garman influenced the lives of many students. Such diverse individuals as Supreme Court Chief Justice Harlan Fisk Stone, U.S. Ambassador to Mexico Dwight Morrow and Phillips-Andover Academy Headmaster Alfred E. Stearns would write of their affection and admiration for Garman. In *The Autobiography of Calvin Coolidge* (1929), the taciturn former president would lavish the most praise on his former teacher. "We looked upon Garman as a man who walked with God . . . To Garman was given a power which took his class up into a high mountain of spiritual life and left them alone with God . . . Truly he drew men out." According to Coolidge, "We were not only learning about the human mind but learning how to use it, learning how to think. A problem would often be stated and the class left to attempt to find the solution unaided by the teacher." While textbooks and lectures were part of Garman's teaching, his unique method also included pamphlets that he wrote, edited, and printed in his cellar. The pamphlets were his personal property; students were allowed to borrow them but not permitted to show them to students outside the philosophy program.

Garman required his students to weigh the evidence, question all, and to think and seek the truth. His basic aim as an educator was to develop students with a greater sense of morality, who were willing to be of service to their fellow man. In a book of his letters and lectures that was published two years after his death he states that

. . . there is no such thing as political ethics apart from divine ethics. . . . man has no dual personality; he is not endowed with two minds, the one to be used in the sphere of religion and the other in the sphere of government and society; that man is always and everywhere himself; that he has but one set of principles by which to guide his conduct; that love to God and love to man are, from the point of view of the finite, exactly the same process.

Garman believed that man's struggle as an individual and race consists of a search for the perfect state, where he finds his true relationship to God and his fellow men. He believed that Christianity was the answer to all questions, the essential element in the acts of service to mankind and to God.

To commemorate his twenty-fifth year at Amherst, in 1906 thirteen of his former students wrote in his honor articles that dealt with philosophical and psychological topics. They were published as *Studies in Philosophy and Psychology*.

As a student at Yale, Garman had contracted a throat infection that made him subject to chronic bronchial infections for the rest of his life. Students remembered him keeping the temperature of his classroom high and wearing an overcoat even during the hot summer months. Garman opened his home to students, and lively discussions and conversations were often conducted late into the night. He died in Amherst, Massachusetts.

Garman left few public papers or writings, yet during his teaching career and after his influence was felt at all levels of society, from the White House to corporate offices to classrooms. He taught a philosophy of service to God and to country by means of a methodology that challenged his students to think. Although his name in not remembered outside the field of education, his memory is kept alive by the effect that he had on a generation of civic leaders. On the Garman Memorial Table at Amherst College his former students expressed his life's work: "He chose to write on living men's hearts."

• The Charles Edward Garman Papers, which include correspondence with former students, essays, copies of his pamphlets, lecture notes, notebooks and diaries, can be found at the Amherst College Library. Eliza Miner Garman, *Letters, Lectures and Addresses of Charles Edward Garman* (1909), is the only published collection of his work. The Forbes Library in Northampton, Mass., has a collection of newspaper accounts of the death and funeral of Garman. An obituary and related articles are in the Northampton, Mass., *Daily Hampshire Gazette*, 10–13 Feb. 1907.

JOHN ALMON WATERHOUSE

GARNER, Erroll (15 June 1921–2 Jan. 1977), jazz pianist and composer, was born Earl (as "Erroll" was pronounced) Garner in Pittsburgh, Pennsylvania, the son of Louis Ernest Garner, an electrical worker, cook, musician, and dance- and pool-hall entrepreneur, and Estella Darcus, a dressmaker. At around age two Garner began reproducing on the piano the tunes he heard on the family piano rolls and phonograph. He never learned to read music and could imitate nonmusical sounds on the piano. Fellow musician Eddie Calhoun insisted that Garner could hear sounds "up into an animal range." At age ten Garner became a soloist with the Kan D Kids, an African-American children's troupe performing on radio station KQV. He played for church socials and in neighborhood houses on Friday nights (admission was ten cents). He played tuba for his high school band and tried all the other instruments. Garner later said that he loved big bands so much that he wanted to make his piano sound like an orchestra. By the time he withdrew from Westinghouse High School in 1939, Garner was locally famous. Playing "for no money, hour after hour" at clubs such as the Crawford Grill, run by the owner of the Pittsburgh Crawfords, a leading baseball team in the black leagues, Garner made two local recordings at

age sixteen; he joined LeRoy Brown's small band and visited New York. By 1939 he had briefly led a sextet and was working for Brown's big band.

Short but muscular and massive, with long arms and hands that could reach a thirteenth and with hands that jazz critic Whitney Balliett said "moved like thieves on the keyboard," Garner began to attract wider attention. In 1941 he was an accompanist in New York and spent the next summer at the Edgewater, a Prohibition-era roadhouse in Wanamassas, near Asbury Park, New Jersey. After another year in Pittsburgh he returned there and was "discovered" by Timme Rosenkrantz, a record producer who took him to New York.

By this time Garner's distinctive style had emerged. His sister said, "Erroll's hands had complete independence. . . . It was almost like being able to split your thinking in half." Garner's powerful left hand (an arranger commented that he could probably have played the entire instrument left-handed) provided a swinging beat often likened to a guitar, tuba, or drum. His right hand, improvisational and embellishing, often lagged behind the beat as much as an eighth note. The result was nearly contrapuntal and thoroughly orchestral.

His third 1944 New York date was at Tondelayo's; he was invited to play at Times Hall. When pianist Art Tatum went on vacation in 1945 from his engagement at the Three Deuces on Fifty-second Street, his bassist Slam Stewart recruited Garner as a replacement. When Tatum left for good, they became the Slam Stewart Trio.

By late 1946 Garner had moved to Los Angeles and formed his own trio. His early recordings for small labels such as Signature, Portrait, and Savoy marked the direction he would take from then on. Applying his unique manner to familiar popular songs not usually thought of as jazz standards, such as "Laura," "Penthouse Serenade," and "Stairway to the Stars," he opened with a lengthy, fanciful introduction, virtually in itself a separate composition, then swung into the tune itself. Unlike many jazz virtuosos, Garner left the main tune easily recognizable.

In 1947 Garner recorded with bebop saxophonist Charlie Parker. "Playing with Bird," Garner said, "you never felt that you had to play the same thing you had played the night before." That same year he was named Pianist of the Year in the *Esquire* magazine jazz poll. In 1948 Garner made his first Paris appearance. He returned to New York to perform at the Three Deuces and Birdland, and he became a regular at major jazz clubs in Chicago and San Francisco. His audience widened with the 1951 *Piano Moods* album (Columbia), which included "I'm in the Mood for Love," "The Way You Look Tonight," "I Cover the Waterfront," "Body and Soul," and his own lilting "Play, Piano, Play."

Garner's career altered course permanently when his brother Linton, a swing band trumpeter, pianist, and arranger, introduced him to Martha Glaser, who became his manager. After the 1953 Modern American Jazz Festival, Garner played his first Carnegie Hall concert in 1954 and in 1955 his first Newport Jazz Festival. In the early 1950s Garner was on a plane landing in Denver. Moved by dewdrops on the windows, he composed the impressionistic "Misty," using his knees for a piano keyboard. With lyrics added later, "Misty" was eventually recorded more than 300 times by a host of different performers. After a 1955 date at the Blackhawk in San Francisco that became a duel of trios with the cerebral Dave Brubeck, Garner played in Carmel, California, on 19 September 1955. As his bassist Calhoun recalled, "We were still smokin'." So Glaser reluctantly allowed a nearby army radio station to tape the performance and play it for the soldiers. The result was *The Concert by the Sea* (Columbia, 1956), which sold relentlessly, even to people who ordinarily did not buy jazz records.

Garner made his first appearance with a symphony orchestra in Cleveland in 1956. Readily identifiable by his shiny, slick hair, huge mustache, and infectious, rhythmic growling, Garner became one of the most frequent jazz performers on American television. In 1957 he made his first European tour. The Columbia LP *Other Voices*, adapting Garner's voicings to an entire orchestra, was a bestseller. Such recordings catapulted Garner into mass popularity, although his right-hand embroideries sometimes sounded uncomfortably like the rippling music of "cocktail pianists." Also in 1957 Garner received the Grand Prix du Disque in Paris (where his recording of "Play, Piano, Play" was buried in a time capsule) and the *Down Beat* magazine award as the year's outstanding instrumentalist. He became the first jazz artist to sign with concert impresario Sol Hurok and in 1958 the first jazz artist to sell one million copies of a long-playing record: *The Concert by the Sea*. In 1960, when Columbia released without his approval an LP of previously unused tapes that he considered substandard and damaging to his reputation, Garner became the first artist successfully to enjoin a record company from releasing a record. This was a landmark in bolstering artists' control over their recorded performances.

In 1962 Garner made the first of eleven annual European concert tours and in 1963 composed part of the score for the Paris-set film *A New Kind of Love*. In 1964 he appeared at the New York World's Fair and in 1967 briefly in the German film *Negresco—Eine Tödliche Affaire* (*My Bed Is Not for Sleeping*). In the same year his *That's My Kick* for MGM records captured the flow of one of Garner's all-night recording sessions. In 1970 came Garner's first Asian tour. The same year he played at a Syracuse, New York, high school in order to quiet rioting students. In 1971 his portrait appeared on a stamp issued by the Republic of Mali, and his star was embedded in the Hollywood Boulevard Walk of Fame. The pianist Oscar Peterson recorded "Tribute to Erroll Garner."

Garner's last concert was with the National Symphony Orchestra in Washington, D.C., in 1974. His last public performance was at Mr. Kelly's Club in Chicago in February 1975, the year he was operated on for lung cancer in Los Angeles. Garner, who never married, died in the elevator of a Los Angeles apartment house of emphysema and fluid in his lungs that resulted from his cancer and subsequent surgery. Although Garner spawned imitations and helped extend jazz into the concert halls, he exerted no real influence on pianistic jazz. He started and ended as an original—in Balliett's words, "trapped inside his style," like many another unschooled virtuoso. His last bass player called him "a happy musician who could get a smile out of the piano." Garner remained a man who could be told to stop in the middle of a recording because he had made an obvious mistake and yet roll on to the end, explaining, "I just wanted to see how it would come out."

• James Doran, *Erroll Garner: The Most Happy Piano* (1985), is a treasure-trove of interviews with Garner's family and fellow musicians, as well as a definitive checklist of his performances. Among jazz critics, Whitney Balliett has frequently written evocatively of Garner, at greatest length and depth in *Jelly Roll, Jabbo and Fats* (1983). Jazz drummer Art Taylor's *Notes and Tones: Musician-to-Musician Interviews* (1970) sheds a good deal of light on Garner's creative process. The 3 Jan. 1977 obituary in the *Los Angeles Times* is useful.

JAMES ROSS MOORE

GARNER, John Nance (22 Nov. 1868–7 Nov. 1967), vice president and Speaker of the House, was born in Blossom Prairie, Red River County, Texas, the son of John Nance Garner III and Sarah Guest, farmers. With money he had saved from chores and playing semiprofessional baseball, Garner entered Vanderbilt University in 1886 but soon dropped out to return to Texas, where he read law and set up a practice in Clarksville at the age of twenty-one. The frail Garner contracted tuberculosis, however, and in 1893 moved to the drier climate of Uvalde, west of San Antonio. In Uvalde he joined the firm of Clark and Fuller prior to establishing his own office. Regaining his health, he prospered and became involved in community affairs as a publisher, banker, and county judge, an administrative post. He became a substantial landholder as well. In 1895 Garner married Mariette Rheiner, daughter of a prosperous rancher. They had one child.

In 1898 Garner, a Democrat, was elected to the Texas House of Representatives, where he soon developed a reputation as a man who studied the issues and supported progressive measures to regulate insurance companies and railroads. Garner was not an ideologue, however, and when possible, brokered compromises to provide regulation without stifling business. He was reelected in 1900.

In 1902 Garner was elected to Congress from the new Fifteenth Congressional District, which included Uvalde. In his campaign Garner used his homespun, neighborly style to stress issues such as a graduated income tax and a tariff for revenue only. "Cactus Jack" soon won respect from members of both parties, from the House leadership, and from Presidents Theodore Roosevelt and William Howard Taft. Garner, who became Democratic whip in 1911 and secured a place on the Ways and Means Committee in 1913, was adept at getting things done for his constituents. Most important was the development of a deep-water port for Corpus Christi.

Although he had some differences with Woodrow Wilson, Garner stood for Wilsonian measures such as independence for the Philippines, a graduated income tax, and the Federal Reserve System. For farmers he helped secure improved credit and marketing programs. Garner, however, did not become close to the administration until the United States entered World War I. His support of the war at a time when several influential Democrats voiced opposition elevated Garner in Wilson's esteem, and he proved invaluable as an administration spokesman in securing the enactment of war measures, especially those related to tax and trade questions.

With the return of the Republicans to power in the House following the 1918 elections and to the White House two years later, Garner considered retirement but decided to run again, in part to make clear his opposition to the Ku Klux Klan.

Garner later came to regard the years between 1918 and 1930 as his most useful in Washington. He became senior Democrat on the Ways and Means Committee in 1923. He maintained good relationships with the three Republican presidents of the time, and while he fought for the measures in which he believed, his opposition was constructive. For instance, Garner normally differed with the Republicans on tariff and tax measures, but since he opposed free trade, he was about as likely to dispute fellow Democrats. Although he could make a rousing speech when the occasion demanded, Garner rarely introduced legislation or spoke from the floor, preferring to work behind the scenes.

On many occasions after he became Democratic leader in 1929, Garner acted with his closest friend, Speaker Nicholas Longworth, a Republican, to expedite the passage of legislation. The two operated what was referred to as the Board of Education, so named because in a Capitol hideaway they gave lessons to colleagues about the pointlessness of filibuster and legislative deadlock and the wisdom of compromise.

Garner achieved his ambition of becoming Speaker when the Democrats regained control of the House in 1931. Despite his prestige and the affection of many peers, Garner did not have an easy time of it. His cautious and conservative stand on economic issues during the depression aroused discontent among members of both major parties. Although Garner disagreed with several features of Republican tax policy, his belief in the balanced budget led him to accept a Hoover administration proposal for a national sales tax in 1932. A rebellion among Democrats and progressive Republicans killed the sales tax proposal just as the presidential race was gaining attention and called Garner's leadership into doubt.

Nevertheless, the support of the Hearst press helped win Garner consideration as a contender for the Democratic presidential nomination. A victory in the California primary and his favorite son status in Texas gave him nearly one hundred pledged delegates going into the Democratic convention. Fearing a deadlock and a prolonged floor fight of the sort that had harmed the party in 1924, Garner released his delegates after the third ballot, accepting the vice presidential nomination that Franklin D. Roosevelt offered him in an effort to secure the vote of the Texas delegation.

During Roosevelt's first term, Garner had as much respect and recognition as a vice president could then hope to have, perhaps more. His fairness as presiding officer was widely acknowledged as were his efforts to give new senators from both parties a chance to preside over the Senate in order to help speed their grasp of parliamentary procedures. More conservative than Roosevelt and the New Dealers who came to prominence, he differed with Roosevelt on some issues, such as the extension of diplomatic recognition to the Soviet Union, but he supported many New Deal policies out of party loyalty and was often consulted by the president on legislation. Garner remained on the ticket in 1936, but thereafter his differences with Roosevelt sharpened over matters such as Roosevelt's deficit-spending policies and especially over the president's abortive effort in 1937 to add justices to the Supreme Court. Garner helped engineer passage of a bill to reform the lower courts, a concession that was meant to save face for Roosevelt after the court-packing bill was rejected in the Senate. Roosevelt believed Garner could have done more had he wished.

In 1938 Garner drew further away from Roosevelt when the president tried unsuccessfully to thwart the reelection of conservative Democrats, many of them southerners. Garner became increasingly outspoken in his opposition as he realized that Roosevelt was likely to seek a third term in 1940. Garner made a bid for the nomination but was opposed in Texas by Jesse Jones and other powerful Roosevelt adherents from the state. His hopes for the nomination received a crushing blow when the Democrats' Texas state convention would not come out against a third term. The favorite son status he had at the Democratic party convention in 1940 was meaningless as Roosevelt swept to a first-ballot nomination.

Garner left Washington for Uvalde shortly after the 1941 inauguration and played no further role in national affairs. When asked if he regretted his aid to Roosevelt at the 1932 convention, Garner replied negatively but added that he might have been of more service to Roosevelt and the nation had he remained in the House. In that way he might have been able to restrain Roosevelt. Garner died in Uvalde.

• Garner burned his papers, so all that remains from his own files is a collection of clippings at the Eugene Barker History Center at the University of Texas. However, a considerable amount of Garner material can be found in the Franklin Delano Roosevelt Library. Two key episodes in Garner's career are discussed in Lionel V. Patenaude, "Garner, Sumners, and Connally: The Defeat of the Roosevelt Court Bill in 1937," *Southwestern Historical Quarterly* 74 (July 1970): 36–51; and Jordan A. Schwarz, "John Nance Garner and the Sales Tax Rebellion of 1932," *Journal of Southern History* 30

(May 1964): 162–80. Much information about Garner can be found in Marquis James, *Mr. Garner of Texas* (1939); Bascom N. Timmins, *Garner of Texas: A Personal History* (1948); Ovie Clark Fisher, *Cactus Jack* (1978); and Michael J. Romano, "The Emergence of John Nance Garner as a Figure in American National Politics, 1924–1941" (Ph.D. diss., St. John's Univ., 1974). Also see Arthur Meier Schlesinger, *Age of Roosevelt*, vol. 2: *The Coming of the New Deal* (1988), and vol. 3: *The Politics of Upheaval* (1988). Other pertinent materials are cited in Donald R. Kennon, ed., "John Nance Garner," in *The Speakers of the U.S. House of Representatives: A Bibliography, 1789–1984* (1986); and Herbert S. Parmet and Marie B. Hecht, *Never Again: A President Runs for a Third Term* (1968). An obituary is in the *New York Times*, 8 Nov. 1967.

LLOYD J. GRAYBAR

GARNET, Henry Highland (23 Dec. 1815–13 Feb. 1882), clergyman and abolitionist, was born in New Market, Kent County, Maryland, the son of George and Henrietta (later called Elizabeth), slaves. Henry escaped with his parents and seven siblings to Wilmington, Delaware, in 1824, assisted by the Quaker Thomas Garrett, a key figure in the Underground Railroad. After a brief stay in Bucks County, Pennsylvania, the Garnets settled in New York City, where Henry received a grammar school education at the African Free School.

In 1828 Henry worked as a cabin boy on a ship, making two voyages to Cuba. The next year he returned from working as a cook and steward on board a schooner sailing from New York City to Washington, D.C., to find that his family had been broken up by slave hunters. His sister was tried as a fugitive, but his parents had escaped. Thomas Willis of Jericho, Long Island, took Henry in, and he was indentured to a Captain Smith for two years. Due to an accident, Henry lost the use of his right leg, and it was later amputated. He began studying in 1831 at the High School for Colored Youth in New York City, where he was introduced to the Latin and Greek classics.

In 1833 Garnet came under the influence of Theodore Sedgwick Wright, pastor of the First Colored Presbyterian Church, who baptized him and encouraged him to attend Noyes Academy in Canaan, New Hampshire. Here he met Julia Williams, a former student at Prudence Crandall's boarding school for black girls in Canterbury, Connecticut. Garnet and Julia married in 1841; they had three children, only one of whom survived to adulthood. Crandall's school was closed in 1834 because of antiblack sentiment, and a year later a mob attacked Noyes Academy. Garnet, along with classmates Alexander Crummell and Thomas Sydney, returned to New York City. News that under the leadership of Beriah Green Oneida Institute had opened its doors to all, regardless of race, brought Garnet and his two friends to this pioneering manual labor and abolitionist school in Whitesboro, New York, in 1836. Garnet enrolled in the preparatory department and, according to Crummell, became distinguished for his intuition, wit, brilliance, and rhetorical skills. He graduated in 1839 and the next

year went to Troy, New York, where he taught school, studied theology with New School clergyman Nathan Beman, and held religious meetings in his house. In 1841 he was ordained and became pastor of the Liberty Street Presbyterian Church in Troy.

Garnet supported the temperance movement and became a strong advocate of political antislavery. He joined the American and Foreign Anti-Slavery Society, backed the Liberty party, and fought for the elective franchise for blacks in New York State. He was active in the black state convention movement, harbored fugitive slaves, and supported the free produce movement, which advocated boycotting all products made by slave labor. Garnet achieved particular notoriety for a speech he delivered at the 1843 black national convention held in Buffalo, New York. In his "Address to the Slaves of the United States of America," Garnet counseled, "Hereditary bondsmen, know ye not, who would be free, themselves must strike the blow!" Opposed by Frederick Douglass and others who found it too militant, Garnet's resolution was rejected by a narrow margin by the delegates.

In 1850 Garnet went to Great Britain to lecture on the free produce movement. He then traveled to Sterling, Jamaica, in 1852 as a missionary on behalf of the United Presbyterian Church of Scotland, also continuing to promote the free produce movement. In Jamaica, Julia directed the Female Industrial School. Illness forced Garnet to return in 1855 to New York City where he served Shiloh Presbyterian Church as pastor upon the death of Theodore Wright. Garnet made several appeals to the American Missionary Association, a nonsectarian organization founded by Christian abolitionists, to conduct domestic missions among New York City blacks and was on the executive committee of the association from 1847 to 1848 and from 1856 to 1860.

By the late 1850s, now an advocate of black emigration and mission work in Africa, Garnet supported the African Civilization Society and its British adjunct, the African Aid Society, which sought to establish a West African colony in Yoruba. Although emigration was opposed by other prominent African-American abolitionists, such as Presbyterian clergyman James W. C. Pennington, Garnet maintained an unwavering commitment to the African Civilization Society. In 1861 he journeyed to England to promote the society.

Garnet became pastor of the Fifteenth Street Presbyterian Church in Washington, D.C., in 1864. He helped recruit African-American troops for the U.S. Army during the Civil War and was active in relief work on behalf of the newly freed slaves. In 1865 he became the first African American to preach a sermon in the White House. He became president of Avery College in Pittsburgh in 1868 and returned to Shiloh Presbyterian Church in New York City in 1870. Around 1879 Garnet, whose first wife had died, married Sarah J. Smith Tompkins. Appointed U.S. minister to Liberia in 1881, Garnet died there the following year.

• Some of Garnet's letters can be found in C. Peter Ripley et al., eds., *The Black Abolitionist Papers* (1981–1983), a microfilmed collection that runs to seventeen reels, and some have been published in Ripley et al., eds., *The Black Abolitionist Papers, 1830–1865* (5 vols., 1985–1992). Biographical treatments of Garnet include William M. Brewer, "Henry Highland Garnet," *Journal of Negro History* 13 (Jan. 1928): 36–52; Earl Ofari, *"Let Your Motto Be Resistance": The Life and Thought of Henry Highland Garnet* (1972); Joel Schor, *Henry Highland Garnet: A Voice of Black Radicalism in the Nineteenth Century* (1977); David E. Swift, *Black Prophets of Justice: Activist Clergy before the Civil War* (1989); and Martin Burt Pasternak, "Rise Now and Fly to Arms: The Life of Henry Highland Garnet" (Ph.D. diss., Univ. of Massachusetts, 1981).

MILTON C. SERNETT

GARNET, Sarah Smith Tompkins (31 Aug. 1831–17 Sept. 1911), educator and suffragist, was born Minisarah J. Smith in Queens County, New York, the daughter of Sylvanus Smith and Ann Eliza Springsteel, farmers, who were of mixed Native American, black, and white descent. Although Garnet's great-grandmother had established a school that her father attended, little is known about Garnet's own early schooling other than that she was taught by her father. However, she was a teacher's assistant at age fourteen with a salary of $20 per year while she studied at various normal schools in the Queens County area. By 1854 Garnet (known as Sarah) was teaching in the private African Free School in the Williamsburg section of Brooklyn. In 1863 she became the first African-American principal appointed by the New York Public School System, serving at the all-black P.S. 80 from her appointment until her retirement in 1900.

The annual closing exercises at Garnet's school were well known for the students' various public presentations and performances of excerpts of literature by standard authors. Garnet also founded a night school that taught basic literacy, sewing, homemaking, and vocational skills to adults. Among her school's better-known graduates were the violinist Walter F. Craig and Susan Elizabeth Frazier, the first African-American to be assigned in 1896 to a white-staffed New York City school.

In 1883, when the school board discussed closing three of its African-American schools, Garnet was active in fighting the proposed change. The compromise reached in 1884 allowed students of both races to attend either the previously all-white or all-black schools, and Garnet may have had white students in her school after that date. The staff of P.S. 80 remained all-black, however. Additionally, in 1883 Garnet opened a seamstress shop, which she operated until her death.

Garnet married an Episcopal priest, Samuel Tompkins, early in life and had two children; the three of them predeceased her. In 1879 she married Henry Highland Garnet, an abolitionist and Presbyterian minister, who served as resident minister to Liberia. He died three years later.

Sarah Garnet was consistently active in civic affairs. In the late 1880s, two decades or more before woman suffrage became a popular issue for women in general or in the African-American community, she organized the Equal Suffrage League, the only African-American suffrage organization in Brooklyn. She was active in the National Association of Colored Women's Clubs (NACWC), serving as the superintendent of its suffrage department. At the NACWC convention following her death she was memorialized as "the most noted suffragist of our race."

When the presses of journalist Ida B. Wells's Memphis, Tennessee, newspaper were burned in 1892 because of her antilynching editorials, Garnet and other prominent black women formed a committee to raise the funds to replace them. She also assisted later in the formation of the Brooklyn Home for Aged Colored People.

A few months before her death, Garnet attended the Universal Races Congress in London and brought suffrage literature back home to her suffrage club. Her sister, Susan Smith McKinney Steward, one of the nation's first African-American female physicians, traveled with her to Europe. W. E. B. Du Bois was a guest at a reception held in Garnet's honor after her return. Garnet died at her Brooklyn home.

Garnet is remembered locally for her ground-breaking role as an African-American woman in New York Public School administration and nationally as one of the very earliest African-American suffragists.

• For additional information on Garnet's life and work, see profiles by Floris Barnett Cash in *Black Women in America*, vol. 1, ed. Darlene Clark Hine (1993); Leedell W. Neyland in *Notable American Women, 1607–1950*, vol. 2 (1971); and Maritcha R. Lyons in *Homespun Heroines and Other Women of Distinction*, ed. Hallie Q. Brown (1926; repr. 1992). See also Dorothy Salem, *To Better Our World: Black Women in Organized Reform, 1890–1920* (1990); Charles Harris Wesley, *The History of the National Association of Colored Women's Clubs* (1984); and Sylvia G. L. Dannett, *Profiles of Negro Womanhood*, vol. 1 (1964). An obituary is in the *New York Age*, 21 Sept. 1911.

ELIZABETH L. IHLE

GARNETT, James Mercer (8 June 1770–23 Apr. 1843), congressman, agricultural reformer, and educator, was born at "Mount Pleasant" plantation, near present-day Loretto in Essex County, Virginia, the son of planters Muscoe Garnett and Grace Fenton Mercer. He was privately educated, and in 1793 married his first cousin, Mary Eleanor Dick Mercer. The couple had four daughters and four sons.

Garnett represented Essex County in the Virginia House of Delegates from December 1799 through January 1801. There he voted for the adoption of James Madison's report on the resolutions condemning the Alien and Sedition Acts. Although he decried politicking as "highly improper, and as degrading to the understanding, as it is to the integrity of freemen" (*To the Freeholders of Essex*, 29 Mar. 1798), he was elected to the U.S. House of Representatives in the Ninth and

Tenth Congresses (Mar. 1805–Mar. 1809). He quickly allied himself with John Randolph of Roanoke and the Tertium Quids, a splinter group of congressional Republicans who objected to the nationalistic stance of the Jefferson administration on issues such as the acquisition of Florida, and who contested the presidential aspirations of James Madison. Garnett opposed the embargo and what he termed "the other self-destroying measures" advanced by the Jefferson administration (*Spirit of 'Seventy-Six*, 14 Feb. 1810). In 1807 he served on the grand jury that indicted Aaron Burr for treason.

Although he declined to run for reelection in 1808, Garnett remained in the public eye by engaging his adversaries in the Georgetown *Spirit of 'Seventy-Six*, the Tertium Quids' party organ. Most of his editorial letters centered on the politicized issues of agricultural reform, manufactures, and the embargo. Signing himself "Cornplanter," Garnett attacked Robert R. Livingston and George W. P. Custis for their agricultural fairs. In a series of vitriolic exchanges between February and July 1810, Garnett argued that by promoting American breeds of sheep and domestic manufacturers, the two Federalist reformers were diverting capital from agriculture. In the pages of the same paper he also engaged Mathew Carey in a heated debate on the protection of American manufacturers, which Garnett, an ardent advocate of free trade, opposed. Carey responded with *Three Letters on the Present Calamitous State of Affairs, Addressed to J. M. Garnett* (1820). At an antitariff convention in Baltimore in 1821, Garnett was appointed to summarize the meeting's sentiments; this address was printed in John Stuart Skinner's *American Farmer*. Garnett attended another such antitariff convention in Philadelphia in 1831.

During the War of 1812 Garnett's opposition to Madison's policies led to accusations that the planter was aiding the British. He defended himself against these charges in the circular *Substance of an Address* (17 Apr. 1815).

In October 1818 Garnett founded the Virginia Agricultural Society of Fredericksburg and was chosen as its first president, a post he held for twenty years. In annual addresses to the society and in frequent pieces published in the *American Farmer*, the *Farmer's Register*, and the *Albany Cultivator*, he lamented Virginia's agricultural and commercial decline. Decrying the population drain to the Southwest as a "raging pestilence," he advocated closer cooperation among agricultural reform societies and the implementation of crop rotation. He was instrumental in founding the Virginia State Agricultural Society, and he served as the first president of the United States Agricultural Society. His advocacy and dissemination of information on agricultural reclamation was more significant than any scientific farming or innovation he carried out at his Elmwood plantation, located near present-day Loretto in Essex County. Indeed, in *Virginia Georgics* (1858) Charles Carter Lee slyly noted that "Garnett lectured on / The way to farm, while Waring [Garnett's neighbor] worked his corn."

Although he believed that "universal liberty" was "that most beautiful, most elusive chimera of the imagination" (*An Address Delivered before the Virginia Agricultural Society of Fredericksburg, . . . October 28, 1818*), Garnett favored religious and moral instruction for slaves to make them a more productive work force. In 1838 he served as a vice president of the Virginia Colonization Society, which sought to end America's racial problems and, at the same time, spread democracy and the Gospel by removing freedmen to Liberia.

A strong belief in the pivotal role of women in securing the preservation of the republic through educating their children and through the power of their moral example, combined with a series of financial reverses that necessitated increasing his income, led Garnett to establish a school for girls at his home about 1822. He instructed the scholars in composition, but the bulk of the teaching duties fell on Garnett's wife, unmarried daughters, and widowed daughter-in-law. Several of his addresses to his students were published as *Seven Lectures on Female Education, inscribed to Mrs. Garnett's Pupils, at Elm-Wood* (1824). The ill health of his wife forced Garnett to close the school after eight years; he then hired male instructors and opened a school for boys. He twice enlarged his schoolhouse to accommodate more pupils. According to Garnett, the poor quality of education in Virginia resulted from the poor quality of teachers. The brightest and most talented men were drawn into law and politics. He advocated the improvement of education through the establishment of voluntary associations, the founding of schools to teach the poor, the implementation of state regulation and standardization, and the use of the Bible as a textbook. His clearest enunciations of his philosophy are *A Discourse on Scholastic Reforms, and Amendments in the Modes and General Scope of Parental Instruction* (1833), *An Address on the Subject of Literary Associations to Promote Education* (1834), and "Popular Education," published in the *Southern Literary Messenger* (1842).

Garnett returned to the House of Delegates from November 1824 through February 1825. In 1829 he was one of four men chosen to represent the counties of Caroline, Essex, Hanover, King and Queen, and King William at the state constitutional convention. Although before the assembly convened he issued *Constitutional Charts; or, Comparative Views of the Legislative, Executive and Judiciary Departments, in the Constitutions of all the States in the Union, including that of the United States* (1829), he took little part in the debates. The convention extended the franchise to white male leaseholders and householders, a move Garnett opposed. He died at Elmwood.

• An extensive correspondence exchanged between Garnett and John Randolph survives in the Garnett-Randolph Transcripts in the John Randolph Papers at the Library of Congress. A small collection of twenty-five letters is at the Virginia Historical Society, which also houses in the Hunter Family Papers information on the Garnetts' schools. Garnett's anonymous and pseudonymous essays in the *Farmer's Register* are identified in J. G. de Roulhac Hamilton, ed., "Writers of

Anonymous Articles in *The Farmer's Register*," *Journal of Southern History* 23 (1957): 90–102. Biographical sketches appear in *The South in the Building of the Nation* 11 (1909): 384–85; Hugh Blair Grigsby, *The Virginia Convention of 1829–30. A Discourse Delivered before the Virginia Historical Society, . . . 1853* (1854), pp. 69–71; "An Address by Professor James Mercer Garnett, . . . June 20, 1898," *Southern Historical Society Papers* 26 (1898): 347–58; *Genealogy of the Mercer-Garnett Family of Essex County, Virginia . . .* (1910), pp. 3–18, written by a descendant of Garnett. See also Avery O. Craven, "The Agricultural Reformers of the Ante-Bellum South," *American Historical Review* 33 (Jan. 1928): 302–14.

SARA B. BEARSS

GARNETT, Muscoe Russell Hunter (25 July 1821–14 Feb. 1864), lawyer and congressman, was born in Elmwood, Essex County, Virginia, the son of James Mercer Garnett, Jr., a lawyer who died when Muscoe was three, and Maria Hunter. Garnett was educated at home by his mother and two aunts until he entered the University of Virginia in 1838. After only one year as an undergraduate, he returned to the family home in Elmwood and spent two years reading in his family library, making two trips to Washington to make use of the Library of Congress, and visiting his uncle R. M. T. Hunter, who was then Speaker of the House. In 1841 Garnett returned to Charlottesville to enroll in the University of Virginia law school, where he completed the requirements for a law degree in one year. The following year he was admitted to the Virginia bar and founded his own law practice in Loretto, Essex County. During this time he contributed book reviews to the *Southern Magazine* and the *Southern Literary Messenger*.

Garnett became acquainted with Nathaniel Beverly Tucker, a prominent Virginia judge, a law professor at the College of William and Mary, and one of the earliest Southern nationalists. Under Tucker's influence, Garnett in 1850 published *The Union, Past and Future: How It Works and How to Save It, By a Citizen of Virginia*, an incendiary pamphlet that argued that the South was disadvantaged economically by its ties to the North. It contained a detailed analysis of the relationship of slavery to the national government, concluding that slavery enjoyed a protected legal and constitutional status. Garnett also contended that slavery was a beneficial system, asking his Southern audience, "Shall the labouring classes be an inferior race, so controlled and directed by the superior minds of whites, as continually to progress in material and moral well being, far beyond any point it has ever shown a power of attaining in freedom?" He ended his tract with a call for a Southern nation. The pamphlet, published in Charleston, gained Garnett wide attention throughout the South as a young scholar and statesman. *The Union Past and Future* is regarded as an important tract in the development of ideas of Southern nationalism, and as one of the earliest and most forceful articulations of the theories of government that animated Southern nationalism before the Civil War.

In 1850 and 1851 Garnett was selected as a delegate to the Virginia Constitutional Convention. In the fall of 1853 he was elected to the Virginia House of Delegates, where he headed the committee on finance. As a state representative Garnett developed a reputation as a fiery orator and twice served as a Virginia delegate to the Democratic national conventions, in Baltimore in 1852 and in Cincinnati in 1856. In November 1856 he was elected to the U.S. House of Representatives, representing the First District of Virginia, and was sworn in on 1 December 1856. Garnett served in Congress from 1856 to 1861, winning reelection to the 35th and 36th congresses. In Congress he obtained national recognition as a strict constructionist and as a vociferous defender of slavery. He also remained active in his home state, serving on the board of visitors of the University of Virginia from 1855 to 1859, and as chairman of the library committee. On 26 July 1860 he married Mary Picton Stevens of Hoboken, New Jersey, daughter of Edwin Augustus Stevens, founder of the Stevens Institute of Technology in Hoboken. Together they had two children.

Garnett was a strong advocate of secession in 1860 and 1861 and served as a delegate to the Virginia Secession Convention in 1861. He withdrew from Congress when Virginia seceded in April 1861. He then became a member of the Virginia State Convention, and in November he was elected to represent the First Virginia District in the Confederate House of Representatives. He served in this post until early 1864, when he contracted typhoid fever in Richmond and was granted leave to return to Elmwood, where he died.

Garnett's early death cut short the career of a promising Southern politician, and he is remembered today less for his service in the U.S. and Confederate congresses than for his writings on government and Southern nationalism. Garnett's particular importance is as an early advocate for a Southern state, and as a theorist of the governmental principles supporting its creation.

• Garnett's own writings and political philosophy are in his *The Union Past and Future* and in the *Congressional Globe*, 34th and 36th Cong., especially 36th Cong., 2d sess., pp. 411–16. For considerations of Garnett's writings and years in Congress, see Thomas Alexander and Richard Beringer, *The Anatomy of the Continental Congress* (1972), and John McCardell, *The Idea of a Southern Nation: Southern Nationalists and Southern Nationalism, 1830–1860* (1979). Brief biographies of Garnett include Harry Clemons, *The Home Library of the Garnetts of Elmwood* (1957); M. J. M. Garnett, "Biographical Sketch of Hon. Muscoe Russell Hunter Garnett," *William and Mary College Quarterly*, July–Oct. 1909, reprinted as a pamphlet (1909) with excerpts from his writings; J. M. Garnett, *Genealogy of the Mercer-Garnett Family* (1910); and Garnett's obituary in the *Richmond Enquirer*, 15 Feb. 1864.

DANIEL HAMILTON

GARNETT, Robert Selden (16 Dec. 1819–13 July 1861), army officer, was born in Essex County, Virginia, the son of Robert Selden Garnett, a U.S. congressman, and Olympia DeGouges. He was a cousin of future Confederate general Richard Brooke Garnett.

Garnett received an appointment to the U.S. Military Academy at West Point in 1837, graduated twenty-seventh of fifty-two in the class of 1841, and was appointed a brevet second lieutenant in the Fourth U.S. Artillery. After a stint as an instructor of infantry tactics at West Point in 1843–1844, he saw significant combat in the Mexican War, serving as an aide to John E. Wool and then to Zachary Taylor. He won brevet promotions to captain and major "for gallant conduct" at Monterrey and Buena Vista. Transferred to the Seventh U.S. Infantry as a first lieutenant in 1848, Garnett was soon promoted to captain and saw action in the Indian wars in Florida in 1850. He served as commandant of cadets at West Point from late 1852 to mid-1854, during Robert E. Lee's tenure as superintendent there. Garnett's last antebellum assignment was as major of the Ninth U.S. Infantry from 1855 to early 1861, most notably in command of expeditions against American Indians in Washington Territory. In 1857 he married Mary Neilson, and upon his return from his assignment on the frontier in 1858, he found that she had died along with their only child in his absence. He spent the next year on leave in Europe, returning just before the winter of 1860–1861.

Garnett, who resigned his commission after the secession of his native state, was quickly appointed colonel and adjutant general on the staff of Robert E. Lee, commanding the Virginia State Forces. He served as Lee's chief of staff in practice if not in title during April and May 1861, working to organize troops. Appointed lieutenant colonel of infantry in the Confederate States Army on 24 May 1861, Garnett was promoted to brigadier general on 6 June 1861 and immediately ordered to northwestern Virginia with about 4,000 troops, primarily Virginians, to help defend the western approaches to the Shenandoah Valley.

With little support from his superiors in the way of troops, weapons, supplies, and provisions and even less support from the predominantly Unionist citizenry of the western Virginia mountains, Garnett struggled to carry out his assignment. The Federal forces opposing him, commanded by George B. McClellan, numbered about twice the Confederates' strength, and Garnett accordingly posted his troops in strong defensive positions on Rich Mountain and Laurel Hill. When Rich Mountain was captured on 10 July, exposing Garnett's flank on Laurel Hill, the Confederates retreated and were pursued by the Federals, who forced them to fight a sharp rearguard action on 13 July 1861 at Carrick's Ford on the Cheat River. Garnett, leading by example and trying to coordinate an orderly withdrawal of his troops as they crossed the river, was killed by a volley of Federal musketry, and his force was quickly scattered or captured. His body, which fell into the hands of the enemy, was soon returned under a flag of truce by McClellan, who observed that Garnett "fell while acting the part of a gallant soldier" (*Official Records*, vol. 2, p. 251).

Garnett, the first general officer of either army to be killed in action in the Civil War, was considered by many contemporaries to be one of the most promising officers in the Confederacy. Walter H. Taylor, assistant adjutant general with the Army of Northern Virginia and one of Lee's most trusted staff officers, called Garnett "the best informed and most capable man in military detail that I ever met" and "General Lee's right-hand man in organizing and marshaling" the Virginia state troops in the spring of 1861 (Taylor, p. 22). Edward Porter Alexander, chief of artillery of the First Corps under Lee, remarked: "In Garnett every trait was purely military. Had he lived, I am sure he would have been one of our great generals" (Alexander, *Military Memoirs*, p. 14). In his personal recollections, Alexander even asserted that, "had he lived, I am sure [Garnett] would have won a reputation no whit behind Stonewall Jackson's" (Gallagher, ed., p. 49). As Douglas Southall Freeman, whose biographical sketch of Garnett and account of his campaign in western Virginia is in many respects still the best, commented, "Garnett's fate and the abandonment of the western approaches to the Shenandoah Valley were lamented equally. . . . From the list of those to whom the South looked hopefully, his high name had to be stricken" (Freeman, p. 37). Garnett's extremely brief tenure as a commander prevents any definitive judgments on his generalship, however.

• Garnett's file in Compiled Service Records of Confederate General and Staff Officers and Nonregimental Enlisted Men, War Department Collection of Confederate Records, RG 109, National Archives, Washington, D.C. (available on microfilm as National Archives Microcopy M331), is useful. The most significant source for Garnett's brief Civil War career is *The War of the Rebellion: A Compilation of the Official Records of the Union and Confederate Armies*, vol. 2 (128 vols., 1880–1901), which includes his and other's official reports and correspondence concerning his campaign in northwestern Virginia. A biographical sketch is in Jedediah Hotchkiss, ed., *Virginia*, vol. 3 of Clement A. Evans, ed., *Confederate Military History* (1899). Useful information on Garnett's antebellum career in the U.S. Army is in Francis Heitman, *Historical Register and Dictionary of the United States Army* (1903). See also Henry M. Price, "Rich Mountain in 1861," *Southern Historical Society Papers* 27 (1899): 38–41; Edward Porter Alexander, *Military Memoirs of a Confederate* (1907) and *Fighting for the Confederacy: The Personal Recollections of General Edward Porter Alexander*, ed. Gary W. Gallagher (1989); Walter H. Taylor, *General Lee: His Campaigns in Virginia 1861–1865, with Personal Reminiscences* (1906); and Douglas Southall Freeman, *Lee's Lieutenants: A Study in Command*, vol. 1 (3 vols., 1942–1944).

J. TRACY POWER

GARRARD, James (14 Jan. 1749–19 Jan. 1822), governor and minister, was born in Stafford County, Virginia, the son of William Garrard, a moderately wealthy planter and militia colonel, and Mary Naughty. The Garrards descended from French Huguenots. James was probably educated in one of the local schools of the Fredericksburg–Stafford County area. He learned surveying and was an active member of a "Regular" Baptist church. He assisted his father in farming. In 1769 Garrard married Elizabeth Mountjoy; they had twelve children, three of whom died in infancy.

As a militia captain in 1776, Garrard commanded a schooner that was captured by the British. Offered his freedom in return for military intelligence, he refused. He later managed to escape. Promoted to colonel in the Stafford militia, Garrard most likely saw plenty of active duty during the British invasions of Virginia in 1781 and probably participated with the Virginia militia army in checking British troops at Gloucester during the Yorktown campaign. Garrard served in the Virginia House of Delegates for one session in 1779.

The western country beckoned, and Garrard, with his wife and seven children, moved to what is now Bourbon County, Kentucky. He built a large stone residence, which he named "Mount Lebanon," near present-day Paris, Kentucky. Through the acquisition of military land warrants and exercise of preemption rights, Garrard, by 1790, had possession of 38,000 acres. He prospered as a farmer and raised fine horses and cattle. He was one of the first persons to initiate the making of "sour mash whiskey" from corn. Garrard's bourbon whiskey was in much demand for its superb quality, so much so that in 1787 a county grand jury indicted him for "retailing liquor without a license." Garrard also had salt works, known as James Garrard and Sons, on a 500-acre plot at the mouth of the Kentucky River.

In 1787 Garrard and Augustin Eastin organized the Cooper's Run Baptist Church, and Garrard served as the church's minister for a decade. Garrard also helped to establish other Baptist churches in Kentucky's Bluegrass region. He was moderator of the Elkhorn Association of Baptist churches, 1790–1791. The Cooper's Run Baptist Church lost five of its members to Indian raids the first year. In 1795 it had 119 members but then rapidly declined in numbers; it was dropped by the Baptist association in 1803 for that reason and for the heresy of its members. Garrard, for all purposes, had become a Unitarian by that time, and his liberal theology had rubbed off on other members of his church. As a preacher, Garrard did not have much of a flair for fiery oratory; lacking a "gift of ready speech," he sounded more like a lawyer than a minister of the gospel.

Garrard drifted into politics, which did not sit well with his fellow Baptists, who strictly adhered to the idea of separation between public and religious offices. Some Baptists also did not like his stance on slavery. Although he owned at one time twenty-three slaves, Garrard denounced slavery as a "horrid evil" and called for some form of gradual emancipation.

In 1785 Garrard again served a single term in the Virginia House of Delegates, representing Fayette County, Kentucky. As a legislator he supported the bill for religious freedom (enacted 1786) and introduced the successful measure for creating Bourbon County from Fayette County. He chose the name for the new county and also of Paris, Kentucky. With the establishment of Bourbon County in 1786, Garrard

was appointed the county surveyor and a justice of the peace. For several years the county court met at his residence. He was a member of the Kentucky Society for the Promotion of Useful Knowledge and the board of trustees for Transylvania Seminary. Garrard was colonel and commander of the Bourbon County militia, and he accompanied Benjamin Logan on the Shawnee expedition into the Ohio country in 1786. He served in the Danville conventions that aimed for separation of Kentucky from Virginia in 1784, May and August 1785, 1787, 1788, and 1790. At the July 1790 convention, which provided enabling measures for statehood, Garrard chaired the committee of the whole for most of the session. He served in the same capacity at the 1792 constitutional convention. At this meeting Garrard presented a memorial for abolition of slavery and also one for guaranteeing religious liberty. Garrard opposed a constitutional provision prohibiting the legislature from freeing slaves unless owners were compensated.

Garrard's strong power base in Bourbon County, reputation of unimpeachable integrity, ability to be a conciliator, and unbleached Jeffersonianism were factors that propelled him to become Kentucky's second governor in 1796. Under the Constitution of 1792 an electoral college selected the governor. Garrard and his main rival, Benjamin Logan, were members of this group. In the balloting Logan received 21 votes, Garrard, 16, Thomas Todd, 14, and John Brown, 1 (which was probably cast by Garrard, preferring not to vote for himself). With no one having a majority, the electoral college held a second ballot, in which the Todd electors switched to Garrard, thus giving him the victory. Logan contended that the election was stolen by a corrupt bargain and that the constitution and law did not allow for a second round of voting. The "disputed election of 1796" became a hot issue in Kentucky politics. The Kentucky Senate was asked to resolve the controversy but refused to do so. Garrard did not reward Todd until four years later, then appointing him to the court of appeals.

Garrard supported a second constitutional convention, which met in 1799. The new constitution provided for direct election of the governor and a single term. Garrard was elected by popular vote for a second term in 1800. During the campaign Garrard was attacked for not staying the execution of Henry Field, a prominent Kentuckian who had killed his wife, and for his antislavery stance. Garrard's sympathy for debtors and his antislavery views made him popular among the poor farmers. As governor, Garrard supported increased state expenditures for internal improvements, won revision of criminal and judicial laws, and vigorously condemned the Alien and Sedition Acts of Congress. He obtained legislation to allow settlers to exercise preemption rights and to secure debt relief for farmers in the Green River area, promoted government assistance to business, and called for steering clear of war with France.

After leaving the governorship, Garrard retired from politics. He died, after several years of declining health, at his home, Mount Lebanon. Garrard was the only person to hold two consecutive terms as governor of Kentucky. Garrard County (1796) is named after him. Garrard's success was owing more to his sterling character than to ability. Yet he was a man of courage and decisiveness. In public life, as his biographer notes, he performed in the role of "liberal, nationalist, conciliator, unifier, and republican."

• The Kentucky Department for Libraries and Archives, Frankfort, has the papers of the governors, which include James Garrard: Executive Journals, Official Correspondence, and Enrolled Bills. A full biography is H. E. Everman, *Governor James Garrard* (1981). See also Everman, *The History of Bourbon County, 1785–1865* (1977). For the Garrard family in America, see Louis des Cognets, Jr., *Governor Garrard of Kentucky: His Descendants and Relatives* (1962). The ministry and Baptist connections are covered in John H. Spencer and Burilla B. Spencer, *History of Kentucky Baptists*, vol. 1 (1886). Two works providing substantial treatment of early Kentucky are Lewis Collins and Richard H. Collins, *History of Kentucky* (2 vols., 1874; repr. 1966), and William E. Connelley and E. M. Coulter, *History of Kentucky*, vols. 1–2 (1922). On Garrard's role in the formation of Kentucky government, see Lowell H. Harrison, *Kentucky's Road to Statehood* (1992), and Joan W. Coward, *Kentucky in the New Republic: The Process of Constitution Making* (1979). The elections of 1796 and 1800 are discussed in Charles G. Talbert, *Benjamin Logan: Kentucky Frontiersman* (1962). An obituary is in the *Kentucky Gazette*, 31 Jan. 1822.

HARRY M. WARD

GARRARD, Kenner (30 Sept. 1827–15 May 1879), soldier and businessman, was born in Fairfield, Kentucky, the son of Jeptha Dudley Garrard, a lawyer, and Sarah Bella Ludlow. Garrard, although born in Kentucky at his paternal grandfather's home, was raised in his parents' home in Cincinnati, Ohio. His maternal grandfather, Israel Ludlow, was a prominent real estate investor in Cincinnati. Garrard entered Harvard University at Cambridge, Massachusetts, with the class of 1848 but left after he received an appointment to the U.S. Military Academy at West Point, New York. He graduated from West Point in 1851 and was commissioned in the artillery but transferred to the cavalry in 1852. He served with the First Regiment of Dragoons (a form of mounted infantry) until the outbreak of the Civil War on the frontier.

During the Texas secession crisis, Garrard was captured in San Antonio on 23 April 1861 by forces from the Texas state militia not yet under Confederate command. He was soon paroled and allowed to return to the North, but he was not exchanged until 27 August 1862. In the interim, he was briefly the commissary general of the army and then commandant at West Point. Upon his exchange he was immediately appointed commander of the 146th New York Volunteer Infantry Regiment, assigned to the Army of the Potomac. In 1862 and 1863 he participated in the campaigns of Fredericksburg and Chancellorsville.

On 2 July 1863 Garrard distinguished himself in the critical fighting at Little Round Top, key to the Union army's defense at Gettysburg. After his brigade commander (Stephen H. Weed, commander of the Third Brigade, Second Division, V Corps) was killed, Garrard assumed command of the brigade and defended his position despite furious Confederate assaults. For his action at Gettysburg, he was promoted to brigadier general of volunteers on 23 July 1863. In late 1863 he commanded his brigade in battles at Rappahannock Station and Mine Run. He then served briefly with the cavalry bureau in Washington, D.C.

In 1864 Garrard transferred to the Army of the Cumberland at Chattanooga, where he was assigned command of the Second Cavalry Division then preparing for General William Tecumseh Sherman's campaign against Atlanta. In command of cavalry over rugged terrain and under the more mobile conditions of fighting in the western theater of the war, Garrard did not command with the same effectiveness he had demonstrated at Gettysburg. His cavalry had chronic problems with logistical support and was constantly outmaneuvered by Confederate cavalry under the veteran command of General Joe Wheeler. Nonetheless, Garrard learned as the campaign progressed and received Sherman's personal congratulations for his raid on Covington, Georgia, which cut a major Confederate railroad and resulted in the confiscation of thousands of bales of enemy cotton. For his actions at Covington, he was breveted colonel in the regular army on 22 July 1864.

After the fall of Atlanta in September 1864 Garrard was reassigned to an infantry command, the Second Division of the XVI Corps, to take part in Major General George H. Thomas's defense of central Tennessee. At the battle of Nashville (15–16 Dec. 1864) his division inflicted heavy losses on the Confederates and took much of an entire division prisoner as Confederate general John B. Hood's army disintegrated on the second day of the conflict. For his actions at Nashville, Garrard was breveted major general of volunteers and brigadier general in the regular army.

After Nashville Garrard participated in several other minor actions that extinguished Confederate resistance east of the Mississippi River. He took part in the campaign against Mobile, Alabama, in early 1865, and he commanded at the capture of Blakeley, Alabama, and then the capture of Montgomery, Alabama, during April 1865. He ended the war breveted as a major general in the regular army.

After the Civil War Garrard served only briefly on occupation duty in the South, commanding the District of Mobile until August 1865, when he was mustered out of volunteer service and reverted to the regular army. He served as assistant inspector general of the Department of the Missouri under General Sherman until 9 November 1866, when he resigned from the regular army. Following his resignation, Garrard returned to his family home in Cincinnati, where he was actively involved in managing his family's extensive real estate holdings in the city. For the rest of his life, he promoted cultural activities in Cincinnati, serving as director of the Cincinnati Music Festival and with the Historical and Philosophical Society of Ohio. He died in Cincinnati, having never married.

Garrard's reputation in the Civil War was decidedly mixed. Like any number of other junior commanders in the Army of the Potomac, he demonstrated great courage and tenacity under fire in the infantry fighting at Gettysburg in 1863. Cavalry command in the West required different qualities, however, and a scholar of the Atlanta campaign has commented that Garrard had "little aptitude for it" (Castel, p. 116). Indeed, when he returned to command infantry at the battle of Nashville, his performance was much improved.

• Garrard's actions at the battle of Gettysburg are covered in some detail in Harry W. Pfanz, *Gettysburg: The Second Day* (1987). His role in Sherman's army emerges throughout Albert Castel, *Decision in the West: The Atlanta Campaign of 1864* (1992). Wiley Sword, *Embrace an Angry Wind: The Confederacy's Last Hurrah: Spring Hill, Franklin, and Nashville* (1992), traces the tactical details of Garrard's last significant campaign in the Civil War. See also Ezra J. Warner, *Generals in Blue: Lives of the Union Commanders* (1964). His obituary is in the *Cincinnati Enquirer*, 16 May 1879.

JAMES K. HOGUE

GARREAU, Armand (13 Sept. 1817–28 Mar. 1865), Romantic writer, journalist, and educator, was born Louis-Armand Garreau in Cognac, France, the son of Louis-Armand Garreau, a lawyer and veteran of the Napoleonic wars, and Marie Rose Dumontet, a native of Saint-Pierre, Martinique. Apparently Garreau left home at a very early age to receive a classical education in Paris at the Lycée Henri IV. Financial difficulties prevented him from completing law school, but before he left Paris to take up a teaching position in the department of Gironde he encountered a New Orleanian who impressed him with talk of opportunity in Louisiana.

In 1838 Garreau wed Marie Anaïs Boraud, and in 1841 the couple set out with their young child for the United States. (They would have six children together.) Settling in New Orleans, Garreau opened a private school for boys while his wife directed a school for girls in an adjacent building. With his facility situated on the boundary between the Vieux Carré and the Faubourg Tremé, a section of the city dominated by prosperous Afro-Creoles, Garreau soon developed close ties with the French-speaking free black community because of his dedication to the instruction of their children.

Political refugees from revolutionary upheaval in France and the French Caribbean and Romantic literary artists, both émigré and native, contributed to the vibrant intellectual milieu that greeted Garreau upon his arrival in antebellum New Orleans. Freelance contributions to the *Revue louisianaise*, a popular weekly modeled on European journals, won Garreau entry into the ranks of the resident literati, and in October 1848 his well-received essays prompted the editor to hire Garreau to write a featured column, the "Revue de la semaine." At one point the shrewd and playful Frenchman invited a fellow émigré and journalist,

radical French republican Charles Testut, to write several articles under his byline.

Exhilarated by the 1848 French revolution, Garreau, an ardent republican, set to work on a number of other projects. In October he and French émigré Eugène Supervielle, a fellow radical, launched a weekly, *Le Démocrite*. The provocative paper lasted only a couple of months but long enough to instigate a duel with an actor angered by a harsh theatrical review. The two combatants fought under the famed oaks of City Park until Garreau disabled his opponent with a stab wound to the arm.

With another republican partisan, French émigré Alexandre Barde, Garreau helped establish a newspaper, *Le Créole*, in Saint Martinville, the so-called "Petit Paris de la Louisiane," a name that acknowledged the wealth and aristocratic lineage of the town's dominant Creole planters. He published a notably witty poem in *Le Créole*, "La Dindonnade de Saint-Martinville," and worked on a historical novel, *Louisiana*, which appeared in 1849 in Testut's two-volume prose anthology, *Veillées louisianaises*.

Like many other Romantic writers of the day, Garreau employed his literary skills to advance a sociopolitical agenda. In *Louisiana*, his dramatization of a 1769 New Orleans–centered revolt against Spanish rule served as a vehicle for attacking slavery and promoting republicanism. The book's antislavery sentiments clearly violated an 1830 state law banning inflammatory reading materials under penalty of imprisonment or death. With *Louisiana*'s publication, Garreau and his family returned to France in late 1849.

Eager to support the republican cause, he settled in Barbezieux and founded a newspaper, *Le Narrateur impartial*. In the weekly journal, he serialized a number of short stories, including "Le Nègre marron, Bras coupé," "Un jour de Noces," and "Naïda," as well as a novel, *Ogine* (1852), based on the Charente region's medieval history. A government crackdown halted publication of his third historical novel, *La Maison maudite*, set in eighteenth-century France.

The reactionary forces of Louis Napoleon Bonaparte had already won control of the Second Republic by the time Garreau arrived in France. When the antirepublican regime forced its opponents underground, Garreau joined the secret society of "les Mariannes," an organization that counted Victor Hugo among its members. In 1851, after a raid on the society's offices revealed Garreau's membership in the group, the government forced him to suspend publication of *Le Narrateur*.

When political repression moderated in 1854, Garreau launched yet another journal, the monthly *Légendes et chroniques de l'Angoumois, de la Saintonge et des provinces limitrophes*, in which he completed publication of *La Maison maudite* and two other novels chronicling the history of southern France, *Leudaste* (1854), depicting life in Gaul under the Merovingians, and *Les Péteaux* (1854), based on a sixteenth-century salt tax revolt.

Impressed with Garreau's work, famed Afro-French writer Alexandre Dumas predicted that he would have a distinguished literary career. But local officials of the Second Empire, stung by the ferocity of Garreau's journalistic attacks, made life in Barbezieux impossible. Garreau abandoned publication of *Légendes et chroniques* and fled to Paris. In the suburb of Saint-Denis he opened a boarding school and continued to write. Plagued, however, by financial and political difficulties, he returned to Louisiana with his family in 1858. In New Orleans he resumed teaching in the city's public and private schools and eventually wrote two unpublished plays, "Le Couronal" and "Michel le braçonnier."

Confederate officials conscripted Garreau into the Louisiana militia with the outbreak of the Civil War. Like his Afro-Creole colleagues, however, he remained in the city when the Union army forced the rebels to withdraw from New Orleans in April 1862. Despite the turmoil, he continued to write, and on 15 May 1864 he published a well-received short story, "L'Idiote," in *Renaissance louisianaise*. Still, the war took its toll. Devastated by the death of a son at Vicksburg, Garreau died in New Orleans near the end of the conflict. In a newspaper obituary in the Afro-Creole *Tribune*, an admirer noted that "it is to him [Garreau] that most of our young men owe their instruction." He made no distinction, the writer continued, when "it was a question of spreading the benefits of education." Among those who mourned his death, the obituary concluded, "none regret it more than the numerous friends that this man of true merit has made in the population of color of this city."

• For an overview of Garreau's life and work, see Edward Larocque Tinker, *Les Écrits de langue française en Louisiane aux XIXe siècle* (1932); Auguste Viatte, *Histoire littéraire de l'Amerique française des origines à 1950* (1954) and "Complement à la bibliographie louisianaise d'Edward Larocque Tinker," *Revue de Louisiane* 3 (1974); Ruby Van Allen Caulfeild, *The French Literature of Louisiana* (1929); John Maxwell Jones, Jr., *Slavery and Race in Nineteenth-Century Louisiana-French Literature* (1978); and Charles-Andre Borand, *Un parrainage inconnu du maréchal de Richelieu. Les origines, la vie et les oeuvres de Louis-Armand Garreau* (1939?). For a contemporary view see Charles Testut, *Portraits littéraires de la Nouvelle-Orléans* (1850), and the obituary in the *Tribune de la Nouvelle-Orléans*, 30 Mar. 1865.

CARYN COSSÉ BELL

GARRETSON, James Edmund (18 Oct. 1828–26 Oct. 1895), dentist and oral surgeon, wan born in Wilmington, Delaware, the son of Jacob M. Garretson and Mary A. Powell. After receiving his early education at the Wilmington Classical Academy, Garretson became a student to Dr. Thatcher, a practicing dentist in Wilmington in 1850. Subsequently he practiced dentistry for a short time in Woodbury, New Jersey, after which he attended the Philadelphia College of Dental Surgery, where he obtained his dental degree in 1856. Garretson opened a practice as a dentist in Philadelphia while at the same time attending medical courses

at the University of Pennsylvania Medical School; he obtained his M.D. in 1859. That same year he married Beulah Craft; the couple had two daughters.

Garretson became a demonstrator at the Philadelphia School of Anatomy in 1854 and remained on its staff until 1862. During part of the Civil War, he served as a dentist in the Union army. In 1869 he became an oral surgeon at the Hospital of the University of Pennsylvania. In 1874 Garretson joined the staff of the Philadelphia College of Dental Surgery and served on its faculty until he died. He became a professor of anatomy at the dental college in 1878 and was appointed dean of the faculty in 1880. Garretson also served as professor of clinical surgery at the Medico-Chirurgical College of Philadelphia for a number of years and became the president of the Medical Chirurgical Society of Philadelphia in 1883.

Garretson is recognized as the originator of oral surgery as a specialty and as the most skillful practitioner of that art in his day. He led the trend in performing oral surgery to avoid external incisions if possible. This process resulted in less facial scarring and required complex operations restricted to the inside of the mouth. In 1887 he became the first to apply the dental engine—later known as the dental drill—as modified for surgical operations, and through his efforts this machine subsequently became useful in certain operations within the skull. In 1869 Garretson published *A Treatise on Diseases and Surgery of the Mouth, Jaws, and Associated Parts*. Five later editions of this book were issued under the title *A System of Oral Surgery* (1873). Garretson's textbook was the standard work in the field of oral surgery for many years.

Garretson also wrote on topics other than medicine. Having acquired a religious background from his family, he was interested in spiritualism, Platonism, and Rosencrucianism and spent a great deal of time writing and lecturing on these subjects. He used the pseudonym John Darby in most of these works. In his writing, he attempted to blend concepts of transcendentalism with scientific facts. Examples of his work include *Thinkers and Thinking* (1873), *Two Thousand Years After* (1876), *Hours with John Darby* (1877), *Nineteenth Century Sense* (1887), and *Man of His World* (1889).

Considered the founder of oral surgery as a medical specialty, Garretson helped to transform oral surgery from painful scarring procedures to a more professional and organized process and made technical advancements in this field, such as the dental engine. He encouraged the development of the Hospital of Oral Surgery at the Philadelphia College of Dental Surgery and thereby the training of new professionals. In addition to writing the major text in oral surgery of his day, he produced many books on bringing science and spirituality together. Garretson retired in 1891 and died at his home in Lansdowne, Pennsylvania.

• Materials by Garretson can be found in the *Papers of the Historical Society of Delaware* 19 (1897): 10–23. Works by

Garretson written under the name John Darby include *Odd Hours of a Physician* (1871) and *Brushland* (1882). Secondary sources are Harold L. Faggart, "Dr. James E. Garretson and the First Hospital for Oral Surgery," *Bulletin for the History of Medicine* 17 (1945): 360–76; and B. L. Thorpe, "James Edmund Garretson, Originator of the Specialty of Oral Surgery," *History of Dental Surgery*, ed. Charles Rudolph Edward Koch, vol. 3 (1910), pp. 395–99. An obituary is in the Philadelphia *Public Ledger*, 28 and 29 Oct. 1895.

DAVID Y. COOPER

GARRETT, John Work (31 July 1820–26 Sept. 1884), businessman and railroad president, was born in Baltimore, Maryland, the son of Robert Garrett, a merchant, and Elizabeth Stouffer. Garrett and his older brother Henry enjoyed growing up in the busy harbor town, where after school they did chores in their father's store and warehouse. At age fourteen Garrett attended Lafayette College in Pennsylvania but left after two years to work in his father's firm.

In the fall of 1836 Garrett made his first business trip to western Virginia and Pennsylvania. He collected debts owed to his father and purchased flour, pork, and butter for the store. While John traveled west, Henry spent most of his time in the Baltimore office. Recognizing their growing roles in the company, their father changed the name of the firm in 1839 to Robert Garrett & Sons. As the firm prospered, both John and Henry made modest investments in railroad and state securities. In 1846 John married Rachel Anne Harrison, the daughter of Baltimore merchant Thomas Harrison. They had four children.

During the late 1840s the Garrett firm started to discount commercial paper and deal in British sterling bills of exchange. The firm started a bank and increased its holdings in Baltimore real estate. Before the Civil War the family had holdings of nearly $1 million. Robert Garrett had been an early investor in the Baltimore & Ohio Railroad; Henry became a B&O director in 1852, and John joined the railroad board in 1855.

The Baltimore & Ohio Railroad in the late 1850s was a 500-mile line from Baltimore to Wheeling and Parkersburg on the Virginia side of the Ohio River plus a branch line to Washington, D.C. The board of directors consisted of eighteen public directors representing Baltimore and the state of Maryland and a dozen directors representing private shareholders. The private interests wanted higher freight rates to permit higher dividends. John Garrett, supported by Johns Hopkins, the largest individual shareholder, succeeded in raising freight rates and eventually obtained an increase in dividends. Garrett was elected president of the Baltimore & Ohio on 17 November 1858. The B&O in 1858 represented an investment of $26 million, with an annual revenue of $4 million, a work force of 4,500, and traffic consisting of coal, flour, grain, livestock, and manufactured goods.

Garrett's first challenge as president came with the outbreak of the Civil War in 1861. Because of its location in the border state of Maryland and western Virginia, the B&O was to experience more than its share of violence and destruction. Since the line was in slave territory, with much of its traffic moving to and from free states, both the Confederacy and the Union regarded Garrett and the B&O with suspicion. Garrett at first viewed his railroad as a southern line and called Confederate leaders "our southern friends." However, the destruction of B&O track and equipment during June 1861 by the Confederate raiders soon had Garrett thinking of the Confederates not as misguided friends but rather as dangerous rebels. The main line of the B&O was again broken in September 1862, and between June and July 1863.

In September 1863 Garrett and Tom Scott of the Pennsylvania Railroad were asked by Secretary of War Edwin M. Stanton to move 25,000 Union troops from Washington, D.C., via Wheeling, Indianapolis, and Louisville to Tennessee to break the siege of Chattanooga. The massive movement of thirty trains (700 cars) was completed in about two weeks. The Civil War also brought prosperity to the B&O. In 1865 Garrett reported that during the war freight traffic had tripled, and passenger service had increased fourfold. Main line revenue had climbed from $3 million to $10 million, and dividends had risen to $8 a share.

Between the end of the war and Garrett's death, the B&O system expanded from 520 miles to 1,700 miles, with the new lines in Pennsylvania, Delaware, Virginia, Ohio, Indiana, and Illinois. A line to Pittsburgh was opened in 1871, and a second route to Washington, D.C., was completed in 1873. Two bridges completed in 1871 across the upper Ohio River replaced long-used car ferries. New routes in Ohio gave service to Columbus, Cleveland, and Sandusky. Garrett opened a 263-mile line West to Chicago in 1874. The B&O had a major interest in lines West of Parkersburg that served Cincinnati and St. Louis. Between 1865 and 1884 Garrett doubled his locomotive roster and tripled the number of his freight cars to serve the new mileage. In the same years the total B&O revenue more than doubled while passenger fares and freight rates were greatly reduced. Garrett was expanding his railroad more with borrowed money than with new share capital, and this debt would force the B&O into receivership in the 1890s.

Rate wars were common in the 1870s and 1880s. John Garrett frequently discussed rates with Commodore Cornelius Vanderbilt and J. Edgar Thompson, the presidents of the New York Central and the Pennsylvania. In fact the railroad owners alternated between collusion and competition. Garrett argued that the shorter B&O route and the abundance of coal along the line entitled his railroad to lower rates for the western traffic. Average freight rates did drop from just over two cents a ton-mile in 1865 to about a penny in the 1880s. Garrett sought to improve his service by having the B&O build and operate its own sleeping cars and run its own telegraph and express systems. The panic of 1873 and the following depression caused revenues to drop and the operating ratio to climb on the B&O, but Garrett's railroad escaped receivership that time. Equally serious was the railroad strike of 1877, which followed major wage cuts for rail workers across the nation. Garrett ended the strike with strike-breakers while refusing to lower the yearly $8 dividends. After the strike he made some concessions in train crew responsibilities, and in 1880 he established the B&O Railroad Employees Relief Association.

In the early 1880s the Baltimore & Ohio was a smaller and weaker system than the two trunklines to the North, the Pennsylvania and the New York Central. However, in his 25-year presidency Garrett had given Baltimore a major trunkline railroad to the West. Although Garrett's attitude toward labor was generally tough and unyielding, he was frequently a generous man with gifts to his church, Lafayette College, the Young Men's Christian Association, and other such projects. Soon after his wife's death late in 1883, Garrett turned over the active management of the B&O to his son Robert. John Garrett died in his cottage in Deer Park, Maryland.

• A sizable amount of material on the railroad career of John Garrett can be found in the Robert Garrett Family Papers, Manuscript Division, Library of Congress, Washington, D.C. For the early life of John Garrett and his B&O presidency to 1870, see William B. Catton, "John W. Garrett of the Baltimore and Ohio: A Study in Seaport and Railroad Competition, 1820–74" (Ph.D. diss., Northwestern Univ., 1959). Edward Hungerford, *The Story of the Baltimore and Ohio Railroad, 1827–1927* (1928), gives a full account of Garrett's Civil War years. A detailed history of the Baltimore & Ohio Railroad can be found in John F. Stover, *History of the Baltimore and Ohio Railroad* (1987). An obituary is in the *Railroad Gazette*, 3 Oct. 1884, p. 711.

JOHN F. STOVER

GARRETT, Leroy (26 Nov. 1913–21 July 1980), pioneer radio broadcaster, was born in Talladega County, Alabama, the son of Roy and Edna Garrett, tenant farmers. Although Garrett's father was illiterate, his mother could read and write and was concerned that all of her children had access to education. At age five Garrett was literate and attended school with his siblings. He also helped his brothers and father farm the land they rented.

Not much is known about Garrett's childhood. By the 1940s he lived in Birmingham, Alabama, where he owned a dry cleaning business. Garrett also worked as a disc jockey at "soul" station WVOK and used his personal records and turntables. In 1957, motivated by the opportunity to secure a broadcast frequency and determined to establish a radio station, Garrett moved to Huntsville, Alabama. He was denied a building permit by the city government, however, and was arrested when he began construction.

Garrett protested the city's discriminatory policy and was allowed to continue with his plans. He converted a house trailer into a radio station on Oakwood Avenue. Garrett was one of the first African Americans to own and operate a radio station in the United States. Previously, most radio stations broadcasting black programming were owned by whites who employed both white and black disc jockeys. Often broadcasts presented stereotyped music and program-

ming that owners and managers mistakenly believed appealed to black listeners. Radio stations were concerned with attracting advertising and often ignored black businesses and consumers. African Americans expressed "widespread dissatisfaction" at this black-oriented radio.

Atlanta's WERD became the first black-owned radio station in 1950 when J. B. Blayton, Jr., purchased it. In the early 1950s Alabama's black population enjoyed the programming of WBIL in Tuskegee and Birmingham's WENN, owned by the Booker T. Washington Broadcasting Company. Garrett was influenced by these stations. Black Birmingham entrepreneur A. G. Gaston, a self-made tycoon, encouraged Garrett in his pioneering radio pursuits.

Garrett applied for a Federal Communications Commission (FCC) license, but the call letters he submitted were rejected. After several failed attempts to secure a call sign, a discouraged Garrett desperately sought a suitable name that would appeal to listeners. He looked through local newspapers and saw an advertisement for 7-Up soda and decided to try WEUP. The FCC accepted these call letters, and WEUP-AM was licensed to Garrett Broadcasting, Inc.

On 20 March 1958 Garrett first broadcasted. His 1,000-watt AM station played at the frequency of 1,600 kilocycles from four in the morning to six at night every day of the week. A variety of gospel and popular music programming was interspersed with news and sermons. The *Huntsville Times* noted, "New Broadcast Station On Air WEUP Is Only Negro Station In Vicinity." The newspaper said that the station would reach listeners within a sixty- to seventy-mile radius. WEUP was the fourth radio station established in Huntsville and the only Alabama station north of Birmingham broadcasting primarily for blacks.

Garrett was community minded and attempted to provide wholesome broadcasts for the African-American community. Religious programming dominated WEUP's broadcasts. Hundley Batts, Sr., who bought WEUP after Garrett's death, remembered attending gospel singings at WEUP's auditorium, known as the Syler Tabernacle, as a child. Garrett gave gifts to radio listeners, mainly promotional items such as keychains emblazoned with advertising slogans and the WEUP symbol. Batts recalled that everyone who attended the singings was presented with WEUP trinkets to take home, which was important to blacks in Huntsville and helped secure dedicated listeners.

Garrett hoped that listeners would feel a personal connection with WEUP and that the station would entertain and empower individuals and the African-American community. He wanted to call the station "Magic 1600," but listeners preferred the motto "WEUP is you." Although some groups and people pressured Garrett to use WEUP to voice racial and political concerns, such as police mistreatment of blacks, he refused to misuse his broadcasting power. Acknowledging that segregationist Huntsville was a difficult environment for blacks, Garrett hoped that his station's programming would aid blacks to gain self-esteem and religious strength to counter social problems.

In addition to carefully choosing what WEUP broadcasted, Garrett also selectively hired disc jockeys. He especially was concerned with training minority broadcasters, and WEUP became an educational center for black broadcasters. A "good businessman," Garrett made WEUP profitable. He banked in Huntsville but channeled the bulk of his funds to Birmingham millionaire Gaston, who invested them for him.

Garrett decided that he wanted to improve WEUP by increasing its power and broadcasting twenty-four hours daily. During the 1960s Huntsville had quickly expanded with the arrival of aerospace and military industry. He applied to the FCC for a night broadcast permit in 1968. The FCC denied his request, basing their rejection on technical reasons. Garrett realized that the denial was racially motivated and filed a lawsuit against the FCC, which he believed had been influenced by wealthy white radio competitors. The FCC had waived technical rules for white stations, and Garrett demanded that WEUP be allowed to build facilities for unlimited broadcast time.

The case was argued at the U.S. Court of Appeals, District of Columbia Circuit, on 28 May 1974. Circuit Judge Spottswood W. Robinson III issued his ruling on 2 June 1975. He stated that the "fact that radio station in question was owned and operated by blacks was relevant" and questioned the "inconsistent" actions of the FCC. Robinson commented that the FCC had waived restrictions in other cases and labeled their "arbitrary treatment" as "an abuse of discretion."

Robinson insisted that WEUP be allowed to broadcast at night, asserting that "its black oriented programming would surpass that of older area stations." He emphasized that "WEUP was and is one of the infinitesimal number of black-owned and -operated broadcasting stations to be found anywhere in the United States." Garrett's landmark case decision has been cited by minorities suing against discrimination in communications.

The decision affected federal law. On 2 November 1978 the Ninety-fifth Congress passed Public Law 95-567, amending the Communications Act of 1934. Section 392 (f) stated that the FCC "shall give special consideration to applications which would increase minority and women's ownership of, operation of, and participation in public telecommunications entities." The FCC was also required to inform minorities of available funds and locations needing radio service.

Garret expanded WEUP to an eleven-acre complex with a 5,000-watt capacity. He died in the Huntsville hospital. News of his death was reported in the *New York Times* but ignored by most Alabama newspapers. The Talladega *Advance* stated that the Talladega native had "emerged from the cotton fields" to own the "first black owned and operated radio station in Alabama." Garrett's son Arnold and nephews Emanuel and Bruce, whom he had raised, managed the station.

After Garrett's death, WEUP expanded to four FM stations in north Alabama and Tennessee. In 1987 his widow, Viola M. Garrett, sold the station to Batts and his wife, Virginia Caples, who continued Garrett's tradition of community service and involvement.

• For more on Garrett and his place in the communications industry, see Jannette Dates and William Barlow, eds., *Split Image: African Americans in the Mass Media*, 2d ed. (1993); John Downing, "Ethnic Minority Radio in the USA," *Howard Journal of Communication* 1 (1989): 135–48; *Federal Reporter*, 2d ser., vol. 513 F.2d (1975); and Frank Ferretti, "The White Captivity of Black Radio," *Columbia Journalism Review* 9 (Summer 1970): 35–39. An obituary is in the *New York Times*, 23 July 1980.

ELIZABETH D. SCHAFER

GARRETT, Mary Elizabeth (5 Mar. 1854–3 Apr. 1915), philanthropist, was born in Baltimore, Maryland, the daughter of John Work Garrett and Rachel Ann Harrison. Her father's wealth as president of the Baltimore and Ohio Railroad (B&O) afforded her a secure childhood, and her participation in Gilded Age social rituals put her in contact with social and intellectual elites.

Her father acknowledged her intelligence but did not believe in equal education for women; nonetheless, she resolved to gain knowledge, which she believed was power. She was well educated in private schools and widely read in English and French classics. To study Greek, then a hallmark of superior education, she arranged for her own lessons; her father at first refused to pay, but she did not stop attending, and in the end he had to acquiesce.

As she grew older Mary Garrett often served her father as secretary on the family's trips to Europe. He tutored her in business and finance; she even notated her personal correspondence like business documents. Although she was probably the only one of his four children with the intelligence and interest to run the family business concerns, a woman succeeding her father would have been difficult, if not impossible. Some friends, however, including Women's Christian Temperance Union leader Frances Willard, later urged her to advance her claim.

Garrett's reading and interests and perhaps her own situation, led to a commitment to women's rights. In the fall of 1877, with her childhood friend Julia Rogers and her acquaintances Mamie Gwinn, M. Carey Thomas, and Thomas's cousin Elizabeth King, she formed the Friday Evening. They met biweekly for discussion, exchanges of writing, and planning philanthropic and political activities. With Rogers, Garrett formed an intimate friendship; they studied together, taking and passing the Harvard entrance examinations in 1879 (though neither attended the "Harvard Annex," later Radcliffe College).

Garrett suffered a breakdown after taking the Harvard examination and only gradually recovered her ability to concentrate; she also experienced severe menstrual pain that was diagnosed as resulting from her studies, a not uncommon medical opinion of the era. In 1880, while traveling in Europe, she suffered a severe ankle sprain and tendon pulls, which incapacitated her for months. Her health would never again be strong.

In 1884 John Garrett died, and his daughter inherited a one-third interest in his estate. She began to turn her talents and fortune to the causes and ideas in which she believed. Her first project, undertaken in 1884 with the Friday Evening group, was founding the Bryn Mawr School for Girls, which opened in 1885 in Baltimore. It offered a good college-preparatory education for girls, something none of the Friday Evening members had had. Garrett's money funded the school, and she and the others in the group remained on its board, controlling finances and curriculum for some years. Garrett effectively led the school and through it realized some of her ideas about education for women and girls.

The school was an academic and social success, but tensions flared among the friends directing it, particularly over admitting Jewish students in 1886: Garrett and Rogers insisted on an open policy, while Thomas and Gwinn wanted to impose quotas. There were also disagreements about the expense of the new school building, which Garrett oversaw and built in 1889–1890, donating $300,000. Garrett and Rogers drifted apart, and in 1891 both their intimate friendship and Rogers's tenure on the board ended.

Though now wary of one another, the Friday Evening group had already begun another venture: endowing a medical school for Johns Hopkins University, on condition that it be open to women. The campaign, launched in 1889, involved soliciting a vast network of women educators, professionals, and philanthropists. Garrett was secretary of the central committee in Baltimore and the largest single donor, contributing $47,787 of $111,300 given to the Hopkins board in 1891. When the trustees balked, wanting a total of $500,000 before opening, Garrett offered to donate the difference if certain conditions were met, among them that the medical school be a graduate school requiring college-level study in sciences and languages. Accepted on these terms, her donations led to the opening of the school in October 1893, with women in the first entering class and each subsequent one.

Through this negotiating period, Garrett was often absent; she had suffered another breakdown in early 1891 and sought medical care in the United States and Europe. Thomas handled most of the Baltimore negotiations, but the decisions were clearly Garrett's. More rifts among other Women's Medical School Fund members, however, led to the withdrawal of Bessie King and the end of her friendship with the remaining trio of former Friday Evening intimates.

During the early 1890s Garrett grew closer to Thomas, who was then dean of Bryn Mawr College in Pennsylvania. During protracted discussions over whether Thomas would be named the second president of the college, in 1893 Garrett pledged $10,000 a year to the institution—more than 10 percent of its annual budget—should Thomas become and remain president. Eventually the trustees accepted this offer,

and Thomas completed a long career there. Garrett eventually donated about $450,000 to Bryn Mawr, funding new buildings, remodeling, library acquisitions, and other projects.

In 1895 Garrett sought and obtained a permanent division of her father's estate, estranging her from several family members but giving her clear control of a large fortune. Reverses in B&O stock in the late 1890s eroded this, leading her to shut up her Baltimore estate and spend much of her time traveling abroad or living in the New York City apartment she shared part time with Thomas.

In 1904 Garrett went to live with Thomas at Bryn Mawr, further supporting her in her role as president. Garrett's work for the college, especially on finance and facilities, was recognized by her appointment as director in 1906 (directors were superior to trustees).

Garrett's commitment to women's rights had often centered on education, but as early as the 1890s she also supported woman suffrage. She eventually persuaded Thomas to join in this effort. The two became friendly with suffrage leaders, including Anna Howard Shaw and Susan B. Anthony, and the National American Woman Suffrage Association (NAWSA) held its annual meeting in Baltimore in 1906. When Anthony expressed concerns about the city's conservatism, Garrett opened her house and hosted a reception, and Thomas organized the first "College Evening," where prominent women educational leaders spoke in favor of suffrage. To support NAWSA, Garrett and Thomas organized a fundraising drive that raised a $60,000 endowment by 1911; Garrett donated $2,500. They then helped lead and raise money for the College Equal Suffrage League, which urged college women to support suffrage.

Garrett's health deteriorated further, and in 1912 she was diagnosed with leukemia. Following the removal of her spleen in 1914 she was an invalid; she died of the disease in Bryn Mawr. Her will, leaving the bulk of her estate to Thomas, excited comment, but Garrett probably expected Thomas would continue to give to the institutions they both believed in.

Garrett's associations, particularly with Thomas, meant that her own quieter personality was often submerged, yet despite her outward calm and aloofness, she was a believer in ideas. Her financial and organizational contributions to schools and to suffrage were important and often path breaking for women, as her contemporaries acknowledged, and the collaborations she forged, though sometimes personally difficult, point to a different model than that of the disinterested, check-writing philanthropist. In financing women's advancement Garrett had few peers, and all of the institutions to which she donated continue to thrive and to advance the causes in which she believed.

• Many of Garrett's personal papers, including a draft autobiography and numerous letters and account books, are contained in the M. Carey Thomas Papers, Bryn Mawr College Archives. The Garrett papers in the Maryland Historical Society contain her correspondence between 1883 and 1895. A few letters are in the Garrett Family Papers in the Library of Congress. There are numerous commentaries on her contribution to Johns Hopkins and its conditions; see A. C. K., "Women at Johns Hopkins," *Nation*, 22 Jan. 1891, p. 1334; "Women and Medicine," *Nation*, 12 Feb. 1891, p. 1337; "On the Opening of the Johns Hopkins Medical School to Women," *Century Magazine*, Feb. 1891; and "The Conditions of Miss Garrett's Gift to the Medical School of Johns Hopkins University," *Boston Medical and Surgical Journal* 128 (1893): 3.

Because of her connection to institutions, much material about Garrett is contained in secondary sources. A portrait of her, in relation to her companion, is Helen Lefkowitz Horowitz, *The Power and Passion of M. Carey Thomas* (1994). See also Edith Finch, *Carey Thomas of Bryn Mawr* (1947); Alan Chesney, *The Johns Hopkins Hospital and the Johns Hopkins University School of Medicine: A Chronicle* (2 vols., 1943–1958); and Hugh Hawkins, *Pioneer: A History of the Johns Hopkins University 1874–1889* (1960). Ida Husted Harper, *The Life and Work of Susan B. Anthony*, vol. 3 (1908), provides some information about Garrett's contributions to the suffrage movement. Her obituary is in the *New York Times*, 4 Apr. 1915, and a story about her will is in the issue of 9 Apr. 1915.

CYNTHIA FARR BROWN

GARRETT, Mary Smith (20 June 1839–18 July 1925), educator of deaf children and child welfare advocate, was born in Philadelphia, Pennsylvania, the daughter of Henry Garrett, a prominent Philadelphia businessman, and Caroline Rush Cole. Little is known of Garrett's early life. She began a lifelong career in deaf education in 1881 when she was hired by the Pennsylvania Institution for the Deaf and Dumb to teach at the recently established "Oral Branch" (a separate campus where sign language was prohibited). Her younger sister, Emma Garrett, was the head teacher at the time. Mary Garrett had had no formal training in deaf education; her sister however, instructed her in the teaching methods she had learned from Alexander Graham Bell, a leading advocate of what was known as "pure oralism," which forbade sign language and insisted on the sole use of lip-reading and speech.

The Garrett sisters resigned their positions in 1884 after conflicts with the board of the directors of the Pennsylvania school. For the next four years, Mary operated a small school in Philadelphia, Miss Mary S. Garrett's Private School for Teaching Deaf Children to Speak, while Emma helped establish and became principal of the Pennsylvania Oral School in Scranton. In 1889 Mary joined her sister at the Scranton school.

Both left Scranton to found, in February 1892, the Home for the Training in Speech of Deaf Children Before They Are of School Age, in Philadelphia, with Emma as principal and Mary as secretary and teacher. The Pennsylvania legislature appropriated $15,000 for a building but no operating funds for the school, and the Garretts showed considerable skill at raising funds privately to support the first year of the school. In June 1893 the legislature made the school a state institution, granting it a yearly budget.

In summer 1893 the Garretts brought their school to Chicago as a "living exhibit" in the Children's Building of the World's Columbian Exposition. Mary was awarded a medal for Excellence in Training Deaf Children in Speech. Her address, "The Next Step in the Education of the Deaf," delivered to the Congress of Women in the Woman's Building of the exposition, criticized the "faulty system of training that makes [deaf people] different" and urged the adoption of her system of strict oral training. The Garretts' stay in Chicago ended in tragedy when Emma exhibited signs of mental illness and ultimately committed suicide by leaping from her hotel window. On returning from Chicago, Mary took over as principal of their school, a position she held until her death.

Even among advocates of pure oralism Mary Garrett was controversial. Having found that deaf children often did not succeed in orally taught classes, she came to believe that oral training had to be more consistent and intensive, and begun at an earlier age, than was usually the case. Children were admitted to her school beginning at two years of age and remained, with no vacations permitted, for six years. The school operated on the premise that if deaf children were always spoken to without gestures or non-oral communication of any kind, they would be compelled to develop oral communication skills. "An idea is never conveyed to their brains through any motion or sign," she wrote. "It is thought better for them to go temporarily without understanding until they are able to understand through . . . speech." Even the use of reading and writing was postponed until the "speech habit" was established.

Although Garrett opposed the idea of separate schools for deaf children, she viewed her school as necessary to prepare pupils for their local public school, where they would communicate through lip-reading and speech. Garrett was much more optimistic about this possibility than most educators of the deaf. She looked forward to the day when "family, friends, and the community will so aid the mother by talking to her deaf child exactly as to her hearing one, that we shall not need institutions especially for them."

Garrett was a dedicated and skilled advocate for the oralist philosophy, publishing pamphlets and delivering speeches to further the cause. In 1896 she brought her school to the International Exhibition in Atlanta, Georgia, where she received a gold medal for her work. In 1907 the State Department appointed her as a delegate from the United States to the International Conference of Teachers of the Deaf in Edinburgh.

Although Garrett's career was dedicated to deaf education, she was also active in other causes. She was first vice president of the Pennsylvania Congress of Mothers and of the Philadelphia Child Welfare Association. From 1906 to 1920 she served as chair for legislation of the National Congress of Mothers. She was a member of the National Association for the Study and Education of Exceptional Children, the executive committee of the Pennsylvania Society for the Prevention of Social Disease, the Acorn Club, the New Century Club, and other organizations concerned with child welfare. She testified in opposition to federal child-labor laws before the Interstate Commerce Committee of the U.S. Senate in 1916, arguing that idleness was a greater threat to children than overwork. She also opposed woman suffrage.

Garrett never married and had no children. She died while on vacation in North Conway, New Hampshire, the same day on which her sister Emma had taken her own life thirty-two years earlier.

Garrett was widely influential within the field of deaf education. Sign language had been the predominant means of instruction in schools for the deaf throughout the nineteenth century. Motivated, in part, by eugenics and the belief that sign languages were evolutionary throwbacks, the movement for which Garrett labored was one of many attempts during this period to proscribe the use of languages other than English in the United States. While organizations of deaf people such as the National Association of the Deaf strenuously opposed oralism, and most schools concluded that the pure oralism Garrett advocated was impractical for many deaf students, the oralist movement was nevertheless successful in greatly limiting the use of sign language in deaf education. Only in the 1970s did sign language return to wide use in the schools.

• Some items by and about Garrett between 1881 and 1884 are in the Pennsylvania School for the Deaf Collection, Gallaudet University Archives, Washington, D.C. Lists of Garrett's articles, pamphlets, and addresses are in *Woman's Who's Who of America, 1914–1915* (1914) and the *Sixteenth Report of the Home for the Training in Speech of Deaf Children* (1922). Her address to the Congress of Women at the Chicago exposition, with a brief biographical introduction, is in Mary K. O. Eagle, ed., *The Congress of Women* (1894). Brief accounts of her work are in Clara C. Park, "Mary Garrett," *American Magazine*, Sept. 1912, and Edward A. Fay, *Histories of American Schools for the Deaf, 1817–1893* (1893). As principal, Garrett wrote yearly reports for the Home for the Training in Speech of Deaf Children. Garrett testified before Senate committees on at least two occasions: see U.S. Senate, Committee on Interstate Commerce, Interstate Commerce in Products of Child Labor, 17 Mar. 1916, and U.S. Senate, Committee on Education and Labor, 16 Mar. 1906. For articles by Garrett and brief items about her schools and activities, see indexes in the *Volta Review* (*Association Review* from 1899 to 1909) and the *American Annals of the Deaf*. Obituaries appear in the *Philadelphia Inquirer* and the *Philadelphia Evening Bulletin*, both on 20 July 1925, and in the *Volta Review* 27 (Dec. 1925): 717–18.

DOUGLAS C. BAYNTON

GARRETT, Pat (5 June 1850–29 Feb. 1908), sheriff, was born Patrick Floyd Jarvis Garrett in Chambers County, Alabama, the son of John Lumpkin Garrett and Elizabeth Ann Jarvis, farmers. When Garrett was three, his family moved to Claiborne Parish, Louisiana, and operated a small plantation. There he attended a country school. At the age of nineteen he left home for Lancaster County, Texas, before drifting to the buffalo ranges of Texas and New Mexico. In November 1876 Garrett killed Joe Briscoe, a fellow buffalo hunter, during an argument. Nearby Fort Griffin,

Texas, authorities declined to prosecute him. Garrett next appeared in Fort Sumner, New Mexico, where he likely worked as a cowboy for John Chisum, the Pecos River cattleman. Garrett married Apolinaria Gutierrez in nearby Anton Chico on 14 January 1880; they raised eight children.

New Mexico's Lincoln County War, a mercantile struggle, had ended at the end of July with the fiery five-day battle in Lincoln. Most of the major participants were now either dead or bankrupt, and the hired guns, symbolized by Henry McCarty, alias Henry Antrim, alias Kid Antrim, alias Billy the Kid, were loose and running. Pat Garrett, a late arrival in Lincoln County, had not been involved in the war. Although he probably knew Billy the Kid, perhaps on a first-name basis, there is no evidence of a close friendship. It is true that Garrett drank and gambled, but he also was married. His associates were men of prominence, whereas Billy the Kid was a product of the saloons, and his companions were young stallions, wild and free like himself.

An ambitious man seeking distinction, Garrett campaigned for the Lincoln County position of sheriff, his pledge being to stabilize the region by either driving out, capturing, or killing the outlaws. With Chisum's support, Garrett won the election. On 19 December 1880 Garrett and his posse surprised Billy the Kid and his friends at Stinking Springs. The posse killed Tom O'Folliard, a gang member. Garrett then tracked the desperadoes into the hills, cornered them in a one-room rock house, and forced their surrender after killing Charlie Bowdre, another outlaw. Sheriff Garrett transported Billy the Kid's gang to Santa Fe. Billy the Kid was moved to Mesilla, New Mexico, tried for the earlier murder of Sheriff William Brady, and sentenced to hang at Lincoln. However, the outlaw escaped the Lincoln courthouse jail after killing two guards. He remained free until 14 July 1881, when Garrett and two deputies tracked him to the Fort Sumner home of Pete Maxwell, a local leader. Garrett shot Billy the Kid dead in Maxwell's bedroom at practically the stroke of midnight.

Overnight, Billy the Kid became a folk hero and Sheriff Pat Garrett a black-hearted villain, an image that persists. Garrett's biting personality made him numerous enemies. *The Authentic Life of Billy, the Kid*, by Pat Garrett (a journalist friend, Ash Upson, claimed to have written every word), failed to redeem Garrett's popularity, although it enhanced the outlaw's prestige. Garrett could not even get reelected sheriff of Lincoln County.

Garrett moved to the Texas Panhandle in 1883–1884 and supervised a law enforcement group near Tascosa called the "Pat Garrett Rangers." He next promoted irrigation projects in the Pecos Valley near Roswell, New Mexico. By 1890 he had moved his family to Uvalde, Texas. Garrett became a county commissioner and a close friend and gambling crony of John Nance Garner, who was to be vice president of the United States under President Franklin D. Roosevelt.

Back in Mesilla, New Mexico, Colonel Albert Jennings Fountain, a newspaper publisher, a Republican, and an attorney who had unsuccessfully defended Billy the Kid, was mysteriously murdered in 1896. Governor William T. Thornton coaxed Pat Garrett to Las Cruces, where he (Garrett) became Dona Ana County sheriff, handled the murder investigation, and made arrests. Following several dramatic episodes, the suspects were tried in 1899 and acquitted.

In 1901 President Theodore Roosevelt (1858–1919) appointed Garrett collector of customs in El Paso, Texas. After a controversial four years in office, and after introducing a saloon owner to Roosevelt as a "west Texas cattleman," Garrett failed to secure another two-year appointment from the president. A financially insolvent and depressed Garrett returned to his ranch in Dona Ana County, New Mexico.

On 29 February 1908 Garrett left his ranch near today's White Sands missile range in a buckboard headed for Las Cruces, twenty miles distant. He hoped to sell his property to Jim Miller, a notorious assassin turned Mexican cattle buyer. In the buckboard beside Garrett rode Carl Adamson, Miller's brother-in-law. Wayne Brazel, a local cowboy who had leased portions of Garrett's ranch and stocked it with goats, rode alongside the buckboard on horseback. When the trio stopped to urinate in the sand hills, someone shot Garrett in the back of his head. Wayne Brazel confessed, claimed self-defense, and was acquitted at his murder trial. Garrett's death remains one of New Mexico's greatest murder mysteries.

Garrett was neither a cowboy nor a gunfighter. Shooting Billy the Kid made him famous, but it overshadowed his other accomplishments. A lifelong agnostic, Garrett was surprisingly well read and skilled at visualizing projects, but he was often surly with people and inept in politics. He was a good family man, and his daughter Elizabeth, who was blind, wrote the New Mexico state song. Above all Garrett was a cool-headed, reflective lawman who kept his gun in his pants and tried to practice his trade in an efficient, businesslike manner. He remains one of America's best-known frontier lawmen.

• Garrett's correspondence with author Emerson Hough is in the Iowa State Historical Department, Des Moines. Record Group No. 56 at the National Archives and Records Service has most of the Garrett-Roosevelt correspondence as well as telegrams and citizen complaints. Because Garrett is best known for slaying Billy the Kid, the two representative books are Robert M. Utley, *Billy the Kid: A Short and Violent Life* (1989), and Frederick Nolan, *The Lincoln County War: A Documentary History* (1992). Garrett's career as a buffalo hunter is largely encapsulated in *Willis Skelton Glenn v. The United States and the Comanche Indians*, No. 1892–93, U.S. Court of Claims, Washington, D.C. See also Jack DeMattos, *Garrett and Roosevelt* (1988). Southwestern newspapers of the relevant dates are filled with Garrett references. For the full Garrett story, see Leon C. Metz, *Pat Garrett: The Story of a Western Lawman* (1974).

LEON C. METZ

GARRETT, Robert (2 May 1783–4 Feb. 1857), merchant and financier, was born in Lisburn, County Down, Ireland, the son of John Garrett and Margaret MacMechen. When Garrett was seven years old his family immigrated to the United States, with his father dying in the course of the journey. His newly widowed mother settled with her children on a farm in Cumberland County, Pennsylvania, where young Garrett grew up performing many of the required chores. In 1798 the family moved to another farm in Washington County, Pennsylvania, and in the following year, seeking greater opportunities, Garrett accompanied an older brother on a trading expedition among the Native American tribes of the area. After traveling extensively along the Monongahela and Ohio rivers, the pair was forced by severely cold weather into spending the winter among the Indians near present-day Marietta, Ohio. The trip proved profitable in more ways than one; in addition to the brothers' success in trading their goods for furs, the venture alerted the younger Garrett to the economic opportunities available in the West.

The early years of Garrett's mercantile career are somewhat obscure. At some point after 1800 he moved to Baltimore, Maryland, and entered the produce and commission house of Patrick Dinsmore as a clerk. After some four years in that position, he formed his own partnership; trading under the name Wallace & Garrett, the firm provided Garrett with additional opportunities to engage in western trade. Following the firm's dissolution in 1812, he returned to Washington County and engaged in business for the next several years. He maintained his ties to Baltimore, however, by marrying Elizabeth Stouffer, the daughter of a prominent businessman of that community and a member of its city council, in 1817; the couple had three children.

Returning to Baltimore for good around 1820, Garrett soon took advantage of his accumulated business experience and Baltimore's location. He opened his own business on Franklin Street, specializing in the wholesale grocery, produce, commission, and forwarding business. Later moving his firm to Howard Street, Garrett successfully competed with older, more established firms by initiating direct connections with the East and West Indies (and South America as well) and by concentrating his efforts on those goods that were in the greatest demand by the rapidly developing West. In addition, Garrett put great emphasis on the rapid transportation of his merchandise, which he moved westward on pack horses and later by wagon trains that ran night and day over the turnpikes and plank roads leading to the frontier. Although Baltimore's geographic location was closer to the West than ports such as New York or Boston, it was hampered by the distance that ships had to travel up the Chesapeake Bay to reach port (a point that was driven home to Garrett, who had become the American agent for shipowners both here and in Great Britain, on many occasions). As such, Garrett tirelessly promoted the improvement of transportation facilities to the West, including the development of the Baltimore & Ohio Railroad, in which he invested heavily (his son John Work Garrett later played an even more prominent role in the railroad's development).

Garrett's business, which became known as Robert Garrett & Sons around 1839, continued to grow and develop, establishing connections with financial and exporting firms such as George Peabody & Company of London. Having established its own banking operations to facilitate trade, the firm eventually restricted itself exclusively to financial dealings. With his own financial status secure, Garrett entered wholeheartedly into the development of his adopted hometown, serving as a director of the Baltimore Water Company, the Baltimore Gas Company, the Savings Bank of Baltimore, and the Baltimore Shot Tower Company. In 1836 he helped to organize the Western (later Western National) Bank, for which he served as a director until his death, and in 1847 he took a similar role in the establishment of the Eutaw Savings Bank of Baltimore, serving as a director of that institution until the end of his life as well. Constantly seeking new methods to facilitate trade in Baltimore, Garrett noted the need for improved business-traveler accommodations. Accordingly, he entered the hotel business in 1845 with the purchase of the Eutaw House, which he turned into a first-rate facility, and expanded his interests in the field in 1850 by purchasing the Wheatfield Inn on Howard Street, which he replaced with a new hotel on the same site.

Successful in business nearly all his life, Garrett's last major project ironically flopped. Some time after the end of the Mexican-American War, he became interested in the trade potential of California and, with a view toward exploiting the possibilities, built (in partnership with others) the *Monumental City*, at the time the largest ocean steamship ever constructed in Baltimore. Hopes for regular traffic between Baltimore and San Francisco were dashed when Baltimore's harbor, not yet dredged to its modern depth, proved inadequate to the vessel's draft requirements.

In his later years Garrett resided with his family at the Eutaw House, where he died. While he successfully built up a mercantile career from nothing, his encouragement of the development of western transportation routes (later brought to fulfillment by his son) stands as his greatest legacy.

• The Robert Garrett Papers are held at the Library of Congress. The best secondary sources on Garrett's life and career are J. Thomas Scharf, *History of Baltimore City and County* (1881), and R. H. Spencer, ed., "John Work Garrett," *Genealogical and Memorial Encyclopedia of the State of Maryland* (1919), pp. 359–70. An obituary is in the *Baltimore Sun*, 5 Feb. 1857.

EDWARD L. LACH, JR.

GARRETT, Thomas (21 Aug. 1789–25 Jan. 1871), abolitionist and Underground Railroad activist, was born in Upper Darby, Pennsylvania, the son of Thomas Garrett and Sarah Price, farmers and owners of several mills. Garrett's early life was spent working on the

family farm and at the mills. He also learned the blacksmith trade. In 1813 he married Mary Sharpless; they had five children. Mary died in 1828, and in 1830 Garrett married Rachel Mendinhall (sometimes spelled Mendenhall); they had one child. Rachel died in 1868. In 1822 Garrett moved to Wilmington, Delaware, where he established a successful mercantile iron, coal, and hardware business.

Garrett's parents were members of the Society of Friends (Quakers), and he remained a member throughout his life. According to family lore, his antislavery activity began in 1813 when one of the family servants was kidnapped to be sold into slavery. Thomas pursued the kidnappers to Philadelphia and rescued the victim. The incident added to his growing concern for the slaves, which had been fostered by the antislavery sentiment of his family and other Quakers. His work as an abolitionist and Underground Railroad organizer and operator would result in his national reputation.

While most northern Quakers were moderate in their antislavery views, emphasizing primarily their own rejection of slavery, Garrett went much further, becoming a follower of Boston abolitionist William Lloyd Garrison, who offended some Quakers with his strong language and confrontational style. Like Garrison, Garrett advocated nonviolent resistance to slavery. Working with abolitionists in the Philadelphia area, Garrett organized a network of sympathizers who provided funds, transportation, and sometimes hospitality to slaves who had fled from their masters. During his lengthy involvement with the Underground Railroad, he kept records of 2,700 slaves he had helped escape. His work, along with that of Levi Coffin in Cincinnati, contributed to the perception that a well-organized escape route for slaves extended throughout the nation.

Even though Delaware was a slave state, except for several newspaper attacks Garrett experienced remarkably little opposition to his Underground Railroad activity, especially in the years just prior to the Civil War. In 1856 Garrett wrote a friend: "There is about as much anti-slavery feeling here as in Boston, and quite as freely expressed."

There were a few exceptions, however. On one occasion several southerners tried to throw Garrett off a train on which he was trying to prevent a black woman from being taken into slavery. Although a $10,000 reward was offered by the Maryland legislature for his arrest for "slave stealing," the act was largely symbolic. More serious was the legal suit brought against him and his associate, John Hunn, in 1848 for damages they caused in assisting several slaves to escape. One of the two judges hearing the case was Roger B. Taney, who as chief justice of the U.S. Supreme Court would later author the *Dred Scott* decision. The court ruled against both the abolitionists and assessed damages of $5,400 against Garrett. Later accounts suggesting that Garrett was impoverished by this decision were apparently exaggerated. After a compromise was arranged, Garrett settled by paying $1,500.

Although Garrett as a pacifist never personally endorsed enticing slaves to abscond or entered other southern states to assist fugitives, he provided funds and assistance for such activities to black abolitionist Harriet Tubman. He also worked closely with black abolitionist William Still and the Philadelphia Vigilance Committee. The Civil War tested his commitment to nonviolence, however. After suggesting that a fugitive slave join the Union army, he asked, "Am I naughty, being a professed non-resistant, to advise this poor fellow to serve Father Abraham?"

Garrett lived to see the outlawing of chattel slavery and continued to work for the end of racial discrimination. He also supported the movements for woman suffrage and temperance. Upon ratification of the Fifteenth Amendment in 1870 granting the vote to black males, blacks in Wilmington carried Garrett through the streets in an open carriage with a banner proclaiming, "Our Moses." At word of Garrett's death in Wilmington, William Lloyd Garrison commented, "His rightful place is conspicuously among the benefactors, saviors, martyrs of the human race."

• William Still's *Underground Rail Road: A Record of Facts, Authentic Narratives, Letters, etc.* (1872) contains a biographical sketch of Thomas Garrett and reprints twenty-three of Garrett's letters. Other Garrett letters are in the libraries of Haverford College, Swarthmore College, and Cornell University and at the Historical Society of Pennsylvania, the Boston Public Library, and the Delaware Historical Society. The latter also has a scrapbook of material on his life compiled by his granddaughter, Helen S. Garrett. James A. McGowan, *Station Master on the Underground Railroad* (1977), corrects some of the often-repeated errors about Garrett and reprints all of his known letters. See also Thomas E. Drake, "Thomas Garrett, Quaker Abolitionist," in *Friends in Wilmington* (n.d.). The obituary in the *Wilmington Daily Commercial*, 25 Jan. 1871, is reprinted in the *Friends Intelligencer*, 11 Feb. 1871.

LARRY GARA

GARRETTSON, Freeborn (15 Aug. 1752–26 Sept. 1827), Methodist itinerant minister, was born in Harford County, Maryland, the son of John Garrettson and Sarah Hanson, plantation owners. As a part of the southern colonial gentry, Garrettson received a good education with both practical and classical components. After his mother died when he was only ten, he took his studies seriously. He began earnestly reading the Scriptures and attending the local Anglican church. He also started experiencing religious visions, dreams, and voices. Although his journal tells the story of a young man who later claimed he "loved the world more than God," Garrettson never lost his mystical temperament or his religious sensitivity.

By the time he was twenty-one Garrettson had inherited the plantation and several dozen slaves from his father. His wealth, however, eventually became a spiritual torment, a handicap that forced him to search for a new religious home. He considered joining the Presbyterians or the Quakers but was eventually drawn to the Methodist renewal movement through the preaching of Robert Strawbridge and the mentoring of Francis Asbury. In 1775 he officially joined the local Methodist fellowship.

One of Garrettson's first actions as a Methodist was freeing his slaves. He wrote in his journal that the thought of emancipation "struck my mind, 'it is not right for you to keep your fellow creatures in bondage'" ("Experience and Travels" [1984], p. 48). With this episode Garrettson became a lifelong antislavery advocate. He eventually wrote a book, *A Dialogue between Do-Justice and Professing-Christian* (1820), which argued that slavery violated the tenets of Christianity and the principles on which the American nation was founded. He also counseled slaveholders, urging them to teach their slaves to read the Bible and to treat them well until a gradual emancipation or colonization took place. Garrettson did not advocate complete racial separation but suggested that former slaves should be given the opportunity to colonize land acquired in the Louisiana Purchase. He fought for this position within the Methodist church until his death.

Garrettson's abilities convinced Asbury that Garrettson should become a Methodist circuit rider, and consequently, he was ordained in May 1776. His ordination began a career that continued until Garrettson was well into his seventies. He traveled thousands of miles by horseback, carriage, boat, and foot, organizing Methodist congregations in North Carolina, Virginia, Delaware, New York, New Jersey, Nova Scotia, Pennsylvania, and Maryland. Speaking of his zeal, Asbury once remarked, "Brother Garrettson will let no person escape a religious lecture" ("Experience and Travels" [1984], p. 23).

Garrettson's rise to prominence within American Methodism began during the American Revolution. Methodists were dogged by accusations of disloyalty and treason. Many Methodists were prominent Tories. Most of the Methodist pastors returned to England, and Asbury went into internal exile. Garrettson was appointed by Asbury to oversee the Methodist ministry during the war. Even though Garrettson supported the patriot cause, he was stoned, beaten, almost hanged, and jailed because he refused to bear arms or take an oath of allegiance and because he openly advocated freeing slaves. Despite severe persecution, American Methodism gained thousands of converts in the South—both black and white. By the end of the revolutionary war, 89 percent of American Methodists resided in the South because of Garrettson and his fellow circuit riders' efforts. Their success can be attributed to an anti-Calvinist message of free will, a tone of anti–Anglican establishment, a revivalistic zeal, and an ingenious organizational structure that bound individuals to an egalitarian local fellowship and the local fellowship to a hierarchically controlled church polity.

In 1784 John Wesley, Methodism's founder, sent emissaries charged with forming an American Methodist fellowship (or church) distinct from its British origins. Garrettson was given the task of taking the news to the South. He traveled 1,200 miles in six weeks, calling ministers and laity to the "Christmas Conference" that formed the American Methodist

Episcopal church. At the conference Garrettson was ordained as a missionary to Nova Scotia, a Canadian province that was a refuge for New England Tories. With a small band of missionaries, Garrettson was extraordinarily successful in establishing Methodism as the largest Protestant presence in Nova Scotia.

In 1787 Garrettson was recalled from Nova Scotia and later sent by Asbury to a circuit in New England. Garrettson, however, never made it to Boston. On a stop in New York City, he discovered that both the city and the Hudson River valley were fertile fields for Methodist missions. In the Hudson River valley Garrettson met his future wife, Catherine Livingston, the daughter of a prominent patriot family. Despite the severe reservations of the Livingston family, the couple was married in 1793 and later had a daughter. Catherine gave Garrettson access to some of the most aristocratic members of the Hudson River gentry. Garrettson's friendship with John Jay, for example, led to the latter's conversion to Methodism. Garrettson and the circuit-riding preachers in his charge were extraordinarily successful in New York and the surrounding states. They logged hundreds of miles through stately manors and rugged frontier.

Garrettson spent much of his remaining life in New York. He built a home on the Hudson open to all Methodist itinerants. Asbury dubbed the mansion "Traveler's Rest." He also founded and endowed the Methodist Missionary and Bible Society, as well as a seminary to educate Methodist children. Still, he never stopped traveling. He opened a circuit in Philadelphia in 1799 and continued to travel throughout the Middle Atlantic states and New England until his death in New York City.

Garrettson spent fifty-two years of his life as a pastor and church organizer in the American Methodist Episcopal church. Along with early American Methodist bishop Francis Asbury, Garrettson should be given credit for transforming Methodism from an unpopular and persecuted British sect during the American Revolution to the largest American denomination by the beginning of the Civil War.

• Garrettson's papers, manuscripts, and letters are at the Drew University Library in Madison, N.J. Other than those cited, Garrettson's published works include *A Letter to the Rev. Lyman Beecher* (1816) and *The Experiences and Travels of Mr. Freeborn Garrettson* (1791). Because Garrettson never completely finished his travel journals, Nathan Bangs drew on surviving journals and letters to produce the valuable biography *The Life of the Rev. Freeborn Garrettson*, 3d ed. (1832). See also Garrettson, "The Experience and Travels of Mr. Freeborn Garrettson," in *Social and Religious Life in the U.S. during the Revolutionary and Federal Periods*, ed. Robert Drew Simpson (1984). For more biographical information, see J. Theodore Hughes, *An Historical Sketch of the Life of Freeborn Garrettson, Pioneer Methodist Preacher*, 2d ed. (1984), and Simpson, *Freeborn Garrettson: American Methodist Pioneer* (1954). There are several recent histories of early American Methodism that include Garrettson and place him in the context of the early republic's religious upheavals. These include Russell Richey, *Early American Methodism* (1991); John Wigger, "Taking Heaven by Storm: Methodism

and the Popularization of American Christianity" (Ph.D. diss., Notre Dame Univ., 1994); and Nathan Hatch, *The Democratization of American Christianity* (1989).

SCOTT FLIPSE

GARRIGUE, Jean (8 Dec. 1914–27 Dec. 1972), poet, was born in Evansville, Indiana, the daughter of Gertrude Heath and Allan Colfax Garrigus, a postal inspector and author. (Garrigue and her sister returned to the original French spelling of the family name.) When she was fourteen years old, Garrigue discovered the imagist poets and a literary ambition. She attended the University of Chicago, graduating in 1937, and moved to New York three years later. Her verses were introduced in a 1941 issue of the *Kenyon Review* as part of a "Nine Young Poets" group that included John Ciardi and Howard Nemerov.

During World War II Garrigue worked at various journalist and reviewing jobs and edited a publication sheet for the United Service Organizations (USO). In 1943 she earned an M.A. from the University of Iowa, and thirty-six of her poems appeared in the New Directions anthology *Five Young American Poets* (1944). In 1954 she was awarded a Rockefeller grant, which enabled her to spend the summer in Europe. Upon her return, she moved to Greenwich Village permanently.

Over the next sixteen years, Garrigue taught and lectured at a number of colleges and universities, among them Smith, Bard, and Queens Colleges, and the Universities of Colorado and Connecticut. She also held a Radcliffe Institute for Independent Study fellowship from 1966 to 1968 and then stayed at the institute for another two years as an appointed scholar. In addition to the Rockefeller grant, she had been given a Guggenheim Fellowship in 1960 and a 1962 grant from the National Academy of Arts and Letters.

Garrigue's poetic career evinced equally smooth upward slopes of achievement and public recognition. Influenced by John Keats, Hart Crane, and female colleagues as diverse as Muriel Rukeyser and Marianne Moore, striving to meld the former's social awareness with the latter's intellectual precision, her initial collection, *The Ego and the Centaur*, was published in 1947, followed by *The Monument Rose* (1953). Her main topics were travel and love, often pursued with a Proustian fastidiousness in an effort to articulate ephemeral emotional states and experiences. It is not surprising that her poetic weaknesses tended toward the archaic and the lushly romantic. "I prefer elaborate structures to functional slick ones," she was quoted as saying in Joseph D. McClatchy's *Contemporary American Poetry* anthology (1990).

It was Garrigue's strategic position at the heart of the New York literary scene as well as the academic conventionality of her well-crafted verses that helped secure her consistent, respectful attention from important establishment outlets, especially the *New York Times*, which reviewed her *Water Walk by Villa d'Este* (1959) with high praise, concluding that "there are few poets around who command as noble or impressive a style as she has at her best." The Sunday book review section of the same paper would use her *Country with-out Maps* (1964)—arguably her strongest collection—as an exemplary stick to assault "the current mode of private confession" and labeled "Pays Perdu," its central long work, "a major poem."

Garrigue lived alone and was a professional writer and teacher in almost every positive sense of the term, an admired figure among New York's literati. Besides poetry, she wrote and published several short stories, one of which won a *Kenyon Review* first prize in 1944, and a whimsical novella, *The Animal Hotel* (1966). Her fascination with the technical aspects of verse is richly reflected in the correspondence she maintained with Marianne Moore. In 1965 she produced *Marianne Moore*, a forty-page monograph that Charles Moles-worth, in his biography of Moore, describes as "one of the earliest studies of her entire body of poetry" and "still one of the best critical introductions to her imagination and style" (*Marianne Moore: A Literary Life* [1990], p. 448).

In the spring of 1972 Garrigue accepted a poet-in-residence position at the University of California despite the increasing burden of Hodgkin's disease. By the fall she was back east and teaching at Rhode Island College, but in December her illness forced her into Boston's Massachusetts General Hospital, where she died. Her last months were devoted to completing the manuscript of *Studies for an Actress and Other Poems*, which Macmillan published the year after her death. Garrigue was a minor poet of high intelligence and impressive technical skills, and her baroque, often eloquent verses are more memorable in their parts than as lyric wholes.

• Garrigue's papers are in the Berg Collection of the New York Public Library; her letters to Marianne Moore are in the Moore collection at the Rosenbach Museum and Library, Philadelphia, Pa. Only two of her books remain in print, *Animal Hotel* (1966) and *Chartres and Prose Poems* (1970), confirming the decline in her reputation since her death. However, the publication of Lee Upton's *Jean Garrigue: A Poetics of Plenitude* (1991) might portend a more balanced assessment of her achievement. See also Laurence Lieberman's appreciative essay-reviews of Garrigue's *New and Selected Poems* (1968) and *Studies for an Actress and Other Poems*, which are reprinted in his *Beyond the Muse of Memory: Essays on Contemporary American Poets* (1995). An obituary is in the *New York Times*, 28 Dec. 1972.

EDWARD BUTSCHER

GARRISON, Charles Willis (15 July 1879–26 Aug. 1935), public health official, was born ten miles north of Bastrop, Louisiana, the son of Samuel Harvey Garrison and Hannah Elizabeth Bogar. His father left farming, moved to Texas, and took up bookkeeping, serving as county district clerk in Abilene, Texas, and as secretary of the Merchants' Credit Association. Young Garrison attended Simmons College in Abilene and Southwestern College at Georgetown, Texas. After taking some medical courses at Galveston Medical School, he studied from 1901 until his graduation in 1905 at the First Memphis Hospital Medical School, Memphis, Tennessee.

In 1906 Garrison married Margaret "Vinnie" Farmer Middleton. Nine years his senior, his wife had graduated in nursing in 1899 from the Belle Point Hospital (subsequently Sparks Memorial Hospital) in Fort Smith, Arkansas. After serving as matron (nursing supervisor) at Logan H. Roots Hospital in Little Rock, she became superintendent of nurses at Memphis General Hospital, where they met. The couple moved to Tuscola, Texas, where Garrison established a private practice; in 1908 they moved to Fort Smith. Although the Garrisons had no children of their own, they raised and adopted her niece and nephew.

Vinnie Garrison had a strong interest in public health and imparted that zeal to her husband. In 1911 Charles Garrison succeeded Morgan Smith to become the second Arkansas state director of the Rockefeller Hookworm Commission, a privately funded body charged with reforming southern health practices by promoting sanitary toilets in order to eliminate hookworms. In 1914, one year before the termination of the commission, Garrison was appointed state health director, a position he held until 1933.

Support for public health measures was weak in Arkansas, especially among politicians. After the hookworm commission demonstrated that the worms entered the body through the feet, state legislator Aurelius G. Gray attacked the commission as a northern plot to force southern children to buy shoes. Governor George W. Hays routinely vetoed appropriations for the state health board.

During the 1920s conditions improved. In 1922 Garrison recruited a notable physician, Frances Sage Bradley, to head the Bureau of Child Hygiene. Bradley lobbied the legislature successfully for matching federal funds under the Sheppard-Towner maternity program. Classes for midwives were held around the state, and Bradley produced nine general education pamphlets titled the Arkansas Family Series. Garrison found the pamphlets offensive, and Bradley, disgusted with what she considered an excess of male chauvinism in Arkansas, left the state in late 1923.

Although hampered by state laws that gave the health board little power and left participation in state programs largely up to the counties, Garrison nevertheless managed by 1933 to create county health units in thirty of Arkansas's seventy-five counties. Garrison, who later observed that his agency was built "on floods and droughts" (Scholle, p. 52), used these natural disasters, notably the flood of 1927, which affected 1.5 million persons in fifty-six counties, to overcome local inertia.

Garrison was a champion of government involvement in health, urging the establishment of county health units and predicting an increasing role for the federal government. Until the late 1920s he received generous support from the Arkansas Medical Society. His wife contributed greatly, serving as the first president of the Women's Auxiliary of the Arkansas Medical Society and as an officer in the women's auxiliaries of the Southern Medical Association and the American Medical Association. She helped orchestrate the Arkansas Federation of Women's Clubs in support of public health programs during the crucial early period.

However, during the late 1920s and early 1930s American doctors in general and Arkansas physicians in particular became increasingly hostile to public health programs, fearful they would lose business. Opposition to midwife training was so pronounced that in 1929 Arkansas abandoned its participation in the program. Attacks on "state medicine," subsequently called "socialized medicine," became common. In 1933 Garrison was fired by conservative governor Julius M. Futrell. Besides Garrison's known radical opinions, he was not a native of Futrell's home county, a necessity for holding office under Futrell. One newspaper lauded Garrison's work and lamented his crucifixion, stating he "had a higher regard for service to mankind than to interests and political expediency" (History of Public Health Collection, UAMS Library). Under his successor, a former Missouri Pacific Railroad physician, the number of county nurses promptly declined to eighteen, and every effort was made to limit services. It was not until World War II that the federal government invested in improvements in public health in Arkansas.

Garrison supplemented his meager pay by serving as professor of preventive medicine at the University of Arkansas's medical school from 1913 to 1918 and again from 1922 to 1931. He also served as city health officer of Little Rock. The author of scientific and educational articles on public health, he spelled out his progressive philosophy of preventive medicine in an article titled "Public Health and Democracy" (*Journal of the Arkansas Medical Society* 16 [Apr. 1919]: 80–81). He also authored "The Development of Medicine and Public Health" for David Y. Thomas's *Arkansas and Its People: A History, 1541–1930* (1930).

Garrison was active in numerous state and national organizations. He served as a director of the Arkansas State Tuberculosis Association and as a member of the National Malaria Committee. In 1924 he was appointed one of the two American delegates to the League of Nations Health Conference. Further national recognition came in 1931 when he served as president of the Conference of State and Provincial Health Authorities of North America. At the annual meeting, he called for increased federal funds and uniform medical laws.

After being discharged in 1933, Garrison entered Columbia University's medical school, intending to retrain for private practice. However, a recurrence of tuberculosis forced him to drop out. He took a job as city health officer in Lexington, Kentucky, until his worsening condition led him to enter the Julius Marks Sanitorium in Lexington, where he died of pulmonary tuberculosis. Unverified is the story that he seriously weakened his lungs after World War I experimenting with the use of poison gas on Arkansas's large mosquito population.

Garrison's career typified the problems of southern public health officials. Faced variously with public indifference, ignorance, and even hostility, he had scant support from state authorities. As the Progressive Era waned, even the medical profession abandoned its commitment to public health. Nevertheless, significant reductions occurred in communicable diseases such as malaria and tuberculosis, while yellow fever disappeared entirely. Pellagra and numerous childhood diseases remained, however, and public health officials in the South could point to numerous problems intensified by the Great Depression.

• A few Garrison items are in the History of Public Health in Arkansas Collection at the University of Arkansas for Medical Sciences (UAMS) Historical Research Center. The standard history, Sarah Hudson Scholle, *The Pain of Prevention: A History of Public Health in Arkansas* (1990), is the best source for his professional career. David Moyers, "The Rockefeller Sanitary Commission for the Eradication of Hookworm Disease in Arkansas, 1910–1914" (unpublished paper on file at the UAMS Library), details his early work. His correspondence to the Rockefeller Sanitary Commission is on file at the Rockefeller Archive Center, Tarrytown, N.Y. For biographical data see David Y. Thomas, ed., *Arkansas and Its People: A History, 1541–1930*, vol. 4 (1930), pp. 360–61. Important obituaries include the Little Rock *Arkansas Gazette*, 28 Aug. 1935, and the *Journal of the Arkansas Medical Society* 32 (Oct. 1935): 89.

Garrison's wife wrote *A History of Public Health Service in Arkansas* (1949) and is discussed in Elissa Lane Miller, "Arkansas Nurses, 1895–1920: A Profile," *Arkansas Historical Quarterly* 47 (Summer 1988): 154–71.

MICHAEL B. DOUGAN

GARRISON, Fielding Hudson (5 Nov. 1870–18 Apr. 1935), medical librarian, bibliographer, and historian, was born in Washington, D.C., the son of John Rowzee Garrison II, a comptroller for the federal government, and Jennie Davis. Garrison graduated from Washington Central High School in 1886. After a year's concentration at home on music and college preparation, he matriculated at Johns Hopkins University in 1887. There he focused on classical and modern languages, with some physics and mathematics, graduating in 1890. Garrison's facility in languages and literature was apparent throughout his career and in his correspondence.

Although his motivation is unknown, in 1890 Garrison enrolled in the Medical Department of Georgetown University, attending classes in the evening. He received his M.D. in 1893, having never attended an autopsy, and apparently with no intention of practicing medicine. In March 1891 he was appointed as a clerk in the library of the Surgeon General's Office (which in 1922 became the Army Medical Library, and in 1956 the National Library of Medicine), under the direction of John Shaw Billings. He worked with Billings until the latter's departure in 1895 on the *Index-Catalogue*, a catalog of the library's books and an index to its periodical holdings. Later he assisted the editor, Robert Fletcher, on the *Index Medicus*, an index to current periodicals, which appeared with greater frequency. These two publications of the library made the medical literature accessible to the profession. Garrison helped to organize the citations by name and subject and prepared them for publication, becoming familiar with the literature in the process.

The bibliographical work required to prepare these indexes for publication involved careful attention to detail, speed, and accuracy. By 1899 Garrison progressed to the rank of assistant librarian. As a result of his developing responsibility, on the death of Fletcher in 1912 he was advanced to the level of principal assistant librarian. His responsibilities frequently involved training not only the support staff but also the many military men assigned as librarians. In 1909 Garrison met Clara Augusta Brown, and they were married the following year. The couple had three daughters.

Garrison joined the army in 1917 as a major in the medical section of the Officers Reserve Corps. In July 1918 he was appointed to the rank of lieutenant colonel and in 1920 to the regular Army Medical Corps. He saw no active field duty; his responsibilities during the war consisted of the collection of information for its history.

Following the war Garrison returned to his former position in the library, but in 1922 he was assigned to the Philippines, where he served till 1924. He found it difficult to acclimate, but he admired his chief and enjoyed the variety of his assignments, which included managing a correspondence course for officers in the Far East, compiling statistics on venereal diseases and doing some of the laboratory work, making abstracts of foreign literature, and working up beriberi cases at the Philippine General Hospital. He rose to the rank of colonel by the time of his retirement in 1930.

As in Washington, Garrison spent much of his leisure time in the Philippines reading or with his music, chiefly playing the piano. Music was both a solace and inspiration for him. He was an avid concert-goer and pianist, and knowledgeable about composers and orchestras; a panegyric to Brahms, his favorite composer, was buried in a paper titled "The Medical History of Robert Schumann and His Family," which he gave at least four times and published in the *Bulletin of the New York Academy of Medicine*.

On his return to Washington, D.C., in 1924, Garrison resumed work at the library and assumed full editorship of the *Index Medicus*. The continuing drudgery of bibliographical work led him to propose the amalgamation of *Index Medicus* with the *Quarterly Cumulative Index* of medical literature, issued by the American Medical Association. The first issue of the resulting *Quarterly Cumulative Index Medicus* (*QCIM*) appeared in January 1927, and the last issue of *Index Medicus* in June 1927. He continued as an editor of the *QCIM* through 1929. Garrison was appointed consultant librarian for the New York Academy of Medicine library in 1925. This involved a monthly visit and much writing, including short articles, book reviews, and editorials for the Academy *Bulletin*.

Garrison was a lonely, shy man, punctilious and meticulous in his relationships and in his work. As he grew older he became more sensitive to perceived slights and suffered from what he saw as overtaxing responsibilities associated with editing the library's pub-

lications. Although he sought the position of librarian, it eluded his grasp, and he remained in his last position until his retirement in 1930, when he was appointed librarian of the William H. Welch Medical Library in the Medical School and lecturer in the Institute for the History of Medicine at Johns Hopkins University. Garrison was not an inspiring lecturer; his voice was low and his delivery monotonous. However, in dialogue with others his enthusiasm and erudition charmed and enlightened.

Garrison's medical history endeavors developed naturally from his education and his association with the medical literature, with his first publications in that field appearing in 1906. For an exhibit in the library he drew together significant medical publications, which developed into his list of "Texts Illustrating the History of Medicine" in the *Index-Catalogue* (ser. 2, vol. 11, 1912). This list of classic texts, growing in length and detail over the years, was published in the *Bulletin of the History of Medicine* (1 [1933]) and was later edited by Leslie T. Morton and published separately in three more editions (1943–1984), becoming known as "Garrison and Morton." Widely consulted by medical historians, librarians, and book dealers, the guide later became *Morton's Medical Bibliography* (5th ed., 1991).

The breadth and depth of Garrison's expertise was revealed in the first edition of his *Introduction to the History of Medicine* (1913; 4th ed., 1929), the first American attempt at a comprehensive history of medicine. As Billings had done for current medical literature for practicing physicians, so Garrison did for future medical historians. His shorter historical pieces, some 250 in number, appeared in various journals.

Garrison had a voluminous correspondence with many of the noted medical figures of his day in the United States and abroad, among them E. C. Streeter, M. G. Seelig, Karl Sudhoff, William Osler, Victor Robinson, Harvey Cushing, William Halstead, William Welch, Charles Singer, and Morris Fishbein. He also carried on a substantial correspondence with H. L. Mencken from 1918 till his death. Many asked for his help in their own historical writings, and he was kept busy providing information sources, manuscript reviews, translations, prefaces, and forewords. He was also invited to present papers and lectures.

Garrison held memberships in many European medical historical groups, and in the American Association for the History of Medicine. He was also a member of the American Medical Association and the American College of Surgeons. He died of cancer in Baltimore, Maryland. In 1938 he was honored posthumously by the American Association for the History of Medicine with the creation of the Fielding H. Garrison Lecture, to be given annually to recognize a notable American medical historian.

• Collections of Garrison correspondence are at Yale University (Garrison-Cushing Letters, Archives and Manuscripts, Sterling Memorial Library), at the Wellcome Historical Medical Library (letters to Paul B. Hoeber, Western Manuscripts

Department), and the National Library of Medicine (Garrison Papers, History of Medicine Division). Among Garrison's other major publications are *John Shaw Billings; a Memoir* (1915); *A Physician's Anthology of English and American Poetry*, with Casey A. Wood (1920); *The Principles of Anatomic Illustration before Vesalius* (1926); and "The Medical and Scientific Periodicals of the 17th and 18th Centuries, with a Revised Catalogue and Checklist," *Bulletin of the History of Medicine* 2 (1934): 285–343. His writings for the New York Academy of Medicine were collected in his *Contributions to the History of Medicine* (1966).

Biographies, though not definitive, are Solomon R. Kagan, *Life and Letters of Fielding H. Garrison* (1938) and his *Fielding H. Garrison; a Biography* (1948). A memorial issue of the *Bulletin of the History of Medicine* 5 (Apr. 1937) contains six articles by colleagues, friends, and students on Garrison's military career, musical interests, and literary gifts, as well as photographs and a bibliography. On Garrison's *Introduction to the History of Medicine* see Gert H. Brieger, "Fielding H. Garrison: The Man and His Book," *Transactions and Studies of the College of Physicians*, ser. 5, 3, no. 1 (Mar. 1981): 1–21. Garrison's years at the Library of the Surgeon General's Office are related in Wyndham D. Miles, *A History of the National Library of Medicine: The Nation's Treasury of Medical Knowledge* (1982). See also Leslie T. Morton, "The History of 'Garrison-Morton': A Personal Account," *Health Libraries Review* 4, no. 3 (Sept. 1987): 132–38.

NANCY WHITTEN ZINN

GARRISON, Jim (20 Nov. 1921–21 Oct. 1992), lawyer, was born Earling Carothers Garrison in Dennison, Iowa, the son of Earling R. Garrison and Jane Ann Robinson, a schoolteacher. He legally changed his name to "Jim" as an adult. Garrison's parents divorced when he was three, and the boy was raised by his mother in New Orleans. He enlisted in the U.S. Army in 1940 and served as a military aviator during World War II. He left active duty in 1946 and enrolled at Tulane University to study law.

After graduating with an LL.B. in 1949, Garrison worked as a special agent for the Federal Bureau of Investigation in Seattle and Tacoma, Washington. He found the work "extremely boring" and returned to New Orleans, where he received the LL.M. from Tulane in 1951. Garrison briefly resumed active service in the military but was discharged after army doctors found him to be suffering from "severe and disabling psychoneurosis" that "interfered with his social and professional judgment to a marked degree." Critics later pointed to the evaluation as foreshadowing his sometimes erratic behavior as a public official and his obsession with conspiracy theories. In 1952 Garrison joined a New Orleans law firm, and two years later he became an assistant district attorney. He married Leah Elizabeth Ziegler in 1957. They had five children.

Garrison resigned as assistant district attorney in 1958 to make his first foray into elective politics, an unsuccessful bid for a criminal court judgeship. After another stint in private practice, he announced his candidacy for district attorney in 1961. Garrison campaigned as a reformer and a political outsider, made effective use of television advertising, and emerged the surprise winner in a five-way race.

The new district attorney quickly cracked down on gambling and prostitution in the French Quarter, accompanying police on vice raids with a pistol strapped to his side. The raids attracted press attention and helped cement Garrison's flamboyant reputation. When judges who oversaw the prosecutor's budget rejected some of his funding requests, Garrison suggested they had been swayed by "racketeer influences." The comments led to his conviction for criminal defamation in 1963. The U.S. Supreme Court overturned the verdict in November 1964 and ruled unconstitutional Louisiana's law regarding the defamation of public officials. Garrison easily won reelection in 1965.

In his second term, Garrison embarked on the campaign that would bring him nationwide attention—investigating the 1963 assassination of President John F. Kennedy. Garrison began his inquiry in the fall of 1966, after U.S. senator Russell Long told him the Warren Commission, which placed sole responsibility for the killing on Lee Harvey Oswald, was "dead wrong." Working secretly at first, Garrison set out to uncover coconspirators Oswald might have met during his stay in New Orleans in the spring and summer of 1963. The first suspect was David Ferrie, a pilot and would-be mercenary who died in February 1967 (the coroner ruled that the death was due to a cerebral hemorrhage, but Garrison alleged that Ferrie had committed suicide). Garrison next focused his investigation on Clay Shaw, a New Orleans businessman who denied knowing Oswald or Ferrie. News of the investigation leaked to the press, and in March the district attorney arrested Shaw and charged him with conspiring to kill President Kennedy.

Although some reports depicted Garrison's case as a morass of contradictory and unreliable testimony, he continued his inquiry and widened the scope of his allegations. He sought to establish links between Oswald and opponents of the Cuban Communist Fidel Castro and between those anti-Castro elements and the Central Intelligence Agency (CIA). In January 1968 Garrison declared on the television program "The Tonight Show" that "the Central Intelligence Agency was deeply involved in the assassination." In early 1969 Garrison used Shaw's trial as a forum to attack the findings of the Warren Commission, suggesting that more than one gunman had fired on the president. His case against Shaw, however, fell apart. Important witnesses recanted their testimony or were discredited on the stand, and the jury acquitted Shaw on its first ballot.

The defeat did not end Garrison's political popularity. He was reelected district attorney in November 1969. Four years later, however, his bid for another term in office was derailed when federal prosecutors tried him on charges of accepting bribes from organized crime figures. Garrison maintained his innocence and accused the federal government of persecuting him for his investigation of the Kennedy assassination. Although acquitted in September 1973, Garrison failed to win reelection two months later. He returned to elective politics in 1978, winning a seat on the Louisiana Court of Appeals for the Fourth Circuit. The same year he and his wife divorced. Garrison was reelected to the bench in 1988 but retired three years later because of poor health.

Garrison never lost his interest in the Kennedy assassination. In *A Heritage of Stone* (1970) he charged that the assassination represented a coup d'état by "the strongest forces in the United States government" to prevent Kennedy from withdrawing U.S. troops from Vietnam and de-escalating the Cold War. "John Kennedy was going to be executed because he was the one man who stood in the way of the continued power of the superstate and the continued growth of empire," Garrison wrote. The former prosecutor later detailed his investigation in *On the Trail of the Assassins* (1988). The latter book provided the basis of the 1991 film *JFK*, which portrayed Garrison as a heroic prosecutor confronting an immense conspiracy. Garrison served as an adviser to director Oliver Stone and made a cameo appearance as Earl Warren. The film was a box-office success and brought renewed attention to the former prosecutor and his controversial theories. Garrison died in New Orleans ten months after the film's release.

Garrison was not the first person to question the findings of the Warren Commission, but as a prosecutor he had visibility and official powers that other critics lacked. His investigation and writings helped fuel public interest in the Kennedy assassination and also provide insight into the reasons behind it. Garrison idealized Kennedy and believed that his assassination drastically altered the course of U.S. history—a notion attractive to Americans dissatisfied with subsequent events during the 1960s and 1970s. His attacks on the truthfulness of public officials suited a nation wary of government deceit regarding the Vietnam War and the activities of the CIA.

• No Garrison personal papers are known to exist. In addition to the books mentioned in the text, Garrison wrote *The Star-Spangled Contract* (1976), a novel that revolves around themes of political intrigue and assassination. Like the literature on the Kennedy assassination itself, most assessments of Garrison are sharply partisan. For favorable accounts, see Paris Flammonde, *The Kennedy Conspiracy* (1969), and James D. Eugenio, *Destiny Betrayed: JFK, Cuba, and the Garrison Case* (1992). For a more negative assessment, see Edward Jay Epstein, *Counterplot* (1969) and *The Assassination Chronicles* (1992). Michael L. Kurtz, *Crime of the Century: The Kennedy Assassination from a Historian's Perspective*, 2d ed. (1993), and Gerald Posner, *Case Closed* (1993), provide a more general history of the assassination and inquiries into it. The screenplay of Stone's movie is reprinted in Oliver Stone and Zachary Sklar, *"JFK": The Book of the Film* (1992), which also contains assessments of the film and of Garrison's role published in the popular press in 1991–1992. An obituary is in the *New York Times*, 22 Oct. 1992.

STEPHEN A. WEST

GARRISON, Lindley Miller (28 Nov. 1864–19 Oct. 1932), lawyer and secretary of war, was born in Camden, New Jersey, the son of Joseph Fithian Garrison, an Episcopalian minister, and Elizabeth Vanarsdale, an educated gentlewoman from an old New Jersey family. Garrison was educated in public schools in Philadelphia, attended Phillips Exeter Academy and was a special student at Harvard. He received a law degree from the University of Pennsylvania in 1885. In 1900 he married Margaret Hildeburn of Philadelphia. The number of their children, if any, is unknown.

Garrison practiced law in Camden and in Jersey City from 1886 to 1898 and rose rapidly in state legal affairs. He was appointed vice chancellor of New Jersey in 1904, and he was serving there when Woodrow Wilson was elected governor. After Wilson became president in 1912, Garrison joined his administration as secretary of war.

Garrison succeeded Henry L. Stimson as secretary in the aftermath of a struggle between Chief of Staff Leonard Wood and Adjutant General Fred C. Ainsworth for bureaucratic command and control of the War Department. The controversy between the two former medical doctors had lasted for almost two years. The army was in the midst of an incremental institutional reorganization that had been in motion since the turn of the century, and Wood's "victory" for the office of the chief of staff had been illusionary. Garrison also became entangled in a debate among professional regular army officers, and between them and the National Guard and other civilians with an interest in military affairs, about the current field organization and reserve policies of the army. The controversy raised historic issues of state and federal authority and posed new definitions of citizenship, which expanded the power of the federal government over the individual and revolutionized the traditional political/military policy of the nation.

The organizational issue was a matter of military doctrine, equipment, organization, and planning that most thought best left to professional soldiers. But the reserve question involved differences among regular army officers, some of whom were disciples of the military philosopher Emory Upton, who wanted an "expansible" long service professional force with fully integrated reserves, and some of whom supported the so-called "citizen-soldier" system and championed short service forces with a large nationally controlled reserve force based on universal compulsory peacetime military service similar to those of the major European powers. Both approaches raised conflicts between the regulars and the National Guard, the "soldiers of the states," who insisted that they should continue, as they had in the past, to constitute the first line of defense for the nation. The question of compulsory peacetime military service threatened to divide the nation as no other issue had since the Civil War.

With neither military experience nor initial understanding of either the bureaucratic tensions between the chief of staff and the War Department bureau chiefs, exemplified by the Wood-Ainsworth affair, or the deeper issues involved in the debates about military policy, Garrison managed to repair the damage done during the "War of the Doctors" and to restore at least the appearance of harmony. He supported Wood's efforts to establish voluntary summer training camps for college youth and pressed for modest increases in the military budget. After the war in Europe broke out in August 1914 Garrison loyally supported President Wilson in the latter's efforts to serve as a disinterested mediator of the conflict.

In 1915, after the *Lusitania* crisis, the president ordered Garrison to prepare plans for a larger military establishment. The 1915 plan, prepared by the Army War College and titled "A Proper Military Policy for the United States," proposed expanding the regular army and creating a national reserve "continental army" of 400,000 volunteers enlisted for six years and trained annually on the European model. The "Garrison Plan," as it was called, immediately drew the opposition of the National Guard and those members in Congress who feared that the measure would threaten local control of the militia and change traditional relations between the states and the federal government. Although many citizen groups endorsed the plan, including the members of the Plattsburg Movement, a privately sponsored organization to train reserve army officers and educate the public to the need for a stronger military, General Wood and former president Theodore Roosevelt opposed it and called for compulsory military service. To pass legislation imposing peacetime conscription or even to create a national reserve of volunteers such as Garrison proposed was politically impossible. In early 1916 Representative James Hay of Virginia, an old congressional enemy of the general staff system, introduced a substitute bill in the House of Representatives to strengthen the National Guard and to eliminate Garrison's continental army. Wilson, not doctrinaire on such matters and intent on capturing the "vital center" of the debate, quickly compromised with Hay and his associates. The National Defense Act of 1916 increased the regular army and modified traditional military policies, introducing a "dual oath" of allegiance that made it possible to federalize the National Guard in national emergencies. It also authorized the establishment of the Reserve Officer Training Corps (ROTC) in the nation's colleges and universities.

Garrison was unwilling to abandon the idea of a new volunteer national reserve. He believed that he had been deserted by the president and resigned as a matter of principle on 10 February 1916 to return to the practice of law. He did not speak openly of his days with Wilson for more than a decade. Finally, a few years after the president's death and a few years before his own, Garrison wrote that he had no regrets about his career in the War Department. He acknowledged that he had been politically expendable and that Wilson, like many reformers, was a political animal who suffered from high ideals in theory and few principles in practice. Garrison died in Sea Bright, New Jersey.

• The most significant manuscript materials on Garrison are in the papers of Assistant Secretary of War Henry Breckin-

ridge and in the Garrison folder in the papers of Ray Stannard Baker, both at the Library of Congress. The three books that best cover his years as secretary of war are John Whiteclay Chambers II, *To Raise an Army: The Draft Comes to Modern America* (1987); John Garry Clifford, *The Citizen Soldiers: The Plattsburg Training Camp Movement 1913–1920* (1972); and John P. Finnegan, *Against the Specter of a Dragon: The Campaign for American Military Preparedness, 1914–1917* (1974). An obituary is in the *New York Times*, 20 Oct. 1932.

DANIEL R. BEAVER

GARRISON, Lucy McKim (30 Oct. 1842–11 May 1877), collector of slave songs and musician, was born in Philadelphia, Pennsylvania, the daughter of James Miller McKim, an eminent abolitionist, and Sarah Allibone Speakman, a Quaker, whose father had operated a station on the Underground Railroad in Chester County, Pennsylvania. McKim's father left the Presbyterian ministry for the antislavery lecture platform in 1836, becoming widely recognized in the abolition movement for his good sense and dedication, although his income remained modest. Her brother Charles Follen McKim, an architect, became a partner in the firm of McKim, Mead & White.

Lucy spent her youth among the Philadelphia abolitionists who associated with Lucretia Mott. Little is known of her early education and music lessons, but by April 1857 she was attending Eagleswood School in Perth Amboy, New Jersey. The school was headed by her father's old friend and associate Theodore Dwight Weld, his wife, Angelina Grimké Weld, and her sister, Sarah Grimké, as part of a Fourierist colony called Raritan Bay Union. The following fall, at the age of fifteen, Lucy began teaching piano at home, later returning to Eagleswood to study and to teach and remaining through 1860–1861. She studied violin there with Frederick Mollenhauer, a fine violinist and a friend of Mendelssohn and Schumann, who had trained in Germany before coming to the United States. Her piano teachers in Philadelphia were Benjamin Carr Cross, a local musician, and Carl Wolfsohn, who became widely respected as an interpreter of Beethoven. She was well trained for the time and the only practicing musician among the northerners collecting slave songs during the Civil War.

Lucy's father became general secretary of the Philadelphia Port Royal Relief Committee, formed to assist the freedmen in the area recently captured by the Union along the South Carolina and Georgia coast. In June 1862 he was sent to the Sea Islands off the coast for a firsthand view of conditions, with his daughter as his secretary. During her three-week stay, Lucy was profoundly moved by the songs of the freed blacks and attempted to transcribe them into musical notation.

Back in Philadelphia she made plans to publish a series of "Songs of the Freedmen of Port Royal," but succeeded in publishing only two, arranged for voice and piano, "Poor Rosy, Poor Gal" and "Roll, Jordan, Roll," registered for copyright on 27 December 1862. Among the first slave songs to be published with their music, they represented a gifted amateur's attempt to capture the sound of a music foreign to her experience. "Poor Rosy" was sent to *Dwight's Journal of Music* with a letter that appeared in the issue for 8 November 1862, headlined "Songs of the Port Royal 'Contrabands.'" She described the music with better understanding than many later critics: "It is difficult to express the entire character of these negro ballads by mere musical notes and signs. The odd turns made in the throat; and the curious rhythmic effect produced by single voices chiming in at different irregular intervals, seem almost as impossible to place on score, as the singing of birds, or the tones of an AEolian Harp. . . . The wild, sad strains tell . . . of crushed hopes, keen sorrow, and a dull daily misery. . . . The words breathe a touching faith." Together with an excerpt from her father's report on his trip titled "Negro Songs," these were notable as very early sympathetic discussions of the songs as music rather than focusing on religious or political aspects of slavery. She published no further songs, probably due to the lack of favorable public response.

Lucy McKim spent the balance of the war years teaching piano and studying. In 1864 she became engaged to Wendell Phillips Garrison (son of abolitionist William Lloyd Garrison), who in 1865 became literary editor of a newly established New York weekly, *The Nation*. They were married in Philadelphia in 1865 and in 1866 formed a joint household with her parents in Llewellyn Park, Orange, New Jersey. She had three children there.

Encouraged by her husband, Lucy began to help with editorial work and to review books for *The Nation*. In the spring of 1867 both Garrisons began to gather slave songs for the first comprehensive collection to be published, the outgrowth of her long enthusiasm. Co-editors with Lucy were William Francis Allen, a young historian and frequent contributor to *The Nation*, who wrote the preface, and his cousin Charles Pickard Ware, who contributed the single largest group of songs. Wendell Garrison actively solicited contributions, possibly acting as his wife's deputy during her pregnancy. The resulting publication, *Slave Songs of the United States* (1867; repr. 1929, 1951), remains the best contemporary source on slave music, an important contribution to American folk music.

The amateurs who notated the songs did the best they could at a time when there were few precedents. Social forces were changing the lives of the freedmen so rapidly that eyewitnesses feared many songs might disappear. The editing was well executed, the source of each song identified, both as to collector and place, and variants were noted. Lucy Garrison, at age twenty-five, served as the intellectual catalyst who helped bring together a diverse group of contributors: teachers, missionaries, army officers, and newspaper correspondents who had served in the South during the war.

After the births of her three children but before she was able to resume her intellectual interests she suffered a long illness and died of heart disease in West Orange, New Jersey, leaving behind a pioneer work in American folk music and an even greater promise unfulfilled.

• Letters to, from, and about Lucy Garrison are in the Garrison Family Papers, Sophia Smith Collection, Smith College. Pertinent material can be found in the Garrison papers, Houghton Library, Harvard University, and in the McKim papers, New York Public Library and Cornell University Library. Her music books are in the Music Division, New York Public Library. Letters from contributors to *Slave Songs of the United States* are bound into Wendell Garrison's copy, now at Cornell. Also useful are James Miller McKim, *The Freedmen of South Carolina* (1862), and Charles Moore, *The Life and Times of Charles Follen McKim* (1929). See also Dena J. Epstein, "Lucy McKim Garrison, American Musician," *Bulletin of the New York Public Library* 67 (Oct. 1963): 529–46; Ira V. Brown, "Miller McKim and Pennsylvania Abolitionism," *Pennsylvania History* 30 (Jan. 1963): 56–72; and Margaret Hope Bacon, "Lucy McKim Garrison: Pioneer in Folk Music," *Pennsylvania History*, 54 (Jan. 1989): 1–16.

DENA J. EPSTEIN

GARRISON, Mabel (24 Apr. 1886–20 Aug. 1963), opera singer, was born in Baltimore, Maryland, the only child of Warren Garrison and Helen Ringrose. By age thirteen her piano talent was so outstanding that she was accepted as a student at Western Maryland College and studied there with pianist Leon Sampaix. After graduation in 1903, her music instructors persuaded her to forsake the piano to study voice. Winning a scholarship in voice to the Peabody Conservatory of Music convinced her to become a professional singer. Her first engagements were in three Baltimore churches, where she was a choir soloist. At one of them she met her future husband, pianist George Siemonn, who was then professor of harmony and theory at the conservatory. They were married in 1908. Three years later Garrison received Peabody's first diploma for vocal proficiency.

Because Baltimore offered limited opportunities for vocal advancement, Garrison and her husband moved to New York City only to face countless disappointments until she sang for Claude Erlanger, then producer of the popular operetta *The Count of Luxembourg*. He hired her at $150 a week, but her first and only performance of the leading role was such a triumph that the star, Ann Swinburne, refused to continue if Garrison sang again. Nevertheless Erlanger kept her on the payroll for the next two seasons. This stipend enabled her to afford lessons with Oscar Saenger, who later introduced her to the directors of Boston's Aborn Opera Company, from which she received a contract. Following a successful debut as Philene in Thomas's *Mignon* in April 1912, she sang Gilda, Lucia, Marguerite, Gretel, and Olympia in her two years with the company. Oscar Hammerstein heard her on tour in New York City and offered to star her in his new opera company, but when none of his grandiose plans materialized, Garrison auditioned at the Metropolitan Opera instead and received a contract for $75 a week. She sang first at a Sunday night concert in February 1914 but did not make her official operatic debut as Frasquita in Bizet's *Carmen* until 27

November, though using the name of Martha Greiner she had actually sung the day before as a Flower Maiden in Wagner's *Parsifal*. Despite favorable notices her assignments were secondary roles except for Urbain, which she sang at a few hours' notice and for which she scored a sensation. She continued to sing minor roles in her second season with the Metropolitan, yet in the concert world her fame was escalating through solo and joint recitals and appearances with leading symphonic orchestras.

Garrison's career rose to greater heights during the summer of 1916. She found overwhelming success at the Ravinia Opera in Highland Park, Illinois, singing such roles as Lucia, Gilda, Violetta, and Lady Harriet, none of which had been entrusted to her at the Metropolitan. In August her first Victor Red Seal recordings were released and quickly achieved bestseller status. In the next eight years she recorded exclusively for Victor and became one of their most prestigious artists.

Garrison's third season at the Metropolitan was highlighted by another of those last-minute appearances, this time as Queen of Night, but it was not until after her second acclaimed season at Ravinia in 1918 that she gradually achieved stardom at the Metropolitan. In her three remaining seasons renditions of Gilda, Adina, Rosina, Lucia, and in particular the Queen of Shemakha in Rimsku-Korsakov's *The Golden Cockerel*, brought her the operatic fame she deserved. She left the Metropolitan after an unannounced farewell performance of Lucia on 22 January 1921, supposedly to concentrate on her concert career but actually because she was pregnant. In retrospect Garrison's Metropolitan Opera career was impressive for an American artist at that time: in eight seasons she had sung sixteen roles and given 109 performances.

Several months following her departure from the Metropolitan, Garrison suffered a miscarriage and her child was stillborn. Grief-stricken, she sought a change of scene in Europe where at Salzburg she met and subsequently studied with the legendary Lilli Lehmann, who restored Garrison's desire to sing. Largely through the great diva's influence, Garrison embarked on a successful operatic tour of Germany, Austria, and Spain, but it was not until 1924 that she resumed her career at its previous scale. In addition to extensive concert tours throughout the United States, she sang Olympia with the Washington Opera Company and the title role in *Alglala* at the premiere of De Leone's opera in both Akron and Cleveland. In 1925 she toured the Far East, singing a total of forty concerts. She also sang Rosina with the Chicago Civic Opera Company as well as the title roles in several Handel opera revivals at Smith College. For two years she had her own radio program, "The Maxwell Hour."

After Garrison retired from singing in 1931, she became professor of vocal music in 1933 at Smith College, where she headed the vocal department, a position she held with distinction until 1941. During this time she and her husband vacationed annually at their villa at Eze-sur-mer in the south of France, where through her association with painters Pablo Picasso and Fernand Léger she developed a keen interest in modern French art and began what would become one of the finest private art collections of that genre in the world.

Throughout World War II Garrison rallied to the cause by giving more than fifteen hundred hours of volunteer service to a New York City hospital. After her husband's death in 1952 she devoted her remaining years to their art collection. Before she died in New York City, she had bequeathed the collection of thirty oils and ten pieces of sculpture to the Baltimore Museum of Art in her husband's name. Mabel Garrison's artistry was threefold. Not only was she a singer of incomparable gifts, but she was also a noted voice teacher and a connoisseur of modern French art.

• For a detailed study of Garrison's life and career plus an extensive discography, see Edward Hagelin Pearson, *Record Collector*, Jan.–Mar. 1993. Frederick H. Martens, *The Art of the Prima Donna and Concert Singer* (c. 1923), devotes a chapter to Garrison's vocal techniques. Gordon M. Eby discusses her career in *From the Beauty of Embers* (1981), and Aida Favia-Artsay, *Hobbies*, Oct. 1954, includes a critical discussion of her Victor recordings.

EDWARD HAGELIN PEARSON

GARRISON, William Lloyd (10 Dec. 1805–24 May 1879), editor, abolitionist leader, and religious reformer, was born in Newburyport, Massachusetts, the son of Abijah Garrison, a seaman, and Frances "Fanny" Lloyd, a housekeeper. The poverty, instability, and religiosity of Garrison's childhood exerted a profound, lifelong influence on him, for his career was always shaped by his strong needs for public recognition, for self-vindication, and for expressing his spiritual zeal.

Garrison's father, a heavy drinker, abandoned the family in 1818, leaving Fanny alone to raise three young children while working as a maid. Family resources sometimes became so meager that his mother would dispatch young Garrison to beg table scraps from the kitchens of neighbors. The family moved several times as Fanny searched for apprenticeships for her sons and a respectable position for herself. The eldest son, James, became an alcoholic and left home at fifteen. William Lloyd, by contrast, imbibed deeply the Baptist zealotry of his mother. In 1818 he apprenticed to the owner of the *Newburyport Herald* and began a lifelong calling as an editorial polemicist and religious moralist.

By the mid-1820s, his apprenticeship completed, Garrison attempted to launch his career by editing a series of newspapers in Massachusetts and Vermont. In all of these ventures, Garrison's assertions of moral superiority and his virulent opposition to the "degeneracy" of electoral politics repelled many readers, causing his newspapers to fail. At the same time, his editorial opinions marked him as a censorious advocate of temperance and antislavery. In 1828, when the Quaker abolitionist Benjamin Lundy invited him to Baltimore to coedit *The Genius of Universal Emancipa-*

tion, Garrison had failed in every editorial endeavor to which he had put his hand.

A widely discussed libel suit, filed in 1830 against Garrison soon after he began his collaboration with Lundy in 1829, quickly reversed the young editor's fortunes. His editorial condemning of a leading Massachusetts merchant, Francis Todd, as a "murderer" for participating in the interstate slave trade landed Garrison first in court, then in the Baltimore city jail after failing to pay the fine that resulted from his conviction. For the next forty-nine days, from his prison cell, Garrison publicized his "martyrdom" and asserted his irrepressible dedication to the cause of "immediate emancipation" of America's slaves by issuing press releases and publishing a pamphlet. Though once again unemployed, Garrison had now become a cause célèbre to New England's fledgling abolitionist movement. Arthur and Lewis Tappan, wealthy New York merchants, paid Garrisons's fine and welcomed him as a comrade-in-arms.

The doctrine of immediate emancipation was not original with Garrison, having been developed by the English abolitionist Elizabeth Heyrick, but until Garrison no one had stated it powerfully enough to bring it to life as a religious imperative, capable of inspiring a comprehensive social crusade. Key to this doctrine was the recognition that enslavement was an abomination in God's sight demanding immediate repentance on the part of the enslaver, opposition to slavery by all right-thinking Christians, and immediate liberation of all those held captive.

After returning to Boston in 1830, Garrison made the immediate emancipation doctrine the centerpiece of the *Liberator*, his next editorial venture, which first appeared in January 1831. Promising to be "harsh as truth, and as uncompromising as justice" in pleading the cause of the slave, Garrison also declared in his famous opening editorial: "I will not retreat an inch and I will be heard." In the three decades that followed, as Garrison proved the accuracy of such predictions, he and the *Liberator* became famous on two continents for an unswerving dedication to a range of radical causes.

The appearance of the *Liberator* coincided with the publication of David Walker's *Appeal to the Colored Citizens of the World* and the Nat Turner slave insurrection in Southampton, Virginia. While Walker exhorted African Americans to use violence in securing their freedom, Turner and his cohorts accounted for perhaps thirty deaths in their unsuccessful attempt to begin a mass revolt. Garrison, a pacifist, deplored all appeals to violence, and his reputation as an agitator was greatly enhanced by both developments. Southern politicians and editors issued threats against his life and liberties, condemning him as an "insurrectionist." Meanwhile, the *Liberator*'s subscription list began to swell, thanks largely to the efforts of free northern blacks. Whites, too, especially religiously inspired men and women in Boston, Philadelphia, and New York City, began offering Garrison their support. A radical abolitionist movement began to take shape.

Early in 1832, when Garrison helped found the Boston-based New England Anti-Slavery Society, "immediatism" and complete social equality for all persons regardless of race were made fundamental to the society's creeds. His widely read pamphlet *Thoughts on African Colonization* (1832) mounted a comprehensive attack on the influential American Colonization Society, which called for gradual emancipation and the repatriation of former slaves to Africa. Garrison indicted this approach as a racist delusion, designed by slaveholders to protect their system from serious criticism, a view that added greatly to his unpopularity. Later that year, when Garrison assisted the Quaker abolitionist Prudence Crandall in her attempt to open an integrated academy for young women, critics began adding charges of "racial amalgamation" to their lengthening indictment. In the process, however, Garrison had developed a commitment to racial equality that marks him as one of the truly visionary democrats of his day.

The year 1833, Garrison's year of triumph, also witnessed the opening of a broad abolitionist assault on the South's "peculiar institution." Garrison toured Great Britain, where he received the support of England's most influential abolitionists, such as Thomas Clarkson, William Wilberforce, and Thomas Buxton. Triumphs continued after his return, most notably in December 1833, when leading northern abolitionists convened in Philadelphia to inaugurate the American Anti-Slavery Society. This organization was designed as a national body that would stimulate the creation of abolitionist societies across the North and win support for immediate emancipation. Its founding members, a profile of the larger crusade against slavery, included New York City religious evangelicals such as the Tappan brothers, Joshua Leavitt, and William Jay, Unitarian radicals such as Samuel Sewall and Samuel May, Quakers like John Greenleaf Whittier and Lucretia Mott, and free African Americans such as Robert Purvis and James McCrummell.

Garrison's contribution to the launching of this biracial, gender-inclusive organization was his authorship of the society's *Declaration of Sentiments*, which stressed nonviolence. While condemning the slaveholder as a "manstealer," the *Declaration* announced unshakable opposition to colonization, to all laws upholding slavery, and to all customs and attitudes that enforced racial prejudice. It also pledged abolitionists to "secure" for people of color "all rights and privileges that belong to all Americans for the paths of preferment should be open as widely to them as to persons of white complexion."

To accomplish these formidable tasks, the *Declaration* also urged abolitionists to found newspapers and antislavery societies, launch petition campaigns, send speakers into the countryside, and challenge the moral sensibilities of slaveholders by appeals through the various religious denominations. Through this broad-based program of "moral suasion," as the abolitionists called it, the aim was peacefully to transform public opinion in favor of freeing the slaves and obliterating racial prejudice. While to most white Americans Garrison's *Declaration* reeked of fanaticism by proposing to transform three million slaves into equal citizens, to later generations it has come to represent a landmark of democratic aspiration.

As abolitionists vigorously implemented these programs, popular opposition mounted in all parts of the nation. In the slave states, abolitionists were threatened, harassed, and expelled. In cities across the North mobs interrupted abolitionists' meetings, attacked their homes, and assaulted communities of free blacks. Garrison himself was harried through the streets of Boston by an angry mob in October 1835. In 1837, after a mob in Alton, Illinois, murdered abolitionist Elijah Lovejoy, discouragement and confusion swept through the movement. In the U.S. Congress, abolitionists' petitions were met with rules that prevented their reception. Leaders of all religious denominations, instead of denouncing slavery, denounced the abolitionists. Southern postmasters encouraged mobs to seize and burn abolitionist literature sent through the mails.

To Garrison, these disheartening events forcefully documented the utterly corrupted state of all American values and institutions and the need to adopt new doctrines to effect their overthrow. His thinking, stimulated by conversations with religious visionaries such as John Humphrey Noyes and Angelina Grimké, soon led him to conclude that all secular governments and organized religions were irredeemably tainted and must be opposed by true Christians. He condemned Scripture itself as "superstition," contrary to the "pure religion of Jesus's perfect example," and rejected claims of male supremacy as yet another variety of "godless enslavement." By late 1837 Garrison had embraced a militant blend of religious perfectionism, political anarchism, anticlericalism, and woman's rights as necessary extensions of his abolitionist creed. He divided his editorial attention between abolitionist issues, questions of women's rights, and news of his attempts to found a nonresistance society. As he did so, he encountered new forms of opposition from within the American Anti-Slavery Society as well as from the public.

Recoiling from Garrison's "heretical" new doctrines were some of abolitionism's best-recognized leaders, men who hated slavery just as much as did Garrison but who also believed deeply in orthodox Protestantism, the legitimacy of state power, and the justness of masculine prerogatives. To Lewis and Arthur Tappan, Joshua Leavitt, James Gillespie Birney, Henry Brewster Stanton, and others, it seemed as if Garrison had taken leave of his senses by attempting to associate immediatism with such widely unpopular and ill-considered creeds. For although the abolitionists had provoked great hostility, those very controversies had, in turn, generated publicity, sympathy, and converts. Judged by this standard, the movement was clearly beginning to gain momentum. It was insanity, his critics argued, to jeopardize this progress by associating Garrison's new extremism with the crusade against slavery.

As his opponents organized to expel him from the movement, Garrison himself developed powerful supporters. Female abolitionists, always an essential constituency of the movement, lined up solidly behind his insistence on gender equality in the governance of the American Anti-Slavery Society. Lucretia Mott, Angelina and Sarah Grimké, Abby Kelley, Elizabeth Cady Stanton, and Maria Weston Chapman, all defenders of Garrison, soon became preeminent figures in the emergence of America's first woman's rights movement. Most African-American abolitionists, led by James A. Barbados, Robert Purvis, and James A. Forten, also sided with Garrison, as did a group of Boston's "radical aristocrats," persons of great inherited wealth such as Samuel J. May, Edmund Quincy, Wendell and Ann Phillips, and the Weston sisters—Caroline, Ann, and Deborah. These individuals, as well as a heterogeneous collection of religious perfectionists (Henry C. Wright, Charles C. Burleigh, and Stephen S. Foster, for example), all saw in Garrison's new thinking a visionary call for a "moral revolution" and defended him strongly against his growing legion of enemies.

From 1837 onward abolitionists divided ever more deeply into "Garrisonian" and "anti-Garrisonian" factions. Meetings of the various antislavery societies grew even more rancorous once some of Garrison's opponents began insisting that all abolitionists were duty bound to nominate and support antislavery candidates for political office, a doctrine that struck at the heart of Garrison's feminism (since women were excluded from the franchise) and his opposition to "coercive government." When the American Anti-Slavery Society met in 1840, formal schism was a foregone conclusion. Both factions had packed the meeting, but when Abby Kelley was elected to a position on the executive committee, it was clear that Garrison controlled the most votes. Lewis Tappan and his evangelical supporters seceded to form the American and Foreign Antislavery Society, and still other anti-Garrisonians decided to found an abolitionist third party, the Liberty party, which put forward slates of candidates for office during the 1840s. Garrison retained firm control over a smaller but ideologically purified American Anti-Slavery Society; Garrison was satisfied, as he informed his wife, the former Helen Benson, whom he had married in 1834, that "we have made clean work of everything." In May 1840 Garrison attended the World Anti-Slavery Conference in England. But his new doctrines had cost him significant support. The American delegation, headed by Wendell and Ann Phillips, failed to amend the meeting's by-laws to include women as participants. Many influential British reformers sided with Garrison's American opponents on this issue.

On his return to Boston in late 1840, Garrison discovered that many abolitionists had supported Liberty party candidate James G. Birney or Whig party candidates who promised to legislate against the interests of slavery. Few heeded his argument that voting made abolitionists accessories to an "enslaving" political system. As the 1840s opened, it was clear, whatever Garrison's own estimate, that he had transformed himself from an inspirational spokesman for a powerful, united movement into the prophetic leader of a small and extreme sect.

As Garrison's abolitionist role became more restricted, popular hostility in the North to the influence of slavery in the nation's political life deepened and spread. Such feelings were spurred by the prospect of slavery's westward expansion as a result of the annexation of Texas, by ongoing congressional debates over the reception of antislavery petitions, and by several spectacular fugitive slave cases. Antislavery issues were becoming increasingly entangled with politics. Garrison responded in an equally political fashion when declaring in 1842 that the federal Union must be annulled. The U.S. Constitution, he now insisted, was "a covenant with death—an agreement with hell" that had been designed by the Founding Fathers to secure the perpetuity of slavery. The masthead of the *Liberator* now displayed the motto "No Union with Slaveholders!," and its columns were filled with editorials calling for the free states peacefully to secede. Soon legally trained abolitionists such as Wendell Phillips provided constitutional arguments to support this surprising demand. But for Garrison the idea of northern secession was preeminently a moral imperative, not a legalistic formulation, a prophetic cry, like "immediate emancipation," that would return God's will (and Garrison's) to preeminence in the crusade against slavery.

Throughout the 1840s and 1850s, as the political crisis over slavery's westward expansion deepened, Garrison's espousals of northern disunion, nonresistance, woman's rights, and anticlericalism satisfied his own prophetic purity but left him and his supporters largely removed from the political events that were leading to civil war. At the same time, the term "Garrisonianism" also came to embody the most dangerous tendencies in Yankee political culture, not only for slaveholders but for those who valued the Union above all else. On 4 July 1854, when Garrison burned a copy of the U.S. Constitution, his flamboyant gesture only confirmed a generalized fear of New England extremism that had become commonplace in antebellum political culture. Only after John Brown's raid on Harpers Ferry in 1859 did Garrison begin to retreat from his nonresistant positions, and only after Abraham Lincoln's election in 1860 did he begin to affirm that the Union deserved preserving in the face of southern moves toward secession.

Although Garrison's public ideology changed little in the two decades before the Civil War, his involvement in interracial controversy revealed the strengths and limitations of his personal egalitarianism. Whenever it became obvious that the legal system or the state was acting prejudicially toward the rights and opportunities of African Americans, Garrison could be counted on as one of the strongest protesters. He made strenuous efforts to assist fugitive slaves, and he peacefully opposed laws that required their return to former masters. He was also an ardent foe of segregation, sitting defiantly in "nigger cars" when traveling by train, agitating for repeal of the Massachusetts antimiscegenation laws during the 1830s, organizing boycotts of segregated rail and steamship lines in the 1840s, and working diligently for integration in Boston's public schools by supporting boycotts by black leaders. To local black activists Garrison was deemed a valuable ally and a genuine friend, always willing to devote the *Liberator* to their causes and to speak emphatically on their behalf.

Whenever black colleagues tried to move out of his orbit of leadership, however, Garrison's responses revealed an unattractive paternalism. Never, for example, did he promote an African American to a position of responsibility on the *Liberator*'s staff even though William Nell, a longtime black employee, was well suited for several vacancies and anxious for advancement. And when America's most famous black abolitionist, Frederick Douglass, proposed in 1846 to begin a newspaper of his own, Garrison joined other white abolitionists in Boston in condemning Douglass's independent course in condescendingly racist terms. This rupture began a slow but steady alienation of several leading black activists from the Garrisonian wing of abolitionism throughout the 1840s and 1850s. But even before this trend began, few blacks ever held significant positions in the American or Massachusetts Anti-Slavery societies, another fact that suggests the deeper divisions of class, color, and sensibility in Garrison's crusade. Never could Garrison outgrow the conviction that he, himself, had been appointed guardian of the better interests of America's black population.

After the South had seceded in 1861 and hostilities had commenced, Garrison's paternalism displayed itself increasingly. He was unflinching in demanding complete and rapid emancipation, the recruitment of black soldiers with pay equal to whites, and the necessity of a constitutional amendment outlawing slavery forever. Yet when it came to the question of extending political equality to emancipated slaves, Garrison strongly demurred.

Beginning in 1862, when some of his closest prewar associates, led by Wendell Phillips, harshly criticized Abraham Lincoln for his cautious approach to the problems of emancipation and race equality, Garrison vigorously defended the president. After the promulgation of the Emancipation Proclamation in 1863, Phillips and his supporters began pressing not only for black enfranchisement but also for the military occupation of the defeated Confederacy, the disenfranchisement of leading rebels, and the redistribution of confiscated lands to the freed people. True emancipation, they argued, could only be secured through the legislation of political equality by Congress, accompanied by a massive reshaping of the southern social order to empower the former slaves.

To counter these proposals, Garrison insisted strongly that voting was not a right but rather a privilege that the freedmen must prove worthy to earn by first proving their moral fitness. To secure the vote they must first demonstrate habits of piety, hard work, and personal morality. Within the American Anti-Slavery Society irreparable divisions grew between the supporters of Garrison and Phillips, and by war's end, in 1865, following the ratification of the Thirteenth Amendment, the two factions had gone their separate ways. Garrison, contending that the work of the crusade had ended in glorious triumph, closed the *Liberator* and moved at its annual meeting that the American Anti-Slavery Society disband. When the Phillips faction voted down Garrison's resolutions, Garrison resigned, leaving the presidency to Phillips, and declared his retirement from the crusade. Although he wrote occasional articles throughout the later 1860s and 1870s on such topics as temperance, Chinese labor, spiritualism, and woman's rights, after 1866 his career was effectively at an end. Henceforward he devoted his attention to his family and to the careers of his four sons as well as to the compounding infirmities of his wife. He died in New York and was buried in Massachusetts.

Historians divide deeply when assessing Garrison's influence. Was the nation's failure to abolish slavery peacefully and to embrace racial equality somehow the result of Garrison's extremism, the moral abstraction of his thinking, or the naïveté of his approaches to politics and economics? Or was that failure the nation's and not Garrison's, a result of the inability of the dominant political culture to respond creatively to Garrison's deeper insights about the fundamental immorality of white supremacy and other coercive beliefs? Whatever their view of this question, most historians generally agree that Garrison embodied perhaps better than anyone else the full and complex spirit of America's antebellum reform movements.

• Garrison's papers are for the most part located in the Boston Public Library; the Smith College Library; and the American Antiquarian Society, Worcester, Mass. They have been published in edited form by Louis Ruchames and Walter Merrill, eds., *The Letters of William Lloyd Garrison, 1805–1879* (1970–1979). Large amounts of his correspondence, as well as extensive portions of his journalistic writings, are reprinted in Wendell Phillips Garrison and Francis Jackson Garrison, *The Story of William Lloyd Garrison as Told by His Children, 1805–1879* (1885–1889). The best modern assessments are John L. Thomas, *The Liberator, William Lloyd Garrison: A Biography* (1963); Walter Merrill, *Against Wind and Tide: A Biography of William Lloyd Garrison* (1965); and James Brewer Stewart, *William Lloyd Garrison and the Challenge of Emancipation* (1992).

JAMES BREWER STEWART

GARROWAY, Dave (13 July 1913–21 July 1982), television broadcaster, was born David Cunningham Garroway, Jr., in Schenectady, New York, the son of David Garroway, a mechanical engineer, and Bertha Tanner. Garroway's father worked for General Electric, and the family moved often before settling in St. Louis, Missouri, in 1927. Garroway developed a keen interest in astronomy and built several telescopes before graduating from St. Louis University High School in 1931. He continued his education at Washington University, also in St. Louis, and graduated with a degree in English in 1935. After a brief stay at the Harvard Business School in 1936, Garroway, with the help of a friend, published *You Don't Say, or Do You?*, a pamphlet containing more than 800 English words that are often mispronounced. While selling this publication in New York City two years later, he was hired as a page for the National Broadcasting Company (NBC), earning $16 a week. He steadily advanced within NBC and studied at the network's announcers school (and persisted even though in his first audition at NBC he finished next to last).

After completing the NBC announcers training course in 1939, Garroway joined station KDKA in Pittsburgh and then, the following year, Chicago station WMAQ, both as a special events announcer. During World War II Garroway served in the U.S. Navy. While seeing duty on a mine sweeper and teaching at a yeoman's school for radio technicians he advanced from ensign to navy lieutenant. After the war he returned to WMAQ, where he did his first program as a disc jockey. Called the "11:60 Club," the midnight show, featuring jazz music and casual conversation, was the format in which Garroway honed his distinctively breezy style of broadcasting. By 1947 Garroway was hosting three radio programs at WMAQ, through which he demonstrated his wide range of interests, wry sense of humor, and relaxed delivery and greatly increased his popularity.

In April 1949 Garroway launched "Garroway at Large," a television variety show broadcast from Chicago for NBC affiliates in the East and Midwest. The show, which featured singers, an orchestra, and comics, was the perfect outlet for Garroway's particular hosting talents. The program was praised for its creative use of camera effects, its preference for visual humor, and the absence of a studio audience, as well as for its embodiment of the new medium rather than trying to retain the characteristics of radio or the stage. Garroway transformed his understated radio style to television and in November 1949 was signed to a five-year contract with NBC, thereby becoming established as a premier national broadcaster.

In that same year Sylvester "Pat" Weaver, who was developing programming for NBC television, was planning a morning show. As he told potential sponsors, early morning hours had yet to be tapped by television, and Weaver's idea was to create a program that would feature news as well as entertainment to keep the morning audience abreast of what was going on in the world. Weaver had thought of using Russ Hughes, a popular, fast-talking broadcaster, as host of the show but changed his mind after seeing "Garroway at Large." The host of the show would be broadcasting a vast amount of information on the two-hour program, and Weaver thought Garroway's easy-going style was better suited to the format. As he reasoned, "A calm relaxed guy in the middle of that maniac setting would be better than another maniac."

The "Today" show was first broadcast with Garroway as host on 14 January 1952. Despite the widespread publicity surrounding the show, it was not financially successful in its first year. To increase interest in the program, NBC, especially in the early years, used Garroway as a kind of public relations man, and he helped to sell the show off the air as much as on, his natural appeal becoming a primary factor in the show's increasing success. In his history of the "Today" show, Robert Metz described Garroway's style as "informality in a formal age, intelligent, casual and, at all times, sincere—even with the commercials. He was a reservoir of factual information, dignified in presenting his knowledge and was somehow handsome, peering owlishly through his gigantic horn-rimmed glasses."

Within the confines of NBC television's news division, the "Today" show was looked upon as a frivolous financial drain. Although it was gaining popularity, the program was running a deficit well into its second year. The producers decided to attract younger viewers by putting a baby chimpanzee (named J. Fred Muggs) on the air with Garroway every morning. Garroway was happy to perform, and the gimmick increased the show's national audience, thereby bringing it out of the red. It was Garroway's manner, however, that helped maintain viewership at such an early hour. His relaxed confidence and calm attitude soothed the viewer in preparation for the business of each day. Garroway's many interests, including bird watching, race car driving, photography, astronomy, and gem cutting, provided him with plenty of material to discuss on the air in his casual and amusing style. His signature sign off—he would extend his arm with his open palm facing the camera and say "peace"—made Garroway a fixture in American homes.

Through the 1950s Garroway and "Today" succeeded beyond NBC's expectations, but in May 1961, with an increasing deterioration behind the scenes, and after the suicide of Garroway's second wife, the former Pamela Wilde de Coninck (with whom Garroway had one son, David Garroway, Jr.), Garroway was fired as host of "Today." The firing stemmed from Garroway's erratic behavior due in large part to the overwhelming pressures he was facing in his private life. In the mid-1960s he produced a documentary, "Exploring the Universe," for public television and also appeared on ABC's "Nightlife" as a guest host. His last work on network television was as emcee on "The Newcomers," a short-lived variety series for CBS in 1971.

Garroway lived his final years in near seclusion in Swarthmore, a Philadelphia suburb. He died as the result of a self-inflicted gunshot wound to the head. He had been recuperating from a very painful and difficult open-heart surgery, and the suicide was thought to have been the result of his recent illness. He was survived by his first wife, the former Sarah Lippincott, their children, Michael and Paris, and his son David, Jr. Viewers and friends in television were shocked and saddened by his sudden death. Longtime journalist and colleague Barbara Walters said of Garroway, "I have never seen anyone in this business who could communicate the way he could. He could look at the camera and make you feel he was talking only with you."

• Robert Metz, *The Today Show* (1977), is a useful history of the program that includes an impressive list of Garroway's accomplishments. Also see the article on Garroway in *Colliers Magazine*, 17 Mar. 1951. An obituary is in the *New York Times*, 22 July 1982.

JOHN P. SHIELDS

GARRY, Spokan (1811–14 Jan. 1892), teacher and tribal leader, was born in a village near where Latah Creek flows into the Spokane River in what is now the state of Washington, the son of Chief Illim-Spokanee, head of the Middle Spokans. His mother's name is unknown. The three branches of the Spokans—Lower, Middle, and Upper—numbered about 1,000, all of whom looked up to Illim-Spokanee. Garry's boyhood name is forgotten. At age fourteen he was chosen as one of a group to be educated at the Hudson's Bay Company mission school on the Red River near what is now Winnipeg, Manitoba, Canada. Nicholas Garry was deputy governor of the company. The Spokan chief's son was given his name. The group, mostly sons of chiefs, were subject to the same Spartan discipline that prevailed in English public schools. They were instructed in the reading and writing of English and the religion of the Church of England. Also included was training in agriculture, for the missionaries believed that only by developing a settled agricultural life could the Indians compete with white people. The boys were above average in intelligence, and once the language barrier was overcome, the missionaries had little trouble.

Having made satisfactory progress in scriptural knowledge and his behavior being judged acceptable, Garry was baptized 24 June 1827. The young man who returned home shortly thereafter was quite different from the boy who had left. He had adopted the hairstyle and clothing of whites and had all but forgotten his mother tongue. Soon after returning he started a school to teach what he had learned. His religious teaching was readily accepted and spread rapidly. Garry instituted the practice of morning and evening prayer services and the saying of grace before meals. Other tribes soon heard of this teaching. Chief Lawyer of the Nez Percé was so impressed by what he learned of Christian observances that he sent a delegation of his people to St. Louis in 1831 to ask for missionaries who could instruct his people further in the new religion. Missionaries responded to this call, but they brought with them their denominational differences, with which Garry was not acquainted. This caused him to lose influence with his people as time went on. Garry was called chief by the Upper and Middle Spokans, but in fact the influence of a chief did not go beyond his power of persuasion. Any who opposed his wishes did not feel themselves bound by his decisions.

Other white people followed the missionaries in ever-increasing numbers. Some of the tribes urged war to end the threat. Garry was a peace-loving man, and while his influence was still strong, he kept the Spokans from joining such plans. Also a realist, he knew it would be impossible to oppose the might of the new arrivals and adopted a policy of cautious friendship. The creation of Washington Territory brought Isaac Stevens as first territorial governor in 1853 with additional responsibility for making treaties with the Indians (which would eventually take the greater part of their lands). At first Garry was successful in keeping his tribe from being so treated. Under his leadership at the Walla Walla Council of 1855 the Spokans, Coeur d'Alenes, and Colvilles prevented Stevens from seizing their best lands for white settlement.

As long as the Spokans stayed peaceful, they were prosperous. Unfortunately Garry could not keep his younger braves under control. In spite of all he could do to prevent it, they joined the Coeur d'Alenes and Palouses in the stunning defeat of Lieutenant Colonel E. J. Steptoe's force, which was seeking to punish the murderers of two white miners. This defeat was avenged by the expedition of Colonel George Wright. Because he refused to take part in the fighting, Garry's influence rapidly declined. Still, he was able to keep his tribe from joining the nonreservation Nez Percés in their war of 1877.

Thereafter, under the Donation Act of 1850, whites were able to take some of the best lands without regard for Indian rights. This, together with the increase of disease, reduced the Spokans to destitution. By executive order of 18 January 1881 the Spokan reservation was created. It was a small, hopelessly inadequate area between the Spokane and Columbia rivers along the forty-eighth parallel that attracted only a few Spokans who did not already live nearby. At a meeting of a commission appointed to settle any disputes arising from the creation of the reservation and to attract more of the tribe to it, Garry had his last hurrah. He held the meeting spellbound as he told of the treatment his people had suffered. All he had ever wanted to do was live at peace with all peoples. Now he was being rewarded by being sent to a reservation. He said he would die first. Looking at the commissioners with withering scorn, he left the meeting. A meeting of Spokans and U.S. government officials in March 1887 reached an agreement by which the Spokans ceded all lands lying outside the reservation. Garry became an isolated figure, refusing to move onto the reservation but unable to defend his claim on his own land.

While away with members of his tribe on a fishing expedition Garry got word that white settlers had taken possession of his property. Garry claimed squatter's rights in light of his many years there and his attempts to become a citizen. Soon Garry and his family were reduced to poverty. No action was taken on his claim. When he died just a short distance from where he had been born, his widow never received a cent and was moved to the reservation. With his two wives, Lucy and Nina, he had two daughters and perhaps two sons. Partly by his efforts northeastern Washington was settled by whites more peacefully than many other areas. He had lived to see the city of Spokane incorporated on tribal lands. Unfortunately both the city and the American branch of the church in which he had been baptized ignored him during his lifetime. Some sources list him as a Presbyterian, perhaps because his surviving relatives had become Presbyterians and held his funeral in the First Presbyterian Church of Spokane. After his death, however, he was honored with a small stained-glass window in Spokane's Episcopal Cathedral of St. John the Evangelist.

• The American Board of Commissioners for Foreign Missions letters and papers at the Oregon Historical Society in Portland and the Hudson's Bay Company archives in Winnipeg are the main archival sources for Garry. Thomas E. Jessett, *Chief Spokan Garry, 1811–1892, Christian Statesman and Friend of the White Man* (1960), is the only complete biography and lists the main primary and secondary sources. Garry's achievements are described in the standard local histories, including H. H. Bancroft, *History of Washington, Idaho and Montana* (1890); Elwood Evans, *History of the Pacific Northwest, Oregon and Washington* (1889); and Clinton A. Snowden, *History of Washington* (1909).

FRANK L. GREEN

GARST, Roswell (13 June 1898–5 Nov. 1977), agricultural leader, was the son of Edward Garst and Bertha Goodwin. He was born in Coon Rapids, Iowa, where his father in 1869 had set up a general store and prospered, both as a merchant and as a land speculator. In 1915 Garst began farming with his brother Jonathan on a 200-acre farm just south of Coon Rapids, which became his family homestead. In 1922 he married Elizabeth Henak, a schoolteacher; they had five children. Four years later, leaving the farm in the hands of a tenant, Garst moved his family to Des Moines, where he met Henry A. Wallace, learned about the fledgling hybrid seed corn business, and discovered his penchant for salesmanship. Wallace taught him how tariffs and surpluses affected agriculture and how the corn-hog ratio functioned, an understanding that he would build on in future years.

In 1930 Wallace granted Garst a franchise to sell hybrid seed corn for his Pioneer Hi-Bred Corn Company in northwest Iowa. Garst moved back to his farm in Coon Rapids, began to raise seed corn, and formed a partnership with Charles Thomas, another Coon Rapids farmer. By 1938, thanks to Garst's salesmanship, the Garst and Thomas Hybrid Seed Corn Company had emerged as the dominant firm in the western Corn Belt. As he demonstrated to farmers the benefits of hybrid seeds, their high yields and strong stalks, Garst developed a style that would remain with him throughout his life. He never stopped learning about hybrid corn and agriculture, and he enthusiastically passed along his understanding in his letters, conversations, and speeches to farmer and officials, both at home and abroad.

During the New Deal, Garst worked tirelessly to help sell the federal government's agricultural program to Corn Belt farmers, chairing the Iowa Corn-Hog Committee and then serving on the National Corn-Hog Committee. While his efforts commanded national attention, Garst remained a private citizen in Coon Rapids and began managing farm lands for wealthy Iowans and Chicago residents. In the 1940s Garst was among the first farmers to discern that adding nitrogen in balance with phosphate and potash to the soil could enhance hybrid corn production. This technique, in combination with mechanization, helped meet national needs during World War II. By the end of the 1940s he made another breakthrough, calling for the feeding of protein-enriched cellulose to cattle. Adding cellulose to fodder, combined with hybridization, increased mechanization, and fertilization, became the basis for success in midwestern agriculture in the years following the war. Herbicides, pesticides, and irrigation were subsidiary factors. Garst's message of corn technology attracted increasing attention. His interest in cellulose, for example, brought him into contact with farmers, experiment stations, and universities in the midwest, and his use of corncobs, protein, and vitamin supplements as a diet for cattle attracted visitors to his farm and led to articles about his methods in farm publications.

Beginning in the 1950s Garst expanded his interest in international affairs, and during the Kennedy administration he championed the Food for Peace program, calling for its extension beyond the Iron Curtain. When a delegation of farm leaders from the Soviet Union visited the United States in 1955, Garst arranged for an unofficial visit to his Coon Rapids farm. One of the visitors, Deputy Minister of Agriculture Vladimir Matskevitch, impressed by what he saw, invited Garst to visit the Soviet Union. Thus began in 1955 a series of visits during which Garst lectured and traveled in the Soviet Union, Rumania, and Hungary. In turn, officials and specialists from Eastern European nations visited Coon Rapids to observe Garst's operations. Pioneer seed and parent hybrid seed corn plants left Iowa for Eastern Europe along with farm machinery. Garst's two sons, David and Stephen, oversaw the planting and harvesting of the 1956 crop in Rumania. In all, Garst made seven trips to Eastern Europe and entertained scores of Soviet and Eastern European agriculturalists at his Coon Rapids farm, including Soviet premier (chairman of the Council of Ministers) Nikita Khrushchev, who visited during his 1959 trip to the United States.

During the 1960s Garst expanded his international outlook to include Central and South America, which he toured for the U.S. Agency for International Development in the spring of 1964. He outlined a demonstration farm program for El Salvador that was put into operation by the U.S. Agency for International Development in 1965 and called for similar programs throughout Latin America. He continued his efforts to promote agricultural development in Europe and Latin America in the 1970s, though on a reduced scale. He retired from Garst and Thomas but did not abate his voluminous correspondence and travels throughout the Corn Belt. He also received increasing recognition, and one article described him as "The Salesman Who Changed Agriculture." In October 1963 Garst was diagnosed as having cancer of the throat; his larynx had to be removed, but by using a voice box placed against his throat he was able to resume his active life. Later, in the summer of 1977, his health failed noticeably. He died in Carroll, Iowa.

• Garst's papers are on deposit in the William Robert Parks and Ellen Sorge Parks Library at Iowa State University. An edition of some of his papers can be found in Richard Lowitt and Harold Lee, eds., *Letters from an American Farmer: The Eastern European and Russian Correspondence of Roswell Garst* 1987). Harold Lee, *Roswell Garst: A Biography* (1984), is a careful study by Garst's son-in-law based on extensive use of his papers. An obituary is in the *Des Moines Register*, 6 Nov. 1977.

RICHARD LOWITT

GARTRELL, Lucius Jeremiah (7 Jan. 1821–7 Apr. 1891), soldier and U.S. and Confederate congressman, was born in Wilkes County, Georgia, the son of Joseph Gartrell, Jr., a planter and merchant, and Eliza Boswell. After attending the state university and Randolph-Macon College in Ashland, Virginia, Gartrell read law in the Washington, Georgia, office of another future Confederate commander, Robert Toombs. In 1841 he married Louisiana O. Gideon, with whom he had six children.

Admitted to the bar in 1842, Gartrell became solicitor general of the state's northern circuit the following year. He was elected to the legislature in 1847 and was reelected two years later. Originally a member of the proslavery wing of the Whig party, Gartrell quickly defected to the Democratic fold. In the early 1850s he vehemently opposed the state coalition of Whigs and moderate Democrats that promoted compromise and rejected secession. In 1855, following the death of his first wife, Gartrell wed Antoinette Burke. They had five children.

In 1856 Gartrell was an elector on the James Buchanan ticket. A year later he won election to the lower house of Congress, where he advocated secession as the best means of preserving slavery and states' rights. In January 1861, toward the close of his second term in the House, he joined with other members of the Georgia congressional delegation in urging state officials to reject eleventh-hour compromises—some proposed by southern politicians—as a means of keeping the Union intact. In the present crisis, he said, "Georgia must rely upon herself." Three months later, when the fall of Fort Sumter ushered in open warfare, Gartrell recruited a regiment from the Atlanta area that he attempted to offer directly to the Confederate government. Denied independent status, the outfit eventually became the Seventh Georgia Infantry, and he was its colonel. Soon after its formation, the Seventh joined forces gathering in the Shenandoah Valley under General Joseph E. Johnston.

Despite his lack of military experience, Gartrell performed ably at First Manassas, the initial full-scale battle in the eastern theater. Late in the afternoon of 21 July, his regiment teamed with the Eighth Georgia under the overall command of Colonel Francis Bartow to guard the left flank of "Stonewall" Jackson's brigade. The Georgians helped stem a tide of demoralized comrades, enabling the Confederates to regain the advantage at a critical point in the fight. The battle brought both triumph and tragedy to Gartrell. His leadership won praise, but his son Henry was killed on the field.

Although military success gratified Gartrell, three months after First Manassas he ran for and was elected to the Confederate House of Representatives, a seat he assumed the following February. At the expiration of his two-year term, he applied for a brigadier generalship in the Confederate army, promising President Jefferson Davis "an honest effort for the faithful discharge of all my duties." To qualify for the rank he desired, Gartrell offered to raise four regiments of Georgia reserves for service in or near their state. He made good on his pledge. By late March 1864 he and his newly formed command reported to Major General Howell Cobb at Macon, and from there they were sent to man the defenses of Augusta. Not until August, however, did Gartrell's promised appointment come through.

Gartrell's brigade saw little service beyond trench digging and sentry duty until Major General William T. Sherman's Union armies rolled across Georgia in the fall of 1864, heading for Savannah. Early in December Gartrell and 1,800 effectives joined other forces in opposing one of Sherman's detachments near Coosawhatchie, South Carolina, just across the Georgia line. Although described by their district commander as "very imperfectly organized," the reserves gave a strong account of themselves on the afternoon of the sixth. Holding their ground along the north bank of the Tullifinny River, they delayed the enemy for more than two hours until forced to retreat across the stream.

When other forces counterattacked that evening, Gartrell was criticized for making a feeble effort at support. Three days later, however, his men held their ground near Pocotaligo, forcing their opponents to table plans to break the Charleston & Savannah Railroad. During the fighting on the ninth, Gartrell was wounded in the side by a shell fragment but remained on the field until the enemy withdrew.

After recuperating, Gartrell served quietly at Augusta until war's end. Back in Atlanta by mid-1865, he resumed his legal practice, forging a reputation as one of the ablest criminal lawyers in the state. His most celebrated case was his successful defense in 1876 of Republican governor Rufus B. Bullock, who had been accused of embezzling public funds during Reconstruction. In 1877 Gartrell was a leading member of the Georgia constitutional convention. Five years later he ran unsuccessfully for the governorship, losing to

former Confederate vice president Alexander H. Stephens. Three years before his death Gartrell was married for a third time, to Maud Condon. They had no children. Gartrell died in Atlanta.

Gartrell was an adroit attorney and a formidable politician at both the state and national levels. One biographer described him in his prime as "large, powerful, robust, full of animal spirits, and a ready debater." Another wrote of Gartrell's "marked eloquence" and "personal magnetism," which served him so well as attorney, legislator, and congressman. In the military realm, however, Gartrell lacked the education and experience though not the courage or energy required of a Civil War field commander. He may have sensed these deficiencies, for he chose to spend half the war in the political arena.

When Gartrell received the wreathed stars of a general, many observers expressed doubts about his ability as a field leader. Generals Samuel Jones and John H. Winder faulted his leadership, and the latter agitated for Gartrell's relief from command. Gartrell's civilian superiors also had qualms about his fitness to lead even second-line troops including boys below and men above enlistment age. Repeatedly Gartrell had to implore government officials to live up to the agreement under which, having raised a brigade, he was to be appointed a general officer.

• The only known body of Gartrell's personal correspondence is part of the Lawyers' Papers Collection at the Atlanta Historical Society and relates to his prewar and postwar legal career. A biographical sketch is among the Robert E. Lee Records at the Georgia Department of Archives and History, Atlanta. Other biographical sources include Clement A. Evans, ed., *Confederate Military History*, vol. 6 (11 vols., 1899); William J. Northen, ed., *Men of Mark in Georgia*, vol. 3 (6 vols., 1907–1912); and Kenneth Coleman and Charles S. Gurr, eds., *Dictionary of Georgia Biography*, vol. 1 (2 vols., 1983). Gartrell's prewar political career is traced in Richard H. Shyrock, *Georgia and the Union in 1850* (1926). *The War of the Rebellion: A Compilation of the Official Records of the Union and Confederate Armies* (128 vols., 1880–1901) contains scattered references to his service at First Manassas and in the Savannah campaign. An informative obituary is in the *Atlanta Constitution*, 8 Apr. 1891.

EDWARD G. LONGACRE

GARVAN, Francis Patrick (13 June 1875–7 Nov. 1937), attorney and collector, was born in East Hartford, Connecticut, the son of Patrick Garvan, paper merchant and tobacco farmer, and Mary Carroll. He attended public school in Hartford, then went on to Yale (A.B., 1897), to Catholic University for a year, and to New York University Law School (LL.B., 1899).

In 1901 Garvan was appointed assistant to the district attorney of New York County. He presented the opening statement for the prosecution at the first trial of Pittsburgh millionaire Harry K. Thaw for the murder of the famed architect Stanford White. Garvan had an aptitude for trial law and subsequently spent eight years as head of the Homicide Bureau of the district attorney's office; he was also in charge of prosecuting numerous commercial and insurance fraud cases.

When he entered private practice in 1910, Garvan was associated first with the firm of Garvan and Armstrong and later with Osborne, Lamb and Garvan.

During World War I Garvan was chief of the U.S. Bureau of Investigation in New York until he was called to Washington to serve as alien property custodian. In this position he discovered that nearly all the chemical patents in the United States were held by foreigners. Wartime conditions allowed him to seize dye patents that had enabled German interests to control the American dye industry. He redistributed the patents to American citizens and after the war successfully defended that action in a legal struggle that reached the Supreme Court. In 1919 he founded the Chemical Foundation, Inc., to promote the development of chemicals on a national scale. He served as its president until his death in 1937. His service to the American chemical industry was recognized in 1929 when he was awarded the American Chemical Society's Priestley medal, the only layman ever to receive that honor.

In 1910 Garvan married Mabel Brady, the daughter of Anthony N. Brady of Albany, an archetypal self-made man who made an enormous fortune in successive enterprises that included streetcar lines and the oil industry. The Garvans, who had six children, began collecting antique furnishings on their honeymoon in England, preferring the craftsmanship and beauty of these old pieces for furnishing their home. Their first pieces were English, but before long they discovered that some were fakes and sold them, resolving that from then on they would collect only American antiques. They also began to take the precaution of having their American purchases authenticated by experts.

Once started, Garvan found that it was hard to stop collecting. The collection soon overflowed the family apartment into a downtown warehouse. Because the collection included a number of superb pieces of furniture and silver, Garvan was asked to lend items to important exhibitions of early American decorative and fine arts during the 1920s. It was these requests, he said, "that made Mrs. Garvan and myself realize that our collection did not belong to us." This realization led to a visionary plan: Yale University would be made trustee of the collection, seeing to its upkeep and circulating it throughout the country so that Americans of all stations and regions could enjoy it and learn from it.

Garvan's plan represented the same community-minded, egalitarian attitude that was apparent in his work in the district attorney's office and the Chemical Foundation. Unlike many collectors of his generation, he was not an elitist, hoarding colonial heirlooms in an effort to distance himself from recent immigrants. Rather, his goals were progressive and democratic. Through his gift Garvan intended to force Yale to share his collection "for the benefit of the country at large and not merely for the limited number who happen to go to New Haven to learn something." Any educational institution or community that put in a request would be eligible for a loan exhibition from the Garvan collection.

On 9 June 1930, his twentieth wedding anniversary, Garvan presented his gift to Yale in honor of his wife. Originally totaling about 5,000 objects, the collection grew to about 10,000 by the time of Garvan's death. Included were furniture, silver, pewter and other metals, glass, ceramics, and prints, all selected as excellent representatives of their type. There were masterpieces, of course, particularly in silver, but Garvan's collecting focus, like his aim for the ultimate use of the collection, was democratic. As one curator put it, his interest was "primarily the gathering of material of expressive quality regardless of rarity, sophistication or elaboration of design and execution." He wanted his collection to be diverse and representative of many styles and types, like the country itself. It was an attitude that was far ahead of its time in terms of scope and inclusiveness.

Garvan's farsighted plan never achieved full implementation; depression-related financial reverses curtailed his collecting, and he died from pneumonia in New York City. In his last years he focused on American silver, intending to amass the finest collection of early American silver in existence. With characteristic energy and determination, he met the challenge: the Garvan collection of American silver at Yale has remained unsurpassed.

• Garman's correspondence is in the Archives of American Art, Smithsonian Institution, Washington, D.C. Elizabeth Stillinger, *The Antiquers* (1980), includes a chapter on Garvan. See also Yale University Art Gallery, *Francis P. Garvan, Collector* (1980); Charles F. Montgomery, "Francis P. Garvan: He Would Educate the Nation," *Arts in Virginia*, Spring 1979; Meyric R. Rogers, "Garvan Furniture at Yale," *The Connoisseur Yearbook* (1960); Charles Messer Stow, "This Country Needs Collectors, Is Opinion of Francis P. Garvan," *New York Sun*, 26 July 1930; "Plans a Wide View for American Art/Francis P. Garvan Tells Purposes of Gift to Yale and Founding of Institute," *New York Times*, 22 June 1930. An obituary is in the *New York Times*, 8 Nov. 1937.

ELIZABETH STILLINGER

GARVEY, Amy Euphemia Jacques (31 Dec. 1896–25 July 1973), journalist, Pan-Africanist, and the second wife of black nationalist Marcus Garvey, was born in Kingston, Jamaica, the daughter of George Samuel Jacques, a property owner, and Charlotte (maiden name unknown). Amy Jacques's family was rooted in the Jamaican middle class; thus, she was formally educated at Wolmer's Girls' School, an elite institution in Jamaica. As a young woman she suffered from ailing health due to recurring bouts with malaria. In need of a cooler climate, she emigrated to the United States in 1917 and settled in New York City where she had relatives. After hearing contradictory reports about the Universal Negro Improvement Association (UNIA), recently founded by Garvey, she attended a meeting in Harlem. She was intrigued by the organization and in 1918 became Garvey's private secretary and office manager at UNIA headquarters in New York. She traveled with Garvey throughout the United States on behalf of UNIA, and they developed a relationship based on their mutual commitment to the organization. Marital problems between Garvey and his first wife, Amy Ashwood, had been evident within the first two months of their marriage. Garvey was granted a divorce from Ashwood in June of 1922, and he married Amy Jacques the next month in Baltimore, Maryland.

The couple was constantly tailed by agents of the Federal Bureau of Investigation (FBI) who feared Garvey's revolutionary racial vision. Finally, in 1923 the federal government incarcerated Marcus Garvey for alleged mail fraud. During his rotating periods of imprisonment between 1923 and 1927, Amy Garvey developed as an organizer and activist. She assumed unofficial leadership of UNIA, though she was never elected to an office. Amy Garvey served as the association's chief spokesperson and raised funds for Marcus Garvey's legal defense. In addition, she served as editor of the woman's page, "Our Women and What They Think," in the *Negro World*, UNIA's weekly newspaper published in Harlem. Her editorials and essays demonstrated her political commitment to nationalism through self-determination but also her belief that women should be activists on behalf of their communities.

Marcus Garvey's sentence was eventually commuted to deportation, and he was discharged from Tombs Atlanta Penitentiary in 1927. Amy Garvey followed her husband back to Jamaica. Like many female activists of the period, she delayed motherhood and did not give birth to their two children, both boys, until the early 1930s. Parenting was a joy but also time consuming, and she could no longer devote all of her energies to her husband and UNIA. Marcus Garvey, on the other hand, continued to be a tireless worker for UNIA, often neglecting his family. In fact, he relocated to London in 1935 so that he could be a more effective leader. Ironically, although Marcus Garvey spoke out against female-headed households, Amy Garvey functioned as a single parent in Jamaica for over two years. Finally, in 1937 Marcus sent for his wife and their children. However, the two years apart had generated severe marital strain. In addition, their older son contracted rheumatic fever in his leg, which required a warm climate. Amy Garvey thus returned to Jamaica with her children in 1938. After Marcus Garvey died in London in 1940, she continued to live in Jamaica and serve UNIA, then headquartered in Cleveland, Ohio.

Amy Garvey's edited books, *Philosophy and Opinions of Marcus Garvey*, published in two volumes (1923, 1925), *Garvey and Garveyism* (1963), and *Black Power in America* (1968), helped to stimulate a rebirth of interest in Garveyism. Because of her meticulous records on Marcus Garvey and UNIA, numerous books and articles have been published in the United States. The board of governors at the Institute of Jamaica acknowledged Amy Jacques Garvey's contribution to the dissemination of Garveyism by awarding her the Musgrave Medal in 1971. She died in Kingston, Jamaica.

• Amy Jacques Garvey's personal papers, including her essays and editorials printed in the *Negro World*, are located at the Special Collection Library at Fisk University, Nashville, Tenn. Robert Hill's edited papers on *Marcus Garvey and the Universal Negro Improvement Association* (7 vols., 1983–1990) is an important source. An obituary is in the *Jamaica Daily News*, 7 Aug. 1973.

ULA Y. TAYLOR

GARVEY, Marcus (17 Aug. 1887–10 June 1940), black nationalist, was born Marcus Moziah Garvey in St. Ann's Bay, Jamaica, the son of Marcus Moziah Garvey, a stonemason, and Sarah Jane Richards. He attended the local elementary school and read widely on his own. Difficult family finances forced him into employment at age fourteen as a printer's apprentice. Three years later he moved to Kingston, found work as a printer, and became involved in local union activities. In 1907 he took part in an unsuccessful printers' strike. These early experiences honed his journalistic skills and raised his consciousness about the bleak conditions of the black working class in his native land.

After brief stints working in Costa Rica on a banana plantation and in Panama as the editor of several short-lived radical newspapers, Garvey moved to London, England, in 1912 and continued to work as a printer. The next two years there would profoundly mold his thoughts on black advancement and racial solidarity. He probably studied at the University of London's Birkbeck College; absorbed Booker T. Washington's philosophy of black self-advancement in his autobiographical *Up from Slavery*; and, perhaps most important, met Duse Mohammed Ali, a Sudanese-Egyptian who was working for African self-rule and Egyptian independence. Duse Mohammed published a small magazine, *Africa Times and Orient Review*. He allowed Garvey to write for the magazine and introduced him to other Africans. Garvey left London convinced that blacks worldwide would have to fend for themselves if they were ever to break the shackles of white racism and free the African continent from European colonial rule.

Back home in Jamaica in 1914, Garvey founded the Universal Negro Improvement and Conservation Association and African Communities League, usually known as the Universal Negro Improvement Association (UNIA). The UNIA would be the vehicle for Garvey's efforts at racial advancement for the rest of his life. His initial undertaking, a trade school in Jamaica, did not succeed, and in 1916 he took his organization and cause to the burgeoning "black mecca" of Harlem in New York City.

Over the next few years Garvey's movement experienced extraordinary growth for a number of reasons. With its slogan "One Aim, One God, One Destiny," the UNIA appealed to black American soldiers who had served abroad in World War I and were unhappy returning to a nation still steeped in racism. Harlem was a fortuitous location for Garvey's headquarters, with its sizable working-class black population, large number of West Indian immigrants, and the cultural explosion of the Harlem Renaissance in the 1920s. A pan-African movement was already under way by the early twenties, emphasizing the liberation of the African continent and black racial pride worldwide, and Garvey successfully tapped into this sentiment. Garvey himself was a gifted writer (using his weekly newspaper the *Negro World* as his mouthpiece) and a spellbinding orator in dazzling paramilitary garb.

Garvey's first marriage in 1919, to his secretary Amy Ashwood, was an unhappy relationship that ended in divorce three years later. The couple was childless. In 1922 he married Amy Jacques, his new secretary. They had two sons. Amy Jacques Garvey became a leading worker in her husband's movement.

By the early 1920s the UNIA had probably 65,000 to 75,000 dues-paying members with chapters in some thirty American cities, as well as in the West Indies, Latin America, and Africa. On various occasions Garvey claimed anywhere from 2 to 6 million members. Accurate membership figures are impossible to obtain because of careless record keeping. But unquestionably millions of other blacks were followers in spirit. Auxiliary organizations included the Universal Black Cross Nurses, the Black Eagle Flying Corps, and the Universal African Legion. The *Negro World* had a circulation of some 50,000. In August 1920 the UNIA hosted a huge month-long international convention in New York City, with several thousand black delegates from all parts of the world, complete with uniforms, mass meetings, and parades. Garvey was named president of a fictional but symbolically powerful "Republic of Africa." This latter move reflected Garvey's interest in the regeneration of Africa. He had already been exploring with the government of Liberia a UNIA construction and development project there and the potential for a back-to-Africa colonization movement for American blacks. Unfortunately, this undertaking foundered as his domestic businesses came into increasing difficulty.

Garvey's business enterprises were his proudest achievements and ultimately the source of his undoing. Inspired by Booker T. Washington's support of black businesses, Garvey founded the Negro Factories Corporation to encourage black entrepreneurship in the United States and abroad. The corporation sponsored a number of small businesses in the United States, including a Harlem hotel and a publishing company.

The crown jewel of Garvey's enterprises was the Black Star Line, a steamship company founded in 1919 to carry passengers and trade among Africa, the Caribbean, and the United States. Garvey launched the line with his usual grandiose promises and a stock sale that raised more than $600,000 (at $5 a share) the first year. What followed in the next twenty-four months was a tragic series of mishaps and mismanagement. The Black Star Line consisted of three aging, overpriced vessels that were plagued by mechanical breakdowns, accidents, and incompetent crews. The business side of the operation suffered from sloppy record keeping, inflated claims made to investors, and dishonest and possibly criminal practices on the part of company officers. One of the ships sank; another was auctioned off; the third was abandoned in Cuba.

Some of Garvey's critics, including many blacks, had begun to question his ethics, his business practices, and the whole UNIA operation. Notable among his black opponents was W. E. B. Du Bois of the National Association for the Advancement of Colored People. Garvey's insistence on black self-segregation ran counter to the NAACP's goal of full integration into American society. When Garvey associated openly with leaders of the white racist Ku Klux Klan and declared that the Klan was a better friend of his race than the NAACP "for telling us what they are, and what they mean, thereby giving us a chance to stir for ourselves," thousands of blacks were outraged.

In 1922 Garvey and three other Black Star Line officials were indicted by the U.S. government for using the mails fraudulently to solicit stock for the defunct steamship line. Ever the showman, Garvey used his trial for a flamboyant defense of himself and the larger cause of black advancement, striking a chord with at least some of his remaining followers, who saw him as a victim of white persecution. Unimpressed, the jury convicted Garvey (though not his codefendants), and he was sentenced to five years imprisonment. After a failed appeal to the U.S. Supreme Court, Garvey began his term in February 1925. That he was able to continue running the UNIA from his Atlanta jail cell was a tribute to his influence over his followers.

In 1927 President Calvin Coolidge commuted Garvey's sentence, and he was deported to Jamaica. The remainder of his life was a struggle to rebuild his movement. He attempted to rekindle his cause by getting involved in Jamaican politics but to no avail. He presided over UNIA conventions in Kingston in 1929 and Toronto in the late 1930s, but the grim realities of the Great Depression left most blacks with little interest and fewer resources to support movements such as his. He died of a stroke in London, where he had moved in 1935.

Obituaries of Garvey emphasized his business failures and portrayed him as an irrelevant relic from the past. His real achievement, however, was in creating the first genuine black mass movement in the United States and in extending that influence to millions of blacks abroad. He emphasized racial pride and purity, the proud history of his race, self-respect, and self-reliance. For his millions of poor and working-class American followers, Garvey's message of black pride and solidarity in the early 1920s came at a critical nadir of race relations. Such themes drew on the philosophy of Booker T. Washington as well as Du Bois, his sworn enemy. He was a harbinger of later black nationalist leaders such as Malcolm X, Stokely Carmichael, and Louis Farrakhan. Garvey thus served as an important link between early twentieth-century black leaders and modern spokesmen. Moreover, he inspired modern African nationalist leaders, such as Kwame Nkrumah of Ghana and Jomo Kenyatta of Kenya, in their struggles against European colonialism.

• Garvey's papers and materials from the UNIA can be found in the multivolume *Marcus Garvey and Universal Negro Improvement Association Papers*, ed. Robert A. Hill (1983–). Amy Jacques Garvey, ed., *Philosophy and Opinions of Marcus Garvey* (1968), is a collection of his early writings up to 1925. E. David Cronon, *Black Moses: The Story of Marcus Garvey and the Universal Negro Improvement Association* (1955), is the fullest account of Garvey's life, with an extensive bibliography. Two additional major biographies are Tony Martin, *The Emancipation of a Race* (1973), and Judith Stein, *The World of Marcus Garvey: Race and Class in Modern Society* (1986). Daniel S. Davis, *Marcus Garvey* (1972), although unannotated and for younger readers, is useful and perceptive. Amy Jacques Garvey, *Garvey and Garveyism* (1963), is an insider's view of his movement. Theodore Vincent, *Black Power and the Garvey Movement* (1971), places Garveyism in the larger context of American black history. Mary Frances Berry and John Blassingame, *Long Memory: The Black Experience in America* (1982), has a short but thoughtful essay on Garvey that discusses his influence in Africa and the fear he inspired in British and French colonial officials there. An obituary is in the *New York Times*, 12 June 1940.

WILLIAM F. MUGLESTON

GARVIN, Charles Herbert (27 Oct. 1890–17 July 1968), physician, was born in Jacksonville, Florida, the son of Charles Edward Garvin, a mounted letter carrier, and Theresa De Courcey. He was educated first at Atlanta University and later graduated from Howard University in 1911 and from its medical school in 1915. At Howard, Garvin was recognized as an outstanding student and leader. He served as president of Alpha Phi Alpha fraternity while in the undergraduate chapter and later served as its national president. During his medical school training, Garvin was awarded top honors in obstetrics and physical examinations. In 1916 he moved to Cleveland, Ohio, to begin medical practice. He chose Cleveland at the urging of George Crile, a well-known surgeon with whom he became acquainted while working as a dining-car waiter during the summers when he was at Howard. The city at that time had a rapidly growing black population drawn by the labor demands of the war industry.

When the United States entered World War I, Garvin enlisted and was among the first black physicians to be commissioned in the armed forces. He served in France as captain and commanding officer of the all-black 368th Ambulance Company, Ninety-second Division. Later, in a response to negative reports and what he described as "insidious propaganda" from General Pershing, he described the superior performance, in the face of adversity, of African-American soldiers and officers who served in the war. Garvin's letter was published nationally in black newspapers in 1931. In 1943 he expanded on the role of black medical officers in an article entitled "The Negro in the Special Services of the U.S. Army World War I and II" (*Journal of Negro Education* 12, no. 3 [Summer 1943]: 335–44).

After completing his service in 1920, Garvin married Rosalind West, a native of Charlottesville, Virginia, and graduate of the Howard University Normal School. He then resumed his practice in Cleveland, where he remained until his death. The couple had two sons.

In Cleveland, as in many cities, black physicians had limited access to hospital privileges, so Garvin's patients were treated primarily in the office and at home. However, he held a succession of courtesy appointments at Lakeside Hospital from 1920 until his retirement in 1968. During his years in practice, he was well known and respected both as an expert in urology and as a tireless advocate for increased opportunities for African-American physicians.

Garvin's interest in medicine extended beyond the practice to research and writing. He published at least thirty-six articles in medical journals, most of them in the *Journal of the National Medical Association* (an organization of African-American physicians), with emphasis on urological diseases and disorders. He also published articles in the *Woman's Voice*, a national women's magazine, and *Opportunity Magazine*, the official publication of the national Urban League. His popular articles dealt with another topic that absorbed much of his attention: the historic contributions of Africans and African Americans in medicine. He completed a manuscript on this subject titled "Africa's Contribution to Medicine: The Negroid Peoples Role in Its Evolution," which remains unpublished.

Garvin was also an active businessman and civic leader. He was a founder of the Dunbar Life Insurance Company (1943), and he helped to organize the Quincy Savings and Loan Company, where he served as a director and chairman of the board (1954). Both businesses were established to serve the new wave of black migrants who came north for work during and after World War II, and both businesses prospered during his lifetime. Garvin also was appointed as the first African-American trustee on Cleveland's public library board in 1939 and served as its president during 1940–1941. Other key civic positions included terms as trustee of the nationally recognized Karamu Settlement House, the Urban League, the National Association for the Advancement of Colored People, and Mt. Zion Congregational Church. He was a founding member of Tau Boule of Sigma Pi Phi Fraternity and an active member of the Fraternal Order of the Elks and the Order of Moose. In addition, he served on the board of trustees of Howard University, as a member of its executive committee and in other capacities, from 1932 until 1964. The university's organization of former interns and residents gave him its William A. Warfield Award in 1963 for his contributions to medicine and to the institution.

The Garvin family was thrust into the national spotlight as pioneers in integrated housing in 1926, when Garvin purchased a lot in an exclusive allotment near Western Reserve University. When neighbors learned that a black family was going to build, they vigorously opposed Garvin's plans. In spite of repeated threats of violence and two bombings after the house was built, the Garvins refused to move. These incidents, which were widely covered by the news media, illuminated some of the problems faced by successful African-American families and forecast the continuing racial polarization in housing in Cleveland and other large urban centers during the twentieth century.

Garvin's career as a practicing physician, his contributions to medical research and medical history, and his business and civic activities exemplify the multiple roles that were often required of and assumed by black middle-class leaders during the twentieth century. His experiences as an armed forces officer, a physician, and an African-American citizen also serve as models of resistance against the barriers of racism that plagued American society during an era when two world wars were fought for democracy.

• Garvin's papers, including articles, awards, and citations, are at the Western Reserve Historical Society in Cleveland, Ohio. News reports of the racial incidents involving Garvin in 1926 are included in the Russell Davis Papers at the WRHS. Also see Russell Davis, *Black Americans in Cleveland* (1972), and David Van Tassel and John Grabowski, *The Encyclopedia of Cleveland History* (1987). Obituaries are in the *Cleveland Press* and the *Plain Dealer*, both 18 July 1968, and the *Cleveland Call and Post*, 27 July 1968.

ADRIENNE LASH JONES

GARY, Elbert Henry (8 Oct. 1846–15 Aug. 1927), lawyer and steel industrialist, was born near Wheaton, Illinois, the son of Erastus Gary and Susan Valette, farmers. Raised in a strict Methodist home that stressed the value of education, Gary attended the local public schools and for a time Illinois Institute, later renamed Wheaton College. After a two-month army stint during the Civil War and a term teaching school, Gary turned to the study of law with his maternal uncle, Colonel Henry Valette, and his uncle's partner, Judge Hiram H. Cody, in Naperville, Illinois. He subsequently attended Union College of Law in Chicago, graduating first in the 1868 class. While clerking for the Illinois Superior Court, he married Julia E. Graves in 1869; they had two children. The couple lived in Wheaton from whence he commuted to Chicago during the subsequent thirty years of his legal career. (After his first wife's death in 1902, Gary married Emma Townsend in 1905. They had no children).

Gary set up his own law practice in 1871, going into partnership first with his uncle and subsequently with his brother and Judge Cody after the latter's retirement as a circuit judge. The firm of Gary, Cody & Gary focused its attention on corporate law, working primarily on behalf of railroad and industrial firms. Gary's legal knowledge and reputation for fair play brought him increased standing within the profession. He served as a DuPage County judge from 1882 to 1890, a period during which he earned the nickname "Judge," by which he was known for the remainder of his life. He served as president of the Chicago Bar As-

sociation from 1893 to 1894. Gary was also active in local politics, serving as president of Wheaton's town council (1872–1873) and as the town's first mayor, serving two terms beginning in 1892.

Gary's corporate law work increasingly led him into direct involvement with the iron and steel industry. He provided legal assistance to the several wire-producing companies that combined into Consolidated Steel and Wire Company in 1892 and then to a subsequent consolidation that formed the American Steel and Wire Company of Illinois in 1898. At this time Gary also served as general counsel to the Illinois Steel Company, the first large steel-industry consolidation, originally formed in 1889. This experience led Gary to the conclusion that vertical integration, especially backward to control raw-material sources, was increasingly important for competitive profitability within the steel industry. Gary later approached J. P. Morgan for financial assistance to create a $200 million holding company that in September 1898 became known as the Federal Steel Company. In addition to his legal role, Gary became president of the new company, giving up his lucrative thirty-year law practice. He became increasingly convinced that to remain competitive in the unstable cutthroat environment of the industry Federal Steel would have to further expand its holdings, which led to his third and largest consolidation.

Faced with what Andrew Carnegie described as "a question of the survival of the fittest," Gary joined with Morgan, Charles Schwab, the president of Carnegie Steel, and George W. Perkins, a Morgan partner, to bring together eight major steel producers and fabricators, including Carnegie Steel, to form the United States Steel Corporation in February 1901. Created to stabilize the industry by its control of about 60 percent of the nation's steel production, U.S. Steel was the country's first billion-dollar corporation. Gary was named chair of the executive committee, while Schwab was appointed president with direct responsibility for operating the company.

Gary faced several problems in organizing and running U.S. Steel. The huge enterprise remained a holding company with local management responsible for running individual plants. This arrangement led to tensions between the Gary-led board, which consisted primarily of bankers and lawyers, and the more traditional "competitive" steelmakers dominated by Carnegie's men and Schwab in particular. Supported by Morgan, Gary consolidated his control of U.S. Steel during the next two years, becoming chair of the newly created board of directors in 1903. His rise led Schwab to resign the presidency and buy a controlling interest in Bethlehem Steel. Gary also sought to close inefficient plants and, starting in 1906, to construct the world's largest, fully-integrated steel plant on the shore of Lake Michigan in an area duly named Gary, Indiana. By 1911, the company had expended $78 million on the plant itself and the accompanying town.

The steel industry traditionally had been characterized by destabilizing competition in the form of extensive price cutting. Gary sought to bring long-term economic stability to U.S. Steel and to the industry as a whole by institutionalizing publicly announced fixed prices. At the same time he sought to maintain wage stability. One mechanism he developed to reinforce this strategy was the so-called "Gary dinners," the first of which was held on 20 November 1907. More than fifty executives representing some 90 percent of the industry gathered to hear Gary exhort them to establish a spirit of trust, cooperation, and stability. Gary carefully avoided talking about price "fixing," but his preachments did lead to common "understandings" of appropriate pricing levels within given product lines for certain periods of time. In 1908 Gary founded the American Iron and Steel Institute (AISI) "on the belief that healthy competition is wise and better than destructive competition." He was elected the AISI's president, and the de facto spokesman for the industry, at the organization's first formal meeting in 1910; he remained president until his death.

Because of U.S. Steel's great size, Gary was continually concerned about possible federal antitrust suits. He constantly stressed that the corporation sought only efficient integration, not monopolistic control of the whole industry. In addition to avoiding "savage" competition and even accepting modest declines in market share, he opened the corporation's financial dealings to public scrutiny and its books to government investigation. Despite Gary's best efforts and President Theodore Roosevelt's earlier support, U.S. Steel came under federal indictment in 1911 for its 1907 acquisition of Tennessee Coal and Iron Company (TC&I). U.S. Steel had purchased TC&I during the October panic at Morgan's request as part of an attempt to help stabilize the faltering stock market. Unlike Roosevelt, President William Howard Taft believed that there was more to the acquisition than simply a desire to allay public concern about the stock market. Furious that the government should accuse the corporation of being in restraint of trade, Gary vigorously defended U.S. Steel. He was exonerated at the district-court level in June 1915 and again in March 1920 by the U.S. Supreme Court.

Gary was very much a paternalist in labor relations. He was a strong advocate of the "open shop," making every effort to break strikes and unions whenever they occurred. But he supported welfare capitalism, voluntary paternalistic initiatives by the corporation to improve working conditions and employee morale, which he believed would contribute to bolstering U.S. Steel's image as a "good trust." In conjunction with George Perkins, who had become chair of the finance committee, Gary established an employee bonus and stock-option plan. Of more direct significance to rank-and-file workers were a safety program, an accident insurance plan, and a pension plan, all coordinated under the leadership of Vice President William B. Dickson. In addition, U.S. Steel's welfare reforms included improvements in sanitary facilities and company housing. Gary, however, insisted on preserving the steel industry's twelve-hour, seven-day workweek. He

approved the elimination of Sunday work only in 1910 and did not embrace the eight-hour day until 1923. Gary and U.S. Steel's refusal to bargain with the steelworkers' unions after World War I led to the 1919 steel strike and the union's defeat.

Gary continued to run U.S. Steel and to influence the steel industry as a whole until his death at his Fifth Avenue home in New York City. While Gary has been seen variously as the steel industry's savior and as a paternal monopolist, few deny that he was the industry's dominant figure for three decades. His vision of a large-scale, vertically integrated firm with stable pricing and cooperative relations with other companies was realized at U.S. Steel and came to characterize the steel industry.

• An eight-volume compilation, *Addresses and Statements by E. H. Gary*, put together by the Business History Society, is located in the Baker Library, Harvard School of Business Administration. A sympathetic biography is Ida Tarbell, *The Life of Elbert H. Gary: A Story of Steel* (1925); see also Stephen H. Cutcliffe's biographical essay and Bruce Seely's "United States Steel Corporation" in *Iron and Steel in the Twentieth Century*, ed. Seely (1994), in the Encyclopedia of American Business History and Biography Series. Also helpful for understanding the formation and subsequent history of the U.S. Steel Corporation is William T. Hogan, *Economic History of the Iron and Steel Industry in the United States* (1971). For Gary's role in the area of labor relations see David Brody, *Labor in Crisis: The Steel Strike in 1919* (1965) and *Steelworkers in America: The Nonunion Era* (1960), and Gerald G. Eggert, *Steelmasters and Labor Reform* (1981). Also valuable is Thomas K. McGraw and Forest Reinhardt, "Losing to Win: U.S. Steel's Pricing, Investment Decisions, and Market Share, 1901–1938," *Journal of Economic History* 49 (1989): 593–619. Obituaries and tributes are in the *New York Times*, 16 Aug. 1927, and *Iron Age*, 18 Aug. 1927.

STEPHEN H. CUTCLIFFE

GARY, Martin Witherspoon (25 Mar. 1831–9 Apr. 1881), lawyer, politician, and Confederate general, was born in Cokesbury, South Carolina, the son of Thomas Reeder Gary, a physician, and Mary Anne Porter. Thomas Gary was a wealthy, upcountry slave owner. In addition to practicing medicine, he farmed and represented Abbeville District for two terms in the state legislature. Martin Gary was a pupil at the Cokesbury Methodist Conference school. He attended South Carolina College but was expelled along with others in his junior class for rebelling against an unpopular teacher. He graduated from Harvard with honors in June 1854. In November of that year he went to Edgefield, South Carolina, to study law with Chancellor James P. Carroll and was admitted to the bar in May 1855. Until his death, Gary maintained a highly successful criminal law practice in Edgefield. Reared a Methodist, he joined the Trinity Episcopal Church in Edgefield and became a vestryman.

In 1860 Gary was a freshman state representative, a "fire-eater," and a secessionist leader in the state. With the election of Abraham Lincoln and the debate over secession in the South Carolina legislature, Gary denounced a proposed resolution to delay action until all the southern governors could be consulted and a cooperative plan agreed upon. "Since it fails to protect our property and persons," Gary proclaimed, "this Union must be deliberately, solemnly, fearlessly, and speedily dissolved." He urged South Carolina not to wait for other states to join it in secession. "Do the patriots of the South object to our taking the lead? By the unanimous consent and voice of the South she [South Carolina] has been assigned the post of honor and danger." Similar to many others in the South, Gary's military experience began in the state militia. In 1859 he was elected colonel of the Second Cavalry Regiment of the state militia in Edgefield, and he became an aide-de-camp for Edgefield's militia general R. G. M. Dunovant at Sullivan's Island after the attack on Fort Sumter.

With the call to arms for the Civil War, Gary raised troops for a company to captain. The Watson Guards, named for their Edgefield sponsor, Tilman Watson, became Company B of the infantry battalion of the famed Hampton Legion formed by wealthy South Carolinian Wade Hampton III. The Hampton Legion was sent to defend Virginia, and the Watson Guards played a major role in the first battle at Manassas. Indeed, Gary and the Watson Guards emerged from the thick of the fighting as heroes. Gary was a brilliant soldier, although he could be somewhat of a loose cannon who sometimes ignored standard army procedures. According to a regimental history, at Manassas he ordered a charge that was successful in its advance but put his men beyond their own lines, laying them open to deadly enemy fire and briefly bringing them under fire from their own troops. He commanded part of the legion temporarily after First Manassas, when Hampton was wounded and Lieutenant Colonel Benjamin Jenkins Johnson was killed.

When the Conscription Act of 1862 offered troops the opportunity to elect officers, it left ambiguous the question of whether field officers should be elected. Politicking for military office, Gary led some dissatisfied captains in the Hampton Legion in petitioning for field officer elections. Specifically, Gary electioneered for the coveted position of lieutenant colonel of the infantry, the position held by his friend, sponsor, and fellow Edgefieldian, James B. Griffin. Gary, outgoing, personable, and given to intemperate outbursts of profanity that delighted many enlisted men, won the election. Thirty-six years later Adjutant Theodore Barker still smoldered over Gary's behavior. Replying to a letter from Edward L. Wells, who was soliciting information for a history of the Hampton Legion, Barker said flatly that the Hampton Legion infantry "was stolen by Gary."

The infantry battalion, entitled to a lieutenant colonel's command under existing War Department policies, continued under Gary at that rank until 12 December, when he was promoted to colonel, retroactive from 26 August. By that time the battalion had been increased to ten companies—full regimental strength. Throughout the war Gary continued in command of the Hampton Legion infantry, which was mounted

and included in the cavalry brigade assigned to him upon his promotion to brigadier general to rank from 19 May 1864. Gary fought at Richmond, Second Manassas, Boonsboro, Sharpsburg (Antietam), Fredericksburg, Suffolk, Chickamauga, Bean's Station, Campbell's Station, Knoxville, James River, and Riddle's Shop. When the Watson Guards went into battle, Gary led the way and fought alongside his troops, often winning against great odds. His soldiering earned the compliment of General Robert E. Lee. Gary was also ruthless. Under his orders the Watson Guards took no African-American Union soldiers as prisoners but summarily executed them.

Gary commanded the last Confederate troops to leave Richmond. At Appomattox, after Lee formally relinquished his army on 9 April 1865, Gary's brigade was still shooting. When a Union courier, under a flag of truce, was sent through the lines with news of capitulation, Gary retorted defiantly that South Carolinians never surrendered. He broke through the Federal lines and caught up with President Jefferson Davis at Greensboro, North Carolina, escorting him south to Cokesbury, where one of the last meetings of the Confederate cabinet convened at the home of Gary's mother. Gary never surrendered or requested a pardon, and he was acclaimed as the "Bald Eagle of the Confederacy."

Gary remained in South Carolina after the war. He never married. His sister, the widow of General N. G. "Shank" Evans, moved with her son to Edgefield after the Civil War and lived with Gary, serving as hostess at his postbellum mansion, "Oakley Park." In 1866 General Daniel Sickles arrested Gary and other leading white Edgefield citizens for murder and complicity in murdering African Americans; they got off. Gary was the main force behind the violent overthrow of South Carolina's Reconstruction. He and other former Confederate officers opposed Reconstruction with all the gusto that they had devoted to opposing the Yankees. Although Gary's only official position was Democratic chairman for Edgefield County, he was the organizing genius and the author of the state campaign blueprint, the Edgefield Plan, also known as the Straightout Plan. Hampton had left South Carolina and gone to Mississippi to supervise his most productive cotton lands, but he came back at Gary's request to run for governor in 1876. During the campaign, Confederate officers like Gary and Matthew Calbraith Butler directed the "troops," white civilians (many of whom had served under these officers) who symbolically donned red shirts and formed themselves into armed companies called rifle clubs. Ostensibly organized for home protection, the clubs were highly visible among the electorate. Gary's extremist views led him ultimately to break with Butler and Hampton, and he was twice defeated in races for U.S. senator by his former allies. In 1876 the new Democratic legislature promptly elected Butler to the U.S. Senate, an honor that Gary had wished for himself. Gary counted on the next Senate seat, but that went to Hampton. When Gary hoped to replace Hampton as governor in 1880, another former Confederate general was chosen. After the war Gary served four years in the state senate.

Although he came from a wealthy, upcountry slave-owning family and his father had represented Abbeville in the state legislature, Gary felt aggrieved that he was not fully accepted as one of the Edgefield or South Carolina elite. He was a man on the make, tough and ambitious. He represented a modern type, harbingers of demagogues like his own Edgefield disciple, Benjamin Ryan Tillman, of the postwar era. They appealed directly to the populace, presenting themselves as men of the people. Gary's extreme racist language and contempt for African Americans was successfully adopted by Tillman, who rode agrarian discontent and racism into the governor's office and later the U.S. Senate.

Gary thrived as a successful attorney and acquired large landholdings to become a successful cotton farmer after the Civil War. His Edgefield home became a "Red Shirt Shrine" of Civil War and Reconstruction memorabilia. He died in Edgefield.

• The Gary papers are at the South Caroliniana Library, University of South Carolina, Columbia. Because of his controversial nature, particularly his role in Reconstruction, the Gary family restricted use of materials from those papers. William Arthur Shepard wrote an unpublished manuscript, "The Bald Eagle of Edgefield" (1933, Edgefield County Historical Society). Gary is treated in the context of his place and times in Orville Vernon Burton, *In My Father's House Are Many Mansions: Family and Community in Edgefield, South Carolina* (1985), and Burton and Judith N. McArthur, *"A Gentleman and an Officer": A Military and Social History of James B. Griffin's Civil War* (1996). On Gary and the Hampton Legion see Ron Field, in collaboration with William B. Bynum and Howard Michael Madaus, *South Carolina Volunteers in the Civil War: The Hampton Legion, pt. 1, Regimental History* (1994). On Gary's refusal to surrender at Appomattox, see Frederick Cushman Newhall, *With General Sheridan in Lee's Last Campaign* (1866); Edward L. Boykin, *The Falling Flag, Retreat and Surrender at Appomattox* (1874); W. G. Hinson, "General Sheridan's Reference to M. C. [sic] Gary of South Carolina," *Confederate Veteran* 2 (Sept. 1894); J. H. Doyle, "With Gary's Brigade at Appomattox," *Confederate Veteran* 29 (Sept. 1921). Lewis P. Jones, "Two Roads Tried—and One Detour," *South Carolina Historical Magazine* 79 (July 1978): 206–18, looks at Gary's approach to race relations. Francis Butler Simkins and Robert H. Woody, *South Carolina during Reconstruction* (1932), has some accounts of the Hampton-Gary split. More information on Gary's specific role in Reconstruction is in the "tragedy of Reconstruction" school accounts, including John S. Reynolds, *Reconstruction in South Carolina* (1905), and David D. Wallace, *The History of South Carolina*, vol. 3 (1932). A sustained defense of Gary is William Arthur Sheppard's highly polemical *Red Shirts Remembered: Southern Brigadiers of the Reconstruction Period* (1940), which accuses Hampton of depriving Gary of his deserved political rewards. Complimentary speeches by Gary's political legatees George Tillman and Ben Tillman are in Ulysses R. Brooks, ed., *Stories of the Confederacy* (1912).

ORVILLE VERNON BURTON

GARZA, Catarino Erasmo (25 Nov. 1859–8 Mar. 1895), Texas newspaper editor and Latin American revolutionary leader, nicknamed "Cato," was born near Ma-tamoros, Tamaulipas, Mexico, the son of Don Encarnación and Doña Maria Jesús Rodriquez de la Garza. Catarino was educated at Galahuises, Nuevo Leon, and became a student at San Juan College. He served in the Mexican National Guard. Partly because of his disillusionment with Porfirio Díaz's seizure of the Mexican presidency, Garza emigrated to Brownsville, Texas, in the 1880s. There he edited *El Bien Publico* and sold sewing machines. He worked for the Commercial Livestock Company and was a delegate to the International Stockmen's Convention in St. Louis, Missouri, in 1886, where he headed the Mexican Department. During this period he became a 32° Mason.

Living near Eagle Pass, Texas, Garza edited the anti-Díaz newspaper, *El Libre Pensador* (1887), which opposed all aspects of the *porfiriato*, or dictatorship. In 1888 he was the victim of an assassination attempt similar to that organized by Díaz agents against Ignacio Martínez, editor of *El Mundo*, in Laredo in 1891. Garza insisted on settling the matter with a shoot-out. Local and state authorities confiscated his newspaper. He then moved to Corpus Christi and Palito Blanco, Texas, where he edited *El Comercio Mexicano*. Circulation of all of Garza's newspapers was limited by political considerations.

From 1889 to 1891 Garza was active on the Texas-Mexican border in the episode called the Garza War. The *garcistas* skirmished with both the *porfiristas* and the Texas Rangers, who attempted to enforce the neutrality laws. On 20 September 1891, at San Carlos, Mexico, the *garcistas* formally proclaimed war against the Díaz regime. They demanded a return to the rights of the constitution of 1857 and adherence to the promise of *No Reelección*, by which the president could not succeed himself.

Several expeditions entered Mexico after the San Carlos proclamation. On 7 November 1891 the *pronunciados* crossed opposite Rancho Agua Negra and were defeated at Derramadero de las Ovejas. In December they skirmished near Guerrero. On 22 December, however, Corporal Edstrom of the U.S. Army was killed, which intensified efforts by both Texas and federal authorities to suppress the raids. Garza barely escaped in an encounter with the Rangers in Starr County (now Brooks County) on 29 December 1891. The raiding continued with an attack on Mier in May 1892 and ended with an assault on San Ygnacio in December 1892. The last raid was led by General Francisco Benavides and resulted in the U.S. Supreme Court's decision in *Ornelas v. Ruiz*. The Court held that the *garcistas* were bandits and not entitled to political asylum. Garza himself probably did not participate in the San Ygnacio raid.

At about this time Garza slipped out of the United States via New Orleans to Havana, Cuba. An unlikely story, confirmed only by family tradition, reports that in Cuba he served as secretary of the navy, presumably with José Martí. In 1894 Garza is positively located at Puerto Limón, Costa Rica, where he published the anti-Díaz tract *La era de Tuxtepec en México o sea Rusia en América*. This pamphlet reviews the abuses of the

Díaz regime, such as the "ley fuga" under which political prisoners were shot "while attempting to escape." Garza exposes corruption as well as domination by Mexican clerical, economic, and military interests. He condemns assassination as an instrument of politics as well as Díaz's betrayal of his promises of reform. Much of the critique anticipates the *maderista* opposition to Díaz.

The circumstances of Garza's death are mysterious. Indeed, some *garcistas* said he did not die but returned to Texas. The Colón *Telegram* places his death in Colombia on 8 March 1895 after the storming of the jail in the plaza of Bocas del Toro. This action was part of the liberal rising that followed President Rafael Nuñez's death. The raiders hoped to establish a Pan-American union to include Colombia, Venezuela, Ecuador, and Mexico. Throughout his career Garza supported liberal revolutionary causes in Latin America and opposed the Díaz dictatorship in Mexico. On the Texas-Mexican border a number of *corridos*, or folk ballads, celebrate the *garcistas* and the Garza War.

• Garza's principal surviving publication is *La era de Tuxtepec en México o sea Rusia en América*, and the only located copy is at the Tulane University Library. Of his newspapers, edited in Texas, *El Bien Publico, El Libre Pensador, El Comercio Mexicano*, and *El Correo*, no copies can be located. During most of his career Garza kept a journal, which is now lost. Documentation of Mexican archival sources may be found in Gabriel Saldívar, *Documentos de la rebelión de Catarino E. Garza en la frontera de Tamaulipas y sur de Texas, 1891–1892* (1943). A varying perspective appears in the correspondence in *Foreign Relations of the United States, 1893* (Washington, D.C., 1894), pp. 425–47. For further bibliographic information and interviews with Garza's descendants, see Gilbert M. Cuthbertson, "Catarino Garza and the Garza War," *Texana* 13, no. 4 (1975): 335–48.

GILBERT M. CUTHBERTSON

GASS, Patrick (12 July 1771–2 Apr. 1870), soldier and member of the Lewis and Clark expedition, was born at Falls Springs, near Chambersburg, Pennsylvania, the son of Benjamin Gass, Jr., and Mary McLene (occupations unknown). At the time he joined the Meriwether Lewis and William Clark expedition (1804–1806), Gass was serving in Captain Russell Bissell's company of the First Infantry at Fort Kaskaskia, Illinois. He came to the expedition officially on 1 January 1804 but probably was in active service before that date. He had been in military service off and on since 1792, having seen duty as a volunteer in a Ranger company before joining the infantry in 1799. About this time he was described as being five feet seven inches tall, of dark complexion, with dark hair and gray eyes. After the death of Sergeant Charles Floyd in August 1804, Gass was promoted from private to sergeant by a vote of his fellow soldiers. The selection, affirmed by the captains, attests to his popularity and to his competence. His skill as a carpenter was of great value to the expedition, and he probably served as construction chief for the party's wintering forts in modern North Dakota and Oregon. In all, he was a valued member of the corps who carried out his duties faithfully and cheerfully.

Gass's journal, published in 1807 after considerable alteration by his editor, David McKeehan, was the first account from the expedition to be published. Due to McKeehan's heavy editing and to the loss of the original, Gass's published diary is not as useful to modern readers as it was to his own generation, who anxiously awaited a report from the expedition about the new Louisiana Territory and western hinterlands. The rough, direct language of a frontier army sergeant is lost, as is shown in this titillating passage from McKeehan's edition:

we . . . ought to give some account of the *fair* sex of the Missouri; and entertain [readers] with narratives of feats of love as well as of arms. Though we could furnish a sufficient number of entertaining stories and pleasant anecdotes, we do not think it prudent to swell our Journal with them; as our views are directed to more useful information. . . . It may be observed generally that chastity is not very highly esteemed by these people and that the severe and loathsome effects *of certain French principles* are not uncommon among them.

Yet the sergeant supplements other diaries and occasionally adds details otherwise overlooked. Being a carpenter, Gass provides singular information about expedition forts and native architecture. He describes the first winter's cabins as "huts . . . containing four rooms each, and joined at one end forming an angle." He also mentions upper floors where "puncheons or split plank were laid, and covered with grass and clay; which made a warm loft"—welcome winter quarters on freezing Dakota nights. Again, at the party's Oregon coast encampment, Gass appraised his working materials with a carpenter's eye and declared that the local fir made "the finest puncheons" he had ever seen. Several editions of Gass's book, including printings in London, Paris, and Weimar, appeared before the captains' narrative history was published in 1814. A Philadelphia edition even carried fanciful engravings of expedition scenes.

After his expedition tour, Gass settled for a time in Wellsburg, Virginia (now W.Va.), but soon returned to army life and served in the War of 1812 until, losing an eye in an accident, he was discharged. He then resettled in Wellsburg, married Maria Hamilton at the age of sixty, and had six children still living in 1854. He died in Wellsburg.

Sergeant Patrick Gass outlived every person who served on the Lewis and Clark expedition whose fate is known. He is distinguished also for being the first from the expedition to publish an account of the trip. Having lived so long, Gass is one of the best known of the expedition's enlisted men and has had more written about him than any other man in the Corps of Discovery, except for the two captains.

• Information about Gass's service in the Lewis and Clark expedition is in Gary E. Moulton, ed., *The Journals of the Lewis and Clark Expedition* (8 vols., 1983–); Donald Jackson, ed.,

Letters of the Lewis and Clark Expedition with Related Documents, 1783–1854, 2d ed. (2 vols., 1978); and Patrick Gass, *A Journal of the Voyages and Travels of a Corps of Discovery . . .* (1807). Biographical studies and sketches include Charles G. Clarke, *The Men of the Lewis and Clark Expedition: A Biographical Roster of the Fifty-one Members and a Composite Diary of Their Activities from All Known Sources* (1970); Earle R. Forrest, *Patrick Gass: Lewis and Clark's Last Man* (1950); John G. Jacob, *The Life and Times of Patrick Gass* (1859); Newman F. McGirr, "Patrick Gass and His Journal of the Lewis and Clark Expedition," *West Virginia History* 3 (Apr. 1942): 205–12; and James S. Smith and Kathryn Smith, "Sedulous Sergeant, Patrick Gass," *Montana, the Magazine of Western History* 5 (Summer 1955): 20–27.

GARY E. MOULTON

GASSER, Herbert Spencer (5 July 1888–11 May 1963), physiologist, was born in Platteville, Wisconsin, the son of Herman Gasser, a physician, and Jane Elizabeth Griswold, a teacher. He received his secondary education at the State Normal School in Platteville, where his mother had studied. As a boy, despite poor health, he developed interests in photography, furniture making, and music. He was a voracious reader.

As an undergraduate at the University of Wisconsin, Gasser developed a strong interest in experimental biology. In 1910 he received a bachelor's degree in zoology. Although he had resisted his father's urging to become a physician, Gasser decided to study medicine as preparation for a research career. He obtained an A.M. in anatomy at Wisconsin in 1911, studying physiology with Joseph Erlanger and pharmacology with Arthur Loevenhart. He then enrolled at the Johns Hopkins Medical School, receiving his M.D. in 1915. Returning to Wisconsin, he worked as an instructor for a year. Erlanger had moved to Washington University in St. Louis, and he invited Gasser to join the faculty there in 1916 as an instructor of physiology.

The onset of World War I highlighted the importance of wound treatment, and in 1916 Gasser and Erlanger began studying the relationship between blood loss from wounds and shock. In 1918 Gasser was invited by Loevenhart to join the Armed Forces Chemical Warfare Service in Washington, D.C., where he spent the balance of the war studying the pharmacology of toxic gases.

Gasser then returned to Washington University and considered what area of research to pursue next. The development of the vacuum tube amplifier, a device that amplified electrical currents, provided a focus, as he and a classmate from Johns Hopkins, H. Sydney Newcomer, explored the ability of the instrument to amplify electrical currents within nerve cells so they could be measured. Neurophysiologists understood that nerve impulses were minute electrical currents that traveled along the long portion of the nerve cell, or axon, but they had no instruments that could accurately measure these tiny currents. Newcomer and Gasser developed a three-stage amplifier that brought the current within measurable range, but it introduced distortion. Gasser and Erlanger believed that a cathode ray oscilloscope would produce a distortionless

display of the amplified current. The Western Electric Company was developing a cathode ray tube whose voltage was low enough to be compatible with the amplifier, and Gasser and Erlanger approached the company through contacts of Newcomer's. With an oscilloscope provided by Western Electric, Gasser and Erlanger produced the first measurable signals of electrical activity from nerve cells. The publication of their methods and results in 1922 marked the beginning of a new era in neurophysiology.

In 1921 Gasser had been appointed professor and chair of the department of pharmacology at Washington University. He and Erlanger continued their collaboration and showed that compound, rather than single, impulses followed a stimulus to the nerve, and that these impulses traveled at different speeds along the axon, thus reaching the brain or spinal cord at slightly different times. Further work established that neurons varied in thickness, and that the larger the diameter, the faster the impulse moved along the cell length. Gasser and Erlanger were then able to classify nerve cells: A cells transmitted impulses most quickly, receiving sensory input and carrying information to voluntary muscles; B cells communicated with the viscera; and C cells, the slowest, carried pain sensations.

Gasser's productive work with Erlanger was interrupted when he was offered a Rockefeller Foundation fellowship in 1923 to study at various European laboratories, both to expose him to other research and to improve his knowledge of European languages. Gasser spent two years abroad, visiting the laboratories of A. V. Hill in London, Walter Straub in Munich, and Louis Lapicque in Paris. When he returned to St. Louis in 1925, he resumed his position as professor of pharmacology. In 1931 Gasser was offered a professorship in physiology at Cornell Medical College in New York City, which he accepted in part because it aligned his teaching responsibilities more closely with his research interests.

His move to New York ended his collaboration with Erlanger, but Gasser continued to study nervous transmission. In 1935 he was appointed director of the Rockefeller Institute, the most prestigious medical research institute in the United States. Gasser was the second individual to hold this position, and he was initially apprehensive both about maintaining the institute's high reputation and about taking on administrative duties which would pull his attention away from research. However, he found the administrative staff at the Rockefeller Institute so competent and well organized that he was able to function primarily as a leader of research and to continue his own work. As successor to the institute's first director, Simon Flexner, Gasser made no dramatic changes, although his presence there did broaden the institute's traditional focus on infections disease so as to include more physiological research.

In 1936 Gasser and Erlanger reunited to deliver the Eldridge Reeves Johnson Lectures at the University of Pennsylvania, which had been established to promote the application of physics to biological research. The award of the Nobel Prize in medicine or physiology to Gasser and Erlanger in 1944 was widely understood to recognize not only the significance of their findings about nerve impulses, but also the importance of the introduction of the oscilloscope, which had quickly become a standard tool in studies of the nerve.

Gasser continued as director of the Rockefeller Institute until his retirement in 1953, but he continued his own research after that time. He never married. Although poor health, including migraines, remained a problem throughout his life, he refused to let discomfort keep him from his work. He enjoyed travel, music, and the theater. He died in New York City, where he had continued to live following his retirement.

• Herbert S. Gasser's correspondence with Joseph Erlanger is preserved in the Joseph Erlanger Collection at the Washington University School of Medicine in St. Louis. An autobiographical memoir, written in the third person, is in *Experimental Neurology*, supp. 1 (1964). The experiments with the vacuum tube were reported in Gasser and H. S. Newcomer, "Physiological Action Currents in the Phrenic Nerve: An Application of the Thermionic Vacuum Tube to Nerve Physiology," *American Journal of Physiology* 57 (1921): 1–26. Important articles by Gasser and Erlanger include "A Study of the Action Currents of Nerve with the Cathode Ray Oscillograph," *American Journal of Physiology* 62 (1922): 496–524, and "The Role Played by the Sizes of the Constituent Fibers of a Nerve Trunk in Determining the Force of Its Action Potential Wave," *American Journal of Physiology* 80 (1927): 522–47. Also see Erlanger et al., "The Compound Nature of the Action Current of Nerve as Disclosed by the Cathode Ray Oscillograph," *American Journal of Physiology* 70 (1924): 624–66. The Eldridge Reeves Johnson lectures were published as Erlanger and Gasser, *Electrical Signs of Nervous Activity* (1937). Louise H. Marshall has examined Gasser and Erlanger's collaboration in "The Fecundity of Aggregates: The Axonologists at Washington University, 1922–1942," *Perspectives in Biology and Medicine* 26 (1983): 613–36.

CAROLINE JEAN ACKER

GASSNER, John Waldhorn (30 Jan. 1903–2 Apr. 1967), critic, educator, and author, was born in Szeged, Hungary, the son of Abraham Gassner, a furrier, and Fanny Weinburger. Until age eight he was educated at home while the family moved to Budapest, Vienna, and Rotterdam, emigrating to the United States in 1911.

From New York's DeWitt Clinton High School, Gassner entered Columbia University, graduating Phi Beta Kappa in 1924 with honors in English and German. Awarded a fellowship, he completed his master of arts in English and comparative literature in 1925. While engaged in further postgraduate work, Gassner also lectured on English literature at the Labor Temple School, reviewed for *New York Herald Tribune Books* (1925–1927), and was an auxiliary editor for Simon and Schuster (1925–1929). After another year of study, he left his doctorate uncompleted. Gassner married Mollie Kern in 1926. The couple had one daughter.

Throughout his life Gassner continued multiple careers in teaching, criticism, and editing, adding dramaturgy, authorship, and theatrical production later. From 1928 until 1945 Gassner taught drama, playwriting, and comparative literature at Hunter College in New York. From 1940 to 1949 he also chaired the dramaturgy and theater history department at Erwin Piscator's Dramatic Workshop of the New School for Social Research. Gassner also lectured weekly at Bryn Mawr College in Pennsylvania (1941–1943). Later, he was lecturer in dramatic arts at Columbia (1949–1956) and also professor of English at Queens College (1951–1956).

Gassner pursued simultaneous nonacademic careers as dramaturge and critic. From 1929, the year he became a U.S. citizen, he read plays for the Theatre Guild, chairing the play department from 1931 to 1944. In 1931 Gassner's play *The White Whale*, about Herman Melville, earned an honorable mention for the University of Chicago's Charles A. Sergel Award. For the Theatre Guild, Gassner adapted Emil Ludwig's *Versailles* (produced at Westchester Country Playhouse in 1931 as *Peace Palace*) and Stefan Zweig's *Jeremiah* (produced on Broadway in 1939). Later, he dramatized Robinson Jeffers's *The Tower beyond Tragedy* for a 1940 California production starring Judith Anderson. Other adaptations include modernizations of *Everyman* (n.d.), the Brome Cycle's *Abraham and Isaac* (n.d.), and Philip Massinger's *A New Way to Pay Old Debts*, produced at the New School between 1940 and 1949. Gassner left the Theatre Guild in 1944 and became manager of the play department at Columbia Pictures for three years, resigning to form his own short-lived Broadway production company.

Gassner had become drama critic for the Marxist *New Theatre* magazine in 1934 and associate editor in 1937, the year he also became critic and associate editor for *Direction* (1937–1944) and critic for *One-Act Play* (1937–1941, associate editor 1940–1941). A member of the Drama Critics Circle from 1936, he chose not to write daily newspaper reviews; magazines gave him time and scope for what he later called a "more European" approach (once "Marxist" became a dirty word) that placed productions in a social and historical context rather than commenting only on their artistic and entertainment values. He broadcast radio reviews in 1937 and 1938, later appearing on "Bessie Beatty's Hour" (1944–1946), "Invitation to Learning" (1945), and "Broadway Talks Back" (1946).

Less stridently doctrinaire and more concerned with artistic values than other Marxist critics, Gassner quickly gained the respect of his daily-reviewer colleagues. In a 1937 *New York Herald Tribune* column otherwise condemning Marxist criticism, Richard Watts, Jr., called Gassner "the best left-wing critic in America, . . . in truth, one of the ablest critics in the country, without respect to social and political adherence." To John Mason Brown, Gassner was "one of the most earnest and informed of our reviewers."

Gassner often assumed the role of the gadfly conscience of his colleagues. In the 1940s he charged New York critics with applying stricter standards to serious plays than to musicals and lighter entertainments, discouraging serious work in favor of trivial diversions. In a 1949 *Theatre Time* article, noting critics' squeamishness about *All My Sons* and *Death of a Salesman*, seen by some as attacks on capitalism in those days of Cold-War McCarthyism, Gassner prophetically warned against the "dead" drama that would result if "controversy and conviction were banished . . . by an hysterical public and by frightened or intimidated producers and backers."

Gassner's aversion to censorship was aroused again in 1963: he and John Mason Brown resigned as drama advisers to the Pulitzer Prize Committee after its trustees rejected their recommendation of Edward Albee's *Who's Afraid of Virginia Woolf?* In a later *New York Times* article Gassner condemned the awarding of prizes as "increasingly out-of-control" and employing "meaningless categories" and noted that even the Nobel prizes had become too politicized in a McCarthy era biased against the left.

In 1941 Gassner added *Forum* and *Current History* as outlets; later, he wrote and/or edited for *Drama Critique*, *Theatre Workshop*, *Theatre Arts*, and *Tulane Drama Review*. From 1950 he wrote quarterly commentaries on the Broadway season for the *Educational Theatre Journal*, whose sponsor, the American Educational Theatre Association, gave Gassner its 1959–1960 Award of Merit.

It was as an author and anthologist that Gassner produced his most enduring effect on theatrical culture. A review of his first major book, *Masters of the Drama* (1940), called him "the foremost authority on the history of drama living in America." *Producing the Play* (1941), a unique textbook featuring chapters contributed by professional specialists, was used as a manual by the U.S. Army's wartime play-production program and adopted as a text by many collegiate drama departments. Gassner also authored some twenty other books of criticism, theory, and history, but his awe-inspiring record of editing some one hundred drama anthologies earned him the title "American theater's anthologist-in-chief."

A prestigious Sterling Professorship, Yale's first in playwriting, was created for Gassner when he was invited to join the Yale Drama School faculty in 1956. Teaching courses pioneered by the school's founder, George Pierce Baker, and "generous of himself far beyond any professorial obligations," Gassner inspired students for the next decade while continuing his prolific writing and publication. He died in New Haven, Connecticut. Ralph G. Allen, a former student and collaborator, noted in a tribute that Gassner had had six careers and in each had "achieved a success that by itself would have conferred great honor on a less extraordinary man."

• Some of Gassner's late-career views on himself, his place among other critics, and other issues are heard in a taped interview, part of Evelyn McQueen's research, available at the Rodgers and Hammerstein Archives of Recorded Sound in the New York Public Library for the Performing Arts. The same library's Billy Rose Theatre Collection has an informa-tive clipping file on Gassner. Gassner's most-adopted anthology is the monumental *A Treasury of the Theatre*, expanded c. 1950 from a 1935 edition edited with Burns Mantle; the new version had gone through four multivolume editions by 1967. The last of Gassner's many anthologies in the Best American Plays series, *Best Plays of the Early American Theatre* (c. 1967, with Mollie Gassner), was acclaimed for Gassner's "brilliant" historical introduction and called "necessary to any library claiming a section on the American theatre." *Directions in Modern Theatre and Drama* (1965), an expanded edition of his *Form and Idea in Modern Theatre* (1956), is Gassner's thoughtful sorting-out of the many styles, movements, fads, and fashions that made up twentieth-century theater history. Lists of Gassner's massive published output are found in various standard biographical dictionary entries but none can include his entire catalog. Gassner is the subject of three doctoral dissertations: Raymond E. Carver, "John Gassner: Play Anthologist" (Univ. of Denver, 1970); Charles C. Harbour, "John Gassner: Dramatic Critic" (Univ. of Texas, Austin, 1970); and Evelyn Mary McQueen, "John Gassner: Critic and Teacher" (Univ. of Michigan, 1966).

DANIEL S. KREMPEL

GASSON, Thomas Ignatius (23 Sept. 1859–27 Feb. 1930), Roman Catholic priest and educator, was born in Sevenoaks, Kent, England, the son of Henry Gasson and Arabella Quinnell. The occupation of his parents is unknown, but his family was of the landed gentry. Gasson was tutored by the Reverend Allen T. Edwards and was also educated at St. Stephen's School, Lambeth, London. Gasson emigrated to the United States in 1872, having made plans to live with an older brother in Philadelphia. There he received private tutoring and was befriended by two Catholic women, Catherine Doyle and Anne McGarvey. The extent of their influence became evident in October 1874, when Gasson forsook his father's Huguenot heritage and was received into the Catholic faith by the Reverend Charles Cicaterri, S.J., at the Chapel of the Holy Family (now the Jesuit Church of the Gesu) in Philadelphia. Gasson took his new faith one step further by joining the Society of Jesus (Jesuits) religious order on 17 November 1875, thereby beginning his novitiate.

In 1877 Gasson took simple vows of poverty, chastity, and obedience and commenced a period of classical study at the Jesuit juniorate, the Frederick Novitiate, in Frederick, Maryland, where he remained until 1880, when he undertook the study of philosophy at the College of the Sacred Heart in Woodstock, Maryland. Gasson then taught a range of high school–level subjects at Loyola College in Baltimore, Maryland, from 1883 until 1886, when he moved to the College of St. Francis Xavier in New York City, where he remained until 1888. Completing his tour at St. Francis, Gasson was ordered to the Imperial Royal University at Innsbruck, Austria-Hungary, where he studied theology, cannon law, and church history. His studies culminated in his ordination on 26 July 1891 by the prince-bishop of Brixen at the University Church in Innsbruck. Gasson then remained at Innsbruck for an additional year of theological studies and also assumed the duties of chaplain at a charitable institution in the city.

After returning to the United States in the summer of 1892, Gasson served as an instructor for two years in poetry at the Jesuit juniorate in Frederick and then studied ascetical theology at that institution for a year. In August 1895 he was assigned to Boston College in Massachusetts, where he taught the junior class and also served as pastor of the Church of the Immaculate Conception, which was located next door to the college. Two years later, Gasson was appointed professor of ethics and political economies, which he continued to teach until his appointment as president of the college on 6 January 1907.

Chartered in the spring of 1863 and opened in September 1864, Boston College had been founded in an atmosphere of bigotry that had been generated by the "Know Nothing" nativist movement, but had managed not only to survive but to outgrow its original location at Harrison Avenue in Boston's South End. Hence, within months of assuming office, Gasson initiated a $10 million fundraising drive. Land in the Chestnut Hill section of Newton, Massachusetts, was purchased in late 1907, and the new grounds were formally dedicated on 20 June 1908, with Father Gasson naming the area "University Heights." Lawn parties and fairs were held on the site to raise money, and Gasson also went on an inspection tour of various colleges throughout the East in order to obtain ideas for building designs. The first building, appropriately named Gasson Hall, was opened for classes in March 1913. In the midst of building up the new campus, Gasson also initiated night classes at the postgraduate level in the liberal arts. While the program was later discontinued for lack of resources, it set the stage for graduate programs that developed later at the college. Gasson had also begun the planning for an on-campus faculty residence, but his term of office ended on 11 January 1914, before these plans could be brought to fruition.

Upon completing his presidential term, Gasson was sent to Georgetown University in Washington, D.C., where he served as dean of the Graduate School and also taught sociology and legal ethics. Serving at Georgetown until 1923, he then became the superior of a lay retreat house at Mount Manresa in Staten Island, New York. The following year he was sent to Montreal, Quebec, to assist in the reorganization of the Jesuits there and in the development of a Loyola College in Montreal. After his death in Montreal, Gasson's remains were returned to Boston for a funeral mass at the Immaculate Conception Church before his burial in the cemetery of the College of the Holy Cross in Worcester, Massachusetts.

The primary legacy of Gasson was the growth and development of Boston College into a first-rate academic institution under his leadership. He was honored by Georgetown University by the creation in 1930 of the Thomas I. Gasson Medal, which used to be awarded to the student compiling the highest average in the study of ethics.

• A small amount of Gasson's correspondence is held at both the Boston College Archives and the Georgetown University Library Special Collections. Secondary literature on Gasson is scarce; the best source of information on his life and career is Charles Donovan, S.J., *History of Boston College* (1990). Obituaries are in the *Boston Transcript*, the *Washington Evening Star*, and the *Montreal Gazette*, 28 Feb. 1930.

EDWARD L. LACH, JR.

GASTON, William (3 Oct. 1820–19 Jan. 1894), lawyer, mayor of Boston, and governor of Massachusetts, was born in Killingly, Connecticut, the son of Alexander Gaston, a merchant, and Kesia Arnold. After graduating from Brown University in 1840 he moved to Roxbury, Massachusetts, where his parents had settled two years earlier. In 1844 he passed the bar examination and opened a practice. He married Louisa A. Beecher in 1852; they had three children.

Gaston quickly built his law practice and became politically active. From 1849 to 1853 he served on the Roxbury Common Council, becoming its president in 1852. He was elected to the state legislature in 1853 and 1854 as a Whig; after antislavery controversies led to the breakup of the party, he became a Democrat. Although he was a Yankee, his opposition to the Know-Nothing movement won the support of many Irish voters. He was again elected to the legislature in 1856, and then served as Roxbury city solicitor from 1856 to 1860. Capping his early political career, he served as mayor of Roxbury in 1861–1862, helped to promote the town's annexation by Boston in 1867, and won a seat in the state senate in 1868.

Meanwhile, Gaston's skill as a trial lawyer won him high professional standing, and the firm of Jewell, Gaston & Field, established in 1865, prospered. As a Yankee Democrat with Irish supporters and a fiscal conservative able to attract Republican votes, he was widely popular. He lost a congressional election in 1870, but the Democrats nominated him for mayor of Boston. He won the election and served two terms, 1871–1872. As mayor he tried to strengthen the party by appointing both Irish and Yankee Democrats, but his narrow interpretation of the mayor's executive powers led him to respond less decisively than many Bostonians wanted to the Great Boston Fire of 1872 and the smallpox outbreak that followed, and later in 1872 voters rejected his bid for a third term.

Gaston's political career was not over, however. Although Republicans had dominated state elections since 1852, the Liberal Republican bolt of 1872 weakened the GOP. The following year, Gaston nearly won the gubernatorial race. In 1874 he ran again and won, aided by Republican disunity, the Grant administration scandals, and a national depression. As governor he was moderate and cautious—moderate in resisting pleas from some Democrats that he sweep all Republican appointees from office and cautious in handling the politically dangerous prohibition issue by successfully urging the legislature to pass a local option law. By 1875, however, the Republicans rallied, and he was defeated for reelection.

Gaston did not seek office again. Instead, he vigorously pursued his legal practice into the 1890s. He died in Boston.

• Gaston's papers are at Brown University. J. M. Bugbee, "Boston under the Mayors," in *The Memorial History of Boston*, ed. Justin Windsor, vol. 3 (1881), discusses Gaston's terms as mayor. Dale Baum, *The Civil War Party System: The Case of Massachusetts, 1848–1876* (1984), provides information on party battles during Gaston's gubernatorial career. See also Melvin G. Holli and Peter d'A. Jones, eds., *Biographical Dictionary of American Mayors* (1981). Obituaries are in the *Boston Transcript*, 19 Jan. 1894, and the *New England Historic and Genealogical Register* 48 (July 1894): 351–53.

GERALD W. MCFARLAND

GASTON, William Joseph (19 Sept. 1778–23 Jan. 1844), statesman and jurist, was born in New Bern, North Carolina, the son of Alexander Gaston, a native of Ireland and British Navy surgeon who settled in America, and Margaret Sharpe, an Englishwoman and a dedicated Catholic. Active in the American revolutionary cause, the elder Gaston was killed by a band of Tories in 1781 in the presence of his wife, to whom was left the responsibility of raising the couple's two children, who also witnessed his death. Margaret Gaston exerted a powerful influence on her son, nurtured him in the Catholic faith, and in 1791 sent him to the newly established Georgetown College in Maryland. Ill health, however, soon forced the young Gaston to return home. After studying at the New Bern Academy for a year, he eventually enrolled at Princeton, where in 1796 he graduated at age eighteen with highest honors. Again returning to New Bern, Gaston studied law under Francis Xavier Martin, earned admission to the bar in 1798, and immediately took over the law practice of brother-in-law John Louis Taylor, who had received a judicial post. Gaston soon earned a reputation as a superb lawyer, attracting many students over the next several years.

Gaston's success at law coincided with his rising political fortunes. In 1800 he ran successfully for the state senate as a Federalist; over the next three decades, he served four terms in the senate (1801, 1812, 1818–1819), as well as seven terms in the House of Commons (1808–1809, 1828–1833), including a few years as speaker (1808–1809). Gaston also briefly entered the national political scene. A presidential elector for Charles Pinckney in 1808, Gaston ran unsuccessfully for Congress in 1810 but won two years later and served in the House of Representatives from 1813 until 1817. During his congressional career, the North Carolinian vigorously opposed the War of 1812, and his most famous speech in Congress denounced the loan bill of 1814, which would have appropriated $25 million for the wartime conquest of Canada. In addition, Gaston opposed a huge congressional pay increase (the so-called "Salary Grab") and in a lengthy speech criticized a parliamentary tactic known as the "previous question," which allowed the majority to call for an immediate vote in order to halt debate on a subject. Describing the practice as a threat to the "liberty of speech," Gaston's well-researched argument against the previous question embarrassed and angered House Speaker Henry Clay, who refused to talk to Gaston for the next twenty years. Despite offending some, Gaston earned a reputation as an outstanding legislator, and Daniel Webster referred to him as "the greatest of the great men of the War Congress."

After two terms in the nation's capital, in 1817 Gaston voluntarily retired from Congress, purchased a townhouse in New Bern, and served out the rest of his public career in his home state. He was chair of the Senate Judiciary Committee, which framed the 1818 act creating a state supreme court, and later was the chair of the Finance Committee in the House of Commons. As a legislator and citizen, Gaston took a special interest in internal improvements and education. In 1832 he introduced in the House of Commons the bill to charter the North Carolina Central Railroad, and at an internal improvements convention the following year he chaired a committee that advocated new colleges, railroads, hospitals, and asylums. Gaston served as director of the state institution for the instruction of the deaf and dumb, as a trustee of the Griffin Free School and the University of North Carolina, and as president of the Agricultural Society of Craven County and the Bank of New Bern. Although he owned over 200 slaves at his death, Gaston publicly denounced the institution of slavery and proclaimed his love for the Union during the nullification controversy.

In 1833, in the midst of a democratic assault on the power and influence of the North Carolina Supreme Court, Gaston won election to the state's highest judicial tribunal. Although the state constitution forbade any person who denied "the truth of the Protestant religion" to hold civil office, United States Chief Justice John Marshall and North Carolina Chief Justice Thomas Ruffin both advised that the language of the state constitution did not explicitly prohibit the Catholic Gaston from judicial service. His ascension to the bench lent instant credibility to the court, and democratic reformers subsequently failed to limit the power of the judiciary. In eleven years of judicial service, Gaston earned a national reputation and became best known for his relatively humane decisions in slave cases. In *State v. Negro Will* (1834), Gaston held that a slave had a right to defend himself against an unlawful attempt by his master to deprive him of life. This opinion modified the infamous *State v. Mann* (1829) decision and initiated a humanizing trend in the court's slavery decisions that lasted for the next decade and a half. In *State v. Manuel* (1838), moreover, Gaston held that free blacks and manumitted slaves in the state possessed all rights of citizenship under the North Carolina constitution; U.S. Supreme Court Justice Benjamin R. Curtis later cited the opinion in his dissent in the *Dred Scott* case. Even during the 1840s, when some southern state judges began to limit manumission, Gaston continued to give judicial approval to emancipation of slaves, holding in *Cameron v. Commissioners* (1841) that "it is the declared policy of this

State to promote and encourage [slaves'] emancipation, so that they be removed and kept removed without the State."

In the midst of his supreme court career, Gaston served as a delegate from Craven County to the North Carolina constitutional convention of 1835. There he unsuccessfully opposed the disfranchisement of free blacks and championed representation in the House of Commons on the basis of the federal formula, under which slaves counted as three-fifths of a person. This measure expanded the power of the newly settled western portion of the state. Gaston reserved his most eloquent arguments, though, for the debate over Article 32 of the state constitution, which denied non-Protestants the right to hold office. In a two-day oration, he urged the convention to eliminate from the constitution all religious tests for public office. The convention ultimately refused to abolish the religious requirement altogether; instead, delegates voted simply to replace the word "Protestant" with the word "Christian." Gaston also served on the committee appointed by the convention to draft the proposed amendments to be submitted to the state's voters.

William Gaston's reputation as a statesman, jurist, and orator was national in scope. Over the course of Gaston's career, Chief Justice John Marshall, Justice Joseph Story, Senator Daniel Webster, and Chancellor James Kent all consulted him on matters of legal and constitutional interpretation. Some mentioned the North Carolinian as a possible successor to Marshall upon his death in 1835, and Gaston turned down an offer from President William Henry Harrison to become U.S. attorney general in 1841. A member of the American Philosophical Society and the American Antiquarian Society, Gaston frequently delivered lectures and commencement addresses at colleges and universities throughout the country. Gaston was part of a generation of public figures in the South whose antislavery and nationalistic views did not threaten political orthodoxy within the region; he died before the issues of slavery and sectionalism began to disintegrate the Union.

Gaston was married three times, first in 1803 to Susan Hay, who died within a year of the marriage. In 1805 he married Hannah McClure; before she died in 1813, the couple had two daughters and a son. In 1816, Gaston married Eliza Ann Worthington, with whom he had two daughters. His third wife died in 1819, leaving her 41-year-old husband a widower for the third time. Gaston died in Raleigh, North Carolina.

• The William Gaston Papers, rich in personal and public material from 1791 to 1844, are located in the Southern Historical Collection at the University of North Carolina, Chapel Hill. A much smaller and less valuable collection of Gaston papers can be found at the North Carolina State Archives, Raleigh, while his judicial decisions are contained in the *North Carolina Reports*, vols. 15–33 (1833–1844). Gaston has been the subject of two books, although both are dated. R. D. W. Connor, *William Gaston: A Southern Federalist of the Old School and His Yankee Friends, 1778–1844* (1934),

chronicles Gaston's political career through his correspondence. J. Herman Schauinger, *William Gaston: Carolinian* (1949), is much more comprehensive and useful as a biography. Other biographical studies include Schauinger, "The Domestic Life of William Gaston, Catholic Jurist," *Catholic Historical Review* 30, no. 4 (Jan. 1945): 394–426; Eva Kelly Betz, *William Gaston, Fighter for Justice* (1964); and Steven Stowe, *Intimacy and Power in the Old South* (1981), which includes chapters on Gaston's family life. See also, on Gaston's judicial career, "William Gaston and the Supreme Court of North Carolina," *North Carolina Historical Review* 21 (Apr. 1944): 97–117, and Walter F. Pratt, Jr., "The Struggle for Judicial Independence in Antebellum North Carolina: The Story of Two Judges," *Law and History Review* 4 (1986): 129–59. General biographical sketches include Henry G. Connor, "William Gaston, 1778–1844," in *Great American Lawyers*, vol. 3, ed. William Draper Lewis (1908); and Charles H. Bowman, Jr., "William Gaston," in *Dictionary of North Carolina Biography*, ed. William S. Powell.

TIMOTHY S. HUEBNER

GATCH, Philip (2 Mar. 1751–28 Dec. 1834), Methodist preacher and abolitionist, was born in Baltimore County, Maryland, the son of Conduce Gatch, a Prussian immigrant, and Presocia Burgin, farmers. He received religious instruction at St. Paul's Anglican church in Baltimore and formal education at a neighborhood school. In January 1772 Gatch first encountered Methodism when he heard Nathan Perigo preach. On 26 April 1772 Gatch underwent religious conversion at a Methodist neighborhood prayer meeting, and that summer he experienced entire sanctification—a term for John Wesley's teaching on the experience of "Christian perfection" or "perfect love," which Wesley believed to be obtainable in this life. He first preached at the Evans Meeting House in Baltimore County in July 1773. Thomas Rankin examined Gatch according to Wesley's *General Rules* in the fall of 1773 and appointed him to travel with Methodist preachers in New Jersey. On 25 May 1774 in Philadelphia, at the second Methodist conference held in America, Gatch was taken into full connection as a traveling preacher and sent to the Frederick Circuit in Maryland. Along with William Watters and Philip Ebert, Gatch holds the distinction of being the first nativeborn American to become a full-fledged Methodist itinerant.

During the Revolution, Methodists were accused of being Tories, or Loyalists, because John Wesley had urged his American followers to remain loyal to the Crown. As a result, a mob attacked Gatch while he was serving on the Frederick Circuit during 1775–1776. The boisterous men covered him with a coat of tar and thereby permanently injured one of his eyes.

When Gatch arrived to serve on the Hanover Circuit in Virginia in 1776, he discovered a revival in progress guided by the Methodist George Shadford and the Anglican priest Devereux Jarratt, whom Gatch described as "a nursing Father to me and others" (quoted in Connor, p. 70). The congregations in Gatch's circuit were so large that they had to meet outside.

In 1778 Gatch married Elizabeth Smith, the daughter of prosperous Methodist farmers Thomas Smith and Martha Stovall of Powhatan County, Virginia. The couple had eight children. Due to his ill health and recent marriage, Gatch declined to continue as a traveling preacher. Instead he settled as a farmer near Manakin and served as a local preacher.

At the Fluvanna Conference of 1779 Gatch was a leader of southern Methodists who agreed that itinerant preachers might administer baptism and communion to the communicants in their circuits. Gatch and others formed a presbytery empowered to celebrate the Sacraments and ordain ministers. Their actions met with stiff resistance from Francis Asbury and northern leaders who felt that Methodists should receive Sacraments only from ordained Anglican priests. In 1780 Asbury persuaded Gatch and southern Methodists to suspend the administration of these ordinances for one year until Wesley's opinion could be obtained. Gatch's willingness to reverse this decision helped to preserve Methodism from a devastating schism.

The end of the revolutionary war roughly coincided with the onset of the Second Great Awakening, which commenced in Virginia in 1785; in this period of heightened revivalism, many Methodists became enthusiastic about emancipation schemes. At the Baltimore Christmas Conference of 1784, during which the Methodist Episcopal church had been formed, slaveholding members were given one year to execute a legal instrument that would free every slave in their possession. In 1785 Methodist preachers tried to gain signatures for a petition to the Virginia General Assembly urging the "immediate or gradual emancipation of all slaves." Following the death of her parents, Elizabeth Gatch inherited nine slaves. On 18 December 1788 Philip Gatch manumitted these slaves, stating that he believed "all men are by nature equally free." He also wrote: "Was I a slave to the *Algereans* [sic] I am sure I should want them to set me free" (quoted in Connor, pp. 145, 150). Along with Methodists and Quakers, Gatch belonged to the Humane Society of Richmond for the Abolition of the Slave Trade, which presented an antislavery memorial to Congress in 1791.

In 1793 Gatch sold his almost 500-acre farm near Manakin and over time bought more than a thousand acres in Buckingham County, Virginia. In addition to farming, he preached at Lackland's Chapel. On 10 May 1794 Francis Asbury, by now a bishop (the first Methodist Episcopal bishop in America), ordained Gatch as a local deacon. During this period, Virginia Methodists lost some of their strongest abolitionists to western migration, including Gatch, who gave as his reason for removing to the Northwest Territory in 1798 that "I could not feel satisfied to die and leave my offspring in a land of slavery" (quoted in Connor, p. 167). Gatch settled in present-day Milford, Ohio, where he preached at the first Methodist society in the Northwest Territory. In 1800 he was appointed as justice of the peace for Clermont County. Elected as a delegate to the Ohio Constitutional Convention in 1802, he was gratified that the new state constitution prohibited slavery and provided African Americans the right to claim protections under the law.

In addition to his careers as a preacher and farmer, Gatch served as associate judge of the Court of Common Pleas of Clermont County from 1803 to 1824. Normally when Gatch held court, he preached in his courtroom on Sundays. In 1822 he played a role in clearing the name of William Henry Harrison, who was then running for a seat in the U.S. House of Representatives from Ohio. When opponents accused Harrison of being friendly to slavery, Gatch certified that Harrison had been a fellow member of the abolition society in Richmond. In 1832 the Ohio Conference readmitted Gatch as a superannuated traveling preacher. He died in Milford. Due to the scarcity of records, his autobiography and conference minutes provide important sources of early Methodist history. As a revivalist, abolitionist, statesman, and justice, Gatch had consistently applied his faith to the pressing political and social issues of his day.

• Gatch's papers, including his autobiography, handwritten minutes of the conferences of early American Methodism (1774–1777), sermons, and letters, are in the Methodist Theological School in Ohio Library, Delaware, Ohio. Two early biographies are John McLean, *Sketch of Rev. Philip Gatch* (1854), which is based on Gatch's autobiography; and William B. Sprague, *Annals of the American Pulpit*, vol. 7 (1861). The most-complete modern assessments are Elizabeth Connor, *Methodist Trail Blazer: Philip Gatch* (1970), and Virginia Gatch Markham, *Descendants of Godfrey Gatch of Baltimore County, Maryland* (1973). See also Paul H. Boase, "Philip Gatch, Pioneer," *Bulletin of the Historical and Philosophical Society of Ohio*, Oct. 1955, pp. 286–96, and his "Fortunes of a Circuit Rider," *Ohio History*, Apr. 1963, pp. 91–116. For Gatch's impact on revivals and slavery reform, see John M. Versteeg, *Methodism: Ohio Area (1812–1962)* (1962); William Warren Sweet, *Virginia Methodism: A History* (1955); Gordon Pratt Baker, ed., *Those Incredible Methodists: A History of the Baltimore Conference* (1972); and Arthur Dicken Thomas, Jr., "The Second Great Awakening in Virginia and Slavery Reform, 1785–1837" (Ph.D. diss., Union Theological Seminary in Virginia, 1981). An early obituary is in *Minutes of the Annual Conferences of the Methodist Episcopal Church, 1829–1839* (1840).

ARTHUR DICKEN THOMAS, JR.

GATES, Caleb Frank (18 Oct. 1859–9 Apr. 1946), missionary and college president, was born in Chicago, Illinois, the son of Caleb Foote Gates, a business executive, and Mary Eliza Hutchins. Gates, Sr., was a benefactor of numerous Congregationalist projects, including the Chicago Theological Seminary. Gates was educated by his parents and in private schools, entering the preparatory department of Wheaton College in 1866 and graduating from Beloit College in 1877.

Gates considered studying medicine and law, but his religious convictions, coupled with his father's desire to give a son as well as money to the Chicago Theological Seminary, motivated his matriculation there. Upon graduation in 1881, he was recommended to the American Board of Commissioners for Foreign Missions for a post in Turkey, which was then part of the Ottoman Empire.

Gates was first posted to Mardin, a mission established in 1867. He returned to the United States in 1883 to marry Mary Ellen Moore, his fiancé since his last year of seminary. They had five children. In 1884 he began a successful secondary school in Mardin. Six years later he returned to the United States to seek medical treatment for his wife and to teach Arabic and Greek at the Chicago Theological Seminary. While there, in 1892, he published *A Christian Business Man*, a biography of his recently deceased father.

Returning to Ottoman Turkey in 1894, Gates became president of Euphrates College at Harput, a comprehensive institution offering education from kindergarten to divinity school. The 1895 massacre of Armenians precipitated rioting around Harput and resulted in the plundering and burning of college buildings. Gates became involved in relief work for destroyed Christian villages, in addition to rebuilding the damaged college and doubling its size. He received international recognition when Knox College in Galesburg, Illinois, awarded him an honorary doctorate in 1897 and the University of Edinburgh in 1899. In 1900 he returned to the United States for two years' medical leave.

While there, Gates was offered the presidency of Robert College, a liberal arts school in Constantinople, founded in 1859 by New York merchant Christopher Robert. When Gates took over in 1903, its endowment totaled $200,000. By his retirement in 1932, it had grown to $4.3 million, and he had opened a School of Engineering, the first of its kind in the Middle East.

With the rise of the Young Turk movement in 1908, nationalism began to exert pressures to bring foreign missionary schools more under Ottoman control. These Gates successfully resisted. World War I created additional burdens that became acute with the severing of United States–Ottoman relations in 1917. (Turkey entered the war on the German side in 1914.) While most of the faculty left, Gates insisted on keeping the college open as a means of maintaining credibility. It survived relatively unscathed, a tribute to Gates's political disinterestedness.

Gates again became involved in relief work to deal with the desperate conditions in the war's aftermath. The period after the war was one of ferment. Returning to the United States in 1919, he stopped in Paris in a futile attempt to lobby Colonel Edward M. House, the American representative at the peace talks, on a possible solution to the problem of ethnic minorities in the Ottoman Empire. In the United States, he ran afoul of the Armenian-American community for refusing to advocate the creation of a separate Armenian state.

In November 1922 Gates was invited to serve as an unofficial adviser on schools and ethnic minorities to Admiral Mark Bristol, a U.S. delegate at the Lausanne Conference, which led to a peace treaty between the Allies and Turkey (created from Ottoman territory that remained after World War I) as well as the definition of borders for the newly formed nation. Bristol,

previously high commissioner in Constantinople, functioning there as the U.S. representative, continued to consult Gates even after the latter's return home the following month. During this time, Gates received the Bulgarian Order of Alexander, a companion to the Order of King George that the Greek government had previously conferred upon him.

In the spring of 1923, Gates traveled again to the United States in the first of two unsuccessful efforts to persuade the Senate to ratify the Lausanne Treaty. He did, however, soothe the sensibilities of the Turkish government offended by the failure to ratify and, in the process, educated many influential Americans about Turkey.

While Gates passionately supported the 1923 establishment of the republic, naively assuming that western political values represented the normative way of governmental organization, growing nationalism taxed his abilities as president of Robert College. Laws requiring instruction in Turkish resulted in the loss of some American faculty, including one of his sons. Gates was, however, successful in such activities as helping to write the republic's laws concerning private schools, assuring legal standing to them. In 1927 he obtained Robert College's formal title to its property, previously held in trust by private individuals.

In 1932 Gates retired and left Istanbul, settling at Princeton, New Jersey, near his sons. His final trip to Turkey occurred in 1938, when he returned for Robert College's seventy-fifth anniversary. He was feted by friends and alumni along the way and greeted as a "Friend of Turkey" in Istanbul. In 1939 he completed his autobiography, *Not to Me Only*. He died in Denver, Colorado, where he had moved to be near his son Caleb, Jr., who had become chancellor of the University of Denver.

Gates was typical of the best of Protestant evangelists in the Middle East during the era. Even when offered positions in the United States, he maintained the deep commitment to the gospel that had motivated his initial decision to go to the missions.

Like many other American Protestant missionaries of the period, Gates went to the Middle East with the intention of evangelizing Muslims, found this an impossible task, and redirected his efforts toward the conversion of Orthodox Christians to Protestantism. Nonetheless, he showed a genuine concern for those he served, as evidenced by his commitment to the mastery of Arabic, Armenian, and Turkish.

Gates distinguished himself as president of Robert College during a politically tempestuous era and his influence on international politics also marked him as unique. Though he was naively romantic in his attitude toward the Turkish Republic, especially in his uncritical support of the socialist vision of those who founded it, this flawed understanding was a product of his deep love for the country and his desire to help it materially as well as spiritually.

• Few sources are available on Gates's life. The most comprehensive is his autobiography, *Not to Me Only* (1940). Information about his family background can be found in his biography of his father, *A Christian Business Man: Biography of Deacon C. F. Gates* (1892). A lengthy obituary is in the *New York Times*, 11 Apr. 1946.

F. MICHAEL PERKO

GATES, Frederick Taylor (2 July 1853–6 Feb. 1929), Baptist minister and philanthropic and business adviser, was born near Maine, in Broome County, New York, the son of Granville Gates, a Baptist minister, and Sarah Jane Bowers. During his childhood the Gates family moved frequently as his father changed pulpits. Young Frederick received his education in the public schools, beginning in Centre Lisle, then in Brookton in Tompkins County (1862–1866), and then in Ovid in Seneca County, where he attended two terms of the East Genisee Conference Seminary (1866–1867).

The family struggled financially during the father's pastorates in these towns. When in the spring of 1867 Granville Gates became a missionary for the American Baptist Home Mission Society (ABHMS) in northwest Missouri and northeast Kansas, he moved his family to Forest City, Missouri. That fall Frederick was enrolled in a college preparatory course at Highland University in Highland, Kansas, where his father soon bought a farm. The family's continuing financial plight forced Frederick to attend school intermittently while working a series of jobs to help relieve the family's debt. He taught school during the winters and worked as a store clerk, a bank teller, and a commission salesman peddling a newly patented harrow to Kansas farmers. In 1873 he entered the University of Rochester but soon decided to save money by returning to Kansas, living at home, and pursuing his studies on his own; he rejoined his University of Rochester class as a junior in 1875 and graduated in 1877 with an A.B. Gates contemplated a career in the law but concluded that the field was too crowded; deciding that he could be most useful as a minister, he entered the Rochester Theological Seminary, graduating in 1880.

Gates became the pastor of the Fifth Avenue Baptist Church in Minneapolis, Minnesota, in June 1880. He later recalled that in the early years his was a "youthful, enthusiastic, and zealous ministry" that was hard on "comfortable sinners and easy-going saints" (*Chapters in My Life*, p. 78). But church membership increased, and by the spring of 1884 he had led campaigns to secure a better location and to erect a new building to house the renamed Central Baptist Church. Gates preached salvation by service, not by faith alone; he began to think more independently and to abandon religious orthodoxy in favor of modernism, "bring[ing] the light of common sense, of reason, and of science to the interpretation of religion" (*Chapters*, p. 79).

After two years in Minneapolis, Gates married Lucia Fowler Perkins, a teacher he had met in Rochester. They were wed in 1882, but she died in 1883. Gates and his second wife, Emma Cahoon, were married in 1886 at her home in Racine, Wisconsin. Seven children were born to the couple in the next eleven years.

Gates was active in the statewide work of the denomination; his mission work and his efforts to promote education brought him into collaboration with George A. Pillsbury, a wealthy businessman in Minneapolis. Early in 1888 Pillsbury approached Gates for advice about his planned bequest of $200,000 for the Baptist academy at Owatonna, Minnesota. Believing the academy too weak to merit such a gift, Gates proposed instead a conditional gift of $50,000 and a public campaign to encourage Minnesota Baptists to contribute to the school. If the drive proved successful and improved the school's standing, Gates argued, Pillsbury could then safely bequeath to the school the additional $150,000. In March Gates resigned from his pulpit to lead this fundraising drive and within six weeks had secured pledges for nearly $60,000 for the renamed Pillsbury Academy.

The surprisingly rapid success of this solicitation attracted the attention of national Baptist leaders, and the Reverend Henry L. Morehouse, corresponding secretary of the ABHMS, invited Gates to attend the national conference in May 1888. Morehouse was promoting the formation of a national organization to promote Baptist education and to raise funds to support Baptist schools, but the plan was opposed by the denomination's eastern leaders. Morehouse won the bitter contest and then nominated Gates to lead the new American Baptist Education Society (ABES). With personal ties to both sides of the sectional debate, Gates managed to calm these waters; he then turned his attention to another controversy: whether and where to build a national Baptist university. By October 1888 Gates had decided that Chicago was the best location for such a university; by June 1889 he had developed a plan for the university's development and had secured from the denomination's wealthiest member, John D. Rockefeller, a pledge of $600,000 toward a million-dollar endowment for the new University of Chicago. During the next year Gates worked with Thomas W. Goodspeed to raise the remainder of the funds. He also negotiated a deal with Rockefeller and William Rainey Harper that committed Rockefeller to a larger endowment for the school and committed Harper to the university's presidency.

As head of the ABES, Gates was a central figure in the development of the University of Chicago and in the improvement of other Baptist colleges and academies across the country. He worked closely with Rockefeller, who began to trust Gates's good judgment and common sense to such a degree that he channeled large sums for educational work through the ABES. In March 1891 Rockefeller asked Gates to move his office from Chicago to New York City in order to help manage Rockefeller's benevolent work. By September 1891 Gates had moved his family to Montclair, New Jersey, and was working from rented offices in Manhattan. He continued to work for both the ABES and Rockefeller until 1893, when he resigned from the ABES to work for Rockefeller exclusively.

Gates soon became one of Rockefeller's trusted business associates as well as his major philanthropic adviser. Because Gates often was on the road for the ABES, Rockefeller asked him to check on some of his unseen investments; when Gates's reports showed these investments to be losing propositions, Rockefeller gave Gates the authority to resolve the matter either by selling the properties or by reorganizing and improving them. Gates's most notable success was in the Mesabi iron range in Minnesota, where his astute management enabled Rockefeller to sell his holdings to J. P. Morgan's U.S. Steel Corporation in 1901 for $88.5 million, with an estimated profit of $50 million.

Gates's most significant work, however, was in providing direction and scope for Rockefeller's philanthropy. He brought order to Rockefeller's charitable work by following what he called "the principles of scientific giving." He ended Rockefeller's practice of making gifts to purely local charities across the country and focused instead on municipal, state, and national organizations, knowledgeable about their fields and capable of investigating the worthiness of applicants. In 1897 John D. Rockefeller, Jr., joined his father's office and began to work closely with Gates. Between 1897 and 1913 their collaboration resulted in the creation of several Rockefeller-endowed corporations that would help define American philanthropy and research in both science and medicine. Gates was the visionary force behind each of these institutions.

The first of these, the Rockefeller Institute for Medical Research (1901; renamed Rockefeller University in 1965), was the first institution in the United States devoted solely to biomedical research. Gates was inspired to suggest this enterprise when he read William Osler's *Principles and Practice of Medicine* (1892) and realized "how woefully neglected" medical science was in the United States. Gates also helped to organize the General Education Board (1902; chartered in 1903) for "the promotion of education within the United States, without distinction of race, sex, or creed," and he encouraged its support of scientific agriculture, higher education, and the full-time system in medical education, which entailed that universities employ salaried, specialized professionals in medical teaching and research rather than contract with physicians in private practice for these services. When he learned of Charles W. Stiles's research on hookworm disease, Gates led the formation of the Rockefeller Sanitary Commission for the Eradication of Hookworm Disease (1909) with $1 million for a five-year public health campaign in the South. In 1913 its work was expanded to combat additional diseases worldwide with the creation of the International Health Commission (later the International Health Board) of the Rockefeller Foundation.

As early as 1905 Gates had urged Rockefeller to broaden his approach to philanthropy by creating a series of large funds with specific purposes that would work for the good of humanity. By 1910 this idea had evolved into plans for the Rockefeller Foundation, which, after attempts to secure a charter from Congress failed, was incorporated in New York in 1913 "to promote the well-being of mankind throughout the world." The foundation focused on medicine and public health in its early years; in 1914 it established the China Medical Board, which built the Peking Union Medical College to develop modern western medicine in China.

Gates resigned from Rockefeller's employment in 1912 but continued to serve on the philanthropic boards and to act as an occasional business consultant to the Rockefellers. Between 1912 and 1920 he worked with two of his sons to develop a 20,000-acre farm, "Broadacre," in North Carolina, following the principles of scientific agriculture. He died in Phoenix, Arizona, while visiting a daughter.

• Gates's personal papers are located at the Rockefeller Archive Center, North Tarrytown, N.Y. Much of his professional work is documented in the Rockefeller Family Archives, which also include nine volumes of Gates's personal correspondence (1895–1913), and in the records of Rockefeller University, the General Education Board, the Rockefeller Sanitary Commission, and the Rockefeller Foundation; these records are also at the Rockefeller Archive Center. His autobiography, which he worked on during 1926–1928 and addressed to his children, was published in 1977 as *Chapters in My Life*. Since Gates's career was so closely tied to the Rockefellers, works about John D. Rockefeller and John D. Rockefeller, Jr., also discuss Gates. See Rockefeller's own *Random Reminiscences of Men and Events* (1909); Allan Nevins, *Study in Power: John D. Rockefeller, Industrialist and Philanthropist* (1953); John Ensor Harr and Peter J. Johnson, *The Rockefeller Century* (1988); David Freeman Hawke, *John D.: The Founding Father of the Rockefellers* (1980); Raymond B. Fosdick, *John D. Rockefeller, Jr.: A Portrait* (1956); and James E. Fell, Jr., "Rockefeller's Right-hand Man: Frederick T. Gates and the Northwestern Mining Investments," *Business History Review* 52 (Winter 1978): 537–61. A useful discussion of Gates's religious thought can be found in Albert F. Schenkel, *The Rich Man and the Kingdom: John D. Rockefeller, Jr., and the Protestant Establishment* (1995). Studies of specific aspects of Rockefeller's philanthropy include Thomas W. Goodspeed, *The Story of the University of Chicago 1890–1925* (1925); Richard J. Storr, *Harper's University: The Beginnings* (1966); George W. Corner, *A History of the Rockefeller Institute, 1901–1953: Origins and Growth* (1964); Fosdick, *Adventure in Giving: The Story of the General Education Board* (1962) and *The Story of the Rockefeller Foundation* (1952); and John Ettling, *The Germ of Laziness: Rockefeller Philanthropy and Public Health in the New South* (1981). Obituaries are in the *New York Times*, the *New York Sun*, and other newspapers around the country, 7 Feb. 1929.

KENNETH W. ROSE

GATES, Horatio (Apr.? 1728?–10 Apr. 1806), soldier, was born, according to tradition, in Maldon, England, the son of Robert Gates, a customs collector, and Dorothy Reeve, a housekeeper. His parents were of low rank, and had he not received patronage from powerful mentors he probably would have been doomed to a life of drudgery. Shortly after his birth his father, who worked for the duke of Bolton, was appointed tidesman in the customs service and later customs collector at Greenwich. His mother, previously housekeeper for the duke of Leeds, assumed the same position in the Bolton household. As a lad, Gates probably attended school in Greenwich. In 1745, through Bolton's influence, he was commissioned ensign in the Twentieth Regiment, then transferred immediately as lieutenant to a regiment Bolton was privately raising. He served for a time in Germany and was appointed regimental adjutant. In 1749 he joined Colonel Edward Cornwallis as an aide and came out with the colonel to Nova Scotia. Five years later he married Elizabeth Phillips. They had one child.

In 1755 Gates was promoted to captain in an independent company serving in New York. He joined his command at the outbreak of the Seven Years' War. He was with General Edward Braddock's army in the ambush near Fort Duquesne; badly wounded, he spent the next few months recuperating. After three years of routine duty he joined General John Stanwix as brigade major and in 1761 went with General Robert Monckton on a successful expedition against Martinique. Chosen by Monckton to deliver news of the victory to London, he was rewarded with promotion to major. By that time he had become a master of military administration and an accomplished leader of men in battle. These skills, however, did him little good once the war ended. Living in England with no chance of promotion, he sought surcease for a time in liquor and gambling, but he mastered these vices in the late 1760s and drifted toward republicanism and Methodism. Finally, in 1772, he sold his army commission and moved with his family to Virginia. There, he settled into the life of a quiet middle-class farmer on his estate, "Travellers Rest."

Gates took little part in growing political tensions between America and Britain over the next few years, beyond expressing Whiggish sentiments to men of like mind, such as Charles Lee (1731–1782). After 1775, however, he let it be known that his heart was with the patriots, despite his previous career as a soldier of the king. American revolutionaries, in dire need of skilled soldiers, welcomed him into their ranks, and on 17 June 1775 Congress appointed him adjutant general in the Continental army with the rank of brigadier general. In the following winter he served with General George Washington at the siege of Boston, using his extensive knowledge of army organization to regularize the Continental army's heterogeneous forces. He also carried on an extensive correspondence with numerous persons, John Adams (1735–1826) in particular, regarding matters military and political. In these writings he emerged as a cautious, defensive strategist who felt that the immature American army must not risk too much for fear of losing all. "Our Business," he argued, "is to Defend the main Chance; to Attack only by Detail; and when a precious advantage Offers." This thinking, the hallmark of his generalship, was to be the key to his success against John Burgoyne two years later at Saratoga. Impressed by Gates's military gifts, Washington praised him to Congress, and the legislators, on 16 May 1776, promoted him to major general.

Although Gates was prudent in military matters, he was among the most radical of Americans in politics.

By mid-1775 he was disgusted with colonials who wanted a reconciliation with Britain, and six months later he openly advocated independence. But Gates's political views had no adverse impact upon his military career—in fact, they may have assisted it. In June 1776 he was chosen by Congress to take command of an American army that had invaded Canada in the previous year. Arriving in Albany, he was surprised to find the army no longer in Canada, but in General Philip Schuyler's Northern Department. Because Schuyler asserted a right to command these troops, both officers agreed that Congress must decide the matter. When the legislators ruled in favor of Schuyler, Gates acquiesced only reluctantly. Given command at Fort Ticonderoga, he worked in harmony with Benedict Arnold for the remainder of 1776, helping thwart Guy Carleton's attempt to gain control of Lake Champlain and capture Ticonderoga. At the end of the year he marched with 600 Continentals to reinforce Washington on the Delaware River, then left the army because of illness. After recovering he commanded troops in Philadelphia during the winter, all the time working with friends in Congress to supersede Schuyler in his command. In March 1777 he succeeded and was ordered back to Ticonderoga. As Gates and Schuyler squabbled over command of New York, British General John Burgoyne prepared for invasion of that state from Canada in the summer of 1777.

Despite the enemy threat, the American commanders continued to be more concerned about prerogative than about defending America. On 22 May Schuyler wangled reappointment to his old position, only to have Gates storm the halls of Congress for yet another reversal. That accomplished on 4 August, partly because Schuyler had in the meantime lost Ticonderoga to Burgoyne, Gates returned to the Northern Department. With the command situation clarified, he concentrated upon defeating the enemy—or, more precisely, upon allowing the enemy to defeat himself. Playing a defensive role, he correctly assessed Burgoyne as being an "old gamester" who might "risque all upon one Throw." Therefore, he fortified his army on Bemis Heights and waited for Burgoyne to batter his way through to Albany. In the battles of Freeman's Farm (19 Sept.) and Bemis Heights (7 Oct.), Gates, ably assisted by Daniel Morgan and Benedict Arnold (although the latter was quarreling with Gates), twice thwarted Burgoyne's attempts to turn his left and bypass his entrenched army. Burgoyne, realizing by 9 October that his position was no longer tenable, retreated northward, followed carefully by Gates. Finding his line of withdrawal cut off by John Stark's militiamen, he capitulated on the seventeenth at Saratoga, agreeing to terms that allowed his army to return to England, provided they not serve again in the war. Gates was severely criticized for the liberality of these provisions, but he correctly pointed out that during negotiations with Burgoyne his supply base at Albany had been threatened by an enemy force from New York City, thus forcing him to direct his attention southward. He was also charged with delaying the report of his victory to Washington, but he explained that his messenger, James Wilkinson, had dallied shamelessly in delivering the news. Finally, he was accused of withholding troops from Washington's hard-pressed main army in late 1777, but he correctly noted that he had in fact dispatched more than he safely should have.

All these criticisms, and others as well, now pouring in upon Gates were from admirers of Washington who scrutinized the victor at Saratoga for signs that he lusted to supplant their hero as commander in chief. After all, the triumphant Gates had gloriously prevailed over his enemies while Washington, in glaring contrast, had been defeated in battles against William Howe (1729–1814) and had lost Philadelphia. Surely these facts would lead Gates to conclude that he should be commander in chief. Therefore, he was jealously watched for signs that he was plotting Washington's overthrow as he served on the Board of War during the winter of 1777. Although there was no evidence to support their suspicions (except what they insisted on "seeing"), some of Washington's supporters nevertheless concluded that Gates was conspiring with Thomas Conway and others, in the infamous "Conway Cabal," to take the commander in chief's place. Finally, even Washington himself began to use these rumors against Gates to cement his own shaky position, implying indirectly but scornfully that his subordinate was scheming against him. A bemused and innocent Gates weathered this storm of abuse well but emerged with a fixed aversion to Washington and his admirers; "a most wicked Junto," he growled, had been trying to sacrifice him "to their Idol." Putting these matters behind him, in April 1778 he took command once again in the Hudson River Valley and after fighting a ludicrous pistol duel with Wilkinson, in which Wilkinson fired three times but Gates refused to fire a shot, moved on to Boston. In 1779, after spurning Washington's offer to conduct a campaign against the Mohawk Indians, he served instead at Providence.

In the summer of 1780 Gates was called upon by Congress to take command of the Southern Department after Benjamin Lincoln's (1733–1810) disastrous surrender of Charleston on 12 May. Although not sanguine about his chances of stemming the British tide there, Gates assumed command of his small, motley force at Coxe's Mill on 25 July and ordered a quick march southward toward the enemy at Camden. His advisers were appalled at Gates's haste, but he nonetheless put his army in motion two days later, marching directly across provisionless country rather than by a westward route through lands abounding with supplies. Gates's haste appeared unseemly, but he was following a well-thought-out plan that required great dispatch. Intending to move into a strong, defensive position just north of Camden, which he would fortify and force the enemy to attack at great disadvantage, he must act with alacrity lest his foes be alerted and thwart his intentions. Unfortunately, his plan did not succeed. On the night of 15 August, as he marched toward Camden with his exhausted army, he encountered a British force commanded by Lord Cornwallis marching northward. Compelled to fight, Gates on 16 August opened the battle of Camden with a charge of militiamen against redcoated regulars, and soon his army was routed. His Continentals, led by Johann Kalb (Baron de Kalb) were decimated and their commander killed. Even while his soldiers were still engaged in battle he rode like the wind back to Hillsborough to rally his forces and reorganize, an unfortunate gallop that his political foes never allowed him to forget. Gleefully wrote Alexander Hamilton (1755–1804), "It does admirable credit to . . . a man of his time of life."

Over the next three months Gates worked manfully to get his army back into fighting trim, and also grieved over the recent death of his son, while Congress debated his future. The outcome was never in doubt. On 5 October the legislators voted to call a court of inquiry to examine Gates's conduct at Camden and to allow Washington to appoint Nathanael Greene in his stead. The court was never convened, but Gates had to wait twenty-two months before Congress finally rescinded its resolution and invited him to rejoin the army. With his self-respect restored, he served Washington at Newburgh as second in command during the winter of 1782–1783. While there he played a role in promoting officer unrest by encouraging John Armstrong (1758–1843) to write the inflammatory Newburgh Address, which hinted at mutiny should Congress not redress army grievances. In March 1783 he left the army for the last time, riding home to the bedside of his dying wife. After her death he was lonely and embittered for a number of years, but in 1786 he married a rich widow named Mary Vallance, moved to Manhattan, and resumed an active life. In 1787 he strongly supported the new Constitution. He became an ardent Jeffersonian in his vigorous old age and was elected in 1800 to a term in the New York state legislature. Sensing his approaching death in early 1806, he expressed great satisfaction at having had a part in the founding of America. He died in Manhattan.

• The Gates papers are in the New-York Historical Society, the New York Public Library, National Archives, and the North Carolina Department of Archives and History. James Gregory, ed., *The Horatio Gates Papers, 1726–1828* (1978), microfilm, is extremely useful. Paul David Nelson, *General Horatio Gates: A Biography* (1976), is the standard life. Samuel White Patterson, *Horatio Gates: Defender of American Liberties* (1941), is too uncritical and also poorly footnoted. A short sketch is George A. Billias, "Horatio Gates: Professional Soldier," in *George Washington's Generals*, ed. George A. Billias (1964). An excellent, readable treatment of Gates's role in the Saratoga campaign is Max M. Mintz, *The Generals of Saratoga: John Burgoyne & Horatio Gates* (1990). See also John S. Pancake, *1777: The Year of the Hangman* (1977), and Hoffman Nickerson, *The Turning Point of the Revolution* (1928). Bernhard Knollenberg, *Washington and the Revolution, a Reappraisal: Gates, Conway, and the Continental Congress* (1940), carefully assesses Gates's relations with Washington and his activities in the Conway Cabal and the revolutionary war. His service in the South is treated in Otho Holland Williams, "Narrative of the Campaigns of 1780," an appendix to William Johnson, *Sketches of the Life and Correspondence of Nathanael Greene*, vol. 1 (1822); and John R. Alden, *The South in the Revolution, 1763–1789* (1957). Richard H. Kohn, "The Inside Story of the Newburgh Conspiracy: America and the Coup d'Etat," *William and Mary Quarterly*, 3d ser., 27 (1970): 187–220, discusses the part Gates played in that episode.

PAUL DAVID NELSON

GATES, John Warne (8 May 1855–9 Aug. 1911), businessman, was born in Turner Junction, Illinois, the son of Asel Avery Gates and Mary Warne. His parents' occupations are unknown. Gates was educated in local public schools and at North-Western College in Naperville and received a degree from a six-month commercial course in 1873. He then worked a number of odd jobs and saved his money. In 1876 he married Dellora Baker of St. Charles, Illinois; they had one child. A few years later Gates invested in a local hardware store, where he noticed that barbed wire for fencing had attained a sudden popularity. As wire fencing, it did not demand much wood, which was scarce on the range. The wire was perfect for containing western-range cattle, and it was inexpensive enough so that farmers could purchase it in large lots for the more sizable western ranches.

Gates saw only opportunity in the expanding western frontier and offered in 1878 to join wire manufacturer Isaac L. Ellwood in his business. Ellwood instead hired Gates as a traveling salesman at $25 a week. Gates's first assignment was Texas, where the vast ranges cried out for a wire fence that was unaffected by wind or fire and that could contain large herds of cattle. Gates challenged local ranchers to test it with their strongest steers. At first they resisted the new wire, but the product quickly won them over. Gates saw that the market stood to grow even faster than he and Ellwood first anticipated, and he left Ellwood's employ to take orders for himself. Gates and a partner built a wire plant in St. Louis, only to be greeted by lawsuits from Ellwood for patent infringements. Gates literally moved back and forth across the Mississippi River, exhausting Ellwood's attempts to serve him with an injunction. Ellwood settled out of court in resignation.

Gates had even bigger plans, however. He dreamed of consolidating all the country's wire manufacturing facilities, and by 1898 he had formed the American Steel & Wire Company of New Jersey with $90 million capitalization. Each new consolidation or addition to the Gates "team" caused the value of Gates's stock to rise, but even that did not satisfy him. He issued additional stock that exceeded in par value the assets that it represented. Gates escaped legal action only because the wire and steel business expanded faster than even he could print stock, and the assets quickly matched the stock's par value.

Known to take risks, but supremely confident in his own judgment and abilities, Gates was known in the investment community as "Bet-a-Million" or "Bet-You-a-Million" for placing his considerable fortune where his mouth was. In 1896 he invested in a large Chicago gas enterprise and a year later cleared $12 million in profits. Before long Gates had the reputation as what would in the late twentieth century be called a corporate "raider"; mere rumors of his activities caused a minor panic in 1900. He worked closely with respected Wall Street analyst William R. Walker and created his own market sources that included the use of private detectives.

Gates's interest in iron and steel brought him into contact with the Carnegie Steel Company in the late 1890s, and in 1894 he replaced Jay C. Morse as the president of the Illinois Steel Company in direct competition with the Carnegies. Understanding the benefits of backward integration, Gates quickly put together the steel companies with his wire business, forming Consolidated Steel & Wire Company, a high-yield operation that gave Gates familiarity with iron and steel production. In 1899 he and a group of Chicago investors that included William and James Hobart Moore attempted to purchase Carnegie Steel, which was up for sale at the time. Gates envisioned a $1 billion "supertrust," but the deal collapsed. At that point Gates went on to form the Republic Iron & Steel Company and in 1906 was a member of the syndicate that took over the Tennessee Coal & Iron Company. Gates also organized the American Tin Plate Company, the American Sheet Steel Company, the American Steel Hoop Company, and the National Steel Company.

In 1902 Gates sold his stock in American Steel & Wire to the newly formed U.S. Steel Corporation under the ownership of a syndicate led by J. P. Morgan and subsequently found himself involved in several deals with Morgan, few that worked to his advantage. Gates secretly gained control of the Louisville & Nashville Railroad in 1902 and then sold it to Morgan at what Morgan believed to be an inflated price. In retaliation, Morgan then lured Gates into a speculative deal financed by Morgan's credit line, then forced a plunge in the value of the securities put up by Gates as collateral. Morgan only permitted Gates to settle up by extracting a promise from the wire manufacturer to resign from the New York Stock Exchange. Gates retired from New York and made a few subsequent ventures in Texas oil. He died in Paris, France, where he had purchased a castle.

• For additional information see Larry Schweikart, "John Warne Gates," *Encyclopedia of American Business History and Biography: Iron and Steel in the 19th Century*; Paul F. Paskoff, ed., *Facts on File* (1989); Joseph Wall, *Andrew Carnegie* (1970); and William T. Hogan, *Economic History of the Iron and Steel Industry in the United States*, vol. 1 (1971). An obituary is in the *New York Times*, 10 Aug. 1911.

LARRY SCHWEIKART

GATES, Sir Thomas (?–1621), governor of Virginia, was born in Colyford, Colyton parish, Devonshire, England. Little is known of his early life before his first experience in English colonization in 1585–1586 when he accompanied Sir Francis Drake in an expedition against the Spanish settlements in the Caribbean. After attacks on Cartegena and St. Augustine, the fleet stopped at Roanoke Island and transported the colonists back to England. In these years Gates was principally a soldier, serving under the earl of Essex in Normandy (1591), at Cadiz (1596) where he was knighted, against the Azores (1597), and in Ireland (1597–1598).

Gates's career expanded after Essex's execution. In 1604 he fought with the English forces in the Netherlands under Sir Henry Walton and traveled to Vienna as ambassador. In 1606 Gates was listed first among those who petitioned James I for a charter to settle Virginia. Gates invested £2,000 in the Virginia Company. Soon after, both he and his friend Thomas Dale obtained leave from the Dutch army to pursue their interests in Virginia. Under the new charter issued in 1609, Thomas West, Lord De La Warr, was appointed governor and Gates governor ad interim until De La Warr arrived in the colony. In May 1609 Gates sailed for Virginia on the *Sea Venture* with Sir George Somers and Christopher Newport, admiral and vice admiral respectively, and seven other vessels. Unfortunately, because of dissension among the three men, the leaders of the expedition and the council's instructions were all on the *Sea Venture*. De La Warr was to follow in August, but he did not take his leave until April 1610. The fleet with Gates sailed directly west and then dropped south into the tropics. The heat and a plague took a heavy toll of the passengers; thirty-two were buried at sea before the fleet sailed into a hurricane off the Bahamas. The ships scattered, and the *Sea Venture*, driven before the storm for three days, came to ground on one of the Bermuda islands. The other ships, leaderless, limped into Jamestown in August. The complement of the *Sea Venture* spent the next nine months marooned in Bermuda. Gates immediately set about building a new vessel out of island cedar and the remnants of the old ship, and Somers followed suit with a second vessel. By early May 1610, stocked with meat from the swine that inhabited the island, they continued the voyage to Jamestown. The incident is believed to have inspired Shakespeare's *The Tempest*.

The party arrived before the town on 23 May 1610 to find a scene of desolation. Over the winter the colony had endured what was called the starving time. The 500 settlers alive in the fall of 1609 had been reduced to 60. The town "appeared rather as the ruins of some ancient [for]tification, than that any people living might now inhabit it," wrote Governor De La Warr. "The *Indian as fast killing without as the famine and pestilence within*" (Brown, vol. 1, p. 405). Without supplies or the means to obtain them quickly, or the strength to cow the Indians into yielding them, Gates determined to abandon the colony. As the departing ships dropped down the James River in early June, they were met by the long boat of De La Warr's fleet and were instructed to return to Jamestown.

The arrival of De La Warr supplied the leadership that had been lacking in the colony since Captain John Smith's departure in September 1609. De La Warr or-

ganized the colonists into work parties and began rebuilding the town. He dispatched Somers to Bermuda for pork and fish (where he died) and sent Gates to England for supplies and to report to the company. In England Gates successfully argued for continued support of the colony, and two relief expeditions were planned. The first, under Dale, reached Jamestown in May 1611. The second, under Gates, who with De La Warr's retirement was now governor, arrived in August. Dale had already begun a serious reform of the colony. Both enforced De La Warr's strict work discipline. Following company instructions to shift the center of the colony away from Jamestown, settlements were established along the James as far west as Henrico. Gates pursued a vigorous campaign to subjugate the Indians, which culminated in peace with Powhatan in 1613 and the marriage of John Rolfe and Pocahontas. In order to discipline an unruly populace, Gates had begun the formulation of a strict body of criminal law in 1610. Both De La Warr and Dale added to it, and William Strachey, secretary of the colony, summarized it in 1612 in his *Lawes Devine, Morall, and Martiall*. Although the regime established under these laws was strict, it was probably necessary given the state of the colony. Gates supported Rolfe's effort to cultivate tobacco and place the colony on a firm economic base. When Gates's three-year term in Virginia expired in 1614, he sailed for England with Rolfe's first four bales of tobacco.

In England Gates maintained his interest in the colony, apparently making plans in 1618 to return. Yet in 1619–1620 he sold sixty of his shares in the company. He died apparently in the Low Countries, probably in 1621. He was married (his wife, whose name is unknown, died on the 1611 voyage to Virginia) and was the father of at least four children. In 1637 two daughters and the widow of a son petitioned the Privy Council for Gates's back pay so that they might take up lands in Virginia still listed in his name.

• There are no Gates papers. Traces of his life can be found in *Calendar of State Papers, Domestic Series, 1611–1618* (1858) and *Calendar of State Papers, Colonial Series, 1574–1660* (1860); Alexander Brown, ed., *The Genesis of the United States* (2 vols., 1890); Susan Myra Kingsbury, ed., *The Records of the Virginia Company of London* (4 vols., 1906–1935); William Strachey, "A True Repertory of the Wreck and Redemption of Sir Thomas Gates Knight," reprinted in *A Voyage to Virginia in 1609*, ed. Louis B. Wright (1964); and Ralph Hamor, *A True Discourse of the Present State of Virginia* (1615). See also Wesley Frank Craven, *The Southern Colonies in the Seventeenth Century, 1607–1689* (1949), and Richard L. Morton, *Colonial Virginia* (2 vols., 1960).

BERNARD W. SHEEHAN

GATLING, Richard Jordan (12 Sept. 1818–26 Feb. 1903), inventor and manufacturer, was born in Hertford County, North Carolina, the son of Jordan Gatling, a wealthy planter, and Mary Barnes. He attended the local public schools and as a young man was of some assistance to his father, who had devised machines for sowing cotton seeds and for thinning out young cotton plants. After a short time as a school-teacher when he was nineteen years of age, Gatling owned and operated a country store for several years. He became a full-time inventor at age twenty, developing and testing a screw propeller for vessels, but in 1839 he was denied a patent because another inventor, John Ericsson, had successfully patented a similar device several months before.

Turning his attention to agricultural machines, Gatling invented and patented a device for planting rice in 1839. In 1844, thinking that he would have greater success in a more northerly market, he began manufacturing it in St. Louis, Missouri, while supporting himself as a dry goods clerk. A later adaptation of this implement greatly facilitated the planting of wheat.

By 1845 Gatling was engaged in the full-time manufacturing and sale of his machines. While on a river steamer en route to Pittsburgh, Pennsylvania, in the winter of 1845–1846, he developed smallpox and, without medical assistance, lay untended in his cabin for several weeks while the vessel was frozen in the ice. Determined not to find himself in such straits again, Gatling attended first the Indiana Medical College in Laporte, Indiana, in 1847–1848 and then the Ohio Medical College in Cincinnati, where he secured his M.D. in 1850. He never practiced medicine but was thereafter able to provide for himself and others in emergency situations; subsequently, people referred to him as "Doctor" for much of his life.

Successful in producing agricultural implements, Gatling expanded his business to Indianapolis and then to Springfield, Ohio, and soon placed on the market other machines he had invented and patented, including a hemp-breaking machine (1847, later modified), and a steam plow (1857), which, however, was never widely used. Gatling married Jemima T. Sanders of Indianapolis, Indiana, in 1854. The couple had at least two sons and a daughter.

With the coming of the Civil War, Gatling began working on improvements in weaponry. His first inventions in this area were a marine steam ram and a rapid-fire, or machine gun, with which his name has ever since been identified; both were patented in 1862. The gun may have been invented because of a suggestion of Colonel R. A. Maxwell that the Union army would require just such a specialized weapon during the coming war. Before the end of that same year, he had produced a working model of this weapon, a hand-cranked .58 caliber version with six barrels, rotated around a central axis. Cartridges dropped from a drum atop the gun and were automatically fed into each barrel. The rate of fire was 350 rounds per minute, but there were problems with accuracy, and the weapon sometimes jammed when fired too rapidly. This was owing in large part to the use of the then-common paper cartridges.

Gatling requested a test of his weapon but was turned down by Brevet Brigadier General James Ripley, then the army's chief of ordnance. Ripley strenuously resisted the testing of any new weaponry and sought to simplify combat logistics by refusing to adopt the great variety of foreign and domestic small arms weapons then in use. Ripley and others may also have suspected Gatling of having southern sympathies.

Gatling persisted, however, despite a disastrous fire in 1863 that destroyed the factory of Miles Greenwood and Company of Cincinnati, the makers of his weapon, and all existing copies of the 1862 version. Soon thereafter, McWhinny, Ringe & Company, another Cincinnati firm, completed twelve copies of the 1862 model, in which Gatling employed copper rim-fire cartridge cases instead of paper. A modest number of Gatlings were put to use by the U.S. Navy in 1862. Major General Horatio Wright, Commander of the Department of Ohio, endorsed Gatling's gun, and Major General Benjamin Butler ordered one dozen of them, which saw limited use in the spring of 1864.

Gatling made specifications of his weapon available to foreign governments, and the French evinced considerable interest late in 1863, requesting a single sample. Gatling offered to sell them 100 guns, but the French declined. Soon thereafter, the U.S. government banned the wartime exportation of weapons and ammunition. However, the War Department under Ripley, who was forced to retire late in 1863, and his successor, Brigadier General George Ramsay, who was reassigned late in 1864, did not change its stance, and a direct appeal for testing made by Gatling to President Abraham Lincoln in that same year was unavailing.

Gatling continued to make improvements in his gun, however, and developed a breech-firing model, which was made for him by the Cooper Fire Arms Manufacturing Company of Frankford, Pennsylvania. This version, which eliminated a gas leak problem, was finally tested at the direction of the new army chief of ordnance, Brigadier General Alexander B. Dyer, early in 1865. The results were generally quite favorable, except for recommendations that changes be made in the rifling of the barrel, that the frame supporting the weapon be strengthened, and that the gun's weight be reduced.

After these modifications were made, the army agreed to adopt the weapon in 1866. One hundred guns were ordered, half with a one-inch caliber, the other half with .50 caliber. The Colt Patent Fire Arms firm, with which Gatling was associated for many years, manufactured the guns at its Hartford, Connecticut, facility. Gatling made further modifications, such as substituting center-fire brass casings for the earlier copper ones, and some of the weapons employed ten barrels rather than six. The U.S. Navy also adopted the improved model Gatlings in 1868, and the wartime ban on exports was lifted, permitting extensive sales abroad. Various Gatling models were widely adopted around the world, notably by the British, French, and Russian armies.

In 1883 a positive cartridge-positioning device, designed by James G. Accles, a Colt employee, took the place of the drum-type gravity feed previously utilized. Gatling himself had moved to Hartford in 1870, and he continued to make improvements in his weapon until he sold his patents and manufacturing rights to the Colt firm in the mid-1880s. Later models were designed to fire 1,200 rounds per minute with the hand crank, and 3,000 rounds per minute when fired with a small electric motor. A gas-operated device soon followed, but neither the electric nor the gas-driven models were adopted by the U.S. Army. The army did utilize some crank-operated Gatlings using .30–40 and .30/06 ammunition in Cuba in 1898, but by that time the weapon was approaching obsolescence. The army declared all Gatlings obsolete in 1911.

In 1886 Gatling invented and spent some years at work developing a steel and aluminum alloy suitable for heavy weapons. An eight-inch model cannon embodying his principles, for which Congress had appropriated $40,000 in 1897, was manufactured by the Otis Steel Works in Cleveland, Ohio. It was then tested by the Ordnance Department at its Sandy Hook proving ground in northern New Jersey early in 1899. The weapon failed when the barrel burst. Although the piece had been fabricated under his general superintendence, Gatling remained convinced until his death that the gun's breech had been sabotaged at the factory.

After this experience Gatling left the field of weaponry and began working again on the agricultural machines with which he achieved his initial business success. He set up a new firm in St. Louis to manufacture a motorized plow he had invented in 1900, but the beginning of production was halted by his death in Hartford.

• Some Gatling materials are in the John Love Papers at the Indiana Historical Society Library. Love was involved for a time in the marketing of Gatling guns in the United States and Europe. The Indiana Historical Society also has research materials collected by Lester M. Busby in the 1960s on Gatling and his gun. The U.S. Patent Office has records of Gatling's patent applications. Published sources include F. Roy Johnson and E. Frank Stephenson, Jr., *The Gatling Gun and Flying Machine of Richard and Henry Gatling* (1979), and Stephenson, *Gatling: A Photographic Remembrance* (1993). See also U.S. Army Ordnance Department, *Report of the Board of Officers . . . on Gatling Guns of Large Caliber, Ordnance Memoranda No. 17* (1874); John H. Parker, *Tactical Organization and Uses of Machine Guns in the Field* (1899); George M. Chinn, *The Machine Gun: History, Evolution, and Development*, vol. 1 (1951); Paul Wahl and Donald R. Toppel, *The Gatling Gun* (1965); and John Ellis, *The Social History of the Machine Gun* (1975). An obituary is in the *New York Times*, 27 Feb. 1903.

KEIR B. STERLING

GATSCHET, Albert Samuel (3 Oct. 1832–16 Mar. 1907), linguist, was born in St. Beatenberg, Switzerland, the son of the Reverend Karl Albert Gatschet and Mary Ziegler. Gatschet received linguistic training at the Universities of Bern and Berlin (1852–1858). His first major publication was a study of the etymologies of Swiss place-names (1867).

After moving to New York in 1868, Gatschet was working as a language teacher and freelance journalist when he became interested in the description and classification of North American Indian languages, beginning with compilations and studies of vocabularies collected on Lieutenant George M. Wheeler's Geographical Survey expeditions to the Southwest (1875, 1876) and the first classification and description of the Yuman family of languages (1877–1892). After being hired by Western explorer and ethnologist John Wesley Powell to do linguistic research for the Geographical and Geological Survey of the Rocky Mountain Region in 1877, Gatschet did his first major field research, on the Klamath language. He became an ethnologist with the Bureau of (American) Ethnology of the Smithsonian Institution when it was organized under Powell in 1879 and continued there until his retirement for health reasons in 1905.

Gatschet made extensive efforts to record information on poorly known North American Indian languages in order to fill out the first comprehensive linguistic classification of them, a major goal of the bureau. He was a principal contributor to this classification, which appeared under Powell's name in 1891. His fieldwork on major language families was chiefly concerned with Muskogean and Algonquian. In 1892 he married Louise Horner; they had no children.

Gatschet's field research in Louisiana, Oklahoma, and in the lower Rio Grande region led to the discovery of a number of distinct remnant languages previously known only by name, if at all. These included Atakapa, Biloxi, Chitimacha, Comecrudo, Cotoname, Natchez, Tunica, and Yuchi, most of which represented isolated, single-language families in the Powell classification. The most astonishing discovery of this kind was the substantial vocabulary of the Karankawa language of Texas he recorded in Lynn, Massachusetts, from a white woman who had learned the language as a child in Texas. His recording of a single two-word phrase of Haname from an aged Tonkawa is the sole documentation of another, apparently distinct language of coastal Texas. Gatschet's work on Juan Pareja's early seventeenth-century studies of the extinct Timucua language of Florida established the distinct nature of this language as well. The discovery of these small families substantially increased the degree of linguistic diversity that had to be recognized for aboriginal North America. Gatschet also demonstrated relationships between distant languages that implied major prehistoric migrations of peoples, notably his showing that Biloxi (on the Gulf of Mexico) and Catawba (in South Carolina) were both related to the Siouan family of the western prairies and plains.

Gatschet made extensive studies of Muskogean traditions, ethnology, and history, in which he combined documentary and field research. He wrote numerous articles on general ethnological and linguistic topics in addition to technical papers. He died in Washington, D.C.

• Gatschet's papers are in the National Anthropological Archives, Department of Anthropology, Smithsonian Institution. His major publications include *Zwölf Sprachen aus dem Südwesten Nordamerikas* (1876); "Der Yuma-Sprachstamm nach den neuesten handschriftlichen Quellen," *Zeitschrift für Ethnologie* 9:341–50, 365–418, 15:123–47, 18:97–22, 24:1–18 (1887–1892); *A Migration Legend of the Creek Indians* (1884); "The Klamath Indians of Southwestern Oregon," *Contributions to North American Ethnology* 2, pts. 1 and 2 (1890); "The Karankawa Indians: The Coast People of Texas," *Papers of the Peabody Museum of American Archaeology and Ethnology, Harvard University* 1, no. 2 (1891): 5–103. A brief account of Gatschet's career is in Curtis M. Hinsley, Jr., *Savages and Scientists* (1981), pp. 177–80, 188. A full obituary is in the Washington *Evening Star*, 16 Mar. 1907. An obituary by James Mooney in *American Anthropologist*, n.s., 9 (1907): 561–70, and the biographical notice by Walter Hough in the *Dictionary of American Biography*, include personal reminiscences of his life and character not found elsewhere, and Mooney has a full, annotated bibliography.

IVES GODDARD

GATTI-CASAZZA, Giulio (3 Feb. 1869–2 Sept. 1940), opera impresario, was born in Udine, Italy, the son of Stefano Gatti, a military officer and later a member of the Italian Parliament, and Ernestina Casazza. After a childhood spent in military garrisons throughout central Italy while his father steadily advanced in rank, Giulio was sent to the National College in Milan, where he studied solfeggio and music theory. From there he was sent to the Arnaldi College, a Jesuit academy in Genoa, and subsequently to the Naval Academy in Leghorn in preparation for a career at sea. Failing to make the grade at the academy ("I studied quite carelessly, demonstrating no special aptitude for my chosen career," he admitted in his memoirs), he transferred to the University of Ferrara, where his parents were then living. He received his naval engineering degree there in 1891. By this time his father had become chair of the governing board of the Teatro Communale, the local opera house, one of several civic responsibilities he assumed in Ferrara.

Two years later, in 1893, when Stefano Gatti became a member of the Italian Parliament and could no longer continue as board chair, his colleagues on the Teatro Communale's governing board awarded the position to his son, then twenty-three years old. There Gatti-Casazza formed the management philosophy with which he would eventually guide two of the most renowned theaters of the twentieth century, the Teatra alla Scala in Milan and the Metropolitan Opera Company in New York.

Refining that philosophy while gaining management experience in Ferrara, Gatti (as he was typically called by colleagues and the press) put the Teatro Communale on a sound financial footing while bringing new works to the area. In 1893, his first season as impresario, he brought Puccini's *Manon Lescaut* and Catalani's *La Wally* to Ferrara, both of which were well attended and roundly acclaimed. In the ensuing four seasons, Gatti brought to the Communale additional operas by Puccini (including *Le villi* and *La bohème*), Mascagni (*I Rantzau* and *Cavalleria rus-*

ticana), and other composers in the then-new verismo genre and in the process gained their respect for his precision and fairness.

Their endorsement would prove valuable when, after five successful seasons at the Teatro Communale during which he "lived continually in the opera house," Gatti was nominated for the directorship of the prestigious La Scala opera house in Milan. In his memoirs, Gatti recalled that when he asked his father whether the challenges of such a momentous leadership position would be beyond his reach at age twenty-eight, Stefano Gatti replied, "My dear young fellow, easy things are made for fools and simpletons. You want my advice? If they indeed offer you the position, accept it."

The offer was confirmed and a relationship cemented between Gatti and the Milanese directors of La Scala during the summer of 1898. But as he knew when he accepted their contract, Gatti had neither a thriving theater nor an opera company per se to oversee: La Scala had shut down entirely the previous year, the city government and influential music patrons having refused to continue subsidizing the opera house after too many seasons of low-quality productions. Yet when Gatti arrived, he found the situation far worse than he had been told. His predecessors, he wrote in his memoirs, had "left not a scrap of written information behind them, and [there was] only a short time ahead of us to prepare for the coming season." Fortunately, however, the same patrons who had brought Gatti to La Scala had also named the equally young Arturo Toscanini as its new musical director. From their first production as impresario and conductor (Wagner's *Meistersinger*, in Dec. 1898), the two men set standards of excellence that would characterize their ten-year partnership at La Scala.

A decade later, across the Atlantic, when the board of directors of New York's Metropolitan Opera Company accepted the resignation of general manager Heinrich Conreid, it was Gatti-Casazza whom the board agreed to approach. Although he was initially reluctant to accept the position ("I did not know America or the English language," he later wrote, "and I was reluctant to leave Italy"), a conversation with Toscanini made him reconsider. The previous year the Metropolitan had also approached Toscanini, but he had declined their offer. But now, he assured Gatti, "If you arrive at an agreement that is suitable to you, I will go to the Metropolitan willingly this time."

When Gatti arrived in New York on 1 May 1908, it "could not have [been] to a colder and more indifferent welcome," he wrote in his memoirs. To his chagrin, he learned that as a result of a split among the Metropolitan's financial backers, a favored insider—Andreas Dippel, a longtime member of the Metropolitan administration—had been given, under the innocuous-sounding title of "administrative manager," a level of authority almost equal to Gatti's in artistic matters. It would take two seasons before Gatti could secure Dippel's resignation and consolidate his position. In the meantime, Toscanini extracted performances from singers and orchestra members that surpassed anything heard previously in New York, causing the leading critics to predict, in the words of the *New York Sun*'s W. J. Henderson, "the beginning of an era in the history of Italian opera" (17 Nov. 1908). The prediction proved accurate for Gatti remained at the Metropolitan for twenty-seven years as general manager and in the process staged more than 5,000 performances of 177 works. Several were New York premieres (Puccini's *La fanciulla del West* [1910], *Il trittico* [1918], and *Turandot* [1926] were among many new works heard at the Metropolitan during Gatti's tenure), and a number were new works by American composers.

Over the years, as the opera stars of one generation passed from the scene, Gatti managed to find newcomers to take their places in the repertoire. When Enrico Caruso, the Metropolitan's brightest star, died suddenly in 1921, Gatti distributed his roles to two younger Italian tenors, Giovanni Martinelli and Beniamino Gigli, who dominated their era as Caruso had his. When Amelita Galli-Curci, the reigning coloratura soprano of the First World War era, lost the bloom of her voice, Gatti signed Lily Pons and again made history. American singers were similarly in Gatti's debt during his long tenure. Two of his many discoveries—the California baritone Lawrence Tibbett, who became one of the most popular singers of the 1930s, and Connecticut-born soprano Rosa Ponselle, whom Gatti had recruited from vaudeville and whose voice invited the comparison "Caruso in petticoats"—were ranked with the greatest European singers of their day.

If the Metropolitan under Gatti reached its artistic and economic zenith in the 1920s, his later years cannot be characterized so favorably. The Great Depression years took their toll in every aspect of the Metropolitan's operations. In his memoirs he likened his predicament during those years to "the captain of a ship caught in a storm." Yet he weathered the challenges long enough to see the opera company through the worst of the economic downturn, formally announcing his retirement in the autumn of 1934. Fittingly, his final words to the Metropolitan audience were heard across the nation on radio in the spring of 1935, during one of the Saturday matinee broadcasts from the Metropolitan's stage—broadcasts that he had inaugurated in partnership with the National Broadcasting Company in the 1931–1932 season.

Gatti-Casazza married twice, the first time to the New Zealand–born soprano Frances Alda; they had no children and divorced in 1928. In 1930 he married the Metropolitan's premiere ballerina, Rosina Galli, who returned with him to Italy when he left the Metropolitan at the close of the 1934–1935 season. He died in Ferrara, his boyhood home.

• Gatti's papers documenting his tenure as general manager are at the Metropolitan Opera Archives in New York City. A similar set of papers reflecting his tenure at the Teatra alla Scala are in that theater's archives. The memoirs of Gatti-Casazza, ghost-written by New York critic Howard Taub-man but personally edited and approved by Gatti himself, first appeared in serialized form in the *Saturday Evening Post* (1933) and were subsequently published as a book under the title *Memories of Opera* (1941). His long career as general manager of the Metropolitan is treated at considerable length in Irving Kolodin, *The Story of the Metropolitan Opera, 1883–1950* (1953), and more recently in Robert Tuggle, *The Golden Age of Opera* (1983). An obituary is in the *New York Times*, 3 Sept. 1940.

JAMES A. DRAKE

GATZKE, Hans Wilhelm (10 Dec. 1915–11 Oct. 1987), historian and university professor, was born in Dülken, Germany, the son of Wilhelm Gatzke, a silk manufacturer, and Else Schwab. Orphaned by the age of seven, he lived with relatives and the parents of friends. Upon completing secondary schooling in Wuppertal, he received a stipend from the German Exchange Service to study in 1934–1935 at Williams College, where he developed an affinity for life in America. Although urged by teachers and friends at Williams to remain, he honored the terms of his grant and returned to Germany, where he studied law first at Munich and then at Bonn. He could not conceal his lack of enthusiasm for the Nazi regime, however, and fell out of favor with authorities to such an extent that his lodging was searched and he was called upon by the Exchange Service to give an account of himself.

Disillusioned, Gatzke made arrangements to visit the United States without telling German officials that he intended to remain there. He returned to the United States early in 1937 and applied for citizenship, which he obtained in 1944. He earned a bachelor's degree in 1938 from Williams College and a master's degree in history in 1939 from Harvard, where he studied primarily under William Langer, continued to work toward a doctorate, and served as teaching fellow and tutor. In 1941–1942 he held a Sheldon Traveling Fellowship, and in 1942 he taught history at Williams College.

U.S. involvement in World War II found Gatzke suspended between citizenships. He had to undergo suspicion as an "enemy alien" and rigorous investigation, which was in part a response to his having edited and translated Karl von Clausewitz's *Principles of War* (1942), before being drafted into the U.S. military in 1943. He served in the Psychological Warfare Division of the U.S. Army's European staff headquarters; helped operate a secret radio station broadcasting into Germany, for which he was rewarded with a commission; and entered Germany with the Third Army in 1945. During another year of service, he was primarily responsible for reviving and supervising radio broadcasting in Hessen.

Returning to the United States in 1946, Gatzke received a Ph.D. from Harvard in 1947 and began a long stint on the faculty of Johns Hopkins University, where he was made associate professor in 1951 and full professor in 1956. In 1950 his dissertation was published as *Germany's Drive to the West: A Study of Germany's War Aims during the First World War*. A pioneering interpretation of the connection between domestic socioeconomic relations and foreign policy, it was based on contemporary published sources and foreshadowed later revisionist arguments by German historians who, unlike Gatzke, had access to official documents. The book was noted for its judiciousness and its conclusion that large sections of Germany's ruling elite had held out for an annexationist victory, that is, for extensive conquests, in order to bolster their dominant position in society, or as Gatzke put it, to assure "the continuation of the existing order, to their own advantage, and to the political and economic detriment of the majority of the German people" (p. 294). It won the American Historical Association's Herbert Baxter Adams Prize in 1950 and made Gatzke's reputation.

After the release of documents that had been captured from the German Foreign Office at the end of World War II, Gatzke undertook a comprehensive study of Gustav Stresemann, foreign minister and leading figure in the government of the Weimar Republic between August 1923 and October 1929. In 1954 he published *Stresemann and the Rearmament of Germany*, a critical but fair-minded reassessment of Stresemann's policies, which Gatzke saw as more devious and nationalistic than had earlier critics. Gatzke became recognized as the authority on the subject and wrote bibliographical articles about the Stresemann papers for the *Journal of Modern History* (26, no. 1 [1954]: 49–59, and 36, no. 1 [1964]: 1–13). His interpretation has remained the standard one.

Gatzke wrote no further monographs but remained prolific. He produced several articles on Russo-German relations in the 1920s, which appeared in the *Vierteljahrshefte für Zeitgeschichte* in the mid-1950s, and many book reviews in such journals as the *American Historical Review* and the *Journal of Modern History*, most of which contributed significantly to historiographical debate in such fields as the life of Hitler, psychohistory, German foreign policy, and German politics during the Weimar and Nazi eras. He also worked with William Langer in revising *An Encyclopedia of World History* (1952); wrote a long article on Europe and the League of Nations for the *Propyläen Weltgeschichte*, edited by Golo Mann (1960); and edited *European Diplomacy Between Two Wars, 1919–1939* (1972). In addition he wrote and revised a brief topical study of world history since 1945, *The Present in Perspective* (1957, 1961, 1965), and coauthored a widely used textbook, *Mainstream of Civilization* (1969, 1974, 1979, 1984).

In 1964 Gatzke joined the faculty of Yale University. In 1969 he succeeded Hajo Holborn as American coeditor on the international team editing for publication the captured German documents, which began appearing in 1949 as *Documents on German Foreign Policy, 1918–1945*. Like Holborn, he worked to enhance German-American understanding. He published "The United States and Germany" in *Current History* (38 [1960]: 6–10) and "The United States and Germany on the Eve of World War I" in *Deutschland in der Weltpolitik des 19. Jahrhunderts* (ed. Immanuel Geiss and Bernd J. Wendt [1973], pp. 271–86). In 1980 he appealed to a wide readership by publishing *Germany and the United States: A Special Relationship?*, which treated aspects of life in postwar Germany as well as German-American relations and exemplify Gatzke's approach:

There has been, and continues to be, mutual criticism, but criticism, if constructive, can be a firmer basis for lasting friendship than mutual admiration. . . . It is rare that relations between nations are wholly harmonious and stable, and to ignore their negative aspects may lead to disappointments, which in turn may cause distrust (pp. 5, 282).

Gatzke gathered many professional honors. He was a member of Phi Beta Kappa, a fellow of the Institute for Advanced Studies at Princeton in 1951–1952, and a member of the board of editors of the *Journal of Modern History* from 1954 to 1957. He won fellowships from the Guggenheim Foundation for 1956–1957 and from the Rockefeller Foundation and the American Council of Learned Societies for 1962–1963. He was a member of the American Committee on the History of the Second World War from 1970 to 1976 and of the Committee for the George Louis Beer Prize (American Historical Association) from 1977 to 1980.

In 1985 nine of Gatzke's former students dedicated to him a festschrift, *German Nationalism and the European Response, 1890–1945* (ed. Carole Fink et al.). Together with Annelise Thimme, the contributors honored him as an exacting scholar, a popular and effective undergraduate teacher, and a demanding and generous graduate mentor who "upheld the highest standards of the profession" and whose seminars were "stimulating laboratories of historical investigation in which German history and European diplomacy are cast in a truly international perspective." Gatzke retired the following year.

One of the younger German émigrés of the 1930s to achieve prominence as scholar and teacher in the United States, Gatzke contributed significantly to knowledge about and understanding of Germany and of Europe in the twentieth century. Through his graduate students he left a reverberating impact on American academic life. Another lasting contribution was his endowment of the Paul Birdsall Prize in European Military and Strategic History, which is awarded biennially by the American Historical Association. Characteristically, he stipulated that his connection with it remain anonymous during his lifetime. Gatzke, who shared the last thirty years of his life with David Gregory, died in New Haven.

• For further biographical details and references to Gatzke's most significant articles and reviews, see the tribute and notes by Carole Fink and Annalise Thimme in the festschrift mentioned above (pp. 267–77). An obituary is in *Perspectives* 26, no. 4 (1988): 14.

C. EARL EDMONDSON

GAUSS, Christian Frederick (2 Feb. 1878–1 Nov. 1951), educator, was born in Ann Arbor, Michigan, the son of Christian Gauss, a baker, and Katherine Bischoff. After receiving his early education at local schools, including instruction in German, his first language, Gauss attended the University of Michigan, earning his B.A. in 1898 and his M.A. the following year. He spent the next two years teaching Romance languages at his alma mater before taking an instructor's position in the same subjects at Lehigh University in Bethlehem, Pennsylvania. In 1902 Gauss married Alice Sarah Hussey, with whom he had four children. Promoted to assistant professor in 1903, he remained at Lehigh until 1905, when he moved to the institution where he spent the rest of his long career—Princeton University.

Brought to Princeton by university president Woodrow Wilson, Gauss served for two years as a preceptor (instructor) and was then appointed professor of Romance languages. An effective teacher, Gauss became chair of the department in 1913, holding that position for a total of twenty-six years (1913–1936, 1943–1946). His teaching made a profound impact on countless numbers of Princeton students, among them Harold R. Medina, Edmund "Bunny" Wilson (who later remembered Gauss as the type of instructor "who starts trains of thought that he does not himself guide to conclusions, but leaves in the hands of his students to be carried on by themselves"), and F. Scott Fitzgerald, all of whom remained in contact with Gauss long after their student days. Gauss managed to avoid discrimination in the anti-German years of World War I and was himself opposed to Germany's aggression. Politically liberal, Gauss through his teachings consistently opposed militant nationalism and fought against what he perceived as an excessive emphasis on American culture in higher education. Seeking to replace nationalistic education with what he termed "moral education," he sought "to whet the appetite of the student and leave him the satisfaction of discovering the truth for himself."

In addition to his teaching duties, Gauss served Princeton as literary editor of the *Alumni Weekly* (1914–1920) and as an officer and trustee of the Princeton University Press. His greatest contribution came in his service as dean of the college, a position he held from 1925 until 1945. A solid administrator, he remained personally popular by advocating student control of campus activities while maintaining order and discipline.

As one of the best-known university administrators in the country, Gauss served in numerous leadership roles outside the Princeton community. He was president of the Dante League of America (1918–1920), an executive council member of the Modern Language Association, and on the executive committee of Phi Beta Kappa. A man of wide-ranging interests and near-encyclopedic knowledge, Gauss was also politically active and a longtime champion of civil rights and academic freedoms. He served as honorary chair of the American Association for a Democratic Germany (a

group seeking to encourage democratic factions as a deterrent to future German aggression) following World War II, as an executive committee member of the National Committee for Democracy and Intellectual Freedom, and as a national committee member of the American Civil Liberties Union. Gauss was no stranger to political controversy; he signed a petition (along with 500 scientists) urging neutrality for the United States prior to Pearl Harbor, and in the postwar years he protested against the U.S. House of Representatives Committee on Un-American Activities, signing another letter to Congress urging the abolition of that body.

Despite his numerous duties, Gauss did not allow his own scholarship to lag. He edited *Selections from Jean Jacques Rousseau* (1914); wrote *The German Emperor as Shown in His Public Utterances* and *Through College on Nothing a Year* (both 1915), *Democracy Today: An American Interpretation* (1917), and *Why We Went to War* (1918); translated (with his wife) Jacques Bainville's *History of France* (1926); and wrote *Life in College* and a critical study of *Madame Bovary* (both 1930) and *A Primer for Tomorrow* (1934). The *Primer* won high praise for its criticisms of current American culture, with George S. Counts referring to the book as "a harbinger of social revolution." His later work included translations of Guglielmo Ferrero's *Women of the Caesars* (1935) and *A Short History of French Literature* (with Charles A. Choquette, 1935). He also contributed to *The City of Man* (1940) and published *The Teaching of Religion in American Higher Education* in the year of his death.

Following his retirement in 1946 Gauss, having survived what he humorously referred to as "an unhappy profession" (that of dean), was named to a newly created office—dean of alumni. He remained active until his sudden death in New York City's Pennsylvania Station.

Hailed in a *New York Times* editorial following his death as "a twentieth-century humanist in the best sense of the word," Gauss exercised a profound influence on two generations of Princeton students through his role as teacher and dean and on countless others through his writings and political activism.

• The papers of Gauss are held at the Princeton University archives. See also *The Papers of Christian Gauss*, ed. Katherine Gauss Jackson and Hiram Haydn (1957). The best secondary source remains "Christian Gauss as a Teacher of Literature," in the prologue to Edmund Wilson's *The Shores of Light* (1952). An obituary is on the front page of the *New York Times*, 2 Nov. 1951.

EDWARD L. LACH, JR.

GAUSS, Clarence Edward (12 Jan. 1887–8 Apr. 1960), U.S. Foreign Service officer, was born in Washington, D.C., the son of Herman Gauss, a U.S. civil servant, and Emilie Julia Eisenman. Gauss's interest in government service was inspired by his father, who worked for the U.S. Bureau of Pensions for forty-five years. Raised in a middle-class home, Gauss attended public schools. After graduating from high school in 1903, he worked as a stenographer for a private Washington law firm and for the Invalid Pensions Committee of the U.S. House of Representatives. In 1906 he began his career in the U.S. State Department.

Initially Gauss worked as a clerk in Washington, but in 1907 the State Department sent him to Shanghai, China, as a deputy consul general. In 1909 the department reassigned him to Washington, D.C., for further diplomatic training. After Gauss passed the foreign service exam, he returned to Shanghai in 1912. In 1917 he married Rebecca Louise Barker at a ceremony held in Yokohama, Japan. They had one son.

Excluding brief assignments at the State Department (1931–1933), the U.S. Embassy in Paris in 1935, and a year's appointment as the first U.S. minister to Australia in 1940, Gauss's foreign service career was passed in China. He served at various ranks in diplomatic posts in Tientsin (1916, 1924–1926, 1927–1931), Amoy (1916–1919), Tsinan (1919–1923), Mukden (1923–1924), Shanghai (1926–1927, 1935–1940), and Peking (1933–1935). His superiors consistently praised Gauss's ability and efficiency. Highlighting the first twenty-five years of his career in China were the two years from 1937 to 1939, when Gauss worked as the consul general in Shanghai during the Japanese invasion and occupation of the city. He assisted Americans who were evacuating the International Settlement in Shanghai as the Japanese assumed military control over the Chinese sections of the city. As president of the Court of Consuls, Gauss also led other foreign embassies in Shanghai's International Settlement and French Concession in diplomatic protests against Japan's expanding military presence until Japan exerted pressure in Washington, D.C., forcing him to retreat from his position of firm resistance to the Japanese aggression.

Gauss's foreign service career in China culminated with his appointment as U.S. ambassador to China in February 1941, at the beginning of one of the most critical periods in U.S. relations with China in the twentieth century. During his tenure as ambassador, the United States declared war on imperialist Japan (and the Fascist powers in Europe) and became China's formal ally in the war China had waged against Japan since July 1937. China's war against Japan, however, was complicated by an internal struggle for power waged by the Chinese Communist party and Chinese Nationalist party forces. The Nationalist party, led by Generalissimo Chiang Kai-shek, controlled China's central government, which the United States formally recognized as the legitimate Chinese government. Although the Chinese Communists and Nationalists had agreed to form a united front alliance against Japan in 1937, intense ideological and political rivalries undermined the alliance. Yet U.S. wartime China policy imperatives demanded that China remain united and focused on strengthening its military resistance to Japan to enable the United States, the Soviet Union, and the Western European Allies to focus their combined military strength on the defeat of the European Axis powers alliance.

Gauss supported U.S. China policy with astute reporting that questioned the political strength and reliability of Chiang's government and with judicious recommendations regarding the amount and types of aid the U.S. government should extend to the Chinese Nationalists. Noting pervasive corruption and inertia, he strongly recommended that U.S. aid to China be granted conditionally, contingent on the Chinese Nationalist government implementing political and social reforms. Chiang challenged his recommendations, which did not meet the Chinese Nationalists' military and economic aid demands. Consequently, Washington policy makers often overrode Gauss's recommendations.

Until early 1944, President Franklin Roosevelt and the U.S. War Department believed that China's participation in the war against Japan was critically important to an Allied power victory, and they cultivated Chiang's cooperation. President Roosevelt sent several emissaries to persuade Chiang to comply with the Allied wartime military strategy. These intermediaries between Roosevelt and Chiang, including White House adviser Lauchlin Currie, Vice President Henry Wallace, Wendell Willkie, and U.S. general Joseph Stilwell, rendered Gauss's position as ambassador almost superfluous. Gauss, however, continued to advocate conditional U.S. financial and military support for the Chinese Nationalists. When Washington strategists determined in January 1944 that victory over Japan could be achieved through attacks on Japanese-held islands in the Pacific rather than in China, they became less solicitous of Chiang and more sympathetic to Gauss's China policy recommendations.

In the summer of 1944 Gauss recommended that the Chinese Communist forces opposing the Japanese army, who were subordinate to the Chinese Nationalist military command and who were therefore dependant on the Nationalists for Allied military aid, be placed under the direct command of General Stilwell, allowing the Communists to receive directly U.S. lend-lease aid. The State Department initially endorsed Gauss's proposal and urged him to present it to Chiang. However, Chiang refused to consider American arming of his rivals, the Chinese Communists, and soon demanded that Washington withdraw General Stilwell from the China military command. President Roosevelt sent his personal representative, Patrick J. Hurley, to soothe Chiang's feelings in the fall of 1944. Hurley supported Chiang's demands for Stilwell's recall, ignored Gauss's recommendations, and resurrected the U.S. policy of appeasing Chiang. After Stilwell was recalled, Gauss, in frustration, resigned as U.S. ambassador to China on 1 November 1944.

Gauss returned to Washington, D.C., and retired from the U.S. Foreign Service on 31 May 1945. In December President Harry Truman appointed him as a director to the Export-Import Bank. During his tenure at the Ex-Im Bank, Gauss testified before several congressional committees regarding pro-Communist sympathies among his U.S. Embassy staff in China. In particular, he was asked to testify regarding the loyalty of his staff secretary, State Department officer John Stewart Service, whom Hurley accused of sabotaging U.S. China policy through his advocacy of a wartime power-sharing arrangement between the Chinese Communist and Nationalist forces. Gauss denied Hurley's accusations and defended his embassy staff. The State Department later awarded Gauss the Medal of Freedom in recognition of his long service in China. After retiring from the Ex-Im Bank in 1952, Gauss moved to Santa Barbara, California, where he died.

Although Gauss had very limited impact on U.S. China policy making during the critical World War II era, he provided the State Department with balanced, well-informed, and accurate assessments of the political situation in Nationalist China. Analyzing the failures of U.S. China policy in the 1940s, historians have recognized the shrewdness of Gauss's political judgments.

• Gauss's papers are in the Department of State Records in the National Archives. See also the Stanley K. Hornbeck Papers at the Hoover Institute, Stanford, Calif.; and the Nelson T. Johnson Papers in the Library of Congress. The published record of Gauss's diplomatic dispatches and correspondence is in U.S. Department of State, *Foreign Relations of the United States*, volumes organized by year and region of the world. A detailed description and an analysis of Gauss's tenure as U.S. ambassador to China are in James L. Durrence, "Ambassador Clarence E. Gauss and United States Relations with China, 1941–1944" (Ph.D. diss., Univ. of Georgia, 1971). Other accounts of Gauss's ambassadorial service are in John S. Service, *The Amerasia Papers: Some Problems in the History of US-China Relations* (1971), and Paul A. Varg, *The Closing of the Door, Sino-American Relations 1936–1946* (1973). An obituary is in the *New York Times*, 9 Apr. 1960.

KAREN GARNER

GAUVREAU, Emile Henry (4 Feb. 1891–15 Oct. 1956), journalist, newspaper editor, and author, was born in Centerville, Connecticut, the son of French-Canadian immigrant parents Alphonse Gauvreau, a New Haven gun factory employee, and Malvina Perron. When he was six years old, a Fourth of July prank by adults crippled his right leg permanently. His family moved to Montreal a year or so later, where his father worked in a bakery. Gauvreau attended the Provencher Academy, run by Jesuits. His accident forced him to wear a leg brace for a few years, which made him more sedentary and interested in both French and English books. When the family returned to New Haven, Gauvreau attended public schools, took odd jobs, studied the flute, drew cleverly, and read widely.

Quitting high school after two years, Gauvreau worked on the *New Haven Journal-Courier*, where he pleased his editors by going after sensational stories about political corruption. He even solved a murder before the police managed to do so. In 1916 he married Sarah Welles Joyner, the *Journal-Courier* society editor; the couple had three children. Gauvreau and his wife moved to Hartford, Connecticut, where he wrote for the *Hartford Courant*. He covered lurid events, published exclusives, and became assistant managing editor. In 1919 he became managing editor. His insistence on publishing accounts of the sales of fake medical diplomas caused a rupture with his editor in chief, so Gauvreau resigned and moved to New York City.

Bernarr Macfadden, the flamboyant physical culturist and publisher, asked Gauvreau to help him establish a daily newspaper, which became the *New York Evening Graphic*. First appearing on 15 September 1924, it was so ribald that it was nicknamed the *Porno-graphic*. Gauvreau tried without success to make money for Macfadden but left him in 1929 and was not surprised when the *Graphic* failed three years later. From 1929 until 1935 Gauvreau worked for William Randolph Hearst's *New York Mirror*. As managing editor, he approved the publication of contests, racing information, and scandalous news items, all in a failing effort to compete with the *New York Daily News*. He also clashed with Walter Winchell, the *Mirror*'s popular Broadway columnist. In 1933 Gauvreau visited the Soviet Union as an observer attached to a congressional mission. When Hearst hired Arthur Brisbane in 1934 and made him Gauvreau's editor, the two men had differences of opinion. When Gauvreau published *What So Proudly We Hailed* in 1935, Hearst regarded it as anti-American and procommunist and discharged him.

Gauvreau became an investigator for the House of Representatives Committee on Patents. Shortly after he began to look into the aircraft industry's practice of sharing patented techniques for their mutual profit, he met the controversial General William "Billy" Mitchell, who had been court-martialed in 1925 for criticizing his superiors' mismanagement of America's infant air force. Gauvreau admired the prophetic aviator, who died in 1936, and later coauthored a biography of Mitchell with Lester Cohen, a fellow journalist. The year 1936 was a busy one for Gauvreau: he was hired by Moses Annenberg, owner of the *Philadelphia Inquirer*, he was divorced by Sally Gauvreau, and he married Winifred G. Rollins, his former secretary at the *Mirror* (the couple had no children). Annenberg assigned Gauvreau to produce sensational rotogravure-section feature stories, and two years later appointed him editor of *Click*, a largely pictorial magazine. In 1940 Gauvreau resigned after arguing with his superiors over working conditions and finances.

During his years as a journalist, Gauvreau often traveled abroad and also found time to write books. His first two were novels. *Hot News* (1931), hastily composed, fast-paced, and verbose, dramatizes events in what Gauvreau calls "tabloidia," behind the scenes in the production of tabloid copy out of corruption, crime, and sex. His second novel, *The Scandal Monger* (1932), concerns the rise and fall of a tabloid columnist, pitted against his vicious managing editor. It was immediately seen to include a scathing portrayal of Winchell. In *What So Proudly We Hailed*, equally splenetic, Gauvreau records his favorable impressions of the paradise-like Soviet Union, where workers are happy and loyal, production is efficient, and children anticipate a glorious future. By contrast, the United States is a land of materialism, corruption, dishonest courts, and lynch law. Reviewers noted that in his novels Gauvreau revealed his abhorrence of tabloid tactics but then employed them in *What So Proudly We Hailed.*

After leaving *Click*, Gauvreau wrote *My Last Million Readers* (1941), an autobiography that candidly presents the phases of his varied career. *Billy Mitchell: Founder of Our Air Force and Prophet without Honor* (1942), though superseded by more balanced, technically more informed biographies that came later, is invaluable because of Gauvreau's personal knowledge and intense admiration of Mitchell. It is vitriolic in its condemnation of Mitchell's superiors. Gauvreau followed this with *The Wild Blue Yonder: Sons of the Prophet Carry On* (1944), which vilifies the industrialists and military men responsible for America's near-fatal unpreparedness in 1941. In this work he notes German and Japanese air efficiency, praises Russian and British war efforts, and calls for a Department of Defense to coordinate separate army, navy, and air force branches. Gauvreau's last book, *Dumbbells and Carrot Strips: The Story of Bernarr Macfadden* (1953), was coauthored with Mary Macfadden, the physical culturist's disillusioned third wife.

In his autobiography, Gauvreau described himself as one who spent his life doing what he detested to make money he did not want to buy things he did not need to impress people he did not like. Nevertheless, his career distinguishes him in the field of tabloid journalism as a bold example and a reformer. Late in life Gauvreau developed a deteriorative brain condition. He died in Suffolk, Virginia.

• The following books illuminate aspects of Gauvreau's journalistic work: Oliver Carlson, *Brisbane: A Candid Biography* (1937; repr. 1970); W. A. Swanberg, *Citizen Hearst: A Biography of William Randolph Hearst* (1961); Lester Cohen, *The New York Graphic* (1964); John Bard McNulty, *Older Than the Nation: The Story of the Hartford Courant* (1964); Thomas M. Nickel, *Click: Innovation or Imitation?* (1976); John Cooney, *The Annenbergs* (1982); and Neal Gabler, *Winchell: Gossip, Power and the Culture of Celebrity* (1994). An obituary is in the *New York Times*, 17 Oct. 1956.

ROBERT L. GALE

GAVIN, Frank Stanton Burns (31 Oct. 1890–20 Mar. 1938), Episcopal theologian and church historian, was born in Cincinnati, Ohio, the son of William James Gavin, a physician, and Laura Adelaide Burns. In 1907 he entered the University of Cincinnati, from which he received the A.B. in 1912. While there he also took courses at Xavier University and at Hebrew Union College. In 1912 Gavin entered the General Theological Seminary in New York City; while there he also studied at Columbia University, where he was a University Fellow in Semitics (1913–1914). He received his M.A. in Semitic languages from Columbia in 1915, his S.T.B. from General Theological in 1915, and his Ph.D. from Columbia in 1922. His dissertation, "Aphraates and the Jews: A Study of the Controversial Homilies of the Persian Sage in Their Relation to Jewish Thought," published in the *Journal of the Society of Oriental Research* in 1923, brought him immediate attention as a scholar.

Ordained a deacon on 15 May 1914 and a priest on 7 April 1915, Gavin began his ministry as rector of St. Luke's Church in Cincinnati, serving there from 1915 until 1917 when he began studies at Harvard University. He received an S.T.M. in 1917 and a Th.D. in 1919. While there he was assistant minister at the Church of St. John the Evangelist in Cambridge; at this time he entered the novitiate of the Society of St. John the Evangelist, sometimes called the Cowley Fathers, although he never took vows. Gavin began his professional teaching career at Nashotah House in Wisconsin, where he was warden of the Collegiate Department (1919–1920) and professor of New Testament (1921–1923). When he went to Nashotah in 1919, the plan was for him and several members of the Society of St. John the Evangelist to conduct the Collegiate Department under the governance of St. Thomas Aquinas House of the Society of St. John the Evangelist. They changed the name of the Collegiate Department, which was sometimes called the Preparatory Department, to the Department of Philosophy, and raised the academic standards. In 1920–1921 Gavin studied contemporary Greek theology in Athens. In 1921 he married Eula Christian Groenier; they had five children. In 1922 he gave the Hale Lectures at Western Theological Seminary in Chicago, Illinois, which were published in 1923 as *Some Aspects of Contemporary Greek Orthodox Thought* and established his reputation as a scholar of Greek Orthodoxy.

In 1923 Gavin joined the faculty of the General Theological Seminary as professor of ecclesiastical history; he held that position until his death. While at General he continued to write and publish. In 1928 he published *The Jewish Antecedents of the Christian Sacraments*, which were his 1927 Chapman Lectures at the S. P. C. K. House in London, England. In these lectures he argued that rudimentary sacramentalism, or at any rate the essential and germinal factors in sacramentalism, not only existed but flourished as an essential part of Judaism. Jewish proselyte baptism, a ceremonial self-immersion, was antecedent to Christian baptism, and the beliefs and practices connected with early Christian baptism can be accounted for by reference only to Judaism and not to any of the mystery religions. Furthermore, the fellowship supper of the Jews, the kiddush, anticipated the Christian Eucharist. Primitive Christian sacramentalism can be adequately explained by reference to the Judaism of Jesus the Jew.

Gavin was recognized as a leading authority on the sacraments. In 1928 Charles Gore and several other English scholars edited *A New Commentary on Holy Scripture, Including the Apocrypha*, and Gavin wrote the essay, "Sacraments in the New Testament." In 1932 he published *Selfhood and Sacrifice: The Seven Problems of the Atoning Life, Addresses on the Words from the Cross*, which argued that life as Jesus lived it was essentially atonement, that Jesus died on the cross "that there should be harmony between God and man, man and man, and man and Nature"; as St. Paul wrote: "God was in Christ, reconciling the world unto Himself" (2 Cor. 5:19). Gavin emphasized that Christ is in the Christian still carrying on the same work. In 1934 he published a pamphlet, *The Church and Society in the Second Century*, in a series called New Tracts for New Times. Here he argued that the primitive church had no interest in reforming the world, but that it wanted to be separate from the world and society. The church was over against the culture.

An Anglo-Catholic, Gavin contributed in 1938 an essay to a volume edited by Bernard Iddings Bell called *Affirmations by a Group of American Anglo-Catholics, Clerical and Lay*. His essay, "Revisions," argued that the expression of the Christian faith must always be revised. "The permanent and unchanging in that Faith once for all delivered to the Saints, if it is to remain permanent and unchanging, must continually express itself in new statement" (p. 151). In 1937 he delivered the Spencer Trask Lectures at Princeton University, which were published as *Seven Centuries of the Problem of Church and State* (1938). Here he discussed the different relationships of church and state in Christian history.

Gavin was active in the ecumenical movement, with a special interest in Episcopal-Eastern Orthodox relations. He was an authority on the Eastern Orthodox communions and wore the Cross of Miron Cristea, bestowed by the Romanian patriarch in 1935. He served as a member of the Theological Commission and the Continuation Committee of the World Conference on Faith and Order and became a counselor to the Presiding Bishop's Advisory Commission on Ecumenical Relations. He attended the World Conference on Faith and Order at Edinburgh, Scotland, in 1937. He died of pneumonia in New York City.

• Gavin's papers are in the Archives of St. Mark's Library at the General Theological Seminary in New York City. Among Gavin's other publications are *The Ideas of the Old Testament* (1923), a manual for students of the Society for the Home Study of Holy Scriptures and Church History; "Eastern Orthodoxy and Marriage," in *An Introduction to the Study of Canon 41* (1935); *The New Idol* (1934); *The Church and Foreign Missions* (1933); "The Catholic Idea of the Eucharist in the First Four Centuries," *Theology* 21 (Oct. 1930): 185–99, and (Nov. 1930): 247–59; "Some Notes on Early Christian Baptism," *Journal of the American Oriental Society* 46 (1926): 15–22; "Some Aspects of Greek Church Life To-day," *Church Quarterly Review* 92 (July 1921): 236–51; and "The Rev. Thomas Bradbury Chandler in the Light of His (Unpublished) Diary, 1775–1785," *Church History* 1 (1932): 90–106. *This Holy Fellowship: The Ancient Faith in the Modern Parish* (1939), edited by Edward Rochie Hardy, Jr., and W. Norman Pittenger, is a collection of essays, mainly by former students, dedicated to Gavin. See also two brief studies of his life and work: Francis J. Bloodgood, "Profile of Frank Gavin (1890–1938), Priest and Scholar," *Historical Magazine of the Protestant Episcopal Church* 29 (1960): 50–55; and "Frank Gavin, Priest and Doctor," *New American Church Monthly* 43 (May 1938): 201–5 (no author is named, but it

was written by a former colleague and a former student). Obituaries are *The Living Church* 98 (30 Mar. 1938): 389, and the *New York Times*, 21 Mar. 1938.

DONALD S. ARMENTROUT

GAVIN, James Maurice (22 Mar. 1907–23 Feb. 1990), army officer, was born James Ryan in New York City. His parentage is uncertain, but his mother was probably Katherine Ryan, an Irish immigrant; his father is unknown. A ward of the city, he was adopted in 1909 by Martin Gavin, a coal miner, and his wife, Mary Terrel, of Mount Carmel, Pennsylvania, and given their name. In April 1924 he enlisted in the U.S. Army, and in 1925 he was admitted to the U.S. Military Academy after passing a special entrance examination for enlisted men. He graduated in 1929 and was commissioned a second lieutenant in the infantry. On 5 September 1929 he married Irma Baulsir; they had one daughter.

Gavin was initially assigned to flight school at Brooks Field, Texas, but after failing the flight course he was transferred to the 25th Infantry Regiment at Camp Jones, Arizona, in December 1925. In 1932–1933 he studied at the Infantry School at Fort Benning, Georgia. Beginning in 1933 Gavin served successively with the 29th Infantry Regiment at Fort Sill, Oklahoma, the 57th Infantry Regiment at Fort William McKinley in the Philippine Islands, and the 7th Infantry Regiment at Vancouver Barracks, Washington, Fort Lewis, Washington, and Camp Ord, California. He was made a first lieutenant in 1934 and was promoted to captain in June 1939. He was a tactical instructor at West Point in 1940–1941.

In 1941, convinced of the growing importance of airborne warfare, Gavin decided to be a paratrooper, training at Fort Benning. In August 1941 he was appointed a company commander in a parachute battalion. Soon after he was promoted to major and he made plans and training officer of the Provisional Airborne Group. In this post Gavin wrote the army's first field manual for airborne operations, utilizing information gleaned from the writings and experiences of the Germans and the Russians and his own innovations, especially in training, small-unit tactics, and unit organization up to the regimental level. After the United States entered World War II in December 1941, he completed the accelerated course at the Command and General Staff School at Fort Leavenworth, Kansas, and in the summer of 1942 he was given command of the 505th Parachute Regiment and promoted to colonel. During the next months Gavin practically created the regiment from scratch, putting his men through an intensive training program at Fort Benning and Fort Bragg in North Carolina.

Gavin's regiment was deployed to North Africa in May 1943 as part of the 82d Airborne Division, and in July 1943 he and the regiment made their first combat drop spearheading the Allied invasion of Sicily. Two months later Gavin's regiment participated in the invasion of Italy, dropping onto the beach at Salerno to reinforce the stalled Allied forces. In September 1943 he was promoted to brigadier general, and after briefly serving as assistant commander of the 82d Airborne he went to England to assist in the planning for the airborne phase of the Normandy invasion. He rejoined the 82d Airborne in February 1944, and on 6 June he led the division's assault section in the D-Day invasion, helping to keep German reinforcements from reaching the Allied beachhead and the landing forces to move inward.

In August 1944 Gavin was given command of the 82d Airborne, making him at age thirty-seven the army's youngest division commander, and in September he participated in Operation Market-Garden, a failed combined ground-air offensive in Holland. Thereafter Gavin, who was promoted to major general in October, led his division through the Battle of the Bulge in December 1944–January 1945 and in the Allied drive across Germany until the end of the war in Europe in May 1945.

Gavin returned to Fort Bragg with the 82d Airborne in December 1945 and remained in command until March 1948, when be became chief of staff of the Fifth Army at Chicago, Illinois. In July 1948, his first marriage having ended in divorce the year before, he married Jean Emert Duncan; they had four daughters. In April 1949 Gavin was appointed to the Weapons Systems Evaluation Group in the Office of the Secretary of Defense. Two years later he was named chief of staff of allied forces in southern Europe, headquartered in Naples, Italy, an assignment he held until December 1952. After commanding the Seventh Corps in Germany, Gavin was named assistant chief for plans and operations in the Department of the Army in 1954. The following year, now a lieutenant general, he became the army's chief of research and development. Dissatisfied with President Dwight D. Eisenhower's emphasis on nuclear weapons at the expense of conventional forces, Gavin argued for an expanded limited war capability that would provide the United States with a flexible response to world crises. At the same time he disliked serving under General Maxwell Taylor, the army chief of staff. The two men, both famous paratrooper generals, had long been rivals, and by this time a sharp personality clash had developed between them. Unwilling to acquiesce in Eisenhower's policies and angered by Taylor's refusal to support him in his opposition to the administration, Gavin retired in January 1958 and several months later published *War and Peace in the Space Age*, a summary of his views on the need to strengthen America's conventional forces.

After leaving the army, Gavin became an executive with Arthur D. Little, Inc., an industrial research and management consulting firm. He took leave from Little in 1961 when President John F. Kennedy appointed him ambassador to France, returning to the firm in the fall of 1962 because of the heavy drain the ambassadorship made on his personal finances. As the United States escalated its involvement in the Vietnam War in the 1960s, Gavin, who had resisted intervention while still in the army, was a prominent critic of the American military effort. Advocating an "enclave strategy" as a prelude to withdrawal, a position strongly criticized by Taylor and other supporters of the war, he charged that the nation was committing too many of its resources to the war to the detriment of its global responsibilities and domestic needs, and he urged early negotiations to end the war. In *Crisis Now*, a book he wrote with Arthur Hadley in 1968, Gavin called for America to end the war and to revitalize its decaying cities and help the poor. He retired in 1977. He published *On to Berlin*, an account of his experiences during World War II, in 1978.

Gavin's reputation rests on his service as a paratrooper. He was a pioneer in developing airborne tactics, and in combat he was a skillful, tough-minded, and courageous leader. He died in Baltimore, Maryland.

• Gavin's papers and an oral history are in the U.S. Army Military History Institute, Carlisle Barracks, Pa. His other major published work is *Airborne Warfare* (1947). T. Michael Booth and Duncan Spencer, *Paratrooper: The Life of Gen. James M. Gavin* (1994), is a valuable biography. References to Gavin's service during World War II are in Clay Blair, *Ridgway's Paratroopers: The American Airborne in World War II* (1985), and Gerard Devlin, *Paratrooper* (1979). His opposition to the Vietnam War is discussed in Robert Buzzanco, "The American Military's Rationale against the Vietnam War," *Political Science Quarterly* 101 (1986): 559–76. An obituary is in the *New York Times*, 25 Feb. 1990.

JOHN KENNEDY OHL

GAY, Ebenezer (15 Aug. 1696–18 Mar. 1787), clergyman, was born in Dedham, Massachusetts, the youngest son of Nathaniel Gay, farmer and carpenter, and Lydia Lusher. Nathaniel Gay, a strong supporter of education in the conservative, agrarian community of Dedham, made certain that Ebenezer was thoroughly prepared for Harvard College. In 1710 Gay entered the Harvard of president John Leverett (1662–1724)—an institution very much caught up in the rational, empirical spirit of the early English Enlightenment. Here Gay was exposed to the works of seventeenth-century English Latitudinarians such as Archbishop John Tillotson, as well as to the techniques of scriptural criticism practiced by Dr. Samuel Clarke. Imbued with this "catholick" spirit, Gay graduated in 1714 with a reputation as a serious, hardworking scholar. From 1714 to 1717 he taught in grammar schools in Dedham, Hadley, and Ipswich, returning to Cambridge to take his second degree in 1717. On 11 June 1718 Gay was ordained and settled in the pastorate of the First Parish in Hingham, a prospering town on the South Shore of Massachusetts Bay. In 1719 he married Jerusha Bradford of Duxbury. They had eleven children.

Gay's extraordinarily successful pastorate at Hingham's "Old Ship" church would last for sixty-nine years (1718–1787). Hingham became increasingly commercialized in these years, as its farming economy became secondary to shipping, the fishing industry, and numerous small milling concerns. By 1730 Gay had become an integral member of the commercial, landholding elite that would dominate Hingham's sociopolitical life throughout the eighteenth century. During the 1730s Gay's preaching moved away from its earlier Calvinistic orientation to an increasingly unapologetic Arminianism. This emphasis on human ability and striving meshed very effectively with the South Shore's modernizing economy. Preaching to mariners and merchants, Gay insisted, on the one hand, that all (as on a ship) should keep their proper place, but, on the other hand, he also encouraged those with "superior abilities and attainments" to "outstrip" their fellow Christians (Wilson, p. 199).

Gay's importance in the development of liberal Christianity was acknowledged by nineteenth-century Unitarians such as Theodore Parker, yet Parker and others were a bit unsure about the precise nature of Gay's contributions. The reason for the confusion was that Gay was rarely a controversial figure such as his dear friend and sometimes protégé, Jonathan Mayhew. Instead, he disseminated his rationalist, Arminian theology through the great number of Harvard graduates who, from the 1720s through the 1780s, came to study with him and prepare for their second degree. Many of these younger clergymen were more outspokenly Arminian than their rather austere and reserved mentor.

New England's Great Awakening (1740–1742) propelled Gay out of his relatively peaceful Hingham ministry into the thick of ecclesiastical and theological controversy. Although he controlled and even profited from the religious revival in Hingham, he was appalled by the social disruption that the Awakening engendered. He actively joined with his old friend Charles Chauncy (1705–1787), assistant minister at Boston's First Church, in organizing Old Light opposition to the great revivalist George Whitefield and the "enthusiasts." In January 1745 Gay drafted a condemnation of Whitefield and mobilized many of the South Shore ministers to support it. This "Weymouth Testimony" indicted Whitefield as the "grand source" of the challenge to the social order and its established ministry; it also condemned him for the way in which he "disparag'd *Humane Reason* and *Rational Preaching*" (Wilson, p. 112).

By 1750 Gay had turned the South Shore not only into a bastion of opposition to New Light preaching, but, more significantly, into a region that actively promoted and defended a more liberal version of Christianity. Gay's visibility increased after he was selected to deliver the annual election sermon in 1745 and the convention sermon in 1746. In the latter sermon, he not only condemned lay exhorters and New Light separatism, but he directly attacked Calvinism, defiantly restating the doctrines of grace in Arminian terms. In 1747 Gay preached the ordination sermon when the controversial Mayhew was settled at Boston's West Church. As Gay's influence grew, he made certain that the group of ministers who constituted the Hingham Association (later called the Bay Association) was dominated by young liberals such as Lemuel Briant, the outspokenly Arminian pastor at Braintree.

During the 1750s the struggle between Calvinist orthodoxy and the adherents of "Christian Liberty" intensified. Gay led or participated in a number of ecclesiastical councils in which he defended ministers under attack for their liberal, Arminian views. When Gay, Mayhew, and Chauncy attended these councils, they seemed less concerned with moderating passions than with championing the cause of enlightened Christianity. Gay's reputation reached its zenith in 1759, when he delivered Harvard's Dudleian Lecture on *Natural Religion as Distinguish'd from Revealed. Natural Religion* provided the first comprehensive ideology for the liberal Christian ministry of the eighteenth century. In the lecture Gay defended the importance of an educated ministry, of human ability to exercise free will responsibly, and of the primacy of natural religion over revelation. The Dudleian Lecture further stamped Gay as the éminence grise of the Arminian party.

Gay remained active as a pastor and scholar until his death in Hingham. In the 1780s he permitted William Hazlitt, an avowed Socinian and father of the English critic of the same name, to preach frequently in the Hingham pulpit. Unlike many of his fellow religious liberals, Gay remained openly loyal to the Crown during the revolutionary years. Though he and his family suffered for their loyalism, the old parson managed to retain his pulpit, even living long enough to regain the affection of his flock.

Gay's ministry virtually spanned the eighteenth century. Ordained in the presence of Cotton Mather, Gay moved from a Latitudinarian Calvinism to a fully developed rationalist, Arminian theology and was succeeded in his Hingham pulpit by Henry Ware, Sr. (1764–1845), who would preside over the liberal theological revolution at Harvard in the early nineteenth century. During the mid- to late 1700s, Gay could properly be called the philosopher of Massachusetts rationalism.

• Although Gay's personal manuscript legacy is slender, the Gay family papers, most of which are held in the Special Manuscript Collections of the Butler Library at Columbia University, are quite useful. The Hingham First Church and Parish Records are deposited with the Massachusetts Historical Society. The most complete and recent assessment of Gay's career is Robert J. Wilson III, *The Benevolent Deity: Ebenezer Gay and the Rise of Rational Religion in New England, 1696–1787* (1984). The most useful general study of religious liberalism in eighteenth-century New England remains Conrad Wright, *The Beginnings of Unitarianism in America* (1955).

ROBERT J. WILSON III

GAY, E. Jane (1830–1919), author, was born in Nashua, New Hampshire, the daughter of Ziba Gay and Mary Kennedy, farmers. Jane Gay, who never used her first name, "Eliza" as entered by her father or "Elizabeth" as she wrote in her last will in 1916, left home at the age of twenty. However, she remained devoted to her family. Gay was educated at schools in Troy and Brooklyn, New York, but most notably at

Miss Willard's School in Troy, the most advanced female academy of its day. She taught school in Knoxville, Tennessee, in 1855 and opened a school for young ladies in Macon, Georgia, the following year. She moved in 1860 to Washington, D.C., where she opened a school for small children. A Yankee schoolmarm with strong antislavery feelings, Gay in 1861 worked for Dorothea Dix caring for the Union wounded, gathering the sentiments and information that later infused *The New Yankee Doodle* (1868). She tutored the grandchildren of President Johnson at the White House in 1866.

E. J. Gay's *The New Yankee Doodle* was published by William O. Bourne in New York City and attributed to "Truman Trumbull, A. M." on the title page. It was a 341-page doggerel verse epic in "Yankee Doodle" format featuring detailed day-to-day chronicles of the Civil War by someone who had a close view of the ugliest aspects of the war and was close, as well, to the administration in Washington. The poem, featuring the rude, jingly style and roughness typical of doggerel and of its namesake "Yankee Doodle," was filled with hundreds of documentary footnotes. Gay wrote of the intertwined emotional and political agony of a war bounded by intricate political anomalies and constraints. She commented harshly on prison camps, war events, politics, and atrocities such as the killing of African-American soldiers by Confederates. She wrote of patriotism toward Lincoln as a war president and ardent advocacy of freedom and rights for blacks. At one point in the narrative Old Abe says to farmer patriot Jonathan, "And here again we disagree— / That is the tender spot,— / I'd like to have *all men* go free, / The Copperheads would not. / When I suggested *buying* slaves, / Their scowl did not relax, sir; 'Buy niggers!' was the hue and cry, / they wouldn't pay the tax sir" (p. 198). Claims that Confederates whittled Yankee bones, documented by a Senate report and described by other northern poets, are connected to scenes of Jefferson Davis auditing southern accounts within sound of the groans of the wounded and dying. The strength of the doggerel texture and the documentary history makes this poem compellingly unpalatable. It went unrecognized in its day, and Gay's revised edition, once possessed by Miss Dodge, is now lost.

Gay became a clerk in the Dead Letter Office from 1866 through 1883, "seventeen years in a penitentiary," according to her description. She knew the Nicolay and Adams families among others of the Washington "Cave Dwellers," an inner circle of powerful intelligentsia in the 1860s and 1870s, and she entertained them often in company with her niece and namesake Jane Gay Dodge. In 1888 she reencountered Alice Fletcher, a classmate at a Brooklyn boarding school for girls, and went with her as cook and photographer (since no more formalized job was possible) to the Nez Percé Indian Reservation in Idaho, where they lived from 1889 to 1892. She recorded her observations and experiences in letters, which were then compiled as notes and photographs titled *Choup-nit-ki*, the single bound copy now preserved in the Schlesin-

ger Library at Radcliffe; it was the basis for *With the Nez Perces*, published in 1981 by the University of Nebraska Press in a series of Plains and Indians sociological works. In the letters to her friends at home, which make up the volume, Gay recorded ironically how the Indians were taught the Declaration of Independence (p. 33), confusing them almost as much as having a woman conduct agency business, unlike their own women and "civilized white women," who naturally stayed at home when any matter touching on their own interests was discussed; they were likewise impressed that they were not consulted in the disposition of their own tribal lands (p. 48–49). She concluded that raising the tribal level up to U.S. citizenship would mystify the Kolkartzot tribe similarly because the "[Indian] Agency grip" has "succeeded in gelatinizing the Indian's backbone until he lies limp and inert in his degradation" (p. 116).

With her niece Emma Gay, E. Jane Gay moved to England in 1906, becoming friends with Dr. Caroline Sturge, a leading suffragist. The three lived together in London until 1909 and then removed to Bristol for Gay's health, remaining throughout the war years. Gay was surrounded by devoted friends during her final years, active and vigorous in her sixties and seventies; her niece carefully noted that she wore elegant clothes to please Dr. Sturge and Emma after having been her own seamstress for years. She died in Somerset, Sussex.

In a later era Gay would have numbered among the most forceful intellects of her generation and might have developed a career of some magnitude. In her time she ended her days in obscurity in an English garden. The "American" characteristics of *The New Yankee Doodle* as an epic treatment of the Civil War by a northeasterner and the literary characteristics of the epic as a doggerel verse narrative based on "Yankee Doodle" call for recognition, as do her sociological insights.

• The E. Jane Gay Collection at the Idaho State Historical Society and the Gay collection and Jane Gay Dodge's materials at the Schlesinger Library of Radcliffe College provide significant archives of material, with some letters in the Dorothea Dix Collection at Radcliffe. *With the Nez Perces, Alice Fletcher in the Field, 1889–1892* (1981), contains a valuable introduction and notes by Frederick E. Hoxie and Joan T. Mark. Excerpts from *The New Yankee Doodle* are in David E. E. Sloane, *The Literary Humor of the Urban Northeast, 1830–1890* (1983), pp. 182–201.

DAVID E. E. SLOANE

GAY, Frederick Parker (22 July 1874–14 July 1939), bacteriologist, was born in Boston, Massachusetts, the son of George Frederick Gay, the owner of a wholesale grocery business, and Louisa Maria Parker. After graduating from the Boston Latin School, he matriculated at Harvard University. During the summer of 1894 he accompanied the Arctic explorer Frederick Albert Cook on one of his expeditions and was shipwrecked in Greenland while returning home; he became a minor celebrity in Boston after the account of his ordeal was published in the local newspapers. He received his A.B. in 1897 and enrolled in the Johns Hopkins University Medical School.

In 1899 Gay traveled to the Philippine Islands where, as both a volunteer soldier and a member of the university's Medical Commission, he campaigned against Emilio Aguinaldo's Filipino freedom fighters while conducting field studies of cholera and dysentery. In 1901 he received his M.D. from Johns Hopkins, as well as the first fellowship ever granted by the Rockefeller Institute for Medical Research. The same year he also accepted a position as assistant demonstrator of pathology at the University of Pennsylvania, where he used his fellowship to conduct clinical studies of bacillary dysentery and childhood diarrheal diseases.

In 1903 Gay traveled to Brussels, Belgium, to conduct research in the newly emerging field of immunology at the Pasteur Institute of Brabant with Jules Bordet, the discoverer of immunity factors in blood serum and later winner of the 1919 Nobel Prize for Physiology or Medicine. Except for a brief return to the United States in 1904 to marry Catherine Mills Jones, with whom he had four children, he worked closely with Bordet for the next three years while studying the nature of the antibodies in blood complement that can break down red blood cells as well as kill bacterial intruders. In 1906 he returned to the United States to become the bacteriologist at the Danvers (Mass.) Insane Hospital, and the next year he accepted a position as instructor of pathology at the Harvard Medical School. He continued to study the antibodies in blood complement and in 1908 published several articles that focused on the role they played in anaphylaxis, the phenomenon whereby an organism becomes more susceptible to, rather than immunized against, particular bacteria after being exposed to blood serum containing that bacteria. In 1909 he made a signal contribution to the development in the United States of bacteriology and immunology as disciplines in their own right rather than minor branches of the more general field of pathology by translating Bordet's *Studies in Immunology* into English.

In 1910 Gay accepted a position as professor of pathology at the University of California. Although he conducted investigations into the causes of several infectious diseases, including syphilis and polio, his primary line of research involved developing a means of typhoid immunization. By experimenting extensively with rabbits, he learned how typhoid fever spreads through an organism and was able to develop a vaccine containing several different antibodies that, after a couple of intravenous injections, could treat typhoid fever. The bulk of his work in this regard was published in several articles which were collected and published as *Typhoid Fever Considered as a Problem of Medical Science* (1918). In 1918 he joined the U.S. Army and served during World War I as a major in the Medical Corps, stationed primarily at the Yale University Medical School, until his discharge the next year. In 1921 he engineered a reorganization of his department so that a separate Department of Bacteriology, with himself as its first director, was created.

In 1923 Gay became the executive officer of the Department of Bacteriology at Columbia University and a professor of bacteriology in both the College of Physicians and Surgeons of the Medical School and the Faculty of Pure Science. His own research interests now focused on local and general immunity, and he conducted a number of studies regarding bacterial infection and immunity in streptococcus and other infectious diseases. He also studied the relationship between herpes and encephalitis and offered evidence that in some cases the cause of the former was also the cause of the latter. In the 1930s he returned to the Philippines as part of the Leonard Wood Memorial Commission for the Eradication of Leprosy, a disease transmitted by bacteria, to survey its leper colonies. In 1935 he and his staff at Columbia coauthored *Agents of Disease and Host Resistance*, an exposition of both the problems faced by and the progress achieved in the fields of bacteriology and immunology. His last book-length publication appeared in 1938 when he wrote *The Open Mind*, a biography and collection of the papers and ideas of his longtime collaborator and friend Elmer Ernest Southard. He died in New Hartford, Connecticut.

Gay chaired the National Research Council's Medical Section from 1922 to 1923 and its Medical Fellowship Board from 1922 to 1926. He also served as chairman of the Advisory Committee on Research of the Leonard Wood Memorial Foundation and was made a commander in the Order of the Crown of Belgium. He was elected to the National Academy of Sciences in 1939.

Gay contributed to the advancement of medicine in the United States in three ways. His investigations into the cause and prevention of a number of communicable diseases shed much light on the pathogenic nature of certain bacteria. His development of a vaccine for treating typhoid fever was a major advance in the fight against that deadly disease. His most important contribution was the role he played in establishing the study of bacteriology and immunology as separate disciplines in this country.

• Although Gay's papers have not been collected in a repository, some of his letters can be found in the Rufus Ivory Cole Papers in the American Philosophical Society's archives in Philadelphia, Pa. A good biography and a complete bibliography of his work appear in A. R. Dochez, "Frederick Parker Gay," National Academy of Sciences, *Biographical Memoirs* 28 (1954): 99–116. An obituary is in the *New York Times*, 15 July 1939.

CHARLES W. CAREY, JR.

GAY, Sydney Howard (22 May 1814–25 June 1888), journalist and abolitionist, was born in Hingham, Massachusetts, the son of Ebenezer Gay, a politician and banker, and Mary Alleyne Otis. He was taught respect for his New England heritage and had a sense of civic duty that he found both burdensome and inspiring in later life. Gay's father—a prominent local figure who had great expectations of his children—announced to Gay while Gay was still young that he would enter the legal profession and set him on an appropriate course of study at Hingham's Derby Academy.

Gay enrolled at Harvard in the fall of 1829, but poor health and a recurring sense of melancholy led him to withdraw after his sophomore year. Against his father's wishes, Gay determined to become a merchant, and in 1832 he found employment as a clerk in the Boston mercantile house of Perkins and Company. Despite moderate success there, however, a respiratory ailment forced his resignation in early 1834. His doctors recommended a change of climate, and thus Gay began what would become a long period of wandering: visiting relatives in Charleston, South Carolina (where the evils of slavery made no apparent impression upon him), idling away a year in China, and finally—in the fall of 1836—venturing west with the intention of making his fortune from a family loan. After floundering in business schemes in Illinois, Missouri, and Louisiana, he returned to Hingham in the spring of 1838 with no money, no career, and no apparent aim for the future.

Adrift and well into adulthood, Gay entirely "lacked a set of values—an ideology—to give meaning and purpose to his life" (Goerler, p. 165). But in the winter of 1838–1839, having failed in all his endeavors to gain material wealth, he removed himself "from the temptations of the world and its vanities" (letter to Elizabeth Neall, quoted in Goerler, p. 161) and immersed himself in reading and reflection; he emerged in the spring of 1839—to his family's great surprise—as an abolitionist. Before this time, he had managed to avoid the strong current for reform in Boston, Massachusetts, later claiming that before 1838 he "had never seen an anti-slavery paper, had never read an anti-slavery book" (letter to Edmund Quincy, quoted in Goerler, p. 124). Indeed, he had even been hostile to abolitionists, writing in February 1838, "I look upon every one of this class of fanatics . . . as either fools or knaves" (letter to Frances May, quoted in Goerler, p. 169). Gay's parents had previously expressed some genteel interest in the movement, but they were by no means fully committed; after his conversion, however, their son suddenly emerged from his lethargy to become a radical.

After briefly teaching in Hingham and joining local abolitionist activities—in 1842 he began lecturing for the American Anti-Slavery Society—Gay attended the society's national convention in New York in May 1843. That summer he joined Frederick Douglass and others on an abolitionist crusade in the West, and the open hostility they met there seems only to have strengthened his antislavery conviction.

In May 1844, at the recommendation of Wendell Phillips, Gay took over editorship of the *National Anti-Slavery Standard*, the New York–based journal of the American Anti-Slavery Society. Before Gay's tenure (in 1840) the society's executive committee and therefore the *Standard* itself—which purportedly had the mission of promoting harmony among abolitionists—had come under the control of the radical abolitionists under Boston's William Lloyd Garrison. Still intended to appeal to a broader and more moderate audience than Garrison's own *The Liberator*, the *Standard* nonetheless relied heavily on Garrison's support and therefore had to please both his faction and more moderate readers; as a result of these unusual pressures the paper suffered, going through three managing editors in the four years preceding Gay's tenure. Working feverishly, Gay charted a middle political course and turned the *Standard* around. He maintained the paper's integrity, added a literary page, and boosted sales, winning the praise of the society's leaders.

Relatively happy and secure for the first time, Gay in 1845 married Elizabeth Neall, herself an agent of the Pennsylvania Anti-Slavery Society. Committed in personal as well as professional life, the couple helped fugitive slaves escape into Canada. Together they had three children, the first of whom died in infancy, a loss that contributed greatly to the depression that still occasionally beset Gay. Melancholy, bouts of illness, and overwork all contributed to his decision to resign from the *Standard* in May 1858.

The *New York Tribune*, a powerful Republican paper, immediately offered Gay a position as librarian and occasional editorialist. He was promoted to managing editor in 1862, and, reinvigorated, flung himself into his work during the war years; his great accomplishment at the *Tribune* was to keep the primary slant of the paper prowar despite owner Horace Greeley's continual disparagement of president Abraham Lincoln's administration and eventual questioning of the war effort itself. Gay himself, however, did not always support the president: true to his abolitionist convictions, he took an August 1862 invitation to the White House—intended as a showing of thanks for his support—as an opportunity to criticize Lincoln personally for his ongoing reluctance to declare slavery at an end. While pragmatic in his full support of the federal government's effort to win the war, Gay nonetheless remained faithful to his ideals in writing that "No abolitionist condemns our Northern oppression of negroes one whit less than he does Southern slavery" (*New York Tribune*, 21 Mar. 1862) and in continually reprimanding the Union army for paying black soldiers less than whites. In the summer of 1865, with the war won, Gay—on the verge of a physical breakdown—resigned.

After two years spent on Long Island recovering his health, in 1867 Gay became managing editor of the *Chicago Tribune*, remaining there until 1871. He helped that city recover from its devastating fire of that year, writing the first report of the Chicago Relief Committee, but then returned east as a member of William Cullen Bryant's *New York Evening Post*. He turned his attention to larger projects, collaborating with Bryant on a popular national history and also writing his own study, *James Madison* (1884).

Gay died on Staten Island, New York, but his body was carried to Hingham for burial with the family of which he had long struggled to be worthy. After beginning life aimlessly, he had placed himself at the forefront of the greatest moral issue of his time. While other New York journalists made their compromises with American slavery, Gay led both the peacetime *Standard* and the wartime *Tribune* in a crusade to see it eradicated.

• Gay's papers are at the Massachusetts Historical Society and the New York Public Library; relevant documents are also with the Gay family papers at the Butler Library, Columbia University. Raimund E. Goerler, "Family, Self, and Anti-Slavery: Sydney Howard Gay and the Abolitionist Commitment" (Ph.D. diss., Case Western Reserve Univ., 1975), is a complete history of Gay's private and public evolution into a dedicated activist and also contains a thorough bibliography. Aileen S. Kraditor, *Means and Ends in American Abolitionism: Garrison and His Critics on Strategy and Tactics, 1834–1850* (1967), provides excellent background on the split in the abolitionist movement that preceded the founding of the *Standard*; Gay's years at the *New York Tribune* are chronicled in Louis Starr, *Reporting the Civil War: The Bohemian Brigade in Action* (1954), pp. 104–34.

W. FARRELL O'GORMAN

GAYARRÉ, Charles Étienne Arthur (9 Jan. 1805–11 Feb. 1895), historian and politician, was born Carlos Esteban Gayarré in New Orleans, the Creole son of Don Carlos Gayarré, a wealthy slaveholding planter, and Marie Elizabeth de Boré. He spent his early years on the sugar plantation of his slaveholding maternal grandfather. In 1825 he graduated from the College of Orleans in New Orleans. In 1826 he published a pamphlet favoring a continuation of capital punishment. From 1826 to 1828 he studied law in a law office in Philadelphia, passing the bar there in 1828. A year later he returned to New Orleans, where he passed the Louisiana bar and also prepared his *Essai historique sur la Louisiane* (2 vols., 1830–1831), which was an abridged translation of François-Xavier Martin's *History of Louisiana* (1828). Some six hundred copies were distributed to state school boards by order of the state legislature, to which in 1830 Gayarré was elected to represent New Orleans. He was appointed assistant attorney general in 1831 and the following year became the presiding judge of the New Orleans City Court. For the remainder of his life, he was called "Judge."

Gayarré was elected to the U.S. Senate in 1835. His political career, however, was delayed by bronchial asthma. Unable even to remain seated for short periods in Congress, he sought medical help in France, where he remained until 1843. While abroad he continued research into Louisiana history and collected pertinent documents. He also met King Louis Philippe, who had once visited Boré, Gayarré's grandfather. After returning to Louisiana Gayarré married Annie Sullivan Buchanan, a well-to-do widow, in 1844; they had no children. (In his youth Gayarré had fathered a son by an African-American woman. He gave his name to the boy.) Gayarré was reelected to the

state legislature in 1844 and soon was urging his fellow legislators to vote to annex Texas. From 1846 to 1853, during part of which time he continued to serve in the legislature (until 1848), he was Louisiana's secretary of state, supervising public education, building up the state library, and helping control state banks. In 1847, at his request, the state legislature appropriated $2,000 to buy copies of documents in Spain relating to Louisiana.

Gayarré revised and enlarged his *Essai historique* as *Histoire de la Louisiane* (2 vols., 1846–1847). This work reproduced parts of documents in their original form and laid the extensive groundwork for his slightly fictionalized *Romance of the History of Louisiana: A Series of Lectures* (1848), and for its expansion, titled *Louisiana: Its Colonial History and Romance* (1851). He followed with *Louisiana: Its History as a French Colony* (1852) and incorporated both works into *History of Louisiana* (4 vols., 1854–1866), the fourth volume of which is *History of Louisiana: The American Domination* (1866).

His massive accomplishment was highly regarded by Gayarré's professional peers and proved immensely popular, as is demonstrated by the fact that a second edition appeared in 1866, a third in 1879, a fourth in 1885 (with maps), and a fifth in 1903 (with a biography of Gayarré by his friend, the southern writer Grace Elizabeth King, and a bibliography by William Beer). The first two volumes, later subtitled *The French Domination*, covered the years 1492 to part of 1769; the third volume, subtitled *The Spanish Domination* and considered the best, covered part of 1769 to 1803; and the fourth covered 1804 to 1816 (with annals forming a supplement covering 1816 to 1861). In 1853 Gayarré's political career ended when he was defeated as an independent Democratic candidate for Congress—by fraud, he alleged. He served as president of the Louisiana Historical Society from 1860 to 1888.

Gayarré's *History of Louisiana* ranks with the works of the finest historians of his era, such as George Bancroft (to whom he dedicated the third volume), John Lothrop Motley, Francis Parkman, and William Hickling Prescott. However, in his lifetime Gayarré received less recognition than some of his peers since readers in the northeastern part of the United States were mainly Anglo-Saxon and democratic, and they regarded Louisiana as dominated by Spanish and French elements and oligarchic even after its defeat during the Civil War. All the same, Gayarré's narrative of the development of Louisiana is of permanent, unique value. It is very thorough; Gayarré once estimated that his history cost him $30,000 for travel, research, assistants, and document copying. The result is a dramatic and sometimes witty narrative, with authentic character sketches, insightful analysis and interpretation, and a stately prose style. Later historians have criticized Gayarré for his unscientific approach, his sometimes florid diction, his stress on persons rather than on institutions, and his excessive and occasionally inaccurate quotations.

In 1860 Gayarré made plans to move to Spain and continue archival research there. He and his wife owned $500,000 worth of property, most of which they converted into cash for the move. But when the Civil War began, Gayarré loyally remained in Louisiana. He invested heavily in Confederate bonds, refused to take the oath of allegiance when New Orleans was occupied by Union troops in 1863, and was reduced to poverty by war's end. He sold family books, portraits, furniture, and plate for cash. He occasionally lectured for pay, once feeling obliged to decline a lecture because he lacked suitable attire. He was a state supreme court reporter (1873–1876), and in the 1870s and 1880s he wrote newspaper and magazine articles—some for pay reluctantly taken. His articles appeared in *Bedford's Magazine*, *De Bow's Review*, *Frank Leslie's Popular Monthly*, the *Magazine of American History*, the *New Orleans Democrat*, the *New Orleans Times-Democrat*, and elsewhere. Two of the best are "The Southern Question" (*North American Review*, Nov.–Dec. 1877), in which he presents his "unreconstructed" view of Reconstruction politics; and "A Louisiana Sugar Plantation of the Old Regime" (*Harper's New Monthly Magazine*, Mar. 1887), in which he fondly recalls his boyhood on his grandfather Boré's sugar plantation.

Gayarré's other publications include three novels. *The School for Politics: A Dramatic Novel* (1854) excoriates the vote-getting tactics of Louisiana's corrupt politicians. *Fernando de Lemos—Truth and Fiction: A Novel* (1872) is a partly autobiographical account of his schooldays at the College of Orleans. *Aubert Dubayet; or, The Two Sister Republics* (1882) concerns the revolutions in America and France. In 1865 Gayarré published *Dr. Bluff in Russia; or, The Emperor Nicholas and the American Doctor*, a two-act comedy. His *Philip II. of Spain* (1866) combines research, a picturesque style, and psychological probing. Toward the end of his life, Gayarré and his wife were partially supported by wealthy New Orleans patrons. He died in New Orleans. He is remembered as a would-be politician too patrician to succeed and as an accomplished, devoted narrative historian of his beloved state.

• Most of Gayarré's papers are in the Department of Archives and Manuscripts at Louisiana State University in Baton Rouge, and the Howard-Tilton Library at Tulane University in New Orleans. Many of his letters are in the library of Duke University, in Durham, N.C., and the Xavier University Archives in New Orleans. Edward Larocque Tinker, "Charles Gayarré," *Papers of the Bibliographical Society of America* 27 (1933): 24–64, includes a primary bibliography. The most complete accounts of Gayarré's life are Earl Noland Saucier, "Charles Gayarré, the Creole Historian" (Ph.D. diss., George Peabody Coll. for Teachers, 1935), and Edward Socola, "Charles Gayarré: A Biography" (Ph.D. diss., Univ. of Pennsylvania, 1954). Liliane Crété, *La Vie quotidiene en Louisiane, 1815–1830* (1978), translated by Patrick Gregory as *Daily Life in Louisiana, 1815–1830* (1981), makes use of Gayarré's reminiscences. Grace King, *Memories of a Southern Woman of Letters* (1952), treats King's long friendship with Gayarré, as does Robert Bush, *Grace King: A Southern Destiny* (1983). Jay B. Hubbell, *The South in American Literature,*

1607–1900 (1954), and especially Clement Eaton, *The Waning of the Old South Civilization 1860–1880's* (1968), evaluate Gayarré. Obituaries are in the *New Orleans Daily Picayune*, 11 and 12 Feb. 1895, and the *New Orleans Times-Democrat*, 11 Feb. 1895.

ROBERT L. GALE

GAYE, Marvin (2 Apr. 1939–1 Apr. 1984), singer and songwriter, was born Marvin Pentz Gay, Jr., in Washington, D.C., the son of Marvin Pentz Gay, Sr., a Pentecostal minister, and Alberta (maiden name unknown), a domestic worker. The junior Gaye grew up in Washington, where he began his musical career by singing and playing organ in the choir at his father's church. At Cardoza High School in Washington, Gaye played piano in a doo-wop group called the D.C. Tones. He dropped out after eleventh grade and enlisted in the U.S. Air Force. After a year of openly rebelling against his commanding officers and feigning mental illness, Gaye was discharged in 1957 for inability to serve.

Gaye then returned to Washington and formed a doo-wop group called the Marquees. He sang tenor with the group, which became his first professional singing experience. In 1957 the Marquees recorded a single, "Wyatt Earp" and "Hey, Little School Girl," which was produced by blues singer and songwriter Bo Diddley. The record failed commercially, and Gaye supported himself by working as a dishwasher at a whites-only drugstore lunch counter in Washington.

In 1958 Harvey Fuqua, a successful rhythm-and-blues singer and producer, hired the members of the Marquees to replace his backup singers, the Moonglows. The newly formed Harvey and the Moonglows, with nineteen-year-old Gaye as its tenor, moved to Chicago in 1959. The group toured the United States and made several recordings on the Chess Records label.

In 1960 Gaye and Fuqua left the Moonglows and moved to Detroit in an effort to sing with Berry Gordy, Jr., founder of the fledgling Motown Records label. Gaye was signed to the Motown label soon after arriving in Detroit. He started out as a drummer for the label's star group, the Miracles. In 1961 Gordy agreed to produce an album featuring Gaye as a singer, and *The Soulful Moods of Marvin Gaye*, which marked the official addition of the "e" to his last name, was the result. The album departed from other Motown recordings with its jazz-based sound. It was aimed at the "crossover" white market but failed commercially.

Urged on by Gordy, Gaye changed his approach to appeal to the growing black music market. In 1962 he wrote and recorded "Stubborn Kind of Fellow," a rhythm-and-blues dance song that failed to attract a significant white audience but reached the top ten of the R&B sales chart. "At that point I knew I'd have to travel the same road as all black artists before me—establish a soul audience and then reach beyond that," Gaye said. In 1962 Gaye performed in the first Motortown Revue, a traveling concert featuring Motown's top stars.

Gaye finally broke into the popular music charts in 1963 with "Hitch Hike," which he cowrote and recorded as a Motown single. On Dick Clark's "American Bandstand" television show, he performed a new dance named after the song. The next single he recorded in 1963, "Pride and Joy," reached the top ten of the pop chart. Later that year Gaye married Anna Gordy, the subject of "Pride and Joy," and Berry Gordy's sister. The couple adopted a son, Marvin Pentz Gaye III, in 1965. Gaye's 1963 live album, *Marvin Gaye: Live on Stage*, featured a string of the singer's hits and cemented his position as a leading rhythm-and-blues performer.

Gaye scored a number of hit records for Motown in the mid-1960s, including "How Sweet It Is" and "You're a Wonderful One" in 1964, "Ain't That Peculiar" in 1965, and "It Takes Two," performed with Kim Weston, in 1966. In 1967 Gaye began an extended recording partnership with Tammi Terrell, a young soprano brought into Motown to complement Gaye's smooth tenor. The pair recorded *United* (1967), which featured several hits, including "Ain't No Mountain High Enough" and "Your Precious Love." Over the next two years Gaye and Terrell released three albums, including nine songs that reached the pop and R&B charts. The partnership ended when Terrell died of a brain tumor in 1970. During the late 1960s Gaye also recorded a number of hits as a solo artist, including the hugely successful "I Heard It through the Grapevine," which reached the top of the R&B and pop charts in 1969. By this point in his career, Gaye had mastered three distinct voices—a soothing mid-range, a harsher, gospel-inflected shout, and a satiny falsetto.

Following the string of hits in the late 1960s, Gaye entered a reclusive phase in which he refused to record or perform for more than a year. During this time he trained rigorously in an attempt to join the Detroit Lions football team as a wide receiver. Fearing a lawsuit if he were injured, in 1970 the team's ownership refused to give him a tryout. Gaye's musical experience during this period was limited to producing and writing material for a young R&B group called the Originals.

Gaye's greatest triumph as a musician came in 1971 with the release of *What's Going On*, the first album he wrote, produced, and performed. *What's Going On* broke several conventions for Motown, which initially opposed the project, and for African-American music in general. Written as a thematic suite, the album's lyrics decried American imperialism, urban poverty, police brutality, and ecological destruction. *What's Going On* was one of the first black mainstream recordings to contain an explicit protest message. The album also greatly broadened the form and content of black popular music. To the R&B palette established by Motown in the 1960s, Gaye added layers of string instruments, jazz-style horns, speaking voices, Latin percussion, and scat singing. The result was an extraordinarily lush and complex musical composition. The album was the most commercially successful of

Gaye's career to that point. Three of its songs—"What's Going On," "Mercy Mercy Me," and "Inner City Blues"—reached the top ten on the R&B and pop charts. The album garnered Gaye a number of awards in 1971, including the *Billboard* magazine trendsetter of the year, the *Cashbox* magazine male vocalist of the year, and the National Association for the Advancement of Colored People's Image Award.

Despite his renewed recording success Gaye continued to refuse to perform live until 1 May 1972, four years after his last public performance, when he appeared at the Kennedy Center in Washington, D.C., as part of the city's Marvin Gaye Day. Later that year Gaye released his next album, *Trouble Man*, which served as the soundtrack for a film of the same name. *Trouble Man* contained only one vocal track, the title song, along with jazz instrumentals featuring Gaye on electronic keyboards, Trevor Lawrence on saxophone, and big-band arrangements by trombonist J. J. Johnson.

In 1973 Gaye moved to Los Angeles and released two albums on the Motown label, a duet with Diana Ross titled *Diana and Marvin*, which was a commercial failure, and *Let's Get It On*, a solo effort whose title track shot to number one on the R&B and pop charts. In another departure from Motown tradition, *Let's Get It On* presented an unabashed celebration of sex. The album was Gaye's greatest commercial success, selling more than 5 million copies. Shortly after the release of *Let's Get It On*, Gaye separated from his wife and moved into an isolated, semirural house in Topanga, California, with Janis Hunter, a sixteen-year-old girl. Gaye and Hunter had two children before they were married in 1977. Expanding on the success of *Let's Get It On*, Gaye performed in twenty cities on a national tour in the summer and fall of 1974.

In 1975 Gaye opened the Marvin Gaye Recording Studio in Hollywood and recorded *I Want You*, an album similar to *Let's Get It On* in its frank sexuality and smooth soul sound. Despite its cool reception by critics, *I Want You*, which was released early in 1976, sold more than 1 million copies. Gaye's 1976 performance at the London Palladium, which featured songs from throughout his career, was recorded and released in 1977 as a two-LP album, *Marvin Gaye Live at the London Palladium*. The album included a studio-recorded disco track, "Got to Give It Up," which reached number one on the soul and pop charts.

Gaye's recording career took its strangest turn in 1978 with the release of *Here, My Dear*, an extended musical diatribe against his first wife, Anna, who had won a divorce ruling against him the previous year. Proceeds from sales of the album, which included the song "You Can Leave, but It's Going to Cost You," went to Anna as part of the divorce settlement. The settlement, along with an extravagant cocaine habit, several years of unpaid federal taxes, and a string of disastrous business investments, created a financial crisis from which Gaye never recovered. His 1979 tour was largely undertaken to repay enormous debts to musicians, his first wife, and the federal government.

Forced to sell his house and many of his possessions, in 1980 Gaye lived in a van on a beach in Maui, Hawaii. That year his second wife divorced him. In 1981 a British promoter financed a tour of England and Europe and persuaded a reluctant Gaye to perform. After the tour Gaye remained in London, afraid to return to the United States and face prosecution for tax evasion. In that year, without Gaye's consent, Motown released *In Our Lifetime*, which the singer was in the process of recording.

In the spring of 1981 Gaye renounced his contract with Motown, severing a relationship that had lasted twenty years, and moved from London to Ostend, Belgium, where he and his son were supported by a Belgian businessman. Gaye signed a new recording contract with CBS Records in 1982 and that year released *Midnight Love*, his most successful album since *Let's Get It On*. "Sexual Healing," a reggae-style single from the album, remained number one on the soul charts for four months and made it to number three on the pop charts. The single sold more than 1 million copies, the album more than 2 million. The commercial success of the album emboldened Gaye to return to the United States in the fall of 1982. He returned to Los Angeles and in January 1983, still struggling financially, moved into his parents' home in the Crenshaw district of the city. That year Gaye won Grammy Awards for best male vocal and best instrumental performance in the rhythm-and-blues category for "Sexual Healing."

During the "Sexual Healing" national tour in the spring and summer of 1983, Gaye's cocaine addiction worsened and he developed severe paranoia and depression. Returning from the tour, he secluded himself in his parents' home for several months. On 1 April 1984, following a fight between the two men, Gaye was shot and killed by his father.

Gaye was one of the preeminent soul singers and composers of his generation. His versatile and silken voice and sensitive phrasing made him a singer without superior in the history of American popular music. A leading voice in the Motown sound of the 1960s, Gaye established himself as a virtuoso performer and composer in the 1970s, when his self-produced albums pioneered several new musical and lyrical forms in popular music.

• David Ritz, *Divided Soul: The Life of Marvin Gaye* (1985; repr. 1991), is a complete and highly informative biography. See also Nelson George, *Where Did Our Love Go: The Rise and Fall of the Motown Sound* (1985). Obituaries are in *Rolling Stone*, 10 and 24 May 1984.

THADDEUS RUSSELL

GAYLE, John (11 Sept. 1792–21 July 1859), Alabama governor, U.S. congressman, and Alabama jurist, was born in Sumter District, South Carolina, the son of Mary Rees and Matthew Gayle, farmers. Originally from Virginia, Matthew Gayle moved to South Carolina about the time of the American Revolution and served with Francis Marion. In 1812, while John was being educated in South Carolina, the family moved to Mount Vernon, Alabama, and then to nearby Monroe County, where Matthew was a planter.

John Gayle attended Mt. Bethel Academy in Newberry District, South Carolina, under the direction of Elisha Hammond, father of James Henry Hammond, a future governor of South Carolina. In 1813 Gayle graduated from South Carolina College, where he was president of the Clariosophic Society, a literary and debating organization. In August 1813, a few weeks after the American Indian massacre of settlers at Fort Mims, he arrived in Alabama; others who followed the same path were killed and scalped. He read law with Judge Abner S. Lipscomb at St. Stephens and in 1818 opened a law practice at Claiborne, Alabama. In 1819 he married Sarah Ann Haynsworth; they had six children.

In 1818 President James Monroe nominated Gayle to be a member of the legislative council of the newly organized territorial legislature of the Alabama Territory. Soon after that body met, the legislature elected Gayle in 1819 to be the solicitor of the First Judicial Circuit of Alabama; he was reelected in 1821. In 1822 he was elected to the Alabama House of Representatives from Monroe County and was reelected in 1823. Also in 1823 he became judge of the Third Judicial Circuit and ex officio judge of the state supreme court, resigning in 1828. In 1829 he was elected to the Alabama House of Representatives from Greene County and was chosen Speaker. By 1830 he owned ten slaves.

In 1831 Gayle was elected governor of Alabama as a strong antinullification candidate. He served two terms, leaving office in 1835. During his administration a crisis developed over American Indian removal, and Gayle clashed with his lifelong friend President Andrew Jackson. A confrontation occurred in 1832–1833, when federal troops attempted to remove whites from Creek Indian lands in Russell County. After a white resident was killed, a county grand jury indicted the responsible soldiers for murder, and Gayle insisted on their surrender to state officials. However, the federal commander prevented the sheriff from serving the warrant.

Governor Gayle championed the rights of settlers, protested that federal protection of the Indians was an insult to Alabama's sovereignty, and directed the organizing of a militia. Realizing the possibility of a state of civil war, President Jackson dispatched Francis Scott Key to resolve the quarrel. Key's diplomacy succeeded, and a collision between state and federal authority was averted. Although the immediate crisis ended, the affair had long-term effects in Alabama politics. Jackson's popularity was diminished, Alabamians were alarmed by the increasing power of the federal government, and the foundation was laid for the states' rights movement in Alabama in the 1850s. Thereafter, states' rights sentiment steadily gained strength among Alabamians.

Also during Gayle's administration, the first railroad in Alabama was built. Forty-four miles in length, it extended east across north Alabama from Tuscumbia to Decatur.

By 1835 Governor Gayle was no longer a Jacksonian. When Martin Van Buren was promoted for president in the second Jackson administration, the Whig party was born in Alabama; the issue that ensured its success was the Creek affair that Alabamians interpreted as a states' rights issue. Gayle served as a Whig presidential elector in 1836 and 1840, although he did not declare himself a Whig until 1840.

After his term as governor, Gayle returned to his law practice, this time in Mobile. His wife died in 1835, and in 1837 he married Clarissa Stedman Peck. They had four children.

In 1847 Gayle was elected to the U.S. House of Representatives as a Whig. In Washington, D.C., he lived in a boarding house where John C. Calhoun and his niece also lodged. Gayle's daughter Amelia, who had traveled to Washington with her father, became an especial favorite of Calhoun, accompanying him on his morning walks around the U.S. Capitol. In Congress Gayle focused most often on matters of local concern, such as instructions to the postmaster at Mobile and the granting of public lands to local railroads. On national questions he was most interested in matters related to the expansion of slavery. His strongest expression of his states' rights views came in an 1848 speech during the debate on the creation of a territorial government for Oregon.

After one term in Congress, Gayle did not seek reelection. He returned to Mobile and in 1849 was appointed judge of the U.S. District Court in Alabama. He continued as district judge until his death in Mobile.

• The most significant information about Gayle is in the Governor John Gayle Papers, Alabama Department of Archives and History, Montgomery, and the Gorgas Family Papers, W. S. Hoole Special Collections Library, University of Alabama, Tuscaloosa. See also William Garrett, *Reminiscences of Public Men in Alabama, for Thirty Years* (1872); W. Brewer, *Alabama: Her History, Resources, War Record, and Public Men, from 1540 to 1872* (1872); Thomas McAdory Owen, ed., *Transactions of the Alabama Historical Society, 1899–1903* 4 (1904): 141–65; J. Mills Thornton III, *Politics and Power in a Slave Society: Alabama, 1800–1860* (1978); and Owen, *History of Alabama and Dictionary of Alabama Biography*, vol. 3 (1921). An obituary is in the *Mobile Daily Register*, 22 July 1859.

SARAH WOOLFOLK WIGGINS

GAYLER, Charles (1 Apr. 1820–28 May 1892), playwright, was born in New York City, the son of C. J. Gayler, a hardware merchant. His mother's name is unknown. He studied for a time at an academy in Suffield, Connecticut, then moved west in 1836 to take a position as a schoolteacher in Dayton, Ohio. There, in the hours he was not teaching, Gayler prepared himself for a career in law at a time when many lawyers were self-taught. He was eventually admitted to practice and traveled the Illinois and Ohio circuits. Gayler later became active in Dayton politics and was a vocal

supporter and close friend of Henry Clay, the Whig candidate for president in 1844. His interest in public affairs led him to journalism and he served briefly as editor of the *Cincinnati Evening Dispatch*.

In 1846 Gayler married Grace Christian (with whom he had eight children) and turned to the profession for which he would be best known. For a time he was an actor in the Ohio theaters managed by James W. Bates, undertaking leading roles such as Hamlet, Othello, and Richelieu. One of his first efforts at playwriting, *The Buckeye Gold Hunters*, was produced by Bates in 1849 at Cincinnati's National Theatre. In this melodrama about the gold rush, then at its height, Gayler displayed what would become one of his trademarks, the facile manipulation of contemporary, real-life material for dramatic effect. Buoyed by the success of this production, Gayler returned to New York City, already the center of theatrical activity in the United States, to advance his career. There, while honing his skills as a playwright, he worked variously as a theatrical manager, a critic for the *Tribune* and the *Herald*, and a writer for literary magazines.

Gayler's output of plays was prodigious, and he is remembered as one of the most prolific dramatists of the second half of the nineteenth century. Estimates of the number of his works range from 150 to 400, with 200 probably near the actual mark. He wrote in a remarkable number of genres, including tragedy, comedy, farce, melodrama, minstrel skit, operetta, and spectacle. To many critics, Gayler was merely a hack with a sure feel for the sensational. A *New York Times* review of an 1870 revival of *Taking the Chances; or, Our Cousin from the City* (1856) is typical: the play was judged "threadbare in plot, slender and truthless in characterization, and pointless in dialogue." Despite a nearly continuous barrage of critical ridicule, however, Gayler managed to interest several leading actors in his scripts. *The Son of the Night* (1857), for example, one of many lurid melodramas that Gayler adapted from French sources, became a standard in the repertoire of Lawrence Barrett and E. L. Davenport.

Many of Gayler's plays were written for specific performers; among these were *The Love of a Prince; or, The Court of Prussia* (1857) for Laura Keene; *There's Many a Slip 'twixt the Cup and the Lip* (1859) for Mr. and Mrs. William J. Florence; *The Magic Marriage* (1861) for James W. Wallack; *The Connie Soogah; or, The Jolly Peddler* (1863) for Mr. and Mrs. Barney Williams; *Atonement; or, The Child Stealer* (1866) for Lucille Western; and *With the Tide* (1874) for Katie Mayhew. These flimsy plays succeeded largely because of the personal magnetism of the stars who appeared in them; most disappeared without a trace when the star's career ended. Gayler also devised two sequels to Tom Taylor's *Our American Cousin*; *Our Female American Cousin* (1859) and *Our American Cousin at Home; or, Lord Dundreary Abroad* (1861). Neither came even remotely close to achieving the immense popularity of the distinguished comedy on which they were based.

Few playwrights, though, were as quick as Gayler in dramatizing current events to capitalize on intense public interest. *Bull Run; or, The Sacking of Fairfax Courthouse* premiered in New York on 15 August 1861, less than a month after the actual battle in Virginia. The play's novelty and timeliness earned it a run of four weeks; Gayler's contemporaries joked that the play had been presented even before some Union survivors of the battle had retreated from the scene. Similarly, *Hatteras Inlet; or, Our Naval Victories* was presented on 2 November 1861, a mere three months after the Union army had captured the North Carolina fort.

Although none of Gayler's plays has withstood the test of time, one in particular was immensely popular in its day, *Fritz, Our Cousin German*, which was first presented by variety performer Joseph K. Emmet at Wallack's Theatre in 1870. This play invoked nearly every melodramatic trick in the book, including the hero's rescue of a child who has been strapped to a revolving mill wheel by the villain. Its plot and spectacular elements changed over time as Emmet sought the best showcase for his considerable comedic talents. Presented in an era when the nation's musical genres were struggling to achieve recognition as artistic forms in their own right, the play was also a prototypical musical, with interpolated songs, dances, and burlesque turns loosely attached to its frail melodramatic structure. It spawned many imitations by playwrights seeking to emulate its winning combination of pathos, humor, and melody.

Gayler was among those who sought to strike gold twice. In 1871 *Carl, the Fiddler* appeared, another prototypical musical starring the inimitable Emmet. This play failed to attract an audience, however, and was quickly dropped. In 1873 Gayler's *Dust and Diamonds* was produced at Wallack's Theatre. This hackneyed potboiler centered on a group of ragpickers and an orphan who is later revealed to be an heiress. It was a clumsy adaptation of a French original and typical of Gayler's practice of using whatever materials were at hand to his own commercial advantage. His literary agility may have earned him as much as $200 per play during this period of his career.

Gayler's last major success was *Lights and Shadows of New York*, first produced at the Standard Theatre in 1888. Critics condemned its story as conventional drivel but conceded its popular appeal. By the end of the nineteenth century Gayler's plays were increasingly rejected by sophisticated New York audiences and relegated to small-town opera houses throughout the country. Gayler was well liked by his contemporaries and a fixture in the so-called "bohemian" set who frequented Pfaff's and the other stylish haunts of actors, artists, and authors. He was the recipient of several benefit performances near the end of his career. Gayler died at his daughter's home in Brooklyn.

• Despite the number and influence of Gayler's works, he has been all but ignored by modern writers. This may be because few of his plays are extant; the Library of Congress and the Center for Research Libraries, Chicago, have the best collections. Some details of his career can be gleaned from Arthur Hobson Quinn, *A History of the American Drama from the Civil War to the Present Day* (1936). The fate of several of his plays can be traced in Gerald Bordman, *American Theatre: A Chronicle of Comedy and Drama, 1869–1914* (1994). A partly fictitious portrait of Gayler was published in *Frank Leslie's Illustrated Newspaper*, 9 May 1868. Obituaries that include retrospectives of Gayler's career are in the *New York Times* and the *New York Herald*, both 29 May 1892, and the *Brooklyn Daily Eagle*, 29 May and 2 June 1892.

KRISTAN A. TETENS

GAYLEY, James (11 Oct. 1855–25 Feb. 1920), engineer and inventor, was born in Lock Haven, Pennsylvania, the son of Samuel Alexander Gayley, a Presbyterian minister, and Agnes Malcolm. His parents had emigrated from northern Ireland to the United States, and Samuel Gayley became minister in West Nottingham, Maryland, shortly after his son's birth. James Gayley attended local schools and a preparatory academy in West Nottingham. He went on to Lafayette College in Easton, Pennsylvania, from which he received a degree in mining engineering in 1876. From that year to 1879 Gayley worked as a chemist for the Crane Iron Company in Catasauqua, Pennsylvania. This was a time of great growth in the iron and steel industries in the United States, and new techniques were being introduced by many inventors, often in small companies.

In 1880 Gayley became superintendent of the Missouri Furnace Company in St. Louis. Two years later he was employed by the E. & G. Brooks Iron Company in Birdsboro, Pennsylvania, to manage their blast furnaces for smelting iron from ore. Gayley married Julia Thurston Gardiner in 1884; they had three daughters and were divorced in 1910.

In 1885 Gayley was employed by Edgar Thomson Steel Works in Braddock, Pennsylvania, to manage their blast furnaces. The company, then owned by Carnegie Brothers and Company, Ltd., later became Carnegie Steel Works. The industry had increased production after about 1880 by devising methods that used large amounts of fuel in the furnaces, primarily coke created by distillation of coal. Gayley's ingenuity led him to find economies in production by inventing and improving equipment. He designed charging bins for the raw materials of iron and steel processing and was the first to install a compound condensing engine that supplied an air blast to the furnace. With pride, Gayley described in 1890 the success of a furnace of his company that, with reduced coke fuel, had produced more tonnage of iron than any other furnace to that time (quoted in Swank, p. 457). Among his several patents were a bronze cooling plate for the walls of steel furnaces (1891) and a casting mechanism for the Bessemer steel technique (1896). Beginning in 1894 he developed a method of processing iron and steel by dry air that made possible much greater uniformity in the production by blast furnaces and considerably reduced the amount of fuel required. It was probably his most important contribution to the steel industry, and he continued making improvements on the procedure until 1911. Gayley became managing director of Carnegie Steel Company in 1897. In that capacity he installed a machine to unload ore mechanically at the dock in Conneaut, Ohio, on Lake Erie, and then designed a ship to use the machine effectively.

At the turn of the century, Andrew Carnegie owned the largest steel company in the United States but wanted to retire. John Pierpont Morgan wanted to create a centralized trust to dominate the steel market, so he purchased Carnegie Steel Company in 1901 and established United States Steel Corporation in Pittsburgh, Pennsylvania. It combined many aspects of the industry, including furnaces, ore deposits, railroad companies, and shipping lines.

In the merger Gayley became first vice president of U.S. Steel in 1901, in charge of obtaining and transporting raw materials for producing steel. He retired in 1909 and in New York City served as president of the American Ore Reclamation Company and the Sheffield Iron Corporation until his death in New York City. He was a trustee of Lafayette College from 1892 and in 1902 donated funds for building the Gayley Hall of Chemistry and Metallurgy at that college. He held several offices of the American Institute of Mining Engineers, including its presidency in 1904–1905. He published a number of papers on steel-industry equipment in the *Transactions* of that society.

Gayley received the Elliott Cresson medal of the Franklin Institute in 1908 for his invention of the dry-air furnace and the Perkins Gold Medal of the American Society of Mechanical Engineers in 1913 for his contributions to the steel industry. Elbert H. Gary, chief executive officer of U.S. Steel, considered Gayley "eminently successful. . . . As first vice-president . . . he was respected, trusted and loved" (quoted in *Transactions of AIME*, p. 641).

• An anonymous biographical sketch of Gayley is in *Transactions of the American Institute of Mining Engineers* 67 (1922): 639–40 (the organization later became the American Institute of Mining, Metallurgical and Petroleum Engineers). A useful history of the iron and steel industry is James M. Swank's *History of the Manufacture of Iron in All Ages*, 2d ed. (1892). An obituary is in the *New York Times*, 26 Feb. 1920.

ELIZABETH NOBLE SHOR

GAYLORD, Willis (1792–27 Mar. 1844), agriculturist, was born in Bristol, Connecticut, the son of Lemon Gaylord and Rhoda Plumb, farmers. His family migrated westward in 1801, becoming early settlers of Otisco, Onondaga County, New York. Just a few years later, when he was twelve, Gaylord suffered a debilitating illness that left him with a severe curvature of the spine. This disability was compounded when he permanently injured an arm. Unable to perform any physical labor, he turned to intellectual pursuits. Facing limited opportunities for formal schooling in this frontier community, he acquired most of his learning through home instruction, reading, and correspondence. As a young man he began to write, producing a manuscript history of the War of 1812 (never published) and (though little survives) some poetry and religious literature.

Gaylord found his widest audience as a scientific and agricultural writer, becoming a key figure in the emergence of the American agricultural reform movement in the 1830s. He was a leading advocate of what he called the "New Husbandry," urging farmers to reclaim or maintain soil fertility by intensive use of manure, proper tillage, crop rotation, and by the culture of root and fallow crops. Informing his specific recommendations was a conviction that innovation, empirical observation, capital investment, and scientific experimentation would result in improvements in both agriculture and rural life. He promoted these ideas mainly through his work as a contributor to and later editor of agricultural journals—the *Genesee Farmer* and the Albany *Cultivator*—and in prize-winning essays published in the *Transactions* of the New York State Agricultural Society. These writings show that he was widely read in the scientific literature of the day, and that he was keenly interested in establishing the relevance of science to agriculture. He incorporated his careful observations of practical farming on his home farm in Otisco into these learned treatises and extended his range of practical experience through correspondence with like-minded agriculturists, such as Luther Tucker, all over the state.

Gaylord's thinking exemplified the ambiguous nature of nineteenth-century agricultural reform. On the one hand, his incisive critique of prevailing farming practices received wide attention because it addressed the increasingly obvious problems of waste and of declining soil fertility. On the other, in his enthusiasm for reform he sometimes advocated novelties (for example, raising silkworms) of which practical farmers were justifiably skeptical. Agricultural science was in its infancy and still largely unable to contribute directly to helping the farmer in his everyday work. Nevertheless, he had a significant impact on the direction of American agriculture in the nineteenth and twentieth centuries through his efforts to adapt the best of European methods to American circumstances and through his advocacy of scientific and capitalistic agriculture.

Willis Gaylord was regarded as a charming and entertaining conversationalist, and despite being almost constantly in physical pain, he was cheerful and uncomplaining. Never married, he died in Camillus, Onondaga County, New York, after a brief, acute illness.

• Gaylord's major publications include *American Husbandry: Being a Series of Essays on Agriculture* (1840), written with Luther Tucker; "Geology as Connected with Agriculture," New York State Agricultural Society, *Transactions* 1 (1841): 273–98, also reprinted in Henry Ellsworth, ed., *Improvements in Agriculture, Arts, &c. of the United States* (1843); "On Tillage," New York State Agricultural Society, *Transactions* 1 (1841): 211–20; "Treatise on Insects Injurious to Field Crops, Orchards, Gardens, and Domestic Animals," New York State Agricultural Society, *Transactions* 3 (1843): 129–75; "Analysis of Soils" and "Rotation Versus Summer Fallow," New York State Agricultural Society, *Transactions* 4 (1844): 61–75 and 118–25, respectively; "Influence of Lakes on Autumnal Seasons," *American Journal of Science* 33: 335;

and various contributions to the *Cultivator*, vol. 1 (1834)–n.s., vol. 1 (1844). An obituary is in the *Cultivator*, n.s., 1 (May 1844): 137–38.

SALLY McMURRY

GAYNOR, Janet (6 Oct. 1906–14 Sept. 1984), actress, was born Laura Augusta Gainer (or Gainor) in Philadelphia, Pennsylvania, the daughter of Frank D. Gainer, a paperhanger and amateur actor, and Laura Buhl. Laura, called "Lolly," was raised in Chicago and then San Francisco. Following her high school graduation, the family moved to Los Angeles. Laura's stepfather encouraged her to enter show business and suggested her screen name, Janet Gaynor.

Gaynor and her sister both found work as extras and bit players in silent comedy shorts at the Hal Roach Studios and elsewhere. According to actor Gilbert Roland, Gaynor showed a special spark, even as an extra. In a tribute printed in the *Los Angeles Times* after Gaynor's death, Roland wrote that "she stood out amongst other extra girls. I was infatuated; a silent crush" (22 Sept. 1984).

Gaynor's first substantial role was in *The Johnstown Flood* (1926), a disaster film produced by the newly formed Fox Film Corporation. Gaynor signed a contract with Fox and was cast in a succession of films in which she played forlorn heroines. It quickly became apparent that she was a burgeoning star. She was cast in one of Fox's most ambitious silent films, *Sunrise* (1927), the exquisitely photographed tale of a husband who schemes with another woman to murder his wife. The film was a critical success. A review in *Variety* (28 Sept. 1927), for instance, praised director F. W. Murnau's "resourcefulness of effects" and stated, "the playing of George O'Brien and Janet Gaynor and their associates is generally convincing, and the story unfolds in settings inexpressibly lovely." The same year she was a poor Parisian girl in the sentimental romance *Seventh Heaven*, opposite Charles Farrell, who would be her costar in a total of twelve films. The *New York Herald Tribune* called her work in *Seventh Heaven* "a masterwork of distinctive pantomime that is both romantic and understandable."

Hoping to repeat the success of *Seventh Heaven*, the Fox studio reteamed Gaynor and Farrell in *Street Angel* (1928), in which Gaynor played a poor Italian girl who takes to the streets to support her sick mother. Their frequent screen pairings sparked gossip of a real-life romance between Gaynor and Farrell, but in 1929 she married attorney Lydell Peck. The union ended in divorce in 1933.

On 16 May 1929 the Academy of Motion Picture Arts and Sciences awarded Gaynor with the first Academy Award for best actress for her performances in *Sunrise*, *Seventh Heaven*, and *Street Angel*. Though she could not guess how important the Academy Awards would become to the motion picture industry, she was excited to receive the honor. In a 1980 interview she said, "It was nice of them to honor an actress just starting out, especially since I really didn't know anything about acting. I was a girl who fell into it."

Unlike many other stars of the silent screen era whose careers ended with the advent of talkies, Gaynor continued to thrive when her films began using sound. She later recalled that "the transition to talkies was difficult for a lot of people but not for me. I thought my voice was just terrible, but it went with me and that was the trick."

Reviewing Gaynor's first all-talking feature film, *Sunny Side Up* (1929), the *New York Herald Tribune* said that "when she starts to speak, Miss Gaynor's voice reveals a baby treble that is hardly as poetic as we hoped for, but it is not long before its unaffected honesty recaptures all of her pantomimic charm."

Gaynor starred in an average of three films a year and became Hollywood's highest-paid actress of the time. She fought against being cast in light musical comedies, holding out for serious dramatic roles. She once took a seven-month suspension—losing $44,000 in salary—rather than accept a role she felt beneath her standards.

By 1936 Gaynor's popularity had been eclipsed by the new darling of the Fox lot, Shirley Temple. Gaynor's contract with the studio lapsed, and her career might have slowed to a halt if not for the intervention of David O. Selznick, who cast her in what would be her best-remembered film, *A Star Is Born*. As a farm girl who becomes a movie star, Gaynor won critical acclaim and an Academy Award nomination. She found the role close to her heart: "The story was perfect for me—a little nobody without any great talent who suddenly finds herself a star."

Gaynor made two more films, including the hit comedy *The Young in Heart* (1938) and then shocked the show business community by retiring while still at the top of her profession. She later explained, "I had been working steadily for seventeen long years. I just wanted to have time to know other things. I wanted to fall in love. I wanted to have a child. I wanted to live." She married Metro-Goldwyn-Mayer costume designer Gilbert Adrian in 1939, and they had one son. She was widowed in 1959 and married producer Paul Gregory in 1964.

In the years following her official retirement, Gaynor returned to show business infrequently. She made her television debut in 1953 in a live production of *Dear Cynthia*. In 1957 she returned to the big screen to take on a supporting role in *Bernardine*, her final film. She also appeared in stage productions of *The Midnight Sun* (1959), *Harold and Maude* (1980), and *On Golden Pond* (1981). A talented artist, her paintings were exhibited in New York, Chicago, and Palm Springs.

In 1982 Gaynor was seriously injured in an accident while riding in a taxi with her husband and actress Mary Martin. She survived the accident but was plagued with continuous medical problems brought about by the trauma. She underwent several operations over the next two years before succumbing to pneumonia, a complication of her weakened condition. She died in Palm Springs, California.

Though she practically faded into obscurity, Gaynor was one of Hollywood's greatest stars. Her twelve years of screen stardom bridged both the silent and talkie eras. Dimpled, diminutive, and wholesome-looking, Gaynor's appeal lay in her ability to project naïveté and innocence even when playing characters of ill repute.

• A critical analysis of Gaynor's career is presented in Connie Billips, *Janet Gaynor: A Bio-Bibliography* (1992). The volume includes a biography, annotated bibliography, and information on Gaynor's work in film, radio, television, and stage. James Robert Parish, *The Fox Girls* (1971), includes a lengthy chapter on Gaynor, with several photographs and a filmography. Parish, *Hollywood's Great Love Teams* (1974), includes a section on the films of Gaynor and Charles Farrell. An interview with Gaynor comprises a chapter of Roy Newquist's *Showcase* (1966). Chauncey L. Carr profiled Gaynor in "Janet Gaynor: As a Child-Woman She Was between Mary Pickford's Simplicity and Audrey Hepburn's Sophistication," *Films in Review*, Oct. 1959, pp. 470–77. Other magazine and newspaper articles of note include Walter Ames, "Janet Gaynor, Adrian Find New Life in Brazil," *Los Angeles Times*, 16 Mar. 1959; Peter Buckley, "Janet Gaynor: At 74, a Star Is Reborn," *Los Angeles Times*, 3 Feb. 1980; John Nangle, "A Final Tribute to Janet Gaynor," *Films in Review*, Nov. 1984, p. 563; Richard Roud, "People We Like: Janet Gaynor," *Film Comment*, Jan./Feb. 1974, p. 37; Edwin Schallert, "Star Remains Film Favorite," *Los Angeles Times*, 3 Aug. 1933; Ursula Vils, "Janet Gaynor: Her Oscar Was a First," *Los Angeles Times*, 10 Oct. 1973; and "Where Are They Now?" *Newsweek*, 15 Apr. 1963, p. 20. Obituaries are in the *Los Angeles Times* and the *New York Times*, 15 Sept. 1984, and *Variety*, 19 Sept. 1984.

BRENDA SCOTT ROYCE

GAYNOR, William Jay (2 Feb. 1848–10 Sept. 1913), jurist and mayor, was born in Whitesboro, New York, the son of Keiron K. Gaynor, a blacksmith and farmer, and Elizabeth Handwright. After attending Assumption Academy and De La Salle Institute, both run by the Christian Brothers, a Roman Catholic teaching order, Gaynor entered the order as a novice in 1863 and for four years taught in parochial schools in Baltimore and Saint Louis. In 1868 he gave up teaching and studied law in Utica, New York; he was admitted to the bar in 1871. After a brief stay in Boston, Gaynor moved in 1873 to Brooklyn, New York, and the following year he married Emma Vesta Hyde. The childless marriage ended in divorce in 1881; Gaynor wed Augusta Cole Mayer in 1886 and with her had eight children, seven of whom lived to adulthood.

After moving to Brooklyn in 1873 Gaynor for a couple of years worked as a reporter for the *Brooklyn Argus* and following its demise for the New York *Sun*. Over the next couple of decades he built up a very lucrative law practice and contributed articles to law journals. As a lawyer he was noted for his thorough legal presentations, support of municipal reform, and sharp attacks against corrupt political bosses, most notably Coney Island's John Y. McKane. Although a Democrat in national politics, Gaynor belonged to no local political group, believing, as did reformer Seth Low, that city concerns should be kept separate from nation-

al issues and parties. Lauded for his political independence and reformist bent, he was elected justice of the New York State Supreme Court in 1893 on a Brooklyn Republican ticket that sought to appeal to independent reform voters. In 1905 he was appointed a member of the appellate division of the supreme court and two years later was reelected to the bench. As a judge Gaynor was hardworking, fair, and sharp-tongued, but respected for his efficient and judicious handling of cases. He ardently defended individual rights against the misuse of power by government, especially the police, and by overzealous social reformers seeking to enforce public morality—a task, Gaynor believed, was better left to churches, schools, and homes.

While serving on the court Gaynor often was mentioned as a candidate for elective office. Casting his eye on the New York mayoralty, the fiercely independent Gaynor understood that to be elected he would need the backing of at least one of New York's regular political organizations. In 1909 Tammany Hall was politically battered by exposures of corruption, dismissed officeholders, and rebellion by dissident Democrats. Charles F. Murphy, the Hall's astute, "clean," and at times unpredictable boss, to the consternation of his organization's leaders, tapped the politically popular and respected Gaynor to run for major on a Tammany ticket. A Gaynor victory, the quiet boss reasoned, might not do much for Tammany spoilsmen but would allow him to keep control of the party organization and put the Hall in step with the forces of reform. Throughout the campaign Gaynor refused to repudiate Tammany but argued that as mayor he would remain free of machine control.

To oppose Gaynor the Committee of One Hundred's Republican-fusion forces nominated Otto T. Bannard, a politically unknown banker, conservative Republican party regular, and supporter of various charities. The Civic Alliance, organized by William Randolph Hearst and his supporters, selected the crusading newspaper publisher and perennial candidate for public office, to head its ticket, and endorsed the rest of the fusion slate. Hearst, the foremost champion of municipal ownership of rapid transit and supporter of the rights of labor and other social legislation, had originally promised to support Gaynor for mayor, but during the campaign attacked the judge for accepting a Tammany nomination. Gaynor won the bitterly fought three-cornered mayoralty race, getting 250,678 votes to Bannard's 177,662 and Hearst's 153,843. But Bannard and Hearst together compiled a total vote almost 80,000 larger than the judge's, and this anti-Tammany majority elected the entire fusion slate below mayor except the candidate for president of the borough of Queens.

Mayor Gaynor was talked about as a potential Democratic nominee for governor of New York in 1910 and even for president of the United States in 1912. But in August 1910, at the height of his popularity, when boarding a ship for a European vacation Gaynor was shot in the throat by James J. Gallagher, a discharged city dock worker. Gaynor recovered sufficiently to return to his mayoral duties in two months, but the attempted assassination was a watershed, permanently damaging his physical and emotional health. The bullet remained in his throat, reducing his voice to a raspy whisper and leaving him with a chronic cough. Constantly tired, the always combative Gaynor now was even more irascible. Despite his many mayoral achievements, his last two years in office were marked by political controversy and disappointment.

Gaynor provided New Yorkers a mildly progressive administration. He enhanced the office of mayor and established personal rapport with the public by daily answering—often with great wit and sarcasm—innumerable letters from constituents, including children, and regularly making speeches and presenting memos to the press explaining his policies and appointments. He and the fusion-reform members of the board of estimate cooperated to modernize municipal administration, frequently utilizing experts from outside civic and reform agencies. Gaynor enforced economy measures in the mayor's office, installed time cards, and put into effect an eight-hour day for city employees. For the most part ignoring Tammany's pleas for patronage but somehow managing to retain the good will and friendship of Boss Murphy, who recognized the strength of the fusion-reform forces, Gaynor appointed competent, politically independent business and professional men to head departments and boards, ordering them to make appointments and promotions according to civil service rules and to institute administrative and fiscal reforms. Such reforms included centralizing authority and responsibility; dismissing incompetent, corrupt, and unneeded workers; installing accounting systems; and reducing waste and departmental operating expenses. Most notably, Gaynor supported Comptroller William A. Prendergast's reorganization of the Department of Finance, which included the installation of centralized auditing and inspection procedures and completion of the accounting and budget reforms begun under Prendergast's predecessor. He also buttressed the comptroller's efforts to reconcile the department's accounts with other city agencies, departments, and bureaus; prepare New York's first corporate stock budget; and introduce changes in the methods used to collect taxes and manage the city's debt.

Gaynor partially reformed the police department, improving working conditions and hours, instituting a pension system, and reducing incidents of saloon graft, arbitrary arrests, and police brutality. But well-publicized incidents of police corruption marred his accomplishments. He suffered a political defeat when he failed to secure a revision of the city's charter that would have increased the mayor's executive power. Negotiations for much-needed additional rapid transit dragged on throughout Gaynor's term. He supported what became known as the dual plan, a municipal financial partnership with the Interborough and Brooklyn rapid transit companies to extend their existing lines, which brought him intense criticism from those reformers who called for a municipally owned and operated subway system. These positions late in his administration with respect to police corruption, charter revision, and new rapid transit construction put the mayor at odds with many fusion members of the board of estimate, other reformers, and especially the press.

Gaynor helped poorer citizens by eliminating graft associated with the granting of licenses to pushcart peddlers, fruit and newspaper stand proprietors, and bootblacks; he also promptly reported to the U.S. attorney general any evidence collected by city detectives of bribes taken in connection with the granting of naturalization papers to immigrants. After the terrible Triangle Shirtwaist Company fire of 1911, in which 146 workers died, most of them women, and the sinking of the *Titanic* in 1912, he initiated relief funds for the victims' families. Gaynor approved equal pay for women teachers but opposed woman suffrage, supported labor's right to organize but dismissed striking city workers, and kept the police neutral in labor disputes but denounced labor violence. In culturally diverse New York he resisted reformers' efforts to go beyond the law to curb Sunday drinking and sports, eliminate gambling and prostitution, and censor movies.

In the mayoral election of 1913 Gaynor was rejected by the major parties but was nominated on an independent ticket. Six days later he died aboard the steamship *Baltic* while on a European cruise to regain his health. Mourned by thousands, Gaynor was buried in Brooklyn.

• Gaynor's mayoralty papers are in the Municipal Archives and Records Center, New York City. Biographies of Gaynor include Louis Pink, *Gaynor: The Tammany Mayor Who Swallowed the Tiger* (1931); Mortimer Smith, *William Jay Gaynor: Mayor of New York* (1951); and Lately Thomas, *The Mayor Who Mastered New York* (1969). Useful on Gaynor's mayoral years is William R. Hochman, "William J. Gaynor: The Years of Fruition" (Ph.D. diss., Columbia Univ., 1955). See the bibliographies in Thomas and Hochman for a list of Gaynor's published articles. Gaynor's career still awaits a modern critical historical study. An obituary is in the *New York Times*, 12 Sept. 1913.

AUGUSTUS CERILLO, JR.

GAYOSO DE LEMOS, Manuel (30 May 1747–18 July 1799), Spanish army officer, governor of the Natchez district, and governor general of Louisiana, was born in Oporto, Portugal, the son of Manuel Luis Gayoso de Lemos y Sarmiento, a Spanish consul general, and Theresa Angelica Amorín y Magallanes. Educated in England, he developed a capacity for languages and diplomacy. He entered the army's Lisbon Infantry Regiment as a cadet in 1771 and began a slow rise in rank.

Gayoso was a brevet lieutenant colonel in 1787, when he was selected to be governor of the newly created Natchez district in West Florida, where the Spanish government intended to use American immigrants as counter-colonists. Spain also sent Irish priests to convert the Protestant settlers. In 1789 Gayoso arrived at his post, where his wife, Theresa Margarita Hopman y Pereira, and infant daughter soon died. (The couple had married in 1787.) Governor General Esteban Miró requested and obtained Gayoso's promotion to colonel in order to impress the foreign population with whom he would be dealing.

As governor of the Natchez district, Gayoso faced almost all of the major problems of Spanish Louisiana. He helped to supervise construction of forts on the Mississippi and organized a militia from the civilian population of Natchez. When Governor General Barón de Carondelet restarted the effort to separate Kentucky from the United States, Gayoso corresponded frequently with James Wilkinson, the chief American proponent of separation, before the effort was abandoned. In 1795, while taking workmen and materials to begin Fort San Fernando de las Barrancas (now Memphis), he met with one of the Kentucky conspirators, Benjamin Sebastian, at the mouth of the Ohio River.

Gayoso also educated himself about the Indians and successfully concluded a treaty with the Southern Indians in 1793, in which the Indians formed a confederation and allied themselves with Spain against the United States. He was effective as governor of Natchez and was recognized for his abilities and intelligence. As Carondelet's term as governor general of Louisiana and West Florida ended, Gayoso solicited and obtained the post. In 1795 the Spanish government promoted him to brigadier general.

In 1792 Gayoso had married Elizabeth Watts, daughter of an American planter, without official permission. She died three months after the marriage. Four years later, Gayoso requested official permission to marry his second wife's younger sister, Margaret Cyrilla Watts. A child was born to them before permission arrived; the marriage took place in December 1797, four months after Gayoso had become governor general of Louisiana.

In Gayoso's two years as governor, the Spanish government under Manuel Godoy took little interest in Louisiana. It ordered Gayoso to evacuate the lands ceded to the United States in the Treaty of San Lorenzo (1795), which he did in 1798, when he also began the task of surveying the new boundary line between Spain and the United States. Suspicious of American immigrants, Gayoso tried to discourage them from entering Louisiana, which they nevertheless did, particularly in Upper Louisiana. He took measures to protect Spanish lands in the far north of the colony and attempted to maintain a formidable number of gunboats on the Mississippi. He promoted trade in Louisiana as well.

Gayoso possessed a genial personality and charmed many of his acquaintances, although former governor general Miró later accused him of being *tramposo* (deceitful). Gayoso enjoyed entertaining lavishly. By his own admission he spent more than 4,000 pesos (the equivalent of $4,000) entertaining three royal French princes in New Orleans in 1798, adding to the mountain of debt he already owed. A well-read man, he left a library of 165 works, in 411 volumes, in Spanish, French, and English, remarkable for the time, when he died of yellow fever in New Orleans, Louisiana.

It is difficult to assess Gayoso's governorship. He served only two years and at a time when Godoy, as first minister in the Spanish government, was inclined to abandon the colony. The problems of possible foreign invasion, decreased military strength, inadequate finances to carry out projects, and American settlement in Spanish lands all hindered the governor in successfully carrying out his duties. Gayoso was well liked by Louisiana's inhabitants and an able administrator, but the problems he faced were overwhelming.

• Documentary information on Gayoso is in the Archivo General de Indias, Seville; the Archivo Histórico Nacional, Madrid; the Archivo General de Simancas, near Valladolid; the Archivo General Militar de Segovia; and Special Collections, Howard-Tilton Library, Tulane University. Jack D. L. Holmes's sympathetic biography, *Gayoso: The Life of a Spanish Governor in the Mississippi Valley, 1789–1799* (1965), is the only full-length study of Gayoso to date. It, however, fails to utilize completely the documentation in the Spanish archives and is slanted in favor of Gayoso at the expense of the Barón de Carondelet. Additional information on Gayoso can be obtained from the following works by Gilbert C. Din: "The Immigration Policy of Governor Esteban Miró in Spanish Louisiana" and "Spain's Immigration Policy in Louisiana and the American Penetration, 1792–1803," both in *Southwestern Historical Quarterly* 73 (1969): 155–75, and 76 (1973): 255–76, respectively, and *Francisco Bouligny: A Bourbon Soldier in Spanish Louisiana* (1993). Also see Irving A. Leonard, "A Frontier Library, 1799," *Hispanic American Historical Review* 23 (1943): 21–51, and Arthur Preston Whitaker, *The Spanish American Frontier: 1783–1795: The Westward Movement and the Spanish Retreat in the Mississippi Valley* (1927).

GILBERT C. DIN

GEAR, John Henry (7 Apr. 1825–14 July 1900), governor and senator, was born in Ithaca, New York, the son of Ezekiel Gilbert Gear, a clergyman in the Protestant Episcopal church, and Miranda Cook. In 1836 the Reverend Gear took his family west to the frontier town of Galena, Illinois, and two years later he was appointed chaplain at Fort Snelling in what is today Minnesota. During these years young John Henry received an education from his father and in whatever schools existed at these frontier outposts. In 1843 John Henry moved to Burlington in the Iowa Territory, where he began clerking in a wholesale grocery house. By 1850 he was a partner in the business, and in 1855 he became full owner. During the 1850s and 1860s Gear was a leading business figure in southeastern Iowa, becoming known to storekeepers and merchants throughout the area and promoting the construction of railroads vital to Burlington's development. In 1852 he married Harriet Foote; they had four children.

Business was Gear's chief preoccupation during his first quarter-century in Burlington. He was, however, elected alderman in 1852 and chosen mayor eleven years later. Not until the early 1870s, when he was in his mid-forties, did his political career begin in earnest. In 1871 Gear was elected on the Republican ticket to the state house of representatives, serving in that body for the next six years. In 1874 the house was split evenly between the Anti-Monopolist party and the Republicans, and not until the 137th ballot were the legislators finally able to agree on Gear as Speaker of the house. Two years later he was reelected to this position. An amiable figure who acquired a reputation for his countless personal acquaintances, Gear was a good choice to preside over the sharply divided house of representatives. Throughout his career, he benefited from this ability to make many friends and few enemies, and he often succeeded where more controversial and outspoken figures would have failed.

Following his service as Speaker of the house, Gear occupied the office of governor for four years. As Iowa's chief executive he won a reputation for pruning expenses and reducing the state's debt. He was especially vigilant in cutting costs at the state's penal facilities and was known for his unannounced inspections of state institutions, during which he sought to uncover waste and excessive expenditures. These efforts earned him the sobriquet "Old Business."

Meanwhile, Gear's ties with the forces of big business were strengthening. In 1877 his daughter married Joseph W. Blythe, the general counsel for the Chicago, Burlington, and Quincy Railroad and reportedly one of the kingmakers of Iowa politics. Blythe sought to ensure that nothing happened in Iowa detrimental to the interests of his railroad, and working through political leaders such as Gear, he generally achieved his goals.

In 1882 Gear failed to win a seat in the U.S. Senate, the Republican caucus in the state legislature instead supporting James Falconer Wilson. After a four-year interlude, Gear was elected to the U.S. House of Representatives, serving from 1887 to 1891 and from 1893 to 1895. In the House he was a member of the important Ways and Means Committee, where he aided in framing the McKinley Tariff of 1890. Believing in the benefits of sugar beet cultivation, Gear was responsible for incorporating a federal bounty for sugar producers in the McKinley Bill.

Finally in 1894 Gear fulfilled his ambition to win election to the U.S. Senate. Albert Cummins was the candidate of the more reform-minded Republicans, who chafed under the domination of Blythe and the Burlington railroad. Blythe, however, was able to rally sufficient strength in the legislature to elect his aging but safe father-in-law. Never one to rock the boat, Senator Gear followed the lead of Iowa's distinguished senior senator, William Boyd Allison, and did nothing to offend the interests of his son-in-law. An orthodox Republican, he supported protective tariffs, a sound currency, and the policies of the William McKinley administration in general. Gear rarely spoke on the floor of the Senate and did not indulge in oratorical pyrotechnics. Instead, he faithfully performed his committee work and loyally served the Republican leadership.

By 1900 a heart condition was taking its toll on the aged senator. Each day his wife accompanied him to the Senate chamber to watch from the gallery and make sure he did not overtax himself. Despite Gear's ill health, Blythe and his allies were determined to reelect him to the Senate and prevent the supposedly dangerous Cummins from securing the post. Consequently, in early 1900 the Iowa legislature chose Gear for a second term. In the summer of 1900 Gear died in Washington, D.C.

Though never a major national figure, Gear was a second-string member of the powerful team of Iowa Republicans who wielded disproportionate power in Congress during the late nineteenth and early twentieth centuries. Following the lead of Senator Allison, he faithfully upheld conservative Republican values and proved an amiable front man for the Burlington railroad. A representative of the old business interests of the nineteenth century, Gear died just as the forces of the Progressive Era were gaining strength and preparing to challenge the political tradition that he had long upheld.

• For biographical sketches on Gear, see *Annals of Iowa* 4 (1900): 555–56; and William H. Fleming, "Gov. John Henry Gear," *Annals of Iowa* 5 (1903): 583–600. An account of Gear's years as governor is in Edgar R. Harlan, *A Narrative History of the People of Iowa* (1931). The *Congressional Record*, 1901, vol. 34, pt. 2, 56th Cong., 2d sess., includes a series of memorial addresses on Gear. An obituary is in the *New York Times*, 15 July 1900.

JON C. TEAFORD

GEARY, John White (30 Dec. 1819–8 Feb. 1873), soldier and governor of Kansas Territory and Pennsylvania, was born near Mount Pleasant, Pennsylvania, the son of Richard Geary and Margaret White. After failing in the iron industry, Geary's father opened a school, where he taught for many years. Geary was a student at Jefferson (now Washington and Jefferson) College when his father died. Forced by the family's debts to drop out of college, he opened a school before finally completing college. He then spent several years clerking and studying engineering and law and was admitted to the bar. Until 1846 he worked as an engineer for Kentucky and Pennsylvania railroads. In 1843 he married Margaret Ann Logan, with whom he had two children. By the time of his maturity, Geary was an impressive figure, towering six feet five and a half inches, weighing 260 pounds, with an iron jaw and penetrating gray eyes. When the United States declared war against Mexico, Geary, who for ten years had been active in the state militia, organized a company known as the American Highlanders. They joined the Second Pennsylvania Regiment, in which he was elected lieutenant colonel.

The regiment moved swiftly to the Mexican coast, where it came under the command of Winfield Scott. Geary now became attached to General J. A. Quitman's brigade, and because Colonel W. B. Roberts fell ill, he often commanded the regiment. Geary led the successful assault on Mexico City's strongest military work, Chapultepec castle, and was assigned command of the citadel. On the death of Colonel Roberts, the men elected Geary colonel. He won praise from both Quitman and Scott and returned home with a shining reputation.

Shortly after Geary's return from Mexico, President James K. Polk, on 22 January 1849, appointed him the first postmaster of San Francisco. He had barely begun work when his Whig successor, appointed by the new Zachary Taylor administration, replaced him. Soon thereafter, however, against his inclination, he was unanimously elected first alcalde of San Francisco, still under the Mexican system of government. The military governor added to Geary's numerous duties by appointing him judge of first instance, combining civil, criminal, and admiralty duties. As California moved toward statehood, Geary wielded his influence to insert an antislavery provision in the state constitution. When San Francisco received a charter, he became the city's first mayor. As alcalde and mayor, judge, and chairman of a board to fund the municipal debt, he launched the anarchic city, governance of which was now in a transitional stage between Mexican and U.S. rule, on its way to a sound future. Because of the deteriorating health of his wife, the two returned to their Pennsylvania farm, where she died the following year. Reportedly worth $.5 million, derived from his business ventures and real estate investments, Geary became an operator of coal mines in his state and in Virginia.

In July 1856 President Franklin Pierce appointed him territorial governor of Kansas. By that date "Bleeding Kansas" had become the nation's most urgent issue, influencing the pending presidential election, as Democrats championed congressional noninterference with slavery and Republicans immediate admission under a free-state constitution, threatening the welfare of Geary's party and nation. Assured of the Pierce administration's support and determined to restore peace, Geary in September reached Kansas, where armed bands roved the territory, terrorizing settlers.

Within a few weeks Geary had substantially restored order, disbanding the proslavery militia, organizing a new one subject to his orders, and averting an attack on Lawrence, threatened by a force of proslavery men. The judicial system was a more difficult problem. The federal judges he deemed negligent and incompetent, the U.S. marshal wanting in courage and energy, the attorney general uncooperative. Geary's troubles with securing justice came to a head when Chief Justice Samuel Lecompte twice freed an accused murderer, the marshal refused to arrest the freed man, the U.S. Senate refused to confirm a judge nominated to replace Lecompte, and Secretary of War William L. Marcy asked that Geary explain his earlier condemnation of Lecompte. Kansas was divided into two governments, one favoring slavery, the other a free state. The proslavery legislature equally proved an obstruction to Geary's goal of "equal and exact justice to all men." The governor defused a potential conflict between legislatures by securing the resignation of the free-state "governor," Charles Robinson (1818–1894).

Meeting in early January 1857, the proslavery legislature clashed with Geary and regularly overrode his vetoes, including his veto of a bill providing for a state constitution to be drafted at Lecompton that did not require general ratification by the electorate.

Violence threatened again. William T. Sherrard, appointed sheriff by a county tribunal but refused confirmation by Geary, confronted the governor with insults and a gun; he was himself subsequently shot by a member of Geary's staff. Geary asked that federal troops stationed in Kansas be sent him, only to be refused by the commanding general. Geary's position had become precarious, without support from the legislature, the courts, local officials, the military, and the prosouthern Pierce administration. The arduous six months had weakened his health, and he had bouts of lung hemorrhages. On 4 March 1857 he resigned and proceeded to Washington, where his account of the Kansas troubles stirred heated northern sympathies.

Geary returned to Pennsylvania and married Mary Church Henderson in 1858; they had two children. For the next several years he observed with dismay the widening chasm between North and South. After hearing of the firing on Fort Sumter, he raised the Twenty-eighth Pennsylvania Regiment, which on 28 June was mustered into service under his command. He compiled a distinguished war record, winning Abraham Lincoln's thanks in 1861, two-star rank, and notable victories. In western Virginia in 1861 he repelled rebel forces under Turner Ashby and the next year drove A. P. Hill out of Leesburg. Promoted to brigadier general on 25 April 1862, Geary was wounded at Cedar Mountain and spent nearly two months convalescing. At Chancellorsville, commanding the Second Division of the Twelfth Army Corps, he was again wounded, recuperating in time to see action at Gettysburg, where on the third day his forces recovered Culp's Hill. Transferred with the Twelfth Corps to the western theater in the fall of 1863, he drove the defenders from Lookout Mountain, planting his battle flag on the heights, and participated in the battle of Missionary Ridge. In the "march to the sea," Geary's division led the way into Atlanta and was the first to enter Savannah. Lincoln promoted him to brevet major general "for fitness to command and promptness to execute." He took part in the Carolinas campaign and, after the Confederate surrender, once more returned to Pennsylvania.

As the gubernatorial election of 1866 loomed, Geary joined the Republicans and, backed by Simon Cameron's faction, won the governorship. In his first term he sought to curb the power of the railroads, vetoing a series of special interest bills, and advocated a general railroad law. He excoriated mine owners for selfish disregard of miners' safety. Strong-willed, passionate, and independent, he made many enemies and barely won reelection. In his second term he succeeded in calling a constitutional convention that instituted a series of reforms. He reduced the public debt and abolished the state tax on real estate, salaries, trades, and professions, while increasing expenditures for eleemosynary institutions and education. His gubernatorial service was characterized by repeated conflicts with the legislature and numerous vetoes (he issued 390 in his six years in office). In 1872 he was a contender for the presidential nomination of the Labor Reform convention and actually received the most votes on the first ballot before being defeated by David Davis. Shortly after retiring from office, he died of a heart attack in Harrisburg.

• Geary manuscripts are in the Atlanta Historical Society collection, the Oregon Historical Society Library, the Pennsylvania Historical and Museum Commission, and Yale University Library. Letters appear in *A Politician Goes to War: The Civil War Letters of John White Geary*, ed. William Alan Blair (1995). Geary's papers as territorial governor are in *Transactions of the Kansas State Historical Society*, vols. 4 and 5 (1890, 1986). The best introduction is Harry M. Tinkcom, *John White Geary, Soldier-Statesman* (1940). James A. Rawley, *Race and Politics: "Bleeding Kansas" and the Coming of the Civil War* (1969), treats the Kansas crisis. Much material pertaining to Geary's Civil War activities may be found in *The War of the Rebellion: A Compilation of the Official Records of the Union and Confederate Armies* (128 vols., 1880–1901). Erwin S. Bradley, *The Triumph of Militant Republicanism* (1964), has material on Geary as governor of Pennsylvania.
JAMES A. RAWLEY

GEDDES, James (22 July 1763–19 Aug. 1838), civil engineer, judge, and surveyor, was born of Scottish parents (names unknown) near Carlisle, Pennsylvania. As a youth, Geddes studied mathematics with a tutor and studied languages independently. In 1793 he visited the area that later became New York state's Onondaga County; he moved there the following year. He organized one of the state's first salt works, helping to establish the salt industry, which would dominate the area's economy for many years.

Geddes studied law and was admitted to the bar. He married Lucy Jerome of nearby Fabius, New York, in 1799; the couple had at least one son. In 1800 Geddes was appointed justice of the peace; nine years later he was made judge of the county court and the court of common pleas. An interest in politics led him to run for the New York State Assembly, to which he was elected in 1804 and again in 1822. He was also elected to the U.S. Congress in 1813.

While Geddes was serving his first term as a New York assemblyman, he was approached by the surveyor general of New York, Simeon DeWitt. DeWitt enlisted Geddes in the movement to construct a canal system to link Lakes Ontario and Erie with the Hudson River. Geddes became a champion of this plan, visiting sites across the state to gather topographical and geological information while promoting the construction of the canal system. He carried on an extensive correspondence with land agents and surveyors, collecting as much information as possible about the lay of the land.

Under the appointment of the state surveyor general, Geddes performed the first canal survey in 1808, in spite of his lack of technical training. Before performing these surveys, he had only used a spirit level on

one occasion for only a few hours; this level, given to him by DeWitt, would be used for many years by Geddes, both on New York canals and during his later work on Ohio canals. In his report, submitted to the New York State Legislature on 20 January 1809, Geddes included surveys along several canal routes: from Lake Ontario to Lake Erie, between Mud Creek and Sodus Bay; from Lake Erie to Lake Ontario, by way of a canal from Lewiston up the Niagara Escarpment to the navigable waters above the Falls of Niagara, and from there to Buffalo; and from Oneida Lake to Lake Ontario, via the Oswego River and from Oneida Lake to where the Salmon Creek enters Lake Ontario. He also explored the possibility of constructing an overland route across the state. This route began at Oneida Lake, continued to the Cayuga Marshes and up the Mud Creek valley and across country to the Genesee River; it proceeded to the Tonawanda Swamp and down the Tonawanda Creek to the Niagara River, which connected with Lake Erie. Geddes's report made clear that a canal could be constructed along an interior route nearly identical to that authorized for the Erie Canal eight years later. His entire survey was accomplished at a cost of $673. In 1810 Geddes assisted a state survey commission headed by De Witt Clinton, but with the outbreak of the War of 1812, these efforts were set aside.

In 1815 peace returned, and Clinton intensified his lobbying for the canal, writing a widely distributed pamphlet detailing the benefits of such a waterway. State representatives from the New York City area objected to the project on the grounds that their taxes would increase and upstate communities would prosper at their expense. Nevertheless, the state government authorized the Erie Canal's construction, which began on 4 July 1817.

Geddes, though continuing his duties as judge of Onondaga County, accepted the appointment of engineer on the Erie Canal. Engineering, more to his liking than law, quickly occupied his full attention. He was responsible for overseeing the western section of the canal, which ran from the Seneca River to within eleven miles of the mouth of Tonawanda Creek. In 1818 he was directed to superintend the construction of the middle section of the canal, between Rome and Utica. During this time Geddes also made a "test-level" between Rome and the eastern end of Oneida Lake, a distance of nearly a hundred miles. His work was so accurate that the discrepancy at the junction of the two levels was less than one and a half inches. In the summer of 1818 Geddes was appointed chief engineer of the Champlain Canal; he remained in charge of its construction until 1822.

Geddes came to be known as a competent, energetic engineer of new waterways throughout much of the eastern United States. In 1822, on the recommendation of New York governor De Witt Clinton, Geddes was selected to survey a canal from the Ohio River to Lake Erie. Five years later he was employed by the federal government to examine routes for the Chesapeake and Ohio Canal. In 1828 he served as a consultant for a Pennsylvania canal, and the following year he investigated a canal route in Maine from Sebago Lake to Westbrook.

Geddes left no papers for future chroniclers. He wrote, "I attach no importance to what I have done, having simply performed my duty; therefore I ask no higher place in the public estimation than should be spontaneously given me" (Stuart, p. 45). Nonetheless, his role was notable. Geddes was among those few who, in building the Erie Canal, shaped the course of the future. The area on the western shore of Onondaga Lake, where he settled and dug salt wells and where he died, was named the town of Geddes in his honor in 1848.

• There are collections of Geddes material at the New York State Archives and at the Erie Canal Museum, Syracuse, N.Y. Nobel E. Whitford, *History of the Canal System of the State of New York, together with Brief Histories of the Canals of the United States and Canada* (2 vols., 1906), is an important source on Geddes. C. B. Stuart, *Lives and Works of Civil and Military Engineers of America* (1871), includes a chapter about Geddes. See also Henry Wayland Hill, "An Historical Review of Waterways and Canal Construction in New York State," *Buffalo Historical Society Publications* 12 (1908); and the multiauthored "Canal Enlargement in New York State: Papers on the Barge Canal Campaign and Related Topics," *Buffalo Historical Society Publications* 13 (1909). Other valuable historical works are Elkanah Watson, *History of the Rise, Progress, and Existing Condition of the Western Canals in the State of New York* (1820); Charles Glidden Haines, *Public Documents Relating to the New York Canals* (1821); and De Witt Clinton, *The Canal Policy of the State of New York* (1821).

DANIEL MARTIN DUMYCH

GEDDES, Norman Bel (21 Apr. 1893–8 May 1958), scene and lighting designer, industrial designer, and producer, was born Norman Melancton Geddes in Adrian, Michigan, the son of Clifton Terry Geddes and Gloria Lulu Yingling. He was educated in public schools in Michigan, Ohio, Pennsylvania, and Illinois before attending the Cleveland School of Art and the prestigious Chicago Art Institute by the time he was sixteen years old. When he was in his early twenties, Geddes had his earliest successes as a magazine and poster artist in Detroit, Michigan. He designed his first theatrical production, *Nju* and *Papa*, for the Little Theatre in Los Angeles in 1916, where he truly began his stage career. That same year Geddes married Helen Belle Sneider (and added the "Bel" to his own name), and they had two daughters (one of whom became the successful Broadway actress Barbara Bel Geddes). In 1916 Geddes also developed the first lenses for stage lights and introduced the first focus spot lamps while working at the Little Theatre. His innovations continued in 1919 when he designed the first combined focus and flood lamp unit.

While sitting on a park bench in Los Angeles dismayed about the difficulty he was having in finding challenging work, Geddes picked up a magazine that included an interview with impresario and banker Otto H. Kahn called "Millionaires Should Help Art-ists." Taking Kahn at his word, Geddes sent a telegram and in the return mail received $400 from Kahn to help him travel to New York City. Kahn introduced Geddes to officials of the Metropolitan Opera, which led to three designs for the Met and, ultimately, to his distinguished Broadway career. In 1917 Geddes met American scene designer Robert Edmond Jones, who had been influenced by the design and production concepts coming out of the European modernist theater. Jones inspired Geddes and helped him find a professional design job at a summer stock theater in Milwaukee in 1918. That same year Geddes designed a New York revival of Oscar Wilde's comedy *The Importance of Being Earnest*, which began his long and prolific career as one of Broadway's leading designers, with occasional forays into opera and ballet design, as well as producing and directing. Borrowing on the techniques of European scene and lighting designers, particularly those of Edward Gordon Craig and Adolphe Appia, Geddes removed footlights and installed balcony rail and auditorium lights in the theaters where he worked.

After scoring a Broadway success with *Ermine* (1920), Geddes embarked on a project of vast scope and scale, designs for Dante's *The Divine Comedy*. Although an actual production was never realized, Geddes constructed a model (with miniature lighting) for *The Divine Comedy* that was exhibited widely and featured in a photo study in *Theatre Arts Magazine*. The approving critical response to the project made Geddes well known in international artistic circles—and influenced a generation of young scene designers who attempted to follow his lead.

Under the influence of the "new stagecraft," as the Craig- and Appia-inspired techniques were known, Geddes promoted the idea of an architectural setting lit to create the necessary mood and environment. This was in strong opposition to the traditional painted realistic settings that had predominated on Broadway stages since the nineteenth century. Geddes's acclaimed design for Max Reinhardt's notable production of *The Miracle* in 1924 required gutting New York's Century Theatre to produce an architectural setting that remade the theater as a medieval cathedral. Complete with pews for seating, stained glass windows, and other embellishments, along with evocative and dramatic lighting that made maximum use of the columns and other adornments Geddes worked into his setting, *The Miracle* was one of the most influential designs of the era. Geddes took this approach further with a 1925 Parisian production of *Jeanne D'Arc*, starring and directed by Eva Le Gallienne. In this case he eliminated all scenic embellishments in order to depend completely on architectural structure (enhanced by lighting) as the basis for the setting. In 1929 Geddes served as the designer of illumination and as a consultant for the Agricultural Commission of the Chicago World's Fair.

Geddes was remarkably versatile as a designer. Despite his preference for architectural settings, he could also design effectively in the naturalistic mode, as he demonstrated in his 1935 setting for Sidney Kingsley's successful drama *Dead End*, which featured a highly detailed city street leading to a pier from which characters could dive into an orchestra pit full of water. Geddes is credited with designing over 200 theatrical productions marked by both the quality of each design and the diversity of works represented. These included musicals such as the Gershwins' *Lady Be Good* (1924), the 1925 edition of the Ziegfeld *Follies*, and Cole Porter's *Fifty Million Frenchmen* (1929). He also excelled in dramas such as the acclaimed productions of *The Eternal Road* (1937) and *Sons and Soldiers* (1943). Although remembered mostly as a designer and producer, Geddes also directed over a dozen productions, including *Nathan Hale* (1917), which he also wrote. It was respectfully received by critics, but few of his other directing credits generated much interest. Geddes made a few forays into film, including designs for *Lief the Lucky* (1919), *Feet of Clay* (1924), *The Sorrows of Satan* (1925), *The Pit and the Pendulum* (1925), and *Bermuda* (1933), but few of these were particularly popular. In 1930 Geddes received the Prize for Design from the Ukrainian State Theatre in Kharkov. He and his first wife, Helen, divorced in 1932. Shortly thereafter he married Frances Waite, who died a few years later. They had no children.

In 1926 Geddes founded a successful industrial design company that had as its goal the modernization of industrial products. The iconoclastic firm aimed at making industrial products more efficient and aesthetically pleasing. Geddes was invited to serve as an architectural consultant for the 1933 Chicago World's Fair Exposition. He designed numerous exhibits and facilities that were visionary in conception, but these were never constructed because of the financial constraints of the depression era. In his 1933 book, *Horizons*, Geddes provided a volume of futuristic designs for everything from homes and businesses to automobiles and trains (also cameras, refrigerators, ships, furniture, and board games). Geddes's aim, in both the theater and his industrial designing, was to break new ground. In *Horizons* he wrote, "We are too much inclined to believe, because things have long been done a certain way, that *that* is the best way to do them. Following old grooves of thought is one method of playing safe. But it deprives one of initiative and takes too long. It sacrifices the value of the element of surprise. At times, the only thing to do is to cut loose and *do the unexpected!* It takes more even than imagination to be progressive. It takes vision and courage."

General Motors hired Geddes to design their Futurama Exhibit at the 1939 New York World's Fair. Although he continued to design for the theater until 1945, when he created designs for the successful musical comedy revue *The Seven Lively Arts*, starring Bert Lahr and Beatrice Lillie, Geddes devoted the remainder of his career to industrial design projects. He married for a third time, to Ann Howe Hilliard in 1944, but their marriage ended in divorce. They had no children.

Geddes was married to his fourth wife, Edith Lutyens, who was also a scene designer, director, and producer, when he died in New York while lunching with a friend.

• Books by Geddes include *Magic Motorways* (1940), *Miracle in the Evening: An Autobiography* (1960), and *A Project for a Theatrical Presentation of the Divine Comedy of Dante Alighieri* (1924). For additional information on Geddes, see Lucius Beebe, "From Hamlet to the World's Fair," *New York Herald Tribune*, 28 May 1939; "Bel Geddes," *Fortune*, July 1930; Bruce Bliven, "Norman Bel Geddes: His Art and Ideas," *Theatre Arts Magazine*, July 1919; George Bogusch, "An American in Paris: Norman Bel Geddes Produces 'Jeanne D'Arc,'" *Theatre Design and Technology*, Oct. 1969, pp. 4–11; M. Sanchez Cobos, "Norman Bel Geddes, the Man that Revolutionized Theatre Architecture," *El Diario*, 23 Oct. 1956; Frederick Hunter, "Norman Bel Geddes," *Texas Quarterly* 5 (1962); Hunter, "Norman Bel Geddes: Renaissance Man of the Theatre," in *Innovations in Stage and Theatre Design* (1972); Thomas J. Mikotowicz, ed., *Theatrical Designers: An International Biography* (1993); Hiram Motherwell, "Geddes: An Engineer in the Theatre," *Theatre Guild Magazine*, Nov. 1931; Bobbi Owen, *Scenic Design on Broadway: Designers and Their Credits, 1915–1990* (1991); and Arthur Strawn, "Norman Bel Geddes," *Outlook*, 12 Feb. 1930. Obituaries are in the *New York Times*, 9 May 1958; the *Stage* (London), 15 May 1958; the *Times* (London), 12 May 1958; and *Variety*, 14 May 1958.

JAMES FISHER

GEDDINGS, Eli (1799–9 Oct. 1878), physician and educator, was born in Newberry County, South Carolina. He studied medicine at the Abbeville Academy from 1818 to 1820 and was licensed to practice by the Charleston Examination Board in 1820.

Geddings's early practice was chiefly in Abbeville, in association with Dr. S. E. Davis, but in the winter of 1821–1822 he left to attend medical lectures at the University of Pennsylvania. He then returned to Abbeville and continued in his practice there until moving to Charleston, South Carolina, in September 1824. There he enrolled in the Medical College of South Carolina and in 1825 was among five in the first class of students to graduate from that newly formed institution. Upon graduation, Geddings spent a year working and studying in the hospitals of London and Paris, returning to Charleston in May 1827. He continued at the medical college as demonstrator of anatomy until 1828, while continuing to develop his private practice.

In 1827 Geddings opened the Charleston Academy of Medicine, a successful private school offering lectures on the full range of surgery and medicine, and based on his already considerable collection of several hundred medical and scientific books, many brought back from Europe. The academy was one of many such schools that flourished in a time when the system of medical apprenticeship was the chief means of professional training. It also served as a preparatory school for those who hoped to continue at the new medical college.

Geddings moved to Baltimore in 1831 to become chair of anatomy and physiology at the University of

Maryland. He also served as editor of the quarterly *Baltimore Medical and Surgical Journal and Review* from 1833, transforming it to the monthly *North American Archives of Medical and Surgical Sciences*. These Baltimore years correspond to a time of particularly nasty dissension and disruption over the inept governance of the medical college by the medical society in Charleston. The avoidance of those disputes appears to have motivated at least the timing of Geddings's departure. In 1837 he returned to the reorganized Medical College in Charleston as chair of pathological anatomy and medical jurisprudence, a position especially created for him. From 1849 to 1858 he was chair of surgery.

During the Civil War Geddings served as a surgeon on the Confederate Army Medical Board. When the fall of Charleston seemed imminent, he made the unfortunate decision to move out to the countryside, shipping his valuable library, along with the finished manuscript of his medical textbook, to Columbia for protection from the Union forces. The books were all destroyed when that city was burned by Gen. William T. Sherman, and the remainder of his medical and surgical equipment in Charleston were all stolen during his absence. In the years of Federal occupation, Geddings worked to reestablish the Medical College in Charleston. Having lost everything in the war, he was forced to sell "The Elms," a small estate north of Charleston that he had purchased in 1843, and return to private practice to supplement his teaching. A substantial part of the proceeds of that sale also went to assist the devastated college in its recovery.

Geddings was highly esteemed both for his teaching and his concern for the improvement of American medical schools. In spite of his age, and the ill will that persisted after the recent war, in 1870 he was appointed chair of the American Medical Association committee on medical education. The following year he resigned from his work as regular physician at the medical college, and lectured as chair of clinical medicine until his retirement in 1873. Geddings had married Mrs. Wyatt Grey. They had three sons, all of whom became physicians, and a daughter. He died in Charleston. One of the preeminent medical teachers in South Carolina for almost half a century, Geddings played a crucial role both in the original establishment of quality medical education in South Carolina, and in its reconstruction after the Civil War.

• Joseph I. Waring, *History of Medicine in South Carolina, 1825–1900* (1967), includes a portrait. All of Geddings's published writings date from the 1830s including a brief *Introductory Lecture of the Medical College of the State of South Carolina* (1838) and several essays and editorials in the *Baltimore Journal*, *North American Archives*, and the *American Journal of Medical Sciences* (Philadelphia). The completed manuscript of a medical textbook was destroyed with his library. Contemporary sources are "Biographical Sketch of Eli Geddings, M.D.," *Charleston Medical Journal and Review* 12 (1857), and *In Memoriam, Eli Geddings*, presented to the Medical Society of South Carolina by F. M. Robertson, T. L. Ogier, and J. B. Chazal (c. 1878).

CHARLES D. KAY

GEER, Will (9 Mar. 1902–22 Apr. 1978), actor, was born Willem Aughe Ghere near Frankfort, Indiana, the son of A. Roy Ghere, a postal worker, and Katherine Aughe, a teacher. The family moved to Kentucky, Georgia, and Tennessee before settling in Chicago, where Geer took up high school dramatics.

For a time Geer combined schooling with a professional career, first (1920–1922) with a repertory company specializing in Shakespeare and Ibsen, then (1923–1924) with Doc Bart's Ark Show Boat, mostly along the Ohio River. The showboat years, he later remarked, convinced him that all performers should learn musical instruments. Geer earned a bachelor's degree in horticulture from the University of Chicago in 1924 and later that year studied at Columbia University while working in the university library.

Geer was still with Bart's when he made his New York debut (1924) in *Uncle Tom's Cabin* as Simon Legree, the first of his exuberantly overplayed villains. Between 1924 and 1927 Geer traveled with several stock companies in midwestern and border states, developing a love for folk music. Joining Minnie Maddern Fiske's stock company in 1928, the towering, robust Geer portrayed Pistol on Broadway in *The Merry Wives of Windsor* (1928). When the company disbanded in 1931 after Fiske's death, Geer became a ship's steward on the Panama Pacific Line, joining the Maritime Union. In 1936 Geer married actress Herta Ware, the granddaughter of Ella Bloor, who was a founder of the American Communist party. They had three children.

Geer's film career began in 1932 in *The Misleading Lady*, a knockabout comedy. He remained in Los Angeles through 1934, helping found the Los Angeles New Theatre Group, for which he directed Clifford Odets's *Waiting for Lefty*. In 1935 Geer made his first visit to Russia. Following his return, he helped found the Actors Repertory Theatre in New York, appearing through 1937 in such plays as Irwin Shaw's *Bury the Dead*. For the radical New Theatre League he toured factories and coal mines with folk singers such as Burl Ives, performing agitprop plays. Joe Klein called him "a happy, expansive blowhard of a man . . . at his best on a makeshift stage in front of an audience of workers." During his second visit to Russia in 1937 Geer appeared with an American company at a Moscow theater festival. On his return he created the role of Slim in John Steinbeck's *Of Mice and Men*.

Late in 1937 Geer originated the role of Mr. Mister, the powerful, corrupt capitalist in Marc Blitzstein's musicalization of the recent steel strike, *The Cradle Will Rock*, called by Jane deHart Matthews the "first serious musical drama written in America which provided a new vernacular for the man in the street." Originally a project of the Works Progress Administration Federal Theatre, *The Cradle Will Rock* lost its sponsorship under congressional pressure, an action that cost the producer, John Houseman, and the director, Orson Welles, their theater. On opening night, while 600 ticketholders fidgeted, Geer previewed his scenes on the sidewalk. The crowd eventually marched to an uptown theater, increasing en route to 2,500. Because their union forbade their appearing onstage in an unsanctioned play, the actors performed *The Cradle Will Rock* seated in the auditorium.

One of Geer's 1938 shows was the revue *Sing Out the News*, a commercial relative of the Federal Theatre's Living Newspapers. In George Kaufman and Moss Hart's sketch "A Liberal Education," Geer was a good liberal father cautioning his son, jeered at by rich kids and radicals alike, to keep an open mind. Geer's character is arrested for disturbing the peace.

In 1939 Geer returned to Los Angeles, starring in the documentary film *The Fight for Life* as a doctor teaching pregnant women safe methods of home birth. Directed by Pare Lorentz, the government-produced film was premiered in the White House. While making the film, Geer met folk singer Woody Guthrie. They toured migrant workers' camps in California's central valley, organizing and entertaining. As Guthrie sang "The Philadelphia Lawyer," Geer acted it out; as Geer recited Vachel Lindsay's "The Congo," Guthrie pounded out the rhythm on his guitar.

In 1939 Geer took up the lead in *Tobacco Road* at New York's Forrest Theatre, where he organized a hootenanny evening with folk singers Guthrie, Leadbelly, and the Golden Gate Quartet, benefiting a Steinbeck agriculture-worker committee. Continuing on Broadway, Geer appeared in a 1941 radio soap opera called "Bright Horizon" and with Guthrie, Ives, and others in Alan Lomax's radio folk opera *The Martins and the Coys*, unaired until 1944.

Geer, who had supported Wendell Willkie for the presidency in 1940, and Guthrie toured a "Roosevelt Bandwagon" prior to the 1944 campaign. On Broadway, Geer appeared in *Flamingo Road* (1946), a revival of *The Cradle Will Rock* (1947), and *Hope Is the Thing with Feathers* (1948). Back in California, Geer began to specialize in playing rugged, principled outdoorsmen, appearing in eight films from 1948 to 1951, including *Deep Waters* (1948), William Faulkner's *Intruder in the Dust* (1949), and *Winchester 73* (1950).

On 11 April 1951, a week after Julius and Ethel Rosenberg were sentenced to death as Soviet spies, Geer refused to cooperate with the House Un-American Activities Committee hearings in Los Angeles, asserting that "the word 'Communist' was an emotional word like 'witch' in Salem." Acting under its Waldorf Hotel pact of 1947, the Motion Picture Association blacklisted Geer for the next eleven years.

In 1952 Geer bought property in Topanga Canyon, near Santa Monica; according to Joe Klein, it became "a halfway house of sorts for lost souls and refugees from the political storms of the period," including Guthrie himself. In his backyard, Geer and his friends

"would perform Shakespeare and agitprop for free each Sunday . . . and make a little money on the side selling hot dogs." Geer lectured on theater and taught vegetable growing. In 1952, crossfiling under existing California law for the nominations of three political parties, Geer unsuccessfully ran for the Sixteenth Congressional District seat eventually won by Republican Donald L. Jackson, a supporter of the House Un-American Activities Committee.

John Houseman hired Geer for his 1954 New York productions of *Coriolanus* and *The Seagull*; in the same year Geer helped reestablish the Folksay Theatre, which was born during the depression. Among his Broadway shows between 1955 and 1959 were *The Ponder Heart*, *Cock a Doodle Dandy*, and *No Time for Sergeants*. In 1957 he became a regular at the Shakespearean Festival in Stratford, Connecticut. By 1962 he had played fifteen roles and established in Stratford a garden based on the 1,000 horticultural references in Shakespeare's plays. In 1960–1961 he toured the nation in Stratford's *A Midsummer Night's Dream*. In 1962, as the blacklist crumbled, Geer returned to film playing the Senate minority leader in *Advise and Consent*, a story with strong witchhunting undertones.

In 1962 Geer, who had helped found a repertory company at the University of Michigan, appeared there as Walt Whitman. Between 1960 and 1962 he toured a show based on Mark Twain's writings, and in 1963 he returned to Broadway in *110 in the Shade*, the musical version of *The Rainmaker*, which ran 330 performances and toured for another year. In 1964 Geer appeared in the film *Black Like Me*, the white John Howard Griffin's account of his months posing as an African American. In 1965 Geer was off Broadway as Robert Frost, in 1966 he was in two Shakespearean roles for the Old Globe in San Diego (where he helped establish another Shakespearean garden), and in 1969 he was back on Broadway in *Horseman, Pass By!* His film roles during this period included the coldly sinister administrator of Faustian technology in director John Frankenheimer's *Seconds* (1966), the prosecuting attorney in Truman Capote's *In Cold Blood* (1967), and a rough-hewn, lovable, and wise grandfather in *The Reivers* (1969), another film version of Faulkner.

During the 1970s, while continuing to appear in films, Geer and his son Raleigh turned the Topanga backyard into three theaters amidst another Shakespearean garden. This was Theatricum Botanicum, designed "to provide opportunities for young actors and actresses to learn to act by playing in classics." Geer advocated a theater in everyone's home, where family members could read to each other. In 1972 he assumed the role of the lumber-mill-owning grandfather Zeb Walton in the depression-era television series "The Waltons"; it brought him an Emmy Award in 1975.

In 1977 Geer and many other former blacklistees sent an open letter to Gustav Husak, president of the Czechoslovakian Socialist Republic: "We who fought for socialism in our own land are ashamed and crip-

pled by the violation of socialist legality in your land
. . . During the McCarthy period, when we ourselves
were jailed, blacklisted and harassed, it was international outrage that helped us to regain our rights."
Geer died in a Los Angeles hospital as his family recited Robert Frost's poetry and sang folk songs.

• Various facets of Geer can be glimpsed in John Houseman,
Unfinished Business (1986), Jane deHart Mathews, *The Feder-
al Theatre 1935–1939* (1967), and Joe Klein, *Woody Guthrie:
A Life* (1981), with a fascinating footnote in Studs Terkel,
Hard Times (1970). Larry Ceplair and Steven Englund, *The
Inquisition in Hollywood* (1983), says little about Geer but a
great deal about the HUAC hearings, which can also be fol-
lowed in the pages of the *New York Times* and the *Los Angeles
Times* in Mar. and Apr. 1951. See also Sally Osborne Norton,
"An Historical Study of Actor Will Geer, His Life and Work
in the Context of Twentieth Century American Social, Politi-
cal, and Theatrical History" (Ph.D. diss., Univ. of Southern
California, 1980–1981). Stanley Green, *Broadway Musicals of
the 30s*, regularly brings its subject to life. The Theatricum
Botanicum continued through the 1990s in Topanga, Calif.
An obituary is in the *New York Times*, 24 Apr. 1978.

JAMES ROSS MOORE

GEFFEN, Tobias (1 Aug. 1870–10 Feb. 1970), rabbi
and theologian, was born Tuviah Geffen in Kovno,
Lithuania, the son of Joseph Geffen, a lumber merchant, and Kuna Rela Strauss, the daughter of a prominent Kovno rabbi. He studied in yeshivot in Kovno,
and in Grodno under Rabbi Eliakim Shapiro. In these
contemporary centers of Jewish learning, he gained a
scholarly reputation through learned discussions and
by preparing papers reconciling seemingly conflicting
opinions. He was granted *semicha* (ordination) by
Rabbi Tzvi Hirsch Rabinowitz of Kovno and Rabbi
Moshe Danishevsky of Slobodka, two opponents of
Musar (an intellectual approach that arose as a reaction
against legalism and tradition as well absolute reliance
on the authority of the Talmud, on the one hand, and
the emotionalism of Hasidism on the other) who headed the Keneset Bet Yitzchak yeshivah, and Rabbi Jacob David Willowski (the Ridbaz). Geffen married
Sara Hene Rabinowitz in August 1898; they had eight
children.

In the wake of the 1903 Kishinev pogrom, Geffen
decided to immigrate to New York City with his family and some of his wife's relatives. In 1904, after an
unsuccessful attempt in business, Geffen was chosen
rabbi of Beit Knesset Ahavat Tzedek B'nai Lebedove,
one of the numerous *landsleit* synagogues on the bus-
tling Lower East Side.

In May 1907 Tzvi Hirsch Rabinowitz, head of the
Kovno Kollel Perushim (a school of advanced Jewish
studies for married men), requested Geffen's services
as a *meshulach* (fundraiser). Geffen traveled to various
cities soliciting contributions until Congregation
Agudas Achim in Canton, Ohio, offered him its pulpit. He reconciled conflicts between two small congregations in the community, which boasted a population
of approximately 200 Jewish families. He gave sermons in Yiddish, conducted classes, ran a small yeshivah, settled disputes between members and over

issues of *kashrut* (ritual preparation of food), and authored rabbinic discourses. He served as a delegate of
Mizrachi (the Orthodox Zionist organization) at the
Federation of American Zionists conference in 1910,
when partly for health reasons he accepted a position
at Congregation Shearith Israel in Atlanta, Georgia.
He remained spiritual leader of this congregation for
sixty years. Shearith Israel, with about seventy-five
families, was the smaller of the two East European Orthodox synagogues in the city and had a poorer, less
acculturated clientele.

Geffen supervised community *kashrut* and the *mik-
veh* (ritual bath), conducted daily Talmudic study sessions, and organized and temporarily ran a community Hebrew school. He also provided early religious
instruction, preparing fifteen future rabbis. Jews from
throughout the Southeast sought his assistance to settle religious disputes. He also organized efforts to raise
money for the relief of Jewish war sufferers from
World War I, assisted Jews in local military installations and in the penitentiary, and served in leadership
capacities in most of the Atlanta Jewish social service
agencies.

As Jews began to move to other areas of Atlanta and
its suburbs in the 1920s and 1930s, membership in
Shearith Israel declined. During World War II, Geff-
en, with the aid of his children, was able to revitalize
the religious school and construct a new synagogue.
The congregation increased and moved from Hunter
Street to Washington Street and finally to University
Drive. In the late 1950s Geffen tried to reconcile two
factions of his congregation over the issue of mixed
(men and women) seating. He had attempted to maintain a community steeped in tradition, but the walls
gradually eroded.

Throughout his career Geffen wrote articles for
publications like *HaMassef* (in Jerusalem) and *Yigdal
Torah* (in New York). He also published his sermons
and commentaries in Hebrew, Yiddish, and English,
including *Lev Yosef* (1924), *Karnei Habod* (1935), *Ha-
drat Yosef* (1942), *Nahalat Yosef* (1946), *Nezer Yosef*
(part 1, 1958; part 2, 1963), and *Fifty Years in the Rabbinate—Autobiography* (1951). He served as regional
chairman and board member of Agudat ha-Rabbanim
(Union of Orthodox Rabbis of the United States and
Canada) and was executive committee member (one of
twelve) of the Rabbinical Council of America. He also
presided over the Atlanta chapter of Mizrachi (1930–
1933) and served as vice president of the Atlanta Zionist organization and the city's Jewish National Fund.
He was one of the few people to learn the formula for
Coca-Cola, knowledge required to recommend changes in the mixture to certify it as kosher. He lived a life
of scholarship, teaching, and obedience to *halachah*
(Jewish law) as much in the old world as the new.
Geffen died in Atlanta.

• Geffen's papers, including an autobiography, are located at
the American Jewish Historical Society, Waltham, Mass.
The Geffen family privately published a work (sections of
which appear in English and in Hebrew) that includes a cata-

log of these papers, essays on various aspects of Geffen's life, a sampling of his writings, photographs, a family tree, and a bibliography. Edited by Joel Ziff, it is titled *Lev Tuviah: On the Life and Work of Rabbi Tobias Geffen* (1988). See also Jay Adler, comp. and ed., *Pri HaGeffen* (1995), an anthology in Hebrew of Geffen's writings. M. David Geffen, "The Literary Legacy of Rabbi Tobias Geffen in Atlanta, 1910–1970," *Atlanta Historical Journal* 23 (Fall 1979): 85–90, summarizes the rabbi's written record. Based largely on Geffen's autobiography and collection, Nathan M. Kaganoff, "An Orthodox Rabbinate in the South: Tobias Geffen, 1870–1970," *American Jewish History* 73 (Sept. 1983): 56–70, suggests that Geffen may have been born in 1873 and that, while his career was somewhat unique in the South, it paralleled those of immigrant Orthodox rabbis elsewhere in America. Charles E. Savenor, "Portrait of an Immigrant Rabbi—The Life of Tobias Geffen" (honors thesis, Brandeis Univ., 1991), describes Geffen's activities concerning Jewish marriages and divorces, business disputes, and *kashrut*. Savenor studies Geffen's role in the national and international rabbinic network and sees him as a "defender of the faith" who was nonetheless a pragmatist.

MARK K. BAUMAN

GEHRIG, Lou (19 June 1903–2 June 1941), baseball player, was born in New York City, the son of German immigrants Heinrich Ludwig Gehrig and Christina Fack. Named Heinrich Ludwig at birth, Gehrig grew up in the heavily ethnic Yorkville and Washington Heights sections of Manhattan. His family was poor. His father, a harsh disciplinarian, held numerous odd jobs, while his domineering mother, a domestic worker, was the principal breadwinner. An introverted child, Gehrig spent much of his youth helping his mother with her chores and taking on odd jobs to supplement the family income. He endured boyhood taunts stemming from a physique much larger than others his age and from the anti-German hysteria that accompanied World War I.

His physical attributes eventually paid off in sandlot sports. He played football and baseball with members of Columbia University's Sigma Nu fraternity, where his mother was a cook and housekeeper and his father a handyman. In high school Gehrig was a football and baseball standout. When his New York High School of Commerce team traveled to Chicago in 1920 for an intercity baseball championship game with Lane Tech, the sixteen-year-old Gehrig amazed spectators by hitting an out-of-the-park home run at Wrigley Field.

Although Gehrig pursued a vocational instead of academic curriculum in high school, he entered Columbia in the fall of 1921. Because he had played twelve professional baseball games under the assumed name of Lou Lewis with Hartford, Connecticut, of the Class A Eastern League after a clandestine tryout with the New York Giants, however, Gehrig was declared ineligible to compete in football during his freshman year and baseball during his freshman and sophomore years (though opposing baseball teams on the schedule agreed to ban him only for the freshman season). He starred in both sports in 1922–1923, playing fullback and defensive tackle on the football team and alternat-

ing between pitcher, outfield, and first base on the baseball squad. A .444 batting average and a slugging percentage of .937 with seven home runs caught the attention of New York Yankees' scout Paul Krichell, who signed Gehrig for a $1,500 bonus. Gehrig left school and reported to Hartford where he hit .304 with 24 homers in only 59 games, which led to a September promotion to the Yankees. The next year he hit .369 with 40 homers at Hartford before late season recall. Gehrig opened the 1925 season with the Yankees, and after pinch-hitting on 1 June he did not miss another regular season game until he retired fifteen seasons and a record 2,130 consecutive regular season games later. Although on sixty-eight occasions Gehrig pinch-hit or played briefly to maintain the successive game streak, his remarkable endurance earned him the sobriquet "Iron Horse."

Gehrig's durability was matched by his consistency. For twelve consecutive seasons he hit above .300 and drove in at least 107 runs. Ten times in eleven years he totaled 30 or more home runs. A muscular 6', 210-pound left-handed slugger who struck the ball with awesome power, he hit 493 career homers, leading the league twice and tying with Babe Ruth for a third home run title. Gehrig hit 41 or more home runs five times, set the major league record for grand slams (23), and on 3 June 1932 became the first American Leaguer to hit four home runs in a single game. Although he batted fourth behind Ruth and frequently came to bat with the bases empty after a Ruthian homer, Gehrig led the league in runs batted in four times and tied for the lead once; seven times he drove in more than 150 runs. With a career batting average of .340 and slugging percentage of .632, Gehrig ranks close behind only Ruth and Ted Williams among the hitters in baseball history who best combined proficiency and power.

While principally known for his hitting, Gehrig was a complete player. Deceptively quick and agile for his size, he stole home 15 times and posted an excellent career .991 fielding average. He was also a clutch performer who excelled in World Series competition with a .361 batting average, .731 slugging percentage, 10 home runs, and 35 RBIs along with one error in 322 chances for a .997 fielding average in seven Series (1926–1928, 1932, 1936–1938). After Gehrig led the Yankees to a four-game sweep of Chicago in 1932 by hitting .529 and driving in eight runs while scoring nine, Cubs manager Charlie Grimm declared: "I didn't think I ever would see a ball player that good."

One of the premier players of baseball's golden decades, Gehrig's greatness is clearly revealed by comparisons with his peers. In 1927, playing on what has been widely hailed as the greatest team in baseball history, Gehrig earned Most Valuable Player honors for batting .373 and posting a .765 slugging percentage, hitting 47 homers, accounting for 175 RBIs, and scoring 149 runs. He earned a second MVP in 1934 after the best season of his career in which he not only won the Triple Crown by leading the league in batting (.363), homers (49), and RBIs (165) but also topped other hitters with a .706 slugging average. In addition to receiving a third MVP in 1936, Gehrig was runner-up for the award in 1931 and 32; four other times he finished in the top five in the balloting (no American League award was made in 1929 or 1930). Fittingly, Gehrig was selected to the American League team in the first six All-Star games from 1933 through 1938.

Gehrig's solid and stolid physical appearance belied an often unhappy personal life. He endured his mother's opposition to his marriage to Eleanor Twitchell in 1933 (the couple had no children) and then her interference with his married life. And his association with teammate Ruth was extremely difficult. Ruth and Gehrig were the best hitting tandem in baseball history. As a youth, Gehrig had idolized Ruth, and he was delighted when the Yankee star helped him with his batting during his rookie season. But their relationship deteriorated to the point of contemptuous cordiality. The strain between them was partly a matter of personality (the reserved, self-effacing, moralistic Gehrig could not abide the behavior of the flamboyant, egotistical, amoral Ruth), partly personal (they stopped speaking in 1934 after Gehrig's mother criticized Ruth's family), and partly professional (Ruth fumed at Gehrig's favored status with manager Joe McCarthy, while Gehrig resented being constantly overshadowed by Ruth as a player and public figure). In addition to letting his bat speak loudly, Gehrig vented his frustrations by persistently grousing with umpires, opponents, and teammates who did not seem to share his obsessive quest for perfection.

If Ruth dominated the press, Gehrig was predominant in the clubhouse. "Buster," as he was affectionately called by teammates despite his criticisms, enjoyed near universal respect for his integrity and sincerity. He personified the desired "Yankee image"—proud, dedicated, dignified, and successful—and in 1934 he became the first player since 1925 to be named team captain. As a player and a person, Gehrig was an integral component of the "Yankee legend" since he was the sole link between the Ruth-led teams of the mid-1920s and the Joe DiMaggio-led clubs of the later 1930s.

Always marked by durability and consistency, Gehrig's play steadily declined with his subpar performance in 1938. By the following spring, his motor skills had dissipated. Following a game on 30 April 1939, he told manager McCarthy he was voluntarily removing himself from the lineup. Gehrig never played another regular season game. On 13 June he checked into the Mayo Clinic in Rochester, Minnesota, and within a week was diagnosed as suffering from amyotrophic lateral sclerosis, a rare and incurable neuromuscular disease that causes atrophy and paralysis. The Yankees quickly arranged for a "Lou Gehrig Appreciation Day" in Yankee Stadium. On 4 July 1939, before a capacity crowd of 61,808 and numerous invited guests, including teammates from the 1927 Yankees, Gehrig spoke some of the most famous words in sports history: "Fans, for the past two weeks you have been read-ing about a bad break I got. Yet today I consider myself the luckiest man on the face of the earth."

The sports idol became a national hero because of the courage and gallantry displayed in dealing with the tragedy of a brilliant career suddenly cut short by a fatal illness, known in subsequent years as "Lou Gehrig's Disease." In December 1939 the Baseball Writers Association of America waived the rule that required a candidate for election to the Hall of Fame to be out of baseball as an active player for at least one year and unanimously voted Gehrig's enshrinement in Cooperstown. He was appointed in October 1939 by Mayor Fiorello LaGuardia to the city's parole commission and worked diligently, despite a steady deterioration of his health and an eventual inability to walk, to combat juvenile delinquency until his death in June 1941, weeks shy of his thirty-eighth birthday. The Yankees commemorated him by retiring his uniform number 4 and placing a monument to him at the base of the center field fence in Yankee Stadium. In the year following his death, two popular biographies appeared as well as the hit movie, *The Pride of the Yankees*, starring Gary Cooper as Gehrig. Gehrig's stature as a role model has endured. Since 1955 a Lou Gehrig Award has been presented annually by Phi Delta Theta fraternity in Oxford, Ohio, to the major league player who best exemplifies Gehrig's character and playing ability. In 1989 he became the fourth baseball player to have his likeness appear on a U.S. postage stamp.

• An extensive collection of clippings is in the Lou Gehrig File, National Baseball Library, Cooperstown, N.Y. Important biographies are Paul Gallico, *Lou Gehrig: Pride of the Yankees* (1942), the best of the contemporary biographies and the basis for the movie; Frank Graham, *Lou Gehrig: A Quiet Hero* (1942), a perceptive portrait by the sportswriter who was the unofficial historian of the Yankees; Eleanor Gehrig and Joseph Durso, *My Luke and I* (1976), a personal but revealing remembrance by his wife; and Ray Robinson, *Iron Horse: Lou Gehrig in His Time* (1990), a balanced and comprehensive life. See also Frank Graham, *The New York Yankees: An Informal History* (1943), and John Mosedale, *The Greatest of All: The 1927 New York Yankees* (1974). For a brief biographical sketch and reprints of insightful newspaper articles, see Joseph J. Vecchione, ed., *The* New York Times *Book of Sports Legends* (1991). Gehrig's playing statistics are in Macmillan's *Baseball Encyclopedia*, 9th ed. (1993), and John Thorn and Pete Palmer, eds., *Total Baseball*, 3d ed. (1993). Obituaries are in the *New York Times*, 3 June and 4 June 1941, and the *Sporting News*, 5 June and 12 June 1941.

LARRY R. GERLACH

GEHRINGER, Charlie (11 May 1903–21 Jan. 1993), baseball player and executive, was born Charles Leonard Gehringer in Fowlerville, Michigan, the son of farmers. Preferring that young Charlie would follow the same occupation, his parents discouraged him from playing baseball; however, they did permit Charlie and his brother to construct a rough diamond on the farm. Charlie learned the game well enough to pitch for the Fowlerville High School team, losing only one game at that level. He also played third base for both school and town teams, then enrolled at the University of Michigan. He attended only one year, playing baseball, football, and basketball, but lettering only in the last of these. His batting skill attracted the attention of the Detroit Tigers management, however, and in 1924 he was given a tryout in Detroit supervised by Manager Ty Cobb. Following the audition Cobb arranged for Gehringer's immediate signing with London, Ontario, Canada, the Tigers farm club of the Class B Michigan-Ontario League.

Gehringer spent most of 1924 with London, hitting .292 in 112 games and playing second base. At the end of that season he appeared with the Tigers, hitting .462 in five games. That brief performance prompted Detroit to move him up to Toronto, Ontario, Canada, of the Class AA International League for 1925. He immediately starred with Toronto, hitting .325 in 155 games. He also hit 25 home runs and drove in 108 runs, and led all International League second basemen in fielding. Recalled to Detroit for eight games at the end of the season, he hit only .167, but he was a Tiger to stay.

In 1926, his first full season with Detroit, Gehringer played in 123 games that year, hitting .277. Except for the 1932 season, when he hit .298, Gehringer did not again finish below .300 until 1941. Until 1942 he was the Tigers' regular second baseman, and by any standards his outstanding accomplishments reflected his versatility. In seven seasons he led all American League second basemen in fielding, and in seven different seasons he had 200 or more hits. In 1929 he led the league in hits with 215, in runs scored with 131, in doubles with 45, in triples with 19, and in stolen bases with 27. He also led the league in games played, putouts, and fielding average. Never a slugger in the fashion of Babe Ruth, the 5'11", 180-pound Gehringer nevertheless was much more than the "slap hitter" so common among middle infielders. He hit 40 or more doubles in a season seven times, and he regularly hit 10 or more triples per season. His .371 batting average, the highest average of his major league career, led the league in 1937. That accomplishment earned his election as the league's most valuable player. His lifetime figures, all with the Tigers, include 2,839 hits and a .320 average. In six consecutive years he made the American League All-Star team, and his batting average of .500 ranks first among players participating in five or more All-Star games.

In Gehringer's first few seasons with Detroit, the team never finished better than fourth in the American League, even when led by heavy hitters such as Cobb and Harry Heilmann. (Gehringer called Cobb a "hateful man" who literally did sharpen his spikes in the dugout. However, Cobb also went out of his way to help Gehringer, especially with regard to Gehringer's batting techniques.) But in 1934, under the management of catcher Mickey Cochrane, the Tigers finally won the American League pennant, and they repeated this feat in 1935 and 1940. While losing the 1934 World Series to the St. Louis Cardinals and the Dean brothers, Gehringer led his team in hits with 11 and in batting average with .379, including one home run.

The next year the Tigers defeated the Chicago Cubs, four games to two, and Gehringer was second on his team in both average and number of hits. In the 1940 World Series the Tigers lost four games to three to the Cincinnati Reds, and Gehringer, nearing the end of his career, hit only .214. In spite of that series his consistent play was still apparent; his overall average for three World Series was .321, precisely the same as his lifetime record.

Gehringer played only 45 games in 1942, finishing the season as a coach for the Tigers. He then enlisted in the U.S. Navy's physical fitness program and was discharged at the end of World War II as a lieutenant commander. For a few postwar years Gehringer lived in Detroit, earning a great deal of money working as an auto manufacturer's representative. During these years he made a home for his diabetic mother, delaying his marriage to care for her. In 1950 Gehringer married Josephine (maiden name unknown); they had no children. The following year the Tigers lured him back into baseball as general manager and vice president. After two years he gave up the general manager's job, which he hated, but he remained vice president until 1959. He was elected to the National Baseball Hall of Fame in 1949, and at the time of his death in Bloomfield Hills, Michigan, Gehringer was the oldest living member in the Hall.

Gehringer was a model of consistent performance as well as a natural athlete who made all his play look simple. Manager Cochrane observed that Gehringer said "hello" on opening day, "goodbye" on closing day, and performed superbly in between. In his honor Fowlerville fans held a "day" for him and presented him with a set of right-handed golf clubs. Gehringer, who threw right-handed, but batted left-handed, said nothing to the donors but taught himself to play right-handed, consistently breaking par from that side of the tee.

• A clipping file on Gehringer is at the National Baseball Library, Cooperstown, N.Y. The best performance data about Gehringer is in John Thorn and Pete Palmer, eds., *Total Baseball* (1993). Richard Bak's *Cobb Would Have Caught It* (1991) has a chapter of fine material, apparently from several conversations between Bak and Gehringer. Good, brief summaries supporting one another are in Gene Karst and Martin Jones, *Who's Who in Professional Baseball* (1973); Martin Appel and Burt Goldblatt, *Baseball's Best: The Hall of Fame Gallery* (1977); and Lowell Reidenbaugh, *Cooperstown* (1983). An obituary is in the *New York Times*, 23 Jan. 1993.

THOMAS L. KARNES

GEIGER, Roy Stanley (25 Jan. 1885–23 Jan. 1947), U.S. Marine Corps officer, was born in Middleburg, Florida, the son of Marion Francis Geiger, a county school superintendent and tax assessor, and Josephine Prevatt. Educated in local schools, Geiger attended Florida State Normal School from 1902 to 1904 and obtained a teacher's certificate. In 1907 he received a bachelor of laws degree from John B. Stetson University at Deland, Florida, and was admitted to the bar.

On 2 November 1907, for reasons he never explained, Geiger enlisted in the U.S. Marine Corps. After rising to the rank of corporal, he accepted a commission as second lieutenant in 1909. Geiger spent the next seven years as a line officer, with duty at sea and foreign postings to Nicaragua, Panama, the Philippines, and China.

In March 1916 Geiger began flight training at Pensacola, Florida. Later asked why he decided to transfer to aviation, he responded, "Oh, I just wanted to fly, that's all." In June 1917 he became the fifth marine to be designated as a naval aviator. The following month he married Eunice Renshaw Thompson; they had two children. Geiger went overseas in July 1918 to command one of the four squadrons making up the First Marine Aviation Force. He received the Navy Cross for leading his unit against German targets during the last months of World War I.

The 1920s saw Geiger alternate between command and school assignments. He commanded Marine squadrons on Haiti (1919–1921) and at Quantico, Virginia (1921–1924). In 1925 he graduated from the Command and General Staff School at Fort Leavenworth, Kansas. Four years later he completed the course at the Army War College. Geiger served as director of aviation at Marine Corps headquarters from 1931 to 1935 then spent four years as commander of Marine Air Group One at Quantico. In 1941 he completed the senior and advanced courses at the Naval War College, followed by a two-month tour as assistant naval attaché for air in London, England. Promoted to brigadier general, Geiger took command of the First Marine Aircraft Wing in October 1941.

Known as "rugged Roy" for his physical vitality, Geiger was a prominent figure in marine and naval aviation circles on the eve of American entry into World War II. A strict disciplinarian, he held his subordinates—and himself—to high standards. His tenacity in pursuit of objectives impressed his peers and his superiors.

On 3 September 1942 Geiger assumed command of all air units—navy, marine, and army—on Guadalcanal in the Solomon Islands. Under extremely difficult operational conditions, Geiger led his "Cactus Air Force" (Cactus was the code name for Guadalcanal) against a powerful Japanese enemy. At one point, on 22 September, the 57-year-old aviator flew a combat mission in a Douglas Dauntless dive-bomber (SBD) and dropped a 1,000-pound bomb on a suspected enemy troop concentration. His action may or may not have caused damage to the Japanese, but it certainly boosted the morale of his hard-pressed airmen. By the time Geiger gave up command on 4 November, his Cactus Air Force was in firm control of the skies over Guadalcanal, credited with shooting down 268 Japanese aircraft.

After an assignment in the New Hebrides, Geiger served as director of Marine Corps aviation from March to October 1943. In November he took over the I Marine Amphibious Corps and during the following two months led the unit in combat on Bougainville Island in the Southwest Pacific.

Geiger continued to hold major combat commands as American forces moved across the Pacific toward the Japanese home islands. During July and August 1944, he directed the III Amphibious Corps during the battle to recapture Guam. In September and October of the same year, the III Corps assaulted Peleliu in some of the bloodiest fighting of the war. In April 1945 Geiger led the III Corps ashore at Okinawa. From 18 until 23 June, three days before the end of resistance on the island, Geiger was commander of the Tenth Army after Lieutenant General Simon B. Buckner, Jr., was killed by Japanese artillery fire. Although Geiger held the post for five days only, this marked the first time that a Marine Corps officer had led a field army.

In July 1945, following his promotion to lieutenant general, Geiger took command of the Fleet Marine Force, Pacific. He remained the senior marine commander in the Pacific for the next sixteen months, overseeing the difficult transition from war to peace. He watched with sadness and apprehension as the mighty combat force that had defeated Japan shrank to a fraction of its wartime strength. An inveterate cigar smoker, Geiger fell ill from lung cancer during Christmas leave in 1946; he died the following month in Bethesda, Maryland.

Geiger always considered himself a Marine Corps line officer who happened to have a specialty in aviation. He believed that aviation should be an integral part of the combat mission of the corps and was an advocate of close air support for ground troops. Equally adept at leading air units—as he demonstrated at Guadalcanal—and major ground forces, Geiger has been acknowledged by military historians as one of the most talented and successful senior combat commanders in the history of the U.S. Marine Corps.

• The extensive collection of Geiger's personal papers is housed at the U.S. Marine Corps Historical Center, Washington, D.C. Roger Willock, *Unaccustomed to Fear: A Biography of the Late General Roy S. Geiger, U.S.M.C.* (1968), is the only full-scale biography. The best brief account of Geiger's career is by Joseph G. Dawson III, "Roy Stanley Geiger," in *Dictionary of American Military Biography*, vol. 1, ed. Roger J. Spiller (1984). Geiger's service in World War II is detailed in Robert Sherrod, *History of Marine Corps Aviation in World War II* (1952), and Jeter Isely and Philip A. Crowl, *The U.S. Marines and Amphibious War* (1951). An obituary is in the *New York Times*, 24 Jan. 1947.

WILLIAM M. LEARY

GEIN, Edward (27 Aug. 1906–26 July 1984), whose ghoulish crimes became the basis for Alfred Hitchcock's classic terror film *Psycho*, was born in La Crosse, Wisconsin, the son of George Gein and Augusta Loehrke, farmers. In 1913 the family (which also included Gein's older brother, Henry) moved to a small dairy farm near Camp Douglas, forty miles east of La Crosse. Less than one year later, they relocated again—this time permanently—to a 195-acre farm six miles west of Plainfield, a remote, tiny village in the south central part of the state.

From all available evidence, Gein was subjected to a deeply pathological upbringing. His mother was a hostile, domineering, and fanatically religious woman (the family was Lutheran) who railed incessantly against the sinfulness of her own sex. His ineffectual father alternated between periods of sullen passivity and alcoholic rage. Gein's emotional suffering was undoubtedly exacerbated by the extreme harshness of the environment and the bitter isolation of his life. A pariah even in childhood, he was generally treated as a laughingstock during his school years (which ended with his graduation from eighth grade). Incapable of forming normal social relationships, he grew up in thrall to his ferociously strong-willed mother.

Gein's father died after a lingering illness in 1940. Four years later, Gein's brother perished under ambiguous circumstances while fighting a marsh fire on the family property. At the time his death was attributed to natural causes, though in later years many townspeople came to believe that—in addition to his other outrages—Gein was guilty of fratricide.

The most devastating loss to Gein was his mother's death from a stroke in December 1945. Living alone in the grim, ramshackle farmhouse, he began to retreat into a world of violent fantasy and bizarre ritual. Though he remained tenuously connected to the community—doing odd jobs for neighbors, plowing snow for the county, making occasional trips into town—he was in the grip of a deepening psychosis.

Two years after his mother's death, Gein began making nocturnal raids on local cemeteries, digging up the graves of recently deceased middle-aged or elderly women whose obituaries he had read in the newspapers. His necrophiliac activities continued for at least five years. In 1954 he murdered a middle-aged tavern keeper named Mary Hogan and brought her 200-pound corpse back to his farmhouse.

During this period, rumors started circulating that Gein kept a shrunken head collection in his bedroom, but these stories were dismissed as the colorful imaginings of the village children, who had begun to regard the Gein place as a haunted house. The truth—which proved infinitely more appalling than the hearsay—finally came to light in the fall of 1957.

On Saturday, 16 November (the opening day of deer-hunting season, when the bulk of Plainfield's male population was away in the woods), 58-year-old Bernice Worden disappeared from the hardware store she operated with her son. Suspicion immediately lighted upon Gein, who had been hanging about the store in recent days, paying unwelcome attention to the widow.

Breaking into the summer kitchen abutting Gein's house, police discovered Worden's gutted and beheaded corpse dangling by the heels from a rafter like a butchered farm animal. Inside the house itself, disbelieving investigators uncovered a large collection of unspeakable artifacts: chairs upholstered with human skin, soup bowls fashioned from skulls, a shade-pull made from a pair of lips, a shoebox full of female genitalia, a nipple-belt, faces stuffed with newspaper and mounted like hunting trophies on the bedroom walls, and a "mammary vest" flayed from the torso of a woman. Gein later confessed that, on various occasions, he arrayed himself in this vest and other human-skin garments and pretended he was his mother.

The discovery of these Gothic horrors in the home of a quiet, midwestern farmer during the proverbially bland Eisenhower era jolted—and transfixed—the country. In Wisconsin itself, Gein quickly entered regional folklore. Within weeks of his arrest, macabre jokes called Geiners became a statewide craze—possibly the first documented instance of what has since become a common phenomenon, the seemingly spontaneous appearance of "sick jokes" about particularly appalling tragedies and disasters. The media, which descended in droves on Gein's hard-pressed hometown, turned him into an instant celebrity. During the first week of December 1957, both *Life* and *Time* magazines ran features on Gein, the former devoting nine pages to his "House of Horrors." For a while, Gein's farmstead became a popular tourist attraction, an intolerable development as far as the outraged community was concerned. On the night of 20 March 1958 a mysterious fire broke out in Gein's house. It was not extinguished until the hated place had been reduced to ashes.

In custody, Gein admitted to graverobbing, a claim initially greeted with skepticism but later confirmed when several empty coffins were exhumed in the Plainfield cemetery. He confessed to killing both Mary Hogan and Bernice Worden, though he maintained that their deaths (both women had been shot in the head) were accidental. Diagnosed as schizophrenic, Gein was committed to Central State Hospital for the Criminally Insane in Waupun, Wisconsin. After a pro forma trial in 1968, he was returned to the mental hospital and, in spite of a 1974 effort to win release, remained institutionalized for the rest of his life. A model inmate, he died of cancer at Mendota Mental Health Institute in Madison and was buried beside his mother in Plainfield.

By the time of his death Gein had become a seemingly undying part of American popular culture. In 1959 horror writer Robert Bloch, who was residing in Wisconsin when Gein's story broke, used the sensational case as the basis for his novel *Psycho* (whose protagonist, Norman Bates, is explicitly likened to Gein at one point in the book). The following year, Alfred Hitchcock transformed Bloch's pulp shocker into his cinematic masterpiece. Insofar as *Psycho* initiated the cycle of so-called slasher movies, Gein is regarded by aficionados of horror as a seminal figure, the "Grandfather of Gore." He is the prototype of every knife-, ax-, and cleaver-wielding maniac who has stalked America's movie screens since. Tobe Hooper's midnight-movie classic *The Texas Chain Saw Massacre* (1975) was directly inspired by the Plainfield horrors, and "Buffalo Bill," the skinsuit-wearing serial killer of

Thomas Harris's *The Silence of the Lambs* (1988), was in part modeled on Gein. Horror fan clubs formed around Gein, and his unsettling likeness adorned magazine covers, T-shirts, comic books, and trading cards.

• For a complete account of Gein's life, crimes, and impact on American popular culture, see Harold Schechter, *Deviant: The Shocking True Story of the Original "Psycho"* (1989).

HAROLD SCHECHTER

GEIRINGER, Hilda (28 Sept. 1893–22 Mar. 1973), mathematician, was born in Vienna, Austria, the daughter of Ludwig Geiringer, a textile manufacturer, and Martha Wertheimer. She studied pure mathematics at the University of Vienna with Wilhelm Wirtinger and received her doctorate in 1917. Her thesis dealt with double trigonometric series.

Geiringer then worked under Leon Lichtenstein editing the centrally important *Jahrbuch über die Fortschritte der Mathematik*. In 1921 she went to the newly formed Institute of Applied Mathematics in Berlin as first assistant to the director, Richard von Mises. Under his influence her interests shifted from pure to applied mathematics. She developed an interest in the theory of plasticity, which stands on the borderland between physics and technology and might form some part of the theory of bridge building, for example. That interest led to her formulation of the so-called Geiringer equations for plane plastic distortions. She also pursued probability theory. She was married, briefly, to another mathematician, Felix Pollaczek. They had one child.

In 1927 Geiringer became a lecturer at the University of Berlin; in 1933 the faculty proposed her as an associate professor. She never attained this position, however, because of Adolf Hitler's rise to power. As a Jew, she lost her position at the university, and she fled with her child to Belgium, where she was a research associate at the Institute of Mechanics in Brussels. In 1934 they moved to Turkey, where Geiringer was made professor of mathematics at the University of Istanbul. Like the other German émigrés, Geiringer learned Turkish in order to give her lectures.

However, in 1938 the powerful Turkish leader Kemal Atatürk died, and war was imminent in Europe. Turkey's neutrality seemed unsure, and in 1939 Geiringer went to the United States to be a lecturer at Bryn Mawr College, a post she held until 1944. There she was mentored by mathematician Anna Wheeler, who helped her with English and eased her adjustment to the less hierarchical American teaching style.

In 1943 Geiringer married von Mises, who was teaching at Harvard after a similar flight from Germany via Turkey. The following year she accepted a job as chair of the mathematics department at Wheaton College in Norton, Massachusetts, which was close enough that she could commute to be with her husband on weekends. She became a naturalized citizen in 1945. Wheaton, with its mathematics department of two, was too small to encompass Geiringer's mathematical energies, but attempts to find employment in the Boston area foundered because of her gender. Geiringer explained to the Wheaton administration: "I have to work scientifically, besides my college work. This is a necessity for me; I never stopped it since my student days, it is the deepest need in my life." They excused her from eating her evening meal with the students, thus allowing her the time after 5:00 P.M. to pursue her own researches. These were focused primarily on biometrical problems that she pushed into the abstract reaches of probability theory. She was also again drawn to problems of plasticity.

On 14 July 1953 von Mises died, and Geiringer began to complete and edit his unfinished works. She was given a grant for the task by the Office of Naval Research, and she went to Harvard as a research fellow in mathematics. Although this was not a long-term position, her financial independence increased in 1956, when the University of Berlin elected her professor emeritus with full salary. She retired from Wheaton in July 1959.

Increasingly freed of teaching responsibilities, Geiringer's research prospered. With G. S. Ludford she completed the von Mises manuscript *Mathematical Theory of Compressible Fluid Flow* (1958). At the same time she worked on plasticity with A. M. Freudenthal. Geiringer then turned her attention to probability theory and edited new versions of von Mises's *Probability, Statistics and Truth* (1957) and *Mathematical Theory of Probability and Statistics* (1964), which incorporated new results of both Erhard Tornies and Abraham Wald. Von Mises's inductive approach to probability theory was highly controversial, and until the end of her life Geiringer vigorously defended it in many lectures and articles. Geiringer was a fellow of the American Academy of Arts and Sciences and a member of Sigma Xi. She died in Santa Barbara, California, when visiting her brother, noted musicologist Karl Geiringer.

• Geiringer's papers are in the archives of Harvard University and in the Schlesinger Library at Radcliffe College. Partial lists of her publications can be found in J. C. Poggendorff, *Biographisch-literarisches Handworterbuch der exakten Naturwissenschaften: 1923–1931*, vol. 6 (1936), p. 865, and vol. 7a (1958), pp. 179–80. Contemporary sources on her life and work include a brief article in the *Wheaton Newsletter*, Sept. 1959. She is treated in Louise S. Grinstein and Paul J. Campbell, eds., *Women of Mathematics: A Biobliographic Sourcebook* (1987), pp. 41–46. Reinhard Siegmund-Schultze focuses on her years in Berlin in "Hilda Geiringer-von Mises, Charlier Series, Ideology, and the Human Side of the Emancipation of Applied Mathematics at the University of Berlin during the 1920s," *Historia Mathematica* 20 (1993): 364–81; and Christa Binder considers her early life in the United States in "Hilda Geiringer: Ihre ersten jahre in Amerika," *Amphora: Festschrift für Hans Wussing*, ed. Sergei S. Demidov et al. (1992), pp. 25–53. Obituaries are in the *Boston Sunday Globe* and the *New York Times*, 24 Mar. 1973.

JOAN L. RICHARDS

GEISEL, Theodor Seuss (2 Mar. 1904–24 Sept. 1991), author, known as Dr. Seuss, was born in Springfield, Massachusetts, the son of Theodor Robert Geisel, a brewer, and Henrietta Seuss. Geisel began his literary career by contributing jokes, essays, and cartoons to his high school newspaper and continued it at Dartmouth College, where he edited, wrote, and drew for *Jack-O-Lantern*, the campus humor magazine. In 1925 he received his A.B. from Dartmouth and enrolled in Oxford University's Lincoln College. Seeking a doctorate in English literature, he soon became bored with "the astonishing irrelevance of graduate work" and punctuated his lecture notebooks with drawings of fantastic beasts. Helen Marion Palmer, a fellow American and Oxonian, saw the doodlings in class and urged Geisel to abandon academia and become an illustrator. He left Oxford after his first year to tour Europe and returned to the United States in 1927 to marry Palmer, who became his unofficial editor and colleague.

Settling in New York City, Geisel found a job writing and illustrating for *Judge*, a weekly humor magazine. In 1928, now known professionally as "Dr. Seuss," he signed a lucrative contract with Standard Oil of New Jersey to draw advertising cartoons for the insecticide Flit. Each cartoon featured the bug spray as the butt of a joke above the caption, "Quick, Henry, the Flit!" Before long, the entire country seemed to be repeating the tag line and laughing—and buying Flit. The cartoons' success opened the doors of the popular magazines of the day to Geisel's essays and artwork. Hoping to catch lightning a second time, Standard Oil hired him to publicize Essolube 5-Star motor oil, which he did by creating such dastardly denizens as the Karbo-Nockus and the Moto-Raspus.

In 1931 Geisel was invited to illustrate *Boners*, a sampler of British schoolboy hilarity. Largely because of his artwork, the book topped the *New York Times* nonfiction bestseller list. This success led him to conclude that he could write as well as illustrate a book for children, and so he completed "A Story That No One Can Beat," an outrageous verse, one part comic strip and one part tall tale, about a little boy's runaway imagination. Because the thinking of the time dictated that children's stories should be morally uplifting and educational, twenty-seven publishers rejected the manuscript because its illustrations were too bizarre and its message too amoral. Luckily an old Dartmouth pal who had just become children's editor for Vanguard Press loved the manuscript and in 1937 published it as *And to Think That I Saw It on Mulberry Street*. The book received good reviews and sold moderately well, so Geisel followed it up with two prose efforts, *The Five Hundred Hats of Bartholomew Cubbins* (1938) and *The King's Stilts* (1939). He also published *The Seven Lady Godivas* (1939), a humorous tale for grown-ups, which flopped. Declaring that "adults are obsolete children, and the hell with them," he devoted himself to children's books, and in 1940 he came out with *Horton Hatches the Egg*. Its refrain, "an

elephant's faithful—one hundred per cent!" gave this yarn about a pachyderm who is tricked into sitting on a bird's nest the moral tone that the bulk of his work lacked, and Horton became a hero loved by children and adults alike.

In 1940 Geisel ended his association with Standard Oil and began drawing editorial cartoons for *PM* magazine, many of which ridiculed Nazis in general and Adolf Hitler in particular. In 1943 he joined the U.S. Army Signal Corps as a captain and was sent to Hollywood, California, where, under legendary film director Frank Capra, he produced training movies and newsreels for the military. It was soon discovered that servicemen responded most positively to cartoons, so Geisel and Chuck Jones, an animator for Warner Bros., created Private Snafu to teach the troops the importance of everything from discipline to taking antimalarial pills. In 1944 Geisel produced *Your Job in Germany*, an indoctrination film for the troops who would occupy Germany after the war. While in Europe to screen the film for American generals, he somehow got trapped behind enemy lines during the Battle of the Bulge and drove around for three days before being rescued by the British. In 1946 Lieutenant Colonel Geisel was discharged and awarded the Legion of Merit for "exceptionally meritorious service in planning and producing films."

After the war Geisel settled in La Jolla, California, and wrote movie scripts for Warner Bros. and RKO. With his wife as collaborator, he produced *Design for Death*, a documentary portraying the vanquished Japanese as victims of their own class system; the film won the 1947 Academy Award for best documentary feature. *Gerald McBoing-Boing*, written by Geisel but illustrated by others, won the 1951 Oscar for best animated cartoon. *The 5,000 Fingers of Dr. T.* (1953), essentially a feature-length cartoon with live actors, became a cult classic. At the same time, he continued to turn out children's books. *McElligot's Pool* (1947), perhaps the greatest fish story ever told; *Bartholomew and the Oobleck* (1949), the tale of a grumpy king who learns to appreciate what he has; and *If I Ran the Zoo* (1950), in which lions and tigers are replaced with Mulligatawnys and Flustards, all won distinction as Caldecott Honor Books for their illustrations. But the book that made Dr. Seuss a household name was *The Cat in the Hat*.

The Cat in the Hat was born in the mid-1950s amidst a national debate over growing illiteracy among children. More than one critic demanded a new type of school primer, one that was fun to read and creatively illustrated so that it could better compete with its nemesis, television. William Spaulding, director of Houghton Mifflin's educational book division, challenged Geisel to come up with a primer that would enthrall juveniles and gave him a first-grade vocabulary list of 225 words, none of which were adjectives. Geisel struggled with the list for over a year, trying to find enough words to rhyme in order to write any sort of story. The book that finally emerged was quite different from the typical primer, in which spotlessly clean boys and girls talk and act with unfailing propriety. By contrast, the Cat in the Hat is an anarchist. Sartorially splendid in a red-and-white stovepipe hat and a red bowtie similar to the one Geisel himself preferred, he blithely creates such a chaotic mess in the house of little Sally and her brother that the two children throw the Cat out into the cold, then tremble for fear of how their mother will react until the Cat reappears with a magic cleaning machine and makes everything right once again. Published in 1957 in basic red, white, and blue, the book was hailed by critics, teachers, and parents. More than thirty years later Geisel was still being praised for "the murder of Dick and Jane [the stars of a particularly bad primer], which was a mercy killing of the highest order" (Anna Quindlen, "The One Who Had Fun," *New York Times*, 28 Sept. 1991). Children begged their parents to buy the book, and within three years *The Cat in the Hat* sold more than 1 million copies, an astounding figure for a children's book. Its success launched Beginner Books, a division of Random House with Geisel as its president, and led to the publication of more child-friendly readers by other authors. The success of these titles led Geisel to create the Bright and Early series for preschoolers in 1968.

Next to the Cat, Geisel's most memorable creation was the Grinch. A large, mean, green thing, the Grinch attempts to ruin the Christmas celebration of the diminutive Whos and in the process learns the true meaning of the holiday. Published in 1957, *How the Grinch Stole Christmas!* was adapted for television in 1966 and was broadcast several times during each Christmas season for a number of years.

Several of Geisel's later books addressed political issues, albeit in a Seussian manner. *Yertle the Turtle and Other Stories* (1958), *The Sneetches and Other Stories* (1961), *The Lorax* (1971), and *The Butter Battle Book* (1984) deal with Nazism, racism, pollution, and the nuclear arms race, respectively. Although it is unknown how many children caught the hidden meanings, Geisel knew that much of his audience comprised adults who read to their young offspring, and in these books he spoke to grown-ups as well as children.

After Geisel's wife died in 1967, he married Audrey Stone Dimond the following year. He fathered no children; when asked why not, he responded, "You have 'em, I'll amuse 'em." Geisel won the American Library Association's Laura Ingalls Wilder Award (1980), the Catholic Library Association's Regina Medal (1982), and a Pulitzer Prize for lifetime achievement (1984). In 1981 eight states declared his seventy-seventh birthday Dr. Seuss Day. He died in La Jolla.

Geisel was the most popular and influential children's author of his day. His fifty-five books, all inspired by a juvenile sense of imagination and playfulness, changed dramatically the way in which youngsters learn to read. His greatest contribution is that, for all children, even the obsolete ones, he made reading fun.

- Geisel's papers are located in the archives of the University of California, San Diego; the University of California, Los Angeles; Baker Library, Dartmouth College; Butler Library, Columbia University; Lincoln College, St. Anne's College, and the Bodleian Library, Oxford University; New York Public Library; San Diego Public Library; Springfield, Mass., Public Library; and the Connecticut Valley Historical Museum, Springfield. A biography is Judith Morgan and Neil Morgan, *Dr. Seuss and Mr. Geisel: A Biography* (1995). A complete bibliography and critical analysis of his work appears in Ruth K. MacDonald, *Dr. Seuss* (1988). His obituary is in the *New York Times*, 26 Sept. 1991.

CHARLES W. CAREY, JR.

GEISMAR, Maxwell David (1 Aug. 1909–24 July 1979), literary critic, was born in New York City, the son of Leon Geismar and Mary Feinberg. Geismar earned his B.A. in 1931 from Columbia University, where he was elected to Phi Beta Kappa, and his M.A. in 1932, also from Columbia University; as a graduate student he was a Moncrief Proudfit Fellow in Letters. Geismar married Anne Rosenberg in 1931; they had two children.

After a year at Harvard University as a teaching fellow, Geismar joined the literature faculty at Sarah Lawrence College in 1933, remaining until 1947. His critical essay on the humorist Ring Lardner led to a Guggenheim Fellowship. Its result was *Writers in Crisis: The American Novel, 1925–1940* (1942), the first of Geismar's series "The Novel in America."

Geismar's was a personal and passionate criticism, far removed from the dominant mode of his era, which focused tightly on the inner workings of literature. He believed that writers, as the unacknowledged legislators of the world, were responsible for enhancing their society. In a late work, Geismar wrote, "I hope the essays are biographies of inner conviction. . . . Isn't the work the true life?"

In *Writers in Crisis*, examining Lardner, John Dos Passos, William Faulkner, Ernest Hemingway, and John Steinbeck, Geismar asserted that the "dazzling materialism" of the 1920s had turned them into "hostile critics" of society rather than "integrated artists." The crisis brought about by the depression of the 1930s, he hoped, would bring about "a return to social sanity." Geismar exhorted Hemingway, whom he had accused of abdicating his responsibility, "What could he not show us of living as well as dying, of the positives in our being as well as our destroying forces?"

Geismar's stance as a radical social historian looking at American life through its letters became firm in the product of his Guggenheim, *The Last of the Provincials: The American Novel, 1915–1925* (1944). Geismar took Willa Cather to task, despite her brilliantly observed novels of prairie life. Strongly believing that rampant capitalism was ruining the nation, he accused Cather of retreating from the real issues of her own time: she had ignored "the process of creating wealth." He found Sinclair Lewis deficient in both love and hate. By contrast, F. Scott Fitzgerald perfectly understood his own time, an age "beautiful and damned," Geismar wrote, echoing the title of one of Fitzgerald's novels. The inelegant Sherwood Anderson was Geismar's favorite; Anderson's social concerns had led to brief Communist party membership.

Geismar was often a school of one, freely attacking critics who, he believed, lacked his own moral fervor. In *The Last of the Provincials* he also castigated Lionel Trilling as a critic more interested in English literature than in that of his own land.

Between 1945 and 1950 Geismar served as contributing editor for *The Nation*, a leading liberal journal. In 1952 he edited a selection of the writings of novelist Thomas Wolfe. He seemed particularly at home in the third volume of his history, *Rebels and Ancestors: The American Novel, 1890–1915* (1953). The byproduct of a 1952 grant from the National Academy of Arts and Letters, *Rebels and Ancestors* studied Frank Norris, Stephen Crane, Jack London, Ellen Glasgow, and Theodore Dreiser. Geismar lauded the literature of the era's progressive movement, "the most brilliant and fruitful source of American social criticism yet compiled." Geismar called the age the true source of the flowering of twentieth-century American literature and praised it for its "years of gain" against the "ravages of insensate capitalism." Norris, he wrote, had restored sexuality "to a proper place in human affairs," and Dreiser showed the "most flexible and generous view of evolutionary thinking in national letters."

American Moderns: From Rebellion to Conformity (1960) was a collection of short and often lacerating essays on contemporary authors. Geismar referred to the 1950s as "the age of [Herman] Wouk" (a popular author whose smug high seriousness Geismar found meretricious). In "By [James Gould] Cozzens Possessed" he likened author to era: a return to "conservatism, conformity and the rest—normalcy, decency, sobriety." He added that Cozzens had made all forms of love look destructive: "Good God, has that become dull, too?" He praised Nelson Algren as an "extreme phase of native American realism" and was unable to dismiss J. D. Salinger, even though he found the fiction of *New Yorker* writers effete. Once more he lauded Dreiser: "I still prefer the old Dreiserian view, or Walt Whitman's view, that these dangerous and powerful feelings—our illicit impulses, I mean—are what make life interesting, valuable and instructive. Indeed, they ARE life."

By the late 1950s Geismar was regularly writing for newspaper book-review sections, academic journals, intellectual magazines, and encyclopedias. He edited the short stories of Jack London (1960) and Sherwood Anderson (1962). Geismar's most corrosive book was *Henry James and the Jacobites* (1963). Decrying the sycophantic "cult of Henry James," he asked, "What latent violence of modern life was James ever really familiar with?" Furthermore, the expatriate James was a kind of traitor, giving up his American citizenship. Geismar scorned "the enchanted love affair of James with his Art, the passion of James for James." He concluded that a liking for James was characteristic of the contemporary United States, living in a "fabricated, fantasy life of its own 'leisure class' existence" and un-

able to deal with the impoverished nations of the world.

In 1963 Geismar also edited *The Ring Lardner Reader*, portraying Lardner as a critic of the American middle class. Geismar opposed the Vietnam war; he became senior editor at the radical magazine *Ramparts*. In 1966 he became a fellow at Boston University, remaining until his death. As American society convulsed during the war, Geismar recognized the literary talent of the ex-convict and radical leader Eldridge Cleaver and wrote the introduction for Cleaver's autobiographical *Soul on Ice* (1968). He was a founding editor in 1970 of *Scanlan's Monthly*.

Also in 1970 came *Mark Twain: An American Prophet*, a lengthy, unusual biography based on Twain's writings. Twain, Geismar asserted, was an ideal author, involved with everything that happened around him. Geismar paid particular attention to writings omitted from 1950s editions of Twain's work. Noting that Twain was more popular in Russia, Asia, Africa, and South America than in the United States, Geismar remarked, "What a shameful, wicked, devastating kind of lie was perpetrated in the national consciousness during the Cold War epoch."

Geismar's last full-length work was *Ring Lardner and the Pursuit of Folly* (1972), a warmly written appreciation in which he wrote, "Humor is the final recourse against life." In 1973 he became advisory editor for the *Chicago Review*, remaining until his death, in Harrison, New York.

• Geismar's papers are at the Boston University Archives. One of the most active of literary critics, Geismar is mentioned in many biographies of the authors of his era, including Matthew Bruccoli, *Fitzgerald and Hemingway: A Dangerous Friendship* (1994); Ring Lardner, Jr., *The Lardners: My Family Remembered* (1976); Sergio Perosa, *The Art of F. Scott Fitzgerald* (1965); and Mark Schorer, *Sinclair Lewis: An American Life* (1961). An obituary is in the *New York Times*, 25 July 1979.

JAMES ROSS MOORE

GELB, Ignace Jay (14 Oct. 1907–22 Dec. 1985), Assyriologist, was born Ignace Jerzy Gelb in Tarnow, Poland, the son of Salo Gelb, a soldier, and Regina Issler. He attended the Gymnasium in Tarnow from 1917 to 1925, when he went to Florence, Italy, to study Renaissance art but became interested in Near Eastern studies and historical geography. From 1926 to 1929 he studied Near Eastern languages at the University of Rome under Giorgio Levi della Vida, the Semitist and Arabist, Carlo Nallino, the Arabist, and others, receiving his doctorate summa cum laude in 1929. Invited shortly thereafter by James Breasted to join the staff of the Oriental Institute of the University of Chicago, he became a traveling fellow and, in 1932, a research assistant. He joined the Oriental Institute faculty in 1937 and rose through the academic ranks to professor (1947), Frank P. Hixon Distinguished Service Professor (1965), and emeritus (1980).

In 1932 and 1935 Gelb made archaeological and epigraphic explorations in Anatolia for the purpose of identifying ancient sites and monuments, especially with a view to collecting sources for Hieroglyphic Hittite, an imperfectly understood Anatolian language. The results of his work appeared as *Hittite Hieroglyphs* (3 vols., 1931–1942) and *Inscriptions from Alishar and Vicinity* (1935). He became interested in the non-Semitic, non-Sumerian peoples living in Mesopotamia and published a monograph on two such peoples, *Hurrians and Subarians* (1944). Collaborative research followed on Hurrian onomastics in *Nuzi Personal Names* (1943) and on Amorite in *Computer-Aided Analysis of Amorite* (1980). He never lost interest in field work and served on archaeological expeditions to the Near East again in 1947, 1963, 1965, and 1966.

Gelb's work at Chicago included a half-century association with the Chicago Assyrian Dictionary Project (CAD). Founded in 1921, this project undertook to collect all materials for the Assyrian and Babylonian languages over their 2,500-year history and to publish a multivolume dictionary. Gelb worked as an assistant to this project until his departure for military service in the U.S. Army in 1943. Under the Office of Strategic Services (OSS), Gelb spent 1945 in Germany preparing materials for the Nuremberg trials. Upon his return to Chicago, Gelb reorganized and revitalized the CAD in collaboration with Thorkild Jacobsen and worked out an ambitious program to enlarge its staff, complete the collections, and begin publication. He wrote a standard operating procedure and the first sample articles, copies of which were widely distributed in the profession. For the next decade he devoted considerable time and effort to this enterprise, but when disputes broke out among members of the editorial board as to the best way to proceed, Gelb resigned as editor in chief in 1954. However, he continued to serve the project as an adviser and editor in various capacities until his death. His own research contribution to the collection of materials for the dictionary centered on grammatical questions and on the oldest phases of the Akkadian language. Gelb visited museums around the world in search of Old Akkadian materials and published a glossary of Old Akkadian (1957), a grammar and list of source materials for Old Akkadian (1952; rev. ed., 1961), and four volumes of documents in various collections.

Gelb's interest in early sources for Akkadian drew him into research on Mesopotamian society and economy in the third millennium B.C. In a series of fundamental studies, he sought to describe institutions such as food distribution, land tenure, family structure, labor, and legal status as well as specific groups within Mesopotamian society, including slaves, laborers, votaries, and prisoners of war. The culmination of this line of his research was *Earliest Land Tenure Systems in the Near East*, published posthumously in 1989, jointly with Piotr Steinkeller and Robert Whiting.

Another important research interest of Gelb's was the comparative study of writing, which he called "grammatology." His *Study of Writing* (1952; rev. ed., 1963), translated into six languages, was a pioneering contribution to this subject. Its strength lies in its analysis of Near Eastern writing systems, whereas his study of Chinese, Mayan, and other systems has since been superseded by specialists in those areas. Gelb was also much interested in linguistics and after 1949 held a joint professorship in the linguistics department of the University of Chicago. His *Sequential Reconstruction of Proto-Akkadian* (1969) grew out of his work on Old Akkadian and Amorite.

With the discovery of a hitherto unknown Semitic language written on clay tablets from Ebla, Syria, dating to the last quarter of the third millennium B.C., Gelb, in his last years, threw himself wholeheartedly into the creation of a new discipline in ancient Near Eastern studies. In addition to his work on the Eblaite language and its relationship to other Semitic languages, Gelb took up once again an old research interest of his, the earliest history of the Semitic peoples, and developed a major new hypothesis concerning a northern Mesopotamian Semitic civilization in the mid-third millennium B.C.

Gelb was an inspiring, generous, and demanding teacher. A volume in his honor was compiled for his sixty-fifth birthday; the contents first appeared in *Orientalia* 42 (1973), parts 1 and 2, and then were assembled as a book, *Approaches to the Study of the Ancient Near East* (ed. Giorgio Buccellati, 1974). He opened his enormous personal files of lexical material to all serious students and researchers, and his personal enthusiasm made him an accessible mentor to anyone who sought his advice.

He received numerous academic honors. He was a member of the Société Asiatique, Paris (1936); the Finnish Oriental Society (1949); the Polish Academy of Sciences (1938); the Institute of Asian Studies, Hyderabad, India (1952); the Accademia Nazionale dei Lincei, Rome (1962); and the American Philosophical Society (1975). He served as national president of the American Oriental Society in 1965–1966; president, Middle West Branch, 1959–1960; president of the American Name Society, 1963–1964; delegate for the University of Chicago to the International Congress of Orientalists in 1931, 1954, 1960, and 1973; and was a member of numerous scholarly organizations, such as the American Schools for Oriental Research, the Archaeological Institute of America, the British Academy, the American Historical Association, and the International Linguistic Association. His total published works included more than twenty books and 250 articles and reviews.

In 1938 Gelb married Hester Mokstad, with whom he had two children. His leisure time was spent at a summer home in the Michigan dunes. His high standards of scholarship, his productivity and vision, and above all his love for research made him one of his generation's leading scholars of the ancient Near East. He died in Chicago.

• Gelb's lexical files and other scholarly papers are in the Oriental Institute of the University of Chicago. A bibliography of his publications to 1973 was compiled by John Hayes in *Orientalia* 42 (1973): 1–8. An autobiographical account of Gelb's work with the Chicago Assyrian Dictionary appears in *The Assyrian Dictionary of the Oriental Institute of the University of Chicago*, vol. 1 (1964), pp. vii–xxi. An obituary by Robert Whiting is in *Archiv für Orientforschung* 34 (1987): 249–51.

BENJAMIN R. FOSTER

GELBERT, Charles Saladin, Jr. (24 Dec. 1871–16 Jan. 1936), early football player, was born in Hawley, Pennsylvania, the son of Charles Saladin Gelbert and Barbara Ott (occupations unknown). Gelbert grew up in nearby Scranton. After graduating from Lackawanna High School, he entered the University of Pennsylvania in 1893. He made the Penn football team as a freshman and starred as an end on the 1894–1896 teams, which were rated among the best in the nation. In these years Penn, coached by George Woodruff, won 52 games and lost 4, outscored opponents 1,594 to 130, and won 34 consecutive games before losing to Lafayette College in 1896. The 1895 team shared the national title with Yale University.

A teammate of All-America players George Brooke and Charles "Buck" Wharton, Gelbert at 5'8" and 165 pounds sported a blond handlebar mustache as well as a full head of hair (virtually a necessity because players had no headgear) and was known as "Miracle Man" for his exploits against bigger opponents. He starred on both offense and defense, and while best known as an end, he also played halfback and occasionally guard. One 1895 press account noted that as a defensive end he was "very fast in getting down the field, sure in tackling and quick at breaking up interference." A contemporary account of an 1894 Harvard game notes his "savage tackle" of an opponent, while an 1896 story tells of his blocking a punt against the Carlisle (Pennsylvania) Indian School team, and in Penn's 1896 win over Cornell he tackled the punter in the end zone for a safety.

But contemporary sources more often noted Gelbert's offensive ability. He led Penn's innovative interference with its blockers moving ahead of the runner instead of playing a more traditional role closer to the runner. He also was a brilliant runner with his "pretty displays of sprinting and dodging" in the open field. In the 1895 Harvard game he recovered a blocked punt and ran for a touchdown. In the same game he figured in one of Penn's double-pass offensive plays in which he received a short pass and shuttled it off to a teammate. Contemporary accounts routinely noted his effectiveness on end runs.

Walter Camp selected Gelbert as an end for All-America honors in 1894, 1895, and 1896. In 1960, Gelbert was elected to the National Football Foundation Hall of Fame. A versatile athlete at Penn, he played baseball for two years and was on the gymnastics team, which gave exhibitions before games in 1895–1896.

Gelbert received a doctor of veterinary medicine degree from Pennsylvania in 1899 and practiced in the Ambler, Pennsylvania, area. He married Nida Florence Kelly of Scranton in 1902 and had three children, including a son, Charles, who was a major league

shortstop with the St. Louis Cardinals and several other teams.

In early 1936, Gelbert was diagnosed as suffering from a malignant abdominal tumor, and, in spite of an optimistic prognosis, he committed suicide in a Philadelphia hospital.

• For Gelbert's athletic performances, see the *New York Times*, Oct. and Nov. 1894–1896. Also see Edward R. Bushnell, *The History of Athletics at Pennsylvania* (1909); Ralph Hickok, *Who Was Who in American Sports* (1971), p. 112; and John McCallum and Charles H. Pearson, *College Football USA, 1896–1973* (1973), p. 324. Material on Gelbert can be found in the University of Pennsylvania archives, Philadelphia. An obituary appears in the *New York Times*, 17 Jan. 1936.

DANIEL R. GILBERT

GELLATLY, John (1853–8 Nov. 1931), art collector, was born in New York City, the son of Peter N. Gellatly, a Scottish émigré, and his Irish wife (name unknown). Orphaned at age seven and raised by his uncle William A. Gellatly, a partner in the New York pharmaceutical firm W. H. Shieffelin & Co., John Gellatly grew up with his cousins at Llewellen Park in West Orange, New Jersey. Another uncle, Burt Gellatly, an amateur painter, encouraged John's early interest in art.

John Gellatly went to work as a clerk and salesman for Schieffelin in 1871. He resigned from the firm in 1884 to enter the real estate and insurance business. At about this time he married Julia Edith Rogers, whom he had met while taking art classes; they had no children. She was the daughter of Columbus B. Rogers, a lawyer, and the niece of Jacob S. Rogers, joint owner of the Rogers Locomotive & Machine Works of Paterson, New Jersey. Edith Rogers Gellatly, as she was known, was a painter of still lifes. She was also an art collector, an interest she encouraged in her husband.

Edith Gellatly's wealth enabled John Gellatly to devote himself to cultural pursuits quite apart from the business activities to which he may have given nominal attention. The couple resided first at 20 West Twenty-first Street and then at 34 West Fifty-seventh Street in New York City, where they built a private gallery for their paintings. When Edith Gellatly died in 1913 she left most of her fortune to John Gellatly, who continued to build the collection they had begun together.

Gellatly liked to cultivate the appearance of an art connoisseur by wearing flamboyant clothing. Yet on another level he was quiet and sentimental, a devoted friend to the artists whom he patronized. An avowed love of truth and beauty prompted him to actively seek out works by artists of the so-called American Renaissance who were "in sympathy with the great masters who preceded them," as he put it. Interested in demonstrating the breadth of an artist's work, he assembled large groups of his or her paintings. At one time he owned thirty paintings by Robert Loftin Newman, thirty-one paintings by Thomas Wilmer Dewing, twenty-three paintings by Abbott Handerson Thayer, and seventeen paintings by Albert Pinkham Ryder. To aid comparison of the art of the present with the art of the past, Gellatly also owned nineteen European old masters. The collector also placed contemporary paintings in antique frames to emphasize their connection to the Italian Renaissance. Gellatly looked especially to the example of Abbott Thayer, who painted modern Madonnas such as the celebrated *Virgin Enthroned* (1891, National Museum of American Art). "It is along way from 1500 to 1900 but somehow your pictures seem more akin to my favorite Italian masters than anything else I know," he wrote Thayer (12 May 1903, Archives of the Smithsonian Institution).

Gellatly was a friend of the Detroit industrialist and art patron Charles Lang Freer, whose own 1906 bequest to the Smithsonian Institution probably served as an example for Gellatly's later gift. The two men visited each other's collections, and they shared a voyage to Europe in October 1900. Both were faithful patrons of Abbott Thayer and Thomas Dewing. They also shared a devotion to the art of American painter James McNeill Whistler. Gellatly purchased Whistler's *Valparaiso Harbor* and *Leonora* (both National Museum of American Art, 1866 and c. 1890, respectively). But Freer had also begun to build what would become a world-class Asian art collection, and he likely encouraged Gellatly to expand his collecting interests to include ancient and Asian antiquities.

Among Gellatly's acqusitions of this type is a striking gold canteen from the Ming period that is embellished with a dragon, a Tang tomb figure of a warrior, and a dramatic seated Kwanyin of monumental proportions. He also bought ancient Syrian, Egyptian, and Arabic glass, hundreds of pieces of Renaissance jewelry, a collection of Gothic ivories, medieval champlevé and Battersea enamels, and modern English glass. In 1921 he made his English butler Ralph Seymour curator of his vast and disparate collection. Today Seymour's notes provide much of the information that documents the circumstances and cost of Gellatly's art purchases.

Determined to cull his collection, in 1917 Gellatly returned many paintings to his artist friends, keeping only what he thought were their best works. As early as 1924, Gellatly was planning to donate his collection, writing to the secretary of the Smithsonian, "you might consider (me) as one of the collectors from whom you could expect gifts." So rapidly did he purchase objects at this time that his fortune was depleted. Much of his collection was, in fact, purchased during the decade of 1918–1928, including fifteen paintings by Childe Hassam and twelve paintings by John H. Twachtman. In 1928 Gellatly sold his house to raise money for further art acquisitions and moved to the Hotel Buckingham. He placed his collection in rented quarters in the Heckscher Building, where he displayed it in a carefully decorated setting to specially invited visitors.

That same year, 1928, the 75-year-old Gellatly offered his collection to Columbia University in honor of his father-in-law, who had been an alumnus there.

When Gellatly's stipulations were found excessively binding by Columbia, he made a similar offer to the Corcoran Gallery of Art. Finally, through the agency of painter Gari Melchers, the chairman of the National Gallery of Art Commission, the Gellatly gift came to the National Gallery of Art (today the National Museum of American Art, Smithsonian Institution), which officially accepted his donation of 1,640 items in June 1929.

John Gellatly married actress Charlayne Whitely Plummer on 24 September 1930, although the couple separated immediately and never lived together. He died in New York City.

• John Gellatly's papers are in the registrar's office of the National Museum of American Art and in the Archives of the Smithsonian Institution. Gellatly expressed his own philosophy in his essay "Pathways in Art," a manuscript found in folder 42 in the Gellatly papers of the Archives of the Smithsonian Institution. Thomas Brumbaugh, "The American 19th Century, Part 3: The Gellatly Legacy," *Art News* 67 (Sept. 1968): 48–51, 58–60, discusses in depth the collector's interest in Ryder, Dewing, Thayer, Hassam, and Twachtman. Ralph Seymour's list titled "A Summary of the Gellatly Collection," dated by him to 1932, located in the files of the National Museum of American Art, provides essential data on the cost and circumstances of many purchases. Paul V. Gardner writes of the non-American side of the collection in "Archaeological Highlights in the John Gellatly Collection," *Archaeology* 7, no. 2 (Summer 1954): 66–73. In *The Elegant Auctioneers* (1970), Wesley Towner sketches a picture of Gellatly as a man-about-town, indicating that his fortune at one time amounted to $5 million. Thomas Beggs, a former director of the museum to receive the Gellatly bequest, discusses the gift in *American Legion of Honor Magazine*, Summer 1959. An obituary by Ernest Peixotto, *New York Times*, 22 Nov. 1931, discusses the circumstances of the collector's inherited wealth.

SUSAN HOBBS

GEMUNDER FAMILY, violin makers and dealers, was active in New York City from 1852 to 1946. Johann Georg Heinrich Gemünder (?–1835) (the umlaut over the "u" was dropped by the descendants in America) was the first Gemunder to take up violin making, in the town of Ingelfingen, Württemberg, Germany, where three of his sons, August Martin Ludwig (22 Mar. 1814–7 Sept. 1895), Johann Georg (13 Apr. 1816–15 Jan. 1899), and Albert (1818–after 1867), learned the craft from him. After their father's death the brothers continued the business until 1839, when they closed the shop and each went his own way. Nearly a decade of unsettled life followed.

August and Albert were the first to immigrate to the United States, and they set up an organ building firm in Springfield, Massachusetts, in 1846. Georg apprenticed himself in Pesth, Vienna, Munich, and, most importantly, to the shop of the premier violin maker J. B. Vuillaume in Paris, where he stayed from 1843 to 1847. Extremely gifted, Georg rapidly developed into a superior craftsman able to do repair work on precious Stradivari violins. He had been trained to make high-bellied German violins, which sound sweet at the player's ear but thin at a distance, but after adopting Vuillaume's viewpoint that the best violins were those of the eighteenth-century Italian masters, he only copied the flatter Stradivari and Guarneri models, with their stronger tone and greater carrying power.

In 1847 Georg joined his brothers in Massachusetts. For one season they tried to establish themselves as concert artists, without success. George (as he became known in America) was the first to go back to violin making. He opened a shop in Boston in 1848. Finding that Boston did not offer enough opportunities, he moved to New York City in 1852. The timing was excellent; New York was on its way to becoming the major music center on the East Coast. It was the only city in the United States with a professional orchestra (New York Symphony, founded in 1842, which later became the New York Philharmonic). George was probably the only reliable repairman around, and his business flourished. Moreover, the string quartet that he had entered in the London Exhibition of 1851 won top honors, earning him international recognition. Thereafter his violins were in demand and were bought by the famous violinists of the day: Ludwig Spohr, Henri Vieuxtemps, Ole Bull, August Wilhelmj, and Theodore Thomas (then concertmaster of the New York Symphony, later founder of the Cincinnati and Chicago symphonies).

August and Albert operated their organ building enterprise until 1859, when they closed it and moved to New York to join their more successful brother. Once again the three Gemunders were working together. Then, as now, the crafting of a high-quality violin that reflects the artistry and pride of its maker is worlds apart from assembly line production of lower-grade instruments, and the brothers debated how the business should be reorganized to take advantage of the expanding New York market. George had built his success and fame solely on his own reputation, and he did not want to change. Albert's viewpoint—and fate—are not known; after 1867 all traces of him disappear. August, however, set up his own shop in 1866, and he soon developed it into a modern business modeled after Vuillaume's establishment in which George had worked.

August's shop employed many craftsmen; manufacturing was systematized to produce instruments in five grades of quality, from professional concert calibre to student instruments, according to the firm's standards. This production system, with craftsmen each specializing in one phase, from making separate parts, to assembly, to final adjustment, was first developed in Mittenwald and Markneukirchen in Germany and in Mirecourt, France, where Vuillaume was born and had learned the craft. August was the first to employ the system in America. He also imported violins in the white (i.e., unvarnished) from Central and Eastern Europe and then finished and varnished them in New York. The Gemunders developed their own clear and brilliant varnish, which they used exclusively and to which they attached great acoustical significance. One grade of instruments, marketed as "Art Violins," was

especially successful. The matched quartet of these instruments now held by the Metropolitan Museum of Art in New York was donated by the August Gemunder firm in 1895. These art violins are inexpensive, commercial (i.e., mass-produced) instruments but are also well made and attractive and apparently filled a need in the burgeoning market of the time. The late nineteenth century saw an unprecedented expansion of the music culture. Piano manufacture was the largest industry in the United States until it was replaced by the automobile industry. String instruments shared in this expansion. Orchestras and music schools were founded; concert halls, built.

August's shop carried a large stock of old and new instruments and accessories, had separate repair and sales departments, and employed a sizable staff. Excellent craftsmen, including the bow makers Knopf and Bausch, worked there, and their work was sold under the Gemunder name. August was extremely successful. When his sons took over, in 1890, the firm was renamed August Gemunder & Sons. By then it was the largest violin establishment in New York City and remained as such for a quarter century. George's refusal to go along with his brother's business methods reflects a sentiment of the time. Mass production, though firmly established in the piano industry, does not yield superior results in violin making. The 1910 edition of the *Grove Dictionary of Music and Musicians*, in the article on violin making, contains a paragraph deploring the system that is lacking in the two previous editions.

In the early 1870s George moved his residence to a small farm in Astoria on Long Island. For several years he commuted to Manhattan, but in 1874 he relocated the shop to Astoria. George's fame was well established. In 1885 the *New York Tribune* published an article on "the famous master of Astoria." Four years later, however, he became incapacitated by a stroke from which he did not recover. The move to Astoria was, in the long run, not good for the business. At the time, with Steinway setting up its piano factory in Astoria, moving out of Manhattan across the East River may have looked desirable, but the major expansion of the city's musical activities was northward, first to Times Square, then to Fifty-seventh Street (Carnegie Hall). Traffic patterns left Astoria out of the mainstream. In 1892 a branch was opened in Manhattan, on Union Square, under the name George Gemunder & Sons; it was operated by George Gemunder, Jr. (1857–10 Nov. 1915), until his death. Two other sons also were trained as violin makers, but neither had their father's talent. The shop was founded at a time when August's business was already a major force, and it never managed to compete successfully.

After August's death in New York City, four sons continued his business: August Martin, Jr. (4 May 1862–22 Mar. 1928), Rudolph Friedrich (9 Feb. 1865–9 July 1916), Charles Henry (30 Apr. 1870–1934?), and Oscar Henry (9 Jan. 1872–14 Jan. 1946), all of whom were born in New York City. Among them, August Martin, Jr., was, like his father, an excellent craftsman who made fine violins. Misfortune struck the firm in 1916 with Rudolph's death in Leonia, New Jersey; his widow demanded her share of the business, thus forcing a liquidation sale. The firm was reorganized but never recovered. By the 1920s the shops of Emil Herrmann and Rembert Wurlitzer had become the dominant establishments in New York. August Gemunder & Sons ceased to operate in 1946 with the death of its last active member, Oscar Henry, in New York.

The Gemunders established violin making, which up to then had only been regarded as folk art, as a professional craft of the highest order in the United States. August successfully developed the large, modern violin shop and dealership in the American environment. Of great continuing interest are the concert-quality violins made by George, August Martin, Sr., and August Martin, Jr. That the Gemunders, with their prominent position and superior craftsmanship, chose to follow Vuillaume and copy the Italian masters, notably Stradivari and Guarneri, helped to establish and reinforce the popular notion that the only really good violins are Italian—a belief that influenced violin making well into the twentieth century. The violins made by August Senior and Junior are generally all of high quality, clearly different from the cheaper products sold by their firm. George, in his basically one-man shop, began in later years to sometimes make violins of lesser quality, according to what the customer could pay, so his output is of uneven quality. In his best work, however, George is unsurpassed. During his life his violins fetched top prices. Following his death prices collapsed. Only after about 1960 did interest in Gemunder violins begin to rise again, along with their auction prices.

• Brief references to Gemunder family members can be found in most dictionaries of violin makers. An excellent, extensive discourse that includes technical details and evaluations of noteworthy examples of their craftsmanship is included in the *Universal Dictionary of Violin and Bow Makers*, vol. 2 (1960).

KEES KOOPER

GENET, Edmond Charles (8 Jan. 1763–15 July 1834), French minister to the United States, was born in Versailles, the son of Edmé Jacques Genet, a foreign office specialist in Anglo-American affairs, and Marie Anne Louise Cardon. The Genets moved in *philosophe* circles and knew Benjamin Franklin (1706–1790).

Gifted in languages, Genet inherited his father's office in 1781. His sister was a *femme de chambre* to Marie-Antoinette, and through the queen's patronage he was appointed secretary of legation in St. Petersburg in 1787. Soon after the outbreak of the French Revolution in 1789 he became chargé d'affaires, but his republicanism offended Catherine II the Great, and in 1792 the empress sent him home. There he received an enthusiastic welcome from the Girondin government, which had been in power since the arrest of Louis XVI that August. After the king's execution in

January 1793, Great Britain joined a coalition of monarchies at war with the French Republic.

On 8 April 1793 Genet arrived in Charleston as minister to the United States. The Girondins and Genet believed the two republics should form a fraternal alliance. They did not envision American participation in the European war, but they expected the same treatment France had accorded the Americans during their struggle for independence. Genet's broad objective was to renegotiate the 1778 treaty that declared the United States to be France's ally and committed it to defend French possessions in the West Indies. France sought repayment of part of America's war debt in return for generous trade concessions. Genet had also been instructed to outfit privateers to harass British ships and to issue commissions for an expedition against Spanish Florida and Louisiana.

Before Genet's arrival, President George Washington had been debating American obligations under the 1778 treaty. The president initially had approved of the French Revolution, but his attitude had changed after the arrest and execution of the king and the exile of the marquis de Lafayette. Treasury Secretary Alexander Hamilton (1755–1804), openly sympathetic to monarchies, opposed measures that might damage Anglo-American trade; he insisted that the execution of the king invalidated the treaty and opposed Genet's reception. Secretary of State Thomas Jefferson, who greeted the French Revolution as the inauguration of a new era of universal liberty, argued that treaties were made between nations, rather than sovereigns, and that the treaty therefore was valid. The French ambassador's arrival forced the issue. Washington agreed to receive Genet but issued a proclamation of neutrality in the European conflict, although in deference to Jefferson he avoided the term *neutrality*.

As soon as he arrived in the United States, Genet outfitted privateers and began planning a military expedition against Spanish possessions. On his six-week journey from Charleston to Philadelphia he received enthusiastic greetings at public meetings, hailing the cause of France as the cause of liberty. When he arrived in the capital he was dismayed by the formality of Washington's greeting but gratified by Jefferson's warmth and friendliness. Jefferson soon discovered, however, that Genet interpreted his public reception as proof that the people did not approve of administration policy and that he was impervious to warnings that the presidential ban on outfitting privateers must be obeyed.

In July, Genet exhausted the patience of even Jefferson and his other Republican supporters when he defied a presidential ban by outfitting a captured British ship as a privateer and allowing it to sail from Philadelphia against the British. When Washington was told that Genet in his anger over administration policy was threatening to appeal directly to the people, the president requested that the minister be recalled. In the interest of international and domestic harmony the decision was not made public.

In February 1794 the new minister, Joseph Fauchet, arrived with a warrant for Genet's arrest. Had the ex-minister returned to France, the Jacobins now in power might have executed him. Granted asylum in the United States, he married Cornelia Clinton, daughter of New York governor George Clinton (1739–1812), settled near Albany, and eventually became a U.S. citizen. Cornelia died in 1810; four years later he married Martha Brandon Osgood. He avoided politics and busied himself with publishing unworkable schemes for powered balloons and for using hydraulic power to haul barges over hills. In his unfinished memoirs he blamed Jefferson for his diplomatic failures. He died in Schodack, New York.

• Genet's papers are in the Library of Congress. Alexander DeConde, *Entangling Alliance: Politics and Diplomacy under George Washington* (1958), is a basic scholarly study. Genet's dispatches are in Frederick Jackson Turner, ed., "Correspondence of the French Ministers to the United States, 1791–1797," *Annual Report of the American Historical Association for the Year 1903* (1903). Harry Ammon, *The Genet Mission* (1973), emphasizes his political impact in the United States and includes a comprehensive bibliography.

HARRY AMMON

GENN, Leo (9 Aug. 1905–26 Jan. 1978), actor, was born in London, England, the son of Willie Genn, a prosperous merchant, and Ray Asserson. Genn, who would later be known as the "man with the black velvet voice," studied law at Cambridge where he was a star athlete and captain of both the soccer and tennis teams. He married Marguerite van Praag, but the date of that marriage is unknown. When he had completed his legal studies, he began practicing law at Middle Temple, and in 1930, on the advice of a friend, he joined a theatrical group in order to meet new clients. Although he was a successful lawyer, Genn soon realized that he preferred the theater to the courtroom. Playing a string of lawyers' roles in several amateur productions, Genn was spotted by Leon M. Lion, a well-known actor-manager, and was offered a professional role. Genn's first appearance on the professional stage was at the Devonshire Park Theatre in November 1930, as Peter in *A Marriage Has Been Disarranged*. When Genn balked at giving up law, Lion offered him a three-year contract as an actor and a lawyer. Genn served in this dual capacity, sometimes spending sixteen hours a day at the theater, and pausing from time to time to act as Lion's legal adviser.

From Lion's theater Genn moved to the West End Repertory Theatre, completing his apprenticeship, and in 1934, he went on to the Old Vic Company where he played classics for two years. In 1936 Genn wrote some legal scenes for the film *Jump For Glory*, starring Douglas Fairbanks, Jr., and as a result, he played the part of the lawyer. He returned to the Old Vic Company from February to April in 1937, playing Orsino in *Twelfth Night* and Burgundy in *Henry V*. He traveled to Elsinore with the Old Vic Company in June 1937, playing Horatio in *Hamlet*. He made his Broadway debut early in 1939 in *The Flashing Stream*, playing the same part he had played at the end of the previous year in London.

The play's short run of only eight performances, coming just after Hitler's invasion of Czechoslovakia, convinced Genn to go home. A member of the Officers' Emergency Reserve, Genn qualified for the Royal Artillery and saw combat in an antiaircraft unit. For a time he served as an instructor at a training camp for artillery officers. In 1943 Genn was promoted to lieutenant colonel, and in 1945 he was awarded the croix de guerre. At the end of World War II Genn joined the British unit investigating war crimes at the Belsen concentration camp, later serving as assistant prosecutor at the Nuremberg and Belsen war trials.

Before his legal assignments ended, Genn wangled sixteen days' leave to shoot a part in *Henry V* (1944), the film that marked Lawrence Olivier's 1944 directorial debut. Although the part was small, Genn's subtle, sarcastic portrayal of the Constable of France earned him an invitation to the United States and a part in the 1946 Broadway production of Lillian Hellman's *Another Part of the Forest*. In 1946 Genn was forty-one years of age, suave, and darkly handsome, and the part of Ben Hubbard, the sinister elder son, was one of his greatest stage successes. Brooks Atkinson, who reviewed the play in the *New York Times Magazine* (17 November 1946), lauded Genn for his depiction of the "strength, unscrupulousness and maturity of Ben." From Broadway Genn went to Hollywood, and in 1947 he achieved recognition from American audiences for his portrayal of Captain Adam Brant in Eugene O'Neill's *Mourning Becomes Electra*. The following year he played psychiatrist Dr. Kik in *The Snake Pit* and appeared in four British films during 1949–1950. He received an Oscar nomination for best supporting actor in 1952 for his portrayal of Gaius Petronius, Nero's counselor in the historical pageant *Quo Vadis* (1951). This was one of the most notable roles played by Genn, the distinguished, gentlemanly actor with the resonant voice who excelled at playing such understated characters in supporting roles.

Genn's long career in theater and film achieved almost dizzying proportions. He returned to the Old Vic Company in 1953 as the Duke of Buckingham in Tyrone Guthrie's Coronation Production of *Henry VIII*. Soon he was back on Broadway and maintained an active involvement in the theater on both sides of the Atlantic for the next fifteen years. In England he became a Council member of the Arts Educational Trust, and in the United States he was appointed Distinguished Visiting Professor of Theater Arts at Pennsylvania State University in 1969 and Visiting Professor of Drama at the University of Utah the same year.

Following the success of his performance in *Quo Vadis*, Genn continued to appear regularly in films, playing the part of Sir Clifford Chatterly in a French production of *Lady Chatterly's Lover* (1956). Despite his vast commitment to theater, he found time to act in many films, including *The Longest Day* (1962), *55 Days at Peking* (1963), and *Ten Little Indians* (1965). All in all, he appeared in more than ninety films, making his last, *The Martyr*, two years before his death in London.

Genn enjoyed a successful career that spanned nearly five decades. His love of drama was lifelong, and he portrayed a number of memorable roles both in the theater and in film. When reflecting on his accomplishments, however, Genn characteristically underplayed his own achievement. "Somewhere inside me," he once said, "was an actor trying to be heard" (*New York Times*, 27 Jan. 1978).

• There is a brief article on Genn, "Actor, Lawyer," in the *New Yorker*, 15 Feb. 1947, p. 25. An obituary is in the *New York Times*, 27 Jan. 1978.

MARY HURD

GENOVESE, Vito (21? Nov. 1897–14 Feb. 1969), criminal entrepreneur, was born in Ricigliano, Italy, the son of Philip Anthony Genovese, a building trades worker, and Nancy (maiden name unknown). Genovese received the equivalent of a fifth-grade education in Italy before following his father to New York City in 1913. A petty thief and street tough in the Greenwich Village area of Little Italy, Genovese soon established a reputation for unusual cunning and violence. Frequently arrested on charges of assault and homicide, he was twice convicted of carrying a concealed weapon. More important, he became a collector for the illegal Italian lottery, an indication that he had attracted the attention of locally prominent underworld figures.

In the 1930s Genovese became increasingly prominent in New York criminal circles. While he established a legitimate company handling waste paper and rags, most of his attention seems to have been devoted to illegal enterprises, especially gambling and extortion. In association with Charles "Lucky" Luciano in 1931, he was involved in a series of murders later linked by law enforcement officials with a major power struggle within the Italian underworld. The death in 1931 of Genovese's first wife (name unknown), whom he had married in 1924, apparently attracted considerable attention among gangland associates. Genovese was almost certainly involved in the murder of Gerard Vernotico, whose widow, Anna Petillo, he married two weeks later on 30 March 1932 and with whom he had two children. Genovese's entanglement in an extortion plot in 1934 led to the murder of one co-conspirator, Ferdinand Boccia, and an ongoing police investigation. In 1936, when Thomas E. Dewey won his celebrated conviction of Luciano for compulsory prostitution, the special prosecutor reportedly indicated that Genovese was his next target. Apprehensive about the Boccia case and fearful of Dewey, Genovese fled to Italy in 1937, a year after he had been naturalized.

Genovese lived well in exile. According to one account, he took $750,000 with him when he left the United States. Anna Genovese, who reportedly managed his income in the United States, made frequent visits to Italy, bringing him additional funds. At Nola in southern Italy, Genovese financed the construction of a power plant and also contributed $250,000 for the building of a municipal structure. For these services, the Mussolini government awarded Genovese the Order of the Crown of Italy, a significant civilian honor. As the fighting in Italy ended, Genovese presented himself to the victorious American forces as an interpreter and facilitator. In 1944, however, he was caught in a U.S. army investigation of black marketing in postwar Italy and jailed. While he was incarcerated, word arrived that he had been indicted in the Boccia case. Although authorities returned Genovese to New York in 1945 to face murder charges, the killing of a key witness in the case ultimately led prosecutors to drop the charges.

Back in the United States in the late 1940s, Genovese and his wife joined the movement to suburbia. They purchased and decorated a luxurious house in Atlantic Highlands, New Jersey, which commanded an impressive view of the New York skyline. Genovese cultivated the image of a conservative and civic-minded businessman. He later advised another underworld figure that respectable life in the suburbs required an altered lifestyle. "Make the people in the neighborhood like you. . . . Give to the Boy Scouts and all the charities. Try to make it to church. Don't fool around with the local girls" (quoted in Maas, p. 206).

Discord with his wife, however, contributed materially to Genovese's problems in the 1950s. Charging physical and emotional abuse, Anna Genovese sued her husband for separate maintenance and support. To buttress her case, she testified that Genovese had stashed large sums of money in European accounts and that he grossed between $20,000 and $30,000 a week from the Italian lottery. Her charges, reported in the tabloid press, brought considerable notoriety and embarrassment to Genovese. Ultimately, she won her case, and her husband sold their home and moved into a modest clapboard cottage in Atlantic Highlands.

Genovese's discomfort was compounded by a series of congressional investigations into organized crime in the 1950s. After sensational televised hearings in 1950–1951, a special committee chaired by Senator Estes Kefauver of Tennessee concluded that Genovese was a major figure in the Mafia, a sinister national crime cartel controlled by Italian Americans. In the late 1950s a select Senate committee on improper activities in the labor-management field heard testimony that Genovese had amassed a fortune of up to $30 million, in part from his activities with corrupt unions.

Law enforcement officials also linked Genovese to a series of highly publicized gangland developments. In May 1957 a would-be assassin in New York wounded Frank Costello, said to be Lucky Luciano's successor in the underworld. In October gunmen killed the notorious Albert Anastasia, another widely feared gang leader, in a New York barbershop. Finally, in November state troopers apprehended Genovese and some sixty other underworld figures during an alleged mob convention in Apalachin, New York. While no compelling explanation for these developments was advanced, officials and reported speculated that they involved either a major underworld power struggle or a debate over narcotics trafficking, possibly both. Genovese, said to be eager to assume Costello's mantle, was indicted shortly thereafter on federal narcotics charges. Convicted in 1959, he began serving a fifteen-year sentence in an Atlanta penitentiary in 1960.

Events in prison led to more notoriety for Genovese. His cellmate and longtime subordinate, Joseph Valachi, became convinced that Genovese, paranoid and vindictive, suspected him of betrayal. Fearing for his life, Valachi agreed to cooperate with federal officials. In 1963 he testified before a congressional committee about the inner workings of organized crime. Valachi claimed that even in prison Genovese dominated an enormously powerful but mysterious Italian-American criminal organization called La Cosa Nostra. Valachi's testimony, largely taken uncritically, had a profound impact on law enforcement, policymakers, and popular culture. In the wake of the hearings, officials moved Genovese to federal facilities in Leavenworth, Kansas. He died of heart problems in a prison hospital in Springfield, Missouri.

• The only biography is David Hanna's brief *Vito Genovese* (1974). Peter Maas provides details from the exposés of the 1960s in *The Valachi Papers* (1968). A useful corrective to the popular literature on organized crime is Dwight C. Smith, Jr., *The Mafia Mystique* (1975). An obituary is in the *New York Times*, 15 Feb. 1969.

WILLIAM HOWARD MOORE

GENTH, Frederick Augustus (17 May 1820–2 Feb. 1893), chemist and mineralogist, was born Friedrich August Ludwig Karl Wilhelm Genth in Waechtersbach, Hesse-Cassel, Germany, the son of Georg Friedrich Genth, principal forest warden to Prince Issenburg, and Karoline Amalie, Freyin (Baroness) von Swartzenau. Genth attended the Gymnasium in Hanau, then studied at Heidelberg under Leopold Gmelin, at Giessen with Justus von Liebig, Hermann Kopp, and the analytical chemist C. R. Fresenius, finally receiving his Ph.D. in 1845 at Marburg, where he worked with Robert Wilhelm Bunsen. His thesis dealt with recovery of copper metal from copper-bearing schists: he later expanded it and published it in *Erdmann's Journal für praktische Chemie* (1846). Genth became an instructor at Marburg and acted as Bunsen's assistant for three years. He then emigrated to the United States, settling first in Baltimore, then in Philadelphia, at that time the center of U.S. chemical manufacture. There he set up an analytical laboratory where he also instructed special students. He quickly succeeded in this venture because his European training in analysis and his rapidly-growing knowledge of mineralogy placed him far in advance of U.S.-trained chemists.

In the fall of 1849 Genth closed his laboratory to accept a position as superintendent of the Washington silver mine in Davidson County, North Carolina. He returned to Philadelphia in August 1850 and reopened the laboratory, continuing with analysis and instruction and adding his own research work. During the 1850s, with Oliver Wolcott Gibbs, he resumed work he had begun at Marburg on ammonia adducts of cobalt(III). This appears to have been the first recognition that ammonia could enter into compound formation, producing well-characterized crystals that were initially named according to their colors—for example roseocobalt and purpureocobalt. Gibbs and Genth reported about thirty-six new compounds in an 1856 paper. Two years later they extended their findings to include ammineosmium compounds. Although Genth's output on strictly chemical subjects included about thirty papers, these studies are regarded as his most important.

In mineralogy Genth's researches were of theoretical importance, and some turned out to have commercial value as well. In fifty-four papers he described about 215 minerals, twenty-four of them his own discoveries, including a nickel gymnite that came to be called genthite. His earliest publication in this area was in 1842, with nine papers appearing before he came to the United States; his last paper, submitted in 1891, was published in 1893. Perhaps the most important was "Corundum, Its Alterations and Associated Minerals," read before the American Philosophical Society in 1873. Corundum is an abrasive alumina found in the Appalachian mountain chain from Alabama to Massachusetts, with the richest commercial deposits in North Carolina. Depending on its impurities and its geological history, it has many forms and colors. Genth's paper discussed first the geology of the various deposits, then the minerals found with corundum: spinel, diaspore, beauxite, gibbsite, quartz, opal, and a wide variety of aluminosilicates. His conclusions traced these minerals to corundum deposits that had been chemically altered in many ways.

In 1872 Genth was named professor of chemistry and mineralogy at the University of Pennsylvania, a position he held until 1888, at some financial loss. He was apparently a good teacher, cordial and helpful to hard-working students but sharply impatient with those who wanted reward without effort. In 1874 he was appointed mineralogist to the second Geological Survey of Pennsylvania; he produced two long preliminary reports on the state's minerals. From 1877 to 1884 he was chemist to the Pennsylvania Board of Agriculture; his report on fertilizers is credited with developing agriculture to competitive excellence. In 1888 Genth reopened his analytical laboratory, where he continued to work until his death. He became overweight and asthmatic in his last years, which restricted his activities, but he carried out his own laboratory work.

Genth was elected to the National Academy of Sciences in 1872. He was vice president of the newly-formed American Chemical Society in 1876 and its president in 1880. He was a fellow of the American Academy of Arts and Sciences, and one of the three honorary fellows at the time of the American Association for the Advancement of Science. He married twice: in 1847 to Karolina Jaeger, daughter of the University of Marburg's librarian, who bore him three children; and after her death, in 1852 to Minna Paulina Fischer, by whom he had nine children. Genth died in Philadelphia.

• The most complete biographies are those by George F. Barker in National Academy of Sciences, *Biographical Memoirs* 4 (1901): 201–31, and *Proceedings of the American Philosophical Society* 40 (1901): x–xxii; the former contains a bibliography and a list of minerals discovered by Genth, as does the account by W. M. Meyers and S. Zerfoss, *Journal of the Franklin Institute* 241 (1946): 341–54. Shorter sketches are in *Journal of the Franklin Institute* 135 (1893): 448–52; and *American Journal of Science* 145 (1893): 257–58. Information on the amminecobalts is in G. B. Kauffman, "Frederick Augustus Genth and the Discovery of Cobalt-Ammines," *Journal of Chemical Education* 52 (1975): 155–56. Genth is placed in German context in H. S. van Klooster, "Liebig and His American Pupils," *Journal of Chemical Education* 33 (1956): 493–97.

ROBERT M. HAWTHORNE JR.

GENTHE, Arnold (8 Jan. 1869–9 Aug. 1942), photographer, was born in Berlin, Germany, the son of Hermann Genthe, a professor of Latin and Greek, and Louise Zober. Genthe received his doctorate in philology from the University of Jena in 1894. While in school, he associated with his mother's cousin, the painter Adolf Menzel, and he published *Deutsches Slang* (1892), a book on German slang.

In 1895 Genthe left Germany for San Francisco, California, to tutor the son of Baron Heinrich von Schroeder, a family friend who had married the daughter of American business mogul Peter Donahue. During his spare time Genthe bought a hand camera and took photographs of his surroundings to send back to his family. He became intrigued with Tangrenbu, the Chinese quarter of the city, and took candid shots of residents, merchants, children, and drug addicts on the streets and in the alleys. He often found his subjects reluctant to be photographed, which Genthe attributed to a fear of the "black devil box" but was more likely due to fears of deportation, so he resorted to lurking in doorways and hiding his camera.

Genthe's Chinatown photographs comprise the only photographic documentation of that region before the destruction of the San Francisco earthquake in 1906. Approximately 200 images from 1896 to 1906 have survived. To enhance the exotic nature of the scenes, he occasionally cropped out or retouched references of Western society. For example, in his photograph "The Toy Peddler," Genthe scratched out an English sign reading "Chinese Candies 5 Cts. Per Bag." In other photographs he erased telephone and electric wires, and, in the case of "An Unsuspecting Victim," he deleted other Caucasians on the street. The Christmas 1897 issue of the weekly magazine *The Wave* published Genthe's shots of Chinatown streetlife, and in 1898 he began exhibiting his work at the California Camera Club. His book *Pictures of Old Chinatown* (1908; repr. 1913) was accompanied by text by Will Irwin.

In the late 1890s Genthe opened his own portrait studio. Through his association with von Schroeder,

Genthe knew several of the city's wealthiest matrons, who flocked to his studio for portraits in the fashionable pictorialist style. Rooted in the English aesthetic movement, pictorialism aimed to raise photography to the level of fine art by using painting as a reference to construct imagery and narrative. In this fashion, Genthe said that he tried to make portraits in which "a uniform sharpness would be avoided and emphasis laid on portraying a person's character instead of making a commonplace record of clothes and a photographic mask" (*As I Remember*, p. 261). As his reputation grew, local notables or those visiting the city would stop by Genthe's studio for a portrait, such as actresses Nance O'Neil (1899) and Sarah Bernhardt (1906), and writer Jack London (1900 and 1906).

In addition to his Chinatown and other streetlife photographs, Genthe's portraits were featured in numerous exhibitions, including the Fourth Philadelphia Salon (1901), the London Salon (1901), two San Francisco Salons (1901, 1902), and the Los Angeles Salon (1902, where he won a *Camera Craft* magazine gold medal). His photographs were widely published in West Coast magazines and often illustrated articles he wrote on photographic theory and technique, such as "Rebellion in Photography" for *Overland Monthly* (Aug. 1901). He also exhibited and published photographs from his many travels, including Mexico (1902); Morocco, Germany, Belgium, and Spain (1904); Japan (1908); New Orleans, Louisiana (1925); Guatemala and Cuba (1927); and Greece (1929 and 1930).

On 18 April 1906, the morning of the great San Francisco earthquake, Genthe, with his cameras and studio destroyed, borrowed a hand-held camera and photographed the destruction across the city. Of his over 180 surviving, sharp-focus photographs of San Francisco, probably his most famous image is "San Francisco, April 18th, 1906," which shows a view from Nob Hill, down Sacramento Street. Enormous clouds of smoke ominously approach, buildings' facades have collapse from the quake, and residents stand and sit in the street, in a stupor, calming watching the approaching fire. "Steps that Lead to Nowhere" (also known as "After the Fire") depicts the barren remains of a large house with the lights of the Mission District in the background.

In the winter of 1907–1908 Genthe began experimenting with color photography using the autochrome technique. His image of a rainbow in the Grand Canyon was the first color photograph to appear on the cover of an American magazine (*Collier's*, 1911). In May 1913 *American Magazine* published an article by Irwin about Genthe, illustrated by a number of his color portraits of actors and personalities.

Genthe moved to New York City in 1911 and remained there until he died, working mainly in portraiture. He had several distinguished sitters including Theodore Roosevelt, William H. Taft, Woodrow Wilson, Andrew Mellon, and John D. Rockefeller. Genthe credited himself for jump-starting Greta Garbo's career with the dark, dramatic photographs he took of her just after she arrived in America in 1925. In 1918 Genthe became a U.S. citizen; he never married.

Genthe also specialized in photographing modern dancers. Isadora Duncan, Ruth St. Denis, Anna Pavlova, and other dance pioneers are featured in *The Book of the Dance* (1916). Intending to take only a passport photo, Duncan so enjoyed having her photo taken by Genthe that the session resulted in a series published just after her death in *Isadora Duncan: Twenty-four Studies by Arnold Genthe* (1929). Duncan wrote that Genthe's portraits of her were not "representations of my physical being but representations of conditions of my soul, and one of them is my very soul indeed" (*My Life* [1927], p. 327). For his dance photographs, Genthe aimed to "record in a pictorially interesting manner, and in a diversity of patterns, impressions of the charm of dance movement, of the fleeting magic designs made by the human body, of the nobility of gesture called forth by the dance" (*As I Remember*, p. 196).

Although Genthe had a highly successful portrait career, working until he died of a heart attack while visiting friends in Connecticut, his pictorial style was well out of fashion by the 1930s. In the article "The Last Stylist" (*Coronet Magazine*, Nov. 1938), a reporter described Genthe as representing "a style, a grace, a gesture which has long since sped away." Despite criticism over Genthe's manipulation of his early images, the photographer's major contribution to photography and to history are his pre-1906 photographs of Chinatown and his photographs of San Francisco just after the earthquake. His direct influence can be seen in several West Coast photographers including Consuelo Kanaga, who also completed a series of Chinatown photographs. Exhibitions of Genthe's work include one at the Staten Island Museum, New York, in 1975, and another at the International Center for Photography, New York, in 1984.

• The Library of Congress has the largest collection of Genthe's prints and negatives. Genthe's other books include *Deutsches Slang: beine sammlung familiärer Ausdrücke und Redensarten* (1892); *The Gardens of Kijkuit* (1919); *Impressions of Old New Orleans* (1926); and his well-illustrated autobiography *As I Remember* (1936). On Genthe's early career, see Toby Gersten Quitslund, "Arnold Genthe: A Pictorial Photographer in San Francisco" (Ph.D. diss., George Washington Univ., 1988). Also see John Kuo Wei Tchen, *Genthe's Photographs of San Francisco's Old Chinatown* (1984), and Maxine Hong Kingston, "San Francisco's Chinatown," *American Heritage*, Dec. 1978. An obituary is in the *Washington Evening Star*, 12 Aug. 1942.

MEL BYARS
N. ELIZABETH SCHLATTER

GEORGE, Bill (27 Oct. 1930–30 Sept. 1982), professional football player, was born William George in Waynesburg, Pennsylvania, of Syrian ancestry, the son of Leo G. George. (His mother's name is unknown.) After starring as a wrestler and football player at Waynesburg High School, George attended Wake Forest College (now University), where he helped turn a losing team into a winning one. The 6′2″, 230-pound George played both offense and defense from 1948 through the 1951 season, winning All-America honors as a guard in 1949. An all-around athlete, he also won the Southern Conference and the regional Amateur Athletic Union wrestling championships, and he led his 1952 summer league baseball team in stolen bases, while batting .370.

Drafted as a "future" by the Chicago Bears of the National Football League in 1951, George graduated from Wake Forest College in 1952, before his eligibility expired. He enjoyed a long, stellar career as a professional player. During fourteen seasons with the Bears as a middle guard and linebacker, he was selected to the all-league team eight times and played in eight straight Pro Bowls (1955–1962). During that time he married Lucy (maiden name unknown); they had three children.

Considered a brilliant, intense, and fearless competitor, George played in 124 consecutive games; over that span he intercepted 18 passes and recovered 16 fumbles. He also scored 26 points as a kicker on four field goals and 14 extra points. With George starring at linebacker, the Bears won the Western Conference in 1956, before losing 47–7 to the New York Giants for the league championship. During the 1963 season he anchored a linebacking corps generally considered the best in the NFL that year, as the Bears defeated the Giants 14–10 in the title game.

A powerful man, agile for his size, George excelled as pass rusher, but he is most notable for his football knowledge. His strategic adaptation in a 1954 game changed the nature of defensive play, creating a new position called middle linebacker, which was generally adopted throughout the league and recognized as a standard position by sports writers within three years of its inception. Defenses had traditionally used five defensive linemen, but when the Philadelphia Eagles continually completed short passes over the middle of the line, George left his usual responsibilities in favor of pass coverage and made an interception. The result was the 4-3 defense of three linebackers positioned behind four defensive linemen. Over the next decade, while serving as the Bears' defensive captain, George developed techniques for the new defensive formation and for the middle linebacker position. His pass rushing abilities destroyed the previously effective shotgun offense in which the quarterback is positioned seven or eight yards behind the line of scrimmage. George Allen, who coached the Bears, Los Angeles Rams, and Washington Redskins, claimed that George was the smartest defensive football player he ever coached; Allen listed him among the best 100 players in pro football history. George Halas described him as "one of the greatest players—the key man in our defense, and the shrewdest player in the league." Off the field his teammates described him as "mischievous" but "strong, understanding, and compassionate."

George played for the Bears through 1965 and finished his NFL career with the Los Angeles Rams in 1966. After the 1965 season George assisted George

Allen in charitable efforts on behalf of American Indians in South Dakota. He returned to the Bears as an assistant coach in 1972 and was elected to the Pro Football Hall of Fame in 1974. The team retired his jersey, number 61. His fourteen years with the Bears were the most for any player in club history.

After his retirement from football, George owned an industrial maintenance supply business in South Barrington, Illinois. He was killed in a car crash south of Rockford, Illinois.

• Newspaper clippings about George are in his file at the Pro Football Hall of Fame, Canton, Ohio. Short biographical pieces can be found in Denis J. Harrington, *The Pro Football Hall of Fame* (1991), and William S. Jarrett, *Timetables of Sports History: Football* (1989). See also Don R. Smith, *Pro Football Hall of Fame All-Time Greats* (1988), and Richard Whittingham, *Bears in Their Own Words* (1991). Obituaries are in the *Chicago Tribune* and the *New York Times*, both 1 Oct. 1982.

GERALD R. GEMS

GEORGE, David (c. 1742–1810), lay preacher and African-American émigré to Nova Scotia and Sierra Leone, was born on a Nottoway River plantation in Essex County, Virginia. His parents, slaves known as John and Judith, were of African origin and had nine children. While a youth David labored in the corn and tobacco fields and witnessed frequent whippings of other slaves, including his mother, who was the master's cook.

When he was about nineteen, George ran away to North Carolina, worked for a brief time, but was pursued and fled to South Carolina. He worked as a hired hand for about two years. After hearing that his first master was again pursuing him, George escaped to Central Georgia where he hid among the Creek Indians. George became the personal servant of Chief Blue Salt, who later sold him to the Natchez chief, King Jack.

A trader with the white settlers, King Jack sold George to the Indian trader George Galphin of Silver Bluff, Georgia. Galphin sent George to work for John Miller, his agent. George mended deerskins and took care of Miller's horses until about 1766, when he went to live at Galphin's frontier trading post. Galphin, an Ulsterman who traded with the Creeks and Choctaws, treated George well.

About 1770 George married a woman known only as Phillis. Soon after his marriage he began attending slave prayer meetings led by a slave named Cyrus. George and his wife experienced conversion after hearing the preaching of George Liele, the African-American Baptist who conducted an itinerant ministry on plantations along the Savannah River. As a child, George had known Liele when the two were slaves in Virginia.

George and his wife were baptized about 1777 by Wait Palmer, a radical white Baptist who belonged to the Separate Baptist movement, which was zealously revivalistic, espousing the need for a "new birth." Liele encouraged George to preach with instruction

from Palmer. Galphin employed a schoolmaster who, along with Galphin's children, taught George to read and write. Of learning these skills at the age of thirty, George later said, "The reading so ran in my mind, that I think I learned in my sleep . . . , and I can now read the Bible, so that what I have in my heart, I can see again in the Scriptures."

With assistance from Palmer, George organized a Baptist congregation on Galphin's Silver Bluff plantation that began with eight members; it expanded to about thirty members by 1778. During the revolutionary war, Lord Dunmore offered emancipation to any slaves who sought sanctuary behind British lines. George went to Charleston. When the British evacuated Charleston in 1782, he and his family were among the Charleston refugees who went to New York City and then to Halifax, Nova Scotia.

Finding no opportunity to preach among blacks in Halifax, George settled in Shelburne. Because white justices, fearing civil disorder, would not let him preach in town, George had to content himself with a hut in the woods, where his preaching attracted whites as well as blacks. He soon had fifty members in what was only the second Baptist church organized in Nova Scotia. In 1784 recently disbanded British soldiers, resenting competition from free black laborers, attacked and destroyed many of their houses. George and his family fled to Birchtown. After six months George returned to Shelburne and regained possession of his old meetinghouse. During the next years he conducted missionary trips in the Maritime provinces. Though only a lay preacher, George was known for his rousing sermons and hymns and was responsible for the organization of seven Baptist churches in Nova Scotia before he left for Africa.

In 1791 Lieutenant John Clarkson of the British navy arrived in Nova Scotia to recruit Nova Scotia blacks for the British-sponsored "Free Settlement on the Coast of Africa" at Sierra Leone, West Africa. George was by now forty-eight years old, the father of six, the largest black landowner in Nova Scotia, and the pastor of two churches. He talked privately with Clarkson and became convinced of the merits of the Sierra Leone enterprise. On 15 January 1792 the George family departed Halifax for Cape Sierra Leone with about 1,200 other black Nova Scotians.

Soon after landing, George expressed his evangelical enthusiasm: "I preached the first Lord's Day (it was a blessed time) under a sail, and so I did for several weeks after. We then erected a hovel for a meetinghouse, which is made of posts put into the ground, and poles over our heads, which are covered with grass." George led the formation of the first Baptist church in West Africa at Freetown, Sierra Leone. He and his members supported Clarkson when other settler factions challenged the authority of the British governor. In 1796, however, George opposed Governor Zachary Macaulay because Macaulay issued a decree that restricted the authority to perform marriages to the ordained clergy of the Anglican church and the governor. George was more moderate in his protest of

British authority than some Nova Scotians, as those who had come with Clarkson were known. More strident settlers called George "Macaulay's tool."

While in Sierre Leone, George did limited missionary work among the indigenous Temne. Conflict among the various ethnic groups prevented him from carrying out plans for establishing Baptist churches in areas outside those occupied by the colonists. George and Thomas Peters, another Nova Scotian, were the first unofficial members of the Sierre Leone Legislative Council. George traveled to Britain in December 1792, remaining six months visiting English Baptists and telling his story. After returning to Sierre Leone, George devoted himself to church work, especially as an advocate for the Baptists when opposition arose from Methodists in the colony. He died in Sierre Leone.

• Primary information on David George is drawn from the account of his life that he gave to English Baptists when he visited them in late 1792 and early 1793. It appeared as "An Account of the Life of Mr. David George, from Sierra Leone in Africa," in the *Baptist Annual Register for . . . 1793*, pp. 473–84. Important studies of the black Nova Scotians are Ellen Gibson Wilson, *The Loyal Blacks* (1976), and James W. St. G. Walker, *The Black Loyalists: The Search for a Promised Land in Nova Scotia and Sierra Leone, 1783–1870* (1976). Details about George's missionary labors in Nova Scotia are found in Anthony Kirk-Greene, "David George: The Nova Scotia Experience," *Sierra Leone Studies*, n.s., 14 (1960): 93–120; and Ingraham E. Bill, *Fifty Years with the Baptist Ministers and Churches of the Maritime Provinces of Canada* (1880).

MILTON C. SERNETT

GEORGE, Gladys (13 Sept. 1894?–8 Dec. 1954), stage and film actress, was born Gladys Anna Clare in Patten, Maine, the daughter of Arthur Evans Clare and Alice Josephine Hazen, actors. Her mother was the daughter of a Boston jeweler. George's commonly published birth year, 1904, was a professional fiction: 1909 newspaper clippings reveal that she played a heroine of marriageable age—unlikely casting for a five-year-old. She may also have romanticized other details in later interviews. These tell us that Sir Arthur Clare (supposedly knighted by Edward VII) was a London Shakespearean actor before immigrating to and marrying in the United States. Gladys's stage debut came at age three, acting and singing in Waterbury, Connecticut. Her formal education stopped at the fourth grade; her father tutored her while they toured stock and vaudeville theaters. During her childhood and youth the family was repeatedly stranded without funds, as her parents had been when she was born, owing to Arthur Clare's habit of touring in untried corners of North America. Gladys remembered playing in theaters, barns, medicine-show tents, and even on railroad station platforms.

For a benefit show in Toronto, Arthur Clare wrote a new sketch, *The Dream Doll*, in which a quarreling couple were reunited by a singing, dancing doll (eight-year-old Gladys), who appeared in a shared dream.

Enthusiastic audience response brought a national tour offer, providing Gladys was starred. "The Three Clares" became "Little Gladys George and Company." *The Dream Doll* was their vaudeville vehicle for years, with changes and new songs as Gladys grew older. Her birth year was probably altered during this period to extend her "child star" longevity.

In theatrical stock, George had played hundreds of roles by her teens. In the 1909–1910 season, when the leading lady was hospitalized in mid-tour, understudy George took over the title role in *Lena Rivers*, earning admiring reviews in Pittsburgh, Cleveland, Toledo, Cincinnati, and Syracuse. *The Dream Doll* was touring again in 1914, and by 1918 the Clares were stranded in Llano, Texas. Arthur Clare found a job managing a Dallas theater, with Gladys in the box office. Informed of an English inheritance, the Clares hurried to New York in August but were again stranded when the fortune failed to materialize. In 1918 George landed her first Broadway part but had to work behind a candy counter and as a clothing model until fall rehearsals began.

Maeterlinck's *The Betrothal*, starring Isadora Duncan, opened on 18 November 1918 with Gladys George as Jalline, the beggar's daughter. Next, the Charles Coburns offered her a national tour in their World War I comedy hit, *The Better 'Ole*. When the tour reached Los Angeles in 1919, George was hired by film producer Thomas Ince. She made five films, but her one-year silent-film career ended when a cooking accident burned and hospitalized her for six months.

Recovered, she joined San Francisco's Alcazar Players. In 1922 she married Ben Erway, the juvenile lead in *The Blindness of Virtue*, her greatest success as an Alcazar leading lady. They appeared together in stock, costarring for several years at Denver's Denham Theatre and in other companies from Salt Lake City to Boston. George sued Erway for divorce in 1929. She played leading roles in touring companies of popular farces in major cities from coast to coast and supported Pauline Frederick in the star's 1932 tour of *As Husbands Go*. In 1933 George married millionaire paper manufacturer Edward H. Fowler.

On Broadway in February 1934 Gladys George earned the only good reviews for *Queer People*, which closed after twelve performances. In May, as a fight-manager's mistress in *The Milky Way*, she impressed producer Brock Pemberton, who signed her for his next production. In the meantime, her screen test had not impressed Paramount but won her a contract with Metro-Goldwyn-Mayer (MGM). Her first film co-starred her with Franchot Tone in *Straight Is the Way*, which failed so miserably that MGM happily granted a temporary release when Pemberton recalled her to Broadway.

Pemberton's production of *Personal Appearance* opened on 17 October 1934. George, her name in Broadway lights for the first time, became New York's highest-paid and most-praised actress. *New York Evening Post* critic John Mason Brown found her to be, in the role of blonde "screen siren" Carole Arden, "the most adroit projector of the wisecrack that our stage boasts." He continued, "a more unrelenting or diverting parody of all that is vacuous but warm blooded in the stereotyped movie star could not be found anywhere." Mason also praised her for "never overdoing a part which abounds in opportunities for overplaying." On Broadway and on tour, the play ran for eighty-five weeks and nearly seven hundred performances.

During the run, George's second marriage dissolved in a tabloid-headlined real-life 1930s Hollywood "screwball" comedy. Accused by her husband of backstage misconduct with *Personal Appearance* actor Leonard Penn, George countersued, charging Fowler with multiple infidelities. Alleging that Fowler had sent gangsters to threaten her, she was given police protection. When her witnesses admitted being paid to lie, Fowler won. His August 1935 divorce prohibited George from remarrying in New York for three years, so on 18 September she married Leonard Penn in New Haven, Connecticut.

In 1936 MGM loaned George to Paramount for the title role in *Valiant Is the Word for Carrie*, her most popular film. Her witty, poignant performance earned George her only Academy Award nomination and bitter disappointment: Luise Rainer's more obvious tearjerking in *The Great Ziegfeld* won Rainer the award. Except for occasional "doddering mommers," as she called them in a 1940 interview, Hollywood assigned George variations on stereotypical "harlots," from good-hearted gangster's molls (*The Roaring Twenties*, 1939) to vicious man-destroyers (*The Way of All Flesh*, 1940), in period costume for westerns or for Madame Du Barry in *Marie Antoinette* (1938).

In 1940 Pemberton brought George back to sophisticated comedy and Broadway in Margery Sharp's *Lady in Waiting*. Then, after surprising New York in September 1941 by playing an old woman in *The Distant City*, George returned to Hollywood, "like everyone, for the money." Between films, she appeared on Broadway briefly as Sabina in *The Skin of Our Teeth* (1943), toured Pacific-coast theaters as Sadie Thompson in *Rain* (1944), and made a few other brief stage appearances. She divorced Leonard Penn in 1944 and in 1946 married Kenneth C. Bradley, a 27-year-old Los Angeles bellboy, divorcing him in 1950.

Gladys George's rarely challenging film roles never brought her stardom equal to her Broadway success. In all, she appeared in thirty-seven films. Her performances in *The Maltese Falcon* (1941), *The Best Years of Our Lives* (1946), and *Detective Story* (1951) are noteworthy. When the ailing, reclusive actress died at home in Hollywood, suicide was suspected, but the cause was a massive cerebral hemorrhage. She left no survivors and less than $500 in the bank.

• The Billy Rose Collection at the New York Public Library for the Performing Arts at Lincoln Center contains a file of clippings and photographs. Kyle Crichton's "Life on the Strand," *Collier's*, 9 Mar. 1935, and other interviews during 1935–1936, the only sources for George's early life, contain autobiographical memories in which specifics of her childhood years vary. John Brunas's nine-page article in *Film Fan Monthly*, Mar. 1972, though it repeats her fictional birth year, is the most detailed summary of her early life and film career and includes a complete filmography. An obituary is in the *New York Times*, 9 Dec. 1954. In its obituary, the *Denver Post*, 9 Dec. 1954, took note of her four years, 1921–1925, as a "top stock company favorite" in Denver.

DANIEL KREMPEL

GEORGE, Grace (27 Dec. 1874–19 May 1961), actress, director, and translator/adapter, was born Grace Doughety in Brooklyn, New York, the daughter of George Doughtery and Ellen Kinney (occupations unknown). She changed her name to Grace George in 1892 for professional reasons. George attended a convent school in Fort Lee, New Jersey. In 1893 she enrolled at the American Academy of Dramatic Arts in New York. She made her professional debut in 1894 as a schoolgirl in *The New Boy*, a farce produced by Charles Frohman at the Standard Theatre in New York. She was subsequently given parts in *The Girl I Left Behind Me* and Thomas's *Charley's Aunt*. Theatrical manager William A. Brady cast George in her first important New York role as Juliette, whose marriage plans are derailed by a determined suitor, in a production of *The Turtle* at the Manhattan Theatre in 1898. In 1899 George married Brady, and their professional careers thereafter intertwined; they had one child.

By 1900 George had received star billing in Brady's company as Adelle in *The Countess Chiffon* and as a young queen who falls in love with a commoner in *Her Majesty, the Girl Queen of Nordenmark*. George honed her talents by appearing in a succession of sophisticated comedies, including Melihac and Halévy's *Frou-Frou* in 1902, in which she played Gilberte. She earned acclaim both critically and publically as Peg Woffington in *Pretty Peggy* in 1903, and the following year she played Louise in a revival of *The Two Orphans*. A year later in *The Marriage of William Ashe* she portrayed the flighty Lady Kitty, a character who invariably does the wrong thing at the wrong time. In a 1906 performance of *Clothes*, she enacted Olivia Sherwood, who lives beyond her means trying to impress others. George achieved particular success in 1907 as Cyprienne in Sardou's *Divorcons* at Wallack's Theatre. She made her London debut as Cyprienne the same year and then toured the play throughout the United States. In 1909 she starred as Marion Stanton, who regains the affections of her roving husband, in Buchanan's comedy *A Woman's Way*. Later that year she performed Lady Teazle in a revival of Sheridan's *The School for Scandal*.

In the 1911 inaugural production at Brady's new theater in New York, The Playhouse, George played Kitty Constable in Bonner's *Sauce for the Goose*. She revived Fitch's *The Truth* in 1914, playing Becky Warder, the uncontrollable liar. In 1915 George revived another American classic, Mitchell's *The New York Idea*, directing the production and acting the role of Cynthia Carslake. This was her first known work as a director. While not the norm at this time, it was not uncommon for women to produce, manage, or direct. Also in 1915, she played Barbara Undershaft in the American premiere of Shaw's *Major Barbara* at The Playhouse. While Shaw was at first reluctant to have the genteel actress assay the fiery role, he eventually applauded her work, and George became one of his most influential American supporters. In 1916 George performed Lady Cicely Waynflete in Shaw's *Captain Brassbound's Conversion*, also at The Playhouse.

In 1921 George directed and performed the title role in *Marie Antoinette*. She appreciated French drama, which she believed had moved beyond what she considered the overly detailed scenic effects of American theater. The French, she wrote, "have emerged from the purely temporal evidences of actuality on stage to an understanding of the movement of the drama. They are looking and listening into the heart of the play" (*Forum*, p. 574). George translated and adapted several French comedies, including *To Love* and *The Nest*, both of which played in 1922.

In a 1924 production of *The Merry Wives of Gotham* George played a rich society lady who does not realize that her poor friend is actually her long lost sister. In 1927 George adapted a play by Paul Geraldy into the racy comedy *She Had to Know*, in which she played a neglected wife who flirts with her husband's friends. George achieved success in 1929 with a production of Ervine's *The First Mrs. Fraser*, which she directed and in which she starred as a divorcée romanced by her former husband. Her skills as a director were probably most applauded for this work. In 1932 she costarred with her talented stepdaughter Alice Brady in a Playhouse production of *Mademoiselle*. In 1935 she created one of her last memorable roles as Mary Herries, a gentle spinster trapped by a gang of vicious robbers, in the first-rate melodrama *Kind Lady*. After her performance of Nell Carter in *Spring Again* in 1941, George did not act again on stage until her appearance in *The Velvet Glove* with Walter Hampden in 1949; she earned praise for her portrayal of Mother Hildebrand, a convent teacher who steers her bishop away from firing a worthy instructor. George made her final professional appearance in 1951 as Mrs. Culver in Maugham's *The Constant Wife*, with Katharine Cornell and Brian Aherne.

George played over fifty stage roles, but she made only one movie, *Johnny Come Lately* with James Cagney in 1943, probably because she was near the end of her career and she was known as a stage, not movie, actress whose life centered around New York, not California. She was petite, with light hair and blue eyes. Lacking great passion and emotional power, she combined daintiness, wit, vivacity, and sparkling vocal skills with a wistful quality that made her especially effective in roles that joined comedy and romantic sentiment. Alexander Woollcott, drama critic and an early radio commentator on the theatrical scene, praised her performing skills, calling her "the life of the party" in her *New York Times* obituary but he criticized her comedies as "futile piffle."

Although justly regarded as one of America's leading comediennes in the early twentieth century, George has probably not been given sufficient credit for her diverse skills. She achieved success as a director, translator, and adapter, and she was also instrumental in introducing and popularizing Shaw's plays in the United States. She furthered the careers of Douglas Fairbanks and Helen Hayes by recommending them for lead roles in some of her husband's productions. Some co-workers considered her difficult and temperamental; others regarded her as a demanding perfectionist. George refused to view theater as merely amusement, preferring to see it as restorative recreation. The theater, she wrote in her *Forum* article, "is the place where we can open the small door of our secret emotions and let in the light of suppressed feeling." George believed that the numerous forms of theater, from serious drama to musical extravaganza, exist "to heal some flagrant wounds of our inner lives, all of them aiming to lift the burdens from overwrought humanity." She died in New York.

• For additional insight into George's views of the theater, see her article "The Appeal of the Theatre," *Forum* 58 (Nov. 1917): 571–78. Lewis C. Strang, *Famous Actresses of the Day in America* (1902), provides information on George's early career. Daniel Blum, *Great Stars of the American Stage* (1952), provides a personal profile along with portraits and character photographs. Obituaries are in the *New York Times*, 20 May 1961, and *Variety*, 24 May 1961.

ROGER A. HALL

GEORGE, Henry (2 Sept. 1839–29 Oct. 1897), economist and reformer, was born in Philadelphia, Pennsylvania, the son of Richard Samuel Henry George, a book publisher, and Catherine Pratt Vallance. George was raised in an atmosphere of daily religious exercises and serious reading. His father was a vestryman in the Protestant Episcopal church who, after a career as a dry-goods merchant and customs-house clerk, published books for the church and its related tract societies.

George attended the Episcopal Academy, but was clearly unhappy and inattentive. He persuaded his father to employ a tutor, under whose attention George thrived. He regularly attended lectures at the Franklin Institute and continued to read avidly. In fact, he later had his own son, Henry George, Jr., educated at home and warned him away from colleges.

Between 1852 and 1858 George worked as a store clerk, as a foremast boy on a voyage to Australia and India, and as an apprentice typesetter in Philadelphia. Determined to seek his fortune on the Pacific Coast, he enrolled for a year as a steward of a navy lighthouse ship that sailed around Cape Horn for San Francisco in 1858. Through the intercession of a cousin in that city, George was able to leave the ship before the expiration of his term. He engaged in a futile effort to prospect for gold in British Columbia before returning "dead broke" to San Francisco to become a printer and writer for various newspapers. For four years he tried to resuscitate the *Evening Journal*, of which he had become a partner, only to lose everything in the project.

In 1861, at the lowest ebb of his fortunes, George married Annie Corsina Fox; they had four children. In 1865 George took to the streets to beg so that he might feed his family.

Although George did not see military service during the Civil War, his articles supported the Republican party. He also enrolled in a military expedition to help drive French forces out of Mexico but was prevented from sailing by the navy. His prominence began to rise together with his income, however, when he worked for the *San Francisco Times*, first as a printer, then as a news and editorials writer, and finally as managing editor. In an article published in the *Overland Monthly* in October 1868, titled "What the Railroad Will Bring Us," he first offered in print the view that economic growth brings with it poverty for the many and wealth for the fortunate few.

At the end of 1868 George visited New York on behalf of the *San Francisco Herald*, a newspaper that was trying to break the monopoly control that Western Union and the Associated Press exercised over telegraphic news services. While there, he experienced what he later described as his epiphany: exploring the streets of Manhattan noting its technological marvels, vast wealth, and grinding poverty. Ironically, during this trip, he also wrote for the *New York Tribune* the article that catapulted him to national fame, "The Chinese on the Pacific Coast." Justifying the hostility of white workers in California to the immigration of Chinese, he argued that people from China not only undermined wages but were also "utter heathens, treacherous, sensual, cowardly and cruel." Not only was the article widely reproduced for anti-Chinese agitation in the East, it assured George a hero's welcome and prominence in state politics when he returned to San Francisco.

During the next decade George linked his political fortunes with those of incumbent governor Henry H. Haight, who supported a fusion of Liberal Republicans and Democrats in opposition to the corruption of the Ulysses S. Grant administration, and developed the economic theory that was to make him world famous. Influenced by the critique of federal tax and tariff policies and of state property taxes developed by U.S. Revenue commissioner David A. Wells, George joined the American Free Trade League, used his editorial posts on various newspapers to support Democrats who shared his views on reforming taxes and ending subsidies to railroads, and ran unsuccessfully for the California legislature.

In the midst of this public activity, George published the pamphlet *Our Land and Land Policy, National and State* (1871), which outlined the basic idea to which he devoted the rest of his life: that society's "fundamental mistake is in treating land as private property." Human labor can create wealth, he argued, only when it is applied to natural resources, which he termed "land." Private ownership of land enables its possessors to charge rent from those who need access to land in order to produce income for themselves and society as a whole. That rent by rights belongs to the society whose labors generated it, and its collection by private individuals impoverishes those who produce it. Government should, therefore, commandeer the full value of unimproved land to meet community needs and abolish all other taxes, which injuriously burden both workers and investors of capital.

During the next eight years George devoted himself to elaborating the economic principles implicit in these ideas. The depression that racked the nation between 1873 and 1878 and the fierce strikes that followed railroad lines from Baltimore to San Francisco in July 1877 imbued his undertaking with a sense of urgency. Although his effort to secure the newly created chair in economics at the University of California was rebuffed, the Democratic governor of the state appointed him state inspector of gas meters, thus providing the income that enabled George to apply himself unreservedly to the writing of *Progress and Poverty: An Inquiry into the Causes of Industrial Depressions and of Increase of Want with Increase of Wealth* (1879).

George proclaimed that "the injustice of society, not the niggardliness of nature, is the cause of the want and misery which the current theory attributes to overpopulation." At the heart of his analysis he placed the proposition that rent is "the price of monopoly, arising from the reduction to individual ownership of natural elements which human exertion can neither produce nor increase." Following the English economist David Ricardo, he asserted that rent was "determined by the excess of [land's] produce over that which the same application can secure from the least productive land in use." As economic output increases, rent swells at the expense of wages and interest, which are also fixed by the output of labor and capital at their least productive applications. Even farmers lose control of their own land, because as land becomes more valuable, "it must gravitate from the hands of those who work for a living into the possession of the rich."

Not only do economic and population growth extend the margin of cultivation, he continued, they also encourage speculation in land, which forces the "margin of cultivation farther than required by the necessities of production." Periodically "land values are carried beyond the point at which . . . their accustomed returns would be left to labor and capital. Production, therefore, begins to stop." A downward spiral of earnings and output follows until such time as increased productivity and lowered earnings to labor and capital allow a renewed advance of rents, and another speculative spiral begins.

The only way the promise of economic progress can be realized by society, George concluded, is for society "to collect the ground-rent for the common benefit." This would eliminate the incentive to accumulate land, throwing it on the market for industrial and agricultural use, while also providing governments with the funds to create public transportation, public baths, gardens, playgrounds, and other projects to enrich urban life. Simultaneously it would stimulate private investors and workers to produce goods in abundance. Thus through market-driven mechanisms "the gospel of brotherhood—the Gospel of Christ" could be realized on earth.

Less than a month after the manuscript of *Progress and Poverty* had been mailed to an initially frosty reception at D. Appleton & Co., Rural Ireland erupted in rent boycotts and "monster meetings" demanding "the land for the people." The formation of the Irish National Land League, headed by Charles S. Parnell and Michael Davitt, elicited enthusiastic support from labor organizations and Irish societies in the United States. When George directed his pen toward the dramatic battle against landlords in Ireland, he was paid handsomely by editor Patrick Ford to go with his family to Ireland as correspondent for the *Irish World and American Industrial Liberator*. George arrived amid draconic repression of the antirent movement. Davitt, Parnell, and numerous others were in jail, the writ of habeas corpus had been suspended, and George himself was twice detained under the Suspicious Persons Act. George quickly made an ally of the charismatic Davitt. His reports electrified Irish sympathizers throughout the United States. They hammered home the theme that Ireland was *not* unique: "There is in Ireland nothing that can be called feudal landlordism." Its problem, like America's, was private ownership of the God-given soil.

On his return to New York, George was accorded a tumultuous welcome by the newly created Central Labor Union, and also a banquet attended by leading literary figures. Circulation of his books was subsidized by the elderly philanthropist Francis G. Shaw (and after 1893 also by the soap manufacturer Joseph Fels), and *Frank Leslie's Illustrated Newspaper* solicited from him a series of articles in reply to the appearance of William Graham Sumner's paean to economic individualism, "What the Social Classes Owe to Each Other."

He returned to the British Isles, this time presenting seventy-five speeches in thirty-five cities during 1884–1885. His sponsors were mainly Radical Liberals, who were then demanding taxation of great landed estates, votes for rural laboring men, and slum clearance financed by taxation of urban land values. Scotland was still astir over the bloody eviction of crofters from the Isle of Skye. George found himself and his ideas at the center of discussion in British Liberal politics, Irish and Irish-American popular movements, and elite free-trade circles in the United States.

Back in New York in 1886, he encountered a city embroiled in strikes, boycotts, and police repression. Enraged by the growing roll of prison sentences faced by members of trade unions and the Knights of Labor, and especially by the jailing of five of its own representatives, the Central Labor Union launched a campaign to unseat the city's Democratic administration and asked George to be its candidate for mayor. George welcomed the nomination and participated tirelessly in the "tailboard campaign." The official vote count awarded him 68,110 votes—considerably fewer than the 90,552 won by the victorious Abram S. Hewitt, but more than his other major rival, Theodore Roosevelt.

The constituencies that had made this campaign a high-water mark in the labor politics of the nineteenth century soon unraveled, but the disintegrative process revealed the diversity of George's admirers. The Anti-Poverty Society, organized in the editorial rooms of George's new newspaper, the *Standard*, early in 1887, was led by both Catholic and Protestant clergymen, who found in George's teachings a practical basis for their social gospel. The Reverend Edward McGlynn, most prominent among its orators, was defrocked and later excommunicated by the Catholic church for his activities but enjoyed immense popularity in Irish neighborhoods. Moreover, both the meetings of the society and the indoor rallies of the election campaign were especially noteworthy for the large participation of women.

The Socialist Labor party had provided much of the initiative for the mayoralty campaign, but it fell into sharp disagreement with George during his unsuccessful 1887 attempt to win election as New York's secretary of state under the banner of the United Labor party. Although many socialists for generations to come welcomed George's critique of existing society, their insistence that only collective ownership of the means of production could solve the workers' problems led to increasingly sharp disputes between them and George.

Prominent businessmen and lawyers who had supported George's 1886 effort formed the New York Tax Reform League after the election to argue that "real estate should bear the main burden of taxation." George carried this impulse a step farther after the decisive defeat of his statewide campaign, jettisoning his party and contending that President Grover Cleveland's 1887 message to Congress calling for tariff reform had reopened public debate on the whole question of tax policies and deserved his endorsement. George campaigned for Cleveland's reelection in both 1888 and 1892, while his followers formed the Single Tax League of the United States and inundated Congress with petitions suggesting their alternative to protective tariffs.

In December 1890, at the end of a new round of speaking tours of Britain, Australia, and New Zealand, George suffered a stroke, which left him, in Louis F. Post's words, "a victim to premature old age in his fifties." He turned his attention to writing a comprehensive *Science of Political Economy*, only to be distracted by the drafting of a rejoinder to Pope Leo XIII's encyclical "The Condition of Labor," by his campaigning on behalf of William Jennings Bryan, and by the sudden death of his daughter Jennie. In 1897, with the boroughs of New York about to be consolidated and tax policies a major topic of political discussion, he decided to run for mayor of the enlarged city but died of a stroke four days before the votes were cast.

By means of his vigorous oratorical style and his direct and simple writing, George had popularized a doctrine that combined trenchant criticism of inequality in modern society with celebration of the potential contribution of technological development and individual endeavor to the social welfare. His ideas had powerful, if divergent, meanings for urban workers, Irish rural laborers, political foes of Britain's landed gentry, Catholic and Protestant preachers of a social gospel, women residing in New York's slums, businessmen aspiring to lift taxes from their own enterprises, and literary enthusiasts of global free trade. Adherents of the Single Tax remedy for urban squalor were to appear frequently in the ranks of reformers during the Progressive Era and beyond.

• Henry George's papers are in the New York Public Library. A catalog of the collection and bibliography of works by and about George is provided by Rollin Alger Sawyer, *Henry George and the Single Tax* (1926). Other major works by George include *The Irish Land Question* (1881), *Social Problems* (1883), *Protection or Free Trade?* (1886), *The Condition of Labour: An Open Letter to Pope Leo XIII* (1891), and *A Perplexed Philosopher* (1892). His collected writings were published in ten volumes in 1900. An indispensable source for his career and his times is by his son and confidant, Henry George, Jr., *The Life of Henry George* (1900). Louis Post, *The Prophet of San Francisco: Personal Memories and Interpretations of Henry George* (1930), provides a valuable supplement. Among the many biographies of Henry George, the most useful are Edward J. Rose, *Henry George* (1968); Charles A. Barker, *Henry George* (1955); and Elwood P. Lawrence, *Henry George in the British Isles* (1957). Insightful discussions of his ideas and influence can also be found in Joseph Dorfman, *Economic Mind in American Civilization* (1949); Richard W. Lindholm and Sein Lin, eds., *Henry George and Sun Yat-sen: Application and Evolution of Their Land Use Doctrine* (1977); Peter D'Alroy Jones, *Henry George and British Socialism* (1991); Alexander Saxton, *The Indispensable Enemy: Labor and the Anti-Chinese Movement in California* (1971); and Ernest Teilhac, *Pioneers of American Economic Thought in the Nineteenth Century* (1936). A careful assessment of the extent and limits of his political influence is in Jack Tager, *The Intellectual as Urban Reformer: Brand Whitlock and the Progressive Movement* (1968). For George's relations with the labor movement, see Peter A. Speek, *The Single Tax and the Labor Movement* (1917); Henry J. Browne, *The Catholic Church and the Knights of Labor* (1949); and David Scobey, "Boycotting the Politics Factory: Labor Radicalism and the New York City Mayoral Election of 1886," *Radical History Review* 28–30 (1984): 280–325. An obituary is in the *New York Times*, 30 Oct. 1897.

DAVID MONTGOMERY

GEORGE, James Zachariah (20 Oct. 1826–14 Aug. 1897), lawyer and U.S. senator, was born in Monroe County, Georgia, the son of Joseph Warren George and Mary Chamblis, farmers. During George's early childhood, his father died, and his mother subsequently remarried. In 1834 his family moved to Mississippi, staying two years in Noxubee County before settling on a farm in Carroll County. George worked in the fields and attended the rural schools. At the age of eighteen he moved to Carrollton and studied law in the office of a circuit judge. During the war with Mexico in 1846, he served in a regiment of Mississippi volunteers under the command of Colonel Jefferson Davis.

After returning to Carrollton in 1847, he received his license to practice law. In the same year he married Elizabeth Brooks Young; they had eleven children, nine of whom survived infancy.

While establishing a reputation as an effective young lawyer, George also acquired farmland and became a prosperous cotton planter. Recommended as "a gentleman of character and a prominent member of the Democratic party" (letter from C. S. Tarpley to General Robert Armstrong, 10 July 1852), he was elected reporter of the state's high court in 1854 and was reelected in 1860. At the Mississippi convention in 1861, he served on the committee that drafted the ordinance of secession.

In the Civil War George first held the rank of captain in a Confederate infantry regiment. Captured by Union forces in 1862, he spent seven months in prison on Johnson's Island, Ohio, in Lake Erie. Following his release, he served briefly as brigadier general of the Mississippi militia before returning to battle as colonel of a Confederate cavalry regiment. Recaptured in the fall of 1863, he passed the remaining nineteen months of the war in the prison on Johnson's Island.

After returning to Carrollton, George resumed his law practice. In 1872 he published *Digest of the Reports*, a summary of all past decisions of the state's high court. The following year he moved to Jackson and established a successful law practice there. As chair of the state Democratic party in 1875, he directed its victorious efforts to overthrow Republican rule and to restore the supremacy of whites. Urging compliance with the Fifteenth Amendment, he opposed violence and intimidation of black voters. In a speech to the state Democratic convention in 1877, he declared, "We are now Americans, with no brand of inferiority upon us. Our statesmanship must embrace the whole country, seeking to advance the common interests." After receiving an appointment to the state supreme court in 1879, he presided for two years as chief justice.

George was elected to the U.S. Senate in 1880 and took his seat the following year, resigning from the Mississippi Supreme Court in February 1881. He was reelected to two more terms, serving until his death. Regular in attendance and skilled in the dialectics of law, he took part in all the constitutional debates on the limits of federal powers and served on a number of important committees, including Agriculture, Judiciary, and Labor and Education. Instrumental in securing appropriations to control floods along the Mississippi River, he also helped obtain federal funds for agricultural experiment stations in every state. Along with some Republicans, he fought unsuccessfully in the 1880s for federal aid to education, contending that the South, "wasted and desolated by war," lacked the resources to educate its large illiterate population. "I see in the South millions of unlettered children . . . of both races," he declared, "and of their parents an anxiety that they be educated" (*Congressional Record*, 48th Cong., 1st sess., p. 2515).

Independent of thought, George placed national interest before his party and endorsed the Pendleton Civil Service Act (1882). He also played a major role in shaping the Sherman Anti-Trust Act (1890) and was the only Democrat among its coauthors. Known as the father of the Department of Agriculture, he initiated the move to elevate it to cabinet status (1889). In 1891 he angered farm leaders and risked political defeat by denouncing the subtreasury plan for federal crop loans as impractical and unconstitutional. Many in the South thought it was "a fortunate thing" to have "such a man as Senator George to tackle the . . . [subtreasury] heresies and expose their dangers" (*Tupelo Journal*, 29 Jan. 1892).

A staunch defender of states' rights, in 1887 George successfully challenged a bill to authorize national inquests into violations of political rights on the grounds that it "would be a grave and serious usurpation by Congress of essential powers reserved to the States." At the Mississippi constitutional convention in 1890, believing that disqualifying what were considered the most ignorant elements of the voting population would benefit both races, he led the drafting of suffrage restrictions that provided a legal framework to maintain white rule. Later, in defending Mississippi's new constitution in the Senate, he argued that it differed little from those in the northern states and that none of its provisions conflicted with the Fifteenth Amendment or any other federal limitation on state power.

Illness prevented Senator George from taking his seat in the second session of the Fifty-fourth Congress (1896–1897). He died in Mississippi City, Mississippi, where he had gone to recuperate. He left an unfinished manuscript that his son-in-law William Hayne Leavell later edited and published as *The Political History of Slavery in the United States* (1915). A traditional southern view of American history, it argues that the sectional struggle for power in the Union, rather than the slavery issue, led to the Civil War and that northern efforts to promote racial equality during Reconstruction were not always to help blacks as much as to punish southern whites.

Self-reliant and positive in his convictions, George left an indelible imprint on the laws of Mississippi and the nation. His views on white political supremacy, in contrast to the race-baiters of his day and later, included an obligation to provide educational opportunities and equal protection under the law to all citizens. A Republican colleague, Senator Henry M. Teller of Colorado, declared, "He loved the South . . . but his patriotism was not bound by sectional lines, and he was devoted to the interests of . . . every section of our common country" (*Congressional Record*, 55th Cong., 2d sess., pp. 3662–63).

• A small collection of George's papers and printed copies of his speeches are in the Mississippi Department of Archives and History. He compiled vols. 30–39 of *Mississippi Reports, High Court of Errors and Appeals* (1857–1867). A full-length biography is Lucy Peck, "The Life and Times of James Z. George" (master's thesis, Mississippi State Univ., 1964). A biographical sketch is in Dunbar Rowland, *Courts, Judges, and Lawyers of Mississippi, 1798–1935* (1935). Frank Johnston, "The Public Services of Senator James Z. George," *Publications of the Mississippi Historical Society* 8 (1904): 201–26, and James W. Garner, "The Senatorial Career of J. Z. George," *Publications of the Mississippi Historical Society* 7 (1903): 245–62, are important sources. A recent assessment of his state leadership is in Thomas N. Boschert, "A Family Affair: Mississippi Politics, 1882–1932" (Ph.D. diss., Univ. of Mississippi, 1995). See also William C. Harris, *The Day of the Carpetbagger: Republican Reconstruction in Mississippi* (1979), and Willie D. Halsell, "The Bourbon Period in Mississippi Politics, 1875–1890," *Journal of Southern History* 11 (Nov. 1945): 519–37, on his role in state politics; and May Spencer Ringold, "Senator James Zachariah George and Federal Aid to Common Schools," *Journal of Mississippi History* 20 (Feb. 1958): 30–36, and "Senator James Zachariah George of Mississippi: Bourbon or Liberal?" *Journal of Mississippi History* 16 (July 1954): 164–82, on his senatorial career. An obituary is in the *New York Times*, 15 Aug. 1897.

THOMAS N. BOSCHERT

GEORGE, Samuel (1795–24 Sept. 1873), Onondaga chief and Iroquois Confederacy spokesman, was born into the Wolf clan on the Buffalo Creek Reservation in western New York State. This community, which encompassed much of the present-day city of Buffalo, was the cultural, political, and religious center of Indian life in the state in the years after the American Revolution. Although we know nothing about George's parents, we do know that he grew to manhood during approximately the same period as the spread of a major Iroquois religious revival led by Handsome Lake. A Seneca prophet, Handsome Lake claimed to have experienced three visions in 1799 and 1800, which led to his founding of a new religion that has influenced the Iroquois ever since. The prophet's message, the *Gaiwiio*, urged abstinence from alcohol, rejection of witchcraft, adoption of the nuclear family structure, use of agricultural technology such as the plow, and resistance to the alienation of Indians from their lands. George became a convert to Handsome Lake's preachings.

Despite the prophet's prohibition of Indian participation in the white man's wars, however, George, along with many other Iroquois, served on the American side during the War of 1812. Serving as a runner along the Buffalo-to-Albany corridor during the conflict, George displayed courage, endurance, and physical prowess, all of which helped make him a leader among his people. After the war, George received a pension from the U.S. government for his participation in the conflict.

George and his people faced major difficulties in the three decades after the War of 1812. At the expense of the Indians, the Ogden Land Company and other land speculators conspired with a series of corrupt federal Indian agents to profit from the development of land in western New York following the opening of the Erie Canal. As a result of these efforts, including bribery of some Indians, the Iroquois were dispossessed of their Buffalo Creek Reservation by a treaty signed in 1838. George and most Iroquois leaders opposed this treaty and sought federal compensation for this loss throughout the nineteenth century.

The Iroquois Confederacy's council fire that had burned at Buffalo Creek was rekindled at the Onondaga Reservation just south of Syracuse, New York, in 1847, when the majority of Onondaga from the Buffalo Creek Reservation moved back to their ancient capital, taking with them their sacred wampum. It was there in 1850 that George became a chief, taking the name Hononwirehdonh or Great Wolf, the hereditary keeper of the wampum, which was a position held by a member of the Wolf clan of the Onondaga Nation. His new responsibilities included striving to create consensus and pacify diverse elements within the Iroquois leadership, a role especially important in the 1850s because Indian unity was needed to fight off legislative efforts by New York State to erode the Onondaga land base.

During the Civil War, George was recognized by federal officials as well as by his own people as the spokesman of the Iroquois Confederacy. By 1863, he was given the honorary rank of brevet general and acknowledged as "Principal Chief of the Six Nations" by federal officials. He was also chosen by the grand council of the Iroquois Confederacy to serve as a delegate to protest certain abuses in the Civil War recruitment process. Because most Indians were poor, unscrupulous recruiters were able to entice underage Indians into military service with promises of cash payments. In November 1863 George met with President Abraham Lincoln but met with limited success, securing the release of only thirteen out of forty-three underage Indians in the Union army. The remaining thirty won the right to be discharged but only after they repaid whatever bounty they had received.

Following the war, George continued to serve as Iroquois Confederacy spokesman. He wrote to the governor of New York protesting illegal timber stripping on Indian lands, complaining of delays in annual state payments due to the Onondaga under various agreements, and urging the appointment of a qualified Indian agent. From 1869 to 1873, George, a traditional herbalist, was appointed by the federal government as "physician to the Onondaga." During these years, his gift for oratory and storytelling became well known, and he became a featured speaker at public events. Overall, George's speaking abilities, diplomatic and medical skills, and physical prowess gave him a position of particular influence at the council fires of the Iroquois Confederacy.

George died at the Onondaga Reservation and was buried according to traditional rites. Although he had been one of the major proponents of Indian traditionalism in the nineteenth century, his was a flexible conservatism. He faithfully attended community ceremonies, maintained the Iroquois language, kept herbalist traditions alive, advocated Indian treaty rights and claims, and rejected the alienation of Indians from their lands; nevertheless, he served the American cause in two wars, thus challenging the orthodoxy of Handsome Lake, permitted missions and schools to be operated at Onondaga, and had dealings with outsiders ranging from the president to the governor of New York. In part as a result of his pragmatic leadership, the Iroquois have survived as a distinct people.

• Letters and petitions from George can be found in the correspondence records of the Office of Indian Affairs, National Archives, Washington, D.C. Records of George's War of 1812 military service are in the New York State Archives, Albany. For George's service as a runner during the war, see Orlando Allen, "Personal Recollections of Captain Jones and Parrish," *Buffalo Historical Publications* 6 (1903): 544. For other references to George, see William M. Beauchamp, *Notebook: Sketches of Onondagas of Note*, in William M. Beauchamp Manuscripts, New York State Library, Manuscript Division, Albany, and Laurence M. Hauptman, "Samuel George (1795–1873): A Study of Onondaga Indian Conservatism," *New York History* 70 (Jan. 1989): 5–22.

LAURENCE M. HAUPTMAN

GERARD, James Watson (25 Aug. 1867–6 Sept. 1951), diplomat, politician, and philanthropist, was born in Geneseo, New York, the son of James Watson Gerard, a respected lawyer and author, and Jenny Jones Angel. He studied at Columbia University (A.B., 1890; A.M. in political science, 1891) and the New York Law School (LL.B., 1892). Admitted to the New York bar in 1892, he began a long association with Bowers & Sands, a law firm founded by his grandfather. In 1901 he married Mary "Molly" Daly, daughter of Marcus Daly, the noted Montana copper industrialist. They had no children.

Throughout his life, Gerard was close to the Democratic party and particularly to the New York organization. His early appointment as counsel to the sheriff of New York City and his election in 1907 as associate justice of the New York State Supreme Court (1908–1913) are evidence of his ties to Tammany Hall. Influenced by leading Democrats, President Woodrow Wilson in 1913 appointed Gerard, a substantial campaign contributor, to the post of ambassador to Spain but changed the appointment, sending him instead to Berlin. Gerard's short and difficult tenure as ambassador constituted the most important period of his public life.

In Berlin Gerard pursued his tasks with an unusually forthright attitude, not wholly appreciated by the Germans. Historians and contemporaries have offered varied appraisals of his performance. Even though Johann Heinrich Count von Bernstorff, the imperial German ambassador in Washington, in 1913 called Gerard Wilson's best diplomatic appointment, Wilson's eminent biographer Arthur S. Link, termed him "an incompetent representative," thus perhaps echoing what between 1914 and 1917 increasingly appears to have been the view of Wilson. It was thought that Gerard lacked diplomatic experience and harbored anti-German sentiments. His forthright reactions to the situation in Berlin were seen as less than helpful in the difficult negotiations with the Germans over submarine warfare and other unrewarding issues. The historian Charles Seymour, by contrast, found that

"Gerard was excelled by none in the dignity and capacity with which he maintained the interests and furthered the policy of his Government in the most trying diplomatic situation" (Seymour, vol. 1, p. 190). Gerard's lack of international experience before being appointed to one of the most important diplomatic posts may have prevented him from always finding the correct tone, but undeniably, while serving under extremely difficult conditions in Berlin, he stood up for the interests of the United States. Notwithstanding his family wealth, he seemed to care little for the pomp and circumstance at the imperial court and instead, quite consciously, presented himself in the role of the civilian and democratic citizen.

Wilson's conflict with the Mexican dictator General Victoriano Huerta and imperial Germany's continued refusal to tolerate the Monroe Doctrine and its implications for European designs on Latin America dominated Gerard's early diplomatic activities. While Wilson refused to recognize the Huerta government, the Germans decided to actively support Huerta and supply him with arms. It was Gerard's unrewarding mission to attempt to slow down Berlin's pro-Huerta policy. With the onset of hostilities in Europe in August 1914, other issues took center stage, and the ambassador faced the difficult task of representing the interests of the neutral United States in what, even prior to February 1917, might as well have been enemy territory. Imperial Germany's submarine campaign against British and neutral shipping created a series of crises, such as the sinking in May 1915 of the passenger liner *Lusitania* and the attack in March 1916 on the Channel steamer *Sussex*. Nothing indicates that a more experienced American diplomat could have been more successful in deterring the Germans from their fatal policy that eventually would bring the United States into the war on the side of Berlin's enemies.

Gerard's bluntness often surprised the Germans. When in 1916 a high German official suggested that Washington, in view of some 500,000 German reservists living in the United States, might find itself in trouble in case of war with Germany, Gerard is said to have replied that he could think of 500,000 lampposts to hang them on. He began to visit prisoner-of-war camps and to attempt to improve conditions in them. Having been involved in social work at home, Gerard quickly joined other humanitarian efforts, lending his support to the American Red Cross delegations active on both European fronts; joining Herbert Hoover's International Commission for the Relief of Belgium; and, with representatives of the Rockefeller Foundation, organizing the Commission for the Relief in Poland. One of the more pressing tasks of the U.S. embassy was much-needed assistance to a great number of Americans stranded in Germany at the outbreak of the war who wished nothing more than to return home safely.

Although Gerard cultivated influential German politicians, he could not, in the end, prevent the emperor from declaring unlimited submarine warfare nor from offering Mexico a military alliance against the United States. After Wilson had broken off diplomatic relations with Germany, Gerard, about to depart from Berlin, was pressured by the German Foreign Office to sign papers that would alter the texts of treaties between the United States and Prussia in 1785 and 1828 and thereby protect Germans and German property in the United States in case of war. Gerard refused the unusual German demand and after further official chicanery at the point of departure eventually returned to the United States, if not appreciated in some quarters, certainly a kind of national hero to the public. Wilson's dislike of him and the accusations of some American Irish that he had been an accessory to the misfortune of Sir Roger Casement, agent for the Irish in Germany, did not stop the vibrant lawyer-politician from further engagement in public life.

Following the war, Gerard voiced support for the newly created League of Nations and advocated American membership. He also returned to the law and became a partner in the New York firm of Laughlin, Gerard, Bowers & Halpin (later Laughlin, Gerard, Halpin & Graham), where he stayed until his retirement in 1944. Besides his legal practice he watched over his considerable mining and other properties in Montana. He also returned to Democratic politics. Already in 1914, though tied down in Berlin and unable to participate in the campaign, he had run for U.S. senator from New York and won over Franklin D. Roosevelt in the primaries, only to be defeated at the polls by the Republican James W. Wadsworth, Jr. In 1920 Gerard vied for the presidential nomination and harbored hopes for the vice presidency. He failed on both counts but vigorously campaigned for every Democratic presidential candidate from James M. Cox to Franklin D. Roosevelt and Harry S. Truman. His dedicated work on behalf of the Democratic party and his powerful positions on important party committees made him a significant political figure to contend with on both the New York and the national level.

Gerard also continued to participate in international affairs. In May 1937 he represented President Roosevelt at the coronation ceremonies of George VI in London, and he took an active part in the anti-Hitler campaign in the United States. He became an early and vociferous supporter of American intervention in Europe and later spoke up in favor of the lend-lease program. Shortly before his death at Southampton, Long Island, New York, he served as one of the officials appointed by President Truman to supervise the Point Four program of economic assistance to the underdeveloped countries.

• Gerard's diplomatic correspondence is in the Records of the Department of State in the National Archives in Washington and the Politisches Archiv of the German Foreign Office in Bonn. The James W. Gerard Papers are in the Maureen and Mike Mansfield Library at the University of Montana in Missoula. Numerous collections of the papers of contemporaries, such as the Diaries and Papers of Edward M. House at the Yale University Library, have letters of Gerard. His three autobiographical works are *My Four Years in Germany* (1917), *Face to Face with Kaiserism* (1918), and *My*

First Eighty-three Years in America (1951). Many of his messages from Berlin are included in James B. Scott, ed., *Diplomatic Correspondence between the United States and Germany* (1918), and in the volumes of *Papers Relating to the Foreign Relations of the United States* covering 1914 to 1917. His diplomatic activities during World War I are discussed by Arthur S. Link, *Wilson*, vols. 1–5 (1956–1965), and Charles Seymour, *The Intimate Papers of Colonel House*, vols. 1–2 (1926). An obituary and related reports are in the *New York Times*, 7 Sept., 9 Sept., and 12 Sept. 1951.

REINHARD R. DOERRIES

GERBER, Daniel Frank (6 May 1898–16 Mar. 1974), businessman, was born in Fremont, Michigan, the son of Daniel Frank Gerber, a businessman (who was known by his middle name) and Dora Pauline Pratt. Gerber attended public schools in Fremont and in 1916 graduated from St. John's Military Academy in Delafield, Wisconsin. He entered the army in 1917 and served in France during World War I. He earned the rank of sergeant and in 1918 was awarded the croix de guerre (cross of war) by the French government. Discharged in 1919, he entered the Babson Institute of Business Administration in Wellesley Hills, Massachusetts. In 1920 he joined his father in the family business, the Fremont Canning Company, which the elder Gerber helped to establish in 1901.

Gerber's first job at Fremont was as a salesman. He quickly rose in the hierarchy and by 1928 was first vice president. In 1923 he married Dorothy Marion Scott, with whom he had five children. In 1927 Dorothy Gerber suggested that Fremont Canning Company branch out into strained baby foods. At that time, pediatricians favored a liquid diet for a baby's first year, but baby food was sold in some areas in pharmacies, available on a doctor's orders. The Gerbers' pediatrician had recommended strained fruits and vegetables as part of the Gerber babies' diets, and Dorothy Gerber was preparing the food herself. This time-consuming task led her to ask her husband why baby food could not be manufactured at Fremont Canning.

Daniel Gerber gave his wife's question serious consideration and, through a series of experiments using the machines at the canning company, produced some strained foods. The foods were then tested by nutritionists, physicians, and consumers. Local mothers, including Dorothy Gerber, were enthusiastic about this timesaving convenience and seemed eager to have the product readily available. Praising Gerber's ingenuity, the family pediatrician said, "You don't begin to realize what you have here" (*Suerth*, p. 5).

Encouraged, Gerber touted the response to his father, who had supported the idea of expanding the business into the production of baby food when his son first suggested it. In 1928 five varieties—vegetable soup, carrots, peas, prunes, and spinach—were introduced to the public through advertisements in such magazines as *Good Housekeeping, Children*, and the *Journal of the American Medical Association*. In the ads the company offered six cans of prepared baby food for one dollar and the name of the purchaser's grocer. Company representatives then traveled the nation in vehicles with horns that played "Rock-a-Bye Baby" and distributed their new product into stores. In its first year of producing baby foods, Fremont Canning sold 590,000 cans, and the "Gerber baby," a rough sketch of a cherub-faced infant, became recognizable nationwide.

Gerber worked diligently in the 1930s to establish a worldwide market for his product. He helped acquire a baby food distributorship in Japan and soon thereafter in Canada. The company hired Dr. Lillian Storms, a dietician, who developed many new recipes, and by 1936 six additional varieties were added. Throughout this time of expansion, company representatives continued to call on doctors for additional medical input. By 1941 baby food sales at Fremont Canning exceeded adult food sales, leading the Gerbers to change the company name to Gerber Products Company. Two years later they ceased to produce anything but baby food. By 1943 company sales exceeded $10 million.

During World War II Gerber baby food displays in grocery stores proclaimed "No Points Required" (referring to ration stamps), thus increasing the product's appeal. Even some childless families bought Gerber baby food, modifying recipes and using the products themselves. In 1945 Gerber succeeded his father as president of the company. Sales continued to soar during the 1950s, and the company went public in 1956. Additional food products, such as meats, juices, and bakery products, were added to the Gerber line. Celebrity endorsements, such as those made by singer Kate Smith, added to Gerber's appeal.

In the 1960s the company continued to grow, offering clothing, care products, toys, and even life insurance. Gerber was president of the company until 1964, when he decided to step down. He remained active, however, as a director and as chairman of Gerber's executive committee.

During his tenure with Gerber Products Company, Gerber turned a small-town, family-run business into an international success. From 1959 to 1969 sales of Gerber products rose from $132 million to more than $222 million. Gerber strived to develop and manufacture products that would simplify and improve the lives of families with infants. He focused on research and constantly pushed for improvements in the preparation of the products that bore his name. He was a civic leader, serving as chairman of the Old State Bank of Fremont for many years. He also donated family funds to build the city's Gerber Memorial Hospital. He died in Fremont, Michigan.

• Little biographical information on Gerber is available. See the Biographical Vertical File at the Library of Michigan in Lansing. An article by Jeff Suerth, then editor of company publications for Gerber Products Company, is "Gerber's: A Company Founded through a Frustrating Experience" in *Chronicle* 15, no. 3 (1979), but it is largely concerned with the corporate background. An obituary is in the *New York Times*, 18 Mar. 1974.

LISABETH G. SVENDSGAARD

GERHARD, William Wood (23 July 1809–28 Apr. 1872), physician and pathologist, was born in Philadelphia, Pennsylvania, the son of William Gerhard, a hatter, and Sarah Wood. His parents were Moravians. After graduation from Dickinson College in Carlisle, Pennsylvania, in 1826, Gerhard received his medical degree from the University of Pennsylvania in 1830. His thesis on endermic medication, based on nearly 200 cases that he had observed as a resident pupil in the Philadelphia Almshouse, appeared in the *North American Medical and Surgical Journal* (9 [1830]: 392–402; 10 [1830]: 145–60). In 1831 he went to Paris, where he continued his studies, principally under Pierre-Charles-Alexandre Louis, in private classes and at the Hôpital de la Pitié.

Rejecting the philosophical generalizations and a priori reasoning by which physicians then generally guided their practice and understanding of diseases, Louis taught the importance of careful observation, recording, and analysis of cases. Gerhard eagerly absorbed the lesson. At the great Paris hospitals, notably the Hôpital des Enfans Malades (Hospital for Sick Children), Gerhard recorded hundreds of observations, correlating them with postmortem findings when that was possible. His first paper, written in collaboration with his friend and fellow student Caspar Wistar Pennock, detailed twenty-three specific cases of cholera that they had observed in Paris hospitals in 1832 (*American Journal of the Medical Sciences* 10 (1832): 319–90, 521–22); the work proved instructive for physicians treating the devastating cholera epidemic in American cities that year. The next year Gerhard published a paper on cerebral affections (tuberculous meningitis), in which he expressed in strong terms the principle that guided his research: "few questions can be resolved without a direct appeal to nature; and it is only from facts well established and carefully analyzed that uncontested truths can be deduced." When investigating a disease Gerhard even refused to read what others had written on the subject, lest his observation and analysis be influenced by those opinions. It was his "firm conviction that no other means are capable of establishing what is positive in medicine than the simple observation and comparison of facts" (*American Journal of the Medical Sciences* 13 [1833]: 314). In the Hospital for Sick Children he gathered material for other papers on smallpox, measles, and pneumonia, which he demonstrated was different in children and in adults.

These articles established Gerhard's reputation in Philadelphia, to which he returned in 1833. The next year he was elected a Fellow of the College of Physicians of Philadelphia. In the same year he was appointed a resident physician at the Pennsylvania Hospital, and in 1835 he was named one of the attending physicians of the Philadelphia Almshouse. Appreciating the opportunities the institution offered for pathological research, he persuaded the managers to change its name to Philadelphia Hospital. He lectured at the Philadelphia Medical Institute, a private school that Nathaniel Chapman had founded, and in 1838 was appointed assistant to Samuel Jackson, professor of the institutes of medicine (physiology) at the University of Pennsylvania.

In 1836–1837 Gerhard published the paper on which his fame chiefly rests, "On the Typhus Fever, Which Occurred at Philadelphia in the Spring and Summer of 1836; Illustrated by Clinical Observations at the Philadelphia Hospital; Showing the Distinction between This Form of Disease and . . . the Typhoid Fever with Alteration of the Follicles of the Small Intestine" (*American Journal of the Medical Sciences* 19 [1836]: 289–322; 20 [1837]: 289–322). Based on cases in the Philadelphia Hospital and his own observations in Paris and Edinburgh, the work not only established the difference between typhoid and typhus fever, which had often been confused even by European physicians, it also demonstrated clearly the usefulness of statistics to determine facts in medicine. Gerhard's paper represented a clear break with the theoretical system advanced by Benjamin Rush, his contemporaries, and their disciples, and it proved to be a cornerstone of the new age of scientific medicine that was opening. Professor James Tyson, who had taught general pathology and morbid anatomy in the University of Pennsylvania, compared Gerhard's work with Jenner's discovery of vaccination (Tyson, *Selected Addresses*, p. 194). The paper was promptly reprinted in Dublin, abstracted in London, and translated in Paris.

Gerhard was a tireless worker. The next six or seven years were probably the busiest and most productive of his life. In 1836 he published *On Diagnosis of Diseases of the Chest*, which demonstrated the importance of auscultation and percussion in diagnosis. In 1837, to accompany his lectures, he issued a *Clinical Guide, and Syllabus of a Course of Lectures, on Clinical Medicine and Pathology*. In 1838 he founded and became editor of the *Medical Examiner*, which he employed as a vehicle for publishing his lectures and promoting his ideas. In the same year he organized and was elected first president of the Pathological Society of Philadelphia, patterned on Louis's Société médicale d'Observation, to which he had belonged in Paris. He established a dispensary clinic in 1841; it was taken into the university two years later. In 1840–1841 he edited, "with American notes and additions," Alexander Tweedie's *System of Practical Medicine* (1840). In 1842 he edited, adding notes and lectures of his own, Robert J. Graves's *Clinical Lectures* (1838) and in the same year published his own work, *Diseases of the Chest*, which went through four editions. In all of his publications and clinical lectures, many printed in medical journals, he urged and demonstrated the importance of observation and analysis. He was elected an attending physician at the Pennsylvania Hospital in 1845.

Gerhard neither sought nor received a professorship in either the University of Pennsylvania or Jefferson Medical College but preferred clinical and pathological work. His students appreciated the practical content of his lectures and demonstrations and the clear and vigorous style in which they were delivered: in

1840 they presented a public testimonial to his "unequalled skill in illustrating the diseases of the thoracic organs." In his private practice Gerhard was a brilliant diagnostician, often called into consultation by other physicians. Among his patients were members of the aristocratic Fisher family of Philadelphia. One of them, the fastidious Sidney George Fisher, although inclined to think Gerhard "gross in manners & feelings," judged him "far ahead of any physician of his age in the country" and gratefully characterized the doctor's attendance in the final illness of a niece as calm, kind, prompt, and decisive (Fisher, *Diary*, pp. 38, 207–8, 567).

A minor stroke in 1843 left Gerhard's leg slightly paralyzed and may have been a reason he did little original research thereafter. In 1850 he married Ann Dobbyn, daughter of a retired officer of the British army; they had three children.

In 1863 Gerhard wrote a paper on spotted fever (cerebrospinal meningitis), which was epidemic in Philadelphia and its vicinity that year; he was especially interested in the disease because of its superficial resemblance to typhoid and typhus fever (College of Physicians of Philadelphia, *Summary of the Transactions* 4 [1874]: 41–49). In 1867 at the Pennsylvania Hospital he inaugurated its series of *Reports*, in which he published one of his last lectures, "On the Treatment of Continued Fevers" (1 [1868]: 244–68), which alluded to his early work on typhoid and typhus. He retired from the hospital staff in 1868 and in the same year visited Europe, where he met again his old master, Louis, now eighty-one. On his return to Philadelphia Gerhard fractured a foot; the complications were nearly fatal, and he never wholly recovered; he passed his final years as an invalid. Gerhard died in Philadelphia.

• The College of Physicians of Philadelphia has a small collection of Gerhard's papers, including letters from friends and fellow students in Paris as well as several volumes of Gerhard's student notes and notes of his lectures by his own students in Philadelphia. The principal source on Gerhard, by his friend and colleague Thomas Stewardson, is "Biographical Memoir of William W. Gerhard, M.D.," College of Physicians of Philadelphia, *Summary of the Transactions*, n.s., 4 (1874): 473–81. William S. Middleton, "William Wood Gerhard," *Annals of Medical History*, n.s., 7 (1935): 1–18, gives a fuller account of Gerhard's thought and practice. A few references to Gerhard are in Nicholas B. Wainwright, ed., *A Philadelphia Perspective: The Diary of Sidney George Fisher* (1967). Personal recollections of a younger contemporary are in James Tyson, *Selected Addresses* (1914), pp. 193–96. William Osler, "The Influence of Louis on American Medicine," in *An Alabama Student and Other Biographical Essays* (1908), pp. 189–210, gives an account of the young American "medical Argonauts" in Paris in the 1830s. Richard H. Shryock, *The Development of Modern Medicine* (1947), pp. 170–91, presents the principles of French medicine that Gerhard helped introduce to the United States.

WHITFIELD J. BELL, JR.

GERHART, Emanuel Vogel (13 June 1817–6 May 1904), theologian and educator, was born at Freeburg, Pennsylvania, the son of the Reverend Isaac Gerhart and Sarah Vogel. In 1833 he was enrolled in the Classical School of the German Reformed Church at York, Pennsylvania. In 1835, while Gerhart was a student, the school was moved to Mercersburg, Pennsylvania, and became Marshall College. Gerhart graduated from Marshall in 1838 and enrolled in the Theological Seminary of the Reformed Church, also located in Mercersburg. He completed his theological studies in 1841. During his student years in these institutions he was especially influenced by three of his professors: Frederick Augustus Rauch, Lewis Mayer, and John Williamson Nevin. Rauch introduced Gerhart to Hegelian philosophy and inspired his pedagogical and literary style. Mayer, who was grounded in the Lockean empiricism then popular in America, instructed Gerhart in theological doctrine. Nevin, one of the progenitors of the Mercersburg Theology, taught Gerhart to appreciate Christocentric theology, especially as it was being formulated in Germany.

Gerhart was ordained in August 1842 and became pastor at Grindstone Hill, Franklin County, Pennsylvania, for one year. In 1843 he was wed to Eliza A. Rickenbaugh; they had three children. Also in 1843 he took up pastoral duties in Gettysburg, Pennsylvania, until 1849 when he received an appointment to be a missionary in Cincinnati, Ohio. While serving in Cincinnati, Gerhart made two journeys into Illinois, Indiana, Ohio, Kentucky, and Wisconsin exploring the need for new German Reformed congregations.

In 1851 the Ohio Synod of the German Reformed Church established Heidelberg College and Theological Seminary at Tiffin, Ohio, to supply a properly educated ministry for its expanding church in the West. Gerhart was named the first president and professor of theology of these schools. In addition to his administrative duties he taught courses in dogmatics, homiletics, church history, apologetics, Old Testament, and New Testament in the seminary; and logic, ethics, psychology, natural philosophy, and German in the college. In 1854 Gerhart was named president of Franklin and Marshall College, Lancaster, Pennsylvania, a post he held until his resignation in 1866. During his presidency the college's facilities were improved, and its finances were stabilized. For the next two years he served as a member of the college's faculty as professor of mental and moral philosophy. In 1868 Gerhart was elected professor of didactic and practical theology at the Theological Seminary in Mercersburg. From 1868 until his death, Gerhart also served as the president of the seminary and was influential in moving the school to Lancaster, Pennsylvania, in 1871.

Following the death of his wife in 1864, Gerhart married Mary M. Hunter (d. 1866), and in 1875 Lucia Cobb, who survived him. He died in Lancaster, Pennsylvania.

A leading figure in his denomination, Gerhart served as president of the General Synod of the German Reformed Church in 1869 and was a member of many of the church's most important committees and agencies. He was an active member of the liturgical committee, which devised the much-disputed "Provisional Liturgy" of 1857, a formal ritual that incorporated elements of worship from the earliest Christian church and Protestant liturgies of the sixteenth century. He was also the premier systematic theologian and apologist for the Mercersburg Theology, an antirevivalistic, sacramental theology that had been promulgated in the German Reformed Church by John Williamson Nevin and Philip Schaff. Like them, Gerhart had grave misgivings about the subjectivism and sectarian spirit produced by American Protestant revivalism.

• A large number of Gerhart's unpublished diaries, manuscripts, notebooks, sermons, and letters are in the archives of the Evangelical and Reformed Church, Philip Schaff Library, Lancaster Theological Seminary, Lancaster, Penn. Gerhart was the author of numerous articles and book reviews in *The Mercersburg Review* and the *Reformed Church Messenger* and its successors. His most important books were *An Introduction to the Study of Philosophy with an Outline Treatise on Logic* (1857) and his two-volume systematic theology, *Institutes of the Christian Religion* (1891, 1894). See also Charles Yrigoyen, Jr., "Emanuel V. Gerhart: Churchman, Theologian and First President of Franklin and Marshall College," *Journal of the Lancaster County [Penn.] Historical Society* 60 (1974): 1–28, and "Emanuel V. Gerhart and the Mercersburg Theology," *Journal of Presbyterian History* 57 (1979): 485–500.

CHARLES YRIGOYEN, JR.

GERICKE, Wilhelm (18 Apr. 1845–27 Oct. 1925), musician and conductor, was born in Graz, Styria, Austria, the son of Freidrich Gericke, a merchant and farmer, and Katharina Spitzy, neither of whom were musical. His earliest and simplistic musical schooling was provided by the master of the village school in Schwanberg. He was chiefly self-taught, however, showed early promise, and by the age of ten was playing the organ in the local church. He was sent to Graz to train to be a schoolmaster. He was generally unhappy there, did not pass his second year, and returned home to Schwanberg. His dream was to be a conductor, and he continued to teach himself the piano, violin, cello, and flute. After a year at home he returned to school at Graz and was offered a chair in the violin section of the local theater orchestra. In 1862 he entered the conservatory of the Gesellschaft der Musikfreunde in Vienna and began his studies with Dessoff. Two years later, even before graduating, he began to conduct operas at Laibach. In 1868 he was appointed first Kapellmeister of the Stadt Theater in Linz on the Danube, and in 1874 he was engaged by the Court Opera in Vienna upon the recommendation of his teacher, Dessoff. The following year Hans Richter joined the Royal Court Opera, and a lifetime friendship between Gericke and Richter began to blossom. It was there that he met Wagner and conducted the first Vienna performance of *Tannhäuser*.

In 1880 Gericke followed Brahms as director of the Singverein of the Gesellschaft der Musikfreunde in Vienna and began to gain experience as a symphonic conductor. It was there that he became acquainted with Brahms and conducted the music of Brahms, Bruckner, and Liszt. As a consequence of both his personal relationships and his conducting positions, Gericke became immersed in, and a major interpreter of, the fruit of late Romantic orchestral music.

The Boston Symphony Orchestra, founded by Henry Lee Higginson, presented its first concert on 22 October 1881 under the direction of Georg Henschel. During the fall of 1883 Higginson was in Europe in part to engage a new conductor for the orchestra. While in Vienna he attended a concert conducted by Gericke and afterward asked Julius Epstein to arrange a meeting with the young conductor. Higginson offered Gericke both the baton of the Boston Symphony and total control over its musical activities, and he accepted.

Gericke's first Boston Symphony concert occurred on 18 October 1884. His tenure with the symphony extended over two terms; from 1884 to 1889, and from 1898 to 1906. Higginson's charge to him was to build and develop an orchestra equal to the best in Europe. Gericke toiled tirelessly to raise the standards of the orchestra, sometimes against a backdrop of local criticism. His concerts were considered by some Bostonians to be rather serious and severe. He demanded extra time for rehearsals, began importing musicians from Europe, and terminated those members who did not meet his rising standards. The repertoire became more serious, and he eliminated the lighter music that Henschel had consistently programmed. During those first years, however, it became clear to all that the orchestra was steadily improving, and Gericke enjoyed increasing respect and popularity in Boston. The symphony began to garner a favorable national reputation by both the public and the press after well-received concerts at Steinway Hall in New York in 1887.

In 1889 Gericke was suffering with a throat disease and decided to return to Vienna. In 1890 he again assumed the leadership of the Gesellschaft concerts. A romance ensued, and in 1892 he married Paula Flamm, the daughter of a court physician and a close friend of Brahms. The couple had one daughter. While in Vienna, Gericke never accepted a full-time position; and when Higginson asked him to return to Boston for the 1898 season, he accepted.

Arthur Nikisch and Emil Paur had sustained the quality and reputation of the Boston Symphony during Gericke's sojourn to Europe. Gericke, upon his return, continued to inflate the ranks of the orchestra with musicians from Europe and once again was a severe taskmaster. He rankled some of the membership of the orchestra and again was occasionally criticized for his heavy and conservative programming. But he gained a reputation as a master interpreter of the classical and Romantic repertoire. He consistently performed the works of his friend Brahms and introduced Boston audiences to Mahler and Bruckner. He was largely responsible for instituting the orchestra's pension fund and provided substantial input to the building of Boston's famed Symphony Hall, which opened in October 1900.

Gericke and the symphony management could not come to favorable terms regarding a new contract, and in February 1906 his resignation was announced. His departure from Boston was a warm one; he was showered with gifts and money after the final concert of the season. The Gerickes returned to Europe and settled in Vienna. Wilhelm's early retirement years were full ones with travel, social activities, and an agreeable family life. The First World War, however, found Gericke torn between his native and adopted countries, but his sympathies lay with Germany. Following the war his American friends came to his aid with gifts of food, money, and a benefit concert in Boston, all of which were of immeasurable help to the Gerickes as they struggled through the horrors of the postwar German and Austrian depression. Gericke suffered an attack of angina in 1924 but recovered to celebrate his eightieth birthday. He died in Vienna.

Wilhelm Gericke was also an active composer throughout his life. His compositions include orchestral, vocal, and piano works, but they have generally been forgotten. His greatest achievement, and the one for which he is remembered, was the development of the Boston Symphony Orchestra into one of the most respected orchestras in the world. As was often said in Boston, "Gericke made the Orchestra."

• Most of Gericke's personal papers have been destroyed, but a few of them may be found in the Brown collection at the Boston Public Library and in the archives of the Boston Symphony Orchestra. The best biographical sketch is John N. Burk's "Wilhelm Gericke: A Centennial Retrospect," *Musical Quarterly* 31, no. 2 (Apr. 1945): 163–87. Two works that detail Gericke's association with the Boston Symphony Orchestra are Mark A. deWolfe Howe, *The Boston Symphony Orchestra* (1914), which gives a good perspective of Gericke's tenure from a contemporary, and Bliss Perry, *Life and Letters of Henry Lee Higginson* (1921), which tells of the relationship between Gericke and Higginson. An obituary is in the *New York Times*, 30 Oct. 1925.

R. NICHOLAS TOBIN

GERMER, Adolph (15 Jan 1881–27 May 1966), trade union administrator and leader, was born in Walan, Germany, into a socialist coal mining family (his parents' names are unknown). Germer immigrated with his parents in 1888 to a mining region of southern Illinois populated largely by ethnic Germans, where he began to work in the mines at age eleven. His childhood experiences were shaped by the depression of the 1890s, the early development of the United Mine Workers Union (UMW), which he joined at age thirteen, and a series of strikes in which he and his family took part. A strike at Virden, Illinois, in 1898, in which coal company men killed seven strikers, influenced the seventeen-year-old Germer to commit himself to both industrial unionism, which is the organization of all workers in an industry into a single union as against the American Federation of Labor (AFL) principle of organization by craft, and socialism, which was a growing force among immigrant German workers in the Midwest.

A dedicated organizer, Germer became a full-time UMW activist, prominent Socialist party member, and leading spokesman for socialism inside the UMW before World War I. Rising to the position of vice president of the Illinois District of the UMW, he was ousted from leadership and expelled in 1916 by the fiercely anti-Socialist business union leadership of the UMW.

Germer then became a full-time worker and national leader of the Socialist party, which had reached the peak of its influence four years earlier when Eugene V. Debs received nearly a million votes for president. Germer was also an advocate of the party's opposition to World War I as an imperialist war aimed at conquering foreign markets rather than making the world safe for democracy, a position that invited government repression. As a signer of the Socialist party's antiwar declaration, Germer was convicted along with others and sentenced to twenty years in prison in 1919 for violation of the wartime Espionage Act. His conviction was subsequently overturned by the Supreme Court in 1921, as were the convictions of many but not all opponents of U.S. entry into the war then and subsequently.

As a leader of the Socialist party's right wing, which had engaged in struggles against the Industrial Workers of the World (IWW) and other radicals before the war, Germer opposed the new Soviet Republic and supported the campaign to expel the left socialists who eventually formed the Communist party after 1919. Continuing to work for the Socialist party as an organizer and administrator in the early 1920s, Germer also went back to the union movement, first as an organizer for the Oil Field, Gas Well, and Refinery Workers, later as a leader of the Reorganized Mine Workers of America, a socialist-supported dual union at the end of the decade. Dual unions, or unions competing with established unions like the UMW, were generally frowned on as dividing the labor movement, even if such unions often came into existence when established unions either could not or would not organize workers.

Although he remained a member of the Socialist party until 1934, Germer became increasingly critical of Marxist theory and the leading role of intellectuals in the party and party building. By the 1930s he had come to believe that both were hindering the development of the labor movement and the empowerment of the working class.

In 1934 Germer resigned from the Socialist party in protest over what he saw as the growing influence of left intellectuals within it, and he joined his old UMW business unionist enemy, John L. Lewis, in the development of the Congress of Industrial Organizations (CIO), becoming its first paid staff organizer in 1935. A leading CIO national staff member and trouble-shooter in the late 1930s, Germer used his considerable administrative talents and background in labor movement politics to contain factional differences, reign in radical rank-and-file groups, and broker deals between a wide variety of trade union leadership groups, ranging from Communist party activists to conservative business unionists. In that capacity, he represented the CIO national leadership in campaigns to organize industrial unions among the rubber workers, oil workers, and auto workers, served as the Michigan director of the CIO from 1937 to 1939, and later served as CIO local director in New York City and regional director in the Rocky Mountain and Pacific states in the 1940s and 1950s.

As a key CIO leadership representative to individual unions and regional, state, and local councils in the New Deal years, Germer sought to shape trade union leadership that would follow a centralized command structure and a national CIO leadership with closer ties to the Democratic party, rather than link the labor movement with a third political party, which had been his aim as a socialist. This strategy made him the natural ally of conservative business unionists who feared that the substantial number of Communist activists, who had gained leading positions in CIO unions, were working from within the labor federation to eventually create some Communist-led labor party. In the aftermath of the German-Soviet Non-Aggression Pact of 1939, Germer first attempted to purge Communist and left leadership from the CIO-affiliated International Woodworkers Association in the Pacific Northwest and western Canada from 1940 to 1944.

The Cold War and the passage of the Taft-Hartley Act of 1947, which barred Communists from holding office in trade unions, shattered the popular front alliances inside the CIO, and Germer's role in fighting Communist and left influence in labor expanded. As Pacific States regional director and representative of the CIO national board and CIO president Philip Murray, he played a major role in purging Communists from state and local industrial union councils, which, like the labor assemblies in late nineteenth-century America, had been bastions of both radicalism and worker involvement in larger political issues. For Germer, the influence of Communists, who had won leading positions and in some cases gained majorities in major councils, represented the continuation of the ideological and political unionism that he had rejected when he left the Socialist party.

Germer was also appointed in 1945 as CIO representative to the left-led World Federation of Trade Unions (WFTU) by Murray. There he worked with the U.S. government to support Truman administration foreign policy positions on both European and colonial questions, and he became embroiled in a series of conflicts with Communist and left trade unionists over these positions. Leaving the post in 1947, he lobbied with Murray for the CIO's withdrawal from the

WFTU. In 1948, particularly, Germer acted as CIO representative in enforcing national CIO directives on state and local councils in support of the Marshall Plan and in opposition to the Progressive party presidential campaign of Henry A. Wallace, ousting left-led pro-Wallace and anti-Marshall Plan councils. Germer championed the CIO's withdrawal from the WFTU in 1949 and its formal expulsion of eleven Communist-led unions in 1949–1950.

By the time of his retirement in 1955, Germer, like many others of his generation, had become very critical of the consequences of the general swing to the right and the lack of militancy and vision that had come to characterize the American labor movement. The merger in 1955 of the AFL with the CIO had created what was on paper the strongest labor federation in all of U.S. history—in effect the culmination of everything for which Germer had worked for decades. However, the lack of interest of the AFL-CIO leadership in organizing the unorganized southern and western workers in the Taft-Hartley "right to work" states and the unskilled, minority, and female workers who constituted a large majority of American workers represented an abandonment of Germer's vision of a strong independent labor movement. The ascent of conservative AFL chief George Meany over the AFL-CIO and its stagnation in membership were unanticipated consequences of Germer's successful fight against social unionism.

Unfortunately, the labor machines that Germer helped to shape made it very difficult for the purged labor radicals and grassroots militants to restore the kind of trade unionism that he had represented in his youth and that he, in speeches in the 1950s and 1960s, reminisced about. Surrounded by photographs of such radical and socialist leaders as Eugene Debs, Clarence Darrow, and Mother Jones, Germer died in Rockford, Illinois, as a new wave of mass political protest in the United States, centered on opposition to the Vietnam War and support for civil rights, was gaining strength. Adolph Germer was married to Vivian Marks. The couple had no children.

A lifelong participant in the struggles of the U.S. labor movement, Adolph Germer began as a class-conscious socialist and retired as a trade union functionary. In essence, he reflected the unresolved conflict between socialist revolutionary ideology and decentralized worker control of unions, on the one hand, and the construction of centralized bureaucratic unions that could endure in a world of large corporations, on the other. Ironically, the labor movement that he had fought to free from intellectuals and radicals so that it could grow atrophied when intellectuals and radicals were purged in the postwar period. The anti-Communist consensus that Germer championed in the labor movement created a postwar political climate that weakened all forms of trade union organization except conservative business unionism whose interest was in preserving and profiting from the status quo. In that sense, the postwar purges that were Germer's greatest victories defeated the possibility of a large inclusive industrial labor movement that he had championed.

• The Adolph Germer Papers, which include Germer's diary, are at the State Historical Society of Wisconsin, Madison. The most important secondary source remains Lorin Lee Cary, "Adolph Germer, from Labor Agitator to Labor Professional" (Ph.D. diss., Univ. of Wisconsin, Madison, 1968). See also Cary, "Institutionalized Conservatism in the Early CIO: Adolph Germer, a Case Study," *Labor History* (Fall 1972): 475–504, for Germer's activities in the late 1930s; Melvyn Dubofsky and Warren Van Tine, *John L. Lewis: A Biography* (1977), for references to Germer's involvement with the UMW and the early CIO; and John H. M. Laslett, *Labor and the Left, a Study of Socialism and Radical Influences in the American Labor Movement, 1881–1924* (1970), for background to Socialist party policy in the AFL. An obituary is in the *New York Times*, 28 May 1966.

NORMAN D. MARKOWITZ

GERNSBACK, Hugo (16 Aug. 1884–19 Aug. 1967), publisher and inventor, was born Hugo Gernsbacher in Luxembourg City, Luxembourg, the son of Moritz Gernsbacher, a vintner, and Berta Dürlacher. Gernsback was precociously interested in electricity, and his parents enrolled him in the École Industrielle in Luxembourg; a possibly apocryphal story states that by the age of thirteen he was earning money as an electrical contractor and had received special dispensation from Pope Leo XIII to install electric bells in the Carmelite convent of Luxembourg City. He later studied languages in a Belgian boarding school before spending three years at the Technikum in Bingen, Germany, inventing a dry-cell battery that was the most powerful in the world but too costly to market.

In 1904 Gernsback emigrated to America and began a succession of jobs involving the creation of companies and the manufacture and sale of batteries. In 1905 he established the Electro Importing Company, a mail-order business selling the Telimco Wireless Radio, which he had developed. This device, the first home radio, proved enormously successful; by 1910 Gernsback's company employed sixty workers. The U.S. government banned amateur transmission during World War I, but Gernsback marketed his radios as kits for electrical experimentation. In 1925 he founded the New York radio station WRNY, and in 1928 he pioneered television broadcasting; some 2,000 scanners in the New York area received his images.

In 1908 Gernsback established *Modern Electrics*, a radio catalog that rapidly became a monthly magazine; one of its editorials was instrumental in establishing the Wireless Act of 1912. In April 1911 *Modern Electrics* began serializing Gernsback's *Ralph 124C 41+*, written to exemplify his contention that fiction could serve to teach science. Set in A.D. 2660, the novel is a melodrama in which Ralph 124C 41+, one of ten superminds allowed to add the + to his name, falls in love with the Swiss girl Alice 212B423, rescuing her from the destructive forces of nature, from the lustful clutches of the Martian Llysanorh', and ultimately from death itself. Thoroughly deficient as fiction, the story nevertheless predicts radar, microfilm and microfiche, tape recorders, television, wireless transmission of power, plant hormones, and weather control. Though he claimed to have written it merely to fill some blank pages in *Modern Electrics*, Gernsback took *Ralph 124C 41+* seriously, revising it several times. He followed it with a series of humorous short stories narrated by "I. M. Alier" that featured Baron Munchausen exploring the moon and visiting Mars.

Gernsback claimed to have been exposed to the ideas of science fiction at the age of nine, when he read a German translation of the work of noted astronomer Percival Lowell, and he retained a lifelong interest in extrapolative fiction. His technical periodicals routinely published science fiction, and on 5 March 1926 his Experimenter Publishing Company published the April issue of *Amazing Stories*, the first English-language magazine devoted entirely to science fiction, a term Gernsback adopted after he failed to popularize *scientifiction*. The masthead of *Amazing Stories* proclaimed "Extravagant Fiction Today—Cold Fact Tomorrow," and the magazine's first editorial stated that "scientifiction" should be "a charming romance intermingled with scientific fact and prophetic vision." Gernsback created a sense of community among his scientifiction fans, but he paid his contributors poorly, when he paid them at all, and he succeeded in alienating many of the more popular writers of his day.

On 20 February 1929 Gernsback lost control of his magazines when three parties filed bankruptcy proceedings against the Experimenter Publishing Company, alleging that it had assets of about $150,000 and more than $600,000 in debts. The circumstances surrounding this suit have been extensively debated, one faction claiming that the health faddist and rival publisher Bernarr Macfadden determined to acquire *Amazing Stories* for his own publishing chain and, after failing to buy the magazine, created three proxies to force Gernsback into involuntary bankruptcy; in 1931 Macfadden was indeed one of the publishers of *Amazing Stories*. A second faction states that the creditors were genuine and claims that Gernsback and his older brother Sidney mismanaged their company, diverting business monies to personal use and paying themselves exorbitant salaries (more than $50,000 for Hugo and $39,000 for Sidney) while operating the radio and television stations at a considerable loss ($50,000 in 1928). A third faction also sees no evidence of a Macfadden conspiracy, has Gernsback aware that his companies were in financial trouble, and claims that Gernsback deliberately abandoned his liabilities after first looting them. This faction observes that immediately before the bankruptcy Gernsback abruptly paid his regular writers, stole a copy of the Experimenter Publishing Company's mailing lists, and within three months of the bankruptcy had established the Stellar Publishing Corporation, using the stolen mailing lists to promote the company's four new magazines.

These four magazines—*Air Wonder Stories, Science Wonder Stories, Science Wonder Quarterly,* and *Scientif-*

ic Detective Monthly—were also dominated by Gernsback's belief that fiction could instruct readers in science; Gernsback's first editorial for *Air Wonder Stories* proclaimed that its contents would be "strictly along scientific-mechanical-technical lines." None of these magazines lasted long, and in May 1930 *Air Wonder Stories* and *Science Wonder Stories* were merged to form *Wonder Stories*, which Gernsback sold to Standard Publications in 1936; unofficially he thereupon retired as a science fiction editor. He continued to publish, however, having some success with magazines such as *Radio-Electronics*, *Radio Craft*, *Popular Electronics*, and *Sexology*; in 1940 he published one of the first science fiction comic books, *Superworld Comics*; it lasted three issues. In 1953 he made a last attempt at publishing a science fiction magazine with *Science-Fiction Plus*; it survived but seven issues. Gernsback continued his proselytizing through a self-published pamphlet called *Forecast* that he issued each Christmas; the 1963 *Forecast* predicted that by 1972 African Americans could have white children if they would but let "chemi-geneticists" alter their enzymes. Other predictions included telescoping ramps, collision-proof cars, thermal furniture, and multiscreen televisions.

In 1950 the Veteran Wireless Operators honored Gernsback with the Marconi Memorial Wireless Pioneer Medal. In 1953 the governments of Luxembourg and Belgium awarded him the Gold Medal of Luxembourg and the Silver Jubilee Trophy of the Belgian Society Helios. Finally, in 1953 science fiction fans named their annual literary achievement awards Hugos in his honor; Gernsback himself received an honorary Hugo in 1960.

Gernsback was married three times. In 1906 he married Rose Harvey, with whom he had two children. Following a divorce, he married Dorothy Kantrowitz in 1921, with whom he had three children. Finally, in 1951 he married Mary Hancher, a technical researcher and writer. He died in New York City, leaving his body to the Cornell University Medical School.

Gernsback was an intelligent and gifted inventor, a shrewd but flawed businessman whose successes are in widely disparate areas and whose most significant creations achieved greatness only when utilized by others. In the fields of radio electronics and popular science, his reputation is secure. His inventions were instrumental in the creation and establishment of radio, television, and radar, and he appeared at a time when America was ready for novelty and needed better communications; his gadgets and publications provided both, were marketed in an appealing manner, and have proved enduring. *Modern Electrics* (retitled *Electrical Experimenter* and, later, *Science and Invention*) merged with *Popular Mechanics* in 1931. At his death he held at least thirty-seven patents, and his inventions and gadgets numbered in the hundreds.

Opinions are divided on Gernsback's role in the history of science fiction. One faction hails Gernsback as the "father of modern science fiction" and claims that without him, American science fiction would not have come into existence. Others claim that Gernsback's emphases on technological accuracy and didacticism impeded rather than enhanced the development of science fiction: science fiction existed before Gernsback, and had Gernsback not marginalized the literature in his magazines, science fiction might have been accorded greater critical acceptance. Both factions nevertheless agree that *Amazing Stories* is the cornerstone of what has become a multibillion-dollar industry and that, had Gernsback not recognized the marketability of the new literature, this would not have occurred.

• The literature on Gernsback is voluminous and unintegrated, and much of it has been published in largely inaccessible fan magazines. Histories of the technologies of radio and television thus accord him mention but do not discuss his science-fiction magazines except in passing; conversely, histories of science fiction do not discuss Gernsback's technical inventions and innovations.

Readily accessible biographical articles published while Gernsback was alive include those in *Time*, 3 Jan. 1944 and 6 Mar. 1964, and *Newsweek*, 3 Jan. 1944. Paul O'Neil's "Barnum of the Space Age," *Life*, 26 July 1963, is lengthy and informative, but its data do not always agree with those in other publications.

Gernsback's patents are discussed by David W. Kraeuter in *The U.S. Patents of Alexanderson, Carson, Colpitts, Davis, Gernsback, Hogan, Loomis, Pupin, Rider, Stone, and Stubblefield* (1991); Kraeuter lists 37 patents, but sources as *Time*, 3 Jan. 1944, state 80. The lower figure appears valid.

Science fiction historian Sam Moskowitz is Gernsback's most tireless champion and has written about him in *Explorers of the Infinite* (1963), *The Immortal Storm: A History of Science Fiction Fandom* (1954; repr. 1974), and in numerous articles. Moskowitz's views are repeated in Lester del Rey, *The World of Science Fiction 1926–1976: The History of a Subculture* (1979), David Kyle, *A Pictorial History of Science Fiction* (1986), Mark Siegel, *Hugo Gernsback, Father of Modern Science Fiction* (1988), and, to some extent, Mike Ashley, *The History of the Science Fiction Magazine*, vol. 1, *1926–1935* (1974).

Critical of Gernsback is James Blish, *More Issues at Hand* (1970). Less personal criticism is put forth by Tom Perry, whose "An Amazing Story: Experiment in Bankruptcy," *Amazing Science Fiction Stories*, May 1978, pp. 101–21, refutes Moskowitz line by line. Brian Aldiss and David Wingrove, *Trillion Year Spree* (1986), argue persuasively that Gernsback "was one of the worst disasters ever to hit the science fiction field," as do a number of English critics. Gary Westfahl, "Evolution of Modern Science Fiction: The Textual History of Hugo Gernsback's Ralph 124C 41+," *Science Fiction Studies*, Mar. 1996, pp. 37–82, definitively examines Gernsback's lifelong revisions to his novel. An obituary is in the *New York Times*, 20 Aug. 1967.

RICHARD BLEILER

GERONIMO (c. 1823–17 Feb. 1909), Bedonkohe Apache war leader, also known by his Apache name, Goyahkla (One Who Yawns), was born on the upper Gila River in what is now either Arizona or New Mexico. He was the son of Tàklishim (The Gray One) and Juana, a full-blooded Apache remembered by her Spanish name; his grandfather was the noted chief Mahko. His father died when Geronimo was young, and the boy and his mother went to Sonora, where they joined the Nednhi (or southern Chiricahua Apache) band led by Juh, a chief with whom Geronimo became closely associated. Geronimo married Gee-esh-kizn, the first of his nine wives. On 5 March 1851 a force of Sonoran irregulars led by Colonel José María Carrasco attacked supposed raiders near Janos, Chihuahua, and killed a number of Apaches, among them Geronimo's mother, his wife, and their three children. This confirmed in Geronimo a lifelong hatred of Mexicans, and it was during his persistent raids into Mexico that he received the name by which he is now remembered.

Geronimo early followed the Chihenne leader Mangas Coloradas, but later he operated more frequently with Juh's band. About 1855 Geronimo joined with Juh in winning a "great victory" over the Mexicans near Namiquipa, Chihuahua. Geronimo's success invested him with unique "power" among his people as a shaman and a war leader. He never became a band chief, however, and throughout his career he deferred to the recognized leaders. While the raids into Mexico continued, after the United States secured New Mexico and California by the treaty of Guadalupe Hidalgo in 1848, the Apache world was increasingly shaped by the advance of the white American frontier. Geronimo was involved in the general warfare that broke out between the United States and the Apaches in 1861, reportedly participating in the attack on American troops in Apache Pass, Arizona, on 14–15 July 1862 and probably assisting Juh in a Whetstone Mountains fight in May 1871 in which the noted Lieutenant Howard B. Cushing was killed.

For the remainder of his career Geronimo endeavored to avoid being confined to the reservations being established by the United States, but on 9 January 1877, in southwestern New Mexico, his party was defeated by a force under Lieutenant J. A. Rucker and afterward appeared at Ojo Caliente, where Victorio's Chihenne had settled. There he was arrested by Indian Agent John P. Clum and was transported to Arizona, where Clum wanted him tried for atrocities. He was released four months later by Clum's successor, H. L. Hart, and remained at the San Carlos Reservation in Arizona until 4 April 1878, when he and Juh bolted for the freedom of Mexico. During Victorio's rebellion against the reservation system in 1879–1880, Geronimo raided with Juh, and their activities appeared to complement those of Victorio's band. In late 1879, however, Geronimo and Juh surrendered and settled at San Carlos again. Two years later, unable to adjust to conditions there, they fled once more to Mexico. From the Sierra Madre in April 1882 they led some sixty warriors in the most remarkable feat of Apache arms on record: the forced extraction of several hundred Indians from the San Carlos Reservation and the herding of them to Mexico. The escorted Indians threaded a country coursed by troops and weathered clashes with military units, but most gained the relative security of the Sierra Madre mountains, where in 1883 they were met by General George Crook and persuaded to return to San Carlos.

In May 1885 Geronimo led some followers on a new flight to Mexico, remaining at large for seventeen months. He did little raiding, but the attacks of his associates added to Geronimo's fearsome reputation, however unfairly. In March 1886 he agreed to surrender to Crook but was flushed onto the warpath again by a bootlegger who felt he could profit more from Indian hostility than tranquility. Geronimo was then courageously contacted by Lieutenant Charles B. Gatewood in August 1886 and was persuaded again to surrender, which he did to Nelson Miles, Crook's successor. The Indian was shipped into exile in Florida with other Apaches, hostile and friendly alike. Geronimo remained in nominal confinement in Florida, Alabama, and finally Fort Sill, Oklahoma, where he died. He had been one of the last Indians to surrender to the United States, and he became a monumental public attraction in his last years, his fame far outstripping the deeds by which he had proven himself little more than an able partisan leader. His name is fixed in American mythology, however, and will never be supplanted, nor has interest in him diminished. He fathered a number of children, few if any of whom survived him.

• Considerable literature about Geronimo exists, much of it based on *Geronimo's Story of His Life* (1906). The narrative was translated and transcribed by Asa (Ace) Daklugie, son of Juh, and edited by Stephen Melvil Barrett, an educator otherwise not known for any particular frontier background or knowledge. Although a valuable insight into the Apache mind, the work must be used with caution, since the editor took liberties with the dictated material. The best current biography is Angie Debo, *Geronimo: The Man, His Time, His Place* (1976), but for a discussion of the leadership of the Apache raid on San Carlos in 1882, and as an alternative to the Debo version, see Dan L. Thrapp, *Encyclopedia of Frontier Biography*, vol. 2 (1988), pp. 548–49. Indispensable is Gillett Griswold, comp., "The Fort Sill Apaches: Their Vital Statistics, Tribal Origins, Antecedents," an unpublished manuscript at the U.S. Army Field Artillery and Fort Sill Museum at Fort Sill, Okla. (see pp. 41–43). For a reasonable solution to the problem of the massacre of Geronimo's dependents in 1851, see Edwin R. Sweeney, " 'I Had Lost All': Geronimo and the Carrasco Massacre of 1851," *Journal of Arizona History* 27, no. 1 (1986): 35–52. Other insightful works include Britton Davis, *The Truth about Geronimo* (1929); Thrapp, *Conquest of Apacheria* (1967); Odie B. Faulk, *The Geronimo Campaign* (1969); and Woodward B. Skinner, *The Apache Rock Crumbles: The Captivity of Geronimo's People* (1987).

DAN L. THRAPP

GEROULD, Katharine Fullerton (6 Feb. 1879–27 July 1944), educator and author, was born in Brockton, Massachusetts. Orphaned in infancy, she was adopted by her uncle, Reverend Bradford Morton Fullerton, and his wife, Julia M. Bell Fullerton. She began her education at Miss Folsom's School and received her B.A. (1900) and M.A. (1901) from Radcliffe College. She held a faculty position in English at Bryn Mawr until 1910.

Katharine learned of her adoption in 1903, and in the fall of 1907 became engaged to William Morton Fullerton, whom she had always believed to be her brother. The engagement, however, did not lead immediately to marriage, as Fullerton returned to his residence in Europe. In 1908 Katharine took sabbatical leave from Bryn Mawr and traveled to England and France. While abroad she met several influential people, among them Henry James and Edith Wharton. She returned to America in 1909 still engaged, but in early 1910 she broke off the engagement. In June of that year, she married Gordon Hall Gerould, an assistant professor at Princeton University who later became a Holmes Professor of Belles Lettres. The couple settled at Princeton, where Gerould remained until her death. They had two children.

Katharine Gerould began writing in college; her story "The Poppies in the Wheat" received the *Century Magazine* prize for the best short story by an undergraduate in 1900. The story was published by the magazine in January 1902. She completed her next short story, "Vain Oblations," and sent the manuscript to Edith Wharton, who interceded on her behalf with Scribner's. The story was published in their magazine in March 1911.

Over the next twenty-five years, Gerould wrote and published about fifty stories in magazines such as *Scribner's*, *Century*, *Harper's Monthly*, the *Atlantic Monthly*, and the *Yale Review*. Several of her stories are set in Conradian Africa ("Vain Oblations" is an example), and others take place in equally exotic locales. Gerould also wrote ghost stories, among them "On the Staircase" (*Scribner's*, 1913); stories about parental self-sacrifice, such as "Pearls" (*Harper's*, 1914); and stories dealing with marital relationships, both bad, as in "The Weaker Vessel" (*Century*, 1913), and good, as in "Leda and the Swan" (*Scribner's*, 1915). In 1917 she published "East of Eden" (*Harper's*), a story loosely based on her relationship with Fullerton. Some of Gerould's stories were collected in three volumes: *Vain Oblations* (1914), *The Great Tradition and Other Stories* (1915), and *Valiant Dust* (1922). Edward O'Brien included Gerould's stories in his *Best Short Stories* of 1917, 1920, 1921, 1922, 1925, and in *The Fifty Best Short Stories, 1915–1939*.

Gerould also wrote several novels. Her first attempt, written on her sabbatical in Tours, France, was not completed. Her second, *A Change of Air*, was published in installments in *Scribner's Magazine* (July–Oct. 1917) and in book form later that year. It was followed by *Lost Valley* in 1922, *Conquistador* in 1923, and *The Light That Never Was* in 1931.

In addition to her fiction, Gerould published numerous critical articles and essays on a variety of subjects. In "The American Short Story" (*The Yale Review*, July 1924), she defended the short story as "a perfectly valid criticism of life" in which "some of the most serious human situations can be treated better . . . than in the novel form." She differentiated between American and European fiction by saying that American writers must go beyond the event in fiction because "we are incurably interested in human character."

As a literary critic, she wrote a number of book reviews, including a review of Edith Wharton's *Glimpses of the Moon* (*New York Times Book Review*, 23 July 1922). Her 1936 essay "Feminine Fiction" (*Saturday Review of Literature*, 11 Apr.) sparked a controversy over women's writing; she carefully delineates between serious fiction (such as that written by Charlotte Brontë, George Eliot, and Edith Wharton) and popular "trash and trimmings" fiction: "fiction created by women writers for women readers . . . that you cannot imagine any man's reading for his own pleasure." Gerould's criticism is as much of the audience, which, she writes, allows woman writers "neither unflattering realism nor romantic consistency." Other critical articles include "Miss Alcott's New England" (*Atlantic Monthly*, Aug. 1911) and "The Remarkable Rightness of Rudyard Kipling" (*Atlantic Monthly*, June 1921).

The editors of *Harper's* considered Gerould "an incisive commentator on present-day social conditions" (Feb. 1926). At their request, she wrote "The Plight of the Genteel," in which she bemoaned the fact that in America the genteel "are eliminated. They are simply poor and of no importance" because cash and material possessions are "the sole basis for social distinction." In a later article for the same magazine titled "Ladies and Gentlemen" (Nov. 1926), Gerould's subject was rhetoric, specifically "the attitude of a nation or a tribe to a given word." She found that "there is no term as yet to describe the large group of women who are honorable in the masculine sense" and that "when I most want to call a woman a lady, I hesitate because the word is not good enough for her." Other subjects that Gerould tackled were as varied as "Dress and the Woman" (*Atlantic Monthly*, Nov. 1911), "The Boundaries of Truth" (*Atlantic Monthly*, Oct. 1913), "Can Pacifists be Patriots?" (*Harper's*, Apr. 1934), and "'Ringside Seats'" (*Harper's*, Dec. 1926), an essay on the Dempsey-Tunney championship fight. A number of Gerould's essays have been collected in two volumes: *Modes and Morals*, first published in 1920 and reprinted in 1971, and *Ringside Seats*, published in 1937. Gerould published two other volumes based on her travels: *Hawaii: Scenes and Impressions* (1916) and *The Aristocratic West* (1925).

Reviewers and critics of Gerould's work included James, Wharton, and Conrad as Gerould's literary mentors, and Austin M. Wright classed her as a member of this "older tradition" of writers. What criticism exists of her short stories is general but mostly positive; Fred Lewis Pattee, for example, classed "Vain Oblations" with "those few tales that burn themselves into one's memory like scorpion bites and will not be erased, that become abiding horrors . . . " (p. 326). Cynthia Griffin Wolfe characterized Gerould's novels as "credible" (p. 191), and R. W. B. Lewis described Gerould as "a novelist of some real competence" (p. 4).

Her essays have not fared as well. Stuart P. Sherman, who enjoyed Gerould's short stories, deplored the "pusillanimity of her essays" and "the moral and intellectual bankruptcy of the class to which they are presumably designed to bring comfort and aid" (p. 132–33). There is no doubt that Gerould considered herself a member of the "genteel class," and her supercilious tone does mar some of her writing, but not all her essays should be dismissed on this ground. In "An Essay on Essays" (*North American Review*, Dec. 1935) Gerould wrote that "The basis of the essay is meditation, and it must in a measure admit the reader to the meditative process." She defined a good essay as one that "sets the reader to thinking." Although one may not always like the content of her essays, they do just that.

Gerould disliked inquiries into her personal life. In "The Personal Touch" (*Harper's*, July 1923), she argues against "the 'life and letters' sort of thing," insisting that "the proper thing to do . . . with an author . . . [is] to read his works. . . . " Gerould's publishing history shows her to be a very successful woman writer whose work reflects the lives and views of a certain segment of American society at the turn of the century. She died in Princeton.

• Collections of Gerould's letters are at the Firestone Library at Princeton and Beinecke Library at Yale. Some biographical information about Gerould can be found in the biographies of Edith Wharton by R. W. B. Lewis, *Edith Wharton* (1975) and *The Letters of Edith Wharton* (1988), and Cynthia Griffin Wolfe, *A Feast of Words* (1977). For a brief discussion of Gerould's writing, see Edward J. O'Brien, *The Advance of the American Short Story* (1923); Stuart P. Sherman, *The Genius of America* (1923); Fred Lewis Pattee, *The New American Literature, 1890–1930* (1930); and Austin McGiffert Wright, *The American Short Story in the Twenties* (1961). Kenneth A. Robb provides summaries of several of Gerould's short stories in the *Dictionary of Literary Biography*, vol. 78.

ALTHEA E. RHODES

GERRY, Elbridge (17 July 1744–23 Nov. 1814), statesman, was born in Marblehead, Massachusetts, the son of Thomas Gerry, a merchant, and Elizabeth Greenleaf. His father was a British immigrant who arrived in 1730, settled in Marblehead, and became one of the most successful merchants in Essex County. The brightest of eleven children, Elbridge entered Harvard in 1758, graduated in 1762, and returned in 1765—the year of the Stamp Act—to submit his master's thesis. Already a firebrand at twenty-one, he argued in it the question: "Can the new Prohibitary Duties which make it useless for the people to engage in Commerce, be evaded by them as faithful subjects?" His answer was "Yes."

After completing his studies, Elbridge settled in his hometown and helped his father and brothers in the family business trading fish to Spain and Portugal. He plunged headlong into local politics in 1770, propelled by the Boston Massacre. In 1772 Marblehead elected him as representative to the General Court, where Gerry met his mentor, the restless radical, Samuel Adams.

When a rumor developed in 1772 that judges were to become dependent on the royal payroll for their salaries, Gerry urged Adams to ostracize and shame

them. Adams had a better plan—to form the famous committee of correspondence system, which became one of the great instruments of colonial resistance. After Boston initiated the idea, Marblehead became one of the first Massachusetts towns to join, with Gerry drafting the resolves and joining the local committee. As a member of the Massachusetts Committee of Correspondence in 1773, he drafted the famous circular letter sent to other colonies.

Gerry's rebellious behavior received a setback in 1774 with Marblehead's "Smallpox War," which showed he was no democrat. He was as hostile to popular democracy as to British tyranny. Fearing an inoculation program inaugurated by Gerry and others, a Marblehead mob threatened his life, burned down the hospital he helped build, and rampaged through the streets. Shocked that "the people" represented as great a threat to good government as "tyrannical rulers," Gerry resigned in disgust from the local committee of correspondence, retired from public office, and stayed home to sulk. He returned to public life only after the British Coercive Acts shut down the port of Boston and threw hundreds out of work. Gerry was appointed to handle the relief donations that came pouring in.

In 1774 he was elected a member of the Massachusetts Provincial Congress—an extralegal body—and served on the Committee of Supply and the Executive Committee of Safety. His merchant experience served him in good stead when he gathered military supplies for the minuteman forces then forming. Some military stores were hidden at Lexington and Concord, and Gerry was mentioned in British dispatches as a man to be watched.

On the night of 18 April 1775 Gerry was in Menotomy (later renamed Arlington) performing official duties when General Thomas Gage sent a surprise raiding party to Lexington and Concord. He was sleeping in a tavern located along the route the British were taking and in the middle of the night was forced to flee into a cornfield in his night clothes to escape capture.

Elected to the Continental Congress in 1776, Gerry began a new phase in his political career. He continued to collect military supplies, but now on a national level, acting in both a private and public capacity as a merchant. Energetic and effective, he was scrupulously honest and frowned on anything that smacked of profiteering.

Gerry emerged as one of the earliest and most vigorous advocates of American independence. "If every man here was a Gerry," wrote his congressional colleague John Adams (1735–1826), "the Liberties of America would be safe against the Gates of Earth and Hell." He signed the Declaration of Independence, whose principles he believed in passionately: natural rights, strict separation of powers, honesty and frugality in government, and equal rights.

He practiced these principles during his terms in the Continental Congress (1776–1781 and 1783–1785) and, indeed, throughout the rest of his life. By virtue of his faithful attendance he became one of the most active members of Congress, especially in matters dealing with supply and finance.

Conscious of the historic role he was playing in helping to found the new nation, Gerry was driven by what scholars called the "spur of fame." This term referred to the achievement of immortality in history through public service. Gerry's desire for public fame, however, warred constantly with his wish for a private happiness as a husband and father.

Distinctive in his handsome appearance and manners, Gerry was of middling height and had a large, broad head with a high, prominent forehead and a long, aristocratic nose. A nervous birdlike man, his movements resembled those of the sandpipers that skittered on Marblehead's beaches. He stammered when speaking and developed a facial tic over time.

Gerry remained a bachelor until he was forty-one. In 1786 he married a twenty-year-old New York belle, Ann Thompson, and left Marblehead to settle in Cambridge in an elegant mansion. But that same year Shays's Rebellion put the question of a private versus public life to the test. On the one hand was his beautiful young wife; on the other was the threat to the republic Gerry had sacrificed so much to bring into being. This threat was represented by the grizzled revolutionary war veteran—Daniel Shays. Hoping to halt mortgage foreclosures, the destitute Shays led debt-ridden farmers in western Massachusetts into rebellion. Remembering his Marblehead mob experiences, Gerry was quickly drawn into the political fray and concluded that such popular uprisings must be countered by a stronger central government. He decided, therefore, to attend the Constitutional Convention in 1787.

To Gerry, republicanism represented the middle ground between the extremes of anarchy and despotism. He wanted a government run neither by power-hungry aristocrats nor by the unruly masses, but rather by men of virtue, merit, and character—men like himself. Shays's Rebellion represented to Gerry the threat of anarchy; at the same time, he distrusted certain American elites. He worried that powerful groups or individuals might attempt to establish an aristocracy or monarchy. He feared political demagogues like John Hancock, economic oligarchs like Robert Morris, and militaristic groups like the Society of the Cincinnati. He even viewed George Washington with suspicion, lest he employ the Society to establish a military dictatorship. Gerry's fear that military power would pave the way to aristocracy or monarchy was so great that in the mid-1780s he became the most outspoken foe in Congress to a peacetime military establishment.

Throughout most of the Constitutional Convention Gerry proved to be a middle-of-the-road nationalist. He hoped to strengthen the central government to prevent breakdowns in public order like Shays's Rebellion. Simultaneously, he fought to keep the government from possessing too much power. He remained "a true federalist," advocating a balanced partnership between the central and state governments. Concern about excessive democracy led him to oppose the popular election of both houses of Congress and the president, but he demanded democratic measures such as the annual election of congressmen, enumerated powers for the central government, and—most important—a national bill of rights.

Twice, Gerry helped to rescue the convention from possible disaster. In July, during the deadlock over large- and small-state representation, Gerry chaired the committee that resolved the explosive issue with the famous Connecticut Compromise. When the convention debated the question, Gerry's personal vote prevented Massachusetts from rejecting the compromise: it was approved by the wafer-thin margin of five states to four.

Yet in September he refused to sign the Constitution, listing three major objections. It had no bill of rights; Gerry feared that personal liberties would not be secure. He believed republican government would not work unless sovereignty was more evenly divided between the states and central government. And finally, he believed the central government had been granted too much military power.

Gerry warned that the Constitution would not be ratified without a bill of rights, and he proved to be right. Massachusetts accepted the document, but only with the strong recommendation that a bill of rights be added. Several other states followed suit, and the Constitution was ratified but only with these provisos. Gerry staunchly supported the new government, helped to frame the Bill of Rights, and served as congressman from 1789 to 1793.

In 1797 President John Adams sent Gerry to France along with John Marshall and Charles Cotesworth Pinckney on a mission to settle several long-standing disputes. The underhanded treatment of the American delegates by Talleyrand and his secret agents, called X, Y, and Z, who demanded bribes, caused Gerry's colleagues to leave in disgust. To their annoyance, Gerry disregarded his instructions and remained in Paris; he feared his departure might result in an open rupture and war. His stubborn independence paid off. President Adams later acknowledged that it was Gerry who "brought home . . . assurances upon which . . . peace was made."

From 1810 to 1812 he was governor of Massachusetts. His first term was moderate in tone and characterized by the conciliation and statesmanship that marked much of his career. But his second term proved as stormy as his first had been smooth. Despite his lifelong belief that political parties were boils on the body politic, he was drawn gradually into partisan politics. He became convinced that the Federalists were monarchists and that some were seeking to rejoin Britain.

In his second administration he helped to enact an electoral law that came to be known as the "Gerrymander bill." Massachusetts was subdivided into new senatorial districts in such a way as to consolidate the Federalist vote into a few districts, thus giving Gerry's Democratic-Republicans an undue advantage. The shape of one electoral district on the map resembled a salamander, and one wit promptly dubbed it a "Gerrymander." Hence, the term used today when redistricting results in a concentration of the strength of one political party and a weakening of its opponent's strength. This political practice was not new: it had been used throughout the colonial period by changing county lines to gain political advantage.

In 1812 Gerry, an ardent advocate of the war against Britain, was elected vice president on the ticket with James Madison (1751–1836). During his two years in office he struggled with his continued ambivalence about partisan politics. He presided over the Senate with dignity, dedication, and a fair degree of impartiality. But he refused to relinquish the chair—as was the custom at the close of the session—lest a peace advocate, a Virginia senator, become president pro tem. President Madison was gravely ill, and Gerry himself was in poor health; the presidency might have fallen into the hands of someone who would conduct the War of 1812 differently.

Gerry died in Washington of a hemorrhage of the lungs after complaining about chest pains. By introducing earlier the motion in Congress to name Washington the site of the nation's capital, he had, ironically enough, picked his own final resting place.

• The best collection of primary sources is the Gerry papers at the Massachusetts Historical Society. The Manuscript Division of the Library of Congress has another major collection composed in part of the Gerry Estates Collection, which contains negative photostats of original letters or transcripts deposited by the Gerry family. The Gerry Collection of Elsie O. and Philip D. Sang, at Southern Illinois University in Carbondale, contains valuable items.

There are two printed collections of Gerry letters: C. Harvey Gardiner, *A Study in Dissent: The Warren–Gerry Correspondence, 1776–1792* (1968), and Russell W. Knight, ed., *Elbridge Gerry's Letterbook: Paris, 1797–1798* (1966).

For secondary sources, see James T. Austin, *Life of Elbridge Gerry* (2 vols., 1827–1828); George Athan Billias, *Elbridge Gerry: Founding Father and Republican Statesman* (1976); Samuel Eliot Morison, "Elbridge Gerry, Gentleman-Democrat," *New England Quarterly* 2 (1929): 3–33; and Clifford K. Shipton, "Elbridge Gerry," *Sibley's Harvard Graduates* 15 (1970): 239–59.

GEORGE ATHAN BILLIAS

GERSHENSON, Joseph (12 Jan. 1904–18 Jan. 1988), motion picture music director, film producer, and orchestra conductor, was born in Kishinev, Russia, the son of Louis Gershenson, a musician, and Ida (maiden name unknown). His mother died when he was a toddler. His father remarried, and his stepmother, also named Ida, raised him. His family emigrated to the United States when Joseph was three. When he was five years old and living in New York, his father performed as U.S. Army bandleader, a post that led to his service as bandmaster of the Eighty-seventh Field Artillery at Camp Fort Ethan Allan, Vermont.

Gershenson pursued violin studies when he was a youngster in the United States, playing on a small custom-sized violin that he kept throughout his lifetime.

He graduated from Morris High School in the Bronx. At age thirteen he worked as a runner for an attorney-accountant, the grandfather of Jacqueline Bouvier Kennedy. Gershenson's boss influenced his decision to attend Pace Institute as an accountant-lawyer. His mind served numbers, and his heart served music. Home phonograph records, radio music, and early motion picture musical soundtracks, geared to highlight the on-screen action of horse "opera" chases and drama for movie theater audiences intrigued him. From the age of sixteen he found work playing at Italian and Irish neighborhood party events in New York City. He also became an orchestra leader at traditional Jewish weddings and bar mitzvahs. After filling in as musical conductor for a friend at New York's Shanley Cabaret, young Gershenson switched careers permanently to music.

By 1924 he had impressed the chain of Radio Keith Orpheum (RKO) Theaters in New York, and they hired him as orchestra leader and conductor for the theatrical stage show presentations that accompanied first-run feature films. From 1920 to 1928 was conductor for the B. F. Keith Theaters, which included the prestigious west Bronx Fordham Theater and the legendary New York Palace and Academy of Music theaters. In 1928 Gershenson was appointed assistant general musical director of all RKO theaters throughout the United States and Canada. Radio shows flourished as primary home entertainment, and Gershenson enjoyed popularity on the RKO "Theater of the Air" as its featured orchestra leader. He married New York stage actress Helen Tucker in 1932; they had two children.

In 1933 Gershenson produced his own independent series of motion picture two-reel musical shorts in New York for Mentone, RKO Pictures, Columbia, and Universal Pictures. In 1939, after selling his production company to Universal, he signed a contract to produce a series of musical shorts under the Universal banner at its California studios. As feature-length movies grew in popularity, Universal Pictures invited Gershenson in 1941 to produce the popular genre for them and a spate of feature musicals followed.

Much of the speedily produced product was considered at that time by some Universal executives to lack artistic value while generating profits. This attitude promoted a decision to save the Joseph Gershenson name for credit on its major releases, and the pseudonym Joseph G. Sanford was adopted for several films. Gershenson's supervisory production role with the series of "personality and name band musicals" also allowed him to voluntarily cede his screen title credit to his assistant and friend, Will Cowan.

The orchestra leaders featured in the Gershenson films as the top bands of the 1940s by virtue of their "Lucky Strike Radio Hit Parade" national notoriety, live vaudeville stage appearances, and major hotel ballroom bookings included Henry Busse, Ted Fio Rita, Ted Weems, Ted Lewis, Jack Teagarden, Ozzie Nelson, Carlos Molina, and Feddie Slack.

In 1943 Gershenson was named executive producer for features made for Universal by his own motion picture production unit. He produced *The Runaround* in 1946, directed by Charles Lamont and starring Rod Cameron and Broderick Crawford with Ella Raines and character actor Frank McHugh. That year he also produced the comedy team of Bud Abbott and Lou Costello in *The Time of Their Lives* with cinema favorites Marjorie Reynolds, Gale Sondergaard, and Binnie Barnes, directed by Charles Barton. Gershenson also produced *Little Giant*, which did not receive critical acclaim but affirmed the lasting comedic genius of the starring comedy duo Abbott and Costello and the talent of actress Margaret Dumont (the tall, classic straight woman teamed with the four Marx Brothers in feature-length comedies). The enduring artistic merit of such films, which appealed to later generations of film buffs as classic comedies, leaves the question of their intrinsic value open for discussion. Gershenson parted from Universal Pictures in 1946, again formed an independent motion picture company, and returned two years later.

In 1948 Universal appointed Gershenson general musical director. His role was to supervise and conduct music for all feature films. Gershenson's outstanding synchronization of musical style and faithful scoring translated the signature hallmark big band sound of many famous orchestra leaders onto film soundtracks that captured the original conductor's musical style. Popular recording artist and jazz clarinetist Benny Goodman, trumpeter Harry James, and trombone artist Glenn Miller, although tapped for a biopic of their lives, could not be transposed onto the motion picture screen through old sound recordings. Instead, their distinctive sounds had to be woven into fresh film frames with original orchestrations to score the motion pictures based on their lives. Gershenson, in his role as musical director masterminded the arrangements and conducted the studio musicians off-camera, refuting experts who said it could not be done. Miller, missing in 1944 on a military air plane during World War II, was never found, and Gershenson led studio musicians at Universal in achieving the musical duplication that Miller's widow later approved, recanting her earlier objections and disbelief that the Glenn Miller sound could be accurately replicated.

A mentor for musicians with his vast knowledge, patience, and a sense of humor that overcame the tedious technical difficulties so often involved in the transition from scoring to rehearsals to the actual filming, Gershenson inspired and helped the young Henry Mancini. Mancini, who later won Academy Awards for his original film scores, was hired to make a film short for $43. At a twenty-year testimonial dinner for Gershenson, Mancini noted, "I went in on a two-week deal with Joe and stayed six years." Mancini later credited Gershenson with teaching him all about film music. (Gershenson's manuscript "Music for Film" was finished too late for publication, as film music scoring gave way to new computer technology.) In 1954 Ger-

shenson and Mancini were listed as joint musical directors on *The Glenn Miller Story*. Louis Armstrong, the great jazz trumpeter, and Gene Krupa, renowned drummer, played themselves in the film.

Other films for Universal Pictures produced by Gershenson include *The Incredible Shrinking Man* (1958), *Curse of the Undead* (1959), *Step Down to Terror* (1958; originally made by Alfred Hitchcock in 1943 as *Shadow of a Doubt*), and *The Leech Woman* (1960).

Films made by Gershenson as head of the music department at Universal include *Magnificent Obsession* (1954); *So This Is Paris, Man without a Star, Foxfire* (1955); *The Benny Goodman Story, All That Heaven Allows, There's Always Tomorrow, The Spoilers, Never Say Goodbye, Away All Boats* (1956); *Battle Hymn, Written on the Wind, My Man Godfrey, Man of a Thousand Faces* (1957); *Never Steal Anything Small, Imitation of Life, This Earth Is Mine, Pillow Talk, Operation Petticoat* (1959); *Back Street, Come September* (1961); *Lover Come Back, Spiral Road, Freud* (1962); *Captain Newman M.D., Send Me No Flowers, I'd Rather Be Rich* (1964); *Father Goose, Shenandoah, The Warlord* (1965); *Madame X, Blindfold, Beau Geste* (1966); *Thoroughly Modern Millie* (1967); *Madigan* (1968); and *Sweet Charity* (1969).

Motion pictures shown on television and home video, not limited to the big screen of four-wall exhibition theaters, introduced new generations of film buffs to the work of Gershenson and the heritage he contributed to film music and Universal Pictures. He died in Calabasas, California.

• Oral history and newspaper clippings files are maintained by Lillian Carson and David Gershenson, the children of Joseph Gershenson. Important biographical information is at the Universal Pictures Library and Archives, MCA Universal Research Department, Universal City, Calif.; in the *International Motion Picture Almanac* (1975); and in Ephraim Katz, *The Film Encyclopedia* (1979).

LEONA MAYER MERRIN

GERSHWIN, George (26 Sept. 1898–11 July 1937), pianist and composer of popular and classical music, was born Jacob Gershvin in Brooklyn, New York, the son of Morris Gershovitz and Rose Bruskin, Russian Jewish immigrants. Gershwin's father, who changed the family name to Gershvin and later Gershwin, worked in the leather industry and at various times owned or operated a restaurant, bakery, cigar store, bookmaking establishment, and Russian bath. During Gershwin's boyhood, his family moved more than twenty-five times within the poor neighborhoods of lower Manhattan and Brooklyn.

A public school graduate, Gershwin had little experience with classical music until he happened to hear a version of Anton Rubinstein's Melody in F played on an electric piano at a penny arcade in Harlem. When his family acquired a piano in 1910, Gershwin and his older brother, Ira, both studied with neighborhood teachers. Gershwin continued serious studies with Charles Hambitzer, who recognized his talent and encouraged him to learn the standard piano repertoire; Hambitzer also took him to concerts and encouraged him to study harmony with Edward Kilenyi. Throughout his life Gershwin worked to perfect his musical craft, and he was an occasional student of such important musical figures as Rubin Goldmark (briefly in 1923), Wallingford Riegger (in the late 1920s), Henry Cowell (on and off from 1927 until 1929), and Joseph Schillinger (1932–1936).

In 1912 Gershwin began studying accountancy at the High School of Commerce, but his talents lay in writing and performing popular music. During the summer of 1914 he earned $15 per week as a Catskill Mountains resort pianist. By this time he had already composed two songs, "Since I Found You" and "Ragging the Traumerei." After abandoning his high school studies in 1914 with his mother's permission, he was hired by the music publishing firm Jerome H. Remick & Co. as a song plugger who sold sheet music by playing the piano and singing the song for customers. While at Remick, Gershwin improved his piano technique, gained experience as an accompanist, and earned extra money by cutting more than 125 pianola rolls from 1915 until 1926, using a variety of pseudonyms. In 1916 his "When You Want 'Em, You Can't Get 'Em—When You've Got 'Em, You Don't Want 'Em" was published on the recommendation of singer Sophie Tucker. Gershwin earned $5 for the composition.

In March 1917, tired of the formulas of popular song writing and drawn to the more dramatic music of the stage, Gershwin left Remick and became the rehearsal pianist at the Century Theater for Jerome Kern and Victor Herbert's musical *Miss 1917*, earning $35 per week. Early in 1918 he was hired, solely to write songs, by Max Dreyfus, head of T. B. Harms Publishing Co. In 1919 Dreyfus promoted Gershwin's "Swanee," and the song became a hit. "Swanee" was later recorded by Al Jolson and earned Gershwin more than $10,000 in royalties in 1920. That same year the song was used in the musical *Dere Mabel*, which closed before it could reach New York. Popular revues such as *Ed Wynn's Carnival* (1920) also included Gershwin tunes.

Gershwin composed the music for *La La Lucille*, his first full-length Broadway show, which opened on 26 May 1919 and ran for 104 performances. From 1920 to 1924 he composed the music for five of *George White's Scandals*, an annual revue. He also wrote scores for *A Dangerous Maid* (1921), *Our Nell* (1922), and *Sweet Little Devil* (1924). The success of *The Rainbow* (1923) and *Primrose* (1924) on the London stage contributed to his popularity in the United States. In 1924 he collaborated with his brother, Ira, to write the music and lyrics for the show *Lady, Be Good*, which included the popular title song and "Fascinating Rhythm." Other Gershwin musical comedies from this period included *Tip Toes* (1925), *Oh Kay* (1926), and *Funny Face* (1927).

While Gershwin's earlier songs such as "Swanee" reflected the influence of the solid beat and regular rhythmic structure of stride piano, he quickly developed a more sophisticated approach to syncopated figures and repetition. This is evident in the slow ballads "Someone to Watch Over Me" (1926), "The Man I Love" (1927), "But Not for Me" (1930), and "Embraceable You" (1930), as well as in up-tempo songs like "Fascinating Rhythm" and "I Got Rhythm" (1930), which was first performed in *Girl Crazy* by Ethel Merman.

The year 1922 brought Gershwin continued success as a songwriter. On 20 February two shows opened on Broadway that included his songs, and both shows proved successful. *The French Doll* ran for 120 performances at the Lyceum Theater with acclaim for a rendition of "Do It Again." *For Goodness Sake*, which featured Fred Astaire and Adele Astaire, ran for 103 performances at the Lyric Theater. "Someone" and "Tra-La-La" were George and Ira Gershwin collaborations, with Ira using the name Arthur Francis.

In 1923 Gershwin accompanied Canadian soprano Eva Gauthier in two much-acclaimed performances of a "Recital of Ancient and Modern Music for Voice" in New York and Boston. The final section of the program consisted of popular songs by Irving Berlin, Jerome Kern, Walter Donaldson, and Gershwin. Popular music had come to the concert hall and was being taken seriously in many quarters as the medium through which American composers would find a national musical identity. Critic Henry T. Parker of the *Boston Evening Transcript* characterized Gershwin's participation in the event as "the beginning of the age of sophisticated jazz."

In 1922 Gershwin had made his first attempt to bring together jazz and more traditional musical genres in a short operatic work, originally "Blue Monday," but later called "135th Street." The piece was first performed as part of *George White's Scandals* in August, but it was withdrawn after a single performance because its serious mood undercut White's upbeat revue. Despite its short life, the brief opera brought Gershwin together with orchestra leader Paul Whiteman, who asked him to compose a symphonic piece in what was considered a jazz idiom. The result, *Rhapsody in Blue*, was arranged by Ferde Grofé and first performed in New York's Aeolian Hall by Whiteman's orchestra on 12 February 1924 in a concert promoted as "An Experiment in Modern Music." Immediate critical reactions were mixed. Constant Lambert called the piece "singularly inept" and said the style was "neither good jazz nor good Liszt." Lawrence Gilman, while admiring Gershwin's rhythmic sense and Grofé's colorful use of the orchestra, found the melodic invention and harmonic structure "lifeless" and "stale." Commenting some years later on the loose structure of both *Rhapsody in Blue* and *An American in Paris*, Paul Rosenfeld felt that Gershwin's music lacked organization and an "appropriate distance" from the emotional quality of the source material.

In spite of such reactions, audiences at the time were thrilled by *Rhapsody in Blue*, which remains one of Gershwin's most popular works. His efforts in this idiom probably inspired other European and American composers to experiment with jazz-like elements in their music.

Gershwin continued to compose for the theater, but he devoted much of his effort to additional orchestral works that made use of jazz idioms. These included the Concerto in F (commissioned by director Walter Damrosch for the New York Symphony Orchestra and first performed with Gershwin as soloist on 3 December 1925), "Three Piano Preludes" (1926), *An American in Paris* (written on a trip to Europe in 1928 and first performed in December of that year), *Second Rhapsody* (premiered in January 1932 by the Boston Symphony Orchestra under Serge Koussevitzky with Gershwin at the piano), *Cuban Overture* (1932), and *Variations on "I Got Rhythm"* (1934).

Gershwin never married. He developed a close relationship with Kay Swift, a divorced woman with three children who was a composer and musician in her own right. They met in 1925 while Swift was still married, and the relationship became more serious after Gershwin's return to New York from a European trip in 1926. Because of her training, Swift was able to help him write and edit some of his music. He dedicated his *Song Book* to her. The depth and extent of Gershwin and Swift's relationship remains unclear because she destroyed his letters after his death.

Gershwin's stage hits continued with *Strike Up the Band* (1927), *Girl Crazy* (1930), and *Of Thee I Sing* (1931), a political satire by George S. Kaufman and Morrie Ryskind with lyrics by Ira Gershwin, which was the first musical comedy to win a Pulitzer Prize. Gershwin also performed in concert and on radio, including his own "Music by Gershwin," which aired on the CBS network in 1934 and 1935. In 1936 he moved to Hollywood, where he and Ira composed for such RKO films as *Shall We Dance* (1937), *A Damsel in Distress* (1937), both of which featured the dancing and singing of Fred Astaire, and *The Goldwyn Follies* (1938).

One of Gershwin's most important contributions to American music was the opera *Porgy and Bess* (1935). Combining the dramatic structure of opera and the musical style of jazz and Tin Pan Alley, the work was especially important in the development of American musical theater. Although it did not recoup its investment, *Porgy and Bess* was an outstanding achievement that brought black singers to the Broadway stage in significant roles. *Porgy*, the original novel by DuBose Heyward, was about life on "Catfish Row," the black quarter of Charleston, South Carolina. It had been produced as a play by the Theatre Guild in New York, and in 1933 Heyward and George and Ira Gershwin contracted with the Guild to produce an opera from the story. In hopes of capturing the sounds of African-American culture in tidewater South Carolina, Gershwin traveled to Folly Island near Charleston in the summer of 1934 to listen to local people and to continue composing his opera, begun earlier that spring. He completed the score that summer and started orchestrating in January 1935. *Porgy and Bess*, called "an

American folk opera" in its promotional materials, opened on Broadway in October 1935. Its poignancy and expressiveness have been recognized by critics, and the opera has often been presented in revival. The 1942 version enjoyed the longest Broadway run for a revival to that time. In 1952 an American company took the work to Europe and the Soviet Union, the Middle East, South America, and Mexico. The film of *Porgy and Bess* (1959), reportedly made for $6 million, did not return half that amount at the box office, though the *New York Times* placed it fourth on its top ten list for 1959. More than any of Gershwin's other works, *Porgy and Bess* established him as one of America's most important composers.

At the height of his creativity and popularity in 1937, Gershwin began to suffer from dizziness and despondency; he ignored these signs and continued to compose. He was working on a ballet score, "Swing Symphony," for *The Goldwyn Follies* when he became ill. He fell into a coma with what was diagnosed as a brain tumor and died two days later in Los Angeles. In later years his music became a central feature in a number of films, among them *Rhapsody in Blue* (1945), a fictionalized biographical picture, and *An American in Paris* (1951), *Funny Face* (1957), and *Manhattan* (1979).

Gershwin's songs, written for the stage, nightclubs, and films, are among the most popular and often-played standards from the great age (1900–1950) of American popular music. Many of his longer works, especially *Rhapsody in Blue*, *An American in Paris*, and *Porgy and Bess*, are widely known and admired. Yet Gershwin's standing as a "serious" composer has never been firmly established. The composer Arnold Schoenberg offered this assessment of his American colleague: "Many musicians do not consider George Gershwin a serious composer. But they should understand that, serious or not, he is a composer—that is, a man who lives in music and expresses everything, serious or not, sound or superficial, by means of music, because it is his native language."

• Gershwin's life and music have been treated in a number of biographies, including Isaac Goldberg's *George Gershwin: A Study in American Music* (1931; rev. and enlarged ed., 1958); David Ewen, *The Story of George Gershwin* (1943) and *George Gershwin: His Journey to Greatness* (1956); Merle Armitage, *George Gershwin: Man and Legend* (1958); R. Payne, *Gershwin* (1960); C. M. Schwartz, *Gershwin: His Life and Music* (1973); D. Jeambar, *George Gershwin* (1982); and Alan Kendall, *George Gershwin: A Biography* (1987). Other studies are discussed in C. M. Schwartz, *George Gershwin: A Selective Bibliography and Discography* (1974). Gershwin's obituary is in the *New York Times*, 12 July 1937.

BARBARA L. TISCHLER

GERSHWIN, Ira (6 Dec. 1896–15 Aug. 1983), song lyricist, was born in Brooklyn, New York, the son of Morris Gershvin (written Gershwine; originally Gershovitz), a leather worker, later a businessman, and Rose Bruskin. His childhood was spent mostly on the Lower East Side of Manhattan. Although his father's business ventures were often unsuccessful, the Gershwins were of comfortable means compared with many of their Russian-Jewish immigrant peers.

The oldest of four children, Ira, called Izzy (often believed to be short for Isadore, though his birth name was in fact Israel), was considered the scholar of the family, as opposed to his younger brother George Gershwin, who hated school. He took piano lessons from his aunt for a time and displayed some talent in drawing, an ability that he and George shared. In 1910 he entered Townsend Harris Hall, a selective preparatory school for the College of the City of New York. He attended college for two years, during which his activities centered on the school literary weekly. He contributed a regular column, "Much Ado," in collaboration with another future lyricist, Isidore "Yip" Hochberg, later known as E. Y. Harburg.

After college, Ira Gershwin worked in various jobs, some in family enterprises. He also continued to write and in 1917 published a piece in the *Smart Set*, a magazine edited by George Jean Nathan and H. L. Mencken, for which he was paid one dollar. His interest in musical theater grew as his brother's involvement increased; he reviewed vaudeville acts for the show business paper the *Clipper* and around 1917 began to contribute lyrics to some of George's songs. The Gershwins' first joint success came in 1918 when "The Real American Folk Song (Is a Rag)" was introduced by the vaudeville singer Nora Bayes in the revue *Ladies First*. Here, however, and in other early lyrics, Gershwin used the pseudonym Arthur Francis, coined from the names of his youngest brother Arthur and his sister Frances, herself a singer. He used his own name beginning in 1924, first with the show *Primrose*, for which he wrote half the lyrics, and then with *Lady Be Good*, for which he wrote them all.

Arguably the greatest songwriting team in history, George and Ira Gershwin distinguished themselves in every genre in which they worked, from the revues of the 1920s, to the musical comedies and operettas of the early 1930s (including *Of Thee I Sing*, which won a Pulitzer Prize), to *Porgy and Bess*, to the final film scores (*Shall We Dance?*, *A Damsel in Distress*, *The Goldwyn Follies*). Two more film scores, *The Shocking Miss Pilgrim* (1946) and *Kiss Me, Stupid* (1964), with music taken posthumously from George's notebooks, would come later. A list of the Gershwins' hit songs alone would fill pages, and for every one of those there is at least one of lesser renown that deserves to be rediscovered. One of these, "Hi Ho," originally meant for Fred Astaire in *Shall We Dance?* but not used, exists in a private recording done at a party, with Ira himself singing and Harold Arlen at the piano. The song was published in 1967.

Through his brother Ira met Leonore Strunsky, the sister-in-law of George's friend and erstwhile lyricist Lou Paley; the couple married in 1926 and had no children. The Gershwins had lived together before Ira's marriage and maintained adjoining residences afterwards—first in New York, then in Beverly Hills.

Leonore Gershwin effectively became the third member of the team, a role that evidently suited her.

Less well known than Gershwin's partnership with his brother is his work with other composers, which took place not just after his brother's death, but throughout the years of their partnership. In the 1920s, for example, Gershwin was lyricist or co-lyricist for three complete shows plus about twenty individual songs, with music by Vincent Youmans, Philip Charig, and others. Of the shows, *Two Little Girls in Blue* and *Be Yourself* (the latter with book co-written by George S. Kaufman) opened on Broadway in 1921 and 1924, respectively, while *That's a Good Girl* was produced in London in 1928. In 1934 Gershwin and his college friend Harburg wrote the lyrics to *Life Begins at 8:40*, a series of vignettes containing sixteen songs, with music by Harold Arlen. Twenty years later, Gershwin and Arlen, who were longtime friends, wrote the scores to two popular musical films, *A Star Is Born* (including "The Man That Got Away") and *The Country Girl*.

There were several other significant collaborations. One was with Vernon Duke (like George Gershwin, a student of music theorist Joseph Schillinger) on the *Ziegfeld Follies of 1936*, which included the standard "I Can't Get Started," and on the score for the film *The Goldwyn Follies* (1938), which his brother had left unfinished when he died. Duke's work on this show included one complete song, "Spring Again," plus the anonymous completion of some or all of the verses to the Gershwin songs, among them "Love Walked In" and "Love Is Here to Stay."

Ira Gershwin's next major work was with the playwright Moss Hart and the composer Kurt Weill, who had just begun the American phase of his career. Hart's play, initially titled *I Am Listening*, became the musical *Lady in the Dark*, with music by Weill and lyrics by Gershwin. The unconventional musical about a woman in psychoanalysis was a hit with both critics and audience; it opened on Broadway early in 1941 and had 467 performances. The best-known song from this show, "My Ship," illustrates the simpler, more sentimental side of both Weill and Gershwin.

A similar feeling pervades "Long Ago (and Far Away)," from the score to the film *Cover Girl* (1944), with music by Jerome Kern. Though he rightly thought the tune to be one of Kern's finest, Gershwin remained somewhat embarrassed by the simplicity of the lyrics. Nevertheless, the song was, by his own recollection, his biggest hit in any given year.

Gershwin and Weill, meanwhile, wrote two more musicals together. One was the film *Where Do We Go from Here?* (1945), with screenplay by Morrie Ryskind (who, with George S. Kaufman, wrote the book for *Of Thee I Sing* and for its sequel *Let 'Em Eat Cake*). This story of a young man who yearns for military service despite his 4-F classification included a series of fantasy sequences set in past and future times. In these sequences, Weill and Gershwin sought to integrate music, lyrics, and drama in operatic fashion. This film was followed by a stage work, *The Firebrand of Florence* (also 1945), an ambitious operetta based on Edwin Justus Mayer's play about the life of Benvenuto Cellini (whose original 1924 production included one of Ira Gershwin's songs); its run on Broadway was unfortunately brief.

Of less real importance, though of interest nonetheless, was *The North Star*, released in October of 1943, which coupled Gershwin's lyrics with the music of Aaron Copland. Produced by Samuel Goldwyn, with screenplay by Lillian Hellman, *The North Star* was a sympathetic portrayal of Communist Russia, which faded into obscurity with the advent of the Cold War. In this instance, in contrast to the way he and his brother usually had worked, Gershwin wrote the lyrics first, with Copland providing the settings later. Gershwin, in fact, did not even hear the music until after the film was released.

Despite all this activity, the myth persists that Ira Gershwin's success depended on that of his brother. Yet any such contention is refuted, not only by the strength of his lyrics themselves, which uniquely blended verbal sophistication with an uncommon degree of warmth and empathy, but by his personal contribution to the Gershwin partnership. He was both his brother's keeper and the duo's manager; after George's death in 1937 he became its executor. He organized the Gershwin manuscripts, donating most of them, scrupulously annotated, to the Library of Congress, and remained an invaluable source to younger performers and scholars who were interested in the Gershwins' work. After an extended period of reclusion, he died peacefully at the family home in Beverly Hills.

• Philip Furia, *Ira Gershwin: The Art of the Lyricist* (1997), is a key source of information. See also Edward Jablonski's account of George's life and career, *Gershwin: A Biography* (1987), especially the section titled "Epilogue: The Myths of Ira Gershwin," pp. 327–71; and Deena Rosenberg, *Fascinating Rhythm: The Collaboration of George and Ira Gershwin* (1991). A taste of Ira Gershwin's writing can be found in his own *Lyrics on Several Occasions* (1973).

STEVEN E. GILBERT

GERSON, Noel Bertram (6 Nov. 1914–20 Nov. 1988), journalist and author, was born in Chicago, Illinois, the son of Samuel Philip Gerson, a newspaperman and later a director of the Shubert theaters in Chicago, and Rosa Anna Noel. Gerson graduated from the University of Chicago with an A.B. in 1934 and the following year earned an M.A. in American history. While at the university, he served as campus correspondent for the *Chicago Herald-Examiner*. After graduating, he continued to work for the newspaper as a reporter and a rewriteman until 1936, when he took a job as publicity writer for the Chicago radio station WGN. He later became the station's talent director and main scriptwriter. During World War II, he served as a captain in military intelligence.

After the war, Gerson continued writing scripts for radio and later, until 1951, for television. He published his first book, *Savage Gentleman*, in 1950. Set in

the eighteenth century during the French and Indian War, the historical novel was favorably reviewed for its color and action. After the success of a second novel, *The Mohawk Ladder*, in 1951, he became a full-time writer.

When asked in an interview about when he started writing, Gerson remarked, "at the age of five, when I wrote a play—a casual work consisting of some two lines of dialogue." Gerson never wrote for the theater, but he did master the art of writing historical and biographical novels, drawing on his background in the study of history and employing his insight into what an audience would enjoy reading about.

Gerson would often take a single, not necessarily well-known historical event and then weave a story around it, mixing fictional heroes, heroines, and villains with actual people. For example, *The Golden Eagle* (1953) is set in Mexico, and the fictional spy-hero maps Vera Cruz for the actual invasion by General Winfield Scott. The action of *The Imposter* (1954) takes place in seventeenth-century New York and Jamaica. Background information on the Maroon community is evidence of Gerson's careful research into his subject. Gerson's 1955 novel *The Highwayman* (set in Kittery, Maine; Boston, Massachusetts; and Cape Breton Island, Nova Scotia) is about the successful expedition of colonial troops against the French fortress of Louisbourg in 1745. To the actual historical figures of Lieutenant General Sir William Pepperall, Governor General William Shirley of the Massachusetts Bay Colony, and Rear Admiral Sir Peter Warren, Gerson added a beautiful and spirited heroine, an Indian maiden, a steady Maine hero, and a dashing French highwayman-spy. Combining interesting characters, action, a good plot, and historical accuracy, Gerson became an expert in writing this type of novel. He would often provide additional historical material for the novels with prefaces or postscripts.

In the articles he wrote for the *Writer* and courses he taught at the Indiana Writers Conference in novel writing and nonfiction writing, Gerson stressed accuracy. He stated that a writer should never falsify factual data for the sake of a story and never invent situations that were not historically true.

Gerson's biographical novels also followed his own guidelines for accuracy and covered a wide range of subjects from Nathan Hale to Mary Shelley to Theodore Roosevelt. His book *TR: A Biographical Novel* (1970) is a result of his lifelong interest in Theodore Roosevelt. Gerson's father had been present at Roosevelt's inauguration. Gerson read all of Roosevelt's adventure books as a child and felt he could best write about him in a biographical novel, acknowledging that "it would have been presumptuous" to compete with Henry Pringle's Pulitzer Prize–winning biography. Like all Gerson's novels, the book is well documented, and, as Gerson stated in the preface, the dialogue reflects Roosevelt's "actual views, as expressed in public or private statements, correspondence and other sources."

Another biographical portrait that was popular and received good reviews—not always the case with Gerson's books—was *Daughter of Earth and Water: A Biography of Mary Wollstonecraft Shelley* (1973). Gerson was always careful to select a subject who would appeal to an audience and had not been "overdone." This novel, described by critic Susan Brownmiller as "well paced," was ahead of the developing interest in Mary Shelley.

Perhaps in an attempt to disguise the seemingly incredible number of books he was producing, Gerson wrote under a number of pseudonyms, including Michael Burgess, Ann Marie Burgess, Paul Lewis, Leon Phillips, and Carter A. Vaughan. Under the pseudonym Samuel Edwards he wrote *The Naked Maja* (1959), a biographical novel about the artist Francisco Goya and his lover the duchess of Alba, who was his subject for a number of portraits and sketches. The novel was made into a film with the same title by MGM, starring Anthony Franciosa and Ava Gardner. Again under the name Edwards, Gerson wrote the novel *55 Days at Peking* (1963), based on the screenplay by Philip Yordan and Bernard Gordon. Gerson also wrote the Wagons West series under the name of Dana Fuller Ross and the White Indian series under the name Donald Clayton Porter. Both series are for juvenile readers.

Gerson married Cynthia Ann Vautier; they had one child. His second wife was Marilyn Allen Hammond. After he left Chicago, he lived in New York City and later in Clinton, Connecticut. He moved to Boca Raton, Florida, where he died.

Gerson wrote 325 books. Although not highly regarded by the critics, he was popular with his readers, who expected a good story, engaging characters, and some historical information—and they were not disappointed. Ranging from the contemporary novel to the historical novel, from the biographical novel to biography and even the western, Gerson appealed to a wide audience.

• Gerson's manuscripts and correspondence are in the Mugar Library, Boston University. The entry in *Something about the Author* (1981) provides biographical information as well as a list of his work, under all of his pseudonyms. Obituaries are in the *Chicago Tribune*, 24 Nov. 1988, and the *New York Times*, 23 Nov. 1988.

MARCIA B. DINNEEN

GERSTEN, Berta (1894–10 Sept. 1972), actress in American Yiddish theater, was born in Cracow, Poland, the daughter of Abraham Gerstein, a Hebrew teacher, and Mesha Timberg, a dressmaker. Gersten's name was also transliterated from the Yiddish as Bertha Gerstein. She came to the United States when she was three years old and was educated in New York public schools, attending through high school. She made her theatrical debut at the age of three, when one of her mother's customers cast her in a Yiddish vaudeville performance requiring a toddler. Gersten went on to perform frequently in the popular Yiddish vaudeville of the Lower East Side.

When as a teenager Gersten began acting in serious dramas, she appeared with the leading actors of the Jewish theater who were striving to transform immigrant audience interest from the popular to the literary, including Boris Tomashevsky at the National Theatre and Maurice Schwartz at the Yiddish Art Theatre. At Schwartz's Yiddish Art Theatre she appeared with many other notable performers, including Celia Adler and Ludwig Satz, performing on and off with this theater for over twenty years. Gersten also frequently played starring roles opposite her first husband, the renowned Yiddish actor Jacob Ben-Ami, the founder of the short-lived Jewish Art Theatre.

Gersten, who was often praised for her physical beauty, performed in Yiddish versions of foreign plays by Ibsen, such as *A Doll's House* (advertised in 1918 as *Nora*) and *Hedda Gabler*, Shakespeare, Strindberg, and Chekhov, as well as in many famous Yiddish dramas, including *Yoshe Kalb*, based on I. J. Singer's novel, Gordin's *God, Man, and Devil*, and *Mirele Efros* (also known as *The Jewish Queen Lear*). Among the many other Yiddish productions she appeared in were *Warsaw at Night* (1938), *Salvation* (1939), *Day of Judgment* (1941), and *Yosele the Nightingale* (1949). In 1939 Gersten starred in a Yiddish film version of the *Mirele Efros*, which was made in New York. Gersten was especially renowned for her portrayals of suffering matriarchal figures. Gersten performed throughout New York City, often playing in the boroughs outside of Manhattan. She also toured abroad, traveling to South America in 1949 and London in 1952.

Gersten's debut in an English-speaking role was in the 1954 Chicago production of *The World of Sholem Aleichem*, which also starred Jacob Ben-Ami. On 28 December 1954 she opened on Broadway in Clifford Odets's *The Flowering Peach*, a retelling of the story of Noah; Gersten played Noah's wife Esther opposite the renowned Yiddish actor Menashe Skulnik. Brooks Atkinson praised Gersten's performance: "Berta Gersten also contributes a notable performance. As Noah's wife, she plays with sardonic sharpness of speech, but with fortitude, patience and forgiveness as the matriarch of the race. She has stature and homely eloquence" (*New York Times*, 29 Dec. 1954). In a follow-up review, Atkinson was even more effusive in his praise of her performance: "Although Miss Gersten is comic, she acts with a magnetism that pulls the whole play together. Without her personal force to serve as contrast, Mr. Skulnik's Noah might get random and discursive" (*New York Times*, 9 Jan. 1955).

In 1963 Gersten played Sophie Tucker's mother in Steve Allen's Broadway musical *Sophie*. In 1959 she understudied Gertrude Berg for the Broadway production of *Majority of One*, and, when Berg fell ill, Gersten took over the national tour in 1962, starring with Sir Cedric Hardwicke. Gersten appeared in the film *The Benny Goodman Story* (1955). The Yiddish star also acted in teleplays for "Playhouse 90" and "Omnibus."

Gersten's second husband was Professor Irwin H. Fenn of Brooklyn Polytechnic Institute. She had a son, Albert Fenn, who was on the photography staff of *Life Magazine*. Gersten died in New York City.

• Information can be found in the Berta Gersten Clipping File in the Billy Rose Theatre Collection at the New York Public Library for the Performing Arts, Lincoln Center. Articles on Gersten can be found in Martin Banham, ed., *The Cambridge Guide to Theatre* (1995), and Don B. Wilmeth and Tice L. Miller, eds., *Cambridge Guide to American Theatre* (1993). General information on Gersten can also be found in David S. Lifson, *The Yiddish Theatre in America* (1965), and Nahma Sandrow, *Vagabond Stars: A World History of Yiddish Theater* (1977). An obituary is in *Variety Obituaries* (1988).

ALVIN GOLDFARB

GERSTER, Arpad Geyza Charles (22 Dec. 1848–11 Mar. 1923), surgeon and medical educator, was born in Kassa, Hungary (later Slovakia), the son of Nicholas Gerster, a master chandler, and Caroline Schmidt-Sándy. At age seventeen he graduated from the Kassa Gymnasium. Robert Ultzmann, a local medical student, drew his interest to medicine, and Gerster entered the University of Vienna in October 1866 to study for that profession. The noted Theodor Billroth was his professor of surgery. In March 1872 Gerster graduated with the degrees of doctor of medicine, master of obstetrics, and doctor of surgery.

Under the universal military service plan, Gerster began his tour in the Austro-Hungarian Army in October 1872. He was a second lieutenant and assistant surgeon in two units, including the Seventh Field Artillery Regiment, before his release in September 1873. Back home, he obtained an appointment as head of the pathology department of the Kassa city hospital.

Eager to seek his fortune in America, Gerster left for the United States in early 1874. En route to Bremen, Germany, he spent several days at Alfred Wilhelm Volkmann's clinic in Halle, learning the new Listerian methods of controlling wound infections. Sailing from Bremen on 21 February 1874, he met his future wife, Anna Barnard Wynne, an American from Cincinnati. They were married on 14 December 1875, and would have three sons.

Gerster arrived in New York City on 9 March 1874 with letters of introduction from Billroth and others; he visited a former classmate and a number of physicians in area hospitals. He settled in Brooklyn, where he took over the general practice of a German physician who was returning home. Two new physician friends, Ernst Krackowizer and Frederick Zinsser, referred him patients, and he assisted Krackowizer in surgery at German Hospital (later Lenox Hill) and in private cases. Through another friend, Gerster was appointed surgeon in a new outpatient department at St. Peter's Hospital.

Gerster's arrival brought to the New York medical community a pioneer exponent of Lister's new sterilizing methods during surgery. While credited with an early, if not the first, report of the use of these techniques, Gerster later modestly acknowledged that some of his New York colleagues had traveled abroad to learn Lister's antiseptic methods and had probably started using them about the same time.

In 1877 Gerster moved from Brooklyn to Manhattan, where he specialized in surgery for the balance of his career. Shortly after his relocation he became a member of the German Dispensary in October, and then surgical division chief in December. The next year he was appointed attending surgeon, and in 1880 he received a similar appointment at Mount Sinai Hospital, a relatively rare distinction for a gentile.

Gerster's surgical abilities were further recognized in 1882 when he became surgeon and professor of surgery in the New York Polyclinic Medical School and Hospital. Described in an 1889–1890 announcement as the "first school of graduates in medicine independent of an undergraduate college," its program attracted students from throughout the United States. Gerster profoundly influenced his students, and his teaching of antiseptic surgery was well received. An early pupil, William J. Mayo (cofounder of the Mayo Clinic), later acknowledged the important role that Gerster played in the dissemination of antiseptic principles in America. Mayo remembered Gerster as "a physician first, and a surgeon second, for he regarded the patient from the broad standpoint of general medicine rather than from the narrower standpoint of surgery" (Mayo, p. 583).

In 1888 Gerster published *Rules of Aseptic and Antiseptic Surgery*, in response to numerous requests. It was the first textbook on the revolutionary subject to appear in the United States and went through three editions before Gerster decided its message was no longer needed. The volume contained halftone illustrations (then relatively rare) made from the author's own photographic plates, a process he learned to illustrate the work.

Gerster held the Polyclinic chair until 1894, when he was made an emeritus professor. Two years later he became consulting surgeon at German Hospital. In 1902 he turned down a chair in surgery at the University of Budapest, saying that he had become "heart and soul an American." From 1910 until 1914 he served as professor of clinical surgery at the College of Physicians and Surgeons, Columbia University, after which he became consulting surgeon at Mount Sinai Hospital. His professional honors included the presidency of New York Surgical Society (1891) and the American Surgical Association (1911–1912). He was also a trustee of New York Academy of Medicine from 1916 until his death.

In surgery, Gerster was noted as a skillful operator who demanded his associates' attention and praised their achievements. Outside of surgery, he loved nature and was a trustee of Association for the Protection of the Adirondacks. His paintings, sketches, and engravings often featured outdoor scenes. A sister, Etelka, was a prominent opera singer, and he had a deep interest in classical music. He was also a bibliophile and a linguist. He died in New York City.

• Gerster published *Recollections of a New York Surgeon: An Autobiography* (1917) and more than eighty medical papers. The major appraisal of his career is William J. Mayo, "Arpad Geza Charles Gerster," *Surgery, Gynecology and Obstetrics* (Apr. 1925): 582–84. See also W. Morgan Hartshorn, ed., *History of the New York Polyclinic Medical School and Hospital* (1942). An obituary is in the *New York Times*, 12 Mar. 1923.

CLARK W. NELSON

GESCHWIND, Norman (8 Jan. 1926–4 Nov. 1984), neurologist and neuroscientist, was born in New York City, the son of Morris Geschwind and Hanna Ruth Blau. Geschwind lost his father when he was four; his mother raised him and his elder brother Irving, who also became a prominent medical researcher. Geschwind attended the Etz Chaim Yeshiva and then the Boys' High School in Brooklyn. At the age of sixteen he was admitted to Harvard College on a full scholarship, but he was soon drafted into the infantry during World War II. He returned to Harvard to receive an A.B. in 1947, magna cum laude, and an M.D. in 1951, cum laude. A Moseley Travelling Fellowship and then a U.S. Public Health Service Fellowship allowed him to spend three years with Sir Charles Symonds at the National Hospital in London. There he met Patricia Dougan, whom he married in 1956; they had three children.

In 1955 Geschwind returned to the United States as chief resident in Derek Denny-Brown's neurology department at Boston City Hospital. He was a research associate at the Massachusetts Institute of Technology from 1956 to 1958 and then joined Fred Quadfasel's department at the Boston Veterans Administration Hospital, serving there until 1966. He was appointed chairman of neurology at Boston University School of Medicine in 1966, James Jackson Putnam Professor at Harvard Medical School and director of the neurological unit at Boston City Hospital in 1969, and neurologist in chief at the Beth Israel Hospital when the Harvard department had to move out of Boston City Hospital in 1976. His interest in the psychological aspects of brain function started in high school and college but developed into a lifelong career under the influence of Symonds, Denny-Brown, and Quadfasel.

Although neurologists and psychiatrists were in fundamental agreement that the brain is the organ of mind and behavior, the period immediately following World War II witnessed a remarkable indifference to the scientific investigation of mind-brain interactions, especially in the clinical departments of American medical schools. The heritage of the great nineteenth-century European neurologists had not yet resurfaced from the devastation of the war. Psychiatric clinics were dominated by psychoanalytic theories that overlooked the role of the brain, and American neurology was turning into a routine medical subspecialty that treated the brain as an organ similar to the liver or heart, without making any concessions to its uniqueness as the site of thought, intellect, and emotion. Geschwind played a major role in changing this state of affairs: he developed a field known as "behavioral neurology," in which neurology, neuroscience, psychology, and psychiatry converged to explore the relationships between mind and brain. In the 1960s there were hardly any behavioral neurologists in the United States, but by his death hundreds listed this field as their specialty, and many among these pointed to Geschwind as their teacher or as their teacher's teacher.

In "Disconnexion Syndromes" (*Brain* 88 [1965]: 237–94, 585–644) Geschwind offered a scientific explanation for many complex behavioral deficits that result from localized brain damage. He showed that the information processing necessary for language, perceptual recognition, and mentally guided motor acts requires orderly connections from one area of the brain to another. The disruption of these connections (rather than the destruction of dedicated centers) results in the behavioral disorders known as aphasia, apraxia, and agnosia. This review, based on his personal observations as a neurologist, a survey of the literature on pertinent animal experiments, and his readings of the European researchers Dejerine, Wernicke, Liepmann, and Goldstein, represents a milestone in the post–World War II development of behavioral neurology and in the related reinvigoration of neuropsychiatry and neuropsychology.

Geschwind's subsequent work emphasized the neurological foundations of cerebral dominance, learning disabilities, and psychiatric disorders. He showed (with Walter Levitsky) that brain regions specialized for language tend to be larger in the left side of the brain than in the right. This finding, consistent with the known left-hemisphere dominance for language, rekindled an interest in investigating the biology of distinctly human functions such as language. His clinical lectures and papers on temporal lobe epilepsy helped to show how a neurological disruption of the limbic system in the human brain can lead to psychiatric symptoms. During the last years of his life, Geschwind was intensely preoccupied with an ambitious monograph synthesizing diverse interactions among brain asymmetry, autoimmunity, and sex hormones. He suggested that testosterone inhibits certain aspects of brain development and immune responses. He thought that this relationship helped to explain why males are more vulnerable to learning disabilities, why females are more prone to autoimmune disorders, and also why immune disorders, left-handedness, and dyslexia may tend to cluster with each other. He died before he had a chance to refine this theory, which remains the least established of his contributions.

Geschwind started to teach and write at a time when the assumption that the brain was also the organ of the mind was neither rejected nor espoused, but just ignored. His work rekindled an interest in this area at a time when powerful tools were becoming available for studying the structure and physiology of the brain. When he died suddenly from a massive heart attack in Boston, unraveling the inextricable relationship between brain and mental function had become one of the most exciting fields of research. He was one of the most charismatic and enthusiastic orchestrators of this transformation.

• Geschwind's most significant articles are collected in his *Selected Papers on Language and the Brain* (1974). See also O. Devinsky and S. C. Schachter, *Norman Geschwind: Selected Publications on Language, Behavior and Epilepsy* (1997). An obituary by M.-M. Mesulam is in *Annals of Neurology* 18 (1985): 98–100.

M.-MARSEL MESULAM

GESELL, Arnold Lucius (21 June 1880–29 May 1961), psychologist and pediatrician, was born in Alma, Wisconsin, the son of Gerhard Gesell, a photographer, and Christine Giesen, a teacher. After graduating from Stevens Point State Normal School in 1899, he studied under Frederick Jackson Turner at the University of Wisconsin (B.Ph., 1903), where he devoted his commencement oration to the problem of child labor. He then taught high school in Stevens Point (1898–1901) and was a principal in Chippewa Falls (1903–1904). Next Gesell followed the example of his normal school psychology instructor and enrolled in Clark University's Department of Psychology, where he began a lifelong friendship with fellow student Lewis Terman and was deeply influenced by G. Stanley Hall's child study movement.

Gesell's dissertation (Ph.D., 1906) analyzed jealousy in animals and humans from a Darwinian perspective, drawing upon novels, philosophical accounts, and questionnaire responses from young women at two normal schools. It also offered a "pedagogy of control" for parents whose children showed an excess of the jealous instinct: "Develop in your children a robust spirit of self-worth . . . let them have a hobby . . . [as] a haven of consolation, when buffeted by rivalry . . . [so that they may] say after reflection, 'I am glad to be myself.'" This philosophy, that maturation could be aided by a thoughtfully engineered environment, became Gesell's message to the world.

After finishing at Clark, Gesell moved to New York, where he taught elementary school at night and lived at the East Side Settlement House. There he was inspired by Edmond Kelly and Edith Kelly, whose anti-aristocratic temperament and evolutionary socialism resonated with the republican and humanitarian values Gesell had learned from his parents.

With the help of Lewis Terman, Gesell obtained a professorship at Los Angeles State Normal School (Jan. 1908), where he married fellow teacher Beatrice Chandler in 1909. They wrote *The Normal Child and Primary Education* (1912) and had two children. To study intelligence testing Gesell visited the Vineland Training School in New Jersey in 1909 and began a long friendship and collaboration with its director Henry H. Goddard. Returning to Los Angeles State, he decided to seek a medical degree. He studied at the University of Wisconsin (1910–1911), then Yale University (M.D., 1915), where he taught part-time in the Department of Education. Shortly after arriving at Yale he obtained a room at the New Haven Dispensary, where he examined children with developmental,

learning, and discipline problems. Calling his room a "psycho-clinic," he began to offer advice to parents and social agencies.

As the country's schools coped with an increased immigrant population, a number of states saw the need for an expert to coordinate intelligence testing and the handling of low-scoring children. In 1915 Gesell accepted such a position in Connecticut, while continuing to teach part-time at Yale. After a two-year sabbatical recovering from tuberculosis, he provided psychological services to the Connecticut Board of Education and the New Haven schools. In 1918 he used an offer from California to induce Yale to convert his professorship (in child hygiene) to a full-time position. Meanwhile, he consulted to the management of a local rubber plant and was a founding member of the American Association of Clinical Psychology.

While continuing to work with problem children, Gesell next adopted a research subject that would transform his career: the normal, preschool child. Before the war he had called for public hygiene campaigns to be extended to schools, using a preventive approach grounded in research on normal development. Then, in 1919, he brought a small group of preschoolers into his clinic and began to record their abilities at ten stages of growth. While collecting this data, Gesell argued for a national system of nursery schools and kindergartens employing experts in "child development"—a biomedical version of child psychology. In his progressivist vision, such expertise would add social control to the chaotic school system and safeguard the mental health of the individual child.

As Gesell explained in *School and Society* (1921, pp. 559–64; 1924, pp. 644–52), preschoolers needed to be placed under "medical oversight and educational observation" in kindergartens that would function as "a kind of Ellis Island" for elementary schools. Aligning himself with children's bureaus and illness prevention campaigns, Gesell warned that the malleability of the child's personality required vigilance by both parents and teachers. "Mental hygiene, like charity, begins at home. But it does not end there," he cautioned. Preschools should educate parents in child rearing and offer children an individualized experience "to help strengthen the home and make up for its deficiencies."

Although his research population remained small and ethnically narrow, Gesell increased the authority of his developmental norms by using motion pictures as illustrations. Inspired by Frank Gilbreth's time motion studies, Gesell's film research began with his helping produce and direct a Pathé newsreel of the Yale clinic in 1923. Characteristically, he gained international fame as a filmmaker without acknowledging work that preceded (John B. Watson's) or was contemporary with (Myrtle McGraw's) his own. From 1930 to 1948 selected babies and mothers were filmed while living in a photographic dome at Yale, creating a scientific version of the silent-era film *Baby's Day*.

In 1925 Gesell was a prominent member of the National Research Council's First Conference on Research in Child Development, having recently published *The Preschool Child from the Standpoint of Public Hygiene and Education* (1923) and *The Mental Growth of the Pre-School Child* (1925). A year later the Laura Spelman Rockefeller Foundation awarded him funds for a new building, more film studies, and a staff of twelve. In 1930 his Yale Clinic of Child Development moved to a wing of the university's Institute for Human Relations (IHR). There Gesell occupied elegant quarters and presided over a staff of thirty-one, which he kept isolated from the IHR's multidisciplinary, neo-Freudian research. With the demise of the IHR in 1940, the clinic was absorbed by the medical school, requiring it to shed its psychologists.

Gesell's widest recognition came from two bestselling guides to child rearing written with Frances Ilg, *Infant and Child in the Culture of Today* (1943) and *The Child from Five to Ten* (1946). In each, behavioral norms for various ages were personified in aphorisms such as "The 3 year old listens well when he is reasoned with"; "FOUR rambles. FIVE knows how to stop"; and "Praise is an elixir to SIX, but correction is a poison."

Upon Gesell's retirement from Yale in 1948, his clinic was disbanded, and staff dispersed. Some stayed and organized the Gesell Institute of Child Development in 1950, with which Gesell was affiliated until his death in New Haven.

In his manners Gesell was formal; some complained of his refusal to answer criticism or provide reasons for his methods. He was known for his "power to attract able, almost fanatically devoted disciples." Gesell possessed superior mechanical abilities and showed a lifelong interest in technology. These qualities and his great attention to detail can be seen in the efficient, simply designed, and meticulously described apparatus he used to assess children. His writing was similar to his deportment: confident, dramatic, and without qualification or compromise. Some criticized its "Olympian" tone and his "preference for long words compounded in the Teutonic manner" (Cedric Fowler, *New Outlook* 165 [1935]: 35). In self-portrayals Gesell adopted a form of autobiographical maturationism, implying that his career unfolded in a benevolent institutional environment, without struggle or ambition.

The issue of Gesell's contributions has been a contentious one within the general field of psychology. Between the two world wars, his work gave a maturationist emphasis to developmental psychology. After his death, critics depicted the years of his greatest influence as the Dark Ages of developmental psychology. Thus Boyd McCandless said that "not until the 1940s did a group of Young Turks . . . come to consider Gesell only as a recorder of norms, neatly labelled and classified but without the explanatory power that is psychology's central issue"; worse, "the harm that has been done by the trusting employment of the [Gesell Developmental Schedules] is incalculable" (pp. 157–58). Others praised Gesell's sensitivity to both maturation and environment, seeing him as "an ethologist of human behavior" and a "sober and reflective

man, innocent of prejudice" (Kessen, p. 211), who was unfortunate to live in a behaviorist era. More recently, Gesell has been recognized as a theorist who anticipated Jean Piaget and Eleanor Gibson. Although pediatricians never claimed any of his developmental tests as their own, modern screening tests borrow freely from the Gesell scales, and *Developmental Diagnosis* (1941) is his most frequently cited work.

• Gesell's papers at the Library of Congress are extensive and comprehensive; they include a chronology of his publications, lectures, and clinic staffing. See also the Laura Spelman Rockefeller Foundation Papers and General Education Board Papers, Rockefeller Archives Center, Pocantico Hills, N.Y. Most of Gesell's films, including outtakes, have been deposited in the Child Development Film Archives at the University of Akron. For background on Gesell's childhood, the State Historical Society of Wisconsin has his father's photographic collection; see also Gesell's eugenical analysis of his hometown, "The Village of a Thousand Souls," *American Magazine*, Oct. 1913, pp. 11–16. Walter R. Miles's entry on Gesell in *Biographical Memoirs, National Academy of Sciences* 37 (1964): 55–96 contains a bibliography and is the best biographical source, although it is uncritical and derivative of Gesell's own essay in *A History of Psychology in Autobiography*, ed. Edwin G. Boring et al., vol. 4 (1952). Psychologists' different perspectives are represented in William Kessen, *The Child* (1965); Boyd McCandless's article on Gesell in *International Encyclopedia of the Social Sciences*, ed. David L. Sills (1968); Esther Thelen and Karen E. Adolph, "Arnold L. Gesell: The Paradox of Nature and Nurture," *Developmental Psychology* 28 (1992): 368–80; and the oral histories summarized in Milton J. E. Senn, *Insights on the Child Development Movement in the United States* (1975). Gesell's intellectual roots, popular writing, and foundation support are illuminated in Steven L. Schlossman, "Before Home Start: Notes toward a History of Parent Education in America, 1897–1929," *Harvard Educational Review* 46 (1976): 436–67; Dorothy Ross, *G. Stanley Hall: The Psychologist as Prophet* (1972); and Hamilton Cravens, "Child Saving in the Age of Professionalism," in *American Childhood: A Research Guide and Handbook,* ed. Joseph M. Hawes and N. Ray Hiner (1985). An obituary is in the *New York Times*, 30 May 1961.

BENJAMIN HARRIS

GESELL, Gerhard Ansel (16 June 1910–19 Feb. 1993), federal judge, was born in Los Angeles, California, the son of Arnold L. Gesell, a physician and founder of the Gesell Institute of Child Psychology, and Beatrice Chandler, a teacher. He was educated at Phillips Andover Academy and received his bachelor's degree (1932) and law degree (1935) from Yale University.

Gesell began his career in 1935 as an attorney for the newly formed Securities and Exchange Commission (SEC). He quickly became an advocate for vigorous enforcement of the securities laws and is widely recognized for helping mold the SEC into a strong regulatory agency. SEC Chairman William O. Douglas, recognizing Gesell's ability, placed him in charge of a major investigation of the New York Stock Exchange and its past president, J. P. Morgan broker Richard Whitney. Only twenty-eight years old when he took on this investigation, Gesell earned frequent comparisons to the young David battling the Goliaths of industry and the stock market. The investigation led to Whitney's guilty plea for misappropriating clients' securities and prompted significant reforms at the New York Stock Exchange. In 1940 Gesell headed the SEC's investigation of the insurance industry in hearings before the Temporary National Economic Committee of Congress.

While at the SEC, Gesell greatly impressed Dean Acheson, who had represented the New York Stock Exchange during Gesell's investigation. In 1940 Acheson recruited Gesell to join him as a partner at Covington & Burling, a prominent Washington, D.C., law firm. When Acheson left the firm for the State Department, Gesell took over Acheson's business for one of the firm's largest clients, E. I. Du Pont de Nemours & Company. He successfully defended Du Pont in a significant antitrust case involving an alleged monopoly of cellophane. When Gesell argued the case before the Supreme Court in October 1955, he handed physical exhibits to the justices to demonstrate the availability of substitute packaging materials. This unusual act, characteristic of Gesell's penchant for the importance of facts, demonstrated how his true love was trial work, not the more academic appellate advocacy. Gesell's work at Covington & Burling, representing Du Pont, General Electric, the *Washington Post*, and others, enhanced his reputation as a trial lawyer and gained him renown as a corporate adviser. In 1954 he advised the *Washington Post* in its acquisition of the rival *Washington Times-Herald*, and in the early 1960s he successfully defended the National Football League in an antitrust action brought by the American Football League. Gesell was also active in Democratic politics in the 1950s and 1960s, serving on the Democratic Central Committee and campaigning actively for Adlai Stevenson in 1956.

In 1945–1946, during the administration of President Harry S. Truman, Gesell had worked with former Attorney General William D. Mitchell on the Joint Congressional Committee investigation into the Pearl Harbor bombing. In 1962 President John F. Kennedy appointed him as chair of the Commission for Equal Opportunity in the Armed Forces. Gesell was a forceful advocate of civil rights in that position, and the commission had lasting influence, integrating military housing and the state National Guards. Gesell was active in community and in alumni organizations, serving as president of the Yale Law School Alumni Association, chair of the board of St. Alban's School in Washington, member of the board of Children's Hospital in Washington, fellow of the American Law Institute, and member of the Lawyers Committee for Civil Rights Under Law. In 1967 the Yale Law School issued him the Citation of Merit, its highest honor for graduates.

In 1967 President Lyndon B. Johnson appointed Gesell to the U.S. District Court for the District of Columbia. He received the American Bar Association's highest rating, and the following commendation from a *Washington Post* editorial (2 Dec. 1967): "His extensive experience in the courtroom, his brilliant legal mind, and his capacity to see all sides of a controversy are precisely the qualities most sought in nominees to the bench." Gesell had a clear vision of the judge's role as a manager as much as a trier of facts, and he combined these roles to become one of the great trial judges in American history.

Owing to both the luck of the draw and the esteem of the District's chief judges, Gesell was able to demonstrate his skill in some of the most significant cases of the twentieth century. An early example of Gesell's judicial boldness was his controversial 1969 decision to strike down the District of Columbia's abortion statute, on grounds of privacy and liberty that the Supreme Court later endorsed in *Roe v. Wade* (1973).

In 1970 Gesell presided over another matter of national significance: the Pentagon Papers case. The *Washington Post* and the *New York Times* had gained access to top-secret documents on U.S. involvement in Vietnam. The Attorney General filed actions against both newspapers to restrain publication, arguing that it would compromise national security. Drawing the case on a Friday afternoon, Gesell refused the government's request, but the Court of Appeals granted a temporary stay of publication and ordered Gesell to hold hearings on Monday. To the consternation of the government, Gesell reviewed the top-secret papers at his home over the weekend, storing them under his sofa pillow at night. He concluded after hearings that there was no national security justification that overrode the First Amendment interest in freedom of the press. Ultimately, the Supreme Court upheld Gesell's view of the law, but he was the only judge of any court—including twenty-nine judges total in both the District of Columbia courts and the Southern District of New York—to refuse to place any prior restraint on publication.

The Pentagon Papers controversy (June–July 1970) eventually led to Gesell's next highly publicized assignment. White House officials intent on retaliation against Daniel Ellsberg, who had leaked the Pentagon Papers, ordered a break-in of his psychiatrist's office to seek incriminating information. Gesell presided over the 1974 trial of the men involved in that break-in and other Watergate conspirators, including John Ehrlichman, Charles Colson, and G. Gordon Liddy. In related actions, Gesell held that President Richard M. Nixon's dismissal of Watergate Special Prosecutor Archibald Cox was illegal; threatened President Nixon with contempt of court for refusing to disclose information requested for the defense of the Watergate conspirators; and restrained Watergate special prosecutor Leon Jaworski from talking to the press about the ongoing trials.

In 1989 Gesell presided over the trial and conviction of Lieutenant Colonel Oliver North in the Iran-Contra affair. This responsibility drew him again into the spotlight and revived public attention to his no-nonsense manner and booming voice, which made him a thundering presence in the courtroom. Always in chambers by 7:00 A.M., Gesell was invariably prepared and thoroughly familiar with the cases before him, and he demanded that lawyers be the same. It was for these qualities, as well as his historic trials and legal rulings, and for his contributions to court management and judicial training, that fellow judges honored Gesell in 1990 with the Edward J. Devitt Distinguished Service to Justice Award.

Gesell lived with his wife, Marion Holliday Pike "Peggy" Gesell, whom he married in 1936, in one of the oldest row houses in the historic Georgetown neighborhood in Washington; they had two children. He was an amateur beekeeper at his farm in Loudoun County, Virginia, and raised vegetables at his summer home on North Haven island in Maine. Gesell trained and inspired twenty-five law clerks, for whom he remained a mentor as they went to positions in government, academia, and private practice of law. He died in Washington, D.C.

• Gesell's papers are at the Library of Congress. The collection includes copies of his unpublished memoirs, titled "My 'Jealous Mistress,'" which provides a delightful account of his legal practice and judicial service. All of his significant judicial opinions are published in the *Federal Reporter*. His training videotape on case management, recorded 22 Jan. 1985, is available from the Federal Judicial Center. Gesell also authored a book on the development and operations of the SEC, *Protecting Your Dollars* (1940). Obituaries are in the *Washington Post* and the *New York Times*, both 21 Feb. 1993.

WILLIAM H. JEFFRESS, JR.
DOROTHY AMES JEFFRESS

GESTEFELD, Ursula Newell (22 Apr. 1845–22 Oct. 1921), metaphysical writer and lecturer, was born in Augusta, Maine. Few details are known of her early life. She spent most of her career in Chicago.

Apparently not plagued by poverty, Gestefeld's childhood household seemed preoccupied with illness. Ursula, like her mother a chronically sickly person, was given little hope of living beyond childhood. Yet, like so many eventually affiliated with New Thought and Christian Science, Gestefeld healed herself through "mind cure," a term that emerged in the United States partly to describe the pioneering work of visionary farmer and healer Phineas Quimby in the 1860s in Gestefeld's home state of Maine. Achieving health and happiness was a constant struggle for the Newells and later for Gestefeld. Her marriage to German-American newspaper editor Theodore Gestefeld in the late 1860s and the strain of bearing and raising four children eventually led her to seek solace in the Church of Christ, Scientist.

In 1884, at age thirty-nine, Gestefeld read Mary Baker Eddy's *Science and Health with Key to the Scriptures* and joined her first instructional class in Chicago. She quickly became an avid adherent to Eddy's message, and Eddy made her a leader in the burgeoning Christian Science movement of the 1880s. Gestefeld's talents as a writer initially fostered Eddy's fast-growing movement. Yet her relation with Eddy was tenuous.

Like people such as Emma Curtis Hopkins, who would become important to New Thought and other metaphysical groups, Gestefeld could not be held within the increasingly authoritarian structure of Eddy's church. By 1888 Gestefeld's talents as a writer and the autonomy from Eddy that she demonstrated in instructional texts such as *Ursula N. Gestefeld's Statement of Christian Science* (1888) and *The Science of the Christ* (1889) fostered a rift and break from Eddy. Eddy ordered George Day, the pastor of the Chicago church, to expel Gestefeld in 1888. After her expulsion, Gestefeld dedicated her life to developing and spreading her own message in writing and speeches and emerged as a leader in the rapidly developing popular religious movement known as New Thought. Gestefeld revealed a strong aversion to the great emphasis on negativism that seemed to pervade Christian Science as well as to the authoritarian control that institutions and individuals could bring to bear over others.

Although it is unclear whether Gestefeld ever joined any of the organizations of the woman's movement, in her writing she found both personal liberation and a sounding board for her feminist views. Like the New Thought movement more generally, she was explicitly apolitical but appealed especially to women and had a general interest in improving society by stamping out ignorance. In two novels, *The Woman Who Dares* (1892) and *The Leprosy of Miriam* (1894), Gestefeld fashioned female characters who overcame the strictures of male-dominated society and became women of strength, courage, and action who reshaped the world around them. Gestefeld also contributed the Deuteronomy chapter to the *Woman's Bible* (2 vols., 1895, 1898), a project directed by Elizabeth Cady Stanton and intended to provide a reinterpretation of the Bible from an egalitarian feminist perspective. It provoked great controversy both in the population at large and among feminists, including the leadership of Stanton's own National Woman's Suffrage Association, which disowned the text.

In her self-help writings, Gestefeld focused on practical methods to make one's life happier, richer, and fuller. Like other emerging New Thought writers of her day, she developed a holistic approach, moving away from a primary emphasis on healing physical ailments. She began calling her message the "Science of Being" and articulated it in writing and in classes for decades in the United States and eventually in Great Britain. To help spread her message and to train others to spread it, Gestefeld also founded in the 1890s the Exodus Club, which was an incorporated church-like organization based in Chicago. Like many New Thought teachers of her day, she also established a "center," calling hers in about 1897 the College of the Science of Being. Her monthly magazine, the *Exodus*, appeared sporadically through 1904 and was one of dozens of national New Thought periodicals to spring up around the end of the century. Her teachings and writings reflected Gestefeld's life of crises and illnesses overcome. Two of her most popular titles during this period were *How We Master Our Fate* (1897) and *How to Control Circumstances* (1901). Gestefeld's institutions were completely nonsectarian, and no member or participant had to make a profession of faith or accept any belief that contradicted his or her sense of reason. One became a member of Exodus for a $25 annual fee for which one could receive written or live instruction from Gestefeld at a lower rate and also be invited to special gatherings and cultural events sponsored by the club. According to an account in *Mind* in January 1902, Gestefeld's Exodus Club had a membership of about three hundred and "a congregation of from five to eight hundred persons."

Yet, like other New Thoughters of her day, Gestefeld's publications brought her much broader influence and fame than did the intimate congregation and club that she had started in Chicago. Through the *Exodus*, her books, and the exposure she received in other New Thought periodicals such as *Mind*, Gestefeld and her ideas came to be known to many thousands of American and British readers, most especially female readers. Perhaps her most important text was the fully polished articulation of her Science of Being, *The Builder and the Plan* (1901). Several of her books were published by the Gestefeld Publishing Company of Pelham, New York, headed by her son Harry Gestefeld.

Readers recognized Gestefeld as a leading light in the national and international New Thought movement. She also played a leading role in several loose-knit national organizations associated with New Thought, including the International Metaphysical League, which she addressed at its first convention in Boston in 1899, and the New Thought Federation, which became the International New Thought Alliance. Gestefeld had also been present at a meeting of the New Thought Federation during the 1904 St. Louis World's Fair that many New Thoughters had hoped would mark the beginning of a stronger institutional program. The turnout was disappointing, but Gestefeld delivered a well-attended speech, "Curing and Healing," in St. Louis.

Although institutional New Thought never quite hit its stride, Gestefeld was typical of other New Thought writers and lecturers who found great personal success. She built her own institutions, including the Science of Being centers in England and the Exodus Club, which became the Church of New Thought in 1904. Gestefeld continued to write and lecture until shortly before her death by toxemia in Kenosha, Wisconsin. Her message spread both in the United States and in Britain, where at least two Gestefeld-related Science of Being centers had been established by the 1920s. While her church did not continue for long after her death, her books continued to be popular in New Thought circles at least into the 1940s.

• For a nearly complete list of book-length published works by Gestefeld, see Charles Braden, *Spirits in Rebellion: The Rise and Development of New Thought* (1963). The text of Braden's work also includes numerous references to Gestefeld's life and career. See also the full treatment by Beryl Satter, "New Thought and the Era of Woman, 1875–1895" (Ph.D. diss., Columbia Univ., 1994), and Catherine Jean Tumber, "A Politics of the Higher Self: Feminism, Progressivism, and Psychotherapeutics, 1875–1900" (Ph.D. diss., Univ. of Rochester, 1992), which includes some useful analysis of Gestefeld. An article by Charles Brodie Patterson, "Ursula N. Gestefeld: A Biographic Sketch," *Mind*, Jan. 1902, is elementary and general but of some use as a reflection of how Gestefeld was viewed in New Thought circles on the eve of that movement's heyday. Similar articles from the period appear in *Arena*, Dec. 1892, and *Catholic World*, Jan. 1893. A short obituary is in the *New York Times*, 25 Oct. 1921.

CLAY BAILEY

GETCHELL, Edith Loring Peirce (25 Jan. 1855–18 Sept. 1940), painter and etcher, was born in Bristol, Pennsylvania, the daughter of Unitarians Joseph S. Peirce, a well-to-do candle manufacturer and politician, and Ann Moore. Peirce's parents sent her in 1874 to study art with Peter Moran at the Philadelphia School of Design for Women, where she specialized in textile design. Returning to Bristol after three years at the school, Peirce designed textiles for Livingston Mills.

Desiring a career as a painter, she studied in New York in the early 1880s with William Sartain and R. Swain Gifford. In Philadelphia she studied painting with Thomas Eakins at the Pennsylvania Academy of the Fine Arts from 1882 to 1884 and joined Gabrielle DeVaux Clements and Blanche Dillaye to study etching with Stephen Parrish in his studio in 1883 and 1884. Peirce set up a studio of her own in Philadelphia in 1883. The next year she made a study tour of Europe.

In April 1885 Peirce married Dr. Albert C. Getchell, a graduate of Philadelphia's Jefferson Medical School who worked in the Worcester, Massachusetts, City Hospital; they were to have two children. Joining him in Worcester, she established a studio and became active in the city's art community. She was a founder of the Worcester Museum of Art and the Worcester Women's Club, was active for fifty years in the Worcester Shakespeare Society, and was a life member of the American Unitarian Association.

Becoming well-known for her etchings as well as her paintings, Peirce Getchell's prints were selected several times for publication by Frederick Keppel of New York, W. K. Vickery of San Francisco, Robert M. Lindsay of Philadelphia, and the Philadelphia Art Union. Her *Solitude* was included in the New York Etching Club's deluxe portfolio, *Twenty Original American Etchings*, in 1885. Cassell & Co. used etchings from that publication in *Gems of the American Etchers*, which they published later that year. The New York Etching Club published *A Souvenir—The Old South Church, Worcester* in its 1888 exhibition catalog, and her *Path to the Wreck* was one of two original etchings used to illustrate the Union League Club version of the *Women Etchers of America* exhibition catalog in 1888. She exhibited fifty-nine impressions in that show.

Getchell exhibited in shows at the National Academy of Design, the Pennsylvania Academy of the Fine Arts, the Philadelphia School of Design for Women, the Philadelphia Society of Artists, the Paris Salon, the American Water Color Society, the Boston Museum of

Fine Arts, London's Royal Society of Painter-Etchers, the Boston Art Club, and the New York Etching Club and at the Williams & Everett Gallery in Boston and the Galerie Durand-Ruel in Paris with Mary Cassatt and Stephen Parrish. She exhibited as well at the 1888 Ohio Valley Centennial Exposition, the 1893 World's Columbian Exposition in Chicago, the 1904 Louisiana Purchase Exposition in St. Louis, and the 1915 Panama-Pacific Exposition in San Francisco. Other exhibitions in the twentieth century included those of the Boston Water Color Club, the Chicago and California Societies of Etchers, Albert Roullier's Art Galleries in Boston, and the Worcester Art Museum, which held a solo exhibition of Getchell's etchings in 1908 and featured her work in its 1912 *Exhibition of American Etchings*.

Along with Mary Nimmo Moran, Getchell was one of the two women members of the New York Etching Club. She was also a member of the Philadelphia Society of Artists, the Philadelphia Sketch Club, and the Chicago and California Societies of Etchers.

Also like Moran and the other prominent artists of the 1880s etching revival, Getchell was primarily a landscape etcher and painter. She painted in watercolor and oil directly from nature. For her etchings, she translated the watercolor into black and white, experimenting with drypoint and using linear, acid biting, and inking techniques to achieve painterly effects. Getchell's work is praised by Will Jenkins in *Modern Etchings and Engravings: Special Summer Number of "The Studio"* (1902) for its "brilliant use of line," vigor, originality, and beautiful atmospheric qualities, which she achieved experimenting with retroussage in which she carefully wiped ink across the plate. The wide range of tones in her etchings creates quiet, somber landscapes that provoke thought about the mysteries of nature. An unidentified author in Sylvester Koehler's *Gems of American Etchers* describes her *Solitude* as "the highest achievement of landscape to work thus upon the feelings—an achievement which lifts it from the mere reproduction of outward forms to the level of lyrical poetry."

Of the more than seventy active women etchers in the 1880s, Peirce Getchell was one of the few who married. Despite her commitment to her family she built a career in landscape painting and etching for which she was known nationally. Getchell died at her home in Worcester.

• A few newspaper clippings and exhibition catalogs on Getchell are in the Worcester Historical Museum and the Worcester Public Library. Her etchings are in collections at the Worcester Art Museum, the Boston Museum of Fine Art, and the Library of Congress. The Worcester Art Museum has the largest collection of her paintings. See also Worcester Art Museum, *Exhibition of Etchings by Edith Loring Getchell, December 5 to December 14, Nineteen Hundred and Eight*. Phyllis Peet, *The Emergence of American Women Printmakers in the Late Nineteenth Century* (Ph.D. diss., Univ. of California at Los Angeles, 1987) and *American Women of the Etching Revival* (1988), are the most thorough sources. An obituary is in the *New York Times*, 19 Sept. 1940.

PHYLLIS PEET

GETTY, George Washington (2 Oct. 1819–1 Oct. 1901), soldier, was born in Georgetown, District of Columbia, the son of Robert Getty and Margaret Wilmot. Entering the U.S. Military Academy at West Point at the age of sixteen, he was a classmate of William T. Sherman and George H. Thomas. He graduated fifteenth in the 42-man class of 1840 and was commissioned a second lieutenant in the Fourth Artillery. Five years later he was promoted to first lieutenant. In the Mexican War, Getty was assigned to General Winfield Scott's army, which landed at Veracruz and advanced inland to Mexico City. Getty took part in the battles of Contreras, Molino del Rey, and Chapultepec and received the brevet rank of captain for gallant conduct.

In Staunton, Virginia, shortly after his return from the war, Getty married Elizabeth Graham Stevenson. (No record exists of any children.) The next year he was off to war again, this time against the Seminoles in Florida, where he served for two years. In 1853 he received regular (not brevet) promotion to captain (still in the Fourth Artillery), and in 1856 it was back to Florida for another two-year stint fighting the Seminoles.

When the Civil War broke out, Getty was stationed at Fort Randall, Dakota Territory. On 14 May 1861 he was transferred to the Fifth Artillery and for a time was stationed at Fort Monroe, on the end of the Virginia Peninsula. On 28 September he was commissioned lieutenant colonel of volunteers. That fall he served as chief of artillery to General Joseph Hooker's division, deployed along the Lower Potomac. In the Peninsula campaign the following spring, he commanded a four-battery brigade of the artillery reserve in the siege of Yorktown and the battles of Gaines' Mill and Malvern Hill. When Confederate general Robert E. Lee invaded Maryland that fall, Getty was involved in the resulting battles of South Mountain and Antietam, where he served as chief of artillery for General Ambrose Burnside's IX Corps. Union artillery performed well at Antietam, prompting their opposite numbers in the Confederate army, their chief targets, to dub the battle "artillery hell." Getty was recognized for his part in this success with promotion to brigadier general of volunteers on 25 September 1862, just eight days after the battle. The next month he took command of one of the infantry divisions of the IX Corps, which he led at the battle of Fredericksburg, 13 December 1862.

In March 1863 Getty was transferred to Suffolk, on the southeastern Virginia coast, where he commanded a division of the VII Corps. The line he held defended the crucial southern approaches to Norfolk and Hampton Roads. In April Confederate forces under General James Longstreet attacked the Suffolk line and then initiated siege operations. Getty performed well throughout the campaign. On 19 April he personally led a successful counterattack against the Confederate siege works, known as Battery Huger. For this service he received a brevet promotion in the regular army. In early May Lee recalled Longstreet to northern Virginia, breaking off the siege of Suffolk. Thereafter, Getty spent several weeks directing the construction of a line of fortifications to cover Norfolk and Portsmouth. Then, with Lee's army far to the north on its summer 1863 invasion of Pennsylvania, Getty led a raid against Confederate supply and communications installations in the vicinity of the South Anna River, creating considerable consternation in Richmond. On 1 August 1863 he was promoted to the regular army rank of major of the Fifth artillery, though he continued to serve in his volunteer rank of brigadier general.

In January 1864 Getty was back with the Army of the Potomac, this time as inspector general. On 25 March he was given command of a division of the VI Corps. On 4 May the Army of the Potomac crossed the Rapidan to open its final campaign against Lee and within hours was engaged in fierce battle in an area known as the Wilderness. In the opening stages of the battle, Getty trotted back and forth with his mounted staff officers across a narrow forest road to create the appearance of cavalry and bluff the enemy into delaying assault until his division was in position. On the second day of the battle, 6 May, he was severely wounded.

By 28 June Getty was back in command of his division, now entrenched before Petersburg, Virginia, in a siege that was already two weeks old. In July Grant ordered the VI Corps north to Washington to counter a Confederate move by troops under General Jubal A. Early. Having accomplished this mission, it then became part of General Philip Sheridan's Army of the Shenandoah. Sheridan launched a campaign aimed at disposing of Early and the Shenandoah Valley itself once and for all. In the fighting that followed, Getty won a brevet in the volunteer service for his gallantry at the battles of Third Winchester and Fisher's Hill. At Cedar Creek, 19 October 1864, when VI Corps commander Horatio Wright was briefly incapacitated by a minor wound, Getty led the corps for several hours. That winter the VI Corps returned to the Petersburg lines. When Lee's lines finally collapsed on 2 April 1865, it was Getty's division that made the first breakthrough. For this, he won a regular army brevet promotion to brigadier general. For his service throughout the war he was brevetted a regular major general.

Getty was mustered out of the volunteer service as a major general, 9 October 1866, and was appointed colonel of the Thirty-eighth Infantry. He continued in that assignment until 1871, when he transferred back to his old branch of the service, becoming colonel of the Third Artillery. He commanded the artillery school at Fort Monroe for six years (1871–1877). In 1878 and 1879 he sat on the board that overturned the

court-martial of General Fitz John Porter, a general falsely accused, convicted, and cashiered fifteen years before in a political vendetta by the Radicals. In 1883 Getty retired from the army and moved to a farm near Forest Glen, Maryland, where he died. He is buried in Arlington National Cemetery.

• For further information on Getty see Bruce Catton, *A Stillness at Appomattox* (1953); U.S. War Department, *The War of the Rebellion: A Compilation of the Official Records of the Union and Confederate Armies* (128 vols., 1880–1901); and Ezra Warner, *Generals in Blue: The Lives of the Union Commanders* (1964).

STEVEN E. WOODWORTH

GETTY, J. Paul (15 Dec. 1892–6 June 1976), petroleum entrepreneur, was born Jean Paul Getty in Minneapolis, Minnesota, the son of George Franklin Getty, an attorney and oil investor, and Sarah Catherine McPherson Risher. Getty's father invested in oil in Bartlesville, Indian Territory (now Okla.), with the company incorporated as the Minnehoma Oil Company. The business struck oil in 1903, and young Getty accompanied his father to Indian Territory, during which time he developed a fascination for the oil industry. Getty attended Emerson Grammar School in Minneapolis and then, after the family moved, attended Harvard Military Academy in Los Angeles while working in his father's oil fields during summer vacations. Other oil strikes at Tulsa and Glenn Pool added to the family's wealth, but Getty's father moved to California more for the climate and personal reasons than for business. Getty graduated from high school in 1909 and agreed to work for his father, saying he wanted to "start at the bottom." He entered the University of Southern California to study political science and economics and then transferred to the University of California at Berkeley in 1911, only to resign from his courses without graduating that year. He then studied at Oxford, sat for a noncollegiate diploma in economics and political science in June 1913, and graduated. After graduation he traveled in Europe and then returned to the United States.

By that time, the Minnehoma Oil Company had grown, and Getty's father intended for Getty to take over the business, even though Getty himself still wanted to travel. Nevertheless, in September 1914 he took a job for his father scouting oil fields in Oklahoma. At the same time, he started to invest in his own wells. In May 1916 Getty and his father incorporated Getty Oil Company, by which time Getty was a "paper millionaire." He abruptly decided to leave the oil business.

After a brief hiatus, during which he made the Los Angeles social scene, Getty returned to activities in the Getty Oil Company in 1918. The company's drills continued to hit gushers in Oklahoma, and soon an industry glut of oil drove prices down, so much so that the Gettys had to borrow $50,000 to survive. At that point, Getty convinced his father to concentrate on new areas in California, which started to pay off by

1922. In March 1923 Getty's father suffered a heart attack, and Getty established himself as the supervisor at the fields, which alienated many of the laborers loyal to his father. When his father recovered, he separated his interests from Getty's, starting a bitter tension between the two. A similar distance appeared between Getty and his mother.

Getty's father died in 1930, leaving Getty as president of George F. Getty, Inc.; in addition he had already purchased shares of Pacific Western Oil Company, which he consolidated with his father's holdings in 1932. After disputes over purchases he wanted to make, he resigned from the board in 1933 but retained his stock. He purchased 18,000 shares of the George F. Getty stock from his mother in 1933, acquiring control of the entire operation. However, in the process he owed her more than $3 million. Harassed by Getty, who did not want to repay the debts, his mother in 1934 established the Sarah C. Getty Trust with $2.5 million of her own money and an additional $1 million of George F. Getty, Inc., funds supplied by Getty.

Getty conducted several campaigns to acquire other oil companies in the 1930s, led by his attempted takeover of the Tide Water Associated Oil Company (finally completed in 1951) and his successful acquisition of Skelly Oil in 1937. A subsidiary of Skelly, Spartan Aircraft, also was absorbed and contributed to the war effort during World War II. Getty operated from 1946 to 1961 as the president and general manager of a holding company under the new name of Mennehoma Financial Corporation. After the war Getty, advised that the Spartan company could not compete in the commercial aircraft industry, agreed to refocus the business on mobile homes, where it prospered.

Getty's company Pacific Western also invested in Middle Eastern oil fields in the Neutral Zone in competition with Aminoil. Whereas Getty once had acquired vast, rich leases for a few hundred dollars, his deals with the Saudis required that he build a mosque, housing, office accommodations, post offices, telephone facilities, and water-supply systems; provide educational facilities for Saudi children; and build a 12,000-barrel refinery, whether or not Getty's drillers struck oil. By 1952 Getty had spent $18 million specifically on drilling (and it was estimated that all the partners had invested a total of $30 million) without finding a drop of oil.

Getty's fortunes turned, however, in 1953. By 1956 estimates of the reserves in Saudi Arabia exceeded 13 billion barrels. Even with the temporary disruptions brought by the Suez Crisis of 1956, the middle eastern production continued to produce profits. When combined with the stock value of Getty Oil (merged with Pacific Western in 1956) and Tidewater (with its Skelly holdings and Minnehoma), Getty's holdings placed him on *Fortune*'s list of the wealthiest people in the world. The magazine estimated his fortune at a billion dollars in 1957, leading Getty to utter his famous quip that "a billion dollars isn't what it used to be."

By that time, Getty, like his counterpart Howard Hughes, had developed a reputation for eccentricities,

such as putting twice the required amount of stamps on envelopes to ensure their delivery; keeping his business papers in cardboard boxes tied with string; and cultivating a habit of scowling at cameras to enhance his Scrooge image. Yet many of the stories of his miserliness were much embellished or even fabricated. Once accused of taking a party of sixteen people to a swank Paris restaurant, then refusing to pay the 140,000-franc bill, in reality Getty was only an invited member of the party. The host schemed to have the bill presented to Getty, and indeed, Getty refused to pay it. The notion that Getty had mountains of cash on hand prompted thousands of letters begging for funds. Once, when he sent an Australian nun a check for $10, newspapers picked up the story and ridiculed him.

Getty, in fact, contributed heavily—but anonymously—to the World Wildlife Fund and the American Hospital in Paris. He did not give $1 million a year to charity, as he claimed. He did, however, abide by his dictum that "the best form of charity I know is the art of meeting a payroll" (Miller, p. 221). Still, the Scrooge references did not abate.

Getty's middle eastern investments combined with his European romantic affairs to make him a vagabond. Between 1949 and 1960 he lived almost his entire existence in hotel rooms before finally residing at "Sutton Place," a large estate in Surrey, England. There the company that owned Sutton Place had installed a pay telephone for its numerous workers, and the story that the richest man in the world had a pay phone in his mansion was reported relentlessly. A BBC interview with Getty added further evidence that money had brought nothing but despair and unhappiness to Getty. Others, however, knew a humorous, often frivolous Getty, who, while taking friends on tours through his gardens, assumed poses to show them how a statue might look. Getty entertained guests with outlandish impressions of Hitler at Nazi youth rallies, or of English snobs, and he thought less of money than perhaps most people in the world. Most of his "wealth" was tied up in corporate structures and oil in the ground, and Getty admitted that he did not carry cash.

Nevertheless, Getty clearly lacked the ability to maintain relationships, whether with his wives or his children. He married five times and had four children: Jeannette Demont (married in 1923, one child; divorced in 1925); Allene Ashby (married in 1926, divorced in 1928); Adolphine Helmle (married in 1928, one child, divorced in 1932); Ann Rork (married in 1932, two children, divorced in 1935); and Louise Lynch (married in 1939, divorced in 1958). His and Jeannette's son, George F. Getty II, was groomed to take over the business but developed sharp differences with his father over the direction of Getty Oil. George died after a fall at a barbecue party in 1973. Getty had other sons to run the business, but Jean Ronald, Adolphine's son, proved incapable, and Gordon Peter, one of Ann's sons, wanted to sing and compose operas. Worse, Gordon had fought Getty over the relatively low payments from the Sarah Getty Trust that the children received. In 1962 Gordon asked for an increase, and in 1966 he filed a "friendly" suit against his father, claiming $7.4 million in unpaid dividends from the trust. Getty had resisted making payments in large part to avoid tax penalties.

In July 1973 Getty's grandson J. Paul Getty III (Eugene Paul's son) was kidnapped, and the ransom demanded was $17 million. Getty refused to pay, contending that kidnappers would then have an incentive to take each of his fourteen grandchildren. He eventually agreed to loan Eugene Paul $850,000 at interest to complete a $1 million ransom offer, which the kidnappers accepted.

Getty nourished an appreciation for fine art, which he collected at both his California and his Surrey homes. In 1970 work began in Malibu on the J. Paul Getty Museum, designed to be a replica of the Villa dei Papyri on the slopes of Mount Vesuvius. Completed in 1974, the museum opened to less than enthusiastic reviews. Getty had established the museum with a $40 million endowment and a $2 million annual operating budget.

By the time the museum opened, Getty's empire consisted of 200 companies, 12,000 employees, and annual profits of $142 million. Most of his close associates noticed a change had occurred after George's death, and Getty gave up hope of having any of his sons take over the business. Gordon managed Getty Oil but fought with the board and eventually sold it to Texaco during a bitter litigation between Pennzoil and Texaco. Gordon, who negotiated the sale to Texaco, was not involved substantially in the Getty board's earlier decision to sell to Pennzoil. However, Gordon extracted an indemnification letter from Texaco, leaving the oil giant to bear the brunt of Pennzoil's $11 billion breach-of-contract suit.

In his final years, Getty grew increasingly isolated at Sutton Place, and, much like Hughes, surrounded himself with only a few associates who connected him to the outside world. Of his extensive family, only his son Gordon and Gordon's mother Ann saw Getty in his last days. He died at Sutton Place. His fortune and estate (including his personal 20 percent holding in Getty Oil) was bequeathed to his museum, while remaining shares of Getty Oil went to the Sarah Getty Trust, which held 42 percent. The museum experienced a phenomenal windfall, with final share prices increasing the endowment to $1.2 billion. Getty's death had endowed one of the wealthiest art museums in the world and sparked a bitter series of lawsuits contesting various aspects of his will. Even in death, the richest man in the world found that his money continued to foster unhappiness.

• Getty does not have an authorized collection of papers. However, extensive primary sources include the voluminous divorce cases, business acquisitions, and probate litigation of the Getty family. Getty's books include *The History of the Oil Business of George F. Getty and J. Paul Getty, 1903 to 1939* (1941), *Europe in the Eighteenth Century* (1949), *My Life and*

Fortunes (1963), *How to Be Rich* (1965), *The Golden Age* (1968), *The Joys of Collecting* (1965), *How to Be a Successful Executive* (1971), and *As I See It* (1976). The best two secondary sources on Getty are Robert Lenzner, *The Great Getty* (1985), and Russell Miller, *The House of Getty* (1985). *Life* magazine published "The Getty Legacy," Dec. 1985, pp. 112–26; his friend Robina Lund wrote *The Getty I Knew* (1977); and the Getty Museum published several scholarly journals. For information on the oil industry, especially relating to Getty, see Thomas Petzinger, Jr., *Oil and Honor: The Texaco-Pennzoil Wars* (1987), Steve Coll, *The Taking of Getty Oil* (1987), and Anthony Sampson, *The Seven Sisters* (1975).

LARRY SCHWEIKART

GETZ, Stan (2 Feb. 1927–6 June 1991), jazz tenor saxophonist and bandleader, was born Stanley Getz in Philadelphia, Pennsylvania, the son of Alexander Getz, a tailor, and Goldie (maiden name unknown). Alexander's surname had been shortened from Gayetzsky when the family emigrated from Russia. Stan Getz was raised in the Bronx from age six. He played harmonica at age twelve, switched to string bass six months later, and then to alto saxophone after another half year. He received a few lessons on the saxophone but was mainly self-taught. To play in the James Monroe High School orchestra, he doubled on bassoon and made such rapid progress that he was named to the All-City High School Orchestra, which entitled him to free lessons from Simon Kovar of the New York Philharmonic Orchestra. At age fifteen he was playing saxophone professionally in Dick Rogers's dance band at Roseland Ballroom in Manhattan, and shortly after his sixteenth birthday he dropped out of high school to tour for nine months with trombonist Jack Teagarden's big band; Teagarden became Getz's guardian to satisfy the school truancy officer.

Getz left the band in Los Angeles in December 1943 and worked in a haberdashery while waiting to qualify for a local musician's union card. Getz brought his parents out West. "They still had ads in the *L.A. Times* for renting apartments, reading 'no children, no pets, no Jews,'" he told interviewer Josef Woodard. He added, "We lived in the back of a barbershop until we found a Jewish building owner." Getz joined Bob Chester's big band and then played with bassist Dale Jones's group. From March 1944 to March 1945 he toured with pianist Stan Kenton's big band. He was a subtle and melodic player, especially devoted at this point in his career to tenor saxophonist Lester Young's understated style, and he despised Kenton's brassy, overblown music. He quit the band during a midwestern tour.

At around this time Getz became addicted to heroin. He toured with Jimmy Dorsey briefly, but by September 1945 he was back in Hollywood, leading a trio at the Swing Club. He played in Benny Goodman's big band intermittently from November 1945 to February 1946. Getz may have left to join drummer Gene Krupa's big band in March 1946, but by another account he joined trombonist Buddy Morrow's big band and then toured with trumpeter Randy Brooks's orchestra while dating Brooks's singer, Beverly Stewart.

A tour with Herbie Fields's big band followed in July. Getz married Stewart around this time; they had three children.

After rejoining Goodman from May to June 1947, Getz worked with singer and baritone saxophonist Butch Stone in Los Angeles. While in New York the previous year, Getz had been involved in Gene Roland's experiments in writing for a section of four tenor saxophones. In Los Angeles in the summer of 1947, Getz left Stone to join an octet comprising trumpeter Roland, four tenor saxes, and a rhythm section, with Beverly Getz as singer, at Pete Pontrelli's Spanish Ballroom. From this experience emerged the "four brothers" saxophone section of Woody Herman's big band.

With great fondness Getz recalled Herman's Second Herd, formed in September. With this group at year's end Getz made his first great recordings: "Four Brothers," featuring tenor saxophonists Getz, Herbie Steward (formerly with Stone), and Zoot Sims and baritone saxophonist Serge Chaloff; and "Summer Sequence, Part IV," a heady ballad solo for Getz. Almost exactly one year later, in December 1948, the latter title was developed further as "Early Autumn." On this recording, a landmark of the cool jazz style, the tenor saxophone has an unprecedented pure tone that Getz himself likened to the sound of a bass flute. Getz left Herman's band in late March or early April 1949.

On 15 December 1949 Birdland opened in New York City. The club took its name from alto saxophonist Charlie Parker (known as "Bird"), who performed that night, as did Getz, and over the next two years when Parker was not working, Getz would borrow his rhythm section, including pianist Al Haig. Continuing in the path of "Early Autumn," many of Getz's recordings from this period are characterized by quiet volume, technical prowess, purity of sound, consistency of timbre, and an ascetic sense of melody. These include "Too Marvelous for Words," "My Old Flame," "Gone with the Wind," "Yesterdays" (all from 1950); "It Might as Well be Spring" (1951), with pianist Horace Silver, who had joined Getz late in 1950; and "Prelude to a Kiss" (1951), recorded in Stockholm during a Scandinavian tour. His most celebrated tracks of the early 1950s are from a performance at Storyville Club in Boston with a quintet that included Haig and guitarist Jimmy Raney; some titles from this collection find him already moving away from the cool jazz mold.

In an effort to be with his family, Getz joined the staff of the National Broadcasting System in 1952, but he hated commercial studio work and returned to steady work as a bandleader. Notable among his many recordings are "Moonlight in Vermont," as co-leader with guitarist Johnny Smith (1952); "Crazy Rhythm," as co-leader with trombonist Bob Brookmeyer (1953); the sextet session *Diz and Getz*, co-led with trumpeter Dizzy Gillespie and incorporating pianist Oscar Peterson's trio and drummer Max Roach (1953); and "Lover Man," from a concert including Brookmeyer at the Shrine Auditorium in Los Angeles (Nov. 1954). By the time of this last date Getz was in deep trouble, having been arrested for using a toy pistol to try to steal narcotics from a Seattle drugstore. The case was dismissed, but Getz was soon rearrested as an addict and sentenced to six months in jail. His marriage broke up, and his three children went to live with relatives.

In the summer of 1955, while performing in the movie *The Benny Goodman Story*, Getz led a quintet at Zardi's in Los Angeles. He recorded *Hamp and Getz* as co-leader with vibraphonist Lionel Hampton and *West Coast Jazz* with the Zardi's group; the latter album includes "Shine," one of Getz's most exuberant performances. After filming ended, he flew to Sweden to see Monica Silferskiold, whom he had met a few months earlier while she was studying at the Foreign Service School at Georgetown University. In Sweden, Getz developed pneumonia and pleurisy. Treated by Silferskiold's father, a doctor, and then sent off for recuperation in Kenya, Getz returned to Sweden and then to the United States, where in 1956 he married Silferskiold. They had two children.

Getz became the first ex-addict musician to regain his New York City police cabaret card, enabling him to work in local clubs. He also toured with Jazz at the Philharmonic. This all-star assemblage was known for its propensity for musical overstatement. Getz, despite his reputation, fit into the energetic context (though always tastefully), and Peterson remarked: "You ain't from the cool school, you're the Steamer." Albums from these years include *For Musicians Only*, with Gillespie and alto saxophonist Sonny Stitt (1956); *The Steamer* (1956); and *Stan Getz and J. J. Johnson at the Opera House* (1957).

After a European tour with Jazz at the Philharmonic in the spring of 1958, Getz remained abroad, living mainly in Hensingor, twenty-five miles north of Copenhagen, Denmark. That summer he was recorded at a concert in Paris; "Ghost of a Chance" summarizes the steps he had taken that decade in bringing a hard edge into his beautiful ballad playing. After working with Jazz at the Philharmonic in Europe late in 1960, he returned to New York in January 1961, but in his first year back he found little success, his playing being considered old-fashioned. In what can only seem mind-boggling to fans from later generations, Getz's quartet, including the extraordinary bassist Scott LaFaro, performed to sparse audiences at the Village Vanguard in June. Discouraged but persistent, Getz continued in his own way. He recorded *Focus*, a set of improvisations over Eddie Sauter's arrangements for string quartet, string bass, and drums; this album is often cited as one of the most convincing examples of the integration of jazz and classical music.

In 1961 guitarist Charlie Byrd performed on a Brazilian tour and brought back bossa nova recordings for Getz, who showed an immediate and astonishingly perfect understanding of the music. In February 1962 Getz and co-leader Byrd recorded *Jazz Samba*. Their version of composer Antonio Carlos Jobim's "Desafinado" crossed over to rock-and-roll stations and carried the album to second place on the then-new stereo-LP sales charts, behind only Leonard Bernstein's *West Side Story.* The next year, as co-leader with Brazilian singer, guitarist, and composer João Gilberto, Getz recorded *Getz/Gilberto,* which included an even bigger hit, "The Girl from Ipanema." In these and following years, Getz brought to bossa nova an American jazzman's great talent for lyrical improvisation and demonstrated its potential as instrumental music of profound depth. But for many musicians this potential found only infrequent realization and more often took a backseat to crass commercialization. Getz himself became cynical and took to announcing "Desafinado" as "Dis Here Finado" in a parody of pianist Bobby Timmons's breezy soul-jazz hit "Dis Here."

After working in London in the spring of 1964, Getz recorded the album *Bob Brookmeyer and His Friends,* including vibraphonist Gary Burton. From mid-1964 through 1966 Burton, bassist Steve Swallow, and drummer Roy Haynes accompanied Getz. In 1967 pianist Chick Corea replaced Burton. That March, Getz and Corea were joined by bassist Ron Carter and drummer Grady Tate for the album *Sweet Rain,* because Swallow and Haynes were ill. Such are the vagaries of the jazz profession: one of the great jazz albums, a moment of unusual creativity and spontaneity, brought on by the flu.

From about 1968 to 1971 Getz's quartet included musicians who pushed him somewhat uncomfortably toward an avant-garde style. At this time he was also troubled by the deterioration of American schools, and around 1969 he left the country. He enrolled his youngest children in schools in London and resided there and in Spain on the Costa Del Sol while commuting internationally for performances.

Early in 1972, with Corea—now playing piano and electric piano—electric bass guitarist Stanley Clarke, and drummer Airto Moreira, Getz performed at the Rainbow Room in New York. In March Moreira switched to percussion, and drummer Tony Williams joined for the album *Captain Marvel.*

Getz often employed pianist Albert Dailey in the early to mid-1970s, and from 1974 into the 1980s drummer Billy Hart worked in his groups. Getz also performed with pianist and singer Jimmy Rowles, co-leader of *The Peacocks,* recorded in 1975. Pianist JoAnne Brackeen joined Getz in 1975. In January 1977 she contributed to his album *Live at Montmartre.* Shortly thereafter keyboardist Andy Laverne replaced Brackeen. Owing in part to Laverne's influence, Getz cautiously explored electronic sounds over the next few years.

In 1981 Getz filed for divorce, accusing Monica of infidelity and of an attempt to poison him. In turn she sought financial payments and protection, citing abuse and unfaithfulness stemming from his alcoholism and drug addiction. In 1987, the same year that doctors removed a malignant tumor from behind Getz's heart, the divorce was granted. Following the requisite court actions, the Supreme Court refused to hear Monica's appeal.

Getz's career flourished in the 1980s. Rejecting electronic sounds, he recorded *The Dolphin* (1981), *Pure Getz* (1982), and *Poetry* (1983). From 1985 he was artist in residence at Stanford University, giving concerts, talking to students, and helping to raise funds. At this time pianist Kenny Barron and drummer Victor Lewis were in his quartet with bassist George Mraz, heard on *Voyage* (1986), or Rufus Reid, on *Anniversary* (1987).

In 1988 Getz contributed a solo on the rock video "Small World" by Huey Lewis and the News. That same year he settled in Malibu, California. *Apasionado,* an electrified big-band session produced by trumpeter Herb Alpert in 1989, provided Getz with yet another hit recording. Shortly before his death he recorded singer Abbey Lincoln's *You Gotta Pay the Band* (Feb. 1991) and a duo with Barron, *People Time* (Mar. 1991). These discs find him playing as well as ever. He died of liver cancer at his home in Malibu.

Throughout his career Getz exhibited a consistent sense of melodic beauty and perfection; these qualities help account for his popular successes beyond the usual jazz marketplace. From the days of "Summer Sequence, Part IV" and "Early Autumn" onward, the magnificent delicacy and purity of his tenor saxophone sound were matched by the depth of his improvisatory ideas on ballads and mildly swinging tunes, but at faster tempos he had a tendency to fall into melodic routines that were exciting but somewhat insubstantial. In the course of his career he addressed this problem. He also changed his sound. He added a heftier edge to the cool base, and even on a pretty ballad he might throw in honking sounds in the instrument's lowest register, rather than sticking to a smooth, subtone timbre as he had initially. He also developed a muffled cry that further personalized his playing. Perhaps most importantly, despite his own misgivings about the consequences of a union of Brazilian bossa nova and American jazz, he created here a new style, and in this style he had no equal. Because his creativity emerged in these diverse ways, and at different paces, Getz's stature as a jazz musician grew gradually as the decades went by. He is now widely regarded as one of the greatest jazz tenor saxophonists.

• Biographical information on Getz is in Richard Palmer, *Stan Getz* (1988), and Hans-Jürgen Schaal, *Stan Getz: sein Leben, seine Musik, seine Schallplatten* (1994). Further detail appears in the following articles, surveys, and interviews: Leonard Feather, "The Resurgence of Stan Getz," *Down Beat,* 28 Feb. 1963, pp. 16–17; Michael James, "The Cool Deviations," *Jazz Monthly* 10 (Apr. 1964): 11–15; Les Tomkins, "It Feels Good to Flex Your Muscles, Says Stan Getz," *Crescendo* 2 (July 1964): 24–26; George Hoefer, "Stan Getz: Always a Melodist," *Down Beat,* 20 May 1965, pp. 14–16; Don DeMichael, "A Long Look at Stan Getz," *Down Beat,* 19 May 1966, pp. 17–20, and 2 June 1966, pp. 15–17; and Palmer, "Stan Getz in the Sixties," *Jazz Journal* 23 (Feb. 1970): 10–11. Other useful sources include Tomkins, "Stan Getz: On Leaving the States, His LP Dates, the Jazz Fates," *Crescendo International* 10 (Nov. 1971): 6–7; Arnold Jay Smith, "Influentially Yours, Stan Getz," *Down Beat,* 12 Aug. 1976, pp. 17–18; Richard Williams, "Presenting . . . the

Stanley Steamer of the '80s: Stan Getz," *Down Beat*, 12 Jan. 1978, pp. 17–18, 52–53, 62; Palmer's three-part "Stan Getz," *Jazz Journal International* 36 (Dec. 1983): 8–11, 37 (Jan. 1984): 14–15, and (Mar. 1984): 18–19; Palmer, "Stan Getz at Sixty," *Jazz Journal International* 40 (July 1987): 8–10; Feather, "Stan Getz: 'A Master at Work,'" *Jazz Times* (Oct. 1988): 36–38; Kevin Whitehead, "Getz Serious," *Down Beat* 57 (June 1990): 34–35; Josef Woodard, "Stan Getz: Back on the Beach," *Down Beat* 57 (July 1990): 20–21; and Thomas Owens, *Bebop: The Music and Its Players* (1995), pp. 79–84. A catalog of recordings is Arne Astrup, *The Stan Getz Discography* (1978), *The Revised Stan Getz Discography* (1984), and *The New Revised Stan Getz Discography* (1991). For further details of his affiliations with big bands, see James A. Treichel, *Keeper of the Flame: Woody Herman and the Second Herd, 1947–1949* (1978); D. Russell Connor, *Benny Goodman: Listen to His Legacy* (1988); and William D. Clancy with Audree Coke Kenton, *Woody Herman: Chronicles of the Herds* (1995). Obituaries are in the *San Francisco Examiner*, 7 June 1991, and the *New York Times*, 8 June 1991.

BARRY KERNFELD

GEYER, Henry Sheffie (9 Dec. 1790–5 Mar. 1859), lawyer and U.S. senator, was born in Frederick, Maryland, the son of John Geyer, a native of Prussia, and Elizabeth Sheffie. He studied law with his maternal uncle Daniel Sheffie and was admitted to the bar in 1811. The following year he volunteered for military duty in the War of 1812, rising to the rank of captain and serving as the regimental paymaster of the Thirty-eighth Infantry.

Following his discharge in 1815, Geyer moved to St. Louis and resumed the practice of law. He quickly became an expert in the exceedingly complex title disputes growing out of Spanish land grants and the disastrous New Madrid earthquake of 1811, which crowded the courts at the time and for many years thereafter. In the noted land case of *Strother v. Lucas*, which he argued before the U.S. Supreme Court, he won the admiration of Chief Justice John Marshall, who remarked at Geyer's legal acumen in a private conversation. In 1817 he compiled and published a digest of the territorial laws of Missouri.

The following year Geyer was elected to the territorial legislature on a nonpartisan ticket. After Missouri became a state in 1821, he was elected to the lower house of the first General Assembly, which promptly chose him Speaker. He continued in the legislature intermittently for the next two decades, assuming major responsibility for the revision of Missouri's statute law in 1825 and 1835. A staunch Whig and admirer of Henry Clay, he, nevertheless, gained the respect of colleagues in both parties.

When the Democrats in the Missouri legislature deadlocked over the reelection of U.S. Senator Thomas Hart Benton (1782–1858) in 1851, Geyer was chosen to fill the seat by a coalition of Whigs and proslavery Democrats. During his single term in the Senate (1851–1857), he sided consistently with the proslavery element. Together with his fellow senator from Missouri, David Rice Atchison, he condemned the attempts of the New England Emigrant Aid Society to colonize Kansas Territory.

Geyer made a major contribution to the proslavery cause on the judicial front. His most noted case, *Dred Scott v. Sandford* was argued before the U.S. Supreme Court near the end of his Senate term. Geyer and Reverdy Johnson represented Dred Scott's nominal owner, John F. A. Sanford, without legal fee. Indeed, one noted historian has claimed that "the real client" the two represented was "the slaveholding South" (Fehrenbacher, p. 288). Geyer, who led the defense effort, elaborated the major arguments upon which Chief Justice Roger B. Taney later drew in presenting the Court's decision in 1857: Scott's ineligibility to sue because as a black he held no citizenship, Scott's forfeiture of whatever freedom he might have acquired by living in Illinois and Wisconsin Territory through his return to Missouri, and the unconstitutionality of the Missouri Compromise.

Geyer retired to St. Louis at the close of his Senate term and died at his home there. He was married three times: on 1 January 1818 to Clarissa B. Starr, on 26 April 1831 to Joanna (Easton) Quarles, and on 12 February 1850 to Jane (Stoddard) Charless.

Contemporaries described Geyer as "a bold, logical, fluent, and argumentative speaker" (Bay, p. 148). Cold and reserved in his demeanor, he, nevertheless, commanded wide respect because of his legal acumen. He was a dominant figure of the Missouri bar throughout his career, and few cases in the thicket of land law were decided without his consultation. His southern background led him to take a strong stand in defense of slavery as his actions in the Senate and the *Dred Scott* case indicate.

• Geyer has yet to find a biographer, perhaps because no body of Geyer's papers is known to exist. The best biographical sketch of Geyer is in J. Thomas Scharf, *History of Saint Louis City and County*, vol. 2 (1883). Accounts of his various court cases may be found in W. V. N. Bay, *Reminiscences of the Bench and Bar in Missouri* (1878), and John F. Darby, *Personal Recollections* (1880). For Geyer's role in the *Dred Scott* case, see Don E. Fehrenbacher, *The Dred Scott Case: Its Significance in American Law and Politics* (1978).

WILLIAM E. PARRISH

GHENT, William James (29 Apr. 1866–10 July 1942), socialist and author, was born in Frankfort, Indiana, the son of Ira Keith Ghent and Mary Elizabeth Palmer, farmers. As a child Ghent lived in Kansas, where his parents struggled to establish a homestead, but after six years Ghent's father moved the family back to Frankfort and opened a drugstore. Ghent went to work at age thirteen, starting as a printer's devil on a local paper. Before long he had become a skilled typesetter and began traveling around the country as an itinerant printer.

Early in the 1890s Ghent settled in New York City, where he started writing on social issues. He became a socialist and worked closely with other middle-class reformers such as the American Fabians and the Nationalist followers of Edward Bellamy. Denying the inevitability of class struggle, Ghent fought the influence of Marxians like Daniel DeLeon during the 1892 Populist party campaign in New York. In 1894 he helped organize the Social Reform Club of New York City, which sought to improve labor conditions by fostering cooperation between workers and middle-class intellectuals. In 1897 he became editor of the *American Fabian*, but he was forced out in 1898 for supporting the Spanish-American War. He then worked briefly for reform mayor Samuel M. "Golden Rule" Jones of Toledo, serving as literary manager in Jones's successful campaign for reelection and his unsuccessful campaign for governor.

During the next few years Ghent gained attention in socialist circles with two books. *Our Benevolent Feudalism* (1902) warned that the United States was moving toward a new form of feudalism in which industrial capitalists would lull the masses with economic security while smothering democracy and competition. In *Mass and Class: A Survey of Social Divisions* (1904) he took a more hopeful view, predicting that socialism's goals would be achieved through democratic politics. But he also attacked existing injustices, criticizing employers to whom, as he said, "life is but a bagatelle when it stands in the way of profit." Under these conditions, Ghent suggested, labor's occasional "lawlessness" was justifiable. Many workers, however, could not recognize their own interests. The answer lay in the group he called "retainers," middle-class Americans who currently functioned as tools of the capitalists but whose true interest lay in leading the lower class toward a collectivist commonwealth.

In 1904 Ghent joined the Socialist party, aligning himself with members such as Morris Hillquit and Victor Berger, who stressed politics and education rather than union action and confrontation. He helped organize the Rand School of Social Science in New York City in 1905 and served from 1906 to 1909 as its only full-time administrative employee; he also taught at the school, which was intended to provide workers with education and the Socialist party with an intellectual center. In 1909 he married a member of the Rand clerical staff, Amy Louise Morrison; they had no children. That same year he moved to the presidency of the Rand School, a position he held until 1911. During this period Ghent wrote *Socialism and Success* (1910), arguing among other things that intellectuals had an important contribution to make to socialism. He also became a popular Socialist speaker; middle-class audiences in particular responded to his gradualism and his emphasis on workers' need for middle-class guidance. As he wrote in 1907: "The intelligence that certain men bring to the movement is the social force that wins thousands of workmen, previously unenlightened, to our cause. This intelligence should be rewarded . . . with the responsibility of leadership."

In 1911 Ghent moved to Washington, D.C., where he became secretary to Berger, now a congressman. Working under only the most general direction from Berger, Ghent drafted a variety of legislative proposals, including a pension bill, but none attracted serious attention. By this time the question of labor violence had become a hotly contested issue in the Socialist party, where conservatives like Hillquit and Berger existed in uneasy coalition with radical groups like the Industrial Workers of the World (IWW). At the national convention in 1912 Ghent sponsored an amendment to the party constitution that would expel any member who advocated violence or sabotage. The passage of Ghent's amendment, and its use the following year to force out IWW leader William D. "Big Bill" Haywood, marked a climactic break between the party's right and left wings.

Ghent found Berger difficult to work for, and when Ghent contracted tuberculosis in 1913 he moved west—first to Phoenix, Arizona, and then a year later to Los Angeles, California. He also began editing a newspaper, *California Outlook*, in which he continued to promote socialism. But in 1917 he broke with the Socialist party when it denounced U.S. entry into World War I. His resignation letter to Hillquit ended, "You are my enemy and I am yours." Ghent and other Socialist bolters helped organize the Social Democratic League, which combined a prowar position with reform proposals for after the war, but the group drew little popular support.

The rise of the Bolsheviks in Russia led Ghent to move further right politically, and by the 1920s he was stressing the importance of capitalism as a defense against Communism. A number of his articles were collected in *The Reds Bring Reaction* (1923), which argued that Communist extremism had caused a tragic backlash, provoking the repression of liberals and reversing the trend toward social reform.

In 1922–1923, while working as a reference librarian at the University of California in Los Angeles, Ghent developed an interest in the history of the Old West. He returned to New York City in 1924, and in 1927 moved to Washington, D.C., where he worked for a year on the staff of the *Dictionary of American Biography* (DAB). He continued writing, contributing articles to the DAB and publishing three books, all on western history. He died in Washington.

Ghent's life exemplifies the career of one kind of American socialist—the reformer who hoped to achieve the party's goal of social justice without accepting the inevitability of the class struggle or conceding leadership to the working class. At each stop in his journey across the political spectrum from moderate left to right, Ghent expressed his views with vigor and passion, illuminating a path traveled by numbers of other reformers during the same years.

• Ghent's papers are in the Library of Congress, while the following archives contain materials related to his life: Rand School Papers, Workingmen's Cooperative Publishing Association Papers, and Algernon Lee Papers, Tamiment Library, New York University; Victor L. Berger Collection, Milwaukee County Historical Society; and Morris Hillquit Papers and A. M. Simons Papers, State Historical Society of Wisconsin, Madison. Other publications by Ghent include a series of pamphlets he wrote for New Appeal Socialist Classics in 1916: *The Tactics of Socialism, Socialism and Organized Labor, Socialism and Social Reform*, and *Questions and An-*

swers. He also wrote *The Road to Oregon* (1929), *The Early Far West* (1931), and, with LeRoy R. Hafen, *Broken Hand* (1931). His career is discussed in Donald Drew Egbert and Stow Persons, eds., *Socialism and American Life* (1952); Lawrence Goldman, "W. J. Ghent and the Left," *Studies on the Left* 3 (Summer 1963): 21–40; Ira Kipnis, *The American Socialist Movement, 1897–1912* (1952); Aileen S. Kraditor, *Radical Persuasion, 1890–1917: Aspects of the Intellectual History and the Historiography of Three American Radical Organizations* (1981); Sally M. Miller, *Victor Berger and the Promise of Constructive Socialism, 1910–1920* (1973); David Shannon, *The Socialist Party of America* (1955); Harold S. Smith, "William James Ghent, Reformer and Historian" (Ph.D. diss., Univ. of Wisconsin, 1957); and James Weinstein, *The Decline of Socialism in America, 1912–1925* (1984).

SANDRA OPDYCKE

GHERARDI, Bancroft (6 Apr. 1873–14 Aug. 1941), telephone engineer, was born in San Francisco, California, the son of Bancroft Gherardi, a commander in the U.S. Navy, and Anna Talbot Rockwell. As a "navy brat" he moved frequently with his family, usually every two years, and attended a number of schools before matriculating at the Polytechnic Institute of Brooklyn. After receiving his B.S. in 1891, he enrolled at Cornell University to study mechanical engineering and received his M.E. and M.M.E. in 1893 and 1894, respectively.

After a brief period of unemployment, in 1895 Gherardi joined the Bell System's Metropolitan Telephone and Telegraph Company in Manhattan as an engineering assistant. Although his primary duties involved testing and inspecting telephone lines, he soon turned his attention to the necessity of doing away with overhead wires because of the problem of urban congestion. Underground cables seemed to offer the best solution; however, because standard practice called for the use of medium-gauge wire throughout the system, an underground cable could accommodate only 150 pairs of wire, making its use too costly. He solved this problem when he demonstrated that connecting individual telephones to the local central office with thin-gauge wire and connecting central offices to one another with heavy-gauge wire permitted underground cables to accommodate up to 2,100 pairs of wire without reducing the quality of service.

In 1898 Gherardi married Mary Hornblower Butler; they had no children. Two years later Gherardi was put in charge of the renamed New York Telephone Company's traffic engineering department, the first such department in the country. In this position he developed innovative methods for handling toll calls and designed switching equipment and buildings that could be readily expanded as the demand for telephone service increased. In 1901 he became chief engineer of the New York and New Jersey Telephone Company, the Bell System operating company that served Long Island and suburban New Jersey. The next year he supervised the installation between Brooklyn and Newark of the country's first commercial-use loaded telephone cable, a major advance in telephony because the wire coils with which the cable

was "loaded" reduced distortion in the signal and permitted the use of thinner-gauge wire. In 1906 these two telephone companies consolidated their operations, and Gherardi became the assistant chief engineer of both.

When the American Telephone and Telegraph Company (AT&T), the Bell System's parent company, was reorganized in 1907, Gherardi became its equipment engineer. Two years later he was made engineer of plant development and standardization for the entire Bell System, charged with upgrading and standardizing transmission and switching equipment. Between 1915 and 1918 he invented an interoffice lamp-indicator signaling system for multiplex telephone circuits, a grounding arrangement for avoiding interference in cables, an antiabrasion cable support, and a system for equalizing transmission lines so that signals are not distorted or degraded by noise from various sources in the system. He also became involved in the establishment of transcontinental telephone service and oversaw in 1915 the completion of a telephone connection that used electronic vacuum tubes instead of loading coils to amplify the signal between New York and San Francisco. Gherardi was promoted to acting chief engineer in 1918, chief engineer in 1919, and vice president and chief engineer in 1920. In these capacities he continued to oversee the efforts of the Bell System's subsidiary operating companies as they upgraded and standardized their equipment by integrating new products developed at AT&T's Bell Telephone Laboratories (BTL); he also implemented a system of exchanging people and ideas among the subsidiaries.

After 1925, when he became a member of BTL's board of directors, Gherardi was in the ideal position to encourage the development of new equipment and then oversee its implementation throughout the entire Bell System. His most important contribution in this regard was to recommend and implement the transition from manual to automatic switching of telephone calls; this required the development and installation of mechanical switching equipment and rotary dial telephones, as well as a massive public education campaign to enable the public to accept and use the new system. By the time he retired from AT&T in 1938, more than half of the Bell System's customers were placing their telephone calls by using automatic dialing.

Gherardi served as president of the American Institute of Electrical Engineers (AIEE) from 1927 to 1928. In 1929 he was elected to the first board of directors of the American Standards Association and served as its president in 1931–1932. He was president of Polytechnic's alumni association from 1914 to 1916 and a member of its board of trustees from 1917 to 1923. He also served on Cornell's board of trustees from 1928 to 1941. In 1932 he received the AIEE's Edison Medal and was elected to the National Academy of Sciences in 1933. Gherardi spent his retirement years in Short Hills, New Jersey, and died while vacationing in French River, Ontario, Canada.

Gherardi was one of the foremost authorities on telephone engineering in the world. His greatest contribution was the role he played as architect of a telephone system that would eventually be capable of connecting virtually every home and business in the continental United States.

• A biography of Gherardi, including a bibliography, is Oliver E. Buckley, National Academy of Sciences, *Biographical Memoirs* 30 (1957): 157–77. An obituary is in the *New York Times*, 16 Aug. 1941.

CHARLES W. CAREY, JR.

GHEZZI, Vic (19 Oct. 1910–30 May 1976), professional golfer, was born Victor J. Ghezzi in Rumson, New Jersey, the son of Frank Ghezzi, a gardener, and Rose Zanelli. Ghezzi, who attended public schools in Red Bank, New Jersey, and graduated from Red Bank High School, followed a traditional path to a professional career. After first caddying at the Rumson Country Club, he worked in the pro shop and finally became the head professional.

A tall, handsome man, Ghezzi turned pro in 1934, just as the Professional Golfers Association (PGA) tour was taking shape as a regular circuit. Within a year he posted wins in the Los Angeles Open and the Calvert Open. During the next few years he registered victories in several minor tournaments before winning another important championship, the North-South Open, in 1938. The following year he became a member of the Ryder Cup squad, the first of his three years with the team.

Undoubtedly 1941 was annus mirabilis for Ghezzi. At the Cherry Hills club in Denver, he bested Bryon Nelson in a tense duel for the PGA championship, which was then a match-play event. On reaching the final match, Ghezzi fell three strokes behind Nelson after twenty-seven holes. Ghezzi rallied to go one-up, but he finished in a tie with Nelson. They matched strokes on the thirty-seventh hole and faced each other on the thirty-eighth hole with thirty-inch putts. Nelson, winning a coin flip to determine who would putt first, missed; Ghezzi barely snaked in his putt to win. The PGA victory marked the only major title in his career, one that he would always savor. "I won against one of the finest players we've ever had," he said. "I feel like a kid on Christmas morning."

Ghezzi enlisted in the army in 1942 at the outset of U.S. involvement in World War II. A sergeant in the Signal Corps, he was with the assault force on the Anzio beachhead in 1943 and served for more than four years.

After the war Ghezzi returned to the PGA tour. Soon he experienced the reverse side of the coin of his earlier major victory, joining Nelson and Lloyd Mangrum in the 1946 U.S. Open at the Canterbury Country Club in Cleveland for one of the most dramatic medal playoffs in golfing history. At the end of regulation play, all three were tied at 284, four strokes under par. All three posted 72s in an eighteen-hole playoff and then played another eighteen holes. After thirteen holes, Ghezzi seemed on the verge of victory with a two-stroke lead; however, he bogied the fourteenth and fifteenth holes and relinquished the lead to Mangrum. With rain pelting the course and lightning striking nearby, he missed an eight-foot putt on the eighteenth green to give Mangrum the title. (Ironically, probably the best part of his golf game was his putting skill.) He never came close to winning another major championship. Over the next few years he played less and less frequently, and he closed out his career on the PGA tour in the 1950s. He was one of a number of good players who sustained professional golf before World War II and into the postwar years before Arnold Palmer did so much to popularize the sport late in the 1950s. Altogether, Ghezzi won thirteen PGA tour events and earned about $200,000. He was elected to the PGA Hall of Fame in 1965.

Besides playing on the tour, Ghezzi was a club professional at four clubs in New Jersey and New York: the Rumson Golf Club, the Englewood Golf Club, the Deal Golf and Country Club, and the Inwood (Long Island) Country Club. He also served as president of the New Jersey PGA and as a consultant for a sporting goods company. Investing his modest earnings wisely, he became fairly rich. At his death, his brother, Joseph Ghezzi, asserted, "You could say he was a millionaire."

At his retirement in 1960, Ghezzi moved to the Bal Harbour section of Miami Beach, Florida. He remained active in golf as the chairman of the Golf Committee of the Indian Creek Country Club, where he was immensely popular. Nearly two decades after his death, fellow member Raymond Floyd still had vivid memories of Ghezzi holding court with his tales of golf. Even as he lay dying from cancer, he rejoiced in Floyd's victory in the 1976 Masters tournament. Ghezzi was survived by his wife, Betty Obrecht Ghezzi, and four stepchildren.

• An article on Ghezzi's full career is in Peter Alliss, ed., *The Who's Who of Golf* (1983). The progress of professional golf during his career is discussed in Benjamin G. Rader, *American Sports: From the Age of Folk Games to the Age of Spectators* (1983). See also "Ghezzi Triumphs over Nelson," *New York Times*, 14 July 1941. Personal sources of information for this article include Raymond Floyd and Joseph Ghezzi, Vic Ghezzi's brother. An obituary appears in the *New York Times*, 1 June 1976.

CARL M. BECKER

GHOLSON, Samuel Jameson (19 May 1808–16 Oct. 1883), jurist and general, was born in Madison County, Kentucky. Little is known of his parents, but it is certain that the family moved to Russellville in northern Alabama in 1817. There Gholson studied law with Judge Peter Martin and gained admission to the bar in 1829. A year later, the young lawyer crossed the border into northeastern Mississippi, where he settled in Athens in Monroe County and established a law practice.

Although still relatively unknown in Mississippi, Gholson found some success in a brief political career.

In 1835 he won election as a Democrat to the state legislature, and the following year, upon the death of one of the state's congressmen, Gholson narrowly defeated the much more prominent John A. Quitman in a special election to serve out the remainder of the term. Gholson's brief tenure in Congress expired in March 1837, but after a special session was called during the summer, before the regular congressional election in November, Gholson again won a special election and retained his seat. In a strange turn of events, however, he lost the fall election and reluctantly surrendered his seat after a lengthy controversy. After this abrupt end to a promising political career, Gholson married Margaret Ragsdale in 1838.

Having lost his position in Congress, Gholson began a long but relatively uneventful judicial career. On 13 February 1839 President Martin Van Buren appointed him U.S. district judge for Mississippi. During the first half of the nineteenth century, federal judges lacked the power they were to gain after the Civil War, when a flurry of congressional action and constitutional amendments considerably expanded the jurisdiction of the federal courts. Consequently, Gholson's court heard few cases, most of which involved local matters, and none of the judge's decisions was published by contemporary law reporters. The scant glimpses of his record available from cases appealed to the U.S. Supreme Court are unexceptional. The Supreme Court overruled, for example, Gholson's decision to uphold the rights of white settlers to build schools on lands previously ceded by treaty to Native Americans (*Gaines v. Nicholson* [1850]).

After two decades of judicial service, Gholson returned to the political fray when the sectional crisis gripped the nation. Along with Judge William L. Harris of the state supreme court, Gholson presided over the Mississippi Democratic Convention of 1860 and urged his state's party faithful to take a strong "southern rights" position. When sectional tensions reached a boiling point the following year, Gholson attended the Mississippi secession convention and became a member of the committee to draft an ordinance of secession. Although a strong supporter of slavery and separation from the Union, Gholson, himself a slaveowner, stirred up a bit of controversy among the delegates by proposing a nearly 100 percent increase in the tax on slaves. He reasoned that since slavery had helped bring on the war, slaveholders ought to bear much of the financial burden of southern independence. The convention promptly defeated the proposal. When Mississippi officially seceded in January 1861, Gholson resigned his position as a federal judge and joined his state's militia.

Gholson saw constant action and suffered repeated injuries during his Civil War military career. Beginning as captain of the Monroe County Volunteers (Company 1, Fourteenth Mississippi) in early 1861, he was later promoted to colonel and brigadier general of state troops. In February 1862, at the battle of Fort Donelson, he was wounded in the right lung, taken prisoner, and ultimately exchanged, before being wounded twice more at the battles of Iuka and Corinth later the same year. On his recovery in 1863 and in light of the impending threat to Vicksburg, Gholson was promoted to major general in command of all state troops and was also put in charge of all Mississippi railroads.

Conflict over whether soldiers were under state authority or Confederate command, however, weakened Mississippi's defenses, and even after the fall of Vicksburg and the passage of a new Confederate Conscription Act, Gholson stubbornly refused to surrender his men to Confederate authority. Despite his differences with the Confederate government, he was a close associate of President Jefferson Davis, who referred to Gholson as "a man of sterling integrity . . . fearless in the discharge of every trust." Eventually, in summer 1864, Gholson became a brigadier general in the Confederate army, after having briefly commanded a cavalry brigade in Mississippi and Alabama earlier that year. He was wounded twice in 1864, first during the spring at Jackson and finally in December at Egypt, Mississippi. In this, Gholson's last and most serious brush with death, he lost an arm and retired from military action.

After the war Gholson returned to Monroe County, this time settling in Aberdeen, and practiced law before winning election to the state legislature in 1865. He served as Speaker of the house until 1867, when the Military Reconstruction Act changed the face of Reconstruction state governments across the South. Forced out of power along with other ex-Confederates, in 1870 Gholson became chief of the Monroe County Ku Klux Klan and later defended several fellow Klansmen during the federal government's brief campaign against Klan violence. After conservative white Democrats regained control of Mississippi's government in 1878, Gholson returned to the legislature as Speaker. He died five years later in Aberdeen.

Gholson's career in many respects typified that of the nineteenth-century southern statesman. His rise within the legal profession opened the door to political opportunities throughout his lifetime, and his high standing within the community made him an ideal candidate for a position of military leadership during the war. Gholson was certainly a better general and politician than he was a judge, as he was more committed to the causes of slavery, secession, and the Democratic party than he was to the abstractions of the law.

• In general the biographical record on Gholson is scant. The David W. Haley Papers in the Mississippi Department of Archives and History (Jackson) contain a few letters to and from him, but the main sources of information about his life are scattered biographical sketches and brief mentions in various works on Mississippi history. See, for example, *The Papers of Jefferson Davis*, vol. 2 (1974), p. 204; John K. Bettersworth, *Confederate Mississippi: The People and Policies of a Cotton State in Wartime* (1943); Dunbar Rowland, *History of Mississippi: The Heart of the South*, vol. 2 (1925), pp. 432–33; *Publications of the Mississippi Historical Society, vol. 9 (1906), p. 66; and James D. Lynch, *Bench and Bar of Mississippi* (1881). An obituary is in the *Natchez Democrat*, 24 Oct. 1883.

TIMOTHY S. HUEBNER

GHOLSON, Thomas Saunders (9 Dec. 1808–12 Dec. 1868), jurist and Confederate congressman, was born in Gholsonville, Brunswick County, Virginia, the son of Major William Gholson, a planter, and Mary Saunders. Gholson received his secondary education in Oxford, North Carolina, and then returned to his home state, where he graduated from the University of Virginia in 1827. He practiced law in Brunswick County until 1840, when he moved to Petersburg and formed a partnership with his older brother, James Hubbard Gholson. After his brother's death in 1848, Gholson practiced with Judge James Alfred Jones of Mecklenburg County. By all accounts, Gholson was a skillful advocate and eloquent orator, and he made a name for himself by taking part in many notable cases, including the famous murder trial of William Dandridge Epes, in which Gholson was the prosecutor.

Gholson married his first cousin, Cary Ann Gholson, the daughter of his uncle Thomas Gholson, in 1829, and the couple eventually had four children. During their lengthy residence in Petersburg, Gholson and his wife were active among the city's social elite, while he himself took a vigorous role in public life. He sat on the Board of Visitors of the College of William and Mary, served as president of the Exchange Bank of Petersburg, advocated the development of railroad lines, and played a leading part in founding the Petersburg Library Association. He was also a vestryman in the Blandford Episcopal Church.

A Whig, Gholson never held political office during the antebellum period, but he did make at least two notable forays into the political arena before the Civil War. In 1850 he attended the Nashville Convention, a meeting of southerners concerned about the fate of their region within the federal Union, where he argued against secession and urged southern acceptance of the Compromise of 1850. Five years later, in the midst of the Whig party's collapse, Gholson cautioned Whigs against joining the nativist Know Nothing, or American, party. "Whigs of Virginia," he warned in an influential essay in the *Richmond Enquirer*, "before you enlist under the banner of what is called the American Party, be ye sure that you will not embrace doctrines and principles more dangerous than all the heresies of Democracy." Aside from these episodes, during his early career Gholson largely stayed out of Virginia politics. Instead, in 1859 he accepted an appointment to the state's fifth judicial circuit.

Ultimately, Gholson embraced secession, the Democratic party, and political office. He held his post as circuit judge during the first few years of the Civil War, but in late 1862 narrowly defeated incumbent Charles Fenton Collier in the race for the fourth district of Virginia seat in the second Confederate congress. While in congress from 1863 to 1865, he served on the judiciary committee and gave staunch support to President Jefferson Davis and the Confederate war effort. He favored suspension of the writ of habeas corpus, advocated almost total government control of the economy, and wanted the war department to possess full power over all state forces. In the waning months of the conflict, Gholson urged continued preparation for war and introduced a resolution "to place at once in the Army every man liable under our laws to render military service." On the other hand, he fervently opposed the use of black troops by the Confederacy.

At the war's end, Gholson sought to recoup his financial losses. He fled to Liverpool, England, where he joined his son-in-law, Colonel Norman Stuart Walker, in forming Gholson, Walker, and Company, a successful cotton and tobacco commission house. While on a business trip to the United States in 1868, Gholson died suddenly of heart failure in Savannah, Georgia, on his way to Virginia, whereupon the *Savannah Morning News* eulogized him as "a genial, warm-hearted man, and one of the 'old stock' and type of this country's chivalrous public men and statesmen." Gholson is buried at the Blandford Church Cemetery in Petersburg. He was the cousin of Samuel J. Gholson and William Y. Gholson.

As it was for so many other nineteenth-century Americans, the Civil War was the defining event in Gholson's life and career. Had it not been for the war, he would no doubt have continued to live the quiet life of a competent and comfortable Virginia lawyer. However, the political traumas of sectionalism caused even cautious southern Whigs like Gholson to embrace secession and southern nationalism, while the defeat of the Confederacy presented new problems and possibilities.

• Of the three prominent members of the nineteenth-century Gholson family, the least is known about Thomas Saunders. A small collection of his papers is at the Special Collections Library, Duke University. Only fragments of his record as a public official exist. See the *Southern Quarterly Review*, o.s., 18: 216–23, for his speech at the Nashville Convention, and the *Richmond Enquirer*, 25 Apr. 1855, for his essay on the Know Nothings. The best overall biographical sketch is "A Note on Judge Thomas Saunders Gholson, President of the Petersburg Library Association," *Tyler's Quarterly Historical and Genealogical Magazine* 19 (Oct. 1937): 84–86. See also "Speech of the Hon. Thos. S. Gholson, of Virginia, on the Policy of Employing Negro Troops and the Duty of All Classes to Aid in the Prosecution of the War," *Journal of the House of Representatives of the Second Congress of the Confederate States of America*, vols. 4 and 7 (1865). Useful obituaries appear in the Savannah *Republican* (15 Dec. 1868), Savannah *Morning News* (14 Dec. 1868), Petersburg *Daily Express* (15 and 19 Dec. 1868), and Petersburg *Daily Index* (15 and 22 Dec. 1868).

TIMOTHY S. HUEBNER

GHOLSON, William Yates (25 Dec. 1807–21 Sept. 1870), jurist, was born in Southampton County, Virginia, the son of Thomas Gholson, Jr., a Virginia congressman who died in the War of 1812, and Ann

Yates. In 1825 Gholson graduated from the College of New Jersey (later Princeton) and afterward studied law near Farmville, Virginia, under the state's famous judge and law teacher, Creed Taylor. On Christmas Day 1827 Gholson married Taylor's niece Ann Jane Taylor, and the couple settled on a plantation near Gholsonville in Brunswick County. Gholson's wife died in 1831, and three years later he moved to Mississippi, where he settled in Pontotoc in the northern portion of the state. After being admitted to the bar, he began a successful law practice and in 1839 married Elvira Wright, the daughter of Judge Daniel W. Wright of the Mississippi Supreme Court. In 1844 Gholson assisted in founding the University of Mississippi as a member of the first board of trustees.

For reasons that are unclear, sometime during the mid-1840s Gholson freed his slaves and left his native South to settle in Cincinnati, Ohio. During the next decade he became one of the most prominent attorneys in his new home state. After opening a law office, he was soon appointed city solicitor and later practiced law with the likes of James P. Holcombe, a noted legal writer from Virginia, and Salmon P. Chase, the future chief justice of the U.S. Supreme Court. Gholson participated in a number of key cases, many of which involved the legal issues of patents and copyrights. He defended several individuals accused of infringing on Samuel Morse's telegraph patent (*Morse v. O'Reilly* [1848], *Smith v. Ely* [1849]). Moreover, he helped defend Holcombe when descendants of U.S. Supreme Court justice Joseph Story argued that Holcombe's *Introduction to Equity Jurisprudence, on the Basis of Story's Commentaries* infringed on Story's original copyright (*Story v. Holcombe* [1847]).

The fame Gholson achieved from such cases became apparent in May 1854, when he was elected to the newly created Superior Court of Cincinnati. The tribunal formed by Gholson and Judges Bellamy Storer and Oliver M. Spencer subsequently won high praise from the state's legal community; Ohio lawyer and later president Rutherford B. Hayes referred to the three as "the best bench I ever saw." Here Gholson wrote his most famous judicial opinion, in *Sanderson Robert v. New England Mutual Life Insurance Company* (1857). Gholson's holding, that the failure to pay life insurance premiums at the time stipulated by the policy effectively nullified the policy, was cited widely in American state and federal courts during the nineteenth century.

Gholson's legal talents, as well as a political dispute within the state's Republican party, catapulted him to the Ohio Supreme Court in 1859. After Chief Justice Joseph R. Swan joined with two other members of the court in upholding the constitutionality of the controversial federal fugitive slave law and refusing to interfere with its enforcement in Ohio, angry Republican leaders refused him renomination. Instead, they championed Gholson as a candidate for the state bench, and he was elected in October of that year. On 8 November 1859 the governor appointed him associate justice of the Ohio Supreme Court, but failing

health forced Gholson to resign from the court on 11 December 1863. Despite the brevity of his judicial service, fellow Ohioan Stanley Matthews, later a justice of the U.S. Supreme Court, once observed that Gholson's opinions "rank high for learning and accuracy."

A studious jurist and talented writer, Gholson devoted much of his career to legal writing and public speaking. He joined Holcombe in editing an edition of John William Smith's *Compendium of Commercial Law* (1850) and, after his resignation from the bench, helped compile a *Digest of the Ohio Reports* (1867). In addition, he published addresses on the payment of the federal government's Civil War debt, in which he opposed repaying creditors with greenback dollars, and on the Reconstruction of the southern states, in which he expressed moderate Republican sentiments. He died near Cincinnati.

Gholson's career spanned much of the nineteenth century and reflected the enormous changes that occurred in American law and society during his lifetime. His migration northward perhaps reflected a personal struggle with the larger issues of slavery and sectionalism, while his focus on commercial law mirrored the nation's economic expansion and technological advancement.

• Precious little biographical information exists on Gholson, as there is no major collection of papers from his life and work. His judicial writings offer the keenest insights into his thinking and are contained in the *Reports of Cases Adjudged in the Superior Court of Cincinnati (Disney's Reports)*, vols. 1–2 (1854–1860), and the *Ohio State Reports*, vols. 9–14 (1858–1863). Useful biographical information is available in G. I. Reed, *Bench and Bar of Ohio* (1897); C. T. Greve, *Centennial History of Cincinnati* (1904); Eugene Roseboom and Francis Weisenburger, *A History of Ohio* (1934); James Edmonds Saunders, *Early Settlers of Alabama* (1969); and *Biographical Annals of Ohio, a Handbook of the Government and Institutions of the State of Ohio* (1904–1905), p. 669. Comments on Gholson's judicial abilities by Rutherford B. Hayes and Stanley Matthews appear, respectively, in Charles Richard Williams, *Diary and Letters of Rutherford Birchard Hayes*, vol. 3 (1924), p. 415; and *Disney's Reports*, vol. 2, pp. v–vi.

TIMOTHY S. HUEBNER

GIAMATTI, Bart (4 Apr. 1938–1 Sept. 1989), scholar, college president, and baseball executive, was born Angelo Bartlett Giamatti in Boston, Massachusetts, the son of Valentine Giamatti, a professor of Romance languages at Mount Holyoke College, and Mary Claybaugh Walton. Raised in South Hadley, Giamatti acquired a love for both books and baseball from his father. Much better at academics than athletics, he graduated from Phillips Academy in Andover, Massachusetts, and Yale University, where he received a B.A. in English magna cum laude in 1960 and, as a Woodrow Wilson Fellow, earned a Ph.D. in comparative literature in 1964. In 1960 he had married Toni Smith, with whom he had three children.

Giamatti began his academic career at Princeton in 1964 teaching Italian and comparative literature and returned in 1966 to his alma mater as an assistant professor of English. At Yale he quickly earned distinction as a teacher of English and comparative literature and as a scholar of medieval and Renaissance literature. Promoted to full professor at the age of thirty-three in 1971, he was named Frederick Clifford Ford Professor of English and Comparative Literature in 1976 but relinquished that endowed chair the next year to become the school's first John Hay Whitney Professor.

Giamatti's foremost academic treatise, *The Earthly Paradise and the Renaissance Epic* (1966), is a revision of his doctoral dissertation, in which he analyzed the persistent search for an earthly garden ("the lost state of bliss and innocence") as a theme in the writings of classical, medieval, and Renaissance writers and then its disappearance as a prominent literary theme as mankind "lost that Renaissance sense of tolerance, spaciousness, and inclusiveness; that faith in man, in ourselves, which the earthly paradises . . . always implied." He also authored *The Play of Double Senses: Spenser's "Fairie Queene"* (1975) and an anthology of previously published essays, *Exile and Change in Renaissance Literature* (1984). Giamatti coedited *The Songs of Bernart de Ventadorn* (1965), the *Orlando Furioso of Ariosto* (1966), and *A Variorum Commentary on the Poems of John Milton* (1970), and he was the general editor of a three-volume anthology, *Western Literature* (1971), and of *Dante in America: The First Two Centuries* (1983). A Guggenheim fellow in 1969–1970, he was an officer in such scholarly organizations as the Renaissance Society of America, the Dante Society of America, and the American Comparative Literature Association. Able to discourse easily on popular culture as well as academic topics, Giamatti received national recognition in 1977 for an essay in the *Boston Globe*, "The Green Fields of the Minds" (22 Dec.), in which he exalted baseball as an "enduring national institution," and for two articles in *Harper's*. One was a denunciation of the New York Mets for trading star pitcher Tom Seaver, and the other was an appreciative analysis of Muhammad Ali's psychological and physical demeanor in the boxing ring.

Giamatti performed a variety of administrative assignments at Yale. He served as Master of Ezra Stiles College (1970–1972), director of the Visiting Faculty Program (1974–1976), director of the humanities division in the Faculty of Arts and Sciences (1976–1978), and associate director of the National Humanities Institute at Yale (1977). Largely because of his work during the summer of 1977 on the Priorities Committee that examined the fiscal crisis confronting Yale, he was chosen on 20 December 1977 to become president of Yale, effective 1 July 1978.

Giamatti was a surprise choice as the school's nineteenth president. At age forty, the youngest president in its 282-year history, he was also the first whose ancestry was not wholly Anglo-Saxon and Protestant. An eloquent speaker with a flair for the dramatic and the possessor of a quick and irreverent wit, the personable Giamatti, who regularly wore a Boston Red Sox baseball cap on campus and drove a yellow Volkswagen,

was an immensely popular choice with students and faculty. But many alumni felt the "shortish, chubby, casual and rumpled" professor lacked the appropriately staid, formal demeanor of his predecessors, and they considered him too independent, passionate, and opinionated to be an effective leader.

Giamatti's personal popularity and unquestioned integrity served him well in dealing with the budgetary and curricular problems confronting Yale. He quickly resolved the institution's fiscal crisis. When Giamatti took office Yale had a $16 million operating deficit and had experienced severe cuts in programs and faculty as well as a staff hiring freeze, but in two years the school had a balanced budget for the first time in ten years. His aggressive and enthusiastic approach to fundraising generated unprecedented donations and brought the faculty a 10 percent increase in salary. In 1980 Giamatti negotiated a contract with the university's employees' union without a strike for the first time since 1965; he did so again in 1982, but in the fall of 1984 he endured a rancorous ten-week strike by Local 35, a new union of clerical and technical workers. He also greatly improved relations between Yale and the New Haven community and joined with the city and the Olin Corporation to develop a high-tech industrial park.

Contrary to ideas then popular in higher education, Giamatti, an academic traditionalist who had been raised in the classic Ivy League mold, advocated a structured curriculum with few elective courses and opposed "ungraded" and "pass-fail" courses. "It is not enough to offer a smorgasbord of courses," he declared. "We must insure that students are not just eating at one end of the table." Under Giamatti, Yale tightened its undergraduate curriculum, imposed a foreign language requirement for bachelor's degrees, added pluses and minuses to the grading system, established interdisciplinary majors, and created a universitywide intensive writing program. Opposed to the growing emphasis on vocational training in higher education, Giamatti argued that Yale's mission was "not to make one technically or professionally proficient, but to instill some sense of the love of learning for its own sake, some capacity to analyze any issue as it comes along, the capacity to think and to express the results of one's thinking clearly, regardless of what the subject matter must be."

Giamatti's tenure was not without controversy, as he wrote and spoke out on a wide range of subjects as diverse as sports and politics. In June 1981 he chastised both major league players and owners in a *New York Times* essay for their "utter foolishness" in allowing "the triumph of greed over the spirit of the garden" to result in what ultimately would be a fifty-day baseball strike. "There is no general sympathy for either of your sides," he declared, because "the people of America care about baseball, not about your squalid little squabbles." And three months later, in his welcoming address to the freshman class, he denounced the Moral Majority and similar conservative political groups as "peddlers of coercion" engaged in a "radical assault" on civil rights and cultural pluralism. And his hard-line stance against striking staff workers at Yale in 1984 earned him a reputation as an antilabor union-buster. Whether because of the rancorous strike or weariness with the pressures of the office, he announced in late 1985 his intention to resign the following year to pursue scholarly research.

Instead, in June 1986 Giamatti was elected president of the National League and took office on 11 December. The election was ironic: when asked in August 1977 about his candidacy for the presidency of Yale, life-long Boston Red Sox fan Giamatti had quipped, "The only job I've ever wanted was to be president of the American League." He brought to the National League presidency the exuberance of a fan, a nostalgic attachment to the presumedly lost traditions of the national pastime, and a determination to preserve the integrity of the game. He took strong stands against cheating. During his first season as president, Giamatti suspended Houston outfielder Billy Hatcher for using a corked bat and Philadelphia pitcher Kevin Gross for using sandpaper to scuff the baseball. The next year he suspended Pete Rose for thirty days for shoving an umpire during an argument. He also insisted on strict enforcement of the balk rule to prevent pitchers from deceiving base runners, and he denounced unruly fan behavior in the stands. Contrary to his personal beliefs, Giamatti succumbed to the homophobic fears of owners by dismissing a gay umpire, Dave Pallone, in November 1988.

In large part because of his charismatic personality and public image as a "fan's fan" and "baseball purist," Giamatti was elected commissioner of baseball on 8 September 1988. Unlike his predecessor, Peter Ueberroth, who viewed baseball primarily as a business and worked to enhance the owners' economic interests, Giamatti saw himself as the trustee of the game's fundamental values and an advocate of fan interests. He took office on 1 April 1989 and immediately faced a stern test in dealing with allegations that Rose, a former star player and current manager of the Cincinnati Reds, had bet on baseball games, including those of his own team, from 1985 to 1987. Giamatti and his special counsel, John Dowd, launched a covert investigation that ignored due process in gathering evidence of Rose's gambling activities. In turn, Rose's attorneys attempted to challenge the commissioner's authority in the matter through a series of court cases. After meeting with Giamatti, Rose consented on 24 August 1989 to a written agreement that, while not specifically charging him with betting on games, banned him from organized baseball for life. Giamatti termed the banishment "the sad end of a sorry episode" that demonstrated "that no individual is superior to the game."

A week later Giamatti, a heavy smoker, was stricken with a massive heart attack at his summer home in Edgartown, Massachusetts, and died later that day at a Martha's Vineyard hospital. Some commentators attributed his death to stress from the Rose affair, but that was probably only a contributing factor. Although

he had served only 154 days, Giamatti, the only commissioner to die in office, had a profound impact on the perception of the game. His unabashed exuberance for the game and sentimental notions of its traditions served to counter the growing cynicism and disillusionment of fans with the business of baseball. Fittingly, Giamatti's scholarly and sporting interests were joined in the posthumously published *Take Time for Paradise: Americans and Their Games* (1989), in which he argued that sport was a cultural reenactment of the nation's commitment to both freedom and community and that baseball was truly the national pastime because, more than any other sport, it "fulfills the promise America made to itself to cherish the individual while recognizing the overarching claims of the group."

A scholar whose love of language frequently led to flights of rhetorical fancy and a moralist who exercised authority with a calculated pragmatism, Bart Giamatti neither published enough academic treatises nor held administrative positions of authority long enough for realities to diminish the idealistic perceptions of the man. Giamatti's enduring legacy lay in his giving voice to the ideals and visions of a generation of students, educators, and baseball fans.

• Manuscripts relating to Giamatti's years at Yale are in the Sterling Memorial Library, Yale University, New Haven, Conn., and an extensive file of clippings on his career in baseball is in the National Baseball Library, Cooperstown, N.Y. Biographical pieces on Giamatti include James Reston, Jr., *Collision at Home Plate: The Lives of Pete Rose and Bart Giamatti* (1991), and Anthony Valerio, *Bart: A Life of A. Bartlett Giamatti by Him and about Him* (1991), a revealing documentary. Other useful biographical sketches are William E. Geist, "The Outspoken President of Yale," *New York Times Magazine*, 6 Mar. 1983, pp. 42, 53–56; Charles Siebert, "Baseball's Renaissance Man," *New York Times Magazine*, 4 Sept. 1988, pp. 36–38ff; and Frank Deford, "A Gentleman and a Scholar," *Sports Illustrated*, 17 Apr. 1989, pp. 86–90ff. The Giamatti-Rose episode is told in Pete Rose and Roger Kahn, *Pete Rose: My Story* (1989), but handled much better in Michael Y. Sokolove, *Hustle: The Myth, Life, and Lies of Pete Rose* (1990). For Giamatti's views on higher education, see *The University and the Public Interest* (1981), a collection of his speeches, and *A Free and Ordered Space: The Real World of the University* (1988), an anthology of essays. Important obituaries are in the *New York Times*, 2 Sept. 1989, and the *Sporting News*, 11 Sept. 1989.

LARRY R. GERLACH

GIANCANA, Sam (24 May 1908–19 June 1975), crime syndicate boss, was born Salvatore Giangana in Chicago, Illinois, the son of Antonino Giangana, a fruit peddler, and Antonia DeSimone. Giancana grew up in the tough ethnic ghetto called The Patch in Chicago's Near West Side during the period when legendary gangster Al Capone was at his most notorious. By age fourteen Giancana had become a leader of the vicious juvenile 42 Gang and never earned more than an elementary school education.

While still a teenager, Giancana developed a reputation as a daring "wheelman," or getaway car driver, and was quickly noticed by the Capone mobsters. He came into the favor of two of Capone's top lieutenants, Paul Ricca and Tony Accardo, and became an eager enforcer-killer for the gang throughout the 1920s. Because of his nerve, ruthlessness, and penchant for violence, Giancana was nicknamed "Mooney" or "Momo," corruptions of "Mooner" (one who is crazy). With his lifetime record of over seventy arrests for crimes including assault and battery, damage by violence, and suspicion of bombing, Giancana undoubtedly lived up to this moniker.

Before he was twenty, Giancana was the prime suspect in three unsolved murders, and in 1925 he served his first federal prison term in Joliet, Illinois, for auto theft. He was sent back to Joliet in 1929 for burglary. When he was released in 1933, he married Angeline DeTolve. They had three children. The eldest, Antoinette, would later achieve a measure of fame as the prototype "Mafia Princess."

Giancana was sent to prison a third time in 1939 for moonshining. Upon his release in 1942, he was forced to swear a pauper's oath to pay his fines for violating federal liquor laws. During World War II, when the draft board asked Giancana what he did for a living, he replied, "I steal." He was then perfunctorily classified 4-F as a "constitutional psychopath [with] an inadequate personality and strong anti-social trends" (*Time*, 30 June 1975). For the next dozen years, the ambitious and political Giancana learned the inner workings of the underworld at the side of Ricca and Accardo, and in 1955 the two aging mobsters turned over the day-to-day operations of the entire Chicago syndicate to Giancana.

From 1956 to 1966 Giancana ruled the Chicago Mafia with an iron hand, masterminding the violent takeover of the city's lucrative numbers rackets from black mobsters. This move alone increased the syndicate's income by millions of dollars per year. He also quickly extended his mob's operations to the vast riches of Las Vegas. So strong was Giancana's hold in Nevada that no other Mafia family dared challenge the Chicago syndicate's stranglehold on Las Vegas's wealth during this period.

As the Chicago crime family's income rose, largely because of Giancana's ruthlessly efficient leadership, so did his power, influence, and notoriety. He took full advantage of his newfound prominence and enjoyed moving in celebrity circles. He wore silk suits, drove flashy cars, and carried on affairs with high-profile women, including singers Keeley Smith and Phyllis McGuire. He became close friends with many other Las Vegas entertainers, most notably Joe E. Lewis, Peter Lawford, and especially Frank Sinatra. Lawford was the brother-in-law of presidential candidate John F. Kennedy, and Giancana attended many parties with them in Las Vegas and Palm Springs, California. In the 1960 election Sinatra and Giancana played crucial roles in delivering Chicago (and consequently Illinois) to Kennedy. For a time in 1962 Giancana even shared a mistress, Judith Campbell Exner, with the president of the United States.

Soon after Kennedy's election, the Central Intelligence Agency surreptitiously enlisted the Mafia, led by Giancana, to assassinate Fidel Castro. This plot was attractive to the underworld, since Castro had halted all gambling in Cuba after the 1959 revolution. The scheme, which included poison pills and even poisoned cigars, ultimately failed, but the fact that it was seriously considered at the highest levels of government attests to the importance of Giancana and the Mafia during this period of American history.

By 1965 Giancana's power had begun to erode. In May he was called before a grand jury but refused to testify against the syndicate; he was jailed for contempt of court. In 1967 Ricca and Accardo eased Giancana out of the top leadership position in Chicago, and he moved his base of operations to Mexico. For the next eight years Giancana traveled extensively in South America, setting up gambling casinos and other rackets, all the while living in luxury in the American enclave of Cuernavaca near Mexico City.

Fearing further indictments by federal authorities and reprisals by his many enemies in the underworld, Giancana applied for Mexican citizenship several times in the late 1960s but was turned down. In July 1974 he was summarily deported from Cuernavaca. Even as the grand jury began pressing again, Giancana tried to reestablish himself with the Chicago syndicate. Accardo and other Mafia leaders, however, were worried that Giancana, now in failing health, might talk. While cooking sausages in the basement kitchen of his Oak Park, Illinois, home, Giancana was shot seven times in the head and neck at close range; he died instantly. Leaders of both the syndicate and the CIA denied any part in Giancana's murder.

During his long, bloody career, Giancana rose from the role of an obscure, mindless thug to the position of unquestioned leader of the most powerful criminal organization west of the Mississippi. By 1964, at the height of his power, he was arguably the most influential gangster in the United States. His interests ranged from international gambling to racketeering in vice, numbers, loan sharking, and narcotics, and he held political control over police chiefs, mayors, state legislators, and even federal officials. He accumulated enormous behind-the-scenes power, making deals with the CIA and socializing with movie stars and the future president of the United States. At bottom, however, Sam Giancana was an impulsive, remorseless criminal, directly or indirectly responsible for hundreds of murders and other vicious crimes. In the end, his violent past caught up with him.

• Giancana left no published works. The most comprehensive biography of Giancana is William Brashler, *The Don* (1977). Another book-length study of Giancana's life and especially his death is Sam Giancana and Chuck Giancana, *Double Cross: The Explosive Inside Story of the Mobster Who Controlled America* (1992); the authors are Giancana's godson and brother, respectively. Besides documenting his entire life, with some bias they speculate about the causes and perpetrators of Giancana's 1975 murder. Giancana is also featured in Ronald Brownstein, *The Power and the Glitter*

(1990), in connection with Frank Sinatra, and he is frankly discussed by Judith Campbell Exner in her 1977 biography, *My Story*, excerpted in *Dream Streets*, by Lawrence Di Stasi (1989). See also Kitty Kelley, "The Dark Side of Camelot," *People Weekly*, 29 Feb. 1988, pp. 106–11, and Nicholas Gage, *Mafia, USA* (1972). At the time of his murder, obituary-style articles appeared in *Time*, 30 June 1975, p. 26, and *Newsweek*, 30 June 1975, pp. 17–18. Obituaries are in the *Chicago Tribune* and *New York Times*, both 20 June 1975.

BRUCE L. JANOFF

GIANNINI, Amadeo Peter (6 May 1870–3 June 1949), banker, was born in San Jose, California, the son of Luigi Giannini, an immigrant farmer and hotel operator from Genoa, and Virginia Demartini. His father died in 1877, the victim of a shooting by a disgruntled workman; his mother soon remarried, to Lorenzo Scatena, a self-employed teamster. Scatena moved the family to San Francisco, where, after working for less than a year for a produce firm, he opened his own wholesale business. Giannini began working for his stepfather at age twelve, rising at midnight to go to work, then attending Washington Grammar School. When he finished the eighth grade, he chose to end his formal education with a short course at Heald's Business College; thereafter, he went to work full time for Scatena. A strapping youth of more than six feet, he did much of the produce buying in Napa, Santa Clara, and San Joaquin counties, venturing as far as Los Angeles at times to find supplies. Scatena rewarded him with a partnership when he was only nineteen.

In 1892 Giannini married Clorinda Agnes Cuneo, whose father had made a fortune from real estate; three of their six children survived to adulthood. In 1901 he retired at age thirty-one at a time when the Scatena firm was one of the largest wholesale produce businesses in San Francisco. He already owned some real estate, giving him a monthly income of $250; he sold his half interest for $100,000 to employees, who would pay him from their profits. Declaring he had no desire to be rich, he said this income would be "ample" for his family's needs.

But in 1902 Joseph Cuneo, his father-in-law, died intestate, and the family needed Giannini to manage the half-million dollar estate. The holdings included a few shares in the Columbus Savings and Loan Society in San Francisco's North Beach area, the city's Italian quarter. Giannini also fell heir to Cuneo's seat on the bank's board. He soon discovered that the bank had no interest in small borrowers, and that a competitor, Andrea Sbarboro's Italian-American Bank, was growing rapidly by catering to such customers. Unable to persuade Columbus to attend to the needs of such people, Giannini and five other directors resigned. They, Scatena, and four others organized the Bank of Italy in October 1904, with a capital of $150,000. Giannini opened the first office directly across the street from Columbus Savings in the renovated room of a saloon. Giannini believed that the great opportunity in banking was providing service to "little people," but throughout his career he insisted on serving clients of every stripe, whether of income, class, or nationality.

He willingly made loans to small merchants, farmers, and laborers, who were at first primarily of Italian origin. Unlike typical bankers who never solicited business, he tramped the streets seeking business; needing deposits so he could expand his loan business, he personally asked people to open accounts. He also resorted to advertising aggressively. Though his tactics shocked the banking establishment, he was convinced that his approach was right, and within fifteen months his Bank of Italy was approaching a million dollars in assets.

The great earthquake and subsequent fire of 18 April 1906, destroyed much of San Francisco; it also gave Giannini a unique opportunity to display his toughness, resourcefulness, and commercial acumen. Before the fire reached his offices, he had loaded two wagons borrowed from the Scatena firm, driven through panicking crowds, extracted the bank's assets—more than $2 million in gold and securities—and taken them, hidden under a load of vegetables, to safety in his own home. He then notified all his depositors that their money was safe and, using a wooden plank as his office amid smoldering ruins, began making loans to businessmen to rebuild their establishments days before any other bank attempted to open. Such strength and leadership established his reputation.

In 1907 Giannini correctly anticipated the coming banking panic and accumulated sufficient gold to meet depositor demands. Thus, unlike his competitors who resorted to using clearing-house certificates and limiting withdrawals, the Bank of Italy met all such requests with no limit and in specie. Though this move further enlarged his reputation, it also persuaded Giannini that in the long run only large banks were truly safe. When in 1908 he heard former Treasury Secretary Lyman J. Gage explain the potential of branch banking, he saw the means to build such a large bank. With the adoption in 1909 of a state banking law permitting branch banking, he began expanding rapidly by acquiring small banks and converting them into branches of the Bank of Italy. He thereby created the country's first extensive branch banking system. His success alarmed competitors and led to appeals to the state legislature to limit branch banking, but they came to naught.

In 1919, with twenty-four branches and $93 million in resources, he organized the Bancitaly Corporation as an umbrella within which to carry forward expansion. Through it he acquired a New York City bank, East River National, and then a system of branch banks in Italy. He also acquired a very successful Los Angeles bank, Bank of America. In 1924 he retired as president of the Bank of Italy in order to focus "on major policies"—primarily more acquisitions—from his position as president of Bancitaly.

Responding to the extended regulation of banks in the McFadden Act (passed in 1927), Giannini brought his Bank of Italy, originally state-chartered, into the national banking system, renaming it Bank of Italy National Trust and Savings Association. Exploiting a provision of the McFadden Act governing acquisition of competing banks, Giannini quickly bought a series of banks that had strong branch networks, bringing them together under the Bank of America of California. In 1929 he acquired another Bank of America, this time a long established New York City establishment. Then in 1930, using the holding company Transamerica Corporation that he created in 1928 to succeed Bancitaly, he brought most of his banks together in the Bank of America National Trust and Savings Association. Because banking law prevented absorbing several of his banks into this framework, he also created a new state-charted bank, Bank of America. When the law was changed in 1933, Bank of America N.T. and S.A. absorbed it as well.

Despite the size of his banking empire and his wealth, Giannini continued to emphasize business with small borrowers, giving crop loans to California fruit growers, loaning regular wage-earners up to $300 on their signature alone, and willingly risking loans where others feared to go—in Hollywood to movie producers.

The Great Depression threatened the stability of Giannini's banking system, and he watched in dismay as the president of Transamerica, Elisha Walker, began to sell off some properties. Though ailing, Giannini launched a proxy fight and in 1932 retook control of Transamerica, taking the position of chairman of the board for both Transamerica and Bank of America. Remarkably, the fight also restored his own vitality; working brutally long hours he maneuvered the company through the worst of the banking crisis in 1933, and by 1939 he had doubled the bank's resources to $1.6 billion. The expansion came in the face of continued opposition and criticism from other bankers and, more critically, a strident attack on the bank for exploiting migratory field hands and maintaining a near stranglehold on the farmlands of California through its mortgage holdings. Close investigation revealed that neither accusation was true.

In October 1948 the Federal Reserve Board announced plans for public hearings on antitrust charges against Transamerica, and they were held in Washington and San Francisco from January to March 1949. The investigation led eventually to an order that Transamerica sell all banking stock except that of Bank of America. Giannini did not live to see the dismemberment of his empire; he had continued working virtually until the end. He died at his home, Seven Oaks, in San Mateo. His estate went almost entirely to the Bank of America-Giannini Foundation, which he had created in 1945 to support medical research and scholarships to children of bank employees. He had also given $1.5 million in 1927 to the University of California to establish the Giannini Foundation of Agricultural Economics.

At Giannini's death, Bank of America was the world's largest commercial bank, with assets of more than $6 billion, operating 517 branches in California and international branches in London, Tokyo, Yokohama, Manila, and Kobe, with representatives in New York, Paris, Milan, Zurich, and Shanghai. Transamerica Corporation, a huge holding company owning banks, financial institutions, real estate, and industrial companies, operated an additional 127 banking offices in western states. Though it never reached his goal of a worldwide network of branch banks, Giannini's skill in building a pervasive branch banking system and his demonstration that banking could profitably serve small borrowers, whether merchants, farmers, or laborers, heavily influenced American banking practice for decades. His bank played a central role in the dramatic economic growth of California and the Pacific coast region, which became one of America's most important subeconomies.

• The largest collections of papers on both Giannini and his banks are held in the archives of the Bank of America in San Francisco; important additional materials may be found in the Bancroft Library of the University of California at Berkeley. There are numerous published histories of the bank and several biographies of Giannini, as well as discussions of him and the bank in a number of general regional and business history studies. The most recent, detailed biography is Felice A. Bonadio, *A. P. Giannini: Banker of America* (1994); a briefer, accessible biography is Gerald D. Nash, *A. P. Giannini and the Bank of America* (1992). Julian P. Dana published the first biography, *A. P. Giannini: Giant in the West* (1947), which relied heavily on interviews with Giannini; the interview notes are in the Bancroft Library. Marquis and Bessie R. James's *Biography of a Bank* (1954) is an authorized institutional history that includes extensive discussion of Giannini. His obituary is in the *New York Times*, 4 June 1949.

FRED CARSTENSEN

GIANNINI, Attilio Henry (2 Mar. 1874–7 Feb. 1943), physician, banker, and motion picture executive, was born in San Jose, California, the son of Italian immigrants Luigi Giannini and Virginia Demartini, farmers and ranchers. After the fatal shooting of his father by a disgruntled employee in August 1876, Giannini's mother took over management of their Alviso, California, farm. She married Lorenzo Scatena, and in June 1880 the family moved to San Francisco. While Scatena developed a wholesale produce business, L. Scatena & Co., Giannini attended Washington Grammar School in North Beach.

Giannini received his B.A. from St. Ignatius College of San Francisco in 1894 and his M.D. in 1896 from the University of California. He served as an assistant surgeon for two years in the Spanish-American War and earned distinction for treating smallpox patients in quarantined camps. After the war Giannini established a medical practice in San Francisco, frequently contributing articles to medical journals. He joined the American Medical Association and the Medical Society of the State of California and was elected president of the San Francisco County Medical Society. When in 1906 a typhus epidemic was feared, Giannini volunteered his services and was honored by San Francisco city and county officials for his efforts. He also completed two terms on the board of supervisors of the city and county of San Francisco.

In 1905 Giannini married Leontine Denker, the daughter of a wealthy Los Angeles real estate developer. They moved to the fashionable Los Angeles suburb of Atherton and had one son. Giannini was known as an "intense, volatile, dark-complexioned man of medium height with quick, dark eyes behind steel-rimmed glasses," who indulged his expensive tastes, frequented the best clubs, and dressed in the best suits (Bonadio, p. 48). A lifelong antagonism with his older brother, Amadeo (known as A.P.), did not keep Giannini from joining his brother in establishing the world's largest bank. Giannini terminated his medical practice in 1909 in order to serve as vice president and manager of the Bank of Italy's first branch in San Jose. While A.P. introduced home loans repayable in monthly installments, Giannini, supporting his brother's innovative idea of targeting the working class, outlined a plan for children's savings accounts.

Giannini was the first banker, according to the head of MGM, Louis B. Mayer, to recognize the motion picture industry as a worthy enterprise for lending. "Doc," as he was called, began granting loans to the industry in 1909 and by 1918 confirmed his commitment by lending the unprecedented amount of $50,000 to producers Famous Players–Lasky. He moved in 1919 to New York to serve as president of his brother's newly purchased East River National Bank. By targeting working-class Jews and Italians, the bank's assets grew from $3.5 million to $13 million only nine months after the sale. The bank's proximity to Broadway allowed Giannini to continue building a relationship with the stage and film industry. He extended more than $100 million in loans to pioneering Broadway theater owners and producers such as Cecil B. DeMille, Lewis Selznick, Marcus Lowe, Samuel Goldwyn, Jesse Lasky, Joseph and Nicholas Schenck, and Carl Laemmle.

Because Giannini was willing to accept a negative of a completed film as collateral for a loan to begin production on the next film, by 1921 most of the major film distributing firms had accounts with the Bank of Italy. Giannini's financial backing enabled the production of Charlie Chaplin's *The Kid* (1921), which launched the career of child star Jackie Coogan. The $250,000 Giannini invested was recuperated within six weeks after the film opened. Boasting that the box office produced the quickest cash profit, Giannini corrected those who labeled him a philanthropist.

In 1928 Giannini's brother acquired Bank of America, one of New York's oldest banking institutions, and consolidated his holdings to form the Bank of America National Association. One result of this transaction was that in 1931 the East River National Bank was absorbed by another of A.P.'s holdings, Manhattan's National City Bank. Giannini returned to Los Angeles to serve as the chair of the general executive committee of the Bank of America. He supervised the original branches of the Bank of Italy in southern California and approved lending to Hollywood. He made the first $1 million loan for Samuel Goldwyn's 1932 pro-

duction of *The Kid from Spain* and in 1939 financed the production of *Gone with the Wind*.

Giannini was an invaluable member on the board of several film studios, not only because he was in charge of approving loans to the motion-picture industry but also because he served as a mediator for studio executives when business or personal disputes arose. In 1936 he retired from all major banking positions to serve as president-elect of the financially struggling United Artists. An intimate of the company; Giannini worked to resolve its financial problems, serving on the board of Selznick-International, advising Goldwyn, and acting as associate of Joe Schenck. United Artists earned its largest gross profit in its history in 1937. In March 1938, however, United Artist producer Goldwyn pressured the studio to cancel Giannini's contract because he was not satisfied with Giannini's ability to sell the films the studio produced. Giannini was insulted when the studio asked him to negotiate the employment contract for his successor. He resigned and received a settlement of $168,000.

Giannini continued to be involved in the movie business throughout his retirement. He was a trustee of Universal Pictures and director of Columbia Pictures Corporation, Selznick International Pictures Incorporated, Lesser-Lubitsch and Company, and Fox West Coast Theaters. He led community chest campaigns, sponsored the Philharmonic Orchestra, and was a member of the board of regents of Loyola University, Los Angeles. Giannini died in Los Angeles while attending a regents annual meeting.

Six years after his death, the Giannini family protested when 20th Century–Fox released *House of Strangers*, a film about a venomous Italian-American banking family. The director and co-writer, Joseph Mankiewicz, modeled it on the widely publicized Giannini in-fighting and constructed a set that duplicated Giannini's original San Francisco bank.

• Reference to Giannini's family history and his contribution to his brother's banking can be found in Gerald D. Nash, *A. P. Giannini and the Bank of America* (1992); Marquis James and Bessie Rowland James, *Biography of a Bank: The Story of Bank of America* (1954); and Felice A. Bonadio, *A. P. Giannini: Banker of America* (1994). See Tino Balio, *United Artists: The Company Built by the Stars* (1976), for details on Giannini's lending and executive role. An obituary is in the *New York Times*, 8 Feb. 1943.

BARBARA L. CICCARELLI

GIAUQUE, William Francis (12 May 1895–28 Mar. 1982), chemist and educator, was born in Niagara Falls, Ontario, Canada, the son of William Tecumseh Sherman Giauque, a railroad worker, and Isabella Jane Duncan. Because his parents were U.S. citizens their three children, although born in Canada, also had U.S. citizenship. When Giauque was a boy, the family lived in Michigan, where he attended school until the age of thirteen, when his father died and the family returned to his hometown. That same year Giauque entered the Niagara Falls Collegiate and Vocational Institute, intending to complete the two-year commercial course so that he, as the oldest son, could help support the family. His mother, however, assisted by the family of local chemist John W. Beckman (for whom she worked part time as a seamstress), persuaded Giauque to switch to the five-year college preparatory program. He initially thought that he would pursue a major in electrical engineering, but in order to make some money as well as gain some engineering experience, he worked for two years at the Hooker Electrochemical Company in Niagara Falls, New York, and his experience in the company's laboratory led him to study chemical rather than electrical engineering.

Beckman heard about Giauque's switch in interest to chemical engineering, and in 1916, after Beckman had been transferred to Berkeley, California, Mrs. Beckman wrote to the Giauques of her husband's high opinion of the University of California at Berkeley's College of Chemistry and its renowned dean, Gilbert Newton Lewis. Beckman's recommendation—and the university's modest $10 per semester fee—convinced Giauque to enroll at Berkeley instead of at the Massachusetts Institute of Technology or Rensselaer Polytechnic Institute. At Berkeley Giauque majored in chemistry, but about one-fourth of his courses were in the field of engineering. While carrying out undergraduate research on the measurement of entropy at low temperatures under Professor George Ernest Gibson, he became interested in the third law of thermodynamics. After graduating with a B.S. summa cum laude in 1920, Giauque pursued graduate work at Berkeley, becoming a university fellow (1920–1921) and James M. Goewey Fellow (1921–1922). With a dissertation produced under Gibson's immediate supervision but with the close cooperation of physicist Raymond Birge, Giauque earned a Ph.D. in chemistry with a minor in physics in 1922. Giauque had intended to pursue a career as a chemical engineer in private industry but decided instead on a research career in chemistry, persuaded both by Lewis's offer of a faculty position and by the department's emphasis on research.

Giauque spent the remainder of his career at Berkeley, where he served as instructor of chemistry (1922–1927), assistant professor (1927–1930), associate professor (1930–1934), and professor (1934–1977). He married Muriel Frances Ashley, a Berkeley Ph.D. in physics, who was a spectroscopist and botanist, in 1932; the couple had two sons. During World War II he designed a mobile unit for the production of liquid oxygen. He was elected faculty research lecturer in 1947–1948 and was named professor emeritus in 1962 but that same year was recalled as director of the low-temperature research program, retiring again in 1981, a year before his death in Oakland, California. Giauque published more articles during the last half of his sixty years at Berkeley than during the first thirty. In all, he published 183 articles and trained fifty-one graduate students. Many of his students became scientists active in cryogenics. A cryogenics laboratory on

the Berkeley campus named in his honor opened in 1966.

Giauque's earliest experiments involved entropy at low temperature and the third law of thermodynamics, and he pursued studies of the properties of matter at the lowest attainable temperatures throughout his career. The third law, initially known as the Nernst heat theorem, was first enunciated in 1906 by German chemist Walther Nernst, who postulated that in any reaction involving only solids or liquids, including solutions, the change in entropy (the degree of disorder in matter) approached zero as the temperature approached absolute zero (O K, $-273.16°C$, or $-459.69°F$). In 1911 German physicist Max Planck argued that Nernst's theorem was not valid for solutions and therefore required an adjustment: the assignment of zero entropy to each element at absolute zero. Planck also understood the theorem to mean that all pure solids and liquids are characterized by zero entropy at absolute zero. Lewis and Gibson, however, argued that entropy was a measure of the randomness of a macroscopic state, that some randomness exists in the structure of even a pure solid or liquid, and that therefore zero entropy is possible only in a perfect crystal of a pure solid or liquid at absolute zero. In 1920 they stated the third law as currently accepted, that the entropy of a perfect crystal is zero at absolute zero.

Giauque confirmed Lewis and Gibson's interpretation in both his dissertation and his first publication ("The Third Law of Thermodynamics: Evidence from the Specific Heats of Glycerol That the Entropy of a Glass Exceeds That of a Crystal at the Absolute Zero," *Journal of the American Chemical Society* 45 [1923]: 93–104, with Gibson), showing that glycerol supercooled at 70 K possesses considerably greater entropy than does crystalline glycerol, and he concluded that this difference exists even at absolute zero. During the remainder of the 1920s and the early 1930s he and his students continued these third-law confirmations with a series of studies on diatomic gases, such as hydrogen chloride and carbon monoxide. These experiments displayed Giauque's characteristic thoroughness and accuracy. They also verified the use of quantum statistics and the partition function in calculating entropy.

From 1928 to 1932 Giauque's research focused on the entropies of gases, and it showed that some molecules, including the hydrogen molecule (H_2), crystallize with residual entropy as the temperature approaches absolute zero. The entropy of solid hydrogen results from a disordered nuclear spin alignment of the two protons in the molecule. In 1927 German physicist Werner Heisenberg proposed that hydrogen and other diatomic molecules of elements could exist in two forms—antisymmetrical (ortho) and symmetrical (para). At the suggestion of American physicist Edward U. Condon, Giauque and graduate student Herrick L. Johnston kept 20 grams of pure hydrogen in a steel container at liquid air temperature (85 K) for 197 days and observed a decrease in its vapor pressure of 0.4 mm. The two attributed this decrease to the reversal of the nuclear spins of the higher-energy ortho form to assume the lower-energy para form, and they obtained an entropy difference that supported Lewis and Gibson's third-law interpretation. Karl Bonhoeffer and Paul Harteck first separated ortho- and parahydrogen in 1929, and by the 1930s the existence of molecular hydrogen in two forms had been established unequivocally.

Giauque's most important scientific contribution—the adiabatic magnetic cooling technique—resulted from third-law studies. This technique enabled scientists to obtain temperatures close to absolute zero and thereby to understand better the principles and mechanisms of electrical and thermal conductivity, to determine heat capacities, and to study the behavior of superconductors at very low temperatures. Giauque realized that applying a strong magnetic field to paramagnetic substances would align the random atomic polar axes in one direction, a process that should generate heat; by using a cooling cycle to carry away this heat, removing the magnetic field to disorder the atoms again, and repeating the process, the paramagnetic substance should be cooled to temperatures unattainable by the then-prevailing technique of compression and expansion. Giauque announced this idea at an American Chemical Society meeting on 9 April 1926 and published it in 1927, but funding and technical problems delayed his experiment until 19 March 1933, when he and graduate student Duncan P. MacDougall used an 8,000 gauss magnet to obtain a temperature of 0.53 K in previously cooled gadolinium sulfate octahydrate. With magnets of more than 100,000 gauss Giauque later attained temperatures as low as 0.004 K. At such low temperatures the commonly used constant-volume gas thermometer was useless, so he developed alternative methods of measuring temperatures, finally inventing a very sensitive carbon (lampblack) resistance thermometer for temperatures below 1 K.

In 1929, while studying the entropy of oxygen, Giauque and Johnston were unable to explain some faint lines in its spectrum. Although others might have ignored these minor deviations or ascribed them to impurities or to unknown higher-energy levels, Giauque, with his characteristic attention to detail, pursued the matter until he could explain the discrepancy. After several months of work, he announced that the lines must be due to small amounts of two hitherto unknown isotopes (forms of an element with the same atomic number but different atomic weights, that is, the same number of protons but a different number of neutrons)—oxygen-17 (0.037 percent) and oxygen-18 (0.204 percent), oxygen with atomic weights of 17 and 18, respectively. Because chemists had arbitrarily assigned an exact relative atomic weight of 16.0000 as the standard for atomic weights to what Giauque showed was an unsuspected three-isotope mixture, a small discrepancy was now obvious between the chemists' atomic weight values and those of the physicists (mass spectrometric scale). Conversion from the physicists' to the chemists' scale involved division by

1.00027. Both scales continued in use until 1961, when the International Union of Pure and Applied Chemistry and the International Commission on Atomic Weights abandoned the O = 16.0000 scale and adopted the carbon-12 isotope scale with ^{12}C = 12.0000 as the new standard. Giauque's discovery of oxygen-18 also provided an isotopic tracer that enabled the study of the mechanisms of photosynthesis and respiration and that led Harold C. Urey and his co-workers to discover deuterium (hydrogen-2) in 1931.

In 1949 Giauque was awarded the Nobel Prize in chemistry "for his contributions in the field of classical thermodynamics, particularly concerning the behavior of substances at extremely low temperatures." According to former student William L. Jolly, a quiz had been scheduled for the day after the prize announcement, and when Giauque entered the classroom, all the students clapped. He then said, on one of the rare occasions when he smiled, "All right, but we're still going to have the quiz today." A serious and intense man who abhorred publicity and avoided most social functions, Giauque would have preferred a less ostentatious way of being awarded the Nobel Prize.

Giauque's other awards included the Pacific Division Discovery Prize of the American Association for the Advancement of Science for discovery of the oxygen isotopes (with Johnston, 1929), Lectureship and Medal of Columbia University's Charles Frederick Chandler Foundation (1936), the Franklin Institute's Elliott Cresson Medal (1937), the American Chemical Society Chicago Section's J. Willard Gibbs Medal (1951), and the ACS California Section's Gilbert Newton Lewis Award (1956). He also was a Fellow of the American Physical Society and the American Academy of Arts and Sciences.

Giauque had few outside interests, and because many of his low-temperature experiments were of long duration and required constant attention, during his early career he and his assistants worked as many as sixty hours without sleep. His philosophy was, "Keep the experiment running." He was an adept experimenter, but he did not own an automobile until he succumbed to family pressure after receiving the Nobel Prize. He always refused to drive, however, and was chauffeured by his wife until her death in 1981.

Giauque calculated the entropy and other thermodynamic properties of substances at extremely low temperatures with ten times the accuracy of any previous researcher. These entropies, together with heats of formation, permit calculation of free energies, which can be used to predict the direction and extent of chemical reactions. He was the first to demonstrate the validity of the third law of thermodynamics, he developed an ingenious technique for reaching temperatures near absolute zero, and he discovered two hitherto unrecognized isotopes of oxygen. In the words of Arne Tiselius of the Royal Swedish Academy of Sciences, who presented him with the Nobel Prize, Giauque's achievements constitute "one of the most significant contributions to modern physical chemistry."

• Giauque's extensive papers are in the History of Science and Technology Collection, Bancroft Library Archives, University of California, Berkeley, as is a 61-page oral history (1974), which cannot be viewed by the public because Giauque never signed a release, and four short, unpublished biographical memoirs (1948 and 1949). His work is summarized in his Nobel lecture, "Some Consequences of Low Temperature Research in Chemical Thermodynamics," in *Nobel Lectures: Chemistry 1942–1962* (1964), pp. 227–50, and some of his articles are collected in *Low Temperature Chemical and Magneto Thermodynamics, I. 1923–1949: The Scientific Papers of William F. Giauque* (1969). In addition to entries on Giauque in the standard reference works, biographical articles with summaries of his work include "Giauque Awarded Nobel Prize for Low Temperature Research," *Chemical and Engineering News*, 28 Nov. 1949, p. 3571; D. N. Lyon and K. S. Pitzer, "William Francis Giauque," in *University of California, In Memoriam* (1985), pp. 152–56; "William F. Giauque," in *Nobel Prize Winners*, ed. Tyler Wasson (1987), pp. 374–75 (with photograph); and William L. Jolly, *From Retorts to Lasers: The Story of Chemistry at Berkeley* (1987), pp. 128–31.

GEORGE B. KAUFFMAN

GIBBES, Robert Wilson (8 July 1809–15 Oct. 1866), writer, physician, and scientist, was born in Charleston, South Carolina, the son of William Hasell Gibbes, a lawyer, and Mary Philip Wilson. It was a well-established Charleston family. Gibbes's father achieved considerable notoriety for his achievements in the Revolution, and his grandfather served as chief justice of South Carolina early in the previous century.

Although he was once been expelled for "rebellion," Gibbes graduated from South Carolina College (later the University of South Carolina) in 1827 and continued at the college as an assistant to Thomas Cooper in the department of chemistry, mineralogy, and geology. That same year, he married Carolina Elizabeth Guignard; they had twelve children. Gibbes received his M.D. from the Medical College of the State of South Carolina in 1834, and purchased a private practice in Columbia. He also served two twelve-month terms as intendant (mayor) of the city in 1839 and 1840.

Gibbes established an infirmary for black slaves at the rear of his office, with an adjoining dissecting room, and tended the large number of slaves on the estate of General Wade Hampton. During this time he undertook researches that led to the publication of "On Typhoid Pneumonia" (*American Journal of the Medical Sciences* [1842]), which revolutionized treatment of the disease by arguing against bloodletting. Gen. Hampton claimed that Gibbes saved him over $5,000 a year in lost slaves.

Although he was a practicing physician, Gibbes's interests in geology and paleontology were widely known. He frequently corresponded with Samuel G. Morton on the subject and occasionally visited him in Philadelphia. When teeth and the partial jaw of a fossil animal were discovered near the Carolina coast in 1845, they were sent off to Gibbes in Columbia. His attempt to identify them as part of a new genus, *Dorudon*, led to a debate in the *Proceedings* of the Philadel-

phia Academy of Natural Sciences, with famed English paleontologist Richard Owen apparently having the final negative word. Gibbes persisted in his interest, however, and had several other articles on paleontology published by the Philadelphia Academy and by the Smithsonian Institution.

Gibbes followed Morton as an outspoken opponent of traditional views of biblical creation and an ardent supporter of the new theories of geology and of the origins of humankind. His efforts to promote these views in South Carolina led him into more than one conflict with local clergy. Gibbes objected not just to the brief time frame implied by *Genesis*, but also to the idea of a single origin for humanity. Following the views of another friend and correspondent, Josiah Clark Nott of Mobile, he maintained that there were several distinct origins of the human species, and consequently several distinct human races. Such theories did much to bolster Gibbes's support of slavery and white superiority.

Gibbes was also a writer, businessman, and historian. In 1853 he published his three-volume *Documentary History of the American Revolution*, which continues to be a valuable source for letters and papers dealing with the war in South Carolina. In the settlement of a mortgage debt, Gibbes took over a Columbia newspaper, the *Daily South Carolinian*, in 1852, and served as its editor for the next six years. In 1855 he purchased the Saluda Company, plagued with financial difficulties, and ran it profitably for the next decade as the Columbia Cotton Mill, producing the rough cotton shirting principally used to clothe slaves.

A chronic sufferer from asthma and other lung ailments, Gibbes was forced to spend four months in bed at the end of 1859 and resolved to spend the winter in a more favorable climate. He chose to convalesce in southern Cuba and was so favorably impressed by the island and by his rapid improvement that immediately on returning he wrote *Cuba for Invalids* (1860), a book rich in local color that carefully describes the island's geology, natural history, and people.

Gibbes was elected president of the South Carolina Medical Association in 1857 and 1858 and was appointed surgeon general of South Carolina in 1861, a position he held throughout the Civil War. At one point he was sent by the Confederate Congress to examine the hospitals in Virginia, receiving praise for his work. The end of the war, however, was disastrous for Gibbes. When Columbia was burned in 1865, he lost his newspaper and his home, with its valuable collections of art, minerals, and fossils. The cotton mill failed. The final years of his life were marked by depression and rapidly failing health, and he died in Columbia.

Although he was an outstanding teacher and physician, Gibbes's racism marred much of his scientific, political, and literary work. The war for the cause that he held so dear brought him only sorrow and ruin.

• Gibbes's correspondence with Morton is in Morton's papers at the American Philosophical Society in Philadelphia. The collection of the University of South Carolina contains many of Gibbes's legal and business papers along with several personal letters, a notebook from Cuba, and a manuscript of the *Documentary History*. The *Documentary History* was reprinted in 1972. The life of Gibbes is outlined in Joseph I. Waring, *History of Medicine in South Carolina, 1825–1900* (1967), which includes a portrait; and in A. R. Childs, "Robert Wilson Gibbes, 1809–1866," *Bulletin of the University of South Carolina*, 1 Oct. 1926. His work in paleontology and geology is described in Richard M. Jellison and Phillip S. Swartz, "The Scientific Interests of Robert W. Gibbes," *South Carolina Historical Magazine* 66 (1965): 77–97.

CHARLES D. KAY

GIBBON, John (20 Apr. 1827–6 Feb. 1896), army officer, was born in Holmesburg, Pennsylvania, the third son of John Heysham Gibbon and Catharine Lardner. During John's childhood, the family moved to Charlotte, North Carolina, where his father became chief assayer of the U.S. Mint. There the elder Gibbon became a slaveowner affiliated with the Democratic party. Appointed to the U.S. Military Academy from North Carolina in 1842, John graduated in 1847 in the middle of his class, having repeated his second year due to difficulties with the English course.

As a brevet second lieutenant, Gibbon was dispatched to Mexico where active operations had already ceased. Commissioned in the artillery, the young officer next served in Florida, seeing action against the Seminole Indians and assisting in their evacuation to the Oklahoma Territory. Gibbon's service in this campaign resulted in an enduring sympathy for Native Americans.

In 1855, he returned to West Point as an artillery instructor, and on 16 October of that year, he married Frances North Moale. The marriage produced four children. During his assignment to the U.S. Military Academy, Gibbon was promoted to captain and transformed his artillery lecture notes into a formal text. *The Artillerist's Manual*, published in 1859, was adopted as standard doctrine for the U.S. Army and replaced a previously used French manual.

Ordered to Utah in 1859, Gibbon became controversial during the secession crisis when he had the military band at Fort Crittenden play the rebel tune "Dixie." Three of his fellow officers then brought charges of treason against him. Defended by his commander, Philip St. George Cooke, Gibbon vigorously proclaimed his loyalty to the Union and prevailed. His parents remained in North Carolina and his three brothers would later fight for the Confederacy. Gibbon and his light artillery battery returned east in the summer of 1861 and, on 8 November, joined Irvin McDowell's division in the Army of the Potomac. Gibbon became the division's chief of artillery, and on 2 May 1862, he was appointed brigadier general of volunteers, commanding a brigade of Brigadier General Rufus King's division six days later. On 28 August, Gibbon and his unit encountered the battlewise troops of General Thomas J. ("Stonewall") Jackson at the battle of Groveton, Virginia, where Gibbon lost one-third of his command and had to retreat. With stern discipline, he whipped his organization into fighting trim

and fostered high esprit by allowing it to wear distinctive black hats. Fighting in the battle of South Mountain on 14 September and at Antietam three days later, his unit became known as the "Iron Brigade." Assigned to command the Second Division of John F. Reynolds's I Corps, Gibbon was wounded leading an attack at Fredericksburg on 13 December. After his recovery, the general was given command of the Second Division of Winfield S. Hancock's II Corps where, with one interruption, he served until 1865. He participated in the battle at Chancellorsville and gained considerable fame during the following battle at Gettysburg. It was Gibbon's division that absorbed and repulsed General George E. Pickett's charge on 3 July 1863. In the successful and valiant defense on Cemetery Hill, Gibbon received another wound and was carried from the field. After commanding draft depots in both Cleveland, Ohio, and Philadelphia, Pennsylvania, during his convalescence, the general once again returned to the Army of the Potomac and division command in 1864. In early 1865, he was brevetted major general and given command of a newly formed XXIV Corps, Army of the James. At the surrender of Confederate general Robert E. Lee's Army of Northern Virginia, Gibbon served as one of three Union commissioners.

Reduced in rank following the Civil War, John Gibbon served in the West, participated in Indian campaigns, rose to department command, and was promoted to brigadier general in the regular army on 10 July 1885. In the postwar era, Gibbon commanded both the Thirty-sixth and Seventh Infantry regiments, the latter assignment beginning in 1869. Against the Sioux in 1876, Gibbon's Seventh Infantry recovered the survivors of George A. Custer's Seventh Cavalry at Little Big Horn and buried the dead. Against the Nez Percé in 1877, his command was bested by Chief Joseph in a bloody fight at Big Hole, Montana. There, Gibbon was wounded for the third and last time in his military career. After the battle, the two leaders, Gibbon and Chief Joseph, became friends.

Gibbon wrote *Personal Recollections of the Civil War* in the early 1880s, a book that was not published until 1928. Serving as the commander of the Department of Columbia in 1885, he had to place the city of Seattle under martial law during the anti-Chinese riots the next year. Gibbon retired from the army in 1891, settling in Baltimore, Maryland. During his last years, he became commander in chief, Military Order of the Loyal Legion. He died in Baltimore. Although he had a tendency toward personal disputes with a few of his contemporaries, John Gibbon was a solid and steady battle commander, a firm disciplinarian, a competent writer, and a man who enjoyed a lifelong reputation for honesty and bravery.

• Gibbon's personal and family correspondence can be found at the Historical Society of Pennsylvania (Philadelphia) and the Maryland Historical Society (Baltimore). Wartime official letters and orders are published in *The War of the Rebellion: A Compilation of the Official Records of the Union and*

Confederate Armies. His own account of the war is *Personal Recollections of the Civil War* (1928). The general's encounter with the Sioux is described in William L. English, *With Gibbon against the Sioux in 1876: The Field Diary of Lt. William L. English* (1966). Gibbon's life and career is best detailed in Dennis S. Lavery, "John Gibbon and the Old Army: Portrait of an American Professional Soldier, 1827–1896" (Ph.D. diss., Pennsylvania State Univ., 1974).

ROD PASCHALL

GIBBON, John Heysham, Jr. (29 Sept. 1903–5 Feb. 1973), surgeon, was born in Philadelphia, Pennsylvania, the son of John Heysham Gibbon, a surgeon, and Mary Young. Gibbon received his early education at Penn Charter School. He graduated from Princeton in 1923 at the age of nineteen and went on to study medicine at the Jefferson Medical College. Disillusioned with medical studies, Gibbon almost dropped out of school to become an artist or a poet, but his father discouraged this decision, and Gibbon obtained his M.D. from Jefferson in 1927.

While Gibbon was an intern at the Pennsylvania Hospital, Joseph Hayman stimulated his interest in research by showing him the useful information he obtained in controlled experiments on the effects of sodium versus potassium in the diets of hypertensive patients. Gibbon decided to pursue a career in research and surgery, obtaining a research fellowship with Edward Churchill at the Harvard Medical School. He began his work with Churchill in a small laboratory at the Boston City Hospital in 1930. His first experiments were concerned with the patho-physiology of arterio-venous fistulas.

In February 1931 a patient in the Massachusetts General Hospital had a massive pulmonary embolism following a cholecystectomy. At that time the results of surgical removal of pulmonary emboli tended to be so poor that the Trendelenburg operation was delayed until the patient was practically moribund. When this patient was taken to the operating room, Gibbon was instructed to notify his chief when her condition deteriorated to the point that the dangerous pulmonary embolectomy could be justified. By morning the patient was failing rapidly, and she was operated upon but died. The idea now occurred to Gibbon that if he could have removed the unoxygenated venous blood, lowered its carbon dioxide, oxygenated it, and pumped the oxygenated red blood into the aorta, he could have saved this patient.

While in Massachusetts in 1931, Gibbon married Mary Hopkinson, the daughter of Charles Hopkinson, a prominent portraitist. They had four children.

Gibbon returned to Philadelphia in the spring of 1931 to work in the physiology department of the University of Pennsylvania Medical School, collaborating with Eugene Landis and Hugh Montgomery on the relationship of temperature and tissue pressure to fluid flow through the capillary wall. During the years 1931 and 1932 he also practiced surgery at the Pennsylvania Hospital in the mornings, working in the laboratory in the afternoons. This research and the contact with

Landis had a profound influence on Gibbon's future. He often discussed with Landis the possibility of developing an apparatus for cardiopulmonary bypass. Finally Landis told him, "If you think you can accomplish this feat, you should go back to Churchill at Harvard and work on this problem. You will never be satisfied until you try." Gibbon asked Churchill for a one-year fellowship to start development of a heart-lung machine, and Churchill reluctantly agreed. Gibbon and his wife began work on the machine.

Pumping blood from the venous circulation to the arterial was easily solved. More difficult was obtaining sufficient gas exchange between venous blood and air to sustain life. All of the procedures the team tried failed. Finally, with the aid of a professor of steam engineering at Harvard, Gibbon designed a device that spread blood in a thin film over a revolving vertical cylinder, increasing gas exchange. The Gibbons' first machine was unimpressive in appearance, but it worked: it maintained heart and lung function in a cat.

In 1933 the Gibbons returned to Philadelphia to continue their work in the Harrison Department of Surgical Research at the University of Pennsylvania. A large part of the department's budget was poured into this project by I. S. Ravdin, its director. They built two improved machines, which they named Queen Mary I and II. These allowed them to maintain complete pulmonary cardiac bypass for twenty-five minutes in cats, which survived indefinitely.

The work was discontinued when Gibbon joined the Army Medical Corps during World War II. From 1942 to 1945 he served in the South Pacific and as chief of surgery at the Mayo General Hospital, Galesberg, Illinois. After the war he served for a brief period as an assistant professor of surgery at the University of Pennsylvania and a surgeon at the Pennsylvania Hospital. In 1946 he was appointed director of surgical research at the Jefferson Medical College, where he had his own facilities and assistants to develop the heart-lung machine.

Although Gibbon was able to build a larger machine with greater pumping and gas exchange capacities, he needed an engineer and mechanical shop to design and construct a machine suitable for human use. He interested Thomas J. Watson, president of International Business Machine Corporation (IBM), to aid him with this project. Watson provided the design and engineering talent, and within a short time a machine was built that was capable of carrying the circulation of an adult human. Two assistants, T. Lane Stokes and John Flick, solved the remaining problem of providing sufficient gas exchange for human pulmonary bypass. On 6 May 1953 the IBM heart-lung machine was used at Thomas Jefferson Hospital during successful open-heart surgery on a twelve-year-old girl, Cecelia Bavolek. She was connected to the apparatus for forty-five minutes, while all cardiopulmonary function was taken over by the machine for twenty-five minutes. Gibbon's machine was the first developed that satisfactorily allowed bypass of the heart and lungs with successful oxygenation of blood. All subsequent heart-lung machines are modifications of Gibbon's original.

In 1956 Gibbon was appointed Samuel Gross Professor of Surgery and chairman of the Department of Surgery at the Jefferson Medical College, a position he held until 1967, when he retired to his farm in Media, Pennsylvania. He was elected to the National Academy of Sciences in 1972. He died in Media while playing tennis.

• Gibbon wrote "Application of a Mechanical Heart and Lung Apparatus to Cardiac Surgery," *Minnesota Medicine* 17 (1954): 171–77. Several biographical sketches and tributes appeared after Gibbon's death, including "Memorial Service for John Heysham Gibbon, Jr., M.D.," *Transactions and Studies of the College of Physicians of Philadelphia* 41 (1974): 176–94; Jonathan E. Rhoads, "Memoir of John Heysham Gibbon, Jr., 1903–73," *Transactions and Studies of the College of Physicians of Philadelphia* 41 (1974): 194–97; and Harris B. Shumacker, Jr., "John Heysham Gibbon, Jr., September 29, 1903–February 5, 1973," National Academy of Sciences, *Biographical Memoirs* 53 (1982): 213–47. A good review of the development of the heart-lung machine is given in Richard H. Meade, *A History of Thoracic Surgery* (1961). See also Anthony R. C. Dobell, "Surgery in the Era of Technology," American College of Surgeons, *Bulletin* 75 (Apr. 1990): 6–12. An obituary is in the *New York Times*, 6 Feb. 1973.

DAVID Y. COOPER

GIBBONS, Abigail Hopper (7 Dec. 1801–16 Jan. 1893), prison reformer and abolitionist, was born in Philadelphia, Pennsylvania, the daughter of Isaac Tatem Hopper and Sarah Tatum, Quakers. Her father earned a moderate living as a tailor and later as a bookseller but devoted most of his time to aiding runaway slaves and free blacks. Her mother was a minister in the Society of Friends. Two years after her mother's death in 1822, her father remarried, and in 1829 he moved with most of his family to New York City. Abigail joined them in 1830 and helped support the family by teaching at a Quaker school.

Abigail Hopper married James Sloan Gibbons, a Philadelphia Quaker and a merchant-banker, in 1833; they had six children. They lived for a brief period in Philadelphia, then relocated to New York City, where they were active in numerous social reforms, especially abolition and prison reform. Because of their antislavery activity, both her father and her husband were expelled from the New York Monthly Meeting of Friends in 1841. She resigned from the society publicly a year later, although she never personally abandoned the Quaker plainness of speech and dress.

With the family comfortably supported by James's business, Abigail Gibbons was able to devote considerable energy to her reform efforts. As an organizer of fundraising antislavery fairs for the Manhattan Anti-Slavery Society, she became part of the abolitionist circle that included such well-known figures as William Lloyd Garrison and Lydia Maria Child.

In addition to antislavery, Gibbons joined with her father in his efforts to bring about the rehabilitation of prisoners. In 1845 her father helped found the Prison Association of New York, and she led the Female Department of the association. The next year she helped establish an institution to house female ex-prisoners, later known as the Isaac T. Hopper Home. As one of the first American women to address the concerns of women prisoners, Gibbons undertook with her co-workers to convert female convicts to religion. However, the reformers came increasingly to question the common notion that individual moral failings accounted for women criminals' predicament and, drawing on the antebellum ideology of a shared sense of womanhood, came to see women prisoners not as social outcasts or "fallen women," but as victims of economic and sexual circumstance. In 1853, following a dispute with male colleagues over conflicting prerogatives and over the autonomy of the women's auxiliary, Gibbons joined Catharine M. Sedgwick and others in establishing the separate Women's Prison Association and Home, which offered released prisoners both practical and spiritual aid. In 1859 she headed the German Industrial School, one of many such institutions designed to provide working-class children with employable skills.

After the start of the Civil War, Gibbons and her daughter Sarah traveled to the nation's capital to serve as nurses, remaining for over three years. During her service in Washington, D.C., her home in New York City, like those of other prominent abolitionists, was ransacked in the draft riots of 1863. Accustomed to achieving her goals despite the fact that men were in power and unintimidated by officials, Gibbons used her influence with various politicians to criticize and reform the military's operation of camps and hospitals. She objected strongly to the inefficiency of army hospitals, the use of corporal punishment, and the prevailing racism of those in command.

After the war, Gibbons continued her reform career in various capacities: by finding employment for returning soldiers through the Labor and Aid Society, by providing jobs for Civil War widows, and by helping found the New York Diet Kitchen Association to distribute food to the poor. Meanwhile she also acted as head of the Women's Prison Association from 1877 until her death. Joining with other former abolitionists in the "purity crusade" against the regulation (and, therefore, legal tolerance) of prostitution, Gibbons headed the New York Committee for the Prevention of State Regulation of Vice.

Like other reform women of her generation and class, Gibbons was a practiced lobbyist. In the 1870s she campaigned with Josephine Shaw Lowell for the establishment of separate women's prisons managed by women. Partly due to her efforts, the New York legislature passed a bill in 1890 requiring the employment of police matrons and two years later voted in a measure establishing a women's reformatory in New York City. Gibbons, who had addressed the legislature on behalf of the latter bill at age ninety-one, was enormously gratified by its passage.

Although Gibbons did not devote her energies to the woman suffrage movement, she did serve as a vice president at the Tenth Woman's Rights Convention in

1860 and maintained contact with many leaders of the movement. For Gibbons, distance from electoral politics fit with both her Quaker reticence and her conviction that, as she wrote a year before her death, "I have not needed [the vote] up to this time, as I always *take* what I want."

Abby Hopper Gibbons died in New York City, having bridged the transition in social reform activity from a largely voluntary, religion-based effort to one characterized by the use of professional workers, legislative solutions, and a partnership between upper-class women and the state.

• Civil War letters between Abigail and James Gibbons are in the Gibbons family Civil War Correspondence New-York Historical Society; several letters from Gibbons also appear in the Antislavery Collection at the Boston Public Library. The major source on Gibbons's life is Sarah Hopper Emerson, ed., *Life of Abby Hopper Gibbons, Told Chiefly through Her Correspondence* (2 vols., 1897). Information on Gibbons's prison reform activities can be found in Caroline M. Kirkland, *The Helping Hand: Comprising an Account of the Home for Discharged Female Convicts and an Appeal in Behalf of That Institution* (1853), and in the Women's Prison Association *Annual Reports*. L. P. Brockett and Mary Vaughan, *Woman's Work in the Civil War* (1867), includes information on Gibbons's nursing activity. An obituary is in the *New York Times*, 18 Jan. 1893.

LORI D. GINZBERG

GIBBONS, Euell Theophilus (8 Sept. 1911–29 Dec. 1975), author and naturalist, was born in Clarksville, Texas, the son of Ely Joseph Gibbons, a carpenter, blacksmith, grocer, and rancher, and Laura Augusta Bowers. Gibbons's mother taught him much about identifying edible wild plants. In 1922 the Gibbons family moved to New Mexico, where extreme poverty forced the family to live on scavenged roots and small game. Leaving home at age fifteen, Gibbons worked as a farmhand and carpenter in Texas and New Mexico. From the Navajo Indians in northern New Mexico he further broadened his knowledge of wild foods.

At age twenty-one Gibbons began living as a hobo in California and the Pacific Northwest, catching rides on trains and foraging for his food. After attending a Communist party camp meeting for the homeless, Gibbons joined the organization and began writing and distributing polemical leaflets. He worked intermittently, including a stint as a laborer in a San Jose canning factory. After being fired from the Continental Can Company, Gibbons worked briefly at a federal work camp, but was soon jailed for inciting labor unrest. Joining the army in 1934, he served as a boat builder and carpenter until 1936. During his term of service, he married Anna Swanson in September 1935; they had two children. After his discharge, he worked odd jobs in Washington State, primarily building boats, and became a district organizer for the Communist party. He resigned this position and his membership in the party when the Soviet Union invaded Finland in 1939.

Although Gibbons remained a civilian during the Second World War, he worked for the U.S. Navy at Pearl Harbor, first as a boatbuilder and then as a hospital worker. After the war he remained on Hawaii, living in a thatched hut on the beach and surviving on foraged food for two years. In 1947 Gibbons entered the University of Hawaii to study anthropology and creative writing, supporting himself by writing crossword puzzles in Hawaiian for the *Honolulu Advertiser*. After divorcing his first wife in 1946, Gibbons married Freda Fryer, a teacher, in December 1949; they had no children but obtained custody of the children from Gibbons's first marriage. Gibbons became a Quaker in 1949. He left the University of Hawaii without graduating in 1950, taking up a position teaching carpentry and boat-building at the Maui Vocational School. He taught there until 1953, when he moved to Moorestown, New Jersey, and taught in a Quaker school for one year. He also attended Temple University part time. After this he worked as a farmer in Greenfield, Illinois, helping to found an agricultural commune. Moving to Wallingford, Pennsylvania, in 1955, Gibbons worked on the buildings and ground staff at Pendle Hill, a Quaker study center, for the next five years. He took classes there while on the staff.

In 1960 the Gibbons family moved to a cooperative community near Philadelphia, called Tanguy Homesteads. From 1960 to 1975, with his wife's financial support, Gibbons worked as a full-time writer. He first authored an unsuccessful novel about a teacher and wild food, "Mr. Markel Retires." The literary agent who read it declined to publish it as a novel but suggested that Gibbons rewrite it as a text on wild foods. After some revision and additional research into Native American botany and the journals of early American explorers, the novel became the nonfiction *Stalking the Wild Asparagus* (1962). Combining home-tested recipes with philosophical musings and anecdotes from his life of foraging, *Stalking the Wild Asparagus* was a highly personal and down-to-earth work. Accessible and entertaining, it provided many readers with their first exposure to a multitude of unusual ingredients and wild foods. Instantly successful, it enabled Gibbons to get a job writing and editing for the magazine *Organic Gardening and Farming*.

Gibbons moved to Troxelville, Pennsylvania, in 1963. He continued to write prolifically, publishing *Stalking the Blue-Eyed Scallop* (1964), *Stalking the Healthful Herbs* (1966), *Stalking the Good Life: My Love Affair with Nature* (1971), and *Stalking the Faraway Places* (1973). He also appeared on televised commercials as a spokesman for the cereal Grape-Nuts, a job that ended abruptly when the Federal Trade Commission ruled that his descriptions of edible wild foods might cause children to eat poisonous plants. At the time of Gibbons's death in Beaverstown, Pennsylvania, he was working on *Euell Gibbons's Handbook of Edible Wild Plants*, which was published posthumously in 1979 and cowritten by Gordon Tucker.

• Gibbons's papers are housed at Boston University. For further information on Gibbons, see John McPhee, "Profiles: A Forager," *New Yorker*, 6 Apr. 1968, and "The Forager," *New*

York Times, 10 Jan. 1976; and J. Goldstein, "Blame It All on George's Mom," *Organic Gardening and Farming* (Oct. 1975). An obituary is in the *New York Times*, 30 Dec. 1975.

ELIZABETH ZOE VICARY

GIBBONS, Floyd (16 July 1887–24 Sept. 1939), journalist, foreign correspondent, and newscaster, was born in Washington, D.C., a few blocks from the Capitol, the son of Edward T. Gibbons and Emma Phillips. His father ran a successful butter and egg business in Washington and owned a small chain of stores. As a child Gibbons delivered butter and eggs in the nation's capital.

The family moved to Des Moines, Iowa, when Floyd was eleven and a few years later to Minneapolis; in both cases so that Edward Gibbons could start up new business ventures, in all of which he seemed to be successful. Floyd was sent back east to Georgetown University, but he was expelled for a prank before obtaining a degree. He returned to Minneapolis, where he got a job as a cub reporter on the *Minneapolis Daily News*. Although this venture originally had the approval of his father, shortly thereafter the elder Gibbons visited the paper's editor to ask him to fire Floyd. (Privately, he believed that newspapermen turned out to be either bums or drunks.) But the editor replied, "No, Mr. Gibbons, I won't fire your son. He seems to have a natural nose for news, and the only way he will leave this paper will be by his own volition."

Gibbons, who possessed an irrepressible, ebullient, and outgoing personality, made a highly successful reporter, and between 1907 and 1912 he worked on several other midwestern papers, including the *Milwaukee Free Press* and the *Minneapolis Tribune*. In 1912 he joined the staff of the *Chicago Tribune*, with which he was strongly identified over the next two decades. He quickly gained a reputation as a "headline hunter" and was frequently sent on dangerous assignments. In 1914 he was sent by the *Chicago Tribune* to Mexico to flush out the desperado Pancho Villa, who had been sought without success by the U.S. Army. Gibbons not only found Villa but also became his confidant and followed him from place to place. Also in 1914 Gibbons married Isabelle Pherrman; a childless marriage, it ended in divorce ten years later.

When the United States entered World War I, Gibbons was assigned to head the *Tribune*'s London bureau. He achieved his first nationwide fame, however, even before he landed in London. He was instructed to sail to England on the SS *Frederick VIII*, which was carrying home Count von Bernsdorff, the discredited German ambassador to Washington. The ship had been promised free passage home by the Allies and surely would not be sunk by a German submarine. However, to get a better story Gibbons chose to sail on the Cunard liner SS *Laconia*, which was clearly under threat from the German submarine fleet. The *Laconia* was indeed sunk off the Irish coast; Gibbons was later rescued, along with many others, by a British mine sweeper. But the story he cabled home from Queens-town appeared in papers all over the United States and began his national reputation.

Gibbons was anything but a desk-hugging bureau chief. He followed the Allied Expeditionary Force into Europe and reported on its battles firsthand. Traveling with the Fifth Marine Corps he lost his left eye to a stray bullet in the battle of Belleau Wood; subsequently he wore an eye patch because he had lost his lower eyelid, which could not be restored in these days before plastic surgery, and he was unable to wear a prosthesis. He returned home to find himself a national hero of sorts—the French government would shortly award him several medals, including the croix de guerre and the legion of honor.

Immediately after his recovery Gibbons undertook an ambitious tour to lecture on his travels and military exploits, and he was lionized wherever he went. He also started work on his first book, *And They Thought We Wouldn't Fight* (1918), a robust defense of the Allied Expeditionary Force. During the more placid decades of the 1920s he took up a number of special assignments around the world. Among his well-publicized exploits during these years was a trip across the Sahara on camelback, an expedition supported by the French government. He showed up around the world wherever trouble was brewing. The eye patch he wore following his war injury became his signature.

In 1925 Gibbons began broadcasting for WGN, the radio station owned by the *Chicago Tribune*—this in addition to his fieldwork and writing. He did not broadcast on a regular basis at first, but in time his breathless delivery and sense of storytelling made him a favorite with the public. Soon, however, he sparked the interest of a wider audience, and in 1929 he was invited to develop a news program for the NBC network, a program called "The Headline Hunter." It was heard irregularly and was used mainly to cover late-breaking news stories from the field. On 25 August 1929 Gibbons covered the arrival of the German airship *Graf Zeppelin* at Lakehurst, New Jersey. This was believed to be the first broadcast to the public by walkie-talkie, and it was accomplished by Gibbons wearing a 24-pound transmitter on his chest.

The following year, however, Gibbons established an even more important milestone in broadcasting history. CBS, a puny upstart attempting to go head-to-head with giant NBC, conceived of the idea of a daily radio newscast. Heretofore radio had not challenged newspapers for regular delivery of news and limited itself to special coverage. But on 24 February 1930 Gibbons began broadcasting the nightly news, sponsored by *Literary Digest* magazine. The program was heard in most places at 6:45 P.M., just before "Amos 'n' Andy," then the most popular broadcast on the air. The nightly news delivered in a machine-gun-rapid–style—sometimes as many as 300 words a minute—made Gibbons's voice and name widely familiar to Americans.

Some listeners did not like the rapid-fire delivery, and some found it particularly unsettling at dinnertime, so in the fall of 1930 Gibbons was replaced by

Lowell Thomas, another adventurer-type, but with a more soothing radio style. Gibbons continued his "Headline Hunter" program, however, and now released from the daily grind, he resumed his vigorous role as a field reporter. During the 1930s Gibbons covered, among other things, the Sino–Japanese War, the Italian conquest of Ethiopia, and the Spanish civil war. Gibbons died suddenly of a heart attack in Saylorsburg, Pennsylvania.

• Unfortunately, no collection of Gibbons's major journalism exists. Gibbons himself was the author of several books, including, *The Red Knight of Germany: The Story of Baron von Richthofen* (1927) and *The Red Napoleon* (1929), a novel. *The Red Napoleon* is a futuristic account of the development of a dictatorship in the Soviet Union, an account that turned out to be a remarkably accurate prophecy of the rise of Stalin. A biography, written by his brother Edward Gibbons, is *Floyd Gibbons: Your Headline Hunter* (1953). For an account of Gibbons's place in the rise of radio news, see George H. Douglas, *The Early Days of Radio Broadcasting* (1987). Obituaries are in the *New York Times* and *Chicago Tribune*, 25 Sept. 1939.

GEORGE H. DOUGLAS

GIBBONS, James (23 July 1834–24 Mar. 1921), Roman Catholic cardinal and author, was born in Baltimore, Maryland, the son of Thomas Gibbons, a merchant clerk, and Bridget Walsh. His parents had come to the United States from Ireland about 1829, and they returned to Ireland in 1837, but after his father's death in 1847 the rest of the family moved to New Orleans. There James worked in a grocery store until a Redemptorist retreat inspired him in 1855 to enter St. Charles College, the minor seminary of Baltimore. From there he graduated to the major seminary, St. Mary's, and upon the completion of his studies in theology was ordained priest by Archbishop Francis Patrick Kenrick on 30 June 1861. He was assigned initially to St. Patrick's Parish, Baltimore, as assistant, but he was named six weeks later pastor of St. Bridget's, a mission of St. Patrick's. There he served as chaplain at Fort McHenry during the Civil War.

In 1865 Archbishop Martin John Spalding of Baltimore made Gibbons his secretary. At the Second Plenary Council of Baltimore in 1866, the prelates, at Spalding's prompting, recommended Gibbons to Rome as vicar apostolic of North Carolina. Gibbons was raised to the episcopacy by Spalding on 16 August 1868.

In North Carolina, Gibbons wrote *Faith of Our Fathers* (1876), the most popular apologetical work written by an American Catholic. In 1869–1870 he was the youngest bishop to attend the First Vatican Council. In 1872 he became bishop of Richmond while retaining his charge in North Carolina, and in 1877 he became archbishop of Baltimore.

In his first decade as archbishop Gibbons had neither great plans nor further ambitions. In 1884, however, the pope chose him to preside at the Third Plenary Council of Baltimore, which produced the most comprehensive body of legislation for the Catholic church in the United States in the nineteenth century. In 1886 he was named a cardinal. He received the cardinal's red hat from Pope Leo XIII in Rome on 17 March 1887. A week later, upon taking charge of his titular church, Santa Maria in Trastevere, he delivered a ringing sermon in praise of his native land and its political system.

While in Rome, Gibbons worked with Archbishop John Ireland (1838–1918), Bishop John J. Keane, and Monsignor Denis O'Connell, a group that would later constitute the inner circle of the "Americanizers," to prevent the Holy See from condemning the Knights of Labor as a secret society. As a result, Gibbons was proclaimed a champion of the workingman. Together the four also prevented the public condemnation urged by several bishops of the works of Henry George (1839–1897) as socialistic, won the approval of the Holy See for the Catholic University in Washington, and countered a petition from German Catholics in the United States for a measure of autonomy—a petition highly critical of Irish bishops. When in 1891 the "German question" emerged again, Gibbons preached in Milwaukee before the new German-speaking archbishop, Frederick Katzer, denouncing all who would "sow tares of discord in the fair fields of the Church in America."

Though supportive of parochial schools, Gibbons defended in 1891 the proposal of his friend Archbishop Ireland of St. Paul, Minnesota, to incorporate parochial schools into the public school system, the so-called Faribault plan. The Vatican decreed that the plan could be tolerated but in 1893 sent to the United States an apostolic delegate, Archbishop Francesco Satolli, to resolve the school controversy and other points of conflict. Though originally sympathetic to the "liberal" bishops, of whom Gibbons was the spokesman, Satolli became uneasy over their involvement in the Parliament of Religions in 1893 and their resistance to Rome's condemnation of certain secret societies. In 1895 the apostolic delegate came out for the parochial schools and the Germans.

Despite these defeats, Gibbons continued to support the Americanizers, the proponents of an American Catholic agenda that included an acceptance of the separation of church and state and the adoption of democratic procedures in the church. Irate Catholic conservatives in Europe seized upon a biography of Isaac Hecker, founder of the American Paulists, as a means to discredit the Americanizers, claiming to see in it such errors as a reliance on the Holy Spirit at the expense of external guidance, a promotion of the natural over the supernatural virtues, and a disparagement of religious vows. In the papal letter *Testem benevolentiae* of 22 January 1899, addressed to Gibbons, Pope Leo XIII condemned these ideas as the heresy of "Americanism."

Despite this blow to the Americanizers, Gibbons continued to enjoy the esteem of Catholic and non-Catholic Americans, and his public utterances commanded national and even international attention. Gibbons was often invited to deliver the invocation at nonreligious national events. He was an almost compulsive joiner, his name being among the board members of a host of national and municipal organizations, usually ones dedicated to social improvement.

Though not a man of great literary talents, he had a facile pen that was seldom idle. In addition to *Faith of Our Fathers*, he published *Our Christian Heritage* (1889), *Ambassador of Christ* (1896), *Discourses and Sermons* (1908), *A Retrospect of Fifty Years* (1916), and essays for such journals as the *North American Review* and *Putnam's Monthly*. Protestants looked to him for explanations of the Catholic position on controversial issues. His responses were always calculated to mitigate differences.

Gibbons won the friendship of Presidents Grover Cleveland, William McKinley, William Howard Taft, and especially Theodore Roosevelt (1858–1919). Though he opposed the war with Catholic Spain and initially the imperialism it begot, Gibbons, under the tutelage of Roosevelt and Taft, rallied the American bishops to oppose the Jones Act, which was designed, in effect, to dismantle the American empire. Though he denounced militarism and the arms race as unchristian and urged international arbitration, on the eve of World War I he was a proponent of preparedness and at its outbreak urged an unreserved response to the nation's call. At the state and municipal level Gibbons was a Progressive, a promoter of such reforms as city planning, public health, and the regulation of sweatshops. However, on the national level he opposed many of the Progressive goals, including the Seventeenth, Eighteenth, and Nineteenth amendments. Though publicly nonpartisan, he usually voted Democratic in state and local elections and Republican in national ones. On the fiftieth anniversary of his priesthood in 1911, business in the national capital came to a virtual standstill as almost every important official went to Baltimore to honor him.

"He reigned in Baltimore like a king," said a British admirer, "but he met every man like a comrade." Gibbons was accessible to rich and poor alike, though he evidenced a certain insensitivity to the social and psychic needs of his immigrant charges. He opposed the disfranchisement of blacks in Maryland but had little inclination to contest the color line. He was an opponent of woman suffrage. Even the workingman fared badly in many of the negotiations of the archdiocese involving differences between management and organized labor.

He exercised great power within the American Catholic Church. As archbishop of Baltimore he served as the principal conduit between the Holy See and the American church until the appointment of an apostolic delegate. As ranking prelate from 1886 he presided over all meetings of the archbishops and bishops, who usually took their cue from him rather than from the apostolic delegate. Though Vatican officials were discomfited when he presided over interdenominational marriages, ignored Roman directives, and failed to promote some of the decrees of the Third Plenary Council, and though they also thought ill of

his administrative abilities, they never criticized him openly. The Vatican was grateful for his influence with the American government in the settlement of church-state affairs.

Gibbons was not a "brick-and-mortar" bishop. He saw separate Catholic institutions and organizations as inimical to the movement of immigrant Catholics into the American mainstream. The material growth of his archdiocese resulted, for the most part, from the initiatives of religious orders, pastors, and laymen. In his administrative role Gibbons relied heavily on others, especially the Sulpician superiors of St. Mary's Seminary in Baltimore. At a time when other Catholic dioceses in the United States moved toward consolidation, centralization, bureaucratic efficiency, and greater dependence on the Vatican, Gibbons perpetuated the laissez-faire approach of nineteenth-century American bishops.

In his attachment to American principles, his ecumenism, his sense of public service, and his qualified relationship with the Holy See, Gibbons continued the Maryland tradition begun by John Carroll, the first archbishop of Baltimore, a man whom Gibbons admired. Gibbons was the most likeable of the leaders of the American Catholic church, simple, outgoing, even-tempered, seldom without a smile, sometimes vacillating, but he could be forceful and decisive.

When he died in the cathedral rectory in Baltimore, he had ruled his archdiocese for forty-three and a half years, one of the longest tenures of an American bishop. He was buried in the crypt of the cathedral.

• Though the bulk of Gibbons's papers are in the archives of the archdiocese of Baltimore, much of his correspondence can be found in the archives of other dioceses and curial congregations in Rome and the Vatican City. His unrivaled biography is John Tracy Ellis, *The Life of James Cardinal Gibbons, Archbishop of Baltimore, 1834–1921* (2 vols., 1952). See also Allen Sinclair Will, *Life of Cardinal Gibbons, Archbishop of Baltimore* (2 vols., 1922), and Thomas W. Spalding, *The Premier See: A History of the Archdiocese of Baltimore, 1789–1989* (1989).

THOMAS W. SPALDING

GIBBONS, Thomas (15 Dec. 1757–16 May 1826), planter, lawyer, and steamship owner, was born near Savannah, Georgia, the son of Joseph Gibbons and Hannah Martin, planters. Gibbons was schooled at home and in Charleston, South Carolina, where he also read law. He married Ann Heyword, but the date of the marriage is unknown. They had three children. Throughout his life Gibbons demonstrated a determined spirit. Contemporaries described him as a "high liver," possessing a "strong mind, strong passions, strong prejudices, and strong self-will" (Halsted, pp. 16–17).

Gibbons remained a Tory during the Revolution, although his brothers were staunch Whigs. Like many Georgia families, they divided their loyalties to preserve their property. During the British occupation of Savannah (Dec. 1778–July 1782) Gibbons practiced law there, frequently serving as legal counsel for

Whigs accused of treason. His efforts to remove the stigma of treason once the Whigs returned to power demonstrate the personal and volatile character of late eighteenth-century Georgia politics. Gibbons's former stand as a Tory rankled several Whig leaders, who had him arrested and attempted to banish him and confiscate his property. Savannah lawyer and revolutionary war veteran James Jackson, who may have conflicted with Gibbons earlier in the war, acted as his most persistent opponent. Not until 1787 did Gibbons obtain clemency, perhaps through the influence of powerful friends and family.

Gibbons's freedom did not come easily. He had endured threats of monetary punishment as well as restrictions on his right to vote, to hold office, and to practice law. Once he regained his citizenship, Gibbons appears to have sought out contention. When he helped former Tories regain their property, his enemies questioned his loyalty and circulated a rumor that he had leaked information to the British during the Revolution. Gibbons believed that Jackson stood behind most of these accusations and challenged him to a duel in 1786. Neither received a wound, but the enmity continued.

In spite of his difficulties, Gibbons prospered politically for a brief time. He obtained a seat in the 1787–1788 Georgia General Assembly and served as tax receiver in Savannah in 1788. He attended the 1787 convention to ratify the federal Constitution and helped to write a new state constitution in 1789. But suspicions about his true allegiance continued to plague Gibbons's political aspirations. When he ran for reelection to the assembly in 1789, the new state constitution had reduced Savannah and Chatham County representation in the lower house from fourteen to five delegates. That change alone would have induced a bitter fight among aspiring candidates, but with Gibbons in the race it became a hotbed of contention, one that signified the start of a new era in Georgia politics. Instead of a deferential, behind-the-scenes contest stressing candidates' virtue, social standing, and ability to lead, it became a bitter, public campaign. His enemies charged Gibbons with crimes abhorrent to traditional eighteenth-century republicanism, claiming that he ignored the interests of his constituents, organized a faction of legislators to increase his own influence, and openly campaigned for office. Gibbons lost the election.

Gibbons persevered in his quest for political influence and became a leader of Savannah Federalists during the 1790s. He served as mayor in 1791–1792, 1794–1795, and 1799–1800. Yet his political schemes encountered more difficulties because of his tenacious temperament, unethical tactics, and Federalism. He was again forcefully opposed by Jackson, who led Georgia's Jeffersonian Republicans. In 1791 Jackson challenged Gibbons's management of General Anthony Wayne's campaign for Congress and had Wayne's election overruled. Gibbons won a seat in the Georgia Senate in November 1792, but that body rejected him because of questionable votes in his favor. Gibbons's

name was linked with the scandalous 1795 Yazoo land sale, in which land companies bribed a large percentage of state legislators to approve the act. John Adams appointed Gibbons to a federal judgeship in 1802, but Gibbons either declined or his nomination was revoked by the Jeffersonians. That same year Republican Henry Putnam publicly lambasted Gibbons, accusing him of supplying incriminating information about Putnam's activities to the Federalist party in Washington, D.C. Although his business interests in New York and New Jersey had begun to divert Gibbons's attention away from Georgia politics, he remained a formidable political foe.

Despite these political setbacks, Gibbons prospered economically. He earned up to £3,000 sterling per year in lawyers' fees. Gibbons acquired property in Southeast Georgia and South Carolina and created several rice and cotton plantations, including the extensive development known as "Whitehall," located near Savannah. He extended his ventures to New York and New Jersey and moved to Elizabethtown, New Jersey, by 1811, although he continued to make numerous trips back to Savannah.

In 1817 Gibbons formed a steamboat partnership with Aaron Ogden, a former New Jersey governor, to transport passengers from New York to New Brunswick, New Jersey. It was an uneasy union at best. Both members sought profit in any obtainable form, and both had personal histories of quarrelsome behavior. After one year of operation, Ogden took Gibbons to court for trying to bypass the partnership and run a steamship on his own.

When Gibbons and Ogden had first joined forces, the heirs of Robert R. Livingston and Robert Fulton possessed a state monopoly to operate a steamboat line in New York. The families and the New York courts claimed that the monopoly extended to the shores of New Jersey. In 1819 Gibbons and Ogden ran afoul of that agreement and were sued by a member of the Livingston family. Gibbons and Ogden denied their partnership and insisted that the waters on which they operated lay well within New Jersey. Gibbons further protested that he purchased a U.S. coastal license, which gave him an overriding permit to use any waterways bordering the Atlantic. The case went to the New York Court of Chancery, where Judge James Kent ruled that only Ogden could sail between New York and Elizabethtown Point because he had earlier yielded to the Livingston monopoly in 1815. Gibbons took his case to the New York Court of Errors and to the U.S. Supreme Court. He worked with Cornelius Vanderbilt, master of Gibbons's steamboat, the *Bellona*, and Daniel D. Tompkins, another Livingston-Fulton rival, to interfere with the monopoly whenever possible.

When *Gibbons v. Ogden* came before the Supreme Court in 1824, Gibbons obtained Daniel Webster, Attorney General William Wirt, and David B. Ogden as lawyers. They challenged the right of a state to interfere with the authority of Congress. At the time of the case, the concept of nationalism had become increasingly popular in America. The Livingston-Fulton monopoly caused alarm among Americans who desired free enterprise upon the nation's waterways. The Court decided in favor of Gibbons. Chief Justice John Marshall presented a landmark statement, claiming that the commerce clause in the Constitution empowered Congress to regulate navigation within states when such action concerned foreign and interstate trade. The Court's decision broke the Livingston-Fulton monopoly and in the nineteenth and twentieth centuries enabled Congress to regulate companies that dealt in communication or transportation that crossed state borders.

Gibbons died a millionaire but he was deprived of a happy family life. He quarreled with his daughter, Ann Gibbons Trumbull, and refused to give an inheritance to her children. In 1816 his wife left him and sued for divorce, claiming that Gibbons kept prostitutes in their home. When Gibbons died in New York City, only one son survived him.

• The most complete account of Gibbons's Georgia career appears in George Lamplugh, *Politics on the Periphery: Factions and Parties in Georgia, 1783–1806* (1986). The book places Gibbons's activities within the context of factional and party politics in late eighteenth-century Georgia. Much of this work is restated in Lamplugh, "Up from the Depths: The Career of Thomas Gibbons, 1783–1789," *Atlanta Historical Journal* 25 (1981): 37–44, with some additional comments about Gibbons. George Dangerfield. "The Steamboat Case," in *Quarrels that Have Shaped the Constitution,* ed. John A. Garraty (1966), Charles Warren, *The Supreme Court in United States History,* vol. 1 (1947), and Maurice G. Baxter, *The Steamboat Monopoly: Gibbons v. Ogden, 1824* (1972), provide a solid account of the intricate court battles and the Supreme Court decision concerning *Gibbons v. Ogden.* William Halsted, *A Full Report of the Case of John Den ex dem. Thomas Gibbons Trumbull, John Heyward Trumbull, Ralph Henry Isham, and Ann His Wife, Daniel Coit Ripley, and Sarah His Wife vs. William Gibbons* (1849), provides background information about Gibbons's private and business affairs, as does the Savannah Unit of the Georgia Writers' Project, "Whitehall Plantation," *Georgia Historical Quarterly* 25 (1941): 341–62 and 26 (1942): 40–64. An obituary is in the *Savannah Republican,* 27 May 1826.

CAROL S. EBEL

GIBBONS, William (1750?–27 Sept. 1800), lawyer and politician, was born at Bear Bluff, South Carolina, the son of Joseph Gibbons, a successful rice planter, and Hannah Martin. Young Gibbons read law in Charleston and began his legal practice in Savannah before the Revolution. Georgians, slow to join the revolutionary movement, were split between Whigs and Loyalists, a division reflected in Gibbons's family. William was an ardent Whig, whereas his brother Thomas Gibbons and his brother-in-law Nathaniel Hall were sympathetic to the Loyalists and were listed under the Confiscation and Banishment Act of 1782.

Although there is no record that Gibbons ever served in the military, he held a number of political and administrative positions during the Revolution. In July 1774 he was listed as a member of the committee from Savannah that was scheduled to meet at Tondee's Tavern on 10 August 1774 to organize a provincial congress. In January of the following year, as a delegate from the district of Acton, he pledged to adhere to an association designed to curtail British imports until American grievances were redressed. On 10 May 1775 he was a member of the small band that broke into the king's powder magazine in Savannah and destroyed 600 pounds of powder, a radical action that demonstrated his commitment to the rebellion.

Georgia Whigs were openly divided as to who should lead the revolutionary movement in Georgia after the duel between Button Gwinnett, a patriot leader, and Lachlan McIntosh, a general in the Continental army. The conservative Whigs from Christ Church Parish, like Gibbons, tended to stand behind McIntosh; the radical Whigs, largely from St. John's Parish and the outlying districts, demanded the transferal of McIntosh to another command outside of Georgia. After the fall of Savannah, when a new Whig government was set up in Augusta on 10 July 1779, Gibbons was a member of the supreme executive committee that chose John Wereat as its chairman. In the controversy that ensued, Gibbons was aligned with the conservatives, who were successfully challenged by a rival government led by George Walton, William Glascock, and Richard Howley. In 1783, as a member of the assembly, Gibbons was chosen Speaker, and after peace was negotiated he was a delegate to the Continental Congress, where he served two years.

On returning to Savannah, Gibbons resumed his legal practice and was elected to the state assembly during 1785–1789 and 1791–1793. He was again chosen Speaker during the 1786–1787 session. Gibbons served as president of the state constitutional convention that met in Augusta on 4 May 1789 and brought the state government in line with the newly ratified federal Constitution. Likewise, he served as an associate justice of the Superior Court of Chatham County.

Gibbons, one of the most successful lawyers in Georgia, was also the owner of several rice plantations. In 1788 he bought "Morton Hall" from his mother, who had purchased the 500-acre property from the committee of the legislature overseeing the sale of confiscated estates. At his death, Morton Hall, a rice and cotton plantation, was described as having $300 worth of cotton or seed; 130 barrels of rice valued at $1,340; 43 slaves appraised at $11,345; and cattle and sheep. Gibbons and his wife, Valeria Richardson, were apparently childless.

Gibbons died in Savannah. His obituary observed, "In his private character he was much respected by all who knew him as an honest and honorable man." It is quite understandable why he is a neglected figure in early Georgia history. The major details of his life are sketchy and often confused with those of his uncle and first cousin, both of whom were his contemporaries and also named William Gibbons. He was a devoted advocate for independence almost from the inception of the revolutionary movement in the laggard colony, and for the next twenty-five years he was a dedicated public servant.

• For further information on Gibbons see Gibbons Genealogy, Georgia Historical Society; *Revolutionary Records of the State of Georgia*; the will of William Gibbons, Morton Hall, 14 June 1799, Book A, 1775–1801, Chatham County Court House, Savannah, Ga.; Federal Writers Project, "Richmond Oakgrove Plantation," *Georgia Historical Quarterly* 24 (Mar., June 1940): 22–42, 124–44, and the two-part "Whitehall Plantation," *Georgia Historical Quarterly* 25 (Dec. 1941): 340–63 and 26 (Mar., June 1942): 40–64, 129–55; and S. F. Miller, *Bench and Bar of Georgia*, vol. 2 (1858). An obituary is in the *Columbian Museum and Savannah Advertiser*, 24 Oct. 1800.

R. FRANK SAUNDERS, JR.

GIBBONS, William (10 Aug. 1781–25 July 1845), physician and Quaker reformer, was born in Philadelphia, Pennsylvania, the son of James Gibbons, a teacher, farmer, and conveyancer, and Eleanor Peters. Descended from some of Pennsylvania's first settlers, Gibbons was privately educated and then attended the University of Pennsylvania, from which he received an M.D. in 1805, having studied with Benjamin Rush, and he published his *Inaugural Essay on Hypocondriasis* the same year. When, in 1806, he wed Rebecca Donaldson, a non-Quaker, his Philadelphia meeting struck him from its membership rolls until, having moved to Wilmington, Delaware, he admitted his error five years later; Rebecca then joined the Friends within two years. The couple had thirteen children. Gibbons remained in Wilmington for the rest of his life, practicing medicine and taking an active part in the civic life of both city and state. Cultivating broad interests, he served as the first president of the state temperance society; mastered Hebrew, Greek, Latin, French, and German; dabbled in meteorology, horticulture, and ornithology; and founded the Delaware Academy of Natural Sciences in 1827. Though passionate about the broad implications of science—he held that human beings, once enlightened by rational science, displayed "an almost inexhaustible fund of resources"—he resisted carrying them to what he considered an extreme. Thus in 1829, growing fearful of the influence of freethinkers Robert Dale Owen and Frances Wright, who had lectured in the area, he attacked them forthrightly in his *Exposition of Modern Skepticism*.

A zealous, sometimes combative Quaker, Gibbons secretly assisted Benjamin Ferris in upholding his side of the "Paul and Amicus" dispute in a series of letters that appeared in the city's *Christian Repository* from 1821 to 1823 to the outrage of both Presbyterian and Quaker evangelicals. He then penned *Truth Advocated in Letters Addressed to Presbyterians* (1822), thrusting himself into the thriving local controversy that the Paul and Amicus debate had engendered between Friends and that denomination. Gibbons took a leading role in pursuing what he and a coterie of Friends in Wilmington liked to call a "reformation," by which they hoped to reverse what they regarded as a century of retrogressive retreat to a conventional orthodoxy among leaders of his sect. Embracing the cause of Elias Hicks, a rural Long Islander whose traditional Quaker message aroused strong emotions among urban Quakers, this group emphasized the application of reason to their faith but also stressed individual experience as the hallmark of what they considered traditional Quakerism. Both the Wilmington reformers and their opponents understood that this position undercut the power of well-to-do Philadelphia elders, evangelical adherents of an orthodoxy based on the authority of the Scripture. On hearing Gibbons's notions such as "religion was a progressive work—therefore we ought to be at liberty," these elders detected frightening overtones of "ranterism," the bugaboo of Quakers in positions of authority since the seventeenth century.

To promote the reformation, Gibbons began his polemical periodical *Berean* in 1824. For four years, this biweekly hounded the power brokers in Philadelphia and sharpened the differences between them and those who were becoming known as "Hicksites." Nearly an exact reflection of Gibbons's convictions and factious style, *Berean*'s articles aggressively rejected any example of human authority in religion, including the Bible, and iterated that the light of Christ within each person should be the individual's primary guide. In one issue, orthodoxy was depicted as creeping across the land like "the frogs of Egypt." "Natural religion," the editor explained in another, was "that light which men have independent of books, or of men." Gibbons's commitment to rationality smacked of Unitarianism, but his insistence that truth originated with God rather than in human minds gave his thought its necessary Quaker twist. His support of antislavery, temperance, and peace efforts likewise demonstrated his commitment to Friends' testimonies.

Gibbons's efforts in the reformation cause were recognized after the Philadelphia Yearly Meeting split in 1827, when he became one of two temporary presiding clerks of the Hicksite schismatics, who saw themselves as advancing the reformation against the entrenched power of the elders. Soon, however, he faced a darker side of the free inquiry he championed. Local Quaker dissidents, led by an associate, Benjamin Webb, adopted the ideas of Owen and Wright and in 1831, at Gibbons's irate insistence, were disowned or expelled from membership. Having weathered this storm, Gibbons returned to the quiet of his practice and his orchards. He died in Wilmington. A posthumous book, *A Review and Refutation of Some of the Opprobrious Charges against the Society of Friends* (1847), continued his assault against Orthodox Quakers and attacked the doctrine of the Trinity. Gibbons's emphasis on individual experience, applied with his rationalism, came gradually to characterize the approach of the Hicksite branch and, after the two Philadelphia Yearly Meetings reunited in 1955, that of many modern Friends.

• A few letters of, to, and about Gibbons survive in the papers of Benjamin Ferris in the Friends Historical Library of Swarthmore College. On Gibbons's life, see the typescript

"Dictionary of Quaker Biography" at Haverford College; H. Larry Ingle, *Quakers in Conflict: The Hicksite Reformation* (1986); and Ingle, "'A Ball That Has Rolled Beyond Our Reach': The Consequence of Hicksite Reform," *Delaware History* 21 (1984): 127–37. An obituary is in *Friends' Intelligencer*, 2 Aug. 1845.

H. LARRY INGLE

GIBBS, Arthur Hamilton (9 Mar. 1888–24 May 1964), author, was born in London, England, the son of Henry James Gibbs, a publisher and a prominent member of the local board of education, and Helen Hamilton. He was the youngest of five brothers, including Cosmo Hamilton and Sir Philip Gibbs, both also authors. As a boy Gibbs was sent to the Collége de St. Malo in Brittany, where he remained for four years. Of his schooling in France, Gibbs writes, "I was a French boy, in a French uniform, with brass buttons and a peaked cap, thinking, fighting, eating, smoking—all in French." For a number of his novels, he later drew extensively from his experience in France and his familiarity with French culture. Shortly after his return home in 1904, his father died, and it became necessary for Gibbs to work. His elder brother Sir Philip Gibbs secured for him a job with a firm of assayers and refiners of precious metals.

After three years of work, Gibbs was sent by his eldest brother, Cosmo Hamilton (who dropped his last name), to St. John's College at Oxford. There he rowed on the college crew team and established some amount of notoriety as an amateur boxer. He remained a sportsman throughout his life. While at Oxford Gibbs also decided, against his family's expectations, not to become a barrister and to devote himself to writing. Also at Oxford Gibbs and Cosmo founded and edited the *Tuesday Review*, a weekly in which Gibbs published a series of satirical sketches that he later put together in his first book, *The Compleat Oxford Man* (1911).

In both 1912 and 1913 Gibbs came to the United States playing a minor role in Cosmo's play *The Blindness of Virtue*. In 1914 he enlisted as a trooper in the British Twenty-first Lancers and was soon commissioned as an officer and transferred to the Royal Field Artillery, serving in Egypt, Greece, Serbia, Malta, Mudros, Ireland, and France, where he was reportedly gassed. In 1919 he was demobilized with the rank of major and awarded the Military Cross. Gibbs returned to the United States and in April 1919 married Jeannette Phillips, a writer and practicing attorney in Boston. The couple, who had no children, moved to an old farm with a colonial house in Lakeville, Massachusetts, and, excepting a great deal of travel, Gibbs spent the rest of his life there. He became a U.S. citizen in 1931.

While at the front Gibbs wrote *Gunfodder* (1919), the manuscript of which he carried home in his knapsack. The book tells of his experiences in the war and his sense of profound disillusionment over the motives behind it. Cosmo wrote later in a sketch about Gibbs that *Gunfodder* was written not in ink but "in the blood and anguish, the anger and despair of those of the men who had served with him and would never come home." The book is important for its awareness of and participation in the new age of modernism, marked most significantly for him by a sense of social and political urgency. For Gibbs, as for many, the war was an age-defining experience and signaled a responsibility in younger generations to make use of what had been learned: "We found truth while we practiced war. Let us carry it to the practice of peace." *Gunfodder* remains Gibbs's most important contribution.

Gibbs enjoyed commercial success throughout his career, publishing two books of verse and sixteen novels in all, four of which became bestsellers: *Soundings* (1925), *Labels* (1926), *Harness* (1928), and *Chances* (1930). Serious critical acclaim, however, was harder to come by. *Gunfodder* and *Soundings*, a story about an English girl raised by her artist father, were two of the few books allotted praise in both commercial and critical arenas, the first for its graphic depictions of war and the second for its characterization and willingness to face contemporary social issues. More common, though, were reviews that acknowledged the bestselling quality of Gibbs's work while noting a general assessment of his prose as belonging to the abyss of "mediocrity." Some of his work was specifically denounced for what critics saw as an overdose of "pacifist propaganda." *Harness* for example, though an immediate commercial success, was not taken seriously by the academic community because of its attempt at both storytelling and political sermonizing: "[The novel] is an attempt at both without the fire of the one or the fundamental interest of the other." In an obituary in the *New York Times*, Gibbs is said to have spoken of his wish that he and his brothers be able to write at least one hundred books, "enough to warrant a small wing in a library," and certainly his focus on quantity detracted from any significant sense of innovation in his fiction.

Aside from those mentioned above, Gibbs's publications include *Cheadle and Son* (1911), *Rowlandson's Oxford* (1911), *The Hour of Conflict* (1913), *The Persistent Lovers* (1914), *Bluebottles* (poems, 1919), *Meredew's Right Hand* (1927), *Undertow* (1932), *Rivers Glide On* (1934), *The Need We Have* (1936), *The Young Prince* (1937), *A Half Inch of Candle* (1939), *A Way of Life* (1947), *One Touch of France* (poems, 1953), and *Obedience to the Moon* (1956). Though much of his work remains in the realm of the popular novel, *Gunfodder* is significant indeed. Gibbs died at Massachusetts General Hospital in Boston after collapsing on a golf course.

• Perhaps the most interesting biographical information is in the writings of Gibbs's brother. Cosmo Hamilton, *Unwritten History* (1924) and *People Worth Talking About* (1933), each contain brief chapters on Gibbs. See also Philip Gibbs, *Adventures in Journalism* (1923). Major biographical entries appear in *Living Authors: A Book of Biographies* (1931) and *Twentieth Century Authors*. Little, Brown was Gibbs's publisher throughout his career. Obituaries are in the *New York Times*, 26 May 1964, and *Publishers Weekly*, 22 June 1964, p. 72.

SARA J. FORD

GIBBS, George (7 Jan. 1776–5 Aug. 1833), mineralogist and patron of science, was born in Newport, Rhode Island, the son of George Gibbs, a wealthy merchant, and Mary Channing. Despite his father's exhortations to "give up travelling. . . . fix yourself to business & lead a regular life observing the strictest economy," Gibbs chose extensive travel in his youth and the life of a wealthy gentleman farmer when he did settle down. He adopted the honorary appellation "Colonel" and was usually referred to as "Colonel Gibbs" or just "the Colonel."

Gibbs traveled in Europe between 1801 and 1805, pursuing his interest in mineralogy by meeting and studying with men known for their activities in the discipline, purchasing two mineralogical "cabinets," or collections, and collecting specimens of his own. The resulting mineralogical collection, known thereafter as the "Gibbs Cabinet," was the largest in North America and "better than many in Europe" (Brown, p. 263). Gibbs made his collections available for study by his countrymen, but the final disposition of the collection was an issue of some dispute. Several institutions wanted it but were unwilling to meet Gibbs's stringent requirements for its display. In March 1811 Gibbs offered a portion of the collection to Benjamin Silliman for display at Yale College on the condition that acceptable space and display facilities could be provided—"say a large room of 20 by 30 ft.," he wrote, "with Shelves & glass doors, as minerals when in Drawers are subject to injury from the curious." By the time the collection was actually in place at Yale and open to the public, Gibbs had provided detailed diagrams for the construction of the display cases, specified that the specimens be arranged according to the system of French mineralogist Abbé Haüy, and traveled to New Haven to help arrange the specimens himself. For all this, the Gibbs Cabinet was only on loan from its opening in 1812 to its eventual purchase by the college for $20,000 in 1825.

The presence of the Gibbs Cabinet at Yale assisted the college in several ways. It allowed Silliman to improve his course in mineralogy and add instruction in geology. This, in turn, contributed to the emergence of Yale as a center of scientific learning, especially in the earth sciences, in the first half of the nineteenth century. Beyond its value in formal instruction, however, the cabinet also contributed to the fame and prestige of Yale College, attracting travelers to New Haven and students to the college.

Although the most famous, the Gibbs Cabinet was not Gibbs's only contribution to American mineralogy nor to Yale College. He made ongoing gifts of money and books to be offered as prizes rewarding student achievement, particularly in mineralogy and geology, at Yale. He frequently loaned Silliman scientific books and journals. He published several papers in Archi-

bald Bruce's *American Mineralogical Journal* and, when Bruce was forced to discontinue publication due to ill health, Gibbs suggested that Silliman establish a journal of his own. Gibbs contributed encouragement, concrete advice, financial resources, and material for publication toward the creation and survival of Silliman's *American Journal of Science and the Arts*. Silliman's journal began publication in 1818, and a year later Gibbs convinced Silliman to undertake another, less successful, project to promote American science. Together, the two obtained a charter from the Connecticut legislature and founded the American Geological Society (1819–1821).

In 1810 Gibbs had married Laura Wolcott; they had seven children. In late 1813 Gibbs purchased "Sunswick Farms," a rural estate on Long Island, New York. He died there at the age of fifty-seven, survived by his wife and three of their children.

• There are collections of Gibbs's papers at the Wisconsin Historical Society and at the Newport Historical Society. Gibbs's story is told in most extended biographies of Benjamin Silliman, including Chandos Michael Brown, *Benjamin Silliman: A Life in the Young Republic* (1989), and John F. Fulton and Elizabeth H. Thomson, *Benjamin Silliman, 1779–1864: Pathfinder in American Science* (1947). Silliman himself wrote a brief notice of Gibbs's life and death, which appeared in the *American Journal of Science and the Arts* 25 (1834): 214–15. See also Stephen Dow Beckham, "Colonel George Gibbs," in *Benjamin Silliman and His Circle*, ed. Leonard G. Wilson (1979).

JULIE R. NEWELL

GIBBS, George (17 July 1815–9 Apr. 1873), ethnographer, geologist, and historian, was born at "Sunswick Farms" near Astoria, Long Island, New York, the son of George Gibbs, a gentleman farmer and amateur geologist, and Laura Wolcott. Both of his parents descended from wealthy, old-stock colonial families. At the age of nine, George was sent to the Round Hill School in Northampton, Massachusetts, which was directed by historian George Bancroft. Although his father had planned a military career for his oldest son, the family's staunch support for the Federalist party made an appointment to West Point impossible in Jacksonian America. Instead, in 1832 Gibbs went to Harvard to study law under Joseph Story. Gibbs's paternal grandmother and aunts lived in Boston, and through them and William Ellery Channing, his uncle by marriage, he was introduced to Boston society.

In 1834 Gibbs published his first book, *The Judicial Chronicle*, a list of judges of the common law and chancery in the United States and England. Although he was close to finishing his studies at Harvard, he left for Europe with an aunt that spring and spent the next two years traveling. Upon his return, he settled in New York, where he was joined by his mother and siblings. His father had died while Gibbs was at Harvard. Instead of practicing law, Gibbs decided to write a biography of his maternal grandfather, former secretary of the Treasury Oliver Wolcott, a project that his former teacher Bancroft encouraged. However, the financial panic of 1837 forced Gibbs to take a more practical approach to life, and he returned to law. After receiving his J.D. from Harvard in 1838 without any further studies, Gibbs joined the law practice of Jonathan Prescott Hall.

Gibbs continued to be less than fully committed to law, and he barely earned a living. He loved the outdoors and was interested in natural history and geology. He hunted and fished, mounted a large collection of birds, and collected mineral samples. The latter he donated to Yale College, where his collection joined his father's mineralogical collection. His love of history was nurtured at the New-York Historical Society, which Gibbs joined in 1839. In 1843 he became the society's librarian, cataloging the collection and steering it toward an emphasis on American subjects. Gibbs started a law practice with Henry Hall Ward, a friend from Hall's office, but his work for the historical society absorbed more and more of his time. He also recommended work on his biography of Wolcott, which became *Memoirs of the Administrations of Washington and John Adams* (1846). Working from his grandfather's papers, Gibbs decided to write a political history instead of a biography, but he made no secret of his own political loyalties. In that volume he wrote that he "felt himself not only the vindicator, but in some sort the avenger, of a by-gone party and a buried race" and ominously described the Jeffersonian Republicans as the root of the nation's "demoralization, and the efficient cause of our ruin" (p. ix). Gibbs's book is still an important source of material on the Federal party's ascendancy.

The excitement over the discovery of gold in California finally dislodged Gibbs completely from his law practice, and in 1849 he left New York for St. Louis, Missouri. Joining a march of the Mounted Riflemen, he traveled overland from Fort Leavenworth to Oregon City. On the trip he made many drawings and kept a journal, portions of which were published in New York newspapers. His lively entries described the climate and landscape, life in camp, and encounters with Sioux Indians and emigrants on the Oregon Trail.

Gibbs settled in Astoria, Oregon, near the mouth of the Columbia River. In 1850 he was appointed deputy collector for the port, but he resigned later that year in the aftermath of having embarrassed his superior by an overzealous prosecution of the customs laws. In 1851 he joined Redick McKee on an expedition to draw up land treaties with the Indian tribes west of the Sacramento Valley. In five months McKee's group met with nearly 10,000 Indians and concluded five treaties. Gibbs, who had already been interested in Indian languages, compiled vocabulary lists of fifteen indigenous tongues and worked on maps of the region. In 1852 he tried his hand at prospecting in northern California with less than impressive results. By the end of the year he was back in Astoria, again as a customs collector, but when Franklin Pierce took office in 1853, Gibbs lost this political appointment.

Gibbs soon found other work. In 1853 George B. McClellan hired him as a geologist and ethnologist to help survey a railroad route to the Pacific. In 1854 Gibbs left Oregon for good, settling near Fort Steilacoom in the Washington Territory on a farm he called "Chetlah." He was rarely there, however, continuing his surveying and conducting ethnological research. Working for the Indian commission in the territory, Gibbs helped shape Indian policy. He argued for keeping Native Americans on their traditional homelands to preserve the cultural and linguistic diversity that he knew was dissolving quickly on reservations. He also campaigned for the use of Indian place names, which he often noted on the maps he made. Gibbs served briefly in 1854 as the acting governor of Washington Territory and was appointed brigadier general of the militia in 1855.

In 1857 and 1858 Gibbs was again in the field, this time surveying the forty-ninth parallel between the United States and Canada for the Northwest Boundary Survey. Working for Archibald Campbell, he traversed the border from the Pacific to the Rockies. Gibbs took every opportunity to add to his knowledge of Indian languages and also collected animal, insect, and plant specimens, many of which he sent to scientists like Louis Agassiz and Asa Gray. In 1860 Gibbs finally returned East to write up his field research in Washington. Twelve years in the West had not made him a rich man as he had hoped, but he did have a large store of artifacts and information.

Setting in Washington, D.C., in 1861, Gibbs continued his work on Native American linguistics, and the Smithsonian Institution published several volumes of his work. While Gibbs avoided politics and thought the Republicans had done little to avoid dividing the Union, he was not idle during the Civil War. He was one of the founders of the Union League Club of New York in 1863, joined the Loyal National League, and wrote for the Loyal Publication Society.

In 1865 Gibbs was appointed clerk to a commission investigating British claims in the American Northwest, a position he held until 1869. He also published another book, *Notes on the Tinneh or Chepewyan Indians of British and Russian America*, in 1867. In 1871, at the age of fifty-six, Gibbs married his cousin Mary Kane Gibbs; they had no children. The couple moved to New Haven, Connecticut, where Gibbs continued his research and writing despite ill health. He died, probably from a combination of rheumatic gout and a pulmonary illness, in New Haven. While Gibbs did not have the professional training to be able to analyze his discoveries, his meticulous observations and recording allowed others to do so. His work on Native Americans was useful to the next generation of anthropologists.

• Many of Gibbs's papers, including sketches, are at the Smithsonian Institution. Works by Gibbs not mentioned above include *Alphabetical Vocabularies of the Clallam and the Lummi* (1863) and *Instructions for Research Relative to the Ethnology and Philology of America* (1863). See Osborne Cross,

The March of the Mounted Riflemen (1940), in which Gibbs's 1849 diary entries are reproduced. Stephen Dow Beckham, "George Gibbs, 1815–1873: Historian and Ethnologist" (Ph.D. diss., UCLA, 1970), is a detailed account of Gibbs's life and work.

BETHANY NEUBAUER

GIBBS, George (19 Apr. 1861–19 May 1940), mechanical engineer, was born in Chicago, Illinois, the son of Francis Sarason Gibbs, a grain exporter, and Eliza Gay Hosmer. Following his 1882 graduation as a mechanical engineer from the Stevens Institute of Technology in Hoboken, New Jersey, Gibbs worked for Thomas Edison as a laboratory assistant before becoming superintendent of meters at Edison's Pearl Street electrical generating station in New York City. In 1883 he took the position of chief chemist of the Oxford Nickel and Copper Company at Bergen Point, New Jersey.

Gibbs's career in railroading began in about 1885 when he was engaged by the Chicago, Milwaukee, and St. Paul Railway Company. His first assignment was to organize a new materials testing department. He was also given the added duties of mechanical engineer in charge of machinery and rolling stock design. The technical advances that evolved from this area of his work made the St. Paul a leader in railroad safety at a time when safety was of little active interest elsewhere in the industry.

Gibbs's system for steam heating eliminated the need for coal stoves, which had been a major source of fire in wooden railway cars. In 1888 he patented a fire extinguisher for railway cars, as well as an improved interlocking track switch and signal. Improvements resulting from his patents in 1889 and 1891 for shields and reflectors for incandescent lamps and a complete car electric lighting system all but removed the potential sources of accidental railroad fires.

In addition to his railroad work during the early 1890s, Gibbs and his brother Lucius formed the Gibbs Electric Company for the manufacture of industrial electric motors. It was in the course of his railroad work that he met George Westinghouse, inventor of the railroad air brake and signaling devices, and Samuel Vauclain of the Baldwin Locomotive Works. Both men believed in the practicality of electric heavy traction for railroads, and they eventually persuaded George Gibbs to join them in developing the concept. As part of the arrangement, Westinghouse purchased the brothers' company. Between 1900 and 1902 George Gibbs served as chief engineer for Westinghouse interests in England and Europe, serving both as consultant for and designer of electrification projects.

From 1902 to 1906 Gibbs served as first vice president of the engineering firm Westinghouse, Church, Kerr, and Company. His knowledge of electric traction brought the firm a number of contracts for railroad improvements. As a member of the electric traction commission of the New York Central Railroad, he helped plan the power system for its new Grand Central Terminal in Manhattan. He served as a consulting engineer to the Rapid Transit Construction Company, then building New York City's first subway. During this period he received more than a dozen patents, the majority of which were for railroad safety devices. The patent with the most far-reaching impact was that issued to him in 1903 for the first all-steel railway passenger car. Up to that time, cars were constructed almost entirely of wood, which fared badly in accidents and was subject to fires. The car he designed had both a sturdy steel exterior and an interior finished with nonflammable insulating material.

His most challenging assignment came about as a result of his appointment as one of the four chief engineers of the Pennsylvania Railroad Improvement Project. Beginning in 1902 and lasting until 1910, the Pennsylvania Railroad embarked on a massive undertaking that created a direct rail link between New York City and the west and south. Rail traffic brought through tunnels under the Hudson and East rivers converged at a new station of monumental proportions located in the heart of downtown Manhattan.

Not only was Gibbs placed in charge of the Electric Traction and Station Construction Division, he was named chair of the Locomotive Committee. This group had the task of designing and testing the electric-powered equipment that was needed to bring traffic through the project's long subaqueous tunnels. The committee's efforts resulted in the prototype of the DD-1 class of electric locomotives.

It was while working for Westinghouse in England that Gibbs first met engineer E. Rowland Hill. Impressed by the younger man's skill, Gibbs hired Hill to serve as his assistant on the Pennsylvania project. After the completion of the work in 1911, the two signed an agreement creating the partnership of Gibbs and Hill, consulting engineers. The contract was renewed several times during the ensuing twelve years. Finally, in 1924, the partnership was converted into a corporation.

In 1917, following the collapse of czarist Russia, the provisional democratic government requested U.S. assistance in reorganizing its nearly moribund transportation system. Gibbs was appointed to the U.S. Railway Commission to Russia whose task it was to study and make suggestions as to how the railroads might be rationalized. His seven-month tour of duty in Russia covered some 30,000 miles of railway.

Gibbs and Hill became leaders in the field of railroad electrification during the 1920s. With no new major railroad lines being built, emphasis was placed on upgrading existing systems, mainly by converting to electricity. The hauling capacity of the Virginian Railway, built 1905–1907, was greatly increased when its Mountain Division was electrified. Trains on the Pennsylvania's busy main line between Washington, D.C., and New York City were added to the growing list of those moved by electric power. At the same time, the firm continued work on the Norfolk & Western Railroad line between Bluefield and Iaeger, West Virginia. This was a long-term project that began in

1912 and was completed in 1926. A major undertaking, it included the design and construction of the distribution system as well as power plants.

Economic hardships befalling the firm of Gibbs and Hill were no different from those experienced by other businesses during the economic depression of the 1930s. The firm's biggest contract during that era was with the Pennsylvania Railroad. In a project that lasted from 1936 to 1938, the company carried out its proposal to electrify the line westward from Paoli, through Harrisburg, and on to Enola, Pennsylvania.

Gibbs was a member and past director of the American Society of Civil Engineers. That organization honored him in 1912 with its Norman Medal and in 1931 with the Wellington Medal for a paper on railroad electrification. He was also a member of the British Institution of Civil Engineers, American Society of Consulting Engineers, American Institute of Electrical Engineers, American Society of Mechanical Engineers, American Railway Engineering Association, American Railroad Association, and American Mathematical Society. He belonged to clubs in New York City, Philadelphia, and Canada. His technical writings were numerous and appeared primarily in engineering society publications. Gibbs, who died in New York City, never married and left no children.

• George Gibbs records his family's history and his own in *The Gibbs Family of Rhode Island* (1933). Much of Gibbs's philosophy regarding railroad electrification is revealed in his article "Railway Electrification," *Electrical World*, 8 June 1929, pp. 1189–91. Particulars on his many patents are in the records of the U.S. Patent Office. The high points of Gibbs's professional life are discussed at some length in the company history, *Before the Colors Fade: A Personal History of Gibbs & Hill, Inc.* (1975). This information is further enhanced by the comments of E. Rowland Hill, his longtime partner, in a "Memoir of George Gibbs" that appears in the *Transactions of the American Society of Civil Engineers* (1940). An obituary is in the *New York Times*, 21 May 1940.

WILLIAM E. WORTHINGTON, JR.

GIBBS, Jonathan C. (c. 1827–14 Aug. 1874), clergyman, educator, and politician, was born free in Philadelphia, Pennsylvania, the son of Maria Jackson and Jonathan C. Gibbs, a Methodist minister. He learned carpentry as a youth and followed that trade until the Presbyterian Assembly helped him enroll at Dartmouth College in 1848. Gibbs, who was one of only two black students at Dartmouth, claimed that he had been rejected by eighteen colleges before being accepted. After graduating from Dartmouth in 1852 he attended the Princeton Theological Seminary. He was ordained as a Presbyterian minister and pastored churches in Troy, New York, and in Philadelphia. While in New York Gibbs campaigned for the extension of black suffrage in the state. When he moved to Philadelphia in 1859 he became prominent in the local Underground Railroad. During the Civil War he joined the freedmen's relief efforts, campaigned against segregated city streetcars, encouraged black enlistments in the army, served as vice president of the

Pennsylvania State Equal Rights League, and continued his participation in the black convention movement. He represented Philadelphia at the black national convention in Syracuse in 1864, which severely criticized the Republican party for its failure to endorse black suffrage and which gave birth to the National Equal Rights League.

In April 1865 Gibbs went to Wilmington, North Carolina, to establish churches and schools for freedmen. He cooperated with white missionaries in the area but was deeply troubled by their paternalism and racism. Nevertheless, he saw the last few months of 1865 as a period of remarkable gains for blacks. In 1866 Gibbs exclaimed, "We have progressed a century in a year." In 1867 Gibbs was transferred to Florida to organize churches and schools among former slaves. When the congressional Reconstruction Act of 1867 mandated black suffrage, he concluded that talented black men were as badly needed in politics as in religion and education. Voters elected him as a delegate to the Florida Constitutional Convention, which met in Tallahassee in January 1868. When Republican delegates divided into conservative and radical factions, he joined the latter but did not slavishly support them, and his speeches were generally temperate. He sought a constitution that would protect the rights of both blacks and property owners. Gibbs proved to be an exemplary delegate. Press accounts described him as being of medium build with "a good intelligent yellow African face," an orator, "not a roarer but a convincing, argumentative, pleasant speaker: in this respect the most talented man in the Convention." Many members agreed with the *New York Tribune* reporter who wrote that there was "no fitter man" at the convention, "white or black."

In 1868 Gibbs was appointed secretary of state; working closely with Florida governor Harrison Reed, he became a well-respected public official. In the governor's absence, Gibbs served as chairman pro tem of the Board of Commissioners of Public Institutions with the support and confidence of other cabinet members. Even the Democrats occasionally praised Gibbs for the equitable manner in which he administered government contracts. His impartiality did not shield him from Ku Klux Klan hatred, however. His brother, during a visit to Tallahassee while Gibbs was secretary of state, found him well-armed and sleeping in the attic, ready to defend himself against the Klan, which had threatened his life. Gibbs fought for civil rights and equal economic opportunity. Emphasizing black history at a time when it received little attention, in 1871 he wrote a series of sketches of distinguished blacks for Florida newspapers in an effort to "incite" black youth to "fit themselves for the higher walks of usefulness." The future, he added, is "to the young man of color who is in earnest. Everything is before us; everything to win!"

When Ossian B. Hart succeeded Reed as governor in 1873, he appointed Gibbs as superintendent of public instruction. Florida had no viable system of public education before Republican Reconstruction, and

Gibbs played a large role in placing it on a firm foundation. The manuscript records of superintendent Gibbs reveal him to have been an intelligent, able administrator who was devoted to public education. County superintendents were charged with keeping complete, accurate records, and Gibbs closely supervised their work. He succeeded in securing the adoption of uniform texts for the state. Although the system of public education experienced rapid growth under Gibbs's brief leadership, he was not satisfied, claiming that white fear of integrated schools inhibited the system at the county level. The mental, moral, and physical possibilities of the black man, Gibbs said, "strikes terror to the hearts of men who have so long trampled him underfoot." He was not always so pessimistic, however. In an address to the National Educational Association at Elmira, New York, in August 1873, he acknowledged Florida's educational shortcomings but offered impressive statistics to illustrate the great improvements that had taken place since the Civil War. His speech received flattering notice in New York journals, which seemed to relate with pride that an African American from the South "had delivered with the dignity of an educated gentleman" a speech that in "breadth of thought and liberality of sentiment" marked him as a "worthy son" of Dartmouth.

Gibbs's sudden death in August 1874 was a serious loss to the state. S. B. McLin, his successor as superintendent of public instruction, wrote that blacks "have lost one of their noblest representatives, our State one of its most valued citizens, and our public school system one of its most intelligent advocates and one of its best friends." Gibbs, in apparent good health, had given a rousing speech at a Republican meeting in Tallahassee but died later the same night. Although he probably suffered a heart attack, it was whispered, and widely believed, that he had been poisoned by white enemies. Gibbs was an outstanding African-American leader during the Reconstruction era.

• The only personal papers available for Gibbs are in the Superintendent of Public Instruction Papers, Florida State Archives, Tallahassee. Excerpts of his letters and speeches can be found in Dorothy Sterling, ed., *The Trouble They Seen: Black People Tell the Story of Reconstruction* (1976). The *New York Tribune*, 5 and 10 Feb. 1868, describes his activities at the state constitutional convention. An important Gibbs letter is printed in the *New National Era*, 19 Oct. 1871. Joe M. Richardson, *The Negro in the Reconstruction of Florida* (1965), contains a biographical sketch, as does Richardson, "Jonathan C. Gibbs: Florida's Only Negro Cabinet Member," *Florida Historical Quarterly* 42 (Apr. 1964): 363–68. Mifflin Wistar Gibbs, *Shadow and Light: An Autobiography* (1902), provides some information on the early life of his brother. Obituaries are in the Tallahassee *Weekly Floridian*, 25 Aug. 1874, the Jacksonville *Tri-Weekly Union*, 18 Aug. 1874, and the Jacksonville *New South*, 19 Aug. 1874.

JOE M. RICHARDSON

GIBBS, Josiah Willard (30 Apr. 1790–25 Mar. 1861), philologist, was born in Salem, Massachusetts, the son of Henry Gibbs, a merchant, and Mercy Prescott. He graduated from Yale College in 1809 and then taught

school in Salem. In 1811 he was appointed a tutor at Yale. During this time he was also studying theology; he received his license to preach in 1814. In 1815 he went to Andover Theological Seminary, where he resided in the home of Moses Stuart and fell under the spell of the great teacher. He remained in Andover, serving for a time as librarian of the seminary, and he published a printed *Catalogue of the Library* (1819). He assisted Stuart in the preparation and publication of his *Hebrew Grammar* (1821), based on the work of Gesenius, and he read widely in German biblical scholarship, becoming, by American standards, a "scholar of the German order" (Dwight, p. 266). Gibbs translated Gesenius's *Hebräisches und Chaldäisches Handwörterbuch über das Alte Testament* (1815), which appeared as *A Hebrew and English Lexicon of the Old Testament including the Biblical Chaldee* (1824). This work enjoyed considerable success and was republished in London in 1827. He also prepared an abridged version for students, *A Manual Hebrew and English Lexicon, including the Biblical Chaldee* (1828; 2d ed., 1832). The grammar and dictionaries put Hebrew on a sound philological basis for American students and scholars and marked the beginning of a new era in the study of biblical Hebrew and Aramaic in America.

In 1824 Gibbs returned to Yale to the salaried position of university librarian, with a simultaneous appointment as lecturer in biblical literature. In 1826 he was appointed professor of sacred literature in the Yale Divinity School. Gibbs shared in the many trials of the struggling new school and was its leading scholar. In 1830 Gibbs married Mary Anna Van Cleve; they had five children.

Deeply reserved and lacking in self-confidence, Gibbs was well known for his willingness to consider all possible sides to a question in deliberate, even excruciating, detail. This trait could become a subject of ridicule among his less accomplished colleagues. One of them, Nathaniel Taylor, remarked, "I would rather have ten settled opinions, and nine of them wrong, than to be like my brother Gibbs with none of the ten settled." Gibbs's students considered him a thorough but uninspiring mentor. His articles were short, seldom more than a few paragraphs, and to his colleagues he often seemed to focus his energies on philological minutiae.

In 1833 a revised and expanded edition of Gesenius's dictionary appeared in Halle, *Lexicon Manuale Hebraicum et Chaldaicum*, a notable advance over his earlier work, which Gibbs decided to translate. With great care he checked the references, rearranged some of the entries, and added his own remarks and examples. For four years he labored in lonely intensity on this task and made arrangements for it to be printed, using Hebrew and oriental type fonts that he paid for himself. However, the first 432 pages—representing about a third of the projected whole—were returned by the printer, when Edward Robinson's less elaborate but excellent translation of Gesenius's work appeared (1836). Gibbs never got over his disappointment and after that devoted his efforts to comparative

Indo-European philology. His most substantial work in this area was *Philological Studies with English Illustrations* (1857), a collection of essays on English, followed by *A Latin Analyst on Modern Philological Principles* (1858). He also contributed extensively to W. C. Fowler's *English Grammar* (1850; 2d ed., 1855).

Gibbs achieved national celebrity through his involvement in the *Amistad* slave ship affair in 1839. A group of African slaves had seized a ship and believed they could return to Africa, but their pilot brought them to the United States, where they were captured by a U.S. naval vessel and jailed in New Haven. No one had been able to communicate with the captives until Gibbs induced some of them to teach him to count to ten in their language, which proved to be Mendi. Gibbs went to New York, where he walked among the docks seeking someone who could recognize the words he had learned. He succeeded in locating a speaker of Mendi whom he brought to New Haven. Through him the captives were able to tell their own story for the first time, and they were eventually freed after a trial that claimed international attention. As a result of this experience, Gibbs published brief vocabularies of various African languages that he elicited from native speakers (*American Journal of Science and Arts* 38, 39 [1840]; *Journal of the American Oriental Society* 1 [1849]).

Gibbs was a founding member of the American Oriental Society (1842) and contributed articles on various Semitic and African languages, inscriptions, and literary works to the first five volumes of its *Journal*. He was a significant, pioneering figure in the development of American comparative philology and linguistics. His work represented an advance over the fantastic and amateurish speculations of Noah Webster on the origins and interrelationships of the world's languages, which were prominent in American education in the first half of the nineteenth century, and it helped bring German work in linguistics to the attention of Americans. Although Gibbs was one of the most learned philologists of his time, his reticence and reluctance to publish meant that his accomplishments were fully appreciated by only a small circle of scholars.

Gibbs was deeply interested in the relationship between language and ideas, especially in philosophy and religious belief. He argued that intellectual discourse relies heavily on "faded metaphors" drawn from concrete experience and objects. According to him, the task of the linguist was to seek "absolute truth" through minute study of individual words, for in no other way could religious or philosophical truths be established. This view had important implications for the critical study of the Bible in New England Protestant theology through the teaching of Horace Bushnell, a prominent preacher and lecturer ("Preliminary Dissertation on the Nature of Language" in *God in Christ* [1849]).

Gibbs died in New Haven. One of his children, Josiah Willard, became a professor at Yale and one of America's most original scientific thinkers.

• Gibbs's personal and scholarly papers are in the Manuscripts and Archives of Yale University, Sterling Memorial Library. A memoir, with a select list of his publications, is in Franklin B. Dexter, *Biographical Sketches of the Graduates of Yale College 1805–1815*, 6 (1912): 250–56. Other memoirs include George P. Fisher, *A Discourse Commemorative of the Life and Services of Josiah Willard Gibbs, LL.D.* (1861), also printed in the *New Englander* 19 (1861), 605–20; W. L. Kingsley, *Yale College* 2 (1879): 37–40 (with portrait); Timothy Dwight, *Memories of Yale Life and Men* (1903), pp. 265–77 (with portrait); and James Hadley, *Semi-Centennial Anniversary of the Divinity School of Yale College, May 15th and 16th, 1872* (1872), pp. 82–86. Gibbs's work with Moses Stuart is summarized in Moses Stuart, *A Hebrew Grammar with a Copious Praxis* (1821), p. vii. The role of Gibbs in the *Amistad* affair is described in William A. Owens, *Slave Mutiny: The Revolt on the Schooner Amistad* (1953), pp. 144–45, 193–99. The influence of Gibbs on Bushnell and New England theology is analyzed by Jerry Wayne Brown, *The Rise of Biblical Criticism in America, 1800–1870* (1969), pp. 171–77. A general assessment of Gibbs is Roland Bainton, *Yale and the Ministry* (1957), pp. 87–88, 153–55. Family information is in J. W. Gibbs, *Memoir of the Gibbs Family* (1879), pp. 40–43, but it is not fully reliable.

BENJAMIN R. FOSTER

GIBBS, Josiah Willard (11 Feb. 1839–28 Apr. 1903), physical chemist and mathematician, was born in New Haven, Connecticut, the son of Josiah Willard Gibbs, Sr., professor of sacred literature at Yale Divinity School, and Mary Anna Van Cleve. Both sides of his family had long histories of academic association with Harvard, Yale and Princeton colleges. Gibbs entered Yale in 1854 and graduated in 1858. During his undergraduate years he regularly won prizes for excellence in Latin and mathematics. On 26 November 1858, shortly after he had begun graduate studies at Yale in engineering, he was elected a member of the Connecticut Academy of Arts and Sciences.

Yale was the first American college to offer the Ph.D. degree, and in 1863 Gibbs became Yale's second recipient of the degree in science and the first in engineering. In his dissertation on gear design, he used a geometric approach, presenting his problem and its solution in visualizable form, rather than restricting his treatment to sets of equations. His lifelong predilection for geometric treatments of mathematical problems is evident in his later work on thermodynamics and in his eulogy (1897) of Hubert Anson Newton, Gibbs's professor of mathematics and a longtime friend.

Gibbs was appointed tutor in Latin at Yale in 1863, and in 1865 tutor in natural philosophy. He was interested in practical industrial problems; his invention (patented 17 Apr. 1866) for "An Improved Railway Car Brake" used the inertia of the car moving forward or backward to set the brakes and devised structural methods for increasing brake pressure.

A bequest from his father in 1861 enabled Gibbs to make an extended visit to Europe from 1866 to 1869. In Paris he attended mathematics lectures by Chasles, Duhamel, Liouville, and Serret, as well as lectures in mathematical and experimental physics by Darboux and Bertin. In Berlin (1867–1868) he attended the physics lectures of Magnus, Kundt, and Quincke, and the mathematics lectures of Weierstrass, Kronecker, Foerster, and Kummer. He spent 1868 and 1869 in Heidelberg, where Helmholtz, Kirchhoff, Cantor, and DuBois-Reymond were among the lecturers.

Gibbs returned in 1869 to his New Haven home, which he shared with his unmarried sister Anna and with his married sister Julia and her husband, Addison Van Name, a mathematician. He now had no formal connection with Yale but lived on his modest income working on a variety of physical and mathematical problems.

On 13 July 1871 Gibbs was appointed professor of mathematical physics, a newly-established chair in Yale's department of philosophy and the arts; he served in this capacity until his death. For the first nine years he received no salary. His strong commitment to Yale is evidenced by his rejection of a remunerative offer from Bowdoin College in 1873.

Gibbs published two important papers in the 1873 *Transactions of the Connecticut Academy*: "Graphical Methods in the Thermodynamics of Fluids" and "A Method of Geometrical Representation of the Thermodynamic Properties of Substances by Means of Surfaces." Conventionally, the physical condition of gases had been described by diagrams showing the volume occupied by a given amount of substance as pressure varied at a given temperature or as temperature varied at a given pressure. Such diagrams were not usually used for liquids or solids, which undergo only small changes of volume with variations in temperature or pressure; moreover, water at 4 degrees Celsius expands on either heating or cooling.

Gibbs noted that, in dealing with solids or liquids, energy (heat content) and entropy (molecular disorder) are more useful measurements. In the first 1873 paper he demonstrated the advantages of an entropy-volume diagram over the usual pressure-volume diagram in displaying the properties of fluids. The second paper extended his treatment to a volume-energy-entropy spatial diagram. He described the three-dimensional surface as the entropy-volume plane deformed through the third (energy) dimension. In this diagram, all states of matter, solid, liquid, and gas, could be shown simultaneously, together with the conditions under which changes from one to the other would occur. The familiar pressure-temperature-volume (PTV) relationships were derivable from Gibbs's surfaces. Whereas PTV diagrams are usually drawn for pure substances, Gibbs's new diagrams were easily adaptable to mixtures of variable composition.

Gibbs's insight so impressed James Clerk Maxwell, the premier physicist of the time, that Maxwell constructed three three-dimensional models of the system for water, using Gibbs's coordinates, and sent Gibbs one of them.

Gibbs's 1873 papers provided the mathematical context for his best-known publication, "On the Equilibrium of Heterogeneous Substances," *Transactions of the Connecticut Academy* 3 (1876): 108–248, 3 (1878):

343–524. This paper lays the theoretical groundwork for the predictability of virtually the entire range of possible chemical reactions. It sets forth the methods for determining what reactions are impossible and what substances can or cannot coexist at equilibrium. It provides the mathematics for calculating the energy that drives reactions, and the heat released or absorbed when those reactions occur.

Two new concepts developed in this paper, used from the 1890s until today, are the phase rule and chemical potential.

The phase rule relates the variability of the system, the number of independently controllable components, and the number of distinct phases present. It has become fundamental in the study of metallurgical processes, in the production, by fractional crystallization, of potassium fertilizers from complex ores, and in many high-pressure gas reactions. Wilhelm Ostwald in Germany and Hendrik Willem Backhuis Roozeboom in Holland did much to promote the use of Gibbs's ideas in physical chemistry.

Gibbs's related concepts of chemical potential and free energy were essential elements in the new discipline of chemical thermodynamics. The Second Law of Thermodynamics—in all systems, change is accompanied by an overall increase in entropy—had arisen from studies on the efficiency limits of steam engines. Gibbs reformulated the Second Law in terms which made it applicable to chemical reactions. Although Gibbs was aware of the implications of his theoretical analysis, he expressed little interest in its practical applications.

The importance of this paper and the utility of its concepts were not immediately recognized by Gibbs's contemporaries. This lack of early response has been attributed to the relative obscurity of the journal in which the paper appeared, although Gibbs also published a lengthy abstract of it in the more widely-read *American Journal of Science*, ser. 3, 16 (1878): 441–58. More important in retarding the spread of Gibbs's ideas was the author's terse, rigorous, mathematical style, with a paucity of illustrative examples, making the text formidably difficult reading. Addison E. Verrill, president of the Connecticut Academy, recalled that the publications committee, which included eminent mathematicians, had expressed the opinion that the only person in the world, besides Gibbs, who could understand the paper, was Clerk Maxwell. Maxwell in fact saw the paper and spoke of its significance, but he died shortly thereafter. The English chemist M. M. Pattison Muir, in an 1880 letter to Gibbs, wrote that he did not venture to read the paper until "I found Clerk Maxwell's translation of [the first part of] your paper into ordinary language, in the Science Conference at South Kensington [1876]."

It was not until 1892, when Wilhelm Ostwald translated Gibbs's paper into German, that its impact was strongly felt. The foundation of the journal *Zeitschrift für physikalische Chemie* in 1887 had signaled the appearance of physical chemistry as a distinct discipline, and its readership was able to appreciate Gibbs's contribution. By 1899, when Henri Louis Le Chatelier's French translation appeared, Gibbs's thermodynamic ideas were already well known.

Many British and German physicists who received copies of Gibbs's paper on thermodynamics did not give it the attention it deserved. Only in retrospect did they recognize how much of value lay in Gibbs's monumental work. In 1924, at the centenary celebration of the founding of the Franklin Institute, Frederick George Donnan delivered an address, "The Influence of J. Willard Gibbs on the Science of Physical Chemistry," in which he referred to Gibbs's paper "On the Equilibrium of Heterogeneous Substances" as "one of the mightiest works of genius the human mind has ever produced" (quoted in W. T. Sedgwick and H. W. Tyler, *A Short History of Science* [1939], p. 416). In 1911 Donnan was able to apply Gibbs's work on osmotic pressure and semipermeable membranes to phenomena involving ionic equilibria; ionization was an unknown phenomenon in Gibbs's time.

Although practical applications of Gibbs's work was slow to emerge, formal recognition of his stature as a scientist came more quickly. On 21 April 1879 he was elected to membership in the National Academy of Sciences. In 1880 he was elected to the American Academy of Arts and Sciences of Boston, from which he received the Rumford Medal in 1881.

Early in 1880 Gibbs, who infrequently left New Haven, went to Baltimore at the invitation of Daniel Coit Gilman, the first president of the new Johns Hopkins University, to lecture on analytical mechanics. Shortly thereafter Gilman invited Gibbs to join the faculty at an annual salary of $3,000. Gibbs was inclined to accept the offer, but word of his imminent departure led Yale to offer him $2,000 a year. His colleagues also asked him to stay, and he did.

Although Gibbs continued to publish short papers in the field of chemical thermodynamics, his attention after 1879 was more concentrated on physical problems—for example, the velocity of light—and on the mathematics required to express fundamental relationships in the fields of electricity and magnetism. He became involved in a controversy in the journal *Nature* (1891–1893) over the merits and priority of two related systems of mathematical representation, one developed by Sir William Rowan Hamilton and the other by Hermann Grassmann. Gibbs persuaded the family of Grassmann, who had died in 1877, to find and publish Grassmann's doctoral thesis, proving his priority. Gibbs had used a modification of Grassmann's system in his lectures and during 1881–1884 had distributed printed copies of the calculation procedure to his students in physics. These notes, systematized, expanded, and supplemented by his student Edwin Bidwell Wilson, with Gibbs's approval, were finally published in 1901 as *Vector Analysis*.

Vector analysis was valuable in treating problems in the rapidly-expanding industrial fields of electricity and magnetism, but Gibbs's horizons extended far beyond the mathematics of the immediately useful. He considered vector analysis as part of a larger field which he called "multiple algebra." He spoke on this subject in his vice-presidential address to the section of mathematics and astronomy of the American Association for the Advancement of Science at its 1886 meeting in Buffalo, New York.

During the 1880s Gibbs published several papers on the theory of light. He supported Clerk Maxwell's view that light was an electromagnetic phenomenon and opposed Sir William Thomson's theory of light as a wave transmitted through an elastic ether. In his last papers on the subject (1888), Gibbs pointed out that the properties of light were derivable from known laws of electricity, whereas the ether theory required the invention of increasingly improbable hypotheses to sustain it.

In 1885 Gibbs was elected a corresponding member of the British Association for the Advancement of Science, and in 1886, a foreign member of the Dutch Society of Sciences. He received honorary memberships in the Cambridge (England) Philosophical Society and the Royal Institution of Great Britain (1891); the London Mathematical Society, the Manchester Literary and Philosophical Society and the Royal Academy of Amsterdam (1892); and the American Philosophical Society of Philadelphia (1895). He also received honorary memberships in the Royal Society of London, the Royal Prussian Academy of Sciences (Berlin), the Washington (D.C.) Academy of Sciences, and the Royal Bavarian Academy of Sciences. In 1901 he was awarded the Copley Medal from the Royal Society of London. Arne Westgren, chairman of the Swedish Royal Academy's Nobel committee on chemistry wrote in *Nobel, the Man and His Prizes* (1950), "Gibbs unquestionably deserved to be awarded the [first or second] Nobel Prize for his work on thermodynamics," but "he was never nominated."

Gibbs never married. He died in New Haven, only a short distance from his birthplace.

• Some unpublished papers are in the Gibbs Collection, Yale University Library. Biographical information on Gibbs appears in Henry A. Bumstead, "Josiah Willard Gibbs," *American Journal of Science* ser. 4, 16 (1903); J. G. Crowther, "*Famous American Men of Science*" (1937); Muriel Rukeyser, *Willard Gibbs* (1942); Lynde Phelps Wheeler, *Josiah Willard Gibbs* (1952); and C. Kraus, "Josiah Willard Gibbs," *Great Chemists*, ed. Eduard Farber, vol. 1 (1961), pp. 785–803. Gibbs's collected papers, first published in 1906, were reprinted in 1961. Wilson's edition of Gibbs's *Vector Analysis*, first published in 1909, was also reissued (1960).

CHARLES H. FUCHSMAN

GIBBS, Mifflin Wistar (17 Apr. 1823–11 July 1915), businessman, politician, and race leader, was born in Philadelphia, Pennsylvania, the son of Jonathan C. Gibbs, a Methodist minister, and Maria Jackson. His parents were free blacks. His father died when Mifflin was seven years old, and his mother was an invalid. As a teenager, Mifflin attended the Philomathean Institute, a black men's literary society, and, like his brother Jonathan C. Gibbs (who would serve as secretary of state in Florida during Reconstruction), became a carpenter's apprentice, and subsequently a journeyman contractor. During the 1840s, Mifflin Gibbs aided fugitive slaves by participating in local Underground Railroad efforts and worked with its famous conductor William Still. It was through this work that he became acquainted with the preeminent black abolitionist Frederick Douglass, accompanying him on an 1849 tour of New York State.

During this tour, Gibbs learned that gold had been discovered in California, and he set out to find his fortune. Reaching San Francisco in 1850, he decided that more money could be made in business than in panning for gold. Consequently, along with a black partner, Peter Lester, Gibbs established a clothing and dry goods store. His business prospered, and he quickly became a well-known and successful entrepreneur. He also kept up his interest in the abolitionist movement, attending three state black conventions (1854, 1855, 1857) and in 1855 purchasing and becoming the editor of a local black antislavery newspaper, the *Mirror of the Times*.

During an economic recession in the United States in 1857–1858, Gibbs followed a new gold rush to Victoria, British Columbia, Canada, where he opened another store. He briefly returned to the United States in 1859 to marry Maria A. Alexander, a former Oberlin student who became the mother of their five children. During the next decade, Gibbs repeated his California business success in Canada by speculating in real estate, becoming the director of the Queen Charlotte Island Anthracite Coal Company, and building a wharf and railroad spur to transport coal. His business ventures brought him influence, and in 1866 he was elected to the first of two terms as a member of Victoria's Common Council. After the second term, however, disgruntled by the direction of local politics, he returned to the United States to complete a formal course in law at a business school in Oberlin, Ohio.

Touring the southern states to find a suitable location to establish a law practice, Gibbs settled in the rapidly growing town of Little Rock, Arkansas, in 1871. Beginning as a lawyer, he was later appointed county attorney, and in 1873 he won election as municipal judge of Little Rock, reportedly the first black man in the nation to be so honored. In 1875 when the Democrats returned to power, Gibbs lost the judgeship, but he quickly rose to prominence in the Republican party, attending national Republican conventions and serving as a presidential elector for Arkansas in 1876 and as secretary of the Republican state central committee from 1887 to 1897. In 1877 he was appointed by President Rutherford B. Hayes as register of the U.S. Land Office for the Little Rock District of Arkansas. He served in the land office for twelve years, the last four as receiver of public monies. In 1897 he was appointed U.S. consul to Tamatave, Madagascar (1898–1901).

In 1901 Gibbs returned to Arkansas and the next year published *Shadow and Light, an Autobiography with Reminiscences of the Last and Present Century* (repr. 1968), a lively account of his life and times, with an introduction by the famous black leader Booker T. Washington. That Washington would introduce the book was no accident; Gibbs epitomized Washington's self-help philosophy. In Little Rock, Gibbs not only speculated in real estate but eventually owned a number of brick office buildings and rental properties. In 1903 Gibbs became president of the city's Capital City Savings Bank (it failed after five years) and later bought shares in several local companies while becoming a partner in the Little Rock Electric Light Company. He was also an active member of the National Negro Business League, founded by Washington to encourage entrepreneurship among blacks.

Although closely tied to the Republican machine in Arkansas, Gibbs fought for equal rights for blacks and supported emigration from the South as a cure for racial oppression (a radical stance in the late 1870s). After Theodore Roosevelt (1858–1919) summarily dismissed black soldiers accused of inciting a race riot in Brownsville, Texas, in 1906, Gibbs abandoned the Republican party and endorsed Democrat William Jennings Bryan for the presidency. The common thread linking these diverse elements was Gibbs's commitment to what he termed "the progress of the race." Although he fought for equality and fair treatment, he believed that property acquisition and education were the keys to racial advancement and that African Americans should establish a skilled middle class in order to compete in the marketplace.

During the last decade of his life, using the income from his rental properties, Gibbs lived quietly and comfortably in Little Rock. After an illness of several months, he died at his home. He was survived by several notable children, among them Harriet Gibbs Marshall, who founded the Washington Conservatory of Music, and Ida Gibbs Hunt, who married William Henry Hunt, Gibbs's successor as U.S. consul to Madagascar. A man of education, talent, energy, and property, Gibbs had a remarkably varied career.

• For biographical information on Gibbs, see Tom W. Dillard, "'Golden Prospects and Fraternal Amenities,' Mifflin W. Gibbs's Arkansas Years," *Arkansas Historical Quarterly* 35 (Winter 1976): 307–33. Obituaries are in the *Arkansas Gazette* and *Arkansas Democrat*, 12 July 1915, and in the Washington *Bee*, 17 July 1915.

LOREN SCHWENINGER

GIBBS, William Francis (24 Aug. 1886–6 Sept. 1967), naval architect, was born in Philadelphia, Pennsylvania, the son of William Warren Gibbs, a financier and corporate director, and Frances Ayres Johnson. A sickly childhood permitted him to stay home from school frequently; during these intervals he studied engineering and mathematics. Because his father disliked engineering, Gibbs majored in economics at Harvard before leaving in 1910 after three years. He then studied law at Columbia University, from which he received his LL.B. and M.A. in 1913. He practiced law for one year, continuing to pursue an avocational interest in naval architecture and marine engineering. Although he won his only court appearance, his disillusionment with the law and a prior agreement with his father led to a one-year "sabbatical." During this period Gibbs designed a 1,000-foot, 55,000-ton ocean liner with a design speed of 30 knots capable of shaving ten hours from the transatlantic speed record. He was joined in this venture by his brother Frederick, who handled the economic aspects; their complementary roles in the giant project led to a lifelong fraternal partnership.

After obtaining professional input into their design, the Gibbses presented their ship to Ralph Peters, president of the Long Island Railroad. Peters was sufficiently impressed to sponsor a meeting with financier J. P. Morgan, one of whose enterprises was the International Mercantile Marine Company, a steamship line specializing in the international passenger and immigration trade. Equally impressed, Morgan hired the Gibbses to further develop their ambitious ship for the IMMC, but World War I intervened. Gibbs worked for the IMMC during the war as chief designer, also becoming naval architect for the U.S. Shipping Control Commission. The brothers continued with IMMC for three years, and William Francis rose to the position of chief of construction.

In 1922, at the request of the federal government, the Gibbses formed Gibbs Brothers, Inc., to restore the famous German ocean liner *Leviathan* to its prewar level of luxury. This ship had been seized at the outset of World War I and reconditioned as a U.S. troopship. The ship's German builders demanded $1 million for its original plans, believing that the job could not be undertaken without them; instead, Gibbs produced plans from the ship and refitted it to the highest standard. This high-visibility job brought both a reputation for excellence and more work to Gibbs Brothers. In 1927 Gibbs married Vera Cravath Larkin, who brought a son to the marriage. The couple had two children.

Gibbs's next major job was a commission from the Matson shipping line for construction of the liner *Malolo* in 1927. Displaying Gibbs's strong interest in safety, this design incorporated the novel concept of sliding doors in watertight bulkheads, which allowed free access through lower spaces but could be closed in a collision. Remarkably, Gibbs's theory was tested even before *Malolo* went into service; during its trials off Cape Cod, it was rammed by a freighter. On the bridge at the time, Gibbs himself pressed the button closing off the bulkhead doors, saving the ship without casualties. Sliding bulkhead doors have since become common aboard ship.

The years between the world wars saw a recession in the naval shipbuilding industry, so in 1929 the Gibbses took on a partner, Daniel Hargate Cox, of the famous yacht designers Cox & Stevens, to expand into the luxury end of the business. The company name was changed to Gibbs & Cox, Inc., and the effort was a success. The firm designed or renovated several large yachts and constructed four large luxury liners in 1931 for the Grace Line. Two years later, the U.S. Navy began to upgrade its outdated fleet, and Gibbs was at the forefront of this defense effort. Beginning with a new destroyer, Gibbs provided new naval designs each year, also designing the revolutionary fireboat *Fire Fighter* (1938) for the city of New York. Capable of pumping 20,000 gallons of water per minute and the most powerful fireboat ever built, *Fire Fighter* was still in use in 1994. Gibbs also designed and supervised construction of the world's largest ocean liner, SS *America* (1939) for the United States Lines.

In 1940 the British government requested a Gibbs design for a mass-producible freighter to replace shipping sunk by the Germans. He adapted a British tramp steamer design for welding rather than riveting, and sixty of the 10,000-ton vessels were ordered. However, around the same time the U.S. Maritime Commission requested a similar design for mass production, prompting Gibbs to modify his plans for the British into what became the famous Liberty ship program of World War II. Traditional construction methods and supply sourcing were radically altered for wartime, trimming building times from four years to four days. Under these conditions, the United States constructed 2,712 Liberty ships and 531 ships of the Victory class (a slightly larger, faster, and more advanced freighter). Along with these merchant designs, Gibbs & Cox also worked on plans for aircraft carriers, cruisers, destroyers, destroyer escorts, icebreakers, landing craft, machine-shop ships, mine sweepers, patrol frigates, tankers, tenders, and general transports, for what was described as "some seventy percent of all United States shipbuilding." In 1942 Gibbs was appointed by the War Production Board as controller of shipbuilding, responsible for coordinating the entire nation's military and commercial ship construction programs. He resigned this post the following year after successfully streamlining the overall effort, and in 1946 he produced designs for converting World War II shipping to commercial use.

However, Gibbs still retained his youthful dream of a 1,000-foot luxury ocean liner, occasionally updating his plans in the intervening years. The project culminated in 1951 with the launch of Design 12201, a United States Lines superliner incorporating all of Gibbs's ideas on speed, size, safety, luxury, and military potential. The $78 million SS *United States* was the fastest and largest passenger ship ever built in the nation. Funded by a government subsidy for potential troop ship conversion, the *United States*'s hull design, top speed, and fuel consumption remained secret for decades. Nevertheless, during its trials the superliner achieved a speed of 38.32 knots (44.13 mph) and easily took the Blue Riband of the Atlantic for the fastest transatlantic passage during its 1952 maiden voyage—an honor the ship held its entire career. Measuring 990 feet in length, "the big ship" had twelve decks and could carry 2,008 passengers per voyage. Nearly everything aboard, including furniture and decoration, was metal or synthetic material for fireproofing, and contemporary folklore held that the only wood on board was in the pianos and chefs' chopping blocks. In 1969 *United States* was retired, a victim of air travel and high labor costs; in 1993 it was sold to Turkish owners. Gibbs continued to work on design and refitting projects until his death, but *United States* remained his personal favorite and professional masterpiece.

A self-taught naval architect, William Francis Gibbs provided designs or specifications for more than 6,000 ships during his career, including the principal U.S. merchant and naval vessels of World War II. He also contributed some of the most significant safety innovations and ocean liner designs of the twentieth century, which gained him international respect and acclaim. His talent lay in a contradictory combination of visionary ideas and intense devotion to detail; well grounded in the theoretical, he was utterly dedicated to practical results. A private man in a very public position, he had the largest impact of any individual on modern shipbuilding and design. He died in New York City.

• Portions of Gibbs's personal effects and library, builder's models, and film footage are at the Mariners' Museum, Newport News, Va.; some of his ship designs are at the Smithsonian Institution's National Museum of American History. The only published biography is Frank O. Braynard, *By Their Works Ye Shall Know Them: The Life and Ships of William Francis Gibbs, 1886–1967* (1968), although Gibbs & Cox prepared the 95-page volume *William Francis Gibbs—Naval Architect and Marine Engineer* (c. 1952) for in-house use. His contributions in World War II are discussed in "Technological Revolutionist," *Time,* 28 Sept. 1942, pp. 20–22; *Current Biography* (1944), pp. 227–30; and Alva Johnston, "The Mysterious Mr. Gibbs," *Saturday Evening Post,* 20 Jan., 27 Jan., and 3 Feb. 1945. Various aspects of his life and career are also found in Richard Austin Smith, "The Love Affair of William Francis Gibbs," *Fortune,* Aug. 1957, pp. 136–60; Edward R. Crews, "The Big Ship," *Invention & Technology,* Spring/Summer 1990, pp. 34–41; "William Francis Gibbs: Naval Architect," *Mariners' Museum Journal* 17 (Fall/Winter 1990), passim; and John R. Kane, "The Speed of the SS *United States,*" *Marine Technology* 15 (Apr. 1978): 119–43. An obituary is in the *New York Times,* 7 Sept. 1967.

PAUL FORSYTHE JOHNSTON

GIBBS, Wolcott (21 Feb. 1822–9 Dec. 1908), chemist, was born Oliver Wolcott Gibbs in New York City, the son of Colonel George Gibbs, a wealthy mineralogist and horticulturist, after whom the mineral gibbsite was named, and Laura Wolcott, whose father was secretary of the treasury during the administrations of Presidents George Washington and John Adams. Gibbs entered Columbia College in 1837. During his junior year he published his first scientific paper, an account of a new form of galvanic battery, in which carbon was used, probably for the first time, as the inactive plate. This was a remarkable achievement both because the author was only eighteen and because, as science courses did not yet involve laboratory instruction, the research was performed under extremely adverse conditions, an indication of Gibbs's strong, independent, and persistent character.

On receiving his A.B. degree in 1841, Gibbs became assistant to Robert Hare, professor of chemistry at the University of Pennsylvania. After several months with Hare, he entered the College of Physicians and Surgeons in New York, from which he received an A.M. (1844) and M.D. (1845). His doctoral dissertation involved a natural system for the classification of the chemical elements. Although he never practiced medicine, his medical studies proved useful in his later work on the physiological effects of isomeric organic compounds on animals.

Gibbs then spent several months studying mineralogy and chemistry at Berlin with Karl Friedrich Rammelsberg and a year with Heinrich Rose, a semester with chemist Justus von Liebig at Giessen, and some time in Paris attending the lectures of chemists Auguste Laurent and Jean-Baptiste-André Dumas and the physicist Henri Victor Regnault. He was most impressed with Rose, whom he regarded as his "chemical father."

In 1848 Gibbs returned from abroad and spent a year as assistant professor at the College of Physicians and Surgeons while also lecturing at Delaware College in Newark, Delaware. In 1849 he was appointed professor of chemistry at the newly established Free Academy (now the City College of the City University of New York), where he taught elementary chemistry. Although he had little time to pursue research, he produced two works that established his reputation—his joint monograph with Frederick Augustus Genth on cobalt-ammines (1856) and his articles on the platinum metals. He became an associate editor (1851–1873) of the *American Journal of Science* and began writing a series of abstracts (eventually amounting to about 500 pages) that brought the results of foreign investigations to American readers. As a correspondent (1869–1877) of the German Chemical Society, he abstracted American articles for European scientists. In 1853 he married Josephine Mauran; they had no children.

During this period Gibbs was a candidate for the chair of chemistry at Columbia, but he was not selected because he was a Unitarian and Columbia was under strict sectarian control. In 1863 he was appointed to a more desirable position, the Rumford Professorship of the Application of Science to the Useful Arts at Harvard University, where he lectured on heat and light and took charge of the chemical laboratory of the Lawrence Scientific School (1863–1871). Gibbs was in charge of students who intended to become professional chemists and who worked as individuals rather than in classes. He rarely had more than twenty students at any one time, had an assistant to relieve him of routine work, and devoted himself to research, largely in analytical chemistry, more than he had been able to previously. More than any other person, Gibbs introduced into the United States the German system of using research as a means of chemical instruction. Although a reformer, he never preached reform, and he probably never imagined that his teaching was remarkable. He simply did what was natural and obvious to him.

In 1871, despite rigorous protests from Gibbs and other scientific leaders, chemistry instruction at Harvard University was reorganized. The Lawrence Scientific School laboratory was consolidated with that of Harvard College, relegating Gibbs to the Department of Physics, where he taught a small advanced class on light and heat and lectured on spectroscopy and thermodynamics. His work was limited to that of the Rumford professorship, which gave him more time for research but deprived chemistry students of his teaching. Thus the extended researches for which he is best known date from his earlier and later periods when all his energies were concentrated on his own personal work rather than from the time when he was burdened with laboratory administration and elementary chemistry teaching. Although not a rich man, Gibbs possessed enough money to equip a small personal laboratory and to hire a private assistant. He adapted himself to his reduced circumstances and cared little for instrumental refinements. His modest equipment was reminiscent of the famous kitchen of the great Swedish chemist Jöns Jacob Berzelius. Gibbs's favorite piece of apparatus was a cast-iron cooking stove; precipitates could be dried in it, crucibles could be buried in the coals, and water could be heated on top of it.

In 1887 Gibbs retired to his summer house at Newport, Rhode Island, where he erected a laboratory. With the aid of several assistants he continued his research for a decade and cultivated his garden. He died in Newport.

Gibbs's research was extremely varied. In 1844 he discussed the theory of compound salt radicals (*American Journal of Arts and Sciences* 46 [1844]: 52), and in 1847, during his European studies, he published a number of mineral analyses. In 1850 he noted that compounds that change color on heating do so in the direction of the red portion of the spectrum, and in 1852 he published the first of his articles on analytical chemistry—a separation of manganese from zinc by the use of lead peroxide. None of these early works was of outstanding importance. Gibbs was still searching for a field to which he could devote himself completely.

Gibbs was a true pioneer who was throughout his career attracted to the problem of introducing order to classes of little-explored and poorly understood compounds on the frontier of chemistry. These classes, which included the cobalt-ammines, platinum metal complexes, and complex inorganic acids, were regarded as exceptional compounds. Gibbs, with his extraordinary patience, experimental ingenuity, and innovative analytical techniques, showed that these compounds were representatives of general classes consisting of large numbers of compounds. He showed the vastness of these classes, established the composition of many of their members, and speculated on their natures, work that was taken up by later investigators.

During the first half of the nineteenth century there were few investigations of cobalt-ammonia bases (now termed cobalt-ammines), the colorful and intriguing compounds that Alfred Werner, the first Swiss Nobel laureate in chemistry, used to erect the foundations of coordination chemistry, which became one of the most active research areas of inorganic chemistry. Credit for the first distinct recognition of the existence of perfectly well-defined and crystallized solid salts of cobalt-ammines belongs to F. A. Genth, who published his results in a short "preliminary notice" of 1851. In July 1852 Gibbs, who had prepared one of Genth's compounds, accepted Genth's proposal to collaborate on a detailed study of these substances, which has become famous in the annals of coordination chemistry. In November 1852 Gibbs made his first original contribution to this field by discovering a new series of compounds, xanthocobalt (pentaamminenitrocobalt[III]). He communicated his results to the American Association for the Advancement of Science at its Cleveland meeting (Aug. 1853), but he did not publish them.

It was not until 1856 that Gibbs and Genth's joint results appeared in a 67-page monograph, *Researches on the Ammonia-Cobalt Bases*, which came to the attention of chemists largely through its reprinted version that appeared in the *American Journal of Arts and Sciences* in 1856 and 1857. Several years had been required to complete the research, for the analytical portion of the work was both difficult and protracted. Gibbs and Genth described in detail the preparation, properties, analyses, and reactions of thirty-five salts of four cobalt-ammine series. In eleven cases they reported crystallographic data obtained by J. D. Dana. For the first time closely related salts were clearly differentiated, although Gibbs and Genth erred in supposing them to be isomeric, i.e., to have the same chemical composition. They also discussed in detail the advantages and disadvantages of the different systems for formulating the constitution of their compounds.

Gibbs and Genth laid the foundations for later work and pointed the way to the future by correctly predicting what are now known as coordination compounds in which "one or more equivalents of ammonia" are replaced by "an equal number of equivalents of a compound ammonia, as for example, methylamin, ethylamin, &c." and those in which cobalt could be replaced by other metals. They concluded their elaborate and extended memoir, which American chemist George F. Barker claimed "has always ranked among the highest chemical investigations ever made in this country," with the statement, "we invite the attention of chemists to a class of salts which for beauty of form and color, and for abstract theoretical interest, are almost unequalled either among organic or inorganic compounds." Their invitation was accepted by a number of chemists, particularly by the Swede Christian Wilhelm Blomstrand, the Dane Sophus Mads Jørgensen, who, beginning in 1878, entered the field because of some discrepant analytical data in Gibbs and Genth's monograph, and by Alfred Werner, beginning in 1893. Thus Gibbs and Genth's memoir deserves credit for attracting chemists to a field that did much to elucidate the nature of chemical bonding, one of the most fundamental topics in chemistry. In the late twentieth century, coordination chemistry experienced a renaissance of activity.

Although Gibbs was primarily an experimentalist, he did not avoid or underrate theory. In an 1867 paper on atomicities, as valences were then called, he developed the idea of residual affinities, whereby atoms form more bonds than expected from their valences. He applied this idea to the cobalt-ammines by postulating chains of ammonia molecules (*American Journal of Arts and Sciences* 2d ser., 44 [1867]: 409–16), which was developed more fully, beginning in 1869, by Blomstrand. In 1875 and 1876 Gibbs used his theories in accounting for additional cobalt-ammines that he prepared, including salts of a new cation.

Gibbs's celebrated work on the platinum metals primarily involved analytical methods, a specialty in which he excelled. In this last joint publication (*American Journal of Arts and Sciences* 2d ser., 25 (1858): 248) Gibbs and Genth reinvestigated the osmium compound $[OsO_2(NH_3)_4]Cl_2$ discovered in 1844 by Edmond Frémy. Because he did not have access to "a laboratory in which the separation and collection of osmic hyperoxide, OsO_4, could be effected without serious danger to the air-passages and to the eyes," Gibbs did not report the full results of his analyses until twenty-three years later (*American Chemistry Journal* 3 [1882]: 233). He described "perhaps the most simple and convenient method of obtaining pure metallic osmium," as well as a method for detecting minute quantities of osmium.

In the first of his series of three articles in the *American Journal of Arts and Sciences* titled "Researches on the Platinum Metals" (2d ser., 31 [1861]: 63), Gibbs addressed himself to what had "always been considered among the most difficult problems with which the chemist [had] to deal," *viz.*, the separation of the different platinum metals from each other. In his second paper (2d ser., 34 [1862]: 341) he proposed a separation method based on his research on the reactions of potassium nitrite and sodium nitrite with all six platinum metals, which seems to be the first systematic study of the platinum metal nitro complexes. In his third article (2d ser., 37 [1864]: 57), he presented a second general method for separating four platinum metals (platinum, iridium, rhodium, and ruthenium), which involved hexaamminecobalt(III) chloride, described in great detail in his 1856 monograph with Genth.

From the work of Sir Humphry Davy on the preparation of the alkali and alkaline earth metals early in the nineteenth century, the possibility existed of determining metals quantitatively by electrolysis, but it was not until more than a half century later that Gibbs was the first to apply this method to analysis by weighing the amount of deposited metal, and he is thus regarded as the father of electrogravimetry. He determined both copper and nickel by methods still universally used today (*Zeitschrift für analytische Chemie* 3 [1864]: 334), and he was the first to deposit metals on a mercury cathode and to determine them as amalgams (*Chemical News* 42 [1880]: 291). In addition to devising new analytical methods, he also developed and perfected old ones. He also invented a number of instruments and pieces of apparatus such as the ring burner and the use of porous septa for heating precipitates in gases. With E. R. Taylor he devised a glass and sand filter, which was a forerunner of the crucibles later developed by Gibbs's assistants Charles Edward Munroe and Frank Austin Gooch.

Beginning in 1877 Gibbs began a series of researches on what he called the "complex inorganic acids" (heteropoly acids), a vast, complicated, and almost unexplored field that he pursued until his last published paper (*American Journal of Arts and Sciences* 17 [1894]: 167). While working in his small private laboratory with only one assistant, he described more than fifty series of complex acids and salts involving the elements tungsten, molybdenum, arsenic, phosphorus, vanadium, antimony, tin, platinum, selenium, tellurium, cerium, and uranium. In one of his late articles, published when he was seventy-one, Gibbs described his research on the cerium group of the rare earths, another extremely difficult and complex subject, and he proposed a new method for determining the atomic weights of the rare-earth metals (*Proceedings of the American Academy of Arts and Sciences* 3d ser., 28 [1893]: 26).

In organic chemistry Gibbs discussed the constitution of uric acid and its derivatives (*American Journal of Arts and Sciences* 2d ser., 46 [1868]: 289) and described their products with alkali metal nitrites (1869). In optics he constructed a normal map of the solar spectrum (*AJAS* 2d ser., 43 [1867]: 1) and measured the wavelengths of elementary spectral lines (*AJAS* 2d ser., 45 [1868]: 298; 47 [1869]: 194); in interference phenomena he discovered what he called the interferential constant, which was independent of temperature. During his last years at Newport Gibbs carried out an extensive study of the physiological effects of isomeric organic compounds on animals, first with Hobart A. Hare (*American Chemistry Journal* 11 [1889]: 435; 12 [1890]: 145, 365) and then with Edward T. Reichert (*ACJ* 13 [1891]: 289, 361, 570; 16 [1894]: 443).

Because Gibbs wrote no books and delivered no popular lectures, he was little known by the general public. Within scientific circles, however, he received the highest honors. One of the founders of the National Academy of Sciences, he served as its president (1895–1900) as well as president of the American Association for the Advancement of Science (1897). A member of many scientific societies and an honorary member of the American and English chemical societies and corresponding member of the Prussian Academy of Sciences and the British Association for the Advancement of Science, he was the only American to be elected an honorary member of the German Chemical Society and was the recipient of several honorary degrees. A fervent patriot of the Union cause, during the Civil War he was active in the Sanitary Commission, a forerunner of the Red Cross, and was a founder of the

Union League Club of New York, organized to bring together patriotic citizens of the city.

A true pioneer of research in many fields, Gibbs enjoyed blazing trails through territories on the frontiers of science. He was called "the first great personality in American chemistry" by Ferenc Szabadváry, author of *History of Analytical Chemistry* ([1966], p. 312). He was a thorough and meticulous scholar, devoted to his science and indifferent to popularity. His portrait is sculptured in bas relief on the west entrance doors of the U.S. Capitol in Washington, D.C., and in 1912 the Wolcott Gibbs Memorial Laboratory was erected at Harvard University, funded by his assistant at Newport, Morris Loeb, and Gibbs's students and friends.

• Gibbs's personal papers are preserved in the Franklin Institute in Philadelphia. A short autobiography written two years before his death and published by his nephew is "Wolcott Gibbs," *Science* 28 (1908): 875–76. Biographies with portraits and bibliographies are Frank Wigglesworth Clarke, "Biographical Memoir of Wolcott Gibbs, 1822–1908," National Academy of Sciences, *Biographical Memoirs* 7 (1910): 1–22, and Theodore W. Richards, "Wolcott Gibbs," *Berichte der Deutschen Chemischen Gesellschaft* 42 (1909): 5037–54. Other biographies include Frank Wigglesworth Clarke, "Wolcott Gibbs Memorial Lecture," *Journal of the Chemical Society* 95 (1909): 1299–1312 (with portrait); Charles Loring Jackson, "Wolcott Gibbs," *American Journal of Science* 27 (1909): 253–59; Edgar Fahs Smith, *Chemistry in America: Chapters from the History of the Science in the United States* (1914; repr. 1972), pp. 264–72 (with portrait); and Ann Marie Ladetto, "Oliver Walcott Gibbs 1822–1908," in *American Chemists and Chemical Engineers*, ed. Wyndham Miles (1976), pp. 171–73. Personal reminiscences are in Charles E. Munroe, "Address at the Unveiling of the Bust of Wolcott Gibbs in Rumford Hall, Chemists' Club [New York], November 25, 1911," *Science* 34 (1911): 864–68. A discussion of Gibbs's work on the platinum metals is George B. Kauffman, "An American Pioneer in Platinum Metal Research: The Life and Work of Wolcott Gibbs," *Platinum Metals Review* 16 (1972): 101–4, and a discussion of Gibbs's work on the metal-ammines is George B. Kauffman, "Early Experimental Studies of Cobalt-Ammines," *Isis* 68 (1977): 392–403.

GEORGE B. KAUFFMAN

GIBBS, Wolcott (15 Mar. 1902–16 Aug. 1958), drama critic, editor, and author, was born Oliver Wolcott Gibbs in New York City, the son of Lucius Tuckerman Gibbs, an electrical engineer and inventor, and Angelica Singleton Duer. When Gibbs was six years old his father died, and his alcoholic mother lost custody of Gibbs and his sister. George Gibbs, a bachelor uncle and noted electrical engineer, became the children's primary guardian. An undistinguished student, after attending the Riverdale Country Day School in the Bronx, New York, and the Hill School in Pottstown, Pennsylvania, Gibbs ended his formal education. He then worked at various jobs, most of which were obtained through family connections. These included an unpaid apprenticeship at the architectural firm of McKim, Mead and White, insurance clerk, chauffeur, and brakeman for the Long Island Railroad. In 1923 he was briefly married to the daughter of another railroad employee, whose name is unknown.

Gibbs's writing career began in 1924 when, again through family connections, he was hired as a reporter by the Griscom chain of newspapers on Long Island. The next year he became associate editor of the *Enterprise* in East Norwich, New York. Through the assistance of his relative, the poet-novelist Alice Duer Miller, he joined the staff of the recently established *New Yorker* magazine as a copy reader in 1927. He was soon promoted to associate editor, a more influential position that brought him into close contact with other writers and editors at the magazine, including James Thurber, Katharine and E. B. White, and Harold W. Ross, the magazine's founder. In August 1929 Gibbs married Elizabeth Crawford, a writer in the *New Yorker*'s advertising department. Seven months later Crawford jumped to her death from the window of their New York apartment. Her suicide contributed to Gibbs's pessimistic view of life, an attitude that colored his writings. In 1933 Gibbs married Elinor Mead Sherwin, with whom he had two children.

During his thirty years at the *New Yorker*, Gibbs served in various capacities. He was one of the magazine's most skilled editors, fine-tuning articles by other writers without imposing his own style. A prolific writer, he contributed numerous essays, profiles, short stories, and literary parodies (his experience as an editor made him especially adept at the latter). From 1937 to 1942, as an editorial writer, Gibbs produced a weekly "Notes and Comments" column. He substituted for E. B. White on the "Talk of the Town" column and for a brief period (Dec. 1944–July 1945) was the magazine's film critic. Collected volumes of Gibbs's writings, nearly all of which appeared first in the *New Yorker*, are *Bed of Neuroses* (1937), *Season in the Sun* (1946), and *More in Sorrow* (1958). He also wrote a collection of short stories about a fictitious Antarctic explorer, *Bird Life at the Pole by Commander Christopher Robin* (1931).

Gibbs is most noted for his theater criticism. Succeeding Robert Benchley as the *New Yorker*'s chief drama critic in 1940, he continued in this post for eighteen years. As a critic Gibbs was caustic and hard to please but remarkably perceptive. He sometimes walked out of a play after the first act, deciding that it was not worthy of a review. On those rare times that a play or performer met with his approval, such as Katharine Cornell in *Candida* and Helen Hayes in *Happy Birthday*, his praise was generous. "I've always felt that play criticism was a silly occupation for a grown man," he said. "It's so easy to make fun of bad plays and most plays are bad. Although I don't think I pan more shows than my fellow critics, I will admit that I write more disagreeably than most" (*New York Times*, 15 Oct. 1950).

Gibbs made his own contribution as a playwright with *Season in the Sun*, an autobiographical comedy (based on earlier stories for the *New Yorker*) about a successful but unfulfilled magazine writer who attempts to write a novel while spending the summer with his family on New York's Fire Island. Directed by Burgess Meredith and starring Richard Whorf,

Season in the Sun opened at Broadway's Cort Theatre on 28 September 1950 to mostly favorable reviews and ran for nearly a year. "A glittering comedy of manners, with more than a little substance beneath its satirical surface," wrote Howard Barnes in the *New York Herald Tribune* (29 Sept. 1950). Gibbs was a slow, painstaking writer of fiction. He was encouraged by the success of *Season in the Sun* to write more plays, but he never completed any.

A short, gaunt man with light brown hair and a wispy mustache, Gibbs dressed nattily and smoked and drank heavily. He was noted for his rudeness to all but a few close friends, such as the writer John O'Hara, a frequent contributor to the *New Yorker*. He was an avid surf fisherman, and his oceanside summer home on Fire Island was one of the few subjects of which he spoke with unrestrained affection. In 1954 he cofounded a weekly newspaper, *Fire Islander*, and served as its editor until 1956. Gibbs died at his home on Fire Island.

• Sources of information on Gibbs include Richard B. Gehman, "The Great Dissenter," *Theatre Arts*, Mar. 1949, pp. 20–22; Arthur Gelb, "Critic in the Spotlight," *New York Times*, 15 Oct. 1950; "Critic on the Beach," *Newsweek*, 19 July 1954, p. 60; and Richard Maney, "Notes and Comments on Wolcott Gibbs," *New York Times*, 24 Aug. 1958. Dale Kramer, *Ross and the New Yorker* (1951), and Brendan Gill, *Here at the New Yorker* (1975), provide insight into Gibbs's personality and role at the magazine. See also Gilbert Leigh Bloom, "An Analysis of the Dramatic Criticism of Wolcott Gibbs as It Appeared in *The New Yorker*, 1933–1958" (Ph.D. diss., Univ. of Iowa, 1971). An obituary is in the *New York Times*, 17 Aug. 1958.

MARY C. KALFATOVIC

GIBRAN, Kahlil (6 Jan. 1883–10 Apr. 1931), poet and painter, was born Gibran Khalil Gibran in Besharri, Lebanon, the son of Khalil Gibran, a gambler and olive grove owner, and Kamila Rahme, a peddler. The boy was named by prefacing his father's name Khalil with the surname of his paternal grandfather, thus Gibran Khalil Gibran. Although in later years Gibran fabricated stories of his family's origins and their years in Besharri, factual accounts (particularly Gibran and Gibran, *Kahlil Gibran, His Life and World*) reveal that his ancestors came to Lebanon from Syria and Palestine in the sixteenth century and that Gibran's immediate family was poor. The intermingling of cultures (Syrian, Turkish, Persian, European), religions (Islam, Maronite Christianity, Catholicism), and languages (Semitic, Arabic, Syrian), as well as destitution, filled nineteenth-century Besharri and Gibran's psyche.

Gibran's boyhood was filled with insecurity and loneliness. Although his flirtatious, aggressive mother's love, understanding, and Maronite Christian faith helped build a foundation upon which Gibran's sensitive character could grow, his father's hot temper, vulgarity, hatred for work, and obsessive gambling caused Gibran to recoil and seek solace in the countryside. By the age of five, he went alone to the fields to escape his parents, to daydream, to feel protected by God's presence, and to draw. The hills and fields symbolized a holy sanctuary for Gibran in which his artistic feelings were nurtured, and he remembered and wrote about these retreats in later life.

In this natural setting Gibran contemplated the mysteries of existence; ran naked in storms; invented toys, kite flying machines, water wheels, and fanciful gardens; and made lead casts of gods and goddesses from sardine cans and sand. The creative process became a consuming, cherished, lifelong adventure that often isolated the inquisitive Gibran.

Gibran was given no formal schooling in Besharri, but a teacher-poet-painter-doctor named Selim Dahir taught the quiet, serious child the rudiments of Arabic writing and language, introduced him to history and art, and urged him to become a knowledgeable and enterprising man. Work was separated from family problems and became his passion.

From an early age Gibran identified personal experiences as religious in nature. After he was injured from a fall and placed on a cross for forty days to heal, he compared his convalescence to the suffering of Jesus. This discovery that he could endure pain had a lifelong effect (Haskell, vol. 45). His biographers Jean and Kahlil Gibran wrote, "His early experiences, steeped . . . in the metaphor of the Gospels, served as the link in his poetry between East and West" (*Kahlil Gibran, His Life and World*, p. 19).

In 1891 Gibran's father was found guilty of embezzlement, and the family was left with a sense of shame. In June 1895 the brave Kamila left her husband and took her children—including Gibran—to live with cousins in the impoverished, multicultured South End of Boston, Massachusetts. When Gibran entered the Quincy School on 30 September 1895, a teacher shortened and misspelled his name to Kahlil Gibran, which he kept as his pen name. He learned English while Kamila opened a dry goods store on Beach Street with her son Peter. In 1896 Gibran first drew and appreciated another artist's work, a MacMonnies Baccanale nymph bronze, a work of art that so offended Bostonians that it was later moved to the Metropolitan Museum in New York.

Throughout his life Gibran's handsome appearance, poetical nature, and painting ability fascinated and enthralled women, many of whom became his patrons, admirers, or lovers. One such woman was Jessie Fremont Beale, who convinced the rich, eccentric, avant-garde photographer Fred Holland Day to rescue the boy from poverty by supporting his talent. On 25 November 1896 she wrote to Day, "[Gibran's] future will certainly be that of a street fakir if something is not done for him at once. . . . A drawing which he made . . . of the Bacchante [*sic*] made quite a sensation."

Gibran and Day's relationship led to a rich, socially stimulating life in which Gibran was accepted as an artist and poet by the city's intellectual and artistic elite, including writers Charlotte Teller (who involved Gibran in the women's rights movement) and Josephine Preston Peabody (whose *The Singing Man* of

1911 included a poem in which she called the young Gibran "The Prophet," a title he later used for his bestselling book); teacher Florence Peirce; artist Lilla Cabot Perry; and his patron, confidante, and love—a progressive schoolteacher named Mary Haskell, who rejected Gibran's proposal of marriage. For the rest of his life he was loved by many women, but he never married.

In 1898 Gibran's poetry and drawings were published in *The Critic* and by Copeland & Day. He attended Beirut's Madrasat-al-Hikmah college; in Beirut he also founded with Joseph Hawaiik the magazine *al-Manarah* (*The Beacon*), in which he published controversial articles and poetry. When, after three years of college, his poetry won a merit award, Gibran returned to Boston. On 21 May 1902 Gibran had his first exhibition of drawings at Wellesley College in Massachusetts. Although his work was well reviewed, his mother's death on 28 June devastated him. In 1904 another tragedy occurred when his paintings were destroyed in the Harcourt Studios fire in Boston.

Challenging contemporary immigrant Arabic writers, Gibran publicly accused them of writing for money, not for the soul. Accepting all countries and people as his own, the worldly Gibran wrote of utopias and of life and love; he viewed death as a liberator, freeing people from earthly suffering and pain. In *A Tear and a Smile* the poet wrote, "For [all] the earth . . . is my land. . . . And all mankind my countrymen" (pp. 89–91). While he bridged the philosophies of East and West, his "she-angel" Mary Haskell corrected manuscripts before they were published. In 1905 *Nymphs in the Valley* and *Spirits Rebellious* appeared, and in 1908 she financed his three-year study at the Académie Julian in Paris, where he completed the paintings *The Ages of Women* (1909–1910) and a portrait of *Auguste Rodin* (1910). Afterward he returned to Boston, where, he noted, "everything seem[ed] dead."

Gibran soon became a sought-after member of New York's inventive avant-garde, along with such friends as the painter Albert Pinkham Ryder, and at the same time he aspired to preserve his ethnic identity by publicly speaking on topics such as civil injustices in the Middle East. By 1912 his longest Arabic novella and spiritual autobiography, *The Broken Wings*, was published. In 1914 he finished the story *The Madman* (1918) and also was given a successful Montross Gallery exhibition. Of *The Madman* the New York reviewer for the *Call* wrote, "This book introduces to English readers the work of the greatest poet of Arabia." When *Twenty Drawings* was published by Alfred A. Knopf in 1919, it was reviewed as having drawings "of graceful emotional exposition of form" (*Nation*, 14 Apr. 1922). The books that followed—*Sand and Foam* (1926), *Jesus, the Son of Man* (1928), and *The Earth Gods* (1931)—showed that passion rather than reason often moved Gibran to expression. *The Prophet* (1923), with its distinctive views of marriage and language of love, was Gibran's crowning literary achievement. After Gibran's death it became the all-time bestselling book in America, yet it received less literary attention than *The Madman* and *The Forerunner*. His last work, *The Wanderer* (1932), was of "a man but with a cloak and a staff with a veil of pain upon his face."

When Gibran died of a heart attack in New York City, he was a celebrated man of arts and letters. The public mourned the loss of the artistic poet, who had consoled them with such memorable messages of love.

• An accurate biography is Jean and Kahlil Gibran, *Kahlil Gibran, His Life and World* (1974). For personal letters see the Mary Haskell Papers at Chapel Hill, vols. 32–40, 69–71; Barbara Young, *A Study of Kahlil Gibran: This Man from Lebanon* (1931); and Young, *This man from Lebanon: A Study of Kahlil Gibran* (1945). For his relationship with Haskell see Virginia Hilu, ed., *Beloved Prophet: The Love Letters of Kahlil Gibran and Mary Haskell and Her Private Journal* (1972). For the Wellesley art exhibition see the *Wellesley College News*, 26 May 1909, p. 4. New York critiques of his art include *New York Herald Tribune*, 20 Dec. 1914; Jean Hamilton, "Woman's Influence Is to Be Found . . . behind All the Creations of Man . . . ," *New York Evening Sun*, 28 Dec. 1909; and the *New York Times*, 25 Feb. 1915. Information about Gibran's drawings is in the *Nation*, 10 Apr. 1920. Appraisals of his writing include Marjorie Allen Seiffer, *Poetry* 23 (Jan. 1924): 216–18, and Rollene W. Saal, "Speaking of Books: *The Prophet*," *New York Times Book Review*, 16 May 1965; *New York Herald Tribune Books*, 3 May 1931; and P. W. Wilson, *New York Times Book Review*, 23 Dec. 1928. A useful source on his last published work is Kahlil and Jean Gibran, eds., *Lazarus and His Beloved* (1973). Obituaries are in the *Boston Evening Transcript* and the *Boston Post*, both 14 Apr. 1931; *Publishers Weekly*, 25 Apr. 1931; and *The Syrian World* 5 (Apr.–May 1931).

PATRICIA JOBE PIERCE

GIBSON, Charles Dana (14 Sept. 1867–23 Dec. 1944), illustrator and social cartoonist, was born in Roxbury, Massachusetts, the son of Charles De Wolf Gibson, a salesman, and Josephine Lovett. He showed youthful skill in art, achieving local recognition as a silhouette cutter at the age of five. His parents and teachers encouraged him, and while still a schoolboy, he worked briefly with the sculptor Augustus Saint-Gaudens, but it soon became clear that his talent was not for three-dimensional art. However, while still a youth, he won a small cash prize for a drawing and this early success convinced him that he could make a living as an artist. Consequently, after finishing high school in 1884, he entered the Art Students League in New York, where he studied for two years while supporting himself by commercial art.

It was not until 25 March 1886, however, that Gibson's first drawing was published in the humor magazine *Life*, inaugurating a relationship that would last for more than forty years. While his work appeared with increasing regularity in *Life*, he also contributed political cartoons to a similar magazine, *Tid-Bits*. By 1888 Gibson was earning enough to travel to Europe to further his art training. On his way to Paris, he stopped in London to visit George du Maurier, the British social cartoonist and writer whose work Gibson looked on as a model. Much of du Maurier's work appeared in *Punch*, the humorous weekly on which *Life* was modeled. The ideal woman that du Maurier had invented—aloof, statuesque, and aristocratic—was a prototype for the figure that would make Gibson's name known worldwide. After leaving London, Gibson spent two months at the Académie Julian in Paris, polishing his pen-and-ink technique. Returning to New York, he quickly established himself as an illustrator with the art editors of *Harper's New Monthly Magazine*, *Scribner's Magazine*, and *Century Magazine* while continuing his work for *Life*, where his social cartoons were generally featured on the double pages at the center of the magazine.

By 1890 Gibson's female character had taken on a distinct personality and was becoming popularly known as the "Gibson Girl." Her carriage was erect, her manners and gestures elegant and correct, and her expression imperturbable if not haughty, although she could look adoringly at the square-jawed, clean-shaven, gentlemanly "Gibson man" when he was created a few years later. She was thoroughly modern and staunchly American: athletic—swimming, bicycling, and playing tennis—and self-confident enough not to be impressed by offers of marriage from members of the European nobility. Gibson created a family for her that made it clear she was the daughter of a self-made man and not an aristocrat by birth. All of these qualities embodied the popular vision of the new America of the 1890s, and many young women and men adopted the fashions, deportment, and mores of Gibson's creations, thus affecting American life for at least twenty years. As Henry Pitz wrote in his 1956 article on Gibson (p. 52), "To many they [the Gibson characters] seemed the superior creatures of a better, but not too remote, world. With effort and a bit of luck one might scramble up to their level."

By 1894 Gibson's fame was such that the first of sixteen picture books of collected drawings was published in large folio format to suit the horizontal double-page spreads in which Gibson's work appeared in the magazines. No text other than the original brief captions accompanied the pictures. Among the best known of these were *The Education of Mr. Pip* (1899)—which chronicled the adventures in high society of the recently wealthy but amiable and befuddled Mr. Pip, his socially ambitious wife, and his Gibson Girl daughter—and *A Widow and Her Friends* (1901)—which followed the emergence from mourning of a beautiful young widow and the antics of the six oddly assorted suitors who followed her adoringly in a variety of situations that ended by her taking the veil, only to find that the six followed her into the church.

Although best known for the "Gibson Girl" drawings and their accompanying social commentary, Gibson was also active as an illustrator of books. His first, *The Anglomaniacs* by Mrs. Burton Harrison, drew on his experiences in London in 1888. As was the custom, it was first serialized in *Century Magazine* beginning in the June 1890 issue and was published in book form later that year. Gibson illustrated twenty-one books during his career, including Anthony Hope's *The Pris-* oner of *Zenda* in 1898 and his *Rupert of Hentzau* in 1906. Among others he also illustrated were six of Richard Harding Davis's adventure tales and three of Robert W. Chambers's novels.

Gibson had developed a virtuoso pen technique, varying from the most delicate line to thick, slashing strokes. He used a pen as another artist would a brush, drawing with economy and control on large sheets of paper, but drawing from his arm and shoulder rather than wrist and fingers as earlier pen draughtsmen had done, thus imparting an energy and an immediacy to his work that were unique at the time. These qualities were easily and accurately reproduced by photoengraving, which only recently had supplanted wood engraving as the method by which drawings were printed. Gibson's ability to characterize and his sparkling, decorative contrasts of black and white created by apparently effortless use of texture were copied by many but successfully adapted by only a few followers, such as James Montgomery Flagg and Howard Chandler Christy.

In 1895 Gibson married Irene Langhorne, one of four beautiful daughters of a prominent southern family (her sister, Nancy, became Lady Astor). They had two children, and their marriage was a happy one, ended only by Gibson's death.

In 1898 Gibson was elected to membership in the National Institute of Arts and Letters. In 1902 he joined the newly founded Society of Illustrators, serving as the society's president from 1904 to 1907 and again from 1909 until 1921, then becoming its honorary president. In 1918 he was elected an associate of the National Academy of Design and a full academician in 1932. In 1921 he was elected to the American Academy of Arts and Letters, becoming a director in 1932.

On 23 October 1902 Gibson signed a multiyear contract with *Collier's Weekly* to produce 100 drawings at $1,000 apiece. Not only was the total amount of $100,000 unheard of for a magazine artist, but so was the notion of an artist's contract. Except for staff artists, illustrators and cartoonists had always worked either on speculation or on assignment, subject to the will and approval of an art editor. Gibson's contract contributed greatly to the establishment of professional business practices for illustrators.

With the security of a $65,000 annual income from his work and investments, Gibson, whose experience had been as a black-and-white artist, decided in 1905 to study painting. After two years abroad, the financial panic of 1907 seriously reduced his income and forced him to return to New York and pen and ink work, although *Cosmopolitan*, a magazine devoted to popular literature, also used some of his pastel drawings for color covers. The Gibson Girl continued to be popular; numerous musical comedies and revues featured her, and songs about her were heard abroad as well as in America.

At the onset of the 1914–1918 war in Europe, Gibson's work took on a decidedly political, anti-German tone, and when the United States entered the war, he was made head of the Division of Pictorial Publicity of the Committee of Public Information, convincing artists to donate their talents to the war effort by designing posters, advertising, and other graphic material. Gibson was ill at ease in public, disliking public speaking and mediating arguments, but his respected position and outward calm ensured his success in this difficult administrative position.

As a businessman, however, Gibson was not so fortunate. After his old friend John Ames Mitchell, founder, editor, and owner of *Life*, died in 1918, the magazine was put up for sale in 1920. The loyal Gibson arranged for its purchase and served as its chief owner and president. As an artist, Gibson had not been able to adjust to the liberated "flapper" girl and the new mood of the postwar era. As president he would not allow his magazine to follow the new trends, and a slow decline in circulation and advertising revenue began, ending with Gibson turning over the presidency in 1928 and contributing his last drawing in 1930. *Life* finally ceased publication in 1936 and sold its name to Henry Luce for his new newsmagazine.

In 1932 Gibson turned to painting again. He was given a one-man exhibition at the American Academy of Arts and Letters from November 1934 to May 1935 and was honored by a major retrospective exhibition at the Cincinnati Art Museum in 1943. In the same year, a year before he died in New York City, he was awarded the gold medal of the American Artists Professional League for his distinguished contribution to American art.

One of the best and most influential illustrators of American life, Gibson's drawings helped to define and inspire a generation, and the phrase "Gibson Girl" became part of the language. His work, both as an artist and as president of the Society of Illustrators, contributed greatly to the establishment of illustration as a respected profession.

• The primary monograph on Gibson remains Fairfax Downey, *Portrait of an Era as Drawn by C. D. Gibson* (1936), even though it was written during the subject's lifetime as a popular biography. It includes a listing of books illustrated by Gibson. More recent appraisals can be found in Henry Pitz, "Charles Dana Gibson: Creator of a Mode," *American Artist* 20 (Dec. 1956): 50–55, and Susan E. Meyer, *America's Great Illustrators* (1978). An obituary is in the *New York Times*, 24 Dec. 1944.

ROWLAND P. ELZEA

GIBSON, Hoot (6 Aug. 1892–23 Aug. 1962), motion picture cowboy star, was born Edmund Richard Gibson in Tekamah, Nebraska, the son of Hyram Gibson, a small rancher and grocer, and Ida Belle Richards. Some accounts attribute his nickname to a fondness for hunting owls in the sandhills of Nebraska, but other stories trace its origins to his stint as a bicycle messenger in California for the Owl Drug Company. Although a skilled rider and roper, Hoot was not, as studio publicists would later claim, simply a real-life cowboy who one day rode onto the Silver Screen. In addition to his drugstore job, Gibson worked as a te-

legrapher and an auto mechanic. While repairing cars in Seattle, he decided to enter the 1912 Pendleton Rodeo, where he was named the All-Around Champion Cowboy. During the next several years Gibson continued to compete in rodeos and to play in Wild West shows. In 1917 he volunteered for military service and gained the rank of sergeant in the Tank Corps.

Meanwhile, Gibson had been joining other rodeo and Wild West performers in drifting in and out of the fledgling motion picture business. He and Art Acord, another rodeo and future film cowboy, had wrangled horses and done stunt work for D. W. Griffith. Gibson had also worked as a wrangler for Universal before being signed as a double for Harry Carey, the studio's reigning cowboy star. He also had formed a close friendship with fledgling director John Ford. Shortly before Gibson had entered the military, he had completed a role for Ford in *Shooting Straight* (1917), a Carey vehicle.

After the war Gibson returned to Universal and quickly surpassed Carey as the studio's top western star. In 1921 he gained his first starring role in *Action*, a film directed by Ford. The following year Hoot married Helen Johnson, a vaudeville performer, and in 1924 he signed a three-year contract with Universal that guaranteed him $1 million over three years. In 1926 he starred in *The Flaming Frontier* (1926), an epic on the scale of Ford's *The Iron Horse* (1925) and one of the first Hollywood films based on the legend of Custer's Last Stand. Another three-year contract with Universal even allowed Gibson to run his own production company, but critics soon were complaining about a declining quality in his films.

During this period Gibson's off-screen adventures became the stuff of Hollywood legend. He threw lavish parties; bought several homes; was seen around town with women other than his wife; brawled with fellow movie cowboys, particularly his old rodeo buddy Art Acord; and recklessly raced both motorcycles and airplanes. He also began to stage his own rodeo, the annual "Hoot Gibson Round-up," which provided footage for one of his last silent films, *King of the Rodeo* (1929). An expensive divorce from Helen in 1930 and a brief marriage to Sally Eilers, a former costar, coincided with a precipitous decline in his motion picture fortunes.

Gibson's career as a cowboy star ended almost as quickly as it had begun. His production company faced severe financial problems when Universal's president, Carl Laemmle, forced him to make all his 1930 films as talkies. As an economy move, Gibson liberally inserted old footage from his old silents. Even so, his films still cost far more than the studio's other westerns, and Laemmle decided that Gibson, once his favorite employee, did not merit a contract renewal for 1931. Soon Gibson's marriage to Eilers also began to disintegrate. When Gibson was hospitalized after crashing at the National Air Races of 1933, while trying to match daredevil stunts with fellow film cowboy Ken Maynard, a young starlet, rather than his wife, was conspicuously pictured at his bedside.

By 1933 Gibson was making headlines as a faded figure from the 1920s rather than as a movie star of the 1930s. Though at least two of his later films—*The Last Outlaw* (1936), with Carey, and *Powdersmoke Range* (1935), with Carey, Tom Tyler, and Bob Steele—were first-rate B-productions that featured flashes of Hoot's old comedic and cowboy magic, Gibson in 1936 put aside his screen career in favor of a series of ill-advised business ventures that left him nearly bankrupt. In 1942 he married for a third time, to Dorothy Dunston.

Although Gibson returned to the screen several times, he did not make a real film comeback. In the early 1940s his old rival Maynard helped Gibson secure one last starring role by reluctantly agreeing to appear with him in the "Trail Blazers" series. Maynard later recalled that he had intended to lose weight for this series but changed his mind when Gibson complained that tiny Monogram Studios was not paying either of them enough money to justify a diet. In fact, Maynard and Gibson, two of Hollywood's greatest stars during the roaring twenties, worked for less than $1,000 a picture. One of Gibson's final films for Monogram, *The Utah Kid* (1944), was shot on such a miserly budget that it incorporated footage originally shot at a "Hoot Gibson Round-Up" more than a decade earlier. Many years later, another old friend, John Ford, signed Gibson to a small role in *The Horse Soldiers* (1959); the film, starring John Wayne, was one of Ford's least successful films and did nothing to revive Hoot's moribund film career. Gibson briefly fronted for a fly-by-night enterprise that promised people they could strike it rich by raising chinchillas for pelts in their basements and garages but found his steadiest employment during the 1950s by working as a "greeter" for a Las Vegas casino.

As a celluloid cowboy, Gibson developed a very different image than Tom Mix and Maynard, Hollywood's other great western stars of the 1920s. Both Mix and Maynard drew on their circus and Wild West Show days with elaborate costumes, daredevils stunts, and horses ("Tony" and "Tarzan") who served as their costars. But Gibson, despite his own Wild West Show background, invariably wore nondescript clothing and rode whatever nag seemed close at hand. Gibson's characters rarely sported a gun belt and simply tucked their six-shooters into their belt or one of their boots. "I played just an ordinary cowboy," Gibson later recalled. He died in Woodland Hills, California.

• There is a great deal of material on Hoot Gibson in William K. Everson, *The Hollywood Western: 90 Years of Cowboys and Indians, Train Robbers, Sheriffs and Gunslingers* (1992), but the most complete and accurate account of Gibson's life and film work appears in Jon Tuska, *The Filming of the West* (1976). Gibson's relationship with John Ford is discussed in Tag Gallagher, *John Ford: The Man and His Films* (1986), and there are accounts of Gibson's most substantial films of the 1930s—*The Last Outlaw* and *The Painted Stallion* (1937)—in Tony Thomas, *The West That Never Was: Hollywood's Vision of the Cowboys and Gunfighters* (1989), a volume based on a PBS television series.

NORMAN L. ROSENBERG

GIBSON, Hugh Simons (16 Aug. 1883–12 Dec. 1954), diplomat and author, was born in Los Angeles, California, the son of Frank (Francis) Asbury Gibson, a bank cashier, and Mary Simons. While traveling in Europe with his widowed mother, Gibson decided to pursue a career in the foreign service and earned a diploma from the *École Libre des Sciences Politiques* in Paris in 1907 to obtain the necessary preparation. After returning to the United States, he passed the State Department examination and was appointed secretary of the American legation at Tegucigalpa, Honduras, in 1908. A year later he moved to London as second secretary. After a brief stint as confidential clerk to the assistant secretary of state, in July 1911 he went to Havana as secretary of the American legation in Cuba. During that tour of duty, he was a member of the special mission to observe elections for the Constituent Assembly of Santo Domingo in December 1913.

In 1914 Gibson was transferred to Brussels as secretary of the legation there; he was promoted in grade a year later. With the outbreak of war, he worked with Herbert Hoover as a director of the Commission for the Relief of Belgium and chairman of its executive committee in Brussels. With Ambassador Brand Whitlock, Gibson tried in vain to obtain a lighter punishment for English nurse Edith Cavell who was executed by the Germans as a spy and smuggler. Gibson chronicled these two years in Belgium in *A Journal from Our Legation in Belgium* (1917).

After nine months in London he was ordered back to the Department of State in February 1917. He accompanied the British secretary of state for foreign affairs on his visit to the United States from April to June and the Belgian War Mission from June to August, when he received a promotion to Class One in the foreign service. In February 1918 Gibson was assigned to Paris as first secretary to the American embassy.

Between November 1918 and April 1919 Gibson again joined Hoover, this time as director general of the American Relief Administration, distributing food and other relief supplies to victims of the war in twenty-three countries. At the end of 1918 and the beginning of 1919, Gibson was also a member of the Inter-Allied Mission to the Balkan countries formed from the former Austro-Hungarian Empire. He later became a director of the Belgian-American Education Foundation, a Hoover-initiated group established to use leftover relief monies to encourage educational exchanges between Belgium and the United States.

President Woodrow Wilson named Gibson envoy extraordinary and minister plenipotentiary to newly independent Poland in April 1919; he remained there until 1924. Much of his work in Poland replicated his earlier experiences in relief, but he also facilitated American technical assistance in agriculture and industry in order to help the new Polish government address some of its severe economic problems. Gibson's lifelong sympathy for the Poles reinforced both his antipathy for leftist, communist, and socialist ideologies and his occasional lapses into anti-Semitism. Ambassador Gibson married Ynes Marie Marcelle Reyntiens, daughter of Major Robert Reyntiens, aide-de-camp to the king of Belgium, in 1922; the couple had one child, a son. Mrs. Gibson died in 1950.

While he was American minister to Switzerland from 1924 to 1927 and ambassador to Belgium and minister to Luxembourg from 1927 to 1933, Gibson's major activities focused on disarmament. He attended the Temporary Mixed Commission of the League of Nations in 1924. In 1925 he served as vice chairman of the American delegation to the Conference for Supervision of International Traffic in Arms and Ammunition and Implements of War. He headed the American representation to the Preparatory Commission for the Disarmament Conference in Geneva in 1926 and 1927. Subsequently he led the American delegation and also chaired the Conference for the Limitation of Naval Armaments in Geneva in 1927, and was an observer at the London Naval Conference in 1930, a delegate to the General Disarmament Conference in Geneva in 1932 and 1933, and acting chairman of the American delegation in 1932. Always committed to arms reductions, by 1932 Gibson had become a strong advocate for abolition of all offensive weapons and reduction of other arms by a third. He was also an observer at the conference of experts for the moratorium on intergovernmental debts in London in 1931.

As one of the first American envoys who had been trained for the foreign service, by the 1930s Gibson was among a growing class of such professionals. President Hoover named these career diplomats as U.S. representatives in thirty-three countries. In addition to Gibson's assignment to Belgium and Luxembourg, Hoover made him ambassador-at-large in Europe. But the end of the Hoover administration meant changes for Gibson. In May 1933 President Franklin Roosevelt moved him to Brazil, where he served as ambassador for four years. In *Rio* (1937), Gibson recounted his part in international efforts to end the seven-year-long Chaco War between Bolivia and Paraguay, first at the Chaco Mediation Conference in Buenos Aires, which arranged a truce in 1935, and then at the Chaco Peace Conference in Buenos Aires in 1935 and 1936, which led to a peace agreement in August 1936.

Gibson briefly returned to head the Belgian embassy and Luxembourg ministry in 1937, chronicling his observations in *Belgium* (1939). He retired from government service in 1938 and subsequently became an editor for Doubleday, Doran and Company.

With the outbreak of war in Europe in 1939, Hoover tried to resume relief activities. Gibson became director general for Europe of the Commission for Polish Relief and the Commission for Relief in Belgium. In 1940 and 1941 he spent considerable time in London, struggling in vain to persuade Winston Churchill to allow lifesaving food for the "small democracies" through the British blockade.

After U.S. entry into the war, Gibson again collaborated with the former president, this time on a plan for peacemaking that might prove less fragile than that of the previous war. They published their recommendations as *The Problems of Lasting Peace* (1942), "New Approaches to Lasting Peace" serialized in *Collier's*, and *The Basis of Lasting Peace* (1945). They argued against an armistice and for a cooling-off transition period to establish the economic and political infrastructure that would ensure stability when a formal peace was concluded. One essential of their proposals, creation of a world institution to preserve peace while still pursuing the war effort, was substantially incorporated in the Moscow Declaration. Gibson also wrote *The Road to Foreign Policy* (1944), which argued for greater use of foreign service professionals rather than political appointees to ensure more consistency of policy and increased attention to a realistic assessment of America's relations with other nations.

In the postwar period, Gibson accompanied Hoover on a round-the-world Famine Emergency Survey in 1946. When State Department officials were unwilling to arrange access for Hoover to Argentine president Juan Perón, Gibson, a lifelong Roman Catholic much decorated by church organizations, used those connections to arrange a Hoover-Perón meeting that made Argentine surplus wheat available to starving Europeans. In 1951 the 21-nation Provisional Intergovernmental Committee for the Movement of Migrants from Europe named Gibson its director. He served in that post until his death in Geneva.

Hugh Gibson was the first American diplomat who came to his profession with formal educational preparation for foreign service. He earned a reputation as a wit and raconteur. Enjoying the company of journalists, but unwilling or unable to match the gentlemen of the fourth estate in drinking capacity, he invented the "Gibson cocktail," plain water distinguished from a martini by the addition of an onion instead of the traditional olive. The onion remained the hallmark of the Gibson even when gin replaced the ambassador's secret ingredient. His claims to fame rest on his efforts in disarmament and border negotiations between the wars as well as a lifelong commitment to relief of the victims of war.

• The main body of Gibson's papers has been deposited at the Hoover Institution at Stanford University. Related collections at the Hoover Institution include the Commission for Relief of Belgium, the Belgian American Educational Foundation, and the Commission for Polish Relief. A smaller collection of personal papers may be found at the Herbert Hoover Presidential Library in West Branch, Iowa. The *New York Times* and *Reader's Digest* regularly published his speeches, especially in the 1940s. Gibson's relief work is included in *An American Epic*, four volumes of edited documents with commentary by Herbert Hoover (1959–1964). After his death, old friends and colleagues collected his bons mots in *Hugh Gibson, 1883–1954: Extracts from His Letters and Anecdotes from His Friends*, edited by Perrin C. Galpin and published by the Belgian-American Educational Foundation in 1956. A major obituary is in the *New York Times*, 13 Dec. 1954.

SUSAN ESTABROOK KENNEDY

GIBSON, James Jerome (27 Jan. 1904–11 Dec. 1979), psychologist, was born in McConnelsville, Ohio, the son of Thomas B. Gibson, a railroad surveyor, and Mary Gertrude Stanbery. The Gibsons followed the rails around the upper Midwest before settling in Wilmette, Illinois, where Gibson attended high school. Gibson later remembered that by "the age of eight I knew what the world looked like from a railroad train and how it seemed to flow inward when seen from the rear platform and expand outward when seen from the locomotive" (*Reasons for Realism* [1982], p. 7). He put this experience to good use, becoming the first major visual theorist to make movement central to his account of perception.

Gibson studied at Princeton University (1922–1928) at a time when the science of psychology had finally secured its independence from philosophy and there was a widespread feeling that epistemological problems were finally going to be put to the test. The teacher who exerted the greatest influence on Gibson was psychologist Edwin B. Holt, then considered to be William James's protégé. Holt inspired Gibson's lifelong attempt to develop a naturalistic account of experience, one that acknowledged the insights of European structuralism without falling prey to its subjectivistic and elitist concept of experience. Gibson earned a B.S. in 1925 and an M.A. the following year.

Gibson's Princeton Ph.D. thesis in 1929 was an attack on the Gestalt theory of experience. Where the Gestalt Theorists saw relatively preestablished and fixed structures in experience, Gibson found experience to be adaptable to the changeable environment. This debate deepened in the 1930s after Gibson went in 1928 to Smith College and worked opposite Kurt Koffka, who was then writing his celebrated *Principles of Gestalt Psychology* (1935). In the early 1930s Gibson discovered that prolonged observation of isolated features of the perceptual world can alter the appearance of those features. For example, prolonged observation of a tilted line causes that line to appear straight and erect lines to appear tilted in the opposite direction. On the basis of these phenomena, Gibson hypothesized in 1937 that persisting features of experience tend to become norms of the phenomenal world. Perceptual theory not only had to deal with more complex phenomena than heretofore but also had to consider both environmental factors as well as organismic experience.

Controversial and potentially revolutionary, Gibson's ideas about perception challenged the traditional, representational account of perception that had been a foundation of Western thought since the Renaissance discovery of perspective. Physical stimulation had been viewed as causing changes in receptors, which cause changes in the brain, which interprets these changes as perception. Accordingly, perceivers construct their worlds by interpreting the subjective appearances of their brain states. Unable to accept this subjectivistic account of vision, Gibson demonstrated that vision is not just an interpretation of our sensa-

tions but is the activity of looking around at things, an activity that helps us adapt to our surroundings. Gibson's *Perception of the Visual World* (1950), published one year after he moved to Cornell University (where he remained for the rest of his career), turned this subjectivistic view on its head—arguing that the subjective impressions of the visual field are interpretations of the experience of objects and events in the visual world, not the other way around.

Gibson's *The Senses Considered as Perceptual Systems* (1966) attacked the causal basis of traditional theories of perception. If perceiving is based on exploratory activity, then it does not start with stimuli and sensations, but with an active, motivated observer hunting for meaningful information. Gibson's radical claim was that the environment is comprised of values, of "affordances" for behavior, which are available to active organisms. The affordances do not cause either perception or action, but if information specifying them is available and detected by an observer, then action may ensue. Much of Gibson's last three decades of research was directed toward demonstrating that rich visual information specifying affordances is available to and used by human perceivers. His many experiments and radical reconceptualization of the nature of the environment and of information are summarized in his last book, *The Ecological Approach to Visual Perception* (1979; rev. ed., 1986).

Despite the controversial nature of his ideas, Gibson was widely recognized as an "original, irreplaceable creative genius" (Restle, p. 291). Among his many honors, Gibson was elected to the National Academy of Sciences and received an American Psychological Association Distinguished Scientific Contribution Award in 1961. Gibson's is the only psychological research to appear in Rom Harré's *Twenty Great Scientific Experiments* (1981); and his ideas about active vision, optical texture, and flow, once so revolutionary, are now commonplace in Hollywood and in video arcades, where the optical flows Gibson discovered are widely used.

Gibson had married one of his Smith students, Eleanor Jack, in 1932. In addition to having two children, Eleanor Gibson went on to forge a career as a distinguished scientist in her own right, making major contributions in the areas of human learning and development. The Gibsons rarely worked as a team, however, and often disagreed, Eleanor being more aligned with behavioral theory, and James being more oriented to epistemological questions.

Gibson's life was devoted to putting the theory of knowledge on a scientific footing and to setting it in a new direction. He appreciated the Western philosophical tradition that makes knowers into interpreters who represent the world to themselves, but he thought this a fundamentally flawed understanding of how we encounter our world, one which makes knowledge a private possession of individuals, divorced from everyday life. He scorned the implicit elitism in such a view, offering a more democratic concept of experience.

The fact is that, although different men do not all use their senses in the same way, they *can* all use their senses in the same way. The basis for agreement. . . . exists in the available stimulus information. Men often disagree but they are not fated to do so by their language or culture. Disagreement is not caused by inherent differences [in interpretation]. A man can always reeducate his attention. For that matter, a man can even get others to see what he has newly seen by describing it carefully, and this is a fortunate man. (Gibson [1966] p. 321)

Gibson, who forever changed how we think about perception, vision, and experience, was such a fortunate man.

Gibson continued to work until his death in Ithaca, New York.

• Gibson's papers, including many experimental notes and drafts for published and unpublished writings from 1929 to 1979 are in the Olin Library at Cornell University. Edward S. Reed, *James J. Gibson and the Psychology of Perception* (1988), is a complete intellectual biography and includes a comprehensive bibliography of Gibson's publications. Among Gibson's works not already mentioned is *Motion Picture Testing and Research*, Army Air Forces Psychology Program Research Reports no. 7 (1947). His dissertation was published as "The Reproduction of Visually Perceived Forms," *Journal of Experimental Psychology* 12 (1929): 1–39. Gibson first discussed effect in "Adaptation, After-effect, and Contrast in the Perception of Curved Lines," *Journal of Experimental Psychology* 16 (1933): 1–31, but see also "Adaptation with Negative After-effect," *Psychological Review* 44 (1937): 222–44. A representative selection of Gibson's essays, which includes Gibson's autobiography and a number of previously unpublished works, is in Edward Reed and Rebecca Jones, eds., *Reasons for Realism: Selected Essays of James J. Gibson* (1982). R. B. MacLeod and H. L. Pick, Jr., edited a festschrift for Gibson, *Perception: Essays in Honor of James J. Gibson* (1974). For Frank Restle's comments, see his "The Seer of Ithaca," *Contemporary Psychology* 25 (1980): 291–93. An obituary is in *American Journal of Psychology* 95 (Winter 1982): 692–700.

EDWARD S. REED

GIBSON, John Bannister (8 Nov. 1780–3 May 1853), jurist, was born in Westover Mills, Pennsylvania, the son of George Gibson, an army officer, and Anne West. His mother, a well-educated Scotch-Irish immigrant, supported the family by opening a neighborhood school after her husband's death in 1791. Gibson attributed his lifelong love of learning to her influence. Around 1795 he entered Dickinson College in Carlisle, a major training ground for future state leaders, but apparently withdrew before receiving a degree. He then studied law with Thomas Duncan, a prominent Carlisle attorney, and was admitted to the bar of Cumberland County in March 1803.

Gibson achieved only limited success as a practitioner. Impatient of workaday details and unwilling to engage in flamboyant courtroom pleading, he attracted few clients in his early efforts to build a practice in Beaver, Pennsylvania, and Hagerstown, Maryland. In 1805 he settled permanently in Carlisle but never attained the celebrity of his friend Duncan and other bar

leaders. He owed his public reputation primarily to his service in the Pennsylvania House of Representatives from 1810 to 1812. Elected as a Democrat, he introduced a bill in 1812 that facilitated land transactions by abolishing common-law restraints on the division of land held by joint tenants. He also advocated legislative sponsorship of turnpikes, canal construction, and other internal improvements. But, as chairman of the judiciary committee, he opposed his party's successful efforts to remove Judge Thomas Cooper for ideological reasons. Gibson married Sarah Work Galbraith in 1812; they had eight children.

In July 1813 Governor Simon Snyder appointed Gibson president judge of the court of common pleas for the newly created eleventh judicial district, a backwoods area whose principal town was Wilkes-Barre. The new judge held court in a log house and soon developed a statewide reputation for efficiency and learning. When a vacancy occurred on the Pennsylvania Supreme Court in 1816, Governor Snyder named Gibson associate justice. For the next thirty-seven years Gibson remained on the court, displaying qualities of judicial statesmanship that made him one of the greatest American jurists of the antebellum period. He succeeded William Tilghman as chief justice in May 1827, pursuant to a commission issued by Governor John A. Schultze.

Efforts by Jacksonian politicians to democratize the Pennsylvania judiciary threatened Gibson's position on two occasions. In 1838 a new state constitution reduced the life tenure of supreme court judges to a term of fifteen years and further stipulated that one member of the existing five-man tribunal should retire every three years, in order of seniority. The constitution was to take effect in January 1839, with Gibson's term scheduled to end three years later. On the advice of an associate, Gibson resigned his commission in November 1838, and he was promptly reappointed by Governor Joseph Ritner. This maneuver, which guaranteed his continuance in office until 1854, violated the spirit, if not the letter, of the constitution and provoked strong criticism in both Whig and Democratic newspapers. Gibson, nevertheless, remained popular with the general public. When Pennsylvania adopted a constitutional amendment in 1850 that called for the election of all state judges, voters in the ensuing election of October 1851 returned the "old Chief" to a place on the reconstituted supreme court. Through a new rotation system, however, he now became an associate justice, a position he held until his death two years later.

While on the supreme court, Gibson wrote more than twelve hundred opinions, which appear in seventy volumes of *Pennsylvania Reports*. In addition, he handed down many other unpublished decisions while sitting as a circuit or trial court judge. An advocate of judicial restraint, he espoused a "commonwealth theory" of government that looked to the legislature to promote public welfare through active intervention in the economy. He elaborated his view of judicial power most tellingly in his famous dissent in *Eakin v. Raub*

(1825), which refuted John Marshall's expansive theory of judicial review on equally logical grounds. The power of judges, Gibson argued, may be classified as either political or civil. The political category embraced "every power by which one organ of the government is enabled to control another, or to exert an influence over its acts." In contrast to its inherent civil authority, a court could exercise such political power only as the result of a clear constitutional grant. Since the Pennsylvania constitution did not authorize judges to strike down state laws, the only remedy for wrongful legislative acts lay with the people, the ultimate source of all governmental authority, and the ballot box.

Despite his restrictive view of the judicial function, Gibson acknowledged that the supremacy clause of the U.S. Constitution empowered a Pennsylvania judge to invalidate any state law that infringed the federal Constitution. In reviewing such measures, however, judges should exercise the greatest caution, since the legislature embodied the popular will and its acts were presumptively constitutional. Gibson adhered to these restraining principles throughout his years on the bench. When the framers of the Pennsylvania constitution of 1838 implicitly sanctioned judicial review of state legislation, he acquiesced in *Norris v. Clymer* (1845). But he continued to insist that a court should overturn a state law only on those rare occasions when the legislature had clearly overstepped its powers, as in *De Chastellux v. Fairchild* (1850). There the legislature had attempted to exercise judicial power by ordering a new trial for litigants involved in a land dispute.

Gibson's deference to legislative policy making tended to promote entrepreneurial ventures and the growth of an urban-industrial society in Pennsylvania. Like Massachusetts and New York, Pennsylvania sought to encourage rapid economic development by granting generous charters to private corporations and by participating directly in the construction of major public works. Gibson, an enthusiastic supporter of internal improvements, defended economic legislation against constitutional challenge. In *Harvey v. Thomas* (1840), he upheld a statute authorizing railroads to build across private property in order to connect with public improvements. When opponents charged that the constitution did not empower the legislature to pass such a measure, Gibson responded that the legislature might do anything the constitution did not expressly prohibit. And in *The Case of "The Philadelphia and Trenton Railroad Company"* (1840), he denied compensation to a landowner who claimed that his property rights had been violated when a railroad chartered by the state laid its tracks down the middle of his street. Gibson ruled that the compensation clause of the Pennsylvania constitution did not require payment for such "indirect" injury to property, although he conceded that damages had usually been awarded to claimants in the past, as a matter "of favour, not of right." When no constitutional issue arose in a case, he drew upon common-law doctrines of negligence, as in *Lehigh Bridge Company v. Lehigh Coal*

and Navigation Company (1833), to limit the liability of businesses for harm caused by risk-producing, but socially valuable, activity.

His record in civil liberties cases was more ambiguous. In several early decisions, such as *Wilson v. Belinda* (1817), he narrowly construed the provisions of Pennsylvania's abolition statute to secure freedom for slave litigants. "[E]very . . . particular required by the act, must be strictly complied with," he argued, "and for this single reason, that the act declares the slave shall be free, if it be not." But in the landmark *Hobbs v. Fogg* (1837) he disfranchised the free black population of Pennsylvania by holding that a Negro was not a "freeman," as that term was used in the state constitution, and so was not qualified to vote. There was little evidence to support his position, although he claimed to rely on an unpublished precedent of 1795, which had been reported to him by an elderly Philadelphia practitioner. Gibson's rambling opinion compiled instances of discrimination in the seventeenth and eighteenth centuries to demonstrate the "unconquerable prejudice of caste" that had allegedly motivated the framers of the 1790 constitution. In its dubious historicism and revelation of the author's own racial bias, *Hobbs v. Fogg* anticipated the controversial decision handed down by Roger B. Taney, chief justice of the United States, in the *Dred Scott* case twenty years later. Yet Gibson had not misjudged the temper of white Pennsylvanians in the 1830s, a decade of increasing racial and ethnic violence. *Hobbs* was a unanimous decision, whose popularity was confirmed when the constitution of 1838 included for the first time a provision that expressly restricted the vote to adult white males.

A highly cultivated man whose interests ranged from music to medicine, Gibson often enlivened his opinions with apt allusions to William Shakespeare, his favorite author. Like his distinguished contemporaries John Marshall and Lemuel Shaw, he was a master of the "grand style" of judicial writing, which eschewed detailed analysis of precedents and concentrated instead on the formulation of general principles from which logical inferences might be drawn. His terse and vigorous decisions helped to shape the institutions of a capitalist economy during its formative period. As a leading advocate of judicial restraint, he also contributed significantly to the continuing debate over the proper role of the judiciary in a democratic society. Plagued by ill health after 1850, he died in Philadelphia, where he had gone, against his doctor's advice, to hold court.

• Letters from Gibson are in the papers of the Gibson-Getty-McClure families at the Library of Congress. Thomas P. Roberts's *Memoirs of John Bannister Gibson* (1890), the standard biography, is a pietistic account by Gibson's grandson. Other early studies that provide useful insights into Gibson's career include William A. Porter, *An Essay on the Life, Character and Writings of John B. Gibson, LL.D.* (1855), and Samuel D. Matlack, "John Bannister Gibson," in *Great American Lawyers*, ed. William Draper Lewis 3 (1907): 351–404. Stanley I. Kutler has explored important aspects of Gibson's jurisprudence in two excellent essays: "Pennsylvania Courts, the Abolition Act, and Negro Rights," *Pennsylvania History* 30 (1963): 14–27, and "John Bannister Gibson: Judicial Restraint and the 'Positive State'," *Journal of Public Law* 14 (1965): 181–97. See also Morton J. Horwitz, *The Transformation of American Law, 1780–1860* (1977), for the role of Gibson and other state judges in the refashioning of American private law before the Civil War.

MAXWELL BLOOMFIELD

GIBSON, Josh (21 Dec. 1911–20 Jan. 1947), Negro League baseball player and Hall of Famer, was born Joshua Gibson in Buena Vista, Georgia, the son of sharecroppers Mark Gibson and Nancy Woodlock. The man that many call the greatest Negro League baseball player came north in 1924 after his father left sharecropping for work in a Pittsburgh steel mill. Josh came of age on Pittsburgh's Northside, where he studied the electrical trade at Allegheny Pre-Vocational School and began playing for sandlot and semipro baseball clubs. After stints with the Gimbel Brothers and Westinghouse Airbrake company teams, he was recruited to catch for the Pittsburgh Crawfords in 1927. "The day I saw him," Crawford captain Harold Tinker recalls, "I said 'This boy is a marvel.' Near the end of the game he hit a home run and hit the ball out of existence. They didn't even go after it."

The Crawfords were then made up of young black sandlot ballplayers, most of whom lived in the city's Hill District. With the addition of Gibson, the Crawfords were ready to challenge Cumberland Posey's Homestead Grays, a stellar aggregation of black pros from across the nation that made Homestead, a milltown near Pittsburgh, its home base. But by the 1929 season, Posey had persuaded Gibson to join the Grays as a salaried player.

In 1930, Gibson slugged what might have been the first ball ever hit over the center field fence in Forbes Field. The same year, he hit a home run that several observers said went out of Yankee Stadium. Although documentation for Negro League and independent baseball records is incomplete, Gibson is credited with 75 home runs in 1931 and 69 in 1934. Many of those were against semipro competition. Monte Irvin described Gibson as the "most imposing man I've ever seen as a hitter . . . very strong, broad shouldered, and happy go lucky. Confident. Knew he was good but he didn't flaunt it. He just got out and did what he was supposed to do."

After several seasons with the Grays, during which Gibson began to build his reputation as black baseball's most feared hitter, the young catcher returned to the Pittsburgh Crawfords in 1934. By then, the Crawfords had left the sandlots behind as numbers baron Gus Greenlee took over the club and remade it into black baseball's best team. Greenlee owned the Crawford Grill, a mecca for jazz aficionados and the hub of his many business enterprises. His revenues from numbers allowed Greenlee to add not only Gibson, but future Hall of Famers Satchel Paige, Oscar Charleston, Judy Johnson, and Cool Papa Bell to the Crawfords and to build Greenlee Field, the first black-owned stadium in the country. In 1933 he revived the Negro National League, which had collapsed in 1931.

Gibson and Paige composed what may have been baseball's best battery, and the Crawfords, champions of the Negro National League in 1935, may well have been baseball's best team ever. Monte Irvin called them black baseball's equivalents of the 1927 New York Yankees.

In 1937, Gibson, Paige, Bell, and a handful of their teammates broke their contracts with the Crawfords to play for Ciudad Trujillo in the Dominican Republic. After leading Ciudad Trujillo, a club closely identified with dictator Rafael Trujillo, to the island's summer championship and winning most of the season's batting honors, Gibson returned to Pittsburgh.

Greenlee, whose Crawfords never recovered from the wholesale exodus of players, traded Gibson to the Homestead Grays. As Grays' first baseman Buck Leonard said, "We just took off after that. He put new life into the whole team." Leonard and Gibson were considered black baseball's Lou Gehrig and Babe Ruth, and the Homestead Grays the Negro Leagues' New York Yankees. After Gibson returned, the Grays won an unprecedented nine Negro League pennants in a row. Playing three times a week at Griffith Stadium in Washington, D.C., during the late 1930s and World War II, in addition to their games in Pittsburgh, the Grays were rivaled by only the Kansas City Monarchs during this epoch.

The muscular 6'2" Gibson began to put on weight during these years, but he remained a speedy base runner and a superb defensive catcher with what Monte Irvin calls "a rifle for an arm." A perennial selection to the East-West all-star game, where he batted a cumulative .483 in nine games, Gibson was most remembered for his epic swings at the plate. The *Pittsburgh Courier* reported that Gibson made about $6,000 a season playing for the Grays during the 1940s, more than the major league minimum salary but far less than that of a comparable major league star, and he earned another $3,000 from winter baseball. Gibson hit home runs throughout the United States and the Caribbean basin, almost 800 in all, according to the Hall of Fame. Decades after his death, fans could still be found from Pittsburgh to Havana who attested that some ball that Gibson hit was the longest home run they ever saw.

Credited with a lifetime .362 batting average in Negro League and Caribbean play, the highest of any Negro Leaguer, Gibson won four Negro League batting titles, as well as batting championships, home run titles, and most valuable player awards in the Negro Leagues, Cuba, the Dominican Republic, Puerto Rico, and Mexico. He played virtually every winter somewhere in the Caribbean, and he also played in Mexico during the summers of 1940 and 1941 rather than with Homestead. While winning MVP honors in Puerto Rico in 1941, he hit .480. During all of his years in baseball, Gibson never played for a losing team.

While considered jovial and carefree by his teammates, Gibson, while still a teenager, encountered tragedy when his bride, Helen, died delivering their twin children, Helen and Josh, Jr., in 1930. He later became a heavy drinker and was occasionally hospitalized.

In October 1945, Brooklyn Dodgers president Branch Rickey signed Jackie Robinson to a contract with the Montreal Royals, the Dodgers' leading farm club. Gibson responded with one of his best seasons ever in 1946, but received no offers to join Robinson in "white" baseball. In 1947, the year that Robinson debuted with the Dodgers, Gibson died, possibly from a stroke, in Pittsburgh. The cause of his death remains uncertain, although a brain tumor and possible drug use have been alleged as contributing factors. The *Pittsburgh Courier* reported: "The exact nature of his illness is still shrouded in mystery, but it is generally believed to have been the result of a 'rundown condition.'"

"All he needed was the chance to do it in the majors," teammate Harold Tinker argued, "and he would have been something." It is unlikely that any who saw him play would disagree.

"Josh Gibson was the black Babe Ruth," remembered fellow Hall of Famer Monte Irvin. "All the black players will tell you that Josh was our best. He was our best hitter, our best all-around player . . . , but he died without feeling the thrill of playing in the major leagues."

In 1972, Gibson was elected to the Hall of Fame, the second Negro Leaguer chosen.

• The best biography of Gibson is John B. Holway, *Josh and Satch: The Life and Times of Josh Gibson and Satchel Paige* (1991). See also William Brashler, *Josh Gibson: A Life in the Negro Leagues* (1978), and Rob Ruck, *Sandlot Seasons: Sport in Black Pittsburgh* (1987).

ROB RUCK

GIBSON, Mary Simons (1855?–11 Sept. 1930), reformer and California state commissioner, was born in the Santa Clara valley, California, the daughter of Solon Simons, a commercial merchant from Maine, and Aurilla K. (maiden name unknown). She was educated in the county public schools and taught school there before moving to Los Angeles in 1878.

Simons continued to teach until 1881, when she married Frank Asbury Gibson, a businessman, and devoted herself to household duties and civic work. They had four children, but only one son, Hugh S. Gibson, survived, later entering diplomatic service and becoming ambassador to Belgium. During the early 1880s she and her mother-in-law, also named Mary, helped found the city's first Protestant orphanage, and she served as its secretary. She joined the Friday Morning Club, Los Angeles's premier woman's club, founded in 1891 by Caroline M. Severance, and became one of its most loyal members. With the Severance family and Kate Douglas Wiggin she raised money for the city library and the Unitarian church.

Gibson's husband, who shared many of her reforming instincts, died in 1902.

Gibson focused on advancing the role of women in public life, and she served on the Friday Morning Club's suffrage, municipal reform, and education committees. She worked for birth control and supported Progressives and Hiram Johnson for governor in 1910 because she saw them as the best advocates of women's rights. She campaigned throughout the state for the suffrage bill, and after its passage in 1912 Governor Johnson appointed her to the newly formed Immigration and Housing Commission.

Johnson had established the commission to study immigrant problems in employment and housing. Gibson, the lone woman on the commission, took the leading role in education policy. An assimilationist—views she shared with Jane Addams and Frances Kellor—Gibson steered the commission's education policy toward easing the process of immigrant adjustment. The policy she developed aimed to provide public education for children of migrant farm workers and to Americanize immigrant women through a Home Teacher Act. The first goal proved difficult to implement because of the nature of migrant labor. The second challenged the common perception that the transmission of American middle-class values came from the teacher in the classroom through the child and on to the home. Gibson argued that schools had a duty to instruct immigrant mothers who had few opportunities to become assimilated.

Adequate housing, access to education for children and adults, and citizenship training, Gibson maintained, were prerequisites for assimilation. She conducted investigations, obtained help from civic organizations, and, armed with statistics, began her program to aid immigrant families by bringing education to foreign-born mothers in their homes or workplaces. After six weeks of intense lobbying in Sacramento that required fundraising for a sophisticated publicity campaign, she witnessed the passage of the Home Teacher Act in 1915. Gibson's political reputation soared. Katherine Philips Edson referred to her as the most politically important woman in southern California. Nationally known Progressives hailed her as the fairy godmother of immigrant women, and Kellor asked her to come east to organize a woman's Republican league.

Gibson chose to remain in California, where she convinced influential educators to establish courses in Americanization techniques. By the summer of 1919 the University of California and the newly organized campus in Los Angeles offered teachers classes in immigrant education. Gibson wrote in 1926 that nearly fifty thousand immigrants had been reached by the classes. Yet the next year the commission was disbanded. Regular Republicans had regained leadership over the party and had begun dismantling most of the Progressives' state commissions. (Disappointed with the Regular Republicans' renewed influence, Gibson had resigned from the commission in 1922, five years before it was dissolved.)

Several years before Gibson's resignation she had become disillusioned with the Republican party. In 1918 Will H. Hays, then head of the Republican National Committee, called for a conference of Republican women to discuss the best way to put women to work for Republican candidates. Gibson responded that she would not be patronized. She was angry with her party for its undervaluation of women. Republican men, she argued, failed to put women in leadership roles that they clearly deserved. She severed her ties with the party after the 1920 election over its opposition to the League of Nations.

Gibson served on the boards of many civic and philanthropic organizations. During World War I she directed the Woman's Committee of the California Council of Defense and organized its first food conservation drive. She chaired the General Federation of Women's Clubs' Immigrant Committee and founded the California branch of the League of Women Voters. She joined Dora and John Randolph Haynes in their work with California's American Indians and served as one of the original trustees of the Haynes Foundation. She was appointed to the boards of directors of International House at the University of California, Berkeley, and the Women's Athletic Club in Los Angeles and was instrumental in securing buildings for both institutions. She was also on the boards of the American Indian National Defense Association and the Los Angeles County Health and Tuberculosis Association. In 1927 Gibson compiled the history of the California Federation of Women's Clubs, and in it she depicted her achievements modestly. She died at her Los Angeles home.

• Important letters from Gibson are in the Katherine Philips Edson Papers, Special Collections, University of California, Los Angeles; the Hugh S. Gibson Papers, Hoover Institution Archives, Stanford University; the Simon Lubin Papers and the Chester Rowell Papers, Bancroft Library, University of California, Berkeley. See also Mary Simons Gibson, "Schools for the Whole Family," *Graphic Survey* 56 (June 1926): 301–3, and Friday Morning Club, *Mary S. Gibson, Pioneer* (1930), which is in the Henry E. Huntington Library, San Marino, Calif. For a fuller discussion of Gibson's role in the Home Teacher Act see Judith R. Raftery, *Land of Fair Promise: Politics and Reform in Los Angeles Schools, 1885–1941* (1993), and "Los Angeles Clubwomen and Progressive Reform," in *California Progressives Revisited*, ed. William Deverell and Tom Sitton (1994). An obituary is in the *Los Angeles Times*, 12 Sept. 1930.

JUDITH ROSENBERG RAFTERY

GIBSON, Phil Sheridan (28 Nov. 1888–28 Apr. 1984), jurist, was born in Grant City, Missouri, the son of William Jesse Gibson, a country lawyer and judge, and Mollie Gibson. Gibson worked his way through the University of Missouri getting his A.B. and LL.B. in 1914. He then enrolled in the military, serving first in France as a private. He eventually rose to the rank of first lieutenant before taking his discharge abroad. He did some postgraduate work at the Inns of Court in London before returning to the United States. After a brief sojourn in Wyoming, he joined his brother, a newspaper editor, in Anaheim, California. He was admitted to the California bar in 1923, practicing law in Los Angeles for the next fifteen years, while also teaching intermittently at Southwestern University Law School.

When Culbert Olson was elected governor in 1938, it was the first time a Democrat had held that office in California since 1894. Gibson was active in Olson's campaign, and consequently, Olson appointed him director of finance when he took office in 1939. In that role Gibson had the difficult job of guiding the first Democratic budget through a hostile legislature, although he managed to do so very successfully. Then, in August 1939 Olson appointed Gibson an associate justice of the California Supreme Court to fill the vacancy caused by the death of Associate Justice William H. Langdon. Less than a year later, in June 1940, Chief Justice William H. Waste also died, and Olson appointed Gibson to replace him, a position he held until his retirement in 1964.

Gibson's accomplishments as a jurist were extraordinary. When he became chief justice in 1940, the court had a backlog of more than 600 cases; in two years Gibson had reduced that to twenty-four uncalendared cases, largely by transferring cases to the district courts of appeal. He persuaded the legislature to give to the judicial council, over which he presided, the power to promulgate rules of appellate procedure in 1941, and two years later such rules were adopted in a form that is easily recognized today. Gibson also sponsored a new administrative procedure act governing most statewide agencies in the promulgation of rules and regulations, as well as adjudication procedure in licensing and the like, a statute that became an influential model for other states and the federal government.

Perhaps Gibson's most remarkable administrative accomplishment, however, was the rationalization of the structure of the trial courts in California. There were, when he started, eight separate trial courts below the superior court, with somewhat overlapping jurisdictions. Gibson proposed reducing the number of trial courts to three: a superior court for each county and a municipal court or a justice court for each district within the county, depending upon the population of the district. To succeed in this effort, Gibson spent years traveling up and down the state speaking to almost any group willing to listen. The state legislature passed a law embodying Gibson's proposals in 1950.

Still, Gibson's most influential reform came in 1960 with the creation of a Commission on Judicial Qualifications composed of judges, lawyers, and citizens empowered to discipline or remove judges for misconduct. Before the commission's creation, the only method of judicial discipline was by impeachment, a cumbersome procedure that had not been used for decades and was, in any case, inherently inappropriate for judges whose failings were due mostly to age and the immoderate use of alcohol. Some form of disciplinary machinery similar to California's has since been adopted in every other state and in the federal government.

Gibson also sponsored the creation of the Administrative Office of the California Courts and was instrumental in the passage of a generous retirement program for judges. While the new program did not compel retirement at age seventy, it significantly reduced retirement benefits for judges who served beyond their seventieth birthday.

Gibson was also a well-respected author of judicial opinions, who frequently paired with his colleague and successor as chief justice, Roger Traynor. An early opponent of all forms of racial discrimination, Gibson forbade racial discrimination by a labor union in *James v. Marinship Corp.* (1944) twenty years before the National Labor Relations Board did so. He also condemned and ruled unconstitutional California's alien land laws aimed at excluding Japanese from land ownership. Gibson also proudly claimed to be one of the very few prominent public officials to oppose the relocation of the Japanese during World War II. Thirteen years after they first confronted the issue, however, Gibson and Traynor changed their views and voted to exclude evidence obtained in violation of the Constitution in criminal cases in *People v. Cahan* (1952), an opinion written by Traynor that anticipated the U.S. Supreme Court's decision in *Mapp v. Ohio* by six years.

Gibson's colleague and friend of many years, Associate Justice Stanley Mosk, once wrote that Gibson "was one of the great men in California history. He was intelligent, energetic, innovative. On a personal basis he was warm and charming, possessing that Southern courtesy characteristic of his Missouri background . . . convivial, modest, but not fanatically so."

Gibson was married to Victoria Glennon; they had one son. He died in Carmel, California.

• There is no known collection of Gibson's papers. For further information, see "In Memoriam: Honorable Phil S. Gibson, *Reports of Cases Determined in the Supreme Court of the State of California, September 20, 1984, to February 7, 1985* (1986), pp. 955–69. An obituary is in the *Los Angeles Times*, 29 Apr. 1984.

PREBLE STOLZ

GIBSON, Randall Lee (10 Sept. 1832–15 Dec. 1892), congressman and senator, was born near Versailles, Woodford County, Kentucky, the son of Tobias Gibson, a prosperous Louisiana sugar planter, and Louisiana Hart. The youth received private tutoring at "Live Oaks," his father's Louisiana plantation, in schools in Terrebonne Parish, Louisiana, and in schools in Lexington, Kentucky, where the family maintained a summer residence known as "Spring Hill." After graduating with honors from Yale College in 1853, Gibson read law in the firm of Clark and Bayne in New Orleans and then completed his studies in the Law Department of the University of Louisiana, from which he graduated in 1855. For the next three years, Gibson traveled and studied in Germany, Russia, and Spain, where for six months he worked as attaché to the American embassy in Madrid. Returning to Louisiana, he practiced law and became a successful sugar planter and slaveholder in Thibodaux.

The Civil War interrupted Gibson's business and political ambitions. Enlisting in the Confederate cause, he was appointed aide-de-camp on the staff of Governor Thomas O. Moore. In March 1861 Gibson was commissioned captain in the First Regiment, Louisiana Artillery. Later that year he became colonel of the Thirteenth Regiment, Louisiana Infantry. He fought at Shiloh, Perryville, Murfreesboro (Stones River), and Chickamauga. In 1864, after winning promotion to the rank of brigadier general, he participated in the Atlanta and Nashville campaigns, concluding his military career by defending Spanish Fort near Mobile, Alabama.

Upon the conclusion of the Civil War in 1865, Gibson, finding his plantation in ruins, practiced law in New Orleans with Edward Austin and later with his brother, McKinley Gibson. In 1868 he married Mary Montgomery; they had three sons. Turning his interests toward politics, he sought a seat in the U.S. House of Representatives in 1872 as a Democrat, but he failed to win election. Two years later he succeeded in his endeavor to represent the First District of Louisiana, winning successive reelections in 1876, 1878, and 1880.

Gibson entered the House during the twilight of southern Reconstruction. In the controversy over the disputed presidential election of 1876, between Rutherford B. Hayes and Samuel J. Tilden, Gibson objected to the recognition of the Republican Hayes electors from Louisiana, believing that the Democratic nominee deserved election. Although he opposed Hayes's election, Gibson, secretary of war in the administration of Ulysses S. Grant, developed a close working relationship with President Hayes in their attempts to conciliate the South. In 1882 Gibson was selected by the Louisiana legislature for the U.S. Senate and was reelected in 1888.

During his legislative career, Gibson advocated programs to benefit the South. Despite the state's rights and strict constructionist views of his party, Gibson was a southern Democrat who welcomed federal aid for internal improvements. He sponsored legislation in 1878 that enabled Captain James B. Eads to construct jetties at the mouth of the Mississippi River. Gibson favored the creation of the Mississippi River Commission to explore ways to improve the navigation of the river. He also supported the Blair Bill, an unsuccessful attempt in 1890 to distribute federal funds to states for educational purposes based on illiteracy rates. In one of his speeches, Gibson stated, "The only way to win genuine public confidence is to assert the truth and to insist that the function of the Government is not to enrich the citizen but to uphold justice and to protect life and property" (*Select Speeches of the Hon. Randall Lee Gibson, of Louisiana . . . 1875–1887* [1887], p. 206).

In addition to his political activity, Gibson played a prominent role in higher education in Louisiana.

Through Gibson and his influence, Tulane University of Louisiana was established with the money and ideas of Paul Tulane, a former resident of New Orleans and a friend of Gibson's father and father-in-law. Gibson and Tulane shared a mutual respect for each other, and higher education in Louisiana benefited from their relationship. In 1881 Tulane invited Gibson to his Princeton, New Jersey, home to accept a bequest of property to be used for education in Louisiana. Two years later, with Gibson's backing, William Preston Johnston, the president of Louisiana State University who was Gibson's cousin and former Yale roommate, accepted the presidency of the new institution. In 1884 Governor S. D. McEnery signed the legislation that transferred the University of Louisiana at New Orleans to the Tulane board of administration, thereby renaming the campus Tulane University of Louisiana.

Gibson was chosen as the first president of the Tulane board of administration, a position he enjoyed wholeheartedly. In addition, he was a member of the boards of administration of the Smithsonian Institution in Washington, the Howard Memorial Library in New Orleans, and the Peabody Education Fund. Gibson served as president of the Tulane board until his death in Hot Springs, Arkansas, where he had gone to improve his health.

• Gibson's papers are in four main repositories, Tulane University Library (New Orleans), Louisiana and Lower Mississippi Valley Collections at Louisiana State University (Baton Rouge), Gibson-Humphreys Papers in the Margaret I. King Library of the University of Kentucky (Lexington), and Gibson-Humphreys Family Papers in the Southern Historical Collection of the University of North Carolina Library (Chapel Hill). Other letters are scattered in the collections of contemporaries, such as the Grover Cleveland Papers (Library of Congress) and the William Preston Johnston Papers, Mrs. Mason Barrett Collection, Tulane University Library. The major studies of Gibson are Donald Eugene Dixon, "Randall Lee Gibson of Louisiana, 1832–1892" (M.A. thesis, Louisiana State Univ., 1971); and Mary G. McBride, "Senator Randall Lee Gibson and the Establishment of Tulane University," *Louisiana History* 28 (1987): 245–62. Gibson's speeches are in the *Congressional Record* from 1877 to 1892. Additional material is in *Memorial Addresses on the Life and Character of Randall Lee Gibson . . .* (1894); Arthur Marvin Shaw, *William Preston Johnston: A Transitional Figure of the Confederacy* (1943); Joe Gray Taylor, *Louisiana Reconstructed, 1863–1877* (1974); Joy J. Jackson, *New Orleans in the Gilded Age Politics and Urban Progress, 1880–1896* (1969); and Edwin W. Fay, ed., *The History of Education in Louisiana* (1898). Obituaries are in the *New Orleans Times-Democrat*, 15 Dec. 1892, and the *New Orleans Daily Picayune*, 16 Dec. 1892.

LEONARD SCHLUP

GIBSON, William (14 Mar. 1788–2 Mar. 1868), surgeon, was born in Baltimore, Maryland, the son of John Gibson. Gibson received his early education in Baltimore and attended St. John's College in Annapolis, Maryland, before attending the 1803–1804 session at the College of New Jersey (later Princeton University). Leaving before he obtained a degree, Gibson began to study in the office of John B. Owen of Balti-

more, and in 1806 he attended a course of lectures at the University of Pennsylvania Medical College. In Philadelphia, Gibson for the first time heard the public lectures of Philip Syng Physick, the "Father of American Surgery," whose every word impressed him. Upon completing the lecture course at Pennsylvania, Gibson sailed to Edinburgh, Scotland, where he witnessed the private practice and operations of John Bell, a prominent English surgeon. At this time he attended lectures on botany and natural history, took art lessons, and also devoted attention to studies of hospital practice. In 1809 he graduated from the University of Edinburgh. His thesis was "De Forma Ossium Gentilium," a work describing the various forms of bone observed in the races of mankind, based on anatomical preparations found in Monro's museum.

In 1808 the Peninsular War, Napoleon Bonaparte's campaign into Spain, was raging. With friends, Gibson chartered a boat that took them to Spain in time to see the battle of La Coruña. Through a friend he made the acquaintance of the brother of Sir John Moore, the commander of the British army in Spain who was killed at the battle of La Coruña. Moore's brother arranged for Gibson to examine "in an unofficial capacity" the important cases of gunshot wounds that occurred in that battle. It is probable that it was at this time that Gibson met Sir Charles Bell, a practitioner of surgery in London, who had been assigned to assist in the care of wounded soldiers. From this contact, Gibson became a private pupil of Bell. While in London, Gibson also observed the operations of John Abernathy and Sir Astley Cooper. Also at this time, Gibson was taken on a trip through England by Cooper, who was impressed by the young American and predicted great things of him.

Gibson returned to the United States in 1810 after three years abroad and opened a practice of surgery in Baltimore. Shortly thereafter he became interested in founding a department of medicine at the University of Maryland. The school was successfully begun and Gibson was chosen to fill the chair of surgery at the age of twenty-three. At Maryland he demonstrated his manual dexterity as well as his abilities as a surgical teacher. In 1812 he tied off the common iliac artery to correct aneurysm for the first time, a bold and original procedure but unfortunately unsuccessful. In 1828 Gibson attempted another daring operation, that of tying off the subclavian artery a day after it was ruptured in an attempt to reduce a dislocation. Unfortunately this patient died of erysipelas within a week. A more successful surgical procedure was Gibson's removal of foreign material from the shoulder of General Winfield Scott, who had been wounded at the battle of Lundy's Lane near Niagara Falls.

Gibson served as a surgeon in the Maryland militia in 1814 when the British attacked Baltimore. In 1815 he visited Europe again and, while traveling in the neighborhood of Waterloo, he took part in the famous battle and received a slight wound.

In 1819, after the death of John Syng Dorsey, Gibson was elected to fill the chair of surgery at the University of Pennsylvania, replacing Dorsey's uncle Philip Syng Physick, who shifted to the chair of anatomy. Gibson brought a fine reputation as an operator and a teacher of surgery to the University of Pennsylvania, for he was a clear, dynamic lecturer. He had a melodious delivery and an attractive style of enunciation. His lectures were illustrated with vivid demonstrations using illustrative diagrams and skillful anatomical dissections of normal and diseased structures and fractures, most of which he prepared himself.

Gibson was a dynamic person and a dexterous surgeon who performed many daring operations; descriptions of a number of them were published in various journals. For example, he treated a fracture by a modified Hagedorn's procedure. Particularly instructive was Gibson's demonstrations of the anatomical damage from gunshot wounds. For this purpose he regularly brought a cadaver into the lecture hall, fired a gun into various regions of the body, and then dissected the paths of the bullets through the tissues.

In 1824 Gibson published his *Institutes and Practice of Surgery*, which was a clearly written guide for his medical students. In addition to his *Institutes*, Gibson published *A Sketch of Lithotripsy in 1841 and Rambles in Europe* in 1839. The sketches of surgeons, physicians, hospitals, and medical schools are interesting, lively, and clear. In 1847 Gibson visited Europe again and described these travels as well as surgical experiences to his classes. Gibson married Sarah Charlotte Hollingsworth; they had three sons and two daughters. He married a second time and had three children. He died in Savannah, Georgia.

• Significant treatments of Gibson's life are in R. French Stone, *Biography of Eminent American Physicians and Surgeons* (1894), and Joseph Carson, *A History of the Medical Department of the University of Pennsylvania* (1869).

DAVID Y. COOPER

GIDDINGS, Franklin Henry (23 Mar. 1855–11 June 1931), sociologist, was born in Sherman, Connecticut, the son of Edward Jonathan Giddings, a prominent congregational clergyman and the author of *American Christian Rulers* (1890), and Rebecca Jane Fuller. The young Giddings apparently did not care for religious instruction and spent a lot of time with his two grandfathers. From one grandfather he learned surveying and mechanical drawing and from the other he learned the art of tanning, spending much of his time in the workshop.

By the time Giddings entered Union College in 1873 he already was acquainted with the writings of Herbert Spencer, Thomas Henry Huxley, Charles Darwin, and John Tyndall. A local high school teacher, Henry H. Scott, had introduced Giddings to these writers, and their work influenced Giddings's later views on the evolution of societies. He studied civil engineering at Union College. He became associate editor of the *Winston Connecticut Herald* in 1875 and taught school

in Massachusetts and Connecticut. In 1876 he married Elizabeth Patience Hawes; they had three children. From 1878 to 1885 he was the editor of the *Berkshire Courier* and the *New Milford Connecticut Gazette*. During these years Giddings was mostly known as a writer with the *Springfield Republican* and a literary critic for the *Springfield Union*. In 1885 Giddings worked with the Massachusetts Bureau of Labor Statistics. In 1888 he received his A.B. from Union College as a member of the class of 1877.

Giddings also wrote articles for both academic (*Political Science Quarterly* and the *Massachusetts Bureau of Labor Statistics*) and nonacademic journals. These articles attracted the attention of scholars, and when future president Woodrow Wilson (then an associate professor of history and political science) moved to Wesleyan University from Bryn Mawr in 1888, he invited Giddings to Bryn Mawr as a lecturer on politics. Bryn Mawr rapidly promoted Giddings, and by 1892 he was a full professor. He taught a variety of courses, including political economy and methods and principles of administration. In 1890 he began offering a graduate seminar on theories of sociology. During his last two years at Bryn Mawr (1892–1894) Giddings gave weekly sociology lectures at Columbia University. In 1894 he became a full professor of sociology at Columbia, the first person to achieve full professorship in that discipline in the United States.

Giddings remained at Columbia for the rest of his life; in 1906 he was appointed Carpentier Professor of Sociology and the History of Civilization. During his academic years Giddings served on many committees and helped found many societies. He was one of the founders of the American Academy of Political and Social Science, and for three years he edited the publications of the American Economic Association. He was a fellow of the American Statistical Association and the American Association for the Advancement of Science. He produced more than fifty Ph.D. students and was president of the Institut Internationale de Sociologie and of the *American Sociological Society* (1910–1911).

Giddings believed that human nature is not solely progressive or conservative but rather prone to both tendencies. Whether one or the other comes to predominate at any particular time is a product of the social environment. If there is a fundamental drive in human nature it is "the will to carry on sustained by faith in the possibilities of life" (*Studies in the Theory of Human Society* [1922], p. 10). The peculiarities of human behavior are impossible to know in all their detail. Giddings believed that emotions have played a large role in the development of the human species. These emotions vary but certainly include fear, anger, dread, envy, and jealousy. All of these have to be brought under control if society is to operate effectively.

Like Charles Cooley, Giddings argued that human nature is basically social, plastic, and malleable. Moreover, one's present nature is primarily developed through the use of language and social cooperation.

Giddings developed the notion of "consciousness of kind" to explain the evolution of knowledge and society. Consciousness of kind develops organically over a long period of time and is stimulated by human interaction with nature and other humans. According to Giddings, this consciousness is more developed in humans than in animals and involves one human's recognition of his or her likeness to other humans. It is "that pleasurable state of mind which included organic sympathy, the perception of resemblance, conscious or reflective sympathy, affection, and the desire for recognition" (*Elements* [1898], pp. 100–101). Four processes are active in consciousness of kind. First, an individual makes his or her neighbor's feeling or judgment an object of thought; at the same instant the individual makes his or her own thought an object; the individual then judges that both are identical; and finally the individual acts in total consciousness that others have come to similar conclusions and will act in similar ways (*Inductive Sociology* [1901], p. 99).

Like many other theorists of his generation, Giddings was committed to an evolutionary view of human society. Giddings distinguished four evolutionary stages: zoogenic, anthropogenic, ethnogenic, and demogenic (*Principles of Sociology* [1900], pp. 73–75). In the lower stages of evolution individuals were more susceptible to emotional forces. Modern society (demogenic) is not totally free of emotional effects but it more self-consciously shapes its own destiny. In Giddings's view, modern society has grown "by the light of ideals that reason has created, through critical reflection upon the revelations of experience, and by a comparative study of the relative value of human desires, as tested by experiment" (*Democracy and Empire* [1900], p. 315). Although modern society shows increased differentiation compared to its earlier counterparts, it also tends toward homogeneity based on likemindedness or consciousness of kind.

Giddings also held the view that societies, modern or other, could not exist without certain inequalities. In part, inequality is a result of constitutional or genetic differences. All humans are not born with the same mental and moral endowment. These constitutional differences are the basis for class formations in society. However, economic and political classes are secondary to what Giddings considered to be the real class divisions in society, which are based on vitality, personality, and social skills. For Giddings, these classes represented the natural divisions in society and led to permanent conflicts. These differences have to be controlled through societal organization; in particular, political organizations are created to harmonize various interests. Giddings wrote that "the primary purpose of the state is to perfect social integration" (*The Responsible State* [1918], p. 9).

Giddings also contributed to a sociological critique of morality. He argued that the mistake of most ethical theories since the Protestant Reformation had been to focus on the isolated individual. This focus was a proper attempt to account for the suppression of the individual under the church. But insofar as ethical systems have assumed the individual as the starting point, he contended, these systems have been radically wrong. Giddings argued that both socialists and staunch individualists were wrong about the growth of society. The former believed that the state could do all the same things that private agencies could do, and the latter believed that society could achieve all its goals without authoritative government. He contended that both ideals were right in principle but wrong in fact. They were wrong, Giddings believed, because knowledge of social laws leads people to believe that there is a tendency toward social equilibrium. Both state and society have self-limiting mechanisms that are altered with changing needs and conditions.

Giddings's definition of his discipline had a strong influence on others writing at a time when sociology as a discipline was being formed in the United States. He argued that the task of sociology was to ascertain the conditions under which social stability and social progress depend: "Sociology enables us to attempt a rational and constructive criticism of our social values, and to combine them in a realizable social ideal" (*Democracy and Empire*, pp. 64–65). The practical value of sociology lies in its ability to complete a system of facts that is only partly given in our daily life. Giddings's sociology teaches that consciousness of kind is the basic fact of all social existence. This fact stresses the importance of loyalty and group solidarity. His theories attempt to emancipate the human mind from the fear of social and natural phenomena, teaching the value of social control and, in particular, rational self-control. Finally, Giddings's theories emphasize the value of public opinion, necessary for a republican government. He died in Scarsdale, New York.

• Three universities have special collections of papers on and by Giddings: the Luther Bernard Papers, Special Collections at the Pennsylvania State University Library; the Luther Bernard Papers, Special Collections at the University of Chicago Library; and the Columbia University Faculty Collection, Rare Book and Manuscript Library, Columbia University. A bibliography of Giddings's writings is available in *Bibliography of the Faculty of Political Science* (1931) at Columbia. For appreciations and assessments of Giddings, see Harry Elmer Barnes, ed., *An Introduction to the History of Sociology* (1948); Frank H. Hankins, "Franklin H. Giddings, 1855–1931: Some Aspects of His Sociological Theory," *American Journal of Sociology* 37 (Nov. 1931): 349–67; Leo Davids, "Franklin H. Giddings: An Overview of a Forgotten Pioneer," *Journal of the History of the Behavioral Sciences* 4 (1968): 62–73; and Robert Bierstedt, *American Sociological Theory: A Critical History* (1981). Giddings also is treated in various histories of sociology, among them Charles Hunt Page, *Class and American Sociology: From Ward to Ross* (1969); Roscoe C. Hinkle, *Founding Theory of American Sociology, 1881–1915* (1980); and Ellsworth R. Fuhrman, *The Sociology of Knowledge in America, 1883–1915* (1980).

E. R. FUHRMAN

GIDDINGS, James Louis (10 Apr. 1909–9 Dec. 1964), archaeologist, was born in Caldwell, Texas, the son of James Giddings and Maude Mathews. After spending three years in the mid-1920s studying English and biology at Rice University, Louis Giddings attended a summer school at the University of Colorado before moving to Alaska, where he obtained a bachelor of science degree from the University of Alaska in 1931. Giddings worked as a thawing engineer from 1932 to 1937 and became interested in the new science of dendrochronology (tree-ring dating) as a means of determining the age of spruce logs uncovered during mining operations. Following a year spent at the University of Arizona studying with A. E. Douglass, the developer of dendrochronology, Giddings became a research associate at the University of Alaska in 1938. He would work there until 1949, ultimately as associate professor of anthropology.

In the spring of 1939 Giddings shared lab space with archaeologist Froelich Rainey in the university's museum, where Giddings's quest for old wood to study drew him to some of Rainey's archaeological specimens. Impressed with Giddings's ability to use dendrochronology to cross-date different parts of sites, Rainey invited him to accompany an archaeological expedition that he and Helge Larsen were planning to Point Hope. Giddings had studied some archaeology at the University of Arizona, but Point Hope would be his first excavation. Unencumbered by preconceptions about what a typical Arctic archaeological site should look like, Giddings persuaded Larsen that it might be worthwhile to test a series of almost imperceptible depressions near the site they were already excavating. This led to the most important discovery that summer: the spectacular Ipiutak culture and its fabulous carvings. It also demonstrated an ability Giddings would possess throughout his career: the knack of finding extraordinary sites.

In the summer of 1940 Giddings commenced his own research project, combining archaeology and dendrochronology in the Kobuk River area of Northwestern Alaska, collecting wood samples and locating sites. In 1941, the year he received an M.A. in dendrochronology from the University of Arizona, Giddings returned to the Kobuk to excavate several of the sites, including a fifteenth-century house ruin at a place called Onion Portage. Four microlithic stone tools that he found in the house did not seem exceptional given then-current knowledge of Arctic prehistory, but twenty years later they would bring him back to Onion Portage.

In the spring of 1942 Giddings again traveled the Kobuk, this time on snowshoes and by dog team for the U.S. Army Engineers. He then enlisted in the navy, spending most of the war in the Southwest Pacific. In 1943 he married Ruth Warner, with whom he would have three children.

In 1947 Giddings returned to the Kobuk and, using wood from living trees, driftwood, and archaeological samples, filled in the gaps in his archaeological and dendrochronological sequences, which now extended almost 1,000 years into the past. From 1948 to 1952 he worked in the Norton Sound region to see if his sequences could also be applied there. At a place called Cape Denbigh he excavated a stratified site and unexpectedly found distinctive microlithic stone tools in the lowest layer. Given the name "Denbigh Flint complex," the tools appeared older than and unlike anything previously known from the Arctic.

In 1949 Giddings moved his home but not his research from Alaska to become assistant professor of anthropology and assistant curator of the University Museum at the University of Pennsylvania, where he would also obtain a Ph.D. in anthropology in 1951. In 1956 he became associate professor of anthropology and director of the Haffenreffer Museum at Brown University, becoming full professor in 1959.

Having concluded that the Denbigh Flint complex was too old to date with dendrochronology, Giddings turned in 1956 to another technique not previously used in the Arctic: beach-ridge dating. In a few parts of Alaska the effects of tides and storms have over millennia resulted in the regular addition of new beach ridges. Historically, because of their reliance on sea mammals, Eskimos camped very near the edge of the ocean. Giddings therefore reasoned that the distance of an archaeological site from the present-day shoreline could indicate the site's age; the oldest sites should be found on beach ridges well back from today's shore. At Cape Krusenstern he found an extraordinary site with 114 beaches, almost all containing archaeological remains. This find allowed him to determine with great accuracy the sequence of cultures and, when combined with radiocarbon dating, demonstrated that people had lived there almost continuously for approximately 5,000 years. But inland from the Cape Krusenstern beaches Giddings found an assemblage of artifacts he named "Palisades" that he was convinced was even older.

His beach-ridge dating having proved that microlithic tools went out of use long ago, Giddings remembered the four microliths he had found twenty years earlier at the Onion Portage site and realized that they must have come from an older level into which the builders of the fifteenth-century house had dug. He reasoned that if the site was stratified it might reveal the age of the Palisades material. Between 1961 and 1964 he proved himself correct, and his excavations there, continued until 1970 by his student Douglas Anderson, uncovered the most deeply stratified site in the Arctic with more than thirty separate artifact-producing levels in eighteen feet of deposits, documenting a human occupation of almost 10,000 years. Unfortunately Giddings never learned of the oldest levels at the site, dying in Pawtucket, Rhode Island, following an automobile collision in Seekonk, Massachusetts.

Giddings pioneered two dating techniques that have proved invaluable in Arctic archaeology, and his excavations extended the documented human history of Alaska to almost 7,000 years earlier than previously known. In addition to numerous scholarly articles and reports, at the time of his death he had finished writing *Ancient Men of the Arctic*, a book that vividly synthesizes his knowledge of Arctic prehistory and his memorable experiences of doing fieldwork in that remote region.

• Giddings's unpublished research has been completed as J. L. Giddings and Douglas D. Anderson, *The Archaeology of Cape Krusenstern* (1986), and Anderson, *Onion Portage* (1988). Listings of Giddings's publications at the time of his death are contained in obituaries by Froelich Rainey in *American Anthropologist* 67 (1965): 1503–7, and Helge Larsen in *American Antiquity* 31 (1966): 398–401. The most extensive summary of Giddings's career and contributions is Henry Collins's introduction to Giddings's *Ancient Men of the Arctic* (1967), pp. xix–xxxi. An obituary is in the *New York Times*, 10 Dec. 1964.

ROBERT W. PARK

GIDDINGS, Joshua Reed (6 Oct. 1795–27 May 1864), antislavery congressman, was born in Bradford County, Pennsylvania, the son of Joshua Giddings and Elizabeth Pease, farmers. At the age of ten he moved with his parents to Ashtabula County in Ohio's Western Reserve, where he lived for the rest of his life. In 1819 he married Laura Waters, with whom he had seven children, two of whom died in infancy. Lacking virtually all formal education, Giddings nonetheless studied law with Elisha Whittlesey, later a U.S. representative, and established a successful practice. After losing his considerable investments in western lands in the panic of 1837 and becoming estranged from his former law partner, future U.S. Senator Benjamin Wade, Giddings ceased legal practice. In 1838 he ran successfully on the Whig ticket, succeeding Whittlesey as congressman from Ohio's Sixteenth District, a region settled chiefly by New Englanders. He held the seat until 1859 when he failed to be renominated, in part because of declining health.

In Congress Giddings's antislavery convictions led him to form a close personal and political association with John Quincy Adams (1767–1848) and to join him in a campaign against the congressional "gag rule," a measure designed to silence floor discussion of slavery. Described as "rough, plain, unpolished," Giddings was imbued with inflexible moral and political principles that kept him on an antislavery, antisouthern course throughout his long career. Believing slavery to be exclusively a state matter, he opposed any federal measure that could be construed as supporting it. Thus he called for the end of slavery and the slave trade in the District of Columbia and argued against the Seminole War, which he believed the government waged at the South's behest in order to protect slavery.

Steady agitation on such issues by Giddings and a small group of like-minded congressmen, both northern and southern, did much to disrupt the national parties and to weaken intersectional comity. To halt that dire process, party leaders attempted to silence them. When in 1842 Giddings again defied party regularity by introducing his Creole Resolutions, which asserted the right of slaves on the high seas to rebel, an angry House censured him. Giddings resigned, but within a month his district overwhelmingly reelected

him, and he triumphantly returned to Congress, demonstrating that antislavery politicians could not be stifled nor could sectional politics be prevented.

Now as before he was pressured to silence by the Whig leadership and to greater zeal by abolitionists. It was to the abolitionists that he paid the greater heed. By this time his daughter Lura Maria, with whom he always maintained a close relationship, had become a Garrisonian, and Garrisonians within his district exercised ever greater influence upon him. Giddings attended their meetings, corresponded with them, and became their political spokesman. He was unusual among northern congressmen not only for his radical antislavery views, but also for the support his district gave him.

In the mid-1840s, as what was then called the "slavocracy" appeared more adamant and aggressive, Giddings's positions and rhetoric became more extreme. His opposition to the annexation of Texas and the war with Mexico was unrestrained. Giddings claimed that annexation destroyed the old Union and that therefore the familiar constitutional defense of slavery as a state right no longer applied. He now based his antislavery stance on the higher law, or natural law, rather than on man-made statutes and the Constitution. In the 1850s he became a perfectionist, a spiritualist, and a religious radical. He spoke often of the justice of slave insurrection and the duty of northerners to aid it and vehemently opposed the Fugitive Slave Law of 1850 and its enforcement. When Abraham Lincoln served in Congress in 1847–1849 and lived in the same rooming house as Giddings, the two men argued over the slavery issue, with Giddings taking stands too extreme for Lincoln then to accept.

Giddings failed in his years-long effort to convert the Whig party to his own advanced antislavery position. In 1848, when the party nominated for president Zachary Taylor, hero of the Mexican War, Giddings joined the new Free Soil party. After passage of the Kansas-Nebraska Act in 1854, he helped lead the Free Soilers into the Republican party and campaigned for John C. Frémont in 1856 and Abraham Lincoln in 1860. Although his role in the denouement of the sectional controversy was not central, Giddings played a crucial part in its development. He was rewarded by appointment as consul general to Canada in April 1861, a post he occupied until his death in Montreal three years later.

• The major manuscript sources are the Joshua R. Giddings Papers at the Ohio Historical Society, the Joshua R. Giddings–George W. Julian Papers at the Library of Congress, and the George W. Julian Papers at the Indiana State Library. Published works by Giddings include *An Expose of the Circumstances Which Led to the Resignation by the Hon. Joshua R. Giddings* (1842), *Speeches in Congress* (1842), *The Exiles of Florida; or The Crimes Committed by Our Government against the Maroons* (1858), and *A History of the Rebellion, Its Authors and Causes* (1864). George W. Julian, *The Life of Joshua R. Giddings* (1892), is a memoir by Giddings's son-in-law. The major modern biography is James Brewer Stewart, *Joshua R. Giddings and the Tactics of Radical Politics* (1970). See also

Jane H. Pease and William H. Pease, *Bound with Them in Chains* (1972), and Douglas A. Gamble, "Joshua Giddings and the Ohio Abolitionists," *Ohio History* 88 (Winter 1979): 37–56.

MERTON L. DILLON

GIDEON, Clarence Earl (30 Aug. 1910–18 Jan. 1972), convict whose Supreme Court case guaranteed indigents the right to legal counsel, was born in Hannibal, Missouri, the son of Charles Roscoe Gideon and Virginia Gregory, both employees in a shoe factory. His father died shortly after Gideon's birthday, and his mother remarried two years later. His stepfather also worked at a local shoe factory. Gideon was educated in the Hannibal public school system until he ran away from home at the age of fourteen, "accepting the life of a hobo and tramp in preference to [his] home" (Lewis, *Gideon's Trumpet*, p. 66).

After a year or so of wandering, Gideon returned to Missouri, where he was arrested for stealing clothes from a country store. He was sent to a reformatory and paroled after only a year. While working various low-wage jobs, he married a woman close to his age, although her name and the exact date of the marriage are unknown. According to Gideon, the two did "very well together for better than a year until [he] got without a job and committed some crimes in 1928" (Lewis, *Gideon's Trumpet*, p. 67). Sentenced to ten years in a Missouri prison on three counts of burglary and larceny, he was paroled after only three years and four months.

Until 1961 Gideon's life followed a similar pattern. During this period he served time for three additional felonies and was arrested on several other occasions without being formally charged. Gideon married Virgil Hoff in 1950, Velma Cooper in January 1955, and Ruth Babineaux in October 1955. All of these marriages, like his first, ended in divorce. He had at least four children with Babineaux and for a time acted as stepfather to her children from a previous marriage. Gideon struggled to keep this family intact, and for almost ten years he held odd jobs ranging from a mechanic to a bar proprietor. He was poor, tubercular, and generally down on his luck, and even law enforcement officials considered him "a perfectly harmless human being, rather likeable [*sic*], but . . . tossed aside by life" (Lewis, *Gideon's Trumpet*, p. 6). In and out of hospitals, marriages, and jails with nearly the same frequency, Gideon encountered no one who could have predicted that he would alter the course of constitutional law.

On 3 June 1961 Gideon was arrested and charged with breaking and entering the Bay Harbor Poolroom in Panama City, Florida. Although he had twice pleaded guilty to felonies and had done little to contest his previous convictions, this time he adamantly maintained his innocence. According to Gideon, the charge resulted from a "falling out" with the proprietor over a poker game he was supposed to fix. He demanded that the trial judge appoint a lawyer to represent him. The judge refused Gideon's request on the grounds that "the only time the court can appoint counsel to represent a Defendant is when that person is charged with a capital offense." Gideon argued that "the United States Supreme Court says I am entitled to be represented by counsel." Ultimately, Gideon was denied counsel, convicted, and sentenced to five years.

Ironically, both Gideon and the judge were mistaken. Although the Supreme Court had never ruled that someone like Gideon was automatically entitled to counsel, it did not forbid Florida to appoint counsel in state criminal cases when "special circumstances" would make a fair trial impossible. Because Gideon's case appeared quite simple on the surface, because he was not mentally defective, and because no obvious courtroom bias existed, the right to legal counsel seemed unnecessary. The trial judge even remarked, "In my opinion he did as well as most lawyers could have done in handling his case" (Lewis, *Gideon's Trumpet*, p. 157).

Gideon's argument was not new. In 1932 the Supreme Court ruled in *Powell v. Alabama* that an accused indigent charged with a capital crime was entitled to a court-appointed lawyer. To deny counsel in the face of a possible death sentence, the Court ruled, was to deny the defendant due process as guaranteed by the Fourteenth Amendment. In *Johnson v. Zerbst* (1938) the Court extended the right to counsel to accused indigents in all federal criminal cases. Neither decision, however, confirmed Gideon's claim that he, an indigent charged with a state crime, was entitled to legal counsel.

In fact, the Court ruled in *Betts v. Brady* (1942) that the due process clause of the Fourteenth Amendment did not apply to states. Subsequent opinions made the *Betts v. Brady* rule more specific. Indigents had to prove they faced "special circumstances," more specifically, that they were somehow hindered by lack of intelligence or skills, by the intricacy of the case, by mental illness, by immaturity, or by the prosecutor or judge's behavior, to be entitled to an appointed counsel. Thus, when Gideon petitioned the highest Court of the land to hear his case in forma pauperis, his penciled, handwritten argument claiming that his conviction violated the due process clause of the Fourteenth Amendment was fundamentally flawed.

Nevertheless, on 4 June 1962 the Court agreed to hear Gideon's case with this specific question in mind: "Should this Court's holding in *Betts v. Brady*, 316 U.S. 455, be reconsidered?" (Lewis, *Gideon's Trumpet*, p. 43). Abe Fortas, a high-powered Washington lawyer who later became the first Supreme Court justice to resign in the face of public criticism, was appointed to argue Gideon's case. After reading a transcript of Gideon's original trial, one associate at Fortas's firm said: "We knew as soon as we read the transcript that here was a perfect case to challenge the assumption of *Betts* that a man could have a fair trial without a lawyer. He did very well for a layman, he acted like a layyer. But it was a pitiful effort really . . . . A lawyer—not a great lawyer, just an ordinary, competent lawyer—could have made ashes of the case" (Lewis, *Gideon's Trumpet*, p. 63).

Apparently Fortas's associate was correct. In a landmark decision written by Justice Hugo Black, who had dissented in *Betts*, the Supreme Court unanimously ruled that "in our adversary system of criminal justice, any person haled into court, who is too poor to hire a lawyer, cannot be assured a fair trial unless counsel is provided for him. This seems to us to be an obvious truth" (Lewis, *Gideon's Trumpet*, p. 189). Granted a new trial, Gideon was acquitted with the help of a local, court-appointed lawyer, who did, indeed, "make ashes of" the state's case against Gideon. After his acquittal, when a reporter asked him if he felt like he had accomplished something, Gideon answered with characteristic succinctness, "Well I did."

In a 22-page letter to Fortas written before the Court's decision, Gideon remarked: "I believe that each era finds a [sic] improvement in law [sic] each year brings something new for the benefit of mankind. Maybe this will be one of those small steps forward" (Lewis, *Gideon's Trumpet*, p. 78). It certainly was, and although Gideon spent the remainder of his life pumping gas and staying out of trouble, the consequences of his humble legal battle were monumental. Florida, along with many other states, chose to apply the *Gideon* rule retrospectively, prompting Gideon to proudly proclaim to *Newsweek* (11 Aug. 1969), "Fifty-eight hundred men in Florida prisons, and nearly 2,000 of them were let go." After marrying a woman named Shirley, whose last name is unknown and with whom he had no children, Gideon died in Florida.

• Gideon's correspondence with Fortas, including his 22-page biographical letter, is in Anthony Lewis, *Gideon's Trumpet* (1964), a detailed account of Gideon's case before the Supreme Court that was later made into a film starring Henry Fonda. Two other texts by Lewis are also useful, *The Supreme Court and How It Works: The Story of the "Gideon" Case* (1966), which contains a photocopy of the first page of Gideon's handwritten petition to the Supreme Court, and *Clarence Earl Gideon and the Supreme Court* (1972). Two more recent assessments of the *Gideon* case are Mark E. Dudley, *"Gideon v. Wainwright" (1963): Right to Counsel* (1995), and Victoria Sherrow, *"Gideon v. Wainwright": Free Legal Counsel* (1995). For a detailed discussion of how the *Gideon* decision affected the Fla. penal system, see Charles J. Eichman, *The Impact of the "Gideon" Decision upon Crime and Sentencing in Florida* (1966). A brief article on Gideon's whereabouts after his acquittal is "Where Are They Now," *Newsweek*, 11 Aug. 1969, p. 8. An obituary is in *Newsweek*, 28 Feb. 1972, p. 61.

DONNA GREAR PARKER

GIES, William John (21 Feb. 1872–20 May 1956), biological chemist and patron of modern dentistry, was born in Reisterstown, Maryland, the son of John Gies, Jr. and Ophelia Letitia Ensminger, occupations unknown. His father died when he was two years old, whereupon his mother took him and his infant brother to the small Pennsylvania Dutch town of Manheim, where her father edited and published the local newspaper. At age seven, Gies started delivering the *Manheim Sentinel* and began to learn the printing trade from his grandfather.

Gies received a B.S. from Gettysburg College in 1893 and then entered Yale University, where he obtained a Ph.B. in 1894 and a Ph.D. in chemistry in 1897. After completing his graduate studies, Gies settled in New York City and served on the biological chemistry faculty of the College of Physicians and Surgeons at Columbia University (1898–1937), Teacher's College at Columbia (1909–1928), and New York College of Pharmacy (1904–1922). He also was employed as a consulting pathological chemist at Bellevue Hospital (1910–1922). In 1899 Gies married Mabel Loyetta Lark, with whom he would have four children.

Gies made important contributions in each of the three main spheres of academic life: research, education, and service. He published textbooks in general, organic, and biological chemistry and eight massive volumes of *Biochemical Researches* (1903–1927). Gies also periodically edited a number of scientific journals, including *Proceedings of the Society for Experimental Biology and Medicine*, *Proceedings of the Society of Biological Chemists*, *Biochemical Bulletin*, and *Chemical Abstracts*.

Gies's association with dentistry began in 1909 when a group of New York dentists interested in broadening dental research asked for his help. In the course of undertaking preliminary research on biochemical aspects of dental disease, Gies concluded that the problem was more difficult than anyone realized and that the science of dentistry, which at the time was mainly concerned with prosthetic mechanics, was too limited. He also came to believe that the prevention of dental diseases and the restoration of health in teeth and adjacent oral tissues were of great importance to general health. However, the medical profession at this time paid little attention to dental diseases and disparaged dentistry as "merely a mechanical art." Because of this negative attitude and the unusual mechanical and aesthetic requirements of dental practice, Gies thought that dentistry should develop as a separately organized profession.

Gies's first formal contact with dental education came in the academic year 1916–1917 when he served as chair of the executive committee of the New York School of Dental Hygiene. In the following year he persuaded the school to become a part of a new dental school at Columbia University that he had helped establish.

Gies believed that before dentistry could become a profession, dental journalism had to be freed from the proprietary influence of the dental supply houses, which used the journals to promote their products, and made an instrument of graduate professional education. To this end he founded, promoted, financed, and edited the *Journal of Dental Research* (1919–1937). He also edited the *Journal of the American College of Dentists* and organized the independent American Association of Dental Editors. In 1920 he founded the International Association for Dental Research and helped guide its affairs for many years. In 1937 he handed over the *Journal of Dental Research* to this association and was a member of its editorial board for many years.

In 1921 the Carnegie Foundation for the Advancement of Teaching selected Gies to make a survey of dental education in the United States and Canada. With the aid of the Dental Educational Council of America, Gies produced a 692-page report that revealed dentistry's glaring defects and the steps needed to correct them (Carnegie Foundation for the Advancement of Teaching, *Bulletin 19, Dental Education in the United States and Canada* [1926]). The report signaled the death knell of commercialism in dental education and secured dentistry's place as another university branch of higher learning. By 1926 there were only three privately operated dental schools, but many university schools were "conducted in the commercial spirit of proprietary schools" (*Bulletin 19*, p. 141). While undertaking this landmark study, Gies successfully led the effort to unite four separate dental education groups into the American Association of Dental Schools (1923). Throughout his life Gies worked to end the divisions that existed in dentistry and to make dentistry the full health care service equivalent of an oral specialty of medical practice.

As a young boy Gies developed a deep and abiding affection for nature and a love of baseball. He played on his college baseball team and, for one summer, for the Manheim Baseball Club, and he umpired games up until 1898. Gies was the consulting chemist for the New York Botanical Gardens for nearly twenty years and a member of its board of scientific directors for seventeen years. On reaching the customary retirement age of sixty-five, Gies gave up his faculty position but remained professionally active. He died in Lancaster, Pennsylvania.

Gies is one of the most revered figures in the history of American dentistry. The dental profession paid tribute to him by dedicating the December 1937 issue of the *Journal of the American College of Dentists* to "William John Gies, leader and champion of modern dentistry, guardian of professional ideals, molder of far-reaching plans, [and] tireless worker in the cause of dental education and research." More than any of his important individual contributions, it was Gies's unflagging commitment to the promotion and welfare of dentistry that endeared him to those who shared his dream of making dentistry a modern profession based on the highest ideals of health care service.

• There is a collection of Gies papers at Columbia University. Gies authored more than 600 works, of which 100 deal with dentistry. The most informative articles about Gies are H. Edmund Friesell, "William John Gies, a Biographical Sketch," *Journal of the American College of Dentists* 4 (1937): 164–68; George L. Heighes, "William John Gies, Manheim Boy," *Pennsylvania Dental Journal* 18 (1951): 273–76; N. Kobrin, "Builders of Modern Dentistry: William J. Gies— the Good Citizen," *Dental Outlook* 28 (1941): 315–18; Leuman M. Waugh, "Burkhart Memorial Scroll to William J. Gies," *New York State Dental Journal* 18 (1952): 330–36; and

Charles B. Millstein, "Dr. William J. Gies's Contribution to Dental Research, Education, and Journalism," *Journal of the Massachusetts Dental Society* 40 (Summer 1991): 131–34. An obituary is in the *New York Times*, 21 May 1956.

STUART GALISHOFF

GIFFORD, Gene (31 May 1908–12 Nov. 1970), jazz and dance band arranger, composer, and musician, was born Harold Eugene Gifford in Americus, Georgia. Details of his parents are unknown. Raised in Memphis, he played banjo and wrote his first arrangements for a high school band. His early professional experience as a banjoist and guitarist was with little-known bandleaders. He played with Bob Foster in El Dorado, Arkansas, and toured with Lloyd Williams, Watson's Bell Hops, Blue Steele (Gene Staples), and Henry Cato.

In Detroit Gifford began writing for bands working under the name of Jean Goldkette, and in 1929 he began playing with one such group, the Orange Blossoms, directed by Hank Biagnini. The Orange Blossoms were scheduled to play a new Canadian nightclub, the Casa Loma, which never opened. Still, several bandmembers took its name when they formed a cooperative big band without Biagnini, and in October 1929 the Casa Loma Orchestra arrived in New York City for recordings, as well as performances at Roseland Ballroom.

Gifford strummed guitar and banjo with the big band until December 1933, when Jacques Blanchette took his place. Nevertheless, his historically significant contribution was as the orchestra's principal arranger and composer, rather than as a performer. Notable among his energetic jazz scores are "San Sue Strut," recorded by the Casa Loma group in February 1930; "Casa Loma Stomp," recorded by that group in December 1930, by Fletcher Henderson's Orchestra in 1932, and again by the Casa Loma band in 1937; "White Jazz," "Black Jazz," and "Maniac's Ball," all from 1931; "Blue Jazz," 1932; "Wild Goose Chase," 1933; and "Stompin' Around," 1934. In contrast to these pieces, Gifford also created sensuous ballads for slow dancing, especially "Smoke Rings," recorded in 1932 and again in 1937, and "Drifting Apart," from December 1937. Apart from the recording studio, Gifford's creations reached a large public via the radio show "Camel Caravan," which featured the Casa Loma Orchestra from 1933 to 1934 and used "Smoke Rings" as the show's theme song. Gifford also received attention through the band's summertime residencies at Glen Island Casino and its wintertime residencies in the Colonnades of New York's Essex House.

Accounts of Gifford's departure from the orchestra are conflicting. In May 1935 his only recording session as a leader included a version of his piece "Nothin' but the Blues," featuring trumpeter Bunny Berigan. According to writer George Simon, during this same time, Gifford had become unreliable, for unstated reasons, and arranger Larry Clinton took his place. On the basis of Gifford's own reply in a questionnaire for *The Encyclopedia of Jazz* (1960), writer Leonard

Feather states that Gifford continued with the orchestra until 1939, when founding member and cooperative president Glen Gray took over the band under his own name. Simon and writer Albert McCarthy, however, date this event as 1937. The previously mentioned recording of "Drifting Apart" from December 1937 testifies that at the very least Gifford was contributing to the band through this year.

In the late 1930s and early 1940s Gifford worked as a freelance arranger for big bands, collaborating with clarinetist Irving Fazola on the staff of WWL radio in New Orleans in 1945. After participating in USO tours in 1945 and 1946, he joined Gray's revived Casa Loma Orchestra from 1948 to 1949. Gifford then settled in New York and worked mainly as an audio consultant and a radio engineer, although he continued to write arrangements. In the last year of his life he returned home to teach music in Memphis, where he died.

The Casa Loma Orchestra was the most popular big band of the early 1930s, especially for college students. This popularity can be attributed in part to the sugary sweet crooning of singer Kenny Sargent and in part to the band's meticulous performances of challenging scores written by Gifford, who contributed a few of the most original arrangements in big band jazz and dance music. His dreamy "Smoke Rings" provides a pioneering example of the type of slow-paced, sentimental ballad that trombonist Tommy Dorsey would feature a few years later, and his fast-paced arrangements offer numerous creative touches, of which the most striking are a brilliantly screwy loping and leaping saxophone line at the start of "White Jazz" and a series of irresistibly rhythmic sectional riffs filling the final portion of "Casa Loma Stomp."

Musical analyst Gunther Schuller argues that Gifford was strongly influenced by African-American arranger John Nesbitt of McKinney's Cotton Pickers while the two men were based in Detroit, and he documents a resemblance between Nesbitt's arrangement of "Chinatown" (1929) and Gifford's subsequent "Casa Loma Stomp." Schuller writes, "Because of its great popularity with a broad segment of the (mostly white) audience, Gifford's *Casa Loma Stomp* did more than any other piece in the early thirties to advance the idea of jazz instrumentals, at least in the guise of frenetic 'killer-dillers,' meant to be listened to *as* music, rather than as background for dancing. More importantly . . . Gifford's *Stomp* brought jazz as an orchestral instrumental music (not mere *dance* music) out of its previous exclusively black domain over to white audiences, musicians and record companies" (Schuller, p. 634–35).

• The Robert Gray Dodge Library of Northeastern University holds arrangements written by Gifford for the Casa Loma Orchestra. For a survey of his career see George Hoefer, Jr., "The Hot Box," *Down Beat*, 2 July 1947, p. 12. George T. Simon, *The Big Bands*, 4th. ed. (1981), gives further details of Gifford's years with Casa Loma. For Surveys of his jazz-oriented contributions to that band see Albert McCarthy, *Big Band Jazz* (1974), and Gunther Schuller, *The Swing Era: The Development of Jazz, 1930–1945* (1989). See also Marshall W. Stearns, *The Story of Jazz*, 2d ed. (1958), and Richard M. Sudhalter et al., *Bix: Man & Legend* (1974). An obituary is in *Down Beat*, 7 Jan. 1971, p. 11.

BARRY KERNFELD

GIFFORD, Robert Swain (23 Dec. 1840–15 Jan. 1905), artist, was born on Nonamesset Island near Wood's Hole, Massachusetts, the son of William Tillinghast Gifford, a boatman, and Annie Eldridge. He was named for Robert Swain, the late invalid son of William W. Swain, a prosperous New Bedford merchant who employed Gifford's father. When he was two, Gifford's family moved to Fairhaven, Massachusetts, where he spent his youth attending the local school and working around the wharves. As the son of an impecunious waterman, Gifford would have had an education limited to the grammar school of Fairhaven had it not been for the kindly encouragement of Mrs. Swain, who saw to it that he studied French, literature, and music and acquired the manners and bearing of a gentleman.

At an early age, Gifford took an interest in drawing, choosing as his principal subject the waterfront activities that he knew very well. Initially self-taught, he became acquainted in 1854 with Albert Van Beest, the well-trained Dutch marine painter brought to New Bedford by the then developing marine artist William Bradford as his teacher. Van Beest took an interest in the youthful Gifford and invited him into the studio he shared with Bradford. Gifford became a frequent visitor, receiving instruction and encouragement. They collaborated on some work, and when Van Beest returned to New York in 1857, Gifford accompanied him, returning to New Bedford after a brief stay. Typical examples of Gifford's early marine painting are *Island of Mount Desert from the Mainland* (1864, Hudson River Museum) and *Fishing Boat on Coast of Grand Manan* (1864, Old Dartmouth Historical Society). Also in 1864 Gifford moved to Boston, but he soon concluded that New York was the best place for an artist to make his way. There he went in 1865, securing a place in Samuel Colman's studio.

For the next five years Gifford worked in New York during the winters, returning to New Bedford or traveling along the coast to Maine and Grand Manan, an island at the mouth of the Bay of Fundy, during the summers to gather material for the marine and coastal subjects in which he initially specialized. He developed habits of industry and frugality that enabled him not only to meet his expenses but also to contribute something to the support of his parents. Gradually, recognition came to him in the form both of sales of pictures and of developing friendships with the leading artists of the day. In 1867 he was elected an associate of the National Academy, with full membership coming in 1878.

Like many artists of his day, Gifford supplemented his income from the sales of paintings with commissions for illustrations in books and periodicals. One of his more important commissions came in 1869—illustrations for three articles in *Picturesque America*, a 48-part serial edited by William Cullen Bryant. This assignment provided the occasion for Gifford's first trip to the West Coast, during which he benefited greatly from the opportunity to see the grand scenery of the West.

In 1870 Gifford embarked on a tour of Europe and North Africa with his friend Louis C. Tiffany. The scenes he saw there became his principal subject for the next few years, particularly those of boats and mosques along the Nile, including one titled *Nile* (1871, Hudson River Museum). Following his marriage in 1873 to Frances Eliot, the daughter of Thomas Dawes Eliot, a judge and congressman from New Bedford—a marriage that eventually produced seven children—the couple traveled abroad, primarily in North Africa, returning to New York in 1875.

Gifford was by then a mature artist, and during the next few years he advanced to the forefront of his profession. In 1876 his painting *The Mosque of Mohammed Ali* won a medal of honor at the Centennial Exposition in Philadelphia. In 1885 his painting *Near the Coast* was one of the four winners of the first Prize Fund Exhibition of the American Art Association and was acquired by the Metropolitan Museum of Art. Somber scenes of the Massachusetts coast constituted Gifford's principal subject matter, of which representative examples include *October on the Coast of Massachusetts* (1873, Corcoran Gallery), *Near the Ocean* (1879, National Museum of American Art), *Near the Marsh* (1880, Brooklyn Museum), and *Padanaram Salt Vats* and *Willows of Padanaram* (1904 and c. 1904, respectively, both at the Old Dartmouth Historical Society).

The amiable and industrious Gifford was a welcome member of many of the artists' clubs and associations in New York. In addition to belonging to the Century Association, the Tile Club, and the Society of American Artists, he was a founder of the New York Etching Club and the American Watercolor Society (in both of which media he produced excellent work), a Patron in Perpetuity of the Metropolitan Museum of Art, and one of the first Americans to be elected to the Society of Painter-Etchers in London. These associations together with his artistic ability resulted in frequent requests for him to serve on juries for exhibitions and advisory committees for various artistic undertakings, including the Advisory Committee on Fine Arts for the State of New York for the World's Columbian Exposition in 1893 and the Awards Committee for the St. Louis World's Fair in 1904. A teacher at the Cooper Union from 1877, he became director of all arts activities there in 1896 and was said to be popular with both students and administration. Gifford died in New York City.

There was a memorial exhibition of Gifford's work at the Century Association in 1905. The next major exhibition of his work did not take place until 1974, but that show, at the Old Dartmouth Historical Society, did much to rescue him from relative obscurity. In addition to his proficiency in painting both in oil and watercolor and his skill as an etcher, his contribution to art in America lies in his participation in the art world of his day through teaching, encouraging others, and working with and for numerous organizations to foster the fine arts.

• Gifford's papers, including correspondence, sketchbooks, proofs of illustrations, articles about him, reviews of exhibitions, and photographs, are in the Old Dartmouth Historical Society, New Bedford, Mass. Much of the collection has been microfilmed by the Archives of American Art, Smithsonian Institution, Washington, D.C. *R. Swain Gifford, 1840–1905*, a catalog of the 1974 exhibition, was published by the Old Dartmouth Historical Society. An account of his etched work is Elton W. Hall, "R. Swain Gifford and the New York Etching Club," in *Prints and Printmakers of New York State, 1825–1940* (1986).

ELTON W. HALL

GIFFORD, Sanford Robinson (10 July 1823–29 Aug. 1880), landscape painter, was born in Greenfield, Saratoga County, New York, the son of Elihu Gifford and Eliza Robinson Starbuck, the descendant of a prosperous whaling family of Nantucket, Massachusetts. Shortly after the birth of Sanford, the fourth of eleven children, his father moved the family to Hudson, New York, where he invested in and built iron foundries and operated banks.

Gifford, who became one of the leading members of the second generation of the Hudson River School, attended Hudson Academy, then Brown University for three semesters in 1842–1844. Several factors and advantages affected his attraction to art. Gifford himself cited his older brother Charles's enthusiasm for the fine arts, manifested chiefly in a collection Charles had gathered of engravings of Old Master paintings whose perusal Gifford called "one of the greatest pleasures of my boyhood" (Gifford to O. B. Frothingham, 6 Nov. 1874). Shortly after quitting Brown, Gifford moved to New York City and studied figure drawing and perspective with the well-known instructor John Rubens Smith and took the antique and life classes at the National Academy of Design. However, his early interest in figural art and portraiture soon shifted to landscape painting. In the summer of 1846 he began sketching in the Catskills and the Berkshire Mountains. It was at the same time and place that his future colleague Frederic E. Church was concluding his training in landscape painting with Thomas Cole, the founder of the Hudson River School, who lived in Catskill just across the river from Hudson. Gifford later attributed his devotion to landscape painting to Cole's work, but it must also have been encouraged by Henry Ary, a local portrait and landscape painter, who gave art instruction and sold his work to Gifford's siblings. Ary had known Cole since the 1830s, and he sketched with Gifford at least once in the field, in the summer of 1849.

As he was training in New York, Gifford also advanced himself socially in the artistic circle of the city. There is evidence that he joined the New York Sketch Club, a society whose regular meetings focused on spontaneous composition drawing around designated themes. He began submitting paintings to the exhibitions of both the National Academy of Design and the American Art Union in 1847, and he continued to contribute several works to each show annually. In the summers he widened his circuit of natural sites in the Northeast to include Lake George and the Adirondacks, the Wyoming Valley and the Susquehanna River in Pennsylvania, Conway Valley and the White Mountains in New Hampshire, and Cape May in New Jersey. His visits often either coincided or were shared with those of other New York painters, such as Asher B. Durand, then president of the National Academy of Design, John Frederick Kensett, Richard William Hubbard, David Johnson, William Trost Richards, Samuel Colman, and Aaron D. Shattuck. In 1851 Gifford was elected an associate of the academy; in 1854 he was elevated to full academician.

With family support and several commissions for paintings, Gifford embarked on a two-year tour of Europe in May 1855. This trip and a return journey to Europe and the Middle East in 1868–1869 are the best-documented periods of Gifford's life, since he faithfully maintained a journal of his experiences in the form of letters to his family that have been preserved in transcript form. In Britain, Gifford visited the National Gallery and admired the classical landscapes of Claude Lorrain and J. M. W. Turner. He called on John Ruskin, the author of *Modern Painters*, to evaluate Turner's accomplishment. In the summer Gifford toured England and Scotland, then moved on to France. He spent most of his time in Paris but visited Barbizon, where he met Jean François Millet and admired the landscape paintings of the Barbizon school. In May and June 1856 Gifford journeyed through the Netherlands to the art colony of Düsseldorf, Germany, where he was welcomed by the leader of the American art colony there, Emanuel Leutze, and by a future colleague, Worthington Whittredge. During the summer Gifford descended the banks of the Rhine on foot and walked throughout Switzerland and the northern Italian lake district. In September, following two weeks in Florence, he headed for Rome, linking up with several American painters who preceded him there, including Whittredge and Albert Bierstadt. During the fall and winter of 1856–1857 Gifford worked on commissions in Rome and sketched in the Campagna, often with his compatriots, and in May 1857 began a sketching tour on foot with Bierstadt into southern Italy, particularly around Naples. Returning north in July, he spent almost two weeks in Venice, then toured Austria and Prussia before returning to London in September to catch a steamer home.

Gifford's mature career commenced after his return to New York. He was fortunate to obtain excellent studio and living quarters at the new Studio Building on Tenth Street, which over the next two decades became the residence of many Hudson River School painters. Gifford gained membership in the Century Club, the principal literary and artistic association of New York, in 1859. He resumed annual summer sketching tours in the Northeast, most regularly in the Catskills near the family homestead in Hudson, frequently camping and working in the mountains with Jervis McEntee, Whittredge, and Hubbard. His special fondness for the Catskills is reflected in the preponderance of Catskill subjects in his oeuvre. His paintings soon became marked stylistically for colored light, hazy atmosphere, and broad spatial effects, and they frequently included a visible radiant sun. These features were inspired in great measure by Turner. The dreamy *Kauterskill Clove* (Metropolitan Museum of Art) of 1862 is a fine example of Gifford's idealizing vision, which was evident even in his earliest major canvas of an American subject, *Mansfield Mountain* (private collection) of 1859, showing Vermont's highest peak, and in *The Wilderness* (Toledo Museum of Art) of 1860, which portrays Mount Katahdin in Maine. Gifford later termed his enterprise "air-painting," reportedly achieved in part by repeated applications of "boiled varnish" to the painted image, which enhanced the effect of the dusty, amber light that distinguishes many of his paintings.

Expressively, Gifford's light and atmospheric effects have been interpreted as a nostalgic evasion of the realities of the Civil War, which coincided with the growth of his career. If so, the sentiment could only have been heightened by the artist's voluntary participation in the war effort, as a member of the Seventh Regiment, New York National Guard, from 1861 to 1863, protecting the cities of Washington, D.C., and Baltimore. This duty normally was limited to several months of each year, permitting Gifford to continue working on pictures and to exhibit annually. After the war the artist began to develop an alternative style or manner, less idealizing in composition and less atmospheric in effect. The stark and haunting *Hunter Mountain, Twilight* (Terra Museum of American Art) of 1866 is Gifford's masterpiece of this style. This and another painting were selected to represent the artist at the Paris Exposition in 1867; *Hunter Mountain* was said to have been widely admired by French critics, one of them citing its "poetic repose."

In 1868 Gifford embarked on his second tour abroad, revisiting many Swiss and Italian locales and adding an excursion to Sicily. In Rome and vicinity he worked with McEntee and spent time with Church and William Stanley Haseltine, among other artists. In January 1869 Gifford left Italy for Egypt and the Mideast, fulfilling the ultimate goal of this trip. He sailed the Nile for several weeks, visited Cairo and Thebes, and continued through Jerusalem, Lebanon, Syria, Turkey, and Greece. By early May Gifford was at Athens, making sketches of the Acropolis for what would become one of the crowning achievements of his career, *Ruins of the Parthenon* (1880, Corcoran Gallery of Art), painted more than a decade later. Following a rapturous six-week stopover in Venice, he went to Paris and returned to America in early September.

In late 1869 and early 1870 Gifford participated with his colleagues in the formation of the Metropolitan Museum of Art. In the summer he made his first trip to the Far West, accompanying Kensett and Whittredge to Denver, then leaving them to join the geological survey expedition of Ferdinand V. Hayden along the old Oregon Trail through Wyoming and Utah. In the summer of 1874 he extended his range west to California, Oregon, Vancouver, and southern Alaska. Relatively little painting resulted from his western sojourns, however. In the 1870s Gifford's subjects were mostly of sites in Europe and the Catskills, where he continued to rove almost every autumn with family members and artist companions. For the Centennial Exposition in Philadelphia in 1876, thirteen of his paintings were selected, more than by any other American artist. Seven were awarded distinction for landscape painting; all but one of the latter group were of European subjects, including *The Golden Horn, Constantinople* (1872 or 1873, unlocated) and *Tivoli* (1869, Metropolitan Museum of Art). This circumstance undoubtedly reflected America's emerging cosmopolitanism after the Civil War, a trend that fostered Gifford's preferences in subject even as his colleagues Church and Bierstadt increasingly were criticized for their spectacular frontier canvases.

By the last decade of his life Gifford's professional success was so secure and his lifestyle so simple that he sometimes spent entire summers fishing in New York and Canada. In 1877 he secretly married Mary Canfield, the "widow of an old friend and schoolmate" (Gifford to John Ferguson Weir, 12 Dec. 1877; quoted in Weiss, *Poetic Landscape*, p. 148) and only gradually introduced her to his colleagues and friends. In the summer of the next year and in 1879 he joined several of his artist friends at a campground owned by Church on Lake Millinocket at the foot of Mount Katahdin in Maine. Gifford visited Lake Superior in the summer of 1880 hoping to shake off a viral ailment but returned to New York seriously ill. His condition became complicated by pneumonia, and he died in New York in late August. His funeral and burial took place in Hudson.

The response to Gifford's passing was remarkable. A memorial meeting of the Century Association on 19 November 1880 was accompanied by an exhibition of sixty-two of his pictures. It was followed that winter by a retrospective exhibition of 160 paintings at the Metropolitan Museum of Art. The tributes culminated in a *Memorial Catalogue* of 731 paintings published by the museum that same year.

The admiration for Gifford as an artist was at least equaled by the regard for him as a man. His "simplicity, gentleness, generosity, and sincerity" (*Art Journal* 6 [1880]) were compared by his contemporaries to the qualities of his recently deceased colleague John Frederick Kensett. He readily socialized at home, in the field, and abroad; he hosted small dinner parties in his studio and was noted more than once for his "chivalric" demeanor with women. In contrast to Kensett, Gifford maintained a distinctive reserve that suggested to John Ferguson Weir "cavernous depths of shade" in his personality. The verbal impression of him seems verified by the long, noble features and serene expression depicted in the several portraits of Gifford made by affectionate colleagues. A sensitive bust portrait of

the artist in oil on academy board by Eastman Johnson, dated 1880, and an almost equally impressive bronze portrait bust by Launt Thompson, dated 1871, are both in the Metropolitan Museum of Art. In his art, too, Gifford then and now compares with Kensett in qualities of observation, rendering, and expression. Kensett is more refined in touch and delicate in tone, Gifford more saturated with color and quiet poetic yearning. Surely they existed on a near par professionally, at the top of their field among the landscape painters who did not—as did Church and Bierstadt—specialize in monumental pictures. For the sake of his reputation, Gifford's death may have been the most timely of all the Hudson River School painters, since his style was then beginning to represent "an almost outgrown phase of American art" (Maria van Rensselaer, "Sanford Robinson Gifford," *American Architect and Building News*, 11 Feb. 1882) in the eyes of younger critics and artists who sympathized with Continental academic trends. Along with the reputations of the other Hudson River School painters, Gifford's lapsed into obscurity in the late 1880s, not to be revived for about seventy years. Today his art has recaptured an appeal comparable to his reputation in the heyday of American landscape painting.

• The transcripts of Gifford's "European Letters," in three volumes, are on microfilm at the Archives of American Art, as is the majority of his surviving correspondence. Other correspondence is in the Department of Rare Books and Manuscripts, Boston Public Library, Mass. Gifford is the subject of a published doctoral dissertation and a thoroughly documented monograph, both by Ila S. Weiss, *Sanford Robinson Gifford (1823–1880)* (Columbia Univ., 1968; repr. 1977) and *Poetic Landscape: The Art and Experience of Sanford R. Gifford* (1988). The artist had one retrospective exhibition in the twentieth century, organized by Nicolai Cikovsky, Jr., who wrote the catalog, *Sanford Robinson Gifford (1823–1880)* (1970). Among nineteenth-century sources, the most useful and revealing are Henry T. Tuckerman, *Book of the Artists* (1867; repr. 1967); George Sheldon, "How One Landscape Painter Paints," *Art Journal*, n.s., 2 (1877): 284–85, and *American Painters* (1878; rev. ed., 1881; repr. 1972); S. G. W. Benjamin, *Our American Artists* (1879) and *Art in America* (1880); and Century Association, *Gifford Memorial Meeting of the Century* (1880). Obituaries are in *American Art Review* 1 (1880): 551; *Art Journal* 6 (1880): 319–20; and the *New York Times*, 30 Aug. 1880.

KEVIN AVERY

GIFFORD, Walter Sherman (10 Jan. 1885–7 May 1966), telephone company executive, was born in Salem, Massachusetts, the son of Nathan Poole Gifford, a lumber merchant, and Harriet Maria Spinney, a schoolteacher. Gifford entered Harvard University in 1901 and completed his course work in three years, but he chose to take his degree with the class of 1905. Gifford started work in 1904 as a clerk at the Western Electric Company, the manufacturing subsidiary of the American Telephone & Telegraph Company (AT&T). In 1905 he transferred to Western Electric's New York headquarters and became its assistant secretary and assistant treasurer. Gifford's statistical reports attracted the attention of AT&T president Theodore N. Vail, who brought him to the parent company as a statistician in 1908. Gifford left the telephone company briefly in 1911 to manage a copper mine in Arizona but at the behest of Vail returned to AT&T after six months to become the company's chief statistician.

The outbreak of World War I led Gifford to enroll in 1915 in the military training school in Plattsburgh, New York, and he was appointed supervising director of the Committee on Industrial Preparedness of the Naval Consulting Board in 1916. Later that year he became director of the Council of National Defense. That same year he also married Florence Pitman; the couple had two children but divorced in 1929. In 1944 Gifford married a widow, Augustine Lloyd Perry; no children were born to this later marriage.

After the war ended, Gifford worked briefly with the Allied peace negotiators at Paris on the Inter-Allied Munitions Committee. He returned to AT&T as its comptroller in late 1918, became its vice president of finance in 1920, and was elected to its board of directors in 1922. He became executive vice president in 1923 and succeeded Harry Bates Thayer as AT&T president on 20 January 1925. For the next two decades Gifford headed AT&T, working closely with trusted subordinates Charles Proctor Cooper, who handled much of the operations side, and Arthur W. Page, who handled public relations.

Gifford's first major policy decisions were in response to a threatened antitrust prosecution stemming from the company's predominant role in the radio industry. Although AT&T had pioneered in radio broadcasting and created the first radio network, Gifford removed AT&T from the ranks of radio broadcasters to avoid prosecution. He sold its seventeen radio stations to the National Broadcasting Corporation (NBC) and limited its role in radio to leasing the long-distance lines that made nationwide radio networks possible. Gifford also divested AT&T of its foreign telephone operations, which were sold to International Telephone & Telegraph Company (IT&T) in 1925. AT&T also divested itself of most other nontelephone operations, although it soon acquired new teletype and telephoto firms.

The start of Gifford's presidency coincided with the consolidation of all of AT&T's research departments into a single entity, Bell Telephone Laboratories (Bell Labs), which became one of the nation's major research centers. Scientists at Bell Labs developed television technology and in 1927 conducted the first public television broadcast in the United States, Commerce Secretary Herbert Hoover speaking from Washington, D.C., to an audience in New York City. Bell Labs also developed the coaxial cable, which could carry a much greater volume of telephone calls (and eventually television programs) than could traditional copper wire lines. Bell Labs' research in acoustics made AT&T a pioneer in motion picture sound technology in the 1930s. Its Electrical Research Products, Inc., subsidiary (collaborating with the Vita-

phone subsidiary of Warner Bros. Studios) was the industry leader until overtaken by RCA's rival sound system in the mid-1930s.

Gifford also lessened AT&T's dependence on investment banks as a source of corporate funds by initiating direct sales of AT&T stock to current stockholders. His policy of $9 annual dividends, regardless of the price of the stock, made AT&T a "blue chip" stock throughout the 1920s and 1930s. AT&T became the largest corporation in America, with more than 600,000 stockholders.

The depression and the New Deal led to new federal legislation that allowed the employees of AT&T's operating companies to become unionized, largely by the International Telephone Workers of America. Congress also enacted the Communications Act of 1934, which Gifford strongly opposed, and created the Federal Communications Commission (FCC). Federal regulatory oversight of interstate telephones rates was established, at least in theory. One of the FCC's first official actions was the institution of a lengthy investigation of AT&T's revenues and its relationship with its subsidiaries.

During the 1930s Gifford also initiated the automation of AT&T's operations, replacing manual telephones and operator-staffed switchboards with dial telephones and automated switchboards. AT&T also shifted its basic marketing strategy, which traditionally had been aimed at business users and the small strata of upper-class households, to market telephones to the larger number of middle-class households, for social purposes as well as business calls. When Gifford took over AT&T, there were approximately twelve million telephones in the Bell System; when he left the company the number had grown to thirty-two million.

Soon after American entry into World War II, federal mobilization agencies imposed orders that prohibited new nonmilitary installations of telephones. Much of Bell Labs' efforts in research and development were directed into radar and microwave technology, which, ironically, would later provide the technological bases for AT&T's new long-distance competitors in the postwar era. Gifford played a substantial role in the wartime mobilization effort, as a member of the War Resources Board and as chairman of the Industry Advisory Committee of the Board of War Communications.

After the war, pent-up demand for telephone service ballooned the number of new installations, and AT&T revenues increased rapidly. The company's annual revenues had been $737 million in 1925; several years later, AT&T became the first corporation to post annual revenues of $1 billion. By the time Gifford left the AT&T presidency in 1948, annual revenues had increased to $2.7 billion.

Gifford began easing himself out of direct operations in the late 1940s. In 1948 he named vice president Leroy A. Wilson as his successor and moved into the newly created position of chairman of the board. He relinquished his remaining operating responsibilities the following year and took on the title of honorary chairman of the board.

In November 1950 President Harry Truman appointed Gifford as U.S. ambassador to Great Britain. He represented the United States in several conferences involving the implementation of the Marshall Plan, the creation of the North Atlantic Treaty Organization, and the negotiation of the Japanese Peace Treaty. After returning to the United States in 1953, Gifford spent the next thirteen years in retirement at his home in North Castle, New York, a Westchester County suburb. He died in New York City.

• Gifford's papers and relevant AT&T records are at the AT&T corporate archives in Warren, N.J. For his life and career see Arthur W. Page, *The Bell Telephone System* (1941), and John Brooks, *Telephone: The First One Hundred Years* (1976). AT&T's changing policies regarding its marketing of telephone service are described in Claude Fischer, *America Calling: A Social History of the Telephone to 1940* (1992). An obituary is in the *New York Times*, 8 May 1966.

STEPHEN G. MARSHALL

GIHON, Albert Leary (28 Sept. 1833–17 Nov. 1901), naval surgeon, was born in Philadelphia, Pennsylvania, the son of John Hancock Gihon, a physician, and Mary J. (maiden name unknown). He received his early education at the Central High School in Philadelphia and was the first student to graduate with an A.B. under its collegiate program. He graduated from the College of Medicine and Surgery in Philadelphia with an M.D. in 1852, at the age of nineteen. In 1854 Gihon was granted an A.M. by Princeton University.

Except for the years 1853–1854, which he spent as a professor of chemistry and toxicology at the Philadelphia Medical College and Surgery, Gihon devoted his entire medical career to the U.S. Navy as a surgeon and medical administrator. In 1855 Gihon enlisted in the navy as an assistant surgeon aboard the receiving-ship *Union*, stationed in Philadelphia. The following year he was assigned to his first foreign post aboard the sloop of war *Levant*, attached to the East India station. Gihon was transferred to the sloop of war *Portsmouth* on 15 November 1856, in the midst of a crisis between British and Chinese forces. He participated in the capture of the barrier forts on the Pearl River near Canton, China, after his ship was fired on.

With mounting social and political tensions in South and Central America, Gihon was transferred to the *Dolphin*, of the Brazil Squadron in 1858. During the unauthorized military campaign of American adventurer William Walker to establish a slave society in Nicaragua, he was assigned to the *Preble*, for duty off the coast of Central America and Panama. He married Clara Monfort Campfield in 1860; two of their three children survived to maturity.

On 1 May 1860 Gihon received his permanent grade of assistant surgeon while on duty at the U.S. Naval Hospital in Brooklyn, New York. He was promoted to the rank of surgeon on 1 August 1861. With the advent of the Civil War he was transferred to the *St. Louis*, on which, except for the period in 1864 when he partici-

pated in the blockade of South Carolina, he spent the entire war, as the vessel cruised the Atlantic islands in search of Confederate privateers. At the end of the war he was appointed senior medical officer at the Portsmouth, New Hampshire, Navy Yard and served in that capacity until 1868.

In 1868 Gihon was assigned to the first navy hospital ship (*Idaho*) of the Asiatic Squadron, stationed at Nagasaki, Japan. While he was on duty on 21 September 1869, the ship was shipwrecked during a typhoon. In 1870 he was placed on special duty in the United States and served in Brooklyn, New York, and Philadelphia; he was also a member of the Naval Medical Board of Examiners. On 7 November 1872 Gihon was assigned medical inspector to the Bureau of Medicine and Surgery of the Medical Department in Washington, D.C. Promoted to fleet surgeon in 1874, he served on the flagship *Wabash* on the European station and then aboard the flagship *Franklin*.

In 1875 Gihon was exempted from further sea duty because of age and rank. He was then chosen to head the medical department of the Naval Academy at Annapolis, Maryland. During this tour of duty, at the request of the chief of the Bureau of Medicine and Surgery, he designed and constructed the model of a hospital ship for the 1876 Centennial Exposition at Philadelphia. Also exhibited was the "Gihon ambulance cot," which was approved for navy use in 1877.

On 27 August 1879 Gihon was appointed medical director, and for the next fifteen years he was in charge of the naval hospitals in Norfolk, Virginia; Washington, D.C.; Mare Island, California; and Brooklyn, New York. After forty years of service he attained the rank of commodore on 1 May 1895 and was retired that September from the U.S. Navy because of his age.

Gihon was the author of several books on sanitation and public health. His earliest book, *Practical Suggestions in Naval Hygiene* (1871), published before the modern age of bacteriology, gave insights into the problems that developed from the unsanitary conditions existing in that period: the unhealthy environment, overcrowding, overwork, lack of proper ventilation, disregard for good personal hygiene, poor diet, etc. In 1877 he published *The Need for Sanitary Reform in Ship Life* and *Sanitary Commonplaces Applied to the Navy* and in 1882, *Prevention of Venereal Diseases by Legislation*. He wrote numerous articles on naval hygiene, medical education, vital statistics, state medicine, medical demography, and climatology. Gihon served for six years as the editor of the *Annual of the Universal Medical Science*.

Beginning in 1876, Gihon represented the medical department of the navy at medical, sanitary, and climatological association meetings and international medical congresses. He was a member of numerous American and international medical, public health, scientific, and historical societies. In 1876 Gihon was elected a member of the executive board of the American Public Health Association and in 1883, its eleventh president. During his presidency, Gihon proposed that a council of state health officers be organized as a section of the association. The formation of such a council was proposed as early as 1879, but as many organizational and policy questions had not been fully addressed, no action was taken until Gihon's proposal had been accepted. A 1953 survey taken by the American Public Health Association placed Gihon on a master list of public health pioneers for his work in the control of syphilis. Gihon also served as vice president of the Association of Military Surgeons in 1895 and as president of the American Academy of Medicine. Gihon was the originator and for many years one of the sponsors in the effort to build a monument in Washington, D.C., to honor Benjamin Rush, pioneering physician and signer of the Declaration of Independence. Gihon died in New York City.

• For Gihon's contributions to public health, see Mazyck P. Ravenel, "The American Public Health Association: Past, Present, Future" in *A Half Century of Public Health*, ed. M. P. Ravenel (1921), pp. 13–55; and Wilson G. Smillie, *Public Health: Its Promise for the Future* (1955), pp. 303, 329, 477. Obituaries are in the *New York Times*, 18 Nov. 1901; and the *Journal of the American Medical Association* 37 (1901): 1404–5.

SAM ALEWITZ